LET TV MOVIES
ENTERTAIN YOU!

Tonight's the night to enjoy a movie on TV. Today's the day to consult the indispensable book to help you pick the best of the best.

All the legendary films are here—hundreds of great new super releases, thousands of golden oldies, all of your all-time favorites. Shoot 'em up westerns. Tuneful musicals. War sagas. Science fiction. Comedies. Foreign films. Enjoy them more with this handy, alphabetized guide. It will let you know in advance which stars are appearing, what the story is about—and whether the picture is worth watching.

· Check your daily newspaper for time and channel.
· Consult **MOVIES ON TV** to help you select the movie to entertain you—tonight.

ENJOY!

Revised and Updated

MOVIES ON TV

1982-1983 Edition

Formerly published as
TV KEY MOVIE GUIDE

Edited by Stephen H. Scheuer

BANTAM BOOKS
TORONTO · NEW YORK · LONDON · SYDNEY

MOVIES ON TV 1982-83
A Bantam Book

Original Bantam edition/November 1958
25 printings through August 1978
Ninth revised edition/November 1981

ISBN 0-553-14806-0

Published simultaneously in the United States and Canada

PRINTED IN THE UNITED STATES OF AMERICA

0 9 8 7 6 5 4 3 2

Preface

This is the ninth edition of MOVIES ON TV. This updated, revised and expanded reference work includes approximately three thousand new reviews. Two thousand of them are reviews of new and old films reviewed for the first time, and about one thousand are totally revised reviews of films reviewed in earlier editions.

The first edition of MOVIES ON TV was published in November 1958 under the title TV Movie Almanac and Ratings. It was the first book ever published reviewing movies shown on television. Updated editions of MOVIES ON TV followed at various intervals throughout the 1960's and 1970's. For this ninth edition, about a thousand of the more important and enduring films of the past six decades have been re-examined and re-reviewed. These totally revised reviews reflect my opinions and those of my colleagues, based on the critical criteria and perspectives of the 1980's rather than those of the 1950's or '60's. They also reflect the dramatically expanded choice of entertainment now available to tens of millions of Americans, thanks largely to the vast channel capacity of cable television.

As always I have one principal objective in mind—to make the viewing of feature films on television more enjoyable and rewarding by enabling movie lovers as well as occasional viewers the opportunity to be better informed and more selective when deciding what to watch on TV. In addition to the exciting new offerings on cable television and Pay-TV, home audiences presently have an ever-increasing menu available via video cassettes and the burgeoning new field of video discs. Millions of Americans are more anxious than ever before to have the information necessary to be more discriminating viewers.

In the past few years virtually every good film—and thousands of poor ones—made during the 1970's and in 1980 have been broadcast on American television. *Gone With the Wind, Jaws* and *The Godfather,* three of the all-time box office champions, have been telecast. *The Godfather* fetched a record price—ten million dollars for one showcasing. At this writing almost the only big box office hits that are not yet signed for network commercial TV are *Star Wars*, its sequel *The Empire Strikes Back* and the 1981 box office smash hit, *Raiders of the Lost Ark*. CBS reportedly offered twenty million dollars for one showing of *Star Wars*, and got turned down.

Most of the broadcast time that local TV stations and cable operators devoted to feature films is filled by movies of comparatively recent vintage, primarily those made during the 1960's and 1970's. For reasons of space, and to permit the inclusion of the aforementioned three thousand new reviews, I have omitted some of the undistinguished films of the thirties, forties and fifties. Also for reasons of space, I have eliminated the critical comments on some of the worst films of the past decade and simply noted the title, cast, director, year of release and the star ratings indicating briefly our critical estimate of each movie.

In the almost twenty-five years since the first edition of MOVIES ON TV was published, there have been many changes regarding the pattern of releasing movies to television. In the early sixties when theatrical films started showing up during prime time on the three commercial networks, those movies were invariably at least five years old. By the 1970's, the time gap between showing in local movie houses and TV showcasing had been dramatically shortened. Mediocre movies were showing up on television within one year of their theatrical release. In the latter part of the 1970's, pay television began to develop quickly thanks largely to the huge success of the satellite-delivered cable TV pay service Home Box Office, which was, and is, almost entirely dependent on movies. With the arrival of Pay TV, theatrical films were shown on Pay TV before they were shown on network commercial television. Now, with the burgeoning market for pre-recorded video cassettes and, perhaps, for the even cheaper video discs, some hit movies are being released on video cassettes and discs *simultaneously* with their release in theaters where they can be appreciated by paying customers. If the income derived from the home market, i.e. pre-recorded cassettes and discs, increases substantially, the movie companies may delay the release of hit films to the pay cable networks because they do not want owners of video cassette recorders to have the opportunity to tape such movies for free off the air on Home Box Office or Showtime until such time as the market for purchase of cassettes and discs has been substantially exhausted. Companies manufacturing new hardware and technology for cable television are working overtime to perfect the devices necessary to charge customers for particular programs they want to watch. Motion picture producers are drooling over the prospect of being able to reap ten or twenty million dollars overnight by charging millions of willing households two, three or four dollars to watch a major movie. (Pay TV customers were charged $20.00 to see the Duran-Leonard fight "live," and a couple of hundred thousand families in the Los Angeles area were delighted to pay the fee.)

There are other recent noteworthy developments concerning movies on TV. The quality of the best of the made-for-television movies is appreciably higher today than in the mid-1970's. Notable examples of the made-for-TV genre like *Friendly Fire* and *A Question of Love* are superior to many movies released in theaters and produced on far larger budgets. There have been numerous examples of movies showing up on network commercial TV with added footage not found in either its theatrical release or subsequent showings on Pay TV. Discarded out-takes from the theatre film are reinserted to pad the movie for a two-part showing on network TV. *The Deep* and *Beyond the Poseidon Adventure* are two such examples. The extraneous footage may detract from the movie's impact, but it means more commercial breaks for the networks.

The proliferating cable networks like Home Box Office, Showtime, The Movie Channel, and the new CBS Cable network are showing many more rewarding foreign films than were formerly available to American TV audiences. That is one of the reasons this edition contains several hundred new reviews of foreign entries. TV can also react far more quickly than motion pictures to current news stories which provide the basis for a good drama or comedy based on a real event. In the spring of 1981, a two-part version of *The People vs Jean Harris,* based on the transcripts of the real courtroom trial, was broadcast on network television within a few months of the trial itself. Movies simply cannot produce a film and get it into the theatres in such a short period of time. Film biographies, once a Hollywood staple, are now produced for the most part as made-for-tv movies.

The extraordinary success of such subscription TV movie networks as Home Box Office is due in large measure to their eliminating two of the three reasons why millions of movie lovers, myself included, often hate watching movies on commercial TV—the endless interruptions for commercials, and the fact that the original film was often mutilated, censored and otherwise diminished when shown on network TV. The remaining problem, the tiny size of TV sets, has not been solved, but some relief is in sight. When you watch a theatrical film on a 21- or 26-inch TV set, you are seeing less than one percent of the full image or picture created by the director and cinematographer designed to be seen on huge screens. But the quality of big screen projection TV sets is far better in 1981 than it was a few short years ago, and still bigger and brighter pictures are on the engineering drawing boards.

Curiously enough, the advantages of being able to see on Pay-TV exactly the same film seen in theaters is bringing in its wake some predictable problems and serious questions of free speech and censorship. Certain American obscenities and colloquialisms have always been banned from commercial network television, but are now routinely heard on theatrical movies seen on such outlets as Home Box Office, Showtime or The Movie Channel. Self-appointed vigilante groups like the Moral Majority are busily mobilizing to purge the airways of what they consider to be offensive or un-American programs, offered by the three commercial networks. Cable TV and various subscription services are already the subject of their simple-minded censorial wrath. This issue will become ever more volatile in the mid-1980's as cable TV is purchased by over a third of all American households.

All the reviews in this book are written by myself and my fellow critics. They are almost always based upon the original complete versions seen in movie theaters. We have no way of knowing what havoc a slothful film editor will wreak on a sophisticated film shown on local TV when he/she has to squeeze a two-hour film into a ninety-minute time period. Your enjoyment of certain movies seen on local outlets will often depend upon what time you tune in. You're much more likely to see a full-length non-edited version of any given feature during the late evening hours. It doesn't matter much whether a station concludes a feature showing at 12:57 or 1:33 a.m. But it is imperative that shows end at a precise pre-determined time during the rest of the broadcast day, usually on the hour or half-hour.

And a final bit of advice for voyeurs throughout the land! There are no present plans for CBS, ABC or NBC to telecast either *Deep Throat* or *The Devil in Miss Jones*. If you simply can't wait for them to show up on cable TV, you can rush out and buy them on pre-recorded video cassettes and watch them to your heart's content in the privacy of your home via your own video cassette recorder.

STEVEN H. SCHEUER

New York City
October, 1981

Special thanks are due to John Goudas, Linda Sandahl, Viana Muller, and Peter Neumann.

I am particularly grateful to five Chicago Reader and Los Angeles Reader contributors, whose capsule film reviews appeared in the first printing of this edition without permission or acknowledgment. Several hundred of the capsule reviews reprinted here are the work of Dave Kehr, film critic of the Chicago Reader; many others were written by Carol Bahoric, Don Druker, Chris Morris, and Dan Sallitt. Their credits were omitted from the first printing of this edition, for which I apologize.

I also wish to thank Myron Meisel, former Los Angeles Reader film critic, for permission to use a substantial number of his reviews in this edition.

Note: In this expanded edition of our guide, you will notice many new reviews of interesting and important films, old and new. With the recent phenomenal growth of cable and 24-hour movie channels, we feel that the variety of films available for general viewing will, in the future, be enormous. We at *Movies on TV* agree with our publishers that our present paperback format is most convenient for the book's users; therefore we faced some hard choices when it came to including literally hundreds of new entries. For purely practical reasons, we had to do some pruning. We decided, in the interests of fairness, to use *quality* as our criterion. So, in this ninth edition, all films rated less than two stars will not be reviewed. We will continue to list the film's date of release, cast, director, and length, but the low rating means that, in our opinion, the film itself is not worth further discussion. We were reluctant to do even this much cutting, but it was necessary if we were to bring you a wealth of new material.

Key to ratings:

**** Excellent	** Fair
***½ Very Good	*½ Poor
*** Good	* Bad
**½ Pretty Good	½ Abysmal

All the "A's" and "The's" are listed under the second word: "A Day at the Races," under "Day at the Races, A"; but if the title is not in English, the film is listed strictly alphabetically: "Les Visiteurs du Soir" under "L".

TV Movie Reviews and Ratings

À Nous la Liberté (France, 1931)****
Raymond Cordy, Henri Marchand, Rolla
France. French comedies directed by René
Clair were the best from anywhere in the
early '30s. This is a romp about freedom
in an industrial state and there's not a
heavy moment in it. Chaplin borrowed
the assembly line gags for "Modern
Times"; it's a tribute to both artists that
the scene is equally inspired in both films.
(97 mins.)

À Propos de Nice (France, 1929)****
Director Jean Vigo's first intimation of
genius—a document, rather than a documentary, about the Las Vegas of the Riviera. The film has a mordant poetry as it
examines aristocrat, tourist, pauper, making oblique social observations without
comment. The images are far too charged
to be assigned meanings so simple as satire. Brilliant, though hardly a masterpiece
like later Vigo films, the film's violent
and subversive contrasts were appropri-
ated by filmmakers for decades after. (42
mins.)

Aaron Slick from Punkin Crick (1952)**
Alan Young, Robert Merrill, Dinah Shore,
Guy Mitchell. A city slicker tries to fleece
a poor widow out West. A rather tedious
musical comedy. (Dir: Claude Binyon, 95
mins.)

Abandon Ship (1957)*** Tyrone Power,
Mai Zetterling, Lloyd Nolan. Tense and
terrifying drama about the fate of 26 survivors of a luxury liner disaster all
crammed into a life boat that can only
hold 12 safely. Tyrone Power is fine. (Dir:
Richard Sale, 100 mins.)

Abandoned (1949)**½ Dennis O'Keefe, Gale
Storm, Raymond Burr, Jeff Chandler.
Sensationalized drama centering around
baby-adoption rackets and how a determined girl and a newspaper man help to
crack them. (Dir: Joe Newman, 79 mins.)

Abbott and Costello Go to Mars (1953)**
Bud Abbott, Lou Costello, Mari Blanchard.
For the duo's fans: All their slapstick and
double talk routines are evident in this
silly space comedy about an accidental
trip to Mars. (Dir: Charles Lamont, 77
mins.)

Abbott and Costello in Hollywood (1945)**
Bud Abbott, Lou Costello, Frances
Rafferty. Bud and Lou run a barbershop
in Hollywood; the usual, with lots of
opportunities for clowning. (Dir: S. Sylvan Simon, 83 mins.)

Abbott and Costello in the Foreign Legion
(1950)** Bud Abbott, Lou Costello,
Patricia Medina. The boys don Foreign
Legionnaires' duds in this moderately funny farce about intrigue amid the sand
dunes of Algiers. (Dir: Charles Lamont,
80 mins.)

Abbott and Costello Meet Captain Kidd
(1952)*½ Bud Abbott, Lou Costello,
Charles Laughton, Hillary Brooke, Leif
Erickson. Color. (Dir: Charles Lamont, 70
mins.)

Abbott and Costello Meet Dr. Jekyll and
Mr. Hyde (1953)**½ Bud Abbott, Lou
Costello, Boris Karloff. Abbott and
Costello fans will enjoy this comedy-horror
film which has them playing a couple of
American detectives in London during the
late 1800's. (Dir: Charles Lamont, 76
mins.)

Abbott and Costello Meet Frankenstein
(1948)***½ Bud Abbott, Lou Costello, Lon
Chaney, Bela Lugosi. This is really a
horror-film parody, with Chaney as the
Wolfman and Lugosi as the Count. The
antics tend to be side-splitting. Need I
warn, it's very lowbrow? (Dir: Charles
Barton, 83 mins.)

Abbott and Costello Meet the Invisible
Man (1951)** Abbott and Costello, Nancy
Guild. A lightweight farce in which
Abbott and Costello play a couple of de-
tectives who are hired by a unique
client—an invisible man. (Dir: Charles
Lamont, 82 mins.)

Abbott and Costello Meet the Keystone
Kops (1955)*** Bud Abbott, Lou Costello,
Fred Clark, Lynn Bari. A & C are in the
movie business circa '12 this time. In be-
tween pies in the face, there's a wild chase
complete with the famous Keystone Kops.
Mack Sennett makes a guest appearance.
(Dir: Charles Lamont, 80 mins.)

Abbott and Costello Meet the Killer
(1949)** Abbott and Costello, Boris
Karloff. A silly excursion into murder and
mirth with the comedy team as a pair of
amateur sleuths who almost get themselves killed in order to solve a murder.
(Dir: Charles Barton, 94 mins.)

Abbott and Costello Meet the Mummy
(1955)** Abbott and Costello, Marie
Windsor. Bud and Lou are treasure
hunters in this yarn about Egyptian tombs
and the many crooks who want to get
their hands on a valuable hoard of gold
and jewels. (Dir: Charles Lamont, 80
mins.)

Abdication, The (Great Britain, 1974)*½
Liv Ullmann, Peter Finch, Cyril Cusack.
(Dir: Anthony Harvey, 102 mins.)

Abduction of Saint Anne, The (MTV
1975)**½ E. G. Marshall, Robert Wagner,
Lloyd Nelson. A young girl is reputed to
have healing powers, and the Catholic
Church wants to have her miracles certified. But there's a hitch . . . she's being held
a virtual prisoner in her gangland father's
estate. Enter the Bishop and the private
detective (Marshall and Wagner respectively). (Dir: Harry Falk, 72 mins.)

Abductors, The (1957)**½ Victor McLaglen, Fay Spain. Fairly well done crime
tale based on true story. Concerns attempt
to rob Lincoln's grave; reasonably inter-

esting. (Dir: Andrew McLaglen, 80 mins.)

Abe Lincoln in Illinois (1940)**** Raymond Massey and Ruth Gordon star in this moving, wonderfully acted version of Robert E. Sherwood's Broadway play. The 16th President's life, his ill-fated love for Ann Rutledge, and his marriage to Mary Todd. (Dir: John Cromwell, 110 mins.)

Able's Irish Rose (1946)* (Dir: A. Edward Sutherland, 96 mins.)

Abilene Town (1945)*** Randolph Scott, Ann Dvorak, Rhonda Fleming. The marshal of Abilene has his hands full separating the cattlemen from the homesteaders in 1870. Fast, well-produced western. (Dir: Edwin Marin, 89 mins.)

Abominable Dr. Phibes, The (Great Britain, 1971)*** Vincent Price, Joseph Cotten, Virginia North. An engaging parody of Victorian horror films by Robert Fuest, the director responsible for the earnestly absurd flavor of "The Avengers" TV series. Price enjoys himself as a mad doctor who revenges the death of his wife by visiting variations of the plagues of Egypt on those he believes responsible—including Cotten, Hugh Griffith, and Terry-Thomas. A former art director, Fuest gives the film a preposterously lush, Ken Russellish look. (93 mins.)

Abominable Snowman of the Himalayas, The (1957)**½ Forrest Tucker, Peter Cushing, Maureen Connell. Better than average horror/science fiction yarn about the legendary Snowman of the Himalayas. (Dir: Val Guest, 85 mins.)

About Face (1952)** Gordon MacRae, Eddie Bracken, Phyllis Kirk. Cadet musical with lavish, over-produced production numbers. This is remake of "Brother Rat" with tunes added. (Dir: Roy Del Ruth, 94 mins.)

About Mrs. Leslie (1954)**½ Shirley Booth, Robert Ryan. When a tycoon dies and leaves a boarding house owner some money, her secret love affair is recalled. Unadorned soap opera, partly compensated for by fine acting. (Dir: Daniel Mann, 104 mins.)

Above and Beyond (1952)*** Robert Taylor, Eleanor Parker. An absorbing subject well handled. Robert Taylor gives a nicely etched performance as the officer who piloted the plane which dropped the atom bomb on Hiroshima, and gets good support from Eleanor Parker. (Dirs: Melvin Frank, Norman Panama, 122 mins.)

Above Suspicion (1943)**½ Joan Crawford, Fred MacMurray, Basil Rathbone. Fast-moving chase melodrama with Fred and Joan trying to aid the British secret service while they honeymoon in Paris. (Dir: Richard Thorpe, 90 mins.)

Above Us the Waves (Great Britain, 1956)*** John Mills, John Gregson. High-tension war drama of midget submarines and the stalking of German battleships. Fine acting and excellent photography. (Dir: Ralph Thomas, 99 mins.)

Abraham Lincoln (1930)*** Walter Huston, Una Merkel, Kay Hammond. Screenplay by Stephen St. Vincent Benét. Biographical drama about the great president. (Dir: D. W. Griffith, 97 mins.)

Abroad with Two Yanks (1944)*** Dennis O'Keefe, William Bendix, John Loder, Helen Walker. Two wacky Marines turn Australia inside out in their escapades over a girl. Wild, frequently hilarious comedy. (Dir: Allan Dwan, 80 mins.)

Absent-Minded Professor, The (1961)**½ Fred MacMurray, Nancy Olson, Tommy Kirk, Ed Wynn, Keenan Wynn. The kids should get a kick out of this vintage Disney production. It's all simple-minded fun as MacMurray bumbles his way through the title role, where his accidental discovery of a formula makes his old Model T Ford fly. (Dir: Robert Stevenson, 104 mins.)

Accattone! (Italy, 1961)*** The life and fate of a young Roman parasite, told in grimly neo-realistic style by director Pasolini. Somewhat remote emotionally, but the squalor of the locale is graphically captured. Well acted by Franco Citti as the wastrel, and a nonprofessional cast. (Dir: Pier Paolo Pasolini, 120 mins.)

Accident (Great Britain, 1967)***½ Dirk Bogarde, Stanley Baker, Jacqueline Sassard. A fascinating, if uneven, study of a married college professor who becomes involved with one of his attractive female students. It's not as simple as it sounds. The complexities are many, and the shadings of Dirk Bogarde's characterization as the professor are superbly etched. The entire cast is top drawer. (Dir: Joseph Losey, 105 mins.)

Accident, The (Italy, 1962)* Magali Noel, Georges Riviere. (Dir: Edmond T. Greville, 85 mins.)

Accidental Death (Great Britain, 1964)** John Carson, Jacqueline Ellis. Former intelligence agents set death traps for each other. Average suspense drama. (Dir: Geoffrey Nethercott, 57 mins.)

Accursed, The (1958)**½ Donald Wolfit, Robert Bray. A fairly interesting mystery involving the guests of a onetime colonel of the Resistance forces at the annual reunion held at his home. (Dir: Michael McCarthy, 78 mins.)

Accused, The (1948)*** Loretta Young, Robert Cummings, Wendell Corey. Schoolteacher accidentally kills an amorous student, tries to cover her crime. Well-made drama. (Dir: William Dieterle, 101 mins.)

Accused of Murder (1956)** Vera Ralston, David Brian. Homicide officer falls for a night club singer suspected of killing a gangland lawyer. Ordinary mystery. (Dir: Joseph Kane, 80 mins.)

Ace, The—See: **Great Santini, The**

Ace Eli and Rodger of the Skies (1973)*½ Cliff Robertson, Pamela Franklin, Eric Shea, Bernadette Peters. (Dir: Bill Sampson [John Erman], 92 mins.)

Ace High (Italy, 1968)**½ Eli Wallach,

2

Brock Peters, Kevin McCarthy. Occasionally interesting spaghetti western which spoofs the genre. Wallach plays a sly bandit in Mexico, who gets the loot no matter what obstacles are in his way. Fine supporting cast makes this an above-average adventure. (Dir: Giuseppe Colizzi, 120 mins.)

Ace in the Hole—See: **Big Carnival, The**

Aces High (Great Britain, 1976)*** Malcolm McDowell, Simon Ward, Peter Firth, Christopher Plummer, Ray Milland. Virtually an all-star cast in a remake of the early sound classic "Journey's End," based on R. C. Sherriff's '29 play. It's the old story about WW I aerial combat, with the young squadron leader (McDowell) sending men to fight and perhaps to die. The dogfights are excellent, and the characterizations, despite the stereotypes, are sound. (Dir: Jack Gold, (103 mins., U.S.; original running time 114 mins.)

Acorn People, The (MTV 1981)*** Ted Bessell, Cloris Leachman, LeVar Burton, Dolph Sweet. A tale set at a summer camp for severely handicapped kids seen through the eyes of a bleeding-heart camp counselor and his associates. At first, the show is not easy to take but the kids grow on you and so do the counselors. (Dir: Joan Tewkesbury, 104 mins.)

Across 110th Street (1972)** Anthony Quinn, Anthony Franciosa, Yaphet Kotto. Violent crime drama shot in Harlem. Infighting among the Mafia and small-time hoods regarding a theft of syndicate cash amounting to close to a half a million. Most of the performances seem arch and contrived, except for Yaphet Kotto's policeman-sidekick of Quinn's veteran cop. (Dir: Barry Shear, 102 mins.)

Across the Bridge (Great Britain, 1957)*** Rod Steiger, David Knight. Crooked tycoon on the lam from Scotland Yard is cornered in Mexico. Considerable suspense in this drama; good performances, especially Steiger's. (Dir: Ken Annakin, 103 mins.)

Across the Great Divide (1976)***½ Robert Logan, George Flower, Heather Rattray, Mark Edward Hall. An unusually well done children's film with no objectionable violence or language. Two spunky orphans have plenty of adventures and hardships en route to their new home in Oregon in the old West. Filmed on location. (Dir: Stewart Raffill, 89 mins.)

Across the Pacific (1942)*** Humphrey Bogart, Mary Astor, Sydney Greenstreet. John Huston directs this comedy adventure which reunited three of the leads of "The Maltese Falcon." Bogart plays an undercover agent trying to entrap Japanese sympathizer Greenstreet during a boat trip from Canada to Panama, falling for Astor along the way. The pleasantly spontaneous comic interaction between Bogart and Astor makes the film well worth seeing, although its virtues are otherwise modest. Script is by Richard Macauley, montage sequences by Don Siegel. (97 mins.)

Across the Wide Missouri (1951)**½ Clark Gable, Ricardo Montalbán, Adolphe Menjou, John Hodiak, J. Carroll Naish. An unusual western set in the 1820's. Clark Gable plays a trapper married to an Indian girl. William A. Wellman directed with less than his usual over-elaboration. (78 mins.)

Act of Love (1953)***½ Kirk Douglas, Dany Robin. American soldier has a tragic affair with a poor girl in occupied Paris. Powerful love story, excellently acted, filmed in France. (Dir: Anatole Litvak, 105 mins.)

Act of Love (MTV 1980)**½ Ron Howard, Robert Foxworth. Howard shows another side of his acting ability in this sentimental drama about the mercy killing of a paralyzed family member. Howard, suffering along with a brother who has been crippled in a motorcycle accident, answers his request to end his misery. The state doesn't consider this an "act of love," so attorney Foxworth arrives to rescue Howard. Based loosely on Paige Mitchell's nonfiction book; explores fascinating emotional issues in the courtroom. (Dir: Jud Taylor, 104 mins.)

Act of Murder, An (1948)***½ Fredric March, Edmond O'Brien, Florence Eldridge. Judge is tried for the mercy killing of his wife. Grim and unrelenting, but finely done drama deserves praise. Alternate title: **Live Today for Tomorrow.** (Dir: Michael Gordon, 91 mins.)

Act of Reprisal, An (1965)*½ Ina Balin, Jeremy Brett. (87 mins.)

Act of the Heart (Canada, 1970)*** Genevieve Bujold, Donald Sutherland, Bill Mitchell. An often moving, superbly acted, independently made low-budget entry that is profoundly marred by a preposterous, unbelievable ending. Young former farm girl arrives in Montreal and falls in love with a priest while developing what turns out to be a fatal case of religious hysteria. (Dir: Paul Almond, 103 mins.)

Act of Violence (1948)**½ Van Heflin, Janet Leigh, Robert Ryan. Well acted and directed but routine chase melodrama about a guy who betrayed his buddies in a Nazi prison camp. (Dir: Fred Zinnemann, 82 mins.)

Act of Violence (MTV 1979)*** Elizabeth Montgomery, James Sloyan, Sean Frye. Ms. Montgomery in a provocative tale about mugging in a big city. Liz plays the liberal, protected divorcée who works for a TV show and is attacked one night at her doorstep. Her change in attitude after the mugging and attempted rape—to fear and often hate—and her arguments with a fellow worker over street violence give the thriller added depth. (Dir: Paul Wendkos, 104 mins.)

Act One (1963)*** George Hamilton, Jason Robards, Eli Wallach. If you have never read Moss Hart's sentimental, best-selling novel about his youthful love affair with the Broadway theater, this watered-down film version will entertain you. (Dir: Doré Schary, 110 mins.)

Action in the North Atlantic (1943)***½ Humphrey Bogart, Raymond Massey. Forget that it was originally war propaganda, relax and enjoy this exciting dramatic tribute to the Merchant Marine. (Dir: Lloyd Bacon, 127 mins.)

Action Man (France, 1967)** Jean Gabin, Robert Stack. Confused tale of a criminal and an American adventurer out to rob a bank. Saved by the always watchable Jean Gabin. Low-budget entry. (Dir: Jean Delannoy, 95 mins.)

Action of the Tiger (1957)**½ Van Johnson, Martine Carol, Herbert Lom. Routine adventure yarn with all the clichés intact—an American adventurer on foreign soil meets a glamorous lady with dangerous plans. Nothing new here, but action fans might enjoy it. (Dir: Terence Young, 92 mins.)

Actors and Sin (1952)*** Edward G. Robinson, Eddie Albert, Marsha Hunt. Two stories by Ben Hecht: "Woman of Sin," hilarious Hollywood burlesque about a child who writes a geat screenplay, and "Actor's Blood," drama of a beautiful actress whose strange death implicates many people. All in all, an entertaining package. (Dir: Ben Hecht, 86 mins.)

Actor's Holiday (1969)** James Franciscus and his family take a vacation in Puerto Rico, in the Dominican Republic, and on other islands. A few picturesque sights along the way. (60 mins.)

Actor's Revenge, An (Japan, 1963)***½ Kazuo Hasegawa, Ayako Wakao, Ganjiro Nakamura, Raizo Ichikawa, Shintaro Katsu, Fujiko Yamamoto. Delightful experimental entertainment from Kon Ichikawa (*Enjo, Fires on the Plain*) concerning a female impersonator who plots a sinister revenge. Kazuo Hasegawa, a star of Japanese film since silent days, is deliciously ironic and superbly histrionic, a mixture of Maverick and the Count of Monte Cristo. Ichikawa experiments with jump cutting and theatricalization of space in bold, exhilarating ways. (Dir: Kon Ichikawa, 113 mins.)

Actress, The (1953)*** Spencer Tracy, Jean Simmons, Teresa Wright, Anthony Perkins (debut), Kay Williams. The autobiography of Ruth Gordon, as directed by George Cukor. Simmons, in a memorable performance, stars as the young New England girl who dreams of going to Broadway—against the strong wishes of her practical, hard-working father (Tracy). The film is saved from coy nostalgia by Cukor's deep appreciation of the issues involved. Its charm is well earned. Screenplay by Gordon, based on her play "Years Ago." (91 mins.)

Ada (1961)** Susan Hayward, Dean Martin. Guitar-playing sheriff is persuaded to run for governor, but his attraction to a good-time girl threatens his political career. Unconvincing. (Dir: Daniel Mann, 109 mins.)

Adalen 31 (Sweden, 1969)**** Peter Schildt, Roland Hedlund, Martin Widerberg, Marie de Geer. Director Bo Widerberg's beautiful, perceptive drama played out against the background of a real event in Swedish history—the 1931 strike in the town of Adalen. Five workers were killed when soldiers fired on the peaceful protesters. Focuses on one family, whose working father is one of the leaders of the strike. Visually breathtaking film about politics, love, and lots more. Widerberg also wrote the screenplay. English subtitles. (115 mins.)

Adam and Evalyn (Great Britain, 1949)**½ Stewart Granger, Jean Simmons. Handsome gambler adopts the daughter of a deceased friend, finds she's pretty enough to fall for. Mildly entertaining romance. (Dir: Harold French, 90 mins.)

Adam and Eve (Mexico, 1956)** Carlos Baena, Christiane Martel. Unsuccessful adaptation of the Book of Genesis, brought to life occasionally by the camerawork of Alex Phillips, one of Mexico's finest cameramen. Acting is only fair. Miss Martel was Miss Universe 1953. (Dir: Albert Gout, 76 mins.)

Adam at 6 A.M. (1970)*** Michael Douglas, Joe Don Baker, Lee Purcell. A good idea that works much of the time. Douglas is a hip California college professor who starts questioning his life-style and takes some time off to get in touch with the "real" world. His odyssey brings him to Missouri, where he meets a variety of "just plain folks" who eventually let him down. The performances are good. (Dir: Robert Sheerer, 100 mins.)

Adam Had Four Sons (1941)*** Ingrid Bergman, Warner Baxter, Susan Hayward. Family governess looks after four children after the mistress of the house dies. Well-acted drama. (Dir: Gregory Ratoff, 81 mins.)

Adam's Rib (1949)**** Spencer Tracy, Katharine Hepburn, Judy Holliday, Jean Hagen, Tom Ewell, David Wayne. One of the best of the Tracy-Hepburn cycle, written by Garson Kanin and Ruth Gordon. Tracy is an assistant D.A. in New York prosecuting a woman accused of shooting her husband, while wife Hepburn defends her. Wayne is hilarious in a small part; Ewell and Holliday do well as the husband and wife—but the show belongs to Tracy and Hepburn. (Dir: George Cukor, 101 mins.)

Adam's Woman (Australia, 1968)* Beau Bridges, John Mills, Jane Merrow. (Dir: Philip Leacock, 95 mins.)

Adding Machine, The (Great Britain-U.S.A., 1969)**½ Phyllis Diller, Milo O'Shea, Billie Whitelaw. Erratic film version of Elmer Rice's brilliant expressionist play of 1923. An overworked accountant murders his boss when he learns he is to be replaced by a machine. The play has been softened, but the impact remains. (Dir: Jerome Epstein, 100 mins.)

Address Unknown (1944)*** Paul Lukas, Carl Esmond. Businessman in Germany embraces the Nazi cause, but his partner in America has his revenge. Interestingly produced drama. (Dir: William Cameron Menzies, 72 mins.)

Adieu, Voyages Lents (France, 1978)** Virginie Thevenet, Michele Simmonet, Jean-François Stevenin. Three-part film explores from different perspectives the lives of a married couple caught in the throes of their own passion. (Dir: Marie-Genevieve Ripeau.)

Adios Amigo (1975)** Fred Williamson, Richard Pryor, Thalmus Rasulala, James L. Brown, Mike Henry. A pallid western comedy with a mostly black cast. Williamson wrote, directed, produced, and stars as the patsy to con man Pryor. It's clean and nonexploitative, exemplary in every aspect but execution. (87 mins.)

Adios Gringo (Italy, 1965)* Montgomery Wood (i.e., Giuliano Gemma), Evelyn Stewart, Pierre Cressoy. (Dir: Giorgio Stegani, 98 mins.)

Adios Sabata (Italy, 1971)**½ Yul Brynner. Another violent, grotesque—but engaging—spaghetti western. Brynner plays the tough hombre out to get a $1 million bag of gold dust from a villainous Austrian colonel. Carnage instead of plot. Sequel to the '70 entry "Sabata." "Frank Kramer" is a pseudonym for Italian writer Giancarlo Parolini, a disciple of spaghetti-western father Sergio Leone. As director, Parolini combines camera style (zooms, whip-pans, dizzy camera gyrations) with a wild imagination for thoroughly improbable stories. (106 mins.)

Admirable Crichton, The—See: **Paradise Lagoon**

Admiral Was a Lady, The (1950)** Four ex-GI's living on their wits meet an ex-Wave, vie for her hand. Edmond O'Brien, Wanda Hendrix, Rudy Vallee. Mild, amusing comedy. (Dir: Sidney Salkow, 87 mins.)

Adolescent, The (France, 1978)**½ Simone Signoret. Jeanne Moreau's second film as a director shows a considerable advance in technical skill, though the project is a hackneyed one about a young girl's coming of age during a rural summer just before WW II. Moreau is observant without being insightful, and her characters are so stock that they could have inhabited a French film of 30 years ago, and did. Signoret plays the wise grandmother like an omniscient cat, and she helps Moreau make these leftovers palatable. (90 mins.)

Adorable Creatures (France, 1956)*** Danielle Darrieux, Martine Carol. Delightful romance taking a young man through many affairs with a variety of beauties and finally to the proverbial "girl next door." Well acted by a top French cast. (Dir: Christian-Jaque, 108 mins.)

Adorable Julia (France, 1962)** Lilli Palmer, Charles Boyer, Jean Sorel. Glamorous actress of the London stage embarks on one last fling with a younger man, soon regrets it. Based on a Somerset Maugham play, is rather flat when it should have bubbled. (Dir: Alfred Heidenmann, 94 mins.)

Adorable Menteuse (France, 1962)* Marina Vlady, Macha Meril. (Dir: Michel Deville, 110 mins.)

Adrift (Czechoslovakia, 1970)*** Rade Markovic, Milena Dravic, Paula Pritchett. Director Janos Kadar started this film just as Soviet screws tightened in Czechoslovakia, and it took him nearly two years to finish it. Some interesting touches, but Kadar is a lazy filmmaker short on inspiration. Pritchett gives the film a touch of western exoticism. (108 mins.)

Adulteress, The (France, 1958)**½ Simone Signoret, Raf Vallone, Sylvie. Somewhat simple story of a woman who kills her husband for her lover, and the ensuing blackmail by a young sailor. Marcel Carne directed and adapted the screenplay from the Emile Zola story "Therese Raquin." Saved by the acting of Miss Signoret. (Dir: Marcel Carne, 106 mins.)

Advance to the Rear (1964)**½ Glenn Ford, Stella Stevens, Melvyn Douglas, Civil War comedy about a band of Union Army goldbricks who are transferred to the wild and wooly West. (Dir: George Marshall, 97 mins.)

Adventure (1945)*½ Clark Gable, Greer Garson, Joan Blondell. (Dir: Victor Fleming, 125 mins.)

Adventure in Baltimore (1948)** Robert Young, Shirley Temple. Minister's daughter has modern views for the 1900 period, keeps her father in hot water by sticking by them. Mild, slow little comedy-drama. (Dir: Richard Wallace, 89 mins.)

Adventure in Indo-China (1957)* Jean Gaven, Dominique Wilms. (Dir: André Pergament, 85 mins.)

Adventure Island (1947)** Rory Calhoun, Rhonda Fleming. Pitiful version of the story about shipwrecked sailors on an island ruled by a madman. Remake of **Ebb Tide**. (Dir: Peter Stewart, 66 mins.)

Adventure of Sherlock Holmes' Smarter Brother, The (Great Britain, 1975)***½ Gene Wilder, Madeline Kahn, Marty Feldman, Dom DeLuise. Impressive debut indeed by Gene Wilder who, in addition to starring in this low-brow slapstick romp, also wrote and directed the deft yarn. Wilder plays Sigi Holmes, Sherlock's younger brother. Laughs throughout, with a riotous cast of top bananas. (Atmospheric sets by Peter Howett and deliciously funny score by John Morris. Dir: Gene Wilder, 91 mins.)

Adventurer of Seville, The (France-Spain, 1954)*½ Luis Mariano, Lolita Sevilla. (Dir: Ladislao Vajda, 90 mins.)

Adventurer of Tortuga (Italy, 1964)* Guy Madison, Nadia Gray. Low-budget entry. (Dir: Luigi Capuano, 100 mins.)

5

Adventurers, The (1970)* Bekim Fehmiu, Candice Bergen, Olivia de Havilland, Anna Moffo. (Dir: Lewis Gilbert, 171 mins.)

Adventures in Silverado (1948)** William Bishop, Forrest Tucker. A stage driver captures a hooded holdup man in the Old West, thereby clearing himself. Based on a Robert Louis Stevenson true story. Routine western. (Dir: Phil Karlson, 75 mins.)

Adventures of a Young Man (1962)** Richard Beymer, Paul Newman, Dan Dailey, Arthur Kennedy, Susan Strasberg. Devotees of Ernest Hemingway's works will find a great deal wrong with this film based on a number of his short stories on the life of his fictional hero, Nick Adams. Richard Beymer is awful in the title role. Paul Newman as a scarred, punchy ex-boxer is excellent. Alternate title: **Hemingway's Adventures of a Young Man**. (Dir: Martin Ritt, 145 mins.)

Adventures of Arsene Lupin (1957)** Robert Lamoureux, Lilo Pulver, O. E. Hasse. The gentleman thief after the gems again, and after a wealthy princess too. French-made, English-dubbed romantic adventure has pleasant period (1912) atmosphere but a slow-moving story. (Dir: Jacques Becker, 97 mins.)

Adventures of Captain Fabian (1951)*½ Errol Flynn, Micheline Prelle, Vincent Price. (Dir: William Marshall, 100 mins.)

Adventures of Casanova (1947)*½ Arturo de Cordova, Turhan Bey, John Sutton, Lucille Bremer, Noreen Nash. (Dir: Roberto Gavaldon, 83 mins.)

Adventures of Don Juan (1948)** Errol Flynn, Viveca Lindfors. Title notwithstanding, this is just another Errol Flynn "swashbuckler" with Errol as the great Don Juan. (Dir: Vincent Sherman, 110 mins.)

Adventures of Freddie (MTV 1977)** Michael Burns, Harry Morgan, Tom Poston. A second-generation inventor comes up with a fabulous "energy disk" which could save the world. As expected, his bosses can only see the "profit motive" of his invention, and there hangs the premise. Alternate title: **Magnificent Magical Magnet of Santa Mesa**. (Dir: Hy Averback, 83 mins.)

Adventures of Frontier Fremont, The (1976)**½ Dan Haggerty, Denver Pyle. Remember "The Life and Times of Grizzly Adams"? Well, here's a sort of sequel with different character names but the same leading man, Dan Haggerty. A tinsmith in the 1830's gets tired of his lot in St. Louis and decides to head for the hills and the simple life. He then encounters bears, rattlesnakes, and cougars. (Dir: Richard Freidenberg, 106 mins.)

Adventures of Gallant Bess (1948)** Cameron Mitchell, Audrey Long. Rodeo performer captures a wild mare, enters it for prize money. Ordinary outdoor drama. (Dir: Lew Landers, 73 mins.)

Adventures of Gil Blas, The (France-Spain, 1955)* Georges Marchal, Susana Canales. (Dir: Rene Jolivet, 95 mins.)

Adventures of Hajji Baba, The (1954)*½ John Derek, Elaine Stewart. (Dir: Don Weis, 94 mins.)

Adventures of Huckleberry Finn (1939)** Mickey Rooney, William Frawley, Walter Connolly. Strictly for the youngsters is this flavorless adaptation of the Mark Twain story. (Dir: Richard Thorpe, 110 mins.)

Adventures of Huckleberry Finn, The (1960)**½ Tony Randall, Eddie Hodges. In this version of the Mark Twain classic the Twain atmosphere is occasionally captured. A good cast including Eddie Hodges as Huck, Tony Randall, Judy Canova, Andy Devine, and former champ Archie Moore help to overcome the deficiencies of the adaptation. (Dir: Michael Curtiz, 107 mins.)

Adventures of Mandrin, The (Italy, 1952)** Raf Vallone, Silvana Pampanini. Soldier of fortune organizes a band of outlaws to fight oppression in a Spanish dukedom. Usual swashbuckler with a better than usual cast. English-dubbed. Alternate title: **Captain Adventure**. (Dir: Mario Soldati, 85 mins.)

Adventures of Marco Polo (1938)**½ Gary Cooper, Sigrid Gurie, Basil Rathbone. Sprawling adventure film with extravagant production detail, but still somewhat of a miss as entertainment. (Dir: Archie Mayo, 101 mins.)

Adventures of Mark Twain (1944)*** Fredric March, Alexis Smith. Biographical sketch of America's great humorist falls short of its goal and cannot be ranked with the great screen biographies. More informative than entertaining. (Dir: Irving Rapper, 130 mins.)

Adventures of Martin Eden (1942)*** Glenn Ford, Evelyn Keyes, Claire Trevor. A seaman struggles to become a successful author. Well-done drama based on Jack London's novel. Well acted. (Dir: Sidney Salkow, 87 mins.)

Adventures of Michael Strogoff (1937)*** Anton Walbrook, Akim Tamiroff. In 1870, a messenger of the Czar imperils his life to warn of invading hordes. Crammed full of action, this Jules Verne story should satisfy the most demanding adventure fan. (Also called **Soldier and the Lady**.) (Dir: George Nicholls, Jr., 90 mins.)

Adventures of Mr. Wonderbird (France, 1952)*** Animated cartoon feature tells the tales of a princess and a handsome chimneysweep. Ideal for the children. Voices of Claire Bloom and Peter Ustinov are heard. (Dir: Pierre Grimault, 70 mins.)

Adventures of Nick Carter, The (MTV 1972)** Robert Conrad, Shelley Winters, Broderick Crawford, Dean Stockwell. A famous private eye of the early 1900's. Flavor of the era is nicely captured in this glossy production, but it's familiar gangster stuff. (Dir: Paul Krasny, 72 mins.)

Adventures of Robin Hood, The (1938)*** Errol Flynn, Olivia de Havilland, Basil Rathbone, Claude Rains. The film that, more than any other, epitomized Warner Bros. supremacy in the production of rousing, elaborately staged, immaculately costumed adventure films. Directed by two of Warner's most popular hack directors (Michael Curtiz and William Keighley), the film starred Flynn at his peak. Color. (106 mins.)

Adventures of Robinson Crusoe (Mexico, 1954)**** Dan O'Herlihy, James Fernandez. A superb adaptation of the Defoe classic starring the superb O'Herlihy. Even when using a realistic plot, director Luis Buñuel manages to introduce surrealist subtleties: the erotic fanatasies of Crusoe as he constructs a scarecrow to chase birds away from his wheat crop; the moment when Friday discovers women's clothing in Crusoe's plunder from the sunken ship. A wonderful adventure film. Color. (90 mins.)

Adventures of Sadie (Great Britain, 1955)*** Joan Collins, Kenneth More. Curvaceous and beautiful Joan Collins is stranded on a tropic island with three males and the situation becomes hilarious. Well-done comedy. Hermione Gingold is seen briefly, and she's funny. (Dir: Noel Langley, 88 mins.)

Adventures of Scaramouche, The (France, 1963)** Gerard Barray, Gianna Maria Canale, Michele Girardon. Traveling clown learns he is really a nobleman, goes after the wicked duke trying to usurp his title. Standard swashbuckling melodramatics. Dubbed in English. (Dir: Antonio Isomendi, 98 mins.)

Adventures of Sherlock Holmes (1939)*** Basil Rathbone, Nigel Bruce, Ida Lupino. Holmes stops the attempt to steal the Crown Jewels of England. Good Holmes mystery, well made and exciting. (Dir: Alfred Werker, 85 mins.)

Adventures of Tartu, The (Great Britain, 1943)**½ Robert Donat, Valerie Hobson. A British spy's adventures in Czechoslovakia during World War II. (Dir: Harold Bucquet, 102 mins.)

Adventures of the Queen (MTV 1975)** Robert Stack, Ralph Bellamy, David Hedison, Bradford Dillman. It's the old bomb plot, set on a cruise ship, with a whiz-bang explosion, dazzling fire-and-rescue number. Special effects crew deserves top billing, along with the ship Queen Mary. (Dir: David Lowell Rich, 100 mins.)

Adventures of the Wilderness Family (1975)*** Robert Logan, Susan Damante Shaw. A convincing piece of family fare. Shot in the Utah mountains. A beleaguered family, led by a disillusioned construction worker, jettisons their urban existence for life on the land. Good-natured. (Dir: Stewart Raffill, 101 mins.)

Adventures of Tom Sawyer, The (1938)***½ Tommy Kelly, May Robson,

Victor Jory. The Twain story is patently inferior to "Huckleberry Finn," yet this flawed David O. Selznick production is probably the best Twain on screen—a crime that ought to be remedied. The early Technicolor is interesting, with James Wong Howe doing some fascinating lighting experiments in the cavern scenes. Effective entertainment that I just loved as a boy. Color. (Dir: Norman Taurog, 93 mins.)

Adventures of Ulysses, The (Italy, 1974)** Bekim Fehmiu, Irene Papas. Another variation of the Ulysses legend, with Fehmiu as the hero and Papas as his patient wife, Penelope. Production looks good, but it's been done before and better. (Dir: Franco Rossi, 106 mins.)

Adventuress, The (Great Britain, 1947)**** Deborah Kerr, Trevor Howard. An Irish lassie, traditionally hating the English, unwittingly becomes the tool of Nazi agents. Thoroughly delightful comic espionage thriller, with Miss Kerr giving an utterly charming performance. Excellent. (Dir: Frank Launder, 98 mins.)

Advise and Consent (1962)**** Henry Fonda, Charles Laughton, Walter Pidgeon, Don Murray, Burgess Meredith. Allen Drury's ponderous Washington novel was transformed by director Otto Preminger into a masterpiece of ambiguity, imposing an orderly and analytical vision on goings-on of deMillean proportions while preserving innumerable opportunities for flamboyant star turns by his large, hammy cast, who are almost all excellent. Laughton's last film. (140 mins.)

Aelita (U.S.S.R., 1924)***½ Nikolai Batalov, Yulia Solntseva. An unusual film for Soviet Russia in the '20s, this science fiction fantasy mixes Marxist entertainment with design principles that director Yakov Protazanov learned during his exile in Paris and Berlin for a few years after '17. Batalov plays a Russian soldier who lands on Mars in a rocket designed by a Soviet engineer, where he organizes the enslaved masses to rebel against their ruler, Queen Aelita (Solntseva). The meshing of realistic scenes of life in Moscow during the period of the New Economic Policy and the visions of technological liberation capture this viewer's fancy. (80 mins.)

Affair, The (MTV 1973)**½ Natalie Wood, Robert Wagner, Bruce Davison. An old-fashioned love story with some modern twists. An insulated lyricist of 30-plus who had polio as a kid, and walks with the aid of canes. The dialogue doesn't always ring true, but the sentimental theme is not without interest. (Dir: Gilbert Cates, 74 mins.)

Affair at Ischia (Germany, 1961)* Tony Sailer, Eva Astor. (Dir: Helmut Weiss, 90 mins.)

Affair in Havana (1957)**½ John Cassavetes, Raymond Burr, Sara Shane. The actors are better than their material in

7

this outing, and they make this somewhat melodramatic opus palatable. It's a love story, triangular-fashion, and the setting adds to the mood of the film. (Dir: Laslo Benedek, 80 mins.)

Affair in Monte Carlo (1953)** Merle Oberon, Richard Todd. British-made drama of a wealthy young widow attempting to reform a gambler. Nice backgrounds, but with the sluggish story it's all bets off. (Dir: Victor Saville, 75 mins.)

Affair in Reno (1957)**½ John Lund, Doris Singleton. Public relations man falls for a lady detective hired as his bodyguard. Pleasant little comedy. (Dir: R. G. Springsteen, 80 mins.)

Affair in Trinidad (1952)**½ Glenn Ford, Rita Hayworth, Valerie Bettis. Intrigue and romance in the tropics with Rita Hayworth cast as a valuable pawn in the deadly game of espionage. Rita also has a dance number. (Dir: Vincent Sherman, 98 mins.)

Affair of State, An (W. Germany, 1966)* Curt Jurgens, Lilli Palmer. (Dir: Sammy Drechsel, 95 mins.)

Affair of Susan, The (1935)** ZaSu Pitts, Hugh O'Connell. Humorous yarn about two depressed people who journey to Coney Island in search of soul mates. They land in jail in a most unusual manner. (Dir: Kurt Neumann, 70 mins.)

Affair to Remember, An (1957)***½ Cary Grant, Deborah Kerr, Richard Denning. Leo McCarey's remake of his own "Love Affair" attempts to penetrate the hysterical core of the material to find its emotional fundamentals. Plenty of emotion and tragedy before Grant and Kerr come together. Grant's acting, by the way, is more interior and subjective than Charles Boyer's was with Irene Dunne in the '39 version. (115 mins.)

Affair with a Killer (Canada, 1965)** Stephen Young, Austin Willis. Mediocre suspense as two investigators looking into U.S.-Canadian smuggling reopen a challenging case when their prime suspect is murdered. Low-budget entry. (Dir: George McCowan, 90 mins.)

Affair with a Stranger (1953)*** Jean Simmons, Victor Mature. Successful playwright and wife plan to divorce, but later manage to solve their problems. Well acted romantic drama. (Dir: Roy Rowland, 89 mins.)

Affairs in Versailles (France, 1954)**½ Claudette Colbert, Gerard Philippe, Orson Welles. Sacha Guitry's colorful and ambitious film about the court affairs and naughty intrigues during the time of Louis XIV. Good cast but film is overdone and lacks continuity. (Dir: Sacha Guitry, 152 mins.)

Affairs of Dobie Gillis (1953)**½ Debbie Reynolds, Bobby Van, Bob Fosse. Light comedy with musical numbers about the young and their carefree antics. Bobby Van dances well and is competent as

"Dobie." Debbie is bouncy as ever as his special girl. (Dir: Don Weis, 73 mins.)

Affairs of Dr. Holl (Germany, 1954)** Maria Schell, Dieter Borsche. Young doctor finds a millionaire's daughter has fallen for him. Undistinguished drama. Alternate title: **Angelika.** (Dir: Rolf Hansen, 99 mins.)

Affairs of Julie, The (W. Germany, 1957)*½ Lilo Pulver, Paul Hubschmid. (Dir: Helmut Kautner, 88 mins.)

Affairs of Martha, The (1942)**½ Marsha Hunt, Richard Carlson, Spring Byington. A maid turns a small town upside down when she writes a book about her employers. Diverting comedy. (Dir: Jules Dassin, 66 mins.)

Affairs of Messalina (Italy, 1953)**½ Maria Felix, Georges Marchal. Ornate, but overproduced, over-acted, and over-long spectacle about the evil temptress of the Ancient Roman Empire. (Dir: Carmine Gallone, 120 mins.)

Affairs of Susan, The (1945)**½ Joan Fontaine, Dennis O'Keefe, George Brent. Occasionally amusing, but overdone, romantic comedy about an actress who changes character to match the requirements of her suitors. (Dir: William A. Seiter, 110 mins.)

Affectionately Yours (1941)** Rita Hayworth, Merle Oberon, Dennis Morgan. Forced, weak little comedy about a man trying to woo back his ex-wife. (Dir: Lloyd Bacon, 90 mins.)

Africa Addido (Italy, 1966)** Inflammatory, provocative feature-length documentary about African culture and history, written, directed, conceived, and edited by Gualtiero Jacopetti. Scenes of violence juxtaposed with lurid sex scenes, animal slaughter, etc. Some question about the authenticity of various scenes. (122 mins.)

Africa Screams (1949)*½ Bud Abbott, Lou Costello, Frank Buck. (Dir: Charles Burton, 80 mins.)

Africa—Texas Style (1966)**½ Hugh O'Brian, John Mills, Tom Nardini. Authentic African locales add to this otherwise slow-moving adventure about a cowboy who hunts and tames wild game. The photography is splendid, lensed in Kenya. (Dir: Andrew Marton, 106 mins.)

African Manhunt (1955)* Myron Healey, Karin Booth. (Dir: Seymour Friedman, 80 mins.)

African Queen, The (1951)**** Humphrey Bogart, Katharine Hepburn, Robert Morley, Theodore Bikel. Director John Huston's odyssey theme in comic garb, as Bogart (who won an Oscar) cavorts like a monkey and Hepburn exploits a latent strain of Eleanor Roosevelt in this immensely popular version of the C. S. Forester novel. It's '15, and Hepburn gradually persuades drunken captain Bogart to attack the German Navy with his broken-down tub. James Agee collaborated on the screenplay, and Morley is memorable in an early cameo. (105 mins.)

African Sanctus *** The story of a remarkable 2000-mile journey through modern Africa and Arabia by composer-explorer David Fanshawe. It inspired a composition of his that incorporates field recordings of native music with a Latin mass.

After the Ball (Great Britain, 1957)** Pat Kirkwood, Laurence Harvey. Biography of English music hall girl Vesta Tilley, who became the toast of two continents. Plodding, old-fashioned musical, pretty mild. (Dir: Compton Bennett, 89 mins.)

After the Fox (U.S.-Great Britain-Italy, 1966)**½ Peter Sellers, Britt Ekland, Victor Mature. Funny tale about an ingenious convict (Peter Sellers) who gets involved in moviemaking in order to cover a big caper. Victor Mature plays an American has-been movie star and he hams it up all the way for the film's biggest laughs. Neil Simon wrote the script and Vittorio De Sica directed. (103 mins.)

After the Thin Man (1936)*** William Powell, Myrna Loy, James Stewart, Joseph Calleia, Elissa Landi. Though it lacks the inventive excitement of the original, the first of several sequels to "The Thin Man" is smoothly acted and well plotted, and W. S. Van Dyke's direction is at its most professional and least careless. Powell and Loy have moved to San Francisco, Asta in tow, and their interplay is effervescent—the happiest married couple in screen history. Suspects and players include a newly minted Stewart, and Calleia (a superb gangster). (110 mins.)

After Tonight (1933)*½ Constance Bennett, Gilbert Roland. (Dir: George Archainbaud, 80 mins.)

After You, Comrade (South Africa, 1966)** Jamie Uys, Bob Courtney. At a world conference in Athens, a small utopian country proposes that the United States and Russian delegates hold a footrace in order to avoid World War III. Good comedy idea with no substantial development. Written and directed by Jamie Uys. (84 mins.)

Against a Crooked Sky (1975)*½ Richard Boone, Stewart Peterson. (Dir: Earl Bellamy, 89 mins.)

Against All Flags (1952)** Errol Flynn, Maureen O'Hara, Anthony Quinn. Flynn the dauntless officer vs. Quinn the brazen Caribbean pirate in a thoroughly routine adventure yarn. (Dir: George Sherman, 84 mins.)

Against the Wind (Great Britain, 1948)***½ Simone Signoret, Jack Warner. British agents parachute into occupied France to aid the resistance movement in their fight against the Nazis. Tense, exciting war melodrama, well done. (Dir: Charles Crichton, 95 mins.)

Agatha (Great Britain, 1979)**½ Dustin Hoffman, Vanessa Redgrave. Despite professional production design by Shirley Russell and supple lighting effects by Vittorio Storaro, this exercise in mystification lacks the payoff to validate the long, slow buildup. It suggests a solution to the unsolved disappearance of mystery novelist Agatha Christie after she was jilted by her caddish husband (Timothy Dalton); but the solution is simply not very interesting. Redgrave does wonders with her underwritten character; the Hoffman role is so shadowy that "underwritten" overstates it. (Dir: Michael Apted, 98 mins.)

Age of Infidelity (Spain, 1955)*** Lucia Bose, Alberto Closas. Flawed, complex morality play which concerns two lovers who accidentally injure a man on a motorcycle and leave him to die, fearing publicity about their love affair. Alternate title: **Death of a Cyclist.** (Dir: Juan Bardem, 86 mins.)

Age of the Medici, The (Italy, MTV 1973)**** Director Roberto Rossellini's trilogy on Renaissance Italy ties together the parallel stories of two distinguished figures, Cosimo de Medici, banker and merchant, and Leon Battista Alberti, architect, humanist, and patron, and through them shows what took place in Florence during one of the greatest periods in the history of art (1430–50). Rossellini calls the film "educational." It is, and more—vivid, concise, and insight-filled retellings of history graced by one of the most fertile cinematic imaginations of our time.

Agent 8¾ (Great Britain, 1964)** Dirk Bogarde, Sylva Koscina, Robert Morley. Promising idea—Bogarde plays a rather witless guy, out of a job, who's sent to Czechoslovakia on U.S. "business." Finds himself embroiled in international espionage. Alternate title: **Hot Enough for June.** (Dir: Ralph Thomas, 98 mins.)

Agent for H.A.R.M. (1965)** Mark Richman, Wendell Corey. Secret agent is assigned to protect the life of a defecting scientist. Routine Iron Curtain cloak-and-dagger melodrama. (Dir: Gerd Oswald, 84 mins.)

Agent for Panic (W. Germany, 1964)*½ Brad Newman, Eric Douglas. Routine. (86 mins.)

Agent for the Plaintiff (1968)** Gene Barry, Susan Saint James, Honor Blackman, Brian Bedford. Publisher Glenn Howard framed by an unethical woman lawyer trying to gain money for her boyfriend. Nothing new or exciting. (74 mins.)

Agent of Doom (France-Belgium, 1963)**½ Annette Stroyberg, Michel le Royer, Jean Servais, Pierre Brasseur. Scientist recovers from an accident in a strange house. Involved spy thriller begins well, soon becomes routine. Dubbed in English. (Dir: Yvan Govar, 90 mins.)

Agent 3S3/Passport to Hell (Italy-France-Spain, 1965)* George Ardisson, Georges Riviere. (Dir: Sergio Solima, 101 mins.)

Agent Z55/Desperate Mission (Japan, 1964)* Jerry Cobb, Yoko Tani. (Dir: Roberto Bianchi Montero, 112 mins.)

Agony and the Ecstasy, The (1965)**½

9

Charlton Heston, Rex Harrison. The agony refers to Michelangelo's troubles during the painting of the Sistine Chapel, but there's a lot of irritations and historical inaccuracies along the way in this over-blown and finally tiresome account of the Italian artistic genius. Irving Stone's best-selling novel. (Dir: Carol Reed, 140 mins.)

Aguirre, the Wrath of God (West Germany, 1972)***½ Klaus Kinski, Ruy Guerra, Helena Rojo. Director Werner Herzog's film shows a party of Spanish conquistadors gradually succumbing to Herzog's animistic vision of nature as they plow through the Brazilian jungles in search of El Dorado. Rife with the disquieting, surrealistic images that are the purest expression of Herzog's considerable talent. (95 mins.)

Ah Wilderness (1935)***½ Lionel Barrymore, Mickey Rooney, Wallace Beery. O'Neill's poignant, yet warm story of a boy breaking through the shackles of adolescence receives an excellent screen treatment. May appear dated but only because adolescents have changed since 1906 when film takes place. (Dir: Clarence Brown, 100 mins.)

Aida (Italy, 1954)**½ Sophia Loren, Lois Maxwell. If you can overcome your reaction to the humorous sight of Miss Loren pretending to sing, you will enjoy this first color version of Verdi's excellent opera. The voices include Tebaldi and Campora. (Dir: Clemente Fracassi, 96 mins.)

Ain't Misbehavin' (1955)**½ Rory Calhoun, Piper Laurie, Jack Carson. Mildly amusing comedy about a sexy chorine (Miss Laurie) who marries a millionaire tycoon and then has to learn how to get along in high society. Every girl should have Piper's problems! (Dir: Edward Buzzell, 82 mins.)

Ain't No Time for Glory (1957)** Barry Sullivan, Gene Barry. American officer tries to take a German-held fortress. Talky World War II drama, originally produced as a "Playhouse 90" TV feature. (78 mins.)

Air Cadet (1951)** Stephen McNally, Gail Russell. Another routine drama about the training of a group of jet air cadets, and how they finally turn into flying aces. (Dir: Joseph Pevney, 94 mins.)

Air Force (1943)*** John Garfield, Arthur Kennedy, Faye Emerson. Another exciting war story about an army plane which takes off for the Pacific, December 6, 1941. Again, forget the propaganda, and watch an exciting film. (Dir: Howard Hawks, 124 mins.)

Air Patrol (1962)* Willard Parker, Merry Anders. (Dir: Maury Dexter, 70 mins.)

Air Strike (1955)** Richard Denning, Gloria Jean. A navy commander tries to mold a jet fighting unit into an efficient fighting machine. Cheaply-made service melodrama, about average. (Dir: Cy Roth, 63 mins.)

Airborne (1962)* Bobby Diamond, Robert Christan. (Dir: James Landis, 80 mins.)

Airport (1970)*** Burt Lancaster, Dean Martin, Helen Hayes, Jacqueline Bisset, Jean Seberg, Van Heflin. Entertaining film and a big box-office hit. Miss Hayes is so memorable as an unlikely stowaway of 70 who manages to visit her daughter whenever the spirit moves her, she's worth the film. Add to her performance the scene of a busy bustling metropolitan airport, beset not only with tracking her down, but by the tragic madness of a passenger whose attache case holds a bomb. Hayes won a supporting Oscar. (Dir: George Seaton, 137 mins.)

Airport 1975 (1974)** Charlton Heston, Karen Black, George Kennedy, Efrem Zimbalist, Jr., Helen Reddy, Sid Caesar. A tacky successor to "Airport." Heston plays an airline troubleshooter whose derring-do involves transferring from a helicopter to the cockpit of a disabled 747 being flown by stewardess Karen Black. Most of the acting and all of the writing is terrible, but the cinematography and special effects are well done. (Dir: Jack Smight, 106 mins.)

Airport '77 (1977)**½ Jack Lemmon, Lee Grant, Olivia de Havilland, Joseph Cotten, James Stewart. First-rate schlock: overlong and incredibly stupid, but that's part of the formula. An executive jet, piloted by Lemmon, is the victim of incompetent hijackers who run it into an offshore oil rig, sending a planeload of panic-stricken character actors to the bottom of the sea. As McGavin says, "The depletion of the oxygen supply could become a crucial factor in survival." Albert Whitlock's special effects are a show in themselves. (Dir: Jerry Jameson, 113 mins.)

Aku Aku (1959)*** Generally interesting documentary despite the amateurish camerawork, as Thor Heyerdahl, of "Kon Tiki" fame, explores Easter Island and makes some fascinating discoveries. (60 mins.)

Al Capone (1959)***½ Rod Steiger, Fay Spain, Martin Balsam. An excellent performance by Rod Steiger raises this crime drama several notches above the average fare. The setting is the Prohibition area in Chicago when Capone controlled everything. (Dir: Richard Wilson, 104 mins.)

Alakazam the Great (1961)*** Nice little cartoon feature for the younger set. About a smart monkey who fancies himself brighter than humans until he learns otherwise. Originally Japanese-made; voices heard include Jonathan Winters, Frankie Avalon, Dodie Stevens. (Dir: Lee Kresel, 84 mins.)

Alambrista! (1978)*** Domingo Ambriz, Linda Gillin, Ned Beatty, Trinidad Silva. Originally produced as part of the public TV series "Visions," director Robert M. Young's examinations of Mexican farmworkers who enter the United States illegally to find work is characteristic of his direct approach. Winner of the Camera d'Or Award at the '78 Cannes Film Festival.

Alamo, The (1960)*½ John Wayne, Richard Widmark, Laurence Harvey. (Dir: John Wayne, 192 mins.)

Alarm on 83rd Street (1965)*½ George Nader, Sylvia Pascal. (Dir: Edward Bernds, 91 mins.)

Alaska Passage (1959)*½ Bill Williams, Nora Hayden. (Dir: Edward Bernds, 72 mins.)

Alaska Seas (1954)** Robert Ryan, Gene Barry, Jan Sterling, Brian Keith. Exjailbird is given a chance by his former partner in an Alaskan salmon cannery, but joins a gang of robbers. Lukewarm remake of "Spawn of the North." (Dir: Jerry Hopper, 78 mins.)

Albert Schweitzer (1957)*** Documentary story of the famed doctor and his African medical work. Continually interesting, good narration spoken by Fredric March. (Dir: Jerome Hill, 80 mins.)

Alcatraz Express (1962)**½ Robert Stack, Neville Brand. From "The Untouchables" series, this tells of Al Capone's ride to Atlanta Penitentiary after a conviction for income-tax evasion, and of Eliot Ness making sure he gets there. It still looks like a TV show, but manages to whip up a good amount of suspense. (96 mins.)

Alcatraz: The Whole Shocking Story (MTV 1980)*½ Michael Beck, Telly Savalas.(Dir: Paul Krasny, 104 mins.)

Alex and the Gypsy (1976)½ Jack Lemmon, Genevieve Bujold, James Woods. (Dir: John Korty, 99 mins.)

Alex in Wonderland (1970)**½ Donald Sutherland, Ellen Burstyn, Federico Fellini, Jeanne Moreau, Paul Mazursky. Director Mazursky's film is a mess and a failure, but many parts are worth seeing. Sutherland plays a director who has one hit behind him and doesn't know what to do next. Neither, apparently, did Mazursky, evidently suffering from Fellini-on-the-brain (Fellini plays a bit part). Some of the scenes between Sutherland and wife Burstyn achieve a behavioral tenderness unusual in any film. (109 mins.)

Alexander Nevsky (U.S.S.R., 1938)**** Nikolai Cherkassov. Sergei Eisenstein produced and directed this film opera on the great Russian prince's repulse of the Teutonic Knights as an exercise in visual and aural counterpoint. Edward Tisse's superb photography and Sergei Prokofiev's stirring musical score set up a rhythm and a tension, culminating in the great battle on the ice, that is irresistible. A turning point for Eisenstein, from the masses as hero to the individual in his isolation. (112 mins.)

Alexander the Great (1956)***½ Richard Burton, Fredric March, Claire Bloom. Lavish spectacle that just misses being a truly good film. Burton is brilliant in several of his major scenes. (Dir: Robert Rossen, 141 mins.)

Alexander the Great (1968)*½ William Shatner, John Cassavetes, Joseph Cotten, Simon Oakland. Produced in 1964, shown in 1968. (Dir: Phil Karlson, 60 mins.)

Alexander: The Other Side of Dawn (MTV 1977)**½ Eve Plumb, Leigh McCloskey. Good-looking Alexander (Leigh McCloskey), hustles women and men on Hollywood Boulevard because he can't land a job. The homosexual aspect is treated with relative care. (Dir: John Erman, 106 mins.)

Alexander's Ragtime Band (1938)***½ Tyrone Power, Alice Faye, Don Ameche, Ethel Merman. Sentimental story of some performers taking them from 1911–1938, serves as a nice excuse for 26 Irving Berlin all-time hits. (Dir: Henry King, 105 mins.)

Alfie (Great Britain, 1966)**** Michael Caine, Shelley Winters, Millicent Martin. This is the film which catapulted Michael Caine to stardom and his performance as an unscrupulous womanizing male is excellent. Alfie is a lecher and he lets you know it right from the start (Caine's talking to the audience really works). The romantic excursions are consistently and honestly portrayed. (Dir: Lewis Gilbert, 114 mins.)

Alfred Nobel Story, The (Germany, 1952)**½ Dieter Borsche, Hilde Krahl. English-dubbed biography of the discoverer of dynamite and initiator of the Peace Prize. Fairly well done. Alternative title: **No Greater Love.** (Dir: Harold Braun, 91 mins.)

Alfred the Great (Great Britain, 1969)* David Hemmings, Michael York, Prunella Ransome. (Dir: Clive Donner, 122 mins.)

Alfredo, Alfredo (Italy, 1973)***½ Dustin Hoffman, Stefania Sandrelli, Carla Gravina. Hoffman (dubbed into Italian and subtitled back into English) is wonderful as an amiable bank clerk who escapes one harrowing marriage only to land in another in director Pietro Germi's domestic comedy. Most of the film is stylish and funny. (97 mins.)

Algiers (1938)*** Charles Boyer, Hedy Lamarr, Sigrid Gurie. The story of Pepe LeMoko, the crook who sought refuge from the police in the Casbah of North Africa, perhaps Boyer's most famous role. (Dir: John Cromwell, 100 mins.)

Ali-Baba (French, 1954)** Fernandel, Samia Gamal. The Gallic funny-faced comic seems out of place romping around in this Arabian Nights tale. Some amusing moments, not enough. (Dir: Jacques Becker, 80 mins.)

Ali Baba and the Forty Thieves (1944)*½ Jon Hall, Turhan Bey, Andy Devine, Maria Montez, Frank Puglia. (Dir: Arthur Lubin, 87 mins.)

Ali Baba and the Sacred Crown (1963)*½ Rod Flash, Celia Cortez. (Dir: Emimmo Salvi, 95 mins.)

Ali Baba and the Seven Saracens (Italy,

1965)* Dan Harrison, Bella Cortez, Gordon Mitchell. Dubbed in English. (Dir: Emimmo Salvi, 83 mins.)

Ali Baba Goes to Town (1937)**½ Eddie Cantor, Tony Martin, June Lang, Gypsy Rose Lee, Roland Young. Another musical Cantor romp, with Eddie in the time of the Arabian Nights. The usual monkey business, plus a young Martin's fine singing. (Dir: David Butler, 81 mins.)

Ali: Fear Eats the Soul (West Germany, 1974)*** El Hedi, Ben Salem, Brigitte Mira, Rainer Werner Fassbinder (as Eugen). Director Fassbinder presents a May-December romance between an aging German hausfrau and a Moroccan immigrant laborer. The visual style emphasizes artificially cheerful primary colors and frames within the frame. The zomboid emotions are pure Fassbinder—never has banality been so devastating. (93 mins.)

Alias a Gentleman (1948)** Wallace Beery, Tom Drake. Reformed crook's ex-partner hires a girl to pose as his former confederate's daughter. Ordinary film. (Dir: Harry Beaumont, 76 mins.)

Alias Jesse James (1959)*** Bob Hope, Rhonda Fleming, Wendell Corey. Eastern insurance company sends its worst agent out West to protect a client, who turns out to be the notorious outlaw. Diverting Hope spoof of Westerns; some gags miss the mark, but most land on the funnybone. Particularly funny ending. (Dir: Norman McLeod, 92 mins.)

Alias John Preston (Great Britain, 1955)** Betta St. John, Alexander Knox, Christopher Lee. Mysterious young man becomes the pillar of a small-town community, but begins to be bothered by strange dreams. Unexceptional, psychological drama. (Dir: David Macdonald, 66 mins.)

Alias Nick Beal (1949)***½ Ray Milland, Thomas Mitchell, Audrey Totter. Honest district attorney is sidetracked in his crime crusade by a mysterious stranger. Absorbing fantasy with fine performances. (Dir: John Farrow, 93 mins.)

Alias Smith & Jones (MTV 1971)*½ Pete Duel, Ben Murphy. (Dir: Gene Levitt, 72 mins.)

Alibi for Death, An (W. Germany, 1964)** Peter Van Eyck, Ruth Leuwerik. Interesting if unlikely saga of a man accused of a hit-and-run killing. He claims the dead man was pushed in front of his truck. While most of the movie is routine, the ending is rather original. (Dir: Alfred Vohrer, 97 mins.)

Alice Adams (1935)**** Katharine Hepburn, Fred MacMurray, Evelyn Venable. Director George Stevens broke into the big time with his single masterpiece, this adaptation of Booth Tarkington's novel. The slow buildup cultivated by Stevens in his Roach comedies is brilliantly embroidered into the painful social comedy of pretentious Hepburn putting on airs and paying in anguish for her aspirations. The consequences of middle-class failure

are conveyed with compassion and objectivity. (99 mins.)

Alice Doesn't Live Here Anymore (1974)**** Ellen Burstyn, Kris Kristofferson, Alfred Lutter, Jodie Foster. Memorable, poignant, often funny comedy-drama about a 35-year-old widow who finds her identity while being obliged to cope with the sometimes harsh reality of economic survival. Burstyn is wonderful playing Alice and deservedly won an Academy Award for her many-shaded portrait of an itinerant ex-housewife turned waitress-singer trying to support herself and her 12-year-old son, winningly played by Lutter. Shot on location throughout New Mexico and the Southwest, the film's impact is based largely on fine acting, good direction from Martin Scorsese, and an unusually deft, original screenplay by Robert Getchell. The basis of the TV series "Alice" and its spinoff "Flo." (112 mins.)

Alice in the Cities (West Germany, 1974)***½ Rudiger Vogeler, Yella Rottlander, Elizabeth Kreuzer. Breakthrough film for director Wim Wenders, about an alienated German journalist trying to Hunter Thompson his way through the East Coast of America and ending up with a small girl in tow. Possible winsomenesses of the plot complications are refreshingly sidestepped. (110 mins.)

Alice in the Navy (Greece, 1965)* Aliki Vouyouclaki, Dimitri Papamichael. (Dir: Alekos Sakelarios, 90 mins.)

Alice in Wonderland (1933)*** W. C. Fields, All-Star Cast. Ambitious film version of the classic fantasy; but lovers of the book will not find the film satisfactory. (Dir: Norman McLeod, 80 mins.)

Alice in Wonderland (British, 1950)**½ Carole Marsh, Pamela Brown, Bunin Puppets. Combination of live action and puppets is interesting, faithful to Lewis Carroll's book, but the film is rather disjointed. (Dir: Dallas Bower, 83 mins.)

Alice in Wonderland (1951)***½ Animated. Taken, of course, from Lewis Carroll's classic. Though not as popular when first released as Disney's other animated features, it has grown steadily in favor. Wonderfully entertaining, and children will never forget that Cheshire Cat! With the voices of Ed Wynn as the Mad Hatter; Sterling Holloway, Cheshire Cat; Jerry Colonna, March Hare; Kathryn Beaumont, Alice. (Dirs: Clyde Geronimi, Hamilton Luske, Wilfred Jackson, 75 mins.)

Alice Sweet Alice (1976)***½ Linda Miller, Paula Sheppard, Brooke Shields, Lillian Roth. Put together on a Woolworth budget and shot in suburban New Jersey, this sleeper broaches more serious moral issues than most American films even dream of. This thriller concerns a childhood trauma which leads to murder. Alfred Sole is a director to watch, if he ever moves up in budget. Re-released as **Holy Terror** in 1981. (108 mins.)

12

Alice's Adventures in Wonderland (Great Britain, 1972)* Fiona Fullerton, Ralph Richardson, Peter Sellers. (Dir: William Sterling, 100 mins.)

Alice's Restaurant (1969)**** Arlo Guthrie, Pat Quinn, James Broderick. Director Arthur Penn's film is loose, episodic, and deeply felt. Based on Arlo Guthrie's best-selling LP, which recounted his adventures and subsequent arrest for littering. This scene and a remarkably funny one where Arlo is momentarily inducted into the U.S. Army help sustain this striking film, a commentary on how some of our youth felt about our society in the late '60s. Arlo is appealing in his movie debut. (111 mins.)

Alien (1979)** Sigourney Weaver, Ian Holm, Yaphet Kotto, Tom Skerritt, Veronica Cartwright. About a spaceship crew menaced by a deadly creature the ship has taken aboard. This amalgam of "Star Wars" and "The Exorcist" has a distinctive look due to director Ridley Scott, but it's a thin thriller, overly dependent on slimy gruesomeness and badly milked suspense. Scott uses little finesse in building tension and is too unconventional to carry off a genre number with conviction. The excellent cast has little to do. (124 mins.)

Alien, The (The Netherlands, 1980)½ Director Rudolf van den Berg's offensive documentary purports to ask Jews what their sense of identity consists of and twists the answers to serve a blatantly anti-Zionist purpose. This kind of sophistry is unlikely to calm tempers, and, however well intentioned, provides fodder for the argument that all anti-Zionism is racist.

Aliens Are Coming, The (MTV 1980)*½ Tom Mason, Melinda Fee, Max Gail, Caroline McWilliams. (Dir: Harvey Hart, 104 mins.)

Alive and Kicking (Great Britain, 1958)*** Sybil Thorndike, Kathleen Harrison, Estelle Winwood, Stanley Holloway. Genial comedy about three cronies at an old ladies' home who run away when they learn they are to be moved. Good cast, pleasant fun. (Dir: Cyril Frankel, 94 mins.)

All About Eve (1950)**** Bette Davis, Anne Baxter, George Sanders, Celeste Holm, Gary Merrill, Thelma Ritter, Marilyn Monroe. One of the best comedy-dramas of all time. Witty, sophisticated and thoroughly entertaining film dealing with the theater and those who toil in it. Multiprize winner including 7 Oscars. Don't miss this one. (Dir: Joseph L. Mankiewicz, 138 mins.)

All American, The (1953)** Tony Curtis, Lori Nelson, Mamie Van Doren. Stilted drama about college football heroes and their problems. (Dir: Jesse Hibbs, 80 mins.)

All American Boy, The (1973)** Jon Voight, Carol Androsky, Anne Archer. Voight skillfully plays an alienated boxer who desperately wants to leave his town, but does not want to commit himself to anything or anyone. Some nice touches scattered along the way, but clumsy. (Writer-Dir: Charles Eastman, 118 mins.)

All Around Reduced Personality (Redupers), The (West Germany, 1978)**½ Helke Sander, Joachim Baumann, Andrea Malkowsky. Story of a commercial photographer who joins a feminist group for a study of contemporary Berlin. Moderately interesting. Grand prizewinner at the '78 Berlin Film Festival. (Dir: Helke Sander, 98 mins.)

All Ashore (1953)** Mickey Rooney, Dick Haymes, Peggy Ryan. Same old musical about three sailors on leave and their adventures. Dick Haymes sings some ballads in his usual fine style. (Dir: Richard Quine, 80 mins.)

All at Sea (Great Britain, 1958)***½ Alec Guinness, Irene Browne. An often hilarious comedy about a seasick skipper, who finds himself in charge of one of the most unusual vessels ever seen. (Dir: Charles Frend, 83 mins.)

All at Sea (Great Britain, 1969)* Gary Smith, Steven Mallett. (Dir: Ken Fairbairn, 60 mins.)

All Fall Down (1962)**½ Eva Marie Saint, Warren Beatty, Karl Malden, Angela Lansbury. Wild lad with a way with women is attracted to a girl in town for a visit. Implausible drama, generally well acted. (Dir: John Frankenheimer, 110 mins.)

All for Mary (Great Britain, 1955)** Nigel Patrick, Kathleen Harrison. Old woman straightens out a romance at a Swiss hotel. Dull comedy doesn't do right by the players. (Dir: Wendy Toye, 79 mins.)

All God's Children (MTV 1980)**½ Richard Widmark, Ned Beatty, Ossie Davis, Ruby Dee, Trish Van Devere. Dramatic impact of an important and topical issue—forced busing to achieve racial equality in education—squandered by a screenplay wasting time on phony plot distractions; despite a top-notch cast, the script bogs down the story, allowing only Widmark's sage judge to overcome the mediocrity. Centers on the lives of a black family, a white family, and one son from each family. The sons are best friends. (Dir: Jerry Thorpe, 104 mins.)

All Hands on Deck (1961)*½ Pat Boone, Buddy Hackett, Barbara Eden, Dennis O'Keefe. (Dir: Norman Taurog, 98 mins.)

All I Desire (1953)***½ Barbara Stanwyck, Richard Carlson, Maureen O'Sullivan, Lyle Bettger, Lori Nelson. A failed actress and mother of three (Stanwyck) returns to the husband (Carlson) and family she deserted years before, in director Douglas Sirk's superior and very personal reworking of a standard soap opera plot. A biting assessment of the value of survival in the face of small-town meanness and prejudice. (70 mins.)

All in a Night's Work (1961)*** Shirley MacLaine, Dean Martin, Cliff Robertson.

When a tycoon dies under mysterious circumstances, his nephew inherits the empire. Sophisticated comedy, brightly paced, pleasant performances. (Dir: Joseph Anthony, 94 mins.)

All Mine to Give (1957)**½ Glynis Johns, Cameron Mitchell. Long, sad saga of a brave pioneer family and their hardships in early Wisconsin. Good performances give some spark to the tale. (Dir: Allen Reisner, 102 mins.)

All My Darling Daughters (MTV 1972)**½ Robert Young. Enjoyable family fare finds Robert Young playing the kindly father, watching his four daughters marry in a single ceremony. Star Young has Raymond Massey as a caustic father-in-law for grownup company. (Dir: David Lowell Rich, 72 mins.)

All My Sons (1948)***½ Edward G. Robinson, Burt Lancaster, Howard Duff. Wealthy man's son accuses him of war profiteering. Frequently gripping, based on Broadway play by Arthur Miller. Well acted. (Dir: Irving Reis, 94 mins.)

All Night Long (1981)*** Gene Hackman, Barbra Streisand, Dennis Quaid, Kevin Dobson, Diane Ladd. An inspired comedy from a highly original talent, Jean-Claude Tramont, a Belgian director making his American feature debut. A gentle comedy of contrasts quite unlike anything we've seen before. Gene Hackman is brilliantly attuned to Tramont's off-center view of American society; his executive-on-the-skids resurrects the neglected skills of character mime in a naturalistic context. It's tonic to experience a comedy concerned with texture and line, with sight gags and aural jokes instead of one-liners, and with *mise-en-scene* as the conveyer of personal expression in a comedy. Barbra Streisand is restrained almost beyond recognition. (Dir: Jean-Claude Tramont).

All Night Long (Great Britain, 1962)*** Patrick McGoohan, Betsy Blair, Paul Harris, Richard Attenborough. "Othello" in a modern jazz background. An ambitious drummer sets out to discredit a top jazzman by compromising his wife. Some fine swingin' music by top players such as Brubeck, Dankworth, Mingus, etc. (Dir: Michael Relph, 95 mins.)

All Nudity Shall Be Punished (Brazil, 1973)**** Darlene Gloria, Paulo Porto, Paulo Sacks. Wonderful, bawdy, satiric, and imaginative comedy about an unlikely love affair between a middle-aged bourgeois and a spunky prostitute gloriously acted by Darlene Gloria. This is one of the most inventive and telling comedies in years. English subtitles. (Writer-Dir: Arnaldo Jabor, 97 mins.)

All Over the Town (Great Britain, 1949)***½ Sarah Churchill, Norman Wooland. Young newspaper editor battles a powerful advertiser. Mildly pleasant romantic comedy-drama. (Dir: Derek Twist, 88 mins.)

All Quiet on the Western Front (1930)**** Lew Ayres, Louis Wolheim, Ben Alexander. Lewis Milestone's Oscar-winning adaptation of Erich Maria Remarque's classic novel has a long overinflated critical reputation but still retains its naive passion, and even when it's being obvious, it's potent. The film lurches stylistically without a coherent visual plan, but Wolheim's noncom dominates the action and transcends the cinematic limitations. There were more personally expressive antiwar films in its wake, but this one's the chairman of the board. (130 mins.)

All Quiet on the Western Front (MTV 1979)**** Richard Thomas, Ernest Borgnine, Ian Holm, Donald Pleasence, Patricia Neal. Remarque's classic novel about WW I from the German point of view. This retelling, as seen through the eyes of the young, idealistic student-turned-soldier, is very good indeed. Thomas, in the leading role, manages an appealing validity and earnestness. Stunning photography, done on location in Europe. One of the best made-for-TV movies of the '70s. (Dir: Delbert Mann, 155 mins.)

All Screwed Up (Italy, 1973)***½ Luigi Diberti, Lina Polito, Isa Danieli. Excellent minor comedy directed by Lina Wertmuller, shorter than usual on big ideas but more concrete in their development. About a group of young people who come to the big city and industrialized urban living. Weird prose, trying for poetry, and the usual Wertmuller mixture of bad taste, spastic cutting, and mordant wit. Polito is especially affecting. (105 mins.)

All That Heaven Allows (1955)*** Jane Wyman, Rock Hudson, Agnes Moorehead, Conrad Nagel, Virginia Grey. The story (which Rainer Werner Fassbinder remade as "Ali—Fear Eats the Soul") concerns a romance between a middle-aged, middle-class widow and a brawny young gardener—the stuff of a standard weepie, you might think, until director Douglas Sirk's camera begins to draw a deeply disturbing, deeply compassionate portrait of a woman trapped by stifling moral and social codes. (89 mins.)

All That Jazz (1979)**½ Roy Scheider, Jessica Lange, Ann Reinking. Scheider is superb as Joe Gideon, a womanizing, chain-smoking, pill-popping director-choreographer of a Broadway musical. Bob Fosse directed this surrealistic film loosely based on his own life. The opening number, "On Broadway," and the closing number, "Bye, Bye Life," are brilliant. There are some marvelous dance numbers, but much of the screenplay coauthored by Fosse and writer Robert Alan Aurthur is sophomoric, sentimental, egomaniacal drivel. Oscars for costume design, adaptation, score. (119 mins.)

All That Money Can Buy—See: **Devil and Daniel Webster, The**

All the Brothers Were Valiant (1953)**½

14

Robert Taylor, Stewart Granger, Ann Blyth. Two strong-willed New England whaling captains, come to grips when one decides to go after lost treasure rather than blubber. Ann Blyth co-stars as Taylor's new bride, whose presence on the vessel adds to the trouble. Plenty of action. (Dir: Richard Thorpe, 95 mins.)

All the Fine Young Cannibals (1960)** Natalie Wood, Robert Wagner, Susan Kohner, Pearl Bailey, George Hamilton. Muddled soap opera about a headstrong girl who is loved by one lad but marries another. (Dir: Michael Anderson, 112 mins.)

All the Kind Strangers (MTV 1974)**½ Stacy Keach, Samantha Eggar, John Savage, Robby Benson. This tale of quiet terror begins with photographer-journalist Keach giving a young boy a ride to his secluded farmhouse...There, he meets the rest of the kids and a young woman (Eggar) whom they call mother. (Dir: Burt Kennedy, 72 mins.)

All the King's Horses (1935)*½ Carl Brisson, Mary Ellis. (Dir: Frank Tuttle, 87 mins.)

All the King's Men (1949)***½ Broderick Crawford, Mercedes McCambridge, Joanne Dru, John Ireland, John Derek. Though Robert Rossen's direction tends to become oppressive in its mood of high seriousness and strenuous import, the performances of Crawford (as the Huey Long-like redneck politician who climbs into the seat of power and abruptly sinks into the sewer of corruption) and McCambridge (as his tough-talking assistant) break through the film's murky veil. The rest of the cast are excellent. Oscars for Crawford, Best Actor; McCambridge, Supporting Actress; Best Film. (109 mins.)

All the Loving Couples (1969)** Norman Alden, Gloria Manon, Paul Lambert. An interesting item from the old days of softcore porno, this garnered some favorable critical notices upon its release. The plot concerns a mate-swapping party at the home of an impotent John Bircher and his bisexual wife in the San Fernando Valley. The games start with spin the bottle and move on from there. My guess is that it would hardly garner an X rating today. Mack Bing directed, and I smell a pseudonym. (76 mins.)

All the President's Men (1976)**** Dustin Hoffman, Robert Redford, Jason Robards, Jr., Jane Alexander, Martin Balsam, Jack Warden. One of the triumphs of this spellbinding political thriller about the Watergate-related events leading to the resignation of President Nixon is that the audience is constantly fascinated and involved, despite the fact that we already know, to use a metaphor of the Old West, who the villain is, and that he will be captured by the posse but never brought fully to justice. Thanks to all concerned, especially to director Alan J. Pakula, there is nary a false note in this entire real-life

melodrama. The astonishingly high level of the ensemble acting is extraordinary. Jason Robards, Jr., giving his best film performance in years, won and deserved the Academy Award for supporting actor. Hoffman and Redford come across like dogged professional newspapermen, not Hollywood superstars imitating political reporters. Expertly adapted from the Woodward and Bernstein book by William Goldman. (Dir: Alan J. Pakula, 136 mins.)

All the Way Home (1963)***½ Jean Simmons, Robert Preston, Pat Hingle, Michael Kearney. Adapted from Tad Mosel's prize-winning play, which in turn was based on James Agee's Pulitzer Prize-winning novel about the death of the head of a family in rural America during the early 1900's and its effects upon his small son. Acting is uneven, but much of it is poignant and moving. (Dir: Alex Segal, 103 mins.)

All the Young Men (1960)**½ Alan Ladd, Sidney Poitier, James Darren. All the young men are types you met in so many other war films set in Korea. (Dir: Hal Bartlett, 87 mins.)

All These Women (Sweden, 1964)**½ Bibi Andersson, Carl Billquist. Director Ingmar Bergman's first film in color is disappointing. A critic makes a deal with a concert cellist to write his autobiography if the cellist will play the critic's compositions. The pacing is slow, even for Bergman, but all the actors deliver excellent performances. (Dir: Ingmar Bergman, 80 mins.)

All Things Bright and Beautiful (Great Britain, 1978)*** John Alderton, Lisa Harrow, Colin Blakely. One of several films based on the autobiographical books of James Herriot, a vet in the magnificent north Yorkshire dales. Set just before WW II, with Alderton and Harrow as newlyweds, and newcomers to the region. Low-key, gentle, well acted. (Dir: Eric Till, 94 mins.)

All This and Heaven, Too (1940)** Bette Davis, Charles Boyer, Barbara O'Neil. Big, long, yet not florid enough rendition of a trashy best-seller, with Boyer as a 19th-century French aristocrat who murders his wife (O'Neil, stealing the picture) to run off with the governess (Davis). Sudses up a storm, and while director Anatole Litvak can make individually impressive directorial decisions, the project reeks of just too, too much. Adapted by Casey Robinson from the Rachel Field novel, with photography by Ernest Haller and music by the redoubtable Max Steiner. (143 mins.)

All Through the Night (1942)*** Humphrey Bogart, Conrad Veidt, Peter Lorre, Judith Anderson, Jackie Gleason, Phil Silvers. Sheer fun and games, with Bogart breaking up a Nazi spy ring. All nonsense, no art, a gas. Vincent Sherman directed this screwy mix of genres; he does a lot of things wrong, but it all comes out in the

15

wash. One of TV's Sgt. Bilko's early movie efforts. (107 mins.)

All Together Now (MTV 1975)**½ Bill Macy, Jane Withers, John Rubinstein, Glynnis O'Connor. A family of four orphans decides to go it alone with their older brother at the head of the household, and they have to convince their relatives they can make it. (Dir: Randall Kleiser, 72 mins.)

All Women Have Secrets (1940)*½ Jean Cagney, Joseph Allen. (Dir: Kurt Neumann, 74 mins.)

Allegro Non Troppo (Italy, 1977)***½ Easily the most graceful, intelligent, and imaginative animated film of the last 20 years. Director Bruno Bozzetto's feature uses the classical music format of "Fantasia" to create a beautiful but pointed fantasy that satirizes life in the machine age. Bozzetto effortlessly transcends Disney's naturalistic bias to discover a breathtaking freedom of color and movement. Slightly marred by clumsy live-action sequences. (85 mins.)

Alligator (1980)**½ Robert Forster, Robin Riker. A thoroughly pleasant, modestly entertaining exploitation film that moves along amiably. With some wit and no cant, it may be the best low-budget monster movie since "Piranha," of which it is a virtual remake. Forster and Riker are good; there are obvious cameos by Michael Gazzo, Henry Silva, Jack Carter, and Dean Jagger. Good jobs by Brandon Chase, producer, and Lewis Teague, director.

Alligator Named Daisy, An (Great Britain, 1955)**½ Diana Dors, Donald Sinden. Young man gets saddled with a pet alligator, meets a girl who loves 'em both. Fairly pleasant comedy. (Dir: J. Lee Thompson, 88 mins.)

Alligator People, The (1959)*½ Beverly Garland, Lon Chaney, Bruce Bennett. (Dir: Roy Del Ruth, 74 mins.)

Almost Human—See: **Shock Wave**

Almost Perfect Affair, An (1979)*** Keith Carradine, Monica Vitti, Raf Vallone, Dick Anthony Williams. Pleasant light romance against the backdrop of the Cannes Film Festival. Lots of local color, most of it imported. Carradine is an innocent abroad who has an affair with the wife of a producing magnate (Vallone). Vitti again displays her chic flair for comedy, and Williams is a delightful hustler. Michael Ritchie directed; this shows he's getting better all the time. (93 mins.)

Almost Summer (1978)***½ Bruno Kirby, Lee Purcell, John Friedrich, Didi Conn, Tim Matheson. The best teen pic in a long time. Universal spent enough for the gloss to seem slightly sinful, but the writing is astute and witty, the story (crooked politics in a student council election) engrossing, and the acting, especially by Kirby, Friedrich, and Matheson, full of conviction and subtlety. Martin Davidson directs gracefully. As for Conn, to quote Luis

Alberni in "Easy Living," "Too much is enough." (88 mins.)

Aloha, Bobby and Rose (1975)* Paul Le Mat, Dianne Hull, Martine Bartlett. (Dir: Floyd Mutrux, 89 mins.)

Aloha Means Goodbye (MTV 1974)* Sally Struthers, James Franciscus, Joanna Miles, Henry Darrow. (Dir: David Lowell Rich, 100 mins.)

Aloma of the South Seas (1941)*½ Dorothy Lamour, Jon Hall. (Dir: Alfred Santell, 77 mins.)

Alone Against Rome (Italy, 1962)*½ Lang Jeffries, Rossana Podesta, Philippe Leroy. (Dir: Herbert Wise, 100 mins.)

Along Came a Spider (1970)**½ Suzanne Pleshette, Ed Nelson. A young widow goes to incredible lengths to prove that a prof. was responsible for her scientist-husband's death. (Dir: Lee Katzin, 72 mins.)

Along Came Jones (1945)***½ Gary Cooper, Loretta Young, Dan Duryea. A mild-mannered cowpoke is mistaken for a notorious killer, nearly gets killed by both sides of the law. Humorous, enjoyable western, a good show. (Dir: Stuart Heisler, 90 mins.)

Along Came Youth (1931)* Buddy Rogers, Frances Dee, Stuart Erwin. (Dirs: Lloyd Corrigan, Norman McLeod, 72 mins.)

Along the Great Divide (1951)**½ Kirk Douglas, Virginia Mayo, Walter Brennan. Slow paced but interesting western drama about the capture and return to justice of an escaped criminal. Excellent desert photography. (Dir: Raoul Walsh, 88 mins.)

Along the Mohawk Trail (1956)*½ John Hart, Lon Chaney. (89 mins.)

Alpha Beta (Great Britain, 1973)***½ Albert Finney, Rachel Roberts. Lacerating drama, based on the British hit play by E. A. Whitehead. Superb performances by the two stars as they torment and torture each other during the course of a rotting marriage. Finney is magnificent, whether taunting his wife or contemplating his bleak future. (Dir: Anthony Page, 67 mins.)

Alpha Caper, The (MTV 1973)**½ Henry Fonda, Larry Hagman, Leonard Nimoy, James McEachin. A knowledgeable probation officer, forced to retire, uses excons to heist a huge shipment of gold ingots. (Dir: Robert Lewis, 90 mins.)

Alphabet Murders, The (Great Britain, 1966)** Tony Randall, Anita Ekberg, Robert Morley. (Dir: Frank Tashlin, 90 mins.)

Alphaville (France, 1965)**½ Eddie Constantine, Anna Karina, Akim Tamiroff. Pretentious juvenile fantasy about a troubleshooter sent to a distant planet where the dictator has a race of robots doing his bidding. Typically Gallic idea of American sci-fi tough-guy style. Visually, director Jean-Luc Godard's most striking early film. (100 mins.)

Altered States (1980)*** Blair Brown, William Hurt, Charles Haid. Paddy

Chayefsky had his name removed from the credits, although his novel is still listed as source material. Director Ken Russell plunges in with abandon. He attempts to overcome the built-in unreadability of Chayefsky's dialogue by having his players deliver their lines at breakneck pace, but it doesn't work. Little more than a spectacular head trip grafted onto a monster-movie plot. Bombastic, yet sustains interest with its elaborate production values. Light, laughable romantic comedy. (Dir: Ralph Smart, 83 mins.)

Alvarez Kelly (1966)*** William Holden, Richard Widmark, Janice Rule. Southern guerrilla officer Widmark decides to rustle some 2500 head of cattle for his side and meets up with adventurer Alvarez Kelly (William Holden). (Dir: Edward Dmytryk, 116 mins.)

Always a Bride (Great Britain, 1953)*** Peggy Cummins, Terence Morgan. Stuffy Treasury official gets mixed up with a confidence ring, including an attractive blonde. Light, laughable romantic comedy. (Dir: Ralph Smart, 83 mins.)

Always for Pleasure (1978)*** A good motto for musical documentarian Les Blank, who here directs the musical traditions of Mardi Gras for your toe-tapping joy. Performers include Professor Longhair ("the Bach of Rock"), the Wild Tchoupitoulas (with the Neville Brothers), Art Ryder's Electric Street Band, the Olympia Brass Band, and Kid Thomas Valentine. (000 mins.)

Always in My Heart (1942)**½ Walter Huston, Kay Francis. A man comes home after a long, unjust prison stretch and wins his daughter's love although she does not know his true identity. (Dir: Jo Graham, 92 mins.)

Always Leave Them Laughing (1949)**½ Milton Berle, Virginia Mayo. Milton is well cast as a comedian who rides to the top on everybody's jokes. Bert Lahr is wonderful in some old sketches. (Dir: Roy Del Ruth, 116 mins.)

Amarcord (Italy-France, 1973)**** Magali Noel, Bruno Zanin, Luigi Rossi. A joyous, beautiful film. Fellini's semi-autobiographical look back at life in the Italian provinces in the 1930's. Set in the seaside town of Rimini, Fellini is concerned with Italian fascism of the '30's under Mussolini. The screen is filled with an unending succession of dazzling, remarkable images which few other living directors can match. Screenplay by Fellini and Tonino Guerra. (Dir: Federico Fellini, 127 mins.)

Amateur Night at the Dixie Bar and Grill (MTV 1979)***½ Henry Gibson, Tanya Tucker, Candy Clark. Engaging melodrama set in a Dixie roadhouse which focuses on the crowd that hangs out there and the help that serves them booze and small talk. Director Schumacher, who also wrote the deft yarn which has moments of parody—as well as moments of homage to Altman's *Nashville*—skillfully guides a uniformly good cast which does not boast any big names. Screenplay has some snap to it, and it's one of the best made-for-TV films of the decade. (Dir: Joel Schumacher, 104 mins.)

Amazing Colossal Man (1957)** Glen Langan, Cathy Downs. Atomic effects make a guy grow and grow and grow. Science-fiction script drags. (Dir: Bert Gordon, 80 mins.)

Amazing Dr. Clitterhouse (1938)***½ Edward G. Robinson, Claire Trevor, Humphrey Bogart. Entertaining, amusing story of a psychiatrist who becomes a crook to study the criminal mind. (Dir: Anatole Litvak, 90 mins.)

Amazing Dr. G., The (Italy, 1965)** Franco Franchi, Gloria Paul, Fernando Rey, Ciccio Ingrassia. A creaky takeoff on the James Bond movies. Francho and Ciccio are a team, à la Martin and Lewis. (Dir: Giorgio C. Simonelli, 85 mins.)

Amazing Grace (1974)* Moms Mabley, Slappy White, Stepin Fetchit, Butterfly McQueen. (Dir: Stan Lathan, 99 mins.)

Amazing Howard Hughes, The (MTV 1977)*** Tommy Lee Jones, Ed Flanders, James Hampton, Tovah Feldshuh, Lee Purcell. An engrossing study of the puzzling eccentric who had an eye for Hollywood beauties but really preferred airplanes and gadgets to people. The movie becomes an account of a deteriorating human in need of psychiatric help, and rich enough to indulge in his eccentricities. The behind-the-scenes drama, supposedly authentic, offers a revealing portrait of a fascinating psychotic. (Dir: William Graham, 210 mins.)

Amazing Mrs. Holliday, The (1943)**½ Deanna Durbin, Edmond O'Brien, Barry Fitzgerald. A silly comedy with dramatic overtones about an American schoolteacher and a group of refugee children. (Dir: Bruce Manning, 96 mins.)

Amazing Transparent Man, The (1960)** Marguerite Chapman, Douglas Kennedy. Fair science-fiction yarn coupled with a crime story. A scientist tries his serum, which makes men transparent, on an ex-con who is dispatched to rob a bank. A neat trick that doesn't quite come off. (Dir: Edgar Ulmer, 59 mins.)

Amazons of Rome (Italy-France, 1963)* Louis Jourdan, Sylvia Syms, Nicole Courcel. Dubbed. (Dirs: Carlo L. Bragaglia, Vittorio Cottafavi, 93 mins.)

Ambassador's Daughter (1956)**½ Olivia de Havilland, John Forsythe, Myrna Loy. GI in Paris falls for ambassador's daughter. Strained comedy isn't as funny as it might have been. (Dir: Norman Krasna, 102 mins.)

Amber Waves (MTV 1980)***½ Dennis Weaver, Kurt Russell, Mare Winningham, Fran Brill. Moving drama transcends the soap opera overtones of the plot. Russell creates a thoroughly credible portrait of a brash, egocentric New York model thrown into the raw world of Midwest wheat harvesting, in contrast to the strong-willed yet surprisingly worldly farmer, perfectly played by Weaver. (Dir: Joseph Sargent, 104 mins.)

Ambush (1950)** Robert Taylor, Arlene Dahl, John Hodiak. (Dir: Sam Wood, 88 mins.)

Ambush at Cimarron Pass (1958)** Scott Brady, Clint Eastwood, Margia Dean. (Dir: Jodie Copelon, 73 mins.)

Ambush at Tomahawk Gap (1953)*** John Hodiak, John Derek, David Brian. Off-beat Western with a good story about four ex-convicts who band together to find some buried stolen money. Exciting climax. Good performances by all. (Dir: Fred Sears, 73 mins.)

Ambush Bay (1966)**½ Hugh O'Brian, Mickey Rooney, James Mitchum. A familiar WW II drama about two-fisted Marines in the Philippines on a special mission; well played by O'Brian and Rooney. Filmed on location. (Dir: Ron Winston, 109 mins.)

Ambush in Leopard Street (Great Britain, 1959)*½ James Kenney, Michael Brennan. (Dir: J Henry Piperno, 60 mins.)

Ambushers, The (1967)* Dean Martin, Senta Berger. (Dir: Henry Levin, 102 mins.)

Amelia Earhart (MTV 1976)*** Susan Clark, John Forsythe, Stephen Macht, Susan Oliver. Clark won an Emmy for her performance as Babe Didrikson Zaharias, one of the world's greatest athletes. She delivers the goods again as the much-publicized Amelia Earhart, America's heroine of the '20's and '30's who loved to fly but hated performing as a celebrity. Pretty good portrait of the good old days when the country abounded in larger-than-life heroes and heroines. Sequences transmit a surprising feeling for flying, explaining why pioneer Amelia and others, past and present, were so goofy about seat-of-your-pants aviation. Aerial sequences staged by Frank Tallman. (Dir: George Schaefer, 162 mins.)

Amelie (France, 1960)** Jean Sorel, Marie-Jose Nat. Girl returns to her childhood home, to find romance and tragedy. Brooding drama gets the arty treatment. Slow, confused. Dubbed. Alternate title: **A Time to Die.** (Dir: Michel Drach, 111 mins.)

America (1924)**** Neil Hamilton, Carol Dempster, Erville Alderson, Lionel Barrymore. Director D. W. Griffith's silent Revolutionary War epic is his most Dickensian film, both in its Victorian morality and its precise narrative structure. The family unit, the usual center of value in Griffith's work, here takes on new dimensions as the final shot transforms George Washington (Arthur Dewey) into a hauntingly literal "father" of his country. (120 mins.)

America, America (1963)**** Stathis Giallelis, Lou Antonio, John Marley. Written, produced and directed by Elia Kazan,

this is an eloquent tribute to Kazan's forebears, and to generations of immigrants who struggled to pursue their vision of the American dream. "America" focuses on one young Greek boy who works his way to the U.S. in the late 1890's. Using both professional and nonprofessional actors, Kazan captures much of the anguish and hope that drove millions to these shores. Enduring cinema valentine to all immigrants. (Dir: Elia Kazan, 174 mins.)

American Christmas Carol, An (MTV 1979)** Henry Winkler, David Wayne, Chris Wiggins. TV producers are always intrigued by the Dickens public domain classic about Scrooge and his transformation from a penny-pinching old codger to a generous soul. In this incarnation, Winkler is weighted down with makeup as old Mr. Slade (alias Scrooge), and time and place have been switched to the depression years in New England. The flashbacks are the only time the story comes alive. (Dir: Eric Till, 104 mins.)

American Dream, An (1966)**½ Stuart Whitman, Janet Leigh, Eleanor Parker. Norman Mailer's offbeat novel served as the basis for this film adaptation. Eleanor Parker, as the hero's bitter, drunken ex-wife, makes the first few scenes memorable, but Stuart Whitman just looks dumb throughout as the tough TV commentator. (Dir: Robert Gist, 103 mins.)

American Friend, The (West Germany, 1977)*** Dennis Hopper, Bruno Ganz, Lisa Kreuzer. The films directed by Wim Wenders are about life lived on the edge; this is one of his edgiest. Based on a Patricia Highsmith novel, *Ripley's Game*, this American-style thriller turns back on itself with deadly European irony. Hopper, an international art smuggler, and Ganz, a dying Hamburg craftsman, commit a murder together and become, briefly, friends. Ganz is excellent in his taciturn, reactive hero's role. Interesting bits by such directors as Nicholas Ray, Samuel Fuller, Gerard Blain, and Jean Eustache. Dialogue is in English, French, and German. (127 mins.)

American Game, The (1979)***½ Perceptive documentary on two high-schoolers who play basketball. Other than that, the worlds of Brian Walker from Lebanon, Indiana, and Arthur (Stretch) Graham, a ghetto black from Brooklyn, are vastly different. The Indiana boy lives almost in a fantasy land, in comparison to Graham's rough-and-tough existence. A rock score by Richie Havens punctuates the action. (Dirs: Jay Freund, David Wolf, Robert Elfstrom, Peter Powell, 85 mins.)

American Gigolo (1980)**½ Richard Gere, Lauren Hutton, Hector Elizondo, Nina Van Pallandt, Macdonald Carey. As usual, director Paul Schrader plays all 12 apostles to his own suffering Jesus. Gere is the Schrader surrogate in search of salvation—he's a high-class lovemaker to rich women. A bedeviling, passionate, constipated work that hits only the targets it doesn't aim at. (117 mins.)

American Graffiti (1973)**** Richard Dreyfuss, Ronny Howard, Cindy Williams, Candy Clark, Mackenzie Phillips, Harrison Ford, Wolfman Jack, Suzanne Somers. A remarkable film about the American car culture and what it was like to be a teenager in a small town in northern California in the fall of '62. Director George Lucas's film is almost beyond criticism, so pervasive has been its influence. It refined nostalgia as a marketable commodity and established a new narrative style, with locale replacing plot, that has been imitated unto redundancy. Produced on a low budget with high marks for all the talent including producer Francis Ford Coppola. Received several Academy Award nominations for Best Picture and Director, and for Miss Clark's memorable portrayal of a blond kewpie doll. (109 mins.)

American Guerrilla in the Philippines, An (1950)** Tyrone Power, Micheline Presle, Tom Ewell. A routine but effective war movie in color which would have been an honorable accomplishment for any director but Fritz Lang. Little of Lang's personality is in evidence as Power awaits the return of Douglas MacArthur by working with the Filipino underground. (105 mins.)

American Hot Wax (1978)***½ Tim McIntire, Fran Drescher, Laraine Newman, Chuck Berry, Jerry Lee Lewis. Director Floyd Mutrux has accomplished what many have claimed and few have evoked: the poetry of experience represented by rock and roll. Alan Freed's landmark Brooklyn concert is the focal point. Mutrux understands that indigenous American pathos derives best from verbal slapstick. There is more lively throwaway byplay than in any American film for a long time, and the wistful quality of McIntire's Alan Freed takes on heroic internal dimensions. Also recommended for William A. Fraker's photography, his best to date. (91 mins.)

American in Paris, An (1951)**** Gene Kelly, Leslie Caron, Oscar Levant. This Oscar-winning film musical written by Alan Jay Lerner, with a George & Ira Gershwin score, and Gene Kelly's brilliant, ambitious choreography, is a must. Leslie Caron made her film debut in this story about an American ex-G.I. (Kelly) who stays in Paris after WW II to make it as an artist. The mood of the city comes across with great charm. The musical numbers are the main attraction. One of the finest American musicals ever made. (Dir: Vincente Minnelli, 113 mins.)

American Madness (1932)*** Walter Huston, Pat O'Brien, Constance Cummings. Director Frank Capra claims he discovered the secret of effective dialogue direction in this story of bank panic: in essence, to speed up the delivery. (By contrast, his earlier "Platinum Blonde" dallied over the

bons mots till the freshness faded.) The first film fully in the patented Capra style—with its spark of contemporary urgency, the masses of crowds arrayed against the decent individual working for their benefit, the attempt to harmonize personal value and common weal, all with a fast-paced, montage-dominated approach. Huston incarnates rectitude without stuffiness as the town banker. (81 mins.)

American Dream, The (MTV 1981)*** Stephen Macht, Karen Carlson, Michael Hershewe, Tim Waldrip. A typical middle-class American family is choking in its pursuit of the American dream. The family of three children is about to increase by one and they can't afford a bigger house. So they move from suburbia to a racially integrated neighborhood in Chicago. The entire cast is first rate. So is the script. (Dir: Mel Damski, 78 mind.)

American Pop (1981)**½ Voices of Ron Thompson, Marya Small, Jerry Holland, Lisa Jane Persky, Jeffrey Lippa, Roz Kelly. Director Ralph Bakshi's attempt to tell through animation the history of American popular songs, from the turn of the century to new wave rock, is a vulgar, trivial exercise in pointless indulgence. The scenario has nothing to say, and, although the selection of songs is good, they aren't illuminated with any purpose or communicated feeling. Bakshi strains for anti-cliche and comes up banal. Derivative but extremely flashy effects. (98 mins.)

American Soldier, The (West Germany, 1970)***½ Karl Scheydt, Elge Sorbas, Jan George, Margarethe von Trotta, Rainer Werner Fassbinder. Described by director Fassbinder as "what's left in the minds of the German people who see a lot of American gangster films," this film follows Ricky, ex-soldier and professional hit man, as he returns to the Munich of his childhood and finds the man he has contracted to kill. Bold and compelling. (80 mins.)

American Tragedy, An (1931)***½ Phillips Holmes, Sylvia Sidney, Frances Dee. Josef von Sternberg's version of Theodore Dreiser's novel emphasizes personal, emotional causes of the tragedy over social ones, thereby obliterating Dreiser's perspective. Holmes makes a haunted George, while Sidney creates a rich character from the doomed poor girl he seduces. Dee plays the rich debutante, getting a fraction of the attention later accorded Elizabeth Taylor in George Stevens's version, "A Place in the Sun." (95 mins.)

Americanization of Emily, The (1964)*** James Garner, Julie Andrews, Melvyn Douglas. Paddy Chayefsky's skillful screenplay is adapted from William Bradford Huie's book about a navy officer whose main job during WW II is to supply his superiors with a variety of the creature comforts, including girls. Julie Andrews gives a beguiling portrayal of a British war widow who can't help falling in love with him. Entertaining, and if you listen, the film actually has something pertinent to say. (Dir: Arthur Hiller, 117 mins.)

Americano, The (1916)*** Douglas Fairbanks, Alma Rubens, Tom Wilson, Charles Stevens. A robust Douglas Fairbanks vehicle in which he squelches a Latin American revolution with fine imperialist fettle. Supervised by D. W. Griffith. Screenplay by John Emerson and Anita Loos, based on Richard Harding Davis's *The Dictator*. Photographed by later major director Victor Fleming (Dir: John Emerson, 60 mins.)

Americano, The (1954)**½ Glenn Ford, Frank Lovejoy. Texas cowboy gets mixed up with bandits in Brazil. Good cast helps this below-the-equator western over the familiar road. (Dir: William Castle, 85 mins.)

Americathon (1979)*** John Ritter, Harvey Korman, Alma Morgan, Meat Loaf. The biggest joke in this film on the bankruptcy of the American economy is that it was substantially financed with West German tax shelter money. A lot of bright ideas float around, some of them funny but virtually none having to do with satire. Since satire is what the film is trying to achieve, there are some arid stretches. A textbook example of the difference between cleverness and wit. There is something dashing about the tacky, terrible production numbers, but the rest is frenzy. (Dir: Neil Israel, 85 mins.)

Amityville Horror, The (1979)*½ James Brolin, Margot Kidder, Rod Steiger, Don Stroud. (Dir: Stuart Rosenberg, 117 mins.)

Among the Headhunters (Great Britain, 1955)*** Documentary of the Armand and Michaela Denis expedition to the island of New Guinea. Well done. (Dir: Armand and Michaela Denis, 92 mins.)

Among the Living (1941)**½ Albert Dekker, Susan Hayward. Man is wrongfully accused when his insane twin brother escapes and commits murder. Strong thriller; good direction and performances. (Dir: Stuart Heisler, 68 mins.)

Amorous Adventures of Moll Flanders, The (Great Britain, 1965)*** Kim Novak, Richard Johnson, George Sanders. Daniel Defoe's classic tale about a gorgeous 18th-century female who stops at nothing to achieve money and social position comes off as a poor man's "Tom Jones" but it's fun all the same. Superb costumes and atmospheric settings. (Dir: Terence Young, 126 mins.)

Amorous Mr. Prawn, The (Great Britain, 1962)**½ Joan Greenwood, Cecil Parker, Ian Carmichael, Dennis Price. General about to retire hasn't enough money, so while he's away his wife converts his HQ into a vacation spot for salmon fishermen. Mildly amusing comedy with some agreeable performers, some amusing scenes. (Dir: Anthony Kimmins, 89 mins.)

Amphibian Man, The (USSR, 1961)*

William Koren, Anastasia Virten. (Dirs: Gennady Kazansky, Vladimir Chebotaryev, 86 mins.)

Amsterdam Kill, The (1978)**½ Robert Mitchum, Bradford Dillman, Keye Luke, Leslie Nielsen, Richard Egan. Drug traffic drama, with Mitchum as a narc busted for embezzling to support a habit of his own. The film opens with some well-tempoed plotting before losing itself in pointless, arbitrary action sequences: Director Robert Clouse's potential appears to have withered. Toiling too many years in the action-exploitation area offshore can do that to you. Mitchum retains his dignity, as do the rest of the cast, including an interestingly aging Egan. (93 mins.)

Amy Prentiss: Baptism of Fire (MTV 1974)** Jessica Walter, William Shatner, Peter Haskell. A woman chief of detectives takes on two cases involving industrial espionage, and a mad bomber about to blow up San Francisco. Standard, but with a little less violence than usual, and the script well-paced. (Dir: Jeffrey Hayden, 72 mins.)

Anastasia (1956)***½ Ingrid Bergman, Yul Brynner, Helen Hayes. Absorbing drama of an amnesiac girl in Germany who may or may not be the daughter of Czar Nicholas II of Russia. Excellently acted, won Miss Bergman her second Oscar award. (Dir: Anatole Litvak, 105 mins.)

Anatomist, The (Great Britain, 1961)**½ Alastair Sim, George Cole. Gruesome story of a Scots doctor who procures bodies for his medical experiments. Good cast, good fare for thriller fans. (Dir: Leonard William, 73 mins.)

Anatomy of a Marriage (France-Italy, 1964)** Marie-Jose Nat, Jacques Charrier. A failed marriage from two points of view. Over-long, superficial, but intermittently interesting. (Dir: Andre Cayatte, 112 mins.)

Anatomy of a Murder (1959)**** James Stewart, Lee Remick, George C. Scott, Ben Gazzara, Joseph N. Welch. Director Otto Preminger's hit seemed a good deal racier in '59, but it's still the best courtroom spellbinder ever made. Stewart is superb as a small-town Michigan lawyer (he won the New York Film Critics Award) defending an army lieutenant (Gazzara) on a charge of murdering his wife's rapist. Remick is marvelous as the sexpot wife who may or may not have been raped, though the spotlight was stolen by Boston attorney Welch, another of Preminger's publicity and casting coups. Score by Duke Ellington. (160 mins.)

Anatomy of a Psycho (1961)* Ronnie Burns, Pamela Lincoln. (Dir. Brooke L. Peters, 75 mins.)

Anatomy of a Seduction (MTV 1979)**½ Susan Flannery, Jameson Parker, Rita Moreno. An older woman–younger man love affair is explored in this glossy soap opera, with a couple of moments of genuine emotion. Flannery heads the cast as a beautiful 40-year-old divorced mother who takes up with her best friend's 20-year-old son. Parker, as the young man home from Princeton for the summer, shows the stuff that stars are made of—poise, good looks, sensitivity, and a personal appeal. Screenplay by Alison Cross. (Dir: Steven Hillard Stern, 104 mins.)

Anatomy of the Syndicate—See: **Big Operator, The**

Anchors Aweigh (1945)*** Gene Kelly, Frank Sinatra, Kathryn Grayson, Dean Stockwell, Jose Iturbi. Even director George Sidney can't mix audacity and simple lack of taste to put over all of this MGM musical about two sailors on leave; but Sinatra and Kelly manage to sell a bit of it, especially when Sinatra sings the great Jule Styne–Sammy Cahn hit "I Fall in Love Too Easily" and Kelly dances with Jerry the cartoon mouse. Oscar to Georgie Stoll, Best Scoring of a Musical. (140 mins.)

And Baby Makes Six (MTV 1979)**½ Colleen Dewhurst, Warren Oates, Mildred Dunnock, Maggie Cooper. Dewhurst plays Mother Earth splendidly. Her Anna, a middle-aged mother with grown children, is pregnant. Loving husband doesn't want another child; Anna, who does, is strong, loving, touching, well read, the family peacemaker—in short, the ideal mom. Almost too ideal. Written by Shelley List. (Dir: Warris Hussein, 104 mins.)

And Baby Makes Three (1949)** Robert Young, Barbara Hale. Foolish comedy about a recently divorced couple who discover that they are to be parents. Good performances. (Dir: Henry Lewis, 83 mins.)

And God Created Woman (France, 1957)**½ Brigitte Bardot, Curt Jurgens, Jean-Louis Trintignant. B.B. was an immediate hit in this tale of a family of sexually preoccupied men who openly and understandably lust after her. Director and cameraman primarily concerned with Brigitte's shape in various states of dress and undress. (Dir: Roger Vadim, 92 mins.)

And Hope to Die (France, 1972)* Robert Ryan, Jean-Louis Trintignant, Aldo Ray. (Dir: Rene Clement, 99 mins.)

And I Alone Survived (MTV 1978)**½ Blair Brown, David Ackroyd, Maggie Cooper. A show for the hardy. True story about a gutsy young lady who survived an air crash in the Sierra Nevadas in the spring of '76. Written by the survivor, Lauren Elder, adapted by Lane Slate. Brown does her best to re-create Lauren's nightmare descent down the side of an icy precipice. (Dir: Billy Graham, 104 mins.)

...And Justice for All (1979)**½ Al Pacino, Jack Warden, John Forsythe, Christine Lahti, Lee Strasberg. I know something about how the court system functions, and I can assure you that this bundle of half-truths and phoniness is not onto it. Pacino's role serves as a focal point for audience self-gratification; the movie panders so much to the moronic side of its audience that its moral posturings amount to the ethical insights of a gnat. Adding to the general cynicism is no way to foster reform. Norman Jewison directed, without a worthwhile idea in his head. (118 mins.)

And Millions Will Die (1973)** Richard Basehart, Susan Strasberg, Leslie Nielsen. Adventure yarn supplies some suspense as a team of scientists try to unearth a dead madman's plan to destroy Hong Kong. The stars are competent enough, but they take a back seat to the exotic locations in Hong Kong, Singapore, and Australia. (Dir: Leslie Martinson, 104 mins.)

And No One Could Save Her (MTV 1973)** Lee Remick, Milo O'Shea. Dublin locations. A wealthy American woman comes to Ireland looking for her husband, who has disappeared. (Dir: Kevin Billington, 74 mins.)

And Now for Something Completely Different (Great Britain, 1972)***½ Graham Chapman, John Cleese, Eric Idle, Terry Jones, Michael Palin. A spinoff from the successful BBC-TV series "Monty Python's Flying Circus," the film is not exactly social satire and not exactly burlesque—it's the kind of Oxbridge humor that looks at normal human activities from radically oblique angles. Most of the pieces are deliciously bright, brash, and amusing. (Dir: Ian McNaughton, 89 mins.)

And Now Miguel (1966)*** Pat Cardi, Michael Ansara, Guy Stockwell. Young son of a sheepherder tries to prove that he's old enough to go along on grazing treks. Refreshing; pleasant entertainment for all the family. (Dir: James Clark, 95 mins.)

And Now, My Love (France, 1975)*** Charles Denner, Marthe Keller, Andre Dussollier. As cute as can be, this tidy little love story directed by Claude Lelouch ends with the lovers meeting for the first time. The film offers some cozy comforts and more than a few inside filmmaking jokes. It's at its best when the gyroscopes and the dollies are put away. (121 mins.)

And Now the Screaming Starts (Great Britain, 1973)**½ Peter Cushing, Herbert Lom, Patrick Magee, Stephanie Beacham. A curse involving a severed hand hangs heavy over the pregnant bride of the lord of a British manor house. Veteran horror director Roy Ward Baker creates a suitable Gothic mood. (Dir: Roy Ward Baker, 91 mins.)

And Now Tomorrow (1944)**½ Loretta Young, Alan Ladd. Corny story about a romance between a deaf girl and her doctor. (Dir: Irving Pichel, 85 mins.)

And So They Were Married (1944)*** Simone Simon, James Ellison. Screwball comedy about a girl who finds that too many keys to her apartment had been given out during wartime, the romantic complications that ensue. Cute, sometimes highly original. Watch for Robert Mitchum in a bit role. Theatrical title: "Johnny Doesn't Live Here Anymore." (Dir: Joe May, 79 mins.)

And Soon the Darkness (Great Britain, 1970)** Pamela Franklin, Michele Dotrice. Two British girls are alone on a bicycle holiday in France. When one girl is missing, the other girl panics. The buildup is breathtaking, but with no definitive denouement the film fizzles into disappointment. (Dir: Robert Fuest, 98 mins.)

And Sudden Death (1936)*½ Randolph Scott, Frances Drake. (Dir: Charles Barton, 70 mins.)

And the Angels Sing (1944)**½ Betty Hutton, Fred MacMurray. Story of some singing sisters and the band leader who discovers them. Routine musical but Betty sings one of her biggest hits, "My Rocking Horse Ran Away." (Dir: George Marshall, 96 mins.)

And the Wild, Wild Women (1960)*** Anna Magnani, Giulietta Masina. This Italian film drama about a women's prison is altered a great deal for this dubbed version but it still has two of Italy's great film stars—Anna Magnani and Giulietta Masina—to make it worthwhile. (Dir: Renato Castellani, 85 mins.)

And Then There Were None (1945)**** Barry Fitzgerald, Walter Huston, Louis Hayward, Judith Anderson. Ten people are invited to a remote, deserted island where they are killed off mysteriously, one by one. Excellent thriller, with René Clair's direction mixing humor and mystery with skillful touches. Fine performances from a grand cast—which was stupidly listed so that the credit order can be used to figure out the mystery. (98 mins.)

And Your Name Is Jonah (MTV 1979)*** Sally Struthers, James Woods, Jeffrey Bravin. A heartbreaking, sometimes poignant story about a seven-year-old deaf child originally diagnosed as mentally retarded. Bravin, a deaf youngster in real life, gives a moving performance as the untrained, undisciplined Jonah, whose mom (Struthers) painfully discovers the best way to treat the deaf. Woods is effective as the boy's traumatized father who is unable to cope with the situation, but the film belongs to young Jeffrey. (Dir: Richard Michaels, 104 mins.)

Anderson Tapes, The (1971)*** Sean Connery, Dyan Cannon, Martin Balsam, Alan King. Lively, suspenseful crime caper with a gimmick. Thief plans to rob an entire Fifth Avenue apartment house. Exciting; the acting is uniformly good. Director Sidney Lumet uses New York well. (98 mins.)

Andrea Chenier (Italy, 1955)** Antonella Lualdi, Raf Vallone. Dubbed tale of the French Revolution, a patriot, and the daughter of a count. (Dir: Clemente Fracassi, 110 mins.)

Andrei Rublev (U.S.S.R., 1969)**½ Anatoli Solonitzine, Ivan Lapikov, Irma Raouch.

Director Andrei Tarkovsky's massive, attentively detailed study of a medieval Russian painter and icon-maker has rarely been shown at full length here, despite worldwide acclaim. Tarkovsky himself has been subjected to intermittent harassment by Soviet authorities, apparently as much for his artistic expressiveness as his political unorthodoxy. The film is determinedly an objet d'art, with tortured wide-screen compositions and twin impulses toward contemplation and the epic. Stiff, stodgy; but some viewers might be substantially moved. Unquestionably a major work. (146 mins.)

Andrews' Raiders—See: **Great Locomotive Chase, The**

Androcles and the Lion (1952)*** Alan Young, Jean Simmons, Victor Mature, Robert Newton, Maurice Evans. Hardly Shaw at his best, and Chester Erskine's direction is pedestrian, but as a child I found the combination of physical comedy and epigrammatic discourse stimulating. A superb ensemble give the maximum in droll line readings. (98 mins.)

Andromeda Strain, The (1971)***½ James Olson, Arthur Hill. Excellent sci-fi tale based on the popular novel by Michael Crichton. A remote spot in New Mexico is contaminated when a satellite crashes there and a team of four top scientists fight the clock trying to analyze the lethal organism and discover a solution. Interesting throughout. Excellent cast. (Dir: Robert Wise, 130 mins.)

Andy (1965)**½ Norman Alden, Ann Wedgeworth. Mentally retarded son of Greek immigrants struggles to communicate with people. Some powerful moments, deserves credit for trying. (Dir: Richard Sarafian, 86 mins.)

Andy Hardy Comes Home (1958)**½ Mickey Rooney, Pat Breslin. Andy Hardy is all grown up and a successful lawyer when he returns to his home town. Andy Hardy film fans will get a kick out of seeing Fay Holden (mother), Sara Haden (aunt) and Cecilia Parker (sister) once again. (Dir: Howard Koch, 80 mins.)

Andy Hardy Meets a Debutante (1940)**½ Mickey Rooney, Judy Garland. Mickey is still chasing attractive MGM starlets in this one. Good Andy Hardy comedy. (Dir: George Seitz, 86 mins.)

Andy Hardy's Blonde Trouble (1944)** Mickey Rooney, Lewis Stone. Andy's college days are complicated by a pair of luscious blonde co-eds who happen to be twins. (Dir: George Seitz, 107 mins.)

Andy Hardy's Double Life (1942)** Mickey Rooney, Lewis Stone. Andy goes to college in this one. The series has lost all its charm and the only important thing about this one is that one of Andy's flirtations is a screen newcomer, Esther Williams. (Dir: George Seitz, 92 mins.)

Andy Hardy's Private Secretary (1941)**½ Mickey Rooney, Lewis Stone. Andy gets out of high school in this one and his secretary is played by a lovely newcomer with a delightful voice named Kathryn Grayson. (Dir: George Seitz, 101 mins.)

Andy Warhol's Bad (1976)**½ Carroll Baker, Perry King, Susan Tyrrell. A delightfully gross comedy of chic disgust, with Baker a housewife who's head of a gang of assassins for hire: all spacy ingenues. Not for all tastes, and quite slick compared to early Warhol galleries of grotesquery, but if approached in the right spirit the film evokes high comedy in the lowest depths. Directed by the able Jed Johnson. (105 mins.)

Andy Warhol's Dracula (Italy-U.S., 1974)**½ Joe Dallesandro, Udo Kier, Vittorio de Sica, Roman Polanski. Another bit of blood-drenched whimsy from the fertile mind of writer-director Paul Morrissey. In this one, vampirism stands for the parasitic death throes of the aristocracy, while virginity represents its ultimate hypocrisy. If religion is the opiate of the masses, Morrissey seems to be saying, then sex is the amphetamine of the classes. Dallesandro is on hand again, to deflower the last upper-class virgin just before Dracula rejuvenates himself on her unsullied blood. All families are unhappy in the same way. (106 mins.)

Angel (1937)** Marlene Dietrich, Herbert Marshall, Melvyn Douglas. A diplomat's wife has an affair with a stranger and then meets him again. This one will disappoint you. (Dir: Ernst Lubitsch, 90 mins.)

Angel and the Badman (1946)***½ John Wayne, Gail Russell. A notorious gunslinger is reformed by the love of a Quaker girl. Western has action, fine scenery, and a good plot; superior entertainment of its type. (Dir: James Edward Grant, 100 mins.)

Angel Baby (1961)** Salome Jens, George Hamilton, Mercedes McCambridge. Effective drama about the tent-circuit evangelists who travel through small towns preaching salvation for sinners. Miss Jens is impressive as a mute who miraculously gets her voice back and falls in love with the young preacher who she thinks is responsible for her recovery. (Dir: Paul Wendkos, 97 mins.)

Angel City (1977)*** Robert Glaudini, Winifred Golden, Pierce Del Rue, Kathleen Kramer. Independent filmmaker Jon Jost has put together elaborate experimental narrative features on what can only be called a strand of a shoestring. This is the best known of his four, a private-eye parody that features a comic Philip Marlowe variant named Frank Goya (played by Glaudini), whose investigation of a murder is set against a detailed economic and social critique of Los Angeles. The film includes a sequence featuring a screen test of a Hollywood remake of "Triumph of the Will." Director Jost is concerned with formal and political problems. (70 mins.)

Angel City (MTV 1980)*** Ralph Waite, Paul Winfield, Mitch Ryan. The lives of West Virginia mountain folk working the fields of Florida are a cruel series of misfortunes and deceptions. There seems no way out for the migrant workers entrapped by cruel labor contracts. Waite and Winfield (from the TV series "The Waltons" portray the proud, downtrodden workers, and Mitch Ryan is properly evil as the labor boss. Several effective scenes. (Dir: Philip Leacock, also credited to Steve Carver, 104 mins.)

Angel Dusted (MTV 1981)**½ Jean Stapleton, John Putch. Jean Stapleton is hard to resist as worried, understanding, frightened Mom whose boy goes berserk after an encounter with angel dust. This becomes a course in proper medical and psychiatric treatment for an angel-dust victim with steadfast Mom by his side. Miss Stapleton gains your sympathy with her anxiety, and her son, John Putch, doesn't embarrass Mom in his TV debut.

Angel Face (1952)***½ Robert Mitchum, Jean Simmons, Herbert Marshall, Mona Freeman. Director Otto Preminger's study in perversity reverses the usual schema of domination and manipulation: the woman (Simmons) calls the shots on her helpless lover (Mitchum). It's so well measured in minute calibrations of lighting and framing that the essential shallowness of the sexual premise is never overcome by the intensity of the implacable style. (90 mins.)

Angel from Texas, An (1940)**½ Jane Wyman, Ronald Reagan, Eddie Albert. Occasionally cute, Grade B comedy about the yokels who take the city slickers. (Dir: Ray Enright, 69 mins.)

Angel in Exile (1948)*** John Carroll, Adele Mara. Crooks plan to hide stolen gold in a small town and then "discover" it, but the townspeople look upon the gold as a miracle. Good melodrama. (Dirs: Allan Dwan, Philip Ford, 90 mins.)

Angel in My Pocket (1969)**½ Andy Griffith, Lee Meriwether. A mid-western town's many problems become Reverend Andy's personal responsibilities. TV faces in the supporting cast including Jerry Van Dyke, Kay Medford, and Edgar Buchanan. (Dir: Alan Rafkin, 105 mins.)

Angel Levine, The (1970)** Zero Mostel, Harry Belafonte. A black angel comes to earth to redeem an aging Jew who has lost his faith. Overdrawn performances, abundance of supersentimentality. (Dir: Jan Kadar, 104 mins.)

Angel on Earth (Germany-France, 1960)** Romy Schneider, Jean-Paul Belmondo, Henri Vidal. A beautiful angel comes to earth to keep an eye on a racing driver. Some amusement, not enough. Dubbed. (Dir: Geza Radvanyi, 88 mins.)

Angel on My Shoulder (1946)*** Paul Muni, Claude Rains, Anne Baxter. A deceased gangster makes a deal with the

23

Devil to return to earth. Enjoyable fantasy. (Dir: Archie Mayo, 101 mins.)

Angel on My Shoulder (MTV 1980)** Peter Strauss, Richard Kiley, Barbara Hershey, Janis Paige. A remake of the '46 Paul Muni movie. Older is better! Strauss plays a '40s gangster who is executed and comes back to earth today in the body of a look-alike D.A. He gives it a valiant try, but the coyness of the material defeats him. (Dir: John Berry, 104 mins.)

Angel on the Amazon (1948)*½ George Brent, Vera Ralston, Brian Aherne. (Dir: John Auer, 86 mins.)

Angel Who Pawned Her Harp (Great Britain 1956)*** Diane Cilento, Felix Aylmer. Romantic fantasy with lovely and talented Diane Cilento cast as an angel. Excellent performances by all. (Dir: Alan Bromly, 73 mins.)

Angel with a Trumpet, The (Great Britain, 1950)***½ Eileen Herlie, Basil Sydney. The panoramic story of a Viennese family, from the last century to Hitler's time. Carefully produced, fine performances. (Dir: Anthony Bushell, 98 mins.)

Angel Wore Red, The (1960)** Ava Gardner, Dirk Bogarde, Joseph Cotten. A serious attempt to mount a love story against the turmoil of the Spanish Civil War of the 1930's. Disappointing despite a fairly literate script and earnest performances. Bogarde plays a Catholic priest who gives up his beliefs and returns to the everyday world. (Dir: Nunnally Johnson, 99 mins.)

Angela Davis: The Web *** Director Jean-Daniel Simon's lengthy portrait of the revolutionary pedagogue attempts to place Davis within the cultural maelstrom of the late '60s, although it is fundamentally a character sketch.

Angela—Portrait of a Revolutionary (1971)*** Enlightening if technically primitive documentary about political revolutionary Angela Davis. Film follows Angela beginning 1969, before she went to prison in late 1970, and then picks her up again after the trial where she was acquitted. Filmmaker was student of Davis' at college. (Dir: Yolande du Luart, 80 mins.)

Angelika—See: **Affairs of Dr. Holl**

Angels in the Outfield (1951)***½ Paul Douglas, Janet Leigh, Keenan Wynn. Enjoyable comedy fantasy about a baseball team and an orphan who sees angels. (Dir: Clarence Brown, 99 mins.)

Angels of Darkness (Italy, 1957)**½ Linda Darnell, Anthony Quinn, Giulietta Masina. Frank adult film of "loose" women in Rome. Morbid and dull. (Dir: Giuseppe Amato, 84 mins.)

Angels One Five (Great Britain, 1952)*** Jack Hawkins, Michael Denison. Story of the Royal Air Force in the dark days of 1940. Authentic, well-made war drama. (Dir: George O'Ferrall, 98 mins.)

Angels Over Broadway (1940)***½ Rita Hayworth, Douglas Fairbanks, Jr., Thomas Mitchell. Good performances and top notch Ben Hecht screenplay make this story about a group of oddballs in a Broadway cafe, fascinating viewing. (Dir: Ben Hecht, 80 mins.)

Angels Wash Their Faces (1939)**½ Ann Sheridan, Dead End Kids. Mildly entertaining drama featuring the Dead End Kids. (Dir: Ray Enright, 90 mins.)

Angels with Dirty Faces (1938)***½ James Cagney, Pat O'Brien, Humphrey Bogart, Ann Sheridan, the Dead End Kids. The classic late-'30s environmentalist crime film, the film stars Cagney and O'Brien as two boyhood pals from the slums who grow up to be a gangster (Cagney) and a priest (O'Brien), and meet their respective rewards on the old turf. Though it meanders a bit in its exposition, director Michael Curtiz's film is strikingly directed and photographed. (97 mins.)

Angi Vera (Hungary, 1978)**** Veronika Papp, Tamas Dunai, Erzsi Pasztor, Eva Szabo. A remarkable political document and a deeply moving drama of ill-fated lovers. One of the most searing indictments ever filmed of the oppressive intellectual and moral climate in a Communist society. That this film was made in Hungary, about the repressive nature of the Communist party structure and activities there three decades earlier, makes it all the more powerful. Focuses on an upwardly mobile 18-year-old girl trying to climb the political ladder in the Stalinist regime in '48. Papp is brilliant, as are the direction and screenplay by Pal Gabor. Based on a novel by Endre Veszi. (96 mins.)

Angry Breed, The (1969)* Jan Sterling, James MacArthur, William Windom. (89 mins.)

Angry Hills, The (Great Britain, 1959)**½ Robert Mitchum, Gia Scala, Stanley Baker. Based on a lesser-known Leon (Exodus) Uris novel, this tale concerns the Greek Resistance during WW II. Predictable, but a good international cast keeps things moving. (Dir: Robert Aldrich, 105 mins.)

Angry Red Planet, The (1960)*½ Gerald Mohr, Les Tremayne, Nora Hayden.

Angry Silence, The (Great Britain, 1960)**** Pier Angeli, Richard Attenborough, Michael Craig. Hard-hitting, absorbing drama beautifully played. One man's stand against a labor union. (Dir: Guy Green, 95 mins.)

Anguish (Spain, 1974)**½ Paco Rabal, Ana Belen. Version of the Benito Pérez Galdós novel, in which a fortune hunter returns from America with riches to excite the greed of a cousin anxious to marry off his daughter. Our parvenu, however, takes a fancy to the maid, despite the girl's clandestine affair with a priest. (Dir: Pedro Olea.)

Animal Crackers (1930)**** The Four Marx Brothers, Margaret Dumont. Worth watching just to see Groucho strut his way through one of his great numbers, "Hooray for Captain Spaulding." Wacky screenplay by Morrie Ryskind, based on the hit Broadway musical he wrote with George S. Kaufman. (Dir: Victor Heerman, 98 mins.)

Animal Farm (Great Britain, 1954)** This animated version of Orwell's satire on Soviet history tends to emphasize the old-maid aspects of his leftward criticism, while banalizing his marvelous imagery. Strictly from "Cliff Notes." Louis de Rochemont produced, and his reputation was kept intact. (Dirs: John Halas, Joy Batchelor, 75 mins.)

Animal House—See: **National Lampoon's Animal House**

Animals, The (1972)**½ Henry Silva, Keenan Wynn, Michele Carey. Tale of the old West features Carey as an abducted lady left to die, who teams with Apache Silva to track down the criminals, Excessive carnage and profane language detract from the finely crafted story written by producer Richard Bakalyan. (Dir: Ron Joy, 86 mins.)

Anna (Italy, 1951)** Silvana Mangano, Raf Vallone, Vittorio Gassman. Night-club singer who has become a nun thinks over the reason for her doing so. Glum, rather shoddy drama, dubbed. (Dir: Alberto Lattuada, 95 mins.)

Anna and the King of Siam (1946)**** Irene Dunne, Rex Harrison, Linda Darnell, Lee J. Cobb. Margaret Landon's book done straight, without songs, by Harrison and Dunne, who outdo Yul Brynner and Deborah Kerr in the musical film of '56. John Cromwell's direction is both attentive to nuance and poky; the charm of the story and the central relationship carry the film along, though without much inspiration. Technical credits are top-notch, from Arthur Miller's camerawork to Bernard Herrmann's music. (128 mins.)

Anna and Toto (West Germany, 1977)**½ Renate Heilmeyer, Franco Lantieri. Film directed by Wolfgang Petersen about a woman made uncomfortable by the visit of a Sicilian man whom she met on vacation.

Anna Christie (1930)*** Greta Garbo, Charles Bickford, Marie Dressler. This is where Garbo first spoke, saying "Gif me a viskey, ginger ale on the side, and don't be stingy, baby." The Eugene O'Neill play was always a pain, with the tag phrase "that old debbil sea" incanted almost as often as the words "pipe dream" in "The Iceman Cometh." Slow but well acted by Garbo and the rest. (Dir: Clarence Brown, 90 mins.)

Anna Karenina (1935)*** Greta Garbo, Fredric March, Basil Rathbone, Freddie Bartholomew, Maureen O'Sullivan. The second of two versions of Tolstoy's novel starring Garbo (the first was "Love" in '27). Clarence Brown directs ploddingly, but at least lights Garbo well. Rathbone provides some relief from the prevalent tone of deathly good taste with a wonderfully fruity performance as Karenin. (95 mins.)

Anna Karenina (Great Britain, 1948)*** Vivien Leigh, Ralph Richardson. Tolstoy's immortal classic of the life and loves of a lady in old Russia. Elaborately produced, well acted drama. (Dir: Julien Duvivier, 110 mins.)

Anna Lucasta (1958)**½ Eartha Kitt, Sammy Davis, Jr. The hit Broadway show about a loose woman who tries to go straight when she falls for a sailor. The play starred an all-Negro cast as does this film version. (Dir: Arnold Laven, 97 mins.)

Annapolis Story (1955)** John Derek, Diana Lynn. Two brothers, both midshipmen at Annapolis, vie for the same girl. Familiar. (Dir: Don Siegel, 81 mins.)

Annapurna (Great Britain, 1953)**** Fascinating documentary account of the Herzog expedition's ascent of the Himalayan peak. Ideal for armchair adventurers. (Dir: Marcel Ichac, 60 mins.)

Anne of Green Gables (1934)*** Anne Shirley, Helen Westley, Tom Brown. A young girl begins to grow up when she must go live with her aunt in rural Nova Scotia. Entertaining version of the popular children's book by L. M. Montgomery. (Dir: George Nicholls, Jr., 79 mins.)

Anne of the Indies (1951)**½ Jean Peters, Louis Jourdan, Debra Paget. Lady pirate comes to the aid of a French ex-naval officer. Smart direction and some fast action; good fare for adventure devotees. (Dir: Jacques Tourneur, 81 mins.)

Anne of the Thousand Days (Great Britain, 1969)*** Richard Burton, Genevieve Bujold, Irene Papas, Anthony Quayle. Effective historical drama about England's King Henry the Eighth and his legendary romance with Anne Boleyn, quite wonderfully acted by Genevieve Bujold. A lavish, civilized and rather genteel depiction of one of history's great romances. One of Richard Burton's best performances. Adapted by Bridget Boland and John Hale from the 1948 play by Maxwell Anderson. Produced by Hal Wallis. (Dir: Charles Jarrott, 146 mins.)

Annie Get Your Gun (1950)*** Betty Hutton, Howard Keel, Keenan Wynn. Film version of the hit Broadway musical, relating the story of sharpshooter Annie Oakley and her rise to fame and fortune. The Irving Berlin tunes are great, the production lavish—and if the leading roles leave something to be desired, the displays of song and dance largely atone for it. (Dir: George Sidney, 107 mins.)

Annie Hall (1977)**** Woody Allen, Diane Keaton, Shelley Duvall. This is an absolutely marvelous film, directed and co-authored by the extravagantly talented Woody Allen. "Annie" is not only one of the funniest and wisest film comedies ever made, it's also a courageous, poignant, perceptive and perfectly acted film. This is more of an autobiographical film than any of Allen's earlier entries. Our red-headed hero Alvy Singer has been in analysis for fifteen years, loves New York, and falls in love with Diane Keaton. Woody and co-author Marshall Brickman fire off an enormous number of comic salvos; the one-liners and the sight gags pay off brilliantly. A joy from start to finish! (Dir: Woody Allen, 94 mins.)

Annie Mae: Brave-Hearted Woman (1979)***½ A tender yet chilling documentary, directed by Lan Brooks Ritz, about a modern-day "squaw warrior" who suffers both in her personal life and through continued persecution by whites until she is condemned to a brutal death for defending the rights of her people.

Annie Oakley (1935)*** Barbara Stanwyck, Preston Foster, Melvyn Douglas, Pert Kelton, Andy Clyde. A modest, pleasant star vehicle for Stanwyck, with a soupçon of something extra by director George Stevens. As usual with Stevens, the plot (about the famous sharpshooter's romance) goes by the wayside, though individual sequences are memorable. (88 mins.)

Anniversary, The (Great Britain, 1968)*½ Bette Davis, Sheila Hancock. (Dir: Roy Ward Baker, 95 mins.)

Anonymous Venetian, The (Italy 1970)* Tony Musante, Florinda Bolkan. (Dir: Enrico Maria Salerno, 91 mins.)

Another Man, Another Chance (France-U.S., 1977)**½ James Caan, Genevieve Bujold, Jennifer Warren, Susan Tyrrell. Talented director Claude Lelouch comes a cropper in this muddled, pretentious yarn (the first few bars of Beethoven's Fifth Symphony are heard often) set in the American West in the 1870's. Caan, playing a widower whose wife has been raped and slain, meets Bujold, the young French widow of a murdered photographer. Their scenes together give this entry more believability than it deserves. (128 mins.)

Another Man's Poison (Great Britain, 1952)*** Bette Davis, Gary Merrill. A blackmailer enters the scene with proof that a woman has murdered her husband, and forces her to do his bidding. Fairly interesting melodrama, good cast. Emlyn Williams. (Dir: Irving Rapper, 89 mins.)

Another Part of the Forest (1948)*** Fredric March, Ann Blyth, Dan Duryea. Lillian Hellman's absorbing story of the fabulous Hubbard family, a band of ruthless Southern industrialists who hated each other but loved money. This story takes place before Miss Hellman's "The Little Foxes." (Dir: Michael Gordon, 107 mins.)

Another Thin Man (1939)*** William Powell, Myrna Loy. Not as sharp as the earlier efforts, but Powell and Loy were and still are the most delightful of screen sleuths. A guy who dreams of deaths before they happen is causing the trouble in this one. The third entry in the series is highlighted by the birth of Nick, Jr. (Dir: W. S. Van Dyke II, 105 mins.)

Another Time, Another Place (Great Britain, 1958)** Lana Turner, Barry Sullivan, Sean Connery. Soapy stuff about a lady correspondent during World War II who engages in a hopeless love affair with a married man, suffers a breakdown when he's killed. (Dir: Lewis Allen, 98 mins.)

Antarctic Crossing (Great Britain, 1958)** Documentary recounting the crossing of the Antarctic by Sir Vivian Fuchs, and his intense rivalry with fellow explorer Sir Edmund Hillary. Creates enough personal tension to relieve the endless parade of panning shots of the snowy wilderness. (50 mins.)

Anthony Adverse (1936)** Fredric March, Olivia de Havilland, Claude Rains, Gale Sondergaard, Louis Hayward. The sprawl at least adds some vitality to the tired best-seller format. It's way too long, ludicrously unfocused, and badly acted, though you can at least suspect that some tongues were in cheeks. Sondergaard won the first Oscar for Best Supporting Actress—a first calumny among many. (Dir: Mervyn Le Roy, 136 mins.)

Antonia: A Portrait of the Woman (1974)**** Antonia Brico. Directors Jill Godmilow and Judy Collins paint an engrossing portrait of indomitable symphony conductor Brico, with the artifact quality of an early attempt to promote the forgotten history of women in American high culture. Brico's resilience in the face of blatant sexism in the concert music business is the focus of the film; the mixture of humor and bitterness she carried with her is commanding. An Academy Award nominee. (58 mins.)

Antonio and the Mayor (MTV 1975)*** Diego Gonzales, Gregory Sierra. Howard Rodman's offbeat, touching little drama of the 1920's, filmed in Mexico, is the story of a bright Mexican boy who infuriates the mayor of his village because of his ability to handle a bicycle that the mayor can't manage. (Dir: Jerry Thorpe, 72 mins.)

Antonio Das Mortes (Brazil, 1970)**** Mauricio do Valle, Odete Lara, Othon Bastos. Part epic, part folklore, part political allegory, director Glauber Rocha's reflection on the role played by legend, myth, and tradition in Brazil's social and political realities is a complex and powerful drama. Antonio (hired by the government, but acting partly out of religious conviction) tracks down and kills the members of a guerrilla band, only to realize, after killing the last rebel in ritualistic combat, that he belongs with the dispossessed country folk against the landowners. Rocha makes Antonio (played by do Valle) very much a contemporary figure (even equating him with Che Guevara), and uses folksongs, rhymed verse, and lush color to fashion a stunning call to arms for the Brazilians and one of the most memorable of all the films of the Cinema Novo. (100 mins.)

Any Gun Can Play (Italy-Spain, 1967)*½ Gilbert Roland, Edd Byrnes. (Dir: Enzo G. Castellari, 103 mins.)

Any Number Can Play (1949)*** Clark Gable, Alexis Smith, Wendell Corey. Well done drama about a gambler who faces a series of crises in the matter of a few hours. Good cast supports Gable in this fast-moving story. (Dir: Mervyn Le Roy, 103 mins.)

Any Number Can Win (France, 1963)**½ Jean Gabin, Alain Delon. Viviane Romance, Jose de Villalonga. Big plans to rob the Cannes gambling casino. Elaborate but overlong. (Dir: Henri Verneuil, 112 mins.)

Any Second Now (MTV 1969)*½ Stewart Granger, Lois Nettleton, Joseph Campanella. (Dir: Gene Levitt, 100 mins.)

Any Wednesday (1966)***½ Jane Fonda, Jason Robards, Jr., Dean Jones. The successful Broadway comedy about a kept girl, her married lover, his wife, and an out-of-town salesman who acts as a catalyst, comes to the screen improved, thanks to Miss Fonda's bright performance. (Dir: Robert Miller, 109 mins.)

Any Which Way You Can (1980)*** Clint Eastwood, Sondra Locke, Geoffrey Lewis, Ruth Gordon. Eastwood's sequel to his biggest hit, "Every Which Way But Loose," repeats an evocation of life-style among the familiar characters, although the edge of nastiness of "Loose" is now shrouded in an air of breezy, benign generosity. It's broad, crude, sometimes funny, and low on intellectual candlepower, but it's professionally designed for its audience. It proves that you can work intelligently for the undiscriminating audience with no loss of self-respect or craft and that the reason for stupid movies is stupidity, not demographics. Eastwood looks great and does his usual array of wonderful things, lean acting that accomplishes more than is readily apparent. Buddy Van Horn directed, doing a strong, efficient job. (105 mins.)

Anyone Can Play (Italy, 1967)** Ursula Andress, Virna Lisi, Marisa Mell, Claudine Auger. Mediocre comedy about four women trying to solve their varied problems; blackmail, bad marriages, and even worse! (Dir: Luigi Zampa, 88 mins.)

Anything Can Happen (1952)***½ Jose Ferrer, Kim Hunter. Delightfully played comedy about an immigrant who accustoms himself to America and finds himself a wife. (Dir: George Seaton, 107 mins.)

Anything for Love—See: **11 Harrowhouse**

Anything Goes (1936)**½ Bing Crosby, Ethel Merman. The original Porter score makes this watered-down production moderately entertaining. "You're the Top" number with Ethel is the limit. TV title: **Tops Is the Limit.** (Dir: Lewis Milestone, 100 mins.)

Anything Goes (1956)**½ Bing Crosby,

Donald O'Connor, Jeanmaire, Mitzi Gaynor. Musical comedy co-stars in Europe try to sign a leading lady for their show. The film needs more sparkle. Great Cole Porter score. (Dir: Robert Lewis, 106 mins.)

Anzio (1968)** Robert Mitchum, Peter Falk, Arthur Kennedy, Robert Ryan. Fabricated account of the decisive World War II battle of the Italian campaign. Even the location filming doesn't raise it above the commonplace. (Dir: Edward Dmytryk, 117 mins.)

Apache (1954)** Burt Lancaster, Jean Peters. A peace-seeking Indian, forced to turn renegade in this action-filled western. (Dir: Robert Aldrich, 91 mins.)

Apache Ambush (1955)** Bill Williams, Richard Jaeckel. Action-filled but routine Western—hero fights unreconstructed Confederate soldiers, Mexican banditos, and, of course, the Apaches. (Dir: Fred Sears, 70 mins.)

Apache Drums (1951)** Stephen McNally, Coleen Gray. Familiar western fare. A gambler with a bad reputation who shows he's made of sterner stuff when the chips are down. (Dir: Hugo Fregonese, 75 mins.)

Apache Fury (Spain, 1963)*½ Frank Latimore, George Gordon, Liza Moreno. Alternate title: **Fury of the Apache.** (Dir: Joseph De Lancy [Jose Maria Elorrieta], 84 mins.)

Apache Rifles (1964)** Audie Murphy, Michael Dante, Linda Lawson. Cavalry captain struggles to bring peace when the Apaches go on the warpath. (Dir: William Witney, 92 mins.)

Apache Territory (1958)** Rory Calhoun, Barbara Bates. A group of survivors of an Indian attack led to safety by a brave cowboy. (Dir: Ray Nazarro, 75 mins.)

Apache Uprising (1966)*½ Rory Calhoun, Corinne Calvet. (Dir: R. G. Springsteen, 90 mins.)

Apache War Smoke (1952)** Gilbert Roland, Robert Horton. Indians, cavalry, stagecoaches, and romance. Familiar. (Dir: Harold Kress, 65 mins.)

Apache Warrior (1957)** Keith Larsen, Jim Davis. Routine Indian adventure. (Dir: Elmo Williams, 74 mins.)

Apache Woman (1955)** Joan Taylor, Lloyd Bridges. Crimes are being blamed on the Apaches—government investigator looks into it. (Dir: Roger Corman, 83 mins.)

Aparajito (The Unvanquished) (India, 1958)**** The second installment of director Satyajit Ray's incomparable Apu trilogy is a transitional work, with more modest merits than the other two films. The pace picks up, since Apu is now living with his parents in Calcutta, where he starts school. Where the first film ("Pather Panchali") dealt with the growth of physical awareness of the world, this one imparts the development of social awareness.The last feature ("The World of Apu") will bring Apu to the point of suffering and moral awareness. (127 mins.)

Apartment, The (1960)**** Jack Lemmon, Shirley MacLaine, Fred MacMurray. Billy Wilder's bitterly funny view of modern urban morality won the Oscar as the best film of its year. A young wheeler-dealer "lends" his apartment to senior executives who wish to do a bit of cheating on the side. Witty adult fare. (125 mins.)

Apartment for Peggy (1948)*** Jeanne Crain, William Holden, Edmund Gwenn. Dated story about married vets struggling to get through college. Warm, humorous and charming. (Dirs: Henry Koster, George Seaton, 98 mins.)

Ape Man of the Jungle (Italy, 1962)* Ralph Hudson, Rita Clein. (Dir: Charlie Foster, 80 mins.)

Ape Woman, The (France-Italy, 1964)*** Ugo Tognazzi, Annie Girardot. Director Marco Ferreri's fifth film is about an opportunist who starts a sideshow featuring a woman covered with hair; he has to marry her to retain her services. Ferreri treats grotesque subjects with a low-key, naturalistic comedy style. The Italian version, with its brutally cynical ending, was never exported, and the ending that we'll see was reshot for foreign distribution. Some scenes are both poignant and funny. (97 mins.)

Aphrodite, Goddess of Love (Italy, 1958)*½ Isabel Cory, Ivo Garrani. (Dir: Mario Bonnard, 86 mins.)

Apocalypse Now (1979)***½ Martin Sheen, Marlon Brando, Robert Duvall, Dennis Hopper, Frederic Forrest. Intended to be the definitive filmic epic about war in general, and the hell of the Vietnam War in particular. A flawed masterpiece, which does have some of the most remarkable scenes ever photographed, especially a helicopter attack on a Vietcong village with a sound track blaring Wagner's "Ride of the Valkyries." (Much of the shattering impact of scenes like this will be lost on a home TV screen.) Loosely inspired by Conrad's novel *Heart of Darkness*, director Francis Ford Coppola's $31 million stunner was shot in the Philippines. The protagonist is a U.S. Army captain (Sheen) assigned to the dangerous mission of running down a renegade Green Berets colonel (Brando) who has taken refuge in the Cambodian jungles. Brando's one brief scene is poorly written and developed. Duvall is chilling as a Vietnam War version of General Patton. Coppola coauthored the screen play with John Milius. Writer Michael Herr, who wrote the stunning "Dispatches" about the Vietnam War, contributed to the narration. The miraculous Academy Award-winning camerawork is by Vittorio Storaro. (153 mins.)

Appaloosa, The (1966)** Marlon Brando, Anjanette Comer, John Saxon. Pretentious western yarn. A wronged buffalo hunter meets with adversity at every turn. The story has Brando pitted against a Mexican bandit, and their many confrontations becoming tiresome long before the shoot-out at the finale. (Dir: Sidney J. Furie, 98 mins.)

Applause (1929)** Helen Morgan, Joan Peers. Early talkie about a burlesque star who almost forsakes her daughter for success. (Dir: Rouben Mamoulian, 87 mins.)

Apple Dumpling Gang, The (1975)** Bill Bixby, Susan Clark. A story for kids about a trio of orphans who find a huge gold nugget in a seemingly tapped-out mine during the 1870's. The kids are adorable, of course. (Dir: Norman Tokar, 104 mins.)

Apple Dumpling Gang Rides Again, The (1979)** Tim Conway, Don Knotts, Tim Matheson, Kenneth Mars, Elyssa Davalos. Innocuous family entertainment from Disney. Sequel to a '75 film. (Dir: Vincent McEveety, 89 mins.)

Appointment, The (1969)* Omar Sharif, Anouk Aimee. (Dir: Sidney Lumet, 100 mins.)

Appointment for Love (1941)*** Charles Boyer, Margaret Sullavan, Reginald Denny. Marital mix-ups get a big play in this sometimes clever, sometimes silly comedy-romance. (Dir: William Seiter, 89 mins.)

Appointment in Honduras (1953)** Glenn Ford, Ann Sheridan, Zachary Scott. Adventurer goes on a dangerous trek through the jungles. Melodrama moves slowly and has banal plot. (Dir: Jacques Tourneur, 79 mins.)

Appointment in London (Great Britain, 1953)***½ Dirk Bogarde, Ian Hunter, Dinah Sheridan. An RAF bomber command during the dark days of 1943, climaxing with a raid over Germany. Intelligent, well acted and directed drama, worthwhile. (Dir: Philip Leacock, 96 mins.)

Appointment with a Shadow (1958)** George Nader, Joanna Moore, Brian Keith. Alcoholic reporter is given a chance at a big story, finds himself target for a killer. Undistinguished crime melodrama. (Dir: Joseph Pevney, 72 mins.)

Appointment with Danger (1951)*** Alan Ladd, Phyllis Calvert, Jack Webb. Post office investigator gets some aid from unexpected sources while foiling a mail robbery. Good crime melodrama. (Dir: Lewis Allen, 88 mins.)

Apprenticeship of Duddy Kravitz, The (Canada, 1974)**** Richard Dreyfuss, Randy Quaid, Joseph Wiseman, Jack Warden, Denholm Elliot, Micheline Lanctot. An exuberant, hilarious, sometimes sad film. Richard Dreyfuss is excellent playing a hustling Jewish teenager on the make in Montreal. One of the many strengths of "Duddy" is the near perfect screenplay by Mordecai Richler, nominated for an Academy Award, based on his own novel and adapted by Lionel Chetwynd. (Dir: Ted Kotcheff, 121 mins.)

April Fools, The (1969)**½ Jack Lemmon,

Catherine Deneuve, Sally Kellerman, Jack Weston, Charles Boyer, Myrna Loy. A good idea for a romantic romp with comedy as its base—but, alas, it doesn't really come off. Lemmon falls in love with his boss' beautiful wife (Miss Deneuve), and gets in and out of improbable messes until the final scene, when true love triumphs. (Dir: Stuart Rosenberg, 95 mins.)

April in Paris (1953)**½ Doris Day, Ray Bolger, Claude Dauphin. A chorus girl named "Dynamite" (Doris, of course) invited to Paris Arts Festival (by mistake) as the representative of the American Theatre. (Dir: David Butler, 101 mins.)

April Love (1957)**½ Pat Boone, Shirley Jones. A young man arrives on a farm in Kentucky and immediately is up to his blue jeans in romance and song. Shirley Jones is the sweet young love interest. (Dir: Henry Levin, 99 mins.)

April Showers (1948)**½ Jack Carson, Ann Sothern. The old vaudeville backstage theme receives an undistinguished treatment in this musical. (Dir: James Kern, 94 mins.)

Aquarians, The (1970)**½ Ricardo Montalbán, Jose Ferrer, Tom Simcox, Kate Woodville. A team of deep sea laboratory scientists stumble upon a group of opportunists bent on salvaging a wrecked vessel with a cargo of poison nerve gas. The underwater photography is superb. (Dir: Don McDougall, 102 mins.)

Arabella (Italy, 1967)**½ Virna Lisi, Margaret Rutherford, James Fox, Terry-Thomas. Mild romantic comedy set in Italy in the 1920's. Virna Lisi tries to extract money from men in order to help her aunt pay off taxes dating back to 1895. Weak script. (Dir: Mauro Bolognini, 105 mins.)

Arabesque (1966)**½ Gregory Peck, Sophia Loren. A contrived, not altogether successful chase melodrama with handsome Greg Peck and beautiful Sophia Loren amid lavish international settings. A language expert (Peck) unwillingly gets involved in intrigue. The sights are more absorbing than any dialogue you'll hear. (Dir: Stanley Donen, 104 mins.)

Arabian Nights (1942)** Maria Montez, Jon Hall, Sabu. Corny but elaborately produced spectacle about the days of dancing slave girls, tent cities, and the Caliph of Baghdad. (Dir: John Rawlins, 86 mins.)

Arabian Nights (Italy-France, 1974)**½ Ninetto Davoli, Franco Merli, Ines Pellegrini. Director Pier Paolo Pasolini's adaptation of the old Arab classic is a pure piece of storytellng, eschewing such modern conceits as artistic coherence, psychological realism, and credibility. Supernatural events are treated with nonchalance, and the story line shifts at random to new areas of interest. Sometimes it is difficult to tell the difference between Pasolini's meticulously recreated 16th-century aesthetic and bad 20th-century filmmaking. Much of the film plays remarkably like contemporary pornography—which is, of course, the best preserved of all prehistoric art forms. (155 mins.)

Arch of Triumph (1948)**½ Charles Boyer, Ingrid Bergman, Charles Laughton. A refugee doctor and a girl with a past in Paris, just before the Nazis take over. From Remarque's novel. Long, rather emotionless drama. (Dir: Lewis Milestone, 120 mins.)

Archangels, The (Italy, 1963)** Roberto Bisacco, Virginia Onorato. Girl in Rome to seek her brother's aid is caught up in the life led by him and his city friends. Slow. Dubbed. (Dir: Enzo Battaglia, 102 mins.)

Arctic Flight (1952)**½ Wayne Morris, Lola Albright. Bush pilot battles foreign agents way up North. Not bad little action melodrama—good location scenes. (Dir: Lew Landers, 75 mins.)

Are Husbands Necessary? (1942)** Ray Milland, Betty Field. Contrived, forced farce about the problems of newlyweds. Rarely funny, often embarrassing. (Dir: Norman Taurog, 75 mins.)

Are You in the House Alone? (MTV 1978)*½ Kathleen Beller, Blythe Danner. (Dir: Walter Grauman, 104 mins.)

Are You There? (Great Britain, 1930)**** Beatrice Lillie. A comic masterpiece (also released as "Exit Laughing") that contains one of the most excruciatingly funny scenes ever recorded on film—the great Lady Peel (Lillie) wooing a recalcitrant suitor while swirling a huge chain of beads. If you ever get a chance to see this comedy gem do so. Your sides will hurt from laughing. (Dir: Hamilton MacFadden, 57 mins.)

Are You With It? (1948)*** Donald O'Connor, Olga San Juan. Mathematician leaves his job and joins a traveling carnival. Cute and pleasant musical, with some good work by O'Connor. (Dir: Jack Hively, 90 mins.)

Arena (1953)** Gig Young, Polly Bergen. Story of cowboys competing for prizes in the Tucson rodeo—but there's not much story. Ordinary stuff. (Dir: Richard Fleischer, 70 mins.)

Arena, The (1974)*½ Pam Grier, Margaret Markov, Lucretia Love, Paul Muller. (Dir: Steve Carver, 83 mins.)

Arise My Love (1940)*** Claudette Colbert, Ray Milland, Walter Abel, Dennis O'Keefe, Dick Durcell. Important, nearly forgotten comedy-melodrama, with Colbert and Milland as two American reporters in Europe as WW II impends. Backdrops include the Spanish Civil War and the sinking of the Athenia. Then-current headlines are gracefully employed. Billy Wilder and Charles Brackett wrote the script; the top-notch photography was by Charles Lang, Jr., with a strong Victor Young score. Abel in his most famous role, as the irascible editor in Paris who intones, "I'm not happy. I'm not happy at all...." (Dir: Mitchell Leisen, 113 mins.)

29

Aristocats, The (1970)***½ Full of invention and character, which has always distinguished Disney products. A mama cat and three of her babies who are kidnapped and left in the country by a mean butler. Everything is set magnificently in Paris in 1910. Especially distinctive are the voices; Eva Gabor, Phil Harris, Sterling Holloway, Ruth Buzzi—and Maurice Chevalier singing the title tune. Pleasant family fare. (Dir: Wolfgang Reitherman, 78 mins.)

Arizona (1940)**½ William Holden, Jean Arthur. Western gal has trouble when her rivals have her wagon trains attached. Some fine action scenes; but it's just too darn long. (Dir: Wesley Ruggles, 122 mins.)

Arizona Bushwhackers (1968)** Standard western has a gunslinger-spy (Howard Keel) aid-taming during the Civil War. Good cast including Yvonne DeCarlo, Scott Brady, John Ireland, Marilyn Maxwell, Barton MacLane, Brian Donlevy, James Craig, Roy Rogers, Jr. Narrator: James Cagney! (Dir: Lesley Selander, 86 mins.)

Arizona Mission (1956)** James Arness, Angie Dickinson, Harry Carey, Jr. The stars give good performances in an otherwise run of the mill western drama. Theatrical title: *Gun the Man Down.* (Dir: Andrew V. McLaglen, 78 mins.)

Armored Attack (1943)**½ Anne Baxter, Walter Huston, Dana Andrews. Russian villagers defend their land when the Nazis invade. Only occasionally effective. Theatrical title: *The North Star.* (Dir: Lewis Milestone, 105 mins.)

Armored Car Robbery (1950)***½ Charles McGraw, William Talman. Four participants in an armored car robbery kill a cop. Tough, exciting, extremely well-made melodrama. (Dir: Richard Fleischer, 67 mins.)

Armored Command (1961)** Howard Keel, Tina Louise, Earl Holliman. Routine war film with a romance thrown in. Predictable. (Dir: Byron Haskin, 99 mins.)

Arms and the Man (West Germany, 1958)*** O. W. Fischer, Lilo Pulver. Nicely executed German version of Shaw's memorable play about a Swiss mercenary, fleeing the enemy in the Balkans, who takes refuge in a girl's bedroom. (Dir: Franz Peter Wirth, 96 mins.)

Around the World (1943)**½ Kay Kyser, Joan Davis. Kyser's orchestra takes a round-the-world tour to cheer up fighting men in battle areas. Dull musical. (Dir: Allan Dwan, 80 mins.)

Around the World in 80 Days (1956)**** David Niven, Shirley MacLaine, Cantinflas. Delightful rendition of the Jules Verne tale. Phileas Fogg (Niven) bets his London club that he can do it in 80 days, and away we go. An odds-on favorite all the way. (Dir: Michael Anderson, 170 mins.)

Around the World under the Sea (1966)** David McCallum, Brian Kelly, Marshall Thompson, Lloyd Bridges. Scientists explore the ocean deep to determine the course of tidal waves and such. Strictly for the juvenile trade. (Dir: Andrew Marton, 117 mins.)

Arrangement, The (1968)**½ Kirk Douglas, Faye Dunaway, Deborah Kerr. Uneven treatment of Elia Kazan's novel about the search for meaning by a successful ad agency exec, and the resistance he encounters from those closest to him. Director Kazan allowed himself to wax poetic too often in this weakly constructed self-analysis. (Dir: Elia Kazan, 127 mins.)

Arrivederci, Baby! (1966)*** Tony Curtis, Rosanna Schiaffino. An amusing comedy about a money-hungry young man who keeps discarding guardians and wives for their fortunes. He meets his match in Rosanna Schiaffino, the widow of a nobleman. (Dir: Ken Hughes, 105 mins.)

Arrow In the Dust (1954)** Sterling Hayden, Coleen Gray. Wagon train dependent on one strong man—this time it's Sterling Hayden and he's a cavalry trooper who impersonates a major. (Dir: Lesley Selander, 80 mins.)

Arrowhead (1953)**½ Charlton Heston, Jack Palance, Katy Jurado. Trouble in the Southwest when a Cavalry unit attempts to sign a peace treaty with the Apaches. Well-made but routine western. (Dir: Charles Warren, 105 mins.)

Arrowsmith (1931)***½ Ronald Colman, Helen Hayes, Richard Bennett, Myrna Loy. From Sinclair Lewis's beautiful novel about dedicated medical researcher (Colman) who remains true to his ideals despite the loss of his beloved wife (Hayes) and the temptation of a rich girl's love (Loy). An absorbing film drama, thanks to an exceptional screenplay by Sidney Howard and John Ford's intelligent direction. Hayes is lovely in one of her few film roles in the earlier part of her distinguished stage career. (108 mins.)

Arsène Lupin (1932)**½ John Barrymore, Lionel Barrymore, Karen Morley, John Miljan. It's John vs. Lionel in this fairly turgid film about the famed gentleman thief. Jack had already essayed Raffles in his late teens on stage and film; he breezes through this part lightly as Lionel ponders through his as a prefect of police. Jack Conway directed, with care yet inattention to matters of pace, character, and style. (84 mins.)

Arsène Lupin Returns (1938)** Melvyn Douglas, Warren William, Virginia Bruce, Monty Woolley. This MGM sequel teams the interesting pair of Douglas and William as the gentleman thief and the detective who pursues him. Bruce is the love interest. (Dir: George Fitzmaurice, 81 mins.)

Arsenic and Old Lace (1944)*½ Cary Grant, Priscilla Lane, Josephine Hull, Jean Adair, Raymond Massey, Peter Lorre, Jack Carson, John Ridgely, James Gleason, Edward Everett Horton. A funny hit play and the number one comedy director in Hollywood should have been a madcap classic. Well, it's not what it should have been. Lorre's giggling, guzzling Dr. Einstein and the two delightful maiden aunts steal every scene, even from such experts as Carson, Gleason, and Horton. (Dir: Frank Capra, 116 mins.)

Arson for Hire (1959)*½ Steve Brodie, Tom Hubbard. (Dir: Thor Brooks, 67 mins.)

Art of Crime, The (MTV 1975)**½ Ron Leibman, Jose Ferrer, David Hedison, Jill Clayburgh. Writers Martin Smith and Bill Davidson, basing their material on the novel *Gypsy in Amber*, dip into gypsy culture and reveal interesting tidbits on the art of fooling the antique-buying public. A slick and slightly different product. (Dir: Richard Irving, 72 mins.)

Art of Love, The (1965)**½ James Garner, Dick Van Dyke, Elke Sommer, Angie Dickinson. Deciding that dead artists are the only ones who sell well, a painter and his buddy decide to fake a suicide. (Dir: Norman Jewison, 98 mins.)   •

Art of Vision, The (1966)***½ Director Stan Brakhage's experimental film which includes all of his "Dog Star Man" (prelude and Parts 1–4), made between '61 and '65. He has been a dominant figure in American experimental cinema since the '50s, and this 4½-hour film may be his most acclaimed work. (207 mins.)

Artists and Models (1937)*** Jack Benny, Ida Lupino, Gail Patrick. Jack runs a down-and-out advertising agency, and if he can find the right model, he lands a big account. Plenty of specialty numbers performed by Martha Raye, Connee Boswell, and Louis Armstrong. (Dir: Raoul Walsh, 97 mins.)

Artists and Models (1955)**½ Dean Martin, Jerry Lewis, Shirley MacLaine, Dorothy Malone. Artist lands a big job doing comic strips, inspired by his goofy partner's dreams. Some fun, but it goes on too long. (Dir: Frank Tashlin, 109 mins.)

Artur Rubinstein—Love of Life (1975)**** A beguiling portrait of the great pianist near retirement, musically supple and anecdotally engrossing. Rubinstein remained an incomparable raconteur and even as blindness kept him from public performance after his late 80s, the insight of his playing deepened continually. François Reichenbach and S. G. Patris directed this Oscar-winning documentary. (91 mins.)

Arturo's Island (Italy, 1963)**½ Vanni de Maigret, Key Meersman, Reginald Kernan. Somber tale of a boy who's left alone in a huge house on his father's island. (Dir: Damiano Damiani, 93 mins.)

As If It Were Raining (France, 1960)*½ Eddie Constantine, Elisa Montes. (Dir: Jose Monter, 85 mins.)

As Long as They're Happy (Great Britain, 1955)**½ Jack Buchanan, Janette Scott. Englishman's daughter swoons for a visiting American crooner. Amusing. (Dir: J. Lee Thompson, 76 mins.)

As Long as You're Near Me (Germany, 1956)** Maria Schell, O. W. Fischer. Story of a girl who lived her love life twice. Excellent performances by two of Germany's leading actors, Miss Schell and Mr. Fischer. (Dir: Harald Braun, 101 mins.)

As the Sea Rages (1960)*½ Maria Schell, Cliff Robertson. (Dir: Horst Haechler, 74 mins.)

As You Desire Me (1932)*** Greta Garbo, Erich von Stroheim, Melvyn Douglas. Garbo, as MGM's reigning star, demanded and got von Stroheim to play opposite her in this adaptation of the Pirandello play about a lovely amnesiac who is rescued from the clutches of a sadistic writer by a husband she keeps forgetting she has. These elements should have led to a better film than this heavy-breathing embalmed melodrama in which the stars do astute byplay in the mode of domination and submission; director George Fitzmaurice brings little more than a stylish visual gloss to the proceedings. (71 mins.)

As You Like It (Great Britain, 1936)***½ Laurence Olivier, Elisabeth Bergner, Felix Aylmer. The art direction, as is its wont, overpowers the Shakespeare in this overmounted production, which is nonetheless notable for the Viennese-accented Rosalind of gamine Bergner and a young Olivier as Orlando, the classic goof. Produced and directed by Paul Czinner, Bergner's husband; music by William Walton. (97 mins.)

As You Like It (Great Britain, MTV 1978)**** Helen Mirren, Angharad Rees, Brian Stirner, Richard Pasco, Clive Francis, James Bolam, Victoria Plucknett. Taking Shakespeare's imaginative comedy outdoors proves an inspiration which lifts the quality and appeal of this BBC production (in the ambitious series of the Bard's complete works). Played to the hilt, with a luminous Helen Mirren as Rosalind, and a handsome if stolid Brian Stirner as Orlando, the charm and spirit of the tale seldom lose momentum. The banishment and subsequent flight of Rosalind, a noble lady disguised as a youth, to the wondrous forest of Arden hold the interest. The idyllic romances of the main characters are meaningfully contrasted with more sober examples of the bitterness of false love and misanthropy, in two superbly acted smaller roles, Touchstone (James Bolam), and the "melancholy" Jacques (Richard Pasco). There is never thoughtless humor in Shakespeare. (Dir: Basil Coleman, 150 mins.)

As Young as We Are (1958)** Pippa Scott, Robert Harland. Schoolteacher falls in love with one of her pupils. Sincere performances. (Dir: Bernard Girard, 76 mins.)

As Young as You Feel (1951)** Monty

31

Woolley, Thelma Ritter, David Wayne, Jean Peters, Marilyn Monroe, Constance Bennett. Zany family and their madcap shenanigans. It doesn't come off despite the starring line-up. (Dir: Harmon Jones, 77 mins.)

Ascent to Heaven—See: **Mexican Bus Ride**

Ash Wednesday (1973)* Elizabeth Taylor, Henry Fonda, Helmut Berger. (Dir: Larry Peerce, 99 mins.)

Ashanti (Switzerland, 1979)*½ Michael Caine, Omar Sharif, Peter Ustinov, Rex Harrison, William Holden, Beverly Johnson. (Dir: Richard Fleischer, 117 mins.)

Ashes and Diamonds (Poland, 1958)**** Zbigniew Cybulski. This film, based on a controversial post-war Polish novel, is about the last day of war and the first day of peace in Warsaw, and the mixed-up loyalties and emotions of a young Polish partisan. (Dir: Andrzej Wajda, 104 mins.)

Ask Any Girl (1959)**½ David Niven, Shirley MacLaine, Gig Young. An attractive cast of expert screen comics adds stature to this feather-weight story about the plight of the single girl in the big city. (Dir: Charles Walters, 98 mins.)

Asphalt Jungle, The (1950)**** Sterling Hayden, Sam Jaffe, Marc Lawrence, Jean Hagen, Louis Calhern, Marilyn Monroe. Director John Huston's theses of collective effort and nihilist failure were never more starkly dramatized than in this genre-creating caper film, which makes crime look like something in line for an SBA loan. Uniformly well acted by a nonpareil gallery of small-bracket losers; Lawrence was never better. Screenplay by Huston and Ben Maddow, photographed by Harold Rosson. (112 mins.)

Asphyx, The (Great Britain, 1972)*** Robert Powell, Robert Stephens, Jane Lapotaire. Not a bad little thriller, with a premise that's certainly unusual. A Victorian scientist (Stephens) discovers that death can occur only when a spiritlike creature called the asphyx escapes from the body. He decides to trap the asphyx and thus create eternal life. This has, of course, disastrous results ("there are *some* things man is not meant to know"). The story is greatly aided by strong performances by Stephens, Powell as his understandably disenchanted son, and Lapotaire as a victim of his experiments. It has a tricky ending, too. (Dir: Peter Newbrook, 99 mins.)

Assassin, The (Great Britain, 1953)**½ Richard Todd, Eva Bartok. Good European backgrounds, routine chase story as detective tracks down a man supposed to be dead. (Dir: Ralph Thomas, 90 mins.)

Assassination Bureau, The (Great Britain, 1969)*** Oliver Reed, Diana Rigg, Telly Savalas, Curt Jurgens, Beryl Reid. Rigg is on assignment for a London newspaper as she gets the goods on a professional outfit headed by ambivalent hero Reed. Together they smash villains Jurgens and

Savalas, while escaping fates worse than death in Reid's Parisian House of Pleasure. Too much pseudo-Victorian whimsy, but just the right amount of Rigg. Basil Dearden directed, a little better than usual. (106 mins.)

Assassination of Trotsky, The (France-Italy-Great Britain, 1972)*** Richard Burton, Alain Delon, Romy Schneider. The killing of Trotsky, the famous Russian revolutionary leader, is documented. Laced with symbolism and psychological insight. The acting is good, and the direction is intense and atmospheric. You may either hate or love this film, but you will react. (Dir: Joseph Losey, 103 mins.)

Assault on a Queen (1966)* Frank Sinatra, Virna Lisi, Tony Franciosa. (Dir: Jack Donohue, 106 mins.)

Assault on Precinct 13 (1976)*** Austin Stoker, Darwin Joston, Laurie Zimmer. First-rate paranoia, third-rate motivation in this exceedingly violent reworking of Howard Hawks's "Rio Bravo" set in a police station in a forsaken neighborhood of Los Angeles. For all the frank borrowings, the film is genuinely reimagined by writer-director John Carpenter ("Halloween") as an urban horror film. (When the editing is credited to one John T. Chance, the character played by John Wayne in "Rio Bravo," one must assume that means Carpenter, too.) (91 mins.)

Assault on the Wayne (MTV 1971)*½ Leonard Nimoy, Lloyd Haynes, William Windom. (Dir: Marvin Chomsky, 74 mins.)

Assignment Abroad (1955)* Robert Alda. (73 mins.)

Assignment in Paris (1952)**½ Dana Andrews, Marta Toren, George Sanders. A reporter is captured and imprisoned when he comes into possession of some important microfilm. (Dir: Robert Parrish, 85 mins.)

Assignment K (Great Britain, 1968)** Stephen Boyd, Camilla Sparv, Michael Redgrave (good in a thankless bit), Leo McKern, Jeremy Kemp. Spies and counterspies all over Europe, with an intrepid British intelligence agent played for a patsy. (Dir: Val Guest, 97 mins.)

Assignment Munich (MTV 1972)**½ Roy Scheider, Richard Basehart, Lesley Warren, Robert Reed. Here's the pilot for the TV series "Assignment Vienna" (there was a change in the location, plus). Scheider stars as Jake Webster, a worldly guy who runs a bar in Munich and does odd jobs for the American military division connected with Interpol. Scheider creates a character in the old Bogart mold, the offbeat adventurer with more than a shade of larceny in his soul and a keen eye for a pretty femme. The plot's a chase story, involving assorted types looking for millions in cached-away gold, and on-location European sites add to the enjoyment. (Dir: David Lowell Rich, 104 mins.)

Assignment Outer Space (Italy, 1960)½

Archie Savage, Rik Von Nutter. (Dir: Antonio Margheriti, 79 mins.)

Assignment to Kill (1968)*½ Patrick O'Neal, Joan Hackett, Herbert Lom. (Dir: Sheldon Reynolds, 102 mins.)

Astonished Heart, The (Great Britain, 1950)**½ Noel Coward, Margaret Leighton, Celia Johnson. Married psychiatrist falls for an old friend, the affair leading to tragedy. Overdone drama. (Dirs: Anthony Darnborough, Terence Fisher, 92 mins.)

Astounding She Monster (1959)* Robert Clarke, Marilyn Harvey. (Dir: Ronnie Ashcroft, 59 mins.)

Astronaut, The (MTV 1972)**½ Monte Markham, Susan Clark. After an astronaut dies during a Mars landing, space officials use the old masquerade trick, hoping to deceive the world with a double. (Dir: Robert Michael Lewis, 72 mins.)

Asylum—See: **House of Crazies**

Asylum (1972)**** Involving documentary about mentally disturbed patients living in a "community" under the guiding aegis of the distinguished British psychiatrist R. D. Laing. Several of the patients are clearly psychotic, but director-producer Peter Robinson never exploits them. Filmed in London at Laing's "community" clinic. (Dir: Peter Robinson, 95 mins.)

Asylum (Great Britain, 1972)**½ Peter Cushing, Herbert Lom, Richard Todd, Barbara Parkins. A chilling quartet of tales—"Frozen Fear," "The Weird Tailor," "Lucy Comes to Stay," and "Mannikins of Horror"—are told to a visiting doctor at an asylum. Entertaining. Written by Robert Bloch. (Dir: Roy Ward Baker, 88 mins.)

Asylum for a Spy (MTV 1967)*½ Robert Stack, Felicia Farr, Martin Milner. (Dir: Stuart Rosenberg, 90 mins.)

At Dawn We Die (Great Britain, 1943)** John Clements, Godfrey Tearle, Greta Gynt. Another version of French Underground versus Nazis. (Dir: George King, 78 mins.)

At Gunpoint (1955)**½ Fred MacMurray, Dorothy Malone. A good cast and good production makes this western drama entertaining. A peaceful man who does his duty as a citizen ends up being stalked by a band of outlaws. (Dir: Alfred Werker, 81 mins.)

At Long Last Love (1975)* Burt Reynolds, Cybill Shepherd, Madeline Kahn, Eileen Brennan, Duilio Del Prete, John Hillerman. (Dir: Peter Bogdanovich, 115 mins.)

At Sword's Point (1952)*** Cornel Wilde, Maureen O'Hara. The sons of the Three Musketeers save their queen from intrigue. Lively costume melodrama. (Dir: Lewis Allen, 81 mins.)

At the Circus (1939)*** The Marx Brothers, Margaret Dumont, Florence Rice, Kenny Baker, Eve Arden. The Marx Brothers in unmistakable decline. Nothing they could do would be without laughs or interest, but the level of zaniness is often less than inspired. Groucho has his moments, as always, singing of "Lydia the Tattooed Lady," and he and Dumont have their act down to a stylized duet of sublime interplay. Harold Arlen did the songs. (Dir: Edward Buzzell, 87 mins.)

At the Earth's Core (Great Britain, 1976)**½ Doug McClure, Peter Cushing, Cy Grant. A sequel to the 1974 "The Land that Time Forgot." Occasionally entertaining blend of fantasy, humor and chills based on the 1923 novel by Edgar Rice Burroughs. Cushing bores through to the center of the earth. (Dir: Kevin Connor, 90 mins.)

At the Stroke of Nine (Great Britain, 1957)** Patricia Dainton, Stephen Murray. A slow but interesting drama about the kidnapping of a newspaper woman. (Dir: Lance Comfort, 72 mins.)

At War with the Army (1950)**½ Dean Martin, Jerry Lewis, Polly Bergen. Sergeant tries to get a dumb PFC to help him out of some girl trouble. Despite the fact that this farce shot Martin & Lewis to fame as a screen comedy team, it doesn't happen to be terribly funny. (Dir: Hal Walker, 93 mins.)

Athena (1954)*½ Jane Powell, Debbie Reynolds, Edmund Purdom, Vic Damone, Linda Christian, Louis Calhern. (Dir: Richard Thorpe, 96 mins.)

Atlantic City (1944)** Constance Moore, Brad Taylor, Stanley Brown, Jerry Colonna. An idea man and his girl, build an enterprise out of some useless swampland. Just fair. (Dir: Ray McCarey, 87 mins.)

Atlantic City (1981)**** Burt Lancaster, Susan Sarandon, Robert Joy, Kate Reid, Hollis McLaren. An absolutely stunning film by Louis Malle, this English-language production is riveting from its first few shots and never lets it up. It has the kind of rhythmically precise direction that bespeaks absolute artistic command, eliciting the maximum impact from the smallest of expressed emotions. The scene is the title town, where the glory days have gone to seed and a new dawn of opportunism is breaking. The drama focuses on a series of losers and fools, pursuing their fantasies and facing the harsh dangers of the ruthless real world. Everyone involved is superlative, from Burt Lancaster and Susan Sarandon to the newcomer Robert Joy (who plays a new breed of punk kid to make your skin creep). The supple screenplay is by playwright John Guare. (105 mins.)

Atlantic Convoy (1942)**½ Bruce Bennett, Virginia Field, John Beal. A man is suspected of aiding the Nazis and must redeem himself. (Dir: Lew Landers, 70 mins.)

Atlantis, the Lost Continent (1961)** Anthony Hall, Joyce Taylor. Costume adventure tale about a mythical lost continent in the days of the Roman Empire. (Dir: George Pal, 90 mins.)

Atlas (1961)** Michael Forrest, Frank

Wolff. Cheap costume catastrophe; made in Greece. (Dir: Roger Corman, 84 mins.)

Atlas Against the Cyclops (Italy, 1961)* Gordon Mitchell, Chelo Alonso.(Dir: Antonio Leonviola, 100 mins.)

Atlas Against the Czar (Italy, 1964)* Kirk Morris, Glória Milland. Alternate title: **Maciste Against the Czar.** (Dir: Amerigo Anton, 90 mins.)

Atoll K—See: **Utopia**

Atom Age Vampire (Italy, 1961)*½ Alberto Lupo, Susanne Loret. (Dir: Richard McNamara, 87 mins.)

Atomic Agent (France, 1959)* Martine Carol, Felix Marten, Dany Saval. (Dir: Henri Decoin, 85 mins.)

Atomic City (1952)*** Gene Barry, Lydia Clarke, Milburn Stone. Son of a physicist is kidnapped. Suspenseful melodrama with an unusual locale, thoughtful script, nice performances. (Dir: Jerry Hopper, 85 mins.)

Atomic Kid (1954)** Mickey Rooney, Robert Strauss, Elaine Davis. Guy survives an atomic blast but becomes radioactive. Fair comedy. (Dir: Leslie Martinson, 86 mins.)

Atomic Man, The (1956)** Gene Nelson, Faith Domergue. A reporter and his girl stumble on a mystery concerning a shady scientist. (Dir: Ken Hughes, 78 mins.)

Atomic Rulers of the World (Japan, 1957)* Ken Utsui. (Dir: Teruo Ishii, 83 mins.)

Atomic Submarine (1960)*½ Arthur Franz, Dick Foran. (Dir: Spencer Bennet, 72 mins.)

Atomic War Bride (Yugoslavia, 1960)* Anton Voldak, Eva Krewskan. (Dir: Veljko Bulajic, 77 mins.)

Atragon (Japan, 1964)* Tadao Takashima, Yoko Fujiyama, Yu Fujiki. (Dir: Inoshiro Honda, 96 mins.)

Attack! (1956)**** Jack Palance, Lee Marvin, Eddie Albert, Buddy Ebsen, Richard Jaeckel. An antiwar film directed by Robert Aldrich. It has always been the most popular of his works, because it is one of his few films with an overt social message. Still, his real interest seems to lie in the war of nerves waged between hard-nosed Lieutenant Palance and chicken Colonel Albert; his obsessive theme has always been the personal divisiveness of men united by action, and it is realized here to grinding effect. (107 mins.)

Attack and Retreat (U.S.S.R.-Italy, 1964)**½ Arthur Kennedy, Peter Falk, Tatiana Samilova. Sprawling World War II story of Italian soldiers and their experiences on the Russian front. (Dir: Giuseppe De Santis, 156 mins.)

Attack of the Crab Monsters (1957)*½ Richard Garland, Pamela Duncan. (Dir: Roger Corman, 70 mins.)

Attack of the 50-Foot Woman (1958)** Allison Hayes, William Hudson. The giantess of the title manages to create quite a fuss. (Dir: Nathan Juran, 65 mins.)

Attack of the Giant Leeches (1959)** Ken Clark, Yvette Vickers. Routine horror tale about outsized leeches. Released as: *"The*

Giant Leeches." (Dir: Bernard L. Kowalski, 62 mins.)

Attack of the Killer Tomatoes! (1978)** David Miller, George Wilson, Sharon Taylor, Jack Riley. Some guys will do anything for laughs. And not get them. Screenplay by Costa Dillon, Steve Peacke, and director John de Bello. Spoof of horror pix in which seemingly ordinary objects (guess what) become sinister menaces. (87 mins.)

Attack of the Mayan Mummy (Mexico-U.S., 1963)* Nina Knight, Richard Webb. (Dir: Jerry Warren, 77 mins.)

Attack of the Moors (Italy, 1960)* Rik Bataglia, Chelo Alonso. (Dir: Mario Costa, 80 mins.)

Attack of the Mushroom People (Japan, 1964)*½ Akira Kubo. (Dir: Inoshiro Honda, 89 mins.)

Attack of the Normans (Italy, 1962)*½ Cameron Mitchell, Genevieve Grad. Dubbed. (Dir: Mario Bava, 90 mins.)

Attack of the Puppet People (1958)*½ John Agar, June Kenney. (Dir: Bert Gordon, 79 mins.)

Attack of the Robots (France-Spain, 1967)* Eddie Constantine, Fernando Rey. (Dir: J. Franco, 88 mins.)

Attack on Terror: The FBI versus the Ku Klux Klan (MTV 1975)**½ Rip Torn, George Grizzard. Compelling recreation of the 1964 murder of three civil-rights workers in Mississippi. The movie romanticizes the real performance of the FBI in the Deep South during the '50's and '60's, but it's still worth seeing. Originally shown in two parts as a four-hour drama. (Dir: Marvin Chomsky, 215 mins.)

Attack on the Iron Coast (Great Britain, 1968)**½ Lloyd Bridges, Andrew Keir, Sue Lloyd, Mark Eden. Commandos attempt a daring raid on German installations during World War II. Competently handled. (Dir: Paul Wendkos, 89 mins.)

Attack Squadron (Japan, 1963)** Toshiro Mifune. Dubbed. The war from enemy viewpoint, as a Japanese officer fights in vain to replace an air attack unit in 1944. (Dir: Shue Matsubayashi, 102 mins.)

Attempt to Kill (Great Britain, 1962)* Derek Farr, Freda Jackson. (Dir: Royston Morley, 57 mins.)

Attica (1974)**** An impassioned, altogether splendid documentary by Cinda Firestone about the prison revolt and the subsequent murders ordered by Nelson Rockefeller. Lest we forget or lest we tire. Effective use of interviews with prisoners and outside civilian participants trying to help end the stalemate which turned into a slaughter. (Dir: Cinda Firestone, 80 mins.)

Attica (MTV 1980)**** George Grizzard, Charles Durning, Henry Darrow, Morgan Freeman, Anthony Zerbe. "The firing continued for six minutes. When the shooting ended, there were 39 people dead, 10 hostages and 29 inmates. Three hostages and 85 inmates were seriously wounded. It was the largest number of casualties in any single engagement between Americans since the Civil War." This is from journalist Tom Wicker's book *A Time to Die*, about the unnecessary slaughter at Attica prison in the fall of 1971 after Governor Nelson Rockefeller sent in the New York state troopers. This docudrama is one of the best of the genre ever made for American TV, and it would have been even more powerful if three, not two, hours, had been allotted to its presentation on ABC. The writer and director had to make changes demanded by the network—one of which made the film less critical of Rockefeller—but it remains a searing, powerful indictment of our prison system and of Rockefeller's decision to send in the troops. Performances are uniformly excellent, including Grizzard as Wicker and Zerbe portraying—not too flatteringly—attorney William Kunstler. Written by James Henerson and directed by one of TV's best, Marvin J. Chomsky, who directed much of "Roots" and all of "Holocaust." TV docudramas have frequently been exploitative, misleading, or both. This one reminds us that they can be valid history and exciting theater. (104 mins.)

Attila (France-Italy, 1955)*½ Anthony Quinn, Sophia Loren, Irene Papas. (Dir: Pietro Francisci, 83 mins.)

Attila 1974: The Rape of Cyprus (Greece, 1975)***½ Powerfully felt documentary directed by Michael Cacoyannis (the Euripides trilogy; "Zorba the Greek") about the Turkish incursion that effectively partitioned the island and precipitated the overthrow of the Greek military junta. The characters are the movers of history: Archbishop Makarios, Nikos Sampson, Glafkos Clerides. Angry yet humanistic, the film evidences a respectful appreciation for the ambiguities of history—where aggression against some means liberation for others. (103 mins.)

Au Hasard Balthazar (France-Sweden, 1966)**** Anne Wiazemsky, François Lafarge, Philippe Asselin. "Everyone who sees this film will be absolutely astonished," said Jean-Luc Godard, "because this film is really the world in an hour and a half." Director Robert Bresson's masterpiece defies conventional analysis, telling a story of sin and redemption by following Balthazar, a donkey, as he passes through the hands of a number of masters, including a peasant girl, a satanic delinquent, and a saintly fool. Not to be missed. (96 mins.)

Audrey Rose (1977)*½ Marsha Mason, Anthony Hopkins, John Beck, Norman Lloyd, Susan Swift. (112 mins.)

August without the Emperor (Japan, 1978)*** Tetsuro Tamba, Rentaro Mikuni, Shin Saburi. A political thriller from Japan, with implications of official corruption that are not easily made in that authority-respecting country. Director Satsuo Yamamoto has made a career of commercial leftism. About political terrorists who hold 350 hostages on a speeding train. The main actors play a trio of officials.

Augustine of Hippo (Italy, 1972)**** Deri Berkani. Another chapter in director Roberto Rossellini's filmed history of civilization. Begins with St. Augustine's appointment as bishop of Hippo Regius in North Africa and follows his attempts to preserve the moral focus of his life as the Roman Empire enters its decline. Rossellini said of the film, "The idea of a civilization that is dying, and that, nevertheless, preserves and projects into the future something of itself—that deeply fascinates me." Stimulating and remarkable. (120 mins.)

Aunt Mary (MTV 1979)*** Jean Stapleton, Martin Balsam, Harold Gould, Dolph Sweet, Anthony Cafiso. A true "you can do anything you want" story, based on the experiences of Baltimore's Mary Dobkin (a chipper old maid who coaches a sandlot baseball team). Writer Burt Prelutsky injects enough spice into the dialogue to keep it from being overly sentimental. Miss Stapleton is terrific playing a lady who knows how to handle kids. Although the baseball scenes are typically Hollywood, she gets good support from child actor Cafiso, who looks and sounds as if he came from the street. Quality, heartwarming fluff. (Dir: Peter Werner, 98 mins.)

Auntie Mame (1958)**½ Rosalind Russell, Forrest Tucker, Peggy Cass, Coral Browne. All of the raucous incidents from the bestseller and the hit play are repeated in the screen version. Roz Russell works like a dynamo in a role tailor-made for her talents. (Dir: Morton DaCosta, 143 mins.)

Autobiography of Miss Jane Pittman, The (MTV 1974)**** Cicely Tyson, Odetta, Michael Murphy, Collin Wilxoc. One of the best movies ever made for American TV. Cicely Tyson won a richly deserved Emmy award for her triumphant performance in the role of a 110-year-old woman who was an ex-slave, and lived to take part in a civil rights demonstration in 1962. Extensive use of flashbacks depicting various episodes in the life of Miss Jane, a fictional character; but the incidents are based on real incidents that happened throughout the South after the Civil War. Adapted from Ernest J. Gaines' novel. Director John Korty, screenwriter Tracy Keenan Wynn both won Emmy awards. (102 mins.)

Autopsy of a Criminal (Spain, 1962)*½ Daniele Godel, Francisco Rabal. (Dir: Ricardo Blasco, 92 mins.)

Autumn Leaves (1956)*** Joan Crawford, Cliff Robertson, Lorne Greene, Vera Miles, Ruth Donnelly. In this interesting example of star masochism, Crawford is a middle-aged spinster who is romanced by a mentally unstable young man prone to fits of violence (Robertson). The material could go tawdry at any point, but doesn't, largely because director Robert Aldrich provides a meaningful visual context for the relationship and also because the two leads play in surprisingly persuasive harmony. (110 mins.)

Autumn Sonata (Sweden, 1978)**** Ingrid Bergman, Liv Ullmann, Lena Nyman. Director Ingmar Bergman painfully evokes the cruelty of unforgiveness, with Ullmann the resentful daughter trying, futilely, to settle old scores with her self-absorbed mother, a concert pianist of international rank, played with uncommon candor by Ingrid Bergman. The usual Ingmar Bergman longueurs are undeniably present—he is the most erratic of the great directors—but the overwhelming compassion for human frailty expressed here compels a like generosity in the viewer. (97 mins.)

Avalanche (1978)½ Rock Hudson, Mia Farrow, Robert Forster. (Dir: Corey Allen, 91 mins.)

Avalanche Express (1979)* Lee Marvin, Robert Shaw, Maximilian Schell, Linda Evans, Mike Connors. (Dirs: Mark Robson, Monte Hellman, 88 mins.)

Avanti! (1972)*** Jack Lemmon, Juliet Mills. Not one of director Billy Wilder's best, but entertaining nevertheless. A successful businessman who goes to Italy to arrange for the return of his tycoon-father's body only to discover dad died with his mistress of long standing. (144 mins.)

Avenger, The (Germany, 1961)*½ Heinz Drache, Ingrid Bergen. (Dir: Karl Anton, 102 mins.)

Avenger, The (Steve Reeves)—See: **Last Glory of Troy, The**

Avenger of the Seven Seas (Italy, 1961)* Richard Harrison, Walter Barnes. (Dir: Domenico Paolella, 94 mins.)

Avenger of Venice (Italy, 1963)* Brett Halsey. (Dir: Riccardo Freda, 90 mins.)

Avengers, The (1950)*½ John Carroll, Adele Mara, Fernando Lamas. (Dir: John H. Auer, 90 mins.)

Avenging Conscience, The (1914)***½ Henry B. Walthall, Blanche Sweet. Pre-*Birth of a Nation* feature by D. W. Griffith, composed of bits and pieces of Poe's short stories, shows Griffith's technical mastery on the eve of his most influential production. (Dir: D. W. Griffith, 60 mins.)

Awakening, The (Italy, 1956)***½ Anna Magnani, Eleonora Rossi-Drago. A heartwarming and touching film. A nun becomes attached to a little boy who has run away from his mother. (Dir: Mario Camerini, 97 mins.)

Away All Boats (1956)**½ Jeff Chandler, George Nader, Julia Adams. Overproduced naval war drama; outrageous displays of heroics. (Dir: Joseph Pevney, 114 mins.)

Awful Dr. Orlof, The (Spain 1962)* Howard Vernon, Conrado San Martin, Diana Lorys. (Dir: Jess Franco, 95 mins.)

Awful Truth, The (1937)**** Cary Grant, Irene Dunne, Ralph Bellamy. Director Leo McCarey's largely improvised film is one of the funniest screwball comedies and one of the most serious at heart. Grant and Dunne are a pair of world-weary socialites who decide to drop the pretense of their wide-open marriage, but fate and Bellamy draw them together again. The awful truth is that they need each other, and McCarey, with his profound faith in monogamy, leads them gradually and hilariously to that discovery. The issues deepen in a subtle, natural way; the film begins as a trifle and ends as something beautiful and affirmative. McCarey won the Best Director Oscar. (Cinephiles will recognize the fox terrier as Asta in the Thin Man movies.) (90 mins.)

B.A.D. Cats, The (MTV 1980)* Asher Brauner, Steve Hanks, Jimmie Walker, Vic Morrow. (Dir: Bernie Kowalski, 78 mins.)

Babbitt (1934)*** Guy Kibbee, Aline MacMahon, Claire Dodd. They lost the bite of the Sinclair Lewis novel, but the performances, especially Mr. Kibbee's, help you forget the weak adaptation. (Dir: William Keighley, 74 mins.)

Babe (MTV 1975)*** Susan Clark, Alex Karras. Babe Didrikson Zaharias was one of the greatest female athletes of all time, and it was inevitable that a movie would be made about her life. Two solid performances by Clark, as Babe, and Karras, as her husband George Zaharias. Worth watching. (Dir: Buzz Kulik, 106 mins.)

Babe Ruth Story, The (1948)** William Bendix, Claire Trevor, Charles Bickford. Sentimental, mediocre biography of the mighty Babe. Run-of-the-mill. (Dir: Roy Del Ruth, 106 mins.)

Babes in Arms (1939)**½ Mickey Rooney, Judy Garland. Not much of Busby Berkeley's visual dynamism is in evidence in this MGM juvenile musical, with Mickey Rooney and Judy Garland leading a gang of ex-vaudeville stars' kids in putting on a fund-raising show to save their parents from bankruptcy. In general, it's pretty hard to take, but Berkeley's crane work is sublime during the title number, which in itself is a somewhat unintentional parody of mob-rule propaganda films. Rooney is so peripatetic that it's surprising he didn't o.d. on amphetamines; this unmodulated exercise in unbridled energy actually netted him an Oscar nomination for Best Actor. (Dir: Busby Berkeley, 97 mins.)

Babes in Bagdad (1952)* Paulette Goddard, Gypsy Rose Lee. (Dir: Edgar Ulmer, 79 mins.)

Babes in Toyland—See: **March of the Wooden Soldiers.**

Babes on Broadway (1941)**½ Mickey Rooney, Judy Garland. Young hopefuls on Broadway. Only the musical numbers merit any attention. (Dir: Busby Berkeley, 118 mins.)

Babette Goes to War (France, 1960)**½

Brigitte Bardot, Jacques Charrier. A WW II spy yarn with lovely B.B. assigned to prowl behind enemy lines for the French army. (Dir: Christian-Jaque, 103 mins.)

Baby, The (1973)**½ Anjanette Comer, Ruth Roman, Marianna Hill, Suzanne Zenor, David Manzy. Starting out as a social document about a kinky family and a dedicated welfare worker, this develops into a full-fledged horror film. Sweet but determined, Comer becomes interested in Baby, fully grown but with the mind of an infant. Acting by Comer, and Roman as the nasty mother, is OK. Slick and sick, with a twist ending. (Dir: Ted Post, 86 mins.)

Baby and the Battleship, The (Great Britain, 1955)**½ John Mills, Richard Attenborough. Fast and rowdy comedy; a couple of sailors smuggle a baby aboard their ship. (Dir: Jay Lewis, 96 mins.)

Baby Blue Marine (1976)*½ Jan-Michael Vincent, Glynnis O'Connor, Katherine Helmond. (Dir: John Hancock, 89 mins.)

Baby Doll (1956)***½ Carroll Baker, Eli Wallach, Karl Malden. Tennessee Williams' tale about a child bride, her possessive but foolish husband, and a stranger who dupes them both. Works most of the time, thanks to Elia Kazan's direction and a good cast. (Dir: Elia Kazan, 114 mins.)

Baby Face Nelson (1957)*** Mickey Rooney, Carolyn Jones, Cedric Hardwicke. Action-crammed story of stickups, bank robberies, ruthless killings, and prison breaks. (Dir: Don Siegel, 85 mins.)

Baby Love (Great Britain, 1969)** Linda Hayden, Keith Barron. A sleazy tale about a nymphet who uses her wiles and body to sexually enslave a household. (Dir: Alastair Reid, 98 mins.)

Baby, the Rain Must Fall (1965)** Lee Remick, Steve McQueen, Don Murray. Soggy drama of a noble wife who tries to live with her moody, guitar-twanging, hotheaded husband. Pretentious, heavy-handed. (Dir: Robert Mulligan, 100 mins.)

Babymaker, The (1970)**½ Barbara Hershey, Sam Groom, Collin Wilcox-Horne. A young, free-spirited girl agrees to bear a child, fathered by the husband of a childless couple. Offbeat drama, successful most of the way. (Dir: James Bridges, 107 mins.)

Babysitter, The (MTV 1980)*½ William Shatner, Patty Duke Astin, Stephanie Zimbalist, Quinn Cummings. A troubled married couple (superbly played by Shatner and Astin) hire an attractive teenager (Zimbalist) to take care of their house and younger daughter (Cummings). Shortly thereafter, the babysitter seemingly takes over the family with spellbinding effect and eventually tries to kill them. It takes kindly neighbor John Houseman to unravel the evil doings next door. A good cast and a rousing conclusion help here. (Dir: Peter Medak, 104 mins.)

Bacchantes, The (France-Italy, 1961)** Taina Elg, Akim Tamiroff. Run-of-the-mill fare of this kind (Italian-made, English dubbed). (Dir: Giorgio Ferroni, 100 mins.)

Bachelor and the Bobby-Soxer, The (1947)**½ Cary Grant, Myrna Loy, Shirley Temple, Rudy Vallee. Rather pallid comedy that can't coast far enough on Grant's charm. In an embarrassing role he is the man who is sentenced by Judge Loy to squire her adolescent sister (Temple), who has a crush on him. This is the screenplay by Sidney Sheldon that beat Ruth Gordon and Garson Kanin ("A Double Life"), Cesare Zavattini ("Shoeshine"), Abraham Polonsky ("Body and Soul"), and Charles Chaplin ("Monsieur Verdoux") for the 1947 Original Screenplay Oscar. None of the losers have ever been voted one, and that's justice for you. Vallee supplies this film briefly. (Dir: Irving Reis, 95 mins.)

Bachelor Bait (1934)**½ Stuart Erwin, Rochelle Hudson, Pert Kelton, Skeets Gallagher. Breezy, early George Stevens-directed comedy draws on his experience making two-reelers. A civil servant starts a marriage brokerage and ends up entangled in the complications. Strong cast. (75 mins.)

Bachelor Flat (1962)**½ Terry-Thomas, Tuesday Weld, Richard Beymer. A shy professor of archeology is caught in a romantic complication with a forthright teenager. Amusing. (Dir: Frank Tashlin, 91 mins.)

Bachelor in Paradise (1961)*** Bob Hope, Lana Turner, Paula Prentiss, Jim Hutton. Author upsets a suburban community when he moves in to write about life there. Pleasing comedy. (Dir: Jack Arnold, 109 mins.)

Bachelor Mother (1939)**** Ginger Rogers, David Niven, Charles Coburn. Delightful comedy directed by Garson Kanin, with Rogers, everyone's favorite shopgirl, as recipient of an abandoned baby. Of course, nobody believes that one, but the store owner's son (Niven) is most understanding. His father (Coburn) doesn't believe Sonny is motivated purely by altruism and dotes on his new grandson. With all that, Frank Albertson still manages to steal the movie as Ginger's co-worker on the make. No larger meanings or genuine comic vision, but about as good and workmanlike a comedy as has ever been made. Remade as "Bundle of Joy" (1956). (81 mins.)

Bachelor of Hearts (Great Britain, 1958)**½ Hardy Kruger, Sylvia Syms. Pleasant comedy about a romantic undergraduate student and his escapades. (Dir: Wolf Rilla, 97 mins.)

Bachelor Party (1957)***½ Don Murray, E. G. Marshall, Larry Blyden, Carolyn Jones, Philip Abbott, Jack Warden. Paddy Chayefsky's TV play is expanded in this entertaining film. The acting is top-notch. (Dir: Delbert Mann, 93 mins.)

Back at the Front (1952)**½ Tom Ewell, Harvey Lembeck, Mari Blanchard. Bill

37

Mauldin's wacky G.I. creations—Willie and Joe—find themselves back in uniform and in trouble with the M.P.'s. (Dir: George Sherman, 87 mins.)

Back from Eternity (1956)**½ Robert Ryan, Anita Ekberg, Rod Steiger. Plane forced down in the jungle can return to safety with only five passengers. *Five Came Back* (1939). (Dir: John Farrow, 97 mins.)

Backroads (Australia, 1981)**½ Bill Hunter, Gary Foley. A couple of down-and-out criminals steal a car and make their way across the Australian outback. One of them is a boorish, abrasive white with a violent temper and racist tendencies; the other is an aborigine portrayed as a basically decent chap who provides us with some political education. The two pick up an assortment of motley characters along the way, and there are a few interesting moments involving the juxtaposition of the utterly different life styles and interests of the members of the group. The dialogue seems to be largely improvised and will not make Neil Simon look to his laurels. A difficult film to get excited about. (Dir: Philip Noyce, 94 mins.)

Back Street (1941)*** Charles Boyer, Margaret Sullavan, Tim Holt, Richard Carlson. The second time around for the classic Fannie Hurst soaper about the lifelong love of a woman for a married man is almost as good as John M. Stahl's original. Boyer and Sullavan make a marvelous pair of aging lovers, and Holt is properly snotty and unbearable as Boyer's self-righteous son. Director Robert Stevenson, who has since gone on to his reward (making family pictures for Disney), handles the sentiment tastefully; although the dialogue scarcely varies from the first picture, I lean toward Stahl's version, if only for its conviction. (89 mins.)

Back Street (1961)** Susan Hayward, John Gavin, Vera Miles. Third version of Fannie Hurst's tearful tale of love on the sly. Not up to the standards of the previous versions. (Dir: David Miller, 107 mins.)

Back to Bataan (1945)*** John Wayne, Anthony Quinn. American colonel forms a guerrilla army in the Philippines to fight the Japanese. Well made, exciting war drama. (Dir: Edward Dmytryk, 95 mins.)

Back to God's Country (1954)** Rock Hudson, Marcia Henderson, Steve Cochran. Adventure yarn about a couple who face tremendous obstacles. Takes place in Canada. (Dir: Joseph Pevney, 78 mins.)

Back to the Wall (France, 1958)***½ Jeanne Moreau, Gerard Oury. Excellent suspense film dealing with a jealous husband's clever plan for revenge on his faithless wife. Top French cast. (Dir: Edouard Molinaro, 94 mins.)

Backfire (1950)** Virginia Mayo, Gordon MacRae, Dane Clark. Routine drama. Poor script but cast gives it a good try. (Dir: Vincent Sherman, 91 mins.)

Backfire! (Great Britain, 1962)*½ Alfred Burke, Zena Marshall. (Dir: Paul Almond, 59 mins.)

Backfire (France, 1964)**½ Jean-Paul Belmondo, Jean Seberg, Gert Frobe. Good comedy and action. Free-lance smuggler Belmondo trying to transport a car to Lebanon. (Dir: Jean Becker, 97 mins.)

Background to Danger (1943)**½ George Brent, Brenda Marshall. Spy story set in Turkey. You will enjoy the two menaces, Lorre and Greenstreet, working against each other. (Dir: Raoul Walsh, 80 mins.)

Backlash (1956)**½ Richard Widmark, Donna Reed. Two people set out to solve the mystery surrounding an Apache massacre of five people—two of whom were never identified. (Dir: John Sturges, 84 mins.)

Backtrack (1969)* Neville Brand, James Drury, Doug McClure, Ida Lupino. (Dir: Earl Bellamy, 95 mins.)

Bad and the Beautiful, The (1953)***½ Barry Sullivan, Lana Turner, Dick Powell, Kirk Douglas, Walter Pidgeon, Gloria Grahame. Charles Schnee's somewhat too-pat script tells the flashback stories of a director (Sullivan), a star (Turner), and a writer (Powell), who were all at some point screwed over by the film's antihero, producer Jonathan Shields (Douglas). Director Vincente Minnelli's earlier films had revealed his passion for re-creating reality in the image of his emotions, but here he began to explore the logical reaction of characters who live in such a world—psychosis. This theme is more of a subtext here than in the films to follow, but even a casual observer can note that no director ever stood closer to his characters' feelings than Minnelli. You can decide whether the film is pro- or anti-Hollywood. Grahame won an Oscar for her portrayal of a southern belle. (118 mins.)

Bad Bascomb (1946)** Wallace Beery, Margaret O'Brien. Run-of-the-mill western. Little Margaret tames outlaw Beery. (Dir: Sylvan Simon, 110 mins.)

Bad Boy (1949)***½ Audie Murphy, Lloyd Nolan. The head of a boys' rehabilitation ranch makes a man of a youth considered to be a hopeless criminal. Good melodrama, well done in every department. (Dir: Kurt Neumann, 86 mins.)

Bad Boys (Japan, 1961)***½ Director Susumu Hani's film mixes a documentary grittiness with a panoply of New Wave lyricisms, in an impressive combination that may be his best work. The film is superficially a conventional social document about a delinquent's reform under the influence of a benign camp environment, but Hani's stylistic complicity with his characters strikes off personally expressive sparks along with the social perorations. The film goes irretrievably sanguine in its last 20 minutes—the sappy liberalism doesn't ring true. The real-life story provided an ironic counterpoint: the delinquent boy who played the alienated hero made a few more films and then dropped back into the petty criminal milieu. But most of this film compares quite favorably with "The 400 Blows." (90 mins.)

Bad Company (1972)**** Jeff Bridges, Barry Brown, Jim Davis, John Savage, Jerry Houser. The cogently written story of boyish outlawry, by David Newman and Robert Benton and expertly realized by Benton in his directorial debut, has a fine novelistic grain. As in all works springing from a deep-seated Americanism, strains of Hawthorne and Melville are evident. Brown is the lad of priggishly good Ohio stock, dodging the Civil War draft, who links up with street-wise primitive Bridges, less out of genuine friendship than the need to survive in a parlous society. One of the most sadly neglected major American films of the '70s, photographed in muddy green by Gordon Willis. (93 mins.)

Bad Day at Black Rock (1954)**** Spencer Tracy, Robert Ryan, Anne Francis, Ernest Borgnine, Lee Marvin, John Ericson, Walter Brennan. An excellent cast enhances this powerful story about a well guarded town secret and the stranger who uncovers it. (Dir: John Sturges, 81 mins.)

Bad for Each Other (1954)** Charlton Heston, Lizabeth Scott, Dianne Foster. Wealthy socialite tries to convince young doctor to practice among the town's exclusive clientele. Dull soap opera. (Dir: Irving Rapper, 80 mins.)

Bad Lord Byron (Great Britain, 1949)*½ Dennis Price, Joan Greenwood, Mai Zetterling. (Dir: David Macdonald, 85 mins.)

Bad News Bears, The (1976)**** Walter Matthau, Tatum O'Neal, Vic Morrow, Joyce Van Patten, Brandon Cruz, Jackie Earle Haley. Sparkling comedy. Morris Buttermaker, a former minor-league ballplayer who presently cleans swimming pools, signs on to coach a team with lots of enthusiasm, but little skill. His solution is to recruit the meanest spitball pitcher in the state, an 11-year-old girl. The screenplay is endearing for its unsentimental approach. Screenplay by Bill Lancaster (Burt's son). (Dir: Michael Ritchie, 105 mins.)

Bad News Bears Go to Japan, The (1978)*½ Tony Curtis, Jackie Earle Haley, Lonny Chapman, Erin Blunt. (Dir: John Berry, 91 mins.)

Bad News Bears in Breaking Training, The (1977)** William Devane, Clifton James, Jimmy Baio, Chris Barnes. The first lackluster sequel to the delightful box-office hit about a team of young baseball misfits. This one, which takes the Bears to the Houston Astrodome, lacks the cast and quality of the original. Devane coaches the bunch of adorable kids, led by Barnes. (Dir: Michael Pressman, 103 mins.)

Bad Ronald (MTV 1978)**½ Scott Jacoby, Kim Hunter, Pippa Scott. Macabre little tale about a young boy living in a secret room in an old Victorian house and slowly going mad. Interesting. (Dir: Buzz Kulik, 72 mins.)

Bad Sister (Great Britain, 1947)** Margaret Lockwood, Joan Greenwood, Ian Hunter. The warden of a home for delinquent girls takes one of them under her wing, tries to straighten her out. Long, talky, trite drama. (Dir: Bernard Knowles, 97 mins.)

Bad Sleep Well, The (Japan, 1960)*** Toshiro Mifune, Takeshi Kato, Masayuki Mori. Director Akira Kurosawa's presage of the Lockheed scandal, with Mifune fighting corporate corruption, is a well-done thriller. (151 mins.; U.S. version, 135 mins.)

Bad Timing/A Sensual Obsession (Great Britain, 1980)*** Art Garfunkel, Theresa Russell, Harvey Keitel, Daniel Massey, Denholm Elliott. For all their calculated artiness and chic fragmentation, most of director Nicolas Roeg's cinematic ideas in this intermittently interesting failure are relatively simple: dissimilar images are juxtaposed to suggest a relation between them. Though the film has a complex construction, it is basically simpleminded. Garfunkel plays a research psychoanalyst in Vienna who has a stormy affair with mercurial Russell, a Holly Golightly for the '80s. Roeg dissipates most of his attentions on a shopworn doppelgänger theme, with Keitel an officious police detective out to establish Gerfunkel's responsibility for the possible success of Russell's suicide attempt. The film is greatly inferior to "Petulia," (which Roeg photographed). Russell, however, is brilliant, her performance ablaze with fragments of compelling original behavior. (123 mins.)

Badge 373 (1973)* Robert Duvall, Verna Bloom, Henry Darrow, Eddie Egan. Screenplay by Pete Hamill, based on the adventures of real-life cop Eddie Egan. (Dir: Howard W. Koch, 116 mins.)

Badlanders, The (1958)**½ Alan Ladd, Ernest Borgnine, Katy Jurado. A remake of "Asphalt Jungle" on horseback as Ladd and Borgnine plan a big gold robbery. Good action. (Dir: Delmer Daves, 83 mins.)

Badlands (1974)**** Sissy Spacek, Martin Sheen, Warren Oates. A remarkable directorial debut by Terrence Malick, who also wrote and produced this perceptive, beautifully observed film about two young, vapid lovers who go on a killing spree in the 1950's before being apprehended. Based on the real-life killing spree of Charles Starkweather and Caril Fugate. The two leads are very convincingly played by Sheen and Spacek. (Dir: Terrence Malick, 95 mins.)

Badman's Country (1958)** George Montgomery, Neville Brand, Buster Crabbe. Pat Garrett forsakes retirement to team with Wyatt Earp and Buffalo Bill (Malcolm Atterbury) to snare outlaws led by Butch Cassidy. Routine western. (Dir: Fred Sears, 68 mins.)

Badman's Territory (1946)*** Randolph Scott, Ann Richards. Marshal has to put up with the most notorious outlaws in the west in a territory outside the control of the government. Good western. (Dir: Tim Whelan, 97 mins.)

Badmen of Missouri (1941)*** Dennis Morgan, Jane Wyman, Arthur Kennedy. Exploits of the infamous Younger brothers. (Dir: Ray Enright, 71 mins.)

Bagdad (1949)** Maureen O'Hara, Paul Christian, (Paul Hubschmid), Vincent Price. The British-educated daughter of a tribal leader of the desert returns to her people after her father is murdered. (Dir: Charles Lamont, 82 mins.)

Bahama Passage (1941)*½ Madeleine Carroll, Sterling Hayden. (Dir: Edward Griffith, 83 mins.)

Bahia (Portugal, 1978)***½ Mira Fonseca, Zeni Persira, Maria Viana, Antonio Pitanga. In this story of the picaresque escapades of a young prostitute, Marcel Camus mines the same exotic vein he tapped in his *Black Orpheus*. From a short story by Jorge Amado *(Way for a Sailor, Gabriella Clove and Cinnamon)*. (Dir: Marcel Camus, 94 mins.)

Ball Out at 43,000 (1957)** John Payne, Karen Steele, Paul Kelly. Routine flying film about pilots and their affairs. Performances are adequate. (Dir: Francis Lyon, 73 mins.)

Bait (1954)** Hugo Haas, Cleo Moore, John Agar. Haas is an old prospector married to a sexy blonde, trying to kill his partner. (Dir: Hugo Haas, 80 mins.)

Bait, The (MTV 1973)** Donna Mills. Miss Mills plays a policewoman acting as bait to catch a demented murderer. Michael Constantine, William Devane, Arlene Golonka. (Dir: Leonard Horn, 73 mins.)

Baker's Wife, The (France, 1938)**** Raimu. A truly great actor (Raimu) in a superb story that makes a quite perfect and profoundly poignant movie. There's not a false note in director Marcel Pagnol's adaptation. Raimu is sad, funny, and altogether wonderful. (Dir: Marcel Pagnol, 98 mins.)

Bal Tabarin (1952)*½ Muriel Lawrence, William Ching. Poor melodrama. (Dir: Philip Ford, 84 mins.)

Balalaika (1939)** Nelson Eddy, Ilona Massey. Pretentious, dull operetta set in Russia during World War I and about the time of the Revolution. (Dir: Reinhold Schunzel, 102 mins.)

Balcony, The (1963)*** Shelley Winters, Peter Falk, Lee Grant, Leonard Nimoy. Uneven but frequently interesting adaptation by screenwriter Ben Maddow of French auteur Jean Genet's difficult, disturbing symbolic play about life in a Parisian brothel. Shelley plays a coarse madam, and Peter Falk provides a few light touches as the police chief of the mythical state. (Dir: Joseph Strick, 84 mins.)

Ball at Anjo House, A (Japan, 1948)**½ Setsuko Hara, Masayuki Mori, Osamu Takizawa. Director Kozaburo Yoshimura is a critical favorite in Japan because his style changes to suit the material on which he is working. A Tradition of Quality hand, without a personality of his own. This exercise about the fall of an aristocratic family after WW II makes an earnest case for postbellum pragmatism. The cast tends toward the careful and obvious style of cinematic acting popular at the time. Hara instills her usual beauty and freshness of temperament.

Ball of Fire (1941)***½ Gary Cooper, Barbara Stanwyck. One of director Howard Hawks's most eccentric projects. Script by Billy Wilder and Charles Brackett, about what happens when a group of seven professors, who have retreated from the world to write an encyclopedia, face the intrusion of a nightclub singer and gun moll, Stanwyck. The youngest of the professors, played by Cooper, answers the call of nature, but Stanwyck's gangster friends intervene. Wilder's characteristically sentimental view of the seven professors is blunted by Hawks, who just as characteristically gives everyone in the film a measure of underplayed dignity. The most appealing and illuminating scene is a rendition of "Genevieve" in memory of one's dead wife, a resigned contemplation of mortality. Remade as "A Song Is Born." (111 mins.)

Ballad in Blue—See: **Blues for Lovers**

Ballad of a Gunfighter (1963)* Marty Robbins, Joyce Redd. (Dir: Bill Ward, 84 mins.)

Ballad of a Soldier (U.S.S.R., 1960)**** This is a hauntingly beautiful and tender story of a young Russian soldier's attempts to get home to see his mother during a leave from the Army during World War II; unspoiled by any propaganda whatever and could have been made anywhere. Wonderfully directed and photographed. (Dir: Grigori Chukhrai, 89 mins.)

Ballad of Andy Crocker, The (MTV 1969)*** Lee Majors, Joey Heatherton. A Vietnam war hero comes home to find nothing but disappointment and despair. His sweetheart has married another guy and his motorcycle repair business has been run to the ground by his lazy partner. The final scene is jolting. (Dir: George McCowan, 73 mins.)

Ballad of Cable Hogue, The (1970)***½ Jason Robards, Stella Stevens, David Warner. Director Sam Peckinpah's ambitious, romantic elegy about capitalism and the Old West. Droll, offbeat screenplay written by John Crawford and Edmund Penney. Robards is a worn-out prospector who talks to God. Stevens plays a prostitute who takes up with Robards, and Warner plays a disturbed preacher with style and detachment. (Dir: Sam Peckinpah, 121 mins.)

Ballad of Josie, The (1968)*½ Doris Day,

Peter Graves. Doris's last film. (Dir: Andrew McLaglen, 102 mins.)

Ballad of Narayama (Japan, 1958)*** Kinuyo Tanaka. The subject of "What Shall We Do with Our Old?" has been treated by the cinema since Griffith's film of that name in '11, and director Keisuke Kinoshita's wide-screen drama approaches it using stylized techniques adapted from Kabuki theater. Tanaka plays an old woman who insists on being taken to the mountaintop to die rather than remain and cause her son's family to starve. The material would be laughably overwrought were it not for Kinoshita's astute recasting of the story in theatrical terms. The film has dignity without severity, and precision of emotion rather than bathos. Despite its pretension to being an objet d'art film, the drama carries a charge of personal involvement. (98 mins.)

Ballerina (France, 1951)** Violette Verdy, Henri Guisol. Young dancer's sleep is interrupted by three telephone calls, bringing on a trio of dreams. Fairish drama, dubbed. Alternate title: **Dream Ballerina**. (Dir: Ludwig Berger, 78 mins.)

Ballerina (W. Germany, 1958)** Willy Birgel, Elisabeth Mueller. Polio strikes a prima ballerina who is so heartbroken she can't dance. (Dir: G.W. Pabst, 91 mins.)

Baltimore Bullet, The (1980)**½ James Coburn, Bruce Boxleitner, Omar Sharif, Ronee Blakely, Michael Lerner. A vulgar tale of two hustlers (Coburn and Boxleitner) on the road, trying to set up a big game with legendary gambler Sharif. It's all plot with no shading, grain, or content, though the pull of narrative is enough to keep the attention until the denouement, which is something of a cheat. Robert Ellis Miller directed; he was quoted as saying that he didn't see any difference between directing for television and for the big screen, and from the look of the film I can see that he doesn't. Blakely has a pointless role. (103 mins.)

Bambi (1942)***½ Animated. A children's classic, beautifully done by Walt Disney's Studios. Story of a fawn's life and his forest friends, lovely. The voices of most of the young woodland creatures, by the way, are those of nonprofessional children. Music by Frank Churchill, Edward H. Plumb. From the book by Felix Salten. Color. (Dirs: David Hand, Perce Pearce, 69 mins.)

Bambole (France-Italy, 1965)** Monica Vitti, Elke Sommer, Franco Rossi, Gina Lollobrigida. Mundane quartet of stories on Italian life. "Monsignor Cupid" episode based on a Boccaccio story directed by Mauro Bolognini. "The Soup" directed by Franco Rossi. "Treatise in Eugenics" directed by Luigi Comencini. "The Telephone Call" directed by Dino Risi. Alternate title: **Four Kinds of Love.** (111 mins.)

Bamboo Prison, The (1954)*** Robert Francis, Brian Keith, Dianne Foster. A young sergeant is accused of collaborat- ing with the Communists during the Korean War. Well-handled. (Dir: Lewis Seiler, 80 mins.)

Bamboo Saucer, The (1968)* Dan Duryea, John Ericson, Lois Nettleton. Alternate title: **Collision Course.** (Dir: Frank Telford, 100 mins.)

Banacek (MTV 1972)**½ George Peppard. The pilot for the series. The plot revolves around the disappearance, between Oklahoma and Texas borders, of an armored truck with a million-dollar-plus gold cargo. Enter Banacek. (Dir: Jack Smight, 104 mins.)

Banacek: Horse of a Slightly Different Color (MTV 1974)*½ George Peppard, Anne Francis. Nothing special. (Dir: Herschel Daugherty, 72 mins.)

Banacek: No Sign of the Cross (MTV 1972)** George Peppard, Broderick Crawford. Entertaining where-is-it? Peppard must recover a jeweled cross valued at a million bucks. (Dir: Daryl Duke, 72 mins.)

Banacek: No Stone Unturned (MTV 1973)** George Peppard, Christine Belford. Banacek is faced with another case involving the disappearance of an art treasure. (Dir: Dick Heffron, 72 mins.)

Banacek: Now You See Me—Now You Don't (MTV 1974)*½ George Peppard, Ralph Manza. (Dir: Bernard McEveety, 72 mins.)

Banacek: Project Phoenix (MTV 1972)** George Peppard. This one involves a missing experimental automobile valued at five million dollars. (Dir: Richard T. Heffron, 73 mins.)

Banacek: The Greatest Collection of Them All (1973)*½ George Peppard, Penny Fuller. (Dir: George McCowan, 72 mins.)

Banacek: The Two Million Clams of Cap'n Jack (MTV 1973)* George Peppard, Andrew Duggan, Jessica Walter. (Dir: Dick Heffron, 72 mins.)

Banacek, The Vanishing Chalice (MTV 1974)*½ George Peppard, Cesar Romero, John Saxon. (Dir: Bernie Kowalski, 72 mins.)

Banacek: To Steal a King (MTV 1972)*½ (Dir: Lou Antonio, 73 mins.)

Banana Peel (France-Italy, 1964)**½ Jeanne Moreau, Jean-Paul Belmondo, Gert Frobe, Claude Brasseur, Jean-Pierre Marielle. It takes some effort to recognize the director of "The Sorrow and the Pity" and "The Memory of Justice" in this lightweight French farce. But even Marcel Ophuls had to start somewhere. Frequently entertaining comedy, as a pair of scoundrels cheat a millionaire out of a large bankroll on the French Riviera. Ophuls coscripted with Claude Sautet. (97 mins.)

Bananas (1971)**** Woody Allen, Louise Lasser, Howard Cosell, Carlos Montalban. Allen is an inspired lunatic. So many of the jokes and sight gags are hilarious it doesn't matter—and probably can't be helped—that a few of them bomb out. Woody runs off to South America and

41

becomes a revolutionary leader, and it's the only American film within memory that makes clear that J. Edgar Hoover really was a black woman. (Dir: Woody Allen, 82 mins.)

Band of Angels (1957)**½ Clark Gable, Yvonne DeCarlo, Sidney Poitier. Gable in the role of a New Orleans gentleman with a past. Sidney Poitier easily walks off with the acting honors as an educated slave. (Dir: Raoul Walsh, 127 mins.)

Band of Assassins (Japan, 1970)** Toshiro Mifune, Keiju Kobayashi. Starring Mifune in his 100th screen appearance, this action-filled film deals with the organization of a paramilitary assassin force, Shinsen, which took upon itself the defense of the tottering shogunate during the late 19th century. (Dir: Tadashi Sawajima, 122 mins.)

Band of Outsiders (France, 1964)***½ Claude Brasseur, Sami Frey, Anna Karina. A gangster story, sort of, by director Jean-Luc Godard, who supposedly told his backers that he was going to make a sequel to "Breathless," and then delivered this mix of musical comedy, slapstick, violence, and incidental observations on politics and philosophy. The leading players make fairly inept burglars, but they do a wonderful version of the "Steam Heat" number from Stanley Donen's "The Pajama Game." This remains one of Godard's most appealing and underrated films, relatively relaxed and strangely optimistic. (97 mins.)

Band Wagon, The (1953)**** Fred Astaire, Cyd Charisse, Jack Buchanan, Oscar Levant, Nanette Fabray. For many, the epiphany of the American musical. Astaire is a washed-up Hollywood star, Fabray and Levant are a husband-and-wife team, and Buchanan is an artsy Broadway director, sort of a cross between Minelli himself and Orson Welles. The musical becomes a meditation on popular vs. high art, coming down hard on the side of the former. Rife with great numbers, including the incomparable "Triplets." Screen play by Betty Comden and Adolph Green. (112 mins.)

Bande à Part—See: Band of Outsiders

Bandido (1956)**½ Robert Mitchum, Ursula Thiess, Zachary Scott. American adventurers cross the border into Mexico during the revolt of 1916 to sell weapons. (Dir: Richard Fleischer, 92 mins.)

Bandit and the Princess, The (German, 1962)*½ Helmut Lohner, Peter Weck. Dubbed. (Dir: Franz Antel, 95 mins.)

Bandit of Sherwood Forest (1946)** Cornel Wilde, Anita Louise, Jill Esmond, Henry Daniell. The son of Robin Hood comes to the aid of the Queen. Elaborate but uninspired. (Dirs: George Sherman, Clifford Sanforth, 86 mins.)

Bandit of Zhobe, The (Great Britain, 1959)** Victor Mature, Anne Aubrey, Anthony Newley. Routine desert adventure. (Dir: John Gilling, 80 mins.)

Bandits of Corsica (1953)** Richard Greene, Paula Raymond, Raymond Burr. Twins overthrow a villainous tyrant in Corsica. Humdrum costume melodrama, based on Dumas' "Corsican Brothers." (Dir: Ray Nazarro, 82 mins.)

Bandits vs Samurai Squadron (Japan, 1980)***½ Tatsuya Nakadai, Shima Iwashita. Despite the unwieldy title, this is a superbly dramatized, complex Japanese period picture directed by Hideo Gosha, probably the major upholder of the tradition of the classical action work as practiced by such great artists as Raoul Walsh. Nakadai plays an outlaw in '22, with Iwashita as a widow and aristocrat who earns her membership in the gang. The film has ambitions it doesn't entirely achieve, but it's sumptuous, fatalistic, ironic, action-packed—and incredibly dense despite its length. Gosha ("Hunter in the Dark," "Three Outlaw Samurai") knows how to let visuals describe the action, and the action expresses profound ideas about society, metaphysics, and ethics. (163 mins.)

Bandolero! (1968)*½ James Stewart, Dean Martin, Raquel Welch. (Dir: Andrew V. McLaglen, 106 mins.)

Bang, Bang Kid, The (US-Spain-Italy, 1968)*** Guy Madison, Sandra Milo, Tom Bosley. Tight comedy approach to absurd tale of a feudal Westerner who gets his comeuppance when a robot incites his people to insurgency. Written by Howard Berk. (Dir: Stanley Prager, 90 mins.)

Bang the Drum Slowly (1973)**** Robert De Niro, Michael Moriarty. Mark Harris' poignant 1956 novel is splendidly translated to the screen. De Niro is touching as an average baseball player dying of Hodgkin's Disease, who wants to play just one more season. Moriarty shines as his friend and teammate. Harris wrote his own screenplay. (Dir: John Hancock, 98 mins.)

Bang! You're Dead (Great Britain, 1954)**½ Jack Warner, Derek Farr, Veronica Hurst, Anthony Richmond. Young boy shoots a man in rural England and is tracked down by police. Slow suspense. (Dir: Lance Comfort, 88 mins.)

Banjo Hackett (MTV 1976)**½ Don Meredith, Ike Eisenmann, Jennifer Warren, Chuck Connors. Meredith becomes an 1880's horse trader with a good heart, whisking his nephew out of an orphanage with the intention of giving the boy a prize mare. (Dir: Andrew McLaglen, 103 mins.)

Banjo on My Knee (1936)**½ Joel McCrea, Barbara Stanwyck, Walter Brennan. Story of the folks who live along the banks of the Mississippi. (Dir: John Cromwell, 80 mins.)

Bank Dick, The (1940)**** W.C. Fields. One of the genuinely great movie comedians has a field day in this still wonderfully funny romp. As a reward for accidentally capturing a bank robber, Egbert Sousé is made a bank guard. (Dir: Eddie Cline, 74 mins.)

Bank Holiday (Great Britain, 1938)*** John Lodge, Margaret Lockwood. Good, low-key British drama; nurse flees her lover to save the suicidally distraught husband of a dead patient. Rich characterizations, varied locales. (Dir: Carol Reed, 86 mins.)

Bank Raiders, The (Great Britain, 1958)**½ Peter Reynolds, Sandra Dorne. An above average British cops and bank robbers yarn. (Dir: Maxwell Munden, 60 mins.)

Bank Shot (1974)* George C. Scott, Joanna Cassidy, Clifton James. (Dir: Gower Champion, 83 mins.)

Bannerline (1951)** Keefe Brasselle, Sally Forrest, Lionel Barrymore. Routine newspaper story about an aggressive small town reporter who tries to launch a one-man campaign against corruption. (Dir: Don Weis, 86 mins.)

Banning (1967)*½ Robert Wagner, Jill St. John, James Farentino, Anjanette Comer. (Dir: Ron Winston, 102 mins.)

Banyon (1971)**½ Robert Forster, Anjanette Comer. A tough John Garfield-type private-eye hero (Robert Forster) who drinks tea instead of booze, tinkers with an erector set, and plays it cool with the ladies, can hardly keep up with the killings after a hood is released from prison. Jose Férrer, Herb Edelman, Darren McGavin. (Dir: Robert Daly, 100 mins.).

Bar Mitzvah Boy (Great Britain, 1976)***½ Jeremy Steyn, Maria Charles, Adrienne Posta. One of the most honored and popular BBC-produced dramas, this mounting of Jack Rosenthal's play is about a boy who runs away on the day of his bar mitzvah. Michael Tuchner ("Villain") directed.

Barabbas (Italy, 1962)***½ Anthony Quinn, Silvana Mangano, Arthur Kennedy, Jack Palance, Ernest Borgnine. Lavish spectacle concerning the thief whom Jesus replaced on the cross; his life in the mines, his victories as a gladiator. Far superior to the usual run of its kind. Literate dialogue by Christopher Fry, excellent performances by a large cast. (Dir: Richard Fleischer, 134 mins.)

Barbarella (France-Italy, 1968)*½ Jane Fonda, Milo O'Shea, Terence Stamp, John Philip Law, Marcel Marceau, David Hemmings, Anita Pallenberg. (Dir: Roger Vadim, 98 mins.)

Barbarian and the Geisha, The (1958)* John Wayne, Sam Jaffe. (Dir: John Huston (re-cut without the director's permission by Wayne), 105 mins.)

Barbarian King, The (Bulgaria, 1964)*½ Victor Stoichev, Ginka Stancheva.

Barbarians, The (Italy, 1953)*½ Helene Remy, Pierre Cressoy. Alternate title: "The Pagans." (Dir: Ferrucio Cerio, 101 mins.)

Barbary Coast (1935)** Joel McCrea, Edward G. Robinson, Miriam Hopkins. Drama about the tough Barbary Coast during the late 1800's. Two fine supporting performances by Walter Brennan and Brian Donlevy. (Dir: Howard Hawks, 100 mins.)

Barbary Coast, The (MTV 1975)**½ William Shatner, Dennis Cole, Lynda Day George, John Vernon. Shatner plays an undercover agent skulking about San Francisco's muddy streets of iniquity. Hokum amidst fairly gaudy surroundings. (Dir: Bill Bixby, 100 mins.)

Barber of Seville (Italy, 1947)** Tito Gobbi, Nelly Corradi, Ferruccio Tagliavini. Another version of Rossini's comic opera. For the dedicated! (Dir: Mario Costa, 110 mins.)

Barefoot Battalion (Greece, 1954)** Maria Costi, Nicos Fermas. Orphans band together to fight the invading Nazis during World War II. (Dir: Gregg Tallas, Dubbed. 89 mins.)

Barefoot Contessa, The (1954)*** Humphrey Bogart, Ava Gardner, Rossano Brazzi, Edmond O'Brien. The life and times of an unhappy glamour girl: her beginnings, her rise to stardom, her loneliness, her tragedy. Splendid production and cast, occasional witty dialogue—but too talky, often obscure drama. (Dir: Joseph L. Mankiewicz, 128 mins.)

Barefoot Executive, The (1971)*** Kurt Russell, Joe Flynn, Harry Morgan, Wally Cox. Walt Disney spoofs TV ratings with an amiable comedy for kids about a chimpanzee who is able to predict programs with good ratings. (Dir: Robert Butler, 96 mins.)

Barefoot in the Park (1967)***½ Robert Redford, Jane Fonda, Charles Boyer. Neil Simon's romantic, funny froth was a Broadway smash hit. Has survived the transfer to the big screen reasonably well. Benefits from Robert Redford, who repeats his Broadway role and Jane Fonda who does not, setting up Manhattan housekeeping with more ideas than money. (Dir: Gene Saks, 104 mins.)

Barefoot Mailman, The (1951)**½ Robert Cummings, Terry Moore. Genial confidence man and a school girl try to swindle some yokels with shady railroad stock. (Dir: Earl McEvoy, 83 mins.)

Barefoot Savage (formerly "Sensualita") (Italy, 1954)** Eleonora Rossi-Drago, Amadeo Nazzari. Female without morals sets two brothers against each other. Dubbed. (Dir: Clemente Fracassi, 72 mins.)

Barkleys of Broadway, The (1949)**½ Fred Astaire, Ginger Rogers. After a hiatus of ten years, Astaire and Rogers teamed up one last time for this so-so movie about a husband-and-wife dance team who bicker incessantly backstage. It isn't very witty—although it's supposed to be—and it isn't really a satire like "Singin' in the Rain" or "The Band Wagon." Nor were Astaire and Rogers "the Lunt and Fontanne of musicals." Even the shift to MGM couldn't furnish the necessary gloss. Still, Astaire's "Shoes with Wings On" number is terrific, and the film has the Gershwin's "They Can't Take That Away from Me." (Dir: Charles Walters, 109 mins.)

Barnacle Bill (1941)** Wallace Beery, Marjorie Main. He's a no good fisherman and she's the widow out to get him. (Dir: Richard Thorpe, 98 mins.)

Barocco (France, 1978)*** Isabelle Adjani, Marie-France Pisier, Gerard Depardieu (in a double role). Director Techine's sensuous, flamboyant, poetic, silly, parodistic thriller combines the improbable with the paroxysmal in a moving meditation on themes of love and morbidity, doppelgängers and guilt, and style as the carrier of emotion. Adjani and Pisier are particularly impressive as contrasting types, and Techine's precious self-consciousness redeems his outsized feelings rather than constricting them.

Baron Blood (Italy, 1972)½ Joseph Cotten, Elke Sommer, Massimo Girotti. (Dir: Mario Bava, 90 mins.)

Baron of Arizona, The (1950)** Vincent Price, Ellen Drew. The story of James Addison Reavis, who once tried to swindle the government out of Arizona Territory by means of a fantastic scheme. Based on fact. Beulah Bondi. (Dir: Samuel Fuller, 97 mins.)

Baron's African War, The (1943-66)**½ Rod Cameron, Joan Marsh, Duncan Renaldo. Nazi poses as Arab leader to influence tribesmen during World War II, is battled by an American agent working with the French. Well done for what it is. (Dir: Spencer Bennet, 100 mins.)

Barracuda (MTV 1978)** Wayne David Crawford, Jason Evers, Roberta Leighton. Fair drama about the pollution of a river in a small Florida community. The script has good intentions, but it's heavy-handed. (Dir: Harry Kerwin, 93 mins.)

Barren Lives (Brazil 1963)***½ Athila Iorio, Maria Riberio. Small budget film about the lives of Brazil's peasant farmers packs a powerful punch. Sensitively written and directed by Nelson Pereira dos Santos. One of the first and best films from Brazil's Cinema Novo movement. Subtitles. (100 mins.)

Barretts of Wimpole Street, The (1934)**½ Norma Shearer, Fredric March, Charles Laughton. The romance of Elizabeth Barrett (Shearer) and Robert Browning (March), despite the tyrannical opposition of her father (Laughton), is given a respectful, stiff treatment by director Sidney Franklin and producer Irving Thalberg. This is the quintessential Thalberg film: overanxious about respectability, stuffed with production value, and having little to do with anything artful about movies. (110 mins.)

Barretts of Wimpole Street, The (Great Britain, 1957)**½ Jennifer Jones, William Travers, John Gielgud. Sensitive but dull remake of the luminous love story between Elizabeth Barrett and Robert Browning. (Dir: Sidney Franklin, 105 mins.)

Barricade (1950)** Ruth Roman, Dane Clark. Routine Western drama with a mining camp setting. Uninspired. (Dir: Peter Godfrey, 75 mins.)

Barrier (Poland, 1966)*** Jan Nowicki, Joanna Szcerbic. Crazy, satirical, surreal experimental adventure by young Polish filmmaker Jerzy Skolimowski, who directed. Wry humor and a good deal of social commentary are trotted out in the process of a young medical student's irrational trip through the city of Warsaw. (83 mins.)

Barrier of the Law (Italy, 1953)*½ Rossano Brazzi, Jacques Sernas, Lea Padovani. Dubbed. (Dir: Piero Costa, 77 mins.)

Barry Lyndon (Great Britain, 1975)***½ Ryan O'Neal, Marisa Berenson, Patrick Magee, Hardy Kruger, Michael Hordern. Stanley Kubrick's tenth feature film is a lavish, visually ravishing, elegant adaptation of the Thackeray novel. Rarely has the 18th century been so painstakingly depicted—from rich Irish landscapes to lush interiors of European castles. The texture of the film, however, is one of cold detachment. Lyndon, passive but likable Irish lad, becomes a socially fashionable peer after his marriage to a rich widow (Berenson), who is exquisitely photographed at every turn. O'Neal's brand of unemotional stoicism lends itself well to the role of the naive fledgling who learns quickly how to become a successful opportunist. Kubrick also did the adaptation. Some critics called it boring, some a masterpiece. The film is greatly diminished when seen on the tiny TV screen. (185 mins.)

Bartleby (Great Britain, 1970)***½ Paul Scofield, John McEnery. Updating of Herman Melville's novella redefines the main character of Bartleby as a symbol of modern, alienated man who is slowly giving up. Paul Scofield plays the boss who has empathy with Bartleby, but must fire him. Bartleby won't go and once taken away he no longer has the will to live. The acting is superb. (Dir: Anthony Friedman, 79 mins.)

Bashful Elephant, The (1962)** Molly McGowan, Kai Fischer. Story about a little girl and her elephant. Circus background offers good scenery. Filmed in Austria. (Dirs: Dorrell and Stuart McGowan, 82 mins.)

Basic Training (1971)***½ Documentary by American filmmaker Frederick Wiseman about the induction procedure in the American army, the tension between obedience and resistance, etc. This arresting film provides numerous insights about the experience of basic training while simultaneously reinforcing many existing movie clichés about army life and personnel. (Dir: Frederick Wiseman, 80 mins.)

Bat, The (1959)*½ Vincent Price, Agnes Moorehead. (Dir: Crane Wilbur, 80 mins.)

Bat People, The (1974)* Stewart Moss,

Marianne McAndrew. (Dir: Jerry Jameson, 95 mins.)

Bataan (1943)*** Robert Taylor, Thomas Mitchell. Good story of the heroes who endured one of our early World War II defeats. A grim reminder and a realistic melodrama. (Dir: Tay Garnett, 114 mins.)

Bathing Beauty (1944)**½ Esther Williams, Red Skelton, Basil Rathbone, Harry James, Xavier Cugat. An early Williams vehicle, and an early George Sidney directorial effort—and for all its lavish production values, an unfunny drag. Skelton is a songwriter who wants to retire with fiancée Williams, only to have his publisher (Rathbone) scheme to break them up. Brilliant color; flashy musical numbers. (101 mins.)

Batman (1966)* Adam West, Burt Ward, Lee Meriwether, Frank Gorshin, Burgess Meredith, Cesar Romero, Alan Napier. (Dir: Leslie Martinson, 105 mins.)

Batman of Africa (1936-66)*½ Clyde Beatty, Elaine Shepard. (Dir: B. Reeves Eason, 100 mins.)

Battered (MTV 1978)** Karen Grassle, LeVar Burton, Mike Farrell. Supposedly nice, ambitious, clean-cut husbands are hauling off and whacking their wives in the face. Drama of wife beaters researched and coauthored by Karen Grassle, best known for her role in the NBC series "Little House on the Prairie," and her collaborator Cynthia Lovelace Sears. Burton and Farrell, an actor always cast in amiable roles, suddenly turn into villains, along with beefy Howard Duff. Grassle and Chip Fields play the victims who find safety in a refuge. A bit bumpy in construction perhaps, but explains some of the problems in law enforcement about this nationwide, until recently neglected problem. (Dir: Peter Werner, 104 mins.)

Battle at Apache Pass (1952)**½ John Lund, Jeff Chandler. Jeff Chandler repeats his characterization of the Indian Chieftain Cochise, which he originated in the film "Broken Arrow," in this rousing western adventure. (Dir: George Sherman, 85 mins.)

Battle at Bloody Beach (1961)** Audie Murphy, Dolores Michaels. Gary Crosby. American joins guerrillas in holding off Japanese in the Pacific during World War II. On the dull side. (Dir: Herbert Coleman, 83 mins.)

Battle Beneath the Earth (Great Britain, 1968)* Kerwin Mathews, Viviane Ventura. (Dir: Montgomery Tully, 92 mins.)

Battle Beyond the Stars (1980)*** Richard Thomas, George Peppard, Robert ("Teenage Caveman") Vaughn. John Saxon, Darleanne Fluegel. New World Pictures' answer to "Star Wars" is a pleasantly good-natured sci-fi epic, undaunted by budgetary restrictions. At this level of filmmaking, eagerness to entertain counts for a great deal, and the film's dog-eared frankness is endearing. Based loosely on "The Seven Samurai," it has occasionally witty asides from screenwriter John Syles, and director Jimmy T. Murakami has pitched the action at an amiable clip. An honestly enjoyable film with a strong sense of its roots in Roger Corman's films of the '50s. Includes a wonderful assortment of alien forms. (104 mins.)

Battle Beyond the Sun (U.S.S.R., 1959)*½ Arla Powell, Andy Stewart. (Dir: Thomas Colchart, 75 mins.)

Battle Circus (1953)** Humphrey Bogart, June Allyson. Love amid the holocaust of war serves as the plot line in this maudlin drama. Poor script and uninspired performances. (Dir: Richard Brooks, 90 mins.)

Battle Command—See: **Eagles over London.**

Battle Cry (1955)**½ Van Heflin, Aldo Ray, Dorothy Malone, Tab Hunter, Nancy Olson. This film should be seen if only for the marvelous moment when Malone undresses while sitting sideways in an armchair that barely keeps her within the confines of the Production Code. A film that provides an acid test of one's admiration for director Raoul Walsh, whose love of pure, elemental drama sometimes required a sacrifice of verisimilitude and evenness of tone. The rather episodic script, written by Leon Uris from his own novel, tells about a group of WW II marine recruits before and during action, with heavy emphasis on romantic and sexual dilemmas. (149 mins.)

Battle Cry (1978)—See: **Tokkan**

Battle Flame (1959)** Scott Brady, Elaine Edwards. Brady plays a Lt. who meets his former love when he is wounded—you guessed it—she's a nurse. (Dir: R. G. Springsteen, 78 mins.)

Battle for the Planet of the Apes (1973)** Roddy McDowall, Claude Akins, John Huston. The plot, for those who still care, is another case of crass human beings vs. the more intelligent simians. (Dir: J. Lee Thompson, 86 mins.)

Battle Hell (Great Britain, 1957)*** Richard Todd, Akim Tamiroff. A fine film about the daring escape of a British ship which has run aground in the Yangtze river during the Chinese Civil War. Excellent performances, notably by Akim Tamiroff. (Dir: Michael Anderson, 113 mins.)

Battle Hymn (1957)*** Rock Hudson, Martha Hyer. Director Douglas Sirk explores the paradox of the title—the religion of warfare—in a melodrama that is a fine example of Sirk's ironic technique, giving the audience the expected piety while subtly mocking the self-righteous Christian hero. But Sirk doesn't go far enough; the film lacks the deep tensions that make masterpieces of his "Tarnished Angels" and "Imitation of Life." Hudson plays a WW II chaplain whose adventure earn him many honors. Based on a true story. (108 mins.)

Battle in Outer Space (Japan, 1960)*½ (Dir: Inoshiro Honda, 74 mins.)

Battle of Algiers (Italy-Algeria, 1967)**** Brahim Haggiag, Jean Martin. Director Gillo Pontecorvo recreated the events leading up to the Algerians' independence from France without using any actual newsreel footage, but imparting to the entire film a quality of astonishing realism. The nonprofessional actors are superb, as is the technical work on the film including the texture of the film itself. Pontecorvo's triumph includes his sympathetic handling of **both** sides of this agonizing, brutal struggle for independence. Quite simply a movie masterpiece. (Dir: Gillo Pontecorvo, 123 mins.)

Battle of Austerlitz (France, 1960)** Leslie Caron, Jack Palance, Vittorio De Sica, Claudia Cardinale. Lavishly produced story of Napoleon and his ambitions as ruler. Badly marred by excessive cutting. (Dir: Abel Gance, 73 mins.)

Battle of Blood Island (1960)**½ Ron Kennedy, Richard Devon. Two GIs, survivors of a Japanese attack, endeavor to stay alive on a Pacific island during World War II. (Dir: Joel Rapp, 64 mins.)

Battle of Britain (Great Britain, 1969)** Michael Caine, Laurence Olivier, Trevor Howard. All the cliche characters from the war movies of the '40's are back. As for the actual fighting of the Battle of Britain, it's squeezed in as a break from the melodrama of the one-dimensional story line. Fine cast wasted. (Dir: Guy Hamilton, 130 mins.)

Battle of Chile, The (Chile-Cuba, 1977)**** A landmark, altogether remarkable political documentary shot by a team of committed filmmakers recording the overthrow of the government of Salvador Allende in 1973. The filmmaking took place over a ten-month period up to and including the political coup that overthrew and killed Allende. One of the strengths of this invaluable historical record is, as one critic noted, *"The Battle of Chile is a Marxist analysis of the overthrow of Allende's Chilean government by the political right; as such it makes no specious pretense to objectivity. Its structure, however, qualifies it as the most informative documentary on the subject and the one which, strangely, may provide a picture (as opposed to an analysis of that picture) acceptable to both ends of the political spectrum."* Produced and edited over a four-year period by the Chilean filmmakers, headed by director Patricio Guzman, and Cuban filmmakers and editors in Havana. B&W. (Dir: Patricio Guzman, 191 mins.)

Battle of Culloden, The (1964)**** Brilliant documentary about the battle waged by the pretender to the British throne, Bonnie Prince Charlie, against George II in 1746, stressing the personal rather than the epic proportions of the battle. (Dir: Peter Watkins.)

Battle of El Alamein, The (Italy-France, 1968)**½ Frederick Stafford, Ettore Manni, George Hilton, Robert Hossein,

Michael Rennie. Lots of action and a good plot enhance this tale of Rommel's defeat late in '42. Twist is that the Italians are the heroes, the Germans their uneasy allies, and the British are the villains. Hossein, a French actor, impersonates Rommel, and Rennie is a rather unsympathetic Field Marshal Montgomery. Not too well dubbed. (Dir: Calvin Jackson Padget (Giorgio Ferroni), 105 mins.)

Battle of Neretva, The (Yugoslavia-U.S.-Italy-Germany, 1969)** Yul Brynner, Sergei Bondarchuk, Curt Jurgens, Sylva Koscina, Hardy Kruger, Orson Welles. Tale of Yugoslavians facing a 1943 invasion by the Germans and Italians. When cut for American release, it lost much of its impact and coherence. (Dir: Veljko Bulajic, 102 mins.)

Battle of Rogue River (1954)** George Montgomery, Martha Hyer. Indians and the admittance of Oregon as a state. Average. (Dir: William Castle, 70 mins.)

Battle of the Bulge (1965)** Henry Fonda, Robert Ryan, Pier Angeli. Muddled WW II film. The performances are secondary to the battle scenes, and they're nothing special. (Dir: Ken Annakin, 162 mins.)

Battle of the Coral Sea (1959)** Cliff Robertson, Gia Scala. Robertson is a submarine officer who is captured by the Japanese and escapes from an island. (Dir: Paul Wendkos, 100 mins.)

Battle of the Sexes, The (Great Britain, 1960)*** Peter Sellers, Robert Morley, Constance Cummings. It's curious to see James Thurber transplanted to the British middle class, and this comedy, though unsuccessful, has many points of interest as it wavers between banal farce and piquant satire. Sellers plays the worm who turns, Morley, his gout-ridden, sybaritic boss, and the underrated Cummings is a career woman executive on the rise. The film's view of women in business is something short of enlightened. (Dir: Charles Crichton, 88 mins.)

Battle of the Villa Fiorita, The (1965)** Maureen O'Hara, Richard Todd, Rossano Brazzi. When their mother runs off with her lover her children try to get her back with pater. (Dir: Delmer Daves, 111 mins.)

Battle of the Worlds (Italy, 1961)*½ Claude Rains, Bill Carter. (Dir: Anthony Dawson, 84 mins.)

Battle Stations (1956)** William Bendix, Richard Boone, John Lund. A naval aircraft carrier during WWII. (Dir: Lewis Seiler, 90 mins.)

Battle Taxi (1954)** Sterling Hayden, Arthur Franz. Young officer learns the value of the helicopter rescue service in Korea. (Dir: Herbert Strock, 80 mins.)

Battle Zone (1952)** John Hodiak, Stephen McNally. Buddies and their exploits. (Dir: Lesley Selander, 82 mins.)

Battleaxe, The (Great Britain, 1961)** Jill Ireland, Francis Matthews. A lock company employs ex-cons who are safe-cracking experts. Mildly amusing. (Dir: Godfrey Grayson, 66 mins.)

Battleground (1949)*** Van Johnson, John Hodiak, Ricardo Montalban, George Murphy. Although a critical and commercial success, this story of the Battle of the Bulge has only intermittent patches of strong direction and forceful dialogue. A doggedly artful movie that stumbles more into self-consciousness than expressiveness. Intelligence is everywhere evident, but inspiration is conspicuously lacking. James Whitmore's quiet authenticity stands out in his first showy role. William A. Wellman directed from a screenplay by Robert Pirosh. Retains interest for Wellman's gritty, abstract schematism, but he fails to reach the pinnnacle set by his "Story of G. I. Joe." (118 mins.)

Battlestar Galactica (MTV 1978)*** Lorne Greene, Richard Hatch, Dirk Benedict, Maren Jensen. Designed as TV's answer to "Star Wars," this is the series' premiere episode that was later released theatrically. A sci-fi blockbuster about a huge spacecraft (the title is its name) which escapes destruction by human-hating robots, the Cyclons. Leading a caravan of 220 space vehicles, the "Galactica" hopes to find the unknown planet Earth. Plenty of action with space battles and exploding heavens; the characters work well together, but after this opening extravaganza, the series and its revival—"Galactica 1980"—fizzled. (Dir: Richard A. Colla, 152 mins.)

Battling Bellhop, The—See: **Kid Galahad** (1937)

Battling Butler (1926)**** Buster Keaton, Sally O'Neil, Francis McDonald, Snitz Edwards. Strange and disquieting Buster Keaton comedy that at times I have dared to think his best. Buster directs and once again plays the part of a spoiled rich youth, but ends up suffering brutally for his callowness and deceptions when he poses as a roundhouse fighter with the same surname as his own. The emotional dynamic of the film seems to link physical pain with a sort of purification that makes love possible; while much of the movie is very funny, it is unstinting in its theme of class redemption. Not for all tastes, or for all Keaton fans, it still must be classed a masterpiece, along with many of his films that are easier to love. (70 mins.)

Bawdy Adventures of Tom Jones, The (Great Britain, 1975)* Nicky Henson, Trevor Howard, Georgia Brown. (Dir: Cliff Owen, 94 mins.)

Baxter (Great Britain, 1972)**½ Patricia Neal, Jean-Pierre Cassel, Britt Ekland, Scott Jacoby, Lynn Carlin. Moving drama of a boy's breakdown after his parents divorce. Based on the novel "The Boy Who Could Make Himself Disappear," and adapted by Reginald Rose. The acting is remarkably sensitive, especially Scott Jacoby in the title role. (Dir: Lionel Jeffries, 105 mins.)

Bay of Angels (France, 1963)**½ Jeanne Moreau, Claude Mann. Director Jacques Demy reportedly wrote the script for his second feature in three days while he was sitting out a production delay on his first, "The Umbrellas of Cherbourg." Moreau stars as a compulsive gambler who falls in love with a bank clerk on holiday in Nice. The tone is mainly lighthearted and light-headed, but Demy finds some room for his customary ironies. Worth seeing for the wonderfully seedy performance by Moreau. B&W. (85 mins.)

Be Beautiful But Shut Up (France, 1958)** Mylene Demongeot, Henri Vidal. (Dir: Henri Verneuil, 94 mins.)

Be Yourself (1930)* Fanny Brice, Robert Armstrong, Harry Green, Gertrude Astor. (Dir: Thornton Freeland, 77 mins.)

Beach Blanket Bingo (1965)**½ Frankie Avalon, Annette Funicello, Deborah Walley, Paul Lynde. Beach adventure with the typical muscle-bound boys and the bikini-clad girls. Paul Lynde, as a press agent, has some funny moments. (Dir: William Asher, 98 mins.)

Beach Casanova (Italy, 1963)**½ Curt Jurgens, Martine Carol, Capucine. Italian soap opera about the goings-on of the rich and the not-so-rich on the Riviera. (Dir: Vittorio Sala, 85 mins.)

Beach Party (1963)** Dorothy Malone, Robert Cummings, Frankie Avalon. Robert Cummings has some good moments as a professor. There's a funny motorcycle gang leader named Eric Von Zipper by Harvey Lembeck. (Dir: William Asher, 101 mins.)

Beach Party—Italian Style (Italy, 1963)*½ Catherine Spaak, Luisa Mattoli, Lisa Gastoni. Alternate title: **Eighteen in the Sun.** (Dir: Camillo Mastrocinque, 85 mins.)

Beach Patrol (MTV 1979)*½ Christine DeLisle, Richard Hill, Jonathan Frakes. (Dir: Robert Kelljan, 90 mins.)

Beach Red (1967)*** Cornel Wilde, Rip Torn, Burr De Benning. Sincere and moving. A group of Marines try to capture a Japanese held island near the Phillippines. Shot on location in the Philippines and Japan, based on the well-known novel by Peter Bowman. (Dir: Cornel Wilde, 105 mins.)

Beachcomber, The (Great Britain,1938)***½ Charles Laughton, Elsa Lanchester. Man of a shiftless disposition becomes respectable when a lady missionary sets out to reform him. Delightful comedy-drama based on Somerset Maugham's story. (Dir: Erich Pommer, 90 mins.)

Beachcomber, The (1955)**½ Robert Newton, Glynis Johns. Bum meets missionary's sister on a tropical island and his life is changed. A bit over-acted, but absorbing film. (Dir: Muriel Box, 82 mins.)

Beachhead (1954)**½ Tony Curtis, Frank Lovejoy, Mary Murphy. Four Marines are assigned to locate Jap mine fields off Bougainville. Routine. (Dir: Stuart Heisler, 89 mins.)

Bear, The (France, 1960)*** Renato Rascal, Francis Blanche. A talking bear and his keeper raise havoc in Paris Zoo. Different, well acted, good fun. (Dir: Edmond Séchan. 85 mins.)

Bear Island (Canada-Great Britain, 1979)*½ Vanessa Redgrave, Donald Sutherland, Richard Widmark, Christopher Lee. (Dir: Don Sharp, 118 mins.)

Beast, The (France, 1975)***½ Sirpa Lane, Lisbeth Hummel, Pierre Benedetti, Guy Tréjan. Walerian Borowczyk ("Story of Sin," "Immoral Tales") has directed a witty, graphic, erotic fable based on the old story of Beauty and the Beast, and this version, while as elegant as Jean Cocteau's, eschews aestheticism for randiness. You've never seen such gigantic penises (well, hardly ever). An American heiress discovers the joys of bestiality when she goes to France to marry into an eccentric old aristocratic family. Her beau turns out to be tall and dark, anyhow. Recommended, but not for the finicky. (102 mins.)

Beast from Haunted Cave, The (1959)*½ Sheila Carol, Michael Forrest, Frank Wolff. (Dir: Monte Hellman, 65 mins.)

Beast from 20,000 Fathoms, The (1953)**½ Paul Christian, Paula Raymond, Cecil Kellaway, Donald Woods, Lee Van Cleef. In the standard early-'50s wrinkle, radiation from an atom-bomb test in the Arctic thaws out a prehistoric rhedosaurus that slouches toward the Big Apple to create havoc. At least it knows where the action is. Dull sci-fi, in which the monster doesn't appear for the longest time, and with weak special effects, the presence of master Ray Harryhausen notwithstanding. Designer Eugene Lourie directed; of the cast, only Kellaway as a professor gobbled up in his bathysphere is of note. (80 mins.)

Beast of Babylon Against the Son of Hercules—See: **Hero of Babylon**

Beast of Budapest, The (1958)** Gerald Milton, Greta Thyssen. A father and son conflict in their beliefs as to Hungary's fight for freedom from the Communists. (Dir: Harmon Jones, 74 mins.)

Beast of Hollow Mountain (1956)**½ Guy Madison, Patricia Medina. A routine western with a bit of science fiction. Interesting. (Dir: Edward Nassour, 79 mins.)

Beast of Morocco (1967)* William Sylvester, Diane Clare, Alizia Gur. Alternate title: *The Hand of Night*. (Dir: Frederic Goode, 88 mins.)

Beast with Five Fingers, The (1946)**½ Peter Lorre, Robert Alda, Andrea King. As in most of the middle-rung horror films, there is a lot of bad to take with the genuinely tingling. This story of a pianist's severed hands running amok has some fine images, and a good performance by Lorre, but it drags a lot in between. Robert Florey, a good director out of the Warners' stable, gets credit, but Luis Buñuel reportedly worked on some of the effects—his only screen work in the 20

years between his early surreal period ('27–'32) and his Mexican resurgence ('47). (88 mins.)

Beasts Are in the Street, The (MTV 1978)* Carol Lynley, Dale Robinette. (Dir: Peter Hunt, 104 mins.)

Beasts of Marseilles (Great Britain, 1957)*** Stephen Boyd, Anna Gaylor. English soldiers hide from the Nazis in Occupied France. Good direction and performances. (Dir: Hugo Fregonese, 100 mins.)

Beat Generation, The (1959)*½ Mamie Van Doren, Steve Cochran, Ray Danton. Alternate title: "This Rebel Age." (Dir: Charles Haas, 93 mins.)

Beat Girl (Great Britain, 1959)**½ David Farrar, Noelle Adam, Christopher Lee. A real archival find, a 1959 British teenpic. Including Adam Faith (later the road manager of "Stardust"), and introducing Gillian Hills as an angry teenager whose resentment of her attractive stepmother has made her determined to destroy her father's happy marriage. She takes up with a group of beatniks and joins them in typically delinquent activities—including a drag race and a game of "chicken" with players placing their heads on railroad tracks. With Oliver Reed as one of the beats, in one of his earliest roles. Of course, stepmama has a sordid past as a stripper, or didn't you know? Of all people, Edmond T. Greville, upholder of a genteel hack tradition in British cinema, directed. (92 mins.)

Beat the Devil (1954)**** Humphrey Bogart, Jennifer Jones, Gina Lollobrigida, Peter Lorre, Robert Morley. Director John Huston's offbeat thriller was so offbeat that it didn't die at the box office—it never even breathed. Bogart starred and put his own money into it—he didn't work with Huston after this. But it's a funny movie that spoofs the spy thriller genre in tricky, interesting ways, and Jones, Lorre, Morley, and Edward Underdown are quite hilarious. However, Bogart doesn't seem to get the joke. (92 mins.)

Beatniks, The (1958)*½ Peter Breck, Tony Travis. (Dir: Paul Frees, 73 mins.)

Beats, The: An Existential Comedy** Venice, California, poet and director Philomene Long conceived this film as a tribute to Stuart Z. Perkoff, whose offbeat poetry of living spanned 15 years—from the early days of the Venice West/Gas House scene until his death in '74. Long filmed encounters with Perkoff's friends and fellow poets Aya, Frank Rios, and Jack Hirschman, as well as memories of Shirley Clarke, Viva, Lawrence Ferlinghetti, and Allen Ginsberg. Long attempts to create the spirit of Perkoff's beat as the film moves back and forth between '58 and the present. Unflinching nonconformism tempered by wit and laughter. For special tastes.

Beau Brummell (1924)**½ John Barrymore, Irene Rich, Carmel Myers, Mary

Astor. This John Barrymore melodrama, one of the biggest grossers of the year, was the first of a series he would do, including the superior "Don Juan" and the fruitily designed "Beloved Rogue." Based on a play by Clyde Fitch (he wrote it for himself on Broadway in 1916), the story is about a British officer who, jilted in love, decides to become what was then known as a "gay bachelor." Astor has one of her first starring roles. Directed by the hack Harry Beaumont. (110 mins.)

Beau Geste (1939)***½ Gary Cooper, Ray Milland, Robert Preston, Brian Donlevy, J. Carrol Naish. Percival Wren's incomparable boys' fantasy is brought to the screen with a superlative cast, and director William Wellman brings off the set pieces with impressive flair, though the picture tends to be filled with romantic hot air. Cooper, Milland, and Preston are the brothers Geste, though the film is easily stolen by Donlevy's martinet and Naish's informer. With Susan Hayward, Broderick Crawford, and Albert Dekker. (120 mins.)

Beau Geste (1966)**½ Doug McClure, Guy Stockwell, Telly Savalas. Another go-round for this plot of brothers in the Foreign Legion. Pretty slack retelling. (Dir: Douglas Heyes, 103 mins.)

Beau James (1957)*** Bob Hope, Vera Miles, Paul Douglas, Alexis Smith. Hope as the dapper Mayor James Walker, in the life and times of New York's favorite politician and gay blade of the dizzy decade of the 1920s. Good entertainment. (Dir: Melville Shavelson, 105 mins.).

Beauties of the Night (France, 1952)***½ Gina Lollobrigida, Gerard Philipe, Martine Carol. A whimsical and charming fantasy. A struggling young composer takes refuge in a dream world. A very bright performance by Gerard Philippe. Alternate title: **Les Belles-de-Nuit.** (Dir: Rene Clair, 84 mins.)

Beautiful Blonde from Bashful Bend, The (1949)**½ Betty Grable, Cesar Romero, Rudy Vallee, Hugh Herbert, Margaret Hamilton. Director Preston Sturges's last Hollywood film hasn't the brashness or the inventiveness of his earlier masterworks—it seems tired and uncommitted. It's possible to imagine Sturges making something raucous of the farcical premise, but the film is distinctive without distinction. Grable is a saloon canary who shoots a sheriff and hides out as a schoolmarm. (77 mins.)

Beautiful But Dangerous (Italy, 1958)*½ Gina Lollobrigida, Vitorio Gassman, Robert Alda. Alternate title: **The Most Beautiful Woman in the World!** (Dir: Robert Z. Leonard, 103 mins.)

Beautiful but Deadly—See: **Don is Dead, The**

Beauty and the Beast (France, 1946)**** Josette Day, Jean Marais. A lavish, surrealistic film of great interest. Cocteau's wild imagination never lets up as he follows the heroine through her unconventional love story with the Beast. Brilliant. (Dir: Jean Cocteau, 90 mins.)

Beauty and the Bullfighter—See: **Love in a Hot Climate**

Bebo's Girl (Italy, 1964)**½ Claudia Cardinale, George Chakiris. Romance about a village girl and a former war hero who is now wanted by the police. Offers some interest. Dubbed. (Dir: Luigi Comencini, 106 mins.)

Because of Him (1946)*** Deanna Durbin, Franchot Tone, Charles Laughton. An innocent and delightful comedy-romance. Charles Laughton does his usual best. (Dir: Richard Wallace, 88 mins.)

Because of You (1952)**½ Loretta Young, Jeff Chandler. A woman serves a prison term for being an accessory to a crime and is determined to pick up the pieces of her life when she is paroled. (Dir: Joseph Pevney, 95 mins.)

Because They're Young (1960)**½ Dick Clark, Tuesday Weld. New high school teacher asks for trouble when he takes an active interest in the destinies of his pupils. (Dir: Paul Wendkos, 102 mins.)

Because You're Mine (1952)*** Mario Lanza, James Whitmore, Doretta Morrow. A drafted opera singer falls for the sister of his tough Army sergeant. One of Lanza's pleasanter vehicles. Paula Corday, Dean Miller. (Dir: Alexander Hall, 103 mins.)

Becket (Great Britain, 1964)**** Richard Burton, Peter O'Toole. About the remarkable 12th century Englishman, Thomas Becket, and his turbulent relationship with King Henry II of England. Based on the wonderful play by Frenchman Jean Anouilh. A thrilling pageant and a valuable history lesson. Sumptuously costumed and flawlessly directed by Peter Glenville. (148 mins.)

Becket Affair, The (Italy, 1966)* Lang Jeffries, Ivan Desny. (Dir: Osvaldo Civirani, 89 mins.)

Becky Sharp (1935)**½ Miriam Hopkins, Cedric Hardwicke, Billie Burke. Director Rouben Mamoulian's forgettable adaptation of Thackeray's "Vanity Fair" was the first feature to be photographed in the perfected Technicolor process. Miriam Hopkins acquits herself fairly well under the weight of the flashy direction, and Pat Nixon appears as an extra in a ballroom sequence (although you'll have to look hard and fast to spot her). (83 mins.)

Bed and Board (France-Italy, 1970)**** Jean-Pierre Leaud, Claude Jade, Hiroko Berghauer. One of director Francois Truffaut's most glowing commentaries on life and love, and the fourth in his partly autobiographical series which began with Antoine Doinel (Leaud) in "The 400 Blows." (Then came "Love at Twenty" and "Stolen Kisses.") His true love (Jade) has now become Antoine's wife and the film covers the first few years of their marriage. Subtitles. (Dir: Francois Truffaut, 95 mins.)

Bed of Roses (1933)*** Constance Bennett, Joel McCrea, Pert Kelton, Franklin Pangborn, John Halliday. Little-known, acerbic comedy about the early years of the Depression. Director Gregory La Cava also contributed to the script. (67 mins.)

Bed Sitting Room, The (Great Britain, 1969)***½ Rita Tushingham, Ralph Richardson, Spike Milligan, Peter Cook, Dudley Moore. In '68 United Artists gave director Richard Lester a million-dollar budget and a free rein, and he made what must have been the most noncommercial film he could imagine. In the aftermath of WW III (which lasts 2 minutes and 28 seconds), Richardson finds himself mutating into a furnished apartment, Rita Tushingham gives birth to something or other, the BBC makes house calls, the British middle class spends its dying days riding in circles through the remains of the Underground, and civil defense officers Cook and Moore periodically descend from a balloon to exhort the populace to "Keep moving! Keep moving!" Lester, not too surprisingly, didn't work again for five years, but this is one of his best efforts, a sharp, deadly satire. (91 mins.)

Bedazzled (Great Britain, 1967)***½ Peter Cook, Dudley Moore, Eleanor Bron, Raquel Welch. A comedy based on the Faustian legend. It doesn't all work, but the jokes, both visual and verbal—are hurled at a rapid nonstop pace, and enough of them are sufficiently inventive and outrageous to reward any enterprising viewer. Directed by Stanley Donen. (107 mins.)

Bedelia (Great Britain, 1946)**½ Margaret Lockwood, Ian Hunter. Engineer weds a previously married woman, suspects her to be a notorious poisoner. (Dir: Lance Comfort, 85 mins.)

Bedeviled (1955)** Anne Baxter, Steve Forrest. Muddled melodrama about a young American preparing for the clergy and his encounter with a femme fatale in Paris. (Dir: Mitchell Leisen, 85 mins.)

Bedford Incident, The (1965)*** Richard Widmark, Sidney Poitier. The dilemma which arises aboard a U.S. Navy destroyer after an unidentified submarine is discovered in the North Atlantic. Widmark's performance plus a fine production should hold your attention. (Dir: James Harris, 102 mins.)

Bedknobs and Broomsticks (1971)**½ Angela Lansbury, David Tomlinson, Roddy McDowall, Sam Jaffe. An elaborate Disney musical fantasy with animated sequences, as Lansbury practices the white arts against evil Nazis. Rather more sophisticated than the run of Disney products, the film lacks the inventiveness that could endow it with genuine charm. Directed by standard-bearer Robert Stevenson. (117 mins.)

Bedlam (1946)**½ Boris Karloff, Anna Lee, Billy House, Richard Fraser. The last of Val Lewton's legendary RKO horror films, set in an 18th-century madhouse ruled by Karloff. Lewton's vaunted taste and discretion were beginning to get the best of him by the end of the series; the mise-en-scène here is based on Hogarth, and the entire film has a stolid, stagy quality absent from the fluid best of Lewton's work. Perhaps that's the fault of director Mark Robson, who lacks the lyrical imagination of Lewton's best collaborator, Jacques Tourneur ("I Walked with a Zombie," "The Leopard Man"). Still, Nicholas Musuraca's excellent cinematography contributes a number of fine effects, and there is a strange and witty aside on the invention of movies. (79 mins.)

Bedtime for Bonzo (1951)**½ Ronald Reagan, Diana Lynn, Walter Slezak. Silly comedy has some appeal. Professor Reagan experiments with a chimp. (Dir: Frederick de Cordova, 83 mins.)

Bedtime Story (1941)***½ Fredric March, Loretta Young. Actress wants to retire, but her playwright-husband has other ideas. Sparkling comedy. (Dir: Alexander Hall, 85 mins.)

Bedtime Story (1964)**½ Marlon Brando, David Niven, Shirley Jones. Wolfish GI and a smooth con man vie for the affections of a visiting soap queen in Europe. Provides some moments of fun. (Dir: Ralph Levy, 99 mins.)

Bees, The (1978)* John Saxon, Angel Tompkins, John Carradine. (Dir: Alfredo Zacharias, 82 mins.)

Before and After (MTV 1979)**½ Patty Duke Astin, Bradford Dillman, Barbara Feldon. Attention, ladies, who are overweight and always promise to start a new diet on Monday—here's your story! Astin is terrific as a pudgy married woman and mother who sees her marriage disintegrating right before her girdle. Wisecracking and self-deprecating, she finally embarks on a diet and exercise routine, eventually emerging as a new, trim, confident person. There are clichés galore in the script, but the talented Astin makes it all work reasonably well. (Dir: Kim Friedman, 104 mins.)

Before the Revolution (France, 1964)***½ Adriana Asti, Francesco Barilli. An absorbing, astonishing film about European politics and Marxism. One of the most surprising things about it is that Bernardo Bertolucci was only twenty-two when he directed this richly textured, excellently acted drama. Asti is outstanding as a neurotic young aunt suffering from guilt complexes. Original screenplay by Bertolucci. Loosely based on Stendhal's "The Charterhouse of Parma." (112 mins.)

Before Winter Comes (Great Britain, 1969)**½ David Niven, Topol, Anna Karina. Comedy about the use of democratic or autocratic means in dispatching prisoners East and West after WWII; a multi-lingual con man gets into the action. But top honors go to the droll Israeli, Topol, as the linguist. Based on a New

Yorker magazine short story by Frederick I. Keefe called "The Interpreter." (Dir: J. Lee Thompson, 108 mins.)

Beg, Borrow or Steal (MTV 1973)**½ Michael Cole, Michael Connors, Kent McCord. Offbeat heist film. Handicapped buddies find it rough staying legit, and decide to execute a robbery. (Dir: David Lowell Rich, 72 mins.)

Beggar Student, The (W. Germany, 1958)** Gerhard Riedmann, Waltraut Haas. Operetta. Students protest against the King in turn-of-the-century Germany. Close your eyes, and open your ears. (Dir: Werner Jacobs, 97 mins.)

Beggar's Opera, The (Great Britain, 1953)***½ Laurence Olivier, Hugh Griffith, Dorothy Tutin, Stanley Holloway, George Devine. Jonathan Swift called John Gay's show a "Newgate pastoral," and this smash hit of the 18th century marked the birth of the modern musical. Short of the mordant cruelty of Brecht's character, Olivier makes a dashing Macheath, working instead in the parodistic mode he revels in. A very young Peter Brook directed, Olivier and Herbert Wilcox co-produced. Screenplay by Christopher Fry. (94 mins.)

Beginning or the End, The (1947)**½ Brian Donlevy, Robert Walker. Ambitious film which strives to tell the story of the first A-Bomb. Too many clichés. (Dir: Norman Taurog, 112 mins.)

Beginning of the End (1957)*½ Peter Graves, Peggie Castle. (Dir: Bert Gordon, 74 mins.)

Beguiled, The (1971)***½ Clint Eastwood, Geraldine Page, Elizabeth Hartman. Director Siegel's Civil War gothic horror tale is one of his best films, containing what is probably Eastwood's finest performance as a wounded Union soldier taking refuge in a girls' school under the knowing hand of mistress Page. At first the women go into a sexual panic reminiscent of the nuns in "Black Narcissus," but there's no doubt that for all of Eastwood's tattered swagger, he is more the prey than the hunter. Evocative, frightening (but not violent), the film springs out of the best of Bierce and Poe—an art film in the most entertaining sense of the term. Siegel proves that he need not work in the action format to give full rein to his distinctive personality; though atypical, the film is as personally expressive as anything he has done. Significantly, it is Eastwood's only box-office flop since he reached certifiable stardom. (109 mins.)

Behave Yourself (1951)**½ Shelley Winters, Farley Granger. Young couple find a dog that's wanted by crooks. (Dir: George Beck, 81 mins.)

Behind Locked Doors (1948)*** Richard Carlson, Lucille Bremer. Investigator goes to a sanitarium where a missing judge is being held captive. Suspenseful, well-acted thriller. (Dir: Oscar (Budd) Buetticher, 61 mins.)

Behind the Badge—See: **Killing Affair, A**

Behind the High Wall (1956)*½ Tom Tully, Sylvia Sidney. (Dir: Abner Biberman, 85 mins.)

Behind the Mask (Great Britain, 1959)*** Michael Redgrave, Tony Britton. Behind the scenes drama of a London hospital, highlighting the conflict between two surgeons. Fine performances. (Dir: John Francis Dillon, 70 mins.)

Behind the Mask of Zorro (Italy, 1964)*½ Tony Russel. (102 mins.)

Behind the Rising Sun (1943)*** Tom Neal, Margo, Robert Ryan. Japanese publisher alienates his son with his extreme political views. Well acted war drama. (Dir: Edward Dmytryk, 89 mins.)

Behind the Wall (Poland, 1971)**** Maja Komorowska, Zbigniew Zapasiewicz. Moving story of loneliness and need. Young female chemist, on the edge of a breakdown, tries to confide in a neighbor in her apartment, while simultaneously asking him for a job. Beautifully acted. (Dir: Krzystof Zanussi, 70 mins.)

Behold a Pale Horse (1964)**½ Gregory Peck, Anthony Quinn, Omar Sharif. Renegade Loyalist continues to harass the Spanish regime, police captain sees a chance to trap him. Vague, cloudy, slow. (Dir: Fred Zinnemann, 118 mins.)

Being There (1979)**** Peter Sellers, Shirley MacLaine, Melvyn Douglas, Jack Warden, Richard Dysart. Director Hal Ashby has rendered Jerzy Kosinski's delicate apologue in terms somewhat different from the novel; it is unmistakably a Hal Ashby film, but he has been faithful to the material. Sellers gives one of his finest portrayals, as an untutored victim of enviromental isolation who has lived all his life inside the walls of a Washington house and its garden. When forced to enter the world, this simple soul becomes by a series of delightful ironies the toast of the town. The gentle allegory is deftly maintained at a high level of sophistication, wit, and humanism. Douglas won a well-deserved Oscar for this one. (107 mins.)

Belated Flowers (U.S.S.R., 1972)*** Olga Zhizneva, Irina Lavrentyeva, Alexander Lazarev. Charming, romantic story based on Chekhov's novella, "Late-Blooming Flowers." A royal family is on its uppers, and the young princess dreams of love while dying of consumption. (Dir: Abram Room, 100 mins.)

Believe in Me (1971)* Michael Sarrazin, Jacqueline Bisset, Allen Garfield. Directed by Stuart Hagmann, John G. Avidsen was brought in. (90 mins.)

Bell Antonio (France-Italy, 1960)**½ Marcello Mastroianni. Comedy about a man-about-town. Dubbed. Funny and heartfelt. (Dir: Mauro Bolognini, 101 mins.)

Bell, Book & Candle (1959)*** James

Stewart, Kim Novak, Jack Lemmon, Ernie Kovacs. This wacky B'way play is delightfully brought to the screen. Zany characters include a whimsical warlock, a high priestess of magic, and Ernie Kovacs as an eccentric author. It's fun all the way! (Dir: Richard Quine, 106 mins.)

Bell for Adano, A (1945)***½ John Hodiak, William Bendix, Gene Tierney. John Hersey's story of the American occupation of a small Italian town is beautifully brought to life on the screen. Believable and sensitively handled. (Dir: Henry King, 103 mins.)

Bell Jar, The (1979)* Marilyn Hassett, Julie Harris, Barbara Barrie, Anne Jackson. From Sylvia Plath's autobiographical novel. (Dir: Larry Peerce, 112 mins.)

Bellboy, The (1960)**½ Lewis's first film as a writer-director, in which he runs riot through Miami's Fontainebleau Hotel. No good can come of trying to explain Lewis's considerable virtues as a filmmaker (the precision of his shots is uncanny) to those who simply do not like him as a performer—which, by this point, must include most of humanity. Jerry is Jerry, alas and hooray. (72 mins.)

Belle de Jour (France-Italy, 1967)**** Catherine Deneuve, Jean Sorel, Genevieve Page, Michel Piccoli. A remarkably beautiful film by Luis Bunuel. A frigid young housewife decides to spend her midweek afternoons as a prostitute. Bunuel's familiar obsessions with anticlericism and hypocritical society, and a preoccupation with erotica, are all here. Comments on our sexual fantasies and hang-ups are humorous and perceptive. Based on Joseph Kessel's novel. (Dir: Luis Bunuel, 100 mins.)

Belle Le Grand (1951)*½ Vera Ralston, John Carroll. (Dir: Allan Dwan, 90 mins.)

Belle of New York, The (1952)**½ Fred Astaire, Vera-Ellen. Turn-of-the-century comedy about a stage door Johnny who falls in love. The dancing's the thing and Astaire and Vera-Ellen make a good team. (Dir: Charles Walters, 80 mins.)

Belle of Old Mexico (1950)** Estelita Rodriguez, Robert Rockwell. (Dir: R.G. Springsteen, 70 mins.)

Belle of the Nineties (1934)**½ Mae West, Roger Pryor, John Mack Brown, Katherine De Mille; Duke Ellington and his Orchestra. Amusing satire on life in the Gay Nineties. Song: "My Old Flame," by Arthur Johnston and Sam Coslow. (Dir: Leo McCarey, 75 mins.)

Belle of the Yukon (1944)** Gypsy Rose Lee, Randolph Scott, Dinah Shore. (Dir: William Seiter, 84 mins.)

Belle Sommers (1962)** Polly Bergen, David Janssen. (Dir: Elliott Silverstein, 62 mins.)

Belle Starr (1941)**½ Gene Tierney, Randolph Scott, Dana Andrews. Tierney isn't exactly a raunchy outlaw, but then this isn't exactly the story of the real Belle Starr. Your basically absurd

Hollywood laundry job. Lamar Trotti wrote it. Color. (Dir: Irving Cummings, 87 mins.)

Belle Starr (MTV 1980)**½ Elizabeth Montgomery, Cliff Potts, Michael Cavanaugh, Gary Combs. The talented Ms. Montgomery is Belle Starr, the bandit lady with an itch to steal cattle and rob trains alongside the James boys, the Youngers, and the Daltons. Liz's Belle is an attractive woman with a large sexual appetite and a yen for Cole Younger (Potts). Belle's ready to turn against her own boyfriend to be off with her outlaw buddies. Ms. Montgomery dominates, and she has an entertaining, if predictable, script to work with; another plus is the camerawork, with director John A. Alonzo displaying an appreciative eye for the land and Liz. A chichi western—a short-lived genre, we hope. (104 mins.)

Belles and Ballets (France, 1960)**½ Members of the Paris Ballet De L'Etoile perform varied numbers. For balletomaniacs worthy fare, well done. (52 mins.)

Belles-de-Nuits, Les—See: **Beauties of the Night**

Belles of St. Trinian's (Great Britain, 1954)*** Alastair Sim, George Cole, Joyce Grenfell, Hermione Baddeley. An enormously popular version of Ronald Searle's awful schoolgirl cartoons, in which the bankrupt institution (presided over by Sim in drag) plays host to little darlings who play the horses, terrorize the natives, and indulge in assorted grotesqueries. Frank Launder and Sidney Gilliat wrote, Launder directed, and the film spawned three sequels. Farce with numerous laughs. (89 mins.)

Belles on Their Toes (1952)**½ Jeanne Crain, Myrna Loy, Debra Paget, Jeffrey Hunter. Sequel to "Cheaper By the Dozen." Some funny scenes involving the further adventures of the large Gilbreth family. (Dir: Henry Levin, 89 mins.)

Bellissima (Italy, 1951)**½ Anna Magnani, Walter Chairi, Tina Apicella. Seldom seen outside Italy, this is one of director Luchino Visconti's few determinedly light works, a comedy set in the studios of Cinecitta, where a contest is being held to find "the prettiest child in Rome." Magnani, an earnestly néorealist mother, enters her daughter and is caught up in a stampede. The story is by Cesare Zavattini, De Sica's wily collaborator on "Bicycle Thief." (95 mins.)

Bells Are Ringing (1960)***½ Judy Holliday, Dean Martin, Fred Clark, Jean Stapleton, Eddie Foy, Jr. A first-rate film reconception of the Broadway musical, in which theatrical conceits are brilliantly realized in formal film terms. One of director Vincente Minnelli's most impressive achievements. Holliday gives probably her best (and last) performance as a meddlesome answering-service operator who finds love with a songwriter (Martin) who has a creative block—a psychological quirk not unknown among Minnelli artist-protagonists. The score is likable but forgettable. This may have been the last gasp of the big-budget musicals as a vehicle for rich personal expression. (127 mins.)

Bells of St. Mary's (1945)***½ Bing Crosby, Ingrid Bergman. Priest and Mother Superior make plans to entice a wealthy skinflint to build them new surroundings. Sequel to "Going My Way." Still entertaining. (Dir: Leo McCarey, 126 mins.)

Beloved Enemy (1936)*** David Niven, Brian Aherne, Merle Oberon. Well done drama about people caught in the Irish Rebellion. Good cast. (Dir: H. C. Potter, 90 mins.)

Beloved Infidel (1959)**½ Gregory Peck, Deborah Kerr, Eddie Albert. The story of writer F. Scott Fitzgerald, his last years as a Hollywood scenarist, his love for columnist Sheilah Graham. Excellent performance by Miss Kerr. (Dir: Henry King, 123 mins.)

Beloved Rogue (1927)**** John Barrymore, Conrad Veidt, Marceline Day. The fictional story of medieval French poet François Villon (of whom almost nothing is really known) and his battles with King Louis XI. An exceptionally beautiful film, gorgeously photographed (B&W); also one of Barrymore's best performances in a silent, at once touching and funny, with that special antic spirit. Veidt makes a marvelously witty king, and Day is lovely as the noblewoman whose love Villon wins. (Dir: Alan Crosland, 99 mins.)

Belstone Fox, The—See: Free Spirit

Ben (1972)* Lee Harcourt Montgomery. (Dir: Phil Karlson, 75 mins.)

Ben Hur (1925)**½ Ramon Novarro, Francis X. Bushman, May McAvoy, Betty Bronson, Carmel Myers. Navarro drives the chariot in this production of the Roman epic based on Lew Wallace's bestselling novel. With a supposed $6 million budget (stupefying for the times), it was one of the first international successes, but never turned a profit. (Dir: Fred Niblo, 133 mins.)

Ben Hur (1959)**** Charlton Heston, Stephen Boyd. Spectacular screen version of the celebrated novel about the conflict between the Jews and the Romans in Jerusalem during the lifetime of Jesus. Charlton Heston is excellent in his Academy Award-winning role as Ben Hur, an aristocratic Jew who suffers grievously at the hands of the Romans for his defense of his people, and is drawn to Jesus in scenes before and during the Crucifixion. The film is meticulously produced and there are numerous sequences of awesome proportions. Special credit due to second unit directors Andrew Marton and Yakima Canutt who directed the spectacular chariot-race sequence. (Dir: William Wyler, 217 mins.)

Bend of the River (1952)*** James Stewart, Rock Hudson, Arthur Kennedy. Sprawling western adventure. Stewart and Kennedy are pitted against each other in this tale of big men in the big country. Rock Hudson has a small featured role. (Dir: Anthony Mann, 91 mins.)

Beneath the Planet of the Apes (1970)**½ James Franciscus, Charlton Heston, Kim Hunter, Roddy McDowall. Astronaut Franciscus is sent on a rescue mission, and things really get hairy. A race of mutated humans living "beneath" the planet and the continuing presence of Hunter's Zira character are featured. (Dir: Ted Post, 108 mins.)

Beneath the Twelve-Mile Reef (1953)**½ Robert Wagner, Terry Moore, Gilbert Roland. Fine underwater photography in this adventure about Greek sponge divers. Shot on location off the coast of Florida. (Dir: Robert Webb, 101 mins.)

Beneath the Valley of the Ultravixens (1979)*** Francesca Natividad, Ann Marie, Ken Kerr. After nearly ten years of increasingly involuted self-parody, director Russ Meyer finally made a film that pays off; it's his best since "Cherry, Harry and Raquel." Roger Ebert, hiding behind a pseudonym, has penned a delirious, delicious parody of "Our Town," with dirty old man Stuart Lancaster as the cracker-barrel master of ceremonies. Once again Meyer has constructed an artificial world of dumfounding unpersuasiveness, populated by the most libidinous creatures this side of Al Capp. Not for prudish grandma! (93 mins.)

Bengal Brigade (1954)** Rock Hudson, Arlene Dahl, Ursula Thiess. A wronged British officer in the Bengal troops in India sets out to clear his reputation. Miss Dahl is exquisite. (Dir: Laslo Benedek, 87 mins.)

Ben-Gurion Remembers (Israel, 1972)***½ Absorbing feature-length documentary about one of the most remarkable political leaders of the 20th century—David Ben-Gurion. Extensive documentary footage dealing with Jews in Eastern Europe, the founding of the state of Israel, and the fascinating personal reminiscences of this dynamic octogenarian. (Dir: Simon Hesera, 82 mins.)

Benjamin (France, 1968)*** Michele Morgan, Catherine Deneuve, Pierre Clementi. Elegantly photographed adventures of a dashing young rake and his conquests in 18th-century France. Dubbed. (Dir: Michel Deville, 100 mins.)

Benji (1974)*** Patsy Garrett, Allen Fiuzat, Cynthia Smith, Peter Breck. Benji outshines his human supporting players. Simple story has the hound saving two kids from kidnappers and earning a place in their grateful parents' home. (Dir: Joe Camp, 89 mins.)

Benny and Barney: Las Vegas Undercover (1977)*½ Jack Cassidy, Terry Kiser, Timothy Thomerson. (Dir: Ron Stalof, 86 mins.)

Benny Goodman Story, The (1956)**½ Steve Allen, Donna Reed. Typical Hollywood version of a bandleader's life and loves. Harry James, Gene Krupa and others make guest appearances. (Dir: Valentine Davies, 116 mins.)

Berkeley Square (Great Britain, 1933)**** Leslie Howard, Heather Angel, Irene Browne. One of the best romantic fantasies of the '30's, greatly aided by a gloriously stylish performance from Howard; wearing clothes of the 18th or the 20th century, he's a joy. Remade as **I'll Never Forget You** (1951) (Dir: Frank "Calvacade" Lloyd, 87 mins.)

Berlin Affair (1970)**½ Darren McGavin, Claude Dauphin, Brian Kelly. An honest, durable hero looking for an old friend suspected of countless things. (Dir: David Lowell Rich, 104 mins.)

Berlin Express (1948)***½ Merle Oberon, Robert Ryan. Allied group in Europe battle a band of Nazi fanatics. Exciting, well written spy thriller. (Dir: Jacques Tourneur, 86 mins.)

Berlin Tunnel 21 (MTV 1981)**½ Richard Thomas, Horst Bucholtz, Ute Christensen, Jose Ferrer. A slow-starting but interesting escape drama set in East and West Berlin during the Cold War. The story gets underway in 1961 when communists erected the Berlin Wall. A group of characters plan to escape by digging an elaborate tunnel complex. None of the individual stories of the characters involved are as interesting as the digging operation. (Dir: Richard Michaels, 184 mins.)

Bermuda Affair (1956)**½ Kim Hunter, Gary Merrill. Grim but interesting film about the disintegration of a marriage. (88 mins.)

Bermuda Depths, The (MTV 1978)*½ Leigh McCloskey, Connie Sellecca. (Dir: Tom Kotani, 104 mins.)

Bermuda Triangle, The (1978)**½ Narrated by Brad Crandall. Speculation on what the Bermuda Triangle may really contain is based on the best-selling novel (disguised as nonfiction) by Charles Berlitz. This polygon in the Atlantic Ocean has as its vertices Bermuda, Miami, and Puerto Rico and has supposedly been the scene of the disappearance of hundreds of people since 1945. There has been a suggestion that outer space beings might be involved. Judge for yourself, if you want to. (Dir: Richard Friedenberg, 93 mins.)

Bernadette of Lourdes (France, 1961)*** Daniele Ajoret, Robert Arnoux. Dubbed. The story of the simple peasant girl who became a Saint. (Dir: Robert Darene, 90 mins.)

Bernadine (1957)*½ Pat Boone, Terry Moore, Janet Gaynor. (Dir: Henry Levin, 97 mins.)

Berserk! (Great Britain, 1968)** Joan Crawford, Ty Hardin, Judy Geeson. (Dir: Jim O'Connolly, 96 mins.)

Best Boy (1979)**** Academy Award-winning documentary of Philly Wohl, 52-year-old retarded cousin of filmmaker Ira Wohl, is deeply moving and impressive. Made over a span of more than three years, following the friendly Philly's relations with his elderly parents (both now deceased) and his efforts to learn simple tasks. A highlight is his encounter with the late Zero Mostel after a revival performance of **Fiddler on the Roof.** Wohl uses his camera as a perceptive, unobtrusive observer, and the participants show a remarkable degree of naturalness as they cope with their best boy. (Dir: Ira Wohl, 104 mins.)

Best Foot Forward (1943)*** Lucille Ball, June Allyson, William Gaxton. Lively, entertaining adaptation of the musical about a boy who induces a screen star to be his date at the military-school prom. (Dir: Edward Buzzell, 95 mins.)

Best House in London, The (Great Britain, 1969)*½ David Hemmings, Joanna Pettet, George Sanders, Dany Robin. (Dir: Philip Saville, 105 mins.)

Best Little Girl in the World, The (MTV 1981)** Jennifer Jason Leigh, Charles Durning, Jason Miller, Eva Marie Saint. The subject of anorexia nervosa, the psychological malady that causes young women to starve themselves almost to death in order to be thin. The superficial plot shows how one teenager, who feels misunderstood and ignored by her parents, becomes an anorectic, but it's all so pat that it really doesn't enlist our sympathy. (Dir: Sam O'Steen, 104 mins.)

Best Man, The (1964)**** Cliff Robertson, Henry Fonda, Lee Tracy. Based on Gore Vidal's perceptive and outspoken play, it deals with the hot-and-heavy fight between two leading contenders of the Presidential nomination of their party. Excellent performances from Cliff Robertson and Henry Fonda as the political rivals, and a tour de force by Lee Tracy in the role of an ex-President. One of the best American movies about politics. (Dir: Franklin Schaffner, 102 mins.)

Best of Enemies, The (Great Britain-Italy, 1962)*** David Niven, Alberto Sordi, Michael Wilding. Comedy drama about the grudging respect that develops between a British and an Italian Captain in North Africa during World War II. (Dir: Guy Hamilton, 104 mins.)

Best of Everything, The (1959)**½ Hope Lange, Suzy Parker, Joan Crawford, Louis Jourdan. The loves of office workers and the higher-ups. Unabashedly trashy, taken from a trashy novel. (Dir: Jean Negulesco, 127 mins.)

Best Place to Be, The (MTV 1979)** Donna Reed, Efrem Zimbalist, Jr., Betty White, Timothy Hutton. Glossy, sudsy woman's show, produced by Ross Hunter, brings Ms. Reed out of retirement to play a protected widow forced to discover what life is all about. Author Helen Van Slyke has the formula down pat. Ms. Reed has a genteel affair with a tall young man and is forced to face problems with her teenage son and hippie daughter. Made as a two-part, four-hour miniseries. (Dir: David Miller, 202 mins.)

Best Things in Life Are Free, The (1956)**½ Gordon MacRae, Sheree North, Dan Dailey, Ernest Borgnine. MacRae, Borgnine, and Dailey portray the hit song-smiths DeSylva, Brown and Henderson. It's the tunes that make up the best part of the film. Songs include: "Good News," "Sonny Boy," "Sunnyside Up," and "Birth of the Blues." (Dir: Michael Curtiz, 104 mins.)

Best Way, The (France, 1976)*** Patrick Dewaere, Patrick Bouchitey. An auspicious directorial debut by writer-director Claude Miller, who has worked as an assistant to such masters as Godard and Truffaut. A tale of two young counselors at a boys' summer camp circa '60—athletic Dewaere, sensitive Bouchitey, and their involved relationship. Dramatic insights and sardonic humor maintain interest. (85 mins.)

Best Way to Walk, The—See: **Best Way, The**

Best Years of Our Lives, The (1946)**** Fredric March, Myrna Loy, Dana Andrews, Teresa Wright, Harold Russell. Perceived on release (to the tune of nine Academy Awards) as a sign that the movies had finally "grown up," director William Wyler's study of a group of men returning to civilian life after WW II was an early "problem picture" and helped create Hollywood's postwar highbrow style of pseudorealism and social concern. The film is very proud of itself, exuding a stifling piety at times; it works as well as it does thanks to accomplished performances by March, Loy, and Andrews. Gregg Toland's deep-focus photography is of primary interest to today's audiences. Remade as a TV movie, "Returning Home." (172 mins.)

Betrayal, The (1958)**½ Phillip Friend, Diana Decker. Blind Canadian ex-officer hears the voice of the one who betrayed him in prison camp during the war. Neat melodrama. (Dir: Ernest Morris, 82 mins.)

Betrayal MTV 1974)**½ Amanda Blake, Tisha Sterling. Fairly suspenseful drama. A wealthy widow who falls into the manipulative hands of a pair of con artists. The girl in the duo has second thoughts about preying on kindly Amanda Blake. (Dir: Gordon Hessler, 78 mins.)

Betrayal (MTV 1978)**½ Lesley Ann Warren, Rip Torn, Richard Masur, Ron Silver. A true story, of a psychiatrist who had an affair with a patient in the name of therapy, becomes a sudsy movie. Sexy Warren plays the victim, and Torn as the villainous psychiatrist has a field day. (Dir: Paul Wendkos, 104 mins.)

Betrayed (formerly "When Strangers Marry," 1944)***½ One of the best "surprise" films ever made. Suspenseful melodrama of a wife whose husband of a few days is suspected of murder. Kim Hunter, Dean Jagger, Bob Mitchum. (Dir: William Castle, 67 mins.)

Betrayed (1954)** Clark Gable, Lana Turner, Victor Mature. Routine spy meller. (Dir: Gottfried Reinhardt, 108 mins.)

Betrayed Women (1955)*½ Tom Drake, Beverly Michaels. (Dir: Edward Cahn, 70 mins.)

Betsy, The (1978)**½ Laurence Olivier, Robert Duvall, Katharine Ross, Tommy Lee Jones. Tame hokum about a car-manufacturing dynasty presided over by a lascivious, power-hungry Olivier. Based on Harold Robbins's potboiler, the screenplay would embarrass most soap opera writers, but Olivier and a top-notch cast throw themselves into it with abandon. (Dir: Daniel Petrie, 119 mins.)

Better a Widow (Italy-France, 1968)*½ Peter McEnery, Virna Lisi. (Dir: Duccio Tessari, 105 mins.)

Better Late Than Never (MTV 1979)**½ Harold Gould, Strother Martin, Harry Morgan, Victor Buono, Donald Pleasance. Old folks revel in a retirement home under the leadership of a spry and canny newcomer. Gould's Harry Landers can't stand being treated like a child subjected to silly rules, and he soon has the inmates behind him for stolen rides in a bus and a train. Diverting fare, though at times a bit far-fetched. (Dir: Richard Crenna, 104 mins.)

Between Heaven and Hell (1956)**½ Robert Wagner, Terry Moore, Broderick Crawford. War tale about a group of less than exemplary soldiers. Wagner plays a spoiled Southerner who learns things the hard way. (Dir: Richard Fleischer, 93 mins.)

Between Midnight and Dawn (1950)** Edmond O'Brien, Gale Storm, Mark Stevens. Two cops love the same gal; a mobster kills one off. Routine. (Dir: Gordon Douglas, 90 mins.)

Between the Lines (1977)***½ John Heard, Lindsay Crouse, Jeff Goldblum, Jill Eikenberry, Gwen Welles. An appealing, perceptive comedy about the problems and pressures of publishing a youth-oriented anti-establishment weekly newspaper. Marvelous ensemble acting from the non-star cast. Sardonic, skillful screenplay by Fred Barron. (Dir: Joan Micklin Silver, 101 mins.)

Between Time and Eternity (Germany, 1960)** Lilli Palmer, Carlos Thompson. Woman with an incurable disease decides to have one last fling. Sudsy, dubbed drama. (Dir: Arthur Maria Rabenalt, 98 mins.)

Between Two Women (1944)** Van Johnson, Gloria De Haven. Another in the Dr. Gillespie series. Lionel Barrymore is the same as ever. (Dir: Willis Goldbeck, 83 mins.)

Between Two Worlds (1944)**½ John Garfield, Edmund Gwenn, Eleanor Parker. Second and weaker version of Sutton Vane's play "Outward Bound." People who don't know they're dead, sailing to meet their destiny. Gwenn is excellent as the ship's steward. (Dir: Edward Blatt, 112 mins.)

Beware, My Lovely (1952)**½ Ida Lupino, Robert Ryan. Young war widow is menaced by a sinister handyman. Suspenseful. (Dir: Harry Horner, 77 mins.)

Beware of Blondie (1950)** Penny Singleton, Arthur Lake, Adele Jergens, Douglas Fowley. Dagwood is left in charge of his boss' construction company. Fair comedy. (Dir: Edward Bernds, 66 mins.)

Beware of Children (Great Britain, 1961)** Leslie Phillips, Julia Lockwood, Geraldine McEwan. Young couple turn property into a holiday home for disturbed children. Mild. (Dir: Gerald Thomas, 80 mins.)

Beware of the Brethren—See: **Fiend, The**

Beware of the Holy Whore (West Germany, 1970)*** Though structurally overambitious and thematically unfocused, this early effort by director Rainer Werner Fassbinder strikes a responsive chord. Members of a film troupe stranded in Barcelona, where they are about to start one of those coproduced international genre films, play out their internecine conflicts in an atmosphere of boredom and uncertainty.

Beware! The Blob (1972)*½ Robert Walker, Godfrey Cambridge, Shelley Berman. (Dir: Larry Hagman, 88 mins.)

Bewitched (1944)**½ Phyllis Thaxter, Edmund Gwenn. Generally interesting psychological melodrama about a girl with a split personality. (Dir: Arch Oboler, 65 mins.)

Beyond a Reasonable Doubt (1956)***½ Dana Andrews, Joan Fontaine, Sidney Blackmer, Barbara Nichols. Director Fritz Lang's last American film, shot in a stripped-down, almost anonymous style that seems to befit its bitterness and disillusion. Reporter Andrews has himself framed for the murder of a stripper in order to expose the incompetence of the police and the fallacy of capital punishment. Then, after he's sentenced, the evidence that will clear him is lost when his editor is killed in an accident. Once he's raised the standard social issues, Lang destroys them all with a shatteringly nihilistic conclusion. Fontaine is the Lang heroine to end (literally) all Lang heroines. (80 mins.)

Beyond All Limits (1959)* Jack Palance, Maria Felix, Pedro Armendariz. Alternate title: **Spoilers of the Sea.** (Dir: Robert Gavaldon, 100 mins.)

Beyond Evil (1980)*½ John Saxon, Lynda Day George. (Dir: Herb Freed, 94 mins.)

Beyond Glory (1948)**½ Alan Ladd, Donna Reed. West Point drama has some good moments. (Dir: John Farrow)

Beyond Mombasa (Great Britain, 1957)** Cornel Wilde, Donna Reed, Leo Genn. Mediocre adventure film set in Africa. (Dir: George Marshall, 100 mins.)

Beyond Sing the Woods—See: **Duel with Death.**

Beyond the Bermuda Triangle (MTV 1975)* Fred MacMurray, Sam Groom, Donna Mills. (Dir: William A. Graham, 78 mins.)

Beyond the Blue Horizon (1942)*½ Dorothy Lamour, Richard Denning. (Dir: Alfred Santell, 76 mins.)

Beyond the Curtain (Great Britain, 1960)*½ Richard Greene, Eva Bartok, Marius Goring. Stewardess eludes East German police while searching for her brother. Entertaining. (Dir: Compton Bennett, 88 mins.)

Beyond the Forest (1949)*** Bette Davis, Joseph Cotten, David Brian, Dona Drake. Two masters of hysteria, Davis and director King Vidor, combine for a hurricane of frenzy. This is the film they talk about in "Who's Afraid of Virginia Woolf?" where Bette says, "What a dump." The movie is fiercely trashy but is made impressive by Davis's bravura intensity and Vidor's almost mystical apprehension of his star's excesses. Close to good art, and definitely great camp. (96 mins.)

Beyond the Law (Italy, 1973)* Lee Van Cleef, Lionel Stander, Antonio Sabato. Dubbed. (Dir: Giorgio Stegani, 98 mins.)

Beyond the Law (1968)***½ Rip Torn, George Plimpton, Norman Mailer, Jose Torres, Beverly Bentley. Tough, frequently absorbing film is off-beat, original movie-making. It's Mailer's version, and vision, of a modern big city police lieutenant (Mailer) and his interrogations in the course of a single evening. Script improvised by members of the cast based on an idea of Mailer's. (Dir: Norman Mailer, 110 mins.)

Beyond the Poseidon Adventure (1979)*½ Michael Caine, Sally Field, Telly Savalas, Peter Boyle, Shirley Jones. (Dir: Irwin Allen, 114 mins.)

Beyond the Time Barrier (1960)*½ Robert Clarke, Darlene Tompkins. (Dir: Edgar Ulmer, 75 mins.)

Beyond the Valley of the Dolls (1970)** Edy Williams, Dolly Reed. Roger Ebert's script wanders into the ironic mode at times, which isn't director Russ Meyer's strong suit. With its final orgy of violence, this is more a horror film than a skin flick, which makes it vintage Meyer territory. Lots of good stuff, if none too coherent. See Michael Blodgett get his, as always. Based on Jacqueline Susann's best-selling trashy novel. (93 mins.)

B. F.'s Daughter (1948)*½ Barbara Stanwyck, Van Heflin, Charles Coburn. (Dir: Robert Z. Leonard, 108 mins.)

Bhowani Junction (Great Britain, 1956)**½ Ava Gardner, Stewart Granger, Bill Travers. Drama mixing love with political intrigue. Ava Gardner plays an Anglo-Indian girl who is torn between her loyalty for the British and the Indians. (Dir: George Cukor, 110 mins.)

Bible, The ... In the Beginning (U.S.-Italy, 1966)*** George C. Scott, John Huston,

Peter O'Toole, Michael Parks, Richard Harris. Dino de Laurentiis once told me that the idea for this movie came to him in a flash: "I wake up inna middle of night, I say to myself, 'Whatsa greatest book ever wrote?' The Bible! So I make a movie of the Bible!" He hired John Huston—"the greatest director inna world!"—to shoot it. Huston, happily, only made it to the middle of Genesis, and the results are superior to what might have been expected. Wildly uneven, the film achieves genuine grandeur in the concluding sequence about patriarch Abraham (Scott). Huston also plays a raggedy Noah in high-camp style, with O'Toole an angel of death. Much of the rest is lousy, but there's some real chance taking and ambition in what could be called a godforsaken project. (194 mins.)

Bicycle Thief, The (Italy, 1949)**** Enzo Staiola, Lamberto Maggiorani. Tragic story of a poor man whose needed bicycle is stolen, his search through Rome with his small son to find the thief. Superbly directed by Vittorio De Sica, a touching, heart-gripping drama. Won the Oscar for Best Foreign Film. (90 mins.)

Big Bad Mama (1974)** Angie Dickinson, William Shatner, Tom Skerritt. (Dir: Steve Carver, 85 mins.)

Big Beat, The (1958)** William Reynolds, Gogi Grant. Musical with pop tunes and a thin background story about the record business. (Dir: Will Cowan, 85 mins.)

Big Bluff, The (1955)*½ John Bromfield, Martha Vickers. (Dir: W. Lee Wilder, 70 mins.)

Big Bob Johnson and His Fantastic Speed Circus (1978)*½ Charles Napier, Maud Adams, Connie Forslund. A "greasy" story about the adventures of an auto-racing team, complete with lady mechanic. A rich kid hires the team for a head-to-head Rolls Royce race against uncle for the family booty. This one's for sappy kids or auto nuts. The wrenches and the transmissions give the best performances. (Dir: Jack Starrett, 104 mins.)

Big Boodle, The (1957)** Errol Flynn, Pedro Armendariz, Gia Scala. Counterfeiters pass phony bills in casino in Havana. (Dir: Richard Wilson, 83 mins.)

Big Bounce, The (1969)* Ryan O'Neal, Leigh Taylor-Young, Lee Grant, James Daly, Van Heflin. (Dir: Alex March, 102 mins.)

Big Broadcast of 1938, The (1938)*** W. C. Fields, Dorothy Lamour, Bob Hope, Shirley Ross. Fields' golf and billiards routines plus Bob and Shirley singing "Thanks for the Memory" are all this film offers—but it's enough. (Dir: Mitchell Leisen, 100 mins.)

Big Broadcast of 1937, The (1936)**½ Jack Benny, George Burns, Gracie Allen, Martha Raye, Shirley Ross; Benny Goodman and his Orchestra, Leopold Stokowski and his Symphony Orchestra. Entertaining variety show which provides a fair satire on the radio industry. Songs: "La Bomba," "Here's Love in Your Eye" by Leo Robin and Ralph Rainger. (Dir: Mitchell Leisen, 100 mins.)

Big Brown Eyes (1936)***½ Cary Grant, Joan Bennett, Alan Baxter, Lloyd Nolan, Walter Pidgeon. This terrific sleeper is one of the best light detective vehicles ever, a major '30s film directed by Raoul Walsh with much of the same savvy dialogue direction and visual efficiency as "Me and My Gal" ('32). Grant, fresh from his moment of self-discovery in George Cukor's "Sylvia Scarlett" (a stiff young leading man turns into the most graceful light comedian in movies before your eyes), is a suave private eye; Bennett, moving out from ingenue roles, is his sardonic girlfriend. The movie is only apparently trivial—it represents the aspects of the art of movies that are most important: grace, tone, line, speed, and heart. (77 mins.)

Big Bus, The (1976)** Joseph Bologna, Stockard Channing, Rene Auberjonois, Lynn Redgrave, Ruth Gordon. This parody of disaster pics is so self-conscious that it misses the comic mark. The usual nuts sign on for the first nuclear-powered bus trip from New York to Denver. Jabs are awash in a sea of crude humor and contrivance. (Dir: James Frawley, 88 mins.)

Big Caper, The (1957)** Rory Calhoun, Mary Costa. Crooked couple decide to mend their ways after a taste of small town friendliness, but the gang has other ideas. (Dir: Robert Stevens, 84 mins.)

Big Carnival, The (1951)**** Kirk Douglas, Jan Sterling. Terrific drama. Grim tale of a big city reporter who capitalizes on a disaster to ride himself back to the big time. Unrelenting in its cynicism, superb performances. Alternate title: **Ace in the Hole** (Dir: Billy Wilder, 112 mins.)

Big Cat, The (1949)*** Preston Foster, Lon McCallister, Forrest Tucker. City lad in the mountain country aids in the tracking down of a killer cougar. Exciting outdoor story. (Dir: Phil Karlson, 76 mins.)

Big Chance, The (Great Britain, 1957)** Adrienne Corri. A man gives in to temptation, and gets nothing but trouble. (Dir: Peter Graham Scott, 61 mins.)

Big Circus, The (1959)**½ Victor Mature, Red Buttons, Rhonda Fleming. Sprawling film about behind-the-scenes activities of the clowns, aerialists, bareback riders, etc. Tough circus boss has his hands full with performers and their problems. (Dir: Joseph Newman, 109 mins.)

Big City (1947)*½ Margaret O'Brien, Danny Thomas, Robert Preston. (Dir: Norman Taurog, 103 mins.)

Big Clock, The (1948)***½ Ray Milland, Charles Laughton, Maureen O'Sullivan, Elsa Lanchester. Suspenseful drama about a man who follows a murderer's clues and finds they lead directly to him. Top mystery entertainment. (Dir: John Farrow, 75 mins.)

Big Combo, The (1955)***½ Cornel Wilde, Jean Wallace, Richard Conte. Wilde plays a pathological cop on the trail of the mob in this brilliant exercise in film noir styling by director Joseph H. Lewis and cinematographer John Alton. Lewis had a feel for the vitality of American violence that made him one of its best interpreters. First-rate all the way, on a low budget. Written by Philip Yordan and scored by David Raksin. (89 mins.)

Big Country, The (1958)*** Gregory Peck, Charlton Heston, Jean Simmons, Burl Ives (Oscar winner), Charles Bickford. Director William Wyler's large-scale antiwestern has some sweep and persuasiveness despite its overly studied avoidance of genre conventions. Peck is a Pacific seacaptain who comes home with bride Simmons to meet discord on the range. He faces opposition from his competitor in love (Heston), his adversary in business (Ives), and his skeptical father-in-law (Bickford). Wyler's punctilious visual style helps sustain interest over the long running time. (165 mins.)

Big Cube, The (Mexico-U.S., 1969)** Lana Turner, George Chakiris, Dan O'Herlihy. Uninspired melodrama. A stepdaughter resents her stepmother and tries to do away with her. (Dir: Tito Davison, 91 mins.)

Big Deal on Madonna Street, The (Italy, 1958)**** A motley gang of bungling crooks make a mess of trying to rob a pawn shop. Film buffs think this is among the funniest films made in the last twenty years and they're dead right. (Dir: Mario Monicelli, 91 mins.)

Big Fix, The (1978)**½ Richard Dreyfuss. Where have all the flowers gone? The notion of a Berkeley-bred private eye should be fresh, but comes across stale with overexpository dialogue composed of a string of knee-jerk "buzz words." Dreyfuss makes an ingratiating Moses Wine, but with incipient signs of George Segalitis (a serious actor's impulse toward terminal cuteness). Although Jeremy Paul Kagan's direction is not terrifically evident, the ring-around-a-rosy poolside to the tune of "We Shall Not Be Moved" is worth a lot of mediocrity. (108 mins.)

Big Frame, The (Great Britain, 1953)** Mark Stevens, Jean Kent. American pilot attends an RAF reunion, finds he's a murder suspect. Routine. (Dir: David MacDonald, 67 mins.)

Big Freeze, The—See: **On Thin Ice**

Big Gamble, The (1961)** Stephen Boyd, Juliette Greco, David Wayne. An Irishman, his bride and a meek cousin seek their fortune on the Ivory Coast. Pretty mild stuff. (Dir: Richard Fleischer, 100 mins.)

Big Gundown, The (Italy, 1968)** Gunman chases after an elusive bandit. Only Van Cleef's steely presence is worthwhile. (Dir: Sergio Sollima, 90 mins.)

Big Gusher, The (1951)** Preston Foster,

Wayne Morris. Against all odds, two buddies strike it rich with black gold. Routine. (Dir: Lew Landers, 68 mins.)

Big Hand for the Little Lady, A (1966)***½ Joanne Woodward, Henry Fonda, Jason Robards, Jr. Clever, well-played yarn; Fonda and his wife arrive in Laredo during an annual big-stakes poker game, and before you can shuffle a deck, Fonda is in the game. A surprise ending. Don't miss it. (Dir: Fielder Cook, 95 mins.)

Big Hangover, The (1950)**½ Elizabeth Taylor, Van Johnson. Sometimes funny comedy about a lawyer who has a peculiar drinking problem. Johnson tends to mug more than is necessary. (Dir: Norman Krasna, 82 mins.)

Big Heat, The (1953)**** Glenn Ford, Alexander Scourby, Lee Marvin, Gloria Grahame. This sizzling film noir directed by Fritz Lang features Ford (in his best performance) as an anguished cop out to smash a maddeningly effete mobster (Scourby) and break his hold on a corrupt city administration. With sensational support from Marvin as a sadistic hood and Grahame as Marvin's bad/good girlfriend whose reward for hanging around is a faceful of scalding coffee. Brutal, atmospheric, and exciting—highly recommended. (90 mins.)

Big House, The (1930)*** Robert Montgomery, Chester Morris, Wallace Beery, Lewis Stone. Desperate convicts try prison break. This early example of prison melodrama is still entertaining. (Dir: George Hill, 88 mins.)

Big House, USA (1955)*** Broderick Crawford, Ralph Meeker. The FBI is called in to track down a brutal kidnap gang. Strong crime melodrama. (Dir: Howard Koch, 82 mins.)

Big Jack (1949)**½ Wallace Beery, Marjorie Main, Richard Conte. Fast moving comedy-drama about a renegade bandit and his misadventures with a young doctor he saves from an angry mob. Beery's last film. (Dir: Richard Thorpe, 85 mins.)

Big Jake (1971)**½ John Wayne, Richard Boone, Maureen O'Hara. Tall-in-the-saddle John Wayne rides to the rescue of his kidnapped grandson. A western that tries to be a comedy. (Dir: George Sherman, 110 mins.)

Big Jim McLain (1952)** John Wayne, Nancy Olson, James Arness. The setting is Hawaii and Wayne, as a special agent, arrives on the scene to investigate a report about a ring of terrorists. (Dir: Edward Ludwig, 90 mins.)

Big Job, The (Great Britain, 1965)** Sidney James, Sylvia Syms. Bungling ex-cons try to retrieve cash hidden in a tree now situated in the front yard of a police station. (Dir: Gerald Thomas, 88 mins.)

Big Knife, The (1955)***½ Jack Palance, Ida Lupino, Wendell Corey, Shelley Winters, Rod Steiger. A Hollywood star tries to break with a grasping producer. Well acted. (Dir: Robert Aldrich, 111 mins.)

Big Land, The (1957)**½ Alan Ladd, Virginia Mayo, Edmond O'Brien. Cattleman and wheat growers combine to have a railroad built near their land. Doesn't blaze any new trails. (Dir: Gordon Douglas, 92 mins.)

Big Leaguer (1953)** Edward G. Robinson, Vera-Ellen, Jeff Richards. Routine baseball film centering on the bush leagues. (Dir: Robert Aldrich, 70 mins.)

Big Lift, The (1950)** Montgomery Clift, Paul Douglas. Factual story of the Berlin Airlift filmed on the spot. (Dir: George Seaton, 120 mins.)

Big Mo—See: **Maurie**

Big Money, The (Great Britain, 1956)** Ian Carmichael, Belinda Lee. Offspring of a family of thieves tries his wings. Mild comedy. (Dir: John Paddy Carstairs, 86 mins.)

Big Mouth, The (1967)** Jerry Lewis, Harold J. Stone, Susan Bay. The big mouth is after diamonds and the gangsters are after Jerry. (Dir: Jerry Lewis, 107 mins.)

Big Night, The (1951)*** John Barrymore, Jr., Preston Foster. A young kid goes looking for the man who mercilessly beat his father, intending to kill him. Moody, grim drama has a lot to recommend it. (Dir: Joseph Losey, 75 mins.)

Big Night, The (1960)**½ Randy Sparks, Venetia Stevenson, Dick Foran. Young couple come upon money stolen in a hold-up, become the targets of crooks. Above average melodrama. (Dir: Sidney Salkow, 74 mins.)

Big Operator, The (1959)*½ Mickey Rooney, Steve Cochran, Mamie Van Doren. Remake of *Joe Smith, American* (1942). Alternate title: **Anatomy of the Syndicate**. (Dir: Charles Haas, 91 mins.)

Big Parade, The (1925)**** John Gilbert, Renée Adorée. A masterpiece, director King Vidor's film about WW I accomplishes what few war epics have, capturing the immense sweep of events while maintaining its focus on the ordinary people whose lives are forever changed by those events. Gilbert stars in his finest performance, as a young American soldier who finds peace with a French girl amid the dirt and horror of war. (126 mins.)

Big Red (1962)**½ Walter Pidgeon, Gilles Payant. Walter Pidgeon owns Big Red and little Gilles Payant exercises him. Filmed against the vast backdrop of the Canadian wilderness in Quebec. Naturally, Big Red escapes while on his way to be sold, goes in search of the little boy he loves. O.K. fare for the kids. (Dir: Norman Tokar, 89 mins.)

Big Red One, The (1980)***½ Lee Marvin, Marie Hamill, Bobby DiCicco, Mark Carradine, Kelly Ward. Director Samuel Fuller's most personal film profoundly comprehends the effect of war on men.

Story of a squad (WW II, Europe) headed by an anonymous sergeant (Marvin) and his four "horsemen" who survive the war over the bodies of the "wet-nose" replacements who facelessly arrive and die. Rivals the war poetry of Wilfred Owen and Siegfried Sassoon in its passionate intensity. The movie may be at times too private for easy accessibility, but Fuller's accomplishment and sagacity dwarf the paltry ambitions of most other filmmakers. (113 mins.)

Big Ripoff, The (MTV 1975)**½ Tony Curtis, Brenda Vaccaro, Larry Hagman, Roscoe Lee Browne. Curtis stars as a stylish con man hired by a millionaire to recover a huge ransom paid to kidnappers. Calculated but fairly interesting. (Dir: Dean Hargrove, 72 mins.)

Big Rose (MTV 1974)** Shelley Winters, Barry Primus. A pair of detectives hired by a wealthy contractor to find out who is out to do him in. (Dir: Paul Krasny, 78 mins.)

Big Shot, The (1942)**½ Humphrey Bogart, Irene Manning. Bogart is fine in the title role but the plot leaves much to be desired. (Dir: Lewis Seiler, 82 mins.)

Big Show, The (1961)** Esther Williams, Cliff Robertson, Nehemiah Persoff, Robert Vaughn. Son takes the rap for domineering circus father's negligence, returns from prison to find forces working against him. (Dir: James Clark, 113 mins.)

Big Sky, The (1952)***½ Kirk Douglas, Dewey Martin, Arthur Hunnicutt, Elizabeth Threatt. A perverse version of A. B. Guthrie's Pulitzer prizewinning novel by director Howard Hawks. Douglas and Martin are fur traders and pals who get into an odd sexual rivalry over an Indian princess. With Douglas's famous finger amputation scene, played for laughs—and getting them—and, if only incidentally, fine B&W panoramic vistas. A Hawks comedy posing as an epic, and excellent. (122 mins.)

Big Sleep, The (1946)***½ Humphrey Bogart, Lauren Bacall, Martha Vickers. A near-masterpiece directed by Howard Hawks, full of corruption, annihilation, and efficient wit. Bogart is a tough private eye, Bacall a shady society broad whose nymphomaniac sister sucks her thumb. The atmosphere is like a chronic hangover, with action and scenes mostly there for their own sake. The plot is impossible to follow, having been muddled by William Faulkner, among others. To this day, no one connected with the film knows who committed one of the murders. It doesn't really matter. (114 mins.)

Big Sleep, The (Great Britain, 1978)*½ Robert Mitchum, Sarah Miles, Richard Boone, Candy Clark, James Stewart. Updated re-make of the 1946 film; from Raymond Chandler's novel. (Dir: Michael Winner, 99 mins.)

Big Steal, The (1949)*** Robert Mitchum, Jane Greer, William Bendix, Ramon

Novarro. This relatively early work of director Don Siegel ("The Killers," "Dirty Harry") is a slightly screwy thriller with four sets of characters chasing one another through Mexico. An interesting formal work, comprised almost exclusively of intercut car interiors shot in front of back-projection machines. Though the story is simple, the crosscutting can get mighty complex. Mitchum prompted a halt to production when he was hauled off to jail on a marijuana charge, but Siegel smoothed over the gaps in the narrative with his usual aplomb, if not with a completely straight face. All in all, a fascinating film of no significance whatever, and very likable. (71 mins.)

Big Store, The (1941)*** The Marx Brothers, Margaret Dumont, Douglass Dumbrille as a fine villain, Tony Martin. Far too conventional in its comedy for much of its length, but this largely pallid Marx Brothers feature (their last for MGM) has some passages of devilishly good whimsy. It opens like a return to old form, and the closing chase isn't bad, either. (Dir: Charles Reisner, 80 mins.)

Big Street, The (1942)**½ Henry Fonda, Lucille Ball. Busboy falls for a crippled nitery singer. Maudlin Damon Runyon drama; some good moments. (Dir: Irving Reis, 88 mins.)

Big Tip Off (1955)** Richard Conte, Constance Smith. Newsman exposes a charity fund racket. Slow-moving crime melodrama. (Dir: Frank McDonald, 70 mins.)

Big Trail, The (1930)*** John Wayne, Marguerite Churchill, Tyrone Power, Sr., Ian Keith, Ward Bond. Epic western of a Missouri-to-Oregon wagon trek casts Wayne in his first starring role as the scout. Although his presence here could've made him a major star at 23, he had to wait until "Stagecoach" ('39) for that, because the acceptance of this film was hindered by a wide-screen presentation that few theaters could then afford. The Wayne philosophy is much in evidence, and the dirty villain is played by Tyrone Power, Sr., father of the famed star, in his last role. Doesn't dwell on action, but thrilling nevertheless. (Dir: Raoul Walsh, 110 mins.)

Big Trees, The (1952)** Kirk Douglas, Patrice Wymore. Dull logging epic. Remake of *Valley of the Giants* (1938). (Dir: Felix Feist, 89 mins.)

Big Wave, The (1961)**½ Sessue Hayakawa, Mickey Curtis. Pearl Buck's story of a Japanese fishing village hit by a tidal wave. Spoken in English, filmed in Japan. Well acted. (Dir: Tad Danielewski, 73 mins.)

Big Wednesday (1978)**½ Jan-Michael Vincent, Garey Busey, William Katt. Director John Milius's paean to the art and discipline of hot-dog surfing is marred by pushy philosophizing and a fair number of overripe lines, but its sincerity is deep and seductive. Three surfing buddies who grow up but never entirely outgrow their sport reunite to face the once-in-a-lifetime challenge of a giant ocean swell. In the context of the subculture the film deftly recreates, a number of ostensibly dead macho myths take on the aura of eternal values. The surfing footage is breathtaking. (125 mins.)

Big Wheel, The (1949)**½ Mickey Rooney, Thomas Mitchell. Hot-shot auto racer nearly causes tragedy. Excellent Indianapolis racing scenes. (Dir: Edward Ludwig, 92 mins.)

Bigamist, The (1953)*** Edmond O'Brien, Joan Fontaine, Ida Lupino. Businessman married to a career woman is discovered to have another wife in another city. (Dir: Ida Lupino, 80 mins.)

Bigfoot, The Mysterious Monsters (1975)* (Dir: Robert Guenette, 76 mins.)

Bigger Than Life (1956)***½ James Mason, Barbara Rush, Walter Matthau. A frightening tale about a man who is given a new wonder drug (cortisone) and becomes a veritable madman when he starts taking overdoses. James Mason is superb. (Dir: Nicholas Ray, 95 mins.)

Biggest Bundle of Them All, The (U.S.-Italy, 1967)** Robert Wagner, Raquel Welch, Edward G. Robinson. A group of bumbling kidnappers abduct an exiled American hood living in Italy. (Dir: Ken Annakin, 110 mins.)

Bike Boy (1967)*** Joe Spencer, Brigid Polk, Ingrid Superstar, Valerie Solanis. This Andy Warhol feature is typically zonked-out, funny, dispassionate, and compassionate. A motorcyclist arrives in the Big Apple from California. He takes a shower and slowly combs his hair. He visits a men's boutique and tries on underwear, to the delight of the male staff, etcetera...Finally, he gives in to the browbeating of Viva, who could seduce a stone, and here does. Spencer is the bike boy, and the women include, briefly, Solaris, who was later to shoot Warhol. Warhol wrote, produced, and directed, letting Paul Morrissey run the camera. (96 mins.)

Bikini Beach (1964)**½ Frankie Avalon, Annette Funicello, Martha Hyer. Familiar beach movie. Some drag strip racing is thrown in. (Dir: William Aster, 100 mins.)

Bill of Divorcement (1932)*** John Barrymore, Katharine Hepburn, David Manners, Billie Burke. Director George Cukor introduced Hepburn to the screen with a stunning staircase shot in this melodrama. Hepburn plays a socialite who rejects her fiancé in order to care for her shell-shocked father. The story is the sort that Cukor would enliven effortlessly a decade later; at this early point in his career, the strain shows. But it's worth a look...and when Barrymore's quivering mingles with Hepburn's tremulous tautness, it's a ham sonata for virtuosos. (76 mins.)

Billie (1965)** Patty Duke, Jim Backus, Warren Berlinger. Family comedy about a young miss who's a wizard in all athletic endeavors. Her prowess on the track field makes her unpopular with the boys. (Dir: Don Weis, 87 mins.)

Billion Dollar Brain (Great Britain, 1967)** Michael Caine, Karl Malden, Ed Begley. Secret agent Palmer, crossing and doublecrossing the enemy in Finland. Francoise Dorleac, Oscar Homolka. (Dir: Ken Russell, 111 mins.)

Billion Dollar Hobo, The (1978)**½ Tim Conway, Will Geer, John Myhers, Victoria Carroll. Mild kid comedy has bungling drifter (or drifting bungler) Conway sole heir to the fortune of Geer, who insists that Conway must prove himself by retracing Geer's steps as a hobo during the depression. Conway wrote the screenplay with Roger Beatty and director/coproducer Stuart E. McGowan. Geer's last theatrical feature. (96 mins.)

Billion Dollar Threat, The (1979)** Dale Robinette, Patrick MacNee, Ralph Bellamy. James Bond should sue! A blatant ripoff of the 007 yarns. The agent is an American named Robert Sands, but his derring-do follows the Bond mode, down to an adversary who threatens to pierce the earth's ozone layer. Naturally, there is also a parade of pulchritude on hand. (Dir: Barry Shear, 104 mins.)

Billy Budd (Great Britain, 1962)***½ Peter Ustinov, Robert Ryan, Terence Stamp, Melvyn Douglas. Well-produced film based on Herman Melville's classic allegorical tale of treachery in the 18th century British navy. Ustinov directed and adapted from the Broadway play. (112 mins.)

Billy Jack (1971)** Tom Laughlin, Delores Taylor, Clark Howat, Bert Freed. This neofascist little morality play has charmed a lot of critics and made a fortune; but its strained argument—that violence is the ticket for all misunderstood flower children and shiftless Viet vets—conjures up memories of "Triumph of the Will." Drama about youth vs. the establishment had a unique distribution history. When first released in 1971, it got lackluster reviews, but was developing a growing audience response. Rereleased in 1973 it became a huge grosser, mostly among the young. Laughlin stars as Billy Jack, a loner, an idealistic young Indian who is committed to aiding a "freedom school" after the young students are harassed by small-town western bigots. Laughlin's real-life wife Taylor is genuinely appealing as the school head. Laughlin directed, using the pseudonym T. C. Frank (the same pseudonym he used when he directed "Born Losers" in '67). Filmed on location in Arizona and New Mexico. Also written and produced by Mr. and Mrs. Laughlin. (112 mins.)

Billy Jack Goes to Washington (1977)** Tom Laughlin, Delores Taylor, Sam Wanamaker, Lucie Arnaz. Clumsy remake of Frank Capra's 1939 classic, "Mr. Smith Goes to Washington." Billy Jack is fighting political corruption. Vacuous and overlong. (Dir: Tom Laughlin, 155 mins.)

Billy Liar (Great Britain, 1963)*** Tim Courtenay, Julie Christie, Mona Washbourne. The Hall-Waterhouse farce has had seemingly indestructible life in its many incarnations over the years—on stage, in print, in movies, and on television. This youthful British Walter Mitty has always seemed to me a strained concept, and the film, which had fresh perspective in '63, dates badly today. Courtenay acquits himself well as the fantasizing Bill—he should be accorded far more comic opportunities onscreen. The film remains notable for the first incarnation of the Christie personality; her star quality is evident. (Dir: John Schlesinger, 96 mins.)

Billy: Portrait of a Street Kid (MTV 1977)**½ LeVar Burton, Ossie Davis, Michael Constantine. Burton offers an honest and at times touching performance as a sullen kid caged in by the ghetto. Director Steven Gethers, who also wrote this fairly antiromantic (for Hollywood) version of the street, surrounds Burton with a solid supporting cast. This better-than-average slice of reality deserves attention. (112 mins.)

Billy Rose's Diamond Horseshoe (1945)**½ Betty Grable, Dick Haymes, Phil Silvers, William Gaxton, Margaret Dumont. Grable plays nightclub singer, this time in love with medical student Haymes, in this comedy-drama directed and written by George Seaton. Haymes sings "The More I See You" beautifully. Tongue-in-cheek writing and a showy production. (Dir: George Seaton, 104 mins.)

Billy Rose's Jumbo (1962)**½ Doris Day, Stephen Boyd, Jimmy Durante, Martha Raye. It was a great spectacle in the '30s when Billy Rose's musical extravaganza, with book by Ben Hecht and Charles McArthur and music and lyrics by Rodgers and Hart, opened at the (no pun intended) Hippodrome Theatre. Real, live elephants on stage! The film version isn't nearly as impressive, although its elephant jokes are superior to those of "Smokey and the Bandit II." A cop stops Durante as he escapes from the circus with the eponymous pachyderm. "Where you going with that elephant?" "What elephant?" A disposable piece of musical entertainment, but for fringe benefits you have superb songs and the last film choreography by Busby Berkeley. (Dir: Charles Walters, 125 mins.)

Billy the Kid (1930)** Johnny Mack Brown, Wallace Beery. Director King Vidor's version of the Billy the Kid myth has the naive lyricism of a folktale. Brown is an appropriately otherworldly hero, Beery is his old gruff self as Pat Garrett. Originally photographed in prototypical 65-mm wide-screen process, the film contains several startling pre-Welles experiments with deep focus. (98 mins.)

Billy the Kid (1941)**½ Robert Taylor, Brian Donlevy. Good western adventure based on the life of the famous outlaw. (Dir: David Miller, 95 mins.)

Billy the Kid Vs. Dracula (1966)* Chuck Courtney, John Carradine, Melinda Plowman. (Dir: William Beaudine, 72 mins.)

Billy Two Hats—See: **Lady and the Outlaw, The**

Bimbo the Great (Germany, 1960)** A film about the circus, sentimental and corny at times. Dubbed. (Dir: Harald Philipp, 96 mins.)

Bingo Long Traveling All-Stars and Motor Kings, The (1976)*** Billy Dee Williams, James Earl Jones, Richard Pryor. High-spirited, charming tale of a barnstorming black baseball team of 1939, who have abandoned the Negro National League in favor of lighting out on their own. Good blend of show business and the struggle for survival. (Dir: John Badham, 111 mins.)

Birch Interval (1976)*** Eddie Albert, Rip Torn, Ann Wedgeworth, Susan McClung, Anne Revere. Sensitive, "uplifting" tale of a troubled family in Pennsylvania around 1947: a young girl (McClung) goes to live with relatives in the Pennsylvania Amish country and has some painful learning experiences. Albert is fine as her troubled grandfather, and Torn is a standout as her beloved but mentally unstable uncle. Based on a well-known young people's novel by Joanna Crawford. (Dir: Delbert Mann, 103 mins.)

Bird of Paradise (1932)*** Dolores Del Rio, Joel McCrea, Skeets Gallagher, John Halliday. This South Seas romancer is an unconvincing drama, but director King Vidor shoots with an eye for sensual detail and exotic eroticism, and some of the images are ravishing in a way disturbing for those accustomed to the style of the time. Although I cannot recommend the film, it lingers in the mind. McCrea is the adventurer who marries native princess Del Rio, and there is some nonsense about sacrifices to the volcano god. Photographed brilliantly by Clyde de Vinna. (80 mins.)

Bird of Paradise (1951)** Debra Paget, Louis Jourdan, Jeff Chandler. South Sea natives have big sacrificial rituals and offer a virgin to an angry volcano. (Dir: Delmer Daves, 100 mins.)

Bird with the Crystal Plumage, The (Italy, 1970)*½ Tony Musante, Suzy Kendall. (Dir: Dario Argento, 98 mins.)

Birdman of Alcatraz (1962)**** Burt Lancaster, Karl Malden, Thelma Ritter, Betty Field, Neville Brand. Gripping true story of convict Robert Stroud, who became an expert on birdlife while serving time for murder. Superior adult drama. (Dir: John Frankenheimer, 147 mins.)

Birdmen, The (MTV 1971)*** Doug McClure, Richard Basehart, Chuck Connors, Max Baer. Tense, well-produced prisoner-of-war escape drama. This junior-grade "great escape" yarn is based on a WW II incident in Germany. You'll be rooting for McClure and his fellow prisoners as they painstakingly construct a two-man glider in the attic chambers of their German castle-prison-fortress, run by gentlemanly Nazi commandant Basehart. The finale is a literal cliff-hanger, and the cast plays it for all it's worth. (Dir: Philip Leacock, 78 mins.)

Birds, The (1963)**** Tippi Hedren, Rod Taylor, Suzanne Pleshette, Jessica Tandy. Director Alfred Hitchcock's masterpiece presents a horrifying vision of present disaster, refracted through a character study of a patrician woman (Hedren) that is as much moral as character biography. The famous last shot blends complete insecurity with unyielding hope. Flawless in every respect, even to the somewhat problematically superficial performances, which are just what the vision requires. (120 mins.)

Birds and the Bees, The (1956)** George Gobel, Mitzi Gaynor, David Niven. Millionaire innocent is snared by a lady card sharp. Remake of "The Lady Eve." (Dir: Norman Taurog, 94 mins.)

Birds, the Bees and the Italians, The (Italy-France, 1966)***½ Virna Lisi, Gastone Moschin, Nora Ricci. Extremely humorous sex farce involving a local café set. (Dir: Pietro Germi, 115 mins.)

Birds Do It (1966)** Soupy Sales, Tab Hunter, Arthur O'Connell. A Cape Kennedy janitor enters an off-limits room. (Dir: Andrew Marlon, 95 mins.)

Birds in Peru (France, 1968)* Maurice Ronet, Pierre Brasseur, Danielle Darrieux. (Dir: Romain Gary, 95 mins.)

Birds of a Feather—See: **Cage aux Folles**

Birds of Prey (MTV 1973)** David Janssen. Airwatch pilot who chases bank robbers. Unusual aerial footage. (Dir: William Graham, 78 mins.)

Birth of a Nation, The (1915)**** Lillian Gish, Henry B. Walthall, Mae Marsh. This might as well be titled "The Birth of the Movies." Director D. W. Griffith's silent about the Civil War and Reconstruction was the first great commercial success among American feature films. It cost $5 million to make, and that's '15 dollars. At the time, it was also the longest film ever made. Seen today, it is an odd combination of the most delicate sentiment and, in its racism, the most brutal insensibility. Griffith made the mistake of glamorizing the Ku Klux Klan. Griffith's subsequent work was unquestionably superior, so don't judge on this alone—though any lesser genius should be flattered to be so judged. (157 mins.)

Birth of the Beatles (MTV 1979)*** Stephen MacKenna, Rod Culbertson, John Altman, Ray Ashcroft. Well-done dramatization of the Beatles' early career as they climbed the unsteady ladder of success from Liverpool to Hamburg to international superstardom. Four British actors play the "Fab Four," while the Beatles' musical sounds are re-created by the group Rain. Besides the familiar backstage story, there are some little-publicized facts about the death, at age 21, of the "fifth Beatle" and the replacement of the original drummer, Pete Best, by Ringo Starr, just prior to the group's skyrocketing to the top. Made before the senseless, awful slaying of Beatle John Lennon in December '80. (Dir: Richard Marquand, 104 mins.)

Birth of the Blues (1941)***½ Bing Crosby, Mary Martin. Minor story of a trumpet player who supposedly organized the first Dixieland jazz band. A delightful score and good performances. (Dir: Victor Schertzinger, 85 mins.)

Birthday Party, The (Great Britain, 1968)**** Robert Shaw, Dandy Nichols. Stimulating, well acted version of Harold Pinter's enigmatic play. A boarder in a British seaside dwelling is taken away by two strangers, who've come to give him a birthday party. (Dir: William Friedkin, 127 mins.)

Birthday Present (Great Britain, 1957)*** Tony Britton, Sylvia Syms. Salesman tries to smuggle a German watch through customs. Well-made drama. (Dir: Pat Jackson, 100 mins.)

Biscuit Eater, The (1972)** Johnny Whitaker, Lew Ayres, Godfrey Cambridge. Disney story about a boy and his dog. Two youngsters try to train a mutt into a champion bird dog. (Dir: Vincent McEveety, 90 mins.)

Bishop's Wife, The (1947)*½ Cary Grant, David Niven, Loretta Young, Edmund Gwenn. (Dir: Henry Koster, 108 mins.)

Bite the Bullet (1975)*** Gene Hackman, James Coburn, Candice Bergen. Written, directed and produced by Richard Brooks. An unconventional, entertaining western about the cruel endurance horseraces that were customary in the West between 1880 and 1910. Coburn and Hackman are marvelous and there's a happy, believable ending. (Dir: Richard Brooks, 131 mins.)

Bitter Creek (1954)*½ Wild Bill Elliot, Carleton Young. (Dir: Thomas Carr, 74 mins.)

Bitter Harvest (MTV 1981)*** Ron Howard, Art Carney, Richard Dysart. Scary, uncomfortable, life-on-the-farm story based on a true incident. Everything goes wrong for a young dairy farmer, frantically looking for reasons why his herd is sick and dying. Howard is splendid as the panicky, gutsy farmer who battles bureaucracy, before discovering a fat-soluble chemical in his dairy feed. Beginning with the birth of a calf, the show conveys an unusual feel for farm life. A well-made film that has a valuable message—be careful with chemicals! (Dir: Roger Young, 104 mins.)

Bitter Harvest (Great Britain, 1963)** Janet Munro, John Stride, Alan Badel. Village girl goes to the big city and is soon caught in a web of vice and corruption. Fine performance by Miss Munro. (Dir: Peter Graham Scott, 96 mins.)

Bitter Reunion (France, 1959)*** Gerard Blain, Jean-Claude Brialy. A reunion of two childhood friends after ten years of separation. Excellent performances. (Dir: Claude Chabrol, 105 mins.)

Bitter Rice (1950)*** Silvana Mangano. Italian film, with English dialogue very poorly dubbed. About workers in the rice fields who toil for grain. Earthy, shocking drama. Adults only. (Dir: Giuseppe De Santis, 107 mins.)

Bitter Springs (Australia, 1950)***½ Tommy Trinder, Chips Rafferty. Pioneer attempts to settle the Australian wilderness. Different, exciting historical melodrama, with fine photography. (Dir: Ralph Smart, 89 mins.)

Bitter Tea of General Yen, The (1933)***½ Barbara Stanwyck, Nils Asther, Walter Connolly. An American woman (Stanwyck) falls in love with the warlord (Asther) who takes her prisoner. An eccentric, moody melodrama, directed in Sternbergian shadows by Frank Capra (of all people). A genuine curiosity, utterly atypical of Capra, it is marvelously crafted and pulsates with forbidden sex. (89 mins.)

Bitter Tears of Petra Von Kant, The (West Germany, 1972)***½ Margit Carstensen, Hanna Schygulla, Irm Hermann. Try to discard preconceptions about how quickly a film should move or about the differences between film and theater before seeing Director Rainer Werner Fassbinder's film version of his own play. In five acts, action is entirely confined to one lavishly decorated room. The actors speak with a deliberate, wicked self-awareness that underlines rather than hides the film's theatrical origins. A prestigious fashion designer falls in love with an aspiring actress (the breathtaking Schygulla) and sees the power balance of the relationship shift terrifyingly away from her. A masterpiece that may require two viewings for proper appreciation. (119 mins.)

Bitter Victory (Great Britain, 1957)***½ Richard Burton, Curt Jurgens, Ruth Roman. Mangled by its producers and never formally released in the U.S., director Nicholas Ray's film is very nearly a masterpiece. The film uses its CinemaScope frame to establish a spatial correlative to a moral struggle between two officers (Burton and Jurgens) lost in the North African desert after a commando raid. Burton, feverish and poetic, captures the doomed, romantic side of Ray in the finest acting Burton has done onscreen. When he surveys a 13th-century Berber village and complains that it is too modern for him, the remark has an absurd plausibility. (83 mins.)

Bittersweet (1940)**½ Jeanette MacDonald,

63

Nelson Eddy, George Sanders, Herman Bing. This bowdlerization of Noël Coward's show convinced him to withhold his musicals from Hollywood, and we're much the poorer. It's one of the most worthwhile MacDonald-Eddy vehicles, but what's interesting in the film comes from the original material, which has been gutted. The songs beat the usual Victor Herbert stuff. Oliver Marsh's color photography (three-strip) is excellent, and Bing has a standout bit as an innkeeper. (Dir: W. S. Van Dyke, 92 mins.)

Bizarre, Bizarre (France, 1937)***½ Michel Simon, Louis Jouvet, Francoise Rosay, Jean-Louis Barrault, Jean-Pierre Aumont. Superb comedy, scripted by Jacques Prevert and directed by Marcel Carne, far from their patented form of fatalistic glumness. Michel Simon plays an English mystery writer with a block, and the best French farceurs of the age all gang up on him, from Louis Jouvet to Francoise Rosay, a young Jean-Louis Barrault as a madman fan, and Jean-Pierre Aumont as a whimsical milkman. It's all quite droll and holds up very well. Alternate title: **Drole de Drame.** (Dir: Marcel Carne, 109 mins.)

Black and White in Color (France-Africa, 1976)***½ Jacques Spiesser, Jean Carmet, Catherine Rouvel. Surprise Oscar winner as Best Foreign Film. A first film by director Jean-Jacques Annaud, who wrote the screenplay with Georges Conchon, it examines the reactions of two groups, one French and one German, stationed in West Africa at the outbreak of WW I. Its perceptive look at patriotism contains truths which can't be overlooked. Filmed in Africa. (91 mins.)

Black Angel (1946)*** Dan Duryea, June Vincent, Peter Lorre, Broderick Crawford. Absorbing mystery, with Vincent trying to clear her husband of an unjust murder charge. Imaginative directing produces a chilling atmosphere. (Dir: Roy William Neill, 80 mins.)

Black Arrow, The (1948)*** Louis Hayward, Janet Blair. Above average swashbuckler. Set around England's famous War of the Roses. (Dir: Gordon Douglas, 76 mins.)

Black Beauty (MTV 1978)** Edward Albert, Eileen Brennan, William Devane. This faithful five-part adaptation of Anna Sewell's enduring 1877 saga of the beautiful black colt traveling from owner to owner, some kindly, some mean, is recommended for the kiddies. Competently produced, with lots of recognizable TV names (Dir: Daniel Haller, 260 mins.)

Black Bird, The (1975)**½ George Segal, Stephane Audran, Lionel Stander, Signe Hasso, Elisha Cook. Occasionally funny updated parody of "The Maltese Falcon." Some of the jokes are very "inside" and will only mean anything to trivia buffs who know the Dashiell Hammett novel and the Huston film in their sleep. (E.g., do you know who Floyd Thursby is?) Sam Spade is still a grumpy, second-rate detective. Film-trivia buffs please note that Elisha Cook Jr. is back playing the same role. Lee Patrick again plays Spade's secretary. (Dir: David Giler, 98 mins.)

Black Book, The—See: **Reign of Terror**

Black Caesar (1973)** Fred Williamson, Art Lund, Julius Harris. Larry Cohen, that erratic but undeniable talent, wrote and directed this black version of the classic gangster saga. It's tough, tawdry, cheapjack, with patches of definite strength. (92 mins.)

Black Castle, The (1952)** Richard Greene, Boris Karloff, Stephen McNally, Lon Chaney, Jr., Paula Corday. Sinister castles, unscrupulous counts, and strange happenings. (Dir: Nathan Juran, 81 mins.)

Black Cat, The (1934)** Boris Karloff, Bela Lugosi, David Manners, Jacqueline Wells (Julie Bishop). Lugosi is on the side of law and order, Karloff is a practitioner of black rites. (Dir: Edgar G. Ulmer, 70 mins.)

Black Cat, The (1941)**½ Broderick Crawford, Hugh Herbert, Basil Rathbone, Gale Sondergaard. A real estate promoter and a goofy antique collector intrude upon the reading of a will in a gloomy old mansion. Neat mixture of comedy and shudders. (Dir: Albert Rogell, 70 mins.)

Black Chapel (France-Italy, 1959)** Peter Van Eyck, Dawn Addams. A journalist is given a document to deliver to an agent in Rome, but finds the agent murdered. Fair suspense. Dubbed. (Dir: Ralph Habib, 88 mins.)

Black Cobra, The (Germany, 1964)*½ Adrian Hoven, Ann Smyrner. A bore. (Dir: Rudolf Zehetgruber, 95 mins.)

Black Dakotas, The (1954)** Gary Merrill, Wanda Hendrix. Peace with the Sioux Nation is endangered by a couple of ruthless hi-jackers. (Dir: Ray Nazarro, 70 mins.)

Black Devils of Kali (Italy, 1954)* Lex Barker, Jane Maxwell. Alternate title: **Mystery of the Black Jungle.** (Dir: Ralph Murphy, 72 mins.)

Black Dragon of Manzanar (1943-66)**½ Rod Cameron, Constance Worth. G-Man extraordinary goes after a ring of Black Dragon agents. Wild and woolly. (Dir: William Witney, 100 mins.)

Black Duke, The (Italy-Spain, 1963)*½ Cameron Mitchell, Gloria Milland. (Dir: Pino Mercanti, 105 mins.)

Black Flowers for the Bride—See: **Something for Everyone.**

Black Fox, The (1962)*** Unusually interesting documentary of Hitler and his rise to power, paralleled by the Goethe fable of Reynard the Fox, symbol of political ruthlessness. Different. Narration by Marlene Dietrich. (Dir: Louis Clyde Stoumen, 89 mins.)

Black Fury (1935)*** Paul Muni, William Gargan, Akim Tamiroff, Karen Morley. Good Warner Bros. social drama, set in a hellish Pennsylvania coal mine where the workers are struggling to organize. Muni,

64

the voice of centrist reason, prevails. Michael Curtiz directed this ideological juggling act with a blind eye to the political implications but a good fix on pace and character. (100 mins.)

Black Girl (Senegal-France, 1969)***½ Mbissine Therese Diop, Anne-Marie Jelinck. A remarkable directorial effort by the African novelist Ousmane Sembene, who also wrote the screenplay, based on his book. A young black girl from Dakar hired to be a maid in France. Filmed in both Africa and France. Chronicles the unhappy life of an unsophisticated, lonely girl trying to cope with an alien culture. Dubbed. (Dir: Ousmane Sembene, 60 mins.)

Black Glove, The (Great Britain, 1954)**½ Alex Nicol, Eleanor Summerfield. American musician in London becomes involved in murder. Fair mystery; good jazz music background. (Dir: Terence Fisher, 84 mins.)

Black Gold (1947)*** Anthony Quinn, Katherine De Mille. An Indian gives permission to drill for oil on his property to obtain money enough to raise horses. Excellent performances turn this into an interesting drama. (Dir: Phil Karlson, 90 mins.)

Black Gold (1963)** Philip Carey, Diane McBain, James Best, Fay Spain. Routine drama of an adventurer betting all on a big oil strike. (Dir: Leslie Martinson, 98 mins.)

Black Hand (1950)**½ Gene Kelly, J. Carrol Naish, Teresa Celli. Interesting drama about the activities of the Mafia or Black Hand as it was known at the turn of the century. (Dir: Richard Thorpe, 93 mins.)

Black Hole, The (1979)*** Maximilian Schell, Anthony Perkins, Ernest Borgnine, Yvette Mimieux, Robert Forster. This science fiction effort from the Walt Disney Studios is less a "Star Wars" clone than an attempt to recapture the kiddie-show magic of such past classics as "Twenty Thousand Leagues Under the Sea." It has a lively sense of menace, and in some of its fruitier moments it is reminiscent of the more traumatic passages in the Brothers Grimm. Gary Nelson's direction is bad, the writing is weak, and the acting is campy at best—but Peter Ellenshaw's production design strikes the right balance of vastness and seductive detail. His spaceship owes more to Christopher Wren than to Stanley Kubrick: an elaborate gothic structure, with spires, vaulted ceilings, and endless corridors populated by scurrying, hooded figures. (97 mins.)

Black Holiday (Italy, 1973)**** Adalberto Maria Merli, Adolfo Celi, John Steiner, Milena Vukotic. About a college professor during the early years of Mussolini's dictatorship who refused to cooperate with the Fascists and was sent to a detention center on a small island in the Mediterranean. Superb understated performance from Merli as the idealistic professor. Directed by Marco Leto. Subtitles. (110 mins.)

Black Horse Canyon (1954)**½ Joel McCrea, Mari Blanchard. A group of people try to recapture a wild stallion who has taken to the hills. (Dir: Jesse Hibbs, 81 mins.)

Black Ice (Great Britain, 1957)** Paul Carpenter, Kim Parker. Submarine rushed to save sinking trawler. Routine melodrama. (Dir: Godfrey Grayson, 51 mins.)

Black Invaders, The (Italy, 1960)* Daniele de Metz, Amedeo Nazzari. (90 mins.)

Black Knight, The (Great Britain, 1954)** Alan Ladd, Patricia Medina. Fast but disappointing tale of knighthood in the days of King Arthur. (Dir: Tay Garnett, 90 mins.)

Black Lancers, The (Italy, 1963)** Mel Ferrer, Yvonne Furneaux. Wicked queen will stop at nothing to keep a kingdom under her control. Dubbed. (Dir: Giacomo Gentilomo, 95 mins.)

Black Legion (1936)**½ Humphrey Bogart, Ann Sheridan, Dick Foran, Erin O'Brien Moore. Honest worker is duped into joining a terrorist Ku Klux Klan-type organization. Based on fact. (Dir: Archie Mayo, 83 mins.)

Black Like Me (1964)**½ James Whitmore, Clifton James, Roscoe Lee Browne. Based on fact. A writer poses as a Negro by chemically changing the color of his skin. Sincere but rambling. (Dir: Carl Lerner, 107 mins.)

Black Magic (1949)** Orson Welles, Nancy Guild. The evil plans of Cagliostro the magician are thwarted. Heavy melodrama. Produced in Italy. (Dir: Gregory Ratoff, 105 mins.)

Black Marble, The (1980)*** Robert Foxworth, Paula Prentiss, Harry Dean Stanton, Barbara Babcock, John Hancock. For cop novelist Joseph Wambaugh a departure into bizarre romantic comedy—and a welcome one, since it provides a context in which his observations on the pressures that bedevil police officers can take artistic shape. The amatory proclamations of Foxworth and Prentiss get unbearably repetitious, but the rigorously small-bracket milieu makes up for it. Stanton adds another consummate portrayal to his growing gallery of cheesy losers—his dog trainer at the end of his tether is memorable, hilarious, and pathetic. Harold Becker directs better than he did in "The Onion Field," though it may be because Owen Roizman handles the photography better than Charles Rosher did. (110 mins.)

Black Market Baby (MTV 1977)**½ Linda Purl, Desi Arnaz, Jr., Bill Bixby, Jessica Walter, David Doyle. An original plot for a change: an unorthodox adoption agency preys on young college girls who are pregnant and don't want to have an abortion. However, when a wealthy couple visit its director, played with oily detachment by Bill Bixby, a new plan is tried as they select the mother-to-be, hire a young man to seduce her, and then convince her to give up the baby. Naturally, all does not go according to plan. Purl, one of TV's better young actresses, is wonderful as the innocent victim, and it's really her film. (Dir: Robert Day, 104 mins.)

Black Monocle, The (France, 1961)*½ Paul Meurisse, Elga Anderson. (Dir: Georges Lautner, 87 mins.)

Black Moon (France-West Germany, 1975)**½ Cathryn Harrison, Therese Giese, Alexandra Stewart, Joe Dallesandro. Challenging, uneven, sometimes pretentious and then dazzling. Young girl flees from a civil war in which the men are battling the women. Bizarre, self-indulgent, difficult. Louis Malle co-authored the screenplay with Ghislain Uhry and Joyce Bunuel. Wonderful photography by Sven Nykvist. (Dir: Louis Malle, 92 mins.)

Black Narcissus (Great Britain, 1947)***½ Deborah Kerr, Flora Robson, David Farrar. Another oddball film from those subversive purveyors of seemingly conventional culture, directors Michael Powell and Emeric Pressburger. This one involves a man's man who sets the hearts of nuns in a Himalayan convent aflutter. The fox-in-the-henhouse theme is piquantly realized in ravishing color, and one might wonder what this perverse intelligence is all about. (99 mins.)

Black Orchid, The (1959)**½ Sophia Loren, Anthony Quinn, Ina Balin. Gangster's widow tries to overcome barriers when she falls in love again. Weepy drama. (Dir: Martin Ritt, 95 mins.)

Black Orpheus (France-Portugal, 1959)**** Breno Mello, Marpessa Dawn. Excellent Portuguese language film based on the Orpheus-Eurydice legend. Updated and played against the colorful background of carnival time in Brazil, complete with dancing, lovemaking, and black witchcraft. A hauntingly beautiful score. Oscar as Best Foreign Film. (Dir: Marcel Camus, 98 mins.)

Black Panther of Ratana (Germany, 1963)* Brad Harris, Marianne Cook, Heinz Drache. (Dir: Jurgen Roland, 94 mins.)

Black Patch (1957)** George Montgomery, Diane Brewster. Horses and wholesome folk have their problems. (Dir: Allen Miner, 83 mins.)

Black Pearl, The (1977)** Gilbert Roland, Mario Custodio, Carl Anderson, Perla Cristal. Novel by Scott O'Dell has been turned into a mediocre feature for children. Story of a Mexican boy's discovery of a fabulous black pearl, guarded by a deadly manta ray, is marred by inadequate special effects. Custodio is effective in his first professional role, and veteran Roland shines in a few brief scenes. Made in Malta Spain. (Dir: Saul Swimmer, 96 mins.)

Black Peter (Czechoslovakia, 1964)***½ Ladislav Jakim, Pavla Martinkova. Czech teen-ager isn't making much headway with his girl friend or his new job of store detective in a supermarket. Coauthored by Milos Forman. He had a keen eye for the hesitancies and insecurity of adolescents. Black and white. (Dir: Milos Forman, 85 mins.)

Black Pirate, The (1926)*** Douglas Fairbanks, Sr., Billie Dove, Donald Crisp. Fairbanks as a swashbuckling pirate on the high seas. The original film had experimental color, and the sweep and action were impeccably staged. Very beguiling, and one of the best Fairbanks films. Directed by Albert Parker, who, although not generally highly regarded, does an admirable job. Lots of fun. (94 mins.)

Black Pit of Dr. M (Mexico, 1959)* Gaston Santos, Mapita Cortes. (Dir: Fernando Méndez, 71 mins.)

Black Rodeo (1972)**½ Muhammad Ali, Woody Strode. Documentary of black rodeo held in New York. Made relevant by commentary concerning the role of the black in winning the West. Ali and Strode clown with the participants. An excellent soundtrack. (Dir: Jeff Kanew, 87 mins.)

Black Roots (1970)*** Rev. Frederick Douglass Kirkpatrick, Rev. Gary Davis, Florynce Kennedy. A generally interesting, straight-forward documentary about the black experience in America. Mostly interviews, some very moving indeed. Aided by some wonderful music. (Dir: Lionel Rogosin, 60 mins.)

Black Rose, The (1950)** Cecile Aubrey, Tyrone Power, Orson Welles, Jack Hawkins, Herbert Lom. Good action scenes and lots of phony local color enliven this saga of a Saxon warrior on oriental travels in the 13th century—a good time to go abroad. As a movie it's negligible, though it's hardly ever boring. Directed with a sure hand and an unengaged heart. (Dir: Henry Hathaway, 120 mins.)

Black Rose (Japan, 1969)**½ Akihiro Maruyama, Eitaro Ozawa. This may be your only chance of the day to see a tall, willowy Japanese female impersonator. She sings and dances and drives men to distraction, while occasionally warbling Latin tunes of the '40s! Better directed than most. (Dir: Kinji Fukasaku, 90 mins.)

Black Sabbath (Italy, 1964)*** Boris Karloff, Mark Damon, Susy Andersen. Boris acts as m.c. and performs in the third of a trio of terror tales: "The Wurdalak," "A Drop of Water" and "The Telephone." Above average. (Dir: Mario Bava, 99 mins.)

Black Scorpion (1957)* Richard Denning, Mara Corday. (Dir: Edward Ludwig, 88 mins.)

Black Shield of Falworth, The (1954)**½ Tony Curtis, Janet Leigh. Swashbuckling adventure set in medieval times. (Dir: Rudolph Mate, 99 mins.)

Black Sleep, The (1956)** Basil Rathbone, Akim Tamiroff, Lon Chaney, Jr., Bela Lugosi, John Carradine. Scientist uses a drug that brings on a sleep resembling death. Fair horror thriller. (Dir: Reginald Le Borg, 81 mins.)

Black Stallion, The (1979)**** Kelly Reno, Mickey Rooney, Teri Garr. Director D. Carroll Ballard's hypnotic film tackles the making of a myth about a boy and his horse, and largely succeeds in drawing us into their mystical bond. Though some of the early footage succumbs to self-conscious beauty, the intensity of the central relationship is conveyed with precision and grace, so that when they return to civilization together, our own world seems to us the world apart. One of the loveliest children's films ever made, and an auspicious debut indeed for the director. With Mickey Rooney in some delicate, laconic work and Clarence Muse in his last role. (127 mins.)

Black Star (Italy, 1966)* Robert Woods, Elga Anderson. (Dir: Giovanni Grimaldi, 93 mins.)

Black Sun (France, 1966)* Michele Mercier, Daniel Gelin. (Dir: Denys de La Patellière, 90 mins.)

Black Sunday (Italy, 1961)** Barbara Steele, John Richardson, Andrea Checchi. Witch returns from her grave to seek revenge after being burned at the stake. Atmospheric horror thriller, better than usual. (Dir: Mario Bava, 83 mins.)

Black Sunday (1977)***½ Robert Shaw, Bruce Dern, Marthe Keller, Fritz Weaver. The Arab guerrilla terrorist organization Black September plans to intimidate America by blowing up the Super Bowl while the President is in attendance. Exciting shootout between police helicopters and the loonies who've stolen the Goodyear blimp. Based on the best-selling suspense novel by Thomas Harris. (Dir: John Frankenheimer, 145 mins.)

Black Swan, The (1942)**½ Tyrone Power, Maureen O'Hara, George Sanders, Laird Cregar, Anthony Quinn. Swashbuckling adventure directed by cinematic veteran and part-time Catholic mystic Henry King. It's lively and light, though never deft enough. The script, a Ben Hecht rehash of situations he used in more customary locales, is distinguished, as is the accomplished lighting of Leon Shamroy in Technicolor, which deserved its Oscar. Power stars rather fecklessly, but his lack of zip is more than compensated for by hammy Cregar, slimy Sanders, streaming-red-tressed O'Hara. (85 mins.)

Black Thirteen (Great Britain, 1953)** Peter Reynolds, Rona Anderson. The son of a college professor has gotten involved with some petty thieves. Well paced. (Dir: Ken Hughes, 75 mins.)

Black Tide (Great Britain, 1956)*½ John Ireland, Joy Webster. (79 mins.)

Black Torment, The (Great Britain, 1964)**½ Heather Sears, John Turner, Ann Lynn. Nobleman returns to his estate to find ghostly goings-on and accusa-

tions of witchcraft. Spooky costume thriller. (Dir: Robert Hartford-Davis, 85 mins.)

Black Tuesday (1954)*** Edward G. Robinson. Condemned killer masterminds his escape from the death house. Good gangster film. (Dir: Hugo Fregonese, 80 mins.)

Black Veil for Lisa, A (Italy-West Germany, 1968)** John Mills, Luciana Paluzzi, Robert Hoffman. A narcotics agent spends more time tailing his flirtatious wife than a gang of suspected drug smugglers. (Dir: Massimo Dallamano, 88 mins.)

Black Water Gold (1970)** Keir Dullea, Ricardo Montalban, Bradford Dillman. Beautiful Bahama location. Story is a mish-mash about sunken treasure, etc. (Dir: Alan Landsburg, 75 mins.)

Black Widow (1954)**½ Van Heflin, Ginger Rogers, Gene Tierney, Peggy Ann Garner. Interesting whodunit. An ambitious girl comes to the big city and ends up being murdered. Through a series of flashbacks, the pieces are fitted into the puzzling murder case by detective George Raft. (Dir: Nunnally Johnson, 94 mins.)

Black Windmill, The (1974)** Michael Caine, Janet Suzman, Donald Pleasence, Delphine Seyrig. Espionage potboiler loses steam midway. A British agent's son is kidnapped as part of a bigger plan to discredit him. A bright spot is Clive Revill's caustic Scotland Yard inspector. Based on the novel "Seven Days to a Killing." (Dir: Don Siegel, 106 mins.)

Black Zoo (1963)** Michael Gough, Jeanne Cooper, Virginia Grey. Proprietor of a private zoo turns murderer. (Dir: Robert Gordon, 88 mins.)

Blackbeard the Pirate (1952)**½ Robert Newton, Linda Darnell, William Bendix. A color adventure film from master director Raoul Walsh, this rambunctious quickie isn't very masterful. Newton is broad indeed as the antihero, and Walsh isn't able to elicit his usual values as he did in a number of burned-ash studio adventure films of the period. For cognoscenti only. (98 mins.)

Blackboard Jungle, The (1955)*** Sidney Poitier, Vic Morrow, Glenn Ford, Anne Francis, Richard Kiley. The song "Rock Around the Clock" entered the mainstream consciousness of America in this indictment of juvenile delinquency and adult failure of responsibility. It also ensured that rock and roll would be associated with dropouts and hoods, which did wonders for its lexicon. Morrow is a Brando heavy and Ford is the dedicated teacher who reaches his kids, tentatively, through visual aids and tape recorders. Well acted and hard-hitting, though grievously dated. Richard Brooks once again directs better than he writes. Debut parts of Paul Mazursky and Jamie Farr. This is the film for which Lenny Baker auditioned in "Next Stop, Greenwich Village." (101 mins.)

Blackjack Ketchum, Desperado (1956)**

Victor Jory, Howard Duff. A one time gunslinger's efforts to restore peace in Oxhorn. (Dir: Earl Bellamy, 76 mins.)

Blackmail (Great Britain, 1929)*** Anny Ondra, John Longden, Cyril Ritchard, Sara Allgood. A woman murders her would-be fiancé, a Scotland Yard inspector. Not aesthetically fascinating, but this was director Alfred Hitchcock's first sound film. Given the technical limitations (Ondra couldn't speak English and had to lip-sync to a British actress standing off-frame), the aggressive experimentation with the sound track is remarkably effective. A sign of things to come rather than Hitchcock at his height, but it shouldn't be missed. (78 mins.)

Blackmailers, The (Spain, 1963)*½ Manuel Benitez, Alberto de Mendoza. (Dir: Rafael Gil, 86 mins.)

Blackout (Great Britain, 1954)** Dane Clark, Belinda Lee. A man awakens from a drunk with blood on his clothes, finds he may have committed murder. So-so melodrama. (Dir: Terence Fisher, 87 mins.)

Blackout (Canada, 1978)*½ Jim Mitchum, June Allyson, Ray Milland, Belinda Montgomery, Jean-Pierre Aumont. Set in Manhattan during the second big power blackout, but made in Canada, this violent actioner has a decent cast to offset its excessive brutality. (Dir: Eddy Matalon, 90 mins.)

Blacks Britannica (1978)*** Powerful exposé of race prejudice in Great Britain. The film is very direct and angry, made by a U.S. filmmaker. (Dir: David Koff, 57 mins.)

Blackwell Story, The (1957)***½ Joanne Dru, Dan O'Herlihy. Story of the early career of Elizabeth Blackwell, the first woman in America to be accepted into medical school in 1856 and finally become a doctor. Depicts an intelligent, committed woman. Accurate portrayal of the prejudice and obstacles male-oriented-and-dominated society of the time imposed on women who tried to break the professional sex barrier. One of the first American films to have a heroine defined by her professional competence rather than her role as a romantic object. (Dir: James Neilson, 74 mins.)

Blacula (1972)**½ William Marshall, Vonetta McGee, Emily Yancy, Thalmus Rasulala. This film has a certain style to it if you like horror films. It tells the story of an African prince who is turned into a vampire by the original Count Dracula. Two hundred years later he turns up in Los Angeles. At first he rampages freely among the unsuspecting populace. Naturally he must meet the end of all vampires, and be vanquished eventually by the forces of good! Quite a lot of blood is spilled along the way, along with a few campy laughs. William Marshall is scary as the black vampire, Mamuwalde. (Dir: William Crain, 92 mins.)

Blaise Pascal (Italy, MTV 1973)**** Not a biography of Pascal so much as a panoramic vision of his era. One of the best episodes in the monumental historical project that occupied the last years of director Roberto Rossellini's career. Made for Italian television, it dramatizes the struggle between reason and faith that informed the 17th century, but it does so with no obvious dramatic devices or any sense that the action has been manipulated to prove a thesis. In Rossellini's films, observation becomes a high art. (120 mins.)

Blanche Fury (Great Britain, 1948)**½ Valerie Hobson, Stewart Granger. Grasping girl about to marry her uncle's son carries on an affair with a steward, resulting in murder. Hard-breathing costume drama is heavy, but nicely acted, tastefully produced. (Dir: Marc Allegret, 93 mins.)

Blancheville Monster (Spain, 1963)**½ Joan Hills, Richard Davis. Young girl is terrorized in a spooky castle as an ancient family legend says her life must be sacrificed. Fairly effective English-dubbed horror thriller. (Dir: Alberto de Martino (Martin Herbert) 89 mins.)

Blast of Silence (1961)** Allen Baron, Molly McCarthy. Professional assassin works himself up to get in the mood for bumping off a racketeer. New York-made, low-budget drama has some effective moments, but mostly comes off as a pretentious try for artiness. Produced by unknowns, it's a better-luck-next-time sort of film. (Dir: Allen Baron, 77 mins.)

Blaze of Noon (1947)**½ William Holden, Anne Baxter. Drama about a pilot in love with the sky who gets married. Plays like a corny "B" movie, but the kids may like its air scenes. (Dir: John Farrow, 91 mins.)

Blazing Forest, The (1952)** John Payne, Susan Morrow, William Demarest. A dull story of the big men who fell the big trees for big stakes. As the title implies, there is a big forest fire sequence. (Dir: Edward Ludwig, 90 mins.)

Blazing Saddles (1974)**** Mel Brooks, Cleavon Little, Gene Wilder, Madeline Kahn. Director Brooks' maniacal, uneven, but often wildly funny spoof of westerns that was accurately described in a promotional ad for the pic: "Ridin', Ropin', Wranglin', and all that Western Bullshit pulled together by Mel Brooks in his new Comedy Classic Blazing Saddles, brought to you by Warner Bros.—the people that gave you 'The Jazz Singer.'" Some of the jokes are hysterical, some sophomoric, but they keep coming so fast you'll forgive the clinkers. There's a spectacularly funny sequence featuring Kahn in a devastating takeoff of Marlene Dietrich while playing the character of Lili Von Shtupp. There are takeoffs on other western film classics including "High Noon." The ending peters out, but it's often lunacy of a high order with some great sight gags. (Dir: Mel Brooks, 93 mins.)

Blazing Sand (Israel-Germany, 1960)**

Daliah Lavi, Gert Guenter Hoffman. Selfish girl tries to persuade four men to undertake a perilous mission to save her lover, lying trapped and helpless in a tomb. Unusual locale is far superior to the trite melodramatic story. Dubbed in English. (Dir: Raphael Nussbaum, 98 mins.)

Bless the Beasts and Children (1971)**½ Billy Mumy, Barry Robins. Glendon Swarthout's novel serves as the basis for this interesting if not totally successful story about a group of problem boys from an expensive ranch-camp who set out to free some captive buffalo earmarked to be shot for sport. To get the message across and still be entertaining is a tall order, and director Stanley Kramer almost pulls it off. Mumy, known to TV fans from "Lost in Space," is quite good as the true rebel of the group, and the western locations add greatly to the atmosphere. (Dir: Stanley Kramer, 106 mins.)

Blind Date—See: **Chance Meeting** (1959)

Blind Goddess (Great Britain, 1948)**½ Eric Portman, Anne Crawford. A young diplomat is involved in a romantic affair that eventually brings on a nasty courtroom trial. Occasionally interesting but extremely verbose drama; well acted. (Dir: Harold French, 88 mins.)

Blind Justice (Germany, 1961)**½ Peter Van Eyck. A somewhat complicated multiple murder drama in which Peter Van Eyck plays a prosecuting attorney who almost destroys himself in his relentless search for the facts in a closed case. Good shots of German night life adds interest when the story gets too heavy-handed. Alternate title: **Whole Truth, The**. (97 mins.)

Blind Man's Bluff—See: **Cauldron of Blood**

Blind Spot (1947)*** Chester Morris, Constance Dowling. Writer on a drunk is accused of the murder of his publisher. Well done mystery. (Dir: Robert Gordon, 73 mins.)

Blind Spot (Great Britain, 1958)** Robert Mackenzie, Delphi Lawrence. Blinded officer becomes involved in a smuggling ring. Ordinary melodrama. (Dir: Peter Maxwell, 71 mins.)

Blinded by the Light (MTV 1980)** Kristy McNichol, James Vincent McNichol, Anne Jackson, Michael McGuire, Keith Andes, Sandy McPeak, Jenny O'Hara, Ben Bottoms. The subject is brainwashing in religious cults—luring young people primarily. However, this script which casts Kristy McNichol and her brother James Vincent (formerly Jimmy) McNichol as siblings facing the problem, only taps a small number of the fascinating, disturbing issues involved. Kristy is wonderful as the sister who can't understand her brother's motives in joining the Light of Salvation, but James has one vacant expression to express every emotion. If the subject interests you, tune in, but don't expect any meaningful insights. (Dir: John Alonzo, 104 mins.)

Blindfold (1966)*** Rock Hudson, Claudia Cardinale, Jack Warden. Psychologist is contacted by a security officer to treat a mentally disturbed scientist, which involves the headshrinker in an international plot. One of the more enjoyable secret-agent suspense thrillers, never takes itself too seriously, has good performances and direction. (Dir: Philip Dunne, 102 mins.)

Bliss of Mrs. Blossom, The (Great Britain, 1968)*** Far-out farce about a bored wife (Shirley MacLaine) of a brassière manufacturer (Richard Attenborough) who stashes away a lover (James Booth) in the attic. Slyly amusing, once the spirit of the thing makes itself evident; amazingly, it's based on fact. Good fun. (Dir: Joe McGrath, 93 mins.)

Blithe Spirit (Great Britain, 1945)***½ Rex Harrison, Constance Cummings, Kay Hammond, Margaret Rutherford. Enchanting, astringent supernatural farce, from the play by Noël Coward. A widower (Harrison) remarries and finds himself haunted by the slinky ghost of his first wife (Hammond). His new wife (Cummings) is not amused. Delightful performances by an expert cast; fascinating color effects by Ronald Neame. Good fun. (Dir: David Lean, 96 mins.)

Blitz on Britain (Great Britain, 1960)**½ Documentary narrated by Alistair Cooke of the Nazi air attack of World War II. Has been seen before, but still interesting. (Dir: Harry Booth, 71 mins.)

Blob, The (1958)*½ Steve McQueen, Aneta Corseaut. (Dir: Irvin Yeaworth, 85 mins.)

Blockade (1938)***½ Henry Fonda, Madeleine Carroll. An adventuress meets and loves a member of the Loyalist forces in Civil War-torn Spain. Well-made, excellently acted. (Dir: William Dieterle, 90 mins.)

Blonde Bait (Great Britain, 1956)*½ Beverly Michaels, Jim Davis. (Dir: Elmo Williams, 71 mins.)

Blonde Blackmailer (Great Britain, 1958)* Richard Arlen, Constance Leigh. (Dir: Charles Deane, 58 mins.)

Blonde Bombshell (1933)*** Jean Harlow, Lee Tracy, Franchot Tone, Frank Morgan, Pat O'Brien. Raucous Hollywood comedy about a movie star, with snappy line readings and not-too-sluggish direction from Victor Fleming. Harlow and Tracy are well matched in this screwy farce—vintage racy, since it was made just before the Code lowered the boom. Loaded with tangy bits and players. Hardly great comic art, but a prime example of quality entertainment from the tolerable end of the MGM production schedule. (91 mins.)

Blonde in a White Car—See: **Nude in a White Car**

Blonde Ransom (1946)*½ Donald Cook, Virginia Grey. (Dir: William Beaudine, 68 mins.)

Blonde Venus (1932)**½ Marlene Dietrich,

69

Cary Grant, Herbert Marshall, Sidney Toler. This is the one campy Josef von Sternberg-Dietrich collaboration (of their five) and the most problematic. Drawn in director von Sternberg's characteristic chiaroscuro, the film seems to offer nothing beneath the elegant surfaces (an observation that does not apply to the other masterpieces of the series). Open to charges of superciliousness, despite the cathartic camp of Dietrich in an ape suit singing "Hot Voodoo." The only sympathetic role Dietrich played for von Sternberg—as a woman who leaves her husband because she thinks she's no good for him—seems full of melodramatic pathos, unsuited to von Sternberg's ironic sensibilities. (80 mins.)

Blondie (1938)****½** Penny Singleton, Arthur Lake, Larry Simms, Jonathan Hale. Snappy comedy, first one in the series based on the popular comic strip. Blondie and Dagwood have problems paying off their furniture installments when he gets stuck with a loan shark's note. Pleasing introduction to the Bumstead family. (Dir: Frank R. Strayer, 80 mins.)

Blondie Brings Up Baby (1939)****½** Penny Singleton, Arthur Lake, Larry Simms. A salesman tells Blondie that Baby Dumpling has a high IQ, so he's enrolled in school. Good share of laughs in this series comedy. Well done. (Dir: Frank R. Strayer, 70 mins.)

Blondie Goes Latin (1941)****½** Penny Singleton, Arthur Lake, Tito Guizar, Ruth Terry. The Bumsteads are on the way to South America for a business deal with some frantic byplay on shipboard. Singleton has a chance to sing and dance here—it's a good musical as well as an up-to-standard entry in the series. (Dir: Frank Strayer, 69 mins.)

Blondie Goes to College (1942)****** Penny Singleton, Arthur Lake, Janet Blair, Larry Parks. Blondie and Dagwood decide to go to college, concealing their marriage. Series comedy moves more slowly than some others but is still fair fun. At the end of this one Dagwood learns he's to become a father again. (Dir: Frank Strayer, 74 mins.)

Blondie in Society (1941)******* Penny Singleton, Arthur Lake, William Frawley. Dagwood's in the dog house when he accepts a Great Dane as payment for a loan and Blondie enters it in a dog show. Series comedy has more laughs than many higher-budgeted shows. Good fun. (Dir: Frank Strayer, 75 mins.)

Blondie Knows Best (1946)****½** Penny Singleton, Arthur Lake, Shemp Howard. Dagwood gets himself in hot water when he has to impersonate his boss to corner a client. Amusing series comedy, with a funny bit by Shemp Howard as a process server. (Dir: Abby Berlin, 69 mins.)

Blondie Meets the Boss (1939)****½** Penny Singleton, Arthur Lake, Jonathan Hale. Dagwood loses his job and Blondie takes his place at the office. Second in the series, keeps up the fast moving amusement set by its predecessor. (Dir: Frank Strayer, 80 mins.)

Blondie on a Budget (1940)******* Penny Singleton, Arthur Lake, Rita Hayworth. Blondie wants a fur coat, Dagwood wants to join the Trout Club; complications become even more clouded when Dagwood's ex-girl enters the picture. Enjoyable series comedy has good gags, the presence of Hayworth at her most glamorous. (Dir: Frank Strayer, 73 mins.)

Blondie Plays Cupid (1940)****½** Penny Singleton, Arthur Lake, Glenn Ford. En route to a vacation, Blondie and Dagwood help out an eloping couple. Pleasant comedy in the series, with the added attraction of Ford in his salad days. (Dir: Frank Strayer, 68 mins.)

Blondie Takes a Vacation (1939)****½** Penny Singleton, Arthur Lake, Donald MacBride. The Bumsteads take over a rundown resort hotel and try to put it on a paying basis. Chucklesome comedy in the series, some good laughs. (Dir: Frank Strayer, 70 mins.)

Blondie's Anniversary (1947)****** Penny Singleton, Arthur Lake, Adele Jergens, William Frawley. Dagwood inadvertently gives Blondie the wrong package for her anniversary present, which means more trouble. (Dir: Abby Berlin, 75 mins.)

Blondie's Blessed Event (1942)******* Penny Singleton, Arthur Lake, Hans Conried. When the strain of Blondie's expectant motherhood begins to show on Dagwood, he's sent to a Chicago convention, where he encounters an impoverished arty playwright. Many laughs in this series comedy, largely due to a gem of a performance by Conried. (Dir: Frank Strayer, 75 mins.)

Blondie's Reward (1948)****** Penny Singleton, Arthur Lake, Chick Chandler, Frank Jenks. Dagwood buys a swamp instead of the property he was supposed to purchase. Mild comedy in the series. (Dir: Abby Berlin, 67 mins.)

Blondie's Secret (1948)****** Penny Singleton, Arthur Lake, Thurston Hall. While waiting for Dagwood so they can start their postponed vacation, Blondie chances upon some counterfeit money. Mild comedy in the series. (Dir: Edward Bernds, 68 mins.)

Blood Alley (1955)****** John Wayne, Lauren Bacall, Anita Ekberg. He-man adventurer John Wayne fights off Chinese Communists single handed and still finds time for Lauren Bacall. Anita Ekberg is disguised in this one, plays refugee clad in burlap. Strictly for the undiscriminating. (Dir: William Wellman, 115 mins.)

Blood and Black Lace (Italy, 1964)****** Cameron Mitchell, Eva Bartok. Grisly shocker concerning some mysterious murders of fashion models. Not for the squeamish, with its multitude of gruesome sequences. Horror fans should give it a passing mark. English dubbed. (Dir: Mario Bava, 88 mins.)

70

Blood and Defiance (Italy, 1962)* Gerard Landry, Jose Greci. (Dir: Nick Nostro, 92 mins.)

Blood and Roses (France, 1961)** Mel Ferrer, Annette Vadim, Elsa Martinelli. English dialogue; jealous girl's body becomes possessed, commits murders as a vampire. Colorful backgrounds and photography can't overcome a hazy plot—just fair horror thriller. (Dir: Roger Vadim, 74 mins.)

Blood and Sand (1922)**½ Rudolph Valentino, Lila Lee, Nita Naldi. Valentino set hearts ablaze in those days as a bullfighter torn between sweet Lee and vampish Naldi. Though laughable in spots, the film holds up rather well, under Fred Niblo's expert direction. Niblo guided Garbo through some of her best American silents—and here he gains in the action scenes what he loses in the love scenes. (80 mins.)

Blood and Sand (1941)** Tyrone Power, Nazimova, Anthony Quinn, Linda Darnell, Rita Hayworth. Director Rouben Mamoulian concentrates more on color and spectacle than on drama in this remake of the Ibáñez chestnut. Power is always a bit ridiculous doing Latins, but the color is something to see, having been photographed by Ernest Palmer and the ubiquitous Ray Rennahan. (123 mins.)

Blood and Steel (1959)** John Lupton, Brett Halsey, Ziva Rodann. Navy Seabees under fire on an enemy-held island are helped by a native girl. Unimportant but competent World War II drama, with its briefness an asset. (Dir: Bernard Kowalski, 63 mins.)

Blood Beast Terror, The (Great Britain, 1968)** Peter Cushing, Robert Flemyng, Wanda Ventham, Vanessa Howard. Another in the long line of Cushing bloodcurdlers, in which he's brought into the case of a young woman on the prowl, who delivers a kiss of instant and horrifying death. Seems that she's an entomologist's daughter who is changing into a giant death's-head moth. (Dir: Vernon Sewell, 88 mins.)

Blood Demon, The—See: **Torture Chamber of Dr. Sadism.**

Blood Feud (Italy, 1979)**½ Sophia Loren, Marcello Mastroianni, Giancarlo Giannini. Director Lina Wertmuller never follows through on any of her ideas—political, cinematic, sexual—and it's apparent that her directionless energy is flagging of its own accord. This drama hasn't an iconoclastic moment that isn't also thoroughly familiar, and Wertmuller relies on the star power of her leads to carry our interest along. Wertmuller is smart enough to avoid undercutting their emotionalism with her freneticism. The result is standard Italian comedy, with hyperkinetic eyestrain. (100 mins.)

Blood Fiend—See: **Theatre of Death**

Blood of a Poet, The (France, 1930)**½

Enrico Ribero, Lee Miller, Jean Desbordes. A landmark film, Cocteau's first, written and narrated by him. "Poet" is constructed as a series of episodic, enigmatic, frequently autobiographical imaginary events, revelations and transformations. From the opening scene when the poet, while drawing, creates a real mouth to the final scene when the poet shoots himself, Cocteau fills the screen with an unending collage of remarkable allegories and images including some fantastic masks. (Dir: Jean Cocteau, 53 mins.)

Blood of Dracula (1957)* Sandra Harrison, Louise Lewis. (Dir: Herbert L. Strock, 69 mins.)

Blood of Nostradamus, The (Mexico, 1959)* Jermon Robles, Julio Aleman. (Dir: Federico Curiel, Alberto Mariscal, 98 mins.)

Blood of the Condor (Bolivia, 1969)**** Marcelino Yanahuaya, Benedicta Mendoza Huanca, Vicente Salinas. Extremely moving film, totally without artifice, concerning the plight of the impoverished Quechua Indians, who are cheated and dehumanized at every turn by whites and mestizos of mixed blood. Fictional story about the "Progress Corps" (the American Peace Corps) and efforts to sterilize the Indian women. The story line doesn't matter here. What does come through is the overwhelming commitment of the director to use this film as a consciousness-raising tool among suffering Bolivian peasants. The film has a naked power, raw power that is undeniable even for educated urbanites from other cultures. Banned in Bolivia, and its talented director exiled, but you should see this cinematic plea for justice if you have an opportunity. (Dir: Jorge Sanjines, 74 mins.)

Blood on His Sword (France, 1961)** Jean Marais, Rosanna Schiaffino. Dashing hero saves the King's goddaughter from charges of witchcraft. Lavishly produced, rather naive costume adventure. Some good action. English-dubbed. (Dir: Andre Hunebelle, 126 mins.)

Blood on Satan's Claw (Great Britain, 1970)**½ Patrick Wymark, Linda Hayden, Barry Andrews. Rural England circa 1670 is the setting for witch trials and an atmosphere of suspense. Better-than-average horror, complete with a girl who grows claws. Not for the squeamish. Hayden gives best performance. (Dir: Piers Haggard, 93 mins.)

Blood on the Arrow (1965)** Dale Robertson, Martha Hyer, Wendell Corey. Lone survivor of an Indian attack is taken care of by the wife of a trader who is involved with outlaws. Typical western. (Dir: Sidney Salkow, 91 mins.)

Blood on the Moon (1948)**½ Robert Mitchum, Walter Brennan, Robert Preston, Barbara Bel Geddes. Murky, violent postwar western. Worth seeing, although of questionable merit. Directed by Robert

71

Wise, in the gutsy days of "Born to Kill." (88 mins.)

Blood on the Sun (1945)*** James Cagney, Sylvia Sidney. In pre-war Japan, an American newspaperman foresees the threat to democracy posed by the ruling warlords, who try to silence him. Fast-paced, suspenseful melodrama. Plenty of Cagney action. (Dir: Frank Lloyd, 94 mins.)

Blood Sisters—See: **Sisters**

Blood Suckers, The—See: **Dr. Terror's House of Horrors**

Bloodbrothers (1978)*** Paul Sorvino, Tony Lo Bianco, Richard Gere. Solid, classical direction by Hollywood vet Robert Mulligan ("Inside Daisy Clover," "Summer of '42"). The story of a Bronx teenager (Gere) struggling to escape the emotional limitations of his oppressive Italian family may lack something in subtlety, but the film makes up for it in craft, intensity, and a fine sense of the divided loyalties that pull people apart. Mulligan remains a master of subjective cinema. (116 mins.)

Bloodhounds of Broadway (1952)**½ Mitzi Gaynor, Scott Brady. A comedy with music in the "Guys & Dolls" tradition, but not nearly as effective. Miss Gaynor plays a hillbilly who comes to the city and turns into a curvaceous Broadway babe. The plot revolves around a crime investigating committee and the various sharpies who spend most of their time dodging the law. (Dir: Harmon Jones, 90 mins.)

Bloodline (1979)*½ Audrey Hepburn, Ben Gazzara, James Mason, Irene Papas, Omar Sharif. Also known as "Sidney Sheldon's Bloodline." (Dir: Terence Young, 116 mins.)

Bloodlust (1961)* Wilton Graff, Robert Reed, Lilyan Chauvin. Based on *The Most Dangerous Game* by Richard Connell. (Dir: Ralph Brooke, 68 mins.)

Bloodsport (1973)*** Ben Johnson, Larry Hagman, Gary Busey. Johnson charges this drama with tension and appeal in the role of a small-town worker who sees nothing but big-time gridiron glory for his hot-shot high-school-star son. The father pushes and pushes and the son is strained and pulled taut, and the confrontation-climax, as well as the entire attitude of the film, is truthful and direct. Made-for-TV. (Dir: Jerold Freedman, 78 mins.)

Bloody Mama (1970)*** Shelley Winters, Pat Hingle, Robert DeNiro. Tough crime saga about Ma Barker and her brood of disturbed sons will be appreciated by some, dismissed by others. It's a brutal, machine-gun-paced account of the criminal rise and fall of the Barker brood. Miss Winters' blatant vulgarity as the dominant Ma Barker is perfectly suited to this movie treatment of the legendary public enemy of the Depression era, while Don Stroud, as her bad-tempered son Herman, and Pat Hingle, as a kidnapped banker, also register with strong performances. The bloody finale is virtually choreo-

graphed, and is a stunner. (Dir: Roger Corman, 92 mins.)

Bloody Vampire, The (Mexico, 1963)* Carlos Agosti, Adrias Roel. (Dir: Michael Morayta, 98 mins.)

Blossoms in the Dust (1941)** Greer Garson, Walter Pidgeon, Marsha Hunt, Fay Holden. What might have been a strong, noble subject—the founding of an orphanage by a woman who has lost her husband and child—founders in the glossy, phony MGM treatment. Matters are not helped by the false uplift of Garson's performance—the lady had poise but no grace, and Pidgeon brought out the worst in her. The issues of illegitimacy are avoided with a vengeance. (Dir: Mervyn Le Roy, 100 mins.)

Blow-Up (Great Britain-Italy, 1966)**** David Hemmings, Vanessa Redgrave. Director Michelangelo Antonioni's fascinating psychological puzzler of the young photographer (David Hemmings) who believes he's an accidental witness to a murder. (The small screen won't help clarify the filmmaker's intent.) Viewers may find the story baffling, but should hold on and catch incandescent Vanessa Redgrave, and assorted models who fill the photographer's nightmarish world. (Dir: Michelangelo Antonioni, 111 mins.)

Blowing Wild (1953)**½ Barbara Stanwyck, Gary Cooper, Anthony Quinn. Power-crazy gal tries to gain control in Mexican oil fields. Well done but hardly worth the trouble. (Dir: Hugo Fregonese, 90 mins.)

Blue (1968)* Terence Stamp, Joanna Pettet. (Dir: Silvio Narizzano, 113 mins.)

Blue Angel, The (Germany, 1930)**** Marlene Dietrich, Emil Jannings. The first film collaboration between director Josef von Sternberg and Dietrich. Reeks with the atmosphere of decay and sexuality. Jannings plays the professor who tries to stop his students from visiting night-club singer Lola Lola (Dietrich) and ends up succumbing to her plump charms. The professor is a repressed little prig whose first sexual encounter results in his total destruction. A riveting performance by Dietrich, which made her a European star and prompted her invitation to Hollywood. (90 mins.)

Blue Angel, The (1959)**½ May Britt, Curt Jurgens. Remake of the 1930 classic which made Marlene Dietrich an international star. Nowhere near as good as the original, but those who aren't familiar with the Dietrich opus will probably enjoy it. Curt Jurgens is very good as a German school teacher who succumbs to the slinky nightclub singer named Lola-Lola. Miss Britt is physically attractive, but she's not convincing as the temptress who leads the professor to near destruction. (Dir: Edward Dmytryk, 107 mins.)

Blue Bird, The (1940)*½ Shirley Temple, Spring Byington. From Maeterlinck's moralistic children's book. (Dir: Walter Lang, 88 mins.)

72

Blue Bird, The (U.S.-U.S.S.R., 1976)** Elizabeth Taylor, Cicely Tyson, Jane Fonda, Ava Gardner Robert Morley. One of maybe half a dozen disappointing films that George Cukor has directed in a long career—but considering the problems that befell Cukor on location in Russia, it's a miracle that it's as good as it is. A musical fantasy done in by a terrible score and atrocious art direction, the film has two or three moments that are genuinely—and unaccountably—affecting. For hard-core Cukorites only. The first Soviet-American movie coproduction. Based on the Maurice Maeterlinck fantasy. (100 mins.)

Blue Blood (1951)**½ Bill Williams, Jane Nigh. Veteran horse trainer persuades a wealthy girl to let him train a former winner headed for oblivion. Refreshing racing story, pleasantly handled. (Dir: Lew Landers, 72 mins.)

Blue Collar (1978)**** Richard Pryor, Yaphet Kotto, Harvey Keitel. Paul Schrader, the screenwriter of "Taxi Driver" and "Obsession," premiered well as a director with this downbeat tale of workday oppression. The union squeezes from one side, the bosses from another, and three auto workers are caught in the contradictions of capitalism. Schrader's cold, deliberate camera style plays a subtle counterpoint to the story of breakdown and despair. An intelligent, controlled, well-observed film, with excellent performances. (110 mins.)

Blue Continent (Italy, 1954)** Documentary of an expedition to the depths of the Red Sea to explore marine life. Average amount of interest in a subject which has been covered more thoroughly and better by Cousteau and others. Narration in English. Produced by diver Bruno Vailati. (Dir: Folco Quilici, 95 mins.)

Blue Country (France, 1978)***½ Brigitte Fossey, Jacques Serres. Written and directed by Jean-Charles Tacchella as a follow-up to his enormously successful "Cousin, Cousine." This bright joyous comedy has much of the charm of its predecessor, plus the beautiful French countryside. The leads are a couple who try to retain their independence while carrying on a lengthy love affair; some of the scenes are marvelous. (104 mins.)

Blue Dahlia, The (1946)**½ Alan Ladd, William Bendix, Veronica Lake, Doris Dowling. Raymond Chandler wrote this directly for the screen, the only original story he ever did for Hollywood. The plot is tough to a fault; the air of disillusioned cynicism is plausibly conveyed; and the characters are rounded, neurotic, and honestly drawn. Still, this story of a vet who comes home to his unfaithful wife only to find her murdered doesn't succeed; the director struggled manfully, but hadn't the heart to be heartless. Produced by John Houseman. (Dir: George Marshall, 96 mins.)

Blue Denim (1959)**½ Carol Lynley, Brandon de Wilde. Another one about misunderstood youth and the consequences of premature love. Well acted but says nothing especially profound. (Dir: Philip Dunne, 89 mins.)

Blue Gardenia (1953)**½ Anne Baxter, Richard Conte, Ann Sothern. Slick, but slow moving mystery-drama about a girl wrongly accused of murder and her efforts to prove her innocence. Good performances. (Dir: Fritz Lang, 90 mins.)

Blue Grass of Kentucky (1950)**½ Bill Williams, Jane Nigh. Daughter of a rival race horse owner allows breeding with her boyfriend's nag, with a fine-running colt the result. Horseflesh fanciers should enjoy this. Well done. (Dir: William Beaudine, 71 mins.)

Blue Hawaii (1961)** Elvis Presley, Joan Blackman, Angela Lansbury. Returning soldier bucks a job with a tourist agency against his parent's wishes, makes good. As goes Elvis, so goes this mild musical. Pretty pictures do not always a movie make—and this one has little else except Presley. (Dir: Norman Taurog, 101 mins.)

Blue Knight, The (MTV 1975)**½ George Kennedy, Alex Rocco. George Kennedy plays Joseph Wambaugh's Bumper Morgan (a role beautifully acted by William Holden in the previous TV mini-series), with his big-bear warmth. Shootouts, chases, and all that Hollywood jazz are missing, as Bumper tracks down a cop-killer while making human contact on the street. There's a feeling of reality to this pilot film. (Dir: J. Lee Thompson, 73 mins.)

Blue Lagoon, The (Great Britain, 1948)** Jean Simmons, Donald Houston. Boy and girl are shipwrecked on a tropic isle, grow to maturity and love each other. Picturesque scenery doesn't overcome the weakness of the tale; moderate adventure drama. (Dir: Frank Launder, 101 mins.)

Blue Lagoon, The (1980)** Brooke Shields, Christopher Atkins, Leo McKern, William Daniels. H. de Vere Stacpoole's novel (first filmed by Frank Launder in '48 with Jean Simmons) stars Shields and Atkins as two youngsters in a lush Fiji paradise. Director Randal Kleiser's evident faith in his story helps him sustain the attitude of naïveté that is essential if the tale is to work, but his visual sense is merely pretty and his feelings are meager. The film is not all that different from "Grease" in its comedy of adolescent sparring, and the tone is just as vulgar, attempting to hype a spurious conceit with stupid, fawning significances. Shields is astonishingly beautiful. (104 mins.)

Blue Lamp, The (Great Britain, 1950)*** Jack Warner, Dirk Bogarde. A young recruit nabs a robber after he has killed a fellow-policeman. Glorifying the British bobby, this is exciting as well as having an authentic documentary-like flavor. (Dir: Basil Dearden, 84 mins.)

Blue Max, The (1966)**½ George Peppard,

Ursula Andress, James Mason. Overblown World War I flying epic that is at its best during some superbly photographed and staged aerial battle sequences featuring vintage planes. George Peppard is well cast as a fastidious German pilot who is eager to become a war ace, and James Mason delivers one of his familiar German-officer performances. For added interest there's Ursula Andress in the role of a glamorous countess. (Dir: John Guillermin, 156 mins.)

Blue Murder at St. Trinians (Great Britain, 1958)**½ Alastair Sim, Joyce Grenfell, Terry-Thomas. Foolish comedy about a jewel thief hiding from the law in a girls' school. The events leading to his eventual capture are pure slapstick. The delightful cast of performers are at the poor script's mercy, but Sim still gets his share of laughs. (Dir: Frank Launder, 88 mins.)

Blue Skies (1946)*** Bing Crosby, Fred Astaire, Joan Caulfield. Bing, Fred and 20 Irving Berlin tunes add up to pleasant entertainment. Plot is corny, but it doesn't get in the way. (Dir: Stuart Heisler, 104 mins.)

Blue Veil, The (1951)**½ Jane Wyman, Charles Laughton, Joan Blondell. Young woman matured by love finds happiness in being a children's nurse. Long, tearful drama, mainly for the ladies. (Dir: Curtis Bernhardt, 114 mins.)

Blue Water, White Death (1971)***½ Underwater-photography buffs and adventurers of all ages will not want to miss this exciting odyssey in search of a Great White Shark, also known as White Death. Peter Gimbel, adventurer, underwater-photography expert and documentary filmmaker, assembled a crew of ten divers and photographers and set out to find the White Shark in a journey which took them from South Africa to Ceylon, India and finally to the coast of Australia. Builds to an unforgettable crescendo. The last 15 or 20 minutes showing the elusive and terrifying Great White Shark battering the aluminum cage in a frenzied attempt to destroy any people and cameras in its path, is one of the most thrilling, awesome sequences ever captured on film. (Dir: Peter Gimbel, 100 mins.)

Blue, White and Perfect (1941)**½ Lloyd Nolan, Mary Beth Hughes. Detective Michael Shayne gets in the war effort by chasing foreign agents who've been stealing industrial diamonds. Good B film. (Dir: Herbert I. Leeds, 78 mins.)

Bluebeard (1944)*** John Carradine, Jean Parker. A puppeteer who strangles girls as a sideline falls for a beautiful dress shopowner, which is his downfall. Suspenseful thriller. Carradine is restrained, very good. (Dir: Edgar Ulmer, 73 mins.)

Bluebeard (France-Italy-W. Germany, 1972)*½ Richard Burton, Raquel Welch, Joey Heatherton. (Dir: Edward Dmytryk, 124 mins.)

Bluebeard's Eighth Wife (1938)*** David Niven, Gary Cooper, Claudette Colbert. Highly problematical Ernst Lubitsch-directed comedy, in which the emotions are uncharacteristically inelegant. Cooper is an American millionaire who runs through wives until he meets determinedly emasculating Colbert, who wants to keep him, whatever the price in sexual humiliation. The moral issues become confused, opting for sentimentality over the hard-edged clarity that Lubitsch had exhibited in "Angel on Balance." (85 mins.)

Bluebeard's Ten Honeymoons (Great Britain, 1960)**½ George Sanders, Corinne Calvet. George Sanders is so suave that he could probably get away with multiple murders as he does in this modern version of Bluebeard. The women fall under George's charming spell and end up done in. (Dir: W. Lee Wilder, 93 mins.)

Blueprint for Murder, A (1953)** Joseph Cotten, Jean Peters. Contrived "perfect crime" melodrama which may keep some viewers guessing as to whether the beautiful Miss Peters is guilty or not. The clues are plentiful and the action predictable for most mystery fans. (Dir: Andrew Stone, 76 mins.)

Blueprint for Robbery (1961)** J. Pat O'Malley, Robert Wilke, Robert Gist. Fair suspense drama as a gang of thieves attempt to rob a Brink's truck of $2 million. Character actor O'Malley is the main attraction, playing the head of the bandits. (Dir: Jerry Hopper, 87 mins.)

Blues Brothers, The (1980)*½ John Belushi, Dan Ackroyd, Aretha Franklin, James Brown. (Dir: John Landis, 133 mins.)

Blues for Lovers (Great Britain, 1965)** Ray Charles, Tom Bell, Mary Peach, Dawn Addams. Dull, restrained melodrama about a blind boy's friendship with a blind American jazz musician. Jazz-pianist Ray Charles performs well enough in his screen debut, but the music is best—an attractive mixture of American jazz and English-ballad blues. Charles' songs include "Cry," "Talking about You," and "Lucky Old Sun." (Dir: Paul Henreid, 89 mins.)

Blues in the Night (1941)*** Priscilla Lane, Richard Whorf. A wonderful score by Harold Arlen and Johnny Mercer, plus an occasionally moving plot combine for good entertainment. With a little more work this could have been a great motion picture. (Dir: Anatole Litvak, 88 mins.)

Blume in Love (1973)***½ George Segal, Susan Anspach, Kris Kristofferson, Shelley Winters, Marsha Mason. Director Paul Mazursky's best comedy is a madcap update on screwball comedies where the philandering husband goes to the ends of the earth to get his wife back. This was the last time Segal achieved a witty, multileveled performance, before lapsing into coy freneticism and spastic catatonia. Mazursky perfectly captures the dopey ambience of southern California in the early '70s, when it was still possible to be laid-back and yet to care passionately about everything. (117 mins.)

Boardwalk (1979)**½ Lee Strasberg, Ruth Gordon, Janet Leigh, Eli Mintz, Joe Silver. Well-acted tearjerker that doesn't succeed. Drama with comic and violent overtones about an elderly Jewish couple, Gordon and Strasberg, who are about to celebrate their 50th anniversary. The wife is dying of cancer, their grown children have problems, and their life is being threatened by a street gang, in this Coney Island setting. Depressing, but the acting lifts the Stephen Verona-Leigh Chapman screenplay above the soap opera level. Cameos by singer-actress Lillian Roth, composer Sammy Cahn, and Linda Manz (of "Days of Heaven"). (Dir: Stephen Verona, 98 mins.)

Boatniks, The (1970)**½ Phil Silvers, Norman Fell, Mickey Shaughnessy, Robert Morse. Another Walt Disney comedy about bumbling crooks and lovable kooks. This time Morse is the adorable coast guard officer who must pursue a trio of vaudevillian jewel robbers (Silvers, Fell, and Shaughnessy) until they finally throw their booty overboard. Stefanie Powers is around for the love interest, and Don Ameche plays the commander, who is also inept. Disney antics for the family. (Dir: Norman Tokar, 104 mins.)

Bob and Carol and Ted and Alice (1969)***½ Elliott Gould, Dyan Cannon, Natalie Wood, Robert Culp. Paul Mazursky's directorial debut was a shrewd blend of satire and commercial calculation, a mixture of sharp gags and mushy sentiment. When the film works, it works very well; when it doesn't, it dies. Gould and Cannon were better attuned to the spirit of the enterprise than Wood and Culp. Today I suspect the film looks like a relic from a time capsule. (105 mins.)

Bob Mathias Story, The (1954)**½ Bob Mathias, Ann Doran. Low budget, entertaining biography of the decathlon champ of the 1948 and 1952 Olympics. Good for the youngsters. (Dir: Francis Lyon, 80 mins.)

Bobbikins (Great Britain, 1960)**½ Max Bygraves, Shirley Jones. Young couple are amazed to discover their 14-month baby talking like an adult, and giving stock market tips too. Pleasant fantasy has some chuckles, clever manipulating of baby to give the effect of speech. (Dir: Robert Day, 89 mins.)

Bobby Deerfield (1977)*½ Al Pacino, Marthe Keller, Anny Duperey. Adapted by Alvin Sargent from Erich Maria Remarque's novel, "Heaven Has No Favorites." (Dir: Sydney Pollack, 124 mins.)

Bobby Ware Is Missing (1955)**½ Neville Brand, Arthur Franz. An offbeat drama about the search for a young teen age boy who has an accident and doesn't come home. The performances are better than average for a Grade "B" film. (Dir: Thomas Carr, 66 mins.)

Bobo, The (Great Britain, 1967)** Peter Sellers, Britt Ekland, Rossano Brazzi. Sellers as an inept matador who can land a singing job, providing he's able to seduce a courtesan (Ekland). Once in a while Sellers gets a few chuckles, but the script of "The Bobo" is surfeited with boo-boos! (Dir: Robert Parrish, 105 mins.)

Boccaccio '70 (Italy, 1962)***½ Sophia Loren, Anita Ekberg, Romy Schneider. Three naughty tales—"The Temptation of Dr. Antonio," with Ekberg as a poster come to life in a satire on prudishness; "The Job," with Schneider as a discontented wife; and "The Raffle," with Loren as the big prize in a love lottery. One's liking for the stories will vary; Sophia is ravishing in "The Raffle," and this segment is extremely funny; all are well acted. Dubbed in English. (Dirs: Fellini, Visconti, De Sica, 165 mins.)

Body and Soul (1947)**** John Garfield, Lilli Palmer. A guy from the slums battles his way to the top of the fight racket, only to learn that the crooked way isn't necessarily the best. Hard-hitting melodrama, crisp and rugged, with some excellent prizefight sequences. Palmer is near-perfect; Garfield gives his best performance. Robert Rossen directed from Abraham Polonsky's screenplay, and with James Wong Howe filming the fights from roller skates, the film has verbal poetry and visual excitement. Nearly everyone on the set later directed: Howe, Polonsky, Joseph Pevney, and Robert Aldrich. The closing line, Garfield's rejoinder to a gangster's threat: "What are you going to do? Kill me? Everybody dies!" is perhaps the most sublimely absurd nugget of poetic moralism ever delivered. (104 mins.)

Body Disappears, The (1941)** Jane Wyman, Jeffrey Lynn. Daffy little forced comedy in the "Topper" tradition but not in the same league. Disappearing people as a comedy device is old hat. (Dir: Ross Lederman, 72 mins.)

Body Is Missing, The (France, 1962)*½ Elke Sommer, Darry Cowl. Alternate title: **Who Stole the Body?** (Dir: Girault, 92 mins.)

Body Snatcher (1945)***½ Boris Karloff, Bela Lugosi, Henry Daniell. A doctor is blackmailed by a villainous coachman when he wishes to stop securing bodies for medical research in Scotland of the 19th century. For horror fans, this is one of the best; for others, a good and chilling version of Robert Louis Stevenson's tale. (Dir: Robert Wise, 77 mins.)

Body Stealers, The—See: **Thin Air**

Bodyhold (1950)** Willard Parker, Lola Albright. The wrestling game is exposed in this dull story of the sport's managers and flunkies. (Dir: Seymour Friedman, 63 mins.)

Boeing-Boeing (1965)** Tony Curtis, Jerry Lewis. The London stage success is Amer-

75

icanized for the screen, hypoed by casting Curtis and Lewis as a pair of calculating Romeos who figure out an elaborate plan involving a bachelor pad with airline stewardesses coming and going. It still comes out, as you might expect, loud and unfunny. (Dir: John Rich, 102 mins.)

Bofors Gun, The (Great Britain, 1968)***½ Grim sessions at a British army camp in postwar Germany, with a superb performance by Nicol Williamson as a tragically misfit Irish soldier. Builds to a poignant climax. Well directed (Jack Gold), excellent cast. Ian Holm, David Warner. Inexcusably, the salty dialogue has been toned down on the TV prints. (Dir: Jack Gold, 106 mins.)

Bogie (MTV 1980)** Kevin O'Connor, Kathryn Harrold, Ann Wedgeworth. A fan magazine view of the life and loves of Humphrey Bogart. O'Connor resembles the late actor, yet reveals little. It's to O'Connor's credit that he only occasionally punches up the familiar speech pattern. More time is allotted to Bogie's stormy marriage to Mayo Methot (his third wife) than to the big love of his life, Lauren Bacall. Wedgeworth is quite good as the manic, hard-drinking, two-fisted Mayo, but Harrold is out-and-out bad as the young Bacall. (Dir: Vincent Sherman, 104 mins.)

Bold Adventure, The (France-Germany, 1956)** Gerard Philipe, Jean Vilar. Lavish, colorful, but drowsy costume adventure about a frivolous Robin Hood battling the Spanish Inquisition in Flemish Belgium. Based on the "Till Eulenspiegel" legend, directed by the star—could have had more dash, pace. Dubbed in English. (Dirs: Gerard Philipe, Joris Ivens, 87 mins.)

Bold and the Brave (1956)***½ Mickey Rooney, Wendell Corey, Don Taylor. Better than average war film with many touches of comedy, the best being a "crap game" sequence in which Mickey Rooney is marvelously funny. (Dir: Lewis Foster, 87 mins.)

Bomb at 10:10 (1967)** George Montgomery. Routine war drama about an escape from a concentration camp and the heroics of the escapees in their bouts with the Nazis. George Montgomery and a European cast do well, but it's all too familiar. (Dir: Charles Damic, 86 mins.)

Bomb for a Dictator, A (France, 1957)** Pierre Fresnay, Michel Auclair. Revolutionists plan to eliminate a dictator via an elaborate plan, which backfires. Talky drama dubbed in English—good performers struggle with the material. (Dir: Alex Joffé, 73 mins.)

Bomb in the High Street (Great Britain, 1963)*½ Ronald Howard, Terry Palmer. (Dirs: Peter Bezencenet, Terence Bishop, 60 mins.)

Bombardier (1943)*** Pat O'Brien, Randolph Scott. Men are trained for missions in the flying fortresses in raids over Ja-

pan. Good war melodrama, well done. (Dir: Richard Wallace, 99 mins.)

Bombers B-52 (1957)** Natalie Wood, Karl Malden, Efrem Zimbalist, Jr. So-so romance and airplane drama. Malden plays Natalie's father who opposes her seeing Col. Zimbalist. After almost 2 hours running time, all, no one will be surprised to learn, ends well. (Dir: Gordon Douglas, 106 mins.)

Bombshell—See: **Blonde Bombshell**

Bon Voyage, Charlie Brown (And Don't Come Back!) (1980)***½ A new "Peanuts" animated feature from the studio of Lee Mendelson and Bill Melendez. The latter directed, as always, and of course Mr. Schulz does the inimitable writing. Droll fun for the kids. (70 mins.)

Bonjour Tristesse (1958)*** Deborah Kerr, David Niven, Jean Seberg, Mylene Demongeot. Director Otto Preminger transformed François Sagan's incisive novelette into a masterpiece of ambiguity, with a piercing, yet compassionate moral stance. Seberg, the young daughter of a Riviera sybarite (Niven, at his best), comes of age one summer while ridding her father's house of a threatening influence, the warm and mature Kerr. It's a film about shallow people that achieves a depth of feeling far beyond their narrow emotional ranges. Preminger's use of widescreen CinemaScope is nothing short of brilliant; this was the first film where I could see how much the shape of a frame can completely inform and alter the meanings of a movie. (94 mins.)

Bonnie and Clyde (1967)**** Warren Beatty, Faye Dunaway, Estelle Parsons, Gene Hackman, Michael J. Pollard. A seminal work for the art and the industry. It has dated only to the extent that its impact has been assimilated by later movies. Part myth, part farce, full of despair and existential dust, the film survives as another poem on mortality from director Arthur Penn. Another film version of the story of Bonnie Parker and Clyde Barrow, tough, psychotic young bank robbers who terrorized the Midwest in the early '30s. Beatty, who also produced, turns in his best movie performance. The film established Dunaway as a major screen personality, and Parsons won an Academy Award for her supporting role as Clyde's sister-in-law. (111 mins.)

Bonnie Parker Story (1958)** Dorothy Provine, Richard Bakalyan. Bloodspattered story of the infamous gal desperado of the public enemy era of the 1930s. Some fast action, otherwise second rate. (Dir: William Whitney, 80 mins.)

Bonzo Goes to College (1952)** Maureen O'Sullivan, Edmund Gwenn. Sequel to "Bedtime for Bonzo," the zany comedy that introduced the misadventures of the mischievous chimp known as Bonzo. This was Universal's attempt to repeat the box-office jingle set by the "Francis" films.

The human actors can't help but appear ridiculous. (Dir: Frederick de Cordova, 80 mins.)

Booby Trap (Great Britain, 1957)**½ Sydney Tafler, Patti Morgan. A fountain pen "bomb" is stolen, and passes from hand to hand. Wildly plotted comedy is fairly amusing fun. (Dir: Henry Cass, 71 mins.)

Boom! (U.S.-Great Britain, 1968)** Elizabeth Taylor, Richard Burton, Noel Coward. Considering all the major talents involved in this opulent opus based on Tennessee Williams's play "The Milk Train Doesn't Stop Here Anymore," it's a big disappointment. However, if you're in the mood for a "campy" exercise dominated by Miss Taylor's beauty, clothes, jewelry and overacting, you might enjoy this story about a coarse, dying millionairess who forms an unholy alliance with a stranger known as the "Angel of Death" (Burton). Miss Taylor is miscast—she's much too young and beautiful to be believable. (Dir: Joseph Losey, 113 mins.)

Boom Town (1940)*** Clark Gable, Spencer Tracy, Hedy Lamarr, Claudette Colbert. A good cast in a rousing tale about a pair of roughnecks who strike it rich in the oil fields. Entertaining and exciting although not a first rate film. (Dir: Jack Conway, 116 mins.)

Boomerang (1947)**** Dana Andrews, Jane Wyatt, Lee J. Cobb, Arthur Kennedy, Sam Levene. The third film directed by Elia Kazan, and one of producer Louis de Rochemont's cycle of quasi-documentaries for 20th Century-Fox in the '40s and '50s. An innocent man is arrested after the killing of a New England priest, and a district attorney works to keep him from being convicted. The plot resolution is unorthodox for the film's time. Exciting; based on a real case. (88 mins.)

Boots Malone (1952)*** William Holden, Johnny Stewart. Fast paced racetrack story with good performances. William Holden plays a somewhat shady character with a good heart. (Dir: William Dieterle, 103 mins.)

Border Incident (1949)**½ Ricardo Montalban, George Murphy, Howard da Silva. Interesting drama about "wetbacks" and murder. Montalban effectively plays an immigration agent who is used as a decoy to break up a large "slave trading" market. (Dir: Anthony Mann, 92 mins.)

Borderline (1950)** Fred MacMurray, Claire Trevor. A policewoman is sent to get the goods on dope smugglers working from Los Angeles to Mexico. Uncertain melodrama wavers between seriousness and farce, is successful at neither. (Dir: William A. Seiter, 88 mins.)

Bordertown (1935)**½ Paul Muni, Bette Davis, Eugene Pallette. Muni looks properly seedy as a degenerate lawyer who gets involved with more than he can handle when he tangles with the bored wife (Davis) of a local businessman (Pallette).

Though the film is turgid and generally undistinguished, there is a fair amount of mood and sexual tension, and the result is fairly engrossing. Muni shows what he could do with an underwritten part before he became Warners' resident esteemed personage. Photographer: Tony Gaudio. (Dir: Archie Mayo, 100 mins.)

Borgia Stick, The (1966)** Don Murray, Inger Stevens, Barry Nelson, Fritz Weaver. Far-fetched story of two pawns in a super-crime syndicate who try to break with the organization. First half is interesting, giving a unique interpretation of modern-day gangsterism; made for TV feature. (Dir: David Lowell Rich, 100 mins.)

Born Free (Great Britain, 1966)**** Bill Travers, Virginia McKenna. A treat for the whole family. Even if you don't particularly care for films about animals, you'll be won over by the touching tale of Elsa, the lion cub raised in captivity, who then must learn to fend for herself in the jungle wilds of Kenya. Bill Travers and Virginia McKenna play a game warden and his wife who supervise the retraining of Elsa when they find out she's too big to remain a pet and might be shipped to the confinement of a zoo. The scenes of Elsa's efforts to return to the jungle are memorable. (Dir: James Hill, 96 mins.)

Born Innocent (MTV 1974)**½ Linda Blair, Joanna Miles, Kim Hunter. Capitalizing on her notoriety from "The Exorcist," 15-year-old Linda Blair is cast as a runaway teenager facing the cruelties of a juvenile detention home. Though the subject matter may put many people off, the hardy should find merit in Joanna Miles' portrayal of the home's understanding teacher and Miss Blair's capable handling of the unfortunate youngster. Filmed on location in Albuquerque, New Mexico. A vivid rape sequence showing Blair being raped by a broomstick was inexplicably included for its first TV showing and has now been toned down for this re-edited version. (Dir: Donald Wrye, 100 mins.)

Born Losers (1967)*½ Elizabeth James, Jane Russell, Tom Laughlin. Laughlin *is* Billy Jack in this. (Dir: Tom Laughlin, 112 mins.)

Born Reckless (1959)*½ Mamie Van Doren, Jeff Richards. (Dir: Howard Koch, 79 mins.)

Born to Be Bad (1950)*** Joan Fontaine, Robert Ryan, Zachary Scott. Ruthless female hides behind an innocent exterior, but eventually reveals her true self. Fashionable romantic drama, good for the ladies. (Dir: Nicholas Ray, 94 mins.)

Born to Be Loved (1959)** Carol Morris, Hugo Haas. Leisurely, mild little drama finds elderly music teacher taking a plain-looking seamstress in hand and making her popular and wanted. We're happy Hugo was so kind to Carol in this particular situation, but the long range implications of this kind of thoughtfulness are worrisome—the decimation of the drab spinster population would put a further and perhaps intolerable strain on this nation's already overburdened maternity wards and public schools system. (Dir: Hugo Haas, 82 mins.)

Born to Dance (1936)** Eleanor Powell, James Stewart, Buddy Ebsen, Reginald Gardiner, Virginia Bruce. Powell (wind her up and she taps) dominates a musical that comes alive in its musical numbers but is otherwise lame. Cole Porter wrote the songs, including "I've Got You Under My Skin" and "Easy to Love." The plot is sailor-meets-girl. (Dir: Roy Del Ruth, 105 mins.)

Born to Kill (1947)*½ Claire Trevor, Walter Slezak, Lawrence Tierney. (Dir: Robert Wise, 92 mins.)

Born to Sing (1941)** Virginia Weidler, Leo Gorcey, Ray McDonald. Juvenile cast is surrounded by juvenile plot in this Grade B nonsense with music thrown in. Picture's one fine moment is a rendition of "Ballad for Americans." (Dir: Busby Berkeley, 82 mins.)

Born Yesterday (1950)**** Broderick Crawford, William Holden, Judy Holliday. Upwardly mobile gangster Crawford hires professor Holden to teach his mistress, Holliday, how to talk like a high-class dame. George Cukor directed a little impersonally, for him. The focus of Garson Kanin's script is on the tender soul that lies under Holliday's platinum exterior, but she's not much fun when she stops playing tough. Cukor had a second chance at the story when he directed "My Fair Lady." Holliday won an Oscar for her hilarious performance as Billie the dumb blonde to end all dumb blondes. (103 mins.)

Borrowers, The (MTV 1973)*** Eddie Albert, Tammy Grimes, Judith Anderson, Dennis Larson. A pleasant fable for young and old. A little boy who has come to convalesce at his great-aunt Sophie's house is overwhelmed with loneliness until he makes a marvelous discovery. Under the floorboards of the house, a fascinating family of tiny little people have made their home by borrowing bits and pieces of stray furnishings to make themselves comfortable and tiny amounts of food to keep themselves alive. (Dir: Walter C. Miller, 78 mins.)

Borsalino (France-Italy, 1970)*** Jean-Paul Belmondo, Alain Delon, Mirielle Darc. A French tribute to the gangster films of the Hollywood 1930's! But the setting has been shifted from Beverly Hills to Marseilles in the 30's. Belmondo and Delon, teamed together for the first time, play two small-time hoodlums on the make. The main virtue of the film is not the familiar story, but the costumes, settings and musical backdrop which really do capture the look and mood of the period. The obligatory cars are on display, as are some garish whores. Engaging if you don't take it too seriously. Based on the book "Bandits of Marseilles." (Dir: Jacques Deray, 126 mins.)

Boss, The (1956)*** John Payne, William Bishop, Doe Avedon. A power-hungry politician takes over a city in the U. S. with frightening results. He joins forces with the rackets and is responsible for the murder of 4 federal agents and innocent bystanders. John Payne gives one of the best performances of his career. (Dir: Byron Haskin, 89 mins.)

Boss's Son, The (1978)*** Asher Brauner, Henry G. Sanders, James Darren, Rita Moreno, Piper Laurie. Director Bobby Roth's autobiographical drama has an appealing directness. A somewhat pampered boy starts to work in his father's carpet-manufacturing business as a delivery trucker and learns some of the contradictions between privilege and labor, and between responsibility and fraternity. A small, very independent film, faltering on story points and hazy on its protagonist, yet dealing with recognizable human situations with compassion, and possessing a practical visual style that overcomes budget limitations. Sanders is superb, and Richie Havens is surprisingly effective. (102 mins.)

Boston Strangler, The (1968)**½ Tony Curtis, Henry Fonda. Despite its lapses, this is a reasonably absorbing screen treatment of Gerold Frank's best-selling account of the Boston murders of a group of women, allegedly committed by a schizophrenic plumber named Albert De Salvo. Tony Curtis is convincing as the deranged De Salvo and Henry Fonda, with mustache, adds to the credibility of director Richard Fleischer's direct, documentary-like approach. (120 mins.)

Botany Bay (1953)** Alan Ladd, James Mason, Patricia Medina. Unjustly convicted man suffers aboard a convict ship bound for Australia, under the wheel of a cruel captain. Fancy but undistinguished costume melodrama. Ladd and Mason in stereotyped roles. (Dir: John Farrow, 94 mins.)

Both Sides of the Law (Great Britain, 1953)*** Anne Crawford, Peggy Cummins. Details the work of a London policewoman who takes on a multitude of cases daily. Good episodic melodrama, holds the interest. (Dir: Muriel Box, 94 mins.)

Bottom of the Bottle (1956)**½ Van Johnson, Joseph Cotten, Ruth Roman, Jack Carson. Melodrama all the way—Van Johnson is an escaped convict. He invades his brother's (Joseph Cotten) comfortable world and asks for help. Old tensions arise while confused wife (Ruth Roman) looks on. A fairly exciting climax puts things in order. (Dir: Henry Hathaway, 88 mins.)

Bottoms Up (Great Britain, 1960)** Jimmy Edwards, Martita Hunt. Headmaster of a school for boys has his hands full when his charges try to take over the place. Some farcical fun here, but not as much as intended. (Dir: Mario Zampi, 89 mins.)

Boulevard Nights (1979)**½ Richard Yniguez, Danny de la Paz. An American subculture can be said to have dipped its toes into the mainstream when a wholly conventional narrative feature can be made about it. Despite some tangy ethnic detail, there isn't an unpredictable moment in this film. Desmond Nakano's screenplay is so workmanlike it's like reading a blueprint, while Michael Pressman directed with a good eye but no sense of pace. Not bad, but a graveyard of opportunities that never knocked. (102 mins.)

Bound for Glory (1976)**** David Carradine, Ronny Cox, Melinda Dillon. A generally excellent biography of Woody Guthrie, one of America's greatest folksingers. Woody's left-wing politics have been toned down somewhat in this, the first major screen story of how Woody left his dust-devastated Texas home in the 30's to find work, and discovered the oppression, suffering and strength of the working people of America during the Great Depression. Carradine gives a superb, intelligent performance as Guthrie, and the supporting cast is excellent. Photography by Haskell Wexler is outstanding and deservedly won an Academy Award. Screenplay by Robert Getchell based on Guthrie's autobiography. (Dir: Hal Ashby, 147 mins.)

Bounty Hunter, The (1954)** Randolph Scott, Dolores Dorn. For Randolph Scott fans—he's a bounty hunter this time, out to capture three criminals. (Dir: Andre de Toth, 79 mins.)

Bounty Killer, The (1965)*½ Dan Duryea, Rod Cameron, Audrey Dalton. (Dir. Spencer G. Bennet, 92 mins.)

Bounty Man, The (MTV 1972)** Clint Walker, Richard Basehart, Margot Kidder. Granite-like Clint Walker rides the vengeance trail once again in this western yarn. It's the same old story—a man sets out to find the varmint who caused his wife's death, and falls in love in the process. (Dir: John Llewelyn-Moxey, 72 mins.)

Bowery, The (1933)***½ George Raft, Wallace Beery, Jackie Cooper, Pert Kelton, Fay Wray. An excellent turn-of-the-century saloon drama, drawn from director Raoul Walsh's childhood memories, including Steve Brodie's (Raft's) historic leap from the Brooklyn Bridge. Walsh would later elaborate this into a masterpiece with "Gentleman Jim." (110 mins.)

Boxcar Bertha (1972)*** David Carradine, Barbara Hershey, Barry Primus. Often interesting drama, based on a book, "Sister of the Road." About a woman labor organizer in Arkansas during the violence-filled Depression era of the early '30's. Rabble-rousing union man (Carradine) fights the railroad establishment aided by the remarkable real-life character Boxcar Bertha (Hershey). Well directed by Martin Scorsese before his '73 hit "Mean Streets." (88 mins.)

Boy (Japan, 1969)*** Tetsuo Abe, Fumio Watanabe, Akiko Koyama. Director Nagisa Oshima got his inspiration for this story from a newspaper account of a family that staged auto accidents. Using their young boy as a decoy, the family then extorted money from the frightened drivers. The examination of a family engaged in this treacherous con game is graphic, probing and disturbing in its morbid fascination. (97 mins.)

Boy and His Dog, A (1975)** Don Johnson, Susanne Benton, Tiger, Jason Robards, Charles McGraw. Not Walt Disney, but a science fiction film based on Harlan Ellison's WW III novel. The survivors of a nuclear holocaust are divided into two camps—the roving bands of scavengers on the surface, and the passionately bourgeois citizens of "Topeka," an artificial community buried five miles underground. L. Q. Jones, the director, worked as an actor in several films directed by Sam Peckinpah, whose influence is obvious on several levels. But this film lacks Peckinpah's density. It seems too schematic and its satire too blunt. (87 mins.)

Boy and the Pirates, The (1960)** Charles Herbert, Susan Gordon, Murvyn Vye. Strictly for the young tots. A long dream sequence in which a boy imagines he's involved with pirates and buried treasure. (Dir: Bert Gordon, 82 mins.)

Boy Cried Murder, The (Great Britain-Germany-Yugoslavia, 1966)**½ Veronica Hurst, Phil Brown, Fraser MacIntosh. Boy with a vivid imagination witnesses a murder, but nobody will believe him. Remake of "The Window" still carries some effective suspense. (Dir: George Breakston, 86 mins.)

Boy, Did I Get a Wrong Number (1966)* Bob Hope, Elke Sommer, Phyllis Diller. (Dir: George Marshall, 99 mins.)

Boy Friend, The (Great Britain, 1971)*** Twiggy, Christopher Gable, Tommy Tune, Glenda Jackson (guest appearance as the star of the show). Producer-director-scenarist Ken Russell mounted the simple boy-meets-girl musical with enough production values and cinema clichés for a Cecil B. deMille epic. But somehow most of it works. Twiggy is the assistant stage manager who gets her big chance to go on when the prima donna fractures her ankle. Musical numbers are campy and wonderful, with Tune a dancing standout and Gable a perfect singing-and-dancing leading man. It's Busby Berkeley, gone mad. Julie Andrews starred in the '54 Sandy Wilson stage version. Twiggy gives it a jolly good try. (108 mins.)

Boy from Oklahoma, The (1954)*** Will Rogers, Jr., Nancy Olson. Will Rogers, Jr. has more acting ability than his famous father displayed in his early films. In this charming western comedy-drama, he is cast as a quiet, peace loving sheriff of a town called Bluerock, which is run by a group of desperadoes. (Dir: Michael Curtiz, 88 mins.)

Boy in the Plastic Bubble, The (MTV 1976)**½ John Travolta, Robert Reed, Diana Hyland. A fascinating, disturbing subject is given a sensitive airing in this provocative story about a boy, born with immunity deficiencies, who grows up in a special plastic-bound controlled environment. Popular TV teen idol John Travolta (Barbarino in "Welcome Back, Kotter") discards his wise-guy image and comes up with a believable portrait of a lad on the brink of manhood, who suddenly finds his germ-free plastic home a prison. The TV film is interesting throughout. The ending will draw a tear or two. Diana Hyland and Robert Reed, as the boy's parents, are good in smaller roles, and Glynnis O'Connor registers as the blossoming, slightly selfish teenager who lives next door. (Dir: Randal Kleiser, 106 mins.)

Boy Meets Girl (1938)*** Pat O'Brien, Marie Wilson, James Cagney. Slightly antiquated today but still a delightful spoof of the movie business. Forerunner of hundreds of imitations. (Dir: Lloyd Bacon, 90 mins.)

Boy Named Charlie Brown, A (1970)**½ The famous comic strip, "Peanuts," which has inspired endless TV specials, serves as the basis for this full-blown, animated theatrical feature. While charming in its own way, the film merely becomes a series of vignettes played with gusto by the familiar cast of characters, including the winsome Charlie Brown and the abrasive Lucy. Voices fit the drawings for the most part, but the Rod McKuen score doesn't. The film seemed too small for the big screen when it was theatrically released. Now, it's right where it belongs—on television. (Dir: Bill Melendez, 85 mins.)

Boy Next Door, The— (See; To Find a Man)

Boy on a Dolphin (1957)**½ Alan Ladd, Sophia Loren, Clifton Webb. The best things about this adventure film are visual—great on location photographic splendor of the blue Aegean, the Greek islands, the majestic city of Athens, plus the physical beauty of the amply endowed Sophia Loren. The plot about the discovery of a sunken work of art is on an elementary level and offers no surprises. (Dir: Jean Negulesco, 113 mins.)

Boy Ten Feet Tall, A (Great Britain, 1963)***½ Edward G. Robinson, Fergus McClelland, Constance Cummings, Harry H. Corbett. Nice family entertainment, thanks to the exotic locale and a good human interest story of a young lad (Fergus M.) trying to cross Africa alone to reach his aunt. Old pro Robinson is first rate and the youngster is charmingly played. (Dir: Alexander Mackendrick, 88 mins.)

Boy Who Caught a Crook, The (1961)*½ Wanda Hendrix, Roger Mobley, Don Beddoe. (Dir: Edward Cahn, 72 mins.)

Boy Who Drank Too Much, The (MTV 1980)**½ Scott Baio, Lance Kerwin, Ed Lauter, Mariclare Costello. Teen idol Baio is a high-school hockey star who turns to alcohol when things get too much for him. He lives with his drunken father, who really doesn't care about him, and it's up to his friend (Kerwin) to help him with his problem. Gets the message across (Dir: Jerrold Freedman, 100 mins.)

Boy Who Stole a Million (Great Britain, 1960)** Maurice Reyna. Virgilio Texera. Boy steals from a bank to help his father pay some bills, becomes object in a search by the police and the underworld. Good Spanish locations, rambling story that never quite makes its point. Mild drama. (Dir: Charles Crichton, 64 mins.)

Boy Who Talked To Badgers, The (MTV 1975)**½ Christian Juttner, Carl Betz, Salome Jens. Lovely Alberta, Canada, scenery is a help to this Disney adventure about a lost 6-year-old boy who survives out on the prairie thanks to a friendly badger. Scenes in which the animal provides food for the boy should please the youngsters. Betz portrays the boy's stiff, unyielding Dad. (Dir: Gary Nelson, 100 mins.)

Boy with Green Hair (1948)*** Pat O'Brien, Dean Stockwell. War orphan becomes an outcast when he finds his hair has suddenly turned green. Fanciful drama has a message, delivered not too well, but impressive nevertheless. (Dir: Joseph Losey, 82 mins.)

Boys, The (Great Britain, 1962)**½ Richard Todd, Robert Morley, Jess Conrad. Four teenagers go on trial for murder and robbery. Juvenile-delinquency courtroom drama adds little to the subject that is not familiar but is well enough done. Todd and Morley are good as the opposing counsels. (Dir: Sidney Furie, 82 mins.)

Boys from Brazil, The (1978)**½ Gregory Peck, Laurence Olivier, Uta Hagen, Rosemary Harris. Director Franklin Schaffner gives Ira Levin's gimmicky thriller the big treatment, so that its small virtues tend to get lost. Peck as Nazi war criminal Josef Mengele is ludicrously off his beat. Olivier is brilliant, doing a fussy Albert Basserman imitation as the hero modeled, loosely, on Nazi-hunter Simon Wiesenthal, with no palpable anger or implacability. The whole film bears attention, despite relentless pointlessness and rampant failures of judgment. (123 mins.)

Boys from Syracuse, The (1940)*** Joe Penner, Allan Jones, Martha Raye. Two sets of twins cause confusion and havoc in ancient Greece. Entertaining musical comedy based on the Broadway show. Fine Rodgers and Hart songs. (Dir: A. Edward Sutherland, 73 mins.)

Boys In Company C, The (1978)*½ Stan Shaw, Andrew Stevens, James Canning, Michael Lembeck. (Dir: Sidney J. Furie, 125 mins.)

Boys in the Band, The (1970)**** Cliff Gorman, Laurence Luckinbill, Kenneth Nelson, Leonard Frey. It doesn't sound like much to say that "Boys in the Band" is the most honest, revealing and poignant American film made about homosexuality up until 1970, but it is intended to be a genuine, admiring compliment. Mart Crowley has adapted his own acclaimed award-winning play, retaining much of the qualities of pathos, bitchiness, loneliness and jealousy that so enriched the play. Remarkably well acted, incidentally, by the leading players, some of whom are heterosexuals in real life. Under William Friedkin's generally sensitive guiding hand, "Boys" is often hilarious and builds to a powerful climax. The TV commercial networks have, in recent years, exploited the theme of homosexuality along with many other subjects, so see this moving film in its original version if you get a chance. (Dir: William Friedkin, 118 mins.)

Boys' Night Out (1962)*** Kim Novak, James Garner, Tony Randall, Howard Duff, Howard Morris. Entertaining comedy about a quartet of executives who want a little fun and scheme to lease an apartment for their shenanigans. Kim Novak, if you can imagine, is a college student doing research in s-e-x who is their prime target. Generally harmless, some good chuckles. (Dir: Michael Gordon, 115 mins.)

Boys of Paul Street, The (U. S.-Hungary, 1968)*** Anthony Kemp, William Burleigh. War's futility is examined in this story of boys squabbling over rights to a vacant lot. Points a moral, is well acted by the lads. (Dir: Zoltan Fabri, 108 mins.)

Boys' Ranch (1946)**½ Butch Jenkins, James Craig. Highly recommended for the youngsters is this cute story about delinquents who are given a chance to reform by working on a cattle ranch. (Dir: Roy Rowland, 97 mins.)

Boys' Town (1938)*** Spencer Tracy, Mickey Rooney. Punk Rooney and Spencer Tracy make this film good entertainment. Story of Father Flanagan's Boys' Town and how his motto, "There is no such thing as a bad boy," is almost destroyed by an incorrigible youngster is too sentimental but is still rewarding film fare. Tracy won an Oscar. (Dir: Norman Taurog, 90 mins.)

Brady Girls Get Married, The (MTV 1981) ** Robert Reed, Florence Henderson, Maureen McCormick, Eve Plumb, Jerry Houser, Ron Kuhlman. Everyone's grown up and two of the girls—Marcia and Jan —are actually getting married. The entire cast of the series is back for the nostalgic update. Strictly for "Brady Bunch" fans. (Dir: Peter Baldwin, 104 mins.)

Brain, The (Great Britain, 1964)**½ Anne Heywood, Peter Van Eyck, Cecil Parker, Bernard Lee. (Dir. Freddie Francis, 85 mins.)

Brain, The (France-Italy, 1969)* David Niven, Jean-Paul Belmondo, Bourvil, Eli Wallach. (Dir: Berard Oury.)

Brain Eaters, The (1958)** Edwin Nelson. Another thing from outer space terrorizes a town. Well, it's better than some of these sci-fi time-wasters. (Dir: Bruno VeSota, 60 mins.)

Brain from Planet Arous, The (1957)*½ John Agar, Joyce Meadows. (Dir: Nathan Juran, 71 mins.)

Brain That Wouldn't Die (1962)*½ Jason Evers, Virginia Leith. (Dir: Joseph Green, 81 mins.)

Brainiac, The (Mexico, 1963)* Abel Salazar, Carmen Montejo. (Dir: Chano Urueta, 77 mins.)

Brainsnatchers, The—See **Man Who Changed His Mind, The**

Brainstorm (1965)**½ Jeffrey Hunter, Anne Francis, Viveca Lindfors. Nicely played suspense yarn about a pair of lovers who work out a plan to get rid of the lady's husband. It's old hat, as far as plot goes, but a good cast breathes new life into it. (Dir: William Conrad, 114 mins.)

Brainwashed (Germany, 1961)** Curt Jurgens, Claire Bloom. A German aristocrat is imprisoned by the Nazis and struggles to keep his sanity in this English-dialogued drama. Good performances cannot overcome the static nature of the tale. (Dir: Gerd Oswald, 102 mins.)

Bramble Bush, The (1960)** Richard Burton, Barbara Rush, Jack Carson, Angie Dickinson. Small-town sinful dramatics reminiscent of "Peyton Place" as a doctor returns home to find all sorts of physical, mental, and moral complications. It's all quite distasteful, but soap opera fans will probably sit enthralled. (Dir: Daniel Petrie, 105 mins.)

Brand New Life, A (1973)***½ Cloris Leachman, Martin Balsam. Among the best made-for-TV films. Honest, touching, thoroughly human story about a couple, married for 18 years (she's going to be 41 and he'll be 46), who discover they are about to become parents for the first time. The drama examines various reactions to the situation, especially in two candidly outspoken scenes—one with star Cloris Leachman and her worldly friend, beautifully played by Marge Redmond, and another with Miss Leachman and her brutally honest mother (Mildren Dunnock). Cloris Leachman has never been better, and her performance earned her an Emmy. (Dir: Sam O. Steen, 74 mins.)

Branded (1950)**½ Alan Ladd, Mona Freeman, Charles Bickford. Crooks pick a wanderer to pose as heir to a wealthy rancher. Leisurely western needs more pace, but has a story that holds the interest. (Dir: Rudolph Mate, 104 mins.)

Brandy for the Parson (Great Britain, 1952)***½ James Donald, Jean Lodge, Kenneth More. Young couple on a boating trip become involved with some whiskey smuggling. Refreshing comedy, good fun. (Dir: John Eldridge, 78 mins.)

Brannigan (Great Britain, 1975)**½ John Wayne, Richard Attenborough. John Wayne in London town! He's an Irish cop from Chicago who journeys to London to bring back a criminal who has fled there.

81

Wayne's American tactics clash with Scotland Yard's Richard Attenborough and the two actors work well together in counterpoint. Action includes the old Wayne staples, a barroom brawl and plenty of fisticuffs. (Dir: Douglas Hickox, 111 mins.)

Brasher Doubloon, The (1947)** George Montgomery, Nancy Guild, Florence Bates, Conrad Janis, Fritz Kortner. "The High Window" was one of Raymond Chandler's most satisfying novels, so it is disappointing that it was adapted into the weakest film of any of his books. Montgomery is callow enough for Philip Marlowe, but lacks the reserves Dick Powell could muster when needed. The budget limits the film to a fuzzily detailed realm, and John Brahm, a director who could bring some of these films off with style ("The Lodger," "Hangover Square") fails to ignite the material. (72 mins.)

Brass Bottle, The (1964)** Tony Randall, Burl Ives, Barbara Eden. Oops! The one about the inferior man who finds an old lamp with a genie in it. Although Barbara Eden of "I Dream of Jeannie" is in the cast, it's Burl Ives who plays the helpful spirit. Familiar stuff by now, and pretty mild at that. (Dir: Harvey Keller, 89 mins.)

Brass Legend, The (1956)** Hugh O'Brian, Raymond Burr, Nancy Gates. Sheriff Hugh O'Brian tracks down and shoots it out with desperado Raymond Burr. Involved western drama. (Dir: Gerd Oswald, 79 mins.)

Brass Target (1978)*½ Sophia Loren, John Cassavetes, George Kennedy, Max von Sydow, Robert Vaughn, Edward Herrmann, Patrick McGoohan. (Dir: John Hough, 111 mins.)

Bravados, The (1958)** Gregory Peck, Joan Collins, Stephen Boyd. Rambling western about a man bent on revenge for his wife's murder. More than half of the film is dedicated to the tracking down of the quartet of despicable murderers and it becomes tedious. Peck is as stoic as ever and Joan Collins is beautiful but rides a horse badly. (Dir: Henry King, 98 mins.)

Brave Bulls, The (1951)**** Mel Ferrer, Anthony Quinn, Miroslava. Superb screenplay about the life, both private and public, of a famed matador. Probing photography makes it a penetrating study. Performances are top caliber, except for Mel Ferrer—even Ferrer is not as dull as usual. (Dir: Robert Rossen, 108 mins.)

Brave Don't Cry, The (Great Britain, 1952)*** John Gregson, Meg Buchanan. Sober, attention-holding story of a mine cave-in, the rescue attempts. Done almost documentary-style; good acting. (Dir: Philip Leacock, 93 mins.)

Brave New World (MTV 1980)** Julie Cobb, Bud Cort, Keir Dullea, Ron O'Neal. Aldous Huxley's influential and controversial British novel about a controlled society 600 years from now receives a three-hour production. We urge you to read Huxley's book and decide for yourself if this "Star Trek campy" TV version has any of the impact of the original story. (Dir: Burt Brinckerhoff, 152 mins.)

Brave One! The (1956)*** Michel Ray, Rodolfo Hoyos. Young boy is attached to his pet bull, runs away to Mexico City to find the beast when he's sold. Charming drama won an Oscar for original story—and original it is. Good entertainment. Written by Dalton Trumbo. (Dir: Irving Rapper, 100 mins.)

Brave Warrior (1952)** Jon Hall, Michael Ansara. History gets in the way of the action in this western set in the time of the War of 1812. (Dir: Spencer Bennet, 73 mins.)

Bravos, The (MTV 1971)* George Peppard, Peter Duel, Pernell Roberts. (Dir: Ted Post, 100 mins.)

Bread and Chocolate (Italy, 1974)**** Nino Manfredi, Anna Karina. A deliciously witty, insightful, and deeply compassionate comedy about the frustrations of Everyman trying to better his lot in life—in this case an uneducated workingman from Naples who arrives in condescending Switzerland and becomes simultaneously a waiter, a resident alien, an illegal immigrant, and an inspired comic hero. Manfredi is wonderful in the leading role. Deftly directed by Franco Brusati, who also wrote the screenplay with Manfredi and Iaia Fiastri. (86 mins.)

Bread, Love and Dreams (Italy, 1954)*** Vittorio De Sica, Gina Lollobrigida. English dubbing detracts a bit from this amusing comedy about a small town law officer and his troubles with a spirited girl, but the fun still maintains a pretty high level. (Dir: Luigi Comencini, 90 mins.)

Bread Peddler, The (France-Italy, 1962)** Suzanne Flon, Philippe Noiret. Woman escapes prison, finds a job as bread deliverer, eventually proves her innocence. Long-drawn-out drama has some occasionally stirring moments. Dubbed in English. (Dir: Maurice Cloche, 122 mins.)

Break in the Circle (Great Britain, 1957)*½ Forrest Tucker, Eva Bartok. (Dir: Val Guest, 69 mins.)

Break of Hearts (1935)*** Katharine Hepburn, Charles Boyer. Female musician falls in love with an orchestra leader. Good romantic drama. (Dir: Philip Moeller, 80 mins.)

Break to Freedom (1955)*** Anthony Steel, Jack Warner. British prisoners in a German camp construct a life-size dummy to cover an escape. Intriguing war drama, good suspense. (Dir: Lewis Gilbert, 88 mins.)

Breakaway (Great Britain, 1956)** Tom Conway, Honor Blackman. An average mystery dealing with racketeer's attempt to obtain a secret formula used to eliminate fatigue in jet flying. (Dir: Henry Cass, 72 mins.)

Breakdown (Great Britain, 1953)*½ Michael Conrad, Lila Graham. (64 mins.)

Breaker Morant (Australia, 1979)*** Edward Woodward, Jack Thompson, John Waters, Charles Tingwell. This true tale of military injustice (three officers of colonial forces fighting the Boer in South Africa were railroaded as scapegoats for the larger imperial purpose) raises discomfiting parallels to My Lai in heroic context. Director-co-writer Bruce Beresford's crisp handling rehabilitates the movie's theatrical origins, but fails to achieve the pungent anger of "Paths of Glory" or the complex inquiry of the best military justice film of all, John Ford's "Sergeant Rutledge." Woodward does a good textbook acting job as the bluff defense counsel. Passable entertainment with no food for thought. (107 mins.)

Breakfast at Tiffany's (1961)***½ Audrey Hepburn, George Peppard, Patricia Neal, Buddy Ebsen, Martin Balsam. Truman Capote's wispily wistful story of a young writer who becomes involved with a madcap New York playgirl. All-out attempt at wacky sophistication should please the cosmopolite, but others may wonder if they didn't go too far over the edge. Nevertheless some fine performances, with the exception of a badly miscast Mickey Rooney, and some hilarious sequences. (Dir: Blake Edwards, 114 mins.)

Breakfast in Bed (Germany, 1963)** Lilo Pulver, O. W. Fischer, Lex Barker. Busy editor neglects his wife, who takes a handsome yoga teacher in retaliation. Then he makes passes at an attractive authoress, and it's off to the divorce court. English-dubbed comedy is reminiscent of the U. S. farces of the 1930s, without their charm. (Dir: Axel von Ambesser, 90 mins.)

Breakheart Pass (1976)*** Charles Bronson, Richard Crenna. A nice, action-packed (but not violent) Charles Bronson film for all ages. It involves a train crossing the Rockies in the 1870's, carrying territorial Governor Fairchild (Richard Crenna), Marshal Nathan Pearce (Ben Johnson), his mysterious prisoner John Deakin (Charles Bronson), Major Claremont (Ed Lauter), and a beautiful lady, Marcia Scoville (Jill Ireland). The train is bringing relief from a diphtheria epidemic when some unnatural deaths occur. There are some real surprises, and the acting keeps you guessing. Like train wrecks? There's a good one here. Screenplay by Alistair MacLean from his own novel. And Miss Ireland and Mr. Bronson get together at the end! (Dir: Tom Gries, 95 mins.)

Breaking Away (1979)**** Dennis Christopher, Dennis Quaid, Barbara Barrie, Paul Dooley. A breath of refreshing cinematic fresh air about four Indiana working-class teenagers looking for a sense of direction after graduating from high school. Shot entirely in Bloomington, Indiana, this charming, tender film follows Dave Stoller's (Christopher's) dogged efforts to become a champion Italian bike racer, which include talking and acting like an Italian, which rouses understandable concern from his parents (perfectly played by Dooley and Barrie). The foursome are much aware of the influence and snobbery of the Indiana college students, a feeling that culminates in the bike-race finale. The engaging yarn benefits from the believable characters in Steven Tesich's Academy Awardwinning screenplay. Director Peter Yates has a sure hand here. (99 mins.)

Breaking Glass (1980)** Hazel O'Connor, Phil Daniels, Jon Finch, Jonathan Pryce. There's probably some underlying hypocrisy in a film that espouses a punk anti-commercialism philosophy and conveys its message with the glitzy manipulative techniques of ultracommercial cinema. Hazel O'Connor plays an idealistic new wave singer-composer who hooks up with a manager and forms a group that starts moving to the top. But the nasty record industry corrupts O'Connor and the characters are polarized into the self-righteous wounded and the callous climbers. Overwrought. (Dir. Brian Gibson, 94 mins.)

Breaking Point, The (1950)***½ John Garfield, Patricia Neal, Phyllis Thaxter, Juano Hernandez, Wallace Ford. The first attempt to do a straight version of Hemingway's potboiler "To Have and Have Not." (Howard Hawks's version had no relation to the original, while John Huston stole the ending for his "Key Largo.") Almost totally neglected by film historians, this may be the best Hemingway adaptation ever filmed. Garfield arguably gives his most rounded performance as the charter boat owner who gets involved with criminals, and director Michael Curtiz never elicited more thematic values than he did in this story of loyalty, moral commitment, and adventure. The sexual triangle of Garfield, Neal, and Thaxter is handled with intelligent sensuality, while Hernandez makes a full-blooded character of what might have been a stereotype. Adapted by Ranald MacDougall. Remade in '58 as "The Gun Runners." (97 mins.)

Breaking the Sound Barrier (Great Britain, 1952)**** Ralph Richardson, Ann Todd, Nigel Patrick. An aircraft manufacturer endures personal grief in his quest to produce a plane that can travel faster than the speed of sound. Truly marvelous aerial drama with a stirring story, superb performances, breathtaking photography. (Dir: David Lean, 115 mins.)

Breaking Up (MTV 1978)**½ Lee Remick, Granville Van Dusen. As the song tells us, "breaking up is hard to do." In this drama about contemporary divorce, "breaking up" is almost impossible. The husband (Van Dusen) turns to his wife (Remick) during a quiet moment on a family outing and tells her he wants to leave home. The rest of the movie is a parade of arguments, legal negotiations, strained visiting days with the kids, unsuccessful job interviews, clumsy passes by old friends, and a general state of controlled hysteria. The script tries too hard to cover all the bases, resulting in a fragmented drama. After a tentative start Remick does quite well as a woman set adrift after having invested 16 years in what she thought was a successful marriage. (Dir: Delbert Mann, 104 mins.)

Breaking Up Is Hard to Do (MTV 1979)*** Ted Bessell, Jeff Conaway, Billy Crystal, Robert Conrad, Tony Musante. Here's a probing, honest, and often engrossing look at six male friends, all involved in show biz in one way or another, who share a beach house one summer—the summer of their discontent. The guys have various opinions and sensitivities about love, sex, marriage, divorce, and the meaning of macho. (Dir: Lou Antonio, 198 mins.)

Breakout (Great Britain, 1959)**½ Richard Todd, Richard Attenborough. British soldiers about to break out of an Italian POW camp realize there's a traitor among them. Well done war thriller, in a familiar sort of way. Alternate title: **Danger Within.** (Dir: Don Chaffey, 99 mins.)

Breakout (Great Britain, 1959)** Lee Patterson, Billie Whitelaw, Hazel Court. Unassuming office worker is contacted by a gang to devise a daring escape from prison. Standard crime melodrama. (Dir: Peter Graham Scott, 62 mins.)

Breakout (MTV 1971)** James Drury, Kathryn Hays. Prison drama takes a different twist as bank robber James Drury becomes thwarted in various escape plans. Wooden dialogue and character follow predictable turns with comic support from Red Buttons as Pipes, the pickpocket con. But the show, at least, breaks out of Folsom prison, with much of the action taking place in the High Sierras near Reno. Woody Strode, Red Buttons, and Sean Garrison add little to cliché material. (Dir: Richard Irving, (100 mins.)

Breakout (1975)* Charles Bronson, Robert Duvall, Jill Ireland, John Huston. (Dir: Tom Gries, 96 mins.)

Breakthrough (1950)** David Brian, Frank Lovejoy, John Agar. Run of the mill glory-drenched war story with time out for occasional romance. Competent performances. (Dir: Lewis Seller, 91 mins.)

Breath of Scandal, A (1959)** Sophia Loren, Maurice Chevalier, John Gavin. Young American in Vienna rescues a princess, falls for her, is hampered by court protocol. Stale romance despite pretty costumes, production. Loren and Chevalier the sole assets otherwise. (Dir: Michael Curtiz, 98 mins.)

Breathless (1960)**** Jean-Paul Belmondo, Jean Seberg. There is no better place to start with the films directed by Jean-Luc Godard than this, his first full-length feature and one of the genuinely seminal films, not only of the French New Wave, but of the modern cinema. Godard's derisive, quixotic, calculatedly jumbled style of recounting the tale of a small-time gangster (Belmondo, in his first screen

role) and his ambiguous girlfriend (Seberg) introduced the notion that film is a composite language. Thus, in a confused world, Godard employed a variety of styles, from melodramatic to comic, from tragic to farcical, with a multitude of quotes from American films. B&W. (89 mins.)

Breezy (1973)** William Holden, Kay Lenz, Roger C. Carmel, Marj Dusay, Sudsy, romantic film about a weary, middle-aged man (Holden) who regains his lust for life through an affair with a "flower child" (Lenz). The scene is sun-drenched California; the obligatory cute dog completes the menage a trois; the villains are the ex-wife and other nasty adults. Of interest only to romanticists and film freaks following Clint Eastwood's dreary directorial career. (Dir: Clint Eastwood, 108 mins.)

Brenda Starr (MTV 1976)*½ Jill St. John, Jed Allan, Victor Buono. (Dir: Mel Stuart, 72 mins.)

Brennus, Enemy of Rome (Italy 1964)* Gordon Mitchell, Tony Kendall. (Dir: Giacomo Gentilomo, 90 mins.)

Brewster McCloud (1970)*** Bud Cort, Sally Kellerman, Shelley Duvall, Stacy Keach, Michael Murphy, Jennifer Salt. The running pictorial image in Brewster is bird crap, and the "hero" of this slapstick is a retarded young gent who thinks he can fly. Obviously not for every genteel taste, but there are some funny, gross, inventive scenes and Cort (remember him from "Harold and Maude"?) is appropriately spacey. We all get our rocks off in various and surprising ways, Altman tells us, and pretty Jennifer Salt, e.g., has an orgasmic response to just watching our crazed hero do pushups. Written by Doran William Cannon. (Dir: Robert Altman, 104 mins.)

Brewster's Millions (1945)**½ Dennis O'Keefe, June Havoc. Young man inherits a million dollars, but has to spend it in two months in order to claim an even larger fortune. Amusing comedy. (Dir: Allan Dwan, 79 mins.)

Brian's Song (MTV 1971)**** James Caan, Billy Dee Williams. Beautifully adapted true story about Brian Piccolo, the Chicago Bears football player who shared a unique friendship with teammate Gale Sayers before cancer claimed Piccolo's life at the age of 26. For a tale dealing with death, this film is bursting with life, particularly in the impeccable, perfectly matched performances of Caan, as the warm and witty Piccolo, and Williams, as the more serious Sayers. William Blinn's thoughtful screenplay is at its best in presenting the growing friendship between the first black-and-white roommates on the Chicago team. You may choke up in the final scenes. (Dir: Buzz Kulik 71 mins.)

Bribe, The (1949)** Robert Taylor, Ava Gardner, Charles Laughton, Vincent Price. Corny, cheap melodrama about the government agent chasing crooks in the Caribbean who falls in love with the seductive wife of one of the bad men. Dir: Robert Z. Leonard, 98 mins.)

Bridal Path, The (Great Britain, 1959)**½
Bill Travers, Bernadette O'Farrell, George
Cole. Young and innocent Scotsman goes
on the hunt for a suitable wife in a leisurely but amusing comedy, full of local
atmosphere. (Dir: Frank Launder, 95 mins.)

Bride and the Beast, The (1958)* Charlotte
Austin, Lance Fuller. (Dir: Adrian Weiss,
78 mins.)

Bride by Mistake (1944)**½ Laraine Day,
Alan Marshal. Millionaire's daughter falls
for a dashing Air Force pilot. Amusing
comedy. (Dir: Richard Wallace, 81 mins.)

Bride Came C.O.D., The (1941)*** James
Cagney, Bette Davis. Cagney and Davis
dig all the laughs possible out of the script
and succeed in making it funny. Plot is
all in the title with Cagney as the flying
delivery boy and Bette as the bride. Jimmy is better than his co-star but it was
Miss Davis' first attempt at comedy, a
field where she later proved her skill.
(Dir: William Keighley, 92 mins.)

Bride Comes Home, The (1935)**½
Claudette Colbert, Fred MacMurray,
Robert Young. Routine romantic triangle
comedy, well played by its stars. (Dir:
Wesley Ruggles. 85 mins.)

Bride for Frank, A (Italy 1956)** Walter
Chiari, Gino Cervi. Rich man returns from
America and proceeds to try to marry his
son off to a local belle. Fair comedy,
English-dubbed. (Dir: Leonardo De Mitri,
90 mins.)

Bride for Sale (1949)**½ Claudette Colbert,
Robert Young, George Brent. Head of an
accounting firm finds his ace female tax
expert is marriage-minded, so he persuades his handsome friend to go to work
on her. Romantic comedy acted by old
masters, even if the material is thin. (Dir:
William D. Russell, 87 mins.)

Bride Goes Wild, The (1948)**½ Van
Johnson, June Allyson, Hume Cronyn.
Van, who hates kids, has to get Butch
Jenkins to pose as his son and the result
is an occasionally amusing farce. (Dir:
Norman Taurog, 98 mins.)

Bride Is Much Too Beautiful, The (France,
1957)** Brigitte Bardot, Louis Jourdan,
Micheline, Presle. Cover girl (Brigitte, who
else?) is publicized into a fake romance,
but she really loves a photographer. Mild
for Bardot—or anyone else. (Dir: Fred
Surin, 90 mins.)

Bride of Frankenstein, The (1935)***½
Boris Karloff, Elsa Lanchester, Colin
Clive, Ernest Thesiger, Dwight Frye, Valerie Hobson. Director James Whale's
quirky, ironic self-parody is, by common
consent, superior to his earlier "Frankenstein". He added an element of playful
sexuality in this version, and used a bizarre visual framework that makes the
film a good deal more surreal than the
earlier work. Lanchester is the reluctant
bride; Karloff returns as the love-starved
monster. Weird and funny. (80 mins.)

Bride Wore Black, The (France, 1967)***½

Jeanne Moreau, Jean-Claude Brialy,
Charles Denner. An entertaining murder
melodrama, dedicated to Alfred Hitchcock,
whom director François Truffaut so
enormously admires and about whom he
has written so knowledgeably. Moreau is
out to revenge the death of her bridegroom. Jean-Luc Godard used the same
story for "Made in U.S.A.," which made
Truffaut want to do it all the more.
Screenplay by Truffaut and Jean Louis
Richard based on a 1940 novel by William
Irish (Cornell Woolrich). (107 mins.)

Bride Wore Red, The (1937)** Joan
Crawford, Franchot Tone, Robert Young,
Billie Burke, Reginald Owen. Director
Dorothy Arzner wrings some feminist issues out of this otherwise tired MGM
soap opera. A peasant girl who seeks a
chance to marry rich and aristocratic. It
isn't a good film, but the unusual
undertext makes it interesting watching.
A Ferencz Molnár play lies somewhere
beneath the script; you wouldn't know it
from Arzner's sober seriousness. (103 mins.)

Brides of Dracula, The (Great Britain,
1960)**½ Peter Cushing, David Peel,
Martita Hunt, Freda Jackson. A vampire
with an unusual ally seeks victims in
19th-century England. An above-average
Hammer horror flick; atmospheric and entertaining. (Dir: Terence Fisher, 85 mins.)

Brides of Fu Manchu, The (Great Britain,
1966)* Christopher Lee, Douglas Wilmer,
Marie Versini. (Dir: Don Sharp, 94 mins.)

Bridge, The (West Germany, 1959)****
Fritz Wepper, Volker Bohnet. One of the
most powerful antiwar films ever made.
Taut direction by Swiss director Bernhard
Wicki. Based on a true story about a
group of German youths killed two days
before the end of WW II in Europe, in a
hopeless attempt to stall the Allied advance before the Nazi regime surrendered.
One of the few notable features to emerge
from the moribund German cinema of the
'50s. Subtitles. (100 mins.)

Bridge at Remagen, The (1969)**½ George
Segal, Robert Vaughn, Ben Gazzara,
Bradford Dillman, E. G. Marshall. Based
on fact, an account of the efforts by Allied
soldiers to commandeer an important tac-
tical bridge from German hands before
it's destroyed. Familiar war plot; excellent camera work in the action scenes.
(Dir: John Guillermin, 116 mins.)

Bridge of San Luis Rey, The (1944)** Lynn
Bari, Nazimova, Louis Calhern, Francis
Lederer. Rowland V. Lee, who specialized
early in Fu Manchu programmers, and
later in assorted swashbucklers ("The
Count of Monte Cristo," "Captain Kidd")
directed this slow-moving rendition of
Thornton Wilder's tale of five travelers
who meet their deaths when a Peruvian
bridge collapses. (85 mins.)

Bridge on the River Kwai, The (Great Britain, 1957)**** William Holden, Alec
Guinness, Jack Hawkins, Sessue Hayakawa. Mammoth, magnificent war dra-

ma directed by David Lean, a superb motion picture; about a hardened, resolute British officer, captive of the Japanese, who drives his men to build a bridge as therapy, and the attempt of an escaped prisoner to demolish it. Performances, production, script, all deserve the highest praise.. Not to be missed. (Dir: David Lean, 161 mins.)

Bridge Too Far, A (1977)**½ Robert Redford, Ryan O'Neal, Gene Hackman, Laurence Olivier, Sean Connery, Liv Ullmann, James Caan, Dirk Bogarde, Anthony Hopkins. "A Bridge Too Far" is a movie much, much too long. This almost three-hour mammoth production, costing $25 million, re-creates the disastrous Allied parachute push into the Netherlands in September '44. Based on the exhaustive book by Cornelius Ryan, this epic becomes exhausting. You feel as if you've seen all those battle scenes before. A tragic, costly battle becomes the backdrop for a series of cameo-star turns. Hopkins is particularly good as the British officer assigned to capture a critical bridge at Arnhem. (Dir: Richard Attenborough, 175 mins.)

Bridge to the Sun (1961)***½ Carroll Baker, James Shigeta. Based on Gwen Terasaki's autobiography, this compelling drama relates the difficulties of a young woman married to a Japanese diplomat during World War II, victim of suspicion and animosity from her husband's government. Capable performances add to the interest, as do the actual location sequences. (Dir: Etienne Perier, 113 mins.)

Bridger (MTV 1976)*½ James Wainwright, Sally Field, Ben Murphy. (Dir: David Lowell Rich, 104 mins.)

Bridges at Toko-Ri, The (1954)***½ William Holden, Grace Kelly, Fredric March, Mickey Rooney. Jet pilot takes off on a dangerous mission during the Korean conflict, while his wife waits patiently for his return. Based on James Michener's book, filmed professionally, powerfully, with fine performances. Superior of its kind. (Dir: Mark Robson, 110 mins.)

Brief Encounter (Great Britain, 1946)**** Celia Johnson, Trevor Howard, Cyril Raymond, Stanley Holloway. A mature married woman suddenly begins an affair with a chance acquaintance, unknown to her husband. Sensitively directed, finely acted. The love scenes between Johnson and Howard are among the most touching ever filmed. This is the film that established director David Lean's reputation. Though based on a short play (and screenplay) by Noël Coward that rarely rises above the level of '40s women's magazines, this tale does zero in on some of the more depressing aspects of English middle-class life, and thus survives more as a social document than as a compelling drama. (85 mins.)

Brief Vacation, A (Italy-Spain 1974)**** Florinda Bolkan. This posthumously released film by Vittorio de Sica (*Bicycle Thieves, Umberto D, Two Women*) stars the exquisite Florinda Bolkan as a tubercular Cinderella transported by the Italian government from her factory job to a luxurious mountain resort, where contact with a wide range of women causes her to blossom into a new self-awareness. Part fable, part neo-realist object-lesson, the film is quintessential de Sica. (Dir: Vittorio de Sica, 106 mins.)

Brigadoon (1954)*** Gene Kelly, Cyd Charisse, Van Johnson. This is not my favorite MGM musical, despite the stars, the artwork of Cedric Gibbons and Preston Ames, the fine Lerner-Loewe score, and the directorial presence of Vincente Minnelli. The film—about two Americans on holiday in Scotland who discover a magical village on the one day each century that it comes to life—is heavy when it should be whimsical, flat when it should be colorful, and curiously uninspired given the delightful premise. Fun, but not thrilling. (108 mins.)

Brigand, The (1952)**½ Anthony Dexter, Jody Lawrance, Anthony Quinn. Anthony Dexter plays a dual role in this predictable adventure film about intrigue in the Spanish royal court. Anthony Quinn's talents are completely wasted. (Dir: Phil Karlson, 94 mins.)

Brigand of Kandahar, The (Great Britain, 1965)*½ Ronald Lewis, Oliver Reed, Yvonne Romain. (Director: John Gilling, 81 mins.)

Brigham Young, Frontiersman (1940)*½ Tyrone Power, Dean Jagger, Mary Astor, Linda Darnell. (Dir: Henry Hathaway, 114 mins.)

Bright Leaf (1950)**½ Gary Cooper, Lauren Bacall, Patricia Neal. A fine cast tells the story of one man's rise to wealth in the early days of tobacco growing. Well acted but a bit overlong. (Dir: Michael Curtiz, 110 mins.)

Bright Road (1953)** Dorothy Dandridge, Robert Horton, Harry Belafonte. New fourth-grade teacher takes an interest in a lad who is antagonistic. Story of a Negro boy and his teacher has sincerity but lacks that necessary spark. (Dir: Gerald Mayer, 68 mins.)

Bright Victory (1951)***½ Arthur Kennedy, Peggy Dow. Touching film about the crisis-laden rehabilitation of a WW II soldier who is blinded in battle. Arthur Kennedy gives one of the best performances of his career as the victim and Peggy Dow is perfect as the understanding girl who finally gives him the courage he needs to go on. Excellent direction. (Dir: Mark Robson, 97 mins.)

Brighthaven Express (Great Britain, 1952) *½ John Bentley, Carol Marsh. (Dir: Maclean Rogers, 75 mins.)

Brighton Rock—See: Young Scarface

Brighton Strangler, The (1945)**½ John Loder, June Duprez. Unusually good B picture about an actor who plays a murderer, and ends up taking his part too seriously. Interesting locale at the misty English seaside. (Dir: Max Nosseck, 67 mins.)

Brighty of the Grand Canyon (1967)** Joseph Cotten, Dick Foran. Brighty is a mule who befriends an old prospector (Foran) who has discovered a mother lode of gold. The Grand Canyon steals the film from the mule. (Director: Norman Foster, 89 mins.)

Brimstone (1949)*** Rod Cameron, Adrian Booth, Walter Brennan. Undercover marshal tangles with a cattleman who has turned outlaw with his sons. Good performances and some rugged action lift this western above the usual run. (Dir: Joseph Kane, 90 mins.)

Bring Me the Head of Alfredo Garcia (1974)**½ Warren Oates, Gig Young, Kris Kristofferson, Isela Vega. Eerie dovetailing of obsession from director Sam Peckinpah. A film in some ways ludicrously flawed and yet with oddments of genius. Oates is excellent as a seedy piano player who comes into possession of the head in question, for which a Mexican landowner has set a fabulous price. The concepts of honor and revenge have never been dramatized with more brutal grimness, and the harsh absurdism of Oates in his rundown car with a bag that draws flies disturbs in original ways. Incoherent at its climax, the film is one of the more maddening works of this major artist, here teetering just before his decline. (112 mins.)

Bring Me the Vampire (Mexico, 1960)* Charles Riquelme, Mary Eugenia St. Martin. (Dir: Alfredo B. Crevenna, 80 mins.)

Bring Your Smile Along (1955)**½ Keefe Brasselle, Frankie Laine, Constance Towers. Frankie Laine fans will enjoy this musical romance in which he sings many songs. The lightweight story is about a female high school teacher who writes lyrics for her composer boy friend's music. (Dir: Blake Edwards, 83 mins.)

Bringing Up Baby (1938)**** Katharine Hepburn, Cary Grant, Barry Fitzgerald, Charlie Ruggles, May Robson. This Howard Hawks-directed classic is perhaps the screwiest of the '30s screwball comedies. Features Grant as an absent-minded paleontologist beleaguered by a persistently kooky Hepburn (and her pet leopard, Baby). The film integrates visual style and viewpoint in the context of its own narrative logic. It's also a scream. (102 mins.)

Brink's Job, The (1978)*** Peter Falk, Peter Boyle, Allen Goorwitz, Warren Oates. Director William Friedkin mixes his customary harsh location grittiness with loutish humor in this re-creation of the famous '50 Boston heist, but his scorn for narrative clarity unravels the film in its second half. The story isn't helped by the circumstances of the actual robbery: they just walked in and took the money. Good, idiosyncratic acting. Oates excels as the

quirky, paranoid weak link. Superb photography by Norman Leigh and excellent production design. (118 mins.)

Brink's: The Great Robbery (MTV 1976)** Darren McGavin, Cliff Gorman, Jenny O'Hara, Leslie Nielsen, Carl Betz. Lengthy recreation of the famous 1950 Boston robbery which took years to solve. First half-hour centers on Boston's small-time crooks wrangling over the best approach to the job, while the remainder deals with the FBI's patient efforts to make some member of the gang sing. The drama of law versus crooks feuding among themselves sounds more exciting than it really is. Darren McGavin's lock expert and his girl Maggie (O'Hara) dominate. (Dir: Marvin Chomsky, 102 mins.)

Broadway (1942)*** George Raft, Janet Blair, Broderick Crawford. George Raft plays himself in this entertaining period piece of the speakeasy era, gangsters, and bootleggers. A highlight of the film is Raft's dancing. (Dir: William Seiter, 91 mins.)

Broadway Bad (1933)**½ Joan Blondell, Ricardo Cortez, Ginger Rogers. Blondell effective as a chorus girl who, when slandered by her husband, uses the publicity to get ahead. Stylish melodrama. (Dir: Sidney Lanfield, 61 mins.)

Broadway Bill (1934)*** Warner Baxter, Walter Connolly, Myrna Loy, Helen Vinson, Lynne Overman. Runyonesque racetrack comedy, breezily directed by Frank Capra in his positive, wisecracking, all-American style. Good performances; young Myrna is lovely. Story by Mark Hellinger. A remake, also directed by Capra, was called "Riding High." (103 mins.)

Broadway Melody, The (1929)**½ Bessie Love, Anita Page, Charles King. The screen's first all-talking musical, this MGM film established the genre's most familiar plot, the putting-on-a-show format. The songs are by Arthur Freed and Nacio Herb Brown. The first sound film to win an Oscar as Best Picture. (Dir: Harry Beaumont, 104 mins.)

Broadway Melody of 1936, The (1935)*** Jack Benny, Robert Taylor, Eleanor Powell. It's Benny vs. Taylor in this sequel. Benny's a columnist, loosely modeled on Winchell (weren't they all?), who's lambasting Taylor's vain producer. The team of Vilma and Buddy Ebsen enliven each sequence in which they appear. Original story by Moss Hart. A top-rate score, Powell's dancing, and the old reliable show-biz plot are perfectly blended in an entertaining musical. Songs by Arthur Freed and Nacio Herb Brown include "You Are My Lucky Star" and "I Got A Feelin' You're Foolin'." (Dir: Roy Del Ruth, 103 mins.)

Broadway Melody of 1938 (1937)*** Judy Garland, Robert Taylor, George Murphy, Eleanor Powell, Sophie Tucker, Buddy Ebsen. A likable, predictable musical that appeals despite the big production, particularly with ingratiatingly low-key performers like Ebsen. It chafes only when a powerhouse bore like Tucker takes over. The story revolves around Powell, that smiling dancing machine, with Taylor and Murphy as the love interests. Garland made the strongest impression with her rendition of "Please Mr. Gable (You Made Me Love You)." (Dir: Roy Del Ruth, 110 mins.)

Broadway Melody of 1940 (1940)***½ Fred Astaire, Eleanor Powell, George Murphy, Frank Morgan, Ian Hunter. Astaire and Powell, in their only teaming, dominate this entertaining musical with a strong Cole Porter score (including "Begin the Beguine"). Astaire is in this rivalry with Murphy (no contest), and the plot is a tad of a nuisance, but the dance numbers are good and there are plenty of them. Not surprisingly, the proficient Miss Powell is not the most alluring of partners for Astaire; they tend to solo in tandem. (Dir: Norman Taurog, 101 mins.)

Broadway Rhythm (1943)**½ Gloria De Haven, Ginny Simms, Ben Blue, George Murphy. Some good individual numbers by people like Lena Horne but generally just a lavish piece of nothing. (Dir: Roy Del Ruth, 114 mins.)

Broadway Thru a Keyhole (1933)** Constance Cummings, Paul Kelly. Very dated musical comedy but a rare chance to see and hear the late Russ Columbo, the famous crooner of the 30's. (Dir: Lowell Sherman, 100 mins.)

Brock's Last Case (MTV 1973)**½ Richard Widmark. This pilot film about a New York detective quitting the force to raise oranges in California led to Widmark's brief "Madigan" series. Brock (or Madigan, out West) is entertaining. Everything goes wrong for the retired cop; still he manfully springs his Indian foreman loose from a murder rap. Overlong plot, but the dialogue is above average; and Widmark, Henry Darrow, and the whole cast add a nice touch. (Dir: David Lowell Rich, 100 mins.)

Broken Arrow (1950)**½ James Stewart, Jeff Chandler, Debra Paget, Will Geer, Arthur Hunnicutt. Ecumenical western, the most successful of the series with red men as heroes. Chandler (who won an Oscar nomination) plays Cochise, who makes a blood brother of Indian agent Stewart. It's less than rousing, but it does make you feel warm and liberal. Delmer Daves directed from Michael Blankfort's screenplay. (93 mins.)

Broken Blossoms (1919)**** Lillian Gish, Richard Barthelmess, Donald Crisp. The celebrated D. W. Griffith classic love story of a young woman and a Chinese gentleman can still tug at the heartstrings and draw a tear or two. Director Griffith allowed Gish and Barthelmess to play the romantic duo with realistic enthusiasm. The result is very moving when the tragic aspects of the stars take over. Crisp, one of Hollywood's most distinguished character actors, is hateful and menacing as

Gish's vicious ex-prizefighter father. (89 mins.)

Broken Horseshoe, The (Great Britain, 1952)*** Robert Beatty, Elizabeth Sellars. A hit-and-run accident victim puts police on the trail of a narcotics ring. Good melodrama, well acted. (Dir: Martyn C. Webster, 79 mins.)

Broken Journey (Great Britain, 1948)*** Phyllis Calvert, James Donald. Survivors of a plane crash in the Alps attempt to reach safety. Tense, well acted melodrama. (Dir: Ken Annakin, 89 mins.)

Broken Lance (1954)**½ Spencer Tracy, Richard Widmark, Robert Wagner, Earl Holliman, Jean Peters. The remake of Joseph L. Mankiewicz's "House of Strangers" as a western, with Tracy performing well as the tyrannical papa riding hard on three rebellious sons, unaccountably won Philip Yordan the Oscar for Best Story. The movie meanders to very little point, and the drama is overheated and without conviction. If you wonder why, look at the director credit. With Katy Jurado (strong). (Dir: Edward Dmytryk, 96 mins.)

Broken Promise (MTV 1981)*** Melissa Michaelson, Chris Sarandon. Here's one that will leave you moist eyed. Five youngsters, left stranded by their parents, are separated, going to different foster homes. However, twelve-year-old Patty, the family leader, battles against the bureaucracy to keep the brood together. Steely, suspicious Patty is played with unexpected skill by Melissa Michaelson. (Dir: Don Taylor, 104 mins.)

Broken Strings (1940)**½ Clarence Muse, Stymie Beard. Muse stars in his own all-black melodrama about a concert violinist whose hands are destroyed. Beard was the black kid in all those "Our Gang" shorts. (Dir: Bernard Ray, 60 mins.)

Broken Treaty at Battle Mountain (1975)***½ The efforts of the federal government to reclaim 24 million acres of Nevada land granted by treaty to the Shoshone people. Narrated by Robert Redford, this lucid documentary makes an effective case. (Dir: Joel L. Freedman, 60 mins.)

Broken Wings, The (Lebanon, 1964)**½ Pierre Bordey, Saladin Nader, Philip Akiki. The first film from Lebanon ever released in this country, made in black and white. It's based on the world-famous book by Kahlil Gibran, **The Prophet**. It may strike you as moving and profound, or pretentious and silly. We won't guess which! If you like old-fashioned romantic melodramatic love stories, you'll be in Arabic heaven with this one. Subtitles. (Dir: Yusuf Malouf, 90 mins.)

Bronco Billy (1980)*** Clint Eastwood, Sondra Locke, Geoffrey Lewis, Scatman Crothers, Sam Bottoms. Actor-director Eastwood continues to vary quirkily against his established persona with this winsome comedy about a small-bracket Wild West show presided over by Eastwood's sappy prince of delusion, but the results are more often screwy than screwball. The comedy timing often falters, and Eastwood swings wide for his laughs, but the film has a coherence of vision that makes it more satisfying as a whole than in its parts. Not as stylistically audacious as "The Gauntlet" or "The Outlaw Josey Wales." (116 mins.)

Bronco Buster (1952)**½ Scott Brady, John Lund, Joyce Holden. Some good touches in this unassuming yarn about a champ rodeo rider who takes a young hopeful in hand and trains him. Frequently quite amusing, good performances. (Dir: Budd Boetticher, 90 mins.)

Brood, The (1979)** Oliver Reed, Samantha Eggar, Art Hindle. Canada's director David Cronenberg is the latest cult darling among movie academics, and much of the case for his work rests on this oddball horror film. Reed plays the charismatic head of a psychiatric institute; his cure depends on a physical manifestation—welts, scars, dripping growths—of the patient's repressed emotions. The idea is vivid, original, and suitably repulsive, but Cronenberg's talents don't go much beyond conception: in the playing, the picture is gray, tepid, and blocky. (91 mins.)

Broth of a Boy (Great Britain, 1959)*** Barry Fitzgerald, Tony Wright, June Thorburn. Entertaining comedy about a TV producer who discovers the oldest man in the world, tries to get him on his video show. Top honors to Fitzgerald for his crusty Irish portrayal. (Dir: George Polleck, 77 mins.)

Brother, Can You Spare a Dime? (Great Britain, 1975)*** An unusual documentary collage about the Depression Era in America, using contemporary film and newsreel footage, made by Australian Philippe Mora. There are some remarkable clips rarely seen anywhere else, of FDR, film stars, bread lines, strikes, gangsters, etc., and the soundtrack is equally interesting. Definitely worth seeing. (Dir: Philippe Mora, 103 mins.)

Brother John (1971)** Sidney Poitier, Beverly Todd, Will Geer, Bradford Dillman. Here's a lesser Poitier effort. He plays an angel (that's right) who returns to his hometown in Alabama to see how the folk are faring in this day and age of hate and violence. It's not a bad idea, but before you can say "Gabriel," the clichés are flying and the southern stereotypes are parading in front of the camera. The plot revolves around a strike at the town's big plant but it really doesn't matter. (Dir: James Goldstone, 94 mins.)

Brother Orchid (1940)***½ Edward G. Robinson, Ann Sothern, Humphrey Bogart, Donald Crisp. Hysterically funny film about a gangster who takes refuge in a monastery and learns some things about life. You'll have a lot of fun with this one especially if you happen to catch it after

exposure to some of the rough gangster pictures of the era. (Dir: Lloyd Bacon, 91 mins.)

Brother Rat (1938)***½ Eddie Albert, Wayne Morris, Priscilla Lane, Ronald Reagan, Jane Wyman. Side-splitting comedy about life in a military school. A tremendous hit on Broadway and equally good in this screen version. Remade as a musical *About Face* (1952). (Dir: William Keighley, 90 mins.)

Brother Rat and a Baby (1940)** Eddie Albert, Jane Wyman, Ronald Reagan. Good performances don't help this weak script cash in on the success of "Brother Rat." (Dir: Ray Enright, 87 mins.)

Brother Sun, Sister Moon (1973)**½ Alec Guinness, Graham Faulkner, Judi Bowker, Valentina Cortese. OK, it is sappy spiritual gunk, but the production values are sumptuous and sedulous, which compensates for a story about a monk. Lina Wertmuller was one of the scriptwriters, Franco Zeffirelli directed—neither of them doing much to write home about. As for Bowker, take pen in hand. One of those pleasant, dumfounding works spawned full bloom from a mutant strain of flower children. Songs by Donovan. (121 mins.)

Brotherhood, The (1968)**½ Kirk Douglas, Alex Cord, Irene Pappas, Susan Strasberg. Highly charged drama about the passions and intrigues of an Italian family connected with the Mafia. K. Douglas, complete with dark hair and handlebar moustache, gives a very strong performance as a syndicate leader who has to run away to Sicily after killing his younger brother's father-in-law. Alex Cord is also effective as Douglas' brother, who, years later, is dispatched to Sicily with a contract on his brother's life. The supporting cast is top-notch, with Luther Adler a standout as Cord's double-crossing father-in-law. (Dir: Martin Ritt, 96 mins.)

Brotherhood of the Bell, The (1970)**½ Glenn Ford. Interesting made-for-TV feature film. Professor Glenn Ford loses his young wife, father, all his possessions and his reputation in a one-sided battle aimed at exposing a secret college fraternity whose members apparently control the business world. The idea of a secret Mafia-like organization originating in a Catholic college may be hard to swallow at first, but David Karp's script gains plausibility over the distance. Ford plays the harassed professor displaying wild, frustrated anger fighting an invisible force, but he can't cover up the tale's weak point—the professor's obvious naïveté in waging an amateur counterattack. (Dir: Paul Wendkos, 100 mins.)

Brotherhood of Satan (1971)** Strother Martin, L. Q. Jones. Martin has a field day in this devil-go-round horror movie set in the Southwest. A local coven needs only one more possessed child to continue their Satan-filled activities . . . and thereby hangs the tale. Some surprising bits of horror, at least enough to get you shivering. (Dir: Bernard McEveety, 92 mins.)

Brotherhood of the Yakuza, The—See Yakuza, The

Brotherly Love (Great Britain, 1970)*** Peter O'Toole, Susannah York, Michael Craig, Harry Andrews, Brian Blessed. Unhappy tale of a Scottish nobleman's descent into insanity. O'Toole is brilliant as the unbalanced peer; York is fine as his abnormally beloved sister. This film was advertised as being about incest; it is not. It is an examination of the painful decisions that have to be made when a relative becomes incompetent. James Kennaway, who based the script on his own novel "Household Guests" and play "Country Dance," makes the story essentially tragic but touched with humor. Involving, grim, beautifully acted. (Dir: J. Lee Thompson, 112 mins.)

Brothers (1977)*½ Bernie Casey, Vonetta McGee, Ron O'Neal. (Dir: Arthur Barron, 104 mins.)

Brothers-in-Law (Great Britain, 1957)**½ Ian Carmichael, Terry-Thomas. Zany but only occasionally funny comedy about big business and love. Two lawyers vie for the same girl but both lose out to a third party. (Dir: Roy Boulting, 94 mins.)

Brothers Karamazov, The (1958)*** Yul Brynner, Maria Schell, Lee J. Cobb, Claire Bloom. Handsomely mounted drama, based on Dostoyevsky's classic. The cast is very good, particularly Lee Cobb. Film is overlong and episodic. Fans of the book will probably find fault with Richard Brooks' screenplay, but still better than most. (Dir: Richard Brooks, 146 mins.)

Brothers Karamazov, The (Russia, 1970)*** Dostoyevsky lovers everywhere wince at the thought of a two-hour version of *Karamazov*, but at least this one's not a network miniseries. It is, rather, a 1970 version written and directed by Ivan Pyriev, best known for his musical comedies of the thirties and forties. Pyriev died in 1968; Mikhail Ulyanov and Kirill Lavrov completed the film after his death. (Dirs: Ivan Pyriev, Mikhail Ulyanov.)

Brothers Rico, The (1957)**½ Richard Conte, Dianne Foster. Fairly well done crime drama with good performances by the principals. Plenty of action. Remade as TV movie *The Family Rico*. (Dir: Phil Karlson, 100 mins.)

Browning Version, The (Great Britain, 1951)**** Michael Redgrave, Jean Kent, Nigel Patrick. An extraordinarily brilliant and moving performance by Michael Redgrave in the title role makes this Terence Rattigan story a touching and memorable film. About a stuffy professor of English at a boys' school who learns of his wife's affair with another teacher as he prepares to leave the school for another teaching post. Supporting roles uniformly well handled. (Dir: Anthony Asquith, 90 mins.)

Brubaker (1980)**½ Robert Redford, Yaphet Kotto, Jane Alexander. Redford stars as a loner-hero, an idealistic warden who attempts to reform prison conditions only to torpedo his own efforts for the sake of an obscure moral principle. In the end, he simply prefers to keep clean rather than get dirty with the real issues confronting the men for whom he takes responsibility. Director Stuart Rosenberg came in on virtually no advance notice after Bob Rafelson was summarily dismissed, and surprisingly, some passages have rudiments of effective visual style. But Rosenberg seems incapable of dealing with a serious idea without reducing it to the simplest possible banality, and the large cast of excellent actors (many from the New York stage) are left with a thesis movie that has no valid, let alone coherent, point. Film based on the experiences of Thomas O. Murlan, dismissed as superintendent of the Arkansas State Penitentiary in 1968 after his humane prison reforms embarrassed then Gov. Winthrop Rockefeller. Screenplay by W. D. Richter. (130 mins.)

Brute Force (1947)***½ Burt Lancaster, Yvonne DeCarlo, Howard Duff, Ann Blyth, Hume Cronyn. Prisoners plan a daring break, and to get even with a sadistic guard captain. Prison drama offers nothing new, but is well done within its own limits. Fine cast. (Dir: Jules Dassin, 98 mins.)

B.S. I Love You (1971)**½ Peter Kastner, Jo Anna Cameron, Louise Sorel, Gary Burghoff. Saucy little flick spotlighting an ad man (Kastner) lost among the spice of life—a financee, an 18-year-old temptress and her mother, his boss (Joanna Barnes). Revolving-door sex but always rather proper. Cast is attractive, but labors with Canadian director Steven Stern's screenplay. (99 mins.)

Buccaneer, The (1938)**½ Fredric March, Franciska Gaal, Akim Tamiroff, Walter Brennan. Director Cecil B. De Mille's strong suits—sex, spectacle, and patriotism—come together in this swashbuckler about Jean Lafitte's battle against the British in 1812. March, as the pirate turned freedom fighter, hams it up as usual, strapping on an impenetrable French accent, but his bravado is in high character. The action finale, a guerrilla attack led from the swamps, is one of deMille's most fluid and atmospheric pieces. (124 mins.)

Buccaneer, The (1958)*** Yul Brynner, Inger Stevens, Charlton Heston, Charles Boyer, Claire Bloom. Jean Lafitte the pirate comes to the aid of Andy Jackson during the War of 1812. Remake of De Mille's early version with Fredric March as Lafitte, this swashbuckler could have used more movement and action. However, the big cast, generally good performances and lavish production make it good big-scale adventure stuff. This was directed by Anthony Quinn, produced by

Cecil B. De Mille—his last such. (120 mins.)

Buccaneer's Girl (1950)** Yvonne DeCarlo, Philip Friend. Typical pirate yarn with dashing buccaneers and the women who love and chase them. Action fans will enjoy the battle scenes. (Dir: Frederick de Cordova, 77 mins.)

Buchanan Rides Alone (1958)*** Randolph Scott, Craig Stevens, Jennifer Holden. Rugged western with strong plot, good cast and generally far more entertaining than usual western film fare. (Dir: Budd Boetticher, 78 mins.)

Buck and the Preacher (1972)*** Sidney Poitier, Harry Belafonte, Ruby Dee. Poitier and Belafonte work well together, but the mood is odd. Starts as drama, mood lightens, and becomes more entertaining. The duo play escaped slaves heading West, and Cameron Mitchell plays the sly villain. Well acted, but the plot has as many holes as Swiss cheese. Poitier's first directional effort. (102 mins.)

Buck Benny Rides Again (1940)**½ Jack Benny, Ellen Drew. Routine comedy that employed Jack's radio character Buck Benny. Film is loosely put together and only occasionally funny. (Dir: Mark Sandrich, 82 mins.)

Buck Privates (1941)*** Bud Abbott, Lou Costello, the Andrews Sisters, Shemp Howard. This film certified Abbott and Costello as topflight stars, and although there isn't a fresh joke in the movie, the recycled burlesque routines are still funny. In fact, their constant repetition, both before and since this film was made, hasn't dimmed their awfulness or their hilarity. (Dir: Arthur Lubin, 84 mins.)

Buck Privates Come Home (1947)** Abbott & Costello, Tom Brown. Ex-GIs take care of a French war orphan. Typical A & C slapstick. (Dir: Charles Barton, 77 mins.)

Buck Rogers in the 25th Century (1979)* Gil Gerard, Erin Gray, Pamela Hensley. (Dir: Daniel Haller, 88 mins.)

Bucket of Blood, A (1959)**½ Dick Miller. Barboura Morris. Far-out sculptor gets a macabre idea on how to improve his artwork. Sick, sick, sick horror-comedy that's interesting, in a repulsive way. (Dir: Roger Corman, 66 mins.)

Buckskin (1968)*½ Barry Sullivan, Wendell Corey, Joan Caulfield, Lon Chaney (Dir: Michael Moore, 98 mins.)

Buckstone County Prison (1978)** Earl Owensby, Don "Red" Barry, Sunset Carson. Owensby stars as a legendary, mystical figure who is sentenced to a term on the county work farm and who must recapture escapees to win his freedom from the brutal guards and unscrupulous warden (played by the late Don "Red" Barry in this penultimate film). Shot on location in and around Shelby, North Carolina. (Dir: Jimmy Huston)

Bud and Lou (MTV 1978)*** Buddy Hackett, Harvey Korman, Michele Lee, Robert Reed. The laughs the title conjures up never come through. The backstage lives and tumultuous careers of the famous comedy team of Abbott and Costello, beginning with their burlesque and vaudeville days, through their successful movie career. A sad, sometimes revealing narrative. Offers a reasonably candid glimpse, especially at Lou Costello's troublesome and unsavory character. Hackett excels as the rotund Costello; Korman is equally good as his browbeaten partner. The famous "Who's on First" sketch is re-created by Hackett and Korman. Written by George Leffers, based on a book by Bob Thomas. (Dir: Robert C. Thompson, 104 mins.)

Buddenbrooks (Germany, 1959)**½ Liselotte Pulver, Nadja Tiller, Hansjorg Felmy. Rather compressed version of Thomas Mann's novel about the dynasty of a mercantile family and its problems. Moves slowly, with occasional good scenes, able performances. Dubbed-in English. (Dir: Alfred Weidenmann, 199 mins.)

Buddy Holly Story, The (1978)***½ Gary Busey, Conrad Janis, Don Stroud, Maria Richwine, Charles Martin Smith. The plotting is contrived, and director Steve Rash's feeling for Buddy Holly's time and place is virtually nil, but Gary Busey's performance is astonishing—less as a great interpretation than as a total physical transformation. Since Holly's life offers few cinematically gripping conflicts, the filmmakers are obliged to invent some, and they tend to distort, rather than illuminate, Holly's career (in fact, some of Holly's original group, the Crickets, are suing the filmmakers for defamation of character). Still, the dramatic high point comes when Busey makes the epochal transition from wire to horn-rimmed glasses, and a star is born. (Dir: Steve Rash, 114 mins.)

Buffalo Bill (1944)**½ Joel McCrea, Maureen O'Hara, Linda Darnell, Anthony Quinn, Thomas Mitchell. One of the first epic westerns in color, this is a spectacle without much drama. The Indian battle is loosely constructed, like the charge on the ice in Sergei Eisenstein's "Alexander Nevsky." William A. Wellman, crude and vigorous, directed, apparently with much distaste for the cloying ending. (90 mins.)

Buffalo Bill and the Indians or Sitting Bull's History Lesson (1976)***½ Paul Newman, Joel Grey, Shelley Duvall, Geraldine Chaplin, Burt Lancaster, Kevin McCarthy, E. L. Doctorow. Robert Altman's eccentric, ambitious, flawed but invariably interesting Bicentennial offering, a visually stunning celebration of his understandable conviction that the business of America is and has been, for a long time, show business! Virtually nothing is left of playwright Arthur Kopit's Broadway play, "Indians," about Buffalo Bill, played here with style and flourish by Paul Newman. Screenplay by Altman and Alan Rudolph presents a different version of William F. Cody's exploits during the Presidency of Grover Cleveland than you have seen in Hollywood films before. (Dir: Robert Altman, 125 mins.)

Buffalo Gun (1962)* Marty Robbins, Wayne Morris, Mary Ellen Kay. (Dir: Albert C. Gannaway, 72 mins.)

Bugles in the Afternoon (1952)*** Ray Milland, Helena Carter. Fast moving cavalry western about an officer who is demoted but rejoins the service as a private and goes on to become a hero. Good performances. (Dir: Roy Rowland, 85 mins.)

Bugs Bunny/Road Runner Movie, The (1979)**½ Animated compilation of some of the best Warner Bros. cartoons, whose excellence is acknowledged by any serious cartoon fancier. Bugs himself, in new footage, hosts the selection of madcap examples of Chuck Jones's work, featuring Daffy Duck, Porky Pig, Elmer Fudd, Pepe Le Pew, and the interminable Road Runner vs. Coyote shorts. For those who haven't been oversaturated with these gems on kiddie TV. Voices by Mel Blanc. Produced and directed by Chuck Jones. (97 mins.)

Bugs Bunny, Superstar (1975)*** Fine collection of the best works of the immortal rabbit. Even those who have never been fans of Warner Brothers' classic cartoons made between 1940-1948 will be entranced by the artistry of the "old-fashioned," realistic animation technique, as well as the ageless wisecracking humor. They don't make them like this anymore. Too bad they could only fit in ten cartoons. Narrated by Orson Welles. Brief appearances by famed animation directors Tex Avery, Bob Clampett, Friz Freleng. (Dir: Larry Jackson, 90 mins.)

Build-Up, The (Japan, 1958)*** Yasuzo Masumura keeps very, very productive in the Japanese assembly-line manner, so that only about one in three of his films merits consideration as a personal work. Yet Masumura, who has made more than 50 films in just over twenty years, has amassed a formidable body of accomplished art despite the high factor of commissioned projects. This satire on the advertising game was one of his earliest distinctive efforts; it's only slightly dated in its social criticism, and very funny. (Dir: Yasuzo Masumura.)

Bulldog Breed (Great Britain, 1960)**½ Norman Wisdom, Ian Hunter. Slapstick-comedian Wisdom up to his ears in catastrophes, as he stubbornly bungles his way through life—from the Navy into Outer Space. Fun if you like this style. (Dir: Robert Asher, 97 mins.)

Bulldog Drummond (1929)**½ Ronald Colman, Joan Bennett, Claude Allister. Colman is a debonair ex-war hero searching for adventure in this early talkie, the first of many Drummond films. The plot involves a man being held prisoner in a fake nursing home, with Drummond enlisted by the man's niece (Bennett) to investigate. Allister is Drummond's sidekick, Algy. Script by Sidney Howard. (Dir: F. Richard Jones, 90 mins.)

Bulldog Drummond Comes Back (1937)**½ John Barrymore, John Howard, Reginald Denny, J. Carroll Naish, Louise Campbell. Though Ronald Colman originated the role in talkies for Goldwyn, a series was launched afterward at Paramount in the late '30s, starring Howard, a comedown from Colman, as Drummond, and with Barrymore earning a living by playing Inspector Neilson of Scotland Yard. Denny made an appealing Algy, with E. E. Clive as the butler, Tenny. In this one Naish is the villain, and Campbell the girl on whom Drummond has his eye. (Dir: Louis King, 64 mins.)

Bulldog Drummond Strikes Back (1934)**** Ronald Colman, Loretta Young, C. Aubrey Smith, Warner Oland. An excellent comedy-suspense film that holds up well today. One of the best of the "Drummond" series that started in 1930; based on the novel entitled (I kid you not) "Bulldog Drummond: The Adventures of a Demobilized Officer Who Found Peace Dull." You won't find this detective yarn at all dull. (Dir: Roy Del Ruth, 83 mins.)

Bulldog Jack (Great Britain, 1935)*** Ralph Richardson, Jack Hulbert, Claude Hulbert, Fay Wray. Semi-classic mild British comedy-thriller about a playboy (Jack Hulbert) who poses as Bulldog Drummond when the real man is sidelined with an injury; the dandy catches the thieves and rescues the girl. There is an exciting chase through the British Museum. For all its derivativeness, the film has charm. Sidney Gilliat was one of many collaborators on the script. (Dir: Walter Forde, 73 mins.)

Bullet for a Badman (1964)** Audie Murphy, Darren McGavin, Ruta Lee. Ex-ranger is menaced by an outlaw who threatens to kill him for marrying his ex-wife. Passable western has the standard ingredients of action and suspense. (Dir: R. G. Springsteen, 80 mins.)

Bullet for Joey, A (1955)** Edward G. Robinson, George Raft. Ex-gangster is hired to kidnap a scientist. Routine melodrama. (Dir: Lewis Allen, 85 mins.)

Bullet for Pretty Boy, A (1970)* Fabian Forte, Jocelyn Lane. (Dir: Larry Buchanan, 88 mins.)

Bullet for the General, A (Italy, 1967)* Giana Maria Volonte, Klaus Kinski. (Dir: Damiano Damiani, 115 mins.)

Bullet Is Waiting, A (1954)**½ Rory Calhoun, Jean Simmons, Stephen McNally, Brian Aherne. Suspense when a lawman and his prisoner are marooned with an old man and his daughter. Melodrama begins well, falls off as it progresses. Performances by the small cast help. (Dir: John Farrow, 90 mins.)

Bullets or Ballots (1936)*** Edward G. Robinson, Joan Blondell, Humphrey Bogart. Good racketeering story with customary top drawer, tough guy performance by Mr. Robinson (Dir: William Keighley, 77 mins.)

Bullfight Spain, 1956)***½ Documentary story of bullfighting, from pre-Christian days up to the present. Highly interesting, includes many scenes of modern matadors, plus some fascinating older material. (Dir: Pierre Braunberger, 76 mins.)

Bullfighter and the Lady (1951)***½ Robert Stack, Joy Page, Gilbert Roland. American sportsman visiting in Mexico is intrigued by bullfighting, gets a matador to help him become one. Absorbing drama of the bullring, with suspenseful ring scenes, fine performances. (Dir: Budd Boetticher, 87 mins.)

Bullitt (1968)*** Steve McQueen, Robert Vaughn, Jacqueline Bisset. Excellent chase finale would make this film worthwhile by itself but it has more to recommend it . . . not the least being Steve McQueen's aggressive performance as a tough, modern-day police detective involved in the middle of Mafia dealings and political intervention. If fast-paced crime dramas-plus are your preference, here's one to savor. Well directed by Peter Yates. (113 mins.)

Bullwhip (1958)**½ Guy Madison, Rhonda Fleming. Guy Madison accepts a shotgun wedding to avoid the gallows in this western, which seems a fair exchange, especially when the bride is lovely Rhonda Fleming. (Dir: Harmon Jones, 80 mins.)

Bundle of Joy (1956)**½ Debbie Reynolds, Eddie Fisher. Love and songs amid a big department store setting in this light and occasionally amusing comedy. Debbie's cute and Eddie sings. Remake of old Ginger Rogers comedy "Bachelor Mother." (Dir: Norman Taurog, 98 mins.)

Bunker, The (MTV 1981)*½ Anthony Hopkins, Cliff Gorman, Michael Lonsdale. A semi-fictional re-creation of the last days of the Third Reich. (Dir: George Schaefer, 180 mins.)

Bunny Lake Is Missing (1965)**½ Laurence Olivier, Keir Dullea, Carol Lynley, Noël Coward. Murky claptrap imbued with corrosive ambiguity by director Otto Preminger's unique ability to stage for CinemaScope, shown in his use of long takes and wide space. What would have paled in almost anyone else's hands nags at the intellect and insinuates itself into the nerve endings. Mystery-drama: Lynley goes through one nightmare after another as a harried young mother who enlists the aid of Scotland Yard to find her missing daughter. Dullea joins his sister in her search, as inspector Olivier begins to doubt that Bunny Lake ever existed. The surprise ending is played for chills. (107 mins.)

Bunny O'Hare (1971)*½ Bette Davis, Ernest Borgnine, Jack Cassidy. (Dir: Gerd Oswald, 92 mins.)

Buona Sera, Mrs. Campbell (1968)**½ Gina Lollobrigida, Peter Lawford, Shelley Winters, Phil Silvers. A diverting comedy premise, well handled by old pro Melvin Frank. Gina, an Italian mother of a lovely young daughter, has been getting checks from 3 former WW II American romances who each think they are the father of her child. Some twenty years later, the Air Force veterans come back for a squadron reunion and the fun starts. Good performances all the way around. (Dir: Melvin Frank, 111 mins.)

Bureau of Missing Persons (1933)**½ Bette Davis, Pat O'Brien, Lewis Stone, Glenda Farrell. Supposed inside story of Missing Persons Bureau never stays in one direction and gets lost itself. Comedy portion is much more entertaining than dramatic segment. (Dir: Roy Del Ruth, 73 mins.)

Burglar, The (1957)*½ Dan Duryea, Jayne Mansfield. (Dir: Paul Wendkos, 90 mins.)

Burglars, The (France-Italy, 1971)**½ Jean-Paul Belmondo, Omar Sharif, Dyan Cannon. Above-average heist film with an attractive cast of stars, a lush Greek setting, and exciting work from the stuntmen in a car chase. Belmondo is the head crook, who steals a fortune in emeralds; Sharif is the dishonest and sadistic policeman out to get the jewels for himself; and Cannon is a woman whose loyalties waver between the two of them. Remake of *The Burglar*. (Dir: Henri Verneuil, 120 mins.)

Burmese Harp, The See: **Harp of Burma**

Burn! (France-Italy, 1970)*** Marlon Brando. Ambitious film about an island in the Caribbean during the mid-19th century, but made in Italy by the Italian director Gillo Pontecorvo, who directed the remarkable "Battle of Algiers." Story concerns the troubled course of a slave revolt and a small island's battle for nationhood while brutalized and exploited by a succession of colonial powers. Brando plays a manipulative Britisher who betrays the islanders. Timely and important subject, marred by inconsistencies in the script, but gifted director Pontecorvo maintains interest. (Dir: Gillo Pontecorvo, 112 mins.)

Burn, Witch, Burn (Great Britain, 1962)**½ Janet Blair, Peter Wyngarde. Professor's wife becomes obsessed with witchcraft, is convinced she must die in his place. Well-made supernatural thriller gets good direction helping the plot through its more far-fetched phases. Remake of *Weird Woman*, 1944. (Dir: Sidney Hayers, 90 mins.)

Burning Court, The (France-Italy-West Germany, 1962)** Nadja Tiller, Jean-Claude Brialy. John Dickson Carr's suspense novel of mystery and the occult about an eccentric man awaiting inevitable death, peters out into this unconvincing, badly dubbed screen rendition, occasionally sparked by fantastic effects. (Dir: Julien Duvivier, 102 mins.)

Burning Hills, The (1956)*½ Natalie Wood, Tab Hunter. (Dir: Stuart Heisler, 94 mins.)

Burning Train, The ** Dharmendra, Hema Malina. A big, splashy, three-hour-plus Indian blockbuster featuring (surprise) a runaway train on fire. The situations may be absurd, and the whole first hour mostly a musical, but that's entertainment, India-style. The special effects were managed by two wizards from Fox, Paul Wurtzel and Jerry Endler. Ravi Chopra handled the melodramatics as director, and R. D. Burman did the music. With Dharmendra as the son of a bankrupt millionaire, Hema Malina as his estranged lover, Danny as the unstable villain, and Simi as a singing nun. (Dir: Ravi Chopra, 185 mins.)

Burnt Offerings (1976)* Oliver Reed, Karen Black, Burgess Meredith, Eileen Heckart, Bette Davis. (106 mins.)

Bus Is Coming, The (1971)***½ Mike Simms, Stephanie Faulkner, Morgan Jones. Impressive, intelligent low-budget independently produced drama that was overlooked and underrated at the time of its brief and limited release. Made by a group of blacks faced with the issue of school integration in a small California town. Fine effort from writer-director Horace Jackson. (107 mins.)

Bus Riley's Back In Town (1965)** Ann-Margret, Michael Parks, Janet Margolin. Youth returns to his home from the Navy determined to make good, resumes an affair with an old flame from the high-rent district. Plodding drama made of artificialities—Parks tries to act like James Dean, the script sounds like William Inge (who did write it, but refused credit), the direction imitation Kazan. The result: mild. (Dir: Harvey Hart, 93 mins.)

Bus Stop (1956)*** Don Murray, Arthur O'Connell, Marilyn Monroe. Critics began to recognize Monroe's acting talent in this version of the William Inge play, although she had projected the same strength and vulnerability in Otto Preminger's "River of No Return" two years before. This small-scale romance between a galoot of a cowboy and an untalented club singer has its tender moments, despite some overly raucous comedy situations. Murray is sensitive as the naive cowboy; O'Connell is his sidekick. Joshua Logan directed, and the signs of incipient vulgarity are disquieting. (96 mins.)

Bush Christmas (Australia, 1974)*** Chips Rafferty. Some school kids run afoul of a couple of thieves on Christmas Day. Highly unusual drama, depicting Yuletide life Down Under. Recommended. (Dir: Ralph Smart, 80 mins.)

Bushman (1972)** Semidocumentary about the cultural and social conflicts facing a young black college student from Nigeria when he arrives in San Francisco to attend college. The actor-student was deported, later permitted to return. Low-budget independent film. B&W (Dir: David Schikele, 75 mins.)

Buster and Billie (1974)**½ Jan-Michael Vincent, Joan Goodfellow. An uneven, occasionally perceptive story about a gang-bang among high-school students in rural Georgia, circa 1948, long before most Americans ever heard of Plains. Sometimes poignant screenplay by Ron Turbeville who based the story on his own high-school days. Joan Goodfellow is quite touching as the acquiescent but disinterested town tramp who finally falls for Buster, played with strength and charm by Jan-Michael Vincent. (Dir: Daniel Petrie, 100 mins.)

Buster Keaton Story, The (1957)** Donald O'Connor, Ann Blyth, Rhonda Fleming, Peter Lorre. Screen biography of the brilliant movie comedian disregards facts flagrantly, presents an almost totally false impression of Hollywood and its brilliant subject. O'Connor tries hard, is responsible for what little success the film has. (Dir: Sidney Sheldon, 91 mins.)

Busting (1973)*** Elliott Gould, Robert Blake, Allen Garfield. Commendable attempt to realistically portray the seamy lives of two Los Angeles vice-squad cops. Gould and Blake are the cynical detectives, forced to arrest (or "bust") the small-time addicts and hookers instead of the real kingpins of organized crime because their police department superiors are getting paid off by the big guys. Well acted by Gould and Blake who go their merry way, flaunting all the rules, seeking revenge on everybody. Peter Hyams, a TV director and screenwriter, makes his feature film debut both directing and writing this one. (Dir: Peter Hyams, 92 mins.)

Busy Body, The (1967)**½ Sid Caesar, Robert Ryan, Anne Baxter. This fairly funny comedy about bumbling gangsters has Sid Caesar in a role which seems tailored for Jerry Lewis. In fact, the whole thing seems like a Jerry Lewis film, which means heavy slapstick antics and joke-filled dialogue. Some clever moments, a good supporting cast. Once again, Caesar's superb talents have been wasted by Hollywood. (Dir: William Castle, 90 mins.)

But, I Don't Want to Get Married (1970)**½ Herschel Bernardi, Shirley Jones, Nanette Fabray. This made-for-TV comedy has two things going for it . . . Herschel Bernardi as a recent widower who is thrust once again into the world of eager women looking for husbands, and a fairly good script. Bernardi's perplexed face in dealing with various ladies (including a brash Shirley Jones, an impossible Nanette Fabray, and an obvious Sue Lyon, among others) keeps the film funny most of the way. The ending at a PTA meeting at which Bernardi encounters a handsome widow (June Lockhart) has a great deal of charm. (Dir: Jerry Paris, 72 mins.)

But Not for Me (1975)**½ Clark Gable, Carroll Baker, Lilli Palmer. Middle-aged Broadway producer is chased by a young secretary, who doesn't think the difference in age matters. Remake of "Accent on Youth" starts promisingly, loses steam as it progresses. Gable is good, as usual, the net result mildly amusing. (Dir: Walter Lang, 105 mins.)

But Where Is Daniel Vax? (Israel, 1972)*** Some funny and ironic scenes in this insightful story about an Israeli pop singer, with an American wife, who returns to Israel to visit some of his old schoolmates, and unexpectedly becomes involved in the difficult task of trying to locate one of them. English subtitles. (Dir: Avram Heffner, 95 mins.)

Butch and Sundance: The Early Days (1979)*** William Katt, Tom Berenger, Jeff Corey, John Schuck, Hill Eikenberry. Muted retrospective imagining of the buddies before the events for which they were immortalized in George Roy Hill's blockbuster ("Butch Cassidy and the Sundance Kid"). The film has little narrative drive, but director Richard Lester imparts an aura of knowing tentativeness. Katt and Berenger struggle manfully with characters that are based on other actors' personalities; (Newman and Redford) they acquit themselves respectably. A film of humor, steady style, and intimations of maturity in search of something resembling a subject. (110 mins.)

Butch Cassidy and the Sundance Kid (1969)**** Paul Newman, Robert Redford, Katharine Ross. An enormously appealing anti-western directed with great flair by George Roy Hill. Newman and Redford give such ingratiating performances that it's easy to overlook some shortcomings in the original screenplay by William Goldman based on two legendary bank and train robbers who clowned their way through much of the 1890's before fleeing to South America. These are certainly the drollest and most sophisticated gunmen you've seen in any American western in a long time. The movie starts out promisingly with Katharine Ross taking her clothes off, but does **not** lose interest after that. Graced with a catchy musical score including the award-winning tune "Raindrops Keep Fallin' on My Head." (Dir: George Roy Hill, 112 mins.)

Butch Minds the Baby (1942)**½ Broderick Crawford, Virginia Bruce. A softhearted mug helps out a mother and her baby when rough times approach. Damon Runyon story has some good moments, some laughs, some tears. (Dir: Albert S. Rogell, 76 mins.)

Butley (Great Britain, 1973)**** Alan Bates, Jessica Tandy, Richard O'Callaghan. Alan Bates is absolutely marvelous in this filmed version of Simon Gray's witty, award-winning play about a masochistic, joyfully malicious English university professor dealing rather badly with his onrushing male menopause. Bates is an actor of great range and technical virtuosity, and this is a valuable permanent record of one of the best acting performances of the decade. The brilliant playwright Harold Pinter, incidentally, makes an extremely auspicious directorial debut, skillfully guiding Gray's own screenplay. Bates' bitchy, witty, slashing tirades are a joy to behold. (Dir: Harold Pinter, 127 mins.)

Butterfield 8 (1960)**½ Elizabeth Taylor, Laurence Harvey, Eddie Fisher. Elizabeth Taylor won her first Oscar for her portrayal in this melodrama. (Some say she received the award for sentimental reasons. She'd been so sick.) Based on John O'Hara's best seller about a misguided gal who lets herself go whenever a man enters the scene. Miss Taylor has given far better performances in better films, but there's a glamorous aura about the slick yarn and Laurence Harvey cuts a good romantic figure as Liz's once-in-a-lifetime, deep love. The supporting cast boasts such stalwarts as Dina Merrill, Mildred Dunnock, Betty Field, and George Voskovec. (Dir: Daniel Mann, 109 mins.)

Butterflies Are Free (1972)*** Goldie Hawn, Edward Albert, Eileen Heckart. The funny and credible Broadway play has been turned into a top-entertainment film, Goldie Hawn is perfectly cast as a fledgling actress who stumbles into the life of self-sufficient blind boy Edward Albert. Enter the boy's over-protective but genuinely loving mother, brilliantly played by Eileen Heckart (she won an Oscar for this role), and doubts creep into the relationship. (Dir: Milton Katselas, 109 mins.)

By Love Possessed (1961)**½ Lana Turner, Efrem Zimbalist Jr., Thomas Mitchell, Jason Robards Jr., George Hamilton. Wealthy attorney realizes his domestic life is not all it should be, is drawn into an affair with the equally lonely and discontented wife of his crippled partner. Controversial novel made into a lackluster film suffering mainly from script trouble. Performances as good as can be expected. (Dir: John Sturges, 115 mins.)

By the Light of the Silvery Moon (1953)*** Doris Day, Gordon MacRae. Songs, dances, and a good amount of nostalgia in this turn of the century musical comedy. Doris and Gordon are a likeable team and make sweet music together. (Dir: David Butler, 102 mins.)

Bye Bye Birdie (1963)***½ Dick Van Dyke, Janet Leigh, Ann-Margret. What happens when a teenage singing idol about to be drafted gives his final TV performance. Musical based on the Broadway stage success. Some tuneful songs, sharp performances by Van Dyke as a songwriter, Paul Lynde as a small-town father, Maureen Stapleton as a domineering mom. Sprightly fun. (Dir: George Sidney, 111 mins.)

Bye Bye Braverman (1968)*** George Segal, Jack Warden, Alan King, Godfrey Cambridge. Based on Wallace Marfield's "To an Early Grave." Interesting if not completely successful attempt by director

Sidney Lumet to create a comedy on the mores of would-be Jewish intellectuals in New York City. focuses on a day when a group of friends attend Braverman's funeral. Part of the movie was filmed in Brooklyn. Lumet gets what humor there may be from the funeral itself. Brightest vignettes are contributed by such character actors as Joseph Wiseman and Sorrell Booke. (94 mins.)

Bye Bye Brazil (1980)*** Jose Wilker, Betty Faria. Carlos Diegues's lush travelogue on modern-day Brazil traverses sufficiently variegated terrain to keep its rather thin saga of a traveling carnival troupe engaging. There are some grand theatrical flourishes to the threadbare showbiz of the Lord Gypsy and his Salome, Queen of the Rhumba. The naivete of the young couple who join up with them is a bit tiresome, though Diegues's view of his native land is never sentimental. While the contrast of old and new cultures is strongly conveyed, the film is too mild in its never-say-die good spirits to register ideas more than vaguely. (Dir: Carlos Diegues)

Cabaret (1972)**** Liza Minnelli, Joel Grey, Michael York. A knockout. One of the most brilliant musicals ever made and certainly the definitive version of Sally Bowles, the original character in Christopher Isherwood's 1939 book about life in pre-World War Two Berlin. Far better than the Broadway musical, thanks largely to the bravura performance of Liza Minnelli playing Sally. Liza can act better than her mother (Judy Garland) and already seems equally accomplished with the songs. Joel Grey won an Academy Award for his dazzling decadence playing a nightclub m.c., the same role he created on Broadway. Liza also won an Oscar. Its handling of the political material during the time of Hitler's rise to power is done with style and integrity. Bob Fosse's direction is inspired throughout. (Dir: Bob Fosse, 124 mins.)

Cabin in the Cotton (1932)**½ Richard Barthelmess, Bette Davis, Henry B. Walthall, Dorothy Jordan, Tully Marshall. Barthelmess stars effectively as a poor sharecropper who is almost brought to ruin when he starts to run with rich-bitch southern belle Davis (in her best early performance). The film's attitudes are severely dated, but the sadistic twinge in director Michael Curtiz's style holds up remarkably well. A chestnut with a life of its own. (77 mins.)

Cabin in the Sky (1943)*** Eddie Anderson, Ethel Waters. For his first shot at directing, Vincente Minnelli was given a throwaway MGM property with an all-black cast. Anderson gets his one great chance to act and perform and he is ably matched by Waters. Specialty numbers

are worked in for John W. Bubbles, Lena Horne, Duke Ellington, Cab Calloway, and Louis Armstrong, and the roots of Minnelli's themes can be discerned in embryonic form. (99 mins.)

Cabinet of Dr. Caligari (Germany, 1919)*** Werner Krauss, Conrad Veidt. Robert Wiene's classic is, after the films of Griffith, Murnau, and Eisenstein, probably the most influential silent film ever made. Whenever you hear the word "expressionism" or think of nightmarish, distorted sets and jagged, moody lighting, you're thinking of all the thousands of films influenced by this 1919 German ponderoso about a mad doctor and the "somnambulist" who does his murderous bidding. Werner Krauss stars as Caligari, and Conrad Veidt is still, after more than half a century, a terror as Cesare the monster. It's pretty dreadful, but it *is* cinematic history. (Dir: Robert Wiene, 69 mins.)

Cable Car Murder, The (MTV 1971)**½ Robert Hooks. Well-made San Francisco cops-and-robbers film features a '70's style murder story. Will interest action fans. Unusual camera views of the city give the show an extra edge as black Inspector Louis Van Alsdale (Hooks) takes on the Establishment over the murder of a shipping magnate's son. Of particular interest is the menacing atmosphere created in a confrontation between the black cop and black bad guys. Cool and strong, Hooks' character shows courage throughout. (Dir: Jerry Thorpe, 78 mins.)

Cactus Flower (1969)**½ Walter Matthau, Ingrid Bergman, Goldie Hawn. Disappointing adaptation of the Broadway hit comedy of Abe Burrows, despite an enchanting co-starring debut by Goldie Hawn for which she won the Academy Award for best supporting actress. Matthau plays a dentist who is having an affair with Goldie, while not admitting to himself that he **really** loves his nurse played by Ingrid. Bergman is too mature for this kind of role. Could use more of Quincy Jones' musical score, and less stilted dialogue. (Dir: Gene Saks, 103 mins.)

Caddie (Australia, 1976)** Helen Morse, Takis Emmanuel, Jack Thompson, Jacki Weaver, Melissa Jaffer. Australian drama based on yet another passive feminist heroine. This story, about the tribulations of a middle-class woman evicted from her home by her philandering husband and her efforts to support her children as a barmaid, should have had more punch than this. Helen Morse makes the heroine a repository of class superiority even in dreary circumstances, and director Donald Crombie's visual style delights in the decorously irrelevant. The film seeks out artistic safety with such alacrity that it seems to want to be petted, as a reward for denuding its story of challenge and anger. Written by Joan Long from an anonymous memoir. (Dir: Donald Crombie, 107 mins.)

Caddy, The (1953)**½ Dean Martin, Jerry Lewis, Donna Reed. Jerry's a golf hopeful who's afraid of crowds in this one. Not the team's best, but should please the partisans. (Dir: Norman Taurog, 95 mins.)

Caddyshack (1980)*½ Michael O'Keefe, Chevy Chase, Rodney Dangerfield, Ted Knight, Bill Murray. (Dir: Harold Ramis, 90 mins.)

Cadet Girl (1941)* Carole Landis, George Montgomery. (Dir: Ray McCarey, 69 mins.)

Cadets on Parade (1942)** Freddie Bartholomew, Jimmy Lydon. Boy runs away from a military academy, is befriended by a poor newsboy. Fair melodrama. (Dir: Lew Landers, 63 mins.)

Caesar Against the Pirates (1960)*½ Gordon Mitchell, Abbe Lane. (Dir: Gabriel Pascal, 127 mins.)

Caesar and Cleopatra (Great Britain, 1945) *** Vivien Leigh, Claude Rains, Stewart Granger. Bernard Shaw's intellectual joke about the aging Roman conqueror and the beautiful but slightly addle-brained beauty of the Nile. Some of the Shavian wit has been preserved, but there are dull stretches. (Dir: Gabriel Pascal, 127 mins.)

Caesar, the Conquerer (1963)*½ Cameron Mitchell. (Dir: Amerigo Anton, 103 mins.)

Café Metropole (1937)*** Tyrone Power, Loretta Young, Adelphe Menjou. Amusing comedy about a young man who is forced to pose as a prince in order to make good on a gambling debt. The phony prince, played by Tyrone, is ordered by his creditor to woo and win an heiress, played by Loretta (Dir: Edward H. Griffith, 83 mins.)

Cage aux Folles, La (France, 1978)**** Ugo Tognazzi, Michel Serrault, Michel Galabru. Tognazzi and Serrault play, with enormous charm and dexterity, a happily settled gay couple that is forced to pass as straight when Tognazzi's son, from a previous moment of heterosexual abandon, brings home his prospective in-laws. There are moments that are excruciatingly funny and one or two others that are genuinely heartbreaking as one of the protagonists, trying to make a fine impression while dressed in a most conservative suit, can't quite figure out what to do with his hands. This comedy was one of the most successful foreign-language films ever at American box offices. (Dir: Edouard Molinaro, 110 mins.)

Cage of Gold (Great Britain, 1950)**½ Jean Simmons, David Farrar. An old flame, who's a scoundrel, returns to blackmail a girl now happily married. Good performances manage to overcome a familiar plot to make this acceptable melodrama. (Dir: Basil Dearden, 83 mins.)

Cage Without a Key (MTV 1975)**½ Susan Dey, Michael Brandon, Sam Bottoms. The theme of this film—how a poorly run juvenile detention home can turn teenagers into hardened criminals—is placed in director Buzz Kulik's careful hands, and his treatment of the material and the cast keeps this shocker from going awry. Sweet ingenue Susan Dey plays a naive youngster, making the transition into a tough little monkey, thanks to her fellow in mates. (Dir: Buzz Kulik, 100 mins.)

Caged (1950)***½ Eleanor Parker, Hope Emerson, Jan Sterling. Gripping drama of women's prison. Eleanor Parker runs the gamut from young innocent bystander sentenced for the theft to hard and bitter convict. Hope Emerson, as the cruel police matron, equals Parker's great performance. Remade as *House of Women, 1962.* (Dir: John Cromwell, 91 mins.)

Caged Heat (1974)** Juanita Brown, Roberta Collins, Erica Gavin, Barbara Steele. I can't exactly recommend this parody of a Roger Corman girl-gang movie, but director Jonathan Demme, who would later do the fine "Fighting Mad" and "Citizen's Band," evinces some genial humor. As good an example of the debased genre as you're likely to find. (83 mins.)

Cahill: U.S. Marshal (1973)*½ John Wayne, Gary Grimes, George Kennedy, Neville Brand. (Dir: Andrew V. McLaglen, 102 mins.)

Cain and Mabel (1936)**½ Marion Davies, Clark Gable, Guy Kibbee. Showgirl Davies meets Gable, and surprise! They fall in love. It's a hackneyed story, but it gives you a chance to see Miss Davies's considerable charm. B&W. (Dir: Lloyd Bacon, 90 mins.)

Caine Mutiny, (1954)***½ Humphrey Bogart, Fred McMurray. Edward Dmytryk's sluggish and undifferentiated direction nearly sinks this great yarn, but the superb cast carries on in fine style. Humphrey Bogart probably gives his most intently crafted characterization as the paranoid Captain Queeg. Fred MacMurray is an unctuous nemesis, Van Johnson the cats paw in the mutiny, and Jose Ferrer the skillful advocate who despises his clients. Somehow Tom Tully got an Oscar nomination, though he's nearly invisible. Based on Herman Wouk's novel. (Dir: Edward Dmytryk, 125 mins.)

Cairo (United States-Great Britain, 1963)*½ George Sanders, Richard Johnson, Faten Hamama. (Dir: Wolf Rilla, 91 mins.)

Calamity Jane (1953)*** Doris Day, Howard Keel, Allyn Ann McLerie, Phil Carey. Day does this in lieu of "Annie Get Your Gun," as Bette Davis did "Jezebel" in lieu of "Gone With the Wind." A sassy, entertaining, excessively loud musical, with the song "Secret Love" a big hit and Oscar winner. (Dir: David Butler, 101 mins.)

Calamity Jane & Sam Bass (1949)*½

Yvonne DeCarlo, Howard Duff. (Dir: George Sherman, 85 mins.)

California (1947)*** Ray Milland, Barbara Stanwyck, Anthony Quinn. Rip-roaring western set in early California when greedy men did not want the territory to become a state. (Dir: John Farrow, 97 mins.)

California (1963)*½ Jock Mahoney, Faith Domergue, Michael Pate. (Dir: Hamil Petroff, 86 mins.)

California Conquest (1952)**½ Cornel Wilde, Teresa Wright, Alfonso Bedoya. Spanish Californians, under Mexican rule, almost end up in the hands of the Russians in this fast paced but not too exciting western drama. (Dir: Lew Landers, 79 mins.)

California Dreaming (1979)* Seymour Cassel, Glynis O'Connor, Dennis Christopher. (Dir: John Hitchcock, 92 mins.)

California Kid, The (MTV 1974)**½ Martin Sheen, Vic Morrow, Michelle Phillips, Stuart Margolin. Sheen and Morrow are pitted against each other throughout this tense drama about a sheriff who is a one-man judge, jury, and executioner in dealing with speeders on the highway. Morrow plays the small-town lawman, and Sheen is the brother of one of the dead speeders. The action of the duel-race-to-the-death at the end is worth waiting for. (Dir: Richard Heffron, 72 mins.)

California Split (1974)**** Elliott Gould, George Segal, Ann Prentiss, Gwen Welles. California Split is western-slang jargon for cutthroat high-low poker and Robert Altman has fashioned here one of his most entertaining,compelling and powerful films. Taut original screenplay by Joseph Walsh about a pair of parasitical California gamblers, who become pals after getting mugged. Gould and Segal work beautifully together, and the scenes in the poker parlor capture the compulsive quality of the frenzied, possessed souls down on their luck, hoping for a reprieve, but obliged to bet on virtually everything including the names of the Seven Dwarfs, There's a funny, touching scene where two amiable semi-hookers, wonderfully played by Ann Prentiss and Gwen Welles, serve the stars breakfast consisting of beer and Froot Loops cereal. Altman's unique vision and his sense of character, pacing and detail combine to produce a multitextured essay that is funny, and genuinely moving. (Dir: Robert Altman, 111 mins.)

California Suite (1978)**** Michael Caine, Maggie Smith, Jane Fonda, Alan Alda, Walter Matthau, Elaine May, Richard Pryor, Bill Cosby. An all-star cast in an excellent adaptation of Neil Simon's play by Simon himself. Four stories about guests at the Beverly Hills Hotel are intertwined, the best being the bittersweet relationship between actress Smith and her (gay) antique dealer husband Caine. Smith won an Oscar (best supporting actress) for her role as a movie star who ironically fails to get an Academy Award in the film. Caine is wonderful in this poignant, acerbic segment. Fonda and Alda compliment each other as a warring ex-married couple, while Matthau and May have fun with their roles as philandering husband and wife. Only the portion with Cosby and Pryor as Chicago doctors sharing an outing with their wives fails to rise above the slapstick level. A grand (hotel) of a show. (Dir: Herbert Ross, 103 mins.)

Call Her Mom (MTV 1972)*½ Connie Stevens, Van Johnson. (Dir: Jerry Paris, 73 mins.)

Call Her Savage (1932)* Clara Bow, Gilbert Roland, Monroe Owsley, Thelma Todd. (Dir: John Francis Dillon, 88 mins.)

Call Me Bwana (Great Britain, 1963)**½ Bob Hope, Anita Ekberg, Edie Adams. Hope chased by foreign agents once more as he tries to recover a lost capsule. It all has the ring of familiarity, but Hope springs eternal and he has some good gags. (Dir: Gordon Douglas, 103 mins.)

Call Me Genius (Great Britain, 1961)**½ Tony Hancock, George Sanders. London office clerk becomes a mad painter in the Paris artists' quarter. Hancock is a popular English clown—his comedy is a matter of taste. For those who may take to him, there are some funny moments here. (Dir: Robert Day, 105 mins.)

Call Me Madame (1953)***½ Ethel Merman, Donald O'Connor, George Sanders, Vera-Ellen. It's Merman and Irving Berlin all the way in this picturization of the snappy stage musical about the free-wheeling Washington "hostess with the mostess." The tunes are fine, the production colorful; Merman fans will be in heaven, of course. (Dir: Walter Lang, 117 mins.)

Call Me Mister (1951)**½ Betty Grable, Dan Dailey, Danny Thomas, Dale Robertson. Dailey was always playing song-and-dance men who had to make up with their wives, and if he made the sinful life plausible, he also made it wholesome, usually because the wife was Grable. His easy energy makes this a passable musical. Set in Japan during what is tactfully not referred to as "the occupation." Thomas and Robertson co-star so you've been warned. Lloyd Bacon directed, and doesn't get in the way. (95 mins.)

Call Northside 777 (1948)***½ James Stewart, Lee J. Cobb, Helen Walker, Betty Garde. Chicago newspaperman Stewart investigates a murder. Director Henry Hathaway, specialized in these true-life dramas; like most of his work, this is convincing, engaging, and ultimately forgettable. With photography by Joe McDonald. (111 mins.)

Call of the Wild (1935)*** Clark Gable, Loretta Young, Jack Oakie, Reginald Owen, Frank Conroy. Overtame version of the Jack London classic, altered to accommodate the romantic interest of virile Gable and scrumptious Young (when she was still proud of it.) It's ingratiating nonsense. William A. Wellman directs saucily if none too carefully. (100 mins.)

Call of the Yukon (1938)** Richard Arlen, Beverly Roberts, Lyle Talbot. James Oliver Curwood's novel "Swift Lightning," about parallel romances in Northern Alaska—one canine, the other human—watered down for the Hollywood version, is an antique by now, but harmless enough. (Dir: B. Reeves Eason, 70 mins.)

Call Out the Marines (1942)**½ Edmund Lowe, Victor McLaglen. Two thickheads round up foreign agents. Funny comedy, boisterous and bawdy. (Dirs: Frank Ryan, William Hamilton, 67 mins.)

Call to Danger (MTV 1973)**½ Peter Graves. Slick outing by "Mission: Impossible" writer-producer Laurence Heath, featuring "Mission" star Peter Graves as a Justice Department sleuth. Diving out of windows and kissing sexy models, Graves retrieves a mobster kidnapped by thugs during crime hearings held in Washington. (Dir: Tom Gries, 73 mins.)

Calling Bulldog Drummond (Great Britain, 1951)**½ Walter Pidgeon, Margaret Leighton. Drummond comes out of retirement and with the aid of a policewoman smashes a crime ring. Pretty fair detective story given better production than the usual run. (Dir: Victor Saville, 80 mins.)

Calling Doctor Death (1943)*** Lon Chaney, Patricia Morison. Effective little thriller, with Chaney as a distinguished doctor whose wife has a yen for other fellows. When the cheating wife is murdered, there are suspects a-plenty. (Dir: Reginald Le Borg, 63 mins.)

Calling Homicide (1956)**½ William Elliot, Kathleen Case. Cop investigating the death of a fellow policeman uncovers blackmail in a modeling school. Neat little mystery merits praise for achievement on a small budget. (Dir: Edward Bernds, 61 mins.)

Callaway Went Thataway (1951)*** Fred MacMurray, Dorothy McGuire, Howard Keel. Funny film about a western hero whose career is revitalized by TV showings of his early films. This has been done before but the cast of pros make it work. (Dirs: Norman Panama, Melvin Frank, 81 mins.)

Caltiki, the Immortal Monster (Italy, 1960)** John Merivale. This time it's archeologists and corpses of Mayans from the seventh century who come to grips. The kids who like their chills on the wild side might enjoy this one. (Dir: Robert Hampton, 76 mins.)

Calypso Heat Wave (1957)*½ Johnny Desmond, Merry Anders. (Dir: Fred F. Sears, 90 mins.)

Calypso Joe (1957)*½ Angie Dickinson,

Edward Kemmer, Herb Jeffries. (Dir: Edward Dein, 76 mins.)

Camelot (1967)*** Richard Harris, Vanessa Redgrave, David Hemmings, Franco Nero. Opulent, generally well-acted version of the Broadway Lerner & Loewe musical. About the Knight's of the Round Table in Hollywood's—and author T. H. White's—version of life in the Middle Ages. Joshua Logan's plodding direction of this $15 million epic is relieved by the magnetic performances of the two British stars Harris and Redgrave, with the latter displaying her special magical brand of beauty, femininity, and strength. Harris, incidentally, really does sing his own songs. The costume designer John Truscott deserves a special accolade for his ravishing creations. (Dir: Joshua Logan, 179 mins.)

Cameraman, The (1928)**** Buster Keaton, Marceline Day, Harold Goodwin, Harry Gribbon. Keaton's silent movie about the problems and principles of making movies: he tries to become a newsreel cameraman for the Hearst newsreel company. Makes a marvelous companion piece to Keaton's other film-about-film, "Sherlock, Jr." You'll see an inspired pantomime sequence as Buster journeys to what was then an empty, newly built Yankee Stadium. (Dir: Edward Sedgwick, 78 mins.)

Camille (1936)***½ Greta Garbo, Robert Taylor, Lionel Barrymore, Henry Daniell, Laura Hope Crews. Garbo's greatest performance, as the dying woman salvaged by her love for a callow youth (Taylor). Director George Cukor allowed uncharacteristic lapses of taste by his supporting cast (Crews, Barrymore), but Daniell as the baron is a masterful study in self-irony. The show is Garbo's and if you've never seen her flush in perfect confidence in the tightest and most luminous of close-ups, this is not an experience to miss. (108 mins.)

Camouflage (Poland, 1976)**½ Piotr Garlicki, Zbigniew Zapasiewicz. Muddled, occasionally interesting drama about the bureaucratic infighting and crushed idealism among university faculty. The protagonists are members of the summer faculty of a graduate linguistics seminar. (Dir: Krzysztof Zanussi, 106 mins.)

Campbell's Kingdom (Great Britain, 1957)*** Dirk Bogarde, Stanley Baker. Young landowner battles a crooked contractor who wants to build a dam across it. Typical western plot transplanted to Canada—still plenty of action, elaborate production values. (Dir: Ralph Thomas, 102 mins.)

Can-Can (1960)**½ Frank Sinatra, Shirley MacLaine, Maurice Chevalier, Louis Jourdan. Lawyer protects a cafe owner when she's accused of presenting the Can-Can, a supposedly lewd dance. Cole Porter musical lumbers across the screen with emphasis upon the dazzle, but the score isn't one of his best and the script lacks true wit. Sinatra fans and lovers of musicals will approve, even though it really isn't up to par. (Dir: Walter Lang, 131 mins.)

Can Ellen Be Saved? (MTV 1974)**½ Kathy Cannon, Michael Parks. Based on a spate of newspaper articles about kids who become "Jesus freaks" and have to be literally kidnapped by their parents and deprogrammed by experts. Young girl gets caught up with a religious group who live and work on a commune until her worried parents enlist help. The script is a bit tacky, especially in the commune scenes. Parks is seen as the self-appointed guru of the pack. (Dir: Harvey Hart, 72 mins.)

Can Hieronymus Merkin Ever Forget Mercy Humppe and Find True Happiness? (Great Britain, 1969)* Anthony Newley, Milton Berle, Joan Collins, George Jessel, Bruce Forsyth. (Dir: Anthony Newley, 106 mins.)

Can You Hear the Laughter? The Story of Freddie Prinze (MTV 1979)*** Ira Angustain, Kevin Hooks, Julie Carmen. Screen biography of the Puerto Rican comic who rose from the barrio to superstardom in TV in a short time, and then took his life. Much of it plays like one of those old Hollywood backstage stories, but the young comic's drug problem is not glossed over. For the most part, a fitting tribute to a wasted talent. Angustain is impressive as Prinze. (Dir: Burt Brinkerhoff, 106 mins.)

Canadian Pacific (1949)**½ Randolph Scott, Jane Wyatt. A surveyor fights all odds to get the railroad through the wilderness. Outdoor melodrama has enough action to receive a passing grade. (Dir: Edwin L. Marin, 95 mins.)

Canadians, The (Great Britain, 1961)*½ Robert Ryan, John Dehner, Teresa Stratas. (Dir: Burt Kennedy, 85 mins.)

Canal Zone (1977)** Be forewarned, this documentary does not deal in any way with whether we should have surrendered control over the Panama Canal. Producer-director Frederick Wiseman is arguably the most gifted documentary filmmaker currently working in American television, but this overlong and self-indulgent essay is one of his least successful and most exasperating efforts. His report focuses on the incredibly boring lives of most of the American military and civilian personnel who live and work in the Canal zone. There are some memorable, sharply etched and poignant vignettes, but capturing boredom on film is a most delicate task, and few contemporary filmmakers other than Antonioni have done it successfully. *Canal Zone* has some rewarding moments, but it is far too long for the subject covered, and is poorly edited. (Dir: Frederick Wiseman, 180 mins.)

Candidate, The (1972)**** Robert Redford, Melvyn Douglas, Peter Boyle, Karen Carlson, Allen Garfield. Refreshing, earnest, unprofound, and quite entertaining. Redford as the vacuous U.S. Senate candidate who gradually becomes aware of his vacuity—not too many steps ahead of the audience, but way ahead of the voting public—turns in one of his best performances. Boyle's intensely squinting campaign Machiavelli and Garfield's media specialist are accurate. Many of those involved, including director Michael Ritchie and screenwriter Jeremy Larner, were in real political campaigns during the late '60s, and they've captured some of the look and feel of such campaigns. (109 mins.)

Candidate for Murder (Great Britain, 1960)** Michael Gough, Erica Remberg, John Justin. Professional killer is hired to do away with a man's wife but fears he will be the victim of a doublecross. Minor but compact melodrama from an Edgar Wallace story—well acted. (Dir: David Villiers, 60 mins.)

Candide (France, 1960)**½ Jean-Pierre Cassel, Dahlia Lavi, Pierre Brasseur, Nadia Gray, Michel Simon. Inconsistent updating of Voltaire's classic satire on optimism in the face of worldly strife, which places the brightly positive hero Candide in a world threatened by atomic holocaust. Ironies fail to jell, though there are some fine grotesque moments. (Dir: Norbert Carbonnaux, 90 mins.)

Candide (MTV Great Britain, 1973)**** Ian Ogilvy, Angela Richards, Frank Finlay. A lively rendition of the Voltaire classic, whose satire could perhaps be fresh again in the context of '70s self-indulgent ingenuousness. James McTaggart translated, adapted, and directed for the BBC; the cast is superb.

Candleshoe (1977)** Jodie Foster, David Niven, Helen Hayes. Foster uncovers some strange doings in an English country home in this Walt Disney effort. Bland and undistinguished fare for the kids. (Dir: Norman Tokar, 101 mins.)

Candy (U.S.-Italy-France, 1968)* Ewa Aulin, Marlon Brando, Richard Burton. (Dir: Christian Marquand, 119 mins.)

Candy Man, The (1969)* George Sanders, Leslie Parrish, directed by Herbert J. Leder. (97 mins.)

Cangaceiro—the Story of an Outlaw Bandit (Brazil, 1953)*** Marisa Prado, Alberto Ruschel. Interesting for its novelty alone, this rugged tale of an outlaw and his downfall has been dubbed into English in okay fashion. Plot gets rather bloody at times. Generally well done. (Dir: Lima Barreto, 91 mins.)

Cannibal Attack (1954)*½ Johnny Weissmuller, David Bruce. (Dir: Lee Sholem, 69 mins.)

Cannon (MTV 1971)**½ William Conrad, Vera Miles, Barry Sullivan. Stocky William Conrad with those hard blue eyes stars as a private investigator who travels to New Mexico to solve a war buddy's murder. Playing for realism, producer Quinn Martin often uses hand-held cameras while filming near Las Cruces, New Mexico, where his hero Cannon, a stranger, faces small-town antagonism. When plot complications tend to wear the viewer down, Martin shores it up with fine location work, Conrad's imposing presence, and a supporting cast featuring J.D. Cannon, Keenan Wynn, and Earl Holliman. (Dir: George McCowan, 99 mins.)

Cannon: He Who Digs a Grave (MTV 1973)** William Conrad, Anne Baxter, Barry Sullivan, David Janssen. Sniper bullets, a horse stampede and a fire don't deter our rotund hero, Frank Cannon, from helping an old war buddy who's been arrested on two counts of murder in a small cattle town. The location scenes in Grass Valley, California, and the performances by the guest stars add gloss to this routine tale. (Dir: Richard Donner, 106 mins.)

Cannon City (1948)*** Scott Brady, Jeff Cory, Whit Bissell. True story of an escape from the Colorado prison told in semi-documentary style and filmed where it happened. Not as good as top prison fiction—but exciting. (Dir: Crane Wilbur, 82 mins.)

Cannonball (1976)*** David and Bob Carradine, Sylvester Stallone, Mary Woronov, Judy Canova. The enormously talented director Paul Bartel followed up his "Death Race 2000" with the saga of an illegal cross-country race. Not up to his other work, but utterly devoid of redeeming social value and makes for a helluva good time. Los Angeles to New York with no holds barred: car wrecks, kung fu, bombings, shootings, country music, Cole Porter impressions, CB radios—all this and more, served up in the distinctively wanton New World Pictures style. (93 mins.)

Can't Help Singing (1944)**½ Deanna Durbin, Robert Paige. Strong-willed girl trails her sweetheart west. Pleasant but uneven costume musical. Jerome Kern tunes help. (Dir: Frank Ryan, 89 mins.)

Can't Stop the Music (1980)** The Village People, Valerie Perrine, Bruce Jenner, Barbara Rush. Not as terrible as its reputation. Compulsively watchable for its awful, sunny crassness. Jenner emerges as the most appealing comic performer; Rush looks utterly fantastic. Allan Carr is the primary perpetrator, while Nancy Walker must take the blame for the inadequate direction. Subject and stars are the Village People, a gay group for straights. (118 mins.)

Canterbury Tales, The (Italy, 1972)*½ Hugh Griffith, Josephine Chaplin, Jenny Runacre, Tom Bell, Tom Baker, Pier Paolo Pasolini. (Dir: Pier Paolo Pasolini, 111 mins.)

Canterville Ghost, The (1944)*** Charles Laughton, Robert Young, Margaret O'Brien. Amusing little whimsy about a cowardly ghost who can only be released from his haunting chores when a descendant performs a deed of bravery. Laughton is wonderful as the ghost. (Dir: Jules Dassin, 96 mins.)

Canyon Crossroads (1955)**½ Richard Basehart, Phyllis Kirk. Uranium prospectors are beset by crooks when they make a strike. Interesting western with a modern touch. (Dir: Alfred L. Werker, 84 mins.)

Canyon Passage (1946)*** Dana Andrews, Susan Hayward, Brian Donlevy. Good western. Dana loves Susan who is his buddy Brian's fiancee. Brian gets into trouble, is almost hanged. There's an Indian battle and, of course, Donlevy obligingly dies to let Dana kiss Susan. Lots of action. (Dir: Jacques Tourneur, 99 mins.)

Canyon River (1956)*½ George Montgomery, Marcia Henderson. (Dir: Harmon Jones, 80 mins.)

Cape Canaveral Monsters (1960)* Scott Peters, Linda Connell. (Dir: Phil Tucker, 69 mins.)

Cape Fear (1962)*** Gregory Peck, Robert Mitchum, Polly Bergen. Brutal tale of a revenge-seeking convict preying upon the sensibilities of the lawyer who sent him to prison. Excellent performances, with a brilliant study in sadism by Mitchum as the meanie. Not for the kiddies, but this is often very powerful. (Dir: J. Lee Thompson, 105 mins.)

Caper of the Golden Bulls, The (1967)**½ Stephen Boyd, Yvette Mimieux, Giovanna Ralli. The familiar plot of having a group of professional crooks combine their talents to pull a big caper is trotted out again for this handsomely mounted production. The Spanish setting is beautifully photographed, and some suspense is generated. (Dir: Russell Rouse, 104 mins.)

Capetown Affair, The (1967)*½ Claire Trevor, James Brolin, Jacqueline Bisset. Remake of *Pickup on South Street*. (Dir: Robert D. Webb, 103 mins.)

Capone (1975)** Ben Gazzara, Susan Blakely, John Cassavetes. Just what we don't need—another movie about the rise and fall of Chicago mobster Al Capone. Gazzara plays Capone with imagination and a case of hypertension. Blakely is a flashy girl who hangs out with the hoods, and Sylvester ("Rocky") Stallone has a small role as Frank Nitti, one of Capone's henchmen. Excessive shootouts and violence. (Dir: Steve Carver, 101 mins.)

Caprice (1967)** Doris Day, Richard Harris. Pure escapist film fare. Doris Day is the same bouncy blonde she plays in all her films, but her leading man in this one is none other than Richard Harris, and he manages to inject some life into the generally witless proceedings. The plot involves espionage, complete with double agents, undercover men, and a lineup of international villains. (Dir: Frank Tashlin, 98 mins.)

Caprice of "Dear Caroline" (France, 1950)** Martine Carol. Continuing the romantic escapades of the "Forever Amber" of the French Court. English-dubbed costume drama, overstuffed as usual. (Dir: Jean Devairre, 90 mins.)

Capricious Summer (Czechoslovakia, 1968)*** Rudolf Hrusinsky, Mila Myslikova. A gentle, visually lovely film, written and directed by Jiri Menzel, the director of "Closely Watched Trains." The slight but perceptive story concerns three middle-aged Czech men on a summer vacation, interrupted by the arrival in a small town of a circus tightrope walker (Menzel) and his fetching young female assistant. A touching, beautifully acted fable for those of you who don't demand constant action. English subtitles. (Dir: Jiri Menzel, 75 mins.)

Capricorn One (1978)** James Brolin, Elliott Gould, Sam Waterston, O.J. Simpson, Brenda Vaccaro. Watergate paranoia extends to the space program as a Mars mission turns out to be a fake. The screenplay, by director Peter Hyams, is dreadful—diffuse and devoid of characterization. But a few clever touches in the visuals, along with some snappy editing, help to pull it out. (127 mins.)

Captain Adventure—See: **Adventures of Mandrin, The**

Captain Blood (1935)***½ Erroll Flynn, Olivia de Havilland. Exciting adaptation of the Sabatini adventure story. This was Mr. Flynn's first major starring picture and he was happily welcomed by critics and fans. It's a top drawer pirate tale. (Dir: Michael Curtiz, 99 mins.)

Captain Boycott (Great Britain, 1947)***½ Stewart Granger, Kathleen Ryan, Cecil Parker. When a wealthy landowner in Ireland threatens his tenants with eviction, the farmers decide to fight. Lusty historical melodrama moves with speed, has fine performances. (Dir: Frank Launder, 92 mins.)

Captain Carey, U.S.A. (1950)**½ Alan Ladd, Wanda Hendrix, Francis Lederer. OSS agent returns to Italy after World War II to track down the man who had betrayed him to the Nazis. Unexceptional suspense drama has a typical Ladd action look. Fairly competent; also includes the Oscar-winning hit song "Mona Lisa." (Dir: Mitchell Leisen, 85 mins.)

Captain Caution (1940)** Victor Mature, Louise Platt, Bruce Cabot. A girl takes over her father's ship and battles the British during the War of 1812. Lots of action here, and if you don't blink you'll see Alan Ladd in a small role. (Dir: Richard Wallace, 85 mins.)

Captain Eddie (1945)**½ Fred MacMurray, Lynn Bari. Famous aviator's life is used as an excuse for a routine sentimental comedy-drama covering most of this century. Don't expect Rickenbacker's story

and film is pleasant enough. (Dir: Lloyd Bacon, 107 mins.)

Captain Falcon (Italy, 1964)*½ Lex Barker, Rosanna Rory. (Dir: Carlo Campogalliani, 97 mins.)

Captain from Castile (1947)**½ Tyrone Power, Jean Peters, Lee J. Cobb, Cesar Romero, Thomas Gomez, Alan Mowbray, Barbara Lawrence, Antonio Moreno, George Zucco, Marc Lawrence. Henry King directed this overlong, stodgy color adventure saga starring Tyrone Power as an ambitious man out to strike it rich in the New World. Lamar Trotti wrote and produced. I have little patience with failed epics of this type, but there is a lot of spectacle (including a real smoking volcano in the background) and a ground-breaking score by Alfred Newman. (Dir: Henry King, 140 mins.)

Captain from Koepenick (Germany, 1956)***½ Heinz Ruhmann. Criminal poses as an officer in order to get the one thing he wants most. It's a perceptive satire and commentary on civilian reaction to the military any time or place and features an extraordinarily moving performance as the would-be officer by Ruhmann. This is a frequently poignant though episodic film. (Dir: Helmut Kautner, 93 mins.)

Captain Fury (1939)*** Brian Aherne, Paul Lukas, Victor McLaglen. A brave soldier of fortune fights the villainous heads of early Australia's penal colony. Rousing action film, highly enjoyable. (Dir: Hal Roach, 90 mins.)

Captain Horatio Hornblower (1951)***½ Gregory Peck, Virginia Mayo, Robert Beatty, James Robertson-Justice. Director Raoul Walsh's predilection for anecdote over plot is given full rein. Peck makes a toy-sailor hero in his ridiculous costume, but Mayo is rightly attuned to the Walsh metabolism. Like the later "The Wind and the Lion," the film examines the roots of little-boy enthusiasts. The first film in which Walsh attempted some conscious use of Technicolor. (117 mins.)

Captain Is a Lady, The (1940)** Charles Coburn, Beulah Bondi. Well acted but minor comedy about an old man who insists on being with his wife in an old ladies' home. (Dir: Robert B. Sinclair, 63 mins.)

Captain January (1936)** Shirley Temple, Guy Kibbee. Shirley is an orphan again and the mean old law is trying to take her away from her wonderful guardian. Real junk but Shirley is cute. (Dir: David Butler, 75 mins.)

Captain John Smith and Pocahontas (1953)*½ Anthony Dexter, Jody Lawrance. (Dir: Lew Landers, 76 mins.)

Captain Kidd (1945)*½ Charles Laughton, Randolph Scott. (Dir: Rowland V. Lee, 89 mins.)

Captain Kidd and the Slave Girl (1954)* Anthony Dexter, Eva Gabor. (Dir: Lew Landers, 85 mins.)

Captain Kronos, Vampire Hunter (Great Britain, 1974)**½ Horst Janson, Caroline Munro, Shane Briant. Rarely exhibited horror film. Captain Kronos (Janson), assisted by Professor Grost (John Cater) attempts to rescue a 19th-century village from a band of vampires. The film was intended to inaugurate a series, but failed commercially. (Dir: Brian Clemens, 91 mins.)

Captain Lightfoot (1955)**½ Rock Hudson, Barbara Rush. Beautifully filmed period adventure about rebellion in Old Ireland of the 1800's. Rock Hudson fits his adventurer's role to a T and Miss Rush offers fine feminine support. (Dir: Douglas Sirk, 90 mins.)

Captain Mephisto and the Transformation Machine (1945-66)**½ Richard Bailey, Linda Stirling, Roy Barcroft. Feature version of serial "Manhunt of Mystery Island." Unknown villain poses as a pirate of old while holding a scientist prisoner in seeking radium deposits. Way, way out serial turned into a kookie feature—lots of action, good camp enjoyment. (Dir: Spencer Bennet, 100 mins.)

Captain Nemo and the Underwater City (Great Britain, 1970)** Robert Ryan, Chuck Connors, Nanette Newman. The underwater special effects of this movie may seem a bit dull, but there are enough spurts of action, wondrous sights, and music to keep this nautical children's tale fairly entertaining. Ryan is Captain Nemo, whose underwater empire is visited by shipwrecked people, including a U.S. Senator (Connors) and a feminist (Miss Newman). (Dir: James Hill, 106 mins.)

Captain Newman, M.D. (1963)*** Gregory Peck, Tony Curtis, Angie Dickinson, Eddie Albert, Bobby Darin. Interesting drama of an air-force psychiatrist whose duty is to his patients first, the military brass second. Well-done vignettes are used as a substitute for any strong plot line, with some good performances helping considerably. (Dir: David Miller, 126 mins.)

Captain Sinbad (1962)* Guy Williams, Pedro Armendariz. (Dir: Byron Haskin, 85 mins.)

Captains and the Kings (MTV 1976)**½ Richard Jordan, Perry King, Patty Duke Astin, Ray Bolger, Charles Durning, Joanna Pettet, Barbara Parkins. Good, old-fashioned, yeasty epic drama opens this nine-hour serialized adaptation of Taylor Caldwell's best-selling novel. Irish immigrants in mid-19th-century America include young, orphaned Joseph Armagh (Jordan), absolutely determined to provide for his sister and brother. He learns that the secret of success in America is money, and catches on fast. Jordan is surrounded by fine actors (especially Bolger and Durning) and lovely women (especially Pettet and Parkins). There's something for everyone here—rough tough days for Irishmen in the coal mines, contrasted with the protected life of the wealthy.

Astin got an Emmy. (Dirs: Douglas Heyes and Allen Reisner, 468 mins.)

Captains Courageous (1937)*** Spencer Tracy, Freddie Bartholomew, Lionel Barrymore, Mickey Rooney, Melvyn Douglas. Rudyard Kipling's popular story of a spoiled rich boy who falls overboard from an ocean liner and gets picked up by fishermen who teach him humility and the value of honest toil. Victor Fleming, who directed, was a macho type with much affinity for the subject matter, but his personality was not decisive enough to overcome the embalming impulses of MGM studio style. Bartholomew is the lad who grows up, but Tracy, with a stage-Portuguese accent, won the Oscar for Best Actor. (116 mins.)

Captains Courageous (MTV 1977)**½ Karl Malden, Jonathan Kahn, Johnny Doran. A remake of the wonderful '37 movie. More faithful to Kipling, but lacks the excitement of the earlier film. As the boy, Kahn (seen as Sarah Miles's son in "The Sailor Who Fell from Grace with the Sea," is properly arch and annoying at the start, and his transition to becoming one of the guys is believable. Malden, complete with beard and New England accent, is fine as the salty captain of the fishing vessel. (Dir: Harvey Hart, 104 mins.)

Captains of the Clouds (1942)*** James Cagney, Dennis Morgan. Some good moments in this fairly exciting melodramatic salute to the RCAF. Cagney may be a bum for the first few reels but he literally comes through with flying colors at the end. (Dir: Michael Curtiz, 113 mins.)

Captain's Paradise, The (British, 1953)**** Alec Guinness, Celia Johnson, Yvonne DeCarlo. A ferry-boat captain between Gibraltar and Algiers establishes the perfect formula for living by having two wives, one in each port, of opposite personalities. Another merry Guinness romp; delightful comedy, adult, witty, grand fun. (Dir: Anthony Kimmins, 80 mins.)

Captain's Table, The (British, 1959)**½ John Gregson, Peggy Cummins. Captain of a cargo vessel is given a trial command of a luxury liner, with the expected comic complications resulting. Pleasing little comedy gets a fair share of grins. (Dir: Jack Lee, 90 mins.)

Captive City, The (1952)***½ John Forsythe, Joan Camden. A fearless newspaper editor and his wife are threatened when they intend to expose a gangland syndicate. Suspenseful, intelligent crime melodrama, well above average. (Dir: Robert Wise, 91 mins.)

Captive Heart, The (Great Britain, 1946)**** Michael Redgrave, Rachel Kempson. Czech officer posing as a British officer killed in action writes to his wife from a concentration camp, and they fall in love with each other through the letters. Finely done war drama, excellent in every way. (Dir: Basil Dearden, 86 mins.)

Captive Wild Woman (1943)** Acquanetta, John Carradine, Milburn Stone. Mad doctor transforms an orang-utang into a beautiful girl. Horror thriller isn't as bad as it sounds, but is cheaply made. (Dir: Edward Dmytryk, 61 mins.)

Captive's Island (Japan, 1966)***½ Akira Nitta, Rentaro Mikuni, Shima Iwashita. A film directed by Masahiro Shinoda in which a reform-school graduate seeks revenge on the guard who brutalized him as a child. A classical Japanese theme on the futility of revenge. Music by Toru Takemitsu.

Capture, The (1950)***½ Lew Ayres, Teresa Wright. In Mexico a man unjustly becomes a fugitive. Good melodrama, well acted. (Dir: John Sturges, 91 mins.)

Capture That Capsule—See: **Spy Squad**

Car, The (1977)** James Brolin, Kathleen Lloyd, John Marley, Ronny Cox, John Rubinstein. Possessed by the devil, a customized luxury sedan terrorizes a New Mexico town. As silly as it sounds, and dull. Brolin stars and Elliott Silverstein directs, both with painfully straight faces. (95 mins.)

Car Wash (1976)** Richard Pryor, Irwin Corey, Franklyn Ajaye, George Carlin, Sully Boyar. The title tells all: a day in the life of a Los Angeles car wash, loosely structured in "American Graffiti"-style vignettes by director Michael Schultz (author of another "Graffiti" carbon, "Cooley High"). Despite Schultz's frenzied mise en scène, the going is tedious, the gags mostly scatological, the moralizing heavy-handed. (97 mins.)

Caravan (Great Britain, 1946)**½ Stewart Granger, Jean Kent. Adventurer sent to deliver a valuable necklace in Spain is waylaid by enemies, found and cared for by a gypsy girl. Costume melodrama has moments of excitement, as well as some warm love scenes. (Dir: Arthur Crabtree, 80 mins.)

Caravans (1978)** Anthony Quinn, Jennifer O'Neill, Michael Sarrazin, Christopher Lee, Barry Sullivan. Plodding '40s-type adventure made in Iran, takes place in '48. O'Neill is an American senator's daughter who has joined Quinn's nomadic Kochi tribe. It's up to young diplomat Sarrazin to get her back. Some action, and a lot of good scenery, beautifully photographed by cinematographer Douglas Slocombe. Based on James Michener's long novel. (Dir: James Fargo, 127 mins.)

Carbine Williams (1952)*** James Stewart, Jean Hagen, Wendell Corey. Based on fact, this is an engrossing personal drama of the man who invented and improved the Carbine Rifle for use by the Armed Forces. Stewart is effective in the lead role. (Dir: Richard Thorpe, 92 mins.)

Cardinal, The (1963)*** Tom Tryon, Carol Lynley, John Huston, Romy Schneider. Handsomely produced, if overlong and episodic saga about the personal life and religious career of a dedicated young Catholic priest who rises to the lofty position of cardinal. Tom Tryon is very attractive as the young cleric, but he plays his role in too stoic a fashion for a person who believed in and cared for people as much as the film indicates. The large supporting cast is uniformly good with the best performances delivered by John Huston as a rather gruff and outspoken cardinal, and Burgess Meredith as the priest of a very poor parish. (Dir: Otto Preminger, 175 mins.)

Career (1959)***½ Dean Martin, Anthony Franciosa, Shirley MacLaine, Carolyn Jones. Strong drama about an actor whose ambition and unwillingness to quit enables him to surmount obstacles in getting to the top of his profession. Story stacks the cards against him a bit too much, but the film is continually absorbing, has fine performances by Franciosa and Martin. (Dir: Joseph Anthony, 105 mins.)

Carefree (1938)*** Fred Astaire, Ginger Rogers. Astaire is a psychiatrist treating radio singing star Rogers in this effort that verges more toward screwball comedy than musical comedy. Features only four numbers, but one is the sensational "Since They Turned 'Lock Lomond' into Swing," in which Astaire plays the harmonica while dancing, tees off half a dozen golf balls in perfect rhythm, and does a Highland fling over two crossed golf clubs. But it's more Rogers's film than Astaire's. (Dir: Mark Sandrich, 83 mins.)

Careful—Soft Shoulder (1942)**½ Virginia Bruce, James Ellison. Nitwit Washington society girl gets involved with a Nazi spy. Surprisingly entertaining comedy, only the wartime background dating it. Pleasing fun. (Dir: Oliver H.P. Garrett, 69 mins.)

Caretaker, The—See **Guest, The**

Caretakers, The (1963)*½ Robert Stack, Joan Crawford, Polly Bergen, Janis Paige. (Dir: Hall Bartlett, 97 mins.)

Carey Treatment, The (1972)**½ James Coburn, Jennifer O'Neill, Skye Aubrey, Regis Toomey. Director Blake Edwards's medical murder story in which hip pathologist Coburn clears a buddy charged with a messy abortion on the chief surgeon's 15-year-old daughter. Some remarkable bits of Edwardian business, but the early part is miserably paced and edited. Never approaches the achievement of Edwards's "Gunn," which it resembles in form. (100 mins.)

Cargo to Capetown (1950)**½ Broderick Crawford, Ellen Drew, John Ireland. Personal drama gets in the way of the action in this adventure film about two tanker tramps in love with the same girl. (Dir: Earl McEvoy, 80 mins.)

Carib Gold (1957)** Ethel Waters, Coley Wallace, Geoffrey Holder. The things that happen when a shrimp boat discovers a sunken treasure. Miss Waters and the Negro cast enhance matters considerably, although the production often has an amateur look. (71 mins.)

Caribbean (1952)** John Payne, Arlene Dahl, Cedric Hardwicke. Mild adventure yarn about the days of pirates, land grants, and the slave trade in the Caribbean. John Payne is heroic and Arlene Dahl serenely beautiful. (Dir: Edward Ludwig, 97 mins.)

Caribbean Hawk (Italy, 1963)*½ Johnny Desmond, Yvonne Monlaur. (Dir: Piero Regnoli, 115 mins.)

Cariboo Trail, The (1950)**½ Randolph Scott, "Gabby" Hayes, Bill Williams. Up in Canada in the 1890's, a cattleman turns to gold prospecting accidentally while searching for land. Above average western has a good story, performances. (Dir: Edwin L. Marin, 81 mins.)

Carmen Jones (1954)***½ Dorothy Dandridge, Harry Belafonte, Pearl Bailey. The story of the femme fatale "Carmen," adapted by Oscar Hammerstein II updating the Bizet music, and directed by Otto Preminger. Despite some faults, it packs quite a bit of power. Well sung by dubbed voices for the principals. The late Miss Dandridge is a spectacularly beautiful dish in this entry. (Dir: Otto Preminger, 105 mins.)

Carnaby, M.D. (Great Britain, 1966)** Leslie Phillips, James Robertson Justice, Shirley Ann Field. Sixth entry in the "doctor" series has Justice once again playing Sir Lancelot Spratt trying to train a young doctor. Phillips is hardly as effective as other young apprentices in the series, who include Dirk Bogarde and Kenneth More. Also released as "Doctor in Clover." (Dir: Ralph Thomas, 95 mins.)

Carnal Knowledge (1971)***½ Jack Nicholson, Arthur Garfunkel, Ann-Margret, Candice Bergen. Two gifted artists, writer Jules Feiffer and director Mike Nichols, have created a funny, perceptive, and sometimes painfully accurate account of the sexual mores and hang-ups of American males over two decades. Nicholson and Garfunkel are Amherst college students in the late 40s who share a dormitory room and a blond virgin from nearby Smith (Bergen). Nicholson plays such a reprehensible louse that it's hard to give a damn about him, but so much of the movie is fresh and revealing that you'll overlook its defects. Ann-Margret is surprisingly effective as a 30-ish TV model, as is Garfunkel in his debut, co-starring role. The ending is modern poetic justice: the stud is punished with impotence. (97 mins.)

Carnation Frank (Germany, 1961)* Chris Howland, Dagmar Hanks. (Dir: Stanley Haynes, 93 mins.)

Carnegie Hall (1947)*** Marsha Hunt, William Prince, Frank McHugh. Director Edgar G. Ulmer has a budget above poverty row for once in this concert film with musical performances set against the story of an immigrant cleaning woman whose son becomes a concert pianist. Music by Bruno Walter, Leopold Stokowski, Arthur Rubenstein, Jascha Heifetz, Lily Pons, Risë Stevens, and the New York Philharmonic—and for filler, Ezio Pinza, Jan Peerce, Harry James, and Vaughan Monroe. (134 mins.)

Carnival in Flanders (France, 1935)**½ In the early 17th century a small Belgian town is occupied by a division of the Spanish army. The men desert the village, leaving their wives to make peace with the enemy by celebrating the takeover with a carnival. Director Jacques Feyder's naïve fable on the virtues of nonviolence failed to please the warring political factions at the time of its release: French patriots thought it approved collaboration, while it was banned by the Nazis who saw themselves parodied in the Spanish soldiers.

Carnival of Souls (1962)**½ Candance Hilligoss, Frances Feist, Herk Harvey. Victim of auto accident has her spirit continue to live. Made in Lawrence, Kansas. Despite some crudities, it's pretty good for Lawrence—it's good for Kansas City while we're at it. (Dir: Herk Harvey, 80 mins.)

Carnival of Thrills (MTV 1980)* John Schneider, Tom Wopat, Robin Mattson, Sorrell Brooke. (Dir: Dick Moder, 104 mins.)

Carnival Story (1954)**½ Anne Baxter, Steve Cochran, George Nader. Tragedy ensues when two men love a beautiful carnival high-diving star. Heavy-handed drama; good performances. (Dir: Kurt Neumann, 95 mins.)

Carny (1980)*** Gary Busey, Jodie Foster, Robbie Robertson, Meg Foster. This tale of two friends who work for the carnival and the runaway girl who comes between them is worth seeing for Busey's vivid performance as a "bozo" who insults customers to get them to pay to throw baseballs at him. Director Robert Kaylor pulls off nice moments but wavers between the roles of documentarist and dramatist. Robertson's heralded acting debut and Foster's first adult characterization are impressive. (105 mins.)

Carolina Cannonball (1955)*½ Judy Canova, Andy Clyde. (Dir: Charles Lamont, 80 mins.)

Carousel (1956)***½ Gordon MacRae, Shirley Jones. Tastefully produced version of the fantasy "Liliom," with the Rodgers & Hammerstein evergreen score. Concerns the marriage of a swaggering carnival barker and a shy girl, and the tragic consequences when he takes drastic steps to provide for their child. Nicely sung, beautiful Maine locale. (Dir: Henry King, 128 mins.)

Carpet of Horror, The (German, 1962)*½ Joachim Fuchsberger Eleonora Rossi-Drago. (Dir: Harald Reinl, 93 mins.)

Carpetbaggers, The (1964)*½ Carroll Baker, George Peppard, Alan Ladd. (Dir: Edward Dmytryk, 150 mins.)

Carrie (1952)*** Jennifer Jones, Laurence

Olivier, Eddie Albert, Miriam Hopkins. This adaptation of Dreiser's "Sister Carrie" has good casting, with Olivier turning in one of his richest screen performances as the man who ruins himself for the upwardly mobile Carrie (Jones). But the screenplay lacks Dreiser's obsessive passion, and the direction by William Wyler is merely attentive without inspiration. (118 mins.)

Carrie (1961)*** Sissy Spacek, Piper Laurie, John Travolta, Betty Buckley. Stylish thriller about a sheltered high-school girl who discovers she has telekinetic powers. Spacek is excellent as the eccentric girl with the weirdo, fanatically religious mother (played to the hilt by Laurie). Carrie is invited as a joke to the high-school prom by one of the most popular, handsome boys in the school; when her dream-come-true turns into a nightmare she turns on her powers, bringing havoc and destruction. The finale is pure Grand Guignol. Eerie and entertaining. (Dir: Brian De Palma, 97 mins.)

Carry On Again, Doctor (Great Britain, 1969)*½ Kenneth Williams, Jim Dale. (Dir: Gerald Thomas, 89 mins.)

Carry On Cabby (Great Britain, 1963)** Sidney James, Hattie Jacques. Another in the long line of English "Carry On" films. A taxicab company competes against a rival that's owned by the boss's neglected wife. Doesn't export too well. (Director: Gerald Thomas, 91 mins.)

Carry on Camping (Great Britain, 1969)*½ Sidney James, Kenneth Williams, Joan Sims, Barbara Windsor. (Dir: Gerald Thomas, 89 mins.)

Carry On Cleo (Great Britain, 1965)**½ Amanda Barrie, Sidney James, Kenneth Connor. Corned-up take-off on the Cleopatra legend, with some comics scampering around, like an old blackout skit prolonged. Despite the crudity, it's reasonably amusing. (Dir: Gerald Thomas, 92 mins.)

Carry On Constable (Great Britain, 1960)** Sidney James, Eric Barker, Kenneth Connor. Group of bungling police rookies manage to gum up the works but redeem themselves. Broad comedy depends on a bunch of old wheezes for laughs, sometimes hits the mark. (Dir: Gerald Thomas, 86 mins.)

Carry On Cruising (Great Britain, 1962)** Sidney James, Kenneth Williams, Kenneth Connor, Liz Frazer. Skipper of a Mediterranean cruising ship is inflicted with a group of inept crewmen gumming up the works. One moth-eaten slapstick gag after another, but this lowbrow comedy manages to keep afloat. (Dir: Gerald Thomas, 89 mins.)

Carry on Jack—See **Carry on Venus**

Carry On Nurse (Great Britain, 1959)**½ Kenneth Connor, Shirley Eaton, Wilfrid Hyde-White. Fun and games in an English hospital—and that's all there is to it. No plot, just a string of farcical sight gags, some of them very funny. (Dir: Gerald Thomas, 90 mins.)

Carry On Regardless (Great Britain, 1961)** Sidney James, Kenneth Connor, Joan Sims, Liz Frazer. Head of an employment agency assigns various bunglers to jobs. Sheer persistence makes some of the ancient gags in this broad farce seem occasionally amusing. (Dir: Gerald Thomas, 86 mins.)

Carry On Sergeant (Great Britain, 1958)**½ William Hartnell, Bob Monkhouse, Shirley Eaton. Tough sergeant about to retire wants his last platoon to be a crack one—but the members are mostly cracked. All the old army routines are crammed into this low-brow comedy. Some of it is funny. (Dir: Gerald Thomas, 88 mins.)

Carry On Spying (Great Britain, 1964)**½ Kenneth Williams, Barbara Windsor, Bernard Cribbins. B.O.S.H. Security Headquarters sends some inept agents to Vienna to combat the villainous activities of S.T.E.N.C.H.—which gives you the idea of the subtle humor involved here. Nevertheless, frequent hearty chuckles are provided. (Dir: Gerald Thomas, 88 mins.)

Carry On Teacher (Great Britain, 1959)**½ Ted Ray, Kenneth Connor, Joan Sims. Dean of a private school wants a better position, but his students and classmates wish him to stay, so they sabotage a scheduled inspection to make him look bad. Practically a textbook of ancient gags, some of which are still funny. (Dir: Gerald Thomas, 86 mins.)

Carry on TV (Great Britain, 1961)*½ Bob Monkhouse, Kenneth Connor. Alternate titles: **Dentist On the Job, Get On With It!** (Dir: C. M. Pennington Richards, 88 mins.)

Carry On Venus (Great Britain, 1963)**½ Bernard Cribbins, Juliet Mills, Kenneth Williams. More royal messing up as a bunch of deadheads nearly manage to upset the Royal Navy. Burlesque of all those sea dramas manages to shape up a nice covey of chuckles. Alternate title: **Carry On Jack.** (Dir: Gerald Thomas, 91 mins.)

Carson City (1952)**½ Randolph Scott, Raymond Massey, Lucille Norman. Railroad engineer fights those who don't want the thing built. Well made western. (Dir: Andre de Toth, 87 mins.)

Carter's Army (MTV 1970)**½ Stephen Boyd, Robert Hooks, Susan Oliver. Often interesting feature which benefits greatly from the fine performance by Robert Hooks as the lieutenant in charge of an all black outfit during WW II. Stephen Boyd plays a white southern officer who clashes with Hooks and his men while trying to carry off a dangerous mission behind enemy lines involving a strategic bridge marked for demolition by the Nazis. Richard Pryor, as a terrified G.I., and Moses Gunn, as a college professor turned foot soldier, are the standouts in a uniformly fine supporting cast. (72 mins.)

Carthage in Flames (France-Italy, 1960)**

Anne Heywood, Jose Suarez, Pierre Brasseur, Daniel Gelin. Carthaginian warrior rescues a young slave girl during the Third Punic War, and she eventually is instrumental in avenging his death. Elaborate costume spectacle dubbed in English has the advantage of a better-than-average cast, some impressive mass scenes. (Dir: Carmine Gallone, 96 mins.)

Cartouche (U.S.A.-France-Italy, 1956)** Richard Basehart, Patricia Roc, Akim Tamiroff. Nobleman's son returns to France to clear himself of a crime. Average costume adventure, nothing new. (Dir: Steve Sekely, 73 mins.)

Cartouche (France, 1964)*** Jean-Paul Belmondo, Claudia Cardinale. Generally amusing swashbuckling spoof, with the athletic Mr. Belmondo as a sort of Gallic Robin Hood. Cardinale is pretty, the pace is fast, so. . . (Dir: Philippe de Broca, 115 mins.)

Carve Her Name With Pride (Great Britain, 1958)**** Virginia McKenna, Paul Scofield. Inspiring true story of Violette Szabo, who braved death while working for the French Resistance in World War II. Excellent performances from McKenna and Scofield. Also noteworthy because this is one of the few films to date made by Scofield, who happens to be second only to Laurence Olivier, about the greatest actor alive. (Dir: Lewis Gilbert, 116 mins.)

Casa Ricordi (Italy, 1954)** Roland Alexandre, Marta Toren. Long, draggy saga of the famous Italian publishing house. Lots of operatic arias, dubbed English dialogue. (Dir: Carmine Gallone, 117 mins.)

Casablanca (1942)***½ Humphrey Bogart, Ingrid Bergman, Paul Henreid. This one is famous for the song, "As Time Goes By," plus a wonderful cast but try not to forget that overall it's a very dull melodrama of intrigue. You'll enjoy it if you can overlook its faults and keep track (between commercials) of its stream of characters. Oscar as Best Film. (Dir: Michael Curtiz, 102 mins.)

Casanova (Italy-France, 1954)*½ Georges Marchal, Corinne Calvet, Marina Vlady. (Dir: Steno, 90 mins.)

Casanova and Company—See: Some Like It Cool

Casanova Brown (1944)**½ Gary Cooper, Teresa Wright. College professor, whose marriage has been annulled, finds that he's a father as he is about to marry again. Fairly amusing comedy, but could have been better. (Dir: Sam Wood, 94 mins.)

Casanova '70 (Italy-France, 1965)*** Marcello Mastroianni, Virna Lisi, Michele Mercier, Marisa Mell. Attractive wolf has psychological difficulty with his love affairs, becoming even more complicated when he meets the real love for him. The best of Mastroianni's films still has some good laughs, and he's always a joy to behold. (Dir: Mario Monicelli, 113 mins.)

Casanova's Big Night (1954)** Bob Hope,

Joan Fontaine, Basil Rathbone, Vincent Price. Hope as a tailor's apprentice who poses as the great lover and finds himself in the middle of court intrigue. Not on a par with other Hope farces—some laughs, but too much tedium in between. (Dir: Norman Z. McLeod, 86 mins.)

Casbah (1948)**½ Yvonne DeCarlo, Tony Martin, Peter Lorre. Another version of the saga of Pepe LeMoko, the criminal who hides from the law in the Casbah section of Algiers, until the love of a woman forces him to the outside world and his doom. Not bad; Martin is convincing as an actor, and the production is good. (Dir: John Berry, 94 mins.)

Case Against Brooklyn, The (1958)** Darren McGavin, Maggie Hayes. A hard hitting, forceful but highly fictionalized account of one rookie cop's attempt to single-handedly break a big gambling syndicate in Brooklyn. McGavin is a good actor but is totally wasted in this overdone police story. (Dir: Paul Wendkos, 82 mins.)

Case Against Ferro, The (France, 1976)** Yves Montand, François Perier, Stefania Sandrelli, Simone Signoret. A poky French detective thriller. Montand, a police inspector, heads the investigation of a murder where he is the suspect being sought. Takes off on the great premise of "The Big Clock," in which the hero's efforts to evade capture are complicated by the guilt of his superior. Takes too long. (125 mins.)

Case of Dr. Laurent, The France, (1957)**** Jean Gabin, Nicole Courcel. An excellent French film (dubbed) about a country doctor who is a dedicated man with an abundance of compassion for his patients. There is a superb birth sequence which is both educational and dramatic, though it may not be intact by the time the TV butchers with the editing scissors get finished. (Dir: Jean-Paul Chanois, 92 mins.)

Case of Mrs. Loring (Great Britain, 1959)** Julie London, Anthony Steel. Provocative theme poorly handled. Wife realizing her husband is sterile submits to artificial insemination and thereby loses her husband in the process. This theme deserves better acting and writing. Julie London is so luscious it makes things even more confusing. Alternate title: **A Question of Adultery.** (Dir: Don Chaffey, 90 mins.)

Case of Patty Smith, The (1962)** Dani Lynn, Merry Anders, J. Edward McKinley. Controversial movie when it appeared, because it was a plea for legalized abortion. Impregnated rape victim, rebuffed by all, seeks a criminal abortion. Overly dramatic, suffers also from Miss Lynn's poor acting. Written, produced and directed by Leo Handel. (93 mins.)

Case of Rape, A (1974)***½ Elizabeth Montgomery. A provocative, controversial subject is treated with candor in this fine dramatization about a married woman who is raped twice by the same young man, and then suffers indignities and personal loss when she goes to court. Miss Montgomery buries her "Bewitched" cuteness and gives a thoughtful, believable performance as the lovely woman subjected to the nightmare of rape. The script introduces little-publicized legal facts about rape cases which will surprise you, and the ending does not make any compromises. Worthwhile. (Dir: Boris Sagal, 104 mins.)

Case of the Red Monkey (Great Britain, 1953)*½ Richard Conte, Rona Anderson. (Dir: Ken Hughes, 73 mins.)

Case 33: Antwerp (Germany, 1965)*½ Adrian Hoven, Corny Collins. (85 mins.)

Casey's Shadow (1978)***½ Walter Matthau, Alexis Smith, Robert Webber, Murray Hamilton. Appealing sentimental and rather touching comedy-drama about quarter-horse raising. Matthau is almost the whole show as the opportunistic horse trainer who would just about sacrifice his three young sons' affections if he could come up with a winner. A brace of teen talent makes good impressions—Andrew A. Rubin, Stephan Burns, Susan Myers, and Michael Hershewe as Casey—while Smith, as a wealthy horse owner, and the colorful race at Duidoso, New Mexico, provide added interest. A lovely "family film, for young and old." (Dir: Martin Ritt, 116 mins.)

Cash McCall (1959)**½ Natalie Wood, James Garner. The best selling novel about big business and the people who play at it. Glossily produced. The attractive stars go through the motions but the script defeats any true development of characters. This film is reminiscent of the 1940's product which has since come to be known as "the typical Hollywood film." (Dir: Joseph Pevney, 102 mins.)

Cash on Demand (Great Britain, 1961)* Peter Cushing, Andre Morell. (Dir: Quentin Lawrence, 84 mins.)

Casino de Paris (France-Italy-Germany, 1957)** Caterina Valente, Vittorio De Sica. Lothario-playwright has designs on a glamorous star, invites her to his villa. She arrives with her family. Mild musical comedy provides only fair fun. Dubbed in English. (Dir: Andre Hunebelle, 85 mins.)

Casino Murder Case, The (1935)**½ Paul Lukas, Alison Skipworth, Donald Cook, Rosalind Russell. Three studios churned out adaptations of S. S. Van Dine's Philo Vance detective novels in the '30s. This was the second MGM attempt, with Lukas playing Vance. (Dir: Edwin L. Marin, 85 mins.)

Casino Royale (Great Britain, 1967)**½ Peter Sellers, Ursula Andress, David Niven. An overblown, lavish production and an array of big-name guest stars such as William Holden, Charles Boyer, Deborah Kerr, Orson Welles, Jean-Paul Belmondo and Woody Allen in the leads are the come-ons for this one. It's a spoof of all the James Bond spy adventures and there are more Bonds than you can keep

track of—but what the picture really needs is Sean Connery and he's conspicuously missing. The special effects are stunning and the gambling casino finale is well staged. No less than five directors had a hand in this not so royale romp. (Dirs: John Huston, Ken Hughes, Robert Parrish, Joe McGrath, Val Guest, 100 mins.)

Cass Timberlane (1947)**½ Spencer Tracy, Lana Turner, Zachary Scott. One of Sinclair Lewis' weakest novels receives a sincere adaptation and is fairly good commercial screen fare. Story is about a respectable midwestern judge who marries a beautiful immature bride and has trouble keeping pace with her youth. (Dir: George Sidney, 119 mins.)

Cassandra Crossing, The (1977)*½ Sophia Loren, Burt Lancaster, Richard Harris, Ava Gardner. (Dir: George Pan Cosmatos, 125 mins.)

Cast a Dark Shadow (Great Britain, 1957)**½ Dirk Bogarde, Margaret Lockwood. Scoundrel after cash marries a woman—object: matrimony, then murder. Unevenly paced thriller has some good suspense, sturdy performances. (Dir: Lewis Gilbert, 84 mins.)

Cast a Giant Shadow (1966)**½ Kirk Douglas, Senta Berger, Angie Dickinson, Topol. Highly romanticized but interesting tale about the Israeli-Arab conflict in the days when Israel first became a state. Kirk Douglas is cast as Col. Marcus, the legendary American soldier who helps shape up Israel's fighting force in 1948. There's action galore, and even a love story for the ladies, plus cameo roles played by none other than John Wayne, Frank Sinatra and Yul Brynner. (Topol is fine playing a Bedouin partial to the Israeli cause. Topol's major star with his glorious lead performance in "Fiddler on the Roof.") (Dir: Melville Shavelson, 142 mins.)

Cast a Long Shadow (1959)*½ Audie Murphy, Terry Moore. (Dir: Thomas Carr, 82 mins.)

Casta Diva (Italy-France, 1955)** Maurice Ronet, Nadia Gray. Another musical biography, this time it's operatic composer Bellini. Dubbed in English, only the music hath charms. (Dir: Carmine Gallone, 100 mins.)

Castaway Cowboy, The (1947)*** James Garner, Vera Miles. Amiable family fare which bears the authentic stamp of Disney quality. James Garner is a Texan who finds himself in Hawaii in 1850 where he gives in to the pleadings of a widow and her charming son to turn their farm into a cattle ranch. The Hawaiian locale and the Western yarn work well in tandem and the cast is fine, notably James Garner, young Eric Shea, and capable Vera Miles. (Dir: Vincent McEveety, 91 mins.)

Castilian, The (Spain, 1963)** Cesar Romero, Broderick Crawford, Alida Valli. Castilian nobleman comes out of exile to lead his people against the Moors. Some fine scenery, big action scenes, but the usual ragged scripting and some inferior performances defeat this European-made spectacle. (Dir: Javier Seto, 129 mins.)

Castle, The (Switzerland-West Germany, 1968)***½ Maximilian Schell, Cordula Trantow. Generally absorbing adaptation of Franz Kafka's uncompleted novel about a land surveyor who comes to a village, and can't make contact with the people in "the castle" who control the town. Beautiful photography by Rudolph Noelte and fine acting by Schell playing K, the surveyor, make this a graphic study of man in hopeless conflict with bureaucracy. (Dir: Rudolf Noelte, 93 mins.)

Castle in the Air (Great Britain, 1955)**½ David Tomlinson, Margaret Rutherford. Scottish earl without funds tries to sell his castle. Amusing comedy. (Dir: Henry Cass, 89 mins.)

Castle Keep (1969)**½ Burt Lancaster, Peter Falk, Patrick O'Neal. Uneven, ambitious film directed by Sydney Pollack. Offbeat, well-produced WW II story set in a Belgian castle where a great many art treasures are kept. Lancaster is the Major who has to hold off a German attack from the castle, and he comes to grips with the Count (Jean-Pierre Aumont), who can't stand by and see the priceless art be destroyed. Too talky at times but good performances keep your attention. (105 mins)

Castle of Evil (1966)* Scott Brady, Virginia Mayo, David Brian. (Dir: Francis D. Lyon, 81 mins.)

Castle of Purity (Mexico, 1974)**** Claudio Brook, Rita Macedo. Fascinating. chilling, powerful psychological drama about a neurotic husband who keeps his wife and children virtual prisoners in their own home. (Dir: Arturo Ripstein, 116 mins.)

Castle of Terror (Italy, 1963)** Barbara Steele, Georges Rivière. Man makes a bet that he can spend the night in a castle from which no living soul has ever returned. Dubbed-English horror thriller has its share of creepy moments, along with some ridiculous ones. (Dir: Anthony Dawson, 77 mins.)

Castle of the Living Dead (Italy, 1964)*½ Christopher Lee, Rossana Podesta, Georges Rivière. Alternate title: **Horror Castle.** (Dirs: Anthony Dawson, Richard McNamara, 83 mins.)

Castle on the Hudson (1940)**½ John Garfield, Ann Sheridan, Pat O'Brien, Burgess Meredith. Of course the acting is top drawer, but you've seen this tired old prison movie plot a million times. Remake of *20,000 Years in Sing Sing*, 1933. (Dir: Anatole Litvak, 77 mins.)

Castles in Spain (France, 1954)** Danielle Darrieux, Maurice Ronet. Soggy story of a bullfighter's love for a French belle, English-dubbed. Attractive cast, but the plot's a lot of bull. (Dir: René Wheeler, 90 mins.)

Cat, The (France, 1958)**½ Françoise Arnoul, Bernard Blier. Love and intrigue in the French underground during the Second World War. Sexy Françoise Arnoul makes a good impression as Cora. (Dir: Henri Decoin, 108 mins.)

Cat! (1966)**½ Roger Perry, Peggy Ann Garner, Barry Coe. Youngsters may like this outdoor tale of a boy who makes friends with a wildcat that eventually saves him from a rustler. Pleasantly done. (Dir: Ellis Kadison, 87 mins.)

Cat and Mouse (West Germany, 1969)** Lars Brandt, Peter Brandt, Claudia Brener. Gunter Grass's novel was adapted by director Hansjurgen Pohland with its penchant for the grotesque intact. Another coming-of-age story in Nazi Germany, but this time the subject is not a demented dwarf ("The Tin Drum"), but two teenage boys, played by the sons of ex-chancellor Willy Brandt. (92 mins.)

Cat and Mouse (France, 1975)**½ Michele Morgan, Jean-Pierre Aumont, Serge Reggiani. One of director Claude Lelouch's more tolerable efforts, with some clever character work to compensate for his inability to handle a camera or cut film. Reggiani happily mugs his way through the part of a Paris police inspector on the trail of a murderer. His name is Lechet, and naturally, he has a dog. (107 mins.)

Cat and the Fiddle, The (1934)*** Ramon Novarro, Frank Morgan, Jeanette MacDonald. Charming, visually inventive version of the Jerome Kern-Oscar Hammerstein operetta, directed by William K. Howard. Not far below the level of Rouben Mamoulian's "Love Me Tonight." An aspiring young singer is waylaid in her love for a temperamental composer by her big break. The songs include "She Didn't Say Yes." Lots of style and cheek in a musical made just before the Production Code purged sex from the genre. (90 mins.)

Cat Ballou (1965)**** Lee Marvin, Jane Fonda, Michael Callan. A very funny offbeat western yarn with a magnificent comedy performance by Lee Marvin as a grizzled, has-been gunslinger who is called back into duty to do away with a lookalike villain. Marvin plays both roles. Marvin won an Oscar for this role. His performances are the major interest in the film, but the funny screenplay deserves a good deal of the credit, too. Well directed. (Dir: Elliot Silverstein, 96 mins.)

Cat Creature, The (MTV 1973)** Stuart Whitman, Meredith Baxter, Gale Sondergaard, Kent Smith, John Carradine. When you subtract tension and discovery from a thriller, there isn't much left. So it is with this tale of prowling cats, Egyptian curses, and reincarnation. Pack these elements tightly around Whitman as a detective and you're in for nothing more than you expect. (Dir: Curtis Harrington, 73 mins.)

Cat from Outer Space, The (1978)** Ken Berry, Sandy Duncan, Harry Morgan.

Harmless kiddie comedy about a feline named Jake from another world, with a collar that gives him extraordinary powers. The cast is pleasant and includes the usual Disney quota of old-timers. Written by Ted Key, the cartoonist who created "Hazel." (Dir: Norman Tokar, 103 mins.)

Cat Girl (1958)** Barbara Shelley, Kay Callard. Beauty suddenly turns feline, murders result. British-made and cheap, but Shelley is a good actress, better than the material. (Dir: Alfred Shaunessy, 69 mins.)

Cat o' Nine Tails (France-Germany-Italy, 1971)* Karl Malden, James Franciscus, Catherine Spaak. (Dir: Dario Argento, 112 mins.)

Cat on a Hot Tin Roof (1958)**** Elizabeth Taylor, Paul Newman, Burl Ives. One of Tennessee Williams' most powerful studies of a southern family is successfully filmed by adaptor-director Richard Brooks. Elizabeth Taylor gives a very fine performance as the wife of a former hero (Paul Newman), who is dominated by his father and has taken to drink. Newman is very good, and Ives masterfully recreates his stage portrayal of massive "Big Daddy." Potent drama. (Dir: Richard Brooks, 108 mins.)

Catch As Catch Can (Italy, 1967)** Vittorio Gassman, Martha Hyer. Moderately bawdy satire features Gassman as a billboard advertising model being harassed by every sort of beast and bug. Improbable 'bugging' is overdone—satire of advertising/political idolization is better—but Gassman is finally overcome by the endless situations. (Dir: Franco Indovina, 95 mins.)

Catch-22 (1970)***½ Alan Arkin, Martin Balsam, Richard Benjamin, Arthur Garfunkel, Jack Gilford, Bob Newhart, Anthony Perkins, Jon Voight. Joseph Heller's black comedy about war and all it really means to the common man has been turned into a flawed masterpiece by director Mike Nichols and the adapter-writer Buck Henry. The setting for Heller's anti-war crusade against the war profiteers is a bombardier group stationed in Italy during WW II, and his gallery of lunatic characters are vividly brought to life, for the most part, by a wonderful cast headed by Alan Arkin as the very sane Yossarian who tried desperately to be certified mad so that he can stop flying missions. The film starts off brilliantly but the various sequences, no matter how well played, come off as isolated anecdotes that don't fully pay off. But it's well worth seeing and Arkin is wonderful. (Dir: Mike Nichols, 120 mins.)

Catcher, The (MTV 1972)*½ Michael Witney. (Dir: Allen H. Miner, 99 mins.)

Catered Affair, The (1956)*** Bette Davis, Ernest Borgnine, Debbie Reynolds, Rod Taylor, Barry Fitzgerald. In the mid-'50s the movies were sufficiently afraid of TV to cannibalize its successes, and this is one of those big-screen adaptations of "little-people" dramas that were to give social realism a bad name. Still, Gore Vidal's adaptation of Paddy Chayefsky's TV play is skillful, and Richard Brooks's direction dignifies the material with visual coherence. Davis is cast against type as a Bronx housewife who attempts to mount a bigger wedding for her daughter than her taxi driver husband (Borgnine) can afford. (93 mins.)

Catherine of Russia (Italy, 1962)** Hildegarde Neff, Sergio Fantoni. Empress Catherine and how she got that way—by overthrowing Peter of Russia and taking the throne. Overstuffed costume drama dubbed in English. (Dir: Umberto Lenzi, 105 mins.)

Catherine the Great (Great Britain, 1934)**½ Elisabeth Bergner, Douglas Fairbanks Jr. The Empress of Russia is forced into a marriage that she does not wish, with resulting unhappiness. Elaborate but heavy, slow historical drama. (Dir: Paul Czinner, 100 mins.)

Catholics (MTV 1973)***½ Trevor Howard, Cyril Cusack, Martin Sheen. Splendid adaptation of Brian Moore's novel about simple worship in an ancient Irish monastery, threatened by increasing permissiveness in the Mother Church. Filmed against the rugged Irish coast, the striking opening scene of this provocative, brooding drama offers the melodic sound of the Latin Mass being offered by an old Irish monk (Cusack) before a tremendous crowd of worshippers, held spellbound by the experience. A memorable performance by Trevor Howard, as the wise, wistful abbot of the institution. Superior. (Dir: Jack Gold. 100 mins.)

Cathy Tippel (The Netherlands, 1975)**** Monique van der Ven, Rutger Hauer, Eddie Brugman. The family of a free-spirited girl force her into prostitution to support them in 1881 Amsterdam. A worthy resurrection of early 20th-century social fiction; exhibits detail, wit, and conscience. Lusciously shot, and glimmeringly performed by van der Ven in the title role. (Dir: Paul Verhoeven, 104 mins.)

Catlow, (Great Britain, 1971)**½ Yul Brynner, Richard Crenna, Leonard Nimoy. Unpretentious action western as Brynner plays a post-Civil War outlaw-drifter hunted down by friend and marshal Crenna. The Spanish desert looks as fine as ever. (Dir: Sam Wanamaker, 101 mins.)

Cattle Drive (1951)**½ Joel McCrea, Dean Stockwell. Interesting western with good performances by McCrea and Stockwell as a saddle worn cowhand and a young upstart, respectively, who team up on a cattle drive and become fast friends. (Dir: Kurt Neumann, 77 mins.)

Cattle Empire (1958)**½ Joel McCrea, Gloria Talbott. Another western tale in which the hero is believed to be a renegade but turns out all right after all, but done with finesse. Better than average. (Dir: Charles Marquis Warren, 83 mins.)

Cattle King (1963)*½ Robert Taylor, Joan Caulfield, Robert Loggia, William Windom. Strife and blazing guns in a tired western about fence-rights conflicts between cattlemen and farmers. Set in Wyoming, 1880s. (Dir: Tay Garnett, 88 mins.)

Cattle Queen of Montana (1954)** Barbara Stanwyck, Ronald Reagan. When her pop is murdered, a lone gal fights an unscrupulous land grabber. Slow; not very believable western. (Dir: Allan Dwan, 88 mins.)

Caught (1949)*** James Mason, Barbara Bel Geddes, Robert Ryan. Model marries neurotic millionaire, is unhappy until a young doctor comes to her aid. Good melodrama, well acted. (Dir: Max Ophuls, 88 mins.)

Caught in the Draft (1941)***½ Bob Hope, Dorothy Lamour. The Army may have changed since 1941, but this picture about a draft-dodging movie star who is finally caught and placed in the Army is grand fun. (Dir: David Butler, 82 mins.)

Cauldron of Blood (Spain-U.S., 1968)* Jean-Pierre Aumont, Boris Karloff, Viveca Lindfors. (Dir: Edward Mann, 101 mins.)

Cause for Alarm (1951)** Loretta Young, Barry Sullivan. This over dramatic story about a woman being terrorized by her husband who suspects her of infidelity is like an expanded TV show. (Dir: Tay Garnett, 74 mins.)

Cavalcade (1933)*** Diana Wynyard, Clive Brook, Una O'Connor, Margaret Lindsay. Elegant adaptation of Noel Coward's play traces the Marryot family from 1899 to 1932. Rich characterizations bring alive the sorrows and triumphs which befall the family during World War I and the Depression. Coward's wonderful songs are left intact. An Oscar-winner for best direction. (Dir: Frank Lloyd, 110 mins.)

Cavalier In Devil's Castle (Italy, 1959)*½ Massimo Serato, Irene Tunc. (Dir: Mario Costa, 85 mins.)

Cavalleria Rusticana (Italy, 1952)** Mario Del Monico, Rina Telli. Mascagni's opera, sung in Italian with English narration. For opera lovers. (Dir: Carlo Vinti, Marion Rhodes, 53 mins.)

Cavalry Command (1963)*½ John Agar, Richard Arlen. (Dir: Eddie Romero, 80 mins.)

Cave of Outlaws (1951)** Macdonald Carey, Alexis Smith. Routine western about hidden gold and the lengths men go to uncover the secret hiding place. (Dir: William Castle, 75 mins.)

Caveman (1981)*** Ringo Starr, Dennis Quaid, Shelley Long, Jack Gilford, John Matuszak. A prehistoric comedy, an older subgenre than you might imagine: Chaplain, Keaton, and Laurel and Hardy all did one! Anyhow, this one is the brainchild of Carl Gottlieb, who directed and co-wrote the script with Rudy deLuca (all fifteen words of dialogue). Silly, lighthearted, and often hilarious. Ringo invents rock n' roll —with real rocks, and one unexpected scene-stealer is the most charming dinosaur you'll ever see! (Dir: Carl Gottlieb, 94 mins.)

Cavern, The (1965)** John Saxon, Brian Aherne, Rosanna Schiaffino. World War II adventure about six men and a woman trapped in a German munitions dump— the cavern of the title. Tensions are high, death is near and escape remote—you can fill in the rest. Directed by veteran Hollywood director Edgar G. Ulmer ("The Black Cat"). (100 mins.)

C.C. and Company (1970)* Ann-Margret, Joe Namath. (Dir: Seymour Robbie, 94 mins.)

Cease Fire (1953)*** Different sort of war film, using a cast of nonprofessionals, showing the activities of an infantry company in Korea prior to the peace talks. Filmed there with real GIs, it has the stamp of authenticity, should still be of interest. (Dir: Owen Crump, 75 mins.)

Ceddo (Nigeria, 1977)**** Director Ousmane Sembene's film tells of a village in Senegal under onerous demands from its colonial masters when WW I breaks out. Long, hypnotic in its discourse, this film is a genuine effort at crafting a Third World cinema. Compelling and consciously ritualistic. A harsh attack on Islamic doctrines and preaching.

Ceiling Zero (1935)***½ James Cagney, Pat O'Brien. The planes may look like antiques but this is still as exciting an aviation story as today's film makers can produce at supersonic speeds. (Dir: Howard Hawks, 95 mins.)

Cell 2455, Death Row (1955)**½ William Campbell, Kathryn Grant. Based on Caryl Chessman's book about his life in prison and the events leading up to it. Frank and sometimes effective. (Dir: Fred F. Sears, 80 mins.)

Cemetery Girls (1979)*½ (among independent features).

Centennial Summer (1946)*** Linda Darnell, Jeanne Crain, Constance Bennett, Walter Brennan, Cornel Wilde. About a family in Philadelphia in 1876 during the Centennial Exposition. A respectable imitation of "Meet me in St. Louis," well directed by Otto Preminger, who one might have thought ill suited for this fluff. Pleasant Jerome Kern-Oscar Hammerstein songs. (102 mins.)

Centurion, The (France, Italy, 1962)*½ John Drew Barrymore, Jacques Sernas. (Dir: Mario Costa, 77 mins.)

Ceremony, The (Japan, 1971)***½ Director Nagisha Oshima's best work to reach this country. A deadly parody of Japan's most beloved genre, the family saga, the film uses the story of the Sakurada clan to mirror the cultural decay of Japan after WW II. An outrageous blend of incest, violence, and looting. (122 mins.)

Ceremony, The (U.S.A.-Spain, 1964)**

111

Sarah Miles, Laurence Harvey, Robert Walker, John Ireland. A try for suspense, detailing efforts to spring a criminal from a Tangier prison. Harvey stars and directs—one task too many, for this cinema ceremony. Good moments offset by uneven treatment. (Dir: Laurence Harvey, 105 mins.)

Certain Smile, A (1958)**½ Rossano Brazzi, Joan Fontaine, Bradford Dillman, Christine Carere. Romantic melodrama for the ladies. Francoise Sagan's novel about a young girl's adventures in affairs of the heart with a suave, middle-aged Frenchman (played by Brazzi as if he were remembering all the early Boyer films) and a rebellious youth (played by Dillman as if he never saw an early Boyer film) is given a sumptuous production that spills all over with the beauty of the French Riviera. (Dir: Jean Negulesco, 104 mins.)

César (France, 1936)**** Raimu, Crane Desmazis, Pierre Fresnay. Director-writer-producer Marcel Pagnol ends his trilogy with a culminating masterpiece, full of audacious experiments with long takes in close-up and simple formalism that anticipate the New Wave by two decades. Marius returns to Marseilles after a 20-year absence to find the child he left with Fanny. The emotional impact is overwhelming. (117 mins.)

Cesar and Rosalie (France, 1972)***½ Yves Montand, Sami Frey, Romy Schneider. An intelligent, objective handling of the classic ménage à trois by French director Claude Sautet ("Classe Tous les Risques"), with a dynamic performance from Montand and good support from Frey and Schneider. (104 mins.)

Chad Hanna (1940)** Henry Fonda, Dorothy Lamour, Linda Darnell, Guy Kibbee. Overlong drama of a young man who joins the circus in the 19th century. The cast of fine actors have little to do. Color. (Dir: Henry King, 86 mins.)

Chadwick Family, The (MTV 1974)**½ Fred MacMurray, Kathleen Maguire. MacMurray stars in a family-oriented film. He's the editor and publisher of a newspaper, thinking of moving to Chicago to head a new national magazine. Crises in his family call for a last-minute change of plans. Cast is good, with Barry Bostwick, playing MacMurray's colorful son-in-law, coming off best. (Dir: David Lowell Rich, 78 mins.)

Chain Lightning (1950)**½ Humphrey Bogart, Eleanor Parker, Raymond Massey. Good shots of jet planes and air action but unfortunately pilot Bogart lands and fights a losing battle with a hackneyed script. (Dir: Stuart Heisler, 94 mins.)

Chain of Evidence (1957)** William Elliott, James Lydon. An amnesia victim is arrested for murder, but a clever cop proves otherwise. Average "B" mystery. (Dir: Paul Landres, 63 mins.)

Chained (1934)** Joan Crawford, Clark Gable, Stuart Erwin. Trite little love triangle. And you'll know before the first reel that Joan will end up with the dashing Gable. (Dir: Clarence Brown, 71 mins.)

Chairman, The (Great Britain, 1969)** Gregory Peck, Anne Heywood, Arthur Hill. Picture if you will Gregory Peck behind the Chinese bamboo curtain on a spy mission, with an explosive device sewn into his head ready to be detonated. Farfetched? Yes, indeed. In this one the Russians are our friends! Title refers to Chairman Mao. (Dir: J. Lee Thompson, 102 mins.)

Chalk Garden, The (British, 1964)***½ Deborah Kerr, Hayley Mills, John Mills, Edith Evans. Tender story of a governess who tries to provide the love her charge, a disturbed 16-year-old girl, needs so badly. Sensitively written and directed, with fine performances by all. It's a superior drama for discriminating audiences, and Edith Evans is superb. (Dir: Ronald Neame, 106 mins.)

Challenge, The (1960)—See: **It Takes a Thief**

Challenge, The (MTV 1970)* Darren McGavin, Broderick Crawford, Mako, James Whitmore. (Dir: Allen Smithee, 73 mins.)

Challenge for Robin Hood, A (Great Britain, 1967)*** Barrie Ingham, Leon Greene. Yet another recounting of the fun and games in Sherwood Forest, but this retelling is better than most, and recommended for the kids who haven't seen it all many times before. There are some songs thrown in for good measure and director C. M. Pennington-Richards for those who treasure such monikers has kept things moving at a lively clip. (Dir: C. M. Pennington-Richards, 85 mins.)

Challenge of the Gladiator (Italy, 1965)*½ Rock Stevens, Gloria Milland. (Dir: Domenico Paolella, 80 mins.)

Challenge to Be Free (1972)* Mike Mazurki. (Dirs: Tay Garnett and Ford Beebe, 88 mins.)

Challenge to Lassie (1949)**½ Edmund Gwenn, Donald Crisp, Lassie. Good family picture starring the famous collie. Veteran actors Edmund Gwenn and Donald Crisp make the somewhat sentimental story ring true. (Dir: Richard Thorpe, 76 mins.)

Challengers, The (1969)**½ Darren McGavin, Sean Garrison, Nico Minardos, Susan Clark. A car-racing drama with all the pat characters and situations. The racing sequences are excitingly photographed, but the triangular love story between racer Garrison, heiress Susan Clark, and playboy-racer Minardos gets a bit too obvious to sustain interest. Originally produced as a possible TV series pilot film, it has a "guest star" lineup including Anne Baxter, Farley Granger, Richard Conte and Juliet Mills. (Dir: Leslie Martinson, 99 mins.)

Chamber of Horrors (1966)** Patrick O'Neal, Suzy Parker. Horror film fans may enjoy this opus about a mass killer loose in Baltimore of the 1880's. All others will probably laugh at the wrong places. Patrick O'Neal rolls his eyes a great deal as the notorious madman. (Dir: Hy Averback, 99 mins.)

Champ, The (1931)*** Wallace Beery, Jackie Cooper, Irene Rich. Director King Vidor's sentimental story of a washed-up boxer and his doting son living the happy lowlife in Tijuana. Rich's performance is accomplished as the mother who has abandoned them. Some unbelievable hokum. Beery shared an Oscar with Fredric March. (87 mins.)

Champ, The (1979)*** Jon Voight, Faye Dunaway, Ricky Schroder, Joan Blondell. Update of the classic four-hankie tale of a broken-down fighter, his adoring son, and the ex-wife who wants custody of the boy she never really knew. Schroder is adorable as the boy. Director Franco Zeffirelli's first American-produced entry. (121 mins.)

Champ for a Day (1953)*** Alex Nicol, Audrey Totter. Prize fighter investigates the disappearance of his manager. Good melodrama has some unusual plot twists. (Dir: William Seiter, 90 mins.)

Champagne for Caesar (1950)***½ Ronald Colman, Celeste Holm, Vincent Price. An unemployed genius gets on a quiz show and proceeds to take the sponsor for all he's worth. Rollicking comedy never lets up for a minute! And Vincent Price as a mad soap tycoon is just about the funniest thing in ages. (Dir: Richard Whorf, 99 mins.)

Champagne Murders, The (France, 1967)** Is the eccentric playboy (Anthony Perkins) a murderer as well? Seems that way, but you never know. Too many other things are unclear in this Gallic-made whodunit, wherein director Claude Chabrol dallies by the wayside too long. Maurice Ronet, Yvonne Furneaux, Stephane Audran, and a particularly silly, unresolved ending. (Dir: Claude Chabrol, 98 mins.)

Champagne Waltz (1937)*** Fred MacMurray, Gladys Swarthout. Jazz musician incurs the wrath of a Viennese waltz enthusiast, but all is well at the end because of the old man's pretty granddaughter. Good musical. (Dir: A. Edward Sutherland, 100 mins.)

Champion (1949)**** Kirk Douglas, Arthur Kennedy, Lola Albright, Ruth Roman, Marilyn Maxwell. Douglas punched his way to stardom as the boxing heel in this rather free adaptation of Ring Lardner's mordant short story. When Douglas socks his crippled younger brother (Kennedy), we cringe, but we also cheer the slugging of a sanctimonious scrounge. Albright is remarkably sensual. (Carl Foreman scripted, launching his own considerable career.) (Dir: Stanley Kramer, 99 mins.)

Champions: A Love Story (MTV 1979)***

James Vincent McNichol, Joy LeDuc, Tony LoBianco. Uneven but touching tale of adolescent puppy love against a backdrop of amateur skating competitions. Better acted than most made-for-TV films. Toward the end, the film gets bogged down in sentiment. John A. Alonzo, who is a marvelous cinematographer, serves in that capacity and directs. (104 mins.)

Chance Meeting (Great Britain, 1954)**½ David Knight, Odile Versois, Theodore Bikel. American Embassy worker falls for the daughter of an Iron Curtain diplomat. Good idea marred by inconclusive, fence-straddling treatment. Some tender, romantic moments, well acted by Bikel. (Dir: Anthony Asquith, 96 mins.)

Chance Meeting (Great Britain, 1959)**½ Hardy Kruger, Stanley Baker, Micheline Presle. It looks bad for a painter who is arrested for a girl's murder although he insists he's innocent. Good performances in a mystery that never grips as it should. Alternate title: **Blind Date.** (Dir: Joseph Losey, 95 mins.)

Chance to Live, A (MTV 1978)** David Cassidy, Gloria De Haven, Anne Lockhart. Cassidy stars in the pilot of the short-lived TV series "Man Undercover." He's an undercover cop who poses as a high-school student to ferret out drug pushers. Manages to illustrate the attitudes, ranging from devil-may-care to worried, of the students involved in the racket. (Dir: Corey Allen, 104 mins.)

Chandler (1971)* Warren Oates, Leslie Caron. (Dir: Paul Magwood, 95 mins.)

Chandu the Magician (1932)** Bela Lugosi, Edmund Lowe, Irene Ware. One of the most creative talents in American cinema, William Cameron Menzies, who directed this film, is generally regarded as a designer. ("The Adventures of Tom Sawyer," "Gone with the Wind," "Around the World in Eighty Days") or art director. Aside from the design, this film is mostly unfortunate. (71 mins.)

Chang (1927)*** Kru, Chantui. Marian C. Cooper and Ernest Schoedsack directed this dramatic documentary in the wilds of Siam (Thailand.) Does not fully deserve its classic status. (73 mins.)

Change of Habit (1970)** Elvis Presley, Mary Tyler Moore. Presley plays a doctor, no less, who heads a clinic in a poor section of town, and Miss Moore plays one of a trio of nuns who offer their services to help out Presley's cause in this mild film. Oh yes, Presley does sing a song or two along the way, in this his 31st film. (Dir: William Graham, 93 mins.)

Change of Mind (1969)** Raymond St. Jacques, Susan Oliver. Absurd premise—the brain of a prominent white DA, dying of cancer, is transplanted into the body of a black listed as virtually DOA after an auto accident—gets a mounting here. The problems the transplant generate are numerous, of course, and they are not uninteresting . . . but you have to be

113

ready to accept the idea and that's asking too much to begin with. Music by Duke Ellington. (Dir: Robert Stevens, 103 mins.)

Change of Seasons, A (1980)**Shirley MacLaine,, Anthony Hopkins, Bo Derek, Michael Brandon, Mary Beth Hurt. Shirley MacLaine's intelligent performance as the betrayed wife of a philandering professor is the only bright spot in this insincere, conventional comedy. The others try, but the foolish, sniggering script gives them nothing coherent to go on. You might watch if you're a big fan of Shirley's—or if you want to see Bo Derek in a hot-tub! (Dirs: Noel Black, Richard Lang, 102 mins.)

Change Partners (Great Britain, 1966)*½ Zena Walker, Kenneth Cope, Basil Henson. (Dir: Robert Lynn, 63 mins.)

Changeling, The (Canada, 1979)*** George C. Scott, Trish Van Devere, Melvyn Douglas, Jean Marsh, John Colicos. Generally well calculated gothic thriller. It's the parents who are evil this time, not the kids—a major shakeup for the genre. Peter Medak's direction is too tricky, but pretty entertaining, full of Dutch angles and corny, sinister tracking shots. The film overstays its welcome by at least half an hour. (113 mins.)

Chant of Jimmie Blacksmith, The (Australia, 1978)*** This film chronicles the rampage by a half-breed aboriginal at the turn of the century. Based on a novel by Thomas Keneally, it seeks both epic sweep and ironic comment and does middling well with each. Although the action is familiar, some of the insights are original, as we see Jimmie try to emulate the white people only to find that they won't give him a chance to achieve what they promise if he's a good boy. He declares one-man war on white possessions—both their women and property. Much of the character detail is excitingly individual, and director Fred Schlepisi has an effective, large canvas. It's not a major film, but it shows considerable talent. (Dir: Fred Schlepisi, 122 mins.)

Chapman Report, The (1962)**½ Jane Fonda, Efrem Zimbalist, Jr., Claire Bloom, Glynis Johns, Shelley Winters. The best-selling novel inspired by the Kinsey Report on the sexual mores of suburban women is brought to the screen as a glossy soap opera. Zimbalist is all cool authority as a research psychologist who becomes entangled with Jane Fonda, a young woman suffering from emotional frigidity. Of the group, Glynis Johns delivers the best performance as a scatterbrained housewife with a secret. (Dir: George Cukor, 125 mins.)

Chappaqua (1967)***½ Jean-Louis Barrault, Allen Ginsberg. Ambitious, underrated vision of what a drug addict feels and sees. Accomplished first directorial effort by Conrad Rooks, who wrote and produced this film over a four-year period, in addition to playing the role of Russell Harwick. (Rooks is himself a drug user who quit). Through stunning photographic effects he manages to suggest the eerie, dazzling, dangerous world of drug takers; includes LSD. Not completely successful, but it's a memorable psychedelic tour with scenes shot in France and India, and boasting a marvelous score by Ravi Shankar. (Dir: Conrad Rooks, 92 mins.)

Charade (1963)***½ Cary Grant, Audrey Hepburn, James Coburn, Walter Matthau. Slick and sophisticated as its two charming stars. It seems Miss Hepburn's late husband swindled his cronies out of a quarter of a million dollars in gold coins, and they think Audrey knows where it's stashed. Enter the suave Mr. Grant, as an undercover C.I.A. agent, and they're off on a wild chase amid the marvelous European settings. After all is said and done, it's a lightweight affair, but the stars and the stylish direction by Stanley Donen keep it alive. (Dir: Stanley Donen, 114 mins.)

Charades (1952)*½ James Mason, Pamela Mason, Scott Forbes. (Dir: Roy Kellino, 86 mins.)

Charge at Feather River (1953)** Guy Madison, Vera Miles, Frank Lovejoy. Just another western adventure—originally made in 3-D but without the optical effects the gimmicks misfire. (Dir: Gordon Douglas, 96 mins.)

Charge of the Lancers (1954)** Paulette Goddard, Jean-Pierre Aumont. Mediocre adventure pic about a gypsy girl and an officer who fight a major portion of the Crimean War. (Dir: William Castle, 80 mins.)

Charge of the Light Brigade, The (France, 1936) Errol Flynn, Olivia de Havilland, David Niven. A splendid gung-ho adventure, with Flynn romancing de Havilland before the fatal assault. The climactic sally is a supreme example of Hollywood craft. (Dir: Michael Curtiz, 115 mins.)

Charge of the Light Brigade (Great Britain, 1968)***½ Trevor Howard, Vanessa Redgrave, David Hemmings, John Gielgud. Director Tony Richardson's withering, stimulating polemic about the stupidity and brutality of the military mind, and societies that not only condone but also glorify war. This fifth movie version—the last was the 1936 entry starring Errol Flynn—of the historic 1854 battle at Balaclava, Turkey, when the English Brigade was decimated by the Russian army, is superlatively acted by an all-star cast in this "thinking man's" spectacle film. No false heroics here, and there's excellent use made of special animated sequences done by Richard Williams. (Dir: Tony Richardson, 116 mins.)

Chariots of the Gods? (West Germany, 1971)*½ (Dir: Harald Reini, 97 mins.)

Charles Dead or Alive (Switzerland, 1972)***½ Francois Simon, Marcel Robert. Absorbing drama of a rich watch manufacturer who is fed up with the materialism that encases his emptiness. He runs off to live with a young married couple, but society and his family find him and commit him to a mental hospital. Francois Simon (Marcel Simon's son) is touching as the manufacturer, his life very relevant to our time. (Dir: Alain Tanner, 110 mins.)

Charles et Lucie (France, 1979)*½ Daniel Ceccaldi, Ginette Garcin. (Dir: Nelly Kaplan, 97 mins.)

Charley and the Angel (1973)*½ Fred MacMurray, Cloris Leachman, Harry Morgan. (Dir: Vincent McEveety, 93 mins.)

Charley Moon (Great Britain, 1956)** Max Bygraves, Dennis Price. Old army buddy starts his friend on a show-business career. Hackneyed backstage story that doesn't come off. (Dir: Guy Hamilton, 92 mins.)

Charley Varrick (1973)***½ Walter Matthau, Joe Don Baker. Very slick, entertaining crime yarn sparked by Matthau's deft performance as a crop-duster pilot who dabbles in bank robbing on the side. Director Don Siegel is right on the beam with the action, and his casting in the smaller supporting roles is perfect—Andy Robinson as a greedy sidekick of Matthau's; Sheree North as an accommodating photographer; Joe Don Baker as a Mafia man; and John Vernon as a banker. Matthau specializes in small bank heists until he accidentally steals some Mafia funds and thereby hangs the story line—a good one that will keep you going until the end. (Dir: Don Siegel, 111 mins.)

Charley's Aunt (1941)*** Jack Benny, Kay Francis. Perennial comedy about the man who poses as an old lady to help his roommate out of a jam is a good vehicle for Jack. (Dir: Archie Mayo, 81 mins.)

Charlie Bubbles (Great Britain, 1968)***½ Albert Finney, Liza Minnelli. Tantalizing, uneven, offbeat movie finds the celebrated British actor Albert Finney doing double duty. As director of the film, as well as its star, Mr. Finney is wonderfully resourceful in creating the image of a young man of very modest circumstances who is catapulted out of his station and into fame, fortune, and an excessive boredom he simply cannot bear. The emptiness of his life is beautifully reflected in scenes of his electronically gadget-filled house, making robots of everyone within. Actually, however, the novelty of the atmosphere wears thin even before he leaves it in a vain effort to go home again to his wife and son. As for the ending, it's either an imaginative cop-out or an irritating one, depending on your point of view. (Dir: Albert Finney, 91 mins.)

Charlie Chan and the Curse of the Dragon Queen (1981)** Peter Ustinov, Richard Hatch, Lee Grant, Angie Dickinson, Brian Keith, Roddy McDowall, Rachel Roberts. Clive Donner is one of the saddest cases of directorial decline in the seventies. He has descended into facetious camp. This slapstick update of the Earl Derr Biggers's character has some inventive gags, all for the most part staged with the timing a hair off, but it hasn't an iota of soul or conviction to it. Peter Ustinov barely attempts to create the Chan character, and the focus is entirely on his young grandson, a comic bumbler with good intentions. Since the film obviously doesn't care about its mystery, neither do we. (Dir: Clive Donner)

Charlie Chan at the Opera (1936)*** Warner Oland, Boris Karloff. The Chan films were among the best B movies, and this is one of the most enjoyable, with Oland's Chan supported by Karloff and fast, if loose, direction by Bruce Humberstone. (66 mins.)

Charlie Chan (Happiness Is a Warm Clue) (MTV 1970)* Ross Martin, Rocky Gunn, Virginia Ann Lee. Alternate title: **The Return of Charlie Chan.** Made in 1970; TV debut, 1978. (Dir: Leslie Martinson, 97 mins.)

Charlie Chan in Egypt (1935)**½ Warner Oland, Rita Hayworth, Stepin Fetchit, Frank Conroy, "Pat" Paterson. Tutmania with Chan, in an above-average entry in the long-running series. (Dir: Louis King, 65 mins.)

Charlie Chan in Paris (1945)**½ Warner Oland, Mary Brian, Erik Rhodes. One of the better Chan mysteries finds the inspector in the City of Light. The solution to the murders involves disguises. (Dir: Lewis Seiler, 71 mins.)

Charlie Chaplin Carnival (1916-17)**** Four Chaplin shorts: "Behind the Screen," "The Count," "The Vagabond," "The Fireman." Good old-fashioned slapstick from one of cinema's authentic geniuses. (Dir: Charles Chaplin, 75 mins.)

Charlie Chaplin Cavalcade (1916-17)**** Four Chaplin comedies: "One A.M.," "The Rink," "The Pawnshop," "The Floorwalker." Still stupendous. (Dir: Charles Chaplin, 72 mins.)

Charlie Chaplin Festival (1916-17)**** Four Chaplin comedies: "The Immigrant," "The Adventurer," "The Cure," "Easy Street." As funny as ever. (Dir: Charles Chaplin, 75 mins.)

Charlie Cobb: Nice Night for a Hanging (MTV 1977)** Clu Gulager, Ralph Bellamy, Blair Brown, Stella Stevens. Gulager, an ingratiating actor who seems to get better with age, is an 1880's Western private eye named Charlie Cobb, who is taken for a greenhorn by everyone when he turns up with a rancher's daughter. The prodigal daughter isn't exactly welcomed by the rancher's second wife, a lady with a murderous scheme. Good cast, fair story. (Dir: Richard Michaels, 100 mins.)

Charlotte (France, 1974)*½ Roger Vadim, Sirpa Lane. (Dir: Roger Vadim, 100 mins.)

Charlotte's Web (1973)***½ Heartwarming animated version of children's classic by E. B. White about a pig who's afraid he's going to be turned into bacon, and a spider who saves him through her magic web. The voices, all marvelous, include Debbie Reynolds, Paul Lynde, Henry Gibson, and Agnes Moorehead. Well animated with an excellently constructed narrative and good climax. For the whole family. (Dirs: Charles Nichols and Iwao Takamoto, 93 mins.)

Charly (1968)*** Cliff Robertson, Claire Bloom, Lilia Skala. The superlative Academy Award-winning performance of Cliff Robertson playing a mentally retarded bakery worker is reason enough to see this one. The rest of the film is appreciably less successful, including a questionable romance between Charly (Robertson) and a bright, beautiful woman (Bloom) after surgery has drastically improved Charly's I.Q. Director Ralph Nelson includes some attractive shots of Boston, a welter of split screens and other "new" camera techniques, but it's Robertson's sensitive handling of the title role, first performed by him on TV, that makes this worth your time. (Dir: Ralph Nelson, 103 mins.)

Charro! (1969)* Elvis Presley, Ina Balin, Victor French. (Dir: Charles Marquis Warren, 98 mins.)

Chartroose Caboose (1960)** Molly Bee, Ben Cooper, Edgar Buchanan. A sugary and sentimental tale (with musical numbers added) about an old railroader who takes in stray people in trouble and is rewarded handsomely for his kindness in the end. You will not be equally rewarded. (Dir: William 'Red' Reynolds, 75 mins.)

Chase, The (1966)** Marlon Brando, Jane Fonda, Robert Redford, E. G. Marshall, Angie Dickinson. Despite a fine cast, a screenplay that bears Lillian Hellman's name, though others were involved, and the directorial talents of Arthur Penn, this story about sex and sin in a small Texas town is an unending compendium of film cliches! Producer Sam Spiegel kept interfering with and overruling Penn during production, and the final jumbled film is evidence of various unresolved points of view. Dickinson and Brando are both as convincing as possible under the trying circumstances. (Dir: Arthur Penn, 135 mins.)

Chase a Crooked Shadow (Great Britain, 1958)**½ Anne Baxter, Richard Todd. Performances make up for many of the inconsistencies in this drama. Miss Baxter becomes the victim of a diabolical plot that is set up to do her out of her sizable inheritance. (Dir: Michael Anderson, 87 mins.)

Chase Me Charlie (1914-32)*** Charlie Chaplin, Edna Purviance, Ben Turpin. Old Chaplin short subjects strung together to form a thin narrative about Charlie's quest for work to win his girl. Antiquated in technique and presentation. The Chaplin comedy genius breaks through occasionally. (Dir: Charles Chaplin, 61 mins.)

Chasers, The (France, 1959)**½ Jacques Charrier, Charles Aznavour. A not very profound but occasionally interesting look at rootless youths in Paris, their search for love, partners, company. First film for director Jean-Pierre Mocky is disappointing. (75 mins.)

Chastity (1969)* Cher, Barbara London. (Dir: Alessio De Paola, 85 mins.)

Chato's Land (1972)*½ Charles Bronson, Jack Palance. (Dir: Michael Winner, 108 mins.)

Chatterbox (1943)**½ Judy Canova, Joe E. Brown. A timid radio cowboy goes to a dude ranch, where he becomes a hero with the aid of the ranch's handy girl. Amusing comedy. (Dir: Joseph Santley, 76 mins.)

Che! (1969)* Omar Sharif, Jack Palance. (Dir: Richard Fleischer, 96 mins.)

Cheap Detective, The (1978)*** Peter Falk, Ann-Margret, Sid Caesar, Louise Fletcher, Nicol Williamson. Neil Simon's parody of "The Maltese Falcon" and "Casablanca" is a little wittier than the film it was cloned from, "Murder by Death," and a handsome, fairly atmospheric production. Still, a spoof is a spoof, and this random collection of one-liners and intentionally flat characters is only superficially engaging. An hour after, you'll want to see a real movie. Falk mumbles through his Bogart impression. Robert Moore directed—his timing isn't up to Simon's, and several laughs are muffled. (92 mins.)

Cheaper by the Dozen (1950)*** Clifton Webb, Jeanne Crain, Myrna Loy. Heartwarming and funny comedy drama about a very large family ruled by Papa Webb. Nostalgic and corny at the same time. One of Webb's best performances. Based on the best-selling novel of the same name. There was a sequel to this film a few years later entitled "Belles on Their Toes" but it wasn't half as good due to the fact that Webb died in the original. (Dir: Walter Lang, 85 mins.)

Cheaters, The (1945)*** Joseph Schildkraut, Billie Burke. A broken-down ham actor comes to a household of snobs at Christmas-time, makes human beings of them. Delightful comedy-drama, excellently acted. (Dir: Joseph Kane, 87 mins.)

Cheaters, The (France, 1958)** Pascale Petit, Jacques Charrier. English-dubbed drama of teenagers on the loose, as a university student becomes involved with the fast-living set. Long and tiresome. A few good moments. (Dir: Marcel Carné, 117 mins.)

Cheers for Miss Bishop (1941)*** Martha Scott, William Gargan. The story of the long life span of a midwest schoolteacher, her loves, sorrows. Heartwarming drama, excellently acted, written. Marsha Hunt. (Dir: Tay Garnett, 95 mins.)

Cherry Harry and Raquel (1969)*** Linda Ashton, Charles Napier, Larissa Ely. Genuinely extraordinary work from Russ Meyer, pioneer nudie filmmaker, replete with such typical gambits as narcotics traffic, necrophilia, lesbianism, frenetic violence, and incest. The stroy was calculated comic strip back when it wasn't fashionable. Highly recommended for anyone who can approach cinema without snobbery. (Dir: Russ Meyer, 71 mins.)

Chess Players (India, 1977))** Richard Attenborough, Saeed Jaffrey. A major disappointment from director Satyajit Ray. An allegorical study of British Raj in 1856, the film contrasts the never-ending chess rivalry of two bickering friends with the power play of a British general to take over a local government. The execution of the idea is too diffuse, and not made visual. (129 mins.)

Cheyenne—See: **Wyoming Kid, The**

Cheyenne Autumn (1964)***½ Richard Widmark, Carroll Baker, Karl Malden, James Stewart. Director John Ford, one of Hollywood's best western film makers, really came up with a winner in this epic retelling of a true incident in frontier history. It's about the migration of a tribe of half-starved Cheyenne Indians from their barren reservation in Oklahoma to their home ground in Wyoming. The treacherous journey tests the Cheyenne's courage and stamina, and their trek is further endangered as the Calvary sets out to prevent their exodus. The cast is a large one, and they are all good, including Richard Widmark, Karl Malden, Carroll Baker, Dolores Del Rio, and, in cameo appearances, James Stewart and Edward G. Robinson. (160 mins.)

Cheyenne Social Club, The (1970)*½ James Stewart, Henry Fonda, Shirley Jones. (Dir: Gene Kelly, 103 mins.)

Chicago Calling (1952)** Dan Duryea, Mary Anderson. A man hears that his estranged wife and daughter have been injured in a motor accident, is unable to contact them via telephone. Slim story, but plenty of human interest in this drama, practically a one-man show by Duryea. (Dir: John Reinhardt, 74 mins.)

Chicago Confidential (1957)**½ Brian Keith, Beverly Garland. Hollywood seems to think that there should be a motion picture about every city in the United States with the tag "confidential" after it. This is one of them. Crime exposés, gangster war lords, etc. (Dir: Sidney Salkow, 74 mins.)

Chicago Deadline (1949)**½ Alan Ladd, Donna Reed, Arthur Kennedy. Routine newspaper yarn about crusading reporter who gets involved with murder and the underworld. Alan Ladd plays it in his usual wooden style. Remade as TV feature *Fame Is the Name of the Game*, 1966. (Dir: Lewis Allen, 87 mins.)

Chicago Story, The (MTV 1981)** Vincent Baggetta, Jack Kehoe, Craig T. Nelson. It's about the senseless killing of a youngster as seen from the viewpoint of the cops, the doctors and the lawyers. The city remains the star of this one, although

the police characters exude a nice flavor. (Dir: Jerry London, 104 mins.)

Chicago Syndicate (1955)** Dennis O'Keefe, Abbe Lane, Paul Stewart. Unbelievable drama about one man's attempt to smash the ten billion dollar crime network of the "Chicago Syndicate." Abbe Lane sings to a mambo beat supplied by Xavier Cugat's orchestra. (Dir: Fred F. Sears, 90 mins.)

Chicken Chronicles, The (1977)**½ Phil Silvers, Ed Lauter, Steve Guttenberg, Lisa Reeves, Kuttee, Gino Baffa. An interesting look at affluent southern California society through the eyes of a group of well-to-do teenagers. The main characters work after school at a fast-food shop (run by Phil Silvers, excellent in a semi-serious role.) The frustration, confusion, and restlessness of these kids' lives is well captured in a screenplay by Paul Diamond (son of I.A.L. Diamond) and by the cast of largely unknown young actors. (Dir: Francis Simon, 92 mins.)

Chicken Every Sunday (1949)**½ Dan Dailey, Celeste Holm, Alan Young. As homespun as a sampler and as nostalgic as blueberry pie cooling off on the window sill. Plot involves a small town dreamer (Dailey) who's always going to strike it big and always ends up losing his shirt. Celeste Holm is good as his patient wife. Good turn of the century music is played behind the action. (Dir: George Seaton, 91 mins.)

Chief Crazy Horse (1955)**½ Victor Mature, Suzan Ball, John Lund. An interesting yarn about one of the greatest Indian chiefs of all time—Crazy Horse, here played by athletic Victor Mature. The plot concerns his alliance with a cavalry major and their eventually necessary parting. (Dir: George Sherman, 86 mins.)

Child and the Killer (Great Britain, 1959)** Pat Driscoll, Robert Arden. GI murderer escapes to the backwoods, is helped by an unknowing child. Average melodrama. (Dir: Max Varnel, 64 mins.)

Child in the House (Great Britain, 1956)*** Phyllis Calvert, Eric Portman, Mandy Miller, Stanley Baker. Intelligent drama of a youngster from a broken home and the change she brings into the lives of her aunt and uncle. Could have been soap opera but the treatment saves it. (Dirs: Cy Endfield, Charles de la Tour, 88 mins.)

Child Is Born, A (1940)**½ Jeffrey Lynn, Geraldine Fitzgerald. Remake of "Life Begins" is well done but the maternity hospital drama is still too morbid and heavy to be called entertaining. (Dir: Lloyd Bacon, 79 mins.)

Child Is Waiting, A (1963)*** Burt Lancaster, Judy Garland. Frequently gripping story of a music teacher and a psychologist on the staff of a school for retarded children. Strong stuff, not for the sensitive, the film uses actual retarded youngsters in the cast, develops a great deal of poignancy despite some weak spots in script and direction. (Dir: John Cassavetes, 102 mins.)

Child Stealer, The (MTV 1979)***½ Beau Bridges, Blair Brown, David Groh. The subject of a divorced parent abducting his children from his ex-wife is given honest, compelling treatment. Brown is heart-wrenching as the ex-wife. Bridges outdoes himself as the ex-husband who feels his two daughters' love for him is being usurped by a new man in Brown's life. (Dir: Mel Damski, 104 mins.)

Children of An Lac, The (MTV 1980)*** Shirley Jones, Ina Balin, Beulah Quo. Compelling drama based on the real-life evacuation and airlift of 219 Vietnamese orphans from the An Lac ("Happy Place") orphanage in Saigon just before the city fell to the Communists in April 1975. This finely acted movie focuses on the determination of Betty Tisdale (Jones) and Balin (played by herself) to negotiate the release of the children and fly them to the United States. Jones, Balin, and Quo (playing Madama Ngai, the Vietnamese woman who started the orphanage) persuasively convey the anguish, frustration, and hope in trying to accomplish a seemingly impossible mission in only 2½ days. (Dir: John Llewellyn Moxey, 104 mins.)

Children of Divorce (MTV 1980)**½ Billy Dee Williams, Olivia Cole, Kim Fields, Barbara Feldon, Stella Stevens. Drama about the offspring of couples who seek divorce. The kids of three households try to understand why and how their world has been torn apart. A good cast helps the story along, but the segmented plotting, divided among the many characters, detracts somewhat from the impact. (Dir: Joanna Lee, 104 mins.)

Children of Paradise (France, 1945)**** Jean-Louis Barrault, Arletty, Pierre Brasseur. Set in the 1840s and filmed under the Occupation in Paris. Marcel Carne's masterpiece about the undying love of Garance (Arletty) and the mime Deburau (Jean-Louis Barrault) is a breathtaking study of the series of relationships between life and theater, mime and tragedy, the real and the imaginary, sound and silence. (Dir: Marcel Carne, 188 mins.)

Children of Rage (Great Britain-Israel, 1975)*½ Simon Ward, Cyril Sucask, Helmut Griem. Clumsy, simplistic, if well-intentioned drama trying to explain both sides of the Arab-Israeli conflict. Considered by many to be an apologia for the Palestinian terrorists, the film is generally tendentious, dreary, and often offensive. (Dir: Arthur Seidelman, 106 mins.)

Children of Sanchez, The (1978)** Anthony Quinn, Dolores Del Rio, Katy Jurado, Lupita Ferrer, Stathis Giallelis. Slow-moving, unperceptive drama of Mexican laborer Quinn's attempts to keep his many offspring, some illegitimate, together. The film does have the ever beautiful Del Rio

as grandmother, plus Chuck Mangione's great score, but it should have been and could have been much better. From the landmark book by sociologist Oscar Lewis. (Dir: Hall Bartless, 126 mins.)

Children of the Damned (Great Britain, 1964)**½ Ian Hendry, Barbara Ferris. Here's the sequel to the infinitely superior "Village of the Damned" horror film. The menacing children with the strange luminous eyes are back in another sci-fi excursion. The children are really feeling their power in this outing ... they set their target as the destruction of the world. (Dir: Anton M. Leader, 90 mins.)

Children of the Lotus Eaters—See: Psychiatrist: God Bless the Children, The

Children's Hour (1962)*** Audrey Hepburn, Shirley MacLaine, James Garner, Miriam Hopkins, Fay Bainter. In 1936, William Wyler made his first attempt to film this initial dramatic success by Lillian Hellman. Titled *These Three*, the lesbian overtones were replaced by allegations of a more conventional affair. It was a good film, but Wyler's remake was heavily slammed by critics who called it lugubrious, sensational, and turgid. They weren't so much wrong as beside the point. What else did they expect from a William Wyler movie? I have always liked the picture, a distinct minority view. It seems to me passionately detached, rigid, yet emotional— an example of Wyler's limited virtues given full rein. The treatment is necessarily dated, but the character definition is underlined by Wyler's meticulous camera style. Miriam Hopkins played the lead in *These Three*. Here she is sensationally unsympathetic. (Dir: William Wyler, 107 mins.)

Child's Play (Great Britain, 1954)** Mona Washbourne, Peter Martyn. A comedy sparked with some drama concerning the escapades of a group of quiz kids and their experiments in an atomic plant. (Dir: Margaret Thomson, 68 mins.)

Child's Play (1972)***½ James Mason, Robert Preston, Beau Bridges. Is Mr. Malley (James Mason) paranoid? Is there really a conspiracy against him by the boys of St. Charles boarding school? Dynamite ending. Direction is atmospheric to create the obligatory demonic and suspenseful mood. Acting is exemplary, led by Preston as the teacher suspected of leading the conspiracy. (Dir: Sidney Lumet, 100 mins.)

China Clipper (1936)*** Pat O'Brien, Beverly Roberts. Well acted and written story of the first flight of Pan American's China Clipper. Sticks to the facts and avoids the wornout cliches of air stories. If you want to see how far we've come, take a look at what was considered amazing in 1936. (Dir: Raymond Enright, 100 mins.)

China Corsair (1951)* Jon Hall, Lisa Ferraday. (Dir: Ray Nazarro, 67 mins.)

China Doll (1958)*½ Victor Mature, Lili Hua. (Dir: Frank Borzage, 88 mins.)

China Gate (1957)** Gene Barry, Angie Dickinson. TV's Bat Masterson in a contrived bit of action concerning France's troubles in Indo-China. If you'd like to believe that the Foreign Legion is still glamorous, take a look. Nat King Cole throws in a song or two, and even does a nice job as a Legionnaire. (Dir: Samuel Fuller, 97 mins.)

China Is Near (Italy, 1967)*** Elda Tattoli, Glauco Mauri. An uneven, yet occasionally brilliant film from the talented young Italian director Marco Bellocchio. (Bellocchio's first film was "Fist in His Pocket.") Story concerns the affairs of an Italian politician's family, and most of it is a satire on left-wing Italian politics, with a few darts thrown at Italian sexual mores. English sub-titles. (Dir: Marco Bellocchio, 108 mins.)

China Seas (1935)*** Clark Gable, Jean Harlow, Wallace Beery, Rosalind Russell. A rousing melodrama about pirates in the China Seas trying to defeat Captain Gable. The stars give a good account of themselves, although the film is an undistinguished, entertaining adventure story. (Dir: Tay Garnett, 89 mins.)

China Venture (1953)**½ Edmond O'Brien, Barry Sullivan, Jocelyn Brando. WW II adventure story about two officers and a navy nurse who try to rescue an Admiral held captive by Chinese Guerrillas. Some exciting sequences. (Dir: Don Siegel, 83 mins.)

Chinatown (1974)**** Jack Nicholson, Faye Dunaway. Excellent crime drama, set in the Los Angeles of the thirties, which evokes those wonderful Bogart films while remaining true to its own spirit and energy. Jack Nicholson is superb as a small-time private eye who stumbles on a big case which involves graft over valuable land and water rights, murder, incest and other attention-getting devices. They're all put in their proper place by writer Robert Towne in an intricate, entertaining screenplay. Director Roman Polanski (he's seen in a bit part as a sadistic, knife-wielding hood) has kept a keen and knowing eye on his cast, including Faye Dunaway as a highly dramatic femme fatale and John Huston as a despicable villain. (130 mins.)

Chip Off the Old Block (1944)*** Donald O'Connor, Ann Blyth. Teenager goes through misunderstandings with the young daughter of a musical comedy star. Neat, breezy comedy with music. (Dir: Charles Lamont, 82 mins.)

Chisum (1970)**½ John Wayne, Forrest Tucker, Christopher George, Ben Johnson. Slam-bang action westerns ride again with tall-in-the-saddle John Wayne as a cattle baron fighting off the treacherous land barons. He's helped by a fine cast who follow the golden rule, "Actions speak louder than words." (Dir: Andrew V. McLaglen, 118 mins.)

Chitty, Chitty, Bang, Bang (Great Britain, 1968)**½ Dick Van Dyke, Sally Ann Howes, Anna Quayle. Intended by the director to repeat the artistic triumph and financial bonanza of "Those Magnificent Men in Their Flying Machines," he flops on both counts. This $10-million production does provide a few laughs for the kids, but it's pretty sophomoric most of the way and bogged down by some really terrible songs. The car-star does eventually get airborne, though the picture itself never takes off. (Dir: Ken Hughes, 142 mins.)

Chloe in the Afternoon (France, 1972)**** Bernard Verley, Zouzou, Francoise Verley, Francoise Fabian, Beatrice Romand. The fourth of Rohmer's feature-length films and the concluding part of his cycle of romantic comedies he calls "Six Moral Fables." A featherweight, beautifully crafted look at monogamous marriage and the foibles of imperfect man. Verley struggles to avoid being unfaithful with "Chloe," charmingly played by singer-actress Zouzou. Written and directed by Eric Rohmer. (97 mins.)

Chocolate Soldier, The (1941)*** Nelson Eddy, Rise Stevens. Score from "The Chocolate Soldier," plus plot of Molnar's "The Guardsman," tempered with good debut performance of Miss Stevens adds up to a nice package for operetta fans. (Dir: Roy Del Ruth, 102 mins.)

Choice, The (MTV 1981)**½ Susan Clark, Mitchell Ryan, Jennifer Warren. Susan Clark is such a good actress that she makes almost anything work, including this turgid drama about a mother who finds her daughter caught in almost the same dilemma which she recently faced herself. Should her pregnant daughter have an abortion in order to keep her relationship with her lover? (Dir: David Greene, 104 mins.)

Choirboys, The (1977)*** Perry King, Don Stroud, James Woods, Randy Quaid, Charles Durning. An accomplished black comedy directed by Robert Aldrich, the greatest surviving master of film noir. The episodic narrative is loosely centered on a group of cops who meet in MacArthur Park every Friday night to blow off steam. (119 mins.)

Choppers, The (1961)*½ Arch Hall Jr., Tom Brown, Marianne Gaba. (Dir: Leigh Jason, 66 mins.)

Christina (Canada, 1974)*½ Barbara Parkins, Peter Haskell, James McEachin, Marlyn Mason. (Dir: Paul Krasny, 98 mins.)

Christine (France-Italy, 1958)**½ Romy Schneider, Alain Delon. A terribly romantic French language film based on a Schnitzler play about a pair of starcrossed lovers, the dashing young officer and the beautiful opera singer. Miss Schneider and Mr. Delon make a perfect pair of lovers, but the dubbing detracts from their performances. (Dir: Pierre Gaspard-Huit, 109 mins.)

Christmas Carol, A (1938)*** Reginald Owen, Gene Lockhart. Sincere, well-acted adaptation of the Dickens classic. (Dir: Edwin L. Marin, 70 mins.)

Christmas Carol, A (Great Britain, 1951)***½ Alastair Sim, Kathleen Harrison. Another version of the classic Dickens tale of miser Scrooge who was turned into a human being by the spirit of Yuletide. Well done. (Dir: Brian Desmond Hurst, 86 mins.)

Christmas Eve—See: **Sinner's Holiday**

Christmas Holiday (1944)*** Deanna Durbin, Gene Kelly. Nice girl marries a ne'er-do-well whose weakness turns him to crime. Sordid tale receives classy direction, good performances to make it above average. (Dir: Robert Siodmak, 92 mins.)

Christmas in Connecticut (1945)**½ Barbara Stanwyck, Dennis Morgan. Occasionally funny farce about a newspaper columnist who is instructed by her boss to have a war hero as her family's guest for Christmas dinner. Of course, she has no family...and by that thread the film hangs. (Dir: Peter Godfrey, 101 mins.)

Christmas in July (1940)**** Dick Powell, Ellen Drew. Guy mistakenly thinks he has won a coffee slogan contest, starts buying everything on credit. Often hilarious comedy, written and directed by Preston Sturges with an unerring hand. Great fun. (Dir: Preston Sturges, 70 mins.)

Christmas Kid, The (U.S.-Spain, 1966)** Jeffrey Hunter, Louis Hayward, Gustavo Rojo, Perla Cristal. Offbeat western short on action, but tries to develop a decent character study. Hunter, born on Christmas Day and attended by three wise men (a mayor, a judge, and a doctor), grows up wild because his father rejects him. Enter Hayward, a charming villain who intends to take over the town. Filmed in and around Madrid, with a lush score by Fernando Garcia Morciello. (Dir: Sidney Pink, 87 mins.)

Christmas to Remember, A (MTV 1978)***½ Jason Robards, Jr., Eva Marie Saint, George Parry, Joanne Woodward. Robards is in top form playing a cantankerous, ailing old Minnesota depression farmer who is angry with God for taking his son away in WW I and treats his city-bred grandson with derision. Saint may be a bit young to play the grandmother, but as the go-between for Robards and grandson Parry, she has the spirit to stand up when it counts. A moving script and splendid acting turn this into quality fare. Adapted by Steward Stern, based on a novel by Glendon Swarthout. (Dir: George Englund, 104 mins.)

Christmas Tree, The (France-Italy, 1969)** William Holden, Virna Lisi, Brook Fuller, Bourvil. A strained lunge for the tear ducts, in a tale of a father's attempt to make the last days happy for his son,

dying of leukemia. Too obvious to be effective. Filmed in France. (Dir: Terence Young, 110 mins.)

Christmas Without Snow, A (MTV 1980)*** Michael Learned, John Houseman, Calvin Level. Offbeat film for the holiday season. A church choir is rehearsing Handel's "Messiah," and we get to know the singers during rehearsals. Learned's divorced man and Level's ghetto college student are the most intriguing characters. Houseman gives his patented performance as the officious choirmaster. (Dir: John Korty, 96 mins.)

Christopher Columbus (Great Britain, 1949)**½ Fredric March, Florence Eldridge. Lavish but empty production concerning the attempts of the explorer to get permission from the Spanish court to sail to the New World. Very slow, talky, dull. (Dir: David MacDonald, 104 mins.)

Christopher Strong (1933)**** Katharine Hepburn, Colin Clive, Billie Burke, Helen Chandler. A superior feminist drama from 1933, directed by the sole female Hollywood director of that era, Dorothy Arzner. Hepburn is perfectly cast as the aviatrix hemmed in by the competing demands of love and career. The sensitivity to the emotional components of the problems facing professional women is remarkable, the drama incisive, though undue attention will be drawn to the boggling gold lame outfit Kate dons for a dance. (Dir: Dorothy Arzner, 77 mins.)

Chronicle of Anna Magdalena Bach (Italy West Germany, 1968)**½ Gustav Leonhardt, Christiane Lang. A somber account of the final years of the great composer Johann Sebastian Bach, of particular interest to serious music students, as the bulk of "Chronicle" is devoted to performances of Bach works including several cantatas. Film details Bach's poverty prior to his death in 1750. Unfortunately the acting, and much of the direction, is poverty-stricken as well. Subtitles. (Dir: Jean-Marie Straus, 94 mins.)

Chubasco (1968)*½ Richard Egan, Susan Strasberg, Christopher Jones. (Dir: Allen H. Miner, 99 mins.)

Chuka (1967)*½ Rod Taylor, Ernest Borgnine, John Mills. (Dir: Gordon Douglas, 105 mins)

Cigarettes, Whiskey and Wild Women (France, 1958)*½ Nadine Tellier, Annie Cordy. (Dir: Maurice Régamey, 90 mins.)

Cimarron (1960)*** Glenn Ford, Maria Schell, Anne Baxter, Arthur O'Connell. Director Anthony Mann's remake of the Edna Ferber novel, originally filmed badly in 1931. The protagonists are a carefree survivor of the Old West (Ford) and his relentlessly civilizing wife (Schell). Mann's epic land rush rivals that of John Ford in the silent "Three Bad Men." Of course, Mann has CinemaScope at his disposal. (140 mins.)

Cimarron Kid, The (1951)** Audie Murphy, Yvette Dugay. Routine western fare with Audie Murphy playing the "Cimarron Kid," an ex-con who tries to go straight against tremendous odds. (Dir: Budd Boetticher, 84 mins.)

Cincinnati Kid, The (1965)*** Steve McQueen, Edward G. Robinson, Ann-Margret, Tuesday Weld. Fine performances by McQueen and Robinson. Their confrontation in a superbly staged card game finale is a highlight in this adventure based on Richard Jessup's novel. McQueen, in the title role, is an itinerant card shark who travels from one big game to the next, stopping along the way up with various girls, including Ann-Margret and Tuesday Weld. Director Norman Jewison has a good eye for detail and the technical end of the film evokes the depression period, in which the story is laid. (Dir: Norman Jewison, 113 mins.)

Cinderella (1950)** Walt Disney's penchant for adorableness, for effect piled on technical effect, reaches apotheosis in this elephantine release. Somewhere beneath the laboriously decorative visual elaboration lies the classic fairy tale. (Dirs: Wilfred Jackson, Hamilton Luske, Clyde Geronomi, 75 mins.)

Cinderella Jones (1946)** Joan Leslie, Robert Alda. Silly triviality about a dumb but pretty little scatterbrain who must marry an intelligent man to be eligible for a million-dollar legacy. (Dir: Busby Berkeley, 88 mins.)

Cinderella Liberty (1973)*** James Caan, Marsha Mason. Good performances by Caan, as an offbeat sailor with a sense of responsibility, and Mason, as an unorthodox bar girl with a street-toughened 11-year-old whose black sailor father ran away before his birth. (Dir: Mark Rydell, 117 mins.)

Cinderfella (1960)** Jerry Lewis, Anna Maria Alberghetti, Ed Wynn. The fairytale adapted to suit the talents of Lewis. A misguided venture—tasteless, ornately dull musical fantasy should appeal to fans of the comic, but no one else. (Dir: Frank Tashlin, 91 mins.)

Cindy (MTV 1978)*** Charlaine Woodward, Scoey Mitchell, Mae Mercer. Don't be put off. The Cinderella fairy tale, with a black cast of principals, is reset in Harlem, circa '43. Newcomer Woodward strikes the right note as a pigtailed girl who comes from South Carolina to live with her daddy, stepmother, and stepsisters in Harlem. She has excellent comic timing. A twist on the happy ending should leave everyone smiling. Music and lyrics by Stan Daniels. (Dir: William Graham, 104 mins.)

Circle of Children, A (MTV 1977)***½ Jane Alexander, Rachel Roberts, David Ogden Stiers, Nan Martin. Luminous adaptation of Mary McCracken's novel about a financially poor, spiritually rich private school for emotionally disturbed children. The most talented of the understanding teachers is Helga, a woman with a marked German accent, unschooled, but a "thera-peutic genius," who inspires an affluent suburban woman to volunteer at the school. Rachel Roberts is wonderful as Helga and Jane Alexander is moving in her worship of this incomparable teacher. You'll be especially dazzled by the children with whom Jane Alexander must prove her worth. (Dir: Don Taylor, 100 mins.)

Circle of Danger (Great Britain, 1951)*** Ray Milland, Patricia Roc. American returns to Europe to investigate the mysterious death of his brother during World War II. Interesting melodrama keeps the viewer in suspense. (Dir: Jacques Tourneur, 86 mins.)

Circle of Death (Mexico, 1955)** Sarita Montiel, Raul Remirez. Businessman stoops to murder to gain control of his wife's fortune. Undistinguished melodrama dubbed in English. (Dir: Alfredo B. Crevenna, 79 mins.)

Circle of Deception (Great Britain, 1961)**½ Bradford Dillman, Suzy Parker. Intelligence agent is assigned a dangerous mission in Germany, is captured and spills the beans. War melodrama has a suspenseful twist but doesn't bring it off too well. However, it has its moments. (Dir: Jack Lee, 100 mins.)

Circle of Iron (1979)** David Carradine, Jeff Cooper, Christopher Lee, Roddy McDowall, Eli Wallach. A Kung Fu fantasy shot in Israel, better produced than the usual chop-'em-sock-'em flicks. Carradine has four roles, and Wallach has a bit as a man in oil. Cooper is awful in his first big role. (Dir: Richard Moore, 102 mins.)

Circle of Love (France-Italy, 1964)*½ Marie Dubois, Claude Giraud, Jean-Claude Brialy, Jane Fonda. (Dir: Roger Vadim, 105 mins.)

Circular Triangle (Germany, 1964)** Lilli Palmer, Sylva Koscina. Battle for industrial power brings on three murders. Fair drama saved by some good acting. Dubbed in English. (Dir: Pierre Kast, 112 mins.)

Circumstantial Evidence (Great Britain, 1954)** Patrick Holt, Rona Anderson. Doctor is placed on trial for murder when his fiancée's ex-husband is found dead. Average courtroom drama. (Dir: John Larkin, 68 mins.)

Circus, The (1928)**** Charles Chaplin, Merna Kennedy, Betty Morrissey. Some marvelous sight gags and other glimpses of the Chaplin genius in this little-known film. In one notable sequence Chaplin is a circus tramp who is chased through a hall of mirrors by a policeman. The characters are right out of the melodramas of the time, wicked father, an ailing daughter, etc. Original story and theme song written by Chaplin, who produced and directed. (60 mins.)

Circus of Fear (Great Britain, 1967)** Leo Genn, Christopher Lee, Suzy Kendall, Cecil Parker, Eddi Arent. Robbery clues lead to a circus, where the bodies and the film begin to pile up. Involved plot, but enough red herrings strewn along the way to interest mystery fans. (Dir: John Moxey, 65 mins.)

Circus of Horrors (British, 1960)**½ Anton Diffring, Erica Remberg. Well done horror film about a plastic surgeon who finds temporary shelter from flight in a traveling circus. The circus background serves well for the surgeon's experiments. Good cast adds to the film. (Dir: Sidney Hayers, 89 mins.)

Circus of Love (West Germany, 1954)** Eva Bartok, Curt Jurgens. Mediocre carnival melodrama as a woman is caught between emotions for two men. An English-language version ("Carnival Story") was made simultaneously, and some of the stars of the American version (Anne Baxter, Steve Cochran) appear here as extras. English subtitles. (Dir: Kurt Neumann, 93 mins.)

Circus World (1964)**½ John Wayne, Claudia Cardinale, Rita Hayworth. The large-scale excitement of the big top, the presence of John Wayne, Rita Hayworth and Claudia Cardinale in starring roles, plus excellent Spanish locations help to overcome the shortcomings of the script. Wayne is the head of a combination wild west and circus show which is in financial straits, and if that isn't enough plot, there are two or three romantic involvements thrown in. Don't expect another "Trapeze" and you'll enjoy it. (Dir: Henry Hathaway, 135 mins.)

Cisco Pike (1971)**½ Gene Hackman, Kris Kristofferson. Narcotics agent (Hackman) blackmails a washed-up rock star (Kristofferson) into dealing off $10,000 worth of Acapulco Gold. The plot's predictable but Kristofferson is fascinating to watch in a role which seems to be an extension of himself. (Dir: Bill L. Norton, 94 mins.)

Citadel, The (British, 1938)**** Robert Donat, Rosalind Russell, Rex Harrison, Ralph Richardson. Cronin's novel about a young dedicated Scots physician who almost loses his way in life is a brilliantly acted gem which almost improves on the wonderful book. (Dir: King Vidor, 113 mins.)

Citizen Kane (1941)**** Orson Welles, Joseph Cotten, Everett Sloane, Agnes Moorehead, George Coulouris. This story of a brilliant tyrant who built up a vast chain of newspapers, sacrificing his personal happiness along the way, was directed by the youthful Welles four decades ago and still stands up as one of the most remarkable films ever made. Welles, as well as being a wonderful actor, opened up whole new vistas for motion pictures. Unequaled in Welles's later career, though he came close with "The Magnificent Ambersons," "Falstaff," and "Touch of Evil." Herman J. Mankiewicz penned the script, but it's Orson's movie all the way. (119 mins.)

Citizens Band—See: **Handle with Care**

City, The (MTV 1977)* Robert Forster, Don Johnson, Jimmy Dean. (Dir: Harvey Hart, 72 mins.)

City, The (MTV 1971)*½ Anthony Quinn, E.G. Marshall, Robert Reed. (Dir: Daniel Petrie, 104 mins.)

City Across the River (1949)**½ Stephen McNally, Peter Fernendez, Thelma Ritter. Irving Shulman's explosive book on juvenile delinquency in Brooklyn, "The Amboy Dukes," makes a tough movie. The "kids" of the streets are depicted in melodramatic terms, but there's enough bite left to retain your interest. (Dir: Maxwell Shane, 90 mins.)

City After Midnight—See: **That Woman Opposite**

City Beneath the Sea (1953)**½ Robert Ryan, Anthony Quinn, Mala Powers. Two-fisted adventure about big men in the big business of treasure hunting beneath the sea. The plot's predictable but Quinn and Ryan are convincing leads and carry the show. (Dir: Budd Boetticher, 87 mins.)

City Beneath the Sea (1971)**½ Stuart Whitman, Robert Wagner, Richard Basehart. Science-fiction fans take note—futuristic underwater storyteller Irwin Allen is at it again. His made-for-TV film is a scenic-effects wonder starring Stuart Whitman and Robert Wagner, Tells of an undersea city, Pacifica, in the year 2053. When its co-creator Mathews (Whitman) returns under Presidential orders, he faces a fistful of crises during shipments of gold and nuclear H-128 from Fort Knox. (Dir: Irwin Allen, 99 mins.)

City for Conquest (1940)*** James Cagney, Ann Sheridan. Sentimental story of a boxer who goes blind making sacrifices for his brother. There's a lot of corn here but it's well seasoned and expertly served. A newcomer named Arthur Kennedy does a nice job as Cagney's brother and you'll also see Elia Kazan, one of America's most talented directors, in a minor role. (Dir: Anatole Litvak, 101 mins.)

City in Fear (MTV 1980)*½ David Janssen, Robert Vaughn, Penny King, Susan Sullivan. Based on a novel by Linda Stewart. (Dir: Jud Taylor, 104 mins.)

City Lights (1931)**** Charlie Chaplin, Virginia Cherrill, Florence Lee. Perhaps Chaplin's greatest comedy, which means that it is one of the great works in the history of cinema. The last of Chaplin's silent films, thanks to Chaplin's refusal to make this a talkie after he had been preparing it for two years. Touching and hilarious tale of the "Little Tramp" who falls in love with a blind flower girl and gets money for an operation to restore her sight. The sequence when Chaplin becomes a boxer is one of his most remarkable. If the ending of this classic doesn't move you, when the Little Tramp peers through the window of a flower shop and sees the hitherto blind girl, you'd better have your heart and your head examined. Written and directed by Chaplin. (90 mins.)

122

City of Bad Men (1953)**½ Dale Robertson, Jeanne Crain, Richard Boone, Lloyd Bridges. Outlaws ride into Carson City and plan to rob the proceeds from the Corbett-Fitzsimmons prizefight. Pleasant western with a slightly different twist. (Dir: Harmon Jones, 82 mins.)

City of Fear (1959)**½ Vince Edwards. One of the many "B" films Vince Edwards made before he became famous as TV's sullen medic "Ben Casey." This one has him cast as an escaped convict who steals a metal container he believes is filled with heroin but actually contains a dangerous, radioactive powder called cobalt 60. Neatly made on a small budget. (Dir: Irving Lerner, 81 mins.)

City of Fear (Great Britain, 1965)*½ Paul Maxwell, Terry Moore. (Dir: Peter Bezencenet, 90 mins.)

City of Women (Italy, 1980)*** Marcello Mastroianni, Ettore Manni, Anna Prucnal, Donatella Damiani, Katren Gebelein. Director Federico Fellini outshouts the women's movement with his own hysterical brand of cinematic rhetoric. The movie starts promisingly, with Mastroianni wandering through a stylishly bizarre world of feminist conferences and womanly provocations, but it degenerates quickly into interminable pretexts for Fellinian fantasies, which are sometimes charming but mostly meaningless. Impressive production design. (138 mins.)

City on a Hunt (1953)** Lew Ayres, Sonny Tufts. Routine mystery, innocent victim of a murder charge uncovering the real culprit. San Francisco background. Cast superior to material. Alternate title: "No Escape." (Dir: Charles Bennett, 76 mins.)

City on Fire (Canada, 1979)*½ Barry Newman, Susan Clark, Shelley Winters, Ava Gardner, Leslie Nielsen, Henry Fonda. (Dir: Alvin Rakoff, 101 mins.)

City Stands Trial, The (Italy, 1954)**½ Silvana Pampanini, Eduardo Ciannelli. Police investigate a double murder, combat an underworld syndicate controlling the city. Period crime story of Naples at the turn of the century has a documentary-like atmosphere, some good moments. English-dubbed. (Dir: Luigi Zampa, 95 mins.)

City Streets (1931)** Gary Cooper, Sylvia Sidney, Paul Lukas, William Boyd (of the stage), Guy Kibbee. Story by Dashiell Hammett. No need to comment on this routine gangster film, as the curious will want to see a 1931 Gary Cooper playing "the Kid." (Dir: Rouben Mamoulian, 82 mins.)

City That Never Sleeps (1953)*** Gig Young, Mala Powers. Policeman nearly strays off the straight and narrow because of a cafe entertainer. Well made crime melodrama with some good performances. (Dir: John H. Auer, 90 mins.)

Clair de Femme (France, 1979)*** Yves Montand, Romy Schneider, Romolo Valli, Heinz Bennent. Costa Gavras tackles a love story, and there are no better screen lovers around today than Yves Montand and Romy Schneider. From a novel by Romain Gary. (Dir: Constantin Costa Gavras, 105 mins.)

Claire's Knee (France, 1970)**** Jean-Claude Brialy, Aurora Cornu, Beatrice Romand, Laurence de Monaghan. The fifth of writer-director Eric Rohmer's series of "Six Moral Tales" is one of the best films of the '70s. Brialy plays a man on summer vacation in the south of France who develops an interest in two young half sisters (Romand and de Monaghan) and by summer's end makes most of the mistakes that men make about women. Rohmer's genius is for capturing the mood of a location, the immediacy of the moment, and the implacable passage of time. (103 mins.)

Clambake (1967)* Elvis Presley, Shelley Fabares, Bill Bixby. (Dir: Arthur H. Nadel, 100 mins.)

Clarence, the Cross-Eyed Lion (1965)**½ Marshall Thompson, Betsy Drake. Another in the string of nature movies resembling "Born Free." Clarence can't focus on his prey when hunting, and he is taken to the Study Center for Animal Behavior in Africa, where he becomes a pet by the daughter of a doctor. Clarence also aids in capturing ape poachers. The television series "Daktari" was based on this film. (Dir: Andrew Marton, 98 mins.)

Clash by Night (1952)***½ Barbara Stanwyck, Robert Ryan, Paul Douglas, J. Carrol Naish, Marilyn Monroe. A brooding love tringle—homecoming wanton Stanwyck, simple fishing-boat owner Douglas, and corrosively cynical projectionist Ryan—set in a scruffy seaport town. The Clifford Odets material roused the sleeping realist in director Fritz Lang: the backwater atmosphere is as authentic as it is oppressive. (105 mins.)

Clash of Steel (France, 1964) *½ Gerard Barray, Gianna Maria Canale. (Dir: Bernard Borderie, 79 mins.)

Clash of the Wolves (1925)*½ Rin Tin Tin, June Marlowe, Charles Farrell. (Dir: Noel Mason Smith, 76 mins.)

Class of '44 (1973)** Gary Grimes, Jerry Houser, Oilver Conant, William Atherton. A disappointing sequel to the much better "Summer of '42," with the same three boys—Hermie, Osey and Benjie—now a little older and graduating from high school. It's also less well acted than "Summer of '42." Benjie disappears early, off to war, while the others go on to college—fraternity hazings, cheating on exams, proms, etc. The whole thing seems terribly contrived, with a serious climax that comes out of nowhere. Fails to generate much emotional impact. Screenplay by Herman Raucher. (Dir: Paul Bogart, 95 mins.)

Class of Miss MacMichael, The (Great Britain, 1978)*½ Glenda Jackson, Oliver

Reed, Michael Murphy, Rosalind Cash. (Dir: Silvio Narizzano, 93 mins.)

Class of '63 (MTV 1973)***½ Joan Hackett, James Brolin. This class-reunion story turns a surprisingly effective emotional drama. Talented actress Joan Hackett delivers a stunning performance as the unhappy wife who meets her old campus flame. What could be soap-opera material about a jealous husband and a wandering wife becomes an absorbing conflict played against fraternity foolishness. Miss Hackett is worth seeing, and so is Cliff Gorman as her husband. (Dir: John Korty, 73 mins.)

Claudelle Inglish (1961)** Diane McBain, Arthur Kennedy, Will Hutchins. Novel by Erskine Caldwell about a teenager, a sharecropper's daughter, who drives men mad, eventually comes to a sad end. Miss McBain and her director try to make something of it, to little avail—pretty drab. (Dir: Gordon Douglas, 99 mins.)

Claudia (1943)***½ Dorothy McGuire, Robert Young. If you've never seen Rose Franken's almost classical story of a child bride who grows up, you're in for a treat. Funny but not hilarious, sentimental but not corny. A delightful story. (Dir: Edmund Goulding, 91 mins.)

Claudia and David (1946)*** Dorothy McGuire, Robert Young. Not as delightful as "Claudia," but this sequel about their baby and life in suburban Connecticut is easy to take. (Dir: Walter Lang, 78 mins.)

Claudine (1974)***½ James Earl Jones, Diahann Carroll, Lawrence Hinton-Jacobs. Charming, skillful comedy-drama about two attractive people in love. Jones and Carroll are delightful together. The film is about blacks on welfare in Harlem. In the early '70s black actor Richard Roundtree said: "What we want in our movies from now on is to show black people winning because they use their heads, not because they do violence with their hands." A welcome relief from the spate of black super-stud movies. Skillful screenplay by Lester and Tina Pine. (Dir: John Berry, 94 mins.)

Claw Monsters, The (1955-66)** Phyllis Coates, Myron Healey. Feature version of serial "Panther Girl of the Kongo." Jungle girl combats a scientist using a monster to scare the natives away from his diamond mine. Serial fans might go for this lowbrow but actionful adventure. (Dir: Franklin Adreon, 100 mins.)

Clear and Present Danger, A (1970)**½ Hal Holbrook, E. G. Marshall, Joseph Campanella. The pilot film for "The Senator" TV series starring Hal Holbrook. His performance, plus a thoughful script about air pollution, should keep your interest. Holbrook is a candidate for the U.S. Senate who sacrifices his political aspirations in order to combat a smog crisis and its repercussions. (Dir: James Goldstone, 99 mins.)

Cleo from Five to Seven (France, 1962)**½

Corinne Marchand, Dorothea Blank. The second feature film directed by Agnes Varda. Two hours in the life of a Parisian pop singer who has become fed up with her life and is awaiting a doctor's report to confirm its end. A walk through the city streets rekindles her joie de vivre—not very convincingly, I'm afraid. Daring in its time, the film now looks rather hackneyed. (90 mins.)

Cleopatra (1934)*** Claudette Colbert, Henry Wilcoxon, Warren William, C. Aubrey Smith, Joseph Schildkraut. Director Cecil B. deMille's film is often appealing and even delightful although it is theatrically blocked and stodgily paced. The miscasting is severe. (101 mins.)

Cleopatra (1963)*** Elizabeth Taylor, Richard Burton, Rex Harrison. As a spectacle, this elaborate production has few equals, but much of it is lost on the TV screen. As historical drama it leaves something to be desired. The acting ranges from brilliant (Harrison as Caesar) to uneven (Taylor as Cleopatra, and Burton as Antony). Overlong, but most viewers will stay to the end. Writer-director Joseph L. Mankiewicz came in after Rouben Mamoulian left and revamped the project in his inimitable way in very little time. (243 mins.)

Cleopatra Jones (1973)* Tamara Dobson, Bernie Casey, Brenda Sykes, Shelley Winters, Antonio Fargas. (Dir: Jack Starrett, 89 mins.)

Cleopatra Jones and the Casino of Gold (1975)*½ Tamara Dobson, Stella Stevens, Norman Fell, Caro Kenyatta. (Dir: Chuck Bail, 96 mins.)

Cleopatra's Daughter (Italy, 1961)*½ Debra Paget, Robert Alda. (Dir: Richard MacNamara, 102 mins.)

Climats (France, 1961)**½ Marina Vlady, Jean-Pierre Marielle, Emmanuela Riva. Leisurely drama of an ill-matched married couple who divorce, and their eventual emotional entanglements thereafter. Sensitive performances, but the delicate theme needed more understanding treatment. Dubbed in English. (Dir: Stellio Lorenzi).

Climb an Angry Mountain (MTV 1972)** Barry Nelson, Fess Parker. Since so many TV heroes pack guns it seemed logical for Fess Parker to become a low-keyed country sheriff. Filmed around Mount Shasta country, lawman Parker, a widower who raises his kids on a ranch, reluctantly goes after a local Indian on the run for a murder rap. The real star is the Shasta scenery, aided by an assist from football's Joe Kapp as the running Indian. (Dir: Leonard Horn, 97 mins.)

Climbers, The (France-Italy, 1959)* Edmund O'Brien, Richard Basehart. (Dir: Yves Allegret, 85 mins.)

Cloak and Dagger (1946)*** Gary Cooper, Lilli Palmer, Robert Alda. University professor works on a secret mission for the OSS inside Germany. Loosely constructed but tense espionage melodrama, well acted. (Dir: Fritz Lang, 106 mins.)

Clock, The (1945)***½ Judy Garland, Robert Walker, James Gleason, Lucille Gleason, Keenan Wynn. Director Vincente Minnelli wanted to create a vehicle for his wife Judy Garland that would show off her considerable acting talent. They chose this magical love story of a soldier on leave in New York City and the office girl he meets, marries, and leaves behind—all in 48 hours. Walker is cast as the shy young hick, and Garland is radiant as the girl. Romantic comedy-melodrama as it should be done. (90 mins.)

Clockmaker, The (France, 1974)***½ Philippe Noiret. An astonishing, perceptive first feature film directed by former critic Bertrand Tavernier and based on a novel by Georges Simenon. Protagonist is a watchmaker in Lyon who is mortified to learn that his grown-up son has committed a political murder, though the son is not politically involved. Philippe Noiret is remarkable playing the watchmaker, inspecting and analyzing the developments as if he were looking through his magnifying glass. A complex, beautifully observed film directed with great restraint, uniformly well acted. The character of the young killer is never adequately dealt with, but "Clockmaker" does finally understand. (Dir: Bertrand Tavernier, 100 mins.)

Clockwork Orange, A (Great Britain, 1971)**** Malcolm McDowell, Patrick Magee, Adrienne Corri. A shattering political allegory about a loathsome, violent anti-hero in a modern society where gangs of young punks run amok and peaceful citizens are imprisoned in their own homes. Produced, written and directed by Stanley Kubrick, based on the novel by Anthony Burgess. (The novel is partially autobiographical, as Burgess' own wife was robbed, raped and severely beaten by three G.I. deserters during a London WWII blackout, and subsequently died of these injuries.) "Clockwork" is loaded with fascinating cinematic images, including some of the most repellent scenes ever, but in Kubrick's masterful hands it builds to a devastating finale. Nominated for Academy Awards for best picture, best direction, and best screenplay. Malcolm McDowell is altogether chilling playing a pathological toughie. After the initial release, Kubrick re-edited "Clockwork" slightly to make it less violent. An unforgettable cinema masterpiece with an appalling message of immorality. (Dir: Stanley Kubrick, 135 mins.)

Clone Master (MTV 1978)*** Art Hindle, Ralph Bellamy, Robyn Douglas. One might have expected, after all the media coverage about cloning and test-tube babies, that the screen version would be just another ho-hum mystery in which the bad guys muscle in on brainy scientists. But it's not so. John D. F. Black, one of our better mystery writers not only dramatizes the act of cloning, but considers how clones—all of them being alike—can go through an identity crisis. This mystery-science fiction entry merits a look because of its script, production, and stars. (Dir: Don Medford, 104 mins.)

Clones, The (1973)** Michael Greene, Gregory Sierra. A strange sci-fi thriller that tries, without much luck, for laughs. There's this scientist, see, who wants to kill this doctor, so makes a clone (duplicate) to replace the doctor, but the clone ... Woody Allen did it far better in his sci-fi film "Sleeper." (Dirs: Paul Hunt and Lamar Card, 94 mins.)

Clonus Horror, The (1979)*½ Tim Donnelly, Dick Sargent, Peter Graves, Paulette Breen, Keenan Wynn, Lurene Tuttle. (Dir: Robert S. Fiveson, 90 mins.)

Close Encounters of the Third Kind (1977)**** Richard Dreyfuss, François Truffaut, Melinda Dillion, Teri Garr, Cary Guffey. Though director Steven Spielberg has added footage depicting the inside of the alien spacecraft, overall the film is less about extraterrestrial visitors than about an obsession with images. I like the middle third of the film best—the compulsion driving Dreyfuss to build his muddy model is quite moving. Spielberg nibbles at paranoia, but in the resolution the universe is seen as profoundly benign. (137 mins.)

Close to My Heart (1951)**½ Gene Tierney, Ray Milland, Fay Bainter. Soap opera plot about a couple who adopt the baby of a convicted murderer and prove there's nothing in heredity. Well acted by a good cast. (Dir: William Keighley, 90 mins.)

Close-Up (1948)**½ Alan Baxter, Virginia Gilmore. Newsreel photographer finds plenty of trouble when he accidentally catches a picture of a wanted Nazi criminal. Fairly good melodrama moves at a fast clip. Filmed in New York City. (Dir: Jack Donohue, 76 mins.)

Closely Watched Trains (Czechoslovakia, 1966)***½ Vaclav Neckar, Jitka Bendova. Gentle, touching film directed by Jiri Menzel, about a shy sexually inexperienced train dispatcher during the period of the German occupation during World War II. Made during a period of increasing artistic freedom in Czechoslovakia, this comedy-drama shows how the decent instincts in people can survive during difficult times, and there is one delicious scene showing a novel use for the posterior of an obliging country wench. Menzel's perceptive hand is evident throughout as this slight story builds to the unhappy finale. Dubbed. (Dir:Jiri Menzel, 89 mins.)

Cloudburst (Great Britain, 1952)** Robert Preston, Elizabeth Sellars. An inoffensive little item from England with good actor Robert Preston completely wasted as an adventurer who can't seem to stay away from trouble. (Dir: Francis Searle, 83 mins.)

Clouded Yellow (Great Britain, 1951)*** Jean Simmons, Trevor Howard. Secret service agent demoted to cataloguing butterflies, aids a girl wrongly accused of murder. Mystery begins slowly but picks up as it progresses to a suspenseful climax. (Dir: Ralph Thomas, 96 mins.)

Clouds Over Europe—See: **Q Planes**

Clouds Over Israel (Israel, 1962)**½ Yiftach Spector, Shimon Israeli, Dina Doronne. Compelling, unpretentious picture about a human confrontation between Israeli military men and an Arab family during the 1956 hostilities. The growth of mutual respect and friendship is nicely told, technical shortcomings and awkward script notwithstanding. (Dir: Ivan Lengyel, 85 mins.)

Clown, The (1953)*** Red Skelton, Jane Greer, Tim Considine. If you're a Red Skelton fan, you might be surprised to see him act in this one—a drama about a comedy performer who loses his wife through divorce and almost loses his son's love. Remake of **The Champ**, 1931. (Dir: Robert Z. Leonard, 89 mins.)

Clowns, The (Italy-France, 1971)***½ Mayo Morin, Lima Alberti, Alvaro Vitali, Gasparmo. Three rings of spectacle, slapstick, and sensation invade the screen in this piece from the master Italian director Federico Fellini. Clowns race to and from in a fantasy circus world of Fellini's youth which is approached as a documentary-within-a-film. Fellini appears in the film as the head of the camera crew and if you ask what it all means you may be hit with the same bucket of water as the journalist who asked the question in the film. Without Fellini's usually amazing substance, but the surface glows with spirit throughout. English subtitles. (90 mins.)

Clowns, The (Italy, 1971)*½ Riccardo Billi, Tino Scotti, Fanfulla. (Dir: Federico Fellini, 90 mins.)

Clue of the New Pin, The (Great Britain, 1962)** Paul Daneman, Bernard Archard. Sleuth investigates the murder of a millionaire whose body is found in a locked vault. Old-fashioned-style whodunit based on an Edgar Wallace story. Should satisfy mystery fans. (Dir:Allan Davis, 58 mins.)

Clue of the Silver Key, The (Great Britain, 1962)** Bernard Lee, Finlay Currie. Scotland Yard investigates the murder of a wealthy moneylender. Typical Edgar Wallace mystery for the sleuthing devotees. (Dir: Gerald Glaister, 59 mins.)

Clue of the Twisted Candle, The (Great Britain, 1960)** Bernard Lee, David Knight. Wealthy man who fears for his life is implicated in murder. Okay Edgar Wallace mystery. (Dir: Allan Davis, 61 mins.)

Cluny Brown (1946)***½ Jennifer Jones, Charles Boyer. Pleasant comedy, superbly acted and directed, about the turbulent career of a plumber's niece and a Czech refugee in England during the war. A satirical spoof of the first-order. (Dir: Ernest Lubitsch, 100 mins.)

Coach of the Year (MTV 1980)**½ Robert Conrad, Red West, David Hubbard, Daphne Maxwell. Macho man Conrad delivers a warm, genuine performance as a Vietnam paraplegic, a former football star who tries to coach kids behind bars. The hip toughs refuse to play buddy-buddy with the coach and make plans to skip the day of the big game. Chicago locations are a plus. (Dirs: Don Medford (football sequences), Andy Sidaris, 104 mins.)

Coal Miner's Daughter (1980)**** Sissy Spacek, Tommy Lee Jones, Beverly D'Angelo, Levon Helm, Phyllis Boyens. Drama and musical biography don't mix; writer Tom Rickman and director Michael Apted wisely concentrate on the atmosphere and the characters, content to let the plot tag along. Spacek's incarnation of country singer Loretta Lynn shows remarkable emotional range and consummate control; Jones, as her supportive husband, surmounts an odd makeup job with subtle, intelligent choices. Quietly observant and warm. (125 mins.)

Coast of Skeletons (Great Britain, 1965)* Richard Todd, Dale Robertson, Heinz Drache. (Dir: Robert Lynn, 90 mins.)

Coast to Coast (1980)** Dyan Cannon, Robert Blake, Quinn Redeker. The genre is screwball comedy in the "Bringing Up Baby" tradition, but the writers are too willing to distort or ignore character for the sake of a gag. Director Joseph Sargent does a respectable job of trying to overcome the script. Cannon plays a woman stashed in a mental institution by her evil husband. She escapes and wangles a cross-country ride with a dense trucker (Blake) whose vehicle is about to be repossessed. The ensuing pursuit is tiresome, but with a smattering of nice moments. (95 mins.)

Cobra (1925)*** Rudolph Valentino, Nita Naldi, Gertrude Olmstead. A rarely seen, classy Valentino silent; he's a young Italian count who has inherited a debt-ridden palace on the Bay of Naples. He goes to work, and falls in love with an efficient secretary, only to be pursued by gold-digging socialites who don't believe he's penniless. There's a lot of hand wringing and a rousing hotel fire, and Valentino doesn't get the girl. Costumes by Adrian. Directed by Joseph Henabery, who played Lincoln in "The Birth of a Nation." (77 mins.)

Cobweb, The (1955)***½ Richard Widmark, Lauren Bacall, Charles Boyer, Gloria Grahame, Susan Strasberg, John Kerr, Lillian Gish. A stellar cast brings William Gibson's dramatic novel about a modern mental institution to the screen with conviction. Miss Gish and Mr. Boyer are standouts as the institution's business manager and head administrator respectively. (Dir: Vincente Minnelli, 124 mins.)

Cockeyed Cowboys of Calico County, The

(MTV 1970)*½ Dan Blocker, Nanette Fabray, Jack Cassidy, Mickey Rooney. (Dir: Tony Leader, 99 mins.)

Cockeyed Miracle, The (1946)** Frank Morgan, Keenan Wynn, Audrey Totter. Cockeyed little fantasy about a couple of ghosts trying to straighten out those they left behind is completely dependent on the cast. (Dir: Sylvan Simon, 81 mins.)

Cockleshell Heroes (Great Britain, 1955)***½ Jose Ferrer, Trevor Howard. Tense suspense tale about one of the most dangerous missions of WW II. "Operation Cockleshell" is the name given to the canoe invasion by a handful of volunteers of an enemy-held French port in order to destroy a group of battleships. Good invasion sequence with "edge-of-sofa" excitement. (Dir: Jose Ferrer, 110 mins.)

Cocktail Molotov (France, 1981)**½ Elise Caron, Philippe Lebas, Francoise Cluzet. Comedy about a 17-year-old French girl coming of age in the turmoil of the late 60's. Three students travel from Paris to Venice in the spring of 1968, become involved with some half-hearted anarchists, and find that the revolution has started without them at home. Visually unexciting (except for the European locales) but charming, sentimental and funny. Miss Caron is particularly engaging. (Dir: Diane Kurys, 100 mins.)

Cocoanuts, The (1929)***½ The Marx Brothers, Margaret Dumont, Kay Francis, the Gamby Hall Girls (dancing bellhops). An eminently watchable antique. The Brothers' first film—a literal recording of their Broadway smash hit. Ponderous, but shows the Marxes at their freshest.Of the two directors, Groucho later remarked: "One of them didn't understand English, and the other didn't understand Harpo." (Dirs: Joseph Santley, Robert Florey, 96 mins.)

Code Name: Diamond Head (MTV 1977)* Roy Thinnes, France Nuyen. (Dir: Jeannot Szware, 79 mins.)

Code Name: Red Roses (Italy, 1969)* James Daly, Pier Angeli, Peter Van Eyck. (Dir: Fernando Di Leo, 96 mins.)

Code Name: Tiger (France-Italian, 1964)*½ Roger Hanin, Daniela Bianchi. (Dir: Claude Chabrol, 86 mins.)

Code of Silence—See: **Killer's Cage**

Code 7, Victim 5! (Great Britain, 1964)*½ Lex Barker, Ronald Fraser. (Dir: Robert Lynn, 88 mins.)

Code 645 (1947-66)*½ Clayton Moore, Ramsay Ames, Roy Barcroft. (Dir: Fred Brannon, 100 mins.)

Code Two (1953)*½ Ralph Meeker, Sally Forrest, Keenan Wynn. Routine cops-and-robbers yarn about the L.A. police division. (Dir: Fred M. Wilcox, 69 mins.)

Coffee, Tea or Me? (MTV 1973)**½ Karen Valentine, John Davidson, Michael Anderson. This lighthearted comedy leans heavily on the perkiness of Karen Valentine. Karen is an airline stewardess with a weakness for strays which leads to a double life, commuting between two husbands in Los Angeles and London. Alec Guinness charmed movie fans in a similar plot in "Captain's Paradise," and it works fairly well in this revamped format. Davidson and Anderson supply the right measure of charm as the young cuckolds. (Dir: Norman Panama, 90 mins.)

Coffin From Hong Kong (Germany, 1964)*½ Heinz Drache, Elga Andersen. (Dir: Manfred R. Kohler, 93 mins.)

Coffy (1973)* Pam Grier, Booker Bradshaw, Rober DoQui. (Dir: Jack Hill, 91 mins.)

Cold Night's Death (MTV1973)*** Eli Wallach, Robert Culp. Culp, Wallach, and a supporting cast of monkeys! Strange forces disrupt experiments being made on monkeys in a snowbound mountain lab. Working in isolation with the animals, scientists blame each other for weird acts of vandalism. Could the culprit be the Abominable Snowman? Takes its time building up the dilemma, scattering occasional clues, but it's worth hanging on for the unpredictable solution. (Dir: Jerrold Freedman, 73 mins.)

Cold Sweat (British, 1974)* Liv Ullmann, Charles Bronson, James Mason. (Dir: Terence Young, 94 mins.)

Cold Turkey (1971)*** Dick Van Dyke, Pippa Scott, Tom Poston. Uneven but often funny comedy about a small Midwestern town trying to win a 25 million dollar reward if everyone in the town will go "cold turkey" for thirty days, i.e. give up smoking cigarettes. Van Dyke plays a preacher urging his flock to avoid the weed. Produced, directed and co-authored by Norman Lear, responsible for the hit TV series "All In The Family." (102 mins.)

Cold Wind in August, A (1961)***½ Lola Albright, Scott Marlowe, Herschel Bernardi. A very moving drama of a lonely burlesque stripper in her thirties and her friendship which turns into a love affair, with a 17-year-old boy. Lola Albright, under the sensitive directorial hand of Alexander Singer, gives a beautifully shaded, poignant, convincing performance playing the stripper searching for affection. Albright, who conclusively proves here that she's a most gifted actress, has never been seen to such good advantage in films since. Scott Marlowe impresses as the young boy. Screenplay by Burton Wohl based on his novel "Cold Wind in August." One of the best American films dealing with adolescent love, especially that of a young boy for an older woman. (Dir: Alexander Singer, 80 mins.)

Colditz Story (Great Britain, 1957)*** John Mills, Eric Portman. Offbeat comedy-drama about British prisoners of war in a German castle fortress (WW II). Excellent performance by Eric Portman. (Dir: Guy Hamilton, 97 mins.)

Cole Younger, Gunfighter (1958)** Frank Lovejoy, James Best. The young cowboy fans will go for this rough and tough western about the notorious gunslinger, Cole Younger, and a couple of men who cross his path. Lovejoy's last film. (Dir: R. G. Springsteen, 79 mins.)

Collectionneuse, La (France, 1967)***½ Patrick Bauchau, Haydee Politoff, Daniel Pommerulle. The third of Eric Rohmer's *Six Moral Tales* was made before both *My Night at Maud's* and *Claire's Knee*, although it has reached these shores much later. *La Collectionneuse* is the young Haydee, who sleeps around but never at home with two intellectual prigs whom she lives with. Far less subtle than the two later works, the film is nonetheless delicious in its ironies and languorous in its lazy, hazy tempo. (Dir: Erich Rohmer, 88 mins.)

Collector, The (U.S.-Great Britain, 1965)**½ Terence Stamp, Samantha Eggar, Mona Washbourne. Misguided adaptation of the John Fowles novel about a young lepidopterist who holds a young woman captive in the hope that she will learn to love him. The film takes a clinical viewpoint that is at odds with the novelist's, and William Wyler's direction is too unstressed. Stamp and Eggar are excellent. (119 mins.)

Colleen (1936)**½ Ruby Keeler, Dick Powell, Jack Oakie. Typical 1936 Dick Powell musical. Hugh Herbert's portrayal of an eccentric millionaire is the only redeeming feature. (Dir: Alfred E. Green, 100 mins.)

College (1927)***½ Buster Keaton. One of the few Keaton features to equal the persistent invention of his gag-laden shorts. He is a brainy but inept young man who pursues his girl to college (though he must work his way through as a soda jerk). He fails ignobly at every sport only to perform the same feats with precision and grace when he dashes to the girl's rescue. Keaton surpasses Harold Lloyd on his own turf. (Dir: James W. Horne, 65 mins.)

College Confidential (1960)*½ Steve Allen, Jayne Meadows, Mamie Van Doren. (Dir: Albert Zugsmith, 91 mins.)

Collision Course (1968)—See: **Bamboo Saucer, The**

Colonel Blimp—See: **Life and Death of Colonel Blimp, The**

Colonel Effingham's Raid (1945)*** Charles Coburn, Joan Bennett. A retired Southern colonel decides to use his military background to straighten out a town. Good comedy thanks to Coburn. (Dir: Irving Pichel, 70 mins.)

Color Me Dead (Australia, 1969)*½ Tom Tryon, Carolyn Jones. (Dir: Eddie Davis, 97 mins.)

Color of Pomegranates, The (Armenia)***½ Directed by Sergei Paradjanov, this film tells the story of Arutin Sayadian, an eighteenth-century Armenian poet-musician who became court minstrel of Herakle XI, King of Georgia. Subsequently banished to a monastery, he became a bishop and finally an archbishop. In 1795

the Shah of Persia invaded Georgia and besieged Sayadian's cathedral, demanding that he renounce Christianity for Mohammedanism or die. He chose death. Paradjanov's film has reportedly been censored by both the Russians and by agents of the ex-Shah of Iran. At least thirty minutes are missing, but what remains has some remarkable scenes. Alternate title: **Sayat Nova**. (Dir: Sergei Paradjanov).

Colorado Territory (1949)**** Joel McCrea, Virginia Mayo, Dorothy Malone, Henry Hull, John Archer. Smashing western remake by director Raoul Walsh of his own "High Sierra." McCrea is the outlaw who escapes from prison and sets out to commit one last robbery; Mayo is his ragtag companion, and Dorothy Malone is the "good" girl who hasn't the moral fiber of Mayo. Walsh's late visual style is epigrammatic and intense; the climax is a knockout. (94 mins.)

Colossus and the Amazon Queen (Italy, 1960)* Ed Fury, Rod Taylor. (Dir: Vittorio Sala, 96 mins.)

Colossus and the Headhunters (Italy, 1960)* Kirk Morris, Laura Brown. (Dir: Guido Malatesta, 85 mins.)

Colossus and the Huns (Italy, 1962)*½ Jerome Courtland, Lisa Gastoni. (Dir: Roberto Bianchi Montero, 90 mins.)

Colossus of New York, The (1958)* John Baragrey, Otto Kruger, Mala Powers, Ross Martin. (Dir: Eugene Lourie, 70 mins.)

Colossus of Rhodes, The (France-Spain-Italy, 1961)** Rory Calhoun, Lea Massari. Better than usual spear-and-sandal effort. Lots of action as heroes try to destroy a huge statue guarding the port of Rhodes. (Dir: Sergio Leone, 128 mins.)

Colossus of the Arena (Italy, 1962)*½ Mark Forest, Scilla Gabel. (Dir: Michele Lupo, 100 mins.)

Colossus: The Forbin Project (1970)**½ Eric Braeden, Susan Clark, William Schallert. Computer runs amok, pits wits against scientists in attempt to take over. Intelligent story, adequately told. Alternate title: **The Forbin Project**. (Dir: Joseph Sargent, 100 mins.)

Colt .45—See: **Thunder cloud**

Columbo: An Exercise in Fatality (MTV 1974)**½ Peter Falk, Robert Conrad. Features a complicated duel of wits between Peter Falk's sloppy Columbo and a nasty physical fitness character (Robert Conrad), an expert at manipulating taped telephone conversations as an alibi for murder. Columbo takes out a 30-day introductory membership to one of the health spas the guy owns. (Dir: Bernard Kowalski, 98 mins.)

Columbo: Death Lends a Hand (MTV 1971)**½ Peter Falk, Robert Culp. Peter Falk's characterization of the seemingly clumsy detective with the brain of Sherlock Holmes is a joy to watch, and he's provided here with a fine adversary in the person of Robert Culp. Culp, who heads up a super-investigative agency, accidentally kills the wife of a client who, in turn, hires Culp's firm to augment the regular police force. The cat-and-mouse game is great fun. (Dir: Bernard Kowalski, 72 mins.)

Columbo: Double Shock (MTV 1973)**½ Peter Falk, Jeanette Nolan, Julie Newmar, Martin Landau. Peter Falk's usually unflappable Columbo has a hard time making the grade with Jeanette Nolan's officious housekeeper, while trying to determine how and by whom her aging, wealthy physical-fitness addict of an employer was murdered. (Dir: Robert Butler, 72 mins.)

Columbo: Swan Song (MTV 1974)**½ Peter Falk, Johnny Cash, Ida Lupino. This can be called a flying musical-murder story. It gains interest from the casting of gravel-throated country-western star Johnny Cash. He plays a former convict-turned-pop-star with the help of his wife, well played by Ida Lupino. (Dir: Nicholas Colasanto, 106 mins.)

Columbo: Troubled Waters (MTV 1975)** Peter Falk, Robert Vaughn, Dean Stockwell. Even when Peter Falk's Columbo goes on a much-needed vacation he's confronted with murder, blackmail and the usual quota of guest-starring suspects. The sleuth boards the "Sun Princess," a cruise ship en route to Mexico. Shortly after they raise ancor, the exotic band singer is found dead. The director is a better actor. (Dir: Ben Gazzara, 98 mins.)

Column South (1953)** Audie Murphy, Joan Evans, Robert Sterling. Slow moving Civil War yarn with Murphy playing a young cavalry officer who averts an all-out Navajo uprising. Miss Evans supplies the necessary romance. (Dir: Frederick de Cordova, 85 mins.)

Coma (1978)**½ Genevieve Bujold, Michael Douglas, Elizabeth Ashley, Rip Torn, Richard Widmark. Bujold thinks something strange is going on at the hospital where she works and she is right. Plot is not as well developed as you'd like. Director Michael Crichton's slow thriller must have begun with something to say about the morality of the medical profession, but it's lost in the shuffle of unnecessary narrative detail. (113 mins.)

Comanche (1956)** Dana Andrews, Linda Cristal, Kent Smith. Indians raid a Mexican town and kidnap the daughter of a Spanish aristocrat among others. Cavalry Scout Andrews has a rough time before he convinces chief that he is on a peace mission. Some good battle scenes. (Dir: George Sherman, 87 mins.)

Comanche Station (1960)*** Randolph Scott, Nancy Gates. Lawman guides a woman and three desperadoes through hostile Indian country. These Scott westerns are usually better than average, and this one is no exception; well-made and exciting. (Dir: Budd Boetticher, 74 mins.)

Comanche Territory (1950)** Maureen O'Hara, Macdonald Carey. Another retelling of the adventures of famed Jim Bowie and his encounter with the Apaches. Macdonald Carey isn't quite up to the image of Bowie but he gives it the old college try. Maureen O'Hara is, as always, Maureen O'Hara. (Dir: George Sherman, 76 mins.)

Comancheros, The (1961)*** John Wayne, Stuart Whitman, Ina Balin, Lee Marvin, Nehemiah Persoff. Generally enjoyable big-scale western about a ranger who infiltrates a gang supplying guns and firewater to the Indians. Played for fun by Wayne, Whitman, Marvin and others; some good action at the end. (Dir: Michael Curtiz, 107 mins.)

Combat Squad (1953)** John Ireland, Lon McCallister, Hal March. During the Korean War, a young, frightened boy finds the courage to become a man in the eyes of his buddies. Familiar war story. (Dir: Cy Roth, 72 mins.)

Come and Get It (1936)**½ Edward Arnold, Joel McCrea, Frances Farmer, Walter Brennan. Edna Ferber's saga of a logging mogul and his efforts to woo the daughter of the woman he loved and left (one of Farmer's strongest performances). Arnold displays manliness and a credible (if fallible) love interest; this excellent actor had range that was untapped in most of his films. Brennan won the first Best Supporting Actor Oscar for his role. Samuel Goldwyn took director Hawks off the picture and replaced him with William Wyler, but only the last ten minutes or so look to be Wyler's. (99 mins.)

Come Back, Africa (1960)***½ Zachariah Mgabi. Semi-documentary, surreptitiously filmed in South Africa, describes the stifling, often violent lives of blacks in that divided society. Unprofessional cast is mostly awkward but Mgabi, the lead, is extraordinary, his performance evoking the helpless despair of being perpetually harassed. Squalid settings evoke the reality best. (Dir: Lionel Rogosin, 90 mins.)

Come Back Charleston Blue (1972)** Godfrey Cambridge, Raymond St. Jacques, Jonelle Allen, Coffin Ed Johnson and Grave Digger Jones return in this sequel to the amusing "Cotton Comes to Harlem." Unfortunately, the gritty frivolity that made "Cotton" a joy is missing in this opus concerning the fight between the black and white gangs that hope to control the Harlem heroin trade. Many may find the hip lingo incomprehensible, and everyone will notice the lack of continuity in the plot. Based on the novel, "The Heat's On," by Chester Himes. The co-author of the screenplay is listed as "Bontche Schweig." It's a Sholom Aleichem character-name used by the gifted TV writer Ernest Kinoy, though this is certainly not a sample of the award-winning Kinoy's best work. (Dir: Mark Warren, 100 mins.)

Come Back, Little Sheba (1952)**** Shirley Booth, Burt Lancaster, Terry

Moore. Splendid performance by Shirley Booth, who won an Oscar, as a slatternly middle-aged housewife, an equally effective one by Lancaster as her alcoholic husband in this absorbing adaptation of the hit play by William Inge. Emotionally searing drama of an unhappy marriage for those who insist on top-quality filmmaking. TV's Hazel fans will be reminded what a moving actress Miss Booth can be. (Dir: Daniel Mann, 99 mins.)

Come Blow Your Horn (1963)*** Frank Sinatra, Lee J. Cobb, Barbara Rush. Neil Simon's Broadway comedy about a Jewish family in New York City is successfully brought to the screen with Sinatra well cast as a playboy and Tony Bill as his hero-worshipping younger brother. Lee J. Cobb and Molly Picon, as the parents, supply the humor of the original script. (Dir: Bud Yorkin, 112 mins.)

Come Dance With Me (France, 1959)*½ Brigitte Bardot, Henri Vidal. (Dir: Michel Boisrond, 91 mins.)

Come Fill the Cup (1951)*** James Cagney, Phyllis Thaxter, Gig Young. James Cagney in another fine performance as an alcoholic ex-newspaper reporter and his struggle to reconstruct his shattered life. Fine performances throughout. (Dir: Gordon Douglas, 112 mins.)

Come Fly With Me (U.S.A.-Great Britain, 1963)** Dolores Hart, Hugh O'Brian, Karl Malden, Pamela Tiffin, Lois Nettleton. Typical empty romantic yarn about a trio of attractive girls who share secrets and troubles—this time they're three overseas airline hostesses, and the objects of their affection are a pilot, a titled jewel thief and a Texas millionaire (what else)! (Dir: Henry Levin, 109 mins.)

Come Live With Me (1941)** James Stewart, Hedy Lamarr. Hedy marries Jimmy to avoid being deported and if you can't guess how it ends you haen't seen many movies. (Dir: Clarence Brown, 86 mins.)

Come Next Spring (1956)***½ Ann Sheridan, Steve Cochran, Walter Brennan, Sonny Tufts. Arkansas man returns home to his wife and family after eight years of wandering. Touching drama with excellent performances, a good script. (Dir: R. G. Springsteen, 92 mins.)

Come September (1961)**½ Rock Hudson, Gina Lollobrigida, Sandra Dee, Bobby Darin. Splendid Italian scenery grafted to a frothy little comedy plot about a millionaire who discovers his caretaker is using his villa as a hotel when he's away. None of the starring players are exactly comedy whizzes, but it's all pleasant enough and Lollo is yummy to look at. With Walter Slezak as the caretaker. (Dir: Robert Mulligan, 112 mins.)

Come Spy with Me (1967)** Troy Donahue, Andrea Dromm, Albert Dekker. Silly spy spoof with nice Jamaican locales. One of the few bright notes is Allen's energetic performance as a daffy lady covering a skin-diving competition. Peter Finch has a cameo as a clerk. (Dir: Marshall Stone, 85 mins.)

Come to the Stable (1949)*** Loretta Young, Celeste Holm. Warm, human story about two French nuns and their efforts to build a children's hospital in America. Loretta Young and Celeste Holm, both nominated for Oscars, play the nuns with taste and charm. (Dir: Henry Koster, 94 mins.)

Comeback Kid, The (MTV 1980)**½ John Ritter, Susan Dey, Rod Gist. Ritter is Bubba Newman, a flashy ex-minor-league pitcher who lands a job coaching a playground of dispirited kids. After dogged practice and misuse of playground funds, Bubba rejoins his team as a batter, but feels uncomfortable about the kids he left behind. Ritter is charming playing a basically unattractive character, but the story turns into very sweet syrup. (Dir: Peter Levin, 104 mins.)

Comedians, The (U.S.A.-France; 1967)**½ Richard Burton, Elizabeth Taylor, Peter Ustinov, Alec Guinness. Graham Greene's novel of unrest in Haiti transferred to the screen as a vehicle for Mr. & Mrs. Burton. The basic material of the novel is interesting but the splendid cast is hampered by Peter Glenville's sluggish direction, and a script that dwells too long on unnecessary detail. Fine supporting performances from Lillian Gish and Paul Ford. (160 mins.)

Comedy Company, The (MTV 1978)** Jack Albertson, Lawrence-Hilton Jacobs, Michael Brandon. Two nightclubs, the Improv (New York City) and the Comedy Store (Hollywood), which let young comics try out their material, spawned some of the best new comics of the '70s. The film tries to duplicate the atmosphere of the clubs, but fails. Albertson plays an ex-vaudevillian who runs the Comedy Company. Part drama, part comedy routines. (Dir: Lee Philips, 104 mins.)

Comedy Man, The (Great Britain, 1963)**** Kenneth More, Cecil Parker, Billie Whitelaw, Dennis Price. Soundly sketched portrait of a small-time actor trying to make the big-time London stage before age catches up with him. Some racy adult sequences, realistic backstage atmosphere, excellent performances. (Dir: Alvin Rakoff, 92 mins.)

Comedy of Terrors, The (1964)*** Vincent Price, Peter Lorre, Boris Karloff, Basil Rathbone. An outstanding cast of masters of the horror-film genre have fun spoofing the type of film they used to work in with nary a smile on their faces. The whole thing concerns a funeral home and a unique scheme for garnering more business. (Dir: Jacques Tourneur, 111 mins.)

Comes a Horseman (1978)*** James Caan, Jane Fonda, Jason Robards, Jr., Richard Farnsworth. A curious feminist parable cum paranoid thriller from director Alan J. Pakula, who knows about both genres.

It's a western, too: Fonda is the lady rancher, Robards the land baron after her spread, Caan the horseman who rides, however ambiguously, to the rescue. Fine in parts but never quite coheres. (118 mins.)

Comic, The (1969)***½ Dick Van Dyke, Mickey Rooney, Michele Lee, Cornel Wilde. Those of you who revere the comedy greats of silent films will particularly enjoy this fine, incisive portrait by Dick Van Dyke of a silent-film comedian. Authentic Hollywood atmosphere, hilarious scenes blended with pathos; youngsters will also delight in this worthy entry, somewhat underrated at the time of its release. Special high praise to writer-producer-director Carl Reiner who also plays a bit part. Pert Kelton is seen to good advantage in a cameo role in her last role. (Dir: Carl Reiner, 94 mins.)

Comin' Round the Mountain (1951)** Bud Abbott, Lou Costello, Dorothy Shay. The feudin', fussin', and a fightin' gets an added slapstick touch as A & C head for them there hills in this cornball comedy about hillbilly hostility. The kids will find it painless. (Dir: Charles Lamont, 77 mins.)

Coming Home (1978)**** Jon Voight, Jane Fonda, Bruce Dern, Robert Carradine. A deeply moving and courageous movie that works on several levels that are normally incompatible. It is, among other things, an unusually touching love story, while also being perhaps the most powerful anti-Vietnam War statement released by a major Hollywood movie company. Voight plays (superbly) a paraplegic veteran who, after returning to a veterans hospital in the States, gradually falls in love with another man's wife (Fonda). Voight and Fonda won Academy Awards. Historian Arthur Schlesinger, Jr., said of this film: "It recalls the horrid waste and destructiveness of the most shameful war in American history, the worst years of our lives. I salute Jane Fonda for insisting that it be made." (Dir: Hal Ashby, 128 mins.)

Coming Out Party, A (Great Britain, 1962)*** James Robertson Justice, Leslie Phillips. Crusty radar expert is captured and imprisoned by the Germans incognito, devises a daring escape from prison camp. World War II story played for comedy, it succeeds because of witty bits of business and the performance etched in acid by Justice. (Dir: Ken Annakin, 90 mins.)

Command, The (1953)** Guy Madison, Joan Weldon, James Whitmore. The first CinemaScope western—which calls for a big "So What?" for TV. Generally formula Cavalry vs. Indians plot about a medic who takes over a fighting outfit. (Dir: David Butler, 120 mins.)

Command Decision (1948)***½ Clark Gable, Walter Pidgeon, Van Johnson. Interesting insight into the emotions of military brass who must send men to their deaths to win battles. A fine cast does very well in this adaptation of the Broadway hit. (Dir: Sam Wood, 112 mins.)

Commando (Belgium-Spain-Germany-Italy, 1963)**½ Stewart Granger, Dorian Gray. Foreign Legionnaires embark on a dangerous mission to capture the leader of an Algerian resistance movement. Fairly well-done action drama has some good moments. Dubbed in English. (Dir: Frank Wisbar. 98 mins.)

Commandos (Italy, 1972)* Lee Van Cleef, Jack Kelly. (Dir: Armando Crispino, 89 mins.)

Commandos Strike at Dawn (1942)*** Paul Muni, Anna Lee. When the Nazis invade Norway, partisans resist and pave the way for a Commando raid. Occasionally exciting war drama. (Dir: John Farrow, 98 mins.)

Committee, The (1968)** The San Francisco improvisational comedy group in a straight performance of sketches. Almost a TV variety show in concept, but some very amusing bits. Cast includes Peter Bonerz, Barbara Bosson, Gary Goodrow. Alternate Title: **A Session with the Committee.** (Dir: Del Jack, 88 mins.)

Communion—See: **Alice Sweet Alice**

Companions in Nightmare (1968)**½ Melvyn Douglas, Gig Young, Anne Baxter, Dana Wynter, Patrick O'Neal. An interesting made-for-TV feature which starts out promisingly, but reverts to melodrama. Various types undergoing group therapy become suspects when one of their kind is murdered. Douglas is very good as a leading psychiatrist who takes things into his own hands to uncover the culprit. (Dir: Norman Lloyd, 99 mins.)

Company of Killers (MTV 1970)**½ Van Johnson, Ray Milland, John Saxon, Diana Lynn. Above-average thriller about a man being harassed by a newspaperman and later the police, after having muttered in a fit of delirium that he is a hired killer. Some suspense and lots of plot. Notable primarily as Diana Lynn's last film, as she died not long after this was completed. Made for TV, but released theatrically first. (Dir: Jerry Thorpe, 86 mins.)

Competition, The (1980)** Richard Dreyfuss, Amy Irving, Lee Remick, Sam Wanamaker. Vulgar, crass drama with material drawn from a "New Yorker" profile on the Leventritt competition. This story of a difficult romance between rival pianists lacks dramaturgic plausibility. Writer-director Joel Oliansky coarsens every aspect of the story. (129 mins.)

Compulsion (1959)*** Dean Stockwell, Bradford Dillman, Orson Welles. Unrelenting account of the murder trial of two twisted youths for a "thrill" murder, based on the Loeb-Leopold case of the 20's. Has a certain horrific fascination, a bravura performance by Welles as the defense lawyer; but remains a rather cold, detached film. (Dir: Richard Fleischer, 103 mins.)

Comrade X (1940)*** Clark Gable, Hedy

Lamarr, Cute, slapstick anti-Russian comedy in the "Ninotchka" vein but not half as good. Hedy's a Russian street car conductor and Clark's an American newspaperman. (Dir: King Vidor, 90 mins.)

Concert for Bangladesh (197)*** Bob Dylan, Ravi Shankar, George Harrison, Eric Clapton, Leon Russell. Straightforward film record of the historic benefit concert at Madison Square Garden in August 1971. Ravi Shankar opens with a series of pieces which are likely to seem overlong to many movie watchers. But there are glorious renditions of Dylan standards, including "Blowing in the Wind," and the concert builds to a powerful close with ex-Beatle Harrison playing his own tunes, "Something" and "Bangladesh." Few trick camera shots here, or unending "crowd" shots—just a faithful rendition of the driving, spirited music. (Dir: Saul Swimmer, 99 mins.)

Concert of Intrigue (Italy, 1954)*½ Brigitte Bardot, Lucia Bose, Pierre Cressoy. Alternate title: **Night of Love**. (Dir: Mario Bonnard, 93 mins.)

Concorde—Airport '79, The (1979)* Alain Delon, Susan Blakely, Robert Wagner, Sylvia Kristel, Cicely Tyson, Martha Raye, Charo, Bibi Andersson, George Kennedy, Eddie Albert. (Dir: David Lowell Rich, 123 mins.)

Concrete Cowboys, The (MTV 1979)* Jerry Reed, Tom Selleck, Morgan Fairchild. (Dir: Burt Kennedy, 104 mins.)

Concrete Jungle, The (Great Britain, 1960)** Stanley Baker, Sam Wanamaker, Margit Saad. Hoodlum pulls a racetrack robbery and goes to prison after burying the loot. His attempts to retrieve it fail due to some double-crossing. Crime drama has evidence of careful production but is disjointed, severely abrupt in its storytelling. Good performances. (Dir: Joseph Losey, 86 mins.)

Condemned (1929)** Ronald Colman, Ann Harding. Early talkie which is very dated today. The stars aren't able to make much of this routine Devil's Island yarn. (Dir: Wesley Ruggles, 100 mins.)

Condemned of Altona, The (1963)*** Sophia Loren, Maximillan Schell, Fredric March, Robert Wagner. Confused, but often interesting drama based on a play by Jean-Paul Sartre, which tells the story of a strange family living in postwar Germany. March builds ships, and his son (Schell) is a madman living in the attic rooms of their estate wearing his Nazi officer's uniform. (Dir: Vittorio De Sica, 114 mins.)

Condemned to Life (Great Britain, 1962)—See: **Walk in the Shadow**

Conduct Unbecoming (Great Britain, 1975)*** Michael York, Richard Attenborough, Trevor Howard, Stacy Keach, Susannah York. Really quite set-bound, but the acting is so good and the plot so intricate that you don't really notice the lack of action. The film is an actor's holiday and the cast is uniformly excellent. About a scandal in a British officers' mess in Northwest India circa 1878, and their notions about honor, women and civility. Unfortunately, once the mystery is revealed it seems rather silly, but up until that time you've enjoyed the suspense. Based on the hit play by Barry England. (Dir: Michael Anderson, 107 mins.)

Coney Island (1943)*** Betty Garble. Cesar Romero, George Montgomery. Betty is at her leggy best in this gay, though routine, musical set in Coney Island at the turn of the century. George and Cesar fight over Betty's affections and who can blame them. Remade by Grable as *Wabash Avenue*. (Dir: Walter Lang, 96 mins.)

Confess Dr. Corda (Germany, 1958)** Hardy Kruger, Elisabeth Mueller. Doctor has a blackout, finds he's suspect in a girl's murder. Kruger is too stodgy for this occasionally interesting whodunit. (Dir Joseph Van Baky, 101 mins.)

Confession (1937)** Kay Francis, Basil Rathbone, Jane Bryan, Ian Hunter, Donald Crisp. The best film in director Joe May's undistinguished American career, a soaper in which Francis is tried for the murder of concert pianist Rathbone. (86 mins.)

Confession, The (France, 1970)**** Yves Montand, Simone Signoret, Emotionally shattering drama about contemporary politics, brilliantly directed by Costa-Gavras. Stands as one of the most powerful and intellectually compelling anti-Communist films ever made. Based on a book by a survivor of the 1952 purges in Czechoslovakia. Montand, giving one of the most restrained and moving performances of his distinguished career, depicts a top party bureaucrat tortured and dehumanized by his beloved Communist party leaders into giving a false confession. You'll not find any of the puerile sloganeering or oversimplifications found in most American "anti-Communist films" such as John Wayne's drivel **The Green Berets**. With this searing essay following upon "Z," Costa-Gavras emerges as one of the most important new directors in world cinema. (Dir: Constantin Costa-Gavras, 138 mins.)

Confessions of a Nazi Spy (1939)*** Edward G. Robinson. Francis Lederer. Well done propaganda melodrama about a weak link in the Nazi spy network. Dated but for all its flag waving speeches, still a grim reminder. (Dir: Anatole Litvak, 102 mins.)

Confessions of a Police Captain (Italy, 1971)**½ Martin Balsam, Franco Nero, Marilu Tolo. Martin Balsam gives a fine performance in this film detailing a policeman's fight to bring in criminals who seem above the reach of the law. Franco Nero is equally fine as the D.A. who is first suspected of corruption, and then leads the investigation. (Dir: Damiano Damiani, 92 mins.)

Confessions of an Opium Eater (1962)* Vincent Price, Linda Ho, Richard Loo,

Philip Ahn. Alternate title: **Souls for Sale.** (Dir: Albert Zugsmith, 85 mins.)

Confessions of Felix Krull (Germany 1958)**½ Horst Buchholz, Lisa Pulver. The amours and experiences of a young opportunist. Better things could have been done with Mann's novel, but the results are satisfactory. (Dir: Kurt Hoffman, 107 mins.)

Confidential Agent (1945)*** Charles Boyer, Lauren Bacall. Exciting intrigue adventure with the Spanish Civil War as background in this slick adaptation of a Graham Greene story. (Dir: Herman Shumlin, 118 mins.)

Confidential Report—See: **Mr. Arkadin.**

Confidentially Connie (1953)** Van Johnson, Janet Leigh, Walter Slezak, Louis Calhern. Teacher in a small Maine college is thrown into the middle of a terrific uproar, all because his wife loves steaks, which come high. Skinny little story. (Dir: Edward Buzzell, 71 mins.)

Confirm or Deny (1941)**½ Don Ameche, Joan Bennett. War correspondent finds love in a London blackout and it mixes up his whole life. Some excitement but a bit dated. (Dir: Archio Mayo, 73 mins.)

Conflagration—See: **Enjo.**

Conflict (1945)*** Humphrey Bogart, Alexis Smith, Sydney Greenstreet. Humphrey kills his wife in this one and spends most of the film in a battle of wits with Greenstreet who tries to break the perfect alibi. Without the fine cast it would be a routine melodrama. (Dir: Curtis Bernhardt, 86 mins.)

Conflict of Wings (Great Britain, 1954)*** John Gregson, Muriel Pavlow, Kieron Moore. The RAF wants to use a small island as site for testing rockets, but the townspeople prefer to let the birds which have nested there for generations remain. Pleasant comedy-drama. (Dir: John Eldridge, 84 mins.)

Conformist, The (Italy-France-West Germany, 1970)**** Jean-Louis Trintignant, Stefania Sandrelli, Dominique Sanda. A fascinating study of decadence and Fascism during Mussolini's reign in Italy in 1938, based on the novel by Alberto Moravia, and written and directed by Bernardo Bertolucci. Brilliantly captures the mood, texture and look of the 1930's, and it's extraordinarily well acted by Trintignant, Sandrelli and Sanda. Trintignant plays a philosophy professor reflecting on his past life. Nominated for major awards for best screenplay and director, Sanda for best actress, and for the stunning cinematography by Vittorio Storaro. (Dir: Bernardo Bertolucci, 115 mins.)

Confrontation, The (Hungary, 1971)** Andrea Drahota, Kati Kovacs. Occasionally interesting story about the political and ideological fighting occurring amongst a group of college-age students in Hungary in 1947, after the assumption of power by the Communists. Westerners, lacking an intimate knowledge of Hungarian politics, will be puzzled by some of the political plot twists. Directed by Miklos Jancso, who made the superior **Red Psalm**. (86 mins.)

Congo Crossing (1936)** Virginia Mayo, George Nader, Peter Lorre. A predictable tale of fugitives from the law who congregate in a West African city where extradition laws are not practiced. Peter Lorre is the best thing in the film. (Dir: Joseph Pevney, 85 mins.)

Congratulations, It's a Boy (MTV 1971)**½ Bill Bixby, Diane Baker, Jack Albertson, Ann Sothern. Comedy-drama about an over-35 swinger who is visited by a 17-year-old lad claiming to be his son. Makes good use of its premise at the outset, but soon settles for predictably silly comedy scenes. Bixby's boyish good looks get in the way of the daddy image. (Dir: William A. Graham, 78 mins.)

Conjugal Bed, The (Italy, 1963)**** Ugo Tognazzi, Marina Vlady. The original title translation for this was *The Queen Bee*, which explains all. It's about a 40-year-old bachelor who marries a virtuous young girl who—literally—loves him to death. Taken seriously, it could be a fine horror story; taken in the manner intended, it's a funny, ribald comedy-drama. Dubbed in English. For adults only. (Dir: Marco Ferreri, 90 mins.)

Connecticut Yankee in King Arthur's Court, A (1949)*** Bing Crosby, Rhonda Fleming, Cedric Hardwicke. The Mark Twain tale of a blacksmith who is transported back to the time of King Arthur, uses modern methods to overcome obstacles. Lavish musical fits Crosby like a glove; good fun. (Dir: Tay Garnett, 107 mins.)

Connection, The (1967)*** William Redfield, Warren Finnerty, Roscoe Lee Browne, Barbara Winchester. The beat aesthetic is rather dated now, but the film has some clever touches. Director Shirley Clarke's movie is about a documentary maker who gets too involved with his subject, a circle of strung-out jazz musicians. The film we're watching is the film he's "making"—as he's talked into trying a taste of heroin himself, his cameramen ignore his orders to stop shooting. Too tricky for its own good and fairly clichéd at its heart, it's still an intriguing evocation of a bygone milieu. (103 mins.)

Connection, The (MTV 1973)**½ Charles Durning. If you like tough, hard-boiled New York characters who have hearts of gold you'll enjoy the lead in this film. Durning's casual acting style fits his character in a tale concerning a daring hotel robbery, and a deal between the crooks and the insurance companies. (Dir: Tom Gries, 73 mins.)

Conquered City (Italy, 1962)**½ David Niven, Ben Gazzara, Martin Balsam, Michael Craig. After the Nazis are chased from Athens, a British major is ordered to hold a hotel at all costs to prevent a cache of arms from falling into the hands of

133

Greek rebels. A passably interesting melodrama. (Dir: Joseph Anthony, 91 mins.)

Conqueror of Atlantis (Italy-Egypt 1963)* Kirk Morris, Luciana Gilli. (Dir: Alfonso Brescia, 93 mins.)

Conqueror of Maracaibo (Italy-Spain, 1961)*½ Hans Barsody, Brigit Corey. (Dir: Jean Martin, 92 mins.)

Conqueror of the Orient (Italy, 1961)*½ Rik Battaglia, Gianna Maria Canale. (Dir: Tanio Boccia, 86 mins.)

Conqueror Worm, The (Great Britain, 1968)* Ian Ogilvy, Hilary Dwyer, Vincent Price. Alternate title: **Witchfinder General.** (Dir: Michael Reeves, 98 mins.)

Conquerors, The (1932)*½ Richard Dix, Ann Harding, Edna May Oliver, Guy Kibbee. (80 mins.)

Conquest (1937)***½ Greta Garbo, Charles Boyer, Reginald Owen, Leif Erickson, Dame May Whitty. Amiably second-rate, though the performances of Boyer and Garbo are detailed and observant, and Maria Ouspenskaya etches one of her most effective bits. Dramatization of the relationship of Napoleon and Marie Walewska of Poland. For once, the MGM costume style isn't too stuffed. Probably the most creditable of the collaborations between Garbo and her favored director, Clarence Brown. (112 mins.)

Conquest of Cochise (1953)** John Hodiak, Robert Stack, Joy Page. Mediocre Cowboys and Indians yarn hampered greatly by miscasting of John Hodiak as Cochise. (Dir: William Castle, 80 mins.)

Conquest of Mycene (Italy-France, 1964)*½ Gordon Scott, Rosalba Neri. (Dir: Giorgio Ferroni, 102 mins.)

Conquest of Space (1955)**½ Eric Fleming, Walter Brooke, Phil Foster. Army space explorers set out to make a landing on Mars. Clever production effects by George Pal, along with a rather bloodless narrative. (Dir: Byron Haskin, 80 mins.)

Conquest of the Air (Great Britain, 1936)** Laurence Olivier, Valentine Dyall. Documentary story of aviation from man's early struggles to his final triumph. Scrappy—could have been better (Dirs: Zoltan Korda, Alexander Esway, Donald Taylor, Alexander Shaw, John Monk Saunders, 74 mins.)

Conquest of the Planet of the Apes (1972)*** Roddy McDowall, Don Murray, Ricardo Montalban. The fourth of the big box-office "ape" films. Roddy McDowall once again plays an ape with leadership qualities, and he's comfortable in the mask as well as the role by now. The time is 1990 and the apes are being used as slaves. One of the best ape entries. Once again, screenwriter Paul Dehn has concocted an absorbing sci-fi tale. (Dir: J. Lee Thompson, 86 mins.)

Conrack (1974)*** Jon Voight, Paul Winfield, Madge Sinclair, Hume Cronyn. A gentle, moving story about a young white schoolteacher who goes to help a group of culturally deprived black youngsters on an island off the coast of South Carolina. This is a particularly appealing film for children, and has many of the same qualities as "Sounder," which was also directed by Martin Ritt. Set in 1969, and based on the non-fiction book "The Water Is Wide," Jon Voight is convincing as he gradually reaches the children with his stories and activities. The last part of the film doesn't quite come together, but there are moments of tenderness and decency, rare commodities in the mid-70's filmmaking world. (Dir: Martin Ritt, 106 mins.)

Conspiracy of Hearts (Great Britain, 1960)*** Lilli Palmer, Sylvia Syms. Group of nuns hide Jewish children from the Nazis. Well done drama, keeps the suspense pretty much on high throughout. (Dir: Ralph Thomas, 116 mins.)

Conspiracy of Terror (MTV 1975)*½ Michael Constantine, Barbarea Rhoades. (Dir: John Llewellyn Moxey, 104 mins.)

Conspiracy of the Borgias (Italy, 1958)*½ Frank Latimore, Constance Smith. (Dir: Antonio Racciöppi, 93 mins.)

Conspirator (1949)**½ Elizabeth Taylor, Robert Taylor. Interesting but not altogether engrossing drama about a beautiful girl who discovers the alarming fact that her new husband, a British army officer, is working with the Communists. Robert Taylor is properly sober as the agent and Elizabeth Taylor is more decorative than dramatic. Remember, this was Miss Taylor's first grown-up role in films; she was seventeen at the time. (Dir: Victor Saville, 85 mins.)

Conspirators, The (1944)* Hedy Lamarr, Paul Henreid. (Dir: Jean Negulesco, 101 mins.)

Constant Husband, The (Great Britain, 1955)*** Rex Harrison, Margaret Leighton, Kay Kendall. Man about to be wed discovers he has already been married—seven times. Amusing, well-acted comedy. (Dir: Sidney Gilliat, 88 mins.)

Constant Nymph, The (1943)**½ Joan Fontaine, Charles Boyer, Alexis Smith, Charles Coburn. A poor young musician must choose between two wealthy sisters; one loves him, the other doesn't. Seems like an easy choice! The performances are fine in this romance. B&W. (Dir: Edmund Goulding, 112 mins.)

Constantine and the Cross (Italy, 1960)*½ Cornel Wilde, Christine Kaufman. Filmed in Yugoslavia. (Dir: Lionello de Felice, 120 mins.)

Contempt (France-Italy, 1963)**** Brigitte Bardot, Jack Palance, Fritz Lang, Michael Piccoli, Georgia Moll. A masterpiece, whose exultant formalism would doubtless be anathema to director Jean-Luc Godard today. About an Italian filming of "The Odyssey," with Piccoli as scriptwriter, Lang as director, and Palance as an American producer, each with his own interpretation of the Greek classic. Action centers on the breakup of dramatist Piccoli's marriage to Bardot—her "contempt" for him is only one of the causes. (103 mins.)

Contest Girl (Great Britain, 1965)** Janette Scott, Ian Hendry, Edmund Purdom. Nicely acted and directed exposé of the beauty-contest racket, as a pretty typist enters a contest, and finds herself caught up in a whirl of deceit and disappointments. Makes its point cleanly, holds interest throughout. (Dir: Val Guest, 82 mins.)

Contraband Spain (Great Britain, 1955)** Richard Greene, Anouk Aimee. Greene discards his "Robin Hood" garb but not his "Robin Hood" attitude in this adventure crammed story of smugglers and intrigue in Barcelona. Usual plot twists with predictable outcome. (Dir: Lawrence Huntington, 82 mins.)

Contract on Cherry Street (MTV 1977)*** Frank Sinatra, Verna Bloom, Harry Guardino, Martin Balsam. Sinatra's TV-movie debut turns out to be a good one. He plays an angry, frustrated New York police inspector who begins cleaning out the mob with his own men after a buddy is killed. It's the old vigilante story with Frankie knowing it's only a matter of time before the revenge tactics get out of control. (Dir: William A. Graham, 156 mins.)

Conversation, The (1974)**** Gene Hackman, John Cazale, Allen Garfield, Frederick Forrest, Cindy Williams. A shattering mystery-drama shot in San Francisco about surveillance and wiretapping in America, produced, written, and directed by Francis Ford Coppola. Bugging expert Hackman slowly discovers that a tape he made contains the secret of a murder. Hackman is marvelous—displaying little emotion most of the time as the guilt-ridden Catholic trying to keep his sanity. Extraordinary scene at the end: Hackman destroys his own apartment as the bugger becomes bugged. Fine support from Garfield as an alternately amiable and desperately envious colleague, plus a superb sound track (vital to the action) by Walter Murch. (113 mins.)

Conversation Piece (Italy-France, 1975)***½ Burt Lancaster, Silvana Mangano, Helmut Berger, Claudia Cardinale. One of director Luchino Visconti's most interesting works. Lancaster limns a retired professor, a man of intellect confronted with his absurdity when he befriends a group of rich young hedonistic leeches (headed by a sullen Berger). (122 mins.)

Convicted (1950)*** Glenn Ford, Broderick Crawford, Dorothy Malone. Prison life gets a candid look in this good screen play about a prisoner and his personal relationship with a warden's daughter. The cast is fine. (Dir: Henry Levin, 91 mins.)

Convicts Four (1962)**½ Ben Gazzara, Stuart Whitman, Sammy Davis Jr., Vincent Price. Based on fact—the story of a prisoner who is rehabilitated through his love for painting. Starts off well, soon becomes cloudy in motivation, uncertain in treatment. Good cast, including bits by Broderick Crawford. Rod Steiger, others. (Dir: Millard Kaufman, 105 mins.)

Convoy (1978)**½ Kris Kristofferson, Ali MacGraw, Ernest Borgnine, Burt Young. The CB fad never took off in movies, and director Sam Peckinpah was left high and dry with this southwestern trucking epic, a potboiler based (so to speak) on the hit single by C. W. McCall. Sam can stage a fight scene better than anyone, and the obligatory car crashes are included, but the core of the movie is empty. (111 mins.)

Coogan's Bluff (1968)***½ Clint Eastwood, Susan Clark, Don Stroud, Lee J. Cobb. Director Don Siegel's hilarious, action-packed study of an Arizona deputy sheriff (Eastwood) set loose in New York City on the trail of an escaped prisoner (Stroud). Eastwood brings to the part a sure knowledge of the deputy's obvious strengths and not-so-obvious failings. Able support from Cobb as the suffering detective whose rules Eastwood can't avoid. An exciting variation on the lone-wolf genre. (94 mins.)

Cool and the Crazy (1958)** Scott Marlowe, Gigi Perreau. Reform school graduate goes to high school—to hook students on dope. Some good acting here. Subject matter has by now become quite routine, alas! (Dir: William Witney, 78 mins.)

Cool Breeze (1972)* Thalmus Rasulala, Judy Pace, Raymond St. Jacques. Substandard heist drama, based, like so many others, on John Huston's "The Asphalt Jungle." (Dir: Barry Pollack, 101 mins.)

Cool Hand Luke (1967)**** Paul Newman, George Kennedy, Dennis Hopper. Taut, honest drama greatly aided by Stuart Rosenberg's direction and a marvelously controlled and artful performance by Paul Newman as a gutsy prisoner on a chain gang. Matching Newman's stunning acting is George Kennedy's Academy Award-winning performance as the brutal leader of the chain-gang crew, a notable musical score by Lalo Schifrin, and the spare screenplay written by Donn Pearce and Frank R. Pierson. Newman's loner-hero with an insatiable appetite for freedom and the ability to do "his own thing" with or without the approval of society is one of the most memorable screen portraits in years. "Cool Hand Luke" deals you a winner. (Dir: Stuart Rosenberg, 126 mins.)

Cool Million (MTV 1972)**½ James Farentino, John Vernon, Barbara Bouchet. Expensively mounted pilot which introduce's Jefferson Keyes (Farentino), a slick operator whose investigating talents command a flat fee of $1 million. (That limits his clientele somewhat.) Keyes chases all over the playgrounds of the idle rich in Greece, Italy, and Switzerland, trying to locate the long-lost daughter of a prominent millionaire. Farentino's personal charm make it mildly entertaining escapist fare. (Dir: Gene Levitt, 104 mins.)

Cool Million: Assault on Gravaloni

(1972)**½ A puzzler that keeps crackling along at a swift pace. Jefferson Keyes (James Farentino) invades the almost impregnable world of a Greek multimillionaire in order to replace a valuable painting with a copy. This dexterous sleight-of-hand takes every bit of finesse Keyes possesses. The cast includes Ilka Chase as a terribly chatty member of the jet set. Made-for-TV. (Dir: John Badham, 72 mins.)

Cool Ones, The (1967)* Roddy McDowall, Debbie Watson, Phil Harris. (Dir: Gene Nelson, 95 mins.)

Cool World, The (1964)***½ Gloria Foster, Hampton Clanton, Carl Lee, George Burke. A powerful film with outstanding direction by Shirley Clarke. Almost all of the remarkable cast were from the junior high schools of Harlem. A semidocumentary look at the horrors of ghetto slum life filled with drugs, violence, human misery, and a sense of despair due to the racial prejudices of American society. No patronizing of the blacks in this cinematic cry for justice. This pioneering cinema verité entry was produced by Frederick Wiseman, who has since emerged as one of America's most gifted documentary filmmakers. (105 mins.)

Cooley High (1975)* Glynn Turman, Lawrence-Hilton Jacobs, Garrett Morris. A series of comic-strip incidents paraded under the doubtful label of "authenticity." Under Michael Schultz's direction, the film alternately lurches and collapses. A masterful performance by Turman means the time wasted watching this movie is still time well spent. (107 mins.)

Coonskin (1975)**½ Voices of Barry White, Charles Gordone, Scatman Crothers. Cartoon feature by Ralph Bakshi ("Heavy Traffic," "Fritz the Cat") loses itself in a muddled narrative and Bakshi's discount nihilism. Technically it was his best work to date, with several passages of first-rate animation and a well-orchestrated voice track. (83 mins.)

Cop Hater (1958)**½ Robert Loggia, Gerald O'Loughlin. Mild meller about a cop killer. Based on an Ed McBain novel. Routine acting and direction, but the finale is fine. New York locations are used to good advantage. (Dir: William Berke, 75 mins.)

Copper Canyon (1950)** Ray Milland, Hedy Lamarr, Macdonald Carey. Gunman helps Civil War vets build new homes in the untamed west. Mild western never achieves the lively pace it needs. (Dir: John Farrow, 83 mins.)

Cops and Robbers (1973)*** Cliff Gorman, Joe Bologna, Shepperd Strudwick. A genial blend of suburban social observation and caper comedy that, sadly, never finds its focus. Gorman and Bologna are fine as two New York cops who plot a sensational securities rip-off to get out from under the stifling security blanket of mortgage payments, 7 a.m. traffic jams, and nauseating backyard barbecues. (Dir: Aram Avakian, 89 mins.)

Cops and Robin, The (MTV 1978)** Ernest Borgnine, John Amos, Michael Shannon. Remember a short-lived series on ABC called "Future Cop"? Well, here's another 2-hour pilot with the same characters—Borgnine and Amos as two policemen who work with a robot cop (Shannon). The "future cop" is assigned to protect a little girl whose mother is set to testify against a mobster. Routine all the way except for the "robot" gimmick. (Dir: Allen Reisner, 104 mins.)

Corey: For the People (MTV 1977)**½ John Rubinstein, Eugene Roche, Frank Campanella. Pretty fair lawyer pilot with Rubinstein as a feisty assistant D.A. investigating the shooting of a doctor by his wife, who claims self-defense. Pressured from all sides, he goes ahead with the case. Fast-paced direction by Buzz Kulik. (78 mins.)

Corky (1971)** Charlotte Rampling, Robert Blake, Patrick O'Neal. Robert Blake almost manages to save this film, but he gets bogged down before too long. A routine version of the country boy who wants to make it big as a stock-car racer. Texas and Georgia locations help a little. Alternate title: **Lookin' Good**. (Dir: Leonard Horn, 88 mins.)

Corn Is Green, The (1945)***½ Bette Davis, John Dall (film debut), Joan Lorring, Rhys Williams, Nigel Bruce. Davis was, if anything, a bit too young for the part of the idealistic schoolmistress who finds one lad in a Welsh mining village with the spark of creativity to seek finer things in life. She gives her customary careful performance, although Dall steals the picture as the student distrustful of the accouterments of learning. Lorring has a standout part as the girl, impregnated by the boy, who could mire him down in a dead-end marriage. Emlyn Williams's semiautobiographical play was adapted by Casey Robinson and Frank Cavett. (Dir: Irving Rapper, 114 mins.)

Corn Is Green, The (MTV 1979)***½ Katharine Hepburn, Ian Saynor, Bill Fraser, Anna Massey. Star Hepburn and director George Cukor combine forces again in this remake. Hepburn may be a bit too old, but her portrayal captures the nuances of a woman who will not be deterred from her goals. Saynor shines in the difficult role of her gifted special student. The supporting cast is perfect. The production, shot on-location in north Wales, adds greatly to the atmosphere of the touching story. (104 mins.)

Cornered (1945)**** Dick Powell, Micheleine Cheirel, Walter Slezak. Airman goes seeking those responsible for the death of his French wife during the war. Excellent drama, fast, tough, fine performances. (Dir: Edward Dmytryk, 102 mins.)

Corpse Came C.O.D. (1947)** George

Brent, Joan Blondell. Grade B mystery about a couple of Hollywood reporters out to solve some moviedom murders. (Dir: Henry Levin, 87 mins.)

Correction Please—Or How We Got into Pictures (1980)***½ Noel Burch is a highly idiosyncratic, often invaluable, occasionally impenetrable film theorist and teacher, who is especially illuminating in his analysis of alternative film grammars. Now he has put his preachings into practice with his film *Correction Please—Or How We Got into Pictures.* The film delves into the mysteries of early cinema to demonstrate "how the mechanics of certain primitive films (made prior to 1906) shed light on the language of cinema and the audience attitudes associated with it." To present his thesis, Burch makes use of three elements: a story retold five times in the styles of five different peiods of film history; excerpts from ten short works from the earliest period of filmmaking that illustrate the development of the so-called "commercial" mode of film language; and quick vignettes of a bearded, old, voyeuristic "peeper" whose visions at the keyhole recapitulate the lessons of the preceding scenes—and sometimes, those to come. A fascinating exercise by a usefully eccentric thinker. (Dir; Noel Burch.)

Corridor of Mirrors (Great Britain, 1948)*** Edana Romney, Eric Portman. A girl meets a mysterious man who lives in the past, and marries him, but their happiness is shattered by murder. Well done melodrama holds the attention. (Dir: Terence Young, 96 mins.)

Corridors of Blood (Great Britain, 1962)** Boris Karloff, Betta St. John. Surgeon in 19th Century London seeks the key to an anesthetic, but becomes a narcotics addict in doing so. Passable horror thriller, with Karloff giving a good performance. (Dir: Robert Day, 87 mins.)

Corrupt Ones, The (1966)** Robert Stack, Nancy Kwan, Elke Sommer. Everybody hustles after a Chinese medallion holding the key to the treasure. Exotic but familiar adventure tale, aided by interesting location shots of Macao and Hong Kong. (Dir: James Hill, 92 mins.)

Corruption (Great Britain, 1968)** Peter Cushing, Sue Lloyd, Kate O'Mara. Intriguing but one-dimensional story of plastic surgeon who atones for his guilt in causing his fiancée to be permanently scarred in an auto accident. The catch—he has to steal glands from strangers! Another psyco doctor on the loose! (Dir: Robert Hartford-Davis, 91 mins.)

Corsican Brothers, The (1941)**½ Douglas Fairbanks Jr., Akim Tamiroff. Ruth Warrick. The classic tale of Siamese twin brothers separated at birth but still joined by a mental bond. Lively costume melodrama. (Dir: Gregory Ratoff, 112 mins.)

Corsican Brothers, The (Italy-France, 1961)** Geoffrey Horne, Jean Servais. The Dumas novel of twins who are reunited to avenge the murder of their family. Not too successfully done, just passable costume melodrama dubbed in English. (Dir: Anton Guilio Majano, 85 mins.)

Corvette K-225 (1943)***½ Randolph Scott, Ella Raines. Canadian Naval officer's courage and fighting spirit prevents destruction of a convoy. Excellent war drama with many scenes actually photographed in combat. (Dir: Richard Rosson, 99 mins.)

Corvette Summer (1978)**½ Mark Hamill, Annie Potts, Kim Milford. Hamill is a convincing high-school car freak (although he does look strangley wizened in close-up) whose class project, a customized Corvette, is stolen. He sets out for Las Vegas to find it, but instead discovers an adult world of hypocrisy and greed—and, as a consolation, women. Matthew Robbins directs with a fine sense of psychological displacement. (104 mins.)

Cosh Boy (Great Britain, 1953)** James Kenney, Joan Collins, Hermione Gingold. Sensationalized London street life, with the accent on violence—delivered in broad Cockney. About a "cosh" youth who goes around molesting ladies of all ages. Kenney is effectively cocky and uninhibited as the boy, and Gingold is outstanding in a small supporting role as a street-walker. (Dir: Lewis Gilbert, 75 mins.)

Cosmic Man, The (1958)* Bruce Bennett, John Carradine. (Dir: Herbert Greene, 72 mins.)

Cosmic Monsters (Great Britain, 1958)** Forrest Tucker, Gaby Andre. Muddled science fiction thriller with the mad scientist and the giant insects and the world in constant danger of complete annihilation. (Dir: Gilbert Gunn, 75 mins.)

Cotton Candy (MTV 1978)**½ Charles Martin Smith, Clint Howard. This teenage tale about high-school kids who form a rock band is a pleasant surprise—simple and honest. Directed by Ron Howard of "Happy Days" and written by his younger brother Clint.(104 mins.)

Cotton Comes to Harlem (1970)**** Godfrey Cambridge, Raymond St. Jacques, Calvin Lockhart, Redd Foxx. Raucous, racy, funny treatment of Chester Himes' fictional black detectives, Grave Digger Jones and Coffin Ed Johnson, and their exploits in Harlem. Cambridge and St. Jacques give perfectly matched performances as Grave Digger and Coffin Ed hot on the trail of a bogus Reverend and his scheme to milk his people out of money. The collected bundle of cash disappears and it's a free-for-all search from then on. (Director: Ossie Davis, 92 mins.)

Couch, The (1962)** Grant Williams, Shirley Knight. Psychotic is released from prison, undergoes treatment, but commits crimes while doing so. Plodding suspense melodrama has been done before in more capable fashion. Strictly routine. (Dir: Owen Crump, 100 mins.)

Counsellor at Law (1933)***½ John

Barrymore, Bebe Daniels, Melvyn Douglas. Barrymore is oddly cast as a Jewish lawyer who has educated himself up from poverty (Paul Muni played the part on stage), but this is one of the best proofs extant (meaning on film) of his acting prowess. The character is completely realized and thoroughly externalized. Elmer Rice's play has dated somewhat, but William Wyler's aggressive direction helps keep the story moving despite the limited setting. (82 mins.)

Count Five and Die (Great Britain, 1958)**½ Jeffrey Hunter, Annemarie Dueringer, Nigel Patrick. American undercover agent works with the British to convince the Germans the Allied landing will be in Holland, thus misleading them. Pretty fair spy thriller is well worked out, has some suspenseful moments. (Dir: Victor Vicas, 100 mins.)

Count of Monte Cristo, The (1934)***½ Robert Donat, Elissa Landi. The classic adventure tale of Dumas about the unjustly imprisoned patriot who makes a spectacular escape during the Napoleonic era. A notable film achievement. (Dir: Rowland V. Lee, 113 mins.)

Count of Monte Cristo, The (France, 1955)*½ Pierre-Richard Wilm, Michele Alfa. (Dir: Robert Vernay, 97 mins.)

Count of Monte Cristo, The (Great Britain, 1977)** Richard Chamberlain, Tony Curtis, Trevor Howard. The old Dumas war-horse trotted out again. Competent, but dated. (Dir: David Greene, 104 mins.)

Count the Hours (1953)** Teresa Wright, Macdonald Carey. Ranch worker and wife are accused of murdering ranchowners; he confesses to spare his pregnant wife. Muddled melodrama. (Dir: Don Siegel, 74 mins.)

Count Three and Pray (1955)***½ Van Heflin, Joanne Woodward, Raymond Burr. First rate western drama about a Civil War veteran and his influence on a small town when he becomes a self-ordained minister. Joanne Woodward is excellent in her first major role. (Dir: George Sherman, 120 mins.)

Count Yorga, Vampire (1970)* Robert Quarry, Roger Perry. (Directed by Robert Kelljan. (92 mins.)

Count Your Blessings (1959)**½ Deborah Kerr, Rossano Brazzi, Maurice Chevalier. A slight comedy which totally relies on the trio of stars' charm and attractiveness to carry it off. The plot has a British Miss Kerr sharing a civilized long-distance marriage arrangement with Brazzi until she decides to shorten the gap. M. Chevalier plays his usual role of romantic mentor. (Dir: Jean Negulesco, 120 mins.)

Countdown (1968)**½ James Caan, Robert Duvall. Drama about space shots to the moon may be dated by now, but it has some good moments. If you can be patient through the soap opera of the spacemen's private lives, the finale delivers the goods. Caan and Duvall lead years before their

costarring assignments in "The Godfather." (Dir: Robert Altman, 101 mins.)

Counter-Attack (1945)**½ Paul Muni, Marguerite Chapman, Larry Parks. Russian paratroopers land behind enemy lines and attack German headquarters. Passing fair war melodrama, a bit too slow. (Dir: Zoltan Korda, 90 mins.)

Counterfeit Killer, The (1968)* Jack Lord, Shirley Knight, Mercedes McCambridge, Jack Weston. (Dir: Joseph Leytes, 95 mins.)

Counterfeit Traitor, The (1962)***½ William Holden, Lilli Palmer, Hugh Griffith. Suspenseful tale based on fact of a businessman approached by the British to pose as sympathetic to the Nazis, in reality spying for England. Fascinating details of espionage, some tense situations, excellent performances by Holden and Palmer. (Dir: George Seaton, 140 mins.)

Counterplot (1959)*½ Forrest Tucker, Allison Hayes. (Dir: Kurt Neumann, 76 mins.)

Counterpoint (1968)* Charlton Heston, Kathryn Hays, Maximilian Schell. (Dir: Ralph Nelson, 107 mins.)

Countess from Hong Kong, A (1967)**½ Marlon Brando, Sophia Loren, Patrick Cargill, Margaret Rutherford, Sydney Chaplin. Director Charles Chaplin's last film. The comedy is urbane without attaining sophistication; the limitations of the leads in executing Chaplinesque business torpedo the enterprise. (108 mins.)

Country Girl, The (1954)**** Bing Crosby, Grace Kelly, William Holden. Superlative performances in a dynamic drama about a performer wallowing in self-pity who has a chance to make a comeback. Kelly won the Oscar for her portrayal, but Crosby is no less effective, gives the acting effort of his long career. Fine film. (Dir: George Seaton, 104 mins.)

Country Music Holiday (1958)*½ Ferlin Husky, Zsa Zsa Gabor, Rocky Graziano. (Dir: Alvin Ganzer, 81 mins.)

County Fair (1950)**½ Jane Nigh, Rory Calhoun. Generally pleasant, if uneventful tale of romance and racing. (Dir: William Beaudine, 76 mins.)

Coup de Grace (West Germany-France, 1976)***½ Margarethe von Trotta, Matthias Habich. A complex, often involving parable of the collapse on one order while a new one unfolds, set in Latvia just after WW I. A German army unit is billeted on a formerly opulent but now rundown estate belonging to one of the officers. Based on the novel by Marguerite Yourcenar. B&W. (Dir: Volker Schlondorff, 96 mins.)

Coup de Tête—See: Hothead

Couple Takes a Wife, The (MTV 1972)*** Bill Bixby, Paula Prentiss. Entertaining, brittle. Concerns a modern married couple who reach an impasse after nine years of wedded bliss, and try to assert their individuality with the aid of a hired "wife".

The "wife" turns out to be a young super-combination governess-cook-housekeeper-confidante. Writer Susan Silver has given her characters good dialogue, wisely avoiding the obvious pitfalls. Cast is first-rate, especially Miss Prentiss as the bright wife-mother who wants to get back into the swing of life, and sexy Valerie Perrine as the offbeat young Ms. who takes on the unique job. (Dir: Jerry Paris, 73 mins.)

Courage to Kavik, the Wolf Dog, The (MTV 1980)** Ronny Cox, Andrew Ian McMillan, John Ireland. The old story of a dog making an agonizing trek back to the family he loves. A champion sled dog, taken to Seattle by a wealthy fool, makes a 2000-mile trip back to Alaska and his young master. The Alaskan scenery and the sled dog outshine the people in this Disney-type offering. (Dir: Peter Carter, 104 mins.)

Courage of Lassie (1945)**½ Elizabeth Taylor, Frank Morgan. Good Lassie adventure with the famous collie becoming a war hero and then, after discharge, he's as confused as any veteran. (Dir: Fred Wilcox, 92 mins.)

Courage of the People (Bolivia-Italy, 1971)***½ The infamous "Night of San Juan"—a Bolivian army reprisal against striking miners and their families. Directed by Jorge Sanjines, a leading Latin American filmmaker. In Quechua and Spanish, with subtitles. An unusually powerful docudrama. (94 mins.)

Courageous Mr. Penn (Great Britain, 1941)*** Clifford Evans, Deborah Kerr. The story of William Penn the Quaker, and how he pioneered the American wilderness while seeking religious freedom. Thoughtful, well acted drama. Also called *Penn of Pennsylvania*. (Dir: Lance Comfort, 79 mins.)

Court Jester, The (1956)*** Danny Kaye, Glynis Johns, Basil Rathbone. Circus clown gets involved with a band of outlaws trying to overthrow the king. Kaye's comedy is an asset in this pleasing spoof of costume epics. (Dir: Norman Panama, 101 mins.)

Court Martial (Great Britain, 1955)***½ David Niven, Margaret Leighton. Army major is court-martialed for taking company funds and being AWOL, and he fights against unjust treatment. Finely acted, tightly directed drama maintains interest on high. (Dir: Anthony Asquith, 105 mins.)

Court Martial of Billy Mitchell (1955)***½ Gary Cooper, Rod Steiger. Excellent, true story of one of the most controversial American military leaders of this country. Film concentrates on Billy Mitchell's defiance of military brass when they called him a crackpot for ideas that might have cut World War II in half. A fascinating film. (Dir: Otto Preminger, 100 mins.)

Court Martial of Major Keller, The (Great Britain, 1961)**½ Laurence Payne, Susan

Stephen. Army has to prove that an officer was incompetent and a coward during battle. Passable service drama; well acted. (Dir: Ernest Morris, 69 mins.)

Courtney Affair, The (Great Britain, 1947)**½ Anna Neagle, Michael Wilding. The son of a rich family falls for the scullery maid. Sugary romantic drama. (Dir: Herbert Wilcox, 120 mins.)

Courtship of Eddie's Father, The (1963)*** Glenn Ford, Shirley Jones, Stella Stevens, Ronny Howard. Frequently charming comedy drama about a widower who tries to bring up his motherless son—and vice-versa. Nice balance between humor and poignancy, well acted by a superior cast, with Stella Stevens standing out—literally—with an excellent comedy job. Good fun. (Dir: Vincente Minnelli, 117 mins.)

Cousin Angelica (Spain, 1974)**** Jose Luis Lopez Vazquez, Lina Canalejas, Maria Clara Fernandez, Fernando Delgado. A remarkable Carlos Saura film about a middle-aged man (Jose Luis Lopez Vazquez) with infantile memories of the Civil War era in Spain. The *coup de théâtre* is that in his memories, though he might crawl about the floor, he is the man he is now, balding and plaintive. For once, Saura's allegorical bent seems well within subjective control, and Vazquez's magnificent performance helps us to penetrate the usually obscure poignancies of the Saura style. With Lina Canalejas as his long lost child-love. (Dir: Carlos Saura, 100 mins.)

Cousin, Cousine (France, 1975)**½ Marie-Christine Barrault (niece of Jean-Louis), Victor Lanoux, Marie-France Pisier. A pair of semimoronic lovers leave their unfaithful spouses for a bout of motorcycle riding, romping through fields, and shocking the bourgeoisie. The language barrier lends a healthy distance. If you need this much reassurance about adultery, you should probably forgo it. (Dir: Jean-Charles Tacchella, 95 mins.)

Cousins, The (France, 1959)***½ Jean-Claude Brialy, Gerard Blain. Director Claude Chabrol has fashioned a marvelous study of the contrasting personalities of two young male cousins, both law students at the Sorbonne. Blain is a country lad with an unsophisticated manner who comes to stay with his egomaniacal and decadent cousin, brilliantly played by Jean-Claude Brialy. It's not so much what happens in the way of plot, but more in the almost hypnotic way the story unfolds. Dubbing works very well here. (Dir: Claude Chabrol, 112 mins.)

Covenant with Death, A (1967)** George Maharis, Laura Devon, Katy Jurado. Muddled, often silly dramatization of the best-selling book by Stephen Becker about a condemned murderer who is instrumental in another man's death while awaiting execution. George Maharis is better than the script as a young Mexican-American judge faced with a sticky decision. Promising material never delivers real impact. (Dir: Lamont Johnson, 97 mins.)

Cover Girl (1944)***½ Gene Kelly, Rita Hayworth. Chorus girl achieves fame and glory when she becomes a top cover girl. Lavish musical with some swell Jerome Kern tunes, spectacular dances by Kelly. It's more effective in color. (Dir: Charles Vidor, 107 mins.)

Cover Girls (MTV 1977)* Jayne Kennedy, Cornelia Sharpe. (Dir: Jerry London, 79 mins.)

Cover Up (1949)*** William Bendix, Dennis O'Keefe. An insurance investigator comes to a small town to check on a doctor's death, and finds that nobody wants to talk about it; hence, foul play is suspected. Nicely-turned mystery. O'Keefe helped write this one, and a good job it is. (Dir: Alfred E. Green, 82 mins.)

Cow and I, The (France, 1960)*** Fernandel. One of Fernandel's better films. The story concerns a French prisoner of war who escapes from a German labor farm and encounters a series of adventures en route to France. There are many charming sequences in this off-beat comedy. (Dir: Henri Verneuil, 98 mins.)

Cowboy, The (1954)***½ Documentary feature of the way of life of our American cowboys, their work, recreations, day-to-day happenings. Made by Elmo Williams, who worked on "High Noon." Narrated by William Conrad, Tex Ritter, John Dehner, Larry Dobkin. Authentic, sincere, a true picture of the west today. Recommended. (Dir: Elmo Williams, 69 mins.)

Cowboy (1958)*** Glenn Ford, Jack Lemmon. Refreshing, generally entertaining western story, based on the experiences of a young Frank Harris—a dude goes west and learns the ways of the range. (Dir: Delmar Daves, 92 mins.)

Cowboy and the Lady, The (1938)** Gary Cooper, Merle Oberon, Walter Brennan. Just exactly what the title suggests—a routine romance between a cowpoke and a rich city girl. Some of the comedy falls flat by today's standards. (Dir: H. C. Potter, 90 mins.)

Cowboys, The (1972)* John Wayne, Slim Pickens, Roscoe Lee Browne, Colleen Dewhurst. (Dir: Mark Rydell, 120 mins.)

Crack in the Mirror (1960)** Orson Welles, Juliette Greco, Bradford Dillman. Unpalatable involvements about a team of lawyers defending two plaintiffs in a murder trial, whose lives parallel those of their clients. Not helped by the three main actors playing dual roles, a trick that doesn't come off. (Dir: Richard Fleischer, 97 mins.)

Crack in the World (1965)**½ Dana Andrews, Janette Scott. A science-fiction tale that seems very credible and registers a good amount of suspense. A group of scientists are attempting to reach the earth's core and in their efforts, they ex-

plode some nuclear bombs causing "a crack in the world." Filmed in Spain. (Dir: Andrew Marton, 96 mins.)

Crack-Up (1946)*** Pat O'Brien, Claire Trevor, Herbert Marshall. Art museum curator is framed into thinking he was in a train wreck by art forgers. Involved but successful mystery. (Dir: Irving Reis, 93 mins.)

Cracked Nuts (1941)*½ Stuart Erwin, Una Merkel, Mischa Auer. (Dir: Edward Cline, 62 mins.)

Cracker Factory, The (MTV 1979)*** Natalie Wood, Perry King, Peter Haskell. Natalie Wood does a tour-de-force as an attractive woman who takes refuge in drink and abrasive action to cover her neurotic needs. The cracker factory of the title is the nickname she gives the psychiatric section of a hospital where she is taken after a screaming, drunken attack on her husband. Confusing, but absorbing. (Dir: Burt Brinkerhoff, 104 mins.)

Cracksman, The (Great Britain, 1963)** Charlie Drake, George Sanders. Innocent locksmith gets mixed up with two rival gangs of crooks. Drake is a local slapstick comedian and may be too far out for most tastes; the comedy is wild, but not particularly inspired. (Dir: Peter Graham Scott, 112 mins.)

Craig's Wife (1936)*** Rosalind Russell, John Boles, Billie Burke. George Kelly's Pulitzer prize-winning play about a ruthlessly ambitious middle-class housewife with a compulsion for home over husband achieves some intriguing ambiguities under Dorothy Arzner's direction. Harriet Craig is generally played as a monster, but Arzner and Russell creditably suggest the forces behind her destructive passions without blunting their edge. Not a compelling piece of cinema, but the drama comes off convincingly. (80 mins.)

Crash (MTV 1978)**½ William Shatner, Eddie Albert, Adrienne Barbeau. Another plane-crash story based on a real incident (over 70 people survived). It often descends to melodramatic soap opera because so many stories are told as vignettes. The crash footage is a plus for those who enjoy "jeopardy" yarns. Written by Steve Brown and Donald S. Sanford, based on a book by Rob and Sarah Elder. (Dir: Barry Shear, 104 mins.)

Crash Dive (1943)**½ Tyronne Power, Dana Andrews, Anne Baxter. Routine war story of a submarine in the North Atlantic and the officers who love the same girl. Why aren't there ever enough girls to go around? (Dir: Archie Mayo, 105 mins.)

Crash Landing (1958)*½ Gary Merrill, Nancy Davis, Roger Smith. (Dir: Fred F. Sears, 77 mins.)

Crash of Silence—See: **Mandy**

Crashout (1955)*** William Bendix, Arthur Kennedy. Six convicts make a break for freedom. Familiar but fast, gutsy melodrama, better than usual for this sort of thing. (Dir: Lewis R. Foster, 91 mins.)

Crawling Eye (British, 1958)** Forrest

Tucker, Janet Munro. Once more we are confronted with oversized deadly menaces, this time a "crawling eye" and once more a group of scientists save the world. (Dir: Quentin Lawrence, 85 mins.)

Crawling Hand, The (1963)* Peter Breck, Kent Taylor, Arline Judge. (Dir: Herbert L. Strock, 89 mins.)

Crawling Monster, The—See: Creeping Terror, The

Crawlspace (MTV 1972)**½ Arthur Kennedy, Teresa Wright, Tom Happer. Interesting, if not altogether successful drama, about a middle-aged couple who take in a strange young man prone to violence. Fine performances by the trio of actors, including newcomer Tom Happer as the weird youth, keep the story from falling apart earlier than it does. (Dir: John Newland, 72 mins.)

Craze (Great Britain, 1974)* Jack Palance, Diana Dors, Julie Edge, Hugh Griffith, Trevor Howard, Edith Evans. (Dir: Freddie Francis, 95 mins.)

Crazy Desire (Italy, 1964)*** Ugo Tognazzi, Catherine Spaak. Charming comedy-drama about a middle-aged man trying momentarily to recapture his youth, as an engineer encounters some teenagers on the road and tries to keep abreast of their fast pace. Many amusing as well as poignant moments, although a trifle overlong. Dubbed in English. (Dir: Luciano Salce, 108 mins.)

Crazy for Love (France, 1955)*½ Bourvil, Brigitte Bardot. (Dir: Jean Boyer, 84 mins.)

Crazy House (1943)**½ Olsen and Johnson, Cass Daley. The two comics arrive in Hollywood to make a movie, form their own company and all hell breaks loose. Amusing nonsensical comedy. (Dir: Edward F. Cline, 80 mins.)

Crazy Joe (1974)** Peter Boyle, Paula Prentiss, Rip Torn. The ads for this gangster saga about real-life hood Joey Gallo read "Who was Crazy Joe?" Well, after seeing this film, you might be prompted to answer, "He's one-third imitation Edward G. Robinson, one-third bogus Humphrey Bogart, and one-third warmed-over James Cagney." Nothing about this film is original . . . it's clichéd all the way and Boyle, a good actor, fails to give his character any conviction. (Dir: Carlo Lizzani, 100 mins.)

Crazy Mama (1975)** Cloris Leachman, Stuart Whitman, Ann Sothern, Tisha Sterling. Perhaps the first substantial effort of director Jonathan Demme ("Fighting Mad," "Last Embrace"); also, his last lousy film. Leachman is the murderous mama trying to make ends meet during the depression. It's a gangster movie, kind of sexy in a campy, arch way—a flighty exploitationer. (82 mins.)

Crazy Quilt (1966)***½ Tom Rosqui, Ina Mela. Surprisingly sophisticated and sensitive first film written, produced, directed, photographed and edited by multi-talented John Korty, on an ambitious subject—the 50-year span of a marriage. Fresh, witty treatment, beautifully acted interpretations make this seemingly pat tale—a pragmatic man marrying a romantic dreamer—a meaningful contemporary fable. San Fransico locales are nicely used. Filmed on a tiny budget of $70,000. Director Korty has gone on to make several other fine films. (75 mins.)

Crazy World of Julius Vrooder, The (1974)** Timothy Bottoms, Barbara Seagull (Hershey), Lawrence Pressman, George Marshall. Attempt to make a comedy about hospitalized Vietnam war veterans misfires. Timothy Bottoms gives an attractive performance but it's not enough. Film trivia buffs, please note the appearance of veteran director George Marshall playing Corky, a wizened veteran of WW I. (Dir: Arthur Hiller, 100 mins.)

Crazylegs (1953)*** Elroy Hirsch, Lloyd Nolan. Biography of the famous football star has two advantages—"Crazylegs" plays himself, and he's a pretty good actor. Sports fans should love it, while others will find it a pleasant film. (Dir: Francis D. Lyon, 88 mins.)

Creation of the Humanoids (1962)* Don Megowan, Erica Elliot. (Dir: Wesley E. Barry, 75 mins.)

Creature from the Black Lagoon (1954)**½ Richard Carlson, Julia Adams. Originally produced in 3-D, this better-than-average science fiction tale has more than its share of visual gimmicks. The plot, complete with bewildered scientists and love interest, appears no innovation, but fans of this genre will enjoy it. (Dir: Jack Arnold, 79 mins.)

Creature from the Haunted Sea (1961)**½ Anthony Carbone, Betsy Jones-Moreland. Low-budget item turns out to be a spoof of horror thrillers mixing gangsters, fleeing revolutionaries and a sea beast. Some good hip dialogue, good-natured kidding of the genre. (Dir: Roger Corman, Monte Hellman, 60 mins.)

Creature of the Walking Dead (Mexico, 1960)*½ Rock Madison, Ann Wells. (Dirs: Fernando Cortez, Jerry Warren.)

Creature Walks Among Us, The (1956)*½ Jeff Morrow, Rex Reason. (Dir: John Sherwood, 80 mins.)

Creature with the Atom Brain (1955)** Richard Denning, Angela Stevens. Overdone science fiction story about a deported mobster who "bumps off" the people who testified against him with the aid of a mad scientist. The method by which the victims meet their end has something to do with "atomic brains." (Dir: Edward L. Cahn, 70 mins.)

Creatures of Darkness (1969)* Bill Williams, Aron Kincaid. (Dir: Bill Williams, 83 mins.)

Creeping Flesh, The (Great Britain, 1970)**½ Peter Cushing, Christopher Lee, Lorna Heilbron. Here's still another "scientist tampering with unknown forces," starring the deadly duo of British horror flicks, Lee and Cushing. It's slickly produced and might even provoke a chill or two if you care for this sort of thing. The plot, if it can be defined at all, concerns a scientist absolutely obsessed with harnessing the "essence of evil"—an ambitious and lofty dedication. (Dir: Freddie Francis, 89 mins.)

Creeping Unkown, The (Great Britain, 1956)**½ Brian Donlevy, Jack Warner, Margia Dean, Richard Wordsworth, Thora Hird, Gordon Jackson. Nigel Kneale's popular British television science-fiction serial was the subject of three feature films, of which this was the first. Brian Donlevy plays Dr. Quartermass, who must deal with the scientific and ethical problems of treating an astronaut who has become infected with a rare disease in space, which may be turning him into a malignant alien. Released in Great Britain as *The Quartermass Experiment*. Decent for sci-fi fans. (Dir: Val Guest, 78 mins.)

Cremator, The (Czechoslovakia, 1968)***½ Rudolph Hrusinsky, Vlasta Chramostova. Ghoulish, gripping, grotesque horror tale. Protagonist is the director of a crematorium who comes to believe in his work (1937) and turns Nazi sympathizer. When Hitler's armies invade and take over Czechoslovakia he is promoted. Subtle, scary performance from Hrusinsky as the crazed mass killer, and you won't soon forget the scenes of him chasing his relatives in the huge crematorium, his place of "business." (Dir: Juraj Herz, 90 mins.)

Crescendo (Great Britain, 1972)*½ Stefanie Powers, James Olson, Margaretta Scott. (Dir: Alan Gibson, 83 mins.)

Crest of the Wave (1954)**½ Gene Kelly, Jeff Richards, John Justin. Interesting but slow-moving war film made in England. Gene Kelly seems miscast in a straight non-dancing role. (Dirs: John & Roy Boulting, 90 mins.)

Cria! (Spain, 1975)*** Geraldine Chaplin, Ana Torrent, Conchi Perez, German Cobos. A discreet, ambitious but unstructured psychological thriller from Spain's director Carlos Saura. Chaplin and Torrent act out a morbid rondelet of memory and desire about a schoolgirl who may or may not have murdered her parents. An obvious intelligence is at work here, but the ideas remain elusive.(110 mins.)

Cries and Whispers (Sweden, 1972)**** Liv Ullmann, Ingrid Thulin, Harriet Andersson. A searing, devastating masterpiece written, directed and produced by Ingmar Bergman. This shattering drama about the relationships of three sisters in a Swedish manor house was voted the best film of the year by the New York Film Critics. It is, quite simply, one of the great films of the decade. Agnes (Andersson) is dying of cancer, circa 1900, and her older and younger sister come to her home for the deathwatch. The sense of pain and suffering is portrayed so realistically as to become almost unendurable, and the acting throughout is faultless. The great cinematographer Sven Nykvist is at the top of his form. Some of the closeup images are as powerful and beautifully composed as anything in modern cinema. Only Bergman, of today's filmmakers, could, successfully, hold a closeup for such a long period of time. A work of genius. (94 mins.)

Crime Against Joe (1956)*** John Broomfield, Julie London. Painter is accused of a girl's murder. Compact mystery has some surprises; nice pace. (Dir: Lee Sholem, 69 mins.)

Crime and Punishment (1935)**½ Edward Arnold, Peter Lorre, Marian Marsh. Hollywood's version of Dostoyevsky's classic novel casts a subtly neurotic Peter Lorre as the haunted student-murderer. Arnold's portrayal of the inspector, who doggedly tracks him down, is overblown. Sternberg's direction is full of flavor and invention. (Dir: Josef von Sternberg, 88 mins.)

Crime and Punishment (France, 1958)*** Jean Gabin, Robert Hossein. Inspector breaks down the will of a murderer. One of the many versions of this crime tale, and rather well done. (Dir: George Lampin, 108 mins.)

Crime and Punishment (U.S.S.R., 1970)** Georgi Taratorkin, Innokenti Smoktunovsky. Adaptations of this classic tend to be dull and stolid, and this may be the stolidest—and longest at nearly 3½ hours. The essential problem is how to incarnate Raskolnikov; only Peter Lorre seemed to have any handle on the role. Porfiry is easier, as Harry Baur, Edward Arnold, and Smoktunovsky ("Uncle Vanya") have shown. Directed ponderously by Lev Kulidzhanov. (200 mins.)

Crime and Punishment, USA (1959)** George Hamilton, Mary Murphy. A good idea that never quite jells and a good deal of blame can be attributed to George Hamilton's stoic performance. As the title suggests, this is an updated version of the classic "Crime and Punishment." (Dir: Denis Sanders, 95 mins.)

Crime by Night (1944)**½ Jane Wyman, Faye Emerson, Eleanor Parker. Private eye on vacation suddenly finds himself investigating an axe murder. Satisfying mystery with Jerome Cowan as the detective. (Dir: Geoffrey Homes, 72 mins.)

Crime Club (MTV 1973)** Lloyd Bridges, Victor Buono, Paul Burke, William Devane, David Hedison, Cloris Leachman, Barbara Rush, Martin Sheen. When the exposition is finally over, about the formation of a crime club by a retired judge to investigate the murder or suicide of a wealthy youngster, the show becomes a fairly interesting mystery story. Bridges and Buono are the self-appointed police, and a wide range of suspects are played by guest stars. No relation to another

MTV of the same name ('75). (Dir: David Lowell Rich, 78 mins.)

Crime in the Streets (1956)*** John Cassavetes, James Whitmore, Sal Mineo. A familiar '50s urban street-gang opus. The film is ultimately an unsatisfying drama in spite of a lot of craftsmanship, with a startling shot here by Sam Leavitt, a fresh piece of performance there by any of the stars, some sharp writing by Reginald Rose in his adaptation of his TV play, and the consistently intelligent direction of Don Siegel. Everyone went on to do better work (91 mins.)

Crime of Dr. Hallett, The (1938)** Ralph Bellamy, Josephine Hutchinson, William Gargan. A researcher in the jungle seeks a cure for a tropical disease and finds romantic complications. Performances, especially by Gargan, lend interest. B&W (Dir: S. Sylvan Simon, 68 mins.)

Crime of M. Lange, The (France, 1935)**** Jean Lefevre, Jules Berry. A masterpiece directed by Jean Renoir. Monsieur Lange (Lefevre), a writer of pulp fiction, is exploited by his boss, capitalist evil incarnate, Batala (Berry). Lange helps form a publishing cooperative after Batala disappears, saving the firm from ruin. When Batala returns, Renoir constructs a convincing moral argument for his murder. Renoir's irony and taste for paradox flourish, abetted by an excellent Jacques Prévert screenplay. (85 mins.)

Crime of Passion (1957)**½ Barbara Stanwyck, Sterling Hayden, Raymond Burr. A wife's ambition for her husband leads to murder. Barbara Stanwyck tends to over-act. (Dir: Gerd Oswald, 84 mins.)

Crime School (1938)*½ Humphrey Bogart, and the "Dead End Kids." Warden Bogart reforms the "kids" in this tired melodrama. (Dir: Lewis Seiler, 90 mins.)

Crime Wave (1954)** Sterling Hayden, Gene Nelson, Charles Bronson. Dancer Gene Nelson plays a straight dramatic role in this average cops and crooks "meller." Not too effective on all counts. (Dir: Andre de Toth, 74 mins.)

Crime Without Passion (1934)***½ Claude Rains, Margo. Story of a lawyer who gets involved in crime and tries to clear himself by criminal methods. Rains is superb as the sadistic lawyer and Margo scores in the role of the girl he thinks he's murdered. (Dirs: Ben Hecht, Charles MacArthur, 80 mins.)

Criminal, The (Great Britain, 1960)*** Stanley Baker, Sam Wanamaker, Margit Saad, Patrick Magee. Imprisonment and betrayal, two of director Joseph Losey's favorite themes, in a film noir about a convict who escapes and turns on a pal. Baker contributes a memorable performance. (97 mins.)

Criminal Life of Archibaldo de la Cruz, The (Mexico, 1955)**** Ernesto Alonso, Miroslava. Despite nagging limitations of budget and style imposed by the exigencies of commercial Mexican filmmaking

in the mid-fifties, this last film from Luis Buñuel's journeyman period in Mexico is nonetheless a superbly Buñuelian fantasy. A man is obsessed with the notion that as a child he had the power to kill people with his music box, and he lives out his guilt and his power in bizarre and funny ways. Very sly about the Latin male's temperament, the film transforms prudery into liberation with its subterranean surrealism. Also known as *Rehearsal for a Crime*. Recommended. (Dir: Luis Buñuel, 91 mins.)

Crimson Altar, The—See: **Crimson Cult, The**

Crimson Blade, The (Great Britain, 1963)** Lionel Jeffries, Oliver Reed, Jack Hedley. Swashbuckler concerning a love affair between the daughter of one of Cromwell's strongest supporters and a Royalist. The emphasis is on character and the cast is uniformly good. Oliver Reed is especially effective. Written and directed by John Gilling. (83 mins.)

Crimson Canary (1945)**½ Noah Beery Jr., John Litel, Lois Collier. Members of a jazz combo are suspected when a singer is murdered. Neat little mystery with a good jazz background. (Dir: John Hoffman, 64 mins.)

Crimson Cult, The (British, 1968)* Boris Karloff, Christopher Lee, Barbara Steele. Alternate titles: **The Crimson Altar; Curse of the Crimson Altar.** (Dir: Vernon Sewell, 81 mins.)

Crimson Kimono, The (1959)*** Glenn Corbett, Victoria Shaw, James Shigeta. Director Samuel Fuller's crime melodrama is loaded with his unique blend of aggressive tracks and shock cuts. The story uses a lot of night locations in Little Tokyo (Los Angeles) and deals bluntly with issues of racism and miscegenation. Graphic and fascinating, but not a major film. (82 mins.)

Crimson Pirate, The (1952)*** Burt Lancaster, Eva Bartok. Adventure on the high seas with Lancaster buckling every swash in sight. Lancaster and circus acrobat Nick Cravat execute some tricky gymnastics in their effort to overthrow tyranny. (Dir: Robert Siodmak, 104 mins.)

Cripple Creek (1952)** George Montgomery, Jerome Courtland, Karin Booth. Two government agents join a band of gold mine thieves to crack a case in this familiar plot. (Dir: Ray Nazarro, 78 mins.)

Crisis (1950)*** Cary Grant, Signe Hasso, Paula Raymond, Ramon Novarro, José Ferrer. A bit arid and talky, but an absorbing drama that generates real tension. Grant is an American surgeon dragooned into performing delicate brain work on a dying dictator (Ferrer), and political morality gets an entertaining workout. (96 mins.)

Crisis at Sun Valley (MTV 1978)** Dale Robinette, Bo Hopkins, Ken Swofford. The dashing skiing sheriff of Sun Valley (Robinette) deals with mountain-climbing teenagers and a way-out conservationist. Robinette was an Olympic skier, but can't act to save his life. (Dir: Paul Stanley, 104 mins.)

Crisis in Mid-Air (MTV 1979)** George Peppard, Desi Arnaz, Jr., Karen Grassle. Here we are again in the crisis-ridden airport. The predictable drama is played in the aircraft, in the traffic control center, and on the landing strip. (Dir: Walter Grauman, 104 mins.)

Criss Cross (1949)***½ Burt Lancaster, Yvonne DeCarlo, Dan Duryea. Probably the best of director Robert Siodmak's films noirs. Lancaster plays a pathetic yet powerful loser whose fatal weakness is his attachment to his treacherous ex-wife (DeCarlo). Franz Planer photographed, giving a classy sheen to the cheap look and Anthony (Tony) Curtis has a bit part—his film debut. (87 mins.)

Critic's Choice (1963)**½ Bob Hope, Lucille Ball. Even the expert comedy talents of Hope and Ball can't save this contrived tale about a New York drama critic whose wife writes a play. Based on the Broadway play with the same title, the screen adaption was altered to suit the talents of the leads but it doesn't really help. (Dir: Don Weis, 100 mins.)

Cromwell (Great Britain, 1970)** Richard Harris, Alec Guinness, Robert Morley. A toneless, cramped spectacle, written and directed by Ken Hughes with a decided lack of historical sense and marked by a grumpy, foolish performance by Harris as England's lord protector. (141 mins.)

Cronaca di un Amore (Italy, 1950)*** Lucia Bose, Massimo Girotti. Director Michelangelo Antonioni's first feature introduces some of his basic concerns—the ironic relationship between knowledge and certainty, and the oblique nature of love. An industrialist unwittingly renews the love affair between his wife and a mechanic when he hires a detective to investigate her past. (96 mins.)

Crook, The (France-Italy, 1970)***½ Jean-Louis Trintignant, Christine Lelouch. Claude Lelouch, director of "A Man and a Woman," casts his romantic eye on crime. Trintignant plays a criminal out to commit an elaborate kidnapping of a bank employee's son and collect ransom from the bank, which would then profit from the publicity. The plan works until a subtle plot twist. Slick, and cynical. First-rate entertainment, and Trintignant is splendid. (73 mins.)

Crooked Hearts, The (MTV 1972)**½ Rosalind Russell, Douglas Fairbanks, Jr. The stars add class to this tale about film-flam amid the geriatric set. Miss Russell corresponds with the elegant Mr. Fairbanks via a lonely hearts club and they strike up a romance—each thinking the other is enormously wealthy. Predictable story, but Miss Russell is always interesting to watch. (Dir: Jay Sandrich, 74 mins.)

Crooked Road, The (Great Britain, 1964)* Robert Ryan, Stewart Granger, Nadia Gray. (Dir: Don Chaffey, 86 mins.)

Crooked Sky, The (Great Britain 1957)*½ Wayne Morris, Karin Booth. (Dir: Henry Cass, 77 mins.)

Crooked Web, The (1955)** Frank Lovejoy, Mari Blanchard. Undercover agents go to great lengths to trap a wartime criminal into a confession. A slow moving film. (Dir: Nathan Juran, 80 mins.)

Crooks Anonymous (Great Britain, 1962)** Julie Christie, Leslie Phillips, Wilfred Hyde-White. Petty thief tries to mend his ways, joins an organization dedicated to the reformation of criminals. Cute idea, mediocre handling. (Dir: Ken Annakin, 87 mins.)

Cross My Heart (1946)** Betty Hutton, Sonny Tufts. Silly comedy about a girl who rarely tells the truth. The young lady confesses to a murder thinking it will help her boy friend, but the scheme backfires. Remake of *True Confession*, 1937. (Dir: John Berry, 83 mins.)

Cross of Iron (Great Britain-West Germany, 1977)** James Coburn, Maximilian Schell, James Mason, David Warner. Despite some formidable action sequences, notably in the tank battles near the end, this film represents director Sam Peckinpah in decline. The characterizations are superficial, which is no fault of the good actors. Needless to say, with its heroic German soldiers, it was a substantial hit in the fatherland. (120 mins.)

Cross of Lorraine, The (1943)*** Jean-Pierre Aumont, Gene Kelly, Sir Cedric Hardwicke. An exceptionally good anti-Nazi film about a group of Frenchmen who surrender too easily, go to a prison camp and learn how the Nazis really operate. Grim, but a picture that may remind you of things you have no right to forget. (Dir: Tay Garnett, 90 mins.)

Crosswinds (1951)** John Payne, Rhonda Fleming, Forrest Tucker. John Payne is the victim of a double cross and other villainous deeds in this average tale of island intrigues. Rhonda Fleming almost loses her head (literally) when a band of head-hunters capture her. (Dir: Lewis R. Foster, 93 mins.)

Crossed Swords (1954)*½ Errol Flynn, Gina Lollobrigida, (Dir: Nato de Angelis, 84 mins.)

Crossed Swords (Great Britain, 1977)*** Oliver Reed, Mark Lester, Raquel Welch, Ernest Borgnine, George C. Scott. Another version of Mark Twain's "The Prince and the Pauper." Richard Fleischer directs a handsomely mounted swashbuckler with a few comic touches. Scott is a plus, Heston a minus. Perfectly respectable entertainment. (113 mins.)

Crossfire (1947)***½ Robert Ryan, Robert Mitchum, Robert Young, Gloria Grahame, Sam Levene. This B pic with a social angle deserves credit for it, though it is hardly the artistic sleeper that critics and the Academy took it for. In the novel ("The Brick Foxhole" by Richard Brooks) the victim was a homosexual; here he is made Jewish. However, hates are not interchangeable. The cast's work is sharp. (86 mins.)

Crossroads (1942)** William Powell, Hedy Lamarr, Basil Rathbone, Claire Trevor. Suspense film about an amnesia victim who is uncertain of his former life is well played. Has some good moments but, overall, is not effective drama. (Dir: Jack Conway, 84 mins.)

Crossroads: South Africa (1980)*** A courageous documentary about the shantytowns set up by blacks about to be relocated to the barren Transvaal from their homes in the city of Capetown, and how they resist the systematic destruction of their homes and dispersal of their families. The film is unsophisticated and it needs tighter editing, but the power of the personalities of those interviewed and the red-hot anger of the footage, which had to be smuggled out of the country, overcome the occasional repetition of image or idea. (Dir: Jonathan Wacks)

Crossroads to Crime (Great Britain, 1960)** Anthony Oliver, Patricia Henegan. Policeman on his own goes after a gang of hijackers. Passable Edgar Wallace mystery. (Dir: Gerry Anderson, 57 mins.)

Crosstrap (Great Britain, 1960)** Laurence Payne, Jill Adams. Writer and his wife on honeymoon in a bungalow run across murder. Average mystery. (Dir: Robert Hartford-Davis, 62 mins.)

Crossup—See: **Tiger by the Tail**

Crowd, The (1928)**** James Murray, Eleanor Boardman, Bert Roach, Estelle Clark. Director King Vidor's silent masterpiece about a little man lost in the crowd of day-to-day living. His expressionistic film is still essential viewing. (98 mins.)

Crowded Paradise (1956)**½ Hume Cronyn, Nancy Kelly. Janitor has a crazy hatred for his Puerto Rican tenants. Lowbudget film has some good scenes. (Dir: Fred Pressburger, 94 mins.)

Crowded Sky, The (1960)**½ Dana Andrews, Rhonda Fleming, Efrem Zimbalist, Troy Donahue. This airplane drama will strike you as a bit familiar and rightly so—it is a slightly altered retelling of "The High and the Mighty" with some new characters thrown in. The large cast does what it can with the episodic script. (Dir: Joseph Pevney, 105 mins.)

Crowhaven Farm (MTV 1970)**½ Hope Lange, Paul Burke, Lloyd Bochner. Thriller dealing with witchcraft and the supernatural. Hope Lange and Paul Burke inherit a farm, which becomes the setting for some very strange happenings. Although most of the plot becomes transparent before too long, you'll probably stay with it to the end. (Dir: Walter Grauman, 73 mins.)

Crowning Experience, The (1960)** Muriel Smith, Ann Buckles. Religious film made for Moral Rearmament—the biography of educator Mary McLeod Bethune. Good performance by Muriel Smith in the role. As a drama, not as effective as it should be—simplistic approach detracts from the power of the narrative. (Dir: Marion Clayton Anderson, 102 mins.)

Crucible, The (France, 1958)***½ Simone Signoret, Yves Montand, Mylene Demongeot. A gripping version of Arthur Miller's memorable play about the Salem witch trials and how a young girl's jealousy caused innocent people to be condemned to death. Miller's play, based on events in Massachusetts almost three hundred years ago, was written as a searing commentary on the evils of McCarthyism in America in the 1950's. This movie was ultimately made in France because the prize-winning playwright was blacklisted in America and blackballed by Hollywood at that time. Alternate title: **Witches of Salem**. (Dir: Raymond Rouleau, 120 mins.)

Crucible of Horror (Great Britain, 1970)*** Michael Gough, Yvonne Mitchell, Sharon Gurney. Tight, chilling tingler. Mother and daughter plan murder of sadistic father. Top-flight suspense, biting and original. Well-acted by a small cast. Ending disappoints. (Dir: Viktors Ritelis, 91 mins.)

Cruel Sea. The (Great Britain, 1953)**** Jack Hawkins, Donald Sinden. Story of the officers and men of the Compass Rose, who faced the dangers of the Nazi subs during World War II. Superbly produced war drama, deserves praise in all departments. (Dir: Charles Frend, 140 mins.)

Cruel Swamp (1956)*½ Beverly Garland, Marie Windsor, Carole Matthews. (Dir: Roger Corman, 73 mins.)

Cruel Tower (1956)*** John Ericson, Mari Blanchard. Drifter takes a job as a steeplejack, incurs jealousy over a girl. Suspenseful melodrama with some hairraising scenes showing the steeplejacks at their work. (Dir: Lew Landers, 80 mins.)

Cruisin' Down the River (1953)** Dick Haymes, Audrey Totter, Billy Daniels. Dick Haymes' singing makes this otherwise dull musical comedy worthwhile. Story is about a riverboat that's turned into a floating nightclub by enterprising ancestors of the original owners. (Dir: Richard Quine, 90 mins.)

Cruising (1980)**½ Al Pacino, Paul Sorvino, Karen Allen, Richard Cox, Don Scardino. Never had so many people trashed a film that they haven't seen. After a pair of horrible murders in the gay leather world, Pacino, a painfully vulnerable cop with no knowledge of what he is getting into, is sent undercover as a decoy. The basic narrative idea is that our growing discomfort with Pacino's convincing integration into his new environment and our growing fear that he may be developing some homicidal impulses of his own—both are inextricably linked to the

145

exhilaration of our release from fear as Pacino's savvy and power increase. Lurid, brutal, dehumanizing, but it does succeed in searing the audience. Script by Friedkin. (Dir: William Friedkin, 106 mins.)

Crusades, The (1935)**½ Loretta Young, Henry Wilcoxon. De Mille epic about the third crusade is lavish, exciting and fairly entertaining. History is twisted a bit too much in favor of romance. (Dir: C. B. De Mille, 123 min.)

Cry Baby Killer (1958)**½ Jack Nicholson, Brett Halsey. Teenager thinks he has killed, holds up in a storeroom with hostages, holding police at bay. Not much to this grim little tale of juvenile delinquents, but what there is is well done. Alert direction, capable acting. Nicholson's debut. (Dir: Justus Addiss, 62 mins.)

Cry Danger (1951)***½ Dick Powell, Rhonda Fleming. Released from prison, a man attempts to prove he was innocent of robbery. Fast, tough melodrama, very good. (Dir: Richard Parrish, 79 mins.)

Cry for Happy (1961)**½ Glenn Ford. Donald O'Connor, Miyoshi Umeki. Through a misunderstanding a group of Navy men living it up in a geisha house is forced to turn its paradise into an orphanage to cool the brass. Mildly amusing service comedy is pleasant enough despite a few misfires on the laugh situations. (Dir: George Marshall, 110 mins.)

Cry for Help, A (MTV 1975)**½ Robert Culp, Elayne Heilveil, Chuck McCann. Follows a sardonic, ex-drunk radio phone-show host (Culp) as he starts a normal day of putting down the parade of kooks who call his early AM show. When an 18-year-old girl indicates she's about to pack it in and do away with herself, he sloughs her off, and a barrage of calls starts a race with the clock to find the mystery girl. Well done. (Dir: Daryl Duke, 72 mins.)

Cry for Love, A (MTV 1980)*** Susan Blakely, Powers Boothe. Hollywood divorcee, daughter of a famous dad, pops pills and finds her equal in a clever alcoholic. There are high times together, but hitting the skids is not necessarily rewarding entertainment. Susan Blakely becomes a convincing bundle of jangled nerves, and Powers Boothe plays the drunk with a flair. Toward the end it becomes a nightmare, which is the point of the flick. Tune out if these sick-os become too depressing, because little is spared. From Jill Robinson's *Bed/Time/Story*. The two leads give fine performances.

Cry Freedom (Philippines, 1959)** Pancho Magalona, Rosa Rosal. Out-of-the-ordinary World War II movie views war from the Philippine perspective—a disparate group of commandos, led by a bus driver, battle the Japanese occupiers. Technically crude, amateurish in other respects. Sequel to **Cat People.** (Dir: Lamberto V. Avellana, 93 mins.)

Cry from the Streets, A (Great Britain, 1959)*** Max Bygraves, Barbara Murray. Often effective drama of homeless children and the welfare workers who try to give them a reason for living. Miss Murray is most effective. (Dir: Lewis Gilbert, 100 mins.)

Cry Havoc (1943)**½ Margaret Sullavan, Ann Sothern. All-female cast in this occasionally moving war melodrama about women who served tirelessly as nurses during our defeat on Bataan. (Dir: Richard Thorpe, 97 mins.)

Cry in the Night, A (1956)** Edmond O'Brien, Natalie Wood, Brien Donlevy, Raymond Burr. A mentally unbalanced man kidnaps the daughter of a policeman, and police try to track them down before it's too late. Only fair melodrama misses on the suspense. (Dir: Frank Tuttle, 75 mins.)

Cry in the Wilderness, A (MTV, 1974)* George Kennedy, Paul Sorenson, Irene Tedrow. (Dir:Gordon Hessler, 90 mins.)

Cry of Battle (1963)** Van Heflin, Rita Moreno, James MacArthur. Wealthy lad earns his mettle when he joins a guerilla unit in the Pilippines during World War II. War drama never gets out of the routine rut despite local color, fairly effective performances. Filmed near Manila. (Dir: Irving Lerner, 99 mins.)

Cry of the Banshee (British, 1970)**½ Vincent Price rolls his eyes and snarls in his inimitable fashion in still another chiller-diller horror film. In this one, he's a British magistrate who dabbles in heinous deeds during his off-hours. (Dir: Gordon Hessler, 87 mins.)

Cry of the Bewitched (Mexico, 1957)*½ Ninon Sevilla, Ramon Gay. Alternate title: **Young and Evil.** (Dir: Alfredo B. Crevenna, 79 mins.)

Cry of the City (1948)*** Richard Conte, Victor Mature, Shelley Winters, Debra Paget. Atmosphere is everything (the script is a drag) in this remake of "Manhattan Melodrama" in which two pals from the slums grow up on opposite sides of the law. Though director Robert Siodmak's films lack lasting impact, his style is striking and effective. (96 mins.)

Cry of the Hunted (1953)**½ Vittorio Gassman, Polly Bergen, Barry Sullivan. Gassman's performance as an escaped convict trudging through the swamps gives some credulity to this otherwise melodramatic yarn about the hunter and the hunted. (Dir: Joseph H. Lewis, 79 mins.)

Cry of the Innocent (MTV 1980)**½ Rod Taylor, Joanna Pettet, Cyril Cusack, Nigel Davenport. A fair action yarn by expert Frederick Forsyth is enhanced by Irish actors like Cusack and lovely scenic views of Ireland. Tale of a man whose family is wiped out by a plane crash. Watery-eyed Taylor and Pettet are to be commended. (Dir: Michael O'Herlihy, 104 mins.)

Cry of the Penguins (Great Britain, 1971)*** John Hurt, Hayley Mills, Dudley

Sutton, Tony Britton. Unusual film revolving around a self-centered youth's study of penguin life in the Antarctic. Doesn't sould like much, but the brash character played by Hurt gives it a lot of zest, and there are fascinating shots of the penguins and their gull adversaries. Originally directed by Al Viola, with wildlife sequences by the renowned Arne Sucksdorff. The framing story, set in Lonon and featuring Mills, was added by Roy Boulting to give Hurt's character added depth. (101 mins.)

Cry of the Wild (Canada, 1972)***½ A superior animal documentary about Canadian wolves. The best parts of the film are those in the middle made by the National Film Board of Canada. Some of the wolves are captured and tamed while living in with the director-photographer Bill Mason. Good scenes in the Canadian Artic and some truly remarkable shots at the end, filmed in a large enclosure where the wolves do not run wild, of the courtship of two wolves and the following scenes of the female wolf with her litter. (90 mins.)

Cry Panic (MTV 1974)*** John Forsythe, Anne Francis, Earl Holliman. Good mystery which will have you rooting for the poor hero, played by Forsythe. He accidentally hits and kills a man on a highway, but when he leaves the scene of the accident to call the police, the body disappears and he's thrown into a complicated web of events. The audience is let in on the reasons for the strange happenings in the small town where Forsythe is detained, but it subtracts from your sustained interst in the proceedings. (Dir: James Goldstone, 78 mins.)

Cry Rape! (MTV 1973)** Andrea Marcovicci, Peter Coffield. A worthy theme, the indignities a rape victim has to endure at the police station, is mishandled. Based on a true story, it veers away from the rape problem to the innocent man wrongly identified in the lineup, and simply becomes a variation on the old plot about a look-alike with the added twist that the suspect is also saddled with the wrong kind of lawyer. (Dir: Corey Allen, 90 mins.)

Cry Terror! (1958)**½ James Mason, Inger Stevens, Rod Steiger, Angie Dickinson. Crafty criminal forces an electronics expert to aid him in an elaborate extortion plot. Occasionally suspenseful crime drama stretches things too far at times but has a good share of thrills. Aided by intersecting New York locations. (Dir: Andrew L. Stone, 96 mins.)

Cry the Beloved Country (Great Britain, 1951)***½ Canada Lee, Charles Carson. Negro Reverend in the back country of South Africa journeys to the city, only to find his people living in squalor, and his son a criminal. Powerful drama of Africa has many gripping moments. (Dir: Zoltan Korda, 105 mins.)

Cry Tough (1959)**½ John Saxon, Linda Cristal. Only moderately interesting drama about the young juvenile delinquent element which springs up in minority groups due to racial hatred. The performances are better than the material. (Dir: Paul Stanley, 83 mins.)

Cry Vengeance (1954)*** Mark Stevens, Martha Hyer. Detective seeks revenge for the murder of his wife and child. Tense, well-directed (by Stevens) crime drama with some new plot twists. (Dir: Mark Stevens, 83 mins.)

Cry Wolf (1947)**½ Errol Flynn, Barbara Stanwyck, Richard Basehart, Geraldine Page. Woman has a creepy time when she goes to her late husband's estate to claim her inheritance. Hackneyed thriller. (Dir: Peter Godfrey, 83 mins.)

Cry Wolf (Great Britain, 1968)**½ Anthony Kemp, Judy Cornwell. Good adventure yarn for the kids—the old fable about the boy who cried wolf once too often is set in contemporary Britain, among diplomats instead of sheep. Resourcefulness of the young hero makes for a happier ending. (Dir: John Davis, 58 mins.)

Crystal Ball (1943)** Paulette Goddard, Ray Milland. A gal from Texas takes a job as a fortune-teller's assistant, where she snags her man. Just passable comedy, with the players better than the script. (Dir: Elliott Nugent, 81 mins.)

Cuba (1979)**½ Sean Connery, Brooke Adams, Chris Sarandon, Jack Weston, Hector Elizondo. (Dir: Richard Lester, 122 mins.)

Cuban Love Song (1931)** Lawrence Tibbett, Lupe Velez, Jimmy Durante, Ernest Torrence. Tibbett has an outstanding supporting cast—but the energy level is minimal. Story of a marine on leave in Cuba; he returns years later to claim his illegitimate child, whose mother has died. (Dir: W.S. Van Dyke II, 86 mins.)

Cuban Rebel Girls (1959)*½ Errol Flynn, Beverly Aadland. (Dir: Barry Mahon, 68 mins.)

Cul-de-Sac (Great Britain, 1966)*** Donald Pleasence, Lionel Stander, Jack MacGowran, Françoise Dorleac. Director Roman Polanski's second British film is a tart, absurdist study of sexual humiliation and exhilaration, with Pleasence giving a smashing performance as George, an effeminate innkeeper who finds expiation in violence, or if adrenalin falters, transvestism. Stander is a gangster gorging on raw eggs, and the wondrous MacGowran makes his turn into unadulterated Beckett. Bizarre, to say the least, but essential Polanski. (111 mins.)

Culpepper Cattle Company, The (1972)**½ Gary Grimes, Billy "Green" Bush, Luke Askew, Bo Hopkins. A great deal of effort on the part of the cameramen and art directors has been expended to give this Western an authentic look, even though it isn't much more than a routine yarn about the "coming of age," in post-Civil War Texas, of a young man who signs on

147

as a cook's helper on a huge cattle drive. Gary Grimes is properly green as the kid who is forced to become a man when he is confronted by killing and rustling. Directorial debut by Dick Richards, who had been a director of TV commercials and sometimes it shows. Screenplay by Eric Bercovici and Gregory Prentiss, based on a story by Richards. (92 mins.)

Cult of the Cobra (1955)** Faith Domergue, Richard Long. Combination murder mystery-horror film about superstitions and curses. Faith Domergue plays a mysterious woman who has the power to change into a snake. (Dir: Francis D. Lyon, 90 mins.)

Cure for Love (Great Britain, 1950)**½ Robert Donat, Renee Asherson. A returning soldier finds romantic complications in his home town. Pleasant comedy. (Dir: Robert Donat, 97 mins.)

Curly Top (1935)*** Shirley Temple, John Boles, Rochelle Hudson, Jane Darwell, Arthur Treacher. An orphaned moppet (Shirley) is adopted by a handsome millionaire (Boles) who falls in love with her beautiful sister (Hudson). He also happens to be a songwriter, and Shirley sings "Animal Crackers in My Soup." One of the better Temples. B&W. (Dir: Irving Cummings, 74 mins.)

Curse of Dracula, The—See: **Return of Dracula**

Curse of Frankenstein, The (Great Britain, 1957)** Peter Cushing, Christopher Lee. The dynamic duo of British horror films, Cushing and Lee, join forces in another installment in the saga of a certain mad scientist and his creature, who both often go under the same name—Frankenstein. (Dir: Freddie Francis, 93 mins.)

Curse of King Tut's Tomb, The (MTV 1980)** Raymond Burr, Eva Marie Saint, Wendy Hiller. Hard to take seriously. Chuckles and terror, as cobras strike and scorpions attack. Burr in dark make-up, wearing a towel on his head, sets the tone as the scheming villain. Parts filmed on location in Egypt's valley of the kings. (Dir: Philip Leacock, 98 mins.)

Curse of Nostradamus, The (Mexico, 1962)* Domingo Soler, Jermon Robles. (Dirs: Federico Curiel, Alberto Mariscal, 77 mins.)

Curse of the Black Widow (MTV 1977)*½ June Allyson, Tony Franciosa, Patty Duke Astin. Lots of TV names—Donna Mills, June Lockhart, Max Gail, Vic Morrow, Sid Caesar, Roz Kelly—do what little they can in this familar murder mystery in which a series of people are killed in the same bizarre fashion. (Dir: Dan Curtis, 104 mins.)

Curse of the Cat People (1944)*** Simone Simon, Kent Smith. Child whose mother was cursed is regarded as strange by her playmates and parents. Odd little drama has moments of genuine quality. Sequel to "Cat People." (Dirs: Gunther Fritsch & Robert Wise, 70 mins.)

Curse of the Crimson Altar—See: **Crimson Cult, The**

Curse of the Crying Woman, The (Mexico, 1961)* Rosita Arenas, Abel Salazar. (Dir: Rafael Baledon, 74 mins.)

Curse of the Demon (Great Britain, 1958)*** Dana Andrews, Peggy Cummins. A major work in a minor genre, a consummate achievement of that genteel visual stylist, director Jacques Tourneur ("I Walked with a Zombie". Marred only by one shot of a cheesy monster insisted upon by the producer and by the obvious alcoholic problems of lead actor Andrews, this film is everything "The Exorcist" wanted to be but wasn't. (95 mins.)

Curse of the Doll People (Mexico, 1960)* Elvira Quintana, Ramon Gay. (Dirs: Paul Nagle, Benito Alazraki, 83 mins.)

Curse of the Faceless Man (1958)* Richard Anderson, Elaine Edwards. (Dir: Edward L. Cahn, 66 mins.)

Curse of the Fly, The (British, 1965)* (Dir: Don Sharp, 85 mins.)

Curse of the Hidden Vault, The (Germany, 1964)*½ Judith Dornys, Harald Lieb. (Dir: Franz Josef Gottlieb, 91 mins.)

Curse of the Mummy's Tomb, The (Great Britain 1964)** Terence Morgan, Ronald Howard. Mummy returns to life to commence a reign of terror. Undistinguished horror thriller. (Dir: Michael Carreras, 80 mins.)

Curse of the Stone Hand (Mexico, U.S.A., 1965)* John Carradine, Sheila Bon. (Dirs: Jerry Warren, Carl Schleipper, 72 mins.)

Curse of the Undead (1959)** Eric Fleming, Kathleen Crowley, Michael Pate. Intriguing mixture of western and "Dracula"-type horror yarn as a vampire stalks the west. Not too successful in execution but deserves credit for trying something different. (Dir: Edward Dein, 79 mins.)

Curse of the Voodoo (U.S.A.-Great Britain, 1965)** Bryant Halliday, Dennis Price, Lisa Daniely. White hunter is the recipient of a curse when he ventures into forbidden territory. Fairish thriller has the asset of some well-constructed suspense scenes. (Dir: Lindsay Shonteff, 77 mins.)

Curse of the Werewolf (Great Britain, 1961)*** Clifford Evans, Oliver Reed. Young lad with questionable antecedents is discovered to be a werewolf. Superior shocker, with more adult ramifications than usual in the plotting. Gruesome, but good. (Dir: Terence Fisher, 91 mins.)

Curse of the Yellow Snake (Germany, 1963)*½ Joachim Berger, Pinkas Braun. (Dir: Frank Gottlieb, 99 mins.)

Curtain Call of Cactus Creek (1950)**½ Donald O'Connor, Gale Storm, Eve Arden, Vincent Price. Amusing romp about a traveling troupe of actors who run into trouble wherever they set up to perform. The melodramas staged by the troupe are the funniest things in the movies. The cast plays it broadly and that's how it should be done. (Dir: Charles Lamont, 86 mins.)

Curtain Up (Great Britain 1952)**½ Robert Morley, Margaret Rutherford. Small theatre group is plagued by an old lady, aunt of the backer, who has written a very bad play. Pleasing comedy that doesn't come off as it should. (Dir: Ralph Smart, 81 mins.)

Curucu, Beast of the Amazon (1956)** John Bromfield, Beverly Garland. Plantation foreman sets out to track down a legendary monster who is killing and terrorizing the natives. Routine thriller yarn is picturesque. (Dir: Curt Siodmak, 76 mins.)

Custer of the West (1968)**½ Robert Shaw, Mary Ure, Robert Ryan. Robert Siodmak directed his first western as his last film. Story of the 7th Cavalry general who was wiped out at Little Big Horn. Made in Spain; sprawling narrative redeemed somewhat by Shaw's thespic capabilities as Custer. Some good big-scale action scenes. (146 mins.)

Customs Agent (1950)** William Eythe, Marjorie Reynolds, Jim Bachus. A U. S. Customs Agent poses as a dope peddler in order to crack a drug smuggling outfit. Plenty of action. (Dir: Seymour Friedman, 80 mins.)

Cutter (MTV 1972)* Peter De Anda, Cameron Mitchell, Barbara Rush, Robert Webber. De Anda plays a low-keyed black private eye who knows the terrain and the people to question when he's assigned to locate a missing pro football player. Naturally, the syndicate is in on it. Chicago location photography. (Dir: Richard Irving, 78 mins.)

Cutter and Bone (1981)*** Jeff Bridges, John Heard, Lisa Eichorn, Ann Dusenberry, Stephen Elliott. Interesting, offbeat mystery. A clique of middle-class drifters are forced to take action when one of them is wrongly accused of murder. The performances are particularly interesting, especially Bridges, as Bone, a good-natured eccentric almost too laid-back for his own good, and Heard as Cutter, his extremely tense Vietnam vet friend, whose plot to prove Bone's innocence causes near havoc. Strong atmosphere, involving story. (Dir: Ivan Passer, 109 mins.)

Cutter's Trail (MTV 1971)* John Gavin, Manuel Padilla, Jr., Marisa Pavan, Beverly Garland, Joseph Cotten. Formula western about U.S. marshal who returns to his town to find it nearly destroyed by Mexican bandits, and vows to track 'em down. (Dir: Vincent McEveety, 104 mins.)

Cyborg 2087 (1966)* Michael Rennie, Wendell Corey. (Dir: Franklin Andreon, 86 mins.)

Cycle, The (Iran, 1974)**½ Ezat Entezami, Frouzan, Ali Nassiriane. Now that the Iranian cinema is functionally extinct, the work of director Dariush Mehrjui is preeminent in its short, troubled history. This lively comedy, which implies that corruption is at the root of all strata of Iranian society, was banned by the shah; it's hard to see how its libertine sardonicism would be welcomed by Khomeini. The film exhibits an active intelligence, but the direction is so uninflected that its satiric points stew in their own lazy juice. In Farsi with English subtitles. (102 mins.)

Cyclops (1957)*½ Gloria Talbott, James Craig, Lon Chaney, Jr., Tom Drake. (Dir: Bert I. Gordon, 75 mins.)

Cyclotrode "X" (1946-66)**½ Charles Quigley, Linda Stirling, Clayton Moore. Feature version of serial "The Crimson Ghost." Masked villain is out to steal an atomic device, and the hero is out to stop him. Good action sequences give this feature cliffhanger a lift. (Dir: William Witney, 100 mins.)

Cynara (1932)**½ Ronald Colman, Kay Francis. Dated romantic drama based on a play has Ronald Colman's excellent performance to recommend it. (Dir: King Vidor, 90 mins.)

Cynthia (1947)** Elizabeth Taylor, Gene Lockhart, George Murphy. Syrupy tale of a sickly girl who proves she's normal and, by so doing, solves everybody's problems. (Dir: Robert Z. Leonard, 99 mins.)

Cyrano de Bergerac (1950)***½ Jose Ferrer, Mala Powers. The classic play about the soldier of fortune with the oversize proboscis, and of his unrequited love for the beautiful Roxanne. Ferrer won the Academy Award for this, but production shortcomings and uninspired casting of other roles mitigate against its effectiveness. Ferrer's performance is properly flamboyant and very moving, and makes this perennial well worth seeing. (Dir: Michael Gordon, 112 mins.)

D-Day, the Sixth of June (1956)*** Robert Taylor, Dana Wynter, Richard Todd. The usual plot of two officers loving one girl, but presented with a bit more credibility than is customary. Good production values, including WW II scenes. With Edmond O'Brien, John Williams, Jerry Paris. (Dir: Henry Koster, 106 mins.)

D.A.—Conspiracy to Kill, The (MTV 1970)*½ Robert Conrad, William Conrad, Belinda Montgomery. (Dir: Jack Webb, 99 mins.)

D.A.: Murder One, The (1969)**½ Howard Duff, Robert Conrad, Diane Baker. A made-for-TV murder mystery produced by Jack Webb which should appeal to fans of the "Dragnet" TV series. The two hours are filled with painstaking detective work as the D.A.'s office tries to trap an attractive nurse (Diane Baker) suspected of multiple murders. The D.A.s are Robert Conrad and Howard Duff, and the capable supporting cast includes J. D. Cannon, David Opatoshu, and Alfred Ryder. (Dir: Jack Webb, 99 mins.)

Daddy, I Don't Like It Like This (MTV 1978)*** Talia Shire, Burt Young, Doug McKeon. Often perceptive handling of a depressing, downbeat subject. About the drab lives of a lower-middle-class family. Written by actor Young, who plays the laborer father, it centers on the bickering of the married couple and effect it has on their young sensitive son (McKeon). Who gives the film's best performance. The focus of the film defeats everyone long before the fade-out. Impressive first effort by director Adell Aldrich, daughter of veteran director Robert Aldrich. (104 mins.)

Daddy Long Legs (1955)***½ Fred Astaire, Leslie Caron. Delightful musical romance. Debonair Fred Astaire has seldom had a better dancing partner than charming and graceful Leslie Caron—their numbers are the film's highlights. The plot borders on modern fairy tale—a French orphan (Miss Caron) is subsidized by a wealthy bachelor with the stipulation that his identity be kept secret. (Dir: Jean Negulesco, 126 mins.)

Daddy-O (1959)* Dick Contino, Sandra Giles. (Dir: Lou Place, 74 mins.)

Daddy's Gone A-Hunting (1969)**½ Carol White, Paul Burke, Scott Hylands. A pretty lively suspense tale. Carol White has her hands full when her ex-lover shows up bent on revenge because she had an abortion during their time together. The mad young man (Scott Hylands) kidnaps the now happily married Miss White's new baby and the chase is on. Exciting photography during the final moments of the chase adds to the tension. (Dir: Mark Robson, 108 mins.)

Daggers Drawn (France, 1963)*½ Françoise Arnoul, Pierre Mondy, Petula Clark. (Dir: Charles Girard, 85 mins.)

Daggers of Blood—See: With Fire and Sword

Dagora, the Space Monster (Japan, 1964)* Yosuke Natsuki. (Dir: Ishiro Honda, 80 mins.)

Daguerreotypes (France, 1975)*** Director Agnes Varda's witty, compassionate film about the inhabitants of the rue Daguerre, Paris, who were among the first subjects of the pioneer photographer of the same name.

Dain Curse, The (MTV 1978)**½ James Coburn, Hector Elizondo, Jason Miller, Jean Simmons, Dave Stewart. Dashiell Hammett wrote this mystery yarn 50 years ago. The film won the Edgar award: the production is first class, and the cast is above average for TV fare, but the story about multiple murders, an alleged family curse, and bogus religious cults only comes alive in spurts. Coburn seldom leaves the screen as the private investigator assigned to check into a small diamond theft which balloons into a bizarre trail of murder and mayhem. The rest of the characters are too eccentric to arouse sympathy. Originally shown as a three-

parter. (Dir: E. W. Swackhamer, 312 mins.)

Daisy Kenyon (1947)**½ Joan Crawford, Henry Fonda, Dana Andrews. A woman must choose between her lover, who has a wife and family, and the man she married on the rebound. Well done film but a bore. (Dir: Otto Preminger, 99 mins.)

Daisy Miller (1974)*** Cybill Shepherd, Barry Brown, Mildred Natwick, Cloris Leachman, Eileen Brennan. An intelligent, visually stunning but curiously uninvolving adaptation of Henry Miller's superb novella about expatriate Americans in Europe and a nouveau riche American girl from Schenectady, colliding with European high society circa 1879. Part of the problem is that Shepherd is simply not a talented enough actress with sufficient range to develop a fully rounded portrait of Daisy. But she does look exquisite, and exactly right—a Renoir vision as captured by cinematographer Alberto Spagnoli. Screenplay by Frederic Raphael. (Dir: Peter Bogdanovich, 91 mins.)

Dakota Incident (1956)**½ Linda Darnell, Dale Robertson, John Lund. Stagecoach wards off Indian attacks. Fairly good western; good performances. (Dir: Lewis R. Foster, 88 mins.)

Dakota Lil (1950)**½ George Montgomery, Rod Cameron, Marie Windsor. Secret agent poses as an outlaw, enlists the aid of a beautiful lady forger to trap a bandit gang. Lively western has the stuff to attract the oats fanciers. (Dir: Lesley Selander, 88 mins.)

Daleks—Invasion Earth 2150 A.D.—See: Invasion Earth 2150 A.D.

Dallas (1950)**½ Gary Cooper, Ruth Roman, Steve Cochran. Cooper plays a man who comes to Dallas for revenge, in this moderately entertaining western drama. Ruth Roman supplies the necessary love interest and Steve Cochran does very well as one of Cooper's intended victims. (Dir: Stuart Heisler, 94 mins.)

Dalton Girls (1957)*½ John Russell, Merry Anders. (Dir: Reginald LeBorg, 71 mins.)

Dam Busters, The (Great Britain, 1955)**** Richard Todd, Michael Redgrave. Excellent war drama about one of the most dangerous missions of WW II. Effective cast and fine script make this one worth your while. (Dir: Michael Anderson, 102 mins.)

Dames (1934)*** Joan Blondell, Ruby Keeler, Dick Powell, ZaSu Pitts, Hugh Herbert. A good Warner Bros. musical. Pitts adds a little variety; Busby Berkeley did the production numbers, which include "When You Were a Smile on Mother's Lips and a Twinkle in Your Daddy's Eye." (Dir: Ray Enright, 90 mins.)

Damn Citizen (1958)**½ Keith Andes, Maggie Hayes, Gene Evans. Story based on fact of a World War II vet who is given a free hand to clean up crime and corruption in a state police organization. Done in documentary fashion, has a fairly good share of interest. (Dir: Robert Gordon, 88 mins.)

Damn the Defiant! (Great Britain, 1962)*** Alec Guinness, Dirk Bogarde, Anthony Quayle. Commander of a fighting vessel faces the opposition of his second in command, a sadistic and cruel officer hated by the crew. Salty maritime costume drama with performances of high standard, interest maintained throughout. (Dir: Lewis Gilbert, 101 mins.)

Damn Yankees (1958)**½ Gwen Verdon, Tab Hunter, Ray Walston. The hit B'dway musical reaches the screen with one big change—Tab Hunter is cast in one of the leads. It's a mistake. He seems out of his element dancing and singing with pro Gwen Verdon. Miss Verdon is best when dancing and she dances most of the time. Ray Walston as the "Devil" has some funny moments. (Dir: George Abbott, 110 mins.)

Damnation Alley (1977)* Jan-Michael Vincent, George Peppard, Dominique Sanda, Paul Winfield. (Dir: Jack Smight, 91 mins.)

Damned, The (1963)—See: **These Are the Damned**

Damned, The (Italy-West Germany, 1969)***½ Dirk Bogarde, Ingrid Thulin, Helmut Grien, Helmut Berger, Charlotte Rampling, Rene Koldehoff. Director Luchino Visconti's excessively operatic view of the rise of Nazism within a social climate of complete decadence. Bogarde and Thulin are corrupt munitions manufacturers done in by the perversions and machinations of young Berger, who does a drag shtick with panache. Shrill and overblown, but a lot of raunchy spectacle. Grien and Koldehoff are very good. (155 mins.)

Damned Don't Cry, The (1950)**½ Joan Crawford, David Brian, Steve Cochran. Joan Crawford finds herself up to her mink in crime and corruption. Heavy David Brian makes the going rougher for her but she knows the "damned don't cry." You might, though. (Dir: Vincent Sherman, 103 mins.)

Damsel in Distress, A (1937)**½ Fred Astaire, George Burns, Gracie Allen, Joan Fontaine, Ray Noble. RKO gave Astaire and Rogers a vacation from each other, she making "Stage Door," and he this somewhat stodgy George Gershwin-scored musical set in England. Fontaine is the rather wan and young (18) lead, playing an heiress Astaire thinks is a chorus girl. Burns and Allen are on hand in abundance, and even get to sing and dance. The songs, including "A Foggy Day" and "Nice Work If You Can Get It," are superb, and Astaire's closing tap dance on a set of drums is terrific. Hermes Pan's choreography won an Academy Award. (Dir: George Stevens, 101 mins.)

Dance, Girl, Dance (1940)*** Maureen O'Hara, Lucille Ball, Louis Hayward, Virginia Field, Ralph Bellamy. Ball plays a burlesque queen; O'Hara is her friend and colleague, a would-be ballerina. The themes are female friendship and a woman's fulfillment, and it is one of director Dorothy Arzner's most coherent and accomplished films. Original screen story by Vicki Baum. (90 mins.)

Dance Hall (Great Britain, 1950)**½ Natasha Parry, Jane Hylton, Diana Dors, Petula Clark, Kay Kendall. Four factory girls break away from their squalid lives at night when they hang out at the local dance hall. Loosely told melodrama manages some good moments, but is too rambling in structure. (Dir: Charles Crichton, 78 mins.)

Dance Little Lady (Great Britain, 1954)**½ Mai Zetterling, Terence Morgan. Ballerina's career is halted by an accident, but she sees her daughter take up where she left off. Slightly tedious drama is aided by good performances. (Dir: Val Guest, 87 mins.)

Dance of Death (France, 1959)*½ Felix Marten, Michele Mercier. (Dir: Jacques Nahum, 86 mins.)

Dance of Death (Great Britain, 1968)**** Laurence Olivier, Geraldine McEwan, Robert Lang, Carolyn Jones. A filmed record of Laurence Olivier's farewell theatrical performance as the canny, psychotic captain of the August Strindberg play. Though some effort is made to render the treatment cinematic, the effects are pedestrian and the production is marred by some shaky casting in the supporting roles. But Olivier's incarnation of an obsessed man hemorrhaging in his mind is memorable—he seems not to play for the camera but for the gallery, making this perhaps his most accurate transcription of a giant stage role. Not to be missed. (Dir: David Giles, 149 mins.)

Dance of Life, The (1929)**½ Hal Skelly, Nancy Carroll, Dorothy Revier, Ralph Theodore, Oscar Levant. Don't hold your breath for the next time this rarity is on. Based on the Broadway hit "Burlesque," the film does not use the actress who made herself a star with the role on stage—Barbara Stanwyck—instead giving the plum part to the less incisive Carroll. Codirectors John Cromwell and Edward Sutherland have bit parts as a doorkeeper and theater attendant, respectively. Often remade, officially and otherwise, it's a hackneyed plot that could only be redeemed by the best acting. (120 mins.)

Dance with Me, Henry (1956)*½ Bud Abbott, Lou Costello, Gigi Perreau. Last Abbott and Costello film. (Dir: Charles Barton, 79 mins.)

Dancing Co-ed (1939)** Lana Turner, Richard Carlson. Nothing here but Lana Turner in dancing clothes back in 1939 and that should be enough to stir memories in many a red-blooded American male. (Dir: S. Sylvan Simon, 80 mins.)

Dancing Heart, The (W. Germany, 1958)*½

Dancing in Manhattan (1944)**½ Fred Brady, Jeff Donnell. Garbage man finds $5,000, doesn't know the bills are marked to trap blackmailers. Amusing little comedy. (Dir: Henry Levin, 60 mins.)

Dancing in the Dark (1949)*** William Powell, Betsy Drake, Mark Stevens. Powell's delightfully droll performance as an ex-ham turned talent scout gives this musical a big lift. Betsy Drake, as his discovery, is hardly a song-and-dance girl, but no matter—Powell steals the show. (Dir: Irving Reis, 92 mins.)

Dancing Lady (1933)**½ Joan Crawford, Clark Gable, Franchot Tone, Fred Astaire, The Three Stooges, Nelson Eddy. This smart and light Crawford vehicle was the biggest hit of her early career. She climbs the ladder from chorus girl to Broadway star while debating the relative merits of suitors Gable and Tone. In the final production number she gets an assist from a fresh-faced kid from New York—Astaire, in his first screen appearance. Robert Z. Leonard directed, better than usual. (82 mins.)

Dancing on a Dime (1940)**½ Grace McDonald, Robert Paige, Peter Lind Hayes. Out-of-work performers live in an abandoned theatre, try to put on their big show. Likable musical is pleasing fun. (Dir: Joseph Santley, 74 mins.)

Dandy in Aspic, A (Great Britain, 1968)* Laurence Harvey, Mia Farrow. (Dirs: Anthony Mann, Laurence Harvey, 107 mins.)

Dandy, the All-American Girl—See: **Sweet Revenge**

Danger: Diabolik (Italy, 1968)* John Philip Law, Marisa Mell, Michel Piccoli, Terry-Thomas. (Dir: Mario Bava, 99 mins.)

Danger in Paradise (MTV 1977)*½ John Dehner, Ina Balin, Cliff Potts. (Dir: Marvin Chomsky, 106 mins.)

Danger in the Middle East (France, 1959)*½ Françoise Arnoul, Michel Piccoli. (Dir: Michel Clement, 85 mins.)

Danger By My Side (Great Britain, 1962)*½ Maureen Connell, Anthony Oliver. (Dir: Charles Saunders, 63 mins.)

Danger Route (Great Britain, 1968)** Richard Johnson, Carol Lynley. British secret agent ordered to kill a Russian scientist who has defected to the Americans. The agent gets his man (his 31st), but a chase ensues with more double crosses than a game of tick tack toe. (Dir: Seth Holt, 91 mins.)

Danger Signal (1945)** Faye Emerson, Zachary Scott. Corny, Grade B melodrama about a fortune-hunting heel, his women and murder. (Dir: Robert Florey, 78 mins.)

Danger Tomorrow (Great Britain, 1960)** Zena Walker, Robert Urquhart. Strange occurrences threaten a woman's sanity. Fair mystery. (Dir: Terry Bishop, 61 mins.)

Danger Within—See: **Breakout**

Dangerous (1935)**½ Bette Davis, Franchot Tone, Alison Skipworth. Davis plays an alcoholic actress loosely inspired by Jeanne Eagels (Davis would later be loosely inspired by Tallulah Bankhead and Ethel Barrymore, among many). Alfred E. Green's direction is awfully dim, and Hollywood tradition has it that Davis only won her first Oscar as compensation for being denied a nomination the year before for "Of Human Bondage," establishing early on the Academy preference for hindsight over insight. (78 mins.)

Dangerous Age, A (Canada, 1957)** Ben Piazza, Anne Pearson. Young couple in love have difficulty adjusting to the world and its demands. Sincere problem drama adds little to the case, becomes just another picture. (Dir: Sidney J. Furie, 70 mins.)

Dangerous Agent (France, 1953)*½ Eddie Constantine, Colette Dereal. (Dir: Jean Sacha, 88 mins.)

Dangerous Assignment (Great Britain, 1950)*½ Lionel Murton, Pamela Deeming. (Dir: Ben R. Hart, 58 mins.)

Dangerous Blondes (1943)*** Allyn Joslyn, Evelyn Keyes. Mystery writer helps his wife solve the murder of a wealthy matron. More laughs than thrills in this comedy-mystery; well done. (Dir: Leigh Jason, 80 mins.)

Dangerous Charter (1962)*½ Chris Warfield, Sally Fraser. (Dir: Robert Gottschalk, 76 mins.)

Dangerous Crossing (1953)**½ Jeanne Crain, Michael Rennie. Mystery drama which takes place on an ocean liner. Miss Crain is cast as a bride whose husband disappears during the first few hours after they set sail. Some suspense and the acting's good. (Dir: Joseph M. Newman, 75 mins.)

Dangerous Days of Kiowa Jones, The (MTV 1966)** Robert Horton, Diane Baker, Sal Mineo, Nehemiah Persoff. Draggy western about a wandering cowpoke who accedes to the request of a dying lawman to take in two killers. (Dir: Alex March, 83 mins.)

Dangerous Exile (Great Britain, 1957)**½ Louis Jourdan, Belinda Lee. During the Revolution, the small son of Marie Antoinette is secretly smuggled into Wales. Typical over-blown costume drama. (Dir: Brian Desmond Hurst, 90 mins.)

Dangerous Female (1931)** Bebe Daniels, Ricardo Cortez. Earliest version of "The Maltese Falcon," with Cortez as private eye Sam Spade after the mysterious black bird and avenging the death of his partner. Despite antiquated technique Hammett's original plot is strong enough to hold it up. Alternate title: "The Maltese Falcon." (Dir: Roy Del Ruth, 80 mins.)

Dangerous Games (France, 1958)** Jean Servais, Pascale Audret. Teenagers get involved in kidnapping and murder. Fair English-dubbed melodrama. (Dir: Pierre Chenal, 90 mins.)

Dangerous Mission (1954)** Victor Mature, Piper Laurie, William Bendix, Vincent Price, Dennis Weaver. Girl witnesses a gangland killing, flees to Glacier National Park, with both the crooks and the law after her. Good scenery, otherwise mild melodrama. (Dir: Louis King, 75 mins.)

Dangerous Moonlight (Great Britain, 1941)**** Anton Walbrook, Sally Gray. Polish pianist flies for the RAF, is implored by his loved one to stick to music. Superb war drama, finely acted, with excellent music sequences ("Warsaw Concerto"). (Dir: Brian Desmond Hurst, 83 mins.)

Dangerous Partners (1945)**½ James Craig, Signe Hasso. Fairly good Grade B chase melodrama with the object in question a mere four million dollars worth of bonds. (Dir: Edward L. Cahn, 74 mins.)

Dangerous Profession, A (1949)** George Raft, Ella Raines, Pat O'Brien. Bail bondsman clashes with the underworld after a killing. Confused, slow crime melodrama. (Dir: Ted Tetzlaff, 79 mins.)

Dangerous When Wet (1953)** Esther Williams, Fernando Lamas, Jack Carson. Williams swims the English Channel, supported by her cloyingly eccentric all-American family (William Demarest, Charlotte Greenwood, Barbara Whiting) and encouraged by hubby-to-be Lamas. Directed by Charles Walters, an intermittently interesting filmmaker who spent too much of his career on trash like this. (95 mins.)

Dangerous Woman, A (1929)** Olga Baclanova, Clive Brook, Neil Hamilton, Snitz Edwards. The plot of this early Paramount talkie resembles the kind of overheated melodrama that flourished in the silents, but which was to find the added realism of the synchronized sound track a formidable obstacle. Baclanova plays a Russian femme fatale in central East Africa who makes the lives of her husband and assorted other men miserable until they take vigilante action. Rowland V. Lee ("Zoo in Budapest") directed; John Farrow, later an excellent director in his own right, adapted. With Edwards, the great Jewish comedian beloved by all fans of Buster Keaton's '20s features. (66 mins.)

Dangerous Years (1947)** Juvenile delinquent William Halop is on trial for murder, learns that he's really the D.A.'s son. In a very small role can be seen Marilyn Monroe, if one watches closely. Fair juvenile delinquency drama. (Dir: Arthur Pierson, 62 mins.)

Dangerous Youth (Great Britain, 1957)* Frankie Vaughan, George Baker. (Dir: Herbert Wilcox, 98 mins.)

Daniel Boone, Trail Blazer (1956)*½ Bruce Bennett, Lon Chaney. (Dir: Albert C. Gannaway, 90 mins.)

Dante's Inferno (1935)**½ Spencer Tracy, Claire Trevor, Henry B. Walthall. A routine Tracy vehicle with Tracy as a shady promoter—memorable mainly for its ten-minute depiction of a descent into hell and for the spectacular fire set off by two whirling Spanish dancers (one of whom, Rita Cansino, later became Rita Hayworth). (Dir: Harry Lachman, 88 mins.)

Dante's Inferno (Great Britain, MTV 1967)*** Oliver Reed, Christopher Logue, Judith Paris. Ken Russell made his iconoclastic mark first on British television in this fantasy on biographical themes of Dante Gabriel Rossetti, poet and leader of the pre-Raphaelite movement—which, had it not existed, Russell would have had to invent. He does his share of inventing, anyway. Made in 1967, before Russell was expected to shock and outrage, the excesses seem imperatives of his own artistic expression. He hadn't quite found his style yet, but the verve is extraordinary.

Darby O'Gill and the Little People (1959)**½ Albert Sharpe, Janet Munro, Sean Connery, Jimmy O'Dea. Disney presents Irish folklore. Estate caretaker-storyteller Darby O'Gill (Sharpe) is involved in sundry adventures with the leprechauns. Kids might not catch all the dialogue because of the rolling brogue, but the color and attractive decors should hold their interest. (Dir: Robert Stevenson, 93 mins.)

Darby's Rangers (1958)** James Garner, Etchika Choureau. Uneven war drama about a band of heroes led by the hero of them all, Major Wm. Darby, played by James Garner. The supporting cast includes the entire Warner Bros. TV talent roster at that time. (Dir: William Wellman, 121 mins.)

Daredevil, The (1972)** George Montgomery, Terry Moore, Bill Kelly, Cyril Poitier. A heel of a racer becomes a go-between for a dope ring. Montgomery registers strongly as the antihero, and the action scenes are well staged. Cheap production and poor acting by the featured players (with the notable exception of Kelly as the one-armed Huck) keeps this from being a good offbeat item. A novelty is a black mortician (Poitier) as the chief menace. Music by the Brooklyn Bridge group. (Dir: Robert W. Stringer, 70 mins.)

Daring Game (1968)** Lloyd Bridges underwater again, and in the air too, as he messes in a Caribbean political plot. Kids will like it best. With Michael Ansara, Joan Blackman and Nico Minardos. (Dir: Laslo Benedek, 100 mins.)

Daring Young Man (1942)** Joe E. Brown, Marguerite Chapman. Joe E., rejected for military service, becomes a hero by outwitting Nazi spies. O.K. for kids and Joe E. Brown's many fans. (Dir: Frank Strayer, 73 mins.)

Dark, The (1979)**½ William Devane, Cathy Lee Crosby, Vivian Blaine. Gory story of an alien zombie terrorizing Los Angeles also has a psychic theme. Revolves around Devane, a writer of stories

153

of the occult, whose daughter is a victim. Not badly done for its type. (Dir: John Bud Cardos, 92 mins.)

Dark Angel, The (1935)*** Fredric March, Merle Oberon, Herbert Marshall. Remake of a silent film drama about a pair of lovers whose lives are all but destroyed by blindness. Good performances by the cast. (Dir: Sidney Franklin, 110 mins.)

Dark at the Top of the Stairs, The (1960)*** Robert Preston, Dorothy McGuire, Shirley Knight, Angela Lansbury, Eve Arden. William Inge's theatrical reputation has shimmied up and down the critical barometer, and this slightly scrubbed version of his midwestern vision is a faithful representation of an academic version of one of his better works. Delbert Mann's direction is overly careful and deliberate—Inge plays better with a dash of hysteria. The cast is impeccable. The Ravetches adapted. (123 mins.)

Dark City (1950)**½ Charlton Heston, Lizabeth Scott, Viveca Lindfors, Jack Webb. Overblown melodrama about a gambler who becomes a target for murder. Good performances by Heston (his first major film) and Jack Webb lift it above routine. (Dir: William Dieterle, 110 mins.)

Dark Command (1940)***½ John Wayne, Claire Trevor, Walter Pidgeon, Roy Rogers. After the Civil War, the Southwest is terrorized by Quantrill's raiders, until one man puts a stop to it. Big, actionful western drama, colorful, fine cast. (Dir: Raoul Walsh, 94 mins.)

Dark Corner, The (1946)*** Mark Stevens, Lucille Ball, Clifton Webb. A detective is neatly framed for murder in this well played and generally interesting melodrama. Lucy has some good comedy lines as the detective's secretary. (Dir: Henry Hathaway, 99 mins.)

Dark Delusion (1947)**½ Lionel Barrymore, James Craig. One of Dr. Gillespie's assistants cures a girl of mental disorder. Likeable medical drama. (Dir: Willis Goldbeck, 90 mins.)

Dark Eyes of London (Great Britain, 1939)** Bela Lugosi, Hugh Williams, Greta Gynt. An Edgar Wallace potboiler forms the basis for this low-budget horror film, which has quite a reputation among genre fans and admirers of Lugosi, who plays a proprietor of a home for the blind who is involved in an elaborate plot to murder victims for their insurance; his modus operandi is a giant who drowns them. Gynt is the lady in distress. (Dir: Walter Summers, 73 mins.)

Dark Horse, The (1946)**½ Philip Terry, Ann Savage. War vet innocently becomes a political contender, makes it rough for the big boss. Pleasant comedy with a fine comedy performance by Donald MacBride as the big shot. (Dir: Will Jason, 59 mins.)

Dark Intruder (1965)** Leslie Nielsen, Judi Meredith. Sleuth steps in to aid the police in solving a mysterious series of murders.

Okay vest-pocket mystery, short in running time, looks as if it were made for a TV series. (Dir: Harvey Hart, 59 mins.)

Dark Man, The (Great Britain, 1951)**½ Maxwell Reed, Natasha Parry. A witness to a murder committed during a robbery is chased by the killer, since she is the only one alive who can identify him. Okay thriller has its share of suspense. (Dir: Jeffrey Dell, 91 mins.)

Dark Mirror, The (1946)***½ Olivia de Havilland, Lew Ayres. A doctor has to figure out which twin sister is normal, and which is a demented murderess. Tight, suspenseful mystery, excellent. (Dir: Robert Siodmak, 101 mins.)

Dark of the Sun (Great Britain, 1968)** Congo mercenary (Rod Taylor) undertakes a dangerous mission: rescue citizens of a besieged town, and bring back valuable diamonds. Plenty of action helps a threadbare script. With Jim Brown, Yvette Mimieux, Kenneth More. (Dir: Jack Cardiff, 101 mins.)

Dark Passage (1947)**½ Humphrey Bogart, Lauren Bacall, Bruce Bennett, Agnes Moorehead. Pretty dumb, but properly moody and atmospheric late '40s thriller, with escaped convict Bogart undergoing a ridiculous brand of plastic surgery and recuperating in Bacall's apartment until he can prove himself innocent of murdering his wife. Delmer Daves directs with an overabundance of film noir zeal. (106 mins.)

Dark Past (1949)*** William Holden, Lee J. Cobb, Nina Foch. Psychiatrist breaks down the resistance of a desperate killer holding him captive. Remake of "Blind Alley" has plenty of suspense, good performances. (Dir: Rudolph Maté, 75 mins.)

Dark Purpose (U.S.A.-Italy-France, 1963)* Shirley Jones, Rossano Brazzi, George Sanders, Micheline Presle. (Dir: George Marshall, Vittorio Sala, 97 mins.)

Dark Side of Innocence (MTV 1976)* Joanna Pettet, Anne Archer, John Anderson, Lawrence Casey, Kim Hunter. (Dir: Jerry Thorpe, 72 mins.)

Dark Victory (1939)*** Bette Davis, George Brent, Humphrey Bogart, Geraldine Fitzgerald, Ronald Reagan. For better or worse, this is what most people mean when they refer to a "Bette Davis movie." She stars as a spoiled Long Island socialite who discovers she's dying of a brain tumor and packs a lifetime into one glorious summer. It's trash, but Davis finds the emotional validity in the character, and director Edmund Goulding is well attuned to the quirkier tendencies of the material. Bogart is wildly miscast as a Lawrencian stable groom. (106 mins.)

Dark Victory (MTV 1976)*** Elizabeth Montgomery, Anthony Hopkins. Elizabeth Montgomery chose the role of the doomed heroine in Bette Davis's weepy 1939 melodrama as a vehicle for her talents. It's been dusted off, brought up to date and given a handsome production. Concerns a successful, beautiful television executive who discovers she has a short time to live and falls in love with her doctor (British actor Anthony Hopkins). Don't be misled, the film isn't all that downbeat. Ms. Montgomery has seldom been better, and the script avoids making too many excursions into mawkish sentimentality. (Dir: Robert Butler, 144 mins.)

Dark Waters (1944)**½ Merle Oberon, Franchot Tone, Thomas Mitchell. A girl returns to her Southern mansion after a shipboard disaster, where she becomes convinced someone is trying to drive her insane. Occasionally suspenseful, generally undistinguished thriller. (Dir: Andre de Toth, 90 mins.)

Darker Than Amber (1970)***½ Rod Taylor, Suzy Kendall, Theodore Bikel. Tough mystery action with more brawn than brain as Taylor plays author John D. MacDonald's character Travis McGee, who lives on a houseboat in Florida and only comes out to play detective or gain revenge on a criminal. Travis falls in love with a girl whose life is endangered by some mobsters, and in true form takes off after them. Well directed by Robert Clouse. Colorful location filming in Florida and the Caribbean add extra flavor. (Dir: Robert Clouse, 97 mins.)

Darling (Great Britain, 1965)**** Julie Christie, Dirk Bogarde, Laurence Harvey. A quite remarkable film commenting on the manners, morals and mores of our time and richly deserving of all the awards it got, including the Academy Award for Julie Christie's stunning performance which was given, and the Academy Award for best film which it did not receive. Perceptive, cynical, deftly written portrait of a young London model who decides to climb the social ladder quickly by jumping, in rather unceremonious fashion, in and out of assorted beds. Brilliantly directed by John Schlesinger, imaginatively edited, and featuring the radiant performance of the ravishing Miss Christie, this is a moving, often amusing and invariably honest film. (Dir: John Schlesinger, 122 mins.)

Darling, How Could You (1951)** Joan Fontaine, John Lund, Mona Freeman. Sentimental drama of an imaginative girl whose fantasies nearly wreck her parents' domestic life. Inoffensive but overly sweet, slow-moving. (Dir: Mitchell Leisen, 96 mins.)

Darling Lili (1970)½ Julie Andrews, Rock Hudson, Jeremy Kemp, Lance Percival. (Dir: Blake Edwards, 136 mins.)

Date at Midnight (Great Britain, 1959)** Paul Carpenter, Jean Aubrey. Man with a past is suspected of foul play when a tragedy occurs. Ordinary melodrama. (Dir: Godfrey Grayson, 57 mins.)

Date Bait (1960)* Gary Clarke, Marlo Ryan. Filmed in Missouri. (Dir: O'Dale Ireland, 71 mins.)

Date with Death, A (1959)* Robert Clarke, Liz Renay, Gerald Mohr. (Dir: Harold Daniels, 81 mins.)

Date with Judy, A (1948)**½ Elizabeth Taylor, Jane Powell, Wallace Beery. The youngsters may enjoy this juvenile comedy but outside of some good musical numbers and the sight of Elizabeth Taylor as she reached physical maturity, it's not much of a film. (Dir: Richard Thorpe, 113 mins.)

Daughter of Dr. Jekyll (1957)* Gloria Talbott, Arthur Shields. (Dir: Edgar Ulmer, 69 mins.)

Daughter of Mata Hari, The—See: **Mata Hari's Daughter**

Daughter of Rosie O'Grady, The (1950)**½ June Haver, Gordon MacRae, James Barton. A gay, tuneful turn of the century musical comedy film. Miss Haver and Mr. MacRae sing and dance delightfully and take care of the romance department. James Barton plays June Haver's father, who forbids her to seek a career on the stage. Look for Debbie Reynolds in a small role as June's sister. (Dir: David Butler, 104 mins.)

Daughter of the Mind (MTV 1969)**½ Gene Tierney, Ray Milland, Don Murray, Ed Asner, John Carradine. Feature based on Paul Gallico's book "The Hand of Mary Constable." Ray Milland is cast as a professor of cybernetics who claims he is visited by his recently killed young daughter's spirit. The plot thickens when government officials become involved and a professor of parapsychology (Don Murray) also enters the picture. (Dir: Walter Grauman, 73 mins.)

Daughters Courageous (1939)*** John Garfield, Claude Rains, Lane Sisters. Trying to cash in on the box office success of "Four Daughters," they assembled the same cast and put them through their paces again. They would have made a sequel but they killed Garfield in the original. Good acting still makes it passable. (Dir: Michael Curtiz, 120 mins.)

Daughters of Darkness (Belgium-France-West Germany-Italy, 1971)*** Delphine Seyrig, Daniele Ouimet, Andrea Rau. Stylish vampire nonsense, with a deluxe high-camp performance by Seyrig as the well-accoutered Bloody Countess who takes on a newlywed (and very Aryan) couple for her sanguinary lease on life. The Belgian director Harry Kumel skillfully manipulates decor, blood, and the day's standards of porn. Rau, fresh off the cover of "Lui," strikingly portrays Seyrig's conscientious assistant. (96 mins.)

Daughters of Destiny (France, 1955)** Claudette Colbert, Michele Morgan, Martine Carol. Triple tale of three women of history and how their fortunes are changed—Queen Elizabeth, Joan of Arc, and Lysistrata. Elaborate production negated by plodding script, sluggish movement. (Dir: Marcel Dagliero, 94 mins.)

Daughters of Joshua Cabe (MTV 1972)** Buddy Ebsen, Sandra Dee, Lesley Warren, Karen Valentine, Jack Elam. Moderately entertaining Western comedy-drama, with Ebsen as a rancher-trapper who has to come up with three long-lost daughters in order to keep his land when a new homesteaders' law is passed. Elam, as a grizzled sidekick of Ebsen's, steals the show. (Dir: Philip Leacock, 72 mins.)

Daughters of Joshua Cabe Return, The (MTV 1975)** Dan Dailey, Dub Taylor, Ronne Troup, Carl Betz. If you enjoyed the antics of the three less-than-respectable girls who are hired to portray the daughters of a wily rancher in the first film, here's the follow-up with a complete cast change. Dan Dailey heads the cast in the role of the rancher, created by Buddy Ebsen the first time around. (Dir: David Lowell Rich, 72 mins.)

Daughters of Satan (1972)*½ Tom Selleck, Barra Grant. (Dir: Hollingsworth Morse, 90 mins.)

David and Bathsheba (1951)**½ Gregory Peck, Susan Hayward. Typical Biblical epic with all the stops pulled—lavish sets, sumptuous costumes, posing actors and wooden dialogue. Women will buy the love story aspects of the tale of King David (Greg Peck) and the ravishing Bathsheba (Susan Hayward) and the adventure-seeking males have a few battle scenes to keep their attention. (Dir: Henry King, 116 mins.)

David and Goliath (Italy, 1961)** Orson Welles, Ivo Payer. Italian-made version of the Biblical tale. Usual stuff. (Dirs: Richard Pottier, Ferdinando Baldi, 95 mins.)

David and Lisa (1962)**** Keir Dullea, Janet Margolin. Sensitively written, beautifully acted and altogether touching story of two mentally disturbed youngsters finding happiness and faith. Low budget "sleeper" was Academy Award nominee for first time director Frank Perry. (94 mins.)

David Copperfield (1935)***½ W. C. Fields, Lionel Barrymore, Edna May Oliver, Basil Rathbone, Roland Young, Freddie Bartholomew. There are enough character epiphanies emergent under George Cukor's direction to make this among the most memorable of Dickens adaptations, though sometimes lapsing into tasteful dullness. Fields is Micawber, Rathbone is Murdstone, Young is Heep, and Oliver is Aunt Betsy. Even Barrymore's Barkis is palatable. (133 mins.)

David Copperfield (Great Britain, 1970)*** Ralph Richardson, Michael Redgrave, Edith Evans. Marvelous film. Charles Dickens' novel comes to life with inspired casting in a first-class production. (W. C. Fields fans may even forget the master's Mr. Micawber in the old MGM picture.) There are flaws in this adaptation, and Dickens purists may object to some of it, but most viewers—young and old alike—will be enthralled. The cast of British

stalwarts are almost all superb. (Dir: Delbert Mann, 100 mins.)

David Holzman's Diary (1968)*** David Holzman, Eileen Dietz, Louise Levine. An imaginative low-budget black and white independently made feature about movie-making and movie-makers. There's one perceptive street-corner interview with a tart, and inventive touches throughout. Written, produced and directed by Jim McBride on location in New York. (74 mins.)

Davy Crockett, Indian Scout (1950)** George Montgomery, Ellen Drew. Army scout looks into a series of wagon train attacks. Average out-door action drama, those marauding Injuns again. (Dir: Lew Landers, 71 mins.)

Dawn at Socorro (1954)**½ Piper Laurie, Rory Calhoun, David Brian. A good cast and a better than average western plot make this one entertaining. Calhoun plays a gunfighter who's forced to think about his life when his health, if not his trigger finger, starts to slip. (Dir: George Sherman, 81 mins.)

Dawn of the Dead (1979)* Gaylen Ross, Ken Foree, Scott Reiniger, David Emge. (Dir: George A. Romero, 125 mins.)

Dawn Patrol, The (1930)**** Richard Barthelmess, Douglas Fairbanks, Jr., Neil Hamilton. Seldom seen American classic. First sound film of the great director Howard Hawks, and the first of his extraordinary '30s dramas in which characters placed in hellish environments (here, WW I in France) cope by quietly and unobtrusively repressing emotion, with the narrative mimicking their stoicism. The aerial scenes are truly spectacular. (112 mins.)

Dawn Patrol, The (1938)***½ Errol Flynn, Basil Rathbone, David Niven. Exciting tale of the men of Britain's Royal Flying Corps during World War I. Conflict concerns the torment of making command decisions and sending your comrades to certain death just to gain an objective. Remake of 1930 film. (Dir: Edmund Goulding, 120 mins.)

Dawn: Portrait of a Teenage Runaway (MTV 1976)**½ Eve Plumb, Bo Hopkins, William Schallert. A film set on Hollywood Boulevard with all its seaminess and oddball characters, focusing on what may happen to teenagers who come to Hollywood and can't find work. About a teeny-bopper (Plumb) and her pimp (Hopkins). (Dir: Randal Kleiser, 102 mins.)

Day and the Hour, The (France-Italy, 1963)*** Simone Signoret, Stuart Whitman, Genevieve Page. Old-fashioned, uneven, but frequently absorbing thanks to veteran director Rene Clement. Melodrama set in Nazi-occupied France during World War II. Signoret's husband has been nailed by the Nazis and she befriends Whitman. Exciting scene aboard the train to Toulouse. Film buffs please note—one of the two assistant directors on this film was the brilliant Costa-Gavras who went on to helm "Z" and "The Confession." Partially dubbed. (Dir: Rene Clement, 115 mins.)

Day at the Races, A (1937)***½ The Marx Brothers, Maureen O'Sullivan, Allan Jones, Margaret Dumont. The first sign of the Marx Brothers' decline. Often very good when Groucho is given a free hand, and often very bad when there is no one in evidence to say, "Cut!" (Dir: Sam Wood, 111 mins.)

Day Christ Died, The (MTV 1980)**½ Chris Sarandon, Colin Blakely, Keith Michell, Jonathan Price, Barrie Houghton, Hope Lange. Reasonably interesting, well-acted docudrama about the events of the few days before Christ's crucifixion. This is a less reverential, rather more daring portrait of Jesus than some other efforts. There has been some controversy about the historical accuracy of this interpretation. Watch it and decide for yourself. Filmed on location in Tunisia. (Dir: James Cellan Jones, 104 mins.)

Day For Night (France, 1972)**** Francois Truffaut, Jacqueline Bisset, Jean-Pierre Léaud, Valentina Cortesa, Jean-Pierre Aumont. Francois Truffaut's joyous, exhilarating comedy, an affectionate satire on the art and madness of making movies. Truffaut himself plays a film director named Ferrand and he tells his crew, "Before starting I hope to make a fine movie. Halfway through, I hope to make a movie." Well, the movie in a movie is called "Meet Pamela," and we don't ever see the finished version. But the complete "Day For Night" is a lighthearted, charming beauty, faultlessly acted by Truffaut himself and the rest of a carefully chosen cast. Truffaut co-authored the screenplay. Oscar as Best Foreign Film. (116 mins.)

Day in the Death of Joe Egg, A (Great Britain, 1972)**½ Alan Bates, Janet Suzman, Peter Bowles. What worked exultantly on the stage flounders into kitchen sink rancor that isn't ameliorated by let's-joke-our-way-through-a-heartbreaking-situation sentimentality. The parents of a spastic child make cruel jokes, and it's really just a black-humored variant on the stiff upper lip. Bates and Suzman do fine work, but the impact of the roles is dwarfed by the proximity of the camera, whereas on stage, flamboyance can carry the day. (Dir: Peter Medak, 106 mins.)

Day of Fury, A (1956)** Dale Robertson, Jock Mahoney. The old plot gimmick of the marshal and an outlaw being friends from the past gets more mileage in this slow moving opus. Robertson is well cast as a charming villain who finally gets his comeuppance. (Dir: Harmon Jones, 80 mins.)

Day of the Animals (1977)* Christopher George, Leslie Nielsen, Michael Ansara. Yarn about how aerosol sprays turn some animals into man-killers. George and Ansara play the fearless leaders of a wilderness tour. Pointless and repulsive. (Dir: William Girdler, 95 mins.)

Day of the Bad Man (1958)** Fred MacMurray, Joan Weldon, John Ericson. Circuit judge has to sentence a convicted killer to death and face the rage of the man's brothers. Western goes in for suspense, succeeds in being merely routine. (Dir: Harry Keller, 81 mins.)

Day of the Dolphin, The (1973)**½ George C. Scott, Trish Van Devere, Paul Sorvino, Fritz Weaver. Misguided fable about the efforts of a dedicated scientist (Scott) trying to train a dolphin to talk, while simultaneously participating in a counter-intelligence scheme involving political assassination. Buck Henry's screenplay touches a number of genres without securing a firm foothold in any particular one—the result is occasional comedy or suspense but never genuine audience involvement. Some extraordinary scenes give the real life sounds made by dolphins swimming and playing and "communicating with each other." (Dir: Mike Nichols, 104 mins.)

Day of the Evil Gun (MTV 1968)**½ Glenn Ford, Arthur Kennedy, Dean Jagger, Nico Minardos. Reasonably suspenseful western about a search for women kidnaped by Apaches. Good performances. A made-for-TV pic, although this was actually released to theaters first. (Dir: Jerry Thorpe, 93 mins.)

Day of the Jackal, The (Great Britain-France, 1973)***½ Edward Fox, Cyril Cusack, Delphine Seyrig. High suspense as an assassin (Fox) is hired by French generals to kill Charles de Gaulle. Intensive manhunt is juxtaposed with Fox's preparation for the killing. Acting and the fine European locations are the highpoints. Fox's portrait of the ruthless, anonymous killer is necessarily unemotional, and he's backed by a strong international cast. (Dir: Fred Zinnemann, 141 mins.)

Day of the Locust, The (1975)***½ Donald Sutherland, Karen Black, Burgess Meredith, William Atherton, Geraldine Page. Memorable, harrowing, long-awaited adaptation of Nathanael West's 1939 novel, a crystalization of his long Hollywood experience as a screen writer. There are shortcomings in "Locust"—Karen Black is far too old, e.g., to play the vulnerable, 17-year-old heroine of West's novel. William Atherton is impressive in his debut in a major role playing an impressionable "civilized" young Yale screen writer trying to cope and succeed in Hollywood circa '38. Schlesinger builds to an unforgettable climax of a movie premiere which becomes a riotous nightmare. Burgess Meredith won an Academy nomination for his endearing performance as a washed-up vaudevillian still selling dreams. Cinematographer Conrad Hall deserves special credit, and got an Academy Award nomination for his work. Screenplay by Waldo Salt. (Dir: John Schlesinger, 140 mins.)

Day of the Outlaw (1959)** Robert Ryan, Burl Ives, Tina Louise. Outlaws, with their leader seriously wounded and the Cavalry in hot pursuit, take over a western community and terrorize the townspeople. Gloomy western, some good blizzard scenes, adequate performances. (Dir: Andre de Toth, 90 mins.)

Day of the Triffids (Great Britain, 1963)** Howard Keel, Nicole Maurey, Janette Scott, Keron Moore. Intelligent dialogue and interesting direction (by Steve Sekely) have earned this science fiction film a good reputation. Blinding meteor showers rain seeds upon the earth, which grow into man-eating plants. Screenplay by Philip Yordan, based on a story by John Wyndham. Good special effects. (93 mins.)

Day of Wrath (Denmark, 1943)**** Lisbeth Movin, Thorkild Roose. Director Carl Dreyer's exploration of the persecution of witches in the 17th century has staggering atmospheric concentration and formal beauty. Critics have found the film ambiguous in its treatment of the reality of evil; but considerations of directorial conviction cannot mar the film's immense power and brilliantly realized sense of torment. (105 mins.)

Day that Shook the World, The (Italy-Yugoslavia, 1976)*½ Christopher Plummer, Florinda Bolkan, Maximilian Schell. (Dir: Veljko Bulajic, 111 mins.)

Day the Earth Caught Fire, The (Great Britain, 1962)***½ Edward Judd, Janet Munro, Leo McKern. In the front rank of sci-fi thrillers, this one is almost too realistic for comfort. Nuclear tests at the North and South Poles shift the earth's orbit, send the planet plummeting toward the sun. The tension runs high throughout, thanks to expert scripting and direction. (Dir: Val Guest, 90 mins.)

Day the Earth Moved, The (MTV 1974)** Jackie Cooper, Cleavon Little, William Windom, Beverly Garland. Another crisis film about a series of unexplained earthquakes. Jackie Cooper and Cleavon Little are a pair of aerial photographers who notice some suspicious blurs in photos they have taken. Moderately engrossing. (Dir: Robert Michael Lewis, 72 mins.)

Day the Earth Stood Still, The (1951)*** Michael Rennie, Patricia Neal, Hugh Marlowe, Sam Jaffe. Like most of the work of director Robert Wise, this slickly constructed science fiction film falls in the middle range of excellence. Rennie, though, was born to play his part, essentially a nonacting, sleekly tailored visitor from another planet whose mission to Earth carries a warning with it. Smooth and atmospheric. (92 mins.)

Day the Fish Came Out, The (Greece-Great Britain, 1967)* Tom Courtenay, Candice Bergen, Sam Wanamaker, Colin Blakely. (Dir: Michael Cacoyannis, 109 mins.)

Day the Sky Exploded, The (Germany, 1958)*½ Paul Hubschmid, Madeleine Fischer. (Dir: Paolo Heusch, 80 mins.)

Day the World Ended, The (1956)*½ Richard Denning, Lori Nelson. (Dir: Roger Corman, 81 mins.)

Day They Robbed the Bank of England, The (Great Britain, 1960)*** Peter O'Toole, Hugh Griffith, Elizabeth Sellars, Aldo Ray. "They" are Irish dissidents, who try the big heist in 1901. Considerable suspense in this crime yarn. O'Toole shows the promise fulfilled later, portraying the arm of the law. (Dir: John Guillermin, 85 mins.)

Day to Remember, A (Great Britain, 1953)**½ Joan Rice, Donald Sinden. The part-time owner of an English pub prepares for an outing to France. Very British, mild comedy. (Dir: Ralph Thomas, 92 mins.)

Daybreak (Great Britain, 1946)** Ann Todd, Eric Portman. The life and loves of an executioner are on exhibition in this melodrama. Dull film fare. (Dir: Compton Bennett, 81 mins.)

Daydreamer, The (1966)*** Cyril Ritchard, Paul O'Keefe, Ray Bolger. A very entertaining animated and live musical adventure. Paul O'Keefe plays a young Hans Christian Andersen who has many adventures with a series of wonderful characters from the Andersen fairy tales. Voices are supplied by such stars as Tallulah Bankhead, Victor Borge, Burl Ives, and Terry-Thomas. (Dir: Jules Bass, 98 mins.)

Daydreamer, The (Le Distrait) (France, 1975)**½ Pierre Richard, Bernard Blier, Marie Christine Barrault, Maria Pacome. Pierre Richard wrote, directed, and starred in this comedy about a young man whose apprenticeship at a Paris ad agency leads to bumbling chaos. When Richard reins in his tendency to cute pathos, he can be an adept physical comedian and plausible romantic leading man, a potent combination. Not quite Cary Grant, but how many have we got these days, with Gene Wilder vulgarizing himself out of consideration? (90 mins.)

Days and Nights in the Forest (India, 1969)***½ One of the most interesting works of Indian director Satyajit Ray (the Apu trilogy). Tells the story of four young men from the city who take a vacation in the country, meet two young women, and generally reveal themselves to be representatives of modern India torn between tradition and contemporary society. Ray accumulates many nice small moments. (120 mins.)

Days of Glory (1944)**½ Gregory Peck, Tamara Toumanova. Russian guerrillas beat back the Nazi enemy. Slow moving war drama. Well acted. Peck's film debut. (Dir: Jacques Tourneur, 86 mins.)

Days of Heaven (1978)**** Richard Gere, Brooke Adams, Linda Manz, Sam Shepard, Robert Wilke. Superbly photographed work of art (Nestor Almendros and

Haskell Wexler) in which the visual images dwarf the simple story line. Writer-director Terrence Malick, in his second film ("Badlands" was his first stunner), uses the two cinematographers to achieve a visual quality rarely seen in American films. Set in Texas in 1916 (and shot in Alberta, Canada), it is the story of a group of farmworkers and their relations with the sickly owner of the land. A locust plague is a stunning highlight. Manz narrates and co-stars. Excellent use of sound. (95 mins.)

Days of 36 (Greece, 1972)** George Kiritsis, Tharos Grammenos. Tries, without much success, to repeat the techniques of "Z" in this story of a political episode in Athens in 1936 at the beginning of the dictatorship. Does create some feeling of how a mood of terror and neo-fascism is created in a populace. Written and directed by Theo Angelopoulos. English subtitles. (110 mins.)

Days of Thrills and Laughter (1961)***½ Third compilation film made by Robert Youngson featuring silent movie clips, and some of it is fabulous. Scenes of comedy and excitement, ranging from Charlie Chaplin, Laurel and Hardy, the Keystone Kops and Fatty Arbuckle to Douglas Fairbanks and Pearl White. Some little-seen gems in this collection of early movie chuckles and thrills. (93 mins.)

Days of Wine and Roses (1962)***½ Lee Remick, Jack Lemmon, Charles Bickford, Jack Klugman. Director Blake Edwards's somber study of alcoholism striking the perfect American couple (Remick and Lemmon) seems far removed from his comic masterpieces, but the theme is the same: how to live in a hostile world. The first part of the film, developing the couple's courtship, is richer than the later bathos and slow descent, though the performances of the four principals are perfect. (117 mins.)

Dayton's Devils (1968)** Leslie Nielsen, Lainie Kazan, Rory Calhoun. Action and romantic interest. An ex-Army colonel trains a team of experts in order to pull a $1.5 million heist at a Strategic Air Command base. Routine. This was, unfortunately, Lainie Kazan's film debut, but she comes off well singing "Sunny." (Dir: Jack Shea, 103 mins.)

De L'Amour (France, 1965)**½ Anna Karina, Michel Piccoli, Elsa Martinelli, Jean Sorel. Free adaptation of Stendhal's book to a modern-day setting: a series of vignettes on love and seduction. Amusing fluff. (Dir: Jean Aurel, 90 mins.)

Dead Are Not Silent, The (1978)*** The two most publicized crimes of the Pinochet regime, the murder of de Toha by starvation in a Chilean hospital and the assassination of Orlando Letelier in downtown Washington, are powerfully exposed in this documentary.

Dead Don't Die, The (MTV 1975)½ George Hamilton, Ray Milland, Joan Blondell,

Linda Cristal, Ralph Meeker. (Dir: Curtis Harrington, 72 mins.)

Dead End (1937)***½ Sylvia Sidney, Joel McCrea, Humphrey Bogart, the Dead End Kids (who later became the Bowery Boys), Claire Trevor, Marjorie Main. The key film in Hollywood's shift from romanticizing gangsters to blaming the environment for producing delinquency. Sidney Kingsley's popular play became, under William Wyler's directorial hand, a series of vignettes about "real life" in the Hollywoodized, studio-built streets (where little girls stick their tongues out at little boys, little boys stick their tongues out at cops, and young men say things like "What chance has a guy got in a place like this?"). (93 mins.)

Dead Eyes of London (Germany, 1961)*½ Karin Baal, Joachim Fuchsberger. (Dir: Alfred Vohrer, 104 mins.)

Dead Heat on a Merry-Go-Round (1966)***½ James Coburn, Camilla Sparv. James Coburn is well cast as one of the great con artists of all time. After he manages to win a parole from prison, Coburn sets up an ingenious bank heist, marries a gorgeous girl, impersonates about half-a-dozen characters, robs some wealthy dames, pulls off the bank job and, of course, gets away with it all. It's entertaining from start to finish, thanks to Coburn's flip, charming performance, and to writer-director Bernard Girard. (104 mins.)

Dead Man on the Run (MTV 1975)** Peter Graves, Tom Rosqui, Mills Watson. Graves stars in this violent action series pilot, filmed in New Orleans. The personable Mr. Graves gives chase around the old, colorful river city. (Dir: Bruce Bilson, 72 mins.)

Dead Man's Chest (Great Britain, 1965)** John Thaw, Ann Firbank, John Meillon. Two young journalists devise a publicity stunt wherein one is to play dead in a trunk. But the trunk is stolen, leading to a charge of murder. Competent mystery melodrama provides enough twists in its short running time. (Dir: Patrick Dromgoole, 59 mins.)

Dead Men Tell No Tales (MTV 1971)** Christopher George, Judy Carne. As an attractive young couple, George and Miss Carne play hide-and-seek with hoods in this moderately entertaining film. (Dir: Walter Grauman, 73 mins.)

Dead of Night (Great Britain, 1946)**** Michael Redgrave, Googie Withers, Mervyn Johns. A man who has had a strange dream visits the country, where other guests relate how some dream of theirs has had its basis in fact. Fine spine-tingling episodic thriller, a true suspense-rouser. The sequence with Redgrave is especially spellbinding. (Dirs: Cavalcanti, Charles Crichton, Basil Dearden, Robert Hamer, 102 mins.)

Dead Pigeon on Beethoven Street (1973)**½ Glenn Corbett, Christa Lang, Anton

Diffring. A film by the creator of "cinema-fist," director Sam Fuller. Made in Germany on a tiny budget, and only released for one or two dates in the Midwest. Director Sam Fuller is an audacious specialist in violence (a shoot-out in a maternity ward), political sloganeering, and backwoods existentialism. Corbett stars as a detective trying to break up an international blackmail ring; Stephane Audran makes a brief appearance as a lesbian named (ominously) Dr. Bogdanovich. With Christa Lang (Fuller's wife). (90 mins.)

Dead Reckoning (1947)**½ Humphrey Bogart, Lizabeth Scott. Director John Cromwell's waxworks mise-en-scène spoils most of the fun in this minor film noir, with Bogart donning raincoat to track the killer of his war buddy. Scott is no Lauren Bacall. (100 mins.)

Dead Ringer (1964)**½ Bette Davis, Karl Malden, Jean Hagen, Peter Lawford, Phil Carey. Paul Henreid, Davis's romantic co-star, directed a piece of guignol with Davis in another double role; the director has one of the two killed off with an ax. It all calls for some high style that is lacking in this rambling narrative. (115 mins.)

Dead Run (France-Italy, 1969)**½ Peter Lawford, Ira Furstenberg. There's enough plot in this superspy versus spy versus CIA agent yarn for a dozen films. Peter Lawford is the topcoat-clad agent who is hot on the trail of an international crime organization which steals top U.S. documents for resale to an enemy power. The on-location filming in Berlin, Munich, and Paris at least offers a vicarious scenic tour for home viewers. (Director: Christian-Jaque, 97 mins.)

Dead to the World (1961)* Reedy Talton, Jana Pearce. (Dir: Nicholas Webster, 87 mins.)

Deadfall (Great Britain, 1968)*½ Michael Caine, Giovanna Ralli. With Eric Portman, Nanette Newman. (Dir: Bryan Forbes, 120 mins.)

Deadlier Than the Male (France, 1957)**½ Jean Gabin, Daniele Delorme. Well acted (mainly by Gabin) drama about a young girl who plots to marry and murder her mother's ex-husband. Sounds provocative but not in the league of top French suspense shockers. (Dir: Julien Duvivier, 104 mins.)

Deadlier Than the Male (Great Britain, 1967)**½ Richard Johnson, Elke Sommer, Sylva Koscina. The return of Bulldog Drummond (Johnson) as the hardy sleuth comes up against a pair of beautiful but deadly assassins (Sommer & Koscina). Amusing in a lowbrow bulldog way. (Ronald Colman first played Bulldog in the 1929 opus "Bulldog Drummond"). With Suzanna Leigh, Steve Carlson. (Dir: Ralph Thomas, 101 mins.)

Deadliest Season, The (MTV 1977)**½ Michael Moriarty, Kevin Conway, Meryl Streep, Andrew Duggan, Patrick O'Neal,

Sully Boyar. Provocative drama, extremely well written by Ernest Kinoy, about the world of professional ice hockey and the bloodthirsty, violent sport it has become to attract paying audiences and TV watchers. Moriarty gives a well-rounded performance as the run-of-the-mill hockey player who decides to become a "goon"—someone who incites mayhem and violence during a game. When he accidentally kills another player during a game, he is arrested and tried. One of the few dramas to deal with the way TV is brutalizing our sports and our society. (Dir: Robert Markowitz, 110 mins.)

Deadliest Sin (Great Britain, 1955)** Sydney Chaplin, Audrey Dalton. A man is marked for death when he attempts to confess an accidental shooting. Grim, slow melodrama. (Dir: Ken Hughes, 75 mins.)

Deadline, U.S.A. (1952)*** Humphrey Bogart, Kim Hunter, Ethel Barrymore. Engrossing newspaper drama without the usual "city room" phoniness. Bogart is excellent as the editor of a large city paper who has to fight the underworld and keep the paper's publisher, superbly portrayed by the late Miss Barrymore, from throwing in the towel and selling out. The scenes between these two stars are standouts. Kim Hunter is wasted in a small role as Bogart's ex-wife. (Dir: Richard Brooks, 87 mins.)

Deadlock (1969)*** Leslie Nielsen, Hari Rhodes. Better-than-average, hard-hitting police drama about racial tensions in the ghetto of a large west coast city. Well produced action yarn with a good feel for earthy jargon and strong performances by Leslie Nielsen as a fair but firm police lieutenant, and Hari Rhodes as the ambitious Negro district attorney with his eye on the Senate. The scenes between Rhodes and Nielsen are the meatiest of the film, but watch for talented Ruby Dee in one scene playing a prostitute being questioned about the murder. Made as a pilot film for a TV series. (Dir: Lamont Johnson, 99 mins.)

Deadly Affair (Great Britain, 1967)*** James Mason, Simone Signoret, Maximilian Schell, Lynn Redgrave. Engrossing detective drama set amid the world of espionage and agents. James Mason is excellent as a British agent who sets out to uncover the hidden facts behind a British government employee's suicide. The plot twists and turns and, although you may be a bit ahead of the action at times, the film sustains interest. In addition to Mason, other top performances include Simone Signoret as a deeply troubled woman and Harry Andrews as a detective. Sidney Lumet directed the yarn based on the John le Carré novel "Call for the Dead." (Dir: Sidney Lumet, 107 mins.)

Deadly Bees, The (Great Britain, 1967)**½ Frank Finlay, Suzanna Leigh. Based on H. F. Heard's horror classic "A Taste for Honey," this starts off well, but disintegrates into stark melodrama before the finale. It's all about a beekeeper who trains a swarm of giant killer bees, and a young lady who almost becomes a victim. (Dir: Freddie Francis, 85 mins.)

Deadly Companions, The (1961)*** Maureen O'Hara, Brian Keith, Steve Cochran. A gunslinger escorts a dance hall hostess through Apache territory on a perilous journey. Good western with a script above the usual run, expert direction, capable performances. (Dir: Sam Peckinpah, 90 mins.)

Deadly Decision (Germany, 1957)**½ O. E. Hasse, Adrian Hoven. Well-made film telling the remarkable true story of Canaris, a top spy who had the Nazis fooled. O. E. Hasse and a fine German cast make the film tense and exciting. (Dir: Alfred Weidenmann, 93 mins.)

Deadly Decoy, The (France, 1962)*½ Roger Hanin, Roger Dumas. Dubbed in English. (Dir: Maurice Labro, 90 mins.)

Deadly Dream, The (MTV 1971)**½ Lloyd Bridges, Janet Leigh, Carl Betz, Leif Erickson. Bridges wanders through a nightmare world and his own seemingly real one . . . but the question posed here is "which world is the real one?" The strange film builds interest following Bridges, a brilliant scientist, as he goes slowly mad. Leigh, as his wife, looks sensational. (Dir: Alf Kjellin, 72 mins.)

Deadly Game, The (MTV 1976)**½ David Birney, Allen Garfield, Walter McGinn, Lane Bradbury. A pilot for a TV series with Birney taking over the role of Serpico, the famous New York cop who had the nerve to finger corruption within the Police Department. Birney is no Al Pacino, but he's no slouch here either, working from the inside on a drug smuggling racket among dock workers! (Dir: Robert Collins, 98 mins.)

Deadly Game, The (MTV 1977)** Andy Griffith, Sharon Spelman, Dan O'Herlihy. Griffith fans will enjoy his easygoing police work as he delves into the mysterious deaths of two old people, caused by the transport of a shipment of deadly chemicals. The U.S. government and the army are trying to keep the incident under wraps. Except for O'Herlihy, the supporting cast is mostly new faces, and that's a plus. (Dir: Lane Slate, 104 mins.)

Deadly Harvest (MTV 1972)*** Richard Boone, Patty Duke. Interesting chase drama filmed in California's Napa Valley benefits greatly from good performances by Boone and Miss Duke. Boone supplies the tang, playing a taciturn, suspicious old wine-grower who defected from an Iron Curtain country years ago, and is now marked for assassination. Duke is a wandering songwriter who sticks with the old winegrower during the murder attempts, and their growing relationship merits attention. (Dir: Michael O'Herlihy, 73 mins.)

Deadly Hero (1976)**½ Don Murray, Diahn Williams, James Earl Jones. Murray gives an excellent performance in this above-average thriller. A psychotic New York City police officer harasses a female mugging victim (Williams) after she witnesses Murray's brutal way of dealing with her predicament. Filmed entirely on location in the Big Apple. (Dir: Ivan Nagy, 99 mins.)

Deadly Hunt, The (MTV 1971)** Tony Franciosa, Peter Lawford, Anjanette Comer, Jim Hutton. Pretty interesting action movie starring killers Franciosa and Lawford, hired to rub out a wealthy lady in the Vancouver woods. Franciosa as the gunman, grinning in anticipation and savoring his comely target, and the polished, meticulous Lawford, help the show, and leisurely footage of the Vancouver bay area and woods, and a snapping forest fire sequence, supply visual support. (Dir: John Newland, 78 mins.)

Deadly Mantis, The (1957)**½ Craig Stevens, William Hopper. Scientist works feverishly to stop a giant mantis heading south from the polar regions. As these thrillers go, it's a fairly good one—clever special effects, should please the horror fans. (Dir: Nathan Juran, 78 mins.)

Deadly Record (Great Britain, 1959)** Lee Patterson, Barbara Shelley. Pilot is accused of murdering his estranged wife, escapes and sets out to clear himself. Routine whodunit, no surprises. (Dir: Lawrence Huntington, 58 mins.)

Deadly Strangers (Great Britain, 1975)** Hayley Mills, Simon Ward, Sterling Hayden. Two people with deep secrets meet accidentally on the road and share a ride. It gradually develops that one is an escaped homicidal maniac, but is it the one you suspect? The suspense is contrived, and the ending is ridiculous. Hayden plays an eccentric who puts in a late appearance. (Dir: Sidney Hayers, 93 mins.)

Deadly Tower, The (MTV 1975)* Kurt Russell, Ned Beatty, John Forsythe, Richard Yniguez. (Dir: Jerry Jameson, 105 mins.)

Deadly Trackers, The (1973)** Richard Harris, Rod Taylor, Isela Vega. (Dir: Barry Shear, 104 mins.)

Deadly Trap, The (1971)** Faye Dunaway, Frank Langella, Barbara Parkins. Muddled thriller directed by France's René Clément. Dunaway is a troubled wife and mother who appears to be suffering a mental breakdown, but there's more to it than meets the eye. Langella is Faye's preoccupied husband, and both he and Faye, at least, are nice to look at. (97 mins.)

Deadly Triangle, The (1977)** Dale Robinette, Diana Muldaur, Robert Lansing. Another pilot film which has one advantage over most of the others—the gorgeous location scenery of Sun Valley, Idaho. Dale Robinette stars as a former Olympic downhill skiing champion who takes to the slopes as the sheriff of Sun Valley. A member of a ski team training in the area is killed, and Sheriff Robinette is called in to investigate. (Dir: Charles S. Dubin, 79 mins.)

Deadman's Curve (MTV 1978)**½ Richard Hatch, Bruce Davison. A sleeper for rock-and-roll fans, based on the true story of a pair of California kids, Jan and Dean, who became famous in the late '50s with a string of surfing song hits. Hatch turns in a sensitive performance as cocky Jan, later crippled by an idiotic auto smashup at the height of his career. The first half focuses on the fun-loving kids striking it rich, followed by a study of a crash victim struggling to retrain his damaged brain and muscles. (Dir: Richard Compton, 104 mins.)

Deadwood '76 (1965)* Arch Hall Jr., Robert Dix. Poor all around. (Dir: James Landis, 100 mins.)

Dealing: Or the Berkeley-to-Boston-Forty-Brick-Lost-Bag-Blues (1972)** Robert F. Lyons, Barbara Hershey, John Lithgow. Based on the novel by Michael and Douglas Crichton dealing with Peter, a bored Harvard Law student (Lyons) who moves grass from Berkeley to Boston for dealer John (Lithgow). Underwearless girl friend Susan (Hershey) gets busted helping and Peter attempts to blackmail a crooked detective to free her. No assertion of values makes for little drama. Lyons' dreary performance doesn't help matters. (Dir: Paul Williams, 88 mins.)

Dear Brigitte (1965)**½ James Stewart, Glynis Johns. Homey family comedy that doesn't come off as successfully as it should have. Papa Stewart tries to cope with his young son's problem—it seems that he has developed a big crush on Brigitte Bardot and keeps sending her fan letters. Finally Stewart and his little boy go to Paris and visit the celebrated French star. (Dir: Henry Koster, 100 mins.)

Dear Caroline—See: **Caprice of Dear Caroline**

➡**Dear Dead Delilah** (1972)** Agnes Moorehead, Will Greer, Patricia Carmichael. Grisly thriller shot in Nashville. The heirs to an old southern mansion are being axed to death over a hidden fortune. Moorehead, in her last screen appearance, delivers as the dying matriarch of the family, but it's Carmichael, an unknown, who makes the most vivid impression as a former mental patient. The situations are perverse, and interesting enough to overcome some of their sillier aspects. Well written by John Farris, who also directed. (95 mins.)

Dear Detective (France, 1978)***½ Annie Girardot, Philippe Noiret, Paulette Dubost. Comedy and mystery are deftly blended in this entertaining tale of a lady detective who falls in love with an old friend, a professor of Greek, while attempting to solve a series of murders involving the Chamber of Deputies. Both Girardot and Noiret are in top form. Alternate title: **Dear Inspector.** (Dir: Philippe De Broca, 105 mins.)

Dear Detective (MTV 1979)**½ Brenda Vaccaro, Arlen Dean Snyder, Ron Silver. Vaccaro again tries to hit the pilot bull's-eye for a TV series, and again she's better than her material. Inspired by a French film by director Philippe De Broca, Brenda plays a police detective sergeant who meets a professor and embarks on an offbeat romance while continuing her investigation of a multiple murder. (Dir: Dean Hargrove, 104 mins.)

Dear Heart (1965)*** Glenn Ford, Geraldine Page, Angela Lansbury. This is the type of sentimental romance which earns the label of "heartwarming" without even trying too hard. Ford is a salesman who meets and woos spinster postmistress Geraldine Page in New York City during a convention. There's more gushing sentiment than need be, but the good cast keeps things under control. Page is customarily expert. (Dir: Delbert Mann, 114 mins.)

Dear Inspector—See: **Dear Detective**

Dear Murderer (Great Britain, 1947)** Eric Portman, Greta Gynt. A businessman murders his unfaithful wife's lover, but finds that the solution isn't as simple as all that. Passable melodrama, definitely not for Junior. Dennis Price. (Dir: Arthur Crabtree, 94 mins.)

Dear Ruth (1947)**½ Joan Caulfield, William Holden. Topical farce of 1947 is now rather obvious comedy about a youngster who has a hot correspondence with a soldier while posing as her older, attractive sister. (Dir: William D. Russell, 95 mins.)

Dear Wife (1949)*** William Holden, Joan Caulfield, Mona Freeman, Billy DeWolfe. "Dear Ruth" is now married, and her teenage sister launches a campaign to get her husband to the State Senate, which disrupts things. Some good laughs in this cleverly directed domestic comedy. (Dir: Richard Haydn, 88 mins.)

Death Among Friends (MTV 1975)* Kate Reid, Martin Balsam, Jack Cassidy, Paul Henreid. Alternate title: **Mrs. R: Death Among Friends.** (Dir: Paul Wendkos, 72 mins.)

Death at Love House (MTV 1976)*½ Robert Wagner, Kate Jackson, Sylvia Sidney, Joan Blondell. (Dir: E. W. Swackhamer, 72 mins.)

Death Be Not Proud (MTV 1975)***½ Arthur Hill, Jane Alexander, Robby Benson. A moving film based on a memoir by John Gunther, in which he wrote about his teenaged son's valiant bout with cancer and the effect the boy's unflagging efforts to beat the unbeatable had on his divorced parents. Although this is a story dealing with death, it is not downbeat. The scenes in which Arthur Hill, as Gunther, and Jane Alexander, as the boy's mother, do their best to cope with the daily agony of their lives, watching their son holding on to hope, are poignant. Robby Benson, in the pivotal, difficult role of Johnny Gunther, is excellent, and the scene in which he comes forth to accept his diploma at his high school graduation will leave you limp. (Dir: Donald Wrye, 100 mins.)

Death Collector—See: **Family Enforcer**

Death Corps—See: **Shock Waves**

Death Cruise (MTV 1974)*½ Richard Long, Polly Bergen, Edward Albert, Kate Jackson, Celeste Holm. (Dir: Ralph Senensky, 72 mins.)

Death In Canaan, A (MTV 1978)**** Stefanie Powers, Paul Clemens, Conchata Ferrell, Tom Atkins. A gripping re-creation of the real-life incident in which young Peter Reilly was accused of brutally murdering his mother in a small Connecticut town in '73. Police brainwashed the confused and frightened lad into signing a confession. The townspeople rallied to Peter's defense, aided by writer Joan Barthel and a group of famous people, including playwright Arthur Miller, until justice triumphed. The acting overall is fine: newcomer Clemens, as the victimized Peter, gives a thoroughly convincing portrayal. You'll come away with the fear that what befell poor Peter Reilly could happen to anyone. (Dir: Tony Richardson, 130 mins.)

Death In Small Doses (1957)** Peter Graves, Mala Powers, Chuck Conners. When "pep" pills cause accidents among truck drivers, an investigation is started. Pep pill yarn may put you to sleep. (Dir: Joseph M. Newman, 79 mins.)

Death In This Garden (France-Mexico, 1956)***½ Simone Signoret, Michel Piccoli, Charles Vanel. The garden of the title is a terrifying South American jungle, through which an international cast of refugees flee after a surprise banana republic revolution. This coproduction was obviously designed as escapist entertainment, but in the hands of director Luis Buñuel it becomes a little more than that. As things get curiouser and curiouser, it's interesting to see how close Buñuel's surrealist vision is to the expected extravagances of genre filmmaking. No masterpiece, but a prime example of subversive cinema. (97 mins.)

Death In Venice (Italy, 1971)*** Dirk Bogarde, Bjorn Andresen, Silvana Mangano, Marisa Berenson. It may not simply be possible to really do full cinematic justice to Thomas Mann's classic, complicated, richly textured novella published in 1913. But Visconti has assuredly captured the visual quality, the look and feel of Venice circa 1911, a city dying of a secret pestilence. Bogarde plays, with great restraint, an aging, world-famous homosexual writer who has developed an uncontrollable passion for a ravishing young boy (Andresen). Andresen is ravishing, so is Visconti's cinematic eye. Directed and co-authored by Luchino Visconti. Venice

has never looked more beautiful or decadent. (130 mins.)

Death Is a Woman (Great Britain, 1965)** Mark Burns, William Dexter. Mediocre under cover-agent story set in the Mediterranean. There are no name stars in this one, and the plot is merely serviceable. Alternate title: **Love Is a Woman.** (Dir: Frederic Goode, 88 mins.)

Death Is Called Engelchen (Czechoslovakia, 1963)*** The story of an embittered partisan in Nazi-occupied Czechoslovakia, told in flashbacks. The Oscar-winning team of Jan Kadar and Elmar Klos directed this film, which was widely attacked in Czechoslovakia for insufficiently praising the Russian role in the liberation.

Death Line (Great Britain, 1972)**½ Donald Pleasence, Norman Rossington, Christopher Lee. Weird shocker from Britain, macabre and horrible. The story, engrossing if far-fetched, is about some victims of a subway construction accident trapped beneath the streets of London in 1892 who survive, most unnaturally, into the present. If you object to seeing pieces of dead bodies lying around being nibbled by rats, this picture is not for you. Well directed by newcomer Gary Sherman. (87 mins.)

Death Moon (MTV 1978)** Robert Foxworth, Joe Penny, Barbara Trentham, France Nuyen. Foxworth tries, but can't overcome the trite predictability of a yarn about the supernatural beliefs of Hawaiian natives. Foxworth is a businessman enjoying a romantic island interlude until the mid-Pacific version of voodoo begins. (Dir: Bruce Kessler, 104 mins.)

Death of a Bureaucrat (Cuba, 1966)***½ Salvador Wood, Silvia Planas, Manuel Estanillo. This satire didn't get an American release until '79. It's a savage and very funny indictment of conditions which make it almost impossible for the hero (Wood) to exhume the body of his late uncle and then to rebury him. The humor, full of homages to Laurel and Hardy and to Buñuel, is engaging. The Cuban government contended that the film was too critical of the way the country was being run, and suppressed it. B&W. (Dir: Tomas Gutierrez Alea, 87 mins.)

Death of a Cyclist—See: **Age of Infidelity**

Death of a Gunfighter (1969)**½ Richard Widmark, Lena Horne. Don't let the title fool you if you're a western action fan—this is a slow-moving character study of a small-town marshal (R. Widmark) who is no longer needed by the townspeople. Widmark is effective in the leading role. Lena Horne, neglected by Hollywood during the 1960's, is cast in the non-singing role of his long-standing mistress. Offbeat, quiet western. Movie buffs please note that this is one of the few films in recent years to have been directed by two people—Robert Totten, who shot the first part of the movie, and Don Siegel, responsible for the last section. (Dir: credited to Allen Smithee, 100 mins.)

Death of a Salesman (1952)**** Fredric March, Mildred Dunnock, Kevin McCarthy. A very moving and forceful filmization of Arthur Miller's Pulitzer Prize winning play about fading salesman Willy Loman and his emotionally charged relationships with his family. Superb performances and interesting film technique add to its appeal. March, one of our handful of genuinely distinguished stage actors, is at the top of his charm. (Dir: Laslo Benedek, 115 mins.)

Death of a Scoundrel (1956)** George Sanders, Zsa Zsa Gabor, Yvonne DeCarlo. A silly and obvious drama about a suave scoundrel who lives by his charm. Zsa Zsa Gabor plays one of the victims which certainly is a switch. (Dir: Charles Martin, 119 mins.)

Death of Her Innocence (1974)** Pamela Sue Martin, Parker Stevenson, Betsy Slade. Released as **Our Time**. This nostalgic soap opera about a fancy girls' school in 1955 cast TV's Hardy Boy and Nancy Drew as young lovers before they went on to brief TV fame. It's a harmless nostalgia trip about a more disciplined time, but the plot is all too predictable, with the young girls' awakening to sex and its melodramatic consequences. Well acted by Pamela Sue Martin, Parker Stevenson, and especially Betsy Slade. Written by Jane C. Stanton, based on her experiences at a posh girls' boarding school. (Dir: Peter Hyams, 90 mins.)

Death of Innocence (MTV 1971)**½ Shelley Winters, Tisha Sterling. Playing a Utah mother, Miss Winters arrives in New York with husband to attend daughter's murder trial, certain it's all a mistake. Mom slowly faces the idea her daughter might be guilty. Filmed partly in New York, with scenes in the old Women's Detention Home and city streets, the show delivers solid performances from cast. Good support from Tisha Sterling, Arthur Kennedy, Ann Sothern, and newcomer Richard Bright. (Dir: Paul Wendkos, 73 mins.)

Death of Me Yet, The (MTV 1971)**½ Doug McClure, Darren McGavin. Rosemary Forsyth, Richard Basehart, Meg Foster. This fairly suspenseful film opens in a typical American community with average people going about their daily business; then we discover that it's a detailed reproduction of such a community in the U.S.S.R. McClure, one of the town's citizens, is dispatched to the U.S. as an infiltrator, but he runs away, takes on a new identity, and lives for six years as a happily married newspaper editor. McClure is at his best, and the supporting cast is effective. (Dir: John Llewellyn Moxey, 78 mins.)

Death of Ocean View Park, The (MTV 1979)*** Mike Connors, Martin Landau, Caroline McWilliams, Diana Canova. Exciting disaster drama about an amusement park which is doomed. The climactic scenes of the park's destruction are very realistic, since the producers were lucky enough to find an actual park which was set for demolition. The plot centers on a large Fourth of July park opening which has been plagued by mysterious, unexplained occurrences. The managers are further alerted to pending disaster when a park employee's pregnant wife foresees in a dream the park being demolished by a fire. (Dir: E. W. Swackhamer, 106 mins.)

Death of Ritchie, The (MTV 1977)***½ Ben Gazzara, Robby Benson, Eileen Brennan. Here's a sleeper—a well-made emotional drama about a teenaged drug addict who can't give up the habit. Robby Benson is quite believable as the kid on drugs, needing help from his parents and from group therapy, since he can't cope on his own. Gazzara plays the father, a man too busy to take the time to really deal with his son's addiction, but one who attempts too late to reach out to the hooked teenager. Watch this show because it spells out the horrors of drugs. Based on a real case history. (Dir: Paul Wendkos, 103 mins.)

Death of Tarzan, The (Czechoslovakia, 1962)*** Rudolph Hrusinsky, Jana Stepankova. Don't be put off by the title. This deft Czech satire has nothing whatever to do with the moronic "Tarzan" films based on the Edgar Rice Burroughs character. An odd, winning combination of farce and drama generated by yet another (Jaroslav Balik) director of the ill-fated Czech film renaissance. Modern morality play, about a half-man, half-gorilla introduced into modern Czech aristocracy. Beautifully acted with some stunning visual sequences. Subtitles. Alternate title: **Death of the Ape-Man.** (Dir: Jaroslav Balik, 72 mins.)

Death of the Ape-Man—See: **Death of Tarzan, The**

Death Penalty (MTV 1980)*** Colleen Dewhurst, David Labiosa, Dana Elcar. A 15-year-old Puerto Rican kills two Anglo kids in a playground. Should he get the chair? A lady psychiatrist says no and the prosecution counters. A rattling good, realistic drama. It is also the story of a psychiatrist changing a raging teenager's attitude, only to learn she is no longer needed. Thought-provoking material, perhaps slanted a bit in the boy's direction, but a decided change from the customary pap. (Dir: Waris Hussein, 104 mins.)

Death Race (MTV 1973)**½ Lloyd Bridges, Doug McClure, Roy Thinnes, Eric Braeden. A good cast fight it out in the dust and sand of this WW II story about Rommel's retreat from El Alamein. A Nazi tank commander (Bridges) stalks American fighter pilots caught in a crippled P-40 plane that is unable to take off. Desert chase scenes filmed among the sand dunes of El Centro, Calif., with stunt segments by Frank Tallman in his old P-40. (Dir: David Lowell Rich, 90 mins.)

Death Race 2000 (1975)***½ David Carradine, Sylvester Stallone, Louisa Moritz, Mary Woronov, Simone Griffith. A quasi-classic exploitation film, and probably one of the key low-budget works of art of seventies cinema. It works on innumerable levels simultaneously—genre, action, parody, politics, entertainment. Bartel preserves his sophistication even as he panders to the mob. The premise of a cross-country road race set in the near future has often been pilfered since, but never rendered with greater verve or density—for which the script, credited to the late Robert Thom, is a big asset. Photographed by Tak Fujimoto. Based on a 1956 short story by Ib Melchior. (Dir: Paul Bartel, 80 mins.)

Death Rides a Horse (Italy, 1968)*½ Lee Van Cleef, John Phillip Law. (Dir: Giulio Petroni, 114 mins.)

Death Scream (MTV 1975)**½ Raul Julia, Tina Louise, Cloris Leachman, Art Carney. Effective, updated version of the real-life Kitty Genovese murder on a Brooklyn street years ago, in which the victim screamed for help for close to half an hour, fighting off her attacker while no one came to her aid. This story makes the victim a lesbian, adding some depth to the investigation, headed by Raul Julia as Lt. Rodriguez. Uses TV stars as witnesses. Tina Louise shines in the brief interrogation scene, playing a former lover of the victim. The subject is involving and the script doesn't cheat. (Dir: Richard T. Heffron, 100 mins.)

Death Sentence (MTV 1974)**½ Cloris Leachman, Laurence Luckinbill. Cloris Leachman has made a specialty out of playing women driven to the brink of disaster by circumstances out of her control, and here's another. This gifted actress tries to overcome some of the plot's more obvious loopholes in this story which has her playing a juror who realizes halfway through a murder trial that her own husband may be the real culprit. Laurence Luckinbill is well cast as Miss Leachman's suspected spouse. (Dir: E. W. Swackhamer, 72 mins.)

Death Squad, The (MTV 1973)**½ Robert Forster, Melvyn Douglas. Strong police yarn about a group of vigilante cops who secretly take the law into their own hands and murder criminals. Forster crisply plays a poor man's "Serpico," a cop who was kicked off the force but is brought back to get to the bottom of the rash of killings. A fine supporting cast helps the action. (Director: Harry Falk, 78 mins.)

Death Stalk (MTV 1975)** Vic Morrow, Vince Edwards, Anjanette Comer, Carol Lynley, Robert Webber. Crisis drama borrows liberally from the movie "Deliverance" for its plot. Focuses on two couples enjoying an outdoors vacation riding the rapids in rafts, when they are pounced upon by four escaped convicts who abduct the wives and leave the two husbands behind. Vic Morrow, leading the pack of escaped convicts, generates a bit of heat in his scenes with Anjanette Comer. (Dir: Robert Day, 72 mins.)

Death Takes a Holiday (1934)***½ Fredric March, Evelyn Venable, Kathleen Harrison. Fascinating drama. Mr. March, as Death, decides to assume human form and take a vacation. Interesting, well played and worth seeing. (Dir: Mitchell Leisen, 90 mins.)

Death Trap (Great Britain, 1962)** Albert Lieven, Barbara Shelley. Girl learns her deceased sister drew some money from the bank before her death, but it seems to have disappeared. Fairly interesting Edgar Wallace mystery. (Dir: John Moxey, 56 mins.)

Death Wish (1974)* Charles Bronson, Hope Lange, Vincent Gardenia. From the novel by Brian Garfield, who unsuccessfully sued the filmmakers because they distorted his intentions. (Dir: Michael Winner, 93 mins.)

Decameron (Italy, 1971)** Franco Citti, Ninetto Davoli, Angela Luce, Pier Paolo Pasolini. Director Pasolini's film is weak in narrative development, rich in the smelly visual metaphors that distinguish his previous works. Very slow going for the relatively simpleminded payoff. Pasolini plays the artist Giotto. (Dir:

Decameron Nights (Great Britain, 1953)*** Joan Fontaine, Louis Jourdan, Joan Collins. Author Boccaccio follows his lady-love, tries to win her affection by telling her two spicy tales. Good-natured costume adventure, made in Italy. Pleasant fun. (Dir: Hugo Fregonese, 85 mins.)

Deception (1946)*½ Bette Davis, Paul Henreid, Claude Rains. (Dir: Irving Rapper, 112 mins.)

Decision Against Time (Great Britain, 1957)**½ Jack Hawkins, Elizabeth Sellars. Test pilot is determined to bring his troubled ship in for a safe landing. Fairly suspenseful drama, well-made. (Dir: Charles Crichton, 87 mins.)

Decision at Sundown (1957)***½ Randolph Scott, Karen Steele, John Carroll. Exceptionally good, adult-slanted western manages to break most of the accepted hoss-opera rules advantageously. Randy is out for revenge again—but the plot gets a novel twist this time. (Dir: Budd Boetticher, 77 mins.)

Decision Before Dawn (1951)**½ Oskar Werner, Richard Basehart, Gary Merrill. A very fine performance by German actor Oskar Werner as "Happy" makes up for some of the shortcomings of the script of this World War II espionage drama. Good on-location photography and a capable supporting cast including Basehart, Merrill and Hildegarde Neff also make this worthwhile but it's Werner's show. (Dir: Anatole Litvak, 119 mins.)

Decision of Christopher Blake (1948)**½

Alexis Smith, Robert Douglas. Good play about the effect a divorce trial has on a small boy becomes an episodic, meaningless story in this screen treatment with Ted Donaldson as the boy. (Dir: Peter Godfrey, 75 mins.)

Decks Ran Red, The (1958)** James Mason, Dorothy Dandridge, Broderick Crawford, Stuart Whitman. Foolish film about a captain endeavoring to thwart a mutiny engineered by two nasty seamen. The dialogue is hollow, the suspense isn't, and the acting only occasionally effective. (Dir: Andrew L. Stone, 84 mins.)

Decline and Fall of a Bird Watcher (Great Britain, 1968)** Genevieve Page, Colin Blakely, Leo McKern, Robin Philips. This adaptation of one of Evelyn Waugh's biting satires on English manners and mores begins well as the callow hero (Philips) gets a position at a weirdly run boys' school. Thereafter the fun becomes cumbersome, off-target, and runs downhill quickly. (Dir: John Krish, 113 mins.)

Deep, The (1977)** Robert Shaw, Nick Nolte, Jacqueline Bisset. This box-office hit, based on Peter "Jaws" Benchley's best seller, is a mechanical thriller that barely gets by as acceptable entertainment. Three sketchily characterized skin divers face every known underwater cliché as they search for sunken treasure. Peter Yates's direction lurches along from one predictable danger to another. The ABC-TV screening added an hour of footage shot but cut in the theatrical release. (123 mins.)

Deep Blue Sea, The (Great Britain, 1955)** Vivien Leigh, Kenneth More. Terence Rattigan's stage success of an emotionally unstable woman's affair with a man beneath her station, rather cumbersomely adapted for the screen. Defects in direction, performances detract from the drama. (Dir: Anatole Litvak, 99 mins.)

Deep End (West Germany-Great Britain, 1970)***½ Jane Asher, John Moulder-Brown, Diana Dors. Intelligent, powerful fable of a young boy's first love. Moulder-Brown epitomizes the adolescent who will not be deterred by the obstacles he faces in courting a nubile bathhouse attendant. His dedicated pursuit sees him overcoming the girl's indifference, as well as triumphing over her fiancé and lover. The affectionately subdued directing conveys all of the high spirits and aspirations of a building passion. Skolomowsky also helped write the screenplay. (Dir: Jerzy Skolomowsky, 87 mins.)

Deep in My Heart (1954)** José Ferrer, Merle Oberon, Walter Pidgeon, Doe Avedon, Helen Traubel, Paul Henreid. Ferrer makes a glum Sigmund Romberg in an excessively long, moderately embarrassing musical biography directed with none of his usual panache by Stanley Donen. Even the best scene will make you wince, as Ferrer tries to pull off a Donald

O'Connor number. Many guest stars. (132 mins.)

Deep Red (Italy, 1975)**½ David Hemmings, Daria Nocolodi, Macha Meril. A noted psychic detects a mad killer in the audience of a press conference. She is murdered (with a meat cleaver) and Hemmings tries to find out who did it. A gory, better-than-average thriller with some classy visual effects. In English. (Dir: Dario Argento, 98 mins.)

Deep Six, The (1958)** Alan Ladd, William Bendix, Joey Bishop, Dianne Foster, James Whitmore. Naval lieutenant whose religious beliefs are Quaker loses the respect of his men but regains it through an act of heroism. World War II drama is thoroughly routine, runs far too long. (Dir: Rudolph Mate, 108 mins.)

Deep Valley (1947)*** Ida Lupino, Dane Clark. Girl living an unhappy life on a farm is attracted to a convict working on a construction job. Excellently acted drama—grim but good. (Dir: Jean Negulesco, 104 mins.)

Deep Waters (1948)** Dana Andrews, Jean Peters. This one may remind you of a dull one-hour TV play. Maine fishing village girl wants man to work on shore. Man likes fishing. An orphan taken care of by girl but likes to fish with man. Familiar? (Dir: Henry King, 85 mins.)

Deer Hunter, The (1978)**** Robert De Niro, Meryl Streep, Christopher Walken, John Cazale, John Savage. It examines the mindless horrors of the Vietnam War without the customary political rhetoric or cant found in other films. Director Michael Cimino adroitly makes clear his affection for these mill workers suddenly thrust into the hell of Vietnam—a war about which they were profoundly ignorant—resulting in incalculable damage not only to the American fighting men and the hapless Vietnamese, but also, in a more subtle way, to the soul and conscience of America. A movie masterpiece. Try and see an unedited print. (183 mins.)

Deerslayer, The (1957)*½ Lex Barker, Forrest Tucker, Rita Moreno. (Dir: Kurt Neumann, 78 mins.)

Deerslayer, The (MTV 1978)** Steve Forrest, Ned Romero. James Fenimore Cooper's intrepid Hawkeye (Forrest) and his Indian blood brother (Romero) slip through the woods, out to rescue cousin Wa-Tah-Wa from the Hurons. A clumsy adaptation which emphasizes action rather than acting or dialogue. (Dir: Dick Friedenberg, 78 mins.)

Defeat of Hannibal, The (Italy 1937)* Annibale Ninchi, Isa Miranda, Francesca Braggiotti. Alternate title: **Scipio Africanus.** (Dir: Carmine Gallone, 109 mins.)

Defection of Simas Kudirka, The (MTV 1978)**** Alan Arkin, Richard Jordan, Donald Pleasence, Shirley Knight. One of TV's best docudramas in recent years: a powerful dramatic essay about man's unquenchable thirst for freedom. The multitalented Arkin is superb as Russian seaman Simas Kudirka, who defected to an American coast guard cutter in '70 and was, through a series of stupefying bureaucratic blunders by naval and federal authorities, turned back to the Russians. From the opening sequence of Kudirka frolicking with his family in Lithuania to the final tense, poignant countryside reunion with his loyal wife, movingly portrayed by Knight, author Bruce Feldman has avoided the temptation to be maudlin or melodramatic. Arkin's rousing speech while being tried for treason in a Russian courtroom is a cry for freedom you won't soon forget. Well directed. (Dir: David Lowell Rich, 104 mins.)

Defector, The (Germany-France, 1966)***½ Montgomery Clift, Hardy Kruger. A fairly engrossing espionage yarn which benefits from good on-location atmosphere in Berlin, and a fine performance by Montgomery Clift as an American professor of physics who gets involved with cold-war intrigues. Hardy Kruger, as the German working for the communists, is constantly in opposition to Clift, the amateur spy on a dangerous mission involving the defection of Russian scientist to the West. The story gets a bit muddled towards the end, but fans of this sort of film will not be disappointed. Incidentally, this was the last film Clift made before his death, and that is the brilliant French film director Jean-Luc Godard playing the small role of a tourist spy. (Dir: Raoul Levy, 106 mins.)

Defiance (1980)* Jan-Michael Vincent, Art Carney, Danny Aiello. (Dir: John Flynn, 103 mins.)

Defiant Daughters (Switzerland-Germany 1961)** Barbara Rutting, Luise Ulrich. Housemistress of a girls' reformatory tries to save a young rebellious girl from a life of misery. Sometimes interesting, mostly heavyhanded delinquency drama dubbed in English. Alternate title: **The Shadows Grow Longer.** (Dir: Ladislao Vajda, 91 mins.)

Defiant Ones, The (1958)**** Tony Curtis, Sidney Poitier, Theodore Bikel, Cara Williams. Provocative, honest racial drama of two escaping chain-gang convicts, white and Negro, whose differences make their flight more difficult because they are literally chained together. Still packs quite a punch, has superb performances, potent Stanley Kramer direction. Fine mature fare. (97 mins.)

Delancey Street: The Crisis Within (1975)**½ Walter McGinn, Lou Gossett. Fairly interesting dramatic version of San Francisco's successful rehabilitation center, Delancey Street, in which ex-cons, junkies and dropouts live together and learn new skills. McGinn exudes force and energy as Delancey's free-wheeling innovator, while action focuses on inmates battling problems. Positive, earthy, up-

beat! Alternate title: **The Sinner.** (Dir: James Frawley, 72 mins.)

Delicate Balance, A (1973)***½ Paul Scofield, Kate Reid, Katharine Hepburn, Lee Remick. Adaptation of the somewhat pretentious Edward Albee play. This filmed play is brilliantly realized as the shifting interplay of focal changes within the frame, layers of implication expressed by precise visual means. An aging, civilized couple try to make living together tolerable. Some of the acting, like the themes, is dense and obscure, yet for once Paul Scofield displays his muffled subtlety to full effect before a camera, Reid steals the show as a sharp-tongued alcoholic. (Dir: Tony Richardson, 134 mins.)

Delicate Delinquent, The (1957)*** Jerry Lewis, Darren McGavin, Martha Hyer. Scapegoat Jerry joins the police force and has a hard time proving himself as a rookie cop. One of the better Lewis offerings. He's restrained, the story is logical, the laughs come frequently. (Dir: Don McGuire, 101 mins.)

Deliver Us from Evil (MTV 1973)*** George Kennedy, Jan-Michael Vincent, Bradford Dillman. Mount Hood, Oregon, which stands over 11,000 feet high, is the real star of this adventure drama filmed on location. Spectacular photography adds to the tale of five men who set out, with the aid of a guide, to spend three days in the Oregon wilderness (shades of "Deliverance") but end up trying to survive the rugged terrain when their guide is killed. Tension builds as the men come across a skyjacker with his fortune in ransom money. The cast, especially Jim Davis in a brief role, is very good. (Dir: Boris Sagal, 90 mins.)

Deliverance (1972)**** Jon Voight, Burt Reynolds, Ned Beatty, Ronny Cox. James Dickey's novel has been excitingly brought to the screen by director John Boorman, earning Academy Award nominations for best picture, direction and editing. Four businessmen—Voight, Reynolds, Beatty and Cox—set out on a canoe trip down a wild Georgia river and look forward to nothing more hazardous than riding the rapids, but their adventure becomes a nightmare of survival. They encounter two demented hillbillies, one of whom physically violates Beatty, and the innocent nature trek turns into a struggle laced with killing. Strong stuff, superbly acted by the entire cast, particularly Voight as the sensitive man who finds he wants to release his primitive instincts when his own life is at stake. (109 mins.)

Delphi Bureau, The (MTV 1972)*½ Laurence Luckinbill, Joanna Pettet, Celeste Holm. (Dir: Paul Wendkos, 72 mins.)

Delta County (MTV 1977)*½ Peter Donat, Joanna Miles, Jeff Conway. (Dir: Glenn Jordan, 106 mins.)

Delta Factor, The (1971)½ Christopher

George, Yvette Mimieux, Diane McBain. (91 mins.)

Dementia 13 (1963)*** Patrick Magee, William Campbell, Luana Anders. Unusually well-crafted low-budget horror film with Magee as a suspected murderer with a predilection for the aristocracy. Though often wrongly identified as director Francis Ford Coppola's first film, this was at least his third. It shows his great promise. (81 mins.)

Demetrius and the Gladiators (1954)**½ Susan Hayward, Victor Mature, Richard Egan. A sequel to TC Fox's successful film "The Robe." Not as good in any department. Probably the only reason it was made was to utilize the very expensive sets and costumes left over from "The Robe." Action fans might like the scenes in the arena where the gladiators do their stuff. (Dir: Delmer Daves, 101 mins.)

Demon, The (1977)**½ Tony Lo Bianco, Sandy Dennis, Deborah Raffin, Sam Levene, Sylvia Sidney. Story of a wave of mass murders striking New York. It's a pity Larry Cohen's talents as a director don't match his audacity as a screenwriter—this could have been a sleaze classic. Too confused and clumsy to be more than a novelty item. (95 mins.)

Demon Planet, The (Italy, 1965)*½ Barry Sullivan, Norma Bengell. Alternate title: **Planet of the Vampires.** (Dir: Mario Bava, 86 mins.)

Demon Pond. (Japan)**½ Tamasaburo Bando, a Kabuki star with a talent for drag, stars. Masahiro Shinoda's elaborate ghost film boasts spectacular special effects and lush, colorful production, but the material is little better than a conventional potboiler. One senses the director retreating into his genre forms rather than confronting them; this is a film that radiates fear of personal expression. It's odd, since Shinoda has been among the most individualistic of Japanese directors, although it's hard to imagine that such an eccentric story was merely a commissioned project. It attempts to be in a league with "Ugetsu" or even "Kaneto Shindo" ("Kuroneko", "Onibaba"), and it is certainly worth seeing, but is scarcely a major work from this major director. Based on a drama by Kyoka Izumi, with electric color work from Masao Kosugi (with Noritaka Sakamoto).

Demon Seed, The (1977)*½ Julie Christie, Fritz Weaver, Gerrit Graham. (Dir: Donald Cammell, 94 mins.)

Demoniac (France, 1957)***½ Jeanne Moreau, Micheline Presle, Francois Perier. Taut and baffling mystery drama of mistaken identities during W.W. II in France. Fascinating and suspenseful throughout. (Dir: Luis Saslavsky, 97 mins.)

Demons of the Mind (Great Britain, 1972)** Paul Jones, Gillian Hills, Robert Hardy, Patrick Magee, Michael Hordern. In 19th-century Austria a baron, convinced that insanity runs in his family, keeps his son and daughter virtual prisoners for fear of what harm they might do. Pioneer psychiatrist Dr. Falkenberg (charismatically played by Magee) finds some surprises in the family's history, but then the film turns into a mess of chases, murders, and horror clichés. (Dir: Peter Sykes, 89 mins.)

Dentist in the Chair (Great Britain, 1961)*½ Bob Monkhouse, Peggy Cummins. (Dir: Don Chaffey, 84 mins.)

Dentist on the Job—See: **Carry On TV**

Denver and Rio Grande, The (1952)**½ Edmond O'Brien, Sterling Hayden, Dean Jagger. Plenty of rough-house action in this western about two rival railroads battling to see who gets through the Royal Gorge first. Outdoor fans should find it routinely entertaining. (Dir: Byron Haskin, 89 mins.)

Deported (1950)**½ Marta Toren, Jeff Chandler, Claude Dauphin. Over-sentimentalized tale of a deported American gangster and his reformation in the hands of a beautiful Italian Countess. Chandler does very well as the gangster who's deported to Italy and gets involved with the black market. (Dir: Robert Siodmak, 89 mins.)

Derby (1971)***½ Mike Snell, Butch Snell, Janet Earp, Eddie Krebs. Enlightening, entertaining documentary about the great American pastime, the Roller Derby. Some of the scenes are stage-managed, while the film pretends to be a cinema-verité report of what happens to the generally sad, dispirited characters trying to make their dream come true in this tacky, tawdry "sport." Directed and photographed by Robert Kaylor. (91 mins.)

Derby Day (Great Britain, 1952)*** Anna Neagle, Michael Wilding. Four stories revolving about the big horse race at Epsom, where the various spectators all have their little plots to unfold. Mildly entertaining package of comedy and drama. (Dir: Herbert Wilcox, 84 mins.)

Dersu Uzala (U.S.S.R.-Japan, 1974)***½ Maxim Munzuk, Yuri Solomin. A fascinating, overlong epic about the struggles of hardy souls to chart the wilderness of Siberia around 1900. The second part of this absorbing survival picture is directed by Japan's wonderful Akira Kurosawa, and is appreciably better than the balance of the film, directed by a Russian colleague. Based on the journals of a Russian, Vladmir Arseniev, "Dersu"'s remarkable photography and the performance of Munzuk as an old native hunter carry this most of the way. (140 mins.)

Desert Attack (Great Britain, 1959)*** John Mills, Sylvia Syms, Anthony Quayle. Tank commander has his hands full in North Africa carrying two nurses to safety and combating a German spy. Originally, a rattling good war story; American version is severely cut, obscuring some of the sense. However, good performances, exciting scenes still make it worthwhile. Alternative title: **Ice Cold In Alex** (Dir: J. Lee Thompson, 80 mins.)

Desert Desperadoes (Italy, MTV 1956)*½ Ruth Roman, Otello Toso, Akim Tamiroff. (Dir: Steve Sekely, 73 mins.)

Desert Fighters (France, 1954)*½ Michel Auclair, Emma Penella, Dalio, Dany Carrel. (Dir: Rene Chanas, 94 mins.)

Desert Fox, The (1951)***½ James Mason, Jessica Tandy. Exciting war drama about the African campaign of Rommel. James Mason is nothing short of great as the Nazi general. Good desert photography. Mason repeated his characterization of Rommel in another film, "The Desert Rats," which showed the other side of the coin regarding the German military tactics under Rommel's command. (Dir: Henry Hathaway, 88 mins.)

Desert Fury (1947)** John Hodiak, Burt Lancaster, Lizabeth Scott, Mary Astor. Good cast in confusing melodrama about gambling. Everybody in the film has a shady past, and the result is a shady motion picture. (Dir: Lewis Allen, 75 mins.)

Desert Hawk, The (1950)** Yvonne DeCarlo, Richard Greene. The only interesting thing about this stale tale of an Arabian Nights adventure is Jackie Gleason in the supporting role of Aladdin. No one really takes the film seriously, especially the pre-rich Gleason. (Dir: Frederick de Cordova, 78 mins.)

Desert Hell (1958)*½ Brian Keith, Barbara Hale, Richard Denning. (Dir: Charles Marquis Warren, 82 mins.)

Desert Legion (1953)** Alan Ladd, Arlene Dahl, Richard Conte. Can you imagine Alan Ladd as a French Foreign Legionnaire? This adventure yarn has super heroics and beautiful desert princesses. (Dir: Joseph Pevney, 86 mins.)

Desert Mice (Great Britain, 1959)**½ Alfred Marks, Sidney James, Dora Bryan. Engaging comedy about British vaudevillian entertainers who performed for British troops during World War II. Nonstellar cast is uniformly fine, especially James as an unfunny boss comic. (Dir: Basil Dearden, 83 mins.)

Desert Pursuit (1952)** Wayne Morris, Virginia Grey. Prospector and a lady gambler are chased by a murderous gang after gold. Western with a gimmick—the baddies are Arabs and use camels instead of horses. Twist makes this one okay. (Dir: George Blair, 71 mins.)

Desert Raiders (Italy, 1964)* Kirk Morris, Helene Chanel. (Dir: Amerigo Anton, 87 mins.)

Desert Rats, The (1953)*** James Mason, Richard Burton, Robert Newton. Good war drama about the turbulent siege at Tobruk during World War II. James Mason once again effectively portrays Gen. Rommel, "The Desert Fox," leader of the Nazi troops. Richard Burton is fine as the commander of the Australian forces; and

Robert Newton gives a standout performance as a professor turned soldier. (Dir: Robert Wise, 88 mins.)

Desert Song, The (1953)** Kathryn Grayson, Gordon MacRae. Still another version of the "never say die" operetta. Kathryn Grayson and Gordon MacRae play the duetting stars this time around and they're no better nor worse than any of their predecessors. The score contains the familiar "Riff Song," among others. (Dir: H. Bruce Humberstone, 110 mins.)

Desert War (Italy, 1962)*½ Peter Baldwin, Chelo Alonso. (Dir: Luigi Filippo d'Amico, 83 mins.)

Desert Warrior, The (Italy-Spain, 1958)** Ricardo Montalban, Carmen Sevilla. Spanish-made, English-dubbed Arabian adventure yarn that benefits somewhat from Ricardo Montalban's ability to perform heroic feats without seeming ridiculous. (Dirs: Fernando Cerchio, Goffredo Alessandrini, Leon Klimovsky, Gianni Vernuccio, Ricardo Munoz Suay, 87 mins.)

Deserter, The (Italy-Yugoslavia-U.S., 1970)** John Huston, Richard Crenna, Ricardo Montalban, Bekim Fehmiu. A fair Western yarn set in 1886. Army officer is out for revenge after the Apaches mutilated his wife—but a good cast of pros, including John Huston, Richard Crenna, Ricardo Montalban and Bekim Fehmiu (remember him as Dax in "The Adventurers"?) help it along. (Dir: Burt Kennedy, 99 mins.)

Design for Living (1933)**½ Gary Cooper, Fredric March, Miriam Hopkins. Noel Coward's delightful comedy receives an unsuccessful screen treatment. Story of three "sensible" people involved in a love triangle was too sophisticated for a movie. The stars are very attractive, though. (Dir: Ernst Lubitsch, 90 mins.)

Design for Loving (Great Britain, 1962)*½ June Thurburn, Pete Murray. (Dir: Godfrey Grayson, 68 mins.)

Design for Scandal (1941)**½ Rosalind Russell, Walter Pidgeon, Edward Arnold. Some good fun in this comedy about an upstanding lady judge and the scoundrel who sets out to smear her good name. (Dir: Norman Taurog, 85 mins.)

Designing Woman (1951)*** Gregory Peck, Lauren Bacall, Dolores Gray, Sam Levene, Chuck Connors. Sportswriter Peck impulsively marries fashion designer Bacall, and a battle of the brows ensues—high against low. Peck, though more limber than usual, is hopeless, but Bacall is perfectly cast. A solid, enjoyable film—but short of major work. (Dir: Vincente Minnelli, 117 mins.)

Desire (1936)*** Marlene Dietrich, Gary Cooper. Familiar but delightful. Lovely jewel thief takes advantage of innocent young man and he becomes her unwitting accomplice in smuggling a stolen necklace. She must now seduce him to regain her prize. (Dir: Frank Borzage, 100 mins.)

Desire in the Dust (1960)** Raymond Burr, Martha Hyer, Joan Bennett. Tyrannical landowner with plenty of skeletons in his closet sees his political ambitions in jeopardy, tries unscrupulous means to rid himself of his troubles. A dose of lust and desire in a southern town, but it's a long way from Faulkner. Burr does well, better than his material. (Dir: William F. Claxton, 102 mins.)

Desire Under the Elms (1958)**½ Sophia Loren, Anthony Perkins, Burl Ives. O'Neill's play concerning the passions of a farmer's young son and the wife of the elderly man misses something in its transference to the screen. Some powerful dramatic moments, mostly unrelieved gloom, meandering pace. (Dir: Delbert Mann, 111 mins.)

Desiree (1954)**½ Marlon Brando, Jean Simmons, Merle Oberon. With this elaborately produced historical drama, Mr. Brando adds Napoleon to his list of screen portrayals, but it does not rank with his best. Jean Simmons is vividly beautiful and, as always, competent in the title role as Napoleon's love before he becomes Emperor. Merle Oberon as Josephine has few scenes, but she makes them count. Michael Rennie completes the starring lineup in this adventure film which sacrifices historical accuracy in favor of romantic flair. (Dir: Henry Koster, 110 mins.)

Desk Set (1957)**½ Spencer Tracy, Katharine Hepburn, Gig Young, Joan Blondell, Dina Merrill. Tired comedy fueled exclusively by the Tracy-Hepburn confrontations. She is the head of the reference department of a major broadcaster and he is the efficiency expert sent in to size up the operation for computerization. The Broadway origins show too mechanically. (Dir: Walter Lang, 103 mins.)

Desperadoes, The (1969)* Jack Palance, Vince Edwards, George Maharis, Neville Brand. (Dir: Henry Levin, 90 mins.)

Desperate (1947)*** Steve Brodie, Nan Leslie. Truckdriver becomes a fugitive when his vehicle is used in a robbery. Above average melodrama. (Dir: Anthony Mann, 73 mins.)

Desperate Characters (1971)*** Shirley MacLaine, Kenneth Mars, Gerald O'Loughlin, Sada Thompson. Well-written character study of a day in the life of an urban couple who face a decaying New York that they are helpless to change. Features fine performances by Miss MacLaine and Mars as the white middle-class pair insulated against their crumbling city in a renovated brownstone. Shares some of the same vision as "Little Murders," but without the humor. Novel by Paula Fox was adapted by Pulitzer Prize-winning author Frank Gilroy, who made an impressive directorial debut as well! (Dir: Frank Gilroy, 88 mins.)

Desperate Hours, The (1955)*** Humphrey Bogart, Fredric March, Arthur Kennedy, Gig Young, Martha Scott, Dewey Martin, Robert Middleton. William Wyler wasn't the best choice to do this kind of suspense-genre entry, essentially a fifties suburban update by Humphrey Bogart of his *Petrified Forest* role, and he hasn't the anarchic temperament or stylistic command to avoid a certain portentousness that is anathema to this sort of story. Still, Fredric March is impressive as the hostage head of the family, and Bogart's last "classical" performance shows that he hadn't forgotten how to play a gangster after all those reluctant hero roles. With the usual solid craft from cameraman Lee Garmes. Joseph Hayes adapted from his novel and play. (112 mins.)

Desperate Journey (1942)**½ Errol Flynn, Ronald Reagan, Raymond Massey. One of the pictures made when Errol was winning the war single-handed. Today, stripped of its propaganda value, it's just a good action story. (Dir: Raoul Walsh, 107 mins.)

Desperate Miles, The (MTV 1975)½ Tony Musante, Joanna Pettet, Jeanette Nolan. (Dir: Dan Haller, 72 mins.)

Desperate Mission (MTV 1971)* Ricardo Montalban, Slim Pickens, Earl Holliman. (Dir: Earl Bellamy, 100 mins.)

Desperate Moment (Great Britain, 1953)***½ Dirk Bogarde, Mai Zetterling. Displaced person in Europe is tricked into confessing to a murder he didn't commit, and his girl tries to help track down the guilty party. Exciting, tense melodrama; excellent performances. (Dir: Compton Bennett, 88 mins.)

Desperate Ones, The (Spain-U.S., 1967)** Maximilian Schell, Raf Vallone, Irene Papas, Theodore Bikel, Maria Perschy. O.K. World War II melodrama. Two Polish brothers escape a Siberian labor camp. Along the way to the Afghanistan border, Schell and Vallone meet Papas and Perschy, and a weak romantic subplot ensues. Alexander Ramati authored the original novel, "Beyond the Mountains," as well as producing, scripting and directing. (Dir: Alexander Ramati, 104 mins.)

Desperate Search (1953)**½ Howard Keel, Jane Greer, Patricia Medina. Moderately interesting drama about the efforts of a search party to bring back two young survivors of a plane crash in the Canadian mountains. Personal drama enters the picture as Keel's ex-wife (Miss Medina) shows up to complicate matters. (Dir: Joseph H. Lewis, 71 mins.)

Desperate Siege (1951)**½ Tyrone Power, Susan Hayward. This routine western drama is sparked by the acting of Tyrone Power and Susan Hayward. The two stars find themselves in the desperate position of being held prisoners in a remote stagecoach station by a band of outlaws. Most of the action unfolds slowly except for one or two tense gun-play sequences. Released as **Rawhide.** Remake of **Show Them No**

Mercy (1935), a gangster film. (Dir: Henry Hathaway, 86 mins.)

Desperate Voyage (MTV 1980)**½ Christopher Plummer, Christine Belford, Cliff Potts, Lara Parker. Plummer convincingly plays a villainous modern-day pirate who waits for SOS signals and then gives the troubled seamen anything but help. Potts and Belford are co-starred as a yachting pair whose pleasure cruise turns into a nightmare of survival. The suspense holds up for most of the picture. (Dir: Michael O'Herlihy, 104 mins.)

Destination Death (Germany, 1961)** Hannes Messemer, Armin Dahlen. German sergeant saves 40 military prisoners who are being transported to their doom during the final days of World War II. Occasionally suspenseful war drama dubbed in English. (Dir: Jurgen Roland, 93 mins.)

Destination Fury (France-Italy, 1964)** Eddie Constantine, Renato Rascel, Dorian Gray. Police inspector appointed to Interpol in Rome is ordered to Paris to bring back a notorious gangster, gets involved in an illegal drug operation. Mild gangster story mixes laughs with thrills in fair fashion. Dubbed in English. (Dir: Giorgio Bianchi, 85 mins.)

Destination Gobi (1953)**½ Richard Widmark, Don Taylor. A notch or two above the average heroic war story. Good photography and some solid acting make up for some of the shortcomings of the script. (Dir: Robert Wise, 89 mins.)

Destination Inner Space (1966)*½ Scott Brady, Sheree North, Gary Merrill. (Dir: Francis D. Lyon, 82 mins.)

Destination Moon (1950)*** Warner Anderson, John Archer. An American space ship takes off to reach the moon. Science-fiction drama is not as fantastic as when it was first released; good detail, imaginative special effects. (Dir: Irving Pichel, 91 mins.)

Destination Tokyo (1943)** Cary Grant, John Garfield, Alan Hale, Dane Clark, Warner Anderson. Archetypal wartime submarine picture, with Grant as the patrician captain on a mission underwater to Tokyo and Garfield as the rebellious sailor. Goes on forever. Delmer Daves directed—and wrote, with Albert Maltz. (135 mins.)

Destiny (1944)** Alan Curtis, Gloria Jean. Escaped prisoner takes refuge in a farm owned by a man with a blind daughter. Uneven drama, with some sequences much better than others. Originally was a sequence for **Flesh and Fantasy**; was expanded. (Dir: Reginald Le Borg, 65 mins.)

Destiny of a Spy (1969)**½ Lorne Greene, Rachel Roberts. This made-for-TV feature film has two things going for it—an excellent British supporting cast and the fine on-location photography of London. Lorne Greene's fans will probably have some trouble accepting him as a Russian spy

who is taken out of mothballs to complete just one more dangerous mission involving a frightened British scientist, a German informer, and the development of a sophisticated counter-radar system. The yarn spins along with few surprises but is richly enhanced by Patrick Magee as a demented witness, Harry Andrews as a compassionate but efficient intelligence officer and Anthony Quayle as Greene's superior. (Dir: Boris Sagal, 99 mins.)

Destroy All Monsters (Japan, 1969)* Akira Kubo, Jun Tazaki. (Dir: Ishiro Honda, 87 mins.)

Destructors, The (Great Britain, 1974)* Anthony Quinn, Michael Caine, James Mason. (Dir: Robert Parrish, 89 mins.)

Destry (1954)**½ Audie Murphy, Mari Blanchard. Not altogether successful remake of the Stewart-Dietrich vehicle made 15 years earlier. Murphy is very good as the gunless Sheriff, but Mari Blanchard is a bust as a replacement for marvelous Marlene. The plot still holds a certain fascination. (Dir: George Marshall, 95 mins.)

Destry Rides Again (1939)***½ James Stewart, Marlene Dietrich, Brian Donlevy, Billy Gilbert, Charles Winninger. An enjoyable film that marks Dietrich's emergence into her shrouded mystique of the '30s into the raucous personality of the '40s. Stewart is the gunslinger without guns, and Donlevy, Gilbert, and especially Winninger as a drunken sheriff are funny and fine, but Dietrich's catfight and rendition of "See What the Boys in the Back Room Will Have" are what you will remember. (94 mins.)

Detective, The (Great Britain, 1954)*** Alec Guinness, Joan Greenwood. Guinness is delightful as a priest who fancies himself a top flight amateur detective. The picture is not among his best but has some pleasant moments as Father Brown tries to trap an art thief. (Dir: Robert Hamer, 100 mins.)

Detective, The (1968)*** Frank Sinatra, Lee Remick, Jack Klugman. Screenwriter Abby Mann has written some pungent, realistic dialogue for this well above-average drama about a hard-bitten New York City police detective investigating a messy murder of a young homosexual. It's your only chance of the night, perhaps, to see Horace McMahon playing a police officer, and there's an attractive performance from Jacqueline Bisset. (When Frankie leaves the environs of New York for a short drive and shows up at a beach house that looks suspiciously like California, don't trade in your glasses! It really *was* California used in the location sequences by the lazy producer.) (Dir: Gordon Douglas, 114 mins.)

Detective Story (1951)**** Kirk Douglas, Eleanor Parker, William Bendix. Sidney Kingsley's Broadway play is excellently adapted to the screen by director William Wyler. Kirk Douglas gives one of his fin-

171

est screen performances as a detective whose personal code becomes twisted from dealing with criminals over a number of years. Most of the action takes place in a New York precinct on one day with assorted "supporting" thieves getting some good scenes, particularly Joseph Wiseman as a burglar, and Lee Grant as a shoplifter. (103 mins.)

Detour (1945)*** Tom Neal, Ann Savage. What can you say about a grade-Z production starring a catatonic unknown (Neal) and the most metaphysically grotesque actress ever to grace an American film (Savage) that takes place mainly in front of a rear-projection screen and a progression of minimally rendered motel rooms and roadside diners, except that it's one of the most daring, perverse works of art ever to come out of Hollywood? Director Edgar G. Ulmer was a master of stylization whose achievement is only now beginning to be appreciated. Screenplay by Martin Goldsmith. (70 mins.)

Detour (Bulgaria, 1969)***½ Nevena Kokanova, Ivan Andonov. Bittersweet, poignant two-character love story of a brief encounter. Engineer driving to the airport at Sofia gives a ride to an archeologist who turns out to be his first love from their university days. (Dirs: Grisha Ostrovski, Tudor Stoyanov, 78 mins.)

Detroit 9000—See: **Police Call 9000**

Devil and Daniel Webster, The (1941)**** Walter Huston, Edward Arnold, James Craig, Ann Shirley. One of the best films ever made. Superb fantasy set in early New England, as a man sells his soul to the devil in return for riches. Alternate title: **All That Money Can Buy**. (Dir: William Dieterle, 106 mins.)

Devil and Miss Jones (1941)*** Jean Arthur, Robert Cummings, Charles Coburn. Pleasant comedy about a department store tycoon who takes a job, incognito, in his own store. Dated but fun. (Dir: Sam Wood, 92 mins.)

Devil and Miss Sarah (MTV 1971)* Gene Barry, James Drury, Janice Rule, Slim Pickens. (Dir: Michael Caffey, 72 mins.)

Devil at 4 O'Clock, The (1961)**½ Spencer Tracy, Frank Sinatra, Kerwin Mathews, Jean-Pierre Aumont. Aging priest and three convicts undertake a perilous rescue mission when a tropic island is threatened by a volcano eruption. Uneven drama has the two stars lending their talents to a weak script, occasionally overcoming the routine situations, direction. (Dir: Mervyn Le Roy, 126 mins.)

Devil at My Heels (France, 1966)*½ Sami Frey, Francoise Hardy, Spiros Focas. (Dir: Jean-Daniel Pollet, 91 mins.)

Devil Doll (1936)***½ Lionel Barrymore. Director Tod Browning's terrific horror thriller about the revenge of a man framed for murder by three business rivals. Marvelous, scary special effects. (80 mins.)

Devil Doll (Great Britain, 1964)** Bryant Haliday, William Sylvester, Yvonne Romain. Hypnotist who uses a wooden dummy in his act is suspected by an investigating reporter of having some dire secret. Adequate thriller has some slightly offbeat angles to keep the interest. (Dir: Lindsay Shonteff, 80 mins.)

Devil In Love, The (Italy, 1966)**½ Vittorio Gassman, Mickey Rooney, Claudine Auger. Surprisingly entertaining film. Gassman and Rooney are sent as envoys from Archdevil Beelzebub circa 1478 to foment war between Rome and Florence during the Renaissance. Refreshing approach to period farce, exuberant cast make this an amusing outing. (Dir: Ettore Scola, 72 mins.)

Devil In the Flesh (France, 1949)***½ Gerard Philippe, Micheline Presle. English-dubbed. Beautifully acted tragic tale of a young student's affair with a mature married woman during World War I. Dubbed dialogue detracts a bit from the drama, but it's still well worthwhile adult drama. (Dir: Claude Autant-Lara, 110 mins.)

Devil Is a Sissy, The (1936)**½ Mickey Rooney, Jackie Cooper, Freddie Bartholomew. Occasionally entertaining juvenile delinquency story featuring the top three young male stars of the era. (Dir: W. S. Van Dyke, 92 mins.)

Devil Is a Woman, The (1935)** Marlene Dietrich, Cesar Romero, Lionel Atwill. Story of an older man who permits himself to be destroyed by the demands of a lovely woman. A bit stilted for modern tastes and you may find it boring. (Dir: Josef von Sternberg, 85 mins.)

Devil Made a Woman, The—See: **Girl Against Napoleon, A**

Devil Makes Three, The (1952)**½ Gene Kelly, Pier Angeli. American GI in post-war Germany becomes involved in black market smuggling after meeting a night club girl. Familiar melodrama given a lift by on-the-spot locations in Germany. (Dir: Andrew Marton, 90 mins.)

Devil of the Desert Against the Son of Hercules (Italy-Spain, 1965)*½ Kirk Morris, Michele Girardon. (Dir: Antonio Margheriti, 93 mins.)

Devil on Horseback (Great Britain, 1954)** Googie Withers, John McCallum, Jeremy Spenser. A young miner's son becomes a winning jockey, but is responsible for the death of a horse when he fouls another jockey in a race. Slow-moving racing melodrama. (Dir: Cyril Frankel, 88 mins.)

Devil Pays Off, The (1941)*** J. Edward Bromberg, Osa Massen. A civilian agent exposes a shipping magnate about to sell his fleet to a foreign power. Well-made, exciting melodrama; noteworthy are John Auer's direction, John Alton's photography. (Dir: John H. Auer, 56 mins.)

Devil Rides Out, The—See: **Devil's Bride, The**

Devil Strikes at Night (Germany, 1958)*** Mario Adorf, Claus Holm. Penetrating study of a psychopathic murderer during

172

the war in Germany. Gestapo enters the case with fascinating results. Mario Adorf is magnificent as the homicidal maniac. (Dir: Robert Siodmak, 105 mins.)

Devil to Pay, The (1931)** Ronald Colman, Loretta Young, Myrna Loy. A not too successful adaptation of a Lonsdale comedy of manners. A bit too stiff and artificial for today's audiences. (Dir: George Fitzmaurice, 80 mins.)

Devil's Agent, The (Great Britain, 1962)** Macdonald Carey, Peter Van Eyck, Christopher Lee. Wine merchant used as an informer by both sides of the Iron Curtain is shot down in Vienna. Average spy thriller with a better than average cast. (Dir: John Paddy Carstairs, 77 mins.)

Devil's Bedroom, The (1964)* John Lupton, Dick Jones, Valerie Allen. (Dir: L. Q. Jones, 78 mins.)

Devil's Bride, The (Great Britain, 1968)**½ Christopher Lee, Charles Gray, Nike Arrighi. Above average horror chiller, with Lee razor-sharp in a switch to the good-guy role—fending off the gathering powers of evil aroused by a group of Satanists. Alternate title: "The Devil Rides Out." (Dir: Terence Fisher, 95 mins.)

Devil's Brigade, The (1968)**½ William Holden, Cliff Robertson, Vince Edwards, Michael Rennie, Dana Andrews. Misfit American GIs join efficient Canadian troops for commando tactics during World War II. Competent if familiar heroics. (Dir: Andrew McLaglen, 130 mins.)

Devil's Brother, The (1933)** Laurel and Hardy, Dennis King, Thelma Todd, James Finlayson. The first Laurel and Hardy operetta (the victim is an 1830 work, "Fra Diavolo," by Auber). There's one classic sequence in which the boys attempt to bottle some wine, but the film suffers from the second-fiddle status conferred on the stars by the script—which has them playing servants to one of the period's ubiquitous sappy tenors (King). (Dirs: Hal Roach and Charles Rogers, 88 mins.)

Devil's Canyon (1953)**½ Virginia Mayo, Dale Robertson. Ex-marshal is sent to prison where he becomes involved with mutineers against his will. Passable combination of western and prison melodrama. (Dir: Alfred L. Werker, 91 mins.)

Devil's Daughter, The (MTV 1972)* Shelley Winters, Belinda Montgomery. (Dir: Jeannot Szwarc, 74 mins.)

Devil's Disciple (Great Britain, 1959)***½ Kirk Douglas, Burt Lancaster, Laurence Olivier. Not the best screen translation of a George Bernard Shaw work, but a rousing good try. Kirk Douglas energetically portrays "Dick Dudgeon," the rebellious and romantic rogue; Burt Lancaster, miscast once again, pompously plays a New England pastor; and Olivier makes the most of his few scenes as the very grand and very opinionated British General Burgoyne. (Dir: Guy Hamilton, 82 mins.)

Devil's Doorway, The (1950)*** Robert Taylor, Louis Calhern. An Indian veteran of the Civil War returns to find injustice and tragedy for his people, fights to aid them. Well-done western drama takes the Indian's point of view, does a good job of it. Direction and photography especially noteworthy, performances good. (Dir: Anthony Mann, 84 mins.)

Devil's Eight, The (1969)** Christopher George, Ralph Meeker, Fabian. Action meller which turns out to be a poor man's "Dirty Dozen." George is a federal agent who enlists the services of a motley crew of prisoners to bust a big moonshining syndicate. (Dir: Burt Topper, 97 mins.)

Devil's Eye, The (Sweden, 1960)*** Jarl Kulle, Bibi Andersson. Bits of the Bergman elegance and insight, snips of humor and captivating paradoxical detail. Story is reminiscent of G. B. Shaw's "Don Juan in Hell": the Devil gets a sty in his eye and resurrects his captive, Don Juan, to deal with its cause—the irritating chastity of a young woman up on earth. One of Bergman's few comedies. Written and directed by Ingmar Bergman. (90 mins.)

Devil's General (Germany, 1956)***½ Curt Jurgens, Marianne Cook. Famous wartime flyer gradually becomes disgusted with the Nazis, and the hopelessness of World War II. Talkative, but engrossing drama, with superb performances, direction. (Dir: Helmut Kautner, 119 mins.)

Devil's Hairpin, The (1957)**½ Cornel Wilde, Jean Wallace, Mary Astor. Champion sports-car racer's disregard of safety is responsible for the crippling of his brother—he tries to reform. As usual, the racing scenes are the main attraction—story line holds up fairly well. (Dir: Cornel Wilde, 82 mins.)

Devil's Hand, The (1961)* Robert Alda, Linda Christian. (Dir: William J. Hole, Jr., 71 mins.)

Devil's Messenger, The (1962)*½ Lon Chaney, Karen Kadler. (Dir: Herbert L. Strock, 72 mins.)

Devil's Own, The (Great Britain, 1966)**½ Joan Fontaine, Kay Walsh, Ingrid Brett. Teacher (Fontaine) at an English private school comes across witchcraft and voodoo rites. Suspense fans will come across a few chills. Marvelous actor Alec McCowen wasted. (Dir: Cyril Frankel, 90 mins.)

Devil's Partner, The (1961)** Edwin Nelson, Jean Allison, Edgar Buchanan. Stranger shows up in a small town, then weird things begin to happen. Unbelievable thriller has good acting to help it. (Dir: Charles R. Rondeau, 75 mins.)

Devil's Rain, The (1975)* Ernest Borgnine, Eddie Albert, Ida Lupino, William Shatner, Keenan Wynn, John Travolta. (Dir: Robert Fuest, 85 mins.)

Devil's Wanton, The (Sweden, 1949)**½ Doris Svedlund, Birger Malmsten. Director Ingmar Bergman's theory of Hell on earth, told from the viewpoint of a girl who tries to find happiness with a man deserted by his wife after her lover has had their baby killed. Often more artiness than art;

gloomy drama for devotees of the Swedish director. English-dubbed. (Dir: Ingmar Bergman, 72 mins.)

Devil's Widow, The—See: **Tam Lin**

Devotion (1946)**½ Ida Lupino, Paul Henreid, Olivia de Havilland. The genius of the Bronte sisters receives a Hollywood treatment in this photoplay. Excellent acting rescues the film but they should have called it "Distortion." (Dir: Curtis Bernhardt, 107 mins.)

D.I., The (1957)** Jack Webb, Don Dubbins, Monica Lewis. Webb portrays a very tough drill instructor in the marines. We see him take a group through the rigorous routines and it gets a little boring. In addition to starring, Webb produced and directed this opus. (106 mins.)

Diabolically Yours (France, 1968)** Senta Berger, Alain Delon. Middling mystery about an amnesiac (Delon) who attempts to unravel the secret of his forgotten memory. Miss Berger is a mysterious woman who helps treat him. Never sustains its suspense. (Dir: Ralph Baum, 101 mins.)

Diabolique (France, 1955)**** Simone Signoret, Vera Clouzot. Excellent, scary murder mystery, as the mistress of a schoolmaster and his wife plan an elaborate murder. One of Simone Signoret's finest performances, the film contains scenes that will leave you on the edge of your seat. Superb direction by Henri-Georges Clouzot. (107 mins.)

Dial Hot Line (MTV 1969)* Vince Edwards, Chelsea Brown, Kim Hunter. (Dir: Jerry Thorpe, 100 mins.)

Dial M for Murder (1954)***½ Ray Milland, Grace Kelly, Robert Cummings, John Williams, Anthony Dawson. Kelly is suspected of murdering a man she didn't even know—or did she? This version of Frederick Knott's hit play uncannily contains many of the usual Hitchcock stylistic devices—the action around the staircase, the transference of guilt, the trade of murders, the intimations of breakdown. Director Hitchcock ignores the play's single-set restriction, proving that imaginative direction can be cinematic without "going" anywhere. John Williams steals scenes as the unflappable police inspector (Dir: Alfred Hitchcock, 105 mins.)

Dial 1119 (1950)**½ Marshall Thompson, Keefe Brasselle. Good suspense thriller that keeps your interest. The cast is primarily made up of no name stars but do very nicely. The setting is a bar where a killer keeps a group trapped. (Dir: Gerald Mayer, 74 mins.)

Dial Red O (1955)**½ William Elliott, Keith Larsen. Smart detective proves the innocence of a disturbed war vet accused of murder. Neat little detective story made on a small budget. (Dir: Daniel B. Ullman, 62 mins.)

Diamond Earrings, The (French, 1953)** Charles Boyer, Danielle Darrieux, Vittorio De Sica. A sometimes tragic and most times confusing "merry-go-round" giving and receiving of a pair of diamond earrings. Stars cannot rise above the script. Alternate title: **The Earrings of Madame De.** (Dir: Max Ophuls, 105 mins.)

Diamond Head (1962)** Charlton Heston, Yvette Mimieux, George Chakiris. Strictly for fans who like their soap opera lavishly mounted and star-studded with Hollywood names. Charlton Heston is a bigger-than-life plantation owner in Hawaii who wants everything his way. His sister (Yvette Mimieux) is equally independent and announces she is going to marry a Hawaiian native (James Darren). The conflict rages on to the finale with Heston baring his chest and teeth at the entire supporting cast. The Hawaiian locations are more interesting than the cardboard characters. (Dir: Guy Green, 107 mins.)

Diamond Jim (1935)*** Edward Arnold, Binnie Barnes, Jean Arthur. Story of "Diamond Jim" Brady, the millionaire sportsman and man-about-town of the gay nineties. Well done period drama. (Dir: A. Edward Sutherland, 100 mins.)

Diamond Queen, The (1953)**½ Fernando Lamas, Arlene Dahl, Gilbert Roland. Two soldiers of fortune in India bargain with a treacherous Mogul for a fabulous blue diamond. Routine adventure. (Dir: John Brahm, 80 mins.)

Diamond Safari (1958)*½ Kevin McCarthy, Andre Morell. (Dir: Woolf Phillips, 67 mins.)

Diamond Wizard, The (Great Britain, 1954)**½ Dennis O'Keefe, Margaret Sheridan. T-Man traces a stolen million to England, ties it in with diamond thievery. Okay crime melodrama. (Dir: Dennis O'Keefe, 83 mins.)

Diamonds (U.S.-Israel, 1976)*½ Robert Shaw, Richard Roundtree, Barbara Seagull. (106 mins.)

Diamonds Are Forever (Great Britain, 1971)***½ Sean Connery, Jill St. John, Charles Gray, Bruce Cabot. Terrific escapist James Bond fun. This is the eighth 007 entry, the sixth to star Connery, and the first to utilize American locations—Los Angeles, Palm Springs, Reno, etc. The basic setting is Las Vegas, the quarry is another evil villain willing and eager to rule the world. Maestro Bond's libido, drollery, and extensive gadgetry foil the rascals, of course. Connery returns to the role of Bond after an absence of four years and he's wonderful—far better than George Lazenby or Roger Moore. Deft screenplay by Richard Maibaum and Tom Mankiewicz, based, of course, on the novel by Ian Fleming. (Dir: Guy Hamilton, 119 mins.)

Diamonds of the Night (Czechoslovakia, 1964)***½ A remarkable directorial debut by 27-year-old Jan Nemec. A bleak, alternately realistic and hallucinatory examination of four days in the lives of two young escapees from the Nazis. Its mood of desperation and paranoia works a grim magic.

Diane (1956)** Lana Turner, Pedro Armendariz, Roger Moore. King's son about to be married to an Italian princess is enamoured of a glamorous French countess. Overstuffed costume drama. (Dir: David Miller, 102 mins.)

Diary of a Bad Girl (France, 1958)*½ Anne Vernon, Danik Patisson. (Dir: Leonide Moguy, 87 mins.)

Diary of a Chambermaid (1946)*** Paulette Goddard, Burgess Meredith. A bewitching chambermaid is hired by a family of eccentrics, where she is involved in amorous byplay and finally murder. Odd, uneven comedy-drama. Some interesting moments, but all rather uncertain. (Dir: Jean Renoir, 86 mins.)

Diary of a High School Bride (1959)** Anita Sands, Ronald Foster. When a teenager marries a young law student, her mother and ex-boyfriend do all they can to break it up. Sincerely done despite the lurid title, but doesn't quite succeed. Some good moments. (Dir: Burt Topper, 72 mins.)

Diary of a Mad Housewife (1970)**** Richard Benjamin, Carrie Snodgress, Frank Langella. Entertaining, perceptive drama boasts marvelous performance by Carrie Snodgress as a bored New York housewife-mother, and Frank Langella as a dashing, successful, and thoroughly selfish writer with whom she has an affair. Richard Benjamin is less interesting in the role of Miss Snodgress's fastidious lawyer-husband who wants to be part of the New York chic scene. Excellent dissection of a modern urban marriage. (Dir: Frank Perry, 94 mins.)

Diary of a Madman (1963)**½ Vincent Price, Nancy Kovack. More of Vincent Price's flamboyant overacting. He plays a French judge who finds he's possessed by a demon, decides life's not worth living. Based on a story by Guy de Maupassant. (Dir: Reginald Le Borg, 96 mins.)

Diary of a Teacher (Italy, 1972)***½ Bruno Cirino, Marisa Fabbri, Mico Cundari. Ambitious and lengthy—over 4½ hours—documentary drama written and directed by Vittorio De Seta and produced by RAI, Italian TV. Frequently moving and perceptive story based on the book "A Year in Petralata," chronicling the attempts of a young, committed teacher and his attempts to involve and intellectually stimulate "problem" youngsters born of impoverished, poorly educated parents. Director decided to "reconstruct, relive, and film from reality, from the authentic teaching experience." Italian dialogue with frequent English narration. Example of imaginative innovative TV, so seldom undertaken by the American TV industry. "Diary" is TV debut for De Seta, responsible for the 1960 "Bandits of Orgosolo." (272 mins.)

Diary of Anne Frank, The (1959)***½ Joseph Schildkraut, Millie Perkins, Shelley Winters. Faithful screen translation of the hit Broadway play about the true, harrowing experiences of the Jewish Frank family and their friends when they are forced to hide from the Nazis in a factory attic in Amsterdam for two long years. Millie Perkins is visually perfect as the young Anne Frank whose spirit gives the group the courage to go on when they lose all hope, but her thesping leaves much to be desired. Of the good supporting cast, Joseph Schildkraut as Anne's strong father and Shelley Winters, as the terrified Mrs. Van Daan, are standouts. Winters won a Supporting Oscar. (Dir: George Stevens, 170 mins.)

Diary of Anne Frank, The (MTV 1980)**** Melissa Gilbert, Maximilian Schell, Joan Plowright, James Coco, Clive Revill. The cast, led by Gilbert as Anne Frank and Schell, is first-rate. The saga of Jews hiding in Nazi-occupied Amsterdam during WW II could be the story of any group of human beings forced to live in fear, while giving way to irritations caused by constricted conditions. It reflects how we all love and hate, change our minds, feel sorry for ourselves, and face adversity as a unity. Contains more life and emotion than the earlier movie version. (Dir: Boris Sagal, 104 mins.)

Dick Tracy (1945)** Morgan Conway, Anne Jeffreys, Mike Mazurki, Jane Greer. Sleuth tracks down Splitface, a maniacal killer bent on revenge. Acceptable comic-strip heroics. (Dir: William Berke, 62 mins.)

Dick Tracy Meets Gruesome (1947)**½ Ralph Byrd, Boris Karloff, Anne Gwynne, Edward Ashley. Sleuth goes after a quartet of bank robbers, using a new kind of paralyzing gas. Fast moving comic-strip melodrama, with Karloff giving it added allure. (Dir: John Rawlins, 65 mins.)

Dictator's Guns, The (Italy-France, 1965)*½ Sylva Koscina, Leo Gordon, Lino Ventura. (Dir: Claude Sautet, 105 mins.)

Did You Hear the One About the Traveling Saleslady? (1968)* Phyllis Diller. (Dir: Don Weis, 97 mins.)

Die! Die! My Darling (Great Britain, 1965)**½ Tallulah Bankhead, Stefanie Powers. Demented woman keeps a young American girl prisoner because she was the fiancée of her dead son. Standard shocker, with Bankhead giving a ripe performance. Thriller fans should give it a passing shudder. Miss Powers was TV's "Girl from U.N.C.L.E." (Dir: Silvio Narizzano, 97 mins.)

Die .Laughing (1980)* Robby Benson, Linda Grosvenor, Charles Durning. (Dir: Jeff Werner, 108 mins.)

Die, Monster, Die (Great Britain, 1965)** Boris Karloff, Nick Adams, Suzi Farmer. Young American arrives in Britain to visit his fiancée, finds her living in a house of horror. Slow-moving thriller can boast of Karloff's customary fine performance, a certain air of suspense. (Dir: Daniel Haller, 80 mins.)

Dillinger (1945)**½ Lawrence Tierney, Anne Jeffreys. Story of the 20th Century's most notorious public enemy hardly does his career justice but is an above average gangster film. (Dir: Max Nosseck, 89 mins.)

Dillinger (1973)**½ Warren Oates, Ben Johnson, Cloris Leachman, Richard Dreyfuss. Hard-driving rhythm of this narrative, supposedly the truth about John Dillinger, Public Enemy No. 1 of the Depression years, keeps interest, but the gratuitous violence finally overwhelms the film. Warren Oates gives a fine performance as Dillinger, but the script leaves no room for insight into the character and thus makes him merely a cartoon book villain. Written and directed by John Milius, then 29 years old. Impressive debut in some ways. (107 mins.)

Dime with a Halo (1963)*½ Barbara Luna, Roger Mobley. (Dir: Boris Sagal, 97 mins.)

Dimples (1936)**½ Shirley Temple, Frank Morgan. Set right before the Civil War on New York's Bowery, this one has Shirley practically selling herself to a rich lady to save her poor daddy. There's a happy, tearful ending for the faithful. (Dir: William A. Seiter, 78 mins.)

Dingaka (Great Britain, 1965)**½ Stanley Baker, Juliet Prowse, Ken Gampu. Attorney takes the case of a tribesman up for murdering a rival whom he believes killed his daughter. Fairly interesting drama filmed in Africa, with the local color partially compensating for a rather sketchy plot. (Dir: Jamie Uys, 98 mins.)

Dinner at Eight (1933)***½ John Barrymore, Jean Harlow, Marie Dressler, Billie Burke, Lionel Barrymore, Wallace Beery, Roland Young. The best of the MGM all-star vehicles of the '30s. Delightful comedy-drama that makes the most of its cumbersome structure by good casting of sharply drawn characters whose dramas comment on one another. Director George Cukor transforms the shopworn anecdotal material into meaningful expression. (113 mins.)

Dinner at the Ritz (Great Britain, 1937)**½ Annabella, Paul Lukas, David Niven. A girl sets out to find her father's murderer, runs into a swindling gang in her quest. Good melodrama keeps the interest. (Dir: Harold D. Schuster, 80 mins.)

Dino (1957)*** Sal Mineo, Susan Kohner, Brian Keith. Sometimes moving drama about a young hood with a chip on his shoulder. Played with a sneer by Sal Mineo. Brian Keith gives a good performance as a social worker who tries to help the hostile youth. Based on a TV play by Reginald Rose. (Dir: Thomas Carr, 96 mins.)

Diplomatic Courier (1952)**½ Tyrone Power, Patricia Neal, Hildegarde Neff. Cloak-and-dagger yarn with good performances by Power and Hildegarde Neff.

Plot offers no new twists but keeps the pace fast and suspenseful. (Dir: Henry Hathaway, 97 mins.)

Dirigible (1931)**½ Jack Holt, Fay Wray, Ralph Graves, Hobart Bosworth, Roscoe Karns. I can't help it, but those damn blimps have always fascinated me, especially the gigantic ocean liners of the sky that were as luxurious as the QE II. This is a limber, entertaining action movie set in 1931, when dirigibles seemed a viable competitor to the airplane for passengers, and it features a most spectacular air disaster near, of all places, the North Pole. It's said that when the cows of Ireland spotted these airships they ran in terror, and from their perspective, it was no wonder. Story by Frank Wead. (Dir: Frank Capra, 93 mins.)

Dirty Dingus Magee (1970)* Frank Sinatra, George Kennedy, Anne Jackson. (Dir: Burt Kennedy, 91 mins.)

Dirty Dozen, The (1967)***½ Lee Marvin, Jim Brown, Ernest Borgnine, John Cassavetes. If you're a devotee of rugged wartime adventure stories filled with lots of tough guys and fights, this is your dream picture. Director Robert Aldrich may have filmed this in Britain, but what's on the screen is an unmistakably American vision of authority and army life, and the nature of the violence in the soldiers is dealt with on some interesting levels. Concerns a gang of convicted G.I.s who are reprieved, only to be trained and turned into more efficient killers. (149 mins.)

Dirty Game, The (France-Italy-West Germany, 1965)* Henry Fonda, Vittorio Gassman, Robert Ryan, Annie Girardot. Alternate title: **The Secret Agents**. (Dirs: Terence Young, Christian-Jaque, Carlo Lizzani, Werner Klingler, 91 mins.)

Dirty Hands (France-West Germany-Italy, 1975)** Rod Steiger, Romy Schneider, Paolo Giusti, Jean Rochefort. Schneider and Steiger are a vacuous upper-class couple involved in a murderous love triangle. The American version lacks a half hour of director Claude Chabrol's original footage. The film seems weak and overwrought for the usually meticulous Chabrol. Based on Richard Neely's book "Damned Innocents." (125 mins.)

Dirty Harry (1971)* Clint Eastwood, Harry Guardino. (Dir: Don Siegel, 102 mins.)

Dirty Mary, Crazy Larry (1974)** Peter Fonda, Vic Morrow, Susan George. If your tastes run to multiple car crashes, highspeed car chases and race car heroesturned-thieves, this is for you. Peter Fonda is a small-time car racer with dreams for the big time. He and his buddy rob a supermarket, and spend the rest of the film running from the law. A perky, sexy, thrill-crazy girl joins them and it's full throttle from start to finish. (Dir: John Hough, 93 mins.)

Disappearance of Aimee, The (MTV 1976)**½ Faye Dunaway, Bette Davis,

James Sloyan. Dunaway plays the glamorous evangelist Aimee Semple McPherson who vanished into the Mexican desert for five weeks in '26 and reappeared claiming she had been kidnapped. The main drama is the hearing her skeptical mother (Davis) and suspicious police officials put her through as she lies in bed recuperating. Dunaway does a creditable job without much support from the superficial script and Davis turns her blistering, suspicious gaze into an effective character device. (Dir: Anthony Harvey, 104 mins.)

Disappearance of Flight 412, The (MTV 1974)**½ Glenn Ford, Bradford Dillman, Guy Stockwell. For sci-fi fans. Air Force personnel become involved with a missing aircraft which might have tangled with UFO's. It's played straight and the production values are good. (Dir: Jud Taylor, 72 mins.)

Disappeared, The (Cuba-Sweden, 1979)***½ One of the most heartwrenching political atrocities of recent years, the 30,000 Chilean citizens who disappeared after the junta seized power from Salvador Allende in '73. The film is a dramatization, but it is not fiction. A necessary "sequel" to "The Battle of Chile." (Dir: Sergio Castilla.)

Discreet Charm of the Bourgeoisie, The (France, 1972)**** Delphine Seyrig, Fernando Rey, Stephane Audran, Jean-Pierre Cassel. The great master-writer-director Luis Bunuel, at age 72 helming his 29th film, has produced one of his most dazzling films ever—wry, stylish, serious, ebullient, funny and profound—all at different times in the same delicious film. Bunuel here savages the upper and middle classes with better humor than usual, but no less brilliance. About some South American diplomats from a tiny country, posted to Paris. Bunuel thrusts at many of his usual targets—politics, the church, the army and the foibles of all mankind. Co-authored by Bunuel and Jean Claude Carriere. (100 mins.)

Disembodied, The (1957)** Paul Burke, Allison Hayes. Combination horror-mystery film with some sci-fi phenomena thrown in. The kids may go for this tale set in the jungle. If you're not in the jungle, you can do better. (Dir: Walter Grauman, 65 mins.)

Dishonorable Discharge (France, 1958)** Eddie Constantine. Another Eddie Constantine Grade B drama with the keynote on action. He plays a wrongly accused ex-Navy officer who manages to clear his name after some action-filled complications. English-dubbed. (Dir: Bernard Borderie, 105 mins.)

Dishonored (1931)*** Marlene Dietrich, Victor McLaglen, Warner Oland. Story by Josef von Sternberg. Dated spy drama but you'll enjoy secret agent Marlene's encounter with General Oland. As usual, La Dietrich is gorgeous. (Dir: Josef von Sternberg, 91 mins.)

Disobedient (Great Britain, 1955)*½ Marian Spencer, Russell Enoch. Alternative title: **Intimate Relations.** (Dir: Charles Frank, 86 mins.)

Disorder (France-Italy, 1962)*½ Louis Jourdan, Susan Strasberg, Curt Jurgens, Alida Valli. (Dir: Franco Brusati, 105 mins.)

Disorderly Orderly, The (1964)** Jerry Lewis, Susan Oliver. Routine Jerry Lewis fun fare. In this excursion, Jerry works as a hospital orderly, the setting for his frenzied slapstick. Familiar faces in the supporting cast include veterans Alice Pearce, Kathleen Freeman and Glenda Farrell. If only Lewis had had the discipline and sense to have a gifted director, and then listen to him! (Dir: Frank Tashlin, 90 mins.)

Dispatch from Reuters (1940)*** Edward G. Robinson, Eddie Albert. Story of the founder of the world-famous British news agency is informative, well produced and acted but sorely lacking in dramatic content. (Dir: William Dieterle, 89 mins.)

Disraeli (1929)*** George Arliss, Joan Bennett. The wily and brilliant Prime Minister of England paves the way for the Suez Canal. Despite its primitive movie technique, this historical drama contains a still gripping, Oscar-winning, authoritative performance by Arliss. (Dir: Alfred E. Green, 90 mins.)

Distant Drums (1951)*** Gary Cooper. Drama of Seminole Indian uprising in Florida is loaded with action and must be classified as good entertainment for adventure fans. (Dir: Raoul Walsh, 101 mins.)

Distant Trumpet, A (1964)** Troy Donahue, Suzanne Pleshette. A dull cavalry western with every cliché about the personal problems of those stationed at a frontier outpost. The scenery is fine. Oh, yes, there are Indians waiting in the wings. (Dir: Raoul Walsh, 117 mins.)

Dive Bomber (1941)*** Errol Flynn, Fred MacMurray, Alexis Smith, Ralph Bellamy. Interesting, well played story about medical problems concerning flying in 1941. Even though it's dated today, there's still a certain amount of historical interest. (Dir: Michael Curtiz, 133 mins.)

Divided Heart, The (Great Britain, 1954)***½ Theodore Bikel, Alexander Knox. An absorbing drama about the story of a boy torn between two mothers who love and want him. Good performances. Set in Europe after World War II. (Dir: Charles Crichton, 100 mins.)

Divided Trail, The (1980)*** The Indian migrations continue, from the reservations to the city. Shot during eight years, this film chronicles the gradual disintegration of a group of Chippewas who come to Chicago and urban alienation. A fascinating subject handled with appropriate commitment by director Jerry Aronson with Mical Goldman.

Divine Madness (1980)***½ Bette Midler.

Midler's concert act was filmed during a three-night stand at the Pasadena Civic Auditorium. A distant third to "The Last Waltz," and "Richard Pryor in Concert." Midler's energy as a performer is undeniable, and she can sing some and tell jokes even better, but she is much less impressive on screen than in person. Producer-director Michael Ritchie has probably captured as much of the excitement of her act as technology will allow. (94 mins.)

Divorce American Style (1967)***½ Dick Van Dyke, Debbie Reynolds, Jason Robards, Jean Simmons. One of the very few deft satires produced by the American film industry in recent years. Stylish script by producer Norman Lear casts a perceptive and jaundiced eye on the American institution of marriage in suburbia. Dick and Debbie are splitting up after many years, and friend Robards, divorced from Jean Simmons, comes up with a far-fetched scheme to fix everything. Director Bud Yorkin gets good performances from all concerned. (109 mins.)

Divorce His; Divorce Hers (MTV 1973)** Richard Burton, Elizabeth Taylor. Weak vehicle for Taylor and Burton. Intended to be a brittle analysis of the events leading up to the disintegration of a marriage, holds interest when the break-up is viewed from both sides. Movie's first half is the story as seen by Burton; second half has Miss Taylor's Jane as the focal point. (Dir: Waris Hussein, 144 mins.)

Divorce—Italian Style (Italy, 1962)**** Marcello Mastroianni, Daniela Rocca. One of the most brilliant modern film comedies. Tremendous performance by Mastroianni as a decadent Sicilian nobleman who wants to get rid of his wife, but can't—the law, you know. Excellent satire on modern Italian manners and mores. Expertly directed, a biting satiric joy throughout. Don't miss it. (Dir: Pietro Germi, 104 mins.)

Divorce of Lady X, The (Great Britain, 1938)*** Merle Oberon, Laurence Olivier, Binnie Barnes, Ralph Richardson. A London barrister allows a pretty miss to spend the night (innocently) in his flat, then discovers he may be named corespondent in a divorce action. Pleasant sophisticated comedy, some good laughs. (Dir: Tim Whelan, 91 mins.)

Divorcee, The (1930)**½ Norma Shearer, Chester Morris, Robert Montgomery. Shearer should never have won a Best Actress Oscar over Greta Garbo and Gloria Swanson, but her performance and this film are surprisingly good. She plays a woman who discovers her husband's infidelity, lets her marriage go by the boards, and takes a crack at the wild life herself. Robert Z. Leonard directed well enough to make one wonder about his otherwise mediocre career. Based on Ursula Parrott's novel "Ex-Wife." (83 mins.)

Dixie (1943)**½ Bing Crosby, Dorothy Lamour. Some good minstrel numbers in this fictitious biography of a famous minstrel man, but story is weak and tiresome. (Dir: A. Edward Sutherland, 89 mins.)

Do Not Disturb (1965)** Doris Day, Rod Taylor. Another Doris Day romantic comedy which her immediate family will no doubt enjoy. All others, be forewarned—it's overly cute. In this one, Miss Day is married to Rod Taylor. They go to England where a series of madcap adventures threaten their marital bliss. Script gives no indication of whether Doris is or is not a virgin in this opus. (Dir: Ralph Levy, 102 mins.)

Do You Know This Voice? (Great Britain, 1964)**½ Dan Duryea, Isa Miranda, Gwen Watford. Fair enough suspense item about a couple who find their son has been kidnaped, with tragic consequences. Some good performances. (80 mins.)

Do You Love Me? (1946)**½ Maureen O'Hara, Dick Haymes, Harry James. Harmless musical about a prudish girl's romance with a crooner. Plenty of swing music for those who want to see what was the rage in '46. (Dir: Gregory Ratoff, 91 mins.)

Do You Take This Stranger? (MTV 1970)* Gene Barry, Lloyd Bridges, Diane Baker. (Dir: Richard Heffron, 100 mins.)

D.O.A. (1949)***½ Edmond O'Brien, Pamela Britton. When he is slipped a dose of slow-acting poison, a man sets out to find his own murderer. Terrifically taut melodrama with suspense on high throughout. Remade as **Color Me Dead**, 1969. (Dir: Rudolph Mate, 83 mins.)

Doberman Gang, The (1973)* Byron Mabe, Julie Parrish. (Dir: Byron Chudnow, 87 mins.)

Doc (1971)**½ Stacy Keach, Faye Dunaway, Harris Yulin. Disappointing, offbeat western. Wyatt Earp gets his face smashed in and Doc Holliday is incapacitated by coughing spasms in this shake-up-the-myth reworking of OK Corral. Wyatt (Yulin) is small and droopy-eyed and Doc (Keach) is self-conscious and brooding. Collectively they will manage to remain standing after the shooting, which takes only seven seconds in what is otherwise a slickly paced character study. If you're looking for a slambanger, this isn't it. (Dir: Frank Perry, 122 mins.)

Dock Brief, The—See: **Trial and Error**

Docks of New York, The (1928)**** George Bancroft, Betty Compson, Olga Baclanova, Clyde Cook. Bancroft is a rowdy stoker who finds love (of a sort) when he rescues a dejected prostitute (Compson) who has thrown herself into the water of the harbor. Director Josef von Sternberg's silent masterpiece has his usual visual splendor; he evokes subtle emotions through highly stylized gestures, with the actors no less than with the lighting. Completely satisfying emotionally. (79 mins.)

Doctor—See also **Dr.**

Doctor and the Girl, The (1949)**½ Glenn Ford, Janet Leigh, Gloria De Haven,

Charles Coburn. Pure soap opera but well done. Glenn Ford plays the doctor son of Park Ave. doctor who decides he wants to earn his way in the medical life and sets up his own practice on the Lower East side of N. Y. The cast does well with the crisis-ridden script. (Dir: Curtis Bernhardt, 98 mins.)

Doctor at Large (Great Britain, 1957)**½ Dirk Bogarde, James Robertson Justice. Amusing comedy about a young doctor's efforts to get into a hospital on staff, over the protest of the superintendent. One of a series, up to the standard of its predecessors. (Dir: Ralph Thomas, 98 mins.)

Doctor at Sea (Great Britain, 1956)*** Dirk Bogarde, Brigitte Bardot. Another in the film series about the adventures of a young doctor. Brigitte Bardot is aboard for this amusing trip. (Dir: Ralph Thomas, 93 mins.)

Doctor Dolittle (1967)** Rex Harrison, Samantha Eggar, Richard Attenborough, Anthony Newley. Elephantine musical that utterly misses the charm of the Hugh Lofting stories which I loved as a boy. Robert Surtees's color work is strong, and Attenborough has a moment or two, but the score, direction, and cast are leaden. Script and lyrics by the baneful Leslie Bricusse. The film almost bankrupted Fox; got a Best Picture Oscar nomination, though I've yet to find a soul who liked it. (Dir: Richard Fleischer, 152 mins.)

Doctor Faustus (Great Britain, 1967)*½ Richard Burton, Elizabeth Taylor. (Dir: Richard Burton, 93 mins.)

Doctor in Clover—See: **Carnaby, M.D.**

Doctor in Distress (Great Britain, 1963)*** Dirk Bogarde, Samantha Eggar, James Robertson Justice. Continuing the medical shenanigans in this series, the grumpy head of a hospital becomes a changed man when he falls in love, and his young aide has his own problems with a glamorous model. Good performers and some amusing situations make this comedy a good entry. (Dir: Ralph Thomas, 103 mins.)

Doctor in Love (Great Britain, 1960)** Michael Craig, Virginia Maskell. Young doctor romances a nurse who disappears only to return at a most inopportune moment. Mild comedy doesn't hit the laugh mark set by others in this series. (Dir: Ralph Thomas, 93 mins.)

Doctor in the House (Great Britain, 1954)*** Kay Kendall, Dirk Bogarde. Highly amusing comedy about the hectic and hilarious life of a medical student. Stars shine. (Dir: Ralph Thomas, 92 mins.)

Doctor of Doom (Mexico, 1962)* Armando Silvestre, Lorena Velasquez. Dubbed in English. (Dir: Rene Cardona, 77 mins.)

Doctor Paul Joseph Goebbels (1962)**½ Documentary study of Hitler's propaganda chief. Well-compiled material, should interest World War II historians.

Doctor Rhythm (1938)**½ Bing Crosby, Beatrice Lillie, Mary Carlisle. Forced, unfunny comedy about a doctor who pinch-hits for a policeman friend on a "routine" bodyguard job. The Lady Peel's many fans will enjoy watching several of her delightful routines. (Dir: Frank Tuttle, 80 mins.)

Doctor Satan's Robot (1940-66)**½ Eduardo Ciannelli, Robert Wilcox, Ella Neal. Feature version of serial "Mysterious Doctor Satan." Mad doctor plans an army of robots, is thwarted by a masked hero. Juvenile nonsense, but has a lickety split pace, plenty of action. Good fun. (Dirs: William Witney, John English, 100 mins.)

Doctor Socrates (1935)*** Paul Muni, Ann Dvorak. Mr. Muni raises this ordinary story of a doctor who patches up a criminal at gunpoint out of the commonplace. (Dir: William Dieterle, 80 mins.)

Doctor Takes a Wife (1940)*** Loretta Young, Ray Milland. Professor and authoress are forced to make the best of it when people get the impression they're married. Entertaining romantic comedy. (Dir: Alexander Hall, 89 mins.)

Doctor Without Scruples (Germany, 1960)** Barbara Rutting, Cornell Borchers. Doctor successfully experimenting in heart surgery is placed under a cloud of suspicion when his assistant proves to be a former Nazi. Mildly interesting drama dubbed in English. (Dir: Falk Harnack, 96 mins.)

Doctor, You've Got to Be Kidding (1967)* George Hamilton, Sandra Dee. (Dir: Peter Tewksbury, 94 mins.)

Doctor Zhivago (Great Britain, 1965)***½ Julie Christie, Omar Sharif, Tom Courtenay. The prize-winning novel of Boris Pasternak about life in Russia before and during the Russian Revolution. Directed by the master David Lean, this mammoth spectacle, filmed partially on location in Spain, not Russia, is too long and episodic, but it's still an impressive and pretty consistently absorbing account of one of the most fascinating and important periods in human history. The screenplay by Robert Bolt is much superior to the screenwriting normally found in such historical dramas, and it takes fewer liberties with the facts of history. Courtenay is an impoverished revolutionary, and he gives one of his best performances to date. (197 mins.)

Doctors, The (France, 1956)*** Jeanne Moreau, Raymond Pellegrin. Well made French drama about the growth of a young doctor. Excellently acted by a top French cast. (Dir: Ralph Habib, 92 mins.)

Doctor's Dilemma, The (Great Britain, 1969)***½ Leslie Caron, Dirk Bogarde, Robert Morley. George Bernard Shaw's thoroughly delightful comedy is excellently brought to the screen with an almost perfect cast. The adventures of a young devoted wife who consults a number of physicians regarding her husband's failing health makes fascinating entertainment. (Dir: Anthony Asquith, 99 mins.)

Doctors' Private Lives (MTV 1978)*½ John Gavin, Donna Mills, Ed Nelson. (Dir: Steve Stern, 104 mins.)

Doctors' Wives (1971)* Gene Hackman, Richard Crenna, Carroll O'Connor, Diana Sands. (Dir: George Schaefer, 100 mins.)

Dodge City (1939)*** Errol Flynn, Olivia de Havilland, Ann Sheridan. Fairly good 1939 version of today's CinemaScope outdoor epics.

Dodsworth (1936)**** Walter Huston, Ruth Chatterton, David Niven, Paul Lukas, Mary Astor, Spring Byington, John Payne, Maria Ouspenskaya. Outstanding film based on Sinclair Lewis's classic novel. Dodsworth, excellently portrayed by Walter Huston, is an archetype of the American self-made man. After a long trip to Europe he finds he is in danger of losing his wife and the peace he thought he had secured. Excellent supporting cast. (Dir: William Wyler, 101 mins.)

Dog Day Afternoon (1975)*** Al Pacino, John Cazale, Charles Durning, Carol Kane. Gripping, funny, sometimes grotesque true story about a Brooklyn bank robbery on August 22, 1972. Robbery ringleader, with a wife and two children, sticks up the joint to get money for a sex-change operation for his drag-queen lover. Al Pacino is stunning playing the bossy hoodlum who revels in being an "instant TV news celebrity" while he negotiates the release of his hostages. There's a wonderful phone conversation between Pacino and his male lover (Chris Sarandon). Sidney Lumet has accurately and perceptively captured part of New York's life-giving frenzy and the diversity of its street people. (130 mins.)

Dog of Flanders, A (1959)**** David Ladd, Donald Crisp, Theodore Bikel. One of the loveliest children's films ever made, the third film version of the famous novel by Ouida written in 1872. About a young Dutch boy, his grandfather, and the stray dog they adopt. Beautifully photographed in color against the Dutch and Belgian countryside with fine performances from all the humans, plus the dog scene stealer Patrasche. (Movie-dog buffs may remember that this is the same foxy mutt that got such good reviews in the '58 film "Old Yeller.") Tastefully produced by Robert Radnitz. (Dir: James B. Clark, 96 mins.)

Doll Face (1945)**½ Vivian Blaine, Dennis O'Keefe, Perry Como. Story of a burlesque girl and her boy friend is routine. But Perry is around and Vivian looks good. (Dir: Lewis Seiler, 80 mins.)

Doll That Took the Town, The (Italy 1957)*½ Virna Lisi, Haya Harareet, Serge Reggiani. (Dir: Francesco Maselli, 81 mins.)

$ (Dollars) (1971)**½ Warren Beatty, Goldie Hawn. Bank robbery in Germany masterminded by Beatty, a bank employee out to steal $1.5 million. Hawn plays a "dippy hooker" and his accessory to the crime. The pacing is slow, but there are a few brief moments of suspense and humor. Good chase as a climax. Casting is odd; Beatty is too subtle an actor for this part and he has difficulty working with Miss Hawn. (Dir: Richard Brooks, 120 mins.)

Doll's House, A (Great Britain, 1973)*** Jane Fonda, Trevor Howard, David Warner, Edward Fox. Women's lib, 19th-century style. Ms. Fonda gives an uneven performance as Nora, Ibsen's doll-like wife and mother who suddenly and dramatically asserts her independence when she is confronted with her husband's arrogant male immorality. The rest of the cast fare much better under director Joseph Losey's steady hand. Interesting note: although the film was produced for theatrical release, it made its debut on TV. (87 mins.)

Dolly Sisters, The (1945)**½ Betty Grable, John Payne, June Haver. Some nice legs and a good score are the only assets of this fictionalized story of the famous sister act. (Dir: Irving Cummings, 114 mins.)

Don Is Dead, The (1973)**½ Anthony Quinn, Robert Forster, Frederic Forrest, Al Lettieri. "Godfather" imitation but well acted. Once again, the Mafiosa families are fighting for control of their interests in Las Vegas, and their code of honor among thieves gets a workout here. Anthony Quinn is perfect as the older Mafia boss and Frederic Forrest scores as a modern-day member of a Mafia family who wants out but can't manage the feat. The dialogue seems natural and the story, though familiar from all those other Mafia movies, still works. Alternate title: **Beautiful But Deadly.** (Dir: Richard Fleischer, 115 mins.)

Don Juan (1926)***½ John Barrymore, Mary Astor, Myrna Loy, Estelle Taylor, Warner Oland. Thrilling, swashbuckling action on balustrade and in boudoir, as Barrymore, still untouched by the ravages of drink, flourishes his respective rapiers. There's no sour grapes Freudianism in this version of the legendary lover, only healthy, ravenous sexuality. Director Alan Crosland keeps the derring-do believable and engrossing, and this is the one Barrymore star vehicle of the '20s that isn't choked by elaborate sets. A silent, but has a sound-synchronized soundtrack. (110 mins.)

Don Juan Quilligan (1945)**½ William Bendix, Joan Blondell, Phil Silvers. Comedy about a bigamist is similar to "Captain's Paradise" only it lacks the wit of the Guinness film. Bendix is married to a girl in Brooklyn and one in upstate New York. Some laughs but not enough. (Dir: Frank Tuttle, 75 mins.)

Dona Flor and Her Two Husbands (Brazil 1978)***½ Sonia Braga. A generally effective sex comedy, distinguished by its origins (Brazil) and the considerable appeal of its star, Sonia Braga. Widowed when her carousing husband dies under the strain of excess debauchery, Flor marries a staid pharmacist. But her memories of the wild life conjure her first husband back from the beyond, and he takes up where he left off. Bruno Barreto's direction is somewhat pokey, but he handles the fantasy element with an interesting matter-of-factness. (Dir: Bruno Barreto, 106 mins.)

Dondi (1960)*½ David Janssen, Patti Page, David Kory. (Dir: Albert Zugsmith, 100 mins.)

Donner Pass: The Road to Survival (MTV 1978)*½ Robert Fuller, Andrew Prine, Michael Callan, Diane McBain. (Dir: James L Conway, 104 mins.)

Donovan's Brain (1953)*** Lew Ayres, Gene Evans, Nancy Davis. Scientist keeps the brain tissue of a dead millionaire alive, but the brain overcomes him and causes him to do its bidding. Suspenseful, well-made melodrama. (Dir: Felix Feist, 83 mins.)

Donovan's Reef (1963)*** John Wayne, Elizabeth Allen, Lee Marvin, Dorothy Lamour, Jack Warden. What happens when a stuffy Boston girl arrives on a South Pacific isle in search of her father forms the basis of this light-hearted, frequently light-headed comedy directed by John Ford as if he were enjoying a vacation. Art it isn't, but there's lots of fun, outrageously played in broad style by the entire cast. Scenic values are superb. (109 mins.)

Don't Answer the Phone! (1980)** James Westmoreland, Flo Gerrish, Ben Frank, Nicholas Worth. Alternate title: **The Hollywood Strangler**. (Dir: Robert Hammer, 94 mins.)

Don't Be Afraid of the Dark (MTV 1973)** Kim Darby, Jim Hutton, Barbara Anderson. A film for fans of horror stories laced with the supernatural. Miss Darby and Hutton play a young couple whose house seems to be inhabited by little demons intent on drawing Kim into their web. (Dir: John Newland, 74 mins.)

Don't Blame the Stork (Great Britain, 1954)** Ian Hunter, Veronica Hurst. Famous actor finds himself an unexpected father when a baby is left on his doorstep. Fairly amusing comedy with a good cast. (Dir: Akos Rathony, 80 mins.)

Don't Bother to Knock (1952)** Marilyn Monroe, Richard Widmark, Anne Bancroft. This was the first dramatic part Marilyn did after her sensational sex-queen build-up and she didn't come off too well. It isn't entirely her fault—the script about a mentally disturbed girl who takes a job as a baby sitter in a large hotel is very weak and often laughable. Widmark, in a familiar role as a tough guy with a good heart, tries to overcome the script but can't. Anne Bancroft, in the thankless role of Widmark's girl, is entirely wasted. (Dir: Robert Baker, 76 mins.)

Don't Cry With Your Mouth Full (France, 1973)**** Annie Cole, Bernard Menez, Frederic Duru. Charming, perceptive comedy about a nubile young girl in provincial France, reminiscent of the early work of Jean Renoir, but not quite as good. You'll see three generations of one French family and their differing manners, mores and morals. Affecting portrayal from Annie Cole as the 15-year-old teenager before and after her first affair. Skillful performance by Menez. (Dir: Pascal Thomas, 116 mins.)

Don't Drink the Water (1969)**½ Jackie Gleason, Estelle Parsons. A Jewish caterer being accused of spying in a Communist country and taking refuge with his family in the American embassy formed the premise of Woody Allen's hilarious but uneven stage play. The timing, pace, and direction of the work have been altered to fit the frame of Jackie Gleason as the caterer. The results may delight Gleason fans, but they will surely outrage Allen fans. Fortunately Allen's comic genius will out, so there are a few chuckles and guffaws for all. (Dir: Howard Morris, 97 mins.)

Don't Give Up the Ship (1959)** Jerry Lewis, Dina Merrill. Jerry in the Navy accomplishes the amazing feat of losing a destroyer, and the big brass would sincerely like to know where he misplaced it. Mild service comedy; some laughs, but Jerry's done better. (Dir: Norman Taurog, 85 mins.)

Don't Go in the House (1980)**½ Dan Grimaldi, Robert Osth, Ruth Dardick. The most gruesome, tortuous murder scene I've ever witnessed comes at the opening of this film, setting the scene for less stomach-retching but equally bizarre demises. The story of a perverted loner, his large Victorian house, and loads of Catholic guilt, together with a disco disfigurement, qualify this as an imaginative entry into the subgenre. Joseph R. Masefield wrote the story and co-scripted with Ellen Hammill. (Dir: Ellen Hammill, 82 mins.)

Don't Go Near the Water (1957)**½ Glenn Ford, Anne Francis, Gia Scala, Earl Holliman, Eva Gabor. Fast paced, amusing service comedy about the goings-on in a naval installation on a South Pacific tropical paradise complete with friendly, curvaceous natives. Ford gets a good share of the laughs and is ably supported by an excellent cast of actors. Based on novel by William Brinkley. (Dir: Charles Walters, 107 mins.)

Don't Just Stand There! (1968)** Robert Wagner, Mary Tyler Moore, Glynis Johns. Not too funny comedy about a group of sophisticated would-be novelist-adventurers who can't seem to stay out of trouble. If you don't look too closely at the plot, you might enjoy some of the shenanigans. One good thing, the ladies—Mary Tyler Moore, Glynis Johns and statuesque Barbara Rhoades—are nice to look at. (Dir: Ron Winston, 100 mins.)

Don't Knock the Twist (1962)*½ Chubby Checker, Linda Scott. (Dir: Oscar Rudolph, 87 mins.)

Don't Look Back (1967)***½ Bob Dylan, Joan Baez, Donovan. Unique documentary about folk-singer Bob Dylan's tour of England in 1965, and a rare opportunity to watch this remarkable young musician on stage and off. You'll see Dylan toying with some simple-minded newspapermen, shots of Dylan's manager, generally get a better idea of what this guarded young artist cares about. Much of the credit for the film goes to the director-editor D. A. Pennebaker. (96 mins.)

Don't Look Back (MTV 1981)**½ Louis Gossett, Jr., Beverly Todd, Ossie Davis. A routine biography of baseball's Leroy "Satchel" Paige. Gossett, a fine actor, is sincere and convincing as the gifted pitcher who fought the color barrier in baseball during the twenties and thirties and finally got to play in the major (white) leagues in 1948. Like many made-for-TV movies, this one lacks subtleties of emotions and character development. Paige's formative years in a reformatory, his struggle for success in black baseball, and his relationship with his wife, Lahoma, seem too pat and simplistic. Ossie Davis is a standout as Chuffy Russell. (Dir: Richard A. Colla, 113 mins.)

Don't Look Now (Great Britain-Italy, 1973)***½ Julie Christie, Donald Sutherland, Hilary Mason, Clelia Matania. Stylistically beautiful thriller about psychic phenomenon0hat works, thanks partially to the haunting visual quality of Venice as photographed by director Nicolas Roeg. The baroque images dominate what could be a straightforward suspense story about a young British married couple who, shortly ioter their daughter's accidental death, make contact with the child through a blind medium. The eeriness of Venice in winter magnificently captured, and Christie and Sutherland are extremely good. Based on a short story by Daphne du Maurier. (110 mins.)

Don't Make Waves (1967)* Tony Curtis, Claudia Cardinale, Sharon Tate. (Dir: Alexander Mackendrick, 97 mins.)

Don't Push, I'll Charge When I'm Ready (MTV 1969)* Sue Lyon, Cesar Romero, Soupy Sales. (Dir: Nathaniel Lande, 100 mins.)

Don't Raise the Bridge, Lower the River (Great Britain, 1968)** Jerry Lewis, Terry-Thomas, Jacqueline Pearce, Patricia Routledge. Jerry Lewis plays it more or less straight as an American in England trying to hold on to his wife. Soft-pedaling of Lewis rates praise under any conditions, but otherwise it's only mild amusement. Screenplay by Max Wilk is better than most of Jerry's scripts. (Dir: Jerry Paris, 99 mins.)

Don't Take It to Heart (Great Britain, 1945)***½ Richard Greene, Patricia

Medina. Young lawyer falls for the daughter of the owner of a rundown castle, stays in the small town to help out the victims of a wealthy skinflint. Exceptionally ingenious romantic comedy, has those little clever touches that mean so much. (Dir: Jeffrey Dell, 89 mins.)

Don't Tempt the Devil (France-Italy, 1963)** Marina Vlady, Virna Lisi, Bourvil, Pierre Brasseur. Ironic mystery-suspense tale features Vlady as a cool, calculating widow and Lisi as the tearful nurse of a murdered man. A few suspenseful moments! (Dir: Christian-Jaque, 106 mins.)

Don't Trust Your Husband (1948)** Fred MacMurray, Madeleine Carroll. The wife of an ad agency exec. doesn't like his after-office hours dealings with a glamorous client, so she decides to make him jealous. Fair comedy which doesn't do right by the players. (Dir: Lloyd Bacon, 90 mins.)

Don't Turn 'Em Loose (1936)**½ Lewis Stone, Bruce Cabot, Betty Grable. Parole board member sees his own son turn out to be a criminal. Interesting crime melodrama. (Dir: Ben Stoloff, 65 mins.)

Doomsday Flight, The (MTV 1966)**½ Van Johnson, Jack Lord, Edmond O'Brien, John Saxon. Familiar but suspenseful melodrama—frantic search for a bomb placed aboard a passenger airliner, to find it before it goes off. Nicely written (Rod Serling), competently acted. Another feature. (Dir: William Graham, 100 mins.)

Doomsday Voyage (1972)* Joseph Cotten, John Gabriel, Ann Randall. (Dir: John Vidette, 88 mins.)

Door with Seven Locks (Germany, 1962)*½ Heinz Drache, Sabina Sesselman. (Dir: Alfred Vohrer, 96 mins.)

Dorian Gray (Italy-Liechtenstein-West Germany, 1970)** Helmet Berger, Herbert Lom, Richard Todd. The second, definitely inferior filming of Oscar Wilde's classic novel about late 19th-century perversions and mores and a painting which ages, updated to London, 1970. Most of the terror, ghastliness and artistry of the original is lost. (Dir: Massimo Dallamano, 93 mins.)

Double, The (Great Britain, 1960)** Jeanette Sterke, Jane Griffiths, Robert Brown. Scoundrel returns to England to assume his partner's identity to claim an inheritance, but his plot runs into a snag. Fair Edgar Wallace mystery melodrama produced on a low budget. (Dir: Lionel Harris, 56 mins.)

Double Agents, The (France, 1959)** Marina Vlady, Robert Hossein. It's a case of whose spy is whose as a young man and a girl suspect each other of being enemy agents. Involved and verbose melodrama dubbed in English. Alternate title: **Night Encounter.** (Dir: Robert Hossein, 80 mins.)

Double Bunk (Great Britain, 1960)**½ Ian Carmichael, Janette Scott. Amusing comedy about newlyweds who buy a broken-down houseboat. Some clever comedy moments. (Dir: C. M. Pennington-Richards, 92 mins.)

Double Con, The (1973)** Mel Stewart, Kiel Martin. Originally released to theaters as "Trick Baby," this was a black-exploitation film that didn't overdo the sex and violence. You might call it a black "Sting," as two con men, one a light-skinned black passing for white, the other his slick black buddy, work their game in an inner-city land deal. However, the pair makes the fatal mistake of involving the relative of a Mafia boss in one of their cons and they in turn become victims. Martin and Stewart are fine in the leading roles and the script makes some interesting comments about race relations. (Dir: Larry Yust, 89 mins.)

Double Confession (Great Britain, 1951)** Derek Farr, Peter Lorre, William Hartnell. A seaside resort is disrupted by murder and blackmail. Sluggish crime drama has only the performances to recommend it. (Dir: Harry Reynolds, 86 mins.)

Double Cross (Great Britain, 1956)** Donald Houston, Fay Compton. Boatman accepts plenty of trouble when he agrees to take some people across the channel. Fair. (Dir: Anthony Squire, 71 mins.)

Double Crossbones (1951)**½ Donald O'Connor, Helena Carter. The kids will probably get many laughs out of this comedy tale of would-be pirates and their misadventures. O'Connor is very agile and funny as the bumpkin turned buccaneer. Hope Emerson stands out in the supporting cast in the role of a colorful lady captain. (Dir: Charles Barton, 76 mins.)

Double Deception (France, 1960)** Jacques Riberolles, Alice and Ellen Kessler. Young man becomes involved with twin entertainers; one of them is murdered; which one? Whodunit takes too long to get to the point. (Dir: Serge Friedman, 101 mins.)

Double Dynamite (1951)**½ Jane Russell, Groucho Marx, Frank Sinatra. Bank clerk saves a gangster's life, is suspected of being in on a theft. Fairly amusing comedy. (Dir: Irving Cummings, Jr., 80 mins.)

Double Exposure (Great Britain, 1954)**½ John Bentley, Rona Anderson. Private eye looking for a missing girl runs into murder. Standard mystery is competently done. (Dir: John Gilling, 63 mins.)

Double Indemnity (1944)**** Fred MacMurray, Barbara Stanwyck, Edward G. Robinson. Deliberate murder receives a microscopic examination in this tense, exciting, well-acted adaptation of the James Cain novel. (Dir: Billy Wilder, 106 mins.)

Double Indemnity (MTV 1973)**½ Richard Crenna, Samantha Eggar, Lee J. Cobb. This remake of Fred MacMurray's film classic hasn't the old oomph, but James Cain's clever story will hold one's interest. Crenna plays the uncertain insurance man, conned into murder by a calculating wife who wants to polish off her husband. As for Miss Eggar's Phyllis, the trouble-

maker, she somehow doesn't seem worth the big risks. (Dir: Jack Smight, 73 mins.)

Double Life, A (1947)**** Ronald Colman, Signe Hasso, Edmond O'Brien, Shelley Winters. A noted actor finds the role of "Othello" taking over his off-stage life. Superb melodrama, suspenseful, excellently written, directed, acted. Highly recommended. (Dir: George Cukor, 104 mins.)

Double Man, The (Great Britain, 1967)*** Yul Brynner, Britt Ekland, Clive Revill, Anton Diffring, Lloyd Nolan. A CIA agent meets danger when he investigates the death of his son in a skiing accident. Novel twists in this spy thriller, well-played and directed. (Dir: Franklin Schaffner, 105 mins.)

Double Suicide (Japan, 1969)*** Kichiemon Nakamura, Shima Iwashita. Absorbing black and white drama from a play written in the early 18th century. The plot involves a married man, his wife, and the prostitute he is in love with. It is almost impossible for an Occidental to understand the emotional progress leading to the end, the "Double Suicide," yet the enduring play is one of the most popular in Japan. The acting is superb—especially Shima Iwashita, who plays both the plain wife and the gorgeous prostitute. There are some strong sexual scenes, and the ending is not for the squeamish. (Dir: Masahiro Shinoda, 104 mins.)

Double Trouble (1967)** Elvis Presley, Annette Day. Typical Presley fare for his fans, but better than most of his earlier vehicles. This time he's a rock singer (what a surprise) who finds love with an English heiress whose life is threatened at every turn. The songs interrupt the action on the average of every ten minutes or so. (Dir: Norman Taurog, 92 mins.)

Double Verdict (France, 1960)** Roger Sauvion, Paul Frankeur, Magli de Vendeuil. Man acquitted of murdering his wife marries the daughter of the jury foreman, and history nearly repeats itself. Fairly interesting drama gets some good performances. Dubbed in English. (Dir: Roger Saltel, 102 mins.)

Double Wedding (1937)**½ William Powell, Myrna Loy. If daffy slapstick is your cup of tea, you'll get plenty of laughs out of this screwball romance which, in spite of severe script trouble, is expertly played by its stars. (Dir: Richard Thorpe, 90 mins.)

Doughgirls, The (1944)*** Ann Sheridan, Jane Wyman, Jack Carson. Fair screen adaptation of the excellent Broadway play about wartime Washington. Eve Arden is wonderful as a lady Russian guerrilla. (Dir: James V. Kern, 102 mins.)

Down Among the Sheltering Palms (1953)** Mitzi Gaynor, Gloria De Haven, David Wayne, William Lundigan, Jane Greer, and Jack Paar. Palm trees, Army officers (post WW II), beautiful native girls, beautiful American girls, songs, comedy (well, almost) and Jack Paar in a small role—who would ask for anything more? Pure escapist fare—entertaining in spots. (Dir: Edmund Goulding, 87 mins.)

Down Argentine Way (1940)** Betty Grable, Don Ameche, Carmen Miranda. A lot of talent is wasted in this silly musical about the romance of an American heiress and a South American cowboy. Ends with a big horse race and you'll be glad to see it end. (Dir: Irving Cummings, 94 mins.)

Down 3 Dark Streets (1954)*** Broderick Crawford, Ruth Roman. FBI man works on three cases at the same time and, naturally, they all come out together at the end. Well-done, entertaining cops-and-robbers tale. (Dir: Arnold Laven, 85 mins.)

Down to Earth (1947)*** Rita Hayworth, Larry Parks. Miss Hayworth, 1947 vintage, appropriately plays the goddess of dance. She takes a part in Producer Parks' musical posing as a mortal. Pleasant, uninspired musical. (Dir: Alexander Hall, 101 mins.)

Down to the Sea in Ships (1949)*** Richard Widmark, Lionel Barrymore, Dean Stockwell. Life on the New England whaling boats seen through the eyes of a very young Dean Stockwell. It's overlong, but Lionel Barrymore creates an exceptional portrait of the salty sea captain. (Dir: Henry Hathaway, 120 mins.)

Downfall (Great Britain, 1963)** Maurice Denham, Nadja Regin. Lawyer wins acquittal for a pathological murderer then hires him as a chauffeur, having his own reasons. Adequate crime melodrama with a good performance by Denham. (Dir: John Moxey, 59 mins.)

Downhill Racer (1969)**** Robert Redford, Gene Hackman, Camilla Sparv. All the skiing enthusiasts in the audience will thrill to the superb sequences, filmed in famous European ski locations, which make up a goodly portion of this movie. It's a quiet drama about a ski champion, played with understated passion by Redford, who finds himself part of an American team competing for the honor of going to the Olympics. He's aloof and arrogant. His coach, well played by Hackman, warns him that he will never be a true champion if all he wants to do is break records. Sparv is around for romantic window dressing, but it's Redford and the skiing sequences that fascinate. (Dir: Michael Ritchie, 101 mins.)

Dr.—See also **Doctor**

Dr. Black Mr. Hyde—See: **Watts Monster, The**

Dr. Broadway (1942)*** Macdonald Carey, Jean Phillips. Broadway doctor becomes involved in the slaying of a reformed gangster. Good melodrama has a script containing bright dialogue, a fast pace. Carey's film debut, Anthony Mann's first as director. (68 mins.)

Dr. Cook's Garden (MTV 1971)*** Bing Crosby, Frank Converse, Blythe Danner. Better than average made-for-TV film.

Bing Crosby is very good as the venerable small-town New England doctor who has worked out a unique and frightening plan to keep the town's population as perfect as his beautiful prize-winning garden. Frank Converse is also effective as a young doctor who comes back home and uncovers Dr. Cook's diabolical plot. Although the action unfolds slowly, stay with it for Crosby's restrained performance, the splendid New England photography, and the surprise ending. Robert Markell, one of TV drama's finest producers, makes this better than most of the junk made for TV. (Dir: Ted Post, 73 mins.)

Dr. Crippen (Great Britain, 1963)**½ Donald Pleasence, Samantha Eggar, Donald Wolfit. For those who prefer their thriller-killers based on fact. About the 1910 crime case of an accused wife murderer (Pleasence) and his mistress (Samantha). There's a new invention in this one—London 1910—as the suspect is apprehended thanks to a new gadget called the wireless. Donald Pleasence is an extraordinary actor, and he's effective in this English why-did-he-dun-it. (Dir: Robert Lynn, 97 mins.)

Dr. Cyclops (1940)**½ Albert Dekker, Janice Logan, Thomas Gley. Dekker raves and froths as the mad scientist in a manner that oddly suggests Hitler. This story of men shrunk to doll size isn't very well made, but delivers the creeps in early Technicolor. (75 mins.)

Dr. Ehrlich's Magic Bullet (1940)**** Edward G. Robinson, Ruth Gordon. Another one of those great biographical films which Hollywood occasionally makes. Story of the man who discovered the first cure for syphilis and forced the medical profession to take notice of it as a disease is beautifully told. Robinson is wonderful as the doctor and Ruth Gordon matches him every step of the way as his wife. (Dir: William Dieterle, 103 mins.)

Dr. Gillespie's Assistant (1942)** Lionel Barrymore, Van Johnson, Susan Peters. Usual run-of-the-mill medical drama but MGM introduced a newcomer named Van Johnson in the title role. (Dir: Willis Goldbeck, 87 mins.)

Dr. Gillespie's Criminal Case (1943)** Lionel Barrymore, Van Johnson, Donna Reed. Same old formula medical melodrama with Mr. Barrymore bellowing and Van Johnson struggling to learn how to act in a film. (Dir: Willis Goldbeck, 89 mins.)

Dr. Goldfoot and the Bikini Machine (1965)* Vincent Price, Frankie Avalon, Dwayne Hickman, Annette Funicello. (Dir: Norman Taurog, 90 mins.)

Dr. Goldfoot and the Girl Bombs (U.S.-Italy, 1966)*½ Vincent Price, Fabian, Franco Franchi. (Dir: Mario Bava, 85 mins.)

Dr. Jack (1922)***½ Harold Lloyd, Mildred Davis, Eric Mayne. Very effective minor comedy where Lloyd is a doctor (based on the Coué fad) who believes most illness can be cured by affirmative psychology. As is often true with Lloyd, the buildup of the situation is funnier than the working-out of the romantic story. Beware the recut and shortened version—a practice that is psychologically hazardous, and artistically criminal. The film has been shorn to tone down some racial humor in the haunted-spook finale. Such censorship is more pernicious than exposure to outdated racial stereotypes. (Dir: Fred Newmeyer, 55 mins.)

Dr. Jekyll and Mr. Hyde (1920)***½ John Barrymore, Nita Naldi, Louis Wolheim. Worth watching just to see a truly great actor at work, before alcohol finally destroyed his prodigious gifts. This version of the famous Robert Louis Stevenson story "The Strange Case of Dr. Jekyll and Mr. Hyde" was based on a New York play version and adapted by Clara S. Beranger. A fascinating bravura performance by Barrymore, and you will see the 'great profile' as he gazes at Nita Naldi when visiting a London music hall. Forget about the film's shortcomings and revel in this charismatic actor pulling out all the stops. (Dir: John S. Robertson, 63 mins.)

Dr. Jekyll and Mr. Hyde (1931)***½ Fredric March, Miriam Hopkins, Rose Hobart. Director Rouben Mamoulian's third feature is a surprisingly frank treatment of the sexual implications of the good doctor's dual nature. Far more delirious than the discreetly psychoanalytic version Victor Fleming made with Spencer Tracy in '41. March shared a Best Actor Oscar. Grandiose and fluid camerawork by Karl Struss. (93 mins.)

Dr. Jekyll and Mr. Hyde (1941)***½ Spencer Tracy, Ingrid Bergman, Lana Turner, Donald Crisp, Barton McLane. Tracy played the title role in Robert Louis Stevenson's classic; Bergman and Turner were originally cast as the good girl and the slut respectively, but Bergman got the brass to exchange the roles and played her first whore. The production is geared for psychological rather than physical horror, and features a couple of Freudian dream sequences. (Dir: Victor Fleming, 127 mins.)

Dr. Kildare Goes Home (1940)** Lew Ayres, Lionel Barrymore, Laraine Day. Sure he's got a family other than kindly old Doctor Gillespie. This one was made to appease those who thought Kildare was born in the hospital. (Dir: Harold S. Bucquet, 78 mins.)

Dr. Kildare's Victory (1941)** Lionel Barrymore, Lew Ayres. Kildare performs his usual astounding medical feats on a beautiful debutante and comes up with a new heart throb. (Dir: W. S. Van Dyke, 92 mins.)

Dr. Kildare's Wedding Day (1940)** Lew Ayres, Lionel Barrymore, Laraine Day. He's finally going to marry nurse Laraine in this one but, as she doesn't want to

make any more Kildare pictures, she gracefully dies. (Dir: Harold S. Bucquet, 82 mins.)

Dr. Mabuse vs. Scotland Yard (Germany, 1963)*½ Peter Van Eyck, Dieter Borsche. (Dir: Paul May, 90 mins.)

Dr. Maniac—See: **Man Who Changed His Mind, The**

Dr. Max (MTV 1974)**½ Lee J. Cobb, Janet Ward. Another medical drama, but Lee J. Cobb deserves your attention as Dr. Max, a Baltimore doctor and weary fighter who takes one day at a time, and doesn't try to play the hero in his authentic on-location surroundings. Dr. Max battles death, and applies a sense of naturalness and anger to the standard moments of crisis that come his way. (Dir: James Goldstone, 72 mins.)

Dr. No (Great Britain, 1962)**** Sean Connery, Ursula Andress. First of the James Bond extravaganzas, with Sean Connery as the super-agent combating a fiend (Joseph Wiseman) out to control the world. Wildly flamboyant, this still possesses the novelty values that made the series so popular. Great tongue-in-cheek fun. With Jack Lord, Bernard Lee, Lois Maxwell, Anthony Dawson. (Dir: Terence Young, 111 mins.)

Dr. Phibes Rises Again (Great Britain, 1972)**½ Vincent Price, Peter Cushing, Beryl Reid, Terry-Thomas. As campy a horror film as you are likely to see. Vincent Price is back from the dead and off to Egypt to do his thing—murder and mayhem. It's all ridiculous, entertaining and better than the first "Phibes." (Dir: Robert Fuest, 89 mins.)

Dr. Strangelove: Or, How I Learned to Stop Worrying and Love the Bomb (1964)**** Peter Sellers, Sterling Hayden, George C. Scott, Keenan Wynn. This masterpiece was produced and directed by Stanley Kubrick, who, along with Terry Southern and Peter George, also had a hand in the screenplay. It is quite simply one of the greatest, funniest, and most shattering motion pictures ever made. Kubrick casts a jaundiced and perceptive eye on a crazed U.S. Air Force general who is determined to save the free world personally from an imagined Communist takeover and nearly starts WW III in the process. Kubrick comments unsparingly—and hilariously—on our alienated, self-righteous society, and supplies bitter humor, great excitement, and a number of marvelous acting performances. Peter Sellers plays three roles brilliantly, and even Sellers has never been more ludicrous or amusing. Sterling Hayden, portraying the general, gives the best performance of his career, and reminds us how foolishly this actor has been wasted in most of his other films. A cinema classic that makes a personal, pertinent, and devastating statement about our troubled society. (93 mins.)

Dr. Terror's House of Horrors (U.S.-Great

Britain, 1965)*** Peter Cushing, Christopher Lee, Donald Sutherland. Five creepy tales of the macabre are dealt out in the Tarot cards of a mysterious doctor who reads the fortunes of his companions in a railway car. Veterans Cushing and Lee deliver the chills and thrills under the able direction of Francis. Gruesome fun. Alternate title: **The Blood Suckers.** (Dir: Freddie Francis, 98 mins.)

Dr. Who and the Daleks (Great Britain, 1965)**½ Peter Cushing, Roy Castle. Kids are the likeliest audience for this science-fiction yarn about a planet of the future with good guys (Thals) and bad guys (Daleks who live in metal shields to protect them against radiation). A scientist, the Dr. Who of the title, gets himself, his two daughters and a friend transported to the planet when his time machine goes berserk. (Dir: Gordon Flemyng, 85 mins.)

Dracula (1931)*** Bela Lugosi, Helen Chandler, David Manners. The Universal classic version. Offers the satisfying spectacle of Lugosi packing six volumes of innuendo into the line, "I never drink ...wine." The opening scenes, set in Dracula's castle, are magnificent—grave, stately, and severe. But the film becomes unbearably static once the action moves to England, and much of the morbid sexual tension is dissipated. Director Tod Browning can be flat, dull, and clumsy, but at best his films light up with a diabolical grace. (75 mins.)

Dracula (MTV 1973)** Jack Palance, Simon Ward, Nigel Davenport, Pamela Brown. The premise of the original Bram Stoker novel forms the basis and the strength of this gothic tale of the "nosferatu" (undead). Palance, as the terrifying Count, captures both the sensitivity and the aristocratic evil of the character, and the on-location filming in Yugoslavia and England supports the mood and atmosphere of eerie ritual. The supporting cast contributes to this entertaining effort. (Dir: Dan Curtis, 100 mins.)

Dracula A.D. 1972 (Great Britain, 1972)* Christopher Lee, Peter Cushing, Stephanie Beacham. (Dir: Alan Gibson, 95 mins.)

Dracula Has Risen from the Grave (Great Britain, 1969)* Christopher Lee. (Dir: Freddie Francis, 92 mins.)

Dracula—Prince of Darkness (Great Britain, 1968)** Christopher Lee, Barbara Shelley. If your tastes run toward tales of vampires and helpless victims being scared out of their wits, this is for you. The British do this sort of thing best and Lee, one of the veterans of British horror films, is on hand as Dracula. (Dir: Terence Fisher, 90 mins.)

Dracula's Daughter (1936)**½ Otto Kruger, Marguerite Churchill, Gloria Holden. A notable sequel to the stilted original with Holden strangely effective as the cursed offspring who falls in love, and tries to hold her man by putting a spell on his fiancée. (Dir: Lambert Hillyer, 72 mins.)

Dragnet (1954)**½ Jack Webb, Richard Boone, Ben Alexander. Feature version of the old TV success. Cops Friday (Webb) and Smith (Alexander) are after a crafty killer. The by-now-standardized technique works satisfactorily. Virginia Gregg is excellent in a poignant bit part. (Dir: Jack Webb, 89 mins.)

Dragnet (1969)**½ Jack Webb, Harry Morgan. Full-length feature film based on popular TV series. Fans of the series will enjoy watching Sgt. Friday and Officer Gannon take more time solving the mysterious murders of beautiful young models. There's an especially suspense-filled climax. (Dir: Jack Webb, 97 mins.)

Dragon Seed (1944)*** Katharine Hepburn, Walter Huston, Agnes Moorehead, Akim Tamiroff. Occasionally gripping adaptation of Pearl Buck's novel about the impact of the Japanese invasion on a small Chinese community. The subject matter and the production make up for many of the film's shortcomings. Miss Hepburn has done better work. (Dirs: Jack Conway, Harold S. Bucquet, 145 mins.)

Dragonfly Squadron (1954)**½ John Hodiak, Barbara Britton. Air Force major is sent to train the South Koreans. Satisfactory war drama. (Dir: Lesley Selander, 83 mins.)

Dragon's Blood, The (Italy, 1959)*½ Rolf Tasna, Katharina Mayberg. (Dir: Giacomo Gentilomo, 97 mins.)

Dragonwyck (1946)** Gene Tierney, Vincent Price, Glenn Langan, Walter Huston, Spring Byington. A Fox gothic, in which Tierney is menaced by her sinister husband (Price). Never a strong visual stylist, director Joseph L. Mankiewicz overcompensates by laying on the atmosphere with a trowel. As always, he seems to enjoy the insane complications of his plot. (103 mins.)

Dragoon Wells Massacre (1957)*** Barry Sullivan, Dennis O'Keefe, Mona Freeman. An ill-assorted group finds itself stranded in the desert with Apaches on the prowl. Above-average western with fine performances and direction. (Dir: Harold Schuster, 88 mins.)

Dragstrip Girl (1957)*½ Fay Spain, Steve Terrell. (Dir: Edward L. Cahn, 69 mins.)

Dragstrip Riot (1958)*½ Gary Clarke, Yvonne Lime, Fay Wray. (Dir: David Bradley, 68 mins.)

Drama of Jealousy, A (Italy-Spain, 1970)** Marcello Mastroianni, Monica Vitti. Despite the high-powered stars of this Italian film, it is merely a labored comedy-drama about the obvious repercussions involving a love triangle. Dubbed in English, the film loses most of its original flavor, little as it has to begin with. Alternate title: **The Pizza Triangle.** (Dir: Ettore Scola, 99 mins.)

Drango (1957)**½ Jeff Chandler, Joanne Dru, Julie London. Top budgeted but otherwise routine western with plenty of two-fisted action to keep viewers awake. Good performances by the cast. (Dir: Hall Bartlett, 96 mins.)

Dream for Christmas, A (MTV 1973)*** Hari Rhodes, Beah Richards, George Spell. Earl Hamner, author of the TV hit "The Waltons," has created a moving film about a black minister's family rebuilding in a rundown Los Angeles pastorate in the early 1950's. Drama emphasizes family togetherness under duress, as the kids go to new schools; wife and grandmother do day work; and the college-trained minister looks for a job to keep going. Author Hamner, who likes sentiment and happy endings, says be good, be kind, be strong, and everything will work out. His Christmas finale is a rouser and should make everyone feel teary and warm inside. The cast does well, but young George Spell is particularly effective as son Joey. (Dir: Ralph Senensky, 100 mins.)

Dream Girl (1948)** Betty Hutton, Macdonald Carey. Pitiful screen treatment of the delightful Elmer Rice play about a girl who daydreams too much. (Dir: Mitchell Leisen, 85 mins.)

Dream Maker, The (Great Britain, 1963)*½ Tommy Steele, Michael Medwin. (Dir: Don Sharp, 86 mins.)

Dream Makers, The (MTV 1975)**½ James Franciscus, Diane Baker, John Astin. Franciscus reveals unexpected emotional flair, playing a hot-shot executive in a topsy-turvy record business. He's most effective turning on the melodramatic valves when his record biggie is fired and he discovers that he himself is out of favor. Offers an interesting exposé of the seamy side of the pop music industry. (Dir: Boris Sagal, 72 mins.)

Dream Wife (1953)**½ Cary Grant, Deborah Kerr, Walter Pidgeon. A happy merry-go-round of a comedy about the capers of a very eligible bachelor who is involved with a modern career woman and a Middle-Eastern beauty. Performances by the stars are in the right groove. (Dir: Sidney Sheldon, 99 mins.)

Dreamboat (1952)**½ Ginger Rogers, Clifton Webb, Jeffrey Hunter, Anne Francis, Elsa Lanchester. A silent-screen star (Webb) is embarrassed when his old movies turn up on the new medium of television. Rogers is the love interest for Webb, and they make an interesting pair. Writer-director Claude Binyon satirizes silent films more than the tube, and that's not satire, that's safe. (83 mins.)

Dressed to Kill (1941)**½ Lloyd Nolan, Mary Beth Hughes. Michael Shayne private eye adventure is well paced thanks to glib dialogue and Lloyd Nolan. (Dir: Eugene Forde, 74 mins.)

Drive a Crooked Road (1954)***½ Mickey Rooney, Dianne Foster, Kevin McCarthy. A little runt of a guy who races cars gets involved with a bank robbery and murder all because of a girl. Mickey Rooney gives a fine account of himself as the pint-sized

Eddie, and the film itself is in the "sleeper" class. (Dir: Richard Quine, 90 mins.)

Drive Hard, Drive Fast (MTV 1973)**½ Joan Collins, Brian Kelly, Henry Silva, and Joseph Campanella play handsome murder targets in an auto drama geared to scare. Racing pilot Kelly drives a lady home to New Orleans from Mexico City in her husband's sports car, and is tailed all the way. Silva, glowering with satisfaction, is the menacing pursuer who listens to all of the couple's car conversations through a hidden bugging device. (Dir: Douglas Heyes, 73 mins.)

Drôle de Drame—See: **Bizarre, Bizarre**

Drum (1976)* Warren Oates, Pam Grier, Fiona Lewis, Yaphet Kotto, Ken Norton. (Dir: Steve Carver, 100 mins.)

Drum Beat (1954)**½ Alan Ladd, Marisa Pavan, Charles Bronson. Alan Ladd tries to make peace with the Modoc Indians. Slightly more meat than the average Indian tale, thanks to writer-director Delmer Daves ("Broken Arrow"). With Audrey Dalton, Robert Keith. (111 mins.)

Drums (Great Britain, 1938)*** Sabu, Raymond Massey. A lad saves the British regiment in India from being slaughtered by a tyrant. Picturesque, colorful, action-packed melodrama, highly enjoyable. (Dir: Zoltan Korda, 100 mins.)

Drums Along the Mohawk (1939)***½ Henry Fonda, Claudette Colbert, Edna May Oliver. Director John Ford's "western" is set in upstate New York during the French and Indian War. He has respect both for the civilized and the savage. With the Ford stock company. (103 mins.)

Drums in the Deep South (1951)**½ James Craig, Guy Madison. Buddies at West Point find themselves on opposite sides when the Civil War breaks out. Fairly exciting historical drama. (Dir: William Cameron Menzies, 87 mins.)

Drums of Tahiti (1954)** Dennis O'Keefe, Patricia Medina. Tahiti is about to become a French possession in 1877 but an American adventurer and a show girl smuggle guns to be used in the fight for independence. Fast moving but nothing new. (Dir: William Castle, 80 mins.)

Drunken Angel (Japan, 1948)***½ Toshiro Mifune, Takashi Shimura, Michiyo Kogure. Mifune is a small-time gangster told by an idealistic slum doctor (Shimura) that he's dying of tuberculosis. Director Akira Kurosawa develops the moral struggle between the two men—the doctor arguing for treatment and rehabilitation, the gangster determined to continue as he is. An odd blend of American film noir and Italian neorealism. (102 mins.)

Du Barry Was a Lady (1943)**½ Red Skelton, Lucille Ball, Gene Kelly, Zero Mostel, Virginia O'Brien. They scrapped all of Cole Porter's score except for "Friendship," and Skelton is no Bert Lahr, but this desecration is still a passably entertaining musical. The premise is the same: Skelton imagines himself in the court of Louis XIV. Directed by the amiable, competent Roy Del Ruth. (101 mins.)

Duchess and the Dirtwater Fox, The (1976)* Goldie Hawn, George Segal.(Dir: Melvin Frank, 104 mins.)

Duchess of Idaho (1950)** Esther Williams, Van Johnson, John Lund. Swimming star (who else?) has romantic complications with a playboy and a band leader in Sun Valley. If you like Williams in the water, okay; otherwise, pretty tedious romantic comedy. Couple of good musical specialties by Lena Horne and Eleanor Powell thrown in. (Dir: Robert Z. Leonard, 98 mins.)

Duck Soup (1933)**** The Marx Brothers, Louis Calhern, Margaret Dumont. This, the most immortal of the Marx Brothers' madnesses, is about the small nation of Freedonia (Land of the Spree and the Home of the Knave). Groucho (Rufus T. Firefly) is given complete power to restore order, but hasn't counted on two enemy spies (Chico and Harpo) and one sappy tenor (Zeppo), though he is more than a match for villain Calhern. Director Leo McCarey makes some comic coherence out of the outrageous puns and sight gags. (Dir: Leo McCarey, 68 mins.)

Duel (MTV 1971)*** Dennis Weaver. A highway game of death between a salesman in a compact car and a gasoline truck sustains its suspense for the full 90 minutes. Salesman Weaver, rolling along on California backroads, can't shake the menacing truck intent on bagging the compact. All attempts to call for help from police and bystanders prove fruitless, and the duel between machine and man reaches a showdown. Young director Steve Spielberg's camera work gives Richard Matheson's story a fine sense of reality, and he has achieved a nerve-racking driver's bad dream in color. (73 mins.)

Duel at Apache Wells (1957)** Anna Maria Alberghetti, Ben Cooper. Lad returns home to save his father's ranch from crooks. Slow western. (Dir: Joe Kane, 70 mins.)

Duel at Diablo (1966)*** James Garner, Sidney Poitier, Dennis Weaver, Bibi Andersson. A tough, sometimes effective western, not for the squeamish. About a fight between the plainsmen and the Apaches. The subplots are plentiful and they're all presented in realistic terms, making for some bloody sequences. Garner is very good as an Indian scout who seeks revenge for his wife's death and Poitier is equally as good in an offbeat role of an ex-Army sergeant. Film also benefits by fine musical score of jazz composer Neal Hefti. (Dir: Ralph Nelson, 103 mins.)

Duel in Durango (1957)** George Montgomery, Ann Robinson. Average "horse opera" with the law pitted against the lawless. Montgomery is comfortable in this type of role and he sets the tone for the rest of the gun-toters. Alternate title:

Gun Duel in Durango. (Dir: Sidney Salkow, 73 mins.)

Duel in the Forest (Germany, 1958)**½ Curt Jurgens, Maria Schell. A well-photographed costume drama set in Germany during the feudal era. Jurgens cuts a dashing figure as the Hessian Robin Hood and Miss Schell adequately fills the bill as his love. (Dir: Helmut Kautner, 112 mins.)

Duel in the Jungle (Great Britain, 1954)*½ Dana Andrews, Jeanne Crain, David Farrar. (Dir: George Marshall, 102 mins.)

Duel in the Sun (1946)***½ Jennifer Jones, Gregory Peck, Joseph Cotten, Charles Bickford, Lillian Gish, Walter Huston, Lionel Barrymore. An extravagant entertainment, bombastic and compelling. After a mass of directors worked on it piecemeal for producer David Selznick, who was aiming for a western "Gone with the Wind," King Vidor made him a delirious epic of *l'amour fou*. Waggishly labeled "Lust in the Dust" for the steamy, horny, destructive love affair between Jones and Peck. (138 mins.)

Duel of Champions (Italy-Spain, 1960)** Alan Ladd, Robert Keith. Dull Italian production done in the epic groove—English dubbed. Alan Ladd appears rather foolish in this adventure. (Dirs: Ferdinando Baldi, Terence Young, 105 mins.)

Duel of Fire (Italy, 1962)*½ Fernando Lamas, Liana Orfei. (Dir: Umberto Lenzi, 85 mins.)

Duel of the Titans (1961)* Steve Reeves, Gordon Scott, Virna Lisi. (Dir: Sergio Corbucci, 88 mins.)

Duel on the Mississippi (1955)** Lex Barker, Patricia Medina. Tempers flare and passions are unleashed in this cliched adventure pic about Louisiana plantations and river pirates. (Dir: William Castle, 72 mins.)

Duel With Death (Austria, 1959)** Gert Frobe, Mai-Britt Nilsson. Proud man knows only his own law but is forced to come to grips with the world. Fair drama localed in Norway, dubbed in English. Alternate title: **Beyond Sing the Woods.** (Dir: Paul May, 103 mins.)

Duellists, The (Great Britain, 1977)**** Keith Carradine, Harvey Keitel, Albert Finney, John McEnery. Superb, eccentric rendering of the Joseph Conrad story about an inexplicable, impassioned feud between two officers of the Napoleonic army. Carradine and Keitel are oddly cast but each is better than ever before. Director Ridley Scott ("Alien") makes an impressive debut. (100 mins.)

Duffy (1968)** James Coburn, James Mason, Susannah York. Another "heist-caper-escapade" film, peopled with handsome men, a beautiful girl, and played against a sumptuous Spanish beach setting...all of which amounts to very little. The cast is better than average for this type of chic adventure but they can't seem to rise above the plodding script. (Dir: Robert Parrish, 101 mins.)

Duffy's Tavern (1945)*** All-Star Cast. Popular 1945 radio show is used as a frame that permits every star on the Paramount lot to perform. Some of it is excellent and the balance, routine. (Dir: Hal Walker, 97 mins.)

Duke Wore Jeans, The (Great Britain, 1958)** Tommy Steele, June Laverick, Michael Medwin. British rock star Tommy Steele, in his second picture, plays a look-alike twosome—an uppercrust noble and a brazen Cockney lad! Breezy comedy with fun and music. (Dir: Gerald Thomas, 90 mins.)

Dulcimer Street (Great Britain, 1947)**** Alastair Sim, Richard Attenborough. Tenants of a boarding house get signatures on a petition to save a boy from paying the murder penalty. Elaborate, at once comic and dramatic tale of London; excellent. (Dir: Sidney Gilliat, 112 mins.)

Dumbo (1941)***½ The story of the little elephant with big ears who learns to fly is still the most charming of the Disney features. Gets back to the freshness, exuberance, and innocence of the short cartoons of the '30s. (Dir: Ben Sharpsteen, 64 mins.)

Dummy (1979)***½ Paul Sorvino, LeVar Burton, Rose Gregorio, Brian Dennehy. Poignant story about a young black teenager (Burton) who is deaf-mute and virtually illiterate. Charged with the murder of a Chicago prostitute, he is represented by a white lawyer (Sorvino) who tries to prove his client's innocence despite the enormous problem of trying to get a statement and proof of innocence from someone who cannot speak and does not understand everything the attorneys say. (Dir: Frank Perry, 102 mins.)

Dungeons of Horror (1964)* Russ Harvey, Helen Hogan. Alternate title: **Dungeons of Harrow.** (Dir: Pat Boyette, 74 mins.)

Dunkirk (Great Britain, 1958)***½ John Mills, Richard Attenborough. Story of the gallant British rescue operation in early World War II. Graphically done, almost documentary-fashion; excellent performances by a fine cast, authentic recreation of the event. (Dir: Leslie Norman, 115 mins.)

Dunwich Horror, The (1970)** Dean Stockwell, Sandra Dee, Ed Begley. Having used up the exploitable works of Edgar Allan Poe, American-International turned to H. P. Lovecraft for this tale of devil worship in a small New England town. The film is not faithful to its source: Lovecraft was the most explicit of horror writers, but instead, director Daniel Haller resorts to the obscurantism of fog filters and slow motion. Begley is as satanic a sweet old man as ever existed. (90 mins.)

Durant Affair, The (Great Britain, 1962)** Jane Griffiths, Conrad Phillips. Young woman becomes enmeshed in a legal battle. Good performances help this rather slow drama. (Dir: Godfrey Grayson, 73 mins.)

Dust Be My Destiny (1939)**½ John Garfield, Priscilla Lane. John and Priscilla have plenty of trouble in this saga of a man trying to find his destiny but the smooth acting and production should entertain you. (Dir: Lewis Seiler, 100 mins.)

Dutchman (Great Britain, 1966)***½ Al Freeman, Jr., Shirley Knight. Lean, taut, well-acted rendition of the play by LeRoi Jones (Imamu Amiri Baraka). It was nearly a period piece when released, but Jones's vision comes through brutally clear. (Dir: Anthony Harvey, 56 mins.)

Dying Room Only (MTV 1973)**½ Cloris Leachman, Ross Martin. The first 15 minutes or so of this made-for-TV suspense film will fascinate. Miss Leachman goes through a harrowing experience at a deserted roadside cafe where her husband disappears when he goes to the men's room. You will probably figure out what's going on before long, but Leachman has a good opportunity to emote in a highly charged drama. (Dir: Philip Leacock, 74 mins.)

Dynamiters, The (Great Britain, 1956)** Wayne Morris, Patrick Holt, Simone Silva. Sleuth tracks down a gang of safecrackers and killers. Crime melodrama without a bang. (Dir: Terence Fisher, 74 mins.)

Each Dawn I Die (1939)**½ James Cagney, George Raft, Jane Bryan, George Bancroft, Maxie Rosenbloom. The Warner Bros. prison pictures were getting pretty tired by this time, but the presence of three generations of screen gangsters—Bancroft, Cagney, and Raft—keeps it tangy until the outrageous, incredible contrivance of the second half. (Dir: William Keighley, 84 mins.)

Each Other (France-Israel, 1979)*** Michal Bat-Adam, Brigitte Catillon, Assaf Dayan. Sensitive portrayal of the affection between two women, an Israeli and an attractive French divorcee and photographer. Their friendship ripens into love, which they are able to share with a man who eventually marries the Israeli but can't accept the women's fondness for each other. A top Israeli actress, Bat-Adam functions as writer-director-star here, excelling at all, although the drama is never as moving as it could be. Shot in Jerusalem in French and Hebrew. (92 mins.)

Eagle, The (1925)** Rudolph Valentino, Vilma Banky, Louise Dresser. Valentino is an aristocrat-turned-outlaw in a ponderous silent costumer. Under Clarence Brown's restraining direction, Valentino holds his bulging eyeballs in check for once. Dresser, as a castrating Catherine the Great, adds the touch of S&M without which no Valentino vehicle would be complete. (75 mins.)

Eagle and the Hawk, The (1933)*** Fredric

March, Cary Grant, Carole Lombard, Jack Oakie. Grim, realistic story of World War I air fighting. A bit dated by our standards but well ahead of its time. Comparable in many ways to "Dawn Patrol." (Dir: Stuart Walker, 68 mins.)

Eagle Has Landed, The (Great Britain, 1976)**½ Michael Caine, Donald Sutherland, Robert Duvall. The talents of the cast are wasted in this improbable film about a group of kindhearted Nazis who parachute into England in a bungled attempt to kill Winston Churchill. A superfluous love affair bogs down the story. Despite all the flaws, the suspense builds. (Dir: John Sturges, 123 mins.)

Eagle in a Cage (U.S.-Yugoslavia, 1970)**½ John Gielgud, Ralph Richardson, Kenneth Haigh. The exiled Napoleon's escapades on the island of St. Helena. Adapted from the TV production, an uninspired look at the private man behind the emperor. However, Gielgud and Richardson offer superb, complementary performances as two highly placed officials. (Dir: Fielder Cook, 92 mins.)

Eagle Squadron (1942)*** Robert Stack, Jon Hall, Eddie Albert. In 1940, a handful of Americans join the RAF to fight the Nazis. Good war melodrama with some exciting action scenes. (Dir: Arthur Lubin, 109 mins.)

Eagles Attack at Dawn (Israel, 1974)**½ Rick Jason, Peter Brown, Michal Bat-Adam. Action-filled saga of the Middle Eastern conflict has Jason, as an Israeli, escaping from an inhumane Arab prison and returning to free his comrades. Builds some suspense. (Dir: Menahem Golan, 90 mins.)

Earl Carroll Vanities (1945)**½ Dennis O'Keefe, Constance Moore. A princess traveling incognito accidentally becomes a hit in a show, falls for a young song writer. Typical musical, nothing important, but fair enough. (Dir: Joseph Santley, 91 mins.)

Earl of Chicago, The (1940)***½ Robert Montgomery, Edward Arnold. Plenty of fun in this story of a Chicago gangster who becomes an English peer after the death of a long-lost relative. Cast is excellent. (Dir: Richard Thorpe, 85 mins.)

Early Bird, The (Great Britain, 1965)*½ Norman Wisdom, Edward Chapman, Jerry Desmonde. (Dir: Robert Asher, 98 mins.)

Early Summer (Japan, 1951)**½ Ichiro Sugai, Chishu Ryu. Yasujiro Ozu is one of Japan's top directors, and this is a good example of his work. Movie concentrates on the emotional problems of a family trying to hold on to the ancient traditions despite the overwhelming tide of changes that sweep their lives. For some, the action may seem too slow, but the drama builds nicely. (Dir: Yasujiro Ozu, 150 mins.)

Earrings of Madame De, The—See: **Diamond Earrings, The**

Earth (Russia, 1930)**** Mikola Nademsky,

Stepan Shkurat. Most of the so-called classics of Soviet cinema are stodgy, formalist works, of which this saga of a peasant's love for his tractor would seem to be a woebegone part. Yet under the animistic direction of that mythic folklorist, Alexander Dovzhenko, the film is transformed into a lyrical evocation of the vitality of birth, life, love, and even death. In short, it is true peasant poetry that transcends the nominal plot about the formation of a collective farm in the Ukraine—it is visual expression raised to sublime heights through subtle and telling details. It sounds boring, I know, but it **is** beautiful silent cinema, though perhaps not quite as compelling as his **Aerograd** or **Arsenal**. Also known as **Soil**. (63 mins.)

Earth Cries Out, The (Italy, 1949)** Marina Berti, Andrea Checchi. When fighting in Palestine breaks out, former wartime buddies choose different paths—one a British officer, one an immigrant, one a terrorist. Slow-moving drama originally had topicality as an asset. English-dubbed. (Dir: Duilio Coletti, 79 mins.)

Earth II (MTV 1971)** Gary Lockwood, Anthony Franciosa. Science-fiction fans may enjoy this mini-sized "space odyssey" about the adventures of the first manned orbiting space station, known as "Earth II." The technical effects are excellent but the drama played out in the futuristic sets seems dwarfed by comparison. Note the dialogue which says that Communist China doesn't have to abide by interspace rules because it is not a member of the United Nations! (Dir: Tom Gries, 100 mins.)

Earth vs. the Flying Saucers (1956)** Hugh Marlowe, Joan Taylor, Morris Ankrum. The title tells it all. About the only point of interest is the special effects work of Ray Harryhausen. The title tells it all. (Dir: Fred F. Sears, 83 mins.)

Earthling, The (1981)**½ William Holden, Ricky Schroder, Jack Thompson, Olivia Hamnett. William Holden stars as an experience-hardened loner dying of cancer, who is thrown together with Ricky Schroder, a pampered city boy, in the Australian bush country where they must learn to survive and trust and love. Shot entirely on location in the isolated Barrington Tops region of New South Wales. Harsh, strident, and undistinguished. This film has been extensively recut since its original Australian release. Photographed by Don McAlpine. (Dir: Peter Collinson.)

Earthquake (1974)**½ Charlton Heston, Richard Roundtree, Genevieve Bujold, Ava Gardner, Marjoe Gortner, Anthony Perkins. An engaging schlock remake of "The Ten Commandments," with the San Andreas Fault standing in for the Red Sea. Heston is still in charge; God makes a more surreptitious appearance, whisking away the morally flawed characters with the help of Universal's crack special effects department. Robson directs well, but a little absentmindedly—halfway through the film, Roundtree rides off on his motorcycle to look for help and is not heard from again. (129 mins.)

East of Eden (1955)**** James Dean, Julie Harris, Raymond Massey, Jo Van Fleet, Lois Smith. John Steinbeck's painfully biblical allegory, with Genesis replayed in Monterey, California, circa '17, is more palatable on screen because of the expressive anguish of the players, led by Dean in his starring debut. Director Elia Kazan gets a little drunk with the possibilities of baroque camera angles but everyone was trying to lick the problems of CinemaScope composition in 1955, and at least Kazan was imaginatively misguided. Raymond Massey and Van Fleet (who won an Oscar) both battle nobly with the impossible roles of Adam and Eve, but it's the tortured empathy of Dean's screen personality that dominates, brilliantly. (115 mins.)

East of Kilimanjaro (U.S.A.-Great Britain-Italy, 1957)*½ Marshall Thompson, Gaby Andre. (Dirs: Arnold Belgard, Edoardo Capolino, 75 mins.)

East of Sudan (Great Britain, 1964)**½ Anthony Quayle, Sylvia Syms. Action drama which doesn't aspire to be anything else. Adventure fans will go along with the treacherous journey taken by a small group of British and Moslem survivors of a brutal Moslem attack on a British outpost located a couple of hundred miles from Khartoum. The time is the latter part of the nineteenth century and the party includes Anthony Quayle as a seasoned soldier and Sylvia Syms as a very proper governess. (Dir: Nathan Juran, 84 mins.)

East of Sumatra (1953)**½ Jeff Chandler, Marilyn Maxwell, Anthony Quinn. Two-fisted adventure film bolstered by performances of Chandler and Quinn as opponents in an effort to set up a tin mining project. Plenty of action and romance. (Dir: Budd Boetticher, 90 mins.)

East of the River (1940)**½ John Garfield, Brenda Marshall. Typical Garfield yarn about the ex-con who, when put to the test, is a nice guy. It's a pity that a talent like Garfield's had to be wasted in so many of these cliche films. (Dir: Alfred E. Green, 73 mins.)

East Side of Heaven (1939)*** Bing Crosby, Joan Blondell. Singing taxi driver finds himself custodian of a baby left by a young mother. Tuneful light comedy, pleasingly done. (Dir: David Butler, 100 mins.)

East Side, West Side (1949)**½ James Mason, Barbara Stanwyck, Ava Gardner, Van Heflin, and Cyd Charisse. Slickly mounted soap opera set in the chic world of the wealthy social set of New York. Miss Stanwyck overacts in her role of a wife who stops pretending her husband still loves her and Ava slinks in and out of the proceedings as a femme fatale. (Dir: Mervyn Le Roy, 108 mins.)

Easter Parade (1948)**** Fred Astaire, Ann Miller, Judy Garland. Excellent, gracefully conceived MGM musical. Astaire plays a dancer with a partner (Miller) getting too big for her tap shoes, so he grooms Garland as a replacement. Astaire and Garland, in their only picture together, play well off each other; as one number puts it, they're a coupla swells. The Irving Berlin score is bright, and director Charles Walters knows how to showcase Astaire to maximum advantage. (109 mins.)

Easy Come, Easy Go (1947)**½ Barry Fitzgerald, Diana Lynn. Barry is wonderful, but the picture is so bad it weighs him down. Story of a lazy, horse-playing Irishman whose sole occupation is stopping his daughter from getting married. (Dir: John Farrow, 77 mins.)

Easy Come, Easy Go (1967)** Elvis Presley, Dodie Marshall. Elvis' fans may enjoy this aimless musical adventure yarn which has the singer playing a Navy frogman who thinks he may have stumbled upon a sunken treasure. Naturally, there are songs and girls galore. Elvis' acting, incidentally, is better than the dopey script. (Dir: John Rich, 95 mins.)

Easy Life, The (Italy, 1963)**** Vittorio Gassman, Jean-Louis Trintignant, Catherine Spaak. Offbeat, absorbing drama of a happy-go-lucky extrovert who has an effect on a serious young law student when they are thrown together by chance. Sharp observation of contrasting personalities, story holds the attention tightly all the way. Fine performances. English-dubbed. (Dir: Dino Risi, 105 mins.)

Easy Living (1937)**** Jean Arthur, Ray Milland, Edward Arnold, Franklin Pangborn, William Demarest. A delightful Preston Sturges-scripted film about a grumpy millionaire (Arnold) who throws his wife's mink out the window. It lands on a poor working girl (Arthur) with whom Arnold's son (Milland) falls in love. Typically Sturges and typically joyful, wry, and accurate. (Dir: Mitchell Leisen, 91 mins.)

Easy Money (Great Britain, 1948)**½ Dennis Price, Edward Rigby. Episodic stories about the effects of sudden riches upon the winners of a football pool. Amusing, with the last episode a comedy gem. (Dir: Bernard Knowles, 94 mins.)

Easy Rider (1969)**** Dennis Hopper, Peter Fonda, Jack Nicholson, Karen Black, Robert Walker, Jr. A devastating, original film that has something truthful and compelling to say about our gun-happy nation. In this box-office smash, made for less than $400,000, two "hippie" motorcyclists sell some dope in southern California, stash their grubstake away in the gas tank, and take off for a jaunt across the Southwest headed for New Orleans. Hopper makes a stunning directorial debut. Acting honors go to Nicholson's virtuoso portrayal of an alcoholic small-town southern lawyer. Much of the dialogue is vapid banalities spoken by inarticulate people. (94 mins.)

Easy to Love (1953)** Esther Williams, Van Johnson, Tony Martin. The spectacular water ballets staged by Busby Berkeley for Esther Williams are really the only attraction to this pallid musical set against Cypress Gardens. (Dir: Charles Walters, 96 mins.)

Easy to Wed (1946)** Van Johnson, Esther Williams, Lucille Ball, Keenan Wynn, Cecil Kellaway. Inferior remake of "Libeled Lady." The film has only Johnson instead of Spencer Tracy, Williams instead of Myrna Loy, Ball instead of Jean Harlow, Wynn instead of William Powell. About a ruthless editor's use of his fiancé to get the goods on an heiress. Edward Buzzell directs without fanfare or flourish. (110 mins.)

Easy Way, The—See; **Room For One More**

Eat My Dust (1976)** Ron Howard, Christopher Norris, Warren Kemmerling. Drive-in movie, for drag-racing and demolition derby freaks only. It's pretty inoffensive but just one long chase. Howard looks cheerful. (Dir: Charles Griffith, 90 mins.)

Ebirah, Horror of the Deep—See: **Godzilla vs. the Sea Monster**

Eboli (Italy-France, 1980)**** Gian Maria Volonte, Paolo Bonacelli, Alain Cuny. Francesco Rosi directed this adaptation of writer-painter Carlo Levi's book about his two years of exile in the mountain village of Lucania for anti-Fascist activities in '35. The village is beyond the influence of much of the modern age: Volonte gives an eloquent, powerful performance as Levi. Rosi's approach may have been too commercial, but this is an engrossing, often lovely film. (120 mins.)

Ebony, Ivory and Jade (MTV 1979)** Bert Convy, Debbie Allen, Martha Smith. Action adventure for fans of *Charlie's Angels*. This slickly produced pilot has Bert Convy playing Nick Jade, a special agent working with a flashy singing duo (beautiful, black Debbie Allen and gorgeous blonde Martha Smith). The girls are reluctant to play spies, but they always give in to Nick's persuasive charm. (Dir: John L. Moxey, 78 mins.)

Eddie Cantor Story, The (1954)** Keefe Brasselle, Marilyn Erskine. Disappointing biography of the famed "Banjo Eyes" rise to fame and fortune. All the stops are pulled to inject pathos and sympathy for the obstacles which befell Cantor in this retelling of his life. Keefe Brasselle goes at it tooth and nail but fails to make an impression. (Dir: Alfred E. Green, 116 mins.)

Eddy Duchin Story, The (1956)**½ Tyrone Power, Kim Novak, Victoria Shaw, James Whitmore, Rex Thompson. On the surface, this is a long, glossy, superficial tearjerker about the early demise from leukemia of a society piano player. However, to afficionados of George Sidney and Kim Novak in their opulent CinemaScope period, there are visual stratagems sufficient to maintain renegade auteurist interest. (Dir: George Sidney, 123 mins.)

Edge, The (1968)*** Jack Rader, Tom Griffin. Visually static, but a maddening, stimulating tract about contemporary American politics and society. Written and directed by Robert Kramer, one of the most gifted of the film world's "underground" directors. Technically sloppy film due to a minuscule budget-film shot for less than $15,000—"Edge" is noteworthy because it's one of the few times that the convictions of the radical young left in our country have been captured on film. Much of the dialogue may strike political sophisticates as puerile, but if you pay more attention to what you hear rather than what you see, you'll find Kramer's film disturbing and involving. Kramer later directed the searing blueprint for a revolution called "Ice." (105 min.)

Edge of Darkness (1943)*** Errol Flynn, Ann Sheridan, Walter Huston, Ruth Gordon. Errol tries to liberate Norway in this but all he manages to do is assist a good cast in making another top flight war drama. (Dir: Lewis Milestone, 120 mins.)

Edge of Eternity (1959)*** Cornel Wilde, Victoria Shaw. Frequently suspenseful "cops and robbers" stuff with Cornel Wilde as a deputy sheriff who's hot on the trail of a murderer who operates around the Grand Canyon resort area. (Dir: Don Siegel, 80 mins.)

Edge of Fear (Spain, 1964)*½ May Heatherly, Virgilio Teixeira. English dialogue. Alternate title: **Night of Fear**. (Dir: Leon Klimovsky, 90 mins.)

Edge of Fury (1958)* Michael Higgins, Lois Holmes. (Dir: Robert Gurney, 77 mins.)

Edge of Hell (1956)* Hugo Haas, Francesca de Scaffa. (Dir: Hugo Haas, 78 mins.)

Edge of the City (1957)***½ John Cassavetes, Sidney Poitier, Jack Warden. Based on Robert Alan Aurthur's memorable TV play "A Man Is Ten Feet Tall," this filmed-on-location along the dock fronts in New York is an exciting, moving film about two longshoremen whose growing friendship is threatened by a bullying bigot. Poitier and Warden, playing a notably repellent punk, are terrific and there's a rousing "claw" fight toward the end of the film. First directorial effort, and a good one, of Martin Ritt, now one of Hollywood's best. Also first feature produced by David Susskind. (Dir: Martin Ritt, 85 mins.)

Edison the Man (1940)*** Spencer Tracy, Charles Coburn. Tracy is perfect as the most famous of all American inventors. His portrayal compensates for certain shortcomings in the script and makes the film a fine tribute to Edison's genius. (See: "Young Tom Edison") (Dir: Clarence Brown, 107 mins.)

Edvard Munch (Norway-Sweden, 1976)**** Geir Westby, Gro Fraas. Director Peter

Watkins's study of the tortured Expressionist painter is obsessively detailed (and meticulously researched); through jittery, subjective montage it creates a life and madness of its own. (167 mins.)

Edward My Son (British, 1949)*** Spencer Tracy, Deborah Kerr. Story of a man who builds a fortune for his son through some shady deeds. Is a compelling film but lacks the superb stage acting of Robert Morley. (Dir: George Cukor, 112 mins.)

Eegah! (1962)* Arch Hall Jr., Richard Kiel, Marilyn Manning. (Dir: Arch Hall, Sr., 90 mins.)

Effect of Gamma Rays on Man-in-the-Moon Marigolds, The (1972)*** Joanne Woodward, Nell Potts, Roberta Wallach, Judith Lowry. Adapted from Paul Zindel's Pulitzer Prize-winning play, this tale of Beatrice Hunsdorfer, the gallant loser whose dreams are unfulfilled, gets an adequate expansion onto the screen. Highlight of the tale is Miss Woodward's performance, which captures all of the desperate dreams of a widow with two children who has not resigned herself to obscurity. The daughter's winning of the science prize, and the ensuing household tension, evoke shock and sympathy. Roberta Wallach is also excellent. At its best in capturing the seemingly chance encounters and dialogues that shape destinies. (Nell Potts is Woodward's real daughter.) (Dir: Paul Newman, 101 mins.)

Effi Briest (West Germany, 1974)*** Hanna Schygulla, Wolfgang Schenck, Ulli Lommel, Lilo Pempeit. Adapted from Theodor Fontane's 19th-century social novel. This story of a 16-year-old girl locked in the boredom of a loveless marriage is perfectly suited to director Rainer Werner Fassbinder's stifling mise en scène. The slow, deliberate pace is sometimes taxing. (140 mins.)

Egg and I, The (1947)*** Claudette Colbert, Fred MacMurray, Marjorie Main. A memorably funny comedy about trials and tribulations on a chicken farm. This picture introduced the characters of Ma and Pa Kettle (Marjorie Main and Percy Kilbride). Claudette Colbert is excellent. Based on Betty McDonald's best seller. (Dir: Chester Erskine, 108 mins.)

Egyptian, The (1954)** Edmund Purdom, Victor Mature, Peter Ustinov, Bella Darvi, Gene Tierney, Michael Wilding. Typical '50s Hollywood biblical spectacular, designed to lure audiences from the tube to the big CinemaScope screen. Based on a best-seller by Mika Waltari, much of the film is wooden and ludicrous, although Leon Shamroy's cinematography and Bernard Herrmann's score are first-rate. The once great Michael Curtiz directed, his flair sorely diminished, and the script is unadulterated hackwork. (140 mins.)

Eiger Sanction, The (1975)**½ Clint Eastwood, George Kennedy, Jack Cassidy. The Eiger is a Swiss mountain peak, and if you wait long enough there is an exciting sequence involving climbers in the Swiss peaks. But there are a lot of lows along the way, thanks to the rambling story based on the best-selling novel by Trevanian. Eastwood plays a college art professor who also happens to be an assassin for a secret U.S. government agency known in this film as CII. Eastwood directs himself for the third time and he allegedly did his own mountain climbing as well. It took three writers to turn out the jumbled, sophomoric screenplay. (128 mins.)

8½ (Italy, 1963)**** Marcello Mastroianni, Claudia Cardinale, Sandra Milo, Anouk Aimee. A stupendous, brilliant and sometimes baffling film, properly deemed one of the truly great films of modern times. Is a stunningly edited semi-autobiographical filmic psychoanalysis by director Federico Fellini as he records the fantasies and real life happenings of a noted filmmaker who is having artistic difficulties completing his new project. Boasts superb performances not only from Mastroianni but also right down to the smallest bit parts. Technically dazzling as Fellini's complete mastery of the film medium seems to make him start his films on a creative level where other directors end up. A complex, stimulating adventurous masterpiece. (135 mins.)

800 Leagues Over the Amazon (Mexico, 1958)*½ Carlos Moctezuma, Elvira Quintana. (Dir: Emilio Gomez Muriel, 78 mins.)

Eight Iron Men (1952)***½ Bonar Colleano, Lee Marvin, Arthur Franz. Absorbing drama of the war in Italy, and a squad of soldiers tied down by heavy enemy fire. Good character sketches, some welcome moments of grim humor. Fine performances. (Dir: Edward Dmytryk, 80 mins.)

Eight O'Clock Walk (Great Britain, 1954)*** Richard Attenborough, Cathy O'Donnell. An innocent young taxi driver is placed on trial for the murder of an eight-year-old girl. Tense mystery, above average. (Dir: Lance Comfort, 87 mins.)

Eight on the Lam (1967)* Bob Hope, Jonathan Winters, Jill St. John, Phyllis Diller. (Dir: George Marshall, 106 mins.)

Eighteen and Anxious (1957)** Martha Scott, Jackie Coogan. A girl has a wild fling despite her mother's overprotective ways and almost winds up dead. Pure soap opera all the way. (Dir: Joe Parker, 93 mins.)

Eighteen in the Sun—See: **Beach Party—Italian Style**

8th Day of the Week, The (Poland-Germany, 1958)**** Sonja Ziemann, Zbigniew Cybulski. A prize-winning Polish film, sensitively acted and superbly directed. A young pair of lovers try to fight against the bitterness and sordidness left by the war. Powerful stuff. (Dir: Aleksander Ford, 84 mins.)

Eighty Steps to Jonah (1969)** Wayne Newton. Overly sentimental tale about a young man (Newton) who is on the run from the police and comes across a camp for blind children. A chorus of violins in the background, and you can take it from there.... (Dir: Gerd Oswald, 107 mins.)

80,000 Suspects (Great Britain, 1963)*** Claire Bloom, Richard Johnson. Occasionally gripping drama showing the attempts to track down smallpox carriers when an epidemic hits a town. Realistic atmosphere sometimes marred by intrusion of a sub-plot about a doctor trying to save his marriage, but the medical suspense elements are well handled. Good performance. (Dir: Val Guest, 113 mins.)

El—See: **This Strange Passion**

El Cid (1961)**½ Charlton Heston, Sophia Loren. This film spectacle is about as opulent as they come and fans of this type of adventure get a full quota of great battle scenes, superb Spanish settings, magnificent costumes and the attractive presence of stars Charlton Heston and Sophia Loren. The saga of the hero, El Cid, who became a legend in Spanish history, is more for the eye than the ear and the final scenes of the film, in which a mortally wounded El Cid is strapped to his mount and sent to ride against his adversaries is a splashy bit of derring do. Much of the visual splendor of this kind of pageant film is lost on your small home screen. (Dir: Anthony Mann, 184 mins.)

El Condor (1970)½ Jim Brown, Lee Van Cleef. (Dir: John Guillermin, 102 mins.)

El Dorado (1967)***½ John Wayne, Robert Mitchum, Christopher George (very good), Arthur Hunnicutt, Michele Carey, Charlene Holt. Ripsnortin' old-fashioned Howard Hawks-directed western fun. Gunfighter (Wayne) helps a whiskey-sodden sheriff (Mitchum) redeem himself and clean up the baddies. Good-natured shenanigans with lots of old pros showing how it's done. (127 mins.)

El Greco (Italy-France, 1964)** Mel Ferrer, Rosanna Schiaffino, Adolfo Celi. When you wake up after watching Mel Ferrer's soporific performance, you may be hard to convince that good films about great artistic geniuses have been and will be made. (Laughton as Rembrandt and Kirk Douglas in "Lust for Life" among others.) But here Mel's in an Italian-French co-production made in Spain about a Greek who speaks English. Theoretically it's about the legendary painter, but there actually are some lovely sequences filmed in Toledo—Spain, not Ohio! (Dir: Luciano Salce, 95 mins.)

El Topo (Mexico, 1971)**** Aléxandro Jodorowsky, Mara Lorenzio, David Silva. An ambitious, fascinating, violence-filled allegorical western, the second film made by Jodorowsky, a Chilean-Russian stage director who once worked for Marcel Marceau. It's also a filmed homage to director Louis Bunuel, as writer-director-editor Jodorowsky sums up the Old Testament and man's search for meaning in his life—all the while filling the screen with a dazzling, decadent panorama of flagellation, assorted grotesqueries, and an altogether remarkable visual style. It doesn't all work but you won't soon forget this cinematic assault on all your senses. Not for the squeamish. Early in the film Jodorowsky explains the title by noting the parable of the mole, which spends its whole life digging toward the light, only to be blinded, in the end, by the sun. English subtitles. (Dir: Alexandro Jodorowsky, 123 mins.)

Eleanor and Franklin (MTV 1976)**** Jane Alexander, Edward Herrmann, Ed Flanders, Rosemary Murphy. Screenwriter James Costigan has adapted Joseph P. Lash's Pulitzer Prize-winning book illuminating the special relationship between plain Eleanor and her more dynamic, dashing cousin, Franklin Delano Roosevelt. Since Eleanor is the focal point of the show, the opening is devoted to her painful, lonely childhood, her adolescent years at school, and her eventual proper courtship with Franklin. The title roles are brilliantly realized by Jane Alexander, who never resorts to parody either in voice or mannerism; and Edward Herrmann, a relative newcomer, who all but steals the film with his portrayal of FDR. In supporting roles, Miss Murphy as FDR's mother and Flanders as Louis Howe, FDR's political manager, are both excellent. Ms. Alexander will break your heart when she discovers a love letter to her husband written by her personal secretary. All in all, a fine personal drama about famous historical figures. Originally shown in two parts. (Dir: Dan Petrie, 208 mins.)

Eleanor and Franklin: The White House Years (MTV 1977)**** Jane Alexander, Edward Herrmann, Priscilla Pointer. More of the public and personal history of Eleanor and Franklin Roosevelt, dramatizing sections of Joseph Lash's book. The best scenes are those dealing with WW II, particularly a scene in which Eleanor visits a hospital ward in the South Pacific and shares a touching moment with a Marine amputee. Miss Alexander and Herrmann are even better than they were in the original "Eleanor and Franklin," having honed their portrayals to perfection. In the large supporting cast, Walter McGinn, taking over the role of Louis Howe from Ed Flanders, comes off best. (Dir: Daniel Petrie, 144 mins.)

Eleanor Roosevelt Story, The (1965)**** Eloquent, truly inspiring documentary biography of Mrs. FDR, graphically portrayed in newsreel and still pictures and especially in the words of Archibald MacLeish's brilliant narrative. Beautifully done, deserves the lavish praise bestowed upon it. (Dir: Richard Kaplan, 91 mins.)

Electric Horseman, The (1979)*** Robert Redford, Jane Fonda, Valerie Perrine, Willie Nelson. This very well-made film failed to grip me for more than a few moments. The direction is skilled; the performances are intelligent and idiomatic; the technical aspects are in good order. But the story—about a beat-up cowboy become cereal huckster for a conglomerate who fights back against the system—is just a newfangled cliché. Fonda and Redford play comfortably together. Director Sydney Pollack, whose talent is so large, ought to be doing better things. (121 mins.)

Electronic Monster, The (Great Britain, 1960) ** Rod Cameron, Mary Murphy. Interesting science-fiction yarn about a group of experimenting scientists who work with dream-inducing devices. (Dir: Montgomery Tully, 72 mins.)

Elephant Boy (Great Britain, 1937)***½ Sabu (debut), W. E. Holloway, Walter Hudd. Documentarian Robert Flaherty shot a great deal of footage; this engrossing drama combines Flaherty authenticity with the narrative coherence of codirector Zoltan Korda. (80 mins.)

Elephant Called Slowly, An (Great Britain, 1970)** Virginia McKenna, Bill Travers, George Adamson. McKenna and Travers return to Africa, in a dramatized travelogue to the scene of their previous "Born Free," for a vacation, and to house-sit in the African bush. They make some elephant friends, visit former lion friends. Nice pictures of the animals. (Dir: James Hill, 91 mins.)

Elephant Man, The (Great Britain, 1980)**½ Anthony Hopkins, John Hurt, Anne Bancroft, John Gielgud, Wendy Hiller. Pietistic presentation of the life of deformed John Merrick. The film's appeals for compassion are more an exercise in congratulating the audience for its presumed tolerance. Hurt wears massive makeup and plays unrelievedly for heart throbs, Bancroft postures. (Dir: David Lynch, 123 mins.)

Elephant Walk (1954)**½ Elizabeth Taylor, Peter Finch, Dana Andrews. A muddled soap opera played out against the splendor of Ceylon. Miss Taylor is ravishingly beautiful as the young English bride who comes to her new husband's (Peter Finch) tea plantation in Ceylon and finds the adjustment to a new life difficult. Action fans will enjoy the large elephant stampede which comes at the film's climax. (Dir: William Dieterle, 103 mins.)

Elevator, The (MTV 1974)** James Farentino, Roddy McDowall, Craig Stevens, Carol Lynley, Myrna Loy. Still another familiar "trapped" melodrama. An elevator stalls following a robbery in a high-rise office building, trapping the thief and seven passengers. Thief James Farentino carries the brunt of the soap opera with an interesting cast supplying the range of expected histrionics. (Dir: Jerry Jameson, 78 mins.)

11 Harrowhouse (1974)** Charles Grodin, Candice Bergen, John Gielgud, James Ma-

son. Muddled, contrived robbery caper. Grodin is a diamond salesman enlisted by a mad millionaire (Trevor Howard) to steal millions of dollars' worth of diamonds. Candice Bergen is one of those flighty, bored heiresses who crave adventure with a capital A. The great supporting cast—John Gielgud, James Mason, Howard—is largely wasted. Also, a flip voice-over narration by Grodin seems jarringly out of place with what is going on in the film. Occasional nice touches, but this is not as rewarding as Avakian's "Cops and Robbers." Now known as **Anything for Love.** (Dir: Aram Avakian, 95 mins.)

11th Victim (MTV 1979)**½ Bess Armstrong, Maxwell Gail, Harold Gould, Eric Burdon. Earnest telefeature about a young lady who leaves her job as a TV newswoman in the Midwest and goes to Hollywood, where she teams up with a police investigator to get to the bottom of her younger sister's murder. Melodramatic all the way. (Dir: Jon Kaplan, 104 mins.)

Elizabeth the Queen—See: **Private Lives of Elizabeth and Essex**

Ellery Queen (MTV 1975)** Jim Hutton, David Wayne, Ray Milland, Kim Hunter, Monte Markham. The popular mystery writer-sleuth again. Boyish, lanky Jim Hutton plays an absent-minded, bumbling "Ellery" in an investigation of the murder of a man's mistress. Hutton, Wayne, and supporting actors all work hard, unsuccessfully trying for a light touch. (Dir: David Greene, 100 mins.)

Ellery Queen: Don't Look Behind You (MTV 1971)**½ Peter Lawford. The sophisticated finesse of Lawford is compatible with the character of Ellery Queen, the worldly American criminologist-author. In this film, Lawford and his American uncle, played with a staccato delivery by Harry Morgan, team up to crack an ominous multiple-murder case. Mystery fans will enjoy following Queen's clever analysis of the hidden clues. Credit director Barry Shear with a stylish production, particularly the New York City location shots. (Dir: Barry Shear, 100 mins.)

Elmer Gantry (1960)**** Burt Lancaster, Jean Simmons, Dean Jagger, Arthur Kennedy, Shirley Jones. Sinclair Lewis's preaching hustler is impersonated by Lancaster at the top of his rousting form: shallow, highly pitched, yet immensely effective. Simmons brings a lot of detail and pathos to the role of the healer exploited by Gantry, and everyone was so shocked at Jones playing a hooker that they gave her an Oscar. Richard Brooks adapted and directed, and an absence of irony purges the film of his accustomed righteousness. (145 mins.)

Elopement (1951)** Clifton Webb, Anne Francis, William Lundigan. Crusty individual gets involved with young love. Another sneering Webb portrayal, if you like 'em. (Dir: Henry Koster, 82 mins.)

Elusive Corporal, The (France, 1962) Jean-Pierre Cassel, Claude Brasseur, Claude Rich. A masterpiece from director Jean Renoir, varying on the situation in "Grand Illusion." This time Frenchmen are in a WW II prison camp. An ironic comedy of fake French heroics and real French heroism. Delicate and witty, with masterly performances by Cassel and Rich. (108 mins.)

Elvira Madigan (Sweden, 1967)**** Pia Degermark, Thommy Berggren. One of the most exquisite, romantic movies ever made. It is exquisite in a quite literal sense, as the color photography provides some of the most ravishing, beautiful scenes ever filmed, thanks to cinematographer Jorgen Persson and the multi-talented Bo Widerberg who wrote, directed and edited this remarkable love story. Based on a true story about a young Swedish army officer around 1900 who runs off with Elvira, a lovely young circus artist. The leads are most attractive, but most of all it is Widerberg's triumph as he offers some of the most glorious images and tones ever seen. English dubbed. (89 mins.)

Elvis! (MTV 1979)***½ Kurt Russell, Season Hubley, Shelley Winters. The first of what may be an unending series of films about Elvis Presley. Kurt Russell, a dark horse for the role, is adept at re-creating Elvis in manner, appearance, speech, and performance. Purists will argue, of course. Takes us from Elvis's meager beginning to the triumphant '71 comeback engagement in Las Vegas. Elvis's songs are sung by Ronnie McDowell. (Dir: John Carpenter, 104 mins.)

Elvis and the Beauty Queen (MTV 1981)** Don Johnson, Stephanie Zimbalist. Another Presley drama that's mildly interesting. Don Johnson plays Elvis who is enchanted by Linda Thompson, a Memphis beauty queen. Linda's job during the five-year affair is to keep Elvis from drugs, but mostly it's a losing battle. This is Linda's side of the story. Stephanie Zimbalist, who may be a shade too sweet for the part, must carry the load. (Dir: Gus Trikonis, 104 mins.)

Elvis! Elvis! (Sweden, 1977)**½ Lele Dorazio, Lena Pia Berhardsson. The story of a seven-year-old's struggle to define himself as a human being and achieve some measure of personal acceptance by his mother and the adult world. Written by Kay Pollak and Maria Gripe; based on Gripe's books about an actual child, Elvis Karlsson. (Dir: Kay Pollak)

Elvis: That's the Way It Is (1970)*** Elvis Presley. Good backstage examination of Presley preparing his club act and taking it on the road. Not too objective, but useful and informative about the anatomy of showmanship. (Dir: Denis Sanders, 97 mins.)

Embezzled Heaven (Austria, 1959)** Annie Rosar, Hans Holt. Mawkish drama about a cook who tries to buy a seat in Heaven, by helping a nephew to become a priest. Good intentions, weak execution. English-dubbed. (Dir: Ernst Marischka, 91 mins.)

Emergency (MTV 1972)** Robert Fuller, Julie London. Fire trucks race through Los Angeles streets as the rescue squad covers a barrage of accidents——auto crashes, a tunnel cave-in, and even a high-wire accident victim. This is director Jack Webb's two-hour pilot for the TV series. (Dir: Christian Nyby, 100 mins.)

Emergency (MTV 1979)** Randy Mantooth, Kevin Tighe, Deidre Lenihan, Patty McCormack. Gage and DeSoto are reunited. This time they are attending a paramedics' convention in San Francisco and become involved with two female paramedics from the Bay Area. Same action, different locale. (Dir: Georg Fenady, 100 mins.)

Emergency Ward—See: **Carey Treatment, The**

Emergency Wedding (1950)** Larry Parks, Barbara Hale. Silly little comedy about a couple who love each other but don't like each other enough to make a go of their marriage. (Dir: Edward Buzzell, 78 mins.)

Emigrants, The (Sweden, 1971)**** Max von Sydow, Liv Ullmann, Eddie Axberg, Svenolof Bern. Profoundly touching story about the hardships of a Swedish peasant family who came to America's Midwest in the middle of the 19th century. Pace is slow and lyrical. Acting by everyone is subtle and emotional. A stirring reaffirmation of the faith, bravery, and inner strength of human beings. Directed, photographed, and coscripted by Jan Troell. (148 mins.)

Emitaï (Senegal, 1973)*** Ibou Camara, Ousmane Camara, Pierre Blanchard, Robert Fontaine, Michel Renaudeau. The title of Ousmane Sembene's Senegalese film means "god of thunder"—the god to whom a tribal village prays when the French colonial government commandeers the rice supply. Set during World War II, the film dramatizes the effect of European ideology on African traditions. At once an allegory and a study of people driven to violence by events in a world beyond their ken, this rarely shown film carries a charge of novelistic ambiguity. (103 mins.)

Emperor Jones, The (1933)***½ Paul Robeson, Dudley Digges, Frank Wilson, Moms Mabley (bit). Adaptation of the expressionistic O'Neill play, with the great Robeson. This was the first film to star a Negro, and it was the last for a long, long time. Director Dudley Murphy added a lot of material explaining how hustler Jones got to be an emperor; surprisingly, these realistic details of a southern black on the make and on the road are the best parts of the film. The O'Neill stuff doesn't play all that well. Robeson was criticized for making the Negro proud, tough, and superstitious; today these seem courageous decisions. (72 mins.)

Emperor of the North Pole (1973)**½ Lee Marvin, Ernest Borgnine, Keith Carradine, Malcolm Atterbury. Most of this set aboard a freight train circa '33. Marvin stars as A-Number-One, king of the hobos, whose ultimate act of self-assertion will be to ride the train of the murderous Shack, a railroad cop. A brutal, vital film, because of the way director Robert Aldrich resolutely undercuts all the myths men contrive to rationalize their fight for naked survival. Alternate title: **Emperor of the North.** (118 mins.)

Emperor Waltz, The (1948)*** Bing Crosby, Joan Fontaine. Pleasing operetta finds Bing as a phonograph salesman trying to sell one to Emperor Franz Joseph of Austria, and wooing a countess on the side. (Dir: Billy Wilder, 106 mins.)

Empire in the Sun (Italy, 1956)*** Engrossing documentary exploring the life and habits of the Peruvian Indians. Fascinating scenes of unfamiliar peoples, should interest all. (Dirs: Mario Craveri, Enrico Gras, 88 mins.)

Empire of Passion, The (France-Japan, 1976)*** Tatsuya Fuji, Eiko Matsuda, Aoi Nakajima, Meika Seri. Japan's most compulsive commercial avant-gardist, Nagisa Oshima (*Boy, The Ceremony*), makes a companion piece to his *In the Realm of the Senses* that is punctiliously traditional. It's a rendition of the *Double Indemnity* plot told as a Japanese ghost story. Oshima has a way of transmuting the genre conventions even as he invokes them. There is an ominous portent in the lush gorgeousness of the images (pictorialism is the dotage of great Japanese directors), but nothing in an Oshima image means just what it appears to mean. The story makes little sense apart from the *mise en scène*, which is part of the point, and it is to the film's credit that it sends shivers up your spine, even as it provokes doubts of a kind more timid thrillers seek to discourage. It dares you to suspend disbelief. (105 mins.)

Empire Strikes Back, The (1980)**** Mark Hamill, Harrison Ford, Carrie Fisher, Billy Dee Williams, Alec Guinness, Frank Oz, David Prowse, Anthony Daniels. Continuation of the "Star Wars" saga is engrossing entertainment and almost nonstop action. All the familiar characters are back, including Ben Kenobi (Alec Guinness) in a cameo. Princess Leia (Fisher) falls in love with brash Han (Ford), Luke (Hamill) learns how to use the Force, Darth Vader (Prowse) reveals a shocking secret, C-3PO (Daniels) manages to fall apart and be put back together. New characters include Yoda (Oz), who tutors Luke, and space dude Lando Calrissian (Williams), a treacherous friend indeed. Doesn't quite have the heart or humor of "Star Wars," but a masterpiece of special effects is rendered by a team of experts, and almost everything an action fantasy should be. The film will have far less impact on TV than on a big theater screen. (Dir: Irvin Kershner, 118 mins.)

Empress Yang Kwei Fei (1955)***½ The first color film by the great Japanese director Kenji Mizoguchi, produced as a big-budget spectacular by the Shaw Brothers of Hong Kong (who were later responsible for the kung fu craze). The film is not as resolutely personal as "Ugetsu" or "Sansho," yet Mizoguchi is able to navigate the commercial requirements gracefully. It has the aura of a fairy tale—in 18th-century China an emperor falls in love with a servant girl—yet the emotions it provokes are anything but simple. (125 mins.)

Empty Canvas, The (France-Italy, 1963)*½ Bette Davis, Horst Buchholz, Catherine Spaak. (Dir: Damiano Damiani, 118 mins.)

Enchanted Cottage (1945)***½ Robert Young, Dorothy McGuire. Two people are thrown together and find love in their mutual unhappiness. Sensitive, touching romantic drama. (Dir: John Cromwell, 91 mins.)

Enchanted Island (1958)*½ Jane Powell, Dana Andrews. (Dir: Allan Dwan, 94 mins.)

Enchantment (1948)*** David Niven, Teresa Wright, Evelyn Keyes, Farley Granger. Occasionally interesting story about a doddering old colonel (Niven) who relives his romantic past via the reverie route. Vintage World War I. The flashbacks are triggered by Niven's grandson's romantic problems. The ladies will love this one. (Dir: Irving Reis, 102 mins.)

Encore (Great Britain, 1952)**** Glynis Johns, Kay Walsh, Nigel Patrick. Three Somerset Maugham stories—a playboy tries to get money from his brother; a spinster makes things rough on ship passengers; and a high-dive artist has a fear of an accident. Excellent entertainment. (Dir: Pat Jackson, 90 mins.)

Encounter with Disaster—See: **13 Great Disasters That Shook the World**

End, The (1978)*** Burt Reynolds, Joanne Woodward, Dom De Luise, Sally Field, Myrna Loy. Reynolds as a director can't manage the problems of tone posed by Jerry Belson's slapsticky script about death. But much of the film is funny, original, and blissfully tasteless. With a nearly bearable performance by De Luise. (106 mins.)

End of August at the Hotel Ozone, The (Czechoslovakia, 1967)*** Ondrej Jariabek, Beta Ponicanova, Magda Seidlerova. An old lady leads eight young women through the ruins of a post-WW III Czechoslovakia in director Jan Schmidt's austere, prize-winning science fiction film. What they're looking for is what I've heard tell is often sought after in pre-WW III Los Angeles. Often involving. (85 mins.)

End of Desire (France, 1959)**½ Maria Schell, Christian Marquand. Wealthy girl discovers her husband has married her to pay off his debts and is carrying on with a servant girl. Slow, occasionally interesting costume drama based on a story by De Maupassant. English-dubbed. (Dir: Alexander Astruc, 86 mins.)

End of St. Petersburg, The (U.S.S.R., 1927)***½ V. I. Pudovkin. Commissioned by the Soviet government to celebrate the tenth anniversary of the revolution (along with Eisenstein's "Oktober"), Pudovkin's film (codirected with Mikhail Doller) traces the last three years of czarist rule through a peasant who comes to St. Petersburg, gets involved in a factory strike and becomes a scab, and is drafted. The social comments may be ham-handed Soviet, but the stories of proletarian destinies are strongly individual and moving. (100 mins.)

End of the Affair, The (Great Britain 1955)*** Deborah Kerr, Van Johnson, John Mills. Well acted, although overlong story of a love affair between an American and the wife of a British civil servant. Based on a Graham Greene novel. (Dir: Edward Dmytryk, 106 mins.)

End of the Dialogue (South Africa, 1970)**** A devastating short documentary, secretly filmed in South Africa, showing how the practice of apartheid affects and degrades the black population of the country. The list of horrors shown is endless—the appalling conditions under which blacks live and work, their denial of basic amenities, and the general hopelessness of their condition without a profound change—most unlikely at the time the film was made—in the whole structure of the oppressive government. Ends with a crawl of blacks murdered or imprisoned for long terms by the government. (Dir: Nana Mahomo, 50 mins.)

End of the Line (Great Britain, 1958)** Alan Baxter, Barbara Shelley. Evil woman induces a man to commit murder for her. Performances help this crime melodrama. (Dir: Charles Saunders, 64 mins.)

End of the Road (Great Britain, 1954)**½ Finlay Currie. Veteran British character actor Finlay Currie gives an excellent performance as "Mick-Mack" in this well made, heartwarming story of an old man and his grandson. (Dir: Wolf Rilla, 76 mins.)

End of the World in Our Usual Bed in A Night Full of Rain, The (Italy-U.S. 1978)* Candice Bergen, Giancarlo Giannini. Lina Wertmuller's English-language debut aborted her Hollywood future, which is a little ironic since the film plays very much like her heralded Italian work. The same babel-like chorus and frantic activity obscuring an intellectual aridity. Actually, the meretriciousness aside, the characterizations of Candice Bergen (quite good) and Giancarlo Giannini invest the goings-on with some genuine pathos. The two stars are a husband and wife whose relationship is dissected. He's a male chauvinist and a Communist journalist, and she's an American feminist and photographer. The arguments may be dumb and the camerawork epileptic, but Wertmuller retains a formidable screenplay mind obscured by her inability to discern between the banal and the sensational. Not as bad as the critics said, but neither were her other works as good as the claims made for them. (104 mins.)

Endless Summer, The (1966)***½ This lovely feature-length documentary about the joys of surfing around the world is a good one. Director, cinematographer, writer Bruce Brown is largely responsible for the glorious, lyrical footage which captures the exhilaration and the danger of this increasingly popular sport among youngsters. A charming musical score and a disarming narrative nicely complement the scenes of two carefree surfers looking for the perfect wave. If you're already a fan of surfing, or are still wondering what all the excitement is about, "The Endless Summer" is a treat! (Dir: Bruce Brown, 95 mins.)

Enemy Below, The (1957)*** Robert Mitchum, Curt Jurgens. Interesting WW II drama in which an American destroyer and a German U-boat play cat and mouse in the Atlantic ocean. Good photography heightens the action. Superior performances. (Dir: Dick Powell, 98 mins.)

Enemy from Space (Great Britain, 1957)* Brian Donlevy, Vera Day. (Dir: Val Guest, 84 mins.)

Enemy General, The (1960)** Van Johnson, Jean-Pierre Aumont. Fair World War II drama set on the European Front. Good performances by the principals. (Dir: George Sherman, 74 mins.)

Enforcer, The (1951)*** Humphrey Bogart, Zero Mostel, Everett Sloane, Ted de Corsia, Bob Steele. Bogart plays a crusading D.A. running down Sloane's mob, which includes hoods de Corsia and Mostel. Bretaigne Windust's finest effort, marred only by persistent rumors that codirector Raoul Walsh did the best scenes. (87 mins.)

Enforcer, The (1976)½ Clint Eastwood, Harry Guardino, Bradford Dillman, Tyne Daly. (Dir: James Fargo, 96 mins.)

England Made Me (Great Britain, 1972)*** Peter Finch, Michael York, Hildegard Neil, Michael Hordern. Graham Greene's prescient, ironic first novel, published in 1935, has received an intelligent treatment on the screen. Richly evocative of pre-WW II Berlin, the film focuses on the moral conflict between an innocent British idealist (York) and the decadent Germany he visits in 1935, especially as personified in a corrupt industrialist (Finch). Though most every detail echoes the theme of disaster just around the corner, the acting, especially Hordern's washed-up newspaper reporter, keeps the film from being too ponderous. (Dir: Peter Duffell, 100 mins.)

Enjo (Conflagration) (Japan, 1958)**** Raizo Ichikawa, Ganjiro Nakamura, Tatsuya Nakadai. Superb adaptation of Yukio Mishima's "Temple of the Golden Pavilion," directed with brutal precision by Kon Ichikawa. A high-strung young man destroys the architectural beauty he so passionately admires. An incisive, awesomely involving work, a gradual crescendo of anguished rage. With Ichikawa as the tortured youth. (96 mins.)

Enola Gay: The Men, the Mission, the Atomic Bomb (MTV 1980)** Patrick Duffy, Billy Crystal, Kim Darby, Gregory Harrison. The decision to drop the atomic bomb on Hiroshima, the secrecy surrounding the mission, the training of the men, and finally the flight of the "Enola Gay" on August 6, 1945, comes to TV. Familiar TV faces such as "Soap"'s Crystal, "Dallas"'s Duffy, and "Trapper John"'s Harrison play airmen but add little to the proceedings. A carefully documented, well-intentioned history lesson that drones on endlessly, and it's a pity considering the importance of the subject. (Dir: David Lowell Rich, 156 mins.)

Ensign Pulver (1964)** Robert Walker, Burl Ives, Millie Perkins. Director Joshua Logan, who guided "Mr. Roberts" to success, hoped to repeat the feat but failed. It's slapstick comedy all the way, and even pros like Burl Ives, Walter Matthau, and Kay Medford can't rise above the sinking material. (Dir: Joshua Logan, 104 mins.)

Enter Inspector Maigret (France-W. Germany, 1966)**½ Heinz Ruhmann, Eddi Arent. Georges Simenon's famous detective Inspector Maigret investigates the case of a Van Gogh painting stolen from a Paris art museum. Mild suspense, tricky dubbing. (Dir: Alfred Weidenmann, 90 mins.)

Enter Laughing (1967)*** Shelley Winters, Elaine May, Jose Ferrer, Reni Santoni. Carl Reiner's funny Broadway lark about a young Jewish boy from the Bronx who wants to be a star of stage 'n screen made a star out of Alan Arkin, but it didn't do the same for Reni Santoni who plays the young would-be actor here. And that's the principal shortcoming of this picture, because newcomer Santoni has neither the range nor the warmth to do justice to this meaty role. But Reiner's romp is still a funny vehicle and there are a lot of laughs along the way, especially from such proven laugh getters as Elaine May and Jack Gilford. (Dir: Carl Reiner, 112 mins.)

Enter the Dragon (1973)** Bruce Lee, John Saxon, Jim Kelly, Ahna Capri. Quite enjoyable, with muscular direction by Robert Clouse. Completed shortly before martial arts expert Lee's death at 32. (Since then, bits and pieces of his work have been fleshed out into features, and there has been a horde of imitators.) Strictly cartoon action with Lee on a big budget; production values run riot. Bruce Lee is probably inimitable, and co-star Capri is always a sufficient reason for moviegoing. Filmed in Hong Kong. (98 mins.)

Entertainer, The (Great Britain, 1960)**** Laurence Olivier, Joan Plowright, Brenda de Banzie. Story about an unpleasant, third-rate British music-hall performer on the skids, photographed against the backdrop of a depressing English seaside resort. Olivier's bravura performance is one of the most brilliant and exciting ever filmed. Olivier captures all the shabbiness, banality, pathos, and false hope of the hero. De Banzie (his comforting wife) is outstanding in a fine supporting cast, which includes Albert Finney in a small part. John Osborne wrote the screenplay from his play, which also starred Olivier, and the perceptive direction is by Tony Richardson. (97 mins.)

Entertainer, The (MTV 1976)**½ Jack Lemmon, Sada Thompson, Ray Bolger. It's easy to understand why Jack Lemmon would be drawn to the role of Archie Rice in John Osborne's play, a role so brilliantly created on stage and film by Laurence Olivier. Lemmon gives a quite moving and varied performance, which is reason enough to see this version. The overall effect is curiously diminished, partly due to some lacklustre performances, notably Sada Thompson as Archie's harassed, embittered wife. The locale has been foolishly changed from Brighton, England, to Santa Cruz, California; Ray Bolger is effective playing Archie's showbiz dad; but it's Jack Lemmon's performance that's the main attraction. Released theatrically abroad. (Dir: Donald Wrye, 98 mins.)

Entertaining Mr. Sloane (Great Britain, 1976)***½ Beryl Reid, Harry Andrews, Peter McEnery. Fine, literate black comedy based on Joe Orton's play. McEnery plays Mr. Sloane, a young hustler who is boarded by the blowsy, kittenish Kate. But complications arise when Ed, Kate's latently homosexual brother, also lusts for the young boy. Nontype casting of Andrews as Ed and Miss Reid as Kate make the farce shine. Some devastating social insight. (Dir: Douglas Hickox, 94 mins.)

Epic That Never Was, The (Great Britain, MTV)***½ Charles Laughton, Merle Oberon, Emlyn Williams. BBC documentary on how the movie "I, Claudius" was abandoned in the '30s. Some interesting interviews—including what is probably the only filmed interview with Josef von Sternberg—and, of course, the 20 or so minutes of footage that survive of "I, Claudius." It could have been one of von Sternberg's most beautiful films, and the remains are more than worth viewing. Worth seeing for the amazing scenes by Laughton as Claudius. (Dir: Bill Duncalf, 60 mins.)

Equus (Great Britain, 1977)**½ Richard Burton, Peter Firth, Colin Blakely, Joan Plowright, Jenny Agutter, Harry Andrews. A psychiatrist (Burton) is obsessed with his "lack of passion" as he treats a young man (Firth) accused of blinding six horses in a sexual frenzy. The original play's nonsensical equation of schizophrenia and lust for life seems even more spurious under Sidney Lumet's passionless direction. Burton is far superior to this material; he holds your interest single-handedly. (137 mins.)

Eraserhead (1977)** Jack Nance, Charlotte Stewart, Jeanne Bates, Allen Josephs, Laurel Near. Director David Lynch's blend of nightmare imagery, Grand Guignol, and camp humor is technically more accomplished than other films seen on the midnight show circuit. Some of it is disturbing, some embarrassingly flat. (100 mins.)

Eric (MTV 1975)*** John Savage, Patricia Neal, Claude Akins, Mark Hamill, Eileen McDonough. Doris Lund's best-selling book about her son Eric's brave struggle with cancer becomes a sound and emotional drama. Miss Neal plays the boy's mother with restraint and dignity, allowing her son to set up his own ground rules in his bout with leukemia. Savage, as Eric, maintains that fine line between optimism and resignation with remarkable credibility, continuing his studies and even playing soccer as long as he is able to. The brief but touching scene in which Eric's little sister gives him her baby-sitting earnings for his birthday is just one of several that build to a compelling finale. (Dir: James Goldstone, 100 mins.)

Erik the Conqueror (Italy, 1963)*½ Cameron Mitchell, Alice and Ellen Kessler, Francoise Christophe. (Dir: Mario Bava, 81 mins.)

Errand Boy, The (1961)**½ Jerry Lewis. Strictly for fans of Lewis. He's a goofy paper hanger who gets involved in a Hollywood studio management mix-up. The Hollywood setting triggers many sight gags. (Dir: Jerry Lewis, 92 mins.)

Escapade (Great Britain, 1957)** John Mills, Yvonne Mitchell, Alastair Sim. Three boys run away from school and endeavor to show the adults how to make the world peaceful. Verbose comedy-drama moves too leisurely. (Dir: Philip Leacock, 87 mins.)

Escapade in Japan (1957)*** Teresa Wright, Cameron Mitchell, Jon Provost. American boy's plane is forced down, so he joins with a Japanese lad to reach his parents. Attention-holding benefits from fascinating Japan locations, good performances. (Dir: Arthur Lubin, 92 mins.)

Escape (1940)*** Norma Shearer, Robert Taylor. Good exciting melodrama based on a best selling novel. Story is about an American trying to get his mother out of a concentration camp in pre-war Nazi Germany. (Dir: Mervyn Le Roy, 104 mins.)

Escape (Great Britain, 1948)*** Rex Harrison, Peggy Cummins. (Dir: Joseph Mankiewicz, 78 mins.)

Escape (MTV 1980)**½ Timothy Bottoms, Kay Lenz. A suspenseful true prison escape yarn about a young American who intends to be the first man to walk out of Mexico's Lecumberri Prison since Pancho Villa did it in '13. Bottoms and Lenz play Dwight and Barbara Worker, a couple who were married in prison just before his escape. Harsh life inside a Mexican prison, the bribery system, romance and suspense add up to an engrossing movie. There's an important message too—kids carrying drugs, stay out of Mexico! (Dir: Robert Lewis, 104 mins.)

Escape by Night (Italy, 1960)**½ Leo Genn, Peter Baldwin. Three escaped prisoners of war, an American, an Englishman, and a Russian, are befriended and helped by an Italian girl during World War II. Drama directed by Roberto Rossellini lacks his usual flair, becomes a mildly interesting, somewhat choppy war drama dubbed in English. (120 mins.)

Escape from Alcatraz (1979)*** Clint Eastwood, Patrick McGoohan. One of the better prison films, based on fact and the book by J. Campbell Bruce. It casts Clint as Frank Norris, a prisoner who attempted to escape from the Rock with two other inmates in '62 and was never heard from again. Eastwood is ideal in this type of role, and McGoohan is equally forceful as the tough warden. Don Siegel's direction is fine. (112 mins.)

Escape from Bogen County (MTV 1977)** Jaclyn Smith, Mitchell Ryan, Michael Parks. Familiar yarn about a ruthless small-town politician who makes his wife a virtual prisoner in her own home. Ryan is up to the demands of the role of the heartless Texas politico, and Parks plays a sympathetic character who aids lovely Jaclyn in her plight. Good production values and location shooting. (Dir: Steven Stern, 104 mins.)

Escape from Colditz (1977)**½ Robert Wagner, David McCallum. Compiled from a hit British TV series about a German prison camp and the Allied POWs who kept the Nazis busy with daring escape attempts and unorthodox behavior. Excellent British supporting cast. (Dirs: W. Slater, P. Gregreen, 104 mins.)

Escape from East Berlin (U.S.A.-West Germany, 1962)**½ Don Murray, Christine Kaufmann. Based on a true story, this drama generates a good deal of suspense. Don Murray plays a man who engineers an escape tunnel leading to the western sector of Berlin and safety. Miss Kaufmann plays a determined young girl in on the plan. (Dir: Robert Siodmak, 94 mins.)

Escape from Fort Bravo (1953)*** Eleanor Parker, William Holden, John Forsythe. Good western film set during the Civil War. The plot concerns the relationship between the Union Captain (Holden) and the people in Fort Bravo. There's a very exciting sequence towards the end of the film in which a large group of hostile Indians pin down a party, escaping from the fort. (Dir: John Sturges, 98 mins.)

Escape from Hell Island (1963)** Mark

Stevens, Jack Donner, Linda Scott. Captain of a charter boat saves a pretty refugee from Castro's Cuba, but becomes a target for death. Stevens is actor and director of this meller; also has some nice Florida location scenes. (Dir: Mark Stevens, 80 mins.)

Escape from Red Rock (1957)** Brian Donlevy, Eilene Janssen. Run-of-the-treadmill western with Donlevy leading a gang of no-goods. Nothing new, but good action and average acting. (Dir: Edward Bernds, 75 mins.)

Escape from Sahara (Germany, 1957)** Hildegarde Neff, Harry Meyer. Three legionnaires decide to desert, force the pilot to change course; the plane crash-lands. Passable desert drama gets a good performance from Neff as a nurse. English-dubbed. (Dir: Wolfgang Staudte, 95 mins.)

Escape from Saigon (France, 1957)*** Jean Chevrier, Barbara Laage. Occasionally suspenseful, lively melodrama about an engineer who rescues his wife from a ruthless trader and flees to safety. Dubbed in English. (Dir: Maurice Labro, 85 mins.)

Escape from Terror (1960)* Jackie Coogan, Mona Knox. (Dirs: Jackie and George Coogan, 71 mins.)

Escape from the Planet of the Apes (1971)*** Roddy McDowall, Kim Hunter, Bradford Dillman, Sal Mineo. The third in the simian cycle of films and a fairly good sci-fi story. Hunter and McDowall, in ape makeup, escape from their planet in the very spaceship that brought Charlton Heston to their world two films before...but they go back in time to the present, the 1970's. Needless to say their arrival in California causes an uproar, and their adventure in our society is both entertaining and, at times, surprisingly meaningful. (Dir: Don Taylor, 98 mins.)

Escape from Zahrain (1962)**½ Yul Brynner, Sal Mineo, Jack Warden, Madlyn Rhue. Rebel leader in an Arab oil state escapes along with some fellow-convicts, and they make a dash for the border. Typical action opus. (Dir: Ronald Neame, 93 mins.)

Escape in the Desert (1945)**½ Helmut Dantine, Jean Sullivan, Philip Dorn. If you want to see what is meant by the Hollywood touch, take a look at this hopped up version of "The Petrified Forest." They removed the original's depth, added some Nazis for timeliness and come up with a mediocre adventure tale. (Dir: Edward A. Blatt, 81 mins.)

Escape to Athena (Great Britain, 1979)** Roger Moore, David Niven, Elliott Gould, Stefanie Powers, Richard Roundtree. This bungled WW II adventure yarn, filmed in Greece, can't decide whether it's comedy or drama. The lighter moments are occasionally funny. An amazing number of explosions in one film, but they don't bring it to life. (Dir: George P. Cosmatos, 117 mins.)

Escape to Burma (1955)*½ Barbara Stanwyck, Robert Ryan. (Dir: Allan Dwan, 86 mins.)

Escape to Mindanao (MTV 1968)**½ George Maharis, Willi Koopman, Nehemiah Persoff, James Shigeta. Good adventure. George Maharis stars in a drama about a prisoner-of-war back in 1942, who's perfectly happy to spend the rest of the war simply staying alive in the camp. A good setup—a reluctant anti-hero, a chase via train, car and ship, a pretty girl, and some absorbing if standard characters—combine to make this better-than-average entertainment. (Dir: Don McDougall, 95 mins.)

Escape to the Sun (Israel, 1972)* Laurence Harvey, Josephine Chaplin, John Ireland, Jack Hawkins. Directed by Menahem Golan. (105 mins.)

Escape to Witch Mountain (1975)*½ Kim Richards, Ike Eisenmann, Ray Milland, Eddie Albert. (Dir: John Hough, 104 mins.)

Escort for Hire (Great Britain, 1962)** June Thorburn, Peter Murray. Man hired as an escort gets mixed up in a murder case. Average mystery melodrama. (Dir: Godfrey Grayson, 66 mins.)

Esther and the King (1960)*½ Joan Collins, Richard Egan, Daniella Rocca. (Dir: Raoul Walsh, 109 mins.)

Essene (1972)*** Documentary by Frederick Wiseman about an Anglican monastery in the Middle West. The members of the monastery are very reserved in their quest for a meaningful group relationship to counter the loneliness of their personal lives. Some of the footage is purely drab and unemotional. In many ways, "Essene" is Wiseman's least accessible, and in some other ways, least interesting essay on American institutions. But you do learn a lot of recondite data about the austere life of these members of a sect which began in the second century B.C. (86 mins.)

Eternal Chains (Italy, 1956)** Marcello Mastroianni and Gianna Maria Canale. An Italian soap opera. Mastroianni plays the leading role of a man who falls in love with his brother's wife. The plot takes on typical melodramatic overtones. Made in 1951. (Dir: Anton Giulio Majano)

Eternal Sea, The (1955)**½ Sterling Hayden, Alexis Smith, Dean Jagger. True story of a Navy officer who continues to serve, despite an artificial limb. Factual but overlong war drama. (Dir: John H. Auer, 110 mins.)

Eternal Waltz (Germany, 1959)** Bernhard Wicki, Hilde Krahl. Ponderous biography of the waltz king, Johann Strauss. For the music-minded, okay. Dubbed-English dialogue. (Dir: Paul Werhoeven, 97 mins.)

Eternally Yours (1939)** Ladies, if you ever plan to marry a magician, watch what happens to Loretta Young when she falls for trickster David Niven. Broderick Crawford is also on hand in this romantic comedy. Good cast wasted on trite material. (Dir: Tay Garnett, 110 mins.)

Eureka Stockade (Australia, 1949)***

Chips Rafferty, Jane Barrett, Peter Finch. Four gold-seekers in early Australia band together to fight a despotic governor, get public sentiment on their side. Impressive historical drama contains plenty of action. (Dir: Harry Watt, 103 mins.)

Europa '51 (Italy, 1951)*** Ingrid Bergman, Alexander Knox, Giulietta Masina. Director Roberto Rossellini's portrait of postwar Europe, about a society woman (Bergman) who struggles to understand the collapsing world around her after the suicide of her son. In the end, her impassive husband (Knox) has her committed to a sanatorium. As in most of his films with Bergman, Rossellini presents extreme melodrama—which may really be something more. (116 mins.)

Europe, the Mighty Continent: The Day of Empires Has Arrived *** Documentary examination of the ruling houses of Europe at the turn of the century, showing the intertwining of Queen Victoria's influence with the vast intermarriages of her relatives in the kingdoms of Germany, Austro-Hungary, and Russia. To Victoria it was unthinkable that war could arise in Europe, since it would be largely a family affair. Included are some interesting early motion pictures of life at the time.

Europeans, The (1979)**½ Lee Remick, Robin Ellis, Lisa Eichhorn, Wesley Addy, Tim Woodward, Kristin Griffith. Miserably mounted adaptation of Henry James, looking for all the world like some fugitive from Masterpiece Theatre. The actors are looking in the wrong direction, the lighting is abysmal, and the music uninspired. The actors, while valiant, seem to make all the wrong inflections. For all that, there is enough interest in the story, even as bowdlerized as it is, that the film plays itself out without boredom, just chagrin. James Ivory, Ishmail Merchant, and Ruth Prawer Jhabvala are the perpetrators. Ivory had one misleadingly interesting film (*Shakespeare Wallah*), which in retrospect seems to have worked solely on the originality of its premise. (90 mins.)

Eve (Great Britain, 1969)*½ Herbert Lom, Celeste Yarnall, Robert Walker, Fred Clark, Christopher Lee. Alternate title: **The Face of Eve.** (Dir: Jeremy Summers, 94 mins.)

Eve of St. Mark, The (1944)*** Anne Baxter, William Eythe. Maxwell Anderson's poetic commentary on war is an often moving, occasionally stilted film. (Dir: John M. Stahl, 96 mins.)

Evel Knievel (1971)*** George Hamilton, Sue Lyon. There's a certain inherent interest in watching a story about an egomaniac who flirts with death, and makes a fortune doing it. Evel Knievel is an American folk hero who's performed some of the most daring death-defying stunts ever executed on a motorcycle. How accurate a portrait of his personal life this film presents is open to question, but Hamilton evokes the cocksure flamboyance

necessary to play the spectacular daredevil who dresses like a rock star and basks in the adoration of his fans. (Dir: Marvin Chomsky, 90 mins.)

Seven Dwarfs Started Small (West Germany, 1970)***½ Helmut Doring, Gerd Gickel, Paul Glauer. Director Werner Herzog's second feature is a frightening, eccentric study of the disservices revolutionaries do their revolutions. Twenty-seven dwarfs are in a "reformatory" grotesquely constructed for average-sized inmates and ruled by a fatuous dwarf who should know better. The inmates stage a protest that quickly degenerates into aimless, pitifully malicious bouts of random violence. Not a vicious denial of the legitimacy of revolt (as too many critics have charged). (96 mins.)

Evening with the Royal Ballet, An (Great Britain, 1963)***½ Margot Fonteyn, Rudolf Nureyev. The young Nureyev and the ageless Fonteyn perform beautifully together to the music of Ravel, Chopin, and Tchaikovsky. Valuable cinematic record. (Dirs: Anthony Have x-Allan, Anthony Asquith, 85 mins.)

Event, An (Yugoslavia, 1969)***½ Pavle Vujisic, Serdjo Mimica. Deeply moving story set in Yugoslavia during World War II, loosely based on a story by Anton Chekhov. Directed by Vatroslav Mimica, story concerns an old peasant and his grandson who set out to sell their decrepit horse. One of the numerous rewarding features made in recent years by the increasingly impressive film industry of this small country. (93 mins.)

Evergreen (Great Britain, 1934)***½ Jessie Mathews, Sonnie Hale, Betty Balfour. Musical comedy with a score by Rodgers and Hart, gargantuan production numbers, and a then fashionable theme ("monkey gland" rejuvenation). Wildly improbable plot about a young lady who poses as her mother, a former stage star. She then falls in love with the man who is pretending to be her son! Made by one of the most polished and underrated British directors, Victor Saville. Screenplay by Emlyn Williams and Marjarie Gaffney. (90 mins.)

Every Girl Should Be Married (1948)**½ Cary Grant, Betsy Drake, Franchot Tone, Diana Lynn. A shopgirl uses her wiles to land a bachelor doctor. Disappointingly mild, undistinguished comedy. (Dir: Don Hartman, 85 mins.)

Every Little Crook and Nanny (1972)*½ Victor Mature, Lynn Redgrave, Paul Sand, Maggie Blye, Austin Pendleton, John Astin, Dom DeLuise. (Dir: Cy Howard, 92 mins.)

Every Man for Himself (France, 1980)**** Jacques Dutronc, Nathalie Baye, Isabelle Huppert. What Jean-Luc Godard calls his second "first film" marks less a return to his sixties work than a resumption of the process of cinematic discovery he has pursued throughout his career, even unto dead-ends. This new film is so intensely poetic in its imagery, so piercing in its deeply felt pursuit of truth through images, that the essentially banal nature of its surface ideas doesn't scant the richness and mystery of its real achievement. Even the best films today don't try this hard to penetrate the soul of our times, but *Every Man for Himself* manages to cut to the heart of what the cinematic image can express. While in some ways the film is about nothing in particular, it's a movie that really grapples with ideas and feelings in exciting ways. The temperament expressed is largely that of a bruised man near burnout, yet the tentative, almost modest array of images that constitute his search for truth belies the tone of self-pity. Alternate title: **Sauve Qui Peut/La Vie.** (Dir: Jean-Luc Godard, 88 mins.)

Every Man for Himself and God Against All—See: **Mystery of Kaspar Hauser, The**

Every Man Needs One (MTV 1972)* Ken Berry, Connie Stevens. (Dir: Jerry Paris, 88 mins.)

Every Minute Counts (France, 1957)*½ Dominique Wilms, Barbara Laage. Alternate title: **Every Second Counts.** (Dir: Alex Joffe, 90 mins.)

Every Which Way But Loose (1978)**½ Clint Eastwood, Sondra Locke, Geoffrey Lewis, Beverly D'Angelo, Ruth Gordon. Clint Eastwood's most eccentric project has also become his biggest hit, although it is less interesting and more equivocal than *The Gauntlet.* Eastwood continues to project an ironic, waspish sensibility that plays off his macho image in cruel, illuminating ways. Eastwood is a muscular fool, whose notions of gallantry are moronically out of place in these freewheeling times. The moral grain of the film is often intricate, with severe lapses of humanism, just as the action itself basically languishes between stretches of bewildering intelligence. The material so obviously engages Eastwood that one wonders why he didn't direct himself, although James Fargo serves the intentions of the vehicle as well as any house director could. The best acting is by the orangutan named Clyde. More humorous touches than most other Eastwood films. (Dir: James Fargo, 115 mins.)

Everybody Does It (1949)***½ Paul Douglas, Linda Darnell, Celeste Holm. A businessman takes up singing, discovers he really has a voice—with Douglas in the role, it's a howl from beginning to end. Sharp dialogue helps, too. Remake of *Wife, Husband, and Friend,* 1939. (Dir: Edmund Goulding, 98 mins.)

Everybody Sing (1938)** Judy Garland, Fanny Brice, Allan Jones, Billie Burke, Reginald Owen. An MGM musical about an eccentric family that puts on a musical show. Director Edwin L. Marin didn't earn his reputation here. (80 mins.)

Everything for Sale (Poland, 1968)**½ Daniel Olbrychski, Andrzej Lapicki. Director Andrzej Wajda's film, in spite of its many adherents, is full of self-reflexive mannerisms and laborious, obvious revelations. The film is about making a film about a charismatic and rebellious actor who ultimately dies trying to catch a moving train. Lapicki is an uncanny Wajda surrogate. (105 mins.)

Everything Happens at Night (1939)*** Ray Milland, Robert Cummings, Sonja Henie. Thanks to good playing by its leading men, this film about two reporters trying to find a Nobel Prize winner is good entertainment. Sonja does some skating between scenes. (Dir: Irving Cummings, 77 mins.)

Everything I Have Is Yours (1952)**½ Marge & Gower Champion, Dennis O'Keefe. Wedded song and dance team find married life interfering with their stage careers. Aside from the dancing of the Champions, nothing particularly novel about this routine musical. (Dir: Robert Z. Leonard, 92 mins.)

Everything You Always Wanted to Know About Sex, But Were Afraid to Ask (1972)**** Woody Allen, Lou Jacobi, Anthony Quayle, Gene Wilder, Burt Reynolds, Tony Randall. The most important and inventive comedy talent in American film has borrowed the title of Dr. David Reuben's best-selling rip-off book about sex, and transformed it into a series of lunatic, hysterical sketches. They don't all work, but it doesn't matter because ordinary Allen is funnier than virtually anything else around. A number of sketches (Woody does not appear in all of them, though he has conceived of and directed the whole mad lot) are excruciatingly funny. Gene Wilder plays a mild-mannered doctor falling head over heels in love with one of his patients—an Armenian sheep named Daisy. Besides that it's your only other chance of the filmic week to see a 40-feet-high female breast, Lynn Redgrave wearing a chastity belt, and a wondrous bit of madness which finds Woody playing a sperm. (87 mins.)

Everything You Know Is Wrong (1974)*** Lively topical comedy from the Firesign Theater Company. From the album of the same name. Interesting, witty record of what were at the time the most deserving subjects for barbs and put-downs.

Everything's Ducky (1961)** Mickey Rooney, Buddy Hackett, Jackie Cooper, Joanie Sommers. Two sailors and a talking duck—fill in the rest. Rooney and Hackett try hard for laughs, which aren't there. (Dir: Don Taylor, 81 mins.)

Evictors, The (1979)** Michael Parks, Jessica Harper, Vic Morrow, Sue Ane Langdon. Southern period gothic from writer-director Charles B. Pierce. Essentially the same plot as "The Amityville Horror": a young couple (Parks and Harper) move into a house that turns out to have a haunted, bloody history. One of those easily predictable triple surprise endings. (92 mins.)

Evil, The (1978)**½ Richard Crenna,

Joanna Pettet, Andrew Prine. Crenna stumbles on the devil himself in a crumbling mansion. Surprisingly decent entry, considering its low production budget. (Dir: Gus Trikonis, 89 mins.)

Evil Eye, The (Italy, 1964)**½ John Saxon, Leticia Roman, Valentina Cortesa. Young doctor and a frightened girl uncover a series of unsolved murders when she fears the worst has happened to her aunt. Suspenseful thriller made in Italy serves up the shudders in interesting fashion. (Dir: Mario Bava, 92 mins.)

Evil of Frankenstein, The (Great Britain, 1964)** Peter Cushing, Peter Woodthorpe. Baron Frankenstein returns to his castle, finds his homemade creature encased in ice, and starts all over again. He shouldn't have bothered. (Dir: Freddie Francis, 87 mins.)

Evil Roy Slade (1972)** John Astin. A crazy, offbeat comedy that might amuse the youngsters. Astin plays the title role of a mean, unremorseful outlaw who has never been loved. While robbing a bank he meets and kisses curvy but pure Pamela Austin, and love hits Evil Roy. Some scenes are quite funny. The film was apparently intended as a pilot for a TV series. Other funny performances are delivered by Dick Shawn as a singing marshal and Dom DeLuise as a psychiatrist trying to help Slade reform. (Dir: Jerry Paris, 100 mins.)

Ex-Champ (1939)**½ Victor McLaglen, Constance Moore, Tom Brown. Former champ turned doorman undertakes to train a young boxer. Fairly interesting melodrama. (Dir: Phil Rosen, 64 mins.)

Ex-Lady (1933)**½ Bette Davis, Gene Raymond, Claire Dodd, Frank McHugh. One of the films that made Davis a star. She plays a young heartbreaker who wants love but not marriage; Raymond's is the heart she breaks. Even then audiences found it less shocking than Warners and director Robert Florey intended, but they loved Bette. (65 mins.)

Ex-Mrs. Bradford, The (1936)***½ William Powell, Jean Arthur. Amateur sleuth with the aid of his ex-wife solves some race track murders. Delightful comedy-mystery, smooth and sophisticated. (Dir: Stephen Roberts, 100 mins.)

Excalibur (1981)**** Nigel Terry, Helen Mirren, Nicol Williamson, Nicholas Clay, Cherie Lunghi, Paul Geoffrey. John Boorman's visually impressive rendering of the Arthurian legend brilliantly preserves its full mythic force, rendering the allusive aspects of the saga fully credible to a modern audience and illuminating why the tales have survived so vividly in our imaginations. Director Boorman's bravura for once matches the magnitude and tone of his subject. There's some hamminess in performance, and the characters remain emotionally remote, but that's the price one pays for sticking to the archetypes. Boorman is after restoration of nobility and classical severity and, if he ultimately falters, the film nevertheless is a tonic corrective to the puny cinema without ambition that dominates both art and entertainment films. (140 mins.)

Excuse My Dust (1951)**½ Red Skelton, Macdonald Carey, Sally Forrest. Amusing Skelton comedy about the days of the "Horseless Carriage." Some good gags, pleasant performers. (Dir: Roy Rowland, 82 mins.)

Execution of Private Slovik, The (MTV 1974)**** Martin Sheen, Mariclare Costello, Ned Beatty, Gary Busey. Sheen's performance as WW II soldier Eddie Slovik, the first serviceman to be executed for desertion since the Civil War, is profoundly moving. Eddie walks through life as if through a lost continent, saved only by his love for the girl who becomes his wife (Miss Costello). Slovik's battle experience makes firing a rifle an impossible duty and leads to his desertion and execution. Richard Levinson and William Link adapted the William Bradford Huie book. (Dir: Lamont Johnson, 104 mins.)

Executioner, The (Great Britain, 1970)**½ George Peppard, Joan Collins, Nigel Patrick. Enjoyable spy-chase-adventure thriller, which uses plot turns to advantage. Suave George Peppard is an American-trained British agent who, along with the necessary quota of sidekicks, must track down the traitor involved in a massacre at a country estate. The landscape from London to Athens is lush, and the action remains tense throughout. Well directed by actor-director Sam Wanamaker. (107 mins.)

Executioners, The (West Germany, 1958)**½ Documentary showing the reign of Nazi terror, its eventual downfall. It's been compiled before and better done, but still worth seeing. Alternate title: **Hitler's Executioners.** (Dir: Felix von Podmanitzky, 78 mins.)

Executive Suite (1954)*** William Holden, June Allyson, Fredric March, Barbara Stanwyck, Shelley Winters, Paul Douglas, Walter Pidgeon. A big cast effectively brings this best-selling novel about big business to the screen. There are many subplots which tend to get in the way of the main theme (the struggle of a group of V.P.s to take over control of a major furniture-manufacturing firm). The best performances are delivered by William Holden, Fredric March, Dean Jagger and Nina Foch. (Dir: Robert Wise, 104 mins.)

Exhibition (France, 1975)** Claudine Beccarie, Benoit Archenoul, Frederique Barral. A documentary about a porno star. Conversations are mixed with hard-core sequences; thus a double dose of filmic reality. Eventually the sex scenes and the actress's preening self-justifications add up to the same sordid, banal truth. (Dir: Jean-François Davy, 96 mins.)

Exile, The (1947)***½ Douglas Fairbanks, Jr., Maria Montez, Paule Croset (AKA Rita Corday), Henry Daniell, Nigel Bruce.

The sublimely European director Max Ophuls made this Fairbanks swashbuckler during his post-WW II tour of duty in the U.S. For once Ophuls had the resources of a well-stocked American studio to play with, and the meeting of modern technology and romantic tradition produced a number of beautiful moments. (95 mins.)

Exit Laughing—See: **Are You There?**

Exit Smiling (1926)**** Beatrice Lillie, Jack Pickford, Franklin Pangborn, Doris Lloyd. A wonderfully funny silent comedy, presumed lost but recovered recently by the American Film Institute. Lillie can do more funny things with a string of pearls than most performers can do with ten pages of dialogue and a hundred props. The film has its sentimentalities, but it is finely tuned, effective character comedy. Reminds us how tragically the motion-picture industry wasted Lillie's superb talents over the years. (Dir: Sam Taylor, 72 mins.)

Exodus (1960)***½ Paul Newman, Eva Marie Saint, Lee J. Cobb, Sal Mineo. Producer-director Otto Preminger put considerable stress on scope and pictorial splendor in bringing Leon Uris' bestselling novel about the hardships of Jewish refugees in the new Israel to the screen. Shows perils of getting to Israel and running the British blockade, and there's an exciting post-Cyprus scene in Israel toward the end of the film. Episodic but generally exciting, well acted and of considerable historic interest about a fascinating and exasperating period in post-war Europe. (213 mins.)

Exo-Man (MTV 1977)** David Ackroyd, Anne Schedeen, Harry Morgan, José Ferrer. Paralyzed from the waist down by mob goons before appearing on the witness stand, a young physics professor constructs a contraption to get around, and then goes after the mobsters. The professor's desire for revenge is clear—he sees to it that the hoods can't cope with either the exo-suit, or the good guy inside. (Dir: Richard Irving, 104 mins.)

Exorcist, The (1973)***½ Ellen Burstyn, Max von Sydow, Lee J. Cobb, Jason Miller, Linda Blair. Welcome back from Mars if you haven't heard about this one yet. It's devilishly clever and involving, and virtually impossible to summarize adequately in a few lines. The story of a 12-year-old girl in a prosperous home in Georgetown, Washington, D.C., who becomes possessed by demons and is finally saved when the vile spirits are exorcised and driven from her body. The implications may not be encouraging for American sociologists but it's easy to understand why this drama had such staggering audience appeal, making it one of the very top grossing films in the history of cinema. Based on author William Peter Blatty's best-selling novel, the film takes itself quite seriously, even though its primary purpose is to scare hell out of the audience, and it certainly succeeds. It succeeds partly because it sometimes is more repellent than scary—when the afflicted girl spews vomit in the Jesuit priests' faces, for example. In some ways it's a familiar blood-and-thunder horror film, but it's undeniably more compelling than almost any other of this genre because it is remarkably well made by the talented director William Friedkin. You momentarily believe the levitations and the swiveling heads, and it's uniformly well acted throughout. Miss Blair is convincing as the deranged child and playwright Jason Miller is effective as the supportive priest. Mercedes McCambridge provides the Voice of the Demon. (122 mins.)

Exorcist II: The Heretic (1977)½ Linda Blair, Richard Burton, Louise Fletcher, James Earl Jones. (Dir: John Boorman, 117 mins.)

Experiment in Terror (1962)*** Glenn Ford, Lee Remick, Stefanie Powers, Ross Martin. FBI agent Ford tries to save Remick from a psychopath (Martin) who has been terrorizing her into helping him rob the bank where she works. A good excuse to explore locations in San Francisco, including, at the climax, Candlestick Park. Nice work, but director Blake Edwards has done better. (123 mins.)

Experiment Perilous (1944)*** Hedy Lamarr, George Brent, Paul Lukas. Doctor investigates the death of a wealthy philanthropist's sister, suspects foul play. Well done mystery. (Dir: Jacques Tourneur, 91 mins.)

Explosive Generation, The (1961)*** Patty McCormack, William Shatner. When a high-school teacher is expelled for teaching sex education, his students rush to his defense. Give this one credit—it tries to say something important and does so in an efficient manner, despite production failings. Unusual adult drama. (Dir: Buzz Kulik, 89 mins.)

Expresso Bongo (Great Britain, 1960)**** Laurence Harvey, Sylvia Syms, Cliff Richard. Delightful mixture of fantasy and realism, as a small-time agent uses any means to push a teenage singer into the big time. Great stylish performance by Harvey as the agent; excellent script with witty dialogue. For adults, fine entertainment. (Dir: Val Guest, 109 mins.)

Expulsion from Paradise (West Germany, 1976)*** Herb Andress, Elke Haltaufderheid. Written, directed, and edited by Niklaus Schilling, this is a satirical look at the new West German film industry, loaded with in-jokes that will amuse filmmakers and filmgoers everywhere. Andress plays a bit actor out to make a name for himself; he encounters the flotsam and jetsam of the Munich film business, from commercials to porn, from bankrupt producers to starlets. Haltaufderheid also produced.

Exterminating Angel, The (Mexico, 1962)**** Silvia Pinal, Enrique Rambal, Claudio

Brook. Director Luis Buñuel turns the Mexican proverb "After twenty-four hours, corpses and guests smell bad" into a satire on the life of the bourgeoisie. Augusto Benedico gives a sumptuous party, but when the guests try to leave, they discover they are locked in the music room. After a few days they are reduced to eating raw sheep. When they finally escape and go to church to celebrate their deliverance, the whole thing starts again. Essential viewing. (91 mins.)

Extra Day, The (Great Britain, 1956)*** Richard Basehart, Simone Simon. Adventures and aspirations of a bit player in a film studio. Well acted, different comedy-drama. (Dir: William Fairchild, 83 mins.)

Extraordinary Seaman, The (1969)** David Niven, Faye Dunaway, Alan Alda, Mickey Rooney. This film, directed by John Frankenheimer ("The Manchurian Candidate" and "Grand Prix"), was released without any publicity and died at the box office. It's a supposedly whimsical, nautical tale set in the Pacific of WW II. Take a look and see if Hollywood made the correct decision in scuttling the hoopla for this film. P.S. We would have done the same. (80 mins.)

Eye for an Eye, An (1966)**½ Robert Lansing, Pat Wayne. An offbeat western yarn which benefits from a good performance by Robert Lansing. Revenge is the keynote of this tale, which has Lansing teaming up with the blinded Pat Wayne as the two prepare for a shootout with villains. (Dir: Michael Moore, 92 mins.)

Eye for an Eye, An —See: **Eyes of the Sahara**

Eye of the Cat (1969)**½ Eleanor Parker, Michael Sarrazin, Gayle Hunnicutt. A macabre outing manages some frightening visual effects involving cats. Tale revolves around wealthy invalid Eleanor Parker (who has numerous cats as pets) and her nephew's (Sarrazin) scheme to get her money. It's both predictable, and implausible, straight through, but Miss Parker and her feline protectors may interest you. (Dir: David Lowell Rich, 102 mins.)

Eye of the Devil (Great Britain, 1967)*½ Deborah Kerr, David Niven, Emlyn Williams, Donald Pleasence, Sharon Tate. (Dir: J. Lee Thompson, 92 mins.)

Eye of the Monocle, The (France, 1962)*½ Paul Meurisse, Elga Anderson. (Dir: Georges Lautner, 102 mins.)

Eye of the Needle, The (Italy-France, 1963)*** Vittorio Gassman, Annette Stroyberg, Gerard Blain. Broad, on-target satire of everything Sicilian, from marriage mores to Mafioso tactics. Follows the legal acrobatics necessary to restore tranquillity to a small town when two local youths deflower a local innocent. (Dir: Marcello Andrei, 97 mins.)

Eye Witness (Great Britain, 1949)*** Robert Montgomery, Patricia Wayne (Patricia Cutts). An American lawyer goes to England to save a friend from a murder charge. Neat melodrama, well played, nicely directed by Montgomery himself. (Dir: Robert Montgomery, 104 mins.)

Eyes of a Stranger (1981)** Lauren Tewes, Jennifer Jason Leigh, John DiSanti. A distasteful, exploitative mad-killer film that aims for commercial appeal in crass ways, this piece nevertheless is capably directed by Ken Wiederhorn, who has too much talent to waste on fundamental trash like this. There isn't a great deal of graphic violence, but the violence is used in particularly unpleasant ways, generally in conjunction with sexual aggression. Nevertheless, Wiederhorn displays some professional flair, and the film has good visual organization. (85 mins.)

Eyes of Annie Jones, The (U.S.-Great Britain, 1964)* Richard Conte, Joyce Carey. (Dir: Reginald LeBorg, 73 mins.)

Eyes of Charles Sand, The (MTV 1972)**½ Peter Haskell, Sharon Farrell, Barbara Rush, Brad Dillman. Splashy melodrama about the rich has the characters working at a highly emotional pitch acting demented and running about brandishing butcher knives. Young business success Charles Sand (Haskell) inherits a gift of visionary sight—seeing quick flashes of old hags and bodies behind crumbling walls—and is soon besieged by a babbling redhead crying for help. Escapist fare, with the actors having more fun than the audience. (Dir: Reza Badiyi, 75 mins.)

Eyes of Laura Mars, The (1978)**½ Faye Dunaway, Tommy Lee Jones, Brad Dourif. Irvin Kershner's coldly directed thriller begins interestingly but slides into a fairly conventional, and fairly disappointing, psychological murder mystery. A fashion photographer (Dunaway) specializes in murkily stated sex and violence only to find her photographs coming to life (or death). (104 mins.)

Eyes of the Sahara (France, 1957)** Curt Jurgens, Lea Padovani, Folco Lulli. Arab native seeks revenge upon a neglectful doctor who was responsible for the death of his wife. Grim, well-acted drama becomes too involved with vague symbolism for complete success. Dubbed-in English. Alternate title: **An Eye for an Eye**. (Dir: Andre Cayatte, 79 mins.)

Eyes Without a Face—See: **Horror Chamber of Dr. Faustus, The**

Eyewitness (1981)**½ William Hurt, Sigourney Weaver, Christopher Plummer, James Woods, Irene Worth, Steven Hill, Morgan Freeman. A genuine disappointment from director Peter Yates and screenwriter Steve Tesich after **Breaking Away**, this potpourri of eccentric character bits never finds a satisfying structure that would give it a story to tell, Tesich's writing has good moments, and a way with the oddball line or trait, but the mystery plot mostly seems an excuse for a mixed bag of riffs without a drama. Yates's direction, meanwhile, adds no inspiration. William Hurt once again impresses as an obsessive type, although his obsession with news-hen Sigourney Weaver is never forthrightly dramatized. They make a good team at a loss for a vehicle.

F for Fake (France, 1973)*** Orson Welles directed this semidocumentary about such liars, fakers, and charlatans as author Clifford Irving of the Howard Hughes book contract scam and art forger Elmyr de Hory. Uneven—some of it spurious, some engaging. Welles' only film of the decade. In English. (85 mins.)

F. Scott Fitzgerald and "The Last of the Belles" (MTV 1974)**½ Richard Chamberlain, Blythe Danner, Susan Sarandon, David Huffman. Interesting, uneven attempt to dramatize a portion of Fitzgerald's life and his short story, "The Last of the Belles." The action is intercut between two separate dramas, with the short story, about a small-town flirt who keeps a steady flow of WW I Army officers buzzing around her, coming off best. Chamberlain and Danner, as Scott and Zelda, are one-dimensional, but Susan Sarandon as the wide-eyed, drawling darling, and Huffman, as the lovestruck soldier, keep things moving. (Dir: George Schaefer, 98 mins.)

F. Scott Fitzgerald In Hollywood (MTV 1976)** Jason Miller, Tuesday Weld, Julia Foster. Hollywood has always been intrigued with the legend that was F. Scott Fitzgerald, and this is still another chapter in the saga of Zelda and Scott, those enduring icons of the Jazz Age. Miller's humorless performance as the writing genius gone sour is strictly one-note, but Tuesday Weld, in an all-too-brief appearance as the mothlike Zelda, teetering on the brink of madness, fares much better. Julia Foster, as the young Sheilah Graham, also scores in a confessional scene in which she pours her heart out to Scott about her upbringing in the poverty of London slums. The character of Dorothy Parker, played by Dolores Sutton, keeps popping in and out, uttering quotable one-liners. Writer James Costigan has fashioned an ordinary script, and British director Anthony Page has done little to enhance the material. (98 mins.)

Fabulous Baron Munchausen, The (Czechoslovakia, 1962)***½ Milos Kopecky, Jana Brejchova. That great liar Baron Munchausen has long been a popular figure of fantasy. See the baron ride a cannonball and travel to the moon as Czech animator/director Karel Zeman applies his considerable talents to set in motion the drawings and conceptions of 19th-century illustrator Gustave Doré. Zeman had much influence on animators (especially British) of the late '60s. (84 mins.)

Fabulous Dorseys, The (1947)** Tommy and Jimmy Dorsey, Janet Blair. The biography of the famous bandleaders who fought each other as they fought to the top. Mild musical; good tunes, not much on plot. (Dir: Alfred E. Green, 88 mins.)

Fabulous World of Jules Verne, The (Czechoslovakia, 1961)*** Louis Tock, Ernest NaVara. An enormously stylish animation enterprise, using contemporary engravings and ornate models to tell several of Verne's fantastic stories. Czech master director Karel Zeman displays a distinctive Eastern European wit and superlative draftsmanship, but the film is a bit too suffocating to convey the expansive, lighthearted spirit of Verne. (83 mins.)

Face Behind the Mask, The (1941)*** Peter Lorre, Evelyn Keyes. Often exciting thriller, thanks to Lorre's able performance as a hideously scarred criminal who falls in love with a gentle blind girl (Keyes). (Dir: Robert Florey, 69 mins.)

Face in the Crowd, A (1957)***½ Andy Griffith, Patricia Neal, Anthony Franciosa. An excellent screenplay by Budd Schulberg is well directed by Elia Kazan and gives Andy Griffith the best role of his career, as a backwoods, guitar playing bum who becomes a national TV personality. Patricia Neal is equally as good as a reporter who discovers and protests and finally destroys the big man. A considerably under-rated film when first released. (125 mins.)

Face in the Rain, A (1963)*** Rory Calhoun, Marina Berti. During World War II an American boy is sheltered from the enemy by the mistress of a German commandant. Suspenseful melodrama, made in Italy. Better than average of its type. (Dir: Irvin Kershner, 91 mins.)

Face in the Sky (1933)**½ Spencer Tracy, Marion Nixon, Lila Lee. The hard-working Tracy made six films that were released in 1933, including "20,000 Years in Sing Sing." An unusual but consistently enjoyable outing that changes from romance down on the farm to life, love, and music in the big city. (Dir: Harry Lachman, 73 mins.)

Face of a Fugitive (1959)**½ Fred MacMurray, Lin McCarthy. Good western with better than average performances by MacMurray and a good supporting cast. MacMurray, falsely accused of murder, changes his identity when he decides to settle in a town, but trouble follows his trail. (Dir: Paul Wendkos, 81 mins.)

Face of Another, The (Japan, 1966)**½ Tatsuya Nakadai, Machiko Kyo, Kyoko Kishida. A film by Hiroshi Teshigahara, the director of "Woman in the Dunes." A factory worker loses his face in an accident. Getting another through plastic surgery, he sets out to seduce his wife as a stranger. (124 mins.)

Face of Eve, The—See: **Eve**

Face of Fear—See: **Peeping Tom**

Face of Fire (1959)**½ Cameron Mitchell, James Whitmore, Bettye Ackerman. Disfigured in a fire, a well-liked local handyman becomes a social outcast. Odd little drama produced in Sweden; but well-acted, often photographically beautiful. (Dir: Albert Band, 83 mins.)

Face of Fu Manchu, The (Great Britain, 1965)** Christopher Lee, Nigel Green, James Robertson-Justice, Tsai Chin. Horror film fiend Lee returns as the unstoppable Dr. Fu, out to destroy the world again and stocking up on poison in the mountains of Tibet. (The film was made entirely in and around Dublin.) (Dir: Don Sharp, 96 mins.)

Face of War, A (1968)**** A memorable documentary directed and photographed by Eugene S. Jones in Vietnam during 1966. Jones, who was wounded twice during the filming, captures the particular horror of the war as seen by the front line troops—in this case foot soldiers of the Seventh Marine Regiment. It is a compassionate, searing account of this and most other wars fought by the front-line troops, and it is mercifully devoid of the chauvinism that was such a standard ingredient for a long period of many American TV documentaries and coverage about the Vietnam War. A chilling, unforgettable document. (72 mins.)

Face to Face (1952)***½ Package of two stories: "The Secret Sharer" (James Mason), a shipboard drama, and "Bride Comes to Yellow Sky" (Robert Preston, Marjorie Steele), a tale of a sheriff in a small western town. Both tastefully produced, literate, well acted. (Dirs: John Brahm, Bretaigne Windust, 90 mins.)

Face to Face (Sweden, 1975)**** Liv Ullmann, Erland Josephson. A devastating masterpiece, Bergman's 39th film, featuring one of the most remarkable acting performances (Ullmann's) in modern cinema. This award-winning drama is about a psychiatrist (Ullmann) who goes through a nervous breakdown on camera. There are very few other contemporary actresses who could be so convincing and convey so many varied emotions and passions. She is remarkable, and so is virtually everything else about "Face to Face." Original screenplay by Bergman himself. Originally made as a four-part series for Swedish TV. (Dir: Ingmar Bergman, 136 mins.)

Faces (1968)**** John Marley, Gena Rowlands, Lynn Cardin, Seymour Cassel. John Cassavetes' brilliant moving drama is one of the most important American films in years, and richly deserves all the awards it got including three Academy Award nominations. (One for Cassavetes' screenplay, one for supporting actress Lynn Carlin, one for supporting actor Seymour Cassel.) Concerns the disintegration of the marriage, after a fourteen-year period, of a middle-class couple in California. What is unique about this document is not the plot line, which is familiar enough, but the revelatory nature of the experience, watching the actors who suggest an improvisatory quality about their work that almost makes the audience feel you are improperly eavesdropping on the most personal of conversations. A stunning, perceptive study of American manners and morals. (Dir: John Cassavetes, 129 mins.)

Faces of Love (Switzerland, 1978)*** Jean-Louis Trintignant, Delphine Seyrig, Lea Massari, Valerie Mairesse. An often involving film by Swiss director Michel Soutter, about a summer production of Chekhov's *The Three Sisters*, directed by Jean-Louis Trintignant. That's reason enough. (Dir: Michel Soutter, 91 mins.)

Facts of Life, The (1960)*** Lucille Ball, Bob Hope. Two of show business' funniest comics are teamed in this laugh filled comedy about the many sides of marriage. Many scenes border on slapstick but they're skillfully carried off by the two old pros. (Dir: Melvin Frank, 103 mins.)

Facts of Murder, The (Italy, 1959)*** Claudia Cardinale, Pietro Germi, Franco Fabrizi, Eleanora Rossi-Drago. Absorbing story of a humanistic police inspector investigating an ugly murder case, his reactions to the people he meets during its course. Good as whodunit or straight drama, well acted, English dubbed. (Dir: Pietro Germi, 110 mins.)

Fade In (1968)** Burt Reynolds, Barbara Loden. Of some note. Reynolds and Miss Loden appeared in this drama about the movie business and the people involved in an on-location film shooting, but it never was released theatrically in the U.S. Tune in and judge for yourself. (Dir: Jud Taylor, 93 mins.)

Fahrenheit 451 (Great Britain, 1966)***½ Oskar Werner, Julie Christie, Cyril Cusack. One of the best, though perhaps the least appreciated of director François Truffaut's films. About a future where books are burned and their readers are hunted down. Adapted from a Ray Bradbury story. Superb Bernard Herrmann score. (111 mins.)

Fail Safe (1964)***½ Henry Fonda, Dan O'Herlihy, Walter Matthau. Nightmarish problem drama of what might happen when, through an error, a SAC plane is ordered to bomb Moscow. This develops into a gripping, suspenseful tale of something that could possibly happen. Excellent performances, Sidney Lumet direction, no punches spared. (111 mins.)

Falling of Raymond, The (MTV 1971)**½ Jane Wyman, Dean Stockwell. It's Miss Wyman in a role which suits her dignified style. She plays a schoolteacher who is thinking of retiring when an old student who failed an important test a few years past shows up with vengeance on his mind. (Dir: Boris Sagal, 73 mins.)

Fair Wind to Java (1953)*** Fred MacMurray, Vera Ralston. Sea captain battles a pirate chief on the high seas. Well made adventure melodrama contains a lot of action, plenty of excitement. (Dir: Joseph Kane, 92 mins.)

Faisons un Rêve (France, 1936)***½ Sacha Guitry, Raimu, Jacqueline Delubac, Michel Simon. A true archaeological find, an early Guitry-directed comedy, adapted from a play of his about the seduction of a married woman. Guitry's comedy is verbal and intricate, and immensely amusing on film. (86 mins.)

Faithful City (Israel, 1952)*** Jamie Smith, Rachel Markus. Frequently effective drama of the rehabilitation of wartime youngsters in Israel. English dialogue. Sometimes crude technically, but generally interesting. (Dir: Josef Leytes, 86 mins.)

Faithful in My Fashion (1946)*** Donna Reed, Tom Drake. Sergeant returns to his shoe-clerking job after the war and falls for a pretty salesgirl. Modest but light, ingratiating comedy, good fun. (Dir: Sidney Salkow, 81 mins.)

Fake, The (Great Britain, 1953)**½ Dennis O'Keefe, Coleen Gray. Private eye in London cracks down on art forgers. Fairly good mystery. (Dir: Godfrey Grayson, 80 mins.)

Falcon and the Co-Eds (1943)*** Tom Conway, Jean Brooks. The Falcon goes to a girls' school to look into the death of an instructress. Above average mystery, well done. (Dir: William Clemens, 68 mins.)

Falcon in Mexico (1944)**½ Tom Conway, Mona Maris. The Falcon trails a killer from New York to Mexico. Pleasant mystery with good backgrounds. (Dir: William Berke, 70 mins.)

Falcon Out West (1944)**½ Tom Conway, Barbara Hale. A cowboy is murdered in an eastern night club, causing the Falcon to head west to find the killer. Okay mystery. (Dir: William Clemens, 64 mins.)

Falcon Strikes Back (1943)**½ Tom Conway, Harriet Hilliard. The Falcon avoids a trap set for him by a gang of criminals. Neat mystery with a surprise solution. (Dir: Edward Dmytryk, 66 mins.)

Falcon Takes Over, The (1942)**½ George Sanders, Lynn Bari, Ward Bond, James Gleason. Anne Revere, Hans Conried, and Helen Gilbert This is probably the best of the series featuring Sanders as the detective created by Michael Arlen. The story, credited to a novel by Raymond Chandler, is "Farewell My Lovely," with the Falcon replacing Philip Marlowe. Witty script, sophisticated acting. (Dir: Irving Reis, 63 mins.)

Fall, The (Brazil, 1978)**½ Nelson Xavier, Lima Duarte. Eminent *cinema novo* director Ruy Guerra directed this story about construction workers fighting for minimum safety standards. Music by Milton Mascimento. (120 mins.)

Fall of Rome (Italy, 1962)** Carl Mohner, Jim Dolen. Brave centurion comes to the aid of Christians when they're persecuted. A notch above the usual Italian spear-and-sandal spectacle. English-dubbed. (Dir: Antonio Margheriti, 89 mins.)

Fall of the Roman Empire (1964)*** Stephen Boyd, Alec Guinness, Christopher Plummer, Sophia Loren, James Mason. Story of the decadence of Rome after the death of Marcus Aurelius, a gargantuan spectacle dramatized with brilliant visual discipline by Anthony Mann, directing his last epic along with Yakima Canutt and Andrew Marton. When a giant hand is wheeled into the arena for the bloody climactic confrontation, we know that we are in Mann-land, not Rome. (188 mins.)

Fall of the Romanov Dynasty, The (U.S.S.R., 1927)*** Director Esfir Shub's first feature may be the first compilation film, a reediting of vast amounts of newsreel footage to re-create the Russian Revolution for its tenth anniversary. (100 mins.)

Fallen Angel (1945)**½ Alice Faye, Dana Andrews, Linda Darnell. Dana marries Alice for her money, hoping to latch on to Linda after he gets some dough. But, alas, Linda is murdered and he's a suspect. Fair drama but not too effective. (Dir: Otto Preminger, 97 mins.)

Fallen Angel (MTV 1981)** Richard Masur, Dana Hill, Melinda Dillon, Ronny Cox. A 13-year-old girl with family problems becomes prey to a child molester, a coach of a girls' softball team. This frank, often exploitative and frightening material works due in large part to Richard Masur's performance as the molester posing as a friend, the understanding grownup. Masur's molester (with his "mother didn't really want you" approach) is so skillful, viewers are able to understand how a youngster (Dana Hill) could easily become a trusting victim. (Dir: Robert Lewis, 104 mins.)

Fallen Idol, The (Great Britain, 1949)**** Ralph Richardson, Michele Morgan, Bobby Henrey. An ambassador's small son idolizes a servant, who has a nagging wife but loves an embassy clerk. When the wife is accidentally killed, the boy innocently points suspicion toward the servant. Superb drama of an adult world seen through the eyes of a child; merits praise in every respect. Directed by Carol Reed, written by Graham Greene. (94 mins.)

Fallen Sparrow (1943)***½ John Garfield, Maureen O'Hara. Survivor of a Spanish Brigade returns to America to tangle with Nazi spies. Smooth, excellently produced melodrama. (Dir: Richard Wallace, 94 mins.)

False Face—See: **Scalpel**

Fame (1980)***½ Irene Cara, Eddie Barth, Maureen Teefy, Lee Curreri, Anne Meara. Director Alan Parker's cross section of four years at New York's High School for the Performing Arts is exciting in spite of some nasty plot contrivances. Unabashedly dedicated to virtues of toil, talent, and upward mobility. Has a host of indefatigable young talents. An overlong good-time movie. (134 mins.)

Fame Is the Name of the Game (MTV 1966)** Tony Franciosa, Jill St. John, Jack Klugman, Susan Saint James. Involved melodrama about a magazine writer who gets his lumps when he investigates the supposed suicide of a girl. Slick production, but scripting and performances seldom rise above the routine. Incidentally, this is a remake of 1949's "Chicago Deadline," with Alan Ladd. (Dir: Stuart Rosenberg, 100 mins.)

Fame Is the Spur (Great Britain, 1949)***½ Michael Redgrave, Rosamund John. The saga of a liberal English statesman who refuses to sacrifice his ideals. Thoughtful, finely performed and directed drama. (Dirs: John and Roy Boulting, 116 mins.)

Family, The (1973)½ Charles Bronson, Telly

Savalas. (Dir: Sergio Sollima, 100 mins.)

Family Affair, A (1937)**½ Lionel Barrymore, Spring Byington, Mickey Rooney. This mild little comedy was the start of the Hardy series. Mr. Barrymore gave way to Lewis Stone in the later editions, however. Catch this one and see if you could have seen its box office potential. (Dir: George B. Seitz, 80 mins.)

Family Diary (Italy, 1962)** Marcello Mastroianni, Sylvie, Jacques Perrin. Saga of two brothers who are separated at birth. One lives in poverty (Mastroianni), the other (Perrin) in comfort. They are reunited, but inevitably split. Outstanding cast helps breathe some life into plodding script. (Dir: Valerio Zurlini, 115 mins.)

Family Enforcer (1976)** Joseph Cortese, Joe Pesci, Anne Johns. This cheaply made urban-gangster melodrama is competently crafted in the Martin Scorsese style—perhaps too much so—by director Ralph de Vito. Story of a fledgling mafioso learning his trade in the slums of Jersey City sports accurate Jersey accents, a nice feel for sleaze, and some predictable but effective ironies. (85 mins.)

Family Flight (MTV 1972)**½ Rod Taylor, Dina Merrill. Out of the old desert plane-crash plot comes a pretty fair flying show. A strained San Diego, Calif., family develops togetherness and maturity when they work their way out of a tight spot. Taylor pulls the family through and straightens out his defeatist son. The flying sequences, particularly in the last act crisis, are good. (Dir: Marvin Chomsky, 73 mins.)

Family Honeymoon (1948)**½ Claudette Colbert, Fred MacMurray, Gigi Perreau. One joke is stretched too far in this thin comedy. A widow with three children takes her brood with her on her second honeymoon. Some funny scenes. (Dir: Claude Binyon, 80 mins.)

Family Jewels, The (1965)*½ Jerry Lewis, Sebastian Cabot, Donna Butterworth, Anne Baxter. Lewis's often fascinating obsession with split personalities (generally, his own) reaches unmanageable dimensions in this exercise, which finds Lewis playing six parts as well as directing. The film drowns in a sea of empty virtuosity, and the gags—more childish than childlike—are no help. (100 mins.)

Family Life—See: **Wednesday's Child**

Family Man, The (MTV 1979)*** Ed Asner, Meredith Baxter Birney, Anne Jackson. Asner and Birney are delightful in this adult tale of a middle-aged married man who falls for a younger woman. Asner is an Irishman who strays for the first time, while his uneasy wife (Jackson) fears she's lost her man. A fine script by William Hanley gives the actors a chance to shine. (Dir: Glenn Jordan, 104 mins.)

Family Nobody Wanted, The (MTV 1975)**½ Shirley Jones, James Olson, Katherine Helmond. Heartwarming, sentimental story of a minister and his loving wife, and the brood of kids they adopt. The twist is that the bids are of mixed ethnic background. Shirley Jones strikes the right note as the minister's wife and James Olson adds his customary authority as the patient husband. A true story, based on Helen Doss' book about her family. (Dir: Ralph Senensky, 72 mins.)

Family Plot (1976)**** Karen Black, Bruce Dern, Barbara Harris, Cathleen Nesbitt, William Devane. Director Alfred Hitchcock's 53d film is another masterpiece. Follows two couples through two apparently unrelated stories, gradually winding the strands together: a fake medium (Harris) and her taxi-driver boyfriend (Dern) are trying to track down the lost heir to a family fortune—but the wayward son, now a professional kidnapper, doesn't want to be found. Hitchcock directs with unmatched skill and precision. (120 mins.)

Family Rico, The (MTV 1972)**½ Ben Gazzara, James Farentino. Adaptation of a Georges Simenon novel avoids gangland shooting and gore in "The Godfather" style, and focuses on a character study of a crime syndicate chief instead. Gazzara stars as a big-time hood, brought up in the old school. Good supporting cast includes Jo Van Fleet, Dane Clark, John Marley, and James Farentino. Remake of the feature **The Brothers Rico** (1957). (Dir: Paul Wendkos, 73 mins.)

Family Secret, The (1951)**½ John Derek, Lee J. Cobb, Jody Lawrance. A young man accidentally kills his best friend and doesn't report it to the police. Strange circumstances keep the suspense mounting until the climax. Some interesting moments. (Dir: Henry Levin, 85 mins.)

Family Upside Down, A (MTV 1978)*** Fred Astaire, Helen Hayes. Astaire and Hayes make it hard to resist this drama about the problems of growing old. Astaire is a retired house painter, shattered by heart attacks, who ends up in a rest home while his wife (Hayes) frets over their separation. The early scenes tend to be syrupy, and both actors overplay occasionally, but they're a pleasure to watch. (Dir: David Lowell Rich, 104 mins.)

Family Way, The (Great Britain, 1967)***½ Hayley Mills, John Mills, Hywel Bennett. Compassionate look at the troubles of young newlyweds (Miss Mills and Bennett). Fine performances by all. John Mills and Marjorie Rhodes are the parents. (Dirs: John and Roy Boulting, 115 mins.)

Fan, The (1949)**½ Jeanne Crain, Madeleine Carroll, George Sanders. Oscar Wilde's comedy of manners, about a lady with a past who uses her daughter to crash society. Attractive production enhances the slightly old-fashioned sentiments of the story. (Dir: Otto Preminger, 89 mins.)

Fanatics, The (Great Britain, 1963)** Craig Stevens, Eugene Deckers. Correspondent matches wits with a gang bent on assassination. Average melodrama based on "Man of the World" TV series. (87 mins.)

Fancy Pants (1950)*** Bob Hope, Lucille

Ball. Bob poses as a gentlemen's gentleman in this hyped-up version of "Ruggles of Red Gap." Could have been funnier, but the stars help it over the rough spots. (Dir: George Marshall, 92 mins.)

Fangs of the Arctic (1953)* Kirby Grant, Lorna Hansen. Chinook is the dog. (Dir: Rex Bailey, 62 mins.)

Fanny (France, 1932)***½ Raimu, Orane Desmazis, Charpin, Pierre Fresnay. The middle panel of the great Marcel Pagnol Marseilles trilogy. Although the weakest of the three under the hand of director Marc Allegret, it displays the same virtues of temperament, observation, and performance as the other two parts. In this one, the pregnant Fanny marries the wealthy Panisse and learns to love him despite feelings for her Marius, who has left to go to sea. As usual, it is Raimu's Cesar who dominates the proceedings, with his emotional range and subtlety the rival of Chaplin's. A feast of robust humor. (Dir: Marc Allegret, 120 mins.)

Fanny (1961)*** Leslie Caron, Horst Buchholz, Maurice Chevalier, Charles Boyer. The earthy magnificence of Marseilles, the personal charm of Charles Boyer and Maurice Chevalier, and the attractiveness of Leslie Caron and Horst Buchholz all help to make this love story entertaining. The tale about young lovers parting, a marriage of convenience, and a reunion which almost destroys everyone's life is a bit overlong but works fairly well most of the time. Director Joshua Logan chose to eliminate the songs from this straight film version based on the Broadway musical, but he uses the familiar score as background music. (133 mins.)

Fanny by Gaslight—See: **Man of Evil**

Fantasia (1940)***½ Mickey Mouse, Leopold Stokowski, The Philadelphia Orchestra. Walt Disney represents classics from Bach to Stravinsky in animation. A classic of brilliant kitsch, with color, depth, grace, and appalling taste. On TV, you'll miss the original stereo sound. (Dirs: 12 credited, 120 mins.)

Fantastic Invention, The—See: **Fabulous World of Jules Verne, The**

Fantastic Planet (France-Czechoslovakia, 1973)*** Voices of Barry Bostwick, Nora Heflin, Cynthia Alder. A Czech animated feature, directed by a Frenchman (René Laloux) and scripted by a Pole (Roland Topor) Tells of a race of 39-foot giants with red eyes (the Draags) and their war and conciliation with a subjugated race—tiny humanlike pets (the Oms). The film has a flat quality that is not entirely overcome by the sensational animation. (71 mins.)

Fantastic Voyage (1966)**½ Stephen Boyd, Raquel Welch, Edmond O'Brien, Arthur Kennedy, Arthur O'Connell, Donald Pleasence. Dumb, dumb, dumb, but impressive superspecial effects by Art Cruikshank make us believe Welch and crew are actually shrunk like an adenoid and sent through the bloodstream of a patient. It is

nonetheless a mad Hollywood revenge for all those educational "Hemo the Magnificent" programs. Boyd is perfectly cast. Oscars for visual effects and art direction. (Dir: Richard Fleischer, 100 mins.)

Fantasy Island (MTV 1977)**½ Bill Bixby, Sandra Dee, Peter Lawford, Hugh O'Brian, Loretta Swit. Pure escapist fare which usually works on some level. Remember "Westworld" and "Futureworld"? Well, here's ABC's made-for-TV answer to those films. A group of adventurous souls come to a private island where they have been promised they can live out their wildest fantasies. Then dreams soon turn into nightmares. Pilot for the hit series. (Dir: Richard Lang, 98 mins.)

Far Country, The (1955)*** James Stewart, Ruth Roman, Corinne Calvet. Lively adventure about cattle rustling, Alaska-style. Stewart plays all the stops as a peaceful cowpoke who gets trampled on at every turn until he just explodes. Walter Brennan, as Stewart's sidekick, gives another good performance. (Dir: Anthony Mann, 97 mins.)

Far from the Madding Crowd (Great Britain, 1967)*** Julie Christie, Alan Bates, Terence Stamp, Peter Finch. Thomas Hardy's novel about a beautiful girl who manages to make a shambles out of three men's lives is not completely successful as brought to the big screen by director John Schlesinger ("Midnight Cowboy" & "Darling"). Julie Christie never finds quite the right beat as the willful farm girl who betters her station in life but can't seem to find love. Of the three male stars, only Alan Bates emerges with a definite character. There is some glorious color photography in this long saga which runs almost three hours. (Dir: John Schlesinger, 169 mins.)

Far from Vietnam (France, 1967)***½ Ambitious, very uneven anti-war documentary made by many members of the French film industry who contributed their time and talent. This intellectualized propaganda film condemning the American action and presence in Vietnam includes 12 different sequences directed by Alain Resnais, Jean-Luc Godard, Agnes Varda, and others. The various sequences differ in quality and content and they are moving, maddening, unfair, accurate, etc., depending, to some degree, on your own political convictions. However, it's well worth seeing, as the subject of the Vietnam War has been with few exceptions, studiously avoided by the American film industry. (Dir: Alain Resnais, William Klein, Joris Ivens, Agnes Varda, Claude Lelouch, Jean-Luc Godard, 90 mins.)

Far Horizons, The (1955)**½ Charlton Heston, Fred MacMurray, Donna Reed. Hollywood's version of the historical Lewis & Clark Expedition with a stress on the romance between Clark and the Indian guide, Sacajawea. Good photography. (Dir: Rudolph Maté, 108 mins.)

Far Road, The (Japan, 1977)***½ Sachiko Hidari. Hidari, one of Japan's finest actresses, produces, directs and stars in this saga of railway workers financed by their union. The film had a big impact on the perception of labor relations in Japan, and is also an affecting family drama with good insight into working-class marriage. (115 mins.)

Farewell Again (Great Britain, 1937)*** Leslie Banks, Flora Robson. Following the events that befall men who are given six hours' leave before their troopship sails. Interesting, frequently absorbing drama, well acted. (Dir: Tim Whelan, 90 mins.)

Farewell Friend (1968)**½ Alain Delon, Charles Bronson. Seen-it-all-before saga of former mercenaries who chum up to rob company vaults. Delon's handsome and Bronson's tough, so together there's romance and action. (Dir: Jean Herman, 119 mins.)

Farewell, My Lovely (1975)**½ Robert Mitchum, John Ireland, Charlotte Rampling, Sylvia Miles. This is the third filmization of Raymond Chandler's popular detective yarn set in the 40s and it's seen better days. Robert Mitchum is Philip Marlow in this edition. Although he's cast well, there's something missing. The low-life characters he encounters in his quest to locate the girlfriend of an ex-con make for interesting individual scenes, but the tale never quite hangs together. An earlier version, the 1944 *Murder, My Sweet*, with Dick Powell as Marlowe, worked better. Sylvester Stallone has a bit part as a hood. (Dir: Dick Richards, 97 mins.)

Farewell to Arms, A (1932)**** Helen Hayes, Gary Cooper. Director Frank Borzage supposedly shot a happy ending to replace Hemingway's ending, but the existing prints end with eternal, spiritual love mourning the death of earthly love. Hayes gives a moving performance as the nurse with whom ambulance driver Cooper has an ill-fated affair in WW I Italy. Oscars for photography and sound recording. (78 mins.)

Farewell to Arms, A (1957)**½ Rock Hudson, Jennifer Jones, Vittorio De Sica, Mercedes McCambridge, Oscar Homolka. Hudson drives the ambulance in this remake of the Hemingway novel. David O. Selznick's exaggerated production values overrun everything, including director Charles Vidor, who hardly seems to know which way to turn. Jones is still alluring at the end of her star period. Filmed in Italy. (152 mins.)

Farewell to Manzanar (MTV 1976)***½ Yuki Shimoda, Nobu McCarthy, Akemi Kikumura, Clyde Kusatsu, Mako. A superb TV drama. The time is California in World War II, and the government is edgy about all those Japanese in coastal areas. Will the Japanese blow up everything in the name of the Rising Sun? To prevent such an occurrence, all Japanese, American-born or not, were sent to detention camps, families split up, and property confiscated. It's a sorry chapter in American history, and it comes to life as we watch a peaceful fisherman's family being incarcerated in Camp Manzanar. An Oriental cast plays the Wakatsuki family in this true story, and

they will arouse sympathy and guilt in abundance. Director John Korty ("The Autobiography of Miss Jane Pittman") helped to write this tale of bitterness and sorrow, and turned it into one of the better TV movies. (98 mins.)

Farmer Takes a Wife, The (1953)** Betty Grable, Dale Robertson, John Carroll, Eddie Foy, Jr., Thelma Ritter. This inferior remake is about a young girl shipping up and down the Erie Canal in the 1820s who fights and finds security in the arms of a stolid if sexy farmer. Stylized sets are used to good advantage. Cast is short on character candlepower. Henry Levin directed, with his usual lack of flair. (81 mins.)

Farmer's Daughter, The (1947)**½ Loretta Young, Joseph Cotten, Rose Hobart, Lex Barker, James Arness. Swedish maid Young revolts against her boss and beau (Cotten) by running for his seat in Congress. Young won an Academy Award, although she is far from her best. H. C. Potter directs with bland pleasantness, and the film needs more. Later a TV series. (97 mins.)

Faro Document, The (Sweden, 1970)***½ Ingmar Bergman's documentary on the people of the North Sea island where the director lived until his emigration to Los Angeles. Bergman interviews his neighbors and friends, focusing on the ways in which they've preserved the traditional life styles of the island in spite of the pressures of modern Swedish industrial society. (Ingmar Bergman.)

Faro Document 1979, The (Sweden, 1979)*** In '69 Ingmar Bergman directed a pessimistic feature documentary about the Baltic island where he lived and shot many of his films; this sequel notes that many of the young who deserted the island are returning. The inhabitants are the protagonists of the film, along with their familiar landscapes. (103 mins.)

Farrebique (France, 1946)*** Enthralling, intimate documentary look at the life of a provincial French farming family, culled from a year of living with and photographing three generations, and the sprawling acreage, vineyards, livestock that comprise the farm, "Farrebique." Sensitive view of nature and traditions. (Dir: George Rouquier, 100 mins.)

Fashions of 1934 (1934)*** William Powell, Bette Davis, Verree Teasdale. Charming nonsense about a notorious fashion bootlegger (Powell) who, with his assistant (Davis), tries to take over the Paris fashion scene. Powell's charm carries the film up to Busby Berkeley's extravagant, colossal production number "Spin a Little Web of Dreams." William Dieterle directed in amiable hack fashion. (78 mins.)

Fascist, The (Italy, 1961)*** Ugo Tognazzi, Georges Wilson. A hardcore Fascist is ordered to capture a famous professor who's a thorn in the side of the enemy, and he does—but the tables are turned before the professor can be brought back. Mildly amusing comedy-drama has some clever sequences, nice performances. Dubbed in English. (Dir: Luciano Salce, 102 mins.)

Fast and Loose (1930)**½ Miriam Hopkins, Frank Morgan, Carole Lombard. Flaming youth, directed by Harold Lloyd's onetime assistant Fred Newmeyer and written by a young, innocent Preston Sturges. Hopkins's film debut. (75 mins.)

Fast and Loose (Great Britain, 1954)**½ Kay Kendall, Brian Reece, Stanley Holloway. Husband is stranded in the country with a glamor girl, wife becomes suspicious. Pleasant comedy. (Dir: Gordon Parry, 75 mins.)

Fast and Sexy (Italy, 1960)** Gina Lollobrigida, Dale Robertson. A good comedy idea that gets bogged down with sentiment. Gina is a joy to behold but Dale Robertson as an Italian is a little much. (Dir: Vittorio De Sica, 98 mins.)

Fast Charlie—the Moonbeam Rider (1979)** David Carradine, Brenda Vaccaro, L. Q. Jones. Inconsequential story of motorcycle racers just after WW I. The personable cast make the most of a slight story about a war veteran who is tempted to fix a race. The "Moonbeam" of the title is the name of a custom-built cycle. (Dir: Steve Carver, 99 mins.)

Fast Company (1953)**½ Howard Keel, Polly Bergen. Trainer has a knack of making a certain horse win, goes into partnership with a pretty owner. Amusing racing comedy. (Dir: John Sturges, 67 mins.)

Fast Friends (MTV 1979)**½ Edie Adams, Dick Shawn, Carrie Snodgress, Mackenzie Phillips. Behind-the-scenes look at a network TV talk show presided over by a not-so-nice host. The story is played out through the initiation of a new assistant talent coordinator on the show. Shawn is perfectly cast as the host, and Adams is good as a Judy Garlandish singer. (Dir: Steven H. Stern, 104 mins.)

Faster Pussycat...Kill! Kill! (1966)**½ Susan Bernard. A Russ Meyer-directed violence opera which seemed distasteful and disgusting on first viewing. On second viewing it succeeded on the level of sheer stylistic folly. Recommended for its audacity.

Fastest Guitar Alive, The (1967)** Roy Orbison, Sammy Jackson, Maggie Pierce, Lyle Bettger, Joan Freeman. Misadventures of a couple of Confederate operators (Roy Orbison, Sammy Jackson) out to rob a mint. Simple Civil War comedy with songs; harmless enough. (Dir: Michael Moore, 87 mins.)

Fastest Gun Alive, The (1956)**½ Glenn Ford, Broderick Crawford, Jeanne Crain. Storekeeper gets a reputation as a fast gun, is challenged by a gunman to a duel. Fairly suspenseful western flamboyantly acted by Ford and Crawford. (Dir: Russell Rouse, 92 mins.)

Fat City (1972)**** Stacy Keach, Jeff Bridges, Susan Tyrell. Director John Huston's deeply moving drama about a washed-up 31-year-old boxer (Keach)—his best film in many years. Filmed on location in and around Stockton, Calif. Benefits greatly from the superb, lean, compassionate screenplay of Leonard Gardner, based on his novel. The protagonist is a boxer but this heartbreaking film is not essentially about boxing—it's about the lonely, empty life of some of the urban poor and their limited expectations. "Before you get rollin', your life makes a beeline for the drain" sums up Keach's attitude. Bridges is fine, and there's a really remarkable supporting performance by Susan Tyrell that earned her an Oscar nomination for her portrayal of a sherry-drinking, alcoholic floozie. She's convincing and heartbreaking. Keach is one of our most gifted young actors and he's memorable. No false bravado in this one as he takes his place among the most affecting losers in recent films. (Dir: John Huston, 96 mins.)

Fat Man, The (1951)** J. Scott Smart, Julie London, Rock Hudson. Radio's famed serial reaches the screen and plays like a radio show; that is, heavy on exposition and slow on action. It's interesting to note that the love interest is supplied by Rock Hudson and Julie London, who have since increased their marquee value somewhat. Emmett Kelly, the famous clown, plays a dramatic role in the film. (Dir: William Castle, 77 mins.)

Fata Morgana (West Germany, 1971)*** Cold, documentarylike images of the Gobi Desert are used in a grotesque retelling of the story of Creation in director Werner Herzog's experimental feature. The landing of a jet plane, repeated nine or ten times, becomes an odd spiritual symbol, at once banal and mysterious. You'll either be bored to death or fascinated. (78 mins.)

Fate Is the Hunter (1964)**½ Glenn Ford, Nancy Kwan, Rod Taylor, Suzanne Pleshette. A sometimes exciting drama which has Ford playing an airlines investigator who leaves no stone unturned in trying to piece together the why and wherefores of a fatal crash which took more than fifty lives. The flashback technique works well, and the cast is competent. There's an excellent climax which maintains the tension. (Dir: Ralph Nelson, 106 mins.)

Fate Takes a Hand (Great Britain, 1962)*½ Ronald Howard, Christina Gregg, (Dir: Max Varnel, 72 mins.)

Father (Hungary, 1966)***½ Andras Balint, Miklos Gabor, Kati Solyom. Post-Stalin Hungarian films are distinguished by a certain philosophical quality, intelligence, and a rich suggestiveness that assails on both political and personal fronts. Istvan Szabo's second film displays these qualities, arguing the overriding need of a true conception of one's history and heritage, as a boy finally accepts the realities of his father's past. Movie is both a parable of Stalinism, and a tale of human error and growth. Lightly told, sensitively acted. Written and directed by Istvan Szabo. (95 mins.)

Father Brown, Detective—See: Detective, The

Father Damien: The Leper Priest (MTV 1980)** Ken Howard, Mike Farrell, Wilfrid Hyde-White. TV series star Ken Howard is miscast as Father Damien, the Roman Catholic priest who gave his life to improve the conditions of a leper colony in Hawaii a century ago, bucking government officials and the church itself in his crusade. (Dir: Steven Gethers, 104 mins.)

Father Figure (MTV 1980)**½ Hal Linden, Timothy Hutton, Martha Scott, Jeremy Licht. Linden is trying to make friends with his two sons, from whom he has been separated for five years. After a rocky start, things warm up in a slow-moving yet well-meaning film. Superior acting: Hutton and Licht are great as the sons who are not sure how to react to their own father. Adapted by William Hanley from Richard Peck's novel. (Dir: Jerry London, 104 mins.)

Father Goose (1964)**½ Cary Grant, Leslie Caron. Cary Grant is always worth seeing, even in a lukewarm comedy effort such as this. Grant forgoes his customary polish and trim wardrobe for the role of a genial, fun-loving drifter named Walter who assists the Australian Navy during World War II by becoming a plane spotter on a remote atoll in the South Seas. Leslie Caron, as a French schoolteacher with a group of her young pupils in tow, descends upon the island, and Grant's peaceful mission turns into a free-for-all. (Dir: Ralph Nelson, 115 mins.)

Father Is a Bachelor (1950)** William Holden, Coleen Gray, Charles Winninger. Lightweight comedy about a roustabout bachelor and his involvement with five orphans, a lovable old medicine showman, and a judge's daughter. (Dir: Norman Foster, 84 mins.)

Father Knows Best Reunion (MTV 1977)**½ Robert Young, Jane Wyatt, Elinor Donahue, Billy Gray, Lauren Chapin. It's been a long time since the Anderson family got together around the old dining-room table in the famous TV series. Young and Wyatt (both very effective) are about to celebrate their 35th wedding anniversary, and since she feels lonely, he sends for the kids. Fine, sensitive moments between father and son, mother and daughter. (Dir: Marc Daniels, 78 mins.)

Father of the Bride (1950)** Spencer Tracy, Elizabeth Taylor, Joan Bennett, Don Taylor, Billie Burke. This ostensibly lighthearted film about the Kafkaesque complications that beset Tracy in bringing off his daughter's wedding is one of the bleakest films of a bleak decade. Director Vincente Minnelli follows Tracy through a seemingly endless series of humiliations culminating in a nightmare sequence that may be too intense for young daughters. (93 mins.)

Father Was a Fullback (1949)** Fred MacMurray, Maureen O'Hara, Thelma Ritter. Football coach's efforts to win the Big Game and solve his family problems simultaneously. Bright comic touches by Thelma Ritter. (Dir: John M. Stahl, 84 mins.)

Father's Dilemma (Italy, 1952)**** Aldo Fabrizi, Gaby Morlay. A very funny comedy revolving around a communion dress and a father's efforts to find it after he has lost it. Hilarious situations arise. The father is superbly played by Aldo Fabrizi. (Dir: Alessandro Blasetti, 88 mins.)

Father's Estate (Iceland-Sweden, 1980)**½ A harsh view of rural life in remote Iceland, and how the sudden death of a father affects the family. One of the children is retarded, another seeks a university education in Reykjavik, another is forced to stay with the farm and to battle unsuccessfully against the financial bosses of the cooperative movement. Hrafn Gunnlaughsson, writer-director, a major young Icelandic literary figure, also has made a half dozen films for national television; this is his feature debut. Technically, a co-production with Sweden. In color. (Dir: Hrafn Gunnlaughsson)

Father's Little Dividend (1951)***½ Elizabeth Taylor, Spencer Tracy, Joan Bennett. Refreshing sequel to "Father of the Bride," all the characters are present and the laughs come fast and furious. What an excellent farceur Spencer Tracy is—see this one if you like well done family comedies. (Dir: Vincente Minnelli, 82 mins.)

Fathom (1967)**½ Raquel Welch, Tony Franciosa. Entertaining, mindless spy spoof with the title role being bikinied rather than acted by the truly ravishing Raquel Welch. She's a superwoman who can do almost anything, and she gets a chance to try skin diving, sky diving, swimming (bikini-clad, of course) and other vigorous stunts. The plot is as busy as Miss Welch, involving a stolen figurine and the parade of villains who are after it. The coastline of Spain is glorious to behold if the males in the audience can keep their eyes off Raquel. (Dir: Leslie H. Martinson, 90 mins.)

FBI Code 98 (1964)** Jack Kelly, Ray Danton, Andrew Duggan. Philip Carey, Peggy McCay, Jack Cassidy. Hoover's heroes investigate an unexploded bomb—sabotage, or some other motive? Routine FBI story. (Dir: Leslie H. Martinson, 104 mins.)

FBI Story, The (1959)** James Stewart, Vera Miles, Murray Hamilton, Nick Adams. The film trades its soul for Bureau approval. Neither the personal story, nor Stewart as an agent, nor the "factual" material coalesce. Under Mervyn Le Roy's lackluster direction, the film meanders without drama, inspiration, or truth. (149 mins.)

FBI Story: The FBI Versus Alvin Karpis, Public Enemy Number One, The (MTV 1974)** Robert Foxworth, Harris Yulin,

Eileen Heckart. Submachine gun blasts fill the screen as 30's killer Alvin Karpis and his gang run rampant, kidnapping and robbing banks and trains. It takes J. Edgar Hoover, the new head of the FBI, to nail the cold-eyed hoodlum, but not before Karpis and his following shoot at innocents as easily as shooting at birds. Takes pains not to glamorize Karpis, effectively portrayed by Robert Foxworth. Eileen Heckart is Ma Barker, a lady hood with a weakness for white gloves. (Dir: Marvin Chomsky, 100 mins.)

F.D.R., the Last Year (MTV 1980)***½ Jason Robards, Jr., Eileen Heckart, Edward Binns, Larry Gates, Kim Hunter. Account of the last 12 wartime months of the president's life. Seated in a wheelchair, decked out in pinstripes, glasses, and bow tie, Robards focuses on Roosevelt's resiliency despite congestive heart failure, presenting him as a buoyant spirit beaten down at times, but never giving up. (Dir: Anthony Page, 153 mins.)

Fear (Germany, 1955)** Ingrid Bergman, Mathias Wieman, Kurt Kreuger. English-dubbed. An indiscreet woman is black-mailed by her lover's ex-girl, then worries that her husband will find out. Names of Bergman and director Roberto Rossellini should have meant a better film than this dull drama. (Dir: Roberto Rossellini, 84 mins.)

Fear in the Night (1947)*** Paul Kelly, De Forest Kelley. An innocent dupe is made to think he has murdered by use of hypnosis. Tense mystery, well above average. Remade as **Nightmare**, 1956. (Dir: Maxwell Shane, 72 mins.)

Fear in the Night (Great Britain, 1972)*** Ralph Bates, Judy Geeson, Peter Cushing, Joan Collins. Tingly psychological thriller from Hammer Films. A neurotic young woman, just married, goes to stay at the lonely boys' school where her husband teaches. Strange things start to happen and she begins to fear for her sanity. (Dir: Jimmy Sangster, 85 mins.)

Fear Is the Key (Great Britain, 1972)* Barry Newman, Suzy Kendall. (Dir: Michael Tuchner, 103 mins.)

Fear No Evil (1969)*** Louis Jourdan, Lynda Day, Bradford Dillman. Fans of the supernatural will enjoy this well produced chiller about a young lady (Lynda Day) who keeps a nightly rendezvous with her dead fiancé (Bradford Dillman). Louis Jourdan is very effective as the handsome psychiatrist who becomes interested in the girl's strange plight, and Miss Day makes an attractive, convincing heroine. The absorbing story delves into the macabre world of the occult which worships evil demons, and the finale involving an enchanted full-length mirror may jolt you. (Dir: Paul Wendkos, 98 mins.)

Fear No More (1961)** Mala Powers, Jacques Bergerac. Girl accused of murder escapes the law and with help from a good samaritan finds the real killer. Passable

mystery: enough plot twists to keep it going. (Dir: Bernard Wiesen, 80 mins.)

Fear on Trial (MTV 1975)***½ William Devane, George C. Scott. John Henry Faulk's book about the infamous black-listing in TV in the 50's and how it ruined his most promising radio and TV career finally has been made into a film, and a surprisingly good one at that. Devane plays the homespun radio personality whose name appears on the powerful AWARE bulletin, a publication created by two vicious businessmen who took it upon themselves to "safeguard" the entertainment industry from infiltration by leftwingers in the McCarthy era. The facts are all here, with some names changed to protect the guilty. The screenplay pays attention to details of the time. Scott enhances every scene he's in, playing the successful lawyer, Louis Nizer, who took on Faulk's case, dedicating over five years to the project. A film to be seen. (Dir: Lamont Johnson, 100 mins.)

Fear Strikes Out (1957)**** Anthony Perkins, Karl Malden, Norma Moore. Don't miss this fine drama with Anthony Perkins giving his best screen performance to date as baseball player Jim Piersall. The film deals mostly with Piersall's personal problems which contributed to his nervous breakdown. Karl Malden is excellent as Piersall's pushy father. (Dir: Robert Mulligan, 100 mins.)

Fearless Frank (1969)* Jon Voight, Monique Van Vooren, Severn Darden. Alternate title: **Frank's Greatest Adventure.** (Dir: Philip Kaufman, 78 mins.)

Fearless Vampire Killers, The (U.S.-Great Britain, 1967)** Roman Polanski, Sharon Tate. Polanski, who scored with "Rosemary's Baby" a year after this film, not only directed this meandering comedy-horror story but also played one of the leads. He is the familiar assistant to the equally familiar mad professor who come to Transylvania to obliterate the local vampires. Sharon Tate is the sexy lass who has been kidnapped by the bloodthirsty throng and she supplies the only diverting moments in the film. Don't expect much. (Dir: Roman Polanski, 110 mins.)

Fearmakers, The (1958)** Dana Andrews, Mel Torme, Dick Foran. A mixed-up drama about crime and violence tied in with political intrigue. Some action but mostly talk. The cast is adequate. (Dir: Jacques Tourneur, 83 mins.)

Feast of Flesh—See: **Night of the Living Dead**

Feather and Father (MTV 1977)**½ Stefanie Powers, Harold Gould. Pilot for a TV series. Gould is charming as the ex-con artist who keeps tending to revert; Powers as Feather, the righteous lawyer, is less than adequate. Feather is working on a case when Father and his cronies start a big-time con to help her cause. (Dir: Buzz Kulik, 78 mins.)

Fedora (West Germany, 1979)*** William Holden, Marthe Keller, José Ferrer, Hildegard Neff, Michael York, Henry Fonda. It's about time director Billy Wilder, curdled cynic, was recognized for the compassionate romantic he has always been. An aging Hollywood director meets a reclusive retired star and finds her beauty mysteriously unchanged. Here Wilder mediates on celebrity, the vanity of art, and shows us characters in the throes of raging against the dying of their light. Recommended. (113 mins.)

Fellini's roma (Italy-France, 1972) Peter Gonzales, Stefano Majore, Anna Magnani, Gore Vidal. Fellini is the first important director to insert his own name into the title of a film, and he certainly hasn't chosen his best film to memorialize himself for the first time. But mediocre Fellini is more involving and inventive filmmaking than the best efforts of most other directors, so this "nostalgic, carefree diary," as Fellini describes it, is worth seeing. It is a grab bab of comedy, drama, fantasy moving from childhood to the present day, intended to be a sardonic commentary on the collapse of Rome and of Western Europe. If you're a devotee of film whores this film is the promised land—fat whores, skinny ones, beautiful ones, grotesques ones, old harlots, young ones, black ones, white ones. There is a wonderful sequence recreating a World War II music hall. Fellini has offered us many of these dazzling, baroque images before but some of the new ones are worth seeing. (Dir: Federico Fellini, 113 mins.)

Fellini's Satyricon (Italy-France, 1969)**½ Martin Potter, Hiram Keller, Capucine, Donyale Luna, Lucia Bose, Gordon Mitchell, Alain Cuny. Flawed Fellini is, of course, more interesting than the best work of virtually all other directors. Once again, Fellini dazzles the eye with a series of ghastly, picaresque, beautiful, freaky, ravishing, bestial images as he turns his attention to recreating the world of Petronius Arbiter, Rome circa 50-66 A.D. But movie math finds that in this "Satyricon" the whole adds up to less than the sum of its parts. One film reference book provides an illuminating list of subjects dealt with in "Fellini's Satyricon." They include, among others, freaks, royalty, hedonism, sorcerers, dwarfs, male homosexuality, perfidy, impotence, priapism, nymphomania, hermaphroditism, mutilation, cannibalism, slavery, suicide, flagellation, orgies, tombs, theater, deserts, ships, Lupercalia and Rome. A phantasmagorical, grotesque dream, a Pagan Dolce Vita. Fellini co-authored the screenplay. (Dir: Federico Fellini, 120 mins.)

Fellini's Casanova (Italy, 1976)**½ Donald Sutherland, Tina Aumont, Cicely Browne. An enormously disappointing, overlong narrative about the celebrated 18th-century Venetian rake, Giovanni Jacopo Casanova de Seingat. Starting with the very first frame of the picture, Fellini provides the eye with some spectacular, bizarre pictorial images—but alas, there is little reward for the mind or the ear! Donald Sutherland plays the fornicating, elegant dandy who is reduced eventually to a whining librarian. He's as good as possible, but it's not enough. (Dir: Federico Fellini, 166 mins.)

Female Animal, The (1958)** Hedy Lamarr, Jane Powell, Jan Sterling, George Nader. Romantic melodrama. A Hollywood star, Miss Lamarr, is saved from death by a handsome extra, Nader. Fouled up by the wooden acting of Nader and the trite, storybook ending. Jan Sterling is best as a has-been actress. (Dir: Harry Keller, 83 mins.)

Female Artillery (MTV 1973)**½ Dennis Weaver, Ida Lupino. Western yarn, shot on location in Antelope Valley, Calif. A group of unescorted women and children traveling West by wagon train meet up with a stranger on the run, played by Weaver. On the distaff side, there's Ida Lupino, Nina Foch, Sally Anne Howes, and Linda Evans. (Dir: Marvin Chomsky, 73 mins.)

Female on the Beach (1955)**½ Joan Crawford, Jeff Chandler, Jan Sterling. Widow falls for a mysterious man who may be out to do away with her for her money. Drama would be suspenseful if it weren't so obvious. However, Crawford handles a tailor-made role with aplomb, so the ladies should like it. (Dir: Joseph Pevney, 97 mins.)

Female Trap—See: **The Name of the Game Is Kill!**

Feminine Touch, The (1941)**½ Rosalind Russell, Don Ameche, Van Heflin. Miss Russell enjoys a romp in this occasionally funny comedy about a professor who brings his wife to New York and discovers the woman in her. (Dir: W. S. Van Dyke, 97 mins.)

Femmes au Soleil (France, 1974)*** Juliette Mayniel, Genevieve Fontanel, Nathalie Chantrel. The dreams, flirtations, and frustrations of several women, braless and clothed, as they idle away their August holiday in the ever brilliant sunshine of southern France, around the swimming pool of a country estate. Often observant, evocative, languid but not boring. Marred by a melodramatic, inconclusive ending. Impressive entry from the young director Lilliane Dreyfus who also wrote and produced. (93 mins.)

Femmes Fatales (France, 1978)***½ Jean-Pierre Mareille, Jean Rochefort. Director Bertrand Blier's second feature is a mordant fantasy: a gynecologist (Mareille) and a pimp (Rochefort) decide that they have had it with women and sex and repair to the countryside to get smelly and celibate. The revolution spreads, the women strike back in force . . . the film ends as science fiction, which gives you the idea. Vulgar, sexist, provocative comedy, the product of a wild, intelligent vision trying to face some difficult issues truthfully and fearlessly.

Fer-de-Lance (MTV 1974)½ David Janssen, Hope Lange. (Dir: Russ Mayberry, 100 mins.)

Ferry To Hong Kong (Great Britain, 1960)** Curt Jurgens, Orson Welles, Sylvia Syms. Slow-moving, outdated melodrama about a drifter who winds up aboard a ferryboat and turns hero when the ship is attacked. Welles overacts as the skipper. (Dir: Lewis Gilbert, 103 mins.)

Festival (1967)*** Feature-length documentary of various performers playing at the Newport Folk Festival in 1963-66. Uneven, but there are some magical moments, including Bob Dylan's first appearance singing a rock version of "Maggie's Farm." Other performers include Joan Baez, Johnny Cash, Judy Collins, Odetta, and Peter, Paul, and Mary. Important historical record of this period in the development of American "folk" music. (Dir: Murray Lerner, 98 mins.)

Feudin' Fussin' and A-Fightin' (1948)** Donald O'Connor, Marjorie Main, Penny Edwards. Take a little of "Hatfield and McCoy Feud" and a lot of "Li'l Abner," add plenty of corn and you have "Feudin' Fussin' and a-Fightin'," (Dir: George Sherman, 78 mins.)

Fever Heat (1968)** Nick Adams, Jeannine Riley. Race driver Ace Jones wants to work his way into the life of a widow of a dead driver so that he can use her inherited garage. Ace is as crooked as a pretzel, but that doesn't make the movie any more interesting. Spiced with subplots of the lives of the other drivers. (Dir: Russell Doughten, Jr., 109 mins.)

Fever in the Blood, A (1961)**½ Efrem Zimbalist, Jr., Angie Dickinson, Jack Kelly, Don Ameche. A judge, a D.A., and a senator all have their eye on the governor's chair, and a murder trial is used to further their political ambitions. Drama of political maneuvering is salty enough to hold the attention, although the casting and the script could have been better. (Dir: Vincent Sherman, 117 mins.)

ffolkes (Great Britain, 1980)*** Roger Moore, James Mason, Anthony Perkins, Michael Parks, Jeremy Clyde. This film with an unpronounceable title (somehow deemed better than "Esther, Ruth and Jennifer," the novel on which it is based), is directed by the perennial good-spirited hack Andrew V. McLaglen. Not a bad caper comedy-thriller. Gruff Moore, in a character role as a woman-hating commando, has to stop Perkins and cohorts from blowing up a costly oil platform in the North Sea or pay a 25-million-pound ransom. Mason is effective as a befuddled admiral, and Clyde, once of the singing team Chad and Jeremy, is good in support. (92 mins.)

Fiancés, The (Italy, 1963)**½ J. Carlo Cabrini, Anna Canzli. Simple tale of an engaged couple who are separated when he must go north to find work. Director Ermanno Olmi exhibits visual control and solicitude for the feelings of the working classes, yet his vision seems willfully circumscribed. Here we deal with nothing more than the loftiest form of termite art. (85 mins.)

Fiction-Makers, The (1967)*½ Roger Moore, Sylvia Syms. (Dir: Roy Baker, 102 mins.)

Fiddler On The Roof (1971)**** Topol, Molly Picon, Norma Crane, Leonard Frey. The long-running, prize-winning Broadway musical hit based on the stories of Sholem Aleichem survives the transfer to the big screen quite well. Set in a small Ukranian village in 1905, "Fiddler" is carried by a splendid score including such rousing songs as "If I Were A Rich Man" and "Tevye's Dream." Director Norman Jewison is fairly literal minded about transferring this stage property to the wide screen but, perhaps surprisingly, it works quite well. Topol does not have the brilliance of Zero Mostel's Broadway "Topol" but he is engaging enough. The rooftop violin solo you see and hear is played by Isaac Stern. (180 mins.)

Fidel (1970)***½ Continuously interesting, frequently amusing feature-length documentary about Cuban leader Fidel Castro. Made in Cuba in 1968, it records some of the changes in Cuban life since Castro came to power in 1959. Written, produced, and directed by Saul Landau, this is an unusually revealing study of this charismatic political figure. It shows Castro speaking to crowds, playing baseball, chatting with peasants, discussing farm policies, etc. Some of the footage was used in a TV documentary broadcast in June '69. (96 mins.)

Fiend, The (Great Britain, 1972)** Ann Todd, Patrick Magee, Tony Beckley. Odd, rather unpleasant shocker about a weird religious sect and the psychotics who belong to it. Some suspense on the way to a very nasty climax. Well acted, ugly; not for children. (Dir: Robert Hartford-Davis, 87 mins.)

Fiend Who Walked the West, The (1958)** Hugh O'Brian, Robert Evans, Dolores Michaels. Ex-cellmate of an escaped killer is freed to help track him down, then finds his life and family's welfare threatened by the "fiend." O'Brian is the put-upon hero, and Evans, later a big exec at Paramount, is the sadistic killer. (Dir: Gordon Douglas, 101 mins.)

Fiend Without a Face (Great Britain, 1958)* Marshall Thompson, Terence Kilburn. Poor science fiction meller in which scientists combat monsters created as a result of experiments by the U.S. Air Force in Canada. (Dir: Arthur Crabtree, 74 mins.)

Fiercest Heart, The (1961)** Stuart Whitman, Juliet Prowse, Raymond Massey, Geraldine Fitzgerald. Army deserters in South Africa (1837) join some

Boers on a trek, protect them from warring Zulus. Good cast wasted in a dismal adventure which uses a lot of stock footage from the Tyrone Power film "Untamed." (Dir: George Sherman, 91 mins.)

Fiesta (1947)** Esther Williams, Ricardo Montalban, Akim Tamiroff, Mary Astor, Cyd Charisse, John Carroll. Esther Williams plays a lady bullfighter in this piece of MGM Latin-American folderol with lots of colorfully inauthentic dancing. Color. (Dir: Richard Thorpe, 104 mins.)

Fifth Avenue Girl (1939)** Ginger Rogers, Walter Connolly, James Ellison. Millionaire arranges a romance between his son and a plain Jane. Strained, dull comedy. (Dir: Gregory La Cava, 83 mins.)

5th Day of Peace, The (Italy, 1972)**½ Richard Johnson, Franco Nero. Prisoner-of-war story which starts out interestingly but soon falters into obvious plot twists. Johnson adds some dignity to the proceedings and Nero supplies the necessary he-man gloss. (Dir: Giuliano Montaldo, 100 mins.)

Fifth Floor, The (1980)*½ Dianne Hull, Bo Hopkins, Patti D'Arbanville. Horror thriller about a disco waitress. From a story by Howard Avedis, producer and director, and exec producer Marlene Schmidt. (90 mins.)

Fifth Horseman Is Fear, The (Czechoslovakia, 1965)**** Powerfully presented story of a Jewish doctor (Miroslav Machacek) harboring a fugitive in Nazi-occupied Prague. Grim, strong sequences stay in the memory. An excellent example of the capabilities of the heretofore neglected Czechoslovakian filmmakers. Fine direction by Zbynek Brynych, superb performances. Subtitles. (100 mins.)

Fifth Musketeer, The (Austria-Great Britain, 1979)** Beau Bridges, Sylvia Kristel, Ursula Andress, Cornel Wilde, Rex Harrison. Still another version of Alexandre Dumas's "Man In the Iron Mask." Offers nothing new; despite a capable supporting cast, Bridges, in the dual role of King Louis XIV and his twin brother Philippe, falls short of the antic heroics needed to carry off the title role with style and conviction. (Dir: Ken Annakin, 103 mins.)

55 Days at Peking (1963)**½ Charlton Heston, Ava Gardner, David Niven, Flora Robson, Leo Genn. Nicholas Ray planned and started directing this blockbuster spectacle set during the Boxer Rebellion (Andrew Marton finished it). Good action uncoils within an intelligent political context. (150 mins.)

Fighter, The (1951)***½ Richard Conte, Vanessa Brown, Lee J. Cobb. In revolution-torn Mexico of 1910, a young patriot offers his services as a boxer to raise money for the cause. Good fight melodrama, well done throughout. (Dir: Herbert Kline, 78 mins.)

Fighter Attack (1953)**½ Sterling Hayden, Joy Page. Another war yarn with Sterling

Hayden cast as a heroic Major who leads an important mission before the film runs its course. Action fans might find this too slow for their tastes but if you stick it out, there's a bang-up climax. (Dir: Lesley Selander, 80 mins.)

Fighting Back (MTV 1980)**½ Robert Urich, Bonnie Bedelia, Richard Herd, Howard Cosell. True story of Pittsburgh Steeler Rocky Bleier's miraculous football comeback after he was seriously injured in Vietnam. As presented, it only works sporadically; not until halfway through does the pace pick up and allow Urich's Rocky to come to life. Real football footage is skillfully edited. (Dir: Robert Lieberman, 104 mins.)

Fighting Father Dunne (1948)***½ Pat O'Brien, Darryl Hickman. A St. Louis priest establishes a home for orphan newsboys. Sincere, well-made drama, good entertainment. (Dir: Ted Tetzlaff, 93 mins.)

Fighting Kentuckian, The (1949)**½ John Wayne, Vera Ralston, Oliver Hardy. Frontiersman courting an aristocrat's daughter foils a plot to steal land from French settlers. Action melodrama is a big production with some good action, but this only partially compensates for script and directorial shortcomings. (Dir: George Waggner, 100 mins.)

Fighting Lady, The (1945)**½ Color documentary made during WW II. Its picture of shipboard life and naval combat is compelling. James Agee thought it reminded him of a box of chocolates filled with plasma. (Dir: William Wyler, 61 mins.)

Fighting Lawman, The (1953)** Wayne Morris, Virginia Grey. Routine western fare about a lawman who comes under a wicked woman's influence but everything turns out for the best. (Dir: Thomas Carr, 71 mins.)

Fighting Mad (1976)***½ Peter Fonda, Lynn Lowry, Philip Carey, John Doucette. An overlooked B picture of genuine merit, directed by Jonathan Demme (*Handle With Care*). Coming at the end of the revenge cycle inspired by *Walking Tall*, its considerable qualities were swamped by generic backlash. Gentler, more honestly felt, and made with much more craft than most of the other entries in the genre, *Fighting Mad* courts an effective ecological lyricism in its story of a returning farmboy (Peter Fonda) who finds that his ancestral home is being threatened by a gigantic real-estate development. Demme has become a director to watch; this was his first sign of real talent: *Fighting Mad* calls to mind, of all people, George Stevens at his best. (90 mins.)

Fighting Rats of Tobruk (Australia, 1945)**½ Chips Rafferty, Grant Taylor, Peter Finch. Story of the dramatic siege during World War II, when the Anzacs held the Nazi hordes off for months under cruel fire. A bit ragged production-wise, but sincere, occasionally exciting. (Dir: Charles Chauvel, 71 mins.)

Fighting Seabees, The (1944)***½ John Wayne, Susan Hayward, Dennis O'Keefe. Tough construction foreman and a Navy man organize a work battalion to repair installations close to Japanese lines. Rousing war melodrama, loaded with action. (Dir: Edward Ludwig, 100 mins.)

Fighting 69th, The (1940)***½ James Cagney, Pat O'Brien. This picture is as corny as they come but is one of the most stirring war pictures you'll ever see. It lacks the dignity of an "All Quiet on the Western Front" but what it lacks in dignity and sensitivity it makes up for in spirit. Top-flight entertainment. (Dir: William Keighley, 89 mins.)

Fighting Sullivans, The—See: **Sullivans, The**

Fighting Wildcats (Great Britain, 1957)** Keefe Brasselle, Kay Callard. Dynamite expert is hired to plant a time bomb to kill an Arab leader. Passable melodrama. (Dir: Arthur Crabtree, 74 mins.)

Figures in a Landscape (Great Britain, 1971)*** Robert Shaw, Malcolm McDowell. A commissioned project, directed in Spain by Joseph Losey, that was largely rewritten by star Shaw during production. An overly conscious and allegorical work of art, but saved by the concreteness of its rugged action. (110 mins.)

File of the Golden Goose, The (Great Britain, 1969)** Yul Brynner, Charles Gray, Edward Woodward. American secret agent, played in an obvious manner by Brynner, infiltrates a counterfeiting ring with the help of Scotland Yard. Nononsense script sticks to the story which is plodding and clichéd. London locations add color, and there's a good sequence of assassination in the Burlington shopping arcade. Well acted by Woodward, in particular, and Gray. (Dir: Sam Wanamaker, 105 mins.)

File on Thelma Jordon, The (1950)**½ Barbara Stanwyck, Wendell Corey, Paul Kelly, Joan Tetzel. This Robert Siodmak-directed film has a contrived melodramatic plot (a D.A. falls in love with a murder suspect and throws the case to save her), a lot of nice film noir touches, and a typically professional portrayal by Stanwyck. Written by Ketti Frings, produced by Hal Wallis, and photographed by George Barnes. (100 mins.)

Fillmore (1972)***½ Last days of the Fillmore West in San Francisco are documented, mainly focusing on the great acts that appeared there and their music. Included are Santana, the Grateful Dead, the New Riders of the Purple Sage, the Jefferson Airplane, Hot Tuna, and the Quicksilver Messenger Service. Most fascinating are the shots of Bill Graham, owner of the Fillmore, which reveal him as a dedicated man with a fine sense of ironic humor. (Dir: Richard T. Heffron, 105 mins.)

Film About Jimi Hendrix, A (1972)**½ A comprehensive look at the life and career of the pre-eminent rock guitarist, with interviews and concert footage. Valuable archival record but not one of the best concert films.

Film Novel—Three Sisters (Hungary, 1978)**½ Zsuzsa Szakacs, Maria Himmer, Eszter Bognar. A large-scale attempt to integrate the story of three real sisters into an overall view of women as an underprivileged class. Nonprofessional players act out situations similar to their own lives: an interesting concept, not completely successful. (Dirs: Istvan Darday, Gyorgyi Szalai, 270 mins.)

Filming of Othello, The (1977)*** Orson Welles shot his version of Shakespeare's *Othello* over what was certainly a record schedule for a low-budget quickie: four weeks spread over four years (1948–1952). The anecdotal material is illuminating and entertaining, as Welles himself recalls and interviews other participants some 25 years later. This latest in Welles's new film-essay stage sounds like a replay of *Citizen Kane*, this time as frank and devious nonfiction, establishing the continuity that marks this artist as the persistently vital force he has been and remains after 40 years. It is regrettable that he prefers much of his most prolific period to remain invisible, and one hopes that is a temporary stinginess in this generous talent. (Dir: Orson Welles, 90 mins.)

Final Chapter—Walking Tall (1977)* Bo Svenson, Margaret Blye, Forrest Tucker. Saga of real-life Tennessee sheriff Buford Pusser, who died under mysterious circumstances after crusading against vice and corruption, comes to an end in this third film about his exploits. It's bloody and boring, and Svenson never manages to overcome the script's many inadequacies. (Dir: Jack Starrett, 112 mins.)

Final Countdown, The (1979)*** Kirk Douglas, Martin Sheen, Katharine Ross, James Farentino. Caught in a time warp, the commanders aboard today's carrier U.S.S. "Nimitz" must decide whether to prevent the bombing of Pearl Harbor in '41. The premise, which surprisingly is believable, combines with the photography, special effects, and a surprise ending to make an entertaining film. (Dir: Don Taylor, 103 mins.)

Final Crash—See: **Steelyard Blues**

Final Programme, The—See: **Last Days of Man on Earth, The**

Final Test, The (Great Britain, 1953)***½ Jack Warner, Robert Morley. Star cricket batsman is dismayed when he finds his son wants to be a poet. Witty, finely written comedy-drama. Recommended. (Dir: Anthony Asquith, 84 mins.)

Find the Lady (Great Britain, 1956)** Donald Houston. A lady disappears and this starts a merry chase for a young doctor and a pretty model. Uneven but brief British film. (Dir: Charles Saunders, 56 mins.)

Finders Keepers (1952)**½ Tom Ewell, Julia Adams. Tom Ewell makes this wacky comedy seem better than it really is. He plays an ex-con who wants to go legit but his two year old son's innocent habits almost land him back in stir. Broad comedy played for belly laughs. (Dir: Frederick de Cordova, 74 mins.)

Finders Keepers, Lovers Weepers (1968)** Anne Chapman, Paul Lockwood, Gordon Wescourt, Duncan McLeod. (Dir: Russ Meyer, 71 mins.)

Fine Madness, A (1966)***½ Sean Connery, Joanne Woodward, Jean Seberg. Sean Connery gives a very fine performance as a bold, outspoken, radical poet who gets caught up in his own momentum. Joanne Woodward as his waitress-wife is brash and funny, and the rest of the cast, mostly made up of Broadway actors, adds greatly to the inventive screwball comedy. Unconventional fun. (Dir: Irvin Kershner, 104 mins.)

Fine Pair, A (Italy, 1968)* Rock Hudson, Claudia Cardinale, Thomas Milian. (Dir: Francesco Maselli, 89 mins.)

Finest Hours, The (Great Britain, 1964)***½ An exhilarating history lesson about Winston Spencer Churchill. This prize-winning documentary is stunning on several counts—scenes of Churchill's childhood, his early adventures in India and South Africa, followed by his remarkable career which thrust him into the heart of most of the great events of this century. F.D.R., Hitler, Mussolini, Stalin, Chamberlain et al appear in vignettes. Churchill's own memorable speeches are heard, as well as the glories of Orson Welles' voice as narrator. Young and old should enjoy this wondrous saga together. (Dir: Peter Baylis, 114 mins.)

Finger Man (1955)**½ Frank Lovejoy, Forrest Tucker. Criminal is released from prison to get the goods on an underworld boss. Fast moving crime melodrama. (Dir: Harold Schuster, 82 mins.)

Finger of Guilt (Great Britain, 1956)**½ Richard Basehart, Mary Murphy, Mervyn Johns, Constance Cummings. Blacklisted, Joseph Losey fled to England, where he directed this self-conscious thriller under the name of Joseph Walton. Basehart plays an American producer who has been driven to England to find work; there he encounters a mysterious woman (Murphy) who claims to have been his lover in Hollywood. The script, by "Peter Howard," is the work of Howard Koch, another refugee. (84 mins.)

Finian's Rainbow (1968)*** Fred Astaire, Petula Clark, Tommy Steele, Al Freeman, Jr., Keenan Wynn. This broke ground when it opened as a Broadway musical in the late '40s, but was dated by the time Francis Ford Coppola directed it for the screen. The best that can be said about this musical, concerned with leprechauns and racism, is Astaire in the leading role; he's funny, and even dances and sings a bit. Clark and especially Steele are also "sort of grandish" in the other leads, and the words and music, by E. Y. Harburg and Burton Lane, are superb. (145 mins.)

Finnegans Wake (1967)**½ Martin J. Kelly, Jane Reilly, Peter Haskell. Director Mary Ellen Bute's "reaction" to James Joyce's poetic masterpiece ('39) is no cause for rejoycing. Joyce's words compete with her images rather than complement them; the result is neither wholly filmic nor wholly intelligent. Filmed partly in Dublin. (97 mins.)

Fire!—See: Irwin Allen's Production of Fire!

Fire and Ice (France-Italy, 1963)*** Romy Schneider, Jean-Louis Trintignant. Unbalanced young would-be assassin swears revenge upon the organization leader who has made a fool of him. Uneven, rambling melodrama dubbed in English. Good performances, but lacks the necessary tension. Supervised by Louis Malle. (Dir: Alain Cavalier, 105 mins.)

Fire Down Below (1957)*** Rita Hayworth, Robert Mitchum, Jack Lemmon. Mitchum and Lemmon are two adventurers who meet and fall for Rita, a shady lady. A ship's explosion traps Lemmon in the debris and Mitchum risks his life to save him. Lemmon is excellent but Hayworth fares less successfully. (Dir: Robert Parrish 110 mins.)

Fire in the Sky, A (MTV 1978)**½ Richard Crenna, Elizabeth Ashley. Pretty fair disaster movie. A comet seems to be headed straight for Phoenix, Arizona, but city officials dally over evacuation plans. When the panic button is pushed the show takes off with good special effects and crowd scenes in Phoenix. (Dir: Jerry Jameson, 156 mins.)

Fire over Africa (Great Britain, 1954)** Maureen O'Hara, Macdonald Carey. Undercover agents work against great odds to smash a smuggling ring operating in Tangier. Mild melodrama. (Dir: Richard Sale, 84 mins.)

Fire over England (Great Britain, 1937)** Laurence Olivier, Vivien Leigh, Flora Robson, Raymond Massey, Leslie Banks. One of the British film industry's periodic attempts to break Hollywood's stranglehold on the world market. Naturally, they hired an American director, William K. Howard, but Howard was mostly a tired journeyman, and this film lacks excitement despite the dashing Olivier as a bold courtier serving Queen Elizabeth I as the Spanish Armada (read: Hitler) threatens. (89 mins.)

Fire Sale (1977)½ Alan Arkin, Rob Reiner, Sid Caesar, Anjanette Comer, Kay Medford, Vincent Gardenia. (Dir: Alan Arkin, 88 mins.)

Fire Under Her Skin (France, 1954)* Giselle Pascal, Raymond Pellegrin. (Dir: Marcel Blistene, 90 mins.)

Fire Within, The (France-Italy, 1963)****

Maurice Ronet, Lena Skerla, Yvonne Clech, Jeanne Moreau, Alexandra Stewart. Director Louis Malle's portrait of the last 24 hours in the life of a man emerging from an alcoholism cure is a moving, penetrating study of a man at the end of his rope. (121 mins.)

Fireball, The (1950)** Mickey Rooney, Pat O'Brien, Marilyn Monroe. An orphan kid becomes a hot-shot roller skater, but his ego gets the best of him. Typical Rooney plot; good roller derby scenes; and The Monroe! (Dir: Tay Garnett, 84 mins.)

Fireball 500 (1966)*½ Frankie Avalon, Annette Funicello, Fabian, Chill Wills. (Dir: William Asher, 92 mins.)

Fireball Forward (MTV 1972)**½ Ben Gazzara, Eddie Albert, Edward Binns, Ricardo Montalban. World War II drama, by the "Patton" writing-producing team, actually uses excess battle footage taken while shooting that movie. Story focuses on command problems after a major general takes charge of a division plagued by bad luck and poor morale. The "Patton" battle sequences are cleverly inserted, but the main interest in the film is Gazzara's major general, a tough dogface up from the ranks. Sporting a close-clipped haircut, Gazzara uses his strong presence to turn his short cigar-smoking general into a believable authority figure. (Dir: Marvin Chomsky, 100 mins.)

Firechasers, The (Great Britain, 1970)*½ Chad Everett, Anjanette Comer. (Dir: Sidney Hayers, 101 mins.)

Firecreek (1968)**½ Henry Fonda, James Stewart. It's the timid sheriff (James Stewart) against the gangleader (Henry Fonda), whose men are terrorizing the town. Traditional western tale gets the heavy treatment. Unduly protracted, but some good performances. With Inger Stevens, Gary Lockwood, Dean Jagger, Ed Begley, Jay C. Flippen, Jack Elam. (Dir: Vincent McEveety, 104 mins.)

Firefly, The (1937)** Jeanette MacDonald, Allan Jones, Warren William. MacDonald asked Louis B. Mayer for a vacation from Nelson Eddy and found herself saddled with MGM's second-string sappy tenor, Jones (who sings "Donkey Serenade").Ogden Nash labored on the screenplay (based on a '12 operetta by Rudolf Friml) to no avail. Robert Z. Leonard directed, giving the film his patented leaden touch. (131 mins.)

Firehouse (MTV 1972)**½ Richard Roundtree, Vince Edwards. Drama about racism in an all-white fire-engine company. Benefits from a decent script, realistic surroundings, and good performances by the stars. An Archie Bunker-type blue-collar fireman (Edwards) leads his close-knit company in the hazing of a new black recruit (Roundtree). The duel between Edwards' hard-eyed station leader and Roundtree's smoldering black man is generally effective, thanks to Frank Cucci's script. (Dir: Alex March, 73 mins.)

Fireman, Save My Child (1954)** Spike Jones, Buddy Hackett. A turn of the century comedy-musical about a group of misfit firemen who are more trouble than a four alarmer. If your tastes lean towards slaphappy slapstick, this is right up your hook and ladder. (Dir: Leslie Goodwins, 80 mins.)

Firemen's Ball, The (Czechoslovakia, 1967)**** Vaclav Stockel, Josef Svet. Director Milos Forman has directed and helped write a wonderfully funny, touching, and observant study of petty bureaucratic minds and people in a small Czechoslovakian town. Simple story concerns the effort to honor a fire chief who is retiring at the ripe old age of 86. The ceremony is turned into a shambles and the film makes its points about politics, life and art in understated but unerringly accurate terms. (No big name stars here—just superb actors portraying recognizable people and constantly offering both humor and insight. Dubbed. (Dir: Milos Forman, 73 mins.)

Firepower (Great Britain, 1979)** Sophia Loren, James Coburn, O. J. Simpson, Eli Wallach, Anthony Franciosa. Involved thriller, with luscious Loren and nice Caribbean scenery, but makes little sense. Three leads are determined to get at wealthy George Touliatos, well guarded in a secluded fortress, for various reasons. People like tiny Billy Barty and Victor Mature, in a last-scene bit, keep turning up as you tune out. (Dir: Michael Winner, 104 mins.)

Fires on the Plain (Japan, 1959)*** Eiji Funakoshi, Osamu Takizawa, Mickey Curtis. Director Kon Ichikawa's absurdist humor almost salvages this antiwar indictment in which routed Japanese soldiers on Leyte resort to cannibalism in order to survive. The film is harsh, forceful, yet recalcitrantly arty in mostly wrongheaded ways. (105 mins.)

First Legion, The (1951)**** Charles Boyer, William Demarest, Barbara Rush. A Jesuit seminary in a small town is the center of attraction when a miracle seemingly occurs, but it is disbelieved by one of the priests. This is a really fine, sensitive drama, wonderfully well acted, directed, written. (Dir: Douglas Sirk, 86 mins.)

First Love (1939)***½ Deanna Durbin, Robert Stack, Eugene Pallette. A Cinderella story complete with the big ball at the end and Prince Charming (none other than Robert Stack). Young Deanna Durbin got her first screen kiss by Stack in this film. Stack's debut. (Dir: Henry Koster, 90 mins.)

First Love (1977)** William Katt, Susan Dey, John Heard, Beverly D'Angelo, Robert Loggia. Joan Darling, who made a name directing "Mary Hartman, Mary Hartman" on TV, broke into feature films directing this story of a college romance complicated by the girl's affair with an older man. The film is more than a little bogged down in sentiment, and it gets worse as the plot thickens. Dey is pretty good. (92 mins.)

First Man into Space (Great Britain, 1959)** Marshall Thompson, Marla Landi. Considering all the factual and advanced information compiled since this science-fiction film was made, the science details are dated. The fiction part is taken care of by the introduction of a monster-creature from out-of-space. Strictly for the kiddies and very young kiddies at that. (Dir: Robert Day, 77 mins.)

First Men in the Moon (Great Britain, 1964)** Lionel Jeffries, Martha Hyer. A mediocre version of the H.G. Wells novel, in which a Victorian eccentric is forced into a moon voyage and then is stranded there. The attitude toward the material is appropriately larky, but the film has no distinction. With special effects by Ray Harryhausen, and with Peter Finch in an uncredited cameo as a process server. (Dir: Nathan Juran, 103 mins.)

First Spaceship on Venus (East Germany-Poland, 1960)* Yoko Tani, Oldrich Lukes. Science fiction film made in Germany with poor production values. (Dir: Kurt Maetzig, 78 mins.)

First Texan, The (1956)** Joel McCrea, Felicia Farr. Lively western about the days when Texas fought for and gained independence from Mexico. History may be altered a bit here and there but it's all for entertainment's sake. (Dir: Byron Haskin, 82 mins.)

First 36 Hours of Dr. Durant, The (MTV 1975)**½ Scott Hylands, Katherine Helmond, Lawrence Pressman, Peter Donat, Dana Andrews. Stirling Silliphant ("Route 66," "Naked City," "Longstreet"), turned out this medical pilot film on hospital life seen through the eyes of a young resident. Except for a nurse suing the hospital for discrimination, and hero Durant battling against "ghost surgery," it's not radically different from its predecessors. (Dir: Alexander Singer, 72 mins.)

First Time, The (1952)*** Robert Cummings, Barbara Hale. Fast and funny comedy dealing with the financial woes of a newly married couple. Cummings is excellent as the male in the middle. (Dir: Frank Tashlin, 89 mins.)

First Time, The (France, 1978)*** Alain Cohen, Charles Denner, Zorica Lozic. More of writer-director Claude Berri's examination of his early life, with young Cohen as a teenaged version of the Claude Langmann he played in "The Two of Us" ('68). Claude is now 16 and attempting to have his first romantic conquest. Pleasant Gallic humor. (85 mins.)

First to Fight (1967)*½ Chad Everett, Marilyn Devin. (Dir: Christian Nyby V, 97 mins.)

First Traveling Saleslady, The (1956)** Ginger Rogers, Carol Channing, James Arness. Ginger Rogers takes to the West

selling corsets during the turn-of-the-century in this light comedy. Some funny situations but most is labored visual jokes. (Dir: Arthur Lubin, 92 mins.)

First You Cry (MTV 1978)**** Mary Tyler Moore, Anthony Perkins, Florence Eldridge, Jennifer Warren, Richard Crenna. TV newswoman Betty Rollin's candid book about her mastectomy and the readjustment period following the operation makes a poignant film with Mary submerging her patented TV personality to honestly convey the anxiety, depression, and torment of the situation, going from stoicism to tears to rage before beginning to build a new life for herself. One of the best made-for-TV films of the decade. (Dir: George Schaefer, 104 mins.)

Fish That Saved Pittsburgh, The (1979)* Julius Erving, Stockard Channing, Jonathan Winters. Comedy about a woebegone pro basketball team that uses astrology to win a championship. Film is woebegone too. (Dir: Gilbert Moses, 102 mins.)

F.I.S.T. (1978)*** Sylvester Stallone, Rod Steiger, Peter Boyle, Melinda Dillon, Tony Lo Bianco, Kevin Conway. Overlong but engrossing drama about a Jimmy Hoffa-like character who rises to union prominence and power the hard way. Title stands for Federation of Inter-State Truckers. Stallone and Joe Eszterhas did the screenplay from the latter's story, and Norman Jewison directed interestingly. (145 mins.)

Fist in His Pocket (Italy, 1966)***½ Lou Castel, Paola Pitagora, Marino Mase. A young director (Marco Bellocchio) made his first film about a decaying family into a grim, frequently grotesque study of rampant psychopathology. A morbidly fascinating drama, well acted. English subtitles. (Dir: Marco Bellocchio, 105 mins.)

Fistful of Dollars (Italy-Spain-West Germany, 1964)**½ Clint Eastwood, Marianne Koch, Gian Maria Volonte. This was to Italian westerns what "The Great Train Robbery" was to westerns. Director Sergio Leone sketched in the themes to come and the film made a lot of money. It also made Eastwood an international star. (96 mins.)

Fistful of Dynamite, A (Italy, 1972)**½ Rod Steiger, James Coburn, Romolo Valli, Maria Monte. Wide-open, true-to-form Sergio Leone-directed spaghetti western. Coburn talks reluctant petty crook Steiger into joining his side of a revolution. Reasonably diverting, frivolous shoot-'em-up. (139 mins.)

Fitzwilly (1967)**½ Dick Van Dyke, Edith Evans, Barbara Feldon, John McGiver, Harry Townes. Van Dyke plays a butler whose stuffy exterior hides a heart of pure larceny, culminating in a try for a heist of Gimbel's department store. Amusing bit of whimsy, helped by a fine cast. (Dir: Delbert Mann, 102 mins.)

Five (1951)* James Anderson, Charles

Lampkin, William Phipps. Pretentious nonsense about the survivors of a nuclear holocaust. The pieties are deadlier than the fallout. Arch Oboler, a good man, wrote and directed, both badly. (93 mins.)

Five Against the House (1955)***½ Kim Novak, Guy Madison, Brian Keith. Engrossing drama about four college students and a glamorous night club singer who plan to hold up a large gambling casino in Reno, merely as an experiment. Good performance by Brian Keith as Brick. (Dir: Phil Karlson, 84 mins.)

Five Bloody Graves (1971)* Robert Dix, John Carradine. (Dir: Al Adamson, 88 mins.)

Five Bold Women (1959)*½ Jeff Morrow, Merry Anders, Irish McCalla. (Dir: Jorge Lopez-Portillo, 82 mins.)

Five Branded Women (1960)** Silvana Mangano, Van Heflin, Barbara Bel Geddes, Vera Miles. Five girls suffer the wrath of the people when they are found to be friendly to the Nazis, but redeem themselves in the Underground. Clumsy WW II drama set in Yugoslavia, never arouses complete sympathy for the characters. (Dir: Martin Ritt, 106 mins.)

Five Came Back (1939)*** Chester Morris, Wendy Barrie. Plane crashes in the jungle, and is able to take off with only five passengers. Suspenseful melodrama. Remade as *Back from Eternity* (1956). (Dir: John Farrow, 75 mins.)

Five Card Stud (1968)**½ Dean Martin, Robert Mitchum. Somebody's been eliminating the participants in a poker session that ended in violence. Dean Martin attempts the western whodunit. Obvious tale has people like Robert Mitchum, Inger Stevens, Roddy McDowall, and John Anderson around to help it over the bumpy spots, of which there are more than a few. (Dir: Henry Hathaway, 103 mins.)

Five Days from Home (1978)**½ George Peppard, Neville Brand, Sherry Boucher. OK drama, produced and directed by Peppard, casts him as an ex-lawman convicted of manslaughter for killing his wife's lover. With only six days left on his sentence, he breaks out of a Louisiana prison to see his critically injured son. Action-oriented script by William Moore. (109 mins.)

Five Easy Pieces (1970)**** Jack Nicholson, Karen Black, Susan Anspach, Fannie Flagg. An impressive, beautifully observed film about a dropout from middle-class America (Nicholson) who picks up work along the way on oil-rigs when his life isn't spent in a squalid succession of bars, motels, and other points along the way in northwest America. Inspired in some ways by "Easy Rider," Nicholson gives a bravura performance....He's in virtually every scene. This is one of the best-acted American films in years. Karen Black playing Nicholson's waitress-girl friend is gauche, vulnerable, and altogether winning. Miss Anspach is equally fine playing the sym-

pathetic, cultivated fiancee of Nicholson's brother. And Helena Kallianiotes is devastating in one scene as a butch hitchhiker complaining about the air and moral pollution of America. Perceptive screenplay by Adrien Joyce. Outstanding direction from Bob Rafelson. The title incidentally refers not to the five women Nicholson has affairs with along the way, but to five musical compositions played at his family's gracious home. (Dir: Bob Rafelson, 96 mins.)

Five Evenings (U.S.S.R., 1979)***½ Ludmila Gurchenko, Stanislav Lubshin. In director Nikita Mikhalkov's impressive film, a middle-aged man on vacation in Moscow revisits the house in which he lived some 17 years before and spends five days with the love of his youth. He's become a bitter, guarded, posturing sort of man, successful within the Soviet system but morally undermined by it. She's been chewed by the system, too, but has remained with her integrity intact—she's too marginal to be destroyed. Much of the film is technically shoddy, but the cumulative power of the couple's renewed relationship is extraordinary. One of the few Soviet films that is reasonably honest about the nature of Soviet life. (120 mins.)

Five Finger Exercise (1962)** Rosalind Russell, Jack Hawkins, Maximilian Schell. Another domineering woman role for Russell, in a sluggish drama about a silly demanding wife who nearly wrecks her family's existence. Based on a Broadway play, which was far better, film emerges as talky, unconvincing. (Dir: Daniel Mann, 109 mins.)

Five Fingers (Operation Cicero) (1952)**** James Mason, Danielle Darrieux. A superb film in the class of "39 Steps" and "Saboteur." One of the most daring espionage agents' deeds is shown with an almost documentary reality. James Mason excels in a fine cast. Suspenseful and engrossing all the way. Don't miss. (Dir: Joseph L. Mankiewicz, 108 mins.)

Five Gates to Hell (1959)* Neville Brand, Patricia Owens, Dolores Michaels. (Dir: James Clavell, 98 mins.)

Five Golden Dragons (Great Britain, 1967)* Bob Cummings, Rupert Davies. (Dir: Jeremy Summers, 70 mins.)

Five Golden Hours (Great Britain, 1961)**½ Ernie Kovacs, Cyd Charisse, George Sanders. Professional "mourner" who consoles widows and is not above a bit of crookery, teams with a beautiful baroness in a swindling scheme, which backfires. Attempt at offbeat comedy misses for the most part; a few humorous scenes offset by unsteady treatment. (Dir: Mario Zampi, 90 mins.)

Five Graves to Cairo (1943)***½ Franchot Tone, Anne Baxter, Erich Von Stroheim, Akin Tamiroff. Fortunio Bonanova, Peter van Eyck. Billy Wilder's wartime melodrama is a complex, intelligent transversal of themes that are usually rife with cliché. It's about the Rommel campaign in North Africa. Erich von Stroheim makes a memorable Field Marshal, drawn more from *Grand Illusion* than history, though the remainder of the cast performs incisively. A model of a well-constructed screenplay, superbly photographed by John Seitz. (Dir: Billy Wilder, 96 mins.)

500-Pound Jerk, The (MTV 1973)** James Franciscus, Alex Karras. Perhaps the only way the U.S. can win an Olympic gold medal in heavyweight weightlifting is to make a light comedy like this on the subject. Starts out in terribly hokey fashion with a hillbilly being groomed as an Olympic hopeful, but picks up steam when the scene shifts to Munich and Olympic action blends into the story. The Olympics footage is worth catching, and old Detroit Lions tackle Karras slowly turns into an ingratiating strong man, after a rocky beginning. (Dir: William Kronick, 73 mins.)

Five Man Army, The (Italy, 1969)*½ Peter Graves, James Daly. (Dir: Don Taylor, 105 mins.)

Five Miles to Midnight (U.S.A.-France-Italy, 1962)** Sophia Loren, Anthony Perkins, Gig Young. Young scoundrel survives a plane crash and goes into hiding, forcing his wife to carry out his plan to collect from the insurance company. Even Loren's looks and the Parisian locale can't save this one. (Dir: Anatole Litvak, 110 mins.)

Five Million Years to Earth (Great Britain, 1967)*** James Donald, Andrew Keir, Barbara Shelley. Are creatures from outer space menacing modern London? The old sci-fi question is suspensefully examined in a good one for the buffs. (Dir: Raymond Baker, 98 mins.)

Five of Me, The (MTV 1981)***½ David Birney, Dee Wallace, Mitchell Ryan. Fascinating multiple-personality story, a relatively rare male case history. Handsome David Birney plays the split personality victim with considerable skill, a Korean War veteran who may turn into a sadistic animal or a child in the blink of an eye. The beginning is a bit disjointed, but the drama builds intensity because the victim is always changing, gentle and loving one second, beating up his bride the next. Psychiatric therapy comes near the end, a painful ordeal revealing the cause, scenes Birney pulls off without going overboard. (Dir: Paul Wendkos, 104 mins.)

Five Pennies, The (1959)*** Danny Kaye, Barbara Bel Geddes, Tuesday Weld. The music's the thing here—pleasant biography of jazzman Red Nichols, a good change of pace for Kaye. But the sound track glistens with solos by Nichols himself, Bob Crosby, and notably Louis Armstrong. A treat for the jazz buffs, entertaining for others. (Dir: Melville Shavelson, 117 mins.)

Five Scouts (Japan, 1939)*** This anecdotal film directed by Tomotaka Tasaka is about five Japanese soldiers on a patrol in Manchuria in '37. The portrayal of army life and combat is notably realistic, and humanism, though mixed with an implicit strain of militarism, took a lot of courage at the time. Retains a certain intensity despite the arty mise-en-scène.

Five Thousand Fingers of Dr. T., The (1953)**½ Hans Conried, Tommy Rettig, Mary Healy, Peter Lind Hayes. A curious film fantasy about a boy who hates piano lessons and dreams about the tortures inflicted by his teacher. The picture is odd enough to have attracted some adherents, but seems mostly lame and literal. Some of the dream sequences break out with eccentric outrageousness. Rudolph Sternad, art director, is the true star. (Dir: Roy Rowland, 89 mins.)

$5.20 an Hour Dream, The (MTV 1980)*** Linda Lavin, Richard Jaeckel, Nicholas Pryor. Takes a serious look at a divorced woman who fights the system in order to get a top-paying job usually given to men on an assembly line. The scenes in the engine factory are authentic and bleak. Ms. Lavin is appealing in her strength and vulnerability as she tries to do the best she can for herself and her 12-year-old daughter. (Dir: Russ Mayberry, 104 mins.)

Five Weeks in a Balloon (1962)** Red Buttons, Fabian, Barbara Eden, Cedric Hardwicke, Peter Lorre. Lightweight, heavy-handed adaptation of an early Jules Verne novel; a balloon-propelled gondola is dispatched by the British government to lay claim to some East African territory. Meant to parody balloon adventures, but is itself a series of well-worn clichés. (Dir: Irwin Allen, 101 mins.)

Fixed Bayonets (1951)**½ Richard Basehart, Gene Evans, Richard Hylton. Interesting and often graphic account of a group of American soldiers in Korea during the hard winter of 1951. Many scenes have a documentary flavor and Basehart is very good as a Cpl. who has a chance to be a hero. (Dir: Samuel Fuller, 92 mins.)

Fixer, The (1968)**** Alan Bates, Dirk Bogarde, Georgia Brown. A deeply moving drama about anti-Semitism in tsarist Russia around 1911, based on Bernard Malamud's Pulitzer Prize-winning novel. As directed by John Frankenheimer, this is one of the better novel-to-screen adaptations of recent years. Based on a true story of a Russian Jewish peasant (Bates) who was wrongly imprisoned for a most unlikely crime—the "ritual murder" of a Gentile child in Kiev. Much of the film, detailing the protagonist's life in prison, is unrelenting, but it pays off as we see the peasant-handyman gain in dignity as the efforts to humiliate him and make him confess fail. Bates is impressive in the title role, and Bogarde is exceptionally good playing a sympathetic tsarist defense attorney. Screenplay by Dalton Trumbo. Photographed on location in rural Hungary. (132 mins.)

Flame, The (1947)*** John Carroll, Vera Ralston, Broderick Crawford. Penniless playboy hits upon an elaborate plan of getting rid of his brother so he will inherit a fortune. Capable melodrama keeps the interest. (Dir: John H. Auer, 97 mins.)

Flame and the Arrow, The (1950)*** Burt Lancaster, Virginia Mayo, Robert Douglas, Aline MacMahon, Nick Cravat. A genuine sleeper—a rousing acrobatic adventure story with a subtle visual style. It seems to me every bit as satisfying on the matinee level as the later *Crimson Pirate*, with the added dividend of Tourneur's harmonious visual patterning and thematic density. Waldo Salt wrote the screenplay, and some of the Robin Hood revolutionary stuff has what you might call consciousness 'about it. Recommended. (Dir: Jacques Tourneur, 88 mins.)

Flame and the Flesh, The (1954)** Lana Turner, Pier Angeli, Carlos Thompson. A corny, over-done tale of an unfortunate woman whose luck has just about run out. Filmed in Europe, the background is about the best thing in the film. Lana Turner is sorely miscast and is almost unrecognizable under a black wig. (Dir: Richard Thorpe, 104 mins.)

Flame Barrier, The (1958)** Arthur Franz, Kathleen Crowley. Scientist disappears in the Yucatan jungles while searching for a lost satellite, so his wife hires two adventurers to locate him. Passable science-fiction, some suspenseful moments. (Dir: Paul Landres, 70 mins.)

Flame in the Streets (Great Britain, 1961)** John Mills, Sylvia Syms, Johnny Sekka. Sober drama of racial conflict in Britain. A white girl announces her plans to marry a black West Indian. Presents a real problem honestly. Well-acted, but the direction is uninteresting. (Dir: Roy Ward Baker, 93 mins.)

Flame is Love, The (MTV 1979)**½ Linda Purl, Shane Briant, Timothy Dalton. Barbara Cartland's romantic novels, set in the turn-of-the-century splendor of the titled and wealthy, are strictly for those who want to read about idealized love. This film adaptation, about the adventures of a young American heiress who travels to Europe for a trousseau but ends up experiencing more than she bargained for, won't disappoint her legions of readers. (Dir: Michael O'Herlihy, 104 mins.)

Flame of Araby (1952)*½ Maureen O'Hara, Jeff Chandler. (Dir: Charles Lamont, 77 mins.)

Flame of Calcutta (1953)* Denise Darcel, Patric Knowles. (Dir: Seymour Friedman, 70 mins.)

Flame of New Orleans, The (1941)*** Marlene Dietrich, Bruce Cabot. Glamorous doll chooses wealthy suitor rather than the adventurous rogue she loves. Romantic tale is not among Dietrich's best but it's still Dietrich. (Dir: Rene Clair, 78 mins.)

Flame of Barbary Coast (1945)**½ John Wayne, Ann Dvorak, Joseph Schildkraut. Montana cattleman falls for a San Francisco saloon singer and opens his own gambling hall. Standard period melodrama, not much action but holds the interest fairly well. (Dir: Joseph Kane, 91 mins.)

Flame of the Islands (1955)**½ Yvonne DeCarlo, Howard Duff, Zachary Scott, James Arness. Many men fight for the love of a beautiful but dangerous night club singer. Overly involved but interesting melodrama; good Bahama locations. (Dir: Edward Ludwig, 90 mins.)

Flame Over India (Great Britain, 1959)***½ Kenneth More, Lauren Bacall, Herbert Lom. Exciting adventure melodrama about a soldier assigned to rescue a Hindu prince and his American governess when rebellion breaks out. Practically the entire film is one big, rousing chase aboard a train, with action aplenty. Superior escapist fare. (Dir: J. Lee Thompson, 130 mins.)

Flaming Frontier (Germany-Yugoslavia, 1965)*½ Stewart Granger, Pierre Brice, Larry Pennell, Leticia Roman, Mario Girotti. (Dir: Alfred Vohrer, 93 mins.)

Flaming Fury (1949)**½ Roy Roberts, George Cooper. Head of the Arson Bureau looks into a mysterious series of fires, uncovers dirty work. Neat little melodrama, speedy and well made. (Dir: George Blair, 60 mins.)

Flaming Star (1960)*** Elvis Presley, Steve Forrest, Barbara Eden, Dolores Del Rio, John McIntire. Grim, well-done outdoor drama gives Presley a good role, and he makes the most of it. He's a part-Kiowa lad who tries to put a halt to bloodshed between Indians and settlers. Script makes some cogent points concerning peace among men, and the direction and performances are better than you might expect. (Dir: Don Siegel, 101 mins.)

Flamingo Road (1949)** Joan Crawford, David Brian, Sidney Greenstreet, Zachary Scott, Gladys George. Classic Crawford vehicle about a carny dancer, ditched in a small town, who takes an interest in civics. Photographed by Ted McCord, music by Max Steiner, adapted by Robert Wilder from his and Sally Wilder's play. This is the film that tipped Crawford's career from the melodramatic into the lurid. (Dir: Michael Curtiz, 94 mins.)

Flamingo Road (MTV 1980)*½ Kevin McCarthy, Barbara Rush, Morgan Fairchild, Woody Brown, Howard Duff, Mark Harmon. A pilot on a rich Florida family from Lorimar, producers of *Dallas* and *Knots Landing* for CBS. The formula is down pat—aristocrats act like commoners to get their way in business and in romance. Experienced Kevin McCarthy, Barbara Rush, and young 'uns Morgan Fairchild and Woody Brown comprise the top drawer Weldon family. Howard Duff is the local sheriff, and clean-cut Mark Harmon, the law school graduate about to marry into the family. (Dir: Gus Trikonis, 104 mins.)

Flap (1970)½ Anthony Quinn, Shelley Winters, Tony Bill. (Dir: Carol Reed, 106 mins.)

Flareup (1969)* Raquel Welch, James Stacy. (Dir: James Neilson, 100 mins.)

Flash and the Firecat (1978)½ Roger Davis, Dub Taylor, Joan Shawlee, Richard Kiel, Tricia Sembera. (Dirs: Ferd and Beverly Sebastian, 84 mins.)

Flash Gordon (1980)*** Sam Jones, Max von Sydow, Melody Anderson, Topol, Ornella Muti, Timothy Dalton, Brian Blessed, Peter Wyngarde. A delightful romp, light-years ahead of the tiresome '30s sci-fi serial. Director Mike Hodges and screenwriter Lorenzo Semple, Jr., keep a straight face only intermittently as they try to keep the scripts up in the air. They succeed through a blend of sophistication and unabashedness. The film hasn't the emotional depth of "Star Wars" or the cosmopolitan air of "Superman," but it's consistently engaging. The acting is quite good except for Jones as Flash. Danilo Donati's production design and costumes are delicious, always a shade of awful with a wink in the background. Music by the very popular rock band, Queen. (110 mins.)

Flatbed Annie & Sweetiepie: Lady Truckers (MTV 1979)**½ Annie Potts, Kim Darby, Harry Dean Stanton, Arthur Godfrey. Darby and newcomer Potts make an ingratiating pair of big-rig drivers. Potts is excellent as she teaches neophyte Sweetiepie (Darby) the tricks of the road. Godfrey is helpful as a sympathetic uncle. (Dir: Robert Greenwald, 104 mins.)

Flea in Her Ear, A (U.S.-France, 1968)** Rex Harrison, Rosemary Harris, Louis Jourdan, Rachel Roberts, John Williams. Flatfooted French farce, with the philandering spouse (Rex Harrison), the vengeful wife (Rosemary Harris), numerous misunderstandings, much running around. Superb cast wasted. Dir: Jacques Charon, 94 mins.)

Fleet's In, The (1942)**½ Dorothy Lamour, William Holden, Betty Hutton. Some good specialty numbers and lively direction make this silly film passable entertainment. Story concerns the "lover" of the Navy's attempts to score with a virtuous gal. (Dir: Victor Schertzinger, 93 mins.)

Flesh (1969)** Joe Dallesandro, Geraldine Smith, Barry Brown, Candy Darling, Jackie Curtis. The first film credited to director Paul Morrissey ("Trash," "Heat"), this features a lot of wandering about the streets of New York by a desultory male hustler. Funny in a deadpan way. (105 mins.)

Flesh and Blood (Great Britain, 1949)** Richard Todd, Glynis Johns. Love, death and medicine in the generations of a turbulent family. Hard to follow, but interesting drama. (Dir: Anthony Kimmins, 102 mins.)

Flesh and Blood (MTV 1979)*** Suzanne Pleshette, Tom Berenger, Mitchell Ryan, Kristin Griffith. Pete Hamill's best-seller about Bobby Fallon, a street-wise punk who rises to become a heavyweight contender, has turned into an even better film. Berenger electrifying as Bobby, the brawling, troubled, yet appealing young man who enters into a short-lived alliance with his still attractive young mother, perfectly realized by Pleshette. (Dir: Jud Taylor, 104 mins.)

Flesh and Fantasy (1943)***½ Charles Boyer, Edward G. Robinson, Barbara Stanwyck. Three exciting and mysterious tales all well acted and gripping. The one starring Robinson as a man told by a fortune teller that his palm says "Murder" is the best but they're all quite good. (Dir: Julien Duvivier, 93 mins.)

Flesh and Flame—See: **Night of the Quarter Moon**

Flesh and Fury (1952)**½ Tony Curtis, Jan Sterling, Mona Freeman. Tony Curtis shows the first signs of acting talent in this prize fighting yarn. He plays a deaf mute who stumbles into the boxing game and winds up a champion. The Misses Sterling and Freeman play the women in his life. (Dir: Joseph Pevney, 82 mins.)

Flesh and the Devil (1926)**½ Greta Garbo, John Gilbert, Lars Hanson. A melodrama of frustrated desire played out in an endless succession of sumptuously curtained boudoirs. The film established Garbo as the silent era's most alluring enigma, but like so many Garbo films, this Clarence Brown-directed effort is mediocre. Turgid and stiff, it finds the magic only occasionally. (109 mins.)

Flesh and the Fiends (Great Britain, 1960)*** Peter Cushing, Donald Pleasence, George Rose. Dastardly grave robbers supply bodies for medical experiments in old Scotland. Horror thriller has some fine performances, should satisfy the fans—too gruesome for the timid! Alternate title: **Mania.** (Dir: John Gilling, 87 mins.)

Flesh and the Woman (Italy, 1958)** Gina Lollobrigida. "Lollo" is cast as a "lady of easy virtue" once again in this mild story of Foreign Legionnaires and their loves. (Dir: Robert Siodmak, 102 mins.)

Flight from Ashiya (1964)** Yul Brynner, Richard Widmark, George Chakiris, Suzy Parker, Shirley Knight. With the Air Rescue Service, looking for survivors and recalling their pasts. Airborne soap opera. Sags. (Dir: Michael Anderson, 100 mins.)

Flight from Destiny (1941)*** Thomas Mitchell, Geraldine Fitzgerald. An offbeat story of a man with only six months to live. Thomas Mitchell's superb acting gives this story a tremendous wallop if you're willing to accept his actions. (Dir: Vincent Sherman, 73 mins.)

Flight from Singapore (Great Britain, 1962)* Patrick Allen, Patrick Holt, Jane Rodgers. (Dir: Dudley Birch, 74 mins.)

Flight from Treason (Great Britain, 1960)**

John Gregson, Robert Brown. Man is blackmailed by spies into stealing atomic plans, fights treason charges. Fair spy melodrama. (60 mins.)

Flight from Vienna (Great Britain, 1956)*½ John Bentley, Theodore Bikel. (Dir: Denis Kavanagh, 58 mins.)

Flight Nurse (1953)** Joan Leslie, Forrest Tucker. Two pilots both love the same nurse, and if this sounds familiar don't blame us. (Dir: Allan Dwan, 90 mins.)

Flight of the Doves (Great Britain, 1971)*** Ron Moody, Jack Wild, Dorothy McGuire, Stanley Holloway. Fun film for the kids as Moody has a virtuoso role playing a detective of many disguises trying to track down two young orphans who have been given a large inheritance. Good Irish scenery, but the plot is slowed by some sentimental songs. (Dir: Ralph Nelson, 105 mins.)

Flight of the Lost Balloon, The (1961)*½ Marshall Thompson, Mala Powers. (Dir: Nathan Juran, 91 mins.)

Flight of the Phoenix, The (1965)***½ James Stewart, Richard Attenborough, Peter Finch, Hardy Kruger. An exciting old-fashioned adventure about a group of plane crash survivors who fight the desert and other awesome odds in order to rebuild their plane and save themselves. The characters are mostly stereotyped, but an excellent cast overcomes the shortcomings of the script. Director Robert Aldrich stages a fantastic finale which generates edge-of-the-seat suspense. (Dir: Robert Aldrich, 147 mins.)

Flight to Hong Kong (1956)** Rory Calhoun, Barbara Rush, Dolores Donlon. Hollywood once more uses Hong Kong as the background for adventure. This tale of intrigue is no more nor less successful than any of its predecessors. Two attractive girls, the Misses Rush and Donlon, are very pleasing to the eyes. (Dir: Joseph Newman, 88 mins.)

Flight to Holocaust (MTV 1977)*½ Patrick Wayne, Chris Mitchum, Desi Arnaz, Jr. (Dir: Bernard Kowalski, 106 mins.)

Flim Flam Man, The (1967)**½ George C. Scott, Michael Sarrazin, Sue Lyon, Harry Morgan, Jack Albertson. A robust ingratiating performance by George C. Scott as a rural con artist makes this picture seem better than it really is. Scott, made up to look old, obviously enjoys himself as he winks, chortles and exudes charm and rascality. Tale about the adventures of a con man and his protégé, a young Army deserter, winningly played by Michael Sarrazin. There is a terrific automobile chase scene that should be noted by those who cherish this kind of cinema hijinks. (Dir: Irvin Kershner, 104 mins.)

Flipper (1963)**½ Chuck Connors, Luke Halpin, Flipper. Youthful fans of the TV series will get a bang out of this film on which it was based. As everybody knows, Flipper is the remarkable dolphin whose relationship with young Luke blossoms

into a real friendship when he saves the wounded dolphin's life. (Dir: James Clark, 90 mins.)

Flipper's New Adventure (1964)**½ Luke Halpin, Flipper, Pamela Franklin. Second "Flipper" feature is again nice kiddie fare, as boy and dolphin head out to sea rather than be separated. They wind up combating extortionists on a deserted isle to help out a marooned mother and daughters. Tale isn't water-tight, but Flipper is gurglingly delightful. (Dir: Leon Benson, 92 mins.)

Flirtation Walk (1934)**½ Ruby Keeler, Dick Powell, Pat O'Brien. Dick goes to West Point for this one and it is fair entertainment. A little bit too long, it still comes out an interesting West Point story with some pleasant music for diversion. (Dir: Frank Borzage, 97 mins.)

Flood! (MTV 1976)**½ Robrt Culp, Richard Basehart, Teresa Wright. Irwin Allen, the producer who brought movie audiences big-budgeted disaster films such as "Poseidon Adventure" and "Towering Inferno," turns his attention to the small screen with a yarn about a collapsing dam which destroys a small town. The vignettes which show people in peril as the flood rises range from predictable to well done. (Dir: Earl Bellamy, 106 mins.)

Flood Tide (1958)** George Nader, Cornell Borchers. Man tries to convince authorities that a crippled youngster whose testimony has convicted a man of murder is a habitual liar. Undistinguished melodrama. (Dir: Abner Biberman, 82 mins.)

Floods of Fear (Great Britain, 1958)**½ Howard Keel, Anne Heywood. Wrongly convicted of murder, a man escapes during a flood and proves his innocence. Frequently exciting melodrama—an English film located in the U.S., and atmospherically well done. (Dir: Charles Crichton, 82 mins.)

Floor Show (1978)*** Director Richard Myers teaches cinematography at Kent State. This film is autobiographical, with dream images that are interwoven with excerpts from Hollywood films. (85 mins.)

Flower Drum Song (1961)*** Nancy Kwan, James Shigeta, Miyoshi Umeki. The Rodgers & Hammerstein musical play about a Chinese picture-bride in San Francisco falling for another is colorfully decked out on film, with some capable players and good song numbers. It runs too long and may pall before it's over, but all in all it's worthwhile. (Dir: Henry Koster, 133 mins.)

Flowers of St. Francis, The (Italy, 1950)**** The monks of Nocere Inferiori Monastery, Aldo Fabrizi. Director Roberto Rossellini's buoyant masterpiece, showing Franciscan monks at Assisi. A great film, all the more impressive for being apparently effortless. (75 mins.)

Fluffy (1965)** Tony Randall, Shirley Jones. Professor gets into a lot of trouble when he escorts a tame lion around. Mild

227

comedy on the silly side; the lion gets most of the laughs. (Dir: Earl Bellamy, 92 mins.)

Flute and the Arrow, The (Sweden, 1958)**½ Ginju, Riga, Chendru. Director Arne Sucksdorff's documentary cum fiction portrays the primitive rites of the Muria tribe in India, based on their belief in pantheistic gods, guardians, and evil demons in dangerous animals. The villagers fight against a leopard and sacrifice Ginju's life to appease the gods and drive away the animal. The camerawork is lovely, but Sucksdorff fails to create believable characters. Instead, the animals make the strongest impression. (78 mins.)

Fly, The (1958)**½ Vincent Price, Herbert Marshall, Al Hedison. Slightly above average fifties' science fiction, enlivened by a nearly literate script by James Clavell ("Shogun"). Al Hedison (before he changed his name to David and became a TV star) is a scientist who, while meddling with a strange theory of molecular exchange, accidentally trades heads with a fly. (Dir: Kurt Neumann, 94 mins.)

Fly by Night (1942)**½ Nancy Kelly, Richard Carlson. Slick little Grade "B" spy story about an interne who becomes involved in espionage. (Dir: Robert Siodmak, 74 mins.)

Flying Deuces, The (1939)*** Stan Laurel, Oliver Hardy, Reginald Gardiner, Jean Parker. Laurel and Hardy join the Foreign Legion, sing and dance "Shine On, Harvest Moon," and Ollie ends up reincarnated as a mule. Conventional wisdom incorrectly says the comedians had gone downhill by '39. (Dir: A. Edward Sutherland, 65 mins.)

Flying Down to Rio (1933)*** Dolores Del Rio, Gene Raymond, Fred Astaire, Ginger Rogers. Audiences in 1933 were paying to see Del Rio and Raymond; as a bonus they got the first screen teaming of Astaire and Rogers—not enough of them for audiences today. The nifty, interminable "Carioca" number is too much of a good thing. (Dir: Thornton Freeland, 89 mins.)

Flying Irishman (1939)*** Doug Corrigan, Paul Kelly. Story of "Wrong Way" Corrigan, who made a spectacular flight—in reverse. Entertaining, amusing comedy-drama. (Dir: Leigh Jason, 72 mins.)

Flying Leathernecks (1951)** John Wayne, Robert Ryan. Strict Marine officer is disliked by his squadron, but in wartime all is forgotten. Badly written, slow war drama; some good actual battle scenes. (Dir: Nicholas Ray, 102 mins.)

Flying Missile, The (1951)** Glenn Ford, Viveca Lindfors. Grim and superficial drama about guided missiles and the men who build and test them. Cliché script prevents actors from doing anything with their roles. (Dir: Henry Levin, 93 mins.)

Flying Saucer (Italy, 1964)** Alberto Sordi, Monica Vitti, Silvana Mangano. An account of what happens when an inva-sion from Mars is threatened. Science-fiction opus is a field day for Sordi, playing four separate roles; but the fun is relatively sparse. Dubbed in English. (Dir: Tinto Brass, 95 mins.)

Flying Tigers (1942)***½ John Wayne, John Carroll, Anna Lee. Squadron leader and his reckless buddy vie for the affections of a pretty nurse while fighting the Japanese. Familiar but lively, well-produced war melodrama; fine special effects. (Dir: David Miller, 102 mins.)

FM (1978)* Michael Brandon, Eileen Brennan, Martin Mull, Cassie Yates, Alex Karras, Cleavon Little. (Dir: John Alonzo, 110 mins.)

Fog, The (1980)**½ Adrienne Barbeau, Hal Holbrook, Janet Leigh, Jamie Lee Curtis, John Houseman. Though for most of its length a crackerjack ghost story, this tall tale confirms director John Carpenter's skill and talent, but no more. With a spooky scene-setter from a grizzled Houseman. (91 mins.)

Fog over Frisco (1934)**½ Donald Woods, Lyle Talbot, Robert Barrat, Margaret Lindsay, Bette Davis. Davis has a vivid role (briefly) as a murdered heiress; Lindsay plays her sister out to catch the killer. Barrat is outstanding. You wonder why director William Dieterle forsook sharp, dynamic work for his dull, dull, stuffy biopics. (68 mins.)

Folies Bergere (1935)**½ Maurice Chevalier, Ann Sothern, Merle Oberon, Eric Blore. The charming, talented Chevalier plays a tycoon who hires a double—a music hall entertainer—to impersonate him, only to find that his wife and his mistress don't quite appreciate the gag. The musical numbers, choreographed by Dave Gould, are spectacular, "Ann" Sothern has what may have been her best soubrette role, and Chevalier is, well, himself. (Dir: Roy Del Ruth, 84 mins.)

Folies Bergere (France, 1957)** Jeanmaire, Eddie Constantine. Ex-GI remains in Paris to seek a singing career, romances a gorgeous folies girl. American-style musical done the French way, not too well. Some nice numbers, otherwise tepid. English-dubbed. (Dir: Henri Decoin, 90 mins.)

Follow a Star (Great Britain, 1959)**½ Norman Wisdom, June Laverick. Cleaning store employee who wants a stage career is duped by a scheming popular singer into using his voice. Slapstick comedy has some amusing scenes, but Wisdom for non-British audiences is a matter of taste. (Dir: Robert Asher, 93 mins.)

Follow Me Quietly (1949)*** William Lundigan, Dorothy Patrick. Detective traps a psychopathic killer. Well made, exciting melodrama. (Dir: Richard Fleischer, 59 mins.)

Follow That Camel (Great Britain, 1967)** Phil Silvers, Kenneth William, Jim Dale. Fun in the Foreign Legion as Sergeant Phil Silvers is forced to aid a friend in a whacky plan. Vaudeville in the desert. (Dir: Gerald Thomas, 95 mins.)

Follow That Dream (1962)**½ Elvis Presley, Arthur O'Connell, Joanna Moore. Strictly for Presley fans! He sings, drawls and gets into plenty of trouble in this comedy about a group of hillbilly home-steaders who settle in a small Florida town which turns into a fairly thriving community. (Dir: Gordon Douglas, 110 mins.)

Follow the Boys (1944)*** George Raft, Vera Zorina, Guest Stars. A hoofer does his bit for the war effort by entertaining with the USO. Slender story is helped by many stars making brief appearances, best of which is a routine by W. C. Fields. (Dir: A. Edward Sutherland, 122 mins.)

Follow the Boys (1963)** Connie Francis, Paula Prentiss, Janis Paige, Russ Tamblyn. American girls at large on the French Riviera. All right if you're a big fan of Francis (not a bad actress, by the way). Otherwise, it's dull. (Dir: Richard Thorpe, 95 mins.)

Follow the Fleet (1936)**** Fred Astaire, Ginger Rogers, Lucille Ball, Randolph Scott, Harriet Hilliard. Song and dance man joins the Navy when his girl turns him down. Fine musical, Astaire and Rogers in top form, as are Berlin tunes. (Dir: Mark Sandrich, 110 mins.)

Follow the Sun (1951)**½ Glenn Ford, Anne Baxter, Dennis O'Keefe. The biog-raphy of golfer Ben Hogan, his ups and downs. Golf fans will vote it great—others, the usual sports saga. (Dir: Sidney Lanfield, 93 mins.)

Folly to Be Wise (Great Britain, 1953)***½ Alastair Sim, Roland Culver. The trials and tribulations of an Army chaplain make a delightfully witty comedy. (Dir: Frank Launder, 91 mins.)

Fool Killer, The (1965)**½ Anthony Perkins, Salome Jens, Dana Elcar, Edward Albert. Runaway boy teams with a tormented Civil War veteran who has lost his memory, and together they are involved in a mysterious murder. A try for a mood piece that becomes simply moody, this arty drama nevertheless has its moments. Good performances. (Dir: Servando Gonzalez, 103 mins.)

Fools (1970)* Jason Robards, Jr., Katharine Ross, Scott Hylands. (Dir: Tom Gries, 93 mins.)

Fools Parade (1971)**½ James Stewart, George Kennedy. Stewart is very good in this tale about a man who is released from prison after serving 40 years and has plans to open a business with the $25,000 he earned while behind bars. However, bad guy George Kennedy, who plays a guard at the prison, has other plans for the money. Anne Baxter also offers a colorful, brief appearance as a flashy madam. (Dir: Andrew McLaglen, 98 mins.)

Footlight Parade (1933)***½ James Cagney, Busby Berkeley, Joan Blondell,

Dick Powell, Ruby Keeler. Top Warner Bros. show-biz musical, with Cagney dynamic as an enterprising hustler and Busby Berkeley contributing some of his most engagingly bizarre production num-bers. Blondell, Powell, and Keeler ("Old Leadfoot") lend their usual strong support. A delight. (Dir: Lloyd Bacon, 100 mins.)

Footlight Serenade (1942)**½ John Payne, Betty Grable, Victor Mature. Routine backstage musical with uninspired score. TV's Phil Silvers is in there to hold up the comedy. (Dir: Gregory Ratoff, 80 mins.)

Footsteps (MTV 1972)**½ Richard Crenna, Joanna Pettet. Better-than-average foot-ball yarn with Crenna as the hero-villain, a skillful defense coach who cuts corners to win. Saddled with a shady past, Crenna's character aims for the big time, coldly using players, ladies, and friends to climb up the ladder. Action clips, well-staged practice sessions, and knowledge-able football talk blend with the charac-ter study, and Miss Pettet, Clu Gulager, Forrest Tucker, and Bill Overton back up Crenna. (Dir: Paul Wendkos, 73 mins.)

Footsteps in the Dark (1941)**½ Errol Flynn, Brenda Marshall. Occasionally amusing comedy-drama with Errol as a slick detective. One of the amusing scenes is contributed by William Frawley. (Dir: Lloyd Bacon, 96 mins.)

Footsteps in the Fog (British, 1955)** Stewart Granger, Jean Simmons. Medio-cre costume melodrama about an ambi-tious servant girl and her diabolical employer. Well played by the cast. (Dir: Arthur Lubin, 90 mins.)

Footsteps in the Night (1957)**½ Bill Elliott, Don Haggerty, Douglas Dick. Policeman investigates a motel murder, saves an innocent man. Good low-budget mystery developed logically and in-terestingly. (Dir: Jean Yarbrough, 62 mins.)

For a Few Dollars More (Italy, 1967)* Clint Eastwood, Lee Van Cleef. (Dir: Sergio Leone, 131 mins.)

For Better, for Worse (1974)**½ Gene Hackman, Liv Ullmann, Susan Tyrrell, Eileen Heckart. This frontier story directed by Jan Troell about a California rancher (Hackman) and the mail-order bride (Ullmann) he overworks, abuses, and ever-so-gradually grows to love might have been a genuine American epic. But about 40 minutes have been cut out with a hatchet, leaving picture, though visually awesome, choppy and at times ridiculous. There is practically no exposition, and the characteristic Troell touches—the meticu-lous laying on of precise details, the stately pacing of the scenes between characters, the emotional shadings in the per-formances—are practically absent. A shame. (116 mins.)

For Heaven's Sake (1926)*** Harold Lloyd, Jobyna Ralston, Noah Young. Almost unknown Lloyd feature of considerable quality, as in the opening scenes, in which spoiled rich kid Harold demolishes two new flivvers in a matter of minutes. Later the film drags as Harold falls under the spell of a mission girl (Ralston) and reforms a gang of roughnecks, but Lloyd's comic skill, even when dealing with less than promising material, is impressive. (Dir: Sam Taylor, 62 mins.)

For Heaven's Sake (1950)**½ Clifton Webb, Joan Bennett, Robert Cummings, Joan Blondell, Edmund Gwenn, Gigi Perreau. Whimsical comedy about a couple of aging angels (Webb & Edmund Gwenn) who come to earth to save a marriage. They manage to create quite a fuss during their visit. Webb & Gwenn are a good team and the rest of the star-filled cast do their best. (Dir: George Seaton, 92 mins.)

For Love of Ivy (1968)**½ Sidney Poitier, Abbey Lincoln, Beau Bridges. A promising story idea conceived by Sidney Poitier—to place him in a romantic situation with a black girl and to show a young Negro woman with some pride and dignity—has gone astray, thanks to a well-meaning if muddled screenplay and some pedestrian direction. Story concerns a young domestic who decides to quit being a maid and go to secretarial school. Principal virtue of "Ivy" is the engaging performance of Abbey Lincoln in the title role. (Dir: Daniel Mann, 102 mins.)

For Love or Money (1963)**½ Kirk Douglas, Mitzi Gaynor, Gig Young, Thelma Ritter. Attorney is hired by a wealthy widow to act as matchmaker for her three gorgeous daughters and the men she has selected for their mates. Douglas tries comedy for a change of pace, which may be good for him, if not the audience. He gets by, and so does the film, in a routine sort of way. (Dir: Michael Gordon, 108 mins.)

For Me and My Gal (1942)*** Judy Garland, Gene Kelly, George Murphy. For his film debut, Kelly is a hoofer who's all heel, even unto mutilating himself to escape the draft (rough stuff in '42). Garland teams well with the newcomer; Busby Berkeley's direction is attentive and fluid; and if the script had taken Kelly a bit further the film might have been extraordinary instead of merely good. Songs include "Ballin' the Jack," "Oh, You Beautiful Doll," and "Smiles." (104 mins.)

For Men Only—See: Tall Lie, The

For Pete's Sake (1974)**½ Barbra Streisand, Michael Sarrazin, Estelle Parsons, Molly Picon. An uneven attempt at screwball comedy. Streisand is a young Brooklyn matron who manages to dress and live exquisitely, although her husband is making no money driving a cab. But never mind; she gets mixed up with the Mafia, goofs miserably as a call girl, and winds up in the middle of a rampaging herd of rustled cattle in downtown Brooklyn. Some good laughs along the way. (Dir: Peter Yates, 90 mins.)

For Singles Only (1968)* John Saxon, Mary Ann Mobley, Lana Wood. (Dir: Arthur Dreifuss, 91 mins.)

For the First Time (U.S.A.-West Germany-Italy, 1959)** Mario Lanza, Johanna von Koczian, Zsa Zsa Gabor. Opera star (Lanza) finds romance with a deaf girl (von Koczian). Mario sings plenty, and that's about it! Filmed in Europe. Lanza's last film. (Dir: Rudy Mate, 97 mins.)

For the Love of It (MTV 1980)**½ Deborah Raffin, Jeff Conaway, Adam West, Don Rickles, Eve Arden. If you like your comedies on the frantic side, you'll enjoy this wacky excursion which finds gorgeous model Raffin on the run after she accidentally acquires some Soviet plans. TV's Conaway of "Taxi" co-stars with Deborah and they make a handsome couple. (Dir: Hal Kanter, 104 mins.)

For the Love of Mary (1948)**½ Deanna Durbin, Edmond O'Brien, Don Taylor. Deanna Durbin is a switchboard operator at the White House and meets many men not solely involved with politics. Charming little comedy. (Dir: Frederick de Cordova, 90 mins.)

For Those Who Think Young (1964)* James Darren, Pamela Tiffin, Tina Louise. (Dir: Leslie Martinson, 96 mins.)

For Whom the Bell Tolls (1943)*** Gary Cooper, Ingrid Bergman, Akim Tamiroff, Katina Paxinou (Oscar winner), Vladimir Sokoloff. Turgid realization of the Hemingway novel, but noteworthy for depth in casting and performance. Cooper is again an admirable Hemingway hero; Bergman evokes both the dream and reality in the novel's conception. Color. (Dir: Sam Wood, 170 mins.)

Forbidden (1932)*** Barbara Stanwyck, Adolphe Menjou. Stanwyck is in love with newspaper editor Menjou; when she discovers he is married she opts to remain his mistress, and goes gray while Menjou rises to political prominence with her unacknowledged help. Menjou dies at the end, and Stanwyck walks out a door to nowhere. Director Frank Capra takes the edge off the tear-jerking with a playful, improvisatory style that works against the grain of the plot. (A few years later he would prove less prudent with his own sentimental stories than he had been with other people's.) (83 mins.)

Forbidden (1954)** Tony Curtis, Joanne Dru. Adventure set in Macao (where else?) where two old flames (Curtis and Dru) rekindle their passion only to have their love and lives threatened by big time racketeers. Good actors at the mercy of the gangsters and the script. (Dir: Rudolph Mate, 85 mins.)

Forbidden (Italy, 1955)** Mel Ferrer, Lea Massari. A young priest comes home to assume his new post as parish priest and gets involved with feudal hostilities. Second-rate Italian-made film. (Dir: Mario Monicelli, 90 mins.)

Forbidden Alliance—See: **Barretts of Wimpole Street, The** (1934).

Forbidden Cargo (Great Britain, 1954)*** Nigel Patrick, Elizabeth Sellars. Complaints send a private investigator to a coastal town, where he uncovers a smuggling racket. Well-done melodrama, at once amusing and suspenseful. (Dir: Harold French, 83 mins.)

Forbidden Fruit (France, 1958)**½ Fernandel, Francoise Arnoul. Fernandel is cast in a dramatic role as middle-aged married man who has an affair with a pretty young girl. He doesn't quite come off as a dramatic actor, you wait for him to do something funny. (Dir: Henri Verneuil, 97 mins.)

Forbidden Games (France, 1952)**** Brigitte Fossey, Georges Poujouly. Superb, poignant film about a poor family who take in a little girl whose parents are killed in an air raid. The youngest son and the little girl become great friends and learn to rely on one another for understanding. Many comic touches are supplied by the noisy neighbors. This film contains one of the most shatteringly dramatic climaxes ever filmed. (Dir: René Clement, 87 mins.)

Forbidden Planet (1956)*** Walter Pidgeon, Anne Francis, Leslie Nielsen, Warren Stevens, Robby the Robot. An engaging science fiction gloss of Shakespeare's "The Tempest," with a ship full of American astronauts landing on a mysterious planet where Pidgeon and his miniskirted daughter (Francis) guard the remains of a lost civilization. It's great to look at, even as the s-f clichés fall fast and heavy, thanks to the MGM sumptuousness of the sets and fine animation and matte work by the Walt Disney Studios. (Dir: Fred M. Wilcox, 98 mins.)

Forbidden Street, The (1949)** Dana Andrews, Maureen O'Hara. Melodrama set in London slums with soap opera tendencies. Nice performance by Dame Sybil Thorndike as a crusty old witch. (Dir: Jean Negulesco, 91 mins.)

Forbin Project, The—See: **Colossus: The Forbin Project**

Force Five (MTV 1975)* Gerald Gordon, Nick Pryor, William Lucking. (Dir: Walter Grauman, 72 mins.)

Force of Arms (1951)**½ William Holden, Nancy Olson, Frank Lovejoy. An Army officer and a young WAC meet and fall in love in the midst of war (WW II). Very reminiscent of "A Farewell to Arms" but not as effective. Good performances by the stars. (Dir: Michael Curtiz, 100 mins.)

Force of Evil (1948)**** John Garfield, Beatrice Pearson, Thomas Gomez. Director-writer Abraham Polonsky's superior melodrama about the numbers racket. Poetic, terse, beautifully exact—film noir at its best. (78 mins.)

Force of One, A (1979)**½ Jennifer O'Neill, Chuck Norris, Clu Gulager, James Whitmore, Jr., Ron O'Neal. As in most martial arts pictures, nuances of mood and character continuity are absent from the script, but director Paul Aaron wrings enough charm out of the actors to make the movie watchable. Norris is rather inhibited for a karate star, but muddles through with a little help from the rest of the cast. For what it's worth, the plot involves a narcotics ring systematically wiping out undercover police, who ask Norris for a helping hand. (96 mins.)

Force 10 from Navarone (Great Britain, 1978)** Robert Shaw, Edward Fox, Harrison Ford, Franco Nero, Barbara Bach. Sequel-of-sorts to the excellent "The Guns of Navarone," using a couple of Alistair MacLean characters to poor advantage. Carl Foreman, producer-writer of the first screenplay, did the story of a group of WW II commandos who must destroy a bridge in Yugoslavia that is vital to the Germans. Shaw, who died after the film, looks haggard, and the action and miniature work are secondrate. (Dir: Guy Hamilton, 118 mins.)

Foreign Affair, A (1948)***½ Marlene Dietrich, Jean Arthur, John Lund. Director Billy Wilder's satire on post-WW II American puritanism vis-à-vis the defeated Germans is deft, delightful, and less nasty than its reputation. Stars Arthur as an Iowa congresswoman on a junket to wicked Berlin, Lund as the officer who tries to cope with her moralizing, and Dietrich as an ex-Nazi chanteuse. (116 mins.)

Foreign Correspondent (1940)**** Joel McCrea, Laraine Day, Herbert Marshall, George Sanders, Albert Basserman. Much like an Alfred Hitchcock's British film of the '30s, gussied up with Hollywood gloss and rather the better for it. McCrea is an American reporter in pre-WW II London who gets involved with a Nazi spy ring and the kidnapping of a European political figure (Basserman). It's worth noting that director Hitchcock was one of the pioneers of the disaster film. The plane crash here is a honey. (119 mins.)

Foreign Exchange (1970)** Robert Horton, Sebastian Cabot, Jill St. John. One of two made-for-TV features starring Robert Horton as former British agent John Smith, adventurer and fatalist. Horton is customarily expressionless as the put-upon ex-agent who gets involved in a prisoner-exchange plot which backfires. (Dir: Roy Baker, 72 mins.)

Foreign Intrigue (1956)*** Robert Mitchum and Genevieve Page. Overlong but sometimes exciting melodrama written and directed by Sheldon Reynolds who created the TV series. Press agent finds plenty of surprises when he checks into the past of his deceased employer. Filmed in Europe. (Dir: Sheldon Reynolds, 100 mins.)

Foreigner, The (1978)**½ Debbie Harry, Patti Astor, The Erasers, The Cramps. A punk feature that combines elements of

231

Hitchcock, Warhol, Godard, and *film noir* in a Blank Generation nightmare. As the Chicago Reader's B. Ruby Rich put it: ".... really two films in uneasy combination. On the one hand, it is a conspiracy nightmare modeled on the classic filmmaking of the 30s-40s-50s *auteurs;* perhaps it is modeled more specifically on the fashionable European remakes and homages to these originals. Its cinematic influences ride the surface like flashy tattoos.... On the other hand, though, [it] is an old-fashioned underground home movie of the New York avant-garde scene, at least that corner of it currently courting punk. Many of the stars are themselves artists or art-world denizens, knowledgeable in the art of parlaying a fine black-leather body suit into an effective cameo role." With music by Ivan Kral.

Foreman Went to France, The (Great Britain, 1942)***½ Tommy Trinder, Clifford Evans, Constance Cummings, Robert Morley. A factory foreman is trapped in France by the onrush of the Nazis, joins with two Tommies and a girl to escape across the channel. One of the best of its kind, a fast, thrilling "chase" melodrama. Recommended. (Dir: Charles Frend, 88 mins.)

Forest Rangers, The (1942)**½ Fred MacMurray, Susan Hayward, Paulette Goddard. When a forest ranger marries a socialite, his former girl tries to show her up. Mildly pleasant comedy-drama, but the cast is better than the material. (Dir: George Marshall, 87 mins.)

Forever (1978)** Stephanie Zimbalist, Dean Butler. The best thing about this bittersweet teenage love story is the performance of the lovely, talented Zimbalist. But even so worthy a director as John Korty can't avoid the tedium that comes from watching a pair of handsome youngsters kiss and smile, kiss and smile, for what seems like forever. (104 mins.)

Forever Amber (1947)**½ Linda Darnell, Cornell Wilde, George Sanders, Richard Greene, Jessica Tandy. As entertainment it's flashy, splashy, and silly, if that's enough. Peggy Cummins was fired after shooting began, and Darnell was rushed in to fill the title role of the lively wench who sacrifices love and honor to get ahead at the court of Charles II (Sanders). Good color from cinematographer Leon Shamroy and well-staged action by director Otto Preminger (more miscast than the heroine) help the time pass pleasantly. Screenplay by Philip Dunne and Ring Lardner, Jr. (138 mins.)

Forever and a Day (1943)**** Ida Lupino, Charles Laughton, Merle Oberon, Brian Aherne, Ray Milland, all-star cast. The saga of a house in London, and of the generations who lived in it. Each sequence shows care, fine casting, direction, writing. (Dirs: René Clair, Edmund Goulding, Cedric Hardwicke, Frank Lloyd, Victor Saville, Robert Stevenson, Herbert Wilcox, 104 mins.)

Forever Darling (1956)** Lucille Ball, Desi Arnaz, James Mason. Silliness about a guardian angel who comes to earth to save a marriage, isn't worthy of the talents of the cast. For Lucy addicts primarily. (Dir: Alexander Hall, 96 mins.)

Forever My Love (Austria, 1955)** Romy Schneider, Karl Boehm. Three films compressed into one, recounting the life and love of Elizabeth of Bavaria (Schneider) and Franz Josef (Boehm). Like Viennese pastry, nice and sweet, but a lot of it makes you sick. (Dir: Ernst Marischka, 147 mins.)

Forever Young, Forever Free (1976)** Karen Valentine, José Ferrer. Filmed on location in Africa; the photography is the chief inducement to watch this sentimental story about a white orphan boy and his African herdboy pal. Valentine plays a meddling, well-meaning Peace Corps worker, but it's the two boys, Norman Knox as the orphan and Muntu Ndebele as the African lad, who give the film some life. (Dir: Ashley Lazarus, 78 mins.)

Forgiven Sinner, The (France, 1962)***½ Jean-Paul Belmondo, Emmanuele Riva. Disillusioned, bitter war widow is helped by the understanding of a kindly priest during World War II. Meticulously detailed, well-acted drama, sober and thoughtful. Slow pace may bother some, but the film is well worthwhile. Dubbed in English. (Dir: Jean-Pierre Melville, 101 mins.)

Formula, The (1980)**½ Marlon Brando, George C. Scott, Marthe Keller, Beatrice Straight, John Gielgud, G. D. Spradlin. And formula is what it is—an elaborate production with terrific locations, and high-caliber stars. All to hide a story that is a simplistic piece of dramaturgy propelled by pompous talk instead of narrative drive. Director John G. Avildsen comes up with some strong pictorial effects to mask the incessant gab and no action of producer Steve Shagan's screenplay about the supression of a formula for extremely cheap oil. (117 mins.)

Forsaking All Others (1934)**½ Joan Crawford, Clark Gable, Robert Montgomery, Charles Butterworth, Billie Burke, Rosalind Russell, Frances Drake. This M-G-M comedy-drama got mediocre reviews when it came out and has no special reputation to speak of, but some film buffs I know have been recommending it to me over the years, and it might be worth checking out. Joan Crawford finds Clark Gable slightly dull as a companion (plausibility problems right there), and she almost goes off with Robert Montgomery. W.S. Van Kyke directed, and he could be very good, or very sloppy, or both, in this period. Other points of interest include a screenplay by Joseph L. Mankiewicz and photography by Gregg

Toland and George Folsey. (Dir: W.S. Van Kyke, 84 mins.)

Fort Apache (1948)***½ John Wayne, Henry Fonda, Shirley Temple, Pedro Armendariz, Ward Bond. A martinet commander (modeled on General Custer) leads his command to defeat by Indians. Fonda plays the megalomaniac, with Wayne, beginning to mature as an actor, an effective counterweight as a pragmatic officer. The implication that Fonda dies a hero regardless of his folly is hard to accept. There is no more piercing moment in director John Ford's films than when Anna Lee, straining to see the troops on the way to a massacre, shouts, "All I can see is the flags!" (127 mins.)

Fort Apache, The Bronx (1981)**** Paul Newman, Edward Asner, Kathleen Beller, Rachel Ticotin. A notable film which works on numerous levels—it's alternately deeply moving, entertaining, searing, provocative, and disturbing. Newman plays a well-intentioned policeman on the beat in the squalid, largely devastated South Bronx of New York City where most of the film was shot. Focuses on the way the police interact and respond to the civilian population and the inevitable process of both parties being brutalized and doing brutalizing things themselves. Screenplay by Heywood Gould deals with the way the poverty, and high rate of unemployment and crime, in the area affects the citizens. *Apache* was picketed at the time of release by law-abiding, working parents from the neighborhood who felt the film slandered the whole area and its residents. (Dir: Daniel Petrie, 125 mins.)

Fort Defiance (1951)*** Dane Clark, Ben Johnson. Above average Grade "B" western with Johnson out to avenge again Clark for deserting during the Civil War. Plenty of action and a passable production. (Dir: John Rawlins, 81 mins.)

Fort Dobbs (1958)** Clint Walker, Virginia Mayo, Brian Keith. An average western epic with the cowboys and Indians fighting it out. Walker, of TV cowboy fame, fits well into the hero groove. (Dir: Gordon Douglas, 90 mins.)

Fort Massacre (1958)** Joel McCrea, Forrest Tucker, Susan Cabot. Joel McCrea's in the saddle again and trouble's not far from his behind. Good action scenes with plenty of gun smoke and Indian warfare. The kids will enjoy this more than their parents. (Dir: Joseph Newman, 80 mins.)

Fort Ti (1953)** George Montgomery, Joan Vohs. An Indian scout joins with the English forces to capture the French-held Fort Ticonderoga. Routine western. Originally in 3-D. (Dir: William Castle, 73 mins.)

Fort Utah (1967)* John Ireland, Virginia Mayo, Robert Strauss. (Dir: Lesley Selander, 84 mins.)

Fortress of the Dead (1965)**½ John Hackett, Conrad Parkham. Man returning to the Philippines after 20 years cannot shake his guilty actions which began at Corregidor during the Japanese invasion. On-the-spot shooting gives this drama a realistic air, which aids it considerably. (74 mins.)

Fortune, The (1975)*** Warren Beatty, Jack Nicholson, Stockard Channing. Director Mike Nichols obviously loved the screwball comedies of the '30s and tried to create a '70s valentine to them. Beatty and Nicholson are bumbling con artists who lure an heiress, Channing, from her father's home and plan to wed, bed, and kill her—not necessarily in that order. The laughs keep flowing, and Channing makes an auspicious debut. Deft, witty screenplay by Adrien Joyce. (86 mins.)

Fortune and Men's Eyes (Canada-U.S., 1971)***½ Wendell Burton, Zooey Hall, Michael Greer. Harrowing, shocking account of homosexuality in prison. Harvey Hart directs with brilliant economy and force. Well acted, especially by Greer as the tough Queenie. Screenplay by John Herbert, based on his stage play. (102 mins.)

Fortune Cookie, The (1966)***½ Jack Lemmon, Walter Matthau. Walter Matthau's Academy Award-winning performance as best supporting actor is a joy, and carries this uneven Billy Wilder comedy. Jack Lemmon takes a back seat, or more literally a wheel chair, to Matthau's portrayal as his money-hungry brother-in-law, who sees a chance to score big when Lemmon is knocked down by a football player while performing his job as a TV cameraman during a Cleveland Browns game. Billy Wilder gets his satiric licks in, but Matthau's is the only completely successful characterization that emerges. Matthau's windup harrangue when he touches on a number of things including some variations on the theme of civil rights and civil liberties is one of the funniest individual scenes in recent years. (Dir: Billy Wilder, 125 mins.)

Fortune in Diamonds (Great Britain, 1951)**½ Jack Hawkins, Dennis Price. Four men trek into the South African jungle to retrieve a cache of diamonds hidden away. Slow-moving adventure melodrama, bolstered by good location scenes. (Dir: David MacDonald, 74 mins.)

Fortunes of Captain Blood (1950)**½ Louis Hayward, Patricia Medina. The dashing Captain Peter Blood, the Spanish Main's most feared buccaneer, is with us once more, this time in the guise of Louis Hayward. Same plot and outcome as in Errol Flynn's swashbuckling days. (Dir: Gordon Douglas, 91 mins.)

Forty Carats (1973)**½ Liv Ullmann, Edward Albert, Gene Kelly, Binnie Barnes, Nancy Walker. The Broadway success about an older woman and a young lover plays like glossy soap opera on the screen. However, if charm can suffice, this film is loaded with it. Liv Ullmann uses only about ⅓ of her acting talent as the 40-year-old divorcée who falls under the spell of a 22-year-old (Albert) while vacationing in Greece. Gene Kelly is quite adroit with his Noel Coward lines as her ex-husband, and Binnie Barnes, in a return to the screen after many years, scores as Liv's sophisticated mother. Escapist fare! (Dir: Milton Katselas, 110 mins.)

48 Hours to Live (Great Britain-Sweden, 1959)*½ Anthony Steel, Marlies Behrens. (Dir: Peter Bourne, 75 mins.)

48-Hour Mile, The (MTV 1970)** Darren McGavin, William Windom, Kathy Brown, Carrie Snodgress. McGavin plays yet another private eye, this time on an assignment involving two women in love with the same man. Good acting helps. This is two episodes from *The Outsider*. (Dir: Gene Levitt, 97 mins.)

Forty Guns (1957)*** Barbara Stanwyck, Barry Sullivan, Gene Barry, John Ericson, Dean Jagger. Director Sam Fuller's original title for this western was "Woman with a Whip" (it survives in the title song), and its perverse overtones remain in this tale of a lady rancher (Stanwyck) who lets her id run rampant over the plains. Greatly admired by the French, it remains a B classic. (80 mins.)

Forty-Niners, The (1954)**½ Bill Elliott, Virginia Grey, Harry Morgan. Marshal makes friends with a gambler in order to track down some killers. Well-done western. (Dir: Thomas Carr, 71 mins.)

49th Man, The (1953)**½ John Ireland, Suzanne Dalbert. Fast moving spy film about U. S. Security Investigators' tracking down of an A-Bomb parts smuggling outfit. Tense climax. (Dir: Fred F. Sears, 73 mins.)

49th Parallel, The (Great Britain, 1941) ***½ Laurence Olivier, Leslie Howard, Raymond Massey, Eric Portman, Glynis Johns. Gripping war drama of a German U-Boat sunk off Canada, its survivors trying to reach safety in neutral territory. Superb cast, with Olivier, Howard, and Massey in for "guest" appearances. The manhunt is exciting, picturesque, with actual background shooting. Alternate title: **Invaders, The.** (Dir: Michael Powell, 105 mins.)

40 Pounds of Trouble (1963)** Tony Curtis, Phil Silvers, Suzanne Pleshette, Claire Wilcox. Limp reworking of Shirley Temple's "Little Miss Marker," the one about the woman-hating gambler who takes a tyke under his wing and softens up. The cast tries hard, but the results are often cloying, saccharine. (Dir: Norman Jewison, 106 mins.)

42nd Street (1933)*** Dick Powell, Ruby Keeler, Ginger Rogers, Warner Baxter, Una Merkel. The archetypal backstage musical, complete with the young understudy going on after the star breaks her leg a few hours before the big opening

and, of course, Busby Berkeley extravaganzas. Baxter is the producer who rushes around and moves the hackneyed plot along. Less impressive than many Warner Bros. musicals, but "Shuffle Off to Buffalo" has panache. (Dir: Lloyd Bacon, 98 mins.)

47 Ronin, The (Japan, 1942)** Director Kenji Mizoguchi's sublime film is one of two dozen screen versions of Japan's most popular samurai tale. Supposedly made to bolster morale during WW II, the film traces the story of the 47 soldiers' revenge on the nobleman who insulted their leader. The nuances of protocol and the finer points of honor may be incomprehensible to Americans, but Mizoguchi's camera defines the underlying emotions with breathtaking skill. (240 mins.)

Forty Thousand Horsemen (Australia, 1941)*** Grant Taylor, Betty Bryant. Saga of the Anzacs in Jerusalem, fighting the Germans during World War I. Lusty, rip-roaring action drama, featuring truly spectacular battle scenes. (Dir: Charles Chauvel, 78 mins.)

42:6 (Ben Gurion) (Switzerland, 1969)* Arieh Mandelblit, David Muchtar, Rolf Brin. (Dir: David Perlov, 103 mins.)

Foster and Laurie (MTV 1975)*** Perry King, Dorian Harewood. Excellently produced, well-acted police film based on the true life slaying of two cops, Gregory Foster and Rocco Laurie, in New York City, 1972. Begins with the street ambush of the patrolmen and, through flashbacks, the lives of the two men are played out. Effective cross-cutting between the personal married lives of the black Foster and the Italian-American Laurie. On-the-job vignettes help make the men real people and, by the time the brutal killing is shown again, we've grown to care about them. Perry King, as Rocco Laurie, and Dorian Harewood, as Gregory Foster, couldn't be better in the leading roles. Director John Llewelyn Moxey also deserves a share of the credit for this hard-hitting police drama. (Dir: John Llewelyn Moxey, 98 mins.)

Foul Play (1978)***½ Goldie Hawn, Chevy Chase, Dudley Moore, Burgess Meredith, Marilyn Sokol. Very funny comedy thriller using San Francisco backdrops as bewildered librarian Hawn witnesses murder and mayhem and can't seem to prove what she's seen. Chase, in his first major role, gets laughs as the smooth detective who becomes both protector and lover. Meredith has a nice scene with a pet snake, and Sokol hits home as Goldie's friend, equipped with all the protection a lady needs. The plot, which gets a bit melodramatic at times, concerns an assassination attempt on the pope while he is attending a performance of "The Mikado." (Dir: Colin Higgins, 116 mins.)

Foul Play (Poland, 1978)*** Lean, propulsive Polish film noir, derivative and hardly above the level of a well-made episode of a TV cop show. Director Marek Piwowski must seem more original in Poland. (90 mins.)

Fountainhead, The (1949)*** Gary Cooper, Patricia Neal, Raymond Massey, Kent Smith, Robert Douglas. Cooper stars as Ayn Rand's archetypal individualist, an architect modeled on Frank Lloyd Wright who is willing to blow up his own work rather than see it perverted by public housing bureaucrats. Vidor's firm commitment to the single human being's right to make his own way in an impersonal world turn this film from a proto-fascist parable into a celebration of freedom and integrity. Elaborate and highly stylized, the film's humanist virtues shine through. Massey and Neal are excellent (Dir: King Vidor, 114 mins.)

Four Bags Full (France, 1957)*** Jean Gabin, Bouvril. Award winning French film combining comedy with a good dramatic plot about two men who take great risks during the Nazi occupation in Paris. Excellent performances. (Dir: Claude Autant-Lara, 84 mins.)

Four Daughters (1938)**** Claude Rains, John Garfield, Gale Page, 3 Lane Sisters. Beautifully acted adaptation of the Fannie Hurst story. One of the year's best, this made the late John Garfield a star. A tragic, moving drama. (Dir: Michael Curtiz, 90 mins.)

Four Days in Dallas—See: **Ruby and Oswald**

Four Days' Leave (Switzerland, 1949)**½ Cornel Wilde, Josette Day, Simone Signoret. A sailor on tour in Switzerland falls for the girl in the watch shop, enters in a skiing contest, wins both. Highly amusing, pleasant comedy with beautiful scenery. (Dir: Leopold Lindtberg, 98 mins.)

Four Days of Naples, The (U.S.-Italy, 1962)***½ Regina Bianchi, Jean Sorel, Lea Massari. Epic reenactment chronicling the spontaneous anti-Nazi uprising in Naples, which liberated the city after WW II. Reminiscent of the early Soviet revolutionary opuses, film has a biting intensity and power. Mostly nonprofessional cast performs admirably. Nominated for an Academy Award for a foreign language film. (Dir: Nanni Loy, 116 mins.)

Four Desperate Men (Australia, 1960)*** Aldo Ray, Heather Sears. Cornered criminals hole up on an island off Sydney, Australia, and threaten to blow up the entire town if they're not permitted to escape. Tense drama with the on-scene shooting (both varieties) adding to the suspense. Well acted. (Dir: Harry Watt, 104 mins.)

Four Feathers, The (1929)**½ Richard Arlen, Fay Wray, Clive Brook, William Powell. This late silent, filmed in Africa, was the first fictional feature of the Ernest Schoedsack-Merian C. Cooper team (who would later give us "King Kong"), and it's an effective version of the A.E.W. Mason story with first-rate location work and a good sense of narrative coherence. Arlen is the lad who must prove his bravery to fiancée Wray and friends Brook and Powell. Codirected by Lothar Mendes, with Schoedsack also manning a camera and editing. (80 mins.)

Four Feathers (Great Britain, 1939)***½ Ralph Richardson, John Clements, June Duprez, C. Aubrey Smith. The best of imperialistic epics, directed with verve and precision by Zoltan Korda, whose attack of the Fuzzy-Wuzzies is superb. A young aristocrat (Clements) isn't cut out for a military career, so when he resigns his commission on the eve of the expedition to the Sudan, he is branded a coward by his friends and sweetheart and must set the disgrace right. Richardson contributes an eccentric portrayal as a blinded officer, and Duprez is lovely. Remade as "Storm over the Nile." (115 mins., originally 140 mins.)

Four for Texas (1963)*½ Frank Sinatra, Dean Martin, Anita Ekberg, Ursula Andress. (Dir: Robert Aldrich, 124 mins.)

Four Frightened People (1934)*** Claudette Colbert, Herbert Marshall, Mary Boland, William Gargan. Four shipwreck survivors wash ashore in Malaya, where progress through an allegorical jungle leads to moral and spiritual improvement—naturally, since this is directed by Cecil B. deMille. Small-scale and modestly budgeted, this was one of deMille's few box-office flops. It was also his last small-scale, modestly budgeted film. (Dir: Cecil B. deMille, 78 mins.)

Four Girls in Town (1957)***½ Julia Adams, Elsa Martinelli, Sydney Chaplin, George Nader. Hollywood story about four hopeful misses who arrive to make good in the flicks. Offbeat handling of the usual success story makes this one stand out; pleasant surprise twists, nice insight into the cinema capital. (Dir: Jack Sher, 85 mins.)

Four Guns to the Border (1954)** Rory Calhoun, Colleen Miller, George Nader. Western fare served with all the necessary ingredients intact. Action fans will enjoy the Apache raids and the gun duels. (Dir: Richard Carlson, 82 mins.)

Four Horsemen of the Apocalypse, The (1921)**** Rudolph Valentino, Alice Terry, Alan Hale, Wallace Beery. This silent version of the Blasco Ibanez potboiler launched Rudolph Valentino as a sultry star capable of executing a mean tango, but it is also one of the great silent films. Director Rex Ingram takes the broad narrative expanse of the novel and invests its bold, primary emotions with impressive visual sweep and discerning selection of detail. From the Argentine pampas to the Paris of WW I, the film aspires to saga and achieves it—even the fruity central metaphor of the Four Horsemen is literally, and impressively, rendered. Valentino himself shows sensitivity as an actor and is particularly well deployed by Ingram, and the rest of the cast, including

Alice Terry (Ingram's wife), Alan Hale, and Wallace Beery, who is fine. Ingram straddles the Griffith tradition and the later pictorial European school; he is the master who David Lean acknowledges as his true antecedent. (Dir: Rex Ingram, 120 mins.)

Four Horsemen of the Apocalypse, The (1961)**½ Glenn Ford, Ingrid Thulin, Charles Boyer, Lee J. Cobb, Paul Henreid. Elephantine drama of an Argentine family and their involvements in World War II, updated but hardly improved from the old silent version, which made a star of Valentino. In this one, Ford's no Rudy, but in fairness he receives little help from script or director. Some of the other performances are okay, but the film runs too long to maintain interest. (Dir: Vincente Minnelli, 153 mins.)

400 Blows, The (France, 1959)**** Jean-Pierre Leaud. Memorable study of an adolescent boy, neglected by his selfish parents, who discovers some unpleasant facts about life. The boy is played with great sensitivity by Jean-Pierre Leaud. The excellent photography and superb editing set the mood for this touching film. (Dir: Francois Truffaut, 99 mins.)

400 Million, The (The Netherlands, 1939)***½ Narrated by Fredric March. A report on the Japanese invasion of China, directed by the Dutch documentarist Joris Ivens (with John Ferno). Financed by a group of Hollywood liberals, among them March, Franchot Tone, and Dudley Nichols, who wrote the commentary. (60 mins.)

Four in a Jeep (Switzerland, 1951)**** Ralph Meeker, Viveca Lindfors. Dramatic story of the international MP patrol in Vienna, and of a girl who needs their help. Excellently done, actually filmed on the spot, with many fine scenes. (Dir: Leopold Lindtberg, 97 mins.)

Four Jills in a Jeep (1944)** Kay Francis, Carole Landis, Martha Raye, Phil Silvers. A big cast in a boring, inept musical about the experiences of its female stars when they went overseas for the USO. Ignore the name performers. This is a below-average "B." (Dir: William Seiter, 89 mins.)

Four Kinds of Love (Italy, 1965)—See: **Bambole**

Four Musketeers, The (1975)**** Raquel Welch, Oliver Reed, Richard Chamberlain, Faye Dunaway, Michael York, Charlton Heston, Simon Ward, Geraldine Chaplin. This is not a sequel to the delightful "Three Musketeers" of director Richard Lester, released in 1973. "The Four Musketeers" was always planned by Lester as a two-part romp and was lensed at the same time as "Three Musketeers" by an unsuspecting cast. (The complexities of international film financing being what they are, one film reference source cites Panama as the producing nation.) On screen, however, it's more joyous escapades

of rogues, gallant damsels, derring-do and swordplay. Loaded with more marvelous sight gags. Huge fun for all. (Dir: Richard Lester, 107 mins.)

Four Nights of a Dreamer (France, 1971)**** Isabel Weingarten, Guillaume des Forets, Jean Maurice Monnoyer. An adaptation of Dostoevski's "White Nights," Director Robert Bresson's film is an exploration of romantic love rendered in a precise, austere style. (91 mins.)

Four Poster, The (1952)*** Rex Harrison, Lilli Palmer. Fine screen treatment of hilarious Broadway comedy about a married couple who go through their lives in scenes played in and around their four-poster bed. Excellent performances by the stars. (Dir: Irving Reis, 103 mins.)

Four Seasons, The (1981)**** Alan Alda, Carol Burnett. Perceptive, amusing and often poignant story about marriage in urban America. Multi-talented Alan Alda also wrote and directed this observant essay about life and love in the suburbs. (117 mins.)

Four Skulls of Jonathan Drake (1959)* Eduard Franz, Valerie French, Grant Richards. (Dir: Edward L. Cahn, 70 mins.)

Four Sons (1940)**½ Don Ameche, Eugenie Leontovich. Drama of a Czech family ripped apart by the Nazi invasion is almost a fine film but reaches for more than it is able to give. Still worth seeing as an anti-war story. Remake of a silent classic. (Dir: Archie Mayo, 89 mins.)

Four Ways Out (Italy, 1954)** Gina Lollobrigida, Renato Baldini. Four men who have held up a cashier's office are tracked down. Ordinary crime melodrama, not helped by English dubbing. (Dir: Pietro Germi, 77 mins.)

Four Wives (1939)**½ Lane Sisters, Claude Rains. The four daughters ride again, this time as wives and mothers. But this time they ran out of breath and came up with a very ordinary movie. (Dir: Michael Curtiz. 110 mins.)

Four's a Crowd (1938)**½ Errol Flynn, Olivia de Havilland, Rosalind Russell. A lot of funny situations help this not-so-funny comedy about a wealthy heiress and her beaus. (Dir: Michael Curtiz, 100 mins.)

Fourteen Hours (1951)*** Richard Basehart, Barbara Bel Geddes, Paul Douglas. Director Henry Hathaway keeps the suspense sharply in focus in this drama about a mentally disturbed man who stands on a ledge of a Manhattan hotel threatening to jump for a period of 14 hours. A few subplots are interwoven into the action involving various spectators (Grace Kelly, Jeffrey Hunter, Debra Paget). Basehart is very effective as the troubled man and Barbara Bel Geddes has some touching moments as his girl friend. This drama is based on a true life incident. Kelly's film debut. (Dir: Henry Hathaway, 92 mins.)

Fourth for Marriage, A (1964)* Tommy

Holden, Marilyn Manning. Alternate title: **What's Up Front.** (Dir: Bob Wehling, 83 mins.)

Fourth Square, The (Great Britain, 1961)** Conrad Phillips, Natasha Parry. Lawyer turns sleuth when his client is involved in robbery and murder. Adequate mystery based on an Edgar Wallace story. (Dir: Allan Davis, 58 mins.)

Fox, The (1968)*** Sandy Dennis, Keir Dullea, Anne Heywood. Sensitive dramatization of D. H. Lawrence's novella about a relationship between two young lesbians. For those of you who care there is a heterosexual liaison between Dullea and Miss Heywood, but the brooding story, filmed largely in rural Canada, benefits greatly from the restrained, moving performances from the three leads. Britain's Anne Heywood is seen to particularly good advantage, and TV-director-actor Mark Rydell has done a commendable job in directing his first feature, tackling this challenging material which could so easily have been vulgarized and distorted. (Dir: Mark Rydell, 110 mins.)

Foxes (1980)**½ Jodie Foster, Sally Kellerman, Cherie Currie, Randy Quaid, Scott Baio. About four young girls who share an apartment in suburban Los Angeles. The plot registers little more than an excuse for some facile, and some disquieting, sociological inquiry. Director Adrian Lyne never achieves a consistent style, but has attentive eyes and ears. Foster is mesmerizing as always, although the sainted mother/sister/goddess she incarnates here would have been an intolerable invention if anyone else had played her. (106 mins.)

Foxes of Harrow, The (1947)*** Rex Harrison, Maureen O'Hara. Fans of historical fiction will be disappointed with this dime-novel tale but there's enough excitement in some of the episodes to please less discerning viewers. Tells of the rise to fame and fortune of an adventurer in 1820 New Orleans. (Dir: John M. Stahl, 117 mins.)

Foxfire (1955)**½ Jane Russell, Jeff Chandler, Dan Duryea. Anya Seton's novel is brought to the screen as a glossy love story with overtones of adventure. Jeff Chandler is well cast as the dedicated mining engineer who has to learn to understand his new socialite wife (Jane Russell in the casting error of many years). (Dir: Joseph Pevney, 92 mins.)

Foxhole in Cairo (Great Britain, 1961)** Peter Van Eyck, James Robertson Justice, Adrian Hoven. British Intelligence trails a German agent sent to Cairo by Rommel to determine the Allied line of defense. Routinely interesting World War II espionage thriller; nothing new, but fairly well done. (Dir: John Moxey, 79 mins.)

Foxiest Girl in Paris, The (France, 1957)**½ Martine Carol, Mischa Auer. French fashion model gets involved with jewel thieves and murder and sets out to crack the case with little or no assistance from the gendarmes. Some laughs. (Dir: Roger De Broin, 100 mins.)

Fra Diavolo—See: **Devil's Brother, The**

Fragment of Fear (Great Britain, 1970)**½ David Hemmings, Gayle Hunnicutt, Flora Robson, Wilfred Hyde White. Suspense as former drug addict Hemmings goes through a slow emotional breakdown. Strange, unexplainable events lead him to question his own sanity. O.K. whodunit! (Dir: Richard C. Sarafian, 95 mins.)

Framed (1947)*** Glenn Ford, Janis Carter, Barry Sullivan. Man is marked for death by two crooks who wish to steal money from a bank. Suspenseful melodrama with a good cast. (Dir: Richard Wallace, 82 mins.)

Francis (1950)**½ Donald O'Connor, Patricia Medina. This was the first of a series of films which featured the box-office-winning gimmick, Francis, The Talking Mule. Donald O'Connor takes a back seat to the bellowing burro (Chill Wills supplies Francis's voice). (Dir: Arthur Lubin, 91 mins.)

Francis Covers the Big Town (1953)**½ Donald O'Connor, Nancy Guild. It's inevitable that Francis, The Talking Mule should become involved with detective work and this is the film in which he does it. He and sidekick Donald O'Connor go through a series of narrow escapes as they get a scoop for the papers on underworld activities. (Dir: Arthur Lubin, 86 mins.)

Francis Gary Powers: The True Story of the U-2 Spy Incident (MTV 1976)**½ Lee Majors, Nehemiah Persoff, Noah Beery, Jr., Lew Ayres. Moderately interesting account of how Powers (a Lockheed employee working for the CIA) was shot down over Russia in 1960, tried for espionage, and sentenced to a prison term. Director Delbert Mann works with care to re-create history, and his sequences with Khrushchev, Eisenhower, and the CIA's Allen Dulles really spark the show. Majors tries hard to make the starring role believable. (104 mins.)

Francis Goes to the Races (1951)**½ Donald O'Connor, Piper Laurie. The Talking Mule gets information from his equine relatives and causes his innocent master, O'Connor, a great deal of trouble. Piper Laurie is wasted as the love interest. (Dir: Arthur Lubin, 88 mins.)

Francis Goes to West Point (1952)**½ Donald O'Connor, Lori Nelson. O'Connor and his talking-mule sidekick end up at West Point after they become heroes in a sabotage plot. The usual shenanigans prevail as O'Connor gets in and out of trouble because of his four-legged "pal."(Dir: Arthur Lubin, 81 mins.)

Francis in the Haunted House (1956)** Mickey Rooney, Virginia Welles. When Donald O'Connor screamed "no" to any more Francis epics, Universal tried once again with Mickey Rooney as the mule's confidant but without much success. Only moderately funny acting with Rooney mugging his way as a bumpkin nobody believes. (Dir: Charles Lamont, 80 mins.)

Francis in the Navy (1955)** Donald O'Connor, Martha Hyer. The last "Francis" film starring Donald O'Connor and not the funniest. After a go at West Point and the Wacs in previous films, Francis makes some choice comments about the nautical division of our armed services. Martha Hyer supplies the obligatory love interest. (Dir: Arthur Lubin, 80 mins.)

Francis Joins the Wacs (1954)**½ Donald O'Connor, Julie Adams. Silly, but Francis' fans will enjoy the hijinks that he and Donald O'Connor go through when a mistake sends Don back into the service—as a Wac recruit! (Dir: Arthur Lubin, 94 mins.)

Francis of Assisi (1961)** Bradford Dillman, Dolores Hart, Stuart Whitman. Cumbersome, frequently inept narrative of St. Francis and the founding of his order in the 13th century. Lavish production should have meant a far better film. (Dir: Michael Curtiz, 111 mins.)

Frankenstein (1931)**** Boris Karloff, Colin Clive, Mae Clarke, John Boles. Mary Shelley's story is altered (giving the monster the brain of a madman) to produce one of the most deservedly famous and chilling horror films of all time. Karloff's acting as the monster, and James Whale's direction (he was to top this with "Bride of Frankenstein" in '35) combine to create an effectively frightening mood. (Dir: James Whale, 71 mins.)

Frankenstein Conquers the World (U.S.-Japan, 1966)** Nick Adams, Tadao Takashima, Kumi Mizuno. An American revamping of a Japanese horror film directed by Inoshiro Honda ("Rodan," "Godzilla"). A sealed box containing the living heart of the Frankenstein monster is shipped from Nazi Germany to Japan, only to be caught in the Hiroshima blast. Later, a wild boy is found living in the wilderness. Parts of the film were recycled in Honda's "Destroy All Monsters." (87 mins.)

Frankenstein Created Woman (Great Britain, 1967)* Peter Cushing, Susan Denberg. (Dir: Terence Fisher, 92 mins.)

Frankenstein Meets the Space Monster (1965)* James Karen, Nancy Marshall. (Dir: Robert Gaffney, 78 mins.)

Frankenstein Meets the Wolf Man (1943)**½ Bela Lugosi, Lon Chaney. It's only natural that these two cutups should get to know each other, and when they do meet, the countryside is crowded with corpses. Pretty lively horror film. (Dir: Roy William Neill, 72 mins.)

Frankenstein Must Be Destroyed (Great Britain, 1969)½ Peter Cushing, Simon Ward, Veronica Carlson. (Dir: Terence Fisher, 97 mins.)

Frankenstein—1970 (1958)** Boris Karloff,

Charlotte Austin. The real Baron Von Frankenstein would turn in his crypt if he saw what they're doing to his castle in this film—A TV troupe is using it as the locale of a horror show. Is nothing sacred? If you take your horror films seriously you can skip this one.—However, it's good for a few laughs. (Dir: Howard W. Koch, 83 mins.)

Frankenstein: The True Story (MTV 1973)*** James Mason, David McCallum, Michael Sarrazin, John Gielgud. Despite its over three-hour length, the quality of performance is so uniformly high in this version of the Frankenstein tale, based on Mary Shelley's gothic novel, that it holds your interest and casts a tantalizing spell of horror, mixed with wonder and suspense. Most convincing are Leonard Whiting's Dr. Frankenstein and Sarrazin's compelling figure of the Creature (Dir: Jack Smight, 200 mins.)

Frankenstein's Daughter (1958)* John Ashley, Sandra Knight. (Dir: Richard Cunha, 85 mins.)

Frankie and Johnny (1966)* Elvis Presley, Donna Douglas. (Dir: Frederick de Cordova, 87 mins.)

Frank's Greatest Adventure—See: **Fearless Frank**

Frantic (1958)**½ Jeanne Moreau, Maurice Ronet. A suspense tale (French-English dubbed) that just misses being very good. A couple of people plan what appears to be an almost perfect crime but as it always happens, things don't turn out that way. The first half is better than the windup. Moreau carries film anyway. (Dir: Serge Friedman, 94 mins.)

Fraternity Row (1977)**½ Peter Fox, Gregory Harrison, Nancy Morgan, Scott Newman. Not a bad film about a '50s college fraternity hazing which ends tragically. Harrison and Morgan come off best; Scott Newman, Paul Newman's late son, plays a gung-ho fraternity brother on the villainous side. (Dir: Thomas J. Tobin, 104 mins.)

Fraulein (1958)*½ Dana Wynter, Mel Ferrer. (Dir: Henry Koster, 98 mins.)

Fraulein Doktor (Italy-Yugoslavia, 1968)*½ Suzy Kendall, Kenneth More, Capucine. (Dir: Alberto Lattuada, 102 mins.)

Freaks (1932)***½ Leila Hyams, Olga Baclanova, Harry Earles, Wallace Ford. A cult classic, this unusual picture is a terrifying vision of life among the weird inhabitants of the sideshow world. The performers are real freaks, and this film is not for the squeamish. (Dir: Tod Browning, 64 mins.)

Freaky Friday (1976)** Jodie Foster, Barbara Harris, Sorrell Booke, John Astin, Patsy Kelly. I've always thought Foster and Harris would be worth watching in anything, but this may be the ultimate test. A mother and daughter switch personalities for a day—since this is a Disney film, certain possibilities are scrupulously avoided. Best left to the kiddies and other forgiving types. Screenplay by Mary Rodgers. (Dir: Gary Nelson, 95 mins.)

Freckles (1960)** Martin West, Carol Christensen. Lad gets a job in a lumber camp, proves the lack of one hand doesn't mean a total handicap. Unexceptional outdoor drama might get by with juvenile audiences. (Dir: Andrew V. McLaglen, 84 mins.)

Free for All (1949)** Ann Blyth, Robert Cummings. An innocent bit of nonsense about an inventor who comes up with a tablet that supposedly turns water into gasoline. Cummings mugs his way through the proceedings and Miss Blyth looks startled and wide-eyed which she mistakenly thinks is the only way to play comedy. (Dir: Charles Barton, 83 mins.)

Free Soul, A (1931)*** Norma Shearer, Lionel Barrymore, Clark Gable, Leslie Howard. Shearer works as a reporter to support her drunken father (Barrymore copped an Oscar), a brilliant attorney who defends mobster Gable, with whom she falls in love. Clarence Brown, a director of sensibility and uneven talents, is at his peak. (91 mins.)

Free Spirit (Great Britain, 1973)**½ Eric Porter, Rachel Roberts, Bill Travers. Offbeat tale of a fox raised with hounds by a professional huntsman, later becoming a menace as he outwits both hunter and hound. Travers, unrecognizable as a bearded woodsman, has a great character part. James Hill directed and adapted the David Rook novel "The Ballad of the Belstone Fox." (88 mins.)

Free Woman, A (West Germany, 1972)***½ Margarethe von Trotta. Director Volker Schloendorff's "Summer Lightning," retitled and shortened a bit, remains a powerful if sometimes too didactic exploration of the problems of freedom for a young woman in a society that preaches more about liberation than it is willing to accept. Van Trotta, Schloendorff's wife and coauthor, is a standout as a German divorcee trying to make a life for herself. (100 mins.)

Freebie and the Bean (1974)* Alan Arkin, James Caan, Valerie Harper, Loretta Swit. (Dir: Richard Rush, 113 mins.)

Freedom Road (MTV 1979)**½ Muhammad Ali, Kris Kristofferson, Ron O'Neal. The former heavyweight champ plays an ex-slave who becomes a U.S. senator from South Carolina during Reconstruction in this earnest, slow-paced version of the Howard Fast novel. Gideon Jackson, who teaches himself to read and write after attending a constitutional convention, realizes that a black man can only be free through education and land ownership, and pulls it off despite the outraged white gentry and their Ku Klux Klan. A study of courage and determination, somewhat flawed in the handling. Ali, who needs some acting lessons, has a modicum of power and dignity. (Dir: Jan Kadar, 208 mins.)

French Cancan (France, 1955)**** Jean Gabin, Francoise Arnoul, Maria Felix, Dora Doll, Valentine Tessier. Jean Renoir's tribute to the great Parisian dance wonder is a deceptively exhilarating musical that sneaks up on some profound ideas about the nature of theater and of art. It's a standard tale of an impresario (Jean Gabin) down on his luck and trying to get a show mounted despite the financial odds. His bistro becomes the talk of Paris, and deservedly. Renoir makes his simple story a dazzlingly complex meditation and still delivers the goods as straight entertainment. A triumphant example of how to inoculate the richest values into generic material. (Dir: Jean Renoir, 93 mins.)

French Connection, The (1971)**** Gene Hackman, Fernando Rey, Roy Scheider, Eddie Egan, Sonny Grosso. Marvelously exciting yarn about a New York cop (Hackman) busting a huge international narcotics ring smuggling vast quantities of heroin into the U.S. Based on the book by Robin Moore; the real narcotics squad officers who broke the case in 1961 (Egan & Grosso) play bit parts in the film. Action takes place in Marseilles, Washington, and New York, and there's one of the best chase sequences in the history of film as Hackman tries to catch his prey on a subway, following by auto. It's an exciting zinger all the way. (Dir: William Friedkin, 104 mins.)

French Connection II (1975)***½ Gene Hackman, Fernando Rey. The sequel to the Academy Award-winning film about New York cop Popeye Doyle and his adventures with the international narcotics ring doesn't pack the punch of the original, but it's still exciting. Gene Hackman is Popeye once again, on the trail of the elusive Kingpin of the French narcotics syndicate (Fernando Rey also repeats his role from the original), and the action set in Marseilles adds to the chase drama. Less complex, more brutal than "F.C." #1—there's a rousing finale in the harbor in Marseille. Frankenheimer back in stride. (Dir: John Frankenheimer, 118 mins.)

French Conspiracy, The (France, 1973)**½ Jean-Louis Trintignant, Jean Seberg, Philippe Noiret, Roy Scheider. A not very thrilling French espionage thriller based on the real-life disappearance in '65 of left-wing leader Ben Barka of Morocco. The underrated Trintignant goes through his paces as the '70s answer to Humphrey Bogart with superb, weary grace. Hear Seberg's wonderful Iowa twanging through her excellent French. (Dir: Yves Boisset, 125 mins.)

French Detective, The (France, 1978)** Lino Ventura, Patrick Dewaere, Victor Lanoux. Meller about two dedicated French cops out to stop a ruthless politician. The charismatic Ventura, always worth watching, is the old-school tough-guy type, and Dewaere is his young, cynical assistant. Hackwork entertainment from director Pierre Granier-Deferre. (93 mins.)

French Key, The (1946)*** Albert Dekker, Mike Mazurki. Smart-talking amateur sleuth and his brawny assistant find a corpse in their hotel room. Good, well-paced mystery, above average. (Dir: Walter Colmes, 64 mins.)

French Line, The (1954)** Gilbert Roland, Jane Russell. Multi-millionairess travels to Paris posing as a model, falls in love with a dashing Frenchman. Boring musical. (Dir: Lloyd Bacon, 102 mins.)

French Mistress, A (Great Britain, 1960)** Cecil Parker, James Robertson Justice, Agnes Laurent, Ian Bannen. Droll fluff. An alluring woman gets teaching post at a British boys' school. Inoffensive, mild comedy! (Dir: Roy Boulting, 98 mins.)

French Postcards (1979)** Marie-France Pisier, Miles Chapin, Blanche Baker. Sometimes pleasant, often plodding comedy about American exchange students in Paris and their introduction to life and love. Carroll Baker's young daughter Blanche has an impossible role, while French star Pisier charms her way throughout the film as codirector of the private academy to which Americans in Paris are sent. Some funny subtitles translate into English the Americans' massacre of French. (Dir: Willard Huyck, 95 mins.)

French Provincial (France, 1974)*** Jeanne Moreau, Marie-France Pisier. Forty years in the history of a small-town manufacturing dynasty, chronicling its takeover by a working-class seamstress (Moreau) and an upper-class adventuress (Pisier). Structured in short, elliptical scenes, it handles its political and emotional themes with art and insight. Director André Techine's long-take, deep-focus style is extraordinarily precise. (91 mins.)

French, They Are a Funny Race, The (France, 1957)**½ Martine Carol, Jack Buchanan. Fast and funny spoof on the French people as seen through the eyes of an English novelist, retired from the British Army and residing in Paris with his glamorous French wife. (Dir: Preston Sturges, 83 mins.)

French Without Tears (Great Britain, 1939)*½ Ray Milland, Ellen Drew. (Dir: Anthony Asquith, 67 mins.)

Frenchie (1951)** Joel McCrea, Shelley Winters. Comedy and drama are juggled in this awkward western about a gal who comes back to the town which sent her away to settle a few scores. McCrea is the town's easygoing sheriff and Miss Winters is Frenchie, of course. (Dir: Louis King, 81 mins.)

Frenchman's Creek (1944)**½ Joan Fontaine, Basil Rathbone, Arturo de Cordova, Nigel Bruce. Costume film about an unholy alliance between an English lady and a French pirate. Swashbuckling

and romantic! (Dir: Mitchell Leisen, 113 mins.)

Frenzy (Great Britain, 1972)**** Jon Finch, Alec McCowen, Vivien Merchant, Barry Foster, Barbara Leigh-Hunt. A marvelous suspense film directed by that master of the genre, Alfred Hitchcock. Taut screenplay by Anthony Shaffer based on the novel "Goodbye Piccadilly, Farewell Leicester Square." Hitchcock's best effort in years, with a faultless cast of nonstars. The wrong man becomes the chief suspect when his wife is murdered—we've seen this plot before but Hitchcock, the old magician, keeps the pace spinning with humor and invention. (Dir: Alfred Hitchcock, 116 mins.)

Freshman, The (1925)*** Harold Lloyd, Jobyna Ralston. Lloyd's biggest-grossing silent comedy is a cut below his best work. He plays an erstwhile Ivy Leaguer at a southern university, where he struggles to make the football team and to keep his pipe lit. Lloyd's ingenuity with gags was unparalleled but he lacked irony about his screen persona. (Dir: Sam Taylor, 76 mins.)

Freud (1962)*** Montgomery Clift, Susannah York, Larry Parks. The early struggle for recognition and the general work of Sigmund Freud, the founder of modern psychiatry, are depicted in often interesting fashion in this drama directed by John Huston. Some inventive montage sequences used to show meaning of dreams, etc. Main storyline involved Freud's treatment of a young patient, well played by Miss York. (Dir: John Huston, 139 mins.)

Friday Foster (1975)½ Pam Grier, Yaphet Kotto, Eartha Kitt, Jim Backus, Godfrey Cambridge. Based on the comic strip of the same name, this is a standard Grier action extravaganza, glutted indiscriminately with sex and death, as she tracks down the sinister Black Sunday organization that's plotting the murder of all of America's black leaders. Screenplay by Orville Hampton from story by director Arthur Marks. (89 mins.)

Friday the 13th (1980)** Betsy Palmer, Harry Crosby, Adrienne King. The kids who attempt to reopen a summer camp where grisly murders occurred two decades before are set up to be sequential victims of an arbitrary scenario. This popular low-budget horror film is close to a copy of "Halloween" with an ending cribbed from "Carrie." Producer-director Sean S. Cunningham's technique is crude. (91 mins.)

Frieda (Great Britain, 1947)***½ Mai Zetterling, David Farrar, Glynis Johns. RAF officer brings his German war bride to his home town, where she is looked upon with suspicion and hatred. Powerful drama, intelligently handled, excellently acted. (Dir: Basil Dearden, 97 mins.)

Friendly Fire (MTV 1979)**** Carol Burnett, Ned Beatty, Sam Waterston. With a few exceptions like "Sticks and

Bones," during the '60s and nearly all of the '70s, the TV networks shamefully refused to broadcast significant dramas about the Vietnam War. This is a deeply moving, poignant film based on C. D. B. Bryan's nonfiction book about an Iowa farm family who turn against the war after their son dies in Vietnam and they learn that he died from "friendly fire"—accidental shelling by American artillery. Burnett turns in her best acting performance to date. (Dir: David Greene, 162 mins.)

Friendly Persuasion (1956)**** Gary Cooper, Dorothy McGuire, Tony Perkins. Touching and often amusing story about a family of Quakers who live in peace and contentment on their land in Indiana until the Civil War breaks out and disrupts their lives. Dorothy McGuire and Gary Cooper are perfectly cast in their roles as the parents. The standout performance in the film is delivered by Tony Perkins as their son who is faced with the realities of war. Well-produced and directed. (Dir: William Wyler, 139 mins.)

Friends (Great Britain, 1971)* Sean Bury, Anicee Alvina. (Dir: Lewis Gilbert, 101 mins.)

Friends of Eddie Coyle, The (1973)**** Robert Mitchum, Peter Boyle, Richard Jordan. A tough, unsentimental, first-rate drama about a Boston hoodlum, which boasts Mitchum giving perhaps the best performance of his career. Mitchum plays Eddie Coyle, a small-time mobster who winds up turning stoolie. Well adapted by Paul Monash based on the novel by George V. Higgins. Skillfully directed by Peter Yates. (102 mins.)

Friendships, Secrets, and Lies (MTV 1979)** Cathryn Damon, Tina Louise, Paula Prentiss, Stella Stevens, Loretta Swit. Nary a man is in sight in this tale of sexual repression—written, acted, directed, and produced by women. Sorority sisters become suspects when a baby's skeleton is discovered after being buried for 20 years. The soap opera material is a bit bumpy at first, but interest picks up as the characters talk about their fears, their dependence on men, and their romantic naïveté. (Dirs: Ann Zane Shanks, Marlena Laird, 104 mins.)

Fright (1956)*½ Eric Fleming, Nancy Malone. Alternate title: **Spell of the Hypnotist.**

Fright (Great Britain, 1971)*** Susan George, Ian Bannen, Honor Blackman. Baby-sitter George is terrorized by strange happenings in a deserted house. The top-notch British actors are all frightening, but the most terrifying performance comes from Bannen. Not for children. (Dir: Peter Collinson, 87 mins.)

Frightened Bride, The (Great Britain, 1952)**½ Mai Zetterling, Michael Denison. A family tries to escape the past when one of the sons is convicted of

murdering a girl, sees it start all over again with the younger son. Occasionally interesting but unconvincing melodrama. Some good moments. (Dir: Terence Young, 75 mins.)

Frightened City, The (Great Britain, 1962)*½ Herbert Lom, John Gregson, Sean Connery. Imitation-American gangster story. (Dir: John Lemont, 97 mins.)

Frisco Kid (1935)*** James Cagney, Margaret Lindsay. Typical, fast moving Cagney melodrama. Plenty of fighting in this tale of revenge on the Barbary Coast. (Dir: Lloyd Bacon, 80 mins.)

Frisco Kid, The (1979)**½ Gene Wilder, Harrison Ford, William Smith, Ramon Bieri, Penny Peyser. The premise of a Polish rabbi making his way across the United States to join a congregation in gold-rush San Francisco is a potentially intriguing one, and every once in a while the sage Jewish wit that might have redeemed the movie surfaces, notably in a well-wrought climax. But aside from the opportunity to experience Gene Wilder in a real character (though he is more surface than one might have hoped), the film never finds a style or direction. Robert Aldrich mixes some very good direction with some very uncertain work, but where the balance tipped in his favor on *The Choirboys*, this film ultimately comes off pointless—the director is simply too miscast. (Dir: Robert Aldrich, 122 mins.)

Frisco Sal (1945)**½ Susanna Foster, Turhan Bey, Alan Curtis. Girl gets a job as a singer in a Barbary Coast saloon while seeking the killers of her brother. Oft-told but nicely produced costume melodrama with music. (Dir: George Waggner, 63 mins.)

Frisky (Italy, 1954)**½ Gina Lollobrigida, Vittorio De Sica. Gossipy small towners concoct an affair between an official and a gorgeous local belle. Mildly amusing comedy, pleasantly performed. Dubbed-in English. (Dir: Luigi Comencini, 98 mins.)

Fritz the Cat (1972)***½ Perhaps the first X-rated animated feature, based on the successful "underground" comic strip by social satirist Robert Crumb. Director, designer, writer Ralph Bakshi has done appreciably more than make a "dirty" cartoon—he and his raunchy on-screen characters puncture just about every myth and sacred cow they swing at. Reminds one of comic Mort Sahl's ingenuous query "Is there anyone I haven't offended?" There are anti-Jewish, anti-black jibes and a wide variety of other generally funny slams and put-downs. It doesn't all work and it seems like a one-note joke before the end, but if you've got an open mind, it's worth seeing. (Dir: Ralph Bakshi, 77 mins.)

Frogmen, The (1951)**½ Richard Widmark, Dana Andrews, Jeffrey Hunter, Robert Wagner. Slow-paced story of the Navy's heroes of the deep and their dangerous exploits during the war. Interesting underwater photography. (Dir: Lloyd Bacon, 96 mins.)

Frogs (1972)** Ray Milland, Sam Elliot, Joan Van Ark. This film has a certain inane appeal. It is a straightforward rip-off of "Willard," using amphibians instead of rodents. There is a nice, swampy atmosphere, and some cheerful, tongue-in-cheek acting. If you don't like monster movies, stay away. (Dir: George McCowan, 91 mins.)

From Hell It Came (1957)* Tod Andrews, Tina Carver. (Dir: Dan Milner, 71 mins.)

From Hell to Borneo (1964)** George Montgomery, Torin Thatcher, Julie Gregg. Soldier of fortune fights to keep control of his private island when he's menaced by pirates and a notorious gangster. Lively Philippine-made actioner makes up in movement what it lacks in finesse. (Dir: George Montgomery, 96 mins.)

From Hell to Texas (1958)**½ Don Murray, Diane Varsi. Interesting Western drama about a young cowboy, nicely played by Murray, who tries to mind his own business and avoid trouble during a time when gunmen ruled the territory. (Dir: Henry Hathaway, 100 mins.)

From Here to Eternity (1953)**** Burt Lancaster, Montgomery Clift, Deborah Kerr, Frank Sinatra, and Donna Reed. An excellent drama taken from James Jones' superb novel about the few days before the bombing of Pearl Harbor, in the lives of five people. This film won the Oscar for best film and Sinatra and Reed won supporting Oscars for their performances. One of the best American films made in the fifties. (Dir: Fred Zinnemann, 118 mins.)

From Istanbul—Orders to Kill (European, 1965)*½ Christopher Logan, Geraldine Pearsall. (Dir: Alex Butler, 88 mins.)

From Mao to Mozart: Isaac Stern in China (1980)**** A marvelous Academy Award winning documentary covering the trip to China, in the summer of 1979, of America's musical dynamo Isaac Stern. Not only is Stern one of the greatest violinists of our time, he is a brilliant communicator and teacher of music. The scenes showing Stern instructing young talented Chinese musicians are superb, as are some visually stunning sequences of China and her vibrant people. Movie credits are sometimes misleading or downright wrong. Murray Lerner, who receives billing as producer and director, was actually fired from the film more than a year before it was completed. Special credit goes to artistic supervisor Alan Miller and executive producer Walter Scheuer. (88 mins.)

From Noon til Three (1976)** Charles Bronson, Jill Ireland. Uneven, offbeat satire directed and written by Frank D. Gilroy, based on his novel. The complex plot deals with the unusual relationship between a drifter turned bank robber

(Bronson) and a rich widow (Ireland) in a tragicomic exploration of our culture, which has perpetuated some of the legends and romantic folklore of the old West. (104 mins.)

From Russia, with Love (Great Britain, 1964)***½ Sean Connery, Lotte Lenya, Daniela Bianchi. High class, diverting hokum. Perhaps the best of the James Bond adventures, so far. Agent 007 is on a tricky mission and he executes more narrow escapes than you can count. There's a dandy encounter with a muscular blond enemy agent (played by Robert Shaw) on a European train. Lotte Lenya is an evil spy out to get Bond. Of course, Sean Connery is, as always, suave, indestructible, and a wow with the ladies. (Dir: Terence Young, 118 mins.)

From the Earth to the Moon (1958)**½ Joseph Cotten, George Sanders, Debra Paget. Scientist discovering a new source of energy plans to send a rocket to the moon. Jules Verne sci-fi adventure; predictably, the special effects take top honors. (Dir: Byron Haskin, 100 mins.)

From the Mixed-Up Files of Mrs. Basil E. Frankweiler (1973)*½ Ingrid Bergman, Sally Prager, George Rose, Johnny Doran, Madeline Kahn. Alternate title: **The Hideaways.** (Dir: Fielder Cook, 105 mins.)

From the Terrace (1960)*** Paul Newman, Joanne Woodward, Myrna Loy. John O'Hara's mammoth novel about big business, social strata, and marriage problems turned into an overlength but well-acted film drama, helped by steady performances, good production. (Dir: Mark Robson, 144 mins.)

From This Day Forward (1946)*** Joan Fontaine, Mark Stevens. Young couple tries hard to adjust to the post-war world. Well-acted, interesting drama. (Dir: John Berry, 95 mins.)

Front, The (1976)***½ Woody Allen, Zero Mostel, Andrea Marcovicci, Joshua Shelley, Georgann Johnson. Woody Allen did not invent this bizarre horror story—the blacklisting in films and TV of the 1950's—he just plays the leading role, and very well, too, of a pal fronting for a blacklisted writer. For the newborn, blacklisting was the abhorrent practice of denying actors, directors, writers, etc., the right to work because of their alleged left-wing political views. The top executives of the TV industry in the early 50's could have quickly ended this loathsome industry-wide practice, but they did not have the elementary decency to do so. Walter Bernstein's original screenplay, which was nominated for an Academy Award, doesn't hold up all the way, but it does bring some humor to a nightmare-real situation full of anguish and suffering. There is a lot of expertise on the subject of blacklisting involved with "The Front." Performers Mostel and Shelley were blackballed for a long time, as were

242

writer Bernstein and director Ritt. This is not the definitive film of the squalid, demoralizing McCarthy days, but it's the only major movie that deals honestly with the aberration of blacklisting, and we must be grateful for that. (Dir: Martin Ritt, 94 mins.)

Front Page, The (1931)***½ Pat O'Brien, Adolphe Menjou, Frank McHugh, Edward Everett Horton, Mary Brian. A film classic. Fast and furious action and dialogue, as reporter O'Brien and editor Menjou battle corruption (and each other). Fascinatingly filmed by director Lewis Milestone, with a cast of stalwarts. (Dir: Lewis Milestone, 101 mins.)

Front Page, The (1974)**½ Jack Lemmon, Walter Matthau, Carol Burnett, Susan Sarandon, David Wayne. Here's the third movie version of the Ben Hecht-Charles MacArthur hit play of the late '20s about the Chicago newspaper world and the city-room gang. Billy Wilder manages to get some steam out of the love-hate relationship between unscrupulous editor Matthau and ace reporter Lemmon. As a nostalgic romp, this film can be enjoyed on its own level, but much of the humor is awfully dated and everyone, except the flawless Mr. Matthau, punches across their lines with an urgency that seems misplaced. Even Carol Burnett in a juicy cameo role as a hooker is surprisingly bad. (Dir: Billy Wilder, 105 mins.)

Front Page Story (British, 1954)***½ Jack Hawkins, Elizabeth Allan, Eva Bartok. A day in the life of a daily newspaper, pointing up a woman on trial for murder, a mother killed in an accident, etc. Dramatic, absorbing, well acted. (Dir: Gordon Parry, 95 mins.)

Front Page Woman (1935)**½ Bette Davis, George Brent, Roscoe Karns, Winifred Shaw. Reporter Davis tries to prove that a woman can be as good a "newsman" as any male; she solves a murder and scoops her boyfriend in the process. O.K. comedy-drama from Warner Bros., with a good mystery to keep you guessing. (Dir: Michael Curtiz, 80 mins.)

Frontier Gal (1945)*** Yvonne DeCarlo, Rod Cameron, Andy Devine. Fast, brawling Western with many comic touches. Yvonne DeCarlo, as a saloon operator, marries Rod Cameron, a fugitive wanted by the law, and the trouble begins. (Dir: Charles Lamont, 84 mins.)

Frontier Uprising (1961)*½ Jim Davis, Nancy Hadley. (Dir: Edward L. Cahn, 68 mins.)

Frozen Alive (Great Britain-West Germany, 1964)*½ Mark Stevens, Marianne Koch. (Dir: Bernard Knowles, 80 mins.)

Frozen Dead, The (Great Britain, 1967)** Dana Andrews. Gruesome experiments involving resuscitation of frozen bodies lead to murder. Routine thriller. (Dir: Herbert J. Leder, 95 mins.)

Frozen Ghost, The (1945)** Lon Chaney. A hypnotist, working in a wax museum, uncovers a murder plot. Typical melodramatics, with a harried performance by Chaney. (Dir: Harold Young, 61 mins.)

Fugitive, The (1947)**** Henry Fonda, Pedro Armendariz, Dolores Del Rio. In Mexico, a priest refuses to support the anti-cleric government. Gripping, superbly directed by John Ford. Fine drama. (Dir: John Ford, 104 mins.)

Fugitive Family (MTV 1980)** Richard Crenna, Mel Ferrer, Eli Wallach. An undercover agent and his family begin a new life in the Napa Valley wine country after testifying against a mobster. Crenna is the wary ex-agent; Ferrer, the mobster seeking revenge. Scenery, Crenna, and winery partner Wallach add patina to a predictable suspense yarn. (Dir: Paul Krasny, 99 mins.)

Fugitive in Belgrade (1966)*½ Jose Laurence, Sven Belik. (180 mins.)

Fugitive in Saigon (France, 1957)** Daniel Gelin, Ann Mechard. Frenchman escapes, lands in Saigon, redeems himself by aiding villagers and a native girl with whom he has fallen in love. English-dubbed drama has good location scenes but the plot dawdles. (Dir: Marcel Camus, 100 mins.)

Fugitive Kind, The (1960)** Anna Magnani, Marlon Brando, Joanne Woodward, Victor Jory. Woeful misfire of Tennessee Williams's "Orpheus Descending," with a blond Brando as a guitar-playing drifter. Magnani is too earthy and offbeat to mix with Brando's quicksilver irony. Woodward and Jory fare better, but this is essentially hooey. (Dir: Sidney Lumet, 135 mins.)

Full Confession (1939)*** Victor McLaglen, Joseph Calleia, Sally Eilers. A priest hears a murderer's confession, cannot divulge the information. Gripping, well-done drama. (Dir: John Farrow, 73 mins.)

Full Day's Work, A (France, 1979)**½ Jacques Douffilo, André Falcon, Vittorio Caprioli. Written and directed by the intelligent actor Jean-Louis Trintignant in a mixture of the zany, the macabre, and the terrifying. Douffilo stars as a young village baker who works at his father's side until, one sunny morning, he puts mom in his motorcycle sidecar and roars off on a murderous rampage, which he approaches as methodically as he approaches the kneading of bread.

Full Hearts and Empty Pockets (Germany, 1964)**½ Thomas Fritsch, Senta Berger, Linda Christian. Opportunistic young man uses blackmail and double-dealing as a means of succeeding in business (he really tries). Pretty fair drama in the spirit of "Room at the Top," not as good, but it holds the interest. English-dubbed. (Dir: Camillo Mastrocinque, 88 mins.)

Full Life, A (Japan)***½ Ineko Arima. Story of a young, liberated woman in Japan of the '60s. Impressive directorial

243

debut by Susumu Hani that makes a striking contrast to recent Hollywood films on the same theme. Arima previously played very polite Japanese ingenues; her performance, like the film, is intelligent, uncompromising, insistent. The style is like Godard without posturing, but a little too quietly ideological for dramatic effectiveness. (102 mins.)

Full of Life (1957)***½ Judy Holliday, Richard Conte, Salvatore Baccaloni. Charming and heartwarming comedy-drama about a young couple of newlyweds who move in with the husband's father when the wife announces she's going to have a baby. Miss Holliday is perfect as the perplexed mother-to-be and Conte matches her performance but Salvatore Baccaloni almost steals the picture with his magnificent portrait of Judy's Italian father-in-law. (Dir: Richard Quine, 91 mins.)

Fuller Brush Girl, The (1950)*** Lucille Ball, Eddie Albert, Lee Patrick. Ball was cast in the Red Skelton part in this sequel to "The Fuller Brush Man." One of the few starring movie roles where Ball reveals even a particle of her comic talent, largely due to the inspired slapstick inventions of scripter Frank Tashlin (rumor has it he directed much of the picture rather than the credited Lloyd Bacon). (85 mins.)

Fuller Brush Man, The (1948)*** Red Skelton, Janet Blair. Salesman stumbles into a murder mystery, traps the hoodlums. Wild and woolly slapstick, well done. (Dir: S. Sylvan Simon, 93 mins.)

Fun and Games (MTV 1980)**½ Valerie Harper, Max Gail, Cliff DeYoung. The title suggests a mindless comedy, but this is an earnest, if oversimplified, attempt to examine sexual harassment on the job. Harper is thoroughly believable as a divorced factory worker who resists the advances of her foreman (Gail), is passed over for a promotion as a result, and decides to fight for her rights. (Dir: Alan Smithee, 104 mins.)

Fun in Acapulco (1963)** Elvis Presley, Ursula Andress, Paul Lukas. What distinguishes this one from the myriad of other Presley films is some nifty scenery. Scenic beauty of a different kind is amply provided as the cameras explore the topographies of Ursula Andress and Elsa Cardenas. (Dir: Richard Thorpe, 97 mins.)

Fun with Dick and Jane (1977)*** Jane Fonda, George Segal, Ed McMahon. Parts of this comedy about contemporary life are quite funny and zany, others are serious and contemptible. The writers and director never seem to have quite made up their minds whether they wanted to produce a satire or an apologia for some of the more repellent values of American middle-class life. Segal plays an unemployed aerospace executive who, quite casually, turns to armed robbery to maintain his luxurious life-style. There are numerous writing credits in this erratic caper which evidently started out as a serious statement, then was turned into a jape, and finally given to the splendid Canadian writer Mordecai Richler for polishing. (Richler worked with director Kotcheff on "The Apprenticeship of Duddy Kravitz.") Fonda and Segal help over the rough spots in this wacky, irritating comedy-drama. Deft, surprising ending finds Segal again back in the corporate driver's seat. (Dir: Ted Kotcheff, 95 mins.)

Funeral in Berlin (1967)**½ Michael Caine, Oscar Homolka. This sequel to the highly successful film "The Ipcress File" again stars Michael Caine as Harry Palmer, spy. Though it's not quite up to the original, it's still good adventure. Shot on location in Berlin, the authentic footage—showing the Berlin Wall—adds to the suspense of the story about the possible defection of the head of Russian security (Homolka). (Dir: Guy Hamilton, 102 mins.)

Funniest Man in the World (1969)* Charles Chaplin. (Dir: Vernon P. Becker, 95 mins.)

Funny Face (1957)**** Fred Astaire, Audrey Hepburn, Kay Thompson. Astaire at his best, top George Gershwin tunes, colorful Parisian scenics, all combine to make a sprightly musical about a fashion photographer who turns a girl working in a bookstore into a high-fashion model. Top entertainment. (Dir: Stanley Donen, 103 mins.)

Funny Girl (1968)**** Barbra Streisand, Omar Sharif, Walter Pidgeon, Kay Medford. The nifty musical in which Barbra plays the famous Broadway star, Fanny Brice. Barbra is quite simply fabulous, giving one of the most triumphant and brilliant performances in the long history of musical films. If you've ever wondered what constitutes "star" quality in motion pictures, just tune in and watch this magical performer provide a definitive answer. Several of the supporting performances are fine, particularly Kay Medford playing Barbra's Jewish momma, who deserved the Oscar nomination she received. Barbra belts out some good songs and she makes them sound great, especially the most recorded song in the show, the Styne-Merrill hit "People." Director William Wyler deserves credit for having handled Barbra's film debut so superbly, for which she won an Oscar. (Dir: William Wyler, 155 mins.)

Funny Lady (1975)***½ Barbra Streisand, James Caan, Omar Sharif, Ben Vereen. This is "Funny Girl 2," but not quite as good overall, though when Barbra's singing it's magic all the way. The talking scenes get in the way and slow things down. Barbra is Fanny Brice, a big star on Broadway in the 30's, but a luckless lady in the offstage happiness department. James Caan playing the pushy Billy Rose works nicely with Barbra, and her spiffy songs include "It's Gonna Be A Great Day," which is a great number, and the enduring ballad, "Me and My Shadow." Ben Vereen is dynamite in a big, flashy dance routine. Screenplay by Jay Presson Allen and Arnold Schulman. (Dir: Herbert Ross, 140 mins.)

Funny Thing Happened on the Way to the Forum, A (1966)******* Zero Mostel, Phil Silvers, Jack Gilford, Michael Crawford, Michael Hordern, Buster Keaton. The mad, bawdy Broadway musical set in ancient Rome with the great Mostel playing a sly, eager-to-be-free slave is transferred to the screen with zest and style. It's burlesque at its best, and director Richard Lester keeps the cast working at a breakneck pace for laughs. The musical numbers are fun, but many have been deleted from the original score by Stephen Sondheim. Reminds us of how the movies neglected and wasted the enormous talents of the three lead comics. (99 mins.)

Funnyman (1967)*** Peter Bonerz. Director John Korty's film, about an actor in San Francisco's improvisational comedy group, the "Committee" and his attempts to make money, good, and girls. Some fun with ad execs, cartoonists, and insecticide commercials. (120 mins.)

Furies, The (1950)**½ Barbara Stanwyck, Walter Huston, Wendell Corey, Gilbert Roland, Judith Anderson. Stanwyck battles with her cattle baron father (Huston) in this Freudian western. Director Anthony Mann was classically trained and had long dreamed of doing a westernized "King Lear." This cluttered, oppressive film was as close as he came. Huston's last picture—he died before its release—and his last line in it is "There'll never be another like me." How true! B&W. (109 mins.)

Further Perils of Laurel and Hardy, The (1967)***½ Expert Robert Youngson's compilation of some hilarious sequences from Stan and Ollie's silent film period. Contains the kind of bellylaughs one experiences all too seldom these days. (Dir: Robert Youngson, 99 mins.)

Furtivos (Spain, 1975)**½ Lola Gaos, Ovidi Montllor. A political allegory, sufficiently muddled to pass the Spanish censors. A governor gathers a group of cronies at a country house for a weekend of hunting, but they spend most of their time symbolically exploiting the lower classes. Director José Luis Borau has introduced a strange sexual subtext about a housekeeper and her painfully repressed son, but it goes for naught. Shallow and more than a little stupefying, though Gaos's limns a role as the mother-housekeeper is worthy of her talents. Title means "poachers." (83 mins.)

Fury (1936)******* Spencer Tracy, Sylvia Sidney, Bruce Cabot, Walter Abel, Walter Brennan. Director Fritz Lang's first American film is a sharp, terrifying study of mob hysteria as a town tries to lynch an innocent murder suspect. Tracy survives, however, and returns to take revenge. Sidney, Brennan, and Cabot (as a near-Neanderthal) are outstanding. (94 mins.)

Fury, The (1978)** Kirk Douglas, Carrie Snodgress, Amy Irving, Charles Durning, Carol Rossen, John Cassavetes. What can you say about a picture in which Douglas gives the most restrained performance? Brian De Palma's ostentatious misdirection spoils a promising screenplay by John Farris and turns the film into an endless series of shock effects, of which the early ones work better than the later. Savvy performances by Rossen and Cassavetes. (117 mins.)

Fury at Showdown (1957)*½ John Derek, John Smith, Nick Adams. (Dir: Gerd Oswald, 75 mins.)

Fury at Smugglers' Bay (Great Britain, 1962)** Peter Cushing, Bernard Lee, Michele Mercier. Head of a cutthroat band of ship wreckers holds a community in the grip of terror. Swashbuckler is on the lengthy side, with a good cast saving inferior material from seeming even worse. (Dir: John Gilling, 92 mins.)

Fury in Paradise (U.S.-Mexico, 1955)* Peter Thompson, Rea Iturbide, Carlos Rivas. (Dirs: George Bruce, Rolando Aguilar, 77 mins.)

Fury of Achilles (Italy, 1962)*½ Jacques Bergerac, Gordon Mitchell. (Dir: Marino Girolami, 116 mins.)

Fury of Hercules (Italy, 1960)*½ Brad Harris, Alan Steel. (Dir: V. Scega, 95 mins.)

Fury of the Apache—See: Apache Fury

Fury of the Pagans (Italy, 1962)*½ Edmund Purdom, Rossana Podesta. (Dir: Guido Malatesta, 86 mins.)

Future Cop (MTV 1976)*½ Ernest Borgnine, Michael Shannon, John Amos. (Dir: Jud Taylor, 72 mins.)

Futureworld (1976)**½ Peter Fonda, Arthur Hill, Blythe Danner. An enjoyable stupid sequel to "Westworld," with Fonda as a hard-nosed reporter investigating a robot-staffed resort complex headed by Hill—who, to no one's surprise, is out to take over the world. Looks good, thanks to shrewd location shooting at modernistic shopping centers and Hyatt hotels. Danner helps. (Dir: Richard Heffron, 104 mins.)

Futz (1969)*** Seth Allen, John Bakos, Mari-Claire Charba. You won't be seeing this far-out allegory on prime-time commercial TV. Ever wanted to see a film about an Appalachian farmer who likes making love to a pig? This is your only chance! It's director Tom O'Horgan's surrealistic vision of Rochelle Owens' award-winning Off-Broadway play. Grotesque, demanding, sometimes rewarding. A film for special tastes for cable TV audiences. "Futz" may be smuts to some. (Dir: Tom O'Horgan, 92 mins.)

Fuzz (1972)**½ Burt Reynolds, Yul Brynner, Raquel Welch. Uneven and scatterbrained police yarn which relies on the easygoing style and charm of Reynolds, as a police detective, and the under-played villainy of Brynner as a culprit with a penchant for bombings. Miss Welch is also on hand as a policewoman who has trouble getting the guys to treat her as just one of the fellas. The cops tend to play each situation for laughs but there are enough serious moments to satisfy crime-story fans. In the fine supporting cast, Tom Skerritt registers strongest as Reynolds' cop-buddy. (Dir: Richard Colla, 92 mins.)

Fuzzy Pink Nightgown, The (1957)** Jane Russell, Ralph Meeker, Keenan Wynn. Jane Russell, as a movie star with blonde hair, is kidnapped by two clumsy but nice guys and the fun begins. Good for a few chuckles. (Dir: Norman Taurog, 87 mins.)

FX 18, Secret Agent (Italy-France-Spain, 1964)* Ken Clark, Jany Clair. (Dir: Maurice Cloche, 95 mins.)

G-Men (1935)*** James Cagney, Lloyd Nolan. Exciting crime-busting story with Cagney on the side of the law for a change. (Dir: William Keighley, 85 mins.)

Gable and Lombard (1976)½ Jill Clayburgh, James Brolin, Red Buttons. (Dir: Sidney J. Furie, 131 mins.)

Gaby (1956)**½ Leslie Caron, John Kerr. A somewhat weak remake of the romantic tale "Waterloo Bridge." The story is about a young soldier who falls in love with a ballerina before he's shipped to the front during WW II. Miss Caron is wistful in the title role but the melodramatic script doesn't help. (Dir: Curtis Bernhardt, 97 mins.)

Gaily, Gaily (1969)***½ Beau Bridges, Melina Mercouri, Brian Keith, George Kennedy, Margot Kidder, Wilfred Hyde-White, Hume Cronyn. Norman Jewison produced and directed this uneven but generally appealing comedy based on Ben Hecht's autobiographical reminiscences of his days as a youthful cub reporter on a Chicago paper. The period is 1910, and the corruption in Chicago is second to none when young bumpkin Ben Harvey, engagingly played by Beau Bridges, comes to town and lands at the jolliest bordello in town. Mercouri is well cast in another of her lovable madam roles and the rest of the supporting cast is good. Bridges is charming, conveying a quality of manly innocence and vulnerability. (117 mins.)

Gal Who Took the West, The (1949)** Yvonne DeCarlo, Charles Coburn, Scott Brady. Amusing comedy-drama set in the wild and woolly west. Miss DeCarlo plays an entertainer who takes the Arizona frontier by storm. (Dir: Frederick de Cordova, 84 mins.)

Gal Young Un (1979)*** Dana Preu, David Peck, J. Smith. Based on a good short story by Marjorie Kinnan Rawlings, produced on a shoestring, and written, directed, photographed, and edited by Victor Nuñez, the film has impeccable artistic credentials. Nuñez's exposition is slow and he has a maddening tendency to repeat his tiniest dramatic points. About a middle-aged woman victimized by a fast-talking hustler: Preu carries herself with dignity, charm, and not a little savvy, but Peck fails to convince as her seducer. (105 mins.)

Galileo (Great Britain-Canada, 1974)*** Topol, Edward Fox, John Gielgud, Clive Revill. Uneven but often absorbing version of Bertolt Brecht's stimulating play as adapted by, and earlier played on the stage by Charles Laughton. Opens in 1609 in Padua with an impoverished Galileo seeking funds both to support his family and his scientific research, which scandalized the intellectual and political establishment of the time. Director Joseph Losey had wanted to direct this project for years, and rounded up an illustrious supporting cast with generally fine performances. But Topol playing Galileo is simply not an actor of enough range and power to play such a demanding role, and the film suffers finally because somehow the events of Galileo do not seem as important as they should. But there is enough of interest to hold thoughtful viewers. (Dir: Joseph Losey, 145 mins.)

Gallant Hours, The (1960)**½ James Cagney. Cagney's restrained performance as "Admiral Halsey" is a far cry from his raucous "Captain" in "Mr. Roberts," but it is the only worthwhile thing about this otherwise routine war film, based on actual events in the South Pacific Campaign during World War II.(Dir: Robert Montgomery, 111 mins.)

Gallant Journey (1946)**½ Glenn Ford, Janet Blair. Biography of the man who contributed to aviation by experimenting with glider planes. Factual but not very exciting drama. (Dir: William Wellman, 85 mins.)

Gallant Lady (1934)*** Ann Harding, Clive Brook, Otto Kruger, Dickie Moore. Predictable but beguiling tale of a purposeful mother who contrives to regain her son born out of wedlock. Sentimental, though less so than was customary then, and stylish. (Dir: Gregory La Cava, 81 mins.)

Gallant Legion, The (1948)*** William Elliott, Adrian Booth, Bruce Cabot. Texas Ranger fights the leader of a powerful group desiring to split Texas into sections. Exciting western, well done. (Dir: Joseph Kane, 88 mins.)

Gallant Sons (1940)** Jackie Cooper, Bonita Granville. Good juvenile mystery for the kids as three youngsters turn detectives and solve a crime. (Dir: George B. Seitz, 76 mins.)

Galloping Major, The (Great Britain, 1951)*** Basil Radford, Jimmy Hanley. A retired major has his eye on a race horse, but when bidding time comes he buys a broken-down temperamental nag by mistake. This one gets very funny at times; one of the better comedies. (Dir: Henry Cornelius, 82 mins.)

Gambit (1966)*** Shirley MacLaine, Michael Caine, Herbert Lom. Shirley MacLaine as a Eurasian lady of intrigue, Michael Caine as an ambitious, but not very effective crook, and a jaunty story about a proposed theft of a valuable art treasure add up to fun. However, be forewarned, the plot fluctuates between subtle comedy, out-and-out spoofing, and serious business. With a little more care, this film could have been very good indeed but it's still entertaining as is. Directed by Ronald Neame, it may remind you occasionally of some of Jules Dassin's spiffy crime films. (108 mins.)

Gambler, The (1974)*** James Caan, Paul Sorvino, Lauren Hutton. James Caan is very good in this story of a compulsive gambler who eventually gets what he seems to be striving for, humiliation and a brutal beating. Along the way, the educated college professor with the double life cons and uses everyone from his bewildered mother to a girl who cares for him. You can't help but feel exasperation as the anti-hero keeps taking risk after risk, never knowing when to call it quits. Director Karel Reisz keeps it all sharply in focus. (111 mins.)

Gambler from Natchez, The (1954)** Dale Robertson, Debra Paget. Adventurer goes after the varmint who killed his pa. Churns a well-worn path down that old celluloid river. (Dir: Henry Levin, 88 mins.)

Game for Three Losers (Great Britain, 1965)** Michael Gough, Mark Eden. Prominent politician becomes enmeshed in an extortion plot. Routine but competent crime melodrama. (Dir: Gerry O'Hara, 55 mins.)

Game of Danger (Great Britain, 1954)**½ Jack Warner, Veronica Hurst. Two little boys playing cops 'n' robbers accidentally kill a man. Out of the ordinary melodrama, but routine handling prevents it from being anything more. (Dir: Lance Comfort, 88 mins.)

Game of Death, A (1945)**½ John Loder, Audrey Long, Edgar Barrier. Big-game hunter is shipwrecked on an island owned by a madman who makes sport of hunting human prey. Exciting version of famous story, "The Most Dangerous Game"; thriller fans should like. (Dir: Robert Wise, 72 mins.)

Games (1967)*** Simone Signoret, Katharine Ross, James Caan. Offbeat, macabre drama which won't be everyone's cup of tea, but there certainly are novel and ghoulish plot turns along the way. The attractive Katharine Ross, who played Dustin Hoffman's young girlfriend in "The Graduate," is convincing playing a young wife, quite rightfully worried about her well being. Newcomer James Caan, playing her husband, is about as animated as a totem pole. Curtis Harrington directed from a story of his own creation. You've got to pay attention to this intellectual chiller-diller about a warped, rich young couple who indulge in way out "games" of a kind not condoned by civilized society. (Dir: Curtis Harrington, 100 mins.)

Games, The (Great Britain, 1969)**½ Ryan O'Neal, Michael Crawford, Charles Aznavour. Hugh Atkinson's novel "The Games," about the grueling preparation of long-distance runners for the Olympic marathon race, makes an episodic drama enlivened by the great race itself at the end of the film. Erich Segal, who is himself an enthusiastic and quite good marathon runner, wrote the screenplay. The character of Vendek, played by Aznavour, is clearly based on the great Czech long-distance runner, Emil Zatopek, who won this race in the 1950's. (Dir: Michael Winner, 96 mins.)

Gamma People, The (Great Britain, 1956)** Paul Douglas, Eva Bartok. Moderate drama with science-fiction and political overtones concerning a gamma ray invention by which people are transformed into either geniuses or imbeciles. (Dir: John Gilling, 79 mins.)

Gammera the Invincible (U.S.-Japan, 1966)* Brian Donlevy, Albert Dekker, John Baragrey. (Dir: Noriaki Yuasi, 88 mins.)

Gang That Couldn't Shoot Straight, The (1971)½ Jerry Orbach, Leigh Taylor-Young, Jo Van Fleet, Robert De Niro, Lionel Stander. (96 mins.)

Gang War (1958)**½ Charles Bronson, Kent Taylor. Teacher's wife is slain by hoodlums, he becomes a one-man vengeance committee. Good performances lift this from the gangster rut. (Dir: Gene Fowler, Jr., 75 mins.)

Gang's All Here, The (1943)*** Alice Faye, Benny Goodman and His Band, Carmen Miranda, Eugene Pallette, Edward Everett Horton, Shelia Ryan, Charlotte Greenwood, James Elliton. Director Busby Berkeley's most audacious film—an exploration of the possibilities of movement and color that moves into the realm of pure abstraction. The sexual symbolism is at its most blatant (what can you say about a film that features 60 girls waving gigantic bananas?) and Berkeley's tendency to disembody reaches its apotheosis when the heads of all the principals float about on a field of amber and gold. (103 mins.)

Gangster, The (1947)*** Barry Sullivan, Belita, John Ireland. The leader of a mob lets his inner fear and insecurity get the best of him, loses his gang; is finally mowed down by a rival outfit. Interesting psychological study of a hoodlum, strong, well acted. (Dir: Gordon Wiles, 84 mins.)

Gangster Boss (France, 1961)** Fernandel. Timid professor unwittingly carries a bag stuffed with money, becomes involved with criminals. Typical Fernandel comedy, with the horse-faced comedian supplying some mild chuckles. Dubbed in English. (Dir: Henry Verneuil, 100 mins.)

Gangster Story (1960)* Walter Matthau, Carol Grace. (Dir: Walter Matthau, 65 mins.)

Gangway (Great Britain, 1937)** Jessie Matthews, Barry Mackay, Noel Madison, Alastair Sim. Second-rate Jessie Matthews vehicle redeemed by the lady's considerable charm and hoofing prowess. (Dir: Sonnie Hale, 85 mins.)

Garden of Allah (1936)**½ Marlene Dietrich, Charles Boyer, Basil Rathbone, Joseph Schildkraut, John Carradine. Superplush clichéd production with sultry temptress Dietrich rejecting one man after another until she meets ascetic dream man Boyer. Set in the Algerian desert, the film's real star is early Technicolor. (Dir: Richard Boleslawski, 90 mins.)

Garden of Delights, The (Spain, 1970)*** Jose Luis Lopez Vazquez, Luchy Soto, Geraldine Chaplin (cameo). Spanish director Carlos Saura's fantasy about a crippled, amnesiac industrialist whose relatives stage grotesque psychodramas from his childhood in order to unlock the secret of his Swiss bank account. All the members of the family end up in wheelchairs. Academic surrealism with moments of superb whimsy and chilling austerity. (99 mins.)

Garden of Evil (1954)**½ Hugh Marlowe, Cameron Mitchell, Gary Cooper, Richard Widmark, Susan Hayward. Too much scowling and glowering in this interesting but misguided western, in which director Henry Hathaway builds to a simmering anticlimax. Ex-sheriff Cooper and gambler Richard Widmark team up to rescue a woman's husband from a mine, only to be trapped by an Indian attack. Hayward projects her usual disquieting sensuality. Excellent score by Bernard Herrmann. (100 mins.)

Garden of the Finzi Continis, The (Italy-West Germany, 1970)**** Dominique Sanda, Lino Capolicchio, Helmut Berger, Fabio Testi. The late director Vittorio De Sica's finest film since the post-war years is a melancholy, slowly-paced rendering of an aristocratic Jewish family's downfall in Mussolini's Italy. As patricians living in a walled estate, the family is impervious to the political events that will engulf them. The acting is flawless— Dominique Sanda's enigmatic portrayal of Micol, the eldest daughter involved in an affair with a gentile, and Helmut Berger's moving performance as her sickly brother, are the two standouts in a uniformly superb cast. De Sica directs in hazy colors which give an air of sentimen-

tality, but in combining personal tragedy with the rising political fervor that will provide the "final solution," De Sica has achieved a rare subtlety. Based on Giorgio Bassani's autobiographical novel. (95 mins.)

Gargoyles (MTV 1972)* Cornel Wilde. (Dir: B. W. L. Norton, 74 mins.)

Garibaldi (Italy-France, 1961)** Renzo Ricci, Paolo Stoppa, Tina Louise. Biography of patriotic Italian leader, soldier, and statesman who fought forces of oppression and saved the country. Elaborately produced, filmed by Roberto Rossellini, but quite lengthy, leisurely in movement. Dubbed in English. Alternate Title: **Viva L' Italia**. (110 mins.)

Garment Jungle, The (1957)*** Lee J. Cobb, Kerwin Mathews, Gia Scala. Forceful drama about the control by the rackets of the garment industry in a big city. Performances are good with a standout bit by Robert Loggia as a brave union organizer who meets with opposition by the thugs. (Dir: Vincent Sherman, 88 mins.)

Gas-Oil (France, 1957)** Jean Gabin, Jeanne Moreau. A truck driver becomes involved in a killing, clears himself. The above rating is solely for the talents of the principal players, who don't deserve this tired old crime story. English-dubbed. Alternate title: **Hi-Jack Highway**. (Dir: Gilles Grangier, 122 mins.)

Gaslight (1944)*** Charles Boyer, Ingrid Bergman, Joseph Cotten. Exciting psychological melodrama about a man who is trying to drive his wife to insanity. Not as good as the Broadway hit "Angel Street" but still good entertainment. (Dir: George Cukor, 114 mins.)

Gaslight Follies (1945)** Nostalgic roundup of films of yesteryear includes glimpses of such luminaries as Mary Pickford, Tom Mix, Chaplin, etc. As well as some old newsreel clips. Narrated by Milton Cross. Passable as a novelty. This was the first production effort of Joe ("Hercules") Levine, who's gone on to bigger and richer productions. (110 mins.)

Gas-s-s....Or It May Become Necessary to Destroy The World in Order to Save It! (1970)**½ Robert Corff, Elaine Giftos, Ben Vereen, Bud Cort, Cindy Williams, Talia Coppola. Some effective scenes in this end-of-the-world youth survival tale, that had a cult following for a while as the time of its release. Country Joe and the Fish supply most of the music. The screenplay, written by George Armitage, tries to be hip and cool! Story line about a defense plant in Alaska which springs a gas main, and everyone over their twenties perishes. Survivors have some spacey experiences back in the U.S. of A. Director Roger Corman has elicited deft performances from a number of troupers who went on to achieve substantial recognition later. Note Talia "Rocky" Shire playing Coralie, and still using the name Coppola. (79 mins.)

248

Gate of Hell (Japan, 1954)*** Kazuo Hasegawa, Machiko Kyo. Winner of both the Grand Prix at Cannes and the Academy Award, this Japanese film is somewhat overrated in the West. About the bloody consequences of a soldier's lust for a noblewoman, which she does not return, but is ill equipped to reject. Kyo is lovely and perplexed as the ruffled love object. Director Teinosuke Kinugasa serves up the choreographed battles and delicate, intelligent color that are cliché virtues of Japanese cinema. (89 mins.)

Gates of Paris (France, 1957)***½ Pierre Brasseur, Henri Vidal. Loafer hides a hunted criminal. Beautiful performances and fine direction of Rene Clair make this comedy drama a standout import that packs a wallop in its own quiet way. (103 mins.)

Gathering, The (MTV 1977)*** Edward Asner, Maureen Stapleton, Lawrence Pressman. Powerful performance by Asner in a nice old-fashioned family drama. A successful engineer discovers he's dying; when his estranged wife discovers his secret, she suggests a Christmas reunion of the whole family. They plan not to tell the children the real reason for the reunion, but of course it leaks out and sets the stage for superb individual scenes. Stapleton shines as the wife and Pressman is excellent as the oldest son. (Dir: Randal Kleiser, 104 mins.)

Gathering, Part II, The (MTV 1979)*** Maureen Stapleton, Rebecca Balding, Jameson Parker, Efrem Zimbalist, Jr. Picks up the action two years after the father's death. Stapleton again plays the strong Kate Thornton, who takes over her husband's business and has to deal with her children's reactions to her new romance at another Christmas family reunion. Most of the cast of "The Gathering" is back. Well-acted drama. (Dir: Charles S. Dubin, 104 mins.)

Gathering of Eagles, A (1963)**½ Rock Hudson, Mary Peach, Rod Taylor. It's the Strategic Air Command this time, with the stern officer whose devotion to duty causes complications in his home life. Some fine aerial camerawork and good performances, along with a story that suffers from slowness when it's on the ground. (Dir: Delbert Mann, 115 mins.)

Gator (1976)** Burt Reynolds, Lauren Hutton, Jerry Reed, Jack Weston. Reynolds's direction is reasonably competent on his first time out. This sequel to "White Lightning" has all the elements of the southern formula: bootleggers, corrupt cops, car chases, and a seducible northern woman (Hutton). (116 mins.)

Gauguin the Savage (MTV 1980)** David Carradine, Lynn Redgrave, Barrie Houghton. Disappointing, handsomely mounted production on the life of painter Paul Gauguin filmed in France and Tahiti. A rebel himself, bony David Carradine plays short, round Gauguin, a genius with

color on a canvas. Writer J. P. Miller's Gauguin is a selfish, carousing fellow, when it comes to wife and friends, like the mad Vincent Van Gogh, but the man could paint. Carradine, generally a good actor is surprisingly wooden. A misfire from numerous talented people. (Dir: Fielder Cook, 131 mins.)

Gauntlet, The (1977)*** Clint Eastwood, Sondra Locke, Pat Hingle, William Prince. Director Eastwood's tale of a down-and-out cop who takes on the mob and his own Phoenix police force to bring in a murder witness (Locke) is full of audaciously stylized action. Quirky and uncompromisingly personal. (109 mins.)

Gay Deceivers, The (1969)* Kevin Coughlin, Larry Casey, Brooke Bundy. (Dir: Bruce Kessler, 91 mins.)

Gay Divorcee, The (1934)**** Fred Astaire, Ginger Rogers, Edward Everett Horton. Astaire and Rogers star together for the first time. It works beautifully, with great Cole Porter songs like "Night and Day," and Con Conrad and Herb Magidson's "The Continental." (Dir: Mark Sandrich, 107 mins.)

Gay Lady (Great Britain, 1949)*** Jean Kent, James Donald. A music hall entertainer makes the grade when she marries a young duke. Pleasant turn of-the-century romance, well acted. Alternate title: **Trottie True**. (Dir: Brian Desmond Hurst, 91 mins.)

Gay Purr-ee (1962)**½ Pleasant animated cartoon about a pussycat who goes to Paris, is saved from the villain, etc. Voices of Judy Garland and Robert Goulet and the songs of Harold Arlen are assets; there are some cute moments, for the younger set. (Dir: Abe Levitow, 86 mins.)

Gay Sisters (1942)** Barbara Stanwyck, George Brent, Geraldine Fitzgerald, Gig Young, Nancy Coleman. Long, dull, tiresome melodrama about one of Hollywood's favorite topics, the bad apple in a fine family. (Dir: Irving Rapper, 108 mins.)

Gay USA (1977)**½ Centered on the 1977 Gay Pride Parade in San Francisco. Though not quite a triumph, it offers a lot of points-of-view within its viewpoint.

Gazebo, The (1959)*** Glenn Ford, Debbie Reynolds, Carl Reiner, John McGiver. When a TV mystery writer is blackmailed, he decides on murder as the way out, takes a shot at a shadowy figure in his home, later discovers the real blackmailer has been murdered—so who did he kill? Wacky comedy gets the laughs—Ford works hard, and there's an adroit performance by McGiver. (Dir: George Marshall, 100 mins.)

Geisha, A (Japan, 1953)**** A late masterpiece by the preeminent Japanese director, Kenji Mizoguchi, who treats his perennial theme—woman, and her problematical place in a society that both exploits and idealizes her—through a story of a young girl's education as a geisha, and her conflicts with an older sister. One of the few Mizoguchi films of the fifties with a contemporary setting, its *mise en scène* is no less eternal than that of *Ugetsu* or *Sansho the Bailiff*. (87 mins.)

Geisha Boy, The (1958)**½ Jerry Lewis, Marie McDonald, Suzanne Pleshette, Sessue Hayakawa. Jerry as an inept magician who joins a USO unit touring the Orient works mightily to produce some laughs in this comedy and succeeds to a fair degree. Some clever gags stand out, while the film has nice visual backgrounds. (Dir: Frank Tashlin, 98 mins.)

Gemini Man (MTV 1976)* Ben Murphy, Katherine Crawford, Richard Dysart, Dana Elcar. (Dir: Alan Levi, 98 mins.)

Gene Krupa Story, The (1960)** Sal Mineo, Susan Kohner, James Darren. Corny, highly fictionalized account of the rise to fame by drummer Gene Krupa. One of he worst scenes is a bit of hokum which describes how Krupa got in with a fast crowd and started smoking marijuana. The casting of Sal Mineo as Krupa is another stroke of idiocy. (Dir: Don Weis, 101 mins.)

General, The (1927)**** Buster Keaton, Marion Mack. Director Keaton is a locomotive engineer in the Civil War South whose train is hijacked by Union spies; his attempts to bring her back become a strangely moving, very funny account of a man's love for the fruits of his work. (74 mins.)

General Della Rovere (Italy, 1960)**** Sandra Milo, Hannes Messemer, Vittorio De Sica. Roberto Rossellini directs a compelling and moving drama of heroism thrust upon an unlikely hero. De Sica gives the performance of his life as a threadbare con man who is forced into martyrdom when he impersonates an Italian resistance leader. (129 mins.)

General Died at Dawn, The (1936)*** Gary Cooper, Madeleine Carroll, Akim Tamiroff, Dudley Digges, Porter Hall. Clifford Odets wrote the script of this exotic adventure, well directed by Lewis Milestone, about a mercenary in China (Cooper) falling in love with a spy (Carroll) and clashing with an evil warlord (Tamiroff). Novelist John O'Hara has a small role. (100 mins.)

Generation (1969)** David Janssen, Kim Darby, Carl Reiner. Unsuccessful filming of the moderately entertaining play about the relationship between a rebellious young couple and her establishment father. Henry Fonda gave a fine, low-key performance on stage, but David Janssen seems totally out of touch with the role, a dogmatic dad determined to have his pregnant daughter deliver his grandchild as he sees fit. Even Kim Darby's usually beguiling manner gets tiresome here. (Dir: George Schaefer, 104 mins.)

Generations of Resistance (1980)***½ UN-sponsored, dramatic story of the rise of black nationalism in South Africa. Director Peter Davis uses rare and illuminating archival footage and the insightful testimony of some who led and participated in resistance to apartheid.

Genesis II (MTV 1973)**½ Alex Cord. Fans of Gene Roddenberry's imaginative science-fiction series "Star Trek" might enjoy this science-fiction film. Alex Cord stars as a 20th-century space scientist who is discovered almost two centuries later in a natural catastrophe. Sci-fi hocus-pocus, served up with a straight face as warring tribes seek to pick the scientist's brain. (Dir: John Llewellyn Moxey, 97 mins.)

Genevieve (Great Britain, 1953)**** John Gregson, Kenneth More, Dinah Sheridan, Kay Kendall. A divinely funny romp about two English couples who are old-car buffs and enter their trophies in a cross-country race. In addition to the glories of the old four-wheeled beauties, a large number of which were collected for this race, you also see Kay Kandall, who was not only sublimely pretty but also a high comedy farceuse of enormous skill. There are numerous delicious sequences in this consistently inventive comedy and if you don't enjoy it immensely you should have your sense of humor checked under Medicare. (Dir: Henry Cornelius, 86 mins.)

Genghis Khan (Philippines, 1953)*** Manuel Conde, Elvira Reyes. A Mongol tribesman rises to be a powerful ruler by overcoming all opposition. Unusual novelty offering has plenty of well-staged action scenes to compensate for some technical weaknesses. (Dir: Manuel Conde, 90 mins.)

Genghis Khan (U.S.-British-German-Yugoslavian, 1965)** Omar Sharif, Stephen Boyd, James Mason, Eli Wallach, Mongol youth grows up to be the mighty Genghis Khan, seeking vengeance upon the rival chieftain who killed his father. Largescale spectacle has the action, but the story and acting are little better than the usual for this type of film. (Dir: Henry Levin, 124 mins.)

Gentle Annie (1944)**½ James Craig, Donna Reed, Marjorie Main. Entertaining little western with Miss Main playing the part of a lovable train robber. Based on a MacKinlay Kantor novel, this offers slightly different types of bad men. (Dir: Andrew Marton, 80 mins.)

Gentle Giant (1967)**½ Dennis Weaver, Vera Miles, Ralph Meeker, Clint Howard, Huntz Hall. Youngsters may go for this uncomplicated tale of a boy and a bear which led to the TV series "Gentle Ben." Adults may sit through it without flinching. (Dir: James Neilson, 93 mins.)

Gentle Gunman, The (Great Britain, 1952)*** John Mills, Dirk Bogarde. A gunman for the Irish rebels believes in more peaceful means for obtaining their goal. Good melodrama. (Dir: Basil Dearden, 86 mins.)

Gentle Rain, The (U.S.-Brazil, 1966)*½ Christopher George, Lynda Day, Fay Spain. (Dir: Burt Balaban, 94 mins.)

Gentle Sex, The (Great Britain, 1943)**½ Lilli Palmer, Jean Gillie. Dramatic story of women in wartime in Britain doing their bit for the eventual victory. Nicely done, some good moments. (Dirs: Leslie Howard, Maurice Elvey, 93 mins.)

Gentleman after Dark, A (1942)*½ Brian Donlevy, Miriam Hopkins, Preston Foster. (Dir: Edwin L. Marin, 77 mins.)

Gentleman at Heart, A (1942)**½ Cesar Romero, Carole Landis, Milton Berle. Fairly amusing comedy about a racketeer who goes into the art business. Berle and Romero are partners in crime and when the material is passable, they'll make you laugh. (Dir: Ray McCarey, 66 mins.)

Gentleman Jim (1942)***½ Errol Flynn, Jack Carson, Alexis Smith. Errol took time out from winning the war to play Jim Corbett in this exciting biography of the suave boxer which also presents an interesting panorama of boxing's early years as an outlawed sport. (Dir: Raoul Walsh, 104 mins.)

Gentleman Tramp, The (1975)***½ Charles Chaplin. Documentary on the career of the immortal Chaplin, written, directed, and edited by Richard Patterson. An affectionate tribute, with music by Chaplin himself and new footage along with the old. Narrated by Laurence Olivier, Jack Lemmon, and Walter Matthau. Color and B&W. (80 mins.)

Gentleman's Agreement (1947)*** Gregory Peck, Dorothy McGuire, John Garfield, Anne Revere, Celeste Holm. Darryl F. Zanuck got kudos for producing this exposé of anti-Semitism, and though the moral issues were presented in such a manner as to make little sense. Based on a bestseller by Laura Z. Hobson, Moss Hart's adaptation makes Peck as a magazine writer who masquerades as a Jew in order to report firsthand on high-society discrimination. It's contrived nonsense, though director Elia Kazan puts his excellent cast through the paces efficiently. Oscars for Best Picture, Director, Supporting Actress (Holm). (118 mins.)

Gentlemen Marry Brunettes (1955)**½ Jane Russell, Jeanne Crain. Beautiful sisters on the loose in Paris is the inviting theme of this dull musical. The girls are fun to look at, but the picture doesn't match their charms. (Dir: Richard Sale, 97 mins.)

Gentlemen of the Night (Italy, 1963)*½ Guy Madison, Lisa Gastoni. (Dir: Pino Mercanti, 98 mins.)

Gentlemen Prefer Blondes (1953)**** Marilyn Monroe, Jane Russell, Tommy Noonan, Charles Coburn, George "Foghorn" Winslow. Director Howard Hawks's grand, brassy musical about two girls from Little Rock—Monroe and Russell—gone gold-digging in Paris. The male sex is represented by Noonan as a nerd, Coburn as a dirty old man, and the unforgettable Winslow as a 12-year-old voyeur. The opening shot—Russell and Monroe in sequins standing against a screaming red drape—is enough to knock you out of your seat, and the pace hardly lets up from there, as Russell romances the entire U.S. Olympic Team to the tune of "Ain't There Anyone Here for Love?" and Hawks keeps topping perversity with perversity. Astonishing. (91 mins.)

George Raft Story, The (1961)**½ Ray Danton, Julie London, Jayne Mansfield. Biography of the screen badman, his rise from hoofer to movie star. Not as bad as might be expected; doesn't stick too close to facts, but Danton delivers well in the title role, while the story is continually attention-holding. (Dir: Joseph M. Newman, 106 mins.)

George Washington Slept Here (1942)*** Jack Benny, Ann Sheridan. Jack has fun in this screen adaptation of the Broadway hit about a city dwelling family which buys a Pennsylvania farmhouse—not in Gettysburg. Ending is weary but there's a lot of fun before it. (Dir: William Keighley, 93 mins.)

Georgy Girl (Great Britain, 1966)**** Lynn Redgrave, Alan Bates, James Mason, Charlotte Rampling. A very touching, charming, and thoroughly entertaining comedy-drama with top-notch characterizations played superbly by the cast. Lynn Redgrave, in the title role of the frumpy British lass who's satisfied with living life vicariously with her swinging London roommate, is quite marvelous and deeply moving. Many things happen to Georgy before she makes a final compromise. Sensitive direction by Silvio Narizzano. Miss Redgrave makes her first starring role a memorable one that richly deserved all the honors it received, and a few that she didn't receive as well. (100 mins.)

Germany, Pale Mother (West Germany, 1979)*** Eva Mattes. Eva Mattes's gargantuan performance as a bourgeois Mother Courage of postwar Germany carries the lengthy and morally suspect dramatic ideas of this elaborate melodrama by Helma Sanders-Brahms. Eva is married just as Poland is invaded, and her husband is drafted for the duration. When he comes home, brutal and alienated, she learns her battle for survival has not yet ended. Sanders-Brahms has thought extensively about her subject, but her ultimate argument—that Germans cannot be held accountable for what was done if they are too young to remember it—beggars the fundamental moral questions raised by her work. The film is ultimately spurious, overlong, and unremittingly depressing, but Mattes brilliantly creates a character who endures not only the hardships of history, but also the demands of her *auteur*. (Dir: Helma Sanders-Brahms.)

Germany, Year Zero (Italy, 1948)***½ Roberto Rossellini followed *Open City* and *Paisan* with this film, the final chapter in what's come to be known as his "War

Trilogy." Filmed in the bombed-out city of Berlin in 1947, it deals with the aftermath of the war, a pervading moral crisis and the fate of a young German boy. To the critics of the time, it seemed that Rossellini had betrayed the tenets of neorealism by introducing melodrama, an elliptical narrative, and intimations of a Christian consciousness. It now appears as Rossellini's first mature work, pointing to his masterpieces of the fifties. (74 mins.)

Geronimo (1940)** Preston Foster, Ellen Drew. The kids may like this childish dramatization of the white man's scrapes with the Apaches, but it's not particularly good for a top budget western. (Dir: Paul H. Sloane, 89 mins.)

Geronimo (1962)**½ Chuck Connors, Ross Martin, Pat Conway. Fairly well-done western, made in Mexico, about the legendary Apache chief and his bandit days south of the border. Once you get over the initial discomfort of seeing Connors play Geronimo, the actioner becomes more interesting. (Dir: Arnold Laven, 101 mins.)

Gervaise (France, 1957)*** Maria Schell, François Perier. Zola's tale of a woman's misfortunes as she tries to provide for her family, care for her alcoholic husband. Excellent performances, direction. English-dubbed. (Dir: Rene Clement, 116 mins.)

Get Carter (Great Britain, 1971)*** Michael Caine, Britt Ekland, Ian Hendry. British gangster film set in the north of England in the '70's. The inspiration is Hollywood 1940's. Compelling entry written and directed by English TV director Michael Hodges, making a promising switch to the big screen. Caine is a cheap hood who returns home to investigate his brother's death. One of Caine's best performances, and Hodges captures the dreary quality of life in the industrial towns. (111 mins.)

Get Christie Love! (1974)**½ Teresa Graves, Harry Guardino. Even TV films get remade. Here's a reworking of an earlier pilot ("Bait") about a lady special investigator dedicated to her job. The sexy and resourceful police detective is played by Miss Graves. The plot keeps her busy, her major target being a large drug-dealing operation connected with the underworld. (Dir: William Graham, 100 mins.)

Get on with It!—See: Carry On TV

Get Out of Town (1960)*½ Douglas Wilson, Jeanne Baird. (Dir: Charles Davis, 62 mins.)

Get Out Your Handkerchiefs (France-Belgium, 1978)***½ Gerard Depardieu, Patrick Dewaere, Carole Laure. Ribald comedy about the roles of the sexes in the emotional revolution, a droll work of incisive intellect. The famous disgruntled remark of Freud, "What is it a woman wants?" is elaborated with shaggy dog ferocity. The answer, of course, is that she knows it when she finds it. Academy Award for Best Foreign Film. (Dir: Bertrand Bliez, 108 mins.)

Get to Know Your Rabbit (1972)***½ Tom Smothers, Orson Welles. Ad exec Smothers learns to be a tap-dancing magician from Welles, acquiring an appropriately seedy trade to drop out on. Director Brian De Palma was wittier and more inventive when he was a bit less sure of himself. (91 mins.)

Get Yourself a College Girl (1964)½ Mary Ann Mobley, Chad Everett, Nancy Sinatra, Stan Getz. (Dir: Sidney Miller, 87 mins.)

Getaway, The (1972)**½ Steve McQueen, Ali MacGraw, Ben Johnson, Sally Struthers. Bank robbers, shotguns, beauty, all slowed down, distorted, and re-sorted by director Sam Peckinpah to smash out a brand of adventurous excitement that is commercially successful. McQueen and MacGraw look so fine together that we can easily ignore their "roles" as an ex-con and his wife frolicking through money and cops. MacGraw's acting is nonexistent. In a fine, excruciatingly explicit moment, McQueen levels a police car with a shotgun—slowly, with impact—Peckinpah-style. (122 mins.)

Getting Away from It All (MTV 1972)** Larry Hagman, Barbara Feldon, Gary Collins, E. J. Peaker. Lighthearted comedy about two New York couples who buy a small island in Maine. Thanks to Hagman's charm, and bits by town justice Burgess Meredith and Paul Hartman, the movie bounces along, overcoming the slight story line. (Dir: Lee Philips, 74 mins.)

Getting Gertie's Garter (1945)**½ The efforts of Dennis O'Keefe to retrieve a garter from Marie McDonald that would get him in trouble with sweetie Sheila Ryan. Comedy has many good chuckles. (Dir: Allan Dwan, 72 mins.)

Getting Married (MTV 1978)**½ Richard Thomas, Bess Armstrong, Mark Harmon, Katherine Helmond, Van Johnson. Predictable romantic comedy with a cast of familir TV personalities. Concerns an up-and-coming songwriter's fancy for a pretty TV newscaster, and his no-holds-barred efforts to break up her forthcoming wedding to another guy. (Dir: Steven Hillard Stern, 104 mins.)

Getting of Wisdom, The (Australia, 1977)**½ Susannah Fowle. Fowle's amused restraint as a talented Australian girl who goes off to a strict boarding school is pleasing, but it's hard to be sympathetic toward a film that takes so few risks. Director Bruce Beresford and screenwriter Eleanor Whitcomb make a mild caricature of everything that happens, thereby avoiding the danger of raw reality. (101 mins.)

Getting Straight (1970)** Elliott Gould, Candice Bergen, Robert F. Lyons. Hippiedom alienation at its shallowest except when Gould, as Harry Bailey—an ex-vet finishing his master's in education—asserts himself. Bailey, trying to tiptoe between the administration and radical students at Everywhere University, succeeds only in reducing deeply felt principles to melodramatic pap. The campus riot is perverse in its slapstick appearance with police looking like Keystone cops and the students throwing pies. The script and Gould take hold only once, at Harry's oral exam where obscene limericks meet a professor's claim that F. Scott Fitzgerald was a homosexual. Oh, and Candice Bergen is quite beautiful. (Dir: Richard Rush, 124 mins.)

Ghidrah, the Three-Headed Monster (Japan, 1965)** Together for the first time, Godzilla, Mothra, and Rodan save Tokyo from the ravages of this parvenu from the provinces. Inoshiro Honda directs, shamelessly. (85 mins.)

Ghost and Mr. Chicken, The (1966)** Don Knotts, Joan Staley. Typesetter who wants to be a reporter stumbles into a murder case. As a vehicle for Knotts, this comedy should please his fans; for others, it's pretty silly. (Dir: Alan Rafkin, 90 mins.)

Ghost and Mrs. Muir, The (1947)*** Gene Tierney, Rex Harrison, George Sanders, Edna Best. Much better than the TV series it inspired, this charming, frothy comedy-romance about a widow (Tierney) who rents an old house and finds she's sharing it with the ghost of its former owner (a salty sea captain marvelously embodied by Harrison) was directed by Joseph L. Mankiewicz before his humor turned cold-blooded. (104 mins.)

Ghost Breakers (1940)*** Bob Hope, Paulette Goddard. Good Hope comedy, which combines chills with laughs. Bob goes along to Cuba to help Paulette claim a haunted castle. (Dir: George Marshall, 82 mins.)

Ghost Catchers (1944)**½ Olsen and Johnson, Gloria Jean. Ole and Chic run a night club next door to a house hired by a southern colonel in town to produce a show, and the house is said to be haunted. Entertaining, zany comedy-mystery. (Dir: Edward F. Cline, 67 mins.)

Ghost Goes West, The (Great Britain, 1935)***½ Robert Donat, Jean Parker. The spirit of a Scottish rogue returns to modern times to help a young member of the family. Charming fantasy-comedy, written by Robert E. Sherwood. (Dir: Rene Clair, 100 mins.)

Ghost in the Invisible Bikini (1966)*½ Tommy Kirk, Deborah Walley, Susan Hart, Boris Karloff, Basil Rathbone. (Dir: Don Weis, 82 mins.)

Ghost of Cypress Swamp, The (MTV 1977)**½ Vic Morrow, Jeff East. The Disney camp's first made-for-TV effort. Expertly utilizes all the ingredients which make the Disney features a family affair. Young Lenny, played by Jeff East, tracks a wounded black panther through the interior of the forbidden Great Cypress Swamp and finds a hermit. (Dir: Vincent McEveety, 106 mins.)

Ghost of Flight 401, The (MTV 1978)** Ernest Borgnine; Gary Lockwood, Robert F. Lyons. Strictly for ghost story fans. Borgnine gives it the old school try as a flight officer who was killed in a Miami plane crash in '72, keeps turning up on flights, warning crews of engine failure. (Dir: Steven Stern, 104 mins.)

Ghost Ship, The (1943)*** Mark Robson, Richard Dix. A long-lost Val Lewton-produced feature (because of a plagiarism suit). One of the first, low-budget efforts of director Robson, it has lots of atmospherics, decent pace, no fat, successful eeriness. Dix is very pleasant. (69 mins.)

Ghosts—Italian Style (France-Italy, 1969)** Sophia Loren, Vittorio Gassman, Marlo Adorf. Loren and Gassman, two very capable actors who can switch from comedy to drama, fail to ignite this silly, empty Italian farce about a married couple down on their luck who move into a cavernous palazzo at the request of the owner to dispel the rumors that the place is haunted. The supporting cast consists of a leering old man and a colorful prostitute, and alas, they're more interesting than the stars. (Dir: Renato Castellani, 92 mins.)

Ghosts of Rome (Italy, 1961)*** Marcello Mastroianni, Sandro Milo, Vittorio Gassman. Spirits "living" in an old house with an eccentric prince seek to right things when the old boy dies and the house is to be sold by his nephew. Fantasy has a fine cast in its favor, although the whimsy becomes a bit repetitious after awhile. Dubbed in English. (Dir: Antonio Pietrangeli, 105 mins.)

GI Blues (1960)**½ Elvis Presley, Juliet Prowse. Tank sergeant becomes the number-one contender to break down the resistance of an iceberg night-club dancer. Pleasant Presley musical should satisfy his fans, while others should find some fun along the way. (Dir: Norman Taurog, 104 mins.)

Giant (1956)**½ James Dean, Rock Hudson, Elizabeth Taylor, Carroll Baker, Dennis Hopper. Monstrous, sprawling pseudo-epic about the death of old Texas and the rise of the oil millionaires. Director George Stevens dwarfs the theme by massive straining after visual effects. Dean's last performance, hints that had he lived, he might have been just another good actor. (198 mins.)

Giant Behemoth, The (Great Britain, 1959)** Gene Evans, Andre Morell. Another prehistoric monster epic and again it rises from the sea and flips its giant lid before it is itself destroyed. Par for the course. (Dir: Eugene Lourie, 80 mins.)

Giant From the Unknown (1958)** Buddy Baer, Sally Fraser. Low-budget shocker with few surprises. Superstitious California villagers think a spirit from the past is seeking revenge and thereby hangs the yarn. (Dir: Richard E. Cunha, 77 mins.)

Giant of Metropolis, The (Italy, 1962)*½

Gordon Mitchell, Bella Cortez. (Dir: Umberto Scarpelli, 92 mins.)

Giant of the Evil Island (Italy, 1964)* Rock Stevens, Dina De Santis. (Dir: Piero Pierotti, 80 mins.)

Gideon of Scotland Yard (Great Britain, 1959)*** Jack Hawkins. Police inspector has a multitude of assorted crimes on his hands, all part of police routine. Done in leisurely John Ford style, a pleasing addition to the ranks of genteel crime stories. Hawkins is very English and very good. (Dir: John Ford, 91 mins.)

Gideon's Trumpet (MTV 1980)**** Henry Fonda, José Ferrer, John Houseman, Fay Wray. Based on the book by award-winning reporter Anthony Lewis. The real-life story of Clarence Earl Gideon (Fonda), a drifter with little education, who was arrested in the early '60s for breaking and entering. The Supreme Court decided he was entitled to a lawyer, although he could not afford to pay for one. (Dir: Robert Collins, 104 mins.)

Gidget (1959)** Sandra Dee, Cliff Robertson. The original in the "Gidget" films—strictly for the teen set. Miss Dee is pert and Robertson is wasted. (Dir: Paul Wendkos, 95 mins.)

Gidget Gets Married (MTV 1971)*½ Monie Ellis, Michael Burns, Don Ameche. (Dir: James Sheldon, 72 mins.)

Gidget Goes Hawaiian (1961)** Deborah Walley, James Darren, Carl Reiner, Peggy Cass. Walley (succeeding to the role Sandra Dee created two years before) pursues Darren while on vacation with her family. Paul Wendkos directed, and with no dishonor to him. (102 mins.)

Gidget Goes to Rome (1963)** Cindy Carol, James Darren. The teenager does as it says in the title, gets involved in some romantic complications. Comedy mainly for the pre-adult set; others can look at the scenery. (Dir: Paul Wendkos, 101 mins.)

Gidget Grows Up (1969)**½ Karen Valentine, Robert Cummings, Edward Mulhare. Gidget just keeps going on and on! A made-for-TV feature which shows the all-American teenager grown up, having an innocent affair with an older man (Mulhare). Karen Valentine supplies the energy for Gidget but the script doesn't help her much. The best thing about the film is a high-camp performance by Paul Lynde as a Greenwich Village landlord whose avocation is the films of the thirties. (Dir: James Sheldon, 75 mins.)

Gift, The (MTV 1979)*** Gary Frank, Julie Harris, Allison Argo, Glenn Ford. Adaptation of Pete Hamill's book about a young man coming of age in the '50s. Frank is excellent as a Brooklyn lad who joins the navy and grows up while on Christmas leave. Ford is good as his tight-lipped, hard-drinking, bitter laborer-father who lost a leg years before and never was able to relate to his family. Somber, but ultimately touching. (Dir: Don Taylor, 99 mins.)

Gift for Heidi, A (1959)*½ Sandy Descher, Douglas Fowley. (71 mins.)

Gift of Love (1958)** Lauren Bacall, Robert Stack, Evelyn Rudie. A remake of the four-handkerchiefer "Sentimental Journey." Unlike its predecessor, this version doesn't even come up with a hit tune. Overly sentimental and sticky plot concerns a childless couple who adopt a strange little girl. Pure soap opera that should appeal to the ladies—gentlemen, beware! (Dir: Jean Negulesco, 105 mins.)

Gift of the Magi (MTV 1978)** Debby Boone, John Rubinstein. Another, not very accomplished version of O. Henry's famous tale, with a musical score. Debby breaks into song at every plot turn about the two deeply-in-love young immigrants. Rubinstein supplies the acting strength as the up-and-coming lawyer. JoAnne Worley, white-haired Peter Graves as O. Henry, and Jim Backus round out the cast. (Dir: Marc Daniels, 78 mins.)

Gigantis, the Fire Monster (Japan, 1959)** Japanese made science-fiction saga about two giant, prehistoric monsters who try to gobble the world. The kids may find it exciting. (Dir: Motoyoshi Odo, 78 mins.)

Gigi (1958)***½ Maurice Chevalier, Louis Jourdan, Leslie Caron. Lerner and Loewe have turned Colette's novel into the archetypal "Gallic romp," but while their score often falters, director Vincente Minnelli's mise-en-scène does not. Chevalier sings "Thank Heaven for Little Girls," Jourdan and Caron make competent lovers, and it's Academy Awards (eight to be exact) all around. (116 mins.)

Gigot (1962)**½ Jackie Gleason, Katherine Kath. A somewhat moving performance by Jackie Gleason as a Chaplinesque mute in Paris who becomes the protector of a French streetwalker and her little daughter, is the best feature of this maudlin entry. The plot is steeped in obvious attempts to tug at your heart, and only about half of it works. Gene Kelly directed with a wavering hand. Filmed in Paris. (104 mins.)

Gilda (1946)**½ Rita Hayworth, Glenn Ford, George Macready, Steven Geray. Director Charles Vidor's film is one of the high points of postwar romanticism, snide and sentimental at the same time. Macready, slimy owner of a South American casino, hires the out-of-luck American Ford to tend the crap tables, unaware (or is he?) that Ford was once in love with his wife (Hayworth). (110 mins.)

Gilda Live (1980)**½ Gilda Radner, Don Novello, Paul Shaffer, Candy Slice, Rouge. Faithfully mounted filmization of Radner's rather pallid Broadway showcase. Radner's material is so thin that it demands allegiance from its viewers as a prerequisite to amusement. With Novello providing a few dry moments as Father Guido Sarducci, rock critic and gossip columnist for the Vatican newspaper. (Dir: Mike Nichols, 96 mins.)

Gilded Lily, The (1935)*** Claudette Colbert, Fred MacMurray, Ray Milland. Amusing romantic comedy about a girl who achieves fame and notoriety by turning down a titled suitor. Fred came into his own with this one. (Dir: Wesley Ruggles, 90 mins.)

Gimme Shelter (1970)**** Mick Jagger, Charlie Watts, Melvin Belli. A stunning documentary by Albert and David Maysles about the rock star Mick Jagger and his Rolling Stones group, including the climactic concert in December 1969 at Altamont which wound up with an on-camera real-life knife slaying. The final concert took place at the Altamont Speedway in California before a crowd of 300,000. There are lots of bad vibes captured by the cinema verite-style filmmakers coming from the huge throng responding to Jagger's bisexual performing style, and the feeling of spiritual and emotional malignancy is pervasive. Disturbing, powerful essay on one aspect of the rock and drug culture at the end of the 1960's. (Dirs: David Maysles, Albert Maysles, and Charlotte Zwerin, 91 mins.)

Gina (France, Mexico, 1956)** Simone Signoret, Charles Vanel. Six ill-assorted seekers of a lost diamond mine face the jungle and greed. Grim, unpleasant drama, although it's well acted. Dubbed in English. (Dir: Luis Buñuel, 92 mins.)

Ginger in the Morning (1973)*½ Monte Markham, Sissy Spacek, Susan Oliver. (Dir: Gordon Wiles, 93 mins.)

Girl, a Guy and a Gob, A (1941)*** Lucille Ball, Edmond O'Brien, George Murphy. Secretary is in love with her boss, but is engaged to a sailor. Cute comedy produced by Harold Lloyd, has some good laughs. (Dir: Richard Jones, 91 mins.)

Girl Against Napoleon, A (Spain, 1959)** Sarita Montiel. A mixture of historical misinformation and adventure served up for the action fan. Miss Montiel is a looker and makes the viewing palatable. English-dubbed. Based on the opera *Carmen*. Alternate title: **The Devil Made a Woman.** (Dir: Tulio Demicheli, 87 mins.)

Girl and the Legend, The (Germany, 1957)** Romy Schneider, Horst Buchholz. Author of the famous "Robinson Crusoe" helps to make some youths happy before his death. Slow-moving, rather saccharine costume drama dubbed in English. (Dir: Josef von Baky, 90 mins.)

Girl and the Palio, The (Italy, 1958)**½ Diana Dors, Vittorio Gassman. American girl wins trip to Italy, and the romantic adventures begin. Played against background pageantry of the colorful Sienese "Palio," a traditional, biennial horse race, film offers a fast-paced plot, plenty of excitement. Alternate title: **The Love Specialist.** (Dir: Luigi Zampa, 104 mins.)

Girl Called Hatter Fox, The (MTV 1977)**½ Ronny Cox, Joanelle Romero, Conchata Ferrell. A biting drama directed by George Schaefer, a man with a sharp eye. Romero makes a promising screen debut as Hatter, a half-crazed New Mexico Indian girl who's been kicked from pillar to post, an orphan wracked by fear and hate. Cox, as a stubborn low-keyed doctor searching for clues to her animal behavior, gives his best TV performance, backed by Ferrell, a tough nurse. (104 mins.)

Girl Can't Help It, The (1956)***½ Tom Ewell, Edmond O'Brien, Jayne Mansfield. One of director Frank Tashlin's exercises in comic-strip vulgarity with a moral. In the idiotic plot, an alcoholic press agent (Ewell) is hired by a gangster (O'Brien) to groom his architecturally unbelievable, but talentless girlfriend (Mansfield) for stardom; but the girl yearns for domesticity, falls in love with Ewell, and the gangster becomes a famous rock-and-roll singer. Hilarious and genuinely appealing. (99 mins.)

Girl Crazy (1943)***½ Mickey Rooney, Judy Garland, June Allyson, Nancy Walker. Mickey and Judy have it all to themselves and they make the Gershwin score a pure delight. Story of the rich young Easterner whose dad exiles him to a small school out west, never gets in the way of the Rooney-Garland talent. Remade as **When the Boys Meet the Girls**, 1965. (Dir: Norman Taurog, 99 mins.)

Girl Friends (1978)***½ Melanie Mayron, Eli Wallach, Bob Balaban, Anita Skinner, Viveca Lindfors. Perceptive, poignant low budget entry. Melanie Mayron as a young photographer out to make it on her own in Manhattan, light years past Marjorie Morningstar. Very authentic in locale, detail, and emotion, the film makes squirrelly virtues out of its low-budget purity, but its affection for even the satirized characters overcomes a certain stinginess of ambition. With Eli Wallach doing his best screen work in many years as a rabbi sincerely tempted by Mayron's sexy decency. Impressive directorial debut for the talented young Claudia Weill, who is beautiful enough herself to be a star in front of the cameras as well. Written by Vicki Polon. (86 mins.)

Girl from Flanders, The (Germany, 1956)** Nicole Berger, Maximillian Schell, Gert Frobe. Orphan girl is wrongly accused of stealing arms during World War I, escapes to work in a night club, is finally rescued by a soldier. Leisurely, rather mild drama dubbed in English—some good detail, performances help it. (Dir: Helmut Kautner, 105 mins.)

Girl From Hong Kong (Germany, 1961)*½ Akiko, Helmut Greim. (Dir: Franz Peter Wirth, 95 mins.)

Girl from Jones Beach, The (1949)**½ Virginia Mayo, Eddie Bracken, Ronald Reagan. Mild comedy about an artist's amusing search for the perfect female model. Miss Mayo in a bathing suit is certainly a worth-while attraction for male viewers. (Dir: Peter Godfrey, 78 mins.)

Girl from Missouri, The (1934)*½ Jean Harlow, Lionel Barrymore, Franchot Tone. Cute, harmless comedy about a young lady from Missouri who by use of her physical assets achieves success in the big city. (Dir: Jack Conway, 80 mins.)

Girl from Petrovka (1974)*½ Goldie Hawn, Hal Holbrook, Anthony Hopkins. (Dir: Robert Ellis Miller, 104 mins.)

Girl-Getters, The (Great Britain, 1964)*** Oliver Reed, Jane Merrow. Girlchasing photographer has phenomenal success in his conquests, but the tables are turned when he meets a glamor girl one summer. Well-done drama of life and love among the younger set. Thick dialect may cause some confusion, but performances are very good, the story interesting. (Dir: Michael Winner, 79 mins.)

Girl Happy (1965)** Elvis Presley, Shelley Fabares. Typical Presley film for his fans. Elvis is a nightclub entertainer who finds love in Fort Lauderdale during those raucous college Easter vacations. For the record, there are twelve songs delivered by Elvis and cast. (Dir: Boris Sagal, 96 mins.)

Girl He Left Behind, The (1956)** Tab Hunter, Natalie Wood, Jim Backus. Silly comedy about a young boy who is drafted into the peacetime army. The events depicted are artificial and what's worse, not very funny. Natalie Wood, as the girl in the title, also gets left behind when it comes to a part. (Dir: David Butler, 103 mins.)

Girl Hunters, The (Great Britain, 1963)** Mickey Spillane, Shirley Eaton, Lloyd Nolan. Mike Hammer beats his way through assorted mayhem while trying to locate his missing secretary. Unique in a trashy sort of way—Spillane plays his own fictional creation, not too badly; British-made American backgrounds are accurate; when it comes, the action is fast and bloody. (Dir: Roy Rowland, 103 mins.)

Girl in Black Stockings, The (1957)**½ Anne Bancroft, Mamie Van Doren, Lex Barker. Some gorgeous suspects in a double murder. Passable whodunit, with nicely filled stockings. (Dir: Howard W. Koch, 73 mins.)

Girl in Every Port, A (1952)** Groucho Marx, William Bendix, Marie Wilson. Navy pals acquire two race horses and try to conceal them on board ship. Tame comedy isn't what one would expect of the talent involved. (Dir: Chester Erskine, 86 mins.)

Girl in His Pocket (1957)** Jean Marais, Genevieve Page. A wacky French language film about a handsome scientist whose experiments lead to wild results— he concocts a solution which reduces people to 3" in size. More silly than funny. (Dir: Pierre Kast, 82 mins.)

Girl in Lovers Lane, The (1960)* Joyce

Meadows, Brett Halsey, Jack Elam. (Dir: Charles R. Rondeau, 78 mins.)

Girl in Room 13, The (1960)*½ Brian Donlevy, Andrea Bayard. (Dir: Richard Cunha, 79 mins.)

Girl in the Bikini, The (France, 1952)*½ Brigitte Bardot, Jean-Francois Calvé. (Dir: Willy Rozier, 76 mins.)

Girl in the Kremlin, The (1957)*½ Lex Barker, Zsa Zsa Gabor. (Dir: Russell Birdwell, 81 mins.)

Girl in the Painting, The (Great Britain, 1948)*** Mai Zetterling, Guy Rolfe, Robert Beatty. Army major runs into a spy plot when he tries to help a girl regain her memory. Good melodrama. (Dir: Terence Fisher, 89 mins.)

Girl in the Part, The—See: **Sanctuary of Fear**

Girl in the Red Velvet Swing, The (1955)**½ Ray Milland, Joan Collins, Farley Granger. One of the most sensational murders of the early 1900's was millionaire Harry K. Thaw's killing of famed architect Stanford White over his wife Evelyn Nesbitt Thaw. Their story is brought to the screen in an elaborate production and a good cast who do very nicely despite the soap opera overtones of the script. (Dir: Richard Fleischer, 109 mins.)

Girl in White (1952)** June Allyson, Gary Merrill, Arthur Kennedy. A soap opera about one of the first women doctors to invade a man's world. Miss Allyson weeps, smiles, and looks bewildered throughout the "sudsy" drama. (Dir: John Sturges, 93 mins.)

Girl Most Likely, The (1957)*** Jane Powell, Cliff Robertson, Kaye Ballard. Girl has a tough time choosing her dream man, for she has three from which to choose. Musical version of a successful Ginger Rogers film (**Tom, Dick and Harry**) is helped considerably by ingenious production numbers staged by Gower Champion. Good entertainment. (Dir: Mitchell Leisen, 98 mins.)

Girl Most Likely to..., The (MTV 1973)**½ Stockard Channing, Edward Asner, Joe Flynn, Jim Backus, Chuck McCann. Bizarre comedy about a homely, dumpy college girl who is transformed into a lovely, sexy dish after a car accident and plastic surgery. The twist here is the new Miriam harbors the old Miriam's hate and goes about seeking revenge in no uncertain terms. Talented Miss Channing has a plum leading role, and the makeup men responsible for Miriam's "before-and-after transformation" deserve a special nod. Comic Joan Rivers, with an assist from Agnes Gallin, wrote the script. (Dir: Lee Philips, 74 mins.)

Girl Named Sooner, A (MTV 1975)*** Cloris Leachman, Richard Crenna, Lee Remick, Susan Deer. Cloris Leachman is superb as a mean, unwashed, brittle, shabby, old and shrewd hill-country woman, knowing where a dollar can be turned from her illegally made whiskey.

Concerns her neglected, mistreated 8-year-old granddaughter (Sooner), but it's Cloris who dominates, with her plan to disown the child in exchange for a government handout. (Dir: Delbert Mann, 98 mins.)

Girl Named Tamiko, A (1962)**½ Laurence Harvey, France Nuyen. Moderately interesting drama which has Harvey playing a Eurasian who is a bitter expatriate from Tokyo eager to gain admission to the United States. Harvey is good but he gets little help from the script. (Dir: John Sturges, 110 mins.)

Girl Next Door, The (1953)** Dan Dailey, June Haver, Dennis Day. Night club star falls for a cartoonist, whose offspring complicates matters. Nothing to sing or draw about. (Dir: Richard Sale, 92 mins.)

Girl of the Golden West (1938)** Jeanette MacDonald, Nelson Eddy, Walter Pidgeon, Leo Carrillo, Buddy Ebsen. Glum rendition of the Sigmund Romberg-Gus Kahn operetta from the heyday of David Belasco is the worst of MacDonald-Eddy vehicle ever. Girl loves guy on lam from Mounties—get it? (Dir: Robert Z. Leonard, 120 mins.)

Girl of the Night (1960)*½ Anne Francis, Lloyd Nolan, Kay Medford, Julius Monk, John Kerr. (Dir: Joseph Cates, 93 mins.)

Girl on the Motorcycle, The—See: **Naked Under Leather**

Girl on Approval (Great Britain, 1962)** Rachel Roberts, James Maxwell. Even Rachel Roberts' good performance can't save this well-worn soap opera about a woman who defies her family and friends in her efforts to help a young orphan. (Dir: Charles Frend, 75 mins.)

Girl Rush, The (1955)** Rosalind Russell, Fernando Lamas, Eddie Albert, Gloria De Haven. Museum employee arrives in Las Vegas to claim partnership in a hotel left by her gambler-father. Try for musical gaiety that fizzles for the most part. Musical numbers below par, the comedy rather tired. (Dir: Robert Pirosh, 85 mins.)

Girl, the Gold Watch & Everything, The (MTV 1980)**½ Robert Hays, Pam Dawber, Jill Ireland, Maurice Evans. Tale revolves around Kirby Winter (Hays), who inherits a magic gold watch from his multimillionaire uncle. Hays is affable and handsome, and comedienne Dawber is pretty and surprisingly talented, but Lampert, in a hilarious supporting role as the secretary of the hero's uncle, almost runs off with the film. (Dir: William Wiard, 104 mins.)

Girl Who Came Gift Wrapped, The (MTV 1974)**½ Karen Valentine, Richard Long, Dave Madden, Farrah Fawcett. Harmless comedy casting Miss Valentine as a young lady who is thrust upon a successful man-about-town publisher of a sophisticated girlie magazine. Count the possibilities, and then see how many are trotted out. (Dir: Bruce Bilson, 78 mins.)

Girl Who Had Everything, The (1953)** Elizabeth Taylor, Fernando Lamas, William Powell, Gig Young. Criminal lawyer's daughter becomes infatuated with a suave crook. Old-hat melodrama with very little. Remake of **A Free Soul**, 1931 (Dir: Richard Thorpe, 69 mins.)

Girl Who Knew Too Much, The (1969)* Nancy Kwan, Adam West, Robert Alda. (Dir: Francis D. Lyon, 95 mins.)

Girl With a Suitcase (France-Italy, 1961)***½ Claudia Cardinale, Jacques Perrin. A thoroughly absorbing and sensitively played Italian language drama about a 16-year-old boy and his innocent and brief romance with a beautiful, sensual girl who lives by her wits. Director Valerio Zurlini captures the mood of the poignant episode and uses his camera to the best advantage in the location shooting of Parma and the Italian Riviera. (Dir: Valerio Zurlini, 96 mins.)

Girl with Green Eyes, The (Great Britain, 1964)*** Rita Tushingham, Peter Finch, Lynn Redgrave. Edna O'Brien's touching novella, "The Lonely Girl," receives a diffuse treatment from director Desmond Davis. It's sensitivities are almost entirely communicated by the excellent trio of players. The material about a writer's affair with a country girl, verges on the trite, and the extensive location shooting in Ireland, while attractive, tends to the familiar. A lot of tenderness and good intentions. (91 mins.)

Girls' Dormitory (1936)**½ Simono Simon, Herbert Marshall, Ruth Chatterton, Tyrone Power. Simone is outstanding in her first American film. Story of a girl in love with the headmaster of her school isn't too well written. (Dir: Irving Cummings, 66 mins.)

Girls! Girls! Girls! (1962)** Elvis Presley, Stella Stevens, Benson Fong. A trivial comedy. Elvis is trying to choose among a bevy of beauties, and the suspense is nil. (Dir: Norman Taurog, 105 mins.)

Girls in the Office, The (MTV 1979)**½ Susan Saint James, Barbara Eden, Tony Roberts, David Wayne. Glossy glimpse of women trying to rise in the hierarchy of a large department store. Saint James is effective as an ambitious worker who pays a big price to see her dreams realized. The rest of the cast are also pretty good. Predictable, but not boring. Based on a book by Jack Olsen. (Dir: Ted Post, 104 mins.)

Girls of Huntington House, The (MTV 1973)**½ Sweet Shirley Jones proves she can handle a dramatic role as the new teacher in a small school for unwed mothers. Shirley and Mercedes McCambridge provide the grownup histrionics. Sparkled by good performances from Sissy Spacek and Pamela Sue Martin. (Dir: Alf Kjellin, 73 mins.)

Girls on the Beach (1964)** Lana Wood, The Beach Boys, Noreen Corcoran. "Sally Sorority" (Miss Corcoran) promises her sisters the Beatles at a benefit performance to pay off the mortgage on their boardinghouse. The Beach Boys, the Crickets, and Lesley Gore do nicely. Humor and acting on a low level. (Dir: William N. Witney, 80 mins.)

Girls' Town (1959)* Mamie Van Doren, Mel Torme, Paul Anka. Alternate title: **Innocent and the Damned.** (Dir: Charles Haas, 92 mins.)

Git! (1965)** Jack Chaplain, Heather North. Runaway orphan trains an English setter to become a fine hunting dog. Harmless little boy-and-dog drama; children will like it best. (Dir: Ellis Kadison, 92 mins.)

Giuseppe Verdi (Italy, 1953)** Pierre Cressoy, Anna Maria Ferraro. Biography of the composer and patriot. Some good operatic selections sung by Del Monaco, Gobbi, etc. Otherwise competent. (Dir: Raffaello Matarazzo, 110 mins.)

Give a Girl a Break (1953)** Debbie Reynolds, Marge and Gower Champion. Director Stanley Donen disowns this early musical, and with its saccharine story and saccharine players (Reynolds, for one) it's easy to see why. Still, the film has its points, including a madly overdone production number involving balloons, confetti, reverse motion, and an impossibly young Bob Fosse at the start of his career. (82 mins.)

Give 'Em Hell, Harry (1975)***½ This is basically a photographed stage play, but James Whitmore is so splendid impersonating Harry Truman (without makeup), and Truman's words and personality are so rousing, that "Give 'Em Hell" is a joy. Whitmore dares a great deal, undertaking a one-man show with no help from film technique, makeup or props, and he succeeds. A compelling tribute to a President more and more Americans think was rough, honest, perceptive, and responsible. (Dir: Peter H. Hunt, 104 mins.)

Give My Regards to Broadway (1948)** Dan Dailey, Charles Winninger. A father who is waiting for vaudeville to come back and the romances of his kids make up the ingredients for this pitiful film. Some good standard songs, well done by Dailey, are the only redeeming features. (Dir: Lloyd Bacon, 89 mins.)

Gizmo! (1980)**** Hilarious documentary demonstrating many crazy (some not so bad) inventions and why they never caught on. Mostly B&W, with some NASA color footage. Will be enjoyed by all members of the family. (Dir: Howard Smith, 79 mins.)

Glacier Fox, The (Japan, 1978)*** Engrossing documentary on the foxes of the Japanese island of Hokkaido. Attractive nature documentary, directed by Koreyoshi Kurahara slightly more rigorously than the popular Disney model. Reedited with a narration by Arthur Hill for American audiences. (90 mins.)

Glass Alibi, The (1946)**½ Paul Kelly, Anne Gwynne, Douglas Fowley. An unscrupulous reporter sees a chance to commit a perfect crime, but fate trips him

up. Sturdy crime drama, showing what brains can do with a small budget. (Dir: W. Lee Wilder, 70 mins.)

Glass Bottom Boat, The (1966)*½ Doris Day, Rod Taylor, Arthur Godfrey. (Dir: Frank Tashlin, 109 mins.)

Glass Cage, The (1963)** John Hoyt, Arline Sax, Robert Kelljan. Detective becomes involved with a strange girl who has a dominating elder sister and a sinister father. Fair psychological melodrama makes an attempt to be different. (Dir: Antonio Santean, 78 mins.)

Glass House, The (MTV 1972)***½ Vic Morrow, Alan Alda, Clu Gulager. As a deterrent to crime, this Truman Capote prison drama is hard to beat—a shocker to the core, besides being a savage indictment of our penal system. In filming it at Utah State Prison in semidocumentary style, director Tom Gries trains his cameras on a new guard, a college professor up for manslaughter, and a kid doing time on a drug rap. Their initiation into the system, with guards looking the other way as a con boss runs "The Glass House," turns into a reign of terror. Bucking the con leader means death by stabbing, going along means homosexual attacks. Raw and gutsy by TV standards. The cast is splendid. (Dir: Tom Gries, 73 mins.)

Glass Key, The (1935)*** Edward Arnold, George Raft, Ray Milland. Good, exciting Dashiell Hammett melodrama about crime, murder and politics. Characters are superbly drawn and over-shadow the routine plot. (Dir: Frank Tuttle, 80 mins.)

Glass Key, The (1942)*** Alan Ladd, Veronica Lake, Brian Donlevy, Robert Preston, William Bendix. Remake of the Dashiell Hammett novel about a good-natured, crooked politician saved from a murder frame-up by his taciturn henchman. The action, under Stuart Heisler's direction, captures some of the gritty atmosphere. (85 mins.)

Glass Menagerie, The (1950)** Arthur Kennedy, Gertrude Lawrence, Jane Wyman, Kirk Douglas. A Tennessee Williams play, filmed without magic—which means without point. Kennedy is good in the easy role, but Lawrence is miscast as the mother, and Wyman and Douglas are likable but out of their league. (Dir: Irving Rapper, 107 mins.)

Glass Menagerie, The (MTV 1973)**** Kathrine Hepburn, Sam Waterston, Joanna Miles, Michael Moriarty. A generally wonderful production of Tennessee Williams' early masterwork, in many ways superior to the original 1950 version starring Gertrude Lawrence. The cast infuses the play with real human beings you come to care about in this classic of the American theater. Katherine Hepburn shines as Amanda Wingfield, the fading, domineering southern belle desperately trying to instill confidence in her sad crippled daughter (Miles) while steering her poetry-writing son toward a more remunerative career. Actually Hepburn is such a strong, charismatic presence on screen that you occasionally doubt her stated inability to straighten out and improve their lives, but it's a moving portrait nonetheless. Waterston scores as Tom, the tortured son, torn between love for his mother and sister and a strong desire to simply pick up and leave; Miles is touching as the fragile and frightened Laura, who collects equally delicate glass animals; and Moriarty, who may be the best young actor in America, is a wonderfully refreshing and convincing "gentleman caller" who serves as the catalyst in the play. Anthony Harvey directed with unerring taste and skill, and mercifully few cuts have been made in the original full-length play. (100 mins.)

Glass Mountain, The (Great Britain, 1950)**½ Michael Denison, Dulcie Gray, Valentina Cortesa. A composer writes an opera inspired by a beautiful Italian girl, but finds he has lost interest in his wife in doing so. Well done romantic drama with fine musical score, performances. (Dir: Henry Cass, 94 mins.)

Glass Slipper, The (1955)*** Leslie Caron, Michael Wilding. Lovely Leslie Caron is perfectly cast as Cinderella in this musical fantasy-which works most of the way. Don't look for anything but a fairy tale, exquisitely mounted, and you'll be entertained. Michael Wilding is the Prince Charming in this opus. (Dir: Charles Walters, 94 mins.)

Glass Sphinx, The (Egypt-Italy-Spain, 1967)* Robert Taylor, Anita Ekberg. (Dir: Luigi Scattini, 91 mins.)

Glass Tomb, The (Great Britain, 1955)**½ John Ireland, Honor Blackman. Carnival people are suspected when a murder is committed there. Neat mystery. (Dir: Montgomery Tully, 59 mins.)

Glass Tower, The (Germany, 1957)** Lilli Palmer, O. E. Hasse, Peter Van Eyck. German-made soap opera about an actress who is virtually kept a prisoner by her wealthy husband in a specially built glass palace. (Dir: Harold Braun, 93 mins.)

Glass Wall, The (1953)*** Vittorio Gassman, Gloria Grahame. Interesting off-beat story about a foreigner who jumps ship in New York after he is refused entry. His exploits in the big city lead him to the U. N. building—the glass wall—where he almost kills himself. Vittorio Gassman is fine as the desperate Peter. (Dir: Maxwell Shane, 80 mins.)

Glass Web, The (1953)**½ Edward G. Robinson, John Forsythe. Strictly for the whodunit fans. A murder mystery involving members of the staff of a weekly TV show titled "Crime-of-the-Week." Get the picture? A good cast keeps it from becoming silly. (Dir: Jack Arnold, 81 mins.)

Glen and Randa (1971)*** Steven Curry, Shelley Plimpton. An ambitious, seriously flawed, but often provocative apocalyptic vision of two survivors of an atomic holocaust. Third film, but first commercial release for the talented but undisciplined writer-director Jim McBride, who also co-authored the biting screenplay. Woodrow Chambliss, a little-known British character actor, is excellent playing an old man who befriends Plimpton and Curry. (McBride's first two films were the experimental "David Holzman's Diary" and "My Girlfriend's Wedding.") Cuts were made in "Glen and Randa," not approved by McBride. (94 mins.)

Glen or Glenda (1953)½ Bela Lugosi, Lyle Talbot, Dolores Fuller, Daniel Davis. This dumbfounding artifact is a serious plea for understanding transvestism, intercut with noxious commentary by Bela Lugosi in occult drag. Glen (director Edward D. Wood, Jr., under the name Daniel Davis) sports double-breasted suits when he really wants to wear double breasts. As the narrator intones: "Yes, in all other ways, Glen was a normal man..." but Glen does get embarrassed when his blond girlfriend finds him in her wardrobe. Meanwhile, Lugosi chortles: "And vat are leetle boys made hov? Snails and puppy dog tails? Or...perhaps it is brassieres! High-heel shoes! Girdles! Ha-ha-ha-ha-ha!" It is to die. (67 mins.)

Glenn Miller Story, The (1954)*** James Stewart, June Allyson. Highly romanticized biography of the famed band leader who was lost during World War II. Immensely successful when first released, the personal charm of James Stewart as Glenn Miller, and June Allyson, as his loving wife, did a great deal to carry the film's more sentimental sequences. Plenty of music in the tradition of the big band sound. (Dir: Anthony Mann, 116 mins.)

Global Affair, A (1964)** Bob Hope, Lilo Pulver, Yvonne DeCarlo. A featherweight comedy not worthy of Hope's talents. He's a United Nations staff member who becomes the temporary guardian of an abandoned baby left at the U.N. A cast of international females try to convince Hope their various countries should adopt the infant. Thereby hangs the thin diaper. (Dir: Jack Arnold, 84 mins.)

Gloria (1980)***½ Gena Rowlands, Juan Adames. A former gangster's moll (Rowlands, inimitable) is on the run with a Puerto Rican kid marked for death by the mob; although she doesn't like the kid, she is willing and able to kill to protect him. Director John Cassavetes, in collaboration with cinematographer Fred Schuler, has found a new way of looking at the landscape of New York City, and his rhythms are consistently fresh and illuminating. (121 mins.)

Glory (1956)*½ Margaret O'Brien, Walter Brennan, Charlotte Greenwood. (Dir: David Butler, 100 mins.)

Glory Alley (1952)*** Ralph Meeker, Leslie Caron, Gilbert Roland. Conventional film noir script about a corrupt boxer (Meeker) who yearns for one last taste of integrity when he returns to New Orleans. Director Raoul Walsh does some unusual visual styling, but the French Quarter atmosphere is irreconcilable with the seedy goings-on. With occasional music by Louis Armstrong. (79 mins.)

Glory at Sea (Great Britain, 1952)*** Trevor Howard, Richard Attenborough, Sonny Tufts. Captain of a lend-lease ship during World War II earns the respect of his crew after committing some errors. Good war melodrama has excitement, compactness, fine performances. (Dir: Compton Bennett, 88 mins.)

Glory Brigade, The (1953)*** Victor Mature, Lee Marvin, Richard Egan. Unpretentious but well made, fast moving story of Greek UN forces in war-torn Korea. Different sort of war plot, above average. (Dir: Robert D. Webb, 82 mins.)

Glory Guys, The (1965)** Tom Tryon, Senta Berger, Andrew Duggan, James Caan. Soldier Tom Tryon is forced by an order from his commanding officer to send raw recruits into action against the Sioux. One-dimensional plot gives way to better action. Screenplay by director Sam Peckinpah. Based on the novel "Dice of God." (Dir: Arnold Laven, 112 mins.)

Glory Stompers, The (1967)* Dennis Hooper, Jody McCrea, Chris Noel, Jock Mahoney. (Dir: Anthony M. Lanza, 85 mins.)

Gnome-Mobile, The (1967)**½ Walter Brennan, Ed Wynn. Walt Disney treat for the kids. Brennan plays the dual role of a wealthy businessman and a gnome who must find a wife for his grandson-gnome. A cute yarn with a pleasant musical score and good special effects. The cast includes Mathew Garber and Karen Dotrice, the charming tots of "Mary Poppins." (Dir: Robert Stevenson, 104 mins.)

Go Ask Alice (1973)*** Jamie Smith Jackson. Provocative fare. The disturbing subject of the indiscriminate use of drugs by high-school kids has seldom been portrayed with more honesty and validity than in this made-for-TV film. Based on the real-life diary of a young girl caught up in addiction from the age of 15, and adapted with sensitivity and restraint by Ellen Violett, the story of Alice, an average teen-ager with a craving for popularity that starts her on the road to severe drug addiction, should be seen by high-school students and their parents. Newcomer Jackson registers in the difficult title role. (Dir: John Korty, 73 mins.)

Go-Between, The (1971)**** Julie Christie, Alan Bates, Dominic Guard, Michael Redgrave, Margaret Leighton. Harold Pinter (with his dramatic sense intact and his penchant for murkiness missing), adapted the L. P. Hartley novel about a young boy's involvement as a go-between in an illicit Victorian love affair and how it causes his personality as an adult to disintegrate. Perfect performances by Leighton and Guard. The best film of director Joseph Losey. (116 mins.)

Go for Broke (1951)*** Van Johnson. The exploits of the 442nd Regimental Combat Team which was comprised of Nisei (Americans of Japanese ancestry) are graphically portrayed in this above average drama set in Italy and France during WW-II. Johnson is joined by a competent cast. (Dir: Robert Pirosh, 92 mins.)

Go Go Mania (Great Britain, 1965)*½ (Dir: Frederic Goode, 70 mins.)

Go Into Your Dance (1935)**½ Al Jolson, Ruby Keeler. A fairly pedestrian musical. Keeler, then Jolson's wife, makes a game effort to dance and is charmingly clumsy. Jolson, dominates the vehicle, and the "I'm a Latin from Manhattan" and "About a Quarter to Nine" numbers are memorable. The plot is forgettable. Archie Mayo directed, if that's what you call it. (89 mins.)

Go, Man, Go (1954)**½ Dane Clark, Sidney Poitier, Pat Breslin. Promoter gets an idea for an all-Negro basketball team, which becomes the Harlem Globetrotters. Sports fans should get a boot out of the fast court scenes; for others, an interesting drama. (Dir: James Wong Howe, 82 mins.)

Go Naked in the World (1961)*½ Gina Lollobrigida, Anthony Franciosa, Ernest Borgnine. (Dir: Ranald MacDougall, 103 mins.)

Go Tell the Spartans (1978)***½ Burt Lancaster, Craig Wasson, Marc Singer. Lean, intelligent movie about the early days of American advisers in Vietnam. Superlative acting by the three leads, and straightforward job-of-work direction by Ted Post. A genuine sleeper whose very limitations of budget and ambition become major virtues. "Incident at Muc Wa," a novel by Daniel Ford. (114 mins.)

Go West (1925)*** Buster Keaton, Howard Truesdale, Kathleen Myers. Not the best of the Keaton-directed comedies, but one that shows him in a rare display of pure pathos. Buster is befriended by a cow (of whom he continued to speak fondly in his old age) on his odyssey, and averts a stampede in downtown Los Angeles by donning a red devil's costume (an unusual color gag for the time). (70 mins.)

Go West (1940)**½ Marx Brothers, John Carroll, Robert Barrat. There's a funny opening bit in a ticket office and a systematic disassembling of a moving train at the climax, but the film contains much of the Marx Brothers' weakest material. They are never without interest, although they test the limits of their fans' patience. (Dir: Edward Buzzell, 81 mins.)

Go West, Young Girl (MTV 1978)**½ Karen Valentine, Sandra Will, Stuart Whitman. Valentine and newcomer Will star in this busted comedy pilot set in the old West. They play a pair of adventurous ladies who set out to find Billy the Kid. Ms. Valentine is adept at this sort of role and she's particularly winning in a saloon poker game scene. Filmed in Tucson. (Dir: Alan J. Levi, 78 mins.)

Go West, Young Man (1936)**½ Mae West, Warren William, Randolph Scott, Una Merkel, Elizabeth Risdon. Moderately entertaining comedy about what happens when a screen star makes a personal appearance and is forced to mingle with the common folk. (Dir: Henry Hathaway, 90 mins.)

Goalie's Anxiety at the Penalty Kick, The (West Germany-Austria, 1971)** Arthur Brauss, Kai Fischer, Marie Bardischewski, Erika Pluhar. An early Wim Wenders feature based on a script by Peter Handke. The goalie commits a meaningless murder, only to find that you only get out of murder what you put into it. Alienation (as Kierkegaard knew) thrives on boredom, and out of it comes the drive to do anything to avoid that gnawing sense of nothing happening. This picture understands that, too; painfully, it only adds to it. You can see where Wenders and Handke were going; both of them have since gotten there. But in case you are in the middle of this picture wondering if something is going to happen, let me perform the act of mercy and tell you: nope. (Dir: Wim Wenders, 101 mins.)

Goat Horn, The (Bulgaria, 1972)**** Anton Gortchev, Milene Penev, Katia Paskaleva. Powerful drama set in the Balkans of the 17th century when what is now Bulgaria was part of the Ottoman Empire and under the brutal reign of the Turks. A shepherd's wife is raped and murdered by swaggering local Turkish officials and the shepherd methodically gets his revenge by killing each of them. Little dialogue but the action builds to a compelling climax aided by the lyrical cinematography of Dimo Lolarov and the taut direction of Metodi Andonov. Uses some of the techniques from the best dramas of the silent days, but the film is convincing and modern in every detail. English subtitles. (95 mins.)

God Bless the Children—See: Psychiatrist: God Bless the Children, The

God Is My Co-Pilot (1945)**½ Dennis Morgan, Dane Clark, Raymond Massey. Tribute to the famous Flying Tigers is very trite and only occasionally exciting. (Dir: Robert Florey, 90 mins.)

God Told Me To—See: Demon

Godchild, The (MTV 1974)**½ Jack Palance, Jack Warden, Jose Perez. Rousing remake of the 1948 John Ford-John Wayne film, "Three Godfathers," which told the story of three Civil War prisoners who are running from the Confederates and Apaches, and come across a dying woman about to give birth. (Dir: John Badham, 72 mins.)

Goddess, The (1958)***½ Kim Stanley, Lloyd Bridges, Steven Hill. An original screenplay by TV's Paddy Chayefsky about a lonely girl who becomes "a love goddess of the silver screen," just like you read about in the fan magazines. Except in this case the lady finds phonies and misses happiness, but it lasts long enough to unwind a striking and powerful performance by Kim Stanley, certainly one of the half dozen most gifted American actresses of today, and one largely ignored by Hollywood before and since this film. Parts of the film may be high-class soap opera, but it's an infrequent opportunity to watch the splendid Miss Stanley at work. (Dir: John Cromwell, 105 mins.)

Godfather, The (1972)**** Marlon Brando, Al Pacino, James Caan, Sterling Hayden, Robert Duvall. One of the most riveting American movies of the decade which also happens to be a superlative gangster film. An absolutely superb performance by Brando as the aging head of a powerful Mafia clan, with fine performances from the supporting cast especially Al Pacino playing Brando's youngest son. Set in 1945 on Long Island with other sequences shot on location in Sicily. Based on the best selling novel by Mario Puzo, this is one of the few times where the film is an improvement on the book. Francis Ford Coppola co-authored the screenplay with Puzo and brilliantly directed this exciting drama. Brando won an Oscar. (175 mins.)

Godfather, The, Part II (1974)**** Al Pacino, Robert De Niro, Robert Duvall, Diane Keaton, Talia Shire, Lee Strasberg, Michael V. Gazzo. Won the Academy Award for best picture and is even better in many ways than Godfather I, as this blockbuster, which begins where Godfather I ended, completes what is surely the greatest gangster saga ever filmed. Michael Corleone (Pacino) has consolidated the power handed to him by his father (Brando) while Godfather II flashes back and forth between the early life of the late Don Vito, and the ongoing story of his embattled family after his death. Pacino and De Niro are customarily excellent, and there's an effective supporting performance by the great method-acting teacher Lee Strasberg playing a Meyer-Lansky type of Jewish, brainy Mafioso. Again written by Coppola and Mario Puzo and marvelously directed by Coppola, who won the Academy Award for best direction. De Niro won an Oscar for best supporting actor and Pacino and Shire got nominated. (200 mins.)

God's Little Acre (1958)**½ Robert Ryan, Aldo Ray, Tina Louise. Erskine Caldwell's famous novel about the Walden family of dirt farmers in Georgia and their endless earthy conflicts reaches the screen with some of the passion diluted. Robert Ryan is most effective as the head of the Walden clan, whose mad obsession that there's gold on his land leads him to near tragedy. Tina Louise is properly seductive as Jack Lord's cheating wife, and Aldo Ray, Buddy Hackett, Vic Morrow and Fay Spain deliver good performances. (Dir: Anthony Mann, 110 mins.)

Godson, The (French, 1972)***½ Alain Delon, Nathalie Delon. Don't be put off by the title, which stems from the distributors' hope to cash in on the huge success of "The Godfather" in 1972. Alain Delon plays a contract killer caught between the police and the syndicate. His isolation is poignantly brought out by the distinguished French director Jean-Pierre Melville. The dubbing is inane (everyone sounds like a Brooklyn cab driver); Alain Delon is perfect, always impassive and fatalistic. The chase in the subway is terrifically exciting. (Dir: Jean-Pierre Melville, 103 mins.)

Godspell (1973)*** Victor Garber, David Haskell. Jesus as a hermaphroditic circus clown. The long-running American rock musical, an international hit, comes to the screen as a stimulating if rather long vaudeville turn...based on the gospel according to St. Matthew, book writer John-Michael Tebelak, and composer-lyricist Stephen Schwartz. Tells the story of Jesus and his disciples in one musical number after another, imaginatively filmed against the fabulous backdrop of New York City. It starts out very interestingly but soon gets somewhat monotonous. The cast of young singers-dancers-actors does very well and the Schwartz score is always listenable. Special credit to cinematographer Richard G. Helmann for his glorious paean to the magic of New York. (Dir: David Greene, 103 mins.)

Godzilla, King of the Monsters (Japan, 1956)* Raymond Burr, Inoshiro Honda. A prehistoric monster threatens Tokyo. But shouldn't monsters be scary? B&W. (Dir: Terry Morse, 80 mins.)

Godzilla vs. the Sea Monster (Japan, 1966)** Akira Takarada, Toru Watanabe. The kids will enjoy this tale of the giant prehistoric monster who goes around doing good. In this one he and the special effects men wage a battle with an evil sea monster. Technically good science-fiction fare on a juvenile level. Alternate title: **Ebirah, Horror of the Deep.** (Dir: Jun Fukuda, 88 mins.)

Goin' South (1978)**½ Jack Nicholson, Mary Steenburgen, Christopher Lloyd, John Belushi. Nicholson directs this often charming romantic Western and plays a death-row thief saved from the gallows by a prudish woman (Steenburgen) who is willing to marry him so he can work in a mine she owns. Time is just after the Civil War. Steenburgen's debut is auspicious. (105 mins.)

Goin' to Town (1935)***½ Mae West, Paul Cavanagh. A Texas oil heiress crashes Newport society. The highlight of this one, besides seeing Mae ride a horse, is her singing (honestly) scenes from Massenet's opera *Samson and Delilah.* You should see Samson! A very funny picture. (Dir: Alexander Hall, 74 mins.)

Going Home (1971)** Robert Mitchum, Brenda Vaccaro, Jan-Michael Vincent. Ineffective drama tries to analyze the effect on a boy of seeing his mother die after being stabbed by his father. Performances by Mitchum, Vaccaro and Vincent help but can't save this entry, the first directorial effort by producer Herbert B. Leonard. (At the time of release Leonard complained his work had been mutilated by the then-President of MGM, James Aubrey, who chopped 12 minutes out of the completed film.) (97 mins.)

Going in Style (1979)***½ George Burns, Art Carney, Lee Strasberg. Director Martin Brest brings a deadpan rhythm to this story of three old men who plan and execute a bank robbery. The leads are excellent, and while there are laughs, the film is primarily a compassionate straight drama. (97 mins.)

Going My Way (1944)***½ Bing Crosby, Barry Fitzgerald. Director Leo McCarey's improvisatory style rescues this light comedy from excessive coyness. The most sentimental sequences (such as the teary reunion of old priest Fitzgerald with his mother from Ireland) are filmed in an unaffected manner that downplays the pathos. (130 mins.)

Going Places (France, 1974)***½ Jeanne Moreau, Gerard Depardieu, Patrick Dewaere, Miou-Miou, Brigitte Fossey. A compelling, maddening comedy-drama about two Rabelaisian louts who steal, fornicate, and generally act like swine all over France. But somehow director Bertrand Blier has managed to combine many disparate elements into a disturbing, provocative tapestry. With a screenplay by Blier and Philippe Dumarcay based on Blier's famous novel (in France) "Les Valseuses," "Places" is alternately tender and brutal, compassionate and misogynistic, crude, lyrical, sexy, and enraging. One of the two hoodlums is shot in the groin, but they both worry about their virility. Miss Moreau, looking quite beautiful playing a woman back in circulation after a ten-year prison stint, appears briefly in the middle of the film and gives it a performing authority it lacks elsewhere. It's an antiestablishment film about the alienation of the young, and the bankruptcy of their lives and goals. English subtitles. (117 mins.)

Going Steady (1958)**½ Molly Bee, Alan Reed Jr. High school seniors keep their marriage a secret until the bride becomes pregnant. Cute comedy-drama, nothing sensational but entertaining. (Dir: Fred F. Sears, 79 mins.)

Gold (Great Britain, 1974)* Roger Moore, Susannah York, Bradford Dillman, Ray Milland, John Gielgud. (Dir: Peter Hunt, 120 mins.)

Gold Diggers of 1933 (1933)*** Warren William, Joan Blondell, Aline MacMahon, Ruby Keeler, Dick Powell, Ginger Rogers. The movie for which Busby Berkeley designed some of his best-known mad dance numbers. It's a pure thirties musical about show girls, well helmed by Mervyn Le Roy. Berkeley's inspirations include pattern dancing with neon violins and the famous "Remember My Forgotten Man" finale. Blondell and William make a surprisingly steamy team, MacMahon slings the wisecracks, Keeler and Powell are in love, and Ginger Rogers sings "We're in the Money" in pig Latin. And yes, there's also "Pettin' in the Park." (Dir: Mervyn Le Roy, 96 mins.)

Gold Diggers of 1935 (1935)**½ Dick Powell, Adolphe Menjou, Alice Brady. The plot crackles and sputters, and the precision dance numbers carry the show in the first feature entirely directed by Busby Berkeley. The nonpareil "Lullaby of Broadway" sequence ends with the heroine, a young girl, plunging to her death from the top of a skyscraper. (98 mins.)

Gold Diggers of 1937 (1936)**½ Dick Powell, Joan Blondell, Victor Moore, Jane Wyman, Osgood Perkins. Above-average musical with a fair score and a good assist from Moore as a none-too-healthy millionaire. (Dir: Lloyd Bacon, 101 mins.)

Gold of Naples (Italy, 1955)***½ Sophia Loren, Vittorio De Sica, Toto, Silvana Mangano. Four generally well done stories about life in Naples. The luscious Sophia should hold male viewers throughout. Dubbed in English. (Dir: Vittorio De Sica, 107 mins.)

Gold of the Amazon Woman (MTV 1979)½ Anita Ekberg, Bo Svenson, Donald Pleasence. (Dir: Mark Lester, 104 mins.)

Gold of the Seven Saints (1961)*½ Clint Walker, Roger Moore, Chill Wills, Leticia Roman. Several bands of outlaws chase a pair of rich trappers over hill and dale. For diehard Western chase fans only. Filmed in Utah. B&W. (Dir: Gordon Douglas, 88 mins.)

Gold Rush, The (1925)**** Charles Chaplin, Mack Swain, Tom Murray. Written and directed by Chaplin. One of the greatest comedies ever. Using the backdrop of the Klondike, Chaplin combines a touching love scene with some of the most inventive and funniest scenes ever filmed. Includes the classic dance where Chaplin uses two bread rolls, and the pantomime sequence where he eats an old shoe. Quintessential Charlie. (100 mins.)

Golden Age of Comedy, The (1957)**** A welcome nostalgic glimpse of some of the screen's funniest scenes featuring the all-time great clowns of Hollywood—Charlie Chaplin, Laurel & Hardy, Keystone Kops, Will Rogers, plus others. What makes this collection of film clips better than most movies of this kind are a superb editing job and the excellent choice of clips. (Dir: Robert Youngson, 79 mins.)

Golden Arrow, The (Italy, 1964)* Tab Hunter, Rossana Podesta. (Dir: Antonio Margheriti, 91 mins.)

Golden Blade, The (1953)** Rock Hudson,

Piper Laurie. Costume nonsense in old Bagdad with Rock seeking to avenge the death of his father and meeting Princess Piper—all this and a magic sword, yet. (Dir: Nathan Juran, 81 mins.)

Golden Boy (1939)*** William Holden, Barbara Stanwyck, Adolphe Menjou, Lee J. Cobb. Clifford Odets' brilliant fight drama has lost some of its wallop in 40 years. Still worth seeing for direction and performances, particularly from the supporting cast. This was Holden's first big break. (Dir: Rouben Mamoulian, 100 mins.)

Golden Breed (1968)*** Dale Davis, Butch Van Artsdalen, Mickey Dora. Vivid documentary about surfing, full of towering waves and the glinting, "golden breed" of surfers. Filmed in Hawaii, California and Mexico. (Dir: Dale Davis, 88 mins.)

Golden Coach, The (Italy-Great Britain, 1953)**** Anna Magnani. Camilla (Magnani), head of a commedia dell'arte troupe touring Peru, plays with her lovers, but finally goes back to her real love, the theater, in director Jean Renoir's luxuriant, tender little fable, which disguises its nobility with a tone of biting irony. (105 mins.)

Golden Demon (Japan, 1956)**½ Jun Negami, Fujiko Yamamoto. A young girl loves a poor student but is forced into marrying a rich man. Soap opera, Japanese style, but done rather well. English-dubbed. (Dir: Koji Shima, 95 mins.)

Golden Earrings (1947)**½ Ray Milland, Marlene Dietrich. A British spy is hidden by a gypsy girl in this aimless comedy which was quite successful when it was released. (Dir: Mitchell Leisen, 95 mins.)

Golden Gate Murders, The (MTV 1979)** David Janssen, Susannah York. The murder mystery aspects of this film are routine, but romance blossoms between a hard-nosed detective (Janssen) and a nun (York). (Dir: Walter Grauman, 104 mins.)

Golden Girl (1951)**½ Mitzi Gaynor, Dale Robertson, Dennis Day, James Barton. If you disregard the cornball plot about the ups and downs a dancer named Lotta Crabtree (Miss Gaynor) has during the Civil War and just watch Mitzi dance and listen to Dennis Day sing, this film can be fun. (Dir: Lloyd Bacon, 108 mins.)

Golden Goddess of Rio Beni (Germany-Spain-France, 1964)*½ Pierre Brice, Harald Juhnke, Gillian Hill. (Dir: Eugen Martin, 93 mins.)

Golden Heist, The—See: **Inside Out**

Golden Horde, The (1951)** Ann Blyth, David Farrar. Overproduced epic about the barbaric sweep of Genghis Khan out of Asia. Miss Blyth is sorely miscast as a voluptuous princess of Samarkand who falls in love with a visiting crusader named Sir Guy (David Farrar). (Dir: George Sherman, 77 mins.)

Golden Madonna, The (Great Britain, 1949) Artist and a girl attempt to retrieve a valuable painting that was accidentally sold in Italy. Pleasant romantic comedy-drama. (Dir: Ladislas Vajda, 88 mins.)

Golden Mask, The (Great Britain, 1952)**½ Van Heflin, Wanda Hendrix, Eric Portman. Reporter accompanies an expedition seeking buried treasure in North Africa. Fairly exciting melodrama with fine location backgrounds. (Dir: Jack Lee, 88 mins.)

Golden Mistress, The (1954)**½ John Agar, Rosemarie Bowe. Treasure hunters incur voodoo vengeance when they steal an idol. Frequently exciting melodrama takes advantage of Haiti locations. (Dir: Joel Judge, 83 mins.)

Golden Moment, The (MTV 1980)*½ Stephanie Zimbalist, David Keith, Richard Lawson, Victor French, Jack Palance. (Dir: Richard C. Sarafian, 109 mins.)

Golden Needles (1974)* Elizabeth Ashley, Burgess Meredith, Joe Don Baker, Ann Sothern. (Dir: Robert Clouse, 92 mins.)

Golden Patsy, The (Germany, 1962)** Gert Frobe. Family man teaches his clan the meaning of money when he announces everything's been lost and they'll have to live like paupers. Mild comedy-drama with a capable performance by Frobe. Dubbed in English.

Golden Salamander, The (Great Britain, 1950)*** Trevor Howard, Anouk Aimée. British archaeologist goes to North Africa to collect valuable antiques, gets mixed up in gun running. Exciting, well made melodrama. (Dir: Ronald Neame, 96 mins.)

Golden Voyage of Sinbad, The (Great Britain, 1974)**½ John Phillip Law. Made-in-Spain adventure yarn detailing the exploits of the mythical sailor in search of a golden crown, as he meets an evil sorcerer, a beautiful slave girl, a six-armed dueling goddess, and a one-eyed centaur. Lots of special effects, exciting for kids. (Dir: Gordon Hessler, 105 mins.)

Goldengirl (1979)** Susan Anton, Curt Jurgens, Harry Guardino, James Coburn, Leslie Caron. Anton is adequate—though ravishing—in her starring debut focusing on a scientist (Jurgens) who subjects his daughter to dangerous drugs, transforming her into an abnormally tall Olympic track star, but with tragic results. Coburn walks through this one as her lover. (Dir: Joseph Sargent, 104 mins.)

Goldenrod (MTV 1977)**½ Tony Lo Bianco, Gloria Carlin. Story about a rodeo star on the Canadian circuit, circa 1950's, whose career experiences ups, downs, and ups. Tony Lo Bianco is good as the champion who takes his wife for granted. (Dir: Harvey Hart, 106 mins.)

Goldfinger (Great Britain, 1964)**½ Sean Connery, Gert Frobe, Honor Blackman. A spectacular heist is planned of the gold deposits in Fort Knox. This is the James Bond picture that really took in the gold, but also the one that signaled the series' creative bankruptcy. A few clever touches fail to obscure the barrenness of the heroics, and the formula becomes painfully

obvious. Blackman makes a fair foil for Connery's 007, but Frobe is less than credible as the world-threatening menace and Guy Hamilton, who took over the director's reins from Terence Young, is no stylist. (108 mins.)

Goldie and the Boxer (MTV 1980)** O.J. Simpson, Melissa Michaelsen, Vincent Gardenia, Gordon Jump. This is O.J.'s first film after his gridiron retirement produced by his own production company. The story, set in the 40s, concerns a down-and-out boxer, Joe Gallagher (O.J.), who returns to the ring managed by a cute little girl (Michaelsen). He becomes champ. A hokey fairy tale drenched in "you can do it" sentimentality. O.J. is a charmer, but he needs some acting lessons. (Dir: David Miller, 104 mins.)

Goldie and the Boxer Go to Hollywood (MTV 1981)**½ O.J. Simpson, Melissa Michaelsen. Here's the sequel to the 1979 TV movie which successfully teamed O.J. Simpson and little Melissa Michaelsen as a boxer and his young, young manager, respectively, of course. The unlikely but loving couple continue their adventures in Tinsel Town while trying to hide from a promoter out to get O.J. and the adoption board. Miss Michaelsen's charm compliments O.J.'s laid-back style, and the two keep the film rolling along.

Goldstein (1965)**½ Lou Gilbert, Ellen Madison, Nelson Algren. The most interesting thing about this offbeat entry is that it is based on an unidentified story by Martin Buber. Symbolic comedy about a bedraggled modern-day prophet who rises out of a lake near Chicago to wander the city streets. Episodic, at times very witty. (Dirs: Benjamin Manaster, Philip Kaufman, 85 mins.)

Goldwyn Follies, The (1938)*** Adolphe Menjou, the Ritz Brothers, Vera Zorina, Kenny Baker, Edgar Bergen, Charlie McCarthy, Bobby Clark. A big musical, without much inspired comedy but with good production-numbers. The last score by George Gershwin, featuring many superb songs, including "Love Walked In," "Love Is Here to Stay," and "Spring Again" (the latter, however, by Kurt Weill). The uneven revue format is poorly handled by director George Marshall. Choreography by George Balanchine. (115 mins.)

Golem, The (Germany, 1920)**** Paul Wegener. Director Wegener's version is the best of the four versions of this perennial horror classic. His hulking claylike monster is an archetype, and the astonishing, angular, teetering sets by Hans Poelzig make the nightmare world of the occult breathtakingly concrete. An extraordinarily vivid, magical, brooding film. (75 mins.)

Goliath and the Barbarians (Italy, 1960)*½ Steve Reeves, Chelo Alonso, Bruce Cabot. (Dir: Carlo Campogalliani, 86 mins.)

Goliath and the Dragon (Italy, 1960)*½ Mark Forrest, Broderick Crawford,

Eleanora Ruffo. (Dir: Vittorio Cottafavi, 87 mins.)

Goliath and the Vampires—See: **Vampires**

Goliath at the Conquest of Damascus (Italy, 1964)* Rock Stevens, Helga Line. (Dir: Domenico Paolella, 80 mins.)

Goliath, the Rebel Slave (Italy-France, 1963)*½ Gordon Scott, Massimo Serrato. (Dir: Mario Caiano)

Gone Are the Days (1963)***½ Ossie Davis, Ruby Dee, Godfrey Cambridge, Alan Alda. Screen version by Ossie Davis of his Broadway hit, "Purlie Victorious"; a brash, satiric swipe at racism and Uncle Tomism in the South by updating Negro folk tales to contemporary struggles. Farcical lampoon, topicality, and energetic acting make for good entertainment. "Amos 'n' Andy" with a potent, civilizing message. (Dir: Nicholas Webster, 100 mins.)

Gone to Earth (Great Britain, 1950)*** Jennifer Jones, Cyril Cusack, Sybil Thorndike, David Farrar. A strange Welsh girl (Jones) in the late 19th century, who is dominated by superstition and an attachment for her pet fox, marries a minister but has stirrings for the manly squire (Farrar). Long dismissed as a failure of producer David O. Selznick and the writer-director team of Michael Powell and Emeric Pressburger, this film is being reassessed. It's ripe material—uneven, but worth seeing. Released in the U.S. ('52) as "The Wild Heart" (82 mins.). (110 mins.)

Gone with the Wind (1939)*** Clark Gable, Vivien Leigh, Leslie Howard, Olivia de Havilland, Hattie McDaniel, Butterfly McQueen, Thomas Mitchell. This landmark film, based on Margaret Mitchell's mammoth novel, won eight Academy Awards. The siege of Atlanta and the hardships of the South during the Civil War are masterfully unfolded in this terrific spectacle. Leigh's performance is fetching as Scarlett O'Hara, Gable still makes the ladies' hearts flutter as Rhett Butler. Part spectacle, part history, a dash of biography, and all smashing entertainment. Although Victor Fleming is credited as director, many other cooks worked on this broth, including George Cukor, William Cameron Menzies, Selznick himself, and Sam Wood. (219 mins.)

Good Against Evil (MTV 1977)* Dack Rambo, Elyssa Davalos, Dan O'Herlihy. (Dir: Paul Wendkos, 79 mins.)

Good Companions, The (Great Britain, 1933)*** Edmund Gwenn, John Gielgud, Jessie Matthews. The popular J. B. Priestley novel about itinerant players in the English countryside is given a charming, cheap mounting. Young dancer Matthews was made a star by this film. Stiff-upper-lip cinema at its most authentic, with the middle-class virtues snug and transcendent. (Dir: Victor Saville, 113 mins.)

Good Companions, The (Great Britain, 1957)**½ Eric Portman, Celia Johnson,

Hugh Griffith. A none too satisfactory remake. The two young leads lack the charm and charisma of the '33 stars. Colorful and moderately entertaining. (Dir: J. Lee Thompson, 104 mins.)

Good Day for a Hanging (1959)** Fred MacMurray, Maggie Hayes, Robert Vaughn. Ex-lawman captures a charming killer, but the townspeople refuse to believe him guilty. Offbeat western moves too slowly, but tries to be different. (Dir: Nathan Juran, 85 mins.)

Good Die Young, The (Great Britain, 1954)**½ Richard Basehart, John Ireland, Gloria Grahame, Margaret Leighton, Laurence Harvey. Four men from assorted backgrounds plan a daring robbery. Rambling melodrama is benefited by a fine cast, some suspense. (Dir: Lewis Gilbert, 100 mins.)

Good Earth, The (1937)**** Paul Muni, Luise Rainer. Pearl Buck's great novel of famine, plague and the fight for survival in China is one of the greatest films Hollywood ever made. Both Muni and Rainer give faultless portrayals in this still wonderful film. (Dir: Sidney Franklin, 138 mins.)

Good Fairy, The (1935)***½ Margaret Sullavan, Herbert Marshall, Frank Morgan, Alan Hale, Beulah Bondi. A delightfully crafted comedy featuring the radiant Sullavan as a do-gooder who tries to bolster Marshall's legal career. The level of romantic whimsy is merrily sustained without cloying. Adapted from a Ferenc Molnár farce by Preston Sturges, the film is directed steadily by William Wyler. (90 mins.)

Good Girls Go to Paris (1939)**½ Joan Blondell, Melvyn Douglas. Waitress with a yen to see Paris tries her wiles on the scion of a social family. Amusing comedy. (Dir: Alexander Hall, 80 mins.)

Good Guys and the Bad Guys, The (1969)**½ Robert Mitchum, George Kennedy. Entertaining Western fare with Mitchum as an aging sheriff who teams with his old enemy Kennedy to ward off a planned train robbery. There's more attention paid to characterization than action, and Mitchum and Kennedy are good in the leading roles, while David Carradine scores as a young outlaw in an energetic performance. The supporting cast is also topnotch, including Lois Nettleton, Marie Windsor and the wily Douglas V. Fowley as a hermit-of-sorts. (Dir: Burt Kennedy, 90 mins.)

Good Humor Man, The (1950)*** Jack Carson, Lola Albright. Slapstick all the way—but many funny moments as Jack Carson gets involved with murderers and blondes and the police. (Dir: Lloyd Bacon, 79 mins.)

Good Morning and Goodbye! (1967)* (Dir: Russ Meyer, 80 mins.)

Good Morning, Miss Dove (1955)**½ Jennifer Jones, Robert Stack. A nostalgic film about a dearly beloved middle-aged

265

school teacher and her effect on her former pupils. The ladies will have two or three good cries during the movie. Miss Jones, with the aid of old-age makeup, is adequate in the title role. (Dir: Henry Koster, 107 mins.)

Good Neighbor Sam (1964)** Jack Lemmon, Romy Schneider, Dorothy Provine. Seemingly endless comedy about an ad man who has to pose as another woman's husband, the consequences therefrom, etc. Lemmon is funny, but he can't do it without help from the writers, which he doesn't receive here. Edward G. Robinson is in for a guest role, to little avail. (Dir: David Swift, 130 mins.)

Good News (1930)** Bessie Love, Cliff Edwards, Mary Lawlor. Like many early sound movies, this is a transcription of a Broadway musical hit with most of the original cast. The scene is Taft College, and the problem is whether the football star will flunk the exam or play in the big game, and whether the guys will get the girls and vice versa. The De Sylva-Brown-Henderson songs are still hummable: "The Best Things in Life Are Free" and "Varsity Drag". (Dirs: Nick Grindle, Edgar J. MacGregor, 90 mins.)

Good News (1947)***½ June Allyson, Peter Lawford, Mel Tormé, Joan McCracken. Crackerjack musical comedy, a stunning debut for young director Charles Walters. It's strictly MGM-land, but the cranework gracefully integrates the numbers into a coherent, seamless whole, and the attitude toward the material kids without mocking. With the extraordinary McCracken doing the "Pass the Peacepipe" showstopper. (95 mins.)

Good Sam (1948)** Gary Cooper, Ann Sheridan, Edmund Lowe. Do-gooder always gets into trouble trying to help others. Good cast can't make up for thin, only occasionally amusing story, produced, directed and cowritten by Leo McCarey. (114 mins.)

Good, the Bad and the Ugly, The (Italy, 1966)*** Clint Eastwood, Eli Wallach, Lee Van Cleef. The third Eastwood spaghetti western racked up huge box-office receipts in the U.S. and Europe. Wallach mugs delightfully, Van Cleef is evil incarnate, and Eastwood is a fine ambiguous hero. Some vaguely Marxist mumblings about the Church and war don't mar the aesthetic power of director Sergio Leone's unrivaled close-ups. (161 mins.)

Good Times (1967)*** Sonny and Cher, George Sanders. Much better than expected. Sonny and Cher, popular recording team, star in their first film, and it's a mad romp in which they play themselves. Sonny wants them to become movie stars, and his fantasies about their would-be films are quite funny. Breezy direction by William Friedkin. (91 mins.)

Goodbye Again (1961)** Ingrid Bergman, Yves Montand, Anthony Perkins. Ingrid as a "mature" interior decorator who enters into an affair with "young American boy" Tony. Romantic drama on the tedious side, based on Françoise Sagan's novel. The Paris locale is aptly captured, but the emotional conflicts border on soap opera. (Dir: Anatole Litvak, 120 mins.)

Goodbye Charlie (1964)* Debbie Reynolds, Tony Curtis, Walter Matthau, Pat Boone. (Dir: Vincente Minnelli, 117 mins.)

Goodbye Columbus (1969)**** Richard Benjamin, Ali MacGraw, Jack Klugman. Unusually successful adaptation of Philip Roth's acclaimed novella about Jewish life in the Bronx in the 1950's. So much of the film is charming, observant, and accurate that one can forgive the lapses from director Larry Peerce. "Columbus" marked the screen debut for Benjamin, deftly playing a college dropout who meets the stylish, stunning Ali at a country club. Excellent screenplay written by Arnold Schulman. Peerce's father, famed opera singer Jan, has a bit part as one of the wedding guests. (105 mins.)

Goodbye, Flickmania! (Japan, 1979)** Takuzo Kawatani, Naohiko Shigeta. Masato Harada has lived as a critic in Los Angeles for a number of years, but he made this film in 1979 in Japan. Set in 1968, the film reworks themes from Hawks's *Red River* in terms of a Japanese social-protest drama, with Takuzo Kawatani a forty-year-old film buff (modeled on John Wayne) and Naohiko Shigeta as a nineteen-year-old buddy who conceives a misguided passion for a prostitute. Lots of references to some good films. (Dir: Masato Harada, 110 mins.)

Goodbye Girl, The (1977)***½ Richard Dreyfuss, Marsha Mason, Quinn Cummings. Dreyfuss and playwright Neil Simon are an unbeatable combination in this enjoyable romantic comedy set in New York. Mason is a Broadway chorine whose lover skipped town and sold his apartment lease to Dreyfuss, a stage actor from Chicago trying to make it in the big city. The trouble is, Mason and her worldly ten-year-old daughter (Cummings) are still in the apartment. Their confrontations make for a lot of funny, witty scenes which naturally lead to romance. The pace is fast and consistently entertaining. (Dir: Herbert Ross, 110 mins.)

Goodbye Mr. Chips (Great Britain, 1939)**** Robert Donat, Greer Garson. Story of the life of an English schoolteacher taken from the James Hilton novel is brilliant screen entertainment. Donat's Oscar-winning portrayal of the lovable Mr. Chips is an acting masterpiece. (Dir: Sam Wood, 114 mins.)

Goodbye, Mr. Chips (1969)** Peter O'Toole, Petula Clark, Michael Redgrave. Mundane musical remake of the original, which starred Robert Donat and Greer Garson. O'Toole plays the shy professor who falls in love with a young girl, Miss Clark. In this version, the young girl is a musical-comedy actress, complete with outlandish friends and a racy past. O'Toole carries the film and even he isn't up to par. The songs are laughable. (Dir: Herbert Ross, 151 mins.)

Goodbye My Fancy (1951)**½ Joan Crawford, Robert Young, Eve Arden. Bright comedy-drama about a lady politician who returns to her alma mater to receive an honorary degree and digs up a lot of old scandals. Based on the Broadway success. (Dir: Vincent Sherman, 107 mins.)

Goodbye, My Lady (1956)**½ Walter Brennan, Brandon de Wilde, Phil Harris. A family movie about an old man, a young boy and a dog. These three live through adventures that would make Huck Finn's mouth water. (Dir: William Wellman, 94 mins.)

Goodnight, My Love (MTV 1972)**½ Richard Boone, Barbara Bain. The nostalgia craze reaches back to the '40's, and all those thrillers with Barbara Bain doubling for Miss Bacall (blond '40's hairdo, shoulder pads, and red, red lipstick); Richard Boone playing an older, more tired, and much heavier version of Bogey's gumshoe; and Michael Dunn cast as his wisecracking dwarf sidekick. Everyone goes around spouting tight-lipped jargon, and even the sinister fat man (Victor Buono) is on hand to complete the picture. (Dir: Peter Hyams, 73 mins.)

Gorath (Japan, 1962)** Ryo Ikebe, Akihiko Hirata. Average sci-fi about an enormous planetary body ("Gorath") hurtling toward the earth. More "scientific" than most of this genre. (Dir: Inoshiro Honda, 83 mins.)

Gordon's War (1973)** Paul Winfield, Carl Lee, David Downing. A black veteran returns home from Vietnam and learns that his wife has died from a drug overdose. Enraged, Gordon (Winfield) declares war on the Harlem drug lords. A rampage of killing follows the predictable route; Winfield is quite good. (Dir: Ossie Davis, 89 mins.)

Gorgeous Hussy, The (1936)** Joan Crawford, Franchot Tone, Robert Taylor. Fictionalized biography of Peggy Eaton, the notorious belle of Washington during Jackson's administration. Picture tells little of her notoriety and emerges as a dull, overly long love story. (Dir: Clarence Brown, 102 mins.)

Gorgo (Great Britain, 1961)*** Bill Travers, William Sylvester, Vincent Winter. Sea monster is captured and put on display in London, but its parent comes after it to wreak havoc on the city. If all those terrible horror thrillers haven't taken the edge off, here's a good one—well-made and exciting. (Dir: Eugene Lourie, 78 mins.)

Gorgon, The (Great Britain, 1964)**½ Peter Cushing, Christopher Lee. Village terrorized when murders occur, the victims turned to stone. Well-made horror thriller has its share of suspenseful sequences. (Dir: Terence Fisher, 83 mins.)

Gorilla at Large (1954)** Anne Bancroft, Cameron Mitchell, Lee J. Cobb, Lee Marvin, Raymond Burr. A murder mystery unfolded amid the gaudy atmosphere of a cheap carnival. Good actors are totally wasted in this routine meller. (Dir: Harmon Jones, 84 mins.)

Gospel According to St. Matthew, The (Italy-France, 1964)**** Enrique Irazoqui, Margherita Caruso. Graphic, rough, fiercely realistic filming of the story of Christ, using only the words and scenes described by Matthew. Director Pier Paolo Pasolini, an avowed Marxist and atheist, portrays Christ as a determined revolutionary. The cast, composed only of non-professionals, including Pasolini's own mother, is persuasive, visually affecting. (136 mins.)

Gossip Columnist, The (MTV 1980)** Kim Cattrall, Bobby Vinton, Robert Vaughn, Martha Raye. Geared for those who enjoy glossy soap operas about glamorous people. Cattrall is a young syndicated gossip columnist who uncovers some unethical moves by a Hollywood figure (Vaughn) with his eye on a political career. Ms. Cattrall is pretty and can act, which is more than can be said for most of the supporting cast. Cameos by many Hollywood luminaries. (Dir: James Sheldon, 104 mins.)

Graduate, The (1967)**** Dustin Hoffman, Anne Bancroft, Katharine Ross. A brilliant, funny, and touching film directed by Mike Nichols, who won an Academy Award for this box-office smash, one of the most successful films of all time. Based on the novel by Charles Webb. In his first major role Hoffman is both hilarious and deeply moving. His first hotel-room tryst with Mrs. Robinson (Bancroft) is one of the most paralyzingly funny scenes ever captured on film. Script by Calder Willingham and Buck Henry concerns a young college graduate who returns to his parents' affluent California swimming-pool world which he despises, and tries to find his own values. (105 mins.)

Grand Central Murder (1942)*** Van Heflin, Cecelia Parker. Private eye solves the murder of an actress in Grand Central Station. Good compact mystery. (Dir: S. Sylvan Simon, 73 mins.)

Grand Hotel (1932)*** John Barrymore, Greta Garbo, Lionel Barrymore, Wallace Beery, Joan Crawford, Lewis Stone. This typical MGM superstar vehicle makes for classy entertainment, with John Barrymore as a jewel thief romancing a very tired ballerina played by Greta Garbo. Lionel Barrymore has but months to live, but is making the most of it despite the soggy presence of boss Wallace Beery, a gross industrialist, who is out to bed stenographer Joan Crawford, while Lewis Stone plays the Eric Sevareid character. Of the pictures nominated for the Oscar for Best Picture of 1931–32, this was the worst, though it was the winner. It's a rare year now when the five nominees are up to the level of *Grand Hotel*. The kinky Edmund Goulding directed, though not as well as in his neglected *Blondie of the Follies* of the same year. (113 mins.)

Grand Illusion (France, 1937)**** Jean Gabin, Pierre Fresnay, Erich von Stroheim, Marcel Dalio, Julien Carette, Dita Parlo, Gaston Modot. An official classic that merits the accolade. Jean Renoir's study of men in war explores the bonds that bind them: be they national, fraternal, or social-class. The conflicts of these bonds are complex and troubling, and Renoir in all his implacable optimism scants none of these ponderables, though his faith was easier held before the second war than after. With superb performances by the cast, and with Jean Daste as the translator of Pindar. (Dir: Jean Renoir, 95 mins.; originally 111 mins.)

Grand Prix (1966)**½ James Garner, Eva Marie Saint, Yves Montand. Sappy story about the European auto racing circuit, greatly aided by some magnificent shots of the racing itself, and what it feels like to be traveling well over 100 miles an hour going around sharp turns. The racing scenes are among the best ever to hit the screen. (Dir: John Frankenheimer, 179 mins.)

Grand Slam (Italy-France-Germany, 1967)*** Edward G. Robinson, Adolfo Celi, Janet Leigh, Robert Hoffman. A professor and a gangster embark on a split-second scheme to heist some diamonds. Perfect-crime capers demand ingenuity and suspense for success, and this has both. (Dir: Giuliano Montaldo, 120 mins.)

Grand Theft Auto (1977)**½ Ron Howard, Nancy Morgan. Too many car chases and crashes, but this is an amiable enough comedy. Howard is eloping with lovely heiress Morgan and the whole city of Los Angeles seems to be in pursuit of the lovebirds. The crashes are well staged, and director-star Howard knows how to pace a film. (89 mins.)

Grande Bouffe, The (France, 1974)**** Marcello Mastroianni, Ugo Tognazzi, Philippe Noiret, Michel Piccoli, Andrea Ferreol. Hilarious, stomach-turning, morbid, breezy, funny, sad fable about four men (Mastroianni, Tognazzi, Noiret, and Piccoli) who shut themselves up in a Parisian villa and gorge themselves to death on gourmet delights, pausing only to sample the charms of three negligible whores and the ample affections of Andrea Ferreol before expiring disgustingly one by one. Marco Ferreri directed this black comedy that satirizes two of France's most cherished institutions: dining and whoring. The fun begins when you realize that each actor is using his or her own real name. Be certain to have dinner at least an hour before you see it. (125 mins.)

Grandma and the Eight Children (Norway, 1977)*** Ann-Cath Vestly. This Norwegian version of *Eight Is Enough* is based on a popular series of children's books by Ann-Cath Vestly, who plays Grandma. The eight kids (whose names all begin with the letter "M") live with their parents in a small two-room flat in the city. When their dad's truck is stolen, the kids recover it and make the thief a friend of the family. Espen Thorstenson wrote and directed this successful film, which spawned a sequel, also by him.

Grandma's Boy (1922)***½ Harold Lloyd, Anna Townsend, Dick Sutherland. Lloyd's favorite among his films—but he made better ones. As usual, Lloyd's confrontation with a bullying tramp (the bearlike Sutherland) becomes a touchstone for psychological maturity through moral aggression. (Dir: Fred Newmeyer, 54 mins.)

Grapes of Wrath, The (1940)**** Henry Fonda, Jane Darwell, John Carradine. John Ford's vision of the ant line of Okies marching across the Depression desert to California was based on John Steinbeck's best seller, and it remains, for better or worse, Ford's best known and most "respectable" film. Ford's admirers have rightly tended to play down this Oscar-winning effort in favor of the director's later and more personal westerns. But there is much to admire here in Gregg Toland's sunbeaten photography and Henry Fonda's meticulous performance as Steinbeck's dashboard saint, Tom Joad. Oscars to Ford and Darwell. (129 mins.)

Grass Is Always Greener over the Septic Tank, The (MTV 1978)*** Carol Burnett, Charles Grodin, Alex Rocco. From Erma Bombeck's witty best-selling novel, which unfortunately reads better than it plays. Writer-mother-wife-and-chief-bottle-washer Dorothy Benson (Burnett), her ad agency exec husband (Grodin), and their two kids leave crowded, dirty, dangerous New York City for the supposedly good life of the suburbs and encounter one pitfall after another. (Dir: Robert Day, 104 mins.)

Grass Is Greener, The (1960)*** Cary Grant, Deborah Kerr, Jean Simmons, Robert Mitchum. Martini-dry comedy about an American millionaire who complicates the wedded bliss of an English couple. Overdose of brittle Noel Coward-ish dialogue makes the pace slow but the cast is good, the production attractive. (Dir: Stanley Donen, 105 mins.)

Grasshopper, The (1970)***½ Jacqueline Bisset, Jim Brown, Joseph Cotten. Remarkable, neglected film about how a young girl eager to enter show business ends up a marginal entertainer, and then a wasted, common whore. Bisset gives her most detailed and affecting performance, and though the film's focus dawdles and occasionally loses itself, director Jerry Paris on the whole turns in a fine, atmospheric job. (95 mins.)

Grateful Dead, The (1977)*** If you're going to like this film, you already know it. Culled from the '74 series of Dead concerts at Winterland in San Francisco. Directed by Jerry Garcia, their lead vocalist-guitarist. You won't get the five-channel sound on TV. (131 mins.)

Gray Lady Down (1978)**½ Charlton Heston, Stacy Keach, David Carradine, Ned Beatty. Technocratic thriller—well mounted, logically paced—about a downed submarine slipping off the continental shelf and the rescue operation attempting against time to raise it. The story was used as early as John Ford's 1930 *Men Without Women*—it still works, as the ghostly underwater silences punctuate the innate hysteria of the situation. Charlton Heston and Stacy Keach star, but the picture is handily stolen by David Carradine and Ned Beatty as a pair of eccentric bathospheric experimenters. David Greene directed competently, as called for. (111 mins.)

Grease (1978)** John Travolta, Olivia Newton-John. Limp, cheaply made version of the Broadway play about growing up cool in the '50s. Director Randal Kleiser has no sense of how a musical is constructed: the songs are bunched together, the production numbers don't move, and the whole film shifts awkwardly between naturalism and stylization. Travolta does little with a pallid part (although he does dance a gratuitous disco number); Newton-John is merely pallid. (110 mins.)

Greased Lightning (1977)*** Richard Pryor, Pam Grier, Beau Bridges, Cleavon Little, Richie Havens. Pryor gives an authoritative performance in this respectful biography of Wendell Scott, the first black professional racing-car driver, who started out running moonshine before WW II and battled prejudice for many years before being allowed to race against whites. There's not enough grit, but there are some wonderful scenes, when Wendell comes home from the war, and his first, hostile meeting with Bridges (who later becomes his close friend). Sincere and enjoyable. Filmed largely on location in Georgia. (Dir: Michael Schultz, 96 mins.)

Greaser's Palace (1972)** Albert Henderson, Michael Sullivan. Robert Downey, gifted director of "Putney Swope," has become self-indulgent. Allegorical story of Jesus. Full of parody and bright ideas which never conquer or compete with the dreariness of the symbolism. The few bright moments are rooted in irreverence: a zoot-suited Jesus, the Holy Ghost running around in a white sheet, and a constipated God who hates his son for being a "homo." The production is glossier than any of Downey's previous productions. (Dir: Robert Downey, 91 mins.)

Great Adventure, The (Sweden, 1955)**** Swedish documentarian Arne Sucksdorff's first feature is an epic depiction of the dispassion of nature, as two children (Sucksdorff's own) enter into the wilderness, capture an otter, and keep it for a pet, only to see it leave them in the spring with no signs of regret. A didactic film in the happiest sense. Sucksdorff's lesson (that nature is more than a playground for man) comes across in the form of a total integration of the filmmaker's sensibility and setting. A nature film that makes the Disney efforts we've all grown up on look puny and dishonest. (Dir: Arne Sucksdorff, 75 mins.)

Great American Beauty Contest, The (MTV 1973)**½ Louis Jourdan, Eleanor Parker, Robert Cummings. Behind-the-scenes drama about the beauty-contest business complete with proposed hanky-panky between judge and contestant. Bob Cummings plays the emcee and show director, anxious to avoid any murmur of scandal, and Miss Parker is the elegant hostess who must deal with Jourdan's Hollywood producer, the troublemaking judge. It's slick soap-opera fare with pretty girls to look at. (Dir: Robert Day, 73 mins.)

Great American Broadcast, The (1941)*** Alice Faye, Jack Oakie, John Payne, Cesar Romero. History of radio (?) is used as a background for a tuneful film, loaded with specialty acts. Jack Oakie is at his best and this one is grand entertainment. (Dir: Archie Mayo, 92 mins.)

Great American Cowboy, The (1974)***½ Larry Mahan, Phil Lyne. Academy Award-winning documentary about the hardships and rewards of the rodeo circuit, follows two stars as they prepare for competition. Rodeo footage well blended with other sequences detailing the off-bronco lives of the two circuit-winning cowboys. Narrated by Joel McCrea. Most of the credit goes to producer, director, editor Kieth Merrill. (90 mins.)

Great American Pastime, The (1956)** Tom Ewell, Anne Francis, Ann Miller, Dean Jones. Moderately entertaining comedy about a suburban lawyer who becomes manager of his son's little-league team. For the kids. (Dir: Herman Hoffman, 89 mins.)

Great American Tragedy, A (MTV 1972)*** George Kennedy, Vera Miles. Story about a successful aerospace engineer whose life undergoes a complete reversal when he's fired from the job he has held for 20 years. This modern-day dilemma has been explored in documentaries, but the dramatic treatment it receives here drives the facts home. Kennedy and Miles are excellent as the couple who face unexpected struggles and challenges when their affluent world crumbles, and the script by Caryl Ledner is adult, believable, and affecting. Above-average. (Dir: J. Lee Thompson, 73 mins.)

Great Balloon Adventure, The—See: Olly Olly Oxen Free

Great Bank Robbery, The (1969)** Kim Novak, Clint Walker, Zero Mostel. Although this comedy western boasts the presence of Mostel as a wily would-be bank robber and a plot that sounds like it can't miss, it peters out long before it gets up a full head of steam. The yarn is about three separate plans to rob a top-security bank in the western town of Friendly, circa 1880. (Dir: Hy Averback, 98 mins.)

Great British Train Robbery, The (West Germany, 1965)*** Horst Tappert, Hans Cossy. Despite the improbable idea of having Germans recreate the famous British train robbery of 1963, the attempt comes off. The German actors could pass for Britons; action is crisp, realistic, well-paced—and non-violent. Horst Tappert is tops as the dispassionate criminal mastermind. Made-for-West German-TV in three ninety-minute segments. (Dirs: John Olden, Claus Peter Witt, 104 mins.)

Great Caruso, The (1951)***½ Mario Lanza, Ann Blyth. Screen biography of the noted opera tenor is a fitting vehicle for Lanza and his powerful voice. Music devotees should revel in the many songs, arias presented. Others should find it a well-made, consistently interesting drama. (Dir: Richard Thorpe, 109 mins.)

Great Catherine (Great Britain, 1968)*** Peter O'Toole, Jeanne Moreau, Zero Mostel, Jack Hawkins. Mostel is marvelously funny in this entertaining adaptation of George Bernard Shaw's one-act play, "Whom Glory Still Adores." Moreau playing Catherine is overshadowed by the maniacal Mostel, but she does join an illustrious list of screen actresses who have portrayed the notorious mother of all the Russias, including Pola Negri, Elisabeth Bergner, Marlene Dietrich, Tallulah Bankhead, and Bette Davis. It's not all Shavian gems, but there is a reenactment of the Battle of Bunker Hill and Voltaire is denounced, so . . . (Dir: Gordon Flemyng, 98 mins.)

Great Chase, The (1962)**½ Compilation of old films stressing the action elements; scenes of Fairbanks, William S. Hart, Lillian Gish, many others. Lengthy sequence from Buster Keaton's "The General." Pleasant if uninspired nostalgia. (Compiled by Paul Killiam, 77 mins.)

Great Dan Patch, The (1949)** Dennis O'Keefe, Gail Russell. The story of the greatest trotting horse of them all, told through the family who owned him. Mild, slow, but of some interest to horse lovers. (Dir: Joseph M. Newman, 94 mins.)

Great Day (Great Britain, 1945)** Eric Portman, Flora Robson. English village makes preparations for a visit from Mrs. Roosevelt during World War II. Mild drama. (Dir: Lance Comfort, 94 mins.)

Great Day in the Morning (1956)**½ Virginia Mayo, Robert Stack, Ruth Roman, Raymond Burr. The loyalties of an assortment of townspeople are tested when the Civil War breaks out. Slightly offbeat western drama with good performances, some above-average touches in the direction. (Dir: Jacques Tourneur, 92 mins.)

Great Dictator, The (1940)**** Charlie Chaplin, Jack Oakie, Paulette Goddard. Charlie Chaplin in his famous dual role: as a poor Jew in a ghetto, and as Hynkel, The Great Dictator. There is a mistaken-identity plot, and Jack Oakie is on hand as Napoloni. The picture is like all Chaplin, very funny and very trenchant. The final peroration has been maligned for its political naïveté, but it is strong sentiment and very touching. The best scene, however, comes when Chaplin mimics Hitler's ranting oratory: "Und Garbitsch farshtunk of der Herring." This was his first all-talkie. (Dir: Charlie Chaplin, 128 mins.)

Great Escape, The (1963)***½ Steve McQueen, James Garner, James Coburn, Richard Attenborough, Charles Bronson, David McCallum, Donald Pleasence. A long, long actioner with a cast of hundreds. Manages to generate a bit of humor, some tension, and a lot of suspense as a group of Allied POWs carry out an elaborate escape from a Nazi camp. (Dir: John Sturges, 168 mins.)

Great Expectations (Great Britain, 1946)**** John Mills, Valerie Hobson, Finley Currie, Alec Guinness, Martita Hunt. The Dickens classic of the young orphan lad whose path crosses that of an escaped convict who aids him in the world. Faithfully transcribed, painstakingly produced, superlatively directed, acted, photographed. A film great. (Dir: David Lean, 115 mins.)

Great Flamarion, The (1945)**½ Erich von Stroheim, Mary Beth Hughes, Dan Duryea. A vaudeville trick-shot artist is tricked by a woman into murdering her husband, while she beats it with another man. Standard melodrama, made palatable by Von Stroheim's fine acting. (Dir: Anthony Mann, 78 mins.)

Great Gabbo, The (1929)*** Erich von Stroheim, Betty Compson. This is Von Stroheim's first talking film, and he gives a fascinating performance as a disgruntled ventriloquist. The musical numbers from the burlesque stage are forgettable, but several scenes of Von Stroheim talking to his dummy are memorable. Screenplay by Hugh Herbert based on a story by Ben Hecht. Von Stroheim tried and failed, incidentally, to get the rights for a remake of "Gabbo." (Dir: James Cruze, 96 mins.)

Great Garrick, The (1937)*** Brian Aherne, Olivia de Havilland. Ponderous, moderately entertaining biography of famous actor David Garrick. (Dir: James Whale, 91 mins.)

Great Gatsby, The (1949)**½ Alan Ladd, Betty Field, Barry Sullivan, Ruth Hussey, Macdonald Carey, Shelley Winters. Alan Ladd is not half the actor Robert Redford is, but at least casting him as Gatsby in this version displayed some sensitivity for what the role is all about. This is an intelligent attempt that fails through lack of ambition: It simply avoids the essential problem that Fitzgerald's novel is undramatic; there's no plot development to theatricalize. (Dir: Elliott Nugent, 92 mins.)

Great Gatsby, The (1974)*** Robert Redford, Mia Farrow, Karen Black, Sam Waterston, Bruce Dern. This is Paramount's third film version of F. Scott Fitzgerald's enduring novel about the Beautiful People of rich WASP society in New York and Long Island of the 1920's. To capture the lavish, extravagant look of the palatial estates of the period, director Jack Clayton and David Merrick took their camera crews to one of the great mansions in Newport, R.I., and it works just fine. In this go around Redford plays Gatsby (ne Gatz), the same part played by Alan Ladd in 1949 and Warner Baxter in '26. Redford is such a skillful actor that you tend to overlook the fact that he's a mite too genteel and civilized, given his modest background and hustling business career with bootlegging connections. Critical opinion was sharply divided re Mia Farrow's performance, but the rest of the cast, especially Waterston playing Nick Carraway, is excellent. There are numerous flaws in the film but director Clayton has caught the look and sometimes the feel of this rich if emotionally impoverished crowd, and there are other virtues besides the glorious clothes. Screenplay by Francis Ford Coppola. (144 mins.)

Great Gilbert & Sullivan, The (Great Britain, 1953)***½ Maurice Evans, Robert Morley. The biography of the leading exponents of light operetta who established a legion of worshipers. Elaborately produced, finely portrayed, with many scenes of their most famous works well represented. (Dir: Sidney Gilliat, 105 mins.)

Great Houdinis, The (MTV 1976)**½ Paul Michael Glaser, Sally Struthers. Paul Michael Glaser (half of "Starsky and Hutch") makes his TV-feature debut as Harry Houdini, and he's well cast as the arrogant performer who rose from a third-rate vaudevillian to the ranks of internationally famous escape artist. Sally Struthers, cast as his long-suffering wife, gives a good account of the Catholic girl who married the Jewish magician, and never won acceptance by her husband's unpleasantly stubborn mother (overplayed by Ruth Gordon). A good deal of the film is devoted to Houdini's relentless efforts to contact his dead mother through mediums, and the epilogue has us believe that he himself made contact with his own wife after death. Who can say if this is a definitive biography? It is entertaining. (Dir: Melville Shavelson, 108 mins.)

Great Ice Rip-Off, The (MTV 1974)**½ Lee J. Cobb, Gig Young. Here's a caper film that pits one great actor, Cobb, and one good actor, Young, against each other. Young plays a leader of a small gang of jewel thieves. Cobb is a retired cop. (Dir: Dan Curtis, 72 mins.)

Great Impostor, The (1961)**½ Tony Curtis, Edmond O'Brien, Arthur O'Connell. Based on the life story of Fred Demara, con artist supreme, who takes on different professions and personalities. Curtis has a field day in this uneven but generally satisfying tale. (Dir: Robert Mulligan, 112 mins.)

Great John L., The (1945)*** Greg McClure, Linda Darnell, Barbara Britton. The biography of the great heavyweight champ (John L. Sullivan), as he rises to the top and falls from the heights to drunkenness and disgrace. Nicely done, with exciting, often hilarious ring sequences. (Dir: Frank Tuttle, 96 mins.)

Great Lie, The (1941)**½ Bette Davis, George Brent, Mary Astor. Mary has a child by George, who is Bette's husband and Bette raises the child as her own which is the great lie. Very talky, never compelling but some of the ladies may like it. Astor won a Supporting Actress scar. (Dir: Edmund Goulding, 107 mins.)

Great Locomotive Chase, The (1956)** Fess Parker. Big Fess Parker cuts an imposing figure playing a Union soldier who leads a dangerous mission behind the Confederate lines in order to destroy strategic railroad bridges. Fair Civil War outing. Alternate title: **Andrews' Raiders.** (Dir: Francis D. Lyon, 85 mins.)

Great Lover, The (1949)*** Bob Hope, Rhonda Fleming, Roland Young. Another of Hope's smooth comic performances in this typical funny Hope film filled with intrigue, beautiful women (there are few more gorgeous than luscious Miss Fleming), and enough plot twists to make you dizzy. (Dir: Alexander Hall, 80 mins.)

Great Man, The (1957)*** José Ferrer, Dean Jagger, Julie London. Fairly honest treatment of Al Morgan novel about a ruthless TV personality who was loved by his public and despised by the people who really knew him. Ferrer plays a reporter who sets out to find out about "The Great Man" after his untimely death. Good performances by the entire cast. (Dir: Jose Ferrer, 92 mins.)

Great Man Votes, The (1939)**** John Barrymore, Virginia Weidler. Scholar who has turned to drink reforms when the Children's Society threatens to take away his offspring. Superb drama, with moments of high comedy; fine performances, a gem of a movie. (Dir: Garson Kanin, 70 mins.)

Great Man's Whiskers, The (MTV 1973)**½ Dean Jones, Dennis Weaver. Old-fashioned drama loosely based on a young girl's letter to President Lincoln suggesting he grow whiskers to hide his look of sadness. The best part—an ingratiating meeting between Lincoln and the youngster—comes in the last act. Jones as an earnest teacher dominates the show while Weaver surprises as Lincoln, giving a brief, appealing performance. (Dir: Philip Leacock, 99 mins.)

Great McGinty, The (1940)******** Brian Donlevy, Akim Tamiroff. Preston Sturges's first film is a gentle, perfectly crafted satire on American political corruption in which unemployed drifter eventually becomes governor through the efforts of a corrupt political boss. Sturges was convinced that the American success story was a load of hooey (as they used to say back in the forties), and that a bum like McGinty had just as much chance—and ability—to go to the top as anyone else. All you needed was luck and a bit of larceny. The perfect fusion of Sturges's wit and frenzy. (Dir: Preston Sturges, 81 mins.)

Great Moment, The (1944)****½** Joel McCrea, Betty Field. Story of the Boston dentist who was the first to use ether is well done, but not a particularly outstanding biography. (Dir: Preston Sturges, 83 mins.)

Great Niagara, The (MTV 1974)****½** Richard Boone, Michael Sacks, Randy Quaid. Adventure yarn benefits from the on-location filming at Niagara Falls, Canada. Make no mistake, this is no honeymoon comedy...it's a tale, set in the Depression era, of a prideful old man (Richard Boone) and his dominance over his two sons who **don't** want to follow in their father's footsteps and conquer the great Falls. Exciting rescue scenes! (Dir: William Hale, 72 mins.)

Great Northfield Minnesota Raid, The (1972)*****½** Robert Duvall, Cliff Robertson. Writer-director Philip Kaufman has created a quirky antiwestern about the last hurrah of the James and Younger gangs, when they launched an ill-fated holdup far north of their usual turf. Kaufman's wit, his interweaving of mood, character, and motif, and the mass of bizarre and hilarious detail help to overcome the essentially bland familiarity of the material. Duvall's Jesse James, driven and rigid, is a remarkable performance. (104 mins.)

Great Profile, The (1940)****** John Barrymore, Mary Beth Hughes, John Payne, Anne Baxter. Sad to see the greatest of them all in a Grade B comedy, supposedly about his own backstage shenanigans. If you remember Barrymore, avoid it—if you've never seen him, don't let the opportunity escape. (Dir: Walter Lang, 82 mins.)

Great Race, The (1965)******* Tony Curtis, Jack Lemmon, Natalie Wood, Ross Martin, Dorothy Provine, Peter Falk. Director Blake Edwards's parody of serial melodrama and tribute to slapstick comedy is overlong and insistently hammy, but it's highly inventive. The story of a New York-to-Paris road race (think about that a moment) between the Great Leslie (a white-suited, teeth-flashing Curtis) and the unscrupulous Professor Fate (Lemmon in a Mack Sennett mustache). Very funny and vulgar. (150 mins.)

Great Rupert, The (1950)****½** Jimmy Durante, Terry Moore. Jimmy and a friendly squirrel combine talents to make happiness. Slim story tied to Durante antics. Amusing. (86 mins.)

Great Santini, The (1979)******** Robert Duvall, Blythe Danner, Michael O'Keefe. A powerful, sensitive family drama concerning a professional warrior (Duvall) who finds his only battle plan for dealing with his family during peacetime is evasive action. Duvall's Marine Corps fighter pilot is a vivid, tightly held portrayal of a man who brooks no rebellion at home but is egged on by his own internal contradictions to self-destructive rebellion and revelry within the service. Duvall gives one of the best performances of the year, and oldest son Michael O'Keefe surmounts innumerable emotional pitfalls to register true. *The Great Santini* did not catch on during its first brief release and was quickly sold to pay cable under the title *The Ace*. Reopened in theaters shortly thereafter, it then attracted some of the audience and critical reception it so richly deserved. Based on the novel by Pat Conroy. (Writer-Dir: Lewis John Carlino, 118 mins.)

Great Sinner, The (1949)****½** Gregory Peck, Ava Gardner, Melvyn Douglas, Walter Huston, Ethel Barrymore, Frank Morgan. An impressive cast of stars tells the story of a collection of people whose gambling fever almost ruins their lives. Peck and Gardner make a good love team. (Dir: Robert Siodmak, 110 mins.)

Great Sioux Massacre, The (1965)****** Joseph Cotten, Darren McGavin, Philip Carey. A low-budget western which attempts, once again, to tell the story behind Custer's last stand. Strictly for dyed-in-the-wool western movie fans. (Dir: Sidney Salkow, 91 mins.)

Great Spy Mission, The—See: Operation Crossbow

Great St. Louis Bank Robbery, The (1959)****** David Clarke, Molly McCarthy, Craham Denton. An early Steve McQueen effort—he's a football hero who goes wrong and becomes involved in the plot of the title. Filmed on location, it has a gritty realism, along with slack pacing. (Dirs: Charles Guggenheim, John Stix, 86 mins.)

Great Train Robbery, The (Great Britain, 1979)*****½** Sean Connery, Lesley Anne-Down, Donald Sutherland, Alan Webb. Immensely entertaining fluff about the first train robbery, masterminded by rogue Sean Connery in 1855. Michael Crichton, who directed and adapted his own novel, has a good, workman-like eye and a logical hand with suspense: He stands alone among today's crowd as one of the few competent hacks. The costumes and trains are particularly special, and Lesley Anne-Down is more, even, than that. (111 mins.)

Great Victor Herbert, The (1939)******* Allan Jones, Mary Martin. Inaccurate and bad film biography of the famous composer, but 28 of his songs well performed compensate for the rest of the picture. With Walter Connolly as Herbert. (Dir: Andrew L. Stone, 91 mins.)

Great Waldo Pepper, The (1975)***½ Robert Redford, Bo Svenson, Susan Sarandon, Bo Brundin. An appealing homage, conceived and directed by George Roy Hill, to the boy-men aerial barnstorming pilots of the early 1920's. Redford plays Waldo Pepper, a daredevil who regrets having missed the opportunity to trade shoot-outs with the great German aces of WW I, and senses that America of the mad 20's doesn't share his passions for stunting and aerial acrobatics. Redford gives one of his most winning, unselfish performances, and his charisma, along with some marvelous dogfights using the venerable antique planes, help make this period piece so appealing to non-flyers who do not worship speed and risk. Screenplay by William Goldman. Director Hill's avocation is flying just such vintage planes, and his love for the planes and the pilots of the period is abundantly clear. If you liked even parts of "Hell's Angels" and "The Red Baron," you'll be entranced by "Waldo." (196 mins.)

Great Wallendas, The (MTV 1978)*** Lloyd Bridges, Britt Ekland, Taina Elg, John van Dreelen, Cathy Rigby. This dramatization of the triumphs and tragedies of a unique family of high-wire artists is a rewarding experience. Bridges is superb as the indomitable Karl Wallenda, whose unquenchable spirit breathes life into his clan; we really believe he and his daughter Jenny (Ekland), his brother Herman (van Dreelen), and the other members of the family are up there performing the dangerous seven-person pyramid themselves. (Dir: Larry Elikann, 104 mins.)

Great Waltz, The (1938)*½ Luise Rainer, Fernand Gravet. (Dir: Julien Duvivier, 100 mins.)

Great War, The (Italy, 1961)***½ Vittorio Gassman, Silvana Mangano, Alberto Sordi. Unusual, fascinating mixture of low comedy and high drama, as a couple of stiffs find themselves becoming heroes in WW I. Gassman is particularly good. (Dir: Mario Monicelli, 118 mins.)

Great White Hope, The (1970)***½ James Earl Jones, Jane Alexander, Chester Morris. Hal Holbrook. Film captures much of the passion of the original Broadway play and, most important of all, the dazzling, virtuoso performance of James Earl Jones portraying Jack Johnson, the first black heavyweight boxing champion crowned in 1908. (Many of the issues "White Hope" deals with are the same ones Muhammad Ali was punished for fifty years later, but Hollywood hasn't had the courage to make a meaningful topical film about Cassius Clay.) Playwright Howard Sackler and director Martin Ritt show the way Johnson (Jones) was victimized and humiliated by a racist, white society, and subjected to,

what for Johnson, must have been the ultimate degradation—being forced to take a dive in a fixed championship fight and lose to a white opponent whom he could easily have beaten. Both Jones, and Miss Alexander, playing his white mistress, garnered richly deserved Academy Award nominations for their performances. Jones has been thrilling theater audiences for years. Watch his bravura screen acting as Jack Jefferson and see why. (101 mins.)

Great Ziegfeld, The (1936)**** William Powell, Luise Rainer, Myrna Loy. Story of great American showman is superbly told and the production is in the Ziegfeld manner. It runs three hours and we hope your TV station doesn't cut it. (Dir: Robert Z. Leonard, 184 mins.)

Greatest, The (1977)**½ Muhammad Ali, Ernest Borgnine, John Marley, Lloyd Haynes, Robert Duvall. Biographical film of the celebrated, outspoken heavyweight champ. Ali plays himself reasonably well. Ponderous screenplay trots out too many fight-yarn clichés. (Dir: Tom Gries, 101 mins.)

Greatest Battle, The (1979)** Stacy Keach, Samantha Eggar, Henry Fonda, John Huston, Helmut Berger. Set during the last North African campaign of WW II, with action centering on the German Panzer Corps in Tunisia. A subplot has Keach as a German major and Eggar as the half-Jewish wife with whom he must deal. The stars make this a bit above the dozens of other European-made war pix. (Dir: Humphrey Longan, 97 mins.)

Greatest Gift, The (MTV 1974)*** Glenn Ford, Julie Harris, Lance Kerwin. Don't let the sanctimonious title put you off, this is a lovely made-for-TV movie almost in the same league with "To Kill a Mockingbird." It's all about life in the South back in 1940, as seen through the eyes of a 13-year-old boy who thinks his preacher father is the greatest man in the world. Filmed in Georgia and based on Jack Farris' novel, "Ramey," the film captures the feeling of a boy growing up and being lucky enough to have a wise and understanding father. Glenn Ford, Julie Harris, Harris Yulin, and especially Lance Kerwin, are splendid, thanks in part to a good script and Boris Sagal's astute direction. (100 mins.)

Greatest Love, The—See: Europa '51

Greatest Rescues of Emergency (MTV 1978)** Kevin Tighe, Randolph Mantooth. "Emergency" flashbacks are pieced together to provide an assortment of the TV series' most dramatic rescue operations. The guys all have their moments, but the stunt men and crash experts are the real heroes. (Dir: R. A. Cinader, 104 mins.)

Greatest Show on Earth, The (1952)**** James Stewart, Charlton Heston, Betty Hutton, Cornel Wilde, Dorothy Lamour.... Or, Cecil B. De Mille visits the circus, resulting in the Big Top show to end 'em all. Splendiferous production of circus life captures all the thrills and excitement, plus a story line that holds it all together capably. Many amusing "guest" appearances by top stars in bit roles, dazzling camerawork. Entertainment plus. Oscars: Best Picture, Best Story. (Dir: Cecil B. De Mille, 153 mins.)

Greatest Story Ever Told, The (1965)**½ Max von Sydow, Telly Savalas, Dorothy McGuire, Charlton Heston, José Ferrer, Claude Rains, Van Heflin. Director George Stevens's folly, in its full, elephantine length. An unnerving roster of cameo appearances tends to undermine the sincerity of the biblican proceedings, which are spectacular and spectacularly dull. Even John Wayne gets in the act. The enterprise reeks of self-congratulatory intellectual piety. The acting, however, is generally fine. You might possibly enjoy it if you're in the mood. (225 mins.)

Greatest Thing That Almost Happened, The (MTV 1977)** Jimmie Walker, James Earl Jones, Deborah Allen. Walker flounders in the serious role of a young basketball player stricken with leukemia; Jones is his widowed dad. (Dir: Gilbert Moses, 104 mins.)

Greed (1924)**** Gibson Gowland, Jean Hersholt, ZaSu Pitts. More than a masterpiece. Sets out to tell all the truth about man's lust for wealth. Director Erich von Stroheim's original version ran nine hours, and the studio cut it to less than two. What remains is the finest piece of mad realism ever perpetrated. Stroheim took his actors to Death Valley so that they could really sweat out those climactic passions, and it shows. Pitts does fine work as a tragedienne. (112 mins.)

Greed in the Sun (France-Italy, 1964)** Jean-Paul Belmondo, Lino Ventura, Reginald Kernan. French truck drivers in Northern Africa. Parched scenery, ancient Moroccan villages form stark backgrounds for disjointed tale. (Dir: Henri Verneuil, 122 mins.)

Greek Tycoon, The (1978)** Anthony Quinn, Jacqueline Bisset, Raf Vallone, Edward Albert, Camilla Sparv. Director J. Lee Thompson does his usual slop job on this vapid, tedious film à clef about Jackie and Ari Onassis. The scenery is pretty, but postcards are cheaper. (106 mins.)

Green Berets, The (1968)* John Wayne, David Janssen, Raymond St. Jacques. (Dirs: John Wayne, Ray Kellogg, Mervyn LeRoy, 141 mins.)

Green Dolphin Street (1947)** Lana Turner, Van Heflin, Donna Reed. A girl sails to New Zealand to marry her sister's fellow and sets off a feature-length series of clichés and outlandish gimmicks. It's not the actors' fault, but this one is pretty bad. (Dir: Victor Saville, 141 mins.)

Green Eyes (MTV 1977)*** Paul Winfield, Rita Tushingham, Lemi. Strong, emotional drama about a black American Vietnam-war veteran who returns to Saigon in 1973 to find his son, born to a Vietnamese bar girl. The only clue he has is that his son has green eyes. His relentless odyssey, filmed in Manila, puts him in contact with an ingratiating, street-wise urchin played with beguiling naturalness by a young actor named Lemi. The scenes of overcrowded orphanages and street kids rummaging through garbage for scraps of food are compelling. You'll not easily forget the tender, tragic reunion scene between the ex-soldier and his Vietnamese lover, in which he tells him of the heartbreaking fate of their son. Paul Winfield gives his best performance since "Sounder" as the haunted man with a mission. (Dir: John Erman, 96 mins.)

Green Fingers (Great Britain, 1947)*** Robert Beatty, Nova Pilbeam, Carol Raye. A fisherman who has talent as a bonesetter refuses to study for a degree and goes into practice for society patients. Well-acted drama, with a slightly new plot twist. (Dir: John Harlow, 83 mins.)

Green Fire (1954)**½ Stewart Granger, Grace Kelly, Paul Douglas, John Ericson. Colorful drama about love, adventure, and emerald mining in South America. Princess Grace and Granger have some torrid love scenes in this one. (Dir: Andrew Marton, 100 mins.)

Green for Danger (Great Britain, 1946)**** Alastair Sim, Sally Gray, Leo Genn. Witty, well-written comedy mystery with impeccable British style and well-controlled daffiness. Sim is a model of comic finesse as the inspector who tries to locate a mad killer who is dispatching patients on the operating table. Sidney Gilliat directed and coscripted with Claude Guerney. (93 mins.)

Green Glove, The (1952)**½ Glenn Ford, Geraldine Brooks. Minor little chase drama concerning wartime treasures. European backgrounds are more exciting than the film. (Dir: Rudolph Mate, 88 mins.)

Green Goddess, The (1930)**½ George Arliss, H.B. Warner, Alice Joyce, Ralph Forbes. An early talkie, remake of a 1923 silent film based on the successful stage play, both of which also starred Arliss as an insidious far-Eastern potentate who takes three Britishers hostage when they crash-land in his kingdom. An antique melodrama that reeks with atmosphere, even when it clunks. The crafty Arliss shines. (Dir: Alfred E. Green, 74 mins.)

Green Grass of Wyoming (1948)*** Peggy Cummins, Charles Coburn. Another pleasant horse story for the youngsters. All about wild stallions, frisky mares and even some trotting races. (Dir: Louis King, 89 mins.)

Green Grow the Rushes (Great Britain, 1952)***½ Richard Burton, Honor Blackman. When the government comes snooping around a small village, the natives are afraid their whiskey-smuggling business is in danger. Extremely pleasant, humorous comedy. (Dir: Derek Twist, 77 mins.)

Green Helmet, The (Great Britain, 1961)** Bill Travers, Nancy Walters, Ed Begley, Jack Brabham. Aging race-car driver (Travers) falls in love with a girl who fears for his life. Sentimentality avoided by the cast, who act straight-faced. Some racing scenes shot at Le Mans and Sebring. B&W. (Dir: Michael Forlong, 88 mins.)

Green Man, The (Great Britain, 1957)*** Alastair Sim, George Cole, Terry-Thomas. In the cozy tradition of British little-man comedy, this farce concerns a watchmaker who leads a double life—he's also a paid assassin. With Sim in one of his most characteristic roles, delightful, wicked, and hilarious. (Dir: Robert Day, 80 mins.)

Green Mansions (1959)**½ Audrey Hepburn, Anthony Perkins, Lee J. Cobb. Young man in the jungles of Venezuela meets a strange girl of the forest, falls in love with her. Based on a novel that would be difficult for anyone to film adequately, this fantasy tries hard, manages some affecting scenes, pretty scenery. (Dir: Mel Ferrer, 101 mins.)

Green Pastures (1936)**** Rex Ingram, Eddie Anderson. The Scriptures, as seen by Marc Connelly, with an all-Negro cast. Something different, superbly produced, highly entertaining. (Dirs: Marc Connelly, Wm. Keighley, 93 mins.)

Green Room, The (France, 1978)** François Truffaut, Nathalie Baye. A dour, morbid enterprise full of pompous self-importance. Director Truffaut and Baye play characters obsessed by the honoring of the dead. Based on two stories by Henry James. (94 mins.)

Green Scarf, The (Great Britain, 1954)***½ Ann Todd, Michael Redgrave, Leo Genn. A deaf and blind mute who confesses to an apparently motiveless murder is defended by a wily lawyer. Excellent melodrama; a fine cast, tight direction and a good script all add to the drama. (Dir: George More O'Ferrall, 96 mins.)

Green Slime, The (U.S.-Japan, 1969)* Robert Horton, Luciana Paluzzi. (Dir: Kenji Fukasaku, 90 mins.)

Green Wall, The (Peru, 1972)**½ Plodding but pleasant in its amiable amateurishness. The location shots in the Peruvian jungle are interesting. Urban man tries to get by with wife and child in the jungle, in the teeth of bureaucratic hassles and snakes in the grass. Moral: He who vegetates, gets tossed. (Dir: Armando Robles Godoy, 110 mins.)

Green Years, The (1946)*** Charles Coburn, Tom Drake, Beverly Tyler, Dean Stockwell. Occasionally moving and generally interesting adaptation of A. J. Cronin's novel about an Irish lad who goes to live with his grandparents in Scotland. Coburn as the boy's great-grandfather is a treat. (Dir: Victor Saville, 127 mins.)

Greetings (1968)***½ Robert De Niro, Jonathan Warden, Gerritt Graham. A loosely constructed, episodic film about two young men trying to coach their buddy on how to weird out the army psychiatrist and thereby flunk the draft physical. There's also some strangeness about the Kennedy assassination and a lot of sexual horseplay—all of it directed with zestful, if at times painfully self-indulgent, good humor, and once in a while a fine satirical relish, by Brian De Palma and Charles Hirsch. Winsome and jaunty. (88 mins.)

Greyfriar's Bobby (U.S.-Great Britain, 1961)*** Donald Crisp, Laurence Naismith. Appealing Disney entry for children about a shepherd's faithful Skye terrier who wins the affection of the city of Edinburgh. (Dir: Don Chaffey, 91 mins.)

Griffin and Phoenix: A Love Story (MTV 1976)**½ Peter Falk, Jill Clayburgh. The personal charisma of Falk and Clayburgh carries this predictable, calculated heart-tugger. Falk, estranged from his wife and two boys, discovers he is dying of cancer and splits the scene. Meanwhile, Clayburgh, a young and vital woman, is told she too has a short time to live, and the two doomed individuals meet. The writers would have us believe that the way to get through a terminal illness is to sneak into a movie, try hang-gliding, and steal cars—in other words, do all the things you always wanted to do without regard for the consequences. The movie runs out of sentimental steam long before the fade-out, but the two stars give it a good try. (Dir: Daryl Duke, 98 mins.)

Grisbi (France, 1953)*** Jean Gabin, Rene Dary, Jeanne Moreau. Fast paced story of the Paris underworld and the men who take the big risks for big stakes. Jean Gabin registers strongly as Max. (Dir: Jacques Becker, 94 mins.)

Grissly's Millions (1945)*** Paul Kelly, Virginia Grey. Murder strikes when a group of relatives gather together waiting for a wealthy old man to die so they can receive his fortune. Above-average mystery, well written. (Dir: John English, 54 mins.)

Grissom Gang, The (1971)***½ Scott Wilson, Tony Musante, Irene Dailey, Kim Darby, Robert Lansing. This major film was critically and commercially shunned. Robert Aldrich directed the aggressively unpleasant adaptation of the James Hadley Chase novel "No Orchids for Miss Blandish," about an heiress who is kidnapped and has a love affair with one of her cretinous abductors. Bracingly original. (127 mins.)

Groom Wore Spurs, The (1951)* Ginger Rogers, Jack Carson, Joan Davis. (Dir: Richard Whorf, 80 mins.)

Groove Tube, The (1974)***½ Chevy Chase, Ken Shapiro, Richard Belzer, Buzzy Linhart. A wacky, satirical, scatological series of maniacal sketches that started out life in an off-off Broadway showcase where the sketches were seen on TV screens. Television itself is the target of much of the humor, some of it sophomoric, some excruciatingly funny, including a ribald takeoff of Howard Cosell and the Sexual Olympics. Written by Ken Shapiro and Lane Sarasohn. One of several reasons to tune in is the chance to see Chevy Chase carry on, well before his success and fame on "Saturday Night Live." (Dir: Ken Shapiro, 75 mins.)

Grounds for Marriage (1951)****½** Van Johnson, Kathryn Grayson. Somewhat silly but amusing tale about an opera singer who decides to make a play for her doctor who just so happens to be her ex-husband. Miss Grayson sings a few arias in addition to being cute and coy. (Dir: Robert Z. Leonard, 91 mins.)

Groundstar Conspiracy, The (1972)*****½** George Peppard, Michael Sarrazin, Christine Belford. A topflight thriller. Peppard plays a government agent assigned to uncover a conspiracy which caused the destruction of a vital secret space unit, and left behind a lone survivor (Sarrazin) who's been badly burned. Before this suspense-charged adventure is over, Peppard has him undergo plastic surgery and brainwashing, so he can be set free and trailed. (Dir: Lamont Johnson, 103 mins.)

Group, The (1966)******* Joan Hackett, Jessica Walter, Joanna Pettet, Kathleen Widdoes, Candice Bergen, Shirley Knight, Elizabeth Hartman. The Jimmy Carter of movies—loaded with contradictions and good intentions, vaguely liberal and pietistic. Mary McCarthy's novel about Vassar grads in the '30s is savaged almost as much as she savaged her subject, with producer Sidney Buchman's screenplay reducing most of the characterizations to quick, obvious traits and eliminating all the social and political observations. Sidney Lumet gets more good scenes with less evident control than any other director. (150 mins.)

Groupies (1970)*****½** Joe Cocker and the Grease Band, Ten Years After, Dry Creek Road. Fascinating, honest and profoundly sad documentary showing the loves and lives of assorted "groupies," that special subculture of the rock music scene. The girls'—and a few homosexual boys'—fondest dream is to smoke the best dope, meet all the most "far-out people." To the over-40 set, the hapless groupies may seem pretty far out, as directors Ron Dorfman and Peter Nevard capture the squalid, itinerant life-style of these teenaged hangers-on. The directors artfully avoid any feeling of voyeurism, or exploitation of their young subjects. (92 mins.)

Guadalcanal Diary (1943)*****½** William Bendix, Lloyd Nolan, Preston Foster. A worthy tribute to the men who fought on Guadalcanal is this stirring action film. Of course it has the mock heroics but it's still one of the best war films. (Dir: Lewis Seiler, 93 mins.)

Guardians, The (Norway, 1978)****½** Vibeke Lokkeberg, Helge Reiss, Odd Furoy. Norwegian novelist Amalie Skram attempted to assume the roles of both homemaker and novelist at the turn of the century and ended up in a mental hospital after a nervous breakdown. She wrote two novels on the subject of her experiences. Set in 1895, this film version presents married mother and painter Else Kant who goes off for a few days' rest at a clinic only to find herself committed by the authoritarian professor who runs the clinic. Vibeke Lokkeberg, herself a director (*The Revelation*), stars in this Norwegian film directed by Nicole Mace, who was born in France but has had a prolific career in Norway.

Guardsman, The (1931)******** Alfred Lunt, Lynn Fontanne, Roland Young, ZaSu Pitts. A superior film adaptation of Ferenc Molnar's Broadway hit about the conceited Austrian actor (Lunt) who goes to elaborate lengths to test his wife's (Fontanne's) marital fidelity. This is, alas, the only starring film ever made by Lunt and Fontanne, who were enduring glories of the American theater for nearly half a century. Lunt was one of the truly great actors of his time (matched among theater actors during the '40's and '50's only by Fredric March and Lee J. Cobb), and in this delightful continental conceit you'll see his dazzling range and technical virtuosity. Fontanne was as gifted as her husband but this is essentially his picture. Watch it for the only film record of their brilliance. Remade as *The Chocolate Soldier*, 1941. (Dir: Sidney Franklin, 83 mins.)

Guendalina (France-Italy, 1957)****½** Jacqueline Sassard, Raffaele Mattioli. Guendalina (Sassard) befriends a young student on the Italian Riviera while her parents are planning a divorce. A gentle, sensitive movie looks at adolescence and the awakening to love of both parents and children. Sassard's first starring role is a skillful, unforced etching of the awkwardness of growing up. (Dir: Alberto Lattuada, 95 mins.)

Guerillas in Pink Lace (1964)****** George Montgomery, Joan Shawlee, Valerie Varda. Five showgirls and an adventurer disguised as a priest make an unlikely combination to escape from enemy-held Manila, but they do—only to wind up on an island also held by the enemy. Juvenile but fast-moving wartime adventure, made in the Philippines. (Dir: George Montgomery, 96 mins.)

Guernica (Italy, 1976)*****½** Mariangela Melato. An elaborate phantasm of political scatology directed by Fernando Arrabal from one of his lesser plays. There are arid patches, but the force of the surrealistic anger comes through undiminished. The vision is all; it sears. Melato plays La Pasionaria as the incarnation of murderous sainthood. (110 mins.)

Guerrilla Girl (1953)*½ Helmut Dantine, Marianne. (Dir: John Christian, 81 mins.)

Guess Who's Coming to Dinner? (1967)***½ Spencer Tracy, Katharine Hepburn, Sidney Poitier, Katharine Houghton. Sidney comes to woo Katie's and Spencer's daughter. Result: one frequently sophomoric sentimental screenplay, buoyed up by a glorious bow-out performance by the deservedly legendary screen team. (The Academy Awards went berserk in 1967, nominating Hepburn (who won) and Tracy, which made sense, but also nominating the film for best picture, which was silly, and voting the award for best screenplay to William Rose, which was idiotic.) Poitier's role was inspired equally by Superman and Horatio Alger, and why he wanted to marry the vapid virgin, portrayed by Hepburn's niece Katharine Houghton, is one of the many things about the film, including Stanley Kramer's direction, that you shouldn't quibble about. Just sit back and watch that great artist Tracy at work for the last time. (112 mins.)

Guess Who's Sleeping in My Bed? (MTV 1973)**½ Dean Jones, Barbara Eden, Ken Mars. Fairly good comedy is extracted from a rather ridiculous situation. Ex-husband Jones barges in on his ex-wife, Miss Eden, with his new wife and infant child, and asks to be put up awhile. (Dir: Theodore J. Flicker, 90 mins.)

Guest, The (Great Britain, 1964)*** Donald Pleasence, Alan Bates, Robert Shaw. "The Caretaker," absorbing early play of Harold Pinter, filmed with three superlative actors. About an old derelict (Pleasence) invited to spend the night in a rundown London house, who becomes involved with two neurotic brothers. Screenplay by Harold Pinter. This not very commercially promising entry was financed by a group including Noel Coward, Richard Burton, Peter Sellers, Leslie Caron and Elizabeth Taylor. (Dir: Clive Donner, 105 mins.)

Guest in the House (1944)**½ Anne Baxter, Ralph Bellamy, Marie McDonald. A young girl taken in by an average household sets to poisoning their minds against each other. Psychological melodrama has its moments. (Dir: John Brahm, 121 mins.)

Guest Wife (1945)*** Claudette Colbert, Don Ameche. Married woman is persuaded to pose as a war correspondent's wife to fool his boss. Amusing romantic comedy. (Dir: Sam Wood, 90 mins.)

Guide for the Married Man, A (1967)*** Walter Matthau, Robert Morse, Inger Stevens. Walter Matthau's comedic talents are put to good use in this broad comedy about philandering husbands, and the efforts they expend to keep the news from reaching their wives. Some spirited bedroom chatter helps move things along.

Robert Morse comes off well as an operator with the ladies who advises friend Walter. A shrewd selection of guest stars (Art Carney, Joey Bishop, Terry-Thomas, Jayne Mansfield, Carl Reiner, Lucille Ball and others) adds to the fun. (Dir: Gene Kelly, 89 mins.)

Guide for the Married Woman, A (MTV 1978)** Cybill Shepherd, Barbara Feldon, George Gobel. Predictable yarn about a bored housewife (Shepherd) who takes the advice of a liberated woman friend (Feldon) and tries to put a little adventure in her life. The vignettes that follow cast such recognizable TV faces as Gobel, Peter Marshall, and Bill Dana. The script manages to be moderately amusing. (Dir: Hy Averback, 104 mins.)

Guilt of Janet Ames (1947)*** Rosalind Russell, Melvyn Douglas, Sid Caesar, Nina Foch. Woman embittered by the death of her husband in the war is shown the light by a journalist. Interesting drama. (Dir: Henry Levin, 83 mins.)

Guilty, The (1947)**½ Don Castle, Bonita Granville. Two friends are in love with the same girl, and she has a twin sister. One of them is murdered, and from there it's anybody's guess as to who, what and why. Complicated mystery, but nevertheless attention-holding. (Dir: John Reinhardt, 70 mins.)

Guilty? (Great Britain, 1956)** John Justin, Barbara Laage. French girl is placed on trial for murdering her lover. Slow-moving courtroom drama. (Dir: Edmond T. Greville, 93 mins.)

Guilty Bystander (1950)*** Zachary Scott, Faye Emerson. A private eye down on his luck snaps out of the fog when he finds his little child has been kidnapped. Generally well done mystery, made in New York. Good musical score by Dimitri Tiomkin. (Dir: Joseph Lerner, 92 mins.)

Guilty or Innocent: The Sam Sheppard Murder Case (MTV 1975)**½ George Peppard, Barnard Hughes, Walter McGinn. Lengthy recreation of the bizarre 1954 Cleveland murder case where osteopath Sam Sheppard was accused of murdering his wife. Two trials, circus-like courtroom proceedings, the emergence of defense attorney F. Lee Bailey (McGinn) as a national figure, and the puzzling personality of Sheppard—a ladies' man, a drinker, a professional wrestler—offer melodramatic grist but supply precious few insights as to what actually happened. Good performances, especially by Peppard as Sheppard and Hughes as a defense attorney, key the drama, and the production gives the right feeling for the tempo and the thinking in 1954. (Dir: Robert Michael Lewis, 144 mins.)

Guitars of Love (West Germany, 1954)* Vico Torriani, Elma Karlowa. (Dir: Werner Jacobs, 90 mins.)

Gulliver's Travels (1939)*** Max and Dave Fleischer, the creators of Betty Boop, tried to beat Walt Disney at his own game with this lavish animated feature. Imitating Disney's naturalistic style, they lost much of their characteristic energy and audacity; little of the rowdiness of their short films remains, although there are some finely executed moments. The Fleischers had more flair than Disney all along, but nobody bothered to tell them. For the kids. (Dir: Dave Fleischer, 74 mins.)

Gulliver's Travels Beyond the Moon (1966)***½ Good animated science-fiction feature loosely based on the celebrated Jonathan Swift fantasy tale. The updating has Gulliver and his cohorts traveling in a spaceship and involved with a number of adventures which should delight the young audience. An additional treat is a good score by Milton DeLugg. (Dir: Yoshio Kuroda, 78 mins.)

Gumshoe (Great Britain, 1971)***½ Albert Finney. Stephen Frears's directorial debut stars Finney as a Liverpudlian bingo caller with delusions of Bogart, who discovers that living out his fantasies is not what he expected. A tribute to every private-eye film and film noir ever made, with more references, homages, and direct quotes than early Godard. (88 mins.)

Gun, (MTV 1974)**½ Stephen Elliott, Jean Le Bouvier, Wallace Rooney. Ambitious attempt to show the life of a gun from the day it comes off the assembly line at the weapons factory through its various owners. Ironically, the gun is fired only twice ... at the factory for testing purposes and at the very end. The semi-documentary approach, which works well at the start of the film, soon gives in to melodrama, especially in a rather long segment involving a Spanish car-wash worker who finds the gun and brings it home. A good try! (Dir: John Badham, 72 mins.)

Gun and the Pulpit, The (MTV 1974)*** Marjoe Gortner, Estelle Parsons, Slim Pickens. Marjoe Gortner (who was so compelling in "Marjoe") is well suited for this colorful role of a gunslinger who finds himself in the garb and guise of a small-town preacher while running hard from a posse. The script is full of clever comedy touches in the dialogue. A supporting cast of pros adds to the yarn. (Dir: Dan Petrie, 78 mins.)

Gun Belt (1953)**½ Tab Hunter, George Montgomery, William Bishop. Fairly entertaining, low budget western about an outlaw who wants to go straight and his old "buddies" who have different plans. (Dir: Ray Nazarro, 77 mins.)

Gun Crazy (1950)**** John Dall, Peggy Cummins, Morris Carnovsky. One of the most distinguished B-movie works of art, director Joseph H. Lewis's film tells of an outlaw couple on the run. A gangster film that explores the limits of the genre. (86 mins.)

Gun Fever (1958)*½ Mark Stevens, John Lupton. (Dir: Mark Stevens, 81 mins.)

Gun for a Coward (1957)** Fred MacMur-ray, Jeffrey Hunter, Dean Stockwell, Janice Rule. Rancher faces trouble trying to raise two younger brothers, one a hothead, the other accused of cowardice. Good cast in a standard western. (Dir: Abner Biberman, 73 mins.)

Gun Fury (1953)**½ Rock Hudson, Donna Reed. Rock Hudson's beautiful fiancée (Donna Reed) is kidnapped by a lustful gunslinger and the search for revenge is on. Slow paced but interesting Western drama. (Dir: Raoul Walsh, 83 mins.)

Gun Glory (1957)** Stewart Granger, Rhonda Fleming, Steve Rowland, Chill Wills. A western that offers little that's new. Gunfighter returns to his ranch to find he's hated by his grown son. Granger is the gunfighter and Steve Rowland (son of director Roy Rowland) is his young son. Rhonda is gorgeous, as always. Based on the Philip Yordan novel "Man of the West." (Dir: Roy Rowland, 88 mins.)

Gun Hawk, The (1963)** Rory Calhoun, Rod Cameron, Ruta Lee, Rod Lauren. Outlaw gunman tracked by the sheriff dissuades a youngster from following the same crooked trail. Formula hoss opera for the western devotees. (Dir: Edward Ludwig, 92 mins.)

Gun Runners (1958)**½ Audie Murphy, Eddie Albert, Everett Sloane. Interesting adventure story about a man who risks his life for a big share of profit for illegal gun-running. Murphy is believable in the role of an adventurer and it's a welcome change from his western parts. Based-again-on Hemingway's "To Have and Have Not." (Dir: Don Siegel, 83 mins.)

Gun the Man Down—See: **Arizona Mission**

Gunfight, A (1971)**½ Kirk Douglas, Johnny Cash. There's lots of talk before this offbeat western justifies its title, but a good part of the dialogue is crisp. Also the stars are interesting as a couple of has-been gunfighters who decide to face each other in one last duel—staged in a bullring and attended by a ticket-buying audience. (Dir: Lamont Johnson, 90 mins.)

Gunfight at Dodge City, The (1959)** Joel McCrea, Julie Adams, John McIntire. Bat Masterson is elected Sheriff and proceeds to clean up the town. Should sound familiar, and it is. (Dir: Joseph M. Newman, 81 mins.)

Gunfight at Red Sands (Spain, 1963)** Richard Harrison, Mikaela, Giacomo Rossi Stuart. When a miner is killed and his gold stolen, his adopted son swears vengeance and sets out to find the outlaws. Spanish locations substituting for Mexico add a note of novelty to this English-dubbed western, which compares in passable fashion with our local product. (Dir: Ricardo Blasco, 97 mins.)

Gunfight at the OK Corral (1957)**½ Burt Lancaster, Kirk Douglas, Jo Van Fleet, Rhonda Fleming, John Ireland. Lancaster as Wyatt Earp and Douglas as Doc Holliday in this big-budget Vistavision western that never achieves scope or intensity. Screenplay by Leon Uris. (122 mins.)

Gunfight in Abilene (1967)*½ Bobby Darin, Emily Banks, Leslie Nielsen. (Dir: William Hale, 86 mins.)

Gunfighter, The (1950)**** Gregory Peck, Jean Parker, Karl Malden. One of Peck's best performances as the would-be-retired gunslinger Johnny Ringo. Skip Homeier, determined to grab the "Fastest Gun" title for himself, forces Ringo into one more shoot-out. Very off-beat western for its time. (Dir: Henry King, 84 mins.)

Gunfighters (1947)*** Randolph Scott, Barbara Britton, Forrest Tucker. Gunslinger wants to hang up his pistols, but lands in the middle of a range war. Well-made western with some rugged action. (Dir: George Waggner, 87 mins.)

Gung Ho! (1943)** Randolph Scott, Noah Beery, Jr., Alan Curtis, Robert Mitchum, David Bruce. During WW II the marines raid Japanese-held Makin Island. War melodrama has plenty of action. (Dir: Ray Enright, 88 mins.)

Gunga Din (1939)***½ Douglas Fairbanks, Jr., Cary Grant, Joan Fontaine, Victor McLaglen, Sam Jaffe. Based on Kipling's imperialist paean to the noble Indian water boy who sacrifices his life to save a British regiment. Fairbanks is torn between respectable married life with Fontaine and loyalty to his brawling, boozing comrades, Grant and McLaglen. Good, dirty fun. Director George Stevens's deliberate pacing serves the comedy well, but the action scenes are blunted by too careful compositions and artsy cutting. (117 mins.)

Gunman's Walk (1958)*** Van Heflin, Tab Hunter, Kathryn Grant. Rancher tries to bring his sons up properly, but the black sheep of the family causes tragedy for all. Superior western, especially in the acting and directing departments—good for outdoor fans. (Dir: Phil Karlson, 97 mins.)

Gunn (1967)**½ Laura Devon, Edward Asner, Sherry Jackson. TV's private eye (Craig Stevens) matches wits and fists with gangland and murderers in an actionful mystery feature. Elements are the same, and fans of the video series should enjoy. (Dir: Blake Edwards, 94 mins.)

Guns at Batasi (Great Britain, 1964)***½ Richard Attenborough, Jack Hawkins, Flora Robson. A provocative drama of substance dealing with the strife-ridden climate prevalent in Africa of the early 1960's. Richard Attenborough, as an old school British sergeant major stationed right in the middle of the upheaval, gives a splendid performance, and he's matched by a distinguished supporting cast including Jack Hawkins, Flora Robson and Cecil Parker. The conflict builds to a tense climax in which the natives plan violent action against the British subjects and their supporters. Incidentally, Mia Farrow

is cast as the young love interest in the film. (Dir: John Guillermin, 103 mins.)

Guns for San Sebastian (France-Mexico-Italy, 1967)** Anthony Quinn, Anjanette Comer, Charles Bronson. Plodding adventure yarn set during the 1750's, and filmed in a Mexican village. Quinn plays a renegade who is thrust into the unlikely position of impersonating a priest of a poor mission. The pace is a bit slow, but it picks up when Quinn steps into action against a gang of invading outlaws, led by Charles Bronson. (Dir: Henri Verneuil, 110 mins.)

Guns in the Heather—See: **Spy Busters**

Guns of August, The (1964)***½ Documentary based on Barbara Tuchman's Pulitzer Prize winning book about the causes and effects of WW I. Old newsreel footage compiled in a capable manner. Good for historians, students and WW I buffs. Narrator: Fritz Weaver. (Dir: Nathan Kroll, 99 mins.)

Guns of Darkness (Great Britain, 1962)** David Niven, Leslie Caron. Businessman and his wife are caught in the turmoil of a South American revolution, find themselves helping the overthrown president escape to the border. Drama gets itself tangled in deeper meanings, never quite makes itself clear. Cast tries hard, but the result is no better than fair. (Dir: Anthony Asquith, 95 mins.)

Guns of Fort Petticoat (1957)**½ Audie Murphy, Kathryn Grant. This is a good story idea that could have made a better film if more attention had been paid to the script. Murphy is a deserter during the Civil War who doesn't agree with his power-hungry colonel's ideas about pointless attacks on the Indians. He assembles the women whose men are fighting in the war and trains them so they can be prepared for Indian attacks which would come as a result of the colonel's senseless campaign against the Indian tribes. (Dir: George Marshall, 82 mins.)

Guns of Navarone, The (1961)**** Gregory Peck, David Niven, Anthony Quinn, Anthony Quayle, Irene Papas. One of the best WW II adventure films. A great cast bolsters this superb tension-filled tale involving a group of heterogeneous soldiers and green guerrilla fighters who must destroy one of the most heavily guarded German fortresses in the Aegean. The suspense builds throughout as the yarn unfolds in excellent scenes shot on location in the Greek Isles. Don't miss this marvelous movie. (Dir: J. Lee Thompson, 159 mins.)

Guns of the Black Witch (Italy, 1962)*½ Don Megowan, Silvana Pampanini. (Dir: Domenico Paolella, 83 mins.)

Guns of the Magnificent Seven (1969)**½ George Kennedy, James Whitmore, Monte Markham. Third "Magnificent Seven" film, with Kennedy's character being the only survivor from the original 1960 film. The action and gunplay are just as fast, but the plot has become routine. Set in Mexico in the 1890's, the group attempts to rescue a Mexican Robin Hood who has been caught by the government. Thrilling conclusion. (Dir: Paul Wendkos, 106 mins.)

Guns of the Timberland (1960)** Alan Ladd, Jeanne Crain, Gilbert Roland, Frankie Avalon. Routine action melodrama about a fight between lumbermen and townspeople who don't want the trees cut down. Moves slowly. (Dir: Robert D. Webb, 91 mins.)

Guns of Zangara (1959)**½ Robert Stack, Robert Middleton. Eliot Ness and the "Untouchables" strive to prevent an assassination attempt on President Roosevelt in 1933. Originally seen as a two-part presentation on TV, the feature version carries a fairly good amount of suspense. (90 mins.)

Gunslinger (1956)*½ Beverly Garland, John Ireland. (Dir: Roger Corman, 83 mins.)

Gunsmoke (1953)** Audie Murphy, Susan Cabot. Not to be confused with the long running TV series of the same name. Just another Audie Murphy starrer in which he plays the stranger in town who has to prove his worth before he's accepted. (Dir: Nathan Juran, 79 mins.)

Guru, The (U.S.-India, 1969)*** Michael York, Utpal Dutt, Rita Tushingham. A strange, generally rewarding and magnificently photographed film made in India and directed by James Ivory. One of the themes of the film is the conflict of Eastern & Western cultures. British pop singer (Michael York) arrives in India to study the sitar with an Indian guru. A silly love story is thrown in, but the music is worth listening to. If you're in the mood for a visually stunning, if somewhat slow-moving film, pay attention to this "Guru." The best performance is turned in by Mr. Dutt. (112 mins.)

Gus (1976)** Tim Conway, Don Knotts, Ed Asner, Gary Grimes. Harmless nonsense from the Disney camp. The stars take a back seat to a mule that kicks field goals. The kids can have a good old time rooting for Gus the mule and his human teammates. (Dir: Vincent McEveety, 96 mins.)

Guy Named Joe, A (1943)**½ Spencer Tracy, Van Johnson, Irene Dunne. Tracy plays a cocky WW II flier whose spirit comes back after his death to guide rookie flier Johnson and to bid a long goodbye to Dunne, his love. The climax and ending are designed to put a lump in your throat. Script by Dalton Trumbo, less worrisome than usual. (Dir: Victor Fleming, 118 mins.)

Guy Who Came Back, The (1951)** Paul Douglas, Linda Darnell, Joan Bennett. Soap opera about a former football star who can't seem to make it after his career comes to a standstill due to an injury. Douglas is better than his material in this one. (Dir: Joseph M. Newman, 91 mins.)

Guyana Tragedy: The Story of Jim Jones (MTV 1980)***½ Powers Boothe, Ned Beatty, Veronica Cartwright, Randy Quaid, LeVar Burton. The events that led up to the Guyana tragedy in '78 are dramatized in this absorbing if somewhat oversimplified account of self-styled messiah Jim Jones and his People's Temple. Boothe is excellent as the minister who got sidetracked and drunk with power, aided by drugs and the unquestioning adoration of his flock. Good supporting cast and fine location photography. (Dir: William A. Graham, 208 mins.)

Guys and Dolls (1955)*** Marlon Brando, Jean Simmons, Frank Sinatra, Vivian Blaine. The musical success concerning a gambler who meets a Salvation Army girl, a floating crap game, and an assortment of Damon Runyon's colorful characters. The Frank Loesser songs are marvelous, but Brando's miscast. Production lavish. A big movie, an entertaining one—but no smash. (Dir: Joseph L. Mankiewicz, 138 mins.)

Gypsy (1962)*** Natalie Wood, Rosalind Russell, Karl Malden. Not as good as the Broadway original, but an interesting backstage musical all the same. An excellent score by Jule Styne and Stephen Sondheim enhances the gay film about the stage mother of them all, Rose Hovick, whose daughters grew up to be Gypsy Rose Lee and June Havoc. The dubbed-in singing detracts from the effectiveness of the musical numbers. Miss Russell is a poor substitute indeed for Ethel Merman who created Gypsy's mother on Broadway. (Dir: Mervyn Le Roy, 149 mins.)

Gypsy and the Gentleman (Great Britain, 1958)** Melina Mercouri, Keith Michell, Flora Robson, Patrick McGoohan. Villain tries to cheat his sister out of her inheritance to keep his gypsy lady friend in a proper manner. Wildly theatrical costume drama, may be fun if not taken seriously. (Dir: Joseph Losey, 89 mins.)

Gypsy Colt (1954)**½ Donna Corcoran, Ward Bond, Frances Dee. Appealing tale for the kids, as wonderful-colt Gypsy proves that she and her small mistress can't be kept apart. Remake of *Lassie Come Home*, 1943. (Dir: Andrew Marton, 72 mins.)

Gypsy Girl (Great Britain, 1966)*** Hayley Mills, Ian McShane. A poignant drama which benefits from good English location sites and a sensitive performance by Hayley Mills as a retiring young girl who is looked upon by her village as a trouble maker. A very attractive young actor named Ian McShane also registers as a gypsy lad who saves Hayley from being sent to a home. It's all a bit old hat, but the charm with which it's presented keeps it interesting. (Dir: John Mills, 102 mins.)

Gypsy Moths, The (1969)**½ Deborah Kerr, Burt Lancaster, Gene Hackman. The story about a trio of barnstorming free-fall parachutists and the turmoil they cause when they hit a small Kansas town during the 4th of July holiday is wonderful at times, and unendurably slow-moving at others. Miss Kerr is quite good as an average housewife who falls for the flashy charms of Lancaster's free spirits, and the flying scenes are marvelous. (Dir: John Frankenheimer, 110 mins.)

H-Man, The (Japan, 1959)* (Dir: Inoshiro Honda, 79 mins.)

Hagbard and Signe (Denmark-Sweden-Iceland, 1967)***½ Eva Dahlbeck, Gunnar Bjornstrand, Gitte Haenning, Oleg Vidov. A stark, beautiful color film, shot in Iceland. Almost primitive in its technique, it is, in its own way, startling in its simplicity. A Scandinavian Romeo-Juliet story about young love in the Middle Ages, marred only by some excessive violence in its battle scenes. The love scenes between the two youngsters are sensitively handled. The "Romeo" of this film is Russian. (Dir: Gabriel Axel, 92 mins.)

Hail Hero! (1969)**½ Michael Douglas, Arthur Kennedy, Teresa Wright, Peter Strauss. Muddled point of view in this well-meaning drama about a young man who enlists during the Vietnam War even though he believes strongly in antiwar philosophies. Douglas, in his film debut, does rather well as the complex young man who can't seem to get through to his family. The original ending, all roses, was later altered. (Dir: David Miller, 100 mins.)

Hail the Conquering Hero (1944)**** Eddie Bracken, Ella Raines, William Demarest. Woodrow Lafayette Pershing Truesmith (Bracken) is discharged from the marines for chronic hay fever; but a bunch of marines adopt him and foist him off on his hometown as a war hero. In the ensuing hero worship he is elected mayor in director Preston Sturges's acidly satirical masterpiece on the manners and mores of small-town America. (101 mins.)

Hair (1979)****Treat Williams, John Savage, Beverly D'Angelo, Annie Golden, Nicholas Ray. Based on the hit musical of the '60s by James Rado, Gerome Ragni, and Galt MacDermot, about a young draftee's pre-induction visit to the world of flower-children. Doesn't live up to the exceptional promise of its first 15 minutes but the musical movement is acutely choreographed by Twyla Tharp. (Dir: Milos Forman, 121 mins.)

Hairy Ape, The (1944)*** William Bendix, Susan Hayward. A rough ship's stoker falls for a red-headed wench who uses him as a pawn in her conquest of other men. From the play by Eugene O'Neill, a good production, well acted. (Dir: Alfred Santell, 90 mins.)

Half a Hero (1953)** Red Skelton, Jean Hagen. Writer gets in over his head when he buys a modern home in the country to please the wife. Very mild for Skelton, this comedy has a few chuckles. (Dir: Don Weis, 71 mins.)

Half a Sixpence (Great Britain-U.S., 1967)**½ Tommy Steele, Cyril Ritchard, Julia Foster, Penelope Horner. English star Tommy Steele plays the orphan of Edwardian England who inherits a fortune in this musical adaptation of the 1905 H. G. Wells novel, "Kipps: The Story of a Simple Soul." Occasionally sprightly, with some diverting musical numbers. Kids will enjoy. Ritchard, an enormously talented performer, appears here in a rare film since Alfred Hitchcock's 1929 "Blackmail." (Dir: George Sidney, 148 mins.)

Half Angel (1951)** Loretta Young, Joseph Cotten. For those who've enjoyed Loretta for lo, these many years. The versatile Miss Young plays a nurse who's suffering from split personality and the whole thing's played for comedy. (Dir: Richard Sale, 77 mins.)

Half-Naked Truth, The (1932)**** Lee Tracy, Lupe Velez, Franklin Pangborn. Remarkable comedy based on stories, true or otherwise, about master publicist Harry Reichenbach. Brilliant performances and bright repartee. One of many neglected masterworks by director Gregory La Cava. (77 mins.)

Hallelujah! (1929)***½ Daniel L. Haynes, Nina Mae McKinney. A young man becomes a preacher, but is tempted, goes wrong, and meets tragedy before he can return to his church. One of the first serious films on a black theme, with an all-black cast; a strong, well-acted drama with music. Today Haynes would become a major star, as well as a bundle of dynamite, singer-dancer-actress McKinney. B&W (Dir: King Vidor, 106 mins.)

Hallelujah Trail, The (1965)* Burt Lancaster, Lee Remick. (Dir: John Sturges, 165 mins.)

Halliday Brand, The (1957)**½ Joseph Cotten, Viveca Lindfors, Betsy Blair, Ward Bond. A talented cast makes most of this western drama bearable but for the most part, the script defeats them. (Dir: Joseph H. Lewis, 77 mins.)

Halloween (1978)*** Jamie Lee Curtis, Donald Pleasence, Nancy Loomis. Well-done, low-budget horror hit. It's Halloween and a madman has escaped and is returning to his hometown for a rampage of murders. Director John Carpenter knows how to scare his audience. (90 mins.)

Halls of Anger (1969)**½ Calvin Lockhart, Rob Reiner, Jeff Bridges, Edward Asner. A second helping of "To Sir, With Love." Handsome Calvin Lockhart plays a black high-school vice-principal, who is the focal point of bussed-in white students. The resulting tensions erupt all over the place in episodic fashion. (Dir: Paul Bogart, 103 mins.)

Halls of Montezuma (1951)**½ Richard

Widmark, Jack Palance, Robert Wagner, Karl Malden, Jack Webb, Richard Boone. The Marines are once again as graphically displayed by Hollywood as the roughest, toughest, brawliest, brawniest, and bravest of all the military who ever fought for the preservation of liberty. Glory drenched heroics played to the accompaniment of the "The Marine Hymn." Widmark is effective as are the other players. (Dir: Lewis Milestone, 113 mins.)

Hamlet (Great Britain, 1948)**** Laurence Olivier, Jean Simmons, Basil Sydney, Eileen Herlie. Shakespeare's tragedy of the Danish prince brought to life by Olivier; film-making at its finest, should be seen by all. The greatest play in all literature superbly directed and performed by the greatest actor of his era—a perfect combination. Oscars for Best Picture, Best Actor. (Dir: Laurence Olivier, 153 mins.)

Hamlet (Great Britain, 1969)***½ Nicol Williamson, Judy Parfitt, Anthony Hopkins, Marianne Faithfull. A filmed version of Williamson's riveting stage performance. In director Tony Richardson's version, the court is a barbaric community and Hamlet a complete cynic. Williamson plays Hamlet as a nervous, energetic intellectual, resentful of the role that destiny has imposed on him. The supporting cast ranges from adequate to terrible. Text has been unnecessarily trimmed, even the famous soliloquies. (114 mins.)

Hamlet (Great Britain, MTV 1980)**** Derek Jacobi, Claire Bloom, Lalla Ward, Patrick Stewart, Eric Porter, Robert Swann. In this more than in any other play, the leading actor dictates the tempo and energy of the production. Jacobi's intense portrayal of the vengeful prince gives one a sense of urgency which keeps the astonishly familiar text freshly meaningful. Jacobi is at his best, alternately thoughtful and savage, as he feigns madness for the royal court while carefully setting traps to avenge his father's murder.

The quality of the other players shows the real strength of these TV productions' once-in-a-lifetime casting. No amount of money could bring together such distinguished performers for a theater run. Claire Bloom is intelligent, voluptuous and regal as Gertrude; Stewart makes painfully clear King Claudius' internal struggles between conscience, lust for power, and passion for his guilty queen; Lalla Ward's tormented Ophelia is thrilling and touching. Also of note are Eric Porter, endearing as Polonius, and Swann as Horatio.

Hammerhead (Great Britain, 1968)* Vince Edwards, Judy Geeson. (Dir: David Miller, 93 mins.)

Hammersmith Is Out (1972)**½ Richard Burton, Elizabeth Taylor, Peter Ustinov, Beau Bridges. Uneven, sometimes funny attempt at making the legend of Faust a timely theme. Burton plays Hammersmith,

a lunatic, who promises Bridges he can have anything if he frees Hammersmith. Bridges obliges and receives wealth and Miss Taylor before his inevitable destruction. Occasionaly inventive satirical touches. (Dir: Peter Ustinov, 108 mins.)

Hand, The (Great Britain, 1961)**½ Derek Bond, Ronald Leigh Hunt. Series of one-arm murders grips London, and the motive seems to date back to a World War II prison camp. Gruesome little thriller is well made, should please horror fans. (Dir: Henry Cass, 60 mins.)

Hand in Hand (Great Britain, 1961)***½ Philip Needs, Loretta Parry, Sybil Thorndike. A poignant drama featuring two wonderful performances by child troupers Philip Needs and Loretta Parry. They, together with the deft direction of Philip Leacock, make this a charming, moving story about the evils or religious bigotry and intolerance. An eight-year-old Roman Catholic boy and a Jewish girl of the same age meet in school and become chums. They start hitchhiking to London to meet the Queen, but their friendship is soon tested, and they are taunted by the cruelties of other children. Has some of the same charm of Leacock's enchanting "The Little Kidnappers." A wonderful film, especially for children. (Dir: Philip Leacock, 73 mins.)

Hand of Night, The—See: **Beast of Morocco**

Handle with Care (1958)** Dean Jones, Joan O'Brien, Thomas Mitchell. Young law student persuades his classmates to investigate unethical practices in a small town. Dry little drama tries to put across a message but takes too many words. (Dir: David Friedkin, 82 mins.)

Handle with Care (1977)***½ Paul Le Mat, Candy Clark, Ann Wedgeworth, Marcia Rodd, Ed Begley, Jr. A good-time movie that rises above its exploitation origins thanks to crack direction by Jonathan Demme, about the lives and loves of CB radio users. (98 mins.)

Hands of a Stranger (1962)** Paul Lukather, Joan Harvey. Based on **The Hands of Orlac** by Maurice Renard. (Dir: Newton Arnold, 86 mins.)

Hands of a Strangler (France-Great Britain, 1960)*½ Mel Ferrer, Dany Carrel, Christopher Lee, Donald Wolfit. Alternate title: **Hands of Orlac, The**. (Dir: Edmond T. Greville, 87 mins.)

Hands of the Ripper (Great Britain, 1971)**½ Eric Porter, Angharad Rees, Jane Merrow. Intriguing, if far-fetched, treatment of the Jack the Ripper tale. The novel premise features the daughter of the famous criminal seeking psychiatric help from Porter (a disciple of Freud) when she claims to inherit her father's murderous tendencies. Victorian London subtly hued, with a stunning finale in St. Paul's Cathedral. (Dir: Peter Sasdy, 85 mins.)

Hang 'Em High (1968)**½ Clint Eastwood, Inger Stevens. Steely avenger sets out to take care of those varmints who strung him up and left him for dead. Played in Clint Eastwood's usual flinty manner, should please nondiscriminating western buffs. With Ed Begley, Pat Hingle, Charles McGraw. (Dir: Ted Post, 114 mins.)

Hangar 18 (1980)** Darren McGavin, Robert Vaughn, Gary Collins. Close encounters of the silliest kind. A crashed UFO is discovered and the government covers up the fact that it contains the bodies of aliens. Released by a company that creates its story ideas from computer analysis of consumer research. (Dir: James L. Conway, 93 mins.)

Hanged Man, The (1964)** Robert Culp, Edmond O'Brien, Vera Miles. Gunman out to avenge the murder of a friend traces his quarry to New Orleans during Mardi Gras time. Originally made as a feature-length film for TV; a revamping of "Ride the Pink Horse" that has little of the Robert Montgomery film's finesse. Just a routine crime drama. (Dir: Don Siegel, 87 mins.)

Hanged Man, The (MTV 1974)**½ Steve Forrest, Cameron Mitchell, Sharon Acker. A western-mystical adventure which casts Forrest as James Devlin, a gunslinger who fantastically survives a hanging, and then dedicates himself to truth and justice. A troupe of skilled supporting actors contribute to this far-fetched tale. (Dir: Michael Caffey, 90 mins.)

Hanging by a Thread (MTV 1979)** Patty Duke Astin, Joyce Bulifant, Bert Convy. Producer Irwin Allen, master of disaster, is at it again! A disabled tramcar high above a gorge is the setting, and flash backs tell us the secrets of the trapped group of victims. (Dir: Georg Fenady, 208 mins.)

Hanging Tree, The (1959)***½ Gary Cooper, Maria Schell, Karl Malden. An underrated Western drama when it was first released. Gary Cooper gives a fine performance as a man torn between law and order. The photography helps to sustain the sober mood of the film. Two Broadway actors (George C. Scott and Ben Piazza) who have since made names for themselves are featured in the supporting cast. (Dir: Delmer Daves, 106 mins.)

Hangman, The (1959)** Robert Taylor, Fess Parker, Tina Louise. Grim U.S. marshal is determined to track down a wanted man but finds himself pitted against an entire town. Draggy western doesn't do right by the cast. (Dir: Michael Curtiz, 86 mins.)

Hangman's Knot (1952)*** Randolph Scott, Donna Reed, Lee Marvin. Action filled western with hero Randolph Scott fighting off vigilantes and winning Donna Reed. More carefully made than most. (Dir: Roy Huggins, 81 mins.)

Hangmen Also Die (1943)*** Brian Donlevy, Walter Brennan, Dennis O'Keefe, Anna Lee. A doctor assassinates the notorious Nazi Heydrich, the Hangman, and as a result a wave of terror sweeps occupied Czechoslovakia. Tense, gripping underground melodrama. (Dir: Fritz Lang, 131 mins.)

Hangover Square (1945)***½ George Sanders, Laird Cregar, Merle Oberon, Sara Allgood. Police inspector Sanders tries to discover if a decent, talented composer who suffers from amnesia is a psychotic killer. Fine musical score by Bernard Herrman and excellent atmospheric camerawork, including a sweeping crane shot during the climactic concert scene. (Dir: John Brahm, 77 mins.)

Hannibal (Italy, 1960)** Victor Mature, Rita Gam. An Italian made epic starring Victor Mature as the Carthaginian General, Hannibal. Splendor and spectacle but nothing else. One cliche upon another. Action fans might enjoy the great battle scenes. (Dir: Edgar G. Ulmer, 103 mins.)

Hannibal Brooks (Great Britain, 1969)* Oliver Reed, Michael Pollard, James Donald. (Dir: Michael Winner, 101 mins.)

Hannie Caulder (Great Britain, 1971)** Raquel Welch, Robert Culp, Ernest Borgnine, Strother Martin, Jack Elam. If you want to look at Raquel in a poncho riding the trail of revenge, here's your chance. The story starts as a trio of vermin-ridden villains—Borgnine, Martin and Elam—rape Ms. Welch after killing her husband and setting fire to her home. The resilient Raquel bounces back, learns how to shoot a gun like Jesse James and sets out to get those varmints. Culp is the man who teaches Hannie how to handle the firing iron. Raquel is more beautiful than talented. Director Burt Kennedy co-authored the pedestrian screenplay with David Haft, using the pseudonym Z. X. Jones. I don't blame them for not wanting credit. (Dir: Burt Kennedy, 85 mins.)

Hans Christian Andersen (1952)*** Danny Kaye, Jeanmaire, Farley Granger. Kaye as the teller of fairytales, who falls in love with a beautiful ballerina. Ideal children's entertainment with some spectacular fantasy scenes—adults may become impatient with the excessive amount of sweetness and light. (Dir: Charles Vidor, 120 mins.)

Happening, The (1967)**½ Anthony Quinn, Faye Dunaway, George Maharis, Michael Parks, Milton Berle. A superb idea which isn't fully realized. A group of young beachtype vagrants (Miss Dunaway, Maharis, Parks and Robert Walker) accidentally kidnap former big-time mafia hood Quinn and the plot takes off. However, the scripters and director Elliot ("Cat Ballou") Silverstein can't make up their minds between a way-out comedy, or an off-beat comedy-drama and the emphasis is juggled back and forth. A maddening offbeat entry. (Dir: Elliot Silverstein, 101 mins.)

Happiest Days of Your Life, The (Great Britain, 1950)**** Alastair Sim, Margaret Rutherford. Merry mixups when a group of schoolgirls are billeted at a boys' school by mistake. Hilarious madcap comedy, a laugh a minute! (Dir: Frank Launder, 81 mins.)

Happily Ever After (MTV 1978)**½ Suzanne Somers, Bruce Boxleitner. Lightweight comedy-drama. Everything is done to make TV series star Somers come off well, but she doesn't have the acting ability to make more than a cutout of a vulnerable young singer drowning in the opportunistic world of Las Vegas show business. Boxleitner is winning as a robust, handsome lumberjack who pursues her with relentless glee. (Dir: Robert Scheerer, 104 mins.)

Happy Anniversary (1959)*** David Niven, Mitzi Gaynor. The hit B'dway show about a couple celebrating their 13th (for good luck) anniversary makes a perfect screen comedy and David Niven couldn't be better, as the spouse. Patty Duke is seen in a typical youngster role.(Dir: David Miller, 81 mins.)

Happy Birthday, Gemini (1980)* Robert Viharo, Rita Moreno, Alan Rosenberg, Sarah Holcomb. Writer-director Richard Benner has adapted Albert Innaurato's loutish, homophobic hit comedy so that its edges have been softened but not its derisive nature. Madeline Kahn instills a lot of character into her caricature, but the insistent pathos of the writing and the score sink the best moments of her work. (107 mins.)

Happy Birthday, Wanda June (1971)*** Rod Steiger, Susannah York, George Grizzard, Don Murray. Literal rendering of Kurt Vonnegut's maniacal play onto the screen finds plenty of funny lines plunked in front of a static camera. The satire of the Hemingway macho myth works sometimes. Steiger plays a modern Ulysses, back from an eight-year search for diamonds in Africa, returning to a perky car-hop who has collected a handful of college degrees in his absence. The ensuing re-education of a devout male chauvinist creates the laughs. (Dir: Mark Robson, 105 mins.)

Happy End (Czechoslovakia, 1967)***½ Give this one a pat for trying something different—the story of a love affair with tragic consequences, told backwards from beginning to end (or is it end to beginning?). Little more than a trick, but amusing as directed by Oldrich Lipsky. Vladimir Mensik and Czech cast. English subtitles. (Dir: Oldrich Lipsky, 73 mins.)

Happy Ending (1969)** Jean Simmons, John Forsythe, Shirley Jones, Bobby Darin, Dick Shawn, Lloyd Bridges. Top cast and writing and direction by Richard Brooks leave this still an empty "woman's picture," reminiscent of '40s vehicles for Crawford, Stanwyck, and Davis. Simmons is wonderful as a disillusioned wife after 16 years, and her husband (Forsythe) also performs well. (112 mins.)

Happy Go Lovely (Great Britain, 1951)*** Vera-Ellen, David Niven, Cesar Romero.

American producer in Edinburgh tries to produce a big musical show, and a chorus girl and a millionaire are enticed into the plot. Diverting musical comedy moves along pleasantly. (Dir: H. Bruce Humberstone, 87 mins.)

Happy Go Lucky (1943)**½ Mary Martin, Dick Powell, Betty Hutton. Pleasant, undistinguished musical about a stenographer who saves her money for a big husband-hunting cruise. (Dir: Curtis Bernhardt, 81 mins.)

Happy Hooker, The (1975)** Lynn Redgrave, Jean-Pierre Aumont, Lovelady Powell, Nicholas Pryor, Tom Poston. Xaviera Hollander's experiences as a madam have been turned into a light comedy which ignores the raunchy specifics of the profession in favor of recounting a businesswoman's rise to success. Ms. Redgrave, looking quite lithe, dispenses puns as she's called on to make Hollander seem an amiable professional catering to such clients as industry-magnate Poston with a table-top strip tease. New York locations and a variety of New York stage actors colorfully flavor the unlikely script. Hollander was a tart who could type. Remember, she was voted "secretary of the year" in Holland. (Dir: Nicholas Sgarro, 96 mins.)

Happy Hooker Goes to Washington, The (1977)*½ Joey Heatherton. Doesn't go far.

Happy Is the Bride (Great Britain, 1959)*** Ian Carmichael, Janette Scott. The strain of going through with their wedding almost causes the betrothed couple to call the whole thing off. Amusing little domestic comedy, nicely played. (Dir: Roy Boulting, 84 mins.)

Happy Landing (1938)**½ Sonja Henie, Don Ameche, Cesar Romero. Entertaining, though not outstanding is this little musical about a plane that makes a forced landing in Norway near "you know whose" home. (Dir: Roy Del Ruth, 102 mins.)

Happy Mother's Day, Love, George—See: Run, Stranger, Run

Happy Road, The (1957)*** Gene Kelly, Barbara Laage, Bobby Clark, Brigitte Fossey, Michael Redgrave. Engaging escapades of two youngsters who become fugitives in the French countryside when they run away from their Swiss school, and of their respective parents, a U.S. businessman widower and a French divorcée, in pursuit. The sight gags are fun—and there are some delicious scenes with Michael Redgrave as a NATO commander hot on their trail. Kelly produced and directed, as well as starred, his first such effort. (Dir: Gene Kelly, 100 mins.)

Happy Thieves, The (1962)** Rita Hayworth, Rex Harrison. The attractiveness of the two stars compensates somewhat for this mediocre comedy about sophisticated art thieves. The plot twists are predictable and the supporting cast mugs

Happy Time, The (1952)***½ Charles Boyer, Louis Jourdan, Linda Christian, Bobby Driscoll. A fine comedy about the ups and downs in the daily lives of an eccentric family headed by Charles Boyer. There's a French maid (Linda Christian) and a roué uncle (Louis Jourdan) and many others to make you laugh. (Dir: Richard Fleischer, 94 mins.)

Happy Years, The (1950)**** Dean Stockwell, Darryl Hickman, Leon Ames, Leo G. Carroll. Delightful tale of a mischievous boy and his adventures at a boys' school in the 1890's. Often hilariously funny, with Stockwell giving a superb performance. Fine fare for the entire family. (Dir: William Wellman, 110 mins.)

Harakiri (Japan, 1962)***½ Tatsuya Nakadai, droning and incantory, is magnificent as the man who visits a feudal lord to request the opportunity to commit harakiri. The underlying motive is revenge, and the criticism of the hypocrisy of codes of honor is sharp. Director Masaki Kobayashi's visual style is precise and convoluted. (150 mins.)

Hard Contract (1969)**½ James Coburn, Lee Remick, Sterling Hayden, Karen Black, Lilli Palmer. Interesting but flawed effort of writer-director S. Lee Pogostin to comment on the way in which Americans so readily accept or explain away murder. Coburn, sleek and rugged, portrays an international hit man who has a contract to kill three men—one in Brussels, one in Spain, and the third (Hayden) he must locate. Miss Remmick delivers an attractive performance as a jet-set chick who breaks down Coburn's cool and shakes his calm hand as he stalks his triple prey. Violent in spots, awkward in others. (Dir: S. Lee Pogostin, 106 mins.)

Hard Day's Night, A (Great Britain, 1964)**** The Beatles. During the peak of their popularity the Beatles made their first movie, and to everyone's surprise and delight it turned out to be a stylishly inventive and thoroughly made contemporary comedy classic. There are a good share of laughs, interspersed with a dozen or so of the Beatles' best songs, plus the astonishing range of talent of these four captivating personalities—John Lennon, Ringo Starr, Paul McCartney, and George Harrison. Director Richard Lester filmed the story about the Beatles on tour in England with a sense of frenzy and unabashed humor, much in the style of the early Marx Brothers' Hollywood comedies, and it works from start to finish. (Dir: Richard Lester, 85 mins.)

Hard Driver (1973)**** Jeff Bridges, Valerie Perrine, Art Lund, Geraldine Fitzgerald, Ed Lauter, Gary Busey. (Theatrically released as "The Last American Hero.") Perceptive, involving examination of a real slice of Americana—stock-car racing—in North Carolina that features outstanding performances and a literate script by William Roberts, based on articles by Tom Wolfe. Bridges is marvelous as a young moonshiner, running whiskey past the revenuers, who turns to racing to help his father (Lund) who has been jailed. Perrine is lovely as a tender, amoral, romantic interest. It's more than a standard action yarn: the movie explores the compromises needed to succeed and the vapid car-racing groupies that follow the circuit. Some expert racing footage (all filmed on location in Virginia and the Carolinas) and healthy doses of humor and pathos. Skillfully directed by Lamont Johnson. (95 mins.)

Hard Man, The (1957)**½ Guy Madison, Valerie French. Interesting enough for a western plot. Madison is a strong-willed cowboy who comes into town which is run by one man (indirectly by the man's greedy wife). He gets involved with the woman and almost pays for this mistake with his life. (Dir: George Sherman, 80 mins.)

Hard Times (1975)***½ Charles Bronson, James Coburn, Jill Ireland, Strother Martin. A tough, lean, remarkably effective fable about a bare-knuckle street fighter slugging his way to a couple of paydays in New Orleans during the Depression era of the 1930's. Charles Bronson, as usual, is a laconic stranger, in this case arriving and departing by train as a hobo. Bronson's sullen power works to good advantage. There are three main fights, one in Bayou country, and two in the piers and warehouses of New Orleans. They are surprisingly exciting despite the obvious fact that neither Bronson nor his opponents seem visibly scarred after a pounding that would break knuckles as well as skin on any mortal. But that carping aside, this marks an auspicious directorial debut for screenwriter Walter Hill. Screenplay written by Hill, Bryan Gindorff and Bruce Henstell, captures the aura and the hard times of the early 1930's. To say that this is Bronson's best screen acting is not much of a compliment, but he does energize this no-nonsense melodrama, and plays well with Coburn portraying an on-the-make small-time hustler and boxing promoter. (Dir: Walter Hill, 97 mins.)

Hard Way, The (1942)**½ Ida Lupino, Dennis Morgan, Joan Leslie, Jack Carson. It's an old ambitious girl stepping on everyone in her way plot but Miss Lupino gives it some dignity. The first half is well done but producer's luck runs out in the final reels. (Dir: Vincent Sherman, 109 mins.)

Hardcase (MTV 1971)** Clint Walker, Stefanie Powers, Alex Karras. Offbeat Western has Walker playing a soldier of fortune who helps Mexican revolutionaries, and finds his wife among them. Occasionally credible, but badly paced. (Dir: John Llewellyn Moxey, 74 mins.)

Hardcore (1979)***½ George C. Scott, Season Hubley, Peter Boyle, Leonard Gaines. One of Scott's best and most searing performances as a father who searches for his daughter in the California porno underworld. Admirable restraint by Paul Schrader in his direction, but lack of control over narrative structure in his scenario. (105 mins.)

Harder They Come, The (Jamaica, 1973)***½ Jimmy Cliff, Carl Bradshaw, Janet Barkley. Reggae singing star Cliff is a country bumpkin who comes to Kingston town and finds himself topping both the most-wanted list and the record charts. The tale is told crudely yet vividly. Includes reggae classics by Cliff, Toots and the Maytals, Desmond Dekker, and the Slickers. Don't let the impenetrable Jamaican dialect throw you (the first quarter of the film is subtitled). (Dir: Perry Henzell, 98 mins.)

Harder They Fall, The (1956)***½ Humphrey Bogart, Jan Sterling, Max Baer. In his last role, Bogart, as a sportswriter dragooned into fronting for a mob-controlled boxer, draws effectively on his weary cynicism. The expose of the fight racket, while familiar, has a brutal honesty. Philip Yordan wrote the good, if didactic, screenplay. (Dir: Mark Robson, 109 mins.)

Hardhat and Legs (MTV 1980)**½ Kevin Dobson, Sharon Gless, W. T. Martin, Ray Serra. Cheerful, fun-loving New York tale by old pros Garson Kanin and Ruth Gordon. Gless is the blueblood blonde with great legs, and Dobson is the Italian construction worker intent on crossing class lines to win the girl. First-rate acting manages to overcome last-minute plot problems. There's also a pitch for Gamblers Anonymous, because our boy can't stay away from the horses. (Dir: Lee Philips, 104 mins.)

Harlan County U. S. A. (1977)**** Director Barbara Kopple's powerful documentary on a Kentucky coal miners' strike is muddled on the issues, but earned its Oscar for a dramatic, involving story full of tough and appealing characters. (103 mins.)

Harlem Globetrotters, The (1951)**½ Thomas Gomez, Dorothy Dandridge. A dull story about one of the members of the famous Negro basketball team. The basketball game scenes are the best things in the film, and they're terrific! Dorothy Dandridge has a small non-singing part. (Dir: Phil Brown, 80 mins.)

Harlow (1965)** Carroll Baker, Mike Connors, Peter Lawford. If you're looking for a definitive biography of the late movie queen of the thirties, skip this one. It's strictly for those who prefer to believe what they read in the movie fan magazines. Carroll Baker is unconvincing as the glamorous sex symbol. The best performance in the film is one by Angela Lansbury in the unpalatable role of Mama Jean. (Dir: Gordon Douglas, 125 mins.)

Harness, The (MTV 1971)***½ Lorne Greene, Julie Sommars. A lovely movie version of John Steinbeck's Salinas Valley tale about a withdrawn farmer and his ailing wife. A bearded Greene is most believable as the grumpy, close-mouthed Californian, who endures his wife's illness until a red-haired hippie and her little boy come along and alter his ideas about living. Greene's farmer isn't converted overnight. Literate script plus Boris Sagal's careful direction convey the man's torment in trying to find out who he is. Miss Sommars is a free soul, the farmer's mentor on life: she never makes a false move, handling Greene gently and lightly. (Dir: Boris Sagal, 99 mins.)

Harold and Maude (1971)**** Ruth Gordon, Bud Cort, Vivian Pickles, Ellen Geer. An often wildly funny and original "black comedy" that was largely ignored at the time of its original release, and panned by most of the tiny number of perceptive critics who should have known better. It's a wry lyrical ode to controlled lunacy, boasting an imaginative, stylish screenplay by young writer Colin Higgins, and an equally fine directorial job from Hal Ashby. Young man of 20 (Cort) is a necrophiliac of considerable promise, and he's got a great flair for inspired sight gags, all relating to death. His companion in love and adventures is a wacky 79-year-old gloriously played by Ruth Gordon, who'd be a formidable foe in automobile demolition derbies. Special credit too to Vivian Pickles playing Cort's beleaguered mother—her arch comments on her son's demented behavior are superbly written and masterfully acted. It's a sick comedy all right—but if you go along with the spirit of this farce, it's one of the most inventive American comedy films in years. (Dir: Hal Ashby, 91 mins.)

Harp of Burma (Japan, 1956)*** Director Kon Ichikawa has fashioned a poetic anti-war film which has impact. A Japanese Army private (Shoji Yasui) takes on a personal crusade to bury all the dead soldiers he finds after the end of World War II. Along his journey's trail, the soldier dons the robes of a Buddhist monk. Alternate title: The Burmese Harp. (Dir: Kon Ichikawa, 116 mins.)

Harper (1966)*** Paul Newman, Arthur Hill, Lauren Bacall, Shelley Winters, Julie Harris. Director Jack Smight's film version of Ross Macdonald's "The Moving Target" casts Newman well as the gumchewing, wise-guy detective with a penchant for connecting with the tragedy of the mysteries he unravels. The film moves perhaps too slickly for its own good, but it's good genre work. (121 mins.)

Harper Valley PTA (1978)**½ Barbara Eden, Nanette Fabray, Ronny Cox, Louis Nye. A surprise box-office hit tied to the Jeannie C. Riley song. Eden is sexy Stella Johnson, who is termed an unfit mother by the puritanical PTA of Harper Valley,

Ohio. The comedy of retribution has her getting even by exposing her adversaries' hypocrisies. A hollow story, but a broad, visual comedy good for some laughs. (Dir: Richard Bennett, 93 mins.)

Harpy (MTV 1971)* Hugh O'Brian, Elizabeth Ashley. (Dir: Jerrold Freedman, 99 mins.)

Harriet Craig (1950)*** Joan Crawford, Wendell Corey, Lucile Watson, Allyn Joslyn. Inferior to the '36 version. Crawford's star presence eliminates any semblance of character creation in this remake of George Kelly's "Craig's Wife." Still, it's an effective theatrical piece. Harriet is a grasping middle-class housewife far more devoted to her house and possessions than to her husband and family. (Dir: Vincent Sherman, 94 mins.)

Harry and Tonto (1974)***½ Art Carney, Ellen Burstyn, Larry Hagman, Geraldine Fitzgerald. Art Carney's Academy Award-winning performance as a New York-based septuagenarian who decides to pack his beloved cat Tonto and head across the United States on his last odyssey. It's a lovely trip, filled with adventures, love, disappointment, people, and death. Director Paul Mazursky doesn't shy away from sentiment but, just when it might get too sticky, his camera picks up something else. Carney doesn't look 72, but let's not quibble—it's a splendid performance worthy of the Oscar he received. O.K. for kids, too. (Dir: Paul Mazursky, 115 mins.)

Harry and Walter Go to New York (1976)*½ James Caan, Elliot Gould, Michael Caine, Diane Keaton, Charles Durning. (Dir: Mark Rydell, 123 mins.)

Harry Black and the Tiger (Great Britain, 1958)** Stewart Granger, Barbara Rush. Talky, only occasionally interesting tale about a man who stalks dangerous jungle beasts for profit and thrills. Photography during hunts surpasses the drama's plot. Filmed in India. (Dir: Hugo Fregonese, 107 mins.)

Harry in Your Pocket (1973)**½ James Coburn, Michael Sarrazin, Walter Pidgeon, Trish Van Devere. A slick crime film which explores, at length, the "art" of pickpockets. The Harry of the title is the superdip of them all, and he's played with icy detachment by Coburn. Sarrazin and Miss Van Devere are two new recruits to the world of pickpockets and Walter Pidgeon is a veteran. Pidgeon gives a good account of himself as an aged con-man with contemporary habits (coke sniffing, for instance). The script takes its time as the group travels from one big city to another, plying their "trade." Slow-moving but not uninteresting. If you want to see a good film on this subject try Robert Bresson's "Pickpocket" (1963). Filmed in Washington State. (Dir: Bruce Geller, 103 mins.)

Hart to Hart (MTV 1979)** Robert Wagner, Stefanie Powers, Roddy McDowall, Jill St. John. A TV series was born of this film about a pair of rich, beautiful sleuths. As hubby and wife, Wagner and Powers aim for the debonair, light touch, skulking around a health spa, but the spark is missing in the mystery. (Dir: Tom Mankiewicz, 104 mins.)

Harum Scarum (1965)* Elvis Presley, Mary Ann Mobley. (Dir: Gene Nelson, 95 mins.)

Harvest: 3000 Years (Ethiopia, 1972)** Director Haile Gerima's epic of tenant farmers in Ethiopia. Slow moving, too long, but has considerable interest.

Harvey (1950)**** James Stewart, Josephine Hull, Peggy Dow, Jesse White, Cecil Kellaway. Delightful fable of a gentle tippler and the six-foot invisible "rabbit" he has adopted for a friend. Stewart is excellent as the whimsical Elwood P. Dowd, while Miss Hull is a joy as his straight-laced sister who is continually embarrassed by his actions. Oscar winner as Best Supporting Actress. Only those not sympathetic to fantasy will not enjoy it—others will find it a treat. (Dir: Henry Koster, 104 mins.)

Harvey Girls, The (1945)*** Judy Garland, John Hodiak, Ray Bolger. Good score, nice performers and an ordinary story add up to a fairly good musical. Tale of a group of young ladies who go to the wild west to become waitresses in a Fred Harvey restaurant is a good background for some nice production numbers. (Dir: George Sidney, 104 mins.)

Harvey Middleman, Fireman (1965)** Gene Troobnick, Hermione Gingold, Charles Durning. Writer-director Ernest Pintoff is a talented, inventive maker of short animated films such as "The Critic." But he comes a cropper here with this juvenile, semi-fairy-tale version of a theme dealt with better in Axelrod's "The Seven Year Itch"—the arrested adolescence of many American adult males. Has a nice scene at the New York World's Fair. Most of the best sequences are without dialogue. (Dir: Ernest Pintoff, 90 mins.)

Has Anybody Seen My Gal (1952)**½ Piper Laurie, Rock Hudson, Charles Coburn. Mildly entertaining package of fads, songs and silly antics of the twenties. The Blaisdells come into a large amount of money and it changes their life drastically. Some laughs and the cast is attractive. (Dir: Douglas Sirk, 89 mins.)

Hasty Heart, The (Great Britain, 1949)***½ Richard Todd, Patricia Neal, Ronald Reagan. Heartwarming story of a stubborn Scottish soldier who has a short time to live and the friends he makes in an Army hospital. A beautiful performance by Richard Todd as the kilted "Lochy." Based on the Broadway play. (Dir: Vincent Sherman, 99 mins.)

Hatari! (1962)**** John Wayne, Elsa Martinelli, Bruce Cabot, Red Buttons. The cast have one hell of a good time (and a few tense moments) on the African plains capturing animals for American zoos. This late masterpiece by director Howard

Hawks is brilliantly entertaining and insightful. All this, and Wayne's rendition of "Whiskey, Leave Me Alone" too. (159 mins.)

Hatchet Man, The (1932)*½ Edward G. Robinson, Loretta Young, Dudley Digges. (Dir: William Wellman, 74 mins.)

Hatfields and the McCoys, The (MTV 1975)*½ Jack Palance, Steve Forrest, John Calvin, Richard Hatch. (Dir: Clyde Ware, 72 mins.)

Hatful of Rain, A (1957)**** Eva Marie Saint, Anthony Franciosa, Don Murray, Lloyd Nolan. An excellent film version of Michael Gazzo's hard-hitting B'way play about a junkie and the people who love him and therefore suffer with him. The performances are of a high level from the stars to the supporting cast, with Anthony Franciosa (repeating his stage role as the junkie's brother) a standout. The last scene which has Miss Saint calling the authorities' help is memorable. (Dir: Fred Zinnemann, 109 mins.)

Hatter's Castle (Great Britain, 1941)** James Mason, Emlyn Williams, Deborah Kerr, Robert Newton. A hatter stops at nothing to attain a higher place in society, drives his family mercilessly. Old-fashioned, wheezing costume drama with a fine cast. (Dir: Lance Comfort, 90 mins.)

Haunted and the Hunted, The—See: **Dementia 13**

Haunted Honeymoon (Great Britain, 1940)*** Robert Montgomery, Constance Cummings, Robert Newton, Leslie Banks, Googie Withers. Lovers of Dorothy Sayers' aristocratic sleuth Lord Peter Wimsey beware—the main characters are greatly changed in this Hollywood-ized version of her classic mystery novel. But the otherwise charming performers really give it their all, and the complex, intriguing plot is intact. One strong plus is the young Robert Newton, already ferocious and perfectly cast as sly, flashy Frank Crutchley. Try it, you might like it. (Dir: Arthur B. Woods, 83 mins.)

Haunted Palace, The (1963)** Vincent Price, Debra Page, Lon Chaney, Jr. It's Price sent to chill and thrill. He's a warlock returned from the grave in the person of his descendant, to seek revenge against the villagers who burned him at the stake a century ago. You can't keep a good bogeyman down. (Dir: Roger Corman, 85 mins.)

Haunted Strangler, The (Great Britain, 1958)** Boris Karloff, Anthony Dawson. Silly far-fetched thriller in which Boris is cast as a novelist who does some research on a "grisly" murder case and becomes so immersed, he starts duplicating some of the "violent" acts. (Dir: Robert Day, 81 mins.)

Haunting, The (Great Britain, 1963)***½ Julie Harris, Claire Bloom, Richard Johnson. Director Robert Wise's strenuously eerie translation of Shirley Compton's novel gives both Julie Harris and Claire Bloom ample room to do their archetypical star-turns: the trembling child/woman versus the beautiful, black-clad butch. Stylish, if willfully elaborate, haunted-house tale. (112 mins.)

Haunting of M, The (1979)**½ Sheelagh Gibney, Nini Pitt, Alan Hay. Promising directional debut for director Anna Thomas on a gothic horror yarn in Scotland. Tiny-budget film about a young woman whose hip sister comes up from London for her coming-out party, and how the sister becomes obsessed with a stranger in a photograph. (90 mins.)

Haunts of the Very Rich (MTV 1972)**½ Lloyd Bridges, Cloris Leachman, Anne Francis, Moses Gunn. Remember "Outward Bound" and "No Exit"? Here's a variation of their themes, placing a group of strangers together in a remote spot, which may or may not be hell. Setting is a sumptuous resort on a plush island where the guests trot out their personal hang-ups before too long. Attractive cast. (Dir: Paul Wendkos, 72 mins.)

Hauser's Memory (1970)**½ David McCallum, Susan Strasberg, Lilli Palmer. Above average made-for-TV-feature. Fairly absorbing drama about the risky business of attempting to use a scientific experiment involving a human memory transplant, before the nature of its result has been tested. David McCallum is particularly effective as the young scientist who boldly takes the injection himself in order to prevent his Nobel Prize winning superior from being subjected to its hazards. Cold, impersonal espionage is at the root of the emergency transplant, as well as of the personal drama that follows. (Dir: Boris Sagal, 99 mins.)

Have Rocket, Will Travel (1959)*½ The Three Stooges. (Dir: David Lowell Rich, 76 mins.)

Have You Heard of the San Fransico Mime Troupe? (1963)***½ A generally well-done hour report on the politically oriented, original "guerrilla theater" group in this country. Funny, satirically incisive, this film should look better on TV than it did in theatres. Director of this refreshing American "commedia dell'arte" group is Ronnie Davis. Rewarding, provocative documentary produced and directed by Don Lenzer and Fred Wardenburg. (60 mins.)

Having a Wild Weekend (Great Britain, 1965)**½ Dave Clark Five. The English pop group's first film, and although it doesn't measure up to the Beatles' "A Hard Day's Night," it has a similar kooky appeal. The plot is best not outlined, but the charm of Dave Clark and his group registers nicely. (Dir: John Boorman, 91 mins.)

Having Babies (MTV 1976)**½ Jessica Walter, Vicki Lawrence, Karen Valentine, Desi Arnaz, Jr. A good cast and fine production values help bolster this story about the personal lives of four expectant mothers (three with husbands) who come together while attending classes in the Lamaze method of natural childbirth. Episodic, but you finally come to care about all of them. Jessica Walter is quite good as a not-so-young woman having her first child. The rest ff the cast is competent. A graphic birth sequence at the end is handled with taste. (Dir: Robert Day, 98 mins.)

Having Babies II (MTV 1977)** Tony Bill, Carol Lynley, Lee Meriwether. The second of three movies dealing with the problems and crises of birth, adoption, and first love. The vignettes are well paced, but this is basically a soap opera confined to a hospital. (Dir: Robert Day, 104 mins.)

Having Babies III (MTV 1978)** Patty Duke Astin. A group of pregnant women play out their personal dramas predictably—everyone lives happily ever after. Astin's dilemma about a cancer operation during her pregnancy, to be performed by her ex-husband, is most interesting.(Dir: Jackie Cooper, 104 mins.)

Having Wonderful Crime (1945)*** Pat O'Brien, George Murphy, Carole Landis. A shady lawyer and his two friends turn sleuths and look into the murder of a magician. Fast paced, breezy comedy-mystery. (Dir: A. Edward Sutherland, 70 mins.)

Having Wonderful Time (1938)**½ Ginger Rogers, Douglas Fairbanks Jr., Red Skelton, Lucille Ball. City girl goes to the mountains for a vacation and falls in love there. Pretty mild comedy has some good scenes but isn't what it should have been. (Dir: Alfred Santell, 70 mins.)

Hawaii (1966)*** Julie Andrews, Richard Harris, Max von Sydow. This epic film based on James Michener's rambling narrative about the early (1820) settlers of Hawaii amounts to pure escapist adventure fare rather than historical drama, but it's lavishly produced, well acted, and reasonably entertaining. Sit back and share the exploits of the strict missionary (von Sydow), his friendly, outgoing wife (Andrews), and the dashing sea captain (Harris) who loves the preacher's wife. The scenery is gorgeous, the spectacle impressive. Von Sydow is miscast in the leading role of a young graduate of Yale Divinity School. (Dir: George Roy Hill, 186 mins.)

Hawaii Five-O (MTV 1968)* Jack Lord, Nancy Kwan, Leslie Nielsen, Lew Ayres. (Dir: Leonard Freeman, 96 mins.)

Hawaii Five-O: V for Vashon (MTV 1972)**½ Jack Lord, Luther Adler, Harold Gould. (Dir: Charles S. Dubin, 159 mins.)

Hawaiians, The (1970)**½ Charlton Heston, Geraldine Chaplin. Spectacle, Charlton Heston, Hawaiian history (Hollywood-style, of course), and a cast of thousands (or so it seems) still can't make this old-fashioned saga really work. Based on a portion of James Michener's rambling novel, the story has so much plot and so many big scenes that the actors are dwarfed by the surroundings. However, a pair of Oriental actors, Mako and Tina Chen, register in

the secondary leads. For the record, Charlton Heston's name is Whip and Geraldine Chaplin plays his wife, Purity. Sequel to "Hawaii," covering period 1870-1900.(Dir: Tom Gries, 134 mins.)

Hawkins on Murder (MTV 1973)**½ James Stewart. Given a good script by David Karp to work with, Stewart plays a shrewd murder trial lawyer. Stewart is Hawkins, a country boy in city clothes, who defends a poor little rich girl—the sensitive, withdrawn type—accused of slaying daddy, stepmother, and stepsister. Stewart combines gentleness with probing queries. Occasionally, the pace of the film is sacrificed for the development of character, but the gamble usually pays off. Bonnie Bedelia, as the accused, leads the supporting cast. (Dir: Jud Taylor, 73 mins)

Hawks and the Sparrows, The (Italy, 1966) Toto, Ninetto Davoli. Director Pier Paolo Pasolini relates the tale "Everyman," using Toto (Italy's most famous comic actor) as the father and Davoli as his empty-headed son. There's also a talking crow who says such things as "The age of Brecht and Rossellini is finished." (91 mins.)

Haywire (MTV 1980)***½ Lee Remick, Jason Robards, Jr., Deborah Raffin, Dianne Hull, Linda Gray. Brooke Hayward's forthright memoir of her parents, actress Margaret Sullavan and superagent-producer Leland Hayward, becomes an often involving drama with unusually good performances by Raffin and the two leads. Remick is the actress who keeps saying she would rather be a mother and wife but trots off to make a movie at the drop of an offer, and Robards is the agent who closes million-dollar deals on the phone, but has trouble communicating with his children. (Dir: Michael Tuchner, 156 mins.)

He Ran All the Way (1951)*** John Garfield, Shelley Winters. Exciting, contrived melodrama about a killer who holds a decent family at bay and hides out in their home. Excellent performance by Garfield. His last. (Dir: John Berry, 77 mins.)

He Rides Tall (1964)** Tony Young, Dan Duryea, Jo Morrow. Marshall finds dirty work on the ranch of his foster-father, instigated by a no-good foreman. Routine western. (Dir: R. G. Springsteen, 84 mins.)

He Stayed for Breakfast (1940)** Melvyn Douglas, Loretta Young. Communist man learns about life, love and capitalist luxury from a beautiful American girl. Comedy employing "Ninotchka" theme is forced and only occasionally funny. (Dir: Alexander Hall, 89 mins.)

He Walked by Night (1948)***½ Richard Basehart, Scott Brady, Jack Webb. Semi-documentary chase drama showing how the police stalk a killer is an exciting, tense and absorbing film. Basehart is superb as the killer. (Dir: Alfred L. Werker, 79 mins.)

He Who Gets Slapped (1924)**½ Lon Chaney, Norma Shearer, John Gilbert. Director Victor Sjostrom's silent film features a rare restrained performace by Chaney as a disgraced scientist who works as a circus clown while plotting his revenge. As a director, both in Sweden as Sjostrom and the U.S. as Seastrom, he pioneered a naturalistic style of lyric subtlety. (85 mins.)

He Who Must Die (France, 1957)**** Melina Mercouri, Pierre Vaneck, Jean Servais, Gert Frobe. A great film about the Passion Play, set in a small Cretan village in 1921, based on the riveting novel, "The Greek Passion," by Nikos Kazantzakis. A Greek village, still under Turkish control following World War I, re-enacts the Passion Play for Holy Week, and finds that the roles of Christ, Mary Magdalene and the Apostles still have great meaning for their modern society. A powerful, searing film that won many awards. Mercouri and Vaneck are perfect, as is the rest of the company. (Gert "Goldfinger" Frobe is seen in a small part.) This was Dassin's second film made in France after being blacklisted in Hollywood during the 1950's. An enduring masterpiece. Dassin co-authored the screenplay with Ben Barzman. Filmed in black and white. (Dir: Jules Dassin, 122 mins.)

He Who Rides a Tiger (Great Britain, 1966)***½ Tom Bell, Judi Dench, Paul Rogers, Kay Walsh, Jeremy Spenser. The unlikely love affair between a burglar (Tom Bell) and a young mother (Judi Dench) is compellingly unreeled in this well-directed drama. Good performances. (Dir: Charles Crichton, 103 mins.)

Head (Germany, 1959)** Horst Frank, Michel Simon. A German made (dubbed in English) horror film and a somewhat gruesome affair. Scientists are working on a way to keep a head alive after it has been removed from the rest of the body. (Dir: Victor Trivas, 92 mins.)

Head (1968)** The Monkees cavorting through a harebrained series of plotless incidents. They camp it up to please their devotees. In '68, this was "in." By now, it may be just in-ane. Matter of taste. Includes appearances by Victor Mature, Annette Funicello, Timothy Carey, Vito Scotti, female impersonator T. C. Jones. Interesting to note this was "written" by director Bob Rafelson and actor Jack Nicholson. Rafelson later directed the splendid "Five Easy Pieces." (Dir: Bob Rafelson, 86 mins.)

Head over Heels (1979)***½ John Heard, Mary Beth Hurt, Peter Riegert, Gloria Grahame. Story of a young man (Heard) and his obsessional pursuit of his married ladylove (Hurt). Director Joan Silver has a strikingly sure sense of emphasis and a marvelous offhand skill with actors. Based on Ann Beattie's novel "Chilly Scenes of Winter." (Dir: Joan Micklin Silver, 99 mins.)

Headless Ghost, The (Great Britain, 1958)**½ Clive Revill, Richard Lyon, David Rose. Unusually good effects enliven this better-than-average comic tale of a haunted castle. Teenage students investigate reports of a headless spirit, and meet more real ghosts than they know what to do with. B & W. (Dir: Peter Graham Scott, 63 mins.)

Headlines of Destruction (France, 1959)** Eddie Constantine, Bella Darvi. Newsman is convinced a man is innocent of murder, sets out to nab the real culprit. Adequate imitation American whodunit, dubbed-in English. Written by John Berry. (Dir: Georges Vernier, 85 mins.)

Headquarters State Secret (Germany, 1962)** Gert Frobe, Peter Carsten. German agent receives a plan for the construction of a mine, but his brother thwarts him and aids the Allies. Fairly interesting WW II spy melodrama, dubbed in English. (Dir: Paul Man, 103 mins.)

Healers, The (MTV 1974)**½ John Forsythe, Season Hubley, Pat Harrington. Fairly absorbing pilot film for a proposed series with Forsythe playing the chief of staff of one of those massive medical research complexes where problems abound. Forsythe's Dr. Kier comes face-to-face with money problems, defecting research men, and a decision on the use of an untested drug in a crisis case. Director Tom Gries manages to give the familiar material some freshness. (Dir: Tom Gries, 100 mins.)

Health (1980)*** Glenda Jackson, Carol Burnett, James Garner, Lauren Bacall, Dick Cavett. Director Robert Altman's uneven but often sardonic and incisive look at a four-day health-food conference in Florida. Cavett plays himself covering the convention for his TV talk show. Despite the high-powered name cast and Altman's reputation and following, 20th Century-Fox virtually abandoned the film after its production. (102 mins.)

Hear Me Good (1957)*** Hal March, Joe E. Ross, Merry Anders. Fast-talking promoter finds he has to rig a beauty contest to satisfy a racketeer and his moll. Minor but breezy, fun-filled Runyonesque comedy with frequently sparkling dialogue, wisecracks. Good fun. (Dir: Don McGuire, 80 mins.)

Hearse, The (1980)** Trish Van Devere, Joseph Cotten, Perry Lang. This story of a woman living in an old house who may or may not be pursued by the devil does try to build suspense through the whole film instead of splashing gore around every five minutes, but it's no more competent or capable of pulling together character and action than its sensationalist competitors. (Dir: George Bowers, 100 mins.)

Heart Beat (1979)**½ Nick Nolte, Sissy Spacek, John Heard. Don't expect the real story of the Cassadys and beat novelist Jack Kerouac, for this is a conscious travesty. A suburban wrinkle on "Design for Living," that intermittently works as an inspired comedy. Nolte and Spacek are remarkably well attuned to writer-director John Byrum's freaked-out vision of childish rebellion and equally childish conformity. The look of the film (by Lazslo

Kovacs) is nothing short of brilliant (109 mins.)

Heart Is a Lonely Hunter, The (1968)**** Alan Arkin, Sondra Locke, Stacy Keach Jr., Cicely Tyson. Carson McCullers' beautiful novel about the life of a deaf-mute in a small Southern town is brought to the screen with admirable sensitivity by all those involved. Moving story of loneliness, human boorishness and cruelty never strikes a false note, and features a remarkable prizewinning performance by Alan Arkin in the role of the deaf-mute. Thomas C. Ryan adapted the McCullers novel with special grace and insight, and the performances are fine throughout, including newcomer Sondra Locke as a young girl who befriends the deaf-mute, and the gifted young actor Stacy Keach portraying a town drunk. Filmed largely on location in Alabama. (Dir: Robert Ellis Miller, 125 mins.)

Heart of a Child (Great Britain, 1958)*** Jean Anderson, Richard Williams, Donald Pleasence. Small boy tries to save his St. Bernard during the food shortage in World War I. Corny, but entertaining drama, especially for the younger fry. (Dir: Clive Donner, 77 mins.)

Heart of a Man, The (Great Britain, 1959)*½ Frankie Vaughan, Anne Heywood, Anthony Newley. (Dir: Herbert Wilcox, 92 mins.)

Heart of Glass (West Germany, 1976)*** Josef Bierbichler, Stefan Guttler, Clemens Scheitz, Sonja Skiba. All the actors are performing under hypnosis. Director Werner Herzog has brought off more idiosyncratic experiments than this, but it adds little to the story of a town that goes collectively insane when the secret of its ruby glass industry is lost. An audacious failure. (94 mins.)

Heart of the Matter, The (Great Britain, 1953)***½ Trevor Howard, Elizabeth Allan. From Graham Greene's novel, about a police commissioner in South Africa who falls in love with an Austrian girl, and is threatened with blackmail. Not always effective drama, but fine performances. (Dir: George More O'Ferrall, 100 mins.)

Heartbeat (1946)*** Ginger Rogers, Jean-Pierre Aumont, Basil Rathbone. Lady pickpocket falls for a dancing diplomat, attains her place in society. Pleasant comedy with a good cast, elaborate production. (Dir: Sam Wood, 102 mins.)

Heartbreak Kid, The (1972)**** Cybill Shepherd, Charles Grodin, Jeannie Berlin, Eddie Albert. A unique American comedy, directed by Elaine May, that is alternately hilarious, poignant, and irritating. (Why do the three main parts have to be such vacuous saps, e.g.?) The story is the chronicle of a young New York Jewish couple whose marriage disintegrates on the Florida turnpike, while they head south, just days after the wedding. Miss Berlin, who is Elaine May's daughter and looks and acts like mama, steals the film playing a gross, nagging young-married. She's quite remarkable in a restaurant scene where she's in the process of being ill. Miss Shepherd is the titillating blond WASP love interest from chilly Minnesota. (Dir: Elaine May, 105 mins.)

Heartland (1979)**** Rip Torn, Conchata Ferrell, Lilia Skala. Excellent, carefully researched low-budget entry about the harsh frontier life in the Rockies circa 1910. Denver widow moves to Wyoming with her young daughter to become the housekeeper for a surly Scottish rancher. Based on a journal kept at the time by Elinore Randall Stewart. Skillful screenplay by Beth Ferris. Fine cinematography by Fred Murphy and director Pearce. (Dir: Richard Pearce, 95 mins.)

Hearts and Minds (1974)**** Academy Award-winning documentary brilliantly intertwines interviews, newsreel footage, and scenes from old movies. Director Peter Davis, known for his expert TV special "The Selling of the Pentagon," portrays the Vietnam War as a widening spiral of insanity, a vortex that pulled otherwise rational, decent men and women into the depths of deceit, degradation, and destruction—both moral and physical. A searing, invaluable history lesson. (112 mins.)

Hearts of the West (1975)**** Jeff Bridges, Alan Arkin, Blythe Danner, Andy Griffith. A charming lark paying homage to the myths of the Old West as seen by an aspiring young writer from Iowa in the early 1960's who heads for Titan, Nevada, and winds up in Hollywood. Deft screenplay is stylishly handled by director Howard Zieff, who gets uncommonly good performances from all the cast. Bridges is delightful as the eager, innocent Iowan, and Blythe Danner provides kisses for Bridges and joy for the rest of us. Alan Arkin plays an excitable no-talent director, jerks his director's chair across an office floor, and gets one of many laughs. Andy Griffith is likeable as a durable stuntman in this eccentric, perceptive love letter to Hollywood and Western films. Nice touches throughout, including Bridges asking to get his hair cut exactly like Zane Grey's. Alternate title: **Hollywood Cowboy.** (Dir: Howard Zieff, 103 mins.)

Heat of Anger (MTV 1972)** Susan Hayward, James Stacy, Lee J. Cobb. Ordinary courtroom drama about a clever lady lawyer. Legal beagle Hayward defends establishment contractor Cobb on a murder rap. (Dir: Don Taylor, 74 mins.)

Heat Wave (MTV 1974)** Ben Murphy, Bonnie Bedelia, Lew Ayres. Yet another crisis drama which uses the premise of a heatwave hitting a town not prepared to cope with it. Naturally a leader comes forth from the panicked crowd and helps to create some order out of the chaos. (Dir: Jerry Jameson, 74 mins.)

291

Heat's On, The (1943)** Mae West, William Gaxton, Victor Moore, Xavier Cugat. West's last movie till '70 was a stinker, though the lady's not to blame. Gaxton, a hammy Broadway star, overpowers the proceedings. (Dir: Gregory Ratoff, 80 mins.)

Heaven Can Wait (1943)**** Don Ameche, Gene Tierney, Charles Coburn, Marjorie Main, Eugene Pallette, Laird Cregar. This color valentine from director Ernst Lubitsch is a remarkably gentle story of a rake's progress and his one true love, in the face of death. The movies have never shown mortality in a sweeter light. (113 mins.)

Heaven Knows, Mr. Allison (1957)*** Deborah Kerr, Robert Mitchum. A somewhat incredible story, which places a rugged U.S. Marine corporal and a gentle Roman Catholic nun on a South Pacific island during WW II, is made palatable by the two good performances of its stars, Miss Kerr and Mr. Mitchum. Directed with his customary skill by John Huston. (107 mins.)

Heaven on Earth (Italy, 1960)** Barbara Florian, Charles Fawcett. Count overcomes his resentment of Americans when he guides an Army major and his daughter on a tour of the beauties of Rome. Scenes of the city are an armchair sightseer's delight, some of them filmed for the first time—but the thin plot is a bore. English dialogue. (Dir: Robert Spafford, 84 mins.)

Heaven Only Knows—See: **Montana Mike**

Heaven with a Barbed Wire Fence (1939)**½ Glenn Ford, Nicholas Conte, Jean Rogers. Two drifters team up with a refugee girl and try to make a living. Ford's first role, and Conte's; pleasing little drama. (Dir: Ricardo Cortez, 62 mins.)

Heaven with a Gun (1969)**½ Glenn Ford, Carolyn Jones. Predictable western yarn. Glenn Ford playing a preacher who tries to bring peace (inner and outer) to a small town. There's the usual collection of citizenry and John Anderson makes a good bad guy. (Dir: Lee H. Katzin, 101 mins.)

Heavenly Body (1943)** William Powell, Hedy Lamarr. Bedroom farce is forced comedy and falls short of its goal. Story of an astronomer's wife who believes a fortune teller and almost runs off with a handsome stranger. (Dir: Alexander Hall, 95 mins.)

Heavens Above (Great Britain, 1963)***½ Peter Sellers, Cecil Parker, Isabel Jeans. Sharp, biting satire about a do-gooder clergyman who always manages to make things difficult for his parishioners. For most it will prove to be a wealth of laughs backgrounded by some thoughtful comment. Sellers is superb as the well-meaning reverend. (Dirs: John & Roy Boulting, 105 mins.)

Heaven's Gate (1980)** Kris Kristofferson, Isabelle Huppert, Christopher Walken, John Hurt, Jeff Bridges, Sam Waterston. The most publicized "disaster" film of the era, partially because *Heaven's Gate* was one of the most expensive pictures in the history of film, costing almost $40 million to produce. When it opened in New York for a special run to qualify for Academy Awards, it received such a critical lambasting that, for the first time ever for a film of this consequence, it was immediately withdrawn by the distributors. Story is based on a real range war in the 1890s in Johnson County, Wyoming, when the cattle owners declared war on the immigrants, mostly from Eastern Europe, who were pouring into the area to establish homesteads on the grazing lands. There are some stunning visual moments in the film, both at parties at Harvard in the 1870s, which were actually shot at Oxford, to some panoramic scenes in the West, but very little finally coheres, and you wind up not caring about the central characters or even being able to follow some of the plot twists. This is not a flawed masterpiece. It's a wildly overlong, ill-conceived film with a couple of visually stunning sequences thanks to the cinematographer and director Cimino, who also wrote the inept, poorly constructed screenplay. Was Cimino's first film after the triumphant *The Deer Hunter*. (Dir: Michael Cimino, 225 mins.)

Heavy Traffic (1973)** Joseph Kaufman, Beverly Hope Atkinson, Frank DeKova, Terri Haven. Director Ralph Bakshi moves to New York's Lower East Side in this grotesque cartoon live-action pinball player's fantasy. He manages to offend nearly everyone from transvestites to Mafiosi. (77 mins.)

Hec Ramsey: Scar Tissue (MTV 1974)*½ Richard Boone, Kurt Russell, Harry Morgan. (Dir: Andrew V. McLaglen, 76 mins.)

Hec Ramsey: The Mystery of the Green Feather (MTV 1972)*½ Richard Boone. (Dir: Herschel Daugherty, 72 mins.)

Hec Ramsey: The Mystery of the Yellow Rose (MTV 1973)*½ Richard Boone, Diana Muldaur, Claude Akins. (Dir: Douglas Benton, 72 mins.)

Hedda (Great Britain, 1975)***½ Glenda Jackson, Timothy West, Jennie Linden. Glenda Jackson dominates this powerful film version of a critically acclaimed London stage production, starring Jackson, of Henrik Ibsen's enduring drama about a Nordic femme fatale—a neurotic, controlling, strong-willed woman who is nonetheless alluring to the males in her town. Jackson is an actress of extraordinary range, and this classic stage role is ideally suited to her. The Ibsen text has been trimmed considerably, which eliminates some of the shadings in Hedda's character, but this is a welcome, absorbing production of a fascinating 19th-century play which is very relevant indeed in the mid-20th century. (Dir: Trevor Nunn, 100 mins.)

Heidi (1937)** Shirley Temple, Jean Hersholt. The youngsters should love this adaptation of Johanna Spyri's juvenile classic. Story of a little Swiss girl's adventures as everybody seems to conspire to take her from her grandfather has warmth and charm. (Dir: Allan Dwan, 88 mins.)

Heidi (Switzerland, 1953)*** Elsbeth Sigmund, Heinrich Gretler. The children's classic of the little girl whose grandfather ends his feud with the village so she can receive an education. Well made, especially for children. English dubbed. (Dir: Luigi Comencini, 98 mins.)

Heidi (Austria, 1965)*** Eva-Maria Singhammer, Gertraud Mittermayr. Generally well-acted filming of the beloved children's story about a little mountain girl who is taken to the city but cannot survive there. Straightforward, far better than the 1937 Shirley Temple schmaltz; benefits notably from its authentic Alpine settings. (Dir: Werner Jacobs, 95 mins.)

Heidi and Peter (Switzerland, 1955)** Elspeth Sigmund, Heinrich Gretler. Sugary sequel to "Heidi" continuing the adventures of the Swiss girl and her family. (Dir: Franz Schnyder, 89 mins.)

Heiress, The (1949)***½ Olivia de Havilland, Montgomery Clift, Ralph Richardson, Miriam Hopkins. William Wyler's direction is careful, methodical, slightly arthritic in this version of the play adapted from Henry James's novella "Washington Square." De Havilland won a second Oscar for playing the homely, awkward girl who falls in love with a dashing fortune hunter Clift, but Richardson dominates the movie with his multilayered, passionately restrained portrayal of her ramrod father, Dr. Sloper. Designed by Harry Horner, score by Aaron Copland. (115 mins.)

Heist, The (MTV 1972)** Christopher George. Serviceable action piece about the amateur who must prove his innocence. Accused of being in on a truck robbery, a harried armored guard goes sleuthing on his own, and does nothing right. (Dir: Don McDougall, 73 mins.)

Helen Morgan Story, The (1957)**½ Ann Blyth, Paul Newman, Richard Carlson. Highly fictionalized life story of the famed singer of blues who was very popular during the twenties and early thirties. Ann Blyth is miscast as the torch singer but she has a few believable dramatic moments. Paul Newman, as the man she loves, does very well with a badly written character. Comedian Alan King, as Newman's buddy, gives a good performance. Gogi Grant sings while Miss Blyth mouths the words. (Dir: Michael Curtiz, 118 mins.)

Helen of Troy (1956)** Rossana Podesta, Jack Sernas, Sir Cedric Hardwicke. No expense was spared in bringing this tale of Paris and Helen to the screen. Lavish sets and a cast of thousands are evident but the drama is sorely missing. Miss Podesta is well endowed physically but her Helen leaves much to be desired histrionically and Jack Sernas is as wooden as the horse employed in the great final battle. Brigitte Bardot plays a hand maiden to Helen in a small role. (Dir: Robert Wise, 118 mins.)

Helga (Germany, 1967)** Ruth Gassmann. Sex-education film, tracing a woman's pregnancy from conception to birth. Fairly instructive; could be advertised as something else. (Dirs: Erich F. Bender, Terry Van Tell, 87 mins.)

Hell and High Water (1954)**½ Richard Widmark, David Wayne, Bella Darvi. Although the plot is somewhat far fetched, this high adventure tale about the efforts of a hand picked group of sailors who are assigned the task of breaking up an enemy plan to trigger another major war, has some tense moments and good underwater photographic effects to recommend it. (Dir: Samuel Fuller, 103 mins.)

Hell Below Zero (Great Britain, 1954)** Alan Ladd, Joan Tetzel. Inept drama of erupting emotions and conflicts aboard an Antarctic ice-breaker. (Dir: Mark Robson, 91 mins.)

Hell Bent for Leather (1980)**½ Audie Murphy, Stephen McNally, Felicia Farr. Not bad western—Murphy is a wandering cowpoke who is framed by a glory-seeking marshal for a crime he didn't commit. McNally is particularly good. (Dir: George Sherman, 82 mins.)

Hell Boats (Great Britain, 1970)** James Franciscus, Elizabeth Shepherd. Predictable war drama, with Franciscus as a navy commander who has a plan to save the Mediterranean from the Nazis in WW II. (Dir: Paul Wendkos, 104 mins.)

Hell in Korea (Great Britain, 1956)*** Ronald Lewis, Stephen Boyd, Robert Shaw, Stanley Baker, Michael Caine. War drama about conflict, courage, and cowardice in Korea. Good performances and action-filled battle scenes. (Dir: Julian Amyes, 81 mins.)

Hell in the Pacific (1968)*** Lee Marvin, Toshiro Mifune. Marvin and Mifune are the only characters in this pretentious, visually complex drama about two soldiers marooned on an island during WW II. Despite the insistent allegory, director John Boorman's visual contrasts redeem the UNESCO message, aided by spectacular lensing by Conrad Hall. (103 mins.)

Hell Is a City (Great Britain, 1960)**½ Stanley Baker, John Crawford, Donald Pleasence. Absorbing British crime chase. Police inspector tracks down escaped criminal he has caught once before. Thoroughly English in its pace and use of bleak locales of city rooftops and desolate moors. Well acted. (Dir: Val Guest, 93 mins.)

Hell Is for Heroes (1962)*** Steve McQueen, James Coburn, Robert Darin, Bob Newhart. One of McQueen's best performances in this nihilistic antiwar film directed by Don Siegel. Watch for

Newhart, who gives an extended telephone monologue to justify his presence on the front lines. (90 mins.)

Hell on Frisco Bay (1956)**½ Alan Ladd, Edward G. Robinson, Joanne Dru. Waterfront cop out of prison goes after the gangland big shot who was responsible for framing him. Hard-boiled crime melodrama is reminiscent of the gangster films of the 30's. Okay for the action fans. (Dir: Frank Tuttle, 98 mins.)

Hell Raiders (1965) John Agar, Richard Webb. (Dir: Larry Buchanan, 80 mins.)

Hell Squad (1958)**½ Wally Campo, Brandon Carroll. Better than average war story of the "Lost Patrol" variety; GIs vs Nazis in North Africa. At times, surprisingly good, considering the low budget. (Dir: Burt Topper, 64 mins.)

Hell to Eternity (1960)*** Jeff Hunter, David Janssen, Vic Damone. Effective drama about true-life Marine hero Guy Gabaldon and his war time (WW II) story. Jeff Hunter is well cast as the handsome and tough marine who became a hero in the South Pacific. David Janssen delivers the film's best acting job as Guy's smooth talking and smooth operating buddy. Vic Damone, in a non-singing role, also comes across nicely. The battle scenes are first rate. (Dir: Phil Karlson, 132 mins.)

Hell with Heroes, The (1968)** Rod Taylor, Claudia Cardinale, Harry Guardino. Routine smuggling yarn with a competent cast who can't save it. Taylor runs a small air cargo service and he gets into trouble with the authorities when he accepts a deal to fly some loot for smuggler Guardino. The only good thing to come out of Taylor's trouble is meeting Guardino's girl Claudia Cardinale. (Dir: Joseph Sargent, 95 mins.)

Hellbenders, The (Italy-Spain, 1967)** Joseph Cotten, Norma Bengell. This Civil War tale was produced in Spain. Except for Joseph Cotten, the entire cast is European, and the dubbing is apparent. The plot involves a Confederate major and his family who steal Union money to rebuild the Confederacy. (Dir: Sergio Corbucci, 92 mins.)

Heller in Pink Tights (1960)**½ Sophia Loren, Anthony Quinn. Fairly entertaining western drama about a theatrical troupe touring the untamed frontier in the 1880's. Slightly different plot, some amusing scenes dealing with the backstage life of the era. (Dir: George Cukor, 100 mins.)

Hellfighters (1968)* John Wayne, Katharine Ross, Vera Miles. (Dir: Andrew V. McLaglen, 121 mins.)

Hellfire Club, The (Great Britain, 1963)*½ Keith Michell, Adrienne Corri, Peter Cushing. Set in 1752. (Dir: Robert S. Baker, 93 mins.)

Hellgate (1952)**½ Sterling Hayden, Joan Leslie, Ward Bond. An innocent man is convicted of consorting with Civil War guerrillas and sent to suffer the tortures of Hellgate Prison, in barren New Mexico. Strong western drama, unpleasant for women and children, but well made. (Dir: Charles Marquis Warren, 87 mins.)

Hellions, The (Great Britain, 1962)** Richard Todd, Anne Aubrey. Five outlaws ride into a frontier town, and the lone lawman is hard put to find help to curtail them. Sounds like a western, sounds like "High Noon"; despite the South African setting, that's about what it is—an imitation, competently made but familiar. (Dir: Ken Annakin, 87 mins.)

Hello, Dolly (1969)***½ Barbra Streisand, Walter Matthau, Louis Armstrong. Huge, lavish, Gene Kelly directed "spectacle" based, of course, on the long running hit Broadway musical. The Broadway success was undeserved, and this transfer to the screen depends almost entirely on Barbra's special magic. She is, of course, quite up to the challenge, even though she is miscast—Barbra is much too young and obviously marriageable while portraying a marriage broker to make the story have much sense—but all these legitimate objections, including a generally routine score, are forgotten when Barbra takes over—as take over she does, especially in a big splashy parade sequence. Barbra overpowers everyone in the cast with the exception of the indomitable "Satchmo" Armstrong making a brief appearance with la Belle Streisand to sing the title song "Hello, Dolly!" which Armstrong helped popularize via his own hit recording of the tune. The story, set in Yonkers, New York, circa 1900, was borrowed from Thornton Wilder, who borrowed the basic plot himself. (Dir: Gene Kelly, 118 mins.)

Hello Down There (1969)*½ Tony Randall, Janet Leigh, Ken Berry, Richard Dreyfuss. (Dir: Jack Arnold, 98 mins.)

Hello, Frisco, Hello (1943)*½ John Payne, Alice Faye, Jack Oakie. Oscar-winning song, "You'll Never Know." (Dir: H. Bruce Humberstone, 98 mins.)

Hell's Angels (1930)**½ Ben Lyon, Jean Harlow, James Hall, Lucien Prival, John Darrow. Howard Hughes broke big into the movie business with this aerial extravaganza, started as a silent and then reworked when talkies came in. Hughes himself directed, although both Howard Hawks and James Whale had some part in it. While the dialogue scenes are stiff, the flying footage still remains remarkable today, even compared with all the special-effects wizardry of current films. One scene, where a crew of a zeppelin abandons ship rather than face capture, is so haunting it gives me goosebumps to remember it—images of men dropping into the void. The dogfights have the look of authenticity, since the many stunt fliers employed (several of whom were killed during the filming) were actually pilots in WW I. Harlow is a socialite who lives for the moment: This film, with her immortal line about slipping into something more comfortable, made her a star at 19, a position she held until her untimely death at 26. If the air footage looks familiar, that's due to its being used as stock shots in dozens of other movies. (Dir: Howard Hughes, 135 mins.)

Hell's Five Hours (1958)*½ Stephen McNally, Coleen Gray, Vic Morrow. (Dir: Jack L. Copeland, 73 mins.)

Hell's Half Acre (1954)**½ Wendell Corey, Evelyn Keyes. Woman goes to Honolulu when she suspects a night club owner of being her husband, believed killed at Pearl Harbor. Involved melodrama has interesting Honolulu locations. (Dir: John H. Auer, 91 mins.)

Hell's Island (1955)*** John Payne, Mary Murphy, Francis L. Sullivan. The whereabouts of a stolen ruby sends John Payne on a wild goose chase with murders and plot twists all along the way. Good for action-melodrama fans. (Dir: Phil Karlson, 84 mins.)

Hell's Kitchen (1939)**½ Ronald Reagan, Dead End Kids. Pretty good Dead End Kids melodrama with the boys involved in blackmail, torture and straightening out the rather unsavory situation in Hell's Kitchen. (Dirs: Lewis Seiler, E.A. Dupont, 90 mins.)

Hellstrom Chronicle, The (1971)***½ Lawrence Pressman. Fascinating documentary film on insects, marred only by some inane and inadvertently funny narration by Dr. Hellstrom (Pressman). He tries to make us believe that the creatures will one day conquer the human race. Contains spectacular photography of insects, using varied and new techniques. So ignore the sensationalism of the phony doctor and sit back and watch a remarkable film. (Dir: Walon Green, 90 mins.)

Hellzapoppin (1941)***½ Olsen and Johnson, Mischa Auer, Martha Raye. The two screwballs unfold their own plot when their director tells them they can't make a movie without a story. It depends upon your own particular taste, but for some this hodge-podge will be screamingly funny; as such, recommended. (Dir: H. C. Potter, 84 mins.)

Help! (1965)*** The Beatles. Some funny moments, but much of it is obvious and protracted, and a distinct disappointment to those movie buffs and Beatle fans for whom "A Hard Day's Night" was such a wondrous surprise. Take our word for it that the plot doesn't matter much in this Richard Lester effort. John, Paul, Ringo, and George are still extraordinarily talented, but their scripters let them down in this frenetic farce. (Dir: Richard Lester, 90 mins.)

Helter Skelter (MTV 1976)* George Di Cenzo, Steve Railsback, Nancy Wolfe, Sondra Blake, Skip Homeier. (Dir: Tom Gries, 175 mins.)

Hemingway's Adventure of a Young Man—See: **Adventures of a Young Man**

Henderson Monster, The (MTV 1980)**½ Jason Miller, Christine Lahti, Stephen Collins, David Spielberg. Talkative drama looks into the unknown perils of genetics experiments. Miller plays a brilliant Nobel laureate whose safety procedures are questioned by an ambitious, if slightly prejudiced mayor (Spielberg). Excellent performance by Lahti (as Dr. Henderson's Ph.D. assistant) as she grapples with her conscience, which tells her to be wary of possible safety dangers, while not denying the benefits that scientific research might bring. (Dir: Waris Hussein, 104 mins.)

Hennessy (Great Britain, 1975)**½ Rod Steiger, Lee Remick, Richard Johnson, Trevor Howard, Eric Porter. The Queen of England was enraged. You'll find some suspense. Irish-demolitions-expert Hennessy, who has resigned from the I.R.A., witnesses his wife and daughter killed in a street riot by a British soldier. So he plans to take revenge by single-handedly blowing up Parliament with the Queen in attendance. Scotland Yard is duly alarmed, while the I.R.A. are afraid of the bad publicity. News footage of the Queen is well edited with Hennessy's fictional appearance as a human bomb, but generally this is an apolitical yawn. Story by Richard Johnson, who appears as an impassive Yard man. On-location scenes shot in Belfast. (Dir: Don Sharp, 103 mins.)

Henry VIII (Great Britain, MTV 1978)*** John Stride, Claire Bloom, Timothy West, Ronald Pickup, Barbara Kellerman. Watching this production of Shakespeare's *Henry VIII*, probably the last play he ever wrote, is rather unsettling. So many of the facts in that monarch's life have been dramatized in other versions on stage, screen, and television, that one is apt to be waiting for major developments which never occur here, while other emphases take center stage. Taking all this into consideration, there's much to applaud in the vivid sets, brilliantly designed period costumes, and excellent performances from an altogether top-flight cast. John Stride's Henry VIII is an oil painting come to life; Claire Bloom's Queen Katharine is a picture of constancy and fidelity destroyed; and Timothy West's Cardinal Wolsey is evil incarnate hidden behind the red cloth of his lofty station, a wily old power seeker for whom Shakespeare shows surprising charity after his downfall. All in all, an unexpectedly fascinating drama. (Dir: Kevin Billington, 180 mins.)

Henry VIII and His Six Wives (Great Britain, 1972)*** Keith Michell, Frances Cuka, Charlotte Rampling, Jane Asher, Lynne Frederick. Though based on the famous BBC TV series, this was designed as a feature film and scripted and directed accordingly. Michell's performance as Henry is first-rate. Waris Hussein directs with less than his usual visual flair. (125 mins.)

Henry V (Great Britain, 1945)**** Laurence

295

Olivier, Robert Newton, Leslie Banks, Leo Genn. Olivier's performance is one of the most brilliant ever captured on film, in this, the first film version of Shakespeare's great drama. The entire film is superb in every detail. The distinguished American movie critic James Agee noted, "The one great glory of the film is the language. The seductive power of pacing alone and its shifts and contrasts, in scene after scene, has seldom been equaled in a movie; the adjustments and relationships of tone are just as good. Olivier does many beautiful pieces of reading and playing. There are dozens of large and hundreds of small excellences which Sir Laurence and his associates have developed to sustain Shakespeare's poem." The battle scenes are brilliantly directed by Olivier, the color photography is breathtaking. All in all one of the greatest films ever made. (Dir: Laurence Olivier, 137 mins.)

Henry V (Great Britain, MTV 1979)***½ David Gwillim, Anthony Quale, Bryan Pringle, Alec McCowan, Tim Wylton, Brenda Bruce, Jocelyn Boisseau. Shakespeare's historical quartet of plays, which began with *Richard II* concludes with *Henry V*, the best-known of the four. Henry's maturity finally fits him, and he becomes the wise monarch, the gracious lover, and the brave soldier, as he sets out to conquer France. The play is filled with rich speeches, and David Gwillim's Henry V gives them a ringing tone, especially in the famous St. Crispian's Day address to his soldiers before the battle of Agincourt, which ended in a shattering victory for the English. (Dir: David Giles, 180 mins.)

Henry IV, Part I (Great Britain, MTV 1979)**** Jon Finch, David Gwillim, Anthony Quale, Tim Piggott-Smith, Brenda Bruce, Bruce Purchase. Fans and scholars will be fascinated by the second in the eight-play cycle of historical sagas which began with *Richard II* and ends with *Richard III*. A fine cast brings this bloody and troubled period of English history to memorable life. Shakespeare apparently couldn't write an unreal character; in this sequel to *Richard II*, the victorious Bolingbroke, now king, is prepared to settle down to a peaceful reign, only to be disconcertingly afflicted by turbulence and rebellion, both in his kingdom and in his own family. Jon Finch gives an intelligent, compassionate performance as the embattled sovereign; David Gwillim is also excellent as the playboy Prince, Hal; and Anthony Quale is brilliant as the drunken, endearing old knight, Sir John Falstaff. (Dir: David Giles, 150 mins.)

Henry IV Part II. (Great Britain, MTV 1979)**** Jon Finch, David Gwillim, Anthony Quale, Bryan Pringle, Brenda Bruce, Frances Cuka, Gordon Gostelow, Jack Galloway. If you've been following this historical cycle which began with *Richard II* and ends with *Richard III*, you'll not want to miss this seldom-produced third play in the group. The public and private struggles of Prince Hal's ascendancy to the throne are the themes of Shakespeare's complex drama. The ailing, lonely king is tormented by guilt over the means he used to gain the throne; he longs to have his wayward son at his side, but pride and resentment keep the two apart. History becomes a perfectly comprehensible family conflict. Meanwhile, Hal is teaching himself to be a king by observing and judging his lower-class companions. The boisterous, underworld characters are more serious here than in *Part I*. They drink and joke, but suffer too, as Falstaff heart-rendingly shows when he is necessarily rejected by the newly-crowned King. The accent is on personal relationships, on love, duty, regret, and reconciliation and new hope. The final scene between the dying King and his son is deeply moving, and beautifully played by Jon Finch and David Gwillim. (Dir: David Giles, 180 mins.)

Her Cardboard Lover (1942)*½ Norma Shearer, Robert Taylor. (Dir: George Cukor, 93 mins.)

Her First Mate (1933)** Slim Summerville, ZaSu Pitts, Una Merkel. Relatively early William Wyler-directed comedy about a candy butcher (Summerville) on a night boat up the Hudson River to Albany who dreams of a life of adventure on the high seas. Instead he meets Pitts and Merkel. (66 mins.)

Her First Romance (1951)** Margaret O'Brien, Allen Martin, Jr. Margaret O'Brien's first teen-ager film in which she received her first screen kiss. Routine story about adolescence. (Dir: Seymour Friedman, 73 mins.)

Her Highness and the Bellboy (1945)** Hedy Lamarr, Robert Walker, June Allyson, Agnes Moorehead. Drab comedy about a bellboy (Walker) who attracts the attention of Princess Hedy while he should be courting sweet June. B & W. (Dir: Richard Thorpe, 111 mins.)

Her Husband's Affairs (1947)*½ Franchot Tone, Lucille Ball. (Dir: S. Sylvan Simon, 83 mins.)

Her Panelled Door (Great Britain, 1950)*** Phyllis Calvert, Edward Underdown. A woman found suffering from amnesia tries to retrace her past. Fairly good psychological melodrama. (Dirs: George More O'Ferall, Ladislas Vajda, 84 mins.)

Her Twelve Men (1954)**½ Greer Garson, Robert Ryan, Barry Sullivan. An attempt to make a humorous "Mr. Chips" out of Greer Garson, as a school teacher in a boys' boarding school, just doesn't come off. Greer works hard but the script lets her down. (Dir: Robert Z. Leonard, 91 mins.)

Herbie Goes to Monte Carlo (1977)** Dean Jones, Julie Sommars, Don Knotts. Third Disney "Love Bug" film has Herbie the Volkswagen entering a road race from

Paris to Monte Carlo with his original owner (Jones) as driver. Herbie also finds time to fall in love with a Lancia named Giselle, owned by Jones's rival and sweetheart Sommars, and to dispose of a pair of jewel thieves. Not as good as the first two, but attractively filmed on location. (Dir: Vincent McEveety, 105 mins.)

Herbie Rides Again (1974)*** Helen Hayes, Ken Berry, Stefanie Powers, Keenan Wynn. Good followup to the Disney hit "The Love Bug" finds the lovable Volkswagen in the care of sweet elderly Hayes, whose home—an old San Francisco firehouse—is marked for destruction by greedy developer Wynn. Latter's lawyer-nephew (Berry) falls for Hayes's boarder Powers and turns against Wynn. Slapstick and special effects add to the fun. (Dir: Robert Stevenson, 88 mins.)

Hercule (France, 1937)*½ Fernandel. (Dir: Alexander Esway, 90 mins.)

Hercules (Italy, 1959)** Steve Reeves. Successful Italian epic, English dubbed, starring muscleman Steve Reeves as Hercules. Kids will love it. Box office click "Biblical" Tarzan film cued many later imitations. (Dir: Pietro Francisi, 107 mins.)

Hercules Against the Moon Men (Italy, 1965)* Alan Steel. (Dir: Giacomo Gentilomo, 88 mins.)

Hercules Against the Sons of the Sun (Italy, 1963)* Mark Forrest, Anna Maria Pace. (Dir: Osvaldo Civirani, 91 mins.)

Hercules and the Black Pirates (Italy, 1963)* Alan Steel, Rosalina Neri. (91 mins.)

Hercules and the Captive Women (Italy, 1962)** Reg Park, Fay Spain. (Dir: Vittorio Cottafavi, 87 mins.)

Hercules and the Masked Rider (Italy, 1963)* Alan Steel, Ettore Manni. (Dir: Piero Pierotti, 86 mins.)

Hercules and the Ten Avengers (Italy-France, 1964)* Dan Vadis. (Dir: Alberto DeMartino, 94 mins.)

Hercules and the Treasure of the Incas (Italy, 1961)* Alan Steel. Alternate title: **Lost Treasure of the Aztecs**. (Dir: Piero Pierotti, 87 mins.)

Hercules and the Tyrants of Babylon (Italy, 1964)* Rock Stevens, Helga Line. (Dir: Domenico Paoleila, 86 mins.)

Hercules In the Haunted World (Italy, 1961)* Reg Park, Christopher Lee. (Dir: Mario Bava, 83 mins.)

Hercules in the Vale of Woe (Italy, 1962)*½ Kirk Morris, Frank Gordon. Alternate title: **Machiste Against Hercules in the Vale of Woe**. (Dir: Mario Mattoli, 95 mins.)

Hercules of the Desert (Italy, 1964)* Kirk Morris, Helene Chanel. (Dir: Amerigo Anton, 80 mins.)

Hercules, Prisoner of Evil (Italy, 1964)* Reg Park, Mireille Granelli. (Dir: Anthony Dawson, 90 mins.)

Hercules Unchained (Italy, 1960)** Sequel to Hercules—juvenile adventure epic starring muscleman Steve Reeves and an Italian cast. English dubbed. (Dir: Pietro Francisci, 101 mins.)

Hercules vs Ulysses (Italy-France, 1961)*½ Georges Marchal, Michael Lane. Alternate title: **Ulysses Against the Son of Hercules**. (Dir: Mario Calano, 98 mins.)

Here Come the Girls (1953)**½ Bob Hope, Tony Martin, Arlene Dahl. Chorus boy is shoved into the limelight as leading man of a show when the star is threatened by a killer. Fairly amusing Hope comedy, the comedian up to his usual bag of tricks. (Dir: Claude Binyon, 78 mins.)

Here Come the Waves (1944)*** Bing Crosby, Betty Hutton. Fairly cute nautical musical about a successful crooner who joins the Navy. Best song is "Accentuate the Positive." (Dir: Mark Sandrich, 99 mins.)

Here Comes Mr. Jordan (1941)**** Robert Montgomery, Claude Rains, Evelyn Keyes. Boxer in a plane crash discovers his time isn't up as yet, so the celestial powers have to find him a new body. One of the most unusual, original fantasies ever made; fine entertainment all around. Remade as *Heaven Can Wait*, 1978. (Dir: Alexander Hall, 93 mins.)

Here Comes the Groom (1951)*** Bing Crosby, Jane Wyman, Franchot Tone, Alexis Smith. Likable Frank Capra comedy with songs about a happy-go-lucky reporter who competes with a real-estate dealer for the hand of a girl. Nice songs, general air of good fun. (Dir: Frank Capra, 113 mins.)

Here We Go Round the Mulberry Bush (Great Britain, 1968)*½ Barry Evans, Judy Geeson, Angela Scoular, Denholm Elliott. (Dir: Clive Donner, 96 mins.)

Here's Your Life (Sweden, 1966)**½ Gunnar Bjornstrand, Per Oscarsson, Ulla Sjoberg. How a boy (Eddie Axberg) comes of age during World War I. Slow-paced, but catches some of the real yearnings and frustrations of youth. Well acted. Impressive first feature by young director Jan Troell, who also collaborated on the screenplay. (Dir: Jan Troell, 110 mins.)

Heretic, The—See: **Exorcist, Part 2, The**

Hero, The (Great Britain, 1971)* Richard Harris, Romy Schneider. (Dir: Richard Harris, 97 mins.)

Hero Ain't Nothin' But a Sandwich, A (1978)**½ Paul Winfield, Cicely Tyson. Very committed, very sincere, and very badly made. Winfield and Tyson struggle with the problems of parenting a 12-year-old drug addict in a film that is psychologically dishonest and cinematically inept. Producer Robert Radnitz and director Ralph Nelson are the carpetbaggers responsible. It may be dull, but don't forget, it's good for you. (105 mins.)

Hero at Large (1980)***½ John Ritter, Anne Archer, Kevin McCarthy. Ritter is an unemployed actor whose Captain Avenger costume becomes his real-life character, and Archer is the modern girl next door. Neither is very good, but director Martin Davidson makes the vehicle a pleasant if implausible entertainment. (98 mins.)

Hero of Babylon (Italy, 1963)*½ Gordon Scott, Michael Lane. Alternate title: **Beast of Babylon Against the Son of Hercules.** (Dir: Siro Marcellini, 98 mins.)

Hero of Rome (Italy, 1963)*½ Gordon Scott, Gabriella Pallotta. (89 mins.)

Herod the Great (Italy, 1960)** Edmund Purdom, Sylvia Lopez. One of many Italian made spectacles with sumptuous sets (used over and over again), cliched scripts and confusing dubbed-in-English performances by a mixture of British, American and Italian actors. Also, some scenes may be considered too sexy for family viewing and will probably be snipped for early evening showings. (Dir: Arnaldo Genoino, 93 mins.)

Heroes (1977)** Henry Winkler, Sally Field, Harrison Ford. An early entry in the returning Vietnam-vet cycle is a mush-brained and obscenely long romance, with Henry Winkler escaping from the psycho ward of a VA hospital and pursuing Sally Field across most of the continent. "He's got rainbows," says a supporting character about Winkler, deftly setting the sensitivity-card tone. Winkler's film debut. (Dir: Jeremy Paul Kagan, 119 mins.)

Heroes of Telemark (Great Britain, 1965)**½ Kirk Douglas, Richard Harris, Ulla Jacobson. A true-life WW II incident is turned into a moderately interesting adventure drama. Kirk Douglas heads a group of brave Norwegians who stop at nothing to destroy a Nazi plant producing essential matter for the development of the atomic bomb. The colorful Norwegian locations help make some of the heroics more believable. (Dir: Anthony Mann, 131 mins.)

Hero's Island (1962)*½ James Mason, Neville Brand, Rip Torn. (Dir: Leslie Stevens, 94 mins.)

Herostratus (Great Britain, 1967)**** Michael Gothard, Gabriella Licudi, Malcolm Muggeridge. Despite its occasional obvious faults, this is a remarkable, chilling, and provocative film which never got the American commercial release it so richly deserved. An impoverished, disillusioned young poet who sees a plastic, uncaring, and unfeeling society all around him decides to commit suicide. But he's anxious to get as much publicity as possible for the "event," so he offers his death to the head of an advertising agency to capitalize on. Written, directed, and edited by Don Levy, a young American director working on a miniscule budget of less than $50,000. Much of the dialogue was improvised by the actors as they went along. Some resourceful shots and technical effects. Filmed mostly in black and white. For those of you who have forgotten, Herostratus was the man who burned down the temple at Ephesus to guarantee himself eternal fame. (Dir: Don Levy, 142 mins.)

Hester Street (1975)***½ Carol Kane, Steven Keats. Director Joan Micklin Silver's ingratiating movie is a modestly effective domestic melodrama photographed in a self-consciously quaint B&W. In the New York of the 1890s, Jake (Keats), a Jewish immigrant with five years in America, dreads the arrival of his wife, Gitl (Kane), from the old country. Jake is a "Yankee" now, who resents Gitl's naïveté and superstition. Kane received an Academy Award nomination for her luminous performance. (90 mins.)

Hey, I'm Alive (MTV 1975)**½ Sally Struthers, Edward Asner. In 1963, young Helen Klaban and middle-aged Ralph Flores crashed in the frozen Yukon wilderness and, somehow, managed to survive for 49 days. This harrowing true-life ordeal is a natural for dramatization, and the TV film starring Struthers and Asner is a fairly good one. Since the action is limited and the scenes repetitive, the middle section bogs down a bit. The performances of the stars, especially Asner, keep things interesting. The ending is well handled, and you'll probably find yourself cheering for their rescue. (Dir: Lawrence Schiller, 72 mins.)

Hey, Let's Twist (1961)* Joey Dee, The Starliters, Teddy Randazzo. (Dir: Greg Garrison, 80 mins.)

Hey, Pineapple! (Japan, 1963)*½

Hey, Rookie (1944)**½ Ann Miller, Larry Parks. Big producer is drafted, stages a big Army show. Pleasant comedy musical with some above average material. (Dir: Charles Barton, 77 mins.)

Hey There, It's Yogi Bear (1964)*½ (Dirs: William Hanna, Joseph Barbera, 89 mins.)

Hi-Jack Highway—See: **Gas-Oil**

Hi Mom! (1970)*** Robert De Niro, Allen Garfield, Jennifer Salt. Designed as a sequel to "Greetings," this is an uneven, sometimes frenetic but often lacerating and acerbic series of vignettes about a Vietnam veteran who decides to make dirty movies. Directed and written by Brian De Palma. (87 mins.)

Hiawatha (1952)** Vincent Edwards, Keith Larsen, Yvette Dugay. Indian brave tries to prevent a war among tribes perpetrated by a hot-headed warrior. Mildly entertaining adventure based on Longfellow's poem. (Dir: Kurt Neumann, 80 mins.)

Hickey and Boggs (1972)**½ Robert Culp, Bill Cosby. Everyone's chasing $400,000 of stolen bank loot including detectives Al Hickey (Cosby) and Frank Boggs (Culp). The "I Spy" team work with the same understatement that made them super to watch on TV, but there isn't enough character development in Walter Hill's script to merit their glancing at each other with so much familiarity. Culp's direction paces the film well with shoot-outs and destruction on the streets of LA. (Dir: Robert Culp, 111 mins.)

Hidden Eye, The (1945)*** Edward Arnold, Frances Rafferty. Blind detective uses his powers to save an innocent man and uncover a murder plot. Tightly knit, suspenseful mystery, above average. (Dir: Richard Whorf, 69 mins.)

Hidden Fear (1957)** John Payne, Alexander Knox. Routine crime meller set in Copenhagen has American (Payne) arriving on the scene to investigate his young sister's involvement with a group of "intrigue-soaked" characters. You've seen it all before at least a hundred times. (Dir: Andre de Toth, 83 mins.)

Hidden Fortress, The (Japan, 1959)**½ Toshiro Mifune. A gritty fairy tale directed by Akira Kurosawa, about a loyal general (Mifune) and two comic sidekicks who protect a princess fleeing evil forces who seek her destruction. The film is visually pleasing and, for Kurosawa, comfortably devoid of serious content. (123 mins.)

Hidden Room, The (Great Britain, 1949)***½ Robert Newton, Sally Gray, Phil Brown. A madly jealous doctor captures his wife's paramour and imprisons him in a deserted bomb-site cellar, where he intends to slowly kill him. Tense, excellently acted and directed melodrama. (Dir: Edward Dmytryk, 98 mins.)

Hide and Seek (Great Britain, 1963)**½ Ian Carmichael, Janet Munro, Curt Jurgens. Professor involved in government work becomes a target for spies who want to kidnap him. Agreeable melodrama, played not too seriously, does well with the familiar material. (Dir: Cy Endfield, 90 mins.)

Hide in Plain Sight (1980)***½ James Caan, Jill Eikenberry, Robert Viharo, Danny Aiello, Kenneth McMillan. Caan's directorial debut is simple and direct, telling the story of a workingman whose children are taken from him as part of a government witness relocation program after his ex-wife's second husband rats on the mob. Caan's direction displays many of the qualities he projects as an actor: reticence, intelligence, distrust of emotion, stolidness, simplicity. The actors have a taciturn force, especially Aiello and McMillan. A good, small movie, proud of its homely virtues. Based on a true story. (98 mins.)

Hideout, The (Great Britain, 1948)*** Howard Keel, Valerie Hobson. An escaped criminal forces a young couple to hide him out while the law pursues him. Tense melodrama, Keel does a good acting job in a non-singing role. aka "The Small Voice" (Dir: Fergus McDonnell, 85 mins.)

Hiding Place, The (1975)** Julie Harris, Eileen Heckart, Arthur O'Connell, Jeanette Clift. This seemingly innocuous film is a product of the propaganda arm of evangelist Billy Graham's organization. Based on a true story of two Dutch sisters sent to a Nazi concentration camp for helping Jewish refugees, the film is alternately fervent and febrile. Bad, but not as bad as it sounds. James F. Collier directs competently. (145 mins.)

High and Dry (Great Britain, 1953)*** Paul Douglas, Alex Mackenzie, Hubert Gregg. An American businessman runs afoul of a rickety cargo vessel in Scotland in this wryly amusing comedy with the crafty Ealing Studios touch. (Dir: Alexander Mackendrick, 93 mins.) aka "The Maggie"

High and Low (Japan, 1963)***½ Toshiro Mifune. Director Akira Kurosawa's adaptation of Ed McBain's 87th Precinct novel "King's Ransom" is an interesting interpretation of the American crime genre by Japan's most accomplished action director. The son of a millionaire's chauffeur is mistakenly kidnapped; but a high ransom is still demanded and the millionaire pays. (142 mins.)

High and the Mighty, The (1954)**½ John Wayne, Robert Stack, Robert Newton, Jan Sterling, Claire Trevor. Adapted by Ernest K. Gann from his novel, this is a precursor of the "Airport" films, with passengers and crew reexamining their lives before an anticipated plane crash. William Wellman directs tediously. Sterling is good in her big scene. (147 mins.)

High Anxiety (1977)***½ Mel Brooks, Madeline Kahn, Harvey Korman. Affectionate, funny spoof and homage to Albert Hitchcock and his filmic style. Brooks considers Hitchcock one of the greatest motion-picture directors who ever lived, and gets laughs parodying Hitchcock's patented camerawork and pacing. Plot, such as it is, concerns a doctor (Brooks) trying to understand and deal with his own neurosis. Brooks co-wrote the screenplay. The maniacal Mel also composed, and sings, the title song. (Dir: Mel Brooks, 94 mins.)

High-Ballin' (Canada, 1978)** Peter Fonda, Jerry Reed, Helen Shaver. Another tedious trucker opus, starring Fonda (no stranger to road movies) and country singer Reed as old pals who team up with an offbeat lady trucker (Shaver) in taking on the thugs who are out to crush the independent truckers. (Dir: Peter Carter, 100 mins.)

High Barbaree (1947)*½ Van Johnson, June Allyson, Thomas Mitchell. (Dir: Jack Conway, 91 mins.)

High Bright Sun, The—See: **McGuire Go Home**

High Commissioner, The (Great Britain, 1968)**½ Rod Taylor, Christopher Plummer, Lilli Palmer, Franchot Tone, Camilla Sparv, Daliah Lavi, Leo McKern, Clive Revill. Dogged Australian sleuth (Rod Taylor) arrives in London to arrest a political bigwig for murder. Mystery never quite achieves the mark intended, despite a fine cast. (Dir: Ralph Thomas, 93 mins.)

High Cost of Loving, The (1958)*** Jose Ferrer, Gena Rowlands, Jim Backus. Fine, if somewhat thin, satire of a white-collar worker's insecure job. Ferrer directs and plays Jim Fry, who fears he is going to be fired at the same time he learns his wife is pregnant. Entertaining, but the ending is too predictable. (Dir: Jose Ferrer, 87 mins.)

High Flight (Great Britain, 1958)**½ Ray Milland, Kenneth Haigh. Well acted (particularly by Kenneth Haigh as an arrogant young R.A.F. flyer) drama about the training of R.A.F. jet flying cadets. Personal drama revolves around the relationship of instructor Milland and his most brilliant but stubbornly undisciplined pupil. (Dir: John Gilling, 89 mins.)

High Ice (MTV 1980)** David Janssen, Tony Musante, Madge Sinclair, Dorian Harewood. When four mountain climbers get stuck on a tiny ledge, it's up to Colonel Musante and forest ranger Janssen to save them. The attempted rescues and the fearful climbers on their precarious perch are impressively photographed, but the bulk of the film is long uninteresting discussions between Musante and Janssen. (Dir: Eugene S. Jones, 104 mins.)

High Infidelity (France-Italy, 1964)*** Nino Manfredi, Charles Aznavour, Claire Bloom, Monica Vitti, Jean-Pierre Cassel, Ugo Tognazzi. Four tales of marital "infidelity," minor infractions. Pleasant, often witty quartet, complemented by the performances of some appealing stars. Directors, in order: Mario Monicelli, Elio Petri, Franco Rossi, Luciano Salce. (129 mins.)

High Lonesome (1950)*** John Barrymore Jr., Chill Wills. A mysterious young man wanders into a ranch and sets into motion a series of weird happenings. Expert combination of western and mystery, well above average. (Dir: Alan LeMay, 81 mins.)

High Midnight (MTV 1979)**½ Mike Connors, David Birney. Highly charged revenge drama about a police cover-up. Connors stars as a by-the-book narcotics officer and Birney is the man whose world crumbles when his wife and daughter are killed in a "no-knock" drug raid. (Dir: Daniel Haller, 104 mins.)

High Noon (1952)**** Gary Cooper, Grace Kelly. Well on its way to becoming a western classic; story of a brave lawman who has to face outlaws sworn to kill him on his wedding day. As fine an outdoor drama as one could wish, as witness its numerous awards. Cooper won his second Best Actor Oscar. (Dir: Fred Zinnemann, 85 mins.)

High Noon, Part Two: The Return of Will Kane (MTV 1980)** Lee Majors, David Carradine, Pernell Roberts. Predictable western yarn. Majors cannot live up to the memory of Oscar-winning Gary Cooper in this watered-down sequel to the successful movie "High Noon." Filmed in Tucson. (Dir: Jerry Jameson, 104 mins.)

High Plains Drifter (1973)** Clint Eastwood, Verna Bloom. For bloodthirsty fans of the tough, silent, and sexy sado-superheroics

of Clint Eastwood as a cowboy to reckon with. You could swear Sergio Leone directed this ambling, violence-ridden western but it is Clint himself who called the directorial shots. The stranger (Clint) rides into the town of Lago, killing three varmints, raping a willing wench, and taking over in anticipation of standing up to three other culprits just released from prison. (Dir: Clint Eastwood, 105 mins.)

High-Powered Rifle, The (1960)* Willard Parker, Allison Hayes. (Dir: Maury Dexter, 62 mins.)

High Risk (MTV 1976)** Victor Buono, Joseph Sirola, Don Stroud. Another pilot for an adventure series which starts off well but dissipates before long. A group of former circus performers exercise their penchant for larceny by executing an elaborate plan to steal a jewel-encrusted mask from a foreign embassy in Washington, D.C. The planning is more fun than the actual robbery sequences and besides, it was all done so much better in "Topkapi." (Dir: Sam O'Steen, 72 mins.)

High Rolling (Australia, 1978)** Joseph Bottoms, Grigor Taylor, Judy Davis. The scenery is better than the story as two pals turn to crime in order to get along. Beautiful Australian locales make up for plot shortcomings, although there is a lot of action along with the comedy. (Dir: Igor Auzins, 90 mins.)

High School (1969)**** A brilliant documentary about a middle-class American high school in Philadelphia and the way in which it—and thousands of other schools all over the country—kills the creative spirit in students and graduates uniformed robots. Produced and directed by Frederick Wiseman, the most important and gifted documentary filmmaker at work in America today. This is a chilling statement about the intellectual and moral bankruptcy of so much contemporary education. Should be seen by all adults and students in or above the junior-high-school level. No famous paid actors here—just typical students in joyless classrooms, where banality is encouraged by the generally pitiful, brutalizing faculty. (Dir: Frederick Wiseman, 75 mins.)

High School Confidential (1958)** Russ Tamblyn, Mamie Van Doren, Jan Sterling. Made when a teen hero could be a narc. Tamblyn is out to bust the pushers, and Jerry Lee Lewis does the title tune. Lots of groovy jive talk and good dragstrip scenes. (Dir: Jack Arnold, 85 mins.)

High School Hellcats (1958)*½ Yvonne Lime, Jana Lund. (Dir: Edward Bernds, 70 mins.)

High Sierra (1941)***½ Humphrey Bogart, Ida Lupino, Arthur Kennedy. Tired old killer on the loose theme receives an exciting rejuvenation from this superb cast aided by an excellent script and production. (Dir: Raoul Walsh, 100 mins.)

High Society (1956)*** Bing Crosby, Grace Kelly, Frank Sinatra, Celeste Holm, Louis

Armstrong. Musical version of "The Philadephia Story," about the efforts of a wealthy man to win back his ex-wife who's about to be remarried, and the reporters who become entangled in the romantic complications. With a stellar cast and a Cole Porter score, it should have been better than it is, but somehow it lacks the sparkle of the original. Nevertheless, pleasant fun. (Dir: Charles Walters, 107 mins.)

High Time (1960)*** Bing Crosby, Fabian, Tuesday Weld. What happens when a wealthy widower returns to college to complete his education. Episodic comedy starts excellently but wears thin before the conclusion. Generally good fun. (Dir: Blake Edwards, 103 mins.)

High Treason (Great Britain, 1952)***½ Liam Redmond, Mary Morris. Thrilling spy drama with plot twists that keep the pace fast and tense. Good script. (Dir: Roy Boulting, 93 mins.)

High Wall (1947)*** Robert Taylor, Audrey Totter, Herbert Marshall. Lady doctor helps a man regain his memory, then proves he didn't kill his wife. Suspenseful, well acted mystery melodrama. (Dir: Curtis Bernhardt, 99 mins.)

High, Wide and Handsome (1937)*** Irene Dunne, Randolph Scott, Dorothy Lamour. Musical tale of the robust adventure which surrounded the discovery of oil in Pennsylvania around 1860. Music by Jerome Kern and Oscar Hammerstein II. Not as good as it seems when you study the credits, but enterprising. (Dir: Rouben Mamoulian, 110 mins.)

High Wind in Jamaica, A (U.S.-Great Britain, 1965)***½ Anthony Quinn, James Coburn. Good adventure drama with fine acting by the cast headed by Quinn as the captain of a pirate vessel. There's a great deal of action when Captain Quinn's ship encounters another vessel and takes some children and the crew. It turns into a stark drama before the climax and never lets up until the tragic ending. Based on the famous novel. (Dir: Alexander Mackendrick, 104 mins.)

Higher and Higher (1943)*** Michele Morgan, Jack Haley, Frank Sinatra, Victor Borge. Man unable to pay his servants forms a corporation with them. Entertaining musical comedy. (Dir: Tim Whelan, 90 mins.)

Highly Dangerous (Great Britain, 1951)*** Margaret Lockwood, Dane Clark. Pretty lady scientist and an American reporter risk their necks obtaining vital information behind the Iron Curtain. Exciting, entertaining spy thriller. (Dir: Roy Baker, 88 mins.)

Highway Dragnet (1954)** Joan Bennett, Richard Conte. A routine chase film of an ex-marine, accused of murdering a girl he has just met. Richard Conte gives a good performance despite the weak script. (Dir: Nathan Juran, 71 mins.)

Highway to Battle (Great Britain, 1961)** Gerald Heinz, Margaret Tyzack. Enemy agents search for a political refugee. Standard espionage drama. (Dir: Ernest Morris, 71 mins.)

Hijack (MTV 1973)** David Janssen and Keenan Wynn are the stars of this suspenseful film about two truck drivers, down on their luck, who take on the job of driving a secret cargo from Los Angeles to Houston. On-location footage in the Antelope Valley, near the Mojave Desert, and a number of gripping auto scenes spark the show. (Dir: Leonard Horn, 90 mins.)

Hilda Crane (1956)*½ Jean Simmons, Guy Madison, Jean-Pierre Aumont. (Dir: Philip Dunne, 87 mins.)

Hill, The (Great Britain, 1965)***½ Sean Connery, Harry Andrews, Ossie Davis. Director Sidney Lumet has etched a chilling study of a British military prison in Africa during WW II. The hitch here is that the inmates are British soldiers. Their almost inhuman treatment makes an absorbing and memorable drama. Sean Connery has never been better as an outspoken, tough prisoner and the supporting cast is flawless, especially Harry Andrews as the sinister head of the detention camp. You won't soon forget the scenes of Connery assaulting the ever crumbling "Hill." (Dir: Sidney Lumet, 122 mins.)

Hill 24 Doesn't Answer (1955)***½ Edward Mulhare, Haya Hararit. First feature made in Israel. Story of four Israeli volunteers who defended their homeland at the cost of their lives. Grim drama with numerous moving scenes. (Dir: Thorold Dickinson, 100 mins.)

Hills Have Eyes, The (1977)** James Whitworth, John Steadman, Janus Blythe. An extended family are stranded in the desert when their trailer breaks down, and they are preyed upon by a grisly band of savage genetic mutants, a shocking reverse image of the normal nuclear family. Former literature professor Wes Craven is a director making a serious attempt at social criticism within the horror genre. (90 mins.)

Hills of Home (1948)*** Lassie, Donald Crisp, Janet Leigh, Edmund Gwenn. Sentimental warm tale of a Scottish doctor (Gwenn) and his beloved collie. Certainly the best dog loves man film since "Lassie Come Home." Big difference here is that Gwenn steals the honors from Lassie. (Dir: Fred M. Wilcox, 97 mins.)

Himiko (Japan, 1974)** Shima Iwashita, Rentaro Mikuni, Masao Kusakari. A savage Japanese rendition of national roots. Set in prehistoric Japan, with the island ruled by a matriarchy of half-Korean priestesses, giving the lie to the myth of Japanese racial purity. Cruelty and violence are seen as fundamental to the national character. One of director Masahiro Shinoda's best. Music by Toru Takemitsu and screenplay by the respected woman poet Taeko Tomioka. (100 mins.)

Hindenburg, The (1975)*½ George C. Scott,

Anne Bancroft, William Atherton, Burgess Meredith, Charles Durning. (Dir: Robert Wise, 125 mins.)

Hippodrome (Germany, 1961)** Gerhard Reidmann, Willy Birgel, Margit Nunke. Adventures, romantic and otherwise, of a girl performer in a circus. Ponderous. (Dir: Herbert Gruber, 96 mins.)

Hired Gun, The (1957)** Rory Calhoun, Anne Francis, Vince Edwards, Chuck Connors. Professional gunfighter is offered a large reward to bring back an escaped murderess. Average western with a better than average cast. (Dir: Ray Nazarro, 63 mins.)

Hired Hand, The (1971)**½ Peter Fonda, Verna Bloom, Warren Oates. Uneven, but often sensitive drama set in New Mexico in 1880, and directed by Peter Fonda. Verna Bloom takes the acting honors with a moving performance as the patient wife of Fonda, an itinerant cowhand. Aided by excellent cinematography and an unobtrusive but helpful musical score. (Dir: Peter Fonda, 93 mins.)

Hired Wife (1940)*** Rosalind Russell, Brian Aherne. Super-secretary marries her boss for business reasons, finds domesticity more difficult than work. Entertaining comedy. (Dir: William A. Seiter, 93 mins.)

Hireling, The (Great Britain, 1973)***½ Robert Shaw, Sarah Miles. This adaptation from L. P. Hartley is an affecting tale of passion complicated by the Byzantine intricacies of the British class system circa '20. Shaw is the rigid, class-bound, inwardly raging chauffeur who falls in love with a titled lady, Miles, who seeks only friendship. Alan Bridges directs in an intelligent, unelaborated style that elicits the best from his two leads. (108 mins.)

Hiroshima, Mon Amour (France, 1959)**** Emmanuele Riva, Eiji Okada. Director Alain Resnais's revolutionary film about the "impossible love" between a French actress and a Japanese architect integrates past and present, poetic imagery and documentary footage, music and the eerie poetry of Marguerite Duras's dialogue into a structure that stunned audiences then but is largely old stuff now. (88 mins.)

His Butler's Sister (1943)*** Deanna Durbin, Franchot Tone, Pat O'Brien. A pleasant romantic comedy that has Deanna Durbin's singing to bolster the proceedings. Deanna, as a maid, gets her employer to fall in love with her. (Dir: Frank Borzage, 94 mins.)

His First Flame (1927)**½ Harry Langdon, Ruth Hiatt, Natalie Kingston. The last feature that Langdon made before his disastrous foray into self-production and -direction. Not his best, but a creditable comedy, true to the fundamentals of the Langdon personality (Frank Capra wrote the script with Arthur Ripley). A sister loves college grad Harry for his money, until her sister sets the house on fire to spur him to win her and her true love. (Dir: Harry Edwards, 51 mins.)

His Girl Friday (1940)**** Cary Grant, Rosalind Russell, Ralph Bellamy, Helen Mack, Gene Lockhart. Director Howard Hawks made "Front Page"'s Hildy Johnson into a woman, and that made all the difference. Hawks developed a technique of overlapping the dialogue, with throwaway syllables in front and back, so that the audience could hear every word that counted, and the impression was of even faster delivery. Grant's brilliance as a physical actor has never been so put to the test, and Russell is more than his equal. It's become fashionable to say that they can't make 'em like this anymore, but the truth is, they could—they don't. (92 mins.)

His Kind of Woman (1951)*** Robert Mitchum, Jane Russell, Vincent Price. Fall guy in a plot to bring an expatriated racketeer back to the U. S. gets wise and rounds up the crooks. Long but lively, entertaining melodrama. (Dir: John Farrow, 120 mins.)

His Majesty O'Keefe (Great Britain, 1954)*** Burt Lancaster. Action packed pirate story about the derring-do of a brave adventurer, Burt Lancaster, Joan Rice. Fun for the younger set. (Dir: Byron Haskin, 92 mins.)

History is Made at Night (1937)**½ Charles Boyer, Jean Arthur. The eternal triangle of wife, husband and other man in a curious mixture of comedy and melodrama. Some bright moments, including a finely portrayed shipwreck sequence. (Dir: Frank Borzage, 110 mins.)

History of Mr. Polly, The (Great Britain, 1949)***½ John Mills, Sally Ann Howes. A young draper carries a dream of adventure replacing his placid life, finally achieves the dream. Witty, tastefully done period comedy-drama. Excellent performances. (Dir: Anthony Pelissier, 96 mins.)

Hit! (1973)**½ Billy Dee Williams, Richard Pryor, Paul Hampton, Gwen Welles. Director Sidney J. Furie takes too long, but he can coax amazing improvised performances from his actors. Gable lookalike Williams is the CIA agent fashioning his own private vendetta. Pryor is Williams's hilarious jivey sidekick, and Welles is the strung-out hooker from Barnard. Action-packed (after the first half) and entertaining in a mock-serious sort of way. (134 mins.)

Hit and Run (1957)* Hugo Haas, Cleo Moore, Vince Edwards. Run! (Dir: Hugo Haas, 84 mins.)

Hit Lady (1974)**½ Yvette Mimieux. Yvette Mimieux wrote the screenplay for this predictable but slick gangster drama in which she stars as the beauty playing a cool, collected and deadly hired assassin. The best scenes involve the "hit lady's" setting up of her victims and, for those who don't catch on earlier, there's a twist ending. (Dir: Tracy Keenan Wynn, 72 mins.)

Hit Man (1972)**½ Bernie Casey, Pam

Grier, Sam Laws. A black remake of the British crime film "Get Carter," written and directed by George Armitage. Competent melodrama, somewhat hamstrung by budget limitations. (90 mins.)

Hit the Deck (1955)** Vic Damone, Tony Martin, Jane Powell, Debbie Reynolds, Walter Pidgeon. The attempt to make another "On the Town," this time with three sailors on leave in San Francisco, is foredoomed to failure. Choreography by Hermes Pan. The good songs include Vincent Youmans's "Sometimes I'm Happy" and Billy Rose's "More Than You Know." (Dir: Roy Rowland, 112 mins.)

Hit the Ice (1943)** Bud Abbott, Lou Costello, Ginny Simms. Sidewalk photographers are mistaken for bank robbers, catch up with the real crooks in Sun Valley. One of the funnier A & C comedies; plenty of laughs and fast action. (Dir: Charles Lamont, 73 mins.)

Hitched (MTV 1971)* Tim Matheson, Sally Field, Neville Brand. (Dir: Boris Sagal, 100 mins.)

Hitchhike (MTV 1974)** Cloris Leachman, Richard Brandon, Sherry Jackson. Miss Leachman plays Los Angeles motorist Claire Stephens, who picks up a hitchhiker on her way to San Francisco. Her passenger is on the run after murdering his stepmother. Routine stuff. (Dir: Gordon Hessler, 74 mins.)

Hitchhiker, The (1953)***½ Frank Lovejoy, Edmond O'Brien, William Talman. Two men on a camping trip are waylaid and held by a desperate fugitive. Excellent, spell-binding melodrama, tense and exciting; directed by Ida Lupino. (71 mins.)

Hitler (1962)** Richard Basehart, Maria Emo. Story of the rise to power of the infamous Nazi dictator. Despite the good intentions it has nothing unseen before—and doesn't have the production values necessary for the scope of the tale. Basehart tries, but misses as Adolf. (Dir: Stuart Heisler, 107 mins.)

Hitler: The Last Ten Days (Great Britain-Italy, 1973)* Alec Guinness, Simon Ward, Diane Cilento, Adolfo Celi. (Dir: Ennio de Concini, 106 mins.)

Hitler's Children (1942)*** Tim Holt, Bonita Granville. Two youngsters are caught in the relentless gears of the Nazi war machine. Good drama of wartime Germany. (Dir: Edward Dmytryk, 83 mins.)

Hitler's Executioners—See: **Executioners, The**

Hitler's Gold—See: **Inside Out**

Hitler's Madman (1943)***½ John Carradine, Patricia Morison, Alan Curtis. Director Douglas Sirk shot his first American film in about a week with incomparable visual style. The narrative of the determined Czech resistance to the barbarities of Reinhard Heydrich is compelling (84 mins.)

H. M. Pulham, Esq. (1941)***½ Hedy Lamarr, Robert Young, Ruth Hussey, Van Heflin. The life of a stuffy Bostonian who is momentarily uprooted from his life by a love affair. Tastefully produced, superbly directed drama, with Young giving a superb performance. (Dir: King Vidor, 120 mins.)

Hobbit, The (MTV 1977)***½ Orson Bean, John Huston, Otto Preminger, Richard Boone, Brother Theodore. Enchanting animated dramatization of J. R. R. Tolkien's popular novel. The Hobbit is so sweet and innocent a little being; the world of adventure he is forced to enter is revealed in overpowering, richly colored, imaginative drawings. You'll have a favorite among the dragons and goblins who try to threaten him, but the froglike creature Gollum who calls him "My precious" is definitely ours. For old and young alike. (Dir: Arthur Rankin, Jr., 78 mins.)

Hobson's Choice (Great Britain, 1954)**** Charles Laughton, Brenda de Banzie, John Mills. Delicious working class comedy, with Laughton as a tyrannical bootmaker brought to heel by his plain-spoken daughter and her meek husband. Under David Lean's direction what should have been an innocuous British comedy has style and life. Laughton's bombast is overshadowed by remarkable performances of de Banzie and Mills. (107 mins.)

Hoffman (Great Britain, 1970)**½ Peter Sellers, Sinead Cusack. Certainly not one of Sellers' best entries, but there are some off-beat laughs along the way in this story about a lonely middle-aged man who blackmails a young female typist into spending a week in his apartment. Sellers' character is a little like an aged Benjamin Braddock from "The Graduate." Screenplay by Ernest Gebler from his novel. (Dir: Alvin Rakoff, 113 mins.)

Hold Back the Dawn (1941)***½ Charles Boyer, Olivia de Havilland, Paulette Goddard. Rather exceptional romantic melodrama with a seedy Boyer desperately trying to marry a vulnerable American (de Havilland) in order to enter the United States. Director Mitchell Leisen softened the mordant Billy Wilder-Charles Brackett screenplay. Photographed by Leo Tover. (115 mins.)

Hold Back the Night (1956)**½ John Payne, Mona Freeman. Nothing exceptional but fairly entertaining Korean War story. (Dir: Allan Dwan, 80 mins.)

Hold Back Tomorrow (1955)* Cleo Moore, John Agar. (Dir: Hugo Haas, 75 mins.)

Hold On! (1966)*½ Peter Noone, Shelley Fabares, Herman's Hermits. (Dir: Arthur Lubin, 85 mins.)

Hold That Co-ed (1938)***½ John Barrymore, George Murphy, Joan Davis. Barrymore in a hilarious musical comedy about politics and football. The great man appears as a caricature of all political demagogues and he's magnificent. Good fun. Murphy has since added some comedy to non-Hollywood politics. (Dir: George Marshall, 80 mins.)

Hold That Ghost (1941)*** Bud Abbott, Lou Costello, Joan Davis. A & C get involved with a dead gangster in a supposedly haunted house. One of their better comedies. (Dir: Arthur Lubin, 80 mins.)

Hole in the Head, A (1959)**** Frank Sinatra, Edward G. Robinson, Eleanor Parker, Carolyn Jones, Keenan Wynn, Thelma Ritter. The last brilliant work of director Frank Capra's career. Sinatra gives a rounded performance as a Miami hotel owner on the verge of financial ruin, scampering everywhere to raise enough capital to stay in business. (120 mins.)

Holiday (1938)**** Cary Grant, Katharine Hepburn, Lew Ayres, Edward Everett Horton, Binnie Barnes. Director George Cukor's masterful film adopted from Philip Barry's play about a society girl (Hepburn) who falls for her sister's charming, eccentric fiancé (Grant). The light nonconformist comedy achieves perfection, but beneath it lies Cukor's serious concern for the ways in which we choose to live our lives. There have been a thousand nonconformist comedies, but only one Holiday. (Dir: George Cukor, 93 mins.)

Holiday Affair (1949)**½ Robert Mitchum, Janet Leigh, Wendell Corey. War widow with a small son is faced with having to choose between two suitors. Mildly amusing comedy-drama. (Dir: Don Hartman, 87 mins.)

Holiday Camp (Great Britain, 1947)**½ Flora Robson, Dennis Price, Jack Warner. Typical family has many varied adventures at a vacation resort. Loosely written, uneven comedy-drama. (Dir: Ken Annakin, 97 mins.)

Holiday for Henrietta (France, 1954)***½ Hildegarde Neff, Michel Auclair, Dany Robin. Captivating comedy about the making of a movie, and the participants' inability to distinguish fact from fiction. Plot summary doesn't do justice to the inventive, stylish quality of the film. (Dir: Julian Duvivier, 103 mins.)

Holiday for Lovers (1959)** Clifton Webb, Jane Wyman, Carol Lynley, Gary Crosby. Psychiatrist and his wife face the difficulties of keeping their daughters from romance while on a tour of South America. Lightweight romantic comedy has all been done before. (Dir: Henry Levin, 103 mins.)

Holiday for Sinners (1952)*** Gig Young, Janice Rule, Keenan Wynn. The future and plans of a young doctor are changed when a broken-down prizefighter commits murder. Offbeat drama taking place in New Orleans during the Mardi Gras. Unusual in plotting, presentation—fine performance by Wynn as the fighter. (Dir: Gerald Mayer, 72 mins.)

Holiday in Havana (1949)** Desi Arnaz, Mary Hatcher. A Cuban beat, Desi Arnaz, and you have this mild musical comedy about carnival time in Havana. (Dir: Jean Yarbrough, 73 mins.)

Holiday in Mexico (1946)*** Walter Pidgeon, Jane Powell, Xavier Cugat. Semi-classical music is spiced with some Latin American melodies in this musical treat. Plot about a widowed ambassador to Mexico and his teen-age daughter who tries to run his house doesn't interfere with Miss Powell's singing, Cugat's rhumbas and Jose Iturbi's piano. (Dir: George Sidney, 127 mins.)

Holiday in Spain—See: **Scent of Mystery**

Holiday Inn (1942)***½ Fred Astaire, Bing Crosby. Irving Berlin's finest music ("White Christmas," "Easter Parade," "Be Careful, It's My Heart"), plus Bing and Fred add up to a screen delight. (Dir: Mark Sandrich, 101 mins.)

Hollow Image (MTV 1979)**½ Robert Hooks, Saundra Sharp, Dick Anthony, Hattie Winston. Author Lee Hunkins describes the dilemma of a black woman who is "making it" as a department store fashion buyer, but feels she has lost touch with her black identity. The drama, though flawed by a pat resolution of the heroine's problems, is sound and believable. (Dir: Marvin J. Chomsky, 106 mins.)

Hollow Triumph—See: **Scar, The**

Holly and the Ivy, The (Great Britain, 1953)***½ Ralph Richardson, Celia Johnson, Margaret Leighton, Denholm Elliot. A country parson gathers his family together at Christmas, discovers that because of him they are unhappy. Superlatively acted drama, slowly paced but always absorbing. (Dir: George More O'Ferrall, 80 mins.)

Hollywood Boulevard (1936)** John Halliday, Marsha Hunt, Robert Cummings, Gary Cooper, Francis X. Bushman. Director Robert Florey uses a number of fallen silent stars in bit parts to tell the story of a fading matinee idol's attempt to recapture the spotlight by writing his telltale memoirs. Location shooting on famous, long-gone Hollywood locations: Knickerbocker Hotel, the Trocadero Bar, and Sardi's Restaurant. (68 mins.)

Hollywood Boulevard (1976)** Candice Rialson, Mary Woronov, Rita George, Paul Bartel, Jonathan Kaplan. The ultimate in-joke movie, with a number of Roger Corman alumni (among them Bartel and Kaplan) satirizing themselves and the B movies they make. Incomprehensible to anyone who hasn't been following today's exploitation filmmaking with tremendous care. (Dirs: Joe Dante, Allen Arkush, 83 mins.)

Hollywood Canteen (1944)**½ Bette Davis, Joan Crawford, Jack Carson, Dane Clark. Davis is the chief hostess and just about everybody—Joan Crawford, John Garfield, Ida Lupino, Peter Lorre, Sydney Greenstreet, Alexis Smith, a very young Eleanor Parker, the Andrews Sisters, Barbara Stanwyck, Jack Carson, Eddie Cantor, and Jack Benny—makes a guest appearance in this piece of WW II propaganda. One of the first directorial efforts of Delmer Daves. (124 mins.)

Hollywood Cavalcade (1939)** Don Ameche, Alice Faye, Buster Keaton. Mindless Fox musical set in the early days of the film industry. Keaton, who clawed his way back from alcoholism, appears in a Keystone Kops sequence with Chester Conklin and a few other poignant survivors of the silents. Color. (Dir: Irving Cummings, 96 mins.)

Hollywood Cowboy—See: **Heart of the West**

Hollywood Hotel (1937)***½ Dick Powell, Glenda Farrell, the two Lane sisters (sans Priscilla), Frances Langford, Hugh Herbert, Alan Mowbray, Louella Parsons. Surprise! A genuine sleeper, in fact. One of the least known of the finest Hollywood musicals, this Busby Berkeley effort is limber in a way that anticipates the fifties by fifteen years, and shows that Berkeley's style was neither so obvious nor so rigid as the parodists would have us believe. Though male chauvinistic as all get-out, the story moves, the songs are perky, and the musical numbers are ingenious without being disingenuous (as some of the pattern-choreography of Berkeley's early thirties work was). (Dir: Busby Berkeley, 109 mins.)

Hollywood Knights, The (1980)*½ Fran Drescher, Stuart Pankin, Tony Danza, Michelle Pfeiffer. (Dir: Floyd Mutrux, 94 mins.)

Hollywood or Bust (1956)*** Dean Martin, Jerry Lewis, Anita Ekberg. Director Frank Tashlin's relentlessly, happily vulgar satire on '50s pop culture and breast fetishism. Jerry wins a convertible in a lottery, so he and Dean set out for the glitter capital, hoping to meet Jerry's favorite squiggling starlet. The best of their films. (95 mins.)

Hollywood Party (1934)** Jimmy Durante, Laurel and Hardy, the Three Stooges, Lupe Velez, Arthur Treacher, Robert Young. Everyone on the MGM lot was in this, and nearly every director there did a piece of it. When they put it all together it didn't jell, so they asked director Allan Dwan to look at it and see what he could do. "It's a disaster," he said. A voice beside him in the screening room: "At last, we got a genius." It was Louis B. Mayer, and he wasn't kidding. Dwan concocted a device of having Durante dream the whole mess, so it wouldn't have to seem connected, and for a pretext they had him waiting for his wife to get dressed for the party. "Yeah, but who'll play Durante's wife?" groaned Mayer. "How about his wife?" replied Dwan. "Genius!" said Mayer. Dwan shot two days' footage and got a nice fat check. Songs by Rodgers and Hart, Gus Kahn, and Arthur Freed. (68 mins.)

Hollywood Revue of 1929, The (1929)*½ Jack Benny, Conrad Nagel, Joan Crawford, Buster Keaton, John Gilbert, Norma Shearer, Marion Davies, Laurel and Hardy. (Dir: Charles Reisner, 130 mins.)

Hollywood Strangler, The—See: **Don't Answer the Phone**

Holy Matrimony (1943)***½ Monty Woolley, Gracie Fields. Superbly acted tale of a great artist who poses as his dead valet, gets married and involved in scandal when his wife innocently sells some of his paintings. Wonderful fun. Remake of *His Double Life*, 1933. (Dir: John M. Stahl, 87 mins.)

Holy Mountain, The (U.S.-Mexico, 1973)**½ Alexandro Jodorowsky, Horacio Salinas, Ramona Saunders. Director ("El Topo") Jodorowsky's film about a Jesus-like protagonist who encounters a Zen master/cosmic teacher called the Alchemist (played by the filmmaker). Under The Alchemist's discipline, a group of the most powerful, evil people on earth are drawn together and formed into an egoless commune that assaults the Holy Mountain of ancient legend in order to find the secret of immortality. (126 mins.)

Homage to Chagall—The Colours of Love (Canada, 1976)***½ A visually stunning, understandably admiring tribute to the great 20th-century artist Marc Chagall, written, produced and directed by Canadian documentary filmmaker Harry Rasky. Produced originally for the CBC television, the focus is almost entirely on the paintings and other work of the great Russian-born artist. The luminous paintings, photographed imaginatively in many parts of the world and from many collections, are enough reason to watch and be dazzled. (Dir: Harry Rasky, 88 mins.)

Hombre (1967)***½ Paul Newman, Fredric March, Diane Cilento. Thoughtful, generally absorbing western, starring Paul Newman as a white man raised by Indians. The plot begins to resemble the John Wayne classic "Stagecoach" when Newman boards a stage on which Fredric March and the rest of the principals are passengers, and there is a final shoot out between the good guys (Newman and pals), and the outlaws. However, the screenplay by Irving Ravetch and Harriet Frank, Jr. raises some interesting human and moral issues along the way, and it's all held together by Martin Ritt's taut direction. (Dir: Martin Ritt, 111 mins.)

Home at Seven (Great Britain, 1952)*** Ralph Richardson, Margaret Leighton, Jack Hawkins. A bank clerk returns home to discover he has been missing one day, due to amnesia, and that he is suspect in a murder. Clever mystery melodrama, well acted and directed (by Richardson) and with several twists. (Dir: Ralph Richardson, 85 mins.)

Home Before Dark (1958)**½ Jean Simmons, Dan O'Herlihy, Rhonda Fleming, Efrem Zimbalist, Jr. Jean Simmons gives a fine performance in this drama about a young woman who comes home after being hospitalized for a nervous breakdown. Her struggle to pick up the pieces of her broken life is touchingly portrayed. The film loses its initial punch about halfway through and settles into soap opera. (Dir: Mervyn Le Roy, 136 mins.)

Home for the Holidays (MTV 1972)** Eleanor Parker, Sally Field, Julie Harris, Walter Brennan. Murder melodrama uses all the standard tricks to convey terror. Unhappy daughter returning to their father's bedside for a family get-together, only to become the target of a deranged killer. (Dir: John Llewellyn Moxey, 73 mins.)

Home from the Hill (1960)**** Robert Mitchum, Eleanor Parker, George Peppard, George Hamilton. Powerful yarn of a southern town, a roistering landowner, his son, and the youth whose relationship to the family causes tragedy. Fine characterization builds in interest, makes the drama absorbing throughout its length. Excellent performances, especially by Mitchum and Peppard. Recommended. (Dir: Vincente Minelli, 150 mins.)

Home in Indiana (1944)*** Walter Brennan, Lon McCallister, Jeanne Crain, June Haver. A routine plot but delightful performances and photography make this film about harness racing a pleasure to see. Lon drives a blind filly in the big race and you'll find yourself cheering. (Dir: Henry Hathaway, 103 mins.)

Home Is the Hero (Ireland, 1961)*** Arthur Kennedy, Walter Macken. Based on a well-known play by Macken, this is a leisurely drama about a violent-tempered man who returns to his household after serving a prison sentence for manslaughter, the changes he finds, he tries to make within himself. Some fine acting by the Abbey Players, authentic atmosphere helps the slow pace. (Dir: Fielder Cook, 83 mins.)

Home Movies (1980)***½ Nancy Allen, Keith Gordon, Kirk Douglas, Gerrit Graham, Vincent Gardenia. This maligned comedy is one of Director Brian De Palma's best works. Some of the wacky bits are genuinely inspired, both repulsive and funny. Allen and Gordon are standouts. Gordon is the lad who is subjected to "star therapy," calculated to elevate him from being a mere extra in his own life. Made with the collaboration of students at Sarah Lawrence College. (90 mins.)

Home of the Brave (1949)***½ Lloyd Bridges, Frank Lovejoy, James Edwards. Negro soldier on a dangerous Pacific patrol is made a mental case by the intolerance of his white cohorts. Hard-hitting drama makes its point well, is excellently acted, especially by Edwards. (Dir: Mark Robson, 85 mins.)

Homebodies (1974)**½ Frances Fuller, Peter Frocco, Paula Trueman. Six elderly people who are being evicted from a brownstone to make way for a skyscraper take to murder to defend their home. Strange horror comedy for those seeking the offbeat. (Dir: Larry Yust, 96 mins.)

Homeboys (1978)**½ A documentary about the young Chicanos of Cuarto Flats, a housing project in Boyle Heights. This began as a film about the wall murals of east L.A. and became the story of the muralist. Explodes myths about Chicano culture just when those myths are being revitalized by major studio projects. (Dir: Bill Yahruas).

Homecoming (1948)** Clark Gable, Lana Turner, Anne Baxter, John Hodiak. Clark is married to Anne in this one but through flashbacks he manages to have his torrid box-office dynamite romance with Lana. It has a war background but it's nothing to shout about. (Dir: Mervyn Le Roy, 113 mins.)

Homecoming: A Christmas Story, The (MTV 1971)*** Patricia Neal, Richard Thomas, Edgar Bergan, Ellen Corby. Pilot for "The Waltons." Earl Hamner, Jr.'s play about a Virginia mountain clan preparing for Christmas back during the depression, invests the characters with charm and civility. Neal (the mother) is the guiding light who holds the family together while worrying over the return of her husband, who's been forced to work in another town. Thomas is John-Boy (author Hamner as a youth). (Dir: Fielder Cook, 104 mins.)

Homecoming, The (Great Britain, 1973)**** Cyril Cusack, Ian Holm, Vivien Merchant, Paul Rogers, Michael Jayston. A marvelous adaptation of Harold Pinter's lacerating, fascinating play about the interpersonal relationships of a British working-class family. Peter Hall, who directed the triumphant stage production, repeats the assignment and it's even more savage, if possible, than on stage. The poignant Pinter pauses and exchanges are stunningly acted by many of the original cast members. Paul Rogers, playing Max, a retired butcher who taunts and competes with his three grown sons, is a standout along with Merchant, the playwright's talented ex-wife. Pinter adapted for the screen. An American Film Theatre presentation. (Dir: Peter Hall, 116 mins.)

Homestretch, The (1947)** Cornel Wilde, Maureen O'Hara. Some wonderful horse racing shots from Ascot to Churchill Downs but the story makes you wish they had eliminated the actors and just shown the races. Fancy-free horse owner and disapproving wife is the worn frame. (Dir: H. Bruce Humberstone, 96 mins.)

Hondo (1953)***½ John Wayne, Geraldine Page, James Arness, Ward Bond. One of Hollywood's best adult westerns. Strong in human relationships with a minimum of violence. Broadway actress Geraldine Page makes her starring film debut in this much underrated western. (Dir: John Farrow, 83 mins.)

Honey Pot, The (Great Britain-U.S.-Italy, 1967)*** Rex Harrison, Susan Hayward, Cliff Robertson, Capucine, Edie Adams, Maggie Smith. Even a second-rate Joseph

L. Mankiewicz film is better than most high-style comedies. Here Mankiewicz takes his turn at updating Ben Jonson's "Volpone." Rex Harrison is a wealthy scoundrel who invites three of his former amours (the Misses Hayward, Adams and Capucine) to share his last days in his Venetian showplace and the intrigues begin. It's all a big fraud, as are most of the characters, but Mankiewicz' brittle, sophisticated dialogue, expertly handled by Harrison and company, is worth savoring, and Maggie Smith is a special delight. For those film buffs who care about such matters, Mankiewicz's screenplay was based partially on a play "Mr. Fox of Venice," a novel called "The Evil of the Day," and the aforementioned Ben Jonson, who is not a member of the Screenwriters Guild. Alternate title: **It Comes Up Murder.** (Dir: Joseph L. Mankiewicz, 131 mins.)

Honeymoon (1947)** Shirley Temple, Guy Madison, Franchot Tone. GI has trouble marrying his fiancee, since he only has a three-day pass. Uninspired comedy. (Dir: William Keighley, 74 mins.)

Honeymoon Hotel (1964)** Robert Goulet, Nancy Kwan, Robert Morse. When a guy's wedding breaks up at the altar, his wolfish buddy joins him on the honeymoon trip, and they check in at a hotel—for honeymooners only. Flimsy farce defeats the hard-working players. (Dir: Henry Levin, 89 mins.)

Honeymoon in Bali (1939)** Fred MacMurray, Madeleine Carroll. Witty romantic comedy about a cold, calculating career girl who is conquered by a man. Silly and out of hand in spots, but very entertaining. (Dir: Edward H. Griffith, 100 mins.)

Honeymoon Killers, The (1970)**½ Tony Lo Bianco, Shirley Stoler, Doris Roberts, Mary Jane Higby. Based on the multiple murderers, Martha Beck and Raymond Fernandez, who were executed in 1951. This low-budgeted drama succeeds in many departments where other more ambitiously produced films fail. Tony Lo Bianco and Shirley Stoler portray a pair of ruthless killers who pose as a nurse and her brother, and seek out wealthy women who fall prey to their murderous schemes. Although the plot is rather direct and straightforward, it's the playing, especially by Lo Bianco in his starring debut, which impresses. Photographed in black and white. Written and skillfully directed by Leonard Kastle. (107 mins.)

Honeymoon Machine, The (1961)*** Steve McQueen, Brigid Bazlen, Jim Hutton, Paula Prentiss. Navy officer gets an idea to use an electronic brain on board his vessel to beat the roulette wheel at the Venice casino. Entertaining comedy, with some youthful players getting the chance to show their stuff. Good fun. (Dir: Richard Thorpe, 87 mins.)

Honeymoon with a Stranger (MTV 1969)**½ Janet Leigh, Rossano Brazzi. This is the type of melodramatic opus Joan Crawford and Greer Garson used to suffer through during the forties. This time out, the troubled gal is Janet Leigh, who spends her honeymoon in Spain looking for her husband, who has disappeared, and trying to convince the local police that the man who claims to be her spouse really isn't. It's all complicated and terribly contrived but the scenery, including Miss Leigh, is nice to look at, and for some, the twist at the end will come as a surprise. (Dir: John Peyser, 73 mins.)

Honeymoons Will Kill You (Spain, 1967)*½ Tony Russell. (Dir: Mario Amendola, 91 mins.)

Honeysuckle Rose (1980)*** Willie Nelson, Dyan Cannon, Amy Irving, Slim Pickens. Not much of interest in the old plot line; director Jerry Schatzberg concentrates his energies on atmosphere, milieu, and music. It may not be great drama, yet it boasts some of the best footage in any film this year. Nelson is the married, traveling music legend who can't help straying while off the homestead; his easygoing manner is effective. Acting by the rest is full of niceties, and Robby Muller's camerawork imbues the images with a special glow—the Texas light never looked like this. (119 mins.)

Hong Kong (1951)** Ronald Reagan, Rhonda Fleming. A WW II veteran and a mission schoolteacher tangle with jewel thieves and murderers in this average adventure story. (Dir: Lewis R. Foster, 92 mins.)

Hong Kong Affair (1958)* Jack Kelly, May Wynn. (Dir: Paul F. Heard, 79 mins.)

Hong Kong Confidential (1958)**½ Gene Barry, Beverly Tyler. Another in the expose series of the criminal machines of famous cities. This one is set in the Orient in the port of Hong Kong, where crime runs rampant until our hero, Gene Barry, enters the picture. Fast moving crime drama. (Dir: Edward L. Cahn, 67 mins.)

Hong Kong Hot Harbor (Germany, 1962)* Brad Harris, Marianne Cook, Horst Frank. (Dir: Jurgen Roland, 102 mins.)

Honkers, The (1972)** James Coburn, Lois Nettleton, Slim Pickens. "Honkers" refers to wild bulls and available women in this erratic rodeo tale. Coburn tries hard to overcome a plodding script playing a self-centered, second-rate rodeo performer. "Honkers" was the second and last film directed by Canadian actor Steve "Fuzz" Ihnat, who died after "Honkers" was finished. Some good rodeo action by cinematographer James Crabe. (Dir: Steve Ihnat, 103 mins.)

Honky (1971)** James Neilson, Brenda Sykes. Director William A. Graham has helped define and develop the TV movie. This theatrical feature is one of his periodic efforts to make an exploitation film with something extra; the result is neither satisfying nor provocative. Neilson plays an all-American boy who falls for the blandishments of a swinging black pusher (Sykes). (89 mins.)

Honky Tonk (1941)**½ Clark Gable, Lana Turner, Frank Morgan, Claire Trevor. First screen meeting of Gable and Turner has no originality other than the teaming. He's a gambler, she's a good girl and you know all along where they're headed. Enough action and loving though, to please most of their fans. (Dir: Jack Conway, 105 mins.)

Honor Among Lovers (1931)**½ Claudette Colbert, Fredric March, Monroe Owsley. A comedy directed on the Ernst Lubitsch model by Dorothy Arzner. Story of a private secretary (Colbert) who has to choose between an affair with her boss (March) or marriage to a poor but honest boy. (76 mins.)

Honor Thy Father (MTV 1973)*** Joseph Bologna, Raf Vallone. Interesting, well-cast television adaptation of Gay Talese's book about an underworld family. Moral is that educated sons seldom matched their father's toughness during the questioning '60's, even in the Mafia. The best thing about this true-life account of New York gangland's infighting is the look and performance of playwright-actor Bologna as heir to his father's Cosa Nostra gang. Brought up as a gentleman, the young man can't hold thugs together while questioning old Sicilian feuds. Bologna's performance is effectively supported by Brenda Vaccaro, Richard Castellano, Raf Vallone. (Dir: Paul Wendkos, 99 mins.)

Hoodlum Priest, The (1961)***½ Don Murray, Keir Dullea. Murray stars as Father Charles Dismas Clark, the Jesuit priest who befriended young criminal offenders and tried to help them help themselves. The film centers on one case in particular, that of a young hotheaded and arrogant ex-con who almost makes it with Father Clark's help and friendship. Murray delivers a fine portrait of a determined man with a mission and Keir Dullea makes a deep impression as the youth he befriends. (Dir: Irvin Kershner, 101 mins.)

Hoodlum Soldier, The (Japan, 1965)***½ Shintaro Katsu. Katsu shows his mettle as a small-time gangster who finds the Japanese army more brutal than anything he's encountered in civilian life. A born troublemaker and ruffian, he is commended to the care of a disaffected intellectual, a private who is himself tempted to desert. Their antics provide a sardonic counterpoint to the savage barbarism of life on the Manchurian front. Among the most substantial Japanese war movies, reminiscent of Norman Mailer and James Jones. Directed by the erratic but often brilliant Yasuzo Masumura. (103 mins.)

Hooper (1978)***½ Burt Reynolds, Sally Field, Jan-Michael Vincent, Brian Keith. Stuntman-turned-director Hal Needham has fashioned one of the finest entertainments of recent years about the greatest stuntman in the world, and the hot young challenger to his position. Amiable comedy and earnest feeling are savvily balanced; the elaborate stunt gags are intriguingly staged. (99 mins.)

Hook, The (1963)*** Kirk Douglas, Robert Walker, Nick Adams. Korean war drama poses a problem—what does a man do when he's ordered to kill a prisoner of war, even if it will insure his own safety? The development is somewhat sketchily presented, but it's food for thought. Well acted. (Dir: George Seaton, 98 mins.)

Hook, Line and Sinker (1969)* Jerry Lewis, Peter Lawford, Anne Francis. (Dir: George Marshall, 92 mins.)

Hoppity Goes to Town (1941)** As in his earlier animated "Gulliver's Travels," director Dave Fleischer doesn't have enough invention or plot to sustain a feature-length film. Some charm in the all-insect cast and the bug's-eye view of metropolitan life. (77 mins.)

Hopscotch (1980)*** Walter Matthau, Glenda Jackson, Ned Beatty. Tailored for the pouty charms of Matthau as a renegade CIA man out to expose the dangerous idiocies of the Company. Director Ronald Neame allows the story to poke along, but it's an amiable entertainment. From a novel by Brian Garfield. Music by W. A. Mozart. (104 mins.)

Horizons West (1952)**½ Robert Ryan, Rock Hudson. Familiar story of two brothers returning from the Civil War, one becoming a lawman and the other an outlaw. Better than usual cast and direction gives it a boost for the western fans. (Dir: Budd Boetticher, 81 mins.)

Horizontal Lieutenant, The (1962)**½ Paula Prentiss, Jim Hutton, Jack Carter. A moderately funny service comedy which benefits greatly from the able comedy team of Prentiss and Hutton as a pair of oddballs. There is a subplot involving a missing Japanese official, but Prentiss and Hutton remain in the focal point of the laughs. (Dir: Richard Thorpe, 90 mins.)

Horn Blows at Midnight, The (1945)** Jack Benny, Alexis Smith, Guy Kibbee. Benny used this film as a runing gag for years, claiming in jest that it ruined his movie career. You'll probably agree. (Dir: Raoul Walsh, 78 mins.)

Hornets's Nest (1970)** Rock Hudson, Sylva Koscina. Derring-do during World War II. Hudson plays a U.S. Army Captain who manages, with the aid of a group of Italian orphans and a sexy German lady doctor, to carry out his sabotage mission against incredible odds. (Dir: Phil Karlson, 109 mins.)

Horrible Dr. Hichcock, The (Italy, 1962)*½ Barbara Steele, Robert Flemyng. (Dir: Robert Hampton (Riccardo Freda), 76 mins.)

Horror at 37,000 Feet, The (MTV 1973)* Buddy Ebsen, William Shatner. (Dir: David Lowell Rich, 73 mins.)

Horror Castle—See: **Castle of the Living Dead**

Horror Chamber of Dr. Faustus, The (France, 1958)***½ Pierre Brasseur, Alida Valli, Edith Scob. An exercise in the macabre directed by French horror artist, Georges Franju. Brasseur is a mad scientist trying to perfect skin grafts for his scarred daughter. Beautifully acted. Franju, despite the crass American release title, managed to evolve a style that was both elegant and expressionistic, pure and magical. (84 mins.)

Horror Hospital (Great Britain, 1973)**½ Michael Gough, Robin Askwith, Vanessa Shaw. A campy satire of the usual thrillers, some of it funny. It has a mad doctor, a desolate manor, a sarcastic dwarfish assistant, an unseen monster who prowls by night, and so on. (Dir: Antony Balch, 91 mins.)

Horror Hotel (Great Britain, 1960)**½ Christopher Lee, Betta St. John, Venetia Stevenson. College student doing research in witchcraft stumbles upon a cult in a Massachusetts village. Shuddery little shocker works up some scary moments. Well done of its kind. (Dir: John Moxey, 76 mins.)

Horror of Dracula (Great Britain, 1958)*** Peter Cushing, Christopher Lee, Michael Gough. This was a gory, sexy rendering of the Bram Stoker novel for its time, pitting Lee against the Van Halsing of Cushing. Terence Fisher directed, representing the Hammer Studio style at its best. (82 mins.)

Horror of Frankenstein, The (Great Britain, 1970)*½ Ralph Bates, Kate O'Mara, Dennis Price, John Finch. Set in the 19th century. (Dir: Jimmy Sangster, 95 mins.)

Horror of Party Beach, The (1964)½ John Scott, Alice Lyon. (Dir: Del Tenney, 82 mins.)

Horrors of the Black Museum (Great Britain, 1959)** Michael Gough, Geoffrey Keen. Gruesome thriller about a famous crime writer with a do-it-yourself technique, providing himself with his own material. Script is one on the silly side, but performances and production are effective. For strong stomachs. (Dir: Arthur Crabtree, 95 mins.)

Horse and Carriage (Greece, 1957)** Orestis Makris. Simple, sentimental tale of a father who disowns his no-good son, and the son's repentance upon his father's death. Avoids being saccharine until the 400-violin ending. (Dir: Dino Dimopoulos, 104 mins.)

Horse Feathers (1932)***½ The Marx Brothers. Gets good marx. The first of their films to satirize the depression, and the topics range from education to prostitution to bootlegging. "Whatever it is," Groucho proclaims at his inauguration as president, "I'm against it." This is the one where Harpo gets into the lemonade. (Dir: Norman McLeod, 80 mins.)

Horse in the Gray Flannel Suit, The (1968)** Dean Jones, Diane Baker, Fred Clark. Walt Disney comedy about an ad-vertising exec who comes up with a clever scheme to promote his client's upset-stomach remedy and get his young daughter the horse she dreams about. The horse is named Aspercel after the patent medicine! Flimsy material gets a long ride. (Dir: Norman Tokar, 113 mins.)

Horse Named Comanche, A (1958)** Sal Mineo, Philip Carey, Jerome Cortland, Rafael Campos. For youngsters. Sal Mineo turns up as a young Indian, White Bull, who will do almost anything to own a certain wild stallion. Tribal customs prevent White Bull from such ownership. Interest centers on scenes between the boy and the horse. Released theatrically as *Tonka*. (Dir: Lewis R. Foster, 97 mins.)

Horse Shoes (1927)**½ Monty Banks, Jean Arthur. A romantic gag comedy starring scriptwriter Banks as a young law-school graduate who wins the daughter of a wealthy plutocrat despite misadventures in a sleeping-car berth and a case involving a forged will. Arthur makes one of her earliest comedy appearances. (Dir: Clyde Bruckman, 64 mins.)

Horse Soldiers, The (1959)** John Wayne, William Holden. Sprawling action film set during the Civil War benefits little from its potent casting of Wayne and Holden in the leading roles. They play union officers who have contrasting viewpoints on war. John Ford directed and not very well at that, but his producers and screenwriters are more to blame. (Dir: John Ford, 119 mins.)

Horsemen, The (1971)**½ Jack Palance, Omar Sharif, Leigh Taylor-Young. Action, adventure, and romance on a superficial level but still entertaining. Sharif in still another death-defying desert role—he's the son of an Afghanistan lord's stablemaster, played by Palance. The beautiful cinematography could pass as a travelogue on Afghanistan and Spain! Stilted screenplay from ace scripter Dalton Trumbo. (Dir: John Frankenheimer, 105 mins.)

Horse's Mouth, The (Great Britain, 1958)**** Alec Guinness, Kay Walsh, Ernest Thesiger, Renée Houston, Michael Gough, Robert Coote. Guinness adapted the Joyce Cary novel to star himself as Gulley Jimson, prototypic nonconformist painter. The acting is tremendous, especially Guinness, Walsh as his reluctant cohabitant and Thesiger as his long-suffering old patron. It's a jaunty, raunchy comedy, in fauvist color, well acted. (Dir: Ronald Neame, 93 mins.)

Hospital (1971)*** Magnificent, deeply moving documentary directed by Frederick Wiseman, about the workings of Metropolitan Hospital in New York City, and the overburdened compassionate staff who try to bring some grace and dignity to their task of dealing with the sick and mostly poor people who flood in to the hospital with all kinds of ailments—victims of razor fights, junkies, etc. There is one absolutely heartbreaking scene

309

showing a concerned psychiatrist doing everything he possibly can to make the laborious city bureaucracy respond to the ongoing needs of a disturbed black homosexual. Wiseman's enormous sympathy for the onscreen characters is evident throughout. Another penetrating study of an American Institution from this pioneering documentary filmmaker. (Dir: Frederick Wiseman, 90 mins.)

Hospital, The (1971)**** George C. Scott, Diana Rigg, Richard Dysart, Barnard Hughes. An original screenplay by Paddy Chayefsky got the Academy Award for this funny and devastating, if slightly exaggerated, account of the incompetence and slothfulness in a typical American hospital, in this case Metropolitan Hospital in New York City. Chayefsky's dialogue and the flamboyant performance of Scott, nominated for an Academy Award, are the two choice ingredients. Hughes is scary and very funny playing a mad impostor doctor. Miss Rigg's unquestionable allure handily solves Scott's fear of impotence. (Dir: Arthur Hiller, 103 mins.)

Hostage, The (1966)**½ Danny Martins, Don O'Kelley, John Carradine. A low-budget surprise drama about a runaway boy features unorthodox editing and plenty of character conviction. (Dir: Russell S. Doughten, Jr., 84 mins.)

Hostage Heart (MTV 1977)** Bradford Dillman, Loretta Swit, Vic Morrow. Terrorists break in during a delicate heart operation on a very rich man. A foolish plot with too much shooting. (Dir: Bernard McEveety, 98 mins.)

Hostage Tower, The (MTV 1980)**½ Keir Dullea, Peter Fonda, Douglas Fairbanks, Jr., Billy Dee Williams, Maude Adams. Debonair crooks steal the Eiffel Tower, taking as hostage the president's mom. Stagy thriller with smooth crooks, classy girls, and the latest gadgets. A specialist in this genre, author Alistair MacLean is clever, particularly in the escape planning, but the show never makes the pulse race. (Dir: Claudio Guzman, 104 mins.)

Hostages (1943)** Luise Rainer, William Bendix, Arturo de Cordova. Fair action film pays tribute to the Czech underground. A group of people are held as hostages after a Nazi is murdered. (Dir: Frank Tuttle, 88 mins.)

Hostile Guns (1967)** George Montgomery, Yvonne DeCarlo. Poor western about a U.S. marshal who has to transport a wagonful of prisoners to the state pen. The only interest is the familiar faces of some of the supporting players—Brian Donlevy, Richard Arlen, Don Barry and Fuzzy Knight. (Dir: R. G. Springsteen, 91 mins.)

Hot Angel, The (1958)** Jackie Loughery, Edward Kemmer. Aerial surveyor for a uranium prospector fights off crooks. Routine action melodrama. Good flying scenes. (Dir: Joe Parker, 73 mins.)

Hot Blood (1956)*½ Jane Russell, Cornel Wilde. (Dir: Nicholas Ray, 85 mins.)

Hot Enough for June—See: Agent 8¾

Hot Ice (Great Britain, 1953)*** Barbara Murray, John Justin. Laughs and thrills evenly divided in one of those spooky mansion-type mysteries. Better than average. (Dir: Kenneth Hume, 65 mins.)

Hot Lead and Cold Feet (1978)** Jim Dale, Karen Valentine, Darren McGavin, Don Knotts, Jack Elam. Typically silly Disney comedy-western with star Dale playing three parts—father and two very opposite sons who are involved in a race over the presumably dead dad's inheritance. There are the two obligatory youngsters to keep the kids happy. The brilliant Dale is largely wasted. (Dir: Robert Butler, 90 mins.)

Hot Line, The—See: Day the Hot Line Got Hot, The

Hot Millions (Great Britain, 1968)***½ Peter Ustinov, Maggie Smith. Amusing comedy about a high-class swindling operation, with some of the action set in London and South America. Ustinov at his roguish best and there's a delightful performance from the versatile British star Maggie Smith, who seems to have a virtually unlimited acting range. (Dir: Eric Till, 105 mins.)

Hot Pepper (1933)**½ Victor McLaglen, Edmund Lowe, Lupe Velez. Another sequel to "What Price Glory?" follows Flagg (McLaglen) and Quirt (Lowe) into civilian life as co-owners of a nightclub who fight over the love of Ms. Velez. Old rivalry keeps plot interesting. (Dir: John G. Blystone, 76 mins.)

Hot Rock, The (1972)*** Robert Redford, George Segal, Ron Liebman, Zero Mostel. The picture combines comedy and suspense in a delightful mixture, nicely balanced by director Peter Yates. Redford and Segal are hired to steal a diamond. Most of the picture concerns not the robbery but the bungling of the burglars in losing the gem, and trying to get it back. Uneven script and Mostel are wasted, but there's much fun along the way, especially Liebman as Murch, who claims he can drive anything. (Dir: Peter Yates, 101 mins.)

Hot Rods to Hell (1967)** Dana Andrews, Jeanne Crain, Mimsy Farmer. Family on the road terrorized by a teenage gang. Usual delinquency theme, nothing new. (Dir: John Brahm, 92 mins.)

Hot Spell (1958)*** Shirley Booth, Anthony Quinn, Shirley MacLaine, Earl Holliman. Family drama set in the South with some good acting to recommend it. Miss Booth plays a disillusioned housewife whose family has grown away from her but refuses to face the brutal truth. Marred by phony ending, well directed by Daniel Mann. (85 mins.)

Hot Stuff (1979)** Dom De Luise, Suzanne Pleshette, Jerry Reed. This woeful comedy tries to justify itself with an appeal for law and order that stands slightly to the right of Dirty Harry's, but the funniest scene in the film features De Luise smoking dope. Script by Michael Kane and Donald E. Westlake. (Dir: Dom De Luise, 91 mins.)

Hot Tomorrows (1977)***½ Ken Lerner, Ray Sharkey, Victor Argo, Herve Villechaize, and the Mystic Knights of the Oingo Boingo. Martin Brest made this exceptional short feature for only $33,000 cash while a directing fellow at the American Film Institute. A bleak comedy about a young student obsessed by death, the film is beautifully controlled in its nervy way, with a musical climax that anticipates Bob Fosse's *All That Jazz* on a fraction of the budget (do they make fractions that small?) As a "student" effort, it is exemplary, quirky, original with a deadpan eye for anomie with energy that suggests a laid-back Cassavettes. (Dir: Martin Brest).

Hotel (1967)*** Rod Taylor, Catherine Spaak, Karl Malden, Melvyn Douglas, Merle Oberon, Richard Conte, Michael Rennie, Kevin McCarthy, Carmen McRae. Trials and tribulations at a posh New Orleans hotel, mainly the efforts made to keep it from falling into the wrong hands. Many stars, many plots; familiar, but something cooking all the time. Suspenseful conclusion. (Dir: Richard Quine, 124 mins.)

Hotel Berlin (1945)*** Faye Emerson, Helmut Dantine. Occasionally interesting adaptation of Vicki Baum's novel centered in a Berlin hotel as Hitler's Germany is collapsing. Most of the characters and situations are contrived but there's some good excitement. (Dir: Peter Godfrey, 98 mins.)

Hotel Paradiso (Great Britain, 1966)**½ Gina Lollobrigida, Alec Guinness, Robert Morley. If your tastes lean towards French farce, peppered with British players (Guinness and Morley) and featuring that Italian eyeful Lollobrigida, this amiable and frothy comedy set in Paris during the early 1900's will entertain you. The plot is much too complicated to go into, but most of the action takes place in a fashionable hotel where secret rendezvous and misunderstandings run rampant. The production directed by Peter Glenville is handsomely mounted, and the cast goes through the standard paces with a sense of style and period. (Dir: Peter Glenville, 96 mins.)

Hotel Sahara (Great Britain, 1951)**½ Yvonne DeCarlo, Peter Ustinov. Occasionally amusing satire on the changing attitudes of civilians occupied during a war. Miss DeCarlo is prepared to accept any current winner. English-made film. Not for American taste. (Dir: Ken Annakin, 87 mins.)

Hothead (France, 1979)**½ Patrick Dewaere. Dewaere is winning as a happy-go-lucky soccer player who contravenes the mania of a town for its sport.

The comedy has a sour perspective, running out of steam without a satisfactory denouement. Director Jean-Jacques Annaud works in the tradition of French hackdom.

Houdini (1953)*** Tony Curtis, Janet Leigh. Colorful film based on the life and loves of the world's most famous magician. Tony Curtis brings a great deal of energy to the title role and he gets good support from Janet Leigh, as his faithful wife and Torin Thatcher, as his assistant. The kids will enjoy magic acts. (Dir: George Marshall, 106 mins.)

Hound Dog Man (1959)** Fabian, Carol Lynley, Arthur O'Connell, Stuart Whitman, Betsy Field. Not bad backwoods drama about a boy (Fabian) learning something about adult responsibilities. Director Don Siegel does a calculatedly small movie, with its virtues similarly scaled. (87 mins.)

Hound of the Baskervilles, The (1939)**** Basil Rathbone, Nigel Bruce. Though it had been filmed five times before, this is the standard version. Classic debut of Rathbone and Bruce as Sherlock Holmes and Dr. Watson. The feeling for Victorian London and mist-shrouded Dartmoor is strong. (Dir: Sidney Lanfield, 80 mins.)

Hound of the Baskervilles (Great Britain, 1959)*** Peter Cushing, Christopher Lee. Frightening mystery yarn based on the famous Sherlock Holmes novel reaches the screen in all its macabre fascination with every terror-filled moment intact. Far superior to many horror films. (Dir: Terence Fisher, 84 mins.)

Hound of the Baskervilles, The (MTV 1972)** Stewart Granger, Bernard Fox. Know-it-all Sherlock Holmes emerges once again, baffling follower Dr. Watson with canny insights as the two investigate Baskerville deaths by the legendary hound. Much is made of Holmes' deductive brilliance, spoken crisply by Granger, and Fox plays the stodgy Watson for chuckles. Producer Stan Kallis gave this relic the old college try. (Dir: Barry Crane, 73 mins.)

Hour of Decision (Great Britain, 1957)** Jeff Morrow, Hazel Court. A writer becomes involved in the murder of a gossip columnist. Usual sort of whodunit aided by good performances. (Dir: Pennington Richards, 74 mins.)

Hour of Glory—See: **Small Back Room, The**

Hour of the Furnaces, The (Argentina, 1966-68)**** A propaganda masterpiece, secretly made by underground Argentine filmmakers. A devastating indictment of American and British "imperialism" in Argentina and the rest of South America. This remarkable film, directed by Fernando Solanas, is one of the most powerful and effective propaganda films ever made. Part one deals with neocolonialism and violence, and the final shot, over four hours later in the full version, is a close-up held for well over two minutes of Che

Guevara. In between you'll find a variety of searing images that you'll not soon forget, together with factual material documenting the filmmakers' belief in the inevitability and desirability of violent revolution to achieve justice for South American working masses. Made to be shown to peasants, factory workers, etc., as a "consciousness-raising tool," it is an unforgetable cinematic experience. (Dir: Fernando Solanas, 250 mins.)

Hour of the Gun (1967)**½ James Garner, Jason Robards, Robert Ryan. Mediocre western drama with Garner as Wyatt Earp and Robards as "Doc" Holliday. This tale might be said to be part two of the 1957 film "Gun-fight at the O.K. Corral." Garner and Robards are quite good in their roles and a better-than-average supporting cast gives the film an added boost. (Dir: John Sturges, 100 mins.)

Hour of 13, The (1952)**½ Peter Lawford, Dawn Addams. Satisfactory thriller about a gentleman crook who tracks down a mad killer specializing in policemen. British made, good atmosphere. Remake of *Mystery of Mr. X*, 1934. (Dir: Harold French, 79 mins.)

Hour of Truth (France-Israel, 1966)**½ Corrine Marchand, Karl Boehm, Brett Halsey, Daniel Gelin, Mischa Azeroff. Controversial film about a disguised ex-Nazi concentration-camp commander who is virtually adopted by an Israeli family. When his real history becomes known, the family must deal with a figure at once hated and beloved, and the issue of whether a Nazi criminal can "reform." A difficult, sensitive situation, fairly well handled. (Dir: Henri Calef, 93 mins.)

Hours of Love, The (Italy, 1963)** Ugo Tognazzi, Barbara Steele, Emmanuele Riva. Ecstatic lovers decide on marriage, and then become disillusioned about each other's interests. Slow comedy, clinched with a happy ending. (Dir: Luciano Salce, 89 mins.)

House Across the Bay (1940)**½ Joan Bennett, George Raft, Walter Pidgeon, Lloyd Nolan. While waiting for her jailbird husband to come out, a singer falls for an aircraft designer; hubby hears of this, seeks revenge. Fair melodrama: Nolan is fine as a shady lawyer. (Dir: Archie Mayo, 72 mins.)

House by the Lake, The (Canada, 1977)** Brenda Vaccaro, Don Stroud. Director William Fruet turns to the rape-revenge genre. Vaccaro is the victim, Stroud the victimizer. Lots of broken glass and broken bodies make for an effective, if not honorable 89 minutes.

House by the River (1950)** Louis Hayward, Lee Bowman, Jane Wyatt. Philanderer strangles his maid, implicates his brother in the crime. Well made but otherwise undistinguished costume thriller. (Dir: Fritz Lang, 88 mins.)

House Calls (1978)**** Walter Matthau, Glenda Jackson, Richard Benjamin, Art Carney. Immensely pleasurable comedy, with Matthau—enjoying the newfound sexual freedom of widowerhood—ultimately courting divorcee Glenda Jackson. The exaggeration of hospital satire could have been flat but for deft performances of the stars. Director Howard Ziett shows signs of major comic talent. (96 mins.)

House Hunting—See: **Make Me an Offer**

House I Live In, The (U.S.S.R., 1958)**½ Vladimir Zemlyanikin, Valentina Telegina. Sensitive Russian film follows a family and their neighbors through troubles, marriages, war, by focusing on their apartment. An interesting film, gracefully performed, which stays clear of sentimentality. (Dirs: Lev Koulidjanov, Yakov Segel, 100 mins.)

House Is Not a Home, A (1964)* Shelley Winters, Robert Taylor, Cesar Romero, Ralph Taeger, Broderick Crawford, Kaye Ballard. One of Polly's "girls"—Raquel Welch. Based on the life of Polly Adler—call her "Madam." Whorehouse story unrelieved by finesse. (Dir: Russell Rouse, 95 mins.)

House of Bamboo (1955)*** Robert Stack, Robert Ryan, Shirley Yamaguchi, Sessue Hayakawa, Cameron Mitchell. Stack stars as an American undercover agent who dissembles his way into the good graces of a protection gang in Tokyo, headed by a psychotic American hoodlum (Ryan). A tough, sometimes nasty, but always exciting effort by director Samuel Fuller. (102 mins.)

House of Cards (1968)**½ George Peppard, Inger Stevens, Orson Welles. Action and lush European locations keep this tale of intrigue crackling from beginning to end. George Peppard plays an unlikely tutor in Paris who gets enmeshed in a right-wing operation made up of French aristocrats headed by arch-villain Orson Welles. There's a suspenseful chase at the end and the production values are first-rate. (Dir: John Guillermin, 105 mins.)

House of Crazies (1972)**½ Patrick Magee, Britt Eklund, Herbert Lom, Charlotte Rampling, Peter Cushing. A horror anthology, this Robert Bloch-authored mélange is effectively gruesome, though not on a par with its model, "Dead of Night." (Dir: Roy Ward Baker, 88 mins.)

House of Dark Shadows (1970)** Joan Bennett, Jonathan Frid, Grayson Hall. Fans of the horror-soap "Dark Shadows" will enjoy this theatrical version of the vampire saga. Bloodsucker Jonathan Frid overplays in the accepted grand style of a junior-league Vincent Price, and there are familiar faces from the long-gone but fondly remembered gothic TV soaper. (Dir: Dan Curtis, 98 mins.)

House of Dracula (1945)*½ Lon Chaney, John Carradine, Lionel Atwill. (Dir: Erle C. Kenton, 67 mins.)

House of Frankenstein (1944)** Boris Karloff, Lon Chaney, Jr., John Carradine,

312

J. Carrol Naish, Elena Verdugo. Now Karloff is the scientist, not the monster. Aided by a homicidal maniac, he brings Dracula, the Wolf Man, and the monster back to life. OK for hardened horror fans. (Dir: Erle C. Kenton, 71 mins.)

House of Hanging (Japan, 1980)*** Koji Ishizaka, Junko Sakurada, Masao Kusakari. Director Kon Ichikawa has made a phenomenally successful series of convoluted whodunits based on stories by Masashi Yokomizo, starring Ishizaka as a scruffy provincial investigator similar to our TV Columbo.

House of Intrigue (Italy, 1957)** Dawn Addams, Curt Jurgens. Beautiful spy bewitches a German officer, who eventually helps her out of a tight situation. Good European backgrounds from Barcelona to Holland, but the espionage plot rambles. (Dir: Duilio Coletti, 94 mins.)

House of Numbers (1957)** Jack Palance, Barbara Lang. Strictly for Jack Palance fans. He plays the dual role of a murderer and his look-alike brother. The story concerns a clever plan for the murderer's escape from prison and manages to generate some suspense along the way. (Dir: Russell Rouse, 92 mins.)

House of Rothschild, The (1934)**½ George Arliss, Loretta Young, Robert Young, Boris Karloff. Your basic boring Arliss historical vehicle with the stagy ham being his wily self. This is one of his more colorful films, helped by Loretta Young as his daughter, Robert Young as her suitor, Karloff as the villain, and the Napoleonic wars. (Dir: Albert L. Werker, 86 mins.)

House of Seven Gables (1940)***½ George Sanders, Margaret Lindsay, Vincent Price. Scheming lawyer falsely accuses his sister's sweetheart of murder, but she waits for him for twenty years to be released from prison. Superbly acted; well made drama, version of Hawthorne's classic novel. (Dir: Joe May, 89 mins.)

House of Strangers (1949)***½ Susan Hayward, Edward G. Robinson, Richard Conte. A powerful drama of family conflicts, filled with hatred and revenge. One of the older sons, Richard Conte, has sworn vengeance on his brothers, whom he blames for his father's death. Superb performance by Robinson as the father. (Dir: Joseph L. Mankiewicz, 101 mins.)

House of the Seven Hawks, The (Great Britain, 1959)**½ Robert Taylor, Nicole Maurey, Linda Christian. A straightforward espionage adventure yarn with touches of legitimate suspense. Robert Taylor plays a charter boat captain who gets involved with international thieves and the Dutch police when a mysterious man dies on his vessel. Taylor discovers an important-looking map on the dead man and spends the rest of the film trying to solve its mystery. Nicole Maurey and Linda Christian are the two females in the case, and the British and Dutch locations add necessary atmosphere. (Dir: Richard Thorpe, 92 mins.)

House of Usher (1960)*** Vincent Price, Mark Damon. Liberally adapted from the Edgar Allan Poe story. An idealistic young man (Damon) confronts and destroys a pathetically decadent representative of the older generation (Price). (Dir: Roger Corman, 79 mins.)

House of Wax (1953)**½ Vincent Price, Phyllis Kirk, Carolyn Jones. Originally made as a 3-D movie, it is loaded with visual gimmicks which were specifically tailored for the process. Nevertheless, there's sinister Vincent Price lurking in the shadows of a wax museum of horrors. Phyllis Kirk and Carolyn Jones add to the proceedings by alternately screaming and looking terrified. Remake of *Mystery of the Wax Museum*, 1933. (Dir: Andre de Toth, 88 mins.)

House of Women (1962)** Shirley Knight, Andrew Duggan, Constance Ford. Innocent expectant mother is convicted of robbery and sent to prison, where she undergoes many trials. Remake of "Caged" doesn't measure up—just a formula prison drama. (Dir: Walter Doniger, 85 mins.)

House on Chelouche Street, The (Israel, 1973)*** Gilda Almagor, Michal Bat-Adam, Shai K. Ophir. Israeli director Moshe Mizrahi's first film is a family drama set in the turbulent period just before partition in Palestine. Gains from an attractive performance by Almagor. (120 mins.)

House on Garibaldi Street, The (MTV 1979)***½ Topol, Nick Mancuso, Alfred Burke, Janet Suzman. Re-creates the kidnapping by Israeli agents of major Nazi war criminal Adolf Eichmann from Buenos Aires, where he had lived under an assumed identity for many years after WW II. Director Peter Collinson is to be commended for letting the story unfold in almost documentary fashion and not succumbing to melodrama. The cast is impeccable; Burke is all cold detachment as Eichmann. (104 mins.)

House on Green Apple Road, The (1970)**½ Janet Leigh, Christopher George, Julie Harris, Barry Sullivan. Suspenseful made-for-TV feature which uses flashbacks to fairly good advantage to tell the story of a woman (Miss Leigh) whose extramarital activities lead to murder. The police believe Miss Leigh's been murdered by her distraught husband but they can't come up with a corpse and thereby hangs the mystery. The supporting cast includes many familiar TV guest-star personalities. (Dir: Robert Day, 113 mins.)

House on Haunted Hill (1959)**½ Vincent Price, Carol Ohmart. A horror film with some laughs if you don't take it too seriously. Host Vincent Price rents a haunted house and offers a select group a large reward if they spend the night. Many strange goings-on liven up their stay. The effects are startling enough for the younger set, if they aren't prone to nightmares. (Dir: William Castle, 75 mins.)

House on 92nd Street (1945)***½ William Eythe, Lloyd Nolan, Signe Hasso. The FBI's battle against the fifth column in a fast paced, exciting film. This was the first picture to effectively combine documentary techniques with the dramatic and none of its imitators have topped it. (Dir: Henry Hathaway, 88 mins.)

House on Telegraph Hill (1951)** Richard Basehart, Valentina Cortesa, William Lundigan. Predictable melodrama with a good performance by Richard Basehart to recommend it. Basehart plays a convincing charmer who marries Miss Cortesa, thinking she is someone else. (Dir: Robert Wise, 93 mins.)

House That Dripped Blood, The (Great Britain, 1970)*** Peter Cushing, Christopher Lee, Nyree Dawn Porter, Ingrid Pitt. A series of four British vignettes set in an appropriately eerie estate, centering on the line of consecutive owners. Much better done than most of this genre—some scary, the last amusing. The first yarn involves a hack murder-mystery writer who sees his fictional character, a wild strangler, wandering all around the house. In other segments, the house has been turned into a wax museum with a striking statue of Salome; witches roam the place pitted against an ample serving of young innocence; and a film star puts on a genuine Transylvanian cloak for his vampire role...and suddenly...The cast, all battle-scarred horror movie veterans, provide satisfying chills but no full-blown terror. (Dir: Peter Duffell, 101 mins.)

House That Screamed, The (Spain, 1970)** Lilli Palmer, John Moulder Brown. Mild thriller about a strange reformatory for wayward girls from rich families, located in the south of France and presided over by strict headmistress Palmer. Young Brown scores as her weird teenaged son. (Dir: Narcisco Ibanez Serrador, 94 mins.)

House That Wouldn't Die, The (1970)**½ Barbara Stanwyck, Richard Egan, Katharine Winn. Made-for-TV feature, old-fashioned haunted house yarn provides some chills. Miss Stanwyck inherits an old house and goes there with her niece. Almost at once, strange goings-on begin occurring and it takes a seance to uncover some macabre facts. The cast is very serious, and plays it straight. From the novel *Annie Come Home* by Barbara Michaels. (Dir: John Llewellyn Moxey, 73 mins.)

House Without a Christmas Tree, The (MTV 1972)***½ Jason Robards, Jr., Mildred Natwick, Lisa Lucas. Charming, beautifully played, thoroughly enjoyable family fare. The focus is on a bright little girl of ten named Addie (Lucas); her reserved, widowed, undemonstrative father (Robards); and her warm but decisive grandmother (Natwick). Although tight-fisted, Addie's father gives her everything

she needs; but he can't seem to understand her urgent desire to have a Christmas tree. (Dir: Paul Bogart, 78 mins.)

Houseboat (1958)***½ Cary Grant, Sophia Loren, Martha Hyer. This Grant-Loren vehicle was a great popular success, and they worked well together, though the film is piffle. Directed by Melville Shavelson from the script he wrote with Jack Rose. (110 mins.)

Householder, The (India, 1963)**½ Shashi Kapoor, Leela Naida. Director James Ivory's first film, the story of a young man trying to come to grips with marriage. For a self-styled humanist, Ivory is very cold. (100 mins.)

Housekeeper's Daughter, The (1939)**½ Joan Bennett, Adolphe Menjou, John Hubbard, Victor Mature. A pretty miss helps a mild-mannered man get rid of some racketeers. Mildly amusing comedy with a hilarious finish. Mature's film debut. (Dir: Hal Roach, 80 mins.)

Houston Story, The (1956)** Gene Barry, Barbara Hale, Edward Arnold. Predictable gangster plot has Gene Barry striving for a top position in the syndicate centered in Houston, Texas. There's plenty of action for fans of this type of story. (Dir: William Castle, 79 mins.)

Houston, We've Got a Problem (MTV 1974)** Robert Culp, Clu Gulager, Gary Collins, Sandra Dee. A melodramatic "current events" story is in store for viewers tuning in to this "suspense" saga based on the near-fatal Apollo 13 mission. In this fictionalized version, the astronauts dangle in space after a crippling explosion in their spacecraft, while Mission Control's staff—Culp, Gulager, and Collins—alternate between attempting to get them back down and dealing with their soap-opera problems. (Dir: Lawrence Doheny, 74 mins.)

How Awful About Allan (1970)**½ Anthony Perkins, Julie Harris, Joan Hackett. Made-for-TV feature. A run-of-the-mill horror story aimed, hopefully, at sending chills up your spine. Anthony Perkins plays a young man recently returned from a mental institution who is a victim of psychosomatic blindness resulting from a fire which killed his father and scarred his sister (Julie Harris). We won't give away the plot but mystery fans will have little trouble figuring out the eerie goings-on. (Dir: Curtis Harrington, 73 mins.)

How Do I Love Thee (1970)** Jackie Gleason, Maureen O'Hara, Shelley Winters, Rosemary Forsyth, Rick Lenz. This sometimes sentimental, sometimes comic family drama just doesn't work. Gleason is a businessman who has never connected with his son, well played by Lenz. (Dir: Michael Gordon, 98 mins.)

How Green Was My Valley (1941)**** Donald Crisp, Walter Pidgeon, Maureen O'Hara. A magnificent movie experience. Director John Ford's Oscar winner is a study of stresses, changes, and heroism in a Welsh coal-mining family as it passes from the blissful 19th to the grim 20th century. What on the surface is a tender and sad film becomes joyous and robust. (118 mins.)

How I Spent My Summer Vacation (MTV 1967)** Robert Wagner, Peter Lawford, Jill St. John, Lola Albright, Walter Pidgeon. Cluttered adventure tale about a young ne'er-do-well who thinks he has the goods on a millionaire. It begins well, with some sharply directed scenes played tongue-in-cheek, but soon falls into utter confusion. (Dir: William Hale, 99 mins.)

How I Won the War (Great Britain, 1967)**½ Stumbling attempt to satirize World War II by director Richard Lester, as he tells of a doltish officer who manages to remain alive while his comrades die grisly deaths. Supposed to be funny, and is occasionally. A further deterrent is sometimes unintelligible dialogue. Michael Crawford, (Beatle) John Lennon, Jack MacGowran, Michael Hordern. (Dir: Richard Lester, 109 mins.)

How Sweet It Is! (1968)**½ Debbie Reynolds, James Garner. Mishaps galore dog the steps of a couple on a European vacation. Some genuinely funny sequences in this amiable laughgetter, with Maurice Ronet, Terry-Thomas, Paul Lynde, Elena Verdugo and Vito Scotti (superb in a bit as a cook). (Dir: Jerry Paris, 99 mins.)

How Tasty Was My Little Frenchman (France, 1971)***½ Arduino Colasanti, Ana Maria Magalhaes. Brazilian director Nelson Pereira dos Santos's witty film recounts the story of a French settler captured by cannibals who, despite the Frenchman's acculturation, honor him in the usual way. A lush, richly detailed work set in the 16th century. (80 mins.)

How the West Was Won (1963)*½ Gregory Peck, Henry Fonda, James Stewart, Debbie Reynolds. Directors include Henry Hathaway, John Ford, and George Marshall. (155 mins.)

How to Be Very, Very Popular (1955)*** Betty Grable, Sheree North, Robert Cummings. Two chorus kids on the lam find refuge in a college fraternity whose members hide them. Comedy on the frantic side has some funny lines, pleasant players. Remake of Bing Crosby's *She Loves Me Not*, 1934. (Dir: Nunnally Johnson, 89 mins.)

How to Beat the High Cost of Living (1980)** Susan Saint James, Jessica Lange, Jane Curtin, Richard Benjamin, Eddie Albert. Another crass comedy from the pen of Robert Kaufman, this time about pampered middle-class housewives who commit crimes against property—stealing the booty of a contest. (Dir: Robert Scheerer, 110 mins.)

How to Commit Marriage (1962)* Jackie Gleason, Bob Hope, Jane Wyman. (Dir: Norman Panama, 104 mins.)

How to Make a Monster (1958)*½ Robert H. Harris, Gary Conway. (Dir: Herbert L. Strock, 74 mins.)

How to Marry a Millionaire (1953)**½ Marilyn Monroe, Lauren Bacall, Betty Grable, William Powell, Cameron Mitchell. The first CinemaScope comedy sends three gold diggers out on the town to catch them each a wealthy husband. Since the three are Monroe, Bacall, and Grable, the results aren't too pallid despite the overfamiliarity of the theme. Powell retains his dapper dignity as the object of their attentions. Like most of director Jean Negulesco's '50s work, it is bland and chic. Nunnally Johnson wrote and produced and was the artistic guiding hand, if any. (95 mins.)

How to Murder a Rich Uncle (Great Britain, 1958)**½ Charles Coburn, Nigel Patrick, Wendy Hiller. Only moderately amusing entry in the British "How To" comedy films. Coburn is the wealthy relation in the title and the manipulators of the plot include sly and suave Mr. Patrick and his family. Miss Hiller is totally wasted in this mild fare. (Dir: Nigel Patrick, 80 mins.)

How to Murder Your Wife (1965)*** Jack Lemmon, Virna Lisi, Terry-Thomas. A frantic, often funny farce-comedy tailored to the talents of Jack Lemmon, who is in top form here. He plays a bachelor about town who wakes up one A.M. to find gorgeous Virna Lisi in his bed with a wedding ring on her left hand. The rest of the action is devoted to Lemmon's frantic efforts to get rid of his Italian spouse, even to the point of contemplating murder. The supporting cast matches Lemmon's energy and offer bright performances, particularly Eddie Mayehoff as an accommodating lawyer and Terry-Thomas as a quipping valet. Written and produced by George Axelrod. (Dir: Richard Quine, 118 mins.)

How to Save a Marriage—And Ruin Your Life (1968)**½ Dean Martin, Stella Stevens, Eli Wallach. A bachelor friend tries to save the marriage of an unfaithful husband, with unexpected results. Strains for laughs at times, but generally amusing. With Anne Jackson, Betty Field, Jack Albertson. (Dir: Fielder Cook, 108 mins.)

How to Seduce a Playboy (Austria-France-Italy, 1966)* Peter Alexander, Renato Salvatori, Antonelia Lualdi. (Dir: Michael Pfleghar, 94 mins.)

How to Steal a Million (1966)***½ Audrey Hepburn, Peter O'Toole, Charles Boyer. The grace and charm of the two stars, and William Wyler's deft direction are displayed in this sophisticated suspense story about the heist of a valuable piece of sculpture from a Paris museum. The theft itself is ingenious, on a par with such memorable scenes in "Rififi" and "Topkapi," and there's a particularly good supporting company including Eli Wallach and the always triumphant Welsh actor Hugh Griffith. Also assorted mouth-watering scenes in and around Paris for the benefit of those of you who can't visit the fabled city in person this season. (Dir: William Wyler, 127 mins.)

How to Steal an Airplane (MTV 1971)*½ Peter Duel, Clinton Greyn, Sal Mineo, Claudine Longet. Alternate title: **Only One Day Left Before Tomorrow.** (Dir: Leslie Martinson, 100 mins.)

How to Stuff a Wild Bikini (1965)*½ Frankie Avalon, Annette Funicello, Dwayne Hickman, Mickey Rooney. (Dir: William Asher, 90 mins.)

How to Succeed in Business Without Really Trying (1967)**** Robert Morse, Michele Lee, Rudy Vallee, Sammy Smith. The whole family will have a lot of fun without really trying to watch this long-running Broadway smash transferred to the big screen by David Swift who wrote, directed and produced this adaptation. Robert Morse, playing a Protestant what-makes-Sammy-run with a captivating charm, repeats his Broadway triumph. Rudy Vallee, who was a stiff in the Broadway production, repeats his wooden performance. Morse, who offers an instructive lesson in how to rise quickly up the corporate ladder, sings "The Company Way" and other tunes written by the late Frank Loesser. Cartoonist Virgil Partch is responsible for many of the funny visual sight gags that are to be found in this good-natured romp. (Dir: David Swift, 119 mins.)

How Yukong Moved the Mountains (The Netherlands, 1976)**** A masterwork by the great documentary filmmaker Joris Ivens, who made this monumental record of China filmed between 1972 and 1975 with his colleague Micheline Loridan. They vary in length from short entries to some over two hours long. This whole work is one of the most stunning and ambitious filmed essays ever made at any time or place. (Dirs: Joris Ivens, Micheline Loridan.)

Howards of Virginia, The (1940)***½ Cary Grant, Martha Scott, Sir Cedric Hardwicke. Spirited backwoodsman is married to an aristocratic Virginia girl at the time of the American Revolution. Their story is a fine example of "flag waving"—with taste. (Dir: Frank Lloyd, 122 mins.)

Howling in the Woods, A (MTV 1971)** Barbara Eden, Vera Miles, Larry Hagman, Ruta Lee, John Rubinstein. Pseudo-psychological thriller in which Eden looks horrified whenever she hears the distant wail of wolves—or what sounds like wolves. A time waster with some chills. (Dir: Daniel Petrie, 104 mins.)

Huckleberry Finn (1974)*½ Paul Winfield, Harvey Korman, David Wayne, Jeff East. (Dir: J. Lee Thompson, 113 mins.)

Hucksters, The (1947)*** Clark Gable, Ava Gardner, Deborah Kerr, Sydney Greenstreet. Adaptation of the novel about advertising which set the style for cheap modern novels is not nearly as pungent as the book. You'll still enjoy Ava Gardner in the role that really boosted her Hollywood stock. Kerr's U.S. debut. (Dir: Jack Conway, 115 mins.)

Hud (1963)**** Paul Newman, Patricia Neal, Melvyn Douglas, Brandon de Wilde. A must for movie-drama fans. A superb cast makes this story, about a ruthless young man who tarnishes everything and everyone he touches, ring true from the start to finish. Newman is the perfect embodiment of alienated youth, out for kicks with no regard for the consequences. The drama is deepened by the bitter conflict between the callous Hud and his stern and highly principled father (Douglas). Patricia Neal makes all her scenes count in her Oscar-winning portrayal, as their world-weary housekeeper. Taut direction from Martin Ritt and excellent on-location Texas photography. Douglas won a Best Supporting Actor Oscar. (Dir: Martin Ritt, 112 mins.)

Hudson's Bay (1940)**½ Paul Muni, Gene Tierney. Story of the founding of the famed Hudson Bay Company is a drawn out story, lacking action or motivation. A disappointing film. (Dir: Irving Pichel, 95 mins.)

Hue and Cry (Great Britain, 1947)*** Alastair Sim, Valerie White. A meek detective story writer and a group of kids crack a gang of thieves. Highly enjoyable romp, from the same men who made "The Lavender Hill Mob." Sim, as usual, is grand. (Dir: Charles Crichton, 82 mins.)

Hugs and Kisses (Sweden, 1967)**½ Agneta Ekmanner, Sven-Bertil Taube, Hakan Serner. What happens when a married couple invite a carefree bachelor to stay with them. Domestic comedy with spice never reaches great heights, but is mildly entertaining. (Dir: Jonas Cornell, 93 mins.)

Huk (1956)*** George Montgomery, Mona Freeman. Huks were marauding fanatic guerrillas terrorizing and plundering plantations in Manila. American Montgomery arrives to sell his inherited plantation and stays to fight. Exciting action scenes, and plenty of them. (Dir: John Barnwell, 84 mins.)

Humain, Trop Humain—See: Human, Too Human

Human Comedy, The (1943)**** Mickey Rooney, Frank Morgan, Marsha Hunt, Van Johnson. If you don't like top drawer sentimental hokum, forget this one. William Saroyan's optimistic philosophy on the human race is beautifully expressed in this story which is almost plotless but deep in characterization and sensitivity. It just tells about a small town in California during World War II but see it and reaffirm your faith in people. (Dir: Clarence Brown, 118 mins.)

Human Condition, The, Part I: No Greater Love (Japan, 1959)**** Tatsuya Nakadai. One of the most neglected masterpieces of world cinema here is director Masaki

Kobayashi's three-film, nine-hour-plus version of Jumpei Gomikawa's six-volume novel on WW II in Japanese-occupied Manchuria. All three films are good, and cumulatively they pack a wallop that equals any other war film. Nakadai gives a protean performance as a student who, after conscientious objection, is sent to Manchuria as a civilian to supervise slave labor. He tries but fails to better their lot by working from the inside, and ends up being punished by military conscription. (208 mins.)

Human Desire (1954)*** Glenn Ford, Gloria Grahame, Broderick Crawford. A loose adaptation of Emile Zola's "The Human Beast," about an unfaithful wife (Grahame). Director Fritz Lang's brilliant geometric compositions create a special universe out of the railroad yards. (90 mins.)

Human Duplicators, The (1965)** George Nader, Barbara Nichols, George Macready. Special agent investigates, find superior beings from another world creating a race of robots who will infiltrate key positions paving the way for invasion. Way-out science fiction, not really as bad as it sounds; should entertain the fans. (Dir: Hugo Grimaldi, 82 mins.)

Human Factor, The (U.S.-Italy, 1975)½ George Kennedy, John Mills, Raf Vallone, Rita Tushingham, Barry Sullivan. (Dir: Edward Dmytryk, 96 mins.)

Human Factor, The (1979)*** Richard Attenborough, Derek Jacobi, Robert Morley, Nicol Williamson, Iman. Director Otto Preminger's film of Grahame Greene's novel lacks the richness and depth of Greene's vision. The story concerns a disenchanted veteran secret agent, and the search for a double agent in the ranks. The relationship between Williamson and his African wife (Iman) is obscured by her inexpressive line readings. Preminger preserves his patented ambiguity, although there are persistent hints that in his old age he is making moral judgments, and fine ones, for all the balance of his point of view. Adapted (just barely) by Tom Stoppard. (Dir: Otto Preminger, 115 mins.)

Human Jungle, The (1954)**½ Gary Merrill, Jan Sterling. Exciting cops and robbers yarn with more action than most similar type films. Merrill plays a police Capt. who comes face to face with some very shady characters of the underworld. (Dir: Joseph M. Newman, 82 mins.)

Human Monster, The— See: **Dark Eyes of London**

Human, Too Human (France, 1972)***½ Penetrating and provocative work. Director Louis Malle ("Lacombe, Lucien") takes a documentary look at the problems of technology at a Citroen plant and the Paris auto show. Stunning images show the factory workers actually deriving comfort from the repetition of their tasks, the public fanatically trusting the manufacturers. Like Malle's other documentary,

"Phantom India," this work shows concern with the environmental factors that shape people's lives. A remarkable feat—an absorbing film about boredom. (Dir: Louis Malle, 77 mins.) Alternate title: **Humain, Trop Humain.**

Human Vapor, The (Japan, 1960)**½ Yoshio Tsuchiya, Kaoru Yachigusa. Well-handled Japanese sci-fi about a man who can make himself into vapor at will—variation on the "Invisible Man" theme. His true love, a classical Japanese dancer, provides some attractive side action. (Dir: Inoshiro Honda, 79 mins.)

Humanoids from the Deep (1980)* Doug McClure, Ann Turkel, Vic Morrow, Cindy Weintraub. (Dir: Barbara Peeters, 80 mins.)

Humoresque (1946)**½ John Garfield, Joan Crawford, Robert Blake. Tough kid Blake grows up to become Garfield and a concert violinist, but can't escape the patronage of wealthy society dame Crawford. Director Jean Negulesco displays a certain visual flair, but the film is derivative schlock. Clifford Odets contributed to the screenplay. (125 mins.)

Hunchback of Notre Dame, The (1923)***½ Lon Chaney, Patsy Ruth Miller, Ernest Torrence. Lon Chaney's "Hunchback" is one of the most extraordinary characters anyone has ever gazed on in the history of motion pictures. Not only was his makeup fantastic, including forty pounds of rubber and putty, but Chaney's acting **beneath** all those layers was very inventive and believable. Chaney, with his darting tongue and single eye, looks grotesque, but his movements in the bell tower and elsewhere are remarkably nimble. First major film version of "Hunchback" and based, of course, on Victor Hugo's novel "Notre Dame de Paris." This was a mammoth production for the period, employing, not to very good advantage, thousands of extras. But Chaney dominates throughout, and worth seeing because of him. (Dir: Wallace Worsley, 108 mins.)

Hunchback of Notre Dame, The (1939)*** Charles Laughton, Thomas Mitchell, Cedric Hardwicke, John Carradine, Edmond O'Brien (debut), Maureen O'Hara. Elaborately designed version of the Victor Hugo tale, outlandishly overacted by a large cast headed by Laughton as a witty and urbane Quasimodo. Director William Dieterle shows more solicitude for the sets than the pace. Effective entertainment. (117 mins.)

Hunchback of Notre Dame (France, 1957)*** Anthony Quinn, Gina Lollabrigida. The latest screen version of the classic tale about the deformed bell ringer of Notre Dame and his love for Esmeralda. Quinn's makeup job is grotesque but he has a field day in the role. Gina's "Esmeralda" is the sexiest so far. (Dir: Jean Delannoy, 104 mins.)

Hundred Hour Hunt (Great Britain, 1952)*** Anthony Steel, Jack Warner. A little girl who is an accident victim needs blood plasma that can only be supplied by a sailor, a boxer and a fugitive. Suspenseful melodrama. (Dir: Lewis Gilbert, 90 mins.)

Hungry Hill (Great Britain, 1947)**½ Margaret Lockwood, Dennis Price. Two Irish families feud with each other through the years, bringing despair and poverty. Rambling, drawn out melodrama, has some good moments, some trite ones. (Dir: Brian Desmond Hurst, 92 mins.)

Huns, The (France-Italy, 1960)*½ Chelo Alonso, Jacques Sernas. (Dir: Sergio Grieco, 85 mins.)

Hunt, The (Spain, 1966)**** Ismael Merlo, Alfredo Mayo. Powerful, brutal, haunting film, superbly directed by young Spaniard Carlos Saura. Three middle-aged men, out on a rabbit-hunting party-picnic, are themselves brutalized by the hunt in this searing drama. Depicts how the well-intentioned hunt disintegrates into a setting for an unexpected kind of violence. Memorable film which never got the attention or the distribution it deserves. English subtitles. Dir: Carlos Saura, 93 mins.)

Hunt the Man Down (1951)*** Gig Young, Lynne Roberts. Public defender is asked to solve a killing for which an innocent man is charged. Above average mystery with a good plot. (Dir: George Archainbaud, 68 mins.)

Hunted Lady, The (MTV 1977)** Donna Mills, Andrew Duggan, Robert Reed. Donna Mills stars as an undercover lady who's being framed. Since Donna has uncovered links between the underworld and a political candidate, she's being fed to the wolves. (Dir: Richard Lang, 104 mins.)

Hunter (1971)** John Vernon, Steve Ihnat. Slick, cold, concise bit of hanky-panky, produced by "Mission: Impossible"'s executive producer, Bruce Geller. Involves a government man who assumes the identity of a brainwashed agent, programmed to release a shipment of deadly virus. Made-for-TV. (Dir: Leonard Horn, 73 mins.)

Hunter, The (1980)*½ Steve McQueen, Eli Wallach, Kathryn Harrold, Ben Johnson, LeVar Burton. (Dir: Buzz Kulik, 117 mins.)

Hunter in the Dark (Japan, 1979)***½ Tatsuya Nakadai, Yoshio Harada, Keiko Kishi. This gangster saga is so densely packed with plot, theme, and character that you feel as if you've read a 600-page novel in 138 minutes. Director Hideo Gosha's style is visually charged, violent, brutal, elegant, and erotic. The women characters are as adept at fending for themselves in a physically combative world as the men.

Hunters, The (1958)**½ Robert Mitchum, Robert Wagner, May Britt, Lee Philips. Jet pilots in Korea. More melodrama than action, but the pace picks up when "the boys" are aloft, due to some first-rate aerial photography. Robert Wagner's first

substantial role, and he's on target as a hotshot pilot. (Dir: Dick Powell, 108 mins.)

Hunters Are for Killing (1970)**½ Burt Reynolds, Melvyn Douglas. This made-for-TV feature is a well-done drama with a small-town setting which uses its Napa Valley, California, scenery to full advantage. Lead Burt Reynolds, a man of few words, returns to the wine country aiming to prove his innocence on a murder rap. He is promptly pushed around by the police and adopted dad (Melvyn Douglas), who orders cops about like servants. Reynolds' strong point is the silent treatment, and he's quite believable as the ex-high school hero with a chip on his shoulder, sore at the Establishment and his father. (Dir: Bernard Kowalski, 99 mins.)

Hunting Party, The (Great Britain, 1971)½ Candice Bergen, Oliver Reed, Gene Hackman. (Dir: Don Medford, 108 mins.)

Hurricane, The (1937)***½ Dorothy Lamour, Jon Hall, Mary Astor, Raymond Massey, C. Aubrey Smith, Thomas Mitchell. Director John Ford's South Seas adventure is taut and entertaining (if not too personal). Ford's childlike savages may be offensive to modern audiences, but his lyricism is still impressive. Massey is at his best as a despotic island governor, and the special effects, to coin a phrase, have never been equaled. In later films Hall and Lamour reduced the genre to absurdity. (120 mins.)

Hurricane (MTV 1974)*½ Jessica Walter, Larry Hagman, Frank Sutton, Barry Sullivan. (Dir: Jerry Jameson, 72 mins.) Hurricane Hunters originally aired as *Hurricane*.

Hurricane (1979)*½ Jason Robards, Mia Farrow, Dayton Ka'ne, Max von Sydow, Trevor Howard. (Dir: Jan Troell, 119 mins.)

Hurry Sundown (1967)* Michael Caine, Jane Fonda, Robert Hooks, John Phillip Law. (Dir: Otto Preminger, 142 mins.)

Husbands (1970)**** John Cassavetes, Peter Falk, Ben Gazzara. A poignant film about three middle-aged men who go on a drinking binge when a mutual friend dies. The sadness and despair of their lives pour out as they even go to England to try to escape themselves. Cassavetes, Falk, and Gazzara are all perfect, and much of their dialogue is improvised. Cassavetes directed and as always, his style is personal and intense. (Dir: John Cassavetes, 138 mins.)

Hush...Hush, Sweet Charlotte (1964)*** Bette Davis, Olivia de Havilland, Agnes Moorehead, Mary Astor, Joseph Cotten. Director Robert Aldrich followed up the commercial success of his "Whatever Happened to Baby Jane?" with an even more outrageous exercise in Hollywood necrophilia. (133 mins.)

Hustle (1975)***½ Burt Reynolds, Catherine Deneuve, Ben Johnson, Eddie Albert, Eileen Brennan. A brilliant, chilling film noir directed by Robert Aldrich. Reynolds acts with depth and complexity as an emotionally bankrupt police detective searching for his lost motivation in the rubble of an L.A. shadow world populated by pimps, whores, and killers. Based on the novel "City of Angels." (120 mins.)

Hustler, The (1961)**** Paul Newman, Piper Laurie, George C. Scott, Myron McCormick, Jackie Gleason. Newman has never been better as the pool hustler who challenges the champ (Gleason) and learns that there are many ways to be a winner. Director Robert Rossen's camera finds the pulse of the drama. (135 mins.)

Hustling (MTV 1975)*** Lee Remick, Jill Clayburgh, Monte Markham. Effective drama about the streetwalkers of New York. Fay Kanin's gutsy, seamy sad tale, based on Gail Sheehy's book, portrays the prostitutes as victims, pushed around by just about everybody, including their pimps. Lee Remick is well cast as the straight woman, a reporter digging into all facets of the shabby business by following a scrappy hooker and her pals around. Jill Clayburgh plays the hooker extremely well. (Dir: Joseph Sargent, 100 mins.)

Hypnotic Eye, The (1960)*½ Jacques Bergerac, Merry Anders, Allison Hayes. (Dir: George Blair, 79 mins.)

I Accuse! (Great Britain, 1958)*** Jose Ferrer, Viveca Lindfors, Emlyn Williams, Leo Genn, Anton Walbrook. The famous Capt. Dreyfus trial and conviction is the basis for this drama. Ferrer plays Dreyfus with a commendable restraint and an excellent supporting cast backs him up. (Dir: Jose Ferrer, 99 mins.)

I Aim at the Stars (1960)*** Curt Jurgens, Victoria Shaw. Gripping semi-documentary styled account of how Wernher von Braun, missile expert, came to work for the U.S. after his close association with the Nazis during WW II. Jurgens is ideally cast as von Braun. Proof that some of our Nazis are better than the Nazis the Russians grabbed. Filmed in Germany. (Dir: J. Lee Thompson, 107 mins.)

I Am a Camera (Great Britain, 1955)*** Julie Harris, Laurence Harvey, Shelley Winters. The record of a young author and a hard-living, carefree girl in pre-war Berlin. Literate, excellently acted comedy-drama. Forerunner to *Cabaret.* (Dir: Henry Cornelius, 98 mins.)

I Am a Fugitive from a Chain Gang (1932)***½ Paul Muni. A scathing indictment of life in a Southern chain gang which has become a film classic. The movie and the book on which it was based caused quite a stir at the time and even led to some investigations. Muni is magnificent in the lead and he's ably assisted by a fine cast. (Dir: Mervyn Le Roy, 100 mins.)

I Am Curious (Blue) (Sweden 1969)* Lena Nyman, Vilgot Sjoman. (Dir: Vilgot Sjoman, 103 mins.)

I Am Curious Yellow (Sweden, 1967)**½ Lena Nyman, Borje Ahlstedt, Peter Lindgren. It's hard to believe that this Swedish import about a female sociologist could have created such a storm of moral outrage at the time of its release. Our heroine is concerned with questions of class structure, but the director is equally concerned with ass structure. People are tumbling, not only in and out of bed, but fornicating in trees, in public buildings, in the water, etc. It's good natured enough and not very erotic. Blessedly lacking any of the accoutrements of sadomasochism, violence and drugs found in films made a decade later. (Dir: Vilgot Sjoman, 121 mins.)

I Am the Law (1938)*** Edward G. Robinson, Wendy Barrie. Law professor wages a one-man war against protection racketeers. Well acted, well done crime melodrama. (Dir: Alexander Hall, 90 mins.)

I Became a Criminal (Great Britain, 1947)*** Trevor Howard, Sally Gray. An ex-pilot framed into prison escapes to square the double cross. Tense, exciting melodrama; well acted. (Dir: Alberto Cavalcanti, 80 mins.)

I Believe in You (Great Britain, 1952)*** Cecil Parker, Celia Johnson, Laurence Harvey, Joan Collins. A wayward young girl and a hoodlum are looked after by a kindly probation officer. Interesting drama is well thought out. (Dir: Basil Dearden, 93 mins.)

I Bombed Pearl Harbor (Japan, 1960)** Toshiro Mifune. A Japanese made film about the Japanese outlook of the war. Moderately interesting. (Dir: Shue Matsubayashi, 100 mins.)

I Bury the Living (1958)**½ Richard Boone, Theodore Bikel. Each time a manager sticks a black pin on a community cemetery chart, somebody dies. Three-fourths of a good thriller; falls apart at the end, but prior to that has some very effective moments. (Dir: Albert Band, 76 mins.)

I Can Get It for You Wholesale (1951)**½ Susan Hayward, Dan Dailey, George Sanders. Story of a heel in the garment industry. Well acted, but somehow unsympathetic, at times rather nasty. Alternate title: **Only the Best.** (Dir: Michael Gordon, 90 mins.)

I Can't Give You Anything But Love, Baby (1940)**½ Broderick Crawford, Johnny Downs. Snappy little musical about a hoodlum who kidnaps a young song writer to compose a love song for his moll. Some good laughs. (Dir: Albert S. Rogell, 60 mins.)

I Changed My Sex—See: **Glen or Glenda**

I Confess (1953)**½ Montgomery Clift, Anne Baxter, Karl Malden. Even Alfred Hitchcock has to strike out some time and this is one of those times—a *priest*, well played by Clift, will not *violate* the sanctity of the *confessional* even at his own expense. (Dir: Alfred Hitchcock, 95 mins.)

I Could Go On Singing (Great Britain, 1963)** Judy Garland, Dirk Bogarde, Jack Klugman. Peculiar dissection of a Garland-like singer is played in a coup of poor taste by Garland herself, with Bogarde lurking behind the scenes. Her last film. (Dir: Ronald Neame, 99 mins.)

I Died a Thousand Times (1955)** Jack Palance, Shelley Winters, Lee Marvin. Fair remake of a Humphrey Bogart-Ida Lupino film called "High Sierra." Palance plays a gangster who loves only two things in the whole world, a dog and a clubfooted girl. After he pays for an operation to correct the girl's foot, he is rejected by her and goes almost mad. Palance overacts. (Dir: Stuart Heisler, 109 mins.)

"I Don't Care" Girl, The (1953)**½ Mitzi Gaynor, David Wayne. George Jessel produced this musical biography of Eva Tanguay and the film is about George Jessel's work in getting the facts about Miss Tanguay. If you disregard the extraneous plot gimmicks, you may enjoy the musical numbers executed by Miss Gaynor and Mr. Wayne and singer Bob Graham. (Dir: Lloyd Bacon, 78 mins.)

I Dood It (1943)**½ Red Skelton, Eleanor Powell. Red's many fans may like this zany slapstick but it's not one of his best. Romance of a pants presser and a movie star is loaded with trite situations and forced humor. (Dir: Vincente Minnelli, 102 mins.)

I Dream of Jeannie (1952)** Ray Middleton, Bill Shirley. Story of how Stephen Foster came to write many of his famous tunes. Corny plot, but plenty of ditties for those who care. (Dir: Allan Dwan, 90 mins.)

I Dream Too Much (1935)** Lily Pons, Henry Fonda. Two young music students are happily married until the wife wins success as a singer. Superb vocalizing by Miss Pons is the feature of this pleasant romantic comedy-drama. (Dir: John Cromwell, 110 mins.)

I Even Met Happy Gypsies (Yugoslavia, 1967)*** Gypsy life, far from happy, surveyed with an ingenious eye by director Aleksandar Petrovic. Principal role played by Bekim Fehmiu, later seen to disadvantage in "The Adventurers." Subtitles. (Dir: Aleksandar Petrovic, 90 mins.)

I. F. Stone's Weekly (1973)**** A remarkable low-budget documentary paying rightful tribute to one of the greatest and, for a long time, most ignored newspapermen of our age—the award-winning investigative journalist I. F. Stone. Filmmaker Jerry Bruck has not made an obsequious film about Stone—he captures the flavor of what Stone himself calls his "maniacal zest and idiot zeal." There was no single momentous Watergate-type story uncovered by Izzy Stone, just many scoops, decade after decade, thanks to a first-rate journalist concerned only with

truth, not power. (Dir: Jerry Bruck Jr., 62 mins.)

I Know Where I'm Going (Great Britain, 1945)**** Wendy Hiller, Roger Livesey. An enchanting, touching romance about a rich girl on her way to marry an unwanted suitor, who runs away and finds true love on an island in the Scottish Hebrides. Wendy Hiller, an astonishing actress of seemingly limitless range, often wasted in motion pictures, is an irresistible delight in this sensitively directed film that is an enduring treat. (Dir: Michael Powell, 91 mins.)

I Know Why the Caged Bird Sings (MTV 1979)*** Diahann Carroll, Ruby Dee, Esther Rolle, Madge Sinclair. Growing up black in the dusty southern town of Stamps, Arkansas, during the '30s was poetically explored by author Maya Angelou in her novel of the same name. Young Maya and her brother are shuttled between their paternal grandmother in Arkansas and their divorced mother in St. Louis. Rolle and Sinclair are memorable. (Dir: Fielder Cook, 104 mins.)

I Led Two Lives—See: Glen or Glenda

I Like Money (Great Britain, 1961)** Peter Sellers, Nadia Gray, Herbert Lom. Sellers as an honest schoolteacher who learns that dishonesty pays off. A version of Pagnol's "Topaze." Sellers makes the mistake of directing himself, resulting in a slow, stiff ironic comedy, done much better in the past by such as Barrymore and Fernandel. (Dir: Peter Sellers, 97 mins.)

I Love a Mystery (1945)** Jim Bannon, Nina Foch, George Macready. The first of a short-lived series of films based on the popular radio series. Has a suitably bizarre plot about a secret society that wants to secure the head of a businessman because he is a dead ringer for their deceased founder. (Dir: Henry Levin, 70 mins.)

I Love a Mystery (MTV 1973)** Ida Lupino, David Hartman, Les Crane, Terry-Thomas, Don Knotts. Moldy revival of the old Carlton E. Morse radio series. Three detectives fly to a private island to flush out missing billionaire. (Dir: Leslie Stevens, 99 mins.)

I Love Melvin (1953)**½ Donald O'Connor, Debbie Reynolds. A happy musical with the accent on youth in song and dance. The plot, which serves as an excuse for the many musical numbers, has O'Connor cast as a top magazine photographer and Miss Reynolds as a Broadway chorus girl. (Dir: Don Weis, 76 mins.)

I Love My Wife (1970)**½ Elliott Gould, Brenda Vaccaro. Funny but uneven comedy dealing with modern marriage. It's all about what happens to Gould and Vaccaro's matrimonial bliss when hubby starts to roam and rove. The film gets into trouble with its sudden changes from satirical to serious moments, but the performances are all topnotch. (Dir: Mel Stuart, 95 mins.)

I Love Trouble (1948)*** Franchot Tone, Janet Blair. Tough private eye runs into foul play while searching for a missing girl. Smooth, speedy, well done mystery. (Dir: S. Sylvan Simon, 94 mins.)

I Love You Again (1940)*** Myrna Loy, William Powell. Lots of fun in this silly comedy about a nice, dull husband who, after a bump on the head, recovers from amnesia and becomes his true self, a slick con man. (Dir: W. S. Van Dyke, 99 mins.)

I Love You, Alice B. Toklas (1968)*** Peter Sellers, Leigh Taylor-Young, Jo Van Fleet. A frequently amusing original comedy by Paul Mazursky and Larry Tucker, with a message, believe it or not. Peter Sellers is at his best as a mother-dominated Los Angeles lawyer who leaves his fiancée at the altar not once but twice to seek "the better things in life," as he puts it. One of those better things is lovely Leigh Taylor-Young as a liberated young lady who turns on Peter and makes him into a hippie, complete with crash pad and long hair. There's more here than the frivolity outlined in this capsule synopsis. Worthwhile and funny, too. (Dir: Hy Averback, 93 mins.)

I Love You, Goodbye (MTV 1974)**½ Hope Lange, Earl Holliman. Muddled story about a housewife and mother of 18 years who suddenly craves more meaning in her life and leaves the whole kit and kaboodle to find herself. The dialogue often reverts to cliches associated with the early preachments of the women's lib movement and minimizes the dramatic moments of the story. Patricia Smith has the best written role as a divorcee who seems content with her new life-style and helps friend Hope Lange. (Dir: Sam O'Steen, 74 mins.)

I Married a Communist—See: **Woman on Pier 13, The**

I Married a Monster From Outer Space (1958)** Tom Tryon, Gloria Talbott. The title tells all, as a young bride discovers her husband is really a being from another planet intent on conquering earth. As these sci-fi thrillers go, not bad; has a certain amount of style. (Dir: Gene Fowler, Jr., 78 mins.)

I Married a Witch (1942)**½ Fredric March, Veronica Lake, Cecil Kellaway, Robert Benchley, Susan Hayward. Director René Clair's whimsy becomes a little arthritic, but March and Lake play well together. Susan Hayward has a small role. Robert Pirosh and Marc Connelly's adaptation of a novel by Thorne Smith. (76 mins.)

I Married a Woman (1958)*½ George Gobel, Jessie Royce Landis, Diana Dors. (Dir: Hal Kanter, 84 mins.)

I Married an Angel (1942)** Jeanette MacDonald, Nelson Eddy, Binnie Barnes, Edward Everett Horton. Rodgers and Hart musical is slaughtered in an inept screen treatment. Banker Eddy dreams about courting an angel (MacDonald) and wakes up to find her a guest in his house. Screen-

play by Anita Loos. B&W. (Dir: W. S. Van Dyke II, 84 mins.)

I Met a Murderer (Great Britain, 1939)*** James Mason, Pamela Kellino. Goaded into murdering his shrewish wife, a farmer flees from the police, is sheltered by a young girl. Brooding, suspenseful melodrama, artistically done. Produced by Mason and the Kellinos. (Dir: Roy Kellino, 78 mins.)

I, Mobster (1959)**½ Steve Cochran, Lita Milan. A criminal tells his story—from a young punk to a big time mobster. Effective only at times due to script limitations. Cochran is good. (Dir: Roger Corman, 80 mins.)

I, Monster (Great Britain, 1971)*** Christopher Lee, Peter Cushing, Mike Raven. Adaptation of Robert Louis Stevenson's "Dr. Jekyll and Mr. Hyde." Though the names of the characters are changed, this is more like the novel than some other film versions of the classic horror tale. Lee gives real depth to the unfortunate creature of the title, and his end is harrowing. (Dir: Stephen Weeks, 75 mins.)

I Never Promised You a Rose Garden (1977)*** Kathleen Quinlan, Bibi Andersson, Susan Tyrrell, Signe Hasso, Diane Varsi. The high-school cult novel about a schizophrenic teenager and her sympathetic psychiatrist. Quinlan is intelligent in the lead role, but can't rise above the standard "Snake Pit" stuff—madness is unconvincing in other people's fantasies. Adapted by Lewis Carlino and Gavin Lambert. (Dir: Anthony Page, 96 mins.)

I Never Sang for My Father (1970)***½ Melvyn Douglas, Gene Hackman, Estelle Parsons. Deeply moving drama. Hackman as a 40-year-old still trying to play son to Melvyn Douglas as the father. Based on Robert Anderson's stage play about an 80-year-old father, former mayor of a Long Island suburb, who is tyrannically obsessed with concepts of strength and pride. Douglas and Hackman are profoundly moving. (Dir: Gilbert Cates, 90 mins.)

I Passed for White (1960)*½ James Franciscus, Sonya Wilde. (Dir: Fred M. Wilcox, 93 mins.)

I Remember Mama (1948)*** Irene Dunne, Barbara Bel Geddes, Oscar Homolka, Philip Ober, Ellen Corby, Edgar Bergen, Rudy Vallee. George Stevens, back from WW II, directed this intently observed drama of a mother and her Norwegian immigrant family in San Francisco. Later a long-running TV series. (134 mins.)

I Sailed to Tahiti with an All Girl Crew (1969)* Gardner McKay, Fred Clark, Diane McBain. (Dir: Richard Bare, 95 mins.)

I Saw What You Did (1965)** Joan Crawford, John Ireland. Couple of teenage girls play a telephone prank, which upsets a murderer and makes them candidate for his next crime. Okay suspense drama with Crawford wasted in a minor role. (Dir: William Castle, 82 mins.)

I Shot Jesse James (1949)***½ Preston

Foster, John Ireland, Barbara Britton. Director Sam Fuller's first film is a passionate telling of the story of Bob Ford, the "dirty little coward who shot Mr. Howard" in the back. Agonizing, claustrophobic, and a masterpiece. (81 mins.)

I **Spy, You Spy** (Great Britain, 1966)**½ Tony Randall, Senta Berger, Herbert Lom. American in Morocco suddenly finds himself enmeshed in the sinister deeds of a spy ring and a disappearing corpse. Good performers add zest to an otherwise familiar, routine comedy thriller. Alternate title: **Bang! Bang! You're Dead!** (Dir: Don Sharp, 92 mins.)

I **Take This Woman** (1940)** Spencer Tracy, Hedy Lamarr. A dedicated doctor thinks his wife, a model, doesn't love him, and so on until you fall asleep. Charles MacArthur did the original story. (Dir: W. S. Van Dyke II, 97 mins.)

I **Thank a Fool** (Great Britain, 1962)*½ Susan Hayward, Peter Finch. (Dir: Robert Stevens, 100 mins.)

I, the Jury (1953)** Biff Elliot, Preston Foster, Peggie Castle, Elisha Cook, Jr. Film version of the Mickey Spillane novel with Elliot as Mike Hammer, the tough private eye, lacks violence, sex, and especially excitement. B&W. (Dir: Harry Essex, 87 mins.)

I **Wake Up Screaming** (1941)***½ Betty Grable, Victor Mature, Laird Cregar, Carole Landis, William Gargan. Hard, creepy atmosphere bolstered by sharply etched characterizations. When Landis is murdered (in an eerie foreshadowing of her own demise), her sister (Grable) searches out the killer, with the help of the prime suspect (Mature). The true star of the film is Cregar, whose sarcastic detective is probably his best performance. Director H. Bruce Humberstone never made a better movie. Remade as "Vicki" ('53). (82 mins.)

I **Walk Alone** (1947)** Burt Lancaster, Kirk Douglas, Lizabeth Scott. Man returns from prison to find that things have changed in this grim, weak melodrama. (Dir: Byron Haskin, 98 mins.)

I **Walk the Line** (1970)*** Gregory Peck, Tuesday Weld. Interesting drama set in the moonshine country of Tennessee. Miss Weld's performance as a young girl who captivates married Sheriff Peck is the main inducement for watching this story about bootlegging moonshiners and their constant bouts with the local law. (Dir: John Frankenheimer, 96 mins.)

I **Walked with a Zombie** (1943)*** Frances Dee, Tom Conway, James Ellison. Tale of voodoo and devil worship in the West Indies transcends the conventions of the horror genre. (Dir: Jacques Tourneur, 69 mins.)

I **Wanna Hold Your Hand** (1978)*** Nancy Allen, Bobby DiCicco, Mark McClure. A genuine surprise, a delightfully raucous comedy about six New Jersey teenagers trying to crash the Ed Sullivan Show broadcast the night the Beatles appeared. Robert Zemeckis, director and co-scripter with Bob Gale, obviously has a natural talent for comic situations, and I harbor special fondness for the genial exaggerations of farce that apparently many others don't find funny. There are uncertain passages galore, but the arrival of a fresh talent is cause enough to cheer. The players, all unknown, ought not to stay that way long. (Dir: Robert Zemeckis, 104 mins.)

I **Want Her Dead** (1974)* Twiggy, Dirk Benedict, Michael Witney. (Dir: Richard Quine, 109 mins.)

I **Want to Keep My Baby** (MTV 1976)*** Mariel Hemingway, Susan Anspach, Jack Rader. This is a strong, poignant, if lengthy film about a fifteen-year-old girl who becomes pregnant, is abandoned by her teenage lover, decides to have her baby, and is persuaded by various forces to keep the infant and care for it. Mariel Hemingway is so tantalizingly gripping in the role of the girl, she rivets your attention to the screen even in repetitious scenes. In addition to the fascination of watching the very young Miss Hemingway, a number of serious questions are raised. Most important, perhaps, is whether a teenager with little experience in living is capable of bringing up her baby alone; or whether it would be preferable both for her and the child if the infant were given up for adoption. (Dir: Jerry Thorpe, 106 mins.)

I **Want To Live** (1958)**** Susan Hayward. Susan Hayward's Academy Award winning performance directed by Robert Wise is the main attraction in this film based on the sensational and controversial murder trial of vice girl Barbara Graham. Miss Graham's past prison record and other incriminating evidence worked against her and resulted in her conviction. The final segment dealing with her execution in the gas chamber packs a real wallop. A powerful indictment of capital punishment. (Dir: Robert Wise, 120 mins.)

I **Want You** (1951)** Dana Andrews, Dorothy McGuire, Farley Granger, Peggy Dow. Samuel Goldwyn's effort to have box office lightning strike twice ("Best Years of Our Lives") via this slow moving drama about the effect of the Korean War on a typical American family. Talky, artificial and often boring. (Dir: Mark Robson, 102 mins.)

I **Wanted Wings** (1941)**½ Ray Milland, Bill Holden, Wayne Morris, Veronica Lake. Story of three young men taking our pre-war Air Cadet training is nothing more than dated propaganda today. (Dir: Mitchell Leisen, 131 mins.)

I **Was a Communist for the F.B.I.** (1951)** Frank Lovejoy, Dorothy Hart. The title tells the whole story. Lovejoy plays Matt Cvetic, a real life F.B.I. agent who posed as a Communist in order to inform on the

Reds' activities in the U.S. (Dir: Gordon Douglas, 83 mins.)

I Was a Male War Bride (1949)*** Cary Grant, Ann Sheridan. Director Hawks's loosely constructed, episodic film in which Free French army captain Grant has to disguise himself as a WAC named Florence, in a wig made from a horse's tail, to accompany his WAC bride (Sheridan) to the U.S. Some genuinely funny moments. (105 mins.)

I Was a Parish Priest (France-Spain, 1952)*** Claude Laydu, Francisco Rabal. Well-made drama of the trials and tribulations of a young priest in his first parish assignment. Capable performances, sincere in treatment. English-dubbed. (Dir: Rafael Gil, 87 mins.)

I Was a Teenage Frankenstein (1957)*½ Whit Bissell, Phyllis Coates. (Dir: Herbert L. Strock, 72 mins.)

I Was a Teenage Werewolf (1957)** Michael Landon, Whit Bissell, Yvonne Lime. Evil doctor succeeds in regressing a troubled teenager into a murderous werewolf. Hokey horror story with some unintentional laughs. Landon later became a TV star. (Dir: Gene Fowler, Jr., 76 mins.)

I Was Monty's Double (Great Britain, 1958)***½ John Mills, Cecil Parker, M. E. Clifton-James as title role. Well done British war drama about a great plot involving an actor impersonating a General to confuse the Germans in the North African campaign. Top performances by a good cast. (Dir: John Guillermin, 100 mins.)

I Will, I Will...for Now (1976)* Elliott Gould, Diane Keaton. (Dir: Norman Panema, 107 mins.)

I Wonder Who's Kissing Her Now (1947)*** June Haver, Mark Stevens. Highly fictionalized career of song writer Joe Howard has such a delightful score and so many talented people that we can overlook its childish plot. (Dir: Lloyd Bacon, 104 mins.)

Ice (1970)***½ Provocative, powerful, maddening drama directed in semidocumentary form by radical writer-filmmaker Robert Kramer. Virtually a blueprint-textbook of how the American urban guerrilla revolution will proceed. A motley collection of earnest but intellectually vapid young political activists talk, commit acts of sabotage, and finally blow up part of New York. Because this is virtually the only American-made feature that deals candidly with the question of political revolution in America, it is especially disappointing that the film is so detached, and that the audience learns little about, and cares nothing for, any of the characters. The young rebels in "Ice" are, incidentally, just as repellent and dehumanized as the system they seek to overthrow. Mostly nonprofessional cast, which eats and makes love without humor or joy. Despite its shortcomings, "Ice" is an absorbing, disturbing document. (Dir: Robert Kramer, 132 mins.)

Ice Castles (1978)**½ Robby Benson, Lynn-Holly Johnson, Colleen Dewhurst. A sentimental film that goes overboard and yet maintains its appeal. Get set to cry at least three times as Johnson makes her film debut as Alexis, an ice skater with Olympic potential who suddenly goes blind. Benson also scores as her sympathetic boyfriend. (Dir: Donald Wrye, 113 mins.)

Ice Cold in Alex—See: **Desert Attack**

Ice Follies of 1939 (1939)** Joan Crawford, James Stewart, Lew Ayres, Lewis Stone, Lionel Stander. A real curiosity, with Stewart and Crawford starring on skates. The story is thin. (Dir: Reinhold Schunzel, 90 mins.)

Ice Palace (1960)**½ Richard Burton, Robert Ryan, Carolyn Jones. Edna Ferber's sprawling novel about the formation of Alaska as a state makes a long episodic film with some good performers trying their best to overcome the soap opera tendencies of the script. Burton and Ryan clash in business, private life and finally politics. Miss Jones goes from a young girl in love with Burton to a gray-haired old lady watching out for Burton's granddaughter. (Dir: Vincent Sherman, 143 mins.)

Ice Station Zebra (1968)**½ Rock Hudson, Ernest Borgnine, Patrick McGoohan. Sprawling submarine adventure produced on a grand scale. Rock Hudson is the commander of an elaborate sub sent to the North Pole on a secret mission involving missile data recorded by a Russian space satellite. Enough plot...tune in and enjoy the many intrigues and excellent photography. Some of the film crawls at a snail's pace, but the overall action clips along. Kids are probably the best audience for this submarine yarn. (Dir: John Sturges, 148 mins.)

Iceland (1942)**½ Sonja Henie, John Payne. A fair score, Sonja's skating and that's it for this film. Plot and dialogue about romance of an Iceland girl and a Marine are a disgrace. (Dir: H. B. Humberstone, 79 mins.)

Iceman Cometh, The (1973)**** Fredric March, Lee Marvin, Robert Ryan, Jeff Bridges, Tom Pedi. March is extraordinary as Harry Hope in the Eugene O'Neill masterpiece, which is more than can be said for Marvin as Hickey, the "iceman." Ryan's valedictory performance as Larry transforms the play, which is set in a 1912 waterfront combination saloon and flophouse. (Dir: John Frankenheimer, 239 mins.)

Ichabod and Mr. Toad (1949)*** In *Ichabod* Bing Crosby is the narrator of the story by Washington Irving. Basil Rathbone relates the story of *Mr. Toad*. This was the second half of Walt Disney's two-part 1949 feature, which paired *The Legend of Sleepy Hollow* with this free rendition of Kenneth

Grahame's *Wind in the Willows*, utilizing the incomparable voice of Eric Blore as the Toad. It is by far the superior portion of the film, and some of the highest quality animation ever done by the Disney studio. The direction is particularly inventive. One wonders why the studio never made a series of films starring Toad, Rat, and Mole, as it would later do with the Pooh characters, far less interestingly. (75 mins.)

I'd Climb the Highest Mountain (1951)*** William Lundigan, Susan Hayward, Gene Lockhart, Lynn Bari, Alexander Knox, Rory Calhoun, Barbara Bates, Ruth Donnelly. Sincere, emotionally effective story of a Methodist preacher and his family in the hinterlands of cracker country. Henry King keeps the material from becoming unduly cloying; avoiding the sort of pseudo-piety that makes most of these kind of movies unendurable. (Dir: Henry King, 88 mins.)

I'd Rather Be Rich (1964)**½ Sandra Dee, Robert Goulet, Andy Williams, Maurice Chevalier. Millionaire's granddaughter asks a stranger to pose as her fiancé to please the old man, who is ill. Amusing romantic comedy, thanks largely to Chevalier. It's a remake of an old Deanna Durbin movie, *It Started with Eve*, (1941), but lacks the charm of the original. (Dir: Jack Smight, 96 mins.)

Ideal Husband, An (Great Britain, 1948)**½ Paulette Goddard, Michael Wilding, Glynis Johns. Oscar Wilde's comedy of manners and morals in Victorian England, elaborately produced, but stuffy, dull. (Dir: Alexander Korda, 96 mins.)

Idiot, The (U.S.S.R., 1958)** Yuri Yakovlev, Yulia Borisova. Dostoyevsky's novel of introspection, about a sensitive nobleman who arrives in the harried, corrupt world of 19th-century Moscow and falls in love with a worldly woman, becomes an almost raucous affair in this screen version, full of emoting and sweeping operatic gesture. (Dir: Ivan Pyriev, 95 mins.)

Idiot's Delight (1939)***½ Clark Gable, Norma Shearer. Robert Sherwood's Pulitzer Prize play loses in the screen version but enough is left to make it worthwhile. Written prior to World War II it is worth seeing today because it expresses one of America's great playwright's views on war. Story has enough comedy to keep it going as pure entertainment. (Dir: Clarence Brown, 120 mins.)

Idolmaker, The (1980)**** Ray Sharkey, Peter Gallagher, Paul Land. A rousing, satisfying piece of superslick filmmaking, about a songwriter-promoter (Sharkey) who creates pop idols out of pretty-eyed ethnic kids. Loosely based on the life of Robert Marcucci, who handled Frankie Avalon and Fabian. Taylor Hackford, directing his first feature, has a keen eye and consummate craft. (119 mins.)

If (Great Britain, 1969)**** Malcolm McDowell, David Wood, Richard Warwick, Peter Jeffrey, Christine Noonan. A striking, enormously powerful if episodic drama about life in a repressive boys' boarding school in England. Distinguished documentary film maker Lindsay Anderson, who directed the memorable "This Sporting Life," has skillfully used both professional and non-professional actors to build this ultimately shattering account of how the students finally react to what they believe is senseless discipline and authoritarianism, both from the faculty and the upper-class prefects. (Don't spend any time worrying about the symbolism and meaning of why the film alternates from time to time from color to black-and-white sequences. The producer simply ran out of money while finishing the movie, and black-and-white processing was cheaper than finishing the film completely in color.) (Dir: Lindsay Anderson, 111 mins.)

If a Man Answers (1962)** Sandra Dee, Bobby Darin, John Lund, Stefanie Powers. Playgirl marries a carefree photographer, resorts to extreme measures to keep him in line after they're married. Lightweight romantic comedy comes along about 26 years too late—they did them better in those days. (Dir: Henry Levin, 102 mins.)

If All the Guys in the World...(France, 1956)**½ André Valmy, Jean Gaven, Jean-Louis Trintignant. Amateur radio operators all over Europe come to the aid of the crew of a French fishing trawler when they become ill and signal for help. Based on an actual incident in the North Sea, this drama attempting to depict the "brotherhood of man" nevertheless seems contrived. Dubbed in English. (Dir: Christian-Jacque, 95 mins.)

If Ever I See You Again (1978)** Joe Brooks, Shelley Hack, Jimmy Breslin, George Plimpton. Obscenely fascinating. Probably the most egocentric film from Hollywood since Jerry Lewis's involuntary retirement. Writer, producer, composer, director, and star Brooks doesn't know much about love, but he understands a lot about revenge. Apparently autobiographical, it's the story of a successful writer of commercial jingles who seeks out the woman who made the mistake of rejecting him in college. Hack proves again she has no acting talent. (105 mins.)

If He Hollers, Let Him Go! (1968)*½ Raymond St. Jacques, Kevin McCarthy, Dana Wynter. (Dir: Charles Martin, 106 mins.)

If I Had a Million (1932)***½ W. C. Fields, George Raft, Gary Cooper, Charles Laughton. Eccentric millionaire decides to will his dough to people picked at random from the phone book, and this is about them. Enjoyable multi-storied film, with the Fields and Laughton episodes screamingly funny. (Dirs: Ernst Lubitsch, Norman Taurog, James Cruze, H. Bruce

Humberstone, Stephen Roberts, William A. Seiter, 90 mins.)

If I Were King (1938)*** Ronald Colman, Basil Rathbone, Frances Dee. You'll love Colman as the swashbuckling, romantic Francois Villon, who, in real life, was a rogue but, in reel life is a lovable hero. One might call him the French Robin Hood. Good costume drama, loaded with action. Also made as *The Vagabond King*. (Dir: Frank Lloyd, 110 mins.)

If It's Tuesday, This Must Be Belgium (1969)*** Suzanne Pleshette, Mildred Natwick, Norman Fell. If you've ever been on a package European tour (and even if you haven't) you'll find plenty of laughs in this saga about a group of travelers who race through seven countries in 18 days. The mixture of the vacationers is delightful, including Pleshette as a young miss who finds time for some romance with handsome Britisher Ian McShane; Miss Natwick as an old lady with energy to spare; Fell and Reva Rose as a married couple who get separated; and Sandy Baron as an Italian-American who almost gets married off while visiting relatives in Venice. Deft screenplay by David Shaw. (Dir: Mel Stuart, 98 mins.)

If Things Were Different (MTV 1980)*** Suzanne Pleshette, Don Murray, Tony Roberts, Artie Johnson. Ms. Pleshette is carving out a new life for herself and her two children after her husband suffers a nervous breakdown which leaves him catatonic. Her relationship with her appealing and understanding boss (Roberts) is handled with restraint and without pat answers. (Dir: Robert Lewis, 104 mins.)

If Tomorrow Comes (MTV 1971)** Patty Duke, Frank Liu. A tearjerker for the ladies. Miss Duke plays a young lady who falls for, and secretly marries, a Japanese-American in southern California a few days before Pearl Harbor. Liu as Patty's husband gives a sincere performance, and James Whitmore as Patty's bigoted father, and Anne Baxter as an understanding schoolteacher, are effective. (Dir: George McGowan, 73 mins.)

If Winter Comes (1947)* Walter Pidgeon, Deborah Kerr, Janet Leigh, Angela Lansbury. (Dir: Victor Saville, 97 mins.)

If You Could Only Cook (1935)**½ Jean Arthur, Herbert Marshall. Dated, but mildly entertaining "depression era" comedy, poor girl meets sad millionaire, thinks he's unemployed, helps him get a job. Result: love. (Dir: William A. Seiter, 70 mins.)

If You Knew Susie (1948)** Eddie Cantor, Joan Davis. Vaudeville team discover a famous ancestor and go to Washington to collect seven billion dollars the government owes them. Mild comedy with music. (Dir: Gordon Douglas, 90 mins.)

Ikiru (Japan, 1952)**** Akira Kurosawa has fashioned a haunting portrait of a lonely man who has spent his life working as a civil servant, seen his wife die, alienated his son, and discovers he is dying of cancer. Determined to give his last days over to enjoying himself, he finds it is not enough, and pours his remaining energy into getting a playground built on the site of a sewage dump. Told in flashback, Kurosawa's intense portrait of a man searching for fulfillment is brilliantly fashioned, capped by a memorable, touching final scene. (Dir: Akira Kurosawa, 150 mins.)

I'll Be Seeing You (1944)*** Ginger Rogers, Joseph Cotten, Shirley Temple, Spring Byington, Tom Tully, Chill Wills, John Derek. A film remarkably redolent of its time, this heavily contrived, depressing romance redeems itself completely whenever the title tune comes on the soundtrack. A wounded vet on furlough (Joseph Cotten) meets and falls in love with a convicted killer (Ginger Rogers, who defenestrated her boss when he made an unwelcome pass—talk about forties *Zeitgeist*), also out on Christmas furlough. Not nearly as trashy as it should be; the pervasive air of hope struggling for an outlet against fatalism is very infectious, since it appears utterly in tune with the mood of its intended audience. I've always found this sort of wartime hokum emotionally engaging, and if you don't, you won't get goosebumps as I do. Dore Schary produced for David Selznick; William Dieterle directed, and that song, of course, was by Irving Kahal and Sammy Fain. (Dir: William Dieterle, 85 mins.)

I'll Be Yours (1947)**½ Deanna Durbin, Tom Drake, Adolphe Menjou. Another light and gay Deanna Durbin comedy about a nice girl searching for a niche in the big city. Tom Drake supplies the love interest opposite Deanna. Remake of *The Good Fairy*, 1935. (Dir: William A. Seiter, 93 mins.)

I'll Cry Tomorrow (1955)**** Susan Hayward, Richard Conte, Jo Van Fleet, Eddie Albert. Superb drama based on Lillian Roth's bold and frank story of her days as an alcoholic and her fight to conquer the dreaded disease. Miss Hayward has never been better and she's matched every step of the way by Jo Van Fleet as her bewildered mother. Conte, Albert and Don Taylor play her various husbands. (Dir: Daniel Mann, 117 mins.)

I'll Get By (1950)**½ June Haver, Gloria De Haven, Dennis Day, William Lundigan. Pleasant musical about a couple of song pluggers and a singing sister act. Many songs and dances and some surprise guest stars (Victor Mature, Jeanne Crain, and Dan Dailey). Gloria De Haven comes off the best in the singing department. (Dir: Richard Sale, 83 mins.)

I'll Get You (Great Britain, 1953)** George Raft, Sally Gray. An FBI man, assisted by a pretty MI operator, tracking down foreign agents who smuggle atomic scientists to the Commies. Slow, not very convincing. (Dirs: Seymour Friedman, Peter Graham Scott, 79 mins.)

I'll Never Forget What's 'Is Name (Great Britain, 1967)***½ Oliver Reed, Orson Welles, Carol White. Incisive portrait of a man disillusioned with his shallow life, and the failure of his efforts to change. Alternately witty and uncomfortably real, generally nicely balanced by director Michael Winner. Fine job by Oliver Reed in the main role. Good work by Orson Welles and Harry Andrews. (Dir: Michael Winner, 99 mins.)

I'll Never Forget You (Great Britain, 1951)**½ Tyrone Power, Ann Blyth, Michael Rennie. Based on the play "Berkeley Square," this charming romantic adventure concerns a scientist who goes back to the 18th Century and relives one of his ancestors' adventures. Women will especially enjoy this film. The cast is perfectly suited to their roles. (Dir: Roy Baker, 90 mins.)

I'll See You In Hell (Italy, 1960)*½ John Drew Barrymore, Eva Bartok. (Dir: Piero Regnoli, 83 mins.)

I'll See You In My Dreams (1952)*** Doris Day, Danny Thomas. A romantic biopic on the rise and success of song writer Gus Kahn. Many good standards are heard done by Doris Day, who plays Mrs. Kahn. Danny Thomas is quite believable as the songsmith. (Dir: Michael Curtiz, 110 mins.)

I'll Take Sweden (1965)**½ Bob Hope, Tuesday Weld. Frankie Avalon. If Bob Hope's brand of film comedy is to your liking, you'll have fun watching his antics in this one. Bob is Tuesday Weld's Daddy, and he whisks her off to Sweden when her romance with Frankie Avalon reaches the serious stage. However, things get hotter in Sweden when Jeremy Slate pops into Tuesday's life and Dina Merrill becomes interested in Hope. The pace is fast but the plot doesn't bear too close an examination. (Dir: Frederick de Cordova, 96 mins.)

Illegal (1955)** Edward G. Robinson, Nina Foch. Well acted but poorly scripted story of the rackets and one couple's involvement. Jayne Mansfield has a brief scene. (Dir: Lewis Allen, 88 mins.)

Illegal Cargo (France, 1957)*½ Francoise Arnoul, Jean-Claude Michel. (Dir: Georges Lacombe, 90 mins.)

Illegal Entry (1949)**½ Howard Duff, Marta Toren, George Brent. Fast-paced action drama about the undercover agents who crack open a large scale smuggling operation which deals with illicit border traffic between Mexico and the United States. The cast is more than competent. (Dir: Frederick de Cordova, 84 mins.)

Illustrated Man, The (1969)***½ Rod Steiger, Claire Bloom, Robert Drivas. Interesting allegorical morality play based on a story by sci-fi writer Ray Bradbury. Scene is a rural camping ground in 1933, where a young man (Drivas) meets a completely tattooed fellow (Steiger). The tattoos each represent a story and as Drivas looks at them, they come to life. (Dir: Jack Smight, 104 mins.)

I'm All Right Jack (Great Britain, 1960)**** Ian Carmichael, Peter Sellers, Terry-Thomas. Screamingly funny satire on labor-management relations in England, as an inept young man finds himself caught between the two in trying to run a factory. Sellers is priceless as an oafish labor leader, and the entire cast catches the spirit of the fun. Recommended. (Dirs: John & Roy Boulting, 104 mins.)

I'm from Missouri (1939)*** Bob Burns, Gladys George. Amusing folksy comedy about a small town Missouri man who goes to England on business and turns the peerage upside down and inspires the English war industry. (Dir: Theodore Reed, 90 mins.)

I'm No Angel (1933)***½ Mae West, Cary Grant, Edward Arnold, Gertrude Michael, Kent Taylor. Mae West is the lion tamer, and Cary Grant the lion in Edward Arnold's traveling circus. West is in rare dudgeon, and the lines are still reasonably uncensored, though the film is many cuts below the preceding *She Done Him Wrong*. Funny courtroom scene. (Dir: Wesley Ruggles, 87 mins.)

Images (1972)**½ Susannah York, Rene Auberjonois. Odd film which attempts to explore the schizophrenia of a young woman. Director-author Robert Altman tried to create suspense by not identifying the woman's images as rooted in either illusion or fact. It doesn't work. Miss York is passable in an impossible role. Compensations include the camerawork by Vilmos Zsigmond and the background of beautiful Ireland. (Dir: Robert Altman, 101 mins.)

Imitation General (1958)*** Glenn Ford, Red Buttons, Taina Elg. Fast-paced service comedy that treats the subject of war lightly and makes heroes of buffoons. Red Buttons steals every scene he's in with his very funny portrayal of a corporal who is on a military stratagem which has M/Sgt. Glenn Ford masquerading as a general. (Dir: George Marshall, 88 mins.)

Imitation of Life (1934)** Claudette Colbert, Warren William, Rochelle Hudson, Louise Bearers, Fredi Washington, Ned Sparks. Far more sentimental than Douglas Sirk's later, icy version of this Fannie Hurst soap opera, John Stahl's film (1934), about a working-girl (Claudette Colbert) who makes good and about Colbert's black maid (Louise Beavers) and her daughter (Fredi Washington) who passes for white, is believable in the context of thirties melodrama and as rich visually as Stahl's other thirties triumphs over implausibility, *Back Street* and *Magnificent Obsession*. (Dir: John M. Stahl, 106 mins.)

Imitation of Life (1959)***½ Lana Turner, John Gavin, Sandra Dee. Lana Turner-Sandra Dee weeper about the friendship of two mothers, one white, one black. Director Douglas Sirk raises this far above the level of soap opera. (124 mins.)

Immacolata and Concetta: The Other Jealously (Italian 1981)** Idadi Benedetto, Marceila Michelangeli, Tommaso Blanco. Definitely one of the weirdest films to come along in a while. The title characters are tough women from Southern Italy who meet in jail and become lovers. A lot of the story deals with the dirt-poor town in which the women live and Immacolata's ambition, which necessitates her sleeping with a local bigwig. The content of the love relationship is nil—all the dialogue between the women is lovey-dovey talk delivered with a passion that would be excessive for a forties MGM movie. The set-piece sex scenes are graphic, almost hard-core; the entire film is ponderously dramatic, with lots of big close-ups and emotionalism. The visuals and sound are cheap in the classic B-film manner. (Dir: Salvatore Piscicelli, 94 mins.)

Immediate Disaster—See: **Stranger from Venus**

Immortal, The (1969)**½ Christopher George, Carol Lynley. The fairly original story was the pilot film for a TV series. Christopher George is cast as a young-looking fortyish test-driver-mechanic who discovers he has a unique blood type which slows down his aging process almost to a halt and keeps him from contracting diseases. The whole thing comes out when his aged boss, millionaire tycoon Barry Sullivan, receives a transfusion of George's blood and temporarily feels rejuvenated. Naturally, George becomes a hunted man. The production is first rate and the acting standout is Barry Sullivan as the wealthy old man who can't face dying. (Dir: Joseph Sargent, 75 mins.)

Immortal Bachelor, The (Italy, 1979)** Giancarlo Giannini, Monica Vitti, Vittorio Gassman, Claudia Cardinale. A fine quartet of Italian performers carry this conventional farce. (Dir: Marcello Fondato, 95 mins.)

Immortal Garden, The (U.S.S.R., 1956)*** V. Makarov, V. Emelyanov. Grim, effective WW II film, designed to glorify the Russian soldiers' valor. Follows the defenders of the Brest fortress, where the initial Nazi invasion of Russia occurred, throughout the war, making liberal use of documentary footage. Co-director and cameraman Tisse is best known for his camera work in Eisenstein's movies. (Dirs: Z. Agnanenko, Edward Tisse, 90 mins.)

Immortal Story, The France, MTV 1968)***½ Orson Welles, Jeanne Moreau, Roger Coggio. Based on the story by Isak Dinesen, this has been adapted and directed by Orson Welles, who also plays the role of an elderly merchant in the Portuguese colony of Macao on the coast of China during the end of the 19th century. This is not top drawer Welles, but lesser Welles is still better than most

other film-making, and this is well worth seeing. There's a sailor lucky enough to get paid to sleep with Jeanne Moreau in this curious tale, originally commissioned by French television. (It runs just over one hour.) English dialogue. The color shots of the Orient by cameraman Willy Kurant are a major help in bringing off this bizarre story. (Dir: Orson Welles, 63 mins.)

Impasse (1969)***½ Burt Reynolds, Anne Francis. An adventure film of the sort in which fearless heroes deal with both women and danger at about the same emotional level . . . two steps above stoicism. Burt Reynolds (before he took off as a sex symbol of the '70s in films) plays the organizer of a caper involving buried World War II treasure in the Philippines. (Dir: Richard Benedict, 96 mins.)

Imperfect Angel (Germany, 1958)*½ Peter Van Eyck, Corny Collins. (Dir: Alfred Vohrer, 98 mins.)

Imperfect Lady, The (1947)**½ Ray Milland, Teresa Wright. In order to aid a gentleman who shielded her, a woman must admit an indiscretion and risk exposing her husband to shame and ruin. If that interests you, maybe you'll like this film. (Dir: Lewis Allen, 97 mins.)

Impersonator, The (Great Britain, 1963)** John Crawford, Jane Griffiths. American soldier in London is a suspected molester of women and murderer, but his innocence is proven. Fairly interesting whodunit with a rather unusual plot twist. (Dir: Alfred Shaughnessy, 64 mins.)

Importance of Being Earnest, The (Great Britain, 1952)**** Michael Redgrave, Edith Evans, Dorothy Tutin, Joan Greenwood, Margot Rutherford. Something of a definitive cast in a less than definitive work of cinema. Still the Oscar Wilde play is unlikely to ever be mounted with a more impeccable array of performers. Wilde is so much more than the sum of his epigrams; this is probably the most perfect British comedy since the Restoration. Color. (Dir: Anthony Asquith, 95 mins.)

Impossible Years, The (1968)*½ David Niven, Lola Albright. (Dir: Michael Gordon, 91 mins.)

Impostor, The (1944)**½ Jean Gabin, Ellen Drew. Criminal escapes during an air raid, assumes a new identity and becomes a soldier during World War II. Slow and talky drama, nevertheless has a certain interest. Well acted. Alternate title: **Strange Confession**. (Dir: Julien Duvivier, 95 mins.)

Impostor, The (MTV 1975)* Paul Hecht, Edward Asner, Meredith Baxter, Nancy Kelly. (Dir: Edward M. Abroms, 75 mins.)

In a Lonely Place (1950)***½ Humphrey Bogart, Gloria Grahame, Frank Lovejoy. Gripping story of a Hollywood writer who is under suspicion of murder and his strange romance with his female alibi. Good script with Hollywood background raises the film above the average murder yarn. Bogart great as always. (Dir: Nicholas Ray, 91 mins.)

In a Year with 13 Moons (West Germany, 1980)**** Volker Spengler, Ingrid Caven, Gottfried John, Elisabeth Trissenaar, Eva Mattes. Rainer Werner Fassbinder follows up *The Marriage of Maria Braun* with one of his most difficult, thought-provoking films. Fassbinder follows the life of transexual Elvira Weishaupf through a series of degradations, culminating in her encounter with the man for whom she got her sex-change operation. Fassbinder dares the audience to accept his grotesques on his own terms, intentionally leaving unbridged the gap between the sordid subject matter and the elevated style. Volker Spengler gives an unnervingly honest performance as Elvira, never acting from outside his character. Recommended. (Dir: Rainer Werner Fassbinder, 129 mins.)

In Broad Daylight (MTV 1971)** Richard Boone, Suzanne Pleshette, John Marley, Stella Stevens. Boone, with dark glasses and cane, plays a recently blinded actor about to murder his unfaithful wife. The idea of a blind actor who can fool people with disguises and escape from tight spots by feeling his way down fire escapes is pretty dopey like the flick. (Dir: Richard Day, 78 mins.)

In Celebration (Great Britain-Canada, 1974)**** Alan Bates, James Bolam, Brian Cox, Bill Owen. The marvelous combination of director Lindsay Anderson and writer David Storey that produced the memorable "This Sporting Life" is reunited in this powerful adaptation of Storey's play about a coalminer's family in a drab town in northern England. Three grown sons return to the village to celebrate their parents' fortieth wedding anniversary. The sons, whose jobs are distasteful to them, mock their father about the "significance" of his mining career. Storey has skillfully delineated his major characters, and there's not a false acting note anywhere. Bates is superb in the leading role of Andrew, a failed painter. An American Film Theatre presentation. (Dir: Lindsay Anderson, 131 mins.)

In Cold Blood (1967)***½ Robert Blake, Scott Wilson, John Forsythe, Paul Stewart. Richard Brooks transforms Truman Capote's objective report of the background, commission, and solution of a murder into an uneasy mixture of facile Freudianism and forties expressionism. The harsh documentary style that the material demands clashes with Brooks's nervous liberalism, and the result is a film that alternately grips and bores—more of the former in the first part of the film, more of the latter in the second. Fine performances from Robert Blake and Scott Wilson as the killers. B&W (Dir: Richard Brooks, 134 mins.)

In Dracula's Castle (MTV 1973)** Johnny Whitaker, Scott Kolden, Clu Gulager, Mills Watson. Wholesome youngsters, out shooting a Dracula horror movie, foul up jewel thieves in this detective entry for kids. Whitaker fits the Disney mold as the innocent, ingratiating lad who works the camera. (Dir: Robert Totten, 104 mins.)

In Enemy Country (1968)**½ Tony Franciosa, Anjanette Comer, Paul Hubschmid. Old-fashioned espionage yarn set during WW II. It's the kind of film in which the heroic action never lets up so you're not too bothered by the holes in the script. Tony Franciosa is properly stoic as a French agent who leads a mission into Nazi Germany and manages to carry it off. The finale in a munitions factory generates excitement and the supporting cast, particularly Paul Hubschmid as Miss Comer's Nazi officer husband, is good. (Dir: Harry Keller, 107 mins.)

In Harm's Way (1965)**½ John Wayne, Kirk Douglas, Patricia Neal, Brandon de Wilde. Despite an impressive all-star cast and a fairly interesting WW II setting, this film fails to register a strong impact. There are too many sub-plots and the Japanese attack of Pearl Harbor merely serves as a backdrop to the love stories of the principals. Of the large cast, Burgess Meredith and Patrick O'Neal come across best. (Dir: Otto Preminger, 165 mins.)

In-Laws, The (1979)***½ Peter Falk, Alan Arkin, Richard Libertini, Nancy Dussault. Wacky comedy that succeeds, due largely to the verve of Falk and Arkin and the sharp cinematography of David Walsh. Arthur Hiller directs up to par, for once. (103 mins.)

In Like Flint (1967)*** James Coburn, Lee J. Cobb, Jean Hale. Fun and games, spy-spoof style! This sequel to "Our Man Flint" chronicles the further outrageous adventures of the "coolest" super-spy of them all, Derek Flint, stylishly played by James Coburn. The plot, merely an excuse for displays of Coburn's gymnastic and romantic skills, centers on a diabolical scheme by a group of women to take control of the world. (Dir: Gordon Douglas, 114 mins.)

In Love and War (1958)**½ Robert Wagner, Bradford Dillman, Jeffrey Hunter, Hope Lange, Sheree North, Dana Wynter, France Nuyen. Episodic but entertaining drama about three young marines' adventures "in love and war." The most interesting character is Brad Dillman as a bright, well read, young man who questions life and tries to find some answers. Dana Wynter, as a beautiful mixed-up socialite in love with Dillman have a couple of good scenes. (Dir: Philip Dunne, 111 mins.)

In Name Only (1939)***½ Cary Grant, Carole Lombard, Kay Francis, Charles Coburn, Helen Vinson. A film whose interest and intelligence far outstrip its quality, this sudser is unusually sensitive in its performance and direction. The problem is the script, and the inability of director Cromwell to punch it up with character insights sufficient to redeem it. Nonetheless, the love triangle of Cary Grant, Carole Lombard, and Kay Francis is adult in the melding of the civilized and the hysteric that separates the grown-ups from the juveniles. Even when the film degenerates into soapy garbage, their poise, intelligence, and vulnerability carry claptrap into a realm of performer's art. (Dir: John Cromwell, 102 mins.)

In Name Only (MTV 1969)* Michael Callan, Ann Prentiss, Eve Arden. (Dir: E. W. Swackhamer, 75 mins.)

In Old California (1942)** John Wayne, Binnie Barnes, Albert Dekker. Young pharmacist sets up shop in Sacramento, bucks the outlaw boss of the town. In modern California they can make some dull oaters. (Dir: William McGann, 88 mins.)

In Old Chicago (1938)***½ Tyrone Power, Alice Faye, Don Ameche. Story of the O'Leary family whose cow is credited with starting the great Chicago fire. Fictional story is interesting and builds neatly into the fire spectacle. Good drama of an era. Alice Brady won Best Supporting Actress Oscar. (Dir: Henry King, 115 mins.)

In Old Vienna (Austria, 1956)* Heinz Roettinger, Robert Killich. (72 mins.)

In Praise of Older Women (Canada, 1979)**½ Tom Berenger, Karen Black, Susan Strasberg, Helen Shaver. The sexual odyssey of a young man who prefers to bed older, experienced women. Plays on one-note, but handsome Berenger has the right touch as the amorous Hungarian swain. (Dir: George Kaczender, 108 mins.)

In Search of America (1971)**½ Carl Betz, Vera Miles, Jeff Bridges. Don't let the grandiose title of this offbeat pilot film for a proposed series put you off... it's an entertaining tale with a charming family that takes to the road en masse to experience the land and its variety of people. Jeff Bridges (Lloyd Bridges' younger son) is very good in the leading role of the catalyst of the venture. He convinces his father (Carl Betz), mother (Vera Miles), and grandmother (Ruth McDevitt) to accompany him on a trek around the country in a reconverted vintage passenger bus. The production is first-rate, but the tale goes a bit stale with the introduction of too many fringe characters in a rock festival setting. In any case, it's worth watching. (Dir: Paul Bogart, 72 mins.)

In Search of Gregory (1970)** Julie Christie, Michael Sarrazin, John Hurt. A forgettable adventure which largely wastes the lovely Miss Christie. Confused story about a young girl (Christie) living in Rome, who goes to Geneva to find romance at her father's wedding. Julie's disturbed younger brother isn't much help in her quest. (Dir: Peter Wood, 90 mins.)

In Search of Historic Jesus (1979)** John Rubinstein, John Anderson, Nehemiah Persoff, Royal Dano. Less than edifying examination of the question of Jesus's divinity, with evidence presented ponderously. The Shroud of Turin, which is said to have been wrapped around his body in the tomb and to wear an imprint of his face, is shown. The reenacted portions are unconvincingly done, with Rubinstein as a hippielike Christ. (Dir: Henning Schellerup, 91 mins.)

In Search of Noah's Ark (1976)* (Dir: James L. Conway, 95 mins.)

In Search of the Castaways (U.S.-Great Britain, 1962)*** Hayley Mills, Wilfrid Hyde-White, Maurice Chevalier, George Sanders. Jules Verne classic adventure yarn, well produced in the Disney manner. Stars the young, ingratiating Mills as the daughter of a sea captain who has been abducted. There follows a mind-boggling adventure which pits the cast against earthquakes, floods, and avalanches which are a tribute to Hollywood special effects geniuses. (Dir: Robert Stevenson, 104 mins.)

In Society (1944)** Bud Abbott, Lou Costello, Marion Hutton. Dumb plumbers foil an attempted art theft. Usual A & C slapstick. (Dir: Jean Yarbrough, 64 mins.)

In Tandem (MTV 1974)** Claude Akins, Frank Converse. Truckers side with an orange rancher, pressured to sell his land to an amusement-park group. It may be predictable fare, but Akins and Converse carry it off with their attractive, energetic performances. Pilot for the subsequent series. (Dir: Bernard Kowalski, 74 mins.)

In the Cool of the Day (Great Britain, 1963)**½ Peter Finch, Jane Fonda, Angela Lansbury. It's the performances by a trio of stars that saves this film from being just another soap opera geared for the ladies. Jane Fonda, Peter Finch and Angela Lansbury form a strange triangle amid the landscape of Greece in this tale about a young, bored wife (Miss Fonda) who falls hopelessly in love with the very married Mr. Finch. Miss Lansbury is Finch's emotionally and physically scarred wife. It's all very old fashioned movie drama, but the acting at least keeps you interested. (Dir: Robert Stevens, 89 mins.)

In the Doghouse (Great Britain, 1961)** Leslie Phillips, James Booth, Peggy Cummins. Forced farce about two veterinarians fresh out of college who set up quarters in the same area. Some laughs but thin going. (Dir: Darcy Conyers, 93 mins.)

In the French Style (U.S.-France, 1963)*** Jean Seberg, Stanley Baker. Frequently fascinating study of the post-World War II female expatriate, embodied in a young art student who comes to Paris, remains to become involved in a series of passionate, usually brief, ultimately meaningless love affairs. Incisive Irwin Shaw script, Robert Parrish direction; very good performance by Seberg. Flavorsome Parisian location scenes. (Dir: Robert Parrish, 105 mins.)

In the Glitter Palace (MTV 1977)**½ Chad Everett, David Wayne, Barbara Hershey. Here's a murder mystery with lesbian overtones that turns out to be better than expected. "Medical Center"'s Chad Everett is more than competent as a lawyer digging into a seamy case involving lesbians. The women's side is told with taste and understanding. Robert Butler deserves a plug for his direction, and the supporting cast, from Barbara Hershey to David Wayne, is effective. (Dir: Robert Butler, 106 mins.)

In the Good Old Summertime (1949)*** Judy Garland, Van Johnson, Buster Keaton, Spring Byington, S. Z. Sakall. A must for Judy Garland fans. Warmhearted comedy-romance about two clerks in a music shop who have a mutual secret, without knowing it. Judy sings "I Don't Care" and other delightful tunes. Based on James Stewart-Margaret Sullavan film "The Shop Around the Corner." (Dir: Robert Z. Leonard, 102 mins.)

In the Heat of the Night (1967)**** Sidney Poitier, Rod Steiger, Lee Grant, Warren Oates. Exciting, superbly acted and directed film about prejudice, manners and morals in a small Mississippi town. Poitier, portraying a Philadelphia detective who becomes accidentally involved in trying to solve a murder case, teams with Steiger to create one of the most fascinating duels of wits the screen has offered in a long time. Steiger won a richly deserved Academy Award, as did Stirling Silliphant's adaptation of the novel by John Ball. Director Norman Jewison does an outstanding job in creating the subsurface tension of life in a "sleepy" Southern town, and the supporting performances are uniformly fine. A first-rate film in all respects. The location scenes of Mississippi, incidentally, were filmed in Southern Illinois. (Dir: Norman Jewison, 110 mins.)

In the Matter of Karen Ann Quinlan (MTV 1977)*** Brian Keith, Piper Laurie. Keith and Laurie give sensitive, highly emotional performances as Catholic parents Joe and Julie Quinlan, who sue for the right to permit their irreparably brain-damaged daughter to die a natural death. A real-life story, handled with compassion and restraint. (Dir: Hal Jordan, 104 mins.)

In the Navy (1941)**½ Abbott and Costello, Dick Powell. The youngsters should enjoy this crazy film about a radio singer who seeks refuge in the Navy. (Dir: Arthur Lubin, 85 mins.)

In the Year of the Pig (1969)**** A riveting, informative, and ultimately moving documentary about American involvement in the Vietnam War. Produced and directed by Emile de Antonio, who was responsible for the remarkable '64 documentary "Point of Order." "Pig" is a shattering indictment of American policy in Vietnam and Southeast Asia. Shows through a series of brilliantly edited sequences of stock footage our lying politicians, and the way in which we devastated the land and the people all the while talking about "peace." Probably the finest film yet made about the Vietnam War, and a reminder that the timid American movie industry never honestly dealt with this momentous event in American society. (Dir: Emile de Antonio, 101 mins.)

In This Our Life (1942)**½ Bette Davis, Dennis Morgan, Olivia de Havilland, Charles Coburn, George Brent. Flashes of director John Huston's personality are sprinkled throughout this admittedly commissioned work. Davis plays the neurotic with a vengeance, screwing up her sister, her husband, and herself. Howard Koch's adaption of the Ellen Glasgow novel manages to hold her nefarious deeds within a credible dramatic framework. (97 mins.)

In Which We Serve (Great Britain, 1942)**** Noel Coward, John Mills. Drama of the men of a British destroyer during World War II, from the captain to the crew. Coward wrote, co-directed, composed the music, and plays the leading role, and does a great job in all departments. Stirring, poignant, a great film. (Dirs: Noel Coward, David Lean, 115 mins.)

Inadmissible Evidence (Great Britain, 1968)**** Nicol Williamson, Eleanor Fazan, Jill Bennett, Gillian Hills. John Osborne's searing stage play about a middle-aged English barrister whose emotional disintegration is unsparingly depicted. If the title role of Bill Maitland was poorly or even just competently acted, this could be an exasperating and embarrassing experience. In the hands of British film and stage star Nicol Williamson, it is one of the most overwhelming and moving experiences that films have offered in many years. Williamson is an actor of staggering energy, technical virtuosity, and sheer theatrical magnetism. This film must be seen by anyone who appreciates great acting, and his enormous talents keep the viewer absorbed, even though you may seldom identify with or care about the manic solicitor Williamson portrays. (Dir: Anthony Page, 96 mins.)

Incendiary Blonde (1945)*** Betty Hutton, Arturo de Cordova. Entertaining musical framed in a fictitious screen biography of famous speakeasy hostess, Texas Guinan. Good music from the prohibition era well done by Miss Hutton. (Dir: George Marshall, 113 mins.)

Incident, The (1967)**½ Tony Musante, Martin Sheen, Beau Bridges, Jack Gilford, Thelma Ritter, Ed McMahon, Ruby Dee, Brock Peters. Terror on the New York subway, as two hoodlums molest an assorted group of passengers. May seem overdone to non-New Yorkers, and it is to a considerable extent, but the basic premise—the passivity of people in times of danger—is disturbingly true. If this all sounds familiar to some of you it's because you may have seen the original 1963 TV production of this drama, which was then entitled "Ride With Terror." (Dir: Larry Peerce, 107 mins.)

Incident at Midnight (Great Britain, 1963)** Anton Diffring, William Sylvester. A former Nazi is spotted in a druggist's shop by an undercover member of the narcotics squad. Okay Edgar Wallace mystery. (Dir: Norman Harrison, 56 mins.)

Incident at Phantom Hill (1966)** Robert Fuller, Jocelyn Lane, Dan Duryea. Assorted group engages in a perilous trek to reclaim gold which had been stolen and hidden years before. Undistinguished western. (Dir: Earl Bellamy, 88 mins.)

Incident in Saigon (France, 1960)*½ Odile Versois, Pierre Massima. (Dir: Jean Leduc, 85 mins.)

Incident in San Francisco (1971)** Christopher Connelly, Richard Kiley. Here's another slick pilot film for a proposed big city newspaper TV series, and as these stories go, it's fair. Christopher Connelly has the leading role of the brash young reporter on the San Francisco *Times* who gets deeply involved in the plight of a man (Richard Kiley) who accidentally causes the death of a young punk while coming to the aid of an old man. Familiar yarn about the honest samaritan who has his good deed turn into a nightmare. Cast, especially Kiley as the victim, is more than competent. (Dir: Don Medford, 98 mins.)

Incident on a Dark Street (MTV 1973)** James Olson, Robert Pine. Fair entry on U.S. attorneys who try court cases on dope peddling, and mobsters in the building contracting business. Good legal guys (Olson, David Canary, Pine) are overshadowed by the colorful baddies (Richard Castellano, Gilbert Roland, William Shatner), with Castellano's small-time Italian hood stealing the show. (Dir: Buzz Kulik, 73 mins.)

Incorrigible (France, 1979)** Jean-Paul Belmondo, Genevieve Bujold. One of director Philippe de Broca's typical light star vehicles. If you rarely get dressed, it might charm the pants off you.

Incredible Journey, The (Canada, 1963)*** Emile Genest, John Drainie. Good family picture with all the Disney components. Two dogs and a cat undertake a 250-mile journey through rough Canadian wilderness, encountering a lynx, a mean farm dog, and an inhospitable bear along the way. Beautiful scenery and a heartwarming story make this enjoyable. (Dir: Fletcher Markle, 80 mins.)

Incredible Journey of Doctor Meg Laurel, The (MTV 1979)**½ Lindsay Wagner, Jane Wyman. A determined young woman doctor returns to her roots in Appalachia to try to help the backwoods inhabitants, who are leery of modern medicine. She locks horns with the local healer, Granny Arrowroot, and the drama comes to life. Wyman's Granny takes the acting honors. (Dir: Guy Green, 156 mins.)

Incredible Mr. Limpet, The (1964)** Don Knotts, Carole Cook, Jack Weston. Mr. Knotts as Mr. Limpet, the man who wished he was a fish—and got his wish, becoming the Navy's secret weapon during World War II. Fantasy may provide some moments of amusement, but the viewer has to be either a Knotts fan or pretty fish-happy. (Dir: Arthur Lubin, 102 mins.)

Incredible Petrified World, The (1958)*½ John Carradine, Robert Clarke. (Dir: Jerry Warren, 78 mins.)

Incredible Rocky Mountain Race, The (MTV 1978)** Forrest Tucker, Larry Storch. A broad, slapdash frontier comedy about a feud between Mark Twain and Mike Fink which results in an improbable cross-country race from Missouri to California, dreamed up by the good people of Missouri who want to get rid of the troublemakers. (Dir: Jim Conway, 104 mins.)

Incredible Sarah, The (Great Britain, 1976)* Glenda Jackson, Daniel Massey, Douglas Wilmer, Yvonne Mitchell, Edward Judd. (Dir: Richard Fleischer, 106 mins.)

Incredible Shrinking Man, The (1957)***½ Grant Williams, Randy Stuart, Paul Langton, William Schallert. An important work in a footnote genre, Jack Arnold's 1957 science-fiction film is one of the decade's few to disdain rubber monsters and come close to making the standard s.f. mysticism seem meaningful. A scientist (Grant Williams), exposed to the usual mysterious radiation, finds himself growing smaller and smaller, merging with the universe as a sentient molecule in Arnold's amazing final image. (Dir: Jack Arnold, 81 mins.)

Incredible Shrinking Woman, The (1981)** Lily Tomlin, Charles Grodin, Ned Beatty. What's really incredible is how far this film goes to avoid the ideas, feminist and otherwise, embedded in its promising premise, which has suburban housewife Lily Tomlin starting to shrink when she inhales a noxious combination of domestic chemicals. It must have sounded a little too much like satire, so in the limitless commercial wisdom of the studio, the story jags off into an incredibly stupid contrivance about mad scientists and plots for world domination. The picture gets its biggest laugh from a guy in a gorilla suit (Rick Baker, of *King Kong* fame) giving the finger. The director, Joel Schumacher, was once a costume designer; true to his background, he's put most of his jokes in the clothes. (88 mins.)

Incredibly Strange Creatures Who Stopped Living And Became Mixed-Up Zombies, The (1964)* Cash Flagg, Carolyn Brandt. (Dir: Ray Dennis Steckler [Cash Flagg], 82 mins.)

Indestructible Man, The (1956)* Lon

331

Chaney, Marian Carr. (Dir: Jack Pollexfen, 70 mins.)

Indian Fighter, The (1955)**½ Kirk Douglas. Douglas is the whole show in this western drama about Sioux uprisings in the Oregon Territory circa 1870. Army Scout Douglas is sent on a peace mission deep into Sioux country. Plenty of action. (Dir: Andre de Toth, 88 mins.)

Indian Love Call—See: **Rose Marie** (1936)

Indian Paint (1965)** Johnny Crawford, Jay Silverheels. Oft-told story of an Indian boy's love for a wild colt, but done pleasantly enough. (Dir: Norman Foster, 91 mins.)

Indian Scarf, The (Germany, 1963)*½ Heinz Drache, Corny Collins. (Dir: Alfred Vohrer, 85 mins.)

Indict and Convict (MTV 1974)**½ George Grizzard, Eli Wallach, William Shatner, Myrna Loy. A sensational case of a seamy Los Angeles double murder. When the wife of a deputy district attorney and her lover are found shot, the chief suspect, the D.A., claims to have been miles away at the time. (Dir: Boris Sagal, 100 mins.)

Indiscreet (British, 1958)**** Cary Grant, Ingrid Bergman, Cecil Parker. Delightfully sophisticated comedy about the on-again, off-again romance between a handsome and wealthy American diplomat and a ravishing European actress. Good lines and magnificent sets. Grant and Bergman are perfect as the urbane pair of lovers. Produced and directed by Stanley Donen on location in London. (100 mins.)

Indiscretion of an American Wife (1954)**½ Jennifer Jones, Montgomery Clift, Gino Cervi, Richard Beymer. Botched attempt to make a neorealist art film in the American mode, with David Selznick hiring Vittorio de Sica to direct Jennifer Jones and Montgomery Clift as participants in a brief encounter. None of it works very well, yet it's interesting to watch these artistic minds at work in utter futility. It is barely over an hour long, which is just short enough to sustain the curiosity throughout. (Dir: Vittorio De Sica, 63 mins.)

Inferno (1953)*** Robert Ryan, Rhonda Fleming, William Lundigan. Suspenseful drama about a pair of ruthless lovers who plot the abandonment of the woman's husband in the Mojave Desert. Robert Ryan plays the abandoned millionaire who manages to survive his plotters' deed. Keeps your interest throughout. (Dir: Roy Baker, 83 mins.)

Infiltrator (France, 1955)** Henri Vidal, Monique Van Vooren, Erich Von Stroheim. Slim story of a police agent who penetrates a drug ring and is threatened by the release from prison of a former underworld czar (played by Stroheim in an appearance that briefly enlivens the proceedings). (Dir: Pierre Foucaud, 110 mins.)

Informer, The (1935)**** Victor McLaglen, Preston Foster, Heather Angel, Margot Grahame, Wallace Ford, Una O'Connor. The inflated reputation of this moody, heavily symbolic effort from John Ford has rightly been put into perspective by critics who now recognize that Ford went on to greater things during the next 30 years. Still, if the extravagant praise of it by thirties critics was a bit unwarranted, it is still a Ford film and still very much a work of great stylistic assurance, deep conviction, and great insight into the need of a man (Victor McLaglen) to betray his friend if only to assert his existence as an individual against the rules of society. McLaglen never topped his performance as Gyppo Nolan, the man who rats on a comrade during the Irish troubles; he won an Oscar. Also Oscars to Ford, Best Director; Dudley Nichols, Best Screenplay; and Max Steiner, Best Musical Score. (Dir: John Ford, 91 mins.)

Informers, The (Great Britain, 1964)**½ Nigel Patrick, Catherine Woodville, Margaret Whiting. Police Inspector's informer is killed by a gang of robbers, so he carries on to nab the ring despite orders to leave it alone. Capable crime melodrama breaks no new ground but is well done. (Dir: Ken Annakin, 105 mins.)

Inga (Sweden, 1968)* Marie Liljedahl, Monica Strommerstedt. (Dir: Joseph W. Sarno, 81 mins.)

Inherit the Wind (1960)**** Spencer Tracy, Fredric March, Gene Kelly. The powerful Broadway play dealing with the famous trial in the twenties in which a school teacher was arrested for teaching Darwin's theory of evolution makes exciting screen entertainment. Tracy and March are excellent as defender and prosecutor respectively. Kelly is surprisingly good as the newspaper man who is instrumental in focusing national attention on the court proceedings. (Dir: Stanley Kramer, 127 mins.)

Inheritance, The (Great Britain, 1947)*** Jean Simmons, Derrick DeMarney. Girl attempts to foil a wicked uncle's effort to have her put out of the way so he can claim her inheritance. Theatrical Victorian thriller manages to generate considerable suspense. From the novel *Uncle Silas* by Sheridan Le Fanu. Alternate title: **Uncle Silas.** (Dir: Charles Frank, 90 mins.)

Inheritance, The (Italy, 1978)*** Anthony Quinn, Dominique Sanda, Fabio Testi. Mauro Bolognini, a mediocre *metteur en scene*, poaches on Douglas Sirk territory with this story of a grasping working class girl who marries into a wealthy family, only to engage its aging patriarch in a lecherous relationship. Bolognini is a generally impersonal filmmaker content to zoom incessantly through his overstuffed decor, but this project has elements of delirium that certify it as his best work. It has drama and sex, which lends some life to the lighting and decor. Dominique Sanda and Anthony Quinn co-star, both very sexy, with Adriana Asti in support.

It isn't great art, but it is exceptionally titillating trash. (Dir: Mauro Bolognini, 105 mins.)

Initiation of Sarah, The (MTV 1978)** Kay Lenz, Shelley Winters. Lenz stars as a college student who becomes involved in the demonic rituals of an old sorority, and Winters is around to add her brand of histrionic terror. Some second-generation talents such as Elizabeth Stack, Nora Heflin, Tisa Farrow, and Talia Balsam are coeds. Hardly "The Sweethearts of Sigma Chi." (Dir: Robert Day, 104 mins.)

Inn of the Sixth Happiness, The (Great Britain, 1958)***½ Ingrid Bergman, Curt Jurgens, Robert Donat. Excellently acted drama of a missionary woman in China and her attempts to lead some children to safety on a perilous trek through enemy territory. Runs to excessive length, but has top work by Bergman and Robert Donat as a mandarin, a compelling finale. Donat's last film. (Dir: Mark Robson, 158 mins.)

Inn on Dartmoor, The (Germany, 1964)*½ Heinz Drache, Paul Klinger. (Dir: Rudolf Zehetgruber, 90 mins.)

Innocent, The (Italy, 1976)***½ Giancarlo Giannini, Laura Antonelli, Jennifer O'Neill. Director Luchino Visconti's last film is a haunting account of aristocratic chauvinism and sexual double standards in turn-of-the-century Italy. Giannini is excellent as the psychotic husband whose lust cannot be satisfied, Antonelli is sensitive as his tormented wife, and O'Neill is superb as his cunning, possessive mistress. Sumptuous photography, costuming, and setting—elegant villas in Italy—are a plus. The pace is sometimes slow. (112 mins.)

Innocent and the Damned—See: **Girls' Town** (1959, Mamie Van Doren)

Innocent Bystanders (Great Britain, 1973)** Stanley Baker, Geraldine Chaplin, Donald Pleasence, Dana Andrews. Muddled espionage film which looks and sounds a great deal like an infinitely superior film, "The Spy Who Came in From the Cold." Stanley Baker is the aging agent who is sent on his last assignment to bring back a Russian scientist named Kaplan from his exile in Turkey. (Dir: Peter Collinson, 111 mins.)

Innocent Sinners (Great Britain, 1958)**½ June Archer, Christopher Hey, Brian Hammond, Flora Robson, David Kossoff. Sentimental but often touching screening of Rumer Godden's novel, "An Episode of Sparrows," about a neglected, tough little girl and two street youths, who try to make a garden out of a bombed-out London lot. Fairy-tale motifs in a barren reality are not as fully exploited as in the novel. Ms. Godden co-scripted. (Dir: Philip Leacock, 95 mins.)

Innocents, The (U.S.-Great Britain, 1961)**** Deborah Kerr, Martin Stephens, Pamela Franklin. Henry James' classic tale dealing with the supernatural, "The

Turn of the Screw," becomes a brilliant suspense film. Deborah Kerr is magnificent as the governess who becomes enmeshed in the eerie household in which the two young children appear to be possessed by ghosts. The youngsters, Pamela Franklin and Martin Stephens, complement Miss Kerr's performance and the entire film is flawless in building to the shattering climax. By all means, don't miss this one, directed by Jack Clayton. (100 mins.)

Innocents in Paris (Great Britain, 1953)**½ Alastair Sim, Margaret Rutherford, Claire Bloom, Laurence Harvey. Londoners take off to see Paris for the first time. Lengthy but amusing film. (Dir: Gordon Parry, 93 mins.)

Innocents with Dirty Hands, The—See: **Dirty Hands**

Inserts (Great Britain, 1975)*** Richard Dreyfuss, Jessica Harper, Veronica Cartwright. John Byrum's directorial debut (he also wrote the script) is bad in almost as many ways as it is good, but the good things are what count. The film is set in the '30s. Excellent acting by Dreyfuss as a former boy wonder director and Harper as an eccentric young lady who decides to jolt Dreyfuss out of his withdrawal from life and to cure his chronic impotence. Some of the actors are embarrassing, and the script often becomes thematically obtrusive. Features the cinema's best orgasm. (99 mins.)

Inside a Girls' Dormitory (France, 1953)** Jean Marais, Francoise Arnoul, Jeanne Moreau. A young, handsome detective arrives at a French girls' boarding school to solve a murder. A choice assignment but a dull movie. (Dir: Henri Decoin, 102 mins.)

Inside Daisy Clover (1965)**½ Natalie Wood, Christopher Plummer, Robert Redford. Although the story about a young film star in the Hollywood of the '30s is mostly glossy soap opera, some good performances make it palatable. Christopher Plummer comes off best as a tyrannical studio head, and Robert Redford is effective in the complex role of a deeply troubled motion-picture matinee idol. Natalie Wood is only half as successful as her co-stars in the title role, the waif-turned-star-turned-neurotic. (Dir: Robert Mulligan, 128 mins.)

Inside Detroit (1956)** Dennis O'Keefe, Pat O'Brien. The war for control by the rackets of the unions in the automobile industry comes into focus in this overdone drama. O'Keefe and O'Brien (sounds like a vaudeville team) are competent in their roles as foes. (Dir: Fred F. Sears, 82 mins.)

Inside Moves (1980)*** John Savage, David Morse, Diana Scarwid, Amy Wright, Harold Russell. Director Richard Donner's film about a group of handicapped people who hang out in a local bar. Some authentically observed behavior of the afflicted, who tend to tell outlandish jokes on one another and can be a lot of fun. The film often strains for an upbeat tone. Cinematographer Laszlo Kovacs is fine, as usual. (Dir: Richard Donner, 113 mins.)

Inside North Vietnam (1967)*** Documentary report photographed in North Vietnam by film-maker Felix Greene, which is of interest, among other reasons, because American audiences have seen so little footage taken in North Vietnam itself. Greene is admittedly hostile to the American presence in Vietnam, and his documentary must be viewed in that light, but there are numerous scenes of village life, and life in the capital of Hanoi, which will interest any thoughtful viewer. (Dir: Felix Greene, 85 mins.)

Inside Out (Great Britain-West Germany, 1975)*½ Telly Savalas, Robert Culp, James Mason. Alternate title: **Golden Heist, The.** (Dir: Peter Duffell, 97 mins.)

Inside Story, The (1948)** William Lundigan, Marsha Hunt. During a bank holiday in the depression days of 1933, a thousand dollars is suddenly in circulation, with startling consequences. Mild little comedy-drama. (Dir: Allan Dwan, 87 mins.)

Inside Straight (1951)** David Brian, Arlene Dahl, Mercedes McCambridge. Ruthless man out to make money lets nothing stand in his way. Slow-paced costume melodrama, stereotyped role for Brian as the big tycoon. (Dir: Gerald Mayer, 89 mins.)

Inside the Mafia (1959)** Cameron Mitchell, Elaine Edwards, Robert Strauss. Rival hoods set up a plot to bump off a ganglord arriving for a big power meeting. Obvious crime melodrama relies upon the action to get it over. (Dir: Edward L. Cahn, 72 mins.)

Inspector Calls, An (Great Britain, 1954)*** Alastair Sim, Eileen Moore. A mysterious policeman investigates the family of a girl who has died of poisoning. From J. B. Priestley's mystical drama, this is rather vague, but occasionally interesting. (Dir: Guy Hamilton, 80 mins.)

Inspector Clouseau (Great Britain, 1968)* Alan Arkin, Frank Finlay, Beryl Reid. (Dir: Bud Yorkin, 94 mins.)

Inspector General (1949)**** Danny Kaye, Walter Slezak. Delightful period farce about an illiterate who's mistaken for a friend of Napoleon's. It's a Danny Kaye romp and one of those rare times when the story comes close to matching his artistry. (Dir: Henry Koster, 102 mins.)

Inspector Maigret (France, 1958)**½ Jean Gabin, Annie Girardot. Wily policeman investigates a brutal murder case. They do such things better over here, despite Gabin's fine acting job. Alternate title: **Woman Bait.** (Dir: Jean Delannoy, 110 mins.)

Interiors (1978)***½ Diane Keaton, E. G. Marshall, Geraldine Page, Maureen Stapleton, Sam Waterston, Richard Jordan, Mary Beth Hurt, Kristin Griffith.

Woody Allen picks up the mask, and every character stands in for aspects of his psyche, though that is where the much-vaunted resemblance to Bergman ends. Their styles couldn't be more dissimilar, for Allen uses so many shopworn art mannerisms that his style recalls chopped meat. Still, it's a seriously felt, sly film that encourages the viewer to overlook the howlers in the dialogue. Some of the acting, notably by Mary Beth Hurt and E.G. Marshall, is superlative. Uneven but often moving and involving. Few intentional laughs in this Allen homage to Ingmar Bergman. (Dir: Woody Allen, 93 mins.)

Interlude (1957)**½ June Allyson, Rossano Brazzi. Hankies out, ladies . . . here's a plot about an American librarian in Germany who falls for a married conductor, etc. Soap opera, as usual competent. (Dir: Douglas Sirk, 90 mins.)

Interlude (Great Britain, 1968)** Oskar Werner, Barbara Ferris, Virginia Maskell, Donald Sutherland. The slick tale of an impossible love between a symphony conductor (Oskar Werner) and a newspaperwoman (Barbara Ferris). All gush and nonsense, but shrewdly catered toward the impressionable ladies in the audience. Some good classical music. Remake of 1957 film. (Dir: Kevin Billington, 113 mins.)

Intermezzo (Sweden, 1936)**½ Ingrid Bergman, Gosta Ekman. Effective heart tugger with Bergman a ravishing model of youthful sensuality as a music student in thrall to her teacher (Ekman). Written and directed by Gustav Molander, a major figure in the early sound period in Sweden. Bergman was spotted in this film by producer David O. Selznick, who brought her to Hollywood for a remake. (70 mins.)

Intermezzo (1939)*** Leslie Howard, Ingrid Bergman, John Halliday, Edna Best. Story of a married concert violinist (Howard) who has an affair with his beautiful protégée (Bergman). Gregory Ratoff's direction catches their star qualities, but the story is sometimes more wimpy than weepy. (70 mins.)

International House (1933)*** W. C. Fields, Burns & Allen, Stuart Erwin. Foolish but occasionally hilarious comedy about an inventor. A fine assortment of characters in this film and, in spite of its age, comedy lovers should enjoy it. (Dir: A. Edward Sutherland, 72 mins.)

International Squadron (1941)**½ Ronald Reagan. Mr. Reagan ends up in the RAF changing from an irresponsible bum to a great hero. Trouble is the script makes the change unbelievable. (Dir: Lothar Mendes, 87 mins.)

International Velvet (Great Britain, 1978)**½ Tatum O'Neal, Nanette Newman, Christopher Plummer, Anthony Hopkins. Sequel to "National Velvet" ('44) has the grown Velvet (Newman) coaching her orphaned niece (O'Neal) into becoming a skilled horsewoman who joins the British Olympic riding team and ends up married. The performances and Tony Imi's stunning photography of the Devon countryside make this worthwhile. (Writer-Producr-Dir: Bryan Forbes, 126 mins.)

Internecine Project, The (Great Britain, 1974)** James Coburn, Lee Grant, Harry Andrews. Muddled espionage yarn about a man who will stop at nothing to be appointed to a high-level position in Washington. Coburn and Grant are inadequate. (Dir: Ken Hughes, 89 mins.)

Interns, The (1962)** Michael Callan, Cliff Robertson, Nick Adams, James MacArthur, Stefanie Powers. A workout for several of the younger performers is the only discernible reason for this melange of medical clichés about the problems faced by assorted young interns during their year of apprenticeship. For all the care lavished upon it, it still looks like a daytime TV serial. (Dir: David Swift, 129 mins.)

Interpol Code 8 (Japan, 1965)* Tatsuya Mihashi, (94 mins.)

Interrupted Journey (Great Britain, 1949)**½ Richard Todd, Valerie Hobson. After a spat with his wife, a man takes a train where he is suddenly involved in the murder of a woman. Fair thriller is marred by weak ending. (Dir: Daniel Birt, 80 mins.)

Interrupted Melody (1955)*½ Eleanor Parker, Glenn Ford, Roger Moore, Cecil Kellaway. The story of Marjorie Lawrence, an Australian opera singer stricken by polio. It's hard to sit through this Oscar winner. Eileen Farrell dubbed in as Parker's singing voice. (Dir: Curtis Bernhardt, 106 mins.)

Interval (U.S.-Mexico, 1973)½ Merle Oberon, Robert Wolders. (Dir: Daniel Mann, 84 mins.)

Intimate Lighting (Czechoslovakia, 1966)**** Zdenek Bezusek, Vera Kresadlova, Karel Blazek. Lively social comedy of provincial life in Czechoslovakia. Director and writer Ivan Passer handles the wry, understated humor beautifully. A small treasure. B&W. (71 mins.)

Intimate Relations—See: **Disobedient**

Intolerance (1916)**** Lillian Gish, Robert Harron, Mae Marsh, Constance Talmadge, Bessie Love. Four interconnected stories of injustice in different historical periods are directed with skill (and lavishness) by the great D. W. Griffith. The gigantic palace set in ancient Babylon may be the most elaborate ever built for a film, and it's decorated with scantily clad dancing girls, peacocks, leopards, elephants, and dozens of doves. The performances are strikingly good—especially Marsh and Talmadge. A silent classic. (123 mins.)

Intruder, The (Great Britain, 1953)*** Jack Hawkins, Michael Medwin, George Cole. An army colonel discovers one of his former regiment rifling his house, decides to contact the old wartime crew to find out what made the lad turn thief. Interesting

drama, well done. (Dir: Guy Hamilton, 84 mins.)

Intruder in the Dust (1949)**** David Brian, Claude Jarman Jr., Juano Hernandez. Based on William Faulkner's novel—a lawyer and a lad come to the aid of a Negro when he's accused of murder. Fine dramatic film for the more discriminating; successful both as a straight whodunit, and as more immediate topical fare. Performances and direction are first rate and Hernandez is marvelous. (Dir: Clarence Brown, 87 mins.)

Intruder Within (MTV 1981)* Chad Everett, Joseph Bottoms, Jennifer Warren. (Dir: Peter Carter, 104 mins.)

Intruders, The (1970)**½ Don Murray, Anne Francis, John Saxon. Moderately absorbing made-for-TV western film with a couple of good performances to recommend it—Don Murray as an ex-gunslinger turned marshal and John Saxon as a half-breed Indian trying to cope with prejudice. The action is centered around a small town's preparation for the reported arrival of the notorious Younger Brothers and Jesse James. (Dir: William Graham, 95 mins.)

Invaders, The—See: **49th Parallel, The**

Invaders from Mars (1953)** Jimmy Hunt, Helena Carter, Arthur Franz. The legendary production designer William Cameron Menzies (whose credits include "Gone with the Wind") directed this sci-fi cheapie. A mélange of Freudian symbols, debased expressionism, and screaming Technicolor. (78 mins.)

Invasion (Great Britain, 1965)** Edward Judd, Yoko Tani, Valerie Gearon. Creatures from another planet crash on earth, perpetrate murders and havoc until outwitted by a doctor. Farfetched but occasionally tense sci-fi thriller. Good cast helps. (Dir: Alan Bridges, 82 mins.)

Invasion Earth 2150 A.D. (Great Britain, 1966)**½ Peter Cushing, Bernard Cribbins, Andrew Keir. Fast-paced science fiction pits a small band of freedom fighters against maniacal, super-intelligent robots from outer space, who have been turning humans into programmed slaves. Based on the BBC-TV serial, "Dr. Who," sequel to "Dr. Who and the Daleks." Alternate title: **Daleks—Invasion Earth 2150 A.D.** (Dir: Gordon Flemyng, 84 mins.)

Invasion of Johnson County, The (MTV 1976)**½ Bill Bixby, Bo Hopkins, John Hillerman, Billy Green Bush. Bixby and Hopkins are well cast in this offbeat Western adventure yarn. Bixby is a dapper Bostonian Brahmin who finds himself in the wild and wooly West without any funds. He teams up with cowpoke Hopkins, who confesses he has been hired by a private army of men who plan to take the law into their own hands. (Dir: Jerry Jameson, 98 mins.)

Invasion of the Animal People (U.S.-Sweden, 1962)* Barbara Wilson, John

Carradine. (Dir: Jerry Warren, Virgil Vogel, 55 mins.)

Invasion of the Body Snatchers (1956)***½ Dana Wynter, Kevin McCarthy. Space invaders overcome townspeople, inhabit their bodies. One of the better thrillers; lively, imaginative, suspenseful. Remade in 1978. (Dir: Don Siegel, 80 mins.)

Invasion of the Body Snatchers (1978)**** Donald Sutherland, Brooke Adams, Jeff Goldflum, Veronica Cartwright. A successful remake and rethinking of Don Siegel's '56 classic, set in San Francisco. It's hard to avoid thinking that the pod bods (vegetable replacements of people) have just had their first weekend of est training. Philip Kaufman directed a garrulous, baroque version with a keen sense of local social detail. Superbly performed. (114 mins.)

Invasion of the Body Stealers—See: **Thin Air**

Invasion of the Neptune Men (Japan, 1961)* Shinchi Chiba. (Dir: Koji Ota, 82 mins.)

Invasion of the Saucer-Men (1957)** Steve Terrell, Gloria Castillo, Frank Gorshin. Teenagers battle bulb-headed aliens in a quickie perfunctorily directed by Edward L. Cahn. Pretty awful, but there's one creepy moment with a severed alien hand crawling around the back seat of a car while two teens make out. (69 mins.)

Invasion of the Star Creatures (1962)*½ Bob Ball, Dolores Reed. (Dir: Bruno Ve Sota, 81 mins.)

Invasion of the Vampires, The (Mexico, 1961)* Tito Junco, Erna-Martha Bauman. (Dir: Miguel Morayta, 92 mins.)

Invasion U.S.A. (1952)*½ Dan O'Herlihy, Peggie Castle, Gerald Mohr. (Dir: Alfred E. Green, 74 mins)

Investigation of a Citizen Above Suspicion (Italy, 1970)***½ Florinda Bolkan, Gianni Santuccio, Gian Maria Volonte. Complex satirical parable about politics and Fascist ideology. Smug, mentally unbalanced police chief plants evidence against himself to test his underlings, his own status, and his moral and social superiority. Absorbing throughout and stylishly directed by Elio Petri, who happens to be a Communist. Oscar as Best Foreign Film. (Dir: Elio Petri, 112 mins.)

Investigation of Murder, An—See: **Laughing Policeman, The**

Invincible Brothers Maciste (Italy, 1965)* Richard Lloyd, Claudia Lange. (Dir: Roberto Mauri, 92 mins.)

Invincible Gladiator, The (Italy, 1962)** Richard Harrison, Isabel Corey. Roman warrior is put to the test as he tries to save the oppressed of the city. Lack of finesse partially atoned for by some fast action scenes in this passable spectacle dubbed in English. (Dir: Anthony Momplet, 96 mins.)

Invincible Six (U.S.-Iran, 1968)*½ Stuart Whitman, Elke Sommer, Curt Jurgens,

James Mitchum. (Dir: Jean Negulesco, 96 mins.)

Invisible Avenger (1958)**½ Richard Derr, Mark Daniels. Lamont Cranston (the Shadow) travels to New Orleans to find mystery and adventure. A plot to kill the President of Santa Cruz is foiled, and Lamont learns to be invisible from an Indian sage. OK make-believe. (Dirs: James Wong Howe and John Sledge, 60 mins.)

Invisible Boy, The (1957)**½ Richard Eyer, Philip Abbott. A science-fiction yarn about a young boy and his robot. The kids might enjoy this adventure which incorporates smuggled cargoes of bombs, rocket ships, spies, scientists and hokum. (Dir: Herman Hoffman, 85 mins.)

Invisible Creature (Great Britain, 1960)** Sandra Dorne, Tony Wright. Moderate supernatural story about an unfaithful husband with murder on his mind and his wife, who seems to have a protective ghost on her side. (Dir: Montgomery Tully, 70 mins.)

Invisible Dr. Mabuse, The (Germany, 1962)*½ Lex Barker, Karin Dor. (Dir: Harald Reinl, 89 mins.)

Invisible Man, The (1933)***½ Claude Rains, Henry Travers. Despite its age, this horror classic still captures the imagination. Rains turns in a first-rate performance as the hero of H. G. Wells' tale, a demented scientist who has successfully made himself transparent and now wants to rule the world. Slowmoving but worth-while. Rains's debut. (Dir: James Whale, 80 mins.)

Invisible Man, The (1975)**½ David McCallum, Melinda Fee, Jackie Cooper. A successful pilot film for the subsequent NBC series. David McCallum assumes the title role (played by Claude Rains in the 1933 classic) of the invisible researcher (clad in a blue body-stocking), a man who discovers how to make animals invisible, then plays guinea-pig himself. (Dir: Robert Michael Lewis, 72 mins.)

Invisible Man Returns, The (1940)*** Sir Cedric Hardwicke, Vincent Price, Nan Grey. A sequel to "The Invisible Man," and almost as good in its own way as the original. Technical effects are excellent and the dialogue crisp. Concerns a man who uses invisibility to hunt for his brother's murderer. (Dir: Joe May, 81 mins.)

Invisible Ray, The (1936)** Boris Karloff, Bela Lugosi. Shudder story about a scientist whose touch is deadly. Karloff and Lugosi keep the yarn perking, but it comes off as familiar stuff for horror fans. (Dir: Lambert Hillyer, 90 mins.)

Invisible Terror, The (Germany, 1963)*½ Hannes Schmidhauser, Ellen Schwiers. (Dir: Raphael Nussbaum, 102 mins.)

Invitation (1952)*** Dorothy McGuire, Van Johnson, Ruth Roman, Louis Calhern. Dorothy McGuire gives a glowing performance as an invalid who makes a stab for happiness despite the constant presence of death. The plot often slips to "soap opera" level but Miss McGuire is worth your attention. (Dir: Gottfried Reinhardt, 84 mins.)

Invitation, The (Switzerland-France, 1973)*** Michel Robin, François Simon, Jean-Luc Bideau, Cecille Vassort. Office workers are invited for the afternoon to the home of fellow-worker Remy Placet (Robin), and are surprised to find him ensconced in almost palatial surroundings. It is a sultry summer day: the sprinklers are running constantly and the liquor poured as freely by a cooly capable butler (played by François Simon, son of the late Michel Simon). By the end of the afternoon, in this subtly crafted film, in-office façades and barriers have come dislodged. The wily, expressionless butler Simon, who concocts the brews, is demonic, and an edge of mystery develops. Acting is good, and Miss Vassort is outstanding as a red-haired, flighty, flirty innocent. Impressive work from director Claude Goretta in this, his third feature. Oscar nominee as Best Foreign Film. (Dir: Claude Goretta, 100 mins.)

Invitation to a Gunfighter (1964)** Yul Brynner, Janice Rule, George Segal. Western fans should be forewarned that there's more Freud than Zane Grey in this story of renegades and revenge. The supporting cast doesn't get much of a chance to rise above their stereotyped roles. (Dir: Richard Wilson, 92 mins.)

Invitation to Happiness (1939)**½ Irene Dunne, Fred MacMurray. Well made but minor little tale of an ambitious fighter who neglects his family while rising to the top. The comedy is fairly good, but the drama is routine. (Dir: Wesley Ruggles, 100 mins.)

Invitation to Murder (Great Britain, 1962)** Robert Beatty, Lisa Daniely. American adventurer goes to the French Riviera to check on beneficiaries of a millionaire's will, finds murder. Standard whodunit. (55 mins.)

Invitation to the Dance (1956)** Gene Kelly, Tamara Toumanova, Carol Haney, Tommy Rall, Igor Youskevitch. Director Kelly's attempt to make an all-dancing musical (no talking, no singing) is a valiant but pretentious stab at a popular art film. A colossally expensive commercial flop. (93 mins.)

Iphigenia (Greece, 1977)*** Tatiana Papamoskou, Irene Papas, Costa Kazakos. Director Michael Cacoyannis's most effective installment of the Oresteia. Well acted and anything but dull, but the story of the sacrificial murder of a girl by her father to appease the gods, like all the Greek classics, still awaits the ministrations of a truly epic filmmaker. (129 mins.)

Ipcress File, The (Great Britain, 1965)**** Michael Caine, Nigel Green. First-rate espionage yarn which will keep you fascinated from start to finish. Michael Caine's British agent Harry Palmer is a magnificent example of role and star fitting like a glove and director Sidney J. Furie's exciting camera work heightens the action at every plot twist. Based on Len Deighton's bestseller, the tense and complex spy story has Palmer investigating the kidnaping of scientists detained behind the Iron Curtain and he comes up with information that threatens his life. (Dir: Sidney J. Furie, 108 mins.)

Irish Eyes Are Smiling (1944)**½ June Haver, Dick Haymes, Monty Woolley. Routine musical supposedly about the chap who wrote the title song. Some fine Irish melodies but little else. (Dir: Gregory Ratoff, 90 mins.)

Irish Whiskey Rebellion (1972)** William Devane, Anne Meara, Stephen Joyce. Humdrum meller about rumrunning off Fire Island in '27. Veteran director Chester Erskine used the pseudonym J. G. Works when he saw the finished product. If you view it, you'll understand his decision. (93 mins.)

Irma La Douce (1963)***½ Jack Lemmon, Shirley MacLaine. Talented producer-director-writer Billy Wilder took the hit Broadway musical, extracted the musical numbers, and came up with a delightfully raucous comedy about Paris prostitutes and their procurers. Lemmon is forced into leading a double life in order to keep his love, streetwalker MacLaine, and his energetic performance is among his best. Miss MacLaine is perfect as the sweet tart named Irma, and director Wilder has punched up the proceedings with style and a spirit of fun. (Dir: Billy Wilder, 120 mins.)

Iron Curtain, The (1948)**½ Dana Andrews, Gene Tierney. First major anti-Communist film is based on the Igor Gouzenko incident. He's the Russian who helped round up a Canadian spy ring. Film is confused, episodic and only has a few exciting scenes. (Dir: William Wellman, 87 mins.)

Iron Major, The (1943)*** Pat O'Brien, Robert Ryan. Life story of Frank Cavanaugh, famous football coach and World War I hero. Well done biographical drama. (Dir: Ray Enright, 85 mins.)

Iron Man (1951)**½ Jeff Chandler, Evelyn Keyes, Stephen McNally. A notch or two above the run of the mill boxing yarns. Jeff Chandler is good as the peace loving coal miner turned boxing champ. The whole cast keeps up with the competent pace set by Chandler. Look for Rock Hudson and James Arness in small roles. Remake of the 1931 film. (Dir: Joseph Pevney, 82 mins.)

Iron Mistress, The (1952)**½ Alan Ladd, Virginia Mayo. Action filled, colorful adventure yarn about Jim Bowie, whose primary claim to fame was a special knife he had made which came to be known as the "Bowie Knife." Ladd is as stoic as always but fits well into the hero adventurer mold. (Dir: Gordon Douglas, 110 mins.)

337

Iron Petticoat, The (Great Britain, 1956)*½ Bob Hope, Katharine Hepburn, Noelle Middleton. (Dir: Ralph Thomas, 87 mins.)

Ironside (MTV 1967)**½ Raymond Burr, Geraldine Brooks, Wally Cox, Kim Darby, Don Galloway, Barbara Anderson, Donald Mitchell. Pilot movie for the TV series stars Burr as a gruff, blunt, cantankerous sleuth confined to a wheelchair, crippled by a sniper's bullet. Don Mankiewicz's script provides pungent dialogue, incisive characterizations, and staccato direction. (Dir: James Goldstone, 104 mins.)

Iroquois Trail (1950)**½ George Montgomery, Brenda Marshall. Hunter avenging his brother's death uncovers traitors on the frontier. Plenty of action in this outdoor action drama. (Dir: Phil Karlson, 85 mins.)

Irwin Allen's Production of Fire! (MTV 1977)**½ Ernest Borgnine, Vera Miles, Patty Duke Astin, Alex Cord, Donna Mills, Lloyd Nolan, Neville Brand, Ty Hardin. Yet another one on devastating forest fires, but this Irwin Allen edition filmed around Portland, Oregon, benefits from multiple story lines, a better than average cast, and excellent fire sequences. Stock footage has been held down to a minimum, and various characters face the threat of cremation throughout, creating some suspense. (Dir: Earl Bellamy, 144 mins.)

Is Everybody Happy? (1943)**½ Ted Lewis, Michael Duane, Larry Parks. Based on the career of bandleader Ted Lewis, this tells of the ups and downs of a jazz band. For Lewis fans, good; for others, fairly pleasant. (Dir: Charles Barton, 73 mins.)

Is Paris Burning? (U.S.-France, 1966)** Leslie Caron, Yves Montand, Simone Signoret, Orson Welles, Gert Frobe. The best-selling novel about the efforts to save Paris from Hitler's torch is turned into a dull, episodic drama with a series of cameo roles played by an international roster of film names. The epic story gets lost as each vignette is highlighted to give its star or stars their moment before the camera. (And each vignette may have been scripted by a different writer, considering the half-dozen scribblers involved.) (Dir: Rene Clement, 173 mins.)

Is There Sex After Death? (1971)***½ Buck Henry, Alan Abel, Marshall Efron, Holly Woodlawn. A raunchy, outrageous, but often wildly funny satire that mocks all the other films that take themselves seriously and try to capitalize on the recent "sexual revolution." It's directed, written, and produced by two hoaxers with a flair—Alan and Jeanne Abel. It's a series of not so serious sketches with Earle Doud as a pornographic magician. "Sex" won't show up on network TV Sunday evening following Walt Disney, but it's a funny outing for the nonprudish. (Dirs: Alan and Jeanne Abel, 97 mins.)

Isabel (Canada, 1968)***½ Fine actress Genevieve Bujold and her then-husband, writer-producer-director Paul Almond, join talents to spin an effective weird tale of a girl who returns home to find mystery and fear. Atmospheric Canadian coastal backgrounds, and an eerie, other-worldly quality. Interesting and offbeat. With Marc Strange, Elton Hayes. (Dir: Paul Almond, 108 mins.)

Isadora—See: **Loves of Isadora**

Ishi, the Last of His Tribe (MTV 1978)***½ Dennis Weaver, Eloy Phil Casados. Sympathetic account of the last wild Indian, hounded by California gold miners, who gave himself up in 1911. Befriended by a Berkeley anthropologist (Weaver), Ishi talks of his past through flashbacks while living in a San Francisco museum. (Dir: Robert Ellis Miller, 104 mins.)

Island, The (Japan, 1962)***½ Powerful Japanese film about a family struggling for existence on a remote and barren island. No dialogue, story told through the camera, actions of the principals. Unusual, engrossing drama. (Dir: Kaneto Shindo, 96 mins.)

Island, The (1980)** Michael Caine, David Warner, Angela Punch McGregor. Big-budget Peter Benchley premise of an in-bred band of marauders descended from 17th-century buccaneers. Director Michael Ritchie forgets that action and violence are not interchangeable dishes from columns A and B. (113 mins.)

Island Affair (Italy, 1962)* Dorian Gray, Daniela Rocca, Elaine Stewart. (Dir: Giorgio Bianchi, 85 mins.)

Island at the Top of the World, The (1974)** David Hartman, Donald Sinden, Agneta Eckemyr. Fanciful yarn based on Ian Cameron's novel "The Lost Ones" has aristocrat Sinden leading an airship into the Arctic wastes in 1907 to find his missing son. Special effects overshadow the actors. (Dir: Robert Stevenson, 94 mins.)

Island in the Sky (1953)*** John Wayne, Lloyd Nolan, James Arness. Wayne exchanges the plains for planes in this adventure film about a pilot and a dangerous rescue mission. Photography is a plus factor here. (Dir: William Wellman, 109 mins.)

Island in the Stream (1977)*** George C. Scott, Claire Bloom, Gilbert Roland, David Hemmings. Director Franklin J. Schaffner's film of Hemingway's last novel comes close to greatness. The Hemingway figure (Scott as a painter) lives alone on a tropical island, where he's visited in turn by his three sons and his ex-wife (Bloom). Dialogue is often poor. (110 mins.)

Island in the Sun (1957)**½ James Mason, John Fontaine, Harry Belafonte, Dorothy Dandridge. Alec Waugh's best-seller is watered-down in this screen translation. Revolves around an assorted group of blacks and whites living in the British West Indies, and their political and personal lives. The fact that this film was made in the late fifties limits the portrayal of inter-racial romances (Harry Belafonte and Joan Fontaine—Dorothy Dandridge and John Justin) and the film loses some of its intended impact as a result. (Dir: Robert Rossen, 119 mins.)

Island of Desire (Great Britain, 1952)** Linda Darnell, Tab Hunter. Poorly acted film about a woman and a young Marine shipwrecked on an island during the war. A mature Englishman joins them to complete the triangle. Your desire may be to tune out. (Dir: Stuart Heisler, 103 mins.)

Island of Dr. Moreau, The (1977)** Burt Lancaster, Michael York, Barbara Carrera, Richard Basehart. H. G. Wells's lurid tale of a mad scientist tinkering with the evolutionary process suffers a flat, matter-of-fact retelling by director Don Taylor. The cast are bland. (98 mins.)

Island of Lost Souls (1933)***½ Charles Laughton, Richard Arlen, Leila Hyams, Bela Lugosi, Kathleen Burke. Enormously amusing horror film with Laughton brazenly hammy as the doctor who vivisects animals to create an intermediate breed, half-man, half-thing. (Dir: Erle C. Kenton, 70 mins.)

Island of Lost Women (1959)*½ Jeff Richards, Venetia Stevenson, John Smith. (Dir: Frank Tuttle, 71 mins.)

Island of Love (1963)*** Robert Preston, Tony Randall, Walter Matthau. Bright comedy about a fast-talking promoter who cons a gangster into financing a movie stinker, then promotes a Greek island as a paradise spot. The fun lets down before the end, but there's some funny, crackling dialogue, a wow comedy performance from gangster Matthau. (Dir: Morton Da Costa, 101 mins.)

Island of Terror (Great Britain, 1967)*** Peter Cushing, Edward Judd, Carole Gray. Medical experts journey to an island where they discover shell-like creatures that show a penchant for devouring the bones of victims. Well-done science-fiction thriller summons up a good share of shudders for the addicts. (Dir: Terence Fisher, 90 mins.)

Island of the Blue Dolphins (1964)**½ Celia Kaye, Larry Domasin. Youngsters are left alone on an island, and the girl befriends a wild dog who becomes her protector. The kids should particularly enjoy this pleasant adventure story, with colorful scenery and an adequate amount of interest. (Dir: James B. Clark, 93 mins.)

Island Princess, The (Italy, 1955)*½ Marcello Mastroianni, Silvana Pampanini. (Dir: Paolo Moffa, 98 mins.)

Island Rescue (Great Britain, 1951)**½ David Niven, Glynis Johns. A major is assigned the task of rescuing a prize cow from a British island occupied by the Nazis. Uneven adventure falls midway between comedy and melodrama, never seems to make up its mind which way to turn. (Dir: Ralph Thomas, 87 mins.)

Islander, The (MTV 1978)** Dennis Weaver, Sheldon Leonard. Weaver as a retired

lawyer manages to add a trace of sanity to a complicated plot about mobsters, call girls, and a law partner accused of beating a stewardess. Familiar scenery of Honolulu. Writer and producer: Glen A. Larson. (Dir: Paul Krasny, 104 mins.)

Isle of the Dead (1945)*** Boris Karloff, Ellen Drew. Greek general on a small island is enmeshed with vampires and witchcraft. Eerie thriller has some good effects. (Dir: Mark Robson, 72 mins.)

Isn't It Shocking (1973)**½ Alan Alda, Edmond O'Brien, Will Geer, Lloyd Nolan, Ruth Gordon. Alda and a cast of veteran character actors manage to convey the right mood in this offbeat made-for-TV murder mystery. In the rural New England town of Mount Angel, the elderly are dying but not from old age, and thereby hangs the tale. Louise Lasser and Pat Quinn costar as the ladies in Sheriff Alda's life. (Dir: John Badham, 90 mins.)

Israel Why (France, 1973)***½ Provocative, lengthy (three hours) documentary about the dream of Israel. Director Claude Lanzmann has clearly been inspired by the techniques and film form of Marcel Ophuls' "The Sorrow and the Pity." This work, though not as brilliantly handled as Ophuls' landmark documentary, is an enlightening, probing study of the dynamics of contemporary Israel. Interviews some of the early settlers, along with the young sabras. Edited in terms of various themes, with the filmmaker's point of view sometimes obtrusive. On balance it is a stimulating, if uneven, feature that will hold your interest if you want to learn more about this historic embattled land. (Dir: Claude Lanzmann, 180 mins.)

Istanbul (1957)** Errol Flynn, Cornell Borchers. Adventurer returns to recover a fortune in diamonds, finds his old flame, presumed dead, alive and an amnesia victim. Shopworn melodrama for Flynn fans, who may take to it—but the accent is on the last syllable of the title. Remake of *Singapore*, 1947. (Dir: Joseph Pevney, 84 mins.)

Istanbul Express (1968)**½ Gene Barry, Senta Berger, John Saxon. An entertaining film on two totally different levels. Viewers who've enjoyed previous made-for-television adventure movies will find this tale of intrigue exciting. It follows art dealer Gene Barry aboard a train, journeying to Turkey to buy certain valuable papers for the U.S. government at an international auction. Old-time movie buffs however, weaned on the trains of Alfred Hitchcock and Carol Reed, may find this all rather droll and a bit of cinematic high camp. (Dir: Richard Irving, 94 mins.)

It (Great Britain, 1967)* Roddy McDowall, Jill Haworth, Ernest Clark. (95 mins.)

It Ain't Hay (1943)** Bud Abbott, Lou Costello. Fair A & C comedy about a champion racehorse named Tea Biscuit. (Dir: Erle C. Kenton, 72 mins.)

It All Came True (1940)**½ Humphrey

339

Bogart, Ann Sheridan. Humphrey goes soft in this occasionally entertaining story of a gangster whose spirit is captured by some old-time vaudevillians. (Dir: Lewis Seiler, 97 mins.)

It Always Rains on Sunday (Great Britain, 1947)*** Googie Withers, John McCallum. Story of a family in the slums of London torn apart by crime. Well-made, but grim, unpleasant. (Dir: Robert Hamer, 92 mins.)

It Came from Beneath the Sea (1955)** Donald Curtis, Faith Domergue. A U.S. submarine tangles with a giant octopus which has come from the lower depths of the sea due to the many H-bomb experiments. Fair science-fiction meller—good for younger audience. (Dir: Robert Gordon, 80 mins.)

It Came from Outer Space (1953)**½ Richard Carlson, Barbara Rush. Good photography and a large budget help to make this first-grade sci-fi entertainment. Richard Carlson, an old hand at fighting visitors from beneath the sea and above the stars, is stalwart once again in the face of faceless creatures. Originally in 3-D. (Dir: Jack Arnold, 81 mins.)

It Comes Up Murder—See: Honey Pot, The

It Conquered the World (1956)** Peter Graves, Beverly Garland. Thing from another planet communicates with a scientist who is to help him conquer earth. Science-fiction thriller is average as these things go, with some occasional good moments. (Dir: Roger Corman, 68 mins.)

It Couldn't Happen to a Nicer Guy (MTV 1974)**½ Paul Sorvino, Michael Learned. A silly premise gets a lot of mileage in this comedy, which boasts a better than average cast, including Michael Learned, mother of TV's "The Waltons." Paul Sorvino can't convince anyone that he was forced, at gunpoint, to make love to a very glamorous young lady who picked him up while he was hitchhiking. Try explaining that to your wife? (Dir: Cy Howard, 72 mins.)

It Grows on Trees (1952)**½ Irene Dunne, Dean Jagger, Joan Evans. An amusing idea which doesn't quite live up to its expectations. The Baxter family discover two trees in their yard which sprout money (5 and 10 dollar bills) rather than leaves. Naturally, the situation becomes hectic. Dunne's last film. (Dir: Arthur Lubin, 84 mins.)

It Had to Be You (1947)**½ Ginger Rogers, Cornel Wilde. Socialite always fails to marry at the last moment, until she meets the right man. Amusing comedy. (Dir: Don Hartman, 98 mins.)

It Happened at the World's Fair (1963)** Elvis Presley, Joan O'Brien, Gary Lockwood. Mix Elvis, the Seattle World's Fair, some romance, and a cute Chinese girl together, and out comes a musical tailored for the fans. Hardly inspired, it should serve its purpose with the undiscriminating. (Dir: Norman Taurog, 105 mins.)

It Happened in Athens (1962)* Jayne Mansfield, Trax Colton, Nico Minardos, Bob Mathias. (Dir: Andrew Marton, 92 mins.)

It Happened in Broad Daylight (Switzerland-Germany)**½ Heinz Ruhmann, Michel Simon., Gert Frobe. When a little girl is brutally murdered, a wily police inspector gets on the case and nails the culprit. Uneven mystery drama moves too slowly, but has a fine performance by cop Ruhmann, documentary-like police detail. English-dubbed. (Dir: Ladislao Vajda, 97 mins.)

It Happened in Brooklyn (1947)**½ Frank Sinatra, Kathryn Grayson, Peter Lawford, Jimmy Durante. Pleasant, inconsequential musical about an ex-sailor (Frank) who moves in with a janitor in Brooklyn (Durante) and tries to make the grade in the music business. Uninspired score hurts this film. (Dir: Richard Whorf, 105 mins.)

It Happened One Christmas (MTV 1977)*** Marlo Thomas, Wayne Rogers, Orson Welles, Cloris Leachman. The ingratiating Thomas in a remake of "It's a Wonderful Life," taking the part played by James Stewart! Sentimental story about a small town and its concern for one of its caring citizens. Good supporting cast includes Welles as a flinty old businessman, Leachman as the guardian angel out to earn her wings, and Rogers as Marlo's supportive spouse. (Dir: Donald Wrye, 115 mins.)

It Happened One Night (1934)**** Clark Gable, Claudette Colbert, Walter Connolly. Reporter Gable chases spoiled heiress Colbert across most of the eastern seaboard, pausing between wisecracks to set the definitive tone for '30s romantic comedy. Connolly is excellent. Not director Frank Capra's best, but he's easier to enjoy when, as here, he has nothing to prove. Oscars: Best Picture, Director, Actor, Actress. (110 mins.)

It Happened One Summer (1945)*** Jeanne Crain, Dana Andrews, Dick Haymes, Charles Winninger, Vivian Blaine. The story of an Iowa farm family who encounter love and adventure while at the state fair, graced by the Rodgers & Hammerstein tunes, which are still a delight. Plot's slightness is still evident, but this version is superior to the later remake. Oscar—Best Song, "It Might As Well Be Spring." Alternate title: **State Fair.** (Dir: Walter Lang, 100 mins.)

It Happened to Jane (1959)**½ Doris Day, Jack Lemmon, Ernie Kovacs. Silly but pleasant comedy about a New England business woman dealing in lobsters who manages to throw a wrench into the big-time operations of a railroad. Kovacs all but steals the show as the cigar-chewing, bald-pated railroad tycoon. (Dir: Richard Quine, 98 mins.)

It Happened Tomorrow (1944)***½ Dick Powell, Linda Darnell, Jack Oakie. A reporter manages to get tomorrow's newspaper from a strange little man; then one day he reads his own obituary. Charming fantasy-comedy, with Rene Clair's splendid direction making it a grand show. (Dir: Rene Clair, 84 mins.)

It Happens Every Spring (1949)*** Ray Milland, Jean Peters, Paul Douglas. Funny film about a chemistry professor who discovers a compound which makes baseballs react strangely to bats. His discovery takes him from the lab to the baseball diamond where he quickly becomes a great strike-out pitcher. Ray Milland is good as the prof and gets able support from Paul Douglas as a catcher and Jean Peters as his sweetheart. (Dir: Lloyd Bacon, 80 mins.)

It Happens Every Thursday (1953)**½ Loretta Young, John Forsythe. Simple little comedy-drama about a couple of city dwellers who move to a small California community and try to run the town's weekly newspaper. The comedy stems from the outrageous schemes Forsythe dreams up to bolster circulation. Young's last film. (Dir: Joseph Pevney, 80 mins.)

It Happens in Roma (Italy, 1956)*** Vittorio De Sica, Linda Darnell, Rossano Brazzi. A good comedy idea that doesn't quite materialize—a married couple agrees to allow each other extramarital activities but eventually end up in each other's arms. (Dir: Giuseppe Amato, 89 mins.)

It Lives Again (1978)**½ Frederic Forrest, Kathleen Lloyd, John Ryan. Director Larry Cohen's long-shelved sequel to "It's Alive" with three mutant killer babies on the loose. Cohen is wildly imaginative, but his films falter in the telling. (91 mins.)

It Means That to Me (France, 1961)*½ Eddie Constantine, Bernadette Lafont. (Dir: Pierre Grimblat, 85 mins.)

It Should Happen to You (1953)**** Judy Holliday, Jack Lemmon, Peter Lawford, Michael O'Shea, Constance Bennett. Holliday, an aspiring actress, has her face painted on a billboard over Columbus Circle as a publicity stunt and finds herself an overnight celebrity. Like Holliday herself, the film is brassy but softhearted. Expert direction by George Cukor. (81 mins.)

It Started in Naples (1960)*** Clark Gable, Sophia Loren, Vittorio De Sica. Lawyer resists the efforts of an Italian waif to take him back to America, until love takes a hand in the shape of the lad's sexy aunt. Good-humored comedy drama has beautiful Italian scenery, Gable and Loren in good form. (Dir: Melville Shavelson, 100 mins.)

It Started in Paradise (Great Britain, 1952)*** Jane Hylton, Ian Hunter, Kay Kendall. Young dress designer will stop at nothing to achieve success, makes enemies by the score. Elaborately produced, well-acted drama, especially enticing for the ladies. (Dir: Compton Bennett, 94 mins.)

It Started with a Kiss (1959)**½ Glenn Ford, Debbie Reynolds, Fred Clark. Flimsy but mildly amusing comedy about an Air Force sergeant, his new bride and a fabulous car, highlighted by splendid scenic backgrounds shot in Spain. Nothing wildly hilarious, but entertaining. (Dir: George Marshall, 104 mins.)

It Started with Eve (1941)***½ Deanna Durbin, Charles Laughton, Robert Cummings. Deanna Durbin's best film. Very funny comedy about mistaken identity and its effect on a zany family. Laughton is very good. Remade as *I'd Rather Be Rich*. (Dir: Henry Koster, 90 mins.)

It Takes a Thief (Great Britain, 1960)*½ Jayne Mansfield, Anthony Quayle. Alternate title: **The Challenge**. (Dir: John Gilling, 90 mins.)

It Takes All Kinds (U.S.-Australia, 1969)* Vera Miles, Robert Lansing, Barry Sullivan. (Dir: Eddie Davis, 100 mins.)

It! The Terror from Beyond Space (1958)* Marshall Thompson, Shawn Smith, Kim Spaulding. (Dir: Edward I. Cahn, 69 mins.)

It Won't Rub Off, Baby!—See: **Sweet Love, Bitter**

Italian Job, The (Great Britain, 1969)***½ Michael Caine, Noel Coward, Rossano Brazzi. Caine shines as a criminal who inherits the plans for a $4 million gold robbery in Turin, Italy. Fast and entertaining with a wonderful car chase rivaling "Bullitt" and "Otley." Coward plays a master criminal who has complete control of the prison he's been placed in. Caine and Coward together are a delight. (Dir: Peter Collinson, 101 mins.)

It's a Big Country (1952)**½ Gene Kelly, Janet Leigh, Fredric March. An octet of stories, some better than others, comprise the framework of this film which is a big valentine to America. One of the best episodes stars Kelly as the son of a Greek immigrant who falls in love with the daughter, played by Miss Leigh, of a Hungarian farmer charmingly played by S. Z. Sakall. Among the many stars who appear in the various segments are Van Johnson, James Whitmore, Gary Cooper and Ethel Barrymore. (Dirs: Charles Vidor, Richard Thorpe, John Sturges, Don Hartman, Don Weis, Clarence Brown, William Wellman, 89 mins.)

It's a Bikini World (1965)** Tommy Kirk, Deborah Walley. A silly "bikini" movie in which Tommy Kirk doubles as a shy bespectacled guy when in truth he's quite a ladies' man. Girl watchers will enjoy this one. (Dir: Stephanie Rothman, 86 mins.)

It's a Dog's Life (1955)***½ Jeff Richards, Dean Jagger, Edmund Gwenn. The saga of a dog—a bull terrier from the Bowery who ultimately is entered in a classy dog show. Charming dog story, thanks mainly to a witty, offbeat screenplay and intelligent direction. From the story *The Bar Sinister* by Richard Harding Davis. Plenty of fun, heart-tugs. (Dir: Herman Hoffman, 87 mins.)

It's a Gift (1934)*** W. C. Fields. The "Master" is a family man in this one and he gets the usual share of laughs from his bouts with his shrewish wife. Plenty of fun as Fields holds the film together. Remake of the Fields's silent *It's the Old Army Game*, 1926. (Dir: Norman McLeod, 70 mins.)

It's a Great Feeling (1949)*** Dennis Morgan, Jack Carson, Doris Day. A lot of fun in this off-beat satire about what a ham Carson is and how nobody at the studio wants to direct him. Lot of stars come on for comic bits. (Dir: David Butler, 85 mins.)

It's a Great Life (1943)**½ Penny Singleton, Arthur Lake, Hugh Herbert. Blondie and Dagwood have a horse on their hands, which pleases an eccentric millionaire client of Dagwood's boss. Amusing comedy in the "Blondie" series, with some capable clowning by Herbert. (Dir: Frank Strayer, 75 mins.)

It's a Mad, Mad, Mad, Mad World (1963)** Spencer Tracy, Milton Berle, Mickey Rooney. Here's director Stanley Kramer's tribute to those screen comedy chases of old. He's assembled an all-star cast headed by Tracy. It's a wild, occasionally funny romp about a robbery and the multiple double crosses that follow. The gags are pretty feeble, but there's a rousing car-chase scene. Here's just a partial list of names you'll see on screen in bit parts: Jimmy Durante, Sid Caesar, Edie Adams, Milton Berle, Dick Shawn, Ethel Merman, Phil Silvers, Buddy Hackett, Mickey Rooney, Terry-Thomas, Jonathan Winters, Peter Falk, and even the Three Stooges. (Dir: Stanley Kramer, 154 mins.)

It's a Wonderful Life (1946)***½ James Stewart, Donna Reed, Lionel Barrymore. A man facing ruin, who has had a hard time of it all his life, is sent help from above in the guise of a guardian angel. Charming comedy-drama has scenes of great warmth, humor. Excellent performances. (Dir: Frank Capra, 129 mins.)

It's a Wonderful World (1939)**** James Stewart, Claudette Colbert, Guy Kibbee. Screwball comedy version of "The 39 Steps" (without handcuffs). Stewart is the man falsely accused of murder who kidnaps Colbert. The script, which is what makes it go, is by Ben Hecht and Herman J. Mankiewicz; Swifty Woody (aka W. S. Van Dyke II) directed. (86 mins.)

It's Alive! (1968)* Tommy Kirk, Shirley Bonne. (Dir: Larry Buchanan, 80 mins.)

It's Alive (1974)* John Ryan, Sharon Farrell, Andrew Duggan. (Dir: Larry Cohen, 90 mins.)

It's Always Fair Weather (1955)*** Gene Kelly, Dan Dailey, Cyd Charisse, Michael Kidd, Dolores Gray. For the last of his MGM musicals, codirector Stanley Donen (with Kelly) tried to add a melancholy tone to the genre palette. Three old war buddies (Kelly, Dailey, Kidd) meet for the first time in years and find that life has disappointed their ambitions. Innovative, involving, and, of course, finally optimistic. (102 mins.)

It's Good to Be Alive (MTV 1974)*** Paul Winfield, Ruby Dee, Lou Gossett. Winfield delivers a moving portrait of Brooklyn Dodger catcher Roy Campanella, facing life as a quadraplegic following his tragic 1958 auto accident. Though Winfield bears no resemblance to the squat, boyish "Campy," the actor's luminous face carries this venture. Battling deep depression, a crumbling marriage and the alienation of his son, David, the ballplayer undergoes treatment with therapist Sam Brockington before he learns to survive. The finale is most effective as he tells 80,000 fans in the Los Angeles Coliseum, "It's good to be alive." Michael Landon directed with taste; Ruby Dee is wonderful as Ruthe Campanella, and Lou Gossett scores as the patient Sam Brockington. But it's Winfield's performance and the story itself that are the winners here. (Dir: Michael Landon, 98 mins.)

It's in the Bag (1945)*** Fred Allen, Jack Benny. Back in 1970, I wrote about this comedy: "A funny, silly movie like they couldn't make anymore if they wanted to." Well, the world has taken a couple of turns since, and this is almost a font of intelligence up against the juvenilia of today's screen comedies. This is Fred Allen's best screen comedy, about a flea circus. Though it's not up to Allen's Alley at its peak and light years behind the flea-circus turn in Chaplin's *Limelight*, it's genuinely wacky. Richard Wallace directed, if that's what you do with Fred Allen. (Dir: Richard Wallace, 87 mins.)

It's Love Again (Great Britain, 1936)**½ Jessie Matthews, Robert Young. Capable, entertaining Matthews vehicle. Her music hall style is winsome and knowing, and she can dance up a storm. (Dir: Victor Saville, 84 mins.)

It's Love I'm After (1937)** Bette Davis, Leslie Howard, Olivia de Havilland. About the offstage fights of a stellar acting couple (Davis and Howard). Neither is particularly good. Archie Mayo directed, without panache. (90 mins.)

It's My Turn (1980)*** Jill Clayburgh, Michael Douglas, Charles Grodin, Beverly Garland. Attempts to revive the art of sophisticated comedy with newer feminist attitudes, but simply mints newer stereotypes. Clayburgh, a brilliant mathematics professor, is an indecisive klutz who can't handle her feelings or manage her life. The insecure direction of Claudia Weill stumbles over business as much as Clayburgh does. Some good discussions about needs and relationships near the end, and the open ending is the most honest thing about the film. Douglas and Grodin are quite good. (91 mins.)

It's Never Too Late (Great Britain, 1956)**

342

Phyllis Calvert, Guy Rolfe. Moderately amusing British comedy about a large household who discover that one of its female members is the authoress of a best-selling novel which has been sold to the movies. The idea is better than the resulting film. (Dir: Michael McCarthy, 95 mins.)

It's Only Money (1962)** Jerry Lewis, Zachary Scott, Joan O'Brien. Lewis and his mentor, director Frank Tashlin, in one of their later, less effective teamings. Creaky plot line about private eyes and stolen inheritances, with a few of Tashlin's wonderfully inventive sight gags. (84 mins.)

It's Your Move (Italy-Spain, 1968)*½ Edward G. Robinson, Adolfo Celi, Terry-Thomas. (Dir: Robert Fiz, 93 mins.)

Ivailo the Great (Bulgaria, 1964)*½ Bogomil Simenov, Lona Davidova. (Dir: Nikola Vulcev, 89 mins.)

Ivan, Son of the White Devil (Italy, 1954)** Nadia Gray, Paul Campbell. Love and adventure set in mysterious Turkey are the ingredients in this costume epic. (Dir: Guido Brignone, 75 mins.)

Ivan the Terrible, Part I (U.S.S.R., 1943)**** Nikolai Cherkassov, Ludmila Tselikovskaya. Russian history on a grand scale as interpreted by master Soviet director Sergei Eisenstein. The somber, brooding photography is enhanced by gigantic sets and a stirring score by Sergei Prokofiev. Eisenstein's hieratic study in stasis is visually his most impressive accomplishment. Cherkassov is a splendid Ivan. B&W (96 mins.)

Ivanhoe (1952)***½ Robert Taylor, Elizabeth Taylor, Joan Fontaine, George Sanders. Near-classic spectacular from the days when Robert Taylor was every woman's knight in shining armor and Elizabeth Taylor was every man's dream. Director Richard Thorpe handles the medieval splendor with ease, though the translation of Walter Scott's epic to MGM prose is a bit ragged. Nevertheless, it's a great kids' picture for adults. (106 mins.)

I've Lived Before (1956)** Jock Mahoney, Leigh Snowden. An interesting idea rather amateurishly handled—this film deals with the mystery of reincarnation. Jock Mahoney plays a man who believes he has lived before in another time. (Dir: Richard Bartlett, 82 mins.)

Ivory Ape, The (MTV 1980)** Jack Palance, Steven Keats, Cindy Pickett, Earle Hyman. An albino gorilla shows up in Africa and is captured by a ruthless (what else) promoter who intends to sell the "ivory ape" to the highest bidder. A shipwreck near Bermuda causes unforeseen complications. (Dir: Tom Kotani, 104 mins.)

Ivory Hunter (Great Britain, 1951)***½ Anthony Steel, Dinah Sheridan. A game warden in East Africa tries to preserve wild life, foils some poachers making away with ivory. Authentic African scenes to-gether with a suspenseful story make this adventure rate high. (Dir: Harry Watt, 97 mins.)

Ivy (1947)**½ Joan Fontaine, Herbert Marshall, Patric Knowles, Cedric Hardwicke. Fontaine is the female equivalent of Jack the Ripper, poisoning her way through Victorian London as reconstructed by William Cameron Menzies. Sam Wood directed a perfect stiff-upper-lip cast. (99 mins.)

Ivy League Killers (Canada, 1962)*½ Don Borisenko, Barbara Bricker. (Dir: William Davidson, 70 mins.)

Jabberwocky (Great Britain, 1977)*** Michael Palin, Max Wall, Deborah Fallender. Gory, vulgar, wildly uneven, and occasionally maniacally funny. Palin is a medieval peasant who hunts down a dreadful beast that has been terrorizing the countryside, the Jabberwock. The Jabberwock is all too obviously a man in an animal suit with papier-mâché appendages. Palin, who is always funny, and veteran British comic Wall (who plays King Bruno the Questionable) get most of the laughs. (Dir: Terry Gilliam, 101 mins.)

Jack and the Beanstalk (1952)*½ Bud Abbott, Lou Costello, Buddy Baer. (Dir: Jean Yarbrough, 87 mins.)

Jack Johnson (1971)**** Fascinating documentary biography of the legendary black heavyweight boxing champion. Uses remarkable vintage clips, most of them never seen before, compiled and edited with skill by boxing aficionados Jim Jacobs and William Clayton. Scenes of his great fights against Jess Willard and others, but there's unique footage of Johnson out of the ring as well—with his white brides, in Russia meeting Rasputin, an auto race with Barney Oldfield, etc. Johnson's pride and drive come through in the narration spoken by Brock Peters. (Dir: William Clayton, 90 mins.)

Jack London (1943)*** Michael O'Shea, Susan Hayward, Virginia Mayo, Frank Craven. Biographical adventure story of the illustrious career of Jack London. Strong cast and exciting sequences make for good entertainment. (Dir: Alfred Santell, 94 mins.)

Jack of Diamonds (U.S.-Germany, 1967)** George Hamilton, Joseph Cotten, Marie Laforet. Ordinary adventure about a sophisticated cat-burglar (George Hamilton) and his capers, both at work and at play. Curvaceous Marie Laforet is also cast as a cat-burglar which should give you an idea of the extent of the seriousness of the plot. (Dir: Don Taylor, 105 mins.)

Jack the Ripper (Great Britain, 1959)** Lee Patterson. British made meller with many shock gimmicks—moderately well done. Producer Joseph E. Levine exploited this Grade B film into a big office grosser.

(Dir: Robert Baker, 88 mins.)

Jackie Robinson Story, The (1950)*** Jackie Robinson, Ruby Dee. Interesting biographical film about Jackie's years as the first Negro in organized baseball. Corny, but recommended for the youngsters. (Dir: Alfred E. Green, 76 mins.)

Jackpot, The (1950)***½ James Stewart, Barbara Hale. Average man wins a fabulous radio-quiz jackpot (in pre-scandal days) and finds his life and wife radically changed, but not for the better. Very funny. (Dir: Walter Lang, 85 mins.)

Jackpot (Great Britain, 1960)*½ William Hartnell, Betty McDowell. (Dir: Montgomery Tully, 71 mins.)

Jackson County Jail (1976)*** Yvette Mimieux, Tommy Lee Jones, Robert Carradine, Severn Darden. Suprisingly good drama from the Roger Corman film factory about a young, attractive woman (Mimieux) who stumbles into a nightmare land of hijacking, rape, and other indignities while driving cross-country from California to New York. There's a very explicit, powerful rape scene when Mimieux is assaulted by her jailer after she is thrown in jail on a bum rap in a dinky Western town. Jones plays a fugitive on the lam who escapes from the jail with Mimieux, who soon faces some important moral questions. Written by Donald Stewart. (Dir: Michael Miller, 84 mins.)

Jacob the Liar (East Germany, 1975)*** Vlastimil Brodsky, Manuela Simon. A haunting, heartwarming, poignant drama—with some comic touches—about life in a Jewish ghetto in Poland during the Nazi occupation of World War II. A Jewish prisoner invents lies to keep hope alive among his doomed coreligionists. Magnificently acted by Czech actor Brodsky and unerringly directed by Frank Beyer, with a gentle, perceptive screenplay by Jurek Becker. One particularly notable scene, when the protagonist pretends to be playing a radio for his wide-eyed young niece. Oscar nominee, Best Foreign Film. (95 mins.)

Jacqueline (Great Britain, 1956)*** John Gregson, Kathleen Ryan. His small daughter helps an Irish dock worker obtain work on a farm. Well-made, nicely acted comedy-drama has charm. (Dir: Roy Baker, 92 mins.)

Jacqueline Susann's Once Is Not Enough— See: **Once Is Not Enough**

Jacques Brel Is Alive and Well and Living in Paris (1975)** Elly Stone, Mort Shuman, Joe Masiell, Jacques Brel. Brel's melodramatic vision—replete with images of pain, loss, death, violence, and despair—is probably better off left unvisualized. Director Denis Heroux New Waves it up with leaden specificity. One of the most pretentious films I've ever seen (as opposed to Brel's music, which is charming in small doses). Filmed in France. (98 mins.)

Jailbreakers, The (1960)* Robert Hutton,

Mary Castle. (Dir: Alexander Grasshoff, 64 mins.)

Jailhouse Rock (1957)*** Elvis Presley, Judy Tyler, Dean Jones, Vaughn Taylor. This may be the best Presley musical, with a great Lieber and Stoller score. Elvis is a con who learns to play in the big house and becomes a rock star. (Dir: Richard Thorpe, 96 mins.)

Jam Session (1944)** Ann Miller, Louis Armstrong. Not much plot but plenty of swing (remember?) performed by top performers including the Pied Pipers, Charlie Barnet and, of course, Ann and Louis. (Dir: Charles Barton, 77 mins.)

Jamaica Inn (Great Britain, 1939)***½ Charles Laughton, Maureen O'Hara, Leslie Banks. A country squire is secretly the head of a band of pirates who wreck ships and ransack them. Tense, excellent suspense melodrama. Based on the best-selling novel by Daphne duMaurier. (Dir: Alfred Hitchcock, 90 mins.)

Jamaica Run (1953)** Ray Milland, Arlene Dahl, Wendell Corey. Jumbled drama with family skeletons in every closet of a large mansion in Jamaica inhabited by a strange crew including beautiful Arlene Dahl. Ray Milland is a skipper of a schooner who helps things back to normalcy. (Dir: Lewis R. Foster, 92 mins.)

Jamboree (1957)*½ Kay Medford, Robert Pastene, Connie Francis, Frankie Avalon, Jerry Lee Lewis, Fats Domino. (Dir: Roy Lockwood, 86 mins.)

James at 15 (MTV 1977)*** Lance Kerwin, Kate Jackson, Melissa Sue Anderson. Novelist Dan Wakefield's finely etched portrait of an Oregon boy who must make new friends when dad takes a teaching post in New England. Kerwin does justice to the material as James, a kid with imagination and an ingratiating smile. (Dir: Joseph Hardy, 104 mins.)

James Dean (MTV 1976)**½ Stephen McHattie, Michael Brandon, Meg Foster, Candy Clark. Recollection of the 50's actor's early days by his best friend, Bill Bast (played by Brandon), when the two met at UCLA and struggled together in New York. The show becomes a curiosity piece, therefore, with McHattie striving to capture the essence of the young rebel, refusing to attempt an all-out imitation. Directed with care and feeling, which James Dean's fans will appreciate. (Dir: Robert Butler, 98 mins.)

James Dean Story, The (1957)** Documentary compilation recounts the life of the controversial film star who was killed in an auto crash. Made up of stills, home movies, scenes from his films, interviews with those who knew him. Dean's fans will like it—others will find it scrappy, inconclusive. (Dirs: George W. George and Robert Altman, 82 mins.)

James Michener's Dynasty (MTV 1976)**½ Sarah Miles, Stacy Keach, Harris Yulin. James Michener outlines the saga of an American epoch, the beginning of a family dynasty in Ohio back in the 1820's. It's Michener's contention that the temptation to move West was not the correct one in most cases, and he sets out to prove this in the tale of a threesome—two brothers and a small, bright, ambitious woman, played by Harris Yulin, Stacy Keach and and England's Sarah Miles as Yulin's wife. The acting juices up this TV "epic" with Miles' Jennifer, wife of a good, solid farmer, leading the way as a fighter and a shrewd businesswoman. (Dir: Lee Philips, 98 mins.)

Jamilya (U.S.S.R., 1970)***½ Natalya Arinbasarova, Suimenkul Chkmorov. A lovely, gentle story about love, beautifully directed by Irina Poplavskaya and making wonderful use of a novel setting—a village in eastern Russia near the Chinese border. Story line is simplicity itself—a young boy, a budding painter, watches the developing love of two adults he adores. Shot in both black and white and color, the color used when we see the lad's painting. (Dir: Irina Poplavskaya, 78 mins.)

Jan Hus (Czechoslovakia, 1954)**½ Zdenek Stepanek, Jan Plvec. Occasionally impressive historical drama dubbed in English, about a simple man persecuted for his religious beliefs. Overlong and leisurely in pace, it nevertheless has some impressive sequences. (Dir: Otakar Vavra, 114 mins.)

Jane Eyre (1944)***½ Orson Welles, Joan Fontaine, Elizabeth Taylor, Margaret O'Brien, Peggy Ann Garner. Effective rendition of the Charlotte Brontë novel, with Welles a brooding, compelling Rochester to Fontaine's governess. A very young and prepossessing Taylor outdoes Brooke Shields in every department. Aldous Huxley collaborated on the screenplay; John Houseman produced. Directed by subsequent Disney factotum Robert Stevenson, in what is probably his best work. (96 mins.)

Jane Eyre (MTV 1971)*** George C. Scott, Susannah York, Jack Hawkins. Scott's Rochester overlooms everything else in this acceptable remake of the Brontë novel. (Dir: Delbert Mann, 110 mins.)

Janis (1975)**½ Grainy, often out of focus, and rather pedestrian, this "documentary" on Janis Joplin is really a good deal of concert footage spliced together with a surprisingly meager amount of "candid" interview material and home movies. With no references to Joplin's life, apart from some coy joshing between her and assorted interviewers (plus a bit of silliness at her high school reunion), the film really misses the mark as reportage; but Joplin fans will still be enthralled by her performances—and why shouldn't they be? Films like this are impossible to review as films anyway. (Dirs: Howard Alk, Seaton Findlay, 96 mins.)

Jason and the Argonauts (Great Britain, 1963)*** Todd Armstrong, Nancy Kovack, Honor Blackman. Special effects buffs cite this as Ray Harryhausen's masterpiece: his work does much to enliven the tired plot and vacuous stars (Armstrong, Kovack). Mario Nascimbene's score is one of his finest; Bernard Herrmann conducts the orchestra. (Dir: Don Chaffey, 104 mins.)

Jaws (1975)**** Roy Scheider, Robert Shaw, Richard Dreyfuss, Lorraine Gary, Murray Hamilton. A fabulous finner! In case you were on Mars in the mid '70s, there's this nasty shark off the coast of Martha's Vineyard, see... One of the great box-office hits of all time. Director Steven Spielberg (age 27) builds the tension methodically and unerringly, and it pays off with one of the scariest finales ever. Special credit to the special effects crew who created the great mechanical man-eater. Live shark footage filmed on the Australian Coral Reef is cleverly integrated with the mechanical marvel. Oscar to John Williams for Best Music Score. Adapted from Peter Benchley's best-selling novel. (124 mins.)

Jaws 2 (1978)*** Roy Scheider, Lorraine Gary, Murray Hamilton, Joseph Mascolo, Jeffrey Kramer. More reminiscent of *The Blob* than *Jaws*, inasmuch as this is essentially a teen movie in which the beachside volleyball games are interrupted by an unwelcome intruder. It's not as slickly manipulative as Steve Spielberg's original, but there is plenty of bloody catharsis. The action mechanism works very well. (Dir: Jeannot Szwarc, 117 mins.)

Jayhawkers, The (1959)**½ Jeff Chandler, Fess Parker. Fast-paced western about ruthless men who try to take over control of an entire state after the Civil War. (Dir: Melvin Frank, 100 mins.)

Jazz Ball (1956)** Compilation of musical acts culled from old Paramount short subjects, featuring Betty Hutton, Mills Brothers, Louis Armstrong, etc. No story line. Occasionally interesting memento of what the greats were doing decades ago. (57 mins.)

Jazz Boat (Great Britain, 1960)** Anthony Newley, Anne Aubrey. A British rock 'n roll musical with a good cast but a tiresome script and an equally boring score. (Dir: Ken Hughes, 90 mins.)

Jazz on a Summer's Day (1960)**** The best filmed record of a jazz concert. The Newport Jazz Festival of 1958 is the setting for Bert Stern's superbly edited account of the exciting, festive air generated by a host of talents who held a crew-cut, long-skirted audience spellbound with their artistry. The roster reads like a who's who of pop jazz...the immortal Louis Armstrong, Dinah Washington, Thelonious Monk, Gerry Mulligan, Chuck Berry, Big Maybelle, Anita O'Day and Mahalia Jackson, with Miss Jackson bringing the whole thing to a rousing close with her gospel song. (Dir: Bert Stern, 85 mins.)

Jazz Singer, The (1927)*** Al Jolson,

Warner Oland, May McAvoy. The film that brought sound to the movies to stay. Story of a cantor's son who becomes a stage star. As a film, not so good, and never was; as movie history, of interest and Al Jolson's overpowering stage personality does come through and is still worth seeing for the first time. (Dir: Alan Crosland, 90 mins.)

Jazz Singer, The (1953)*** Danny Thomas, Peggy Lee. Updated version of the old Al Jolson film which revolutionized the motion picture business. This version did not make history but is nevertheless an entertaining story about a Jewish boy who prefers show business to becoming a cantor like his father before him. Danny Thomas is quite good in the title role. (Dir: Michael Curtiz, 107 mins.)

Jazz Singer, The (1980)** Neil Diamond, Laurence Olivier, Lucie Arnaz, Catlin Adams. Remake of Al Jolson's '27 film about the young man whose father wants him to be a Jewish cantor is an expensive vanity production for a pop star (Diamond) out to expand his stardom. Handsome production work canceled out by transparently phony drama. Olivier should stay away from dialect parts—his Yiddish accent often lapses into something close to Scottish. (Dir: Richard Fleischer, 115 mins.)

J.D.'s Revenge (1976)** Glynn Turman, Lou Gossett, Joan Pringle, David McKnight (as J.D.). Fair black actioner is a bit of a surprise from director Arthur Marks, a stiff on his previous outings who has graduated to amiable hackdom. Turman is a law student possessed by the spirit of a man murdered in '42, which gives him the chance to sport a zoot suit as he carves up the heavies. As usual, blood flows freely and gratuitously. (95 mins.)

Jeanne Eagels (1957)**½ Kim Novak, Jeff Chandler, Agnes Moorehead. A glorified yet watered down depiction of the rise and fall of actress Jeanne Eagels. Kim Novak is sorely miscast and overacts throughout. (Dir: George Sidney, 109 mins.)

Jennifer (1978)** Lisa Pelikan, Bert Convy, Nina Foch. Young Virginia hill girl, awarded a scholarship to an exclusive girls' school, uses her power over snakes to combat her tormentors. Not a bad thriller. (Dir: Brice Mack, 90 mins.)

Jennifer: A Woman's Story (MTV 1979)** Elizabeth Montgomery, Bradford Dillman, Scott Hylands. Montgomery is a widow battling for control of her husband's boat-building firm. Based on a British TV series. Most of the males in the film are rats, including the heroine's late philandering husband. (Dir: Guy Green, 104 mins.)

Jennifer on My Mind (1971)** Michael Brandon, Tippy Walker, Peter Bonery. Erich Segal wrote the script, a minus entry on the ledger. Society is responsible for the unhappiness of the wealthy young,

or didn't you know? Noel Black directs, badly. (90 mins.)

Jenny (1970)*½ Marlo Thomas, Alan Alda, Marian Hailey, Elizabeth Wilson, Vincent Gardenia (Dir: George Bloomfield, 93 mins.)

Jeopardy ((1953)**½ Barbara Stanwyck, Barry Sullivan, Ralph Meeker. Woman trying to find help for her injured husband is captured by an escaped killer. Modest little thriller is well made, but remains a minor drama. (Dir: John Sturges, 69 mins.)

Jeremiah Johnson (1972)*** Robert Redford, Will Geer, Stefan Gierasch. Director Sydney Pollack's straightforward film of a man determined to live life deliberately, no matter what the hardships. Redford turns in a sturdy performance as Johnson, a man who goes up into the Rocky Mountains to find the meaning of life in the 1830's. The dialogue is spare, the scenery is the real star. Satisfying. (110 mins.)

Jeremy (1973)***½ Robby Benson, Glynis O'Connor, Leonardo Cimino, Pat Wheel. A love story about two New York high-school teenagers, without the usual overlay of drugs, violence, rape, etc. A tender, often quite sensitive portrayal of first love and sexual awakenings. Robby Benson is enormously appealing as a Jewish would-be cellist, meeting and wooing a Gentile lass who loves the dance. Written by Arthur Barron, a distinguished TV documentary filmmaker, who makes an impressive feature film directorial debut with this sensitive, low-budget entry. "Jeremy" never got the attention it deserved. (Dir: Arthur Barron, 90 mins.)

Jericho (Great Britain, 1937)**½ Paul Robeson, Henry Wilcoxen, Wallace Ford. The charismatic Robeson, in one of the films made during his exile in England, plays a French soldier who deserts to Africa and becomes a sheikh. (Dir: Thorton Freeland, 77 mins.)

Jericho Mile, The (MTV 1979)***½ Peter Strauss, Richard Lawson, Roger E. Mosley, Miguel Pinero. Strauss is a tense, pent-up lifer at Folsom State Penitentiary, who becomes obsessed with running the fastest mile possible. Filmed on location, with smaller roles and extras being actual prisoners. When the prison officials try to clear the way for Strauss to qualify for the Olympic trials, the story really takes off. Director Michael Mann gives the film a strong sense of place and a big-budgeted theatrical look. (104 mins.)

Jerk, The (1979)**½ Steve Martin, Bernadette Peters, Catlin Adams, Jackie Mason. Martin makes his starring debut as the '80s' answer to Jerry Lewis. He and director Carl Reiner lack comic vision, and the result is a boring series of failed gags. Martin plays the white stepchild of black sharecroppers. (93 mins.)

Jerusalem File, The (U.S.-Israel, 1972)**½ Bruce Davison, Zeev Revah, Donald Pleasence, Nicol Williamson, Daria

Halprin. Naive story of student idealism working to solve the Arab-Israeli turmoil. An American archaeology student (Davidson), studying in Israel, attempts to continue and expand his Yale-based friendship with an Arab student leader (Revah) amid a background of militarism and strife. Pleasence and Williamson offer well-drawn characterizations, but the real star is Raoul Coutard's cinematography (he also did "Z"), which breathes a sense of time and place into this simplistic tale. (Dir: John Flynn, 96 mins.)

Jesse James (1939)***½ Tyrone Power, Henry Fonda, Nancy Kelly. A superb cast in a highly fictionalized account of the life of America's most famous outlaw. Glorifies him too much but is real exciting screen entertainment. (Dir: Henry King, 106 mins.)

Jesse James Meets Frankenstein's Daughter (1966)* John Lupton, Cal Bolder, Narda Onyx. (Dir: William Beaudine, 88 mins.)

Jessica (U.S.-French-Italian, 1962)** Angie Dickinson, Maurice Chevalier. When a glamorous midwife turns men's heads in a small Italian village, the women of the town pull a "Lysistrata" and go on "strike." Filmed in Italy, the scenics are the main attraction in this slow-moving comedy. (Dir: Jean Negulesco, 112 mins.)

Jesus Christ Superstar (1973)*** Ted Neeley, Carl Anderson, Joshua Mostel, Yvonne Elliman. Most of director Norman Jewison's films are terrible botches, but this is a significant, substantial achievement. The songs are superbly integrated into a coherent overall approach. Unbearably moving. (107 mins.)

Jesus Trip, The (1971)**½ Robert Porter, Billy Bush, Tippy Walker, Robert Tessier. A bunch of unknowns provide credible performances in a story about a motorcycle gang kidnapping a young nun (Walker). The police begin a relentless search for the gang, and many unusual plot twists develop. (Dir: Russ Mayberry, 84 mins.)

Jet Over the Atlantic (1959)**½ Guy Madison, Virginia Mayo, George Raft. Fairly interesting drama about a plane which is in danger when a bomb is discovered aboard during the flight from Spain to New York. (Dir: Byron Haskin, 95 mins.)

Jet Pilot (1957)** John Wayne, Janet Leigh, Hans Conried. Director Josef von Sternberg's broad comic-book style undermines the cold war hysteria of this delayed-release film made in '49-'50. Leigh is a busty Russian spy pilot captured and eventually married by Wayne. Produced by Howard Hughes. (112 mins.)

Jet Storm (Great Britain, 1959)**½ Stanley Baker, Richard Attenborough, Diane Cilento. Interesting psychological drama as a demented father tries to gain revenge on the man who killed his child. Will he explode the bomb in his suitcase or will he be persuaded by jet-plane passengers to give himself up? Alternate title: **Killing Urge**. (Dir: C. Raker Endfield, 99 mins.)

Jezebel (1938)*** Bette Davis, Henry Fonda, George Brent, Fay Bainter, Margaret Lindsay. Davis won an Oscar as the fiery southern belle who flouts convention while flitting from banker Fonda to dandy Brent. As usual, director William Wyler pays more attention to detail than to style. Bainter deserved the Oscar she got. (103 mins.)

Jigsaw (Great Britain, 1962)**½ Jack Warner, Ronald Lewis, Yolande Donlan. Capable whodunit about police investigating a murder, painstakingly putting the clues together. Done efficiently, semidocumentary style; mystery fans should enjoy. (Dir: Val Guest, 107 mins.)

Jigsaw (1968)**½ Harry Guardino, Hope Lange, Bradford Dillman, Pat Hingle. Fairly engrossing tale about a scientist (Dillman) who thinks he has committed a murder, and hires a private detective to fill in the missing pieces. No real surprises in this mystery but most of it works. (Dir: James Goldstone, 97 mins.)

Jigsaw (1972)**½ James Wainwright, an offbeat, rugged actor in the Lee Marvin groove, plays the leading role of a police detective in this well-paced pilot for the TV series. When Wainwright follows a suspicious-looking character to a hotel, he becomes involved in a mystery. There's an exciting two-car chase across dirt roads, and the supporting cast, including Vera Miles, Richard Kiley, and Irene Dailey, helps Wainwright's earnest, convincing performance. Alternate title: **Man on the Move**. (Dir: William Graham, 99 mins.)

Jim Thorpe, All American (1951)*** Burt Lancaster, Phyllis Thaxter. Burt Lancaster portrays the All-American Indian athlete who rose from an obscure beginning to international fame. Sport fans will enjoy this one. (Dir: Michael Curtiz, 107 mins.)

Jimmy B. & Andre (MTV 1980)**½ Alex Karras, Madge Sinclair, Curtis Yates. A sentimental true-life story in which Karras plays a role that suits him to a T. When he was playing pro football he used to hang out in a bar-restaurant in Detroit run by Greek Jimmy Butsicaris. Jimmy B. became the mentor of a young black street-wise kid who hustled to make an honest buck any way he could. This is their story, and it's a fairly good one. You'll root for Andre, the kid with all the odds stacked against him but one—his friendship with Jimmy B., a guy who cared. (Dir: Guy Green, 104 mins.)

Jimmy the Gent (1934)*** James Cagney, Bette Davis, Alice White. Early Warner Bros. programmer stars Cagney as a shady businessman who feigns honesty to impress a young, fetching Davis. Michael Curtiz (who else) directed this fast-paced, full-of-surprises comedy. (67 mins.)

Jivaro (1954)**½ Fernando Lamas, Rhonda Fleming, Brian Keith. Into the land of head-hunters come the fearless treasure seeking adventurers with Fernando Lamas at the helm and beautiful Rhonda Fleming not far behind. Action filled jungle film. (Dir: Edward Ludwig, 91 mins.)

Joan of Arc (1948)**½ Ingrid Bergman, Jose Ferrer, Ward Bond. Mammoth, lavish production based on the life of the French farm girl who led the French armies against England and was later tried as a heretic. Despite the pretensions, the film is top-heavy, wallows in its own opulence. Performances, including Bergman's, are adequate, no more. May hold the attention, but a classic it isn't. (Dir: Victor Fleming, 100 mins.)

Joan of Paris (1942)***½ Michele Morgan, Paul Henreid, Alan Ladd. French girl sacrifices her life so that the English flyers may escape the Gestapo in occupied France. Gripping suspenseful war drama, excellently acted, well produced. (Dir: Robert Stevenson, 95 mins.)

Joe (1970)***½ Peter Boyle, Dennis Patrick. Savage, powerful, but imperfect film, which benefits greatly from an astonishingly bravura performance by Peter Boyle. Joe is a foul-mouthed, unashamed, reactionary bigot, who hates "niggers" and "hippies" with equal rage. Boyle somehow manages to find some humor in the role. His monologue in a neighborhood bar, where he meets and befriends an affluent advertising executive who is also a murderer, is one of the most compelling scenes in years. The other acting is not on a par with Boyle's and the generally perceptive script by Norman Wexler flounders at the end, but you'll be mesmerized by "Joe" long before this low-budget entry, shot on location in New York, comes to its flawed conclusion. (Dir: John G. Avildsen, 107 mins.)

Joe Butterfly (1957)** Audie Murphy, George Nader, Burgess Meredith. GIs in Japan encounter a shrewd native operator who helps them get out the first edition of "Yank." Disappointing service comedy takes an amusing idea and almost completely botches it. Mild at best. (Dir: Jesse Hibbs, 90 mins.)

Joe Dakota (1957)**½ Jock Mahoney, Luana Patten. Stranger rides into town and finds the populace agog with oil fever, uncovers skullduggery behind the drilling. Pleasant little western carries a good amount of entertainment. (Dir: Richard Bartlett, 79 mins.)

Joe Kidd (1972)**½ Clint Eastwood, Robert Duvall. Moderately interesting Eastwood western with the star giving still another of his "quiet cowboy with a quick gun" portrayals. The setting is New Mexico at the turn of the century. The plot centers on the Spanish-Americans fighting the land barons for what they believe to be their property. In steps Joe Kidd (Eastwood) to aid the Spaniards and the sparks fly in a flashy, violent finale. The on-location photography of the High Sierras

is a spectacular bonus. (Dir: John Sturges, 88 mins.)

Joe Macbeth (Great Britain, 1955)**½ Paul Douglas, Ruth Roman. Egged on by his grasping wife, a gangster kills his way to the top of the mob. Modernized Shakespeare, a noble experiment that doesn't quite succeed. Made in England, but the American locale is fairly accurate. (Dir: Ken Hughes, 90 mins.)

John and Julie (Great Britain, 1955)**½ Moira Lister, Constance Cummings, Noelle Middleton. Warm-hearted British comedy about two children and their adventures in the splendor-filled world of royalty. (Dir; William Fairchild, 82 mins.)

John and Mary (1969)**½ Dustin Hoffman, Mia Farrow. Gentle if sometimes tedious study which treads lightly on a resigned affair between two singles who pick each other up at a bar but don't really swing. Hoffman is "John" and Farrow is "Mary," names revealed only after the night's lovemaking has turned into the morning after's falling in love. The action is painfully confined to an apartment interior (with some flashes outdoors) and the acting is constricted by the screenplay which prefers social commentary to humanism. But it is a "star vehicle" and Hoffman and Farrow are alternately quarrelsome and lovable. (Dir: Peter Yates, 92 mins.)

John F. Kennedy: Years of Lightning, Day of Drums (1964)**** Excellent U.S. Government documentary on the Presidential life, and death, of John F. Kennedy, guarantees to stir up all the old emotions. Memorial tribute, also a propaganda effort, the film was intended for showing abroad and only made available in the U.S. by an act of Congress. It does not attempt a sober reassessment of Kennedy's brief term in office. The narration by Gregory Peck is unobtrusive, yet adds to the compelling, emotional mood. (Dir: Bruce Herschensohn, 88 mins.)

John Goldfarb, Please Come Home (1965)*½ Shirley MacLaine, Peter Ustinov, Richard Crenna. (Dir: J. Lee Thompson, 96 mins.)

John Loves Mary (1949)**½ Ronald Reagan, Patricia Neal, Jack Carson. Stage comedy about a returning soldier trying to sneak a war bride into this country, while his fiancee wants to get married. Loses a lot of its spontaneity. Neal's film debut. (Dir: David Butler, 96 mins.)

John Paul Jones (1959)**½ Robert Stack, Marisa Pavan, Charles Coburn, Bette Davis. Rambling biography of America's first naval hero, moderately well played by Stack against stacked odds—talky script, static direction. Miss Davis makes a token appearance as Empress Catherine of Russia. Battle scenes lend some maritime excitement. Filmed mainly in Spain. (Dir: John Farrow, 126 mins.)

Johnny Allegro (1949)**½ George Raft, Nina Foch. Raft is once again the shady hoodlum who squares himself with the cops by acting as an undercover agent to expose an international smuggling outfit. Plenty of two-fisted action. (Dir: Ted Tetzlaff, 81 mins.)

Johnny Angel (1945)*** George Raft, Claire Trevor. Merchant marine officer unravels the murder of his father, smashes a ring of enemy agents. Well done melodrama with good production values. (Dir: Edwin L. Marin, 79 mins.)

Johnny Apollo (1940)*** Tyrone Power, Dorothy Lamour, Edward Arnold, Lloyd Nolan. Fast paced gangster melodrama with college grad Power choosing a life of crime out of bitterness over his dad's conviction of fraud. Mostly routine but good entertainment. (Dir: Henry Hathaway, 93 mins.)

Johnny Belinda (1948)***½ Jane Wyman, Lew Ayres, Charles Bickford, Agnes Moorhead. Jane Wyman gives an Oscar-award-winning performance as a deaf mute in this sensitive and moving story of a person living in a world of silence. (Dir: Jean Negulesco, 103 mins.)

Johnny Cash: The Man, His World, His Music (1970)*** Johnny Cash, June Carter, Bob Dylan, Don Reed. Quite interesting feature about the famous country-music star. We hear a lot of good Cash tunes, also learn something about Cash himself as we travel with Johnny to his hometown in rural Arkansas where he grew up in poverty. This is a longer version of material first seen as a television documentary. Cash joins Dylan on "One Too Many Mornings" and there's a couple of fine tunes from a young man named Don Reed who auditions for Cash. (Dir: Robert Elfstrom, 94 mins.)

Johnny Come Lately (1943)**½ James Cagney, Grace George. A wandering vagabond stops in a small town and helps an old lady run her newspaper. Mild for Cagney, but generally entertaining comedy-drama. Only film of stage actress George. (Dir: William K. Howard, 97 mins.)

Johnny Concho (1956)** Frank Sinatra, Keenan Wynn, Phyllis Kirk, William Conrad. Sinatra as a cowboy is very hard to take! The plot centers around a coward who must face up to a fast gun. Some good scenes but slow moving and, to be truthful, rather boring. (Dir: Don McGuire, 84 mins.)

Johnny Cool (1963)** Henry Silva, Elizabeth Montgomery. Violent, familiar tale of a mafioso (Silva) seeking revenge in gangsterdom. Studded with guest bit parts including Sammy Davis, Jr., Mort Sahl, Joey Bishop, Telly Savalas. (Dir: William Asher, 101 mins.)

Johnny Dark (1954)*½ Tony Curtis, Piper Laurie, Don Taylor. (Dir: George Sherman, 85 mins.)

Johnny Doesn't Live Here Anymore—See: **And So They Were Married**

Johnny Eager (1941)***½ Robert Taylor, Lana Turner, Van Heflin. Top rate gangster melodrama about a good-looking, egotistical hood. Van Heflin's performance as Taylor's confidante and Greek chorus won him an award (a Supporting Actor Oscar) and stardom. (Dir: Mervyn Le Roy, 107 mins.)

Johnny Guitar (1954)*** Joan Crawford, Sterling Hayden, Scott Brady, Mercedes McCambridge. Gambling house proprietress has built her establishment on a railroad site, earns the resentment of the town. Unusual western tries to be different, which is something to commend, anyway. (Dir: Nicholas Ray, 110 mins.)

Johnny Holiday (1949)***½ William Bendix, Stanley Clements, Hoagy Carmichael, Allen Martin, Jr. Delinquent boy is reformed at the Indiana Boys' School. Authentic, forceful drama has a good air of sincerity. (Dir: Willis Goldbeck, 92 mins.)

Johnny In the Clouds (Great Britain, 1945)***½ Douglass Montgomery, John Mills, Michael Redgrave. Story of a flying field in England during World War II, and the various emotional entanglements of the airmen. Stirring war drama with praiseworthy performance, direction. Alternate title: **The Way to the Stars**. (Dir: Anthony Asquith, 87 mins.)

Johnny Nobody (Great Britain, 1961)*** Nigel Patrick, Aldo Ray, William Bendix, Yvonne Mitchell. When a disliked writer is killed by a mysterious stranger soon known as "Johnny Nobody," the local priest suspects a plot; the villagers are claiming the deed to be a miracle. Offbeat drama has a decidedly unusual story, interesting performances and direction to back it up. Good fare. (Dir: Nigel Patrick, 88 mins.)

Johnny O'Clock (1947)**½ Dick Powell, Evelyn Keyes. Confused, tough tale of an honest gambler who gets accused of murder. Good, rough dialogue but without a purpose. (Dir: Robert Rossen, 95 mins.)

Johnny Stool Pigeon (1949)**½ Howard Duff, Shelley Winters, Dan Duryea, Tony Curtis. Routine but well played crime drama about an ex-con who serves as a "stoolie" for the police in order to uncover a dope ring. Good gangland scenes. (Dir: William Castle, 76 mins.)

Johnny Tiger (1966)**½ Robert Taylor, Geraldine Brooks, Chad Everett, Brenda Scott. Teacher comes to the Seminole Reservation in Florida to instruct the Indian children, finds his task is harder than he bargained for. Different sort of drama makes good use of location scenery, Indian customs. Runs a bit too long, but worth seeing. (Dir: Paul Wendkos, 102 mins.)

Johnny Trouble (1957)** Stuart Whitman, Ethel Barrymore, Carolyn Jones. Guy on the road turns a new leaf when he meets a woman who has never given up hope of her long-lost son's returning. Drama leans toward the maudlin, was done better years ago as "Someone To Remember." Barrymore's last. (Dir: John H. Auer, 80 mins.)

Johnny You're Wanted (Great Britain, 1956)*½ John Slater, Alfred Marks. (Dir: Vernon Sewell, 71 mins.)

Johnny Yuma (Italy, 1966)* Mark Damon, Lawrence Dobkin, Rosalba Neri. (Dir: Romolo Guerrieri, 99 mins.)

Joker Is Wild, The (1957)*** Frank Sinatra, Jeanne Crain, Mitzi Gaynor. The story of nightclub entertainer Joe E. Lewis, who conquered problems with the gang lords of the roaring 20's, and the bottle of today. Played by Sinatra in his standard hipster style, the story has moments of dramatic force, some good nostalgic tunes. (Dir: Charles Vidor, 126 mins.)

Jokers, The (Great Britain, 1967)***½ Michael Crawford, Oliver Reed. A sparkling British comedy that doesn't go for big laughs but keeps you smiling throughout. An attractive pair of well-to-do brothers, charmingly played by Oliver Reed and Michael Crawford, come up with a wild plot to snatch the Crown Jewels and then give them back. They figure all the odds and go through with it. The actual theft is a brilliantly staged sequence, and viewers will find the suspense almost unbearable. There's a twist to the ending which adds to the film's bite, and credit must be paid to the superb photography which heightens the action at all times. Director Michael Winner also thought up this engaging yarn! (94 mins.)

Jolly Bad Fellow, A (Great Britain, 1964)***½ Leo McKern, Janet Munro, Maxine Audley. Wildly amusing comedy about a scoundrelly professor who discovers a poison which will cause painless and untraceable death, decides to use it for his own devices. Anyone who can mix murder and mirth successfully deserves credit, and the participants here have done it. (Dir: Don Chaffey, 94 mins.)

Jolson Sings Again (1949)**** Larry Parks, Barbara Hale. The rest of the Al Jolson Story and as good as its predecessor. Parks once again mouths the songs that made the "Minstrel of Broadway" famous. (Dir: Henry Levin, 96 mins.)

Jolson Story, The (1946)**** Larry Parks, Evelyn Keyes. The film biography of the popular singer from his boyhood to his success on the stage and in talkies. Grand show with Jolson singing his numbers perfectly to Parks' miming. (Dir: Alfred E. Green, 128 mins.)

Jonah—Who Will Be 25 in the Year 2000 (Switzerland-France, 1976)**** Jean-Luc Bideau, Rufus, Miou-Miou, Jacques Denis, Jonah. Director Alain Tanner's affectionate study of a group of '60s radicals trying to make the transition to the '70s. That rare thing, a political film that speaks to the heart as well as the mind. (110 mins.)

Jordan Chance, The (MTV 1978)**½ Raymond Burr, Stella Stevens. Burr plays—you guessed it—a criminal lawyer: Frank Jordan, an ex-con who served time for a crime he didn't commit, and studied law in the pen. He only defends those

he feels have been given a raw deal by the courts. (Dir: Jules Irving, 104 mins.)

Joseph and His Brethren (Italy, 1960)*½ Geoffrey Horne, Robert Morley. (Dir: Irving Rapper, 103 mins.)

Joseph Andrews (Great Britain, 1976)*½ Ann-Margret, Peter Firth, Beryl Reid, Michael Hordern, John Gielgud. When the novel was being born, Samuel Richardson's best-selling "Pamela" was mercilessly burlesqued by Henry Fielding as "Shamela." It took two centuries for the revenge of the Richardsons: director Tony Richardson's "Tom Jones." Not content, he returns to plunder another Fielding novel with a style so maladroit as to leave the original untarnished. This cast has less charm. (104 mins.)

Josephine and Men (Great Britain, 1955)** Glynis Johns, Jack Buchanan, Peter Finch. Girl's mother instincts get her into plenty of trouble with men. Comedy is never as funny as it should be. (Dir: Roy Boulting, 98 mins.)

Journey, The (1959)**½ Deborah Kerr, Yul Brynner, Jason Robards, Jr. Brynner parades around as a Russian officer who mixes business (detaining the evacuation of neutral citizens from revolution-torn Hungary circa 1956) and pleasure (putting the make on pale Deborah Kerr). A good cast, including Robert Morley, E. G. Marshall and Anne Jackson, are at the mercy of a mediocre script. Some mild suspense at the end. Robards's debut. (Dir: Anatole Litvak, 125 mins.)

Journey Beneath the Desert (France-Italy, 1961)*½ Haya Harareet, Rad Fulton, Jean-Louis Trintignant. (Dirs: Edgar Ulmer, Frank Borzage, Guiseppi Masini, 105 mins.)

Journey for Margaret (1942)***½ Robert Young, Laraine Day, Margaret O'Brien. Story of the small, innocent victims of the blitz is splendidly acted, warm melodrama. If this doesn't make you cry, then you simply don't like children. (Dir: W. S. Van Dyke, 81 mins.)

Journey from Berlin/1971 (1980)***½ Annette Michelson, Ilona Halberstadt, Gabor Vernon. Director and ex-dancer Yvonne Rainer's film has two major sections: a psychoanalytic session (featuring theorist Michelson) and a kitchen conversation. The psychoanalysis explores a shifting terrain of anxiety, self-flagellation, questions of power, contradictions between intellect and sexuality, and quirky observations about the private politics of terrorism. (125 mins.)

Journey from Darkness (MTV 1975)**½ Marc Singer, Kay Lenz, Joseph Campanella, William Windom. Marc Singer is effective in this adaptation of a true story about a blind student who doggedly battles his way into medical school, when everyone says that's impossible. The parents don't want to see their boy hurt, college professors spell out the difficulties, and only the student and his girl, well played by Kay

Lenz, remain undaunted. (dir: James Goldstone, 100 mins.)

Journey Into Fear (1942)*** Orson Welles, Joseph Cotten, Dolores Del Rio, Ruth Warrick, Everett Sloane. Welles cowrote the screenplay with Joseph Cotten, designed, and produced. That makes for a lot of influence, and it shows. It's good but has as much in common with the low-budget Mr. Moto and Charlie Chan films of the late thirties as it does with its foggy rendition of the Welles style. An effective version of the Eric Ambler thriller set in WW II Turkey as a U.S. armaments expert is sought by Nazi agents. (Dir: Norman Foster, 69 mins.)

Journey Into Fear (Canada, 1975)** Sam Waterston, Yvette Mimieux, Zero Mostel. An unsuccessful attempt to remake Orson Welles' 1942 film based on Eric Ambler's novel. Sam Waterston is no Welles, and the updating of the espionage yarn set in Turkey and the U.S. to the 70's dilutes the suspense of the original tale. Yvette Mimieux offers something to look at during the dull movie. Filmed in Europe. (Dir: Daniel Mann, 103 mins.)

Journey Into Light (1951)**½ Sterling Hayden, Viveca Lindfors. A minister loses faith, becomes a derelict, is reformed by a blind girl in a Skid Row mission. Slow well acted drama. (Dir: Stuart Heisler, 87 mins.)

Journey Into Nowhere (Great Britain, 1963)**½ Tony Wright, Sonja Ziemann. Odd little suspense drama made in South Africa; man on the lam from hoodlums meets a woman about to go blind, they devise a double indemnity insurance plan, the survivor collecting. Unpolished, but with good acting by the leads. (Dir: Denis Scully, 73 mins.)

Journey of Robert F. Kennedy, The (1970)***½ An engrossing, perceptive and touching portrait of the late Senator Robert F. Kennedy, the man, the politician, the husband and father, and the inspired spokesman for the blacks and the poor. The documentary benefits from the narration written by Arthur Schlesinger, Jr., which presents views from both supporters and opponents of Kennedy, and gives a clear picture of RFK's strong sense of dedication to his work and family as well as his ambition. Through a series of well edited film clips, RFK's political career is traced from the days he managed his brother John F. Kennedy's 1960 Presidential campaign to his own strenuous campaign for the Presidential nomination in 1968, which ended abruptly when he was killed by an assassin. A highlight, among many others, is an interview with civil rights leader Charles Evers, who sums up Robert F. Kennedy as a man who really cared about people. (Dir: Mel Stuart, 75 mins.)

Journey to Freedom (1957)* Jacques Scott, Genevieve Aumont. (Dir: Robert C. Dertano, 60 mins.)

Journey to Jerusalem, A (1968)*** A documentary record of a concert given by violinist Isaac Stern and conducted by Leonard Bernstein. Filmed in Jerusalem several weeks after the end of the Six Day War in 1967. The music, including selections from Mahler and Mendelssohn, is glorious. The filmmaking itself, partially because the film was organized and shot so hurriedly, is less well done. But "Journey" is a moving record of an emotion-filled event, the reunification of Jerusalem. (Dir: Michael Mindlin, Jr., 84 mins.)

Journey to Shiloh (1968)** Michael Sarrazin, Brenda Scott. A cast of young players, including Michael Sarrazin, James Caan, Michael Burns and Brenda Scott, is featured in this western yarn set during the Civil War. Fans get a good amount of action in this tale about a group of green young men who set out for Virginia to join up and fight for the Confederacy. Routine but played with youthful energy. (Dir: William Hale, 101 mins.)

Journey to the Beginning of Time (Czechoslovakia, 1960)**½ Victor Betral, James Lukas, Peter Hermann, Charles Goldsmith. Nice kiddie fare. Four youngsters explore a cave in New York's Central Park after a museum visit, find themselves in prehistoric times. (Dir: Karel Zeman, 87 mins.)

Journey to the Center of the Earth (1959)***½ James Mason, Pat Boone, Arlene Dahl, Diane Baker, Thayer David. Juvenile adventure maintaining a credible tone of silliness throughout that understands the continuing appeal of Jules Verne. Mason is the expedition leader whose entourage includes the actors named and a goose called Gertrude. Has one of Bernard Hermann's most effective scores. Technicolor. (Dir: Henry Levin, 132 mins.)

Journey to the Center of Time (1967)*½ Scott Brady, Gigi Perreau, Anthony Eisley. (Dir: D. L. Hewitt, 82 mins.)

Journey to the Far Side of the Sun (Great Britain, 1969)*½ Roy Thinnes, Lynn Loring, Herbert Lom. (Dir: Robert Parrish, 99 mins.)

Journey to the Lost City (Germany, 1960)*½ Debra Paget, Paul Christian. (Dir: Fritz Lang, 94 mins.)

Journey to the 7th Planet (1962)** John Agar, Greta Thyssen. A group of earthmen come to grips with beautiful women and strange forces on the planet number 7 in this predictable sci-fi entry. (Dir: Sidney Pink, 83 mins.)

Journey's End (1930)***½ Colin Clive, Ian Maclaren, David Manners. Near-perfect rendering of R. C. Sherriff's classic antiwar play. Clive is unforgettable as the alcoholic captain who cracks under the strain of responsibility. (Dir: James Whale, 120 mins.)

Joy House (France, 1964)**½ Jane Fonda, Alain Delon, Lola Albright. French director Rene Clement is only half successful in making this macabre suspense yarn work—but the half that does is worthwhile. Lola Albright is hiding her lover (a criminal) in a chamber in her Riviera villa, while cousin Jane Fonda is trying to seduce chauffeur Alain Delon. They all clash before the surprise ending. (Dir: Rene Clement, 98 mins.)

Joy in the Morning (1965)**½ Richard Chamberlain, Yvette Mimieux. The two attractive stars are earnest in this uneven love story about a young couple who face many of every day's problems during the early days of their marriage. Set in the early 1900's in a college town, the plot reads like a monthly installment in a ladies' magazine, but it's harmless stuff, and the stars are decorative. (Dir: Alex Segal, 103 mins.)

Joy of Living (1938)***½ Irene Dunne, Douglas Fairbanks Jr. Happy-go-lucky globe trotter romances a career-minded stage star. Delightful romantic comedy, with some good Jerome Kern tunes. (Dir: Tay Garnett, 100 mins.)

Joy Ride ((1958)*** Regis Toomey, Ann Doran. Punch-packed little suspense drama about an "average man" who is terrorized by a bunch of young punks, turns the tables on them. Nothing big, but within its own framework quite good, including the performances and script. (Dir: Edward Bernds, 60 mins.)

Joyride (1977)*** Desi Arnaz, Jr., Robert Carradine, Melanie Griffith, Anne Lockhart, Tom Ligon. A group of disaffected adolescents go in search of their lost souls along the Alaska pipeline. Interesting achievement in a minor genre. (Dir: Joseph Ruben, 92 mins.)

Juarez (1939)**** Paul Muni, Brian Aherne, Bette Davis, John Garfield. Brilliantly acted, moving, dramatic story of the great Mexican hero. Muni adds another notch to his record of screen portrayals. (Dir: William Dieterle, 132 mins.)

Jubal (1956)***½ Glenn Ford, Ernest Borgnine, Rod Steiger, Felicia Farr. Superior western. Ford plays a drifter named Jubal Troop who is given a job by rancher (Borgnine) and immediately starts off a chain reaction of jealousy, hate and violence. Rod Steiger's prtrayal of a sadistic cowhand named "Pinky" is outstanding. (Dir: Delmer Daves, 101 mins.)

Jubilee Trail (1953)**½ Vera Ralston, Joan Leslie, Forrest Tucker, Pat O'Brien. Singer helps a young wife overcome skulduggery in old California. Costume drama has plenty of lavish scenes, but a rambling story. (Dir: Joseph Kane, 103 mins.)

Judex (France-Italy, 1964)**½ Channing Pollock, Francine Berge, Michel Vitold. Slow-moving refilming of a 1916 French silent serial about master-criminal Judex, whose main weapons are magic and style (he is protrayed by American magician Channing Pollock), and his arch-enemy, a beautiful woman who strips down to black for her nefarious deeds. Director Franju

has aimed for the unabashed melodrama of the original, and overdoes it. But it's intermittently inventive and absorbing. (Dir: Georges Franju, 96 mins.)

Judge and Jake Wyler, The (1972)**½ Bette Davis, Doug McClure. Although Miss Davis is top-lined in this pilot film for an unsold TV series, it's really McClure's show. He plays an ex-con working for ex-Judge Davis, who runs a detective agency from her fortresslike home. (Dir: David Lowell Rich, 100 mins.)

Judge Dee and the Monastery Murders (MTV 1974)* Khigh Dhiegh. (Dir: Jeremy Kagan, 72 mins.)

Judge Hardy and Son (1939)** Mickey Rooney, Lewis Stone, Cecilia Parker. Sentimental Hardy family entry. Mom gets sick, an old couple is being evicted, and other soap opera situations come to a happy, tearful conclusion. (Dir: George B. Seitz, 90 mins.)

Judge Hardy's Children (1938)**½ Mickey Rooney, Lewis Stone. Andy and the judge are in Washington for this one and Andy saves the day for his dad. Good family entertainment. (Dir: George B. Seitz, 80 mins.)

Judge Horton and the Scottsboro Boys (MTV 1976)*** Arthur Hill, Vera Miles, Lewis J. Stadlen, Ken Kercheval, Ellen Barber. A drama about one of the most shameful miscarriages of justice in American history, the famous case of the "Scottsboro Boys." In Alabama back in 1931, nine poor, young and virtually illiterate black men were arrested and tried for the alleged rape of two promiscuous white women. Despite compelling evidence proving their innocence, they were convicted by several all-white, male juries, and some of them remained incarcerated for almost 20 years—their lives destroyed. This disturbing, absorbing history lesson about racial bigotry in the South at that time focuses on one courageous white judge, who reversed the jury's verdict and may well have saved the young men from being hanged. Hill plays the embattled Judge Horton, heading a generally good cast, skillfully directed by Fielder Cook. Based on the book "The Scottsboro Boys," by Professor Dan T. Carter. (98 mins.)

Judge Priest (1934)***½ Will Rogers, Anita Louise, Stepin Fetchit. Will Rogers stars in John Ford's portrait of life in a small town in the Old South, one of the most deeply felt visions of community in the American cinema. Ford's later partial remake, *The Sun Shines Bright* is a masterpiece, but the accomplishments of this version are impressive enough. In some ways, *Judge Priest* marks the birth of the poet in Ford. By 1931, he had made some forty features, many of the sixty that followed would rank with the finest works of the medium. (Dir: John Ford, 71 mins.)

Judge Steps Out, The (1949)**½ Alexander Knox, Ann Sothern. Probate judge leaves home and finds happiness as a cook in a roadside stand. Occasionally good, generally rather mild comedy-drama. (Dir: Boris Ingster, 91 mins.)

Judgment At Nuremberg (1961)**** Spencer Tracy, Burt Lancaster, Judy Garland, Richard Widmark, Montgomery Clift, Maximilian Schell, Marlene Dietrich. A searing, thoughtful film from producer Stanley Kramer, based on Abby Mann's memorable TV drama of the same name. Concerns the proceedings at the Nazi War Crimes Trials in Nuremberg and explores, among other things, the degree to which an individual or a nation can be held responsible for carrying out the orders of their leaders, however heinous the commands may be. Uniformly well acted with Schell winning, and deservedly so, an Academy Award for his portrayal. Several of the stars appeared for a fraction of their normal salaries and some in small roles, just because they wanted to be in this distinguished, disturbing movie. (Dir: Stanley Kramer, 178 mins.)

Judith (U.S.-Great Britain, 1966)* Sophia Loren, Peter Finch, Jack Hawkins. (Dir: Daniel Mann, 109 mins.)

Juggernaut (Great Britain, 1974)**** Omar Sharif, Richard Harris, David Hemmings, Anthony Hopkins, Shirley Knight, Roy Kinnear. A smashing, very British thriller directed by that master technician Richard Lester. Sharif captains a luxury liner on the Atlantic, and Harris—England's ace bomb defuser—drops in by parachute to take care of the seven large bombs an extortionist who calls himself Juggernaut has placed on board. The film is almost stolen by Kinnear as the terrified little purser whose job it is to keep the spirits of the 1200 seemingly doomed passengers up. (110 mins.)

Juggler, The (1953)*** Kirk Douglas, Milly Vitale. An absorbing drama about the Jewish refugee camps and the fight for rehabilitation; Kirk Douglas gives a powerful performance as a one-time circus juggler. (Dir: Edward Dmytryk, 86 mins.)

Juke Box Rhythm (1959)* Jo Morrow, Brian Donlevy, Jack Jones. (Dir: Arthur Dreifuss, 81 mins.)

Juke Girl (1942)**½ Ann Sheridan, Ronald Reagan, Faye Emerson, Gene Lockhart. This was supposed to be the sordid tale of conditions among Florida's migratory workers but it emerges as a well-acted, tiresome melodrama. (Dir: Curtis Bernhardt, 90 mins.)

Jules and Jim (France, 1962)**** Oskar Werner, Jeanne Moreau, Henri Serre. The pre-WW I era is evoked by the ménage à trois of Jules (Werner), Jim (Serre) and Catherine (the incomparable Moreau). Catherine is willful, maddening, and entirely herself; she incarnates Jules' and Jim's art and friendship, while herself remaining an intransigent, perverse, independent individual. Lovely and lyrical early work by director François Truffaut. (110 mins.)

Julia (1977)**½ Jane Fonda, Vanessa Redgrave, Jason Robards, Jr., Maximilian Schell, Hal Holbrook, Meryl Streep. Not a bad film, only a criminally unambitious one. Directed by Fred Zinnemann, whose reverence for the material does it no service. The spontaneity and verve of Lillian Hellman's memoir are drained out of the film, which is so impeccably mounted it's stuffed. Standouts are Schell as an unassuming but heroic resistance fighter and Robards as Dashiell Hammett. (118 mins.)

Julia Misbehaves (1948)**½ Greer Garson, Walter Pidgeon, Elizabeth Taylor. Farce about an ex-chorus girl who is her estranged husband's guest after an 18-year separation is ridiculous and lowers Miss Garson's dignity. She does manage to squeeze some laughs out of the proceedings, however. (Dir: Jack Conway, 99 mins.)

Julie (1956)** Doris Day, Louis Jourdan, Barry Sullivan. Thoroughly unbelievable melodrama about an airline stewardess who is terrorized by her insane husband, menacingly overplayed by Jourdan. There's an almost laughable climactic sequence in which Miss Day single-handedly brings in an airliner. (Dir: Andrew L. Stone, 99 mins.)

Julie, the Redhead (France, 1959)**½ Pascale Petit, Daniel Gelin. Factory tycoon leaves a share to his former mistress; his son and her niece try to iron things out, love blossoms. Mildly amusing, mildly spicy comedy—some clever scenes, attractive performance by Petit. Dubbed in English. (Dir: Claude Boissol, 100 mins.)

Juliet of the Spirits (France-Italy-West Germany, 1965)***½ Giulietta Masina, Mario Pisu, Sylva Koscina, Lou Gilbert, Valentina Cortese. Masina (wife of director Federico Fellini) stars in his gaudy, voluptuous exploration of a middle-aged woman's longings and fantasies. The Maestro keeps his hurdy-gurdy excesses nearly under control. (148 mins.)

Julius Caesar (1953)*** John Gielgud, Marlon Brando, James Mason, Deborah Kerr, Greer Garson, Edmond O'Brien, Louis Calhern. Gielgud's multileveled Cassius stands out, and Mason (Brutus) and Brando (Marc Antony) are solid. An elaborate, sturdy, intelligent Hollywood adaptation directed by Joseph L. Mankiewicz with a political shrewdness that suits the play. Excellent (and relatively neglected) work by O'Brien as Casca and Calhern as J.C. (120 mins.)

Julius Caesar (Great Britain, 1970)**½ John Gielgud, Jason Robards, Charlton Heston, Richard Chamberlain, Robert Vaughn, Richard Johnson, Diana Rigg. There have been at least five earlier film versions of Shakespeare's political drama, the most recent being the '53 version starring Marlon Brando as Caesar. This version is curiously uneven, despite a generally superior cast. There are some excellent performances, particularly Gielgud playing Caesar and Richard Johnson as

Cassius, but Jason Robards playing Brutus is embarrassingly bad. There still are scenes where you will enjoy the glories of Shakespeare's play. (Dir: Stuart Burge, 117 mins.)

Julius Caesar (Great Britain, MTV 1978)***½ Richard Pasco, David Collings, Charles Gray, Keith Michell, Virginia McKenna, Elizabeth Spriggs. Beautifully spoken against eloquent sets recalling ancient Rome, this BBC production moves in a deliberate pace through the early scenes of conspiracy, to the impassioned ones of Caesar's fateful murder, and the final scenes of bitter war. Shakespeare shows us character rather than action. In this process, Richard Pasco's Brutus leaves, perhaps, the most lasting and troubling impression; Charles Gray's Caesar becomes a majestic, human, and memorable figure; David Collings' almost pitifully envious Cassius and Keith Michell's grief-stricken and vengeful Mark Antony are strong, fascinating characterizations. Virginia McKenna as Brutus's wife Portia also deserves a note of praise for her skillful portrayal of an intelligent woman in despair. (Dir: Herbert Wise, 180 mins.)

Jumping Jacks (1952)** Dean Martin, Jerry Lewis, Mona Freeman. Dean and Jerry play two cabaret entertainers who end up in the paratroop corps, in one of their better early romps. (Dir: Norman Taurog, 96 mins.)

June Bride (1948)*** Bette Davis, Robert Montgomery. Good sophisticated comedy-drama expertly played and chock full of excitement. Not fast and hilarious but enough chuckles to satisfy as Bob plays a magazine writer and Bette his boss. They're doing a June bride feature but the wedding takes place in March so it can make the June issue. (Dir: Bretaigne Windust, 97 mins.)

Jungle Book, The (1942)*** Joseph Calleia, Frank Puglia, Sabu. Alexander Korda's lavish production of the Kipling tales suffers from a certain preciousness of decor, but as family entertainment it works very nicely, capturing a sense of fairy-tale engrossment. Zoltan Korda directs less incisively than usual. (109 mins.)

Jungle Book, The (1967)***½ Voices of Phil Harris, George Sanders, Louis Prima, Sebastian Cabot, Sterling Holloway. Immensely entertaining animated feature, made at a time when the Disney Studio was retrenching on its animation division—some of the footage was redrawn from earlier efforts, particularly "Snow White and the Seven Dwarfs" with the dwarfs reworked as jungle creatures. Sander's evil tiger voice is a magisterial creation. (Dir: Wolfgang Reitherman and four animation directors, 78 mins.)

Jungle Cat (1960)**½ Disney documentary on the feline jaguar, its natural life in the Amazon rain forest fully detailed. Unusual footage includes mating of yellow and black jaguar cats. (Dir: James Algar, 70 mins.)

Jungle Fighters (Great Britain, 1961)***½ Laurence Harvey, Richard Todd, Richard Harris, David McCallum. Rugged war drama about a British patrol in Burma, a nasty private who breaks all the rules, and a dangerous trap set by the Japanese. Grim, mainly for the male audience; excellent performances. Alternate title: **Long, the Short and the Tall, The.** (Dir: Leslie Norman, 105 mins.)

Jungle Gold (1944-66)**½ Linda Stirling, Allan Lane, Duncan Renaldo. Feature version of serial "The Tiger Woman." Outlandish nonsense about a girl Tarzan type who helps the hero battle some wicked oil seekers. Good action for kids; adults may get a kick out of it too. Miss Stirling looks fetching in abbreviated garb. (Dirs: Spencer Bennet, Wallace Grissell, 100 mins.)

Jungle Headhunters (1951)**½ Interesting documentary travelogue, Cotlow expedition into headhunter territory on the Amazon. Good for armchair adventurers. (67 mins.)

Jungle Princess, The (1936)** Dorothy Lamour, Ray Milland, Akim Tamiroff, Lynne Overman. The first in Dottie's long series of native girls clad in silk sarongs. Milland is a pilot downed on an unchartered island, where he discovers her. Pleasant, hokey entertainment. (Dir: William Thiele, 85 mins.)

Junior Bonner (1972)*** Steve McQueen, Robert Preston, Ida Lupino, Ben Johnson, Joe Don Baker. An unassuming major film from director Sam Peckinpah, this rodeo story stars McQueen as the aging star who finds he can't go home again. Fine character vignettes turned in by Preston and Lupino are of a high order, and the movie is filled to overflowing with small, subtle, rowdy beauties. (100 mins.)

Junior Miss (1945)*** Peggy Ann Garner, Allyn Joslyn. Cute little teen-age comedy which should remind us how our youngsters behaved during the '40's. Based on the hit Broadway play. (Dir: George Seaton, 94 mins.)

Jupiter's Darling (1955)** Esther Williams, Howard Keel, Marge & Gower Champion, George Sanders. Gay doings in old Rome, as Hannibal Keel captures gorgeous Esther and stops the battle while they romance. Historical spoof doesn't quite make it, so except for the Champions' dancing it's pretty much of a drag. (Dir: George Sidney, 96 mins.)

Just a Little Inconvenience (MTV 1977)**½ Lee Majors, James Stacy, Barbara Hershey. Stacy, who lost an arm and a leg in a motorcycle accident three years before this entry, returns with friend Majors and Hershey in a story of an embittered war veteran who blames his best friend for his injury. A rehabilitation drama in which Stacy's character learns to ski again. Sequences showing Stacy putting on his skis, getting up, falling down, cursing and trying again, make the show. The love story doesn't work. (Dir: Theodore J. Flicker, 104 mins.)

Just Across the Street (1952)**½ Ann Sheridan, John Lund. An often amusing comedy about mistaken identity and the incidents leading up to the final confrontation and happy conclusion. Miss Sheridan is an old hand at comedy dialogue and a good supporting cast add to the film's appeal. (Dir: Joseph Pevney, 78 mins.)

Just Around the Corner (1938)** Shirley Temple, Joan Davis, Bill Robinson. Shirley dances with "Bojangles" but close your eyes for the rest of this silly film. It's a depression story and it will depress you. (Dir: Irving Cummings, 70 mins.)

Just Be There—See: **Swinging Teachers**

Just for You (1952)**½ Bing Crosby, Jane Wyman, Ethel Barrymore. Pleasant comedy-drama with many musical moments thrown in for good measure. Bing plays a successful B'dway producer who sets out to win his son and daughter's affection after a long period of concentrating only on his career. Miss Wyman plays the woman in Bing's life and young Natalie Wood (age 14) plays Bing's daughter. (Dir: Elliot Nugent, 104 mins.)

Just Great—See: **Tout Va Bien**

Just Imagine (1930)*** John Garrick, El Brendel, Maureen O'Sullivan, Majorie White, Hobart Bosworth, Kenneth Thomson. Beguiling bit of antique musical frumpery, about New York City past, present, future—e.g., 1880, 1930 and 1980. New Yorkers of the 1980's all have numbers instead of names, their own airplanes to get around in, with landing pads all over the many-tiered city. A bizarre trip to Mars is also included, where everything comes double or upside-down. Songs by B. G. De Sylva, Lew Brown, and others. (Dir: David Butler, 102 mins.)

Just Like a Woman (Great Britain, 1966)**½ Wendy Craig, Francis Matthews. Bright, witty dialogue paces this situation comedy about a TV producer and his somewhat eccentric wife as their marriage breaks up. Flimsy plot, but the gags, particularly in-jokes about British TV, abound. Written and directed by Robert Fuest. (89 mins.)

Just Off Broadway (1942)** Lloyd Nolan, Phil Silvers, Marjorie Weaver. Weak Michael Shayne adventure with the great detective serving on a murder jury but solving the case on the side. (Dir: Herbert I. Leeds, 66 mins.)

Just Tell Me What You Want (1980)***½ Ali MacGraw, Alan King, Peter Weller, Myrna Loy, Keenan Wynn. Jay Presson Allen's script is a paean to détente between the sexes. King plays a charismatic self-made man, and MacGraw is his main mistress of many years who rebels when he liquidate's a film production company rather than turn it over to her. It's nonsense, and under the unsteady direction of Sidney Lumet there is no coherent comic approach, but the situations are original and fresh and carry you along. (112 mins.)

Just This Once (1952)**½ Janet Leigh, Peter Lawford. Pleasant comedy about the ins and outs of romance. The attractive stars go through their paces as if they really enjoy their work. (Dir: Don Weis, 90 mins.)

Just You and Me (MTV 1978)**½ Louise Lasser, Charles Grodin. The kooky Lasser of "Mary Hartman, Mary Hartman" fame wrote this and plays Jane, a daffy New Yorker who drives to L.A. with a straight-arrow computer salesman, well played by Grodin. During the four day trip, some of the time Jane scores with offbeat comments, and some of the time a sensitive, self-centered Jane is a big pain. (Dir: John Erman, 104 mins.)

Just You and Me Kid (1979)** George Burns, Brooke Shields, Burl Ives, Lorraine Gary, Ray Bolger. What sounded surefire—Burns as an ex-vaudevillian and Shields as a young runaway hiding from a dope pusher—is disappointing indeed. Burn's patented humor and the TV comedy expertise of director and cowriter Leonard Stern, in his film debut, aren't enough. Occasional moments of bland fun. (93 mins.)

Juvenile Court (1973)**** A remarkable study of a juvenile court in Memphis, Tennessee. You'll see the frightened children, worried about their punishment as well as their crimes, and you'll see a number of the generally sympathetic counselors who take up their cases with gratifying dedication—cases ranging from prostitution, to child abuse, drug addiction and armed robbery. One of the many things you will remember from this insightful look at an American institution is the character of the judge of the court, Kenneth A. Turner. Wiseman clearly believes that the juvenile offender is the victim of the society and therefore its ward, and that children in such courts are the results of institutional neglect and abuse, and of misunderstanding and miseducation on the part of the responsible parents and schools. (Dir: Frederick Wiseman, 135 mins.)

Juvenile Jungle, (1958)*½ Corey Allen Rebecca Welles. (Dir: William Witney, 69 mins.)

J. W. Coop (1972)*** Cliff Robertson, Geraldine Page, Cristina Ferrare, R. G. Armstrong. Robertson cowrote, produced, directed, and stars in this rodeo story about a released con who tries to climb to the top of the rodeo circuit in the face of the more modernized contenders—specialists who fly to rodeos and compete in several a day. The theme of individualism is barely realized, but the locations are apt, and the rodeo details (which make up most of the movie) are fascinating and very well done. An honorable entry in a neglected area. (112 mins.)

Kagemusha (Japan, 1980)***½ Tatsuya Nakadai, Tsutomu Yamazaki, Kenichi Hagiwara. Japan's greatest warlord battles to maintain control of the nation. A confounding epic from director Akira Kurosawa, shot on the biggest budget in Japanese film history. Bizarre artistic decisions regarding camera setups and editing, with some of the weirdest battle footage ever conjured up by a major filmmaker. An old man's film, sparkled by contemplation rather than action. The ideas stimulate even as the emotional core remains deliberately obscured. Indubitably a major work, the film combines much terrible direction with densely textured artistry. (160 mins.)

Kaleidoscope (Great Britain, 1966)** Warren Beatty, Susannah York, Clive Revill, Eric Porter. A playboy (Beatty) tries a cleverly crooked way to beat the European gambling casinos in this visually pretty but placid caper. (Dir: Jack Smight, 103 mins.)

Kanal (Poland, 1957)**** Teresa Izewska. Grim and powerful drama of Polish patriots using the sewers of Warsaw in an attempt to escape from the Nazis during the uprising of 1944. Excellent in direction and performance, unrelieved in its intensity. English-dubbed. (Dir: Andrzej Wajda, 91 mins.)

Kangaroo (1952)** Peter Lawford, Maureen O'Hara. The beautiful on-location photography (Australia) is the best feature of this adventure drama. Lawford is miscast as a sailor who becomes involved in a muddled mistaken identity plot. Miss O'Hara thinks the Australian landscape is the County Cork and plays it accordingly. (Dir: Lewis Milestone, 84 mins.)

Kansas City Bomber (1972)*½ Raquel Welch, Kevin McCarthy. (Dir: Jerrold Freedman, 99 mins.)

Kansas City Confidential (1952)**½ John Payne, Coleen Gray, Preston Foster, Neville Brand. Sharply done crime story of bank robbers. Suspense chase from Kansas City to Guatemala maintains interest and pace. A graphic tale that chickens out for a "nice" ending. (Dir: Phil Karlson, 98 mins.)

Kansas City Massacre, The (MTV 1975)**½ Dale Robertson, Bo Hopkins, Lynn Loring, Scott Brady. Robertson is back playing Melvin Purvis, G-Man, in this tough gangster saga set during the Depression. Has the high production values of the previous made-for-TV film. Follows the events leading up to the infamous Kansas City massacre at the Union Plaza Railroad Station, in which two gunmen and five officers were killed and twelve innocent bystanders were wounded. Robertson is all quiet swagger and authority as the G-Man who's out to nail Pretty Boy Floyd, John Dillinger and Baby Face Nelson. (Dir: Dan Curtis, 100 mins.)

Kansas Raiders (1950)**½ Audie Murphy, Brian Donlevy, Marguerite Chapman. Exciting Western adventure that benefits greatly from an assorted group of young actors playing famous outlaws who joined Quantrill's Raiders and destroyed Lawrence, Kansas. Audie Murphy plays Jesse James, Tony Curtis is Kit Dalton, Dewey Martin and James Best are the Younger Brothers and Richard Long is Frank James. (Dir: Ray Enright, 80 mins.)

Kapo (France-Italy-Yugoslavia, 1960)**½ Susan Strasberg, Emmanuele Riva. Disguised Jewish girl in Nazi prison camps becomes hardened, murderously intent on her own survival. Movie begins well, is effectively graphic about the horrors of the holocaust and imprisonment, with Strasberg apt as a wide-eyed Jewish innocent (reminiscent of the starring Broadway role of Anne Frank that rocketed her to fame); but the subsequent melodramatics prove too much for Strasberg, and the film is not worthy of the momentous realities involved. (Dir: Gillo Pontecorvo, 116 mins.)

Karate (1961)* Joel Holt, Reiko Okada. (Dir: Joel Holt, 80 mins.)

Kate Bliss and the Ticker Tape Kid (MTV 1978)**½ Suzanne Pleshette, Don Meredith, Tony Randall, Burgess Meredith, Harry Morgan. Pleshette plays a turn-of-the-century lady detective who treks west in hot pursuit of wily bandits headed by Dandy Don. Three of the best character actors in the business help the movie. (Dir: Burt Kennedy, 104 mins.)

Kate McShane (MTV 1975)**½ Anne Meara, Christine Belford, Cal Bellini. Comedienne Anne Meara plays a pugnacious Denver, Colorado, lawyer, defending a blueblood in the stabbing of a no-good husband. It's all Kate McShane as she, backed by her Irish dad, battles a pompous D.A., throws snowballs at her Jesuit brother. Despite her efforts, this predictable lady-lawyer pilot never really takes off, although it did result in a TV series. (Dir: Martin Chomsky, 72 mins.)

Katerina Izmailova (U.S.S.R., 1967)***½ Galina Vishnevskaya, N. Boyarsky. Good version of the dramatic opera by Russian composer Dimitri Shostakovich. First performed in 1934, the opera is about a woman whose illicit affair leads to murder and tragedy in Siberia. Bolshoi Opera company star Vishnevskaya is excellent in the title role. (Dir: Mikhail Shapiro, 118 mins.)

Katherine (MTV 1975)*** Art Carney, Sissy Spacek, Henry Winkler, Jane Wyatt. This film about a girl who forsakes her parents and a life of luxury to become an underground political activist is well done. The story never lags, and Spacek is always believable as she goes from idealized liberalism to militant radicalism. Winkler scores as a bearded liberal who starts her on the leftward road. (Dir: Jeremy Paul Kagan, 104 mins.)

Kathleen (1941)*½ Shirley Temple, Herbert

Marshall, Laraine Day. (Dir: Harold S. Bucquet, 88 mins.)

Kathy O' (1958)***½ Patty McCormack, Dan Duryea, Jan Sterling. Publicity man is assigned to a brat of a child movie star, gets involved when she runs away. Plenty of fun in this Hollywood-behind-the-scenes comedy drama. Well played, highly enjoyable. (Dir: Jack Sher, 99 mins.)

Katie Did It (1951)**½ Ann Blyth, Mark Stevens. Moderately entertaining comedy about a small town girl who runs into a New York City slicker who just won't take no for a final answer. Miss Blyth is cute and Stevens has an abundance of persuasive charm. (Dir: Frederick de Cordova, 81 mins.)

Katie: Portrait of a Centerfold (MTV 1978)** Kim Basinger, Vivian Blaine, Dorothy Malone. Basinger, a cutie from Georgia, plays Katie, a Texas lovely whose modeling career turns sour in Hollywood after an assignment as a centerfold piece for a girlie magazine. Miss Basinger has more than good looks, but she can't do much with the material written by Nancy Audley. (Dir: Robert Greenwald, 104 mins.)

Keegans, The (MTV 1976)*½ Adam Roarke, Spencer Milligan, Paul Shenar, Judd Hirsch, Heather Menzies, Tom Clancy, Joan Leslie. (Dir: John Badham, 72 mins.)

Keep 'Em Flying (1941)**½ Bud Abbott and Lou Costello, Martha Raye. Early Abbott & Costello comedy with all the slapstick antics that made the pair famous. Martha Raye plays twin sisters. (Dir: Arthur Lubin, 86 mins.)

Keep It Clean (Great Britain, 1956)*½ Ronald Shiner, Diane Hart. (Dir: David Paltenghi, 75 mins.)

Keep Talking, Baby (France, 1961)* Eddie Constantine, Mariella Gozzi. (Dir: Guy Lefranc, 95 mins.)

Keep Your Powder Dry (1945)** Lana Turner, Laraine Day, Susan Peters, Agnes Moorehead. Adventures of three girls from different walks of life who join the WACs. Dull, ineptly written melodrama. B&W. (Dir: Edward Buzzell, 93 mins.)

Keeper of the Flame (1942)*** Spencer Tracy, Katharine Hepburn. Good drama, superbly acted by one of our better screen teams. Tracy is doing an article on the death of a great American and the excitement mounts when the widow, Miss Hepburn, finally admits that the great American was a fascist. (Dir: George Cukor, 100 mins.)

Keetje Tippel—See: **Cathy Tippel**

Kelly and Me (1957)**½ Van Johnson, Piper Laurie, Martha Hyer. Song-and-dance man hits the big time when he teams up with a smart police dog. Fairly pleasing show-biz drama. (Dir: Robert Z. Leonard, 86 mins.)

Kelly's Heroes (1970)** Clint Eastwood, Don Rickles, Donald Sutherland. Clumsy copy of "The Dirty Dozen." Soldiers, turned plunderers under the command of East-wood, march into German-occupied town to rob the bank during World War II. Sutherland creates an anachronistic role of a spaced-out hippie tank commander which is beautiful to watch, despite the rest of the film. (Dir: Brian Hutton, 149 mins.)

Kennel Murder Case, The (1933)***½ William Powell, Mary Astor, Eugene Pallette. Philo Vance mystery with the customary sealed-room puzzle. Better mounted than most whodunits of the time. Powell is a poised, well-cast Vance with excellent support, and Michael Curtiz's direction is exemplary. (73 mins.)

Kenner (1969)** Jim Brown, Madlyn Rhue, Robert Coote. Brown is a two-fisted adventurer in this predictable yarn about a man out to avenge his partner's murder amid the teeming background of Bombay, India. You've seen it a thousand times before. (Dir: Steve Sekely, 87 mins.)

Kenny Rogers as the Gambler (MTV 1980)** Kenny Rogers, Christine Belford, Bruce Boxleitner. A Rogers hit song inspired this movie starring the singer in his first dramatic role: a shrewd gambler who befriends a younger chance taker (Boxleitner) and encounters a variety of bad guys. Passable fare, and Rogers shows a modest acting flair. (Dir: Dick Lowry, 104 mins.)

Kent State (MTV 1981)*** Talia Balsam, Ellen Barkin. Valuable docudrama about the needless slaughter, on May 4, 1970, by the Ohio National Guard, of four students at Kent State University who were part of a student protest about the Vietnam war. The climax when the students are mowed down is undeniably moving, but the overall impact is diminished considerably because the episodic structure of the narrative and the screenplay, by Gerald Green and Richard Kramer, never adequately explain the background of the protest and the deep passionate intellectual commitment of not only the students but many millions of Americans throughout the country at that time who were bitterly opposed to continued American involvement in the Vietnam war. (Dir: Jim Goldstone, 147 mins.)

Kentuckian, The (1955)**½ Burt Lancaster. Lancaster stars as a two-fisted frontiersman in this adventure tale set in the early 1800's. The plot is filled with rugged action, romance, and an ample amount of comedy. Diana Lynn, as a shy and proper "School Marm," stands out in a good supporting cast which includes Dianne Foster, John McIntire, and Una Merkel. (Dir: Burt Lancaster, 104 mins.)

Kentucky (1938)** Loretta Young, Richard Greene, Walter Brennan. Trite romance set against a horse-breeding background. Young and Greene are the barely star-crossed lovers, and Brennan, in an uninspired turn as a colonel type, won the Best Supporting Actor Oscar against John Garfield, Robert Morley, Basil Rathbone, and Gene Lockhart. Lamar Trotti scripted.

Color. (Dir: David Butler, 94 mins.)

Kentucky Moonshine (1938)*** Ritz Brothers. If you don't like the Ritzes, run for the hills because the boys disguised as Kentucky hillbillies have this all to themselves. (Dir: David Butler, 85 mins.)

Kenya—Country of Treasure (1964)* William Sylvester, June Ritchie. (90 mins.)

Kes (Great Britain, 1970)**** David Bradley, Colin Welland, Lynne Perrie. A beautiful, tender story about a 15-year-old Yorkshire boy who tames and trains his pet—a kestrel hawk. Shooting entirely on location in northern England, with a largely nonprofessional cast, director Ken Loach coaxed some glorious natural performances from these adept scene stealers. Bradley is particularly marvelous while training his beloved "Kes," or listening to various boorish adults including a frustrated athletic coach at his school. Only drawback to this luminous tale is the heavy Yorkshire accents, which are not always intelligible to American audiences. One of the first English-language films where you sometimes yearn for subtitles. A delicate, haunting film with pathos and humor. (Dir: Ken Loach, 110 mins.)

Kettles in the Ozarks, The (1956)** Marjorie Main, Arthur Hunnicutt. This one is without the benefit of Percy Kilbride's (Pa Kettle) special participation. Ma Kettle visits Pa's lazy brother, played in the screen hillbilly tradition by Arthur Hunnicutt, and gets in the middle of a heap of trouble with bootleggers and the law. (Dir: Charles Lamont, 81 mins.)

Kettles on Old MacDonald's Farm, The (1957)** Marjorie Main, Parker Fennelly. Last Kettle epic (without Pa Kettle as played by Percy Kilbride) and the least effective. Some sight gags still work but Percy is sorely missed. (Dir: Virgil Vogel, 80 mins.)

Key, The (Great Britain, 1958)*** Sophia Loren, William Holden, Trevor Howard. A stellar lineup, but this drama doesn't quite deliver the dramatic impact it sets out to. The premise involves a man (Howard) who gives a duplicate key to his friend (Holden) to Sophia Loren's apartment, with the instructions that he must do the same when and if Howard is killed in enemy action during WW II. Trevor Howard is first rate as always and there are enough interesting scenes and issues raised to make this worth seeing. (Dir: Carol Reed, 125 mins.)

Key Largo (1948)*** Humphrey Bogart, Lauren Bacall, Edward G. Robinson, Claire Trevor, Lionel Barrymore. Not a great movie but John Huston manages to get so much out of his wonderful cast that you're bound to be entertained by this gangster melodrama set in Key West, Florida. Trevor won a Best Supporting Actress Oscar. (Dir: John Huston, 101 mins.)

Key Man, The (Great Britain, 1957)*½ Lee

Patterson, Hy Hazell. (Dir: Montgomery Tully, 78 mins.)

Key to the City (1950)**½ Clark Gable, Loretta Young. A light comedy romance for indiscriminating film fans, as small town mayors meet and fall in love during a mayors' convention in San Francisco. The action is predictable but fast paced. (Dir: George Sidney, 99 mins.)

Key West (MTV 1973)*½ Stephen Boyd, Ford Rainey, Tiffany Bolling, Sheree North. (Dir: Anthony Martin, 100 mins.)

Key Witness (1960)**½ Jeffrey Hunter, Pat Crowley. Hard-hitting drama about a man who is a witness to a crime and the terror he and his family face because of it. Some brutal scenes make this strong stuff, not for the squeamish. (Dir: Phil Karlson, 82 mins.)

Keys of the Kingdom, The (1944)*** Gregory Peck, Thomas Mitchell, Roddy McDowall. Slow, rambling, occasionally moving adaptation of A. J. Cronin's novel about the life of a missionary. Peck's first major film and he does a nice job. (Dir: John M. Stahl, 137 mins.)

Khartoum (Great Britain, 1966)***½ Charlton Heston, Laurence Olivier. Some well-directed gigantic battle scenes and Olivier's splendid performance are two of the best features in this better-than-most spectacle film. Major scenes filmed in the desert along the Nile, as historical fact and Hollywood fiction are combined to tell the tale of confrontation in 1883 between British General Charles Gordon (Heston) and the Arab leader named Mahdi (Olivier) involved in the siege of Khartoum in the Sudan. Scene between Heston and Olivier is excellently handled by director Basil Dearden. (134 mins.)

Khyber Patrol (1954)**½ Richard Egan, Dawn Addams. The Empire vs. The Rebels in this familiar English adventure film. O.K. for the kids and action fans. (Dir: Seymour Friedman, 71 mins.)

Kid, The (1921)***½ Charles Chaplin, Jackie Coogan, Edna Purviance. One of director Chaplin's most highly regarded features, but its Victorian sentimentality borders on the supercilious and the dream sequences of Charlie as an angel are cloying. Coogan (age seven) does a priceless set of Chaplin imitations, as the foundling adopted by the tramp, and together they rule the streets with comic skill and ingenuity. (90 mins.)

Kid Boots (1926)*** Eddie Cantor, Clara Bow, Billie Dove. The musical comedy hit that made Cantor a star was made into this silent where he's a tailor's helper paired Bow, already a star but not yet the "It" girl. A buoyant curiosity. (Dir: Frank Tuttle, 95 mins.)

Kid for Two Farthings (Great Britain, 1955)**** Celia Johnson, Diana Dors, Jonathan Ashmore. Lad in the London slums believes a one horned goat is a magic unicorn that will bring him luck. Something different; touching, superbly directed (Carol Reed) comedy-drama, a fine film. (Dir: Carol Reed, 91 mins.)

Kid from Brooklyn, The (1946)*** Danny Kaye, Virginia Mayo, Vera-Ellen. Remake of Harold Lloyd's comedy "The Milky Way" and although not as good, Kaye manages to make it fun. Story concerns a milkman who is turned into a prize fighter. (Dir: Leo McCarey, 113 mins.)

Kid from Left Field, The (1953)**½ Dan Dailey, Anne Bancroft, Lloyd Bridges. Peanut vendor used his son, operating as batboy, to break a baseball team's slump. Pleasant, but doesn't exactly burn up the league. (Dir: Harmon Jones, 80 mins.)

Kid from Left Field, The (MTV 1979)** Gary Coleman, Robert Guillaume, Ed McMahon. In this sugary remake of a '53 Dan Dailey movie, Coleman plays a batboy for the San Diego Padres who is the son of a former second baseman (Guillaume). Rewritten for Gary, who is scarcely taller than the bats he carries. (Dir: Adell Aldrich, 104 mins.)

Kid from Spain, The (1932)*** Eddie Cantor, Robert Young, Lyda Roberti; Paulette Goddard, Betty Grable (chorines). Given the talents of director Leo McCarey and choreographer Busby Berkeley, this Cantor vehicle should have been more of a romp. Eddie plays his usual simpleton who in this one is mistaken for a bullfighter. The dance numbers are opulent in the Goldwyn manner. (110 mins.)

Kid Galahad (1937)***½ Edward G. Robinson, Bette Davis, Humphrey Bogart, Wayne Morris. First-rate boxing melodrama, well acted by an all-star cast. Remade with Elvis Presley in '62, and with Bogart in a reworking called "The Wagons Roll at Night" ('41). (Dir: Michael Curtiz, 101 mins.)

Kid Galahad (1962)**½ Elvis Presley, Gig Young, Charles Bronson, Lola Albright. This remake of a '37 Michael Curtiz film was astute casting for Elvis Presley at a key point in his movie career—he was equal to the limited demands of the dramatic part, and was surrounded by able character actors and a decent story. Elvis is a fresh-faced boxer who encounters the usual temptations from gangster Bronson, and Young and Albright are the world-weary couple who try to keep him straight. Directed, far better than might be expected, by Phil Karlson. (95 mins.)

Kid Glove Killer (1942)*** Van Heflin, Marsha Hunt. A superior Grade B crime film which uses police labs instead of chases and other contrivances. Many of our modern, adult crime stories stem from the type of thinking that went into this film. (Dir: Fred Zinnemann, 74 mins.)

Kid Millions (1934)*** Eddie Cantor, Ethel Merman, Ann Sothern, George Murphy, Warren Hymer. One of Sam Goldwyn's elaborately produced Cantor vehicles. This time, Banjo Eyes is a ghetto youth who comes into a fortune and enjoys himself for some 90 minutes, leading up to a fina-

le in an ice-cream factory. Hymer is amazing. (Dir: Roy Del Ruth, 100 mins.)

Kid Rodelo (1966)** Don Murray, Janet Leigh, Broderick Crawford. Dull western made in Spain. Don Murray's very brave as he tries to fight off the greedy crooks after a cache of stolen gold, and keep an eye on fetching Janet Leigh at the same time. Not worth keeping an eye on this oater. (Dir: Richard Carlson, 91 mins.)

Kidnaped (1938)**½ Freddie Bartholomew, Warner Baxter. Robert Louis Stevenson's classic altered for the screen with just the title and character names maintained. Good juvenile adventure tale. (Dir: Alfred Werker, 90 mins.)

Kidnapped (Great Britain, 1960)**½ Peter Finch, James MacArthur. Straightforward, restrained Disney production of Robert Louis Stevenson's classic about a young heir whose scheming uncle arranges for his kidnapping, and his adventures at sea with a stalwart Jacobite (anti-King George) Scotsman. Movie lacks vigor, excitement of book's previous filmings. It's well acted. The director is not related to the author. (Dir: Robert Stevenson, 97 mins.)

Kidnapped (Great Britain, 1971)*** Michael Caine, Trevor Howard, Jack Hawkins, Donald Pleasence, Walter Matthau. The fourth cinematization of the famous classic by Robert Louis Stevenson, and a lesser-known sequel, "David Balfour." The film deals with the fighting between the English and the Scottish during the end of the 18th century. The main character is the swashbuckling Alan Breck, played with flair by Caine. David Balfour has been nicely woven into the story as an aid in Breck's fight for Scotland. The Scottish highlands steal the show. (Dir: Delbert Mann, 100 mins.)

Kidnappers, The—See: Man on the Run

Kidnapping of the President, The (1980)** William Shatner, Hal Holbrook, Van Johnson, Ava Gardner. While on a state visit to Toronto, the president is kidnapped by an international terrorist and held in an armored truck filled with explosives until a huge ransom is paid. Far-fetched, unconvincing melodrama. (Dir: George Mendeluk, 113 mins.)

Kill a Dragon (1967)** Jack Palance assisted by buddy Aldo Ray, scuffles with Fernando Lamas. Oriental natives hire an adventurer to polish off a mystery man determined to walk off with a deadly cargo of nitro. Far Eastern hokum weighed down by heavy plot and dull actors. (Dir: Michael Moore, 91 mins.)

Kill Her Gently (Great Britain, 1958)** Marc Lawrence, Maureen Connell, Griffith Jones. Two escaped convicts are talked into bumping off the wife of an ex-mental patient. Cheaply made but adequate crime drama. (Dir: Charles Saunders, 73 mins.)

Kill Me If You Can (MTV 1977)**** Alan Alda, Talia Shire, John Hillerman. Alda is a powerhouse portraying Caryl Chessman's 12-year battle to stay out of San Quentin's gas chamber, winning eight stays of execution through the efforts of his attorney Rosalie Asher (Shire). Alda makes a grinning, cocky criminal, proud of his high IQ, as he wages an unceasing legal battle from death row, writing books on the side. A powerful and all too rare polemic against capital punishment, with an unsparing gas chamber sequence right down to the final twitch. (Dir: Buzz Kulik, 104 mins.)

Kill Me Tomorrow (Great Britain, 1957)** Pat O'Brien, Lois Maxwell. Crime reporter needing money for his son's operation smashes a diamond smuggling ring. "Kill Me Tomorrow" is a bore today. (Dir: Terence Fisher, 80 mins.)

Kill or Be Killed (1980)** James Ryan, Charlotte Michelle, Norman Combes. A martial arts olympics held in a desert fortress forms the background for this chop-'em-upper, starring a rare all-Caucasian cast. Karate sequences by Norman Robinson. (Dir: Ivan Hall, 90 mins.)

Kill or Cure (Great Britain, 1962)** Terry-Thomas, Dennis Price, Lionel Jeffries, Moira Redmond. Terry-Thomas as a private sleuth investigating murder at a health resort. The gap-toothed comic finds it difficult to carry a film on his shoulders alone, and gets little help from the script. (Dir: George Pollock, 88 mins.)

Kill the Umpire (1950)**½ William Bendix, Una Merkel. Pretty funny film about an umpire's life—his training, his job and his love of baseball. (Dir: Lloyd Bacon, 78 mins.)

Killdozer (MTV 1974)** Clint Walker, Carl Betz, Neville Brand, and James Wainwright all play construction workers on a desolate island, but stunt man Carey Loftin is the real star of the film. Loftin manages a battle between an unmanned bulldozer and a power shovel in the main act, so if you dig machine duels, tune in. From the novella by Theodore Sturgeon. (Dir: Jerry London, 74 mins.)

Killer Bees (MTV 1974)** Gloria Swanson, Kate Jackson, Edward Albert, Craig Stevens. Old-time movie fans will be curious to see the indomitable Swanson once again in this predictable chiller about a strange family of winegrowers who keep killer bees on the premises. Albert is the prodigal grandson returned with his pregnant fiancee (Miss Jackson), and their visit triggers the macabre finale. It's Miss Swanson's and the bees' show. (Dir: Curtis Harrington, 74 mins.)

Killer by Night (MTV 1971)** Robert Wagner, Diane Baker. One of TV's favorite plots—about the highly communicable disease which invades the city, requiring doctors to find the carrier before an epidemic breaks out—gets a new twist. This time the carrier is an armed, dangerous cop killer, all of which sets up a contrived film peopled by familiar, competent performers. (Dir: Bernard McEveety, 100 mins.)

Killer Elite, The (1975)**½ James Caan,

Robert Duvall, Gig Young, Arthur Hill, Bo Hopkins. Director Sam Peckinpah's talent has shown itself in fits and starts. Caan is betrayed and shot by his partner Duvall as they battle on opposite sides of a mysterious CIA-involved operation. Some good, understated character dramatics in the first half, mostly involving Caan's agonizingly slow recovery from gunshot wounds. The plot is a little far-fetched, and martial arts elements are dragged in by the heels. (123 mins.)

Killer Fish (1979)*½ Lee Majors, Karen Black, James Franciscus, Margaux Hemingway. (Dir: Anthony M. Dawson (Antonio Margheriti), 101 mins.)

Killer Force (1975)*½ Telly Savalas, Peter Fonda, Hugh O'Brien, O. J. Simpson. (Dir: Michael Winner, 100 mins.)

Killer Grizzly—See: Grizzly

Killer Is Loose, The (1956)*** Joseph Cotten, Rhonda Fleming, Wendell Corey. Bank robber vows vengeance upon the detective who nabbed him. Suspenseful, exciting drama. (Dir: Budd Boetticher, 73 mins.)

Killer on Board (MTV 1977)** Claude Akins, Beatrice Straight, George Hamilton. The villain is a virus running amok on a cruise ship. While half of the ship is quarantined, Oscar-winning actress Straight battles passenger panic. (Dir: Philip Leacock, 104 mins.)

Killer Shrews, The (1959)* James Best, Ingrid Goude. (Dir: Ray Kellogg, 69 mins.)

Killer Spy (France, 1958)** Jean Marais, Nadia Tiller. Retired secret agent stumbles across a body and goes to work once again trapping a spy ring. Routine but fairly actionful espionage thriller, with Marais in good form. Dubbed in English. (Dir: Georges Lampin, 82 mins.)

Killer That Stalked New York, The (1950)**½ Evelyn Keyes, Charles Korvin. A diamond smuggler enters the U. S. carrying a contagious disease and the fuse is set in a wild search to save the city from death. Some tense moments. (Dir: Earl McEvoy, 79 mins.)

Killer Who Wouldn't Die, The (MTV 1976)*½ Mike Connors, Gregoire Aslan, Mariette Hartley. (Dir: William Hale, 98 mins.)

Killers, The (1946)*** Burt Lancaster, Ava Gardner, Edmond O'Brien, Sam Levene, Albert Dekker. Director Robert Siodmak's atmospheric rendition of Ernest Hemingway's classic short story proved a success for the young Lancaster (in his first film) as an ex-fighter who double-crosses the fixers and becomes a target of reprisal. As the insurance investigator assigned to the case (O'Brien) pieces together the story of the fighter's rise and fall from grace with the mob, the film becomes an example of film noir at its most expressive. (105 mins.)

Killers, The (1964)***½ Ronald Reagan, Lee Marvin, John Cassavetes, Angie Dickinson. The second film version of

360

Ernest Hemingway's short story, directed by Don Siegel with far more energy than Robert Siodmak could muster for his overrated 1946 effort. This one is a masterpiece, me thinks. Siegel turns the story inside out, taking the point of view of Hemingway's two faceless hit men and following their attempt to find out why one of their victims refused to run. It was planned as one of the first made-for-TV movies, but Siegel, with the perversity of a true auteur, went ahead and shot it in 'scope anyway. Thankfully, Universal decided it was too violent and released it to theaters. With Lee Marvin, Angie Dickinson, and Ronald Reagan, in his final, appropriately loathsome, screen role. (Dir: Don Siegel, 95 mins.)

Killers Are Challenged (Italy, 1965)** Richard Harrison, Wandisa Guida. Undercover agent has a task to recover some important plans. Routine spy thriller dubbed in English, lots of action, little sense. (Dir: Martin Donan, 89 mins.)

Killers' Cage (1960)** Terry Becker, Elisa Loti, Ed Nelson. The FBI wants a former crime syndicate member to return to the U.S. and testify—the mob wants him rubbed out. So-so suspense melodrama made in Mexico. Alternate title: **Code of Silence.** (Dir: Mel Welles, 75 mins.)

Killer's Carnival (1965)** Stewart Granger, Lex Barker. Viennese narcotics smuggling, Roman secret agents, and Brazilian political assassination are on this bland menu of three plodding adventure stories. Low-budget entry. (Dirs: Albert Cardiff, Robert Lynn, and Sheldon Reynolds, 95 mins.)

Killer's Kiss (1955)***½ Jamie Smith, Frank Silvera, Irene Kane. Director Stanley Kubrick's first "official" feature (he disowns "Fear and Desire") is a showoffy and talented lowlife story of a boxer who finds his girlfriend murdered. A climactic chase through a doll factory. Very good for a first try by a nervy kid. (67 mins.)

Killers of Kilimanjaro (Great Britain, 1960)** Robert Taylor, Anne Aubrey. An adventure story set in deepest Africa has Taylor cast as an engineer who is surveying the territory for the eventual building of the first African railway. There are the compulsory shots of wildlife and the close calls on each principal in the cast. (Dir: Richard Thorpe, 91 mins.)

Killers of the East (Italy, 1954)* Lex Barker, Florence Mari, Paul Muller. (Dirs: Gian Paolo Callegari, Ralph Murphy, 75 mins.)

Killers Three (1969)*½ Robert Walker, Diane Varsi, Dick Clark. (Dir: Bruce Kessler, 88 mins.)

Killing, The (1956)*** Sterling Hayden, Coleen Gray. Crooks plan a daring racetrack robbery. Some thrills in this crime meller plus a fine performance by Marie Windsor. Direction by Stanley Kubrick, a newcomer at that time, is unnecessarily

arty but interesting. (Dir: Stanley Kubrick, 83 mins.)

Killing Affair, A (MTV 1977)** O. J. Simpson, Elizabeth Montgomery, Dean Stockwell. Simpson is paired with Montgomery in this cop show. O.J.'s married detective and Liz's Viki Eaton play a homicide team who slide into an off-hours affair. Bedroom and kissing scenes by O.J. and Liz vie with a not very exciting murder case and gratuitous chase sequences. (Dir: Richard C. Sarafian, 104 mins.)

Killing Game, The (France, 1967)**½ Jean-Pierre Cassel, Claudine Auger. An often lovely, yet overly tricky film done in an almost pop-art style. A young couple drive a rich young man to distraction. There are some good scenes, but the overall effect is strained. (Dir: Alain Jessua, 94 mins.)

Killing Kind, The (1973)**½ Ann Sothern, John Savage, Ruth Roman, Cindy Williams. Barely released and rarely shown, this may be director Curtis Harrington's most successful exercise in murderous mood. Savage made a neglected starring debut as a misunderstood mama's boy with a homicidal bent; as his sympathetic mother, Sothern gives a performance refreshingly free of mannerisms. Well paced. (95 mins.)

Killing of Randy Webster, The (MTV 1981)** Hal Holbrook, Dixie Carter, James Whitmore, Jr. A crazy teenager steals a van down in Houston, giving the cops a wild chase, and winds up with a bullet in his head. This is a true story on a Houston police coverup, finally brought out in the open by the victim's parents. Hal Holbrook stars as the father and is effective in the early going playing the tough Dad, angry because his son Randy (Gary McCeery) can't do anything right. The emotional scenes between son and dad are the best part—then the show turns into another exercise in battling the bureaucrats. (Dir: Sam Wanamaker, 104 mins.)

Killing Stone (MTV 1978)**½ Gil Gerard, Nehemiah Persoff, Corinne Michaels. Michael Landon is the writer-director of this pilot about an ex-convict turned newspaper columnist. Gerard is well cast as a man who served ten years before being released on account of new evidence. (104 mins.)

Killing Urge—See: **Jet Storm**

Kim (1950)**½ Errol Flynn, Dean Stockwell, Paul Lukas, Robert Douglas, Thomas Gomez. Rudyard Kipling's best novel rendered in Hollywood schoolboy terms. Nevertheless, a colorful adventure story, with Flynn near the end of his tether and Stockwell as Kim. A trifle stodgily directed by Victor Saville. (113 mins.)

Kimberley Jim (South Africa, 1965)** Jim Reeves, Madeleine Usher, Clive Parnell. Two American con men win a diamond claim and become involved in the conflicts between the town tyrant and everybody else. Naive action drama with plenty of rough edges, but for all that rather pleasant. (Dir: Emil Nofal, 82 mins.)

Kind Hearts and Coronets (Great Britain, 1949)**** Alec Guinness, Dennis Price, Valerie Hobson, Joan Greenwood. Guinness made a sensation with his portrayal of the eight relatives whom Price must eliminate in order to claim a title in this, director Robert Hamer's (and Ealing Studios') most charming comedy. The satire is biting without being nasty, and the inexorable logic of murder unfolds with a delicious verve. (104 mins.)

Kind Lady (1935)*** Aline MacMahon, Basil Rathbone. Murdering criminals take over the house of a recluse, intending to rob and kill her. Suspenseful melodrama. (Dir: George B. Seitz, 80 mins.)

Kind Lady (1951)**½ Ethel Barrymore, Maurice Evans, Angela Lansbury. A chilling mystery about a sinister retinue of servants who invade an old lady's home and terrorize her. Top rate performance by the talented cast. Remake of the 1935 film. (Dir: John Sturges, 78 mins.)

Kind of Loving, A (Great Britain, 1962)***½ Alan Bates, June Ritchie, Thora Hird, James Bolam, Norman Rossiter. Coming near the end of the "kitchen sink" cycle of British realism, this first feature by director John Schlesinger never received due attention. Bates and Ritchie are forced to marry when she becomes pregnant. An old story, but sensitively handled. (112 mins.)

Kindar the Invulnerable (Italy, 1964)* Mark Forest, Rosalba Neri. (Dir: Osvaldo Civirani, 98 mins.)

King: A Filmed Record... Montgomery to Memphis (1970)**** Brilliant, eloquent documentary, recording the remarkable life of Rev. Martin Luther King, Jr. It traces King's leadership from the beginnings of the civil rights movement in 1955 to his tragic assassination in 1968. Packs a terrific emotional wallop including his historic "I have a dream" speech at the Washington Monument, "Bull" Connor the racist sheriff shouting orders to jail "that blind nigger" (singer Al Hibbler), and finally the scenes of Sen. Robert Kennedy at King's funeral. The readings by a variety of cinema stars are superfluous, but the film is one of the important and most moving historical documents of this or any age. Produced originally by Ely Landau as a fund raiser for the Martin Luther King Special Fund. Longer versions run over four hours. Sequences supervised by directors Joseph L. Mankiewicz and Sidney Lumet. (153 mins.)

King and Country (Great Britain, 1964)***½ Dirk Bogarde, Tom Courtenay, Leo McKern. Sensitive private is placed on trial for desertion during World War I, is defended by a Captain convinced of his innocence. Brutal study of the injustices of war may prove too strong for the more delicate viewers; but it packs quite a punch, is excellently acted. (Dir: Joseph Losey, 86 mins.)

King and Four Queens, The (1956)** Clark Gable, Eleanor Parker, Jo Van Fleet. King Gable locks horns with four beautiful would-be-widows and their gun-toting mother-in-law for a prize of $100,000 in gold. Picture jumps from comedy to drama without much conviction. (Dir: Raoul Walsh, 86 mins.)

King and I, The (1956)*** Deborah Kerr, Yul Brynner, Rita Moreno. Typically overproduced Fox filming of the Rodgers and Hammerstein hit, with Yul Brynner doing the Oscar-winning role he is still profiting from 25 years later, and Kerr (dubbed) as the British school teacher come to Siam to educate Brynner's army of children. Too long, too cute, but the score includes such hummables as "Hello Young Lovers," "Getting to Know You," and "Shall We Dance." (Dir: Walter Lang, 133 mins.)

King and the Chorus Girl (1937)***½ Fernand Gravet, Joan Blondell. Excellent comedy about a king who falls in love with a commoner. Very popular subject in 1937. Screen play by Norman Krasna and Groucho Marx. (Dir: Mervyn LeRoy, 100 mins.)

King Creole (1958)**½ Elvis Presley, Dolores Hart, Walter Matthau, Carolyn Jones, Dean Jagger. Who but Hal Wallis would have tailored the one halfway decent Harold Robbins novel, "A Stone for Danny Fisher," as a Presley vehicle? Bad but not too bad, as Elvis shows some mettle under Michael Curtiz's glum, competent direction. Young busboy on the verge of delinquency gets his break when he is forced to sing at a New Orleans nightclub and makes a hit. (116 mins.)

King in New York, A (Great Britain, 1957)**** Charles Chaplin, Dawn Addams, Michael Chaplin. Writer-director Charles Chaplin's last starring film, tinged with his special bitter sweet genius. He plays a deposed European monarch who visits America during the McCarthyist hysteria. Hilarious scene as the king is tricked into appearing on live TV by a sultry pitch-lady (Addams). Serious statements from the mouth of a young "radical" schoolboy, played by Chaplin's son Michael, who informs on his parents' friends, thereby saving his parents' teaching jobs. A remarkable, uneven political satire. (105 mins.)

King in Shadow (Germany, 1957)** O. W. Fischer, Horst Buchholz, Odile Versois. Brain specialist determines that a young king is not mad, but extremely sensitive; his efforts to help him lead to triumph, then tragedy. Heavy English-dubbed historical drama, glum going. (Dir: Harold Braun, 87 mins.)

King Kong (1933)**** Fay Wray, Bruce Cabot, Robert Armstrong, Noble Johnson. The classic monster film, still as much fun as when it came out. It should be noted, however, that audiences of the day weren't anymore naive about the Freudian implications of the giant ape on the building than we are, so don't feel all that superior about it. Today we don't get those kinds of monsters on the tops of buildings. (Dirs: Merian C. Cooper, Ernest B. Schoedsack, 100 mins.)

King Kong (1976)** Jeff Bridges, Jessica Lange, Charles Grodin. Inadequate remake. Director John Guillermin and his screenwriter Lorenzo Semple (of "Batman" fame) replace primal antisocial fantasy with labored puns and self-parody. The much-heralded 40-foot ape robot makes only one brief, unimpressive appearance. A passable $22 million kiddie show. (134 mins.)

King Kong Escapes (Japan, 1967)* Rhodes Reason, Mie Hama. (Dir: Inoshira Honda, Arthur Rankin, Jr., 96 mins.)

King Kong vs. Godzilla (Japan, 1962)*½ Michael Keith, James Yagi. (Dir: Thomas Montgomery, Inoshiro Honda, 90 mins.)

King Lear (Great Britain, 1971)**** Paul Scofield, Irene Worth, Alan Webb, Cyril Cusack, Patrick Magee, Jack MacGowran. Director Peter Brook applied the theories of Jan Kott to his stage production; much of the immediacy is dissipated in the screen version. Scofield's Lear is dead inside, with exquisite dirgelike cadences, his world in constant decomposition. Webb's Gloucester, Worth's Goneril, and especially MacGowran's Fool are among the most complex portrayals in screen Shakespeare. (137 mins.)

King of Burlesque (1936)*** Warner Baxter, Alice Faye, Jack Oakie. A nice score and good performances make this musical entertaining. Story of a burlesque producer who loses his shirt in the arts offers nothing to the film. (Dir: Sidney Lanfield, 83 mins.)

King of Hearts (France-Great Britain, 1967)**½ Alan Bates, Genevieve Bujold, Pierre Brasseur. A gentle, sentimental fable from director Philippe de Broca, in which Bates plays an unknown soldier stranded in an insane asylum abandoned by its staff during WW I. The ironies are comfortably predictable. Astoundingly popular sweet trifle. (102 mins.)

King of Jazz (1930)**½ Bing Crosby, Paul Whiteman. Musical revue in two-color Technicolor, blackout gags, vaudeville turns, Gershwin's "Rhapsody in Blue," assorted production numbers and—to be sure not to miss anything in this early musical—a brief animated cartoon sequence. Lively musical fun with early '30s flavor. (Dir: John Murray Anderson, 120 mins.)

King of Kings, The (1927)*** H. B. Warner, Jacqueline Logan, Ernest Torrence, William Boyd, Joseph Schildkraut. Director Cecil B. deMille's epic of the ministry, crucifixion, and ressurection of Christ. Silent with a music track. (115 mins.)

King of Kings (1961)***½ Jeffrey Hunter, Robert Ryan, Siobhan McKenna, Viveca Lindfors. Excellently produced story of Jesus Christ. Told simply yet with great emotional power, generally well acted. Some may quibble with variations in story, but the overall result is one of a difficult task successfully carried out. (Dir: Nicholas Ray, 161 mins.)

King of Marvin Gardens, The (1972)**½ Jack Nicholson, Bruce Dern, Ellen Burstyn. Nicholson gives a smashing performance as a seedy, philosophical radio personality, and Dern bolsters his reputation as an electric screen presence, but the film sags under the weight of its ponderous sincerity. Director Bob Rafelson has a feeling for the clichés of pop culture, but he tends to do everything too often and for too long—and the result is self-consciously and earnestly arty. (103 mins.)

King of the Coral Sea (Australia, 1953)** Charles Tingwell, Chips Rafferty, Rod Taylor. Smugglers use a pearl diving operation as a front to get aliens into Australia. Crude but fast moving adventure yarn with nice local backgrounds. (Dir: Lee Robinson, 74 mins.)

King of the Gypsies (1978)** Eric Roberts, Sterling Hayden, Annette O'Toole, Brooke Shields, Shelley Winters. No one can accuse writer-director Frank Pierson of romanticizing Gypsies: for all the evocations of close family ties, this film presents Gypsies as dishonest, repressive, narrow-minded anachronisms. The actors are miscast and unconvincing. (112 mins.)

King of the Khyber Rifles (1954)** Tyrone Power, Terry Moore, Michael Rennie. Only occasionally interesting adventure epic set in India during a minor revolution. Power is cast as a half-caste (pun intended) British Captain in the Khyber patrol. Miss Moore is miscast as a young lady caught in the turbulent proceedings. (Dir: Henry King, 109 mins.)

King of the Mongols (Japan, 1964)** Hashizo Okawa, Yoshio Yoshida. Samurai soldier comes to the aid of an emperor besieged by a rebel lord. Childish but spectacular in the true sense of the word, costume adventure. Fun if not taken seriously. Dubbed in English; bears a suspicious resemblance to the Jules Verne adventure "Michael Strogoff." (Dir: Tai Kato, 88 mins.)

King of the Roaring Twenties (1961)**½ David Janssen, Mickey Rooney. David Janssen carries the cumbersome lead of an uneven script and some glaring miscasting and still comes off rather well in the role of racketeer Arnold Rothstein. The film traces his climb to the top of "gangdom." (Dir: Joseph M. Newman, 106 mins.)

King of the Underworld (1939)**½ Humphrey Bogart, Kay Francis. Kay Francis is a lady doctor again in this one but she succeeds in outwitting Bogie who is of course the character in the title. (Dir: Lewis Seiler, 80 mins.)

King of the Vikings (Spain, 1960)* Antonio

Vilar, Marie Mahor. (Dir: Luis Lucia, 81 mins.)

King on Horseback (France, 1957)** Jean Marais, Nadia Tiller, Eleonora Rossi-Drago. English-dubbed costume adventure about some traveling players who aid the French in their war against Austria. Passable, thanks to the cast. (Dir: Georges Lampin, 88 mins.)

King Queen Knave (West Germany-U.S., 1973)**½ David Niven, Gina Lollobrigida, John Moulder Brown, Mario Adorf. This adaptation by director Jerzy Skolimowski of a minor Vladimir Nabokov novel was never regularly released—a pity, since it's an accomplished, if picayune comedy that captures much of the flavor of the mordant Nabokov wit. A burlesque of Freudian oedipal struggle, as a doofus of a boy succeeds to fortune despite his dragooned seduction of his aunt and attempted murder of his uncle. An elegant, sardonic entertainment. (92 mins.)

King Rat (1965)**** George Segal, Tom Courtenay, James Fox. An excellent World War II prisoner-of-war story graphically depicts the everyday existence of British and American POWs confined in a Japanese war camp. The interest of the film lies in the character of a thoroughly unscrupulous opportunist, skillfully played by George Segal, and a standout performance as a young British soldier by James Fox who manages to emerge as an individualist, despite Segal's influence on his survival. Well-paced and directed by Bryan Forbes. (133 mins.)

King Richard and the Crusaders (1954)**½ Rex Harrison, Virginia Mayo, Laurence Harvey, George Sanders. Elaborate costume epic based on Sir Walter Scott's tale of the Crusaders, "The Talisman." Many battle scenes keep the action lively for adventure fans. (Dir: David Butler, 114 mins.)

King Solomon's Mines (Great Britain, 1937)***½ Paul Robeson, Cedric Hardwicke, Roland Young. Not as scenic as the Technicolor remake, but follows the book more closely. The majestic Robeson, as the mysterious African chieftain Umbopa, fills the screen with a star quality seldom captured by Hollywood. The story of the search for a lost diamond mine is often exciting. From the novel by H. Rider Haggard. (Dir: Robert Stevenson, 80 mins.)

King Solomon's Mines (1950)**** Stewart Granger, Deborah Kerr, Richard Carlson, Hugo Haas. Rousing adventure tale of a white hunter guiding a party through darkest Africa in search of a lady's missing husband. Authentic jungle films filmed magnificently; enough action, suspense for all. Excellent entertainment. (Dirs: Compton Bennett, Andrew Marton, 102 mins.)

King Steps Out, The (1936)**½ Grace Moore, Franchot Tone, Walter Connolly. The kind of story that was popular throughout the '20s and '30s—royalty

romancing commoners—but even when the scenario of the musical falters into clay-mouthed operetta, director Josef von Sternberg's camera captures the delicacy, if not the delirium, of a passion beyond the players' capabilities to express. No masterpiece. (85 mins.)

Kingfisher Caper, The (South Africa, 1975)** Hayley Mills, Jon Cypher, David McCallum, Volente Bertotti. Fair actioner about diamond operations off the African coast, in which Cypher attempts to dredge up enough sparklers to pay off ruthless McCallum, and win David's sister, Jon's sweetheart. Hayley gives one of her lesser performances. Some interesting scenes of modern methods for finding diamonds. Bertotti is decorative as Cypher's straying wife/McCallum's uneasy mistress. Adapted by Roy Boulting from the Wilbur Smith novel "Diamond Hunters." (Dir: Dirk De Villiers, 89 mins.)

Kings Go Forth (1958)**½ Frank Sinatra, Tony Curtis, Natalie Wood. Implausible tale mixing war action and racial problems, as a heelish GI romances a beautiful gal with questionable antecedents. Well acted, with Sinatra his usual self, Curtis as the heel, Miss Wood nice to look at—but the story has holes. (Dir: Delmer Daves, 109 mins.)

Kings of the Sun (1963)**½ Yul Brynner, George Chakiris, Shirley Ann Field. Impressively mounted, but empty historical drama about the ancient Mayan civilization. Yul Brynner, wearing little but a loincloth, plays an Indian chief. Production gradually disintegrates into melodrama. (Dir: J. Lee Thompson, 108 mins.)

King's Pirate, The (1967)** Doug McClure, Jill St. John, Guy Stockwell, Mary Ann Mobley. Silly costume comedy-drama about pirates and their adventures, circa eighteenth century. The absurd goings-on set in Madagascar involve a pirate queen (Miss St. John), a British naval officer (McClure), a pirate leader (Stockwell), and an Indian princess a long way from home (Miss Mobley). Nonsense like this made stars thirty years ago, of people like Turhan Bey—to say nothing of exciting personalities like Errol Flynn—but it all seems pretty dated and stilted. Remake of Flynn's *Against All Flags*, 1952. (Dir: Don Weis, 100 mins.)

King's Rhapsody (Great Britain, 1955)** Anna Neagle, Errol Flynn, Patrice Wymore. Stilted and out of date operetta type of story—heir to the throne has to forsake his true love and marry a princess. Sad reminder of Flynn's declining years. (Dir: Herbert Wilcox, 93 mins.)

King's Row (1941)**** Ann Sheridan, Robert Cummings, Ronald Reagan, Charles Coburn, Betty Field. Young doctor sees a small town in all its pettiness and squalor at the turn of the century. Splendid drama, superbly done in all respects. (Dir: Sam Wood, 127 mins.)

King's Story, A (Great Britain, 1965)***

Over-long, absorbing documentary about the early life of the former Edward VIII of Britain, who abdicated his throne in 1936 to marry the woman he loved. Narrated by Orson Welles, the film uses old clips from the late Duke of Windsor's personal records, closes with a moving re-reading, by him, of his abdication speech. (Dir: Harry Booth, 100 mins.)

King's Thief, The (1955)** Edmund Purdom, Ann Blyth, David Niven. Lively but routine costume thriller, dastardly nobleman tries to steal the Crown Jewels. Purdom foils him. David Niven deserves better. (Dir: Robert Z. Leonard, 78 mins.)

Kingston: The Power Play (MTV 1976)**½ Raymond Burr, Bradford Dillman, Dina Merrill. Another Burr pilot, in which he's a top-echelon editor-publisher-reporter who never lets threats get in the way of his getting the story. Plot takes its twists from then current headlines. Burr, sparked by the character, is more animated than usual. (Dir: Robert Day, 104 mins.)

Kipps (Great Britain, 1941)***½ Michael Redgrave, Diana Wynyard, Phyllis Calvert. Fine screen version of H. G. Wells's gentle satirical comedy about a shopkeeper who inherits a fortune and tries to make his way in high society, neglecting the poor girl who loves him. The cast are first-rate all around, and Redgrave is marvelously funny and touching in the title role. (Dir: Carol Reed, 112 mins.)

Kismet (1944)*** Ronald Colman, Marlene Dietrich. If you still care to see this perennial fable of poets and caliphs and poets' daughters this is as good a version as any. (Dir: William Dieterie, 100 mins.)

Kismet (1955)**½ Ann Blyth, Howard Keel, Vic Damone, Dolores Gray, Monty Woolley. The usually brilliant director Vincente Minnelli seems off his feed in this Arabian nights musical fantasy filmed in CinemaScope. The score, after Aleksandr Borodin, is liltingly sung by Keel, Damone, and Blyth, who was classically trained. Gray stops the show with the witty "Bagdad," reprising her Broadway role. (113 mins.)

Kiss, The (1929)***½ Greta Garbo, Conrad Nagel, Lew Ayres. Director Feyder's style was a paradoxical blend of realism and pictorialism, which, at its best, as here, is uniquely affecting. The gleaming twenties décor, by Cedric Gibbons, is outstanding. A striking starring debut for young Lew Ayres, as the youth who precipitates a crisis by falling in love with the unhappily married Garbo. (Dir: Jacques Feyder, 70 mins.)

Kiss and Tell (1945)*** Shirley Temple, Jerome Courtland. Corliss Archer is in more hot water when she is suspected of being a future mother. Pleasant, humorous teenage comedy. (Dir: Richard Wallace, 90 mins.)

Kiss Before Dying, A (1956)*** Robert Wagner, Joanne Woodward, Mary Astor.

Director Gerd Oswald's first film, a graceful, coolly ironic thriller about a psychopath who murders his pregnant girlfriend while his devoted mother looks on. An excellent example of the work of a director whose artistry has, ironically, doomed him to anonymity. (Dir: Gerd Oswald, 94 mins.)

Kiss in the Dark, A (1949)** David Niven, Jane Wyman, Broderick Crawford. Silly nonsense about a stuffed shirt who takes over an apartment house and comes face to face with life. (Dir: Delmer Daves, 87 mins.)

Kiss Me Deadly (1955)*** Ralph Meeker, Albert Dekker, Paul Stewart, Maxine Cooper, Cloris Leachman, Juano Hernandez, Jack Elam, Marian Carr. The end of the world, starring Ralph Meeker (at his sleaziest) as Mickey Spillane's Mike Hammer (at his most neolithic). Director Robert Aldrich's film is in some way the apotheosis of film noir—it's certainly one of the most extreme examples of the genre, brimming with barely suppressed hysteria and set in a world totally without moral order. (Even the credits run upside down.) Also starring a young newcomer, Cloris Leachman (who is lovely and compelling). (Dir: Robert Aldrich, 105 mins.)

Kiss Me Kate (1953)**** Kathryn Grayson, Howard Keel, Ann Miller. Cole Porter's delightful Broadway play is turned into a bright entertainment package with songs, dances, and comedy. The score includes the familiar "Wunderbar," "So in Love," and "Always True to You in My Fashion." The stars are perfectly cast with Ann Miller a standout in what may be her best screen role. A truly great score makes this a musical treat. (Dir: George Sidney, 109 mins.)

Kiss Me, Kill Me (MTV 1976)*½ Stella Stevens, Claude Akins, Pat O'Brien, Robert Vaughn. (Dir: Michael O'Herlihy, 72 mins.)

Kiss Me Stupid (1964)**½ Dean Martin, Kim Novak, Ray Walston. A near masterpiece, marred only by the relative acting limitations of Walston in a role conceived for Peter Sellers. A leering, searing fable about sex, jealousy, loyalty, ambition, and how they play off one another. Director Billy Wilder develops a farcical premise that starts on a level with a "Playboy" joke, investing it with bitter, heartfelt irony. Martin and Novak have never been better. Look for Henry Gibson and Mel Blanc in small roles. (126 mins.)

KISS Meets the Phantom (MTV 1978)** Anthony Zerbe, KISS (Gene Simmons, Peter Criss, Ace Freshley, Paul Stanley). The rock group KISS are a wild bunch: one spits fire, another triggers rays from his eyes as they outwit an amusement park madman played by old reliable Zerbe. Weird optical effects and a concert segment. (Dir: Gordon Hessler, 104 mins.)

Kiss of Death (1947)*** Victor Mature, Brian Donlevy, Richard Widmark, Mildred

Dunnock. Widmark made his remarkable debut as a giggling killer, although his performance has not aged well. Victor Mature, as a hood who can't stay straight, and Gray, as his girl, really outdo Widmark (it's Mature's best leading performance). Still, how can you compete for attention with a grinning Widmark pushing crippled Dunnock down a flight of stairs so she won't squeal? (Dir: Henry Hathaway, 98 mins.)

Kiss of Evil (Great Britain, 1963)**½ Clifford Evans, Noel Willman. Honeymooning couple are ensnared by the owner of a chateau who turns out to be a vampire. Effective horror thriller, well done for those who like 'em. (Alt. title: **Kiss of the Vampire**.) (Dir: Don Sharp, 88 mins.)

Kiss of Fire (1955)**½ Jack Palance, Barbara Rush, Martha Hyer. Adventure with a capital A! All the ingredients of adventure are present in this fast-paced yarn about Spanish traitors, hostile Indians, rebels, renegades, and a Spanish Robin Hood named El Tigre. The cast is uniformly good. (Dir: Joseph Newman, 87 mins.)

Kiss of the Vampire—See: **Kiss of Evil**

Kiss the Blood Off My Hands (1948)** Burt Lancaster, Joan Fontaine, Robert Newton. Muddled melodrama about two ill-fated lovers who each commits an accidental murder for the sake of their love. Weak script and fair performances. (Dir: Norman Foster, 79 mins.)

Kiss the Girls and Make Them Die (Italy, 1966)*½ Mike Connors, Dorothy Provine, Terry-Thomas, Raf Vallone. (Dir: Henry Levin, 106 mins.)

Kiss the Other Sheik—See: **Paranoia**

Kiss Them For Me (1957)** Cary Grant, Jayne Mansfield, Suzy Parker. Even suave Cary Grant can't save this belabored farce about a trio of Navy war heroes who arrive in San Francisco for some rest and recreation, with the accent on the latter. Jayne Mansfield giggles and wiggles appropriately while Suzy Parker proves, once again, she's breathtakingly beautiful, but no actress. (Dir: Stanley Donen, 105 mins.)

Kiss Tomorrow Goodbye (1950)**½ James Cagney, Barbara Payton. Cagney is the whole show in a familiar role of an escaped convict who gets his comeuppance in the last scenes of the fast paced drama. (Dir: Gordon Douglas, 102 mins.)

Kisses for My President (1964)** Fred MacMurray, Polly Bergen, Arlene Dahl. Lightweight, silly comedy about the trials and tribulations of the first lady President of the U.S. Polly Bergen is all crooked-raised-eyebrows as the Commanderess-in-Chief, and Fred MacMurray is bewilderment personified as her spouse. (Dir: Curtis Bernhardt, 113 mins.)

Kissin' Cousins (1964)*½ Elvis Presley, Arthur O'Connell, Pam Austin, Jack Albertson, Glenda Farrell. (Dir: Gene Nelson, 96 mins.)

Kissing Bandit, The (1948)** Frank Sinatra, Kathryn Grayson, J. Carrol Naish, Mildred Natwick, Mikhail Rasumny, Billy Gilbert, Clinton Sundberg. Frank Sinatra has had fun all his career putting down this as his most embarrassing vehicle, and it is embarrassing, yet not all that bad. Sinatra played a young businessman who has to live up to the reputation of his bandit father. On second thought, maybe it is that bad. (Dir: Laslo Benedek, 102 mins.)

Kitten with a Whip (1964)** Ann-Margret, John Forsythe, Peter Brown. Juvenile delinquent gal breaks into the home of an aspiring political figure and nearly ruins his career. Sleazy bit of sensationalism not helped by Ann-Margret's inability to project; direction and the rest of the cast better than the material. (Dir: Douglas Heyes, 83 mins.)

Kitty (1945)**½ Paulette Goddard, Ray Milland. Costume drama about a girl who rises from poverty to fame, fortune and title (set in England) by indiscreet use of her charms. Moderate entertainment. (Dir: Mitchell Leisen, 104 mins.)

Kitty Foyle (1940)**½ Ginger Rogers, Dennis Morgan, James Craig. Ginger Rogers won an Oscar for her tangy performance as an upwardly mobile working girl. Really not up to her work in Gregory La Cava's "The Primrose Path" that same year, or any number of other roles. The film is marred by stodgy attitudinizing, and the Dalton Trumbo-Donald Ogden Stewart adaptation of a Christopher Morley novel is less than a model of lightness. Directed by Sam Wood. (107 mins.)

Kitty: Return to Auschwitz (Great Britain, MTV 1979)**** A lacerating extraordinary documentary produced by Yorkshire Television. Focuses on a now middle-aged woman who miraculously survived the horrors of almost two years in the infamous Nazi concentration camp Auschwitz in 1943 and 1944. She returns with her son to Auschwitz in her native Poland to revisit the camp and try to explain to her son, despite the pain of the awful memories, what life was like for the Jewish victims and how Kitty and her mother managed to survive. The unspeakable hell described by Kitty makes this one of the most important and in its own terms shattering documents ever filmed about the Holocaust. Should be required viewing for every teenager and adult alive. (Producer: Peter Morley, 88 mins.)

Klansman, The (1974)*½ Lee Marvin, Richard Burton, Lola Falana, O. J. Simpson. (Dir: Terence Young, 112 mins.)

Klondike Annie (1936)***½ Mae West, Victor McLaglen, Gene Austin. The meeting of two irresistible forces, West and director Raoul Walsh. West's script is laundered, but the air is still blue. Catch Mae's ditty entitled "I'm an Occidental Woman in an Oriental Mood for Love." She also speaks Chinese. What a gal. McLaglen is Mae's leading man, and for once she's got her hands full. (80 mins.)

Klute (1971)**** Jane Fonda, Donald Sutherland. An absolutely brilliant performance by Jane Fonda, for which she quite deservedly won the Academy Award, carries the day in this psychological thriller. Fonda plays a would-be actress-model. She is a vulnerable, self-aware, articulate, hustling middle-class call girl. Story concerns Klute (Sutherland), a small-town policeman. He comes to New York in search of a missing friend, meets Fonda, and falls in love with her—sort of! But it's Jane's picture all the way under the sure hand of director Alan J. Pakula. Fonda is believable and heartbreaking—whether she is pretending to be interested while she is turning tricks with her paying clients, or talking to her psychiatrist. (Dir: Alan J. Pakula, 114 mins.)

Knack and How to Get It, The (Great Britain, 1965)***½ Rita Tushingham, Ray Brooks, Donal Donnelly, Michael Crawford. Save for the stylish direction Mike Nichols gave Ann Jellicoe's play off-Broadway, the film might never have been made. We should be grateful, since director Richard Lester has completely reimagined the action in the mod terms of the time, creating an enduring comedy. Crawford is the chap who'd like to make it with the birds; his roommate Brooks is the man who has the knack. (84 mins.)

Knickerbocker Holiday (1944)** Nelson Eddy, Charles Coburn. The famous play of Old New York, and of Peter Stuyvesant the governor, and of how love makes a fool out of him. Fine Maxwell Anderson-Kurt Weill songs—including "September Song"—but otherwise, dull, stiffly acted. (Dir: Harry Brown, 85 mins.)

Knife in the Head (West Germany, 1979)***½ Bruno Ganz, Angela Winkler. Absorbing drama about a university professor who is shot by a policeman while visiting his ex-wife. Benefits from a strong performance by Ganz in the leading role. (Dir: Reinhard Hanuff, 108 mins.)

Knife in the Water (Poland, 1962)***½ Leon Niemczyk, Jolanta Umecka, Zygmunt Malanowicz. Director Roman Polanski's doctoral dissertation from the Polish Film School is a typical blend of sexual tension and dramatic attenuation. Some masterful confrontations and even better avoidances of confrontation. A minor official and his wife out for a country weekend pick up a hitchhiker, who picks them up. Good, if overlong and overrated. (94 mins.)

Knight Without Armour (Great Britain, 1937)*** Marlene Dietrich, Robert Donat, Irene Vanbrugh. British movie mogul Alexander Korda imported French director Jacques Feyder for this swashbuckler, then compounded the cultural schizophrenia by casting Donat and Dietrich in the leads. By the way, it takes place in Russia. An aristocratic woman is rescued from the Bolshevik Revolution by a British undercover agent. Atmosphere, romance, and suspense. Based on a novel by James Hilton. (107 mins.)

Knights of the Black Cross (Poland, 1960)*** Ursula Modrynska. Sprawling adventure made in Poland, directed by Aleksander Ford. In its original form, this was a very fine film about the Crusaders, but it's been edited here. Nevertheless, impressive. (Dir: Aleksander Ford, 180 mins.)

Knights of the Round Table (1954)**½ Robert Taylor, Ava Gardner, Mel Ferrer, Stanley Baker, Felix Aylmer. MGM's first production in CinemaScope is one of their typical embalmed costumers, featuring King Arthur, Queen Guinevere, Lancelot, and the lot. Ferrer is a wet charge of powder. (Dir: Richard Thorpe, 115 mins.)

Knightriders (1981)***½ Ed Harris, Gary Lahti, Tom Sauini, Amy Ingersoll. George A. Romero's grafting of the Arthurian cosmology onto the biker picture is a bold, scintillating inspiration, and in the process, he rethinks the sixties counter-culture movie into contemporary terms. *Knightriders* presents a small society existing outside of, and frankly critical of, conventional life-styles. The film treats alternative values and their relationship to madness and fantasy, searching for that point where pragmatism intersects integrity. The film is far too long, and the issues do get muddled along with some of the action, but Romero keeps it lively with his muscular cutting and resolute iconoclasm. After a master-piece like *Dawn of the Dead*, this comes as something of a disappointment, but there are enough intriguing ideas to preserve one's faith in Romero's talent. Well-played by the largely unknown cast. (Dir: George A. Romero, 146 mins.)

Knives of the Avenger (Italy, 1967)** Cameron Mitchell, Fausto Tozzi. Well-done adventure story set among the Vikings. When their king is away, a tribal people are threatened by marauders, until a strange warrior intervenes. Dramatic lighting, tight direction, keep this story jumping. Poor dubbing. (Dir: Mario Bava, 86 mins.)

Knock on Any Door (1949)**½ Humphrey Bogart, John Derek, George Macready, Allene Roberts. The usually brilliant director Nicholas Ray succumbs to social consciousness and pontification in this drab drama about a slum punk on trial for murder. Since he's played by Derek in his starring debut, he's "misunderstood." The opening sequence, a nervous orchestration of intricate cranework on a darkened slum set, suggests what might have been had they scrapped the script. (100 mins.)

Knock on Wood (1954)*** Danny Kaye, Mai Zetterling. Another treat for Danny Kaye fans. Danny's up to his neck in international adventures as a night club puppeteer with a penchant for getting into trouble. Lovely Mai Zetterling adds to the fun. (Dir: Norman Panama, 103 mins.)

Knockout (1941)** Arthur Kennedy, Cornel Wilde, Anthony Quinn. Stereotyped fight picture characters combine to knock out good acting and directing. (Dir: William Clemens, 73 mins.)

Knute Rockne—All American (1940)***½ Pat O'Brien, Ronald Reagan. Good biography of the famous Notre Dame football coach, and contains that now immortal movie line, "Go in there and win it for the Gipper." Fact is mixed in with the corn, but it's still one of the best football films glorifying the old college try. Reagan shows off his shifty movements in this one, long before he started to run for elective office. (Dir: Lloyd Bacon, 98 mins.)

Kojak: The Chinatown Murders (MTV 1974)*½ Telly Savalas, Dan Frazer, Kevin Dobson, Demosthenes. (Dir: Jeannot Szware, 98 mins.)

Koko, a Talking Gorilla (France, 1978)*** This engrossing and eccentric documentary from director Barbet Schroder centers on Penny Patterson, a psychology student who reports that in an experiment at the San Francisco Zoo she taught a gorilla, Koko, how to sign thoughts and responses to human language. The evidence is not thoroughly persuasive, but Schroeder's emphasis is on the drive to communicate and the love that attends that drive.

Kona Coast (1968)**½ Richard Boone as a seaman investigating the death of his teenaged daughter. Ordinary plot highlighted by exotic Hawaiian locations, a superior cast. Joan Blondell, Vera Miles, Steve Ihnat, Chips Rafferty, Kent Smith. (Dir: Lamont Johnson, 93 mins.)

Konga (Great Britain, 1961)** Michael Gough, Margo Johns. The one about the mad scientist who turns a small chimp into a murdering huge gorilla monster. Thriller diehards may take to it, but it reminds one how really good "King Kong" still is. (Dir: John Lemont, 90 mins.)

Kon-Tiki (1951)***½ Documentary of the Thor Heyerdahl expedition, covering 4,300 miles in a raft to the Polynesian Islands. Despite crude photography, an absorbing filmic record of an amazing achievement. Narrated by Ben Grauer. (Dir: Thor Heyerdahl, 73 mins.)

Koroshi (1966)** Patrick McGoohan, Yoko Tani. Actually a two-part adventure based on the TV series "Secret Agent," which has been strung together for theatrical release. Drake, the agent from British Security, is dispatched to Tokyo to get to the bottom of a mystery involving a planned assassination of a U.N. dignitary. (Dirs: Peter Yates, Michael Truman, 93 mins.)

Kotch (1971)**½ Walter Matthau, Deborah Winters, Felicia Farr. Matthau can do almost no wrong in this comedy-drama about an over-70 widower who can't live with his son and daughter-in-law and keep his sanity. He sets out to live his remaining time as a sort of overgrown boy scout, helping out a pregnant teenager. Matthau doesn't look or sound old enough, but he has a certain gruff charm which works. Auspicious directorial debut for actor Jack Lemmon. (114 mins.)

Krakatoa-East of Java (1969)** Maximilian Schell, Diane Baker, Brian Keith, Rossano Brazzi, Sal Mineo, Geoffrey Holder. About the huge volcanic explosion in 1883. They didn't find out that Krakatoa is *west* of Java until the advance publicity was out. Wrong-way script and direction too, the latter featuring perhaps the only known long-held close-up in wide-screen of a sole of a shoe. (Dir: Bernard Kowalski, 135 mins.)

Kramer vs. Kramer (1979)**** Dustin Hoffman, Jane Alexander, Meryl Streep, Justin Henry. Director Robert Benton has astutely adapted Avery Corman's novel about an advertising man who discovers what child raising means after his wife leaves them. Benton's style is direct, fluid, and precise. Hoffman has not been so affecting since "The Graduate." Benton elicits equally extraordinary results from son Henry, wife Streep, and sympathetic neighbor Alexander. The film has problems resolving the plot, but its character truths are persuasive. (105 mins.)

Kremlin Letter, The (1970)***½ George Sanders, Max von Sydow, Bibi Andersson, Orson Welles, Patrick O'Neal. This picture seemed so curdled and despairing when it came out that critics sorely underrated it. Now the film seems finely attuned to director Huston's evolving personal concerns. There are kernels of compassion hidden within the baroque plot complications, though Huston isn't sure that positive values can make any real difference in a cruel, narrow, treacherous world. The letter of the title is sent by a U.S. official to the U.S.S.R. and proposes the annihilation of China. (116 mins.)

Kronos (1957)*½ Jeff Morrow, Barbara Lawrence. (Dir: Kurt Neumann, 78 mins.)

Kung Fu (1972)*** David Carradine. The pilot film for the popular Oriental western TV series. David Carradine stars as a Chinese-American priest trained in discipline, humility, perception, and the art of karate-judo. Hunted for the murder of Chinese royalty, the priest finds work with a railroad crew and he humbles the white villain bosses with his superior ways. Flashbacks to the priest's boyhood training allow the film to avoid using the usual western claptrap. Carradine is very good in the lead and gets fine support from Barry Sullivan and Albert Salmi as the bad guys. (Dir: Jerry Thorpe, 75 mins.)

L-Shaped Room, The (Great Britain, 1962)**** Leslie Caron, Tom Bell, Brock Peters, Cicely Courtneidge, Emlyn Williams. Beautifully done drama of a pregnant girl taking lodgings in a rundown boarding house, and the struggling young writer who meets, helps, loves her. Leslie Caron never better; rest of the cast excellent, with the script and direction by Bryan Forbes superb. Fine adult fare (125 mins.)

La Belle Americaine (France, 1961)*** Robert Dhery, Colette Brosset. Enjoyable comedy about an American automobile, and its meaning to an average Frenchman. Some hilarious moments. (Dir: Robert Dhery, 100 mins.)

La Bête Humaine (France, 1938)*** Jean Gabin, Simone Simon. Director Jean Renoir's generous sensibility seems at odds with the sterile determinism of the Zola novel on which the film is based. Gabin is an epileptic train engineer drawn to the young wife (Simon) of the stationmaster. The married couple murder a man who has tried to seduce her; Gabin witnesses the killing and begins an ambiguos emotional blackmail. Fritz Lang remade this film in 1954 as "Human Desire." A beautiful opening scene, with Gabin at the controls of his train, rushing through the countryside and into the city. (105 mins.)

La Chinoise (France, 1967)**** Anne Wiazemsky, Jean-Pierre Leaud, Francis Jeanson. Continuing some of the themes dealt with in "Masculine-Feminine" (1966), the brilliant Jean-Luc Godard turns out one of his most stimulating films—one of the times when his genius for movie making meshes perfectly with the ideas he is expressing. This is a film about **ideas**, mostly those of a group of anarchic Maoist students in Paris. Subtitles. (Dir: Jean-Luc Godard, 95 mins.)

La Cucaracha—See: **Soldiers of Pancho Villa, The**

La Dolce Vita (Italy, 1960)**** Marcello Mastroianni, Anita Ekberg, Anouk Aimée. Staggering portrayal of decadence, hopelessness amoung the upper crust of Rome. Masterfully directed by Federico Fellini in a series of episodic images literally battering the eye, brain. Strictly for adults, it is absorbing throughout its length, has the elements of greatness. Dubbed in English. (Dir: Federico Fellini, 175 mins.)

La Favorita (Italy, 1952)*½ Gino Sinemberghi, Paolo Silveri, Sophia Loren. (Dir: Cesare Barlacchi, 79 mins.)

La Femme Infidèle (France-Italy, 1969)**** Michel Bouquet, Stephane Audran, Maurice Ronet. Elegant, intelligent, and sensual: never sordid, frequently funny, and very moving. Director Claude Chabrol's classic of adultery and murder is nearly perfect. Chabrol has proved to be the best of the French New Wave, surpassing Truffaut, Resnais, and Godard. (105 mins.)

La Grande Bouffe (France-Italy, 1973)**** Marcello Mastroianni, Ugo Tognazzi, Philippe Noiret, Michel Piccoli, Andrea Ferreol. Hilarious, stomach-turning, sad fable about four men who shut themselves up in a Parisian villa and gorge themselves to death on gourmet delights, pausing only to sample the charms of three negligible whores and the ample affections of Ferreol before expiring disgustingly. Marco Ferreri directed this black comedy that satirizes two of France's most cherished institutions: dining and whoring. Have dinner at least an hour before you see it. (133 mins.)

La Guerre Est Finie (France-Switzerland, 1966)**** Yves Montand, Ingrid Thulin, Genevieve Bujold. A marvelous film about political idealism, superbly directed by Alain Resnais and exquisitely acted by Montand and Thulin. Montand plays, to quiet perfection, the role of an aging revolutionary who fought against Franco in the Spanish Civil War but now knows, and reluctantly understands, that he and his cause will **not** win. Intelligent, perceptive script from screenwriter Jorge Semprun. Miss Thulin plays Montand's sensual, political mistress, and their scenes together are quite magic. (Dir: Alain Resnais, 121 mins.)

La Marseillaise (France, 1937)***½ Pierre Renoir, Louis Jouvet, Julien Carette. Director Jean Renoir's fascinating (but not wholly successful) film parallels the rise of the French Revolution with the spread of its rallying song, the Marseillaise. Louis XVI (played by Pierre Renoir, Jean's brother) is less of a monster than an anachronism, struggling to learn the subtleties of the latest fashions—tomatoes and toothbrushes—while the peasants storm the Bastille. Envisioned by Renoir as a call for national unity against the growing threat of Hitler. (130 mins.)

La Parisienne (France-Italy, 1958)***½ Brigitte Bardot, Charles Boyer. Diplomat's daughter goes to great lengths to make her husband pay attention to her. One of the best Bardot films; a sly, sophisticated comedy that is pleasant all the way. (Dir: Michel Boisrond, 85 mins.)

La Religieuse—See: **The Nun**

La Ronde (France, 1950)**** Anton Walbrook, Simone Signoret, Serge Reggiani. Director Max Ophuls's witty, virtuoso version of Arthur Schnitzler's play, showing love as a bitterly comic merry-go-round. Walbrook acts as master of ceremonies and narrator as one love affair overlaps another and love's roundabout carries the cast full circle. (100 mins.)

La Salamandre (France, 1972)**** Bulle Ogier, Jean-Luc Bideau, Jacques Denis. Writer-director Alain Tanner's compassionate look at two Swiss TV writers and a girl whose life story yields more complications than either can deal with dispassionately. A witty, probing look at Swiss society and the intellectual binds of sophisticated idealism. Exquisitely performed, from a brilliant script by Tanner and critic John Berger. (125 mins.)

La Sonnambula (Italy, 1952)*½ Gino Sinembreghi, Paolo Bertini. (Dir: Cesare Barlacchi, 79 mins.)

La Strada (Italy 1954)**** Anthony Quinn, Giulietta Masina, Richard Basehart. An altogether beautiful movie, both touching and amusing, magnificently acted by Masina and Quinn. A brutal, itinerant performer takes in a pathetic slow-witted waif, and her devotion to him is repaid with insults and indifference. English dubbed. A basically simple story has been turned into one of the most memorable films available on TV. Oscar as Best Foreign Film. (Dir: Federico Fellini, 115 mins.)

La Traviata (Italy, 1966)**½ Gino Bechi, Franco Bonisolli. Verdi's opera, starring Anna Moffo as the ill-fated Violetta. Dignified attempt, but remains staged opera . . . and, to an amateur music critic's ear, not especially well sung. (Dir: Mario Lanfranchi, 106 mins.)

La Viaccia—See: **Love Makers, The**

Lacemaker, The (France, 1978)*** Isabelle Huppert, Yves Beneyton. Huppert is a beautician's apprentice romanced by an emotionally stunted representative of the upper-middle class in a love story cum political allegory directed by Claude Goretta. The ending is too heavy for the film to bear, but there are a number of well-observed moments along the way. (108 mins.)

Lacombe, Lucien (France-Italy-West Germany, 1974)**** Pierre Blaise, Aurore Clément, Holger Lowenadler, Thérèse Giehse. Director Louis Malle's troubling, finely perceived study of a bumbling French peasant's drift into fascism in the last years of WW II makes no blanket condemnations and leaves us with the uneasy notion that, in the definition of "the banality of evil," a major component is ordinary human carelessness. (137 mins.)

Lacy and the Mississippi Queen (MTV 1978)*½ Kathleen Lloyd, Debra Feuer, Jack Elam. (Dir: Robert Butler, 78 mins.)

Lad: A Dog (1962)** Peter Breck, Peggy McCay, Angela Cartwright. How a collie brings love to a crippled girl, and various other saccharine ingredients. For canine lovers and impressionable youngsters exclusively. (Dirs: Leslie H. Martinson, Aram Avakian, 98 mins.)

Ladies First (France, 1963)*½ Eddie Constantine, Christiane Minazzoli, Mischa Auer. (Dir: Raoul Andre, 93 mins.)

Ladies in Love (1936)**½ Janet Gaynor, Loretta Young, Simone Simon. Strictly for the ladies is this overly romantic tale of the affairs of four beautiful girls in Budapest. A load of familiar faces in the cast. (Dir: Edward H. Griffith, 97 mins.)

Ladies in Retirement (1941)***½ Ida Lupino, Louis Hayward, Evelyn Keyes. Housekeeper kills her employer to save her sisters from being put in an asylum. Gripping suspense drama, excellently acted. (Dir: Charles Vidor, 92 mins.)

Ladies' Man, The (1961)**½ Jerry Lewis, Helen Traubel, Pat Stanley, George Raft, Harry James. One of the stranger chapters in director Lewis's continuing psychobiography: the most direct and intimidating confrontation between Lewis's perpetual pre-adolescent character and the wide world of sex. Jerry bungles into a plot line that might have been lifted from an ancient stag movie: he's the handyman at a women's boardinghouse. But Jerry resists the fleshy temptations of the opposite sex with all the blind determination of a six-year-old. Not a screamingly funny film but enlivened by some of Lewis's most audacious camerawork. (106 mins.)

Ladies' Man (France, 1960)** Eddie Constantine, Françoise Brion. Another French-made Grade B crime film with Eddie Constantine playing FBI Agent Lemmy Caution. This time, the action is based on the French Riviera. (Dir: Bernard Bordene, 95 mins.)

Ladies of the Chorus (1949)** Adele Jergens, Marilyn Monroe. Former Burlesque queen sees her daughter become a star. Marilyn's first big chance; good thing she didn't stop there. (Dir: Phil Karlson, 61 mins.)

Ladies Who Do (Great Britain, 1963)** Robert Morley, Peggy Mount, Harry H. Corbett. Rather dawdling comedy about a cleaning woman who begins to make her mark on the Stock Exchange, quite by chance. Amusing, thanks to the players, but seldom rises to any great heights. (Dir: C. M. Pennington-Richards, 85 mins.)

Lady and the Mob (1939)*** Ida Lupino, Fay Bainter, Lee Bowman. Wealthy old eccentric takes harsh steps to rid her town of racketeers. Frequently funny comedy. (Dir: Ben Stoloff, 70 mins.)

Lady and the Outlaw, The (1973)**½ Desi Arnaz, Jr., Gregory Peck. Offbeat western drama casts Arnaz as a half-breed who teams up with a bearded Scotman (Peck, behind that beard and Scottish brogue) to pull a robbery which ends up in murder. The pace is too slow, but the drama is earnest and well played. Photographed in Israel. (Dir: Ted Kotcheff, 80 mins.)

Lady and the Tramp (1955)*** Voices of Peggy Lee, Barbara Luddy, Larry Roberts, Stan Freberg, Verna Felton, Alan Reed. Yet another of Disney's primal fables, not inspired, surely, but very deep. The opening few reels are as poignant a distillation on screen of a young child's experience of rejection upon the birth of a sibling that I can think of; the Disney identification with a toddler's perspective (psychological as well as spatial) was acute. The mating rituals haven't the raw force of *Bambi*, but then what does? Plot concerns a pampered pet Cocker Spaniel—Lady—who eventually falls in love with a street mutt—Tramp. (Dir: Hamilton Luske, 75 mins.)

Lady Be Good (1941)*** Eleanor Powell,

Robert Young, Ann Sothern. Gershwin score, a fine cast and a good production add up to better-than-average screen entertainment. Story of a boy and girl songwriting team isn't much but thanks to Miss Sothern and Mr. Young it doesn't hurt the picture. (Dir: Norman Z. McLeod, 111 mins.)

Lady by Choice (1934)**½ Carole Lombard, May Robson, Roger Pryor. Lombard plays a publicity-mad dancer who attempts to convert old sot Robson into a model of motherly respectability. Scripted by Jo Swerling and Dwight Taylor; directed by the undistinguished David Burton. (78 mins.)

Lady Caroline Lamb (Great Britain-Italy, 1973)*½ Sarah Miles, Jon Finch, Richard Chamberlain, Margaret Leighton, Laurence Olivier, John Mills. (Dir: Robert Bolt, 123 mins.)

Lady Dances, The—See: **Merry Widow, The** (1934)

Lady Doctor (Italy, 1958)** The lady doctor is none other than Abbe Lane in this feather-weight comedy about love's bout with the Hippocratic oath. Vittorio De Sica plays a baffled suitor. (Dir: Camillo Mastrocinque, 97 mins.)

Lady Eve, The (1941)**** Barbara Stanwyck, Henry Fonda, Charles Coburn, William Demarest, Eugene Palette, Eric Blore. Preston Sturges, the best comedy director of the '40s, and he was equally good at light romance, satire, slapstick and even a stray serious moment. This is one of the finest of romantic comedies. Fonda is a beer heir who is interested in snakes; Stanwyck is a gold digger who is interested in Fonda's interest in snakes. A honey all the way (97 mins.)

Lady for a Night (1941)** John Wayne, Joan Blondell. The lady owner of a Mississippi gambling boat is accused of murdering a wealthy socialite. Slow, rather corny costume drama. Wayne looks out of place. (Dir: Leigh Jason, 87 mins.)

Lady from Shanghai (1948)*** Rita Hayworth, Orson Welles, Everett Sloane. Irish sailor accompanies a beautiful woman and her lawyer husband on a cruise, becomes a pawn in murder. Melodrama is saved by Welles touches in direction, turning it into a good thriller. (Dir: Orson Welles, 87 mins.)

Lady from Texas (1951)**½ Josephine Hull, Howard Duff, Mona Freeman. Universal had to come up with a follow up vehicle for Josephine Hull, who won an Oscar the year before for her brilliant performance in "Harvey," and this lightweight Western comedy is it. Miss Hull's special brand of whimsy is wasted on this yarn about an eccentric old lady who turns a whole town upside down, but the film itself is pleasant. Her last film. (Dir: Joseph Pevney, 77 mins.)

Lady Gambles, The (1949)**½ Barbara Stanwyck, Robert Preston, Stephen McNally. Miss Stanwyck gives a good performance in this melodrama about a woman deeply caught in a compulsive trap of gambling. Preston is also fine in the role of her patient husband. (Dir: Michael Gordon, 99 mins.)

Lady Godiva (1955)** Maureen O'Hara, George Nadar. Normans and Saxons are at each other's throats while history adds a bit of a reshuffling in this familiar tale of adventure. Don't expect too much from Lady Godiva's famous ride. (Dir: Arthur Lubin, 89 mins.)

Lady Has Plans, The (1942)** Paulette Goddard, Ray Milland. Spy story is comedy-drama and not outstanding in either department. Paulette is mistaken for a tattooed woman spy when she comes to neutral Lisbon and is immediatley pursued by all sides. (Dir: Sidney Lanfield, 77 mins.)

Lady Ice (1973)*½ Donald Sutherland, Jennifer O'Neill, Robert Duvall, Patrick Magee. (Dir: Tom Gries, 93 mins.)

Lady in a Cage (1964)** Olivia de Havilland, James Caan, Ann Sothern, Jennifer Billingsley. Unpleasant drama about young toughs who keep a woman (Miss de Havilland) trapped in an elavator while they ransack her home. Some good scenes, but generally overplayed. Caan's film debut. (Dir: Walter Grauman, 93 mins.)

Lady in a Jam (1942)** Irene Dunne, Ralph Bellamy, Patric Knowles. Daffy comedy about a crazy mixed-up heiress and her love life, especially her love for her psychiatrist. (Dir: Gregory La Cava, 78 mins.)

Lady in Cement (1968)*½ Frank Sinatra, Raquel Welsh, Dan Blocker, Richard Conte, Lainie Kazan, Martin Gabel. (Dir: Gordon Douglas, 93 mins.)

Lady in Distress (Great Britain, 1939)*** Paul Lukas, Michael Redgrave, Sally Gray. Happily married man brings on trouble when he meets a magician's lovely assistant. Fine performances bolster this mild little dramatic tale, turn it into superior entertainment. (Dir: Herbert Mason, 76 mins.)

Lady in the Car with Glasses and a Gun, The (U.S.-France, 1970)*** Samantha Eggar, Oliver Reed, John McEnery, Stephane Audran. Better than average suspense as secretary Samantha Eggar takes her boss's car for the holiday in the Mediterranean, oddly retracing a journey she has not taken, and is recognized by people she has not met before. When a body turns up in her trunk, things get serious. Miss Eggar delivers an outstanding performance, but the mystery of the film,is limited by its premise. (Dir: Anatole Litvak, 105 mins.)

Lady in the Dark (1944)***½ Ginger Rogers, Ray Milland, Mischa Auer, Warner Baxter, Jon Hall. This wonderful Broadway musical of Moss Hart's was a pioneering production at the time, and if you never saw Gertrude Lawrence in the original you won't have to make any invidious comparisons with Ginger's trouping in this splendid tuneful fantasy about a successful career woman under psychoanalysis. The dream sequences are especially worth seeing in color and there are several good tunes. (Dir: Mitchell Leisen, 100 mins.)

Lady in the Iron Mask (1952)** Louis Hayward, Patricia Medina, John Sutton, Steve Brodie, Alan Hale Jr. Princess is kept a prisoner locked in an iron mask, so her twin sister will inherit the throne. Usual sort of costume melodrama. (Dir: Ralph Murphy, 78 mins.)

Lady in the Lake (1946)**½ Robert Montgomery, Lloyd Nolan, Audrey Totter, Leon Ames, Jayne Meadows. Director Montgomery's adaptation of Raymond Chandler's finest novel is a misguided experiment in subjective cinema, with the camera standing in, literally, for detective Philip Marlowe, smoking cigarettes and punching hoods with mechanical insouciance. Orson Welles planned to make his first film this way—thank God he didn't, or we'd have a very different "Citizen Kane." (103 mins.)

Lady in the Morgue (1938)*** Preston Foster, Frank Jenks. The body of a beautiful woman disappears from the morgue, and private eye Bill Crane has a heck of a time with gals and gangsters before solving the case. High-rating mystery has many clever touches above average. (Dir: Otis Garrett, 80 mins.)

Lady Is Willing, The (1942)*** Marlene Dietrich, Fred MacMurray, Aline MacMahon. Broadway star arranges a marriage of convenience with a baby doctor so she can adopt a child. Nicely done drama. (Dir: Mitchell Leisen, 92 mins.)

Lady L (U.S.-Italy-France, 1965)*** Sophia Loren, Paul Newman, David Niven. Sumptuous settings and Sophia Loren and her male co-stars help shore up this lightweight saga of a laundress who works her way up to a title through a series of wacky misadventures. The tale of Lady L offers Miss Loren the chance to age some fifty or so years and she manages quite nicely, but we prefer her in the early sequences, where she romps about turn-of-the-century Paris with revolutionist Newman and Lord Niven. For those film historians who care about details, Peter Ustinov directed, wrote the screenplay and plays a cameo role. Ustinov took over this project after many other writers and millions of dollars had already been spent on the pre-production required to turn the Romain Gary novel into a workable screenplay. (Dir: Peter Ustinov, 107 mins.)

Lady Liberty (Italy-France, 1971)* Sophia Loren, William Devane, Luigi Proietti. (Dir: Mario Monicelli, 95 mins.)

Lady Luck (1946)*** Robert Young, Barbara Hale, Frank Morgan. Nice girl tries to tame a high-rolling gambler by marrying him. Good comedy-drama, well made and satisfying. (Dir: Edwin L. Marin, 97 mins.)

Lady of Burlesque (1943)*** Barbara Stanwyck, Michael O'Shea, J. Edward Bromberg, Pinky Lee, Iris Adrian. Strippers are strangled backstage, with one of the cuties eventually figuring out the solution. Entertaining, boisterous mystery based on Gypsy Rose Lee's "The G-String Murders." Stanwyck is well cast and William Wellman has the right directing style for this kind of racy potboiler. (91 mins.)

Lady of Lebanon Castle, The—See: **Lebanese Mission**

Lady of the House (MTV 1978)**½ Dyan Cannon, Armand Assante, Zohra Lampert. Cannon shines in this glossy, laundered version of the story of San Francisco's notorious madam, Sally Stanford, who became mayor of the suburb of Sausalito. As Sally tells it, she was clean until her divorce from a classy Bay City attorney (Assante); but after being framed on bordello charges by the police, she took up the trade and prospered. Produced by William Kayden. (Dirs: Ralph Nelson and Vincent Sherman, 104 mins.)

Lady of the Tropics (1939)**½ Robert Taylor, Hedy Lamarr. The ladies may like this torrid romance between the half-native girl and the American millionaire. It's a tragic story which you'll find dated by our standards. (Dir: Jack Conway, 100 mins.)

Lady on a Train (1945)*** Deanna Durbin, Ralph Bellamy, Dan Duryea, Edward Everett Horton, David Bruce. Fairly exciting mystery. A girl sees a man murdered but nobody believes her. Not content to leave well enough alone she follows up what she has seen and becomes involved in an absorbing adventure. (Dir: Charles David, 93 mins.)

Lady Says No, The (1951)** Joan Caulfield, David Niven. Magazine photographer interviews a gal who's written an anti-men book, breaks down her romantic resistance. Ordinary comedy has a good cast that deserves better. (Dir: Frank Ross, 80 mins.)

Lady Sings the Blues (1972)*** Diana Ross, Billy Dee Williams, Richard Pryor. Fictionalized story of great singer Billie Holiday employs enough clichés for a dozen films of this genre, but comes out a winner solely due to the truly luminous performance by Diana Ross as Lady Day, which earned her an Academy Award nomination. Not only does the beautiful Diana recreate the songs of Miss Holiday, duplicating the style without reverting to mimicking, but her dramatic power is surprising and convincing. The story takes many liberties with the facts surrounding the hapless singer's life, such as her being raped as a teenager, her working in a brothel, her severe addiction to heroin, and her tumultuous love life. Ignoring the script superficialities, you will be rewarded by La Ross's bigger than life portrayal of a musical giant. (Dir: Sidney J. Furie, 144 mins.)

Lady Takes a Chance, A (1943)**** Jean Arthur, John Wayne. New York working girl takes a western tour, falls for a brawny cowpoke who doesn't want to be tied down. Fine fun; delightful romantic comedy with some hilarious sequences, capable players. (Dir: William A. Seiter, 86 mins.)

Lady Takes a Flyer, The (1958)** Lana Turner, Jeff Chandler. Attractive stars in a very predictable yarn about a beautiful lady who falls for an aviation ace and the trouble they have reconciling their lives. (Dir: Jack Arnold, 94 mins.)

Lady Takes a Sailor, The (1949)*** Jane Wyman, Dennis Morgan, Eve Arden. Slapstick comedy about an efficient girl who always tells the truth has a lot of laughs in its contrived and comic plot. (Dir: Michael Curtiz, 99 mins.)

Lady Vanishes, The (Great Britain, 1938)**** Margaret Lockwood, Michael Redgrave, Paul Lukas, Dame May Whitty. Director Alfred Hitchcock's masterful spy thriller, with Lockwood and Redgrave searching for kidnapped agent Whitty aboard a trans-European express train, and pursued by sinister Nazi agents. Vintage Hitchcock, with superb pacing and editing. (97 mins.)

Lady Wants Mink, The (1953)*** Dennis O'Keefe, Ruth Hussey, Eve Arden. Accountant's wife causes trouble when she starts a mink farm. Breezy comedy has some good laughs. (Dir: William A. Seiter, 92 mins.)

Lady with a Lamp (Great Britain, 1951)*** Anna Neagle, Michael Wilding. Story of courageous nurse Florence Nightingale. Lavishly produced biography, well acted. (Dir: Herbert Wilcox, 112 mins.)

Lady with Red Hair (1940)**½ Miriam Hopkins, Claude Rains. Inaccurate, occasionally interesting story of the great actress Mrs. Leslie Carter and the famous producer David Belasco. Film is uneven, stodgy and only occasionally entertaining. (Dir: Curtis Bernhardt, 81 mins.)

Lady With the Dog, The (U.S.S.R., 1960)**** Iya Savvina, Aleksey Batalov. A magnificently acted and directed story based on a Chekhov short story. Set in Yalta around 1900, a middle-aged married banker from Moscow meets the unhappy, beautiful young wife of a local petty official. Very low-key, and straightforward. Sensitively directed without a lot of extraneous flourishes by director Iosif Kheyfits, who also wrote the adaptation. (Dir: Iosif Kheyfits, 86 mins.)

Lady Without Passport, A (1950)**½ Hedy Lamarr, John Hodiak. Intrigue and romance in an exotic locale serves as the basis once again for an adventure film starring the beautiful Hedy Lamarr. (Dir: Joseph H. Lewis, 72 mins.)

Lady Without Camellias, The (Italy, 1953)*** Lucia Bose, Andrea Cecchi, Alain Cuny. A little-known, impressive early film directed by Michelangelo Antonioni. About a former Milanese shop girl who has a small part in a low-budget quickie movie, and then dreams of becoming a serious, recognized movie star. Bose's quality of distant, detached glamour is used to good advantage by the fledgling Antonioni, and there are evidences throughout of the striking cinematic techniques that earned him world-wide recognition a decade later. (Dir: Michelangelo Antonioni, 105 mins.)

Ladykillers, The (Great Britain, 1955)**** Alec Guinness, Cecil Parker, Peter Sellers. Menacingly funny, with a sharp script by William Rose and well-keyed direction by Alexander Mackendrick. Black comedy about a gang of cutthroats undone by the sweet obtuseness of a sly little old lady. (94 mins.)

Lady's Morals, A (1930)** Grace Moore, Wallace Beery, Reginald Denny. Moore plays Jenny Lind, the Swedish Nightingale, in this early musical, singing arias from "Norma" and "The Daughter of the Regiment" and ending up with a blind concert pianist (Denny). Beery plays P. T. Barnum, Lind's impresario in the U.S. (Dir: Sidney Franklin, 75 mins.)

Lafayette (France, 1962)** Orson Welles, Jack Hawkins, Edmund Purdom. Muddled historical drama about the French patriot Lafayette. Some action scenes come off nicely, but it moves sluggishly, despite the international cast. (Dir: Jean Dreville, 110 mins.)

Lafayette Escadrille (1958)*½ Tab Hunter, Etchika Choureau, David Janssen. (Dir: William Wellman, 93 mins.)

L'Age d'Or (France, 1930)**** Gaston Modot, Lya Lys, Max Ernst. Here a couple are continually interrupted while making passionate love. Director Luis Buñel's legendary surrealist classic has been generally unavailable since the producer pulled it from circulation 50 years ago in embarrassment over the scandal it caused. Today the film seems hardly scandalous at all, though it retains its provocative manner and fierce inventiveness. It's a revelation to see how fully formed Buñel's anarchic sensibility was so early in his career, and though he would gain in depth and richness, the scabrous attack on all enemies of liberation is here in full dudgeon, in this masterpiece of bullheaded aestheticism. (60 mins.)

L'Amour (1973)** Michael Sklar, Donna Jordan, Jane Forth. Although Paul Morrissey and Jed Johnson are credited as collaborators, this is perhaps the last film to purport to be directed, instead of "presented," by Andy Warhol. Shows signs of "commercialism." Here whininess is not a tool of art but the end of it: Sklar is a disturbingly uningratiating queen for a day. (90 mins.)

Lancelot of the Lake (France-Italy,

1974)**** Luc Simon, Laura Duke Condominas. A severe, cathartic masterpiece that takes up the Arthurian legend where most versions end, with Camelot in fading glory and the ideals of chivalry giving way to a modern, pragmatic mentality. The rhythms are slow and irresistible; director Robert Bresson's clang of armor and heavy breathing of burdened horses, framed at midriff, is daring cinema like no one else's. (85 mins.)

Land of Fury (Great Britain, 1954)**½ Jack Hawkins, Glynis Johns, Noel Purcell. Danger and hardships pioneering in old New Zealand. Well cast, fine outdoor locale, but the plot lacks pace. Alternate title: **The Seekers.** (Dir: Ken Annakin, 82 mins.)

Land of the Pharaohs (1955)*** Jack Hawkins, Joan Collins, Dewey Martin. Director Howard Hawks's background as an engineer comes to the fore in this account of the building of the pyramids. The story is a whopper, with Hawkins a visionary pharaoh saddled with an ambitious wife (Collins, purring up a storm). The film doesn't work, but has more than its share of crazy pleasures. (106 mins.)

Land Raiders (1970)** Telly Savalas, George Maharis, Arlene Dahl. Ordinary western about a feud between two brothers, and the woman they both love. The feud is broken up by rampaging Apaches, and not a moment too soon. George Maharis has a part-time Spanish accent. Filmed in Budapest and Spain. (Dir: Nathan Juran, 101 mins.)

Land That Time Forgot, The (Great Britain, 1974)**½ Doug McClure, Susan Penhaligon, John McEnery. An old-fashioned adventure yarn based on the 1918 novel by Edgar Rice Burroughs which never lets logic get in the way of the action. The time is World War I. A group from a German sub and the survivors of an Allied ship come together and find themselves in a lost world where prehistoric animals still rule the roost! This is the type of movie which had kids screaming and shouting at Saturday matinees during the 40's—BTV (Before TV). There's even a volcano eruption at the film's finale. (Dir: Kevin Connor, 92 mins.)

Landlord, The (1970)**** Beau Bridges, Lee Grant, Pearl Bailey, Diana Sands, Lou Gossett. Alternately hilarious and serious satire on our fouled-up race relations. The entire cast is superb in this story of a young, rich white man who buys a tenement in Brooklyn with dreams of converting it to a showplace home for himself. But he hasn't bargained on the militant black tenants who have no intention of conveniently moving out. The confrontations are very funny, and the satire is devastating. Director Hal Ashby, (in his first effort) and writer William Gunn have produced a gem. Based on the novel by Kristin Hunter. (114 mins.)

Landru (French-Italian, 1962)**½ Charles Denner, Michele Morgan, Danielle Darrieux. Men who've dreamed of having numerous wives and getting rid of them without the bother of a divorce will love this entry. The macabre tale of Bluebeard, the husband who did away with many wives, is told again via this fairly well done French film, dubbed in English. (Dir: Claude Chabrol, 114 mins.)

Lanigan's Rabbi (1976)**½ Art Carney, Stuart Margolin, Janis Paige, Janet Margolin. Character is the key here. A mildly diverting comedy with Carney as a sympathetic police chief who refuses to believe the town Rabbi (Stuart Margolin) is a real murder suspect. Based on the best-seller "Friday the Rabbi Slept Late," the show takes a different tack from the usual cop format, with the detective and the suspect becoming close friends. Carney shoulders the load, and that's good enough part of the time. Made-for-TV. (Dir: Louis Antonio, 98 mins.)

Larceny (1948)**½ John Payne, Shelley Winters, Dan Duryea, Joan Caulfield. Routine crime pic with bad guy turning good guy and the gangster's moll who wants to go legit. Dan Duryea plays Silky, an arch villain, to the hilt. (Dir: George Sherman, 89 mins.)

Larceny, Inc. (1942)*** Edward G. Robinson, Jane Wyman, Broderick Crawford, Anthony Quinn, Jackie Gleason, Jack Carson. Entertaining story about an ex-con who does his best to go straight. This is a fairly amusing little farce which is well played by an expert cast. (Dir: Lloyd Bacon, 95 mins.)

Large Rope, The—See: Long Rope

Large Rope, The (Great Britain, 1953)*** Donald Houston, Susan Shaw. After serving a prison term, a man returns to his home town only to be implicated in a murder. Lengthy but well-done melodrama holds the interest. (Dir: Wolf Rilla, 72 mins.)

Las Vegas Hillbillies (1966)* Ferlin Husky, Jayne Mansfield, Mamie Van Doren. (Dir: Arthur C. Pierce, 90 mins.)

Las Vegas Lady (1976)* Stella Stevens, Stuart Whitman, George Di Cenzo. (Dir: Noel Nosseck, 87 mins.)

Las Vegas Shakedown (1955)** Dennis O'Keefe, Coleen Gray. Ex-convict swears to kill a gambling house owner who testified against him. Fair melodrama tries to tell too much story. (Dir: Sidney Salkow, 79 mins.)

Las Vegas Story (1952)** Jane Russell, Victor Mature, Vincent Price. Married woman meets an old flame in Las Vegas, who saves her husband from a murder charge. Undistinguished melodrama. (Dir: Robert Stevenson, 88 mins.)

Laserblast (1978)* Keenan Wynn, Roddy McDowall, Cheryl Smith. (Dir: Michael Rae, 80 mins.)

Lassie Come Home (1943)***½ Roddy McDowall, Donald Crisp, Lassie. Story of an impoverished family which sells a prize collie is warm, sentimental and beautifully done. Remade as *Gypsy Colt*, 1954. (Dir: Fred M. Wilcox, 88 mins.)

Last Adventure, The (France-Italy, 1967)** Alain Delon, Lino Venturi, Joanna Shimkus. A stunt flyer, a racing mechanic and a girl who's in love with both of them set out on a treasure hunt in the Congo. No riches for the audience. (Dir: Robert Enrico, 102 mins.)

Last American Hero, The—See: **Hard Driver**

Last Angry Man, The (1959)*** Paul Muni, David Wayne, Betsy Palmer. Even Paul Muni can't always raise this story of a dedicated general practitioner in Brooklyn above the level of soap opera. A very uneven script hampers the talented cast. There's a great performance by Luther Adler in the role of a long-time doctor friend of Muni's who became a specialist to raise his standard of living. Muni's last. (Dir: Daniel Mann, 100 mins.)

Last Angry Man, The (MTV 1974)**½ Pat Hingle, Lynn Carlin. Gerald Green's best-selling novel about a lovable old general practitioner was turned into a fairly successful film in 1959 with Paul Muni. In this version, only the title and the central characters remain...the setting is the Brooklyn of 1936 and Hingle brings a dignity and quiet force to the role of Dr. Abelman. Nostalgia and sentiment are the mainstays but the pace is too lethargic at times to sustain involvement. Michael Margotta shines in the role of Frankie, a young tough with a serious illness. (Dir: Jerrold Freedman, 74 mins.)

Last Blitzkrieg, The (1958)** Van Johnson, Kerwin Mathews. Routine war film with some good action shots. The performances are of no help. (Dir: Arthur Dreifuss, 84 mins.)

Last Bridge, The (Germany, 1954)**** Maria Schell. This is the beautiful, profoundly moving film that marked Maria Schell as one of the finest new screen actresses of her generation. A tender story about a nurse during the war (WWII) who has loyalties and affections for individuals on both sides—German and Yugoslav. It's one of the most stirring anti-war arguments you'll ever see or hear. Expertly directed on location in Yugoslavia by Helmut Kautner. (90 mins.)

Last Challenge, The (1967)**½ Glenn Ford, Angie Dickinson. Western fans will not be cheated by this routine but well-played horse opera. Glenn Ford is the former gunslinger turned marshal who has to keep an eager young gun (Chad Everett) from shooting up the town. The tension builds to the inevitable shootout and the supporting cast includes such good actors as Angie Dickinson, Jack Elam and Gary Merrill. (Dir: Richard Thorpe, 105 mins.)

Last Chance, The (Switzerland, 1945)**** E. G. Morrison, John Hoy. American and RAF pilot downed in enemy territory attempt to make their way to Switzerland and freedom. Stirring war drama, superbly written and directed, acted by a nonprofessional cast. (Dir: Leopold Lindtberg, 105 mins.)

Last Chants for a Slow Dance (1980)*** Tom Blair, Jessica St. John, Steve Vooheis, Mary Vollmer. A moody, disturbing look at individual alienation and obsessive desire from independent director Jon Jost, whose concern for formal experiments and political analysis hasn't kept him from making feature-length films on the slimmest of budgets. (88 mins.)

Last Charge, The (Italy, 1962)* Tony Russel, Haya Harareet. Alternate title: **Fra Diavolo.** (Dir: Leopoldo Savona, 84 mins.)

Last Command, The (1955)***½ Sterling Hayden, Anna Maria Alberghetti, Ernest Borgnine, Richard Carlson. Story of Jim Bowie, and the historic battle of the Alamo. Historical action drama has fine battle scenes, a good cast, and holds the interest. (Dir: Frank Lloyd, 110 mins.)

Last Crusade, The (Rumania, 1971)**½ Intended to be an epic saga about the end of the 16th century when the Rumanians struggled under the leadership of Prince Michael the Brave to free themselves from the brutal reign of the Turks. May be your only chance of the day to see someone impaled at the beginning of a movie. Clumsy subtitling doesn't help any. (Dir: Sergui Nicolaescu.)

Last Cry for Help, A (MTV 1979)**½ Linda Purl, Shirley Jones, Tony Lo Bianco. Low-keyed drama about a lonely teenager who tries to be all things to everyone, and ends up trying to take her own life. Purl is very good as the troubled Sharon who meets a young man, also with suicidal tendencies, who might have provided the kind of love she craves. No pat solutions. (Dir: Hal Sitowitz, 104 mins.)

Last Day, The (MTV 1975)½ Richard Widmark, Barbara Rush, Robert Conrad, Loretta Swit. (Dir: Vincent McEveety, 100 mins.)

Last Days of Man on Earth, The (Great Britain, 1973)**½ Jon Finch, Jenny Runacre, Sterling Hayden. Director Robert Fuest goes to work on a Ken Russellish science fiction story about the creation of a technological superman. A lot of nasty fun, though Fuest sometimes seems more interested in the set decorations than the characters. Finch heads an unrestrained cast. (89 mins.)

Last Days of Pompeii (1935)*** Preston Foster, Basil Rathbone, Alan Hale, Dorothy Wilson. Peace-loving blacksmith strives for wealth by becoming a champion gladiator. Average story bolstered by spectacular scenes of the destruction of Pompeii, a technical tour de force. (Dir: Ernest B. Schoedsack, 100 mins.)

Last Days of Pompeii, The (Italy-Spain, 1959)**½ Steve Reeves, Christine Kaufmann. Italian made, English dubbed, spectacle produced for the adventure fans. There's some good photographic effects during the climactic eruption of the volcano, Vesuvius. (Dir: Mario Bonnard, 97 mins.)

Last Detail, The (1973)***½ Jack Nicholson, Otis Young, Randy Quaid. Tough story about two sailors escorting a third to a military prison comes off as an effective drama. Nicholson, as the honcho of the detail, is marvelous as an alternately brawling and sensitive swabbie. Young, as the other shore patrol noncom, and Quaid, as the hapless young prisoner, are also good. The "detail" turns into a sort of last-celebration-of-life for Quaid when his two jailers take pity on him and show him a good time, sailor-liberty-style. (Dir: Hal Ashby, 104 mins.)

Last Embrace (1979)**** Roy Scheider, Janet Margolin, Sam Levene, Marcia Rodd, Christopher Walken. Jonathan Demme finally erupts as a first-rank director. His visual style is remarkably consistent throughout, and it scintillates with imagination and taste. Scheider and Margolin are convincing neuresthenic leads in this thriller, and the character cameos are vivid. (103 mins.)

Last Escape, The (1970)* Stuart Whitman, John Collin. (Dir: Walter Grauman, 90 mins.)

Last Flight of Noah's Ark, The (1980)** Elliott Gould, Genevieve Bujold, Ricky Schroder, Vincent Gardenia. Disney feature operating on the uncomfortable assumption that the lives of human beings are worth risking for the preservation of animals. (Dir: Charles Jarrott, 97 mins.)

Last Frontier, The (1956)** Victor Mature, Anne Bancroft, Robert Preston, Guy Madison, James Whitmore. A frontier outpost is almost destroyed due to the arrogant stubbornness of ruthless colonel. Routine western heroics with plenty of battle scenes. Alternate title: **Savage Wilderness.** (Dir: Anthony Mann, 98 mins.)

Last Gangster, The (1937)*** Edward G. Robinson, James Stewart. Robinson is released after ten years on the rock and finds his world has changed. His futile fight to regain power makes this an interesting, although not superior, film. (Dir: Edward Ludwig, 80 mins.)

Last Giraffe, The (MTV 1979)*** Susan Anspach, Simon Ward, Gordon Jackson. Conservationists and animal lovers will have a field day with this story about the efforts of Ward and Anspach to save the endangered Rothschild giraffe of Kenya. Superb location photography in and around Nairobi enhances the true-life film about safari guide Jock Leslie-Melville and his American photojournalist wife Betty. She adopts one giraffe named Daisy, and spearheads the mammoth job of relocating a large herd of the threatened animals. (Dir: Jack Couffer, 104 mins.)

Last Glory of Troy, The (Italy, 1962)*½ Steve Reeves. Alternate title: **The Aveng-** er. (Dir: Giorgio Rivalta, 100 mins.)

Last Grave at Dimbaza (South Africa, 1975)**** Enormously powerful documentary about the effects of the brutal racist apartheid policies of the government of South Africa. Filmed at great risk by the filmmakers who shot the footage illegally and then smuggled it out of South Africa. One of the many powerful scenes explains how the black men are purposely kept separated from their families for long periods of time. Disturbing, searing film which gives little reason for a peaceful revolution for the embattled native population. (Dir: Nana Mahomo, 65 mins.)

Last Grenade, The (Great Britain, 1970)* Stanley Baker, Honor Blackman, Richard Attenborough, Rafer Johnson, Alex Cord. (Dir: Gordon Flemyng, 93 mins.)

Last Gun, The (Spain, 1964)* Cameron Mitchell. (88 mins.)

Last Gunfight, The (Japan, 1959)*** Toshiro Mifune. Demoted detective is transferred from Tokyo to a city ruled by criminals. Gangster story, Nipponese style—as a novelty, not without interest. Dubbed in English. (Dir: Kihachi Okamoto, 95 mins.)

Last Hard Men, The (1976)** Charlton Heston, James Coburn, Barbara Hershey, Michael Parks, Chris Mitchum, Jorge Rivero. A fossil, one of the few studio westerns of the seventies. While it would be creditable in the context of the fifties, when so many westerns were being made, it isn't nearly substantial enough to stand as an exemplar of the genre in these times. Charlton Heston stars as the aging sheriff who pursues the escaped convict (James Coburn) he had sent up, after the convict kidnaps his daughter (Barbara Hershey) in revenge. Directed by amiable hack Andrew McLaglen. (Dir: Andrew McLaglen, 98 mins.)

Last Holiday (Great Britain, 1950)**** Alec Guinness, Beatrice Campbell, Kay Walsh, Bernard Lee, Wilfred Hyde-White. Man decides to make the time count when he is told he has a short time to live. Excellent comedy-drama with the usual impeccable Guinness performance. Script by J. B. Priestley. (Dir: Henry Cass, 89 mins.)

Last Hours Before Morning (MTV 1975)*½ Ed Lauter, Rhonda Fleming, Robert Alda, Peter Donat. (Dir: Joe Hardy, 74 mins.)

Last Hunt, The (1956)*** Stewart Granger, Robert Taylor, Debra Paget. Engrossing action drama about the last of the big buffalo hunters in the Dakotas during the 1880's. The on-location photography is the film's main asset and the actors are secondary to the action sequences. (Dir: Richard Brooks, 108 mins.)

Last Hurrah, The (1958)**** Spencer Tracy, Jeffrey Hunter, Pat O'Brien, Dianne Foster, Basil Rathbone, John Carradine, Jane Darwell, Donald Crisp, James Gleason. Version of the Edwin O'Connor novel stars Tracy as Frank Skeffington, last of the old-style political bosses, whose last, losing campaign lets director John Ford explore failure of tradition, the wretchedness of modern cultural homogeneity, and the tragic fate that awaits men who choose to stand outside the flow of history. Full of good, rich Irish humor, this is ultimately a sad film. (121 mins.)

Last Laugh, The (Germany, 1924)***½ Emil Jannings, Maly Delschaft. One of the most unusual and interesting of Murnau's films, which shows directorial techniques imitated half a century later by lesser European directors. Jannings plays an elderly hotel doorman forced to retire and surrender his precious uniform, which gave him status in his neighborhood. Jannings is excellent, and there's interesting imagery throughout. (Dir: F. W. Murnau, 72 mins.)

Last Man on Earth, The (U.S.-Italy, 1964)** Vincent Price, Franca Bettoia. Scientist finds himself the sole survivor of a plague that has either killed the earth's population or turned them into subhuman zombies. Adequate sci-fi horror thriller filmed in Italy. Some scary sequences. Remade as *The Omega Man*, 1971. (Dir: Sidney Salkow, 86 mins.)

Last Married Couple in America, The (1980)* George Segal, Natalie Wood, Valerie Harper, Dom DeLuise. (Dir: Gilbert Cates, 97 mins.)

Last Metro, The (1980)***½ Catherine Deneuve, Heinz Bennent, Jean-Louis Richard, Jean Poiret and Sabine Haudepin. Francois Truffaut's entertaining film about a theatrical troupe surviving during the Occupation in Paris boasts smashing performances from Deneuve and Bennent, the latter as a theatrical genius who, because of his Jewish background, is forced into hiding in the theater's basement. From there he supervises new productions unbeknownst to the authorities and even his own troupe (the character is based on Max Ophuls). Truffaut's usual masterly touch with anecdotal material is evident, but so is a disquieting disinclination to seize the opportunities in his promising material. The film might have been a masterpiece, but nothing in it cuts deeply; Truffaut is content with surface originality and avoids any personal implication in the fundamental situation, preferring instead to palm off plot contrivance as a substitute for sustained meditation. (Dir: Francois Truffaut)

Last Mile, The (1958)*#½ Mickey Rooney, Frank Conroy. A good attempt at remaking the famous movie (of 1932) that starred Preston Foster. The years have taken some of the bite of this hard-hitting prison drama. Mickey Rooney tries but never quite comes off. (Dir: Howard W. Koch, 81 mins.)

Last Movie, The (1971)* Dennis Hopper, Julie Adams, Sam Fuller. (Dir: Dennis Hopper, 110 mins.)

Last Musketeer, The (France, 1955)*½ Georges Marchal, Dawn Addams. (Dir: Fernando Cerchio, 95 mins.)

Last of Mrs. Cheyney, The (1937)**½ Robert Montgomery, William Powell, Nigel Bruce, Joan Crawford, Frank Morgan, Benita Hume, Jessie Ralph, Sara Haden, Melville Cooper. Frederick Lonsdale's play had always been a popular cinematic perennial (Norma Shearer did it under Sidney Franklin's direction in 1929), what with the commercial mix of high society and jewel thieves. Joan Crawford limns the part in this film: it was one of her most popular vehicles of the thirties. The production itself was something of a sad affair: Director Richard Boleslawski died during the shooting, and it was finished by Dorothy Arzner (some accounts also contend that George Fitzmaurice did a few days on it). (Dirs: Richard Boleslawski, Dorothy Arzner, 98 mins.)

Last of Sheila, The (1973)** James Coburn, Dyan Cannon, Richard Benjamin, James Mason, Joan Hackett, Raquel Welch, Ian McShane. A nifty, intricate, campy parlor game, set on a yacht on the Riviera, which should keep you absorbed watching for clues. The plot concerns conniving Hollywood-producer Coburn who invites six friends for a cruise, during which he plans to discover which one killed his wife at a party a year ago. The personalities are outrageously colorful: the brash agent, the has-been director, the failed screenwriter, the sex-pot starlet, etc. The script, by Stephen Sondheim and actor Anthony Perkins, is a full-fledged mystery, full of bitchy Hollywood in-jokes. Song "Friends" sung by Bette Midler. (Dir: Herbert Ross, 120 mins.)

Last of the Blue Devils, The (1979)**** Count Basie and Orchestra, Joe Turner, Jay McShann. So the camera is in the wrong place, at least it's on, and I loved every minute of looking at the remnants of the heyday of Kansas City jazz hanging out at the union hall, talking and playing. An invaluable contribution to our culture. (Dir: Bruce Ricker, 91 mins.)

Last of the Comanches (1953)**½ Broderick Crawford, Barbara Hale. A group of courageous men and women are trekking across a desert to Fort Macklin when Indians attack. The cavalry and a young Indian save the day in this fair Western drama. Remake of *Sahara*, 1943. (Dir: Andre de Toth, 85 mins.)

Last of the Cowboys, The—See: **Great Smoky Roadblock, The**

Last of the Fast Guns (1958)**½ Jock Mahoney, Gilbert Roland, Linda Cristal. Gunslinger is hired to find a man's missing brother in Mexico, finds danger in the quest. Neat western moves at a speedy clip. (Dir: George Sherman, 82 mins.)

Last of the Good Guys, The (MTV 1978)**½ Robert Culp, Dennis Dugan. Light-spirited cop show which pits an idealistic rebel cop and his buddies against a tough by-the-book sergeant. The story line stumbles a bit, but newcomer Dugan is a charmer as the young knight in blue, tilting against Culp's tyrannical bad guy. (Dir: Theodore J. Flicker, 104 mins.)

Last of the Mobile Hotshots (1970)*½ James Coburn, Lynn Redgrave, Robert Hooks. (Dir: Sidney Lumet, 108 mins.)

Last of the Mohicans, The (1936)*** Randolph Scott, Binnie Barnes, Heather Angel, Henry Wilcoxen, Bruce Cabot. The famous story of the French-Indian wars, and of the noble redmen who helped turn the tide against their brothers. Exciting, elaborately produced, good action. (Dir: George B. Seitz, 100 mins.)

Last of the Mohicans, The (MTV 1977)** Steve Forrest, Ned Romero, Andrew Prine, Don Shanks. Do you need another inferior version of James Fenimore Cooper's classic frontier yarn about Hawkeye and his Indian friends? Forrest stars as the intrepid white hunter who, with his two Indian blood brothers, Chingachgook (Romero) and Uncas (Shanks), helps a British officer escort two young women safely through hostile Indian country. (Dir: James L. Conway, 104 mins.)

Last of the Red Hot Lovers (1972)**½ Alan Arkin, Sally Kellerman, Paula Prentiss, Renee Taylor. Neil Simon's hit play arrives on the screen jazzed up with fewer laughs and Simon's own screen treatment of his play. Story of Jewish, middle-class Barney Fishman's hopes for an extramarital affair. Arkin plays the Don Juan owner of a seafood restaurant who can't remove the smell of fish from his hands as he tries three assignations using his mother's apartment. Arkin's physical mannerisms are funny and fine in conveying tthe erotic urge and its accompanying guilt. (Dir: Gene Saks, 98 mins.)

Last of the Secret Agents? (1966)** Nancy Sinatra, Marty Allen, Steve Rossi. Comedy team of Allen and Rossi play American tourists mixed up in espionage. Familiar pattern, but a few surprisingly funny moments. (Dir: Norman Abbott, 92 mins.)

Last of the Ski Bums (1969)*** A snow skier's version of "The Endless Summer," except that this world-wide search for perfect powder instead of the perfect wave isn't quite as skillfully done. Several ski bums are shown schussing their favorite mountains in various parts of the world including the Western U.S., Europe and New Zealand. There is some first-rate photography, and the film does capture some of the joy of skiing, and the special nature of the world-wide breed of "ski bum." (Dir: Dick Barrymore, 86 mins.)

Last of the Vikings (France-Italy, 1961)*½ Cameron Mitchell, Edmund Purdom, Isabelle Corey. (Dir: Giacomo Gentilomo, 102 mins.)

Last Outpost, The (1935)*** Cary Grant, Claude Rains, Gertrude Michael. A defense-of-the-British-Empire melodrama with an amazingly corny plot that is enjoyable anyway. Dashing officer Grant falls in love with the man (Rains) who saved his life. Exciting series of narrow escapes during the battles between the Kurds and the British in the Sahara Desert. (Dir: Charles Barton, 75 mins.)

Last Outpost, The (1951)** Ronald Reagan, Rhonda Fleming, Bruce Bennett. Brothers are pitted against each other in this story of the West during the Civil War. Indians add to the confusion. (Dir: Lewis R. Foster, 88 mins.)

Last Picture Show, The (1971)**** Timothy Bottoms, Jeff Bridges, Cybill Shepherd, Ben Johnson, Cloris Leachman. A poignant and deeply moving drama about a young boy growing up in a small town (Archer City) in Texas during the early 1950's. Part of the remarkable quality of director Peter Bogdanovich's masterpiece is that the camera is, quite purposely, **not** the star, and Bogdanovich has further enhanced the simplicity of the story by shooting the film in black and white. Based on the novel by Larry McMurtry, the performances from both established veterans—Leachman, Johnson—and assorted newcomers like Bottoms are uniformly and unerringly perfect. (Both Leachman, playing the vulnerable neglected wife of a high-school football coach, and Johnson, a pool-hall owner, deservedly won Academy Awards for their performances.) Only Bogdanovich's second feature, this won an Academy Award nomination of best picture. One of the finest American films in 20 years. (Dir: Peter Bogdanovich, 118 mins.)

Last Posse, The (1953)*** Broderick Crawford, John Derek, Charles Bickford, Wanda Hendrix. Good western about a ruthless cattle baron who forms a posse to regain $100,000 stolen from him. Performances and script better than average. (Dir: Alfred L. Werker, 73 mins.)

Last Rebel, The (1971)* Joe Namath, Jack Elam, Victoria George. Filmed in Italy. (Dir: Denys McCoy, 89 mins.)

Last Remake of Beau Geste, The (1977)*** Marty Feldman, Ann-Margaret, Michael York, Peter Ustinov, Trevor Howard. Breaking away from Mel Brooks, Feldman cowrote, directed, and starred in a Foreign Legion spoof which is uneven but often enormously funny, and frequently in bad taste—much of it intentional. Gary Cooper is intercut in scenes from the '39 version, not affectionately. (84 mins.)

Last Ride, The (1944)** Richard Travis, Eleanor Parker. Remember the black market in tires? Well, it's the background for this Class "B" melodrama. (Dir: Ross Lederman, 56 mins.)

Last Ride of the Dalton Gang, The (MTV 1979)** Larry Wilcox, Jack Palance, Randy Quaid. According to this long-winded, scenically attractive western, the

Dalton boys were just a bunch of fun-lovin' fellas who stole horses and robbed banks and trains. The law catches up with them when they hit their hometown bank in Coffeyville. (Dir: Dan Curtis, 156 mins.)

Last Ride to Santa Cruz, The (Germany, 1964)*½ Edmund Purdom, Marion Cook, Mario Adorf. (Dir: Rolf Olsen, 99 mins.)

Last Roman, The (West Germany-Rumania, 1968)** Laurence Harvey, Orson Welles, Sylva Koscina, Honor Blackman, Harriet Andersson, Michael Dunn. Lots of action and gore, plus a good international cast. Some interest generated by the Ladislas Fodor script, based on a best-seller by Felix Dahn. Originally made as a two-part spectacular, it casts Harvey as a passionate Roman in 525 A.D. who hopes to turn the Goths and Byzantines against each other and reclaim Rome for Italy. Harvey and Dunn, the dwarf actor, have some good scenes, Welles just a bit part. (Dir: Robert Siodmak, 92 mins.)

Last Run, The (1971)** George C. Scott, Trish Van Devere, Tony Musante. Scott's screen presence is the only decent thing in this chase entry about a retired get-away driver (Scott) who comes back to help a hot-shot hood escape from the police in Spain. John Huston, who was the original director, escaped after a brief spell behind the cameras, and was replaced by the plodding Richard Fleischer. (100 mins.)

Last Safari, The (Great Britain, 1967)**½ Gabriella Licudi, Johnny Sekka, Stewart Granger, Kaz Garas. Safari guide (Stewart Granger) antagonized by a playboy (Kaz Garas), with thrilling African scenery atoning for the lack of plot and a subpar performance from Garas. (Dir: Henry Hathaway, 110 mins.)

Last Summer (1969)**** Barbara Hershey, Richard Thomas, Bruce Davison, Cathy Burns. Perceptive, beautifully acted drama about the experiences of four teenagers during a summer on Long Island's Fire Island. Beautiful, restrained screenplay by Eleanor Perry based on the novel by Evan Hunter. The performances are uniformly fine, and Cathy Burns in particular is marvelous. Alternately funny, poignant, and chilling, it's been sensitively directed by Frank Perry. Powerful finale. (Dir: Frank Perry, 97 mins.)

Last Sunset, The (1961)** Kirk Douglas, Rock Hudson, Dorothy Malone, Joseph Cotten, Carol Lynley. Drifter pursued by a lawman arrives at the ranch of an old sweetheart. Combination of "Rawhide" and "Peyton Place," really gets the emotional relationships a-churning; more silly than dramatic, overwritten, overdirected, overacted. (Dir: Robert Aldrich, 112 mins.)

Last Survivors, The (MTV 1975)* Martin Sheen, Diane Baker, Christopher George, Anne Francis. (Dir: Lee H. Katzin, 89 mins.)

Last Tango in Paris (Italy-France, 1972)****

Marlon Brando, Maria Schneider, Jean-Pierre Leaud. This is, in many ways, a remarkable film, but you won't know why unless you manage to see this much publicized pioneering work unedited on pay cable or some late-evening non-network broadcast. Brando plays a middle-aged American who meets Schneider, a young French girl, while he's apartment hunting. Quickly and silently, they make love. There are other surprises and many revealing moments throughout the rest of the film. (One of the few widely distributed films, incidentally, that clearly depicts anal intercourse.) One critic called "Tango" not a sex film; yet it is the first sex film. Brando gives one of his most moving performances of the decade, which, considering how many terrible films he's appeared in, doesn't sound like much of a compliment, but he remains a very great actor. Director Bernardo Bertolucci also collaborated on the original screenplay. (Dir: Bernardo Bertolucci, 129 mins.)

Last Ten Days, The (Germany, 1956)***½ Oskar Werner, Albin Skoda. A tight, gripping, detailed depiction of the last ten days of Adolph Hitler. Excellent portrayal by Oskar Werner. (Dir: G. W. Pabst, 113 mins.)

Last Time I Saw Archie, The (1961)** Robert Mitchum, Jack Webb, Martha Hyer, France Nuyen. Weak service comedy about a fast-talking "gold brick" and his less confident side-kick, played by Robert Mitchum and Jack Webb, respectively, (Dir: Jack Webb, 98 mins.)

Last Time I Saw Paris, The (1954)**½ Elizabeth Taylor, Van Johnson, Donna Reed, Walter Pidgeon. F. Scott Fitzgerald's short story "Babylon Revisited" is expanded and glossed over in this sumptuous but overly dramatic film. Miss Taylor is as gorgeous as always as Johnson's true love and Donna Reed registers strongly in a climactic scene with Johnson. (Dir: Richard Brooks, 116 mins.)

Last Train from Bombay (1952)** Jon Hall, Lisa Ferraday. An American diplomat gets involved with the intrigues of Bombay. Nothing new in this tired plot. (Dir: Fred F. Sears, 72 mins.)

Last Train from Gun Hill (1959)**½ Kirk Douglas, Anthony Quinn, Earl Holliman, Carolyn Jones. All the action comes at the end of this deliberately paced western drama about a law officer who tries to bring the young killer of his wife to justice. The hitch is the young killer's father and the lawman were the best of friends at one time. Builds to okay payoff. (Dir: John Sturges, 94 mins.)

Last Tycoon, The (1976)**½ Robert De Niro, Tony Curtis, Ingrid Boulting, Robert Mitchum, Jeanne Moreau. Rewarding adaptation of F. Scott Fitzgerald's unfinished tragedy about Hollywood and its movie moguls of the late '20s and '30s. The character of Monroe Stahr is clearly based on the legendary movie producer Irving Thalberg, Robert De Niro is remarkably effective, capturing Stahr's power and influence in a low-key, restrained, subtly shaded performance. But Boulting is lackluster as the heroine. Faithful, skillful screenplay by Harold Pinter. (125 mins.)

Last Valley, The (Great Britain, 1971)** Michael Caine, Omar Sharif, Florinda Bolkan, Nigel Davenport, Arthur O'Connell. Scenery steals the show in this misguided but not altogether uninteresting allegorical adventure epic. The tail end of the Thirty Years War, circa 1641, is the setting for a group of strangers meeting in a hidden valley, where life is tranquil and untouched by the chaos of war. Captain Michael Caine brings his troops into the Eden and meets runaway philosophy professor Omar Sharif. Confusing accents, sophomoric dialogue and a confused plot sabotage the promising premise. Produced, directed and written by James Clavell, bases on the novel by J. B. Pick. Filmed in England and Austria (Dir: James Clavell, 127 mins.)

Last Voyage, The (1960)**½ Robert Stack, Dorothy Malone, Edmond O'Brien, George Sanders. Suspense drama about a liner ripped by an explosion, the efforts of the passengers and crew to abandon ship. Stretches things a bit too far at times, but the sinking scenes are the real thing, quite fascinating. (Dir: Andrew L. Stone, 91 mins.)

Last Wagon, The (1956)**½ Richard Widmark, Felicia Farr, Nick Adams. Tough leader brings a wagon train through perilous country. Okay western, but good cast deserves better. (Dir: Delmer Daves, 99 mins.)

Last Waltz, The (West Germany, 1958)*½ Eva Bartok, Curt Jurgens. (Dir: Arthur Maria Rabenalt, 92 mins.)

Last Waltz, The (1978)**** The Band, Neil Diamond, Bob Dylan, Joni Mitchell, Eric Clapton, Ringo Starr. Director Martin Scorsese, whatever his failings, can never be impersonal, and this elaborate fantasy is anything but a "rockumentary" of the farewell performance of the Band at Winterland in San Francisco. (115 mins.)

Last Warning, The (1938)*** Preston Foster, Frances Robinson. Above average mystery with amusing dialogue. Private detective is hired to catch a kidnapper who calls himself "The Eye." (Dir: Al Rogell, 70 mins.)

Last Wave, The (Australia, 1977)***½ Richard Chamberlain, David Gulpilil, Olivia Hamnett. Director Peter Weir's disquieting mood piece about an Australian lawyer who takes a pro bono assignment defending some aborigines charged with ritual murder. Despite some obscure claptrap, the movie is eerily effective and impeccably controlled. (106 mins.)

Last Woman on Earth, The (1960)** Antony Carbone, Betsy Jones-Moreland. Moderately entertaining film about the

last 3 people left on earth after fallout does everyone else in. The actors are better than the script and the on-location photography in Puerto Rico enhances the film. (Dir: Roger Corman, 71 mins.)

Last Year at Marienbad (France-Italy, 1961)***½ Delphine Seyrig, Giorgio Albertazzi. This is a fascinating, elusive film that was hailed by international critics when it first appeared and has been puzzling and satisfying audiences since that time. Well photographed symbolic, allegorical drama of a trio at a forlorn spa, and the attempts of a man to lure a mysterious woman away with him. A difficult multi-leveled arty entry that is worth the attention of serious discriminating film enthusiasts. (Dir: Alain Resnais, 93 mins.)

L'Atalante (France, 1934)**** Michel Simon, Dita Parlo, Jean Daste. A surrealist masterpiece by the great director Jean Vigo, who died and was buried the same day the film opened. Vigo united realism with poetry in this story of a barge captain (Daste) and the peasant girl he marries (Parlo). (89 mins.)

Late George Apley, The (1947)*** Ronald Colman, Peggy Cummins. J. P. Marquand's pungent satire on stuffy Boston society emerges on the screen as a pleasing family comedy, milder than "Life With Father" and not half as good. (Dir: Joseph L. Mankiewicz, 98 mins.)

Late, Great Planet Earth, The (1977)½ Orson Welles, Hal Lindsey. Narrated by Welles. Sophomoric rubbish about the imminent end of the world. Based on the book by Hal Lindsey, who coauthored the disagreeable screenplay. (Dir: Robert Amram, 86 mins.)

Late Show, The (1977)**** Art Carney, Lily Tomlin, Howard Duff, Bill Macy. A sardonic, affectionate paean to the private-eye genre flicks of the 40's and 50's. It benefits greatly from a touching, nicely underplayed stint by Art Carney playing a washed-up, aging private eye determined to solve one tantalizing biggie. The major credit for the success of the film goes to Robert Benton who not only wrote the wise, knowing original screenplay but makes a most impressive directorial debut as well. Tomlin starts out as Carney's client but soon turns into a dizzy sidekick. They are delicious together. If this occasionally seems like a Robert Altman film, it's because it almost is—he produced this deft winner. (Dir: Robert Benton, 94 mins.)

Lathe of Heaven, The (MTV 1980)*** Bruce Davidson, Kevin Conway. A Public Television cerebral sci-fi yarn set in the not-too-distant future. Davidson, who is plagued by the fact that his dreams come true, must go to a Voluntary Therapy Clinic, where his therapist (Conway) tries to use the young man's power to build a near-utopian world. Of course, it all backfires. Confusing climactic scenes are open to interpretation by the viewer. From the novel by Ursula K. LeGuin. (Dirs: David Loxton, Fred Barzyk, 120 mins.)

Latin Lovers (1953)** Lana Turner, Ricardo Montalban, John Lund. Lana, a very rich girl, arrives in Brazil for a rest and ends up being chased by a dashing rancher, Ricardo. Lana and Ricardo make a torrid pair of "Latin Lovers," but the rest is tepid. (Dir: Mervyn Le Roy, 104 mins.)

L'Atlantide (Germany, 1932)***½ Brigitte Helm. The English-language version of director G. W. Pabst's rare film, adapted from Pierre Benoit's novel "The Lost City of Atlantis" and somehow transposed to the Sahara. Pabst's direction is lucid and psychologically incisive. (90 mins.)

L'Attentat—See: **French Conspiracy, The**

Laughing Policeman, The (1973)**½ Walter Matthau, Lou Gossett, Bruce Dern. Award-winning thriller by Per Wahloo and Maj Sjowall is transplanted from Stockholm to San Francisco in a tense, diffuse film directed by the unsteady Stuart Rosenberg. Forceful work by Matthau and Gosset, and Dern turns in one of his most accomplished, detailed, interpretations. (112 mins.)

Laughter in Paradise (Great Britain, 1951)**** Alastair Sim, Joyce Grenfell, Audrey Hepburn (first major role). A vastly amusing British comedy, blessed with a delightful Michael Pertwee script, about a prankster who leaves his heirs a fortune if they discharge amiably diabolical tasks. Sim tries to get himself arrested, while his fiancée (Joyce Grenfell) is a WAAF described as "an officer and a gentleman." First-rate cast with great depth. (Dir: Mario Zampi, 93 mins.)

Laura (1944)**** Dana Andrews, Gene Tierney, Clifton Webb, Vincent Price, Judith Anderson. Otto Preminger's direction combines a coldly objective temperament and a masterful narrative sense to turn this classical '40's melodrama into something as haunting as its famous theme (by David Raksin). (88 mins.)

Lavender Hill Mob, The (Great Britain, 1951)**** Alec Guinness, Stanley Holloway. A mild-mannered bank employee evolves a fool-proof plan, he thinks, to make away with an armored car gold shipment. Hilarious comedy, fun all the way, another triumph for Guinness. Audrey Hepburn in a bit. Oscar, Best Story and Screenplay (T.E.B. Clarke). (Dir: Charles Crichton, 82 mins.)

L'Avventura (Italy-France, 1960)**** Monica Vitti, Gagriele Ferzetti, Lea Massari. Director Michelangelo Antonioni's studied, enormously perceptive film about empty relationships in an unfeeling world. Story superficially concerns the disappearance of a girl, and the search for her by her lover and her best friend. This is one of Miss Vitti's best performances. The slow pace of the film contributes to its overall impact. (Dir: Michelangelo Antonioni, 145 mins.)

Law, The (MTV 1974)**** Judd Hirsch, John Beck. Here's a rarity . . . an excellent TV film which graphically depicts the everyday workings of the public defender's role in Los Angeles. This is not an ordinary cops-and-crooks yarn with pat conclusions built into the script, but a true-to-life look at a deputy public defender who accidentally latches on to some vital information which could crack a bizarre, unsolved murder case. The first third sets up the job of the public defender, and Judd Hirsch, as Murray Stone, creates a full-blown character who never lets up in his intensity, giving the film its chief interest and appeal. Other performances are also first-rate and the story keeps you riveted from start to finish. (Dir: John Badham, 124 mins.)

Law and Disorder (Great Britain, 1958)*** Michael Redgrave, Robert Morley. Two of England's top theatrical and movie names make this comedy worth your attention. Plot concerns a retired crook who can't seem to stay far enough away from trouble. (Dir: Charles Crichton, 76 mins.)

Law and Disorder (1975)*** Carroll O'Connor, Ernest Borgnine, Karen Black. O'Connor and Borgnine are two lower-middle-class development dwellers who organize a civilian police force with comic and tragic results. Director Ivan Passer doesn't quite seem to know precisely where the film is (though he knows where he wants it to end up). (102 mins.)

Law and Jake Wade, The (1958)**½ Robert Taylor, Richard Widmark, Patricia Owens. Good western. Taylor is well cast as a former outlaw turned marshal in a town in New Mexico. His old buddy, played with all the stops pulled, by Richard Widmark, pops up and things change. The action sequences are excitingly staged. (Dir: John Sturges, 86 mins.)

Law and Order (1953)** Ronald Reagan, Dorothy Malone. Customary western story about the retired U. S. Marshal who couldn't hang up his holster for any length of time. Rather ponderously paced. (Dir: Nathan Juran, 80 mins.)

Law and Order (1969)***½ Documentary essay by Frederick Wiseman about the police force in Kansas City is a compassionate statement about the sometimes dangerous and always delicate task of being a policeman, and the fact that policemen, like the rest of us, are sometimes humane, sometimes cruel, impatient, etc. There's one particularly notable sequence as a truculent, black male teenager is manacled after creating a commotion in an apartment house and how he tries, successfully, to antagonize his white captors while waiting to be taken to the police station. Many viewers will understand why filmmaker Wiseman feels that being a policeman is a difficult and often undesirable job. Also several vivid sequences where ordinary citizens brutalize each other. Another valuable Wiseman

381

study of American institutions. (Dir: Frederick Wiseman, 81 mins.)

Law and Order (MTV 1976)**½ Darren McGavin, Keir Dullea, Robert Reed, James Olson, Teri Garr. Excessively long TV drama based on Dorothy Uhnak's best-seller about a New York Irish family of cops. With abundant use of flashbacks, the capable McGavin displays authority and stubbornness portraying the young and middle-aged cop, Brian O'Malley, warts and all, as he rises in the ranks. While the film concentrates on corruption within the force, its aim is to show policemen as human beings with normal weaknesses, such as an inability to communicate with their kids. (Dir: Marvin J. Chomsky, 144 mins.)

Law Is the Law, The (France-Italy, 1958)**½ Fernandel, Toto. A broad comedy tailored to the talents of France's top comedian, Fernandel, and Italy's top clown, Toto. Each represents opposite sides of the law and it's a tug-of-war all the way. (Dir: Christian-Jaque, 103 mins.)

Law of the Land, The (MTV 1976)* Jim Davis, Barbara Parkins, Glenn Corbett, Andrew Prine, Moses Gunn, Don Johnson, Cal Bellini, Charlie Martin Smith, Nicholas Hammond. (Dir: Virgil Vogel, 98 mins.)

Law of the Lawless (1964)*½ Dale Robertson, Yvonne DeCarlo, William Bendix, Bruce Cabot, Arlen Richard. (Dir: William F. Claxton, 87 mins.)

Law vs. Billy the Kid, The (1954)** Scott Brady, Betta St. John. Another version on the notorious career of Billy the Kid and his good friend Pat Garrett. Nothing new about this Western. (Dir: William Castle, 73 mins.)

Law West of Tombstone (1938)*** Harry Carey, Tim Holt. Ex-outlaw moves into a new town and establishes law and order. Above-average western has a good cast, better story than usual. (Dir: Glenn Tryon, 80 mins.)

Lawless, The (1950)***½ Macdonald Carey, Gail Russell, John Sands. A hard-hitting and gripping story of bigotry against the Mexican-American fruit pickers in California and a crusading newspaperman's fight against it. Well acted. Tab Hunter's first. (Dir: Joseph Losey, 83 mins.)

Lawless Breed, The (1953)** Rock Hudson, Julia Adams. Ordinary western fare with Hudson playing a marked man who finally stops running and serves a long prison term so that he can end his days a free man. Some action but mostly talk. (Dir: Raoul Walsh, 83 mins.)

Lawless Street, A (1955)*** Randolph Scott, Angela Lansbury. Randolph Scott as the marshal has a hard job cleaning up the town of Medicine Bend. Gunplay wins the day. (Dir: Joseph H. Lewis, 78 mins.)

Lawman (1971)** Burt Lancaster, Robert Ryan, Lee J. Cobb, Sheree North, Robert Duvall. The lawman is Lancaster riding into town to arrest cowman Cobb and his

boys for the accidental shooting of an old man. A lot of gore. Good cast wasted on a no-talent director, Michael Winner. (99 mins.)

Lawrence of Arabia (Great Britain, 1962)**** Peter O'Toole, Omar Sharif, Alec Guinness, Anthony Quinn, Jose Ferrer, Jack Hawkins. Director David Lean's marvelous Academy Award-winning spectacle about the legendary British officer and his exploits, military and non-military, in Palestine circa WW I. A remarkable film on many counts: screenwriter Robert Bolt's intelligent screenplay, Peter O'Toole portraying Lawrence making a stunning starring film debut and capturing many of the nuances and character subtleties of this complex homosexual hero; Lean's directorial work and certainly the cinematography. Try if you can to see this film in a **theater** before you watch it on TV. Lean and his colleagues capture the awsome beauty of the desert as it has never been shown before in this kind of a dramatic film. Even on your small-screen TV, however, this is a treat for the eye and ear, and the supporting cast is flawless. (Dir: David Lean, 222 mins.)

Lawyer, The (1970)***½ Barry Newman, Diana Muldaur. A brash, no-holds-barred performance by Newman as a small-town lawyer trying to make it to the top with a local murder case that gets a lot of national attention is the main lure of this film. Loosely based on the true-life murder trial of Dr. Sam Sheppard, the drama focuses more on the attorney than the defendant. In addition, Miss Muldaur has some good scenes as the young lawyer's lovely wife. Character of Petrocelli, Newman's TV series, originated here. (Dir: Sidney J. Furie, 120 mins.)

Lay that Rifle Down (1955)*½ Judy Canova, Robert Lowery. (Dir: Charles Lamont, 70 mins.)

Lazarus Syndrome, The (MTV 1979)**½ Louis Gossett, Jr., Ronald Hunter, E. G. Marshall. In this pilot, Gossett plays a dedicated, compassionate doctor in a major hospital who joins forces with an ex-newspaperman patient (Hunter) to expose the irresponsibility of a highly respected surgeon-administrator. The best scenes are between Gossett and Hunter. (Dir: Jerry Thorpe, 78 mins.)

Le Beau Serge (France, 1958)***½ Jean-Claude Brialy, Gerard Blain, Bernadette Lafont. About a young man who goes back from a city to his own village to help a friend. This companion piece to "Les Cousins" is the first feature directed by Claude Chabrol—the first film of the New Wave. This film is very Catholic in theme and quite controlled in its visual style; it explores the relationships between urban and rural youth in a way that imbues their conflicts with significance beyond the strictures of a situation. (93 mins.)

Le Bonheur (France, 1965)***½ Jean-

Claude Drouot, Claire Drouot, Marie-France Boyer. Director Agnes Varda's self-consciously amoral essay on the nature of happiness, in which an apparently contented family man causes his wife's suicide and goes on living contentedly with his mistress. (87 mins.)

Le Boucher, (France, 1971)**** Stephane Audran, Jean Yanne, Antonio Passallia. Director Claude Chabrol's finest film is set in a French village and tells of a self-possessed schoolteacher (Audran) and the simple butcher (Yanne) who loves her, set against the background of a series of brutal murders in the area. Both suspenseful and serene. (93 mins.)

Le Chagrin et la Pitié—See: **Sorrow and the Pity, The**

Le Distrait—See: **Daydreamer, The**

Le Mans (1971)** Steve McQueen. Racing fans will appreciate this excitingly photographed account of the famous 24-hour Le Mans endurance race and the participants of the annual event. Steve McQueen, who raced in real life, looks right at home in the role of a determined American out to win the big one despite some near-fatal mishaps in his other attempts. There's virtually no plot or dialogue other than in the time-out sequences, but the racing footage is the thing here. Incorporates real footage from the 1969 and 1970 Le Mans races. Repetitive for non-racing freaks. (Dir: Lee H. Katzin, 106 mins.)

Le Sex Shop (France, 1973)**½ Claude Berri, Juliet Berto, Nathalie Delon. Cute, cute, cute. Berri directed and stars in this episodic little farce about a normal bookstore proprietor who goes into the Weird Harold business to avoid bankruptcy and finds his initiation into the world of kinky sex to be more than he can handle. (92 mins.)

Leadbelly (1976)**½ Roger E. Mosley, James E. Brodhead, John McDonald. Mosley gives an impressive impersonation in the Gordon Parks, Sr., dramatization-direction of the life of the legendary bluesman. Depicts a whole lot of fighting, drinking, and singing while maintaining a curious silence on Leadbelly's concert career and the co-opting of his music. The certainly white, presumably liberal, hand of producer David Frost is painfully in evidence. (121 mins.)

League of Gentlemen, The (Great Britain, 1960)**** Jack Hawkins, Richard Attenborough, Nigel Patrick. Fine blend of comedy and suspense, as a retired ex-army officer recruits some of his former men to pull off a big robbery. Writing shows much wit, style—performances excellent, direction perceptive. (Dir: Basil Dearden, 114 mins.)

Learning Tree, The (1969)**½ Kyle Johnson, Alex Clarke, Estelle Evans. Based on his autobiographical novel, director Gordon Parks, Sr.'s film was the first black movie to be backed by a Hollywood major. Not surprisingly, it's conventional and rather toothless—a lyrical look at growing up black and poor. (107 mins.)

Lease of Life (Great Britain, 1955)***½ Robert Donat, Kay Walsh, Denholm Elliott, Adrienne Corri. Moving drama, superbly acted, as always, by the late Robert Donat. About a dying vicar in a small parish. (Dir: Charles French, 93 mins.)

Leather Boys, The (Great Britain, 1964)***½ Rita Tushingham, Dudley Sutton. Moving drama of teenager who marries a serious auto mechanic and then begins to cheat on him. The plot is minor, but the characters are touching. (Dir: Sidney J. Furie, 103 mins.)

Leather Saint, The (1956)** John Derek, Paul Douglas, Cesar Romero. Young minister becomes a fighter to aid polio victims. Undistinguished boxing drama has all the familiar plot ingredients. (Dir: Alvin Ganzer, 86 mins.)

Leave 'Em Laughing (MTV 1981)***½ Mickey Rooney, Anne Jackson, Red Buttons, William Windom. When Mickey Rooney turns on the juices look out! The Mick is devastating playing Chicago clown Jack Thum, a supermarket children's performer who adopts orphans and rejected kids. Whether Mickey the clown is telling corny stories to sad-faced kids, or getting drunk over the news he has cancer, Rooney has his audience by the throat, with nary a word about overdoing the sentimentality. He is surrounded by old pros—Anne Jackson as worried wife Shirlee, Red Buttons playing a fellow hospital patient, Elisha Cook as a failed clown who runs a bar and William Windom, a clown from the big top. This is all Rooney, a rare chance to see Mickey at the top of his game. (Dir: Jackie Cooper, 104 mins.)

Leave Her to Heaven (1945)*** Gene Tierney, Cornel Wilde, Jeanne Crain, Vincent Price, Mary Phillips. American family melodrama at its most neurotic, with Tierney as a gorgeous nut case so intent on securing her husband's attentions that she murders his crippled brother and throws herself downstairs to miscarry her baby, which might compete for her husband's affection. Trashy movie revels in striking imagery and no-holds-barred excess. A lush score by Alfred Newman. (Dir: John M. Stahl, 111 mins.)

Leave It to Blondie (1945)**½ Penny Singleton, Arthur Lake, Chick Chandler, Marjorie Weaver. Dagwood finds himself among the finalists in a song-writing contest, although he didn't write it. Entertaining comedy in the "Blondie" series. (Dir: Abby Berlin, 75 mins.)

Leave Yesterday Behind (MTV 1978)**½ John Ritter, Carrie Fisher. Ritter and Fisher are attractive in a romantic drama where Ritter plays a college polo player who is permanently crippled during a championship game. Bitterness engulfs him until Fisher's attention turns out to be good medicine. (Dir: Richard Michaels, 104 mins.)

Lebanese Mission, The (France, 1956)**½ Jean-Claude Pascal, Jean Servais, Gianna Maria Canale. English-dubbed. Countess becomes involved with two prospectors who have discovered a uranium lode. Occasionally interesting melodrama. Well acted. Alternate title: Lady of Lebanon Castle. (Dir: Richard Pottier, 90 mins.)

Leda—See: Web of Passion

Leech Woman, The (1960)** Coleen Gray, Grant Williams. Scientist's wife discovers the secret of perpetual youth and begins to bump off unsuspecting males for their hormones. Well, that's one way to get them. (Dir: Edward Dein, 77 mins.)

Left Hand of God, The (1955)**½ Humphrey Bogart, Gene Tierney, Lee J. Cobb. Slow-moving adventure yarn made interesting by the performances of the male stars. Bogart is an American who gets caught up in the private wars of a renegade Chinese warlord, played with much bravado by Cobb. (Dir: Edward Dmytryk, 87 mins.)

Left-Handed Gun, The (1958)***½ Paul Newman, John Dehner, Hurd Hatfield. Director Arthur Penn's first feature film was based on Gore Vidal's TV play about Billy the Kid, and although it is ragged cinema, it is strikingly original. Newman plays Billy as a drooling mental defective who becomes enmeshed in a myth-making vise that is both his immortality and his destruction. The film has a shaggy sense of harsh absurdism, with unpredictable, unnerving violence. (102 mins.)

Left, Right and Center (Great Britain, 1960)**½ Alastair Sim, Ian Carmichael, Patricia Bredin. Television personality runs for office on the Conservative ticket and is opposed by a pretty young Laborite—love blossoms. Satire on British politics has its moments, but some of the punch may be lost outside the Commonwealth. (Dir: Sidney Gilliatt, 100 mins.)

Legend of Boggy Creek, The (1973)* (Dir: Charles B. Pierce, 90 mins.)

Legend of Hell House, The (Great Britain, 1973)***½ Clive Revill, Roddy McDowall, Pamela Franklin, Gayle Hunnicutt. Well-acted, suspenseful psychic tale. It is believed that Hell House holds the key to determining if there is life after death. A psychologist (Revill), a mental and a physical medium (Franklin and McDowall), and others set out to explore the house and its secrets. One sequence, a séance conducted in the house, is particularly chilling. Written by Richard Matheson, based on his novel "Hell House." (Dir: John Hough, 93 mins.)

Legend of Lizzie Borden, The (MTV 1975)*** Elizabeth Montgomery, Ed Flanders, Fritz Weaver. Carefully handled version of the famous Lizzie Borden murders, casts no new light on the Massachusetts legend, but entertains, in its fashion. Montgomery gives a tour-de-force

performance playing the celebrated ax-murderess, and capable Ed Flanders scores in the chief supporting role of the prosecuting district attorney. The sets and background detail are worthy of a theatrical feature, and the pacing is tight. (Dir: Paul Wendkos, 100 mins.)

Legend of Lylah Clare, The (1968)**½ Kim Novak, Peter Finch, Ernest Borgnine. Uneven but interesting old-fashioned melodrama about the movies and those by-now-familiar stereotypes who live, eat and breathe film-making. Kim Novak is the sexy starlet who resembles a flamboyant star of the thirties, Lylah Clare (who died mysteriously and tragically on her wedding night) and gets a crack at playing Lylah in a biographical film. Peter Finch is Lylah's real-life director-husband and history repeats itself as he falls for her reincarnation. A great deal of this is pure pap, but there are glimpses of good film-making and Peter Finch's wonderfully tormented characterization. Based on a 1963 TV drama of the same name, directed by Franklin ("Patton") J. Schaffner, which starred Tuesday Weld and Alfred Drake. (Dir: Robert Aldrich, 130 mins.)

Legend of Sleepy Hollow, The (MTV 1980)** Jeff Goldblum, Dick Butkus, Paul Sand, Meg Foster. Another version—a poor one—of Washington Irving's classic story of Ichabod Crane (Goldblum) and the headless horseman. Gary Coleman is an annoying host. (Dir: Henning Schellerup, 104 mins.)

Legend of the Golden Gun (MTV 1979)** Jeff Osterhage, Hal Holbrook, Carl Franklin, Keir Dullea. Western about a farmer who turns into a deadly shot in order to seek revenge against Quantrill and his raiders. Osterhage plays hero John Colton, but the major attraction of the film is Holbrook as fast-draw John Hammer, who teaches Colton the tricks of the trade. Playing fast and loose with history, the story has Colton meeting General Custer, and other legends along the trail of revenge. (Dir: Alan J. Levi, 104 mins.)

Legend of the Lone Ranger, The (1981)** Klinton Spillsbury, Michael Horse, Jason Robards, Christopher Lloyd. Everybody tried very hard and the film would be passable, but everything surrounding the story is wrong, wrong, wrong; there's an effort to produce operatic gravity with operatic music, and a too breezy convention about the film. It lacks conviction and, most crucially, any discernible point. It's a picturesque bore. Klinton Spillsbury (the Lone Ranger) was dubbed; one suspects he was as bad as the dubbing was lousy. The stunts, however, are quite impressive, and Jason Robards does a funny turn as President Grant (holding court in a train car that would have been a *People* magazine dream item circa 1870). Michael Horse and Christopher Lloyd are demented arch-criminals. The films' right-wing

384

stances would be reprehensible if the film had any punch; instead, the audience-pandering Reagan-age homilies are so mechanical as to seem insincere. (Dir: William A. Frakar, 98 mins.)

Legend of the Lost (1957)**½ John Wayne, Sophia Loren, Rossano Brazzi. A powerhouse trio of stars and some excellent photography are the only plus factors of this sprawling, over-produced adventure epic. By the way, Miss Loren has come a long way in the acting department since this opus. (Dir: Henry Hathaway, 109 mins.)

Legend of Valentino, The (MTV 1975)** Franco Nero, Suzanne Pleshette, Judd Hirsch, Yvette Mimieux. Highly romanticized version of the life and loves of Rudolph Valentino, the legendary silent film star! Nero plays the Italian emigrant who rose to Hollywood stardom, and the best thing that can be said about his performance in this cliché-ridden script is that at least he's authentically Italian. According to writer-director Melville Shavelson, Valentino was an unhappy man who never enjoyed his success and became the victim of a line of heartless women, ruthless producers and over-sexed fans. Can be enjoyed on the same level as a fan magazine. (Dir: Melville Shavelson, 98 mins.)

Legendary Champions, The (1968)***½ Documentary of heavyweight boxing champs from John L. Sullivan to Gene Tunney. A natural for ring devotees; others will find it absorbing too. (Dir: Harry Chapin, 77 mins.)

Legion of the Doomed (1958)* Bill Williams, Dawn Richard. (Dir: Thor Brooks, 75 mins.)

Legions of the Nile (Italy-France-Spain, 1960)** Linda Cristal, Georges Marchal. Fast-paced, superficial treatment of Antony and Cleopatra features two-dimensional plot of action and amour. (Dir: Vittorio Cottafavi, 90 mins.)

Lemon Drop Kid, The (1951)*** Bob Hope, Marilyn Maxwell. Hope's delivery makes a natural for this role of a fast talking race track bum who has to come up with a bundle he owes the syndicate or else. The laughs are all there. Remake of the 1934 film with Lee Tracy. (Dir: Sidney Lanfield, 91 mins.)

Lemonade Joe (Czechoslovakia, 1964)*** Karel Fiala, Olga Schoberova. Wild spoof of Yank westerns with the usual pure hero, purer heroine, dirty varmints. At first it's frantically funny, then the hoke palls; but it's certainly a novelty and good fun. Dubbed-in English. (Dir: Oldrich Lipsky, 84 mins.)

Lenny (1974)**** Dustin Hoffman, Valerie Perrine, Jan Miner. Dustin Hoffman's bravura portrayal of the tortured, self-destructive, brilliantly inventive comic Lenny Bruce is enough of a reason to see "Lenny," which garnered several Academy Award nominations, including

ones for Hoffman, Perrine and director Bob Fosse. Drug-addict Lenny Bruce, who died in 1966 after being harassed by the police and courts for years, has been the subject of plays, books and films. This film has the advantage of using material from Bruce's trials which are "performed" by Hoffman as part of his nightclub act. Valerie Perrine is sexy, sad and funny as Lenny's suffering wife. Hoffman is a marvel—overlook some of the weak points and watch dazzling Dustin. (111 mins.)

Lenny Bruce (1967)**** A valuable icon of the 1960's, and this brilliant, visionary, self-destructive, put-upon comedy genius. This is the only film Bruce ever made, an unedited filmed record of a San Francisco nightclub performance in August of 1965. The photography is uneven, as are some of Bruce's routines, but the best of it is astonishing, and it remains the best record of this tormented soul's inspired, bizarre, irreverent and sometimes grotesque humor. Bruce discusses savagely and inventively his trial in New York State for having performed obscene material. Alternate title: **The Lenny Bruce Performance Film.** (Produced by John Magnuson, 68 mins.)

Lenny Bruce Performance Film, The—See: **Lenny Bruce**

Lenny Bruce Without Tears (1975)*** A documentary about the comedian Lenny Bruce, who died in 1966, written and directed by Fred Baker. It contains clips from kinescopes of old Bruce TV appearances, interviews with Bruce himself, and people like Kenneth Tynan and Mort Sahl talking about Bruce and his influence on American comedy and society. Valuable sociological record provides a few insights and some Bruce-generated laughs. (Dir: Fred Baker, 78 mins.)

Leopard, The (U.S.-Italy, 1963)***½ Burt Lancaster, Claudia Cardinale, Alain Delon, Paolo Stoppa. The Lampedusa novel, sumptuously realized as elegy by director Luchino Visconti. Lancaster limns the aging aristocrat who knows that his days are numbered after the risorgimento; Delon is his son who flirts with revolution. Among the most poised of all historical films. *The Leopard*, rarely shown at full length, unspools as a meticulously detailed emotional experience. Music by Nino Rota. Note: The uncut version (above) is most unlikely to be on TV. Unfortunately the dubbing in English is terrible. (205 mins.)

Leopard Man, The (1943)***½ Margo, Dennis O'Keefe, Jean Brooks. Excellent low-budget thriller from the Val Lewton stable, directed with savage poeticism by Jacques Tourneur. About a series of murders attributed to an escaped leopard, from the novel "Black Alibi" by Cornell Woolrich. (66 mins.)

Lepke (1974)*½ Tony Curtis, Anjanette Comer, Michael Callan, Warren Berlinger,

Milton Berle. (Dir: Menahem Golan, 109 mins.)

Les Anges du Péché (France, 1943)*** Jany Holt. The earliest extant film directed by Robert Bresson shows the seeds of his spare, concentrated style in a study of a Dominican nun's obsessive devotion to a female ex-convict who comes to live in her convent. Bresson draws parallels between a life in prison and a life in God, and finds his final image of freedom in a pair of handcuffs. The talky and relatively conventional script by dramatist Jean Giraudoux is balanced by Holt's superbly understated performance as the prisoner. (73 mins.)

Les Carabiniers (France- Italy, 1963)***½ Genevieve Galea, Marino Mase. Ironic, difficult allegory on war which is ultimately worth the trouble necessary to understand it. An important work by one of the masters of movies in the period before he gave up films for polemics. (Dir: Jean-Luc Godard, 80 mins.)

Les Enfants Terribles (France, 1950)**½ Nicole Stephane, Édouard Dermithe, Renée Cosima. Jean-Pierre Melville, selected by Jean Cocteau to direct the film version of his novel, developed a location-based style that strongly influenced the directors of the New Wave generation. The story is typically Cocteau: two adolescents, willfully cutting themselves off from the adult world, bind themselves together through a series of strange, enigmatic games which end in incest and death. (107 mins.)

Les Girls (1957)**** Gene Kelly, Kay Kendall, Mitzi Gaynor, Taina Elg. Very entertaining musical with a talented cast plus a sparkling Cole Porter score. Kelly plays an American hoofer with three beautiful girls in his act. In between musical numbers, he falls in love with his gorgeous co-workers. Kay Kendall steals every scene she's in. A joyous film. (Dir: George Cukor, 114 mins.)

Les Misérables, (1935)**** Fredric March, Charles Laughton, John Beal, Florence Eldridge, Rochelle Hudson, Cedric Hardwicke, John Carradine. From Victor Hugo's classical French novel. Remarkably exciting and moving. Richard Boleslawski directed, and it's just about his most lively work. The performances are searing, with March as Valjean and Laughton as Javert, and Eldridge as the pathetic Fantine. Best of the innumerable versions, including the many French. (108 mins.)

Les Miserables (1952)**½ Michael Rennie, Debra Paget, Robert Newton. Victor Hugo's classic story of an escaped convict and the detective who trails him for a lifetime. Well acted, well enough produced, but there are just too many versions around now, though this isn't a bad one. (Dir: Lewis Milestone, 104 mins.)

Les Miserables (France, 1957)*** Jean Gabin, Bernard Blier, Bourvil. Faithful

adaptation of Victor Hugo's novel of an escaped convict and his relentless police pursuer—so faithful, in fact, that the nearly four-hour version is available in two separate parts. Generally commendable, but doesn't alter the fact that too many versions of this story are already around. This happens to be one of the better ones though. English-dubbing. (Dir: Jean-Paul Le Chanois, 210 mins.)

Les Misérables (MTV 1978)***½ Richard Jordan, Anthony Perkins, John Gielgud, Celia Robson. May be the definitive version of Victor Hugo's classic novel. It's handsomely mounted, filmed for the most part in France, and boasts a screen treatment by John Gay that permits the characterizations to build in depth. Jordan is superb as Jean Valjean, the impoverished man who is imprisoned for stealing a loaf of bread for his sister's starving family. Anthony Perkins is interesting but strained as Inspector Javert, Valjean's nemesis. (Dir: Glenn Jordan, 156 mins.)

Les Visiteurs du Soir (France, 1942)***½ Arletty, Jules Berry, Marie Dea, Alain Cuny, Fernand Ledoux. In the 13th century, the Devil sends his messengers to earth to corrupt and destroy human souls; but one of them is reformed by love. Beautiful, engrossing allegory, Remarkably, this celebration of integrity, fidelity, and resistance was made under the Nazi occupation of France; apparently, the Germans just didn't get it. Very well made on a small budget, but with a grasp of form and style. Arletty is incredibly gorgeous. Alternate title: *The Devil's Envoys*. Written by Jacques prevert, Pierre Laroche. (Dir: Marcel Carné, 110 mins.)

Les Yeux sans Visage—See: **Horror Chamber of Dr. Faustus, The**

Let George Do It (Great Britain, 1940)** George Formby, Phyllis Calvert, Bernard Lee. Several good comic turns in a light spy spoof, as vaudevillian Formby jokes and sings his way past agents of the Third Reich. (Dir: Marcel Varnel, 82 mins.)

Let It Be (Great Britain, 1970)*** John Lennon, Paul McCartney, George Harrison, Ringo Starr. The Beatles pack it in with a sad and wistful record of their final recording sessions. Michael Lindsay-Hogg directed, admirably away from Richard Lester's exuberance. In the Beatles' third and last appearance in a feature film, the music is what matters. Shots of the late John Lennon dancing with his wife Yoko Ono, and George and Ringo playing a few bars of "Octopus Garden." (88 mins.)

Let No Man Write My Epitaph (1960)** Burl Ives, Shelley Winters, James Darren. Badly done sequel to "Knock on Any Door." The performances are on the amateurish side, particularly Shelley Winters, who overacts throughout in the role of a junkie. (Dir: Philip Leacock, 106 mins.)

Let the Good Times Roll (1973)**½ Little

Richard, Bo Diddley, The Shirelles, The Five Satins, Chuck Berry. If you grew up in the 50's with its music blaring in your ear and stacks of 45's spinning in your brain, this nostalgic trip down memory lane, via two filmed concerts of oldies but goodies, will give you a high. Splitscreen devices showing the performers as they were when you were sporting a D.A., upturned collars, pointed shoes, and teased hair, and as they are now (some drastically different), bolsters the endless parade of rock and roll. The lineup of performers includes Little Richard, The Shirelles, The Five Satins, Chuck Berry, Chubby Checker, Fats Domino, Bill Haley and The Comets, and Bo Diddley, among others. (Dirs: Sid Levin, Robert Abel, 99 mins.)

Let Us Live (1939)**½ Henry Fonda, Maureen O'Sullivan. Fiancee of an innocent man about to be executed fights to save his life. Grim, overdone but well-acted drama. (Dir: John Brahm, 70 mins.)

Let's Be Happy (1957)**½ Tony Martin, Vera-Ellen. Vera-Ellen inherits some money and travels to Scotland dancing in the heather all the way. Tony Martin sings. Some lovely on the spot photography. (Dir: Henry Levin, 93 mins.)

Let's Dance (1950)** Fred Astaire, Betty Hutton. Ex-actress and her former partner fight her wealthy mother-in-law when she tries to take away her son. Astaire's superlative dancing gets lost in a sugary, dull plot, and Hutton is hardly his best vis-à-vis in the terpsichore department. (Dir: Norman Z. McLeod, 112 mins.)

Let's Do It Again (1953)**½ Jane Wyman, Ray Milland, Aldo Ray. Footloose comedy about an almost divorced couple and their escapades to make each jealous. Wyman is very funny as the wife. Remake of *The Awful Truth*, 1937. (Dir: Alexander Hall, 95 mins.)

Let's Do It Again (1975)*** Sidney Poitier, Bill Cosby, Calvin Lockhart, John Amos, Jimmie Walker, Ossie Davis, Denise Nicholas, George Foreman. Sequel which is funnier than the original "Uptown Saturday Night." Poitier and Cosby are once again two pals who are involved in shenanigans to raise money for their ailing lodge. This time, Poitier has hypnotic skills which are trained on a puny boxer (hilariously played by Walker) to turn him into a champ. Trouble comes when they confound two gangsters with opposite lifestyles, Amos and Lockhart. High-spirited fun, that might be called a black, lower-middle class version of "The Sting." (Dir: Sidney Poitier, 112 mins.)

Let's Face It (1943)** Bob Hope, Betty Hutton. Undistinguished, but occasionally amusing, Hope vehicle about soldiers who agree to help middle-aged married women avoid becoming lonesome. Complications are obvious, and so is much of the comedy. (Dir: Sidney Lanfield, 76 mins.)

Let's Live a Little (1948)**½ Hedy Lamarr, Robert Cummings. A harassed ad man

falls for a lady psychiatrist, and vice versa. Pleasant romantic comedy. (Dir: Richard Wallace, 85 mins.)

Let's Make It Legal (1951)**½ Claudette Colbert, Macdonald Carey, Marilyn Monroe, Robert Wagner, Zachary Scott. Mildly amusing comedy about a married couple who decide to get a divorce after 20 years of marriage. This throws their children and friends into a frenzy and everyone tries to do his small part in keeping the marriage intact. The cast does well. (Dir: Richard Sale, 77 mins.)

Let's Make Love (1960)**½ Marilyn Monroe, Yves Montand, Tony Randall. The personal appeal of the two stars—Monroe and Montand—should make up for the shortcomings of this lightweight comedy-romance played against a show-business background. Both stars sing a little, act a little and generate a lot of sex appeal. (Dir: George Cukor, 118 mins.)

Let's Make Up (Great Britain, 1955)* Anna Neagle, Errol Flynn, David Farrar. Alternate title: **Lilacs in the Spring.** (Dir: Herbert Wilcox, 94 mins.)

Let's Rock (1958)** Julius La Rosa, Phyllis Newman, Conrad Janis, Paul Anka, Della Reese. Phyllis Newman is the best and only worthwhile thing in this second rate rock 'n roll musical comedy. (Dir: Harry Foster, 79 mins.)

Let's Scare Jessica to Death (1971)** Zohra Lampert, Kevin O'Connor, Mariclaire Costello. Zohra Lampert, an interesting and talented actress, gives this horror yarn whatever allure it has, but alas, it's not enough. Ms. Lampert is Jessica, a former mental patient, who arrives at an old Connecticut house with her husband and their friend, supposedly for a rest. Enter a strange lady. (Dir: John Hancock, 89 mins.)

Let's Switch (MTV 1975)*½ Barbara Feldon, Barbara Eden, George Furth. (Dir: Alan Rafkin, 74 mins.)

Let's Talk About Women (Italy-France, 1964)**** Vittorio Gassman, Eleonora Rossi-Drago, Heidi Strop, Sylva Koscina. A series of sometimes excruciatingly funny vignettes, all of which star Gassman and involve his desire to get into or stay out of bed with some comely wench. The opener, about a gun-slinging stranger making a courtesy call to an isolated farmhouse, is hysterical, and so are a number of the other sketches in this delicious episodic entry. Just sit back and enjoy the almost unending laughs about manners, mores and amour! (Dir: Ettore Scola, 108 mins.)

Letter, The (1940)***½ Bette Davis, Herbert Marshall, James Stephenson, Gale Sondergaard. The height of repressed sexuality onscreen is achieved through the muted tension between Davis and Stephenson in this hothouse drama from W. Somerset Maugham. William Wyler's velvety slick direction obscures the shallowness of the enterprise. Screenplay by Howard Koch. (95 mins.)

Letter for Evie, A (1945)**½ Marsha Hunt, John Carroll, Spring Byington. Fair Grade B film using the familiar plot about the man who sends his handsome friend's picture to the girl he has been courting by mail. Hume Cronyn is excellent as the deceiver. (Dir: Jules Dassin, 89 mins.)

Letter from an Unknown Woman (1948)**** Joan Fontaine, Louis Jourdan, Mady Christians. A breathtaking, bitter, exquisitely orchestrated exploration of love and selfishness. Fontaine has never been better, or lovelier, as the young girl whose lifelong infatuation with a gifted, callow concert pianist (Jourdan) leads to great sorrow. Script by Howard Koch, from the novel by Stefan Zweig. (Dir: Max Ophuls, 89 mins.)

Letter to Three Wives, A (1949)**** Ann Sothern, Linda Darnell, Paul Douglas, Kirk Douglas, Jeanne Crain, and the delectable voice of Celeste Holm. Writer-director Joseph L. Mankiewicz won twin Oscars for this well-constructed suburban comedy-satire about three women who are wickedly advised by a fourth that she has run off with one of their husbands. (102 mins.)

Letters, The (MTV 1973)**½ Barbara Stanwyck, Jane Powell, Dina Merrill, Ida Lupino, Leslie Nielsen. Three soap-operaish short stories are tied together by an old gimmick—a trio of letters that have been lost in the mail for a year, drastically altering the lives of the recipients when delivered. (Dirs: Gene Nelson and Paul Krasny, 73 mins.)

Letters from Frank (MTV 1979)**½ Art Carney, Maureen Stapleton, Mike Farrell, Margaret Hamilton. Always easy to watch, Carney and Stapleton team up for a drama about retirement, with Art chomping at the bit after being replaced by a computer. Hamilton is a delight as the peppery grandmother. (Dir: Edward Parone, 104 mins.)

Letters from Three Lovers (MTV 1973)** June Allyson, Ken Berry, Juliet Mills. Undelivered letters find their way to the addressees a year after they were sent. June Allyson and Robert Sterling share a "brief encounter" and plan to make it a monthly thing, but his letter doesn't reach her in time, etc. Familiar fare! (Dir: John Erman, 72 mins.)

Liane, Jungle Goddess (West Germany, 1956)* Marion Michael, Hardy Kruger. (Dir: Eduard von Borsody, 85 mins.)

Libel (Great Britain, 1959)**½ Olivia de Havilland, Dirk Bogarde, Paul Massie. A wealthy man is accused of being an impostor, sues for libel; some doubt arises in his wife's mind whether or not he's telling the truth. Fairly interesting drama works up good suspense after a slow start. (Dir: Anthony Asquith, 100 mins.)

Libeled Lady (1936)*** Spencer Tracy, Myrna Loy, William Powell, Jean Harlow. A typically overproduced and underdeveloped MGM star vehicle which helps explain why so many great stills and so few good movies came out of that studio in the '30s. Tracy is a newspaper editor trying to pry a scandal out of heiress Loy; Powell and Harlow are bait. A long way from the best of the era's screwball comedies. (Dir: Jack Conway, 98 mins.)

Liberation of L. B. Jones, The (1970)**½ Roscoe Lee Browne, Lola Falana, Anthony Zerbe, Lee J. Cobb, Lee Majors. Tragedy about a black man who divorces his wife for adultery with a white cop. Jesse Hill Ford's novel had real anger, but William Wyler, directing his last feature, wasn't up to such passion. Part of the problem may be the didactic presence of Stirling Silliphant adapting the script. (102 mins.)

License to Kill (France, 1964)*½ Eddie Constantine, Daphne Dayle. (Dir: Henri Decoin, 95 mins.)

Lies My Father Told Me (Canada, 1975)***½ Yossi Yadin, Len Birman, Marilyn Lightstone, Jeffrey Lynas, Ted Allan. A charming, sentimental ethnic memoir about growing up in 1924 in a Jewish "ghetto" in Montreal. It's an autobiographical story of author Ted Allan who wrote the screenplay and also appears as Mr. Baumgarten. Focuses on the relationship of a young boy and his aged grandfather, a robust, free-spirited peddler. A gentle, tender tale suitable for children of all ages. Affectionately directed by Jan Kadar, remembered for his haunting "Shop on Main Street." (102 mins.)

Lieutenant Schuster's Wife (MTV 1972)** Lee Grant. Amateur detective, a New York cop's widow, is determined to clear her husband's good name. In the story, filmed for the most part on New York streets, sleuth Grant runs into the likes of Eartha Kitt at an uptown pool hall, and meets wily Nehemiah Persoff. Miss Grant deserves better. (Dir: David Lowell Rich, 73 mins.)

Lieutenant Wore Skirts, The (1956)**½ Tom Ewell, Sheree North. TV writer gets jealous when his wife is taken back into service. Funny at times, but never quite jells. (Dir: Frank Tashlin, 99 mins.)

Life and Assassination of the Kingfish, The (MTV 1977)*** Edward Asner, Nicholas Pryor, Diane Kagan, Fred Cook. The political saga of Huey P. Long, who rose from small-town lawyer to governor of Louisiana and U.S. Senator, is candidly presented in a well-produced TV feature starring Edward Asner, whose portrayal of the charming rogue who was labeled a demagogue by most of his critics is excellent. Wearing a dark wig and adopting a down-home accent, Asner creates a picture of a man driven by his lust for power, coupled with a strong desire to give the common man a fair shake. Long's personal life is sketchily treated; rather, the film favors the Huey Long who paraded among his puppet-politicians, bending rules and making deals. Though not totally accurate history, the film does spell out the relentless ambition of a man who might have made it to the White House if fate had not intervened in September, 1935, when he was gunned down in Louisiana. (Writer-Dir: Robert Collins, 100 mins.)

Life and Death of Colonel Blimp, The (Great Britain, 1943)**** Roger Livesey, Anton Walbrook, Deborah Kerr. Old-fashioned, pompous British Army officer finds he's out of date when WW II begins. In full-length form, this is a superb portrait of a windbag; a drastically cut version destroys the impact. Color. (Dirs: Michael Powell, Emeric Pressburger, 163 mins.)

Life and Loves of Mozart, The (Germany, 1956)**½ Oskar Werner, Nadja Tiller. The later years of Mozart, his work, and his love for a young singer. Well done but a bit too dramatic in performances. (Dir: Karl Hart, 92 mins.)

Life and Times of Grizzly Adams, The (1974)*½ Dan Haggerty, Marjory Harper, Don Shanks, Lisa Jones. (Dir: Richard Friedenberg, 100 mins.)

Life and Times of Judge Roy Bean, The (1972)** Paul Newman, Anthony Perkins, Ava Gardner, Stacy Keach, Tab Hunter. Director John Huston makes the cardinal error of pontificating over the film's burlesques. The movie huffs and puffs and blows itself down. Paul Newman postures as the self-appointed Texas judge (circa 1880), and the real interest is in the supporting cameos. John Milius penned the screenplay. (124 mins.)

Life at the Top (Great Britain, 1965)**½ Laurence Harvey, Jean Simmons, Honor Blackman. Sequel to the successful "Room at the Top" but not as well done. Has Laurence Harvey repeating his characterization of the opportunist who married the boss' daughter and found true unhappiness. It's competently handled, but too familiar. However, the performances by Harvey and Jean Simmons, as his disappointed wife, are worth watching. (Dir: Ted Kotcheff, 117 mins.)

Life Begins at College (1937)*** Ritz Brothers, Joan Davis, Tony Martin. This zany film will only appeal to the youngsters and the many fans of the Ritz Brothers. It's a crazy football comedy played strictly for slapstick. (Dir: William A. Seiter, 94 mins.)

Life Begins at Eight-thirty (1942)**½ Monty Woolley, Ida Lupino, Cornel Wilde. Well acted but dreary drama of an alcoholic, broken-down actor and his daughter who gives up everything to help him. Too morbid in spite of Woolley's frequent attempts at humor. (Dir: Irving Pichel, 85 mins.)

Life Begins for Andy Hardy (1941)**½ Lewis Stone, Mickey Rooney, Judy Garland. Andy gives New York a fling and he almost misses out on starting college. Wait'll you see the troubles he gets into in the big city. (Dir: George B. Seitz, 100 mins.)

Life for Ruth—See: **Walk in the Shadow**

Life in Emergency Ward 10 (Great Britain, 1959)*½ Michael Craig, Wilfred Hyde White, Dorothy Alison. (Dir: Robert Day, 86 mins.)

Life in the Balance, A (1955)** Ricardo Montalban, Anne Bancroft, Lee Marvin. Despite the good cast, this cheaply made meller about a series of murders and the various suspects generates very little excitement. Mexican locations the chief asset. (Dir: Harry Horner, 74 mins.)

Life of Brian—See: **Monty Python's Life of Brian**

Life of Donizetti (Italy, 1951)** Amadeo Nazzari, Mariella Lotti. The film biography of the great composer of Italian opera. Good operatic sequences sung by Tito Schipa and others, a stilted story. English-dubbed. (Dir: Camillo Mastrocinque, 98 mins.)

Life of Émile Zola (1937)**½ Paul Muni, Joseph Schildkraut. Ho-hum posturing by Muni (as Zola) fails to generate any life in this overstuffed biopic, which is no more palatable for the rightness of its ringing homilies. Schildkraut is the falsely accused Captain Dreyfus. One of Oscar's sadder hours (this won Best Picture). (Dir: William Dieterle, 130 mins.)

Life of Her Own, A (1950)*** Lana Turner, Ray Milland, Tom Ewell, Louis Calhern, Ann Dvorak. Unadulterated soap opera with a shaky script (by Isobel Lennart), but director George Cukor is able to transform it into a drama of some complexity. Turner is surprisingly effective as the farm girl who makes it in the Big Apple as a top model, but Dvorak is the standout in the showy role of an aging model. (108 mins.)

Life of Oharu, The (Japan, 1952)**** Toshiro Mifune, Kinuyo Tanaka. Director Kenji Mizoguchi's masterpiece is resolutely modernist, yet elegantly classical. Tanaka is a samurai girl who descends into prostitution and degradation. (150 mins.)

Life Upside Down (France, 1965)*** Charles Denner, Anna Gaylor. Young Frenchman about to be married causes concern when he suddenly becomes withdrawn, living in another world. English-dubbed drama is a most intriguing study of a man on the verge of insanity but may not be appreciated by all viewers. For those who do, it will prove absorbing, excellently enacted and directed. (Dir: Alain Jessua, 93 mins.)

Life With Blondie (1945)**½ Penny Singleton, Arthur Lake, Ernest Truex. When Daisy becomes a pin-up dog, Blondie and Dagwood have to contend with many inconveniences, including some gangsters. Some good laughs in this entertaining entry in the "Blondie" series. (Dir: Abby Berlin, 75 mins.)

Life with Father (1947)*** William Powell,

Irene Dunne, Elizabeth Taylor, Edmund Gwenn, Zasu Pitts, Martin Milner, Jimmy Lydon. Uncomfortably respectful movie adaptation of Clarence Day's autobiographical play. It's stiff, thin, and sickly charming. Director Michael Curtiz can handle comedy but domestic bliss seems beyond his range. Powell and Dunne are perfectly cast, but the film doesn't work the way it should. (118 mins.)

Life with Henry (1941)****½** Jackie Cooper, Eddie Bracken, Hedda Hopper. Good "Henry Aldrich" comedy as Henry tries to win a trip to Alaska and goes into the soap business. Bracken is a delight as Henry's sidekick. (Dir: Ted Reed, 80 mins.)

Lifeboat (1944)*****½** Tallulah Bankhead, Walter Slezak, William Bendix, John Hodiak, Canada Lee. Director Alfred Hitchcock's briny technical exercise is confined to the boat of the title, with the characters thrashing out the ideological conflicts of WW II as in a John Steinbeck screenplay. Nasty, disquieting, with some political bite. Bankhead has her only substantial movie role. (96 mins.)

Lifeguard (1976)****½** Sam Elliott, Anne Archer, Stephen Young, Parker Stevenson. Aimless movie about a 30-plus-year-old lifeguard in California who thinks the time may have come for him to settle down and live a real life as a car salesman. Sam Elliott is handsome and well-built, but the role doesn't let him go much beyond his handsomeness. Anne Archer has a good scene as his highschool girl friend looking for a rekindling of sorts. A couple of involving sequences. (Dir: Daniel Petrie, 96 mins.)

Light Across the Street (France, 1956)****** Brigitte Bardot, Raymond Pellegrin. An early BB movie before she became the "sex kitten." BB plays the wife of a trucker who switches her affections to a gas station jockey when her husband spends too much time trying to make money. (Dir: Georges Lacombe, 79 mins.)

Light at the Edge of the World, The (U.S.-Spain-Liechtenstein, 1971)***** Kirk Douglas, Yul Brynner, Samantha Eggar. (Dir: Kevin Billington, 101 mins.)

Light Fantastic, The (1962)***½** Dolores McDougal, Barry Bartle, Jean Shepherd. (Dir: Robert McCarty, 85 mins.)

Light Fingers (Great Britain, 1958)****** Guy Rolfe, Roland Culver, Eunice Gayson. Man suspects his wife of being a kleptomaniac, hires a bodyguard for her, who turns out to be a jewel thief. Comedy forces for laughs a bit too hard. (Dir: Terry Bishop, 90 mins.)

Light in the Forest, The (1958)****½** James MacArthur, Carol Lynley. Walt Disney's version of the Conrad Richter novel. Concerns an Indian who learns gradually that he must coexist with the whites. In time he falls in love with a white girl. Good outdoor locations. Bears the superficiality which is Disney's trademark. (Dir: Herschel Daugherty, 93 mins.)

Light in the Piazza (1962)******* Olivia de Havilland, Rossano Brazzi, Yvette Mimieux, George Hamilton. Woman and her childlike daughter travel to Italy, where the mother has fears when a nice young lad falls in love with the beautiful but retarded girl. Delicate and disturbing love story graced by beautiful Italian scenics, good performances. (Dir: Guy Green, 101 mins.)

Light That Failed, The (1939)*****½** Ronald Colman, Ida Lupino, Walter Huston. Superb acting carries this sincere screen version of Kipling's first novel. Story of an artist who is losing his sight is romantic, heroic and often good drama. (Dir: William Wellman, 97 mins.)

Light Touch, The (1951)****½** Stewart Granger, Pier Angeli, George Sanders. Innocent young girl artist unwittingly provides a suave art thief with a copy of a masterpiece with which he plans a swindle. Flavorsome location scenes in Italy provide more interest than the flimsy romantic story. Good cast, pleasant innocuous entertainment. (Dir: Richard Brooks, 110 mins.)

Lightning Strikes Twice (1951)****½** Ruth Roman, Richard Todd, Mercedes McCambridge. Despite a hackneyed script about a man acquitted of his wife's murder, Richard Todd manages to create an interesting characterization and gets able support from the two ladies in the cast. (Dir: King Vidor, 91 mins.)

Like Mom, Like Me (MTV 1978)****½** Linda Lavin, Kristy McNichol, Patrick O'Neal, Max Gail. Slow-moving, occasionally sensitive account of a mother and her teenage daughter whose college professor husband/father has run off with a student. In lesser hands the often soggy material would die, but Lavin and McNichol add a sense of reality. (Dir: Michael Pressman, 104 mins.)

Like Normal People (MTV 1979)******* Shaun Cassidy, Linda Purl, Hope Lange. The poignant, uplifting real-life story of Roger and Virginia Rae Meyers, a determined retarded couple who fell in love and got married, is handled with restraint. Purl is astonishing, capturing the speech and mannerisms of a retarded young lady, and—surprise, surprise after his bubblegum roles—Cassidy gives a valid characterization of the retarded young man. (Dir: Harvey Hart, 104 mins.)

Likely Story, A (1947)*****½** Bill Williams, Barbara Hale. Returned vet thinks he has only a short time to live and gets mixed up with racketeers. Surprisingly good little comedy has many laughs, extremely pleasant players. (Dir: H. C. Potter, 88 mins.)

Li'l Abner (1959)****½** Peter Palmer, Leslie Parrish, Stubby Kaye. The Broadway musical based on the famous cartoon characters of Dogpatch makes a mildly entertaining film. The humor seems forced but the musical numbers are fast paced and colorful. Peter Palmer fills the physical requirements of Li'l Abner and sings well. (Dir: Melvin Frank, 113 mins.)

Lilacs in the Spring—See: **Let's Make Up**

Lili (1953)**** Leslie Caron, Mel Ferrer, Jean-Pierre Aumont, Zsa Zsa Gabor. A thoroughly captivating film for youngsters and adults alike, beautifully scored, performed, and produced. Leslie Caron is utterly captivating in the title role of a French orphan who joins a small traveling carnival, and soon falls for the charms of a sophisticated magician (Jean-Pierre Aumont), very much the ladies' man although he's actually married. An unforgettable highlight of the film is a charming dream sequence in which Lili dances with the life-size replicas of the puppets who magically materialize on the road. (Dir: Charles Walters, 81 mins.)

Lilies of the Field (1963)**** Sidney Poitier, Lilia Skala. Heart-warming drama with an Academy Award-winning performance by Poitier as a handyman who encounters some nuns who have fled from East Germany, winds up building a chapel for them. Originally released with little fanfare, the film became a big hit, deservedly so. In addition to Poitier, there's a splendid job by Miss Skala, understanding direction by Ralph Nelson. See it. (93 mins.)

Liliom (1930)*** Charles Farrell, Rose Hobart, Estelle Taylor, Lee Tracy. The Ferenc Molnár play, which later was made into the musical "Carousel," is congenial material, about a trouble-prone, scalawag hero who dies and is permitted by heaven to return to earth for a single day. Director Frank Borzage unifies the lovers across time and space to add a dimension of visual profundity to Molnár's charismatic conceits. (94 mins.)

Lilith (1964)***½ Warren Beatty, Jean Seberg, Peter Fonda, Kim Hunter, Gene Hackman. Director Robert Rossen creates one of the most intelligent, sensitive portraits of madness ever put on film. The tale is of a trainee therapist (Beatty) whose growing love for a beautiful schizophrenic under his care (Seberg) ends tragically in death and his own madness. Rossen's film captures beautifully the nuances and subtleties of the interior world of the mentally disturbed. (114 mins.)

Lillian Russell (1940)**½ Alice Faye, Don Ameche, Henry Fonda. One of America's fabled stage stars who reigned late in the 19th century deserved better screen treatment than she receives here. Old songs are good but her highly fictionalized romances are dreary. (Dir: Irving Cummings, 127 mins.)

Limbo (1972)** Kate Jackson, Kathleen Nolan, Katherine Justice. Meandering but well-meaning film makes an antiwar statement, centering on the reactions of three wives waiting at an air force base in Florida for their missing husbands in Vietnam, and their eventual trip to Paris to speak with North Vietnamese officials.

The acting by the three ladies is adequate, but director Mark Robson's skill does not match his passion. (112 mins.)

Limbo Line, The (Great Britain, 1968)½ Craig Stevens, Kate O'Mara, Eugene Deckers, Jean Marsh. (Dir: Samuel Gallu, 98 mins.)

Limelight (1952)**** Charles Chaplin, Claire Bloom, Buster Keaton, Sydney Chaplin, Nigel Bruce. Director Chaplin here turns more inward than ever before. Mawkish in places, the film rides over its stilted portions to achieve profundity in the final image of ballet dancer Bloom whirling on the stage after Chaplin's screen death. Chaplin's music hall routines are bitterly comic memories of his early career; Keaton and Chaplin perform together for the first and only time. Chaplin won an Academy Award for his musical score. (144 mins.)

Limit, The (1972)** Yaphet Kotto, Ted Cassidy. Kotto directs with some talent and stars as a tough black cop fighting a gang of cycle toughs. Less brutal, more humane than most films of this genre. (90 mins.)

Lincoln Conspiracy, The (1977)** John Anderson, Bradford Dillman. A new twist to the Lincoln assassination plot: Lincoln's assassin, actor John Wilkes Booth, was in cahoots with some members of the U.S. Senate in trying to get rid of the Great Emancipator. Historical mishmash produced on a low budget comes across with little conviction. (Dir: James L. Conway, 104 mins.)

Linda (MTV 1973)* Stella Stevens, Ed Nelson, John Saxon, John McIntire. (Dir: Jack Smight, 90 mins.)

Lindbergh Kidnapping Case, The (MTV 1976)*** Cliff De Young, Anthony Hopkins, Joseph Cotten, Walter Pidgeon, Sian Barbara Allen, Martin Balsam, David Spielberg. Well-made drama on the sensational 1932 tragedy is cast with care. The talented young De Young appears to be a dead ringer for the famous flyer, gallant Charles Lindbergh, but he finds it tough going trying to portray the stoic Lindy, who carefully masks his emotions during the kidnapping of his baby son and the subsequent trial of Bruno Richard Hauptmann. Welsh actor Anthony Hopkins is more effective as Hauptmann, and Spielberg outshines the principals in the role of prosecuting-attorney Wilentz. It's an earnest, sincere effort to depict an earlier America that's only partly successful. (Dir: Buzz Kulik, 144 mins.)

Line Up, The (1958)***½ Eli Wallach, Robert Keith, Warner Anderson, Richard Jaeckel. Two passionately dedicated San Francisco cops pursue two insanely dedicated professional killers in director Don Siegel's gritty study, which culminates in a brilliantly executed car chase over an unfinished freeway. Expanded from the TV series "San Francisco Beat." (86 mins.)

Links of Justice (Great Britain, 1958)*½

Jack Watling, Sarah Lawson. (Dir: Max Varnel, 68 mins.)

Lion, The (Great Britain, 1962)** William Holden, Trevor Howard, Capucine, Pamela Franklin. Some mighty nice African backgrounds here—and some pretty unconvincing plot motivations. About an American lawyer who comes to Africa to see his remarried wife and their daughter. Fascinating locale offset by weak direction and the confused script. (Dir: Jack Cardiff, 96 mins.)

Lion Is in the Streets, A (1953)*** James Cagney, Barbara Hale, Anne Francis. The rise of a ruthless Southern politician is vividly portrayed by Jimmy Cagney. As a peddler he marries a local schoolteacher and begins his climb by exploiting the local townfolk. Familiar, but still stirring climax as exposed corruption causes the politician's downfall. (Dir: Raoul Walsh, 88 mins.)

Lion in Winter, The (Great Britain, 1968)**** Peter O'Toole, Katharine Hepburn, John Castle, Anthony Hopkins, Jane Merrow. Playwright James Goldman's excellent Broadway play, which was a financial flop despite good notices, is a superb historical drama, marvelously well acted by O'Toole and Hepburn. Katie tied with Barbra Streisand for an Academy Award for her portrayal of the great medieval figure Eleanor of Aquitaine. Narrative starts in 1183 during the reign of King Henry II of England. The luminous Rosemary Harris dominated the Broadway play, but that is not the case in this wide screen version as Hepburn and O'Toole present one of film history's most fascinating pairs of embattled lovers. (Dir: Anthony Harvey, 135 mins.)

Lion of Thebes, The (Italy, 1964)* Mark Forest, Yvonne Furneaux. (Dir: Giorgio Ferroni, 87 mins.)

Lions Are Loose, The (France, 1961)**½ Claudia Cardinale, Michele Morgan, Danielle Darrieux, Lino Ventura. Good international cast can't do much with this labored comedy about a gal from the country who gets entangled in amours in Paris. Nice to look at, but that's all. Dubbed-in English. (Dir: Henri Verneuil, 98 mins.)

Lipstick (1976)½ Margaux Hemingway, Chris Sarandon, Anne Bancroft, Mariel Hemingway. (Dir: Lamont Johnson, 89 mins.)

Liquidator, The (Great Britain, 1966)** Rod Taylor, Trevor Howard, Jill St. John. If your tastes run toward secret missions and handsome spies messing with beautiful redheads on the Riviera and in London, this adventure yarn is definitely for you. Taylor is being trained by British Intelligence for a secret mission involving assassinations and such, but the plot doesn't really interfere with the two-fisted action and lovemaking. A big asset is the fine supporting cast of top-notch character actors. (Dir: Jack Cardiff, 104 mins.)

Lisa (U.S.-Great Britain, 1962)**½ Stephen Boyd, Dolores Hart. If you like chase movies full of suspense and mystery, this one is definitely for you. The plot doesn't always make sense, with too many facts deliberately masked for the sake of building tension, but the excellent European locations, the performances of Dolores Hart and Stephen Boyd, and a better-than-average supporting cast compensate for this flaw. The story concerns a flight across Europe by a disturbed young Jewish refugee right after World War II, and the aid she gets from a police officer who accidentally teams up with her. (Dir: Philip Dunne, 112 mins.)

Lisbon (1956)*** Ray Milland, Maureen O'Hara, Claude Rains. Adventurer is hired by an international scoundrel to act as go-between in a kidnapping. Melodrama has a good bit of dash, pleasant players, and picturesque locale. (Dir: Ray Milland, 90 mins.)

Lisette (1961)*½ John Agar, Greta Chi. (Dir: R. John Hugh, 83 mins.)

List of Adrian Messenger, The (1963)*** George C. Scott, Herbert Marshall, Gladys Cooper, Kirk Douglas, Robert Mitchum, Frank Sinatra. Oddball thriller from director John Huston, with little flair or wit. George C. Scott is the detective seeking a mass murderer who has the knack of bizarre disguises; the trail is littered with red herrings, not least of which are four guest stars in dumbfounding varieties of drag. (98 mins.)

Listen, Darling (1938)**½ Judy Garland, Freddie Bartholomew, Walter Pidgeon, Mary Astor. Cute little tidbit about a couple of youngsters who try to marry off a widow so they can have a mother and father. (Dir: Edwin L. Marin, 80 mins.)

Lisztomania (Great Britain, 1975)** Roger Daltrey, Sara Kestelman, John Justin, Fiona Lewis, Ringo Starr. Director Ken Russell views classical composer Franz Liszt, not inaptly, as the first mass culture hero, like a rock star of today, but Russell's development renders the idea progressively less profound. (104 mins.)

Little Big Horn (1951)*** John Ireland, Lloyd Bridges, Marie Windsor. Saga of a small band of cavalry sent to warn Custer of impending Indian attack. Grim, gripping, excellently acted. (Dir: Charles Marquis Warren, 86 mins.)

Little Big Man (1970)**** Dustin Hoffman, Faye Dunaway, Richard Mulligan, Chief Dan George. Powerful historical film about the development of the West, how the white man treated the Indians (in this case the Cheyennes), climaxing with General George A. Custer's famous last stand at Little Big Horn. This is one of the few American films, up till this time, that didn't patronize or caricature the Indians, and it benefits from a good screenplay by Calder Willingham based on Thomas Berger's novel. Much of the narrative unfolds in the form of flashbacks seen through the eyes of a 121-year-old white man, Jack Crabb (Hoffman), the sole white survivor of Custer's last stand. Custer is portrayed as the psychotic he clearly was. Special credit goes to makeup man Dick Smith for the extraordinary makeup he created for Hoffman. A complex, ambitious, rewarding "western," extremely well directed by Arthur Penn. (147 mins.)

Little Boy Lost (1953)***½ Bing Crosby, Claude Dauphin, Christian Fourcade. War correspondent returns to France in search of his son, born during World War II, whom he has never seen. Tender, touching drama, with Crosby carrying it off in fine style. Should cause the ladies to reach for the hankies. (Dir: George Seaton, 95 mins.)

Little Caesar (1930)***½ Edward G. Robinson, Douglas Fairbanks, Jr., Glenda Farrell, William Collier, Jr., George E. Stone. One of the all-time great gangster movies. By modern standards it's ordinary in many respects, but Robinson's portrayal of a merciless killer is a masterpiece which has withstood years of mimicry. The gangster role that made Edward G. Robinson a star, though the straightforward direction of Mervyn LeRoy pales into relative insignificance next to such contemporary masterpieces as Hawks's *Scarface* or even Rowland Brown's *Quick Millions*. Despite its limited artistry, this is nonetheless a classic. (80 mins.)

Little Cigars (1973)*½ Angel Tompkins. Angel Tompkins is the leader of a gang of midgets who pull off a heist. The film's success is also midget-sized. (Dir: Chris Christenberry, 92 mins.)

Little Colonel, The (1935)**½ Shirley Temple, Lionel Barrymore, Bill Robinson, Evelyn Venable. Corny, contrived Temple vehicle of the old South, but Robinson dances with Shirley! Shirley is adorable. (Dir: David Butler, 80 mins.)

Little Darlings (1980)** Kristy McNichol, Tatum O'Neal, Kris Erickson, Armand Assante. Unabsorbing story of two 15-year-old girls at summer camp who are in a race to be the first to lose their virginity. The subsequent plot developments are incidental. O'Neal is disappointing but McNichol is excellent, skillfully portraying a range of emotions and rising far above the material. (Dir: Ronald Maxwell, 95 mins.)

Little Fauss and Big Halsy (1970)*½ Robert Redford, Michael Pollard, Lauren Hutton. (Dir: Sidney J. Furie, 97 mins.)

Little Foxes, The (1941)**** Bette Davis, Herbert Marshall, Teresa Wright, Dan Duryea, Richard Carlson. Superb film based on Lillian Hellman's strong play about the double dealings of a Southern family presided over by a vixen named Regina, a part tailor-made for Miss Davis' talents. A must for drama fans. Miss Davis is altogether bitchy and quite wonderful. Prequel: *Another Part of the Forest*, 1948. (Dir: William Wyler, 116 mins.)

Little Fugitive, The (1953)***½ Richie Andrusco, Rickie Brewster. Mistakenly thinking he has killed his 12-year-old brother, a little boy runs away, lands at Coney Island. Human, often touching, always amusing little comedy-drama, with a nonprofessional cast. The little boy Andrusco is amazing. (Dir: Ray Ashley, 75 mins.)

Little Game, A (MTV 1971)* Ed Nelson, Diane Baker, Katy Jurado, Howard Duff. (Dir: Paul Wendkos, 72 mins.)

Little Giant (1946)** Bud Abbott & Lou Costello, Elena Verdugo. Costello plays a salesman who bilks the crooked manager (Abbott) of the firm he works for, and wins a prize for his effort. Plenty of slapstick. (Dir: William A. Seiter, 91 mins.)

Little Girl Who Lives Down the Lane, The (U.S.-Canada, MTV 1976)***½ Jodie Foster, Martin Sheen, Alexis Smith, Scott Jacoby, Mort Schuman. Very involving thriller concerning strangely independent adolescent girl threatened by child molester who knows her guilty secret. Jodie Foster's best role to date, she is every doting father's dream. Well acted all around. An excellent script adequately realized by Nicholas Gessner. (94 mins.)

Little House on the Prairie, The (MTV 1974)**½ Michael Landon, Karen Grassle. Landon returns to acting, as well as directing this simple story about a post-Civil War family trekking from Wisconsin to Kansas to open a new life as homesteaders. It's based on the book by Laura Ingalls Wilder, the real-life daughter of the pioneering family. Pilot for subsequent series. (Dir: Michael Landon, 100 mins.)

Little Hut, The (Great Britain, 1957)*** Ava Gardner, Stewart Granger, David Niven. The French play about a wife, her husband and his best friend living a "civilized" existence while shipwrecked on an island makes a frothy, sophisticated film. The stars romp throughout and have at least as much fun as the audience. (Dir: Mark Robson, 78 mins.)

Little Kidnappers, The (Great Britain, 1954)**** Adrienne Corri, Duncan MacRae. Two boys kidnap a baby because they can't have a dog. Brilliant, simple, moving and amusing film. That's all there is to it, but it's a gem. Jon Whiteley and Vincent Winter, the boys, won Special Oscars. (Dir: Philip Leacock, 93 mins.)

Little Ladies of the Night (MTV 1977)**½ David Soul, Lou Gossett, Linda Purl, Clifton Davis, Carolyn Jones, Lana Wood, Dorothy Malone. Linda Purl is quite good playing the role of a very young teenager, around 14, forced into prostitution by some threatening pimps after running away from home and a pair of insensitive parents. David Soul, who became a TV star on "Starsky & Hutch," plays a sympathetic police officer. The squalid world of pimps, young hookers and their loveless clients is handled with reasonable restraint, though of course the language is greatly cleaned up, giving the whole proceeding an air of unreality. (Dir: Marvin Chomsky, 100 mins.)

Little Lord Fauntleroy (1936)***½ Guy Kibbee, Jessie Ralph. Surprisingly uncloying entertainment from producer David O. Selznick and director John Cromwell, with Freddie Bartholomew as the long-lost American heir brought under the tutelage of curmudgeonly C. Aubrey Smith, whose hard heart is tamed by the loveable boy. Dolores Costello makes an affecting mother ("Dearest"), and Mickey Rooney limns his archetypal good-hearted Irish tough. A nice job that I wouldn't have thought I could have been dragged to, let alone enjoy. (Dir: John Cromwell, 98 mins.)

Little Man What Now? (1934)**** Margaret Sullavan, Douglass Montgomery, Alan Hale, Alan Mowbray. Margaret Sullavan in postwar Germany, in the earliest of all of Hollywood's anti-Nazi films. But the film's chief merit lies not in its political content, but in the lyrical quality of its romance which is none the less transcendent for its squalid setting. A major work by Hollywood's master romanticist, Frank Borzage. (90 mins.)

Little Men (1940)**½ Kay Francis, Jack Oakie, George Bancroft. Louisa May Alcott's sequel to her classic "Little Women" is pleasant entertainment for the kids. Francis is very good as the grown-up Jo March, who marries and runs an unconventional school for boys. (Dir: Norman Z. McLeod, 84 mins.)

Little Minister, The (1934)***½ John Beal, Katharine Hepburn, Donald Crisp, Andy Clyde, Dorothy Stickney, Reginald Denny, Beryl Mercer. James M. Barrie's play ought to cloy unto death, but this romance of a Scot minister is charming, subdued and satisfying. (Dir: Richard Wallace, 110 mins.)

Little Miss Broadway (1938)** Shirley Temple, Jimmy Durante, George Murphy. Routine Shirley Temple film carrying her from orphanage to success in her foster home. (Dir: Irving Cummings, 71 mins.)

Little Miss Marker (1934)*** Adolphe Menjou, Charles Bickford, Shirley Temple. A little girl is left with gangsters as security for an IOU. Sentimental Damon Runyon tale was made when Miss Temple was at her cutest. Good entertainment. First of four versions. (Dir: Alexander Hall, 80 mins.)

Little Miss Marker (1980)**½ Walter Matthau, Julie Andrews, Tony Curtis, Sara Stimson, Bob Newhart. Fourth version of the Damon Runyon tale casts Matthau ideally as sour, penny-pinching gambler Sorrowful Jones, who is melted by the warmth of tiny Stimson, left in his keeping as collateral for a bet. Andrews is pleasant as a formerly wealthy socialite and Curtis is a cardboard villain. Slow moving but reasonably pleasant. First directorial effort of Walter Bernstein, who also did the screenplay. (103 mins.)

Little Mo (MTV 1978)**½ Glynnis O'Connor, Michael Learned, Anne Baxter. Story of the tragic death of Maureen Connolly—the women's tennis champ of the early '50s—a little girl from San Diego who was determined to be the best at something. Star O'Connor is no Little Mo on the court, but the tennis sequences are surprisingly good. Learned plays Little Mo's single-minded tennis instructor Eleanor Tennant, and Baxter is effective as Mo's mom. (Dir: Dan Haller, 156 mins.)

Little Mr. Jim (1946)*** Butch Jenkins, James Craig, Frances Gifford. When tragedy strikes his family, a small lad turns to the Chinese cook for companionship. Touching, well done drama. (Dir: Fred Zinnemann, 92 mins.)

Little Murders (1971)***½ Elliott Gould, Marcia Rodd, Vincent Gardenia, Elizabeth Wilson, Alan Arkin as a crazy detective. Jules Feiffer's devastating off-Broadway satire has been turned into an equally impressive movie. Under Alan Arkin's careful directorial eye for capturing the absurd moment without sacrificing the meat of the text, the film emerges as an important document of the violence-ridden New York scene, and what turns the average citizen from apathy to militancy. The story of Alfred, the mild-mannered photographer, brilliantly played by Gould, and his romantic involvement with Patsy, the cockeyed optimist (Rodd) and her outrageous family, can't be summed up . . . it has to be seen and absorbed. The absurdities will keep you laughing until they hit home and make you stop and think in wide-eyed astonishment. Donald Sutherland's lunatic clergyman is extraordinarily funny. (108 mins.)

Little Nellie Kelly (1940)**½ Judy Garland, George Murphy. Granddaughter of a stubborn Irish cop tries to patch up a family feud that has lasted for years. Sentimentality reigns supreme in this Irish-laced comedy-drama. Garland's singing is always worthwhile, Murphy turns in a good job, helping to overcome the mawkishness of the plot; diverting for unsophisticates. (Dir: Norman Taurog, 100 mins.)

Little Night Music, A (Great Britain, 1977)** Elizabeth Taylor, Diana Rigg, Len Cariou, Hermione Gingold, Lesley-Anne Down. Film version of the hit musical play, which was in turn inspired by Ingmar Bergman's "Smiles of a Summer Night." A prime example of a good property gone wrong, but it does contain the now classic tune "Send in the Clowns." (Dir: Harold Prince, 124 mins.)

Little Nuns, The (Italy, 1965)*** Catherine Spaak, Sylva Koscina. Charming, tender comedy drama about the adventures of two nuns who go to the city to protest when the soundwaves of jets overhead threaten to destroy the ancient fresco of their convent. Good entertainment. Dubbed in English. (Dir: Luciano Salce, 101 mins.)

Little Old New York (1940)**½ Alice Faye, Fred MacMurray, Richard Greene. Don't take this story about Fulton and his steamboat too seriously and you may have some fun. It's long, slightly miscast but occasionally entertaining. (Dir: Henry King, 100 mins.)

Little Prince, The (1974)**½ Richard Kiley, Steven Warner, Gene Wilder, Bob Fosse, Clive Revill, Donna McKechnie. Disappointing musical version of the enduring book by Antoine de Saint-Exupery. The talent for this fable about a neurotic aviator and the little boy from outer space, who becomes his mentor about earthly matters like life and love, is impressive. Musical score by Lerner and Loewe, adaptation by Alan Jay Lerner. Director Stanley Donen has made several of the most stylish, charming musicals ever, but "Prince" remains too coy and pretentious. Multi-talented director Bob Fosse steals the show with his nifty Snake. (88 mins.)

Little Princess, The (1939)***½ Shirley Temple, Anita Louise, Ian Hunter, Cesar Romero, Arthur Treacher. Shirley is a rich little girl in Victorian London who is mistreated when her father (and his fortune) is lost in the Boer War. One of the highlights—Shirley and Treacher sing, and dance "The Old Kent Road," a traditional "Pearlie" song. From the children's book by Frances Hodgson Burnett, who also wrote *Little Lord Fauntleroy*. Technicolor. Amazingly effective and enjoyable for all ages—really. (Dir: Walter Lang, 91 mins.)

Little Rebels, The (France, 1955)**½ Jean Gabin, Jacques Moulieres. Gabin gives another fine performance as an understanding judge who takes the time to care and love the young orphans who go the wrong way. (Dir: Jean Delannoy, 93 mins.)

Little Romance, A (U.S.-France, 1979)**** Laurence Olivier, Broderick Crawford, Diane Lane. Delightful romantic comedy about two precocious children who run off to seal their eternal love with a kiss beneath the Bridge of Sighs in Venice at sunset as the bells toll. Despite some manipulative sympathy tugging and a hammy, surface performance by Olivier as a rakish boulevardier who abets their adventure, the touch is deft and delicate throughout, thanks to director George Roy Hill, who never lets his bright and winsome leads be cute. (108 mins.)

Little Savage, The (1959)** Pedro Armendariz, Terry Rango. Strictly for the junior set. A tale of piracy and island adventures seen through the eyes of a little boy. Filmed in Mexico. (Dir: Byron Haskin, 73 mins.)

Little Shepherd of Kingdom Come, The (1961)** Jimmie Rodgers, Luana Patten. Kentucky mountain boy is a wanderer until taken in by a loving family; but he takes the side of the North when the Civil War begins. Pleasing rural tale takes a bit too much time to tell its story. (Dir: Andrew V. McLaglen, 108 mins.)

Little Shop of Horrors, The (1960)*** Jonathan Haze, Jackie Joseph, Mel Welles, Jack Nicholson. The key film in the Roger Corman legend. Shot in two or three days on an invisible budget, this is one of the most grotesque and extreme of black comedies, the story of a poor schlub whose pet plant develops an appetite for human blood, moaning "Feed me! Feeeeed me!" as the hero goes out in search of fresh victims. Not for all tastes, but still a grungy wonder, perhaps director Roger Corman's best film. Nicholson makes an early appearance in a bit as a masochistic dental patient. (70 mins.)

Little Theater of Jean Renoir, The (France-Italy-West Germany, 1969)***½ A delightful, if slight collection of short tales and musical episodes wryly hosted by director Jean Renoir, whose bittersweet, darkly comic view of the human condition bursts with dramatic possibilities. The last episode "Le Roi d'Yvetot," is the best. Originally produced for European TV. Subtitled. (100 mins.)

Little Women (1933)**** Katharine Hepburn, Joan Bennett, Frances Dee, Paul Lukas. It could have been oppressively sweet, but it's one of the best efforts of producer David Selznick and of director George Cukor. Hepburn is amazingly unaffected as Jo, and the whole piece is finely acted. Tasteful but not dull, an effective piece of Americana. (120 mins.)

Little Women (1949)**½ June Allyson, Peter Lawford, Margaret O'Brien, Elizabeth Taylor, Janet Leigh, Mary Astor. Louisa May Alcott's girls Jo, Beth, Amy and Meg return in this re-make about life in Concord at the time of the Civil War. Entertaining when it's light and gay but when they turn on the tears, it's a mess. Those who like to cry at sentimental nonsense will have a good bath here. (Dir: Mervyn Le Roy, 121 mins.)

Little Women (MTV 1978)* Meredith Baxter Birney, Susan Dey, Ann Dusenberry, Eve Plumb, Dorothy McGuire, Greer Garson. (Dir: David Lowell Rich, 208 mins.)

Little World of Don Camillo (France, Italy, 1953)*** Fernandel, Gino Cervi. Priest feuds with the Communist mayor of his town. Enjoyable comedy-drama with good performances. (Dir: Julien Duvivier, 96 mins.)

Littlest Hobo, The (1958)**½ Buddy Hart, Wendy Stuart. Nice story of a dog's adventures, especially for the kiddies. (Dir: Charles Rondeau, 77 mins.)

Littlest Rebel, The (1935)** Shirley Temple, John Boles, Bill Robinson. Another corny film featuring Shirley and Bill Robinson. Shirley is the heroine of the Civil War in this, and your kids will love it. (Dir: David Butler, 70 mins.)

Live a Little, Love a Little (1968)½ Elvis Presley, Michele Carey, Rudy Vallee. (Dir: Norman Taurog, 89 mins.)

Live a Little, Steal a Lot—See: **Murph the Surf**

Live Again, Die Again (MTV 1974)**½ Walter Pidgeon, Donna Mills, Geraldine Page, Vera Miles. How a family reacts to the reemergence of a young mother (Miss Mills), frozen for 30 years. The family—husband Thomas (Pidgeon) in his 70's, middle-aged daughter Marcia (Miss Miles), and the housekeeper (Miss Page)—face a wrenching readjustment to Caroline's youthful 32, largely unprepared thanks to the wonders of cryogenics, the science of freezing which is actually still in the embryonic stage. (Dir: Richard A. Colla, 74 mins.)

Live and Let Die (Great Britain, 1973)*** Roger Moore, Yaphet Kotto, Jane Seymour, Geoffrey Holder. If you're counting, this is number 8 in the James Bond films, and by now they all look and sound remarkably the same. This time out, Roger Moore as Agent 007 tries to unearth a large heroin operation in the Caribbean. Flashy photography, exotic locales, and an ample serving of sexy ladies keep things popping along at a nice clip. Personally, we miss Connery. Title song by Paul McCartney. (Dir: Guy Hamilton, 121 mins.)

Live Fast, Die Young (1958)** Mary Murphy, Michael Connors. Sister searches for a runaway teenager, finds her in time to prevent her from taking part in a robbery. Ordinary crime melodrama. (Dir: Paul Henreid, 82 mins.)

Live for Life (France-Italy, 1967)** Yves Montand, Candice Bergen, Annie Girardot. A TV reporter and his affairs, marital and extramarital, fancied up with pretty photography by the director of "A Man and a Woman," Claude Lelouch. Despite the frills, it never goes anywhere, not even when it tries for relevancy in a Vietnam sequence. (111 mins.)

Lively Set, The (1964)** James Darren, Pamela Tiffin, Doug McClure, Joanie Sommers. Lad shows more interest in racing engines than college, so he quits to devote his time to putt-putts. Teen-age fare exclusively with a lot of noise and a dull story. (Dir: Jack Arnold, 95 mins.)

Lives of a Bengal Lancer (1935)***½ Gary Cooper, Franchot Tone, Richard Cromwell, Sir Guy Standing, C. Aubrey Smith, Douglass Dumbrille, Akim Tamiroff, Monte Blue, Kathleen Burke. Cooper, Tone, and Cromwell are the soldiers three doing their level best on the North-West Indian Frontier. The film is so naively enthusiastic that its dated attitudes can hardly be felt as offensive, though it takes little reflection to find them so. The keynote is adventure, and the film delivers. From the book by P. C. Wren. (110 mins.)

Lives of Jenny Dolan, The (MTV 1975)** Shirley Jones, Dana Wynter, Lynn Carlin, George Grizzard, Ian McShane. Shirley Jones is starred in this slick murder-mystery drama, playing a retired investigative reporter who comes back to work for a crack

at unearthing the sinister plot behind the governor's assassination, and three other deaths which occurred in the same night. Film producer Ross Hunter is billed as executive producer on this one and, as always, he makes sure his leading lady is dressed in an array of top fashions —Ms. Jones wears no less than a dozen chic costumes. Sewing better than the scripting. (Dir: Jerry Jameson, 98 mins.)

Living Coffin, The (Mexico, 1958)* Gaston Santos, Maria Duval. (Dir: Fernando Mendez, 72 mins.)

Living Free (Great Britain, 1972)*** Susan Hampshire, Nigel Davenport. Exotic African scenery and three tiny lion cubs provide pleasant family entertainment in this sequel to "Born Free." Virginia McKenna and Bill Travers have been replaced as the keepers of lions held in captivity. In this picture, Elsa has died and left her young cubs to deal with the problem of learning to fend for themselves. This sequel is overly sentimental, and some of the scenes are patently phony, but the kids won't care. (Dir: Jack Couffer, 91 mins.)

Living in a Big Way (1947)***½ Gene Kelly, Marie McDonald, Charles Winninger, Clifford Sunberg, Phyllis Thaxter, Spring Byington. Director Gregory LaCava's last film mixes too many modes too uncertainly, but there are brilliant passages. Kelly is back from WW II facing the problems of scarce housing and a wealthy wife. With the impressive McDonald, and a brilliant piece of sustained timing by Sunberg as a butler. One of Kelly's most brilliant dance numbers, performed on a construction site. (103 mins.)

Living It Up (1954)** Dean Martin, Jerry Lewis, Janet Leigh. Jerry as a rural attendant whose sinus trouble is mistaken for radiation, becomes a human-interest story with New York at his feet. Martin and Lewis fans will approve, but the shadow of the original "Nothing Sacred" with March and Lombard makes this one shrivel in comparison. (Dir: Norman Taurog, 95 mins.)

Lizzie (1957)** Eleanor Parker, Richard Boone, Joan Blondell. Psychoshenanigans concerning a drab girl who seems to have another self lurking within her. Clumsy development loses the interest. (Dir: Hugo Haas, 81 mins.)

Lloyds of London (1936)***½ Tyrone Power, Madeleine Carroll, Freddie Bartholomew, George Sanders. Engrossing, often exciting story of the famous English insurance and banking firm. This picture tells of its early history and rise to prominence around the time of the battle of Trafalgar. (Dir: Henry King, 101 mins.)

Loan Shark (1952)**½ George Raft, Dorothy Hart, Paul Stewart. An ex-con smashes a vicious loan shark racket that has been plaguing workers in a tire plant. Fast-moving crime melodrama, with Raft at his best. (Dir: Seymour Friedman, 74 mins.)

Lock Stock and Barrel (MTV 1971)**½ Tim Matheson, Belinda Montgomery, Claude Akins. Uneven, well-cast, carefully produced western farce about newlyweds, hustling preachers, and land swindles. Half sincere character study and half leering TV-style sexual innuendo, the show is redeemed by the lighthearted approach of its skillful actors and the willingness of the parent studio (Universal) to spend the money necessary for quality. (Dir: Jerry Thorpe, 78 mins.)

Locker 69 (Great Britain, 1962)** Eddie Byrne, Paul Daneman. Private eye finds his employer dead, but when he tells the police, the body vanishes. Fair Edgar Wallace mystery. (Dir: Norman Harrison, 56 mins.)

Locket, The (1947)** Laraine Day, Brian Aherne, Robert Mitchum. Beautiful but mentally unbalanced girl ruins the lives of the men who love her. Overdone, confused melodrama. (Dir: John Brahm, 86 mins.)

Locusts (MTV 1974)** Ben Johnson, Ron Howard. Grasshoppers here, there and everywhere! A well-meaning but slow-moving account of a young man, washed out of Navy flight school and returned home to Montana farm country in 1943. Demanding father (Ben Johnson) is cutting down son (Ron Howard), and the boy finally gets a chance to win back his father's respect. A good, earnest cast gives the material a valiant try on location in Alberta, Canada. (Dir: Richard Heffron, 72 mins.)

Lodger, The (1944)*** Laird Cregar, Merle Oberon, Cedric Hardwicke, Sara Allgood, George Sanders. The most meticulously appointed of three versions of the Marie Belloc Downes novel (one a silent directed by Alfred Hitchcock). John Brahm directs with a firm command of the suspense elements and a looser rein on the pacing. Cregar is impeccable as the mysterious roomer suspected of being Jack the Ripper. (84 mins.)

Log of the Black Pearl, The (MTV 1975)**½ Ralph Bellamy, Keil Martin, Anne Archer. Here's a ripe old-fashioned sailing melodrama, filmed in Mexican waters and directed by outdoor expert Andy McLaglen, who learned his trade on "Have Gun Will Travel." A young stockbroker inherits a beautiful old sailing ship from his ailing grandfather and hunts for sunken treasure. The plot may not be exciting, but the boat and the scenery are put to good use by director McLaglen. (100 mins.)

Logan's Run (1976)*** Michael York, Richard Jordan, Jenny Agutter, Farrah Fawcett-Majors, Peter Ustinov, Roscoe Lee Browne. A science-fiction film that is less concerned with philosophizing about the future than providing some entertainment with dazzling sets and futuristic gadgets.

Living in a domed-in hedonistic civilization, Logan (York) is a policeman who hunts down "runners" who attempt to escape the society's law that at 30 you must submit to "renewal," which is actually execution. Logan tries to flee the dome and encounters a lonely hermit, played by Ustinov. The technological gimmicks encountered in the year 2274 are enough to sustain interest, if the melodramatic plot is not to your liking. Jerry Goldsmith composed a rousing score to accompany the miles of glass used for sets. Later a brief TV series. (Dir: Michael Anderson, 120 mins.)

Lola (U.S.-Great Britain, 1971)**½ Susan George, Charles Bronson. An adult drama about a May-September romance between a liberated 16-year-old and a close-to-40-year-old American writer who meet, have a tempestuous affair, and make the mistake of marrying. (Dir: Richard Donner, 95 mins.)

Lola Montes (France-West Germany, 1955)**** Martine Carol, Peter Ustinov, Oskar Werner, Anton Walbrook. Extravagant masterpiece (the last film directed by Max Ophuls) tells the story of a courtesan (Carol) who lived with (among others) Franz Liszt and the Austrian emperor and who ended up in a circus ring in New Orleans, selling her kisses and her memories to the masses. (140 mins.)

Lolita (U.S.-Great Britain, 1962)*** James Mason, Peter Sellers, Shelley Winters, Sue Lyon. Controversial story of a man of the world suddenly if not inexplicably infatuated with a "nymphet." Satiric, many good sequences, but not a complete success. Decidedly unusual. Good performances, especially from Sellers. Worth seeing. (Dir: Stanley Kubrick, 152 mins.)

Lollipop Cover, The (1965)*** Don Gordon, Carol Seflinger, John Marley. A thoughtful scenario brightens this low-budget production about a former prize-fighter and an abandoned child who are transformed by their experiences traveling together. (Dir: Everett Chambers, 85 mins.)

Lolly-Madonna XXX (1973)*½ Rod Steiger, Robert Ryan, Jeff Bridges. (Dir: Richard C. Sarafian, 103 mins.)

London Town (Great Britain, 1946)** Sid Field, Greta Gynt, Kay Kendall, Petula Clark. The rise of a comedian from the smalltime to stardom. British imitation of an American musical had a lot of money spent on it but something went wrong somewhere. Mild at best. Alternate title: **My Heart Goes Crazy**. (Dir: Wesley Ruggles, 98 mins.)

Lone Ranger, The (1956)** Clayton Moore, Jay Silverheels, Lyle Bettger, Bonita Granville. The masked man and faithful Tonto uncover dirty work between Indians and whites. Feature version of popular perennial radio and TV show with a more elaborate production and well-known cast names, but it's still the same old Heigh-Yo, Silver. (Dir: Stuart Heisler, 86 mins.)

Lone Ranger and the Lost City of Gold, The (1958)*½ Clayton Moore, Jay Silverheels. (Dir: Lesley Selander, 80 mins.)

Lone Star (1952)**½ Clark Gable, Ava Gardner, Broderick Crawford, Lionel Barrymore. A big Western film with the stress on romance, but why complain when the romantic interest is supplied by Ava Gardner. (Dir: Vincent Sherman, 94 mins.)

Lone Wolf's Spy Hunt, The (1939)*** Warren William, Ida Lupino, Rita Hayworth. Michael Lanyard, a jewel thief who would forgo the goodies for the sake of a damsel in distress, was the hero of a long series of B films from '35 to '49. This was William's first try at the part, and he moved Lanyard to the right side of the law. This is generally considered the best of the series—a fast, chic piece of efficient moviemaking. (67 mins.)

Loneliest Runner, The (MTV 1976)**½ Michael Landon, Brian Keith, DeAnn Mears. Story of a little boy, unable to control his bed-wetting, who grows up to become an Olympic champion marathon runner. The culprit is mom (Mears)—a regular witch—who is positive her growing son is merely weak and lazy. Writerdirector Landon appears at the beginning and the end as the grown-up runner making his final Olympic stadium run before a roaring crowd—a daydream come true. (78 mins.)

Loneliness of the Long-Distance Runner, The (Great Britain, 1962)***½ Tom Courtenay, Michael Redgrave, James Bolam, Alec McCowan. Intellectually suspect drama, redeemed by a masterful expression of alienation and rebellion by Courtenay as the delinquent who can only express his disgust for the values society seeks to inculcate in him. Michael Redgrave co-stars as a fatuous headmaster. The essential problem is the material from the novel by Alan Sillitoe and the grievously unsteady hand of director Tony Richardson. (104 mins.)

Lonely Are the Brave (1962)***½ Kirk Douglas, Walter Matthau, Gena Rowlands, George Kennedy, Carroll O'Connor. As the proverbial last cowboy, Douglas finds himself in deep trouble and unable to pilot his horse past the superhighways and into the wilderness as he is hunted down by truck and helicopter. The cast is phenomenally good. David Miller directed, far better than usual—the film has some real edge and pathos. From the novel "Brave Cowboy" by Edward Abbey. (107 mins.)

Lonely Man, The (1957)**½ Jack Palance, Anthony Perkins, Neville Brand. Triedand-true plot of a gunfighter's attempts to reform against all odds makes for a wellacted if unexceptional western drama. (Dir: Henry Levin, 87 mins.)

Lonely Profession, The (MTV 1969)*** Harry Guardino, Barbara McNair, Dina Merrill. Better-than-average, private eye film with a very good performance by

Harry Guardino as a small-time detective who gets involved in a wild case. (Dir: Douglas Heyes, 96 mins.)

Loners, The (1972)* Dean Stockwell, Pat Stich. (Dir: Sutton Roley, 79 mins.)

Lonelyhearts (1958)**½ Montgomery Clift, Robert Ryan, Myrna Loy, Dolores Hart, Maureen Stapleton. Overlong and brooding story about an "advice to the lovelorn" columnist who gets too involved with his job and ends up questioning himself about values in life and love. The subject matter doesn't come across in this badly written script based on the superb novel "Miss Lonelyhearts" by Nathanael West. The cast flounders with the material but Miss Stapleton fares the best as the wife of a cripple who hungers for a passionate love. (Dir: Vincent J. Donehue, 101 mins.)

Lonesome Cowboys (1968)** Viva, Taylor Mead, Eric Emerson, Joe D'Alessandro. Andy Warhol and company on the range, with antic results. Viva and Mead prance about, improvising peerlessly banal dialogue. Director Warhol's camera imparts meaning to an impassive stare, showing how the expressive qualities of minimalism can be splashed up interminably onscreen. (110 mins.)

Long Ago Tomorrow (Great Britain, 1971)*** Malcolm McDowell, Nanette Newman, Georgia Brown. Though the story is somewhat cliched, the direction by Bryan Forbes and the powerful acting by a well-rounded cast overcome the difficulty. McDowell is impressive as a wheelchair victim who is strengthened by a love affair with another cripple, Miss Newman. She dies in true "Love Story" fashion, but he can overcome the tragedy because his life has been made meaningful. (111 mins.)

Long Dark Hall, The (Great Britain, 1951)**½ Rex Harrison, Lilli Palmer. A married man is accused of the murder of a showgirl, nearly is executed for the crime he didn't commit. Just average mystery melodrama; some good courtroom scenes. (Dir: Anthony Bushell, 86 mins.)

Long Day's Dying, The (Great Britain, 1968)** David Hemmings, Tom Bell, Tony Beckley, Alan Dobie. Grisly incident involving three privates and their German prisoner in no-man's land. War is hell; so is an over-wrought war movie, despite laudable intentions. (Dir: Peter Collinson, 93 mins.)

Long Day's Journey Into Night (1962)**** Katharine Hepburn, Ralph Richardson, Jason Robards Jr., Dean Stockwell. An unrelenting, shattering film, magnificently directed by Sidney Lumet. Eugene O'Neill's triumphant tragedy, largely autobiographical, of a New England family and their relationships alternately wavering between love and hate, guilt and pride. Jason Robards Jr., who captured Broadway with his stunning portrayal of the oldest son, repeats his finely honed portrayal but is matched every step of the way by Katharine Hepburn, giving what must surely be one of the most devastating performances ever offered by an American actress. Ralph Richardson is also splendid but it is this landmark play by the great author and Hepburn's losing battle with drug addiction that will haunt any viewer for a long time. (136 mins.)

Long Days of Summer, The (MTV 1980)** Dean Jones, Joan Hackett, Ronnie Scribner. Director Dan Curtis delves into when he was growing up in Bridgeport, Conn., during the '30s. In this sequel to "When Every Day Was the Fourth of July," Jones again plays an up-and-coming Jewish attorney who has to fight prejudice at every turn. The second Max Schmeling-Joe Louis boxing match serves as a catalytic event which triggers the hate of some bigots and almost ends up in tragedy. (78 mins.)

Long Duel, The (Great Britain, 1967)*** Yul Brynner, Trevor Howard. Brynner and Howard star in this intelligent adventure epic which pits two men of honor against each other. Brynner plays an Indian leader who fights Howard, representing the British in India during the 1920's. Their personal integrity interferes with the call to duty in many instances. Good quota of action. (Dir: Ken Annakin, 115 mins.)

Long Goodbye, The (1973)**** Elliott Gould, Sterling Hayden, Mark Rydell, Nina van Pallandt. A gloriously entertaining and sophisticated detective yarn based on Raymond Chandler's novel about an indolent flatfoot, Philip Marlowe (Gould). Marlowe is hired to find a missing husband, is threatened by a Jewish hoodlum (hysterically played by Rydell), and journeys to Mexico. Style is more important in this Robert Altman-directed winner than plot. There's a slick opening sequence with Marlowe and his cat; nutty scenes where Marlowe, en route to visit his client, can only pass if he listens to the guard's imitations of old movie stars; and shots of Marlowe's neighbors—four luscious girls who are into nude yoga. Gould has a stylish slovenliness about him that is precisely right, as is the cinematography by Vilmos Zsigmond. The ending's been changed, along with some other details. But even Chandler purists will enjoy this one. (Dir: Robert Altman, 111 mins.)

Long Gray Line, The (1955)*** Tyrone Power, Maureen O'Hara. Tyrone Power gives one of his best performances as the Irish immigrant who finds a home and love at West Point. John Ford directed with his usual skill. Film is extremely sentimental. (Dir: John Ford, 138 mins.)

Long Haul, The (Great Britain, 1957)*½ Victor Mature, Diana Dors. (Dir: Ken Hughes, 88 mins.)

Long Hot Summer, The (1958)***½ Paul Newman, Joanne Woodward, Orson Welles, Lee Remick, Anthony Franciosa, and Angela Lansbury. Thanks to a good cast, William Faulkner's novel "The Hamlet" and stories "Barn Burning" and "The Spotted Horses" are brought to the screen with power and conviction. Welles is perfectly cast as the tyrannical head of a Southern family which includes a strong willed daughter (Miss Woodward), a weakling son (Franciosa) and the latter's young, flighty wife (Miss Remick). A stranger (Paul Newman) shows up and things start crackling. Miss Lansbury gives another of her fine supporting performances as Welles' sometime mistress. Poor ending weakens film well directed by Martin Ritt. (117 mins.)

Long John Silver (Australia, 1953)**½ Robert Newton, Kit Taylor, Rod Taylor. The bold buccaneer battles a rival pirate for the spoils of Treasure Island. Entertaining swashbuckling saga, with Newton giving a broadly humorous portrayal. (Dir: Byron Haskin, 109 mins.)

Long Journey Back (MTV 1978)*** Mike Connors, Cloris Leachman, Stephanie Zimbalist, Kathy Kurtzman. Absorbing, uplifting real-life story about a family's long, hard struggle to help a high-school girl recover from a school-bus accident in which she has lost a leg and suffered brain damage. Zimbalist is excellent as the popular, bright senior who is dealt a blow few people can overcome. Leachman and Connors are good as her parents, almost torn apart by the tragedy, and Kurtzman is effective as the younger sister relegated to the background when all the attention and love is heaped upon the victim. (Dir: Mel Damski, 104 mins.)

Long, Long Trailer, The (1954)***½ Lucille Ball, Desi Arnaz, Marjorie Main, Keenan Wynn. Director Vincente Minnelli expresses the last word on '50s situation comedy in this film designed as a vehicle for Ball and Arnaz at the height of their TV popularity, amplifying Lucy's character into the personification of consumer culture—a shrill, castrating harpy who drags the helpless Desi through one humiliation after another in her maniacal pursuit of middle-class bliss. (96 mins.)

Long Memory, The (Great Britain, 1953)** John Mills, Eva Bergh, Elizabeth Sellars. Man wrongly imprisoned for murder is released full of bitterness, redeems himself through the love of a girl. Well acted, frequently exciting melodrama. (Dir: Robert Hamer, 91 mins.)

Long Night, The (1947)** Henry Fonda, Barbara Bel Geddes, Vincent Price, Ann Dvorak. The killer of a shady magician hides out in a hotel room, while his girl pleads with him to give himself up. Dreary, ponderous drama; some good moments. (Dir: Anatole Litvak, 101 mins.)

Long Ride from Hell, A (Italy, 1970)* Steve Reeves, Wayde Preston. (Dir: Alex Burks, 94 mins.)

Long Ride Home, The (1967)**½ Union officer (Glenn Ford) on the trail of escaped Confederate soldiers. Violent western carries an occasional punch. With

George Hamilton, Inger Stevens, Paul Petersen, Max Baer. Alternate title: **A Time for Killing.** (Dir: Phil Karlson, 88 mins.)

Long Riders, The (1980)*** The clans Carradine, Keach, Quaid, and Guest; Pamela Reed, Amy Stryker. Director Walter Hill lays on irony and ambiguity to the point that the moral positions of the film—variations on the story of the James-Younger gang—are obscure, yet his approach enriches the moribund western genre. Dynamite cameos by Reed (as Belle Starr) and Stryker. (98 mins.)

Long Rope, The (1961)**½ Hugh Marlowe, Alan Hale, Chris Robinson. Circuit judge finds himself against an entire town when he tries a man for murder. Okay western drama made on a small budget—it's better than some of the more elaborate ones. (Dir: William Witney, 61 mins.)

Long Ships, The (Great Britain-Yugoslavia, 1964)** Richard Widmark, Sidney Poitier. One of those epics about a brave Viking and his search for a golden bell, opposed by villainous Moors. Good actors usually look silly in these things, and this one is no exception. The two-star rating is for the scenery only. (Dir: Jack Cardiff, 125 mins.)

Long, the Short and the Tall, The—See: Jungle Fighters

Long Voyage Home, The (1940)**** John Wayne, Thomas Mitchell, Barry Fitzgerald, Mildred Natwick. Based on play of Eugene O'Neill. Tale of merchant seamen, their hopes, dreams, close comradeship. Superbly directed by John Ford, a gripping, dramatic, often beautiful film. (Dir: John Ford, 105 mins.)

Long Wait, The (1954)** Anthony Quinn. Dull Mickey Spillane adventure about an amnesia victim falsely accused of murder. Even Spillane fans will be disappointed. (Dir: Victor Saville, 93 mins.)

Longest Day, The (1972)*** John Wayne, Henry Fonda, Robert Ryan, Red Buttons, Richard Burton, Richard Todd, Mel Ferrer, Alexander Knox, Curt Jurgens. This is one of the better samples of the usually not very compelling all-star WW II drama. An account of D day (June 6, '44), when the Allies landed in Normandy. All cameos and vignettes, each too neatly packaged to capture the sense of the moment. Directors are Andrew Marton, highly skilled journeyman; Bernhard Wicki, arty German director; and Ken Annakin, amiable British hack. Guess who prevails. From the book by Cornelius Ryan. (169 mins.)

Longest Hundred Miles, The (MTV 1966)**½ Doug McClure, Katharine Ross, Ricardo Montalban. Young army corporal, a pretty lady lieutenant, a padre, and an assortment of children band together in an attempt to flee the Japanese occupation of the Philippines during World War II. Melodrama is paced swiftly but is cliché-filled, not particularly well acted. (Dir: Don Weis, 93 mins.)

Longest Night, The (MTV 1972)*** David Janssen, James Farentino. Good kidnap yarn based on a case that made headlines years ago. Daughter of a wealthy businessman is abducted by a meticulous, calculating, clever young man and his girl friend, and is subsequently buried alive in a specially constructed box with a battery-operated air supply for one week. Tension reaches nerve-racking stage. Well directed by Jack Smight. Cast, headed by Farentino as the kidnapper and Janssen as the girl's father, couldn't be better. (73 mins.)

Longest Yard, The (1974)*** Burt Reynolds, Eddie Albert, Ed Lauter. About the bitter competition of two football teams—one composed of imprisoned criminals, the other of their guards. Director Robert Aldrich clearly has some heavy notions about self-respect, integrity, and racial harmony, but he is driven more to patness than to exploration. Reynolds gives a fine, intelligent performance; also noteworthy is Lauter's compromised prison guard. (122 mins.)

Longstreet (MTV 1971)*** James Franciscus, Jeanette Nolan. Absorbing drama from start to finish. James Franciscus has seldom been better than he is in this excellently produced pilot film for a proposed series about a top-flight insurance investigator who is blinded in an explosion which kills his wife. Most of the film is taken up with Mike Longstreet's (Franciscus) specialized training program to cope with his blindness and it's interesting. In a uniformly fine cast, the standouts are Jeanette Nolan as Longstreet's intelligent mother and John McIntire as the doctor who uses the human approach in dealing with Longstreet's blindness. (Dir: Joseph Sargent, 93 mins.)

Look Back in Anger (Great Britain, 1959)**** Richard Burton, Claire Bloom, Mary Ure. Englishman John Osborne's famous and important play about an "angry young man" fighting against "the establishment" emerges as a powerful comment on the mood in England in the mid '50's. Richard Burton is a shade too mature for the part of "Jimmy Porter" but he's a glorious actor and has several excellent scenes. (Dir: Tony Richardson, 99 mins.)

Look for the Silver Lining (1949)**½ June Haver, Charles Ruggles, Rosemary DeCamp, Gordon MacRae, S. Z. Sakall. Haver plays Marilyn Miller in a pleasant minor musical of no special distinction. Musical direction by Ray Heindorf, who was nominated for an Academy Award. (Dir: David Butler, 106 mins.)

Look in Any Window (1961)** Paul Anka, Ruth Roman, Alex Nicol. Paul Anka goes dramatic for the first time in this cheap, sensationalized story of parents who set bad examples for their teenage children and then are surprised when they get into trouble. Anka fans might like watching their singing idol play it straight on film. (Dir: William Alland, 87 mins.)

Look What's Happened to Rosemary's Baby—See: **Rosemary's Baby II**

Look Who's Laughing (1941)**½ Lucille Ball, Bergen & McCarthy, Fibber McGee and Molly. Hectic happenings when the famous ventriloquist is forced down in the village of Wistful Vista. Pleasing comedy.

Lookin' Good—See: **Corky**

Looking for Love (1964)* Connie Francis, Jim Hutton, Susan Oliver. (Dir: Don Weis, 83 mins.)

Looking for Mr. Goodbar (1977)**** Diane Keaton, Richard Gere, Tuesday Weld, Tom Berenger. One of Richard Brooks's best films. It has been grievously misunderstood, however, mostly by the puritanical of mind who have assumed that Brooks was passing some moral judgment on promiscuity by allowing the lead character to be murdered. Diane Keaton brings a special sweetness to the tawdry role of a teacher in pursuit of rougher trade; finding someone who could capture the tension between such extremes amounts to a genuine casting coup. The detailing is rather primary and the sociologizing worthless, yet Brooks, in seeking the truth of the lead character's experience, makes a valiant stab at rendering a most elusive temperament without too much psychological pinioning. Keaton is heartbreaking, and *Goodbar* builds to a harrowing, shattering climax. Based on Judith Rossner's best-selling novel. Adapted by Richard Brooks. (135 mins.)

Looking Glass War, The (Great Britain, 1970)**½ Christopher Jones, Pia Degermark, Ralph Richardson, Anthony Hopkins. John le Carre's fine espionage novel has been turned into a mildly entertaining film. It begins with the usual spy jargon, this time in the expert hands of Richardson, Paul Rogers, and Anthony Hopkins...and they soon decide to send a Polish defector (Jones) into East Germany to gain information on a rocket operation. Jones' subsequent adventures, including a love scene or two with Degermark (less effective here than in the haunting "Elvira Madigan"), are predictable. (Dir: Frank R. Pierson, 106 mins.)

Loophole (1954)**½ Barry Sullivan, Dorothy Malone. Bank teller accused of theft clears himself by nabbing the real culprits. Tightly-knit crime melodrama. (Dir: Harold Schuster, 80 mins.)

Loot (Great Britain, 1972)***½ Richard Attenborough, Lee Remick, Milo O'Shea. Black, funny farce, based on a play by the late Joe Orton. Its only fault lies in the failure by the director to open it up from a one-act play. The plot concerns money hidden in a coffin resting in a seedy British hotel. The acting is lively and Remick can be forgiven for her varying Irish brogue. It's rare to find a farce with sympathy for its characters. (Dir: Silvio Narizzano, 92 mins.)

Lord Jim (Great Britain, 1965)*** Peter O'Toole, Eli Wallach, James Mason, Daliah Lavi, Curt Jurgens. A lavish, magnificently photographed and unusually well acted story of a seaman in the Far East based on Joseph Conrad's famous novel written in 1900. You'll probably enjoy this more if you **haven't** read Conrad's rousing tale and you'll appreciate the stunning on-location sequences shot in many areas of the Orient, including Hong Kong, Cambodia and Singapore. Produced, written and directed by the multi-talented Richard Brooks. (154 mins.)

Lord Love a Duck (1966)***½ Tuesday Weld, Roddy McDowall, Lola Albright, Ruth Gordon. Director George Axelrod's mordant satire on high-school life and suburban madness is tempered by an evenhanded compassion. It's slapdash filmmaking (the boom appears in many shots), but compelling. With Weld in perhaps her most scintillating performance. (105 mins.)

Lord of the Flies (Great Britain, 1963)*** James Aubrey, Roger Elwin, Tom Chapin. Offbeat study of English schoolboys, stranded on an island, and their gradual reversion to savagery when left to their own devices. Peter Brook's powerhouse theatrical invention functions unevenly in cinema, and while he may have imaginative approaches to the problem of filming William Golding's allegory, the results are sporadic. The insistent determinism of the camera style tends to stifle the resolute improvisation of the youthful players. It's an interesting, compelling work, though it proves the paradox that a barely adapted play can be true cinema (*Gertrud, Perceval*) and a determinedly overedited, "visual" film like this one can be irretrievably theatrical. With Hugh Edwards, extraordinary as Piggy. One of the few films directed to date by the brilliant English stage director Peter Brook. (91 mins.)

Lord of the Rings, The (1978)*** Animated version of the classic J. R. R. Tolkien tale of Hobbits, Middle-earth, and the ring that gives the holder unlimited, morally ambiguous power. Director Ralph Bakshi used the Rotoscope, beginning with live actors and then animating over them, for startling effects. May not be pure Tolkien, but it should please many Tolkien fans. Biggest drawback is that the film ends with "To Be Continued." (130 mins.)

Lords of Flatbush, The (1974)** Henry Winkler, Perry King, Sylvester Stallone, Susan Blakely. Trip back in time to a Brooklyn high school and the camaraderie of male adolescents eager but ultimately afraid to assert their emerging manhood. The ambience includes pseudo-'50s rock-and-roll songs, the obligatory TV programs in the background ("My Little Margie" and "Ozzie and Harriet"), the ritual appearance of the classic T-Bird, and a lot of making out, drive-ins, Brylcreem, Trojans, and motorcycles. Looks dreadful, but boasts young stars on the threshold, all of them very good here. (Dirs: Stephen F. Verona and Martin Davidson, 85 mins.)

Lorna (1964)***½ Lorna Maitland, Mark Bradley, James Griffith. Excellent early low-budget film from director Russ Meyer says much about rural boredom and American passion. Lorna, married a year to a laborer in the salt mines, is raped by an escaped murderer—whom she then takes for a lover. Steamy, but rather circumspect by today's standards. (77 mins.)

Los Olvidados (The Young and the Damned) (Mexico, 1951)**** Alfonso Mejia, Miguel Inclan, Estela Inda. Director Luis Buñuel's semidocumentary about juvenile gangs in Mexico City. A mind-rending indictment of moral as well as material poverty. (88 mins.)

Los Tarantos (Spain, 1963)*** Carmen Amaya, Antonio Gades, Sara Lezana, Daniel Martin. The Romeo and Juliet-West Side Story idea told to the tune of clicking heels and castanets in this decidedly unusual drama with some fine dancing, flamenco-style. For those who appreciate something different. Dubbed in English. (Dir: Rovira-Beleta, 81 mins.)

Loser Takes All (Great Britain, 1956)**½ Rossano Brazzi, Glynis Johns. Well acted comedy-drama about a young married couple who win at the tables in Monte Carlo but almost lose each other in the process. (Dir: Ken Annakin, 88 mins.)

Losers, The (1970)*½ William Smith, Bernie Hamilton. (Dir: Jack Starrett, 96 mins.)

Loss of Innocence (Great Britain, 1961)**** Kenneth More, Danielle Darrieux, Susannah York. Exquisite drama of a young girl at a vacation hotel in France who becomes a woman through her involvement with a handsome jewel thief. Tender, touching, fine performances, colorful photography of the French countryside. (Dir: Lewis Gilbert, 99 mins.)

Lost (Great Britain, 1955)*** David Farrar. Exciting and tense British drama about a lost child and the clever police work involved in finding him. (Dir: Guy Green, 89 mins.)

Lost and Found (1979)*** George Segal, Glenda Jackson, Paul Sorvino, Maureen Stapleton. Most of the gang from "A Touch of Class" set out to do it again, this time in a marital comedy with a university backdrop. Some nice moments, and Jackson and Segal do have a special chemistry together onscreen, but this "classy" sequel is less successful, though often engaging. Writers: director Melvin Frank, Jack Rose. (102 mins.)

Lost Battalion (1961)** Diane Jergens, Leopold Salcedo. Moderately interesting World War II yarn, filmed in the Philippines, about a group of Americans who go

through the Japanese lines in order to rendezvous with a submarine. Some action sequences for adventure fans. (Dir: Eddie Romero, 83 mins.)

Lost Boundaries (1949)***½ Mel Ferrer, Beatrice Pearson. A lightskinned Negro doctor passes for white in a small New England town. Absorbing drama handles a touchy subject with taste, finesse. Based on fact. (Dir: Alfred L. Werker, 99 mins.)

Lost Command (1966)**½ Anthony Quinn, Alain Delon, George Segal, Claudia Cardinale, Michele Morgan. An all-star cast and well-staged war sequences help keep this action film interesting, despite the pretentious handling of the political and human aspects of the French-Algerian conflict. Best acting is contributed by Alain Delon, playing a dedicated military man whose clashes with the poor leadership and distaste for the endless killing eventually cause him to leave the French army. (Dir: Mark Robson, 129 mins.)

Lost Continent, The (Great Britain, 1968)** Eric Porter, Hildegarde Knef (Neff), Suzanna Leigh, Tony Beckley. Balderdash about storm survivors landing on an uncharted land where weird things occur. Comic-strip stuff, played with grim determination. Some of it is inventive if you care for comic strip characters. (Dirs: Michael Carreras, Leslie Norman, 89 mins.)

Lost Horizon (1937)**** Ronald Colman, Sam Jaffe, Jane Wyatt, H. B. Warner, Edward Everett Horton, Margo, Thomas Mitchell, Isabel Jewell, John Howard. In it's original length. (The studio bosses apparently got cold feet immediately on it's release, and have been snipping away at it ever since). This is a lovely, strange, moving story of four escapees from a revolution, who find refuge of several sorts in a magical valley in which the only law is to "Be kind." Time has taken the elitist edge off of author James Hilton's *utopianism*, and added romance and nostalgia. Capra has actually improved on the novel; making most of the refugees American instead of British mysteriously helps. The acting is uniformly expert to the point of luminosity; standouts are, of course, Colman, Sam Jaffe as the oldest inhabitant, and H. B. Warner, as the mystical bureaucrat, Chang. (Dir: Frank Capra, 118 mins.)

Lost Horizon (1973)*½ Peter Finch, Liv Ullmann, John Gielgud, Olivia Hussey, Charles Boyer, George Kennedy, Sally Kellerman, Bobby Van, James Shigeta. (Dir: Charles Jarrott, 151 mins.)

Lost in a Harem (1944)** Bud Abbott, Lou Costello, Marilyn Maxwell, John Conte. A slice of nothing about a couple of magicians and their adventure in an Oriental land. Strictly for the kids in spite of the misleading title. (Dir: Charles Reisner, 89 mins.)

Lost in Alaska (1952)**½ Bud Abbott, Lou Costello, Tom Ewell. The Klondike inherits the clowning duet in this fast paced comedy about gold, gambling and gals. Plenty of funny sight gags make this a notch or two above average A&C fare. (Dir: Jean Yarbrough, 76 mins.)

Lost in the Stars (1974)**½ Brock Peters, Melba Moore, Raymond St. Jacques, Paul Rogers. Occasionally interesting but ultimately disappointing adaptation of the Broadway musical of Kurt Weill and Maxwell Anderson which in turn was based on Alan Paton's famous novel "Cry the Beloved Country." (The 1951 film starred Canada Lee.) About racial prejudice in South Africa. Black clergyman (Peters) develops a relationship with a white painter (Rogers) after Rogers' son is killed in an attempted robbery. Neither the plodding direction of Daniel Mann nor the screenplay of Alfred Hayes manages to infuse the drama with much excitement, but the basic story of bigotry remains all too relevant and the performances are generally fine. American Film Theatre presentation. (Dir: Daniel Mann, 114 mins.)

Lost Island of Kioga (1938-66)** Herman Brix (later known as Bruce Bennett), Mala. Feature version of serial "Hawk of the Wilderness." Survivors of shipwreck find a muscular ruler on an uncharted island. Farfetched adventure tale, but produced with some flair. (Dirs: William Witney, John English, 100 mins.)

Lost Lagoon (1958)** Jeffrey Lynn, Peter Donat. Castaway on a Caribbean isle begins a new life, but loses the audience. (Dir: John Rawlins, 79 mins.)

Lost Man, The (1969)**½ Sidney Poitier, Joanna Shimkus, Al Freeman, Jr. Sidney Poitier in the off-beat role of a hunted criminal, some interesting scenes involving the civil rights movement in this country, plus the excitement of a continuous chase, make this film palatable. Don't look beyond the surface story, which is loosely based on a far more successful film "Odd Man Out," and you'll probably enjoy it. Poitier is strong, and Miss Shimkus also registers as a social worker who falls in love with the fugitive. The film's best performance is by Al Freeman, Jr., as a questioning civil rights leader. Directed and written by author Robert Alan Aurthur. (122 mins.)

Lost Missile, The (1958)** Robert Loggia, Ellen Parker. As a runaway missile threatens New York, a young scientist works against time to stop its course of destruction. Fair cheaply-made science-fiction thriller manages to work up some suspense. (Dir: Lester Berke, 70 mins.)

Lost Moment, The (1947)***½ Robert Cummings, Susan Hayward, Agnes Moorehead. Young American publisher finds that love letters he has been seeking in Venice cause near-tragedy. Absorbing drama, taken from Henry James' novel; excellent in production and performance. (Dir: Martin Gabel, 88 mins.)

Lost One, The (Italy, 1948)*** Nelly Corradi, Tito Gobbi. Verdi's opera "La Traviata" sung in Italian with narrative portions in English. Nicely staged, well sung; good for opera devotees, interesting for others. (Dir: Carmine Gallone, 82 mins.)

Lost One, The (West Germany, 1951)*** Peter Lorre, Karl John, Helmuth Rudolph. Peter Lorre gives a fine performance portraying a resident doctor in a refugee camp in Germany shortly after the end of World War II. But in many ways the most interesting thing about this little-known film is that it was the only film directed by Lorre, and he turns in a more than creditable job. Lorre also had a hand in the involving screenplay which includes, among other things, commentary about the circumstances that fostered and permitted Nazism. An unusual film to have been made in Germany at that time. (98 mins.)

Lost Patrol (1934)***½ Victor McLaglen, Boris Karloff, Wallace Ford, Reginald Denny, Alan Hale. A British patrol is ambushed by hostile Arabs and picked off one by one. Gripping drama directed by John Ford. (80 mins.)

Lost People, The (Great Britain, 1949)*** Mai Zetterling, Dennis Price, Siobhan McKenna, Richard Attenborough. Problems confronting a British Army captain in post-war Germany, trying to relocate displaced persons. Rambling, but frequently touching, well-acted topical drama. (Dir: Bernard Knowles, Muriel Box, 89 mins.)

Lost Planet Airmen (1949)*½ Tristram Coffin, Mae Clarke. (Dir: Fred Bannon, 65 mins.)

Lost Squadron (1932)*** Joel McCrea, Richard Dix, Erich Von Stroheim, Mary Astor. Tyrannical film director makes his aerial stunt men do perilous tricks, so they band together to stop him. Unusual melodrama has plenty of suspense. (Dir: George Archainbaud, 90 mins.)

Lost Treasure of the Aztecs—See: **Hercules and the Treasure of the Incas**

Lost Weekend, The (1945)**** Ray Milland, Jane Wyman. Grim, brutal, award-winning study of a dipsomaniac based on Charles Jackson's novel. Excellent film. Milland won an Oscar. (Dir: Billy Wilder, 101 mins.)

Lost World, The (1960)**½ Michael Rennie, Fernando Lamas, Jill St. John. Primarily for the youngsters who like their adventure yarns fast and colorful. Good screen version of Sir Arthur Conan Doyle's science-fiction story about an expedition into the deep regions of the Amazon. Visual tricks, such as prehistoric beasts doing battle with a modern helicopter are the film's best features. (Dir: Irwin Allen, 98 mins.)

Lost World of Sinbad, The (Japan, 1964)*½ Toshiro Mifune, Makoto Satoh. (Dir: Senkichi Taniguchi, 95 mins.)

Lotus for Miss Kwen, A (1967)*½ Lang

Jeffries, Werner Peters. (Dir: Jurgen Roland, 92 mins.)

Louis Armstrong—Chicago Style (MTV 1976)*** Ben Vereen, Red Buttons, Margaret Avery, Janet MacLachlan. Based on the early career of the great jazz trumpeter, this film zeroes in on Louis' struggle to avoid playing in a Chicago club run by the mob during the early 30's. Vereen is terrific in the title role, a musical genius who had to buck bigotry and shady characters before he could stand in front of an audience and share his genius with them. Vereen doesn't imitate "Satchmo," but captures the essence of Armstrong's individualistic singing style, and he's marvelous in the dramatic scenes. Also making an impression in supporting roles are Avery as Louis' true love, and Buttons as the trumpet player's opportunistic manager. (Dir: Lee Phillips, 72 mins.)

Louisa (1950)**½ Ronald Reagan, Piper Laurie, Charles Coburn, Spring Byington in title role, Edmund Gwenn. Moderately entertaining film about the trials and tribulations of an average family which has to cope with the young daughter's romantic problems as well as Grandma's. A pleasant cast carries it off nicely. (Dir: Alexander Hall, 90 mins.)

Louisiana Purchase (1941)***½ Bob Hope, Victor Moore, Vera Zorina. Delightful comedy (plus 3 pleasant tunes) about an attempt to frame a senator down Louisiana way. Loads of laughs and Bob's filibuster is a classic. (Dir: Irving Cummings, 98 mins.)

Love (1927)*** Greta Garbo, John Gilbert. An early version of Tolstoy's "Anna Karenina" which has, among other things, a happy ending. Greta Garbo, who later starred in a talking version that stuck closer to the original text, plays the harassed heroine who must choose between maternal love and passionate love. John Gilbert plays the handsome Count. The screen team of Garbo and Gilbert captured the fancy of the 1920's moviegoers. (Dir: Edmund Goulding, 100 mins.)

Love Affair (1939)**** Charles Boyer, Irene Dunne. One of the wittiest and most civilized of the romantic films of the '30's. Couple meet on shipboard, fall in love, but break their engagement and decide to meet again in six months. Touching, wry, and beautifully acted by the two leads; superior direction by Leo McCarey. Remade by McCarey as *An Affair to Remember*. (89 mins.)

Love Affair, A: The Eleanor & Lou Gehrig Story (MTV 1977)*** Edward Herrmann, Blythe Danner. Less a baseball yarn than a love story. Herrmann is becoming one of our finest and most interesting actors though he is miscast as the great Yankee first baseman. But Danner is sensational as Eleanor, and this is her show, playing a woman madly in love with a good, gentle, serious man. Baseball fans will see a few clips of Gehrig and Babe Ruth hitting homers at Yankee Stadium, along with Herrmann's rendition of the dying Gehrig's famous farewell speech. (Dir: Fielder Cook, 104 mins.)

Love Among the Ruins (MTV 1975)**** Katharine Hepburn, Laurence Olivier, Richard Pearson. One of the finest made-for-TV movies. Olivier and Hepburn star in this romantic comedy, written with style by James Costigan, and they're magical together. Olivier plays a prestigious London barrister—London circa 1911—who is defending his client (Hepburn) from a suit brought by a younger man who claims she trifled with his affections and has reneged on her promise to marry him. It's the first time Olivier and Hepburn ever worked together, giving "Love" a touch of class that few, if any, other actors could provide. (Dir: George Cukor, 100 mins.)

Love and Anarchy (Italy, 1972)**** Giancarlo Giannini, Mariangela Melato, Lina Polito. Enormously powerful political drama about Italian fascism during the 1930's, brilliantly written and directed by Lina Wertmuller. Much of the action, before a shattering climax, takes place in a bordello. Anarchist peasant comes to Rome to assassinate Mussolini. There is one astonishing sequence where the assembled prostitutes are dining together and taunting each other, while Miss Wertmuller's sure hand indelibly captures the decadence and moral squalor of that society. Acting splendid throughout. Establishes Ms. Wertmuller as one of the most gifted directors, male or female, to emerge in years. (108 mins.)

Love and Bullets (1979)** Charles Bronson, Jill Ireland, Rod Steiger, Henry Silva, Bradford Dillman. John Huston bowed out of directing this potboiler and Stuart Rosenberg stepped into the breach. Bronson and Ireland (his wife) star in this story of a cop out to bring the wife of a syndicate boss back from Switzerland. Boring dialogue. (103 mins.)

Love and Death (1975)**** Woody Allen, Diane Keaton, Frank Adu, Olga Georges-Picot. One of Woody Allen's funniest, most consistent films. Woody plays a bumbling, to put it mildly, Russian, trying to avoid the draft in the Napoleonic War. Diane Keaton is the pretentious cousin he's loved from afar. Allen take these plot characters and parodies 19th-century politics, philosophy, and war; and makes it funny. It's full of slapstick; and to movie buffs it's twice as funny, because it is full of mocking visual references to every film ever made from a Russian novel, from "The Brothers Karamazov" to "The Twelve Chairs." A treat. (85 mins.)

Love and Kisses (1965)** Rick Nelson, Kristin Nelson, Jack Kelly. A spinoff of the Nelson family situations, this one has father Ozzie directing son Rick and daughter-in-law Kristin in a mild comedy about the problems occurring when a young couple elope. Very mild fare. (Dir: Ozzie Nelson, 87 mins.)

Love and Marriage (Italy, 1964)***½ Lando Buzzanca, Maria Grazia Buccella, Renato Tagliani, Ingeborg Schoener, Sylva Koscina. Uneven but highly amusing compendium of four episodes: lusty love stories with a twist. The first two are the best—beguiling, ribald, clever. The players are energetic, deliciously good-looking. (Dirs: Gianni Puccini, episodes 1 and 4; Mino Guerrini, episodes 2 and 3, 106 mins.)

Love and Pain and the Whole Damned Thing (1972)*** Maggie Smith, Timothy Bottoms, Charles Baxter. An eccentric, humorous love story notable for the glorious performance of lovely Maggie Smith. Smith is a superb actress, cast as a spinster in her late 30's who is running away from her two aunts in England, while Bottoms plays a college student, the son of a Pulitzer Prize-winning author, coming to Europe to flee his tyrannical dad. They meet in Spain, and quickly learn their neuroses complement one another. The affectionate comedy dissolves when Miss Smith reveals she is dying of "Love Story" disease. (Dir: Alan J. Pakula, 110 mins.)

Love and the Frenchwoman (France, 1960)*** Jean-Paul Belmondo, Annie Girardot, Martine Carol, Francois Perier. Seven separate stories detailing exactly what the title implies, dealing in aspects of love in all forms at all ages. As with most compilations, some scenes are better than others, but it all makes an entertaining if lengthy show. Narrated and dubbed in English. (Dirs: Henri Decoin, Jean Delannoy, Michel Boisrond, Rene Clair, Henri Verneuil, Christian-Jaque, Jean Paul Le Chanois, 124 mins.)

Love at First Bite (1979)*** George Hamilton, Susan Saint James, Richard Benjamin, Arte Johnson. Very funny spoof about Count Dracula finding himself caught up in today's disco-swingin' social whirl. George Hamilton, complete with ridiculous Bela Lugosi accent, makes a terrific blood-sucking Count, and the screenplay provides one laugh after another. Richard Benjamin also delivers a top comedy performance as a doctor out to expose Hamilton's voguish vampire. Fun for all. (Dir: Stan Dragoti, 93 mins.)

Love at Twenty (France-Italy-Japan-Poland-West Germany, 1962)***½ Jean-Pierre Leaud, Eleonora Rossi-Drago, Barbara Lass. Five vignettes of love among the young from youthful directors of France (Francois Truffaut), Italy, Japan, Germany, Poland. Varying in quality: French segment has a good deal of charm; the Italian is rather thin in plot; the Japanese is the most bizarre and dramatic; the German has the smoothest technique; and the Polish one is probably the best in all-around quality. English-dubbed. (Dirs: Francois Truffaut, Renzo Rossellini, Shintaro Ishihara, Marcel Ophuls, Andrzej Wajda, 113 mins.)

Love Boat, The (MTV 1976)** Hal Linden, Don Adams, Karen Valentine, Harvey Korman, Florence Henderson. The first pilot (not to be confused with the second and third pilots) for the successful TV series that takes place on a cruise ship. Four separate stories; the accent is on comedy, with an occasional serious moment. (Dir: Richard Kinon, 104 mins.)

Love Boat II (MTV 1977)* Bert Convy, Celeste Holm, Hope Lange, Craig Stevens, Robert Reed. Second pilot film, leading to the hit series. (Dir: Hy Averback, 106 mins.)

Love Bug, The (1969)*** Dean Jones, Michele Lee, Buddy Hackett, David Tomlinson. Many films produced by the Walt Disney organization, responsible for this comedy, have been sentimental tales about a young girl and her horse, or a freckle-faced boy and his favorite pooch. They were called "heart-warming" pictures for the youngsters. This is the same kind of film, intended for the same audience, but the "horse" happens to be a Volkswagen automobile. It's a long commercial for the German manufacturer, with a few mild chuckles provided along the way. This "family film" was a huge commercial success. Despite this parent's rather grumpy response to it, we suspect that the moppets will thoroughly enjoy it. Buddy Hackett provides most of the laughs, along with the cutesy car, as they tootle around San Francisco. Several sequels. (Dir: Robert Stevenson, 107 mins.)

Love Crazy (1941)*** William Powell, Myrna Loy, Gail Patrick, Jack Carson. Myrna finds innocent Bill in a friendly situation with Gail Patrick. She sues for divorce and Bill fights to keep her in this zany comedy. (Dir: Jack Conway, 99 mins.)

Love Finds Andy Hardy (1938)*** Mickey Rooney, Judy Garland, Lewis Stone. Mickey is at his best here and so is Judge Lewis Stone as Andy gets involved with a bevy of young lovelies. Judy was being groomed for stardom by now and the Hardy pictures were so popular they were considered a good showcase for young talent. (Dir: George B. Seitz, 90 mins.)

Love from a Stranger (1947)**½ Sylvia Sidney, John Hodiak. After marriage, a woman suspects her husband to be a mad strangler with herself intended as his next victim. Acceptably exciting suspense melodrama. Remake of the 1937 British film. (Dir: Richard Whorf, 81 mins.)

Love from Paris (Germany, 1957)*** Romy Schneider, Horst Buchholz. Tender, tragic tale of the romance between a young painter and a girl in Paris. Sensitively directed, well played; the ladies should particularly enjoy it. Dubbed in English. Alternate title: **Monpti.** (Dir: Helmut Kautner, 97 mins.)

Love God?, The (1969)* Don Knotts, Anne

405

Francis, Edmond O'Brien. (Dir: Nat Hiken, 101 mins.)

Love Happy (1949)**½ Marx Brothers, Ilona Massey, Vera-Ellen, Marilyn Monroe, Raymond Burr. Harpo befuddles some crooks who are after a precious diamond. The Marxian madness loses some of its magic in this spasmodically funny but uneven farce. (Dir: David Miller, 91 mins.)

Love Has Many Faces (1965)** Lana Turner, Cliff Robertson, Hugh O'Brian, Stefanie Powers. "Peyton Place" comes to Mexico, as a wealthy playgirl—"girl!"—fears she is losing her husband to a young girl. It's soap opera, with the suds a dirty gray. (Dir: Alexander Singer, 105 mins.)

Love Hate Love (MTV 1971)*** Ryan O'Neal, Peter Haskell, Lesley Warren. A good performance by Peter Haskell as a relentless rich man with sadistic tendencies is the main attraction of this suspense film. Haskell loses pretty Lesley Warren to handsome Ryan O'Neal and then makes their lives miserable by dogging their every move, even cross-country to California. The suspense builds nicely and Haskell's menacing presence will send chills up most lady viewers' backs. (Dir: George McCowan, 73 mins.)

Love in a Goldfish Bowl (1961)*** Tommy Sands, Fabian, Jan Sterling. Two students who are thought to be bad influences on each other get together anyway for a wild beach-house party. Nice chuckling adolescent comedy has quite a few bright touches. Watch especially for a hilarious bit by Elizabeth MacRae in a party scene. (Dir: Jack Sher, 88 mins.)

Love in a Hot Climate (France, 1953)*½ Daniel Gelin, Zsa Zsa Gabor. Alternate title: **Beauty and the Bullfighter.** (Dir: Georges Rouquier, 70 mins.)

Love in the Afternoon (1957)*** Audrey Hepburn, Gary Cooper, Maurice Chevalier. Director Billy Wilder, who usually hits a homer each time he is at bat, only manages to get to third base with this sophisticated comedy about the escapades of a middle-aged American playboy in Europe. Audrey Hepburn is, as always, winning as a young music student who falls under the playboy's spell, but Cooper is too old to fit the bill as the "champagne and violins" casanova. (126 mins.)

Love in the City (Italy, 1953)**½ Five documentary stories illustrating typical Italian life. An exploration of a dance hall in Rome; interviews with women who have tried suicide; a survey of matrimonial agencies; story of a young mother; and (the best) male reaction to the female form divine walking the streets. Some moments of high interest, at other times aimless. English narration. (Dirs: Michelangelo Antonioni, Federico Fellini, Alberto Lattuada, Maselli-Zavattini, Dino Risi, 90 mins.)

Love Is a Ball (1963)** Glenn Ford, Hope Lange, Charles Boyer. Pure escapist fare.

Glenn Ford plays a man of the world who gets involved in a scheme initiated by suave matchmaker Charles Boyer. The plot is predictable. Sumptuous French Riviera setting. (Dir: David Swift, 111 mins.)

Love Is a Many-Splendored Thing (1955)**½ Jennifer Jones, William Holden. Female fans will cry and just adore this romantic tale about the love affair between an American war correspondent and a glamorous Eurasian lady doctor. It's a modern "Madame Butterfly" yarn which is based on Han Suyin's autobiographical novel. Oscars: Best Score, Alfred Newman; Best Costume Design, Charles LeMaire; Best Song, title song by Sammy Fain and Paul Francis Webster. (Dir: Henry King, 102 mins.)

Love Is a Woman—See: **Death Is a Woman**

Love Is Better Than Ever (1952)**½ Elizabeth Taylor, Larry Parks. Silly romantic comedy somewhat enhanced by the attractive stars. Miss Taylor plays a Conn. dancing teacher who meets a bachelor about town (Parks) and uses every trick in the book to nab him. (Dir: Stanley Donen, 81 mins.)

Love Is News (1937)** Loretta Young, Tyrone Power, Don Ameche. Forced, contrived comedy about an heiress who decides to marry a reporter because she hates newspapers. A poor film but agreeably played. Remade, with Power, as *That Wonderful Urge,* 1948. (Dir: Tay Garnett, 78 mins.)

Love Is Not Enough (MTV 1978)**½ Bernie Casey, Renee Brown, Stuart K. Robinson. Pilot for the short-lived TV series "Harris and Company." About a fine, upstanding black family run by a strong, caring father (a welcome departure from the successful sitcom formula built around cartoon characters and played for laughs). Casey acts as every father ought to, black or white. (Dir: Ivan Dixon, 104 mins.)

Love Laughs at Andy Hardy (1946)** Mickey Rooney, Lewis Stone, Sara Haden. Post-war Hardy film finds Andy getting out of service and going back to his romances with the same juvenile approach. (Dir: Willis Goldbeck, 93 mins.)

Love Letters (1945)** Jennifer Jones, Joseph Cotten. Contrived, confused and boring love story is only for soap opera fans. A girl develops amnesia when she learns that somebody other than her fellow has been sending her love letters. The real chap shows up, woos her, cures her, wins her. (Dir: William Dieterle, 101 mins.)

Love Lottery, The (Great Britain, 1954)** David Niven, Herbert Lom, Peggy Cummins. David Niven is the lucky ticket holder who wins a movie star in a love lottery in this contrived and not so funny British film. (Dir: Charles Crichton, 89 mins.)

Love Machine, The (1971)½ John Phillip Law, Dyan Cannon, Robert Ryan, David Hemmings, Jackie Cooper. (Dir: Jack Haley, Jr., 108 mins.)

Love Makers, The (France-Italy, 1961)***

Jean-Paul Belmondo, Claudia Cardinale, Pietro Germi. Innocent farm boy goes to the big city where he meets and falls in love with a prostitute. Drama benefits from good performances and production. English-dubbed. Alternate title: **La Viaccia.** (Dir: Mauro Bolognini, 103 mins.)

Love Match, The (Great Britain, 1955)** Arthur Askey, Thora Hird. Little man gets into trouble by disagreeing with a referee at a soccer match. Mild comedy, funnier on the other side of the pond than over here. (Dir: David Paltenghi, 85 mins.)

Love Me—Love Me Not (Great Britain, 1962)** Craig Stevens, Erica Rogers. Roving correspondent runs into plenty of trouble while vacationing on the Riviera. Okay melodrama adapted from "Man of the World" TV series. (86 mins.)

Love Me or Leave Me (1955)***½ Doris Day, James Cagney. The highly dramatic and tune-filled career of singer Ruth Etting becomes the basis for a better than average film biography. Doris Day has seldom been shown to better advantage both vocally and dramatically. James Cagney, as Marty the Gimp, a racketeer who loves Ruth, steals every scene he is in. Oscar: Best Story, Daniel Fuchs. (Dir: Charles Vidor, 122 mins.)

Love Me Tender (1956)** Elvis Presley, Richard Egan, Debra Paget. This familiar Civil War western served to introduce Elvis Presley to film audiences. Except for this dubious distinction, the film has a predictable plot line involving robberies, double-crosses and assorted ingredients found in most westerns. Elvis sings a couple of tunes and has a death scene. (Dir: Robert D. Webb, 89 mins.)

Love Me Tonight (1932)*** Maurice Chevalier, Jeanette MacDonald. A Parisian tailor woos and wins a princess in this tuneful Rodgers and Hart film musical. Dated today but well-directed and a big step forward for its time. (Dir: Rouben Mamoulian, 100 mins.)

Love Nest (1951)** June Haver, William Lundigan, Marilyn Monroe, Jack Paar. Moderately funny comedy about an ex-GI and his wife and their adventures when they buy an apartment house. Among the zany tenants are shapely Marilyn Monroe as an ex-Wac and of all people, Jack Paar in one of his few movie appearances. Explains why Jack never did make the grade in motion pictures. (Dir: Joseph M. Newman, 85 mins.)

Love of Three Queens (France-Italy, 1953)*½ Hedy Lamarr, Massimo Serato, Cathy O'Donnell. (Dirs: Marc Allegret, Edgar Ulmer, 97 mins.)

Love on a Pillow (France-Italy, 1962)* Brigitte Bardot, Robert Hossein, James Robertson-Justice. (Dir: Roger Vadim, 102 mins.)

Love on the Dole (Great Britain, 1941)*** Deborah Kerr, Clifford Evans. The problems of a London slum family during the depression of the 1930s. Grim drama, but well made, well acted. From the novel and play by Walter Greenwood. (Dir: John Baxter, 89 mins.)

Love on the Run (1936)**½ Clark Gable, Joan Crawford, Franchot Tone. As the title indicates, Clark woos Joan from one end of the globe to the other. He and Tone are foreign correspondents so there's a spy plot too in this wild, cliche-heavy, romantic comedy. (Dir: W. S. Van Dyke, 80 mins.)

Love on the Run (France, 1979)*** Jean-Pierre Leaud, Marie-France Pisier, Claude Jade. More adventures of ever adolescent Antoine Doinel, who was introduced in "The 400 Blows" ('59) and played through the years by Leaud. Critics were unkind to this compilation of old and new footage from the Doinel sagas, but it's a pleasant bit of instant nostalgia as the performers are seen over a period of 20 years. (Dir: François Truffaut, 93 mins.)

Love Specialist, The—See: **Girl and the Palio, The**

Love Story (Great Britain, 1946)**½ Margaret Lockwood, Stewart Granger, Patricia Roc. A concert pianist goes away for a rest, falls for a man who is loved by another girl, making a pretty triangle. Ladies should enjoy this overlong but otherwise interesting romance, with excellent piano, orchestral interludes. (Dir: Maurice Ostrer, 108 mins.)

Love Story (1970)**½ Ali MacGraw, Ryan O'Neal, Ray Milland. The box-office bonanza starring MacGraw and O'Neal as the star-crossed lovers who meet, fall in love, marry, struggle until they make it financially, only to be faced with the fact that the wife is dying. It's all high-gloss histrionics, written by Erich Segal, played out against a sentimental score by Francis Lai, and acted with quiet restraint by Miss MacGraw. Audiences loved it when it played in the movie theaters and TV viewers have followed suit. (Dir: Arthur Hiller, 100 mins.)

Love That Brute (1950)**½ Paul Douglas, Jean Peters, Cesar Romero. Gangster puts on a tough front but really has a heart of gold. Pleasant enough comedy, but original version—"Tall, Dark, and Handsome" was better. (Dir: Alexander Hall, 85 mins.)

Love Thy Neighbor (1940)*** Jack Benny, Fred Allen, Mary Martin. Film designed to cash in on the Benny-Allen gag feud of radio days is moderately entertaining. Mary has some good numbers while Jack and Fred trade insults. (Dir: Mark Sandrich, 82 mins.)

Love Trap—See: **Curse of the Black Widow**

Love Under Fire (1937)**½ Loretta Young, Don Ameche, Frances Drake, Sig Ruman, John Carradine. Some bright lines and a few good scenes but this comedy-drama about spies, which is set against the Spanish Civil War, never comes together as a unit. (Dir: George Marshall, 75 mins.)

Love War, The (MTV 1970)½ Lloyd Bridges,

Angie Dickinson, Harry Basch. (Dir: George McCowan, 72 mins.)

Love with the Proper Stranger (1963)*** Natalie Wood, Steve McQueen, Edie Adams, Herschel Bernardi. Good performances by the two leads place this film a notch or two above the average fare. It's a contemporary love story set in New York City, and the on-location scenes add greatly to the film's appeal. McQueen is a musician, very much his own man, until he becomes involved with Miss Wood. (Dir: Robert Mulligan, 100 mins.)

Loved One, The (1965)***½ Robert Morse, Jonathan Winters, Anjanette Comer, Milton Berle, John Gielgud, Rod Steiger, Liberace. Irreverent, uneven black comedy, based on the novel by Evelyn Waugh, concerns the sudden suicide of a Hollywood star and his nephew's problems in paying the exorbitant funeral bill. Macabre humor is well played by a large star-studded cast. Notable is Liberace's grinning portrayal of a funeral director. Deft, sometimes savage screenplay written by Terry Southern and Christopher Isherwood. Co-produced by award-winning cinematographer Haskell Wexler. (Dir: Tony Richardson, 116 mins.)

Love-ins, The (1967)* James MacArthur, Susan Oliver, Richard Todd. (Dir: Arthur Dreifuss, 91 mins.)

Lovely to Look At (1952)**½ Kathryn Grayson, Howard Keel, Red Skelton, Ann Miller, Zsa Zsa Gabor. Entertaining remake of the musical "Roberta," with many of the lovely Jerome Kern tunes, such as "Smoke Gets in Your Eyes." The songs take precedence over the thin plot, set in the haute-couture fashion world of Paris. Kathryn Grayson and Howard Keel are up to their musical assignments. Marge and Gower Champion offer some excellent dance turns. (Dir: Mervyn LeRoy, 105 mins.)

Lovely Way to Die, A (1968)** Kirk Douglas, Sylva Koscina. Detective (Kirk Douglas) guards a woman accused of murder, sets out to prove her innocent. With Eli Wallach, Kenneth Haigh, Martyn Green, Sharon Farrell. Not such a lovely way to waste time. Film debut of Ali MacGraw. (Dir: David Lowell Rich, 103 mins.)

Lovemaker, The (Spain-France, 1956)**½ Betsy Blair, Jose Suarez. Plain, unloved spinster is victimized by a cruel joke that ends tragically. Spanish-made drama is well acted but overlong. (Dir: Juan A. Bardem, 80 mins.)

Lover Boy (Great Britain, 1954)**½ Gerard Philipe, Valerie Hobson, Joan Greenwood. Opportunistic Frenchman in London has a talent for romancing the ladies, uses it—and them—to climb to success and wealth. Savagely bitter comedy packed quite a punch in its original form, but censorship has taken its toll. Nevertheless, t ere are still some splendid moments.

Excellent direction by Rene Clement, performances by the entire cast. (105 mins.)

Lover Come Back (1946)**½ Lucille Ball, George Brent, Vera Zorina. George Brent is a war (WW-II) correspondent whose traveling keeps him away from his wife (Lucille Ball). Trouble comes in the shape of a war photographer (Vera Zorina) and Lucy heads for the divorce courts. Plenty of laughs for Lucy fans. (Dir: William A. Seiter, 90 mins.)

Lover Come Back (1961)*** Doris Day, Rock Hudson, Tony Randall, Edie Adams. Some good laughs in this Day-Hudson battle of the sexes. He's an advertising tycoon, she's a competitor, it's love on the make. Frequent bright dialogue, direction, clever situations, nice supporting performances. (Dir: Delbert Mann, 107 mins.)

Lovers, The (France, 1958)***½ Jeanne Moreau, Jean-Marc Bory, Alain Cuny. Louis Malle's second film, about a beautiful, bored housewife's thirst for a deeper love and a more meaningful life. Controversial at the time, due to some explicit lovemaking. Moving, poetic, vivid, and Moreau is simply superb in the starring role. There are boring stretches between the brilliant pivotal scenes, however. (Dir: Louis Malle, 90 mins.)

Lovers and Lollipops (1956)**½ Lori March, Cathy Dunn, Gerald O'Loughlin. Young widow worries if her daughter will accept a new suitor. Slender tale has some refreshing moments, but remains pretty lightweight. (Dirs: Morris Engel, Ruth Orkin, 80 mins.)

Lovers and Other Strangers (1970)***½ Gig Young, Richard Castellano, Beatrice Arthur. A comedy winner! A raucously funny portrait of two families who come together when the daughter of one (Bonnie Bedelia) and the son of the other (Michael Brandon) announce wedding plans. Miss Arthur and Castellano play the first-generation Italian parents of the lad and they have the lion's share of the funny lines. Also scoring in individual scenes are Gig Young as the father of the bride; Anne Meara and Harry Guardino as a bickering couple; Anne Jackson as a cast-aside mistress; and Marian Hailey as a weepy, whining bridesmaid. (Dir: Cy Howard, 104 mins.)

Lovers and Thieves (France, 1957)***½ Jean Poiret, Michel Serrault. Director Sacha Guitry's last picture maintained the laughing skepticism that was his trademark. This one concerns a thief and his victim who are coincidentally involved with each other in more than a simple robbery. Intelligent and impeccable. (Dir: Sacha Guitry, 81 mins.)

Lovers of Paris (France, 1957)**½ Gerard Philipe, Danielle Darrieux. A Frenchman finds that the easiest way to success entails a short-cut through the proprietress' boudoir. Sexy French bedroom comedy-drama, well acted. Alternate title: **Pot Bouille**. (Dir: Julien Duvivier, 115 mins.)

Lovers on a Tightrope (France, 1960)*½ Annie Girardot, Francois Perier. (Dir: Jean-Charles Dudrumet, 83 mins.)

Love's Dark Ride (MTV 1978)** Cliff Potts, Carrie Snodgress, Jane Seymour, Shelly Novack. Based on a real-life story about a blind man who learns that his real problem lies within. A vehicle for Potts, who scores with his cocky, devilish manner. Accidentally blinded by a gunshot, Potts's character feels sorry for himself. Snodgress is largely wasted as his girlfriend, yet her warmth brings relief. (Dir: Delbert Mann, 104 mins.)

Loves of a Blonde (Czechoslovakia, 1965)**** Hana Brejchova, Vladimir Pucholt. Milos Forman's touching, wry triumph about a shy girl in a small, male-depleted factory town, and her unconquerable romanticism. Uses humor, pathos, desire and sorrow in an original, touching way. The film seemingly moves of its own accord; most of the actors are nonprofessional and enact the situations honestly, often in wholly unexpected ways. Best is the dance scene, where some newly-arrived, middle-aged army reservists are faced by the man-hungry factory girls. (88 mins.)

Loves of Carmen, The (1948)**½ Rita Hayworth, Glenn Ford. Familiar opera about the love of a soldier for a gypsy minus the music. Not a very impressive film, but Miss Hayworth should keep the men awake. (Dir: Charles Vidor, 99 mins.)

Loves of Edgar Allan Poe, The (1942)**½ John Shepperd (later known as Shepperd Strudwick), Linda Darnell, Virginia Gilmore. Interesting but uninspired film biography of one of our greatest writers. Definitely one of the weakest biographical films to come from a major studio. (Dir: Harry Lachman, 67 mins.)

Loves of Isadora, The (Great Britain, 1969)***½ Vanessa Redgrave, James Fox, Jason Robards. The long, rambling story of Isadora Duncan, the celebrated, tormented, passionate, and damned woman whose revolutionary work became the forerunner of modern dance. Flawed in many respects including a lack of continuity, but Vanessa Redgrave's no-holds-barred performance as Isadora is electrifying. Alternate title: **Isadora.** (Dir: Karel Reisz, 131 mins.)

Loves of Joanna Godden, The (Great Britain, 1947)**½ Googie Withers, Jean Kent. Period melodrama, as a woman struggles to keep her home intact, despite the loss of her loved one and the interference of her sister. Leisurely, but commendably acted, directed. Fine music score by Vaughan Williams. (Dir: Charles Frend, 89 mins.)

Love's Savage Fury (MTV 1979)** Jennifer O'Neill, Perry King, Raymond Burr, Vernee Watson. Another ripoff of "Gone with the Wind." The gorgeous O'Neill is the focus of this Civil War saga, playing a southern belle fallen on hard times.

. There's some nonsense about hidden gold and most of the action takes place in a hellhole of a Yankee prison camp. Plenty of romance pulp fiction, and you don't even have to turn the pages. (Dir: Joseph Hardy, 104 mins.)

Lovey: A Circle of Children, Part II (MTV 1978)**** Jane Alexander, Ronny Cox. This extraordinary work is based on the real-life experiences of Mary McCracken, a dedicated teacher of children with severe learning disabilities, to whom we were introduced in "A Circle of Children, Part I." Alexander, the star of both dramatizations, is remarkably effective portraying the dynamic woman, divorced after a 23-year marriage, who has found solace and inspiration in the challenge of reaching these seemingly unmanageable children. The wonders she works on a dirty, tantrum-bound child of eight she calls "Lovey" are enthralling. B&W. (Dir: Jud Taylor, 104 mins.)

Lovin' Molly (1974)**½ Blythe Danner, Anthony Perkins, Beau Bridges, Susan Sarandon. Blythe Danner's luminous performance as a Texas lass who wouldn't let convention stand in the way of loving two men at the same time, for a period covering four decades, is the best thing about this strange little film. Based on Larry McMurtry's novel, "Leaving Cheyenne," the story starts out in 1925 and goes up to the mid-60's, but the earlier scenes are the best since the principals, Ms. Danner, Bridges and Perkins, look silly in old-age makeup. (Dir: Sidney Lumet, 98 mins.)

Loving (1970)***½ George Segal, Eva Marie Saint, Sterling Hayden, Keenan Wynn. A quietly intense movie, humorous, human and insightful, about a New York illustrator whose suburban family, New York mistress and job prospects are veering toward unwanted routine. Movie's final scene is incongruous in its farcical mayhem, but otherwise the film is sensitive, restrained and, grounded in a peculiarly American reality, rings true. Segal gives a fine, multi-level performance as the harassed free-lance artist. Written by Don Devlin. (Dir: Irvin Kershner, 90 mins.)

Loving You (1957)** Elvis Presley, Lizabeth Scott, Wendell Corey, Dolores Hart. Small-town boy becomes an overnight sensation when he's signed by a lady press agent to sing with her ex-husband's country band. Tailormade for Presley and his tunes, the story matters little—too little, if one doesn't dig Elvis. (Dir: Hal Kanter, 101 mins.)

Lt. Robin Crusoe U.S.N. (1966)* Dick Van Dyke, Nancy Kwan. (Dir: Byron Paul, 110 mins.)

Lucan (MTV 1977)** Ned Beatty, Kevin Brophy, Stockard Channing. Here's another version of the old story about the boy raised in a forest with wild animals, attempting to understand modern civilization and the wickedness of man. Kevin Brophy plays the 20-year-old innocent, busy Ned Beatty is his deceitful boss, and Stockard Channing is the boss's friendly daughter, ready to initiate a shy Lucan. MGM production values help, but the story remains predictable. Try Truffaut's "The Wild Child." (Dir: David Greene, 79 mins.)

Lucas Tanner (1974)**½ David Hartman, Rosemary Murphy, Joe Garagiola. In this pilot film for the TV series, lanky, personable David Hartman becomes a midwestern high-school English teacher and his wholesome enthusiasm pays off. Tanner is that rarity, a good, open-minded teacher who understands kids, but battles suspicious parents and jealous cohorts. On-location footage in Webster Groves, Mo., and St. Louis provides a welcome change from the customary California scenery. (Dir: Richard Donner, 74 mins.)

Lucía (Cuba, 1970)***½ Raquel Revuelta, Eslinda Nunez, Adela Legra. A three-part film; in each part a heroine named Lucia engages in a form of struggle peculiar to her era. The first Lucia is from the colonial upper class caught in the Spanish-American War (1848); the second is the companion of an urban guerrilla fighting against Machado in the early '30s; the third is a contemporary Cuban, trying to overcome spousal opposition to her participation in the "revolutionary life." Engrossing third-world cinema, a rare credible example of socialist art. (Dir: Humberto Solas, 161 mins.)

Luck of Ginger Coffey, The (U.S.-Canada, 1964)**** Robert Shaw, Mary Ure. Fine drama of a young Irish immigrant in Montreal with his wife and daughter trying to better himself in the world against all odds, including his own attitude. Excellently acted and directed, with the actual locales adding to the authenticity. (Dir: Irvin Kershner, 100 mins.)

Luck of the Irish, The (1948)**½ Tyrone Power, Anne Baxter, Cecil Kellaway. While trying to choose between his newspaper boss' daughter and a sweet colleen, Tyrone has the invaluable aid of a leprechaun. Whimsical and ordinary film. (Dir: Henry Koster, 99 mins.)

Lucky Jordan (1942)**½ Alan Ladd, Helen Walker. Ladd carries this film about an AWOL soldier who inadvertently becomes a hero by defeating a gang of Nazi agents. (Dir: Frank Tuttle, 84 mins.)

Lucky Lady (1975)* Gene Hackman, Liza Minnelli, Burt Reynolds, Robby Benson, Michael Hordern. (Dir: Stanley Donen, 118 mins.)

Lucky Luciano (Italy-France-U.S., 1973)** Gian Maria Volonte, Rod Steiger, Edmond O'Brien, Charles Siragusa, Vincent Gardenia. Rather clinical look at the life of a crime boss whose career flourished even after deportation to his native Italy. Some violence, but the emphasis is on the atmosphere in which Luciano (Volonte) was

able to operate. Narcotics agent Siragusa, who worked on the Luciano case for years, plays himself quite well. Filmed in New York City and Italy. (Dir: Francesco Rosi, 112 mins.)

Lucky Me (1954)** Doris Day, Bob Cummings, Phil Silvers, Nancy Walker. Disappointing musical comedy with only a few good things in the whole film. Chorus girl and friends out of jobs in Florida. A perfect example of Hollywood's wasting of talent. (Dir: Jack Donohue, 100 mins.)

Lucky Nick Cain (1950)*** George Raft, Coleen Gray. A gambler on vacation on the Riviera is framed for the murder of a T-man, does some sleuthing on his own to break up an international counterfeiting ring. Good speedy melodrama for Raft fans. Made in Italy. (Dir: Joseph M. Newman, 87 mins.)

Lucky Night (1939)*½ Myrna Loy, Robert Taylor, Joseph Allen. Pitiful, contrived little nothing about an heiress who marries a poor poet. The cast is incapable of helping this film because the authors have failed to provide them with decent dialogue. (Dir: Norman Taurog, 82 mins.)

Lucky Partners (1940)**½ Ronald Colman, Ginger Rogers. Artist shares a sweepstakes ticket with a girl, which proves lucky. Occasionally amusing comedy, but could have been better. (Dir: Lewis Milestone, 102 mins.)

Lucky to Be a Woman (Italy, 1958)**½ Sophia Loren, Charles Boyer. Lightweight comedy bolstered by the stars' performances—plot centers around a model and her escapades in the international movie set. (Dir: Alessandro Blassetti, 94 mins.)

Lucy Gallant (1955)**½ Jane Wyman, Charlton Heston, Claire Trevor. Charlton Heston strikes oil and Jane Wyman builds the biggest fashion business in Texas but they find that marriage and careers don't mix. Claire Trevor adds another portrayal as the "heart of gold" saloon keeper to her list. (Dir: Robert Parrish, 104 mins.)

Ludwig (Italy, 1972)*½ Helmut Berger, Trevor Howard, Romy Schneider, Gert Frobe, Silvana Mangano. (Dir: Luchino Visconti, 173 mins.)

Lullaby of Broadway (1951)** Doris Day, Gene Nelson, Gladys George. More backstage nonsense with music and plenty of dancing. Score includes standards by George Gershwin and Cole Porter which help. Gladys George registers as Doris' mother. Broadway was never like this! (Dir: David Butler, 92 mins.)

Luna (Italy, 1978)** Jill Clayburgh, Matthew Barry, Renato Salvatori. Bertolucci's Jungian remake of *High School Confidential*. In this story of an opera singer reaching out to her addicted teenage son by incestuous advances, since there is no confrontation by director Bernardo Bertolucci with his own evidently deeply held feelings, there is no dramatic context for the actors to play against, and Clayburgh and Barry bump against implausibility and vagary. A resolute failure. Pretentious, irritating and tasteless. Salvatori is very funny as a Communist pickup. (141 mins.)

Lupo (Israel, 1970)**½ Yuda Barkan, Gabi Amrani, Esther Greenberg. Sentimental, saccharine lightweight pastry about a middle-aged junk dealer in Tel Aviv. Leading role is played with charm by Barkan, a 25-year-old actor. Shot on location in Tel Aviv, and captures some of the infectious quality of the town's struggling tradesmen. Kids might enjoy. Written and directed by Menahem Golan, who made the lovely "Sallah." English subtitles. (Dir: Menahem Golan, 100 mins.)

Lure of the Wilderness (1952)**½ Jean Peters, Jeffrey Hunter, Walter Brennan. Young man finds an escaped convict and his daughter hiding out in the swamp, helps him prove his innocence. Remake of 1941's "Swamp Water" has the benefit of color but doesn't have the interest of the original. Some good moments, however. (Dir: Jean Negulesco, 92 mins.)

Lured (1947)**½ A dance hall girl disappears in London, so friend Lucille Ball sets out to find her, nearly gets herself killed. With George Sanders, Boris Karloff. Fairly good mystery. (Also called "Personal Column.") (Dir: Douglas Sirk, 102 mins.)

Lust for a Vampire (Great Britain, 1970)**½ Michael Johnson, Suzanna Leigh, Yutte Stensgaard, Ralph Bates, Barbara Jefford. Ravishing young vampirette (Stensgaard) feels pangs of love for a novelist (Johnson) who has come to the old castle where she is a pupil in what is now an exclusive girls' school, to study the supernatural. Racy, high-humored, gory and full of female allures and perversions. Based on characters from J. Sheridan Le Fanu's 19th-century novel "Carmilla" (as were Roger Vadim's "Love and Roses" and Roy Ward Baker's "The Vampire Lovers"). (Dir: Jimmy Sangster, 95 mins.)

Lust for Gold (1949)**** Glenn Ford, Ida Lupino, Gig Young. Excellent film showing how greed and evil take over and ruin basically good people. Edge-of-seat suspense and fine performance by all. A real sleeper! (Dir: S. Sylvan Simon, 90 mins.)

Lust for Gold (U.S.S.R., 1957)** Ivan Pereverzev, Inna Kmit. Greed in the gold fields of prerevolutionary Russia. Several people are wiped out when they let their natural instincts get the better of them. As mundane a piece of anticapitalist propaganda as you'll ever see. (Dir: I. Pravov, 92 mins.)

Lust for Life (1956)**** Kirk Douglas, Anthony Quinn. Superb film about the turbulent personal life of the tormented artist Vincent van Gogh, masterfully played by Kirk Douglas. Anthony Quinn won his second Oscar for his colorful performance as van Gogh's close friend and severest critic, artist Paul Gauguin. A special treat—all those marvelous van Gogh masterpieces. (Dir: Vincente Minnelli, 122 mins.)

Lusty Men, The (1952)***½ Susan Hayward, Robert Mitchum, Arthur Kennedy. When a cowpoke becomes a rodeo star and lets it go to his head, his wife suffers. Very good drama with authentic rodeo atmosphere, solid performances and direction. (Dir: Nicholas Ray, 113 mins.)

Luta Continua, The—See: **Struggle Continues, The**

Luther (1974)*** Stacy Keach, Patrick Magee, Alan Badel, Hugh Griffith. John Osborne's stunning play about the famous 16th-century cleric who changed the course of the world has been shortened and its impact reduced in the move to the screen. Albert Finney is not on hand to recreate his triumphant stage performance, but Stacy Keach, a fine but lesser actor, is increasingly effective as the film builds. Set in Germany in 1506-1533, Luther's actual early stamping grounds are now in East Germany, so this "Luther" was filmed on a "church" set in England. Rewarding historical drama. American Film Theatre presentation. (Dir: Guy Green, 112 mins.)

Luv (1967)**½ Jack Lemmon, Peter Falk, Elaine May, Eddie Mayehoff. Heavy-handed rendering of Murray Schisgal's clever Broadway play about life and loves among a set of middle-class New Yorkers—part of a group much concerned with self-analysis and psychiatric jargon. Although the script and the performances have been cheapened, Elaine May is genuinely funny, and there's enough left to provide a few laughs along the way. If the whole picture had been as well handled as the scene with Elaine and Jack in a Ferris wheel . . . (Dir: Clive Donner, 96 mins.)

Luxury Liner (1948)** George Brent, Jane Powell, Lauritz Melchior. Good voices but nothing else in this musical about a ship's captain and his meddling teen-age daughter. (Dir: Richard Whorf, 98 mins.)

Lydia (1941)***½ Merle Oberon, Joseph Cotten, Edna May Oliver, George Reeves, Alan Marshal. An elderly lady has a reunion with four of her lost loves, relives the romantic past. Sensitive, poignant romantic drama, skillfully directed, acted. (Dir: Julien Duvivier, 104 mins.)

Lydia Bailey (1952)**½ Dale Robertson, Anne Francis, Juanita Moore, William Marshall. American lawyer goes to Haiti to get a girl's signature on a legal document. Becomes involved in a war with Napoleonic forces. Pleasant costume adventure moves at a good pace, has a colorful setting. (Dir: Jean Negulesco, 88 mins.)

M (Germany, 1931)**** Peter Lorre (film debut), Gustav Grundgens, Ellen Widman, Inge Landgut. Suspenseful, psychological crime drama, brilliantly directed by Fritz

Lang. Lorre plays a pitiable, disturbed child murderer in Berlin, and the film offers an intriguing delineation of the painstaking methods employed by the police and the underworld, both out to trap the killer. Remade in the U.S. ('51). (99 mins.)

Ma & Pa Kettle (1949)*** Marjorie Main, Percy Kilbride. The first of the "Ma and Pa Kettle" series and one of the funniest. These rural characters were first introduced in the Claudette Colbert-Fred MacMurray comedy "The Egg and I," and their fan appeal was so great that Universal starred them in their own vehicle. Marjorie Main and Percy Kilbride are a matchless pair as the Kettles. (Dir: Charles Lamont, 75 mins.)

Ma & Pa Kettle at Home (1954)**½ Marjorie Main, Percy Kilbride. "Ma & Pa Kettle" fans will get a kick out of this comedy in which Pa tries to make the dilapidated farm over into an efficient, prosperous operation. Just about everything turns out wrong and the reults provide many laughs. (Dir: Charles Lamont, 81 mins.)

Ma & Pa Kettle at the Fair (1952)**½ Marjorie Main, Percy Klibride. Cornball comedy with Kettles getting into one impossible predicament after another. Pa buys a sick horse, Ma enters him in a race at the county fair by mistake; Rosie, the Kettles' oldest daughter, falls in love. (Dir: Charles Barton, 77 mins.)

Ma & Pa Kettle at Waikiki (1955)**½ Marjorie Main, Percy Kilbride. The Kettles find themselves in Hawaii in this outing. They are invited to that island paradise by another branch of the Kettle clan who has made millions in canned fruit. Many zany incidents occur during the Kettles' stay in Hawaii. (Dir: Lee Sholem, 79 mins.)

Ma & Pa Kettle Back on the Farm (1951)**½ Majorie Main, Percy Kilbride. More fun as the Kettle clan gets involved with false uranium deposits on their property, in-law trouble via their oldest son's wife's parents, and gangsters who think their property is loaded with uranium. (Dir: Edward Sedgwick, 80 mins.)

Ma & Pa Kettle Go to Town (1950)** Marjorie Main, Percy Kilbride. Strictly for the Kettle-clan fans. Ma and Pa win a trip to New York City in a soft-drink-slogan contest and have a series of predictable but amusing adventures. There are gangsters, stolen money, kidnappings and zany chases galore. An added attraction is Marjorie Main's "beauty treatment" at a fashionable New York cosmetic mill. (Dir: Charles Lamont, 80 mins.)

Ma & Pa Kettle on Vacation (1953)**½ Marjorie Main, Percy Kilbride. The "Kettle" fans will have more fun with this broad comedy in which "Ma and Pa" go to Paris on vacation. Naturally, they don't confine their activities to sightseeing and get involved with an international espionage operation. (Dir: Charles Lamont, 75 mins.)

Macabre (1958)** William Prince, Jim Backus. This horror film doesn't rely on monsters for its impact—there are all sorts of fiendish things going on, such as burying people alive, for instance. The cast is better than the vehicle but they seem to enjoy playing at being terrorized. (Dir: William Castle, 72 mins.)

Macahans, The (MTV 1976)**½ James Arness, Eva Marie Saint, Richard Kiley, Bruce Boxleitner. Sprawling Western movie based on the theatrical feature "How the West Was Won," benefits from the cast and production. "Gunsmoke"'s Arness, backed up by Saint and young newcomer Boxleitner, returned to television playing scout Zeb Macahan, leading his brother's family west from Bull Run, Virginia, in time to avoid the Civil War. The trek west is interspersed with Civil War battle scenes involving Zeb's brother and nephew—sequenses culled from other MGM pictures. (Dir: Bernard McEveety, 120 mins.)

Macao (1952)*** Robert Mitchum, Jane Russell, William Bendix, Brad Dexter, Gloria Grahame. Adventurer helps the police to capture a gangster wanted in the U. S. (Dirs: Josef von Sternberg, Nicholas Ray, 80 mins.)

MacArthur (1977)**½ Gregory Peck, Ed Flanders, Dan O'Herlihy. Superficially engaging study of General Douglas MacArthur. The film lacks grandeur, and everyone seems to be invading the same beach six or seven times. Two stirring sequences in the otherwise talky film are MacArthur's return to the Philippines and the signing of the Japanese surrender aboard the U.S.S. "Missouri." (Dir: Joseph Sargent, 130 mins.)

Macbeth (1948)*** Orson Welles, Roddy McDowall, Jeanette Nolan, Dan O'Herlihy, Edgar Barrier. Perhaps director Orson Welles's most problematical film. He attempted to transpose his Shakespearean vision from stage to film by using the economics and logistics of a Republic western: no budget, three-week schedule, papier-mâché sets on the western ranch. Welles's voice is still one of the great theater instruments around, but his Macbeth is inscrutable. O'Herlihy's Macduff and Barrier's Banquo are fine. Nolan is ludicrously incompetent playing Lady M. This was Welles's last Hollywood film for ten years. (105 mins.)

Macbeth (MTV 1960)** Maurice Evans, Judith Anderson. It's hard to imagine how Evans was taken seriously as a Shakespearean actor in America for several decades. His woebegone inadequacy posing as Macbeth gives the classics a bad name. Anderson is a compelling Lady Macbeth, but is given nothing in the way of intelligent context by director George Schaeffer.

Macbeth (Great Britain, MTV 1970)***½

Eric Porter, Janet Suzman. Porter and Suzman portray the sanguinary pair in an adept BBC production, of the play, directed by John Gorrie in a manner well adapted to the visual limitations of TV.

Macbeth (Great Britain, 1971)***½ Jon Finch, Francesca Annis, Martin Shaw, John Stride. In the uproar over the extreme (but not unwarranted) violence and gore in this film, director Roman Polanski's personal life, and the fact that this was Playboy Eneterprises' first production (and that Lady Macbeth did her dream speech in the nude), the merits of the film were largely overlooked. It is a grim, valid conception of the bloody drama. Polanski and his script advisor, Kenneth Tynan, dispense with a great deal of the poetry. (Most of the line readings are rather muffled.) Finch and Miss Annis, the two young leads, expertly portray the murderous couple. (140 mins.)

Machine Gun Kelly (1958)** Charles Bronson, Susan Cabot. Small time hoodlum becomes a public enemy due to the goading of a dame. Bronson's good, the film is less so. (Dir: Roger Corman, 80 mins.)

Machine Gun McCain (1970)** Peter Falk, John Cassavetes, Britt Ekland. Stars are more interesting than this routine crime drama set in the U.S. but shot mostly in Europe. It involves a raid on a Las Vegas casino controlled by the Mafia, and it costs everyone concerned a large price. (Dir: Giuliano Montaldo, 94 mins.)

Machiste Against Hercules in the Vale of Woe—See: Hercules in the Vale of Woe

Machiste in King Solomon's Mines (Italy, 1964)* Reg Park, Wandisa Guida. (Dir: Martin Andrews, 92 mins.)

Machiste, Strongest Man in the World— See: Mole Men Against the Son of Hercules

Macho Callahan (1970)* David Janssen, Jean Seberg, Lee J. Cobb, David Carridine. (Dir: Bernard L. Kowalski, 99 mins.)

Maciste Against the Czar—See: Atlas Against the Czar

Mackenna's Gold (1969)*½ Gregory Peck, Omar Sahrif, Camila Sparv. (Dir: J. Lee Thompson, 128 mins.)

Mackintosh & T.J. (1975)**½ Roy Rogers, Clay O'Brien, Joan Hackett. Corny oater shot in Texas marks the return of western star Rogers to his first starring role in 22 years. He's a philosophical ranch hand who befriends a tough kid (O'Brien), and has difficulty with younger hands whose views clash with his. Rogers's best performance, though that isn't much of a compliment. Music by Waylon Jennings. (Dir: Marvin J. Chomsky, 96 mins.)

Mackintosh Man, The (Great Britain, 1973)**½ Paul Newman, Dominique Sanda, James Mason, Harry Andrews, Michael Horden. Thriller about cold-war espionage—the kind of plot that was quite popular in the '60s when spies were busy coming in from the cold. Not only is the plot outdated, but the excellent supporting actors have been given lightweight roles badly cast. Miss Sanda's French accent belies her portrayal of a young Englishwoman. Newman affects a series of poses as he plays the agent out to trap Mason, a Communist who has infiltrated the top ranks of British intelligence. Enough car chases, escapes, captures and beatings as well as fine photography (by Oswald Morris) of England, Ireland and Malta, to keep fans of the genre occupied. Based on the novel "The Freedom Trap," by Desmond Bagley. (Dir: John Huston, 98 mins.)

Macomber Affair, The (1947)***½ Gregory Peck, Joan Bennett, Robert Preston. Hemingway's tale of the triangular difficulties of a husband, wife and guide on an African hunting expedition. Literate, well acted. (Dir: Zoltan Korda, 89 mins.)

Macon County Line (1974)**½ Alan Vint, Jesse Vint, Max Baer, Cheryl Waters. There is a great deal of violence and some effective drama in this supposedly factual story, about a vengeful southern sheriff who is out for blood after his wife is brutally killed by a pair of drifters. The acting, by Alan and Jesse Vint (brothers in real life), and Baer (he also co-scripted and produced) as the sheriff, is very good. (Dir: Richard Compton, 89 mins.)

Macumba Love (1960)*½ Walter Reed, Ziva Rodann, June Wilkinson. (Dir: Douglas Fowley, 85 mins.)

Macunaima (Brazil, 1970)**½ Grande Otelo, Paulo Jose. Daring Brazilian allegory of a black, 45 years old, who turns white while prancing between the "jungle" and the "city." Wild and far-out fairytale sequences involving cannibalism and incest move the narrative. Sometimes interesting experiment. (Dir: Joaquim Pedro De Andrade, 95 mins.)

Mad About Men (Great Britain, 1954)** Glynis Johns, Donald Sinden, Margaret Rutherford, Dora Bryan. Girl who intends to do good keeps transferring her affections from her husband to her former fiance. Slow-moving comedy needs more sparkle. (Dir: Ralph Thomas, 90 mins.)

Mad About Music (1938)*** Deanna Durbin, Herbert Marshall. Girl attending a swanky Swiss school invents a father to impress classmates. Fine Durbin film, well produced, acted and naturally featuring the lovely voice. (Dir: Norman Taurog, 100 mins.)

Mad Adventures of "Rabbi" Jacob, The (France, 1974)*** Louis De Funes, Suzy Delair, Marcel Dalio. In this catchall slapstick comedy, writer-director Gerard Oury lampoons bigotry, Arab nationalism, gangsterism, the police, and many little conventions that only the Franch would notice—all with total abandon. But the film strains so for laughs, and takes so long to congratulate itself when it gets them, that the humor begins to sour. (96 mins.)

Mad at the World (1955)**½ Frank Lovejoy, Keefe Brasselle, Cathy O'Donnell. When a gang of juvenile delinquents seriously injure a young father's baby, he decides to take the matter in his own hands and goes on the hunt for them. Grim drama, well made. (Dir: Harry Essex, 72 mins.)

Mad Bull, The (MTV 1977)** Alex Karras, Susan Anspach. Supposedly, an inside view of wrestling and its weird fans. Uneven. Karras is an athlete who can act with some finesse, and Anspach, his girl from the grocery store, more than holds her own. (Dirs: Walter Doniger, Len Steckler, 104 mins.)

Mad Dog Coll (1961)*½ John Chandler, Kay Doubleday, Brooke Hayward, Telly Savalas, Vincent Gardenia. (Dir: Burt Balaban, 88 mins.)

Mad Dog Morgan (Australia, 1976)**½ Dennis Hopper, Jack Thompson, David Gulpilil. Dennis Hopper plays the ravaging Australian bandit in a rather weak genre movie. However, the color cinematography by Mike Molley is superb. (Dir: Philippe Mora, 102 mins.)

Mad Dogs and Englishmen (1971)*** Joe Cocker, Leon Russell. Filmed record of Cocker's tour of the U.S. in '70. He is excellent and sings numbers like "Space Captain," "Something," and "Let It Be," adapting all to his unique gravelly voice. Russell is his sideman, and occasionally sings. Shots of Cocker offstage are interesting, if you like Cocker. (Dir: Pierre Adidge, 114 mins.)

Mad Executioners, The (West Germany, 1963)*½ Hansjorg Felmy, Maria Perschy, Dieter Borsche. (Dir: Edwin Zbonek, 93 mins.)

Mad Ghoul, The (1943)**½ David Bruce, Evelyn Ankers. Wild thriller, with an excellent performance by Bruce as a doctor kept in a state of living death. Grisly stuff which horror addicts should enjoy. (Dir: James Hogan, 65 mins.)

Mad Little Island (Grat Britain, 1958)**½ Jeannie Carson, Donald Sinden. Scottish islanders are horrified to learn their home is to be turned into a rocket base. Sort of a sequel to "Tight Little Island," and not nearly as amusing. (Dir: Michael Relph, 87 mins.)

Mad Love (1935)**½ Peter Lorre, Frances Drake, Colin Clive. Mad doctor operates on a pianist mutilated in an accident, grafts the hands of a murderer to him. Over-acted but atmospheric thriller (Dir: Karl Freund, 70 mins.)

Mad Magician, The (1954)**½ Vincent Price, Mary Murphy, Eva Gabor, Patrick O'Neal. Having been a mad wax museum owner in 3-D, Price now turns to magic mixed with murder. On TV, the effect of Price turning a garden hose on the audience in 3-D is lost—unfortunately, because it's more interesting than anything that happens in the story. (Dir: John Brahm, 72 mins.)

Mad Max (Australia, 1980)**** Mel Gibson, Joanne Samuel, Hugh Keays-Byrne, Tim Burns, Roger Ward. About the ultimate gang of motorcycle bandits. Director George Miller's provocative, stimulating cheapie is the best action exploitation film in years, with chases and crashes to satisfy the most jaded thrill seeker. (93 mins.)

Mad Miss Manton (1938)***½ Barbara Stanwyck, Henry Fonda. Society girl turns sleuth and investigates a murder. Fast, funny comedy-mystery, very good fun. (Dir: Leigh Jason, 80 mins.)

Mad Monster Party (1967)*½ (Dir: Jules Bass, 94 mins.)

Mad Room, The (1969)*** Stella Stevens, Shelley Winters. Pretty good remake of 1941 "Ladies in Retirement"—a thriller full of suspense and plot twists to set you on the wrong track. Stevens is quite good as the companion to a wealthy widow (Winters) who brings her brother and sister to live with her after they are released from an asylum. There are some gory scenes but fans of this type of horror story will be fascinated. (Dir: Bernard Girard, 93 mins.)

Mad Wednesday—See: **Sin of Harold Diddlebock, The**

Madame (France, 1963)** Sophia Loren, Robert Hossein. One of Loren's worst films—an inaccurate account of France during Napoleon's reign. Loren is beautiful but the script defeats her efforts at comedy. Nothing, however, quite overcomes her good looks. (Dir: Christian-Jaque, 104 mins.)

Madame Bovary (1949)*** Jennifer Jones, James Mason, Van Heflin, Alf Kjellin, Louis Jourdan. Miss Jones gives a beautiful performance in the title role. The ballroom scene—with Bovary waltzing herself to an epiphany—is one of the most brilliantly designed and edited sequences in any of director Vincente Minnelli's films. (114 mins.)

Madame Curie (1943)***½ Greer Garson, Walter Pidgeon, Henry Travers. Occasionally too slow but generally brilliant screen biography of the discoverers of radium. Garson and Pidgeon's are ideal in this informative and entertaining film. (Dir: Mervyn LeRoy, 124 mins.)

Madame Rosa (France-Israel, 1977)**** Simone Signoret, Claude Dauphin, Samy Ben Youb. Signoret is marvelous as a Jewish ex-prostitute who raises the offspring of working streetwalkers and has a particular affection for a 14-year-old Arab boy. The film has humor, warmth, poignance, and love. Academy Award, Best Foreign Film. (Dir: Moshe Mizrahi, 105 mins.)

Madame Satan (1930)**½ Kay Johnson, Reginald Denny, Lillian Roth, Roland Young. This extravaganza was one of director Cecil B. deMille's few talkies to be set in the dazzling world of the rich. Gaudily outrageous, with a splashy, posh masked ball held in a dirigible and a leap

414

from same into the Central Park reservoir. The film is stiff and pallid as art, though the costumes and sets remain marvels of gilded excess. (105 mins.)

Madame Sin (1972)** Bette Davis, Robert Wagner. With silver-blue eyeshadow splashed over her famous lids, Miss Davis plays an oriental villainness in this handsomely mounted film made in England. The location footage taken on the Isle of Mull and the Scottish coast turns out to be the real star, backed by English supporting actors and Wagner, with Miss Davis appearing content to remain in the background. The plot has Madame Sin kidnapping a U.S. intelligence agent. (Dir: David Greene, 73 mins.)

Madame X (1937)** Gladys George, Warren William, William Henry. Someone named Alexandre Bisson once wrote a play about a mother charged with murder being defended by an attorney who is, unbeknownst to himself, her son. Filmmakers threw themselves on it like poverty on the world; this is one of at least five versions. George plays the long-suffering heroine. Dated, but has a few interesting scenes. (Dir: Sam Wood, 72 mins.)

Madame X (1966)** Lana Turner, John Forsythe, Ricardo Montalban. The ancient tear jerker about the tragic lady who sacrifices all for love and her son, given an updated but not improved treatment. Turner suffers and suffers; the Ross Hunter production is scrumptious, but it's all reminiscent of another day. (Dir: David Lowell Rich, 100 mins.)

Madame X (MTV 1981)**½ Tuesday Weld. This potboiler has been remade many times. Here's the latest re-incarnation with beautiful Tuesday Weld taking the part of the heroine who has to sacrifice her beloved wealthy husband and child when her past comes back to haunt her. She sinks into a life of degradation and finally is put on trial for murder. Lana Turner was the last one to play the part in a 1966 movie version, and Ms. Weld resembles her at times. Soap opera suds abound. (Dir: Robert Miller, 104 mins.)

Mädchen in Uniform (Germany, 1931)***½ Dorothea Wieck, Hertha Thiele, Emilia Unda. A boarding school for the daughters of the Prussian military aristocracy becomes a microcosm of Germany in director Leontine Sagan's remarkable film, which sees a lesbian relationship as the only available alternative to the authoritarian order. Independently made and cooperatively financed, it was one of the few genuine women's films of the '30s. Based on a play by Christa Winsloe and performed by an all-women cast. (110 mins.)

Mädchen in Uniform (France-West Germany, 1958)** Lilli Palmer, Romy Schneider, Christine Kaufmann. Drama of life in a school for girls, and of the relationship between one emotionally sensitive

girl and her teacher. Remake of a famous German film of the early talkie era, but not as potent—draggy, merely passable. Dubbed in English. (Dir: Geza Radvanyi, 91 mins.)

Made for Each Other (1939)**½ Carole Lombard, James Stewart, Charles Coburn, Lucile Watson, Louise Beavers. The appealing Stewart and Lombard are married, and the vicissitudes of the little people have rarely been given a more thorough wringing. Essentially a fraudulent movie. (Dir: John Cromwell, 85 mins.)

Made for Each Other (1971)**** Renee Taylor, Joseph Bologna, Paul Sorvino. Delightful, joyous comedy about a pair of losers in New York who meet at an emergency group-therapy session. Hilarious and touching at the same time. This frenetic love story was shot on location in the Big Apple, and it is surprisingly well directed by newcomer Robert B. Bean. (104 mins.)

Made in Heaven (Great Britain, 1952)**½ David Tomlinson, Petula Clark. Doubting young wife suspects her husband of flirting with an attractive maid. Pleasant little romantic comedy. (Dir: John Paddy Carstairs, 80 mins.)

Made in Italy (Italy-France, 1965)***½ Anna Magnani, Nino Manfredi, Virna Lisi, Sylva Koscina. Thirty-two short vignettes about modern Italian life comprise this funny, often touching film. Anecdotes range foom a tearful nun gazing at wedding gowns to adulterous pursuits. Best is the final episode, starring the expressive Magnani as an imperious mother herding her brood across a crowded intersection. (Dir: Nanni Loy, 101 mins.)

Made in Paris (1966)*½ Ann-Margret, Louis Jourdan. (Dir: Boris Sagal, 101 mins.)

Madeleine (Great Britain, 1949)**** Ann Todd, Norman Wooland. The story of Madeleine Smith, who was tried for poisoning her lover in Scotland in 1857. Superbly directed and performed, absorbing drama from beginning to end. (Dir: David Lean, 101 mins.)

Mademoiselle (France-Great Britain, 1966)**½ Jeanne Moreau, Ettore Manni, Keith Skinner. Moreau is a repressed schoolteacher who cries rape after enjoying an ecstatic night with an immigrant worker in director Tony Richardson's earnestly dull adaptation of Jean Genet's only work written for the screen. (103 mins.)

Madigan (1968)**** Richard Widmark, Henry Fonda, Inger Stevens. A brilliant police thriller directed with sharp-edged verve by Don Siegel. Story of a troubled police commissioner (Fonda) and a maverick police detective (Widmark, in one of his better performances) who is out to get the job done no matter how. (101 mins.)

Madigan: Park Avenue Beat (MTV 1973)*½ Richard Widmark, John Larch. Episode of the "Madigan" series. Concerns a policeman (Larch) thrown off the force after killing a surrendering criminal he mistakenly believed had slain his partner. The plot may be contrived, but it's handled decently. (Dir: Alex March, 72 mins.)

Madigan: The Lisbon Beat (MTV 1973)*½ Richard Widmark. Somewhat off-beat episode; police-detective Madigan (Widmark) first loses a prisoner handcuffed to him, then spends most of his time enjoying the sights of spectacular Lisbon. (Dir: Boris Sagal, 76 mins.)

Madigan: The Naples Beat (MTV 1973)** Richard Widmark, Rossano Brazzi, Raf Vallone. In addition to Widmark, this series episode features Brazzi and Vallone as opposing mobsters. The setting is Naples, and the story concerns drug traffic and gang warfare. (Dir: Boris Sagal, 72 mins.)

Madigan's Millions (Spain-Italy, 1967)*½ Dustin Hoffman, Cesar Romero, Elsa Martinelli. (Dir: Stanley Page, 76 mins.)

Madison Avenue (1962)** Dana Andrews, Eleanor Parker, Jeanne Crain, Eddie Albert. Routine drama supposedly revealing the naked truth about the cutthroat world of big time advertising. All the characters are caricatures, and the plot about the machinations involved in parlaying a small-time dairy into a national trademark is just a local yawn. (Dir: H. Bruce Humberstone, 94 mins.)

Madness of the Heart (Great Britain, 1949)**½ Margaret Lockwood, Paul Dupuis. Beautiful blind girl marries a wealthy Frenchman, meets opposition from the family and friends. Slick romantic drama, familiar but competent. (Dir: Charles Bennett, 74 mins.)

Mado (France, 1976)**** Michel Piccoli, Romy Schneider, Charles Denner, Ottavia Piccolo. Piccoli has a role to match his skills as an actor, playing a shallow man with deep feelings, a businessman forced to the edge and striking back in kind. Excellent support from a fine cast, particularly Piccolo as a prostitute. (Dir: Claude Sautet, 130 mins.)

Madonna of the Seven Moons (Great Britain, 1945)*** Phyllis Calvert, Stewart Granger. An early encounter with a gypsy leaves its mark upon a woman for life, endangers the safety of her daughter. Strong melodrama. Well done. (Dir: Arthur Crabtree, 88 mins.)

Madron (1970)**½ Richard Boone, Leslie Caron. Boone and Caron are far better than this routine western story about a nun and a gunman who team up in a dangerous trek across a desert, stalked by Apaches. filmed in Israel. (Dir: Jerry Hopper, 93 mins.)

Madwoman of Chaillot (Great Britain, 1969)**½ Katharine Hepburn, Yul Brynner, Danny Kaye, Edith Evans, Charles Boyer. John Huston left and was replaced by Bryan Forbes after shooting several weeks of this picture, but it was conceptually flawed from the outset. The

producers foolishly tried to make a huge, opulent, star-studded spectacle out of Jean Giraudoux's bittersweet, small-scale morality fable. Evans scores in a trial scene, and the great Kate is stunning in her series of fantastic flowered bonnets. (132 mins.)

Mafia (Italy-France, 1968)*½ Claudia Cardinale, Lee J. Cobb, Franco Nero. (Dir: Damiano Damiani, 98 mins.)

Mafu Cage, The (1978)*** Lee Grant, Carol Kane, Will Geer, James Olson. Suspense story based on a French play by Eric Westphal, "Toi et Tes Nuages." Uneven but often involving, thanks largely to a notable performance by Kane. (Dir: Karen Arthur, 104 mins.)

Maggie, The—See: **High and Dry**

Magic (1978)'*** Anthony Hopkins, Ann-Margret, Burgess Meredith. An old chestnut: the ventriloquist dominated by his dummy. Hopkins's performance is designed to be overrated, Meredith is excellent in a role that truly demonstrates his range. Ann-Margret finally looks attractive instead of glamorous. Claptrap, but if you respond to the premise, potentially devastating. (Dir: Richard Attenborough, 106 mins.)

Magic Bow, The (Great Britain, 1947)**½ Classical music lovers have a treat in store for them, with this biography of famed violinist Paganini, as portrayed by Stewart Granger. With Phyllis Calvert, Jean Kent, Cecil Parker, Dennis Price. Offscreen violin solos played by concert artist Yehudi Menuhin. (Dir: Bernard Knowles, 105 mins.)

Magic Box, The (Great Britain, 1952)*** Robert Donat, Margaret Johnston, Maria Schell, many others. The story of William Friese-Greene, the inventor of the motion picture camera, whose life was a tragedy through hardships and lack of recognition. Interesting, but rather top-heavy, due to the number of hands invoved. (Dir: John Boulting, 103 mins.)

Magic Carpet, The (1951)** Lucille Ball, Raymond Burr, John Agar. TV's Perry Mason (Burr) and Lucy (Ball) find themselves in the mystical time of Caliphs and Viziers in this corny Arabian Nights farce. (Dir: Lew Landers, 84 mins.)

Magic Carpet (1972)** Susan Saint James is the star of this scenic tour through Italy. She leads a group of Americans as a substitute tour guide. Supporting cast of disgruntled tourists includes Jim and Henny Backus, Abby Dalton, and Wally Cox. Major interest is the footage of Rome, Venice, Florence, Ischia, and Naples. (Dir: William Graham, 99 mins.)

Magic Christian, The (Great Britain, 1969)*½ Peter Sellers, Ringo Starr, Raquel Welch. Adaptation of the Terry Southern novel. In this farce, business baronet Sellars and Ringo whom he has adopted, go off together to prove the corruptibility of the world. Director Joseph McGrath's past achievements don't prepare us for this tasteless, hedonistic mess. Many cameo appearances. (95 mins.)

Magic Face, The (1951)*** Luther Adler, Patricia Knight. Noted actor kills Hitler, then poses as Der Fuhrer, in order to halt Nazi tyranny. Well-done melodrama made in Europe holds the interest. (Dir: Frank Tuttle, 88 mins.)

Magic Fire (1956)** Yvonne DeCarlo, Rita Gam, Alan Badel. Tale of the romantic troubles of composer Richard Wagner. Overdone drama is a victim of ham acting and plodding plot. (Dir: William Dieterle, 95 mins.)

Magic Flute, The (Sweden, 1973)**** Ulrik Gold, Josef Kostlinger. An exquisite adaptation by director Ingmar Bergman of Mozart's opera "The Magic Flute." Most of the time, Bergman simply photographs the action unfolding during a stage production of the Mozart masterwork. Primarily of interest to opera lovers. (134 mins.)

Magic Fountain, The (1961)** Childrens' fairy tale about a hidden magic fountain, narrated by Cedric Hardwicke. OK for the small fry. (Dir: Allan David, 85 mins.)

Magic of Lassie, The (1978)** James Stewart, Mickey Rooney, Alice Faye, Pernell Roberts. Lovable old Stewart steals the show form lovable old Lassie. Grandpa Jimmy doesn't want to sell his vineyards to rich and mean Roberts, so Roberts takes Lassie away. For kids and nostalgic adults. (Dir: Don Chaffey, 90 mins.)

Magic Sword, The (1962)½ Basil Rathbone, Gary Lockwood, Estelle Winwood, Anne Helm, Vampira. (Dir: Bert I. Gordon, 80 mins.)

Magic Town (1947)**½ James Stewart, Jane Wyman, Kent Smith, Donald Meek, Regis Toomey. A pollster publicizes a small town as being statistically accurate in all polls, which only causes trouble for the town's mild way of life. Uneven comedy, misses fire most of the time; just fair. (Dir: William Wellman, 103 mins.)

Magic Voyage of Sinbad, The (U.S.S.R., 1953)* (Dirs: Aleksandr Ptushko, James Landis, 79 mins.)

Magic Weaver, The (U.S.S.R., 1960)*** Mikhail Kuznetsov. Pleasant fairy tale about a returning soldier and his tall tales. Primarily for the youngsters. English-dubbed. (Dir: Aleksandr Rou, 87 mins.)

Magical Mystery Tour (Great Britain, 1969)** The Beatles. Rarely shown, for a good reason: the self-indulgent psychedelic material is almost impossible to watch. Originally made for British TV. Contains a number of Beatles songs. (Dirs: The Beatles, 60 mins.)

Magician, The (Sweden, 1958)**** Max von Sydow, Ingrid Thulin. An early Ingmar Bergman directed film that will tingle your spine and stimulate your brain. The supernatural, comic, mystical and the human mingle in this imaginative tale of a magician and his troupe who are detained in a small Swedish community when their magical powers are disbelieved. Visually rich, gothic atmosphere. (102 mins.)

Magician of Lublin, The (West Germany-Israel, 1979)*** Alan Arkin, Louise Fletcher, Shelley Winters, Valerie Perrine. The wonderful, sexy, wise Isaac Bashevis Singer novel is the first of his works to be filmed. The result is ambitious, but only occasionally successful. Arkin's performance in the title role carries the film most of the way. (Dir: Menachem Golan, 105 mins.)

Magnet, The (Great Britain, 1950)**** Stephen Murray, Kay Walsh, William Fox (later known as James Fox). An imaginative ten-year-old swindles a lad out of a magnet, is convinced the thing is some sort of charm. Delightful comedy, clean and refreshing, sparklingly written. (Dir: Charles Frend, 78 mins.)

Magnificent Ambersons, The (1942)**** Tim Holt, Joseph Cotten, Anne Baxter, Dolores Costello, Richard Bennett. Director Orson Welles's second completed feature is probably his best, partisans of "Citizen Kane" notwithstanding. Lovingly crafted, hauntingly nostalgic portrait of a midwestern town losing its Victorian sensibility to the machine age. Stars the voice of Welles, whose narration is glorious. An awkward studio ending was tacked on while Welles was in South America. Virtually every word of the script is from the Booth Tarkington novel. (88 mins.)

Magnificent Cuckold, The (France-Italy, 1964)**½ Claudia Cardinale, Ugo Tognazzi, Bernard Blier. Racy comedy features Tognazzi as a suspicious husband who spies on his young wife, convinced she's having an affair. Naturally, he's outwitted by his sensual wife. Funny sequences along the way. (Dir: Antonio Pietrangeli, 117 mins.)

Magnificent Doll, The (1946)** Ginger Rogers, David Niven, Burgess Meredith. The story of Dolly Madison, the President's wife whose relationship with Aaron Burr nearly altered the course of American history. Elaborate but heavy, not too well-acted drama. (Dir: Frank Borzage, 95 mins.)

Magnificent Dope, The (1942)*** Henry Fonda, Don Ameche, Lynn Bari. Amusing comedy which has the country boy, as usual, outwitting the city slickers. Fonda and Ameche are a good contrast and the film has its share of laughs. (Dir: Walter Lang, 83 mins.)

Magnificent Fraud, The (1939)** Akim Tamiroff, Lloyd Nolan, Patricia Morison. Loud, yet boring tale of an actor in a mythical South American country, who tries to impersonate an assassinated dictator. (Dir: Robert Florey, 80 mins.)

Magnificent Magical Magnet of Santa Mesa—See: Adventures of Freddie

Magnificent Matador (1955)**½ Anthony Quinn, Maureen O'Hara. Bullfighter runs away on the day of his protégée's entry into the ring. Good bullfight sequences atone somewhat for a hackneyed plot. (Dir: Budd Boetticher, 95 mins.)

Magnificent Obsession (1935)*** Irene Dunne, Robert Taylor, Betty Furness. John M. Stahl, master of melodrama, directs Lloyd Douglas's uplifter about a playboy who becomes a doctor in order to restore the eyesight of a woman whose blindness he caused. (90 mins.)

Magnificent Obession (1954)**½ Jane Wyman, Rock Hudson. Classily produced soap-opera which leans heavily on sentiment and turns out to be a four-handkerchief film for ladies. Lloyd C. Douglas's novel about one man's devotion and faith to a woman whose blindness he caused is handled well by the two stars and a good supporting cast. This is a remake of the 1935 version which starred Irene Dunne and Robert Taylor. (Dir: Douglas Sirk, 108 mins.)

Magnificent Roughnecks (1956)** Jack Carson, Mickey Rooney. Couple of oil men have trouble with rival drillers and rival gals. Two veteran performers in a plot that's also seen long service. (Dir: Sherman A. Rose, 73 mins.)

Magnificent Seven, The (1960)*** Yul Brynner, Steve McQueen, James Coburn, Charles Bronson, Robert Vaughn. American remake of Akira Kurosawa's film "The Seven Samurai," set, of course, in the West. Brynner is a gunfighter who recruits six tough guys to defend a group of Mexican peasants from bandits. John Sturges directs well, though often pretentiously. (126 mins.)

Magnificent Sinner, The (France, 1960)**½ Romy Schneider, Curt Jurgens. Love story of a girl and the czar of Russia, who is not free to marry her, ending tragically in assassination. Some tender scenes, good performances, but mostly murky, slow-moving historical drama. English-dubbed. (Dir: Robert Siodmak, 91 mins.)

Magnificent Yankee, The (1950)***½ Louis Calhern, Ann Harding. Superbly acted biographical drama, the story of Oliver Wendal Holmes, Supreme Court justice and man of legal astuteness. Perhaps a bit too placid for some tastes, it is nevertheless a film of rare refinement, well worthwhile. (Dir: John Sturges, 80 mins.)

Magnum Force (1973)** Clint Eastwood, Hal Holbrook, David Soul. Director Ted Post makes Eastwood's Dirty Harry seem wishy-washy and haggard. The action sequences and Eastwood are fine. Offbeat casting of usually the sweet Holbrook as the leader of the heavies. (122 mins.)

Magus, The (Great Britain, 1968)*** Anthony Quinn, Candice Bergen, Michael Caine, Anna Karina. John Fowles's complex, elliptical novel about a young English schoolteacher (Caine) who arrives on a small Greek island is heady material for a motion picture. But Fowles wrote the screenplay himself, and makes this bizarre story as intelligible as possible. (Dir: Guy Green, 116 mins.)

Mahler (Great Britain, 1974)**½ Robert Powell, Georgina Hale, Rosalie Crutchley, Antonia Ellis. The composer Gustav Mahler, played by Powell, recalls his life and hard times during a fatal train ride. Director Ken Russell finds plenty of room for his patented wretched excess, notably in a dream sequence that features Cosima Wagner (Ellis) as a Nazi pope. (115 mins.)

Mahogany (1975)*½ Diana Ross, Anthony Perkins, Billy Dee Williams. Mediocre picture about a fashion designer (Ross) fighting her way to success, only to find it's lonely at the top. Ross's star power is pleasing, however. Berry Gordy, mogul of Motown, directs, and though no master, he's as credible as many a bankable hack. (109 mins.)

Maid in Paris (France, 1957)**½ Daniel Gelin, Dany Robin. Wacky French comedy about a young girl, whose father is a movie star, and her amours in Gay Paree. Robin is delightful as the willing mademoiselle. (Dir: Gaspard-Huit, 84 mins.)

Maids, The (Great Britain, 1975)***½ Glenda Jackson, Susannah York, Vivien Merchant. Director Christopher Miles's unstable, radically oblique visuals go a long way toward capturing Jean Genet's mood of the confusion of sexual and class hatreds, though Jackson and York always seem to be competing for our attention. Jackson gives an exhausting performance that requires her to go full out (and to maintain one monologue for nearly the whole second act). One of the better American Film Theater presentations. (95 mins.)

Mail Bag Robbery (Great Britain, 1957)** Lee Patterson, Kay Callard. Clever crooks plan a unique setup for robbing a train's gold shipment. Fairly well worked out low-budget crime melodrama. (Dir: Compton Bennett, 70 mins.)

Mail Order Bride (1964)**½ Buddy Ebsen, Keir Dullea, Lois Nettleton, Warren Oates. Early version of the western comedy as practiced by director-writer Burt Kennedy ("Support Your Local Sheriff"). In this one, Ebsen attempts to get Dullea to settle down by marrying him off to Nettleton. Fine supporting cast. (83 mins.)

Main Actor, The (West Germany, 1978)**½ Mario Adorf, Vadim Glowna, Michael Schweiger. Director Reinhard Hauff made a nonprofessional Manfred Reiss, a boy star in "Paule Paulander" ('76). Now he films the ugly consequences, using actors who look like Hauff and Reiss to tell the story. (88 mins.)

Main Attraction, The (Great Britain, 1962)** Pat Boone, Nancy Kwan, Mai Zetterling. Picked up by an older circus woman, a mixed-up youth starts straying in his attentions, rouses ire and jealousy among the circus crowd. Standard plot, corny ending. Zetterling is outstanding as the aging circus performer. (Dir: Daniel Petrie, 85 mins.)

Main Chance, The (Great Britain, 1965)** Gregoire Aslan, Tracy Reed, Edward De Souza. Mastermind organizes a diamond-smuggling scheme, picks an ex-RAF pilot to help him. Standard vest-pocket crime melodrama. (Dir: John Knight, 61 mins.)

Main Event, The (1979)* Barbra Streisand, Ryan O'Neal, Paul Sand. (Dir: Howard Zeiff, 112 mins.)

Main Street to Broadway (1953)** Tom Morton, Mary Murphy. Young playwright refuses to be discouraged in trying to be a success on Broadway. Trite story of theater life, with Broadway and Hollywood luminaries being dragged in briefly for name value. (Dir: Tay Garnett, 102 mins.)

Maitresse (France, 1976)**½ Gerard Depardieu, Bulle Ogier, André Rouyer. Eccentric work from director Barbet Schroeder, with scenes of bondage and flagellation. Seen through the eyes of a sneak thief (Depardieu) who happens upon the salon of master mistress Ogier. (112 mins.)

Major and the Minor, The (1942)*** Ginger Rogers, Ray Milland, Diana Lynn. Rogers plays a broke New York career woman who impersonates a 12-year-old in order to ride half-fare to her home in Iowa. Milland is the officer who tries to take care of Ginger as she falls in love with him. The director Billy Wilder ironies are present in abundance. Remade as "You're Never Too Young." (100 mins.)

Major Barbara (Great Britain, 1941)***½ Wendy Hiller, Rex Harrison, Robert Newton, Robert Morley, Deborah Kerr. George Bernard Shaw did not write the play but collaborated with director Gabriel Pascal on this film version. Hiller stars as the Salvation Army worker, daughter of a munitions manufacturer, who moves from innocence to disillusionment to acceptance of the material and social values of her father's world; Harrison is the good-natured intellectual who joins the Salvation Army to be near Barbara. A bit slow to start, but an enthusiastic and intelligent rendering of the wonderful Shavian wit. (115 mins.)

Major Dundee (1965)**½ Charlton Heston, Richard Harris, James Coburn, Senta Berger. Although the film was taken from director Sam Peckinpah and mangled, it's still loaded with action and meaning. Heston is persuasive as a tough commander who leads a cavalry mission across the Mexican border in pursuit of Indians. Many of his troops are Confederate prisoners of war, whose loyalty is only to their own escape. (134 mins.)

Majority of One, A (1961)**½ Rosalind Russell, Alec Guinness, Ray Danton, Madlyn Rhue. A mild, humorous but stagebound comedy of the romance between a Jewish matron from New York and a Japanese businessman. This film tries for a social consciousness it's really too light-

minded to sustain; but if one takes it for what it is—a sitcom—it's enjoyable indeed. Russell and Guinness run rings around the other actors. (Dir: Mervyn Le Roy, 156 mins.)

Make Haste to Live (1954)*** Dorothy McGuire, Stephen McNally. Husband returns from prison intending to kill his wife, after failing the first time. Suspenseful mystery-melodrama with a good cast. (Dir: William A. Seiter, 90 mins.)

Make Me an Offer (Great Britain, 1954)**½ Peter Finch, Adrienne Corri. Amusing comedy about the buying and selling of antiques. Finch gives a very entertaining performance and Corri is a decorative side kick. (Dir: Cyril Frankel, 89 mins.)

Make Me An Offer (MTV 1980)**½ Susan Blakely, Patrick O'Neal, John Rubinstein. Blakely is effective as a young woman who leaves her cheating husband and gets it together in the glamorous, high-pressure world of Beverly Hills real estate agents. Starting out as a mousy assistant of O'Neal's, she rises quickly in the dog-eat-dog business. The only sour note is the love story angle involving Blakely and a veterinarian played by Rubinstein. (Dir: Jerry Paris, 104 mins.)

Make Mine Mink (Great Britain, 1960)***½ Terry-Thomas, Athene Seyler, Billie Whitelaw. Dowager and an ex-officer team to commit larceny, the proceeds going to charity. The British have a knack for making these crazy comedies, and this is one of the better ones; often screamingly funny, with bright lines, situations. (Dir: Robert Asher, 101 mins.)

Make Way for Lila (Sweden-Germany, 1962)**½ Erica Remberg, Joachim Hansen. Unusual locale adds interest to this slender tale of a girl, raised by Laplanders, who becomes the object of two men's affections. Picturesque scenery, pleasant performances. Dubbed in English. (Dir: Rolf Husberg, 90 mins.)

Make Way for Tomorrow (1937)***½ Victor Moore, Beulah Bondi, Thomas Mitchell. Story of aged parents who have become a burden to their children and must resign themselves to separation. Director Leo McCarey combines tenderness and comedy, amplifying small gestures into poignant moments. Magnificently acted by Moore and Bondi, this is an unrecognized classic of American cinema. (92 mins.)

Make Your Own Bed (1944)*½ Jane Wyman, Jack Carson. (Dir: Peter Godfrey, 82 mins.)

Making It (1971)** Kristoffer Tabori, Joyce Van Patten, Marlyn Mason. Redolent of the hypocrisy implicit in Hollywood's version of New Morality. A 17-year-old stud-about-town reforms when his mother has an abortion and the doctors force him to watch. Notable only for the presence of Tabori, a skilled actor in a badly written part. (Dir: John Erman, 95 mins.)

Malaga (Great Britain, 1960)** Trevor Howard, Dorothy Dandridge, Edmund

419

Purdom. Jewel thief heads for Spain after a partner who has doublecrossed him. Some good players trapped in a vague, cumbersome story, with only the location photography commendable. (Dir: Laslo Benedek, 97 mins.)

Malaya (1949)**½ Spencer Tracy, James Stewart, Valentina Cortesa. Good old-fashioned adventure tale about a pair of daring men of the world who combine their skills to smuggle raw rubber out of occupied Malaya. A good supporting cast includes such stalwarts as Sydney Greenstreet, John Hodiak, Lionel Barrymore, and Gilbert Roland. (Dir: Richard Thorpe, 98 mins.)

Male Animal, The (1942)***½ Henry Fonda, Jack Carson, Olivia de Havilland. Clever, witty comedy about a dull but principled college professor, his wife, and a former football hero friend from their college days who pays them a visit. Long live the memory of co author James Thurber. Remade as "She's Working Her Way Through College." (Dir: Elliott Nugent, 101 mins.)

Male Hunt (France-Italy, 1964)*** Jean-Paul Belmondo, Jean-Claude Brialy, Catherine Deneuve. Young man is determined to get married despite the efforts of assorted people to dissuade him. Sprightly comedy dubbed in English has a number of amusing twists and turns. (Dir: Edouard Molinaro, 92 mins.)

Malicious (Italy, 1973)**½ Laura Antonelli, Turi Ferro, Alessandro Momo, Tina Aumont. A hypocritical, lustful, and devious Sicilian widower hires a stunning young housekeeper, the luscious Antonelli, but his 14-year-old son, to assert his sexual identity, sets out to prove her a whore. That he succeeds, and that the film clearly sympathizes with his success, makes for less-than-appetizing after thoughts. Still, you'll probably laugh—it's beautifully done. (Dir: Salvatore Samperi, 97 mins.)

Malpas Mystery, The (Great Britain, 1961)** Maureen Swanson, Allan Cuthbertson. Girl released from prison works undercover for a detective agency, uncovers a crime ring. OK Edgar Wallace mystery. (Dir: Sidney Hayers, 61 mins.)

Malta Story, The (Great Britain, 1954)**½ Alec Guinness, Jack Hawkins. British pilot falls in love with a Maltese girl on that bomb-stricken isle during war. Fair, but not up to Alec's later high standards. (Dir: Brian Desmond Hurst, 98 mins.)

Maltese Bippy, The (1969)*½ Dan Rowan, Dick Martin, Carol Lynley, Robert Reed. (Dir: Norman Panama, 92 mins.)

Maltese Falcon, The (1931)—See: **Dangerous Female**

Maltese Falcon, The (1941)**** Humphrey Bogart, Mary Astor, Peter Lorre, Sydney Greenstreet (film debut), Walter Huston, Lee Patrick, Elisha Cook, Jr., Jerome Cowan, Barton MacLane. Third adaptation of the Dashiell Hammett yarn about Sam Spade, one of the best private-eye

flicks ever made. The falcon is a jewel-encrusted statuette with a long history and a long list of would-be owners. Director John Huston also wrote the screenplay. (100 mins.)

Mambo (1955)** Silvana Mangano, Shelley Winters, Vittorio Gassman. Salesgirl rises to the heights as a glamorous dancer, becomes involved in complicated love affair. Romantic drama that never quite jells, overlong and sketchily developed. Produced in Italy, English dialogue. (Dir: Robert Rossen, 94 mins.)

Mame (1974)**½ Lucille Ball, Beatrice Arthur, Robert Preston. The wonderful Broadway musical based on the madcap misadventures of marvelous Auntie Mame has been diluted in this screen version starring Ball, who doesn't measure up to the sophisticated grandness and exaggerated madness of the larger-than-life character. Arthur scores in a recreation of her Broadway part of Mame's best friend, Vera Charles, and the production values are first-class, if a bit over ambitious. (Dir: Gene Saks, 131 mins.)

Mamele (Poland, 1938)**½ Molly Picon, Edmund Zayenda, Max Bozyk. Meyer Schwartz's popular Second Avenue comedy was a New York stage triumph for Picon, who repeats her role in this film version directed by actor Joseph Green. Molly plays the youngest sister in a large family, an energetic girl who exercises her creative impulses by matchmaking her sisters' suitors. Comedy and pathos get a strong workout when she herself becomes an object of romantic attention. In Yiddish. (102 mins.)

Mamma Turns 100 (Spain, 1979)*½ Geraldine Chaplin, Amparo Munoz, Fernando Fernan Gomez. Director Carlos Saura's comic sequel to "Anna and the Wolves." Anna, an English girl (Chaplin), returns to the eccentric family where she once taught as a governess, only to have her new husband seduced by one of her daughters. Heavy-handed allegory and satire. (98 mins.)

Man, The (1972)**½ James Earl Jones, Martin Balsam, Lew Ayers, William Windom. Occasionally interesting drama about the first black president of the United States, played by Jones. Thrust into the job after the death of the president and speaker of the House, and the incapacitating stroke of the vice president, he finds himself not taken seriously by the cabinet, so he attempts to assert his power. Script by Rod Serling, form the best seller by Irving Wallace. The dialogue and plot are brittle if somewhat evasive. Jones is fine. (Dir: Joseph Sargent, 93 mins.)

Man, a Woman and a Killer, A (1975)**½ Richard A. Richardson, Caroline Zaremba. Low-budget independent entry. Richardson plays a young man who has paranoid delusions that a man's going to assassinate him. Archetypal San Francisco relationships are hassled out by the actors, most impressively by Zaremba as Richardson's girlfriend. Typical of the film's devices is the use of English subtitles to translate San Francisco dialogue. (Dirs: Richard A. Richardson, Richard R. Schmidt, Wayne Wang, 78 mins.)

Man About the House, A (Great Britain, 1948)*** Margaret Johnston, Kieron Moore, Dulcie Gray. Spinsters take a villa in Italy, and one of them falls for a dashing young man who proves to be up to no good. Well done, frequently absorbing drama. (Dir: Leslie Arliss, 83 mins.)

Man About Town (1930)*** Jack Benny, Rochester, Dorothy Lamour. Jack is a great lover in this one (at least he thinks so) and when the routine musical numbers don't interfere, he and Rochester (Eddie Anderson) have a ball. (Dir: Mark Sandrich, 90 mins.)

Man About Town (France, 1947)**½ Maurice Chevalier, Françoise Perrier. Chevalier as a movie-maker in the old primitive silent days. Leisurely paced, but pleasant comedy dubbed in English. Some amusing insights into the days when movies were young. (Dir: René Clair, 89 mins.)

Man Alive (1945)**½ Pat O'Brien, Ellen Drew, Adolphe Menjou, Rudy Vallee. Husband though dead returns and plays "ghost" to haunt a suitor away from his wife. Amusing farce. (Dir: Ray Enright, 70 mins.)

Man Alone, A (1955)***½ Ray Milland, Mary Murphy, Raymond Burr, Ward Bond. Gunslinger exposes the leader of an outlaw band who massacred a stagecoach party. Different western has plenty of suspense, good direction by Milland. (Dir: Ray Milland, 95 mins.)

Man and a Woman, A (France, 1966)**** Anouk Aimée, Jean-Louis Trintignant. A visually stunning, superbly acted, and ultimately very moving contemporary love story. Aimée makes this seeming soap opera become art, not artifice, and she is aided by the direction and the inventive camera work of Claude Lelouch. Trintignant is also fine playing a racing-car driver who woos Aimée. The setting is various parts of France, but the emotional truths captured here are universal. (102 mins.)

Man and Child (France, 1957)** Eddie Constantine, Juliette Greco, Jacqueline Ventura. When a girl is abducted by a dope ring, an innocent man's daughter is kidnapped by her family as an exchange. Passable crime drama, a bit better than the usual Constantine heroics. Dubbed in English. (Dir: Raoul André, 90 mins.)

Man and the Monster, The (Mexico, 1958)** Enrique Rambol, Marta Roth, (Dir: Rafael Baledon, 78 mins.)

Man at the Carlton Tower (Great Britain, 1961)** Maxine Audley, Lee Montague. Sleuth gets on the trail of a disappearing suspect in a jewel robbery. Mildly entertaining melodrama based on an Edgar Wallace mystery. (Dir: Robert Tronson, 57 mins.)

Man Bait (Great Britain, 1952)*** George Brent, Marguerite Chapman, Diana Dors. An innocent moment off guard with a blonde gets a book dealer into a mess of trouble, including murder. Nicely done melodrama. (Dir: Terence Fisher, 80 mins.)

Man Behind the Gun (1952)** Randolph Scott, Patrice Wymore. Depending on how you feel about the dubious charms of Los Angeles, you are either sore at Scott or beholden to him. According to this hokey western, he built the joint single-handed. (Dir: Felix E. Feist, 81 mins.)

Man Between, The (Great Britain, 1953)***½ James Mason, Claire Bloom, Hildegarde Neff. A Berliner who makes a shady living risks his life to save a kidnapped girl from the Communists. Moody, topical melodrama has tenseness, atmosphere, a fine acting job from Mason. (Dir: Carol Reed, 100 mins.)

Man Called Adam, A (1966)**½ Sammy Davis, Jr., Peter Lawford, Cicely Tyson, Ossie Davis, Louis Armstrong. Davis is excellent in the difficult role of a jazz musician who is filled with bitterness and self-pity. A tragic tale of the jazz world and a black striving for personal acceptance. (Dir: Leo Penn, 102 mins.)

Man Called Dagger, A (1967)* Terry Moore, Sue Ann Langdon, Eileen O'Neill. (Dir: Richard Rush, 86 mins.)

Man Called Gannon, A (1969)*** Tony Franciosa, Michael Sarrazin, Susan Oliver, Gavin MacLeod. A remake of the 1955 film "Man Without a Star." Well-paced western with a good performance by Franciosa as a drifter who takes a young cowpoke (Sarrazin) under his wing and ends up fighting against him in a small range war. There's not a wasted scene in this tale and the characterizations probe a little deeper than usual in this type of film fare. (Dir: James Goldstone, 105 mins.)

Man Called Horse, A (1970)*** Richard Harris, Judith Anderson, Corinna Tsopei. An ambitious, serious film which sometimes gets laughs in the wrong places. Harris convincingly plays a white man captured by the Sioux in 1825, tortured and finally converted to their way of life. Anderson, spouting in the role of his Indian mother-in-law, is ridiculous. Commendable attempt to deal with the Indian culture, doesn't always succeed for white man's eyes. (Dir: Eliot Silverstein, 114 mins.)

Man Called Peter, A (1955)***½ Richard Todd, Jean Peters. A fine performance by Todd as Peter Marshall, the Scotsman who became a minister in the U.S. and rose to the high postition of U.S. senate chaplain, makes this film. Peters capably handles her co-starring assignment as the girl Marshall weds. Todd's sermon scenes are standouts. (Dir: Henry Koster, 119 mins.)

Man Could Get Killed, A (1966)**½ James Garner, Melina Mercouri, Sandra Dee, Tony Franciosa. Businessman in Portugal is mistaken for a secret agent, becomes involved with smugglers. Spoof of secret agent stories isn't as funny as some of the supposedly serious ones, but it has some captivating scenery and a competent cast to atone for the plot deficiencies. Filmed in Rome and Lisbon. (Dirs: Ronald Neame, Cliff Owen, 100 mins.)

Man Detained (Great Britain, 1961)** Bernard Archard, Elvi Hale. Owner of a company from which a large sum of money has been stolen is murdered, and a burglar is accused of the crime. Fair Edgar Wallace mystery. (Dir: Robert Tronson, 59 mins.)

Man Escaped (France, 1957)***½ François Leterrier, Charles Le Clainche. Taut and exciting film about a daring escape by a French Resistance leader who is captured by the Germans during WW II. This film is a multi-prize winner. (Robert Bresson, 94 mins.)

Man for All Seasons, A (Great Britain, 1966)**** Paul Scofield, Robert Shaw. Robert Bolt's literate and penetrating treatment of the conflict waged between Sir Thomas More and King Henry VIII makes a smooth transition to the screen, with excellent performances by Scofield as More, Shaw as Henry VIII, Wendy Hiller as Alice More, Orson Welles as Cardinal Wolsey, and, in a brief role. Vanessa Redgrave as Anne Boleyn. Director Fred Zinnemann has mounted the film with an eye for characterization rather than spectacle, and the result is superior drama. Other Oscars: Best Picture, Best Director, Best Color Cinematography (Ted Moore), Best Screenplay (Bolt), Best Color Costume Design (Elizabeth Haffenden, Joan Bridge.) (120 mins.)

Man Friday (Great Britain, 1975)*½ Peter O'Toole, Richard Roundtree, Peter Cellier. (Dir: Jack Gold, 115 mins.)

Man from Atlantis (MTV 1977)** Patrick Duffy, Belinda J. Montgomery, Victor Buono. Pilot film is humdrum science fiction about a man with gills instead of lungs, a survivor from the lost city of Atlantis. Duffy can't talk, but he swims like a fish, so the navy puts him to work! (Dir: Lee H. Katzin, 104 mins.)

Man from Atlantis: The Death Scouts (1977)** Patrick Duffy, Belinda Montgomery. Remember the water-breathing hero suspected to be the remaining survivor of the lost continent of Atlantis? No? Well, he's back anyway in this sequel for sci-fi fans. Encounters some alien beings reputed to be able to survive underwater, and teams up with the lady oceanographer who originally discovered him. (Dir: Marc Daniels, 106 mins.)

Man from Atlantis: The Disappearances

(MTV 1977)**½ Patrick Duffy, Belinda Montgomery. Duffy shines as Mark Harris, the water-breathing humanoid thought to be the last survivor of the lost continent of Atlantis. Dr. Merrill (Miss Montgomery) is abducted and whisked to a mysterious island off South America, and Mark needs all his special powers to rescue her. For a change, the villain of the piece is a female mad scientist (Darleen Carr)— (Dir: Charles Dubin, 72 mins.)

Man from Atlantis: The Killer Spores (MTV 1977)** Patrick Duffy is a liaison between NASA and some deadly "ectoplasmic spores" capable of destroying the world. (Dir: Reza Badiyi, 106 mins.)

Man from Bitter Ridge, The (1955)** Lex Barker, Mara Corday, Stephen McNally. Ordinary western drama about cattle barons and those who oppose them. The cast just goes through the paces. Grade B movie fare. (Dir: Jack Arnold, 80 mins.)

Man from Button Willow, The (1965)** Animated feature about the alleged adventures of the first government agent, Justin Eagle. The plot centers around Eagle's attempt to rescue a kidnapped senator in the old West. Voices include Dale Robertson, Howard Keel, and Edgar Buchanan. (Dir: David Detiege, 82 mins.)

Man from Cocody (French-Italian, 1965)** Jean Marais, Liselotte Pulver. Diplomat becomes involved in tracking down a secret society and diamond smuggling in Africa. Pleasant players and some sharp direction overcome to some extent the rather silly melodramatic plot. Dubbed in English. (Dir: Christian-Jaque, 84 mins.)

Man from Colorado (1948)*** William Holden, Glenn Ford, Ellen Drew. Sadist becomes a federal judge and runs things his way. Good western has an offbeat portrayal by Ford. (Dir: Henry Levin, 99 mins.)

Man from Del Rio (1956)** Anthony Quinn, Katy Jurado. This western tale starts out well enough but slowly disintegrates into just another horse opera. Quinn is fine when the script isn't fighting him. (Dir: Harry Horner, 82 mins.)

Man from God's Country (1958)** George Montgomery, Randy Stuart. Cattleman gets involved in a land grabbing scheme for a proposed railroad. Nothing new. (Dir: Paul Landres, 72 mins.)

Man from Laramie (1955)*** James Stewart, Arthur Kennedy, Cathy O'Donnell. Above Average western drama about a man who proves he is a tower of strength against the evil forces of a town. Stewart is good, as is the whole cast. (Dir: Anthony Mann, 104 mins.)

Man from Oklahoma, The (West Germany, 1964)* Rick Horn, Sabine Bethmann. (Dir: J. Balcazar, 85 mins.)

Man from Planet X, The (1951)** Robert Clarke, Margaret Field, William Schallert. A friendly alien is betrayed and antagonized by human greed. Director Edgar G.

Ulmer, the Edgar Allen Poe of B (and C and D) movies, concocted one of the first of the 50s alien-visitor plots for this low, low-budget sci-fi film. Full of his bleak spirit—the catatonic acting, the breakaway sets, the cramped exteriors, all contributing to Ulmer's harrowingly consistent vision of a blasted, barren world. The acting of past Screen Actors Guild president Schallert constitutes grounds for impeachment. (70 mins.)

Man from the Alamo, The (1953)**½ Glenn Ford, Julia Adams. Interesting western adventure about the only man to survive the Alamo massacre. Naturally, he's labeled a coward and has to keep silent until he finds out the truth about the mystery surrounding the massacre at Ox-Bow, a town near the Alamo. (Dir: Budd Boetticher, 79 mins.)

Man from the Diner's Club, The (1963)**½ Danny Kaye, Cara Williams, Martha Hyer, Telly Savalas, George Kennedy. Diners Club employee makes out an application for a gangster trying to leave the country, and the troubles begin. Comedy on the silly side is not up to the star's talents but provides some mild amusement along the way. (Dir: Frank Tashlin, 96 mins.)

Man Hunt (1941)***½ Walter Pidgeon, Joan Bennett, George Sanders, Roddy McDowall, John Carradine. Perfectly constructed thriller by director Fritz Lang, from the popular novel "Rogue Male." Pidgeon is a British big-game hunter stalking Adolf Hitler, purely, he thinks, for the sport of it. Soon Gestapo agents begin to hunt Pidgeon. (105 mins.)

Man Hunter, The (MTV 1969)½ Sandra Dee, Roy Thinnes, Al Hirt. (Dir: Don Taylor, 98 mins.)

Man I Love, The (1929)**½ Richard Arlen, Mary Brian, Olga Baclanova, Bruce Bennett, Andrea King, Alun Hale. Arlen plays Dum-Dum Brooks, who splits with his chick (Brian) to New York, where he falls in with the wrong kind of people (namely, the filthy rich). Story and screenplay by Herman J. Mankiewicz. (Dir: William A. Wellman, 74 mins.)

Man I Love, The (1946)**½ Ida Lupino, Robert Alda. Singer visiting her family catches the eye of a nitery owner. Good acting offsets a soapy opera. (Dir: Raoul Walsh, 96 mins.)

Man I Married, The (1940)*** Francis Lederer, Joan Bennett, Lloyd Nolan, Anna Sten. Fascinating anti-Nazi film about an American girl married to a German-American. They visit Germany in '38 and she sees her husband fall for Hitler's doctrines. (Dir: Irving Pichel, 77 mins.)

Man in a Cocked Hat (Great Britain, 1960)**½ Terry-Thomas, Peter Sellers. Inept clerk in the Foreign Office is sent to a small colony where he proceeds to gum up the works. Mildly amusing comedy. (Dirs: Jeffrey Dell, Roy Boulting, 88 mins.)

Man in Grey, The (Great Britain, 1943)*** James Mason, Stewart Granger, Margaret Lockwood. An evil marquis carries on with a hussy while married in name only to another. Purple-passioned costume melodrama is redeemed by good performances, particularly from Mason. (Dir: Leslie Arliss, 116 mins.)

Man in Outer Space (Czechoslovakia, 1961)** Milos Kopecky, Radevan Lukavsky. Accidental space traveler lands on a far planet whose inhabitants help him back to earth, but centuries later; his greed affects the people of the future. Fanciful sci-fi saga is hard to swallow, but does have a slightly different plot, interesting effects. Dubbed in English. (Dirs: Oldrich Lipsky, William Hole, Jr., 85 mins.)

Man in the Attic (1953)** Jack Palance, Constance Smith. Mysterious man takes a room in a lodging house when London is terrorized by Jack the Ripper. Remake of "The Lodger" passes muster, but doesn't add anything to the original. (Dir: Hugo Fregonese, 82 mins.)

Man in the Back Seat, The (Great Britain, 1961)**½ Derren Nesbitt, Carol White. Two young crooks attack a bookmaker carrying money from the racetrack chained to his wrist, are forced to make him a captive. Fairly suspenseful crime melodrama based on an Edgar Wallace story. (Dir: Vernon Sewell, 57 mins.)

Man in the Dark (1953)**½ Edmond O'Brien, Audrey Totter. A somewhat novel approach to an old gangster story. A convict submits to a brain operation which is suppose to free him from his criminal tendencies but just makes him lose his memory instead. (Dir: Lew Landers, 70 mins.)

Man in the Glass Booth, The (1975)**½ Maximilian Schell, Lois Nettleton, Luther Adler. Robert Shaw's moving but flawed play about war criminal Eichmann's trial in Israel is clumsily adapted by Edward Auhatt. Schell is bombastic and sometimes effective. Fine supporting cast. (Dir: Arthur Hiller, 117 mins.)

Man in the Gray Flannel Suit, The (1956)**½ Gregory Peck, Jennifer Jones, Fredric March, Marisa Pavan. Sloan Wilson's best seller is brought to the screen in typical Hollywood style—glossy and melodramatic. Peck is as wooden as ever as the Madison Ave. husband whose past comes back and makes him search for answers. Miss Jones is wasted and March, generally a superb actor, shouts his way through his scenes. (Dir: Nunnally Johnson, 153 mins.)

Man in the Iron Mask, The (1939)*** Louis Hayward, Joan Bennett. The classic tale of intrigue in France, and the twin brother of Louis XIV who was kept in an iron mask so that no one would see his face. Elaborate costume adventure. (Dir: James Whale, 119 mins.)

Man in the Iron Mask, The (MTV 1977)*** Richard Chamberlain, Patrick McGoohan, Ralph Richardson, Louis Jourdan. Lavish production and the timeless Alexandre Dumas story add up to an entertaining family film. Chamberlain has a field day with the dual role of France's King Louis XIV and his twin brother, who is believed to have died at birth. Royal intrigues unfold as the villains, led wonderfully by McGoohan, try to thwart the plans of statesman Richardson and musketeer Jourdan to replace the king with his look-alike brother. (Dir: Mike Newell, 104 mins.)

Man in the Middle, The (1964)**½ Robert Mitchum, France Nuyen, Trevor Howard, Keenan Wynn. Muddled courtroom drama which can't make up its mind where to place the guilt. The story concerns an American lieutenant stationed in India at the end of WW II, who shoots a British sergeant. The question whether the American soldier is sane or not becomes the crux of the case, but you may lose interest long before the end. (Dir: Guy Hamilton, 94 mins.)

Man in the Moon (Great Britain, 1961)*** Kenneth More, Shirley Ann Field. British comedy with a good idea, satirizing the attempts to make a missile shot to the moon. Idea is superior to the execution; however, much of it is still quite droll. (Dir: Basil Dearden, 98 mins.)

Man in the Net, The (1959)*½ Alan Ladd, Carolyn Jones, Stan Moger, Tom Helmore. (Dir: Michael Curtiz, 97 mins.)

Man in the Raincoat (France-Italy, 1957)*** Fernandel, Bernard Blier. One of the better Fernandel movies —this time he is up to his neck in murder and bumbles his way to a hilarious climax. (Dir: Julien Duvivier, 87 mins.)

Man in the Road, The (Great Britain, 1957)** Derek Farr, Ella Raines. Scientist becomes an amnesia victim after an accident, is a target for foreign agents after his secrets. Ordinary spy melodrama. (Dir: Lance Comfort, 83 mins.)

Man in the Saddle (1951)**½ Randolph Scott, Joan Leslie, Ellen Drew. Two women are in love with Scott in this better-than-average western. Don't misunderstand—there's still plenty of shooting and riding for devoted Scott fans. (Dir: Andre de Toth, 87 mins.)

Man in the Santa Claus Suit, The (MTV 1979)**½ Fred Astaire, Gary Burghoff, John Byner. Burghoff, Byner, and Convy each rent a Santa Claus suit from costume shop owner Astaire. Their lives are changed, because the suit is endowed with Fred's magical spell. Astaire mysteriously pops up throughout the story in a number of different roles. (Dir: Corey Allen, 104 mins.)

Man in the Shadow (1957)**½ Jeff Chandler, Orson Welles, Ben Alexander. Sheriff engages in a battle with a tyrannical ranch owner who has ordered a Mexican laborer beaten badly enough to die. Top performers give this routine western drama more than it deserves. (Dir: Jack Arnold 80 minds.)

Man in the Trunk, The (1942)* Lynne Roberts, George Holmes. (Dir: Malcolm St. Clair 70 mins.)

Man in the White Suit, The (Great Britain, 1951)**** Alec Guinness, Joan Greenwood, Cecil Parker. Furor in a textile plant when a young scientist invents a cloth material that never wears, tears or becomes dirty. The industry unites to destroy him and his creation. Top-flight fun. Greenwood almost steals the film from Alec. (Dir: Alexander Mackendrick, 84 mins.)

Man in the Wilderness (1971)*** Richard Harris, John Huston, John Bindon. Based on two actual incidents in the northwest, this adventure yarn of survival in the Dakotas of the 1820s is interesting, if flawed. Harris is an experienced guide who gets mauled by a bear and is left to die by his expedition companions, led by the menacing Huston. The Spanish Pyrenees, where the film was shot, can pass for the U.S. Northwest. (Dir: Richard C. Sarafian, 105 mins.)

Man Inside, The (Great Britain, 1958)**½ Jack Palance, Anita Ekberg, Nigel Patrick. Fairly good drama about a group of international jewel thieves who hit the jackpot when a very valuable diamond comes into their possesion. Palance plays a detective who's on the group's trail. (Dir: John Gilling, 90 mins.)

Man is Armed, The (1956)** Dane Clark, William Talman. Truck driver framed for murder leaves prison with revenge in mind. Fair melodrama. (Dir: Franklin Adreon, 74 mins.)

Man Made Monster (1941)** Lon Chaney, Lionel Atwill. After being used in a series of experiments, a young man finds that he's immune to electric shock. Familiar sci-fi yarn with plenty of technical mumbo-jumbo. (Dir: George Waggner, 60 mins.)

Man Named Rocca, A (France, 1961)** Jean-Paul Belmondo, Christine Kaufmann. Two men imprisoned for a crime they didn't commit volunteer to dig mines in order to earn their freedom. Fair melodrama on the grim side. Dubbed in English. (Dir: Jean Becker, 106 mins.)

Man of Aran (Great Britain, 1934)**** Colman (Tiger) King, Maggie Dillane. A classic. Director Robert Flaherty's brilliant documentary chronicling the barren, meager existence of the inhabitants off the Irish coast remains unparalleled for visual imagery. (77 mins.)

Man of Conquest (1939)**½ Richard Dix, Joan Fontaine, Gail Patrick. The story of Sam Houston, soldier, statesman, hero of Texas. With fine, large scale battle scenes, good performances. (Dir: George Nicholls, Jr., 99 mins.)

Man of Evil (Great Britain, 1944)*½ James Mason, Phyllis Calvert, Stewart Granger. (Dir: Anthony Asquith, 90 mins.)

Man of La Mancha (Italy, 1972)*½ Sophia

Loren, Peter O'Toole, James Coco. (Dir: Arthur Hiller, 140 mins.)

Man of Marble (Poland, 1972)**** Krystyna Janda, Jerzy Radziwiowicz. A young filmmaker, for her graduation film project, decides to investigate the life of a worker-hero in the Stalinst '50s, Birkut (Radziwiowicz), who fell from official favor. Polish censors distorted the political meaning of the film by cutting out the shooting of Birkut by the police, and delayed general release till '77. (Dir: Andrzej Wajda, 150 mins.)

Man of 1000 Faces (1957)***½ James Cagney, Dorothy Malone, Jane Greer. Cagney is superb in the satisfying film biography of Lon Chaney, Sr., the silent screen star who was a make up wizard and created a series of memorable screen characterizations. (Dir: Joseph Pevney, 122 mins.)

Man of the West (1958)**½ Gary Cooper, Julie London, Lee J. Cobb. A good cast makes this otherwise routine western tale interesting. Screenplay by Reginald Rose has the hero, a reformed gunslinger, pitted predictably against his uncle, a notorious outlaw. (Dir: Anthony Mann, 100 mins.)

Man on a String (1960)**½ Ernest Borgnine, Kerwin Mathews. Story of Boris Morros, who served as a double agent to expose Communist espionage. Documentary-type drama has some good moments but never quite hits the mark. (Dir: André de Toth, 92 mins.)

Man on a String (MTV 1972)*½ Christopher George, Joel Grey, Jack Warden. (Dir: Joseph Sargent, 73 mins.)

Man on a Swing (1974)**½ Joel Grey, Cliff Robertson. Director Frank Perry almost pulls off this offbeat crime meller but it falls apart before the finale. Grey, in a dramatic role as a clairvoyant, gives a solid performance, and Robertson is less stoic than usual as the cop trying to solve the sex slaying of a young woman. (109 mins.)

Man on a Tightrope (1953)*** Fredric March, Gloria Grahame, Terry Moore, Cameron Mitchell, Adolphe Menjou. Story of a small German traveling circus troupe. March fares better than the other stars as a jealous husband who loves his unfaithful wife, unconvincingly portrayed by Grahame. Filmed on location in Europe. (Dir: Elia Kazan, 105 mins.)

Man on Fire (1957)**½ Bing Crosby, Inger Stevens, Mary Fickett, E. G. Marshall. One of Crosby's few non muscial films. The crooner plays a man with a custody problem concerning his son and his divorced wife. Melodramatic soap opera. (Dir: Ranald MacDougall, 95 mins.)

Man on the Eiffel Tower, The (1949)***½ Charles Laughton, Franchot Tone, Burgess Meredith. A police inspector craftily breaks down the resistance of a murderer when evidence is lacking. Intelligent, suspenseful melodrama, made in France.

Performances of the principals are standout, as is the hair-raising conclusion. (Dir: Burgess Meredith, 97 mins.)

Man on the Move—See: **Jigsaw (1972)**

Man on the Flying Trapeze, The (1935)***½ W. C. Fields, Mary Brian. Fields is in typical form as a cynical, downtrodden husband and father who, however, gets up and fights. Remake of his silent "Running Wild," with Brian repeating her role as the daughter. (Dir: Clyde Bruckman, 68 mins.)

Man on the Outside (MTV 1975)½ Lorne Greene, Lorraine Gary, James Olson. (Dir: Boris Sagal. 100 mins.)

Man on the Roof (Sweden, 1976)*½ Carl-Gustaf Lindstedt, Hakan Serner, Sven Wollfer. (Dir: Bo Widerberg, 110 mins.)

Man on the Run (1964)** Burgess Meredith, William Phipps. Small son of an American living in Manila is kidnaped, he vainly tries to get the lad back. Fair suspense drama filmed in the Philippines. (Dir: Eddie Romero, 78 mins.)

Man or Gun (1958)*½ Macdonald Carey, Audrey Totter. (Dir: Albert Gannaway, 79 mins.)

Man Outside, The (Great Britain, 1968)* Van Heflin, Heidelinde Weis, Pinkas Braun, Peter Vaughan. (Dir: Sam Gallu, 98 mins.)

Man Proof (1937)**½ Myrna Loy, Rosalind Russell, Franchot Tone, Walter Pidgeon. Big cast plus little story equals ordinary film. Myrna loves Walter who marries wealthy Rosalind but would like to keep little Myrna in his closet. Franchot comes in to give Myrna that fade out kiss. (Dir: Richard Thorpe, 80 mins.)

Man to Man Talk (France, 1958)**½ Yves Montand, Nicole Berger. Pleasant French comedy about a young lad who learns about the birds and the bees despite his over protective and bumbling parents. Good performances. (Dir: Luis Saslavski, 89 mins.)

Man-Trap (1961)* Jeffrey Hunter, Stella Stevens, David Janssen. (Director Edmond O'Brien 93 mins.)

Man Upstairs, The (Great Britain, 1959)*** Richard Attenborough, Virginia Maskell, Donald Houston, Bernard Lee. Attenborough delivers a strong performance as a shattered human being who attempts to kill himself after a series of depressing events. Well-made melodrama. (Dir: Don Chaffey, 88 mins.)

Man Who Came to Dinner, The (1941)*** Monty Woolley, Bette Davis, Ann Sheridan, Jimmy Durante, Reginald Gardiner. And stayed and stayed. Adaptation of the hit comedy by George S. Kaufman and Moss Hart. Davis comes off best since she is not working for laughs, although Gardiner's takeoff on Noël Coward and Durante's on Harpo Marx are effective. Woolley plays the irascible Alexander Woollcott figure. (Dir: William Keighley, 112 mins.)

Man Who Changed His Mind, The (Great Britain, 1936)*½ Boris Karloff, Anna Lee, John Loder. (Dir: Robert Stevenson, 61 mins.)

Man Who Cheated Himself, The (1950)**½ Lee J. Cobb, Jane Wyatt, John Dall. An honest cop meets a cheating dame and forgets his honesty. Just fair crime melodrama; good cast better than the story. (Dir: Felix E. Feist, 81 mins.)

Man Who Could Cheat Death (Great Britain, 1959)**½ Anton Diffring, Hazel Court, Christopher Lee. Man becomes ageless through a gland operation, becomes a murderer when he earns the secret of eternal youth from the doctor. Occasionally effective thriller, remake of "Man in Half Moon Street." Good performances. (Dir: Terence Fisher, 83 mins.)

Man Who Could Talk to Kids, The (MTV 1973)**½ Peter Boyle, Scott Jacoby, Robert Reed, Tyne Daly. A touching subject gets dramatic treatment, but never seems to fullfill the promise of the early scenes. Jacoby is a young teenager whose deep-rooted problems cause him to retreat into his own world except for occasional outbursts of violence. His troubled parents don't know how to cope, so they seek aid of an affable, honest, unorthodox social worker, Boyle. (Dir: Donald Wrye, 73 mins.)

Man Who Could Work Miracles, The (Great Britain, 1936)*** Roland Young, Joan Gardner, Ralph Richardson. Good rendition of an H. G. Wells short story in which a timid department store clerk finds he can do whatever he wants. Dated in all the best ways. (Dir: Lothar Mendes, 82 mins.)

Man Who Died Twice (MTV 1970)**½ Stuart Whitman, Brigitte Fossey, Jeremy Slate, Bernard Lee. Artist presumed dead wanders in Spain, and falls in love with a depressed French girl. Flashbacks of Whitman's previous life prove interesting, thanks to a good supporting cast. (Dir: Joseph Kane, 100 mins.)

Man Who Fell to Earth, The (Great Britain, 1976)*** David Bowie, Buck Henry, Candy Clark, Rip Torn. An extraterrestrial comes to our planet from a distant galaxy, desperately seeking a water supply for his people. Has suspense, intrigue, romance of a sort, even humor. The sci-fi effects are absolutely beautiful. Several scenes show Newtown's (Bowie's) barren home world and its people, and one lovely moment shows him slipping briefly and unobtrusively through a time warp. Leading actors are all good. (Dir: Nicolas Roeg, 140 mins.)

Man Who Finally Died, The (Great Britain, 1962)*½ Stanley Baker, Peter Cushing, Mai Zetterling. (Dir: Quentin Lawrence, 100 mins.)

Man Who Had His Hair Cut Short, The (Belgium, 1966)***½ Senne Rouffaer, Beata Tyszkiewicz. A brilliant dirctorial debut for André Delvaux, this blend of insight and horror follows a timid, lonely teacher (Rouffaer) from an infatuation with one of his pupils (Tyszkiewicz) to a wholly illusory murder with psychological precision. (95 mins.)

Man Who Haunted Himself (Great Britain, 1970)** Roger Moore, Olga Georges-Picot, Hildegard Neil. Venerable sci-fi gambit drama, as Moore plays a businessman who finds that his double has been slowly taking his place in the office, at his club, and at home. Is Moore mad or is there sabotage afoot? Weak ending. (Dir: Basil Dearden, 94 mins.)

Man Who Knew Too Much, The (Great Britain, 1934)** Peter Lorre, Edna Best, Leslie Banks. Not as good as the '56 also by director Alfred Hitchcock. Does have re-creation of the siege of Sidney Street and a villain, impersonated by Lorre with fine flair. (84 mins.)

Man Who Knew Too Much, The (1956)***½ James Stewart, Doris Day. Director Alfred Hitchcock at his best. Stewart and Miss Day star in this exciting suspense yarn of intrigue complete with murder, assassination plots, kidnappings, and a hair-raising climax. The stars do very nicely in their roles of an American couple vacationing in French Morocco who are accidentally drawn into a series of mysterious adventures. Oscar: Best Song, "Que Sera, Sera" (Jay Livingston and Ray Evans). (120 mins.)

Man Who Liked Funerals, The (Great Britain, 1959)** Leslie Phillips. A comedy with numerous unrealized possibilities thanks to the shoddy script. The acting doesn't salvage it either. (Dir: David Eady, 60 mins.)

Man Who Loved Cat Dancing, The (1973)**½ Burt Reynolds, Sarah Miles, Jack Warden, Lee J. Cobb, George Hamilton. About a gruff but inwardly gentle train robber (Reynolds) and the wretchedly unhappy "lady" who learns to love him (Miles). The plot contrivances are sticky. A good example of the western's last gasp. (Dir: Richard Sarafian, 114 mins.)

Man Who Loved Redheads, The (Great Britain, 1955)***½ Moira Shearer, John Justin, Gladys Cooper, Denholm Elliott. Throughout his long life, a man seeks the redhead of his youthful dream, becoming enamored by many carrottops in the process. (Dir: Harold French, 89 mins.)

Man Who Loved Women, The (France, 1977)***½ Charles Denner, Leslie Caron, Nelly Borgeaud. Denver plays a man who will go to any length to chase a well-turned ankle. Director François Truffaut's experiments in narration work well enough but serve to vitiate the emotional strength of the film. (119 mins.)

Man Who Never Was, The (1956)**½ Clifton Webb, Gloria Grahame, Stephen Boyd. Account of Operation Mincemeat, which was instrumental in paving the way for the Allied invasion of Europe in WW II. When the film sticks to the facts, it is engrossing. (Dir: Ronald Neame, 103 mins.)

Man Who Played God, The (1932)**½ George Arliss, Bette Davis, Ray Milland. Arliss vehicle gives that hammy actor the chance to do his star turns. He's a musician turned deaf who overcomes bitterness by helping young people (including Davis and Milland, in early roles). Arliss is awesomely good at this sort of tailor-made tripe—better than Liberace in the remake, "Sincerely Yours." (Dir: John G. Adolfi, 81 mins.)

Man Who Reclaimed His Head, The (1934)*** Claude Rains, Joan Bennett, Lionel Atwill. Effective anti-war picture, despite its improbable title, stars Rains as a brilliant journalist who sells his brains to an unscrupulous politician by ghostwriting for him. Upshot is war, adultery, misery, but Claude finally ... well, you guessed it. Bitter picture doesn't pull its punches. (Dir: Edward Ludwig, 82 mins.)

Man Who Returned to Life, The (1942)**½ John Howard, Ruth Ford. Good B film about a man who leaves a town to get a fresh start and, some years later, learns that they're about to try a man for murdering him. Above-average quickie. (Dir: Lew Landers, 61 mins.)

Man Who Shot Liberty Valance, The (1962)***½ John Wayne, James Stewart, Lee Marvin, Woody Strode, Vera Miles. One of the greatest of director John Ford's memory westerns, a moving bitter meditation of immortality and survival. Stewart is cast as a idealistic lawyer who has becomes famous for killing a notorious badman. Wayne incarnates his own myth with subtle melancholy. *Liberty Valance* culminates Ford's inquiry into the fabric of the social contract that began with the 1939 *Young Mr. Lincoln.* (122 mins.)

Man Who Skied Down Everest, The (Japan, 1975)** Yuichiro Miura. Documentary about a crazed Japanese who spends vast amounts of money and six lives in order to climb Mount Everest and ski—for 2½ minutes—down one of its slopes. An unctuous narrator (Douglas Rain) reads pop-Zen aphorisms from the skier's diary while we see the expedition force gathered around a videotape machine watching "Bonanza" reruns. The scenery, though, is nice, and the scene where he actually skies down Everest is truly breathtaking. Oscar winner for Best Documentary Feature. (Dirs: F. R. Crawley, James Hager, Dale Hartleben, 86 mins.)

Man Who Turned to Stone, The (1957)* Victor Jory, Charlotte Austin. (Dir: Leslie Kardos, 80 mins.)

Man Who Understood Women, The (1959)*** Henry Fonda, Leslie Caron. Hollywood genius makes an aspiring actress a star, marries her, then finds he has no time for her. She looks elsewhere. Unevenly balanced but with plenty to recommend it, including some biting dialogue, Fonda's fine performance. (Dir: Nunnally Johnson, 105 mins.)

Man Who Wagged His Tail, The (Italy-Spain, 1957)**½ Peter Ustinov, Pablito Calvo. Disliked, miserly lawyer is changed by magic into an ugly dog and must find salvation before he can return to human form. Mild fantasy has some amusing moments but is loosely put together. English-dubbed. (Dir: Ladislao Vajda, 91 mins.)

Man Who Wanted to Live Forever, The (MTV 1970)**½ Burl Ives, Sandy Dennis, Stuart Whitman. Fairly gripping drama with a good performance by Ives as a multimillionaire who has built a fantastic medical heart-disease research center for his own sinister purpose. Whitman and Dennis co-star as medical personnel who catch on to Ives's dark plans, and try to escape on skis down treacherous slopes. The escape sequence is beautifully filmed on location in the Canadian Rockies, and provides an exciting finale. (Dir: John Trent, 99 mins.)

Man Who Was Nobody, The (Great Britain, 1960)** Hazel Court, John Crawford. Lady detective joins forces with a sleuth to solve a murder. Fair low-budget Edgar Wallace mystery. (Dir: Montgomery Tully, 58 mins.)

Man Who Would Be King, The (1975)**** Michael Caine, Sean Connery, Christopher Plummer. Excellent, rousing treatment of Rudyard Kipling's yarn of greed and ambition in India, circa 1880. Caine and Connery are fine as the pals who decide to resign from the army and set themselves up as deities in Kafiristan. Given a grand treatment by director John Huston. who co-authored the screenplay with Gladys Hill. (127 mins.)

Man Who Would Not Die, The (1975)* Dorothy Malone, Keenan Wynn, Aldo Ray. (Dir: Robert Arkless, 83 mins.)

Man Who Wouldn't Talk, The (Great Britain, 1957)**½ Anthony Quayle, Anna Neagle, Zsa Zsa Gabor. Man on trial for the murder of a beautiful secret agent refuses to help himself, is defended by a clever lady barrister. Mystery keeps the interest, moves at a fairly good pace. (Dir: Herbert Wilcox, 85 mins.)

Man with a Cloak, The (1951)**½ Joseph Cotten, Barbara Stanwyck, Leslie Caron. An interesting costume drama about a mysterious man who enters two women's lives. The stars do well with this suspense yarn (Dir: Fletcher Markle, 81 mins.)

Man with a Million, (Great Britain, 1954)*** Gregory Peck, Jane Griffith, Ronald Squire, Wilfred Hyde-White, A.E. Matthews. A man who's supposed to be rich becomes famous and powerful proving that money comes to money. Interesting, entertaining film based on a Mark Twain story. Alternate title: **The Million Pound Note.** (Dir: Ronald Neame, 90 mins.)

Man with Bogart's Face, The (1980)*** Robert Sacchi, Michelle Phillips, Franco

Nero. Sacchi's impression of Humphrey Bogart catches the mannerisms without the emotional depth and delicacy. Robert Day's direction is pedestrian, but the film's action is coherent and affectionate, invoking the Bogart myth without messing it up too much. Andrew J. Fenady produced and adapted from his novel. Last film of George Raft (in cameo). (106 mins.)

Man with the Balloons, The (France-Italy, 1964)*½ Marcello Mastroianni, Catherine Spaak, Ugo Tognazzi. (Dir: Marco Ferreri, 85 mins.)

Man with the Golden Arm, The (1955)*** Frank Sinatra, Eleanor Parker, Kim Novack. Nelson Algren's novel of heroin addiction receives director Otto Preminger's usual considered treatment. Jazz score by Elmer Bernstein. (119 mins.)

Man with the Golden Gun, The (Great Britain, 1974)**½ Roger Moore, Christopher Lee, Britt Ekland, Hervé Villechaize. For those still counting, this is the ninth James Bond film, the second starring Roger Moore as agent 007, and the fourth directed by Guy Hamilton. 007 has gone slightly stale. Bond is chasing after a solar energy capsule confiscated by a globe-hopping hit man, played with authority and villainy by Britain's Lee, of all those horror flicks. (125 mins.)

Man with the Golden Keys (France, 1956)** Pierre Fresnay, Annie Girardot. College professor is framed by three students and dismissed in disgrace—he finally gets his revenge. Unexceptional but fairly interesting drama; dubbed-in English. (Dir: Leo Joannon, 90 mins.)

Man with the Green Carnation, The—See: **Trials of Oscar Wilde, The**

Man with the Gun (1955)**½ Robert Mitchum, Jan Sterling, Henry Hull. Absorbing but somewhat ponderous western drama. A good cast does more for the story than the story does for the stars. (Dir: Richard Wilson, 83 mins.)

Man with the Power, The (MTV 1977)* Vic Morrow, Bob Neill. (Dir: Nicholas Sgarro, 106 mins.)

Man with Two Faces (Great Britain, 1964)*½ Tab Hunter, Zena Walker. (Dir: Stanley Goulder, 74 mins.)

Man Without a Country (MTV 1973)*** Cliff Robertson, Robert Ryan. Nice adaptation of the classic story about Philip Nolan, the misguided patriot who sided with Aaron Burr in his plan to join Texas and Mexico to the United States. In his ensuing court martial, he renounced his country and received a sentence never to set foot on American soil again, leading to 60 years of exile on the high seas. Robertson does very well in the title role. To add to the authenticity, much of the footage was shot in Mystic Seaport, Connecticut, aboard vessels of the period. (Dir: Delbert Mann, 78 mins.)

Man Without a Star (1955)*** Kirk Douglas, Jeanne Crain, Claire Trevor. Two-fisted western with Douglas taking center stage and keeping it. He plays a lovable character who uses his fists and guns only when his charm fails to do the job. Crain is properly stiff as the big landowner and Trevor tosses off another big-hearted saloon hostess portrayal. Remade as "A Man Called Cannon." (Dir: King Vidor, 89 mins.)

Man, Woman and Sin (1927)*** John Gilbert, Jeanne Eagels. Remarkable little drama that showcases the mature talents of stage legend Eagels in a sultry, flashy part that suggests her charisma. Gilbert is very good too, as a poor boy who rise's in the newspaper business only to be undone when he gets entangled with the sophisticated Miss Eagels. Film eventually falls into fallen-woman melodrama, but it has tang and atmosphere that keeps it lively and meaningful for modern tastes. (Dir: Monte Bell, 71 mins.)

Manchu Eagle Murder Caper Mystery, The (1975)* Gabriel Dell, Barbara Harris, Will Geer. (80 mins.)

Manchurian Candidate, The (1962)***½ Frank Sinatra, Janet Leigh, Laurence Harvey, Angela Lansbury. Outrageously clever script by George Axelrod, from the novel by Richard Condon, about a Communist plan to use the American right wing as a cover to take over the country. When the liberal senator is assassinated in his kitchen, milk spills instead of blood. Lansbury's best performance. The presence of Sinatra and Leigh is irrelevant. (Dir: John Frankenheimer, 126 mins.)

Mandabi (The Money Order) (Senegal, 1969)*** Mamadou Guye, Ynousse N'Diaye. Early feature from Ousmane Sembene of Senegal, novelist and preeminent director of black Africa is a satire about how "been-tos" (Africans who have been to Europe) condescend to their countrymen. A simple old man receives a money order and the windfall threatens to destroy the traditional fabric of his life; the finger pointing at the intellectual class is acute. (90 mins.)

Mandingo (1975)*½ James Mason, Ken Norton, Susan George, Perry King. (Dir: Richard Fleischer, 127 mins.)

Mandrake (MTV 1979)** Anthony Herrera, Robert Reed, Gretchen Corbett. From the famous comic strip comes Mandrake the Magician, conquering evil with sleight of hand. Herrera, a magician himself, plays the title role with some style. Mandrake tackles a madman villain while coming to the aid of a tycoon who's being blackmailed. For the kids. (Dir: Harry Falk, 104 mins.)

Mandy (Great Britain, 1953)**** Phyllis Calvert, Jack Hawkins, Mandy Miller. Gripping story of a child born deaf and dumb, and of her efforts to adjust herself. Fine drama, superlatively acted by little Miss Miller. (Dir: Alexander Mackendrick, 93 mins.)

Maneater (MTV 1973)** Ben Gazzara, Richard Basehart, Sheree North. Gazzara leads a band of vacationers whose mobile home meets with mechanical difficulty, and accepts help from Basehart, who is a wild-animal trainer. Lions, and tigers, and bears ensue. Predictable all the way. (Dir: Vince Edwards, 74 mins.)

Maneater of Hydra (1969)* Cameron Mitchell, Kai Fischer. (Dir: Mel Welles, 85 mins.)

Man-eater of Kumaon (1948)**½ Sabu, Wendell Corey. Hunter wounds a tiger, then trails him when the beast terrorizes the community. Interesting jungle melodrama. (Dir: Byron Haskin, 79 mins.)

Manhattan (1979)**** Woody Allen, Diane Keaton, Michael Murphy, Meryl Streep, Mariel Hemingway. Director Allen sublimates his gag bent into genuine drama in his most worthwhile film. He jettisons the sweetness of "Annie Hall" and looks at "himself" with a jaundiced eye—the womanizer he plays in this film is a wily manipulator aware of his prowess. I can't think of another movie in which New York has appeared so beautiful. Hemingway establishes herself as the best natural actress in a long time. B&W. (96 mins.)

Manhattan Angel (1949)*½ Gloria Jean, Ross Ford (Dir: Arthur Dreifuss, 68 mins.)

Manhattan Melodrama (1934)**½ Clark Gable, William Powell, Myrna Loy. Bank robber John Dillinger was watching this MGM film loosely inspired by his character at the Biograph Theatre in Chicago just before he was ambushed by the FBI. An absorbing, fraudulent show, well crafted, ephemeral, familiar rather than inspired. Gable and Powell are two pals who grow up to take opposite sides of the law, and Loy is the lovely lady caught in between. Warner Bros. was a lot more adept at these things than MGM, though director W. S. Van Dyke II manages some panache amid the overstuffed art direction. (93 mins.)

Manhunt—See: Italian Connection, The

Manhunt in Space (1954)* Richard Crane, Sally Mansfield. (78 mins.)

Manhunt in the Jungle (1958)** Robin Hughes. Fearless explorer journeys to the Amazon to search for a missing expedition. Locale provides film with only interest. (Dir: Tom McGowan, 79 mins.)

Manhunter (MTV 1974)* Ken Howard, Gary Lockwood, Stefanie Powers, James Olson. (Dir: Walter Grauman, 74 mins.)

Mania—See: Flesh and the Fiends

Maniac (Great Britain, 1963)**½ Kerwin Mathews, Nadia Gray. American artist in France has his life placed in danger when the father of his sweetheart's stepdaughter escapes from a mental institution. Interesting thriller. (Dir: Michael Carreras, 86 mins.)

Maniac (1981)½ Joe Spinell, Caroline Munro. Joe Spinell stars as the title character on the rampage. (Dir: William Lustig)

Manitou, The (1978)**½ Tony Curtis, Michael Ansara, Susan Strasberg, Stella Stevens, Ann Southern. Curtis, sleazier

than ever, is a fake spiritualist desperate to find out why Strasberg is growing a fetus on her back. The answer is worse than he thinks. Undeniably trivial, but made with extravagance and some flair. (Dir: William Girdler, 105 mins.)

Mannequin (1937)**½ Joan Crawford, Spencer Tracy, Alan Curtis. Crawford is a poor girl from New York's Lower East Side, unhappily married to a petty crook, who finds relief with Tracy, a self-made millionaire. Director Frank Borzage's gift for visual metaphor is evident in his use of a flickering light bulb in the stairway of Crawford's tenement apartment as a symbol of dying hope. (95 mins.)

Mannequin (France, 1976)* Nadine Perles, Elton Frame, Alain Schwarte. (Dir: Claude Pessis)

Manpower (1941)*** Marlene Dietrich, Edward G. Robinson, George Raft. Raft and Robinson want Dietrich and the sparks really fly in this rip-roaring adventure about the hazards faced by the men who risk their lives daily repairing high-tensions lines. (Dir: Raoul Walsh, 103 mins.)

Man's Castle (1933)***½ Spencer Tracy, Loretta Young, Glenda Farrell. Tracy and Young are two lovers who transcend the depression in a New York shantytown. Few love stories have achieved such emotional intensity, and most of the others were also directed by Frank Borzage (pronounced BorZAYghee). (75 mins.)

Man's Favorite Sport? (1964)**½ Rock Hudson, Paula Prentiss, Maria Perschy. Outdoorsman-columnist Hudson suddenly finds he has to live up to his reputation in this Howard Hawks- directed comedy that is funnier than it has any right to be. Rock trying to fish (though he has never fished in his life) in order to save his job is quite a sight. Still, two hours is too long for one joke. (120 mins.)

Manster, The (Japan 1962)* Peter Dyneley, Jane Hylton. (Dir: George P. Breakston, Kenneth Crane, 72 mins.)

Man-Trap (1961)* Jeffrey Hunter, Stella Stevens, David Janssen. Director Edmond O'Brien. (93 mins.)

Many Rivers to Cross (1955)*** Robert Taylor, Eleanor Parker, James Arness. Frontier girl goes to extreme lengths to land a marriage-shy adventurer. Outdoor setting, but the emphasis is on comedy rather than action—and it gets rib-tickling quite often. Good fun. (Dir: Roy Rowland, 92 mins.)

Mara Maru (1952)** Errol Flynn, Ruth Roman. He-man adventurer Flynn plays both sides against the middle in this rather dull story of sunken treasures. Roman stands around waiting to be embraced when Errol has a free moment. (Dir: Gordon Douglas, 98 mins.)

Mara of the Wilderness (1965)** Adam West, Linda Saunders. In a variation on Kipling's classic jungle tale "Mowgli," Mara is adopted and raised by Alaskan wolves after the death of her parents, and then rediscovered by civilization. Animal-adventure story for the kids; West, in a pre-"Batman" role, does well as the anthropologist who befriends the young wolf-girl. (Dir: Frank McDonald, 90 mins.)

Maracaibo (1958)**½ Cornel Wilde, Jean Wallace, Abbe Lane, Michael Landon. Top fire fighter discovers an old flame while attempting to put out an oil-well blaze. Not much glow in the thread-bare story, but occasional excitement in the action scenes, resulting in a mildly entertaining melodrama. (Dir: Cornel Wilde, 88 mins.)

Marat/Sade (Great Britain, 1967)***½ Ian Richardson, Glenda Jackson, Patrick Magee. Director Peter Brook's film of his stage production of Peter Weiss's play about revolution, passivity, and responsibility features superb performances from the leads. Brook's use of close-ups substitutes horrifying detail for the crazy mirror of the Charenton asylum. Brilliantly photographed by David Watkin. Complete title: "The Persecution and Assassination of Jean-Paul Marat as Performed by the Inmates of the Asylum of Charenton Under the Direction of the Marquis de Sade." (115 mins.)

Marathon (1980)**½ Bob Newhart, Herb Edelman, Dick Gautier, Anita Gillette, Leigh Taylor-Young. While on a six-mile run in California, middle-aged, married Newhart falls for a pretty jogger (Taylor-Young) and ends up in the New York Marathon just to be with her. You'll hear a Newhart monologue on the phone and catch his character doing all the wrong things—just like watching the "Bob Newhart Show" on TV. (Dir: Jackie Cooper, 104 mins.)

Marathon Man (1976)*** Dustin Hoffman, Laurence Oliver, Marthe Keller, Roy Scheider. Exciting thriller about double agents and elderly Nazis, but it's too heavily plotted and suffers from gratuitous violence—whether it's plain, old-fashioned stabbings or Oliver playing a former dentist who puts his past calling to professional use by torturing Hoffman. Hoffman is customarily splendid, and I'm always glad to glimpse the genius of Oliver, but his Nazi role is really beneath him. Keller is attractive playing Hoffman's love interest. Screenplay by William Goldman from his own novel. (Dir: John Schlesinger, 120 mins.)

Marauders of the Sea (Great Britain, 1962)** Terence Morgan, Jean Kent, Kieron Moore. Sir Francis Drake tries to rescue an English sailor who has hoped to establish himself as king of America. Passing fair costume adventure edited from a good British TV series, "Sir Francis Drake."(85 mins.)

Marcelino—See: **Miracle of Marcelino, The**

March of the Wooden Soldiers (1934)** Stan Laurel, Oliver Hardy, Charlotte Henry. Laurel and Hardy backed by a Victor Herbert operetta ("Babes in Toyland"). Strictly a kiddie show, with little of L & H's usual polish. The climax—giant, slobbering bogeymen invade Toyland—changes the tone from MGM to Universal grotesque. (Dirs: Gus Meins, Charles R. Rogers, 73 mins.)

March on Paris 1914 (of Generaloberst Alexander von Kluck)—and His Memory of Jessee Holladay, The (1977)*** Wulf Gunther Brandes, Jessie Holladay Duane. Offbeat, sometimes charming low-budget independent feature directed by New York iconoclast Walter Gutman, who was 74 when he made this exuberant film. Chronicles the romance of a German officer and an American woman. Photography and special effects by Mike Kuchar. (70 mins.)

March or Die (Great Britain, 1977)** Gene Hackman, Catherine Deneuve, Terence Hill, Max von Sydow. Hymn to machismo seems sadly out of date. Director Dick Richards's Foreign Legion story is beautifully designed and photographed, but the narrative is as flat as the ubiquitous horizon line.(107 mins.)

Marciano (MTV 1979)**½ Tony Lo Bianco, Belinda Montgomery, Vincent Gardenia. The story of Rocky Marciano's rise from obscurity to heavyweight champion of the world is reminiscent of all those fight movies of the '40s and the '50s complete with wavy close-ups signaling flashbacks. Lo Bianco is a bit too old to play Rocky in his early 20's but he has the physical attributes and acting ability to make the gentle fighter with a deadly punch believable. Love story between Rocky and his wife is predictably melodramatic. (Dir: Bernard L. Kowalski, 104 mins.)

Marco Polo (France-Italy, 1962)** Rory Calhoun, Yoko Tani. Nephew of the great khan is rebelling against uncle's wicked prime minister—along comes Marco Polo to help him out. Despite an attempt to treat things tongue in cheek, this costume adventure dubbed in English never manages to rise above the routine. (Dirs: Hugo Fregonese, Piero Pierotti, 90 mins.)

Marco, the Magnificent (Afghanistan-Egypt-France-Italy-Yugoslavia, 1965)* Horst Buchholz, Anthony Quinn, Omar Sharif, Orson Welles. (Dirs: Denys De La Pateliere, Noel Howard, Christian-Jaque, Cliff Lyons, 100 mins.)

Marcus-Nelson Murders, The (1973)***½ Telly Savalas, Marjoe Gortner, José Ferrer, Gene Woodbury. Brooklyn detectives coerce a young black man into confessing to the grisly murder of two New York girls. Savalas's detective is the hero, blowing the whistle on fellow cops as he funnels information to the skilled defense attorney. Authentic New York locations and good performances by the cast, particularly Woodbury as the railroaded suspect, give this controversial material a sharp edge. Pilot for TV's "Kojak." (Dir: Joseph Sargent, 148 mins.)

Marcus Welby, M.D. (1969)**½ Robert Young, Anne Baxter, James Brolin. Pilot.

Young is the last of a dying breed—the dedicated general medical practitioner who makes house calls, gets involved with his patients, and neglects his private life and health in the process. (Dir: David Lowell Rich, 99 mins.)

Mardi Gras (1958)**½ Pat Boone, Christine Carere, Gary Crosby, Sheree North, Tommy Sands. Pure escapist fare, Boone and company sing, dance, march, and act their way through this Technicolor romance with attractive energy. The setting is the Mardi Gras festival in New Orleans. (Dir: Edmund Goulding, 107 mins.)

Margie (1946)***½ Jeanne Crain, Alan Young, Lynn Bari. One of the few period musicals that sustains its charm without compromising its artistry. Crain plays a pretty but painfully shy adolescent in the late '20s in this screenplay by F. Hugh Herbert based on the early chapters of Ruth McKinney's "My Sister Eileen". The tone is delicate rather than coy and the period songs are effective. Henry King's direction is at its best. (94 mins.)

Margin for Error (1943)**½ Joan Bennett, Milton Berle, Otto Preminger. Entertaining but dated comedy-drama about intrigues in the New York office of the German consul before the war. (Dir: Otto Preminger, 74 mins.)

Marie Antoinette (1938)*** Norma Shearer, Tyrone Power, John Barrymore, Robert Morley, Joseph Schildkraut. Opulent costumer directed by breezy, insubstantial W. S. Van Dyke, II. Good performances from Shearer and Barrymore, and a terrific one from youngish Morley as Louis XVI. See if you can recognize Tyrone Power. (160 mins.)

Marie Antoinette (France, 1958)** Michele Morgan, Richard Todd. Story of the girl who rises to power in the French court of Louis XVI and the stormy days of the Revolution is lavishly produced but frequently dull, moves at a slow pace. Cast is good but overwhelmed by the script. Dubbed in English. (Dir: Jean Delannoy, 108 mins.)

Marie of the Isles (Italy, France, 1960)*½ Belinda Lee, Alain Saury, Folco Lulli. (Dir: Georges Combret, 96 mins.)

Marilyn (1963)**½ Marilyn Monroe. Film fans will be interested in this movie-magazine-type review of Monroe's life and career. Rock Hudson narrates the story of the girl who went from sexy starlet to super screen star in a short time. There are clips from 15 of Marilyn's films, including one from her last, uncompleted movie, "Something's Got to Give," which she was working on at the time of her tragic death. (Edited by Pepe Torres, 83 mins.)

Marilyn: The Untold Story (MTV 1980)**½ Catherine Hicks, Jason Miller, Frank Converse, Viveca Lindfors. Hicks makes Marilyn Monroe believable. Marilyn's legend, her story of being left in the lurch by everyone — mom, dad, agent, lovers, husbands is endless. Monroe fans shouldn't miss this one. (Dirs: John Flynn, Jack Arnold, Lawrence Schiller, 156 mins.)

Marines Fly High, The (1940)*** Richard Dix, Chester Morris, Lucille Ball. Marines foil a revolt in Central America. Fast-moving action melodrama. (Dirs: George Nicholls, Jr., Ben Stoloff, 60 mins.)

Marius (France, 1931)**** Raimu, Pierre Fresnay, Charpin, Orane Demazis. Marcel Pagnol's great trilogy opens by introducing us to Marius (a lean and sexy Fresnay), who dreams of going to sea; his love, Fanny (Demazis), who understands his dream; Marius's father, César (Raimu), who runs a Marseilles waterfront bar; and César's wealthy friend Panisse (Charpin). All the actors create miracles of performance. (Dir: Alexander Korda, 120 mins.)

Marjoe (1972)**** A revealing cinema verité-style documentary about Marjoe Gortner, a charismatic former child prodigy on the evangelist revival circuit. We see Gortner in action, hustling gullible "worshipers" in revival meetings filmed in California, Michigan, Texas, and other states. Gortner gave up his "ministry" when this film was released and widely publicized. Conceived and directed by Sarah Kernochan and Howard Smith. (92 mins.)

Marjorie Morningstar (1958)** Natalie Wood, Gene Kelly, Everett Sloane, Claire Trevor, Ed Wynn. Wood plays a suburban Jewish girl out to realize her career ambitions in the Big Apple, only to end up as a happy housewife. Young women today would not be as easily satisfied by a fiction such as Herman Wouk's. Glossy, but essentially boring and valueless. (Dir: Irving Rapper, 123 mins.)

Mark, The (Great Britain, 1961)**** Stuart Whitman, Rod Steiger, Maria Schell. One of the finest psychological dramas ever filmed, played with extraordinary distinction and excitement. It combines an honest awareness of the uses of psychiatric therapy as well as its limitations, as it follows the path of a highly disturbed parolee into the threatening world of reality. (Dir: Guy Green, 127 mins.)

Mark of Cain, The (Great Britain, 1948)**½ Sally Gray, Eric Portman. A notorious crime passionel rocks Victorian London. Leisurely melodrama, but rather interesting. Well acted. (Dir: Brian Desmond Hurst, 88 mins.)

Mark of the Hawk (Great Britain, 1958)** Sidney Poitier, Eartha Kitt, John McIntire. Well-intentioned but rambling, wordy topical drama of a young African politician who is swayed by his terrorist brother, but adheres to nonviolence. Complex background of the good points are bogged down in an unsure scenario. (Dir: Michael Audley, 83 mins.)

Mark of the Phoenix (Great Britain, 1958)*½ Sheldon Lawrence, Julia Arnall. (Dir: Maclean Rogers, 63 mins.)

Mark of the Renegade (1951)**½ Ricardo Montalban, Cyd Charisse, Gilbert Roland. Colorful adventure in southern California during the middle century. Montalban cuts a fine figure as a Spanish renegade and Charisse is ravishing as a Spanish noblewoman. (Dir: Hugo Fregonese, 81 mins.)

Mark of the Vampire (1935)** Lionel Barrymore, Lionel Atwill, Elizabeth Allan, Bela Lugosi. Director Tod Browning's remake of his silent "London after Midnight," for all the shrewd parody and intricate lighting effects (by James Wong Howe), is stilted and unconvincing. Barrymore plays the expert on vampire lore who solves the mystery of vampiric attacks on a young girl in a derelict castle. (61 mins.)

Mark of the Vampire (1957)** John Beal, Coleen Gray. Doctor takes pills given him by a dying scientist; they turn him into a vampire. Passable horror thriller, thanks to Beal's good performance in the lead role. (Dir: Paul Landres, 74 mins.)

Mark of the Whistler (1944)**½ Richard Dix, Janis Carter, Paul Cavanagh. Attempted swindle of an unclaimed bank account. The "Whistler" series was based on a popular radio show and featured the likable Dix, who alternated between victim and perpetrator from one film to the next. It kept audiences guessing. (Dir: William Castle, 61 mins.)

Mark of Zorro, The (1920)*** Douglas Fairbanks, Sr., Marguerite de la Motte, Noah Beery. The first of Fairbank's out-and-out swashbucklers, with sets designed to fit the limitations of his athletic ability. Lots of action, but dull direction by Fred Niblo. (90 mins.)

Mark of Zorro, The (1940)*** Tyrone Power, Basil Rathbone, J. Edward Bromberg, Linda Darnell, Gale Sondergaard, Eugene Pallette. This splashy version has enough good spirits and desire to please to carry it past severe defects. Power makes a good try, though Zorro he ain't. The caliber of swordplay is above average, particularly with the skillful Rathbone swashing. Cinematographer Arthur Miller does first-rate B&W work. (Dir: Rouben Mamoulian, 93 mins.)

Mark of Zorro, The (MTV 1974)**½ Frank Langella, Gilbert Roland, Yvonne DeCarlo, Richardo Montalban, Louise Sorel. Here's a zesty remake of the romantic adventures of Don Diego, a fop by day and the avenging bandit known as Zorro by night. Dashing, handsome Langella is perfectly cast as the hero. (Dir: Don McDougall 74 mins.)

Marked Woman (1937)*** Bette Davis, Humphrey Bogart, Lola Lane, Eduardo Ciannelli. Davis plays a clip-joint hostess who turns informer on high-living Ciannelli (modeled on Lucky Luciano), and Bogart as the Thomas E. Deweyesque public prosecutor in this melodrama. (Dir: Lloyd Bacon, 99 mins.)

Marketa Lazarova (Czechoslovakia, 1966) *½ Wide-screen medieval spectacle. Story of the doomed love between an outlaw and the daughter of a squire has impressively mannered compositions and a fusty period look. Frantisek Vlacil directs, in that heavy, methodical eastern European way that lets you hear the breathing under the armor.

Marlowe (1969)*** James Garner, Gayle Hunnicutt, Carroll O'Connor. Garner plays Philip Marlowe, Raymond Chandler's legendary detective. He's caught under a pile of corpses when he's hired by a mysterious blonde. Pace is fast and tough, but it's the bravura acting that carries the movie. O'Connor is a standout as a cop always two steps behind Marlowe. (Dir: Paul Bogart, 95 mins.)

Marie (West Germany, 1972)*** Maria Schell, Anna Martins, Heinz Bennent. Martins plays a 17-year-old girl whose relationship with her separated parents fluctuates between indifference and anxiety. Her mother (Schell) is a wealthy physician in a small town; Marie lives with her father (Bennent) in a small apartment. When he dies, Marie stays there alone and begins to make discoveries about her parents' relationship. (Dir: Hans W. Geissendorfer.)

Marnie (1964)**** Tippi Hedren, Sean Connery, Diane Baker. Although panned on release, this is one of director Alfred Hitchcock's greatest and darkest achievements. Hedren, in a performance based on a naked, anxious vulnerability, is a compulsive thief; Connery is the neurotically motivated southern gentleman who catches her in the act and forces her into marriage, the alternative being prison. (130 mins.)

Maroc 7 (Great Britain, 1967)** Gene Barry, Elsa Martinelli, Cyd Charisse, Denholm Elliott, Alexandra Stewart. Secret agent (Barry) after clever jewel thieves. Slow chase, nothing exceptional. (Dir: Gerry O'Hara, 91 mins.)

Marooned (1969)**½ Gregory Peck, Gene Hackman, James Franciscus, Lee Grant, Mariette Hartley. A lot of money went into making this adventure story about astronauts marooned in space, but it misfires: personal stories about the astronauts' wives get in the way. (Dir: John Sturges, 134 mins.)

Marmalade Revolution, The (Sweden, 1979)*** Erland Josephson, Bibi Andersson, Marie Goranzon. The second feature directed by Josephson (who starred, scripted, and co-directed with cinematographer Sven Nykvist) is a deft social satire about a middle-aged professor who finally leaves his wife. The last straw: She calls him to task for buying the wrong kind of marmalade. His case becomes a prominent news story.

Marquise of O, The (France-West Germany, 1975)**** Edith Clever, Bruno Ganz, Peter Luhr. Director Eric Rohmer's subtle retelling of a Heinrich von Kleist

432

story about an Italian aristocrat who discovers, unaccountably, that she's pregnant. The film's stately pace and the quiet way in which it makes its points give it the aura of a fading vision of gentility. (102 mins.)

Marriage-Go-Round, The (1960)** Susan Hayward, James Mason, Julie Newmar. Professor finds himself the target of a Swedish student who has selected him as her perfect mate—trouble is, he's married. Comedy tries for sophistication, becomes strained. (Dir: Walter Lang, 98 mins.)

Marriage is a Private Affair (1944)** Lana Turner, James Craig, John Hodiak. Hasty war marriage, boy goes to fight, girl gets restless but all comes to a happy ending in this talky bore. (Dir: Robert Z. Leonard, 116 mins.)

Marriage Is Alive and Well (MTV 1980)* Joe Namath, Jack Albertson, Judd Hirsch, Melinda Dillon. (Dir: Russ Mayberry, 104 mins.)

Marriage Italian Style (Italy, 1964)***½ Sophia Loren, Marcello Mastroianni. Not as funny as "Divorce Italian Style," but the stars carry off this comedy in fine style. About a luscious, happy prostitute and her efforts to trick a wealthy businessman into marriage, and then to hold on to him. Film again makes a meaningful comment on Italy's antiquated laws of marriage and divorce. Dubbed in English. (Dir: Vittorio De Sica, 102 mins.)

Marriage of a Young Stockbroker, The (1971)**½ Richard Benjamin, Joanna Shimkus, Elizabeth Ashley. Occasionally amusing but generally heavy-handed comedy about a young, married, bored stockbroker (Benjamin) who tries to improve his morale by going to porno flicks and ogling any passing young damsels. Based on the novel by Charles Webb, who wrote "The Graduate," and directed by Lawrence Turman, who produced "The Graduate." They tried to repeat the magic formula of that entry, but none of the participants happen to have Mike Nichols' talent. Tiffany Bolling is noteworthy in a supporting role. (Dir: Lawrence Turman, 95 mins.)

Marriage of Convenience, The (Great Britain, 1961)** Harry H. Corbett, John Cairney, Jennifer Daniel. Bank robber escapes prison, finds his girl has married the detective who arrested him. Passable crime drama based on an Edgar Wallace story. (Dir: Clive Donner, 58 mins.)

Marriage of Maria Braun, The (West Germany, 1979)**** Hanna Schygulla, Klaus Lowitsch, Ivan Desny, Gottried John, Ranier Werner Fassbinder. Director Rainer Werner Fassbinder's best film since *Fox and his Friends* is on a woman's rise to wealth and power and takes its metaphoric impetus from the history of postwar Germany. Schygulla, a brilliant actress who makes every advantage out of her limitations of range, plays a girl who loses her husband after one wedded night, and remains steadfastly devoted to the princi-

ple of her marriage through an incredible sequence of events and lovers. (120 mins.)

Marriage on the Rocks (1965)**½ Frank Sinatra, Dean Martin, Deborah Kerr. One of those screwy comedies that almost works—but it's fun anyway. Frank and Deborah are Mr. and Mrs., but they get a Mexican divorce by mistake, and Miss Kerr marries Frank's best friend (Martin). More complications, more switching, and a happy ending. (Dir: Jack Donohue, 109 mins.)

Marriage Playground, The (1929)**½ Fredric March, Mary Brian. The seven children of a fast-living American couple are left to fend for themselves in Europe; the eldest daughter (Brian) takes care of the group and falls in love with another American tourist (March). (Dir: Lothar Mendes, 79 mins.)

Marriage: Year One (MTV 1971)**½ Sally Field, Robert Pratt, William Windom. He's a hard-working, relatively square, dedicated student (Pratt), and she's a modern, involved, anti-establishment type from a wealthy family (Field). Enough touching moments and fine performances to sustain interest. (Dir: William A. Graham, 104 mins.)

Married Woman, The (France, 1964)*** Macha Meril, Philippe Leroy. Director Jean-Luc Godard's witty dissection of Parisian marriage has often been imitated by later filmmakers eager to score with humorous pornography. De Gaulle heartily disapproved of this one, which contributed to its making some money. (94 mins.)

Marry Me (Great Britain, 1949)**½ Derek Bond, Susan Shaw. Couple of elderly spinsters run a marriage bureau, manage to tie together four couples. Pleasing little comedy. (Dir: Terence Fisher, 97 mins.)

Marry Me Again (1953)*** Robert Cummings, Marie Wilson. Girl tries to get her fella to marry her, even if she has more money than he. Enjoyable comedy has some clever gags. (Dir: Frank Tashlin, 73 mins.)

Marry Me! Marry Me! (France, 1968)**** Claude Berri, Elizabeth Wiener, Betsy Blair, Regine. Charming romantic comedy, produced, directed, and written by Claude Berri, who somehow also found time to play the role of Claude, a Jewish encyclopedia salesman in Paris who's inconveniently fallen in love with a pregnant Belgian girl. Gentle, perceptive story about European Jewish families. (96 mins.)

Marrying Kind, The (1952)***½ Judy Holliday, Aldo Ray, Madge Kennedy. An excellent combination of comedy and pathos make this film of marital ups and downs most entertaining. Holliday proves she can act in a serious vein; it's not much of a compliment but Ray gives his best performance. (Dir: George Cukor, 93 mins.)

Mars Needs Women (1968)*½ Tommy

Kirk, Yvonne Craig. (Dir: Larry Buchanan, 80 mins.)

Martin (1978)*** John Amplas. The plight of a demythologized vampire is compared to the slow death-by-recession that plagues the Pittsburgh suburb in which he lives. Low-budget film directed by George Romero.

Marty (1955)*** Ernest Borgnine, Betsy Blair. The pathos and authenticity of Paddy Chayefsky's screenplay—adapted in a movie theater version from his TV-show script—was revolutionary at the time, but now seems merely drab. The tale of a Bronx butcher (Borgnine, in an Oscar-winning performance) finding love is still moving, despite Delbert Mann's dreary direction. (90 mins.)

Martyrs of Love (Czechoslovakia, 1968) ***½ Petr Kopriva, Marta Kubisova, Karel Gott. Three-part surreal comedy directed by the somewhat didactic Jan Nemec is the last film he was allowed to make by Czech authorities. Experimental, severe yet playful. Best episode is the first, "The Junior Clerk's Temptation." (73 mins.)

Mary and Joseph: A Story of Faith (MTV 1979)**½ Blanche Baker, Jeff East, Colleen Dewhurst. Not much is known about Mary and Joseph, so this holiday religious drama takes certain liberties in depicting the courtship and trials of the couple before the birth of Jesus. Mary's belief that she is bearing the Son of God, in contrast to the doubts of young Joseph and the citizenry of Nazareth, is fully explored. (Dir: Eric Till, 104 mins.)

Mary Jane Harper Cried Last Night (MTV 1977)*** Kevin McCarthy, Bernie Casey, Tricia O'Neil. First time a full-length TV movie has dealt with the urgent issue of battered children. Standout performance by O'Neil as a tough Brooklyn-born doctor with a history of child abuse in her own life. Casey also scores as the concerned social worker who won't quit even though it means treading on some high-society toes. Another plus is an ending which doesn't cop out. (Dir: Allen Reisner, 104 mins.)

Mary, Mary (1963)**½ Debbie Reynolds, Barry Nelson, Michael Rennie, Diane McBain. A dashing movie star complicates matters when it appears that a book publisher still loves his ex-wife, and vice versa. Film version of long-running Broadway stage success isn't altered much, retains most of the witty lines—which is also a disadvantage, for it remains a photographed stage play. Should afford a fair amount of fun. (Dir: Mervyn LeRoy, 126 mins.)

Mary of Scotland (1936)*** Katharine Hepburn, Fredric March, Florence Eldridge, John Carradine. Director John Ford does an intriguing, handsomely mounted job with Maxwell Anderson's trivial play. Hepburn is the Catholic pretender making her clumsy play for the English throne, and March is Bothwell, her arrogant, sardonic lover. (140 mins.)

Mary Poppins (1964)***½ Julie Andrews (film debut), Dick Van Dyke, Glynis Johns. Charming outing for the kids. It doesn't have the soft-edged sense of whimsy and wonder that the Pamela Travers books have, but Walt Disney's version of the Mary Poppins stories avoids the worst saccharine excesses, thanks largely to the verve of performances by Van Dyke and everyone's pal, Julie Andrews. Made Andrews a star and won her an Oscar. (Dir: Robert Stevenson, 140 mins.)

Mary, Queen of Scots (Great Britain, 1971)*** Vanessa Redgrave, Glenda Jackson, Nigel Davenport, Trevor Howard. A lame script with plodding direction and not much concern for historical accuracy diffuses the excitement generated by Vanessa Redgrave's Academy Award-nomination performance. The picture really comes alive in the scenes between Jackson and Redgrave, marvelous actresses both, and some lovely costumes and panoramas of the countryside. (Dir: Charles Jarrott, 128 mins.)

Mary White (MTV 1977)***½ Kathleen Beller, Ed Flanders, Fionnuala Flanagan. A lovely, human drama inspired by Pulitzer prizewinning newspaper editor William Allen White's poignant editorial written after the accidental death of his beloved 16-year-old daughter, who had steadfastly sought her own identity, even to the point of annoying many. Beller is luminous, bright, and thoroughly convincing as a young lady well ahead of her time. (Dir: Jud Taylor, 104 mins.)

Maryjane (1968)* Fabian, Patty McCormack, Diane McBain. (Dir: Maury Dexter, 95 mins.)

Maryland (1940)**½ Walter Brennan, Fay Bainter, John Payne. Film about a woman who sells all her horses after her husband is killed in an accident is a fairly good horse story. (Dir: Henry King, 92 mins.)

Masculin Feminine (France-Sweden, 1966)**** Jean-Pierre Leaud, Marlene Jobert, Chantal Goya, Brigitte Bardot. Director Jean-Luc Godard's accomplished and moving examination of Parisian youth, wildly experimental in its day, is now a legitimate classic. (103 mins.)

M*A*S*H (1970)**** Donald Sutherland, Elliott Gould, Sally Kellerman. The two real stars of this extraordinarily funny film about an American army medical unit during the Korean War are screenwriter Ring Lardner, Jr., and director Robert Altman. Academy Award and deservedly won an Academy Award, and director Robert Altman. Generated one of the best series ever done on TV. (116 mins.)

Mask of Dimitrios, The (1944)***½ Peter Lorre, Sydney Greenstreet, Zachary Scott, Faye Emerson. Features Lorre's witty interpretation of a mystery writer investigating the life of a notorious scoundrel (Scott, who is superb). By boldly moving his camera to underline the broad sweeps of the narrative, director Jean Negulesco creates the mood of a dark fable. (95 mins.)

Mask of Fu Manchu, The (1932)** Boris Karloff, Myrna Loy, Lewis Stone. "Classic" version of the Sax Rohmer story is a stodgy, dull bit of work by director Charles Brabin (Charles Vidor, uncredited, is said to have done some of it). If your idea of fun is Karloff in long fingernails and Loy in oriental trousers, this may be for you. Tony Gaudio's lush photography helps, but not enough. (72 mins.)

Mask of the Avenger (1951)** John Derek, Anthony Quinn, Jody Lawrance. The Count of Monte Cristo rides again, but only in name. Young Renato Dimorna (Derek) takes the guise of the count to outwit the evil governor (Quinn) and win back his beloved Maria. You've seen it all before and better done. (Dir: Phil Karlson, 83 mins.)

Mask of the Musketeers (Italy, 1960)*½ Gordon Scott, Jose Greci. (101 mins.)

Masked Conqueror, The (Italy, 1962)* Alberto Lupo, Giorgio Ardisson. (Dir: Luigi Capuano, 94 mins.)

Masked Man Against the Pirates, The (Italy, 1965)* George Hilton, Claude Dantes. (Dir: Vertunio de Angelis, 105 mins.)

Masque of the Red Death, The (Great Britain, 1964)*** Vincent Price, Hazel Court, Jane Asher, Patrick Magee, Nigel Green. Director Roger Corman's sixth adaptation of Edgar Allan Poe is a work of consummate imaginative power and originality. Devil-worshiping Prince Prospero (Price) abducts an innocent village girl to his medieval Italian castle and tries to interest her in his diabolical goings-on while the plague rages outside. (86 mins.)

Masquerade (Great Britain, 1965)***½ Cliff Robertson, Jack Hawkins, Marisa Mell, Michel Piccoli. A delightful spy spoof. Robertson and Hawkins are a pair of Foreign Office emissaries assigned to kidnap a young prince of a country that possesses vast oil deposits. Director Basil Dearden keeps a firm hand on the proceedings, and we're spared much of the farcical mugging and hijinks so often found in this kind of picture. (101 mins.)

Masquerade in Mexico (1945)*½ Dorothy Lamour, Arturo de Cordova. (Dir: Mitchell Leisen, 96 mins.)

Masquerader, The (1933)**½ Ronald Colman, Elissa Landi. Colman plays two parts in the derring-do tale based on a popular novel by Katherine Cecil Thurston. (Dir: Richard Wallace, 78 mins.)

Massacre (1956)** Dane Clark, James Craig. Just another western about the Indians massacring the good guys on our side by using guns sold to them by the bad guys. Set in Mexico. (Dir: Louis King, 76 mins.)

Massacre at Central High (1975)**½ Derrel Maury, Andrew Stevens, Kimberly Beck. Obsessive B movie set in a California high school. Some faults of dialogue and acting. (Dir: Renee Daalder, 85 mins.)

Massacre at Fort Perdition Spain, 1964)** Jerry Cobb, Marta May. Sole survivor of a bloody massacre tells the whole story when he's placed on trial. Slightly offbeat western—filmed abroad, and relatively fresh plot. (Dir: Jose Maria Elorrieta, 92 mins.)

Master Hand (Japan, 1973)**½ Shintaro Kastu, Tatsuya Nakadai. Burly Katsu, familiar as the blind swordsman Ichi, plays a man determined to become champion at Japanese chess. The big showdown with Nakadai makes an offbeat variant on samurai confrontations. (Dir: Horikawa Hiromichi.)

Master of Ballantrae (Great Britain, 1953)**½ Errol Flynn, Yvonne Furneaux. Another swashbuckling role for Flynn as he surmounts danger after danger. Plenty of adventure and romance. (Dir: William Keighley, 89 mins.)

Master of the World (1961)** Vincent Price, Charles Bronson, Mary Webster. Richard Matheson concocted this gloss on several Jules Verne novels, with Price as a megalomaniacal Captain Nemo of the air. Cheaply made film hasn't much drive. (Dir: William Witney, 104 mins.)

Master Plan (Great Britain, 1954)*½ Wayne Morris, Tilda Thamar. (Dir: Cy Endfield, 77 mins.)

Master Race, The (1944)*** George Coulouris, Nancy Gates, Lloyd Bridges, Osa Massea. German officer flees when the Nazi empire starts to collapse. Good war drama. (Dir: Herbert J. Biberman, 96 mins.)

Master Spy (Great Britain, 1963)**½ Stephen Murray, June Thorburn. Communist physicist visits England and asks for political asylum, but is he really a spy? Good performances and several neat plot twists show to advantage in this interesting drama. (Dir: Montgomery Tully, 71 mins.)

Masterson of Kansas (1954)** George Montgomery, Nancy Gates. Some of the famous names of the West show up in this western: Bat Masterson, Doc Holliday, Wyatt Earp. Now if only Montgomery were that colorful! (Dir: William Castle, 73 mins.)

Mata Hari (1931)** Greta Garbo, Ramon Novarro, Lionel Barrymore, Lewis Stone, Karen Morley. Garbo tries to wheedle secrets out of Novarro and Stone in her most ludicrous film. George Fitzmaurice directed without a trace of wit or style. Handsome production. (90 mins.)

Mata Hari's Daughter (Italy, 1955)** Ludmilla Tcherina, Frank Latimore, Erno Crisa. Daughter of the famous spy follows in her mother's footsteps. Fairish espionage melodrama, cast and production better than the material. Dubbed in English. (Dir: Renzo Merusi, 102 mins.)

Matchless (Italy, 1967)* Patrick O'Neal, Ira Furstenberg, Donald Pleasence. (Dir: Alberto Lattuada, 103 mins.)

435

Matchmaker, The (1958)*** Shirley Booth, Tony Perkins, Shirley MacLaine, Robert Morse, Paul Ford. Well-meaning matchmaker assumes the responsibility of finding a wife for a wealthy skinflint of a merchant. Generally amusing version of Thornton Wilder's stage play, perhaps too restricted in technique to be completely successful—but good cast, some funny moments. Story was later turned into Broadway musical success "Hello, Dolly!" (Dir: Joseph Anthony, 101 mins.)

Matilda (1978)* Elliott Gould, Robert Mitchum, Harry Guardino. (Dir: Daniel Mann, 103 mins.)

Mating Game, The (1959)*** Tony Randall, Debbie Reynolds, Paul Douglas. Randall steals the picture with his zany performance as an IRS investigator who comes to check on an unpredictable business man who hasn't paid his taxes and ends up falling in love with the man's pretty daughter (Miss Reynolds). A lot of sight gags, a fast-paced script plus Randall's comedy timing add up to fun. (Dir: George Marshall, 96 mins.)

Mating of Millie, The (1948)**½ Glenn Ford, Evelyn Keyes. Career woman looks for a mate so she can legally adopt an orphan boy. Fairly amusing comedy-drama. (Dir: Henry Levin, 87 mins.)

Mating Season, The (1951)**½ Gene Tierney, John Lund, Thelma Ritter, Miriam Hopkins, Jan Sterling. Plainspoken mother of a man who has married well poses as a servant without letting on her relationship to her social daughter-in-law. Amusing comedy hinges largely on Ritter's acid remarks, and she walks away with the show.(Dir: Mitchell Leisen, 101 mins.)

Matt Helm (MTV 1975)* Tony Franciosa, Laraine Stephens, Ann Turkel. (Dir: Buzz Kulik, 72 mins.)

Mattei Affair, The (Italy, 1973)**** Gian Maria Volonte, Peter Baldwin, Luigi Equarzina. Political thriller about the death of Italy's most notorious tycoon, Enrico Mattei (Volonte) has depth, intelligence, a sense of genuine ambiguity. Director Francesco Rosi structures his film like a '70s version of "Citizen Kane" using documentary footage, flashbacks, and simulated news coverage techniques. (118 mins.)

Matter of Humanities See: **Marcus Welby, M.D.**

Matter of Innocence, A (Great Britain, 1967)** Hayley Mills, Trevor Howard, Shashi Kapoor. A sentimental, clumsily written tale in which Mills has an affair with a dashing Indian gigolo, played with slick charm by Kapoor. The screenplay, based on a Noël Coward short story, follows the transformation of plain Polly (Hayley) to sexy Polly, thanks to the death of her wealthy aunt. Howard is wasted as Polly's ne'er-do-well uncle. The ladies may enjoy it. (Dir: Guy Green, 102 mins)

Matter of Life and Death, A —See: **Stairway to Heaven**

Matter of Life and Death, A (MTV 1981)**½ Linda Lavin, Salome Jens, Peter Donat. Lavin portrays real-life crusading nurse Joy Ufema, who helped set up new methods to treat the terminally ill. The script by Lane Slate tends to be too talky, but that's the nature of the message. (Dir: Russ Mayberry, 104 mins.)

Matter of Morals (U.S.-Sweden, 1960)**½ Patrick O'Neal, Maj-Britt Nilsson, Mogens Wieth, Eva Dahlbeck. American businessman meets Swedish sex, discards his U.S. wife, his business and moral ethics. Alternately compelling and mediocre; the story is mainly mundane—acting, production, backgrounds are more intriguing. (Dir: John Cromwell, 90 mins.)

Matter of Time, A (Italy-U.S., 1976)½ Liza Minnelli, Ingrid Bergman, Charles Boyer, Tina Aumont. (99 mins.)

Matter of Who, A (Great Britain, 1961)**½ Terry-Thomas, Alex Nicol, Sonja Ziemann, Honor Blackman. When a man becomes ill aboard a plane, a conscientious investigator for the World Health Organization looks into the matter and becomes involved in an oil swindle plot. Curious mixture of comedy and suspenseful drama, with a restrained performance by Terry-Thomas. (Dir: Don Chaffey, 90 mins.)

Matter of Wife . . . and Death, A (1975)* Rod Taylor, Dick Butkus, Anne Archer. (Dir: Marvin Chomsky, 72 mins.)

Maurie (1973)** Bernie Casey, Bo Svenson, Janet MacLachlan, Stephanie Edwards. A tearjerker for men. Maurice Stokes, one of Cincinnati's finest basketball players, was mysteriously paralyzed soon after being named Rookie of the Year of the NBA. His teammate, Jack Twyman, spent ten years trying to raise funds to rehabilitate his friend, who finally died. Character development is kept to a minimum. Instead we're given a soap opera. (Dir: Daniel Mann, 113 mins.)

Maurizius Case, The (France, 1953)**½ Daniel Gelin, Eleonora Rossi-Drago, Anton Walbrook. A young lawyer tries to investigate a murder case that sent a man to prison 18 years before. It's talky, but still better than most—thanks to the original book. (Dir: Julien Duvivier, 110 min.)

Maverick Queen, The (1956)**½ Barbara Stanwyck, Barry Sullivan, Scott Brady. Bandit woman falls for a detective working undercover. Adequate western, with cast better than material. (Dir: Joseph Kane, 92 mins.)

Max Havelaar (The Netherlands-Java, 1976)***½ Peter Faber, Sacha Bulthuis, Elang Mohamad Adenan Soesilaningrat. Lush, expansive film based on a classic Dutch Novel. A naïve civil servant, sent to colonial Indonesia, tries to reform the corrupt local system only to be brutally thwarted by his own government and by mercantile interests. (Dir: Fons Rademakers, 165 mins.)

Maxime (France, 1958)** Charles Boyer, Michele Morgan. Impoverished aristocrat is to arrange a romance for a boorish young millionaire, but falls for the lady himself. Costume romance tries for charm, but misses. (Dir: Henri Verneuil, 93 mins.)

Maya (1965)**½ Clint Walker, Jay North, Sajid Khan. Entertaining jungle-adventure tale, filmed on location in India. Two boys team up to deliver a small, sacred white elephant to a jungle temple in India. The two young stars are small but engaging. (Dir: John Berry, 91 mins.)

Maybe I'll Come Home in the Spring (MTV 1971)*** Sally Field, Eleanor Parker, Lane Bradbury, Jackie Cooper. A lovely little movie that doesn't try to take in too much. Another "generation gap" story—pathetic and touching—shot in California's middle-class San Fernando valley by talented director Joe Sargent. Field and Bradbury play the groping daughters, parents are Cooper and Parker, and all give good performances. (73 mins.)

Mayday at 40,000 Feet (MTV 1976)*½ David Janssen, Lynda Day George, Christopher George. (Dir: Robert Butler, 106 mins)

Mayerling (Great Britain-France, 1968)* Omar Sharif, Catherine Deneuve, James Mason, Ava Gardner. (Dir: Terence Young, 140 mins.)

Mayflower: The Pilgrim's Adventure (MTV 1979)**½ Anthony Hopkins, Richard Crenna, Jenny Agutter. Story of the Pilgrims' 60-day crossing of the Atlantic in 1620. Hopkins, a good actor, commands attention as the ship's captain and fetching Agutter provides the love interest as Priscilla Mullens. The action and the waves pick up during the last half. David Dukes is amusing as a vain Capt. John Smith. (Dir: George Schaefer, 97 mins.)

Mayor of 44th Street (1942)**½ George Murphy, Anne Shirley, Richard Barthelmess. Reformed gangster becomes an agent for name bands, has trouble with another not-so-reformed hood. Pleasant musical comedy-drama. (Dir: Alfred E. Green, 86 mins.)

Maytime (1937)**½ Jeanette MacDonald, Nelson Eddy, John Barrymore. Probably the best Eddy-MacDonald vehicle, largely because of the intense performance by Barrymore as MacDonald's jealous husband. There's no doubt where your sympathies will lie as the warblers fight him for their freedom to love and croon "Mammy's Li'l Baby Loves Shortnin' Bread" and Tchaikovsky's Fifth Symphony with sappy lyrics. (Dir: Robert Z. Leonard, 132 mins.)

Maytime in Mayfair (Great Britain, 1949)** Anna Neagle, Michael Wilding. Gay sophisticated comedy about the rivalry between two fashionable dress salons. Elaborate, witty. (Dir: Herbert Wilcox, 94 mins.)

Maze, The (1953)*** Richard Carlson, Veronica Hurst. Originally produced as a 3D feature, this horror film has more than its share of visual gimmicks. The plot concerns a house where a mysterious mutation (an oversized frog) dominates the inhabitants. One of the better films of this genre. (Dir: William Cameron Menzies, 81 mins.)

McCabe & Mrs. Miller (1971)**** Warren Beatty, Julie Christie, Shelley Duvall, Keith Carradine. A stunning, droll yarn about life, whores, and heroism—or the lack of it—in the bleak Northwest around '02. Beatty is affecting as a small-time gambler on the make who amuses himself, and sometimes the townspeople, by pretending that he's a former gunslinging outlaw, while setting up the town's first bordello in what used to be the Presbyterian Church. Christie arrives to manage the prosperous cathouse. Inventively directed by Robert Altman. Co-authored by Altman, based on the novel "McCabe" by Edmund Naughton. (107 mins.)

McCloud: Fifth Man in a String Quartet (MTV 1972)*½ Dennis Weaver, Lilia Skala, Avery Schreiber. (Dir: Russ Mayberry, 79 mins.)

McCloud: Give My Regrets to Broadway (MTV 1972)*½ Dennis Weaver, Milton Berle, Barbara Rush. (Dir: Lou Antonio, 78 mins.))

McCloud: Top of the World, Ma! (MTV 1971)** Dennis Weaver, Bo Svenson, Stefanie Powers. Bo plays a big, shy semi-pro football player who steals his boss's car in Ohio, brings his mother to New York, checks her into the best hotel, and then sets out to collect a $10,000 debt. (Dir: Alex March, 76 mins.)

McCloud: Who Killed Miss U.S.A.? (MTV 1970)** Dennis Weaver, Craig Stevens, Diana Muldaur. Pilot for the TV series. Weaver plays the title role (McCloud, not Miss U.S.A.) of a New Mexico deputy marshal who finds himself in New York City on a murder case. Good on-location photography of New York City adds to the story about a young beauty queen's murder. (Dir: Richard Colla, 99 mins.)

McConnell Story, The (1955)**½ Alan Ladd, June Allyson, James Whitmore. The romanticized story of real-life jet ace McConnell, acted as if he had lockjaw by Ladd. As in many previous films, Allyson winds up weeping in the window for her man. (Dir: Gordon Douglas, 107 mins.)

McGuire, Go Home (Great Britain, 1965)*½ Dirk Bogarde, Susan Strasberg, Denholm Elliott. (Dir: Ralph Thomas, 114 mins.)

McHale's Navy (1964)** Ernest Borgnine, Tim Conway, Joe Flynn. Feature version of a once-popular TV series, this has the nutty PT crew involved in a horse race and some big betting. Too long as a feature; however, the kids should get some laughs. (Dir: Edward J. Montagne, 93 mins.)

McHale's Navy Joins the Air Force (1965)**

Joe Flynn, Tim Conway. TV series expanded to feature form again, this time without Borgnine. Conway receives most of the attention, as he masquerades as an air force looey. Pure slap-stick. (Dir: Edward J. Montagne, 90 mins.)

McKenzie Break, The (Great Britain, 1970)***½ Brian Keith, Helmut Griem. Authentic, vivid WW II drama. Keith gives a tremendous performance as an Irish intelligence agent put in charge of a British prison in Scotland to prevent an escape by captured Germans. Griem as his adversary, the leader of the POWs is also excellent. The screenplay is literate, the direction tough and tight, and the Germans actually speak German. Watch for the suspenseful ending and Keith's last line. (Dir: Lamont Johnson, 108 mins.)

McLintock (1963)**½ John Wayne, Maureen O'Hara. Don't be fooled by the western setting and the presence of Wayne in this film—it's primarily a comedy, amply supplied with slapstick. Wayne is a cattleman who literally pulls no punches in trying to win and woo his wife back. The pace is raucous and wild. (Dir: Andrew V. McLaglen, 127 mins.)

McMillan and Wife: Cop of the Year (MTV 1972)** Rock Hudson, Susan Saint James, John Schuck. McMillan's sidekick Sgt. Enright is in a room arguing with his wife while plenty of people, including Mac, overhear the battle. The lady is then shot. You've seen it before... (Dir: Bob Lewis, 79 mins.)

McMillan and Wife: The Devil, You Say (MTV 1973)** Rock Hudson, Susan Saint James, John Schuck. Suspense builds when Commissioner McMillan discovers there's a cult of Satanists behind the mysterious Hallowe'en gifts. Chiller, thriller, meller! (Dir: Alex March, 72 mins.)

McNaughton's Daughter (MTV 1976)** Susan Clark, Vera Miles, Ralph Bellamy. A mediocre, somewhat different pilot that was partly successful. Clark is a deputy D.A. assigned to prosecute a saintly missionary (Miles) accused of murder. (Dir: Jerry London, 98 mins.)

McQ (1974)** John Wayne, Eddie Albert, Diana Muldaur. Wayne just doesn't look comfortable in modern dress. He is again a law enforcer whose theme song is "My Way." He quits the force when his buddy is killed in order to ride the vengeance trail, by car this time. Boring musical score by Elmer Bernstein. (Dir: John Sturges, 111 mins.)

Me and My Gal (1932)*** Spencer Tracy, Joan Bennett, George Walsh. A rather improbable but engaging concoction teams burlesque and gangster genres, hard-nosed detective Tracy with fine-featured (but gum-chewing) cashier Bennett. A period piece, evocative and witty. (Dir: Raoul Walsh, 78 mins.)

Me and the Colonel (Great Britain, 1958)***½ Danny Kaye, Curt Jurgens, Nicole Maurey. A delightful serious comedy about military capers involved in the safe escape of fleeing refugees. Kaye registers strongly in a change-of-pace role as a Polish Jew pitted against an anti-Semitic colonel during the final days of WW II. Under Peter Glenville's sensitive direction Kaye's restrained performance is most affecting. (109 mins.)

Mean Streets (1973)**** Robert De Niro, Harvey Keitel, David Proval, Amy Robinson, Richard Romanus. Excellent portrait of the small-time hoods in New York City's Little Italy and their special code of ethics. De Niro is wonderful as a hanger-on who is in to a loan shark for a big sum, and tries to get his childhood friend Charlie, a lower-echelon mafioso, to intervene on his behalf. Keitel is effective as Charlie, and the film has a terrific impact. Director Martin Scorsese, who helped write the screenplay based on his own story, grew up in the neighborhood, and he reveals the brutality, competitiveness, and strong family ties of the neighborhood. (110 mins.)

Meanest Man in the World, The (1943)***½ Jack Benny, Eddie "Rochester" Anderson, Priscilla Lane. Benny plays a lawyer who discovers the secret of success: being ruthlessly, relentlessly nasty. Benny's voice, with its slides, crescendos, and precise pauses, is a magnificent comic instrument. (Dir: Sidney Lanfield, 57 mins.)

Measure for Measure (Great Britain, MTV 1978)**** Kenneth Colley, Tim Pigott-Smith, Kate Nelligan, John McEnery, Christopher Stravli. One of the more difficult Shakespeare comedies, set in an exotic, mythical Vienna whose duke gives over the government to Angelo to reform the city's lax sexual morals. Angelo harshly sentences Claudio to death for fornication. How Claudio's sister Isabella, a pure young lady soon to become a nun, argues for her brother's life, and how the mortal man in Angelo responds to the beautiful woman is deeply involving and, in the end, oddly moving. The plot turns are innumerable, but the acting of Colley, Pigott-Smith, and Nelligan will hold your attention to the end. (Dir: Desmond Davis, 150 mins.)

Meat (1976)***½ A documentary about a meat-packing plant in Colorado, but it's really a film about—among other things—ecology, and some of the moral issues raised by the high meat consumption of affluent America. It's also about the process of death—a symphony of slaughter as the animals are stunned, killed, dressed, and packaged in ways unfamiliar to most meat eaters. One of director Frederick Wiseman's most abstract, involved works. (112 mins.)

Meatballs (Canada, 1979)**½ Bill Murray, Kate Lynch, Chris Makepeace. Generous, often gentle summer camp comedy is not very deft. Murray is likable as a head counselor who gruffly plays Wallace Beery to an updated, angst-ridden Jackie Cooper (Makepeace). (92 mins.)

Mechanic, The (1972)*½ Charles Bronson, Jan-Michael Vincent, Keenan Wynn, Jill Ireland. (Dir: Michael Winner, 95 mins.)

Medal for Benny, A (1945)***½ Dorothy Lamour, Arturo de Cordova, J. Carrol Naish. When news reaches a small California town that one of its sons has been killed in action, the town fathers see a chance for some publicity. Touching drama from a Steinbeck story, with fine performances, especially by Naish. (Dir: Irving Pichel, 77 mins.)

Medea (Italy, 1971)** Maria Callas, Giuseppi Gentile, Laurent Terzieff. The heroine murders her children, poisons her husband, practices sorcery, and dabbles in arson on the side—a natural for the only filmed role of opera star Callas under the direction of pagan Pier Paolo Pasolini. The film is turgid, clumsy, and virtually unendurable, though you may want to see the Callas personality in bas-relief. (100 mins.)

Medical Story (MTV) 1975)***½ José Ferrer, Beau Bridges, Carl Reiner. Strong, unusual drama about a hotshot young doctor who discovers negligence, dishonesty, and cover-ups among the staff at a well-known hospital. He must decide whether to risk his career to blow the whistle on unnecessary surgery by a respected gynecologist. Based on a real-life story; script by Abby Mann. (Dir: Gary Nelson, 116 mins.)

Medium, The (1951)***½ Anna Maria Alberghetti, Marie Powers. Menotti's strange, brooding opera, well sung. For specialized tastes, but there is a haunting score and Miss Powers's electric portrayal of a medium-spiritualist. (Dir: Gian-Carlo Menotti, 87 mins.)

Medium Cool (1969)**** Robert Forster, Verna Bloom, Harold Blankenship. Impressive debut for director Haskell Wexler. An amazingly realistic semidocumentary about the 1968 Democratic National Convention in Chicago. (110 mins.)

Medusa Against the Son of Hercules (Italy, 1963)* Richard Harrison, Anna Ranalli. (Dir: Marcello Baldi, 90 mins.)

Medusa Touch, The (Great Britain, 1978)** Richard Burton, Lee Remick, Lino Ventura. Burton uses eyes and voice to suggest telekinesis in a shaggy-dog horror film. Remick is his eminently reasonable psychiatrist, and Ventura (alas, less charismatic in English. Recommended for the curious and tolerant. Based on Peter Van Greenaway's novel. (Dir: Jack Gold, 110 mins.)

Meet Boston Blackie (1941)*** Chester Morris, Rochelle Hudson, Richard Lane, Charles Wagenheim. Morris makes a rambunctious Blackie, in his debut in the series. With Lane as the police chief unshakably convinced that Blackie is up to no good, Wagenheim as the faithful sidekick, and Hudson as the fleeting love

interest. The story is a piece of pulp, but Robert Florey is good at directing low-budget formula films. (61 mins.)

Meet Danny Wilson (1952)**½ Frank Sinatra, Shelley Winters, Alex Nicol, Raymond Burr. Not a bad film but the story line about an entertainer and gangsters does get jumbled to say the least. A big bonus for Sinatra fans is the long list of standards he sings. (Dir: Joseph Pevney, 86 mins.)

Meet John Doe (1941)***½ Gary Cooper, Barbara Stanwyck, Walter Brennan, Edward Arnold, Spring Byington, James Gleason. Cooper plays a hobo who makes news by threatening to commit suicide to protest world conditions. Inspired by the newspapers, the public sets out to change his mind. The plot mechanism becomes impossible to resolve, so the ending is necessarily unsatisfying. Director Frank Capra, with the invaluable assistance of political boss Arnold, creates a convincing portrait of latent American fascism. It is also, rather confoundingly, a romantic comedy. (Dir: Frank Capra, 132 mins.)

Meet Me After the Show (1951)** Betty Grable, Macdonald Carey, Rory Calhoun. Efforts of a producer to get his ex-wife, an amnesia case, back in his show. Grable gams its chief asset. (Dir: Richard Sale, 86 mins.)

Meet Me at the Fair (1953)*** Dan Dailey, Diana Lynn, Chet Allen. Charming film about a traveling medicine man who gets involved with a runaway orphan and the authorities. Dailey is charm personified as the fast-talking con man with a heart of gold and young Allen has a lovely voice. (Dir: Douglas Sirk, 87 mins.)

Meet Me in Las Vegas (1956)**½ Dan Dailey, Cyd Charisse, Agnes Moorhead. Wispy little story about a gambling rancher and the dancer who brings him luck doesn't mean a thing—the big news here is the terpsichore, including a "Frankie and Johnnie" ballet that's a knockout, and the guest appearances of Lena Horne, Frankie Laine, Jerry Colonna, and others. (Dir: Roy Rowland, 112 mins.)

Meet Me in St. Louis (1944)***½ Judy Garland, Margaret O'Brien, Tom Drake, Mary Astor, Leon Ames, Marjorie Main. To a charming, sentimental tale about a family in St. Louis at the turn of the century has been added a wonderful musical score and cast. (Dir: Vincente Minnelli, 113 mins.)

Meet Mr. Lucifer (Great Britain, 1954)*** Stanley Holloway, Peggy Cummins, Kay Kendall. The devil introduces television into three homes to stir up trouble. Neat, amusing fantasy-comedy; some good laughs. (Dir: Anthony Pelissier, 83 mins.)

Meet Peter Foss (West Germany, 1958)**½ O. W. Fischer, Walter Giller. Breezy melodrama featuring a likable scoundrel who outwits both hoodlums and the law in a chase after a fortune. Fischer is very dapper. Dubbed in English. (Dir: Wolfgang Becker, 90 mins.)

Meet the Stewarts (1942)*** William Holden, Frances Dee. Heiress marries a white-collar man, tries to get along on a budget. Pleasing comedy. (Dir: Alfred E. Green, 73 mins.)

Meetings with Remarkable Men (1979)**½ Dragan Maksimovic, Terence Stamp, Athol Fugard, Bruce Myers. Theater maestro Peter Brook directs this tale of G.I. Gurdjieff, an inspirational teacher—or a cultist charlatan—whose influence persists in spiritual covens today. Shot on location in Afghanistan, the film is at least as intriguing for Brook's odyssey among third-world cultures as for Gurdjieff's. Beautiful, but almost never convincing. (Dir: Peter Brook.)

Megara (Greece, 1975)***½ This direct film record of the tyranny of the Greek junta captures more impassioned outrage than the synthetic melodrama of "Z." The regime granted tycoon Stratis Andreadis a concession for an oil refinery, expropriating the land of the town of Megara and evicting the population of 20,000 by force. Their resistance and growing political sophistication culminates in the brutally suppressed students' uprising at the Polytechnic School of Athens in '74, just before the fall of the colonels. Directors Yorgos Tsemberopoulos and Sakis Maniatis made the film secretly and at great peril.

Mein Kampf (Sweden, 1960)***½ Grim documentation of the horrors of the Hitler regime. Technically rough but the harrowing sequences speak for themselves. (Dirs: Erwin Leiser, Ingemar Ejve, Tore Sjoberg, 117 mins.)

Melba (Great Britain, 1953)*** Patrice Munsel, Robert Morley. Phony film biography of Nellie Melba is distinguished by Miss Munsel singing scores of arias. For opera fans only. (Dir: Lewis Milestone, 113 mins.)

Melinda (1972)** Vonetta McGee, Calvin Lockhart. Another violent, predictable black actioner. McGee flickers briefly as the title character, but she must die so that the revenge plot can get under way. Lockhart is an unlikely action hero as the disk jockey out to get her killers. (Dir: Hugh Robertson, 109 mins.)

Melody (Great Britain, 1972)*** Mark Lester, Jack Wild, Tracy Hyde. Appealing tale of an 11-year-old boy who wants to marry a 12-year-old girl so they can always be together. Slightly silly premise saved by marvelous acting. Wild and Lester, who worked so well together in "Oliver!" are a delight as Wild plays Lester's older friend. (Dir: Waris Hussein, 103 mins.)

Melvin Purvis, G-Man (MTV 1974)**½ Dale Robertson, Harris Yulin, Margaret Blye. A good script graphically depicts the cat-and-mouse game between the notorious Machine Gun Kelly and colorful G-man Melvin Purvis. Robertson is right as Purvis and his casual manner adds to the tone of the piece. Yulin also scores as Kelly and Blye has some good scenes as his pretty wife. Slick gangster fare. (Dir: Dan Curtis, 74 mins.)

Member of the Wedding, The (1953)**** Julie Harris, Ethel Waters, Brandon de Wilde. Hit Broadway play by Carson McCullers brought to the screen with great performances by the trio of stars. The theme of adolescence is beautifully treated. You'll not soon forget Harris's touching and beautifully realized growing pains. (Dir: Fred Zinnemann, 91 mins.)

Memories of Underdevelopment (Cuba, 1968)**** Sergio Corrieri, Daisy Granados, Eslinda Nunez, Beatriz Ponchora. Tomas Gutierrez Alea, a director of enormous gifts and international stature, portrays the alienation of Sergio—a 38-year-old living off remunerations from his nationalized property, whose only response to the '62 missile crisis is to watch it through binoculars while his countrymen respond with action. (104 mins.)

Memory of Eva Ryker, The (MTV 1980)**½ Natalie Wood, Ralph Bellamy, Robert Foxworth. An ocean liner was torpedoed at the outbreak of WW II. Years later, a multimillionaire (Bellamy) starts to salvage the liner, on which his beautiful wife and scores of others perished, and the complicated plot unfolds. Wood plays Eva Ryker's mother in the flashbacks and is also quite good as Eva Ryker. Old-fashioned melodrama produced by Irwin Allen. (Dir: Walter E. Grauman, 153 mins.)

Memory of Justice, The (West Germany-U.S., 1976)**** Director Marcel Ophuls's intense, demanding documentary starts with Nuremberg trials of '46 and goes on to Algeria and Vietnam, intercutting newsreel footage and contemporary interviews. (Dir: Marcel Ophuls, 278 mins.)

Men, The (1950)**** Marlon Brando, Teresa Wright, Jack Webb. Paralyzed war vet tries to adjust. Brando's first film, and a superb one. Dramatic, persuasive, with fine work in every department. (Dir: Fred Zinnemann, 85 mins.)

Men Against the Sun (Great Britain, 1954)**½ John Bentley, Zena Marshall. An engineer is persuaded to join the builders of a railroad across darkest Africa. Good backgrounds, but just an average plot. (Dir: Brendan Stafford, 64 mins.)

Men and Wolves (Italy, 1957)** Yves Montand, Silvana Mangano, Pedro Armendariz. Confused drama about a notorious lady-killer who covets another lady-killer's wife. Ably acted. (Dir: Giuseppe De Santis, 98 mins.)

Men Are Not Gods (Great Britain, 1937)** Miriam Hopkins, Gertrude Lawrence, Rex Harrison. A romantic triangle affair brings near-tragedy to three theatrical people. Rather stiff comedy-drama. Well acted. (Dir: Walter Reisch, 82 mins.)

440

Men Can't Be Raped (Finland, 1978)***½ Anna Godenius, Gosta Bredefeldt, Nils Brandt. A woman who has been raped becomes obsessed with avenging herself on her attacker, causing him to be as humiliated as she has been. Jorn Donner directed and adapted the novel by Marta Tikkanen; Billie August photographed. (Dir: Jorn Donner.)

Men in Her Diary (1945)**½ Peggy Ryan, Jon Hall, Louise Albritton. Unattractive secretary keeps a diary of imaginary romances, which gets her in plenty of hot water. Amusing comedy. (Dir: Charles Barton, 73 mins.)

Men in War (1957)*** Robert Ryan, Aldo Ray. Grim, realistic war film about the Korean War. Good performances by Ryan and Ray make the tale palatable. Among the large supporting cast, Nehemiah Persoff, Scott Marlowe, and Vic Morrow stand out. (Dir: Anthony Mann, 104 mins.)

Men of Boys Town (1941)** Spencer Tracy, Mickey Rooney. Sequel to "Boys Town" is just a sentimental rehash of a lot of B movies. Tracy is still good as Father Flanagan but, for the most part, the film is awful. (Dir: Norman Taurog, 106 mins.)

Men of Sherwood Forest (Great Britain, 1954)** Don Taylor, Eileen Moore. Robin Hood and his Merrie Men attempt to restore King Richard to the throne. It's been done before on a larger scale, but this costume adventure has enough action to get by. (Dir: Val Guest, 77 mins.)

Men of the Dragon (MTV 1974)** Jared Martin, Robert Ito, Katie Saylor. Fairly mild martial arts film, with high-flying karate kicks and low-blow kung-fu thrusts. Filmed in Hong Kong; the scenery is good enough but the story is silly. (Dir: Harry Falk, 74 mins.)

Men of the Fighting Lady (1954)**½ Van Johnson, Walter Pidgeon. Routine war film about an aircraft carrier and the men assigned to her. There's the usual cast of stock characters, and some exciting actual war footage. (Dir: Andrew Marton, 80 mins.)

Men of Two Worlds (Great Britain, 1945)**½ Eric Portman, Phyllis Calvert, Robert Adams. Educated native returns to his homeland of East Africa, realizes his people live literally in a different world, tries to persuade them to move from their highly infested area. Carefully produced drama has picturesque scenes, a sincere attempt to cope with pressing problems—but the drama is loose, slow moving. (Dir: Thorold Dickson, 107 mins.)

Men Who Tread on the Tiger's Tail, The (Japan, 1953)*** Hanshiro Iwai, Susumu Fujuta, Ken'ichi Enomoto. Directed by Akira Kurosawa in '45 under impossibly adverse production conditions. He hams up a hoary old Kabuki drama, using comic actor Enomoto as a cowardly porter whose antics comment on the dignified story of honorable retainers. Even as he sends up the material and scores satiric points, Kurosawa preserves the suspense and authority of the original drama. (60 mins.)

Men with Wings (1938)*** Fred MacMurray, Ray Milland, Louise Campbell. Story of two air pioneers, one a stunt flier and war hero, the other a man who dreams of aviation's future. Ambitious film tries to chronicle the history of aviation. Fair entertainment. (Dir: William A. Wellman, 106 mins.)

Menace, The (France, 1960)*½ Robert Hossein, Elsa Martinelli. (Dir: Gerard Oury, 90 mins.)

Menace in the Night (Great Britain, 1958)** Griffith Jones, Lisa Gastoni. Witness to a robbery and murder is threatened by the chief crook if she should go to the police. Ordinary crime melodrama, with a good performance by Miss Gastoni as the terrified witness. (Dir: Lance Comfort, 78 mins.)

Mephisto Waltz, The (1971)*** Alan Alda, Jacqueline Bisset, Curt Jurgens, Barbara Parkins. World-famous pianist Jurgens is dying of a rare blood disease when he grants journalist Alda a rare interview. Satanic possession is involved and Miss Bisset has the strange feeling that husband Alda is changing. Eerie music and sublety are the chief assets of this West Coast "Rosemary's Baby." (Dir: Paul Wendkos, 108 mins.)

Merciless Trap, The (Japan, 1964)*½ Makoto Sato. (79 mins.)

Mermaids of Tiburon, The (1962)* George Rowe, Dianne Webber, Timothy Carey. (Dir: John Lamb, 76 mins.)

Merrill's Marauders (1962)**** Jeff Chandler, Ty Hardin, Will Hutchins, Claude Akins. Splendid WW II film—story of the famous outfit of war-hardened veterans who battled the enemy in Burma under excruciating conditions calling for the limit of human endurance. Rates with the best of them, realistic, tough, ultimately inspiring. Fine performance by Chandler (in his last film, released after his death) and direction by Samuel Fuller. (98 mins.)

Merrily We Go to Hell (1932)*** Sylvia Sidney, Fredric March, Cary Grant. A society girl (Sidney) marries a newspaperman who has great ambitions and a serious drinking problem. Together they thrash out their love and fears and have a good time and some hairy moments. This may be director Dorothy Arzner's best film. (78 mins.)

Merry Andrew (1958)**½ Danny Kaye, Pier Angeli. Pleasant, if not top drawer, Kaye musical comedy vehicle. The setting is a small circus with Danny cast as a schoolteacher who joins the troupe for a brief interval. Mild, entertaining film. (Dir: Michael Kidd, 103 mins.)

Merry Monahans, The (1944)*** Donald O'Connor, Ann Blyth, Jack Oakie. Story of vaudevillians is so well played, including some cute musical numbers, that it

441

rises above its commonplace plot. (Dir: Charles Lamont, 91 mins.)

Merry Widow, The (1925)**** John Gilbert, Mae Murray, Tully Marshall, Roy d'Arcy, Josephine Crowell. Using the Franz Lehár operetta only as a takeoff (the prince must marry the widow of his wealthiest subject in order to keep the money in the kingdom), director Erich von Stroheim creates a delicious portrait of the Hapsburg Empire in final decay. Murray is superlative, as are Gilbert and the despicably creepy supporting cast. (110 mins.)

Merry Widow, The (1934)**** Maurice Chevalier, Jeannette MacDonald, Edward Everett Horton, Una Merkel. Last and finest of director Ernst Lubitsch's musicals, based on the Franz Lehár operetta retooled with lyrics by Lorenz Hart. Chevalier is the prince; MacDonald, on the brink of her fatal meeting with Eddy, is the widow. Charming and poignant. (99 mins.)

Merry Widow, The (1952)* Lana Turner, Fernando Lamas, Una Merkel, Richard Haydn. Third and worst version of the operetta. Color. (Dir: Curtis Bernhardt, 105 mins.)

Mesa of Lost Women, The (1953)** Jackie Coogan, Richard Travis, Mary Hill. Coogan is a mad scientist who plans to create a race of superbeings by combining the superior qualities of deadly spiders with those of beautiful women. (Dirs: Herbert Tevos, Ron Ormond, 70 mins.)

Message from Space (Japan, 1978)*½ Vic Morrow, Sonny Chiba, Peggy Lee Brennan. (Dir: Kinji Fukasaku, 105 mins.)

Message to My Daughter, A (MTV 1973)**½ Kitty Winn, Bonnie Bedelia. Sentimental. Miss Winn is a daughter searching for identity against the background of her dead mother's tape-recorded words of wisdom. Miss Bedelia is the expired mom and she works well, as does Miss Winn. Solid production values, but not provoking enough. (Dir: Robert Michael Lewis, 74 mins.)

Messalina (Italy, 1960)*½ Belinda Lee, Spyros Fokas. (Dir: Vittorio Cottafari, 84 mins.)

Messalina Against the Son of Hercules (Italy, 1965)*½ Richard Harrison, Lisa Gastoni. (Dir: Umberto Lenzi, 98 mins.)

Meteor (1979)**½ Sean Connery, Natalie Wood, Brian Keith, Henry Fonda, Trevor Howard. It's hard to make a rousing adventure film when the heroics are performed by computers and guided missiles, and the humans have nothing to do but push buttons and stare at video screens. Director Ronald Neame brings his impersonal British craftsmanship to the drama so it won't be a complete bust. With Connery in an Al Pacino part, Wood in a nonpart, and Keith miming wittily as a Russian scientist who speaks no English. Fonda once again plays a U.S. President. (107 mins.)

Meteor Monster (1957)* Anne Gwynne, Stuart Wade. (Dir: Jacques Marquette, 73 mins.)

Metropolis (Germany, 1926)*** Brigitte Helm, Alfred Abel, Gustav Froelich, Rudolf Klein-Rogge. Although considered a classic, this evocation of a mechanized utopia run by underground slave labor is simpleminded proletarian-leisure-class cant that was moldy even when it was made. The visual impact of the bizarre geometric sets and the lighting of Karl Freund give this Fritz Land-directed epic some lasting distinction. Far below Lang's Hollywood standard. (120 mins.)

Mexican Bus Ride (Mexico, 1951)***½ By common consent, director Luis Bunnuel's brightest, most pleasant film—the tale of a young man called away on his wedding day to settle the question of his dying mother's legacy and of the bizarre and delightfully nutty bus ride that takes him not only back home but to a new kind of maturity. The surrealism is not forced or obvious, but, as in all Buñuel films, the philosophical jabs are there. (85 mins.)

Mexican Hayride (1948)**½ Bud Abbott, Lou Costello, Luba Malina. Madcap antics get involved with phony silver stock and a lady toreador. Malina is funny as a senorita named Dagmar. (Dir: Charles Barton, 77 mins.)

Mexican Spitfire (1939)**½ Lupe Velez, Leon Errol. Senora's husband is aided by Uncle Matt in saving a big contract. Amusing comedy. (Dir: Leslie Goodwins, 67 mins.)

Mexican Spitfire at Sea (1942)** Lupe Velez, Leon Errol. The spitfire goes after an advertising contract for her husband en route to Honolulu. Mild comedy. (Dir: Leslie Goodwins, 73 mins.)

Mexican Spitfire's Baby (1941)** Lupe Velez, Leon Errol. The spitfire adopts a war orphan, who turns out to be a beautiful French girl. Mild comedy. (Dir: Leslie Goodwins, 69 mins)

Mexican Spitfire's Blessed Event (1943)** Lupe Velez, Leon Errol. The success or failure of a big business deal depends upon a nonexistent baby, so the spitfire tries to get one. Mild comedy. (Dir: Leslie Goodwins, 63 mins.)

Mexican Spitfire's Elephant (1942)** Lupe Velez, Leon Errol. The spitfire gets tangled with crooks who try to smuggle a diamond through customs in a miniature elephant. Mild comedy. (Dir: Leslie Goodwins, 64 mins.)

Miami Exposé (1956)** Lee J. Cobb, Patricia Medina, Edward Arnold. A police lieutenant tracks down and cracks a vice operation in Florida. Fair cops and robbers. This is typical of how Cobb's brilliant acting was wasted by Hollywood film producers. (Dir: Fred F. Sears, 73 mins.)

Miami Story, The (1954)** Barry Sullivan, Luther Adler, Beverly Garland. Miami's syndicate is cracked by an ex-gangster and his girl. Routine crime film. (Dir: Fred F. Sears, 75 mins.)

Michael Kohlhaas (West Germany, 1969)* David Warner, Anna Karina. Dir: Volker Schloendorff, 97 mins.)

Michael Shayne, Private Detective (1940) **½ Lloyd Nolan, Marjorie Weaver. In the capable hands of Mr. Nolan, this fast-talking detective comes to life and is a welcome addition to the list of sleuths found in B films. (Dir: Eugene Forde, 77 mins.)

Mickey One (1965)***½ Warren Beatty, Alexandra Stewart, Hurd Hatfield. An absorbing, imaginative film, with actor Beatty and director Arthur Penn, responsible in their next film for the smash hit "Bonnie and Clyde." Electric performance from Beatty as a struggling nightclub comic who's in a jam with mobsters and goes on the lam. Penn makes good use of various Chicago locations. Supporting cast are unusually good. (93 mins.)

Midas Run (1969)** Fred Astaire, Anne Heywood, Richard Crenna, Roddy McDowall, Ralph Richardson. A routine caper as Astaire organizes a plot to steal a gold shipment leaving England by air. His cronies are Crenna, a college professor fired for pacifism, and Miss Heywood, Crenna's eventual lover. Little credibility, but Astaire retains his charm and Miss Heywood is ravishing. (Dir: Alf Kjellin, 106 mins.)

Middle of the Night (1959)**½ Fredric March, Kim Novak. A not altogether successful filmization of Paddy Chayefsky's hit play, primarily due to miscasting Novak as the girl who finds herself in love with an older man. March is good as the aging widower who finds a new meaning of life when he falls for a girl young enough to be his daughter. The supporting cast are top-notch. (Dir: Delbert Mann, 118 mins.)

Middle of the World, The (Switzerland, 1974)**** Olimpia Carlisi, Philippe Leotard, Juliet Berto. Affecting, intelligent story of a couple trying to forge a nonsexist relationship. He (Leotard) is a small businessman running for parliament; she (Carlisi) is an Italian immigrant waitress. Director Alain Tanner and scripter John Berger have a didactic study that never harangues, but honestly informs and explores. Dialogue in French. (115 mins.)

Middleman, The (India, 1975)***½ Pradip Mukherji, Satya Bannerji. Director Satyajit Ray completes his trilogy on youth in India. A young man fails to take honors and so becomes one of literally a million applicants for limited professional positions. The hard choice presents itself: starve or (horrors!) go into trade. He becomes an avid capitalist, and the moral and cultural issues are substantial. (131 mins.)

Midnight (1939)**** Claudette Colbert, Don Ameche, John Barrymore, Mary Astor, Francis Lederer. Scintillating comedy from Mitchell Leisen from a script by Charles Brackett and Billy Wilder. Colbert is a girl on her uppers in Paris who finds herself enmeshed in the marital tangles of Barrymore and Astor. With Francis Lederer and Don Ameche, this classic demonstrates that personal filmmaking can be wrought through what is apparently little more than masterful craft. Barrymore is incredibly funny and touching. Best scene: Claudette telephones her "daughter." Remade as "Masquerade in Mexico." (94 mins.)

Midnight Cowboy (1969)**** Dustin Hoffman, Jon Voight, Sylvia Miles. A devastating, lacerating, superbly acted drama which deservedly won the Academy Award for Best Picture, Best Director (John Schlesinger), and Best Screenplay (Waldo Salt). Story of a male hustler (Voight) and his decrepit buddy (Hoffman) who dream of making it big in New York and retiring to Florida. Based on the novel by James Leo Herlihy. The two are stunning, and you won't soon forget the sordid, squalid, lost souls who populate New York's still repellent 42nd St. area. (113 mins.)

Midnight Express (Great Britain, 1978)**** Brad Davis, John Hurt, Randy Quaid. Beguilingly downbeat story of Billy Hayes's incarceration in a Turkish prison for hashish smuggling, and his escape. (Dir: Alan Parker, 120 mins.)

Midnight Lace (1960)**½ Doris Day, Rex Harrison, John Gavin. An overproduced mystery-thriller in which most of the footage finds lovely Day being terrorized by an unknown phone caller. It's up to you to guess and you'll probably find it easy. (Dir: David Miller, 108 mins.)

Midnight Lace (MTV 1981)*½ Mary Crosby, Gary Frank. (Dir: Ivan Nagy, 104 mins.)

Midnight Madness (1980)½ David Naughton, Debra Clinger, Ed Deezen. (Dirs: Michael Nankin, David Wechter, 110 mins.)

Midnight Man, The (1974)** Burt Lancaster, Susan Clark, Cameron Mitchell. Lancaster plays a night watchman-turned-detective at a small southern college. On parole from a murder conviction, Lancaster is doggedly persistent tracking down the killer of a campus coed. Plot is confusing, movie too slow. (Dirs: Roland Kibbee and Burt Lancaster, 117 mins.)

Midnight Offerings (MTV 1981)*½ Melissa Sue Anderson, Mary McDonough, Patrick Cassidy. (Dir: Rod Holcomb, 104 mins.)

Midnight Story, The (1957)** Tony Curtis, Marisa Pavan, Gilbert Roland. Traffic cop investigates on his own when he is outraged by the murder of a parish priest. Strictly routine production graced by a good cast. (Dir: Joseph Pevney, 89 mins.)

Midsummer Night's Dream, A (1935)***½ James Cagney, Dick Powell, Olivia de Havilland, Joe E. Brown, Mickey Rooney. This was one of the first attempts to bring Shakespeare to the screen and it was, by and large, successful. Mickey Rooney's Puck is the highlight of the film. (Dirs: Max Reinhardt, William Dieterle, 117 mins.)

Midsummer Night's Dream (Czechoslovakia, 1961)*** Shakespeare's comedy fancifully done with animated puppets, well narrated by Richard Burton. Amusing novelty. (Dir: Jiri Trnka, 74 mins.)

Midsummer Night's Dream, A (1967)***½ Suzanne Farrell, Edward Villella, Patricia McBride, Arthur Mitchell. The enchanting ballet, to music by Felix Mendelssohn, based on Shakespeare's fantasy-comedy. George Ballanchine's choreography, for the New York City Ballet is brought to the screen unaltered. The first feature-length filming of ballet in the U.S. Close-ups reveal the extraordinary, delicate beauty of the company's youngest prima, Farrell, who dances the fairy Queen, Tatiana. (Dir: Dan Eridsen, 93 mins.)

Midsummer Night's Dream, A (Great Britain, 1968)**** Ian Richardson, Judi Dench, Ian Holm, Diana Rigg, Helen Mirren. Directed by the innovative Peter Hall with speeches shot with the actors seen upside down, and the like. Cast of superb actors from the Royal Shakespeare Company. Intensely interesting and entertaining; a must-see if you love Shakespeare. (124 mins.)

Midway (1976)** Charlton Heston, Henry Fonda, James Coburn, Glenn Ford, Edward Albert. The dullest part of a war movie comes when everybody starts explaining strategy, poking at charts, and moving little boats around on maps. And that's about all this is, except for the climactic battle scene, most of which was lifted from old navy documentary footage and an anonymous Japanese production. (Dir: Jack Smight, 132 mins.)

Mighty Crusaders, The (Italy, 1961)*½ Francisco Rabal, Sylva Koscina, Gianna Maria Canale, Rik Battaglia. (Dir: Carlo Ludovico Bragaglia, 87 mins.)

Mighty Joe Young (1949)** Robert Armstrong, Terry Moore, Ben Johnson. Cut-rate "King Kong" is served up by the same producers who made the Academy Award original. Good special effects though the ape is too lovable to inspire terror. (Dir: Ernest B. Schoedsack, 94 mins.)

Mighty Jungle, The (U.S.-Mexico, 1964)*½ Marshall Thompson. (Dirs: David DaLie, Ismael Rodriguez, Arnold Belgard, 88 mins.)

Mighty McGurk, The (1946)** Wallace Beery, Dean Stockwell, Edward Arnold, Cameron Mitchell. Contrived and confused drama about an ex-fighter who befriends an orphan boy. (Dir: John Waters, 85 mins.)

Mighty Ursus (Italy-Spain, 1961)*½ Ed Fury, Cristina Gajoni. (Dir: Carlo Campogalliani, 92 mins.)

Migrants, The (MTV 1974)*** Cloris Leachman, Ron Howard, Sissy Spacek, Cindy Williams. See Leachman's high-caliber portrait of an earth mother who breathes life into her clan even in the face of her own despair. Tennessee Williams's story about the deprivations endured by migratory workers is effectively adapted by Lanford Wilson. Producer-director Tom Gries pays unfailing attention to detail and Howard deserves special mention as the son who wants out. (78 mins.)

Mikado, The (Great Britain, 1939)***½ Kenny Baker, Jean Colin, Martyn Green. The Gilbert and Sullivan operetta of shenanigans in the high court of old Japan, with a wand'ring minstrel wooing a noble lady. Colorfully done, excellently sung. (Dir: Victor Schertzinger, 90 mins.)

Mickey and Nicky (1976)*** Peter Falk, John Cassavetes, Ned Beatty. Experimental feature from director Elaine May ran outrageously over budget and showcases some of the worst lighting, cutting, and sound imaginable. Yet the film has genuine power and feeling. Falk and Cassavetes star as old buddies caught up in a squeeze from the mob. (119 mins.)

Mildred Pierce (1945)*** Joan Crawford, Zachary Scott, Jack Carson, Eve Arden. This adaptation of a James Cain novel was a big hit but it's not a great movie. Oscar winner Crawford is superb but the characters are not too believable. Ann Blyth as Joan's vicious daughter is the character you must accept as real to enjoy the picture. If you can do that, you'll find it an engrossing melodrama. (Dir: Michael Curtiz, 111 mins.)

Miles to Go Before I Sleep (MTV 1975)**½ Martin Balsam, Mackenzie Phillips, Kitty Winn. Can retired people find renewal by helping hardened teenage delinquents? Balsam will charm you as a gentle widower, but 15-year-old Phillips steals the show as Robin, the mercurial delinquent he wants to help. Earnest, well-intentioned reality drama. (Dir: Fielder Cook, 78 mins.)

Milkman, The (1950)** Jimmy Durante, Donald O'Connor, Piper Laurie. A waste of talented people—this lightweight comedy with songs about a couple of milkmen and their escapades offers a few laughs. The stars work hard but the material is mediocre. (Dir: Charles Barton, 87 mins.)

Milky Way, The (1936)**** Harold Lloyd, Adolphe Menjou, Helen Mack. The most impressive Lloyd talkie features an array of deft farceurs. Harold is a milkman who happens to knock down the champion in a brawl, and the gags that develop from the situation are impeccably constructed. Remade as "The Kid from Brooklyn." (Dir: Leo McCarey, 83 mins.)

Milky Way, The (France-Italy, 1969)**** Paul Frankeur, Laurent Terzieff, Edith Scob. Director Luis Buñuel's taut, funny and bitter, peculiarly devout history of the Roman Catholic Church in Europe, told in terms of its progress through heresies and schisms. The old master's surrealistic vision of religion is perfectly realized in this little gem. (105 mins.)

Mill of the Stone Women (France-Italy, 1960)*½ Pierre Brice, Scilla Gabel. (Dir: Giorgio Ferroni, 94 mins.)

Millhouse: A White Comedy (1971)***½ A harsh satire "documentary" about Richard Milhous Nixon released years before he became our first unindicted co-conspirator president. (Dir: Emile de Antonio, 92 mins.)

Million Dollar Baby (1941)** Ronald Reagan, Priscilla Lane, Jeffrey Lynn. If you think girls who are poor and suddenly get a million dollars should give it up so their boyfriend will still love them you may enjoy this Hollywood nonsense. (Dir: Curtis Bernhardt, 100 mins.)

Million Dollar Dixie Deliverance, The (MTV 1978)**½ Brock Peters, Kip Niven. The Disney family formula works again in this pre-Civil War tale. Peters helps five Yankee school kids who have been kidnapped for ransom cross the battle lines. Action-packed yarn with some suspense, overboard at times. (Dir: Russ Mayberry, 104 mins.)

Million Dollar Face (MTV 1981)** Tony Curtis, David Huffman, Herschel Bernardi, Sylvia Kristel, Roddy McDowall. If you enjoy Sidney Sheldon's novels and those movies about rich tycoons and their personal machinations, try this vapid, senseless portrait of the cosmetics business. There's a top model, a new ad campaign, underhanded tactics, illegitimate sons popping up, love intrigues, etc. Tony Curtis is the ruthless tycoon and Sylvia Kristel is the beautiful model with "the million dollar face." (Dir: Michael O'Herlihy, 104 mins.)

Million Dollar Legs (1932)***½ W. C. Fields, Jack Oakie, Susan Fleming, Lyda Roberti, Ben Turpin, Hugh Herbert, Billy Gilbert. An indescribably wild, anarchic farce from Fields and Co., set in a mythical (thank God) country, where the strongest man gets to be President. See Fields lift weights; see Lyda Roberti, the Polish bombshell, sizzle the scenery as the "hottest thing in all Klopstokia," Mata Machree. Somehow they all end up at the 1932 Los Angeles Olympics. Some people hate this picture; others think it's the funniest movie ever made. See what you think. (Dir: Edward Cline, 64 mins.)

Million Dollar Mermaid (1952)*½ Esther Williams, Victor Mature, Walter Pidgeon. (Dir: Mervyn Le Roy, 115 mins.)

Million Dollar Rip-Off, The (MTV 1976)*½ Freddie Prinze, Allen Garfield, Christine Belford, Brooke Mills. (Dir: Alexander Singer, 72 mins.)

Million Eyes of Su-Muru, The (Great Britain, 1967)*½ Shirley Eaton, Frankie Avalon, George Nader. (Dir: Lindsay Shonteff, 84 mins.)

Millionaire, The (MTV 1978)* Robert Quarry, Martin Balsam, Edward Albert. (Dir: Don Weiss, 104 mins.)

Millionaire for Christy, A (1951)** Fred MacMurray, Eleanor Parker. A secretary goes on the make for a millionaire, and lands him. Mild comedy. (Dir: George Marshall, 91 mins.)

Millionairess, The (Great Britain, 1960)** Sophia Loren, Peter Sellers, Alastair Sim, Vittorio De Sica, Dennis Price. First-rate cast in a vulgar scattered rendition of a minor Geroge Bernard Shaw play. Loren plays the richest woman in the world, who falls for a poor Indian doctor, limned by Sellers. Anthony Asquith has directed better on many an occasion. (90 mins.)

Min and Bill (1930)*** Marie Dressler, Wallace Beery, Dorothy Jordan. Charming antique features the dynamite combination of Dressler (won an Oscar) and Beery as waterfront characters trying to hold on to Marie's daughter (Jordan). (Dir: George Hill, 70 mins.)

Mind Benders, The (Great Britain, 1963)**½ Dirk Bogarde, Mary Ure, John Clements. Scientist engages in an experiment to test complete isolation from all the normal senses, emerges a psychological wreck. Drama begins well, slowly goes downhill; good performances. (Dir: Basil Dearden, 101 mins.)

Mind of Mr. Soames, The (Great Britain, 1970)**½ Terence Stamp, Robert Vaughn. Interesting situation marred by false characterizations. Mr. Soames (Stamp) is a 30-year-old man who has been in a coma since birth. He is to be operated on and brought to life by Dr. Bergen (Vaughn). (Dir: Alan Cooke, 95 mins.)

Mind over Murder (MTV 1979)*½ Deborah Raffin, David Ackroyd, Bruce Davison, Andrew Prine. (Dir: Ivan Nagy, 104 mins.)

Mine Own Executioner (Great Britain, 1947)***½ Burgess Meredith, Kieron Moore. A psychiatrist practicing without a medical degree finds trouble in his domestic life as well as with his patients. Well-made drama, informative, with some tense situations. (Dir: Anthony Kimmins, 103 mins.)

Mingus (1968) Bassist Charles Mingus, one of the greatist makers of jazz music, was also an incomparable personality. This documentary is the one visual alternative to his wonderful, lying, brilliant book "Beneath the Undergod." The "Village Voice" calls this "the first jazz film about jazz." (Dir: Thomas Reichman, 60 mins.)

Mini-Skirt Mob, The (1968)* Diane McBain, Jeremy Slate, Sherry Jackson, Patty McCormack. (Dir: Maury Dexter, 82 mins.)

Ministry of Fear (1944)***½ Ray Milland, Marjorie Reynolds. Exciting, offbeat spy melodrama, set in wartime England and based on a Graham Greene novel. Good direction and an interesting, mysterious story. (Dir: Fritz Lang, 86 mins.)

Miniver Story, The (Great Britain, 1950)** Greer Garson, Walter Pidgeon, John Hodiak. Peace comes to England after WW II, but not to the Miniver family—daughter's in the midst of a romantic attatchment, while Mrs. Miniver discovers personal tragedy. Weepy drama, a travesty of the original "Mrs. Miniver" film. (Dir: H. C. Potter, 104 mins.)

Minnesota Clay (Italy-France-Spain, 1966)½ Cameron Mitchell, Ethel Rojo, Georges Riviere. (Dir: Sergio Corbucci, 89 mins.)

Minnie and Moskowitz (1971)***½ Gena Rowlands, Seymour Cassel, Val Avery. Moving study of two disimilar but lonely people whose unlikely romance illuminates the screen, thanks to the fine performances of Rowlands and Cassel. Minnie is an art curator with a duplex apartment and a large library. Moskowitz is a parking lot attendant, and they meet when Minnie's blind date threatens her in Moskowitz's lot. (Dir: John Cassavetes, 114 mins.)

Minotaur, Wild Beast of Crete (Italy, 1961)** Bob Mathias, Rosanna Schiaffino. (Dir: Silvio Amadio, 92 mins.)

Minstrel Man (MTV 1977)*** Glynn Turman, Ted Ross, Stanley Clay, Sanndra Sharp, Art Evans. The old-time minstrel shows were racist, and usually the minstrels were whites got up in blackface. Filmed on location in Mississippi, this compelling teleplay focuses on the efforts of a group of post-Civil War black minstrel performers to form their own troupe and to present material that would be less degrading to blacks. Beautifully acted play about a little-known part of our theatrical history. (Dir: William A. Graham, 104 mins.)

Minute to Pray, A Second to Die, A (U.S.-Italy, 1968)**½ Arthur Kennedy, Alex Cord, Robert Ryan. One of the better Italian oaters. Cord is an outlaw epileptic who hides out in Escondido. He is sought by other outlaws, bounty hunters, territorial lawmen, and the vermin who prey on cripples. Good paranoia amid well-shot vistas. (Dir: Franco Giraldi, 103 mins.)

Miracle, The (1959)**½ Carroll Baker, Roger Moore, Walter Slezak. An ambitious effort to bring Max Reinhardt's epic play about a novice nun and her rebellion with God to the screen. Baker is miscast and the overblown production values can't overcome the empty melodramatics. (Dir: Irving Rapper, 121 mins.)

Miracle in Milan (Italy, 1951)***½ Francesco Golisano, Paolo Stoppa, Emma Gramatica. Vittorio De Sica's directs a powerful neorealistic indictment of conditions in postwar Italy. Based on a novel by Cesare Zevattini, the film tells of the fight of a group of shantytown poor against a rich man who wants to take their land away to exploit the oil underground. Their leader is a young man armed only with his ideals and, for a while, a magic dove. When the fight proves hopeless they all fly off on broomsticks to a better life. (96 mins.)

Miracle in the Rain (1956)**½ Jane Wyman, Van Johnson. Sentimental women's picture about a lonely young woman (Wyman) who meets a young soldier (Johnson) and falls in love. Their joy is interrupted when he ships out but Jane holds on to the hope that he'll come back. The two stars do well and there's a good supporting performance by Eileen Heckart, as Jane's friend. (Dir: Rudolph Maté, 107 mins.)

Miracle of Marcelino, The (France, 1955)**** Pablito Calvo, Rafael Rivelles. A beautiful and heartwarming film about a little orphan boy, who is raised by monks, and is visited by Christ in a miracle. Calvo gives a touching performance as Marcelino. (Dir: Ladislao Vajda, 90 mins.)

Miracle of Morgan's Creek (1944)**** Betty Hutton, Eddie Bracken, Diana Lynn, William Demarest. The real miracle here is director Preston Sturges, and the way in which he was able to deal, comically to be sure, with a theme that would not have been allowed by the censors at the time if it had been depicted solemnly. Small-town girl (Hutton) gets drunk and becomes pregnant, thanks to one of a number of obliging GIs. The problem is that Betty can't remember which soldier is the daddy-to-be. The "miracle" concerns the way in which the problem is resolved. Remade as Jerry Lewis's "Rockabye Baby". (99 mins.)

Miracle of Our Lady of Fatima, The (1952)*** Gilbert Roland, Frank Silvera, Susan Whitney. Story of three peasant children who witnessed a vision in the small Portuguese village of Fatima in '17. Interesting, and well acted by a large cast. (Dir: John Brahm, 102 mins.)

Miracle of the Bells (1948)*½ Fred MacMurray, Valli, Frank Sinatra, Lee J. Cobb. (Dir: Irving Pichel, 120 mins.)

Miracle of the Hills (1959)** Rex Reason, Nan Lelsie. New minister meets plenty of opposition when he attempts to reactivate a parish in a wide-open mining town. Pleasing, unsophisticated western drama. (Dir: Paul Landres, 73 mins.)

Miracle on Ice (MTV 1981)*** Karl Malden, Andrew Stevens, Steve Guttenberg, Jerry Houser. Hollywood attempts to recreate the saga of the 1980 U.S. Olympic Hockey team—a bunch of kids who upset the mighty Russians and then defeated Finland for the gold medal in Lake Placid. The trick is to blend acting sequences with actual Olympic game footage, and not make it too apparent. The game footage is marvelous, and the Hollywood stuff isn't too much of a letdown because Karl Malden puts on a show as the canny, jabbering coach Herb Brooks, who made the kids play way above themselves. (Dir: Steven Hillard Stern, 152 mins.)

Miracle on 34th Street (1947)**** Edmund Gwenn, John Payne, Maureen O'Hara, Natalie Wood. Kris Krigle is hired to play Santa Claus at Macy's and that begins a delightful combination of fantasy, whimsy, and heartwarming humor. For young and old and all who want to believe in Santa. (Dir: George Seaton, 96 mins.)

Miracle on 34th Street (MTV 1973)**½ Sebastian Cabot, Jane Alexander, David Hartman, Roddy McDowall. Remake is less charming than its predecessor, but remains pleasant entertainment. Cabot is Santa, and the hearings on his sanity, with our hero's defense lawyer well played by Hartman, provide the heart of the tale. (Dir: Fielder Cook, 104 mins.)

Miracle Worker, The (1962)**** Anne Bancroft, Patty Duke, Victor Jory, Inga Swenson, Andrew Prine. Superb film version of the brilliant Broadway play by William Gibson dealing with the training of blind, deaf Helen Keller. Miss Bancroft deserved the Oscar she won for the role of Miss Keller's teacher, Annie Sullivan. Duke (Oscar, Best Supporting Actress) is equally effective in the role of young Miss Keller. Fine direction by Arthur Penn. (107 mins.)

Miracle Worker, The (MTV 1979)**** Patty Duke Astin, Melissa Gilbert, Charles Siebert. Astin (who as Patty Duke played the first Broadway and movie versions) gives a superb performance as Helen's magnificent teacher, Anne Sullivan. Gilbert gives a respectable performance as Helen. Unless you're made of stone, the climactic moments of this William Gibson drama, in which Sullivan finally breaks through to her pupil, will leave you drained. (Dir: Paul Aaron, 104 mins.)

Mirage (1965)*** Gregory Peck, Diane Baker, Walter Matthau. Peck stars as an amnesiac who wakens after the first New York power blackout, starts to retrace his past, and becomes involved in a murder plot. Matthau is the rumpled detective he hires to help him, Baker is a mysterious girl, and veteran hack director Edward Dmytryk does about his best work. Peter Stone wrote the screenplay based on a novel by Howard Fast. (107 mins.)

Miranda (Great Britain, 1948)**½ Glynis Johns, Griffith Jones, Margaret Rutherford. Physician on a holiday away from his wife snags an amorous mermaid while fishing. Mildly entertaining fantasy-comedy. (Dir: Ken Annakin, 77 mins.)

Mirror Cracked, The (1980)*** Angela Lansbury, Edward Fox, Elizabeth Taylor, Rock Hudson, Kim Novak, Tony Curtis, Geraldine Chaplin. Rendition of the Agatha Christie novel. This film disorients viewers by casting aged fifties stars as actors in a fifties movie—they all seem so old for 1953. Still, the story has its surprises (if you don't spot the similarity of the plot to the story of Gene Tierney), and everyone acts in an archly bitchy way

that isn't exactly clever, but is passably amusing. Guy Hamilton directed, and the best joke is that for all his satirical gibes at the style of a moviewhodunit-within-the-movie, his own style is completely indistinguishable from the movie-within-the-movie. (97 mins.)

Mirror Has Two Faces, The (France, 1959)** Michele Morgan, Bourvil. Doctor performs plastic surgery on a plain-looking married woman, makes her a beauty and changes her life—not for the better. Slick treatment of an old soap opera idea. English-dubbed. (Dir: André Cayette, 98 mins.)

Mirror, Mirror (MTV 1979)** Loretta Swit, Lee Meriwether, Janet Leigh. Drama for the ladies. Producer-director Joanna Lee gets into female emotional problems, spelling out the good and bad effects of cosmetic surgery. Swit's flat-chested housewife wants a breast implant; Leigh's cutesy widow goes to a quack for a face-lift and almost dies; and Meriwether's model agency prexy submits to an eye-lift to win back an old lover (but Meriwether is too beautiful to require an eye-lift, and looks unchanged after surgery). (104 mins.)

Misfits, The (1961)*** Clark Gable, Marilyn Monroe, Montgomery Clift. Pretentious as hell, but affecting. Arthur Miller's original screenplay about a group of modern-day cowboys and a frightened divorcee is more a curiosity piece than good film drama. A slam-bang wild-horse roundup toward the end compensates somewhat for the faulty script. Clift does the best acting. All three leads died within five years of the film's release, and this was the last film of Gable and Monroe. (Dir: John Huston, 124 mins.)

Miss Grant Takes Richmond (1949)*** Lucille Ball, William Holden. Clever comedy about a secretarial school that is a front for a bookie syndicate. Lucy and Holden make a good comedy team. (Dir: Lloyd Bacon, 87 mins.)

Miss Robin Hood (Great Britain, 1953)**½ Margaret Rutherford, Richard Hearne. A meek writer of girls' adventure stories aids a battle-ax in repossessing her recipe for whiskey, which was stolen by a distiller. Screwball comedy isn't as funny as it was meant to be. (Dir: John Guillermin, 78 mins.)

Miss Sadie Thompson (1953)**½ Rita Hayworth, José Ferrer, Aldo Ray. The sultry saga of sinful Sadie Thompson is on view in this fair remake of Somerset Maugham's "Rain." Rita plays the island sinner this time while Ferrer screams of fire and brimstone. (Dir: Curtis Bernahrdt, 91 mins.)

Miss Susie Slagle's (1945) Sonny Tufts, Joan Caulfield, Lilian Gish, Veronica Lake. Leisurely, pleasant story about a boardinghouse for medical students in Baltimore around 1910. Inoffensive and generally entertaining. (Dir: John Berry, 88 mins.)

Miss Tatlock's Millions (1948)**½ John Lund, Wanda Hendrix, Robert Stack. Lund is a Hollywood stunt man hired to pose as the mentally defective heir to a millionaire's fortune. Charles Brackett's screwball comedy script centers on incest, greed, and insanity, but the graceless cast does it in. (Dir: Richard Haydn, 101 mins.)

Missle Base at Taniak (1953-66)*½ Bill Henry, Susan Morrow, Arthur Space. (Dir: Franklin Adreon, 100 mins.)

Missing Are Deadly, The (MTV 1975)*½ Ed Nelson, Leonard Nimoy, José Ferrer, Gary Morgan. (Dir: Don McDougall, 74 mins.)

Mission Batangas (1968)** Dennis Weaver, Vera Miles, Keith Larsen. Grade B adventure set during WW II in the Philippines. An American pilot stumbles upon a plan to commandeer the Philippine government's sock of gold bullion, but circumstances, both good and bad, interfere. (Dir: Keith Larsen, 100 mins.)

Mission Mars (1968)* Darren McGavin, Nick Adams, Heather Hewitt. (Dir: Nicholas Webster, 95 mins.)

Mission of the Sea Hawk (Great-Britain, 1962)** Terence Morgan, Jean Kent. Sir Francis Drake journeys to France searching for a missing nobleman. Feature version of the TV series "Sir Francis Drake," better produced than the usual run—passable costume adventure. (83 mins.)

Mission over Korea (1953)** John Derek, John Hodiak, Audrey Totter, Maureen O'Sullivan. Typical war story with romantic sidelines. Two officers argue about their jobs in the Korean conflict and later show their true colors to one another. (Dir: Fred F. Sears, 86 mins.)

Mission Stardust (Italy-Spain-West Germany, 1967)* Essy Persson, Lang Jeffries. (Dir: Primo Zeglio, 95 mins.)

Mission to Hell with Secret Agent FX15 (West Germany, 1964)* Paul Hubschmid, Marianne Hold, Horst Frank. (Dir: Frank Kramer, 95 mins.)

Mission to Morocco (1959)*½ Lex Barker, Julie Reding. (79 mins.)

Mission to Moscow (1943)***½ Walter Huston, Eleanor Parker. A fine, well-played movie adaptation from the book by ex-ambassador to Russia Joseph Davies. (Dir: Michael Curtiz, 123 mins.)

Mission to Venice (France-Italy-West Germany, 1963)*½ Sean Flynn, Madeleine Robinson. (Dir: Andre Versini, 88 mins.)

Mississippi (1935)*** Bing Crosby, W. C. Fields, Joan Bennett. Pleasant musical about a young man who refuses to fight a duel and takes refuge as a singer on a showboat. A few good Rodgers and Hart tunes, plus Fields's work as the captain add up to nice entertainment. (Dir: A. Edward Sutherland, 64 mins.)

Mississippi Gambler (1953)*** Tyrone Power, Piper Laurie, Julie Adams. Colorful romantic-adventure with Power perfectly cast as a dashing gambler who plays for high stakes in matters of love, honor, and reputation. Laurie is equally effective as a spirited, headstrong southern belle. Good escapist entertainment. (Dir: Rudolph Maté, 98 mins.)

Mississippi Mermaid (France-Italy, 1969)*** Jean-Paul Belmondo, Catherine Deneuve, Michel Bouquet. What begins as a mildly diverting romantic thriller about a mail-order bride-meanders into confusing melodrama. One of director François Truffaut's most sumptuous-looking films, and minor fun if you don't follow it too closely. (123 mins.)

Mississippi Summer (1968)½ J. A. Preston, Robert Earl Jones. (Dir: William Bayer, 88 mins.)

Missouri Breaks, The (1976)**½ Marlon Brando, Jack Nicholdon, Harry Dean Stanton, Kathleen Lloyd. An enormously disappointing, muddled western set in Montana during the 1880s. The Missouri Breaks are the headwaters of the Missouri River in Montana, but the audience doesn't get many breaks from this one. Director Arthur Penn reportedly had to cater to Brando's every whim, including making inane alterations in the script. Sometimes Marlon sports an Irish brogue, playing a western lawman, sometimes not. Nicholson gives the best performance in the film. Quirkish screenplay by Thomas McGuane. (126 mins.)

Missouri Traveler, The (1958)**½ Brandon de Wilde, Lee Marvin, Gary Merrill. Exaggerated piece of Americana about a young runaway who provides for himself by training race-horses. Thinly plotted, but some good acting by Marvin and de Wilde saves the picture. (Dir: Jerry Hopper, 103 mins.)

Mr. —See Mister

Mr and Mrs Bo Jo Jones (MTV1971)** Desi Arnez, Jr., Christopher Norris, Dan Dailey, Dina Merrill, Tom Bosley. In '58 when our mores were different, a reluctant high-school boy marries his pregnant schoolmate, a blond snubnosed youngster from a well-to-do family. The kids face disappointed parents on both sides and slowly grow as a unit, gaining strength as they push awkwardly through their problems.(Dir: Robert Day, 73 mins.)

Mr. and Mrs. Smith (1941)*** Carole Lombard, Robert Montgomery, Gene Raymond. Director Alfred Hitchcock's screwball comedy about a marriage that develops a legal hitch contains many a Hitchcockian theme and stylistic tic. Adequate farce with good acting. (95 mins.)

Mr. Arkadin (Great Britain, 1955)*** Orson Welles, Michael Redgrave, Katina Paxinou, Akim Tamiroff, Mischa Auer. Director Welles again reviews a rich man's past through the memories of those who loved and hated him. A bit confusing, due to budget stringencies forced on Welles. (99 mins.)

Mr. Belvedere Goes to College (1949)** Clifton Webb, Shirley Temple, Alan Young. Eccentric genius enrolls at a college to get a degree, finds life has its complications. Sequel to Webb's successful "Sitting Pretty"—not up to the original. Mild comedy. (Dir: Elliott Nugent, 83 mins.)

Mr. Belvedere Rings the Bell (1951)*** Clifton Webb, Joanne Dru, Hugh Marlowe. Screen adaptation of a Broadway play about life in an old folks' home. When Webb decides to bring some merriment to the home, the fun begins and hardly lets up throughout the film. (Dir: Henry Koster, 87 mins.)

Mr. Billion (1977)**½ Jackie Gleason, Terence Hill, Valerie Perrine, Slim Pickens. Lighthearted film about a young man from Italy (Hill) who inherits a business empire when his uncle in America dies. To claim his fortune, he must reach San Francisco in 20 days, which means eluding villainous Gleason and Pickens as well as sumptuous Perrine. Predictable but enjoyable comedy-adventure. (Dir: Jonathan Kaplan, 93 mins.)

Mr. Blandings Builds His Dream House (1948)*** Cary Grant, Myrna Loy, Melvyn Douglas. Grant's power to redeem the thinnest material is amply demonstrated in a slight situation comedy about a city couple's determination to build a suburban retreat, against all the expected rural odds. (Dir: H. C. Potter, 94 mins.)

Mister Buddwing (1966)** James Garner, Jean Simmons, Angela Lansbury, Katharine Ross, Suzanne Pleshette. One of those awful movies which you can sit back and enjoy provided you don't take the plot seriously. Garner is an amnesiac running all over New York City (good on-location shots) trying to find out who he is. The ladies who help him along the way include Simmons as a flighty rich lady, Lansbury as a sympathetic woman, Ross as a pretty young thing, and Pleshette as an aspiring actress. (Dir: Delbert Mann, 100 mins.)

Mr. Bug Goes to Town—See: Hoppity Goes to Town

Mister Cory (1957)***½ Tony Curtis, Martha Hyer, Kathryn Grant. Fast, rowdy, fun-filled story of a lad from the Chicago slums who grows up to be a big-time gambler. Slick direction, well-written script, nice performance by Curtis and supporting players. (Dir: Blake Edwards, 92 mins.)

Mr. Deeds Goes to Town (1936)**** Gary Cooper, Jean Arthur, George Bancroft. Director Frank Capra's populist classic is about backwoods poet Longfellow Deeds (Cooper), who inherits a fortune, goes to New York, and meets virtually every kind of big-city corruption and cynicism before he opts for the New Deal solution of sharing the wealth and giving the little guy an economic break. (115 mins.)

Mr. Denning Drives North (Great Britain, 1951)*** John Mills, Phyllis Calvert. An aircraft manufacturer kills a blackmailer, suffers the consequences of conscience until an American lawyer-friend comes to

his aid. Suspenseful melodrama, well acted. (Dir: Anthony Kimmins, 93 mins.)

Mr. Drake's Duck (Great Britain, 1951)*** Douglas Fairbanks, Jr., Yolande Donlan. An American couple buy an English farm, where they encounter a duck that lays uranium eggs. Fast-moving, sprightly comedy, pretty funny. (Dir: Val Guest, 76 mins.)

Mr. Dynamite (1941)**½ Lloyd Noland, J. Carrol Naish, Irene Hervey. Baseball star visiting a carnival matches wits with a gang of enemy agents. Simple but fast-moving, exciting little melodrama gives a good hour's relaxation. (Dir: John Rawlins, 63 mins.)

Mr. 880 (1950)***½ Burt Lancaster, Dorothy McGuire, Edmund Gwenn. Charming real-life story about a T-man and a UN secretary who investigate a lovable old counterfeiter. Gwenn shines as the money-maker. (Dir: Edmund Goulding, 90 mins.)

Mr. Emmanuel (Great Britain, 1945)*** Felix Aylmer, Greta Gynt. A Jewish gentleman braves Nazi Germany in his quest for a lost friend. Well acted, frequently gripping drama. (Dir: Harold French, 93 mins.)

Mister Freedom (France, 1968)* Delphine Seyrig, Philippe Noiret, Donald Pleasence, Yves Montand, Daniel Cohn-Bendit, Simone Signoret. (95 mins.)

Mr. Hobbs Takes a Vacation (1962)**½ James Stewart, Maureen O'Hara, Fabian, Maria Wilson, John Saxon, Reginald Gardiner. Family encounters plenty of trouble when they try to take a vacation in a run-down beach house. Typical father-against-the-world domestic comedy, which Stewart can play in his sleep. Some funny but familiar scenes. (Dir: Henry Koster, 116 mins.)

Mr. Horn (MTV 1979)** David Carradine, Richard Widmark, Karen Black. William Goldman penned this laconic western about the legendary Scott Tom Horn, the man who captured the famous Apache warrior Geronimo. Features plenty of long shots and battle scenes in which Indians fall off cliffs and horses. This western, played in a tight, low-key style, means to correct the white man's hero image. (Dir: Jack Starrett, 208 mins.)

Mr. Imperium (1951)** Lana Turner, Ezio Pinza. An improbable pair try to prove that May-December romances can work in this light romantic comedy. The film doesn't work but Ezio does sing. (Dir: Don Hartman, 87 mins.)

Mr. Inside/Mr. Outside (MTV 1973)**½ Hal Linden, Tony Lo Bianco. A number of factors lift this murder mystery above the usual thriller. It stars two capable actors, and is shot on location in New York City; the original fracas takes place inside a foreign embassy—off limits to the local police force because of diplomatic immunity. (Dir: William Graham, 73 mins.)

Mister Jericho (MTV 1970)**½ Patrick Macnee, Connie Stevens, Herbert Lom.

Jewel thief caper with slick production values, good on-location Riviera backgrounds, and fastpaced gimmicks. Macnee plays ingenious con artist with a flair and he's matched by Lom as an eccentric millionaire. OK time passer. (Dir: Sidney Hayers, 85 mins.)

Mr. Klein (France-Italy, 1976)***½ Alain Delon, Jeanne Moreau, Suzanne Flon. Set in Paris in '42, this is primarily about the Holocaust. Delon gives a startling performance as an art dealer who discovers that his identity is being siphoned off by a Jewish refugee of the same name. Although this is a thriller, director Joseph Losey's approach is more intellectual than emotional and, for all its limitations, a remarkably involving success. (122 mins.)

Mr. Lord Says No (Great Britain, 1952)*** Stanley Holloway, Kathleen Harrison. Mr. Lord defies the British government when they want to demolish his home to make way for a new highway. Highly amusing comedy (Dir: Muriel Box, 76 mins.)

Mr. Lucky (1943)*** Cary Grant, Laraine Day, Charles Bickford, Gladys Cooper, Paul Stewart, Henry Stephenson. Grant is a gambler redeemed by Day on behalf of the war effort. Directed by H. C. Potter in his finest hour. (100 mins.)

Mr. Majestyk (1974)* Charles Bronson, Al Lettieri, Linda Cristal, Alejandro Rey. (Dir: Richard Fleischer, 103 mins.)

Mister Moses (1965)** Robert Mitchum, Carroll Baker. Mitchum and the blond Miss Baker take a back seat to the glorious on-location African scenery in this mild adventure epic. Mitchum is involved in gem smuggling. (Dir: Ronald Neame, 113 mins.)

Mr. Moto Takes a Chance (1938)** Peter Lorre, Rochelle Hudson, That almost-too-clever Japanese sleuth up against intrigue in Indochina. Lorre is good, but the writing isn't as smooth as in the Chan films. (Dir: Norman Foster, 70 mins.)

Mr. Music (1950)**½ Bing Crosby, Nancy Olson, Charles Coburn. Bing as a composer who would rather golf and loaf than work, and the attempts to get him into action. Mild story, below-par tunes, but Crosby carries the load well. (Dir: Richard Haydn, 113 mins.)

Mr. Peabody and the Mermaid (1948)**½ William Powell, Ann Blyth, Irene Hervey, Andrea King. A middle-aged gent has his life changed completely when he comes upon an amorous mermaid one day. Mildly amusing fantasy. (Dir: Irving Pichel, 89 mins.)

Mr. Peek-A-Boo (France, 1951)*** Bourvil, Joan Greenwood. Comedy about a man who has the power to walk through walls. Delightful, with Parisian comic Bourvil a riot. (Dir: Jean Boyer, 74 mins.)

Mr. Perrin and Mr. Traill (Great Britain 1948)***½ David Farrar, Marius Goring. Bitterness develops between an old schoolmaster and a younger teacher when the latter makes a better impression with

his winning ways. Excellent melodrama, with good performances, especially from Goring as the old schoolmaster (Dir: Lawrence Huntington, 92 mins.)

Mr. Potts Goes to Moscow—See: Top Secret

Mr. Quilp (Great Britain, 1975)* Anthony Newley, David Hemmings, David Warner. (Dir: Michael Tuchner, 118 mins.)

Mr. Reckless (1948)*½ William Eythe, Barbara Britton. (Dir. Frank McDonald, 66 mins.)

Mr. Ricco (1975)*½ Dean Martin, Eugene Roche, Denise Nicholas, Cindy Williams, Geraldine Brooks. (Dir: Paul Bogart, 98 mins.)

Mister Roberts (1955)**** Henry Fonda, James Cagney, William Powell, Jack Lemmon, Betsy Palmer. Hilarious film about a combat ship far from the battles of WW II. Time has dimmed the Oscar-winning luster of Lemmon's hamming as opportunistic Ensign Pulver in favor of Cagney's superbly psychotic commanding officer. Fonda is as brilliant as ever in the title role. (Dirs: John Ford, Mervyn LeRoy, 123 mins.)

Mr. Robinson Crusoe (1932)*** Douglas Fairbanks, Sr, Maria Alba. Doug bets he can live on a deserted island for a year, and his athletic prowess overcomes all odds. Lively adventure is rather good fun. (Dir: A. Edward Sutherland, 80 mins.)

Mister Rock 'n Roll (1957)* Alan Freed, Rocky Graziano, Lionel Hampton, Frankie Lymon. and Charles Dublin, 86 mins.)

Mr. Sardonicus (1961)**½ Guy Rolfe, Oscar Homolka, Ronald Lewis, Audrey Dalton. Doctor is called by his former love to a castle to treat her husband, whose face is paralyzed. Thriller brings off the shudders in efficient fashion (Dir: William Castle, 89 mins.)

Mr. Scoutmaster (1953)** Clifton Webb. Even Webb's aplomb doesn't save this comedy about a reluctant scoutmaster and his misadventures with a pack of future eagle scouts. (Dir: Henry Levin, 87 mins.)

Mr. Skeffington (1944)**½ Bette Davis, Claude Rains, Walter Abel. Davis marries a stockbroker (Rains) for his money, but after 30 years of suffering she finds she can't help but love him. Typical lavishly produced Davis vehicle from the '40s. Vincent Sherman's limping direction is a liability. (TV version 127 mins., original running time 146 mins.)

Mr. Smith Goes to Washington (1939)**** James Stewart, Jean Arthur, Thomas Mitchell, Edward Arnold, Claude Rains. A Frank Capra-directed masterpiece, poised deftly between screwball comedy and populist drama. Stewart plays maverick Senator Smith. (130 mins.)

Mr. Soft Touch (1949)**½ Glenn Ford, Evelyn Keyes, John Ireland. A sentimental, corny comedy-drama about a gambler who gets involved with a social worker of a local settlement house. Good performances despite the saccharine script.

450

(Dirs: Henry Levin, Gordon Douglas, 93 mins.)

Mr. Steve (France, 1957)**½ Jeanne Moreau, Philippe Le Maire. Bank clerk is forced by a clever gangster to assist in a daring robbery, falls for the gangster's wife. English-dubbed crime melodrama unfolds fairly interestingly, with good performances. (100 mins.)

Mr. Sycamore (1974)** Jason Robards, Jr., Jean Simmons, Sandy Dennis. Strange comedy about mailman Robards, who wants to escape his drudgery by turning into a tree. Simmons is a librarian and the object of Robards's earthly affection. Director Pancho Kohner and Ketti Frings try to adapted to the latter's '42 play, but are defeated. (87 mins.)

Mister V—See: **Pimpernel Smith**

Mr. Winkle Goes to War (1944)*** Edward G. Robinson, Ruth Warrick. Thirty-eight-year-old bank clerk is drafted, surprises everybody by becoming a hero. Entertaining, novel war melodrama. Dir: Alfred E. Green, 80 mins.)

Mistress, The (Japan, 1953)**½ Hideko Takamine. English-dubbed drama of a girl who sells herself into slavery in order to support her ailing father. Japanese locale has novelty, but the movement is often extremely studied, slow moving. (Dir: Shiro Toyoda, 106 mins.)

Mistress of the World (Italy-France-Germany, 1959)** Martha Hyer, Carlos Thompson, Gino Cervi, Sabu. Wild sci-fi tale of a professor whose invention for controlling the world's magnetic fields is imperiled by Chinese agents. Lavishly produced, first-rate cast stuck in pure junk—but it's fun if not taken seriously. (Dir: William Dieterle, 107 mins.)

Misty (1961)**½ David Ladd, Arthur O'Connell, Pam Smith. Good adventure story for the kids, as two young children try to tame a wild pony. David Ladd (Alan Ladd's son) plays the wholesome young boy. Filmed on location on the islands of Chincoteague and Assateague off the coast of Maryland. From the popular children's story by Marguerite Henry. (Dir: James B. Clark, 92 mins.)

Mix Me a Person (Great Britain, 1961)**½ Anne Baxter, Adam Faith, Donald Sinden. Teenage guitarist finds himself charged with murder when a policeman is killed. Uneven drama has some absorbing scenes, fairly good performances. (Dir: Leslie Norman, 108 mins.)

Mixed Company (1974)*½ Barbara Harris, Joseph Bologna, Tom Bosley. (Dir: Melville Shavelson, 109 mins.)

M.M.M. 83 (Italy, 1965)*½ Pier Angeli, Fred Beir, Gerard Bain. (Dir: Sergio Bergonzelli, 83 mins.)

Moana (1926)*** Ta'avale, Fa'amgase. One of the earliest feature-length documentaries and one of the best ever made. (A new version has just been released with a musical score added.) Moana is a young Polynesian boy on the island of Samoa.

This historic documentary shows typical events in his life. (Dirs: Robert Flaherty, Frances Hubbard Flaherty, 77 mins.)

Mob, The (1951)*** Broderick Crawford, Ernest Borgnine, Richard Kiley. Good gangland film about a policeman who joins the mob in order to get to the big boys. Well acted; snappy dialogue. (Dir: Robert Parrish, 87 mins.)

Moby Dick (1956)*** Gregory Peck, Orson Welles, Harry Andrews, Richard Basehart, James Robertson-Justice. Ray Bradbury's adaptation is only adequate, but director John Huston's grasp of the material is so intense that some sparks of personal art flash throughout. As Captain Ahab, Peck's attempt at smoldering New England rigidity doesn't play. Welles has a strong cameo as the preacher Father Marple. The final whaling scenes are extraordinary by any standard, as action suggests metaphoric force far better than conscious visual symbolism. (116 mins.)

Model and the Marriage Broker, The (1952)*** Jeanne Crain, Thelma Ritter, Scott Brady. The marriage broker is wisecracking Ritter and the model she matches up is lovely Crain. Brady plays the groom-to-be and getting them together takes up most of the running time. Director George Cukor is a master at this kind of sophisticated comedy. (103 mins.)

Model for Murder (Britain 1959)** Keith Andes, Hazel Court. Routine British murder mystery involving a search by an American officer for his dead brother's girlfriend. (Dir: Terry Bishop, 75 mins.)

Model Shop (1969)**½ Anouk Aimée, Gary Lockwood, Alexander Hay. French director Jacques Demy's first U.S. film in English is alternating interesting and monotonous. Lockwood, in the film's best performance, is a troubled youth who runs into Aimée while she is working in one of those L.A. spots where you can photograph models for a fee. The two lost souls share a brief but burning time together. (95 mins.)

Modern Hero, A (1934)**½ Richard Barthelmess, Jean Muir, Marjorie Rambeau. Director G. W. Pabst's only American film, adapted from a Louis Bromfield novel with Barthelmess as a rising young man who becomes a ruthless industrialist, is a bit turgid. Intelligent support from Rambeau. (71 mins.)

Modern Romance (1980)*** Kathryn Harrold, Bruno Kirby, James L. Brooks. Albert Brooks confirms the considerable talent he showed in his *Real Life* with this funny comedy, filled with insight, that exercises all its viciousness on Brooks himself, making it a far more honest examination of relationships than anything Woody Allen has done. Brooks plays Everyman as compulsive asshole, unable to handle emotional jolts, overcome rabid possessiveness or resist the blandishments of canny salesmen. His visual style, featuring long takes and lots of audacious handheld stuff by cinematographer Eric

Saarinen, is distinctively his own, respecting the extended passages in real time that enable his unyielding observation to achieve telling effect. He may be working a dead-end street with scathing comedy of self-abnegation, but there's no doubt that his talent is potentially major. James L. Brooks is the fatuous director who will be recognized by any filmmaker in Hollywood as the ninny he's been dealing with (in one guise or another) all his professional career. (100 mins.)

Modern Times (1936)**** Charles Chaplin, Paulette Goddard. One of the all-time greats, a sensational one-man show by Chaplin, writing, directing, producing, scoring, and starring in this eternal saga of everyman in all times. The Tramp moves from factory worker to department store janitor to singing waiter, as modern times knock him cruelly about. (100 mins.)

Modesty Blaise (Great Britain, 1966)*½ Monica Vitti, Terence Stamp, Dirk Bogarde. (Dir: Joseph Losey, 119 mins.)

Mogambo (1953)*** Clark Gable, Ava Gardner, Grace Kelly, Donald Sinden, Laurence Naismith. Remake of "Red Dust," which starred Gable and Jean Harlow; Gable repeats his role of the white hunter whose life is complicated by two beautiful women. Gardner gives one of her best performances, in a colorful role. (Dir: John Ford, 116 mins.)

Mohammad, Messenger of God (Great Britain, 1976)*½ Anthony Quinn, Irene Papas, Michael Ansara. (Dir: Moustapha Akkad, 179 mins.)

Mole Men Against the Son of Hercules (Italy, 1961)* Mark Forest. (Dir: Antonio Leonviola, 98 mins.)

Molière (France, 1975)*** Philippe Caubert, Josephine Derenne, Brigitte Catillon. Director Ariane Mnouchkine's epic life of Molière, France's greatest playwright, bursts with zest and offers an incisive view of the 17th century in all its enlightenment and hypocrisy. Molière, a fascinating man, provides an ideal means to perceive the nature of his time. Most of the actors are from Mnouchkine's celebrated troupe, the Théâtre du Soleil. (Dir: Ariane Mnouchkine, 270 mins.)

Molly (1950)**½ Gertrude Berg, Philip Loeb. Life with the Goldbergs, as Molly's former suitor pays the family a visit. Mildly amusing. (Dir: Walter Hart, 83 mins.)

Molly and Me (1945)*** Monty Woolley, Gracie Fields, Roddy McDowall. Well-played warm comedy about a maid who straightens out her employer's life. Not hilarious, but a very pleasant diversion. (Dir: Lewis Seller, 76 mins.)

Molly Maguires, The (1969)**½ Sean Connery, Richard Harris, Samantha Eggar. In the 1870s the Molly Maguires tried to improve Pennsylvania coal miners' conditions through terrorism. James McParlan (Harris) is a Pinkerton detective who manages to infiltrate the Molly Maguires. Shot on location in Eckley, Pa.,

which some civic boosters say is the ugliest town in America. Aided by the money Paramount spent to uglify the town, Eckley now considers itself a historical resource and has a mining museum. (Dir: Martin Ritt, 124 mins.)

Moment by Moment (1978)*½ John Travolta, Lily Tomlin. Detailed account of a love relationship. (Dir: Jane Wagner, 102 mins.)

Moment of Truth, The (France, 1952)** Michele Morgan, Jean Gabin, Daniel Gelin. An actress and her doctor husband are celebrating their tenth wedding anniversary when a stranger, who has attempted suicide, disrupts their life. Even the divine Morgan can't triumph over the cumbersome plot. (Dir: Jean Delannoy, 90 mins.)

Moment to Moment (1966)**½ Jean Seberg, Sean Garrison, Honor Blackman. Wanting to end an illicit affair, a young wife accidentally shoots her paramour, then frantically tries to hide the body—which disappears. Creaky plot, with the audience always one step ahead—but the production's pretty and the players are pleasant. (Dir: Mervyn LeRoy, 108 mins.)

Mon Oncle d'Amérique (My Uncle from America) (France, 1980)**** Gerard Depardieu, Nicole Garcia, Roger-Pierre. Unusual movie in which director Alain Resnais returns to his themes of memory and loss, using behavioristic theories to assert that repression of man's innate aggressive instincts creates hierarchical systems. However arrogantly simple the scientific ideas are, Resnais has found a correlation for his elegant formalism in these deterministic notions. Luckily, his filmmaking, like any human motivation, possesses a mystery that defies mere prescriptions. The film is simultaneously witty and melancholic, acute and suspect, and always lovely. (Dir: Alain Resnais, 125 mins.)

Mona Kent (1961)* Sandra Donat, Johnny Olsen. (Dir: Charles J. Hyndt, 75 mins.)

Mondo Cane (Italy, 1962)*½ (105 mins.)

Money from Home (1953)** Dean Martin, Jerry Lewis, Pat Crowley. Dean and Jerry are on the spot when Dino's IOUs start showing up and a mobster tells him to pay up or else help throw a horse race. Strained comedy based on a Damon Runyon story is below par. (Dir: George Marshall, 99 mins.)

Money Movers (Australia, 1978)*** Terence Donovan, Ed Devereaux, Tony Bonner. Interesting Australian real-life thriller (from Devon Minchin's novelistic version "The Money Movers") about the $20 million robbery of a counting house by members of a security company. (Dir: Bruce Beresford, 91 mins.)

Money Order, The—See: Mandabi

Money Talks (1972)**½ Allen Funt of TV's "Candid Camera" produced and directed this film, which puts people in situations where avarice might get the better of them. Using his hidden-camera technique, he photographs such scenes as bowls of free money on the street or girls dropping greenbacks. Amusing diversion (81 mins.)

Money to Burn (MTV 1973)**½ E. G. Marshall, Mildred Natwick, Alejandro Rey, Cleavon Little. Fun. A sympathetic cast portrays a counterfeiting group. The pace, the people, the plot, and the dialogue all have a sense of humorous larceny. (Dir: Robert Michael Lewis, 72 mins.)

Money Trap, The (1965)** Glenn Ford, Elke Sommer, Rita Hayworth, Joseph Cotten, Ricardo Montalban. Familiar fare about an honest cop driven to dishonest deed by his sexy, money-hungry wife. Ford and Sommer fit their roles nicely, but Hayworth comes off best, in a supporting role as an embittered woman who has turned to alcohol for solace. (Dir: Burt Kennedy, 92 mins.)

Money, Women and Guns (1958)**½ Jock Mahoney, Kim Hunter, Tim Hovey. When an old prospector is bushwhacked, his will specifies four beneficiaries: a detective goes after the heirs and the killer. Offbeat western with an element of whodunit, nicely done. (Dir: Richard Bartlett, 80 mins.)

Mongols, The (France-Italy, 1961)**½ Jack Palance, Anita Ekberg. Adventure epic, dubbed in English. Palance is tall and ugly, Anita is tall and pretty, the story is just tall. (Dirs: André de Toth. Leopoldo Savona, Riccardo Freda. 102 mins.)

Mongo's Back in Town (MTV 1971)***½ Joe Don Baker, Sally Field. Unvarnished script by convict E. Richard Johnson. Tough, rough, arresting Christmas yarn about a San Pedro killer who returns to help his brother out of a jam over counterfeit plates. The plot is complicated, but the characters and dialogue, and the acting of Baker as Mongo and of Field are splendid. (Dir: Marvin Chomsky, 73 mins.)

Monitors, The (1969)* Guy Stockwell, Keenan Wynn, Ed Begley. (Dir: Jack Shea, 92 mins.)

Monk, The (MTV 1969)*** George Maharis, Janet Leigh, Carl Betz. Typical private-eye crime tale in which the hero spouts glib dialogue, the plot is incredible, and the writers come up with a plot gimmick every 20 minutes or so. Maharis is fine as the hero, Gus Monk, and gets excellent support from the San Francisco backgrounds. (Dir: George McCowan, 73 mins.)

Monkey Business (1931)***½ The Marx Brothers, Thelma Todd, Ruth Hall. Four Marx Brothers are stowaways on an ocean liner, where Groucho and Zeppo on the one hand, and Chico and Harpo on the other, get involved with rival gangs and mixed up in a kidnapping. Script written by S. J. Perelman. A bit disorganized, it carries hints of surrealism (especially in Harpo's extraordinary performance) that flowered in "Duck Soup". (Dir: Norman Z. McLeod, 77 mins.)

Monkey Business (1952)**** Cary Grant, Ginger Rogers, Marilyn Monroe, Charles Coburn. A chemistry professor (Grant) unknowingly discovers a youth serum. He and his wife (Rogers) psychologically revert to teenagers, then children, as their unspoken impulses come bubbling up under the influence of the drug. Very funny and strangely frightening. (Dir: Howard Hawks, 97 mins.)

Monkey Hustle, The (1976)** Yaphet Kotto, Rosalind Cash, Rudy Ray Moore. Surprisingly softhearted Chicago black exploitationer wouldn't have been half bad if director Arthur Marks had been able to get over his congenital narrative problems. A mess, but a pleasant one. (90 mins.)

Monkey in Winter, A (France, 1962)*** Jean Gabin, Jean-Paul Belmondo. Two great male stars of French cinema discover their are kindred spirits in this mild, unembellished, anecdotal tale of an old and a young man who postpone reality for a day of drinking and dreams. (Dir: Henri Verneuil, 104 mins.)

Monkey Mission, The (MTV 1981)** Robert Blake, Keenan Wynn. A second TV movie for Robert Blake's pugnacious private eye Joe Dancer. Blake soft pedals the hard-nose approach while trying to swipe a museum vase for a client. An agile monkey and Keenan Wynn as an electronics whiz are included to make Blake's hero more likable! A better yarn is needed—not another animal act! (Dir: Russ Mayberry, 104 mins.)

Monkey on My Back (1957)** Cameron Mitchell, Dianne Foster. Often interesting dramatized biography of boxer Barney Ross, his early rise to fame in the ring, his high spending days as a gambler, his heroic career in the marines during WW II, and his narcotics addiction and struggle to kick the habit. Brutal at times in its realism, with helpful performance from Mitchell. (Dir: André de Toth, 93 mins.)

Monkeys, Go Home! (1967)* Dean Jones, Maurice Chevalier, Yvette Mimieux. (Dir: Andrew McLaglen, 101 mins.)

Monocle, The (France, 1964)* Paul Meurisse, Barbara Steele, Marcel Dallo. (Dir: Georges Lautner, 97 mins.)

Monolith Monsters, The (1957)** Grant Williams, Lois Albright, William Shallert. Strange deaths occur after a meteor shatters in the California desert. A geologist discovers why, at the risk of his life. Standard sci-fi thriller. (Dir: John Sherwood, 77 mins.)

Monsieur Beaucaire (1946)*** Bob Hope, Joan Caulfield, Marjorie Reynolds, Patric Knowles, Cecil Kellaway, Joseph Schildkraut. Naturally, the film is somewhat different with Hope in the lead instead of Rudolph Valentino. One of Bob's most inspired romps, as a barber impersonating a dandy in the court of Louis XV. Directed by old-hand George Marshall in his best period. From the novel by Booth Tarkington. (93 mins.)

Monsieur Gangster (France-Italy-West Germany, 1963)**½ Lino Ventura, Sabine Sinjen, Bernard Biler. Small businessman takes over a deceased friend's interests, which prove to be on the shady side of the law, with discontent bubbling among members of his new "gang." Minor but fairly entertaining crime story dubbed in English. (Dir: Georges Lautner, 98 mins.)

Monsieur Hulot's Holiday (France, 1951)**** Jacques Tati. The best slapstick comedy of the '50s. Mostly silent, except for sound effects, the film is a series of well-executed sight gags. Not as great as Keaton or Chaplin, director Tati is nonetheless an endearing performer. Anyone of any age will enjoy this film. (96 mins.)

Monsieur Robinson Crusoe (France, 1959)** Darry Cowl, Beatrice Altariba. Foolish French farce about an amorous street peddler who goes from one adventure to another. (Dir: Jack Pinoteau, 88 mins.)

Monsieur Verdoux (1947)**** Charlie Chaplin, Martha Raye, Marilyn Nash. Chaplin's sardonic "comedy of murders" is a masterpiece. Chaplin (who directed) plays a bank clerk turned bluebeard, murdering lonely women for their money after marrying them, all in order to support his lovely storybook family complete with crippled wife. Chaplin gets chilling humor out of his efforts to kill a victim and still get to the bank before it closes, or in his repeated attempts to sink the unsinkable Raye in a grotesque parody of "An American Tragedy." At this trial, he defends his actions: "If war is the logical extension of diplomacy, then the logical extension of business is murder." (123 mins.)

Monster from a Prehistoric Planet (Japan, 1967)* Tamio Kawaji. (Dir: Itaruyasu Noguchi, 90 mins.)

Monster from Green Hell (1957)** Jim Davis, Barbara Turner. Dull horror filled science fiction story about huge monsters discovered in the jungles of Africa. (Dir: Kenneth Crane, 71 mins.)

Monster from the Surf (1965)* Jon Hall, Sue Casey. (Dir: Jon Hall, 75 mins.)

Monster of Piedras Blancas, The (1961)*½ Les Tremayne, Jeanne Carmen. (Dir: Irvin Berwick, 71 mins.)

Monster on the Campus (1958)**½ Arthur Franz, Joanna Moore, Troy Donahue. Scientist injects himself with blood of an ancient fish, turns into a monster. Shocker that delivers the goods—enough eeriness to keep the nails bitten down. (Dir: Jack Arnold, 76 mins.)

Monster That Challenged the World, The (1957)** Tim Holt, Audrey Dalton. Atomic experiments uncover sea beasts who begin their reign of terror. Standard science fiction horror thriller—better than

some, should please the fans. (Dir: Arnold Laven, 93 mins.)

Montana (1950)** Errol Flynn, Alexis Smith. Cowboys help to make a state of Montana; based on a novel by Ernest Haycox. Smith was almost as pretty as Errol in those days. (Dir: Ray Enright, 76 mins.)

Montana Belle (1952)** Jane Russell, George Brent, Scott Brady. Belle Starr throws in with the Dalton gang, but is persuaded to reform and turn against the outlaws. So-so western, nothing new. (Dir: Allan Dwan, 81 mins.)

Montana Mike (1947)**½ Robert Cummings, Brian Donlevy, Marjorie Reynolds. An angel comes to earth to help reform a western badman. Different kind of western story, pleasant. (Dir: Albert S. Rogell, 95 mins.)

Monte Carlo (1930)**** Jeanette MacDonald, Jack Buchanan, ZaSu Pitts. Wonderfully inventive early sound musical directed by Ernst Lubitsch, in which a chorus of "Beyond the Blue Horizon" is begun by the wheels of a train, picked up by a passenger (MacDonald), and carried by the peasants in every field the train passes. Great stuff, done up in high Paramount gloss. (85 mins.)

Monte Carlo Baby (France, 1952)*½ Audrey Hepburn, Cara Williams, Jules Munshin. (Dirs: Jean Boyer, Jean Jerrold, 70 mins.)

Monte Carlo Story, The (1957)** Marlene Dietrich, Vittorio De Sica, Arthur O'Connell. A fortune hunter and huntress meet in Monte Carlo and foolishly choose love in lieu of wealth. Glamorous settings, including Marlene, are the sole assets of this Riviera trifle. (Dir: Samuel Taylor, 100 mins.)

Monte Walsh (1970)* Lee Marvin, Jeanne Moreau, Jack Palance. (Dir: William A. Fraker, 108 mins.)

Monterey Pop (1969)***½ All-star concert. The first and one of the best of the rock concert films. The acts include Janis Joplin, the Mamas and the Papas, the Jefferson Airplane, Otis Redding (backed by Booker T. and the MGs), Jimi Hendrix, the Who, Country Joe and the Fish, and a finale by Ravi Shankar. (Dir: D. A. Pennebaker, 79 mins.)

Monty Python and the Holy Grail (Great Britain, 1975)*** John Cleese, Graham Chapman, Terry Gilliam, Eric Idle, Terry Jones. Made by the same talented zanies responsible for the Monty Python TV series. Very uneven satiric sketches filmed among the castles, lochs, and moors of Scotland. King Arthur and the Knights of the Round Table have never looked so absurd. (Dirs: Terry Gilliam, Terry Jones, 89 mins.)

Moon and Sixpence, The (1942)***½ George Sanders, Herbert Marshall, Eric Blore, Elena Verdugo, Florence Bates, Albert Basserman. Somerset Maugham's dramatic story of a man with the urge to paint, and how he discards his conventional life to follow his calling. Thoughtfully done, tastefully performed. (Dir: Albert Lewin, 89 mins.)

Moon Is Blue, The (1953)** William Holden, Maggie McNamara, David Niven. When this comedy about a "virgin" and her determined pursuers was first released, it was considered daring for its spicy dialogue and frank depiction of the sexual chase, but by now it's just a mild fizzle. Based on the F. Hugh Herbert Broadway hit. Use of the word "virgin" resulted in the film creating a furor and being banned in many markets in the U.S. (Dir: Otto Preminger, 95 mins.)

Moon Is Down, The (1943)***½ Cedric Hardwicke, Lee J. Cobb, Peter Van Eyck, Dorris Bowden. Dated but powerful version of the Steinbeck story of the Nazi occupation of Norway. Still some moral lessons to be learned from this story. (Dir: Irving Pichel, 90 mins.)

Moon of the Wolf (MTV 1972)** David Janssen, Barbara Rush, Bradford Dillman, John Beradino. Modern-day werewolf tale rekindles some of the chills and menace of the old monster flicks. After the badly torn body of a young lady is discovered, Sheriff Janssen has his work cut out for him. Scenes in which the werewolf appears are played for spine-tingling terror, and they work for the most part. (Dir: Daniel Petrie, 73 mins.)

Moon over Miami (1941)** Don Ameche, Betty Grable, Carole Landis, Robert Cummings. Dumbly enjoyable musical: Betty Grable, Carole Landis, and Charlotte Greenwood go gold digging with Don Ameche, Robert Cummings, and Jack Haley. The color work is especially good. (Dir: Walter Lang, 91 mins.)

Moon Spinners, The (U.S.-Great Britain, 1964)*** Hayley Mills, Joan Greenwood, Eli Wallach. Pleasant Walt Disney production tells the story of a young English girl (Mills) and her aunt (Greenwood), who visit Crete and receive an odd, chilly reception. A tale of thieves and stolen gems. Keep an eye out for silent-screen star Pola Negri, appearing as Madame Habib, a shady buyer of stolen goods. From the suspense novel by Mary Stewart. (Dir: James Neilson, 118 mins.)

Moon Wolf (Finland-West Germany, 1959)** Carl Mohner, Ann Savo. Mildly interesting tale of a savage wolf captured in Alaska and trained to be used in space research. Dubbed in English. (Dir: Martin Nosseck, George Freedland, 85 mins.)

Moon Zero Two (Great Britain, 1969)** James Olson, Catherina Von Schell. Ordinary sci-fi yarn made on a restricted budget. The Moon is now a colonized community and spaceman Olson is transporting a mammoth sapphire to the Moon, but the bad guys have other plans. (Dir: Roy Ward Baker, 100 mins.)

Moonfleet (1955)** Stewart Granger, Viveca Lindfors, Joan Greenwood, George Sanders. A tale of smugglers and blackguards in 18th-century England. Granger plays the dashing adventurer Jeremy Fox, who's always flirting with danger. Despite the good cast, the film is disappointing but it should appeal to adventure fans. (Dir: Fritz Lang, 89 mins.)

Moonlighter, The (1953)½ Barbara Stanwyck, Fred MacMurray. (Dir: Roy Rowland, 77 mins.)

Moonraker, The (Great Britain, 1957)** George Baker, Sylvia Syms, Marius Goring. High adventure and court intrigues set in 17th-century England. Mildly entertaining for swashbuckling fans. Good British cast go through the paces. (Dir: David MacDonald, 82 mins.)

Moonraker (Great Britain, 1979)*** Roger Moore, Lois Chiles, Richard Kiel. The 11th James Bond film. With the help of luscious CIA agent Holly Goodhead (Chiles), Bond (pallidly played by Moore) must stop a madman from destroying the human race and starting over with his own eugenic breed. The film opens with a free-fall fight where Bond and Jaws (Kiel) battle for one parachute, and ends with massed laser gun battle aboard a space station. (Dir: Lewis Gilbert, 126 mins.)

Moonrise (1948)*** Dane Clark, Gail Russell, Ethel Barrymore, Allyn Joslyn, Rex Ingram, Henry (Harry) Morgan, Lloyd Bridges. This was a middling-budgeted Republic picture with a rich, expressionistic style not entirely typical of director Frank Borzage. With its shadows and tension-racked frames, it brings painful guilts to the surface. A young father (Clark) seeks to overcome his heritage of "bad blood" (his father was an executed killer). But he also becomes a murderer in a brawl and flees. (Dir: Frank Borzage, 90 mins.)

Moonrunners, The (1975)** James Mitchum, Waylon Jennings, Joan Blackman. Sour-mash action-comedy about a band of bootleggers, based on the real-life exploits of Jerry Rushing, a North Carolina celebrity who has since had quite an acting career of his own. This film is the basis for the popular TV dreck "The Dukes of Hazzard." (Dir: Gy Waldron, 102 mins.)

Moonshine County Express (1977)** William Conrad, Susan Howard. Moonshiners—Three sexy sisters—try to outrun the law and a big moonshiner who are after a valuable cache of prime drinking "likker." Conrad is a bullying villain, and Howard the brains of the sister act. Car chases take over when the script fails. (Dir: Gus Trikonis, 95 mins.)

Moonshine War, The (1970)**½ Alan Alda, Patrick McGoohan, Richard Widmark, Melodie Johnson. The repeal of Prohibition is only a few months away, so revenue agent McGoohan is interested in getting the 150 bottles of aged moonshine hidden on Alda's property. He's not above bringing in gangster Widmark to try some violence. There's a neat ending, but little

455

Moontide (1942)**½ Jean Gabin, Ida Lupino, Thomas Mitchell. Beautifully acted but generally boring mood drama. A dock worker in a California fishing village prevents a waitress from committing suicide and then falls in love with her. (Dir: Archie Mayo, 94 mins.)

Moonwalk One (1972)***½ A unique documentary record of the Apollo II flight and man's first lunar landing on July 20, 1969. Valuable historical record of the momentous scientific feat, extremely well produced by Francis Thompson. (Dir: Theo Kamecke, 96 mins.)

Moralist, The (Italy, 1959)** Vittorio De Sica, Alberto Sordi, Maria Perschy. A guardian of public morals turns out to be a scoundrel, scamp and swindler. Fair English-dubbed comedy never quite takes advantage of the good cast. (Dir: Giorgio Bianchi, 86 mins.)

Moran of the Lady Letty (1922)** Rudolph Valentino, Dorothy Dalton, Walter Long. Rudolph Valentino made one of his few ventures outside costume drama for this middling sea adventure. (Dir: George Melford, 71 mins.)

More (Luxembourg, 1969)** Mimsy Farmer, Klaus Grunberg, Heinz Engelman. Photographed entirely—and ravishingly—on the Spanish island of Ibiza. It's a kind of a "Days of Wine and Roses" about drug addiction, glamorizing mindless flower generation teenagers as they kill themselves with heroin. Some very perverse sexual numbers in this convincingly acted story, directed and coscripted by Barbet Schroeder. (115 mins.)

More American Graffiti (1979)** Candy Clark, Bo Hopkins, Ron Howard, Cindy Williams. Disappointing sequel, with four stories linked by a common theme of nostalgia and commemoration. (Dir: B. W. L. Norton, 111 mins.)

More Dead Than Alive (1968)*½ Clint Walker, Vincent Price, Anne Francis. (Dir: Robert Sparr, 99 mins.)

More Than a Miracle (Italy-France, 1967)**½ Sophia Loren, Omar Sharif, Dolores Del Rio. Sumptuous fairy tale with the beautiful Loren and the dashing Sharif managing to make the affair a diverting entertainment. The plot, or plots are too fantastic and involved to go into. Suffice it to say, Sophia is a gorgeous peasant girl who goes to any lengths to land her handsome prince. (Dir: Francesco Rosi, 105 mins.)

More Than a Secretary (1936)*** Jean Arthur, George Brent. Girl takes a job as secretary to the publisher of a health magazine, falls for him. Breezy, entertaining comedy. (Dir: Alfred E. Green, 77 mins.)

More Than Friends (MTV 1978)**½ Rob Reiner, Penny Marshall. In casting, producer Reiner gave himself the sympathetic role and cast his real-life wife, Marshall, in the female lead. His lovesick writer is

believable, and she gets an opportunity to play a full-blown character with more than funny one-liners. Presumably some of the material is autobiographical. (Dir: Jim Burrows, 104 mins.)

More the Merrier, The (1943)**** Jean Arthur, Joel McCrea, Charles Coburn. Director George Stevens concocted some brilliant set pieces in this classic comedy that takes place in housing-short WW II Washington. The courting scene on the stoop between McCrea and Arthur is justly famous, but of course the film is stolen by Coburn as the matchmaking Mr. Dingle, and it is a tribute to that fine actor that what might have been insufferable is irresistible. (Dir: George Stevens, 104 mins.)

More Wild Wild West (MTV 1980)**½ Robert Conrad, Ross Martin, Jonathan Winters. Winters plays the crazy professor vs. those TV WWW intelligence agents from the late '60s. Conrad and Martin return to their famous roles in a wild, slapstick adventure. (Dir: Burt Kennedy, 104 mins.)

Morgan (Great Britain, 1966)**** Vanessa Redgrave, David Warner, Robert Stephens. A daffy, dazzling bit of English black comedy with a stunning debut in a major role by Warner, who plays a delightfully mad painter trying to win back the affections of his ex-wife (the gorgeous Vanessa) in decidedly novel fashion. He doesn't succeed, but director Karel Reisz succeeds in keeping the laughs flowing, delivering pathos and truth along the way. (Dir: Karel Reisz, 97 mins.)

Morgan The Pirate (France-Italy, 1960)** Steve Reeves, with his clothes on plus a beard, plays the legendary buccaneer. Action fans will enjoy this action. (Dirs: Primo Zeglio and André de Toth, 95 mins.)

Morituri (1965)**½ Marlon Brando, Yul Brynner. Tangled tale of espionage in WW II aboard a German freighter bringing rubber from the Orient to Germany. Brando is a wealthy German pacifist working for the British and Brynner is the freighter's captain. (Dir: Bernhard Wicki, 123 mins.)

Moritz, Dear Moritz (1978)**½ A stepson of director Hank Bohm plays 15-year-old Moritz, who is troubled by bankrupt parents, tough teachers, a tormented grandmother, and an uncaring, hypocritical world. He fantasizes sadistic revenge fantasies and is tentatively redeemed by a nice blond girl and three tough musicians who become his friends. Strong youth film in semidocumentary style.

Morning After, The (1974)*** Dick Van Dyke, Lynn Carlin. Van Dyke may surprise you with his fine performance as a successful public relations writer who plunges ever deeper into the world of alcoholism at the expense of his wife, kids, and job. Anyone familiar with this dreaded disease will recognize the man's lying promises to quit and destructive acts. (Dir: Richard Heffron, 74 mins.)

Morning Glory (1933)***½ Katharine Hepburn, Douglas Fairbanks, Jr., Adolphe Menjou. Hepburn won her first Oscar in this portrayal of a young girl trying to make it as an actress in the big town. She's arrogant, unmanageable, ruthless; naturally, no one can resist her. Astringency is the main ingredient of the film's charm. (Dir: Lowell Sherman, 80 mins.)

Mortal Storm, The (1939)***½ Margaret Sullavan, James Stewart, Robert Young, Frank Morgan, Robert Stack, Maria Ouspenskaya. After their families are split between Nazis and anti-Nazis after Hitler's takeover in '33, Stewart and Sullavan try to escape from Germany. (Dir: Frank Borzage, 99 mins.)

Moscow Does Not Believe In Tears (1980)**½ Vera Alentova. Just how few people vote for the Foreign Film Oscar was highlighted when this upset *The Last Metro* and *Kagemusha* for the 1980 prize. The only thing this wholly conventional, old-fashioned work demonstrates is that the Russians are every bit as capable of indulging in emotional frauduleance as was heyday Hollywood. Critical dramatic moment is scant while concentration is on the most obvious and fabricated of conflicts. Though the film purports to show ordinary people and their feelings, it is so obviously synthetic and phony that only devotees of Joan Crawford could buy it. The film is also outlandishly long: It's really two films conjoined. Vera Alentov, the star, has genuine presence and poise, and director Vladimir Menshov (her husband) seems competent in the dull Soviet style, but this film is devoid of artistic weight or consequence.

Moses (Great Britain-Italy, 1975)*** Burt Lancaster, Anthony Quayle, Ingrid Thulin, Irene Papas. The script by Anthony Burgess provides a good mixture of epic spectacle and intimate narrative. Lancaster lends his usual steely presence to the role of the lawgiver, but Quayle's talent is wasted as Aaron, and the rest of the international cast are not given much of a chance to develop their characters. (Dir: Gianfranco De Bosio, 141 mins.)

Mosquito Squadron (Great Britain, 1969)** David McCallum, David Buck. McCallum heads RAF squadrons out to destroy a series of tunnels in France where the Nazis are building rockets. Complicating matters, McCallum is in love with the wife of a pilot held captive in the caves. Warmed-over treatment of some old clichés. (Dir: Boris Sagal, 90 mins.)

Moss Rose (1947)*** Ethel Barrymore, Peggy Cummins, Victor Mature, Vincent Price. Slow-moving but well-played and interesting Victorian mystery drama. Story of a blackmailing chorus girl and an aristocratic family involved in murder. (Dir: Gregory Ratoff, 82 mins.

Most Beautiful Woman In the World, The—See: **Beautiful But Dangerous**

Most Dangerous Game, The (1932)*** Joel McCrea, Leslie Banks, Fay Wray. Smashing yarn about a mad big-game hunter who lures men to his island where he can match wits with them as hunter and prey. Crude, but powerful. (Dirs: Ernest B. Schoedsack, Irving Pichel, 63 mins.)

Most Dangerous Man Alive (1961)* Ron Randell, Debra Paget, Elaine Stewart. (Dir: Allan Dwan, 82 mins.)

Most Wanted Man, The (France-Italy, 1953)*½ Zsa Zsa Gabor, David Opatoshu, Nicole Maurey, Fernandel. (Dir: Henri Verneuil, 85 mins.)

Most Wonderful Moment, The (Italy, 1955)**½ Marcello Mastroianni, Giovanna Ralli. A young doctor finds the way to love and peace of mind from the faith given him by a courageous girl. A realistic childbirth sequence is well handled, (Dir: Luciano Emmer, 94 mins.)

Motel Hell (1980)**½ Rory Calhoun, Nancy Parsons, Nina Axelrod. Calhoun is a kindly old farmer whose secret recipe for dried pork fritters includes cured human flesh. With an attractive cast of supporting victims. (Dir: Kevin Connor, 102 mins.)

Mother and Daughter—the Loving War (MTV 1980)**½ Tuesday Weld, Frances Sternhagen, Kathleen Beller. Weld is the whole show in this soap opera that takes a middle-class American woman from her high-school pregnancy to the time she becomes a grandmother. At 27 Weld plays a teenager more convincingly than she plays a 40-year-old. Harry Chapin's songs are monotonous. (Dir: Burt Brinckerhoff, 104 mins.)

Mother and the Whore, The (France, 1973)***½ Jean-Pierre Leaud, Bernadette Lafont, Françoise Lebrun. This emotionally draining but rewarding marathon was written and directed by Jean Eustache. A narcissistic young man is involved with a nurse and an older woman with whom he shares an apartment. The three wind up sharing the same bed in this maddening, perceptive, lyrical film which has an improvisatory quality about much of the writing. The last, lacerating scene with the three lead characters is shattering. B. & W. (215 mins.)

Mother Didn't Tell Me (1950)**½ Dorothy McGuire, William Lundigan. McGuire has a flair for comedy which she seldom gets a chance to display. However, this fast-paced comedy gives her the opportunity to really cut loose in the role of a young bachelorette with a psychosomatic cough. Naturally the doctor turns out to be an eligible, handsome bachelor. (Dir: Claude Binyon, 88 mins.)

Mother Is a Freshman (1949)** Loretta Young, Van Johnson, Rudy Vallee. Young widow joins daughter on campus and falls in love with English professor. Lightweight comedy, stretching one joke too far. (Dir: Lloyd Bacon, 81 mins.)

Mother, Jugs and Speed (1976)*½ Bill

Cosby, Raquel Welch, Harvey Keitel, Allen Garfield, Dick Butkus. (Dir: Peter Yates, 98 mins.)

Mother Kusters Goes to Heaven (West Germany, 1975)*** Birgitta Mira, Ingrid Caven, Armin Meier. A film redeemed by its melodrama and undercut by its satire. Mother Kusters (Mira) is thrust into the role of radical darling when her son goes berserk on the assembly line and is killed. With Caven as a craven nightclub entertainer. (Dir: Rainer Werner Fassbinder, 108 mins.)

Mother on the Quay (Japan, 1976)**½ Tamao Nakamura. Japanese sentimental hit about the love of a mother for her son. Facing hardship after the death of her husband, she considers killing herself and her young son, only to be dissuaded by an elderly gentleman. Years later their lives are happier until the son is sent with the army to Manchuria, and his mother must wait, year after year, for his return. (Dir: Komuri Kenjiro.)

Mother Wore Tights (1947)**½ Betty Grable, Dan Dailey, Connie Marshall. Gentle account of the life of a vaudeville team has some charm, if you haven't seen too many Fox '40s musicals lately. (Dir: Walter Lang, 107 mins.)

Mothra (Japan, 1961)** Franky Sakai. Giant monster threatens the earth. First-class trick work in this otherwise naive thriller. (Dirs: Inoshiro Honda, Lee Kresel, 99 mins.)

Mouchette (France, 1966)**** Nadine Nortier, Marie Cardinal, Paul Hebert. At times unbearably moving story of the last 24 hours in the life of a 14-year-old peasant girl, based on a novel by Georges Bernanos. Nonprofessional cast. (Dir: Robert Bresson.)

Moulin Rouge (Great Britain, 1952)***½ José Ferrer, Colette Marchand, Zsa Zsa Gabor, Eric Pohlman, Suzanne Flon, Christopher Lee. Biography of painter Henri Toulouse-Lautrec, whose physical deformity caused his despair in love, and who frequented the more notorious quarters of Paris. Colorful drama with flash, dash, and excellent performances. (Dir: John Huston, 119 mins.)

Mountain, The (1956)**½ Spencer Tracy, Robert Wagner, Claire Trevor, E. G. Marshall, Anna Kashfi. Two brothers climb an Alpine peak to reach the wreckage of a crashed airliner. Tracy is always good to watch. (Dir: Edward Dmytryk, 105 mins.)

Mountain Man (1977)**½ Denver Pyle, Ken Berry, Cheryl Miller. History and nature are the stars of this family film about a man who moves to the Yosemite Valley in the 1860s and wages an almost single-handed battle of conservation against the lumber czars. Pyle is perfectly cast as the hero who takes his cause all the way to President Lincoln's doorstep. (Dir: David O'Malley, 104 mins.)

Mountain Men, The (1980)*** Charlton Heston, Brian Keith, Victoria Racimo. Boisterous adventure film about a couple of aging trappers in the Wyoming forests. The humor never slips into cuteness, and the brutality of the violence (and the sex) is never hedged. Director Richard Lang conveys enough of the story's epic dimension. (102 mins.)

Mountain Road, The (1960)** James Stewart, Glenn Corbett, Lisa Lu. Drab war drama of personal problems and stopping the enemy in China. Beneath the talents of Stewart and a good cast. (Dir: Daniel Mann, 102 mins.)

Mourning Becomes Electra (1947)*** Rosalind Russell, Leo Genn, Raymond Massey, Kirk Douglas. Eugene O'Neill's tale of hatred and conflict in a New England family in Civil War days. Long, powerful drama. (Dir: Dudley Nichols, 105 mins., TV version; orginal running time 173 mins.)

Mouse on the Moon, The (Great Britain, 1963)**½ Margaret Rutherford, Ron Moody, David Kossoff. Sequel to the hilarious "The Mouse That Roared," again based on a novel by Leonard Wibberly. This spoof of the race to space falls short of the rapid-fire satire of the first film. Rutherford is amusing as the graceless yet grand duchess, and Kossoff repeats his captivating scientist role, here putting some explosive wine to imaginative use. (Dir: Richard Lester, 85 mins.)

Mouse That Roared, The (Great Britain, 1959)***½ Peter Sellers, Jean Seberg, Leo McKern. Satire on the idiocies of foreign policy. The minuscule Grand Duchy of Fenwick declares war on the United States in order to lose and then receive foreign aid. Sellers plays three roles, including the grand duchess. (Dir: Jack Arnold, 83 mins.)

Mousey (MTV 1974)** Kirk Douglas, Jean Seberg, John Vernon. Douglas is a timid biology teacher in Canada who is driven to thoughts of murder by his callous wife (Seberg). It's complicated and not very interesting; there are many corpses before the fade-out, and Douglas' thirst for revenge remains unquenched. He should have waited for a decent script. (Dir: Daniel Petrie, 74 mins.)

Move Over, Darling (1963)** Doris Day, James Garner, Polly Bergen, Chuck Connors. Returning from an airplane crash five years before, a wife discovers her husband about to remarry. Remake of "My Favorite Wife" somehow manages to drain all the fun from the situation, becomes a plodding, strained comedy. (Dir: Michael Gordon, 103 mins.)

Movie Maker, The (MTV 1967)**½ Rod Steiger, Robert Culp, Sally Kellerman. Battle for control of a film studio; Steiger, the last of the bigtime film moguls, takes on Culp, a young company man. Good acting highlights the Rod Serling script. (Dir: Josef Leytes, 91 mins.)

Movie Movie (1978)**** George C. Scott,

Barry Bostwick, Harry Hamlin, Barbara Harris. Successful parody for a change, thanks to the directorial presence of Stanley Donen. A double feature, with actors, lines, plot twists, sets, and shots repeated in both films—a fight picture and a backstage musical. Bostwick and Hamlin are wonderful in juicy roles. Funny, affectionate screenplay by Larry Gelbart and Sheldon Keller. (106 mins.)

Movie Murderer, The (MTV 1970)**½ Arthur Kennedy, Warren Oates, Tom Selleck. Routine but interesting-in-spots feature. Kennedy is very good as an aging insurance company investigator who goes out on a limb to prove that a series of fires involving the destruction of movie films are related. Oates, as a hired arsonist, supplies the film's most interesting sequences as he goes about his business of setting blazes which look like accidents. (Dir: Boris Sagal, 99 mins.)

Mrs. Brown, You've Got a Lovely Daughter (Great Britain, 1968)** Stanley Holloway, Mona Washbourne. Herman's Hermits inherit a dog and try to make a racer of him. Inoffensive and mild. (Dir: Saul Swimmer, 95 mins.)

Mrs. Columbo (MTV 1979)**½ Kate Mulgrew. Peter Falk does not appear as TV's shambling, hang-dog detective Columbo; instead, you'll see his wife, a contrasting personality. Young, vibrant, round-cheeked Mulgrew from Iowa plays Mrs. Columbo, a chic housewife, a mom, and a newspaper stringer, on the move at a fast clip after she overhears people planning a neighborhood murder. (Dir: Boris Sagal, 104 mins.)

Mrs. Mike (1949)*** Dick Powell, Evelyn Keyes. Girl undergoes the hardships of rough living when she marries a Mountie. Entertaining drama. From the popular young people's novel. (Dir: Louis King, 99 mins.)

Mrs. Miniver (1942)**** Greer Garson, Walter Pidgeon, Richard Ney, Dame May Whitty, Teresa Wright, Helmut Dantine. Winner of seven Academy Awards, this dramatic, yet simple story of the courage of the British people as WW II crept into their backyard is a film masterpiece. (Dir: William Wyler, 134 mins.)

Mrs. O'Malley and Mr. Malone (1950)**½ Marjorie Main, James Whitmore. Main, famous for her Ma Kettle characterization, plays a modified version of Ma in this comic murder mystery. The action takes place on a train and involves detectives, cached loot, and chases. Good fun. (Dir: Norman Taurog, 69 mins.)

Mrs. Parkington (1944)*** Greer Garson, Walter Pidgeon, Edward Arnold, Peter Lawford. Fictitious story of the lives of a multimillionaire and the poor girl he wed is well told although episodic and occasionally corny. (Dir: Tay Garnett, 124 mins.)

Mrs. Pollifax—Spy (1971)* Rosalind

Russell, Darren McGavin. (Dir: Leslie Martinson, 110 mins.)

Mrs. R: Death Among Friends—See: **Death Among Friends**

Mrs. R's Daughter (MTV 1979)** Cloris Leachman, Season Hubley. A determined mother battles to bring her daughter's rapist to trial in this version of a real-life story. Although Miss Leachman gives a convincing performance as the mother, the material is tiring. (Dir: Dan Curtis, 104 mins.)

Mrs. Sundance (MTV 1974)**½ Elizabeth Montgomery, Robert Foxworth, L. Q. Jones. Don't look for Robert Redford or Paul Newman in this sequel to "Butch Cassidy and the Sundance Kid"—not even in flashbacks. Sundance's widow, played by Miss Montgomery, has returned to the U.S. from South America, living a quiet life as a small-town teacher until word gets out that Sundance may be alive and waiting at his old hideout. (Dir: Marvin Chomsky, 78 mins.)

Mudhoney (1965)** Hal Hopper, Antoinette Cristiani, John Furlong. One of the small independent rural sexploitation features director Russ Meyer was making in the mid-'60s. Today the film seems circumspect in its pursuit of forbidden thrills. (92 mins.)

Mudlark, The (Great Britain, 1950)*** Irene Dunne, Alec Guinness, Andrew Ray, Finlay Currie, Anthony Steele, Wilfred Hyde-White. Interesting and charming story about a young orphan who manages to smuggle himself into Windsor Castle to meet Queen Victoria. Dunne, with a good makeup job, is quite good as the queen and Ray is perfect as the boy. Guinness as Disraeli has a few well-played scenes with Miss Dunne, plus a long speech that's an actor's dream. (Dir: Jean Negulesco, 99 mins.)

Mugger, The (1958)*½ Kent Smith, James Franciscus. (Dir: William Berke, 74 mins.)

Mulligan's Stew (MTV 1977)**½ Lawrence Pressman, Eliner Donahue, Johnny Whitaker, Alex Karras. Warm tale of a high-school coach and his wife and three kids who take on four more kids when the coach's sister and brother-in-law die in a plane crash. Good acting. (Dir: Noel Black, 72 mins.)

Mummy, The (1932)*** Boris Karloff, Zita Johann, David Manners, Bramwell Fletcher. The charmingly egregious Karloff, as an ancient Egyptian prince brought to life, attempts to take first-rate actress Johann as his mate. (Dir: Karl Freund, 72 mins.)

Mummy, The (Great Britain, 1959)** Christopher Lee, Peter Cushing. Lukewarm remake of the terrifying original with Boris Karloff. Plot concerns an archaeological dig where a mummy comes back to life to deal with the scientists disturbing its rest. (Dir: Terence Fisher, 86 mins.)

Mummy's Ghost, The (1944)** Lon Chaney,

John Carradine. The gauze-wrapped mummy of Prince Kharis is in America, searching for the reincarnation of his ancient love. OK shudder story in the series. (Dir: Reginald Le Borg, 60 mins.)

Mummy's Tomb, The (1942)*½ Lon Chaney, Dick Foran, Turhan Bey. (Dir: Harold Young, 61 mins.)

Munster, Go Home (1966)** Fred Gwynne, Yvonne DeCarlo, Al Lewis, Terry-Thomas. Herman Munster inherits a title, and the family go to England, where they're involved in plenty of creepy doings. Feature based on the TV show will please the fans, but the noninitiated will find it on the silly side. (Dir: Earl Bellamy, 96 mins.)

Munsters' Revenge, The (MTV 1981)*½ Fred Gwynne, Yvonne DeCarlo, Al Lewis, Sid Caesar. (Dir: Don Weis, 104 mins.)

Muppet Movie, The (1979)**** Jim Henson, Frank Oz, Charles Durning, Austin Pendleton. The celebrated TV puppets with many famous guest stars. Kermit the Frog, most appealing musical comedy leading man since Bing Crosby, heads for Hollywood and what he believes is stardom, meeting Miss Piggy along the way. A delight, and a triumph for wizard Muppeteer Jim Henson. (Dir: James Frawley, 98 mins.)

Murder (1930)***½ Herbert Marshall, Norah Baring. This early sound film directed by Alfred Hitchcock is the story of a stage actor (Marshall) who is determined to prove a young girl innocent of a murder that takes place in a theatrical troupe. (92 mins.)

Murder a la Mod (1968)**½ Jared Martin, Margo Norton, Jennifer Salt. A young filmmaker becomes involved in a brutal murder. Young director Brian De Palma, who also wrote and edited this offbeat try, creates some inventive sequences in this low-budget entry, even if the film as a whole is not completely successful. Filmed in New York. (80 mins.)

Murder Ahoy (Great Britain, 1964)*** Margaret Rutherford, Lionel Jeffries. Once again Miss Rutherford is magnificent as Agatha Christie's Miss Marple, the geriatric set's counterpart to James Bond. This time she's cast adrift with an unknown murderer on a British naval cadet training ship. (Dir: George Pollock, 93 mins.)

Murder at 45 RPM (France, 1960)** Danielle Darrieux, Georges Millot. Singing star and her husband are involved in a web of suspicion and muder. Fairish English-dubbed mystery builds up a lot of suspense to a weak letdown. (Dir: Étienne Perier, 99 mins.)

Murder at the Gallop (Great Britain, 1963)*** Margaret Rutherford, Robert Morley. Marvelous Miss Marple, Agatha Christie's 70-plus amateur sleuth brilliantly brought to life by Miss Rutherford, is at it again. She manages to solve a double murder and turn down a proposal of marriage in the bargain. The droll Robert

Morley is excellent. (Dir: George Pollock, 81 mins.)

Murder at the Mardi Gras (MTV 1978)** David Groh, Didi Conn, Barbi Benton, Harry Morgan. Film relies on location atmosphere rather than a good story. New Orleans's free-for-all Mardi Gras is the setting for this murder yarn. A young woman thinks she has witnessed a killing during the festivities. (Dir: Ken Annakin, 104 mins.)

Murder at the World Series (MTV 1977)** Bruce Boxleitner, Hugh O'Brian. Michael Parks, Lynda Day George. Janet Leigh. The Houston Astros are pitted against the Oakland A's at the Houston Astrodome. A young man, bent on revenge for not making the team in the tryouts, kidnaps a top player's wife—but he gets the wrong girl. Boxleitner is good as the demented kidnapper. (Dir: Andrew McLaglen, 106 mins.)

Murder by Contract (1958)**½ Vince Edwards, Philip Pine, Herschel Bernardi. Good low-budget film about a hired killer who painstakingly sets up his victim, a beautiful woman who is a government witness. Tense and interesting. Edwards is coldly arrogant as the hit man. (Dir: Irving Lerner, 81 mins.)

Murder by Death (1976)**** Alec Guinness, Peter Falk, Peter Seller, Maggie Smith, Nancy Walker. Entertaining parody of murder mysteries by master comedy-marksman Neil Simon. Five of the world's most legendary detectives (modeled on Sam Spade, Miss Marple, etc.) are invited to a weekend at an isolated country house to solve a murder at midnight. A triple-reverse, double-whammy ending will leave you gasping. (Dir: Robert Moore, 95 mins.)

Murder by Decree (Canada-Great Britain, 1979)*** Christopher Plummer, James Mason, Donald Sutherland, Genevieve Bujold, David Hemmings, John Gielgud. Sherlock Holmes mystery with Plummer as the supersleuth and Mason as Dr. Watson. These impeccable actors are the best Holmes and Watson ever in a superbly crafted mystery about Jack the Ripper. Not a dull moment, although it does get gory. (Dir: Bob Clark, 120 mins.)

Murder by Natural Causes (MTV 1979) ***½ Hal Holbrook, Katharine Ross, Barry Bostwick. Stylish mystery yarn. Holbrook brings a wonderful restraint to the film as a successful mentalist whose cool-headed wife Allison (Ross) is intricately plotting his death. Bostwick is all emotion as a young actor used by Ross to bolster her plan. Now you can tune in and watch them triple-cross one another. (Dir: Robert Day, 104 mins.)

Murder Can Hurt You (MTV 1980)*½ Victor Buono, John Byner, Tony Danza, Jamie Farr, Gavin McLeod. (Dir: Roger Duchowny, 99 mins.)

Murder, He Says (1945)*** Fred MacMurray, Marjorie Main, Helen Walker. Part brutal horror, part giddy farce. Frequent lapses of taste by director George Marshall contribute to the film's outlandish tone. Hillbilly feud, with insurance salesman MacMurray caught in the middle. Main does a psychotic variation on her Ma Kettle role. (91 mins.)

Murder in Music City (MTV 1979)*½ Sonny Buono, Lee Purcell, Lucille Benson. (Dir: Leo Penn, 104 mins.)

Murder in Peyton Place (MTV 1977)* Ed Nelson, Dorothy Malone, Christopher Connelly, Tim O'Connor. (Dir: Bruce Kessler, 104 mins.)

Murder in Reverse (Great Britain, 1945)*** William Hartnell, Dinah Sheridan, Petula Clark. A man sent to prison for murder gets out to find that the supposed victim is still alive. Very good drama with an unusual twist. (Dir: Montgomery Tully, 88 mins.)

Murder, Inc. (1960)*** Stuart Whitman, Mai Britt, Henry Morgan, Peter Falk. Relatively factual, unpleasant but fascinating story of a big crime syndicate, and how a young couple is caught in its web. Distinguished by a smashing portrayal by Falk of Abe Reles. Should please crime story fanciers. (Dirs: Burt Balaban, Stuart Rosenberg, 103 mins.)

Murder Most Foul (Great Britain, 1964)*** Margaret Rutherford, Ron Moody. The sight of Agatha Christie's engaging grande dame of detectives, Miss Marple, as played by Miss Rutherford, is cause for rejoicing. (Dir: George Pollock, 90 mins.)

Murder My Sweet (1944)**½ Dick Powell, Claire Trevor, Anne Shirley, Otto Kruger, Mike Mazurki. Powell, the sappiest of '30s tenors, became the most motheaten tough guy of the '40s. Humphrey Bogart's Powell hasn't Bogart's irony or force, but as Raymond Chandler's Philip Marlowe, he's droll and thus gets across the literary conception. (Dir: Edward Dmytryk, 95 mins.)

Murder on Approval (Great Britain, 1956)** Tom Conway, Delphi Lawrence. Average British crime "meller" dealing with the search for a rare stamp which leads to violence. (Dir: Bernard Knowles, 70 mins.)

Murder on Flight 502 (MTV 1975)**½ Robert Stack, Hugh O'Brian, Fernando Lamas, Walter Pidgeon, Polly Bergen. Although airplane crisis yarns may be formula drama, they usually work, and this one turns out to be pretty good. A 747 from New York to London has reached the "point of no return" when a letter is discovered that indicates a potential murderer is aboard. Subplots crop up without interfering with the suspense. (Dir: George McCowan, 98 mins.)

Murder on the Orient Express (Great Britain, 1974)**** Albert Finney, Lauren Bacall, Martin Balsam, Ingrid Bergman, Jacqueline Bisset, Sean Connery, John Gielgud, Wendy Hiller, Anthony Perkins, Vanessa Redgrave, Richard Widmark, Michael York. A terrific mystery for everyone, especially Agatha Christie fans.

Set in '34, the complex plot involves a train full of exotic people traveling from Istanbul to Calais. While they are snowbound, one of the passengers is murdered. Fortunately, Hercule Poirot (Finney) is on the train. Soon it turns out that everyone aboard has something to hide, including the victim. (Dir: Sidney Lumet, 127 mins.)

Murder Once Removed (MTV 1971)** John Forsythe, Richard Kiley, Barbara Bain, Joseph Campanella. Bain is the wealthy patient of handsome Dr. Forsythe, who falls for her and considers murdering her husband as a last resort. (Dir: Charles Dubin, 78 mins.)

Murder or Mercy (MTV 1974)**½ Melvyn Douglas, Bradford Dillman, Denver Pyle. This drama about a father-and-son law firm has two things going for it—a good story and that stalwart actor Douglas, playing a doctor accused of administering a lethal dose of morphine to his wife, who is dying of cancer. Good courtroom drama. (Dir: Harvey Hart, 74 mins.)

Murder Party (West Germany, 1961)**½ Magali Noel, Harry Meyen. (Dir: Helmut Ashley, 79 mins.)

Murder Reported (Great Britain, 1957)* Paul Carpenter, Melissa Stribling. (Dir: Charles Saunders, 58 mins.)

Murder She Said (Great Britain, 1961)*** Margaret Rutherford, James Robertson-Justice, Arthur Kennedy. Cheerily preposterous Rutherford embodies Agatha Christie's matronly, home-style detective, Miss Jane Marple. Marple, as adroit and appealing as ever, poses as a housemaid in an estate full of nefarious goings-on. (Dir: George Pollock, 87 mins.)

Murder That Wouldn't Die, The (MTV 1980)* William Conrad, Marj Dusay, Robin Mattson. The fat man, Conrad, is back sleuthing again as Bill Battles, retired L.A. cop. He digs into his brother's murder in Hawaii while doubling as a special-team football coach. The imperturbable Conrad, island scenery, football players, and a dash of murder make a boring package. (Dir: Ron Satlof, 104 mins.)

Murder Will Out (Great Britain, 1952)***½ Valerie Hobson, James Robertson-Justice, Edward Underdown. The after-effects of the murder of a beautiful secretary involve an acid-tongued author, his wife, and a weak radio personality. Suspenseful mystery, intricately plotted, nicely done. (Dir: John Gilling, 83 mins.)

Murder Without Tears (1953)** Craig Stevens, Joyce Holden. A series of murders keeps detective Stevens on his toes in this mediocre crime movie. (Dir: William Beaudine, 64 mins.)

Murderer's Row (1966)**½ Dean Martin, Ann-Margret, Camilla Sparv, Karl Malden. Martin as Matt Helm handles his double-entendre lines well enough, but just doesn't cut it in the supergent class. Ann-Margret is miscast again—this time

461

she's a kidnapped scientist's daughter—and only Malden, overplaying the villian of the piece, comes through with an interesting performance. (Dir: Henry Levin, 108 mins.)

Murders in the Rue Morgue (1932)*½ Bela Lugosi, Sidney Fox. (Dir: Robert Florey, 62 mins.)

Murders in the Rue Morgue (1971)*** Jason Robards, Jr., Herbert Lom, Michael Dunn. Fourth film version transfers Poe's classic tale of murders to a Paris theater at the turn of the century. The only clue is that all the victims were business associates of the theater owner (Robards). The police suspect Lom. Lively chiller filmed in Spain. (Dir: Gordon Hessler, 86 mins.)

Murdock's Gang (MTV 1973)** Alex Dreier, Janet Leigh. Premise is better than its realization. Revolves around a disbarred criminal attorney who decides to employ ex-cons to solve crimes. Dreier, as the attorney, operates out of an impressive office and dominates the proceedings. (Dir: Charles Dubin, 73 mins.)

Muriel (France-Italy, 1963)*** Delphine Seyrig, Jean-Pierre Kerien, Nita Klein. Complex and disturbing film directed by Alain Resnais, with a middle-aged woman trying to connect with her past by returning to her first lover. As intelligent as it is bleak. (115 mins.)

Murieta (Spain, 1965)** Jeffrey Hunter, Arthur Kennedy, Diana Lorys. About a legendary California bandit of the 1849 Gold Rush days Joaquin Murieta, and how anti-Mexican bigotry in the Old West forced him into a Robin Hood role. Bogs down under weight of its grim morality and uninspired performances. (Dir: George Sherman, 108 mins.)

Murmur of the Heart (France, 1971)**** Lea Massari, Daniel Gelin, Benoit Fereux. A suspense film: Will the young hero sleep with his mother or not? Delicate comedy of manners about growing up in the France of Dien Bien Phu days. The lifestyle of the upper-middle class is both satirized and loved. Massari's performance demonstrates that sex is something mysterious and wonderful. (Dir: Louis Malle, 118 mins.)

Murph the Surf (1975)* Robert Conrad, Don Stroud, Donna Mills, Luther Adler. Alternate titles: **Live a Little, Steal a Lot,** and **You Can't Steal Love.** (Dir: Marvin Chomsky, 101 mins.)

Murphy's War (Great Britain, 1971)**½ Peter O'Toole, Sian Phillips, Philippe Noiret. Complex ideological effort about a WW II Irishman who, after the massacre of the crew of his ship by a German U-boat, seeks revenge at all costs. O'Toole, as the sole survivor of the attack, packs a ferocious wallop into his performance. The photography is lush and the direction by Peter Yates adds flavor, yet the film tends to pull apart. (106 mins.)

Muscle Beach Party (1964)** Frankie Avalon, Annette Funicello, Buddy Hackett. Strictly for beach party fans. In addition to the musclemen and the bathing beauties there are many songs. The plot is incidental. (Dir: William Asher, 94 mins.)

Music for Millions (1944)**½ Margaret O'Brien, José Iturbi, June Allyson, Jimmy Durante. Lovers of sentimental corn will adore this tearjerker but others are warned to steer clear. Girl cellist who worries about fighting hubby, with June and Margaret the sob sisters working on your emotions. (Dir: Henry Koster, 117 mins.)

Music in Manhattan (1944)**½ Anne Shirley, Philip Terry, Dennis Day. Boy and girl are forced to pose as man and wife. Pleasant musical comedy. (Dir: John H. Auer, 80 mins.)

Music in My Heart (1940)*** Tony Martin, Rita Hayworth. Singer about to be deported falls for a girl about to enter into an unhappy marriage with a millionaire. Entertaining comedy with music. (Dir: Joseph Santley, 70 mins.)

Music Lovers, The (Great Britain, 1971)*** Richard Chamberlain, Glenda Jackson, Max Adrian. Flamboyant director Ken Russell mixes glorious visual images with nonsense, paying little attention to the historical facts about Russian composer Pëtr Ilich Tchaikovsky. Chamberlain plays the composer in this film with music. If you're turned on by smashed champagne glasses you'll adore this bio. (122 mins.)

Music Man, The (1962)**** Robert Preston, Shirley Jones, Buddy Hackett, Pert Kelton, Ronny Howard, Paul Ford, Hermione Gingold. The saga of Harold Hill, who arrives in River City, Iowa, to organize a boys' band and falls for Marian, the librarian, etc. The Meredith Willson musical hit, filmed with most of its gaiety intact, including Preston's smashing performance and well-whistled tunes. Fun for the whole family. (Dir: Morton Da Costa, 151 mins.)

Musketeers of the Sea (Italy, 1960)*½ Pier Angeli, Robert Alda, Aldo Ray. (Dir: Massimo Patrizi, 116 mins.)

Muss 'Em Up (1936)**½ Preston Foster, Margaret Callahan. Clever detective solves a kidnapping plot. Interesting mystery melodrama. (Dir: Charles Vidor, 68 mins.)

Mustang Country (1976)** Joel McCrea, Patrick Wayne, Nika Mina. McCrea's first major film in years is a disappointing western. Aging rancher and Indian lad (Mina) team up to capture a wild stallion in the Canadian Rockies. Producer-director-writer John Champion shot it in Banff. (79 mins.)

Mutations, The (Great Britain, 1973)½ Donald Pleasence, Tom Baker, Brad Harris, Julie Ege. (Dir: Jack Cardiff, 92 mins.)

Mutiny (1952)*** Mark Stevens, Angela Lansbury. Patriots attempt to run the British blockade and get gold bullion from

France during the War of 1812. Speedy maritime adventure maintains a no-nonsense attitude that helps the action. (Dir: Edward Dmytryk, 77 mins.)

Mutiny in Outer Space (1964)**½ William Leslie, Dolores Faith. Two astronauts return to a space station bearing a deadly fungus which, if brought back, would affect earth. Slightly better than the usual run of sci-fi adventures made on a low-budget; good effects. (Dir: Hugo Grimaldi, 81 mins.)

Mutiny on the Blackhawk (1939)*½ Richard Arlen, Andy Devine, Constance Moore. (Dir: Christy Cabanne, 66 mins.)

Mutiny on the Bounty (1935)**** Clark Gable, Charles Laughton, Franchot Tone. One of the great adventure movies of all time. Laughton's award-winning performance as the infamous Captain Bligh is worth canceling all plans, staying home to watch. Oscar for Best Picture. (Dir: Frank Lloyd, 135 mins.)

Mutiny on the Bounty (1962)*** Marlon Brando, Trevor Howard, Richard Harris. If sheer length and opulence justifies the term "block-buster," this movie remake of the famous Gable-Laughton epic of the midthirties qualifies. However, those who fondly recall its predecessor will find the comparisons unfavorable. Brando's curiously erratic portrayal of Fletcher Christian throws the film off-balance. Howard is excellent as Captain Bligh. The scenic effects are frequently magnificent. (Dirs: Lewis Milestone and Carol Reed, 179 mins.)

My Blood Runs Cold (1965)*½ Troy Donahue, Joey Heatherton, Barry Sullivan. (Dir: William Conrad, 104 mins.)

My Blue Heaven (1950)**½ Betty Grable, Dan Dailey, David Wayne. Fast moving musical with Grable and Dailey tapping and singing their way through. The silly plot, which serves as stage waits between numbers, concerns a show business team and their efforts to adopt a family. (Dir: Henry Koster, 95 mins.)

My Bodyguard (1979)**½ Chris Makepeace, Adam Baldwin, Ruth Gordon. Rather manipulative film in which a rich kid is bullied enough in a Chicago public high school to justify the gleeful sadism of climactic bullying-the-bullies scenes. With a sentimental buddy-buddy romance thrown in and a clutch of lovable eccentrics in the supporting cast. (Dir: Tony Bill, 97 mins.)

My Brilliant Career (Australia, 1979)**** Judy Davis, Sam Neill, Wendy Hughes. Autobiographical novel (circa 1900) of Miles Franklin (a woman's male nom de plume) has been transformed into a charming, perceptive, poignant tale about what it was like then for a young woman writer growing up in rural Australia. Davis is enormously accomplished and touching in the leading role. (Dir: Gilliam Armstrong, 100 mins.)

My Brother Talks to Horses (1946)**½ Butch Jenkins, Peter Lawford, Edward Arnold. Jenkins is adorable as the little chap who asks racehorses if they're going to win, but the charm of the film's basic theme is left at the post. (Dir: Fred Zinnemann, 93 mins.)

My Brother's Keeper (Great Britain, 1948)*** Jack Warner, George Cole. Two convicts escape from prison, and the elder shows the young lad that it pays to go straight. Well-done melodrama. (Dirs: Alfred Roome, and Roy Rich, 96 mins.)

My Cousin Rachel (1952)***½ Olivia de Havilland, Richard Burton, John Sutton, Ronald Squire. The stars are perfect in this fascinating suspense tale based on Daphne du Maurier's novel about a young man who sets out to prove that his cousin is a treacherous woman and ends up hopelessly in love with her. Low-key photography heightens the mood of this mysterious yarn set in 19th-century England. (Dir: Henry Koster, 98 mins.)

My Darling Clementine (1946)**** Henry Fonda, Linda Darnell, Victor Mature, Walter Brennan, Tim Holt, Ward Bond, Alan Mowbray. Western about the Earp-Clanton feud, which climaxed with the epic gunfight at the OK Corral. Stars Fonda as the elegant Earp and Mature as a surprisingly moving Holliday. (Dir: John Ford, 97 mins.)

My Darling Daughters' Anniversary (MTV 1973)**½ Robert Young, Ruth Hussey, Raymond Massey. Sequel to "All My Darling Daughters" in which Young, as a widower-judge, married off his four daughters on the same day. It's a year later and Young is planning his own nuptials to antique dealer Hussey, but the complications and obstacles pile up until they seem almost insurmountable. (Dir: Joseph Pevney, 73 mins.)

My Dear Secretary (1948)*** Laraine Day, Kirk Douglas, Keenan Wynn. A wolfish author meets a secretary who writes a best-seller. Cute comedy, with Wynn especially amusing. (Dir: Charles Martin, 94 mins.)

My Dearest Señorita (Spain, 1972)*** Jose Luis Lopez Vazquez. This black comedy from Franco Spain was Spain's Academy Award nominee for Best Foreign Film. Lopez Vazquez, a magnificent actor, plays a middle-aged spinster who suddenly discovers she is really a man, only to learn that being raised as a woman ill-equips a person to function in a man's world. (Dir: Jaime de Arminan.)

My Dream Is Yours (1949)*** Doris Day, Jack Carson, Lee Bowman, Adolphe Menjou, Eve Arden, Bugs Bunny. Underrated Warner Bros. musical cribs elements from Day's own career story. Director Michael Curtiz adds lots of sour ambience to the radio-themed rise-to-stardom saga. Color. (101 mins.)

My Fair Lady (1964)**** Rex Harrison, Audrey Hepburn, Stanley Holloway, Wilfrid Hyde White, Gladys Cooper, Jeremy Brett, Theodore Bikel. The fabulous Broadway musical makes an entertaining film with most of its magnificent charm intact. Harrison deserved the Oscar he won for his superb performance as Prof. Henry Higgins, the British gentleman who turns the cockney flower seller, Eliza Doolittle, into a gracious lady. Miss Hepburn shines in the second half. The whole cast is a joy, and the sets and costumes resplendent, but it's the lyrics of Alan Jay Lerner and the music of Frederick Loewe that make it all an unforgettable experience. (Dir: George Cukor, 170 mins.)

My Father's House (MTV 1975)** Cliff Robertson, Robert Preston. Muddled attempt at serious drama, bolstered by good performances. Robertson plays the 41-year-old successful businessman-husband-father who suffers a heart attack and does some heavy thinking about his own dad, via many flashbacks. Preston's dominating performance as Robertson's father adds greatly to the sequences about the past. (Dir: Alex Segal, 96 mins.)

My Favorite Blonde (1942)***½ Bob Hope, Madeleine Carroll, Gale Sondergaard, George Zucco. Luscious British spy, Madeleine, is forced to enlist the aid of frightened Bob in carrying out her mission and the result is a barrel of laughs. (Dir: Sidney Lanfield, 78 mins.)

My Favorite Brunette (1947)*** Bob Hope, Dorothy Lamour, Peter Lorre. Photographer Bob turns detective to help Dotty out of a jam, and there you have all the ingredients for another romp for Hope fans. (Dir: Elliott Nugent, 87 mins.)

My Favorite Spy (1942)**½ Kay Kyser, Ellen Drew, Jane Wyman. Bandleader is a flop as a soldier, but is pressed into espionage duty. Pleasant comedy with music. (Dir: Tay Garnett, 86 mins.)

My Favorite Spy (1951)*** Bob Hope, Hedy Lamarr, Francis L. Sullivan. Bob's a small-time burlesque performer who's a double for a spy, with the usual crossed identities. Typical Hope comedy, the sort of thing he does well; fast-paced, generally satisfying. (Dir: Norman Z. McLeod, 93 mins.)

My Favorite Wife (1940)***½ Cary Grant, Irene Dunne, Randolph Scott, Gail Patrick, Ann Shoemaker, Scotty Beckett. Unsuspecting widower Grant marries Patrick but wife no. 1 Dunne shows up for the honeymoon, having been rescued from an island where she was shipwrecked with hunk of man Scott. Writer-director Garson Kanin is clever, light, yet never lively. Remade as "Move Over, Darling." (88 mins.)

My Foolish Heart (1949)*** Susan Hayward, Dana Andrews, Kent Smith, Jesse Royce Landis, Lois Wheeler. Loosely based on one of J. D. Salinger's short stories, "Uncle Wiggily in Connecticut." Tale of a wartime romance between a lonely girl and a pilot. Miss Hayward is excellent, and Andrews plays it at the right level to complement her. Hayward was in her most smoldering period, and her performance has an emotional directness and frank sensuality that redeems the novelettish plot elements. (Dir: Mark Robson, 98 mins.)

My Forbidden Past (1951)** Robert Mitchum, Ava Gardner, Melvyn Douglas. Girl from the wrong part of town inherits a fortune and plans to break up the marriage of the man she loves. Uneven, not-too-good costume melodrama. (Dir: Robert Stevenson, 81 mins.)

My Friend Flicka (1943)*** Roddy McDowall, Preston Foster, Rita Johnson. Devoid of hokum, this story of a boy's love for an outlaw horse is no "Lassie" or "The Yearling" but it's still a beautiful story and among the better animal films. (Dir: Harold Schuster, 89 mins.)

My Friend Irma (1949)** Marie Wilson, Diana Lynn, Dean Martin, Jerry Lewis, John Lund. Based on the once popular radio series, this comedy concerns a girl dimwit whose boyfriend discovers a potential singing talent at an orange-juice stand, the resulting complications. First film for Martin & Lewis. The gags are obvious. (Dir: George Marshall, 103 mins.)

My Friend Irma Goes West (1950)** Marie Wilson, John Lund, Dean Martin, Jerry Lewis, Diana Lynn. Irma and company follow Dean and Jerry when they go to Hollywood to make their fortune. Comedy based on the radio show has some pretty low gags. For fans only. (Dir: Hal Walker, 90 mins.)

My Gal Sal (1942)*** Rita Hayworth, Victor Mature, Carole Landis. Gay '90s musical about a song writer's love for a musical star is a harmless frame for some entertaining oldtime music and production numbers. (Dir: Irving Cummings, 103 mins.)

My Geisha (1962)** Shirley MacLaine, Yves Montand, Edward G. Robinson, Bob Cummings. Lengthy comedy about an actress who is so adept at posing as a geisha girl that her husband, not recognizing her, signs her to play the role of "Madame Butterfly." Assuming one can swallow this premise, there are some beautifully photgraphed scenes of Japan. (Dir: Jack Cardiff, 120 mins.)

My Girl Tisa (1948)**½ Lilli Palmer, Sam Wanamaker. Immigrant girl works to bring her father to New York, and to help her boyfriend become a lawyer. Pleasant but leisurely costume comedy-drama. (Dir: Elliott Nugent, 95 mins.)

My Girlfriend's Wedding (1969)**½ Low-budget, experimental film "diary" of a young Englishwoman talking about her life, her loves, her child, and why, because she needs a visa, she's about to marry a willing anarchist. Interesting offbeat effort, written and directed by Jim McBride. B&W. (60 mins.)

My Heart Goes Crazy—See: **London Town**

My Husband Is Missing (MTV 1978)** Sally Struthers, Tony Musante. Struthers has a noncomedy role: her flyer-husband has been missing in action over Vietnam for six years, so she goes to North Vietnam to see if he's still alive. Accompanying her is a cynical Canadian newspaperman who falls in love with her. (Dir: Richard Michaels, 104 mins.)

My Kidnapper, My Love (MTV 1980)**½ James Stacy, Mickey Rooney, Glynnis O'Connor. Stacy, who lost an arm and a leg years ago in a traffic accident, returns to action as a New Orleans news vendor befriending a young, disturbed runaway (O'Connor). A lively, seamy piece, not like the current rash of heartwarming tales about the courageous handicapped. Stacy is all man with the lost girl and tough when it counts with bookmaker brother Rooney, who wants to kidnap and ditch the girl. (Dir: Sam Wanamaker, 104 mins.)

My Life to Live (France, 1962)*** Anna Karina, Saddy Rebbot, André Labartre. Director Jean-Luc Godard's examination of the life of a prostitute is also his exploration into the mysteries of his then-wife, Karina. Once considered radical and maddening, the film now seems almost quaint. Weakened by that inadvertent prudishness typical of French radicals. (85 mins.)

My Little Chickadee (1940)**½ Mae West, W. C. Fields, Joseph Calleia, Margaret Hamilton. Fields and West's only appearance together in a film is a classic among bad movies. West and Fields wrote their own dialogue, which helps. (Dir: Edward Cline, 83 mins.)

My Love Came Back (1940)*** Olivia de Havilland, Jeffrey Lynn, Jane Wyman. A lot of good music decorates this minor tale of a girl violinist who wants a husband, but if you like good music you should be able to tolerate the inoffensive plot. (Dir: Curtis Bernhardt, 85 mins.)

My Love Has Been Burning (Japan, 1949)*** Kinuyo Tanaka, Mitsuko Mito. The story is about the leader of the postwar feminist movement in Japan, Hidako Mageyama. From a provincial aristocratic family, she goes to Tokyo for a man who turns out to be a government spy. When she marries a man who is active in a democratic movement, she realizes that she is being co-opted and patronized, and leaves him to dedicate her life to women's rights. (Dir: Kenji Mizoguchi.)

My Lucky Star (1938)*** Sonja Henie, Richard Greene, Cesar Romero. Typical Henie vehicle finds her in college, ice skating in a department store, and just about everything else but it's good fun. (Dir: Roy Del Ruth, 84 mins.)

My Man and I (1952)**½ Shelley Winters, Ricardo Montalban, Claire Trevor, Wendell Corey. Mexican boy, a new citizen, has trouble with a stingy rancher and his wife. Uneven drama sometimes slips into second gear, occasionally comes up with a fine moment. OK performances. (Dir: William Wellman, 99 mins.)

My Man Godfrey (1936)***½ Carole Lombard, William Powell, Eugene Pallette, Mischa Auer, Gail Patrick, Alan Mowbray, Alice Brady. Lombard's most unforgettable screwball performance as the madcap heiress who finds gentleman-bum Powell on a garbage heap while on a scavenger hunt. He becomes her family's butler and brings a touch of the common man to the filthy rich. Marvellously funny, and the actors are marvelous too: Pallette is touching as the long-suffering paterfamilias; Mischa Auer a standout as a radical artist who does ape imitations; and William Powell is simply sublime in the title role. (Dir: Gregory La Cava, 90 mins.)

My Man Godfrey (1957)**½ June Allyson, David Niven. Disappointing remake of the sophisticated '30s comedy about a butler who competes for his mistress's romantic attentions. Niven is fine but Miss Allyson is miscast and can't carry off the more subtle comedy aspects of the script. (Dir: Henry Koster, 92 mins.)

My Michael (Israel, 1975)*** Oded Kotler, Bfrat Lavie, Moti Mizrachi. Understated, fragile, often sensitive drama loosely based on the novel by Amos Oz. Study of a boring marriage in Jerusalem in the '50s, as seen from the wife's point of view. (Dir: Dan Wolman, 90 mins.)

My Name Is Ivan—See: **Youngest Spy, The**

My Name Is Julia Ross (1945)*** Nina Foch, May Whitty, George Macready. Gothic thriller in which a family of eccentrics conspire to drive a young woman insane. (Dir: Joseph H. Lewis, 65 mins.)

My Name Is Nobody (Italy-France-West Germany, 1974)*** Henry Fonda, Terence Hill, Jean Martin. Interesting study of an aging gunfighter (Fonda) and the young, up-and-coming cowboy (Hill) he teams with for one last shoot-'em-up before retiring. Based on an idea by Sergio Leone. (Dir: Tonino Valerii, 115 mins.)

My Night at Maud's (France, 1969)**** Jean-Louis Trintignant, Françoise Fabian, Antoine Vitez, Christine Barrault. Marvelously witty and civilized comedy of manners. Maud, a divorced Protestant exquisitely acted by Fabian, invites a visiting Catholic engineer (Trintignant) to spend the night in her nonexistent spare room. Faultlessly written and directed by Eric Rohmer, this is one of the most beautifully realized films in years. B&W. (109 mins.)

My Old Man (MTV 1979)**½ Kristy McNichol, Warren Oates, Eileen Brennan. Racetrack stories seldom work on the big or little screen, but this expanded version of Ernest Hemingway short story "My Old Man" becomes a grand, sentimental backstretch yarn about a seedy trainer (Oates) and his watchful, horse-loving daughter (McNichol). Brennan adds warmth and fun as waitress Marie. Remake of "Under My Skin." (Dir: John Erman, 104 mins.)

My Outlaw Brother (1951)** Mickey Rooney, Robert Preston, Robert Stack, Wanda Hendrix. An eastern kid comes West and finds his brother to be the mysterious leader of an outlaw band. Rooney looks out of place in the saddle, but then so do the rest of the cast. (Dir: Elliott Nugent, 78 mins.)

My Pal Gus (1952)*** Richard Widmark, Joanne Dru, George Winslow. Fay and Michael Kanin have fashioned a warm-hearted comedy drama about a little boy from a divorced home. Little Winslow (with the very deep voice) will capture your heart as Gus. Dru plays the proprietress of a school to which Gus is sent and it's with her help that everything turns out for the best. (Dir: Robert Parrish, 83 mins.)

My Pal Wolf (1944)**½ Sharyn Moffett, Jill Esmond. Little girl deserted by her parents and cared for by a cruel governess attaches herself to a stray dog. Nicely done little drama, entertaining. (Dir: Alfred Werker, 76 mins.)

My Reputation (1946)**½ Barbara Stanwyck, George Brent, Lucile Watson, Eve Arden. Soap opera fans may like this story of a young widow who, in all innocence, dates an army officer and is victimized by gossip and almost loses her sons' love. (Dir: Curtis Bernhardt, 95 mins.)

My Seven Little Sins (France, 1956)** Maurice Chevalier, Paolo Stoppa. Harmless little comedy about an aging Casanova and his antics on the Riviera. For Chevalier fans only. (Dir: Jean Boyer, 98 mins.)

My Side of the Mountain (U.S.-Canada, 1969)*** Ted Eccles, Theodore Bikel. Nice film for children about a Canadian boy who leaves his family to live in the mountains alone. He meets a retired folksinger, played by Bikel, who helps him get adjusted and saves him when he is trapped during the winter. Beautiful nature photography makes this fine family fare. (Dir: James B. Clark, 100 mins.)

My Sister Eileen (1942)**½ Rosalind Russell, Janet Blair, Brian Aherne, George Tobias, Allyn Joslyn, Elizabeth Patterson, and a memorable June Havoc. The old warhorse of a comedy about two girls from Ohio who find love and zaniness in a Greenwich Village apartment. (96 mins.)

My Sister Eileen (1955)*** Janet Leigh, Jack Lemmon, Betty Garrett, Bob Fosse. Musical remake. Garrett, a great comedienne, was used too little in films. (Dir: Richard Quine, 108 mins.)

My Six Convicts (1952)***½ Millard Mitchell, Gilbert Roland, Marshall Thompson. Very funny film about prison life, unlike most such films. Mitchell is a standout in a great cast. Stanley Kramer produced. (Dir: Hugo Fregonese, 104 mins.)

My Six Lovers (1963)*½ Debbie Reynolds, Cliff Robertson, David Janssen. (Dir: Gower Champion, 101 mins.)

My Son John (1952)* Helen Hayes, Robert Walker, Van Heflin, Dean Jagger. (Dir: Leo McCarey, 122 mins.)

My Son, My Son (1940)*** Brian Aherne, Louis Hayward, Madeleine Carroll, Laraine Day. Good vintage drama of a young wastrel who proves his father's faith in him by dying a hero. (Dir: Charles Vidor, 117 mins.)

My Sweet Charlie (MTV 1970)***½ Patty Duke, Al Freeman, Jr. In a remote Louisiana resort area, closed up during the off-season, a young pregnant southern girl, thrown out by her father, takes refuge in a cottage. Her solitary wait for the arrival of her child is broken when a young black lawyer, also on the run, decides to hide out in the same house. Superbly played by Freeman and Duke. (Dir: Lamont Johnson, 97 mins.)

My Uncle (1958)**** Jacques Tati. In a memorable French comedy, Tati the inimitable runs afoul of the modern mechanized world in some inspired pantomime reminiscent of the silent comedy days. Lots of fun. (Dir: Jacques Tati, 110 mins.)

My Uncle from America—See: **Mon Oncle d'Amerique**

My Wife is a Panther (France, 1961)** Jean Richard, Jean Poiret. Young man finds plenty of complications when a panther takes a shine to him. Mild, silly comedy dubbed in English. (Dir: Raymond Bailly, 85 mins.)

My Wife's Best Friend (1952)**½ Anne Baxter, Macdonald Carey. Wife gets an inadvertent confession of philandering from her husband, and the upsets begin. Unimportant but cute romantic comedy. (Dir: Richard Sale, 87 mins.)

My Wild Irish Rose (1947)** Dennis Morgan, Arlene Dahl, George O'Brien. Horrible musical supposedly based on the life of composer Chauncey Olcott. Only redeeming feature is a nice score of standard Irish tunes. (Dir: David Butler, 101 mins.)

Myra Breckinridge (1970)½ Mae West, Raquel Welch, John Huston, Rex Reed, Farrah Fawcett. (Dir: Michael Sarne, 94 mins.)

Mysterians, The (Japan, 1959)** English-dubbed science fiction stuff about a race of intellects from outer space attempting to take over earth when their planet is destroyed. Dubbed dialogue is unintentionally funny, but the production is elaborate, often quite imaginative. (Dir: Inoshiro Honda, 85 mins.)

Mysterious Castles of Clay (1978)***½ This Academy Award-nominated feature documentary presents a vivid view of the insects living in and around that obligatory feature of the African scene, the termite mound. Alan Root produced. Well done of this genre. Narrated by Orson Welles. (90 mins.)

Mysterious Island, The (1929)*½ Lionel Barrymore, Jane Daly, Lloyd Hughes. MGM version of the Jules Verne novel, marred by addition of poorly staged dialogue sequences. Some interesting fantasy passages. (Dirs: Lucien Hubbard, Maurice Tourneur, Benjamin Christensen, 94 mins.)

Mysterious Island, The (Great Britain, 1961)*** Michael Craig, Michael Callan, Herbert Lom, Gary Merrill, Joan Greenwood. There's little of Jules Verne left in this lively adventure, where Craig and Merrill are Confederate escapees from a Yankee prison who sail in a balloon to the eponymous island where they fight some superb Ray Harryhausen creations with the assistance of Lom's Captain Nemo. Cy Endfield here makes perhaps the best of the juvenile fantasies of its period. (101 mins.)

Mysterious Lady, The (1928)**½ Greta Garbo, Conrad Nagel. Another Garbo femme fatale silent film. She's Tania, Russian spy, and the setting is Berlin, 1915, where she uses and then falls for an Austrian army officer. (Dir: Fred Niblo, 96 mins.)

Mysterious Magician, The (West Germany, 1965)*½ Joachim Berger, Heinz Drache. (Dir: Alfred Voher, 95 mins.)

Mystery in Mexico (1948)**½ William Lundigan, Jacqueline White, Ricardo Cortez. American investigators look into a jewel robbery and hijacking in Mexico. Well-made melodrama. (Dir: Robert Wise, 66 mins.)

Mystery of Edwin Drood, The (1935)*** Claude Rains, Heather Angel, Valerie Hobson. This is an adaptation of Charles Dickens's final—and uncompleted—novel. Concerns a choirmaster who leads a double life, giving choir lessons by day, smoking opium by night. Nicely played by Rains, and moderately interesting. (Dir: Stuart Walker, 87 mins.)

Mystery of Kaspar Hauser, The (West Germany, 1976)***½ Bruno S., Walter Ladengast, Brigitte Mira. Strangely sentimental story of a man who has been raised without ever leaving the confines of a small cell. The man-child's efforts to socialize himself are played as elementary social satire, which works well, thanks to director Werner Herzog's audacity in casting a genuine schizophrenic, identified only as "Bruno S.," in the central role. Story is based on a child who appeared in a German town in the 1820s. (110 mins.)

Mystery of Marie Roget (1942)**½ Maria Montez, Patric Knowles, John Litel. Crisp detective thriller, from the short story by Edgar Allan Poe. Medical examiner Paul Dupin tries to find out why a famous actress disappeared from home. (Dir: Phil Rosen, 60 mins.)

Mystery of the Black Jungle—See: Black Devils of Kali

Mystery of the Wax Museum (1933)*** Lionel Atwill, Fay Wray, Glenda Farrell. Historic color-talkie suspense tale about a mad wax sculptor, whose London museum burns down leaving his fingers crippled, which prompts him to find an alternative sculpting method in New York. Disappearing bodies lead to the villian's unmasking. Remade as "House of Wax." (Dir: Michael Curtiz, 77 mins.)

Mystery Street (1950)*** Ricardo Montalban, Sally Forrest, Jan Sterling. Neat mystery about police procedure in tracking down a killer in Boston. Emphasis on police lab work, absorbingly done, flavorsome location scenes, good acting. (Dir: John Sturges, 93 mins.)

Mystery Submarine (1950)* Macdonald Carey, Marta Toren, Robert Douglas. A real stinker. (Dir: Douglas Sirk, 78 mins.)

Naked Africa (1957)**½ Documentary of tribal life in Africa narrated by Quentin Reynolds is interesting fare for travel buffs, should hold the attention of others as well. (Dir: Cedric Worth, 70 mins.)

Naked Alibi (1954)** Sterling Hayden, Gloria Grahame. Fast moving routine crime meller. Sterling Hayden plays an ex-cop who doggedly tracks down a murder suspect. The supporting cast needs a few alibis. (Dir: Jerry Hopper, 86 mins.)

Naked and the Dead, The ((1958)** Aldo Ray, Cliff Robertson, Raymond Massey, Joey Bishop, Lili St. Cyr. Story of combat in the Pacific, and the war of resentment between officers and men, taken from Norman Mailer's best-selling novel. A botched job, unsteadily written and directed, not too well acted, it often becomes a parody of all war dramas. (Dir: Raoul Walsh, 131 mins.)

Naked Brigade, The (U.S.-Greece, 1965)*½ Shirley Eaton, Ken Scott. (Dir: Maury Dexter, 191 mins.)

Naked City (1948)*** Barry Fitzgerald, Howard Duff. New York police investigate a girl's violent death. The "city" is the real star here; fine New York scenes in a conventional plot. Pilot for the TV series of the same name. (Dir: Jules Dassin, 96 mins.)

Naked Dawn, The (1955)***½ Arthur Kennedy, Betta St. John, Roy Engel. A tangled relationship develops between a bandit and the young couple who become his accomplices in a series of capers. Edgar G. Ulmer's knowing, precise direction triumphs over an often faltering screenplay. (82 mins.)

Naked Earth (Great Britain, 1958)** Richard Todd, Juliette Greco. Two lonely people are drawn together in the Africa of last century. Juliette's not naked; it's just the plot that gets exposed. (Dir: Vincent Sherman, 96 mins.)

Naked Edge, The (Great Britain, 1961)**½ Gary Cooper, Deborah Kerr. Absorbing if not altogether successful film adaptation of the suspense novel "First Train to Babylon" by Max Ehrlich. Cooper, in his last film, plays a middle-aged business man whose wife begins to suspect him of murder after the arrival of a strange letter. The supporting cast is fine, including such names as Eric Portman, Diane Cilento, Hermione Gingold, and Michael Wilding. (Dir: Michael Anderson, 100 mins.)

Naked Heart, The (France-Great Britain, 1950)* Michele Morgan, Kieron Moore. (Dir: Marc Allegret, 96 mins.)

Naked Hills, The (1956)** David Wayne, Marcia Henderson, James Barton, Keenan Wynn, Jim Backus. Underground story about the men who caught the gold fever during the gold rush days in California way back in the 1800's. James Barton takes top acting honors as a dreamer who just won't give up. (Dir: Josef Shaftel, 73 mins.)

Naked Jungle, The (1954)*** Charlton Heston, Eleanor Parker, William Conrad, Abraham Sofaer. Heston and wife Parker are besieged on their South American plantation by an invading army of red ants. Director Byron Haskin has managed enough plausibility and humor to make this into model nonsense. (95 mins.)

Naked Kiss, The (1964)***½ Constance Towers, Anthony Eisley, Virginia Grey. This brilliant pulp exercise directed by Samuel Fuller opens with a bald prostitute beating a man unconscious with a telephone. But when she tries to go straight, she only finds that respectable society hides vermin such as child molesters. (93 mins.)

Naked Maja, The (1959)** Ava Gardner, Anthony Franciosa. Elaborately mounted but intrinsically dull drama about the romance between Goya, the painter, and the Duchess of Alba. Miss Gardner is breath-takingly beautiful but the talky script and Franciosa's histronics become tedious. Filmed in Italy. (Dir: Henry Koster, 111 mins.)

Naked Prey, The (1966)*** Cornel Wilde. A striking adventure film which has some brutal scenes. A tale about man versus the jungle. Wilde plays an African safari guide who watches his party of three hunters brutally killed by a tribe who decide to give him a chance for survival. The jungle code allows Wilde, stripped of his clothing, weapons and food, to be hunted like a lion by the tribe's best hunters. Builds suspense. One of Wilde's best performances and he also directed this unusual entry with fine scenes filmed in Africa. (Dir: Cornel Wilde, 94 mins.)

Naked Runner, The Great Britain, 1967)* Frank Sinatra, Peter Vaughan, Derren Nesbitt, Nadia Gray. (Dir: Sidney J. Furie, 104 mins.)

Naked Spur, The (1953)***½ James Stewart, Robert Ryan, Janet Leigh. Stewart is a bounty hunter with obsession and Ryan is his quarry in director Anthony Mann's landmark psychological western, in which the outcroppings of rocks become neurotic extensions of the

character's inner tensions. One of the key films of the genre. (91 mins.)

Naked Street (1955)**½ Farley Granger, Anthony Quinn, Anne Bancroft. Underworld leader gets a cheap hoodlum free from a murder rap so the hood can marry his sister. Satisfactory crime drama, well acted. (Dir: Maxwell Shane, 84 mins.)

Naked Truth, The—See: **Your Past Is Showing**

Naked Under Leather (France-Great Britain, 1968)**½ Alain Delon, Marianne Faithfull, Roger Mutton, Marius Goring. Not half bad, but especially memorable for the opening sequence in which Faithfull, clad in a skintight leather jump suit (zipper in front) rides over the verdant countryside for long minutes, only to leap into the bedroom of a luxurious ranch house and utter the immortal opening line: "Skin me." (Dir: Jack Cardiff, 91 mins.)

Nakia (1974)** Robert Forster, Arthur Kennedy, Linda Evans. Forster strikes a heroic pose as an Indian deputy sheriff in this pilot film for the TV series. It combines action with a message about modern-day Indians. Although it is reasonably well written and well played, it still comes out old sombrero and totally familiar. Filmed on location in Albuquerque, N.M. (Dir: Leonard Horn, 74 mins.)

Name of the Game Is Kill! The (1968)* Jack Lord, Susan Strasberg, Collin Wilcox, T. C. Jones, Tisha Sterling. (Dir: Gunnar Hellstrom, 88 mins.)

Namu, the Killer Whale (1966)** Robert Lansing, Lee Meriwether. For the kiddies who find a killer whale adorable. This Ivan Tors production has a naturalist befriending a whale. Naturally, the fishermen in the vicinity object and cause trouble for both Namu and his master. (Dir: Laslo Benedek, 89 mins.)

Nana (1934)*** Anna Sten, Lionel Atwill, Phillips Holmes. Producer Samuel Goldwyn made a big play to launch Polish actress Sten as the new Garbo in the title role from Emile Zola's novel. Sten is good, and beautiful, but lacks Garbo's ability to instill excitement. Tale of a high-living whore's downfall is generally lucid and intelligent, if uninvolving. (Dir: Dorothy Arzner, 89 mins.)

Nancy Drew, Reporter (1939)**½ Bonita Granville, John Litel. In this one Nancy is putting in a month on a paper covering minor assignments but she manages to get her pretty nose on a murder and we're off again. The kids should enjoy this whole series. (Dir: William Clemens, 70 mins.)

Nancy Drew—Trouble Shooter (1939)*½ Bonita Granville, John Litel, Frankie Thomas. Typical, pretty bad entry in the series featuring Granville as the ingenue sleuth. Edward Stratemeyer created not only Nancy Drew but almost every popular children's adventures series: the Hardy Boys, Tom Swift, the Rover Boys, and the Bobbsey Twins, to name a few. (Dir: William Clemens, 69 mins.)

Nancy Goes to Rio (1950)**½ Jane Powell, Ann Sothern, Barry Sullivan. The plot gets in the way of this otherwise charmingly played musical. Jane Powell and Ann Sothern play daughter and mother respectively. They both toil in the theatre. The film is at its best when Jane and company are singing. (Dir: Robert Z. Leonard, 99 mins.)

Nanny, The (Great Britain, 1965)**½ Bette Davis, William Dix, Jill Bennett, Pamela Franklin. Bette Davis fans will enjoy still another of the star's growing gallery of sinister portraits in macabre yarns. This time out, Miss Davis is cast an an English nanny whose sense of reality is clouded due to some deep dark secret in her past. Her charge, a very disturbed young lad fresh out of a junior asylum and wonderfully well-acted by ten-year old William Dix, is wise to her, but he has trouble making anyone else believe him. Despite the built-in melodrama, Miss Davis's performance is quite restrained and has touches of credibility and pathos. (Dir: Seth Holt, 93 mins.)

Nanook of the North (1922)**** The great documentary about the life and daily hardships of an Eskimo family, still a superb piece of filmmaking. The silent version was modernized with music and narration in '39 and again in the '70's. (Dir: Robert Flaherty, 55 mins.)

Napoleon (France, 1927)**** Albert Dieudonné, Antonin Artaud, Abel Gance. One of the greatest films ever made. Abel Gance composed and directed this visually stunning biography. (Parts of the original have been lost). Starts with Napoleon as a young child at boarding school and follows his early career until his triumphal entry into Italy. Had a triumphant run at New York's Radio City Music Hall in '80, selling out the huge theater. (240 mins.)

Napoleon and Samantha (1972)**½ Michael Douglas, Will Geer, Jodie Foster, Johnny Whitaker, Ellen Corby. A pet lion, two good child actors—Foster and Whitaker—and TV names Douglas and Geer in a entertaining Disney item for kids. The kids want to keep the lion. They start out on an adventurous trek across the Oregon terrain to find their good friend Douglas. There are a few action scenes along the way, but Jodie Foster comes away with the lion's share of the good lines (pardon the pun). (Dir: Bernard McEveety, 91 mins.)

Napoleon II—L'Aiglon (France, 1961)** Jean Marais, Bernard Verley, Georges Marchal. Overstuffed historical drama about the efforts to prevent the son of Napoleon from fulfilling his destiny. Well produced but sluggish. Dubbed in English. (Dir: Claude Boissol, 105 mins.)

Narco Men, The (Spain-Italy, 1968)*½ Tom Tryon, Ana Castor. (Dir: Julio Coll, 95 mins.)

Narrow Margin, The (1952)*** Charles McGraw, Marie Windsor. Detective guards an important grand jury witness aboard a train. Suspenseful crime melodrama. (Dir: Richard Fleischer, 70 mins.)

Nashville (1975)**** Lily Tomlin, Shelley Duvall, Henry Gibson, Ronee Blakley, Karen Black, Geraldine Chaplin, Keenan Wynn, Keith Carradine. A stunning bold work of art commenting on the American dream, while focusing on Nashville, the dream center and cultural capital of country music. A work of audacity and prodigious talent by director Robert Altman. It's a collage, a series of stunning impressions and notes with an extraordinary screenplay by Joan Tewkesbury. The performances are remarkable, including impressive debuts from unknowns like Blakley. Tomlin, in her movie debut, proves that she is a tremendously gifted actress. Chosen as the best picture of the year by the New York Film Critics and the National Society of Film Critics. Won Academy Award nominations for Best Picture, Best Direction, and for support-ing performances by Gibson, Tomlin and Blakley. Won the Academy Award for best original song, "I'm Easy," by Keith Carradine. (159 mins.)

Nasty Habits (Great Britain-U.S., 1976)** Glenda Jackson, Sandy Dennis, Anne Meara, Geraldine Page, Anne Jackson. Weak Watergate comedy reset in a Philadelphia convent, with Jackson as Nixon, Dennis as John Dean, Meara as Ford, and Page and Jackson as Haldeman and Ehrlichman. Says Glenda, "You won't have Sister Alexandra to kick around any more." Ho ho. (Dir: Michael Lindsay-Hogg, 91 mins.)

Nasty Rabbit, The—See:**Spies A-Go-Go**

National Lampoon's Animal House (1978)***½ John Belushi, Tim Matheson, John Vernon. Belushi is the head slob of the Delta fraternity, which occupies a run-down shanty. These dregs of Faber College indulge in wild toga parties, pranks, and confrontations with the dean and the neighboring Omega house. Tasteless, but extremely funny. (Dir: John Landis, 109 mins.)

National Velvet (1944)***½ Mickey Rooney, Elizabeth Taylor, Donald Crisp, Ann Revere, Angela Landsbury, Reginald Owen. The whole family will love this enchanting story of a butcher's daughter and a bum kid who train a horse to win the Grand National. (Dir: Clarence Brown, 123 mins.)

Native Drums (Italy-France, 1955)* Marcello Mastroianni, Pedro Armendariz, Kerima, Charles Vanel. (Dir: Gian Gaspare Napolitane, 100 mins.)

Nativity, The (MTV 1978)**½ Madeline Stowe, John Shea, Jane Wyatt. The story of the Nativity, told from the vantage point of the courtship of Joseph (Shea) betrothed to Mary (Stowe), and the reaction he has to Mary's pregnancy and the virgin birth. Filmed in the desert terrain of Spain, the atmosphere of ancient times is convincing, as are the cast. (Dir: Bernard Kowalski, 104 mins.)

Natural Enemies (1979)* Hal Holbrook, Louise Fletcher, José Ferrer, Viveca Lindfors. (Dir: Jeff Kanew, 100 mins.)

Naughty But Nice (1939)**½ Ann Sheridan, Dick Powell, Ronald Reagan. Pleasant, diverting little musical which lampoons the popular music business and its relationship to the classics. Incidentally, this was near the beginning of Sheridan's "oomph" build-up and she does. (Dir: Ray Enright, 90 mins.)

Naughty Girl (France, 1957)** Brigitte Bardot, Mischa Auer. Silly comedy about a young miss and her involvement with a band of counterfeiters. Bardot is sexy, as usual. (Dir: Michel Boisrond, 77 mins.)

Naughty Marietta (1935)** Nelson Eddy, Jeanette MacDonald, Frank Morgan, Elsa Lanchester. Victor Herbert's operetta served as the excuse for the first pairing of Eddy and MacDonald, the most popular (and now the most notorious) musical team of the '30's. The score includes the parodist's favorite, "Ah, Sweet Mystery of Life," and other numbers too annoying to mention. (Dir: W. S. Van Dyke II, 80 mins.)

Naughty Martine (France, 1953)** Claude Dauphin, Dany Robin, Henri Vidal. Saucy French comedy about the adventures of a beautiful young girl and her pursuit of l'amour, toujours l'amour. Loses a great deal in the dubbing, so brush up on your French. (Dir: E. E. Reinert, 90 mins.)

Naughty Nineties, The (1945)** Bud Abbott & Lou Costello, Rita Johnson. Comics Abbott & Costello invade the old Southern world of showboats and card sharks on the Mississippi. Plenty of sight gags, even if the written jokes don't survive the trip downstream. (Dir: Jean Yarbrough, 76 mins.)

Navajo (1952)*** Documentary story of life among the Indians, as seen through the eyes of a small boy. Excellent; director Norman Foster, producer Hall Bartlett, cameraman Virgil Miller deserve plenty of credit for this warm, human drama. (Dir: Norman Foster, 71 mins.)

Navajo Joe (Italy-Spain, 1966)* Burt Reynolds, Aldo Sanbrell. (Dir: Sergio Corbucci, 89 mins.)

Navigator, The (1924)***½ Buster Keaton, Kathryn McGuire. A rich young couple, who have never had to look after themselves, are stranded on a deserted ocean liner where the ordinary difficulties of life are magnified by the fact that all the amenities are intended not for one person but for a thousand. One of Keaton's most elaborate films, with the gags so rapid and tightly interwoven that it is often difficult to keep up with them. (Dir: Donald Crisp, 62 mins.)

Navy Blue and Gold ((1937)*** Robert Young, James Stewart, Lionel Barrymore. The old Annapolis story in the hands of a fine cast turns into an entertaining film. Stewart is exceptionally good in this one and began to display the charm which made him a star. (Dir: Sam Wood, 94 mins.)

Navy Blues (1941)*** Ann Sheridan, Martha Raye, Jack Oakie, Jack Haley. A lot of talented people, plenty of noise and a few good songs make this zany but not witty musical entertaining. A few surprises in the supporting cast, including Jackie Gleason in his film debut. (Dir: Lloyd Bacon, 108 mins.)

Navy Comes Through, The (1942)*** Pat O'Brien, George Murphy, Jane Wyatt. The merchant marine keeps the sea lanes open during WW II. Exciting melodrama. (Dir: A. Edward Sutherland, 82 mins.)

Navy vs. the Night Monsters, The (1966)** Mamie Van Doren, Bobby Van, Anthony Eisley. Now we know why Antarctica was uninhabited for so long—it's the man-eating plants with mobile roots. Sexy nurse and navy man stand between the revived vegetation and disaster. (Writer-Dir: Michael A. Hoey, 90 mins.)

Nea (A Young Emmanuelle) (France-West Germany, 1976)***½ Samy Frey, Ann Zacharias, Nelly Kaplan, Micheline Presle. The best sex comedy of its year. Zacharias plays an adolescent girl who writes a best-selling pornographic novel. Her collaboration with her editor (Frey) is remarkable, to say the least. Micheline is the model mother who walks through the woods with her daughter as she explains her lesbian affair. (Dir: Nelly Kaplan, 103 mins.)

Nebraskan, The (1953)** Phil Carey, Roberta Haynes. Routine Western about having Army Scout winning the trust of Indian War Chief of the Sioux tribe. Roberta Haynes, a good actress, deserves better, and so do you. (Dir: Fred F. Sears, 68 mins.)

Necromancy (1972)* Orson Welles, Pamela Franklin. (Dir: Bert I. Gordon, 82 mins.)

Ned Kelly (Great Britain, 1970)** Mick Jagger, Tony Richardson, Clarissa Kaye. As the Australian cowboy-turned-bandit, Jagger is only a snarl more convincing than Frank Sinatra's cowpoke in "Johnny Concho." (Dir: Tony Richardson, 100 mins.)

Ned McCobb's Daughter (1929)** Robert Armstrong, Carole Lombard, Irene Rich. A rumrunner (Armstrong) rescues his sister-in-law (Rich) from the consequences when her brother gets mixed up with murder and fast women—one of them a waitress (Lombard). Based on a play by Sidney Howard. (Dir: William J. Cowen, 67 mins.)

Negatives (Great Britain, 1968)*** Diane Cilento, Peter McEnery, Glenda Jackson. Macabre offbeat drama which is not everyone's cup of tea. It's a tale about a couple who thrive on charades for sexual stimulation (they usually play a famous wife-murderer and his victim). Enter a glamorous photographer (Diane Cilento) with an equally warped sense of bedroom play and the film goes off in mad, but interesting tangents. The three actors in the cast—Diane Cilento, Peter McEnery and Glenda Jackson—do very well. Promising directional debut by Peter Medak. (90 mins.)

Nela: The Story of a Painter* The filmmaker's materials are the most painfully personal imaginable—the paintings, diaries, and home movie footage of a talented daughter who died of leukemia at 22. The solemnity of the material compels reflection in the viewer of the sort we cannot think too often about—that our lives are short and days numbered, and that anything worth doing is worth working at now. Hans Conrad Fischer is the director and the father.

Nelson Affair, The (1973)**½ Glenda Jackson, Peter Finch, Michael Jayston, Anthony Quayle, Margaret Leighton, Dominic Guard. The performances of the two leads almost make up for the shortcomings of the pedestrian script about the scandalous love affair between Admiral Lord Nelson (Finch) and Lady Hamilton (Jackson). The narrative moves along at a nice pace, but the inherent melodrama of the piece tends to detract from the actors' fine turns. Talky screenplay by Terence Rattigan from his play "A Bequest to the Nation." Glenda Jackson is a superb actress and an accomplished belcher. (Dir: James Cellan Jones, 115 mins.)

Neon Ceiling, The (MTV 1971)**½ Gig Young, Lee Grant, Denise Nickerson try their best to make this a moving drama but the script often defeats the talented trio. In any case, there are enough dramatic ingredients here to keep viewers interested for the two hours—an adolescent awakening to the ways of the world; a philosophical, beer-drinking loner; and a neurotic woman running away from an unsatisfactory marriage. The neon ceiling of the title refers to the collection of neon signs which Gig Young has assembled on the ceiling of his ramshackle, roadside combination restaurant-gas station. Lee Grant won an Emmy for her performance. (Dir: Frank R. Pierson, 97 mins.)

Neptune Disaster, The (1973)* Ben Gazzara, Yvette Mimieux, Ernest Borgnine, Walter Pidgeon. (Dir: Daniel Petrie, 98 mins.)

Neptune's Daughter (1949)**½ Esther Williams, Ricardo Montalban, Red Skelton, Betty Garrett. Light and tuneful romantic comedy with Esther's swimming and Red Skelton's funny-man antics. Oscar-winning song (by Frank Loesser), "Baby, It's Cold Outside," is from this film. (Dir: Edward Buzzell, 93 mins.)

Nero and the Burning of Rome (Italy, 1953)** Gino Cervi, Steve Barclay, Milly Vitale. Story of the corrupt Roman Emperor whose degradation and degeneracy finally causes his overthrow. Cervi is good in the role, adding to what would otherwise be a typical English-dubbed historical spectacle. (Dir: Primo Zeglio, 97 mins.)

Nero Wolfe (MTV 1979)*** Thayer David, Anne Baxter, Brooke Adams, Tom Mason. David is perfectly cast as Rex Stout's stout, sophisticated sleuth, who manages to mix gourmet cooking with expert detective work. Mason makes a favorable impression as Wolfe's sidekick, Archie Goodwin. (Dir: Frank D. Gilroy, 104 mins.)

Network (1976)**** Faye Dunaway, William Holden, Peter Finch, Robert Duvall, Beatrice Straight. Paddy Chayefsky's searing, perceptive satire of television network news. About a network TV anchorman who's gone bananas, and the avaricious bastards in the executive suites who capitalize on his madness after initially firing him. Finch, playing the role of the maniacal newscaster; Oscars for Straight, as Holden's embittered wife; Dunaway, playing the ambitious program executive who only cares about ratings. (Dir: Sidney Lumet, 121 mins.)

Nevada (1944)**½ Robert Mitchum, Anne Jeffreys. Cowpoke stops crooks after mining claims. Fast moving, well made western. (Dir: Edward Killy, 62 mins.)

Nevada Smith (1966)**½ Steve McQueen, Karl Malden, Suzanne Pleshette, Brian Keith, Arthur Kennedy. The character who appeared in Harold Robbins' "The Carpetbaggers" (Nevada Smith) is given a film of his own. The tale of this half-breed rebel is episodic, but Steve McQueen makes him come alive and a fine supporting cast is helpful. It's primarily a tale of revenge in which Nevada tracks down the killers of his parents. (Dir: Henry Hathaway, 120 mins.)

Nevada Smith (1975)* Lorne Greene, Cliff Potts, Adam West. (Dir: Gordon Douglas, 72 mins.)

Never a Dull Moment (1950)**½ Irene Dunne, Fred MacMurray. New York songwriter marries a rancher, tries to get used to open-air life. Mildly amusing comedy. (Dir: George Marshall, 89 mins.)

Never a Dull Moment (1968)**½ Dick Van Dyke, Edward G. Robinson, Slim Pickens, Dorothy Provine. Enjoyable, often funny. Robinson is a mobster kingpin with a penchant for art and a plan to steal a precious painting. He has hired a professional killer to help him when along comes Van Dyke, an actor who has played gangster parts and is mistaken for the hit man. (Dir: Jerry Paris, 100 mins.)

Never Back Losers (Great Britain, 1961)** Jack Hedley, Jacqueline Ellis. Insurance investigator looks into case of a jockey injured in a car crash after taking out a large policy. Fair Edgar Wallace mystery. (Dir: Robert Tronson, 61 mins.)

Never Give a Sucker an Even Break (1941)***½ W. C. Fields, Gloria Jean, Margaret Dumont, Leon Errol. A Fields nightmare, as he relates a strange tale of romantic adventures in a mythical country to a skeptical movie producer. No use in describing it—plotless farce has some moments of Fields at his best, and a wild car chase at the end. (Dir: Edward Cline, 71 mins.)

Never Give an Inch (1971)*** Paul Newman, Michael Sarrazin, Henry Fonda, Lee Remick, Richard Jaeckel. Theatrically released under the title "Sometimes a Great Notion" (after Ken Kesey's novel), this saga about a logging family in Oregon has good acting and glorious scenery going for it. The Stampers—father Henry Fonda, and sons Paul Newman, Michael Sarrazin and Richard Jaeckel—are a tough group. They defy a local strike by most of the other loggers in the area, and pay dearly for their decision to keep their operation going. The performances are uniformly good. (Dir: Paul Newman, 108 mins.)

Never Let Go (Great Britain, 1960)** Peter Sellers, Richard Todd, Carol White, Elizabeth Sellers. Unpleasant melodrama about car thieves and their bout with the police. Sellars plays it straight and it's a bad job—one of his few film misadventures. (Dir: John Guillermin, 91 mins.)

Never Let Me Go (1953)**½ Clark Gable, Gene Tierney. The two attractive stars make this drama worthwhile. Gable plays an American newspaper correspondent who takes tremendous risks to smuggle his wife out of Communist Russia. There are some exciting scenes involving the actual escape toward the end of the film. (Dir: Delmer Daves, 94 mins.)

Never Love a Stranger (1958)** John Drew Barrymore, Lita Milan, Steve McQueen. Barrymore portrays a young man who chooses the "fast buck," "fast women" path to destruction in this drama based on Harold Robbins' best seller. If you got to go, Barrymore probably has the right idea, but the film is not much. (Dir: Robert Stevens, 91 mins.)

Never Mention Murder (Great Britain, 1964)** Maxine Audley, Dudley Foster. Surgeon discovers his wife loves another man, decides to eliminate him by bungling a cardiac operation. Ordinary crime drama whose main asset is its brevity. Based on an Edgar Wallace story. (Dir: John Nelson Burton, 56 mins.)

Never on Sunday (1960)**** Melina Mercouri, Jules Dassin. Miss Mercouri delighted the movie audiences of the world with her inimitable performance of a carefree *fille de joie* in this film. A tourist named Homer tries to "reform" her, but his attempt to play Pygmalion has its setbacks. Director Dassin made an unfortunate choice in casting himself in the role of Homer, but the magnificent Melina is the stellar attraction here, and she's luminous throughout. Wonderful Greek musical score. (Dir: Jules Dassin, 91 mins.)

N'er Put It in Writing (Great Britain,

1963)½ Pat Boone, Milo O'Shea, Fidelma Murphy. (Dir: Andrew L. Stone, 93 mins.)

Never Say Die (1939)**½ Bob Hope, Martha Raye. Bob tries but this is little more than juvenile slapstick about a hypochondriac millionaire who marries a Texas gal because he thinks he has but two weeks to live. (Dir: Elliott Nugent, 82 mins.)

Never Say Goodbye (1946)**½ Errol Flynn, Eleanor Parker. A few laughs in this familiar farce about a man trying to win back his ex-wife but too much of it is contrived and silly. (Dir: James V. Kern, 97 mins.)

Never Say Goodbye (1956)**½ Rock Hudson, Cornell Borchers, George Sanders. Satisfactory remake of a 1945 film, "This Love of Ours" which starred Merle Oberon in the role played by Cornell Borchers in this version. Story concerns a woman whose husband left her many years ago taking her only daughter with him and how they meet years later and try to pick up the pieces of their torn lives. (Dir: Jerry Hopper, 96 mins.)

Never So Few (1959)**½ Frank Sinatra, Gina Lollobrigida, Peter Lawford, Steve McQueen. Despite an all star cast, this turns out to be just another WW II adventure with heavy romantic overtones. Miss Lollobrigida is a vision and Steve McQueen comes off best among the male contingent. (Dir: John Sturges, 124 mins.)

Never Steal Anything Small (1959)**½ James Cagney, Shirley Jones, Roger Smith, Cara Williams. Cagney as a crooked labor leader who will stop at nothing to become boss of the waterfront. Unlikely blend of satire, song, slapstick never jells, although the cast works hard. (Dir: Charles Lederer, 94 mins.)

Never Take No for an Answer (Great Britain-Italy, 1951)*** Vittorio Manunta, Denis O'Dea. Small boy tries to take his sick donkey to the crypt of St. Francis, where he is sure the animal will recover. Charming Italian story has plenty of good touches, human interest. (Dirs: Maurice Cloche & Ralph Smart, 82 mins.)

Never Too Late (1965)*** Paul Ford, Maureen O'Sullivan, Connie Stevens, Jim Hutton. Broadway comedy hit about a middle-aged couple with a grown, married daughter who discover they are to become parents. Transferred to the screen with all the funny situations intact. However, it becomes labored before the end, even with a truly wonderful performance by blustering Paul Ford as the old man thinking of retiring, and then hit with the news that he's to be a father. Maureen O'Sullivan, who appeared on Broadway along with Ford, is just right as the wife, and Connie Stevens and Jim Hutton supply the young romance of the subplot. (Dir: Bud Yorkin, 104 mins.)

Never Wave at a Wac (1952)**½ Rosalind Russell, Paul Douglas, Marie Wilson. Society hostess doesn't realize what she's in for when she joins the Women's Army

Corps. Mildly amusing comedy, with a cast of seasoned laugh-getters helping it along. (Dir: Norman Z. McLeod, 87 mins.)

New Adventures of Heidi, The (MTV 1978)** Katy Kurtzman, Burl Ives, John Gavin. Musical based on Johanna Spyri's Heidi books, but with all new, contemporary material. There's no sweet sick little girl whose health is restored by her friendship with Heidi and a Swiss Alps diet of goat's milk and cheese. Instead, there's a spoiled rich runaway, whose mother is dead and whose father is too busy, who manages to find a friend and companion in Heidi. Kurtzman makes Heidi a lovely, sensitive little girl. Ten unmemorable songs. (Dir: Ralph Senensky, 104 mins.)

New Avengers: The Eagle's Nest (MTV 1976)**½ Patrick Macnee, Joanna Lumley, Gareth Hunt. Can John Steed's new cohorts, lovely Lumley and sturdy Hunt, ever replace Diana Rigg? They're up to their necks in intrigue as a murder investigation takes them to a barren island which houses a retreat for monks. (Dir: Desmond Davis, 104 mins.)

New Centurions, The (1972)**½ George C. Scott, Stacy Keach, Jane Alexander. Uneven police story, based on the novel by Sgt. Joseph Wambaugh, that falters despite a good acting turn by Scott as a veteran cop who winds up his years of duty and retires. Keach is the hot-shot new cop with new ideas and he gets involved in a series of plot developments that play like separate TV cop shows. The best moment comes as Scott wars with the idleness of retirement and finally commits suicide in a scene that has an air of nobility only Scott can bring to it. Patronizing tone doesn't help. (Dir: Richard Fleischer, 103 mins.)

New Daughters of Joshua Cabe, The (MTV 1976)* John McIntire, Jack Elam, Liberty Williams, Renne Jarrett, Lezlie Dalton. (Dir: Bruce Bilson, 72 mins.)

New Healers, The (MTV 1972)**½ Burgess Meredith, Leif Erickson. A pilot for a proposed series which isn't half bad. A trio of para-medics gravitates to a remote rural area which has one aging, ailing doctor. It takes a while for the populace to accept the new breed of "healers." Veteran actors Burgess Meredith and Leif Erickson shine in their supporting roles. (Dir: Bernard Kowalski, 54 mins.)

New Interns, The (1964)**½ Michael Callan, Barbara Eden, George Segal, Inger Stevens. Fairly interesting drama about hospitals and doctors. There are at least three major plots and as many subplots. Callan plays the wise-guy casanova who tries to interest nurse Barbara Eden in romance. (Dir: John Rich, 123 mins.)

New Kind of Love, A (1963)**½ Paul Newman, Joanne Woodward, Thelma Ritter, Eva Gabor, Maurice Chevalier. The first quarter of this romantic comedy is quite funny, with an amusing opening scene of a department store rush. After that, the plot and the laughs go downhill. Mildly enjoyable fluff about how reporter Paul Newman meets and chases fashion designer Joanne Woodward. (Dir: Melville Shavelson, 110 mins.)

New Land, The (Sweden, 1973)**** Liv Ullmann, Max von Sydow, Eddie Axberg. Superb sequel to deeply moving "The Emigrants"; they were originally intended to be shown together as one film. The saga of the Oskar family documents their hardships in carving a new life in the growing U.S. Their grim experiences range from a fruitless search for gold in the Southwest to their eventual settlement in Minnesota. Ullmann and von Sydow provide a timeless example of the efficacy of married love. A remarkable filmed essay on foreign emigration to America. (Dir: Jan Troell, 161 mins.)

New Leaf, A (1971)***½ Walter Matthau, Elaine May, James Coco, Jack Weston. A large credit is due Miss May, the writer-actor-director whose inventiveness keeps you smiling throughout. Matthau plays a sly snob who's bankrupt and looking for a rich woman to marry within six weeks. He finds Miss May, a rich botanist and one of the world's clumsiest ladies. Laughs and love ensue! May's direction is perfect, never slick, always warm and slightly askew. Incidentally, if you have a feeling that you've heard the musical score before, it's because you **have**. It's lifted from Paramount's '67 release, "Oh Dad, Poor Dad, Mamma's Hung You in the Closet and I'm Feelin' So Sad." (102 mins.)

New Maverick, The (MTV 1978)** James Garner, Charles Frank, Jack Kelly. Pilot which attempted to bring Ben, the latest member of the Maverick clan, back in a new TV series. Frank is appealing as Ben; on hand to introduce him is Garner's Brett, and he's still the whole show. Pace is leisurely, and there's more accent on characterization than on action. (Dir: Hy Averback, 104 mins.)

New Moon (1940)**½ Jeanette MacDonald, Nelson Eddy, Mary Boland. The Sigmund Romberg-Oscar Hammerstein score, as sung by Eddy and MacDonald, and laboring under the heavy touch of director Robert Z. Leonard. (105 mins.)

New, Original Wonder Woman, The (MTV 1975)½ Lynda Carter, Lyle Waggoner. (Dir: Leonard Horn, 72 mins.)

New Orleans (1947)*½ Arturo de Cordova, Dorothy Patrick, Louis Armstrong, Billie Holiday, Woody Herman. Dull story, good music. De Cordova and Patrick have a poor boy-rich girl thing. Holiday, dressed as a maid (God help us), sings "Do You Know What It Means to Miss New Orleans?" (Dir: Arthur Lubin, 89 mins.)

New World, A (Mexico, 1956)*½ Arturo Arias, Lorena Velasquez. (Dir: Rene Cardona, 88 mins.)

New Year's Evil (1980)* Kip Niven, Roz

Kelly, Chris Wallace. Music by Shadow. (Dir: Emmett Alston, 90 mins.)

New York Confidential (1955)**½ Broderick Crawford, Anne Bancroft, Richard Conte. Tense and exciting expose of the big crime syndicate working out of New York. Supposedly based on facts. Anne Bancroft took part in this before her Broadway successes. (Dir: Russell Rouse, 87 mins.)

New York, New York (1977)**½ Liza Minnelli, Robert De Niro, Lionel Stander, Barry Primus, Mary Kay Place. De Niro is an uninvolved, feckless jazz musician with little appeal, except in the eyes of Liza. A sadly arrogant failure, awash with brilliance and feeling and no sense of responsibility toward the audience. The entire film makes no emotional sense, which is especially unnerving since each individual scene does. (Dir: Martin Scorsese, 153 mins.)

New York Town (1941)**½ Fred MacMurray, Mary Martin, Robert Preston. Occasionally amusing comedy about a sidewalk photographer who befriends a homeless lass in the big city. (Dir: Charles Vidor, 94 mins.)

Newman's Law (1974)*½ George Peppard, Roger Robinson, Abe Vigoda. (Dir: Richard Heffron, 98 mins.)

Newsfront (Australia, 1978)***½ Bill Hunter, Wendy Hughes, Gerard Kennedy, Angela Punch. Intercuts history on film with personal history in a slick film about an Australian newsreel cameraman from '48 to '56. Hunter projects a stolid charisma new to the screen. Part B&W, part color. (Dir: Phillip Noyce, 110 mins.)

Next Man, The (1976)*½ Sean Connery, Cornelia Sharpe, Albert Paulsen. (Dir: Richard Sarafian, 108 mins.)

Next of Kin (Great Britain, 1942)***½ Nova Pilbeam, Mervyn Johns, Jack Hawkins. Showing the effects of loose information, how it can lead to enemy ears. Excellent wartime drama. (Dir: Thorold Dickinson, 85 mins.)

Next Stop, Greenwich Village (1976)***½ Lenny Baker, Shelley Winters, Ellen Greene, Mike Kellin, Christopher Walker. Affectionate, engaging, autobiographical Valentine directed and written by Paul Mazursky about his own growing up in New York's Greenwich Village circa 1953. Two unusually winning performances by newcomers Baker and Greene combine to make this film alternately farcical, rueful and wistful. It doesn't all work, but it's an often lovely portrait of the joys and defeats of an aspiring adolescent comedian in the Big Apple! (Dir: Paul Mazursky, 109 mins.)

Next Time We Love (1936)**½ James Stewart, Margaret Sullavan, Ray Milland. Wife gives up her singing job to accompany her husband on a foreign assignment. Fairly good romantic drama. (Dir: Edward H. Griffith, 87 mins.)

Next to No Time (Great Britain, 1958)** Kenneth More, Betsy Drake. Shy factory employee tries to put his plan of automation into practice. Uneven comedy has some clever moments but never quite makes the top. Well acted. (Dir: Henry Cornelius, 89 mins.)

Next Voice You Hear, The (1950)*** James Whitmore, Nancy Davis, Gary Gray. Over-sentimentalized, but nevertheless engrossing drama about a group of people who hear the voice of God on the radio and the effect it has on their lives. (Dir: William Wellman, 82 mins.)

Niagara (1953)**½ Marilyn Monroe, Joseph Cotten, Jean Peters. This film boasts two scenic marvels, Niagara Falls and M.M. in various states of undress. The drama is heavy handed and pretty obvious but La Monroe's undulations and attempt at portraying a faithless wife make it worthwhile. (Primarily for the male viewers.) (Dir: Henry Hathaway, 89 mins.)

Nicaragua: September 1978 (1978)**** An emotionally charged on-the-spot documentary of the Sandinista uprising, taking sides against the brutality of the Somoza regime. (Dir: Frank Diamond.)

Nice Little Bank That Should Be Robbed, A (1958)** Tom Ewell, Mickey Rooney, Dina Merrill. Two amateur crooks bungle an elaborately planned bank robbery. Comedy with a clever idea that doesn't live up to its promise. Just middling fair fun. (Dir: Henry Levin, 87 mins.)

Nichi-Ren (Japan)**½ Kinnosuke Yorozuya, Keiko Matsuzaka, Keinosuke Bayanam. Historical drama about the 13th-century Buddhist religious teacher. Noburo Nakamura directed and adapted a biographical novel by Matsutaro Kawaguchi. Medieval life is painstakingly rendered, as is the quasi-erotic relationship between the holy man (Yorozuya, a Kabuki actor) and his sister (Matsuzaka).

Nicholas and Alexandra (Great Britain, 1971)*** Michael Jayston, Janet Suzman, Laurence Olivier, Jack Hawkins, Tom Baker, Alexander Knox, John Wood. Huge sprawling, uneven, but often interesting historical film about the 14-year period leading up to the Russian Revolution. Film focuses on the royal couple, and there's some particularly good acting by Miss Suzman, whose performance earned her an Academy Award nomination. There are some ravishing costumes by Yvonne Blake and Antonio Castillo of the period, which deservedly did win the Academy Award. (Dir: Franklin J. Schaffner, 183 mins.)

Nicholas Nickleby (Great Britain, 1947)***½ Derek Bond, Cedric Hardwicke, Sally Ann Howes, Bernard Miles. Charles Dickens' classic of a boy who strives to protect himself and his family from an evil, miserly uncle is given a first-class treatment. The director's style is lumpy and dark; perhaps the film's brilliance and emotional power are due to the endless resonance and fascination of Dickens' story, here faithfully transferred. Scenes where young Nicholas attempts to earn a living as a wandering player are movingly and lovingly portrayed. (Dir: Alberto Cavalcanti, 95 mins.)

Nick Carter in Prague—See: **Dinner for Adele**

Nick Carter—Master Detective (1939)** Walter Pidgeon, Rita Johnson, Henry Hull. First American feature of Jacques Tourneur, who would later direct some fine horror films. Typical MGM B movie with Pidgeon as the obnoxious title hero tracking down an industrial spy. (60 mins.)

Nickel Ride, The (1975)***½ Jason Miller, Linda Haynes, Bo Hopkins. Director Robert Mulligan's study of a small-time hood (Jason Miller) suffering a crisis of conscience was hacked into incomprehensibility by 20th Century-Fox's executive in charge of philistinism. Enough of Mulligan's conception survives to create a resonant example of subjective cinema. (99 mins.)

Nickelodeon (1976)*** Ryan O'Neal, Burt Reynolds, Tatum O'Neal, Brian Keith, Stella Stevens, John Ritter, Jane Hitchcock. It was probably a career mistake for director Peter Bogdanovich to tackle such an expensive personal project, but sweet obliviousness is part of this film's considerable charm. The freewheeling adventures of early filmmaking are chronicled here. The closing sequence has genuine grandeur, and one can see the nobility of the slapstick conception even when it is not realized. A failure of the highest order. (121 mins.)

Nicky's World (MTV 1974)**½ Charles Cioffi, George Voskovec, Olympia Dukakis, Mark Shera. Often touching story about a New York Greek family determined to hang on to their storefront bakery despite pressures from a supermarket chain and the local banks to evict them. Fine performance by Shera as a teenager whose pluck and imagination save the day. (Dir: Paul Stanley, 78 mins.)

Night After Night (1932)** George Raft, Constance Cummings, Mae West. Speakeasy owner gets mixed up with high society. Relic of Prohibition still has some interest, largely due to Mae in her film debut. (Dir: Archie Mayo, 75 mins.)

Night Ambush (Great Britain, 1957)*** Dirk Bogarde, Marius Goring. British soldiers sneak into occupied Crete, capture a German general and make it to safety with him. Uneven but different war story has some moments. (Dir: Michael Powell, 93 mins.)

Night and Day (1946)**½ Cary Grant, Alexis Smith, Monty Woolley, Jane Wyman, Eve Arden. A life of Cole Porter, told without truth or wit. There are, however, a lot of songs, including Mary Martin singing "My Heart Belongs to Daddy." Grant also sings, with considerable talent. Directed way off the beam by Michael Curtiz. (128 mins.)

Night and the City (Great Britain,

1950)**** Richard Widmark, Gene Tierney, Hugh Marlowe, Googie Withers, Herbert Lom. Director Jules Dassin's pip of an expressionist thriller, filmed in a London artfully relit to resemble New York's Lower East Side. Widmark gives one of his most underrated performances, nervous and taut, as American lowlife (he is a wrestling promoter) on the lam. Withers and Lom turn in stylish portrayals as underworld figures. (95 mins.)

Night at the Opera, A (1935)**** The Marx Brothers, Kitty Carlisle, Allan Jones, Margaret Dumont. The Marx Brothers' funniest film, except for "Duck Soup." The stateroom scene is one of the greatest continuous laugh inducers ever. The love interest by Jones and Carlisle bores many, but Louis B. Mayer knew they would help the picture make money. (Dir: Sam Wood, 90 mins.)

Night Butterflies (Japan, 1957)**½ Machiko Kyo. An atmospheric character study of professional "hostesses" in the nighttime Tokyo of the Ginza's bars and cabarets. The film tackles a subject customarily treated with derision—the lower-class "madames" are considered pretenders to glamour—seriously, despite a satiric touch or two. (Dir: Kimisaburo Yoshimura.)

Night Call Nurses (1972)** Patricia T. Byrne, Alana Collins, Mittie Lawrence, Clint Kimbrough, Felton Perry, Stack Pierce. (Dir: Johnathan Kaplan, 85 mins.)

Night Caller, The (France-Italy, 1975)** Jean-Paul Belmondo, Charles Denner, Lea Massari. Clumsy French imitation of American crime films, which is badly dubbed to boot. Belmondo plays a police inspector tracking down a lunatic who calls up women on the telephone and then strangles them in person. Enlivened only by a chase across the rooftops of Paris. The producer should have bought Belmondo rubber-soled shoes and a better script. (Dir: Henri Verneuil, 91 mins.)

Night Chase (MTV 1970)**½ David Janssen. Yaphet Kotto. David Janssen is on the run again. He's a world-weary gent taking an all-night cab ride along the California coast after shooting his wife's lover, and he gives cabbie Yaphet Kotto an exasperating time. Kotto's appealing character counters the familiar, tired, defeatist type Janssen specializes in. Even though the trip is much too long, location footage at Del Mar race track, along coastal highways, and at the San Diego Zoo help hold your attention. (Dir: Jack Starret, 99 mins.)

Night Club Scandal (1937)**½ John Barrymore, Lynne Overman, Charles Bickford, Louise Campbell. Well-acted, entertaining little mystery. Not a whodunit but interesting as you know who's guilty and watch the police make the mistakes. (Dir: Ralph Murphy, 74 mins.)

Night Creature (1978)** Donald Pleasence, Nancy Kwan, Ross Hagen. Made in Thailand, with Pleasence as a Hemingwayesque writer, living on an island compound in southeast Asia, who become obsessed with a man-eating black leopard. The film fails to deliver on any of its promised cheap thrills. (Dir: Lee Madden, 83 mins.)

Night Creatures (1962)**½ Peter Cushing, Yvonne Romain, Oliver Reed. Village vicar is in reality the head of a notorious smuggling ring. Lively, suspenseful costume thriller, some spooky scenes, some suspense, some action, all blended together ably. (Dir: Peter Graham Scott, 81 mins.)

Night Cries (MTV 1978)** Susan Saint James, William Conrad, Michael Parks. Saint James stars in this familiar meller about a woman who has lost her child at birth but keeps dreaming he's alive somewhere. A dream therapist (Conrad) tries to convince her she's wrong, and her husband (Parks) is long-suffering, but Susan won't let up. Her probing leads to a startling denouement. (Dir: Richard Lang, 104 mins.)

Night Digger, The (Great Britain, 1971)**½ Patricia Neal, Pamela Brown, Nicholas Clay. Pseudo-psychopathic horror film that is really an understated character study. English spinster Neal is dominated by her frightening blind mother (Brown), who adopted her. Into this tense relationship pops Clay, a young man with intense eyes who is accepted by the mother as a housekeeper. Based on the novel "Nest in a Falling Tree" by Joy Cowley, the screenplay was written for the then partly paralyzed Neal (who had suffered a near-fatal stroke) by her husband, Roald Dahl. (Dir: Alastair Reid, 100 mins.)

Night Drum (Japan, 1958)**½ Director Tadashi Imai chose a successful direct narrative approach for this somber tale set in feudal Japan—about a returning warrior who discovers his wife has committed adultery during his absence. According to the prescribed code, she must be killed to save his honor. (Dir: Tadashi Imai, 95 mins.)

Night Editor (1946)*** William Gargan, Janis Carter. Crooked cop gets involved with luscious but mean dame. Well scripted, well acted B melodrama. (Dir: Henry Levin, 68 mins.)

Night Encounter—See: **Double Agents, The**

Night Fighters (1960)**½ Robert Mitchum, Anne Heywood, Dan O'Herlihy, Richard Harris. The Irish rebellion is the setting of this adventure yarn which has a fine cast of players headed by Robert Mitchum. On-location photography is also an asset. (Dir: Tay Garnett, 85 mins.)

Night Flight From Moscow (France-Italy-West Germany, 1973)** Yul Brynner, Henry Fonda, Dirk Bogarde, Virna Lisi, Philippe Noiret. An international cast of capable actors are bogged down in a plot-heavy espionage tale about double agents and their intricate operations in Western Europe. Brynner has the biggest part as a Soviet KGB official who gives up names of his fellow agents to the CIA and British Intelligence. (Dir: Henri Verneuil, 121 mins.)

Night Freight (1955)**½ Forrest Tucker, Barbara Britton. Railroad operator battles ruthless trucking outfit. Action melodrama manages to whip up some excitement. (Dir: Jean Yarbrough, 79 mins.)

Night Gallery (MTV 1969)**½ Joan Crawford, Richard Kiley, Roddy McDowall, Barry Sullivan, Ossie Davis. Strictly for those who found Rod Serling's "The Twilight Zone" TV series to their liking. This feature is divided into three mystery tales bridged by a trio of portraits. None is really terribly original but a willing audience will probably stick with the suspenseful dramas of the macabre. Joan Crawford tears at the scenery in the second story about a wealthy blind woman who arranges to buy another person's sight and submit to an operation which may give her 10 or 11 hours of vision. The idea got bogged down in melodrama but Miss Crawford gives it her all. The other two tales have Roddy McDowall as an unscrupulous young man who meets his comeuppance, and Richard Kiley as a tortured ex-Nazi hiding out in South America. (Dir: Boris Sagal, 98 mins.)

Night Has a Thousand Eyes, The (1948)**½ Edward G. Robinson, Gail Russell, John Lund, William Demarest, Virginia Bruce. Somewhat portentous rendition of a Cornell Woolrich novelette, with Robinson bug-eyed as a vaudeville mentalist who gradually discovers he has real psychic powers. Interesting script ideas are marred by scattershot execution and lack of consistent development. (Dir: John Farrow, 80 mins.)

Night Heaven Fell, The (France, 1958)*½ Brigitte Bardot, Stephen Boyd, Alida Valli. (Dir: Roger Vadim, 83 mins.)

Night Holds Terror, The (1955)*** Jack Kelly, Vince Edwards, John Cassavetes, Hildy Parks. Creditable low-budget suspense film, with a strong grasp of realistic detail. Kelly is a factory worker who is kidnapped at gunpoint by three thugs, one of them memorably played by Cassavetes. (Dir: Andrew L. Stone, 86 mins.)

Night in Casablanca, A (1946)**½ The Marx Brothers. The boys are involved in North African intrigue, but they get off enough humor to please their most ardent followers. Others beware. (Dir: Archie Mayo, 84 mins.)

Night in Paradise (1946)**½ Merle Oberon, Turhan Bey. In old Greece, dashing Aesop, disguised as an old man, falls for a beautiful princess. Romantic costume spectacle doesn't take itself seriously, which is all for the best. (Dir: Arthur Lubin, 84 mins.)

Night into Morning (1951)**½ Ray Milland, John Hodiak, Nancy Davis. The producers of this film probably thought lightning would strike twice if they cast Ray Milland as a man who turns to the bottle for solace (not unlike Milland's Academy Award-winning "Lost Weekend") but it doesn't work. This time Milland is a college professor whose wife and son are killed in an explosion, thereby triggering his battle with the bottle. (Dir: Fletcher Markle, 86 mins.)

Night Is My Future (Sweden, 1947)****½** Mai Zetterling, Birger Malmsten. Blinded young man meets a girl who tries to bring him happiness. Plodding drama directed by Ingmar Bergman is not up to his best work. English-dubbed. (Dir: Ingmar Bergman, 87 mins.)

Night Kill (1980)****** Robert Mitchum, Jaclyn Smith, Mike Connors, James Franciscus. Smith of TV's "Charlie's Angels" is the unfaithful wife of a wealthy industrialist; she plots his death with her lover, only to have things backfire bizarrely. Produced for theatrical release but sold instead to network TV. Smith's gorgeous, but she's a lousy actress. (Dir: Ted Post, 96 mins.)

Night Monster, The (1942)****** Bela Lugosi, Lionel Atwill, Irene Hervey. A maniac is at work in a creepy mansion, and all of his victims are medical men. Typical horror yarn. (Dir: Ford Beebe, 73 mins.)

Night Moves (1975)****½** Gene Hackman, Susan Clark, Jennifer Warren. One character says, while talking about a local girl-chaser, "He'd fuck a woodpile on the chance there was a snake in it." Well, you won't find that line anywhere when "Night Moves" shows up on network TV, but you will find a disappointing, though sharply observed, melodrama shot on location in California and Florida. I say disappointing because it's the first film in five years from the talented Arthur Penn, but this melodrama about a private eye (Hackman) who goes to Florida to find a runaway girl-drifter never quite jells. Your stomach may curdle, though, at the violent end she meets—beheaded by a marauding seaplane while scuba diving. (Dir: Arthur Penn, 100 mins.)

Night Must Fall (1937)****½** Robert Montgomery, Rosalind Russell, May Whitty. Montgomery, previously cast as a debonair leading man, plays a debonair psychotic killer in the popular Emlyn Williams thriller. Montgomery's victim is a horrible old woman, whom you nonetheless don't want to see murdered. (Dir: Richard Thorpe, 117 mins.)

Night Must Fall (Great Britain, 1964)****½** Albert Finney, Mona Washbourne, Susan Hampshire. Inadequate remake of the 1937 classic film thriller of Emlyn Williams which starred Robert Montgomery. In this reincarnation, talented Albert Finney falls victim to gross overplaying as the psychotic killer who gets in the good graces of his aging invalid employer, only to turn around and do her in. The suspense falters before night falls. (Dir: Karel Reisz, 105 mins.)

Night My Number Came Up, The (Great Britain, 1955)*****½** Michael Redgrave, Alexander Knox. Well acted British drama of an Air Force officer's troubled dreams and their effect on his work. (Dir: Leslie Norman, 94 mins.)

Night of Dark Shadows (1971)***½** David Selby, Lara Parker, Kate Jackson, Grayson Hall. (Dir: Dan Curtis, 96 mins.)

Night of Fear—See: **Edge of Fear**

Night of January 16th (1941)****** Robert Preston, Ellen Drew. Fair little mystery about a sailor who is left a huge legacy but must solve a few mysteries before he can touch the dough. (Dir: William Clemens, 79 mins.)

Night of Love—See: **Concert of Intrigue**

Night of Nights, The (1939)****** Pat O'Brien, Olympe Bradna, Roland Young. A broken down playwright makes a comeback after being reunited with his long-lost daughter. Corny, sentimental trash which is well acted. (Dir: Lewis Milestone, 86 mins.)

Night of San Juan, The (Bolivia, 1971)******** Federico Vallejio, Felicidad Coca. Powerful documentary recreation by gifted Bolivian director Jorge Sanjines, made after his memorable "Blood of the Condor." Reconstructs the 1967 massacre, by the Bolivian Army, of a group of striking, nonviolent, impoverished tin miners. Cast of nonprofessional actors, most of whom were participants in the '67 protest and witnesses to the massacre. Sanjines' passion about changing social and political institutions is evident throughout his earnest film. Financed and produced, interestingly enough, by RAI-TV, Italian television, as one of a series of six films commissioned by RAI and directed by young South American directors to examine today's society in various Latin-American countries. (Dir: Jorge Sanjines.)

Night of Terror (MTV 1972)****** Donna Mills, Martin Balsam. Aims to scare, and often succeeds despite several contrived situations. Seeking a vital piece of information, a killer stalks two girls (Miss Mills and Catherine Burns) who share an apartment. Ex-New York cop Eddie Egan plays the police detective in the case. (Dir: Jeannot Szwarc, 73 mins.)

Night of the Blood Monster (Great Britain, 1972)***** Christopher Lee, Maria Schell, Leo Genn, Margaret Lee. (Dir: Jess Franco, 84 mins.)

Night of the Following Day, The (1969)*****½** Marlon Brando, Richard Boone, Rita Moreno, Pamela Franklin. Hubert Cornfield directed this artsy kidnapping drama, with Brando, lean and sexy again (and blond), as the ringleader. Excellent, complex performance from Moreno as Brando's junkie friend. Based on Lionel White's '53 novel "The Snatchers." Filmed in France. (93 mins.)

Night of the Generals, The (France-Great Britain, 1967)****½** Peter O'Toole, Omar Sharif, Tom Courtenay, Donald Pleasence,

Philippe Noiret. A compelling premise—a Nazi intelligence officer trails a general who murders prostitutes—and a cast to dream about. Hans Helmut Kirst's novel becomes interminable under director Anatole Litvak's ponderous hand. Filmed in Warsaw and Paris. (148 mins.)

Night of the Great Attack, The (Italy, 1960)*½ Agnes Laurent, Fausto Tozzi. (Dir: Giorgio M. Scotese, 91 mins.)

Night of the Grizzly (1966)**½ Clint Walker, Martha Hyer. Predictable adventure about a former lawman who goes to Wyoming with his family in order to start a new life. He encounters a bear who threatens his existence, and he pursues it with a vengeance. The action is slow in starting, but the climax packs some excitement. (Dir: Joseph Pevney, 102 mins.)

Night of the Hunter (1955)**** Robert Mitchum, Lillian Gish, Shelley Winters, Peter Graves, James Gleason. A great film, the only directorial effort by actor Charles Laughton. Nightmarishly haunting parable of children on the run from their evil preacher-stepfather. Mitchum gives his greatest performance as the avaricious false preacher who spellbinds adults and scares children. Scripted by James Agee from the novel by Davis Grubb. (93 mins.)

Night of the Iguana, The (1964)**** Richard Burton, Ava Gardner, Deborah Kerr, Sue Lyon. Thanks to John Huston's expert direction and a faithful and literate screenplay, Tennessee Williams's searing drama about genteel losers down on their luck in Mexico becomes a satisfying, moving film. Burton is perfect as a defrocked clergyman bent on destruction; Kerr is superb playing an anguished spinster; and Gardner, in one of the best performances of her career, plays the proprietress of a seedy resort hotel with a remarkable quality of restrained sensuality. (125 mins.)

Night of the Juggler (1980)** James Brolin, Cliff Gorman, Richard Castellano, Julie Carmen. Brolin plays an ex-cop who chases a maniac all over New York City in a desperate effort to retrieve his kidnapped daughter. Overplotted thriller starts out decently but collapses quickly. (Dir: Robert Collins, 101 mins.)

Night of the Lepus (1972)½ Stuart Whitman, Janet Leigh, Rory Calhoun, DeForest Kelley. (Dir: William Claxton, 89 mins.)

Night of the Living Dead (1968)**½ Judith O'Dea, Russell Streiner, Duane Jones. Director George A. Romero's gruesome low-budget horror film was the first big success on the cult circuit. Shot in Pittsburgh, the film—tawdry, threadbare, and personal—features zombies who devour the entrails of the living. (90 mins.)

Night of the Quarter Moon (1959)* Julie London, John Drew Barrymore, Nat Cole. Alternate title: "Flesh and Flame." (Dir: Hugo Haas, 96 mins.)

Night Passage (1957)**½ James Stewart,

Audie Murphy, Dan Duryea, Dianne Foster, Brandon de Wilde. Fairly interesting western about a railroad trouble shooter trying to recover a stolen payroll. Things get sticky when his brother turns up on the side of the outlaws. (Dir: James Neilson, 90 mins.)

Night People (1954)**½ Gregory Peck, Broderick Crawford, Rita Gam. Interesting cloak and dagger yarn set in Berlin concerning the efforts of the U.S. Army Intelligence Corps to get a young American soldier, who has been kidnapped, out of the Russian sector. (Dir: Nunnally Johnson, 93 mins.)

Night Plane from Chungking (1943)**½ Robert Preston, Ellen Drew. Well done, contrived little B action film about a plane downed in China containing one traitor on its passenger list. (Dir: Ralph Murphy, 69 mins.)

Night Porter, The (Italy-U.S., 1974)***½ Dirk Bogarde, Charlotte Rampling, Isa Miranda. In director Liliana Cavani's exploration of Nazism as erotic ritual, Bogarde plays an ex-concentration camp officer whose chance meeting years later with one of his victims (Rampling) leads to a renewal of their sadomasochistic love affair. A delirious, fascinating work that wanders too much for its own good. (115 mins.)

Night Rider, The (MTV 1979)** David Selby, Percy Rodrigues, Pernell Roberts. Selby is a mild-mannered lawyer who turns into an avenging Zorrolike character when the sun goes down. It's set in the old, old West and the plot is as old as the old, old hills. (Dir: Hy Averback, 90 mins.)

Night Riders (Mexico, 1958)*½ Gaston Santos, Alma Rosa Aguirre. (Dir: Fernando Mendez, 76 mins.)

Night Runner, The (1957)** Ray Danton, Merry Anders. Parolee from a mental hospital goes berserk, turns into a killer. Average suspense melodrama offers little novelty. (Dir: Abner Biberman, 79 mins.)

Night Slaves (MTV 1970)** James Franciscus, Lee Grant, Leslie Nielsen. A muddled sci-fi yarn which generates some suspense during the first few scenes but deteriorates into a somewhat silly plot, involving inhabitants from outer space and their takeover of a small town. Lee Grant deserves better. (Dir: Ted Post, 73 mins.)

Night Stalker, The (MTV 1972)*** Darren McGavin, Carol Lynley, Claude Akins. Exciting piece of foolishness involving a breezy reporter and a fanged vampire in Las Vegas, a perfect setting for the entertainment. In the old tradition of wisecracking newsmen, McGavin shines as a nosy reporter sparring with the Vegas establishment over vampire killings. Result is a lively, violent, and irreverent murder show. (Dir: John Llewellyn Moxey, 73 mins.)

Night Strangler, The (MTV 1973)**½ Darren McGavin, Jo Ann Pflug, Margaret

Hamilton. Sequel to the thriller "The Night Stalker," which stands as one of the highest-rated made-for-TV films. McGavin repeats his newspaper reporter role tracking down a story to Seattle, Wash., where a nocturnal strangler is on the prowl. (Dir: Dan Curtis, 73 mins.)

Night Terror (MTV 1977)*½ Valerie Harper, Richard Romanus, Michael Tolan. (Dir: E. W. Swackhamer, 76 mins.)

Night That Panicked America, The (MTV 1975)*** Paul Shenar, Cliff De Young, Vic Morrow, Eileen Brennan. On October 30th, 1938, the now-famous Orson Welles radio broadcast of H. G. Wells's "War of the Worlds" struck a chord of panic in the hearts of millions of listeners, who mistook the dramatization about an invasion from Mars for the real thing. People actually fled from their homes in New Jersey, the locale of the radio drama. Film recreates the radio show in authentic detail, and speculates about what radio listeners did, in well-constructed fictional vignettes, brought to life by a hand-picked cast. The Mercury Radio players, led by Orson Welles (excellently played without resorting to mimicry by Shenar), are all fine, and the radio show sequences are fascinating. Joseph Sargent has directed with skill and taste. (Dir: Joseph Sargent, 98 mins.)

Night Prowler, The (Australia, 1978)** Kerry Walker, John Frawley, Ruth Cracknell. Odd mixture of psychology and satire has obese, neurotic Walker, a young woman in Sydney of the late '60s, pretending to have been raped by a night prowler so that she can become one herself. A father fixation figures in her problems. Adapted by Patrick White from his own short story and directed by the maker of "The Rocky Horror Picture Show." (Dir: Jim Sharman, 90 mins.)

Night the World Exploded, The (1957)** Kathryn Grant, William Leslie. Pretentious science fiction "meller" dealing with the end of the world by destructive forces found deep in the Earth's crust. (Dir: Fred F. Sears, 64 mins.)

Night They Killed Rasputin, The (Italy-France, 1960)** Edmund Purdom, John Drew Barrymore, Gianna Maria Canale. Young aristocrat attempts to assassinate the power-loving mad monk Rasputin, who is running Russia his own way. Historical drama acted in the old wild-eyed style manages to drum up a fair amount of interest. English-dubbed. (Dir: Pierre Chenal, 87 mins.)

Night They Raided Minsky's, The (1968) ***½ Jason Robards, Bert Lahr, Britt Ekland, Norman Wisdom, Elliott Gould. Forget the silly story line about a pert, innocent Amish girl from the sticks of Pennsylvania (Ekland) who storms Broadway and ends up stripping—in burlesque. Just enjoy the many engaging things in the film, including some nostalgic scenes which capture the attractive, sleazy quality of old-time burlesque, and the comedians whose "racy" material filled out the stage waits between the strippers. Lahr's last film; he died during production and a double was used in some scenes. (Dir: William Friedkin, 99 mins.)

Night They Took Miss Beautiful, The (MTV 1977)*½ Phil Silvers, Stella Stevens, Sheree North, Chuck Connors. (Dir: Robert Michael Lewis, 104 mins.)

Night Tide (1961)**½ Dennis Hopper, Linda Lawson, Launa Anders. A strange film that almost makes it. A young sailor meets a young carnival girl who believes she's really a mermaid transformed into an earthling and she fears her evil streak. The photography is arty but it works to establish mood. The acting is also better than average. (Dir: Curtis Harrington, 84 mins.)

Night to Remember, A (1942)***½ Brian Aherne, Loretta Young, Gale Sondergaard, Sidney Toler, Blanche Yurka. Mystery writer and wife turn detectives when they find a body in their Greenwich Village apartment. Bright comedy-mystery has some hilarious lines, smart performances. (Dir: Richard Wallace, 91 mins.)

Night to Remember, A (Great Britain, 1958)**** Kenneth More, Honor Blackman, David McCallum. Impressive achievement—documentarylike retelling of the ill-fated maiden voyage of the "Titanic," magnificently detailed, authentic, stirring saga of heroism of "grace under pressure." Superb Eric Ambler script, Roy Baker direction, performances by the huge cast. (Dir: Roy Baker, 123 mins.)

Night Train (Great Britain, 1940)***½ Rex Harrison, Margaret Lockwood, Paul Henreid. With the help of the secret service, a scientist's daughter saves a valuable formula from the Nazis. Excellent suspense thriller, one of the best of its kind. Alternate title: **Night Train to Munich**. (Dir: Carol Reed, 93 mins.)

Night Train for Inverness (Great Britain, 1959)** Norman Wooland, Jane Hylton. Diabetic is in great danger unless he's reached in time. Fairly suspenseful drama. (Dir: Ernest Morris, 69 mins.)

Night Train to Milan (Italy, 1963)**½ Jack Palance, Yvonne Furneaux. Passenger recognized as a wanted Nazi commits murder and holds a girl as hostage. Suspense thriller dubbed in English holds the attention pretty well. (Dir: Marcello Baldi, 90 mins.)

Night unto Night (1949)* Ronald Reagan, Broderick Crawford, Viveca Lindfors. (Dir: Don Siegel, 92 mins.)

Night Visitor, The (Great Britain, 1971)*** Max Von Sydow, Liv Ullmann, Trevor Howard. A neat little thriller, which draws its strength from three fine performances and a fast, intricate plot. An ax-murderer is imprisoned, but another crime with the same *modus operandi* is committed—could he have done it? One hint: keep your eye on the bird. (Dir: Laslo Benedek, 106 mins.)

Night Walker, The (1964)**½ Barbara

479

Stanwyck, Robert Taylor. Woman is terrorized by nightmares, which seem to be instigated by her husband who supposedly was killed in a fire. Suspense drama with some spooky moments, all pros Stanwyck and Taylor giving it a professional gloss. (Dir: Willaim Castle, 86 mins.)

Night Watch (Great Britain, 1973)* Elizabeth Taylor, Laurence Harvey, Billie Whitelaw, Robert Lang. (Dir: Brian G. Hutton, 98 mins.)

Night Without Sleep (1952)**½ Linda Darnell, Gary Merrill, Hildegarde Neff. Mentally disturbed man is driven to murder. Minor but well acted little psychothriller. (Dir: Roy Baker, 77 mins.)

Night Without Stars (Great Britain, 1951)**½ David Farrar, Nadia Gray. Blinded man in France becomes involved with black marketeers and murder, returns to England to have his sight restored, so he can solve the mystery. Interesting mystery melodrama. (Dir: Anthony Pelissier, 86 mins.)

Nightcomers, The (Great Britain, 1971)** Marlon Brando, Stephanie Beacham, Harry Andrews, Thora Hird, Verna Harvey. Exercise in nastiness by director Michael Winner. A depraved, filthy Irish lout seduces a proper Victorian lady who turns ravenous in the bedroom. A perfunctory turn of the screw. Based on characters from Henry James. (96 mins.)

Nightfall (1957)**½ Aldo Ray, Brian Keith, Anne Bancroft. Fairly absorbing crime drama. Good performances. Suspenseful tale of an artist chased by robbers for their stolen loot. (Dir: Jacques Tourneur, 78 mins.)

Nighthawks (Great Britain, 1979)**½ Ken Robertson, Tony Westrope, Maureen Dolan. A sober film about a homosexual teacher who stays in the closet by day and searches out lovers by night. Directed with kitchen sink realism by Ron Peck and Paul Hallam. (113 mins.)

Nighthawks (1981)***½ Sylvester Stallone, Rutger Hauer, Billy Dee Williams, Persis Khambatta. This anti-terrorist thriller tries hard to be a *French Connection* for the eighties and in large measure succeeds. Sylvester Stallone plays a New York City cop who is pitted against an international terrorist out to rehabilitate himself with the fraternity by proving his value at garnering publicity in a spectacular manner. As played by Rutger Hauer, making a fabulously impressive American debut, the man is a formidable adversary, which keeps the suspense mechanism tightly coiled. There are several superb chase sequences and some beautiful location work, marking Bruce Malmuth, in his first theatrical feature, a director of considerable accomplishment and a talent to watch. Stallone works well, and though the dialogue scenes creak, there aren't many of them. This is a good, professional action film that delivers. Of course, it has noth-

ing to say about terrorism or politics, glossing over its subject with mindless facility, but such action cinema can often be its own artistic justification. (100 mins.)

Nightmare (1942)**½ Brian Donlevy, Diana Barrymore. Fairly exciting suspense tale. An American gambler stumbles into murder, and finds himself hot on the trail of foreign agents. Donlevy does nicely in the lead. (Dir: Tim Whelan, 81 mins.)

Nightmare (MTV 1973)**½ Richard Crenna, Patty Duke Astin, Vic Morrow. "Rear Window" type thriller. A New Yorker thinks he's witnessed a shooting, and decides to play sleuth when police display skepticism. Fair suspense yarn contains hokey segments along with a climactic chase scene. Crenna delivers a believable performance as the witness, Mrs. Astin handles the screaming bits, and Vic Morrow is the quizzical detective. (Dir: William Hale, 75 mins.)

Nightmare Alley (1947)***½ Tyrone Power, Joan Blondell, Coleen Gray, Helen Walker, Mike Mazurki. A pungent film, this story of a carnival hustler making it as a spiritualist in society circles only to end up a degraded geek is an anomaly in the career of Power. Scriptwriter Jules Furthman rescues much of the nastiness of William Lindsay Gresham's original novel. (Dir: Edmund Goulding, 111 mins.)

Nightmare Castle (Italy, 1965)*½ Barbara Steele, Paul Muller. (Dir: Allan Grunewald, 83 mins.)

Nightmare in Badham County (MTV 1976)**½ Deborah Raffin, Lynne Moody, Chuck Connors. Two college girls driving through the South during their summer vacation are railroaded by a vicious sheriff and a corrupt judge, and sent to a prison farm. (Dir: John Llewellyn Maxey, 104 mins.)

Nightmare in the Sun (1964)*½ Ursula Andress, John Derek, Arthur O'Connell, Aldo Ray, Sammy Davis, Jr. (Dir: Marc Lawrence, 81 mins.)

Night's End (India, 1978)*** This Award-winning work is set in a feudatory state of India in '45 where a schoolmaster's wife is abducted by the son of a wealthy family, and a revolutionary situation develops. (Dir: Shyam Benegal.)

Nights of Cabiria (Italy, 1957)***½ Giulietta Masina. A simple minded prostitute is taken in by every man she meets. Intensely dramatic, grim tale. Finely acted and well directed by Federico Fellini. Basis for the musical "Sweet Charity." Very moving thanks to Mrs. Fellini's sensitive acting. (110 mins.)

Nightwing (1979)*** Nick Mancuso, David Warner, Kathryn Harrold, George Clutesi. An interesting thriller. A plague of infected vampire bats strikes a Hopi-Navajo reservation in the Southwest. Only an Indian sheriff and a maddened scientist can stop it. The locale is interesting, the plotting tense, and the special effects spectacular. From the novel by Martin Cruz Smith. (Dir: Arthur Hiller, 103 mins.)

Nijinsky (Great Britain, 1980)**½ Alan Bates, George de la Pena, Leslie Browne. Director Herbert Ross's life of the great dancer who went mad is handsome, though the drama is shallow. Ross and scenarist Hugh Wheeler stereotype everyone equally, homosexuals and heterosexuals alike. Bates is superbly convincing as impresario Sergei Diaghiley. The dance sequences are disappointing. (129 mins.)

Nina B. Affair, The (France-West Germany, 1961)** Nadia Tiller, Pierre Brasseur. Millionaire's discontented wife plans his death. Slow-moving drama is stretched out past its proper length. Dubbed in English. (Dir: Robert Siodmak, 105 mins.)

Nine Girls (1944)*** Evelyn Keyes, Jinx Falkenburg, Ann Harding, Nina Foch. Hated sorority girl is murdered, and one of the girls turns sleuth to find the killer. Well written, nicely acted and directed mystery. (Dir: Leigh Jason, 78 mins.)

Nine Hours to Rama (U.S.-Great Britain, 1963)***½ Horst Buchholz, Jose Ferrer, Diane Baker. Absorbing, well-mounted political drama about the nine hours leading up to the assassination of India's Mahatma Gandhi, a significant and rarely treated subject in films. Buchholz plays the rebellious Indian youth who is assigned to kill Gandhi, and though his romantic entanglements slow the action, the pace picks up again before the shattering climax. The supporting cast is uniformly fine, and the superb on-location camera work in India adds greatly to the film. Memorable performance by nonprofessional actor J. S. Casshyap playing and looking remarkably like Mahatma Gandhi. (Dir: Mark Robson, 125 mins.)

Nine Lives (Norway, 1958)**½ Documentary reenactment of true story, as a brave resistance fighter braves the perils of the frozen wilderness in an attempt to disrupt Nazi operations during World War II. Fascinating tale suffers from stilted treatment, should have been much better. Native cast, with narration in English by March of Time voice Westbrook Van Voorhees, with Luis Van Rooten supplying additional commentary. Jack Fieldstad stars as real-life Jan Baalsrud. Produced by Louis de Rochemont. (Dir: Arne Skouen, 90 mins.)

9/30/55 (1977)*** Richard Thomas, Susan Tyrrell, Thomas Hulce. It's the date James Dean was killed in an auto accident. Thomas has seldom been better as a young high-school senior who affectionately apes his hero and shares his own adoration with a girlfriend. Offbeat, uneven, affecting. (Dir: James Bridges, 101 mins.)

9 to 5 (1980)**½ Jane Fonda, Lily Tomlin, Dolly Parton, Dabney Coleman, Sterling Hayden, Henry Jones, Marian Mercer, Elizabeth Wilson, Lawrence Pressman. A condescending piece of nonentertainment, pretends to be addressing an important social issue in comic terms. Secretaries gang up on a piggish boss thereby consigning the whole story to easy stereotypes and meaningless satire. The three main players, Fonda, Parton, and Tomlin, are intelligent and appealing, but the film can't escape its own calculated origins. (Dir: Colin Higgins, 111 mins.)

1984 (Great Britain, 1955)*** Edmond O'Brien, Michael Redgrave, Jan Sterling, Donald Pleasence. Orwell's image of what our world will be like in '84 has been converted to an interesting if somewhat confused film. (Dir: Michael Anderson, 91 mins.)

1988: The Remake (1978)*** Ed Nylund, Skip Kovington, Carolyn Zaremba. Dying librarian Nylund holds auditions for a new version of "Showboat." It's all a put-on of cinema verité (Nylund, playing himself, was acting, not dying). (Dir: Richard R. Schmidt, 97 mins.)

1941 (1979)** Dan Aykroyd, Ned Beatty, John Belushi, Lorraine Gary. A raucous film that spends $28 million for a few laughs and much destruction. Farce based on a real incident in which a Japanese sub was allegedly spotted off the coast of southern California six days after the attack on Pearl Harbor. Cars, tanks, planes, and property are obliterated en masse. Aykroyd is notable as a by-the-book tank sergeant. (Dir: Steven Spielberg, 118 mins.)

90 Degrees in the Shade (Czechoslovakia-Great Britain, 1965)***½ Anne Heywood, James Booth, Ann Todd, Donald Wolfit. Married food-store manager has an affair with a stock girl and has been stealing from the liquor supply; it spells tragedy. From Czechoslovakia, extremely well directed, acted by a cast that's partly British. Superior dramatic fare. (Dir: Jiri Weiss, 86 mins.)

92 in the Shade (1975)***½ Peter Fonda, Warren Oates, Elizabeth Ashley, Margot Kidder. Thomas McGuane directed and adapted his own novel about Florida fishing-boat captains. The original tragic ending was toned down in the later release. Well acted. Filmed in Key West. (93 mins.)

99 and 44/100% Dead (1974)** Richard Harris, Edmond O'Brien, Bradford Dillman, Ann Turkel, Chuck Connors. Harris (fatigued acting) is a professional killer brought into a gangland feud by boss O'Brien (overacting) to even the odds against rival boss Dillman and hired sadist Connors. (Dir: John Frankenheimer, 97 mins.)

99 River Street (1953)***½ John Payne, Evelyn Keyes, Peggy Castle, Ian Wolfe, Frank Faylen. Taxi driver is aided by an ambitious actress in extricating him from a robbery in which his wife is involved. Sharp melodrama has superior acting, as well as excellent direction and camera work to make it above average. (Dir: Phil Karlson, 83 mins.)

99 Women (Italy-Spain-West Germany,

481

1969)½ Maria Schell, Mercedes McCambridge, Herbert Lom. (Dir: Jesus Franco, 86 mins.)

Ninotchka (1939)**** Greta Garbo, Melvyn Douglas, Ina Claire, Bela Lugosi, Sig Ruman, Felix Bressart. A sparkling, witty political fairy-tale about a cold (but beautiful) commissar who melts to the bourgeois charms of Paris and Melvyn Douglas, jeopardizing honor and career for love. Garbo fully complements the casual sophistication and stylistic grace of director Ernst Lubitsch. Written by Billy Wilder, along with Charles Brackett and Walter Reisch. Remade as the musical "Silk Stockings." (110 mins.)

Ninth Configuration, The—See: **Twinkle, Twinkle, Killer Kane**

Nitwits, The (1935)*** Bert Wheeler, Robert Woolsey, Betty Grable. Proprietors of a cigar counter solve a murder in a department store. Pretty funny comedy-mystery, one of the better Wheeler-Woolseys. (Dir: George Stevens, 81 mins.)

No Deposit, No Return (1976)** David Niven, Darren McGavin, Kim Richards, Brad Savage, Barbara Feldon. Lackluster Disney comedy in which two rich kids, Kim and Brad, connive to spend an Easter holiday with their busy widowed mom (Feldon). They induce two inept crooks to offer them for ransom to their wealthy grandfather (Niven), who's glad to be rid of the kids for a while. (Dir: Norman Tokar, 112 mins.)

No Down Payment (1957)**½ Joanne Woodward, Tony Randall, Jeffrey Hunter, Barbara Rush, Cameron Mitchell. Problems of four married couples living in a post-war housing project. Sort of a pre-fab Peyton Place, with as much underhand plotting going on. Good performances but the story often misses paying off. (Dir: Martin Ritt, 105 mins.)

No Escape (France, 1958)** Raf Vallone, Magali Noel. An escaped criminal enters the life of a lonely widow, who is dominated by her father-in-law and a mean servant. You've seen it before a hundred times. (Dir: Charles Brabant, 101 mins.)

No Greater Love—See: **Alfred Nobel Story, The**

No Highway in the Sky (Great Britain, 1951)***½ James Stewart, Marlene Dietrich, Glynis John, Jack Hawkins. Absent-minded professor insists a new commercial airline is not safe. Very good mixture of suspense and gentle comedy, excellently played by Stewart and Dietrich, a British cast. (Dir: Henry Koster, 98 mins.)

No Leave, No Love (1946)** Van Johnson, Keenan Wynn. Van's fans may be able to endure this long, forced comedy about a couple of Marines loose in the big city with plenty of money, thanks to a radio appearance. There's a romance, of course, but the picture never really moves. (Dir: Charles Martin, 119 mins.)

No Love for Johnnie (Great Britain, 1961)**** Peter Finch, Stanley Holloway, Mary Peach, Billie Whitelaw. Brilliantly acted drama about a member of parliament whose political and domestic affairs are both failures, and of his love for a young model. Incisive character portrait of a lonely man, frustrated in his attempt to cope with the world. Superior adult fare. (Dir: Ralph Thomas, 96 mins.)

No Man Is An Island (1962)**½ Jeffrey Hunter, Marshall Thompson. Story based on fact about a navy radioman who is trapped by the outbreak of WW II, becomes a guerrilla in the hills of Guam. Done in straightforward manner, with a good performance by Hunter. This nevertheless looks like all the other war films, although the location shooting in the Philippines is an added asset. (Dir: John Monks, Jr., 114 mins.)

No Man of Her Own (1932)**½ Clark Gable, Carole Lombard, Dorothy Mackaill, Grant Mitchell, Elizabeth Patterson. A card shark is reformed by love. Not as potent as it used to be, but then Gable is Gable, and Lombard is pretty to look at. Gable and Lombard's only co-starring film. (Dir: Wesley Ruggles, 85 mins.)

No Man of Her Own (1949)** Barbara Stanwyck, John Lund, Jane Cowl, Lyle Bettger, Phyllis Thaxter, Richard Denning. What could have been an ordinary, if improbable, sudser turns out (through fine acting and, apparently, sheer concentration) to be astonishingly involving and even moving. The plot, from a story by Cornell Woolrich, is certainly nothing to brag about; a down-and-out woman changes identities with a wealthy war widow when the latter is killed in a train wreck. The leads give unusually strong, magnetic performances (Lund was never better), and this is a rare chance to see famous beauty and stage star Jane Cowl, as the protagonist's "mother-in-law," who becomes deeply involved in the complex plot. Recommended. (Dir: Mitchell Leisen, 98 mins.)

No Man's Land (1964)*½ Russ Harvey, Kim Lee. (Dir: Russ Harvey, 72 mins.)

No Man's Woman (1955)** Marie Windsor, John Archer. Double-crossing dame is murdered. Ordinary mystery. (Dir: Franklin Adreon, 70 mins.)

No Maps on My Taps (1978)*** Sandman Sims, Chuck Green, Bunny Briggs. Three great hoofers speak with their feet in this delightful documentary on tap dancing as an expression of black heritage and culture. Features interviews and footage of Briggs (as a child dancer), John W. Bubbles, and the greatest, Bill Robinson. (Dir: George T. Nierenberg.)

No More Excuses (1968)***½ Robert Downey, Allen Abel, Paula Morris. The censorious prudes programming most TV stations probably won't run this sometimes inspired farce written and directed by Robert Downey, but we're going to review it anyway. One critic astutely noted "the whole experience was like watching and listening to a brilliant friend as he free associated with no thought of whether he was making a fool of himself." A collection of sight gags, scatological jokes, and one-liners running the gamut from the assassination of President Garfield to the Society for Indecency to Naked Animals. Downey, who also directed "Putney Swope," plays Private Steward Thompson. Low budget, big talent. (52 mins.)

No, My Darling Daughter (Great Britain, 1961)**½ Michael Redgrave, Juliet Mills, Michael Craig, Roger Livesey. Tycoon realizes his daughter is at that grown-up age, entrusts her to a friend while on a business trip—and the trouble really begins. Performers such as Redgrave, Livesey, and Craig deserve better material than this mild comedy, but they troupe through it capably. (Dir: Betty Box, 97 mins.)

No Name on the Bullet (1959)*** Audie Murphy, Joan Evans, Charles Drake, Virginia Grey, Warren Stevens. Offbeat, grim little western that boasts a strong plot and a remarkable performance by Murphy (always a seriously underrated actor). A hired gunman comes into a small town to kill an unnamed person; everyone has something to hide and the respectable citizens begin to turn on each other. Murphy's eminently professional gunslinger is a fresh, intelligent, chilling conception, very well done. (Dir: Jack Arnold, 77 mins.)

No Nukes (1980)***½ Jane Fonda, Ralph Nader. Jackson Browne, Bruce Springsteen, Carly Simon, Bonnie Raitt, James Taylor, the Doobie Brothers, Crosby, Stills and Nash, and other rock acts in a filmed concert to benefit the antinuclear power forces. (Dirs: Julian Schlossberg, Danny Goldberg, Anthony Potenza, 103 mins.)

No Ordinary Summer (U.S.S.R., 1956)*½ Viktor Korshunov. (Dir: Vladimir Basov, 103 mins.)

No Other Love (MTV 1979)**½ Richard Thomas, Julie Kavner, Elizabeth Allen. Two slightly retarded young adults, while living at a hostel run by a caring couple, fall in love and hope to get married. Thomas and Kavner don't appear retarded enough to warrant the objections raised to their marriage, but this is a commendable effort to present a delicate subject sincerely. (Dir: Richard Pearce, 104 mins.)

No Place Like Homicide (Great Britain, 1961)** Kenneth Connor, Sidney James, Shirley Eaton, Donald Pleasence. The one about all the relatives gathered in a spooky mansion to hear the reading of the will, done for laughs—only it might have been better played straight. Only a fair assortment of thrills and chuckles. Remake of Karloff's "The Ghoul." (Dir: Pat Jackson, 87 mins.)

No Place to Hide (1956)*½ David Brian, Marsha Hunt, Keenan Wynn. (Dir: Josef Shaftel, 71 mins.)

No Place to Hide (MTV 1981)*½ Mariette Hartley, Kathleen Beller, Deir Dullia. (Dir: John Llewellyn Moxey, 104 mins.)

No Place to Run (MTV 1972)**½ Herschel Bernardi, Scott Jacoby. Touching old-man, young-boy drama, helped by the casting of Bernardi and Jacoby. Bernardi may be a shade underage for the over-70 grandfather part, and cameras avoid close-ups, but the skilled actor turns on the warmth and makes a credible character. (Dir: Delbert Mann, 73 mins.)

No Regrets for Our Youth (Japan, 1946)***½ Denjiro Okochi, Eiko Miyoshi, Setsuko Hara. Director Akira Kurosawa's first major work is a meaty drama of the young left faced with the political realities of the fascist Japanese military state of the '30s. Hara gives a psychologically complex performance as a radicalized young woman. (111 mins.)

No Resting Place (Great Britain, 1951)**½ Michael Gough, Eithne Dunne. A drama of Irish vagrants, particularly of one who becomes a fugitive with his family when he accidentally kills a gamekeeper. Grim, beautifully photographed. (Dir: Paul Rotha, 77 mins.)

No Return Address (1961)*½ Harry Lovejoy, Alicia Hammond. (Dir: Alexander Grattan, 76 mins.)

No Room for the Groom (1952)**** Tony Curtis, Piper Laurie, Spring Byington. Don DeFore, Jack Kelly. Curtis and his bride, Laurie, can't sleep together: he gets the measles, recovers in time to be drafted, and gets back to find his house overrun by the most monstrous group of in-laws in film history. Director Douglas Sirk's attitude is summarized in the last shot, which pans from the lovers' embrace to a stuffed fish hanging on the wall behind them. (82 mins.)

No Sad Songs for Me (1950)** Margaret Sullavan, Wendell Corey, Viveca Lindfors, Natalie Wood. Messy soap opera about a woman who starts setting her affairs straight, which includes promoting a love affair for her husband and her friend, when she finds she is dying of cancer. Good performances but limiting script. One of Sullavan's few film leads, and worth seeing largely for that reason; her last film. (Dir: Rudolph Maté, 89 mins.)

No Safety Ahead (Great Britain, 1959)*½ James Kenney, Susan Beaumont. (Dir: Max Varnel, 68 mins.)

No Sun in Venice (France-Italy, 1957)** Francoise Arnoul, Christian Marquand. Plodding, half-baked romance broken up by a villain who is in love with the girl. Good music is provided by the Modern Jazz Quartet. (Dir: Roger Vadim, 97 mins.)

No Survivors Please (West Germany, 1964)* Maria Perschy, Robert Cunningham. (Dirs: Hans Albin, Peter Berneis, 92 mins.)

No Time for Breakfast (France, 1976)*** Annie Girardot, François Perier, Jean-Pierre Cassel, Isabelle Huppert. Girardot, the closest we come nowadays to Joan Crawford and Bette Davis, plays a head of surgery who has to juggle the demands of her profession, her teenage children, her diplomat husband, her lovers, and the news that she may have contracted cancer. Her emotional facility is overwhelming. (Dir: Jean-Louis Bertucelli, 100 mins.)

No Time for Comedy (1940)*** James Stewart, Rosalind Russell, Genevieve Tobin, Charles Ruggles, Allyn Joslyn. Loose adaptation of the S. N. Behrman hit benefits from the cast but loses its satiric bite. As it now stands it's the story of a country boy who becomes a successful writer and must face the accompanying consequences. Stewart and Russell are at their best. (Dir: William Keighley, 93 mins.)

No Time for Flowers (1952)**½ Paul Christian, Viveca Lindfors. An actor is hired by the Communists to test the fidelity of an embassy clerk, but they both foil the Reds. Fairly amusing comedy made in Austria; no "Ninotchka," but pleasant enough. (Dir: Don Siegel, 83 mins.)

No Time for Love (1943)*** Claudette Colbert, Fred MacMurray, Richard Hadyn, Ilka Chase, June Havoc. Amusing comedy about a lady photographer who falls for a sand-hog. Routine tale is superbly told and delightful viewing. (Dir: Mitchell Leisen, 83 mins.)

No Time for Sergeants (1958)*** Andy Griffith, Myron McCormick, Nick Adams. Andy Griffith is the whole show as the Georgia farm boy who gets drafted into the Army and creates mayhem among his superiors and colleagues. It's a virtuoso comedy performance. The supporting cast is fine. (Dir: Mervyn Le Roy, 111 mins.)

No Time for Tears (Great Britain, 1957)*** Anna Neagle, George Baker, Anthony Quayle, Sylvia Syms, Flora Robson. Touching drama of the activities in a children's hospital, an unabashed tearjerker, but adeptly done. Fine performances. (Dir: Cyril Frankel, 86 mins.)

No Time to Be Young (1957)** Robert Vaughn, Roger Smith, Merry Anders. Slight drama about a trio of young men who find their backs are up against the wall and therefore plan a robbery. Cast is adequate considering the script. (Dir: David Lowell Rich, 82 mins.)

No Time to Kill (Great Britain-Sweden-West Germany, 1961)* John Ireland, Ellen Schwiers. (Dir: Tom Younger, 72 mins.)

No Trees in the Street (Great Britain, 1959)**½ Stanley Holloway, Sylvia Syms, Herbert Lom, Ronald Howard. Director J. Lee Thompson makes a good attempt at showing the slum living conditions of pre-war London and the various personalities caught in them. With less stress on the personal dramas, this film could have been a good social commentary. (Dir: J. Lee Thompson, 99 mins.)

No Vietnamese Ever Called Me Nigger (1968)***½ Low-budget black and white documentary about the anti-Vietnam War protests of the mid-60's is a powerful reminder of the moral outrage and passion of so many American citizens, young and old alike, during those embattled years. Has some memorable footage of an anti-war march, and some eloquent interviews with black veterans from "Nam." Produced and directed by David Loeb Weiss, a nonprofessional filmmaker. (76 mins.)

No Way Back (West Germany, 1955)** Ivan Desny, Ruth Niehaus, Lila Kedrova. Russian army officer in Berlin earns the suspicion of his superiors when he searches for a girl who had befriended him during the war. Problem drama doesn't make its point too well—leisurely and sometimes dull. (Dir: Victor Vicas, 87 mins.)

No Way Out (1950)***½ Richard Widmark, Linda Darnell, Sidney Poitier (feature debut). Biting drama about a Negro-hating, cop-hating hoodlum who incites a big race riot and almost ruins a Negro intern's chances of becoming a doctor. Director Joseph L. Mankiewicz gets top performances from his cast. (106 mins.)

No Way to Treat a Lady (1968)***½ Rod Steiger, Lee Remick, George Segal. Neat suspense yarn which affords Rod Steiger a tour-de-force as a psychotic killer who uses ingenious disguises to trick his victims. George Segal does very well as a harassed police detective who gets brief phone calls from the killer and builds a strange alliance as a result. A good show, primarily because it provides Steiger with a showcase to demonstrate his extraordinary acting range and talent. Alec Guinness played 8 roles in "Kind Hearts & Coronets." The versatile Steiger plays 7 roles in this one. (Dir: Jack Smight, 108 mins.)

Noah's Ark (1929-58)** Dolores Costello, George O'Brien. Silent spectacle of Biblical times has been decked out with sound effects and narration. The spectacle is still effective, some scenes have tremendous scope—but the story dates badly. As a novelty, it will suffice. (Dir: Michael Curtiz, 75 mins.)

Nob Hill (1945)** George Raft, Joan Bennett, Vivian Blaine, Peggy Ann Garner. Saloon owner in the brawling San Francisco days breaks down the resistance of a blue-blooded socialite. Pleasant but unimportant drama with music. (Dir: Henry Hathaway, 95 mins.)

Nobi—See: **Fires on the Plain**

Nobody Lives Forever (1946)**½ John Garfield, Geraldine Fitzgerald, Walter Brennan, Faye Emerson, George Tobias. The acting is top drawer but this story of a hustler who comes back from the war and tries to swindle an innocent girl is very weak. Of course he falls for her—Oh, have you seen it too? (Dir: Jean Negulesco, 100 mins.)

Nobody Waved Goodbye (Canada, 1964) ***½ Peter Kastner, Julie Biggs, Claude Rae. Made on a small budget, this film beautifully documents the plight of a young 18-year-old who does not know what he stands for or cares about. Caught between the moral and material values of his parents and the boredom of high school, he steals a car and runs away with his girl friend. Compelling debut performance by Kastner gives the film real emotional impact. Underrated now, and at the time of release. (Writer-Dir: Don Owen, 80 mins.)

Nobody's Perfect (1968)** Doug McClure, Nancy Kwan, James Whitmore, David Hartman. If you are devoted to scatterbrain service comedies in which the hero (Doug McClure, in this case) flits from one impossible situation to another and still manages to fall in love with a beautiful girl (Nancy Kwan in a nurse's uniform), tune in. The plot revolves around a missing Buddha statue, some crazy sailors and a jinxed village. (Dir: Alan Rafkin, 103 mins.)

Nocturna (1979)**½ Nai Bonet, John Carradine, Yvonne DeCarlo, Brother Theodore, Tony Hamilton. Producer Bonet, the granddaughter of elderly Count Dracula (Carradine) is given to disco dancing and stripping at the least provocation. Her love for musician Hamilton, a mere mortal, makes her human too. Bonet's acting is poor, but Carradine and DeCarlo are good as old flames and Theodore is hilarious as a demented servant. (Dir: Harry Tampa [Harry Hurwitz], 83 mins.)

Nocturne (1946)*** George Raft, Lynn Bari. Detective refuses to believe the death of a woman-chasing songwriter was suicide. Smooth mystery, interesting and suspenseful. (Dir: Edwin L. Marin, 88 mins.)

Non-Stop New York (Great Britain, 1937)** John Loder, Anna Lee, Francis L. Sullivan. Fairly intriguing but ultimately disappointing semiscience fiction mystery set aboard the first nonstop transatlantic flight. (Dir: Robert Stevenson, 70 mins.)

None But the Brave (1965)** Frank Sinatra, Clint Walker, Tommy Sands, Tony Bill. Routine World War II action drama set in the Pacific, notable only because Sinatra also tried his hand at directing for the first time. Sinatra's platoon of Marines (he's the company medic) crash on an island occupied by a small band of Japanese soldiers and their many confrontations (some bloody...others peaceful) make up the bulk of the film's two-hour running time. (Dir: Frank Sinatra, 105 mins.)

None But the Lonely Heart (1944)***½ Cary Grant, Ethel Barrymore, June Duprez, Barry Fitzgerald, Jane Wyatt, Dan Duryea, George Coulouris.. A Cockney layabout comes to self-discovery when he learns his mother is dying. Clifford Odets wrote and directed, with shaky technique but basic earnestness. (113 mins.)

None But the Lonely Spy (Italy, 1964)* Ken Clark, Bella Cortez. (Dir: Emimmo Salvi, 90 mins.)

None Shall Escape (1944)***½ Alexander Knox, Marsha Hunt. A Nazi officer is put on trial, and his crimes are reviewed. Gripping drama packs a punch. Set in the future: made during WW II, but taking place *after* the war. (Dir: André de Toth, 85 mins.)

Noose Hangs High, The (1948)** Abbott & Costello, Leon Errol, Cathy Downs. Typical A & C film this time involving $50,000 stolen from the boys by some bad men. O.K. for kids. (Dir: Charles Barton, 77 mins.)

Nora (West Germany, 1973)*** Margit Carstensen. A quickie, shot on videotape by director Rainer Werner Fassbinder. Hothouse rendition of Ibsen's "A Doll's House": mirror shots, tracks around ornate furniture, and suffocatingly long takes in overstuffed rooms. Carstensen doesn't have the directness to play Nora.

Nora Prentiss (1947)** Ann Sheridan, Kent Smith, Robert Alda. Meaningless, hackneyed melodrama about a doctor who almost loses everything just because he meets and falls for Miss Sheridan. (Dir: Vincent Sherman, 111 mins.)

Norliss Tapes, The (MTV 1973)** Roy Thinnes, Angie Dickinson, Claude Akins. Ghost story from horror-story specialist Dan Curtis. A serious Roy Thinnes plays an investigator of the occult involved in tracking down the mystery of a deceased sculptor who appears to be very much alive. (Dir: Dan Curtis, 74 mins.)

Norma Rae (1979)**** Sally Field, Ron Leibman, Beau Bridges, Pat Hingle, Barbara Baxley. Field gives a rousing, Oscar-winning portrayal of a union organizer who whips the textile workers of a small southern town into solidarity, along with itinerant agitator Leibman, a sort of John Garfield with the cutes. Director Martin Ritt is often sluggish and vague, but it's an involving entertainment with a good heart. (113 mins.)

Norman, Is That You? (1976)* Redd Foxx, Pearl Bailey, Dennis Dugan, Michael Warren. (Dir: George Schlatter, 92 mins.)

Norseman, The (1978)** Lee Majors, Mel Ferrer, Cornel Wilde. Low-grade actioner set in 1006, as Viking prince Majors comes to North America in search of his father, King Ferrer. (Dir: Charles B. Pierce, 90 mins.)

North Avenue Irregulars, The (1979)** Edward Herrmann, Susan Clark, Cloris Leachman, Barbara Harris. Inane Disney comedy based on a real-life story. The ladies of the parish of newly arrived minister Herrmann help him combat a local bookie operation. (Dir: Bruce Bilson, 99 mins.)

North by Northwest (1959)**** Cary Grant, Eva Marie Saint, James Mason, Martin Landau, Jessie Royce Landis, Leo G. Carroll. Grant, a martini-sodden advertising director, awakes from a middle-class daydream into an underworld nightmare when he's mistaken for a secret agent. A great and entertaining movie, directed by

Alfred Hitchcock at the height of his powers. (136 mins.)

North Dallas Forty (1979)***½ Nick Nolte, Mac Davis, Dayle Haddon, Bo Svenson, John Matuszak, Steve Forrest, Dabney Coleman. Witty and wise comedy about the battered lives of pro footballers, Nolte's considerable talent is almost matched by Mac Davis, a singer who makes an impressive debut—and for that matter, by pro player John Matuszak, who acts better than many professionals. (Dir: Ted Kotcheff, 120 mins.)

North Sea Is Death Sea (West Germany, 1975)*½ Uwe Enkelmann, Dschingis Bowakow, Marquard Bohm. Would you believe, a children's film? Two young boys run away from home, steal a boat, and set sail for the high seas. (Dir: Hark Bohm, 85 mins.)

North Star, The (1943)**½ Anne Baxter, Dana Andrews, Walter Huston. Russian propaganda on the rocks, from Hollywood (thanks to our WW II alliance with the U.S.S.R.). Lillian Hellman wrote the screenplay in the days when her refusal to compromise seemed far less admirable. Plenty of "For every one that falls, ten will rise to take his place" and "You cannot keel the spirit of a free peepul." An excellent cast is stranded. (105 mins.)

North to Alaska (1960)***½ John Wayne, Stewart Granger, Ernie Kovacs, Capucine, Fabian. Big, brawling, lusty adventure about a couple of prospectors who have woman trouble in addition to their other problems. Lots of rugged action, slapstick laughs played in fun. (Dir: Henry Hathaway, 122 mins.)

Northern Lights (1978)*** Susan Lynch, Robert Behling. Independent feature, set in North Dakota in 1915, depicts the struggle of Norwegian and Swedish immigrants to live off the stark prairie land. The Non-Partisan League, an organization of farmers to fight the railroad and banking trusts, provides a political backdrop for the love story. Sincere intentions, but in a murky, gritty style. (Dirs: Rob Nilsson, John Hanson.)

Northern Pursuit (1943)**½ Errol Flynn, Julie Bishop, Helmut Dantine, Gene Lockhart. Errol, still winning the war single-handed, is a Canadian Mountie in this one pursuing a Nazi aviator who's dashing through Canada bent on sabotage. (Dir: Raoul Walsh, 94 mins.)

Northwest Mounted Police (1940)*** Gary Cooper, Madeleine Carroll, Paulette Goddard, Robert Preston, Preston Foster. DeMille's tribute to the Mounties is a typical lavish, colorful action-packed and shallow story, but if you like sagas, here it is. (Dir: Cecil B. deMille, 125 mins.)

Northwest Outpost (1947)*½ Nelson Eddy, Ilona Massey, Joseph Schildkraut. (Dir: Allan Dwan, 91 mins.)

Northwest Passage (1940)***½ Spencer Tracy, Robert Young, Walter Brennan, Ruth Hussey. Epic-adventure yarn about the triumph of the will over fatigue, hunger, rage, weakness, insubordination, and even cannibalism, as Tracy and his men trek through the Northwest Territory from Idaho, fighting Indians all the way, to carve out a trade route. From the book by Kenneth Roberts. Color. (Dir: King Vidor, 125 mins.)

Norwood (1970)* Glen Campbell, Kim Darby, Joe Namath, Carol Lynley, Pat Hingle. (Dir: Jack Haley, Jr., 95 mins.)

Nosferatu (Germany, 1922)***½ Max Schreck, Alexander Granach, Greta Schroeder. Director F. W. Murnau's is the best version of the Dracula story. Superbly atmospheric, though technically limited. (63 mins.)

Nosferatu the Vampyre (West Germany, 1979)*** Klaus Kinski, Isabelle Adjani, Bruno Ganz. Director Werner Herzog's zomboid dementia is cut to the cloth of the saga of the undead, and unsurprisingly this most hypnotic of directors has created the most obsession-saturated of Dracula films. Kinski's body control, misshapen skull, and measured rhetoric make him an ideal Dracula, exuding a centuries-old weariness that can be overcome only by desire. (105 mins.)

Not as a Stranger (1955)*** Robert Mitchum, Frank Sinatra, Olivia de Havilland, Gloria Grahame. This is a somewhat watered down version of Morton Thompson's best selling novel about doctors and their degrees of dedication to their chosen profession. The operating room scenes are far superior to the soap opera tendencies of the personal drama. Charles Bickford and Lon Chaney are outstanding in a large supporting cast. (Dir: Stanley Kramer, 136 mins.)

Not Reconciled (West Germany, 1965)*** Heinrich Hargesheimer, Carlheinz Hargesheimer. Let Manny Farber speak for me: "Every line of dialogue, compositional gambit, as well as the various compromises made by the Fahmel family members, is made to answer to [director Jean-Marie] Straub's austere attitude about what is or isn't spiritual or intellectual vulgarity. The unusual nature of the film is that it so resists melodrama at every point." A filming of Heinrich Böll's novel "Billiards at Half-Past Nine." (53 mins.)

Not So Dusty (Great Britain, 1956)*½ Leslie Dwyer, Joy Nichols. (Dir: Maclean Rogers, 80 mins.)

Not with My Wife, You Don't (1966)**½ Tony Curtis, Virna Lisi, George C. Scott, Carroll O'Connor. Occasionally diverting marital comedy which has George C. Scott playing a broad funny role for a change—and his fans might want to see this side of him. Also on hand, as handsome window dressing, is Tony Curtis, as a jealous husband-Air Force officer, and Virna Lisi, as his beautiful Italian wife. The plot is familiar fare but you'll get a few laughs out of it. (Dir: Norman Panama, 118 mins.)

Nothing But a Man (1964)**** Ivan Dixon, Abbey Lincoln. Moving, hard-hitting film about a Negro couple who strive for dignity in an Alabama town. Ivan Dixon and Abbey Lincoln are excellent as the newlyweds who meet with more than their share of opposition as they try to make a life for themselves. Most of the film is simple in its narrative style which begins to haunt you even before the movie ends. Low-budget independent entry with a big wallop. (Dir: Michael Roemer, 92 mins.)

Nothing But the Best (1964)***½ Alan Bates, Denholm Elliot, Harry Andrews, Millicent Martin. A vastly underrated comedy gem, with a superb performance by Bates as a British working-class stiff who wants to better his lot and uses his wiles, charm, and wit to reach the "top." Along the way, he encounters obstacles which he disposes of with alacrity and aplomb until he possibly has to resort to murder. Does he or doesn't he? Tune in (when it's on), find out, and have a good time along the way. (Dir: Clive Donner, 99 mins.)

Nothing But the Night (Great Britain, 1972)** Christopher Lee, Peter Cushing, Diana Dors. Odd British shocker starts out as a mystery but strays into mass murder, insanity, illicit experiments, and the search for eternal life. Satisfyingly hammy performances by the leads. (Dir: Peter Sasdy, 90 mins.)

Nothing But the Truth (1941)*** Bob Hope, Paulette Goddard. Bob is good, but much of the story is old hat in this tale of a man who bets that he can tell only the truth for 24 hours. Some laughs, of course, but not Bob's best. (Dir: Elliott Nugent, 90 mins.)

Nothing Personal (1980)*½ Donald Sutherland, Dabney Coleman, Suzanne Somers. (Dir: George Bloomfield, 98 mins.)

Nothing Sacred (1937)**** Carole Lombard, Fredric March, Walter Connolly, Charles Winninger, Sig Ruman, John Qualen, Maxie Rosenbloom, Hattie McDaniel. A girl thought to be dying is turned into the "Sweetheart of New York City" as a newspaper publicity stunt. One of the funniest films ever made. The script is by Ben Hecht, and it shows; he was always at his best writing about the byways of newspaperdom. The pace is crackling, the dialogue hilarious, and the actors electrifying, especially March and Lombard as the wiseacre lovebirds, Winninger as a tippling country doctor, and Connolly as a magnificently irascible editor (listen for March's description of him—one of the funniest lines ever.) A great comedy. (Dir: William Wellman, 77 mins.)

Notorious (1946)**** Cary Grant, Ingrid Bergman, Claude Rains, Louis Calhern. A masterpiece, directed by Alfred Hitchcock, in which spy Grant talks Bergman into marrying Rains, head of a ring of neo-Nazis in South America. Sex is used for both ambiguity and treachery, which means that it is very sexy between Cary and Ingrid. Many moments of breathtaking brilliance. (106 mins.)

Notorious Gentleman, The (Great Britain, 1945)***½ Rex Harrison, Lilli Palmer. The story of a charming but scoundrelly wastrel who goes through life without purpose until love redeems him. Absorbing ironic comedy-drama, with a fine performance from Harrison. (Dir: Frank Launder, 108 mins.)

Notorious Landlady, The (1962)*** Kim Novak, Jack Lemmon, Fred Astaire. Young American in London rents an apartment from a beautiful but mysterious girl whom the police suspect of having murdered her husband, and promptly gets involved. Generally entertaining comedy, thanks to Lemmon's droll antics; the proceedings occasionally become strained, but there's enough flash and dash to the production to satisfy. (Dir: Richard Quine, 123 mins.)

Notorious Mr. Monks (1958)*½ Vera Ralston, Don Kelly. (Dir: Joseph Kane, 70 mins.)

Novel Affair, A (Great Britain, 1957)*** Margaret Leighton, Ralph Richardson, Rossano Brazzi. Witty, sophisticated comedy about a respectably married authoress of a sexy novel and her over-amorous chauffeur. Cast is excellent. (Dir: Muriel Box, 83 mins.)

Now and Forever (1934)**½ Gary Cooper, Carole Lombard, Shirley Temple. Thief Gary sees the light thanks to adorable Shirley. Not a bad film. (Dir: Henry Hathaway, 82 mins.)

Now Voyager (1942)***½ Bette Davis, Paul Henreid, Claude Rains, Gladys Cooper, John Loder, Bonita Granville, Ilka Chase. A repressed, put-upon spinster is awakened to life and love in this most famous of classic tearjerkers. Smoothly told, strongly acted, emotively directed. Rains, as a warmhearted psychiatrist, nearly steals the show, but he has Cooper, the domineering matron, to contend with. The best of its kind, and they sure don't make 'em like this anymore. (Dir: Irving Rapper, 117 mins.)

Now You See Him, Now You Don't (1972)** Kurt Russell, Joe Flynn, Jim Backus, Cesar Romero, William Windom. Sequel to the 1970 "The Computer Wore Tennis Shoes." Disney entry using the old gimmick of invisibility that's strictly for the kids. The stars all participate in a bit of hectic activity to save a nearly bankrupt college. Thanks to an invisible spray, everything disappears, even automobiles. Kids will chuckle. (Dir: Robert Butler, 88 mins.)

Now You See It, Now You Don't (MTV 1968)*½ Jonathan Winters, Luciana Paluzzi, Steve Allen, Jayne Meadows. (Dir: Don Weis, 96 mins.)

Nowhere to Hide (MTV 1977)** Lee Van Cleef, Tony Musante, Edward Anhalt. Some suspense in this Edward Anhalt yarn about the problems of protecting a witness, a former hit man, against a syndicate boss who assures the law he will get the witness before trial. The casting of Tony Musante as the hit man, writer-producer Anhalt as the syndicate boss, and Lee Van Cleef as a U.S. Marshal, add points to a fair action script. (Dir: Jack Starrett, 79 mins.)

Nowhere to Run (MTV 1978)**½ David Janssen, Stefanie Powers. Janssen brings his effectively world-weary presence to a Las Vegas gambling tale. He's worked out a nifty blackjack system with a special goal in mind—to be freed of his awful, unfaithful wife (Powers). The gambling sequences make the show. (Dir: Richard Lang, 104 mins.)

Nude Bomb, The (1980)** Don Adams, Sylvia Kristel, Vittorio Gassman, Rhonda Fleming. If anyone could breathe some stylistic life into this recap of the "Get Smart" TV series, director Clive Donner would be the one. We miss Barbara Feldon. (94 mins.)

Nude in a White Car (France, 1958)**½ Marina Vlady, Robert Hossein. Routine crime meller done by the French in an imitation-Hollywood fashion. Some excitement is generated by the stars but it's mostly familiar fare. (Dir: Robert Hossein, 87 mins.)

Nude Restaurant (1967)** Viva, Taylor Mead, Louis Waldon, Brigid Polk. Andy Warhol wrote, directed, produced, shot, and edited. Nothing much happens. Viva is incomparably original as the waitress who prattles endlessly. (100 mins.)

Number One (1969)* Charlton Heston, Jessica Walter, Diana Muldaur, Al Hirt, John Randolph, Bruce Dern. (Dir: Tom Gries, 105 mins.)

Number 17 (Great Britain, 1932)***½ John Stuart, Anne Casson, Donald Calthrop. Directed by the master, Alfred Hitchcock, before he started to work, within a couple of years, on bigger-budgeted films like "The 39 Steps." A classy entry throughout, with—of course—a splendid chase finale sequence. (83 mins.)

Number Six (Great Britain, 1962)** Ivan Desny, Nadja Regin, Brian Bedford. Crook in London seeks the identity of a secret operative assigned by the police to keep an eye on him. Mildly entertaining Edgar Wallace crime melodrama. (Dir: Robert Tronson, 59 mins.)

Nun, The (France, 1965)**** Anna Karina, Liselotte Pulver, Micheline Presle. Masterful, subdued, intensely dramatic adaptation of French author Diderot's "La Religieuse." Set in a convent, it chronicles the anguish of a young and beautiful sister (Miss Karina) who refuses to take her vows, or Christ, quite seriously enough. First-rate direction from Jacques Rivette, who also co-authored the screenplay. You'll not soon forget this searing comment on religious life and training, and the problems Miss Karina encounters. (140 mins.)

Nun and the Sergeant, The (1962)* Anna Sten, Robert Webber. (Dir: Franklin Adreon, 73 mins.)

Nun's Story, The (1959)**** Audrey Hepburn, Peter Finch. The best selling novel is brought to the screen with taste and skill by a talented cast headed by Audrey Hepburn. The story follows a young girl through her early convent days, her taking of the vows and her work in Africa. Peter Finch gives a fine account of himself as a non-religious doctor working in the Congo. Director Fred Zinnemann gets excellent performances from the whole company. (Dir: Fred Zinnemann, 149 mins.)

Nuremberg and Its Lesson** The Allies edited Joseph Goebbels footage into a document to show the world the full impact of Nazi horror. Still shattering and devastating.

Nurse (MTV 1980)**½ Michael Learned, Robert Reed, Tom Aldredge. Medical drama adapted from Peggy Anderson's best-seller. Learned winningly portrays a doctor's widow who resumes her nursing career, running things in a New York City hospital. She has a hard time, but shares caring moments with a terminally ill ex-cop (Aldredge). (Dir: David Lowell Rich, 98 mins.)

Nurse Edith Cavell (1939)**½ Anna Neagle, George Sanders. Story of the brave nurse who served the allies so gallantly during WW I. Impressive drama, well acted. (Dir: Herbert Wilcox, 98 mins.)

Nurse Sherri (1978)** Jill Jacobson, Geoffrey. A sweet young nurse, raped by an invisible presence, is transformed into a murderess until exorcised by a Haitian physician. (Dir: Al Adamson.)

Nutty, Naughty Chateau (France-Italy, 1963)**½ Monica Vitti, Curt Jurgens, Jean-Claude Brialy, Jean-Louis Trintignant. Excellent cast of stars in slight comedy, concerning a young man who takes refuge in a strange chateau where everyone is dressed in 17th-century garb. Based on a Françoise Sagan play. (Dir: Roger Vadim, 102 mins.)

Nutty Professor, The (1963)*** Jerry Lewis, Stella Stevens, Kathleen Freeman, Howard Morris. Director Jerry Lewis plays Dr. Julius Kelp, an absent-minded chemist who invents a potion that turns him into the irresistible Buddy Love, a character who bears a not wholly coincidental resemblance to Dean Martin. It all depends on whether you find Lewis funny. A technically impeccable work of inspired megalomania. (107 mins.)

Nylon Noose, The West Germany, 1963)*½ Richard Goodman, Laya Raki. (Dir: Rudolf Zehetgruber, 74 min.)

Nyoka and the Lost Secrets of Hippocrates (1942-66)** Kay Aldridge, Clayton Moore. Feature version of serial "Perils of Nyoka." Jungle girl searching for her missing father competes with a villainous rival hand for some priceless tablets. Pretty farfetched stuff, but at least it moves fast. (Dir: William Witney, 100 mins.)

O. Henry's Full House (1952)*** Charles Laughton, David Wayne, Marilyn Monroe, Anne Baxter, Jeanne Crain, Jean Peters, Gregory Ratoff, Farley Granger, Fred Allen, Oscar Levant, Richard Widmark, Dale Robertson. An all-star cast enacts a quintet of O. Henry's short stories, best of which is "The Last Leaf" with Anne Baxter and Gregory Ratoff sharing top acting honors. Each episode was directed by a different director with a different cast. This sort of film omnibus has never really been successfully done by Hollywood. The Italian and French film makers excel in this type of movie. (Dirs: Henry Hathaway, Howard Hawks, Henry King, Henry Koster, Jean Negulesco, 117 mins.)

O Lucky Man! (Great Britain, 1973)**½ Malcolm McDowell, Ralph Richardson, Rachel Roberts, Arthur Lowe, Helen Mirren, Mona Washbourne, Vivian Pickles. McDowell is a salesman trying to rise in a modern society full of sham and corruption. Director Lindsay Anderson's modern "Candide" is valiant, comic, and thoughtful. Good use of Alan Price songs, and the performance level is high, especially Lowe and Richardson. (166 mins.)

Objective Burma (1945)***½ Errol Flynn, William Prince. Another superb war movie. This one is about paratroopers dropped in Burma with their objective being a Jap radar station. It's exciting, realistic entertainment. (Dir: Raoul Walsh, 142 mins.)

Obliging Young Lady (1941)***½ Joan Carroll, Edmond O'Brien, Ruth Warrick, Eve Arden. Young girl involved in a court fight is sent to a mountain resort where complications arise over her parentage. Delightful comedy, many laughs. (Dir: Richard Wallace, 80 mins.)

Oblong Box, The (U.S.-Great Britain, 1969)** Vincent Price, Christopher Lee. Another in the seemingly endless Vincent Price-Edgar Allan Poe horror tales. (This is the eleventh Poe story produced by American International Pictures alone.) This time out, Price is a 19th-century Englishman who does his brother dirt, and lives to regret it. All the expected touches, including coffins, not-dead corpses, mutilations, etc., are present for fans of this genre. (Dir: Gordon Hessler, 91 mins.)

Obsession (France, 1954)**½ Michele Morgan, Raf Vallone. Slow paced well acted melodrama concerned chiefly with a woman's pain in facing the awful truth about the man she loves. (Dir: Kean Delannoy, 103 mins.)

Obsession (1976)**½ Cliff Robertson, Genevieve Bujold. Director Brian De Palma's tribute to Alfred Hitchcock is a crude rehash of Hitchcock images and themes. Robertson is a businessman who feels responsible for his wife's death in a kidnapping plot; 15 years later he meets her double and remarries, hoping to recreate the past. If you've seen "Vertigo," you'll be half an hour ahead of De Palma all the way through. The score, by Bernard Herrmann, is one of his last—and worst. (98 mins.)

Ocean's Eleven (1960)**½ Frank Sinatra, Dean Martin, Sammy Davis, Jr., Joey Bishop, Peter Lawford, Angie Dickinson. Ill-assorted group decides to pull a daring Las Vegas robbery, and it nearly comes off. Members of the so-called Sinatra "Clan" participated in this uneven comedy-crime drama, and it gives the uncomfortable impression of being a big inside joke. Some amusement, but they probably had more fun while making it. (Dir: Lewis Milestone, 127 mins.)

October Man, The (Great Britain, 1947)*** John Mills, Joan Greenwood. Man suffering from a head injury is suspected of murdering a model, proves his innocence. Good mystery has plenty of suspense. (Dir: Roy Baker, 86 mins.)

October—Ten Days That Shook the World (U.S.S.R., 1928)** Thoroughly ignoble and aesthetically wrongheaded. The vaunted innovation of "intellectual montage" succeeds only in taking an expressive art form and using it to convey snide jokes that would just as well have been verbalized. The savage caricaturing of the film's villains lacks perspective and honesty. Director Sergei Eisenstein was a good propagandist, but the world would be better off if there were no good propagandists. (105 mins.)

Odd Couple, The (1968)**** Jack Lemmon, Walter Matthau, Herb Edelman, Carole Shelley, John Fiedler. A marvelously funny comedy. Neil Simon's hit play about two grumpy ex-marrieds (Lemmon and Matthau) who take up housekeeping together in New York. It's one of the few times in Hollywood history where the film version has improved on the Broadway original, and much of the credit for this happy state of affairs goes to director Gene Saks, even though he does have a nearly foolproof screenplay and cast to work with. Later the TV series. (105 mins.)

Odd Man Out (Great Britain, 1947)**** James Mason, Kathleen Ryan, Robert Newton. Gripping story of the last hours of a wounded fugitive from a holdup during the Irish rebellion. Almost painful in its suspense, tragedy, a drama that is not soon forgotten. Remade as "The Lost Man." (Dir: Carol Reed, 113 mins.)

Odds Against Tomorrow (1959)** Robert Ryan, Ed Begley, Harry Belafonte, Shelley Winters, Gloria Grahame. A ridiculous story premise—that three bank robbers fail because two of them are racists who can't handle working with a black man—is given a pretentious visual treatment. Winters and Grahame compete in the blowsiness sweepstakes, and the aggressive cinematography is by Joe Brun. (Dir: Robert Wise, 95 mins.)

Ode to Billy Joe (1976)** Robby Benson, Glynnis O'Connor, Joan Hotchkis. Based on the hit song popularized by Bobby Gentry. The script by Herman Raucher purports to tell you "what the song didn't." Unfortunately, it does. Trivial coming-of-age melodrama. (Dir: Max Baer, 100 mins.)

Odessa File, The (Great Britain-West Germany, 1974)**½ Jon Voight, Maximilian Schell, Mary Tamm, Maria Schell. Frederick Forsyth's novel about an earnest German journalist who stumbles upon the whereabouts of a Nazi war criminal and risks his life to get him, is only moderately successful in transition to the screen. A lugubrious screenplay, heavy on endless exposition, keeps the film from taking off. But Voight's wonderful performance (his German accent is very convincing), and the excellent confrontation scene between him and Maximilian Schell's evil SS officer, compensate for several lesser scenes. (Dir: Ronald Neame, 128 mins.)

Odette (Great Britain, 1950)***½ Anna Neagle, Trevor Howard. The true story of an heroic Frenchwoman who worked underground for the duration of the war fighting the Nazis. Excellent drama, all the more inspiring because it actually happened. From the book by Peter Churchill. (Dir: Herbert Wilcox, 106 mins.)

Odongo (Great Britain, 1956)** Rhonda Fleming, Macdonald Carey. Passion, if little else, is set loose in the jungles of Africa when a Kenya white hunter and a woman doctor find themselves on the same safari. (Dir: John Gilling, 85 mins.)

Oedipus the King (Great Britain, 1967)*** Christopher Plummer, Orson Welles, Lilli Palmer, Richard Johnson, Donald Sutherland. After Sophocles' play about the plague-wracked city of Thebes. If you approach this all-star version of the classic play in terms of a stimulating history-drama class, you'll find it well worth your time. Filmed on location at a ruined Grecian amphitheater at Dodona. Plummer playing King Oedipus gives a striking, if sometimes irritating performance. Notable supporting performances from Lilli Palmer playing Plummer's wife, and from Orson Welles portraying a blind seer. (Dir: Philip Saville, 97 mins.)

Of Human Bondage (1934)*** Bette Davis, Leslie Howard, Kay Johnson, Frances Dee, Reginald Owen. Davis achieved genuine stardom with her overdetailed incarnation of the sluttish waitress Mildred in this uneven adaptation of W. Somerset Maugham's novel. For all the fascination with the showily degenerating Mildred/Bette, the more interesting relationship is the conventional one of Johnson

and Dee. John Cromwell directed, with a certain flair. (83 mins.)

Of Human Bondage (Great Britain, 1964)** Kim Novak, Laurence Harvey. The classic Somerset Maugham novel of a young doctor and his obsessive infatuation with a frowzy waitress was memorably filmed before with Leslie Howard and Bette Davis. This time everybody gives it the old try, but the results are scrappy. Harvey suffers nobly, but Novak deserves credit for a performance that's ineffective but interesting. (Dir: Ken Hughes, 98 mins.)

Of Human Hearts (1938)***½ Walter Huston, James Stewart, Beulah Bondi. You'll like this sensitive, dramatic tale of a backwoods family in Ohio. Story tells of a young physician who is sent for by Lincoln during the Civil War because he has neglected writing to his mother. Picture tells the story of this boy and his family. (Dir: Clarence Brown, 103 mins.)

Of Life and Love (Italy, 1958)*** Anna Magnani. Several romantic plots, including Magnani as a famous screen actress. Skimpy tales but Magnani is customarily convincing. (Dirs: Giorgio Pastina, M. Soldati, Luchino Visconti, Aldo Fabrizi, 103 mins.)

Of Love and Desire (1963)½ Merle Oberon, Steve Cochran, Curt Jurgens. (Dir: Richard Rush, 97 mins.)

Of Mice and Men (1939)**** Burgess Meredith, Lon Chaney, Betty Field. Steinbeck's classic tale of a feeble-minded soul and his protector, set on the migratory farms of the Salinas Valley. A film masterpiece! Excellent all around. (Dir: Lewis Milestone, 107 mins.)

Off Limits (1953)**½ Bob Hope, Mickey Rooney, Marilyn Maxwell. A fight manager is drafted and manages to break all the regulations when he tries to develop a new fighter. Mildly amusing Hope comedy with Rooney lending capable support. (Dir: George Marshall, 89 mins.)

Off the Minnesota Strip (MTV 1980)*** Mare Winningham, Michael Learned, Hal Holbrook. Newcomer Winningham is splendid as Michele, a confused teenager who runs away to New York and becomes a prostitute. She returns to her midwestern home to find her parents and school friends unable to provide the compassion and understanding she so desperately needs. (Dir: Lamont Johnson, 104 mins.)

Offense, The (Great Britain, 1973)***½ Sean Connery, Trevor Howard, Vivien Merchant, Ian Bannen. In return for playing James Bond, United Artists allowed Connery to make two films of his choice—one was this powerful version of John Hopkins' stage play, which makes few compromises for its audience. Tale of a middle-class policeman's crackup is realistic and unsentimental. Connery is extremely moving as a cop who kills a child molester during an interrogation, because the criminal has forced the detective to face himself. Talky at times, betraying its theatrical origins, but one of the hardest hitting films financed by Hollywood in that period. Supporting roles wonderfully acted. (Dir: Sidney Lumet, 118 mins.)

Officer and the Lady (1941)**½ Bruce Bennett, Rochelle Hudson, Roger Pryor. Cop exposes two crooks who have pulled a robbery, even though his girl may be implicated. Fast moving crime melodrama. (Dir: Sam White, 60 mins.)

Oh! Calcutta! (1972)** Bill Macy, Raina Barrett, Margo Sappington. At the end of "Calcutta," someone asks, "Who wrote this piece of shit anyway?" That's a good question under the circumstances, especially because this is a grainy, murky version of what was, in September of 1970, a closed-circuit videotape telecast of the long-running theatrical revue spoofing modern ideas of sex and sensuality. The voyeurs in the audience will be disappointed—there are some scenes photographed in the buff, but it's all pretty hazy, and seems rather tired and dated by now. A few clever sketches along the way written by such clever gents as Jules Feiffer, Dan Greenburg, David Newman and Robert Benton. "Calcutta" was "devised" by the brilliant and audacious English theater critic Kenneth Tynan. Bill Macy seen before his starring days on "Maude." (Dir: Guillaume Martin Aucion, 108 mins.)

Oh Dad, Poor Dad, Mamma's Hung You in the Closet and I'm Feelin' So Sad (1967)* Rosalind Russell, Robert Morse, Jonathan Winters, Barbara Harris. (Dir: Richard Quine, 86 mins.)

Oh God! (1977)**½ George Burns, John Denver, Paul Sorvino, Terri Garr. Burns seems to be warming up for a good Second City sketch on God's return to earth as a rumpled vaudevillian. Then it becomes clear that director Carl Reiner isn't kidding—he thinks his movie is going to save the world. The gags are slighted in favor of John Denver-style homilies, mouthed by Denver, while the film collapses. (110 mins.)

Oh God! Book II (1980)** George Burns, Suzanne Pleshette, David Birney, Louanne. Burns is back to give God a bad name in this sequel to the '77 embarrassment. Story and coscript by Josh Greenfield. (Dir: Gilbert Cates)

Oh Men! Oh Women! (1957)*** David Niven, Tony Randall (debut), Ginger Rogers, Dan Dailey, Barbara Rush. Tony Randall steals the film from the other four stars in the role of a zany patient of psychoanalyst David Niven. As it turns out, they're both in love with the same woman, Barbara Rush. Based on the hit B'way play. Lots of laughs if you like your dialogue with gags about analysts. (Dir: Nunnally Johnson, 90 mins.)

Oh What a Lovely War (Great Britain, 1969)**** Laurence Olivier, Ralph Richardson, John Mills. Oh what a lovely film actor-producer-director Richard Attenborough has made from what was originally little more than a series of inspired sketches about man's continuing folly. Using real songs popular in Britain before and during WW I, Attenborough has skillfully given a cohesive form and narrative to this material, and employed in the process just about every great name in the British theater. One of the most stirring antiwar films ever made. (139 mins.)

Oh, You Beautiful Doll (1949)** June Haver, S. Z. Sakall, Charlotte Greenwood, Mark Stevens, J. C. Flippen. This Fox musical biopic of Fred Fisher is little more than skeletal entertainment. Some charm, from the turn-of-the-century tunes and Haver's presence. (93 mins.)

O'Hara, United States Treasury (MTV 1971)** David Janssen, Lana Wood. Stars customs agent David Janssen chasing narcotics smugglers around the country. This is a vintage blend of Jack Webb and writer Jim Moser. The agents talk in code, using that efficient, manly, clipped, no-smiling technique which has become Webb's TV trademark; but in this pilot film, Treasury jargon is constant and fans may need a few subtitles. Location scenes in San Pedro, Chicago, and aboard a Marine jet fighter—Webb's closing ace for the climatic chase. (Dir: Jack Webb, 99 mins.)

Ohms (MTV 1980)** Ralph Waite, David Birney, Talia Balsam. Farmers are the good guys, the power company and its lawyers are the bad guys, in this acceptable tale about eminent domain. The utility intends to run a million-volt line across farm property, but the farmers fight back in a highly original way, showing that corporate, or government, power can be beaten. (Dir: Dick Lowry, 104 mins.)

Okinawa (1952)** Pat O'Brien, Cameron Mitchell. Action packed war drama about the heroic crew of the destroyer U.S.S. Blake and their part in the invasion of Okinawa (WW II). (Dir: George Brooks, 67 mins.)

Oklahoma! (1955)**½ Gordon Macrae, Shirley Jones, Rod Steiger, Gloria Grahame, Gene Nelson. Director Fred Zinnemann's literalism couldn't be more inappropiate for this sophisticated hokum that revolutionized the American theater. Not nearly folksy enough. Nelson's dancing is good, though the inspiration of Agnes De Mille's choreography is dissipated onscreen. Still a great Rodgers and Hammerstein score. (145 mins.)

Oklahoma Crude (1973)** George C. Scott, Faye Dunaway, John Mills, Jack Palance. Limping formula picture burdened by Stanley Kramer's clubfooted direction. Dunaway is a tough lady wildcatter holding out against the forces of nasty Big Oil (personified by nasty, squinting, cigar-chomping Palance) aided by an erstwhile father (Mills) and a hobo (Scott). (108 mins.)

Oklahoma Kid, The (1939)*** James Cagney, Humphrey Bogart, Rosemary Lane, Donald Crisp, Ward Bond. Pretty good big-budget western sticks closely to the conventions of the genre, goes at a brisk pace. Cagney sings "I Don't Want to Play in Your Yard," a popular comic song of the 1890s. (Dir: Lloyd Bacon, 90 mins.)

Oklahoman, The (1957)** Joel McCrea, Barbara Hale. A quiet western with little action. Joel McCrea fans will enjoy watching the master film cowboy go through the paces as a widower who settles in a small town. (Dir: Francis D. Lyon, 73 mins.)

Old Acquaintance (1943)*** Bette Davis, Miriam Hopkins, Gig Young. Davis writes serious fiction while Hopkins makes a mint with pulp romances. The girls vie for the same men, bitching it up in high style. Davis's affair with a much younger man (Young) is handled intelligently. Directed rather well by Vincent Sherman. (110 mins.)

Old Boyfriends (1979)*** Talia Shire, Keith Carradine, Richard Jordan, John Belushi. Methodical plotting and characterization in the screenplay by the brothers Schrader. There is everywhere evidence of intelligence and care; Shire plays a depressive psychologist who takes to the road to seek out and rectify her past; Carradine renders a small miracle as a psychologically damaged youth. (Dir: Joan Tewkesbury, 103 mins.)

Old Dark House, The (1932)***½ Charles Laughton, Raymond Massey, Boris Karloff, Melvyn Douglas, Lillian Bond, Ernest Thesiger. Highly enjoyable gothic thriller about a group of travelers stranded in a lonely mountain house during a storm. A fantastic cast, impeccably directed by James Whale; literate, scary, funny, and above all, bizarre. (75 mins.)

Old Dark House, The (Great Britain, 1963)**½ Tom Poston, Robert Morley, Janette Scott. American salesman spends the night in a creepy mansion, where the heirs are bumped off one by one. Fairly effective spooky thriller, with a welcome note of lightness and a genuinely surprising ending. (Dir: William Castle, 86 mins.)

Old Dracula (Great Britain, 1975)* David Niven, Teresa Graves, Peter Bayliss. (Dir: Clive Donner, 89 mins.)

Old Fashioned Way, The (1934)***½ W. C. Fields. A "must" for students of comedy as are all of Fields' starring films. Here he's the head of an acting troupe that appropriately performs "The Drunkard." A one-man show. (Dir: William Beaudine, 74 mins.)

Old Los Angeles (1948)*** William Elliott, John Carroll, Catherine McLeod, Joseph Schildkraut, Andy Devine. Man finds that gold miners are being cheated and his brother murdered, tries to find the guilty one. Good western moves at a fast pace. (Dir: Joe Kane, 87 mins.)

Old Maid, The (1939)*** Bette Davis, Miriam Hopkins, Jane Bryan. Davis must give her baby to be raised by her married sister (Hopkins) when her suitor is killed in the Civil War. The late Casey Robinson adapted Zoë Akins's adaptation for the stage of the Edith Wharton novel. What remains is soap opera, but still an awesomely effective tear machine. Director Edmund Goulding is skillful with such material, and Tony Gaudio's photography helps. (100 mins.)

Old Man and the Sea, The (1958)*** Spencer Tracey. Ernest Hemingway's story about a determined Cuban fisherman does not make a great film, but it is a good try. Tracy is excellent in the leading role, which amounts to virtually a monologue during the long passages at sea. Fine camerawork (two of the cinematographers were James Wong Howe and Floyd Crosby) adds to the mood of the film. (Dir: John Sturges, 86 mins.)

Old Man Who Cried Wolf, The (MTV 1970)*** Edward G. Robinson, Martin Balsam, Diane Baker. Skillful performance by Edward G. Robinson as an old man who witnesses the murder of an old friend but can't convince anyone of it. Suspense builds as Robinson risks his life and sanity trying to prove he's right, and the production is first class all the way. The supporting cast is very good, with Percy Rodrigues a standout as a sinister murderer. (Dir: Walter Grauman, 73 mins.)

Old Testament, The (Italy, 1963)*½ Susan Paget, Brad Harris. (Dir: Gianfranco Parolini, 110 mins.)

Old Yeller (1957)*** Dorothy McGuire, Fess Parker, Tommy Kirk, Kevin Corcoran, Chuck Connors. An old Disney classic that the kids will adore. The title character is a terrific mongrel dog, redeemed from his bad ways by the love of a Texas ranch family. McGuire and Parker head the adoptive family, and Kirk and Corcoran are the two kids who get into and out of innumerable scrapes with the help of the faithful "Old Yeller." (Dir: Robert Stevenson, 83 mins.)

Oldest Profession, The (France-West Germany-Italy, 1967)**½ Jeanne Moreau, Jean-Claude Brialy, Raquel Welch, Jacques Charrier, Anna Karina. The prostitute traced from prehistory to future times, in six chronological chapters. The first five are mildly humorous, but sketchy. The final segment, "Anticipation," directed by Godard, is more polished and clever, a look at the future when a visitor from outer space arrives in Paris to discover an oddly programmed sort of love-making. (Dirs: Franco Indovina, Mauro Bolognini, Philippe de Broca, Michael Pfleghar, Claude Autant-Lara, Jean-Luc Godard, 97 mins.)

Olive Trees of Justice, The (France, 1962)*** Pierre Prothon, Jean Pelegri. An Algerian-born Frenchman returns to Algeria where his father lies dying, and comes to grips with the Arab-French hostilities. Directed by American James Blue as propaganda for the French government, but is far from pointed or heavy-handed. Film is a moving, lyrical, incisive document about war and humanitarian concerns, provides a fascinating retrospective on the colonization of Algeria by the French. Based on the book by Jean Pelegri. (90 mins.)

Oliver (Great Britain, 1968)**** Ron Moody, Mark Lester, Shani Wallis, Oliver Reed, Jack Wild, Hugh Griffith. This superlative musical directed by Carol Reed won five Academy Awards including those for Best Picture and Direction. With an assist from Charles Dickens and some new dialogue and songs by Lionel Bart, taken from his smash hit theatrical musical, Reed has given new life to the classic tale about the luckless orphan Oliver Twist. Lester, playing Oliver, is one of the most appealing child actors to come along in a good while; the role of Fagin, acted with great relish by Moody, has been sanitized of the anti-Semitic implications of the original story. You'll be delighted by such songs as "Pick a Pocket or Two," and the magical re-creation of London in the 1830s. (153 mins.)

Oliver Twist (Great Britain, 1948)**** Alec Guinness, John Howard Davies, Robert Newton, Kay Walsh, Anthony Newley. Guinness brings a touch of humor to his portrayal of master pickpocket Fagin and his performance is a joy. The film wasn't allowed into the U.S. because of its alleged anti-Semitic overtones, until most of Guinness's profile close-ups were scissored. Director David Lean's faithfulness to the grimy details of the novel will be a shock to those brought up on the sugary world of "Oliver!" Newley plays the Artful Dodger. (105 mins.)

Oliver's Story (1978)* Ryan O'Neal, Candice Bergen, Ray Milland, Nicola Pagett, Edward Binns. (Dir: John Korty, 92 mins.)

Olly Olly Oxen Free (1978)*** Katharine Hepburn, Kevin McKenzie, Dennis Dimster. What, you ask, is someone of Hepburn's stature doing in a children's movie? Well, she's playing a character part, an eccentric lady who runs a junkyard and helps two small boys in their quest to launch a huge hot-air balloon. The Great Kate provides reason enough to watch. (Dir: Richard A. Colla, 89 mins.)

Olympia (Olympische Spiele) (Germany, 1936)**** Talented Nazi director Leni Riefenstahl edited the 1936 Olympics in Munich to make a great film. She was inhibited by the propaganda requirements of the Third Reich and by the unforgivable four gold medals won by American Negro Jesse Owens, so she opted for the grace and poetry of bodies in motion. A bit long if you're not an enthusiast, but lovely.

The diving sequences are especially stunning. (225 mins.)

Olympic Visions—See: **Visions of Eight**

Omar Khayyam (1957)** Cornel Wilde, Debra Paget, Raymond Massey, Michael Rennie, John Derek. Adventurer and poet battles a gang of assassins who intend to take over Persia. Opulent production gracing the same old plot. (Dir: William Dieterle, 101 mins.)

Omega Man, The (1971)*½ Charlton Heston, Rosalind Cash, Tony Zerbe. (Dir: Boris Sagal, 98 mins.)

Omen, The (1976)*** Gregory Peck, Lee Remick, David Warner, Billie Whitelaw. The devil returns in another big screen performance—this time in the form of a five-year-old boy sired by the devil himself, and inadvertently adopted by a wealthy American couple. Some mystery derives from the boy's father (Peck) hunting for his son's true lineage. Earnest acting, especially by Whitelaw as a maid sent by the devil to care for the boy, and Warner as a photographer whose pictures reveal some disturbing "omens," enhance the chills. (Dir: Richard Donner, 110 mins.)

On a Clear Day You Can See Forever (1970)*** Barbra Streisand, Yves Montand. The combination of a perfectly cast Streisand and a melodic score by Alan Jay Lerner and Burton Lane adds up to pleasant fare if you're not too demanding. Barbra's a young woman who discovers acute ESP powers which send her to sexy psychiatrist Montand. He puts her under hypnosis and off she goes to reenact her past lives. Director Vincente Minnelli is at the top of his form, especially when mounting the sequences taking place amid the pomp and pageantry of 19th-century English aristocracy. Songs include title song, "He Wasn't You," "Come Back to Me," and "Go to Sleep." Barbra makes it worthwhile. (129 mins.)

On an Island with You (1948)**½ Esther Williams, Peter Lawford, Jimmy Durante, Ricardo Montalban, Cyd Charisse. A lot of Esther in bathing suits is what this romance of a naval flyer and an actress offers. If you like to watch Esther swim, this one is for you. (Dir: Richard Thorpe, 107 mins.)

On Approval (Great Britain, 1944)***½ Beatrice Lillie, Googie Withers, Clive Brook, Roland Culver. Droll deadpan farce, featuring a superbly arch quartet of players. The women exchange boyfriends and everyone savors the ironic consequences together. It's all quite civilized and thoroughly barbaric. Withers steals the show, no mean feat when Lillie has incomparable lines like "You will find the dinghy by the jetty." Brook directs well. (80 mins.)

On Borrowed Time (1939)***½ Lionel Barrymore, Cedric Hardwicke, Beulah Bondi. Warm, sentimental fantasy about an old man who isn't ready to die so he chases "Death" up a tree. You'll laugh and cry at this good adaptation of the stage success. (Dir: Harold S. Bucquet, 98 mins.)

On Company Business (1979)***½ Documentary details the workings of the CIA over 30 years. Director Allan Francovich headed a team who culled through a thousand hours of government footage and news documents to piece together this comprehensive portrait. Not many revelations, but the thoroughness and cumulative impact are in themselves revelatory and engrossing. (180 mins.)

On Dangerous Ground (1951)***½ Robert Ryan, Ida Lupino, Ward Bond, Ed Begley. Unusual psychological drama directed by Nicholas Ray, delineating the moral profile of a burnt-out cop (Ryan), who hates humanity because of what he's seen on the street. The resolution (involving a hackneyed city-country opposition and a redemptive blind girl played by Lupino) is disappointing. (82 mins.)

On Foot, on Horse and on Wheels (France, 1957)** Noel-Noel, Denise Grey. A muddled farce that makes a great deal of use out of the transportation problems in Paris. Most of the funnier episodes are too labored. (Dir: Maurice Delbez, 90 mins.)

On Her Majesty's Secret Service (Great Britain, 1969)*** George Lazenby, Diana Rigg, Telly Savalas. Agent 007 James Bond is back again, but Sean Connery has departed. His replacement, Lazenby, is about as animated as Westminster Abbey, but there are enough exciting scenes in this hokum to keep most Bond fans entertained. Some splendid location scenes in Switzerland with a really thrilling ski chase, and our hero also being pursued by the meanies as he navigates down a toboggan course. It may be the longest toboggan race ever, but it's a short, exciting pursuit as handled by the director. The plot concerns the bad guys' plan to conquer the world using a virus. (Dir: Peter Hunt, 140 mins.)

On Moonlight Bay (1951)*** Doris Day, Gordon Macrae, Leon Ames, Billy Gray, Mary Wickes, Rosemary DeCamp. Booth Tarkington's Penrod stories make interesting material for an early Day musical. Day and MacRae are the romancing couple and Ames is her father. (Dir: Roy Del Ruth, 95 mins.)

On Our Merry Way (1948)** Paulette Goddard, Burgess Meredith, Dorothy Lamour, James Stewart, Henry Fonda, Fred MacMurray. Questions asked by an inquiring reporter lead to a series of humorous stories. A good idea that doesn't come off, due to inept scripting. (Dirs: King Vidor, Leslie Fenton, 99 mins.)

On the Avenue (1937)**** Madeleine Carroll, Dick Powell, Alice Faye, the Ritz Brothers. Lively musical with excellent songs by Irving Berlin ("Let's Go Slumming on Park Avenue"). Carroll is an heiress outraged by a revue satirizing her foibles, but she falls in love with its easygoing star (Powell). Later revamped as "Let's Make Love." (Dir: Roy Del Ruth, 89 mins.)

On the Beach (1959)***½ Gregory Peck, Ava Gardner, Fred Astaire, Anthony Perkins. Nevil Shute's searing novel about the last people on earth, who face certain death from radioactivity after WW III. Too much footage for the Peck-Gardner romantic interludes, and Astaire is miscast as a scientist, but the film remains a powerful comment against war. (Dir: Stanley Kramer, 134 mins.)

On the Beat (Great Britain, 1962)*** Norman Wisdom, Jennifer Jayne. Stumbling car cleaner at Scotland Yard wants to be a policeman, gets his chance when he poses as a crook to trap jewel robbers. Amusing farce starring the popular English comic; some rib-tickling situations. (Dir: Robert Asher, 105 mins.)

On the Double (1961)**½ Danny Kaye, Dana Wynter, Margaret Rutherford, Wilfred Hyde-White. Danny's a GI whose impersonations land him in hot water during WW II. The talented Mr. Kaye doesn't get much help from the scriptwriters, but there are some nice moments. (Dir: Melville Shavelson, 92 mins.)

On the Fiddle—See: **Operation Snafu**

On the Nickel (1979)** Donald Moffat, Penelope Allen, James Gammon, Ralph Waite. Woebegone independent feature about life on skid row in L.A. indulges in every sentimentality at a snail's pace. Waite wrote, produced, and directed, and plays the flashiest part. (96 mins.)

On the Riviera (1951)*** Danny Kaye, Gene Tierney, Corinne Calvet. Fast and funny comedy about the international set and their gay escapades on the Riviera, the playground of the rich. Kaye sings, dances, clowns and makes love to Gene Tierney. Watch for Gwen Verdon in a can-can number. (Dir: Walter Lang, 90 mins.)

On the Sidelines (Hungary, 1976)*** Ferenc Kallai won a festival award for his role as an aging bachelor who works a dead-end job in a bakery but comes alive when he referees football games on weekends. (Dir: Peter Szasz.)

On the Town (1949)**** Gene Kelly, Frank Sinatra, Jules Munshin, Vera-Ellen, Ann Miller, Betty Garrett. Adapted from the hit Broadway musical. Kelly, Sinatra, and Munshin are three sailors out for a day in New York; Vera-Ellen, Miller, and Garrett are the girls they spend it with. Brilliant use of locations by directors Kelly and Stanley Donen, coupled with the split-second timing of the principals, make this a genuine classic. (98 mins.)

On the Waterfront (1954)**** Marlon Brando, Eva Marie Saint, Karl Malden, Lee J. Cobb, Rod Steiger. Forceful, super-charged melodrama about the docks of New Jersey—the workers, the bosses, the criminals, and their families. Brilliantly acted by all with Brando a superb standout. Winner of many Oscars including Best Film. Directed by Elia Kazan. Brando's shattering performance is among the finest ever recorded on film, and Steiger got his start to stardom here. The scene between them in an auto is superbly played and directed. Brando and Saint won Oscars (she for Best Supporting Actress). (108 mins.)

On the Yard (1979)***½ John Heard, Thomas Waites, Mike Kellin. Director Raphael D. Silver and Joan Silver's independent production team (Midwest Films) comes up with the most plausible of prison pictures. Waites and Heard are excellent. Based on a novel by Malcolm Braly, who served time at San Quentin; he also scripted. Shot at the State Correctional Facility at Rockview, Pa. (102 mins.)

On Thin Ice (West Germany, 1961)*½ Tony Sailer, Ina Bauer. (Dir: Geza von Cziffra, 90 mins.)

On Your Toes (1939)** Vera Zorina, Eddie Albert. Screen treatment of the Rodgers and Hart musical which first introduced the ballet "Slaughter on Tenth Avenue." Terrible film and absolutely no music except for the ballet. (Dir: Ray Enright, 94 mins.)

Once a Thief (1965)*** Ann-Margret, Alain Delon, Jack Palance. Absorbing crime yarn which benefits from Alain Delon's restrained performance as an ex-con who tries to go straight but has little luck. Ann-Margret is miscast as Delon's wife, but Jack Palance and Van Heflin are fine in the chief supporting roles. (Dir: Ralph Nelson, 107 mins.)

Once Again (Ek Baar Phir) (India, 1980)** Deepte Naval, Suresh Oberoi, Pradeep Barna. A wife leaves her philandering movie star husband for another man—no small feat for a Hindu wife. Some insights into Indian culture, but slowly-paced. (Dir: Vinod Pande)

Once Before I Die (1966)*½ John Derek, Ursula Andress, Ron Ely. (Dir: John Derek, 97 mins.)

Once in a Lifetime (1933)*** Jack Oakie, Sidney Fox, Aline McMahon, ZaSu Pitts. The famous George S. Kaufman-Moss Hart play about the havoc wreaked by the coming of sound movies is given a lively if stage-bound rendition. If Russell Mack hadn't directed, it might have been a classic. (80 mins.)

Once in Paris (1978)*** Wayne Rogers, Jack Lenoir, Gayle Hunnicutt. This bittersweet story of a transient affair is little more than a series of anecdotes, some charming, some dramatic. Rogers is a screenwriter called to Paris to doctor a script; under the tutelage of his shady chauffeur (Lenoir), he comes to a more European attitude about love and friendship. (Writer-Producer-Dir: Frank Gilroy, 100 mins.)

Once Is Not Enough (1975)** Kirk Douglas, Alexis Smith, David Janssen, George Hamilton, Melina Mercouri, Brenda Vaccaro, Deborah Raffin. Chic stupid film, based on the trashy novel about the Beautiful People by Jacqueline Susann. Raffin's complex about daddy Douglas is played against Smith and Mercouri as lesbians, Vaccaro as a nympho editor, and Janssen as Norman Mailer. Director Guy Green has little sense of humor and less control over decor and narrative. (122 mins.)

Once More, My Darling (1949)**½ Robert Montgomery, Ann Blyth. Suave and sophisticated comedy about a young lady who sets her cap for a somewhat older film matinee idol who is recalled to active duty in the Army. Silly in spots but still fun. (Dir: Robert Montgomery, 94 mins.)

Once More, with Feeling (1960)*** Yul Brynner, Kay Kendall. A bit of sophisticated fluff that relies on the charm of its two stars—and they are very winning. Brynner plays an egotistical symphony conductor who discovers he doesn't want his beautiful wife (played by the late Kay Kendall) to divorce him after all. Kendall, as always in her regrettably short career, is a comedic joy. (Dir: Stanley Donen, 92 mins.)

Once upon a Dead Man (MTV 1971)**½ Rock Hudson, Susan Saint James, Jack Albertson, René Auberjonois. Pilot for "McMillan & Wife." You'll like Rock as the rich big-city police commissioner and Susan as his very loving wife. The standard stolen art object plot includes a great bicycle chase. The comedy touches are quite good, thanks to director-writer Leonard Stern. Best supporting-cast performance is by John Schuck as a police sergeant. (104 mins.)

Once upon a Family (MTV 1980)***½ Barry Bostwick, Lee Chamberlain, Nancy Marchand, Elizabeth Wilson. TV's answer to "Kramer vs. Kramer." Bostwick is excellent as a man who suddenly finds himself in the role of father-mother and chief dishwasher when his frustrated wife walks out to seek a life of her own. Later the wife wants the kids. An honest script. (Dir: Richard Michaels, 94 mins.)

Once upon a Honeymoon (1942)**½ Ginger Rogers, Cary Grant, Walter Slezak. Director Leo McCarey's ambitious film is brilliantly conceived and erratically executed. Grant, an American radio correspondent covering the early years of WW II, falls for Rogers, an ex-burlesque queen married to a top Nazi functionary (Slezak). (116 mins.)

Once upon a Horse (1958)** Dan Rowan, Dick Martin, Martha Hyer. Couple of dumb cowboys steal cattle and rob the bank of the beautiful owner of the town, but eventually wish they hadn't. Western satire doesn't come off most of the time, although there are a few funny moments. (Dir: Hal Kanter, 85 mins.)

Once upon a Scoundrel (1973)**½ Zero Mostel, Katy Jurado, Tito Vandis. Mostel's

495

last film, released only after years of litigation, is a fable about the warming up of a Scrooge-like figure. Ocasionally amusing comedy set in Mexico about a land baron who loves a young wench. (Dir: George Schaefer, 90 mins.)

Once upon a Spy (MTV 1980)** Eleanor Parker, Ted Danson, Christopher Lee. Predictable comedy-adventure pilot with a better-than-average cast. Tall, handsome Danson plays a computer expert who becomes a reluctant spy when the villainous Lee manages to steal NASA's ultimate computer, which weighs in excess of 3000 tons. Parker is the head of a highly sophisticated investigation unit assigned the task of finding the computer and thwarting Lee's maniacal plans. (Dir: Ivan Nagy, 104 mins.)

Once upon a Starry Night (MTV 1978)** Dan Haggerty, Denver Pyle, Jack Kruschen, Ken Curtis. Haggerty's Grizzly Adams and his crazy old mountain man, Pyle's Mad Jack, are back with corn pone for the kids. A winter avalanche forces a pair of youngsters and their uncle to take shelter in Grizzly's cabin while Adams goes off to hunt for their parents. That means plenty of time for Mad Jack and Frost-Bite Foley (Kruschen) to spin their yarns. (Dir: Jack B. Hively, 78 mins.)

Once upon a Time (1944)**½ Cary Grant, Janet Blair, Ted Donaldson. Theatrical producer forms a "partnership" with a boy who has a dancing caterpillar. Mild comedy never quite hits the mark intended. (Dir: Alexander Hall, 89 mins)

Once upon a Time in the West (Italy-U.S., 1969)**½ Henry Fonda, Claudia Cardinale, Jason Robards, Jr., Charles Bronson. Director Sergio Leone's epic western, his best film. With Fonda as an utter villain, Bronson as a mysterious avenger, Robards as a good bad man, and Cardinale as a rather nasty lady-in-distress, not to mention a long list of good character actors and Ennio Morricone's score. (165 mins.)

Once You Kiss a Stranger (1969)** Carol Lynley, Paul Burke. Glossy but empty melodrama about the country-club set and their intrigues. Burke suffers as the hero while Lynley, looking terrific, rolls her eyes as an unstable miss bent on using men. Remake of "Strangers on a Train." (Dir: Robert Sparr, 106 mins.)

One and Only, The (1978)** Henry Winkler, Kim Darby, Hervé Villechaize, Gene Saks. Film opens outrageously, but soon lapses into conventional kookiness. Winkler is the egomaniac actor who ends up as a Gorgeous George wrestler, and Darby suffers as his intended. A very funny foul bit by Saks as a fight manager. (Dir: Carl Reiner, 98 mins.)

One and Only, Genuine, Original Family Band, The (1968)* Buddy Ebsen, Lesley Warren, John Davidson, Walter Brennan, Janet Blair. (Dir: Michael O'Herlihy, 117 mins.)

One Day in the Life of Ivan Denisovich
(Great Britain-Norway-U.S., 1971)**** Tom Courtenay, Alfred Burke. A remarkably moving, heart-breaking account, in very straightforward cinematic fashion, of the ongoing indignities and horrors of the Russian prison labor camps. The time is 1950, the setting the Siberian wilderness. Ivan (Courtenay) is in the 8th year of a 10-year sentence. His crime? Having escaped from a German prisoner-of-war camp! Based on the now-celebrated Alexander Solzhenitsyn's novel. Filmed on location near the Arctic Circle in Norway. Courtenay is convincing in his unending struggle to survive. (Dir: Casper Wrede, 100 mins.)

One Desire (1955)**½ Rock Hudson, Anne Baxter, Natalie Wood. A costume soap opera about a gal from the wrong side of the tracks who tries to cross over into the local social register. Based on novel "Tacey Cromwell." Anne Baxter works very hard to make the character more than just a soap opera heroine and she occasionally succeeds. (Dir: Jerry Hopper, 94 mins.)

One-Eyed Jacks (1961)***½ Marlon Brando, Karl Malden, Katy Jurado. Outlaw out of prison goes hunting for the friend who betrayed him. Eccentric, majestic western close to the vest of Brando's temperament, so good one wishes he would direct again. (Stanley Kubrick began as director, only to be fired by the producer-star.) (141 mins.)

One Eyed Soldiers, The (U.S.-Great Britain-Yugoslavia, 1967)* Dale Robertson, Luciana Paluzzi. (Dir: Jean Christophe, 92 mins)

One Flew Over the Cuckoo's Nest (1975)**** Jack Nicholson, Louise Fletcher, Brad Dourif, William Redfield, William Sampson. A stunning adaptation of Ken Kesey's novel that deservedly won Academy Awards for best actor (Nicholson), best picture, best director (Forman) and best actress (Fletcher). This is a far cry from the typical movieland version of mental hospitals. The acting is astonishing throughout. Nicholson is really breathtaking: there's not a false note in his remarkable portrait. Fletcher, playing Nurse Ratched, a constant irritant to Nicholson's deranged character, subtly manages to be almost always unpleasant, often insensitive, but never resorting to caricature. Flawlessly directed by Milos Forman. Splendid screenplay by Laurence Haubman and Bo Goldman. (129 mins.)

One Foot in Heaven (1941)**** Fredric March, Martha Scott, Beulah Bondi, Gene Lockhart. With barely a plot of any consequence, this story of a minister's life is funny, sad, moving and interesting. Superbly acted by Mr. March as the minister and Martha Scott as his devoted wife. (Dir: Irving Rapper, 108 mins.)

One Foot in Hell (1960)**½ Alan Ladd, Don Murray, Dolores Michaels. Revenge-obsessed man takes job as deputy, intending to get even with townspeople responsible for the death of his wife. Fair-enough western with a plot slightly offbeat. (Dir: James B. Clark, 90 mins.)

One Girl's Confession (1953)** Cleo Moore, Hugo Haas, Glenn Langan. Tiresome melodrama about a young girl's predicament caused by her stealing $25,000 from her evil employer. Both of Cleo Moore's assets are well displayed. (Dir: Hugo Bass, 74 mins.)

One Heavenly Night (1931)** Evelyn Laye, John Boles, Leon Errol. One of many operetta-type films made during the early thirties. If you like this type of film stuff, here it is with all the sugar-coated ingredients intact. (Dir: George Fitzmaurice, 80 mins.)

One Hour with You (1932)**½ Maurice Chevalier, Jeanette MacDonald, Roland Young. Oskar Straus's music. Director Ernst Lubitsch's famous touch (George Cukor codirected) and a good cast manage to give some life to this mischievous little operetta. (84 mins.)

101 Dalmatians (1961)*** This Disney feature cartoon was one of his best in decades. Parent dogs fight rousingly to rescue their pups from extermination. Inflation has extinguished this kind of fully executed animation. (Dirs: Wolfgang Reitherman, Hamilton S. Luske, Clyde Geronimi, 80 mins.)

100 Cries of Terror (Mexico, 1965)*½ Adriana Welter, George Martinez. (Dir: Ramon Obon, 96 mins.)

100 Men and a Girl (1937)** Deanne Durbin, Leopold Stokowski, Adolphe Menjou. Durbin was the big-money, reedy-voiced child star who infected a number of late '30s musicals before creeping puberty ended her career. This is one of her more tolerable vehicles. (Dir: Henry Koster, 84 mins.)

100 Rifles (1969)* Jim Brown, Raquel Welch, Burt Reynolds. (Dir: Tom Gries, 110 mins.)

One in a Million (1936)*** Sonja Henie, Don Ameche, Ritz Brothers, Adolphe Menjou. Sonja's first American film and her skating is a treat to watch. Story isn't much but she's surrounded by a lot of good performers. Plot concerns a Swiss girl whose father is training her for the Olympics. (Dir: Sidney Lanfield, 94 mins.)

One in a Million: The Ron LeFlore Story (MTV 1978)**½ LeVar Burton, Madge Sinclair, Paul Benjamin, Billy Martin. Burton is appealing in this drama, based on the real-life story of baseball star Ron LeFlore, which dutifully chronicles the struggle of the young black, desperately poor teenager to escape from the horrors of the ghetto in Detroit where violence, drugs, and lack of interest in learning were all around him. Several scenes, including the death of his drug addict brother, are quite compelling. (Dir: William A. Graham, 104 mins.)

One Is a Lonely Number (1972)*** Trish Van Devere, Monte Markham, Janet Leigh, Melvyn Douglas. Film of a young divorcee in San Francisco (Van Devere) trying to adjust to the breakup of her marriage is quiet, yet effective. (Dir: Mel Stuart, 97 mins.)

One Little Indian (1973)***½ James Garner, Vera Miles, Clay O'Brien, Jodie Foster. Garner, in his regulation antiheroic role as an army deserter sentenced to hang for excessive compassion for Indians and children, and O'Brien as a young white boy raised as an Indian and desperate to return to his tribe make a perfect pair in this Walt Disney studios melodrama. Directed for maximum warmth and humor by Disney stalwart Bernard McEveety, this is one you can feel secure letting the kids see. (90 mins.)

One Machine to Kill Bad People (Italy, 1948)*** One of director Roberto Rossellini's few comedies. A fable about a camera that has the power to kill with a click of the shutter, this could almost be a parody of the political aims of neorealism: The camera captures truth, but truth can be a dangerous thing. Rossellini left before the film was completed; the footage was assembled and released a few years later, without his control.

One Man's China (Great Britain, 1972) ***½ A fascinating pictorial essay directed by veteran journalist-filmmaker Felix Greene that presents the most comprehensive and up-to-date documentary on mainland China that was available at the time of release and for some years thereafter. Released as two separate feature-length films; covers among other things the ethnic minorities, visits to communes, the Chinese educational system, etc. Greene is virtually never critical of any aspect of Chinese society, but nonetheless this is an often visually stunning and rewarding documentary about a vast, important country so little understood by the rest of the world. (189 mins.)

One Man's Way (1964)**½ Don Murray, Diana Hyland. Those who read Norman Vincent Peale's best selling book ("The Power of Positive Thinking") will want to tune in for this Hollywood version of the famed clergyman's life, despite its episodic treatment. Don Murray is very good in the leading role, as is Diana Hyland as his wife. (Dir: Denis Sanders, 105 mins.)

One Million B.C. (1940)** Carole Landis, Victor Mature, Lon Chaney, Jr. Story of the struggle of the cave men for survival in prehistoric times. Often rather ridiculous, sometimes fascinating; at least, it's different. (Dirs: Hal Roach, Hal Roach, Jr., 80 mins.)

One Million Years B.C. (Great Britain, 1966)*½ Racquel Welch, John Richardson. (Dir: Don Chaffey, 95 mins.)

One Minute to Zero (1952)** Robert Mitchum, Ann Blyth. Colonel carries on a romance before leaving for the perils of Korea. Unconvincing war melodrama. (Dir: Tay Garnett, 105 mins.)

497

One More River (1934)*** Colin Clive, Diana Wynyard, C. Aubrey Smith, Jane Wyatt, Mrs. Patrick Campbell. Adapted from the John Galsworthy novel by R. C. Sheriff. A wife runs away with her lover and her husband has them pursued by detectives. (Dir: James Whale, 88 mins.)

One More Time (Great Britain, 1970)* Peter Lawford, Sammy Davis, Jr., Esther Anderson. (Dir: Jerry Lewis, 93 mins.)

One More Tomorrow (1946)** Ann Sheridan, Dennis Morgan, Jane Wyman, Alexis Smith. They're trying to say something about war profiteering but it's poorly presented and emerges as a foolish twisting of Philip Barry's play "The Animal Kingdom." (Dir: Peter Godfrey, 88 mins.)

One More Train to Rob (1971)** George Peppard, Diana Muldaur. The attractiveness of the cast is the chief appeal of this western tale of vengeance set in California of the 1880s. After Peppard is framed for a train robbery and is released from prison, he seeks out his former double-crossing partners, now leading respectable lives, determined to get revenge. (Dir: Andrew McLaglen, 104 mins.)

One Night in Lisbon (1941)**½ Madeleine Carroll, Fred MacMurray, Billie Burke, Patricia Morison, John Loder. Romantic comedy about an American pilot and an aristocratic English girl in wartime Britain has a few scattered laughs. (Dir: Edward H. Griffith, 97 mins.)

One Night in the Tropics (1940)**½ Allan Jones, Nancy Kelly, Robert Cummings, Lou Abbott, Bud Costello. In this movie, Abbott and Costello began as a team, playing second fiddles in the story of overly cautious Cummings who takes out love insurance on his wedding to Kelly, then finds he has a rival in broker Jones. Amusing musical with songs by Jerome Kern, Oscar Hammerstein II, and Dorothy Fields. (Dir: A. Edward Sutherland, 82 mins.)

One Night of Love (1934)**½ Grace Moore, Tullio Carminati, Lyle Talbot. One of those marvelously stupid Moore opera movies. In this one, Grace is an aspiring opera star and Carminati is her demanding teacher. The singing and music stink, but it's all so delirious that no one need care. Believe it or not, the film, Moore, and director Victor Schertzinger got Oscar nominations. (95 mins.)

One of My Wives Is Missing (MTV 1976)**½ Jack Klugman, Elizabeth Ashley, James Franciscus. Although the story is terribly contrived, there are enough plot twists, admirably pulled out of a hat by a talented cast, to sustain interest. Klugman plays a resort-area police detective called by Franciscus to investigate the disappearance of his wife. If you're in the mood for a mystery with good performances, especially by Ms. Ashley, tune in. (Dir: Glenn Jordan, 98 mins.)

One of Our Aircraft Is Missing (Great Britain, 1941)***½ Godfrey Tearle, Eric Portman, Hugh Williams, Pamela Brown, Joyce Redman, Googie Withers. The crew of a downed bomber tries to get back to England from its landing place in Holland. Excellent war melodrama, suspenseful, well acted. (Dirs: Michael Powell, Emeric Pressburger, 106 mins.)

One of Our Dinosaurs Is Missing (Great Britain, 1975)*** Helen Hayes, Peter Ustinov, Clive Revill. Silly but entertaining Disney comedy about a secret formula hidden in a dinosaur skeleton in London's Natural History Museum. Set after WW I, featuring Chinese agents, English nannies, and lots of slapstick. The overplaying, especially by Ustinov as evil Hnup Wan, is very funny. (Dir: Robert Stevenson, 97 mins.)

One of Our Own (MTV 1975)**½ George Peppard, Zohra Lampert, William Daniels, Scott McKay, Oscar Homolka, Strother Martin. Peppard is into the surgery game as chief of services in a major hospital. Hospital crises are rampant. Good supporting cast gives pilot a touch of class. (Dir: Richard Sarafian, 100 mins.)

One on One (1977)**½ Robby Benson, Annette O'Toole. Underscripted college basketball saga is strictly ad-"Rocky." Director Lamont Johnson has fallen sadly short of his early promise. (99 mins.)

One Plus One—See: Sympathy for the Devil

One Potato, Two Potato (1964)**** Barbara Barrie, Bernie Hamilton, Richard Mulligan. Vivid sensitive drama about an interracial courtship and marriage between a hesitant white divorcee and a strong, but mild-mannered black man. Barbara Barrie is magnificent as the woman who hesitates at first but then commits herself fully to the love she feels for the black man, well played by Bernie Hamilton. The climax is a shattering courtroom custody battle for the woman's daughter between Miss Barrie and her ex-husband. You'll probably disagree with the court's decision but tune in for an absorbing drama. (Dir: Larry Pearce, 92 mins.)

One Sings, the Other Doesn't (France-Belgium-Curaçao, 1976)** Valerie Mairesse, Thérèse Liotard. Goopy feminist paean directed by Agnes Varda describing a lifelong friendship between free-floating Mairesse (who sings) and common-law widow Liotard (who doesn't). It's all very cute, full of pretty flowers and nice colors—a suburban matron's notion of liberation." (120 mins.)

One Spy Too Many (MTV 1968)** Robert Vaughn, David McCallum, Rip Torn. Culled from "The Man from UNCLE" series. Ilya and Napoleon Solo employ their super-secret agent tactics to hunt down a mad scientist bent on brainwashing the world via a "will gas." Rip Torn gleefully plays the maniac. (Dir: Joseph Sargent, 100 mins.)

One Step to Eternity (France, 1954)**½ A French roué invites his first wife, his current wife, his mistress and his fiancee to his apartment with the idea of committing murder. Some suspense is generated—however, a good premise doesn't go anywhere. It may give you an idea though for an off-beat party of your own. (Dir: Henri Decoin, 94 mins.)

One Sunday Afternoon (1948)**½ Dennis Morgan, Janis Paige, Don DeFore, Dorothy Malone. James Cagney carried this nostalgic gay '90s tale when it was called "Strawberry Blonde" (also released to TV) but he's not around to support this musical version. (Dir: Raoul Walsh, 90 mins.)

One That Got Away, The (Great Britain, 1957)**** Hardy Kruger, Colin Gordon. Cocky captured German pilot insists on trying to escape. Based on fact, this is a crack suspense drama, finely made and brilliantly acted by Kruger. (Dir: Roy Baker, 106 mins.)

1001 Arabian Nights (1960)**½ Color cartoon feature, with Mr. Magoo, and the voice of Jim Backus, back in old Baghdad. The nearsighted one is a lamp dealer whose nephew, Aladdin, gets the lamp with the genie, etc. Amusingly done, if not outstanding. Some songs, some cute moments—kiddies will like it. (Dir: Jack Kinney, 76 mins.)

One Touch of Venus (1948)**½ Ava Gardner, Robert Walker, Dick Haymes, Eve Arden, Tom Conway. A Greek statue of Venus comes to life in a department store, causes romance and misunderstandings. Mild musical comedy, never quite hits the mark intended. (Dir: William A. Seiter, 81 mins.)

One-Trick Pony (1980)**½ Paul Simon, Blair Brown, Rip Torn. There is something inert about Paul Simon's performance as an aging musician whose career and marriage are going down the drain. Director Robert M. Young's work is likable but lacks force. (98 mins.)

One, Two, Three (1961)**** James Cagney, Pamela Tiffin, Horst Buchholz, Arlene Francis. Cagney is the whole show in this hilarious Billy Wilder-directed satire on Coca-Cola diplomacy in divided Berlin. The plot is something about a Coke executive who has to chaperone the boss's daughter (Tiffin), who is infatuated with one of Berlin's ever-present Communist students (Buchholz). Very funny score by André Previn. (Dir: Billy Wilder, 115 mins.)

One Way Passage (1932)***½ William Powell, Kay Francis, Frank McHugh. Moving drama about the romance of an escaping convict and a girl dying of heart trouble, avoids being corny and emerges as an affecting melodrama. Oscar: Best Original Story, Robert Lord. Remade as "Till We Meet Again." (Dir: Tay Garnett, 69 mins.)

One Way Street (1950)**½ James Mason, Marta Toren, Dan Duryea, William Conrad, Jack Elam. The charm of the stars make up for the inadequacies of the script in this chase melodrama about thieves, lovers and intrigue. (Dir: Hugo Fregonese, 79 mins.)

One Way Wahine (1965)*½ Anthony Eisley, Joy Harmon, Edgar Bergen. (Dir: William O. Brown, 80 mins.)

One Woman's Story (Great Britain, 1949)***½ Ann Todd, Trevor Howard, Claude Rains. Woman married to rich broker meets her former lover in Switzerland, and the affair begins once more. Poignant, sparklingly acted romantic drama. Alternate title: **The Passionate Friends.** (Dir: David Lean, 86 mins.)

Onion Field, The (1979)**½ John Savage, James Woods, Franklyn Seales, Ronny Cox. This true story of a cop killing is an object lesson in the limitations of undiluted naturalism. There is little in this literal adaptation of Wambaugh's nonfiction piece beyond the straight facts, and these facts go largely undramatized. Though James Woods's portrait of a psychopath garnered the critical raves, it is the stooge portrayed by Franklyn Seales that is the genuinely complex creation. (Dir: Harold Becker, 126 mins.)

Onionhead (1958)**½ Andy Griffith, Felicia Farr, Walter Matthau, Joey Bishop. Not as funny as Griffith's army tour in "No Time for Sergeants" but this Coast Guard comedy has its moments. This time, Griffith is the ship's cook aboard a buoy tender. (Dir: Norman Taurog, 110 mins.)

Only a Woman (West Germany, 1962)** Maria Schell, Paul Christian. Young man resents the advice of a lady headshrinker, sets out to prove her wrong and winds up falling for her. Romantic comedy done with a too-heavy hand; dubbed in English. (Dir: Alfred Weidenmann, 86 mins.)

Only Angels Have Wings (1939)**** Cary Grant, Jean Arthur, Richard Barthelmess, Thomas Mitchell, Rita Hayworth. Director Howard Hawk's masterpiece examines the lives and loves of the pilots of a small commercial airline in Latin America. Spare, brittle screenplay by Jules Furthman. Exemplary acting from the large cast. (121 mins.)

Only Game in Town, The (1970)*½ Eizabeth Taylor, Warren Beatty, Charles Braswell. Filmed in Paris and Las Vegas. (Dir: George Stevens, 113 mins.)

Only One Day Left Before Tomorrow— See: **How to Steal an Airplane.**

Only One New York (1964)**½ French-made narrated in English; a roving camera-eye view of New York City, from Coney Island to Harlem and all stops in between. Interesting for what the foreign eye can discern about an American metropolis; also good for those natives who have never visited the place. (Dir: Pierre-Dominique Gaisseau, 72 mins.)

Only the Best—See: **I Can Get It for You Wholesale**

Only the French Can (France, 1954)***½ Jean Gabin, Edith Piaf, Francoise Arnoul. Jean Renoir wrote and directed this thoroughly delightful and entertaining film dealing with the era when the Can-Can first shocked Parisians—long before the same dance upset Khrushchev. (Dir: Jean Renoir, 93 mins.)

Only the Valiant (1951)** Gregory Peck, Barbara Payton, Gig Young, Ward Bond. Peck stars as the misunderstood cavalry officer who must win his men's respect after having lost face in a previous skirmish with hostile Indians. Action galore for horse opera fans and little else in the way of character development or logical plot progression. (Dir: Gordon Douglas, 105 mins.)

Only Two Can Play (Great Britain, 1962)**** Peter Sellers, Mai Zetterling, Richard Attenborough. A comedy delight. Sellers is a frustrated Don Juan who tries some extramarital maneuvering, with disastrous results. Witty performance by Zetterling as the object of his desires. Adapted from Kingsley Amis's novel "That Uncertain Feeling." (Dir: Sidney Gilliat, 106 mins.)

Only When I Larf (Great Britain, 1968)** Richard Attenborough, David Hemmings, Alexandra Stewart. An innocuous caper about a trio of British con artists who try to fleece some African diplomats. Richard Attenborough gives a bravura performance, but the level of the humor explains the title. Man with a spear stuck in him repeatedly remarks it hurts "Only when I larf." (Dir: Basil Dearden, 104 mins.)

Only with Married Men (MTV 1974)*½ David Birney, Michele Lee, Dom DeLuise, Judy Carne, Gavin MacLeod. (Dir: Jerry Paris, 74 mins.)

Open City (Italy, 1945)**** Aldo Fabrizzi, Anna Magnani, Marcello Pagliero, Maria Michi. The story of a group of workers and a priest in Rome in '43-'44, when it was declared an open city by the Nazis. Director Roberto Rossellini's treatment of everyday Italian life was part of the beginning of neorealism. The film, begun only two months after Liberation, astonished audiences all over the world and remains a masterpiece. (101 mins.)

Open the Door and See All the People (1964)** Maybelle Nash, Alec Wilder. Conflict of two households run by elderly sisters, one a crab, the other open and generous. Offbeat whimsical comedy doesn't have the touch necessary for success. (Dir: Jerome Hill, 82 mins.)

Operation Abduction (France, 1957)*½ Frank Villard, Daniele Godet. (Dir: Jean Stelli, 91 mins.)

Operation Amsterdam (Great Britain, 1959)** Alexander Knox, Peter Finch, Eva Bartok. Exciting true-life incident emerges as routine suspense outing about a fran-

tic attempt, in 1940, to smuggle out of Holland a fortune in industrial diamonds before the Nazis arrive. (Dir: Michael McCarthy, 105 mins.)

Operation Atlantis (Italy, 1965)*½ John Ericson, Berna Rock, Maria Granada. (Dir: Paul Fleming, 91 mins.)

Operation Bikini (1963)** Tab Hunter, Frankie Avalon, Scott Brady, Gary Crosby, Eva Six. Demolition squad seeks out an American sub held by the Japanese to destroy new radar equipment on it. War drama filled with the familiar plot clichés; okay for the action fans. (Dir: Anthony Carras, 83 mins.)

Operation Bottleneck (1961)*½ Ron Foster, Miko Taka. (Dir: Edward L. Cahn, 78 mins.)

Operation Bullshine (Great Britain, 1959)**Donald Sinden, Barbara Murray, Dora Bryan. Trouble when a horde of females in uniform descends on a woman-starved remote outpost. Some laughs in this military comedy, but there's little subtlety. All very obvious. (Dir: Gilbert Gunn, 83 mins.)

Operation Camel (Denmark, 1960)* Lou Renard, Nora Hayden. (Dir: Sven Methling, Jr., 72 mins.)

Operation Caviar (France, 1959)** O. W. Fischer, Eva Bartok, Senta Berger. Bank clerk suddenly finds himself with plenty of complications when he becomes a spy. Mildly amusing wartime comedy-melodrama, dubbed in English. (Dir: Geza Radvanyi, 92 mins.)

Operation C.I.A. (1965)*½ Burt Reynolds, Danielle Aubry. (Dir: Christian Nyby, 90 mins.)

Operation Conspiracy (Great Britain, 1956)** Philip Friend, Mary Mackenzie. Undercover operator combats foreign agents after nuclear information, meets an old flame and murder along the way. Routine thriller. (Dir: Joseph Stirling, 69 mins.)

Operation Cross Eagles (U.S.-Yugoslavia, 1969)** Richard Conte, Rory Calhoun. Routine WW II thriller about a commando group behind German lines assigned to capture a German commandant and exchange him for an American captain. (Dir: Richard Conte, 90 mins.)

Operation Crossbow (1965)*** George Peppard, Tom Courtenay, Sophia Loren, Lilli Palmer, Trevor Howard. Rip roaring WW II espionage adventure crammed with as much action as possible. Although Sophia Loren is top-billed, she has a brief role—it's really George Peppard, Tom Courtenay, and Jeremy Kemp as a trio of agents assigned to destroy a heavily guarded Nazi munitions installation who keep things buzzing. Exciting finale. (Dir: Michael Anderson, 116 mins.)

Operation Dames (1959)** Eve Meyer, Chuck Henderson. Entertainers in Korea are trapped behind enemy lines, take a perilous path to safety. War story made on a small budget has nothing new, but

500

gets by. (Dir: Louis Clyde Stoumen, 74 mins.)

Operation Daybreak (Great Britain, 1976)*** Timothy Bottoms, Anthony Andrews, Anton Diffring. Suspenseful drama based on the assassination of brutal Nazi Reinhard Heyrich (Diffring) in WW II, this exciting but overlong melodrama was shot on location in Prague with the cooperation of the government. Czech patriots, trained as commandos in England, succeed in killing Heydrich, but one by one, they are tracked down by the Germans and captured or shot. (Dir: Lewis Gilbert, 118 mins.)

Operation Delilah (U.S.-Spain, 1966)*½ Rory Calhoun, Gia Scala. (Dirs: Luis de los Arcos, Sidney W. Pink, David Elias, 86 mins.)

Operation Diplomat (Great Britain, 1953)**½ Guy Rolfe, Lisa Daniely. A doctor called in to perform an emergency operation at a deserted country house suspects his patient may be an important missing diplomat. OK melodrama moves at a fast clip. (Dir: John Guillermin, 70 mins.)

Operation Diplomatic Passport (France, 1962)*½ Roger Hanin, Christine Minazzoli. (Dir: André Labrousse, 85 mins.)

Operation Disaster (Great Britain, 1950) ***½ John Mills, Nigel Patrick. A submarine on a routine cruise hits an old mine, and sinks to the bottom with twelve men still surviving. Tense, finely written and played story of rescue operations. (Dir: Roy Baker, 102 mins.)

Operation Eichmann (1961)** Werner Klemperer, Ruta Lee. Sensationalized account of the reign of terror in the German concentration camps presided over by Adolf Eichmann (played by Werner Klemperer). This film was made in a hurry to capitalize on Eichmann's trial and can hardly be taken seriously as a documentary of the time. (Dir: R. G. Springsteen, 93 mins.)

Operation Gold Ingot (France, 1963)** Martine Carol, Felix Marten, Francis Blanche. Ex-secret agent and his wife are asked to save a family friend from trouble, chase after gangsters in Barcelona. Average crime melodrama, with a fair pace and picturesque background aiding. Dubbed in English. (Dir: Georges Lautner, 90 mins.)

Operation Hong Kong (West Germany, 1964) Horst Frank, Maria Perschy, Brad Harris. (Dir: Helmut Ashley, 95 mins.)

Operation Kid Brother (Italy, 1967)** The producers of this low-budget quickie tried to capitalize on Sean Connery's success in the Bond films and cast his real-life brother, Neil Connery, in the role of a cosmetic surgeon thrust into the world of espionage. The gimmick doesn't really work, and Neil doesn't generate the type of excitement his older brother does. A poor man's 003½! (Dir: Alberto De Martino, 104 mins.)

Operation Mad Ball (1957)***½ Jack Lemmon, Ernie Kovacs (debut), Mickey Rooney, Arthur O'Connell, Kathryn Grant. Delightful wacky Army comedy about an operator who upsets all rules and regulations in his search for fun for himself and his buddies. Kovacs is great as a bewildered officer and his scenes with Lemmon are gems. (Dir: Richard Quine, 105 mins.)

Operation Manhunt (1954)**½ Harry Townes, Jacques Aubuchon. The story of Igor Gouzenko, Russian code clerk who forsook the Communists and defected to the West. Gouzenko appears briefly. Okay melodrama made in Canada. (Dir: Jack Alexander, 77 mins.)

Operation Mermaid (Great Britain, 1963) *** Mai Zetterling, Keenan Wynn, Ronald Howard. American gathers together a crew of ex-Commandos to search for hidden Nazi treasure. Well-knit melodrama with a good cast, suspense. (Dir: John Ainsworth, 86 mins.)

Operation Pacific (1951)*½ John Wayne, Patricia Neal. (Dir: George Waggner, 109 mins.)

Operation Petticoat (1959)***½ Cary Grant, Tony Curtis, Dina Merrill. A big, big hit comedy highlighting Cary Grant's ageless appeal and Tony Curtis' energetic performing, about a sub and its mad, mad crew and their unbelievable exploits in the South Pacific. Fun for all. Later a TV series. (Dir: Blake Edwards, 124 mins.)

Operation St. Peter's (Italy, 1968)* Edward G. Robinson, Lando Buzzanca. (Dir: Luccio Fulci, 100 mins.)

Operation Secret (1952)*** Cornel Wilde, Phyllis Thaxter, Steve Cochran, Karl Malden. Good espionage thriller about the dangerous activities of the French underground, known as "The Maquis," during WW II. Many narrow escapes and tense situations in well acted adventure. (Dir: Lewis Seiler, 108 mins.)

Operation Snafu (Great Britain, 1961)** Alfred Lynch, Sean Connery, Stanley Holloway, Wilfred Hyde White. Lynch and Connery as a pair of cronies in the RAF, out to swindle fellow soldiers during WW II. Amiable pairing can't break through episodic script based on the R. F. Delderfield novel "Stop at a Winner." (Dir: Cyril Frankel, 97 mins.)

Operation Snatch (Great Britain, 1962)**½ Terry-Thomas, George Sanders. A bungling officer is sent to Gibraltar during WW II to make sure the Barbary apes stay there—legend has it that as long as they do, Gibraltar will remain in the British Empire. English comedy attempt that is only occasionally funny. (Dir: Robert Day, 83 mins.)

Operation Stogie (Great Britain, 1962)*½ John Hewer, Anton Rodgers, Susan Stephen. (Dir: Ernest Morris, 75 mins.)

Operation Thunderbolt (Israel, 1977)**½ Klaus Kinski, Assaf Dayan, Gila Almagor. Wanly efficient depiction of the Entebbe hostage rescue raid, containing some logistical details not available to the American filmmakers who did versions. The heart-tugging Jewish solidarity sequences, milked to the limit, work best. (Dir: Menachem Golan, 120 mins.)

Operator 13 (1933)** Marion Davies, Gary Cooper, Jean Parker, Katherine Alexander. Davies's last vehicle for MGM. The underrated actress who had trouble in talkies with her speech impediment but was a grand comedienne takes on the heavy role of an actress who becomes a Union spy during the Civil War and finds herself involved with Confederate he-man Cooper. Based on a real-life story. (Dir: Richard Boleslawski, 86 mins.)

Operation Warhead—See: **Operation Snafu**

Opposite Sex, The (1956)*** June Allyson, Joan Collins, Dolores Gray, Ann Sheridan, Ann Miller, Joan Blondell. Slickly produced, updated remake of "The Women." Allyson plays the Norma Shearer role this time around and she has a few songs thrown in for good measure. The supporting cast is very good, particularly Collins. (Dir: David Miller, 117 mins.)

Optimists, The (Great Britain, 1974)*** Peter Sellers, Donna Mullane, John Chaffey. Sentimental story of London slum kids befriended by old busker Sellers. Written and directed by Anthony Simmons, from his novel "The Optimists of Nine Elms." With songs by Lionel Bart and music by Beatles' producer George Martin. Deserved more attention than it received. (110 mins.)

Orca (1977)* Richard Harris, Charlotte Rampling, Will Sampson, Bo Derek, Keenan Wynn. (Dir: Michael Anderson. 92 mins.)

Orchestra Rehearsal (Italy-Monaco, 1978)*½ Balduin Baas, Clara Colosimo, Elisabeth Labi, Ronaldo Bonacchi. Director Federico Fellini's film lacks resonance, consistency, and bite. An extended soliloquy by the hapless German conductor confronted by rebellious intrumentalists speaks directly to a core of human feeling, but is undercut by some pat associations of a German accent with totalitarianism. Nino Rota's last score. (72 mins.)

Orchestra Wives (1942)*** Glenn Miller, Ann Rutherford, George Montgomery, Cesar Romero. Silly story about girls married to musicians serves to give the Miller crew a chance to fill the screen with some wonderful arrangements. (Dir: Archie Mayo, 98 mins.)

Orchids and Ernie (1927)*** Colleen Moore, Jack Mulhall, Hedda Hopper. Moore, a delightful comedienne, plays a switchboard operator who yearns for a millionaire but settles for a sexy valet. Some really clever title cards. Watch for the cameo by a nearly infant Mickey Rooney as (what else?) a fully grown midget. (Dir: Alfred Santell, 75 mins.)

Ordeal (MTV 1973)**½ Arthur Hill, Diana Muldaur, James Stacy. Hill is cast in the role of a man who is badly injured and left to fend for himself in the desert by a hateful wife and her lover, in this predictable man-versus-nature drama. Hill generates some interest. (Dir: Lee H. Katzin, 73 mins.)

Ordeal of Patty Hearst, The (MTV 1979)*** Dennis Weaver, Lisa Eilbacher. Good dramatization of the kidnapping in '74 of the heiress who later turned radical, and her eventual arrest by FBI agents. Eilbacher is well cast as Patty in a script that doesn't build undue sympathy for her; Weaver is also very good as Charles Bates, the FBI special agent in charge of the kidnapping case. The Symbionese Liberation Army hideout sequences are graphic—and the producers don't pull any punches. (Dir: Paul Wendkos, 156 mins.)

Orders Are Orders (Great Britain, 1954)**½ Brian Reece, Margot Grahame, Peter Sellers. In his pre-stardom days, Peter Sellers has a small part in this confusing but funny British farce about a movie company descending on an army camp to shoot a film on location. Remake of the '33 film. (Dir: David Paltenghi, 78 mins.)

Orders to Kill (Great Britain, 1958)***½ Eddie Albert, Paul Massie, Lillian Gish, Irene Worth. Engrossing spy thriller concerning an American intelligence agent's mission to kill a supposedly French Nazi collaborator. Tight and tense. Acting is very good. (Dir: Anthony Asquith, 93 mins.)

Ordinary Tenderness (Canada, 1973)**½ Ester Auger, Jocelyn Berube. Overlong, but well-photographed story about two young lovers waiting to get together after a lengthy separation. Little dialogue. Ambitious, but not altogether successful. English subtitles. (Dir: Jacques Leduc, 82 mins.)

Oregon Trail, The (1959)*½ Fred MacMurray, Gloria Talbott. (Dir: Gene Fowler, Jr., 86 mins.)

Oregon Trail, The (MTV 1976)*½ Rod Taylor, Douglas V. Fowley, Blair Brown, Andrew Stevens. (Dir: Boris Sagal, 98 mins.)

Organization, The (1971)*** Sidney Poitier, Barbara McNair, Ron O'Neal. It's the third time round for Poitier's characterization of the low-key detective known as Virgil Tibbs, which he created in the memorable film "In the Heat of the Night," and subsequently played in "They Call Me Mr. Tibbs." In this tale, set in San Francisco, Tibbs reluctantly joins forces with a well-organized vigilante group determined to smash the drug traffic in their area. The action is swift, the performances slick. (Dir: Don Medford, 106 mins.)

Organizer, The (Italy, 1964)**** Marcello Mastroianni, Renato Salvatori, Annie Girardot. Absorbing drama of textile workers involved in a factory strike years ago. Tremendous performances by Mastroianni as a professor who leads them to fight for their rights. Excellent direction keeps the interest high throughout. Fine dramatic fare. Dubbed in English. (Dir: Mario Monicelli, 126 mins.)

Oriental Dream—See: **Kismet** (1944)

Orientals, The (Italy, 1960)* Nagwa Fouad, Nick Kendall. (110 mins.)

Orphan Train (MTV 1979)*** Jill Eikenberry, Kevin Dobson, Linda Manz. A warm, entertaining story set in the late 1850's that recounts the troubled journey of a group of New York City orphans to the Midwest, where, they hope, they will be adopted by farm families. Eikenberry gives a convincing performance as social worker Emma Syms, an orphan herself, who spearheads the venture, and Dobson portrays a tough photojournalist with a soft heart. Top-notch child actors bring life to the story. (Dir: William A. Graham, 156 mins.)

Orphans of the Storm (1922)*** Lillian Gish, Dorothy Gish, Joseph Schildkraut. A remarkable spectacle film directed by D. W. Griffith, based on a play called "Two Orphans" but transformed by Griffith to the period of the French Revolution. Griffith uses and improves upon the standard melodramatic tricks of his time so that Lillian Gish—searching for and finally finding an adopted blind sister—achieves a moving moment even in today's cinema. You name it, Griffith's got it—murder, orgies, kidnappings, hairbreadth escapes, and Lillian Gish saved from the razor-sharp edge of the guillotine. A memorable landmark of the silent era. (120 mins.)

Orpheus (France, 1949)**** Jean Marais, Maria Casares, François Perier, Juliette Greco with the Maenads on motorcycles. Director Jean Cocteau creates his own mythology for his own purposes. Marais is a poet, besieged by admirers, who hears voices from other worlds over the radio and meets Death, black-gloved, when she comes through the mirror. Defies comparison with anything else in cinema. A magical work. (95 mins.)

Osaka Elegy (Japan, 1936)***½ Isuzu Yamada. The first fully mature film of director Kenji Mizoguchi stars Yamada as a young telephone operator who allows herself to be seduced by her boss to aid her family, then ends up alone. A tough-minded story, filmed with sublime compassion.

Oscar, The (1966)** Stephen Boyd, Elke Sommer, Eleanor Parker, Ernest Borgnine, Milton Berle, Tony Bennett, Jill St. John. A big splashy, sexy soap opera about an unscrupulous actor who uses everyone to further his career. There are many stars who do the best they can in their roles as Hollywood types but despite a first-class production, the film is corny and obvious. (Dir: Russel Rouse, 119 mins.)

Oscar Wilde (Great Britain, 1960)*** Robert Morley, John Neville, Ralph Richardson, Phyllis Calvert. One of two British films, made in 1960, about the tragic libel trial of the famed playwright in the 1890's, when he was accused of sodomy and sexual perversion. (Peter Finch starred in "The Trial of Oscar Wilde.") This filming is the harsher. Morley, physically close to the real Wilde, gustily exudes the wit and decay of the man; Richardson is masterful as the Queen's counsel. Some sequences are poorly conceived but, overall, a compelling portrait. B&W. (Dir: Gregory Ratoff, 96 mins.)

Osho—See: **Master Hand**

O.S.S. (1946)*** Alan Ladd, Geraldine Fitzgerald. Fairly exciting drama about a mission by America's cloak and dagger heroes. A bit obvious, but interesting story. (Dir: Irving Pichel, 107 mins.)

Ossessione (Italy, 1942)**** Massimo Girotti, Clare Calamai, Elio Marcuzzo. The first great Italian neo-realist film was unseen in the U.S. for more than 30 years because it was based on James M. Cain's novel "The Postman Always Rings Twice," only it was wartime and they didn't get the rights. A remarkable debut film for director Luchino Visconti. (135 mins.)

Othello (France-U.S., 1951)**** Orson Welles, Micheal MacLiammoir, Fay Compton, Robert Cook, Suzanne Cloutier. Director Orson Welles's first foreign film was shot in snatches over the years, as his editing and soundtrack began to fragment. Othello is compromised by his limitations as an actor; as usual, he makes virtues of his faults. A muscular film, bounding rather than smoldering with jealous energy. Exultantly theatrical and filmic. (91 mins.)

Othello (Great Britain, 1965)*** Laurence Olivier, Frank Finlay, Maggie Smith, Joyce Redman. The fourth filmed version of Shakespeare's masterpiece, and it's a towering achievement, largely due to the genius of Olivier. He is arguably the greatest stage actor of the century, and he does full justice to this most demanding role of the crazed Moor, Othello. There are some surprises here—Olivier plays Othello in blackface, but his interpretation is that of a modern man, sensitive to racial slurs, responsive to contemporary psychological nuances. This is a filmed version of Olivier's legendary stage portrayal, and generations to come must be thankful this wondrous performance has been captured for all ages. Finlay, Smith and Redman, portraying Iago, Desdemona and Emilia, respectively, were all nominated for Academy Awards. Full Shakespeare text presented almost without cuts. (Dir: Stuart Burge, 166 mins.)

Other, The (1972)**** Uta Hagen, Diana Muldaur, Chris Connelly. Director Robert Mulligan crafts a nearly perfect work, based on Thomas Tryon's horrific novel about twin boys who keep changing identities. (100 mins.)

503

Other Love, The (1947)**½ Barbara Stanwyck, David Niven, Richard Conte, Gilbert Roland. A beautiful concert pianist finds she is ill, throws her life away before realizing a doctor is in love with her. Fair romantic drama. Good performances. (Dir: André de Toth, 95 mins.)

Other Man, The (1970)** Roy Thinnes, Joan Hackett, Arthur Hill, Tammy Grimes. This made-for-TV feature goes back to the melodramas of the 1940's for its inspiration and the ladies may enjoy it. Joan Hackett plays a role once limned by Joan Crawford, Bette Davis, Greer Garson (take your pick). She's quite good as the rich married lady who falls hopelessly in love with a notorious playboy (Roy Thinnes). The plot sounds simple, but it's not. Thinnes makes an attractive mysterious mystery man, but it's Miss Hackett's vehicle, and she's up to the task. (Dir: Richard Colla, 99 mins.)

Other Side of Hell, The (MTV 1978)***½ Alan Arkin, Roger E. Mosley, Morgan Woodward. Nightmare about life in a hospital for the criminally insane. A shattering tale of guard brutality, and of patients who must cure themselves. Arkin is superb as Frank Dole, a highly disturbed, intelligent inmate, who is determined to survive. Czech director Jan Kadar excels in conveying moods of inner helplessness. (156 mins.)

Other Side of Midnight, The (1977)* Marie-France Pisier, John Beck, Susan Saradon. (Dir: Charles Jarrott, 110 mins.)

Other Side of the Mountain, The (1975)**½ Marilyn Hassett, Beau Bridges. (Dir: Larry Peerce, 103 mins.)

Other Side of the Mountain, Part II, The (1977)*½ Marilyn Hassett, Timothy Bottoms, Belinda Montgomery. Hassett again plays paralyzed Olympic-hopeful skier Jill Kinmont, in a bout with true love in the person of a truck driver (Bottoms). Sentiment is applied with a trowel, so be forewarned. (Dir: Larry Peerce, 105 mins.)

Other Voices (1969)*** Often interesting documentary about a small clinic in Pennsylvania dealing with mentally disturbed adolescents. Reminds us again of what an inexact science psychiatry is. (Dir: David H. Sawyer, 100 mins.)

Other Woman, The (1954)** Cleo Moore, Hugo Haas. Girl trying to make good in Hollywood plans to blackmail a director. A little more time and effort would have made this drama of the movies much better—as it is, a fairly interesting story. (Dir: Hugo Haas, 81 mins.)

Otley (Great Britain, 1969)*** Tom Courtenay, Romy Schneider, Fiona Lewis, Alan Badel. Engaging secret-agent spoof, and it's a particular pleasure to be able to watch Tom Courtenay play a light role for a change, as he did so well as Billy Liar. (You can see the serious Tom Courtenay in films like "Dr. Zhivago" and "One Day in the Life of Ivan Denisovich.") Courtenay plays an affable drifter who picks up wom-

en and various animate objects that don't belong to him. (Dir: Dick Clement, 90 mins.)

Our Daily Bread (1934)*** Tom Keene, Karen Morley, Barbara Pepper, John Qualen. American classic of, and about, the depression, directed, financed, and coauthored by a master, King Vidor, as a personal statement of his faith in America. A young couple join a commune where each person ideally contributes an individual skill to help everyone. (74 mins.)

Our Dancing Daughters (1928)*** Joan Crawford, Dorothy Sebastian, Anita Page, Johnny Mack Brown. This well-made jazz baby film epitomizes what the '20s thought they were all about. Crawford incarnates the ultimate flapper in the role that made her a genuine star. (Dir: Harry Beaumont, 86 mins.)

Our Hearts Were Growing Up (1946)**½ Diana Lynn, Gail Russell. Silly story about two young girls on a weekend at Princeton University during the 1920s who get mixed up with bootleggers. A few laughs, but mostly forced comedy. (Dir: William D. Russell, 83 mins.)

Our Hearts Were Young and Gay (1944)*** Diana Lynn, Gail Patrick. Delightful little comedy about a trip abroad during the gay year of 1932 by two young, attractive girls. (Dir: Lewis Allen, 81 mins.)

Our Little Girl (1935)**½ Shirley Temple, Joel McCrea, Rosemary Ames. Shirley patches up her parents' troubled marriage by drastic means. Sentimental melodrama; fine if you love Shirley. (Dir: John Robertson, 63 mins.)

Our Man Flint (1966)***½ James Coburn, Lee J. Cobb, Gila Golan. This super-gimmicked, high-style spoof of the James Bond superman, secret agent films benefits from the suave presence of Coburn, as Flint. It's all tongue-in-cheek stuff kept bouncing along at a rapid clip by director Daniel Mann. The plot, if you care, concerns an organization which plans to take over the world with their secret weapon—controlling the weather. Besides, we get a chance to root for the U.S.A. and against the meanies from abroad. (107 mins.)

Our Man Flint: Dead on Target (MTV 1976)** Ray Danton, Sharon Acker. Ray Danton takes over where James Coburn left off in this update of the old, flashy secret-agent spoofs. The action is predictably fast and ridiculous, and Sharon Acker adds a little luster to the production. (Dir: Joseph Scanlon, 72 mins.)

Our Man in Havana (Great Britain, 1960)*** Alec Guinness, Burl Ives, Maureen O'Hara, Noël Coward, Ernie Kovacs. Graham Greene's novel is brought to the screen with many changes. The comedy is stressed in many scenes but the uneven picture fluctuates between out and out comedy and stark drama. The plot concerns a vacuum cleaner salesman who is recruited to become a spy but never receives any instructions about his duties as a spy. The best scenes are those between Alec Guinness (as the spy) and Ernie Kovacs as a Cuban police officer. (Dir: Carol Reed, 107 mins.)

Our Man in Jamaica (Spain-West Germany-Italy, 1965)*½ Larry Pennell, Margarita Scherr. (Dir: Richard Jackson, 96 mins.)

Our Man in the Caribbean (Great Britain, 1962)** Carlos Thompson, Shirley Eaton, Diana Rigg. Soldier of fortune finds himself the target for a swindle, manages to trick the tricksters. Passable melodrama based on a TV series. (85 mins.)

Our Miss Brooks (1956)**½ Eve Arden, Gale Gordon, Richard Crenna. The popular radio and TV series is on the screen. Nothing new and if you were a fan of "Miss Brooks," you'll enjoy this visit with the old crew at Madison High. (Dir: Al Lewis, 85 mins.)

Our Mother's House (Great Britain, 1967)*** Dirk Bogarde, Pamela Franklin, Mark Lester. Entertaining British entry concerns a group of children, the oldest being 13, who decide to conceal their invalid mother's death and carry on as a family unit. Enter wandering no-good dad (Bogarde) and the plot takes on shadings of the unexpected. (Dir: Jack Clayton, 105 mins.)

Our Time—See: **Death of Her Innocence**

Our Town (1940)***½ Frank Craven, William Holden, Martha Scott, Thomas Mitchell, Fay Bainter. Since the stage manager device becomes inept, the Thornton Wilder play loses much of its impact in its screen adaptation. Still folksy and sweet; buoyed by wise performances. (Dir: Sam Wood, 90 mins.)

Our Very Own (1950)** Ann Blyth, Farley Granger, Joan Evans, Donald Cook, Jane Wyatt, Natalie Wood. Melodramatic yarn about a young girl who accidentally discovers she has been adopted. The stars do well but they can't escape the soap opera overtones of the script. There's a good scene between Miss Blyth and her legitimate mother, well played by Ann Dvorak. (Dir: David Miller, 93 mins.)

Our Vines Have Tender Grapes (1945)*** Edward G. Robinson, Margaret O'Brien, Agnes Moorehead. Warm, moving, well-played story about the love people have for each other in a small community. It's a touching theme and it's delivered with a minimum of corn. (Dir: Roy Rowland, 105 mins.)

Our Wife (1941)**½ Melvyn Douglas, Ruth Hussey. Trumpet player wants to marry a socialite, but his divorce isn't final. Lengthy comedy is too drawn out, but is nicely made. (Dir: John M. Stahl, 95 mins.)

Out of Sight (1966)*½ Jonathan Daly, Karen Jensen. (Dir: Lennie Weinrib, 87 mins.)

Out of the Blue (1947)**½ George Brent, Virginia Mayo, Ann Dvorak, Turhan Bey, Carole Landis. A husband is in all sorts of hot water when a shady lady passes out

in his apartment. Cute romantic comedy. (Dir: Leigh Jason, 84 mins.)

Out of the Fog (1941)*** Ida Lupino, John Garfield, Eddie Albert. Movie version of Irwin Shaw's "The Gentle People" benefits from wonderful acting by a top drawer cast and Anatole Litvak's skillful direction. Story of a gangster's preying on innocent people wavers between greatness and mediocrity. (86 mins.)

Out of the Past (1947)***½ Robert Mitchum, Jane Greer, Kirk Douglas, Rhonda Fleming. Gas station owner with a past meets a desperate woman and winds up in murder. The ultimate Robert Mitchum movie. Director Jacques Tourneur has created something close to a masterpiece in this adaptation of a novel by Geoffrey Homes. (97 mins.)

Out of This World (1945)**½ Eddie Bracken, Diana Lynn, Veronica Lake. Good farce plot is poorly handled. Story of a crooner who makes the girls swoon has some funny moments, but is generally forced comedy. Bracken is the crooner, and he borrows a familar voice (Bing Crosby's) for the occasion. (Dir: Hal Walker, 96 mins.)

Out of Towners, The (1970)*** Jack Lemmon, Sandy Dennis, Anthony Holland, Sandy Baron. The "Out-of-Towners" are non-New Yorkers in Neil Simon's uneven but frequently funny and sardonic notion of the perils that await the unwary who choose to visit the demilitarized zone of peacetime New York. Lemmon plays an obnoxious, dyspeptic executive from Ohio visiting "Fun City" for a job audition. "Out-of-Towners" is a discarded playlet from Simon's "Plaza Suite," but he's inserted some lacerating humor in this grim vision of New York, and Anthony Holland is a marvelously funny hotel clerk. (Dir: Arthur Hiller, 97 mins.)

Out West with the Hardys (1938)**½ Mickey Rooney, Lewis Stone. Just as many warm, human problems confront them out west as in their other films. Hardy pictures are always worthy of your attention if you like homespun humor, beautifully acted. (Dir: George B. Seitz, 84 mins.)

Outback (Australia, 1971)*** Gary Bond, Chips Rafferty, Donald Pleasence. Offbeat adventure. A young schoolteacher (Bond) in Australia's barren outback is scheduled to fly to Sydney during vacation. To get the plane, he goes to Yago, a small boomtown, and during the night he loses his money and joins several locals in a vicious hunt and some cheap sex leading to attempted suicide. Pleasence is at his best as a grotesque alcoholic doctor. (Dir: Ted Kotcheff, 99 mins.)

Outcast, The (1954)*** John Derek, Joan Evans, Jim Davis. Young man returns to Colorado intending to obtain a ranch from his uncle which he thinks is rightfully his. Fast, exciting western. (Dir: William Witney, 90 mins.)

Outcast of the Islands (Great Britain,

1951)*** Trevor Howard, Ralph Richardson, Robert Morley, Kerima, Wendy Hiller. A low-minded British trader (superbly played by Howard) infects the innocence of a Malayan village in this adaptation from Joseph Conrad. The scuzzy leonine Howard is fully matched by the heroic declamations of Richardson as the decent captain, and by Morley's complexly realized Almayer. The film is technically stunning, as one would expect from Director Carol Reed, but is also too cold, distanced, and consciously crafted to ignite the passion the material demands. (102 mins.)

Outcasts of Poker Flat, The (1952)**½ Anne Baxter, Dale Robertson, Cameron Mitchell, Miriam Hopkins. Four shady characters are run out of a mining town and marooned in a cabin during a snowstorm. Competent western drama based on a Bret Harte story, some nice performances by Baxter and Mitchell. (Dir: Joseph M. Newman, 81 mins.)

Outcry (Italy, 1957)** Steve Cochran, Alida Valli, Betsy Blair. Slow, muddled drama of a man and the women he loved and left. Arty effort by Antonioni leaves much to be desired. Dubbed in English. (Dir: Michelangelo Antonioni, 115 mins.)

Outer Space Connection, The (1975)* (Dir: Fred Warshofsky, 106 mins.)

Outfit, The (1973)*** Robert Duvall, Karen Black, Robert Ryan, Joe Don Baker, Sheree North. Slick actioner by Chicago director John Flynn stars Duvall and Baker as two small-time toughies out to wreak havoc on—and incidentally rip off—the mob (personified by an obviously dying Ryan). (103 mins.)

Outland (1981)***½ Sean Connery, Peter Boyle, Francis Sternhagen. Writer-director Peter Hyams transplants many commercial elements to the space setting, for the most part successfully. On view here are the cop drama, spectacular gory killings, and, most of all, the Western; and for once the outer-space background adds some textural interest to the drama. The mining colony on a moon of Jupiter is convincingly created so that we genuinely experience the new, grungy frontier amid the technology, which is appropriately taken for granted. Sean Connery is the sheriff who must battle hired assassins without the aid of the people he protects; the "High Noon" climax is well conceived but lacks the punch of the central chase and fight sequence through the colony, which is both exciting and credible. (105 mins.)

Outlaw, The (1943)*½ Walter Huston, Thomas Mitchell, Jane Russell, Jack Beutel. (Dir: Howard Hughes, 103 mins.)

Outlaw Blues (1977)** Peter Fonda, Susan Saint James, John Crawford. Comedy-thriller about a songwriter on the run. Clumsy direction and editing in pedestrian chase entry. (Dir: Richard T. Heffron, 101 mins.)

Outlaw Josey Wales, The (1976)*** Clint Eastwood, Chief Dan George, Sondra Locke. Wales leaves his farm in this 1820s western to seek revenge for his murdered family. Eastwood combines cold pragmatism with strident Old Testament morality. As the director, Eastwood manages the picaresque plot skillfully. His emotional vulnerability as Wales marks another step away from his overcriticized "macho" image. All in all, a very creditable film. (135 mins.)

Outlaws Is Coming, The (1965)** The Three Stooges, Adam West, Nancy Kovack. The three goofs journey west, where Annie Oakley (Kovack) helps them expose a villainous outlaw boss. Kids and fans should get some laughs. B&W. (Dir: Norman Maurer, 89 mins.)

Outpost in Indo-China (France, 1964)** Jacques Harden, Alain Saury. Captain faces the task of securing a fort and evacuating refugees during the Vietnamese fighting. Fairly interesting war drama dubbed in English. (Dir: Leo Joannon, 93 mins.)

Outpost in Malaya (Great Britain, 1952)** Claudette Colbert, Jack Hawkins. Adventure and intrigue on a rubber plantation form the background for this mediocre, often dull, film. (Dir: Ken Annakin, 88 mins.)

Outrage (1964)***½ Paul Newman, Claire Bloom, Laurence Harvey, Edward G. Robinson, William Shatner. Conflicting stories are heard in the aftermath of a crime, as a bandit kidnaps a married couple, molests the wife, murders the husband. Story is taken from Japanese film "Rashomon" and set in our West. Intellectually interesting tale of the elusive nature of "truth" and how it changes in the eyes of the beholder. (Dir: Martin Ritt, 97 mins.)

Outrage (MTV 1973)**½ Robert Culp, Thomas Leopold, Marilyn Mason. Disturbing, thought-provoking story about a group of teen-age boys who menace a new family in an upper-middle-class neighborhood of a small California community. The kids begin with annoying pranks and graduate to real violence, until the man of the house (Culp) takes the law into his own hands. The finale, in which Culp goes on a hard-hitting no-holds-barred vengeance spree, packs a wallop. Incidentally, this story is based on a true-life incident. (Dir: Richard T. Heffron, 74 mins.)

Outrageous! (Canada, 1977)*** Craig Russell, Hollis McLaren, Richert Easley. Female impersonator shacks up chastely with escaped schizophrenic. Russell is even better out of drag. (Dir: Richard Benner, 100 mins.)

Outriders, The (1950)*** Joel McCrea, Arlene Dahl, Barry Sullivan. Rousing action filled western with the expert cowboy Joel McCrea at the helm. Good scenes focusing on the trek of a wagon train across treacherous Indian territory, and a better than usual script. (Dir: Roy Rowland, 93 mins.)

Outside Chance (MTV 1978) *½ Yvette Mimieux. (Dir: Michael Miller, 104 mins.)

Outside Man, The (France-U.S., 1973)** Jean-Louis Trintignant, Ann-Margret, Roy Scheider, and Angie Dickinson. Despite the star-studded cast, this crime melodrama suffers from a lack of cohesive continuity. Trintignant is a hired killer from France who arrives in Los Angeles to eliminate a syndicate biggie. What he doesn't know is that he too is earmarked for assassination by American hit-man Scheider. The chase is on and revenge is the name of the game. Too bad, this one had promise. (Dir: Jacques Deray, 104 mins.)

Outside the Law (1956)* Ray Danton, Leigh Snowden. (Dir: Jack Arnold, 81 mins.)

Outside the Wall (1950)** Richard Basehart, Marilyn Maxwell, Signe Hasso. Basehart's performance is the only recommendable feature of this tiresome tale of an ex-con who finds a job as a laboratory assistant at a sanitarium and encounters all sorts of evil people. (Dir: Crane Wilbur, 80 mins.)

Outsider, The (Great Britain, 1948)*** Richard Attenborough, Bernard Miles. An incorrigible youth is made into a decent citizen at a boys' school. Sensitively done drama of youth, merits praise in writing, direction, performances. (Dir: Roy Boulting, 98 mins.)

Outsider, The (1961)***½ Tony Curtis, James Franciscus. An absorbing film which bogs down a bit in the last third but it doesn't detract from the overall impact of the true story of American-Indian Ira Hayes who was one of the Marines who helped hoist the flag on Iwo Jima. Tony Curtis gives one of his best screen performances. Good screenplay by Stewart Stern. (Dir: Delbert Mann, 108 mins.)

Outsider, The (MTV 1967)*½ Darren McGavin, Ann Sothern, Edmond O'Brien. (Dir: William Graham, 98 mins.)

Outsider, The (1979)*** Craig Wasson, Sterling Hayden, Patricia Quinn. An idealistic American (Wasson) joins the IRA after a tour in Vietnam, only to discover that he is being used as a sacrificial lamb for propaganda purposes. Writer-director Tony Luraschi's refusal to develop legitimate suspense goes beyond artistic integrity into mere stubbornness. Based on Colin Leinster's novel "The Heritage of Michael Flaherty." Filmed in Belfast. (128 mins.)

Over-Exposed (1956)*½ Cleo Moore, Richard Crenna. (Dir: Lewis Seiler, 80 mins.)

Over My Dead Body (1942)** Milton Berle, Mary Beth Hughes. Milton as a writer who never finishes his mystery stories provides a fair amount of comedy in this B film. (Dir: Malcom St. Clair, 68 mins.)

Over the Edge (1979)**½ Michael Kramer, Pamela Ludwig, Matt Dillon. This film is told so subjectively from the viewpoint of a disaffected teenager that it endorses violence as an emotional release from adult repression and adolescent frustration. Director Johnathan Kaplan has a fine feel for the crushing blandness of "planned communities." (95 mins.)

Over the Hill Gang, The (MTV 1969)*½ Edgar Buchanan, Andy Devine, Rick Nelson, Pat O'Brien. (Dir: Jean Yarbrough, 72 mins.)

Over the Hill Gang Rides Again, The (MTV 1970)**½ Walter Brennan, Fred Astaire, Chill Wills, Edgar Buchanan. Sequel to "The Over the Hill Gang," a modest western which relied on a gimmick—the casting of Hollywood veteran actors in the roles of ex-Texas rangers rallying once again. In this outing, Fred Astaire joins the group as a drunken, grizzled ex-lawman (he's really a sight with a five-day growth of whiskers and battered garb) who finds his way back thanks to aid from his old cronies. (Dir: George McCowan, 73 mins.)

Over There 1914-1918 (France, 1963)*** Compilation of old film showing the progress and effects of WW I. Well done, some powerful scenes from the past. Narrated in English. (Dir: Jean Aurel, 90 mins.)

Over 21 (1945)**½ Irene Dunne, Charles Coburn, Alexander Knox. Wartime comedy about a wife who stands by her "aging" hubby through the rigors of officers' candidate school. (Dir: Charles Vidor, 102 mins.)

Overboard (MTV 1978)** Cliff Robertson, Angie Dickinson. Supercharged movie based on a novel by Hank Searles. Cliff and wife Angie embark on a dream vacation, sailing around the world on a yacht, but tragedy intervenes. Flashbacks spell out the past of their life together. (Dir: John Newland, 104 mins.)

Overcoat, The (U.S.S.R., 1959)***½ Roland Bykov, Y. Tolubeyev. Faithful, intelligent adaptation of the classic by Nikolai Gogol, a tragicomic and purely Russian tale of a lowly civil clerk in imperial Russia who dreams only of possessing a new overcoat that will not only warm him, but bolster his dignity and pride. Bykov is excellent as the clerk. B&W. (Dir: Aleksei Batalov, 93 mins.)

Overland Pacific (1954)**½ Jock Mahoney, Peggie Castle. Undercover agent investigates Indian attacks on the railroad, discovers white men behind it all. Exciting western, with rugged action. (Dir: Fred F. Sears, 73 mins.)

Overlanders, The (Australia, 1946)***½ Chips Rafferty, Daphne Campbell. When the Japanese threaten invasion of Australia, brave men undertake a great trek across the continent with precious cattle. Engrossing story of events that actually occurred has the ingredients of a western, war story, and documentary; an unusual film that is worth seeing. (Dir: Harry Watt, 91 mins.)

Owen Marshall, Counsellor at Law (MTV 1971)* Arthur Hill, Vera Miles, Joseph Campanella, Dana Wynter, William Shatner. (Dir: Buzz Kulik, 100 mins.)

Owl and the Pussycat, The (1970)*** Barbra Streisand, George Segal. Call girl (Streisand) hooks up with flunky bookstore clerk (Segal) in a raunchy, boisterous, often funny outing. The Streisand and Segal duet keep you involved even though the story's been done before. Let this one meow ya! (Dir: Herbert Ross, 95 mins.)

Ox-Bow Incident, The (1943)***½ Henry Fonda, Harry Morgan, Dana Andrews, Anthony Quinn. A powerful, relentless anti-lynching drama, with strong performances, especially from Fonda as a cowboy with a conscience. From the novel by Walter Van Telburg Clark. (Dir: William Wellman, 75 mins.)

Pacific Adventure (Australia, 1945)*** Ron Randell, Muriel Steinbeck. True story of Sir Charles Kingsford Smith, pioneer aviator who conquered the Pacific. Factual, authentic atmosphere helps this interesting biographical drama. (Dir: Ken G. Hall, 69 mins.)

Pacific Liner (1939)*** Victor McLaglen, Chester Morris, Wendy Barrie. Ship's doctor tries to stem the spread of cholera aboard an ocean liner, but is hampered by the engineer. Suspenseful melodrama. (Dir: Lew Landers, 76 mins.)

Pack Up Your Troubles (1939)** Ritz Brothers, Jane Withers. The Ritzes provide a few laughs but you'll have to be strong to tolerate the sickly WW I plot about spies and Jane Withers at the front. (Dir: H. Bruce Humberstone, 68 mins.)

Pad (and How to Use It), The (1966)**½ Brian Bedford, Julie Sommars, James Farentino. Comedy about a swinging bachelor and a shy one who team up to woo an unsuspecting young miss, provides a few laughs. Brian Bedford playing the shy member of the duo is especially adroit and amusing. Julie Sommars is adequate as the girl. This film is loosely based on British playwright Peter Shaffer's excellent one-act play "The Private Ear." (Dir: Brian Hutton, 86 mins.)

Paddy the Next Best Thing (1933)*** Janet Gaynor, Warner Baxter, Walter Connolly, Margaret Lindsay. Delightful romantic romp, with Gaynor particularly charming. (Dir: Harry Lachman, 76 mins.)

Pagan Love Song (1950)** Esther Williams, Howard Keel. Strictly for escapists—a tuneful and eye-filling musical with the customary swimming sequences starring the "Queen of the Surf," Miss Williams. Keel's fine voice makes the songs worthwhile. (Dir: Robert Alton, 76 mins.)

Pagans, The—See: **Barbarians, The**

Paid in Full (1950)*½ Robert Cummings, Lizabeth Scott, Diana Lynn, Eve Arden. (Dir: William Dieterle, 105 mins.)

Paint Your Wagon (1969)*½ Lee Marvin, Jean Seberg, Clint Eastwood. (Dir: Joshua Logan, 151 mins.)

Painted Hills, The (1951)**½ Lassie, Paul Kelly, Gary Gray. Typical Lassie adventure with the dog coming out ahead of his human co-stars. The kids will enjoy the villain who is outsmarted by the crafty canine and her young master. Pretty photography an asset. (Dir: Howard F. Kress, 65 mins.)

Painted Veil, The (1934)*** Greta Garbo, Herbert Marshall, George Brent, Warner Oland. Garbo pictures are always a treat and this overly dramatic story of a beautiful woman who is neglected by her husband while in Hong Kong is passable entertainment. Remade as "The Seventh Sin." (Dir: Richard Boleslawski, 86 mins.)

Painting the Clouds with Sunshine (1951)** Virginia Mayo, Dennis Morgan, Gene Nelson. The chorines have moved from Broadway to Las Vegas in this remake of "The Golddiggers." Lively dances. (Dir: David Butler, 87 mins.)

Paisan (Italy, 1946)*** Carmela Sazio, Garmoore, Robert van Loon, Maria Michi, Bill Tubbs. Director Roberto Rossellini's episodic account of the Allied invasion of Italy during WW II is neorealist: precise, zealous in pursuit of truth, doggedly historical in viewpoint. (90 mins.)

Pajama Game, The (1957)*** Doris Day, John Raitt, Carol Heney, Bob Fosse. A lively, infectious musical, about a strike at a pajama factory. The players are engaging, the choreography snappy and original, with dancers Haney and Fosse stand outs in their "Steam Heat." Tunes also include "Hey There You With the Stars in Your Eyes" from the Broadway hit starring Raitt, directed by George Abbott. (Dirs: George Abbott, Stanley Donen, 101 mins.)

Pajama Party (1964)** Tommy Kirk, Annette Funicello, Donna Loren, Elsa Lanchester. This one is sillier than most beach-party films because it has a science fiction bent. Would you believe Kirk as a Martian? (Dir: Don Weis, 85 mins.)

Pal Joey (1957)**½ Frank Sinatra, Rita Hayworth, Kim Novak. Penny candy imitation of the Broadway show—but not a bad musical. How much you like it will depend on your taste for director George Sidney's controlled excesses. Songs by Hart and Rodgers. Novak is hopelessly bad. (111 mins.)

Paleface, The (1948)*** Bob Hope, Jane Russell. Dentist becomes western hero because Calamity Jane is doing the shooting for him in this cute spoof of western films. (Dir: Norman Z. McLeod, 91 mins.)

Palestinians Do Have Rights, The (1977)*½

Palm Beach Story (1942)**** Claudette Colbert, Joel McCrea, Mary Astor, Rudy Vallee. Everything works as it should in this hilarious Preston Sturges-directed comedy. Colbert is the young wife fleeing her husband (McCrea), and winding up in Palm Beach surrounded by dizzy millionaires (including the delightful team of Astor and Vallee). (90 mins.)

Palm Springs Weekend (1963)** Connie Stevens, Ty Hardin, Troy Donahue, Robert Conrad, Stefanie Powers. Strictly for the teen-age audience, about the annual Easter Week invasion of Palm Springs by hordes of college kids and their friends out to have a good time. Hollywood's idea of typical "college types" may give the teen-agers an added chuckle. (Dir: Norman Taurog, 100 mins.)

Palmy Days (1931)**½ Eddie Cantor, George Raft, Charlotte Greenwood. Frantically paced comedy set in a health resort overrun by bathing beauties, circa 1930, and gangsters. Many production numbers staged by Busby Berkeley. Cantor is good and Charlotte Greenwood gets her share of laughs. (Dir: A. Edward Sutherland, 77 mins.)

Palomino, The (1950)** Jerome Courtland, Beverly Tyler. A prize palomino breeding stallion is stolen and as a result the heroine's ranch goes to pot. Fair outdoor adventure story for the youngsters. (Dir: Ray Nazarro, 73 mins.)

Panache (MTV 1976)*½ Rene Auberjonois, David Healy, Charles Frank, Joseph Ruskin. (Dir: Gary Nelson, 72 mins.)

Panama Hattie (1943)**½ Red Skelton, Ann Sothern, Marsha Hunt. Another Broadway musical hit is slaughtered in the screen transition. A fine cast does their best with the plot about blowing up the Canal but the film has no spark. Lena Horne makes her Hollywood debut in this. (Dir: Norman Z. McLeod, 79 mins.)

Pandora and the Flying Dutchman (Great Britain, 1951)*** James Mason, Ava Gardner. A beautiful playgirl is the replica of the girl for whom the legendary Flying Dutchman was condemned to sail the seas forever; off the coast of Spain, she is visited by a mysterious stranger. Fanciful drama, not always successful, but extremely interesting. (Dir: Albert Lewin, 123 mins.)

Pandora's Box (Germany, 1928)**** Louise Brooks, Fritz Kortner, Franz Lederer. Like Alban Berg's opera "Lulu," this is based on Frank Wedekind's play. Story of an amoral woman who proceeds through a series of sexual relationships, ending as a prostitute on the streets of London who takes Jack the Ripper home one night. Director G. W. Pabst was years ahead of his time in making his meditations on character the central focus of his films instead of the story line. Brooks, the incarnation of intelligent eroticism, deserves the cult that has grown up around her; the later decline of her career is one of the cinema's great losses. (110 mins.)

Panhandle (1948)*** Rod Cameron, Cathy Downs. Brawny Cameron mops up a few

western varmints, one a young gun played by Blake Edwards, who's now reformed and turned into a big time movie director. Actionful oats opera, one of the better ones. (Dir: Lesley Selander, 84 mins.)

Panic (Great Britain, 1963)** Janine Gray, Dyson Lovell, Glyn Houston. Girl working for a diamond merchant is hit during a robbery and loses her memory, is taken in by a friendly ex-boxer. Fair crime melodrama. (Dir: John Gilling, 69 mins.)

Panic at Lake Wood Manor—See: It Happened at Lake Wood Manor

Panic Button (1963)** Maurice Chevalier, Michael Connors, Jayne Mansfield, Eleanor Parker. Gangster's son goes to Italy to make a pilot for a TV film, which must be a bad one so that the syndicate can take a tax loss. Mild comedy filmed in Europe unwinds a cast of veteran performers. (Dir: George Sherman, 90 mins.)

Panic in Echo Park (MTV 1977)**½ Dorian Harewood, Robin Gammel, Catlin Adams. Good acting bolsters this routine pilot film for a proposed series about a dedicated black doctor who jeopardizes his career when he delves into a possible epidemic that has broken out in a ghetto community. Dorian Harewood is convincing as Dr. Stoner, a man who puts principles ahead of personal gain, and Robin Gammell, as his superior, opposed to his crusade, makes a good adversary. (Dir: John Llewellyn Moxey, 72 mins.)

Panic in Needle Park, The (1971)*** Al Pacino, Kitty Winn, Alan Vint. Pacino in his first starring role is very effective as a heroin addict who drags a young girl down into his world of hookers, pimps, thieves, and other low-life inhabitants of New York City's "Needle Park." A harrowing film, well observed and decently dramatized. (Dir: Jerry Schatzberg, 110 mins.)

Panic in the City (1968)* Howard Duff, Linda Cristal, Nehemiah Persoff, Dennis Hopper. (Dir: Eddie Davis, 97 mins.)

Panic in the Parlor (1957)** Peggy Mount, Shirley Eaton, Ronald Lewis. Raucous heavy handed British farce about a domineering mother (jarringly played by Peggy Mount) and a screwball family. (Dir: Gordon Parry, 81 mins.)

Panic in the Streets (1950)***½ Richard Widmark, Jack Palance, Paul Douglas, Barbara Bel Geddes, Zero Mostel. A dead body in New Orleans is found to be carrying bubonic plague. A courageous doctor and the police track down the source, leading to an exciting climax. Directed by Elia Kazan with on-the-spot location realism, and a good supporting performance from Mostel. (96 mins.)

Panic in Year Zero (1962)*** Ray Milland, Jean Hagen, Frankie Avalon. Forceful drama about a man trying to survive along with his family when the country is devastated by an atomic attack. Some of the drastic steps he takes may be questioned by the audience, but there's no doubt of the impact of the story. Milland acts well, directs even better. (95 mins.)

Panic on Page One—See: **City In Fear**

Panic on the 5:22 (MTV 1974)** James Sloyan, Ina Balin, Lynda Day George. A private railroad club car is taken over by three thugs out to rob and perhaps kill. Will the large cast make it home in time for the 6:30 news, or will they become victims of Sloyan and his two sidekicks? Or will you feel you've seen it all before? (Dir: Harvey Hart, 78 mins.)

Pantaloons (France, 1956)*** Fernandel, Carmen Sevilla. Fernandel romps through this funny French farce as a valet masquerading as his master, Don Juan. (Dir: John Berry, 93 mins.)

Papa's Delicate Condition (1963)*** Jackie Gleason, Glynis Johns, Charles Ruggles, Elisha Cook, Jr. Slight, entertaining comedy of manners, morals, and proprieties in a small American town at the turn of the century. The "condition" referred to is drunkenness, and Papa's serious-minded wife is not amused. The period atmosphere is carefully created; Gleason is affecting (in a role originally meant for Fred Astaire!). From the autobiography of silent screen star Corinne Griffith. (Dir: George Marshall, 98 mins.)

Paper Chase, The (1973)**** Timothy Bottoms, John Houseman, Lindsay Wagner. Comedy about nose-to-the-grindstone law students tyrannized by an icy classroom martinet, Houseman's droll Kingsfield. Writer-director James Bridges has fashioned an authentic drama. (111 mins.)

Paper Lion (1968)***½ Alan Alda. Engaging, observant dramatization of George Plimpton's bestseller about his experiences in the world of pro football. Designed to capitalize on the huge audience that now sits transfixed, watching pro football every Sunday during the fall, producer Stuart Millar and his screenwriter have skillfully fashioned a believable plot line based on Plimpton's factual report. (Millar also directed much of the last part of the film skillfully, after the director who gets screen credit, Alex March, was fired.) Model-turned-actress Lauren Hutton is both beautiful and charming playing Alda's girlfriend. The scenes of the Detroit Lions training scrimmages, and in the locker room capture the flavor of this tough, fascinating sport. (107 mins.)

Paper Man (MTV 1971)*** Dean Stockwell, James Stacy. Intriguing, imaginative drama about a computer. Group of bright college students, using the university computer, create a fictitious human and go off on a buying spree with the character's credit card. When bills come due, more data is put into the computer. Soon the paper man displays puzzling independent behavior which includes murder. (Dir: Walter Grauman, 73 mins.)

Paper Moon (1973)**** Ryan O'Neal, Tatum O'Neal, Madeline Kahn. Director Peter Bogdanovich is back with another

lovely piece of yesterday in black and white. Finely engraved story of Kansas con man selling Bibles to women just turned widows, with the aid of an innocent nine-year-old determined to be corrupted. The interplay between the con man and his tiny sidekick (a real-life father and daughter) is irresistibly real and sweetly sentimental. Tatum O'Neal steals the movie from her dad while giving one of the most appealing performances by a child actor in many years. Tatum, in her film debut, won a Best Supporting Actress Oscar. (101 mins.)

Paper Tiger (Great Britain, 1974)*½ David Niven, Toshiro Mifune, Ando, Hardy Kruger. (Dir: Ken Annakin, 99 mins.)

Papillon (1973)*** Steve McQueen, Dustin Hoffman, Victor Jory, William Smithers. A generally exciting film based on the best-selling novel about Henri "Papillon" Charriere's real-life escape from the brutal French penal colony of Devil's Island, off the eastern coast of South America. McQueen's escape on a raft is rousing escapist fare. (Dir: Franklin J. Schaffner, 153 mins.)

Parachute Battalion (1941)**½ Robert Preston, Nancy Kelly, Edmond O'Brien. Two trainees in the parachute corps go through the hazardous training and fall for the same girl. Typical but fairly interesting service melodrama. (Dir: Leslie Goodwins, 75 mins.)

Paradine Case, The (1948)***½ Gregory Peck, Charles Laughton, Alida Valli, Ethel Barrymore, Charles Coburn. Permit my minority opinion that this admittedly long, talky film is among the best work of director Alfred Hitchcock and producer-cowriter David O. Selznick. Lawyer Peck falls in love with the beautiful woman he is defending against a murder charge. Based on Robert Hichens's novel. Impeccably performed. (132 mins.)

Paradise Alley (1978)**½ Sylvester Stallone, Armand Assante, Lee Canalito. Stallone is the writer, star, and naive, appallingly fearless debut director of this upbeat film about three brothers in the '40s looking to move out of the slums and onto Easy Street. He figures the best plan is to turn one huge brother (Canalito) into a champion wrestler. (107 mins.)

Paradise Connection, The (MTV 1979)** Buddy Ebsen, Bonnie Ebsen, Marj Dusay. Buddy Ebsen is a Chicago lawyer searching for an estranged son mixed up in drug smuggling. Daughter Bonnie tries hard as a singing waitress, but the flick is flat. Filmed in Hawaii, on the island of Maui. (Dir: Michael Preece, 104 mins.)

Paradise, Hawaiian Style (1966)** Elvis Presley. Typical Presley musical for his fans. This time out, Presley is an airline pilot who returns to Hawaii to interest his buddy, played by James Shigeta, in setting up a shuttle-plane business. Songs, romance, and island cuties. (Dir: Michael Moore, 91 mins.)

Paradise Lagoon (Great Britain, 1957)*** Kenneth More, Sally Ann Howes, Diane Cilento. A funny comedy based on "The Admirable Crichton." The plot concerns a group of ship-wrecked British families who come to rely on the resourcefulness of a butler. The young lady of a respectable family falls for the servant as does a flighty upstairs maid. (Dir: Lewis Gilbert, 94 mins.)

Parallax View, The (1974)***½ Warren Beatty, Paula Prentiss. Fascinating, disturbing story about a political assassination of a senator, not unlike the Kennedys, and one reporter's efforts to get to the bottom of the mystery surrounding the killing by a busboy who himself is killed. Suddenly witnesses at the assassination start dying off, and one of them goes to reporter Beatty who gets on the case. Extremely well directed by Alan Pakula. (102 mins.)

Paranoia (French-Italy, 1965)** Marcello Mastroianni, Virna Lisi, Pamela Tiffin. Three separate tales concerning man, romance, and mentality. Aside from Mastroianni's good looks, Tiffin's charm, and Lisi's glamour, little to recommend; tales never seem to come to a boil. Dubbed in English. (Dir: Luciano Salce, Eduardo de Filippo, 85 mins.)

Paranoia (Italy-France, 1968)* Carroll Baker, Lou Castel. (Dir: Umberto Lenzi, 91 mins.)

Paranoiac (Great Britain, 1963)**½ Janette Scott, Alexander Davion, Oliver Reed. Elaborate, entertaining murder tale; plentiful gore, fanciful props, chilling atmosphere. (Dir: Freddie Francis, 80 mins.)

Paratrooper (Great Britain, 1953)** Alan Ladd, Leo Genn, Susan Stephen. A Canadian joins the paratroopers under an assumed name because he has a fear of responsibility due to an earlier service experience. Muddled action film with drab acting. (Dir: Terence Hill, 87 mins.)

Pardners (1956)** Dean Martin, Jerry Lewis, Agnes Moorehead. Eccentric playboy and a ranch foreman head west with a prize bull, foil varmints bent on taking over the ranch. Dean and Jerry out west in a comedy which, after a good start, slows down to a canter. (Dir: Norman Taurog, 88 mins.)

Pardon Mon Affaire (France, 1976)**½ Jean Rochefort, Anny Duperey, Daniele Delorme. Director and cowriter Yves Robert has made an assured, glossy sex comedy of the Rock Hudson-Doris Day sort. Not very satisfying tripe, though Rochefort is an able farceur and Duperey a magnificent hallucination of femininity. Delorme is too wonderful to play leftover wives. (105 mins.)

Pardon My French (1951)** Merle Oberon, Paul Henreid. A Boston schoolteacher acquires a French chateau, finds it inhabited by miscellaneous squatters, including a dashing composer and five fatherless children. Slender little comedy, not much.

Made in France. (Dir: Bernard Vorhaus, 81 mins.)

Pardon My Past (1945)***½ Fred MacMurray, Marguerite Chapman. Ex-soldier is mistaken for a wealthy playboy who owes money to some gamblers. Delightful comedy-drama, smoothly done and entertaining. (Dir: Leslie Fenton, 88 mins.)

Pardon My Sarong (1942)*** Bud Abbott, Lou Costello, Virginia Bruce, the Ink Spots. Two bus drivers on a playboy's yacht land on a tropic isle, where they thwart villains trying to steal the temple jewels. One of the better Abbott and Costello comedies, with some genuinely amusing bits of business. (Dir: Erie C. Kenton, 84 mins.)

Pardon My Trunk (Italy, 1953)** Vittorio De Sica, Sabu. Vittorio De Sica plays a school teacher who receives a real live elephant as a gift from an Indian Prince whom he has befriended. Sounds hilarious but isn't. On the strength of this film we feel De Sica is a better actor than Sabu. (Dir: Gianni Franciolini, 78 mins.)

Parent Trap, The (1961)*** Hayley Mills, Maureen O'Hara, Brian Keith, Una Merkel, Joanna Barnes. Hayley Mills is simply wonderful playing twins in this family comedy-drama produced by the Walt Disney studio. Miss Mills meets her look-alike at a summer camp and after some detective work, they discover they are twins. Adapted for the screen and directed by David Swift. (124 mins.)

Pariahs of Glory (France, 1964)**½ Curt Jurgens, Maurice Ronet. French soldier meets the German who killed his brother years ago, but the two fight together in Indo-China. War drama has some affecting scenes, but lacks the necessary punch. Dubbed in English. (Dir: Henri Decoin, 95 mins.)

Paris Blues (1961)***½ Paul Newman, Joanne Woodward, Sidney Poitier, Diahann Carroll, Louis Armstrong. Directed on location in Paris by Martin Ritt. This is a frequently effective love story of "Two boys meet two girls." This quartet, however, consists of four supremely attractive performers who bolster the story line. Newman and Poitier play jazz musicians and there's a lot of good music thrown in as a bonus. (Dir: Martin Ritt, 98 mins.)

Paris Does Strange Things (Elena et les Hommes) (France, 1957)**** Ingrid Bergman, Mel Ferrer, Jean Marais, Juliette Greco. Director Jean Renoir's most artificial meditation, about a lovely princess who has a great desire to control everything around her. (86 mins.)

Paris Express (Great Britain, 1952)**½ Claude Rains, Marta Toren, Herbert Lom. Femme fatale plunges a bookkeeper into a web of murder and robbery. Well-acted but complicated melodrama. (Dir: Harold French, 83 mins.)

Paris Holiday (1958)**½ Bob Hope, Fernandel, Anita Ekberg, Martha Hyer,

Preston Sturges. Typical Bob Hope comedy with Bob sharing the clowning honors with France's Fernandel. Not all the jokes come off but there's Anita Ekberg to look at, so who can complain? (Dir: Gerd Oswald, 100 mins.)

Paris Honeymoon (1939)**½ Bing Crosby, Shirley Ross, Franciska Gaal. Pleasant, inconsequential Crosby film about the romance of an American with a French peasant girl. (Dir: Frank Tuttle, 85 mins.)

Paris in the Month of August (France, 1966)**½ Susan Hampshire, Michel De Re. A married clerk finds a bit of extramarital romance with an English girl. Charles Aznavour as a lover, and it's pleasant. (Dir: Pierre Granier-Deferre, 94 mins.)

Paris Model (1953)** Marilyn Maxwell, Paulette Goddard, Eva Gabor. Dull story but a parade of pulchritude to please men of all ages. The "Girls" racket is the film theme. (Dir: Alfred E. Green, 81 mins.)

Paris Que Dort—See: **Crazy Ray, The**

Paris Underground (1945)*** Constance Bennett, Gracie Fields. American and her English companion are caught by the Nazi invasion of France, work for the underground throughout the war. Interesting melodrama, based on fact. (Dir: Gregory Ratoff, 97 mins.)

Paris When It Sizzles (1964)* William Holden, Audrey Hepburn, Noel Coward. (Dir: Richard Quine, 110 mins.)

Park Row (1952)*** Gene Evans, Mary Welch. Melodrama about two competing newspapers. Samuel Fuller's rolling, slugging direction is absolutely convincing. (83 mins.)

Parnell (1937)** Clark Gable, Myrna Loy. One of Gable's worst pre-war films. Story of the great Irish patriot is poorly written and terribly miscast. (Dir: John M. Stahl, 118 mins.)

Parrish (1961)*** Claudette Colbert, Karl Malden, Troy Donahue, Connie Stevens. An entertaining soaper. The plot drags when it centers on the sappy title character (Donahue), but the unlikely romance between his widowed mother (Colbert) and a flashy tycoon (Malden) is interesting and portrayed with conviction by the two experts. Stevens is engaging as a bad girl with a heart of gold. (Dir: Delmer Davies, 140 mins.)

Parson and the Outlaw, The (1957)* Anthony Dexter, Sonny Tufts, Marie Windsor, Charles "Buddy" Rogers. (Dir: Oliver Drake, 71 mins.)

Parson of Panamint, The (1941)*** Charles Ruggles, Ellen Drew. Offbeat western about a wild town that grew up with a gold strike and its young, hard hitting, yet gentle parson, who is almost executed as a murderer. (Dir: William McGann, 84 mins.)

Part-Time Wife (Great Britain, 1961)*½ Anton Rodgers, Nyree Dawn Porter. (Dir: Max Varnel, 70 mins.)

Partner, The (Great Britain, 1963)** Yoko Tani, Guy Doleman. Movie producer gets involved in a swindling plot. Average mystery based on an Edgar Wallace story. (Dir: Gerard Glaister, 58 mins.)

Partners in Crime (Great Britain, 1962)** Bernard Lee, John Van Eyssen. Police investigate the murder of a wealthy businessman and a burglary. Fair Edgar Wallace mystery. (Dir: Peter Duffell, 54 mins.)

Partners in Crime (MTV 1973)** Lee Grant, Harry Guardino, Bob Cummings. Pilot wastes Grant's considerable talents. She plays a judge who resigns to become a detective with an ex-con for her partner. (Dir: Jack Smight, 78 mins.)

Parts: The Clonus Horror—See: **Clonus Horror, The**

Party, The (1968)*** Peter Sellers, Claudine Longet, Marge Champion. Director Blake Edwards's effortless celebration of the sight gag. Indian bit player Sellers, who has just destroyed a remake of "Gunga Din," finds himself at a posh party at his producer's Hollywood home. There are elephants, people falling into swimming pools, and mountains of soapsuds, but somehow the image that lingers in my mind is Sellers feeding "birdie num-nums" to a myna. (99 mins.)

Party Crashers, The (1958)** Mark Damon, Bobby Driscoll, Connie Stevens, Frances Farmer. Teenage gang members get into trouble when they intrude on a party at a roadhouse. Routine juvenile delinquency drama. (Dir: Bernard Girard, 78 mins.)

Party Girl (1958)***½ Robert Taylor, Cyd Charisse, Lee J. Cobb, John Ireland. Taylor is a crippled mouthpiece for the mob who meets his match in cynical vulnerability in Charisse. Cobb is the boss gangster. Nicholas Ray's direction is triumphantly expressive. (98 mins.)

Passage, The (Great Britain, 1979)* Anthony Quinn, James Mason, Patricia Neal, Malcolm McDowell, Christopher Lee. Based on the Novel, "Perilous Passage" by Bruce Nicolayson. (Dir: J. Lee Thompson, 99 mins.)

Passage to Marseille (1944)*** Humphrey Bogart, Claude Rains, Sydney Greenstreet, Peter Lorre, Michele Morgan. Confused but often exciting story of convicts who escape from Devil's Island to join forces with the free French. When it finally gets down to adventure it's not a bad film. (Dir: Michael Curtiz, 110 mins.)

Passenger (Poland, 1963)***½ Aleksandra Slaska. A remarkable if somewhat fragmented film about two women prisoners in Auschwitz, the infamous German concentration camp. Devastating sequences concerning life in the camp made by the gifted director Andrzej Munk, who died in 1961 before finishing the film. Later completed by film-industry colleagues. (60 mins.)

Passenger, The (Italy, 1975)**** Jack Nicholson, Maria Schneider, Jenny Runacre, Ian Hendry. One of director

Michelangelo Antonioni's finest works. Nicholson and Schneider star as a journalist, who trades one identity for another, and the girl who becomes his accomplice. Less a thriller (though the mood of mystery is pervasive) than a meditation. (Dir: Michelangelo Antonioni, 123 mins.)

Passing of the Third Floor Back, The (Great Britain, 1935)*** Conrad Veidt, Anna Lee, René Ray. Odd, interesting filming of the whimsical book by the Victorian novelist Jerome K. Jerome. Episodic story about the effect a stranger has on the lives of some discontented inhabitants of a boardinghouse. Excellent cast, fine production. (Dir: Berthold Viertel, 90 mins.)

Passing Stranger, The (Great Britain, 1954)*** Lee Patterson, Diane Cilento. An American deserter becomes involved deeper and deeper in a smuggling racket, until he decides to take action. Above average, tense drama. (Dir: John Arnold, 67 mins.)

Passion of Anna, The (Sweden, 1969)**** Max von Sydow, Liv Ullmann, Bibi Andersson. Marvelous complex psychological drama about four people on an island in desolation and despair. Von Sydow is Andreas Winkelman, who has taken refuge in a hermit's existence. His actions are the catalyst for uncovering the others' self-deception. A masterwork from director Ingmar Bergman. Colors play a symbolic role and Sven Nykvist, the cameraman, has created amazing hues. (99 mins.)

Passion of Slow Fire, The (France 1961)*** Jean DeSailly, Alexandra Stewart. Sleuth unravels a web of intrigue when a beautiful American girl is found murdered. Involved but intriguing Gallic mystery, done with style. From a Georges Simenon novel. (Dir: Edouard Molinaro, 94 mins.)

Passionate Sentry, The (Great Britain, 1953)*** Nigel Patrick, Peggy Cummins. The romantic story of a palace guard and the girls who chase him. Pleasant comedy. (Dir: Anthony Kimmins, 84 mins.)

Passionate Summer (Great Britain, 1958)** Virginia McKenna, Bill Travers. Tropic schoolmaster's love starved wife makes a play for a young teacher. Overly dramatic story of the tropics; good cast, not much else. (Dir: Rudolph Cartier, 103 mins.)

Passionate Thief, The (Italy, 1962)**½ Anna Magnani, Ben Gazzara. Uneven comedy about a small time bit player who inadvertently keeps thwarting the attempts of a pickpocket on New Year's Eve. Some funny scenes, but it's too protracted. Dubbed in English. (Dir: Mario Monicelli, 105 mins.)

Passport for a Corpse (Italy, 1962)*½ Linda Christian, Albert Lupin. (Dir: Mario Gariazzo, 86 mins.)

Passport to China (Great Britain, 1961)** Richard Basehart, Lisa Gastoni. Adventurer attempts a rescue of an American secret agent and a Formosan pilot missing in Red China. Strictly routine melodrama, little new. (Dir: Michael Carreras, 75 mins.)

Passport to Destiny (1943)** Elsa Lancaster, Lloyd Corrigan. English scrubwoman believes she is guided by a "magic eye," goes to Germany to kill Hitler. Good idea, but routine in the telling; fair comedy-drama. (Dir: Ray McCarey, 64 mins.)

Passport to Pimlico (Great Britain, 1949)**** Stanley Holloway, Margaret Rutherford, Basil Radford, Naunton Wayne, Hermione Baddeley. This little gem manages to parody the not-so-funny situations of postwar England and divided Berlin, while at the same time poke fun at the archaic system of vested interests and status quo proprieties in England. Fish-shop proprietor Holloway unearths an ancient treaty establishing Pimlico (a district in London) as part of Burgundy (thus subject neither to British licensing laws nor to postwar rationing); the inhabitants proceed to make monkeys out of Whitehall. A treat. (Dir: Henry Cornelius, 84 mins.)

Passport to Treason (Great Britain, 1955)** Rod Cameron, Lois Maxwell. Private detective called to help a friend finds him murdered, starts investigating. Average mystery on the complicated side. (Dir: Robert S. Baker, 70 mins.)

Password Is Courage, The (Great Britain, 1962)**½ Dirk Bogarde, Maria Perschy. Reasonably interesting account of the WW II exploits of Charles Coward, a real-life hero who made many daring escapes from Nazi prison camps. Details many of the escapes, and a good cast of English actors adds to the flavor of the story. (Dir: Andrew L. Stone, 116 mins.)

Pastor Hall (Great Britain, 1940)**½ Wilfred Lawson, Nova Pilbeam. A courageous priest speaks out against the Nazis in Germany, is imprisoned, tortured. Strong drama, some gripping moments. (Dir: Roy Boulting, 97 mins.)

Pat and Mike (1952)**** Spencer Tracy, Katharine Hepburn, Aldo Ray, Chuck Connors, Charles Bronson. About a hustling trainer who grooms a gifted gym teacher to be the world's greatest woman athlete. The best Tracy-Hepburn film—see the magnificently relaxed and graceful teamwork of the stars. (Dir: George Cukor, 95 mins.)

Pat Garrett and Billy the Kid (1973)*½ James Coburn, Kris Kristofferson, Bob Dylan, Jason Robards, Jr. (Dir: Sam Peckinpah, 106 mins.)

Patch of Blue, A (1965)***½ Sidney Poitier, Elizabeth Hartman, Shelley Winters. A moving, well-acted film about a sensitive relationship which develops between a blind white girl and a black man. The story is fairly predictable, but Sidney Poitier and Elizabeth Hartman bring a touching credibility to their roles which keeps you interested throughout. Shelley

Winters is seen in her Oscar-winning supporting role as the garish, vulgar, intolerable mother of the blind girl, and Wallace Ford offers a nice bit as Miss Hartman's alcoholic grandfather. (Dir: Guy Green, 105 mins.)

Path of Hope, The (Italy, 1950)**½ Raf Vallone, Elena Varzi. When their mine is closed down and there's no work, inhabitants of a small mining town trek from Italy to France to find a new life. Fairly well done social drama; won some awards when first released, but generally overrated. (Dir: Pietro Germi, 101 mins.)

Pather Panchali (India, 1956)**** Subir Banerji. First film in a mighty trilogy by Indian director Satyajit Ray. Beautifully done story of a poverty stricken family in a Bengali village. Although the locale is exotic, strange to the western eye, the situations should be familiar, as they relate to all of us. Superb performances, mostly by a non-professional cast. English-dubbed. (112 mins.)

Pathfinder and the Mohican, The (1956)*½ John Hart, Lon Chaney. (90 mins.)

Paths of Glory (1957)**** Kirk Douglas, Ralph Meeker, Adolphe Menjou, Wayne Morris, George Macready. A superb film about a French Army division fighting in Verdun during WW I. Kirk Douglas is excellent as an officer who believes in treating his men as human beings as well as soldiers. Stanley Kubrick brilliantly directed a carefully chosen cast. Truly a great film! (66 mins.)

Patrick (Australia, 1978)*** Susan Penhaligon, Robert Helpmann, Julia Blake. A worthy horror entry. Comatose in a third-rate private hospital bed, Patrick passes his time with psychokinetic mischief. The script is unusually bright for this kind of essentially arbitrary thriller, and director Richard Franklin uses a smart montage-oriented approach and largely overcomes the pinch-penny Australian budget. The dubbing destroys any sense of verisimilitude of the performances. (90 mins.)

Patriot Game, The (France, 1978)***½ Illuminating documentary on the struggle to wrest northern Ireland from England and unify it with southern Ireland. Told largely from the point of view of the provisional wing of the IRA. (Dir: Arthur Mac Caig, 97 mins.)

Patsy, The (1964)** Jerry Lewis, Ina Balin, Ed Wynn, Peter Lorre. Yet another Lewis starrer, directed and co-authored by Hollywood's self-appointed actor-producer-director-writer. This particular story line concerns a Hollywood bellboy tapped for movie stardom. The pace is frantic, the slapstick routines ever-present. Jerry did have the good sense to bolster the film with brief appearances from, among others, the late Ed Wynn and Peter Lorre. (101 mins.)

Pattern for Murder (West Germany, 1964)* George Mather, Julie Reding. (80 mins.)

Patterns (1956)***½ Van Heflin, Everett Sloane, Beatrice Straight, Ed Begley. If you didn't see this compelling Rod Serling drama either time it was done on network TV, tune in. Executive becomes involved in power squeeze in large corporation. (Dir: Fielder Cook, 83 mins.)

Patton (1970)**** George C. Scott, Karl Malden. Scott's magnificent performance as General George S. Patton earned him an Oscar, and the film was selected as the best of 1970 by the Academy Award members. It's gutsy, tough, comparatively honest and fascinating portrait of the WW II general whose military bravado and love of war made him a hero, and also caused him to be relieved of his command in Sicily. In addition to Scott's monumental performance, the film boasts a series of brilliantly staged battle sequences, tracing Patton's career in the North African, Sicilian, and European campaigns. Recommended fare. (Dir: Franklin Schaffner, 170 mins.)

Paula (1952)*** Loretta Young, Kent Smith, Tommy Rettig. Paula (Loretta Young) takes a young boy, who is a mute as a result of a "hit and run" accident, into her home. Strange events come into focus as a result. Good acting despite the sometimes stilted script. (Dir: Rudolph Mate, 80 mins.)

Pawnbroker, The (1965)**** Rod Steiger, Geraldine Fitzgerald, Jaime Sanchez. One of the most shattering, powerful and honest films made in America in the sixties. Superbly directed by Sidney Lumet in New York's Harlem. Story concerns a Jewish pawnbroker, victim of Nazi persecution, who loses all faith in his fellow man until he realizes no man is an island. Uniformly fine performances down to the smallest bit part, but Steiger is quite spectacular in his own beautifully controlled performance. A rare experience for discerning adults. (116 mins.)

Pay or Die (1966)*** Ernest Borgnine, Zohra Lampert. Well acted and realistically brutal account of the Mafia's activities in New York City during the years preceding WW I, based on fact. Borgnine gives a strong performance as a detective and is backed by a good supporting cast. Miss Lampert is a remarkably versatile and talented performer. (Dir: Richard Wilson, 111 mins.)

Payday (1972)**** Rip Torn, Elayne Heilveil, Ahna Capri. Observant and deeply moving film about a second-rate country and western singer (Torn) whose road to Mecca—in this case, Nashville, Tenn.—is littered with men and women used and abandoned when he no longer needs them. Honest, knowing screenplay by Don Carpenter; superbly directed by Daryl Duke. The beauty and the poverty of the Alabama countryside are captured by cinematographer Richard C. Glouner and there's a particularly touching performance from Heilveil, playing a young, innocent groupie. (Dir: Daryl Duke, 103 mins.)

Payment in Blood (Italy, 1967)½ Edd Byrnes, Guy Madison. (Dir: Enzo Girolami [E. G. Rowland], 89 mins.)

Payment on Demand (1951)**½ Bette Davis, Barry Sullivan, Jane Cowl. For Bette Davis fans—here's a typical melodrama which makes full use of her "personal" acting style. Miss Davis' marriage to Barry Sullivan is on the rocks and headed toward divorce—but first, we have a series of flashbacks depicting the past and Bette really pours it on—crying, laughing, screaming, strutting, and generally chewing up the scenery. (Dir: Curtis Bernhardt, 87 mins.)

Payroll (Great Britain, 1961)**½ Michael Craig, Françoise Provost, Billie Whitelaw. Wife of a murdered armored-car guard works with the police in trapping a gang of robbers. Tough, fast-paced crime melodrama, well acted. (Dir: Sidney Hayers, 94 mins.)

Pearl, The (1947)**** Pedro Armendariz, Maria Elena Marques. An excellent Mexican film about a poor fisherman who finds a luscious pearl which changes his life. Pedro Armendariz is superb as the bewildered fisherman who can't believe what is happening to him and his wife. Based on a John Steinbeck story. (Dir: Emilio Fernandez, 77 mins.)

Peasants of the Second Fortress, The (Japan, 1971)*** A unique documentary about Japanese farmers trying to block the building of a new airport near Tokyo. Directed over a five-year period by Shinsuke Ogawa, the unedited film runs almost nine hours. A small "war" erupted in Japan over this project, and the film chronicles the efforts—losing ones, ultimately—of farmers to fight the government and keep their land. (143 mins.)

Peeper (1976)** Michael Caine, Natalie Wood, Kitty Winn, Thayer David. Silly, occasionally engaging spoof of private-eye films, with Caine as a British eye in L.A. in '47. Either Wood or Winn may inherit a sizable sum. Based on the novel "Deadfall" by Keith Laumer; screenplay by W. D. Richter. (Dir: Peter Hyams, 87 mins.)

Peeping Tom (Great Britain, 1960)**** Carl Boehm, Moira Shearer, Anna Massey. Insane photographer kills models while photographing their reactions to death. Directed with brilliance and eccentricity by Michael Powell. (109 mins.)

Peer Gynt (1941)** Charlton Heston, Betty Hanisee, Alan Heston, David Bradley. Bradley, not long out of high school, directed a rendition of the Ibsen play with 17-year-old Charlton Heston as Peer. A historical curiosity. (85 mins.)

Peggy (1950)** Diana Lynn, Rock Hudson, Charles Coburn. Silly, unpretentious little comedy about college life, football heroes and the girls who scream over them, and the big Rose Bowl Tournament. (Dir: Frederick de Cordova, 77 mins.)

Peking Express (1951)** Joseph Cotten, Corinne Calvet, Edmund Gwenn. Romance and adventure aboard a speeding train, with a doctor and a wandering lady in the midst of it. Remake of a Dietrich film, "Shanghai Express," and as usual the original was better—routine melodrama. (Dir: William Dieterle, 95 mins.)

Pendulum (1969)*** George Peppard, Jean Seberg, Richard Kiley. Interesting action drama with George Peppard well cast as a Washington, D.C., police captain who becomes a chief suspect when his wife and her lover are murdered. There are many subplots, but TV director George Schaefer, making his film bow with this one, keeps the pace clipping along. Original screenplay by Stanley Niss is more intelligent than most, and raises some stimulating questions about civil liberties and "law and order." (Dir: George Schaefer, 106 mins.)

Penelope (1966)** Natalie Wood, Ian Bannen, Dick Shawn, Peter Falk. Silly, occasionally entertaining comedy in which Natalie Wood plays a zany girl who befuddles even her psychiatrist, when she holds up her husband's bank. Peter Falk, as a detective, gives the film's best performance. (Dir: Arthur Hiller, 97 mins.)

Penn of Pennsylvania—See: **Courageous Mr. Penn**

Penitentiary (1979)*** Leon Isaac Kennedy, Thommy Pollard, Hazel Spears, Badja Djola, Wilbur "Hi-Fi" White. Kennedy, a man unjustly imprisoned, makes his mark in jail with his fast fists. Director Jamaa Fanaka's eye is unceasingly alert for audience payoff. (99 mins.)

Pennies from Heaven (1936)*** Bing Crosby, Madge Evans, Edith Fellows, Louis Armstrong. Wandering drifter befriends a homeless waif, soon has a pretty truant officer on their trail. Outdated but still amusing musical. (Dir: Norman Z. McLeod, 81 mins.)

Penny Serenade (1941)***½ Cary Grant, Irene Dunne, Beulah Bondi. An honorable tearjerker, expertly directed by George Stevens. Grant and Dunne try to hold their marriage together by adopting a child. (120 mins.)

Pennywhistle Blues (Great Britain, 1952)***½ Something different—comedy about a thief who loses his stolen loot, as it passes from hand to hand. Made in South Africa, with a native cast. Utterly delightful, charming, funny. See it. Star Tommy Ramokgopa also did the music. (Dir: Donald Swanson, 63 mins.)

Penthouse, The (Great Britain, 1967)** Suzy Kendall, Terence Morgan. Excessively brutal drama about a day of sadism and terror when two intruders invade a penthouse shared by a married man and his young mistress. Based on the play "The Meter Man," by C. Scott Forbes. Written and directed by Peter Colinson. (97 mins.)

People, The (MTV 1972)*** Kim Darby,

William Shatner, Diane Varsi, Dan O'Herlihy. Pleasant movie filmed in northern California's beautiful redwood country. Adapted from Zenna Henderson's science-fiction novel, the soft, gentle tale takes its time as Melodye (Kim Darby), a new, young schoolteacher, puzzles over an isolated community of stoic, shuffling parents and students who don't laugh, sing, or play games. Melodye's quiet probing into the community's past results in an unusual revelation, and the climactic scenes contain a Thoreaulike message. (Dir: John Korty, 73 mins.)

People Against O'Hara, The (1951)*** Spencer Tracy, Diana Lynn, John Hodiak, Pat O'Brien, James Arness. Good film about lawyers—not merely their performance of duty but their personal involvements. Spencer Tracy is great as always and a competent supporting cast matches him. (Dir: John Sturges, 102 mins.)

People Next Door, The (1970)** Eli Wallach, Julie Harris, Hal Holbrook, Cloris Leachman. One of many films dealing with suburbia and teenage drugs. Some talented actors don't manage to convey much emotion or impact. Harris, for example, is reduced to lighting lots of cigarettes in this occasionally involving story. (Dir: David Greene, 93 mins.)

People That Time Forgot, The (Great Britain, 1977)** Patrick Wayne, Doug McClure. Forgettable lost-civilization movie with prehistoric monsters, raging volcanoes, and primitive cavemen harassing Wayne, who is trying to rescue a marooned comrade, naval officer McClure. Based on a yarn by Edgar Rice Burroughs. (Dir: Kevin Conner, 90 mins.)

People Toys—See: Devil Times Five

People vs Dr. Kildare, The (1941)** Lew Ayres, Lionel Barrymore. It's not Kildare's fault that a leg he operated on is paralyzed but he has to go to court with Gillespie's help to clear himself. (Dir: Harold S. Bucquet, 78 mins.)

People Will Talk (1951)*** Cary Grant, Jeanne Crain, Sidney Blackner, Walter Slezak, Hume Cronyn, Finlay Currie. Remarkably funny, stringent social comedy from producer-director Joseph L. Mankiewicz. Dr. Pretorius, the hero, falls in love with a young lady who is expecting another man's child, and marries her anyway. It doesn't sound funny, but it is! Best scene: Grant's birthday party. (110 mins.)

Pepe (1960)** Cantinflas, Dan Dailey, Shirley Jones, Ernie Kovacs. This monstrous, interminable wheeze was intended to make the popular Mexican comic Cantinflas a star in the U.S., but it finished him off instead. Appearances by several dozen guest stars worked at the box office for Cantinflas's only previous film, "Around the World in Eighty Days," but not this time. (Dir: George Sidney, 195 mins.)

Pépé le Moko (France, 1936)*** Jean Gabin, Mireille Balin, Gabriel Gabrio. Director Julien DuVivier's poetic-realist imagination is at its high point as Gabin personates a Parisian gangster who is lured out of his lair in the Casbah by a fatal passion for a mysterious lady (Balin). (90 mins.)

Pepote (Spain, 1957)*** Pablito Calvo, Antonio Vico. A frequently touching film about an aging onetime toreador and his friendship with a young boy of seven. Acting is top-notch. (Dir: Ladislao Vajda, 85 mins.)

Peppermint Soda (France, 1979)***½ Odile Michel, Elenore Klarwein, Anouk Ferjac. About sisters growing up in the early '60s, discovering men, sex, and lipstick. Kury's eye is so sure and her direction so precise that the film bursts open with familiar truth invested with fresh insight. (Dir: Diane Kurys, 97 mins.)

Perfect Couple, A (1979)** Paul Dooley, Marta Heflin, Titos Vandis, Henry Gibson. Director Robert Altman's sour temperament ill equips him for romantic comedy. The film bogs down in interminable rock-group sequences. (110 mins.)

Perfect Friday (Great Britain, 1970)***½ Stanley Baker, Ursula Andress, David Warner. Deft comedy thriller. Baker plays a British banker who, when faced with customer Andress, realizes he can steal a million dollars. Warner plays an aristocratic loafer, Miss Andress's husband, also involved in the caper. All three actors are marvelous, and Miss Andress, surprisingly, shows comic talent. (Dir: Peter Hall, 94 mins.)

Perfect Furlough, The (1959)*** Tony Curtis, Janet Leigh, Linda Cristal. Service comedy which borders on slapstick most of the way. Curtis works hard as a khaki-clad Lothario who gets into one insane predicament after another. Linda Cristal gets some of the film's best lines as a movie queen involved in a big publicity stunt that backfires. (Dir: Blake Edwards, 93 mins.)

Perfect Gentlemen (MTV 1978)*** Lauren Bacall, Ruth Gordon, Lisa Pelikan, Sandy Dennis. A sprightly comedy caper film with a better-than-average cast. The stars' husbands are all serving time in a country club prison. (Dir: Jackie Cooper, 104 mins.)

Perfect Marriage, The (1947)** Loretta Young, David Niven. Comedy about the problems of a couple who, after ten years of marriage, find they can't stand each other makes a labored, tedious film. (Dir: Lewis Allen, 87 mins.)

Perfect Match, A (MTV 1980)**½ Linda Kelsey, Michael Brandon, Colleen Dewhurst, Charles Durning, Lisa Lucas. A 32-year-old mother can only be saved by a bone marrow transplant from the teenaged daughter she gave up for adoption. The acting enhances the material.

Perfect Strangers (1950)*½ Ginger Rogers, Dennis Morgan, Thelma Ritter. (Dir: Bretaigne Windust, 88 mins.)

Performance (Great Britain, 1970)** Mick Jagger, James Fox, Anita Pallenberg. Jagger presides over a decadent household where gangster-on-the-lam Fox seeks refuge. This film was ahead of its time: audiences didn't know how to respond to its sex, violence, and complicated visual style. Novelist Donald Cammell and cinematographer Nicolas Roeg directed. Repellent but fascinating. (106 mins.)

Perilous Holiday (1946)*** Pat O'Brien, Ruth Warrick, Alan Hale, Edgar Buchanan. Adventurer in Mexico City stumbles upon a counterfeiting ring that doesn't stop at murder. Good melodrama, breezily written, acted. (Dir: Edward H. Griffith, 89 mins.)

Perilous Voyage (MTV 1969)* Michael Parks, William Shatner, Michael Tolan, Louise Sorel. (Dir: William Graham, 97 mins.)

Perils of Pauline, The (1947)** Betty Hutton, John Lund, Billy de Wolfe. Pretended biography of Pearl White, the queen of silent-movie serials. Frantic and loud, with a few good scenes of life on the Hollywood sets. Color. (Dir: George Marshall, 96 mins.)

Perils of Pauline, The (1967)** Pat Boone, Pamela Austin, Terry-Thomas. Originally made as a pilot for a proposed TV series that didn't sell, this forced farce is purely for those who find slapstick antics irresistible. Pamela Austin is all blonde innocence as the put-upon orphan who goes through a series of incredible adventures that would make Alice's wonderland excursion seem predictable. Movie buffs please note this bit of hokum has nothing to do with the 1947 Betty Hutton starrer bearing the same name. (Dirs: Herbert B. Leonard, Joshua Shelley, 99 mins.)

Period of Adjustment (1962)*** Tony Franciosa, Jane Fonda, Jim Hutton, Lois Nettleton, Jack Albertson. A rarity, a Tennessee Williams comedy—not his best work, but as transferred to the screen quite pleasant, refreshing entertainment, well played by a young cast. It's all about the problems of a young married couple in adjusting to the rigors of domestic life, and it has many amusing scenes. (Dir: George Roy Hill, 112 mins.)

Persecution (Great Britain, 1974)* Lana Turner, Ralph Bates, Trevor Howard, Olga Georges-Picot. (Dir: Don Chaffey, 96 mins.)

Persecution and Assassination of Jean-Paul Marat as Performed by the Inmates of the Asylum of Charenton Under the Direction of the Marquis de Sade, The— See: **Marat/Sade**

Persona (Sweden, 1966)**** Liv Ullmann, Bibi Andersson, Gunnr Bjornstrand. Director Ingmar Bergman's masterpiece is less enigmatic today, seeming emotionally direct and thematically accessible. Ullmann is an actress who has decided to remain mute; her babbling nurse is played by Andersson as a surrogate for our decent impulses and petulant disappointments. There is no more moving expression of spiritual anguish in cinema. (81 mins.)

Personal Affair (Great Britain, 1953)**½ Gene Tierney, Leo Genn, Glynis Johns, Pamela Brown. Teacher is implicated when a romantic schoolgirl suddenly disappears. Well-made but conventional drama. (Dir: Anthony Pelissier, 82 mins.)

Personal Column—See: **Lured**

Personal Property (1937)** Jean Harlow, Robert Taylor, Reginald Owen, Una O'Connor. Bob does everything to win Jean in this one. He poses as a butler and a sheriff's deputy but before the first reel is over you know he'll win her. (Dir. W. S. Van Dyke, 84 mins.)

Pete Kelly's Blues (1955)**½ Jack Webb, Janet Leigh, Peggy Lee, Edmond O'Brien, Lee Marvin. Fairly successful reenactment of the people and sounds in the jazz world of the '20s. Jack Webb gives his usual wooden performance in the lead. Peggy Lee went dramatic in this one and surprisingly did very well. Ella Fitzgerald sings a couple of numbers. (Dir: Jack Webb, 95 mins.)

Pete 'n' Tillie (1972)**½ Walter Matthau, Carol Burnett, Geraldine Page, René Auberjonois. Miss Burnett and Mr. Matthau are a pair of middle-aged realists who meet, have an affair, marry, have a child, and have to deal with the fact that the boy is dying. With less talented stars this could have been dismissed as soap opera junk, but they keep it afloat in a sea of pathos. Page's bitchy relief was sufficient to net an Oscar nomination. (Dir: Martin Ritt, 100 mins.)

Pete Seeger—a Song and a Stone (1972)**½ Pete Seeger, Johnny Cash, Lester·Flatt. Seeger is a remarkable man, a talented musician and the star of this disappointing documentary; shows Seeger strummin', singin', and talkin' during a year and a half in various places throughout the U.S. Interesting sequence when Seeger talks about the many years when he was blacklisted by American TV. (Dir: Robert Elfstrom, 85 mins.)

Peter and Paul (MTV 1981)*** Anthony Hopkins, Robert Foxworth, Jon Finch, David Gwillim. Impressive biblical drama chronicles the tortured paths of disciples Peter and Paul preaching Christianity in its infancy. Anthony Hopkins dominates as Paul of Tarsus, who sees the light on the road to Damascus despite whippings, stonings and intense opposition from Jerusalem as he spreads the word of Jesus to kings and gentiles. The language is understandable—its style avoids the Sunday school aura, and Anthony Hopkins with his clipped manner of speech commands attention epitomizing the power of belief in the human being. Robert Foxworth disappoints as Peter. (Dir: Robert Day, 202 mins.)

Peter Ibbetson (1953)*** Gary Cooper, Ann

Harding, John Halliday, Ida Lupino. Weirdly affecting though dated supernatural romance. Though Peter is in jail for life, he and his childhood sweetheart continue to meet in their dreams. From the Edwardian story by George Du Maurier. (Dir: Henry Hathaway, 88 mins.)

Peter Lundy and the Medicine Hat Stallion (MTV 1977)*** Leif Garrett, Mitchell Ryan. A charming movie, aided by author Marguerite Henry's storytelling skills about frontier life. Her hero is a 16-year-old boy who loves his Indian pony. He makes a break from a mother he adores and a stern, embittered father to win a job riding for the Pony Express. The New Mexico scenery and the feeling for land and animals hit the bull's-eye for family entertainment. (Dir: Michael O'Herlihy, 104 mins.)

Petrified Forest, The (1936)***½ Bette Davis, Leslie Howard, Humphrey Bogart, Dick Foran, Genevieve Tobin, Porter Hall, Charley Grapewin. Bogart's first screen success was a re-creation of his stage triumph as Duke Mantee, a southwestern thug who keeps a seedy diner full of people hostage overnight. Among the hostages are a dreamy girl with romantic illusions about the world (Davis) and a melancholy poet (Howard) who is willing to lay down his life to help her preserve those illusions. Robert E. Sherwood's ironic classic looks pretty stagy under Archie Mayo's direction, but the principals are smashing. (83 mins.)

Petticoat Fever (1936)**½ Robert Montgomery, Myrna Loy, Reginald Owen. Perennial summer stock favorite fails to ring the bell as good movie comedy. Bob is all alone in Labrador when Myrna arrives, thanks to a plane crash, with her fiancé. Rest is pretty silly and forced. (Dir: George Fitzmaurice, 81 mins.)

Petty Girl, The (1950)*** Robert Cummings, Joan Caulfield, Elsa Lanchester, Melville Cooper, Mary Wickes. Bob Cummings plays an artist who specializes in glamour girls and his unlikely model is prim school teacher Joan Caulfield. Fun for all, and an early preview of a later TV series of the ageless Cummings. (Dir: Henry Levin, 87 mins.)

Petulia (1968)**** George C. Scott, Julie Christie, Richard Chamberlain, Joseph Cotten, Shirley Knight. A modern masterpiece. Scott is the surgeon with identity problems and Christie is the unhappily married girl who offers him the possibility of some meaning. Finely supported by Knight and Chamberlain. (Dir: Richard Lester, 105 mins.)

Peyton Place (1957)*** Lana Turner, Diane Varsi, Hope Lange, Arthur Kennedy, Lloyd Nolan, Betty Field, Russ Tamblyn, Mildred Dunnock. Here's the original film which served as the basis for the popular TV soap opera. It's actually much better than you may expect. Lana Turner and a fine supporting cast bring to life all the shady secrets of the New England town which made Grace Metalious' book a best seller. Granted this is soap opera, but it's well played and the production is first rate, with excellent photography of a New England autumn adding greatly to the atmosphere. Diane Varsi as Allison and Hope Lange as Selena are the standouts among the young actors in the film. (Dir: Mark Robson, 157 mins.)

Phantasm (1979)** Michael Baldwin, Bill Thornbury, Kathy Lester. Don Coscarelli wrote, directed, photographed, and edited this ragged low-budget horror entry. The narrative is so incoherent that the few imaginative shocks don't register until they're nearly off the screen. (90 mins.)

Phantom Horse, The (Japan, 1956)**½ Ayako Wakao. Pleasantly entertaining drama of a boy's love for a race horse. It's all been done many times before over here, but the different backgrounds make it refreshing. (Dir: Koji Shima, 90 mins.)

Phantom India (France, 1969)**** Director Louis Malle's brilliant, staggering six-hour essay on India, an unending succession of dazzling imagery and cultural shock. From the opening scene of a flock of vultures devouring the anus of a dead cow, Malle's cameras, as much as any movie possibly can, manage to capture the sense and smell of the Indian countryside. There are religious festivals in Madras, a malnourished village giving daily offerings of precious grain to feed rats, and scenes of urban life in Bombay and others. (360 mins.)

Phantom Lady (1944)***½ Franchot Tone, Ella Raines, Thomas Gomez, Elisha Cook, Jr., Regis Toomey. A very intriguing mystery film. A man is convicted of murdering his wife and a few people who believe him innocent try to clear him. Typical plot, but handled so well that you forget you've seen it before. (Dir: Robert Siodmak, 87 mins.)

Phantom of Crestwood, The (1932)** Ricardo Cortez, Karen Morley, Anita Louise. The picture has tired blood. Morley brings the others to a darkened house, object: blackmail. (Dir: J. Walter Ruben, 77 mins.)

Phantom of Hollywood, The (MTV 1974)** Jack Cassidy, Broderick Crawford, Skye Aubrey, Jackie Coogan. High melodrama on the low hokey side. A disfigured actor goes amok when the movie studio back lot (the actor's secret home for 30 years) is torn down. A large name cast cavorts on the MGM studio premises (Dir: Gene Levitt, 74 mins.)

Phantom of Liberty, The (France, 1974)**** Jean-Claude Brialy, Monica Vitti, Adolfo Celi, Michel Piccoli. The phrase "Phantom of Liberty" is from Karl Marx; the genius on screen is director Luis Buñuel. The first episode is set in Spain in the early 19th century and there are some memorable images—a fancy dinner party where guests sit on bathroom toilets and furtively ask permission to go to the dining room. There are dazzling visual images throughout. (104 mins.)

Phantom of the Opera, The (1925)**½ Lon Chaney, Mary Philbin, Norman Kerry. A wronged musician hides in an opera house while plotting revenge. Director Rupert Julian's allegedly classic silent doesn't have much going for it except the famous unmasking scene. (94 mins.)

Phantom of the Opera (1943)**½ Nelson Eddy, Susanna Foster, Claude Rains. This rendition provides almost as much opera as phantom, with Eddy and Foster warbling away, oblivious to the crazed antics of Rains, who makes a good monster. The film looks superb under the color lighting of Hal Mohr, who was awarded a cinematography Oscar. (Dir: Arthur Lubin, 92 mins.)

Phantom of the Opera, The (Great Britain, 1962)*** Herbert Lom, Heather Sears, Edward DeSouza, Michael Gough. Another version of the old Lon Chaney thriller about a hideously scarred creature terrorizing an opera house. This one is nicely produced, succeeds in its purpose of providing shudders. (Dir: Terence Fisher, 84 mins.)

Phantom of the Paradise (1974)**½ Paul Williams, William Finley, Jessica Harper, Gerrit Graham. A Grand Guignol send-up and put-down of the rock business may have seemed a good idea, with a maimed musician haunting a concert hall operated by a malevolent tycoon, but the ideas misfire one after another. Director-writer Brian De Palma's game gets too pretentious and sadistic. (92 mins.)

Phantom of the Rue Morgue (1954)**½ Karl Malden, Patricia Medina, Steve Forrest, Merv Griffin, Erin O'Brien-Moore. Eerie horror film about an insane murderer in Paris and his many coldblooded murders. Based on the story by Edgar Allan Poe. Well made, but pretty rough for the kiddies. Remake of "Murder in the Rue Morgue." (Dir: Roy Del Ruth, 84 mins.)

Phantom Planet (1962)** Dean Fredericks, Coleen Gray. A fairly absorbing Grade B science fiction yarn about a planet of midget sized inhabitants who fight an enemy attack with the aid of an astronaut who lands there. The special photographic gimmicks are good and help the film. (Dir: William Marshall, 82 mins.)

Phantom Tollbooth, The (1970)*** Butch Patrick. A bit of live action and lots of animation are used to bring the Norton Juster novel to the screen. It's charming for young children, as bored Butch takes a trip through the mysterious tollbooth with the Kingdom of Wisdom as a goal. There are seven new songs on the journey, too. (Dirs: Chuck Jones, Abe Levitow, David Monahan, 90 mins.)

Pharaoh's Curse (1957)** Mark Dana, Ziva Rodann. Archeological expedition encounters a monster from thousands of years ago in Egypt. Fair horror thriller has some suspenseful scenes. (Dir: Lee Sholem, 66 mins.)

Phase IV (Great Britain, 1973)*½ Nigel Davenport, Lynne Frederick, Michael Murphy. (Dir: Saul Bass, 83 mins.)

Phenix City Story, The (1955)**½ John McIntire, Kathryn Grant, Richard Kiley, Edward Andrews. Director Phil Karlson's raw film noir is based on the real-life story of Phenix City, Ala.—a vice-ridden small town scrubbed down by a crusading lawyer. Karlson virtually remade this film in '73 as "Walking Tall," making a commercial success out of a lifetime of personal obsession. (100 mins.)

Phffft! (1954)***½ Judy Holliday, Jack Lemmon, Kim Novak, Jack Carson. Judy Holliday and Jack Lemmon make the most hilarious movie team since the days of Jean Arthur & James Stewart in this fast paced, sometimes funny, story of a marriage that almost goes phffft! Kim Novak lays a small but decorative part. (Dir: Mark Robson, 91 mins.)

Philadelphia Story, The (1940)**** Katharine Hepburn, Cary Grant, James Stewart, Ruth Hussey, Virginia Weidler, John Howard, Henry Daniell, Roland Young. Philip Barry's witty comedy of manners about a spoiled rich girl (Hepburn) who longs for romance gets the royal treatment from director George Cukor. There's a splendid supporting cast (Grant as her sardonic ex-husband, Stewart as the streetwise but romantically naive reporter who falls in love with her, and Hussey as Stewart's philosophical partner). Remade as "High Society." (112 mins.)

Phoenix, The (MTV 1981)* Judson Scott, Shelley Smith, E. G. Marshall, Fernando Allende. (Dir: Douglas Hickox, 78 mins.)

Phone Call from a Stranger (1952)*** Shelley Winters, Gary Merrill, Michael Rennie, Bette Davis. Gary Merrill stars in this good episodic drama as the lone survivor of a plane crash who takes it upon himself to contact some of his traveling companions' relatives. Most of the action unfolds via flashbacks. Bette Davis, in a brief role as an invalid, gives the best performance in the film with Keenan Wynn, as her brash salesman of a husband, ranking a close second. (Dir: Jean Negulesco, 96 mins.)

Phone Rings Every Night, The (Germany, 1962)*½ Elke Sommer. (Dir: Geza von Cziffra, 82 mins.)

Phony American, The (West Germany, 1962)** William Bendix, Ron Randell, Christine Kaufmann, Michael Hinz. War orphan is left with a German family by a U.S. Army officer, grows up and tries to enlist in our Air Force. Drama has a certain amount of charm but moves quite slowly. (Dir: Akos Rathony, 72 mins.)

Picasso Summer, The (1969z**½ Albert Finney, Yvette Mimieux. Offbeat romantic tale just misses. It's a strange mixture of surrealism and reality, with Finney and Mimieux playing a couple who adore Picasso and form an alliance based on their mutual love for the great artist's work. When they try to visit the artist in the south of France, the film takes off on a wild tangent and never gets back on course. They never get to meet Pablo either. Story by Ray Bradbury. (Dir: Serge Bourguignon, 96 mins.)

Piccadilly Incident (Great Britain, 1946)*** Anna Neagle, Michael Wilding, Reginald Owen, Frances Mercer. In wartime England, a man thinks his wife has been killed, but she returns after he has married again. Blend of romance and drama is tailor-made for the feminine audience. (Dir: Herbert Wilcox, 88 mins.)

Piccadilly Jim (1936)*** Robert Montgomery, Madge Evans, Billie Burke, Frank Morgan, Robert Benchley. P. G. Wodehouse's story of a cartoonist and his bumbling father is turned into a delightful comedy. Eric Blore almost steals the picture playing, you guessed it, a gentleman's gentleman. (Dir: Robert Z. Leonard, 97 mins.)

Pickpocket (France, 1959)*** Martin LaSalle, Marika Green, Jean Pelegri. An austere meditation written and directed by Robert Bresson, about an educated thief who believes that the road to heaven is paved with bad intentions and that somehow God wants him to steal. Dryly acted by LaSalle, but, as in most of Bresson's other films, the cinematography is languid and exquisite. (Dir: Robert Bressonn 75 mins.)

Pickup (1951)**½ Beverly Michaels, Hugo Haas. Occasionally effective drama about an old man who marries a cheap girl he picks up and the complications that arise when a handsome younger man enters the picture. (Dir: Hugo Haas, 78 mins.)

Pickup Alley (Great Britain, 1957)** Victor Mature, Anita Ekberg, Trevor Howard. Routine crime matter, Mature is a narcotics agent whose sleuthing takes him to London, Lisbon, Athens, Rome, etc. Miss Ekberg dresses up the picture with her presence. (Dir: John Gilling, 92 mins.)

Pickup on South Street (1953)*** Richard Widmark, Thelma Ritter, Jean Peters, Richard Kiley. As a heavy, a pickpocket who accidentally lifts a roll of top-secret microfilm, Widmark draws on the snickering, psychotic style that first made him a star. Director Sam Fuller's flair for chunky, racking violence is fully vented. Ritter gives an excellent, layered performance. (80 mins.)

Pickwick Papers, The (Great Britain, 1953)**** James Hayter, Nigel Patrick, James Donald, Joyce Grenfell, Kathleen Harrison, Hermione Gingold, Alexander Gauge. Simply one of the most delightful movies ever made. Perfectly adapted, set, and acted. In the picturesque 1830's, goodhearted Mr. Pickwick and his friends travel about England in search of adventure.

Touching and hilarious. From the lovely stories by Charles Dickens. (Dir: Noel Langley, 109 mins.)

Picnic (1956)*** William Holden, Kim Novak, Rosalind Russell, Betty Field, Cliff Robertson, Arthur O'Connell, Nick Adams. Unevenly acted film version of William Inge's moving Broadway play about a stranger who arrives in a small Kansas town and changes a number of lives. The acting ranges from good (Holden) to fair (Russell) to inept (Novak). (Dir: Joshua Logan, 113 mins.)

Picnic at Hanging Rock (Australia, 1976)***½ Rachel Roberts, Dominic Guard, Anne Lambert, Helen Morse. Mystical, dreamlike, rather gentle horror film which poses no easy answers to what really happened to a group of Australian schoolgirls who disappeared on Valentine's Day, '00. Based on the novel by Joan Lindsay, the film is a rewarding entry for those who like their thrillers done with a subtle hand. (Dir: Peter Weir, 110 mins.)

Picture Mommy Dead (1966)**½ Don Ameche, Martha Hyer, Zsa Zsa Gabor. A complicated mystery which sustains its interest despite the hokey aspects of the script involving a young girl who loses her memory after the tragic death of her mother. It's all sinister, and a good deal of it works. (Dir: Bert I. Gordon, 88 mins.)

Picture of Dorian Gray, The (1945)*** George Sanders, Hurd Hatfield, Donna Reed, Angela Lansbury, Peter Lawford. Oscar Wilde's novel receives as perceptive a treatment as could be expected from producer-writer-director Albert Lewin. Impeccably epigrammatic deliveries from Hurd Hatfield as Dorian and Sanders as the devil, plus the irresistible pathos of Angela Lansbury's innocent songstress singing of her canary. (110 mins.)

Picture of Dorian Gray, The (MTV 1973)*½ Shane Briant, Charles Aidman, Nigel Davenport. (Dir: Glenn Jordan)

Pie in the Sky—See: **Terror in the City**

Piece of the Action, A (1977)** Sidney Poitier, Bill Cosby, James Earl Jones, Denise Nicholas. Director Poitier's film is embarrassing in its social worker piety and contains—believe it or not—a detailed lecture on the value of common courtesy. Cosby looks lost in the witless screenplay. (Dir: Sidney Poitier, 135 mins.)

Pied Piper, The (1942)***½ Monty Woolley, Anne Baxter, Otto Preminger, Roddy McDowall. Wartime story of a Monty Woolley type Englishman who hates kids and finds himself stuck with a pack of them and trying to escape the Nazis. Warm, amusing, and powerful film. (Dir: Irving Pichel, 86 mins.)

Pied Piper of Hamelin, The (1957)** Van Johnson, Claude Rains, Kay Starr. Musical version of the fairy tale about the piper who rids the town of rats. Originally produced as a TV special, it suffers in comparison with motion picture feature technique; passable for the kiddies. (Dir: Bretaigne Windust, 92 mins.)

Pierrot le Fou (France-Italy, 1965)***½ Jean-Paul Belmondo, Anna Karina, Samuel Fuller. Director Jean-Luc Godard produced this film before his films became Marxist polemics. It deals with a young writer (Belmondo) and his love affair with Marianne (Miss Karina). Beautifully poignant, for as the two despair of each other they find they are both fed up. (110 mins.)

Pigeon, The (MTV 1969)** Sammy Davis, Jr., Pat Boone, Dorothy Malone, Ricardo Montalban. Although Sammy Davis, Jr., works very hard as a private detective, this weighty and cliché feature falls short. Miss Malone is the widow of a former syndicate bigwig who kept a diary and the Mafia wants the little black book. Private eyes Davis and Boone get in on the case and it's fist fights and car chases, until the end. (Dir: Earl Bellamy, 74 mins.)

Pigeon That Took Rome, The (1962)**½ Charlton Heston, Elsa Martinelli, Harry Guardino, Brian Donlevy. Tough infantry officer is sent behind Nazi lines into occupied Rome to see what's cooking, sends pigeons back with messages, finds time for some romance. Heston seems rather grimly determined to be a light comedian in this one, but the laughs come with fair frequency, aided by some good dialogue. (Dir: Melville Shavelson, 101 mins.)

Pillar of Fire, The (Israeli, 1963)*** Michael Shillo, Lawrence Montaigne. In 1948 an Israeli desert outpost sends out a patrol when the Arabs invade the area. Unusual locale aids this war drama filmed in Israel, compensating somewhat for sketchy production values. Spoken in English. (Dir: Larry Frisch, 76 mins.)

Pillars of the Sky (1956)**½ Jeff Chandler, Dorothy Malone, Ward Bond, Lee Marvin. Western fans will buy this tale of a no-account, hard drinking, woman chasin' Sgt. who finally sees the error of his ways after a series of action-packed scenes. Jeff Chandler makes a believable cavalry noncom and the supporting cast is more than competent. (Dir: George Marshall, 95 mins.)

Pillow of Death (1945)** Lon Chaney, Brenda Joyce. Lawyer commits a succession of murders to marry the girl he loves. Fair mystery; the plot is old hat. (Dir: Wallace Fox, 66 mins.)

Pillow Talk (1959)**** Doris Day, Rock Hudson, Tony Randall. Deft light comedy which may be labeled "a typical Doris Day vehicle," i.e. the thirtyish Miss Day has somehow managed to keep both her virginity and such attractive suitors as Rock Hudson. Tony Randall is very funny; Hudson is surprisingly skillful. Frothy dialogue makes this a fine film of its kind. (Dir: Michael Gordon, 105 mins.)

Pilot No. 5 (1943)*½ Franchot Tone, Marsha Hunt, Gene Kelly, Van Johnson. (Dir: George Sidney, 70 mins.)

Pimpernel Smith (Great Britain, 1942)***½ Leslie Howard, Mary Morris, Francis L. Sullivan, Hugh McDermott. Witty, exciting melodrama. A mild-mannered professor becomes an undercover leader against the Nazis. Director Leslie Howard updates his famous role as "The Scarlet Pimpernel" to 1942, smuggling political prisoners out of Germany instead of revolutionary France. (122 mins.)

Pin Up Girl (1944)** Betty Grable, Martha Raye, Joe E. Brown. Promising title produces absolutely nothing. Story of the romance of a sailor and a girl has no comedy, not enough legs and a load of specialty numbers which don't help. (Dir: H. Bruce Humberstone, 83 mins.)

Pine Canyon is Burning (MTV 1977)**½ Kent McCord, Diana Muldaur. Modest fire story attempts to emphasize people against a crisis background. It's a tale about a widowed fireman trying to raise two kids while working out of a lonely fire station. Happily, the characters are a bit more than wooden pieces set against the background of a canyon fire out of control. (Dir: Chris Nyby III, 79 mins.)

Pink Jungle, The (1968)** James Garner, Eva Renzi, George Kennedy. Dull action drama set in a banana republic in South America. The mistaken identity gimmick is used to death in this one as James Garner, a photographer by trade, is taken for an espionage agent. (Dir: Delbert Mann, 104 mins.)

Pink Panther, The (Great Britain, 1964)**** Peter Sellers, David Niven, Robert Wagner, Claudia Cardinale, Capucine. The sophisticated comedy that began the long association of director Blake Edwards and Peter Sellers, with Sellers as the unwitting anarchist Inspector Clouseau, pursuing a jet-set jewel thief (Niven) who's conveniently carrying on an affair with Clouseau's wife (Capucine). (113 mins.)

Pink Panther Strikes Again, The (Great Britain, 1976)**** Peter Sellers, Herbert Lom, Lesley-Ann Down. Fourth farce about addle-brained Inspector Clouseau is tops. This time Sellers is pitted against his former chief, the villainous Dreyfus (Lom), who twitches as the Bondian rascal in control of a device that threatens to destroy the world. Expertly directed by Blake Edwards. (103 mins.)

Pink String and Sealing Wax (Great Britain, 1945)**½ Googie Withers, Gordon Jackson. Tavernkeeper's dissatisfied wife uses a chemist's son in her plan to murder her husband. Period melodrama is graced by good performances to help it along. (Dir: Robert Hamer, 89 mins.)

Pinky (1949)*** Jeanne Crain, Ethel Barrymore, Ethel Waters. Strong racial drama dealing with light-skinned Negro girl who comes home to the South. Director Elia Kazan gets excellent performances all around. (102 mins.)

Pinocchio (1940)**** Voices of Dickie Jones, Cliff Edwards. From Carlo Collodi's

521

story about the puppet boy who becomes human. The Disney version is a marvel: the animation is dazzling and the songs are catchy and clever. Oscars for Best Original Score and Best Original Song. (Supervising Dirs: Ben Sharpsteen, Hamilton Luske, 88 mins.)

Pioneer Builders—See: **The Conquerors**

Pioneer Woman (MTV 1973)**½ William Shatner, Joanna Pettet, David Janssen. There's an old-fashioned quality of noble heroics against great odds in this well produced western adventure. A family uproots itself and sets out for the promised farmland in Nebraska, only to meet with hostility from the squatters and a seemingly endless line of personal defeats. Miss Pettet is well cast as the mother of the clan who must shoulder all the responsibility when her husband is killed. (Dir: Buzz Kulik, 73 mins.)

Pipe Dreams (1976)** Gladys Knight, Barry Hankerson, Bruce French, Sherry Bain. Uninteresting story about a woman chasing her runaway husband through the Alaskan oil fields gives soul singer Knight a chance to show a little charm in her acting debut; the long lyrical montages of snowscapes that director Stephen Verona has substituted for plot give Knight an excuse to sing six songs offscreen, which ain't all bad. (89 mins.)

Piranha (1978)**½ Bradford Dillman, Kevin McCarthy, Heather Menzies. Fast, well-made rip-off of "Jaws" with enough cheap thrills for the action trade. Dillman accidentally releases a tankful of mutant piranhas into a mountain stream, and as they swim downriver they attack Wynn, a summer camp counseled by Paul Bartel, and a beach resort managed by Dick Miller. Joe Dante, the director, betrays hardly a trace of human values. (92 mins.)

Pirate, The (1948)***½ Judy Garland, Gene Kelly, Walter Slezak, Gladys Cooper, George Zucco, the Nicholas Brothers. A rollicking, definitely tongue-in-cheek musical about a girl infatuated with a famed pirate. The audacious, vain, ragged actor who loves her decides to impersonate the buccaneer to impress her. Kelly and Garland are in fine form; Cole Porter's jaunty score includes "Love of My Life" and "Be A Clown"; Kelly does some dynamite specialty numbers with the Nicholas Brothers. Color. (Dir: Vincente Minelli, 102 mins.)

Pirate, The (MTV 1978)** Franco Nero, Eli Wallach, Anne Archer, Christopher Lee. Harold Robbins's best-selling novel makes an ordinary film about an Arab prince brought up in the West and his second marriage to an American sexpot. As the Arab, Nero circles the globe with a blonde (Archer), who gives up her American freedom to be his wife. Ms. Archer is decorative but unconvincing. (Dir: Kenneth Annakin, 208 mins.)

Pirate and the Slave Girl (France-Italy,

1960)*½ Lex Barker, Chelo Alonso. (Dir: Piero Pierotti, 87 mins.)

Pirate of the Black Hawk (France-Italy, 1958)*½ Mijanou Bardot, Gerard Landry. (Dir: Sergio Grieco, 75 mins.)

Pirates of the Coast (Italy, 1960)*½ Lex Barker, Estella Blain. (Dir: Domenico Paolella, 102 mins.)

Pirates of the Mississippi, The (Germany, 1963)*½ Hansjorg Fenny, Horst Frank, Sabine Sinjen. (Dir: Jurgen Roland, 95 mins.)

Pirates of Tortuga (1961)*½ Ken Scott, Leticia Roman, Dave King. (Dir: Robert D. Webb, 97 mins.)

Pit and the Pendulum, The (1961)**½ Vincent Price, John Kerr, Barbara Steele. One of the first and probably still the best of the films based on Edgar Allan Poe tales starring Vincent Price. This thriller has all the stock ingredients inherent to horror yarns including the castle on the hill, a fantastic torture chamber, walled-up coffins and screams in the night. John Kerr plays the young innocent who comes to Price's Spanish castle to investigate his sister's mysterious death and falls prey to the spooky goings-on. (Dir: Roger Corman, 80 mins.)

Pitfall (1948)*** Dick Powell, Lizabeth Scott, Raymond Burr, Jane Wyatt. A grimy, superior film noir directed by André de Toth. Powell is a foursquare family man who enjoys a harmless dalliance with model Scott, unaware that he's risking the wrath of a psychotically jealous private eye (Burr). (84 mins.)

Pittsburgh (1942)** John Wayne, Marlene Dietrich, Randolph Scott. Miner's drive for power costs him his friends and the woman he loves: Capable performers can't do much with this sluggish melodrama. (Dir: Lewis Seiler, 91 mins.)

Pizza Triangle, The—See: **Drama of Jealousy, A**

P.J. (1968)**½ George Peppard, Gayle Hunnicutt, Raymond Burr, Brock Peters, Wilfrid Hyde White, Susan Saint James. Intricate detective yarn starts on a tough note, and maintains a hard-hitting approach up to the finale on a deserted island. Tale involves Peppard as a small-time private eye hired by wealthy tycoon Burr to watch over Burr's beautiful mistress Hunnicutt. There are enough villains around to cast at least five melodramas. (Dir: John Guillermin, 109 mins.)

Place for Lovers, A (Italy-France, 1968)* Faye Dunaway, Marcello Mastroianni. (88 mins.)

Place in the Sun, A (1951)**½ Montgomery Clift, Elizabeth Taylor, Shelley Winters, Keefe Brasselle. Director George Stevens's ponderous adaptation of Theodore Dreiser's "An American Tragedy" exerts a peculiar power in spite of itself. Clift is painfully good, while Winters manages to be painful. The Clift-Taylor love scenes are very hot. (122 mins.)

Place of One's Own, A (Great Britain,

1945)*** Margaret Lockwood, James Mason. Elderly couple buy an old neglected house, take in a girl as companion, find she is influenced by spirits. Entertaining drama, well acted. (Dir: Bernard Knowles, 91 mins.)

Place to Go, A (Great Britain, 1963)** Bernard Lee, Rita Tushingham. Tiresome threadbare drama of an East End London family and their troubles. Miss Tushingham is wasted. (Dir: Basil Dearden, 87 mins.)

Plague (Canada, 1978)**½ Celene Lomez, Daniel Pilon, Kate Reid. Well done sci-fi. Deadly bacteria are created in a genetic research laboratory, spreading a plague that threatens the world. Thought-provoking screenplay by the producers, Ed Hunt and Barry Pearson. (Dir: Ed Hunt, 90 mins.)

Plainsman, The (1936)***½ Gary Cooper, Jean Arthur, Charles Bickford, Porter Hall, Anthony Quinn, James Ellison. Rootin' shootin' western, loaded with story and action. A deMille spectacle, no message but heap good picture. (Dir: C. B. deMille, 113 mins.)

Plainsman, The (1966)** Don Murray, Guy Stockwell, Bradford Dillman, Abby Dalton. Wild Bill Hickok, Buffalo Bill, and Calamity Jane foiling Indians and gun runners. Imitation of the venerable old Gary Cooper-Jean Arthur epic, but nowhere near as good. (Dir: David Lowell Rich, 92 mins.)

Plan 9 from Outer Space (1959)* Bela Lugosi, Vampira. Lugosi's last film, released after his death. (Dir: Edward Wood, Jr., 79 mins.)

Planet Earth (MTV 1974)*** John Saxon, Diana Muldaur, Janet Margolin. Gene Roddenberry is back on the top-flight sci-fi track with this socio-political film incorporating the best elements of his former TV series ("Star Trek") plus an added bonus—it takes place on Earth. After the "Great Catastrophe," 22d-Century Earth has been fragmented into isolated colonies, one of which is PAX, a lofty community of idealists dedicated to bringing the Earth into harmony with itself. The focus is on a PAX team of specialists who come into conflict with a female-dominated society where males are turned into cowering slaves called "dinks." (Dir: Marc Daniels, 75 mins.)

Planet of Blood (1966)** Basil Rathbone, John Saxon, Judi Meredith, Dennis Hopper. Space ship is sent to Mars to investigate a mysterious missile; therein is found a survivor from another world with a passion for human blood. Set in 1990, this sci-fi thriller is way, way out. Fans might get a kick out of it. (Dir: Curtis Harrington, 80 mins.)

Planet of the Apes (1968)**** Charlton Heston, Kim Hunter, Maurice Evans, Roddy McDowall. Exciting science-fiction film based on Pierre Boulle's book "Monkey Planet." This sci-fi thriller even has some political and sociological comment on our troubled times. Four astronauts crash on a distant planet. Director Franklin J. Schaffner used desolate areas of Utah and Arizona to good advantage for his "planet" location scenes, and the makeup men who devised the fantastic ape masks rate a special bow. (112 mins.)

Planet of the Vampires—See: Demon Planet, The

Planets Against Us (Italy-France, 1960)* Jany Clair, Michel Lemoine. (Dir: Romano Ferrara, 83 mins.)

Platinum Blonde (1931)*** Jean Harlow, Loretta Young, Robert Williams. Early screwball comedy, with refreshing dialogue crisply paced, yet compromised by lack of visual verve or style. Confoundingly, Young has the brassy part while Harlow plays the rich bitch—couldn't they have switched? (Dir: Frank Capra, 90 mins.)

Platinum High School (1960)* Mickey Rooney, Terry Moore, Dan Duryea, Yvette Mimieux. (Dir: Charles Haas, 93 mins.)

Play Dirty (Great Britain, 1969)*½ Michael Caine, Harry Andrews, Nigel Davenport. (Dir: André de Toth, 117 mins.)

Play It Again, Sam (1972)*** Woody Allen, Susan Anspach, Diane Keaton, Tony Roberts. Woody Allen fans of today may be slightly disappointed in this early effort—a one-joke affair that stretches on a little too long before the excellent fadeout, a faithful, funny recreation of the farewell scene between Bogart and Bergman in "Casablanca." Woody is a compulsive Bogart fantasizer and it drives his wife (Susan Anspach) out of his life, which drives him into the arms of his best friend's wife, Diane Keaton. Jerry Lacy, in an uncanny Bogart imitation, pops up every now and then as Bogart's spirit, and keeps things bubbling. Allen fans will love it. (Dir: Herbert Ross, 84 mins.)

Play It As It Lays (1972)** Tuesday Weld, Anthony Perkins, Tammy Grimes. Bargain basement social pathology served up with the self-conscious solemnity of a modern-day Spengler by director Frank Perry. Did you know that "creative" movie people have empty lives and even emptier souls? Did you know that the California freeway is a visual metaphor for spiritual and cultural ennui? If not, this film will be a revelation. (99 mins.)

Play It Cool (Great Britain, 1962)*½ Billy Fury, Helen Shapiro, Michael Anderson, Jr., Dennis Price. (Dir: Michael Winner, 74 mins.)

Play Misty for Me (1971)*** Clint Eastwood, Jessica Walter, Donna Mills. Eastwood makes a surprisingly promising directorial debut while starring in this mystery. About a sexy disk jockey on a California radio station, and his involvement with a psychotic lady who keeps requesting that old standard "Misty." Miss Walter is first rate playing the dangerous listener who takes charge of Eastwood's life when he

523

makes the mistake of entering into what he thinks is a casual affair. Roberta Flack's song "The First Time I Ever Saw Your Face" became a hit via this film. (102 mins.)

Playback (Great Britain, 1962)** Margit Saad, Barry Foster. Policeman falls for a married woman, agrees to kill her husband for the insurance. Fair example of "perfect crime" drama, based on an Edgar Wallace story. (Dir: Quentin Lawrence, 62 mins.)

Playboy of the Western World, The (Ireland, 1962)**** Siobhan McKenna, Gary Raymond. Beautiful, lyrical, and long-overdue film of the classic Irish play of J. M. Synge. The actual plot about a young stranger who becomes the idol of a small village is less important than the soaring, poetic language of the play and the lovely performance of Siobhan McKenna, one of the truly great actresses of our time, seldom used to good advantage in films. Miss McKenna truthfully is a few years too old to play the role of Pegeen, but she and the playboy Gary Raymond are both fine, and the Irish brogue is a joy to hear. (Dir: Brian Desmond Hurst, 100 mins.)

Players (1979)* Ali MacGraw, Dean-Paul Martin, Maximilian Schell. (Dir: Anthony Harvey, 120 mins.)

Playgirl (1954)**½ Shelley Winters, Barry Sullivan. Moderately interesting drama about a woman's concern for her young sister's reputation. Miss Winters is fairly good in the role of the overprotective sister. (Dir: Joseph Pevney, 85 mins.)

Playing for Time (MTV 1980)**** Vanessa Redgrave, Jane Alexander. Shattering drama about life in the Auschwitz death camp in Poland, one of the Nazis' most murderous camps for European Jewry. Based on a book by Fania Fenelon, herself a survivor of the camps, and adapted by Arthur Miller. Luminous, bravura performance by Redgrave playing Fenelon. Director Daniel Mann's best work in years.

Playmates (MTV 1972)**½ Alan Alda, Doug McClure, Connie Stevens, Barbara Feldon. About divorce, California-style. Stars Alda and McClure as a pair of fathers who meet with their sons at an amusement park on their visitation days. Despite totally different backgrounds they become friends, and the complications begin. Sharp dialogue and realistic plot twist make it a cut above average. (Dir: Theodore Flicker, 74 mins.)

Playtime (France, 1968)**** Jacques Tati. The most visually inventive film of the '60s is also one of the funniest. Set in the ultramodern part of Paris, all skyscrapers, glass, and computers. Director-star Tati has succeeded in nothing less than a complete reworking of the conventional notions of montage. Certainly the last word on Mies van der Rohe. (108 mins.)

Plaza Suite (1971)***½ Walter Matthau, Maureen Stapleton, Barbara Harris, Lee Grant. Matthau is supplied with three juicy comic roles by playwright Neil Simon in this film version of the hit play—and he's grand in all of them. In the first, he plays a businessman who agrees to try to find the old magic in his 20-year marriage by returning to the scene of the crime—the honeymoon suite at the Plaza—with his wife (Miss Stapleton). In number two, Miss Harris almost steals Matthau's thunder playing an old flame of a Hollywood producer who agrees to a meeting in a hotel room, but only to satisfy her hunger for tidbits about Hollywood. Miss Grant shares the honors in segment three, which has the duo playing the parents of a bride who won't come out of the bathroom in the hotel suite. (Dir: Arthur Hiller, 114 mins.)

Please Believe Me (1950)**½ Deborah Kerr, Robert Walker, Peter Lawford, Mark Stevens. A wacky comedy about a trio of bachelors who give a new heiress the rush. The cast, all pros, have some trouble making the script work. (Dir: Norman Taurog, 87 mins.)

Please Don't Eat the Daisies (1960)*** Doris Day, David Niven, Janis Paige. Friendly comedy about a drama critic, his wife and four children—the critic has problems with his work, the wife has problems with renovating an old house in the country, and things become quite hectic in general. Some good laughs, clever dialogue. (Dir: Charles Walters, 111 mins.)

Please Mr. Balzac (France, 1956)** Brigitte Bardo, Daniel Gelin. Routine comedy whose only asset is the now famous Bardot body. About a girl who writes a scandalous novel, and lams out for Paris when her prudish family objects. (Dir: Marc Allegret, 99 mins.)

Please Murder Me (1955)** Raymond Burr, Angela Lansbury, Lamont Johnson. A brilliant attorney sacrifices his career and scruples to defend a murderess with whom he is in love. Muddled melodrama. (Dir: Peter Godfrey, 78 mins.)

Please Turn Over (1959)** Ted Ray, Jean Kent. Silly comedy done in the British style. The actors are far better than their material. Plot concerns a girl who writes a sexy novel and causes a commotion. (Dir: Gerald Thomas, 86 mins.)

Pleasure Cove (MTV 1979)** Tom Jones, Constance Forslund, Joan Hackett, Harry Guardino. Singer Jones plays a handsome crook in this opus about life at a swanky island resort. The plotting is light, the characters stereotyped. (Dir: Bruce Bilson, 104 mins.)

Pleasure of His Company, The (1961)**½ Fred Astaire, Debbie Reynolds, Lilli Palmer, Tab Hunter. Debonair charmer returns home for his daughter's wedding but tries to break up the couple when he finds her to be attractive. Good cast takes advantage of some witty lines to give this comedy a fair amount of fun. (Dir: George Seaton, 115 mins.)

Pleasure Palace (MTV 1980)**½ Omar Sharif, Hope Lange, José Ferrer, Victoria Principal. Sharif plays a gentlemanly high roller, invited to Las Vegas to save casino owner Lange from a crude Texan and his associates. The glamour side of Sin City is on display, yet the pace meanders. Beautiful girls, the turn of a card, rich surroundings, and Sharif provide effortless viewing. (Dir: Walter Grauman, 104 mins.)

Pleasure Seekers, The (1964)**½ Ann-Margret, Carol Lynley, Pamela Tiffin, Anthony Franciosa, Brian Keith, Gene Tierney. A well-produced remake of "Three Coins in The Fountain" with the locale shifted from Rome to Spain. Three young girls looking for romance find it amid the Spanish architecture. The dialogue has a bite to it at times, but it's mainly a romantic excursion of the variety enjoyed most by the female audience. (Dir: Jean Negulesco, 107 mins.)

Plot to Assassinate Hitler, The (Germany, 1955)**½ Maximilian Schell. Story of the German officers' plan to eliminate the hated Nazi leader unfolds in documentary fashion, is frequently gripping despite the familiarity of the narrative. Dubbed in English. (Dir: Falck Harnack, 90 mins.)

Plough and the Stars, The (1936)** Barbara Stanwyck, Preston Foster, Barry Fitzgerald, Una O'Connor, J.M. Kerrigan. Disappointing version of Sean O'Casey's wonderful play about the months leading up to the Easter Week rising in Dublin in '16. Director John Ford and screenwriter Dudley Nichols hoped to capitalize on the huge success of their earlier Irish film "The Informer." (73 mins.)

Plunder in the Sun (1953)** Glenn Ford, Diana Lynn, Patricia Medina. An Aztec fortune is the prize in this involved modern day treasure hunt. Performances are good but the pace is slow and everybody talks too much. (Dir: John Farrow, 81 mins.)

Plunder Road (1957)***½ Gene Raymond, Wayne Morris. Make a thousand grade B crime tales and you're bound to turn out one gem...this is it! Superior melodrama about an attempted $10 million theft. (Dir: Hubert Cornfield, 76 mins.)

Plunderers, The (1960)**½ Jeff Chandler, John Saxon, Dolores Hart. Sprawling western drama about a group of outlaws and their effect on a town. It's all familiar but played straight by a cast of actors who look comfortable in western garb. (Dir: Joseph Pevney, 94 mins.)

Plunderers of Painted Flats (1959)*½ Corinne Calvet, John Carroll, Skip Homeier. (Dir: Albert C. Gannaway, 77 mins.)

Plutonium Incident, The (MTV 1980)**½ Janet Margolin, Powers Boothe, Bo Hopkins. Occasionally involving yarn about a plutonium-processing plant whose management tries to crush the workers' attempt to unionize and press for better safety conditions. Margolin is a worker who is used in a nefarious plan to cover up everything. (Dir: Richard Michaels, 104 mins.)

Plymouth Adventure (1952)*** Spencer Tracy, Gene Tierney, Van Johnson. Good adventure epic about the Pilgrims' voyage on the Mayflower and the hardships they encounter when they land at Plymouth, Mass. Don't look for historical accuracy—just sit back and enjoy the fine acting of Spencer Tracy and his supporting players. For the record, Van Johnson plays John Alden to Dawn Addams's Priscilla Mullins. (Dir: Clarence Brown, 105 mins.)

Poacher's Daughter, The (Ireland, 1958)**½ Julie Harris, Harry Brogan, Tim Seely. Irresponsible son with an eye on motor bikes and flashy ladies is finally straightened out by a sincere girl. Unlikely premise. Mildly amusing comedy has the Irish flavor for those who like it and the talented and wasted-by-films Miss Harris. (Dir: George Pollack, 74 mins.)

Pocket Money (1972)*** Naive Paul Newman and his alcoholic sidekick Lee Marvin go searching through Mexico to buy a herd of cattle for evil boss Strother Martin. The duo are suckers for every swindler with a bum steer, but their charming presence redeems the screenplay, which is chock full of character development and short on plot. Written by Terry Malick, who went on to write and direct "Badlands." (Dir: Stuart Rosenberg, 102 mins.)

Pocketful of Miracles (1961)*** Glenn Ford, Bette Davis, Hope Lange, Ann-Margret, Peter Falk, Thomas Mitchell, Edward Everett Horton, Jack Elam. Veteran comedy director Frank Capra brings this Damon Runyon yarn to the screen with a liberal mixture of corn, sentiment, and broadly played performances. The plot revolves around a street vendor called Apple Annie (Bette Davis) and the lengths she and her "guys and dolls" friends go to help her masquerade as a society matron when her daughter pays a surprise visit. Not all of it works but there's Miss Davis giving it all she's got and a hilarious performance by Peter Falk as a Broadway type. Remake of "Lady for a Day." (136 mins.)

Point, The (MTV 1971)***½ Charming animated feature musical fantasy that should fascinate the youngsters and keep the adults interested. It tells the story of Oblio, a little boy who is born without a point on his head in a kingdom where everything and everyone has a literal point. His uniqueness eventually causes him to be banished to the pointless forest, a veritable wonderland, where Oblio experiences one great adventure after another before returning home a hero. The images (especially in color) are superb, and the musical score by Harry Nilsson creates the appropriate mood. (Dir: Fred Wolff, 73 mins.)

Point Blank (1967)*** Lee Marvin, Angie Dickinson, Keenan Wynn, Carroll O'Connor. Director John Boorman's well-integrated revenge melodrama. Marvin becomes an agent for the destruction of his enemies in the L.A. underworld, but they die by their own hands. (92 mins.)

Point of Order (1964)**** Brilliant, deeply disturbing documentary about the Army-McCarthy hearings in the spring of 1954. Consists solely of kinescopes from the TV coverage, deftly edited by filmmaker Emile de Antonio. The demagoguery and character assassination techniques of Wisconsin Sen. Joseph McCarthy seem even more chilling in light of the Watergate revelations two decades later. B&W. (Dir: Emile de Antonio, 97 mins.)

Poison (1951)**½ Michel Simon, Sacha Guitry. Unhappily married couple each secretly plan to kill the other. Grim drama, well acted. English-dubbed. (Dir: Sacha Guitry, 83 mins.)

Poison Ivy (1953)** Eddie Constantine. Rousing French-made Grade B crime drama with Eddie Constantine playing a tough FBI agent who's up to his badge in everything from gold smugglers to shark-infested waters. (Dir: Bernard Borderie, 90 mins.)

Police Call 9000 (1973)*** Alex Rocco, Hari Rhodes, Vonetta McGee, Scatman Crothers. Good inner-city police film, set in Detroit. Rhodes is a black detective and the sensational Rocco is the white cop who takes most of the flak while investigating the rip-off of a black gubernatorial candidate's fund-raising dinner. Great use of Motown locations. (Dir: Arthur Marks, 106 mins.)

Police Python .357—See: **Case Against Ferro, The**

Police Story (1973)**½ Vic Morrow, Ed Asner, Chuck Connors, Sandy Baron, Harry Guardino. Gutsy, realistic police drama based on material written by Los Angeles lawman Joseph Wambaugh, who portrays police as human beings—this was a pilot for the anthology TV series. Not the idealized Hollywood version of police chasing bad guys. One cop can almost be compared to the cruel thief he's determined to nail, while an associate openly displays his racism only to be taught a humorous lesson by fellow officers. The characters, the story, and the realistic Los Angeles backgrounds are all first-rate. Good performances. (Dir: William Graham, 74 mins.)

Policeman, The (Israel, 1971)**½ Shai K. Ophir, Zahariva Harifai. Pleasant lark about an Israeli policeman who is going to be retired from the force, after 20 years, unless he can make a big arrest and obtain a promotion. Ophir, a gifted pantomimist, plays the bungling cop well, but the film is too sentimental. Written and directed by leading Israeli humorist Ephraim Kishan. (87 mins.)

Pollyanna (1960)***½ Hayley Mills, Jane Wyman, Agnes Moorehead, Richard Egan, Adolphe Menjou. Enjoyable family fare. Nice, uncluttered tale about a young girl who changes the life of almost everyone she comes in contact with, due to her optimistic outlook on life. Thirteen-year-old Hayley Mills is perfect as Pollyanna, a role which lets her use her cute mannerisms naturally, and the supporting cast is absolutely right...Jane Wyman as Aunt Polly, Agnes Moorehead as a cured hypochondriac. Menjou's last film. (Dir: David Swift, 134 mins.)

Pom Pom Girls, The (1976)** Robert Carradine, Jenifer Ashley, Lisa Reeves. High-school film with a little more sex and less wit than "American Graffiti." (Dir: Joseph Ruben, 90 mins.)

Pony Express (1953)**½ Charlton Heston, Rhonda Fleming, Jan Sterling, Forrest Tucker. Buffalo Bill and Wild Bill Hickok team up to see that the mail goes through. Cast and production distinguish an ordinary western plot (Dir: Jerry Hopper, 101 mins.)

Pony Soldier (1952)**½ Tyrone Power, Cameron Mitchell, Robert Horton. Mountie tries to stop a tribe of rebellious Indians from going on the warpath. Lively action melodrama goes through its familiar paces with speed and dispatch. (Dir: Joseph M. Newman, 82 mins.)

Pool of London (Great Britain, 1951)*** Bonar Colleano, Susan Shaw. A merchant sailor not above a little smuggling gets mixed up with stolen diamonds for which murder was committed. Suspenseful melodrama, well staged and acted. (Dir: Basil Dearden, 85 mins.)

Poor but Beautiful (1957)**½ Marisa Allasio, Renato Salvatori. An Italian film about love and triangles. Some funny scenes and the attractive cast make it worthwhile. (Dir: Dino Risi, 103 mins.)

Poor Cow (Great Britain, 1967)**½ Carol White, Terence Stamp. Life in the Lower Depths, as a girl (Carol White) seeks happiness for her baby and contends with a husband in jail. Generally capable performances. Carol White is particularly impressive in this saga of the sexual mores of the English low-income worker. (Dir: Kenneth Loach, 104 mins.)

Poor Devil (MTV 1973)**½ Sammy Davis, Jr., Jack Klugman, Adam West, Christopher Lee. Pilot film in which Davis plays the devil's bumbling disciple. He's been given a last chance to prove himself to the head man by wooing a San Francisco accountant (Klugman), but Sammy continues to foul up with the best of intentions. Davis fans will enjoy this lighthearted fantasy. (Dir: Robert Scheerer, 78 mins.)

Poor Little Rich Girl, The (1936)*** Shirley Temple, Alice Faye, Jack Haley. Shirley isn't an orphan in this one so she runs away from home and gets picked up by a vaudeville team. Typical Temple vehicle but pleasanter than most. (Dir: Irving Cummings, 79 mins.)

Poor Pretty Eddie—See: **Red Neck County**

Popeye (1980)**½ Robin Williams (Popeye), Shelley Duvall (Olive Oyl), Paul L. Smith (Bluto), Paul Dooley (Wimpy), Wesley Ivan Hurt (Swee'Pea). Jules Feiffer's screenplay misses the spirit of the Segar strip and the Fleischer cartoons, and despite director Robert Altman's efforts to impart an ensemble theatricality to the goings-on, the project just rambles around. (114 mins.)

Popi (1969)*** Alan Arkin, Rita Moreno. Alan Arkin's flawless, luminous performance as the New York Puerto Rican widower who wants a better life for his two sons is the film's main attraction. He will win your heart as he comes up with an outrageous plan to set his boys adrift in a boat off the Florida coast in hopes of their finding a better home with some wealthy people after being rescued. The picture has charm and pathos in well-measured amounts, and Arkin is brilliant. (Dir: Arthur Hiller, 115 mins.)

Poppy (1936)*** W. C. Fields, Rochelle Hudson, Richard Cromwell, Lynne Overman. When W.C. is on screen, this is a delight. Story of a carnival bum who tries to pass his daughter off as a missing heiress. (Dir: A. Edward Sutherland, 74 mins.)

Poppy Is Also a Flower, The (1966)**½ Trevor Howard, E. G. Marshall. First shown on TV as a special on behalf of the UN. A cast of all-stars (Yul Brynner, Omar Sharif, Marcello Mastroianni, Rita Hayworth, Angie Dickinson, and more) fill cameo roles in this dope-smuggling tale, and they weigh it down. However, Howard and Marshall, as agents assigned to follow the illegal operation right from its origin in the poppy fields, do well, and there's an exciting chase sequence in the action-packed last half hour. (Dir: Terence Young, 100 mins.)

Porgy and Bess (1959)***½ Sidney Poitier, Dorothy Dandridge, Sammy Davis, Jr., Pearl Bailey, Diahann Carroll. George Gershwin's opera about the inhabitants of Catfish Row, and a crippled beggar who cares for a beautiful but reckless girl. Lavishly produced by Samuel Goldwyn, with the superb score brilliantly sung. However, the show is staged stiffly, unimaginatively—some of the performances are not on a par with the musical end. All in all, the score's the thing. (Dir: Otto Preminger, 116 mins.)

Pork Chop Hill (1959)*** Gregory Peck. Stark war drama about the last hours of the Korean War. It's hard-hitting and tough with an excellent supporting cast, which includes George Peppard, Harry Guardino, and Rip Torn. Superior war film directed by veteran Lewis Milestone. (97 mins.)

Port Afrique (Great Britain, 1956)** Pier Angeli, Phil Carey, Anthony Newley. French Morocco is the setting for this dull story of revenge and murder. Lovely Pier Angeli plays a nightclub singer involved in the shady goings-on. (Dir: Rudolph Mate, 92 mins.)

Port of New York (1949)*** Scott Brady, Yul Brynner, K. T. Stevens. When a government agent is killed working on a narcotics case, his buddy crashes through to get the goods on the gang. Competent crime melodrama, made in New York. Brynner's film debut, with his own hair. (Dir: Laslo Benedek, 79 mins.)

Port of Revenge (Great Britain, 1961)*½ Dan O'Herlihy, Maurice Teynac. (90 mins.)

Port of Seven Seas (1938)** Wallace Beery, Maureen O'Sullivan, John Beal. An earlier version of the oft-told tale of "Fanny," as a Marseilles girl loves a lad who goes to sea; when babytime is near, her father and an elderly suitor come to the rescue. The Gallic flavor just isn't there. (Dir: James Whale, 81 mins.)

Port Sinister (1953)*½ James Warren, Lynne Roberts. (Dir: Harold Daniels, 65 mins.)

Portnoy's Complaint (1972)* Richard Benjamin, Karen Black, Lee Grant. (Dir: Ernest Lehman, 101 mins.)

Portrait in Black (1960)**½ Lana Turner, Anthony Quinn, Sandra Dee, John Saxon, Richard Basehart, Lloyd Nolan, Anna May Wong. Typical example of slick Hollywood mystery-romance. Ingredients: bedridden tycoon, dissatisfied wife, weak-willed doctor in love with wife, mix well with murder, conscience pangs and revenge. It's all nicely garnished, but still hash. (Dir: Michael Gordon, 112 mins.)

Portrait of a Mobster (1961)**½ Vic Morrow, Leslie Parrish. Strictly for fans of gangster movies who like their action tough and the plot simple. Vic Morrow gives a tight-lipped performance as Dutch Schultz, the notorious hood of the Prohibition era. Lovely Leslie Parrish does quite well in a predictably written role. (Dir: Joseph Pevney, 108 mins.)

Portrait of a Rebel: Margaret Sanger (MTV 1980)*** Bonnie Franklin, David Dukes, Richard Johnson. Time is the early years of the century when Margaret Sanger took on the medical profession, the courts, the Senate, and the Catholic Church in her battle to give women birth control information. Bouncy Bonnie is a trifle girlish in her rendition of Sanger, the scrapper, but the drama is a rewarding history lesson. (Dir: Virgil Vogel, 104 mins.)

Portrait of a Sinner (Great Britain, 1959)** Nadja Tiller, Tony Britton, William Bendix. Temptress keeps a young man and her elderly boss on a string, but really craves the man who did her dirt years before. Unsavory drama has a capable cast and director. (Dir: Robert Siodmak, 96 mins.)

Portrait of a Stripper (MTV 1979)**½ Lesley Ann Warren, Edward Herrmann, Vic Tayback. Warren gives a finely etched performance of a young widow with a son, who begins work in a strip joint to meet her expenses. She quits after one degrading walk down the ramp, only to be confronted by her father-in-law's charge that she is an unfit mother. Melodrama is kept to a minimum. (Dir: John Alonzo, 104 mins.)

Portrait of an Unknown Woman (West Germany, 1954)**½ Ruth Leuwerik, O. W. Fischer. Tasteful treatment of a painter enchanted by a beautiful woman at the opera. When he molds her face on a sculpture, scandal is let loose. You've seen the rest. (Dir: Helmut Kautner, 86 mins.)

Portrait of Jason (1967)***½ Fascinating, haunting documentary portrait of a 33-year-old black male homosexual prostitute who is also a heroin addict. Director Shirley Clarke just turned her cameras on this charismatic, tortured soul as he tells about his past life, orgies, experiences in jail, and does a few pathetic impersonations, etc. You virtually feel Jason Holliday disintegrating right before your eyes. One of the most powerful anti-drug statements ever captured on film. (105 mins.)

Portrait of Jennie (1948)*** Joseph Cotten, Jennifer Jones, Ethel Barrymore, Lillian Gish, David Wayne. Silly story from a Robert Nathan novella about a disillusioned artist (Cotten) who paints the portrait of a strange, doomed girl (Jones), whom he suspects is a ghost. (Dir: William Dieterle, 86 mins.)

Portrait of the Artist as a Young Man, A (Great Britain, 1977)**½ Bosco Hogan, T.P. McKenna, John Gielgud, Rosaleen Linehan, Maureen Potter. After his abominable "Ulysses" and vulgar "Tropic of Cancer," director Joseph Strick attacks another classic novel, with predictable results. However, with Gielgud delivering the hellfire sermon and actors like McKenna and Hogan, there are moments of eloquence and power. Shot on location in Dublin. (92 mins.)

Poseidon Adventure, The (1972)*** Gene Hackman, Ernest Borgnine, Shelley Winters, Stella Stevens. A gripping "Titanic-like" adventure that falls into the category of popular appeal films which score big at the box office, providing vicarious thrill after thrill. It's New Year's Eve on the "Poseidon" when a 90-foot tidal wave turns the huge ocean liner upside-down and the stage is set for the survival of the fittest among the all-star passenger list...including resourceful leader-minister Hackman; detective Borgnine and his ex-prostie-wife Stevens; a middle-aged Jewish couple, Winters and Jack Albertson; terrified pop singer Carol Lynley; and amiable haberdasher-bachelor Red Buttons. Their plight and trek to possible survival is excellently photographed, if slightly on the incredible side. The special effects are the real star of the film. (Dir: Ronald Neame, 117 mins.)

Posse (1975)***½ Kirk Douglas, Bruce Dern, Bo Hopkins, James Stacy. Produced and directed by Douglas, who also stars as an 1890s U.S. marshal determined to advance his political career over the bodies of Texas outlaws. Dern is the outlaw who turns the tables on Douglas's posturing and platitudinizing. (94 mins.)

Posse from Hell (1961)** Audie Murphy, John Saxon, Zohra Lampert, Vic Morrow. Run-of-the-mill western with Audie Murphy riding and shooting once again in his usual brave fashion. No surprises, but action fans will probably stick with it, as a gunslinger goes after four escaped killers. (Dir: Herbert Coleman, 89 mins.)

Possessed (1974)**½ Joan Crawford, Van Heflin. Morbid story of a woman schizophrenic is occasionally interesting but generally too heavy and melodramatic to appeal to anyone but a loyal Crawford fan. (Dir: Curtis Bernhardt, 108 mins.)

Possessed, The (MTV 1977)** James Farentino, Joan Hackett, Claudette Nevins, Diana Scarwid. Farentino plays a defrocked priest who appears at a girls' school to do battle against evil. Poor horror script with good performances. (Dir: Jerry Thorpe, 78 mins.)

Possession of Joel Delaney, The (1972)** Shirley MacLaine, Perry King. OK thriller. New York divorcee MacLaine chases around her kid brother Joel (King) in a laughingly desperate attempt to make him her son. Poor Joel is possessed by the spirit of a deceased Puerto Rican friend who used to chop off girls' heads! The exorcism scene and the New York location shots can really shake you up, but the terror is in slow motion. (Dir: Waris Hussein, 105 mins.)

Possessors, The (1959)**½ Jean Gabin, Pierre Brasseur. Story of a family and their involvement with the stock exchange. Literate French drama, slow moving but well acted. (Dir: Denys De La Patelliere, 94 mins.)

Postman Always Rings Twice, The (1946)***½ John Garfield, Lana Turner, Cecil Kellaway, Hume Cronyn, Leon Ames. Garfield, drifting down the California coast, is waylaid by a shimmering Turner and her plot to murder her husband. Adapted from a novel by America's finest pulp writer, James M. Cain, the film is a key work of the postwar period, drips with demented romanticism and the venom of disillusionment. Tay Garnett directed, finding the pull of obsession in every tracking shot. (113 mins.)

Postman Always Rings Twice, The (1981)**½ Jack Nicholson, Jessica Lange. Why re-make the James M. Cain story if you aren't passionately engaged by the material? At least Neil Diamond cared about *The Jazz Singer*. Bob Rafelson has turned in a professional, self-effacing job as director, and the film looks handsome, but it just lies there, without the demented spark that Cain's prose fired it with. Rafelson peculiarly cuts out of scenes before their payoff, leaving audiences unfamiliar with the tale somewhat stranded. Jack Nicholson, though too old for the low-life lover, inhabits the period convincingly, and Jessica Lange, despite having developed a potentially serious case of method acting, manages to transform Cora from a fantasy projection into a real character. None of it seems to amount to much, though. With John Colicos, Michael Lerner, and Angelica Huston as a lion tamer. (Dir: Bob Rafelson, 97 mins.)

Pot o' Gold (1941)** James Stewart, Paulette Goddard. The gal's rich pop hates dance bands, but nevertheless she lands Horace Heidt's orchestra on pop's program. Pleasant musical comedy. (Dir: George Marshall, 86 mins.)

Potemkin (U.S.S.R., 1925)**** Antonov, Vladamir Barsky. This film has been labeled everything from "one of the best films ever made" to "the greatest film of all time." Director Sergei Eisenstein's masterpiece is a re-creation of the successful sailor revolt aboard the battleship "Potemkin" in Odessa harbor in 1905. The massacre of the civilian population that supported the mutiny, which takes place on the great steps of the city, is one of the most powerful sequences in the history of film. It is a thrilling, shocking, exciting, and overwhelming movie classic. (67 mins.)

Pound (1970)*** Lawrence Wolf, Elsie Downey, Marshall Efron. Rover and Feydeau hang loose in director Robert Downey's erratically insane satire of impounded dogs (played by humans) awaiting an owner or the big sleep—the latter can only come when Con Edison fixes the gas lines. Not Downey's best but a lot of macabre humor, much of it funny. (92 mins.)

Pourquoi Pas! (Why Not!) (France, 1979)** Sami Frey, Christine Murillo, Mario Gonzalez, Nicole Jamet. Pallid but pretty comedy from writer-director Coline Serreau, about a threesome who are emotionally generous enough to welcome a fourth to the ménage. The film is all too taken with its hip ease of affection.

Poverty and Nobility (Italy, 1954)** Sophia Loren, Toto. Poor boy falls for a ballerina from a noble family, causing confusion. Dubbed-English comedy from Loren's salad days. She's good to look at, while the film itself is bearable. (Dir: Mario Mattoli, 83 mins.)

Powder Keg (MTV 1971)** Rod Taylor, Dennis Cole. Railroad blowups, dirty bandits, rape, and a Stutz Bearcat roadster, circa 1914, keep the action barreling along in this film. Writer-producer-director Doug Heyes has thrown everything into the overlong story. Troubleshooters Taylor and Cole get around in the yellow roadster, and they're hired by the railroad to handle Mexican hijackers who hold a train and passengers hostage below the border. (Dir: Doug Heyes, 93 mins.)

Powder River (1953)** Rory Calhoun, Corinne Calvet, Cameron Mitchell. Routine western about a gunman turned marshal and the collection of stock characters with whom he matches wits and/or guns. (Dir: Louis King, 78 mins.)

Power, The (1968)** George Hamilton, Suzanne Pleshette, Michael Rennie, Yvonne DeCarlo. Reasonably interesting, sci-fi yarn about a mind which has fantastic power to do almost anything as long as it's evil! Hamilton tries to oppose this "power" since he too possesses a "powerful" mind. (Dir: Byron Haskin, 109 mins.)

Power (MTV 1980)*** Joe Don Baker, Karen Black, Ralph Bellamy, Brian Keith. Script by Ernest Tidyman on the rise to power of a tough labor leader, patterned after Jimmy Hoffa. Baker is splendid as '30s Chicago meat dock worker Tommy Vanda, who moves up the labor ranks with help from the mob and eventually becomes arrogant and totally corrupt. (Dir: Barry Shear, 200 mins.)

Power and the Glory, The (1933) Spencer Tracy, Colleen Moore, Ralph Morgan, Helen Vinson. Tracy is a tycoon risen from the working classes, with elaborate flashbacks demonstrating how he used everyone on his way to the top. Director William K. Howard is not up to realizing some of the complexities that could have been developed (as they later were in "Citizen Kane"). (Not related to the Graham Greene novel of the same name.) Script by Preston Sturges. (76 mins.)

Power and the Prize, The (1956)**½ Robert Taylor, Elisabeth Mueller, Burl Ives. Slick Hollywood version about the world of big business. Taylor adequately plays the ambitious executive who finds he fought too hard for things he really didn't want after he falls in love with an attractive refugee. Ives is a stereotyped big tycoon. (Dir: Henry Koster, 98 mins.)

Power Man (1979)* Art Hindle, Edward Binns, Joe Rassulo. Silly opus about a man who develops superhuman powers after being struck by lightning. (Dir: John Llewellyn Moxey, 90 mins.)

Power of the Whistler (1945)**½ Janis Carter, Richard Dix. Killer gets amnesia and girl amateur detective discovers his identity. Suspenseful thriller. (Dir: Lew Landers, 66 mins.)

Powers Girl, The (1942)** George Murphy, Anne Shirley, Carole Landis, Dennis Day, Benny Goodman. A fast-talking agent makes a Powers model out a dainty dish, but falls for her sister. Tolerable comedy (Dir: Norman Z. McLeod, 93 mins.)

Practically Yours (1945)** Fred MacMurray, Claudette Colbert, Robert Benchley, Cecil Kellaway, Rosemary DeCamp. A pilot sends a message of love to a girl before he crashes into the Pacific. This "comedy" is about all the confusion caused when a girl thinks he meant her and he turns up alive. Few laughs, silly situation. (Dir: Mitchell Leisen, 89 mins.)

Practice Makes Perfect (France, 1979)**½ Jean Rochefort, Nicole Garcia, Annie Girardot, Danielle Darrieux, Lila Kedrova, Katherine Alric. Another fluff piece from director Philippe de Broca, starring Rochefort as a celebrated concert pianist who tries to juggle his wife, life, career, daughters, ex-wife, and mistress.

Pray for the Wildcats (MTV 1974)*** Andy Griffith, William Shatner, Robert Reed, Marjoe Gortner, Angie Dickinson. An offbeat tale that should keep you engrossed throughout. Griffith, in a change-of-pace casting, plays an unscrupulous tycoon who gleefully manipulates three ad agency execs beyond the point of endurance. The four men go to the Baja California territory on a motorcycle trek, during which they discover their true strengths and inevitable weaknesses. The cast is first-rate and the story strives for originality. (Dir: Robert Michael Lewis, 100 mins.)

Prelude to Fame (Great Britain, 1950)***½ Guy Rolfe, Kathleen Byron, Jeremy Spenser. A boy is found to have musical talent, becomes a child prodigy conductor, but finds fame has its sadness too. Drama, well written and directed, finely acted. (Dir: Fergus McDonnell, 78 mins.)

Premature Burial, The (1962)** Ray Milland, Hazel Court, Heather Angel. Edgar Allan Poe's intricate and engrossing suspense tale about a man who fears he will be buried alive is impoverished by this screen treatment, so packed with contrivances, clichés and gloomy decors as to be absurd, often funny, but not very scary. If you don't know the story and can stand the devices, see it. Better yet, read the original (Dir: Roger Corman, 81 mins.)

Premeditated (France, 1960)** Jean-Claude Pascal, Pascale Roberts. Man goes on trial for the murder of his wife and her lover. Fair English-dubbed courtroom drama. (Dir: André Berthomieu, 90 mins.)

Prescription: Murder (MTV 1968)**½ Peter Falk, Gene Barry. A familiar, old-fashioned murder yarn gets the glossy Universal mounting. Peter Falk plays the cigar-smoking, trench-coat-carrying detective who just can't buy successful Hollywood psychiatrist Gene Barry's airtight alibi. (Dir: Richard Irving, 99 mins.)

Presenting Lily Mars (1943)*** Van Heflin, Judy Garland, Fay Bainter, Richard Carlson, Spring Byington, Marilyn Maxwell. Slight, well-done little tale of a stage-struck girl and her loving, eccentric family. Nothing new, but charmingly told. Heflin is good as the exasperated producer continually hounded by the aspiring actress, and Judy was so lovely at this period. One fine moment: Judy and a theatre cleaning lady discuss life, and sing the turn-of-the-century hit, "Every Little Movement Has a Meaning of Its Own." (Dir: Norman Taurog, 104 mins.)

President's Analyst, The (1967)***½ James Coburn, Godfrey Cambridge. Wacky, rewarding satire written and directed by Theodore J. Flicker. Spy spoof which benefits greatly from the smoothness of James Coburn in the title role. The premise is tremendously original, and although it falters towards the end, the story offers some wild chases, and amusing sequences with analyst Coburn becoming more and more paranoid, thanks to his delicate assignment as secret headshrinker to the President. Even lampoons the FBI. (Dir: Theodore J. Flicker, 104 mins.)

President's Lady, The (1953)**½ Susan Hayward, Charlton Heston, Fay Bainter, Carl Betz, John McIntire. Charlton Heston's effective performance as Andrew Jackson makes this costume drama, based on Irving Stone's best seller about the romance between the young Jackson and a married woman, worthwhile. Miss Hayward is less effective in an overdrawn characterization. (Dir: Henry Levin, 96 mins.)

President's Mistress, The (MTV 1978)** Beau Bridges, Karen Grassle, Larry Hagman, Susan Blanchard. High-style hokum about a beautiful blonde who is having an affair with the president; word flashes out that the lady is a Russian spy. Lots of black limos cruising Washington streets and tight-lipped intelligence men. (Dir: John Llewellyn Moxey, 104 mins.)

President's Plane is Missing, The (MTV 1971)**½ Buddy Ebsen, Peter Graves, Rip Torn, Raymond Massey, Arthur Kennedy. The premise—the threat of a nuclear attack by Red China—was devised before relations improved. The fictional President boards Air Force One, which crashes soon thereafter. Cast brings the stock Washington characters to life in the midst of the ensuing international tension. (Dir: Daryl Duke, 100 mins.)

Pressure Point (1962)*** Sidney Poitier, Bobby Darin, Peter Falk. A black psychiatrist (Poitier) is treating a prison inmate (Darin) who is a racist and a member of the Nazi party. Photographed in razor-like B&W by Ernest Haller. (Dir: Hubert Cornfield, 91 mins.)

Pretender, The (1947)*** Albert Dekker, Catherine Craig. Businessman marries for money, hires a gangster to eliminate his rival; through an error, he finds himself the intended victim. Tight, suspenseful melodrama, well above average. (Dir: W. Lee Wilder, 69 mins.)

Pretty Baby (1950)**½ Dennis Morgan, Betsy Drake, Edmund Gwenn, Zachary Scott. Funny comedy about a resourceful working girl who uses gimmicks to get to the top in her career. Well acted by Drake and Gwenn. (Dir: Bretaigne Windust, 92 mins.)

Pretty Baby (1978)**** Keith Carradine, Brooke Shields, Susan Sarandon, Antonio Vargas. Too careful and excruciatingly tasteful, but an effective inquiry into the passion of a photographer for an 11-year-old prostitute in Storyville, New Orleans. Carradine's physical inarticulateness is immensely effective, and Shields does well with the caprices of the preadolescent whore. Sharp characterization by Fargas as the musician of the brothel. Director Louis Malle's sanity can be cloying, but the film's offhand way with whim and obsession stays in the mind. Shields is astonishingly beautiful. (109 mins.)

Pretty Boy Floyd (1960)** John Ericson, Joan Harvey, Barry Newman. Fictionalized account of one of the nation's big time killers. John Ericson has the physical attractiveness and acting ability to rise above some of the drama's cliched plot twists. Gangster-film fans will find all the familiar episodes to their liking. (Dir: Herbert J. Leder, 96 mins.)

Pretty Boy Floyd (1974)—See: **Story of Pretty Boy Floyd, The**

Pretty Poison (1968)**** Anthony Perkins, Tuesday Weld, Beverly Garland. Absorbing, low-budget psychological drama about a paranoid young man (Perkins) and his girl friend (Weld), underrated critically at the time of its first release, "Poison" boasts first-rate performances from both Weld and Perkins. A notably adroit screenplay by Lorenzo Semple, Jr., and a promising debut from young director Noel Black. We are purposely not going to tell you any more of the story, but this tale of madness in Massachusetts will keep you guessing from beginning to end. (89 mins.)

Price of Fear, The (1956)** Merle Oberon, Lex Barker. Muddled melodrama about a woman who is responsible for a hit and run accident and goes to extremes to keep it a secret. Miss Oberon has had better vehicles and better leading men too. (Dir: Abner Biberman, 79 mins.)

Price of Silence, The (Great Britain, 1960)** Gordon Jackson, June Thorburn. Ex-con takes a job with a real estate company intending to go straight, but a blackmailing former cellmate makes it tough. Routine crime melodrama. (Dir: Montgomery Tully, 73 mins.)

Pride and Prejudice (1940)**** Greer Garson, Laurence Olivier, Edmund Gwenn, Mary Boland, Edna Mae Oliver, Maureen O'Sullivan, Karen Morley, Freida Iniscourt, Frank Lawton. One of the few vindications of the MGM "classic" style that often presented embalmed editions of literary works, this Jane Austen adaptation is lively, gracious, and entertaining. Olivier and Garson are well matched. Robert Z. Leonard's direction, for once, is exemplary. Aldous Huxley worked on the script with Jane Murfin. (116 mins.)

Pride and the Passion, The (1957)**½ Cary Grant, Sophia Loren, Frank Sinatra. Over-produced spectacle set during the Spanish Revolution against Napoleon. The real star of the overlong epic is an enormous cannon which is abandoned by the Spanish Army, and retrieved by the band of guerrillas with the aid of a British naval officer. Grant looks uncomfortable in his role of the naval officer; Sophia Loren is merely decorative as a fiery Spanish girl; and Frank Sinatra is badly miscast as the guerrilla leader, Miguel. (Dir: Stanley Kramer, 132 mins.)

Pride of St. Louis (1952)**½ Dan Dailey, Joanne Dru, Richard Crenna. Sentimentalized biography of Dizzy Dean, baseball pitcher extraordinary, character de luxe. Could have used more authenticity, but Dailey gives the role a good try. (Dir: Harmon Jones, 93 mins.)

Pride of the Blue Grass (1954)** Lloyd Bridges, Vera Miles. Routine race track story with some action on the turf for racing fans. The plot is all too familiar but the kids may enjoy the horses. (Dir: William Beaudine, 71 mins.)

Pride of the Marines (1945)***½ John Garfield, Eleanor Parker, Dane Clark, Rosemary De Camp, John Ridgely. Moving, human story of Al Schmid, the marine who was blinded by a grenade after killing 200 Japanese. It's an account of his adjustment to blindness and it's told with simplicity and taste. Performances are excellent. (Dir: Delmer Daves, 119 mins.)

Pride of the Yankees, The (1942)**½ Gary Cooper, Teresa Wright, Babe Ruth, Walter Brennan, Dan Duryea. Cooper was a good choice to play baseball star Lou Gehrig, but this biopic never surmounts the lack of drama in the screenplay by Jo Swerling and Herman J. Mankiewicz, and Sam Wood's direction is barely adequate. Wright is quite good as Gehrig's wife. (127 mins.)

Priest Killer, The (MTV 1971)*½ George Kennedy, Raymond Burr, Don Galloway. (Dir: Richard Colla, 100 mins.)

Priest's Wife, The (Italy-France, 1970)** Marcello Mastroianni, Sophia Loren. Those stalwart Italian stars of many a tearjerker and comedy, Mastroianni and Miss Loren, team up once again for a piece of frothy nonsense about an earthy singer who falls in love with a man of the cloth. The plot fluctuates between outrageously staged scenes of blatant slapstick and melodrama. The stars have appeared to better advantage in other films. (Dir: Dino Risi, 106 mins.)

Primate (1974)*** Provocative, rewarding documentary directed by Frederick Wiseman, but not for the squeamish. Shows the gruesome details of experiments being performed on animals, mostly monkeys, at the Yerkes Primate Research Center in Atlanta. For interested adults, not for children. (105 mins.)

Prime Cut (1972)*½ Lee Marvin, Gene Hackman, Sissy Spacek. (Dir: Michael Ritchie, 91 mins.)

Prime Minister, The (Great Britain, 1941)** John Gielgud, Diana Wynyard, Fay Compton. Despite the remarkable sets and costumes, and three fine performances, this is an elaborate, reverent bore. You might want to look in anyway to see the great Gielgud as Disraeli; but George Arliss was better. (Dir: Thorold Dickinson, 94 mins.)

Prime of Miss Jean Brodie, The (Great Britain, 1969)**** Maggie Smith, Robert Stephens, Pamela Franklin, Celia Johnson. Don't miss Smith's Academy Award-winning performance as the irrepressible, irresistible, melodramatic, and thoroughly mad teacher at an exclusive girls' school, late '30s. Miss Smith's portrayal is one of those unique experiences in film which must be savored . . . she struts, poses, and mesmerizes you at every turn, as her wide-eyed charges (the "crème de la crème" as she labels them) raptly listen to her speak of her affairs, her misguided allegiances to Mussolini and Franco, and her dedication to love, art, and truth. The plot ends on an unhappy note, but Miss Brodie's contagious joie de vivre and final defeat remain long after the fade-out. (Dir: Ronald Neame, 116 mins.)

Primrose Path, The (1940)*** Ginger Rogers, Joel McCrea, Marjorie Rambeau, Miles Mander, Harry Trevers, Strange little comedy-drama about a girl from the wrong side of the tracks who falls in love with an upper-crust youth. The tone of this film varies pretty extremely from farce to melodrama, but it is oddly involving. Worth seeing. (Dir: Gregory La Cava, 93 mins.)

Prince and the Pauper (1937)***½ Errol Flynn, Claude Rains, Mauch Twins, Alan Hale, Henry Stephenson, Barton MacLane. Exciting, skillful adaptation of Mark Twain's story about a beggar who changes places with a prince. (Dir: William Keighley, 118 mins.)

Prince and the Pauper, The (1938)—See: **Crossed Swords**

Prince and the Showgirl, The (Great Britain, 1957)***½ Laurence Olivier, Marilyn Monroe, Sybil Thorndike, Jeremy Spencer, Richard Wattis. Romantic story of a Balkan prince and an American chorus girl in London at the time of the Coronation of King George V (1912). The plot is slight but the dialogue sprightly, the period setting interesting. Though they apparently loathed each other, the stars are wonderful together; well worth seeing for that reason alone. From the Terrence Rattigan stage hit "The Sleeping Prince". (Dir: Laurence Olivier, 117 mins.)

Prince of Central Park, The (MTV 1977)*** T. J. Hargrave, Ruth Gordon, Lisa Richard, Marc Vahanian. A charming story, based loosely on the novel by Evan H. Rhodes, about a 12-year-old boy and his younger sister, who run away from their foster home and take refuge in a tree house in Central Park. The kids live hand-to-mouth until an old lady, who frequents the park each day, begins leaving them food and notes. Old lady wonderfully played by Gordon. Hargrave is so natural as the resourceful lad that he makes the fairy tale work. (Dir: Harvey Hart, 74 mins.)

Prince of Foxes (1959)*** Tyrone Power, Orson Welles, Wanda Hendrix, Everett Sloane, Katrina Paxinore, Marina Berti. Atmospheric historical drama of a social-climbing artist who throws his lot in with Cesare Borgia, Rennaissence tyrant. Power was always good at playing a con man; Welles is entrancing as the great, if wicked, Cesare (his sister Lucrezia appears, too). Welles seemed to carry around with him a miasma of directorial power; there are some extraordinarily fine battle scenes in this Henry King-directed pageant. From the novel by Samuel Shellabarger. (Dir: Henry King, 107 mins.)

Prince of Pirates (1953)** John Derek, Barbara Rush. John Derek, Prince Roland of Hagen takes to the high seas of adventure to destroy the Spanish Armada. What's on the other channels? (Dir: Sidney Salkow, 80 mins.)

Prince of Players (1955)*** Richard Burton, Maggie McNamara, Raymond Massey, John Derek. An excellent performance by Richard Burton in the role of famous Shakespearean actor Edwin Booth makes this uneven biography worthwhile. Within the framework of Booth's turbulent career and private life, Burton gets the chance to perform scenes from "Romeo and Juliet" with an assist by Eva Le Gallienne. (Dir: Philip Dunne, 102 mins.)

Prince Valiant (1954)*½ James Mason, Janet Leigh, Robert Wagner, Debra Paget, Sterling Hayden. It's colorful enough, with adequate period mounting, but otherwise the attempt to render a live-action comic strip is stilted. Mason is lively as a black knight. (Dir: Henry Hathaway, 100 mins.)

Prince Who Was a Thief, The (1951)** Tony Curtis, Piper Laurie. Typical Hollywood film about the plush pageantry of the Arabian Nights and the colorful Princes and Paupers who lived on opposite sides of The Masques. (Dir: Rudolph Maté, 88 mins.)

Princess and the Pirate, The (1944)*** Bob Hope, Virginia Mayo, Walter Brennan, Victor McLaglen. Typical Bob Hope film which should please his legions of fans. This time out, he's caught up in the sinister machinations of the scourge of the seas—buccaneers! Funny film. (Dir: David Butler, 94 mins.)

Princess Comes Across, The (1936)*** Carole Lombard, Fred MacMurray, William Frawley, Porter Hall, Alison Skipworth. Adventures of a bogus princess as she travels aboard a luxury liner and gets involved in some amusing incidents with a few zany characters. (Dir: William K. Howard, 76 mins.)

Princess O'Rourke (1943)***½ Robert Cummings, Olivia de Havilland, Jane Wyman. A pleasant, diverting comedy about a guy who discovers his fiancee is a queen. The Norman Krasna script is delightfully played and a pleasure to watch. (Dir: Norman Krasna, 94 mins.)

Prisoner, The (Great Britain, 1955)**** Alec Guinness, Jack Hawkins. A cardinal is imprisoned and relentlessly questioned by the police of a communist state. An actor's show; and Guinness and Hawkins display superb performances in this gripping topical drama. (Dir: Peter Glenville, 91 mins.)

Prisoner in the Middle (1974)* David Janssen, Karin Dor, Chris Stone. (Dir: John O'Connor, 91 mins.)

Prisoner of Second Avenue, The (1975)**½ Jack Lemmon, Anne Bancroft. Bancroft is miscast in the role of the wife of a man (Lemmon) who loses his job in an ad agency after 22 years. Their readjustment consists of his having a nervous breakdown and her yelling all over the place. Neil Simon's one-liners aimed at urban woes are often funny. (Dir: Melvin Frank, 99 mins.)

Prisoner of Shark Island, The (1936)*** Warner Baxter, Gloria Stuart, John Carradine, Harry Carey, Ernest Whitman. True story of the doctor who innocently set Booth's injured leg after the Lincoln assassination. The doctor was given a prejudiced trial and sent to Shark Island. Interesting film directed by John Ford. (94 mins.)

Prisoner of the Iron Mask (France-Italy, 1960)*½ Michel Lemoine, Wandisa Guida. (Dir: Francesco De Feo, 80 mins.)

Prisoner of the Jungle (France, 1959)*½ Georges Marchal, Françoise Rasquin. (Dir: Willy Rozier, 82 mins.)

Prisoner of the Volga (Italy, 1960)*½ John Derek, Elsa Martinelli, Dawn Addams. (Dir: W. Tourjansky, 102 mins.)

Prisoner of War (1954)** Ronald Reagan, Steve Forrest. Volunteering to get information on how American prisoners are being treated, an undercover agent suffers in a Korean POW camp. Brutal, not too convincing war story. (Dir: Andrew Marton, 81 mins.)

Prisoner of Zenda, The (1937)***½ Ronald Colman, Madeleine Carroll, Douglas Fairbanks, Jr., David Niven, C. Aubrey Smith, Mary Astor, Raymond Massey. The durable old melodrama of the king's double, who's called in to do an impersonation when the royal one is kidnapped. A swashbuckler to the core, done with great style, lavish production. Superior fun. (Dir: John Cromwell, 120 mins.)

Prisoner of Zenda, The (1952)*** Stewart Granger, James Mason, Deborah Kerr, Robert Coote, Robert Douglas. Remake of the Anthony Hope chestnut follows the '37 version scene by scene, but lacks the panache of the earlier film..The casting is a step down in every part. (Dir: Richard Thorpe, 100 mins.)

Prisoner of Zenda, The (1979)**½ Peter Sellers, Lynne Frederick, Lionel Jeffries,

Elke Sommer, Gregory Sierra. Tongue-in-cheek remake of Anthony Hope's romantic swashdasher, with Sellers in the old Ronald Colman role. Directed by Richard Quine, who has seen better days. Even the brilliant Sellers can't save this creaky vehicle. (108 mins.)

Prisoners of the Casbah (1953)*½ Gloria Grahame, Cesar Romero. (Dir: Richard Bare, 78 mins.)

Private Affairs of Bel Ami, The (1947)*** George Sanders, Angela Lansbury. Ann Dvorak, Frances Dee, John Carradine, Warren William, Albert Basserman. Witty, stringent telling of the Guy de Maupassant story of a charming, ruthless schemer and his victims. Fine script; the marvelous cast of Hollywood pros finally get a chance to do something different and challenging, and they soar. Intelligent and involving. (Dir: Albert Lewin, 112 mins.)

Private Angelo (Great Britain, 1949)*** Peter Ustinov, Maria Denis. A cowardly private in the Italian army manages to pass himself off as a hero to his townspeople. Frequently delightful comedy, good fun. (Dirs: Peter Ustinov, Michael Anderson, 102 mins.)

Private Battle, A (MTV 1980)**½ Jack Warden, Anne Jackson, David Stockton. Another real-life story about a family's struggle with cancer. Irish-American author Cornelius Ryan ("The Longest Day," "A Bridge Too Far") is the victim, and Warden convincingly portrays his changing emotions during his four-year bout with the dreaded disease. John Gay's script even dares to point out that doctors don't always know what they're doing. (Dir: Robert Lewis, 104 mins.)

Private Benjamin (1980)*** Goldie Hawn, Eileen Brennan, Armand Assante, Mary Kay Place. Hawn is engaging as a Jewish princess who ends up enlisting in the army, but the story rambles off into pointlessness and the jokes tend to be unnecessarily cruel, though Goldie's charming pout and big blue eyes carry the action along from one modest tickle to another. (Dir: Howard Zieff, 110 mins.)

Private Buckaroo (1942)*½ Andrews Sisters, Harry James, Joe E. Lewis. (Dir: Edward F. Cline, 68 mins.)

Private Files of J. Edgar Hoover, The (1978)**½ Broderick Crawford, José Ferrer, Michael Parks, Rip Torn, Ronee Blakley. Sometimes enlightening look behind the scenes at Hoover, the FBI, and recent American history. Directed, produced, and written by Larry Cohen. (112 mins.)

Private Hell 36 (1954)**½ Ida Lupino, Steve Cochran, Howard Duff, Dean Jagger, Dorothy Malone. A murky psychological study fraught with artsy pretensions. The title refers to a house trailer, where a crooked cop is holed up with a dame, his ex-partner in hot pursuit. Action doesn't come until too late in the picture. (Dir: Don Siegel, 81 mins.)

Private Life of Don Juan, The (Great Britain, 1934)*** Douglas Fairbanks, Sr., Binnie Barnes, Merle Oberon, Benita Hume, Melville Cooper. Fairbanks's last film, a wry account of the twilight years of the notorious seducer in which the ladies find him disappointing. Audiences were perplexed by the new Doug, hair thinning and waistline spreading, and stayed away—though the picture has more than its share of charming touches. (Dir: Alexander Korda, 90 mins.)

Private Life of Henry VIII, The (Great Britain, 1933)***½ Charles Laughton, Wendy Barry, Miles Mander. Laughton's impersonation of the great monarch is an immortal slice of ham, and director Alexander Korda's lush production showcases the star well. It's British "tradition of quality" near its apex. (97 mins.)

Private Lives (1931)***½ Norma Shearer, Robert Montgomery, Reginald Denny, Una Merkel. Americanizing Noël Coward's comedy works surprisingly well. Shearer is up to the repartee and works well with Montgomery. Denny and Merkel are in fine fettle too as the luckless new spouses. Deft direction from the normally plodding Sidney Franklin compounds the surprises. (84 mins.)

Private Lives of Adam and Eve, The (1960)* Mickey Rooney, Mamie Van Doren, Mel Tormé, Tuesday Weld, Paul Anka. (Dir: Albert Zugsmith, 87 mins.)

Private Lives of Elizabeth and Essex, The (1939)*** Bette Davis, Errol Flynn, Donald Crisp, Olivia de Havilland, Vincent Price. Critics made a fuss about how unhistorical the film was, but Maxwell Anderson's verse play, from which the film was ostensibly adapted, wasn't too keen on accuracy itself (of character or meter). Davis turns in a shaded, detailed performance as Elizabeth I, and Flynn, though mismatched and miscast, keeps his aplomb as a dashing Essex. The early color (by Sol Polito) is good. Michael Curtiz directs with considerable technical skill but not much sympathy for the material. Color. (120 mins.)

Private Navy of Sergeant O'Farrell, The (1968)* Bob Hope, Phyllis Diller, Jeffrey Hunter, Gina Lollobrigida. (Dir: Frank Tashlin, 92 mins.)

Private Number (1936)**½ Robert Taylor, Loretta Young, Basil Rathbone. Corny story of a secret marriage between a housemaid and her boss' son. OK for soap opera fans. (Dir: Roy Del Ruth, 80 mins.)

Private Parts (1972)*** Ayn Ruymen, Lucille Benson, Laurie Main. Teenage girl runs away from home and goes to live with her neurotic aunt who runs a shabby hotel in a rundown part of Los Angeles. The lodgers are as gamey a bunch of perverts and nuts as you'll encounter in a dozen films. Made on a low budget as an independent feature by director Paul Bartel, there are some genuinely surprising twists and scares in this uneven, offbeat psycho-drama. Some wild sexual hang-ups shown quickly for those of you who compile this kind of erotica. (87 mins.)

Private Property (1960)** Corey Allen, Warren Oates, Kate Manx. Two drifters step into the life of a beautiful, neglected housewife; slow-paced sex and seduction, which explodes in a violent finale. Despite the lurid story, Leslie Stevens's first film is occasionally interesting. (Dir: Leslie Stevens, 79 mins.)

Private War of Major Benson, The (1955)*** Charlton Heston, Julie Adams, Tim Hovey, Sal Mineo. Hard-bitten army officer is forced to accept a transfer to a military school as commanding officer. Enjoyable if a bit prolonged comedy is a welcome change of pace for Heston; good share of chuckles. (Dir: Jerry Hopper, 105 mins.)

Private Worlds (1935)**½ Claudette Colbert, Charles Boyer, Joel McCrea, Joan Bennett. Story of intrigue in a mental hospital is antiquated but might interest those who like modern psychiatric stories. Interesting for comparison. (Dir: Gregory LaCava, 84 mins.)

Private's Affair, A (1959)** Sal Mineo, Christine Carere, Barbara Eden, Gary Crosby, Terry Moore, Jim Backus. Four draftees and their girl friends are tapped for a big army show, but complications interfere. Threadbare comedy plot used as a showcase for some younger talent. Nothing much. (Dir: Raoul Walsh, 92 mins.)

Private's Progress (Great Britain, 1956)***½ Dennis Price, Ian Carmichael, Terry-Thomas, Richard Attenborough. An earnest but stumbling young man is called into the army, where he makes a mess of things. Britain's answer to Pvt. Hargrove is a rollicking comedy, often hilariously funny despite the thick dialect. (Dir: John Boulting, 97 mins.)

Privilege (Great Britain, 1967)**½ Paul Jones, Jean Shrimpton. Vintage hysteria about how media packaging of rock stars turns them into near-religious figures with substantial potential for political influence. Peter Watkins directs with the driving johnny-on-the-spot style that is his greatest strength and most appalling weakness. The excellent (and very late '60s) cinematography is by Peter Suschitsky. (101 mins.)

Prize, The (1963)**½ Paul Newman, Elke Sommer, Edward G. Robinson. Writer in Stockholm to accept the Nobel Prize becomes involved in a spy plot to kidnap a scientist. Overlong thriller tries for the Hitchcock touch, only occasionally succeeds. Some suspenseful moments, but the rest is padding. (Dir: Mark Robson, 136 mins.)

Prize of Arms, A (Great Britain, 1962)*** Stanley Baker, Tom Bell, Helmut Schmid. Another good example of the type of crime story the British do so well. A band of men attempt to rob an army payroll in a seemingly perfect crime that goes astray. Suspenseful, well acted. (Dir: Cliff Owen, 105 mins.)

Prize of Gold, A (Great Britain, 1955)*** Richard Widmark, Mai Zetterling. An exciting drama set in occupied Berlin concerning a fabulous scheme to steal a shipment of gold bullion from the Berlin airlift. Fine cast. Zetterling is as talented as she is pretty. (Dir: Mark Robson, 98 mins.)

Prizefighter, The (1979)** Tim Conway, Don Knotts, David Wayne. Dopey, broad comedy about boxing business hokum in the '30s. Conway wrote the story and cowrote the screenplay with John Myhers, who also appears. (Dir: Michael Preece, 99 mins.)

Prizefighter and the Lady (1933)**½ Max Baer, Myrna Loy, Jack Dempsey, Walter Huston. This picture was made to cash in on Baer's popularity after he floored Max Schmeling. Surprise was that Baer could act and the film is reasonably entertaining. (Dir: W. S. Van Dyke, 103 mins.)

Probe (MTV 1971)*½ Hugh O'Brian, Elke Sommer, Burgess Meredith, Sir John Gielgud. (Dir: Russell Mayberry, 97 mins.)

Problem Girls (1953)*½ Susan Morrow, Helen Walker. (Dir: E. A. Dupont, 70 mins.)

Prodigal, The (1955)*½ Lana Turner, Edmund Purdom. (Dir: Richard Thorpe, 114 mins.)

Producers, The (1968)***½ Zero Mostel, Gene Wilder, Dick Shawn, Estelle Winwood. A preposterous, often wildly funny tale about an impoverished Broadway theater producer who stages a ghastly play in the hopes of making his fortune by selling more than 100% of the show to investors. Conceived, written, and directed by Mel Brooks. The show within a show is called "Springtime for Hitler." Wilder's flawless performance as Mostel's nervous henchman earned him an Academy Award nomination. Shawn playing Hitler is very funny too, once you accept the premise of this lunacy, which earned Brooks an Academy Award for his screenplay. (88 mins.)

Professional Soldier (1936)**½ Victor McLaglen, Freddie Bartholomew. The leads are delightful but the story isn't handled well. Tale of a retired colonel who is paid to kidnap the youthful king of a mythical European country had a lot of potential but it didn't come off. (Dir: Tay Garnett, 78 mins.)

Professionals, The (Great Britain, 1961)** William Lucas, Andrew Faulds. Safecracker is hired by a mob for a bank robbery. Passable low-budget crime melodrama. (Dir: Don Sharp, 61 mins.)

Professionals, The (1966)**** Burt Lancaster, Lee Marvin, Claudia Cardinale, Jack Palance, Robert Ryan. Splendid, rip-snorting, old-fashioned adventure yarn, circa 1917, brilliantly brought to pulsating life by a cast of rugged leading men and sensuous Claudia Cardinale. The plot has Ralph Bellamy hiring our he-men to fetch his allegedly kidnapped wife (Claudia) back from Mexico where she has been taken by bandito Jack Palance. The trail to and from Mexico is strewn with marvelously played sequences. Produced, written and directed by Richard Brooks, and he did a notable job in all three departments. (Dir: Richard Brooks, 117 mins.)

Professor Beware (1938)**½ Harold Lloyd, Phyllis Welch, Lionel Stander. It's all Mr. Lloyd and very little script in this silly comedy about a professor trying to unravel a 3000-year-old love story who meets its modern counterpart. Plenty of typical Lloyd chase sequences. (Dir: Elliott Nugent, 93 mins.)

Project: Kill (1977)*½ Leslie Nielsen, Gary Lockwood. A government man (Nielsen) in a CIA-like agency makes a mysterious exit and is hunted down by his ex-partner (Lockwood). Usual secret agent yarn. (Dir: William Girdler, 104 mins.)

Project M-7 (Great Britain, 1953)*** Phyllis Calvet, James Donald, Herbert Lom. At a secret research station, an inventor is designing a plane that will fly at fantastic speeds. One of his colleagues is a spy. Interesting melodrama; good aerial scenes. (Dir: Anthony Asquith, 79 mins.)

Project X (1968)* Christopher George, Greta Baldwin, Monte Markham, Henry Jones. (Dir: William Castle, 97 mins.)

Projectionist, The (1971)**** Chuck McCann, Ina Balin, Rodney Dangerfield. Wacky, appealing, low-budget winner written, directed, produced, and edited by Harry Hurwitz. McCann plays Captain Flash, with impersonations along the way of Bogart, Beery, and Oliver Hardy. The projectionist works in a movie house and has difficulty separating the real world from the movie world. (88 mins.)

Prom Night (1980)*½ Jamie Lee Curtis, Leslie Nielsen, Eddie Benton. (Dir: Paul Lynch, 91 mins.)

Promise, The (1978)** Kathleen Quinlan, Stephen Collins, Beatrice Straight. Clumsy, old-fashioned soap opera. Young Collins and Quinlan are in love, but his tough-minded businesswoman mother, Straight, objects. A convenient auto accident gives Straight the chance to tell her son that Quinlan is dead. They meet again, but he doesn't recognize her, since she's had plastic surgery. (Dir: Gilbert Cates, 97 mins.)

Promise Her Anything (Great Britain, 1966)**½ Warren Beatty, Lionel Stander, Robert Cummings, Hermione Gingold, Keenan Wynn, Leslie Caron. Pleasant romantic comedy set in New York's Greenwich Village, but shot in England. Beatty plays a destitute young filmmaker who sets out to woo and win a young widow (Caron). Beatty turns in a deft, charming performance, and Caron always a delight. (Dir: Arthur Hiller, 98 min..)

535

Promise Him Anything...(MTV 1975)* Frederic Forrest, Meg Foster, Eddie Albert, Tom Ewell. (Dir: Edward Parone, 74 mins.)

Promise of Love (MTV 1980)*½ Valerie Bertinelli. Bertinelli tackles a depressing role—a frightened 28-year-old Vietnam War widow, untrained for much of anything. What do you do with your life? Do you return home to caring parents? Earnest, and tedious. (Dir: Don Taylor, 104 mins.)

Promised Land, The (Chile, 1973)**½ Nelson Villagra, Marcelo Gaete, Rafael Benavente. Occasionally interesting political semidocumentary written and directed by the gifted Chilean filmmaker Miguel Littin. About the various ways in which the Chilean workers are degraded and kept in poverty. Some of the shooting began in rural Chile in 1972, but not finished as planned due to the overthrow of the Allende government. English subtitles. (120 mins.)

Promised Lands (France, 1974)*** A complex, flawed, sometimes maddening, always stimulating docudrama about the cauldron of the Middle East and Israel after the 1973 war. Conceived, written, and directed by Susan Sontag, film utilizes newsreel footage, contemporary interviews, and "cinema-verité" footage to form this impressionistic collage of the embattled lands. Some cogent arguments advanced for the Israeli position by novelist-painter Yoram Kaniuk, and there's some lacerating footage of shell-shocked soldiers being forced to relive the horrors of battle as a therapeutic treatment. (87 mins.)

Promises in the Dark (1979)**½ Kathleen Beller, Marsha Mason, Ned Beatty. A young girl (Beller) is helped to confront her dying of cancer by an understanding doctor (Mason). Good intentions almost carry it through, though the drama remains mired in the drive for a well-wrought story with rounded characters. (Dir: Jerome Hellman, 115 mins.)

Promoter, The (Great Britain, 1952)**** Alec Guinness, Valerie Hobson, Glynis Johns, Petula Clark. Guinness romps his way through the tale of a lad from the slums who pushes his way to success. Witty, always intelligent, always entertaining. (Dir: Ronald Neame, 88 mins.)

Prophecy (1979)** Talia Shire, Robert Foxworth, Armand Assante. Silly, slow-moving horror film directed by John Frankenheimer. The monster suggests an overgrown grizzly with a bad case of acne; the mise-en-scène suggests an inept home movie. (100 mins.)

Proud and the Beautiful (France, 1957)***½ Gérard Philipe, Michele Morgan. Her husband a victim of the plague in Mexico, a woman falls for and revitalizes a drunken doctor. Grim drama, well acted ɑɑd directed. (Dir: Yves Allegret, 94 mins.)

Proud and the Profane, The (1956)*** William Holden, Deborah Kerr, Thelma Ritter. War and soap opera, but well mixed to form a reasonably entertaining film. It's the story of a war widow who meets and falls for a tough marine colonel while serving in the Pacific during WW II. Good performances and superior treatment overcome the triteness of the yarn. (Dir: George Seaton, 111 mins.)

Proud Ones, The (1956)*** Robert Ryan, Virginia Mayo, Jeffrey Hunter. Good western bolstered by a better than average cast. The plot centers around a gun-toting marshal and the men who tried to balk the law. (Dir: Robert D. Webb, 94 mins.)

Proud Rebel, The (1958)***½ Alan Ladd, Olivia de Havilland, David Ladd (debut), Dean Jagger. Touching story of a Civil War veteran and his mute son who go to work for a farm woman as the father hopes to find a doctor who can cure the boy's affliction. Young David Ladd steals the show with a fine portrayal, while his father delivers one of his better performances. Superior family entertainment. (Dir: Michael Curtiz, 103 mins.)

Proud Stallion, The (Czechoslovakia, 1964)**½ Jorga Kotrobova, Rudolph Pruncha. Girl attempts to save a beautiful wild stallion, marked for death. Pleasant English-dubbed outdoor story, especially for the kiddies. (84 mins.)

Proud Valley, The (Great Britain, 1940)*** Paul Robeson, Edward Chapman, Simon Lack. Excellent semimusical about an American seaman who settles in a Welsh coal-mining town. The music ranges from Negro spirituals to "Elijah," sung by an expert Welsh choir and of course the great Robeson (in political exile). (Dir: Pen Tennyson, 76 mins.)

Providence (France-Great Britain-Switzerland, 1977)**½ John Gielgud, Ellen Burstyn, Dirk Bogarde. A dying British novelist (Gielgud) mentally composes a novel during a sleepless night. Gielgud writes and rewrites, using characters based on the members of his own family, sometimes getting the voices and structure confused. Director Alain Resnais's first film in English. (104 mins.)

Prowler, The (1951)***½ Van Heflin, Evelyn Keyes. Patrolman investigating a prowler falls for a disc jockey's wife, plans to do away with him. Strong, gripping melodrama, excellently acted. (Dir: Joseph Losey, 92 mins.)

Prudence and the Pill (Great Britain, 1968)* David Niven, Deborah Kerr, Keith Michell. (Dirs: Fielder Cook, Ronald Neame, 92 mins.)

Psych-Out (1968)*** Jack Nicholson, Susan Strasberg, Dean Stockwell, Bruce Dern, Henry Jaglom, Garry Marshall. Above average drama about Haight-Asbury hippie life (circa 1968) seen through the eyes of deaf Susan Strasberg, who arrives looking for her missing brother. Her adventures depict the world of the lost band experimenting with drugs and the supporting cast is pretty good all the way around. Flawed by a melodramatic ending. (Dir: Richard Rush, 89 mins.)

Psyche 59 (Great Britain, 1964)** Patricia Neal, Curt Jurgens, Samantha Eggar. Blind wife suspects there's something fishy between her husband and her sexy younger sister, and by golly, she's right. Lumbering drama seldom gets out of low gear. (Dir: Alexander Singer, 94 mins.)

Psychiatrist: God Bless the Children, The (MTV 1970)**½ Roy Thinnes, Pete Duel, Barry Brown, Luther Adler. Roy Thinnes stars as a psychiatrist who really cares about his patients. This movie belongs to Duel, playing an uptight ex-junkie with a mad-on for the whole world. Duel's complex character is interesting, and his performance is effective. Duel and Thinnes, patient and doctor, respectively, join forces to combat the growing drug abuse in a small California community. One scene in which Duel confronts the leader of the kids (well played by John Rubinstein) and gets verbally shot down is the film's best. (Dir: Daryl Duke, 98 mins.)

Psychic, The (Italy, 1979)* Jennifer O'Neill, Marc Porel, Evelyn Stewart. Gabriele Ferzetti. (Dir: Lucio Fulci, 89 mins.)

Psychic Killer (1975)* Jim Hutton, Julie Adams, Paul Burke. (Dir: Ray Danton, 90 mins.)

Psycho (1960)**** Anthony Perkins, Janet Leigh, Martin Balsam, Vera Miles, John Gavin. Here Alfred Hitchcock has directed the most profound achievement in the macabre mode, in any of the arts. Perkins appears to be protecting his mother in the murders of a young woman embezzler and a private detective hired to find her. (109 mins.)

Psychomania (1963)*½ Lee Philips, Shepperd Strudwick, Dick Van Patten, Sylvia Miles, James Farentino. (Dir: Richard Hilliard, 92 mins.)

Psychopath, The (Great Britain, 1966)** Patrick Wymark, Margaret Johnston. Serves up all the expected bloody ingredients to satisfy chiller fans. Competent British cast goes through the paces in this tale about multiple murder and a strange German household. (Dir: Freddie Francis, 83 mins.)

PT 109 (1963)**½ Cliff Robertson, Ty Hardin, Robert Culp. The story of John F. Kennedy, naval hero of WW II, and his exploits in the Pacific. Minus the subject of the narrative, this would be a routine war story. Robertson does well in the role. (Dir: Leslie Martinson, 140 mins.)

Public Affair, A (1962)*** Myron McCormick, Edward Binns. Don't overlook this little story of a state senator battling, with legal means, a crime syndicate. Rather straitlaced and leisurely, with the low budget showing through, but done with a sincerity that deserves commendation. (Dir: Bernard Girard, 75 mins.)

Public Enemy, The (1931)***½ James Cagney, Jean Harlow, Joan Blondell, Beryl Mercer, Eddie Woods, Donald Cook, Mae Clarke. Cagney explodes onscreen with his kinetic Irish gangster. Rough stuff, with ragged direction by William A. Wellman. (84 mins.)

Public Eye, The (Great Britain, 1972)*½ Mia Farrow, Topol, Michael Jayston. (Dir: Carol Reed, 95 mins.)

Public Hero No. 1 (1935)*** Lionel Barrymore, Jean Arthur, Chester Morris. Exciting, occasionally amusing drama of the destruction of a gang of outlaws by the then movie favorites, the G-men. Best part of the picture is Joseph Calleia as the gangster. (Dir: J. Walter Rubin, 91 mins.)

Public Pigeon No. 1 (1956)** Red Skelton, Vivian Blaine, Janet Blair. Lunchroom counter man is taken in by a gang of crooks, but he turns the tables on them. Mild little comedy based on a TV show Skelton did; below average. (Dir: Norman Z. McLeod, 79 mins.)

Pueblo (MTV 1973)***½ Hal Holbrook. Absorbing dramatization of the seizure in 1968 by the North Koreans of the U.S.S. "Pueblo," an American naval vessel equipped with sophisticated electronic devices used in spying missions. Holbrook as Commander Bucher creates a whole human being out of his character, and his performance serves as the core of this literate drama. (Dir: Anthony Page, 108 mins.)

Pulp (Great Britain, 1972)*** Michael Caine, Mickey Rooney, Lionel Stander, Lizabeth Scott. Caine is a writer of pulp thrillers who finds that life tends to imitate "art" when he is hired to ghost the memoirs of a retired gangster movie star (Rooney). Good script, nice performances by Stander and Scott (doing a Lauren Bacall number), and crisp direction by Michael Hodges. (95 mins.)

Pumping Iron (1977)**** Arnold Schwarzenegger, Louis Ferrigno, Mike Katz, Franco Columbu. A fascinating, surprisingly engaging documentary about world-champion body-builders. One of the many strengths is that the directors, George Butler and Robert Fiore, have avoided the considerable temptation of making body-building and those dedicated to it seem altogether grotesque. World champion Schwarzenegger has not only a magnificent body but a charming, sardonic sense of humor. Graphically shows the demanding, tortuous, constant weightlifting regimen required of world champions in this sport. (85 mins.)

Pumpkin Eater, The (Great Britain, 1964)***½ Anne Bancroft, Peter Finch, James Mason. Absorbing, brilliantly acted story of a woman's personal insecurity and her crumbling marriage. Famed playwright Harold Pinter has written a stinging, perceptive screenplay based on the novel by Penelope Mortimer. Bancroft contributes a performance of dazzling range and power. Finch's portrayal of her errant husband is equally impressive in a less volatile fashion, and there's a devastating scene in a beauty parlor with an actress named Yootha Joyce. (110 mins.)

Punch and Jody (MTV 1974)** Glenn Ford, Ruth Roman, Pam Griffin. Sentiment is piled on with a trowel. Glenn Ford is a self-made, small-time circus boss who is suddenly made the guardian of a teenaged daughter he didn't know existed. (Dir: Barry Shear, 74 mins.)

Punishment Battalion (Germany, 1960)**½ Werner Peters, Georg Thomas. Doctor is banished to a battalion comprised of officers fallen from favor, experiences bloody battles at the Russian border. Grim WW II drama has some effective scenes, ably produced. Dubbed in English. (Dir: Harold Philipp, 90 mins.)

Punishment Park (1971)**½ Jim Bohan, Van Daniels, Harlan Greene. A maddeningly uneven, prescient drama about dissidents and the American political landscape. Written and directed by Peter Watkins, who misunderstands a great deal about democracy and the political passions of American youth when confronted with a neo-fascist government. Some of the film is simple-minded drivel, parts are chilling indeed. (88 mins.)

Puppet on a Chain (Great Britain, 1970)** Sven-Bertil Taube, Barbara Parkins, Alexander Knox. Routine international smuggling entry, with Swedish actor Taube playing an American narcotics agent tracking down his prey in Amsterdam. Aided by exciting speedboat chase through the canals of glorious Amsterdam, which ends with a larcenous, murderous priest crashing into an impenetrable stone wall. Many shots of beautiful Amsterdam throughout this meller. (Dir: Geoffrey Reeve, 97 mins.)

Pure Hell of St. Trinian's, The (Great Britain, 1960)**½ Joyce Grenfell, Cecil Parker, George Cole. Girls' school full of mischievous lovelies receives a visit from an Eastern potentate with an eye out for harem wives. Free-wheeling nonsensical farce in this series churns up some laughs through its sheer wildness. (Dir: Frank Launder, 94 mins.)

Purple Gang, The (1959)** Barry Sullivan, Robert Blake. Average cops and gangsters yarn. Barry Sullivan represents the law and a group, known as the Purples, make his job a tough one. Robert Blake is very effective as a young hood with a taste for killing. (Dir: Frank McDonald, 85 mins.)

Purple Heart, The (1944)*** Dana Andrews, Richard Conte, Farley Granger, Sam Levene, Richard Loo. Powerful, brutal story of the trial of the crew of a flying fortress shot down by the Japanese during the Tokyo raid. (Dir: Lewis Milestone, 99 mins.)

Purple Hills, The (1961)** Gene Nelson, Kent Taylor, Joanna Barnes. Arizona cowboy kills an outlaw, but a gambler also puts in a claim for the reward; both are menaced by Indians friendly to the outlaw. Minor western just about gets by. (Dir: Maury Dexter, 60 mins.)

Purple Mask, The (1955)**½ Tony Curtis, Coleen Miller, Gene Barry, Angela Lansbury. Tony Curtis is cast in an Errol Flynn-type role as a count who puts on "the Purple Mask" and performs acts of derring-do which have Napoleon baffled. High adventure with some fun. (Dir: H. Bruce Humberstone, 82 mins.)

Purple Noon (France, 1960)***½ Alain Delon, Maurice Ronet, Marie Laforet. Director René Clement has fashioned a tightly paced mystery with an excellent performance by Delon as a fun-loving loafer who gets into an almost unbelievable situation involving a forgery, murder and impersonations. (115 mins.)

Purple Plain, The (Great Britain, 1954)*** Gregory Peck, Brenda De Banzie, Bernard Lee. A flier crashes in the jungle, fights his way back to civilization. Good suspense story, a bit overlong, but well-acted by hero Peck. (Dir: Robert Parrish, 100 mins.)

Pursued (1947)*** Robert Mitchum, Teresa Wright, Judith Anderson, Dean Jagger. Spanish-American War vet seeks the man who killed his father years ago in a family feud. Offbeat western has a different story, good performances. (Dir: Raoul Walsh, 101 mins.)

Pursuers, The (Great Britain, 1961)*½ Cyril Shaps, Francis Matthews. Manhunt is on for a foreign agent. Below-par melodramatics. (Dir: Godfrey Grayson, 63 mins.)

Pursuit (MTV 1972)*** Ben Gazzara, E. G. Marshall, Martin Sheen. Suspenseful thriller based on a novel by Michael Crichton (under the pen name of John Lange). Crichton also makes his directorial debut, and he gets tension out of his tale. About a wealthy leader of an extremist group who plans to destroy a large number of people in a major city (San Diego) via lethal nerve gas. There's a revealing scene in which Gazzara has lunch with his psychiatrist, and the climax of the yarn will have your palms sweating. (73 mins.)

Pursuit Across the Desert (Mexico, 1960)*½ Pedro Armendariz, Tere Velasquez. (Dir: Gilberto Gazcon, 75 mins.)

Pursuit of Happiness, The (1971)**½ Michael Sarrazin, Barbara Hershey, Arthur Hill, E. G. Marshall, Ruth White. Decent tale of a young man who accidentally runs over a jaywalker and, because of his rebellious attitude, faces long imprisonment. Sympathetic attempt to explain why a youth, with so many advantages, goes wrong. White's last film. (Dir: Robert Mulligan, 93 mins.)

Pursuit of the Graf Spee (Great Britain, 1956)*** John Gregson, Anthony Quayle, Peter Finch. True story of the German ship, and its scuttling off South America.

Excellently produced war tale, good factual material. (Dirs: Michael Powell, Emeric Pressburger, 106 mins.)

Pushover (1954)***½ Kim Novak, Fred MacMurray, Dorothy Malone, E. G. Marshall. Pretty good drama about a cop who is seduced into neglecting his duty by a blonde man-trap (Kim Novak). Kim Novak registered in this, her first major film assignment. Her lousy performances come later when she's richer and more famous. (Dir: Richard Quine, 88 mins.)

Putney Swope (1969)***½ Allen Garfield, Alan Abel, Mel Brooks. An irreverent, manic, sometimes hysterically funny satire of various American sacred cows. Some wild put-downs and take-offs of TV commercials, scattered throughout this genuinely hip fable about the rise of a black Madison Ave. advertising agency called Truth and Soul. Not for every taste, but this remains one of the most daring American comedies of the period. Credit due to the writer-director, Robert Downey. (84 mins.)

Puzzle of a Downfall Child (1971)* Faye Dunaway, Barry Primus, Viveca Lindfors, Barry Morse, Roy Scheider. (104 mins.)

Pygmalion (Great Britain, 1938)***½ Leslie Howard, Wendy Hiller, Scott Sunderland, Wilfrid Lawson, Marie Lohr, David Tree, Esmé Percy. This adaptation of the George Bernard Shaw play represents classical British cinema at its best—would it were better! Sterling performances by Howard (Henry Higgins), Hiller (Eliza), and Lawson (Doolittle). Shaw liked the movie, even with the altered ending. (Dirs: Anthony Asquith, Leslie Howard, 96 mins.)

Pyro (1963)** Barry Sullivan, Martha Hyer. Badly burned engineer vows vengeance upon the woman who jealously started the blaze in which his family perished. Grim melodrama made in Spain moves leisurely but does a fair job of keeping the attention. (Dir: Julio Coll, 93 mins.)

Q Planes (Great Britain, 1939)***½ Laurence Olivier, Ralph Richardson, Valerie Hobson. Spies are lurking around Britain's aircraft, but they are foiled by a young test pilot and a crafty Scotland Yard man. Good thriller, with Richardson's policeman's role being delightfully acted. (Dir: Tim Whelan, 78 mins.)

QB VII (Part I) (MTV 1974)*** Ben Gazzara, Anthony Hopkins, Leslie Caron, Lee Remick. Leon Uris's best-seller becomes one of the most ambitious films ever produced for TV; it's nearly six hours long. Filmed on location in Israel, England, Belgium, and the U.S., it tells the story of a knighted Polish expatriate, Dr. Adam Kelno, living in England, and the libel suit he initiated against an American writer for accusing the doctor in his book of performing criminal medical practices in a concentration camp during WW II. In part I, Dr. Kelno's life from the close of the war to the present unfolds in fascinating flashbacks, centering particularly on the years he spent in Kuwait administering medical aid to the Arabs. Hopkins is absolutely superb as Kelno, and it is his portrayal of a difficult role which commands your attention. (Dir: Tom Gries.)

QB VII (Part II) (MTV 1974)*** Although the second half bogs down a little, concentrating on the post-WW II life of the author Abe Cady (Ben Gazzara), it leads to his father's death in the Holy Land, and triggers his interest in the struggle of the Jewish people and the writing of his major novel. The novel, of course, is the impetus for Dr. Kelno's libel suit, and the ensuing courtroom scenes pick up the act considerably. Anthony Hopkins's final scenes in court, with Anthony Quayle matching him as Cady's lawyer, are shattering as the accuser turns accused. (Dir: Tom Gries, 312 mins., complete.)

Quackser Fortune Has a Cousin in the Bronx (1970)**½ Gene Wilder, Margot Kidder. A comedy-drama of easygoing charm, personified in the central character of a free spirit named Quackser Fortune who prefers being a dung collector to joining the sweating masses. His relationship with an American girl attending college in Dublin gives the film a sweetness that adds to its appeal. Wilder and Kidder are wonderful and the on-location photography is good. (Dir: Waris Hussein, 90 mins.)

Quadrophenia (Great Britain, 1979)***½ Phil Daniels, Mark Wingett, Philip Davis, Leslie Ash. Director Franc Roddam's film of the Who's rock opera is an extravagant, involving teen pic with a responsible intellectual grounding. The hero, a jumpy young mod played with commanding intensity by Daniels, achieves a moment of perfect bliss and then self-destructs, in a sentiment straight out of the 19th-century fiction. The fine score of the Who is mixed with period pieces for a firmly underpinned musical subtext. (115 mins.)

Quality Street (1937)*** Katharine Hepburn, Franchot Tone, Fay Bainter. Costume romance showcases Hepburn; Tone, her sweetheart, goes off to the Napolenic wars and fails to recognize her upon his return, so she masquerades as her niece to win him back. Not nearly as arch as the James Barrie play could have been; director George Stevens keeps it mostly in check. The perils were so great and so largely avoided that it is an achievement of sorts. (84 mins.)

Quantez (1957)** Fred MacMurray, Dorothy Malone, Sydney Chaplin, John Gavin. Four men and a woman escape a posse after a bank robbery, hole up in a deserted Mexican town, where their emotions get the better of them. Western depends too much on conversation, slows down the pace. (Dir: Harry Keller, 80 mins.)

Quarantined (MTV 1970)**½ John Dehner, Gary Collins, Sharon Farrell. Pilot for a proposed medical series. John Dehner is the head of a family of doctors (three sons and a psychiatrist daughter-in-law) who run a modern clinic atop a hill near the sea. Just for the record, during the course of the film, there's a threatened cholera epidemic. (Dir: Leo Penn, 73 mins.)

Quare Fellow, The (Great Britain-Ireland, 1962)*** Patrick McGoohan, Sylvia Syms, Walter Macken. A biting, intense prison drama, also packed with the Irish humor which characterized Brendan Behan's original play. Eloquent argument against capital punishment, on emotional rather than intellectual terms. Well acted. "Quare fellow" is Irish jargon for a condemned man. Written and directed by Arthur Dreifuss. (85 mins.)

Quartermass Experiment, The—See: *Creeping Unknown, The*

Quartet (Great Britain, 1948)***½ Dirk Bogarde, Françoise Rosay, Honor Blackman, Cecil Parker, Mai Zetterling. The most satisfying of the Somerset Maugham anthologies. Of the four tales, the opening and closing adaptations by R. C. Sheriff are models of British hackwork at its most civilized and intelligent. (Dirs: Ken Annakin, Ralph Smart, Harold French, Arthur Crabtree, 120 mins.)

Quebec (1951)** Corinne Calvert, Patric Knowles, John Barrymore, Jr., Barbara Rush. When the Canadians rebel against England, fighting for freedom is the wife of the British forces' commander. Corny tale partially atoned for by spectacular battle scenes, plenty of action. (Dir: George Templeton, 85 mins.)

Queen, The (1968)**** Harlow, Jack Doroshow, Andy Warhol, Terry Southern. A remarkable and tasteful documentary about one aspect of the subculture of American male homosexuals. The title refers to the winner of a beauty pageant for transvestites. This prizewinner, directed by Frank Simon, does not mock the hapless souls involved in the proceedings, or treat this beauty contest as a freak show. (68 mins.)

Queen Bee (1955)**½ Joan Crawford, Barry Sullivan, Betsy Palmer, John Ireland, Fay Wray. Joan Crawford, in Dixie dress, chewing up the scenery. A knock-'em-down star turn; Ranald MacDougall writes and directs, far too extremely. (95 mins.)

Queen Christina (1933)*** Greta Garbo, John Gilbert, Ian Keith, Lewis Stone, C. Aubrey Smith. Garbo plays the sexually ambiguous 17th-century Swedish monarch who cast aside the throne to marry her lover, Gilbert—a transparently bad deal. The considerable mythic force of Garbo's personality is given full rein: in the long closing close-up, the play of emotions on her face is as subtle as the viewer's imag-

ination, since director Rouben Mamoulian told her to think of nothing at all—it's eloquent blankness. (101 mins.)

Queen for a Day (1951)*** Phyllis Avery, Adam Williams, Edith Meiser, Darren McGavin. Stories of the contestants of the radio show are presented, some comic, some dramatic. Generally well-done episodic film. (Dir: Arthur Lubin, 107 mins.)

Queen for Caesar, A (France, 1962)**½ Pascale Petit, Gordon Scott, Akim Tamiroff. Another Cleopatra tale as the beauteous princess challenges her brother for the throne. The alluring Miss Petit and some good production values rate this historical drama slightly better than the usual. Dubbed in English. (Dir: Victor Tourjansky, 95 mins.)

Queen of Babylon, The (Italy, 1956)* Rhonda Fleming, Ricardo Montalban. (Dir: Carlo Bragaglia, 98 mins.)

Queen of Outer Space (1958)** Zsa Zsa Gabor, Eric Fleming. Ridiculous outer space yarn. A group of women rule a planet without men. Then a spaceship arrives and the all-male crew are held prisoner. Naturally Zsa Zsa can't stand to see them destroyed. Color. (Dir: Edward Bernds, 80 mins.)

Queen of Sheba, The (Italy, 1953)*½ Gino Cervi, Leonora Ruffo. (Dir: Pietro Francisci, 103 mins.)

Queen of Spades, The (Great Britain, 1948)*** Anton Walbrook, Edith Evans, Ronald Howard. Bizarrely overmounted adaptation of the Pushkin story about a Russian officer who is obsessed with learning the secret of winning at cards. The macabre quality comes on strong, but the civilized restraint of Walbrook as the officer speaks volumes with the dryest of means. (Dir: Thorold Dickenson, 96 mins.)

Queen of the Nile (Italy, 1962)** Jeanne Crain, Edmund Purdom, Vincent Price. Nefertiti's daughter is loved by a young sculptor who escapes execution and fights for her. Dubbed-English costume drama is a bit more logical than most. (Dir: Fernando Cerchio, 85 mins.)

Queen of the Seas (Italy, 1961)*½ Lisa Gastoni, Jerome Courtland. (Dir: Umberto Lenzi, 87 mins.)

Queen of the Stardust Ballroom (MTV 1975)***½ Maureen Stapleton, Charles Durning, Michael Brandon, Michael Strong. Maureen Stapleton's lonely widow with grownup kids, meeting and falling in love with Charles Durning's shy, beer-barrel postman, évokes moments of warmth and sympathy. The over-the-hill couple have much to offer, and their moments together, dancing old '30s steps in a ballroom jammed with lively, wrinkled peers, simply lift one's spirits. Early scenes miss the beat, particularly the use of a song sung by Stapleton, but the bravura performances overshadow any flaws. (Dir: Sam O'Steen, 100 mins.)

Queen's Guards, The (Great Britain, 1961)** Raymond Massey, Robert Stephens, Daniel Massey. Story of the training and hard work that go into the making of an honored group of soldiers. Meticulous detail concerning aspects of soldier life slows up the pace too much. (Dir: Michael Powell, 110 mins.)

Quentin Durward (Great Britain, 1955)*** Robert Taylor, Kay Kendall, Robert Morley. If you're a devotee of costume spectacles, this is better than most. We have the requisite brave adventurer (Taylor) protecting the fair maiden (Kendall—and very fair she is too) from political intrigue. Exciting action scenes. From the novel by Sir Walter Scott (Dir: Richard Thorpe, 101 mins.)

Quest (MTV 1976)**½ Tim Matheson, Kurt Russell, Brian Keith, Keenan Wynn. Surprise—an enjoyable western TV-series pilot with a feeling for those rowdy, freewheeling frontier times. Tracy Keenan Wynn, a careful writer, takes a shot at authenticity in this leisurely tale of brothers separated after an Indian raid—one a city boy training to be a doctor, and the other raised by Indians. As played by Matheson and Russell, the brothers are overshadowed by Brian Keith's Tank Logan, journeyman of the West—cattle thief, gunslinger, con artist, lover of language. (Dir: Lee H. Katzin, 98 mins.)

Question of Adultery, A—See: **Case of Mrs. Loring, The**

Quest for Love (Great Britain, 1971)*** Tom Bell, Joan Collins, Denholm Elliott. Not a love story but a strange, gentle science fiction flick, from a short story by John Wyndham. A physicist, after an accident at his lab, finds himself in a parallel world. Unusual, interesting plot. The acting is excellent: even Collins is good! (Dir: Ralph Thomas, 91 mins.)

Question of Guilt, A (MTV 1978)*½ Tuesday Weld, Ron Liebman, Alex Rocco. Stars the talented Weld in a depressing character assassination drama about a murder chase that's rigged by the police: witnesses are pressured to lie because the suspect is a loose woman. (Dir: Robert Butler, 104 mins.)

Question of Love, A (MTV 1978)*** Gena Rowlands, Jane Alexander, Ned Beatty. Thoughtful, sensitive drama based on a real-life child custody trial opposing a lesbian mother to her ex-husband. Rowlands and Alexander do well as the women who have combined their families and moved in together. The script presents a balanced picture of the proceedings. (Dir: Jerry Thorpe, 104 mins.)

Questor Tapes, The (MTV 1974)***½ Robert Foxworth, Mike Farrell, Dana Wynter, Lew Ayres, John Vernon. Probably the best science-fiction ever made for television. Original, suspenseful, funny and involving. While engaged on a massive project to build an android (a robot with human characteristics), a famous scien-

tist disappears. The creature soon goes after him. Taut script, fine performances, especially Foxworth as the robot. (Dir: Richard A. Colla, 100 mins.)

Quick and the Dead, The (1964)** Larry Mann, Sandy Donigan, Victor French. American patrol is captured but manages to escape. WW II drama made on an infinitesimal budget shows value for the dollar, but it's still just another war picture. (Dir: Robert Totten, 92 mins.)

Quick, Before It Melts (1965)** Robert Morse, George Maharis, Anjanette Comer, Norman Fell. A silly comedy which doesn't come to life, despite some energetic playing by Robert Morse and Michael Constantine in a supporting role as a Russian. Morse and Maharis are a writer and photographer, respectively, who invade a military installation, Little America, and almost cause an international scandal. (Dir: Delbert Mann, 98 mins.)

Quick Gun, The (1964)* Audie Murphy, Merry Anders, James Best. (Dir: Sidney Salkow, 87 mins.)

Quicksand (1950)**½ Mickey Rooney, Jean Cagney, Peter Lorre. A young man "borrows" twenty bucks from a cash register, intending to pay it back, but circumstances pile up to the point where his life is at stake. Neat little melodrama has suspense, a subdued Rooney. (Dir: Irving Pichel, 79 mins.)

Quiet American, The (1958)*** Audie Murphy, Michael Redgrave, Claude Dauphin, Gloria Moll. Graham Greene's angry novel comes to the screen a bit watered down in its approach towards Americans. Audie Murphy is miscast as the hero but a good supporting cast makes up for it. (Dir: Joseph L. Mankiewicz, 120 mins.)

Quiet Man, The (1952)**** John Wayne, Maureen O'Hara, Victor McLaglen, Barry Fitzgerald, Mildred Natwick, Ward Bond, Arthur Shields. Director John Ford's Oscar winner is a tribute to an Ireland that exists in the imaginations of songwriters and poets, a fairy-green place where people say "faith and begorrah." John Wayne is an Irish-American boxer who returns to his native village to claim the family homestead and win the heart and hand (and dowry) of the local beauty (O'Hara) by winning over (and ultimately pommeling into senselessness) her harddrinking brother, McLaglen. Marvelous cast includes Fitzgerald as Wayne's pixieish helper. From the story by Maurice Walsh. (129 mins.)

Quiet Wedding (Great Britain, 1941)** Margaret Lockwood, Derek Farr. Zany comedy about a wedding that turns into a fracas. Lovely fun despite the excess talk. (Dir: Anthony Asquith, 63 mins.)

Quiet Woman, The (Great Britain, 1951)*** Derek Bond, Jane Hylton, Dora Bryan, Dianne Foster. The owner of a seaside pub has her secret revealed when her

541

jailbird husband returns. Good melodrama. (Dir: John Gilling, 69 mins.)

Quiller Memorandum, The (U.S.-Great Britain, 1966)**½ George Segal, Alec Guinness, Max von Sydow, Senta Berger. This uneven spy-drama will appeal to fans of espionage yarns who don't look to be surprised, just entertained. Segal is an American agent in Berlin looking for the head of a neo-Nazi party that is gaining momentum in present-day Germany. There is the usual quota of heavies plus the expected beautiful girl who tangles with our agent. Screenplay by Harold Pinter based on the novel "The Berlin Memorandum" by Adam Hall. (Dir: Michael Anderson, 105 mins.)

Quincannon, Frontier Scout (1956)** Tony Martin, Peggie Castle, John Bromfield. Tony Martin as a cowboy. He seems very uncomfortable not being in a tux in front of a nightclub audience singing Neapolitan songs. Some lively action in this grade B western. (Dir: Lesley Selander, 83 mins.)

Quinns, The (MTV 1977)**½ Barry Bostwick, Susan Browning, Geraldine Fitzgerald. Pilot film about four generations of an Irish clan who work for the New York City Fire Department. Broadway-trained cast is led by Tony award-winner Bostwick, veteran Fitzgerald, and talented Browning—not to mention the Fire Department. (Dir: Daniel Petrie, 78 mins.)

Quo Vadis? (Italy, 1912)*** This may or may not be the first feature-length film. Lavishly produced (for its time). (Dir: Enrico Guazzoni, 80 mins.)

Quo Vadis (1951)***½ Robert Taylor, Deborah Kerr, Leo Genn, Peter Ustinov, Finlay Currie, Abraham Sofaer. A really big one—the Christians are persecuted, Rome burns, Taylor loves Kerr, and just about everything else happens in this splashy spectacle. Some weak moments, notably in the script, but some fine ones too, notably from Ustinov. Lavish throughout. (Dir: Mervyn Le Roy, 171 mins.)

Ra Expeditions, The (1974)***½ Engrossing documentary record of anthropologist Thor Heyerdahl's two ocean voyages aboard a small papyrus boat. Because he was fascinated by the similarity between Egyptian and Latin American pyramids, Heyerdahl set out to prove that pre-Columbian people were capable of crossing the Atlantic. So he sailed with a small crew of experts in a paper boat, identical to those of ancient times. The crew contends with the perils of the high seas—hurricanes, sharks, sickness and mechanical failures. Narrated by Roscoe Lee Browne with comments from Heyerdahl. (Dir: Lennart Ehrenborg, 93 mins.)

Rabbit, Run (1970)**½ James Caan, Jack Albertson, Arthur Hill, Carrie Snodgrass,

Anjanette Comer. John Updike's novel rather faithfully brought to the screen. Scene showing a drunk young wife drowning her baby in the bathwater won't please the "Love Story" crowd. But Caan is well cast and although the film is unsuccessful, it has some effective emotional high points. (Dir: Jack Smight, 94 mins.)

Rabbit Test (1978)* Billy Crystal, Joan Prather, Alex Rocco. (Dir: Joan Rivers, 84 mins.)

Rabbit Trap, The (1959)** Ernest Borgnine, Bethel Leslie, David Brian. Draftsman dominated by his job and boss is called back from a vacation, which proves to change his life. Based on a TV play, this sluggish little drama hoped to be another "Marty" but missed the mark. Mild, at best. (Dir: Philip Leacock, 72 mins.)

Rabid (Canada, 1977)** Marilyn Chambers, Frank Moore, Joe Silver. In this aggressive little horror movie, porn queen Chambers contracts a complicated case of rabies when she wakes up from a skin-graft operation. One of the side effects is a strange compulsion to stick people with a curious fanged phallus that she's grown under her armpit. David Cronenberg directs, with more enthusiasm than skill. (91 mins.)

Race d'Ep (France, 1980)** Chronicle of the last 100 years of gay life, in four segments, about a pornographic photographer (1900); a woman assistant to a German sex researcher ('30s); a 16-year-old liberated gay ('60s); and an American husband exposed to French homosexual love ('80s).

Race for Your Life, Charlie Brown (1977)** Better production values than in the specials made for TV. The "Peanuts" gang are away at summer camp, and young kids will enjoy the climactic river race. (Dir: Bill Melendez, 75 mins.)

Race with the Devil (1975)** Peter Fonda, Warren Oates, Loretta Swit, Lara Parker. A dumb chase melodrama. Oates and Fonda, out for a pleasant excursion in their sumptuous camper, find witchcraft and murder in the unlikeliest Texas towns. Jack Starrett directs an ersatz vehicle that holds the attention until cheap thrills prevail. (88 mins.)

Racers, The (1955)** Kirk Douglas, Gilbert Roland, Bella Darvi, Cesar Romero, Lee J. Cobb. The only redeeming feature of this film is the sports car racing sequences and they have a limited appeal even to fans. The drama is contrived and woven out of the conflicts, both professional and personal, among the breed who thrive in the European sports car racing world. (Dir: Henry Hathaway, 112 mins.)

Rachel and the Stranger (1948)*** Loretta Young, William Holden, Robert Mitchum. Frontier wanderer stops at the cabin of a backwoodsman and wife and settles their problems. Entertaining frontier comedy-drama. (Dir: Norman Foster, 93 mins.)

Rachel, Rachel (1968)**** Joanne Woodward, James Olson, Estelle Parsons, Geraldine Fitzgerald. A beautiful, deeply moving story of a young spinster, thanks largely to a superb screenplay by Stewart Stern and contributions from various members of the Newman family, including producer-director Paul. Woodward gives a restrained, poignant portrayal of the lonely, sexually inhibited schoolteacher living in a small town in Connecticut. (The Newmans' daughter lends a hand by acting Rachel as a child in the various flashback sequences.) Plaudits also to Parsons as Rachel's equally frustrated fellow-schoolmarm. One of the loveliest American films in years. (101 mins.)

Racing Blood (1954)** Bill Williams, Jean Porter, Jimmy Boyd (debut). Colt born with a split hoof is supposed to be destroyed, but a stable boy and his uncle make him a winner. Usual turf story, pleasant in a familiar sort of way. If you have a split hoof in the family, take heart. (Dir: Wesley Barry, 76 mins.)

Racing Fever (1964)* Joe Morrison, Barbara Biggart. (Dir: William Grefe, 90 mins.)

Rack, The (1956)*** Paul Newman, Wendell Corey, Edmond O'Brien, Anne Francis, Walter Pidgeon. A war hero returns from a Korean prison camp and faces trial for treason. Well-acted courtroom drama grips the attention throughout. (Dir: Arnold Laven, 100 mins.)

Racket, The (1951)*** Robert Mitchum, Lizabeth Scott, Robert Ryan. Police captain opposes a big racketeer who stops at nothing. Nicely produced, exciting crime melodrama. (Dir: John Cromwell, 88 mins.)

Racket Busters (1938)** George Brent, Hymphrey Bogart, Penny Singleton. Bogart moves in on the trucking industry, meets opposition from Brent. (Dir: Lloyd Bacon, 71 mins.)

Racket Man, The (1944)**½ Tom Neal, Larry Parks, Hugh Beaumont. Racketeer reformed by the army becomes an undercover agent after black marketeers. Lively, well done action melodrama. (Dir: D. Ross Lederman, 65 mins.)

Rafferty and the Gold Dust Twins—See: Rafferty and the Highway Hustlers

Rafferty and the Highway Hustlers (1975)**½ Sally Kellerman, Mackenzie Phillips, Alan Arkin. Released as "Rafferty and the Gold Dust Twins," but given a more provocative title for TV. Familiar tale about a couple of footloose and fancy-free (and larcenous) females who get men to give them rides at gunpoint. The pair is made up of Kellerman, who wants to be a singer, and Phillips, as a teenage runaway. Their victim is Arkin, playing a not-too-bright driving test inspector. Their escapades en route from Los Angeles to Arizona provide some laughs but the whole thing soon fizzles out. (Dir: Dick Richards, 91 mins.)

Raffles (1939)** Olivia de Havilland, David Niven. Weakly done film about the adventures of an amateur cracksman thief. Primarily a straight drama with obtrusive comedy overtones creeping in every now and then. (Dir: Sam Wood, 72 mins.)

Rage (1966)* Glenn Ford, Stella Stevens. (Dir: Gilberto Gazcon, 103 mins.)

Rage (1972)*½ George C. Scott, Richard Basehart, Martin Sheen. (Dir: George C. Scott, 105 mins.)

Rage in Heaven (1941)** George Sanders, Robert Montgomery, Ingrid Bergman, Lucile Watson, Oscar Homolka, Philip Merivale. Strange, grim mystery about the final dissolution of a psychotic and its effect on his unsuspecting family. Complex, unusual plot, remarkable performance by Montgomery. The denouement is almost too tense. Sanders gets to play a good guy for once. Script by Christopher Isherwood, which sheds new light on the main characters. (Dir: W. S. Van Dyke, II, 83 mins.)

Rage of Paris, The (1938)**½ Danielle Darrieux, Douglas Fairbanks, Jr., Louis Hayward. Frothy comedy about a Parisian girl who sensibly campaigns vigorously to snare a wealthy husband but succumbs to true love. Dated but well played. (Dir: Henry Koster, 78 mins.)

Rage to Live, A (1965)*½ Suzanne Pleshette, Bradford Dillman, Ben Gazzara, Bethel Leslie. (Dir: Walter Grauman, 101 mins.)

Raggedy Ann and Andy (1977)*** Claire Williams. This full-length animated version of the classic children's book by Johnny Gruelle published more than half a century ago contains some superb animated sequences, in this musical adaptation supervised and directed by English animation wizard Richard Williams. The screenwriters—Patricia Thackray and author-TV comedy writer Ray Wilk—have fashioned a plot of sorts: Babette the French doll is captured by pirates and Raggedy Ann and Andy set out to rescue her. (Dir: Richard Williams, 84 mins.)

Raging Bull (1980)**** Robert De Niro, Cathy Moriarty, Joe Pesci, Frank Vincent, Nicholas Colasanto. Film biography of middleweight champion Jake La Motta concentrates on his personal battles. Dynamically detailed performances from De Niro, Pesci, and Colasanto. B&W. (Dir: Martin Scorsese, 128 mins.)

Raging Tide, The (1951)** Richard Conte, Shelley Winters, Stephen McNally, Charles Bickford, Alex Nicol. Predictable crime melodrama which talks itself to death. Conte plays a murderer on the run who learns too late the value of honesty. Miss Winters drifts in and out of the film as Conte's moll. (Dir: George Sherman, 93 mins.)

Raices de Sangre (1979)**½ Popular success produced in the U.S. for the Chicano market here and Latin audiences abroad. Uses the theme of "Norma Rae" to depict the working conditions in textile factories with Chicano and Mexican employees. (Dir: Jesus Trevino.)

Raid, The (1954)**½ Van Heflin, Anne Bancroft, Richard Boone. Interesting and well made western set after the Civil War. A small group of Confederate soldiers escape from a Union prison and plan the burning and sacking of a small Vermont town as partial payment for the destruction of Atlanta. Heflin is very good as the leader of the prisoners. (Dir: Hugo Fregonese, 83 mins.)

Raid on Entebbe (MTV 1976)***½ Peter Finch, Martin Balsam, Horst Bucholz, Jack Warden, Yaphet Kotto, Charles Bronson. Made as a hurried special in the race to be the first drama on the American TV screens to dramatize the heroic rescue at Entebbe by Israeli commandos. Still, a quite accurate and dramatic recount. Starts with the capture of a French plane by four terrorists and follows through to the rescue one week later. Commendably directed by Irving Kershner, considering the time restraints. (118 mins.)

Raid on Rommel (1971)*½ Richard Burton, John Colicos. (Dir: Henry Hathaway, 99 mins.)

Raiders of Leyte Gulf (1963)**½ Michael Parsons, Leopoldo Salcedo. American paratrooper aids the Philippine guerrillas in harassing the Japanese forces. Filmed in the Philippines, this war drama contains plenty of rugged action, which compensates somewhat for the lack of production finesse. (Dir: Eddie Romero, 80 mins.)

Raiders Of The Lost Ark. (1981)**** Harrison Ford, Karen Allen Denholm Elliott, Ronald Lacey, Wolf Kahler, John Rhys-Davies. Zowie! One of the most wildly entertaining *movie-movies* ever made, an inspired tribute to "The Perils of Pauline" and other cliffhanging Saturday-matinee series of the 1930's and 1940's. Our death defying courageous hero is a young idealistic archeologist trying to track down the long missing Ark of the Covenant before the dastardly Nazis unearth it. There are marvelous races, chases and general derring-do involving the repeated rescue of our heroine Marion (Karen Allen), the special effects created for the payoff scene demonstrating the magical powers of the Ark are fantasmagorical. A remarkable achievement from executive producer George Lucas and director Steven Spielberg. Lucas, incidentally, co-authored the original story. Fabulous fun for young and old; Screenplay written by Lawrence Kasdan. (Dir. Steven Spielberg, 115 mins.)

Raiders of the Seven Seas (1953)**½ John Payne, Donna Reed. Bold pirate captures a countess, saves her from the rascal she is to marry. Lively costume adventure, plenty of action. (Dir: Sidney Salkow, 88 mins.)

Raiders of the Spanish Main (Great Britain, 1962)** Terence Morgan, Nanette Newman. En route back from the New World, Sir Francis Drake stops to rescue sailors held prisoner by the Spanish on an island. Adequate costume sea adventure taken from the "Sir Francis Drake" TV series. (88 mins.)

Railroaded (1947)*** John Ireland, Hugh Beaumont, Sheila Ryan. The law gets a desperate criminal who has involved an innocent youth. Tight, suspenseful crime opus, well above average. (Dir: Anthony Mann, 72 mins.)

Rails into Laramie (1954)** John Payne, Mari Blanchard, Dan Duryea. Another passable western about the pioneering group of he-men who tamed the lawless frontier in order to bring the "rails" into "Laramie." (Dir: Jesse Hibbs, 81 mins.)

Railway Children, The (Great Britain, 1970)**** Dinah Sheridan, Jenny Agutter, Sally Thomsett, Gary Warren. Family entertainment. An engaging and entertaining film version of the Edwardian children's classic story about three children who are relocated from London to a Yorkshire village on a railroad line with their mother. A vivid and heartwarming picture of British life at the turn of the century is evoked and the three young actors are superb. (Dir: Lionel Jeffries, 108 mins.)

Rain (1932)**½ Joan Crawford, Walter Huston, William Gargan, Beulah Bondi. Crawford is not a very piquant Sadie Thompson, though she dares some clever gambits with her makeup and hair, but Huston gives a near-definitive portrayal of the ramrod bigot Reverend Davidson. Director Lewis Milestone has little stylistic control. (93 mins.)

Rain People, The (1969)***½ Shirley Knight, James Caan, Robert Duvall. A quiet, modestly conceived art film directed by Francis Ford Coppola. The runaway housewife theme was ahead of its time. A road movie with some brains. (102 mins.)

Rainbow (MTV 1978)*** Andrea McArdle, Michael Parks, Piper Laurie, Martin Balsam, Jack Carter. Nostalgic film about the young Judy Garland is a corny, sentimental treat packaged in the old Hollywood style. McArdle, the Broadway sensation from "Annie," is a workhorse like Judy, singing everything from "Zing Went the Strings of My Heart" to "Gotta Dance," but she sings better than she acts. Based on the book "Rainbow" by Christopher Finch. (Dir: Jackie Cooper, 104 mins.)

Rainbow Jacket, The (Great Britain, 1954)*** Robert Morley, Kay Walsh, Honor Blackman, Wilfrid Hyde-White. Disbarred jockey takes a lad in hand and teaches him the tricks of the trade. Familiar but well constructed racing melodrama. (Dir: Basil Dearden, 99 mins.)

Rainbow 'Round My Shoulder (1952)**½ Frankie Laine, Charlotte Austin, Billy Daniels. Lively musical about a Hollywood studio messenger who gets a screen test and winds up in the movies. (Dir: Richard Quine, 78 mins.)

Rainmaker, The (1956)***½ Katharine Hepburn, Burt Lancaster, Wendell Corey, Lloyd Bridges, Earl Holliman. N. Richard Nash's hit play about a frightened spinster who's transformed into a woman ready for love by a visiting "con man" relies mainly on Hepburn's personal magnetism and is a success only in this area. Lancaster blusters and bellows as Starbuck, the rainmaker who has a drought-ridden town in the palm of his hand, but it's a surface performance with little emotional depth. The supporting cast is up to par. (Dir: Joseph Anthony, 121 mins.)

Rains Came, The (1939)** Tyrone Power, Myrna Loy, George Brent. Well-edited special effects of flood and earthquake enliven an otherwise dolorous film. Power is absurdly cast as a noble Indian physician. Directed carefully but not well by Clarence Brown. Remade as "The Rains of Ranchipur." (104 mins.)

Rains of Ranchipur, The (1955)**½ Lana Turner, Richard Burton, Fred MacMurray, Michael Rennie, Joan Caulfield. Elaborately produced remake of the Myrna Loy-Tyrone Power film "The Rains Came," about the forbidden romance between the wife of an English nobleman (Miss Turner) and a progressive Hindu doctor (Richard Burton). The plot offers nothing new in the way of drama but the pace is smooth, the spectacle lavish and the stars attractive. (Dir: Jean Negulesco, 104 mins.)

Raintree County (1957)**½ Montgomery Clift, Elizabeth Taylor, Eva Marie Saint, Rod Taylor, Lee Marvin. Massively metricious adaptation of the novel by Ross Lockridge, Jr. Edward Dmytryk's heavy direction is wearying beyond measure. Even the interesting sexual ambiguity of Taylor and Clift fails to sustain audience attention. John Green's score is a help. (Dir: Edward Dmytryk, 168 mins., orig. 187 mins.)

Raise the Titanic (1980)* Jason Robards, Richard Jordan, Anne Archer, Alec Guinness. (Dir: Jerry Jameson, 112 mins.)

Raisin in the Sun, A (1961)*** Sidney Poitier, Ruby Dee, Diana Sands, Claudia McNeil, Ivan Dixon. Lorraine Hansberry's play about a black family in the Chicago ghetto trying to make sense of their lives stars sterling role model Poitier as the father. Don Bogle, an authority on black films, characterizes "Raisin" as a disorganized intergrationist melodrama, but it was important in its time for accurately portraying middle-class aspirations of ghetto blacks, and the cast is impeccable. (Dir: Daniel Petrie, 128 mins.)

Rasing a Riot (Great Britain, 1955)*** Kenneth More, Mandy Miller. Delightful comedy about a sailor who comes home on leave and is left in charge of his three energetic children while his wife leaves to go to her mother's sick-bed. The naval commander tries to run his house like a tight ship, which results in laugh provoking situations. (Dir: Wendy Toye, 91 mins.)

Rally Round the Flag, Boys! (1958)** Paul Newman, Joanne Woodward, Joan Collins, Jack Carson, Tuesday Weld. Max Shulman's funny novel about the citizens of Putnam's Landing and their reactions to an army missile base in their backyard gets the Hollywood treatment. The characters, hilarious in the book, appear somewhat ridiculous on the screen. Newman lacks comedy timing and Woodward is fighting the script all the way. (Dir: Leo McCarey, 106 mins.)

Ramona (1936)**½ Loretta Young, Don Ameche, Kent Taylor, Pauline Frederick. Romantic drama set in old California about the trials of the Indian peons, and their Spanish overlords. The performances, especially Frederick's, save this from being an exotic soap opera. From the novel by Helen Hunt Jackson. Color. (Dir: Henry King, 90 mins.)

Rampage (1963)** Robert Mitchum, Elsa Martinelli, Jack Hawkins, Sabu. Fans who like their adventure films with a minimum of plot twists might enjoy this action drama starring Mitchum as a big-game hunter. Mitchum's assignment is to bring back some rare examples of jungle cats from the Malayan wilds with the help of capable Jack Hawkins and lovely Elsa Martinelli. (Dir: Phil Karlson, 98 mins.)

Rampage at Apache Wells (West Germany-Yugoslavia, 1965)* Stewart Granger, Pierre Brice, Macha Meril. (Dir: Harald Philipps, 91 mins.)

Ramparts of Clay (France-Algeria, 1970)**** Lelia Schenna. A stunning, visually breathtaking fictional documentary about the emancipation of a young woman who lives in a desolate, primitive mountain village in Tunisia. Shot on location in Tehouda, Algeria, and based on a book by Jean Duvignaud entitled "Change at Chebika." Schenna, a handsome young actress, is the only professional in the cast. You'll learn more about poverty, ignorance, and religious superstition among these proud peasant peoples than you can find in most books. (Dir: Jean-Louis Bertucelli, 87 mins.)

Ramsbottom Rides Again (Great Britain, 1956)* Arthur Askey, Sabrina. A British western set in Canadian Rockies. Need we say more! (Dir: John Baxter, 82 mins.)

Rancho Deluxe (1975)***½ Jeff Bridges, Elizabeth Ashley, Sam Waterson, Clifton James, Slim Pickens, Helen Craig, Charlene Dallas. Thanks largely to a quirky, wry, picaresque screenplay by talented novelist Thomas McGuane, this Western spoof works quite well most of the time. Bridges and Waterson play two nonchalant cattle rustlers who finally do wind up in the pokey, but they and you will have some droll fun before the final fadeout. (Dir: Frank Perry, 93 mins.)

Rancho Notorious (1952)**** Marlene Dietrich, Mel Ferrer, Arthur Kennedy. A perversely stylized western directed by Fritz Lang, his last and best. Unrestrained Technicolor and painted backdrops remove any sense of reality from this film about a safe haven for gunslingers operated by Dietrich. Then Kennedy arrives, looking for the man who killed his fiancée. (89 mins.)

Random Harvest (1942)*** Ronald Colman, Greer Garson, Susan Peters, Philip Dorn, Bramwell Fletcher, Reginald Owen, Rhys Williams. Colman has amnesia so he must learn to love Garson over again. One of his most popular roles. Lots of sentiment; Mervyn LeRoy directed with technical competence and without finer sensibility. From the novel by James Hilton. (124 mins.)

Rangers, The (MTV 1974)* James G. Richardson, Colby Chester, Jim B. Smith. (Dir: Chris Nyby, Jr., 72 mins.)

Rangers of Fortune (1940)**½ Fred MacMurray, Albert Dekker, Gilbert Roland, Patricia Morison. Off-beat western defies convention, but is a very confusing film. Story of three renegades who help an old man and a young girl. Ambitious try that just doesn't succeed in rising above average. (Dir: Sam Wood, 82 mins.)

Ransom! (1956)**½ Glenn Ford, Donna Reed, Leslie Nielsen. Somewhat hysterical drama of an industrialist who debates whether to pay the ransom when his son is kidnapped. Overwrought performance by Ford, but the story does contain some suspense. (Dir: Alex Segal, 109 mins.)

Ransom for a Dead Man (1971)**½ Peter Falk, Lee Grant. Ended up as the TV series "Columbo." Grant plays a brilliant lawyer who coolly murders her husband, then watches lawmen puzzle over her adroit kidnap-ransom, cover-up scheme. Falk is the bumbling local detective who gets in the way of the pros, but slowly zeroes in on the true picture. (Dir: Richard Irving, 100 mins.)

Ransom for Alice (MTV 1977)* Yvette Mimieux, Gil Gerard, Barnard Hughes. (Dir: David Lowell Rich, 79 mins.)

Rapture (U.S.-France, 1965)** Melvyn Douglas, Dean Stockwell. A romantic drama with pretensions toward art. Douglas plays a retired judge who keeps his beautiful daughter (Patricia Gozzi) isolated from the world; enter Stockwell as a handsome, intelligent fugitive. Have your hankies ready for the finale. (Dir: John Guillermin, 98 mins.)

Rare Breed, The (1966)** James Stewart, Maureen O'Hara, Brian Keith. Cowhand is entrusted to deliver a prize bull, paving the way for romance with its original owner. Pleasant, slow-moving western. (Dir: Andrew V. McLaglen, 97 mins.)

Rashomon (Japan, 1951)*** Toshiro Mifune, Machiko Kyo. The good but overpraised film that introduced Japanese cinema to the western world. The story of a man and his wife who are surprised by a bandit while crossing the forest is told by each participant as well as by a witness, and the theme is the unknowability of truth when all human beings are naturally liars. (Dir: Akira Kurosawa, 90 mins.)

Rasputin and the Empress (1932)** John, Ethel, and Lionel Barrymore, Diana Wynyard, Ralph Morgan. The only film with all three Barrymores. Today Lionel (Rasputin) seems more or less hopeless, while John and Ethel wear impressively well, except when he does self-parody and she plays the grande dame. Directed by Richard Boleslawski, and the shadow of the Moscow Art Theatre hangs heavily over the proceedings. (130 mins.)

Rasputin—The Mad Monk (Great Britain, 1966)**½ Christopher Lee, Barbara Shelley, Richard Pasco, Francis Matthews. Putting historical inaccuracy aside, this is an effective, colorful shocker about Rasputin's insinuation of himself into the last of Russia's royal households, thanks to his uncanny hypnotic powers and sexuality. One of many "Rasputin" films. Lee plays the monk with compelling grossness. Written by the executive producer, Anthony Hinds. (Dir: Don Sharp, 92 mins.)

Rat Race, The (1960)*** Tony Curtis, Debbie Reynolds, Jack Oakie, Kay Medford, Don Rickles. Tough-tender story of the Big City, of a love affair developing between a naive aspiring musician and a brittle-minded dancer. Nice N.Y. atmosphere, some good lines, insight into character. Entertaining. (Dir: Robert Mulligan, 105 mins.)

Raton Pass (1951)**½ Dennis Morgan, Patricia Neal, Steve Cochran. Exciting Western. Husband and wife fight tooth and nail for a cattle empire. (Dir: Edwin L. Marin, 84 mins.)

Rattle of a Simple Man (Great Britain, 1964)**½ Harry H. Corbett, Diane Cilento, Thora Hird. Diverting sex comedy features Corbett as a shy bachelor who has to spend a night with entertainer Cilento to win a bet. Knowing of the wager, the girl graciously helps him. Adapted by Charles Dyer from his hit London play. (Dir: Muriel Box, 96 mins.)

Ravagers (1979)** Richard Harris, Ann Turkel, Art Carney, Ernest Borgnine. It's 1991, and civilization is dead. Of course, with enough films like this, one could make that claim for '79. (Dir: Richard Compton, 91 mins.)

Raven, The (1935)** Boris Karloff, Bela Lugosi. Lurid thriller about a plastic surgeon who adores the works of Edgar Allan Poe. Karloff is effective as a gangster who needs a face-lift, but the film is just so-so. (Dir: Louis Friedlander, aka Lew Landers, 61 mins.)

Ravishing Idiot, A (France-Italy, 1964)*½ Anthony Perkins, Brigitte Bardot. (Dir: Edouard Molinaro, 110 mins.)

Raw Deal (1948)***½ Dennis O'Keefe, Claire Trevor, Marsha Hunt, Raymond Burr. Framed into prison by the mob, a gangster escapes and goes seeking vengeance. Excellent melodrama with fine direction, photography (by John Alton), good performances. (Dir: Anthony Mann, 79 mins.)

Raw Edge (1956)** Rory Calhoun, Yvonne DeCarlo. Just another western with Calhoun and Miss DeCarlo playing parts they could play in their sleep. Setting is Oregon at the time when land barons ruled the frontier. (Dir: John Sherwood, 76 mins.)

Raw Winds in Eden (1958)**½ Esther Williams, Jeff Chandler, Rossana Podesta. A mildly entertaining adventure yarn with an island setting and two-fisted men fighting over statuesque Miss Williams. The plot is predictable but things move fast so you won't get bored. (Dir: Richard Wilson, 89 mins.)

Rawhide—See: **Desperate Siege**

Rawhide Years, The (1956)*** Tony Curtis, Colleen Miller, Arthur Kennedy. Fast, funny western yarn about double crosses and false accusations which cause Tony to become a hunted fugitive bent on clearing his name. Arthur Kennedy delivers the best acting job in the film. (Dir: Rudolph Maté, 85 mins.)

Raymie (1960)**½ David Ladd, Julie Adams, Richard Arlen, John Agar. The charm of this film can be attributed mainly to David Ladd's completely believable performance as a boy who loves animals and fish, especially barracudas. Good family film fare. (Dir: Frank McDonald, 72 mins.)

Razor's Edge, The (1946)**½ Tyrone Power, Gene Tierney, Clifton Webb, Herbert Marshall, Anne Baxter. Claptrap Somerset Maugham novel, glossied up. Highly effective thesping from Baxter (Oscar, Best Supporting Actress) and Tierney. The movie has some substance, showing that coherence isn't necessarily all. (Dir: Edmund Goulding, 146 mins.)

R.C.M.P. and the Treasure of Genghis Khan (1948-66)*½ Jim Bannon, Virginia Belmont. (Dirs: Fred Brannon, Yakima Canutt, 100 mins.)

Reach for Glory (Great Britain, 1962)** Harry Andrews, Oliver Grimm, Michael Anderson, Jr., Martin Tomlinson. Well-meaning allegory that misses. Boys evacuated from London during WW II fashion their own war games. Similar idea to "Lord of the Flies," only much less coherent. Based on the novel "The Custard Boys" by John Rae. (Dir: Philip Leacock, 89 mins.)

Reach for the Sky (GB 1956)***½ Kenneth More, Muriel Pavlos, Alexander Knox, Nigel Green. Amazing true story of Douglas Bader, an ebullient character who became a WW2 flying ace and squadron commander despite having lost both legs in an accident several years earlier. He was also a prisoner of war and, with quintessential British doggedness, kept escaping, much to the Nazi's embarrassment. A fascinating tale, charmingly played. (Dir: Lewis Gilbert, 108 mins.)

Reaching for the Moon (1931)*** Douglas Fairbanks, Sr., Bebe Daniels, Edward Everett Horton, Bing Crosby. Snappy depression comedy with song as an antic, charming Fairbanks leaps all over some shiny art deco sets you won't believe! Still entertaining. Music by Irving Berlin. (Dir: Edmund Goulding, 62 mins.)

Ready for the People (1964)* Simon Oakland, Richard Jordan, Everett Sloane, Anne Helm. (Dir: Buzz Kulik, 54 mins.)

Real American Hero, A (TV 1978)** Brian Dennehy, Forrest Tucker, Ken Howard. Pilot film based on the real-life Tennessee sheriff Buford Pusser, best known from the "Walking Tall" films. Dennehy as the angry sheriff, frustrated by the "technicalities" of the law in trying to put a moonshiner out of business. Filmed in Tennessee. Written and produced by Samuel A. Peeples. (Dir: Lou Antonio, 104 mins.)

Real Glory, The (1939)*** Gary Cooper, David Niven, Andrea Leeds, Broderick Crawford. Rousing action film about three soldiers who aid in trying to squelch the terrorist uprising in the Philippines. (Dir: Henry Hathaway, 96 mins.)

Reap the Wild Wind (1942)*** Ray Milland, John Wayne, Paulette Goddard, Susan Hayward, Robert Preston, Raymond Massey, Hedda Hopper. Lavish deMille adventure tale of an 1840 love triangle off the Florida Keys where the most profitable thing a man could do was wreck ships. Lusty film, loses much of its value on small TV screen. Oscar: Best Special Effects. (Dir: Cecil B. deMille, 124 mins.)

Rear Window (1954)**** James Stewart, Grace Kelly, Raymond Burr, Wendell Corey, Thelma Ritter. Alfred Hitchcock-directed suspense treat—photographer is laid up in his apartment, takes to examining his neighbors through binoculars, witnesses a murder. Nail-biting tension laced with some scenes of sharp sophisticated comedy, a delight from beginning to end. (112 mins.)

Rebecca (1940)**** Joan Fontaine, Laurence Olivier, Judith Anderson, George Sanders. Newlywed Fontaine tries desperately to pierce her aristocratic husband's strange obsession with his recently deceased first wife. Director Alfred Hitchcock's production of the Daphne du Maurier best-seller was his first American picture, and he scrupulously followed David O. Selznick's instructions not to tamper with the novel. Oscar winner as Best Picture. (115 mins.)

Rebecca of Sunnybrook Farm (1938)**½ Shirley Temple, Randolph Scott, Jack Haley, Bill "Bojangles" Robinson, Gloria

Stuart. If you like Shirley you'll love her in this but if you want your kids to see a screen adaptation of the famous children's book—this is not it. (Dir: Allan Dwan, 74 mins.)

Rebel Flight to Cuba (West Germany, 1959)*½ Peter Van Eyck, Linda Christian. (Dir: Gottfried Reinhardt, 92 mins.)

Rebel Without a Cause (1955)***½ James Dean, Natalie Wood, Sal Mineo, Jim Backus, Ann Doran, Dennis Hopper, Nick Adams. Sensitively acted story of a teenager who is not satisfied with a world he never made. Dean's performance is touching and exciting; Wood and Mineo are first-rate. Dean's alienation is perfectly expressed through director-writer Nicholas Ray's vertiginous mise-en-scène. (111 mins.)

Rebellion in Patagonia (Argentina, 1974)***½ Powerful drama by a gifted, little-recognized director, Hector Olivera. About a labor strike in Patagonia (Argentina) and the brutal way it was put down. Masterful re-creation of the period. The political content is dealt with intelligently, including the changes in the character and attitude of the Army commander.

Reckless (1935)** Jean Harlow, William Powell, Franchot Tone, May Robson, Rosalind Russell. Certainly this film is artistically reckless and most of the time it fails miserably, but it's mishmash to reckon with. Harlow rises above most of the nonsense given her to do, as the story, loosely based on the life of Libby Holman, switches from musical to romance to tragedy and back. (Dir: Victor Fleming, 96 mins.)

Reckless Moment (1949)***½ James Mason, Joan Bennett, Geraldine Brooks, Henry O'Neill. A woman who has killed a scoundrel to protect her family finds herself in the clutches of a blackmailer. Well acted and directed, this is a good melodrama. (Dir: Max Ophuls, 82 mins.)

Reckoning, The (Great Britain, 1969)*** Nicol Williamson, Rachel Roberts. Williamson stars as a ruthless businessman who has made a success in southern England but is forced to return to his home in the north to visit his dying father. Drama is frequently effective. Fine supporting cast. (Dir: Jack Gold, 109 mins.)

Red (Canada, 1970)* Daniel Pilon, Genevieve Deloir. (Dir: Gilles Carle, 101 mins.)

Red Alert (MTV 1977)*** William Devane, Ralph Waite, Michael Brandon, Adrienne Barbeau. Gripping suspense drama about troubles within a nuclear power plant. Provokes many questions about nuclear power-plant safety, and our growing dependence upon computer control. Given a strong story, the actors are effective, especially Waite. The film was photographed at Houston's giant Space Lab, and at the NASA Mission Control Center. (Dir: William Hale, 106 mins.)

Red and the Black, The (France, 1957)***½ Gerard Philipe, Danielle Darrieux, Antonella Lualdi. Stendhal's great work is given a sensitive and successful treatment on film, but don't expect all the novel's subtleties. A young man from provincial 19th-century France aspires to greatness, chooses first the Church, then gentleman's employment, and gentlewoman's seduction, to accomplish his ends. Philipe and Darrieux, in the leading roles, give truly splendid performances. (Dir: Claude Autant-Lara, 145 mins.)

Red Badge of Courage, The (1951)**½ Audie Murphy, Bill Mauldin, Arthur Hunnicutt, John Dierkes, Royal Dano, Andy Devine. From Stephen Crane's novel of the Civil War. Terribly mangled by the studio, John Huston's film is still a remarkably powerful discussion of war. Murphy is excellent as usual as the uncertain hero, as is cartoonist Mauldin. Huston reportedly won't even look at this; it isn't what he wanted, but it **is** still fine filmmaking. (69 mins.)

Red Badge of Courage, The (MTV 1974)*** Richard Thomas, Warren Berlinger, Wendell Burton, Charles Aidman. This faithful adaptation of Stephen Crane's classic Civil War novel about fear under fire stars Thomas as Henry Fleming, the youth who questions his courage in battle, runs away, and then fights again in a fit of madness with his tattered company of greenhorns. The braggart, the questioner, and the solid man all have their moments before authentic, bloody battle scenes reveal a regiment learning how to be resolute, in this noble attempt at bringing a poignant story to life. Not as good as the '51 version, but worth seeing. (Dir: Lee Philips, 74 mins.)

Red Ball Express (1952)** Jeff Chandler, Alex Nicol, Sidney Poitier, Hugh O'Brian, Jack Kelly. Routine WW II drama, played in the European combat zone, with all the cliched GI's. Jeff Chandler plays a tough but human leader of the truck division known as the Red Ball Express. (Dir: Budd Boetticher, 83 mins.)

Red Beard (Japan, 1965)***½ Toshiro Mifune, Yuzo Kayama, Yoshio Tsuchiya. Kayama, an impetuous young doctor, conflict's with his aging superior in an impoverished clinic in early 19th-century Japan. Mifune is superb as the older doctor. The film, criticized for excessive sentimentality by some, is a masterful evocation of period and a probing study of the conflict between responsibility and idealism. (Dir: Akira Kurosawa, 185 mins.)

Red Circle, The (Germany, 1960)*½ Karl Georg Saebisch, Renate Ewert. (Dir: Jurgen Roland, 94 mins.)

Red Cloak, The (France-Italy, 1955)*½ Fausto Tozzi, Patricia Medina, Bruce Cabot, Domenico Modugno. (Dir: Giuseppe Maria Scotese, 95 mins.)

Red Culottes, The (France, 1963)** Bourvil, Laurent Terzieff. Story of French

POWs trying to escape holds the interest fairly well, but the story has been done before, and better. Dubbed in English. (Dir: Alexandre Joffe, 105 mins.)

Red Danube, The (1949)**½ Walter Pidgeon, Janet Leigh, Peter Lawford, Ethel Barrymore, Angela Lansbury. Interesting but over-dramatic story of political intrigue and romance in Europe. A handsome British officer and a lovely ballerina are plagued by the Communists. (Dir: George Sidney, 119 mins.)

Red Desert (France-Italy, 1964)*** Monica Vitti, Richard Harris. The film where director Antonioni became Michelangelo. Highly charged use of expressive color in a story of a young woman's dissatisfaction and neuroses. Though a little misty, it's still an intriguing piece of film. (120 mins.)

Red Detachment of Women, The (China, 1970)**½ Ching Ching-hua, Lo Sing Siang, members of the China Ballet Troupe. Combination of European ballet, Chinese folk dance, Peking opera, and acrobatics in the ballet, Nixon was invited to watch on his trip to Peking in '71. No great shakes as a ballet performance, but fairly engaging thanks to the piquancy of its heroine, who turns to the Communist revolution in the '30s after a series of brutal encounters with her evil landlord. (Dir: anonymous, 105 mins.)

Red-Dragon (Italy-West Germany, 1965)* Stewart Granger, Rosanna Schiaffino, Horst Frank. (Dir: Ernst Hofbauer, 89 mins.)

Red Dust (1932)***½ Clark Gable, Jean Harlow, Mary Astor, Gene Raymond. Sexy hothouse comedy-drama, with Gable and Harlow at their easiest together. The film is frank, funny, and not sunk by the dramatics of Astor having an affair with Gable while husband Raymond is out scouting rubber. As entertainment, the film is quite a turn-on, and the two stars show the real talent they were often dismissed as not having. Remade by Gable as "Mogambo." (Dir: Victor Fleming, 83 mins.)

Red Garters (1954)**½ Rosemary Clooney, Jack Carson, Gene Barry, Guy Mitchell. Satire of westerns uses all the standard plot ramifications: man seeks revenge for brother's death, falls for the purty town girl, etc. All done with stylized sets, costumes. It doesn't work but represents a try for something different. Some fair tunes warbled by Clooney, others. (Dir: George Marshall, 91 mins.)

Red Hand, The (West Germany, 1960)*½ Eleonora Rossi-Drago, Paul Hubschmid, Hannes Messemer. (Dir: Kurt Meisel, 98 mins.)

Red-Headed Woman (1932)*** Jean Harlow, Chester Morris, Charles Boyer (Hollywood debut), Lewis Stone. The best, sauciest Anita Loos talkie, ideally tailored to Harlow as a ruthlessly ambitious shopgirl out to climb the social ladder.

Witty and saucy in the pre-Code style. (Dir: Jack Conway, 74 mins.)

Red, Hot and Blue (1949)**½ Betty Hutton, Victor Mature, June Havoc, William Demarest. Girl ambitious to get ahead in the theater is helped by a director and a publicist but runs afoul of gangsters. Pleasant comedy is mainly a showcase for Hutton's brassy talents; songwriter Frank Loesser has a role as a hoodlum, in a bit of offbeat casting. (Dir: John Farrow, 84 mins.)

Red House, The (1947)***½ Edward G. Robinson, Lon McCallister, Judith Anderson, Rory Calhoun, Julie London. A farmer holds a terrifying secret concerning a sinister house in the woods. Excellent suspense thriller. (Dir: Delmer Daves, 100 mins.)

Red Inn, The (France, 1951)** Fernandel, Françoise Rosay. Monk discovers that travelers stopping at an inn are robbed and murdered by the proprietors, tries to save some potential new victims. Grotesque mixture of comedy and murder doesn't quite come off. Some amusing scenes, not enough. English-dubbed. (Dir: Claude Autant-Lara, 90 mins.)

Red Light (1949)** George Raft, Virginia Mayo, Raymond Burr. Another "innocent-man-sent-to-prison" mystery drama, with Raft playing his usual Great Stone Face. Mayo is pretty, in case you haven't heard. (Dir: Roy Del Ruth, 83 mins.)

Red Line 7000 (1965)**½ James Caan, Laura Devon, Charlene Holt. Director Howard Hawks's study of insane ambition on the stock-car racing circuit. The racing footage is flat and dull, but the dialogue scenes have a primitive emotional force in spite or (or perhaps because of) the young, untried cast, headed by Caan. (110 mins.)

Red Menace, The (1949)** Robert Rockwell, Hanne Axman, Barbra Fuller. A Republic Pictures contribution to postwar scare and bait tactics. Rockwell and Fuller star, if you can call it that. (Dir: R. G. Springsteen, 87 mins.)

Red Mountain (1951)**½ Alan Ladd, Lizabeth Scott, John Ireland, Arthur Kennedy. Confederate officer assigned to raider Quantrill discovers the leader is out for himself alone, goes on the hunt for him. Well-made western moves at a fast clip. (Dir: William Dieterle, 84 mins.)

Red Neck County (1975)* Leslie Uggams, Shelley Winters, Michael Christian. (Dir: Richard Robinson, 86 mins.)

Red Planet Mars (1952)** Peter Graves, Andrea King, Herbert Berghof, Marvin Miller. An amazing cold-war artifact. Decoded messages reveal Mars is the base of an interplanetary religious revival, prompting the godless Russkies to interfere. From a dumbfounding script by Anthony Weiller and John L. Balderston. (Dir: Harry Horner, 87 mins.)

Red Pony, The (1949)*** Robert Mitchum, Myrna Loy, Peter Miles. Ranch boy is gifted with a colt, grows to love him but the colt escapes. John Steinbeck story receives a good production, but moves rather leisurely. (Dir: Lewis Milestone, 89 mins.)

Red River (1948)*** John Wayne, Montgomery Clift, Joanne Dru, Walter Brennan. Western about an empire-building cattle baron. Wayne became a major actor in this genuine epic, and Clift suggests something in his nervy angularity that never quite emerged in his later "sensitive" performances. (Dir: Howard Hawks, 125 mins.)

Red Roses for the Führer—See: **Code Name: Red Roses**

Red Sheik, The (Italy, 1962)* Channing Pollock, Mel Welles. (Dir: Fernando Cerchio, 90 mins.)

Red Shoes, The (Great Britain, 1948)*** Moira Shearer, Marius Goring, Robert Helpmann, Anton Walbrook. Director Michael Powell and Emeric Pressburger's film is a cult item for ballet fans; others will probably find its sentimentalism beyond the pale. A strange morbidity is largely the product of the killingly hard-edged use of Technicolor. (133 mins.)

Red Skies of Montana (1952)** Richard Widmark, Jeffrey Hunter, Richard Boone. Adventure yarn about the brave band of forest fire fighters known as "Smoke Jumpers." The fire fighting sequences will please action fans; but the plot involving Hunter's efforts to gain revenge for his father's accidental death in a mission led by Widmark merely serves as a stage wait between holocausts. (Dir: Joseph M. Newman, 99 mins.)

Red Sky at Morning (1971)**½ Richard, Thomas, Claire Bloom, Desi Arnaz, Jr., Richard Crenna. Despite some flaws, this nostalgic excursion about a teen-age boy coming into his own in New Mexico in 1944 works fairly well, thanks largely to Thomas' performance in the leading role. Bloom tends to overact as Thomas' mother and Arnaz is surprisingly good as his buddy. The '40s flavor is there without being self-conscious. (Dir: James Goldstone, 113 mins.)

Red Snow (1952)** Guy Madison, Carole Mathews, Ray Mala (last film). Twin adventure yarn about the Alaskan Air Command; their missions and their loves. Madison is incompetent once again. (Dir: Boris L. Petroff, 75 mins.)

Red Sun (France-Italy-Spain, 1971)* Charles Bronson, Ursula Andress, Alain Delon, Toshiro Mifune, Capucine. (Dir: Terence Young, 112 mins.)

Red Sundown (1956)** Rory Calhoun, Martha Hyer, Dean Jagger. Usual western tale about the lawless renegade turned lawful deputy and the trouble he encounters before and after the transition. Calhoun at least looks believable in the role. (Dir: Jack Arnold, 81 mins.)

Red Tent, The (Italy-U.S.S.R., 1971)**½ Peter Finch, Sean Connery, Hardy Kruger, Claudia Cardinale. Well-acted adventure film about the '28 rescue of the crew of the dirigible "Italia," commanded by General Umberto Nobile (Finch), which crashed during a North Pole flight. Nobile's rescue by a Swedish pilot who had room for only one passenger aroused much controversy. The film bogs down when it tries to analyze the responsibilities of leadership, visualized through the general's sense of guilt. (Dir: Mikhail K. Kalatozov, 121 mins.)

Red Tomahawk (1967)* Howard Keel, Joan Caulfield, Broderick Crawford. (Dir: R. G. Springsteen, 82 mins.)

Red Train, The (Switzerland, 1973)** Pretentious pseudodocumentary which attempts not very successfully to combine, in supposed documentary form, scenes of emigrant Italian workers going home to vote with parables about the legend of William Tell. English subtitles. (Dir: Peter Ammann, 90 mins.)

Red, White and Black, The—See: **Soul Soldier**

Redhead and the Cowboy, The (1950)** Glenn Ford, Rhonda Fleming, Edmond O'Brien. At the close of the Civil War a cowhand is mistaken for a Confederate spy by a beautiful courier, gets himself tangled in espionage. Just fair western, doesn't have the necessary movement for a successful action film. (Dir: Leslie Fenton, 82 mins.)

Redhead from Manhattan (1943)** Lupe Velez, Michael Duane. Theatrical star agrees to impersonate her cousin until the cousin has taken her baby, which causes romantic mix-ups. Ordinary musical comedy. (Dir: Lew Landers, 63 mins.)

Redhead from Wyoming, The (1952)*½ Maureen O'Hara, Alex Nicol, Jack Kelly. (Dir: Lee Sholem, 80 mins.)

Redmen and the Renegades, The (1956)*½ John Hart, Lon Chaney. (89 mins.)

Redneck (Italy-Great Britain, 1972)*½ Franco Nero, Telly Savalas, Mark Lester. (Dir: Silvio Narizzano, 87 mins.)

Reflection of Fear, A (1973)*½ Robert Shaw, Sally Kellerman, Mary Ure, Sondra Locke. (Dir: William A. Fraker, 90 mins.)

Reflections in a Golden Eye (1967)**½ Marlon Brando, Elizabeth Taylor, Brian Keith, Julie Harris, Robert Forster. Novelist Carson McCullers's perceptive novel has been cheapened and distorted in this film version directed by John Huston, but there are some splendid acting performances. Brando, playing a homosexual southern army officer, has trouble with his southern accent at times, but he conveys the personal anguish and indecision of the tortured officer. Other good performances from Forster as the object of Marlon's affection—despite Brando having Taylor in his bedroom each night—and from Keith and Harris. (108 mins.)

Reflections of Murder (MTV 1974)*** Sam Waterston, Tuesday Weld, Joan Hackett. "Diabolique," classic French thriller with a surprise ending, has been remade with

550

an American cast which is up to the demands of the tale. A schoolmaster, who has been mistreating his ill wife, is murdered by her and his former mistress. They put his body in the private school's unused swimming pool, but when they drain the pool some days later, the body is gone and the suspense builds to the fascinating close. A far cry from the original, but it's still a chilling story. (Dir: John Badham, 100 mins.)

Reformer and the Redhead, The (1950)** June Allyson, Dick Powell, David Wayne. Zany comedy bordering on the ridiculous with Allyson as an unpredictable redhead with a nose for trouble and Powell as the patient reformer. (Dir: Norman Panama, 90 mins.)

Rehearsal for a Crime—See: Criminal Life of Archibaldo de la Cruze, The

Reign of Terror (1949)*** Robert Cummings, Richard Hart, Arlene Dahl, Richard Basehart, Beulah Bondi. Director Anthony Mann's baroque rendition of the French Revolution takes a turn into black comedy about halfway through, when the head of the secret police paternalistically advises our hero (Cummings) not to stay out too late at night: "Remember, children, there's a revolution on." An ingratiating little film, droll and surprising. Photographed in striking high contrast by the best film noir cameraman, John Alton. (89 mins.)

Reincarnation of Peter Proud, The (1975)** Michael Sarrazin, Margot Kidder, Jennifer O'Neill. Clunky yarn: university professor Sarrazin has a recurring dream and suddenly discovers, via a TV documentary, his relation to a man killed decades before. Shock ending. (Dir: J. Lee Thompson, 104 mins.)

Reivers, The (1969)**** Steve McQueen, Sharon Farrell, Mitch Vogel, Rupert Crosse. Not all of William Faulkner's novels have survived the transfer to film very well, but this charming tale about the adventures of a 12-year-old boy with some of his older buddies is a notable exception. The journey follows a northward route up to Memphis, and McQueen, giving one of his most winning performances to date, is a big help. So is the direction of Mark Rydell. A particularly good film for teenagers, and a sure-fire hit for all the family. (107 mins.)

Relations (Denmark, 1972)* Bjorn Puggard Muller, Gertie Jung. (Dir: Hans Abramson, 91 mins.)

Relentless (1948)*** Robert Young, Marguerite Chapman, Akim Tamiroff. A cowboy is accused of murder and, after escaping, sets out to clear himself. Well-made western. Color. (Dir: George Sherman, 93 mins.)

Relentless (MTV 1977)**½ Will Sampson, Monte Markham, John Hillerman. Sampson, the imposing Indian actor in "One Flew over the Cuckoo's Nest," sets the tone for this drama about Arizona state troopers' pursuit of a band of bank robbers, led by a former major. The terrain of mountain ranges in Arizona and Utah helps make the proceedings believable. (Dir: Lee H. Katzin, 78 mins.)

Reluctant Astronaut, The (1967)*½ Don Knotts, Arthur O'Connell. (Dir: Edward Montagne, 101 mins.)

Reluctant Debutante, The (1958)*** Rex Harrison, Kay Kendall, Sandra Dee, John Saxon. From William Douglas Home's dinner theater perennial. Harrison and Kendall are the aristocratic Britishers whose daughter (Dee), primed for high society, has gotten involved with an American jazz drummer (Saxon). Kendall, in one of her few full parts, is worth seeing the movie for. (Dir: Vincente Minnelli, 94 mins.)

Reluctant Heroes, The (MTV 1971)** Ken Berry, Jim Hutton. Korean War service comedy-drama owes a lot to the picture "M*A*S*H" for its style and pace. Ken Berry is exceptionally adroit playing the role of Lt. Murphy, a war historian who finds himself heading a dangerous mission against the enemy. The dialogue among the men on the mission is brittle and often funny, providing the fine supporting cast, in which Hutton, Warren Oates, and Cameron Mitchell are standouts, with some good moments. (Dir: Robert Day, 73 mins.)

Reluctant Spy, The (France, 1963)** Jean Marais, Genevieve Page. Suave playboy works undercover for the French Secret Service, gets himself into plenty of scrapes. Mild, lightweight espionage thriller with comedy overtones; passable. Dubbed in English. (Dir: Jean-Charles Dudrumet, 93 mins.)

Remains to Be Seen (1953)**½ June Allyson, Van Johnson, Angela Lansbury, Dorothy Dandridge. Band vocalist and an apartment house manager who wants to be a drummer get tangled in a murder case. Mildly entertaining mystery-comedy, helped by a good supporting cast. (Dir: Don Weis, 89 mins.)

Remarkable Andrew, The (1942)**½ William Holden, Brian Donlevy. Ghosts of our founding fathers come to the aid of a timid young man fighting graft. Interesting, well-played hokum. (Dir: Stuart Heisler, 81 mins.)

Remarkable Mr. Pennypacker, The (1959)** Clifton Webb, Dorothy McGuire, Charles Coburn, Jill St. John, David Nelson. Scalawag specializes in large families and small talk—not much of it very amusing either. Misses capturing elusive charm of Broadway play it's based on. (Dir: Henry Levin, 87 mins.)

Rembrandt (Great Britain, 1936)***½ Charles Laughton, Gertrude Lawrence, Elsa Lanchester. The most intelligent of director Alexander Korda's historical spectacles, but not for art lovers. A lusty, yet emotionally affecting performance by Laughton. (84 mins.)

Remember? (1939)** Robert Taylor, Greer Garson, Lew Ayres. Silly little comedy about a guy who elopes with his friend's fiancée, and then the friend instead of shooting his pal uses the couple for some nonsensical experiment. (Dir: Norman Z. McLeod, 83 mins.)

Remember My Name (1978)**½ Geraldine Chaplin, Tony Perkins, Berry Berenson. Director Alan Rudolph goes fuzzy with the narrative when clarity ought to at least put in a cameo appearance. The film is dreamy, spacy, pointed, yet imprecise. It's Chaplin's finest zombie characterization yet, and Perkins and Berenson are well deployed as a married couple (which they are, in real life). Alberta Hunter's song score embellishes the movie. (96 mins.)

Remember the Day (1941)*** Claudette Colbert, John Payne. The ladies should like this sentimental story of a teacher's life, her guidance of one pupil and her unhappy romance. (Dir: Henry King, 85 mins.)

Remember the Night (1940)***½ Fred MacMurray, Barbara Stanwyck, Beulah Bondi. D.A. MacMurray falls in love with Stanwyck—a problem, since he's prosecuting her for shoplifting. The loose, graceful script is by Preston Sturges (one of his last before he turned to directing). (Dir: Mitchell Leisen, 86 mins.)

Remember When? (1974)** Jack Warden, William Schallert, Jamie Smith Jackson. Writer Herman Raucher, who struck gold with the film "Summer of '42," is still on the '40s nostalgia trail. Here he wrote a pilot for a proposed TV series about the home front during WW II. The setting is Connecticut. (Dir: Buzz Kulik, 96 mins.)

Renaldo and Clara (1978)**½ Bob Dylan, Sara Dylan, Joan Baez, Ronee Blakley, Ronnie Hawkins. Long, repetitious, self-indulgent film written and directed by and with Dylan in which his personality and his relationships are dissected, discussed, and acted out as many musicians (Arlo Guthrie, Roberta Flack, and others) perform with his Rolling Thunder Revue. David Blue, at a pinball machine, comes off well as a commentator on the Dylan mystique. (232 mins.)

Rendezvous Hotel (MTV 1979)** Bill Daily, Jeff J. Redford, Teddy Wilson. Daily becomes manager of a Santa Barbara, Calif., hotel in this drivel. This is known as "madcap comedy," with guests and employees vying for attention. (Dir: Peter Hunt, 104 mins.)

Rendezvous with Annie (1946)**½ Eddie Albert, Faye Marlowe, Gail Patrick. Army pilot flies home secretly to spend a few hours with his wife, but this leads to complications. Light, frothy comedy has many amusing moments. (Dir: Allan Dwan, 89 mins.)

Renegade Gunfighter (1966)* Pier Angeli, Zachary Hatcher, Dick Palmer. (Dir: Silvio Amadio, 76 mins.)

Report to the Commissioner (1975)** Michael Moriarty, Susan Blakely. Some very good actors, writers and the director all seem to have been working at cross-purposes on this film version of James Mills's best-selling novel. Broadway's Moriarty, in his starring debut in films, plays a puddin'-headed rookie cop who is used as a scapegoat by his superiors when he accidentally kills a sexy young lady who is actually an undercover cop, in the apartment of a big-time dope pusher she has been living with. Oh well, Blakely is lovely to look at as the fearless lady cop. (Dir: Milton Katselas, 112 mins.)

Reprisal (1956)**½ Guy Madison, Felicia Farr, Kathryn Grant. Good film with a novel approach to westerns—the plot concerns the racial issue. (Dir: George Sherman, 74 mins.)

Reptilicus (Denmark-U.S., 1961)*½ Carl Ottosen, Ann Smyrner. (Dirs: Sidney Pink, Poul Bang, 81 mins.)

Repulsion (Great Britain, 1965)*** Catherine Deneuve, Ian Hendry, Patrick Wymark, Yvonne Furneaux. Director Roman Polanski's study of the private hell of madness is a bit too clinical. Deneuve is a beautician whose mind is slowly deteriorating—with frightening consequences. (105 mins.)

Requiem for a Gunfighter (1965)*½ Rod Cameron, Stephen McNally, Tim McCoy. (Dir: Spencer G. Bennet, 91 mins.)

Requiem for a Heavyweight (1962)***½ Anthony Quinn, Julie Harris, Jackie Gleason, Mickey Rooney. This drama of a washed-up pug and the employment counselor who tries to help him land a job is based on the highly successful TV presentation. As a film it hasn't been changed much, except for the cast, who contribute excellent performances. Familiar but well done. (Dir: Ralph Nelson, 95 mins.)

Requiem for a Secret Agent (Italy, 1965)*½ Stewart Granger, Daniela Bianchi, Peter Van Eyck. (Dir: Sergio Sollima, 105 mins.)

Rescue from Gilligan's Island (MTV 1978)* Bob Denver, Alan Hale, Jr., Jim Backus, Natalie Schafer. (Dir: Les Martinson, 104 mins.)

Rest Is Silence, The (West Germany, 1959)**½ Hardy Kruger, Peter Van Eyck. Young man seeks to prove his father was murdered by his uncle. Or if you will, "Hamlet" modernized, with specific references to Shakespeare's work. Rather clever in adaptation, with some fairly good performances. Dubbed in English. (Dir: Helmut Kautner, 106 mins.)

Restless Breed, The (1957)** Scott Brady, Anne Bancroft. Routine western drama about a man bent on revenge for his father's murder. Bancroft is wasted as an Indian girl. (Dir: Allan Dwan, 81 mins.)

Restless Years, The (1958)** John Saxon, Sandra Dee, Margaret Lindsay, Teresa Wright. Small-town dressmaker tries to keep her daughter's illegitimacy a secret, but the secret's out. For ladies only, unadorned soap opera. (Dir: Helmut Kautner, 86 mins.)

Resurrection Syndicate—See: **Nothing But the Night**

Retik, the Moon Menace (1952-66)* George Wallace, Aline Towne. (Dir: Fred C. Brannon, 100 mins.)

Retreat, Hell! (1952)** Frank Lovejoy, Richard Carlson, Anita Louise. Undistinguished Korean War drama. (Dir; Joseph H. Lewis, 95 mins.)

Return from the Ashes (Great Britain, 1965)*** Maximilian Schell, Ingrid Thulin and Samantha Eggar plus some interesting plot twists make this weird suspense film worthwhile. After years in a Nazi concentration camp which left her scarred, Miss Thulin undergoes plastic surgery and returns to Paris eager to pick up her life. In the interim, her husband and stepdaughter have become lovers, and a strange twist of fate unites the trio in a diabolical game of wits. (Dir: J. Lee Thompson, 108 mins.)

Return from the Sea (1954)**½ Neville Brand, Jan Sterling. Pleasant film about two lonely people who meet in San Diego and fall in love. Miss Sterling has some very good moments as a plain waitress and Brand registers in a sympathetic role as a seaman. (Dir: Lesley Selander, 80 mins.)

Return from Witch Mountain (1978)** Bette Davis, Christopher Lee, Kim Richards, Ike Eisenmann. Sequel to Walt Disney studio's "Escape to Witch Mountain" has those two cute kids from outer space being used as pawns for the schemes of mad scientist Lee. He wants the supernatural powers of Ike and Kim to help him conquer the world, while accomplice Davis merely wants to use them to get rich quick. Fun only for the kids, with good special effects. (Dir: John Hough, 93 mins.)

Return of a Man Called Horse (1976)*** Richard Harris, Gale Sondergaard, Geoffrey Lewis. English aristocrat (Harris) returns to counter what the whites have been doing to the Indians. Sequel to "A Man Called Horse." Superior in every way to its predecessor, the film does also tend to revel in gratuitous sadism. The largely silent storyline is intelligently and excitingly handled, and while one may quibble with some of the sociological assumptions, it's an incisive and rousing job of visual expression. Recommended. (Dir: Irvin Kershner, 125 mins.)

Return of a Stranger (Great Britain, 1961)**½ John Ireland, Susan Stephen. Mysterious man causes plenty of tense moments for a young couple. Fairish suspense thriller, helped by the performers. (Dir: Max Varnel, 63 mins.)

Return of Charlie Chan, The—See: **Charlie Chan (Happiness Is a Warm Clue)**

Return of Doctor X (1939)*** Humphrey Bogart, Wayne Morris, Rosemary Lane, Dennis Morgan. Sequel to "Doctor X." The whole show here is a funny, chilling, off-beat performance by Bogart as the mad doctor of the title, being pursued by the usual spoil-sports. (Dir: Vincent Sherman, 62 mins.)

Return of Don Camillo, The (France, 1953)***½ Fernandel, Gino Cervi. Fernandel once more delights all as the hilariously unconventional priest Don Camillo. A small village is turned inside out and vastly changed by the pixie padre's arrival. Inventive writing and acting. (Dir: Julien Duvivier, 115 mins.)

Return of Dracula, The (1958)*½ Francis Lederer, Norma Eberhardt. (Dir: Paul Landres, 77 mins.)

Return of Frank James, The (1940)***½ Henry Fonda, Gene Tierney (debut), John Carradine, Jackie Cooper, Henry Hull. Tautly-directed sequel to "Jesse James," which follows Frank as he sets out to find the man who shot his brother in the back, Bob Ford. Humorous, direct, fast-paced, perhaps better than the original. (Dir: Fritz Lang, 92 mins.)

Return of Giant Majin (Japan, 1966)*½ Kojiro Hongo. (Dirs: Kenji Misumi, Yoshiyuki Kuroda, 78 mins.)

Return of Jesse James (1950)**½ John Ireland, Ann Dvorak, Hugh O'Brian. Small-time outlaw is a dead ringer for the late Jesse; he becomes a big-timer by cashing in on the James name. Above-average western. (Dir: Arthur Hilton, 75 mins.)

Return of Joe Forrester, The (MTV 1975)**½ Lloyd Bridges, Pat Crowley, Jim Backus. Bridges stars in this pilot film as Forrester, who returns to his old job as a cop on the beat, where his presence always spelled security to the neighborhood shopkeepers and tenants. The idea of street cop as friend and helper gives the story its appeal. (Dir: Virgil W. Vogel, 78 mins.)

Return of Monte Cristo (1946)**½ Louis Hayward, Barbara Britton, George Macready. Nephew to Edmund Dantes is framed to Devil's Island by enemies who wish to prevent him from claiming the Monte Cristo inheritance. Okay costume melodrama. (Dir: Henry Levin, 91 mins.)

Return of October, The (1948)**½ Glenn Ford, Terry Moore, James Gleason. Girl buys a racehorse because it reminds her of a dead uncle. In spite of corny Kentucky Derby finale, this has some laughs. (Dir: Joseph H. Lewis, 89 mins.)

Return of Peter Grimm (1935)*** Lionel Barrymore, Helen Mack. Man who dominated his household before death returns from the Beyond to find things changed. Interesting, well acted drama. (Dir: George Nicholls, Jr., 82 mins.)

Return of Sabata (Italy, 1971)* Lee Van Cleef. (Dir: Frank Kramer, 106 mins.)

Return of the Fly (1959)** Vincent Price, Brett Halsey. Sequel to the successful box-office thriller "The Fly," this second attempt to construct another macabre tale about a man who turns into a fly during an experiment doesn't live up to its predecessor's chilly sequences. (Dir: Edward L. Bernds, 80 mins.)

Return of the Giant Monsters (Japan, 1967)* Kojiro Hongo, Kichijiro Ueda. (Dir: Noriaki Yuasa, 85 mins.)

Return of the Gunfighter (MTV 1966)**½ Robert Taylor, Chad Everett, Ana Martin. Lively western about a gunslinger who goes looking for the murderers of an old friend. Routine plot but plenty of action, good production, rugged performance by Taylor. (Dir: James Neilson, 98 mins.)

Return of the Incredible Hulk, The (MTV 1977)** Bill Bixby, Lou Ferrigno, Jack Colvin. Second feature based on the comic-book Hulk is no better than the first. Bixby again plays mild-mannered scientist David Banner, who is transformed, whenever he gets angry, into a seven-foot, green, raging creature endowed with incredible strength. (Dir: Alan Levi, 104 mins.)

Return of the Mod Squad, The (1979)**½ Clarence Williams III, Peggy Lipton, Michael Cole, Sugar Ray Robinson. Sequel to the old TV series, about three young undercover police officers. Same old stuff, with the three being plunged into jeopardy at every turn. (Dir: George McCowan, 104 mins.)

Return of the Pink Panther, The (Great Britain, 1975)**** Peter Sellers, Herbert Lom, Christopher Plummer, Catherine Schell. A triumphant return of Sellers (as the exquisitely inept Inspector Clouseau) under the razor-sharp direction of Blake Edwards. (115 mins.)

Return of the Secaucus Seven, The (1980)**** Director John Sayles, making a debut long feature in 16-mm for $60,000, presents another reunion of aging '60s types coping with disillusion. Literate, funny, and engrossing. (106 mins.)

Return of the Seven (1966)* Yul Brynner, Robert Fuller, Jordan Christopher. (Dir: Burt Kennedy, 96 mins.)

Return of the Tall Blond Man with One Black Shoe, The (France, 1974)*** Pierre Richard, Mireille Darc, Jean Rochefort. Frequently funny sequel finds Richard again playing a naive classical musician caught up in the world of espionage. (Dir: Yves Robert, 89 mins.)

Return of the Texan (1952)** Dale Robertson, Joanne Dru, Walter Brennan, Richard Boone. Talky drama about the obstacles faced by a handsome widower who comes back to the homestead where he grew up. Walter Brennan plays a role that may remind you of his "Grandpa McCoy" characterization. (Dir: Delmer Daves, 88 mins.)

Return of the World's Greatest Detective, The (MTV 1976)*½ Larry Hagman, Jenny Colasanto, Nicholas Colasanto, Woodrow Parfey. (Dir: Dean Hargrove, 72 mins.)

Return to Earth (MTV 1976)**½ Cliff Robertson, Shirley Knight, Ralph Bellamy, Stefanie Powers. Edwin "Buzz" Aldrin,

the second man to walk on the moon, is the subject of this moderately engrossing movie. Robertson is excellent as Aldrin; his military carriage, clipped speech and low-key playing get inside the man, showing us how a national hero can suffer severe depression in the aftermath of what was, by his standards, the high point of his life. Knight is also good as Aldrin's wife, Joan, trying to help him but unable to break through his defenses. (Dir: Jud Taylor, 72 mins.)

Return to Fantasy Island (MTV 1978)** Ricardo Montalbán, Hervé Villechaize, Joseph Cotten. Pilot film. People shell out a lot of money to live out their fantasies. (Dir: George McGowan, 104 mins.)

Return to Macon County (1975)**½ Nick Nolte, Don Johnson. Nolte and Johnson, as a pair of itinerant drag-racing bums, are much better than their material as they again get in trouble with the law. A sequel of sorts to "Macon County Line." (Dir: Richard Compton, 104 mins.)

Return to Paradise (1953)**½ Gary Cooper, Roberta Haynes. Slow-moving story of the romance of a bum and a native girl in the South Seas. (Dir: Mark Robson, 100 mins.)

Return to Peyton Place (1961)* Carol Lynley, Jeff Chandler, Eleanor Parker, Mary Astor, Tuesday Weld. (Dir: José Ferrer, 122 mins.)

Return to Sender (Great Britain, 1963)** Nigel Davenport, Yvonne Romain. Tycoon makes an agreement with the underworld to destroy the reputation of the prosecuting attorney who sent him to prison. Fair Edgar Wallace crime-drama. (Dir: Gordon Hales, 61 mins.)

Returning Home (MTV 1975)**½ Dabney Coleman, Tom Selleck, James R. Miller, Whitney Blake, Joan Goodfellow. Remake is not as good as award-winning 1946 film "The Best Years of Our Lives." Tasteful retelling of the wonderful story of three returning WW II veterans, and their adjustment to civilian life. (Dir: Daniel Petrie, 72 mins.)

Reunion in France (1942)*½ Joan Crawford, John Wayne. (Dir: Jules Dassin, 104 mins.)

Reunion in Reno (1951)**½ Mark Stevens, Peggy Dow. Lightweight comedy-drama about a little girl who turns a Reno divorce lawyer's life into a merry-go-round when she decides to investigate the possibility of divorcing her parents. Gigi Perreau plays the nine-year-old with charm. (Dir: Kurt Neumann, 79 mins.)

Reveille with Beverly (1943)** Ann Miller, William Wright, Dick Purcell. Miller is a dynamo as a disk jockey who puts on a big show with Frank Sinatra, Duke Ellington, Count Basie, Bob Crosby, and the Mills Brothers. (Dir: Charles Barton, 78 mins.)

Revenge (Great Britain, 1971)* Joan Collins, James Booth, Sinead Cusack. (Dir: Sidney Hayers, 89 mins.)

Revenge at Daybreak (France, 1958)** Danielle Delorme, Henri Vidal. Ordinary melodrama set during the Irish revolution—young girl sets out to avenge her brother's death. (Dir: Yves Allegret, 84 mins.)

Revenge for a Rape (MTV 1976)½ Mike Connors, Robert Reed, Deanna Lund. (Dir: Timothy Galfas, 106 mins.)

Revenge of Black Eagle (Italy, 1964)*½ Rossano Brazzi, Gianna Maria Canale. (Dir: Riccardo Freda, 97 mins.)

Revenge of Frankenstein, The (Great Britain, 1958)**½ Peter Cushing, Francis Matthews. Another in the series of films made about the creation of the Frankenstein monster. Production is well mounted and very well acted. (Dir: Terence Fisher, 94 mins.)

Revenge of Ivanhoe, The (Italy, 1965)* Clyde Rogers (aka Rik van Nutter), Gilda Lousak. (Dir: Amerigo Anton, 98 mins.)

Revenge of the Barbarians (Italy, 1961)*½ Anthony Steel, Daniella Rocca, Robert Alda. (Dir: Giuseppe Vari, 104 mins.)

Revenge of the Conquered (Italy, 1962)* Burt Nelson, Wandisa Guida. (Dir: Luigi Capuano, 91 mins.)

Revenge of the Creature (1955)** John Agar, Lori Nelson, John Bromfield. The gill-man from the Black Lagoon, on his third outing and looking the worse for wear. Young Clint Eastwood has a bit part. (Dir: Jack Arnold, 82 mins.)

Revenge of the Gladiators (Italy, 1964)* Mickey Hargitay, Jose Greci. (Dir: Luigi Capuano, 90 mins.)

Revenge of the Gladiators (Italy, 1965)** Roger Browne, Scilla Gabel, Gordon Mitchell. Suspense tale in post-Spartacus Rome as slave revolt turns out to be a plot by a Roman senator. Battle scenes are OK. (Dir: Michele Lupo, 100 mins.)

Revenge of the Musketeers (Italy, 1962)* Fernando Lamas, Gloria Milland. (Dir: Fulvio Tulvi, 93 mins.)

Revenge of the Pink Panther (Great Britain, 1978)**½ Peter Sellers, Dyan Cannon, Herbert Lom. In number six of the series Sellers gives an unconscionably sloppy performance as Inspector Clouseau, redeemed only in his scenes with a goofy Cannon. Lom gets better with each Panther picture. (Dir: Blake Edwards, 99 mins.)

Revenge of the Pirates (Italy, 1951)*½ Maria Montez, Jean-Pierre Aumont, Milly Vitale. (Dir: Primo Zeglio, 95 mins.)

Revenge of Ursus (Italy, 1961)* Samson Burke. (Dir: Luigi Capuano, 99 mins.)

Revengers, The (1972)** William Holden, Susan Hayward, Ernest Borgnine. Western riddled with clichés. Holden is bent on revenge and enlists a motley crew of killers. Hayward is around to show that Holden may have a soft spot in his head...we mean heart. (Dir: Daniel Mann, 110 mins.)

Revolt at Fort Laramie (1957)**½ John Dehner, Frances Helm. Army fort is split upon the outbreak of the Civil War, with the commander torn between loyalty to the South and duty as an officer. Pretty fair western, with a somewhat different plot and good acting by Dehner. (Dir: Lesley Selander, 73 mins.)

Revolt in the Big House (1958)**½ Gene Evans, Robert Blake. Cons plan a daring escape headed by a good cast with a good performance by young Blake. (Dir: R. G. Springsteen, 79 mins.)

Revolt of Mamie Stover, The (1956)**½ Jane Russell, Richard Egan, Joan Leslie, Agnes Moorehead. Above-average melodrama of a beautiful young girl, forced to leave town, who goes to Hawaii and earns a small fortune as a dance-hall hostess during WW II. Based on a novel by William Bradford Huie. (Dir: Raoul Walsh, 93 mins.)

Revolt of the Barbarians (Italy, 1964)* Roland Caray, Grazia Maria Spina. (99 mins.)

Revolt of the Mamalukes (Egypt, 1963)*½ Omar Sharif. (Dir: Aatef Salem, 90 mins.)

Revolt of the Mercenaries (Italy-Spain, 1962)*½ Virginia Mayo, Conrad Sammartin. (Dir: Piero Costa, 102 mins.)

Revolt of the Praetorians (Italy, 1965)* Richard Harrison, Moira Orfei. (Dir: Alfonso Brescia, 95 mins.)

Revolt of the Tartars (Italy, 1956)** Curt Jurgens, Genevieve Page. Emissary of the czar undertakes a dangerous trek to deliver a message to the Grand Duke. Lavishly produced, somewhat slow moving. Fair spectacle stuff. English-dubbed. (Dir: Carmine Gallone, 111 mins.)

Reward, The (1965)* Max von Sydow, Yvette Mimieux, Efrem Zimbalist, Jr., Gilbert Roland. (Dir: Serge Bourguignon, 92 mins.)

Reward (MTV 1980)** Michael Parks, Annie McEnroe, Richard Jaeckel. Parks, cast as an ex-cop bent on vindicating his dead partner, is amiable, but you've seen this story before. (Dir: E. W. Swackhamer, 78 mins.)

Rhapsody (1954)** Elizabeth Taylor, Vittorio Gassman, John Ericson, Louis Calhern. Taylor plays a wealthy woman involved with a pianist and a violinist in this long and turgid romance, which isn't redeemed by sequences of classical music dubbed in by Claudio Arrau and Michael Rabin. Adapted by Fay and Michael Kanin from a novel by H. H. Richardson, the film is an unrelieved drag. (Dir: Charles Vidor, 115 mins.)

Rhapsody in Blue (1945)**½ Robert Alda (film debut), Alexis Smith, Oscar Levant. Biopic of George Gershwin shows some care and intelligence, but suffers from the requirements of that boring genre, the musical success-and-heartbreak story. Paul Whiteman performs the complete title tune. (Dir: Irving Rapper, 139 mins.)

Rhino (1964)**½ Robert Culp, Shirley Eaton, Harry Guardino. An exciting show for the younger set. About a zoologist who

555

goes after a rare white rhino. The animal footage is very interesting. The cast really has little to do, but the South African scenery is gorgeous. (Dir: Ivan Tors, 91 mins.)

Rhinoceros (1974)** Zero Mostel, Karen Black, Gene Wilder. Grotesque rendition of Eugene Ionesco's antifascist parable where people turn into rhinoceroses. Director Tom O'Horgan's camera trickery obscures Ionesco's method—which is to let the horror build up in the audience's imagination—opting instead for frenetic spectacle. Wilder is marvelous as a mild man who holds out for his own individuality, but Mostel gives a hysterical exhibition as Wilder's prissy friend who goes out of control with "rhinoceritis." An American Film Theatre presentation. (101 mins.)

Rhubarb (1951)***½ Ray Milland, Jan Sterling, Gene Lockhart. When a millionaire who owns a baseball club passes on, a cat inherits the team; as a mascot the feline leads the club toward a pennant. Zany comedy has plenty of fun and an amazingly well-trained cat actor. From the story by H. Allen Smith. (Dir: Arthur Lubin, 95 mins.)

Rhythm and Blues Review (1955)*** Filmed live at the Apollo, featuring Count Basie, Lionel Hampton, Cab Calloway (doing "Minnie the Moocher"), Sarah Vaughn, Nat King Cole, Big Joe Turner, and the Delta Rhythm Boys. Valuable jazz archive footage. Color. (70 mins.)

Rhythm on the Range (1936)** Bing Crosby, Martha Raye, Bob Burns, Frances Farmer. Cowboy Bing romances an heiress and a prize cow in this forced comic offering. (Dir: Norman Taurog, 88 mins.)

Rhythm on the River (1940)*** Bing Crosby, Mary Martin, Oscar Levant, Basil Rathbone. Nothing turns into something when handled by experts. A couple of successful ghost song writers try and click on their own, but only succeed in falling in love. Pleasant musical. (Dir: Victor Schertzinger, 94 mins.)

Rice Girl (Italy, 1959)** Elsa Martinelli, Michel Auclair. Lust and love in the rice fields, as a girl finds promise of happiness after a hard past. After Mangano and Loren working in the same neighborhood, this drama is pretty mild. Dubbed-in English. (Dir: Raffaello Matarazzo, 90 mins.)

Rich and Strange (Great Britain, 1931)*** Joan Barry, Henry Kendall, Betty Amann. A strange, semi-humorous early Hitchcock where the title really tells it all. A discontented young couple suddenly come into a large sum of money, and decide to take a trip around the world. They go through some wild adventures, find out more than they want to know about each other, and wind up in the middle of a shipwreck. Unexpected and entertaining. (Dir: Alfred Hitchcock, 91 mins.)

Rich Kids (1979)*** Trini Alvarado, John Lithgow, Kathryn Walker, Irene Worth.

Intelligent and pleasant but shallow film about children of divorce. The actors, all from the New York stage, get deeper into their characters than we have grown accustomed to, but do not register comfortably on camera. Walker's bitter wife is a standout, as is the sharp cameo by Worth as her mother. (Dir: Robert M. Young, 96 mins.)

Rich, Young and Pretty (1951)**½ Jane Powell, Vic Damone, Fernando Lamas, Wendell Corey, Danielle Darrieux. A typical MGM musical built around Jane Powell's soprano talents. She's a Texan's daughter who finds her long-lost mom in gay Paree. (Dir: Norman Taurog, 95 mins.)

Richard Pryor Is Back (1979)***½ Richard Pryor. We didn't know he'd been gone! Practically the same concert Pryor gave one day earlier in the same auditorium in "Richard Pryor Live in Concert." So seeing this is like seeing the first film again. If you haven't seen the earlier film, see this one.

Richard Pryor Live in Concert (1979)**** Richard Pryor. Captures Pryor in all his glory, unfettered by mass media restraints. A remarkable document of a brilliant, manically funny act. (Dir: Jeff Margolis, 78 mins.)

Richard II (Great Britain, MTV 1978)**** Derek Jacobi, John Gielgud, Jon Finch, Charles Gray, David Swift, Wendy Hiller, Mary Morris, Janet Maw. Jacobi will fascinate you as the young English king Richard II, who, reigned over medieval England when the Wars of the Roses, lasting nearly one hundred years, were about to erupt. Shakespeare used these history plays as an opportunity to examine the concepts of law, royalty, honor, and duty. His idea of Richard, who was deposed in 1399 by his valorous, determined cousin, Henry Bolingbroke, was of a monarch more poet and playboy than pragmatist or warrior. This series of plays has many important but briefly seen characters, who were as well-known to the Elizabethan audience as George Washington is to us; modern viewers are aided by television under these circumstances, where the same actors will be playing the same roles throughout the eight-play cycle. We might not recognize the titles or names (in fact, some characters are called by several different names in the same play!), but we do get to know the faces. The BBC production displays the playwright's detailed eloquence of word and thought. All the actors are admirable; Jacobi becomes an unforgettably moving figure in his final, despairing hours. (Dir: David Giles, 180 mins.)

Richard III (Great Britain, 1955)**** Laurence Olivier, Claire Bloom, Ralph Richardson, John Gielgud. Olivier is wickedly funny, reveling in the evil ambition of Shakespeare's totally villainous king. Marvelous film of the humpbacked king and his conquests on the battlefield and in the boudoir. (158 mins.)

Richie Brockelman, Private Eye (MTV 1976)** Dennis Dugan, Suzanne Pleshette, Norman Fell. Dugan is an unlikely private detective in this uneven yarn. Husky-voiced Pleshette is good as an amnesiac femme fatale who hires the young would-be Sam Spade to find out who she is. (Dir: Hy Averback, 78 mins.)

Ricochet Romance (1954)** Marjorie Main, Chill Wills, Rudy Vallee. Marjorie Main is back playing her "Ma Kettle" characterization in everything but name. Some funny moments. (Dir: Charles Lamont, 80 mins.)

Riddance (Hungary, 1973)*** Erzesbet Kutvolgyi, Gabor Nagy, Mariann Moor. Often touching love story. A young female factory worker meets a boy from a richer family and feels obliged to claim she's a university student. Miss Kutvolgyi is attractive in the leading role. Communist Hungary hasn't gotten rid of the class system, according to this tale written and sensitively directed by a woman, Marta Meszaros. (84 mins.)

Ride a Crooked Mile (1938)** Akim Tamiroff, Frances Farmer. Corny, overdone drama about a boy who decides to help his growling thief of a father break out of Leavenworth. Some good acting, but the story is more confusing than entertaining. (Dir: Alfred E. Green, 78 mins.)

Ride a Wild Pony (Australia, 1975)** Michael Craig, John Meillon, Eva Griffith. Slow-moving family yarn set in the Edwardian period. Two children claim the same wild pony as their own. A court battle follows. (Dir: Don Chaffey, 104 mins.)

Ride Back, The (1957)*** Anthony Quinn, Lita Milan, William Conrad. Anthony Quinn makes more of this low key western than seems possible. The plot, about a U.S. law officer tracking a wanted murderer in Mexico, unfolds slowly but the actors bring honest characterizations. (Dir: Allen H. Miner, 79 mins.)

Ride Beyond Vengeance (1966)** Chuck Connors, Michael Rennie, Gloria Grahame, Joan Blondell, James MacArthur. Familiar western drama told in flashback by a saloon keeper. Connors returns to his home after getting a stake and is robbed and branded by a band of outlaws. (Dir: Bernard McEveety, 101 mins.)

Ride 'Em Cowboy (1942)**½ Bud Abbott, Lou Costello, Dick Foran, Anne Gwynne. One of the better Abbott and Costello vehicles has them out West on a dude ranch. Features a great chase sequence and the usual antic humor. Songs by the Merry Macs and Ella Fitzgerald are a restful break. (Dir: Arthur Lubin, 82 mins.)

Ride in the Whirlwind (1967)*** Cameron Mitchell, Millie Perkins, Jack Nicholson. With a little bit more work, this western drama could have been memorable. As it

is, it is a better-than-average tale of western justice and the men who fled from it and those who searched for it. The cast is good, with Mitchell delivering the film's best performance. (Dir: Monte Hellman, 82 mins.)

Ride Lonesome (1959)**½ Randolph Scott, Karen Steele, Pernell Roberts. Good Scott western epic which should appeal to his fans. He plays a former sheriff who captures a young renegade and brings him to justice. (Dir: Budd Boetticher, 73 mins.)

Ride Out for Revenge (1957)**½ Rory Calhoun, Gloria Grahame, Lloyd Bridges. A bang-up western with all the clichés nicely fitted into the brief running time of the film. Calhoun upholds the law and meets with a great deal of opposition from the bad guys. (Dir: Bernard Girard, 79 mins.)

Ride the High Country (1962)**** Joel McCrea, Randolph Scott, Mariette Hartley (debut). An absolutely first-rate western, which gives Scott and McCrea, in their last performances as western heroes, the best roles of their lives, and they make the most of it. Directed by Sam Peckinpah in a controlled, subtle way—unlike many of his later violence-laden films. Written by N. B. Stone, Jr., and shot on location in the glorious Inyo National Forest in California. Two old-time lawmen sign on to escort gold from the goldfields to the bank, meeting trouble along the way. (94 mins.)

Ride the High Iron (1957)*½ Don Taylor, Sally Forrest, Raymond Burr. (Dir: Don Weis, 74 mins.)

Ride the High Wind (South Africa, 1965)** Maria Perschy, Albert Lieven, Darren McGavin. Bush pilot (Darren McGavin) sets out to recover long-lost gold. Unusual locale, familiar plot. (Dir: David Millin, 86 mins.)

Ride the Man Down (1952)*** Rod Cameron, Brian Donlevy, Ella Raines. Ranch foreman keeps it from land grabbers while awaiting the new owners. Fast-paced, exciting western with a good cast. (Dir: Joseph Kane, 90 mins.)

Ride the Pink Horse (1947)**** Robert Montgomery, Wanda Hendrix, Thomas Gomez, Andrea King, Fred Clark, Iris Flores. Suspenseful tale of a hoodlum helped by a Mexican girl when he is crossed by his employers. Out of the ordinary crime drama with superb performances and direction by Montgomery. Remade as "The Hanged Man." (101 mins.)

Ride the Wild Surf (1964)** Tab Hunter, Fabian, Barbara Eden. The kids are the best audience for this swinging film about the surfing craze in Hawaii. A group of young bronzed surfers engage in romantic interludes in between their riding the big waves. (Dir: Don Taylor, 101 mins.)

Ride to Hangman's Tree, The (1967)** Jack Lord, James Farentino, Melodie Johnson. A remake, for no discernible reason, of "Black Bart." The original was a humdrum western, and so is this familiar tale about three partners in crime who decide to try and go straight. (Dir: Al Rafkin, 90 mins.)

Ride Vaquero (1953)** Robert Taylor, Ava Gardner, Howard Keel, Anthony Quinn. Sluggish western concerns a smouldering beauty who causes the downfall of some notorious outlaws. Melodramatic situations are too much, making the cast look silly at times. (Dir: John Farrow, 90 mins.)

Rider on a Dead Horse (1962)** John Vivyan, Lisa Lu, Bruce Gordon. Prospector seeks revenge when his partner murders a third and tries to pin it on him. Undistinguished western. (Dir: Herbert L. Strock, 72 mins.)

Rider on the Rain (France-Italy, 1969)*** Charles Bronson, Marlene Jobert, Jill Ireland. Satisfying thriller that suspends credulity and keeps you guessing through neat psychological twists. Mellie (Jobert) has been raped in her home but has dropped her attacker with a shotgun blast. Arrogant investigator Dobbs (Bronson) appears on the trail of an escaped inmate. Sharp dialogue, underplayed acting and deft directorial control blend for fine suspense. Taut screenplay by novelist Sebastien Japrisot. (Dir: Rene Clement, 119 mins.)

Riders to the Stars (1954)**½ William Lundigan, Herbert Marshall, Richard Carlson, Martha Hyer, Dawn Addams. Fair science-fiction thriller about three men sent into outer space to investigate certain meteor behavior. (Dir: Richard Carlson, 81 mins.)

Riding High (1943)*** Dorothy Lamour, Victor Moore, Dick Powell. Big budgeted musical with little entertainment value. Something about a silver mine, a young man who wants to save it, and some musical nothings. (Dir: George Marshall, 89 mins.)

Riding High (1950)**½ Bing Crosby, Coleen Gray, Charles Bickford. Mark Hellinger's story about a businessman who'd rather spend his time at the race track is turned into a pleasant Crosby comedy with songs. Veteran comedy director Frank Capra keeps things snapping and a good supporting cast of pros, like Raymond Walburn, William Demarest and Bickford, give the film an added charm. Remake of "Broadway Bill." (112 mins.)

Riding Shotgun (1954)** Randolph Scott, Wayne Morris. Scott is riding and shooting in his usual manner. (Dir: André de Toth, 74 mins.)

Riff-Raff! (France, 1961)** Robert Hossein, Marina Vlady. Inquest into a girl's death brings forth many surprising discoveries. Long, involved melodrama moves too slowly. English-dubbed. (Dir: Jean Valere, 109 mins.)

Riffraff (1935)** Jean Harlow, Spencer Tracy, Mickey Rooney. Cliché filled, melodramatic story of the tuna fishing indus-

try in California. An insult to its excellent cast. (Dir: J. Walter Ruben, 96 mins.)

Riffraff (1947)*** Pat O'Brien, Anne Jeffreys. Crooks are after an oil field survey in Panama, but are foiled by the local jack-of-all-trades. Well done melodrama holds the interest. (Dir: Ted Tetzlaff, 80 mins.)

Rififi (France, 1954)**** Jean Servais, Carl Mohner, Jules Dassin. There's a classic robbery scene in this exciting story about some crooks whose mutual distrust traps them all. A superior film. Brilliantly directed by American Jules Dassin. (115 mins.)

Rififi in Amsterdam (Italy-Spain, 1966)*½ Roger Browne, Aida Power, Evelyne Stewart. (Dir: Terence Hathaway, 83 mins.)

Right Cross (1950)**½ Dick Powell, June Allyson, Ricardo Montalbán, Lionel Barrymore, Marilyn Monroe. Good prizefighting story about a Mexican boxer who desperately wants to become a champion. Montalbán, as the pugilist, takes top acting honors with Powell a close second as an easy-going sportswriter. (Dir: John Sturges, 90 mins.)

Right Hand of the Devil (1963)*½ Aram Katcher, Lisa McDonald. (Dir: Aram Katcher, 72 mins.)

Right On (1971)***½ Powerful, independent low-budget film. Director Herbert Danska focuses his cameras on three young, activist black poets. Their anger, dreams and concerns seem to burst thru the screen aided by some stunning visual images. Photographed largely in New York's Harlem. (80 mins.)

Right out of History: The Making of Judy Chicago's Dinner Party (1980)*** Documentary record of a much publicized and conceptually bold artistic project—"The Dinner Party," a feminist tribute to great women. Records the team efforts to solve artistic, technical, and financial problems. The artwork itself centers around dinner plates, most of which remind us that the vagina is the source of all life. (Dir: Johanna Demetrakas, 75 mins.)

Ring, The (1952)**½ Gerald Mohr, Lalo Rios, Rita Moreno. Mexican lad from the Los Angeles slums is turned into a boxing prospect, gets too cocky as a result. Smoothly made drama of fighting and racial discrimination, nicely acted. (Dir: Kurt Neumann, 79 mins.)

Ring of Bright Water (Great Britain, 1969)*½ Bill Travers, Virginia McKenna, Peter Jeffrey. (Dir: Jack Couffer, 107 mins.)

Ring of Fear (1954)** Mickey Spillane, Pat O'Brien, Clyde Beatty. Cops and robbers in a circus tent performed mostly by nonactors—Beatty, Spillane, and tamed animals. (Dir: James Grant, 93 mins.)

Ring of Fire (1961)** David Janssen, Joyce Taylor, Frank Gorshin. A try for suspense as some hoodlums capture a lawman and hold him hostage in their flight for freedom. Some nice scenery and a spectacular explosion at the end, but it needs more; weak script, so-so performances. (Dir: Andrew L. Stone, 91 mins.)

Ring of Passion (MTV 1978)***½ Bernie Casey, Stephen Macht, Britt Ekland. A first-rate boxing movie, with Casey as the great heavyweight champion Joe Louis and Macht as a sympathetic Max Schmeling who wanted nothing to do with Hitler's racist madness, but was afraid to speak out. Good fight sequences. (Dir: Robert Michael Lewis, 104 mins.)

Ring of Terror (1962)*½ George Mather, Austin Green. (Dir: Clark Paylow, 72 mins.)

Ring of Treason (1964)**½ Bernard Lee, William Sylvester, Margaret Tyzack. Staccato suspense in this punctuated story of a Russian spy ring in London. Lee is an ex-navy man taken to drink and mixing in with vile people. British in detail and design, and based on Britain's Portland spy case. Exciting finale. (Dir: Robert Tronson, 90 mins.)

Rings on Her Fingers (1942)**½ Henry Fonda, Gene Tierney, Laird Cregar. Well played but overdone tale of a girl who is conned into fronting for swindlers and falls for her first victim. (Dir: Rouben Mamoulian, 85 mins.)

Rio Bravo (1959)**** John Wayne, Dean Martin, Ricky Nelson, Walter Brennan, Ward Bond. Humorous western is a Howard Hawks–directed masterwork. Wayne is sheriff and Martin is drunk. (141 mins.)

Rio Conchos (1964)** Richard Boone, Stuart Whitman, Tony Franciosa. For western action fans who can't get their fill of two-fisted he-men living by their own code in the old West. The cast is a good one, including Jim Brown and Edmond O'Brien. About a group who set out to recover some stolen rifles which are earmarked for sale to the Apaches. (Dir: Gordon Douglas, 107 mins.)

Rio Grande (1950)***½ John Wayne, Maureen O'Hara, Victor McLaglen, Ben Johnson, Harry Carey, Jr. Tough cavalry commander awaits orders to cross a river so he can clean up marauding Indians. John Ford epic western has beautiful scenery, some good action and plenty of human interest. (105 mins.)

Rio Lobo (1970)*½ John Wayne, Jorge Rivero, Jennifer O'Neill, Jack Elam. (Dir: Howard Hawks, 114 mins.)

Rio Rita (1929)*** Bebe Daniels, John Boles, Bert Wheeler, Robert Woolsey. Early talkie, a sagebrush operetta adapted from the Ziegfeld stage hit, is not too bad. Vaudevillians Wheeler and Woolsey were never better. Luther Reed directs without much life. (135 mins.)

Rio Rita (1942)*** Kathryn Grayson, Bud Abbott, Lou Costello. A & C fans and even a few others will enjoy this musical about a ranch which is infested with Nazi spies. (Dir: S. Sylvan Simon, 91 mins.)

Riot (1969)**½ This typical prison drama, in which some up-to-date violence has been thrown in, benefits from the strong acting personalities of Jim Brown and Gene Hackman. The story concerns a group of cons who take over a section of the prison, hold some guards as hostages, and the fireworks begin. (Dir: Buzz Kulik, 97 mins.)

Riot in Cell Block 11 (1954)***½ Neville Brand, Leo Gordon, Emile Meyer. Grim, violent, but thoughful prison drama based on the experiences of producer Walter Wanger (who was incarcerated for shooting Jennings Lang). Brand plays a prisoner who is paranoid but solid, and Gordon contributes perhaps his best incarnation of the angry heavy. (Dir: Don Siegel, 80 mins.)

Riot on Sunset Strip (1967)* Aldo Ray, Mimsy Farmer. (Dir: Arthur Dreifuss, 85 mins.)

Rise and Fall of Legs Diamond, The (1960)*** Ray Danton, Elaine Stewart, Karen Steele, Jesse White, Simon Oakland. Fast-moving and impressive account of the career of a hoodlum who rose to national infamy. Danton slickly portrays the racketeer and there's plenty of pulchritude for the male audience. (Dir: Budd Boetticher, 101 mins.)

Rise and Rise of Casanova, The—See: **Some Like It Cool**

Rise and Shine (1941)*** Jack Oakie, Linda Darnell, Milton Berle, George Murphy, Walter Brennan, Sheldon Leonard. Occassionally hilarious comedy about a dumb football hero's adventures. Oakie is perfect and you should have some fun with this in spite of some uninspired music. (Dir: Allan Dwan, 93 mins.)

Rise of Louis XIV, The (France, 1966)**** Jean-Marie Patte, Raymond Jourdan, Silvagni, Pierre Barrat. One of a series of brilliant historical films directed by Roberto Rossellini for Italian TV. Begins with the last days and death of Mazarin, includes the building of Versailles, and ends as Louis XIV forces his court to watch him devour a 14-course meal. This ravishing photography and the dazzling costumes are a feast for the eye thanks to cinematographer Georges LeClerc. The Sun King is presented as the complex, bizarre figure he surely was. (100 mins.)

Rising of the Moon (Ireland, 1957)*** Frank Lawton, Denis O'Dea, Cyril Cusack, Noel Purcell, Maureen Connell. Trio of Irish tales directed by John Ford. Full of the ould blarney but still charming. Introduced by Tyrone Power. (81 mins.)

Rising Target (1976)*** Documentary of Senator Robert F. Kennedy's campaign in the '68 California presidential primary and his assassination the day of his victory. Director Barbara Frank calls her compilation a thriller about politics, show business, idealism, and murder. Virtually completed in '69, but not released for seven years. Glimpses along the way of wife

Ethel, Jerry Lewis, Gene Kelly, Ted Kennedy, Walter Cronkite, etc. (80 mins.)

Risk, The (Great Britain, 1960)*** Peter Cushing, Tony Britton, Virginia Maskell, Donald Pleasence. When a cure for plague is discovered, then withheld, resentment causes a scientist to become prey for foreign agents after the formula. Tightly knit spy drama holds the attention throughout. (Dirs: Roy & John Boulting, 81 mins.)

Ritual of Evil (MTV 1969)**½ Louis Jourdan, Anne Baxter, Diana Hyland. Entertaining feature starring Jourdan as a psychiatrist interested in the bizarre world of the occult. A young heiress' death brings about Jourdan's investigation of the events leading to the tragedy. A series of good supporting players come on for their scenes. (Dir: Robert Day, 98 mins.)

Ritz, The (Great Britain, 1976)*** Jack Weston, Rita Moreno, Kaye Ballard, F. Murray Abraham, Jerry Stiller. A manic, fast-paced farce, set in a sleazy Manhattan homosexual bathhouse, that is, by turns, very funny, heavy-handed and repetitive. Adapted by Terrence McNally from his Broadway play. Director Richard Lester keeps things going along at a frantic pace. Moreno, playing a hopelessly untalented but very determined pop singer, is hilarious. (91 mins.)

Rivals, The (Great Britain, 1963)** Jack Gwillim, Erica Rogers. Daughter of a wealthy industrialist is kidnapped. Edgar Wallace crime melodrama. (Dir: Max Varnel, 56 mins.)

River, The (Great Britain, 1951)**** Esmond Knight, Nora Swinburne, Patricia Walters. Director Jean Renoir's masterpiece, his first film in color. The story concerns an English family living on the banks of the Ganges, and how the European mind can gradually succumb to the eternal perspectives of Inda. (99 mins.)

River Changes, The (West Germany, 1956)** Rossana Rory, Harold Maresch. A muddled drama about the inhaitants of a small village who are plagued by an army of ruthless men. Plenty of romance and some action. (Dir: Owen Crump, 91 mins.)

River Gang (1945)**½ Gloria Jean, Keefe Brasselle, John Qualen. Waterfront girl who lives in a land of fantasy becomes involved in murder and a crime ring. Offbeat grade B mystery has several above-average touches. (Dir: Charles David, 60 mins.)

River Lady (1948)*½ Yvonne DeCarlo, Rod Cameron, Dan Duryea. Riverboat gambling queen falls for a logger, builds a big logging syndicate. Flamboyantly routine action drama, nothing new. Color. (Dir: George Sherman, 78 mins.)

River of Evil (West Germany-Brazil, 1964)*½ Barbara Rutting, Harold Leipnitz. (Dirs: Helmut M. Backhaus, Franz Eichhorn, 86 mins.)

River of Gold (MTV 1970)*½ Roger Davis,

Suzanne Pleshette, Dack Rambo. (Dir: David Friedkin, 72 mins.)

River of Mystery (MTV 1971)**½ Vic Morrow, Claude Akins, Niall MacGinnis, Louise Sorel, Edmond O'Brien. Adventure tale about a hunt for diamonds in Brazil by a group of seedy characters including such familiar types as the perennial revolutionary leader and the American swindler forced to leave the U.S. Morrow and Akins are fine, Sorel is quite good, and O'Brien is well cast as a swindler. (Dir: Paul Stanley, 104 mins.)

River of No Return (1954)***½ Robert Mitchum, Marilyn Monroe, Rory Calhoun. Monroe and Mitchum search for her missing husband in an excellent western, one of the first films to discover the potential of CinemaScope. (Dir: Otto Preminger, 91 mins.)

River of Three Junks, The (France, 1957)*½ Dominique Wilms, Jean Gavin. (Dir: André Pergament, 93 mins.)

River's Edge, The (1957)*** Anthony Quinn, Ray Milland, Debra Paget. Better than average crime melodrama about a killer who menaces his old girlfriend and her husband's life in an attempt to smuggle a stolen fortune into Mexico. Excitement for action fans. (Dir: Allan Dwan, 87 mins.)

Rivkin: Bounty Hunter (MTV 1981)**½ Ron Leibman, Harry Morgan, Glenn Scarpelli, Harold Gary. Bounty hunting in New York means street chases on foot and via wheels. You've seen it all before. Still this is a carefully produced "streets of New York" number, particularly in the casting. Ron Leibman, a peppery hustler, is a "watch me, watch me" actor and his bounty hunter dominates every scene. You either like Leibman or you don't, there's no middle ground. Support for the compulsive Leibman is very strong, with young Glenn Scarpelli as son Keith, Harry Morgan as a neighborhood priest and New York's Harold Gary playing the realistic bail-bondsman. (Dir: Harry Harris, 104 mins.)

Road House (1948)*** Ida Lupino, Richard Widmark, Cornel Wilde, Celeste Holm. A good cast lifts this routine melodrama out of the ranks of mediocrity. Widmark plays a sadistic road house owner who has his enemy paroled in his custody so he can torture him. (Dir: Jean Negulesco, 95 mins.)

Road Show (1941)**½ Adolphe Menjou, Carole Landis, Patsy Kelly, Charles Butterworth, John Hubbard. A playboy and his screwy friend from an insane asylum join a traveling carnival. Completely mad, amusing farce. (Dirs: Hal Roach, Hal Roach, Jr., Gordon Douglas, 87 mins.)

Road to Bali, The (1952)** Later and lesser Hope-Crosby teaming, back in the South Seas with the spirits flagging and the color unflattering. (Dir: Hal Walker, 90 mins.)

Road to Denver (1955)**½ John Payne,

Mona Freeman, Lee J. Cobb, Skip Homeier, Lee Van Cleef. Cowhand tries to keep his hot-headed brother out of trouble when the kid joins up with the outlaws. Pretty fair western. (Dir: Joseph Kane, 90 mins.)

Road to Glory, The (1936)***½ Fredric March, Warner Baxter, Lionel Barrymore, June Lang. William Faulkner co-wrote the script, with Joel Sayre. Remarkably strong World War I story of a French regiment at the front, and the strains, stresses, and misunderstandings between commanders and men. Baxter and March both give powerful performances as soldiers who strive to finally work together. (Dir: Howard Hawks, 95 mins.)

Road to Hong Kong (1961)*** Bing Crosby, Bob Hope, Joan Collins, Dorothy Lamour. The last of the "Road" pictures, with only a brief appearance by Lamour. The plot centers around a couple of hustlers who find themselves up to their necks in international intrigue and interplanetary hokum. A good supporting cast includes Robert Morley, Joan Collins, and last but not least, Peter Sellers. (Dir: Norman Panama, 91 mins.)

Road to Morocco (1942)*** Bob Hope, Bing Crosby, Dorothy Lamour, Anthony Quinn. Zany Hope-Crosby comedy is a bit too silly, but still gets its share of laughs from their insults and encounters. A few good songs help out. (Dir: David Butler, 83 mins.)

Road to Rio (1947)*** Bob Hope, Bing Crosby, Dorothy Lamour, the Andrews Sisters, Gale Sonderguard. Crazy, delightful antics in Rio de Janeiro expertly handled by experts. Good fun. (Dir: Norman Z. McLeod, 100 mins.)

Road to Singapore (1940)*** Bob Hope, Bing Crosby, Dorothy Lamour, Anthony Quinn, Charles Coburn. First of the "Road" films and not much to offer except for Bob and Bing's presence. Zany tale about two playboys who go to Singapore to forget women. (Dir: Victor Schertzinger, 92 mins.)

Road to Utopia (1945)***½ Bing Crosby, Bob Hope, Dorothy Lamour, Hillary Brooke, Jack LaRue. Vaudeville team involved in search for Alaskan gold mine but—forget the plot—this one is funny. (Dir: Hal Walker, 90 mins.)

Road to Zanzibar (1941)***½ Bob Hope, Bing Crosby, Dorothy Lamour, Una Merkel, Eric Blore. Satire on all jungle pictures is the funniest of the "Road" series. Bing and Bob tour Africa as a couple of carnival hustlers. (Dir: Victor Schertzinger, 92 mins.)

Roadblock (1951)**½ Charles McGraw, Joan Dixon, Milburn Stone. Insurance investigator turns crook to get enough money for his girlfriend. Well acted, suspenseful crime melodrama. (Dir: Harold Daniels, 73 mins.)

Roadie (1980)** Meat Loaf, Art Carney, Blondie, Alice Cooper, Hank Williams, Jr.,

Roy Orbison. A meretricious movie. Director Alan Rudolph has no knack for comedy. The ungainly Meat Loaf, as the Texas boy who can fix anything, carries the movie with genuine star charisma, and he can act too. (105 mins.)

Roaring Twenties, The (1939)**** James Cagney, Priscilla Lane, Gladys George, Humphrey Bogart, Jeffrey Lynn, Frank McHugh. Bootleggers in New York, in one of the best Hollywood gangster films ever. Cagney gives a light, sure performance, and the pace is crisp. Director Raoul Walsh emerged with this film as the Hollywood action man with a lot extra. (106 mins.)

Robber's Roost (1955)*½ George Montgomery, Richard Boone. (Dir: Sidney Salkow, 82 mins.)

Robbery (Great Britain, 1967)**½ Stanley Baker, Joanna Pettet, James Booth, Frank Finlay, Barry Foster. This tense melodrama based on the hijacking of the London night mail train is only partially successful. The plans for the robbery and its actual execution are well handled, but the characterizations are overdrawn and get in the way. Based on the much publicized train robbery in England in '63. (Dir: Peter Yates, 114 mins.)

Robbery, Roman Style (Italy, 1965)** Claudia Mori, Adriano Celentano. Perfectly executed bank robbery goes awry when the crooks battle among themselves. Routine crime melodrama. Dubbed-in English. (Dir: Adriano Celentano, 93 mins.)

Robbery Under Arms (Great Britain, 1957)**½ Peter Finch, Ronald Lewis, David McCallum, Jill Ireland. Two brothers join an outlaw on a cattle-stealing venture in Australia. Well made, but very similar to our westerns. (Dir: Jack Lee, 83 mins.)

Robe, The (1953)*** Richard Burton, Jean Simmons, Victor Mature, Michael Rennie, Richard Boone. Hailed as the first film to be made in the CinemaScope process—which means nothing for TV viewers. The Lloyd C. Douglas religious novel about a Roman tribune ordered to crucify the Messiah, and his conversion to Christianity when he dons the robe of Jesus, is reverent, stately, impressively produced. It is also slow-moving, rather stilted, and not especially well acted. (Dir: Henry Koster, 135 mins.)

Roberta (1935)***½ Irene Dunne, Randolph Scott, Fred Astaire, Ginger Rogers. A sublime score with a dated plot. Astaire and Rogers are second bananas to Dunne and Scott, but probably do their best dance routines in this picture. Irene's singing voice is serviceable in those wondrous Jerome Kern ballads. (Dir: William A. Seiter, 105 mins.)

Robin (1979)** Monica Tidwell, Lee Dorsey, Louis Senesi. Fair drama of a model on the run from a tough pimp. She stops in a small town and is about to pursue an affair with a married lawyer when she is suddenly murdered. Tidwell shows some promise in the lead. (Dir: Hank Aldrich, 100 mins.)

Robin and Marian (Great Britain, 1976)**** Audrey Hepburn, Sean Connery, Robert Shaw, Richard Harris, Nicol Williamson, Denholm Elliott, Ian Holm. Hepburn returns in this historical romance—a revisionist view of medieval history and our friends from Sherwood Forest. But thanks largely to the two stars, this tale of Robin Hood, 20 years after he left Sherwood Forest to join Richard the Lion-Hearted on the Crusades, is a surprisingly affecting and genuinely touching love story. Connery and Hepburn are a magical pairing. Special credit to the photography of David Watkin. (Dir: Richard Lester, 106 mins.)

Robin and the Seven Hoods (1964)*** Frank Sinatra, Dean Martin, Bing Crosby, Sammy Davis, Jr., Barbara Rush, Peter Falk. Entertaining musical spoof of the Prohibition days in Chicago. Sinatra and his cronies are well suited to their roles of small-time hoods who fleece the rich and give to the less affluent, like orphans and such. The original musical score is very good, including a couple of standout songs, "My Kind of Town" and "Style." The entire cast appears to be having a good time and so will you. (Dir: Gordon Douglas, 103 mins.)

Robin Hood and the Pirates (Italy, 1961)*½ Lex Barker. (Dir: Giorgio C. Simonelli, 90 mins.)

Robinson Crusoe (MTV 1974)***½ Stanley Baker, Ram John Holder. Baker is the shipwrecked, resourceful hero of the Daniel Defoe novel. The wrenching aches of solitude are evoked, as are the methodical feats of labor Crusoe devised to keep himself occupied in body and mind. The final scenes of his meeting Friday (played with innocence and charm by Holder) and trying to teach the lad to speak English are involving. (Dir: James MacTaggart, 104 mins.)

Robinson Crusoe of Mystery Island (1936-66)*½ Ray Mala. (Dir: Mack V. Wright, 100 mins.)

Robinson Crusoe on Mars (1964)*** Adam West, Vic Lundin, Paul Mantee. Despite its ridiculous title this is an imaginative and intelligent sci-film about the survival of an American spaceman marooned on Mars. (Dir: Byron Haskin, 109 mins.)

Robot vs. the Aztec Mummy, The (Mexico, 1960)* Ramon Gay, Rosita Arenas. (Dir: Rafael Portillo, 65 mins.)

Rocco and His Brothers (Italy-France, 1960)***½ Alain Delon, Renato Salvatori, Annie Girardot, Katina Paxinou, Claudia Cardinale. Drama of a woman and her sons who come to Milan to find livelihood and the various fates befalling the offspring. Many subplots meticulously woven together to make a broad canvas of contemporary Italy, absorbing despite the length. Dubbed-in English. (Dir: Luchino Visconti, 152 mins.)

Rock-a-Bye Baby (1958)** Jerry Lewis, Marilyn Maxwell, Reginald Gardiner, Hans Conried. Lewis parents a set of unexpected triplets. Director Frank Tashlin manages to slip in a bit of Hollywood parody as Jerry invades the set of a deMille-ish religious spectacular. For Lewis fans and other unbalanced types. (107 mins.)

Rock Around the Clock (1956)** Bill Haley and His Comets, Johnny Johnston. Quickie musical produced to capitalize on the popularity of Haley. Johnston is around to further the plot—which is fairly nonexistent. Rock and roll fans may like to compare this vintage film with the current musical trends. (Dir: Fred F. Sears, 77 mins.)

Rock Around the World (1957)** Tommy Steele. Story—fictional perhaps—of British singing idol Steele. Lots of songs for his fans, nothing else.

Rock 'n' Roll High School (1979)**½ P. J. Soles, Vincent Van Patten, Clint Howard, the Ramones. Amiable, rambunctious film aimed ostensibly at the teen trade but more obliquely and effectively at New Wave fans. It's more cleverly cut than shot—which means that it moves quickly and energetically even as the concepts and characters disintegrate. (Dir: Alan Arkush, 94 mins.)

Rock 'n Roll Revue (1956)*** Duke Ellington, Dinah Washington, Lionel Hampton, Nat King Cole, Big Joe Turner, and the Clovers in a compilation of music acts. Hipsters will dig! (65 mins.)

Rock, Pretty Baby (1957)** John Saxon, Luana Patten, Sal Mineo, Fay Wray. Slight plot about a high-school band leader out to win the big contest tied to vast amount of rock-and-roll numbers. Teenagers should appreciate. (Dir: Richard Bartlett, 89 mins.)

Rock Rock Rock (1956)**½ Alan Freed, Frankie Lymon and the Teenagers, Chuck Berry, La Vern Baker, the Moonglows, the Flamingos, Johnny Burnette, Tuesday Weld (film debut). For rock archivists only; but if you're interested, this is your only chance to see some of these performers. (83 mins.)

Rocket from Calabuch (Spain-Italy, 1956)**½ Edmund Gwenn, Valentina Cortesa. Silly comedy about an old scientist who decides to experiment in rockets. The flavor of the village setting comes through and enhances the otherwise lightweight comedy. Gwenn is funny in the role of the bearded scientist. (Dir: Luis Berlanga, 90 mins.)

Rocket Man, The (1954)*½ Charles Coburn, Anne Francis, George Winslow, Spring Byington. (Dir: Oscar Rudolph, 79 mins.)

Rocket Ship X-M (1950)** Lloyd Bridges, Hugh O'Brian, Osa Massen. This B picture was probably the first to exploit space travel after WW II (beating George Pal's bigger "Destination: Moon" to the screen), and its plot premise is ludicrous: the astronauts set out for the Moon and end up on Mars instead. Music by Ferde Grofé. (Writer-Dir: Kurt Neumann, 77 mins.)

Rockford Files, The (1974)** James Garner, Lindsay Wagner. Pilot film for the TV series starring Garner as a private eye who insists on a $200-a-day fee from his pretty client (Miss Wagner) for fingering the murderer of her wino father. The best thing about the film, involving such familiar ploys as a harrowing car chase, is Garner's performance—he uses his easygoing dry wit to advantage. (Dir: Dick Heffron, 74 mins.)

Rocking Horse Winner, The (Great Britain, 1949)***½ Valerie Hobson, John Mills, John Howard Davies. D. H. Lawrence's superb short story isn't entirely successful in its extended screen adaptation. A boy discovers he can keep his parents together by the money he wins predicting winners at the track. Davies rides his rocking horse (his means of infallible predictions) for all it's worth; his desperate drive suggests the depth of his fears, but it is Hobson, as his beautiful, selfish mother, who steals the picture with a subtle, balanced portrayal. (Writer-Dir: Anthony Pelissier, 91 mins.)

Rocky (1976)**** Sylvester Stallone, Talia Shire, Burgess Meredith, Burt Young, Carl Weathers. Packs a powerful sentimental punch. The Academy Award–winner about a loutish lug who wants to become a boxing champ. John G. Avildsen won the Academy Award for his direction of "Rocky" which features a notable closing fight aided by a deft makeup man. Stallone makes you care for him in the screenplay written by him, and Shire, playing his painfully shy girlfriend, is splendid. Uses the slums of Philadelphia to good advantage for much of the on-location scenes. (119 mins.)

Rocky Horror Picture Show, The (Great Britain, 1975)**½ Tim Curry, Susan Sarandon, Barry Bostwick, Meat Loaf. The midnight show phenomenon is based on a British rock musical which flopped on the U.S. stage. Primarily a spoof of old monster movies, but to update the proceedings the chief weirdo at the castle is a bisexual named Frank N. Furter who wears lipstick and sings. Many cultists have seen the film dozens, even hundreds of times, and you may want to see for yourself what all the shouting is about. (Dir: Him Sharman, 100 mins.)

Rocky Mountain (1950)** Errol Flynn, Patrice Wymore. Opposing forces unite to fight a common enemy, the attacking Indians. You've seen it before, though not always with Mr. & Mrs. Flynn. (Dir: William Keighley, 83 mins.)

Rocky II (1979)**½ Sylvester Stallone, Talia Shire, Burt Young, Burgess Meredith, Carl Weathers. More of the same, literally: Rocky is down on his luck and struggling for another shot at the title.

Shameless manipulation conjures up emotional responses from the earlier film, but it's all mechanics, and implausible to boot. The climactic fight sequence is a rouser, but makes no sense. Stallone may yet make a good writer-director, but he's got to get out from under his own cult tendencies as an actor. (119 mins.)

Rodan (Japan, 1957)** Kenji Sawara. Japanese made science fiction film about a huge flying monster. Technically inferior to American made films of the same insipid nature. (Dir: Inoshiro Honda, 72 mins.)

Rodeo (1952)**½ John Archer, Jane Nigh. Girl takes over a rodeo when the promoter skips with the loot, makes it a success. Pleasant melodrama doesn't try for any heights, manages to be pleasing in its own small way. (Dir: William Beaudine, 70 mins.)

Rodeo Girl (MTV 1980)** Katharine Ross, Bo Hopkins, Candy Clark. Slow-moving story about Ross as a woman who desires to become a rodeo star. Tired of being a housewife, she hits the rodeo circuit with Clark, going against the wishes of husband Hopkins. Little action, much boredom. (Dir: Jackie Cooper, 104 mins.)

Roger Touhy, Gangster (1944)**½ Preston Foster, Victor McLaglen. Fairly good crime film loosely based on Touhy's career. Maybe if he looked like Foster, he would have become an actor. (Dir: Robert Florey, 65 mins.)

Rogue Cop (1954)*** Robert Taylor, Janet Leigh, George Raft, Anna Francis, Steve Forrest. Better than usual cops and robbers yarn. Raft is a standout as a syndicate czar who is more than a bit sadistic and ruthless. Taylor is effective as a detective who's on the take. Miss Francis has two excellent scenes as a young moll who drinks to forget her plight. (Dir: Roy Rowland, 92 mins.)

Rogue River (1950)***½ Rory Calhoun, Peter Graves. A state policeman and his ne'er-do-well cousin become involved in a bank robbery. Exceptionally well-written, lively melodrama, well above average. (Dir: John Rawlins, 81 mins.)

Rogue's Gallery (1968)** Roger Smith, Dennis Morgan, Brian Donlevy. Private-eye yarn that started out as a TV pilot film and wound up not getting a theatrical release. Smith is John Rogue (that's the title, folks) and he goes through a tussle trying to keep his client from killing himself. Movie buffs will spot various old-timers in the supporting cast, including Jackie Coogan, Morgan, Edgar Bergen, and Richard Arlen. (Dir: Leonard Horn, 88 mins.)

Rogue's March (1952)** Peter Lawford, Richard Greene, Janice Rule. Average costume drama about a British regiment stationed in India. Lawford and Greene make dashing soldiers of the Queen, lovely Janice Rule supplies love interest. (Dir: Allan Davies, 84 mins.)

Rogues of Sherwood Forest (1950)** John Derek, Diana Lynn, Alan Hale. Robin Hood rides again! Lavish sets and costumes but the same tired plot. (Dir: Gordon Douglas, 80 mins.)

Rogue's Regiment (1948)*½ Dick Powell, Marta Toren, Vincent Price. Intelligence officer joins the Foreign Legion in search of an escaped Nazi bigwig. Dull melodrama. (Dir: Robert Florey, 86 mins.)

Roland the Mighty (Italy, 1958)*½ Rik Battaglia. (Dir: Pietro Francisci, 98 mins.)

Roll, Freddy, Roll (MTV 1974)** Tim Conway, Jan Murray, Ruta Lee. Tim Conway's adept comedy style adds a freshness to this silly plot about a man who accidentally finds himself a short-term celebrity as he tries to break a Guinness world record for staying on roller skates for more than a week. (Dir: Bill Persky, 74 mins.)

Roller Boogie (1979)** Linda Blair, Jim Bray, Beverly Garland. Talented director Mark L. Lester fails to energize this pallid disco teenpic, even with a big budget (for the genre). Blair fakes her way through. The story is numbing. (103 mins.)

Rollerball (1975)**½ James Caan, Ralph Richardson, John Houseman. The sick '70s by William Harrison. (Dir: Norman Jewison, 123 mins.)

Rollercoaster (1977)**½ George Segal, Richard Widmark, Timothy Bottoms, Susan Strasberg. An excuse for Sensurround—strap a Panavision camera to the front car of a rollercoaster and pound the audience with sound waves, and you can hardly help but generate some cheap but real thrills. The story is disposable, as is James Goldstone's erratic direction. Widmark, with all his right-wing roles, is fast becoming the discount Burt Lancaster. (119 mins.)

Rolling Man (MTV 1972)**½ Dennis Weaver, Agnes Moorehead. A born loser wanders about the country after serving a prison term, looking for his son and dreaming of becoming a successful racetrack driver. Uneven, but has a sense of reality. Prison sequences, sleazy bars, and small-town auto tracks form the sordid background for a colorful collection of characters Weaver encounters along the way. Weaver registers and so do Sheree North, Don Stroud, and Jimmy Dean as a fast-talking operator Weaver meets in jail. (Dir: Peter Hyams, 73 mins.)

Rolling Thunder (1977)** William Devane, Tommy Lee Jones, Linda Haynes. Unnecessarily violent. Devane returns from Vietnam with dead eyes and a hollow soul, snapping to life only when his wife and child are killed in a robbery. As he sets out for vengeance, Devane seems motivated less by love for his family than by an unholy nostalgia for his wartime experiences. Director John Flynn lacks the means to make Devane's madness and masochism come to life, and the ending is traditional revenge melodrama. (99 mins.)

Roman Holiday (1953)**** Gregory Peck, Audrey Hepburn, Eddie Albert. Comedy delight about a newspaperman in Rome who meets and falls for a lonely princess traveling incognito. Oscar-winning performance by Hepburn, smart William Wyler direction, a production with great charm, completely captivating. (119 mins.)

Roman Scandals (1933)**½ Eddie Cantor, Ruth Etting, Gloria Stuart. Adapted from a play by George S. Kaufman and Robert E. Sherwood as an odd little musical, with dances by Busby Berkeley. The songs are not memorable, but among the Goldwyn Girls you can spot Betty Grable, Lucille Ball, and Paulette Goddard. (Dir: Frank Tuttle, 85 mins.)

Roman Spring of Mrs. Stone, The (Great Britain, 1961)*** Vivien Leigh, Warren Beatty, Jill St. John. Based on Tennessee Williams's novel. All the decadence of the takers and the taken along the Via Veneto in Rome is bared in this tale about an aging actress who succumbs to taking a young paid-for lover. Miss Leigh by now, has played this type of role often. Warren Beatty fills the physical requirements of the handsome Italian gigolo but his accent gets in the way. Lotte Lenya, in the role of a ruthless social procurer, adds a sinister note and her performance is, by far, the best in the film. (Dir: José Quintero, 104 mins.)

Romance of a Horsethief (U.S.-Yugoslavia, 1971)*** Yul Brynner, Eli Wallach, Jane Birkin, David Opatoshu. Director Abraham Polonsky's farce of Jewish ghetto life in a Russian village at the turn of the century is far more complex than "Fiddler on the Roof." Funny and charming, the film nonetheless builds toward a revolutionary view of a people and of history. Brynner gives the performance of his career. (100 mins.)

Romance of Rosy Ridge, The (1947)*** Van Johnson, Thomas Mitchell, Janet Leigh (debut). With tensions high after the Civil War, a mysterious stranger is looked upon with suspicion by a southern-sympathizing Missouri farmer. Well made, charming drama. (Dir: Roy Rowland, 106 mins.)

Romance on the High Seas (1948)*** Doris Day, Jack Carson, Janis Paige, Oscar Levant. This was Doris's first film and it made a lot more noise at the box office than with the critics. Light little romantic comedy with a cruise background doesn't interfere too much with a delightful score. (Dir: Michael Curtiz, 99 mins.)

Romanoff and Juliet (1961)***½ Peter Ustinov, Sandra Dee, John Gavin, Akim Tamiroff, John Phillips. Peter Ustinov wrote, directed, and stars in this comedy spoof set in a mythical country in which the daughter of the American ambassador falls in love with the Russian ambassador's son. Some of the lines don't work but the premise is funny enough and there's always Ustinov as a jack-of-all-trades in the mythical country. (103 mins.)

Romantic Englishwoman, The (Great Britain–France, 1975)***½ Glenda Jackson, Michael Caine, Helmut Berger, Nathalie Delon. A pulp novelist (Caine) loves to fantasize about the (nonexistent) infidelities of his wife (Jackson), and pushes her into an absurd affair with a second-rate German gigolo (Berger). Caine despises the banality of "real life"—what he really wants is to live in a bad movie, with himself as the director. Reality and fantasy become hopelessly mixed, and by the end of the film even we, the spectators, don't know for sure where we are. Screenplay by Tom Stoppard and Thomas Wiseman, from Wiseman's book. (Dir: Joseph Losey, 115 mins.)

Rome Adventure (1962)** Troy Donahue, Suzanne Pleshette, Angie Dickinson, Rossano Brazzi. Librarian out to see some fun and a young architectural student meet and romance in Italy. The usual complications ensue, but it all works out fine by the end—and predictably. Gorgeous scenery, but the actors get in front of it too often with the sappy plot. (Dir: Delmer Daves, 119 mins.)

Rome, 1585 (Italy, 1963)* Debra Paget, Daniella Rocca, Livio Lorenzon. (Dir: Mario Bonnard, 85 mins.)

Rome Like Chicago (Italy, 1967)** John Cassavetes is a mobster with revenge on his mind after his partner takes over his business and his wife while he is in prison. Predictable, and produced on a modest budget—which shows. (Dir: Alberto DeMartino, 109 mins.)

Romeo and Juliet (1936)*** Norma Shearer, Leslie Howard, John Barrymore, Basil Rathbone, Edna May Oliver, C. Aubrey Smith, Violet Kemble Cooper, Ralph Forbes, Andy Devine. Irving Thalberg's production stars his wife (Shearer) as a Juliet a bit long in the tooth, and Howard as a poetical Romeo with his sexuality in his throat. George Cukor's direction is intelligent but too much aware of doing a classic. There are points of interest in Barrymore's eccentric Mercutio and Rathbone's fiery Tybalt. (140 mins.)

Romeo and Juliet (Great Britain, 1954)***½ Laurence Harvey, Susan Shentall, Flora Robson, Mervyn Johns, Bill Travers. Shakespeare's tragedy of star-crossed lovers, beautifully filmed (in color) in Italy. Pictorially splendid, but the performances leave something to be desired. (Dir: Renato Castelli, 140 mins.)

Romeo and Juliet (Great Britain, 1966)**** Margot Fonteyn, Rudolph Nureyev, David Blair. Fonteyn belies her advancing age by her radiant, graceful dancing of the young, delicate Juliet, in this filming of the British Royal Ballet's interpretation of Prokofiev's ballet. Nureyev is moving as Romeo, and both he and Blair (Mercutio) make masterful use of mime in their roles, the ballet becoming a physi-

cally expressive blend of acting and dance. Not to be missed. (Dir: Paul Czinner, 126 mins.)

Romeo and Juliet (Great Britain–Italy, 1968)*** Leonard Whiting, Olivia Hussey, Milo O'Shea, Michael York, John McEnery, Robert Stephens. Director Franco Zeffirelli's visually ravishing version of Shakespeare's tragic romance of tender young love. Romeo (17-year-old Whiting) and Juliet (15-year-old Hussey) are right in their youth but not good enough performers. The feel for 15th-century Verona is right and the Mercutio-Tybalt duel is sensational. For those who care, this is the 13th version of "R and J." (152 mins.)

Romeo and Juliet (Great Britain, MTV 1978)**½ Patrick Ryecart, Rebecca Saire, John Gielgud, Michael Hordern, Anthony Andrews, Celia Johnson. This BBC production is lax and unfocused. Saire is a suitable age 14 (Juliet was 13), but she makes her eagerness to love Romeo (Ryecart) seem like an unrealistic adolescent whim. Several performances are eccentric: Andrews tends to make Mercutio a chattering, shallow popinjay; and Hordern's Capulet becomes a doddering if occasionally endearing old fool. However Johnson is magnificent as the loving old nurse. (Dir: Alvin Rakoff, 200 mins.)

Romulus and the Sabines (Italy, 1961)** Roger Moore, Mylene Demongeot, Jean Marais, Rosanna Schiaffino. Romulus and his band raid the neighboring Sabines, carrying off their women, which, as you know, means war. English-dubbed costume spectacular at least has a better cast than customary, in addition to the usual gaucheries. (Dir: Richard Pottier, 101 mins.)

Roof, The (Italy, 1957)*** Gabriella Pallotti, Giorgio Listuzzi. Poverty-stricken young couple overcome red tape in finding a new home and happiness. Gentle drama directed by Vittorio De Sica, some fine moments. English dubbing detracts somewhat. (91 mins.)

Rookie, The (1959)*½ Tommy Noonan, Pete Marshall, Julie Newmar. (Dir: George O'Hanlon, 86 mins.)

Rookies, The (1972)** Darren McGavin, Paul Burke, Cameron Mitchell. Pilot for the TV series. A police show focusing on the new breed of questioning, caring, college-trained recruits. The customary tough, skeptical sergeant puts rookies through training, grudgingly pays respect to the men when they perform well on the streets. Predictable, slickly produced. (Dir: Jud Taylor, 72 mins.)

Room at the Top (Great Britain, 1959)**** Laurence Harvey, Simone Signoret, Heather Sears, Allan Cuthbertson, Donald Wolfit, Hermione Baddeley, Donald Houston. Harvey is a young North Country man-on-the-make who reaches the management level by knocking up the factory owner's daughter, discarding his aging mistress (Signoret, Best Actress Oscar) along the way. Both are good, and get fine support from Cuthbertson and Sears. (Dir: Jack Clayton, 115 mins.)

Room for One More (1952)*** Cary Grant, Betsy Drake, Lurene Tuttle. Modest fare performed with consummate professionalism by Grant and his then-wife, Drake as a couple who cannot resist adopting forsaken children. The sentimentality and homilies get to be too much, but Grant makes the suspect material moving and warm. (Dir: Norman Taurog, 98 mins.)

Room Service (1938)**½ The Marx Brothers, Ann Miller, Lucille Ball. Broke producer and his aides stall from being kicked out of their hotel room. Amusing comedy, but not the Marxes at their best. Remade as musical, "Step Lively." (Dir: William A. Seiter, 78 mins.)

Room 13 (West Germany, 1964)*½ Joachim Fuchsberger, Karin Dor, Walter Rilla. (Dir: Harold Reinl, 82 mins.)

Rooney (1958)*** Barry Fitzgerald, John Gregson. Dublin dustman aids a bedridden man henpecked by his grasping relatives. Delightful Irish comedy, good fun. (Dir: George Pollack, 88 mins.)

Rooster Cogburn (1975)**½ John Wayne, Katharine Hepburn, Anthony Zerbe, Strother Martin. Though not a good picture, this is enjoyable occasionally. Concerns the murder of spinster Eula Goodnight's minister father (shades of "The African Queen"), and the theft by desperadoes of some nitroglycerin. Marshal Rooster Cogburn rides off to catch the miscreants. The star chemistry is the only thing of interest here; Wayne and Hepburn are full of life and spark "Rooster" a little. (Dir: Stuart Millar, 107 mins.)

Roots, The (Mexico, 1957)**½ Beatriz Flores, Juan De La Cruz. Four assorted vignettes of the Mexican people, most of them fairly well done, but brevity of the plots doesn't give one time to become really interested. Dubbed in English. (Dir: Benito Alazraki, 96 mins.)

Roots of Heaven, The (1958)*** Errol Flynn, Juliette Greco, Trevor Howard, Eddie Albert, and Orson Welles. Interesting ambitious film based on Romain Gary's prize-winning novel about a group comprised of adventurers, opportunists, and one idealist who join forces in an effort to protect the African elephant (theatened with destrucion and eventual extinction by ivory hunters). Trevor Howard is a standout as the idealist and there's a colorful contribution by Welles as a TV news personality. (Dir: John Huston, 131 mins.)

Rope (1948)***½ James Stewart, John Dall, Farley Granger, Cedric Hardwicke. With a story related to the Leopold-Loeb case, this truly frightening classic concerns two college boys who kill for thrills. Full of suspense and ingenious camera work from director Alfred Hitchcock. Color. (80 mins.)

Rope Around the Neck (France, 1964)** Jean Richard, Dany Robin, Magali Noel. Man with an increasing desire to murder his wife finally attempts the deed, but finds himself involved in another crime. Tricky whodunit dubbed in English is developed too slowly. (Dir: Joseph Lisbona, 78 mins.)

Rope of Flesh—See: **Mudhoney**

Rope of Sand (1949)**½ Burt Lancaster, Corinne Calvet, Claude Rains, Peter Lorre, Sam Jaffe, Paul Henreid. Adventurer returns to claim a hidden fortune in diamonds, fights off the machinations of a police chief and a diamond-company executive after the cache. Hard-boiled melodrama heavy on the rough stuff; action fans should like it. (Dir: William Dieterle, 104 mins.)

Rosalie (1937)** Eleanor Powell, Nelson Eddy, Frank Morgan, Edna May Oliver, Ray Bolger. Songs by Cole Porter don't salvage this hackneyed musical about a college football hero (Eddy) who falls for an incognito Balkan princess, played by, of all people, Powell. (Dir: W. S. Van Dyke II, 122 mins.)

Rose, The (1979)***½ Bette Midler, Alan Bates, Frederic Forrest. Midler's first major movie is a dramatic account of the life of a Janis Joplin–type singer, with a lot of the Midler personality mixed in. She really shines in the concert scenes, and perhaps surprisingly does good work dramatically, although the Bill Kerby–Bo Goldman screenplay gets very heavy at times. Some deeply moving moments. (Dir: Mark Rydell, 134 mins.)

Rose Bowl Story (1952)** Vera Miles, Marshall Thompson, Natalie Wood. Usual sort of football story, OK for those who love quarterbacks. Natalie plays the kid sister here. (Dir: William Beaudine, 73 mins.)

Rose Marie (1936)**½ Jeanette MacDonald, Nelson Eddy, James Stewart, David Niven, Gilda Gray. MacDonald hunts for her fugitive brother (Stewart) in the wilds of Canada, but finds a partner for duets in Mountie Nelson Eddy. They sing "Indian Love Call" without damaging each other's ears, and Nelson bellows "Songs of the Mounties" all by himself. W. S. Van Dyke II directed this antique in stupefying MGM mid-'30s style. (112 mins.)

Rose Marie (1954)**½ Ann Blyth, Howard Keel, Fernando Lamas, Bert Lahr, Marjorie Main. The story, though changed from the original, is still terrible—now the heroine is a French-Canadian trapper's daughter, instead of an opera star on the lam. But who watches an operetta for the story? The music is lovely, and one has a rare chance to hear Ann Blyth's beautiful voice—Fernando, surprisingly, is pretty good, too. (Dir: Mervyn Le Roy, 105 mins.)

Rose of Washington Square (1939)*** Al Jolson, Alice Faye, Tyrone Power. Alice and Al sing some of the most memorable songs of the twenties and it is, of course, the highlight of an otherwise ordinary film. Backstage plot about a Follies girl who loves a bum is poorly written and not too well acted. (Dir: Gregory Ratoff, 86 mins.)

Rose Tattoo, The (1955)**½ Burt Lancaster, Anna Magnani, Virginia Grey, Ben Cooper, Marisa Pavan. Tennessee Williams play enacted by the actress for whom it was written, Magnani (Oscar, Best Actress). A comedy about a widowed housewife for whom no man can be as good as her late husband (his sexual prowess was as endowed him, after death, with the mantle of sainthood). Magnani gets a rare chance to use her comic skill, and the performance is continuous laughter, in and out of character. Lancaster is woefully miscast as the village idiot. The film is an amazement of black-and-white contrasts in James Wong Howe's photography (Oscar), but the film is stodgy and poorly staged, in the inept hands of director Daniel Mann. (117 mins.)

Roseanna McCoy (1949)** Farley Granger, Joan Evans (debut), Raymond Massey, Richard Basehart. Trite melodrama depicting the legendary feudin' hill families of the Hatfields and the McCoys. The performances range from fine (Basehart) to very poor (Evans in the title role). (Dir: Irving Reis, 89 mins.)

Rosebud (1971)½ Peter O'Toole, Richard Attenborough, Cliff Gorman, John V. Lindsay. (Dir: Otto Preminger, 126 mins.)

Roseland (1977)*** Lou Jacobi, Teresa Wright, Christopher Walken, Geraldine Chaplin. Director James Ivory's threefold story, set around the tattered dance palace near New York's Times Square, uneven, but buoyed by many character vignettes. (103 mins.)

Rosemary (West Germany, 1958)***½ Nadja Tiller, Peter Van Eyck. Devastating German satire on its own middle-class morality, beautifully filmed and suspensefully performed by a superb cast of players. Based on the real-life story of a call girl whose social ambitions become a menace to her admirers, it keeps you glued to the screen from sophisticated beginning to cynical end. (Dir: Rolf Thiele, 99 mins.)

Rosemary's Baby (1968)**** Mia Farrow, Ruth Gordon, John Cassavetes, Ralph Bellamy, Sidney Blackmer. Double-threat Roman Polanski adapted Ira Levin's best-seller about witchcraft as practiced on New York's Central Park West, and also directed this exciting horror film. Oscar: Gordon, Best Supporting Actress. (136 mins.)

Rosemary's Baby II (MTV 1976)**½ Ruth Gordon, Patty Duke Astin, Ray Milland. Rosemary's Baby, Adrian/Andrew, finds himself torn between his human and inhuman sides. Inferior sequel with a good cast, including holdover Gordon, who recreates her role of the next-door witch. (Dir: Sam O'Steen, 104 mins.)

Rosetti and Ryan: Men Who Love Women (MTV 1977)** Tony Roberts, Squire Fridell. The pilot film for the subsequent series. The light touch is the key when a pair of cocky lawyers defends a lady accused of doing in hubbie on the family yacht. Patty Duke Astin is the defendant part of a classy supporting cast that includes Susan Anspach and Bill Dana. (Dir: John Astin, 106 mins.)

Rosie (1967)*½ Rosalind Russell, James Farentino, Sandra Dee, Brian Aherne. (Dir: David Lowell Rich, 98 mins.)

Rosie the Riveter (1980)**** Director Connie Fields spent two years viewing and reassembling footage from WW II and another year interviewing women factory workers from the period to create this stunning documentary. Interviews with five women are intercut with government-produced newsreels, propaganda films from the beginning of WW II urging women out of their homes and into factories, and films from the end of the war suggesting that now a woman's place was in the home. Rosie the Riveter was not a middle-class housewife who came to work out of patriotism but a working-class woman who got a high-paying "male" job in wartime but was shunted back to a low-paying service or office job—or the unemployment line—when the men came home.

Rotten to the Core (Great Britain, 1965)**½ Charlotte Rampling, Ian Bannen, Anton Rogers, Eric Sykes. Sly comedy of a bumbling bunch of crooks who nearly make off with several million pounds. Rogers (who plays the brains behind the caper) highlights with his ingenious impersonations. (Dir: John Boulting, 87 mins.)

Rough Cut (1980)**½ Burt Reynolds, Lesley-Anne Down, David Niven, Patrick Magee, Timothy West. The tired old plot about a jewel thief's yen for a "sophisticated" lady. A movie without content, style, or wit. (Dir: Don Siegel, 112 mins.)

Rough Night in Jericho (1967)* Dean Martin, George Peppard, Jean Simmons. (Dir: Arnold Laven, 97 mins.)

Roughly Speaking (1945)*** Jack Carson, Rosalind Russell, Robert Hutton, Alan Hale, Donald Woods, Jean Sullivan. Ambitious wife struggles to aid her ne'er-do-well husband in his business schemes, while raising a large family. Long but deftly acted, pleasantly done comedy drama. True story, from the autobiography of Louise Randall Pierson. (Dir: Michael Curtiz, 117 mins.)

Rounders, The (1965)*** Glenn Ford, Henry Fonda, Sue Ane Langdon, Chill Wills. Ford and Fonda are a very ingratiating pair of modern-day horse wranglers who share some comical adventures in this engaging tale, written and directed by Burt Kennedy. The two have their hands full when they attempt to break a stubborn horse and this becomes the film's

567

funniest running gag. A good supporting cast of familiar faces—Chill Wills, Edgar Buchanan and Denver Pyle—help keep the comedy rolling briskly along. (85 mins.)

Roustabout (1964)***½ Elvis Presley, Barbara Stanwyck. Another Presley opus for his fans, with Barbara Stanwyck thrown in for good measure. Barbara runs a carnival, and Elvis is a vagabond youth who joins the show and sings in a honky-tonk on the midway. (Dir: John Rich, 101 mins.)

Roxie Hart (1942)*** Ginger Rogers, Adolphe Menjou, George Montgomery, Nigel Bruce, Lynne Overman, Spring Byington, Phil Silvers. This version of Maurine Watkins's "Chicago" is mostly a raucous success, despite lapses in tone. Rogers murders her two-timing boyfriend and gets sprung through the efforts of a simple barefoot mouthpiece, Menjou. (Dir: William Wellman, 75 mins.)

Royal Flash (Great Britain, 1975)***½ Malcolm McDowell, Alan Bates, Florinda Bolkan, Oliver Reed, Britt Ekland. McDowell is Harry Flashman, a captain in Queen Victoria's army—liar, coward, thief, and all-around sonofabitch. It's "The Three Musketeers" updated by a century or two, with plenty of subtle detailing and unsubtle slapstick by director Richard Lester. (98 mins.)

Royal Hunt of the Sun, The (Great Britain, 1969)**½ Robert Shaw, Christopher Plummer, Nigel Davenport. Peter Shaffer's play was effective onstage, but opened up to spectacle proportions, its verbal posturings become silly. Shaw is no more than stolid as Pizarro, but Plummer is in high-camp heaven as the Inca emperor Atahualpa, with sinuous body movements and bird language. An expensive flop. (Dir: Irving Lerner, 110 mins.)

Royal Scandal, A (1945)**½ Tallulah Bankhead, William Eythe, Anne Baxter, Vincent Price, Charles Coburn. Farce about Catherine the Great (Bankhead). Eythe, who died young, sets off sexual energies with the voracious but older Tallulah. Otto Preminger's direction is stylistically maladroit, resulting in a mostly leaden rendition of an epigrammatic screenplay. (94 mins.)

Royal Wedding (1951)*** Fred Astaire, Jane Powell, Sarah Churchill, Peter Lawford. Astaire and Powell are brother and sister, in London to see Queen Elizabeth II marry Prince Philip. One moment, when Fred dances on the ceiling, is an impeccably executed bit of movie magic. (Dir: Stanley Donen, 93 mins.)

"R.P.M." (Revolutions per Minute) (1970)*½ Anthony Quinn, Ann-Margret, Gary Lockwood. (Dir: Stanley Kramer, 92 mins.)

Ruby (1970)*** Earl Tibbets. Independently made study of small-town frustrations and exploration of the life of Ruby, the school-bus driver. Low-budget entry is often perceptive and funny. (Dir: Dick Bartlett.)

Ruby (1977)**½ Piper Laurie, Stuart Whitman, Janit Baldwin, Fred Kohler, Jr. Ambitious, offbeat occult thriller. Laurie, a former gangster's moll who has taken the money and run, operates a drive-in which is visited, in due course, by the vengeful spirit of her dead lover. Director Curtis Harrington treats the camp aspects of the script with what these days could pass for restraint. (85 mins.)

Ruby and Oswald (MTV 1978)** Michael Lerner, Frederic Forrest. Manipulative, heartbreaking "docudrama" based on *some* of the known facts about the murder of Lee Harvey Oswald by Jack Ruby. The audience is shown the real footage of Kennedy's arrival in Dallas and his funeral, interspersed with fictional scenes performed by actors. We do not learn much about Ruby's motives, nor do we get any real insight into Oswald's psychopathic personality. (Dir: Mel Stuart, 156 mins.)

Ruby Gentry (1952)*** Jennifer Jones, Charlton Heston, Karl Malden, Josephine Hutchison. Jones has never been more appealing on the screen than she is in this supercharged drama about a sexy wench who seeks revenge on an elaborate scale when her true love decides to marry a more respected female in the community. The love scenes are torrid and Miss Jones enacts the siren with all stops pulled. (Dir: King Vidor, 82 mins.)

Ruffians, The (France, 1960)** Marina Vlady, Robert Hossein. Man becomes involved with his boss's daughter, suspects she's leading a secret life. Fair drama dubbed in English. (Dir: Maurice Labro, 102 mins.)

Ruggles of Red Gap (1935)**** Charles Laughton, Charlie Ruggles, Mary Boland, Leila Hyams, Roland Young, Zasu Pitts. An English butler (Laughton) finds himself in the Wild West after he is won by an American in a poker game. The high point is Laughton's rendering of the Gettysburg Address to an astonished barroom full of Americans; but the whole film is a delight, with wonderful support from Ruggles and Boland. (Dir: Leo McCarey, 92 mins.)

Rulers of the Sea (1939)*** Margaret Lockwood, Douglas Fairbanks, Jr., Will Fyffe. Interesting drama of the first steam crossing of the Atlantic which led to the beginning of the luxury liner. Not a great epic, but Mr. Fyffe is superb and the tale well told. (Dir: Frank Lloyd, 97 mins.)

Rules of the Game, The (France, 1939)**** Marcel Dalio, Nora Gregor, Roland Toutain, Gaston Modet, Julien Carette, Jean Renoir. The greatest film ever made. Period, no arguments. This masterpiece of masterpieces was booed off the screen at its Paris premiere in 1939, banned by the Nazis, the negative severely damaged by bombs. Restored to its original cut in 1961, it lives. Jean Renoir wept when he saw the reassembled print. The whole of cinema of every kind is contained in this capacious, protean achievement, to be stacked against the best of Shakespeare and Mozart. Based on the play "Les Caprices de Marianne," by Alfred de Musset, the deceptively limpid plot follows a lavish house party at a country château, and the hearts and minds of those present. Renoir himself plays the bearlike Octave, who paves the road to hell with his good intentions. (110 mins.)

Ruling Class, The (Great Britain, 1971)**** Peter O'Toole, Alastair Sim, Harry Andrews, Arthur Lowe, Carol Brown. Biting satire, madcap farce about the English upper classes. O'Toole plays the mad 14th Earl of Gurney, who has inherited his father's huge estate. He thinks he's Jesus Christ and when his family tries to cure him, he becomes Jack the Ripper. Spiced with vaudeville songs and Arthur Lowe as a butler who has inherited $70,000. Wonderful fun, and O'Toole is marvelous in one of his best screen performances. (Dir: Peter Medak, 155 mins.)

Run a Crooked Mile (MTV 1969)**½ Louis Jourdan, Mary Tyler Moore. A muddled feature, greatly enhanced by the charm of Louis Jourdan. Jourdan plays a school teacher who becomes an amnesia victim and lives the life of a wealthy playboy for a two-year period, marrying Moore in the interim. However, it is not a comedy. (Dir: Gene Levitt, 100 mins.)

Run, Angel, Run! (1969)** William Smith, Valerie Starrett, Margaret Markov. Smith is a former member of the Devil's Advocates motorcylce gang and has exposed them in a magazine article. He and Valerie Starrett have to avoid them at all costs. She also wrote the screenplay, as V. A. Furlong. (Dir: Jack Starrett, 95 mins.)

Run for Cover (1955)*** James Cagney, Viveca Lindfors, John Derek, Ernest Borgnine, Jean Hersholt (last film). Taut Western story about a duo of bandits and their reformation. Leads up to an exciting climax. Cagney fine as always with good support by Derek and Lindfors. (Dir: Nicholas Ray, 93 mins.)

Run for the Sun (Great Britain, 1956)** Richard Widmark, Jane Greer, Trevor Howard, Peter Van Eyck. Author and lady reporter crash in the jungle, come upon an English traitor and a wounded Nazi, who hunted them. Chase melodrama has a few thrills. Filmed in Mexico. Color. (Dir: Roy Boulting, 99 mins.)

Run for Your Money, A (Great Britain, 1949)***½ Donald Houston, Alec Guinness, Meredith Edwards, Moira Lister, Hugh Griffith, Joyce Grenfell. Two Welsh coal miners have various misadventures when they visit London. Delightful comedy, raising many chuckles. Excellently acted. (Dir: Charles Frend, 83 mins.)

Run for Your Wife (Italy-France, 1965)**½ Ugo Tognazzi, Marina Vlady, Rhonda Fleming, Juliet Prowse. Nice, frothy comedy about an Italian bachelor visiting the U.S. on business, who decides to stay here by marrying a native. Only she turns out to be more formidable, less predictable, and less inclined to marry than he had expected. (Dir: Gian Luigi Polidoro, 97 mins.)

Run of the Arrow (1957)*** Rod Steiger, Charles Bronson, Brian Keith, Sarita Montiel. Steiger is an unreconstructed ex-Confederate soldier (with, curiously, an Irish accent) who lights out for the territories and joins the Sioux nation, only to find that his real loyalties lie with the beleaguered U.S. calvary. (Dir: Samuel Fuller, 86 mins.)

Run Silent, Run Deep (1958)*** Clark Gable, Burt Lancaster, Don Rickles. An interesting war drama about submarine warfare and the bitter conflict of the sub commander (Gable) and his lieutenant (Lancaster). Exciting photography adds to the suspense. Gable and Lancaster are realistic in their portrayals. (Dir: Robert Wise, 93 mins.)

Run, Simon, Run (MTV 1970)*** Burt Reynolds, Inger Stevens. Reynolds gives a strong performance as an American Indian who returns to the reservation after serving a long prison term for a murder he didn't commit. He patiently waits for his moment of revenge, falling in love with the beautiful Stevens in the meantime. Miss Stevens's character of a rich socialite-turned-social worker is a bit uneven in the writing, but it doesn't detract from the overall effect of the drama. The unexpected ending is still jolting. (Dir: George McCowan, 73 mins.)

Run, Stranger, Run (1973)** Patricia Neal, Cloris Leachman, Bobby Darin, Ron Howard. Gothic horror set in Nova Scotia fails to live up to the beauty of the scenery. Everyone has a skeleton in the closet, and there are several corpses sunken by sub-plots. Interesting to watch is Tessa Dahl, Miss Neal's real-life daughter, as she plays a sexually infatuated youngster. (Dir: Darren McGavin, 90 mins.)

Run Wild, Run Free (Great Britain, 1969)** John Mills, Mark Lester, Gordon Jackson, Sylvia Syms. Mills and young Lester are helpless, caught by another heavy-handed version of "doing your own thing." The boy plays a mute whose salvation comes through his love for a wild pony. Set on the Devonshire moors. (Dir: Richard C. Sarafian, 100 mins.)

Runaround, The (1946)*** Broderick Crawford, Ella Raines, Rod Cameron. Fast-moving comedy about two guys who are hired to trail a runaway heiress who is about to marry a deckhand. Good performances. (Dir: Charles Lamont, 86 mins.)

Runaway (MTV 1973)** Ben Johnson, Ed Nelson, Vera Miles, Martin Milner, Ben Murphy. A ski train roars down a mountainside when the brakes freeze in this story which mixes scares with character bits. Realistic footage is the main ingredient, while the engineer and a trio of helpers struggle to prevent the almost certain crash. (Dir: David Lowell Rich, 73 mins.)

Runaway Barge, The (MTV 1975)*½ Tim Matheson, Bo Hopkins, Jim Davis. (Dir: Boris Sagal, 72 mins.)

Runaway Bus, The (Great Britain, 1954)** Frankie Howerd, Margaret Rutherford, Petula Clark. A bus lost in a London fog commandeered by a screwy driver has an international thief aboard. Very mild comedy, misses fire often. (Dir: Val Guest, 75 mins.)

Runaways, The (MTV 1975)*½ Josh Albee, Dorothy McGuire, Van Williams. (Dir: Harry Harris, 72 mins.)

Runner Stumbles, The (1979)** Dick Van Dyke, Kathleen Quinlan, Maureen Stapleton, Beau Bridges. Muddled melodrama. Van Dyke is a priest who falls in love with a spirited nun. The screenplay is too talky and the characters are stilted. Based on a play by Milan Stitt. (Dir: Stanley Kramer, 99 mins.)

Running (Canada, 1979)**½ Michael Douglas, Susan Anspach, Larry Dane. Me Generation fable about a runner who leaves his family in order to train for the Montreal Olympics. Runner Douglas rants ferociously, but his playing in the lower register isn't convincing. Writer-director Steven H. Stern rightly recognizes the masochism inherent in running, but resorts to stock footage for a fraudulent finale. (103 mins.)

Running Man, The (Great Britain, 1963)*** Laurence Harvey, Lee Remick, Alan Bates. Scoundrel fakes his death in a glider crash, joins with his wife in a plan to defraud the insurance company, but while in Spain they are frightened by the appearance of an insurance investigator. Fairly ordinary story polished by fine performances, Carol Reed's suspenseful direction. Good melodrama. (103 mins.)

Running Target (1956)*** Arthur Franz, Doris Dowling. Different sort of outdoor drama, about a sheriff leading a posse after four escaped convicts. Exceptionally good photography, performances; tense chase scenes, good insight into human character. Above average. (Dir: Marvin Weinstein, 83 mins.)

Running Wild (1955)*½ William Campbell, Mamie Van Doren, Keenan Wynn, John Saxon. (Dir: Abner Biberman, 81 mins.)

Rush to Judgement (1967)**½ A documentary film about the assassination of President Kennedy, conceived by producer Mark Lane as a "brief for the defense" of Lee Harvey Oswald. Film, condemned by most critics at the time of its release, remains a disturbing, if disjointed film, because many of the arguments raised in the film have never been answered satisfactorily—and maybe never will be. (Dir: Emile de Antonio, 122 mins.)

Russia (1972)**½ Earnest if uninspired documentary tour through a dozen of the 15 Soviet Republics. Filmed in 1969 in various parts of Siberia, the Baltic states, Moscow, the Ukraine, etc. Helpful narration written by Soviet expert Harrison Salisbury. Produced, directed, and photographed by Theodore Holcomb. (108 mins.)

Russian Roulette (Canada, 1975)*½ George Segal, Cristina Raines, Denholm Elliott, Louise Fletcher. (Dir: Lou Lombardo, 104 mins.)

Russians Are Coming, the Russians Are Coming, The (1966)***½ Alan Arkin, Paul Ford, Carl Reiner, Theo Bikel, Eva Marie Saint, John Phillip Law, Brian Keith, Jonathan Winters. Wacky amusing comedy about a Russian submarine which runs aground off the shore of Nantucket. Boasts a delightful performance by Arkin as a befuddled Russian sailor. Director Norman Jewison keeps things perking along, despite some holes in the script. (120 mins.)

Rust Never Sleeps (1979)*** Neil Young. Concert from a tour, filmed in continuous time, intermissions, delays, and all. (He directed.) Worth the price of admission for Young's opening number, a forceful, flowing rendition of "Sugar Mountain." Goofy concert format with giant props, gimmicky intros and exits, and roadies dressed up like the Mole Men in the Fantastic Four, but the music is strong. (103 mins.)

Ruthless (1948)***½ Zachary Scott, Diana Lynn, Louis Hayward, Sydney Greenstreet, Lucille Bremer. Director Edgar G. Ulmer chronicles the rise and fall of an arch-heel in high film noir style. Ulmer was a genius with the low budgets he was invariably given to work with, making the restrictions—of acting, scope, and script—into positive virtues through a perverse, minimalist style. While not for all tastes, this is still some kind of a masterpiece. (104 mins.)

Rutles, The (United States–Great Britain, MTV 1978)***½ Eric Idle, Neil Innes, Rikki Fataar, John Halsey. Monty Python's Eric Idle was the mastermind behind this satire of the Beatles. We follow the Rutles through their early days in Liverpool, their trip to America and appearance on the Ed Sullivan show, right through to the group's breakup. Neil Innes wrote the music, which sounds just like the Beatles' most famous tunes. Excellent cameos by George Harrison, Paul Simon, Mick Jagger, and actors from the original TV "Saturday Night Live." (Dirs: Eric Idle, Gary Weiss, 78 mins.)

Rx Murder (Great Britain, 1958)** Rick Jason, Marius Goring, Lisa Gastoni. American doctor arrives in a quiet English seaside resort and soon suspects the local practitioner, whose three previous wives have suddenly died. Passable mystery is well done in a familiar way. (Dir: Derek Twist, 85 mins.)

Ryan's Daughter (Great Britain, 1970)*** Robert Mitchum, Trevor Howard, Sarah Miles, John Mills, Christopher Jones. A wildly cinematic experience, featuring Oscar-winning camerawork roving over Ireland. Unabashedly sentimental tale about a pampered, indulged, married woman (played by Miles) and her desire for a British soldier (Jones). Mitchum plays her school teacher husband with feeling that highlights the film, and Mills won an Oscar for his portrayal of a crippled mute. (Dir: David Lean, 192 mins.)

Saadia (1953)*½ Cornel Wilde, Mel Ferrer, Rita Gam. (Dir: Albert Lewin, 82 mins.)

Sabotage (Great Britain, 1936)*** Sylvia Sidney, John Loder, Oscar Homolka. Adaptation of Joseph Conrad's novel "The Secret Agent." Director Alfred Hitchcock instills this violent, disquieting drama with his own preoccupations. (76 mins.)

Saboteur (1942)***½ Robert Cummings, Priscilla Lane, Otto Kruger, Norman Lloyd. Director Alfred Hitchcock's thriller (often confused with his '36 "Sabotage") follows a typical structure of his comedies: an innocent man, mistaken for a spy, is chased across the country. Along the way he acquires a female accomplice and smokes out the true villain. This time the stars are weak and the chase plot is shapeless: but there is an exciting climax inside the Statue of Liberty. Script by Dorothy Parker. (108 mins.)

Sabre Jet (1953)**½ Robert Stack, Coleen Gray, Richard Arlen, Julie Bishop, Amanda Blake. Wives wait for their husbands to return from Korean missions. Too few air action shots. (Dir: Louis King, 96 mins.)

Sabu and the Magic Ring (1957)** Sabu, Daria Massey. OK fantasy for the kiddies; it's played lightly for laughs, but could have used more. (Dir: George Blair, 61 mins.)

Sacco and Vanzetti (Italy, 1971)*** Gian Maria Volonte, Riccardo Cucciolla, Cyril Cusack. This documents the case of two Italian immigrants, admitted anarchists accused of robbery, but innocent of the crimes—in this film—they are being prosecuted for. Based on the world-famous 1920s court case in Massachusetts. It's still a powerful, sad indictment of American political hysteria. Meant to touch our prejudices, and it does! Well acted. (Dir: Giuliano Montaldo, 120 mins.)

Sacketts, The (MTV 1979)** Sam Elliott, Tom Sellack, Jeff Osterhage, Glenn Ford. It's feuding and hating time out west for the Sackett boys. Up in Colorado gold country, the Bigelows square off against the Sacketts; and down in New Mexico, bigots simmer against the Mexicans. Author Louis L'Amour is a stickler for authenticity, so it isn't Hollywood moralism that's on parade. Cowboy fans won't be disappointed in this brief and lively western. (Dir: Robert Totten, 208 mins.)

Sad Horse, The (1959)** David Ladd, Patrice Wymore, Rex Reason, Chill Wills. A boy and his horse—young Ladd is good but one boy does not a picture make. (Dir: James B. Clark, 78 mins.)

Sad Sack, The (1957)*** Jerry Lewis, David Wayne, Phyllis Kirk, Peter Lorre. Jerry in the army again, as inept as ever, getting mixed up with spies and Arabian intrigue. Among his funnier efforts, with a fast pace and good gags. (Dir: George Marshall, 98 mins.)

Saddle the Wind (1958)**½ Robert Taylor, Julie London, John Cassavetes. Gunman turns in his weapons and becomes a rancher but is forced to return to them to face a showdown with his reckless younger brother. Nicely directed western breaks no new ground but is well done within its own framework. (Dir: Robert Parrish, 84 mins.)

Saddle Tramp (1950)*** Joel McCrea, Wanda Hendrix, Ed Begley, Jeanette Nolan, John McIntire. McCrea plays a lovable "saddle tramp" who doesn't want any trouble but ends up right in the middle of a big scale range war. Entertaining, thanks to McCrea's casual way with a line and some clever dialogue. (Dir: Hugo Fregonese, 77 mins.)

Sadko—See: **Magic Voyage of Sinbad, The**

Safari (Great Britain, 1956)**½ Janet Leigh, Victor Mature, John Justin. Victor Mature as the brave white hunter heads a safari that meets with the savage tribes of the Mau Mau. Tense and action-filled adventure. (Dir: Terence Young, 91 mins.)

Safe at Home (1962)** Mickey Mantle, Roger Maris, Don Collier, Bryan Russell, William Frawley. Little Leaguer runs away to the Yankee spring-training camp to try to get Mantle and Maris to attend a banquet. Thin baseball story might get by with the youngsters. Mantle and Maris are better on the diamond than in front of a camera. (Dir: Walter Doniger, 83 mins.)

Safecracker, The (Great Britain, 1958)** Ray Milland, Barry Jones. Routine spy "meller" with a gimmick. Milland plays a respectable safe expert who turns thief and is imprisoned. During WW II his knowledge is put to use on a dangerous mission. Some suspense along the way. (Dir: Ray Milland, 96 mins.)

Safety Last (1923)***½ Harold Lloyd, Mildred Davis. The last two reels (Lloyd as a human fly) are justly celebrated and contain perhaps the most famous comedy still in film history (Harold hanging from the hands of a clock 12 stories above the streets of downtown Los Angeles). The motivation of the boy to climb the skyscraper is sound, showing that Lloyd was a rich purveyor of character comedy rather than a mere gagman. (Dirs: Fred Newmeyer, Sam Taylor, 71 mins.)

Saga of Hemp Brown, The (1958)** Rory Calhoun, Beverly Garland, John Larch.

Army lieutenant is dismissed from the service when he's framed for a payroll robbery; with the aid of a traveling show he goes after the true culprit. Standard western. (Dir: Richard Carlson, 79 mins.)

Sahara (1943)*** Humphrey Bogart, Dan Duryea, Lloyd Bridges. American tank with an assorted crew outwits the Nazis in the desert. Frequently exciting war drama, well done. Remade as "Last of the Comanches." (Dir: Zoltan Korda, 97 mins.)

Saigon (1948)** Alan Ladd, Veronica Lake, Luther Adler, Morris Carnovsky. Routine adventure story set in Indochina involving a black marketeer and half a million dollars. (Dir: Leslie Fenton, 94 mins.)

Sail a Crooked Ship (1962)** Robert Wagner, Dolores Hart, Ernie Kovacs, Carolyn Jones, Frankie Avalon. Young man gets tangled with a gang of crooks who intend to use an old Liberty ship to pull a bank robbery in Boston. Comedy huffs and puffs for laughs, achieves tedium instead—Kovacs, in his last film, strives mightily to hold it together. (Dir: Irving S. Brecher, 88 mins.)

Sail into Danger (Great Britain, 1957)** Dennis O'Keefe, Kathleen Ryan. Fast paced crime film about a skipper of a motor launch in Barcelona and his clever efforts to defeat a group of art treasure thieves. Poor script. (Dir: Kenneth Hume, 72 mins.)

Sailing Along (Great Britain, 1938)**½ Jack Whiting, Jessie Matthews, Roland Young. This musical was one of the last '30s films to use the British countryside as a background for song and romance. Typically pert and pleasant, and Matthews is a whiz-dancer. (Dir: Sonnie Hale, 94 mins.)

Sailor Beware (1951)**½ Dean Martin, Jerry Lewis, Corinne Calvet. Martin and Lewis in the navy, with Jerry getting a reputation as a lady-killer. Horribly uneven, but some of the shtick scores big. (Dir: Hal Walker, 108 mins.)

Sailor of the King (Great Britain, 1953)**½ Jeffrey Hunter, Michael Rennie, Wendy Hiller. Another World War II drama. It's the British Navy against the Nazi U-Boats in this one. Rennie plays the British commander with commendable restraint while Hunter displays a bit too much energy as the novice who finally gets the chance to show the stuff of which heroes are made. (Dir: Roy Boulting, 83 mins.)

Sailor Who Fell from Grace with the Sea, The (Great Britain, 1976)*** Sarah Miles, Kris Kristofferson, Jonathan Kahn, Margo Cunningham. Yukio Mishima's brooding, erotic novella has been transferred from Japan to a coastal town in England. This is a very uneven but often striking, macabre piece about a group of five young schoolboys who commit a ritual murder upon a visiting sailor. Miles plays a lonely widow who falls in love with Kristofferson before he meets his untimely end. (Dir: Lewis John Carlino, 104 mins.)

St. Benny the Dip (1951)*** Dick Haymes, Nina Foch, Roland Young, Freddie Bartholomew. Three con men hide from the police in a mission, where they are duly reformed. Rather pleasant comedy-drama, nice entertainment. (Dir: Edgar G. Ulmer, 81 mins.)

Saint in London (Great Britain, 1939)**½ George Sanders, Sally Gray. The Saint picks up a wounded man on a road and is plunged into crooked doings. Entertaining mystery. (Dir: John Paddy Carstairs, 72 mins.)

Saint in New York, The (1938)*** Kay Sutton, Louis Hayward, Sig Ruman. The first "Saint" film, featuring the dapper sleuth invented by Leslie Charteris. Stars the smooth Hayward, an actor who always seemed to have a good time coasting on his talents. He helps a civic committee clean up a gang of racketeers. Good melodrama, well made, and exciting. (Dir: Ben Holmes, 71 mins.)

Saint in Palm Springs (1941)**½ George Sanders, Wendy Barrie. The Saint is entrusted to deliver three valuable stamps to a girl for her inheritance. Entertaining mystery. (Dir: Jack Hively, 65 mins.)

St. Ives (1976)** Charles Bronson, Jacqueline Bisset, Maximilian Schell, John Houseman. Bronson is drawn into a murder by scheming Houseman and Bisset. (Dir: J. Lee Thompson, 98 mins.)

Saint Jack (1979)*** Ben Gazzara, Denholm Elliott, James Villiers. An American in Singapore, a pimp with a heart of gold, is played by Gazzara as a thoughtful, sweet character. He tries to survive xenophobia and competition, services servicemen on R and R, and makes a few low-keyed friendships along the way. (Dir: Peter Bogdanovich, 112 mins.)

Saint Joan (1957)**½ Richard Widmark, Richard Todd, John Gielgud, Kenneth Haigh and Jean Seberg. A poor filmization of Shaw's wondrous play "Saint Joan," marred by the performance of inexperienced actress Jean Seberg. Others in the cast range from good to superb, notably John Gielgud; will stand as a monument to the bad judgment of Otto Preminger in giving Jean Seberg the title role. (Seberg has since shown considerable ability in films.) (Dir: Otto Preminger, 110 mins.)

St. Louis Blues (1958)**½ Nat Cole, Eartha Kitt, Pearl Bailey, Cab Calloway, Mahalia Jackson, Ruby Dee. The music's everything in this life story of composer W. C. Handy. Story line never really gets going, but the innumerable tunes are superbly performed by Cole, Kitt, Ella Fitzgerald, others. (Dir: Allen Reisner, 94 mins.)

Saint Meets the Tiger (Great Britain, 1941)**½ Hugh Sinclair, Jean Gillie. The Saint gets on the trail of a gang that has stolen a fortune in gold. Lively detective story. (Dir: Paul Stein, 70 mins.)

Saint Strikes Back (1939)*** George Sanders, Wendy Barrie, Barry Fitzgerald. The

Saint helps a girl trap thieves who have framed her father. Good detective story, well made. (Dir: John Farrow, 64 mins.)

Saint Takes Over (1940)*** George Sanders, Wendy Barrie. The Saint arrives back in America to save a friend from a murder charge. Above average detective story, well done. (Dir: Jack Hively, 69 mins.)

St. Valentine's Day Massacre (1967)** Jason Robards, George Segal, Jean Hale. Fans who adored the early Warner Bros. gangster films starring Raft, Cagney and Edward G. Robinson, might relish this warmed-over version of the Chicago gangland of the late '20s. The famous "massacre" is the highlight of the film, and the cast is appropriately stern-faced and threatening. (Dir: Roger Corman, 100 mins.)

Sainted Sisters, The (1948)**½ Joan Caulfield, Barry Fitzgerald, Veronica Lake. Barry reforms a couple of con girls in this film which completely depends on him for its appeal. (Dir: William Russell, 89 mins.)

Saints and Sinners (Great Britain, 1949)*** Kieron Moore, Christine Norden. A successful businessman returns to his native Irish village to find things changed. Warm comedy-drama with fine work by members of the famous Irish Abbey Theatre. (Dir: Leslie Arliss, 85 mins.)

Saint's Double Trouble (1940)** George Sanders, Helene Whitney, Bela Lugosi. The Saint traps a look-alike who has been engaging in diamond smuggling. Fair mystery. (Dir: Jack Hively, 68 mins.)

Saint's Girl Friday (Great Britain, 1953)** Louis Hayward, Naomi Chance, Diana Dors. The Saint investigates the murder of a socialite friend. Fair mystery. (Dir: Seymour Friedman, 68 mins.)

Sakima and the Masked Marvel (1943-66)**½ William Forrest, Louise Currie, Johnny Arthur. Feature version of serial "The Masked Marvel." Businessman is in league with a Japanese agent intending to sabotage the war effort; a masked crusader thwarts them at every turn. It may not be art, but it's entertaining; lively serial heroics for the kids and camps. (Dir: Spencer Bennet, 100 mins.)

Saladin and the Great Crusades (Egypt, 1963)*½ Ahmed Mazhar, Nadia Lootfi. (Dir: Youssef Shahin, 90 mins.)

Salesman (1969)**** Innovative, revealing; altogether shattering documentary, cinema-verité style, about the lives of several Bible salesmen in the South. Produced, directed, and photographed by the gifted brother team of Albert and David Maysles (with Charlotte Zwerin), this is one of the most extraordinarily honest glimpses of contemporary American life that you have ever seen captured on film. A real-life late 1960's sequel to Arthur Miller's creation of Willy Loman. There are no professional actors here—just real people going through their endless pitches and house calls. This is, in some ways,

one of the saddest American films ever, but it is memorable on many counts, including the editing of Dede Allen. A towering film, made on a tiny budget. (90 mins.)

Sally and Saint Anne (1952)**½ Ann Blyth, Edmund Gwenn, Gregg Palmer, Hugh O'Brian. Corny but heart warming story of a zany family and one member in particular, namely Sally (Ann Blyth) who really believes that Saint Anne is their patron saint. (Dir: Rudolph Mate, 90 mins.)

Salome (1953)**½ Rita Hayworth, Stewart Granger, Charles Laughton, Judith Anderson. Over-produced and over-long story of Salome and the events leading up to her famous dance of the seven veils. Rita sheds the veils while Charles Laughton leers and Judith Anderson flares her talented nostrils. (Dir: William Dieterle, 103 mins.)

Salome, Where She Danced (1945)** Yvonne DeCarlo, Rod Cameron, Albert Dekker. This passed for intentional camp even when it was made, or, as an earlier edition of this book put it, the film is "often unintentionally funny." DeCarlo plays a kootch dancer in Austria who is suspected of spying. She flees to the American West. (Dir: Charles Lamont, 90 mins.)

Salt and Pepper (Great Britain, 1968)** Couple of carefree London club owners (Peter Lawford, Sammy Davis, Jr.) unwittingly and unwillingly become involved in international intrigue. Hipster comedy strains for fun. Michael Bates, Ilona Rodgers. (Dir: Richard Donner, 101 mins.)

Salt of the Earth (1954)*** Will Geer, Mervin Williams. An interesting, seldom exhibited film about labor-management relations and the exploitation of the working class in America. Directed by Herbert Biberman, and partially financed and produced by the International Union of Mine, Mill & Smelter Workers. Shot on location in New Mexico. (104 mins.)

Salty (1974)** Mark Slade, Nina Foch, Julius W. Harris. Innocent yarn about a couple of young guys who team with a black truck driver to try to restore a run-down yacht basin in Florida. Aimed mainly at the kids: the title role is played by a performing seal. (Dir: Ricou Browning, 90 mins.)

Salty O'Rourke (1945)*** Alan Ladd, Gail Russell, Stanley Clements. Gambler hires a crooked jockey to ride for him. Race-track story gets a good production, neat script. (Dir: Raoul Walsh, 97 mins.)

Salut l'Artiste (France-Italy, 1973)***½ Marcello Mastroianni, Francoise Fabian, Jean Rochefort. Mastroianni is marvelous in this charming, affectionate look at the struggles of an unsuccessful bit player. His personal life isn't so hot either. His mistress leaves him, so he tries going back to his wife and family—but it seems his wife is pregnant by another man. But

Nicholas has one thing going for him: he believes in the elusive "glamour" of his profession, no matter how humiliating the acting role. Appealing, sardonic humor focusing on this naive oaf. (Dir: Yves Robert, 96 mins.)

Salvage (MTV 1979)** Andy Griffith, Trish Stewart, Richard Jaeckel. Dull pilot film. Griffith plays an enterprising junkman who goes all the way to the moon for his salvage. Writer: Mike Lloyd Ross. (Dir: Lee Philips, 104 mins.)

Salzburg Connection, The (1972)** Barry Newman, Anna Karina, Karen Jensen. Inept treatment of Helen MacInnes' spy thriller with so many plot twists you have to strain to make the story coherent. Every country in the world has an agent out to steal a box of incriminating Nazi war documents that has fallen into the hands of Anna Karina. Representing the United States and democracy is Barry Newman...democracy's in plenty of trouble...(Dir: Lee H. Katzin, 93 mins.)

Sam Hill—Who Killed the Mysterious Mr. Foster? (1971)**½ Ernest Borgnine, Judy Geeson. Here's a spirited comedy-western, a TV pilot starring Ernest Borgnine as a deputy sheriff who looks dumb but isn't. Borgnine teams up with a little towheaded thief (Stephen Hudis) to find out who poisoned the local minister. Ernie plays his familiar lunkhead character and he's backed up smartly by a good cast including Will Geer, J. D. Cannon, Judy Geeson, and villain Bruce Dern. In lesser hands, the film might fall apart, but this bunch slips in a little fun. (Dir: Fielder Cook, 99 mins.)

Sam Marlow, Private Eye—See: **Man with Bogart's Face, The**

Sam Whiskey (1969)* Burt Reynolds, Clint Walker, Ossie Davis, Angie Dickinson. (Dir: Arnold Laven, 96 mins.)

Samar (1962)*** George Montgomery, Gilbert Roland, Joan O'Brien, Ziva Rodann. Commandant of a penal colony refuses to bow to his strict superiors, breaks with the administration and leads his people through the jungles to freedom. Highly interesting, unusual story well done; rugged adventure fare. (Dir: George Montgomery, 89 mins.)

Same Time Next Year (1978)**** Alan Alda, Ellen Burstyn. Thanks largely to the performances of Alda and Burstyn, the long-running Broadway play by Bernard Slade was turned into one of the gentler, more touching love stories of the late '70s. A couple, not married to each other, have a secret tryst once a year, for two decades. Burstyn won an Academy Award. Their seaside cottage is the Heritage House on the northern California coast at Mendocino. (Dir: Robert Mulligan, 117 mins.)

Sam's Song (1971)** Robert De Niro, Jennifer Warren, Jered Mickey, Terrayne Crawford, Viva. Early De Niro film casts him as a New York film editor working on a documentary about Nixon and spending a weekend with rich friends Warren and Mickey. Blonde Crawford enters their lives and proceeds to disrupt everyone. Arty and pretentious. Excellent photography by Alex Phillips, Jr. (Dir: Jordan Leondopoulos, 92 mins.)

Samson (Italy, 1962)* Brad Harris, Brigitte Corey. (Dir: Gianfranco Parolini, 99 mins.)

Samson Against the Sheik (Italy, 1962)* Ed Fury. (Dir: Domenico Paolella, 95 mins.)

Samson and Delilah (1949)***½ Victor Mature, Hedy Lamarr, George Sanders, Angela Lansbury. Biblical tale of the mighty Samson, whose power was curtailed by the scheming Delilah, given the high-powered deMille treatment. Some truly spectacular effects, action scenes—also the expected naiveté, hokey sequences. All in all, and when compared with some later imported spectacles, it comes off quite well. Oscars: Best Art Direction, Costume Design. (Dir: Cecil B. deMille, 128 mins.)

Samson and the Sea Beasts (Italy, 1963)* Kirk Morris, Margaret Lee. (Dir: Amerigo Anton, 84 mins.)

Samson and the Seven Challenges (Italy, 1964)* Dan Vadis. (100 mins.)

Samson and the Seven Miracles of the World (Italy, 1961)*½ Gordon Scott, Yoko Tani. (Dir: Riccardo Freda, 78 mins.)

Samson and the Slave Queen (Italy, 1964)*½ Alan Steel, Pierre Brice, Moira Orfei, Maria Grazia Spina. (Dir: Umberto Lenzi, 92 mins.)

Samson and the Vampire Woman (Mexico, 1963)* Santo, Lorena Velazquez. (Dir: Alfonso Corona Blake, 89 mins.)

Samson in the Wax Museum (Mexico, 1963)* Santo, Norma Mora. (Dir: Alfonso Corona Blake, 90 mins.)

Samurai (MTV 1979)** Joe Penny, James Shigeta, Beulah Quo. Penny as a young D.A. who often reverts to his martial arts skills to solve his cases. Fernando Lamas, Ron Jacobs, and Danny Thomas admit being the executive producers. (Dir: Lee Katzin, 90 mins.)

Samurai Assassin (Japan, 1965)*** Toshiro Mifune, Keiju Kobayashi, Michiyo Aratama. A swordsman is hired to assassinate a man who he gradually realizes is the father who deserted him. (Dir: Kihachi Okamoto, 123 mins.)

San Antonio (1945)*** Errol Flynn, Alexis Smith, S. Z. Szakall. Conventional grade A western from Warner Bros., handsome but for aficionados of the genre only. (Dirs: David Butler, Raoul Walsh, 111 mins.)

San Francisco (1936)*** Clark Gable, Jeannette MacDonald, Spencer Tracy, Jack Holt. Conflict between the notorious Barbary Coast and snobbish Nob Hill is not resolved by the great '06 earthquake. W. S. Van Dyke II, master of the big-budget quickie, directed not too carefully and all the better for it. (115 mins.)

San Francisco International Airport (MTV

1970)½ Pernell Roberts, Clu Gulager, Van Johnson. If you liked "Airport," you'll like this film. The main plot—a big heist of a cargo plane carrying three million in cash—is well done, and a subplot climaxed by a 14-year-old boy taking a plane up on his own should delight air-minded small fry. Roberts as the airport manager and Gulager as the head airport security officer are excellent. (Dir: John Llewellyn Moxey, 96 mins.)

San Francisco Story (1952)** Joel McCrea, Yvonne DeCarlo. Miner is persuaded by a newspaper editor to help him fight vice in the city. Tale of the Gold Coast in the lusty days doesn't have anything new. (Dir: Robert Parrish, 80 mins.)

San Pedro Bums, The (MTV 1977)**½ Darryl McCullough, John Mark Robinson. The pilot for the series. Five newcomers (at the time) live a carefree existence on their rundown tuna boat. When their good friend, lovingly known as Pop, falls victim to a robbery by some local bullies, they attempt to right the wrong. The plot relies heavily on the appeal of the five male stars—Christopher Murney, Jeffry Druce, John Mark Robinson, Stuart Pankin, and Darryl McCullough. (Dir: Barry Shear, 79 mins.)

San Quentin (1937)** Pat O'Brien, Humphrey Bogart, Ann Sheridan, Barton MacLane. There have been better prison pictures than this tripe. In this one Bogart's sister (Sheridan) falls in love with the warden (O'Brien). MacLane plays a sadistic guard. (Dir: Lloyd Bacon, 70 mins.)

Sanctuary (1961)** Lee Remick, Yves Montand, Odetta, Bradford Dillman. Governor's daughter is seduced by a Cajun, who returns after she's married, to cause her further trouble. It all ends in murder. Faulkner's seamy tale of the South in the 1920s given a distorted, choppy production treatment; even the talented cast is stymied. (Dir: Tony Richardson, 90 mins.)

Sanctuary of Fear (MTV 1979)*** Barnard Hughes, Kay Lenz. Hughes's performance as G. K. Chesterton's Father Brown, detective, is a treat. But the script takes us on a repetitive trip through a young girl's nightmarish experience of unexplained and unmotivated murders and disappearances. (Dir: John Llewellyn Moxey, 104 mins.)

Sand (1949)** Mark Stevens, Coleen Gray, Rory Calhoun. The trials and tribulations of a show horse named Jubilee. Some good photography. (Dir: Louis King, 78 mins.)

Sand Castle, The (1961)***½ Barry Cardwell, Alec Wilder. A diverting try for something away from the usual run, showing an afternoon in a boy's life at the seashore. Whimsical film is often quite charming, should be enjoyed by the discriminating who want something different. (Dir: Jerome Hill, 67 mins.)

Sand, Love and Salt (West Germany-Italy-Yugoslavia, 1956)** Marcello Mastroianni, Jester Naefe, Isabelle Corey. A shipwrecked boat, a beautiful girl, a sunburned sailor, and love. Despite these ingredients, the film falls flat. Made before Mastroianni clicked big in later movies. (Dir: Franz Cap, 89 mins.)

Sand Pebbles, The (1966)**½ Steve McQueen, Richard Attenborough, Candice Bergen, Richard Crenna. A sprawling, over-long adventure drama set in China during the 1920's. McQueen gives a commanding low-key performance as an independent sailor-engineer who clashes with his superiors after he becomes politically aware of the situation around him. The film is much too long, but not without interest. (Dir: Robert Wise, 195 mins.)

Sandcastles (MTV 1972)** Jan-Michael Vincent, Bonnie Bedelia, Mariette Hartley. Good cast helps this trite ghost story. Vincent, Herschel Bernardi, and Bedelia try to bring off this love story about a man who dies in an auto crash, and returns to make amends for a previous act of thievery. If you can accept the idea that Miss Bedelia's character can fall in love with a ghost, the game is won. Miss Bedelia is an interesting actress, and she's backed up by Bernardi's understanding restaurateur. (Dir: Ted Post, 73 mins.)

Sanders (Great Britain–West Germany, 1964)**½ Richard Todd, Marianne Koch, Albert Lieven. Young woman doctor arrives at a remote African outpost and finds a dedicated doctor involved in smuggling diamonds, with a policeman on his trail. Picturesque story of the Dark Continent moves at a fairly good rate. (Dir: Lawrence Huntington, 83 mins.)

Sanders of the River (Great Britain, 1935)*** Paul Robeson, Leslie Banks, Nina Mae McKinney. Robeson lends dignity to an apology for British imperialism in Africa. Well directed by Zoltan Korda. Another reminder of how shamefully the great Robeson was wasted by Hollywood. He sings a traditional African song, gorgeously. Alternate title: **Coast of Skeletons.** (98 mins.)

Sandokan Against the Leopard of Sarawak (Italy, 1964)*½ Ray Danton, Guy Madison. (Dir: Luigi Capuano, 94 mins.)

Sandokan Fights Back (Italy, 1964)*½ Guy Madison, Ray Danton. (Dir: Luigi Capuano, 96 mins.)

Sandpiper, The (1965)** Elizabeth Taylor, Richard Burton, Eva Marie Saint, Charles Bronson. The presence of Elizabeth Taylor and Richard Burton and the grandeur of the great Big Sur location shots don't really make up for this limp and saccharine love story between a liberated artist (Miss Taylor) and a dedicated, married and confused minister (Burton). However, if you want to while away a couple of hours, this sophisticated soap opera peopled by beautiful people will fill the bill. (Dir: Vincente Minnelli, 116 mins.)

Sands of Beersheba (U.S.-Israel, 1965)**½ Diane Baker, David Opatoshu, Tom Bell. American girl in Israel meets the friend of her fiancé, who was killed in the 1948 fighting, soon finds herself caught between love and war. Filmed in Israel, this drama offers little that is new. (Dir: Alexander Ramati, 89 mins.)

Sands of Iwo Jima (1949)***½ John Wayne, John Agar, Forrest Tucker. Officer's son has no liking for the traditions of the Marine Corps, but a tough sergeant makes him see otherwise under stress of battle. Some of the best war scenes ever staged are here, together with a splendid performance by Wayne. (Dir: Allan Dwan, 109 mins.)

Sands of the Kalahari (Great Britain, 1965)*** Stuart Whitman, Stanley Baker, Susannah York, Harry Andrews, Theodore Bikel, Nigel Davenport. A strange he-man adventure involving the survivors of a plane crash in Africa's dangerous Kalahari Desert. Stuart Whitman does very well in the role of an arrogant professional hunter whose desire to prove his strength leads to the destruction of most of his party and eventually himself. There's a fantastic finale in which Whitman pits his prowess against a tribe of wild baboons. (Dir: Cy Endfield, 119 mins.)

Sangaree (1953)** Fernando Lamas, Arlene Dahl, Francis L. Sullivan, Patricia Medina. Sangaree, a Georgia plantation, is the scene of this turbulent drama about pirates and family jealousies. Sangaree is sort of a poor man's Tara without the excitement of the Civil War to enhance it. Besides that Lamas is no Gable. (Dir: Edward Ludwig, 94 mins.)

Sanjuro (Japan, 1962)***½ Toshiro Mifune, Tatsuya Nakadai, Takashi Shimura. A sardonic samurai comedy, with more satisfying because less ambitious work than usual by director Akira Kurosawa. (96 mins.)

Sansho the Bailiff (Japan, 1954)***½ This epic story about a brother and sister who fall into the hands of an unscrupulous slave owner is one of the finest films to come out of Japan. Director Kenji Mizoguchi heightens the inherent drama, the plight of the family being torn apart during 11th-century feudalism, by concentrating on the story and allowing the actors to emote with all stops out. May strike some as Japanese soap opera, but the setting and exquisite production details make it memorable. (Dir: Kenji Mizoguchi, 119 mins.)

Santa Claus Conquers the Martians (1964)** John Call, Leonard Hicks, Donna Conforti. A bad film shot on a low budget in an abandoned Long Island airport hangar. Two children are kidnapped by Martians to advise on the Martians' domestic problems. (Dir: Nicholas Webster, 81 mins.)

Santa Fe Passage (1955)*** John Payne, Faith Domergue, Rod Cameron. Indian-hating scout takes a job with a wagon train. Actionful western, above average. (Dir: William Witney, 90 mins.)

Santa Fe Trail (1940)*** Errol Flynn, Olivia de Havilland, Van Heflin, Ronald Reagan, Raymond Massey. Typical Class A 1940 western. A lot of action, plus an elaborate production was always sure to ring the bell at the box office. The formula hasn't changed much. (Dir: Michael Curtiz, 110 mins.)

Santee (1972)*½ Glenn Ford, Michael Burns, Dana Wynter. (Dir: Gary Nelson, 91 mins.)

Santiago (1956)*** Alan Ladd, Rossana Podesta, Chill Wills, Paul Fix. Remember the "Maine"? In this period tale, Ladd and Nolan are unwilling partners running guns to Cuban revolutionaries, during the island's fight for independence from Spain. This would be a fairly routine actioner, were it not for a mordant and, in spots, extremely risqué script. Nolan, as the slimy baddie, gets all the best lines—listen carefully. (Dir: Gordon Douglas, 93 mins.)

Sapphire (Great Britain, 1959)**** Nigel Patrick, Yvonne Mitchell. The murder of a good-time girl leads police to racial problems in untangling the mystery. A good whodunit further enhanced by some perceptive comments on current social problems; hits the mark either way. First rate screenplay and excellent performances, especially from Yvonne Mitchell, make this English entry a winner. (Dir: Basil Dearden, 92 mins.)

Saps at Sea (1940)**½ Stan Laurel, Oliver Hardy, Ben Turpin. Middle-level Laurel and Hardy in a small boat. Gordon Douglas directs competently. (57 mins.)

Saraband (Great Britain, 1948)*** Stewart Granger, Joan Greenwood. An unhappy girl married to a man in line for the English throne falls in love with an adventurer, but the affair ends tragically. Costume romance has a stylish presentation, especially in the direction. (Dirs: Michael Relph, Basil Dearden, 96 mins.)

Saracen Blade, The (1954)** Ricardo Montalban, Betta St. John. Not many clichés are omitted in this costume adventure about the Crusades and the days of knights and their valiant deeds. (Dir: William Castle, 76 mins.)

Saracens, The (Italy, 1963)*½ Richard Harrison, Ana Mori Ubaldi. (Dir: Roberto Mauri, 89 mins.)

Sarah T.—Portrait of a Teenaged Alcoholic (MTV 1975)*** Linda Blair, Verna Bloom, William Daniels, Larry Hagman. Linda Blair is quite convincing as a mixed-up 15-year-old, hooked on secret drinking. It all begins when Sarah must cope with a new school and surroundings after her mother remarries. Ends on an upbeat note, as Sarah convinces her parents that she's an alcoholic ready for outside help. (Dir: Richard Donner, 100 mins.)

Saratoga (1937)**½ Clark Gable, Jean Harlow, Walter Pidgeon, Lionel Barrymore, Frank Morgan. Gable is a bookie and Harlow is a racing man's daughter in this romantic comedy of the racing world. Miss Harlow died before completing this film. (Dir: Jack Conway, 92 mins.)

Saratoga Trunk (1945)**½ Gary Cooper, Ingrid Bergman, Flora Robson, Jerry Austin, Florence Bates. Elaborate version of Edna Ferber's novel, with the social commentary and local history left out. In an odd bit of casting, Ingrid is a Creole beauty from the wrong side of the tracks, bent on achieving a fortune; Cooper is a rough-edged Texas millionaire. Their romance is slower without the moral ramifications, such as they were, implied in the book, but the sparks between them make it watchable at least. (Dir: Sam Wood, 135 mins.)

Sarge—the Badge or the Cross (MTV 1971)*** George Kennedy, Ricardo Montalban. Thanks to writer Don Mankiewicz, director Richard Colla, and actor George Kennedy, this drama about a cop who turns priest after his wife is killed in a car bombing tragedy manages to avoid the clichés such a plot might trigger, and holds your interest throughout. George Kennedy plays the lead as a big laconic character, given to wearing tinted glasses, and he makes the man believable. Don Mankiewicz keeps the sermonizing down, while priestly good deeds alternate with detective work on the bombing puzzle. Absorbing. (Dir: Richard Colla, 99 mins.)

Saskatchewan (1954)**½ Alan Ladd, Shelley Winters, J. Carrol Naish, Hugh O'Brian. Mountie needs all the help he can muster to drive the Sioux Indians back across the border. Fast-moving if familiar outdoor action tale. (Dir: Raoul Walsh, 87 mins.)

Satan Bug, The (1965)**½ George Maharis, Richard Basehart, Anne Francis, Dana Andrews. Science-fiction fans will buy this one without too many reservations, but drama fans will probably lose interest before the final fadeout. The suspense tale which starts out excitingly, has Richard Basehart playing a diabolical doctor bent on destroying mankind by unleashing stolen virus germs on an unsuspecting populace. Most of the action involves agent George Maharis' attempts to track down the stolen "satan bug" and avert total annihilation. (Dir: John Sturges, 114 mins.)

Satan Met a Lady (1936)*** Warren William, Bette Davis, Alison Skipworth, Arthur Treacher. Second film version of Dashiell Hammett's "The Maltese Falcon" is played tongue in cheek. William is a sublimely seedy detective, unheroic and just half a brain ahead of being a derelict. Davis is well cast as Brigid O'Shaughnessy. (Dir: William Dieterle, 75 mins.)

Satan Never Sleeps (1962)*½ William Holden, Clifton Webb, France Nuyen. Webb's last film. (Dir: Leo McCarey, 126 mins.)

Satan's Satellites (1958)* Judd Holdren, Aline Towne. (Dir: Fred Brannon, 70 mins.)

Satan's School for Girls (MTV 1973)**½ Roy Thinnes, Pamela Franklin, Jo Van Fleet, Lloyd Bochner. Thriller takes its time before getting to the mystery elements. Miss Franklin plays a young lady who enrolls in a private fine-arts school to get to the bottom of her younger sister's suicide. She's soon roaming into dark, hidden rooms. (Dir: David Lowell Rich, 73 mins.)

Satan's Triangle (MTV 1975)**½ Kim Novak, Doug McClure. Melodrama about the infamous "Devil's Triangle," an area where ships, planes and people just disappear off the face of the earth. Helicopter rescue pilots come to the aid of a distressed vessel and find a beautiful woman survivor. The surprise twist at the end is a good one. (Dir: Sutton Rolley, 72 mins.)

Satellite in the Sky (Great Britain, 1956)**½ Kieron Moore, Lois Maxwell. A British made science-fiction tale of the earth satellite. Interesting but often too technical in the dialogue. (Dir: Paul Dickson, 84 mins.)

Saturday Night and Sunday Morning (Great Britain, 1961)**** Albert Finney, Shirley Ann Field. A wonderful, robust film, expertly directed by Tony Richardson, detailing the life and loves of a young working-class rascal from the English midlands. Incisive comment on certain mores of the English working class that captures the mood of such a dreary industrial community. Electric, vital performance of Finney deservedly shot him to stardom. An admirable piece of filmmaking in every detail. (98 mins.)

Saturday Night Fever (1977)**** John Travolta, Karen Lynn Gorney, Donna Pescow. Driving, powerful film, a huge box-office and critical success. Capitalizes on disco fever with Travolta's riveting dancing sequences. Screenplay by Norman Wexler has some perceptive comments to make on the social and sexual rituals of working-class kids in Brooklyn. (Dir: John Badham, 119 mins.)

Saturday Night Kid, The (1929)** Clara Bow, James Hall, Jean Arthur. Bow (on the way down) meets Arthur (on the way up) in this Paramount comedy. Bit part by Jean Harlow. (Dir: Eddie Sutherland, 69 mins.)

Saturday Night Out (Great Britain, 1964)** Heather Sears, Bernard Lee, Nigel Green. Weak tale of a sailor's love has several unconnected episodes strung together. Solid acting, but wooden roles. Lee is the notable exception as a businessman involved with a blackmailing woman. (Dir: Robert Hartford-Davis, 96 mins.)

577

Saturday's Hero (1951)*** John Derek, Donna Reed, Sidney Blackmer, Aldo Ray. A handsome youth tries to rise above his immigrant family's background by going to college on a football scholarship. He finds things aren't all peaches and cream on the other side of the tracks. Better than usual performances from the actors involved. (Dir: David Miller, 111 mins.)

Saturn 3 (Great Britain, 1980)*** Kirk Douglas, Farrah Fawcett, Harvey Keitel. Douglas and Fawcett have made their Malibu in outer space, only to face the intrusion of madman Harvey Keitel and his rogue robot, who upset their plastic paradise by insinuating that they could get down to work, with Earth starving and all. Uneven, and marred by a weak ending. Stanley Donen produced, and stepped into the director's shoes when John Barry died during shooting. (105 mins.)

Savage, The (1952)**½ Charlton Heston, Susan Morrow. Man raised by the Sioux is torn between loyalties when war threatens between the Indians and the whites. Outdoor drama covers familiar ground, is done well enough to please the adventure fans. (Dir: George Marshall, 95 mins.)

Savage (MTV 1972)**½ Martin Landau, Barbara Bain. Landau and Bain are a respected team of TV journalists digging into the questionable background of a Supreme Court nominee. Scripters attempt to keep things fairly authentic. (Dir: Steven Spielberg, 78 mins.)

Savage Bees, The (MTV 1976)** Ben Johnson, Michael Parks. Predictable New Orleans-based drama about the influx of African killer bees brought here by a visiting cargo ship. This is a "disaster" story with the sheriff's dog the initial victim. Do you thrill to the hum of buzzing critters? (Dir: Bruce Geller, 106 mins.)

Savage Eye, The (1961)**** Barbara Baxley. A dramatized documentary about a woman's lonely days following her recent divorce and the series of adventures she forces herself into in order to combat the feeling of desperation. Miss Baxley is excellent and the candid documentary technique works beautifully. An adult treatment of an adult subject. (Dir: Ben Maddow, 68 mins.)

Savage Gringo (Spain, 1965)*½ Ken Clark, Yvonne Bastien, Alfonso Rojas. (Dir: Antony Roman, 82 mins.)

Savage Innocents, The (France-Great Britain-Italy, 1960)*** Anthony Quinn, Yoko Tani, Peter O'Toole. Quinn is superb as an Eskimo who acts as he must, unmindful of the expectations of the government official (O'Toole, dubbed) sent into his territory. Filmed in Greenland and Hudson's Bay. (Dir: Nicholas Ray, 110 mins.; also 89-min. version.)

Savage Is Loose, The (1974)** George C. Scott, Trish Van Devere, John David Carson. Director Scott sees the story of the Garden of Eden as a dialogue between reason and instinct, with instinct winning at a terrible cost. A naturalist and his wife, marooned on a South Sea Island in 1912, must come to grips with the awakening sexuality of their jungle-reared son. Scott's visual style is somber in the extreme, but his handling of the incest theme is curiously hopeful. (114 mins.)

Savage Land, The—See: **This Savage Land**

Savage Pampas (U.S.-Argentina-Spain, 1966)* Robert Taylor, Ron Randell. (Dir: Hugo Fregonese, 99 mins.)

Savage Seven, The (1968)* Robert Walker, Larry Bishop, Joanna Frank. (Dir: Richard Rush, 96 mins.)

Savage Wilderness—See: **Last Frontier, The**

Savages (1972)** Sam Waterston, Kathleen Widdoes, Louis J. Sradlen. Misconceived social satire uses a decadent garden party as a metaphor for the decline of Western civilization. Directed by James Ivory, who hasn't the least notion of how to organize things visually. George W. S. Trow and Michael O'Donoghue wrote the screenplay, and the cast is interestingly eccentric. Pretentious rot. (108 mins.)

Savages (MTV 1974)**½ Andy Griffith, Sam Bottoms, Noah Beery. Andy Griffith takes a holiday from his usual nice-guy roles, to become a despicable menace. He's a New York lawyer who goes to a desert area to hunt bighorn sheep, with young Sam Bottoms as his guide. After Griffith kills an old prospector and pretends it was an animal, he and Sam begin a cat-and-mouse game of life and death in the desert. Suspenseful in parts. (Dir: Lee H. Katzin, 72 mins.)

Save the Tiger (1973)**** Jack Lemmon, Jack Gilford, Laurie Heineman. Lemmon gives the performance of his career as a garment manufacturer at the end of his tether. Remarkable acting by Gilford as Lemmon's suffering partner. (Dir: John G. Avildsen, 99 mins.)

Sawdust and Tinsel (Sweden, 1953)**** Harriet Andersson, Ake Groenberg, Hasse Ekman. Writer-director Ingmar Bergman's 18th film is set in the eerie world of a traveling circus caravan. (95 mins.)

Saxon Charm, The (1948)***½ Robert Montgomery, Audrey Totter, Susan Hayward, John Payne. Montgomery is good in this character study of a vicious Broadway producer. Story is at times hard to believe, but sustains interest throughout. (Dir: Claude Binyon, 88 mins.)

Say Goodbye, Maggie Cole (MTV 1972)**½ Susan Hayward, Darren McGavin. Strong performances by Hayward and McGavin give this one about doctors working in a slum area a boost. It's a tearjerker, with Hayward playing a recently widowed doctor who goes back into practice with McGavin, a gruff but dedicated ghetto G.P. There won't be a dry eye in your house when young leukemia patient Nichele Nichols says goodbye to Dr. Maggie Cole. (Dir: Jud Taylor, 73 mins.)

Say Hello to Yesterday (Great Britain, 1970)**½ Leonard Whiting, Jean Simmons, Evelyn Laye. Modest, simply constructed romance of a suburban housewife, Simmons, and a young mod, played with exuberance by Whiting. They meet and part within the space of her ten-hour trip to London. A twist on "Brief Encounter." Jean Simmons is particularly touching, and Laye is funny as her mother. Written by Alvin Rakoff and Peter King. (Dir: Alvin Rakoff, 92 mins.)

Say One for Me (1959)** Bing Crosby, Debbie Reynolds, Robert Wagner. Bing back in priestly togs again, but this time he's almost defeated by a weak plot about a show-business parish, a chorus girl, and a night club manager with designs on her, all culminating in the Big Benefit Show. (Dir: Frank Tashlin, 119 mins.)

Sayat Nova—See: **Color of Pomegranates, The**

Sayonara (1957)** Marlon Brando, Miyoshi Umoki, Red Buttons, James Garner, Ricardo Montalban. Long, vulgar, obvious soap opera that confirmed that Joshua Logan's promise as a film director was false. The story involves two parallel romances in occupation Japan, and none of the tears are earned. Paul Osborn adapted the James Michener novel. (147 mins.)

Scalawag (1973)** Kirk Douglas, Mark Lester, Neville Brand, Lesley Anne Down. Pirate film with all the clichés on board. Kirk Douglas stars as a bearded peg-leg pirate, and he also directed the opus on a level best appreciated by 10-year-olds who adore comic books. (93 mins.)

Scalpel (1976)**½ Robert Lansing, Judith Chapman, Arlen Dean Snyder. Pretty good, involved Georgia-made thriller. Plastic surgeon Lansing makes over the face of go-go dancer Chapman to resemble his missing daughter so that he can get his hands on the latter's inheritance. A twist ending. (Dir: John Grissmer, 95 mins.)

Scalphunters, The (1968)*** Burt Lancaster, Ossie Davis, Shelley Winters. Entertaining western which mixes excitement with an ample amount of comedy. Lancaster is at his atheltic and charming best as a fur trapper whose pelts are stolen. Enter Ossie Davis as an educated runaway slave and the plot thickens. Telly Savalas and Shelley Winters are colorful as a renegade killer and his woman. Snappy direction by Sydney Pollack. (102 mins.)

Scalplock (1966)*½ Dale Robertson, Diana Hyland. (Dir: James Goldstone, 100 mins.)

Scampolo (West Germany, 1959)** Romy Schneider, Paul Christian, Carlos Thompson. Orphan girl finds happiness with a young architect. Sugary comedy, a bit too much sweetness and light. Dubbed in English. (Dir: Alfred Weidenmann, 95 mins.)

Scandal at Scourie (1953)**½ Greer Garson, Walter Pidgeon. Another Garson-Pidgeon costume drama and not one of their best. The stars are more than adequate but the script is steeped in sentiment and affords little else, as it recounts the problems of a Canadian couple in adopting an orphan. (Dir: Jean Negulesco, 89 mins.)

Scandal in Paris, A (1946)*** George Sanders, Signe Hasso, Akim Tamiroff. The story of Vidocq, the thief and blackguard who cleverly talks his way into becoming Prefect of Police. Tasty costume melodrama intelligently directed, well written and acted. (Dir: Douglas Sirk, 99 mins.)

Scandal Sheet (1952)**½ Broderick Crawford, Donna Reed, John Derek. Over-done newspaper yarn about a couple of reporters who crack a murder case which involves their editor-friend. Energetically played by the principals. (Dir: Phil Karlson, 82 mins.)

Scanners (1981)**½ Jennifer O'Neal, Stephen Lack, Patrick McGoohan. A small group of social misfits are imbued with telepathic powers. The logic of nightmare isn't sufficiently consistent to push this into classic status, but the film is loaded with good ideas (maybe too many), and the execution is intermittently powerful. Like Tod Browning, his director David Cronenberg's technical faculties aren't always up to the forcefulness of his conceptions.

Scapegoat, The (Great Britain, 1959)**½ Alec Guinness, Bette Davis, Nicole Maurey. Uneven comedy-drama about an English schoolteacher whose exact double, a French nobleman, offers him his family and responsibilities. Everything is done well, but it all doesn't seem to mesh. From the novel by Daphne Du Maurier. (Dir: Robert Hamer, 92 mins.)

Scapegoat, The (France, 1963)** Michele Morgan, Jacques Perrin. Not to be confused with Alec Guinness film with the same title. This one is a French made, English-dubbed adventure meller about madness, murder and injustice in 16th Century Venice. Miss Morgan, a fine actress who squandered her talents in too many of these costume films, is merely decorative once again. (Dir: Duccio Tessari, 94 mins.)

Scar, The (1948)*** Paul Henreid, Joan Bennett. A gangster gets a new face, and a girl makes a new personality to go along with it, but too late, for he must pay the penalty. Suspenseful melodrama. Alternate title: **Hollow Triumph.** (Dir: Steve Sekely, 83 mins.)

Scar of Shame, The (1927)*** Harry Henderson, Lucia Lynn Moses, Ann Kennedy. Melodrama produced for the "race" market, treating class divisions within black society as a successful concert pianist marries a woman beneath his station. Produced by The Colored Players Film Corp. of Philadelphia. (Dir: Frank Peregini, 90 mins.)

Scaramouche (1952)*** Stewart Granger, Eleanor Parker, Janet Leigh, Mel Ferrer.

Exciting and colorful adventure drama set in 18th Century France. Granger handsomely fits the role of the swashbuckling and romancing hero and is surrounded by two beautiful ladies, the Misses Parker (sexier than she's ever been) and Leigh (as the patient noblewoman who secretly loves her "Scaramouche"). From the novel by Raphael Sabatini. (Dir: George Sidney, 118 mins.)

Scarecrow (1973)*** Gene Hackman, Al Pacino, Dorothy Tristan, Ann Wedgeworth. In the rash of buddy films produced in the early 70's, this could have been the definitive one, except for a poor climax which robs the drama of lasting emotional impact. Hackman and Pacino are superb as a pair of drifter-losers who team up to travel from California to Philadelphia, where Hackman plans to open up a car wash. It's a foregone conclusion the pair will never make it to Philly. Their encounters along the way solidify their relationship. A kind of 70's version of Steinbeck's "Of Mice and Men." (Dir: Jerry Schatzberg, 104 mins.)

Scared Stiff (1953)*** Dean Martin, Jerry Lewis, Lizabeth Scott, Dorothy Malone. Singer and his busboy friend flee from a murder charge and land on a mysterious island to help an heiress in distress. Remake of Bob Hope's "The Ghost Breakers" works well with Dean and Jerry, blends laughs and chills expertly. (Dir: George Marshall, 108 mins.)

Scared Straight! Another Story (MTV 1980)** Stan Shaw, Don Fullilove, Randy Brooks, Terri Nunn. Often frightening follow-up to the award-winning documentary in which troublemaking kids visit a prison to be scared about life behind bars. Raw scenes get the message across; it's a living hell in there. Shaw (from "Roots") is effective as the convict leader explaining the facts of cell life and the kid actors display an un-Hollywood naturalness. (Dir: Richard Michaels, 104 mins.)

Scarface Mob, The (1962)**½ Robert Stack, Keenan Wynn, Neville Brand. Eliot Ness and a special force of lawmen band into "The Untouchables," out to get the goods on Al Capone and his mob. Originally the opening installments in the TV series, this crime drama of the Aspirin age still looks pretty good in feature form. (Dir: Phil Karlson, 96 mins.)

Scarface: The Shame of the Nation (1932)**** Paul Muni, Ann Dvorak, Karen Morley, George Raft. Dark, exhilaratingly violent work was almost too potent for its time. It holds up startlingly well in ours. Muni gives his best performance as the simian hood Tony Camonte, whose one redeeming virtue is that he loves his sister a lot. Gestures are the clue to character—and to its flaws; the consistency of acting style at service of the director's eccentric vision is virtually unparalleled in cinema. (Dir: Howard Hawks, 99 mins.)

Scarlet Angel (1952)**½ Rock Hudson, Yvonne DeCarlo, Amanda Blake. Adventure yarn with Rock playing a sea captain who is constantly being used by vixen Yvonne. The plot gets very complicated but there are enough bar room brawls and love scenes to keep you awake. (Dir: Sidney Salkow, 81 mins.)

Scarlet Baroness, The (West Germany, 1962)** Dawn Addams, Joachim Fuchsberger. British secret agent is sent to wartime Germany to obtain information about the progress of production of atomic weapons by the Nazis. Passable cloak-and-dagger adventure dubbed in English. (Dir: Rudolf Jugert, 90 mins.)

Scarlet Buccaneer, The—See: **Swashbuckler**

Scarlet Claw, The (1944)*** Basil Rathbone, Nigel Bruce, Arthur Hohl. Of the films set in the present with Rathbone as Sherlock Holmes and Bruce as Dr. Watson, this probably is the most satisfyingly authentic. The setting is the Canadian moors and the mood is patriotic. (Dir: Roy William Neill, 74 mins.)

Scarlet Coat, The (1955)** Cornel Wilde, Michael Wilding, Anne Francis, George Sanders. Heavy-handed historical costume drama about the American Revolution. Anne Francis is lovely as the lady caught in the web of espionage. (Dir: John Sturges, 101 mins.)

Scarlet Empress, The (1934)**** Marlene Dietrich, John Lodge, Sam Jaffe, Louise Dresser. One of director Josef von Sternberg's greatest films, with a rich Dietrich performance as Catherine the Great. Literally overspilling its frame with bric-a-brac and veils, the film avoids political content as it descends into a world of mystery and sensuality. Jaffe and Dresser excel in supporting roles. Uncomprehending leading man Lodge later quit acting to become governor of Connecticut, anticipating Ronald Reagan by two decades. (110 mins.)

Scarlet Pimpernel, The (Great Britain, 1934)***½ Leslie Howard, Merle Oberon, Raymond Massey. Adventure classic mounted in the stiff-jointed British style of the '30s, where visual splendor meant large sets and fussy costumes in films abominably lit and virtually undirected. Still, Howard is nigh perfect casting as that damned, elusive pimpernel, and the romantic heroics are remarkably untainted by sexist biases, though the class assumptions are dismaying. From the novel by Baronness Orczy. (Dir: Harold Young, 110 mins.)

Scarlet Street (1945)**** Edward G. Robinson, Joan Bennett, Dan Duryea. Director Fritz Lang's most harrowing study of guilt and damnation. Robinson plays a quietly suffering bookkeeper who encounters fate in the guise of a calculating prostitute (Bennett) and her pimp (Duryea). (103 mins.)

Scars of Dracula, The (Great Britain,

1970)* Christopher Lee, Denis Waterman, Jenny Hanley. (Dir: Roy Ward Baker, 94 mins.)

Scavengers, The (1959)**½ Vince Edwards, Carol Ohmart. In his pre-Ben Casey days. Edwards gets mixed up with shady women and shadier killers in the Orient. Quite mixed up, but some interest due to actual locales. John Cromwell's direction (79 mins.)

Scenes from a Marriage (Sweden, 1973) **** Liv Ullmann, Erland Josephson, Bibi Andersson. Ingmar Bergman's stunning, telescopic examination of a crumbling marriage, originally made as six 50-minute programs for Swedish TV. Bergman shaped and edited the original footage into this remarkable drama running almost three hours. This superb film dissects different events, quarrels, lovemaking, misunderstandings, etc., over more than ten years of marriage, divorce and a new, more mature relationship. Ullmann is, to no one's surprise, astonishing and Josephson is nearly as remarkable. Written and directed by Ingmar Bergman. (168 mins.)

Scenes from a Murder (Italy, 1972)** Telly Savalas, Anne Heywood. TV's Lt. Kojak used to be on the other side of the law. Here he plays a murderer involved in a cat-and-mouse chase after a beautiful actress. The lovely Heywood is a good foil for Telly's sinister killer. (Dir: Alberto DeMartino, 90 mins.)

Scent of a Woman (Italy, 1975)*** Vittorio Gassman, Agostina Belli, Alessandro Momo. Gassman scores a triumph in this Italian comedy-drama of a blind rogue forced to pursue his quarry through his other senses. Bravura reigns over sense, and the film's values are questionable. (Dir: Dino Risi, 103 mins.)

Scent of Mystery (1960)** Denholm Elliott, Peter Lorre, Beverly Bentley. Discovering that a young American heiress is about to be murdered, an Englishman and a sour-visaged cab driver (Lorre) set about to save her, sight unseen. Good cinematography in ordinary film released in theaters with an accompanying track of scents, such as perfume and tobacco odors, which were triggered mechanically at the right point in the film to serve as clues to the mystery. The process was labeled "Smell-o-vision." Some critics felt that described the film, too. (Dir: Jack Cardiff, 125 mins.)

Scheherazade (France-Italy-Spain, 1963)*½ Fausto Tozzi, Gerald Barray. (Dir: Pierre Gaspard-Huit, 104 mins.)

Schemer, The (France, 1956)** Michel Auclair, Annie Girardot. Art dealer is swindled by thieves, joins them in crime. Good performances help this involved melodrama along. Dubbed-in English. (Dir: Gilles Grangier, 90 mins.)

Schlock (1973)**½ John Landis, Saul Kahan, Joseph Piantadosi. This may be the only monster movie in which the director doubles as the monster. About the rampages of the missing link Schlockthropus. The title tells all. (Dir: John Landis, 80 mins.)

Schloss Vogelod—See: **Haunted Castle, The**

School for Love (France, 1955)*½ Brigitte Bardot, Jean Marais. (Dir: Marc Allegret, 72 mins.)

School for Scoundrels (Great Britain, 1960)*** Ian Carmichael, Alastair Sim, Terry-Thomas. Innocent young man joins a school with an unusual course in successmanship. Enjoyable comedy has some pointed laughs, a cast of capable performers. (Dir: Robert Hamer, 94 mins.)

Scorchy (1976)* Connie Stevens, Cesare Danova, William Smith, Joyce Jameson, Greg Evigan. (Dir: Hikmet Avedis, 99 mins.)

Scorpio (1973)**½ Burt Lancaster, Alain Delon, Paul Scofield. Adequate spy thriller which gives you the impression it should have been better. Lancaster, stoic and stolid, is the agent who is marked for extinction by fellow agent Scorpio (Delon), and the cat-and-mouse chase is on. You've seen it before but Lancaster gives it a slightly added dimension and a fine supporting cast, including Scofield as a Russian agent, John Colicos, and J. D. Cannon, provides substance to this rather flimsy affair. (Dir: Michael Winner, 114 mins.)

Scorpio Letters, The (MTV 1967)* Alex Cord, Shirley Eaton. (Dir: Richard Thorpe, 98 mins.)

Scotch on the Rocks (Great Britain, 1953)*** Ronald Squire, Kathleen Ryan. Natives cause a Parliamentary investigation when they refuse to pay their taxes. Amusing comedy. (Dir: John Eldridge, 83 mins.)

Scott Free (MTV 1976)*½ Michael Brandon, Susan Saint James, Michael Lerner. (Dir: William Wiard, 72 mins.)

Scott Joplin (1977)**½ Billy Dee Williams, Art Carney, Clifton Davis. Williams stars in a production line biopic of the ragtime composer, originally intended for TV. Engages your attention on a low level: highly inaccurate as biography. (Dir: Jeremy Paul Kagan, 96 mins.)

Scott of the Antarctic (Great Britain, 1948)*** John Mills, Derek Bond, Kenneth More, Christopher Lee. An account of the ill-fated British expedition to the South Pole, with stunning photographic effects (in color), authentic narrative, but as drama it's curiously remote, only occasionally affecting. (Dir: Charles Frend, 110 mins.)

Scout's Honor (MTV 1980)**½ Gary Coleman, Katherine Helmond, Pat O'Brien, Wilfrid Hyde-White, Harry Morgan. Friendly, entertaining story stars Coleman as an orphan who yearns to be a Cub Scout. He and the rest of the kids win over the sour grown-ups for a happy ending. The parents of the Scouts are all played by former child TV stars: Jay ("Dennis the Menace") North, Lauren ("Father Knows Best") Chapin, Angela ("Make Room for Daddy") Cartwright, and Paul ("Donna Reed Show") Petersen. First telecast on the 50th anniversary of the Cub Scouts of America. (Dir: Henry Levin, 104 mins.)

Scream and Scream Again (Great Britain, 1970)**½ Vincent Price, Christopher Lee, Peter Cushing. An above-average, somewhat more sophisticated Vincent Price mad-scientist effort revolving around a series of psychotic murders in England. It seems Dr. Browning is gathering bits and pieces of people to build a perfect human being. Woven into this gruesome tale is a subplot of political intrigue. (Dir: Gordon Hessler, 94 mins.)

Scream, Blacula, Scream (1973)**½ William Marshall, Pam Grier, Don Mitchell. Blaxploitation sequel to "Blacula." The black vampire (Marshall) is resurrected to continue his grisly exploits; Mitchell lends strong support. (Dir: Bob Kelljan, 95 mins.)

Scream of Fear (Great Britain, 1961)*** Susan Strasberg, Ronald Lewis, Ann Todd, Christopher Lee. Girl poses as her paralyzed friend to investigate what has happened to her father, nearly loses her life in finding out. Sharply directed thriller works up good amount of suspense, shudders. (Dir: Seth Holt, 81 mins.)

Scream of the Wolf (MTV 1974)** Peter Graves, Clint Walker, Jo Ann Pflug. There's a creature which may or may not be a killer wolf, a rash of killings by an almost superhuman wolflike beast, so author Graves and hunter Walker are called in to solve the mystery. (Dir: Dan Curtis, 74 mins.)

Scream, Pretty Peggy (MTV 1973)**½ Bette Davis, Ted Bessell, Sian Barbara Allen. This melodrama strains a bit to create a few scares, but fans of Miss Davis' horror-movie roles will enjoy watching her over-act. An innocent college student plays part-time housekeeper for Bette's weird family in their creepy mansion. (Dir: Gordon Hessler, 74 mins.)

Screaming Mimi (1958)*½ Anita Ekberg, Phil Carey, Gypsy Rose Lee. (Dir: Gerd Oswald, 79 mins.)

Screaming Skull, The (1958)*½ John Hudson, Peggy Webber, Alex Nicol. (Dir: Alex Nicol, 68 mins.)

Screaming Woman, The (MTV 1972)*** Joseph Cotten, Walter Pidgeon. Sweet Olivia de Havilland, as a wealthy lady recovering from a nervous breakdown, sees a woman buried alive, but nobody believes her. Ray Bradbury's short story will have viewers rooting for Olivia, frantically seeking help from the police, neighbors, little boys, and the killer. Filmed on a grand Santa Barbara estate, by and large, the suspenseful Bradbury plot holds up. (Dir: Jack Smight, 73 mins.)

Scrooge (Great Britain, 1970)**½ Albert Finney, Alec Guinness, Edith Evans. This musical version of Charles Dickens' timeless Christmas yarn about the flinty old miser-turned-philanthropist once he's shown the error of his ways, is as empty as a neglected Christmas stocking. Albert Finney, as Scrooge, plays the cantankerous, stingy businessman with great flair, and is the main bright spot. Music adds nothing and Sir Alec Guinness, painted a ghastly, ghostly gray from bandaged head to manacled foot, is a sight to behold as Marley. Unimaginatively directed by Ronald Neame. (118 mins.)

Scruples (MTV 1981)*½ Shelley Smith, Dirk Benedict, Jessica Walter, Roy Thinnes. (Dir: Robert Day, 104 mins.)

Scudda-Hoo! Scudda-Hay! (1948)** Lon McCallister, June Haver, Walter Brennan, Natalie Wood. Story of a farm boy who gets hold of a pair of mules and then trains them to be the best team around is mild fare. (Dir: F. Hugh Herbert, 95 mins.)

Scum (Great Britain, 1978)***½ Ray Winstone, Phil Daniels, Julian Firth, Mick Ford. The physical, sexual, and psychological violence of Borstal prison for youthful offenders, 20 years after Brendan Behan traversed the same territory. The change is exponentially more shocking. Ray Winstone and Phil Daniels, the rocker and mod stars of "Quadrophenia." Powerful, disturbing, and violent. (Dir: Alan Clarke)

Sea Chase, The (1955)**½ Lana Turner, John Wayne, Tab Hunter, James Arness. Far-fetched tale of adventure and romance. Wayne skippers a renegade freighter which is bound for Valparaiso. On board is an assorted crew and Lana Turner, Wayne's woman. Curious to see Big John as a German officer. (Dir: John Farrow, 117 mins.)

Sea Devils (Great Britain, 1953)**½ Rock Hudson, Yvonne DeCarlo. Fisherman turned smuggler gets involved with a beautiful spy during the Napoleonic era. Standard costume melodramatics get a lift from some action scenes. (Dir: Raoul Walsh, 91 mins.)

Sea Gull, The (U.S.-Great Britain, 1968)***½ Vanessa Redgrave, Simone Signoret, David Warner, James Mason, Harry Andrews, Kathleen Widdoes. Strong adaptation of Anton Chekhov's play about rural Russia during the latter part of the 19th century, an enduring, illuminating masterpiece. Director Sidney Lumet has rounded up a superlative cast of players. "Sea Gull" does seem static at times, but generally an absorbing rendition. (141 mins.)

Sea Gypsies, The (1978)**½ Robert Logan, Mikki Jamison-Olson, Cjon Damitri Patterson. A family movie. Logan plays a widower who sets sail with his two daughters and a female photographer (Jamison-Olson) around the world. Naturally, they wind up stranded on a deserted island near Alaska and set up a new way of life.

The photography is excellent and the plot is based on a true story. (Dir: Stewart Raffill, 101 mins.)

Sea Hawk, The (1940)*** Errol Flynn, Brenda Marshall, Claude Rains, Gilbert Roland, Flora Robson. Exciting, rollicking swashbuckler with Flynn sailing the seas in Her Majesty's service against the Spaniards. Robson is a guileful Queen Elizabeth I. The direction of Michael Curtiz is a prime example of dashing craftsmanship. (127 mins.)

Sea of Grass, The (1947)**½ Spencer Tracy, Katharine Hepburn, Robert Walker, Melvyn Douglas. The cast fights hard but this western about a man who sees New Mexico turning into a dust bowl and fights to save the grass is disappointing. It never stays with any of its many themes long enough to sustain interest and is certainly unworthy of the Tracy-Hepburn combo. (Dir: Elia Kazan, 131 mins.)

Sea Pirate, The (France-Italy-Spain, 1966)* Gerard Barray, Antonella Lualdi, Genevieve Casile. (Dir: Roy Rowland, 85 mins.)

Sea Shall Not Have Them, The (Great Britain, 1954)*** Michael Redgrave, Dirk Bogarde. Rescue launch attempts to save a crew of a downed plane, existing on a rubber raft in the North Sea. Good drama, well acted. (Dir: Lewis Gilbert, 91 mins.)

Sea Wife (Great Britain, 1957)** Joan Collins, Richard Burton, Basil Sydney. Heavy-handed WW II romance. Three men and a woman, survivors of a torpedoed ship, live on a desert island knowing each other by nicknames. After their rescue, Burton searches desperately for his "Sea Wife." The acting is good, but the story is overwrought and pretentious. (Dir: Bob McNaught, 82 mins.)

Sea Wolf, The (1941)**½ Edward G. Robinson, John Garfield, Ida Lupino. Director Michael Curtiz's version of the Jack London novel is brutal and briny, though it has a suffocating visual style. Otherwise, a good Warner Bros. action film, with Robinson the model of a tough tyrant. (90 mins.)

Sealed Cargo (1951)*** Dana Andrews, Carla Balenda, Claude Rains. Fishing vessel rescues the captain of a Danish ship, who is really the commander of a mother ship for Nazi subs. Exciting, suspenseful melodrama. (Dir: Alfred L. Werker, 90 mins.)

Sealed Soil, The (Iran, 1978)**½ The first film of Iran's first (and apparently last) woman filmmaker tells the story of an 18-year-old girl in passive revolt against the role to which her traditional society has relegated her. (Dir: Marva Nabili.)

Seance on a Wet Afternoon (Great Britain, 1964)**** Kim Stanley, Richard Attenborough. Enthralling, brilliantly acted drama of a professional medium near the brink of insanity, who involves her weak husband in a kidnaping plot. Tremendous performances by Miss Stanley

and Attenborough, backed by fine script and direction by Bryan Forbes. Top dramatic fare. (121 mins.)

Search, The (1948)**** Montgomery Clift, Aline MacMahon, Wendell Corey. Moving, sensitive story of a war orphan found in the ruins of post-war Europe. You're made of steel if this one doesn't move you. The cast is superb. (Dir: Fred Zinnemann, 104 mins.)

Search for Bridey Murphy, The (1956)** Louis Hayward, Teresa Wright. Based on M. Bernstein's freak best-seller about a housewife who when under hypnosis recalls a previous life. Quickly made to cash in on the then-current controversy, this drama has only fair entertainment values, except for a good performance by Wright. (Dir: Noel Langley, 84 mins.)

Search for the Gods (MTV 1975)*½ Stephen McHattie, Kurt Russell, Raymond St. Jacques, Ralph Bellamy. (Dir: Jud Taylor, 100 mins.)

Searchers, The (1956)**** John Wayne, Jeffrey Hunter, Natalie Wood. Wood has been missing for years (kidnapped by Indians) and Wayne and Hunter are the searchers. Film has a beauty available only to a supreme visual poet like director John Ford. (119 mins.)

Searching Wind, The (1946)*** Robert Young, Sylvia Sidney. Lillian Hellman's story of a career diplomat who has never taken a firm stand on anything is potentially good drama but never quite makes it. (Dir: William Dieterle, 103 mins.)

Seas Beneath (1931)** George O'Brien, Marion Lessing, Warren Humer. A German submarine and a U.S. sub chaser fight it out like proper WW I gentlemen. (Dir: John Ford, 99 mins.)

Seaside Swingers (Great Britain, 1964)**½ Freddie and the Dreamers, John Leyton, Mike Sarne, Liz Fraser. Zippy, hippy little musical about youngsters at a seaside resort and their problems with romance. Tunes aren't too bad, the players quite pleasant. Good fun for the teenagers. (Dir: James Hill, 94 mins.)

Season of Passion (Australia, 1961)*** Ernest Borgnine, John Mills, Anne Baxter, Angela Lansbury. Sugar-cane cutters find their annual on-the-town vacation in Sydney has changed, financially and romantically. Offbeat drama with a little-known locale, well acted, this drama should satisfy those in search of different fare. (Dir: Leslie Norman, 93 mins.)

Sebastian (Great Britain, 1968)**½ Dirk Bogarde, Susannah York, Lilli Palmer, John Gielgud. Fast faced espionage movie with talented cast members running all over the place deciphering codes, dodging double-agents, and falling in love. Dirk Bogarde sets the tone with his cool demeanor, and the supporting cast boasts such bright names as Lilli Palmer, Margaret Johnston and Nigel Davenport. (Dir: David Greene, 100 mins.)

Second Best Secret Agent, The (Great

Britain, 1965)* Tom Adams, Veronica Hurst. (Dir: Lindsay Shonteff, 96 mins.)

Second Chance (1953)** Robert Mitchum, Linda Darnell, Jack Palance. South-of-the-border western is typical Mitchum. Competently made but of little interest beyond the novelty of 3-D action. (Dir: Rudolph Maté, 81 mins.)

Second Chance (MTV 1972)** Brian Keith, Elizabeth Ashley, Juliet Prowse. Loosely woven, fairly pleasant comedy about a stockbroker who acquires a ghost town and fills it with assorted talent in need of another break. The experimental community works until the locals accuse their benefactor of becoming a dictator. Gentle humor and minor, low-key problems. (Dir: Peter Tewksbury, 73 mins.)

Second Chorus (1940)** Fred Astaire, Paulette Goddard, Burgess Meredith, Charles Butterworth. Cheery third-rate musical. Astaire and Meredith are collegian tooters who aspire to play with Artie Shaw. Goddard is their manager and the love interest, and Butterworth is around for quiet laughs. (Dir: H. C. Potter, 83 mins.)

Second Fiddle (1939)** Sonja Henie, Tyrone Power, Rudy Vallee, Edna May Oliver. Henie plays an ice-skating teacher who leaves the Midwest for Hollywood and stardom. Yech. B&W. (Dir: Sidney Lanfield, 86 mins.)

Second Greatest Sex, The (1955)** Jeanne Crain, George Nader, Kitty Kallen, Bert Lahr. "Lysistrata" gets another revamping in this western musical. The women are tired of the men fighting all the time, so they go on a love-strike. A lot of talent is wasted on this strained comedy effort, particularly Bert Lahr. (Dir: George Marshall, 87 mins.)

Second Time Around, The (1961)*** Debbie Reynolds, Andy Griffith, Steve Forrest, Juliet Prowse. Sprightly western comedy about a young widow and her children who find themselves stranded in an Arizona town—but she soon livens things up when she becomes sheriff. Good fun. (Dir: Vincent Sherman, 99 mins.)

Second Woman, The (1951)*** Robert Young, Betsy Drake. The whole community suspects a man of being responsible for the death of his fiancee, but his new love proves them wrong. Good psychological suspense melodrama. (Dir: James V. Kern, 91 mins.)

Seconds (1966)*** Rock Hudson, Salome Jens, John Randolph, Will Geer. Intriguing premise of this suspenseful drama should be enough to whet your appetite. Rock Hudson is a middle-aged businessman who discovers he can arrange for a secret organization to give him a "second" chance at life. After submitting to surgery, and psychiatric orientation, Rock emerges as a handsome young man with seemingly everything one could ask for. The nightmare begins at this point, and although some of the plot twists may seem

excessive, the imaginative story holds your attention. Directed by John Frankenheimer. (106 mins.)

Secret Agent, The (Great Britain, 1936) ***½ John Gielgud, Madeleine Carroll, Robert Young, Peter Lorre, Lilli Palmer. Adapted from W. Somerset Maugham's "Ashenden." Director Alfred Hitchcock has said the film has too many twists and ironies—what with agent Gielgud assigned to kill a spy, only to kill an innocent tourist, while the real spy (Young) survives and almost manages to kill his assassin. (93 mins.)

Secret Agent Superdragon (Italy-France-West Germany, 1966)* Ray Danton, Marisa Mell. (Dir: Calvin Jackson Padget, 95 mins.)

Secret Agents, The—See: Dirty Game, The

Secret Beyond the Door (1948)**½ Joan Bennett, Michael Redgrave. Usually the temptress, Bennett is now the tempted, as she discovers that her husband (Redgrave) has a deep, dark secret. Suspense drama, certainly not one of director Fritz Lang's best. (98 mins.)

Secret Ceremony (Great Britain, 1968)**½ Elizabeth Taylor, Mia Farrow, Robert Mitchum. Macabre, muddled, but interesting melodrama. The plot concerns a warped and wealthy Miss Farrow who brings a blowsy Miss Taylor home as a substitute mother, not counting on the sudden appearance of stepfather Mitchum. The "edited for TV" version is butchered and watered down. (Dir: Joseph Losey, 101 mins.)

Secret Command (1944)*** Pat O'Brien, Carole Landis, Chester Morris, Ruth Warrick. A two-fisted gent puts a stop to sabotage in the California shipyards. Actionful melodrama, well above average. (Dir: A. Edward Sutherland, 82 mins.)

Secret Conclave, The (Italy, 1953)**½ Henri Vidon, Tullio Carminati. As Pope Pius X prays during WW I, recollections of his life are brought back to him—although he considers himself a simple country priest, he eventually becomes Pope at the meeting of the famed secret conclave. Recommended for Catholic audiences. Others should find this religious drama fairly interesting. (Dir: Umberto Scarpelli, 60 mins.)

Secret Door, The (Great Britain, 1964)*½ Robert Hutton, Sandra Dorne. (Dir: Gilbert Kay, 72 mins.)

Secret File—Hollywood (1962)* Robert Clarke, Francine York. (Dir: Ralph Cushman, 85 mins.)

Secret Fury, The (1950)** Claudette Colbert, Robert Ryan. Bride is claimed to be already married, is sent to an asylum on what looks like a frameup. Just fair mystery moves too slowly. (Dir: Mel Ferrer, 86 mins.)

Secret Garden, The (1949)*** Margaret O'Brien, Dean Stockwell, Herbert Marshall. An eerie, suspenseful drama about two children, Margaret O'Brien and Dean

Stockwell, and their discovery of a magical, secret garden. Well acted by the entire cast, including Miss O'Brien whose grown-up acting performances have been pretty awful. (Dir: Fred M. Wilcox, 92 mins.)

Secret Heart, The (1946)**½ Claudette Colbert, Walter Pidgeon, June Allyson. Cast helps but there's no spark to this dreary psychological study of a girl who worships her dead father and hates her lovely stepmother. Some of the ladies may like this. (Dir: Robert Z. Leonard, 97 mins.)

Secret Invasion (1964)**½ Stewart Granger, Raf Vallone, Edd Byrnes, Mickey Rooney. Though this war film predates the popular film "Dirty Dozen" by a few years, it's basically the same story. A group of criminals are promised a pardon if they'll participate in a dangerous mission involving the infiltration of Nazi-held territory in Yugoslavia during WW II. Though the film has some exciting sequences, the cast isn't strong enough to give it a much-needed sense of adventure. Stewart Granger, as the major in charge of the mission, comes off best. (Dir: Roger Corman, 98 mins.)

Secret Life of an American Wife, The (1968)*½ Walter Matthau, Patrick O'Neal, Edy Williams. (Dir: George Axelrod, 88 mins.)

Secret Life of John Chapman, The (MTV 1976)*** Ralph Waite, Susan Anspach, Brad Davis, Pat Hingle. A curiously affecting "real life" drama based on the notable book "Blue Collar Journal." It's a deft adaptation of the chronicle of the president of Pennsylvania's prestigious Haverford College, during his voluntary sojourn doing odd jobs of manual labor. Waite plays the adventurous college president with ease. The best performance, though, comes from Miss Anspach as a good-natured, harried and vulnerable waitress in a luncheonette. (Dir: David Lowell Rich, 72 mins.)

Secret Life of Plants, The (1980)*** Often interesting documentary, with a fascinating score by Stevie Wonder. (Dir: Walon Green.)

Secret Life of Walter Mitty, The (1947)***½ Danny Kaye, Virginia Mayo, Ann Rutherford, Boris Karloff. Thurber's story of a man who lived in two worlds—the real one and his own fantasy world—makes an entertaining vehicle for Danny Kaye. Some excellent song sequences and sharp comedy lines make this one above average. (Dir: Norman Z. McLeod, 105 mins.)

Secret Mark of D'Artagnan (France-Italy, 1962)*½ George Nader, Magali Noel. (Dir: Siro Marcellini, 95 mins.)

Secret Mission (Great Britain, 1942)**½ James Mason, Stewart Granger, Michael Wilding. British spy drama with excellent actors making the most of the intrigue. (Dir: Harold French, 82 mins.)

Secret Night Caller, The (MTV 1975)*½ Robert Reed, Hope Lange, Elaine Giftos, Michael Constantine. (Dir: Jerry Jameson, 72 mins.)

Secret of Convict Lake, The (1951)**½ Glenn Ford, Gene Tierney, Ethel Barrymore, Zachary Scott, Ann Dvorak. Convicts invade a village inhabited only by women; complications arise. Ethel Barrymore, as matriarch of the village, is the only interesting feature. (Dir: Michael Gordon, 83 mins.)

Secret of Dr. Kildare, The (1939)** Lew Ayres, Lionel Barrymore, Laraine Day. Certainly not one of the best in this series. Kildare continues his long Hollywood internship, Barrymore is still the barking "heart of gold" Gillespie and Laraine continues as Kildare's pretty combination nurse-sweetheart. (Dir: Harold S. Bucquet, 85 mins.)

Secret of Dr. Mabuse (1962)*½ Peter Van Eyck, Leo Genn, Yoko Tani. (Dir: Hugo Fregonese, 90 mins.)

Secret of My Success, The (Great Britain, 1965)*½ Lionel Jeffries, James Booth, Honor Blackman, Stella Stevens, Shirley Jones. (Dir: Andrew L. Stone, 103 mins.)

Secret of Santa Vittoria, The (1969)**½ Anthony Quinn, Anna Magnani, Hardy Kruger, Virna Lisi. Ponderous direction by Stanley Kramer and a screenplay that savors little of the excellent dialogue found in Robert Crichton's novel dissipate most of the potential inherent in this story of Italian hill town at the end of WW II. Anna Magnani, back in a major picture after a lamentably long absence, is reason enough to see this comedy-drama, as she bullies husband Quinn and dominates every scene she is in. The German army never did find the big cache of wine, but you can content yourself with Magnani and a good supporting performance by Hardy Kruger as a German officer. (140 mins.)

Secret of the Black Trunk (West Germany, 1962)*½ Joachim Hansen, Senta Berger. (Dir: Werner Klingler, 96 mins.)

Secret of the Black Widow, The (West Germany, 1963)*½ O. W. Fischer, Karin Dor, Werner Peters. (Dir: F. J. Gottlieb, 107 mins.)

Secret of the Chinese Carnation, The (West Germany, 1965)* Brad Harris, Horst Frank. (Dir: Rudolf Zehetgruber, 95 mins.)

Secret of the Incas (1954)**½ Charlton Heston, Robert Young, Nicole Maurey, Yma Sumac. Adventurer finds a map holding the location of a priceless gold sunburst, arrives to find an archeological expedition already there. Melodrama with enough intrigue and suspense to hold the action fans. (Dir: Jerry Hopper, 101 mins.)

Secret of the Purple Reef, The (1960)** Jeff Richards, Peter Falk, Richard Chamberlain. Two brothers arrive to investigate the mysterious sinking of their father's ship. Passable Grade B melodrama with a couple of TV names who meant less then. Colorful* Caribbean location scenes. (Dir: William Witney, 80 mins.)

Secret of the Red Orchid (West Germany, 1962)** Adrian Hoven, Christopher Lee, Marisa Mell. Scotland Yard teams with an FBI agent to nab a murdering blackmailer. Fair Edgar Wallace mystery dubbed in English—some moments of suspense. (Dir: Helmut Ashley, 94 mins.)

Secret of the Sphinx (Italy-West Germany, 1964)*½ Tony Russel, Maria Perschy. (Dir: Duccio Tessari, 95 mins.)

Secret of the Telegian, The (Japan, 1960)*½ Akihiko Kirata. (Dir: Jun Fukuda, 86 mins.)

Secret of Treasure Mountain (1956)** Raymond Burr, Valerie French. A buried Indian treasure is mysteriously guarded by an old man and his attractive daughter. Routine adventure film. Burr in his pre-Perry Mason days. (Dir: Seymour Friedman, 68 mins.)

Secret Partner (Great Britain, 1961)** Stewart Granger, Haya Harareet. Routine meller with Stewart Granger cast as a man who must prove he is innocent of an embezzlement charge and win back his wife in the process. Haya Harareet woodenly plays Granger's wife. (Dir: Basil Dearden, 91 mins.)

Secret People, The (Great Britain, 1952)**½ Valentina Cortese, Audrey Hepburn, Serge Reggiani. Refugee in London meets her former fiance who persuades her to enter into an espionage plot. Long, leisurely melodrama doesn't have enough spark to lift it much above the ordinary. (Dir: Thorold Dickinson, 87 mins.)

Secret War of Harry Frigg, The (1968)** Paul Newman, Sylva Koscina. In WW II, a rebellious private is called upon to try and free some captured Allied generals. Obvious attempt at service humor, with Paul Newman wasted. Andrew Duggan, Tom Bosley, John Williams. (Dir: Jack Smight, 110 mins.)

Secret Ways, The (1961)**½ Richard Widmark, Sonja Ziemann. Fast-paced but brainless chase thriller behind the Iron Curtain. Widmark tries to smuggle an anti-Communist leader out of Red Hungary. Some exciting narrow-escape sequences. (Dir: Phil Karlson, 112 mins.)

Secret World (France, 1969)**½ Jacqueline Bisset, Jean-Francois Maurin. The combination of Miss Bisset's beauty and an offbeat tale makes this film interesting. A young French boy, scarred by his parents' death in a car crash, becomes deeply infatuated with a beautiful English lady visiting his aunt and uncle's château. When it comes time for Miss Bisset to go back to England, the boy is once again shattered and retreats into himself. (Dirs: Robert Freeman, Paul Feyder, 94 mins.)

Secrets (MTV 1977)* Susan Blakely, Roy Thinnes. (Dir: Paul Wendkos, 106 mins.)

Secrets of Three Hungry Wives (MTV 1978)** Jessica Walter, James Franciscus, Eve Plumb, Gretchen Corbett, Heather MacRae. Franciscus is a playboy who preys on suburban housewives and their offspring in this sudsy whodunit. Walter, Corbett, MacRae, and Plumb all have good reason to murder the rat. (Dir: Gordon Hessler, 104 mins.)

Seduced and Abandoned (Italy, 1964)**** Saro Urzi, Stefania Sandrelli. A wonderfully funny film that takes a sardonic, angry view of Sicilian family life and the hypocrisy which plays such an important part in their lives and mores. Pietro Germi, the same wizard responsible for "Divorce, Italian style," wrote and directed this witty and bitter view of his countrymen. Story is about what happens in a Sicilian town when a young girl is seduced by the fiancé of her sister. English dubbed. (118 mins.)

Seduction of Joe Tynan, The (1979)*** Alan Alda, Meryl Streep, Barbara Harris. A rather facile drama about a charismatic liberal senator (Alda) that hasn't more density than a good Movie of the Week. Alda, who wrote the script, projects a more piquant sense of decency than anyone else in movies, but the dramatic situations are too pat. (Dir: Jerry Schatzberg, 107 mins.)

Seduction of Mimi, The (Italy, 1974)**** Giancarlo Giannini, Mariangela Melato, Agostina Belli. Rollicking mélange of political humor, Sicilian double standards, and sexual fandangos served up by director Lina Wertmuller. Giannini and Melato strike sparks as a metallurgist and his mistress whose concepts of honor diverge tragically. Mangled American reediting job by Fima Noveck. (89 mins.)

Seduction of Miss Leona, The (MTV 1980)** Lynn Redgrave, Brian Dennehy, Conchata Ferrell, Anthony Zerbe. Sentimental three-hankie drama about a prudish, old-fashioned college professor (Redgrave) who falls in love with a married handyman, skillfully played by the large Dennehy. Redgrave's fellow academicians use successful ploys to dampen the blossoming relationship. (Dir: Joseph Hardy, 104 mins.)

See Here, Private Hargrove (1944)*** Robert Walker, Keenan Wynn, Donna Reed, Robert Benchley. Many an ex-Army man will get plenty of laughs out of this fair adaptation of the famous best seller. (Dir: Wesley Ruggles, 101 mins.)

See How She Runs (MTV 1978)***½ Joanne Woodward, John Considine, Lissy Newman. Woodward stars in this extraordinary drama about a woman of 40 who suddenly finds the need to do something for herself, and herself alone, overpowering. A teacher, divorced, with two young daughters and a paralyzed father dependent upon her, she nevertheless takes up jogging at every moment she can spare, until it becomes central to her existence, a fact to which she insists her family must adjust. Skillful development of the protagonist who develops her running skills enough to enter the Boston Marathon and have her family root for her. (Dir: Richard Heffron, 104 mins.)

See How They Run (MTV 1964)** John Forsythe, Senta Berger, Jane Wyatt, Franchot Tone. Three orphaned children are pursued by their father's murderer when they take incriminating evidence with them to South America. Draggy suspense drama offers nothing unusual. (Dir: David Lowell Rich, 99 mins.)

See My Lawyer (1945)**½ Olsen and Johnson, Grace McDonald, Noah Beery, Jr. The two comics want to squirm out of a movie contract, hire three young lawyers to help them. Amusing musical nonsense. (Dir: Eddie Cline, 67 mins.)

See No Evil (Great Britain, 1971)**½ Mia Farrow, Robin Bailey. A suspense thriller which works only part of the way, but the chills are there if you're patient. Farrow plays a blind girl who comes home to her uncle's house after the accident which caused her blindness, and begins living a nightmare. (Dir: Richard Fleischer, 89 mins.)

See the Man Run (MTV 1971)**½ Robert Culp, Angie Dickinson, Eddie Albert, June Allyson. Stock kidnapping plot undergoes a wrenching, far-out twist here. Linked to a kidnapping through a wrong telephone number, an out-of-work actor decides to cut himself in. Culp carries off the idea quite well with a nice assist from Miss Dickinson. (Dir: Corey Allen, 73 mins.)

Seeding of Sarah Burns, The (MTV 1979)**½ Kay Lenz, Martin Balsam, Cliff DeYoung. Lenz is fine as an introspective young woman who volunteers for an embryo transplant (she carries the baby for the mother who conceived the embryo but can't risk the pregnancy). Once the drama settles into the obvious twist of the young woman becoming too attached to the growing infant in her, the whole thing becomes a soap opera. Balsam adds a note of authority as the compassionate doctor on the case. (Writer-dir: Sandor Stern, 104 mins.)

Seekers, The—See: **Land of Fury**

Seems Like Old Times (1980)***½ Chevy Chase, Goldie Hawn, Charles Grodin. Synthetic farce concocted by Neil Simon is nevertheless his most efficient original screenplay. The charm and adeptness of the three lead players make almost every laugh work, and Jay Sandrich's direction is well balanced, if visually uninventive. It doesn't mean a thing, nor has it any of the richness of the thirties comedies it emulates, but you care about the characters and the situations are mostly pretty funny. (102 mins.)

Seizure: The Story of Kathy Morris. (MTV 1980)**½ Penelope Milford, Leonard Nimoy, Christopher Allport. The real-life crisis of young singer Kathy Morris (excellent acting by Milford) is transferred to the screen with taste and a sense of reality. Ms. Morris was struck with a seizure,

resulting in an operation which left her in a coma. The film methodically depicts her courageous struggle against adversity, and her eventual victory. Graphic operating-room sequences are not for the squeamish. (Dir: Gerald Isenberg, 104 mins.)

Sellout, The (1951)**½ Walter Pidgeon, John Hodiak, Audrey Totter, Karl Malden. Okay crime yarn. Pidgeon plays a crusading newspaper editor who tries to overthrow the corrupt local law enforcement. (Dir: Gerald Mayer, 83 mins.)

Semi-Tough (1977)*** Burt Reynolds, Kris Kristofferson, Jill Clayburgh. Pro football players Reynolds and Kristofferson form a triangle with Clayburgh, and Convy does an accurate sendup of a noxious character. The charm of the players makes scriptwriter Walter Bernstein's lines rather funny. Convy is most devastatingly accurate in his sendup of Werner Erhart, founder of est. Director Michael Ritchie, one of the sharper comedy men in Hollywood, is still sloppy. (99 mins.)

Seminole (1953)**½ Rock Hudson, Barbara Hale, Anthony Quinn, Richard Carlson, Hugh O'Brian. A good cast makes this adventure movie seem better than it is. The story of Seminole Indians and their efforts to stay free takes up the bulk of the film and it's interestingly unfolded. (Dir: Budd Boetticher, 87 mins.)

Senator Was Indiscreet, The (1947)***½ William Powell, Ella Raines, Peter Lind Hayes. A bird-brained senator lets a hot political diary get out of his hands, and it may spell doom to his machine. Side-splitting farce comedy. Some biting satire, hilarious dialogue. Don't miss it. (Dir: George S. Kaufman, 81 mins.)

Send Me No Flowers (1964)*** Doris Day, Rock Hudson, Tony Randall, Clint Walker, Paul Lynde. In this, their funniest film together, Day is an average housewife and Hudson her hypochondriac husband. He mistakenly believes he is dying, and keeps trying to fix her up with other men, much to her annoyance. Both are very amusing playing against type—he isn't a he-man, and she isn't a virgin. Good supporting cast. (Dir: Norman Jewison, 100 mins.)

Senechal the Magnificent (France, 1958)** Fernandel, Nadia Gray. Actor is mistaken for an army officer, setting off a wave of misunderstandings and impersonations. Fernandel fans will like, others will merely tolerate this mild English-dubbed comedy. (Dir: Jacques Boyer, 78 mins.)

Senior Prom (1959)** Jill Corey, Jimmie Komack, Paul Hampton, Tom Laughlin, Mitch Miller. Harmless little college musical about a young student who makes a hit recording and becomes "top man on campus." Guest appearances by Connee Boswell, Jose Melis, Louis Prima, Keely Smith and even Ed Sullivan. (Dir: David Lowell Rich, 82 mins.)

Senior Year (MTV 1974)* Gary Frank,

Glynnis O'Connor. (Dir: Dick Donner, 72 mins.)

Sensations (1944)**½ Eleanor Powell, Dennis O'Keefe, W. C. Fields. Dancing star resorts to novel means to obtain publicity. Mild musical; some good moments. (Dir: Andrew L. Stone, 86 mins.)

Sense of Loss, A (1972)*** Enlightening but ultimately disappointing documentary about the fighting, bitterness and religious hatred in northern Ireland. Interviews with people closely involved bring out the mindless futility of the ongoing violence in that embittered land. Moving interview with Bernadette Devlin. Director Marcel Ophuls' concern and innate humanity are evident throughout. (135 mins.)

Sensitive, Passionate Man, A (MTV 1977)*½ Angie Dickinson, David Janssen. (Dir: John Newland, 98 mins.)

Senso—See: Wanton Contessa, The

Sensualita—See: Barefoot Savage, The

Sentinel, The (1977)** Chris Sarandon, Christina Raines, Ava Gardner, José Ferrer, Arthur Kennedy. Director Michael Winner turns his sledgehammer style to a gothic thriller set in a Brooklyn brownstone, where Satan's legions must be held at bay. Some of the most unpleasant shock effects in recent memory. (91 mins.)

Separate Peace, A (1972)**½ Parker Stevenson, John Heyl, William Roerick. Two young men at a private school (Heyl and Stevenson) face the transition to manhood in the last years of WW II. Director Larry Peerce has fashioned a strangely arch, listless film based on John Knowles's 1960 best-seller—the '40s ambience is well done, but Peerce seems as afraid of closeness and commitment as his protagonists. (104 mins.)

Separate Tables (1958)**** Deborah Kerr, Burt Lancaster, David Niven, Rita Hayworth. Faithful film version of Terence Rattigan's two one-act plays about the guests of a British seaside resort and their individual dramas. Miss Kerr & Mr. Niven (he won an Oscar for this performance) come off with the top acting honors as a spinster and a charming ex-colonel who turns out to be a fraud. Wendy Hiller, also an Oscar winner for her work here, plays Mr. Lancaster's long suffering mistress and the proprietress of the establishment. (Dir: Delbert Mann, 98 mins.)

September Affair (1950)*** Joan Fontaine, Joseph Cotten, Jessica Tandy. Engineer and concert pianist miss their plane while sightseeing in Naples; when the plane is reported crashed, they find they have a chance to start life anew together. Romantic drama the ladies should enjoy—well made, generally avoids the maudlin. (Dir: William Dieterle, 104 mins.)

September Storm (1960)*½ Joanne Dru, Mark Stevens. (Dir: Byron Haskin, 99 mins.)

Serenade (1956)**½ Mario Lanza, Joan Fontaine, Vincent Price, Vincent Edwards.

One of Lanza's lesser efforts. He plays a street singer who is discovered by society playgirl (Miss Fontaine) and concert manager (Vincent Price). Overdramatic plot but the opera arias are worthwhile. (Dir: Anthony Mann, 121 mins.)

Serengeti (West Germany, 1959)***½ Absorbing documentary of two zoologists who take a census of wild animals facing extinction on the steppes of Serengeti in Tanganyika. Remarkable animal footage should fascinate everyone. Oscar: Best Documentary. (Dirs: Dr. Bernhard and Michael Grzimek, 84 mins.)

Sergeant, The (France-U.S., 1968)** Rod Steiger, John Phillip Law, Ludmila Mikael. Cut-rate "Reflections in a Golden Eye" set in a dreary army camp in '52 France. Under John Flynn's direction and Steiger's smoldering smoked ham, the film degenerates shrilly. With Law as the love object. (107 mins.)

Sergeant Deadhead (1965)** Frankie Avalon, Deborah Walley, Cesar Romero, Fred Clark, Buster Keaton. Girl-shy GI (Avalon) turns into a wolf and disrupts a missile base. Silly, harmless antics that waste the great Keaton. (Dir: Norman Taurog, 89 mins.)

Sergeant Madden (1939)*** Wallace Beery, Tom Brown, Alan Curtis, Marc Lawrence, Laraine Day. Beery is a sanctimonious cop with two sons—one goes good and one goes bad. Distinguished by a superlative performance by heavy Lawrence and by Josef von Sternberg's haunting direction. (82 mins.)

Sergeant Matlovich vs. the U.S. Air Force (MTV 1978)**½ Brad Dourif, Marc Singer, William Daniels. The role of Sgt. Matlovich, the real-life declared homosexual who battled with the air force to remain in service, tends to be one-dimensional. Brad Dourif, a magnetic, intense actor, does his best to bring the character to life, but little insight is brought to bear on his sexual preference. Daniels is effective as an air force priest who tries to make Matlovich understand himself and his motives. (Writer-Dir: Paul Leaf, 104 mins.)

Sgt. Pepper's Lonely Hearts Club Band (1978)**½ Peter Frampton, the Bee Gees, Alice Cooper, George Burns, Billy Preston, Steve Martin. Fairly stupid, badly filmed rip-off of the music of the Beatles by performers who had nothing to do with it. Frampton isn't too terrible, but the Bee-Gees are vapid, all of them. The only one who scores is Steve Martin singing "Maxwell's Silver Hammer." Rated stars for apparently indestructible Beatles music only. (Dir: Michael Schultz, 111 mins.)

Sergeant Rutledge (1960)**½ Jeffrey Hunter, Constance Towers, Woody Strode. Director John Ford doesn't always come up with winners and this western film is one of his lesser efforts. There's rape, racial prejudice and courtroom dramatics thrown together in this muddled sagebrush drama. (118 mins.)

Sergeant Ryker (1968)** Lee Marvin, Bradford Dillman, Vera Miles, Peter Graves, Lloyd Nolan. Lee Marvin as an army sergeant on trial for treason during the Korean conflict. Fleshed out from a 1963 TV show, this is of ordinary interest aside from Marvin's strong performance. (Dir: Buzz Kulik, 85 mins.)

Sergeant Was a Lady, The (1961)*½ Martin West, Venetia Stevenson, Bill Williams. (Dir: Bernard Glasser, 72 mins.)

Sergeant X of the Foreign Legion (France, 1960)*½ Christian Marquand, Noelle Adam, Paul Guers. (Dir: Ludmilla Goulian, 91 mins.)

Sergeant York (1941)*** Gary Cooper, Walter Brennan, Joan Leslie. The "true" story of Alvin York, a backwoods pacifist who became one of the most decorated soldiers of WW I, provides a shaky basis for a film. The first half documents York's rural upbringing with simplicity and charm, but the second half—the war—degenerates quickly and grotesquely. Cooper won his first Oscar. (Dir: Howard Hawks, 134 mins.)

Sergeants 3 (1962)** Frank Sinatra, Dean Martin, Sammy Davis, Jr. A supposedly high-camp remake of "Gunga Din" to accommodate Frank Sinatra and his buddies. Some of it is diverting, but you'll tire of the jinks of the cavalry bunch, played by F. S. and group, long before Sammy Davis, Jr. gets his chance to be heroic in true Gunga-Din fashion. Other members of the Clan in attendance are Peter Lawford and Joey Bishop. (Dir: John Sturges, 112 mins.)

Serial (1980)*** Martin Mull, Tuesday Weld, Bill Macy, Sally Kellerman, Peter Bonerz, Nita Talbot, Christopher Lee, Tom Smothers. For the benefit of those of us who do not live in California, the screenwriters have changed Cyra McFadden's popular comic novel from a satire of a specific place—Marin County—to a wry look at the American pursuit of A, the "good life" and B, inner peace. Mull and Weld star as a relatively sane couple trying to keep a grip on reality while others about them are losing theirs; both are warm, intelligent screen presences. The best character is a deeply unimpressed little boy named Stokely. (Dir: Bill Persky, 92 mins.)

Serpent, The See: **Night Flight from Moscow**

Serpent of the Nile (1953)** Rhonda Fleming, Raymond Burr, William Lundigan. Foolish drama about the Roman Empire in the days of Cleopatra (Rhonda Fleming) and Mark Antony (Raymond Burr) and their eventual suicides. Rhonda looks ravishing. (Dir: William Castle, 81 mins.)

Serpent's Egg, The (West Germany, 1977)** Liv Ullmann, David Carradine, Gert Frobe, Glynn Turman, James Whitmore. It was an exciting idea: director Ingmar Bergman on a big budget doing a horror story about Germany in the early '20s. Well, it's a lousy film, interesting only for its superb art direction and the colossal wrongheadedness of its errors. Ullmann as a seedy cabaret performer fails to be slutty and irresistible. Carradine's catatonia isn't as reflective as that of Richard Harris (who withdrew shortly before shooting). The great director is painfully vulnerable to the lure of his own clichés. (119 mins.)

Serpico (1973)**** Al Pacino, John Randolph, Jack Kehoe, Tony Roberts, Cornelia Sharpe. Peter Maas's book about real-life honest cop Frank Serpico, whose stories about corruption in the New York City police force led to an investigation, is turned into an excellent film by director Sidney Lumet. Pacino is brilliant in the title role of the cop who couldn't keep his mouth shut after witnessing cops on the take. Another plus is the sense of reality conveyed by the use of good New York location footage, focusing in on the habitués of street crime. (130 mins.)

Servant, The (Great Britain, 1963)***½ Dick Bogarde, Sarah Miles, James Fox, scriptwriter Harold Pinter (bit). Director Joseph Losey's first collaboration with Pinter explores themes of guilt and power as a manservant (Bogarde) corrupts his employer (Fox). Losey's dark, crowded compositions provide the perfect setting for the class war's Pyrrhic victory. (115 mins.)

Session with the Committee, A—See: **Committee, The**

Set This Town on Fire (MTV 1972)** Chuck Connors, Lynda Day. Drama about the pressures placed on a respected newspaper publisher sets a slow pace, but the theme is different and fairly interesting. A publisher (Carl Betz) goes along with close friends in having second thoughts over a local hero imprisoned for manslaughter, and then regrets his change of heart. Doesn't cop out with the expected ending. (Dir: David Lowell Rich, 99 mins.)

Set-up, The (1949)*** Robert Ryan, Audrey Totter, Alan Baxter, George Tobias. Tough if pretentious boxing film about a fighter on the skids who refuses to go crooked, helped by the gritty pugnacity of Ryan in the lead. Good support from Baxter and Tobias, and another overwrought turn by Totter. Robert Wise directs rather well, considering limitations of budget, conception, and talent. (72 mins.)

Set Up, The (Great Britain, 1963)** Maurice Denham, John Carson. Thief is tricked into breaking into a wealthy businessman's home, becomes the target in a murder frame-up. OK Edgar Wallace mystery. (Dir: Gerard Glaister, 58 mins.)

Seven (1979)* William Smith, Barbara Leigh, Guich Koock. Leaden tongue-in-cheek action film. (Writer-Dir: Andy Sidaris, 101 mins.)

Seven Alone (1975)**½ Dewey Martin, Aldo Ray, Anne Collings, Stewart Petersen. Adventure film for family viewing. Based on "On to Oregon" by Honore Morrow, it relates the crisis-filled journey of six young brothers and sisters led by a 13-year-old boy across the wild terrain of America during the 1840's. The Wyoming location adds to the film's appeal. (Dir: Earl Bellamy, 100 mins.)

Seven Angry Men (1955)*** Raymond Massey, Debra Paget, Jeffrey Hunter, Dennis Weaver. Raymond Massey doesn't portray Lincoln in this film about the Civil War, instead he plays John Brown. Tense climax and fine acting throughout bolsters this Civil War western. (Dir: Charles Marquis Warren, 90 mins.)

Seven Beauties (Italy, 1975)**** Giancarlo Giannini, Shirley Stoler, Fernando Rey, Elena Fiore. A remarkable, paradoxical, chilling masterpiece written and directed brilliantly by Lina Wertmuller. "Seven Beauties" is a nickname for a two-bit hoodlum known as the "monster of Naples" before WW II. Giannini's scene in the POW camp where he tries to save his life by making love to the gross German commandant, superbly played by Stoler, is one of the most searing scenes in modern cinema. (115 mins.)

Seven Brides for Seven Brothers (1954)**** Jane Powell, Howard Keel. A rare treat—an original Hollywood musical which works in every department. Based loosely on a story by Stephen Vincent Benet, this tune-filled yarn tells of six fur-trapping brothers who come to town to find wives after their eldest brother (Keel) takes lovely Miss Powell as his bride. There's a kidnapping and a great many musical numbers before the happy conclusion. The dances by Michael Kidd are brilliant, and the entire cast is delightful. Credit must also go to director Stanley Donen for making the whole thing appear as fresh as the accompanying musical score. (103 mins.)

Seven Capital Sins (France-Italy, 1962)*** Jean-Louis Trintignant, Marina Vlady, Eddie Constantine, Jean-Pierre Aumont. The sins as depicted by some notable French directors in an episodic film. As expected, parts better than the whole—but some good sequences. (Dirs: Sylvain Dhomme, Eugene Ionesco, Max Douy, Edouard Molinaro, Philippe de Broca, Jacques Demy, Jean-Luc Godard, Roger Vadim, Claude Chabrol, 113 mins.)

Seven Chances (1925)**** Buster Keaton, T. Roy Barnes, Ruth Dwyer. Brilliant comedy buff from the hoary premise of a poor man who must marry by sunset or lose a fortune. Subtlety and slapstick mingle in perfect harmony in this most sublimely realized of all Keaton-directed fantasies. (60 mins.)

Seven Cities of Gold (1955)** Anthony Quinn, Richard Egan, Jeffrey Hunter, Michael Rennie, Rita Moreno. Routine costume adventure tale about the Spanish Conquistadors' 18th-century expedition to California in search of the lengendary "7 cities of gold." Quinn is well cast as the hot blooded leader of the operation and the rest of the cast is adequate. (Dir: Robert D. Webb, 103 mins.)

Seven Days In May (1964)**** Burt Lancaster, Kirk Douglas, Ava Gardner, Fredric March, Edmond O'Brien. An exciting suspense drama concerned with politics and the problems of sanity and survival in a nuclear age. Benefits from taut screenplay by Rod Serling, and the direction of John Frankenheimer, which artfully builds interest leading to the finale. March is a standout in a uniformly fine cast. (118 mins.)

Seven Days' Leave (1942)**½ Victor Mature, Lucille Ball. Soldiers on leave discover that one of them will inherit a fortune if he can marry a girl who is already engaged. Mildly amusing musical comedy. (Dir: Tim Whelan, 87 mins.)

Seven Days to Noon (Great Britain, 1950)**** Barry Jones, Olive Sloane. Tense melodrama about a deranged atomic scientist who threatens to blow up London if they fail to do his bidding. Excellent thriller; suspense on high throughout. (Dirs: John & Roy Boulting, 93 mins.)

Seven Deadly Sins (France-Italy, 1953)**** Gerard Philipe, Michele Morgan, Françoise Rosay. An episodic yet thoroughly enjoyable film dealing with each of the seven deadly sins. One of the best is the French episode dealing with "Pride," which is brilliantly acted by Michele Morgan. This has everything; comedy, drama, romance and adventure. Not to be missed. (Dirs: Edouard Molinaro, Jean Dreville, Yves Allegret, Roberto Rossellini, Carlo Rim, Claude Autant-Lara, Georges Lacombe, 120 mins.)

711 Ocean Drive (1950)**½ Edmond O'Brien, Joanne Dru. Interesting crime "meller" about an ingenious racketeer and the many tricks he employs to outwit the big gambling syndicate. Edmond O'Brien is fine in the leading role. (Dir: Joseph M. Newman, 102 mins.)

7 Faces of Dr. Lao (1964)*** Tony Randall, Barbara Eden, Arthur O'Connell. Randall's performance is a tour-de-force affair, and it's the best thing about this fantasy set in the last century. He plays Dr. Lao, the mysterious magical Chinese proprietor of a circus that comes to town and generates a wave of good happenings. In addition to playing Dr. Lao, Randall plays six other roles with the aid of elaborate make-up and costumes—all performers in the one-man traveling show—he's great to watch. (Dir: George Pal, 100 mins.)

Seven Golden Men (Italy, 1967)** Philippe Leroy, Rossana Podesta. Familiar heist yarn with a foreign cast, including the attractive Miss Podesta for window dressing. The gold reserve of the Swiss National Bank in Geneva is the object of all the planning and executing by the seven criminals. (Dir: Marco Vicario, 87 mins.)

Seven Guns to Mesa (1958)** Lola Albright, Charles Quinlivan. The outlaws again hold stage-coach passengers as hostages while they wait to rob a gold shipment in this familiar story. Lola Albright is along for the bumpy ride. (Dir: Edward Dein, 69 mins.)

Seven Hills of Rome, The (1957)**½ Mario Lanza, Peggie Castle. Mario singing and romancing a la Roma. Slight plot, with several attractive slices of female Italian pizza displaying some nice hills of their own. Lotsa Lanza lungwork and Renato Rascel ("Arrivederci Roma"). (Dir: Roy Rowland, 104 mins.)

Seven in Darkness (MTV 1969)**½ Milton Berle, Dina Merrill, Sean Garrison. Highly melodramatic tale. Although its plane-crash-survivor theme is familiar, the fact that all the survivors are blind people on their way to a convention adds an interesting gimmick to the film. The on-location production is first-rate. Taking a cue from past films of this genre, the survivors are mostly well played stereotypes—Milton Berle as a gruff businessman not resigned to his blindness, Sean Garrison as the ex-Marine with a secret about an incident in Vietnam, Barry Nelson as a jealous group leader, Lesley Ann Warren as an overprotected blind folk singer, Dina Merrill as a woman blind from birth. (Dir: Michael Caffey, 73 mins.)

Seven in the Sun (Italy, 1960)*½ Frank Latimore, Saro Urzi, Gianna Maria Canale. (Dir: Sergio Bergonzelli, 88 mins.)

Seven Little Foys, The (1955)*** Bob Hope, Milly Vitale. Hope is a bit more reserved in this story about the real life vaudeville family known as the Singing and Dancing Foys. He plays a show business "ham" who has a large family and wants them all to love the stage as much as he does. When his wife dies, he's faced with more problems. Good production numbers and a guest appearance by James Cagney as George M. Cohan. (Dir: Melville Shavelson, 93 mins.)

Seven Minutes, The (1971)** Wayne Maunder, Marianne McAndrew, Philip Carey, Jay C. Flippen, Edy Williams. Seven minutes is the average time it takes a woman to achieve orgasm in this adaptation of an Irving Wallace novel, and it's also the title of a book on trial for obscenity. Maunder is completely forgettable. (Dir: Russ Meyer, 116 mins.)

Seven-Per-Cent-Solution, The (1976)***½ Nicol Williamson, Alan Arkin, Robert Duvall, Laurence Olivier, Joel Grey. An enjoyable lark! What would have happened if Sherlock Holmes had met with Sigmund Freud? According to Nicholas Meyer, who adapted his own novel for the screen, Freud could have cured the sleuth of his fondness for cocaine and Holmes could have solved the mystery of one of the psychiatrist's patients. Splendid cast. (Dir: Herbert Ross, 113 mins.)

Seven Samurai, The (Japan, 1954)**** Toshiro Mifune, Takashi Shimura, Yoshio Inaba. Narrative power, exciting battle scenes, and director Akira Kurosawa's customary richness of imagery make this a classic film. Seven men agree to protect a village from annual attacks by bandits in 16th-century Japan. No matter how many remakes are attempted, Kurosawa's film remains the top entry. (141 mins.)

Seven Seas to Calais (Italy, 1962)** Rod Taylor, Keith Michell, Irene Worth. Admiral Drake, pirate galleons, and war on the high seas make "spaghetti" sea-going version of England's defeat of the Spanish Armada, and her laying claim to the New World, circa 1588. Some good actors in this swashbuckler. (Dirs: Rudolph Maté, Primo Zeglio, 102 mins.)

Seven Sinners (1940)*** Marlene Dietrich, John Wayne, Broderick Crawford. Honky-tonk singer attracts a handsome lieutenant. Trashy tale atoned for by a fine cast, plenty of rugged action. (Dir: Ray Garnett, 87 mins.)

Seven Slaves Against the World (Italy, 1965)* Roger Browne, Gordon Mitchell, Schilla Gabel. (Dir: Michele Lupo, 96 mins.)

Seven Surprises (Canada, 1963)** Compilation of seven short films stressing the more fanciful aspects of life. Varying degree of interest, with some better than others. Might do as novelty, even though it adds up to little more than seven shorts in a row. (Dirs: Claude Jutra, Albert Faille, Eduardo Carpentier, Grant Munro, 77 mins.)

Seven Sweethearts (1942)** Kathryn Grayson, Van Heflin, Marsha Hunt. Frank Borzage, one of the great directors, never made a tolerable musical. In this one, none of the other six daughters can marry until the eldest does. (98 mins.)

Seven Thieves (1960)***½ Edward G. Robinson, Rod Steiger, Joan Collins, Eli Wallach. Tense melodrama about a plot to rob the Monte Carlo gambling vaults. High-gear suspense, fine performances; only drawback is a weak ending, which nevertheless won't hurt the preceding thrills. Well above average. (Dir: Henry Hathaway, 102 mins.)

Seven-Ups, The (1973)** Roy Scheider, Tony Lo Bianco, Richard Lynch. Producer Philip D'Antoni ("The French Connection," "Bullitt") made a shaky transition to director in this undercover cop story. Scheider leads the team of cops out to stop hoods from kidnapping one another. The scenery is well used, but with the exception of a thrilling car chase there is little that reminds you of D'Antoni's past successes. The ruthlessness of the cops is repulsive. (Dir: Philip D'Antoni, 103 mins.)

Seven Ways from Sundown (1960)**½ Audie Murphy, Venetia Stevenson, Barry Sullivan. Well-made western starring

Audie Murphy as a ranger with the strange name of Seven-Ways-from-Sundown Jones, known as Seven for short. The action is plentiful and there's the inevitable shoot-out at the end. (Dir: Harry Keller, 87 mins.)

Seven Women (1965)** Anne Bancroft, Margaret Leighton, Sue Lyon. Absurd China-based western, substituting wily Mongols for the standard complement of Indians. Mission personnel, circa 1935, are trying to protect themselves from a barbaric warlord. (Dir: John Ford, 93 mins.)

Seven Year Itch, The (1955)**** Marilyn Monroe, Tom Ewell, Evelyn Keyes, Sonny Tufts. This is probably Marilyn Monroe's best screen performance. She is ideally cast as a sexy model who lives in the same apartment building as a happily married man (Tom Ewell) who finds himself thinking and living like a bachelor when his wife goes on a prolonged summer vacation. Billy Wilder handles both his stars expertly and the result is high style comedy. Great fun. (105 mins.)

1776 (1972)** Howard da Silva, Ken Howard, William Daniels. Movies like this give American history and G-rated pictures a bad name. According to this view, the Founding Fathers were a collection of prissy nitwits, romantic buffoons, and vainglorious babblers. Miserably directed, with the most forgettable musical score since "Goodbye, Mr. Chips." (Dir: Peter H. Hunt, 150 mins.)

7th Cavalry, The (1956)*** Randolph Scott, Barbara Hale. Above-average Randolph Scott western. Good plot and action kept at a good level. Story concerns a cavalry unit returning to the scene of Custer's massacre. (Dir: Joseph H. Lewis, 75 mins.)

Seventh Commandment (1961)* Jonathan Kidd, Lyn Statten. (Dir: Irvin Berwick, 82 mins.)

Seventh Cross, The (1944)***½ Spencer Tracy, Signe Hasso, Hume Cronyn. This is a truly exciting chase melodrama about an anti-Nazi who escapes from a concentration camp in 1936 and attempts to get out of the country. Beautifully acted. (Dir: Fred Zinnemann, 112 mins.)

Seventh Dawn, The (U.S.-Great Britain, 1964)* William Holden, Capucine, Susannah York. (Dir: Lewis Gilbert, 123 mins.)

Seventh Heaven (1927)*** Janet Gaynor, Charles Farrell, David Butler. Love in a garret in Paris. The famous theme is "Diane." (119 mins.)

Seventh Heaven (1937)*½ Simone Simon, James Stewart, Gale Sondergaard. (Dir: Henry King, 102 mins.)

Seventh Seal, The (Sweden, 1957)**** Max von Sydow, Gunnar Björnstrand, Bibi Andersson. Director Ingmar Bergman's masterpiece about the philosophical dilemmas of modern man. The setting is 14th-century Sweden. A knight (von Sydow) and his squire return from a crusade to find the black plague spreading death across their land. The knight confronts death incarnate to play a game of chess, with the knight's life at stake. Brilliantly directed and photographed. One of the greatest films of the era. (105 mins.)

Seventh Sin, The (1957)** Eleanor Parker, Bill Travers, George Sanders. Wife becomes bored while married to a doctor and begins an affair with a shipping tycoon. Remake of an old Garbo film, "The Painted Veil," but not an improvement. Mostly soap opera. (Dir: Ronald Neame, 94 mins.)

Seventh Sword, The (1962)** Brett Halsey. Spanish-made, English-dubbed adventure epic with heroics running rampant in the person of Brett Halsey as a leader of a band of seven swordsmen. Kids will be pleased with fast-paced action. (Dir: Riccardo Freda, 84 mins.)

Seventh Veil, The (Great Britain, 1945) *** Ann Todd, James Mason, Albert Lieven, Herbert Lom, Hugh McDermott. Superior psychological gothic romance. A beautiful young pianist (Todd) runs away from her tyrannical guardian (Mason—with a limp, yet) and can't choose between her two boyfriends. A friendly psychiatrist steps in. Beautifuly set, fine musical sequences, and Mason's portrayal is archetypical. (Dir: Compton Bennett, 92 mins.)

Seventh Victim, The (1943)**½ Kim Hunter, Tom Conway. Girl in New York looking for her sister finds a mysterious cult of devil worshipers. Suspenseful, eerie, but overly complicated thriller. (Dir: Mark Robson, 71 mins.)

Seventh Voyage of Sinbad, The (1958)** Kerwin Mathews, Kathryn Grant, Torin Thatcher. Resolutely dull Ray Harryhausen fantasy film is about Sinbad's search for a roc's egg to restore his girlfriend to her former height (before she met an evil magician). (Dir: Nathan Juran, 87 mins.)

79 A.D. (Italy, 1963)*½ Brad Harris, Susan Paget, Mara Lane. (Dir: Gianfranco Parolini, 113 mins.)

Severed Head, A (Great Britain, 1971)**½ Lee Remick, Richard Attenborough, Claire Bloom. Talented cast works very hard to be sophisticated and chic in this faithful but awkward adaptation of Iris Murdoch's novel about multiple indiscretions among the British upper crust. The whole thing eventually acquires the taste of flat champagne. (Dir: Dick Clement, 96 mins.)

Sex and the Married Woman (MTV 1977)**½ Joanna Pettet, Barry Newman, Keenan Wynn. Sexual innuendo is all in this comedy about a married lady who writes a book about the sexual experiences of 50 others. First-class cast, including Pettet as the author and Newman as her less-than-happy spouse. (Dir: Jack Arnold, 104 mins.)

Sex and the Single Girl (1964)**½ Tony Curtis, Natalie Wood, Lauren Bacall, Henry Fonda. Helen Gurley Brown's bestseller has been turned into an innocent spoof of the sexual daydreams of Madison

Avenue types and their female counterparts. The cast plays it for laughs that aren't always there. (Dir: Richrd Quine, 114 mins.)

Sex and the Single Parent (MTV 1979)** Mike Farrell, Susan Saint James. Light fare about a pair of divorcees with kids who start going together. Good chemistry between George (Farrell) and Sally (Saint James). Their problems seem inflated, but that's par for TV. (Dir: Jackie Cooper, 104 mins.)

Sex and the Teenager—See: To Find a Man

Sex Kittens Go to College (1960)* Mamie Van Doren, Tuesday Weld, Louis Nye, Martin Milner. (Dir: Albert Zugsmith, 94 mins.)

Sex Symbol, The (MTV 1974)* Connie Stevens, Shelley Winters, Jack Carter. (Dir: David Lowell Rich, 72 mins.)

Sextette (1978)* Mae West, Timothy Dalton, Dom DeLuise, Tony Curtis, Ringo Starr, George Hamilton. (Dirs: Ken Hughes, Irving Rapper, 91 mins.)

Shack Out on 101 (1955)** Frank Lovejoy, Terry Moore, Lee Marvin, Keenan Wynn. Deep-discount production about Commie spies infiltrating a hamburger joint in the middle of nowhere. (Dir: Edward Dein, 80 mins.)

Shadow Box, The (MTV 1980)*** Joanne Woodward, Christopher Plummer, James Broderick, Ben Masters, Melinda Dillon. The Pulitzer prizewinning play by Michael Cristofer works better as a film, thanks to director Paul Newman, who keeps the fragmented drama moving along. Still a flawed, depressing piece about terminal cancer patients in an experimental program in a mountain hospice. We learn about three patients in prolonged melodramatic scenes. Broderick as a blue-collar patient and Woodward as a femme fatale are miscast, but Masters, as the patient Plummer's homosexual companion, and Dillon as the patient Sidney's long-suffering daughter, are outstanding. (111 mins.)

Shadow in the Sky (1951)**½ Ralph Meeker, Nancy Davis, James Whitmore, Jean Hagen. Trouble ensues when a war vet's brother-in-law comes to live with him, after being discharged from a hospital with a psychological disorder. Good writing makes this drama fairly gripping stuff. (Dir: Fred M. Wilcox, 78 mins.)

Shadow in the Street (MTV 1975)**½ Tony LoBianco, Sheree North. Tony LoBianco stars as an ex-con struggling to survive as a sympathetic parole agent. He's dealing with a strict lady officer (Sheree North) and a desperate ex-con; and, though the situation may be predictable, John D. F. Black's script manages to create some suspense, and LoBianco gives it strength. (Dir: Richard D. Donner, 74 mins.)

Shadow Man (Great Britain, 1953)**½ Cesar Romero, Kay Kendall. Good direction sparks this British thriller which has some pretty tense moments as London gambling saloon owner, Romero, gets involved with murder, romance, jealousy and Scotland Yard. (Dir: Richard Vernon, 75 mins.)

Shadow of a Doubt (1942)**** Teresa Wright, Joseph Cotten. Gripping suspense film in the grand Alfred Hitchcock tradition. A niece suspects her uncle of being the Merry Widow murderer. Uniformly good performances. (Dir: Alfred Hitchcock, 108 mins.)

Shadow of Evil (France-Italy, 1964)** Kerwin Mathews, Robert Hossein, Pier Angeli. OSS 117, France's answer to Bond's 007, in his third recasting, here played by Mathews. Flimsy plot concerns mad scientist, plague-contaminated rats in Bangkok. Elaborate production, incoherent yarn. (Dir: André Hunebelle, 92 mins.)

Shadow of Fear (Great Britain, 1955)**½ Mona Freeman, Jean Kent, Maxwell Reed. Melodrama with some suspense but no surprises. A good supporting cast fares better than the stars. (Dir: Albert S. Rogell, 76 mins.)

Shadow of the Hawk (Canada, 1976)* Jan-Michael Vincent, Chief Dan George, Marilyn Hassett. (Dir: George McCowan, 92 mins.)

Shadow of the Thin Man (1941)**½ William Powell, Myrna Loy, Barry Nelson, Donna Reed. Nick is solving a race track crime and, although it lacks the freshness of the others, it's still entertaining. (Dir: W. S. Van Dyke II, 97 mins.)

Shadow of Treason (Great Britain, 1964)* John Bentley, Faten Hamama, Anita West. (94 mins.)

Shadow on the Land (MTV 1968)* Jackie Cooper, John Forsythe, Carol Lynley, Gene Hackman. (Dir: Richard Sarafian, 97 mins.)

Shadow on the Wall (1950)** Ann Sothern, Zachary Scott, Gigi Perreau, Nancy Davis. Unconvincing murder meller—a child is sole witness to a murder for which her father has been unjustly convicted. Change of pace role for Sothern as the murderess, otherwise not much. (Dir: Patrick Jackson, 84 mins.)

Shadow on the Window, The (1957)**½ Philip Carey, Betty Garrett, John Barrymore, Jr. An interesting crime drama about a group of young hoods led by a psychopath (played with a wild intensity by Barrymore, Jr.) who kill a businessman and take his secretary along as hostage. The secretary's ex-husband happens to be a detective and sets out to find her and apprehend the criminals. (Dir: William Asher, 73 mins.)

Shadow over Elveron (MTV 1968)** James Franciscus, Shirley Knight, Leslie Nielsen, Franchot Tone, Don Ameche. Predictable drama about a corrupt law officer in a small town and a dedicated young doctor who faces up to him and the town. The plot borrows from every other film about small-town tyranny and blackmail. (Dir: James Goldstone, 99 mins.)

Shadow Warrior, The—See: **Kagemusha**

Shadows (1959)**** Lelia Goldoni, Ben Carruthers, Hugh Hurd. A seminal work for American independent cinema, director John Cassavetes's first feature parlayed the beat atmosphere of the late '50s into a model for low-budget narrative films bursting with personal expression. Cassavetes examines imperfect relationships—tentative, fervent, and cruel—with skeptical compassion. (87 mins.)

Shadows Grow Longer, The—See: **Defiant Daughters**

Shaft (1971)** Richard Roundtree, Moses Gunn, Charles Cioffi. Black super-dick takes on the Mafia in Harlem. So-so thriller with some nice touches and a nearly perfect last ten minutes. (Dir: Gordon Parks, 106 mins.)

Shaft in Africa (1973)**½ Richard Roundtree, Frank Findlay, Vonetta McGee. John Shaft has moved up (his apartment has a view—and a black parking attendant), out (Harlem never appears, and Shaft gets the hubcaps stolen off his red sports car while he's jogging in Central Park), and in (he has been totally shoehorned into the role of James Bond). Veteran British action hack John Guillermin directs with a polished flair as Shaft infiltrates the Africa-to-France slave market and destroys eight (or was it nine?) assassins. (112 mins.)

Shaggy D.A., The (1976)**½ Dean Jones, Suzanne Pleshette, Tim Conway. Another slick Disney creation, sequel to "The Shaggy Dog." Jones is a district attorney who turns into a canine at embarrassing times. He tries to overcome villain Wynn, and it makes for some pretty hilarious scenes. (Dir: Robert Stevenson, 91 mins.)

Shaggy Dog, The (1959)**½ Fred MacMurray, Jean Hagen, Tommy Kirk, Annette Funicello. One of Disney's first plunges into real-life features. Cheerful tale of a boy's transformation into an old English sheep dog by way of a mystical antique ring. Will hold the attention of the youngsters. (Dir: Charles Barton, 104 mins.)

Shake Hands with the Devil (Great Britain, 1959)**½ James Cagney, Don Murray, Glynis Johns. Cagney plays an IRA leader during the Irish troubles of the '20s. Director Michael Anderson twists the piece into a drab essay on the morality of terrorism, but Cagney keeps some life in it. Filmed in Ireland. (110 mins.)

Shake, Rattle and Rock (1956)*½ Lisa Gaye, Michael Connors. (Dir: Edward L. Cahn, 72 mins.)

Shakedown, The (Great Britain, 1960)* Terence Morgan, Hazel Court, Donald Pleasence. (Dir: John Lemont, 91 mins.)

Shakespeare Wallah (India, 1965)***½ Shashi Kapoor, Felicity Kendal. Gently satiric and deeply humane, the film follows the fortunes of a seedy British troupe of traveling Shakespeare players who discover that they have no real feeling for their native Indian audiences. Script by Ruth Prawer Jhabvala. (115 mins.)

Shakiest Gun in the West, The (1968)*½ Don Knotts, Barbara Rhoades, Jackie Coogan, Donald Barry. (Dir: Alan Rafkin, 101 mins.)

Shalako (Great Britain, 1968)** Sean Connery, Brigitte Bardot, Honor Blackman, Stephen Boyd, Jack Hawkins. Despite a powerhouse cast, this western limps along under the pointless direction of Edward Dmytryk. The premise (European big-game hunters in Indian-infested New Mexico, 1880) never takes hold, though Blackman's death scene is like an oasis in an arid landscape. Filmed in Spain. (114 mins.)

Shall We Dance (1937)*** Fred Astaire, Ginger Rogers, Edward Everett Horton. Longer and more pretentious than most of the Astaire-Rogers musicals, but still a sufficiently sophisticated good time. The Gershwin score includes "They Can't Take That Away from Me" and "Let's Call the Whole Thing Off." (Dir: Mark Sandrich, 116 mins.)

Shame (Sweden, 1968)**** Liv Ullmann, Max von Sydow, Gunnar Bjornstrand. Director Ingmar Bergman focuses on war in modern society, and how it degrades and humiliates us all. Married concert violinists flee to a small island to escape the civil war raging on the mainland. Ullmann is profoundly moving playing von Sydow's wife, trying to hang on to her own dignity while her husband and everyone around her lose theirs. Bergman also wrote the screenplay. Dubbed. B&W. (103 mins.)

Shameless Old Lady, The (France, 1965)**** Sylvie. Delightful, touching award-winning film about a 70-year-old widow who makes a late stab at putting a little fun in her life, after living a very quiet and sedate life. French character actress Sylvie gives one of the most luminous and endearing performances you'll ever hope to see, and her daily encounters as the "shameless" old lady are a delight. A gentle, honest, and altogether beautiful film. (Dir: Rene Allio, 94 mins.)

Shampoo (1975)**** Warren Beatty, Julie Christie, Jack Warden, Goldie Hawn. Insightful, complicated comedy that has something serious to say, often in very acerbic ways, about the morals and manners of our times. Beatty, who cowrote the screenplay with Robert Towne, gives one of his most engaging and expert performances as a hedonistic stud, a Beverly Hills hairdresser out to bed down with as many of his voluptuous customers as time and energy permit. (Dir: Hal Ashby, 112 mins.)

Shamus (1973)**½ Burt Reynolds, Dyan Cannon. Good sport and expert stunt man Reynolds plays a private eye in a confusing action film. All the characters are stock as shamus (detective, that is)

Reynolds smiles, smacks, kisses, and belts his way through a series of thugs, mugs, broads, and cops while trying to get to the bottom of a large export deal involving government arms. Miss Cannon has little to do as one of Reynolds' women. (Dir: Buzz Kulik, 99 mins.)

Shane (1953)**** Alan Ladd, Jean Arthur, Van Heflin, Brandon de Wilde, Jack Palance. Truly epic western, among the best ever made. Simple story of a gunfighter coming to the aid of homesteaders has been filmed with amazing skill by George Stevens, with some of the finest scenic values ever put on film. There's action, drama, fine performances. A winner. (Dir: George Stevens, 118 mins.)

Shanghai Express (1932)**** Marlene Dietrich, Clive Brook, Anna May Wong, Warner Oland. Exciting in scope and delirious in its emotions. Dietrich is Shanghai Lili, riding the train with her jilted love Brook as warlord Oland intercedes. All the characters live on the edge of the abyss. (Dir: Josef von Sternberg, 80 mins.)

Shanghai Gesture, The (1941)** Gene Tierney, Walter Huston, Victor Mature. A tycoon is drawn into a web of evil in an Oriental gambling den, with his daughter as one of the lures. Arty, slow, far-fetched melodrama. (Dir: Josef von Sternberg, 106 mins.)

Shanghai Story, The (1954)**½ Ruth Roman, Edmond O'Brien. Americans in Shanghai are imprisoned by the Communists. Good cast and direction can't quite overcome a familir plot. (Dir: Frank Lloyd, 99 mins.)

Shanks (1974)* Marcel Marceau, Tsilla Chelton, Philippe Clay. (Dir: William Castle, 93 mins.)

Shape of Things to Come, The (Canada, 1979)*½ Jack Palance, Carol Lynley, Barry Morse. (Dir: George McCowan, 95 mins.)

Sharad of Atlantis (1936-66)*½ Ray Corrigan, Lois Wilde, Monte Blue, Lon Chaney, Jr. (Dirs: B. Reeves Eason, Joseph Kane, 100 mins.)

Share Out, The (Great Britain, 1962)**½ Bernard Lee, Alexander Knox, Moira Redmond. Private eye works undercover to smash a blackmail racket. Good cast helps this standard Edgar Wallace mystery. (Dir: Gerald Glaister, 61 mins.)

Shark! (U.S.-Mexico, 1969)*½ Burt Reynolds, Barry Sullivan, Arthur Kennedy. (Dir: Samuel Fuller, 91 mins.)

Shark Kill (MTV 1976)* Richard Yniguez, Phillip Clark, Jennifer Warren. (Dir: William A. Graham, 72 mins.)

Shark River (1953)** Steve Cochran, Carole Mathews, Warren Stevens. Brother accompanies a Civil War vet who has killed a man in the Everglades. Good scenery, but otherwise so-so melodrama. (Dir: John Rawlins, 80 mins.)

Sharkfighters, The (1956)** Victor Mature, Karen Steele, James Olson. A naval research team of scientists headed by Victor Mature set out to find a repellent, which when dissolved around a man in water would keep sharks away. A bit too technical to be entertaining. (Dir: Jerry Hopper, 73 mins.)

Shark's Treasure (1975)*½ Cornel Wilde, Yaphet Kotto. (Dir: Cornel Wilde, 95 mins.)

Sharon: Portrait of a Mistress (MTV 1977)**½ Trish Van Devere, Patrick O'Neal, Sam Groom. Van Devere is appealing in this drama about a woman trapped in the life-style of a mistress. Everything goes along predictably until an unmarried man (Groom) takes an interest in her. O'Neal plays the latest married man in her life. (Dir: Robert Greenwald, 104 mins.)

She (Great Britain, 1965)**½ Ursula Andress, John Richardson, Peter Cushing, Christopher Lee. Lesser but not bad remake of H. Rider Haggard's exotic romance. Color and location filming (not to mention belly dancers) enliven the film. (Dir: Robert Day, 92 mins.)

S*H*E (MTV 1980)** Omar Sharif, Cornelia Sharpe, Anita Ekberg. Slick production values, exotic location shooting, and the beautiful Sharpe as a sexy female James Bond type are the draws here. S*H*E (Securities Hazards Expert) is hot on the trail of international blackmailers who plan to jeopardize the world's oil supply if their demands aren't met. Sharif gives the production a modest touch of class as the head of an old wine-producing family. (Dir: Robert Lewis, 96 mins.)

She Couldn't Say No (1954)*** Robert Mitchum, Jean Simmons. Oil heiress wishes to repay citizens of her home town for childhood kindnesses, disrupts the community in doing so. Pleasant, enjoyable comedy. (Dir: Lloyd Bacon, 89 mins.)

She Cried Murder! (MTV 1973)**½ Telly Savalas, Lynda Day George. Pretty widow witnesses a murder and has to face the killer, who turns out to be the inspector conducting the police investigations. Savalas plays the evil cop, and he's cold and forceful. Mrs. George registers suitable panic, on location in Toronto. (Dir: Herschel Daugherty, 73 mins.)

She Devil (1957)* Mari Blanchard, Jack Kelly, Albert Dekker. (Dir: Kurt Neumann, 77 mins.)

She Done Him Wrong (1933)**** Mae West, Cary Grant, Gilbert Roland. The best West film. Grant is the Salvation Army officer who meets his match in Mae, who tells him bluntly: "You can be had." Based on the play "Diamond Lil" by Mae herself. (66 mins.)

She Lives (MTV 1973)*** Desi Arnaz, Jr., Season Hubley, Anthony Zerbe. An excellent dramatic performance by a relative newcomer, Hubley, and a surprisingly sensitive turn by Arnaz, make this a fine film. It has a "Love Story" theme about a young couple who discover the girl is dying, but unlike Ali MacGraw, Miss

Hubley rages against that good night, refusing to go gently. She and her lover begin a determined search for a doctor who will give them hope. (Dir: Stuart Hagmann, 73 mins.)

She Married Her Boss (1935)***½ Claudette Colbert, Melvyn Douglas, Jean Dixon, Raymond Walburn. Unjustly neglected classic comedy with stars Colbert and Douglas at their impeccable best. Walburn contributes a smashing cameo as a tipsy butler. (Dir: Gregory LaCava, 90 mins.)

She Played with Fire (Great Britain, 1958)**½ Jack Hawkins, Arlene Dahl. Arlene Dahl's attractive presence almost makes up for the inadequacies of this melodrama about a beautiful woman who has a bad influence on men. (Dir: Sidney Gilliat, 95 mins.)

She Stoops to Conquer (Great Britain, 1971)**** Ralph Richardson, Tom Courtenay, Juliet Mills. Oliver Goldsmith's classic comedy does well indeed in this BBC production. (Dir: Michael Elliott, 120 mins.)

She Waits (MTV 1972)** Patty Duke, David McCallum, Dorothy McGuire, Lew Ayres. Ghost-story enthusiasts get still another tale full of curtains rustling, and a mother-in-law warning that evil spirits are lurking about the family mansion. (Dir: Delbert Mann, 73 mins.)

She Wore a Yellow Ribbon (1949)**** John Wayne, Joanne Dru, John Agar. Most elegiac of all westerns, beautiful and subtle. Like its retiring cavalry officer, the film ages well. Wayne is cast against type as a man 20 years older than he was then. (Dir: John Ford, 103 mins.)

Sheba Baby (1975)** Pam Grier, Austin Stoker, D'Urville Martin. Even Grier, as a private detective trying to stop the mob from taking over her father's loan company, gets sandbagged in this clumsy black actioner. William Girdler's direction is anything but lively. (90 mins.)

Sheep Has Five Legs, The (France, 1954)*** Fernandel, Françoise Arnoul. Fernandel plays six rolés in this frequently amusing French comedy about an old wine-grower and his sons. (Dir: Henri Verneuil, 95 mins.)

Sheepman, The (1958)*** Glenn Ford, Shirley MacLaine. Engaging, conventionally heroic western about a sheepman who tries to forge détente in a cattle town. The screenplay by William Bowers and James Edward Grant, has some inspired moments. Ford does his thing as a droll, tough man with a reserve of quiet temper. (Dir: George Marshall, 85 mins.)

Sheik, The (1921)**½ Rudolph Valentino, Agnes Ayres, Adolphe Menjou. Valentino found his definitive screen image in this rape romance, playing a dashing desert vagabond who captures a tempestuous English girl. So popular that a brand of prophylactics was named after it. (Dir: George Melford, 73 mins.)

Sheila Levine Is Dead and Living in New York (1975)*½ Jeannie Berlin, Roy Scheider, Rebecca Dianna Smith. (Dir: Sidney J. Furie, 112 mins.)

Shell Game (MTV 1975)** John Davidson, Tommy Atkins, Jack Kehoe, Robert Sampson. Singer John Davidson stars as a cheerful con man attempting to fleece a rat, in a film more interested in suspense and the light touch than in violence, which is a relief. Davidson performs with a certain ease. (Dir: Glenn Jordan, 72 mins.)

Shell Shock (1964)*½ Carl Crow, Frank Leo, Beach Dickerson. (Dir: John Hayes, 84 mins.)

Shenandoah (1965)**½ James Stewart, Rosemary Forsyth, Doug McClure. Rather one-note and sentimental performance by James Stewart as a farmer dragged into the Civil War when it begins to encroach on his land and family. (Dir: Andrew V. McLaglen, 105 mins.)

Shepherd of the Hills, The (1941)** John Wayne, Betty Field, Harry Carey. Good cast bogged down by sentimentality in the Harold Bell Wright tale of a man who returns to the Ozarks to face his son's hatred. Nice color photography by Charles Lang. (Dir: Henry Hathaway, 98 mins.)

Sheriff, The (MTV 1971)**½ Stars Ossie Davis as an elected black sheriff in a California town. Explosive situation develops when a black girl is raped and a white man is the chief suspect. Featured in the competent supporting cast are Ruby Dee, Moses Gunn, and Ross Martin. (Dir: David Lowell Rich, 73 mins.)

Sheriff of Fractured Jaw, The (Great Britain, 1958)** Kenneth More, Jayne Mansfield, Robert Morley, Henry Hull. Silly western comedy which benefits somewhat by the casting of English actor Kenneth More in the title role. "Ruggles Out West" or "How a British gentleman tries to establish his gunsmith business in the wild and woolly West of frontier days, and ends up sheriff of a lawless town" might be an appropriate subtitle. Miss Mansfield supplies window dressing as a saloon hostess. Connie Francis sings for Mansfield in the musical numbers. (Dir: Raoul Walsh, 102 mins.)

Sheriff Was a Lady, The (West Germany, 1964)* Mamie Van Doren, Rik Battaglia. (Dir: Sobey Martin, 88 mins.)

Sherlock Holmes (1932)*** Clive Brook, Reginald Owen, Ernest Torrence. One of the many Holmes films based on the books of Conan Doyle. This debut is handsomely mounted; Torrence is especially appealing playing Moriarty. (Dir: William K. Howard, 68 mins.)

Sherlock Holmes and the Deadly Necklace (Great Britain-West Germany, 1964)**½ Christopher Lee, Senta Berger, Thorley Walters. Holmes and Dr. Watson once again combat the evil Moriarty, who's after a valuable necklace. Interesting English-German effort, with Lee a perfectly adequate sleuth whom mystery fans, especially Holmes addicts, should appreciate. (Dir: Terence Fisher, 85 mins.)

Sherlock Holmes In New York (MTV 1976)**½ Roger Moore, John Huston, Patrick Macnee, Gig Young, Charlotte Rampling. Sherlock Holmes tale played in the noble tones of the Victorians—meant to draw laughs. Moore as Holmes matches wits with Huston's wily Professor Moriarty over a scheme to steal gold from the major companies. Cast, costuming, and production are conceived in the grand manner, and Boris Sagal's direction makes the film an entertaining diversion. (104 mins.)

Sherlock Jr. (1924)**** Buster Keaton, Kathryn McGuire. Joe Keaton may have made funnier films, or even more profound ones, but nothing touches this, the definitive silent-comedy meditation on the meaning of cinema. Fast-moving and surreal, it hasn't dated a whit in its hilarious dissection of the interface of dreams and appearances. Keaton is an imaginary detective. Wildly hilarious masterpiece. (57 mins.)

She's Back on Broadway (1953)*** Virginia Mayo, Steve Cochran, Gene Nelson, Frank Lovejoy, Patrice Wymore. Neat little backstage melodrama of a movie star returning to the stage, and her ex-lover, now a famous director on the skids. The tight knowledgeably written script, lively musical numbers, good color, and especially two thoughtful, even passionate performances by Cochran and Mayo lift this well above the limits of its type. (Cochran was always underrated as an actor.) Very much worth seeing. (Dir: Gordon Douglas, 95 mins.)

She's Dressed to Kill (MTV 1979)** Eleanor Parker, John Rubinstein, Jessica Walter. Nonsense for those who wish to turn off their minds and wallow in the glossy world of high fashion and contrived murder yarns. Parker is the haute couture designer who plans a big comeback to be staged at her sumptuous mountain home. Naturally, the top beautiful people are invited and the murderer strikes. (Dir: Gus Trikonis, 104 mins.)

She's Working Her Way Through College (1952)** Virginia Mayo, Steve Cochran, Gene Nelson, Ronald Reagan. A burlesque queen goes to college. That's right. The best thing about this movie is the dancing. Remake of "The Male Animal." (Dir: H. Bruce Humberstone, 101 mins.)

Shield for Murder (1954)*** Edmond O'Brien, Marla English, John Agar, Carolyn Jones. Crooked cop kills a bookmaker and hides twenty-five grand. Brutal crime melodrama is well made, nicely acted. (Dirs: Howard Koch, Edmond O'Brien, 80 mins.)

Shinbone Alley (1971)*** Voices of Eddie Bracken, Carol Channing, John Carradine. Feature-length cleverly animated cartoon based on the characters archy the cockroach and mehitabel the cat. Endearing in a lightly racy way, but badly marred by show business sentimentality. Unlike the Don Marquis books, this is not mainly for adults. (Dir: John D. Wilson, 84 mins.)

Shine on Harvest Moon (1944)**½ Ann Sheridan, Dennis Morgan, Jack Carson, Marie Wilson. Some good old songs but not much more in this ridiculously fictionalized biography of entertainers Nora Bayes and Jack Norworth. (Dir: David Butler, 112 mins.)

Shining, The (1980)*** Jack Nicholson, Shelley Duvall, Danny Lloyd, Scatman Crothers, Anne Jackson. Extraordinary horror film directed by Stanley Kubrick. This is a drama in which the devil enlists minions to do his evil mischief, and the concept of sin, predestination, and the path to salvation is very au courant. A cantankerous, willful, unyieldingly controlled movie. Nicholson plays a dangerously unbalanced writer, Duvall his fearful wife, Lloyd their telepathic son. (146 mins.)

Shining Hour, The (1938)***½ Joan Crawford, Margaret Sullavan, Melvyn Douglas, Robert Young. Young, a Wisconsin dairy farmer, goes to New York to try to stop a showgirl (Crawford) from marrying his brother (Douglas). He fails, and falls in love with Crawford himself, prompting his unloved wife (Sullavan) to sacrifice herself in order to clear his way. Almost laughable plot becomes a deeply felt film in the hands of director Frank Borzage. (80 mins.)

Shining Season, A (MTV 1979)*** Timothy Bottoms, Allyn Ann McLerie, Rip Torn. This real-life tale of an Olympic-class miler cut down by cancer is a heart wringer. Bottoms plays Albuquerque's John Baker, always on the move, bursting with life until cancer takes over. Despite pain, he coaches all kinds of kids until the bitter end. Bottoms does a good job, and so does director Stuart Margolin. (104 mins.)

Shining Victory (1941)***½ James Stephenson, Geraldine Fitzgerald, Donald Crisp, Barbara O'Neill, Sig Ruman. A selfless psychiatric researcher is loved by his devoted assistant, and tragedy strikes. This simple, straightforward plot is turned into a magically moving picture, due to fine production values and deeply romantic performances by Fitzgerald, and Stephenson (who died soon afterward—he was wonderful, and this is one of your only chances to see him.) (Dir: Irving Rapper, 80 mins.)

Ship Ahoy (1942)**½ Eleanor Powell, Red Skelton, Bert Lahr, Frank Sinatra. Entertaining but trite little musical about a girl who is unwittingly helping enemy agents. Dancing and music (Tommy Dorsey) are worthwhile. (Dir: Edward Buzzell, 95 mins.)

Ship of Fools (1965)**½ Simone Signoret, Oskar Werner, Lee Marvin, Vivien Leigh, Michael Dunn, George Segal, Elizabeth

Ashley, José Ferrer. Lilia Skala, Karen Verne, Werner Klemperer. Director Stanley Kramer's adaptation of the Katherine Anne Porter novel (and Abby Mann's script) reduces her ironies to bromides on the moral dangers of social appeasement. Still, some star turns recommend the film (there are a few from which recoil is the only gallant response), and the production does have a velvety black and white design. B&W. (149 mins.)

Ship That Died of Shame, The (Great Britain, 1955)*** Richard Attenborough, Virginia McKenna. Drama about the conversion of a one time heroic war ship into a smuggling vessel. Top performances. (Dirs: Michael Relph, Basil Dearden, 91 mins.)

Shipmates Forever (1935)**½ Dick Powell, Ruby Keeler. Musical about Annapolis has a nice score and a tired story. Interesting Annapolis setting and the music make it attractive entertainment. (Dir: Frank Borzage, 108 mins.)

Ships with Wings (Great Britain, 1941)*** John Clements, Michael Wilding, Michael Rennie, Ann Todd. A pilot cashiered from the service becomes a hero aboard an aircraft carrier when WW II breaks out. Good war melodrama, excellent combat scenes. (Dir: Sergei Nolbandov, 89 mins.)

Shipwreck Island (Spain, 1962)**½ Pablito Calvo, Charito Maldonado. Spanish-made, English-dubbed adventure tale about a group of lads shipwrecked on a deserted island and their attempts to survive. Interesting premise, fairly well done. (Dir: Emilio Gomez Muriel, 88 mins.)

Shirts/Skins (MTV 1973)***½ Bill Bixby, Doug McClure, McLean Stevenson, Leonard Frey. Fascinating, forthright story by writer Bruce Paltrow about a group of moderately successful men who turn a weekly basketball match into a hide-and-seek, win-or-lose contest in which two teams hide basketballs somewhere in Los Angeles and then retrieve them. (Dir: William Graham, 73 mins.)

Shock Corridor (1963)*** Peter Breck, Constance Towers, Gene Evans. Director Samuel Fuller again treads the fine line between madness and reality in this story of a newsman's search for a killer in an insane asylum. Stunningly photographed by Stanley Cortez. Don't miss the attack of the nymphomaniacs. (101 mins.)

Shock Treatment (1964)*½ Lauren Bacall, Stuart Whitman, Roddy McDowall, Carol Lynley. (Dir: Denis Sanders, 94 mins.)

Shock Waves (1977)** Peter Cushing, John Carradine, Brooke Adams. More laughs than chills in this silly mystery yarn in which a group of tourists stumble upon a Caribbean island where a former Gestapo officer (Cushing) presides over a small army of half-dead mutant soldiers. Filmed in Miami. (Dir: Ken Wiederhorn, 86 mins.)

Shocking Miss Pilgrim, The (1947)*½ Betty Grable, Dick Haymes. (Dir: George Seaton, 85 mins.)

Shockproof (1949)*** Cornel Wilde, Patricia Knight. Female ex-con falls for her parole officer while trying to go straight. Well-made melodrama with a slightly different slant. Leads were married at the time. (Dir: Douglas Sirk, 79 mins.)

Shoe Shine (Italy, 1946)**** Rinaldo Smerdoni, Franco Interlenghi. Director Vittorio De Sica's best film is a heart tugger of substantial dimensions. Few opportunities for cheap sentiment are scanted in this story of two street kids who want to save up to buy a horse, but overpowering emotion builds to such a climax that all is forgiven. (93 mins.)

Shoes of the Fisherman, The (1968)** Anthony Quinn, Laurence Olivier, Oskar Werner, David Janssen, Vittorio De Sica, John Gielgud. Or, Zorba the Pope. Awful adaptation of an equally awful book by Morris L. West. Quinn is humble Russian cardinal who is elected pope and proceeds to solve the world's problems by giving away the Vatican wealth, straightening out Janssen's marital problems, and mediating between Russian premier Olivier and the young Chinese president. Gielgud has the best role as a corpse, and Werner also gets to die, something he excels at. (Dir: Michael Anderson, 162 mins.)

Shoot, The (West Germany, 1964)** Lex Barker, Ralf Wolter, Marie Versini. Hero and his friend pursue a notorious bandit. Good direction by Robert Siodmak keeps this costume adventure perking. English dubbed. (120 mins.)

Shoot First (Great Britain, 1953)*** Joel McCrea, Evelyn Keyes. American officer thinks he has killed a man while hunting, but becomes involved in a spy plot while clearing himself. Well-knit thriller enlivened by good comedy sequences. (Dir: Robert Parrish, 88 mins.)

Shoot Loud, Louder! I Don't Understand (Italy, 1966)**½ Marcello Mastroianni, Raquel Welch. A zany, if not hilarious, comedy about the wild goings-on in a strange household inhabited by Marcello Mastroianni and his eccentric uncle. Add Raquel Welch, a murder, a disappearance, underworld hoods, and missing money—and you know what you're in for. (Dir: Eduardo de Filippo, 100 mins.)

Shoot Out (1971)** Gregory Peck, Dawn Lyn, Pat Quinn. A tired western, undistinguished but not bad. Based on Will James's novel "The Lone Cowboy." (Dir: Henry Hathaway, 95 mins.)

Shoot-Out at Medicine Bend (1957)*½ Randolph Scott, James Craig, Angie Dickinson, James Garner. Typical Scott oater in which good predictably triumphs over evil. Vengeance is all, and Dickinson suffers nobly. B&W (Dir: Richard L. Bare, 87 mins.)

Shoot the Piano Player (France, 1960)*** Charles Aznavour, Marie Dubois, Nicole

Berger, Michele Mercier, Albert Remy. Director François Truffaut calls this "a pastiche of the Hollywood B film." Ironic story of a timid pianist (magnificently played by Aznavour) who has retreated from the concert stage to play in a second-rate café. Pictorially stunning, with canny use of the scope frame. (92 mins.)

Shooting, The (1967)**½ Millie Perkins, Will Hutchins, Jack Nicholson, Warren Oates. Offbeat western which saves on sets by photographing a long trek with the trio of stars. The plot involves Miss Perkins, bent on revenge, getting two young cowpokes to help her in her deeds. Some good scenes add interest, and the film doesn't drag out the premise, which is another plus. (Dir: Monte Hellman, 82 mins.)

Shootist, The (1976)*** John Wayne, James Stewart, Lauren Bacall. Western drama about an old gunman dying of cancer who decides to "exit" with all guns a-blazin' and take a few mean varmints with him. Wayne's last role (between bouts of the cancer that killed him). Impressive supporting cast includes Stewart in a cameo role. (Dir: Don Siegel, 100 mins.)

Shootout in a One Dog Town (MTV 1973)**½ Richard Crenna, Stefanie Powers, Jack Elam, Arthur O'Connell. Slick western yarn with a twist ending. Crenna is a small-town banker entrusted with a $200,000 deposit and must use all his resources to keep it from being stolen by a gang of desperadoes. Veteran actor Elam scores, as usual, in the role of the town's bartender, who also happens to be the makeshift law officer. (Dir: Burt Kennedy, 74 mins.)

Shop Around the Corner, The (1940)**** Margaret Sullavan, James Stewart, Frank Morgan, Joseph Schildkraut. Lovely romantic comedy, set in Prague, about two shop assistants who fall in love by mail. Stewart and Miss Sullavan are charming together; Schildkraut is a convincing snake in the grass; and Morgan almost steals the picture (as usual) as the sentimental shop owner. Remade as "In the Good Old Summertime." (Dir: Ernst Lubitsch, 97 mins.)

Shop on High Street,The—See: **Shop on Main Street, The**

Shop on Main Street, The (Czechoslovakia, 1965)**** Ida Kaminska, Josef Kroner. One of the most heartrending and moving films ever. A Slovak (Kroner) befriends and protects an elderly Jewess (Kaminska) until he receives a deportation order. Miss Kaminska, playing the old lady, is altogether extraordinary and richly deserved the critical acclaim she received, including an Oscar nomination. Exquisitely directed by Jan Kadar and Elmar Klos. English subtitles by Lindsay Anderson. Oscar: Best Foreign Film. (128 mins.)

Shopworn Angel, The (1938)** Margaret Sullavan, James Stewart, Walter Pidgeon.

Sentimental romance with a 1917 setting which is long on corn and short on sense. Another of those "waste of talent" films. (Dir: H. C. Potter, 85 mins.)

Short Cut to Hell (1957)**½ Robert Ivers, Georgann Johnson. Professional killer is doublecrossed after committing murder, seeks his revenge. Interesting for two reasons: it's a remake of "This Gun for Hire," and it was directed by James Cagney, who handles his task nicely. Film itself moves at a speedy clip, though not up to the original. (87 mins.)

Short Eyes—See: **Slammer**

Short Walk to Daylight (MTV 1972)** James Brolin, Abbey Lincoln. Suspense adventure tale about seven passengers on a New York subway train who try to find their way to safety after an earthquake destroys a good part of the city. If your tastes run to this brand of melodrama... (Dir: Barry Shear, 73 mins.)

Shortest Day, The (Italy, 1963)**½ Franco Franchi, Ciccio Ingrassia. Two zany soldiers accidentally destroy Germany's secret weapon during WW II. War comedy given a lift by an all-star cast supporting the two comics, a rather cheerful burlesque of "The Longest Day." Dubbed in English. (Dir: Sergio Corbucci, 82 mins.)

Shot in the Dark, A (Great Britain, 1964)**** Peter Sellers, Elke Sommer, George Sanders. Best film of the Pink Panther series. The plot is from a Broadway mystery-farce. Blake Edwards directs expertly. Filmed in Paris. (101 mins.)

Shotgun (1955)**½ Sterling Hayden, Yvonne DeCarlo, Zachary Scott. Interesting western, hero out to avenge a brutal murder. Gets a bit bloody at times. (Dir: Lesley Selander, 81 mins.)

Shout, The (Great Britain, 1979)***½ Alan Bates, Susannah York, John Hurt. Implications of menace and sexual aggression are forcefully conveyed by Bates as a scruffy madman, Hurt as a high-strung composer, and York as the wife who comes under a spell cast by the sinister Bates. Based on Robert Graves's short story. (Dir: Jerzy Skolimowski, 87 mins.)

Shout at the Devil (Great Britain, 1976)* Lee Marvin, Roger Moore, Barbara Parkins. Flaccid brawler, with a mugging Marvin and an ossified Moore as African adventurers mixed up in WW I. Planes crash, houses burn, ships blow up, but you have to keep reminding yourself how much "fun" it all is. Filmed in Malta; based on Wilbur Smith's novel. (Dir: Peter Hunt, 147 mins.)

Show Boat (1936)**** Irene Dunne, Allan Jones, Helen Morgan, Paul Robeson, Charles Winninger. Awesomely effective mounting of the classic musical with the famous Jerome Kern melodies like "Old Man River" and "Can't Help Loving That Man." Director James Whale's somber, montage-oriented expressionism heightens the dramatic effectiveness of the material and counteracts its latent maudlin strains. (113 mins.)

Show Boat (1951)*** Kathryn Grayson, Howard Keel, Ava Gardner, Marge & Gower Champion, Joe E. Brown, Agnes Moorehead. The unforgettable Jerome Kern score is still a big asset to this version of the noted musical drama of love aboard a Mississippi show boat. Otherwise, the cast is highly capable, the song numbers put over with zest. All that's lacking is that certain something that distinguishes a great musical from a good one. (Dir: George Sidney, 107 mins.)

Showdown, The (1950)*** William Elliott, Walter Brennan, Marie Windsor, Jim Davis, Harry Morgan. Former state trooper looking for his brother's killer finds suspects in a gambling house. Western with a slightly different twist is well handled throughout. (Dir: Dorrell and Stuart McGowan, 86 mins.)

Showdown (1963)** Audie Murphy, Kathleen Crowley, Charles Drake. Two drifters are imprisoned with some outlaws, who force them to hand over some stolen bonds. Fair western with a complicated plot, will satisfy the outdoor regulars. (Dir: R. G. Springsteen, 79 mins.)

Showdown (1972)**½ Rock Hudson, Dean Martin, Susan Clark. Above-average western, thanks to a screenplay by Theodore Taylor that has flashes of humor. Good-guy Rock is a sheriff who has to track down his old childhood buddy who has chosen the crooked path, played in a smirking, relaxed style by Dean, who again is a western wino. Susan Clark is cast as the woman who is fond of both men, naturally. (Dir: George Seaton, 99 mins.)

Shrike, The (1955)***½ José Ferrer, June Allyson. The impressive B'way play by Joseph Kramm is brought to the screen with some glaring defects which rob it of its total impact—the miscasting of Allyson in the role of the domineering wife who nearly destroys her husband by her love turned to jealousy and a watered down script which reverts to a happy ending. Ferrer repeats his B'way role as the husband and is very effective. (Dir: José Ferrer, 88 mins.)

Shuttered Room, The (Great Britain, 1967)*½ Carol Lynley, Gig Young, Oliver Reed. (Dir: David Greene, 99 mins.)

Sicilian Clan, The (France, 1969)*** Jean Gabin, Alain Delon, Lino Ventura. Heist caper with style and restrained acting. Patriarch Gabin heads a family that lives over a pinball repair store and occasionally indulges in a spectacular crime. They spring an old friend, Delon, and embark on their biggest job yet—stealing a cache of diamonds from a DC-8 en route to New York. Beautifully photographed and directed, with a climax that's tops for a crime drama. (Dir: Henry Verneuil, 116 mins.)

cilians, The (Great Britain, 1964)*½

Robert Hutton, Reginald Marsh, Ursula Howells. (Dir: Ernest Morris, 76 mins.)

Siddhartha (1973)**½ Shashi Kapoor, Simi Garewal, Pinchoo Kapoor. Director Conrad Rooks's faithful version of Hermann Hesse's novel on the search for inner peace. Unless you are attuned to the vagaries of Hinduism, you are likely to find it flat and lethargic. (95 mins.)

Side Street (1949)**½ Farley Granger, Cathy O'Donnell. Although the plot of this low budget gangster drama is old hat, the performances of Granger and Miss O'Donnell as a pair of newly-weds down on their luck give it added dimension. A good supporting cast includes Paul Kelly, James Craig and Jean Hagen. (Dir: Anthony Mann, 83 mins.)

Sidecar Racers (1975)*½ Ben Murphy, Wendy Hughes, John Clayton, Peter Graves. (Dir: Earl Bellamy, 100 mins.)

Sidekicks (MTV 1974)**½ Larry Hagman, Lou Gossett. Amiable feature stars Hagman as the white western hustler who keeps selling his black buddy Gossett as a slave. Mistaken for bank robbers by the law, as well as by a gang of silly thieves, the con men apply the light touch to the broad comedy. A version of the James Garner theatrical release "Skin Game." (Dir: Burt Kennedy, 72 mins.)

Sidewalks of London (Great Britain, 1938)**½ Charles Laughton, Vivien Leigh, Rex Harrison. A London street entertainer picks up a waif and sees her go to stardom, sacrificing his love for her to do so. Well acted, but brittle, unconvincing drama with music. Laughton is fine. Alternate title: **St. Martin's Lane.** (Dir: Tim Whelan, 84 mins.)

Sidewalks of New York (1931)*** Buster Keaton, Anita Page, Cliff Edwards. Buster plays a slumlord who falls in love with a lady of the tenements (Page). The comedy is mostly uninspired; you can see that Keaton had no significant creative control of the film. But some flashes of brilliance, worth watching for. (Dirs: Jules White, Zion Myers, 70 mins.)

Sidewinder 1 (1977)* Michael Parks, Marjoe Gortner, Susan Howard. (Dir: Earl Bellamy, 96 mins.)

Sidney Sheldon's Bloodline (1979)* Audrey Hepburn, James Mason, Ben Gazzara, Omar Sharif, Romy Schneider. (Dir: Terence Young, 116 mins.)

Siege (MTV 1978)**** Martin Balsam, Sylvia Sidney, Dorian Harewood. Gripping story about inner-city gangs that prey on the aged. Conrad Bromberg has written a persuasive, chilling study of a black youth (Harewood) who sets himself up as King Simon, the head of a small band of younger disciples. (Dir: Richard Pearce, 104 mins.)

Siege at Red River, The (1954)**½ Van Johnson, Joanne Dru, Richard Boone. Interesting western with action and history combined to tell the story about the forerunner of the machine gun, the Gatling gun, and how it served to revolutionize warfare. There's also a love story centering around Van Johnson and Joanne Dru. (Dir: Rudolph Mate, 81 mins.)

Siege of Fort Bismarck, The (Japan, 1963)** Makoto Sato. WW I story based on fact, about the first aerial bombardment, as the Allies shatter a German stronghold. Japan was on our side then, remember? Interesting as a novelty. Dubbed in English. (Dir: Kengo Furusawa, 98 mins.)

Siege of Sidney Street, The (Great Britain, 1960)*** Donald Sinden, Nicole Berger, Kieron Moore. Anarchist gang is trapped by police, which develops into one of the bloodiest battles in the annals of British crime. Historical melodrama should interest most viewers. Plenty of action; clever cameo of Winston Churchill played by the film's author, Jimmy Sangster. (Dirs: Robert Baker, Monty Berman, 94 mins.)

Siege of Syracuse (France-Italy, 1960)* Rossano Brazzi, Tina Louise, Sylva Koscina. (Dir: Pietro Francisci, 97 mins.)

Siege of the Saxons (Great Britain, 1963)* Ronald Lewis, Janette Scott. (Dir: Nathan Juran, 85 mins.)

Sigma III (1966)* Jack Taylor, Silvia Solar, Diana Martin. (Dir: Albert W. Whiteman, 90 mins.)

Sign of the Cross, The (1932)**** Fredric March, Claudette Colbert, Charles Laughton, Elissa Landi. Laughton offers the definitive Nero in director Cecil B. deMille's insanely lavish treatise on the decline and fall of Western Civilization. De Mille seizes the opportunity to indulge the full range of his perversity. Nero's wife Poppaea (Claudette Colbert) bathes in ass's milk while lusting after noble centurion March—but he has fallen in love with a humble Christian girl (Landi). Thoroughly mad and immensely enjoyable. (120 mins.)

Sign of the Pagan (1954)** Jeff Chandler, Jack Palance, Rita Gam. Elaborately produced epic that doesn't come off. Chandler plays a Roman centurion who is captured by Attila's barbaric army and escapes to prepare for the large scale battle between the Christians and the Huns. Jack Palance overacts as Attila the Hun and the script becomes particularly muddled when it tries to explain the religious temper of the times. (Dir: Douglas Sirk, 92 mins.)

Sign of the Ram (1948)**½ Susan Peters, Alexander Knox. Invalided wife rules her family with iron hand, not wishing it to elude her grasp. Well acted but generally average drama. (Dir: John Sturges, 84 mins.)

Signed, Arsene Lupin (France, 1959)** Robert Lamoureaux, Alida Valli. Gentleman cracksman gets involved in a case of missing paintings that's been baffling the Paris police. Well produced but sluggish period melodrama. Dubbed in English. (Dir: Yves Robert, 90 mins.)

Signpost to Murder (1964)**½ Joanne Woodward, Stuart Whitman, Edward Mulhare. The cast is far better than the material in this obvious thriller about an escaped criminal who has been certified insane and his involvement with a lady he meets. The psychological delving into the man's past is pretty elementary and you'll probably have the whole thing figured out long before the end. (Dir: George Englund, 74 mins.)

Silence, The (Sweden, 1963)*** Ingrid Thulin, Gunnel Lindblom, Jorgen Lindstrom, Birger Malmsten. Director Ingmar Bergman ends his trilogy on loss of faith. Little artistic coherence in this story of two sisters and their sordid lives. Oppressive atmosphere. Lindblom and Thulin have candlepower between them. (105 mins.)

Silence, The (MTV 1975)*** Richard Thomas, Cliff Gorman. In a superior production, Thomas is most convincing as the real-life West Point cadet, James Pelosi, who was ostracized by the "silent treatment" by all the other cadets for two years, because of an alleged violation of the academy's honor code. The excellent script by Stanley Greenberg is the result of his 70 hours of taped conversations with the actual cadet recalling the experience of his ordeal. (Dir: Joseph Hardy, 72 mins.)

Silencers, The (1966)* Dean Martin, Stella Stevens, Victor Buono, Daliah Lavi, Cyd Charisse. (Dir: Phil Karlson, 102 mins.)

Silent Call, The (1961)**½ Gail Russell, David McLean, Roger Mobley. Wispy little drama of a boy's dog, left behind when the family moves from Nevada to Los Angeles, who breaks away and follows the trail. Within its limits quite entertaining. Good script and direction. Russell's last film. (Dir: John Bushelman, 63 mins.)

Silent Enemy, The (Great Britain, 1958)*** Laurence Harvey, Dawn Addams, John Clements. The story of Lionel Crabb, British frogman of WW II fame, whose underwater exploits in stopping the Italian fleet are recounted. Good suspense, absorbing submarine detail, capably performed. (Dir: William Fairchild, 92 mins.)

Silent Gun, The (MTV 1969)** Lloyd Bridges, John Beck, Ed Begley, Pernell Roberts. Routine western about still another reformed gunman (Bridges) who helps to rid a small town of the bad guys. This film was a pilot for a proposed TV series that didn't make it to the networks. (Dir: Michael Caffey, 74 mins.)

Silent Invasion, The (Great Britain, 1960)** Eric Flynn, Petra Davies. Girl loves an officer of the invading army, until her brother is killed. Average grade B war drama. (Dir: Max Varnel, 70 mins.)

Silent Movie (1976)**** Mel Brooks, Marty Feldman, Dom DeLuise, Harry Ritz. Director Mel Brooks's movie about a director trying to make a comeback in '76 by making a silent movie. Wacky, consistently entertaining, inventive madness. The gags are written out in the form of subtitles. (Dir: Mel Brooks, 88 mins.)

Silent Night, Bloody Night (1973)**½ Patrick O'Neal, Astrid Heeren, John Carradine, Candy Darling. A pretty scary horror movie set in an old mansion in Massachusetts. Director Ted Gershuny keeps the audience right on the edge of its seat with the suspense, and adds some class in his deft handling of some flashback sequences. O'Neal is just right in the lead. (90 mins.)

Silent Night, Evil Night—See: **Black Christmas**

Silent Night, Lonely Night (MTV 1969)**½ Lloyd Bridges, Shirley Jones, Cloris Leachman. Tale about a brief interlude shared by two lonely people during the Christmas holidays in a New England college town. Bridges and Jones are the two strangers who come together while each is trying to cope with his own personal problem—Bridges' wife is a mental patient, and Miss Jones has found out her absent husband has had an affair. Winter location shots at Amherst, Mass., add an authentic note. (Dir: Daniel Petrie, 98 mins.)

Silent Partner, The (Canada, 1978)***½ Elliott Gould, Susannah York, Christopher Plummer. Curtis Hanson has fashioned an effective script for a well-performed tense thriller. The twisty plot concerns a larcenous bank clerk who foolishly crosses a psychotic robber. (Dir: Daryl Duke, 103 mins.)

Silent Running (1972)*** Bruce Dern, Cliff Potts. Spectacular space effects highlight this skillful science-fiction speculation on the state of ecology in the year 2008. Dern plays the head of a rocket crew who have been sent to orbit Saturn with man's only remaining samples of vegetation. Dern is excellent and he is aided by two robots, Huey and Dewey, who have a marvelous scene playing poker. The director, Douglas Trumbull, served his apprenticeship as an assistant to Stanley Kubrick on "2001"—and it shows. (90 mins.)

Silent Scream (1980)**½ Rebecca Balding, Cameron Mitchell, Yvonne DeCarlo, Barbara Steele. Unexceptional horror film, that demands attention for its stylistic conviction. Economical narrative affords functional visual pleasures as it pokes in the corners of his material. Worn old plot involves an old house with a mysterious, murderous secret inhabitant. Good Roger Kellaway score. (Dir: Denny Harris, 87 mins.)

Silent Victory: The Kitty O'Neil Story (MTV 1979)*** Stockard Channing, James Farentino, Colleen Dewhurst. Impressive real-life drama on deaf Kitty O'Neil, the Hollywood stuntwoman who holds the women's world land speed record. Channing is first-rate as the plucky Kitty, driven by a determined mom (Dewhurst) to

act like people with normal hearing. Writer: Steven Gethers. (Dir: Lou Antonio, 104 mins.)

Silent Witness, The (1978)*** Richard Hamer, Sarah Twist, Angela Ellis. Documentary on the Shroud of Turin, believed by many to be the cloth placed on Christ's body in his tomb. Evidence in favor of the Shroud's authenticity comes from France, Israel, Italy, and Turkey. Only some scenes of Christ's being flogged detract from the film. Narrated by Kenneth More. (Dir: David W. Rolfe, 57 mins.)

Silent World, The (France, 1956)**** Wonderful French documentary, Cousteau's exploration of the ocean's depths. Ideal in color. Oscar: Best Documentary. (Dirs: Jacques-Yves Cousteau, Louis Malle, 86 mins.)

Silk Stockings (1957)**½ Fred Astaire, Cyd Charisse, Janis Paige, Peter Lorre. Director Rouben Mamoulian's musical remake of "Ninotchka" is a little sluggish, and the anti-Soviet propaganda is coarse and intrusive. Charisse and Astaire acquit themselves honorably. (117 mins.)

Silken Affair, The (Great Britain, 1956)**½ David Niven, Genevieve Page, Beatrice Straight. Funny comedy that has Niven playing a somewhat sheepish accountant who decides to take a fling. (Dir: Roy Kellino, 96 mins.)

Silver Bears (Great Britain, 1978)**½ Michael Caine, Cybill Shepherd, Louis Jourdan, Stephane Audran, Tom Smothers, Martin Balsam. Complicated comedy about a Las Vegas syndicate boss (Balsam) who sends Caine to Switzerland to buy a bank in order to launder illegal profits. A few funny moments, but too many characters, plot twists, and double crosses. (Dir: Ivan Passer, 113 mins.)

Silver Chalice, The (1954)**½ Paul Newman, Pier Angeli, Jack Palance, Virginia Mayo, Natalie Wood. Based on Thomas B. Costain's novel. This is the story of a Greek youth who makes the "Silver Chalice" of the Last Supper. Many subplots make the film much too long. Newman's film debut. (Dir: Victor Saville, 137 mins.)

Silver City (1951)**½ Yvonne DeCarlo, Edmond O'Brien, Barry Fitzgerald. Assayer trying to escape his past arrives in Silver City to help a girl and her father mine a rich vein, opposed by the owner of the land. Actionful western with plenty of movement for the fans. (Dir: Byron Haskin, 90 mins.)

Silver River (1948)**½ Errol Flynn, Ann Sheridan. Run-of-the-mill western which leans on its name actors for support. Errol is a no-good power-hungry louse in this one but the ladies will still like him. (Dir: Raoul Walsh, 110 mins.)

Silver Streak (1976)*** Gene Wilder, Jill Clayburgh, Richard Pryor, Ned Beatty, Patrick McGoohan. Wilder stars as a tired businessman hoping for a rest while taking the train from Los Angeles to Chicago, but finding adventure, mystery, and romance. Directed with unusual verve by Arthur Hiller. (124 mins.)

Silver Whip, The (1953)*** Dale Robertson, Robert Wagner, Rory Calhoun, Kathleen Crowley. If "action" speaks louder than "dialogue," this is a "noisy" picture. Wagner plays an enthusiastic western youth who wants to ape his two best friends, Sheriff Calhoun and stage guard Robertson, and ends up in trouble. (Dir: Harmon Jones, 73 mins.)

Simba (Great Britain, 1955)***½ Dirk Bogarde, Virginia McKenna. Excellent drama dealing with a man's revenge for his brother's death against the hostile mau mau tribes of Kenya. Some terrifying sequences graphically portrayed. (Dir: Brian Desmond Hurst, 99 mins.)

Simon (1980)*** Alan Arkin, Austin Pendleton, Madeline Kahn, Judy Graubart, Fred Gwynne. Marshall Brickman directs a screenplay (his own) which mistakes smugness and derision for satire. Manages to be anti-intellectual and culturally snobbish at the same time. Arkin is gentle and skillful, and Gwynne is, as always, quite good. (97 mins.)

Simon and Laura (Great Britain, 1955)***½ Kay Kendall, Peter Finch. Amusing British satirical comedy about the "private lives" of a TV husband and wife team. Kendall and Finch are excellent foils as the TV "ideal couple." (Dir: Muriel Box, 91 mins.)

Simon of the Desert (Mexico, 1965)**** Claudio Brook, Silvia Pinal, Hortensia Santovena. The greatest short feature ever made. Director Luis Buñuel's anarchic humor was never more pungent, his visual style never more subtly formal, his gibes at holiness and purity more telling. Simon has been standing on a pillar in the wilderness for 20 years, avoiding temptation; the devil (Pinal) glides over to him in a self-propelling casket. (45 mins.)

Sin of Harold Diddlebock, The (1947)**** Harold Lloyd, Frances Ramsden, Rudy Vallee. Director Preston Sturges, the great satirist of the '40s, coaxed Lloyd out of retirement for this sequel to "The Freshman." In making this film Lloyd takes a brave backward look, with humor and regret, at his career. Alternate title: **Mad Wednesday, The** (90 mins.)

Sin of Mona Kent, The—See: Mona Kent

Sinbad and the Eye of the Tiger (Great Britain, 1977)** Patrick Wayne, Taryn Power, Jane Seymour. Weak scenario. Sinbad searches for a prince who's been transformed into a tiger by a sorceress's evil spell. Ray Harryhausen turns in a lackluster job on special effects. (Dir: Sam Wanamaker, 113 mins.)

Sinbad the Sailor (1947)*** Douglas Fairbanks, Jr., Maureen O'Hara, Anthony Quinn. The seafaring storyteller has adventurous experiences with a secret amulet and a beautiful princess. Ridiculous,

but great fun in this swashbuckling costume entertainment. (Dir: Richard Wallace, 117 mins.)

Since You Went Away (1944)**** Claudette Colbert, Jennifer Jones, Joseph Cotten, Robert Walker, Lionel Barrymore, Shirley Temple, Hattie McDaniel. Director John Cromwell and producer-writer David O. Selznick made this fine film about an idealized family on the home front in WW II. (172 mins.)

Sincerely Yours (1955)** Liberace, Joanne Dru, Dorothy Malone. It's that man with the candelabra in a heart-tugger full of corn and concerts. Liberace is just as obnoxious in feature films as he was on his TV show. Remake of "The Man Who Played God." (Dir: Gordon Douglas, 115 mins.)

Sing and Like it (1934)**½ Nat Pendleton, ZaSu Pitts, Edward Everett Horton. Early screwball comedy offers some laughs. Pendleton, a mother-fixated gangster, overhears Pitts singing a hymn to motherhood and decides to back her in a Broadway musical. He blackmails the city's leading critic (Horton) into giving his show a rave, and it's a hit—at least until Pendleton's own mother shows up, fresh from the slammer. (Dir: William A. Seiter, 72 mins.)

Sing, Boy, Sing (1958)** Tommy Sands, Lili Gentle, Edmond O'Brien, Nick Adams. Rock-and-roll idol's religious training and the pressures of being a star cause him to break under the strain. The songs may hold the teenagers, but the plot is sluggishly developed. Based on a TV drama. (Dir: Henry Ephron, 91 mins.)

Sing You Sinners (1938)***½ Bing Crosby, Fred MacMurray, Donald O'Connor, Ellen Drew. Solid entertainment as Bing cavorts around as a wastrel who strikes it rich at the track. "I've Got a Pocket Full of Dreams" is from this film and, although there's not too much music, Crosby fans should love it. (Dir: Wesley Ruggles, 90 mins.)

Sing Your Worries Away (1942)**½ Bert Lahr, June Havoc, Buddy Ebsen. Entertainers get mixed up with some gangsters trying to pull a swindle. Amusing musical comedy. (Dir: A. Edward Sutherland, 71 mins.)

Singapore (1947)** Fred MacMurray, Ava Gardner. Adventurer returns to Singapore to find his beloved a victim of amnesia, and married. Trite melodrama makes good actors look pretty silly. Remade as "Istanbul." (Dir: John Brahm, 79 mins.)

Singer Not the Song, The (Great Britain, 1961)** John Mills, Dirk Bogarde. Long, glum drama of a priest and a bandit in Mexico, as one tries to reform the other to no avail. Miscast, overwritten, underdirected. (Dir: Roy Baker, 129 mins.)

Singin' in the Rain (1952)**** Gene Kelly, Donald O'Connor, Debbie Reynolds, Cyd Charisse. This spoof of Hollywood in the early days of sound is one of the all-time great film musicals. Book by Betty Comden and Adolph Green. Irresistible songs like "You Are My Lucky Star" and of course the title song. Charisse has a dance specialty with Kelly. (Dirs: Gene Kelly, Stanley Donen, 103 mins.)

Singing Nun, The (1966)** Debbie Reynolds, Greer Garson, Ricardo Montalban, Chad Everett, Agnes Moorehead. A fictionalized, mawkish account of the story behind the real-life nun who became an international celebrity when her recording of the song "Dominique" was released. Debbie Reynolds is bearable as the young nun whose energy becomes contagious when she arrives at a poor convent in Belgium. The plot switches frequently from light-hearted scenes to heavy handed pathos. The musical sequences are OK, and Ed Sullivan is on hand displaying both of his facial expressions. (Dir: Henry Koster, 98 mins.)

Sinister Man, The (Great Britain, 1961)** John Bentley, Jacqueline Ellis. Oxford scholar is found dead and valuable archeological specimens missing. Fair Edgar Wallace mystery. (Dir: Clive Donner, 61 mins.)

Sink the Bismarck! (Great Britain, 1960)*** Kenneth More, Dana Wynter. A maritime battle of wits as the British forces strive to conquer the pride of Hitler's Navy during World War II. Excellent special effects heighten this well done semidocumentary-style war story. (Dir: Lewis Gilbert, 97 mins.)

Sinner, The—See: **Desert Desperados**

Sinner's Holiday (1947)*½ George Raft, George Brent, Randolph Scott, Joan Blondell, Virginia Field. (Formerly "Christmas Eve.") (Dir: Robert Siodmak, 92 mins.)

Sins of Babylon (Italy, 1963)* Mark Forest, Jose Greci. (Dir: Michele Lupo, 90 mins.)

Sins of Lola Montes (France, 1955)*½ Martine Carol, Peter Ustinov, Anton Walbrook. (Dir: Max Ophuls, 110 mins.)

Sins of Rachel Cade, The (1961)**½ Angie Dickinson, Peter Finch, Roger Moore. Although this film is overlong and lapses into corny preaching, it has Angie Dickinson delivering a creditable acting job as an American nurse doing missionary work in the Belgian Congo. Peter Finch brings his usual quiet force to the role of a doctor who loves Miss Dickinson. (Dir: Gordon Douglas, 124 mins.)

Siren of Bagdad (1963)**½ Paul Henried, Patricia Medina, Hans Conried. An Arabian Nights tale done with a flair for comedy—same old story but Hans Conried keeps things going at a bouncy pace. (Dir: Richard Quine, 72 mins.)

Sirocco (1952)** Humphrey Bogart, Marta Toren, Lee J. Cobb, Zero Mostel. Slow moving melodrama about sinister characters and their shady dealings. The stars are the picture's sole virtues. (Dir: Curtis Bernhardt, 98 mins.)

Sis Hopkins (1941)**½ Judy Canova, Susan Hayward, Bob Crosby. Country girl wins out over snooty cats at a girls' school. Amusing comedy. (Dir: Joseph Santley, 98 mins.)

Sister Angele's Secret (France, 1955)** Sophie Desmarets, Raf Vallone. Novice nun sees a murder committed, falls for the killer, tries to persuade him to surrender. Well acted but grim drama dubbed in English. (Dir: Leo Joannon, 90 mins.)

Sister Kenny (1946)***½ Rosalind Russell, Alexander Knox, Dean Jagger. Story of the famous nurse and her fight against infantile paralysis. Frequently stirring drama, excellently acted. (Dir: Dudley Nichols, 116 mins.)

Sisters, The (1938)*** Bette Davis, Errol Flynn, Anita Louise, Jane Bryan, Ian Hunter. Director Anatole Litvak isn't up to the scope and sweep of this tale of three sisters and their marriages at the turn of the century. Davis plays very well against Flynn; Bryan and Louise manage with more subtlety in less flashy roles. San Francisco earthquake scenes are well shot by Tony Gaudio. (120 mins.)

Sisters (1973)*** Jennifer Salt, Margot Kidder, Charles Durning. Director Brian De Palma's comedy-thriller is full of false promise. The tip-offs of a superficial stylist unable to take anything seriously including his own work lie in the relentlessly brutalized characters, including Salt as an impossibly idiotic girl reporter and Kidder as a separated Siamese twin. Filmed on Staten Island, New York. (92 mins.)

Sisters of the Gion (Japan, 1936)**** Isuzu Yamada, Yoko Umemura. A masterpiece directed by Kenji Mizoguchi, subtle, compact, and emotionally devastating. Story of two geisha sisters who hold traditional and modern views. But both end up prisoners to male morality. Stunningly acted.

Sitting Bull (1954)**½ Dale Robertson, Mary Murphy, J. Carrol Naish (title role). Ridiculous inaccurate tale of Sitting Bull and Custer is loaded with phony action and OK for the kids. (Dir: Sidney Salkow, 105 mins.)

Sitting Ducks (1980)*** Zack Norman, Michael Emil, Patrice Townsend. Two oddball players (Norman and Emil) are given a loose, improvisatory context in which to bounce off their speech patterns and petty paranoias. The result is an eccentric comedy that mixes self-congratulation and pointlessness with some genuine behavioral inspiration. The film loiters and meanders but it doesn't bore. Henry Jaglom's makeshift direction keeps you off-balance. (90 mins.)

Sitting Pretty (1948)**½ Clifton Webb, Robert Young, Maureen O'Hara. Webb became a popular comic lead with his fussy creation of Mr. Belvedere, the unflappable babysitter with a firm hand for the brats. His memorable scene of pouring oatmeal over a baby's head charmed millions, causing them to neglect the essential smugness of this overextended material. Young and O'Hara are the couple who hire him. (Dir: Walter Lang, 84 mins.)

Sitting Target (Great Britain, 1972)*½ Oliver Reed, Jill St. John, Ian McShane. (Dir: Douglas Hickox, 93 mins.)

Situation Hopeless—But Not Serious (1965)**½ Robert Redford, Alec Guinness, Michael Connors. An excellent idea that works only part of the way. A lonely German air-raid warden captures two American airmen (Redford and Connors) near the end of WW II, and keeps them prisoner in his cellar long after the war is over. Guinness manages to bring the suitable absurdity required by his character of the captor, but the pace of this satirical spoof is not as crisp as it should have been. (Dir: Gottfried Reinhardt, 97 mins.)

Six Black Horses (1962)** Audie Murphy, Dan Duryea, Joan O'Brien. A cowboy, a girl, and a killer are set upon by Indians in the desert. Ordinary western, with Duryea's familiar baddie performance worth noting; everything else's routine. (Dir: Harry Keller, 80 mins.)

Six Bridges to Cross (1955)*** Tony Curtis, George Nader, Julie Adams, Sal Mineo. Well made gangster film about a loser who keeps getting deeper and deeper into a life of crime until he masterminds a really big caper—knocking over an armored car and getting away with over 2½ million dollars. Loosely based on the Boston Brink's Robbery. Curtis is very good as the hood who couldn't go straight. (Dir: Joseph Pevney, 96 mins.)

633 Squadron (U.S.-Great Britain, 1964) *** George Chakiris, Cliff Robertson. A good action film which doesn't have to have a love story attached, but unfortunately, it has. However, it doesn't dominate the story, which becomes exciting. Chakiris and Robertson are assigned to destroy a very important Nazi stronghold in Norway, but complications set in, and an act of heroism above and beyond the call of duty gets the job done. (Dir: Walter Grauman, 94 mins.)

Six Million Dollar Man, The (1973)*½ Martin Balsam, Lee Majors, Darren McGavin. (Dir: Richard Irving, 73 mins.)

Six of a Kind (1934)**** W. C. Fields, George Burns, Gracie Allen. A cross-country motor trip becomes a laugh riot in the hands of the leads. Don't miss Fields's great pool-shooting routine. (Dir: Leo McCarey, 65 mins.)

Skag (MTV 1980)*** Karl Malden, Piper Laurie, Kathryn Holcomb. Potato-nosed Malden plays middle-aged steel-mill foreman Pete Skagska, who suffers a stroke at the mill. Returning home to recuperate, Skag uncovers family problems alongside worries about his own health and the possibility of impotence. He becomes not an Archie Bunker but a hard-hitting, realistic blue-collar dad—a hero, not a dummy. (Dir: Frank Perry, 152 mins.)

Skatetown, U.S.A. (1979)* Scott Baio, Flip Wilson, Ron Palillo. (Dir: William A. Levey, 98 mins.)

Skezag (1970)**** Powerful, disturbing documentary about a black hustler-heroin addict in New York. Most of it is an interview with Vietnam veteran Wayne Shirley, including scenes of Shirley "shooting up." "Skezag" is a slang expression for heroin. In the beginning, Shirley comes on as a hip, ingratiating, wise-cracking foul-mouthed con man. As time passes you see his bravado fading, as Shirley himself literally wastes away, and the viewer is left with a portrait of the hapless addict, fairly literally committing suicide in front of his eyes. Produced and directed by independent filmmakers Joel L. Freedman and Philip F. Messina. (73 mins.)

Ski Champ, The (West Germany, 1958)** Olympic champ Toby Sailer. Lots of schussing around, little plot, about a skier preparing for a championship race. But Tony's a fabulous skier so....Dubbed in English. (Dir: Hans Grimm, 90 mins.)

Ski Fever (U.S.-Austria-Czechoslovakia, 1967)* Martin Milner, Claudia Martin, Vivi Bach, Tony Sailer. (Dir: Curt Siodmak, 98 mins.)

Ski Lift to Death (MTV 1978)**½ Deborah Raffin, Charles Frank, Suzy Chaffee. Attractive ski resort movie filmed in Canada's Banff National Park and Lake Louise. There's a little of everything in this snow smorgasbord—expert skiing sequences, tempting wenches, a scary gondola accident, and a gun-toting killer out on the slopes. (Dir: William Wiard, 104 mins.)

Ski on the Wild Side (1967)*** Karl Schranz, Nancy Greene, Suzy Chaffee, Roger Staub. A documentary for ski buffs shot on some of the great runs and mountains all over the world including the American Rockies, Europe, New Zealand and Japan. It's not as good as "The Endless Summer" about surfing, but skiers everywhere will enjoy this armchair travelogue. (Dir: Warren Miller, 104 mins.)

Ski Party (1965)** Frankie Avalon, Dwayne Hickman, Deborah Walley. A very poor man's "Some Like It Hot." Avalon and Hickman get into girls' costumes and go on a "ski party" to find out all about the opposite sex and the types of men they adore. The result is a film strictly for kids who probably can follow the plot and talk on the phone at the same time. (Dir: Alan Rafkin, 90 mins.)

Ski Troop Attack (1960)** Michael Forest, Frank Wolff. American ski patrol is trapped behind enemy lines in Germany's Huertgen Forest. Modest but interesting WW II drama makes good use of icy locales, novel settings. (Dir: Roger Corman, 61 mins.)

Skin Game (1971)*** James Garner, Lou Gossett, Susan Clark. James Garner's relaxed charm and winking good humor are put to fine use in this surprisingly agile comedy set in pre-Civil War days. Garner, a con artist, and his sidekick, runaway slave Lou Gossett—also excellent in his role, combine for some funny incidents including the unlikely subject of racism. Incidentally, a TV pilot starring Gossett and Larry Hagman in the leads didn't live up to this original. (Dir: Paul Bogart, 102 mins.)

Skipalong Rosenbloom—See: **Square Shooter, The**

Skippy (1931)** Jackie Cooper, Mitzi Green, Robert Coogan. Appealing nine-year-old imp Cooper played his first major role in this film about Percy Crosby's comic-strip character, the mischievous Skippy. In one scene, when Jackie has to cry over the loss of his dog, he was told by the director (his uncle) that his own dog had actually been killed. So much for screen realism. (Dir: Norman Taurog, 85 mins.)

Skirts Ahoy (1952)**½ Esther Williams, Vivian Blaine, Joan Evans. Typical musical about three sailors and their romances—only this time the sailors are Waves. The male side in the romance dept. is supplied by Barry Sullivan, Keefe Brasselle and Dean Miller. There are specialty numbers by the DeMarco Sisters and Billy Eckstine. (Dir: Sidney Lanfield, 109 mins.)

Skull, The (Great Britain, 1965)** Peter Cushing, Christopher Lee, Jill Bennett, Patrick Wymark. Acting vanguard of horror flicks pep up this improbable saga about the murderous powers of the notorious Marquis de Sade's skull. (Dir: Freddie Francis, 83 mins.)

Skullduggery (1970)* Burt Reynolds, Chips Rafferty, Edward Fox, Susan Clark. (Dir: Gordon Douglas, 103 mins.)

Sky Above and the Mud Below, The (France-Belgium-the Netherlands, 1961)**** Absorbing, frequently harrowing documentary exploration of primitive peoples. Fascinating stuff. French-made and one of best of its kind. Oscar: Best Documentary Feature. (Dir: Pierre-Dominique Gaisseau, 90 mins.)

Sky Above Heaven (France, 1964)*½ Andre Smagghe, Marcel Bozzufi. (Dir: Yves Ciampi, 105 mins.)

Sky Full of Moon (1952)*** Carleton Carpenter, Jan Sterling, Keenan Wynn. Charming film about a young cowboy who comes to Las Vegas during Rodeo Week to strike it big. Carleton Carpenter gives remarkably accurate performance as the novice on-the-town and is aided by a professional supporting cast. (Dir: Norman Foster, 73 mins.)

Sky Hei$t (MTV 1975)*½ Don Meredith, Frank Gorshin, Stefanie Powers. (Dir: Lee H. Katzin, 100 mins.)

Sky Riders (1976)** James Coburn, Susannah York, Robert Culp. Well above—several thousand feet above, as a matter of fact—the level of most mediocre melodramas, thanks entirely to some ex-

citing, well-photographed scenes of the sport of hang-gliding. Here the sport is deftly employed to rescue some hostages held in an abandoned monastery on a high peak in Greece. The plot you've seen before—American industrialist (Culp) has his wife and children kidnapped by a terrorist group. Coburn and his derring-do glider gang ease down for the rescue. Filmed in Athens and the Greek countryside. (Dir: Douglas Hickox, 90 mins.)

Sky Terror (1972)**½ Charlton Heston, Jeanne Crain, Yvette Mimieux, Walter Pidgeon, James Brolin. Also known as "Son of Airport"! This tale about a bomb threat aboard an airplane flown by Heston, who was loved by stewardess Mimieux, is not a bomb. It's a straightforward thriller without any pretensions. Filled with fine ensemble character acting—including Pidgeon as a U.S. senator and Rosey Grier as a cellist. Don't let the subtle title change fool you—moviegoers saw this as "Skyjacked." Based on the novel "Hijacked" by David Harper. (Dir: John Guillermin, 100 mins.)

Sky Trap, The (MTV 1979)**½ Marc McClure, Kitty Ruth, Jim Hutton. Disney adventure yarn with fast-paced chases and escapes and the good guys coming out on top. Sailplane pilot (McClure) gets involved in a dope-smuggling caper against his will. (Dir: Jerome Courtland, 104 mins.)

Sky Without Stars (West Germany, 1955)*** Eva Kotthaus, Erik Schumann, Horst Buchholz. Postwar divided Berlin, from a West German view—and laudably done. (Dir: Helmut Kautner, 105 mins.)

Skydivers, The (1963)*½ Kevin Casey, Marcia Knight, Eric Tomlin. (Dir: Coleman Francis, 75 mins.)

Skyjacked—See: **Sky Terror**

Skylark (1941)*** Claudette Colbert, Ray Milland, Brian Aherne. Amusing little comedy about a wife who gets the "seven-year itch" and has a brief and enlightening interlude with another man. (Dir: Mark Sandrich, 94 mins.)

Sky's the Limit (1943)*** Fred Astaire, Joan Leslie, Robert Ryan, Robert Benchley. War hero spends his leave in New York and falls in love with a girl. Pleasing musical with great Astaire dancing. (Dir: Edward H. Griffith, 89 mins.)

Skyward (MTV 1980)** Bette Davis, Suzy Gilstrap, Howard Hesseman. Sentimental "you can do anything" drama about a 14-year-old paraplegic girl who dreams of flying. Paraplegic Gilstrap stars, with Davis as an ex-stunt pilot and Hesseman as an airfield watchman. Hokey stuff. (Dir: Ron Howard, 104 mins.)

Skywatch (1960)**½ Tommy Steele, Ian Carmichael, Benny Hill. A routine service drama which benefits greatly from its fine British players. Song-and-dance man Steele does well as a renegade serviceman who has a yen for a good time during wartime. (Dir: Lewis Gilbert, 90 mins.)

Skyway to Death (MTV 1974)** Ross Martin, Stefanie Powers, Bobby Sherman, Nancy Malone. Another crisis drama with a host of TV names—Martin, Powers, Sherman, Malone, Joe Campanella, John Astin—coming together in an aerial tramway, kept there by a maniacal saboteur. Of course we get to know them and their hang-ups. It's obvious, to say the least. (Dir: Gordon Hessler, 74 mins.)

Slammer (1977)*** Bruce Davidson, Jose Perez, Joseph Carberry. Miguel Pinero's brilliant play about an accused child molester thrown in the tank with hardened types is given an overly conscientious treatment by director Robert M. Young. Powerhouse performances, especially by Davidson and Carberry. (104 mins.)

Slander (1957)** Van Johnson, Ann Blyth, Steve Cochran. TV star is victimized by the ruthless publisher of a scandal magazine. Weakly written drama misses out on a good idea with inferior treatment. (Dir: Roy Rowland, 81 mins.)

Slap Shot (1977)**** Paul Newman, Strother Martin, Jennifer Warren, Lindsay Crouse, Melinda Dillon. Foulmouthed, funny, authentic, marvelously acted movie about a minor-league hockey team in a seedy Massachusetts mill town. Newman plays an aging player-coach who's a clumsy romantic and a lousy, losing coach until he directs his simpleminded charges to act like crazed hoodlums on the ice. Nancy Dowd has written several juicy supporting parts for the women, touchingly acted by Warren, Crouse, Dillon, and Kathryn Walker. Another fast-paced winner from savvy director George Roy Hill. (122 mins.)

Slattery's Hurricane (1949)**½ Richard Widmark, Linda Darnell, Veronica Lake. Personal drama amid a weather station's reporting of a hurricane. Herman Wouk penned the screenplay before his more successful efforts. Veronica Lake was a real dish in those days. (Dir: André de Toth, 83 mins.)

Slaughter (1972)*½ Jim Brown, Stella Stevens, Rip Torn. (Dir: Jack Starrett, 92 mins.)

Slaughter on Tenth Avenue (1957)*** Richard Egan, Jan Sterling, Dan Duryea, Walter Matthau. Assistant D.A. runs into formidable obstacles when he tries to get the goods on waterfront hoodlums. Compact and informative crime drama, well done. (Dir: Arnold Laven, 103 mins.)

Slaughterhouse-Five (1972)***½ Michael Sacks, Ron Liebman, Sharon Gans, Valerie Perrine. Ambitious film adaptation of Kurt Vonnegut's complex novel, a parable about Billy Pilgrim, an American Everyman. Director George Roy Hill and screenwriter Stephen Geller have a good feel for the fantasy in Vonnegut's work—WW II experiences and mental illness are mixed with other striking images in this demanding if flawed work. Newcomer Sacks is effective playing Billy. Filmed on location in Czechoslovakia and Minnesota. (104 mins.)

Slaughter's Big Rip-off (1973)*½ Jim Brown, Ed McMahon, Brock Peters. (Dir: Gordon Douglas, 93 mins.)

Slave Girl (1947)*** George Brent, Yvonne DeCarlo. Playboy is sent to Tripoli to rescue imprisoned American seamen. Often quite funny satire on adventure films; some good laughs. (Dir: Charles Lamont, 80 mins.)

Slave Girls of Sheba (Italy, 1964)* Linda Cristal, Jose Suarez. (Dirs: Giacomo Gentilomo, Guido Zurli, 92 mins.)

Slave of Love, A (U.S.S.R., 1976)**** Elena Solovei, Rodion Nakhapetov, Alexander Kalyagin. Delightful bittersweet romance about a penny dreadful film company shooting in the Crimea as the postrevolutionary civil war echoes in the distance. Solovei is captivating as the lead actress of the film within the film, a potboiler that is the last gasp of the old order. Recommended. (Writer-Dir: Nikita Mikhalkov, 94 mins.)

Slave Queen of Babylon (Italy, 1962)*½ John Ericson, Yvonne Furneaux. (Dir: Primo Zeglio, 101 mins.)

Slave Trade in the World Today (France-Italy, 1964)*** Bizarre, semidocumentary about the plight of African and European women sold to rich Arabs for their harems. Filmed, often by hidden cameras, throughout Africa, India, and the Middle East. Scenes include young boys and girls being openly traded, a slave market near Khartoum where old sheiks examine nude young girls, a caravan smuggling enslaved children from Chad to Saudi Arabia. (Dirs: Roberto Molenotti and Folco Quilici, 86 mins.)

Slavers (1980)* Trevor Howard, Ray Milland, Cameron Mitchell, Britt Ekland, and Ron Ely. (Dir: Jurgen Goslar.)

Slaves (1969)* Stephen Boyd, Ossie Davis, Barbara Ann Teer, Gale Sondergaard, Dionne Warwick, Nancy Coleman. (Dir: Herbert J. Biberman, 110 mins.)

Slaves of Babylon (1953)** Richard Conte, Linda Christian, Maurice Schwartz. Biblical history suffers another setback with this romanticized nonsense relating how Nebuchadnezzar was defeated by an Israeli shepherd and his army. (Dir: William Castle, 82 mins.)

Slaves of the Invisible Monster (1950-66)* Richard Webb, Aline Towne. (Dir: Fred Bannon, 100 mins.)

Sleep, My Love (1947)*** Claudette Colbert, Don Ameche, Robert Cummings. A husband who wants his wife out of the way tries to get rid of her by driving her insane. Familiar suspense melodrama; well done, but nothing new. (Dir: Douglas Sirk, 97 mins.)

Sleeper (1973)**** Woody Allen, Diane

Keaton, John Beck, Don Keefer. A riotous film directed by the multitalented Allen. It's Woody's inspired, nutty vision of the future. After undergoing an operation Woody is frozen and awakens in 2173 to find himself in a police state, where the government has perfected its torture techniques to the point where hapless victims are forced to watch reruns of Howard Cosell on TV. There are marvelous sight gags, and an unending flow of one-liners, most of them funny. Woody also coauthored the screenplay with Marshall Brickman. (88 mins.)

Sleeping Beauty (1959)***½ Voices of Mary Costa, Bill Shirley, Vera Vague. The most impressive post-WW II Disney animated feature, and the most expensive (in real dollars). For Disney technology at its pinnacle, there is nothing else like it. The look of the fairy tale is based on 15th-century French manuscripts, with a medieval flattened sense of perspective and harsh, angular lines. (Dirs: Clyde Geronimi, Eric Larson, Wolfgang Reitherman, Les Clark, 75 mins.)

Sleeping Car Murder, The (France, 1965)***½ Yves Montand, Simone Signoret, Jean-Louis Trintignant, Jacques Perrin. An intriguing murder mystery mounted with class and taste by Costa-Gavras ("Z"). The cast are all perfect in this complex tale involving a multiple murderer. (Dir: Costa-Gavras, 95 mins.)

Sleeping Car to Trieste (Great Britain, 1948)*** Jean Kent, Albert Lieven. Some spies steal a valuable political diary and take off on the Trieste express, aboard which a famous detective outwits them. Neat spy thriller with some good comedy touches. (Dir: John Paddy Carstairs, 95 mins.)

Sleeping City, The (1950)**½ Richard Conte, Coleen Gray, Peggy Dow, Alex Nicol. Moderately convincing drama about a detective who impersonates an intern in a hospital in order to crack a narcotics ring. Good performances by the cast. (Dir: George Sherman, 85 mins.)

Sleeping Tiger (Great Britain, 1954)***½ Alexis Smith, Dirk Bogarde, Alexander Knox. Psychiatrist brings a criminal to his home for study, but the doctor's wife falls for him. Excellently acted, suspenseful drama, well done throughout. (Dir: Joseph Losey, 89 mins.)

Sleepytime Gal (1942)**½ Judy Canova, Jerry Lester. A cake decorator in Miami enters singing competition, gets mixed up with gangsters. Amusing musical comedy. (Dir: Albert S. Rogell, 84 mins.)

Slender Thread, The (1965)*** Sidney Poitier, Anne Bancroft, Telly Savalas. The appeal of the two stars helps to overcome some of the strained dramatics in this story about a clinic whose sole purpose is to help desperate people via a phone call. Sidney Poitier plays a college student who volunteers his services at the "Crisis Clinic." The action of the film takes place during the time he tries to keep would-be suicide Anne Bancroft on the phone while police attempt to find her whereabouts. Miss Bancroft has the far showier role, but Poitier keeps his characterization crisp and interesting. (Dir: Sydney Pollack, 98 mins.)

Sleuth (1972)**** Laurence Olivier, Michael Caine. Marvelous inventive mystery based on the smash-hit play by Anthony Shaffer. It's a joy to see the great Olivier hamming it up, acting out his own special "games." Caine is equally skillful playing the butt of one of the "games," but it turns out that ... well, we're **not** going to tell you the plot of this stylish thriller briskly directed by Joseph L. Mankiewicz. Just see and enjoy. (137 mins.)

Slight Case of Larceny, A (1953)*** Mickey Rooney, Elaine Stewart. A screwball comedy which almost makes it. Rooney and Eddie Bracken make a good team and it's their performances which are worth the whole film, as they play a couple of ex-GIs in trouble over a get-rich-quick scheme. (Dir: Don Weis, 71 mins.)

Slight Case of Murder, A (1938)***½ Edward G. Robinson, Ruth Donnelly, Jane Bryan. In this screamingly funny satire of gangster films, Rico (Robinson) is a bootlegger who decides to go straight, confounding friends and enemies alike. The performances are all hilarious. Remade as "Stop, You're Killing Me." (Dir: Lloyd Bacon, 90 mins.)

Slightly Dangerous (1943)*½ Lana Turner, Robert Young, Walter Brennan. (Dir: Wesley Ruggles, 94 mins.)

Slightly French (1949)*** Dorothy Lamour, Don Ameche. Film director hires a carnival girl to pose as a new French import. Diverting comedy with good musical numbers, smooth direction. Remake of "Let's Fall in Love." (Dir: Douglas Sirk, 81 mins.)

Slightly Honorable (1939)***½ Pat O'Brien, Broderick Crawford, Ruth Terry, Eve Arden, Edward Arnold, Evelyn Keyes. A murder mystery of the fast and wacky school, as a lawyer tangles with crooked politics and sinister killings. Rapid-paced, with bright dialogue and a great cast, how could it miss? (Dir: Tay Garnett, 83 mins.)

Slightly Scarlet (1956)*** John Payne, Arlene Dahl, Rhonda Fleming. Crook intends to turn the tables on his crime syndicate boss and muscle in himself. Unpleasant but well made, well acted melodrama. (Dir: Allan Dwan, 99 mins.)

Slim Carter (1957)*** Jock Mahoney, Julie Adams, Tim Hovey. Café entertainer becomes a western star and the idol of millions, but it all goes to his head—until an orphan boy takes a hand. Pleasant, slightly different behind-the-scenes comedy-drama, good entertainment. (Dir: Richard Bartlett, 82 mins.)

Slime People, The (1963)* Robert Hutton, Susan Hart. (Dir: Robert Hutton, 76 mins.)

Slipper and the Rose, The (Great Britain,

1976)** Richard Chamberlain, Gemma Craven, Edith Evans. Director Bryan Forbes's tired musical version of the Cinderella story stars the noted terpsichorean Chamberlain and newcomer Craven, not to the great advantage of either. An air of desperation prevails throughout. (146 mins.)

Slither (1973)***½ James Caan, Sally Kellerman, Peter Boyle, Louise Lasser. Very diverting first movie by director Howard Zieff. It's a wild and woolly chase in trailers and campers for a stash of loot, with lots of stops along the way for extravagantly detailed comic vignettes. (97 mins.)

Slow Dancing in the Big City (1978)**½ Paul Sorvino, Anne Ditchburn, Nicolas Coster. Macho film about ballet is too manipulative to wring out eye moisture, but John G. Avildsen's superb direction and editing ekes out considerable entertainment. Sorvino is a lovable lug of a columnist who falls in love with Ditchburn. (101 mins.)

Small Back Room, The (Great Britain, 1949)*** David Farrar, Kathleen Byron. A research scientist has problems both in his work and his home life. Expertly produced, interesting drama. Alternate title: **Hour of Glory.** (Dirs: Michael Powell, Emeric Pressburger, 106 mins.)

Small Change (France, 1976)**** Eva Truffaut, Tania Torrens, Jean-François Stevenin, Philippe Goldmann. A wise, beautiful, poetic comedy about children and a mistreated boy that also happens to be very funny. One of Truffaut's tenderest, most observant works. Written and directed by François Truffaut with Suzanne Schiffman. (104 mins.)

Small Circle of Friends, A (1980)**½ Brad Davis, Jameson Parker, Karen Allen. Could be called "Jules and Jim Go to Harvard." Director Rob Cohen slams everything across without density, depth, or texture. (Dir: Rob Cohen, 112 mins.)

Small Town Girl (1953)** Jane Powell, Farley Granger, Ann Miller, Billie Burke, Nat King Cole. A crafty girl tricks a stranger into marriage when he's drunk and then sets out to win his heart. Bad musical, mostly, with some fine dancing and a few good production numbers like Miller's "I've Got That Beat," staged by Busby Berkeley. (Dir: Leslie Kardos, 93 mins.)

Small Town in Texas, A (1976)* Timothy Bottoms, Susan George, Bo Hopkins. Pretty dull actioner with Bottoms and George battling corrupt cops and a lame script. Director Jack Starrett doesn't start wrecking cars until the last 30 minutes. (95 mins.)

Small Voice, The—See : **Hideout, The**

Small World of Sammy Lee, The (Great Britain, 1963)*** Anthony Newley, Julia Foster, Robert Stephens. Sammy (Newley) is a minor Soho personality who must raise some money or face gang brutality; his reactions are a mixture of terror and his easygoing façade. Neatly crafted suspense, set in the unglamorous, tawdry locales of Soho. Movie is dominated by Newley's sterling performance. Written and directed by Ken Hughes. (105 mins.)

Smallest Show on Earth, The (Great Britain, 1957)*** Peter Sellers, Margaret Rutherford, Bill Travers, Virginia McKenna. Often amusing comedy about a young married couple who inherit a tacky movie theater along with its most improbable staff. The British cast expertly play it for laughs but the lines aren't all that funny. (Dir: Basil Dearden, 81 mins.)

Smart Woman (1948)*** Constance Bennett, Brian Aherne. A lady lawyer has a special prosecutor fall for her. Good melodrama. (Dir: Edward A. Blatt, 93 mins.)

Smash-up: The Story of a Woman (1947)**½ Susan Hayward, Lee Bowman, Eddie Albert, Marsha Hunt. Features Hayward's showy portrayal of an alcoholic, but the film's sensationalism is dated. (Dir: Stuart Heisler, 103 mins.).

Smash-Up Alley (1973)** Darren McGavin, Richard Petty, Noah Beery, Jr. For fans of stock-car racing, the "true" story of the king of the hill, Richard Petty, who plays himself, and his father, Lee, played by McGavin. The emphasis is on action—lots of racing footage—and the competition between father and son. (Dir: Edward J. Lasko, 72 mins.)

Smash-Up on Interstate 5 (MTV 1976)**½ David Groh, Vera Miles, Harriet Nelson. Another "disaster" film. This time it's with 39 cars involved, in which 14 people die and 62 are injured. The footage of the chain-reaction crack-up is superbly photographed, and the sequence both starts the movie and ends it (in slow motion the second time around). In between, flashbacks take viewers back 43 hours earlier and introduce all the characters. The vignettes are predictable and melodramatic, but Miles manages to be quite good as a middle-aged divorcée who shares a brief romantic interlude with an unlikely truck driver (Groh). (Dir: John Llewellyn Moxey, 106 mins.)

Smashing Time (Great Britain, 1967)*** Comic misadventures of two country girls (Lynn Redgrave, Rita Tushingham) in the mod world of London. Often harkens back to the old slapstick days; good-humored, enjoyable, knock-about farce with Michael York, Anna Quayle, Ian Carmichael. Directed with flair by Desmond Davis. (96 mins.)

Smile (1975)***½ Barbara Feldon, Bruce Dern. This could have been a great comedy. It isn't, but a lot of it is droll and satirical. It's a spoof on the biggest goof of all time, the American Beauty Pageant. This one is called the Young American Miss Pageant, and all the expected participants are on hand for the event held in sunny California. There's the sponsor, Bruce Dern's used-car salesman; the den mother, well played by Barbara Feldon; Michael Kidd's sarcastic and bitter Hollywood choreographer down on his luck; and the parade of contestants who give the picture its center. Biting screenplay by Jerry Belson. Fourth feature from the gifted director Michael Ritchie. (113 mins.)

Smile, Jenny, You're Dead (MTV 1974)*** David Janssen, Zalman King, Howard da Silva, Jodie Foster. Janssen plays private eye Harry O (for Orwell), a part created in a similiar pilot film. Janssen is cool and collected as the sleuth who lives a relaxed life in a California beach community and only becomes involved when he chooses. The case which captures his attention involves a model who is being trailed, unbeknown to anyone, by a psychotic photographer. Tight pace, and Janssen's personal brand of laconic charm comes through nicely. (Dir: Jerry Thorpe, 90 mins.)

Smile When You Say "I Do" (MTV 1973)**½ Director Allen Funt uses his candid-camera technique to good advantage in this delightful series of vignettes focusing on the institution of marriage. There's a lot of fun in store in most of the wild and spontaneous situations. There's a segment about a nutty lady (who insists that her dogs be legally married before starting a family) that's a standout. (74 mins.)

Smiles of a Summer Night (Sweden, 1955)**** Ulla Jacobsson, Eva Dahlbeck, Harriet Andersson, Jarl Kulle. Perhaps director Ingmar Bergman's greatest film, a high sex comedy that gradually becomes a contemplation of the inevitable sadness of human relations. The going never gets sticky, as in later Bergman. (108 mins.)

Smiley (Australia, 1957)** Colin Peterson, Ralph Richardson, Chips Rafferty. Youngster trying to raise money for a bicycle gets involved with smugglers. Novel locale is the main asset of this mild little drama. The youngsters will like it best. (Dir: Anthony Kimmins, 97 mins.)

Smiley Gets a Gun (Australia, 1959)** Keith Calvert, Chips Rafferty, Sybil Thorndike. Boy is promised a rifle by the local constabulary, provided he can earn it by doing good deeds. Mild comedy-drama, with the different locale helping somewhat. (Dir: Anthony Kimmins, 89 mins.)

Smilin' Through (1932)*** Norma Shearer, Fredric March, Leslie Howard. Weepy story with Shearer playing an orphan who falls in love with a killer's son. From the old play by Jane Cowl and Jane Murfin. (Dir: Sidney Franklin, 97 mins.)

Smilin' Through (1941)**½ Jeanette MacDonald, Gene Raymond, Brian Aherne. Remake is not very good, despite flickers of cinematic intelligence and a dab of personality here and there. The only screen pairing of real-life husband and wife MacDonald and Raymond (no,

she wasn't married to Nelson Eddy). Color. (Dir: Frank Borzage, 100 mins.)

Smoke (MTV 1970)*** Ronny Howard, Earl Holliman, Andy Devine. Sensitive Disney production deals with a boy who distrusts his new stepfather and extends his love to a stray German shepherd dog. Howard and Holliman are acceptable in the leads of the drama, played at a slow pace. Nice children's fare. (Dir: Vincent McEveety, 98 mins.)

Smokey and the Bandit (1977)***½ Burt Reynolds, Sally Field, Jerry Reed, Jackie Gleason, Paul Williams, Pat McCormick. The top of its class. Two oddly matched Texas millionaires commission ace driver Smokey to race from Georgia to Texas with a load of illegal beer. The acting is tongue-in-cheek and breezy, the action naturally fast; Gleason, hilarious as a sputtering sheriff, and the whole thing curiously irresistible. Country singer Reed also got a pleasant hit song out of it. (Dir: Hal Needham, 97 mins.)

Smokey and the Bandit II (1980)*** Burt Reynolds, Jackie Gleason, Sally Field, Dom DeLuise, Paul Williams. Reynolds's ability to make character points by radiating his personality is all that holds interest in this uninspired sequel. The writing is uncommitted, lazy, and mean-spirited, and Hal Needham's direction is pedestrian. Would you believe an endless skein of elephant jokes? How about pregnant elephant jokes? (101 mins.)

Smoky (1946)*** Fred MacMurray, Anne Baxter, Burl Ives. Story of a man's love for his horse is wonderful film fare for the youngsters and those who like sentimental outdoor drama. Smoother than '34 version. (Dir: Louis King, 87 mins.)

Smoky (1966)**½ Fess Parker, Diana Hyland. This is the third remake of the famous Will James sentimental story about a horse named Smoky and the events, both good and bad, which befall the animal. It's pretty old-fashioned fare by now, but this production is played straight, and therefore works. The kids will be pulling for Smoky from start to finish. (Dir: George Sherman, 103 mins.)

Smooth as Silk (1946)*** Kent Taylor, Virginia Grey. Attorney murders in a jealous rage, then schemes to cover his crime. Well-knit plot, good direction and performances put this "B" into the "A" class. (Dir: Charles Barton, 65 mins.)

Smugglers, The (Great Britain, 1947)**½ Michael Redgrave, Richard Attenborough, Jean Kent, Joan Greenwood, Francis L. Sullivan. A young lad is instrumental in rounding up a gang of smugglers, of which his guardian is the boss. Costume melodrama moves too slowly, and the net result is only fair. (Dir: Bernard Knowles, 90 mins.)

Smugglers, The (MTV 1968)** Shirley Booth, Carol Lynley, Kurt Kasznar, David Opatoshu. Predictable drama. About two American tourists in Europe (Miss Booth and Miss Lynley) who are used as decoys by an international smuggling operation. (Dir: Alfred Hayes, 97 mins.)

Snafu (1945)**½ Robert Benchley, Conrad Janis. Family is upset when "their boy" comes home a hardened teen-age soldier. Amusing comedy. (Dir: Jack Moss, 82 mins.)

Snake Pit, The (1948)**½ Olivia de Havilland, Leo Genn, Mark Stevens, Celeste Holm, Beulah Bondi. Social problem drama about the treatment of the mentally ill makes an idealistic plea for shock therapy that seems shocking itself today. De Havilland suffers madly as the young woman who is committed. Anatole Litvak directs with his usual frustrating overelaboration of basic plot points, not to mention belabored thematic exposition. (108 mins.)

Snatched (MTV 1973)**½ Howard Duff, Barbara Parkins. Fairly effective kidnapping film makes the grade with the help of a solid cast. A mastermind kidnaps the wives of three wealthy men and asks for a cool million for each. (Dir: Sutton Roley, 73 mins.)

Sniper, The (1952)*** Arthur Franz, Adolphe Menjou, Marie Windsor, Richard Kiley. Adult drama about a deranged sniper who baffles police on his trail. Exciting climax. Good performances, particularly by Arthur Franz. (Dir: Edward Dmytryk, 87 mins.)

Sniper's Ridge (1961)**½ Jack Ging, Stanley Clements. Captain orders a last raid before the Korea peace talks in an effort to grab glory for himself. Compact low-budget war drama is better than many bigger films of the same type. (Dir: John Bushelman, 61 mins.)

Snoop Sisters, The (1972)**½ Helen Hayes, Mildred Natwick, Craig Stevens, Jill Clayburgh. Thanks to the professional elan of its stars, Misses Hayes and Natwick, this comedy-murder mystery holds your interest despite some outrageous but amusing plot twists. The Snoop Sisters, who collaborate on writing mystery novels, get involved in solving the murder of a onetime movie star, played in a brief appearance by real-life onetime movie star Paulette Goddard. Art Carney also registers as the sisters' part-time bodyguard. This was the pilot for a TV series. (Dir: Leonard B. Stern, 99 mins.)

Snoopy, Come Home (1972)***½ Don't confuse this "Peanuts" theatrical release with the TV specials, even if they are similar. This was the second theatrical film based on Charles Schulz's wonderful collection of characters including Charlie Brown, Lucy, Linus, Schroeder and, of course, Snoopy, who is the star of this opus. It features a delightful musical score by the Sherman brothers (Robert B. and Richard M.), whose big credit is "Mary Poppins." Story is endearing, dealing with Snoopy's odyssey to find a place where there are no signs bearing the unwelcome greeting "No Dogs Allowed." We also liked the bird, "Woodstock." (Dir: Bill Melendez, 90 mins.)

Snorkel, The (Great Britain, 1958)*** Peter Van Eyck, Betta St. John, Mandy Miller. Clever murder mystery film with good acting by the principals about a "perfect crime" attempt that nearly succeeds. (Dir: Guy Green, 92 mins.)

Snow-Fall (Hungary, 1974)**½ Imre Szabo, Maria Markovicova. A soldier comes home on leave during WW II (remember, Hungary fought as an Axis power aligned with Germany and Italy) to find his family suffering incredible hardships, eking out a living as woodcutters in the mountains. (Writer-Dir: Ferenc Kosa.)

Snow Job (1972)* Jean-Claude Killy, Daniele Gaubert, Vittorio De Sica, Cliff Potts. (Dir: George Englund, 90 mins.)

Snow Treasure (1968)*½ James Franciscus, Ilona Rodgers. (Dir: Irving Jacoby, 95 mins.)

Snow White and the Three Stooges (1961)**½ Carol Heiss, Three Stooges, Patricia Medina. The Snow White fairytale, with the heroine on ice skates and the team of Moe, Curley, and Larry substituting for the Seven Dwarfs. Not really as bad as it sounds—the small fry should love it, while grownups shouldn't have too bad a time. (Dir: Walter Lang, 107 mins.)

Snowbeast (1977)*½ Bo Svenson, Yvette Mimieux, Clint Walker. (Dir: Herb Wallerstein, 106 mins.)

Snowbound (Great Britain, 1948)*** Robert Newton, Dennis Price, Herbert Lom, Stanley Holloway. A movie director undertakes a dangerous mission to recover some gold bullion in the Italian Alps. Good cast, otherwise ordinary thriller. (Dir: David Macdonald, 85 mins.)

Snowfire (1958)**½ Molly McGowan, Don Megowan, Claire Kelly. Family film about a little girl who befriends a wild stallion that is considered dangerous by ranchers who are hunting it down to destroy it. Kids and adults may be touched by the sentimental story. (Dirs: Dorrell and Stuart McGowan, 73 mins.)

Snows of Kilimanjaro, The (1952)*** Gregory Peck, Susan Hayward, Ava Gardner, Hildegarde Neff. Darryl F. Zanuck brings the late Ernest Hemingway's rambling novel to the screen with a powerhouse lineup of stars. The overall result, however, is a bit of a disappointment due to script limitations and uneven performances. There's a bit of melodramatic histrionics by Miss Gardner as she is being carried off a battlefield that is jarringly hammy. Neff does what she can with a skeleton of a part as a Contessa. (Dir: Henry King, 117 mins.)

So Big (1953)*** Jane Wyman, Sterling Hayden. Edna Ferber's sentimental novel, complete with every tearful scene and every sacrifice on the part of Miss Wyman's character. Nancy Olson registers strongly in a top supporting role and the two stars handle their roles expertly. A good family picture. Remake of '32 film. (Dir: Robert Wise, 101 mins.)

So Dark the Night (1946)***½ Steven Geray, Micheline Cheirel, Eugene Borden, Theodore Gottlieb (Brother Theodore). One of the best B films ever made. Geray plays a French detective on leave from his Parisian post, solving a murder in the provincial countryside. Director Joseph H. Lewis is talented and unpretentious. (71 mins.)

So Darling, So Deadly (Italy-West Germany, 1967)* Brad Harris, Barbara Frey, Jennie Kendall. (93 mins.)

So Dear to My Heart (1948)*½ Burl Ives, Beulah Bondi, Bobby Driscoll. Disney nostalgia, laid on heavily, about life on a country farm in '03. The animated sequences only reinforce the live-action treacle. Young children may enjoy it. (Dir: Harold Schuster, 84 mins.)

So Ends Our Night (1941)**** Fredric March, Margaret Sullavan, Glenn Ford, Frances Dee, Erich Von Stroheim. Gripping drama of refugees from the Nazis traveling from country to country without passport. Excellent performances. A fine film. From the novel by Erich Maria Remarque. (Dir: John Cromwell, 117 mins.)

So Evil My Love (1948)**½ Ray Milland, Ann Todd, Geraldine Fitzgerald. Well done, but strangely uninteresting drama of love, murder and blackmail in Victorian England. (Dir: Lewis Allen, 109 mins.)

So Long at the Fair (Great Britain, 1950)***Jean Simmons, Dirk Bogarde, Honor Blackman. In Paris with her brother for the Exposition, a young girl is thrown in panic when he disappears, and everyone who has seen him denies his existence. Interesting melodrama keeps the attention. (Dirs: Terence Fisher, Anthony Darnborough, 86 mins.)

So Proudly We Hail (1943)**½ Claudette Colbert, Paulette Goddard, Veronica Lake, Sonny Tufts (film debut). Picture dedicated to our brave army nurses on Bataan has some effective scenes, but is generally routine drama. (Dir: Mark Sandrich, 126 mins.)

So This is Love (1953)** Kathryn Grayson, Merv Griffin. Contrived biography of opera singer Grace Moore, as artificial as these biographies usually are. Kathryn Grayson miscast as the diva. (Dir: Gordon Douglas, 101 mins.)

So This Is New York (1948)***½ Henry Morgan, Rudy Vallee, Hugh Herbert, Donna Drake. Small town family comes to the big city to find a man for sister, manages to turn the city on its ear. Extremely clever, funny comedy, with many original little touches, good performances. Based on the Ring Lardner novel. (Dir: Richard A. Fleischer, 79 mins.)

So This is Paris (1954)*** Tony Curtis, Gloria De Haven, Gene Nelson, Corinne Calvert. Entertaining musical comedy about three gobs on leave in Paris and their encounters with girls, orphans, Paris society, and the gendarmes. Many musical numbers with Curtis doing surprisingly well in the singing and dancing department. (Dir: Richard Quine, 96 mins.)

So Young, So Bad (1950)**½ Paul Henreid, Catherine McLeod, Anne Francis, Rita Moreno, Anne Jackson. A doctor assigned to a girls' correctional school discovers inhuman conditions prevailing there, fights them. Fairly good melodrama. (Dir: Bernard Vorhaus, 91 mins.)

Socrates (Italy, MTV 1970)***½ Jean Sylvere, Anne Caprile, Richard Palacios. Another first-rate historical drama directed by Roberto Rossellini. Socrates refuses to carry out an order from Critias, one of his former students. Scenes from Socrates's later trial; and his refusal to escape after being condemned to death. Concludes with Socrates drinking hemlock and dying among his friends. Enormously stimulating dialogue, thanks to the script by Rossellini and Marcella Mariani. English subtitles. (120 mins.)

Sodom and Gomorrah (U.S.-France-Italy, 1961)**½ Stewart Granger, Pier Angeli, Stanley Baker, Anouk Aimee, Rossana Podesta. The story of Lot, who leads his people to Sodom, where a cruel queen reigns over a city of sin. Actually, it's all rather tame in structure, although it has the usual made-in-Italy trappings. Some fairly good performances make it a passable Biblical spectacle. (Dir: Robert Aldrich, 154 mins.)

Soft Beds, Hard Battles—See: **Undercovers Hero**

Soft Skin, The (France, 1964)***½ Jean Desailly, Françoise Dorleac, Nelly Benedatti. One of director François Truffaut's best. Desailly plays a typical Truffaut man-child who bumbles through an extramarital affair with stewardess Dorleac. (120 mins.)

Soil—See: **Earth**

Sol Madrid (1968)** Paul Lukas. Narcotics agent (David McCallum) battles the Mafia in Mexico. Thoroughly routine. With Stella Stevens, Telly Savalas, Ricardo Montalban. (Dir: Brian G. Hutton, 90 mins.)

Solaris (U.S.S.R., 1972)*** Natalya Bondarchuk, Donatas Banionis, Yuri Jarvet. Highbrow science fiction film offers half-baked profundities and overworked irony. A group of space scientists, on a base set in the middle of a sentient ocean on a distant planet, are visited by flesh-and-blood specters from their past. (Dir: Andrei Tarkovsky, 165 mins.)

Soldier Blue (1970)*** Candice Bergen, Peter Strauss, Donald Pleasence. Offbeat, violent, ultimately rewarding "western" about the U.S. Army's unhuman treatment of American Indians, based on the real Sand Creek Massacre of Cheyenne warriors and their families, including children. This may be one film where you'll be rooting for the U.S. Cavalry to be wiped out. Based on the novel "Arrow in the Sun" by Theodore V. Olsen, and adapted by John Gay. Bergen gives one of her best performances to date as the liberated young fiancée of an Army officer who sides with the Indians. (Dir: Ralph Nelson, 112 mins.)

Soldier in Skirts—See: **Triple Echo**

Soldier in the Rain (1963)*** Steve McQueen, Jackie Gleason, Tuesday Weld, Tony Bill, Tom Poston. Uneven comedy-drama about the bond of friendship between a wordly-wise master sergeant and his naive worshiper. Always seems on the verge of something great without actually accomplishing it. However, there's a good share of laughs, some heart-tugs, fine performance by Gleason. (Dir: Ralph Nelson, 88 mins.)

Soldier of Fortune (1955)**½ Clark Gable, Susan Hayward, Gene Barry. Just another routine adventure story set in Hong Kong. This production is handsomely mounted and has name stars but it can't disguise the commonplace plot. (Dir: Edward Dmytryk, 96 mins.)

Soldier of Orange (The Netherlands, 1978)**** Rutger Hauer, Paul Verhoeven. An intelligent, sensitive war-adventure movie. Hauer plays a charismatic, disengaged, callow student who grows into heroism during the Nazi occupation of the Netherlands. His classmates reach destinies as diverse as their well-delineated characters. (Dir: Paul Verhoeven.)

Soldiers of Pancho Villa, The (Mexico, 1959)** Dolores Del Rio, Maria Felix, Emilio Fernandez, Pedro Armendariz. Elaborate, frequently colorful, often banal drama of Villa's fight to free Mexico from tyranny. Good cast, better than the material provided. Dubbed in English. (Dir: Ismael Rodriguez, 90 mins.)

Soldiers Three (1951)** Stewart Granger, David Niven, Robert Newton, Walter Pidgeon. With the boys in India, 1890—a trio of army privates get into one mess after another. Try for a "Gunga Din" type of adventure misfires—some action, some amusement, but not enough. (Dir: Tay Garnett, 87 mins.)

Sole Survivor (MTV 1970)**½ Vince Edwards, Richard Basehart, William Shatner. A glossy production, excellent location photography of the Mojave Desert, and a good male cast enhance this feature about a WW II bomber discovered in the Libyan desert 17 years after it has crashed, with the ghosts of the crew hovering over it. An investigation reveals that the plane's navigator and only survivor, now an important general, might have bailed out and falsified his account of the plane's fate. (Dir: Paul Stanley, 100 mins.)

Solid Gold Cadillac, The (1956)** Judy Holliday, Paul Douglas, Fred Clark. A not too sharp George S. Kaufman-Howard Teichmann satirical play on big business becomes hopelessly blunted in the film version. Holliday, a small stockholder, creates havoc at a board meeting over corrupt corporate practices. Narrated by George Burns. (Dir: Richard Quine, 99 mins.)

Solitary Man, The (MTV 1979)**½ Earl Holliman, Carrie Snodgress. Contemporary family drama loses steam before the end. Holliman is better than the script as the man whose wife for 18 years announces that she wants a divorce. (Dir: John Moxey, 104 mins.)

Solo for Sparrow (Great Britain, 1962)** Anthony Newlands, Nadja Regin. Policeman goes after robbers who have committed murder while pulling a heist. OK crime drama based on an Edgar Wallace story. (Dir: Gordon Flemyng, 58 mins.)

Solomon and Sheba (1959)**½ Gina Lollobrigida, Yul Brynner. Good escapist movie fare; lavish spectacle with the emphasis on pictorial splendor and not the script. Miss Lollobrigida is as appealing as ever as the voluptuous Queen of Sheba and Yul Brynner fits comfortably in the role of King Solomon. A large supporting cast includes George Sanders, Marisa Pavan and David Farrar. (Dir: King Vidor, 139 mins.)

Sombra, the Spider Woman (1947-66)*½ Bruce Edwards, Virginia Lindley, Carol Foreman, Brother Theodore. (Dirs: Spencer Bennet, Fred Brannon, 100 mins.)

Sombrero (1953)** Ricardo Montalban, Pier Angeli, Vittorio Gassman, Yvonne DeCarlo, Cyd Charisse. Story of three bachelors in a small Mexican village and their adventures in love. Attempt at something different fails largely because the plots are inclined to wander all over. Some good moments, mostly confusion. (Dir: Norman Foster, 103 mins.)

Some Came Running (1958)**½ Frank Sinatra, Shirley MacLaine, Dean Martin, Martha Hyer, Arthur Kennedy. An all-star cast brings James Jones's novel about life in a small midwestern town after WW II to the screen. Most of the plot falls into the soap opera groove but the performances, especially Shirley MacLaine as a good time gal, should keep your interest. (Dir: Vincente Minnelli, 127 mins.)

Some Kind of a Nut (1969)* Dick Van Dyke, Angie Dickinson, Zohra Lampert. (89 mins.)

Some Kind of Miracle (MTV 1979)*** Andrea Marcovicci, David Dukes. Another wrenching wheelchair drama about a Californian who injures his spine in a body-surfing accident. Dukes is convincing as the quadriplegic making a rare recovery, but Marcovicci steals the show as his distraught fiancée. Based on a book by Jack Willis, a gifted TV documentary filmmaker who was badly hurt surfing on the East Coast in the mid-'70s. (Dir: Jerrold Freeman, 104 mins.)

Some Like It Cool (West Germany-Italy-France, 1977)* Tony Curtis, Britt Eklund,

Sylva Koscina. (Dir: François Legrand, 87 mins.)

Some Like It Hot (1959)**** Tony Curtis, Marilyn Monroe, Jack Lemmon, Joe E. Brown, George Raft, Pat O'Brien. May well be the most hilarious American movie of its generation. Director Billy Wilder puts a flawless cast through improbable, riotous capers. Curtis and Lemmon play two musicians on the lam from Chicago mobsters after witnessing a gangland rubout. Marilyn is altogether edible. Brown delivers the last line as a classic topper. (122 mins.)

Some of My Best Friends Are . . . (1971)**½ Carleton Carpenter, Sylvia Syms, Gil Gerard. This film, set in a Manhattan gay bar on Christmas Eve, is a little artificial, but worthy of a researching glance. (Dir: Mervyn Nelson, 109 mins.)

Some People (Great Britain, 1962)* Kenneth More, David Hemmings, Annika Wills. (Dir: Clive Donner, 83 mins.)

Somebody Killed Her Husband (1978)* Farrah Fawcett, Jeff Bridges, Tammy Grimes, John Wood, John Glover. (Dir: Lamont Johnson, 96 mins.)

Somebody Loves Me (1952)** Betty Hutton, Ralph Meeker. Biography of song-spinners Blossom Seeley and Benny Fields, their ups and downs in show biz. Thoroughly routine musical primarily for the nostalgically-minded. (Dir: Irving Brecher, 97 mins.)

Somebody Up There Likes Me (1956)***½ Paul Newman, Pier Angeli, Everett Sloane, Sal Mineo. The true story of Rocky Graziano's rise from a small time hood to the middle-weight champ of the world. Newman is superb as "Rocky" and he gets top support from Miss Angeli as his wife, Joseph Buloff as a candy store philosopher, Eileen Heckart as his mother and Everett Sloane as a fight promoter. (Dir: Robert Wise, 113 mins.)

Someone Behind the Door (France, 1971)* Charles Bronson, Anthony Perkins, Jill Ireland. (Dir: Nicolas Gessner, 97 mins.)

Someone I Touched (MTV 1975)**½ Cloris Leachman, James Olson, Glynnis O'Connor, Kenneth Mars. Venereal disease, a provocative subject for TV, is explored. Miss Leachman stars as an over-30 wife who finally becomes pregnant, only to discover that both her husband and a pretty young girl he has had a brief fling with have venereal disease. Handled rather well, except for occasional lapses into melodrama. (Dir: Sam O'Steen, 72 mins.)

Someone Is Watching Me (MTV 1978)** Lauren Hutton, David Birney, Adrienne Barbeau. Terror show isn't as scary as it should be. The weak spot is top fashion model Hutton, who plays a TV news director being bugged by phone calls, notes, and presents from a nut who keeps track of her every move. She isn't up to conveying the panic called for by the role. (Writer-Dir: John Carpenter, 104 mins.)

Someone to Remember (1943)*** Mabel Paige, John Craven. Old woman whose son has disappeared years ago becomes a foster mother to some college boys. Touching, well acted drama, recommended. Remade as "Johnny Trouble." (Dir: John H. Auer, 80 mins.)

Something Big (1971)* Dean Martin, Brian Keith, Carol White, Honor Blackman. (Dir: Andrew V. McLaglen, 108 mins.)

Something Evil (MTV 1972)**½ Sandy Dennis, Darren McGavin, Ralph Bellamy. Talented director Steven Spielberg turns to the devil here, and has a ball with scary visual effects. The devil occupies a Pennsylvania farmhouse, eager to assert his powers on new tenants. Spielberg's tricks with the camera make this entry better than the usual ghost-story film. (73 mins.)

Something for a Lonely Man (1968)*** Dan Blocker, Susan Clark, Warren Oates. A very pleasant film. Blocker stars as a man who convinces some settlers to locate in a spot he thinks the railroad will go through. When the train route turns out to be some 20 miles away, he becomes a subject of ridicule. Not fast moving or super-slick, but charming, and well acted by Dan, Clark as the girl who believes in him, and a good supporting cast. (Dir: Don Taylor, 99 mins.)

Something for Everyone (1970)*** Angela Lansbury, Michael York, Anthony Corlan. Bizarre black comedy with an occassional dash of sophistication and wit. It's Noel Coward cross-pollinated with Edgar Allan Poe, and sometimes it works. Michael York is a sexy opportunist in lederhosen who descends upon the castle of the Countess Von Ornstein, which has seen better days, and proceeds to infiltrate everyone's bedroom. York becomes a footman, but soon works his way up the household ladder until he's running things. A surprise ending is delicious, and the cast, especially York and Angela Lansbury as the flamboyant and outspoken countess, is excellent. Screenplay by Hugh Wheeler based on the novel "The Cook," by Harry Kressing. (Dir: Harold Prince, 110 mins.)

Something for Joey (MTV 1977)*** Geraldine Page, Marc Singer, Jeff Lynas. Heartwarming true-life story about Heisman Trophy-winner John Cappelletti and his special relationship with his young brother, Joey, a victim of leukemia. Singer as the college football star Cappelletti gives a sensitive performance, and he's matched by Lynas as Joey. (Dir: Lou Antonio, 108 mins.)

Something for the Birds (1952)**½ Victor Mature, Patricia Neal, Edmund Gwenn. Genial comedy about Washington society. Edmund Gwenn plays an aging engraver in a Washington printing plant who crashes many Washington social functions. The love story revolves around a lobbyist (Victor Mature) and a representative of an ornithology society (Patricia Neal). (Dir: Robert Wise, 81 mins.)

Something for the Boys (1944)*** Vivian Blaine, Phil Silvers, Carmen Miranda. Tuneful, loud musical loaded with feminine pulchritude and set in a home for war wives. Phil is at his best in this one and you'll hear a young newcomer named Perry Como sing "I Wish I Didn't Have To Say Good Night." (Dir: Lewis Seiler, 85 mins.)

Something in the Wind (1947)**½ Deanna Durbin, Donald O'Connor, John Dall. Girl disc jockey is mistaken for the amour of a late multi-millionaire. Slight comedy has Durbin's fine singing to help it. (Dir: Irving Pichel, 89 mins.)

Something Money Can't Buy (Great Britain, 1952)**½ Patricia Roc, Anthony Steel. Discontented young man quits his job, and has his wife nearly beat him to breadwinning. Mildly amusing comedy. (Dir: Pat Jackson, 82 mins.)

Something of Value (1957)*** Rock Hudson, Dana Wynter, Sydney Poitier, Wendy Hiller. Robert Ruark's overwritten but compelling novel about the Mau Mau uprising is transferred to the screen with many of the book's exciting highlights intact. The major conflict of the story centers around Rock Hudson and Sidney Poitier, childhood friends who find themselves on opposite sides of the law. Poitier gives an intense performance as the leader of a Mau Mau band and Hudson shows up to good advantage, too. (Dir: Richard Brooks, 113 mins.)

Something to Live For (1952)*** Ray Milland, Joan Fontaine, Teresa Wright. Deft direction by George Stevens gives added luster to this dramatic story of an alcoholic actress saved by an A.A. member who falls in love with her although he's married. Ladies should enjoy; men will find it interesting too. (89 mins.)

Something to Shout About (1943)**½ Don Ameche, Janet Blair, William Gaxton. Trite backstage plot receives a little support from some Cole Porter music. Best tune: "You'd Be So Nice to Come Home To." (Dir: Gregory Ratoff, 93 mins.)

Something Wild (1961)**½ Carroll Baker, Ralph Meeker, Mildred Dunnock, Jean Stapleton. A strange film that weaves a hypnotic spell at the start but soon sinks into predictable melodrama. Carroll Baker plays an emotionally disturbed young girl who is saved from doing away with herself by a man who turns the incident to his advantage. Ralph Meeker's performance as the guy who brings the frightened girl to his apartment and keeps her prisoner is the best thing about the film. (Dir: Jack Garfein, 112 mins.)

Sometimes a Great Notion—See: **Never Give An Inch**

Somewhere I'll Find You (1942)**½ Clark Gable, Lana Turner. Clark and Lana burn up the screen in a mediocre adventure story which finds them as correspondents running all over the war-torn world. (Dir: Wesley Ruggles, 108 mins.)

Somewhere in Time (1980)** Christopher Reeve, Jane Seymour, Teresa Wright. Reeve stars as a playwright who falls in love with an old photograph of an actress and, after talking to a lunatic expert on time travel, wills himself back to 1912. There he meets and inevitably wins the actress, played by Seymour. Director Jeannot Szwarc and screenwriter Richard Matheson let mysticism substitute for even the vaguest interest in real life—in how people talk, act, get obsessed, fall in love. (103 mins.)

Son of a Gunfighter (U.S.-Spain, 1965)*½ Russ Tamblyn, James Philbrook, Fernando Rey, Mara Granada. (Dir: Paul Landres, 92 mins.)

Son of Ali Baba (1952)** Tony Curtis, Piper Laurie, Hugh O'Brian. Typical Arabian nights adventure with Curtis cast as the son of Ali Baba and Princess Azura. Narrow escapes, colorful sets, and romance abound in this Bagdad opus. (Dir: Kurt Neumann, 75 mins.)

Son of Captain Blood, The (U.S.-Italy-Spain, 1962)** Sean Flynn, Alessandra Panaro, Ann Todd. Back in 1935, Flynn made his major starring debut as a young swashbuckler in "Captain Blood," a rousing tale that earned him instant fame. Son Sean here makes his screen debut, fittingly as the "Son of Blood," embroiled with his Pa's pirate friends in further sea adventures. Unfortunately, Flynn Jr., though as handsome as Dad, has none of his father's acting finesse and assertive charm. Movie itself is given slick production, but stultifying plot and dialogue. (Dir: Tulio Demicheli, 88 mins.)

Son of Dear Caroline, The (France, 1955)** Brigitte Bardot, Jean-Claude Pascal, Magali Noel. Adventures of an orphan boy fighting in Spain who learns he is of French parentage. Elaborate costume drama, novelettish in content. Bardot has a minor role. Dubbed in English. (Dir: Jean Devaivre, 90 mins.)

Son of Dr. Jekyll (1951)** Louis Hayward, Jody Lawrance. Hollywood never lets a commercial gimmick die—so here's still another in the rash of "son of" films. Not so "horrific" as its predecessor, nor as well done. (Dir: Seymour Friedman, 77 mins.)

Son of Dracula (1943)**½ Lon Chaney, Louise Albritton. A strange fellow known as Count Alucard (that's Dracula spelled backwards) comes to stay at an American manse. Unbelievable horror yarn, but fun anyway. (Dir: Robert Siodmak, 79 mins.)

Son of Flubber (1963)**½ Fred MacMurray, Nancy Olson, Tommy Kirk. A family picture from the Disney stable with MacMurray's absentminded professor innocently causing trouble again with his invention known as "flubber," an antigravity substance everyone wants. Much visual slapstick. (Dir: Robert Stevenson, 100 mins.)

Son of Frankenstein (1939)*** Boris Karloff, Basil Rathbone, Bela Lugosi, Lionel Atwill. The new Baron Von Frankenstein learns that his father's monster is running loose, and tries to catch up with the fiend. Lavishly produced, plenty of spine-tingling thrills. (Dir: Rowland V. Lee, 99 mins.)

Son of Fury (1942)*** Tyrone Power, George Sanders, Gene Tierney. No message in this 18th-century drama but an abundance of action and romance. Ty, who's wronged by Uncle George, leaves England, goes to a Pacific island, finds Gene and a bucket of pearls. He goes back for his revenge. Remade as "Treasure of the Golden Condor." From the novel "Benjamin Blake." (Dir: John Cromwell, 98 mins.)

Son of Hercules in the Land of Darkness (Italy, 1963)* Dan Vadis, Carol Brown. (81 mins.)

Son of Hercules in the Land of Fire (Italy, 1963)* Ed Fury, Claudia Mori. (Dir: Giorgio C. Simonelli, 86 mins.)

Son of Kong (1933)*** Robert Armstrong, Helen Mack. Adventurer returns to the island where the mighty King Kong used to dwell, finds another huge gorilla there. Fantastic adventure, a sequel to its famous predecessor, is good fun. (Dir: Ernest B. Schoedsack, 69 mins.)

Son of Lassie (1945)** Peter Lawford, June Lockhart, Donald Crisp. Unlike its magnificent predecessor ("Lassie Come Home") this is little more than a juvenile adventure which will, of course, also appeal to dog lovers. Collie and her master shot down over Germany during the war and so on to the fadeout. (Dir: S. Sylvan Simon, 102 mins.)

Son of Monte Cristo (1940)*** The offspring of Dumas' stalwart hero is portrayed by Louis Hayward, as he foils the dastardly plans of dictator George Sanders and wins the hand of Joan Bennett, whilst dueling all over the place. Entertaining swashbuckling melodrama. (Dir: Rowland V. Lee, 102 mins.)

Son of Paleface (1952)***½ Bob Hope, Jane Russell, Roy Rogers. Sequel is much funnier than "Paleface." Hope repeats as a frontier dentist, and director Frank Tashlin supplies many outrageous visual gags. Color. (Dir: Frank Tashlin, 95 mins.)

Son of Robin Hood, The (Great Britain, 1958)*½ David Hedison, June Laverick, David Farrar. (Dir: George Sherman, 81 mins.)

Son of Sinbad (1953)*½ Dale Robertson, Sally Forrest, Vincent Price, Lili St. Cyr. (Dir: Ted Tetzlaff, 88 mins.)

Son of the Red Corsair (Italy, 1960)*½ Lex Barker, Sylvia Lopez. (Dir: Primo Zeglio, 97 mins.)

Son of the Sheik (1926)***½ Rudolph Valentino, Vilma Banky. A rousing, romantic melodrama, full of sandy fights, chases, and escapes. Valentino in his last film, plays the dual role of father and son. In this sequel to Valentino's colossal hit,

"The Sheik," he remains a remarkable screen presence, and it's easy to understand why he was the screen's earliest sex symbol. (Dir: George Fitzmaurice, 72 mins.)

Son Rise: A Miracle of Love (MTV 1979)**½ James Farentino, Kathryn Harrold. Based on the real-life experience of a couple with an autistic son. Farentino and Harrold star as the courageous, determined parents who won't settle for a negative prognosis. (Dir: Glenn Jordan, 104 mins.)

Song and the Silence, The (1969)*** Harry Rubin, Annita Koutsouveli, Nana Austin. An unusual, surprisingly effective low-budget film about a group of Hasidic Jews in Poland in 1939, filmed by amateur actors in the Catskill Mountains of New York. Produced, directed, written, and photographed by Nathan Cohen, film does capture some of the love, humor and optimism of this sect little understood by the general public. An off-beat, often rewarding American entry. (80 mins.)

Song Is Born, A (1948)**½ Danny Kaye, Virginia Mayo, Steve Cochran, Benny Goodman, Tommy Dorsey. Remake of Gary Cooper comedy titled "Ball of Fire" with music added for good measure. Not up to the original although Kaye tries very hard to rise above the material. (Dir: Howard Hawks, 113 mins.)

Song of Bernadette, The (1943)*** Jennifer Jones, Charles Bickford, Gladys Cooper, Lee J. Cobb, Vincent Price. Adapted from Franz Werfel's book about Bernadette's visions of the Virgin Mary at Lourdes. Despite its colossal length, the film tends to remain tasteful and reasonably effective. The transparent quality of Jones as St. Bernadette won an Oscar. B&W. (Dir: Henry King, 156 mins.)

Song of Freedom (Great Britain, 1937)*** Paul Robeson, Elizabeth Welch, Esmé Percy. Robeson plays a successful American singer who discovers his African origins and returns to take leadership of his tribe. Well-intentioned film is worth seeing for Robeson only. (Dir: J. Elder Wills, 80 mins.)

Song of Love (1947)** Katharine Hepburn, Paul Henreid, Robert Walker, Henry Daniell, Leo G. Carroll. Musical biopic focusing on the romance between Robert and Clara Schumann and their relationship with the young Johannes Brahms. The script is hopeless. Artur Rubinstein lent his pianistic talents offscreen. (Dir: Clarence Brown, 119 mins.)

Song of New Life—See: Earth

Song of Russia (1943)**½ Robert Taylor, Susan Peters, John Hodiak, Robert Benchley. Taylor, a symphony conductor on tour in the U.S.S.R., meets and marries an attractive comrade (Peters); in the background, the country prepares for WW II. Film about our wartime ally was made practically by government request, but during the cold war some of those involved were blacklisted. (Dir: Gregory Ratoff, 107 mins.)

Song of Scheherazade (1947)** Yvonne DeCarlo, Jean-Pierre Aumont, Brian Donlevy, Eve Arden. Far fetched story of Rimsky-Korsakoff and his love for a dance girl named Cara. Elaborate settings and some of Rimsky-Korsakoff's music save the picture from being a stupefying bore. (Dir: Walter Reisch, 106 mins.)

Song of Sister Maria, The (Spain, 1952)*** Dominique Blanchar, Maria Dulco. Sincere, well made drama of a young singer who gives up her career to become a nun. Miss Blanchar is excellent in the role. Dubbed in English. (Dir: Rafael Gil, 81 mins.)

Song of the Islands (1942)*½ Victor Mature, Betty Grable, Jack Oakie. (Dir: Walter Lang, 75 mins.)

Song of the Open Road (1944)**½ Jane Powell (film debut), Edgar Bergen, Bonita Granville. Juvenile movie star runs away and joins youngsters who are saving farm crops. Fairly pleasant musical, with some comedy from Bergen and McCarthy, W. C. Fields. (Dir: S. Sylvan Simon, 93 mins.)

Song of the Sephardi (1980)*** The Jews have two large subgroups, the Ashkenazim from Germany and eastern Europe, and the Sephardim, descendants of the great Jewish culture of Spain. During the Moorish reign in Iberia the Jews were the administrators and physicians, the philosophers and purveyors of culture. Expelled by Christian King Ferdinand in 1492, the Sephardim dispersed to Turkey, Salonika, and Amsterdam. This documentary traces some of their history and culture. (Writer-Dir: David Raphael.)

Song of the Thin Man (1947)**½ William Powell, Myrna Loy. Nick and Nora move in jazz circles as they glibly track down a murderer in this one. Good dialogue but the series has become commonplace and obvious. Last in the series. (Dir: Edward Buzzell, 86 mins.)

Song to Remember, A (1945)*½ Paul Muni, Cornel Wilde, Merle Oberon. Big, overproduced composer biography with Wilde seething as Frédéric Chopin and Oberon simpering as George Sand. Muni devours most of the scenery as Chopin's teacher, and director Charles Vidor juggles the clichés. Color. (113 mins.)

Song Without End (1960)**½ Dirk Bogarde, Genevieve Page, Capucine. Schmaltzy film biography of Franz Liszt. Bogarde pretends to play the piano, and the film is decisively superior to "A Song to Remember," and I mean that to be very, very faint praise. Director Charles Vidor died during production and was replaced by George Cukor. (141 mins.)

Sons and Lovers (U.S.-Great Britain, 1960)**** Trevor Howard, Dean Stockwell, Mary Ure, Wendy Hiller. Absorbing, successful dramatization of D. H. Lawrence's autobiographical novel. Howard is splendid as the gruff coal-mining father of the sensitive, young, would-be artist (Stockwell). Hiller, as the dominant mother, turns in a beautifully controlled and very moving performance, and Stockwell keeps up with this high-powered cast. Extremely well directed by Jack Cardiff, and there's some outstanding cinematography from Freddie Francis. (103 mins.)

Sons of Katie Elder, The (1965)**½ John Wayne, Dean Martin, Martha Hyer. John Wayne and Dean Martin may sound like strange co-stars but they work well together and make this otherwise standard western yarn entertaining. Wayne, Martin, Earl Holliman and Michael Anderson, Jr. are the sons of the title and they all show up at their Ma's funeral determined to make the name of Elder respectable once again. Some of the town bullies have other plans and this sets the stage for brawls-a-plenty with Wayne and company right in the middle. (Dir: Henry Hathaway, 122 mins.)

Sons of the Desert (1933)**** Stan Laurel, Oliver Hardy, Charley Chase, Mae Busch. The funniest L & H feature. The title refers to a fraternal order that provides the boys their only escape from noisy, henpecked married life. To go to the national convention, they concoct an incredible tale about a rare tropical malady Stan has, and the inevitable hilarious complications ensue. (Dir: William A. Seiter, 68 mins.)

Sooner or Later (MTV 1979)**½ Barbara Feldon, Judd Hirsch, Denise Miller, Lynn Redgrave. A young girl enters her teens and yearns to be just a little older so that she can share a romance with a boy who's 17. Director Bruce Hart and Carol Hart's script avoid the clichés as much as possible. Miller stars as Jessie, and Rex Smith (as a 17-year-old rock singer) is the object of her affection and performs many songs. (104 mins.)

Sophie's Place (U.S.-Great Britain, 1969)** Telly Savalas, Edith Evans, Warren Oates, Cesar Romero. A good cast is the main attraction of this crime spoof about a proposed heist at a stately British estate. Hoods Savalas and Oates work in cahoots with a British gang to rob Dame Evans' home. Written and directed by Jim O'Connolly. (106 mins.)

Sorcerer (1977)**½ Roy Scheider, Bruno Cremer, Francisco Rabal. Director William Friedkin's remake of the French thriller "Wages of Fear" is marginally watchable. He senselessly complicates a simple story—four men drive a truckload of nitro through a South American jungle—with a lengthy exposition and some unfortunate existential overtones. (122 mins.)

Sorceress, The (France, 1956)*** Marina Vlady, Maurice Ronet. The strange offbeat story of a beautiful girl who is believed to be a witch and her struggle to find happiness through love. (Dir: André Michel, 97 mins.)

Sorority Girl (1957)*½ Susan Cabot, Dick Miller. (Dir: Roger Corman, 62 mins.)

Sorrow and the Pity, The (Le Chagrin et la Pitié (France-Switzerland-West Germany, 1970)**** Pierre Mendès-France, Louis Grave, Albert Speer, George Bidault, Jacques Duclos, Anthony Eden. One of the most brilliant and shattering films ever made. Documentary about anti-Semitism and the division of France between Nazi occupation and the collaborationist Vichy regime during WW II. Many respectable Frenchmen succumbed to the virus of racial and religious bigotry, as director Marcel Ophuls makes devastatingly clear in dozens of interviews. Focuses on the city of Clermont-Ferrand (under Vichy, '40-'42; German-occupied, '42-'44). B&W. English subtitles and dubbing. (260 mins.)

Sorrowful Jones (1949)**½ Bob Hope, Lucille Ball. Bookie Hope gets involved with racketeers and fixed races in this Damon Runyon story. Ball is more reserved than she is in her "Lucy" characterization. Surprisingly, this film is a remake of an old Shirley Temple movie, "Little Miss Marker." Hope and Lucy still deliver a goodly amount of laughs. (Dir: Sidney Lanfield, 88 mins.)

Sorry Wrong Number (1948)**½ Barbara Stanwyck, Burt Lancaster, Wendell Corey. Overheated, gimicky radio play made into an overheated, gimicky film. Stanwyck invests her harridan in distress with some human dimension; Lancaster plays her murderous husband. Effective melodrama, undignified by any claim to art. (Dir: Anatole Litvak, 89 mins.)

S.O.S. Titanic (MTV 1979)*** David Janssen, Cloris Leachman, Susan Saint James. The real-life sinking of the luxury liner R.M.S. "Titanic" by an iceberg during its maiden voyage in 1912 is vividly re-created. Story begins with the rescue of the survivors and proceeds through flashbacks. (Dir: Billy Hale, 160 mins.)

Soul Kiss, The—See: **Lady's Morals, A**

Soul Soldier (1970)*½ Rafer Johnson, Cesar Romero, Janee Michelle. (Dir: John Cardos, 78 mins.)

Soul to Soul (1971)*** This captivating musical documentary, filmed in cinema verité style, effectively captures the sights and sounds of a 1971 all-night concert by visiting black American soul and gospel artists, along with African musicians as part of the 14th annual Independence Celebration of Ghana, the first black African nation. Director Denis Sanders manages to catch the excitement of the event on film. Stirring performances of such soul stars as Wilson Pickett, Ike and Tina Turner, Roberta Flack, and Les McCann. (96 mins.)

Souls for Sale—See: **Confessions of an Opium Eater**

Sound and the Fury, The (1959)*** Yul Brynner, Joanne Woodward, Stuart Whitman, Ethel Waters. William Faulkner's novel of the decadent South, unevenly filmed—story of a young girl trying to find a life of her own away from the tyrannical rule of her uncle. Some fine moments, too often confused, static. Performances generally excellent. (Dir: Martin Ritt, 117 mins.)

Sound of Anger, The (MTV 1968)** Burl Ives, James Farentino, Guy Stockwell, Dorothy Provine. Pilot for a TV series about two lawyer brothers and their partner. Courtroom case involves a pair of young lovers accused of doing away with the girl's wealthy papa. There's a fairly good surprise climax, but it's all familiar trial fare. (Dir: Michael Ritchie, 100 mins.)

Sound of Music, The (1965)** Julie Andrews, Christopher Plummer, Eleanor Parker. Don't send a lynching party at this late date to my publisher's office, but there were people in the movie business who referred to this bit of filmed treacle as "The Sound of Mucus." I agree! But most of the rest of the world did and does not agree, and made this one of the most popular films in the history of cinema. Julie plays Maria Trapp escaping from Austria and the Nazis with her young children into the haven of Switzerland. Salzburg is a lovely town, and the Swiss Alps serve as a background for the lilting Rodgers and Hammerstein songs. Oscars: Best Picture, Best Director, Best Scoring, Best Editing, Best Sound. (Dir: Robert Wise, 174 mins.)

Sound Off (1952)**½ Mickey Rooney, Anne James. A mild and often amusing comedy with music about a recruit who falls in love with a WAC officer. (Dir: Richard Quine, 83 mins.)

Sounder (1972)**** Cicely Tyson, Paul Winfield, Kevin Hooks, Carmen Mathews. One of the most moving and compassionate films in many years. About a Negro family of sharecroppers (it was Negroes then, not blacks) in rural Louisiana during the depression. (For impoverished blacks it was **always** a depression.) Based on the novel by William H. Armstrong, it has been expertly adapted for the screen by Lonne Elder III, and sensitively and lovingly directed by Martin Ritt. The father is imprisoned for stealing a ham, and injured at the prison work farm before he returns home. Miss Tyson is absolutely marvelous, a combination of warmth, strength, and tenderness as she carries her family through various crises. (105 mins.)

South of Pago Pago (1940)** Victor McLaglen, Jon Hall, Frances Farmer. Sea pirates try to steal the pearls of a tropic isle, but the natives revolt. Dated South Seas melodrama. (Dir: Alfred E. Green, 98 mins.)

South of St. Louis (1949)**½ Joel McCrea, Alexis Smith, Zachary Scott, Dorothy Malone. Three ranch partners face post Civil War troubles, become involved in gun running. Adequately presented western. (Dir: Ray Enright, 88 mins.)

South of Tana River (Denmark, 1964)** Poul Reichardt, Axel Strobye, Charlotte Ernst. Story of a girl, her father, and a game warden in the African wilderness. Interesting scenes of wild life, hokey story. Dubbed in English. (Dirs: Bent Christensen, Sven Methling, 88 mins.)

South Pacific (1958)***½ Mitzi Gaynor, Rossano Brazzi, France Nuyen, Ray Walston, John Kerr. Rodgers and Hammerstein's celebrated 1949 Broadway musical about the love story between a U.S. Navy nurse and a suave French planter in the South Pacific during WW II is given a big, lavish production. Mitzi Gaynor, as the outspoken Nellie Forbush, is excellent in the leading role but Rossano Brazzi doesn't register quite as forcefully as he should. The supporting cast is wonderful and there are all those familiar and enduring songs—"Some Enchanted Evening," "Younger Than Springtime," "There Is Nothing Like a Dame," "Bali Ha'i." Josh Logan, who ruined many other films, directed this one splendidly. (167 mins.)

South Sea Sinner (1950)** Shelley Winters, Macdonald Carey, Frank Lovejoy. This is so bad that, in a macabre way it's fun to sit through. Shelley Winters, complete with feather boa and bleached blonde hair, plays a small time "Sadie Thompson" on an island inhabited by various shady characters. Liberace is seen as "Maestro" the piano playing philosopher who accompanies Miss Winters in her nightclub scenes. (Dir: H. Bruce Humberstone, 88 mins.)

South Sea Woman (1953)*** Burt Lancaster, Virginia Mayo, Chuck Connors. Rollicking, free for all comedy with Lancaster and Connors playing a pair of brawling marines who end up fighting a large part of the Pacific War singlehanded. Virgina Mayo comes between the two buddies and keeps things popping. (Dir: Arthur Lubin, 99 mins.)

South Seas Adventure (1958)**½ Diane Beardmore, Marlene Lizzio. Fifth feature film done in the Cinerama process loses most of its interest on the small screen. Basically a travelogue of the South Seas with an imposed plot about a budding romance. Narration is mundane. Real interest is in the foreign locations. (Dirs: Walter Thompson, Basil Wrangell, Richard Goldstone, Carl Dudley, Frances Lyon, 120 mins.)

Southern Star, The (Great Britain-France, 1969)**½ George Segal, Ursula Andress, Orson Welles. A mixed bag of tricks but an entertaining adventure based on a Jules Verne story about the ups and downs of jewel thieves in the wilds of Africa, circa 1900. Segal makes a capable heroheel and Miss Andress adds visual interest as the lady in the proceedings. Welles has a brief part, but an African actor named Johnny Sekka and the scenery of Senegal are the most interesting ingredients. (Dir: Sidney Hayers, 102 mins.)

Southern Yankee, A (1948)*** Red Skelton, Arlene Dahl, Brian Donlevy. Red's fighting the Civil War in this one and his fans will eat it up. He crawls between the lines carrying a two-sided flag for protection in a really hysterical scene. (Dir: Edward Sedgwick, 90 mins.)

Southerner, The (1945)**** Zachary Scott, Betty Field, J. Carroll Naish. Director Jean Renoir's best American film tries to apply his cool location style to poor Southern rural farmers. A tenant farmer struggles to support his family. Visually astounding, but marred by undigested pieces of unassimilated theatricality. (Dir: Jean Renoir, 91 mins.)

Southside 1-1000 (1950)**½ Don DeFore, Andrea King. A secret service agent tracks down a counterfeiting ring and its mysterious leader. Average crime melodrama. (Dir: Boris Ingster, 72 mins.)

Southwest Passage (1954)**½ John Ireland, Joanne Dru, Rod Cameron. Bank robber joins a caravan testing the value of camels in the desert. Fast moving western with some new plot angles. (Dir: Ray Nazarro, 82 mins.)

Soylent Green (1973)* Charlton Heston, Joseph Cotten, Edward G. Robinson, Leigh Taylor-Young, Chuck Connors. (Dir: Richard Fleischer, 97 mins.)

Space Children, The (1958)* Adam Williams, Peggy Webber, Jackie Coogan. (Dir: Jack Arnold, 69 mins.)

Spanish Affair (1958)**½ Richard Kiley, Carmen Sevilla. Practically nonexistent plot about an American architect falling for a secretary in Spain used as an excuse to show off some breathtaking scenery, places of historical interest in Spain. Lightweight but pleasant, especially for viewers planning a trip to Spain. (Dir: Don Siegel, 92 mins.)

Spanish Gardener (Great Britain, 1956)*** Dirk Bogarde, Jon Whiteley. Diplomat's boy makes friends with a gardener, who changes his outlook and way of living. Well acted, interesting drama. (Dir: Philip Leacock, 94 mins.)

Spanish Main, The (1945)**½ Maureen O'Hara, Paul Henreid, Walter Slezak. Dashing adventurer rescues the girl he loves from the clutches of a villainous nobleman. Colorful pirate melodrama has plenty of action. (Dir: Frank Borzage, 101 mins.)

Spare the Rod (Great Britain, 1961)**½ Max Bygraves, Donald Pleasence, Geoffrey Keen. New young teacher faces obstacles in trying to break through to a group of tough kids. English version of "Blackboard Jungle" type of story has some good supporting performances and a familiar plot. (Dir: Leslie Norman, 93 mins.)

Sparkle (1976)** Philip M. Thomas, Irene Cara, Vonetta McGee. Rise of a black music group, clearly modeled on the Supremes. McGee shows some star power, but dies early in the story. The cinematography, very, very dark, is by Bruce Surtees. (Dir: Sam O'Steen, 98 mins.)

Spartacus (1960)**** Kirk Douglas, Jean Simmons, Laurence Olivier, Tony Curtis, Charles Laughton. This star-studded, lavishly mounted spectacle about a slave revolt against the Romans is a topnotch film for admirers of big spectacles. Director Stanley Kubrick handles the mammoth story without losing sight of the personal drama involved. Dalton Trumbo's literate script avoids the verbal banalities of comparable film epics. Douglas is convincing as Spartacus, the Thracian slave whose thirst for freedom makes him a natural choice to lead the oppressed out of bondage. The film has some exciting and graphic scenes set in a gladiator school and a bloody encounter in the arena. Suffers when seen on a small TV screen, but still thrilling. (161 mins.)

Spartacus and the Ten Gladiators (France-Spain-Italy, 1965)* Dan Vadis, Helga Line. (Dir: Nick Nostro, 96 mins.)

Spawn of the North (1938)*** Henry Fonda, Dorothy Lamour, George Raft, John Barrymore. Good, rousing adventure tale about the days when Russian pirates tried to take over our salmon industry. Well played and loaded with action. (Dir: Henry Hathaway, 110 mins.)

Speaking of Murder (France, 1957)** Jean Gabin, Annie Girardot. Gabin manages to rise above the weak script in this complex crime drama. Annie Girardot doesn't get a chance to show what she can do. (Dir: Gilles Grangier, 90 mins.)

Special Day, A (Italy-Canada, 1977)***½ Sophia Loren, Marcello Mastroianni, John Vernon. Loren and Mastroianni generate nostalgia and drama in this social parable. On the day of a Hitler visit to Fascist Rome two loners (he is a homosexual, waiting to be deported; she is a downtrodden housewife) enjoy a brief encounter. Wistful love story, quite moving. (Dir: Ettore Scola, 106 mins.)

Special Delivery (1976)*½ Cybill Shepherd, Bo Swenson, Sorrell Brooke. (Dir: Paul Wendkos, 99 mins.)

Special Kind of Love, A—See: **Special Olympics**

Special Olympics (MTV 1978)*** Charles Durning, Irene Tedrow, Herb Edelman, George Parry. A retarded youngster named Matt (played by Parry), a cheerful, uncoordinated kid who can't do anything right and drives everyone crazy, finds an outlet in running and jumping, learns, grows, toughens, and finally enters the Special Olympics for the handicapped. Touching family film. (Dir: Lee Philips, 104 mins.)

Special Section (France, 1975)*** Michel Lonsdale, Ivo Garrani, Jacques François. Costa-Gavras directs this scathing, flawed, but involving study of the spineless French Vichy government which collaborated with the Nazis during WW II. About Vichy's

fear of reprisals from the German government after a Nazi officer is killed by terrorist underground forces. (110 mins.)

Specialists, The (MTV 1975)* Robert York, Jack Hogan, Maureen Reagan. (Dir: Richard Quine, 72 mins.)

Specter of the Rose (1946)*** Judith Anderson, Ivan Kirov, Lionel Stander. Strange tale of a young ballet dancer who is slowly losing his mind, and of the girl who loves him. Written and directed by Ben Hecht, this is a wordy, theatrical, but often fascinating, offbeat drama. (90 mins.)

Spectre (MTV 1977)**½ Robert Culp, Gig Young. A slick film by "Star Trek"'s Gene Roddenberry, produced in England with stars Robert Culp and Gig Young, is regretfully mild fare. Roddenberry visualizes a modern Sherlock Holmes (Culp) and his medical associate (Young) confronted by murders at every turn as they delve into power plays by an English financier. Story, dealing with the supernatural, lacks polish. (Dir: Clive Donner, 106 mins.)

Spectre of Freedom, The—See: **Phantom of Liberty, The**

Speedtrap (1978)** Tyne Daly, Joe Don Baker. Routine crime drama about a pair of investigators (well played) who are hot on the trail of a car-theft organization. (Dir: Earl Bellamy, 104 mins.)

Speedway (1968)*½ Elvis Presley, Nancy Sinatra, Bill Bixby, Gale Gordon. (Dir: Norman Taurog, 94 mins.)

Spell, The (MTV 1977)** Lee Grant, James Olson, Susan Myers. Deals with an unhappy high-school girl, the brunt of jokes by her classmates, who starts willing bad things to happen to her enemies. In asking audiences to accept the effects of her concentration, the show inevitably runs into difficulties. Susan Myers, with her innocent face, is a good choice for the 15-year-old daughter. (Dir: Lee Philips, 76 mins.)

Spell of the Hypnotist—See: **Fright**

Spellbound (1945)*** Ingrid Bergman, Gregory Peck, Michael Chekhov. Secondrate thriller. Salvador Dali's dream sequence is visually contrived, but its obsessiveness dovetails stunningly with the ripe healthiness of Bergman and the monotonic shell shock of Peck. Recommended with a grain of salt. (Dir: Alfred Hitchcock, 111 mins.)

Spencer's Mountain (1963)** Henry Fonda, Maureen O'Hara, James MacArthur. A pastoral attempt about a land-loving valley dweller who keeps promising to build another home for his wife and family. Too much sweetness and light becomes quite cloying before long. Cast superior to the material provided. (Dir: Delmer Daves, 119 mins.)

Spider, The (1958)** Ed Kemmer, Gene Persson. A big one comes to life to terrorize a community. Special effects give this one a passing chill. (Dir: Bert I. Gordon, 72 mins.)

Spider and the Fly, The (Great Britain,

1949)*** Guy Rolfe, Eric Portman, Nadia Gray. During WW I, the French espionage service enlists the aid of a safecracker in obtaining important documents from the enemy. Tense, suspenseful spy melodrama, well done. (Dir: Robert Hamer, 87 mins.)

Spider-Man (MTV 1977)** Nicholas Hammond, David White, Michael Pataki. Pilot film for the kids about the comicbook hero who's endowed with superpowers after being bitten by a radioactive spider. Hammond's fancy plastic getup is the best thing about the whole hokey business as he scales skyscrapers to battle evil and corruption. (Dir: E. W. Swackhamer, 78 mins.)

Spider's Stratagem, The (Italy, 1969)***½ Alida Valli, Giulio Brogi. Enormously interesting, convoluted film made by Bertolucci when he was 28 for Italian television, based on a short story, "Theme of the Traitor and Hero," by the Argentinian writer Jorge Luis Borges. A stylish, demanding political whodunit, set in the Po Valley of Italy during the middle 1930's, a time of Mussolini and Italian Fascism. Screenplay by the remarkable Bertolucci. (Dir: Bernardo Bertolucci, 97 mins.)

Spider's Web, The (Great Britain, 1960)*½ Glynis Johns, John Justin. (Dir: Godfrey Grayson, 89 mins.)

Spies-a-Go-Go (1965)* Arch Hall Jr., Mischa Terr. (Dir: James Landis, 85 mins.)

Spikes Gang, The (1974)** Lee Marvin, Ron Howard, Gary Grimes, Charlie Martin Smith. Mediocre western filmed in Spain stars Marvin as an elderly outlaw who takes three young runaway farm boys under his wing and unsuccessfully tries to teach them how to rob banks. They all do their best with a rambling screenplay full of twists and violence. (Dir: Richard Fleischer, 96 mins.)

Spin a Dark Web (Great Britain, 1956)*½ Faith Domergue, Lee Patterson. (Dir: Vernon Sewell, 76 mins.)

Spinout (1966)* Elvis Presley, Shelley Fabares. (Dir: Norman Taurog, 95 mins.)

Spiral Road, The (1962)*** Rock Hudson, Burl Ives, Gena Rowlands. Lengthy but interesting, well acted drama of a doctor in the remote jungles of Batavia and his discovery of both medical progress and faith. Grips the attention, although some sequences could have been shortened to advantage. (Dir: Robert Mulligan, 145 mins.)

Spiral Staircase, The (1946)**½ Dorothy McGuire, George Brent, Ethel Barrymore. Mysterious killer haunts a gothic mansion and threatens mute maid McGuire. Adaptation of a suspense novel by Ethel Lina White. Not very interesting. (Dir: Robert Siodmak, 83 mins.)

Spirit Is Willing, The (1967)** Sid Caesar, Vera Miles, Barry Gordon, John McGiver, Cass Daley. A couple rent a New England house by the sea, and summer vacation soon turns into a ghosthunt. Mild farce. Once again, the talented Caesar is wasted by Hollywood. (Dir: William Castle, 100 mins.)

Spirit of Saint Louis, The (1957)**½ James Stewart, Murray Hamilton, Patricia Smith. Stewart stars as Charles Lindbergh in this sometimes absorbing, sometimes tedious account of his early life and his historic trans-atlantic solo flight. Stewart is good and the supporting cast gives him the necessary assistance. (Dir: Billy Wilder, 138 mins.)

Spirit of the Beehive (Spain, 1973)***½ Fernando Fernan Gomez, Teresa Gimpera, Ana Torrent. Time—1940 in a remote Castilian village in post-Civil War Spain. Two children watch a traveling film show of James Whale's "Frankenstein" and are traumatized by it, with alarming results for one of the children. A fascinating, underplayed drama which builds interest and tension. Expert use of some nonprofessional actors, all expertly directed by Victor Erice, who was also partially responsible for the original story (98 mins.)

Spiritism (Mexico, 1961)* Jose Luis, Nora Veyran. (Dir: Benito Alazraki, 85 mins.)

Spirits of the Dead (France-Italy, 1969)*** Jane Fonda, Peter Fonda, Alain Delon, Brigitte Bardot, Terence Stamp. Based on three tales by Edgar Allan Poe. Roger Vadim's "Metzengerstein," starring the two Fondas, is a tale of medieval love and horror centering on a great black horse. The final segment, "Never Bet the Devil Your Head" or "Toby Dammit," directed by Federico Fellini, is by far the best. An entrancing small girl with a large white ball lures alcoholic actor Stamp to pursuit or escape. Louis Malle is the third director. (117 mins.)

Spitfire (Great Britain, 1942)***½ Leslie Howard, David Niven. The story of the invention of the plane that served so well during WW II, and of its inventor. Fine biographical drama. (Dir: Leslie Howard, 90 mins.)

Splendor (1935)**½ Miriam Hopkins, Joel McCrea, David Niven. Dated romantic epic which seems a bit corny today but there's some good acting especially by Miriam Hopkins. Story by Rachel Crothers. (Dir: Elliott Nugent, 77 mins.)

Splendor in the Grass (1961)***½ Natalie Wood, Warren Beatty (film debut). This absorbing film produced and directed by Elia Kazan, just misses being a classic. Wood and Beatty costar as two young people making the painful and beautiful discovery of love in a small Kansas town prior to the depression of the thirties. Their sensitive performances, along with good ones by Pat Hingle, Zohra Lampert, and Audrey Christie, make this a must for drama fans who're not above shedding a tear or two. The ending is unsatisfactory, but it doesn't ruin the movie. Oscar: William Inge, Best Original Screenplay. (124 mins.)

Split, The (1968)*½ Jim Brown, Diahann Carroll. (Dir: Gordon Flemyng, 91 mins.)

Split Second (1953)***½ Stephen McNally, Alexis Smith, Jan Sterling. Escaped prisoners hold hostages in a Nevada atom-bomb testing area. Terrifically suspenseful, taut melodrama, well done. Directed by Dick Powell. (85 mins.)

Spoilers, The (1942)*** Marlene Dietrich, John Wayne, Randolph Scott, Margaret Lindsay, Richard Barthelmess. John is out to protect his gold mine and his woman in this one. Loaded with action and a great hand-to-hand fight by Wayne and Scott. (Dir: Ray Enright, 87 mins.)

Spoilers, The (1955)**½ Anne Baxter, Jeff Chandler, Rory Calhoun, Barbara Britton, Ray Danton. Rex Beach's classic action yarn about the "spoilers" who turned the Yukon into a claim-jumper's paradise, remade with all the flair and flavor intact. Miss Baxter is very good as Cherry, the classy proprietress of the local saloon, and Chandler fulfills the requirements of western hero. (Dir: Jesse Hibbs, 84 mins.)

Spoilers of the Sea—See: **Beyond All Limits**

Spring In Park Lane (Great Britain, 1948)*** Anna Neagle, Michael Wilding. Delightful comedy concerning romantic complications and mistaken identity. Witty, fun. (Dir: Herbert Wilcox, 90 mins.)

Spring Reunion (1957)** Betty Hutton, Dana Andrews, Jean Hagen, Laura La Plante. Betty Hutton goes dramatic as the spinster who attends her high school class reunion and finds true love at long last. Unbelievable script hampered by awkward acting of Hutton. (Dir: Robert Pirosh, 79 mins.)

Springfield Rifle (1952)*** Gary Cooper, Phyllis Thaxter, Paul Kelly. Bitter Civil War western about spies and schemers, with Cooper as a good traitor and Kelly as a failed Machiavelli. (Dir: André de Toth, 93 mins.)

Sputnik (France, 1961)** Noel-Noel, Mischa Auer. Mildly amusing comedy about a henpecked Frenchman who discovers animals on his farm used by the Russians for rocket experiments, and they try to get them back. Dubbed in English. (Dir: Jean Dreville, 85 mins.)

Spy Busters (1969)**½ Kurt Russell, Patrick Dawson, Glenn Corbett. Disney production values are apparent in this espionage yarn about an American student who attends an Irish university. After he is entrusted with an enigmatic message by a dying agent, the plot takes off with kidnappings, chases, and a beautifully photographed glider grand finale. (Dir: Robert Butler, 90 mins.)

Spy I Love, The (France-Italy-Belgium, 1964)** Jacques Balutin, Virna Lisi. Secret agents investigate the theft of an atomic device. Naive but actionful action thriller dubbed in English. (Dir: Maurice Labro, 98 mins.)

Spy in Your Eye (Italy, 1965)* Brett Halsey, Pier Angeli, Dana Andrews. (Dir: Vittorio Sala, 88 mins.)

Spy Killer, The (MTV 1969)** Robert Horton, Sebastian Cabot, Jill St. John. Horton is an ex-agent who now earns his living as a shady private eye. His old employer, British Security, enlists his aid for another assignment and he reluctantly agrees, for a stiff fee. Predictable espionage fare. (Dir: Roy Baker, 73 mins.)

Spy Smasher Returns (1942-66)**½ Kane Richmond, Marguerite Chapman. Feature version of serial "Spy Smasher." Comic-strip hero and his twin brother go after a master enemy agent, amid fistfights galore, some wild flamboyant action, making this good juvenile fun. (Dir: William Witney, 100 mins.)

Spy Squad (1961)*½ Dick O'Neil, Richard Jordahl, Dick Miller. (Dir: Will Zens, 75 mins.)

Spy Who Came In from the Cold, The (Great Britain, 1965)**** Richard Burton, Claire Bloom, Oskar Werner. The best-selling novel about hypocrisy and betrayal in the world of espionage is brought to the screen with all its grim realities intact. Richard Burton is very effective as a disenchanted agent on his supposedly last assignment and Oskar Werner is a standout as a member of German intelligence. Tautly directed by Martin Ritt. (112 mins.)

Spy Who Loved Me, The (Great Britain, 1977)*** Roger Moore, Barbara Bach, Curt Jurgens, Richard Kiel. Beefed-up production values and a minimum of Moore make this the best of the '70s James Bond movies. Hollow spectacle, but spectacle withal. In this tenth Bond film, 007 must join forces with a beautiful Russian agent (Bach) to stop a mad shipping magnate (Jurgens) from destroying the world. Kiel ("Jaws") is the metal-mouth giant who is continually trying to dispose of our hero. (Dir: Lewis Gilbert, 125 mins.)

Spy with a Cold Nose (Great Britain, 1966)*** Laurence Harvey, Daliah Lavi. Funny, if uneven, spy spoof. Title refers to a dog equipped with a microphone-transmitter, which is given to the Russian prime minister by British intelligence. It's an offbeat idea for a film comedy. Laurence Harvey plays a veterinarian, and Lionel Jeffries is terribly amusing as a bumbling British counter spy. There's one riotous scene towards the end set in an embassy in Moscow. (Dir: Daniel Petrie, 93 mins.)

Spy with My Face, The (1966)*½ Robert Vaughn, Senta Berger, David McCallum. (Dir: John Newland, 86 mins.)

Spylarks (Great Britain, 1965)** Eric Morecambe, Ernie Wise, William Franklyn. British spy spoof which suffers in the trip across the Atlantic. The comedy team of Morecambe and Wise pull their antics all over the place as a pair of inept spies out to crack a sabotage scheme. (Dir: Robert Asher, 104 mins.)

S*P*Y*S (Great Britain, 1974)** Elliott Gould, Donald Sutherland, Zou Zou, Joss

Ackland. Misspelled and misguided attempt to pair that marvelous team from M*A*S*H together again for more comedy. "Gould and Sutherland" (as their names appear in the credits) are CIA agents whom their boss has decided are expendable. They are. Humor derives from their being shot at, beaten up and generally abused. Some funny asides from the two stars, but they're not worth waiting for. (Dir: Irvin Kershner, 87 mins.)

Squad Car (1960)* Paul Bryar, Vici Raaf. (Dir: Ed Leftwich, 62 mins.)

Square Jungle, The (1955)** Tony Curtis, Pat Crowley, Ernest Borgnine, Paul Kelly, David Janssen. Corny prizefight yarn with all the clichés. Tony plays a kid from the wrong side of the tracks who turns to boxing and becomes a temporary champion. The cast struggles with a trite script. (Dir: Jerry Hopper, 86 mins.)

Square of Violence (U.S.-Yugoslavia, 1961)**½ Broderick Crawford, Branko Plesa, Valentina Cortesa, Bibi Andersson. When Yugoslav partisans in WW II kill 30 Nazi officers, 300 innocent men are taken hostage by the Germans. Crawford is the partisan responsible for the bombing, torn between his loyalty to the cause and his concern for the 300. A tense, little-known picture, director Leonardo Bercovici's first. (98 mins.)

Square Shooter, The (1951)**½ Maxie Rosenbloom, Max Baer. Two-gun "Skipalong" Rosenbloom tames feared outlaw "Butcher" Baer in this western burlesque. Crude slapstick, but funny at times. (Dir: Sam Newfield, 72 mins.)

Squeaker, The (West Germany, 1965)** Heinz Drache, Barbara Rutting. Scotland Yard traces a robber-murderer who uses snake venom on his victims. Edgar Wallace mystery leaves a lot of loose ends dangling; some suspenseful scenes. (Dir: Alfred Vohrer, 93 mins.)

Squeeze a Flower (Australia, 1969)* Jack Albertson, Walter Chiari, Dave Allen. (Dir: Marc Daniels, 102 mins.)

SS Strikes at Dawn, The (Yugoslavia, 1966)* Frederick Lake, Joseph Laurentz. (79 mins.)

Sssssss (1973)*½ Strother Martin, Heather Menzies. (Dir: Bernard L. Kowalski, 99 mins.)

SST-Death Flight (MTV 1977)** Lorne Greene, Susan Strasberg, Burgess Meredith. Tale about a planeload of passengers who suddenly are confronted with a life-and-death situation. The maiden trip of the first supersonic plane—and the invited guest list includes celebrities, contest winners, and a scientist carrying a deadly virus. Guess what happens! (Dir: David Lowell Rich, 106 mins.)

St.—See: **Saint**

Stage Door (1937)***½ Katharine Hepburn, Ginger Rogers, Adolphe Menjou, Lucille Ball. RKO made the Edna Ferber-George S. Kaufman play into a vehicle for Hepburn and Rogers; sometimes corny, it nevertheless captures the manic-depressive dormitory atmosphere of young actresses trying to make it in New York. Rogers is pseudo-tough and on the offensive; Hepburn is the starry-eyed rebel, always parrying. Appealing and funny. Gregory LaCava, master of off-the-cuff '30s comedy, directed. (93 mins.)

Stage Door Canteen (1943)**½ Lon McCallister, Cheryl Walker, Sunset Carson, Katharine Cornell, William Terry. Interesting curio set in a WW II USO canteen where the guest celebrities seem to outnumber the servicemen by about ten to one: Tallulah Bankhead, Edgar Bergen, Helen Hayes, Johnny Weissmuller, Katharine Hepburn, Paul Muni, Merle Oberon, Harpo Marx, and others appear, and the nonstop swing soundtrack features Benny Goodman, Count Basie, Xavier Cugat, and, alas, Kay Kyser and Guy Lombardo. (Dir: Frank Borzage, 132 mins.)

Stage Fright (Great Britain, 1950)***½ Marlene Dietrich, Jane Wyman, Michael Wilding, Richard Todd, Alastair Sim. Alfred Hitchcock, back in an English setting for the first time in over a decade, directs an uneven story about a young man (Todd) suspected of murdering an actress's husband. Dietrich is effective in a music hall role (singing "The Laziest Gal in Town"), but Wyman is unequal to the difficult demands of being a Hitchcock heroine. (110 mins.)

Stage Struck (1957)**½ Henry Fonda, Susan Strasberg, Christopher Plummer, Herbert Marshall. Remake of Hepburn's "Morning Glory," relating the tale of a young girl whose ambitions spur her on to become a great actress. Strasberg doesn't live up to the role, which hurts the film; otherwise, some good New York atmosphere, other performances. First film by Plummer, one of our most brilliant stage actors and a movie name thanks to "Sound of Music." (Dir: Sidney Lumet, 95 mins.)

Stage to Thunder Rock (1964)** Barry Sullivan, Marilyn Maxwell, Scott Brady, Lon Chaney, Jr., Keenan Wynn. Standard western item about gunslinger and his prisoner, padded with some pretentious comments on the mercenary side of justice, but tight action pacing, good acting helps. (Dir: William F. Claxton, 82 mins.)

Stage to Tucson (1950)**½ Rod Cameron, Wayne Morris, Sally Eilers. Two Civil War buddies are sent to Tucson to investigate the many stage coach hi-jackings and find more trouble than they bargained for. Action-crammed western. (Dir: Ralph Murphy, 82 mins.)

Stagecoach (1939)**** John Wayne, Claire Trevor, Thomas Mitchell (Oscar), George Bancroft, Andy Devine, John Carradine. The most famous, and the weakest, of director of John Ford's major westerns is burdened with a pretentious Dudley Nichols script (a "cross section of society" is aboard the stagecoach), but its virtues remain intact. The visual contrast of claustrophobic interior spaces (the coach, the various way stations), with the expanse of Monument Valley, provides a vivid physical correlative to the film's thematic push for freedom. (96 mins.)

Stagecoach (1966)**½ Ann-Margret, Alex Cord, Bing Crosby, Red Buttons. An all-star remake of the classic John Ford–John Wayne western. Action is still pretty good the second time around. Gordon Douglas directed. (114 mins.)

Staircase (Great Britain, 1969)***½ Rex Harrison, Richard Burton, Cathleen Nesbitt. Film from the Charles Dyer play was a box-office failure. Director Stanley Donen brings a plaintive note of desperation to this story of two aging, bickering homosexuals who share a London flat. Harrison manages only surfaces, but Burton turns in one of his best performances as the more vulnerably domestic of the two. A bandage about his head, Burton is the very image of morose need. (96 mins.)

Stairway to Heaven (Great Britain, 1946)***½ David Niven, Roger Livesey, Kim Hunter, Raymond Massey. Outrageous fantasy-drama, in which Niven plays a flier whose brain is damaged when he bails out of his plane; he has visions that he has actually been to heaven. Very bad good film. Alternate title: "A Matter of Life and Death." (Writer-Dirs: Michael Powell, Emeric Pressburger, 104 mins.)

Stakeout (1962)*½ Bing Russell, Billy Hughes, Eve Brent. (Dir: James Landis, 81 mins.)

Stalag 17 (1953)**** William Holden, Robert Strauss, Peter Graves. Tale of a POW camp is laced with director Billy Wilder's special brand of cynicism. Holden (Academy Award) plays a sergeant suspected of being a spy. Much funny byplay of men at loose ends. (120 mins.)

Stalk the Wild Child (MTV 1976)**½ David Janssen, Trish Van Devere, Joseph Bottoms, Benjamin Bottoms. A boy found running with a pack of wild dogs is brought to a university medical center for observation and rehabilitation. It gets muddled while behavioral psychologist Janssen and speech therapist Van Devere work to make a full-rounded, socially acceptable person out of the wild boy. Ben Bottoms plays the lad in the early scenes, and his real-life brother Joseph is the grown-up Cal. (Dir: William Hale, 78 mins.)

Stalking Moon, The (1968)**½ Gregory Peck, Eva Marie Saint. Peck and Miss Saint do well in this tightly paced western drama which requires some initial patience before getting into the story. Eva Marie Saint is released after being a prisoner of the Apaches for a number of years, with her nine-year-old half-breed son, but the boy's Indian father stalks them. Primarily a chase film. (Dir: Robert Mulligan, 109 mins.)

Stallion Road (1947)** Ronald Reagan, Alexis Smith, Zachary Scott. Ron is a veterinarian and Alexis a lovely rancher in this dull romantic drama which offers nothing more than some good looking horses. (Dir: James V. Kern, 97 mins.)

Stand at Apache River (1953)**½ Stephen McNally, Julia Adams, Hugh Marlowe, Hugh O'Brian, Jack Kelly. Familiar western yarn about a group of strangers who find themselves stranded in a secluded trading post inn waiting for an inevitable Apache attack. Some suspense. (Dir: Lee Sholem, 77 mins.)

Stand By for Action (1942)**½ Robert Taylor, Brian Donlevy, Walter Brennan, Charles Laughton, Marilyn Maxwell. The snooty wartime naval officer in conflict with the regular navy man, the sinking of a Jap ship, some salty humor create an occasionally entertaining but generally tiresome film. (Dir: Robert Z. Leonard, 109 mins.)

Stand By Your Man (MTV 1981)**½ Annette O'Toole, Cooper Huckabee, Helen Page Camp, James Hampton. This is Tammy Wynette's tale of the Memphis beauty-parlor student who sings her way into the hearts of country music fans, despite electric shock treatment, young 'uns and stormy marriages. Cooper Huckabee and Tim McIntire play Tammy's first and third husbands as the flick conveniently overlooks number two. Parallels are obvious between the big screen "Coal Miner's Daughter" and "Stand By Your Man," with Annette O'Toole convincing as survivor Tammy. (Dir: Jerry Jameson, 104 mins.)

Stand-In (1937)***½ Joan Blondell, Leslie Howard, Humphrey Bogart, Alan Mowbray, Jack Carson. Rollicking screwball farce about a timid but efficient accountant sent to re-organize a bankrupt Hollywood studio. He decides to find out how the place works from the bottom up, and learns the ropes from a sexy but under-employed "stand-in." Fast and funny, with a fine supporting cast, and some electric romancing between the two leads. Bogart, as a cynical director whose best friend is a little black Scottie dog, once again proves he could play any role. (Dir: Tay Garnett, 90 mins.)

Stand Up and Be Counted (1972)**½ Jacqueline Bisset, Stella Stevens, Steve Lawrence, Gary Lockwood, Loretta Swit. Hollywood discovers women's lib, but insists on adding the usual bunch of stereotypes. Miss Bisset plays a fashion magazine journalist who covers the women's lib scene in Denver. The characters she meets are primarily used for old gags that lampoon the tenets of the movement. (Dir: Jackie Cooper, 99 mins.)

Stand Up and Cheer (1934)**½ Warner Baxter, Madge Evans, James Dunn, Shirley Temple. Crazy depression musical has the president creating a cabinet post for the secretary of amusement in the hope of laughing gloom away. Occasionally amusing but very dated. Will Rogers worked on the screenplay. (Dir: Hamilton MacFadden, 80 mins.)

Standing Room Only (1944)**½ Fred MacMurray, Paulette Goddard, Edward Arnold. A secretary books herself and boss on as servants in a Washington home to avoid the hotel room shortage. Funny when it was topical but only mildly amusing today. (Dir: Sidney Lanfield, 83 mins.)

Stanley and Livingstone (1939)*** Spencer Tracy, Cedric Hardwicke, Nancy Kelly, Richard Greene, Walter Brennan. Reasonably intelligent and moderately entertaining historical epic. Location footage from Africa is employed extensively, and Tracy gives his usual professional reading of the intrepid journalist Henry M. Stanley who goes searching for missionary-explorer David Livingstone. (Dir: Henry King, 101 mins.)

Star, The (1952)*** Bette Davis, Sterling Hayden, Natalie Wood. It's mostly Davis in this portrait of an aging Hollywood actress trying for a comeback. Good support from Hayden. Director Stuart Heisler juggles the clichés adroitly. (91 mins.)

Star (1968)** Julie Andrews, Daniel Massey, Richard Crenna, Robert Reed. Disappointing musical based on the life and career of the legendary Broadway theater star, English-born actress Gertrude Lawrence. Directed by Robert Wise and boasting songs by such greats as Cole Porter and Noël Coward, "Star" becomes overly sentimental and winds up depicting Miss Lawrence as a grown-up girl scout modeled on Mary Poppins. The best performance in the film is from Daniel Massey playing Coward. (Dir: Robert Wise, 122 mins.)

Star Crash (1979)** Marjoe Gortner, Christopher Plummer, Caroline Munro. Galactic adventure is uneven, occasionally appealing. Music by John Barry. (Writer-Dir: Lewis Coates, 91 mins.)

Star Dust (1940)**½ Linda Darnell, John Payne, Roland Young. Story of young hopefuls trying to break through in Hollywood is mildly entertaining. (Dir: Walter Lang, 85 mins.)

Star Is Born, A (1937)***½ Fredric March, Janet Gaynor, Adolphe Menjou, Lionel Stander. Here's the original version of the poignant, dramatic story about a famous Hollywood star whose popularity declines as his young actress-wife reaches superstardom. March, as the matinee idol on the skids, and Gaynor, as his loyal wife, are perfectly cast and keep the story from slipping into cheap sentimentality. The direction by William Wellman hits the right note, and the fine screenplay by Dorothy Parker, Alan Campbell and Robert Carson reveals a great deal about Hollywood in the 30's. (Dir: William Wellman, 110 mins.)

Star Is Born, A (1954)**** Judy Garland, James Mason, Charles Bickford, Jack Carson. The clichéd Hollywood story of a husband forced into second place by his wife's career has been often told but it almost doesn't matter thanks to Judy's musical genius and a fine supporting cast. Judy's star was reborn with this film and James Mason adds another moving performance to his list. Garland's songs include "Born in a Trunk" and the sound of Judy's voice is certainly one of the enduring monuments of this century. (Dir: George Cukor, 154 mins.)

Star Is Born, A (1976)*½ Barbra Streisand, Kris Kristofferson. (140 mins.)

Star Spangled Girl, The (1971)*½ Sandy Duncan, Tony Roberts, Todd Susmann. (Dir: Jerry Paris, 93 mins.)

Star-Spangled Rhythm (1942)*** All-star cast. Gigantic variety is loaded with talent, but most of their ammunition is blank. Flimsy plot has little to do with the film, but Victor Moore is good as the studio gate keeper who's supposed to be an executive. (Dir: George Marshall, 99 mins.)

Star Trek—the Motion Picture (1979)** William Shatner, Leonard Nimoy, Stephen Collins, Persis Khambatta, DeForest Kelley. A major sci-fi disappointment. The expensive special effects frequently look substandard, so it still plays like a TV show. Robert Wise directs dully and mechanically. Some philosophical discussions which sound like an intergalactic rendition of Abbott and Costello's "Who's on First" routine. Khambatta is riveting. (132 mins.)

Star Wars (1977)**** Mark Hamill, Harrison Ford, Alec Guinness, Carrie Fisher, Peter Cushing, Anthony Daniels, David Prowse. Zowie! A technically dazzling and enjoyable science fiction film for children of all ages. The plot is the bad guys (the galactic empire) vs. the good guys (the rebels). You'll root for the good guys and hope the beautiful young princess (Fisher) will be rescued by two young Prince Charmings (Hamill and Ford). You'll still enjoy the film on TV, but of course much is lost in the transfer from the big screen. Wizard special effects, and George Lucas's direction is perfection and grace incarnate. (121 mins.)

Stardust (Great Britain, 1974)*** David Essex, Adam Faith, Larry Hagman. Shallow but slick. Director Michael Apted's portrait of a British rock star—from obscurity to fame to pop deification—captures most of the surface sensations of the cult culture of the '60s. Essex is credible as the superstar, and Hagman is just as credible as the American conglomerate builder who packages and markets him; but Faith is the real surprise, with a detailed, compelling performance as the enigmatic road manager. (107 mins.)

Stardust Memories (1980)**** Woody Allen, Charlotte Rampling, Jessica Harper, Marie-Christine Barrault. Autobiographical story of a filmmaker besieged by fans, overanalyzed by critics, and tormented by multiple love affairs reveals

625

the waspish, malcontent side of Allen more than his previous films. The three women in the hero's life get short shrift as he strenuously questions the meaning of life between slashes at his favorite targets. Allen's smugness has previously always been held in check by a genuine concern with the other characters in his films; the wages of self-contemplation for him seem to be disconnected and barely involving narrative. Director Allen's movies about the meaning of love are more effective than his movies about the meaning of life. B&W. (91 mins.)

Starlift (1951)** Doris Day, Gordon MacRae, Virginia Mayo, Gene Nelson, Janice Rule, Ruth Roman, and hosts of stars. All the Warner Brothers stars get together in this one to entertain the troops. Thin plot line serves merely as a wait between acts—and the acts are hardly worth it. (Dir: Roy Del Ruth, 103 mins.)

Stars and Stripes Forever (1952)**½ Clifton Webb, Debra Paget, Robert Wagner, Ruth Hussey, Finlay Currie. Enjoyable musical having practically nothing to do with the life of John Philip Sousa. A friendly little fictional family drama is substituted for biography, but the music is authentic, rousing, and constantly well-performed. (Dir: Henry Koster, 89 mins.)

Stars Are Singing, The (1953)** Rosemary Clooney, Anna Maria Alberghetti, Lauritz Melchior. Singer shelters an escaped immigrant girl, finds she has a fine voice. Syrupy musical with the vocalistics far superior to the script. (Dir: Norman Taurog, 99 mins.)

Stars in My Crown (1950)**½ Joel McCrea, Ellen Drew, Dean Stockwell. There's a quiet charm about this film but it's not enough to overcome the soap-opera plot line about a self-made parson and his effect on a small Southern town. (Dir: Jacques Tourneur, 89 mins)

Stars Look Down, The (Great Britain, 1939)**** Margaret Lockwood, Michael Redgrave. Dramatic tale of the life of Welsh coal miners, the ensuing tragedy. Grimly realistic, finely directed by Carol Reed, well acted. (110 mins.)

Starship Invasions (Canada, 1978)** Robert Vaughn, Christopher Lee, Helen Shaver. Ripoff of the big hit sci-fi films of the last few years made it from theaters to TV in record time. The cast do their best with the subpar script about a UFO expert (Vaughn) who befriends a peaceful group of aliens to stop a villainous alien captain (Lee) from taking over the Earth. (Dir: Ed Hunt, 89 mins.)

Starsky and Hutch (MTV 1975)**½ Paul Michael Glaser, David Soul, Michael Lerner. Another police yarn about undercover cops who face syndicate hit men, but creator William Blinn manages to hold interest because of his ability to develop believable characters. Starsky and Hutch (played by Glaser and Soul, respectively), portray two ingratiating, brave

people. Pilot for the series. (Dir: Barry Shear, 72 mins.)

Start the Revolution Without Me (1970)**½ Donald Sutherland, Gene Wilder, Hugh Griffith, Orson Welles. Sometimes funny farce starts out promisingly. Sutherland and Wilder, two of the movies' better comedy actors, ham it up to the nth degree as a pair of twins (that's right, four of 'em) who are separated at birth (one from each set), with two lads growing up in French aristocracy while the other pair are reared as peasants. The setting for this classic yarn of mistaken identity is the French Revolution. (Dir: Bud Yorkin, 90 mins.)

Starting Over (1979)*** Burt Reynolds, Candice Bergen, Jill Clayburgh, Paul Sorvino, Austin Pendleton. Engaging comedy of modern manners. Basically a love triangle, with writer Burt trying to choose between teacher Clayburgh and ex-wife Bergen, a writer of hideous pop songs. The romance is fun, but the best scenes are with Burt's companions in group therapy. (Dir: Alan J. Pakula, 106 mins.)

State Fair (1933)*** Will Rogers, Janet Gaynor, Lew Ayres. Rogers takes his prize pig, Blue Boy, to the Kansas State Fair in the first and best film version of the Phil Stong novel. Director Henry King elicited some homespun virtues from the material, giving it a credible, warm feeling. (80 mins.)

State Fair (1945)*** Jeanne Crain, Dana Andrews, Charles Winninger. Richard Rodgers and Oscar Hammerstein II wrote original songs for this remake; otherwise the Will Rogers version is superior. Oscar to Rodgers and Hammerstein for Best Original Song, "It Might as Well Be Spring." Color. (Dir: Walter Lang, 100 mins.)

State Fair (1962)** Pat Boone, Ann-Margaret, Bobby Darin, Alice Faye, Tom Ewell. Third time around for this musical tale of a family attending the Iowa State Fair, and the various romantic mixups. This one lacks sparkle, freshness, lags well behind the other two in entertainment values. (Dir: José Ferrer, 118 mins.)

State of Siege (France, 1973)***½ Yves Montand, Renato Salvatori, O. E. Hasse. Director Costa-Gavras's camera work makes it virtually impossible to see anything onscreen clearly, so the film must make its appeal on the basis of content. Piquant political drama about the kidnapping and assassination of an American "technical expert" on police methods in Uruguay; at the time of its release, this was the most direct indictment of American clandestine support for anti-guerrilla fascist activities in Latin America to reach our screens. (120 mins.)

State of the Union (1948)*** Spencer Tracy, Katharine Hepburn, Angela Lansbury, Van Johnson, Adolphe Menjou. An honest businessman is persuaded to run for public office, finds his ideals in danger. Some good satire on the logistics of politics, which haven't changed as much as we think. But this wobbles between comedy and drama. Expert players keep it rolling along, though. (Dir: Frank Capra, 124 mins.)

State Secret (Great Britain, 1950)**** Douglas Fairbanks, Jr., Glynis Johns, Jack Hawkins, Herbert Lom. Noted surgeon is tricked into aiding the head of a European police state, flees with the secret police not far behind. Excellent suspense thriller played lightly; laughs, thrills and fun. (Dir: Sidney Gilliat, 97 mins.)

Station Six Sahara (Great Britain-Germany, 1963)*** Carroll Baker, Peter Van Eyck, Ian Bannen. Into a small group of men running an oil station in the Sahara comes a beautiful blonde who starts the emotions soaring. Lusty melodrama on the sizzling side with a well-written script obscuring the familiarity of the tale, and capable direction and performances adding to it. (Dir: Seth Holt, 99 mins.)

Station West (1948)*** Dick Powell, Jane Greer, Burl Ives, Agnes Moorehead. Army officer goes undercover to trap a gang of hi-jackers and murderers. Good western has enough action, is well acted. (Dir: Sidney Lanfield, 92 mins.)

Statue, The (1971)** David Niven, Virna Lisi, Robert Vaughn. Prudish comedy as domestic bliss is threatened when Miss Lisi carves a nude 18-foot statue of her Nobel Peace Prize-winning husband Niven. The catch—Niven is mad because the bottom half does not resemble him. He searches for the real model thinking his wife has cheated on him. A mawkish, immature mess. (Dir: Ron Amateau, 84 mins.)

Stavisky (France-Italy, 1974)***½ Jean-Paul Belmondo, Charles Boyer, Anny Duperey. Director Alain Resnais's generally absorbing drama about corruption in France in the '30s. Focuses on the famous Stavisky case, a financial swindle conceived by a flamboyant conman (Belmondo) and involving top government officials. Production, thanks partly to costumes by Yves St. Laurent, captures the look of rich, decadent France of that time. (117 mins.)

Stay Hungry (1976)**½ Jeff Bridges, Sally Field, Arnold Schwarzenegger, Scatman Crothers, Joe Santo. Promising premise of a young, privileged boy intent on his independence, and the spunky working girl he lives with, fizzles out due to unmanageable plot strands. Bridges is wonderful as the boy who occupies a Tara-like mansion, and Miss Field's first mature role shows her at her best. The gym club that Bridges invests in is authentically peopled by such brawny iron-pumpers as former Mr. Universe, Arnold Schwarzenegger. Based on the novel by Charles Gaines. Some nice touches from director Bob Rafelson, who needs a firmer hand. (103 mins.)

Steamboat Bill Jr. (1928)**** Buster Keaton, Ernest Torrence, Marion Byron. Keaton, a recent Yale graduate, comes home after many years to find his father, an irascible Mississippi riverboat captain, in deep trouble with a competing big company. Buster saves the day, though he must brave jail and a great hurricane to do it. One of the best comedies ever made. (Dir: Charles F. Reisner, 70 mins.)

Steel Bayonet (Great Britain, 1957)** Leo Genn, Kieron Moore. Fairly well made British war drama. The performances outrank the film's rambling script about the exploits of a division of soldiers assigned a dangerous task. (Dir: Michael Carreras, 84 mins.)

Steel Claw, The (1961)**½ George Montgomery, Charito Luna. Marine about to be discharged because of the loss of a hand organizes guerrillas when the Japanese invade the Philippines. Fine photography, plenty of action compensate for a weak script in this frequently exciting war drama, very capably directed by Montgomery. (96 mins.)

Steel Cowboy (MTV 1978)** James Brolin, Rip Torn, Strother Martin, Jennifer Warren. A trucker about to go broke hauls stolen cattle for a black market bigwig, and manages to outsmart the opposition. Brolin and Torn are the truckers, and the sly Martin is the black marketeer, and a scene stealer. (Dir: Harvey Laidman, 104 mins.)

Steel Fist, The (1952)** Roddy McDowall, Kristine Miller. Good try at serious drama about a U.S. student who's trapped in an Iron Curtain country but it doesn't quite come off. The script is on the pedestrian side and even McDowall's earnest performance can't lift it out of the ordinary adventure groove. (Dir: Wesley Barry, 73 mins.)

Steel Helmet, The (1951)***½ Gene Evans, Robert Hutton, Steve Brodie, James Edwards, Richard Loo. During the Korean War a battle-worn American sergeant (Evans) forms a survival pact with a Korean orphan. Samuel Fuller's powerful direction turns a trite story into a vivid study of national and personal identity. (84 mins.)

Steel Key, The (Great Britain, 1953)*** Terence Morgan, Joan Rice, Dianne Foster. Two scientists working on a secret process for hardening steel die suddenly, and a private investigator tracks down the reason behind it all. Good melodrama moves at a fast pace. (Dir: Robert Baker, 69 mins.)

Steel Town (1952)** Ann Sheridan, John Lund, Howard Duff. Usual drama about two guys vying for the same girl and a top spot in a large steel mill. (Dir: George Sherman, 85 mins.)

Steel Trap, The (1952)***½ Joseph Cotten, Teresa Wright. A banker steals five hundred thousand dollars on a Friday afternoon, and frantically tries to return it by

Monday. Suspenseful melodrama, keeps one guessing, excited. (Dir: Andrew L. Stone, 85 mins.)

Steelyard Blues (1973)** Jane Fonda, Donald Sutherland, Peter Boyle. Director Alan Myerson (with his revue background) made this disjointed, cheaply made jokefest about a bunch of lunatics and their efforts to have a good time. Three nonconformists band together to steal an electrical circuit which will enable them to fly away. Tolerance for pranksterism is required. (93 mins.)

Stella Dallas (1925)**½ Belle Bennett, Ronald Colman, Alice Joyce, Jean Hersholt, Douglas Fairbanks, Jr. Bennett plays the vulgar woman who gives up her daughter so the kid can have the advantages of an upbringing by a wealthy family. Of course, the girl grows up to despise women like her mother. Adaptation of the popular Olive Higgins Prouty novel. (Dir: Henry King, 112 mins.)

Stella Dallas (1937)**½ Barbara Stanwyck, John Boles, Anne Shirley. In this classic tearjerker Stanwyck plays a crude, common woman who marries but can't hold on to blueblood Boles. When she realizes she is an obstacle to the marriage of her beloved daughter Shirley into wealthy society, Stanwyck gives her daughter up. No movie has ever questioned less the desirability of being socially acceptable. (111 mins.)

Step Down to Terror (1959)** Colleen Miller, Charles Drake, Rod Taylor, Jocelyn Brando. So-so remake of "Shadow of a Doubt"—son returns home to his family, is eventually found to be a psychotic killer. Just fair suspense melodrama. (Dir: Harry Keller, 76 mins.)

Step Lively (1944)*** Frank Sinatra, George Murphy, Gloria De Haven. Fast-thinking theatrical producer gets his show on despite financial problems. Lively, enjoyable musical. Remake of "Room Service." (Dir: Tim Whelan, 88 mins.)

Step Out of Line, A (MTV 1971)*** Peter Falk, Peter Lawford, Vic Morrow, Jo Ann Pflug. Amateurs carry out the robbery of a San Francisco money exchange company in exciting fashion, goofing at crucial moments. Falk's role is the toughest, since he must change from a straight-as-an-arrow guy. (Dir: Bernard McEveety, 100 mins.)

Stepford Wives, The (1975)** Katherine Ross, Paula Prentiss, Nanette Newman, Patrick O'Neal, Tina Louise. Ross stars as a young suburban wife whose investigations into the strange transformation of her female neighbors into mindless robots leads to a grisly secret. The cast—with the exception of the always delightful Prentiss—are dreary, and by the time the mystery takes shape, it's hardly possible to care. (Dir: Bryan Forbes, 115 mins.)

Steppenwolf (U.S.-Switzerland, 1974)**½ Max von Sydow, Dominique Sanda, Pierre Clementi. Director Fred Haines tried valiantly to film the Hermann Hesse classic about the dual nature (ordered/animalistic or ascetic/hedonistic) of humanity, but his elliptical style comes across as merely indecisive, and his visual trickery as merely facile. Von Sydow and Sanda rub accents and manage to generate a few dramatic sparks. (105 mins.)

Sterile Cuckoo, The (1969)***½ Liza Minnelli, Wendell Burton. Touching romance of Pookie Adams (Minnelli), a kook who insists upon calling all those who won't participate in her world "weirdos," and the innocent straight (Burton) she captivates. Miss Minnelli is quite remarkable in her heartbreaking portrayal of a neurotic college girl creating obvious games to shut out dealing with the world. Liza was nominated for an Academy Award for this one. The film often plods due to the first directorial effort by Alan J. Pakula, but it finally gets where it was destined to go. Even, quiet, and touching. (107 mins.)

Stevie (Great Britain, 1978)**½ Glenda Jackson, Trevor Howard, Alec McCowen, Mona Washbourne. Tiresome talkfest includes incidents involving, and poems by, Stevie Smith, one of a long line of mild English literary eccentrics. Jackson is unconvincing, but Washbourne does well with her pointless part, and McCowen etches an incisive cameo as the frustrated suitor. (Dir: Robert Enders, 102 mins.)

Stiletto (1969)*** Alex Cord, Britt Ekland, Barbara McNair. Sex and violence fill this disjointed pop movie based on the Harold Robbins novel. Cord is a jet-setter with a posh yacht, beautiful women at his side (Ekland and McNair), and killers out to get him. (Dir: Bernard Kowalski, 108 mins.)

Sting, The (1973)**** Paul Newman, Robert Redford, Robert Shaw. A marvelously entertaining caper about two deft con men (Newman and Redford) operating in and around Chicago circa '36. Director George Roy Hill gives the film a fast pace and a glittering visual style. There are some rollicking Scott Joplin musical rags in this exuberant comedy. Great wrap-up scene as Newman and Redford swindle Shaw out of a big bundle in one of the most inventive schemes ever depicted on screen. Winner of seven Academy Awards. (129 mins.)

Stingray (1978)** Christopher Mitchum, Sherry Jackson, Les Lannom. Weird comedy with lots of action and death, as Mitchum and Lannom are pursued by a murderous gang trying to grab the cache of heroin hidden in their car. Jackson, disguised as a nun, tries hard to be tough as the leader of the cutthroats. Made in and around St. Louis, this one definitely isn't subtle. (Dir: Richard Taylor, 99 mins.)

Stir Crazy (1980)**½ Richard Pryor, Gene Wilder, George Stanford Brown. Uneven but incredibly popular comedy of two inept thieves sent to the Big House. The writing and direction are pretty lumpish, Wilder doesn't have much to do, but Pryor is always wonderful—all he has to do is show his face. (Dir: Sidney Poitier, 111 mins.)

Stitch in Time, A (Great Britain, 1963)** Norman Wisdom, Edward Chapman, Jeanett Sterke. Typical slapstick vehicle for Britain's most popular vaudeville star, Wisdom. Incidental plot keeps the clown cavorting around a hospital where his boss is having an operation for a swallowed watch. (Dir: Robert Asher, 94 mins.)

Stolen Face (Great Britain, 1952)*** Paul Henreid, Lizabeth Scott. A plastic surgeon molds the face of a convict into a replica of his lost love. Interesting drama. (Dir: Terence Fisher, 73 mins.)

Stolen Hours (Great Britain, 1963)** Susan Hayward, Michael Craig, Diane Baker. Poor remake of Bette Davis's "Dark Victory" has Hayward as the darling of the international set until she takes ill. Her whole life takes on new meaning when handsome Dr. Craig enters it. (Dir: Daniel Petrie, 97 mins.)

Stolen Life, A (1946)**½ Bette Davis, Glenn Ford, Dane Clark, Walter Brennan, Charles Ruggles, Bruce Bennett. Bette has a fine time playing twins who are in love with the same man in this soap opera. Then one is killed in an accident and the other takes her place. Pretty far-fetched, but fun to watch, thanks to a troupe of pro's. (Dir: Curtis Bernhardt, 107 mins.)

Stone (MTV 1979)**½ Dennis Weaver, Vic Morrow, Roy Thinnes. Pilot film stars Weaver as Stone, a homicide detective turned famous author. He must track down a mad killer who's following the murder scheme laid out in his book. Writer-producer Stephen J. Cannell comes up with a decent police story. (Dir: Corey Allen, 104 mins.)

Stone Killer, The (1973)** Charles Bronson, Martin Balsam, Ralph Waite, Norman Fell. Violent crime film, based on John Gardner's book "A Complete State of Death." Bronson plays a police officer, who stops at nothing to track down the plans of a crazed underworld figure out for revenge for the gangland assassinations of his cronies in 1931. Exciting finale set in a remote desert fortress, where Vietnam veterans are being trained to kill those remaining men who were responsible for the gangland killings. (Dir: Michael Winner, 97 mins.)

Stonestreet (MTV 1977)* Barbara Eden, Joan Hackett, Richard Basehart. (Dir: Russ Mayberry, 78 mins.)

Stooge, The (1952)** Dean Martin, Jerry Lewis, Polly Bergen. Singer uses a song plugger in his act, treats him badly—then flops when the stooge leaves him. Comedy for Martin and Lewis fans is no great shakes as humor or backstage drama. (Dir: Norman Taurog, 100 mins.)

Stoolie, The (1974)**½ Jackie Mason, Dan Frazer, Marcia Jean Kurtz. Genial, sentimental treatment of a police informer who runs off to Miami Beach with $7,500 lent by the police department of N.Y. As a love story between two less than attractive people, this is quite touching, but as a tale of the underworld, the plotting is laughable. Cluttered by details like a parrot who roller skates. Mason's gritty performance is surprisingly skillful. Directed by John Avildsen ("Rocky") between two more ambitious efforts, "Joe" and "Save the Tiger." (90 mins.)

Stop! Look! and Laugh! (1960)** The Three Stooges, Paul Winchell. Half old footage of The Three Stooges comedies and half new stuff featuring Paul Winchell and his dummy Jerry Mahoney. Verdict: for half-pints. (Dir: Jules White, 78 mins.)

Stop Me Before I Kill (Great Britain, 1961)**½ Claude Dauphin, Diane Cilento, Ronald Lewis. After a crash an auto racer recovers physically but finds himself trying to murder his wife. Fairly entertaining melodrama has enough twists and turns to keep the mystery fans guessing. Good performances. (Dir: Val Guest, 108 mins.)

Stop the World, I Want to Get Off (Great Britain, 1966)**½ Tony Tanner, Millicent Martin. Unfortunately, this literal screen version of the successful Broadway and London musical hit becomes boring before too long, although there are some standout songs including "What Kind of Fool Am I?" Tony Tanner makes a good Littlechap, a sort of everyday Everyman who goes through his life in song, dance and mime. Music and lyrics by Anthony Newley and Leslie Bricuse. Newley starred in the theater and he's a more inventive performer than Tanner. (Dir: Philip Saville, 98 mins.)

Stop Train 349 (France-Italy-West Germany, 1964)** Sean Flynn, Jose Ferrer, Nicole Courcel. Young lieutenant faces the Russians who want to search a train for an East German defector. Merely passable suspense drama suffers from overstated treatment, slowness of pace. (Dir: Rolf Haedrich, 95 mins.)

Stop, You're Killing Me (1952)** Broderick Crawford, Claire Trevor, Virginia Gibson, Bill Hayes. Remake of "A Slight Case of Murder." About a big time beer baron and his cronies. Just doesn't come off. Some tunes are added for good measure. (Dir: Roy Del Ruth, 86 mins.)

Stopover Tokyo (1957)** Robert Wagner, Joan Collins, Edmond O'Brien. The heroes of this spy thriller (Wagner and Ken Scott) behave like two TV series heroes. In other words, they manage to survive against extreme odds; show how brave they really are at the slightest provocation, and have all the beautiful women wish they would give up being Intelligence Agents and settle down. The Orient is the backdrop for murder, intrigues and occasional embraces. (Dir: Richard L. Breen, 100 mins.)

Stork Club, The (1945)**½ Barry Fitzgerald, Betty Hutton. Hat check girl befriends penniless bum who is, naturally, a billionaire. Silly fable is saved by some nice performances. (Dir: Hal Walker, 98 mins.)

Storm Center (1956)**½ Bette Davis, Brian Keith, Kim Hunter. Davis took over from Mary Pickford (in what was to have been Pickford's first film in 23 years) as a small-town librarian who is fired when she refuses to remove a book accused of Communist tendencies from the shelves. Made at the height of popular reaction to McCarthy hysteria, the film trades on liberal impulses in lieu of competent filmmaking. (Dir: Daniel Taradash, 85 mins.)

Storm Fear (1955)**½ Cornel Wilde, Jean Wallace, Dan Duryea. Wounded bank robber shows up at his brother's house to seek shelter. Interesting drama, moves a bit too slowly but is well acted. (Dir: Cornel Wilde, 88 mins.)

Storm in a Teacup (Great Britain, 1937)*** Vivien Leigh, Rex Harrison. Candidate for election in a Scottish town is hurt by an accident with a dog, that is played upon by a young reporter into a national incident. Clever, amusing comedy. Cecil Parker is fine as the pompous politician. (Dirs: Victor Saville, Ian Dalrymple, 86 mins.)

Storm in Jamaica—See: **Passionate Summer**

Storm over the Nile (Great Britain, 1955)**½ Anthony Steel, Laurence Harvey, Mary Ure. Remake of a once great action film, "Four Feathers," is reasonably exciting. Englishman who resigns his army commission goes to the Sudan to prove he is not a coward. (Dirs: Terence Fisher, Zoltan Korda, 107 mins.)

Storm Warning (1950)**½ Ginger Rogers, Ronald Reagan, Doris Day, Steve Cochran. Melodramatic story of a visiting in-law who witnesses a murder by the Ku-Klux-Klan. Good acting by Ginger Rogers. (Dir: Stuart Heisler, 93 mins.)

Stormy Weather (1943)*** Lena Horne, Bill Robinson, Fats Waller, Dooley Wilson. All-Negro musical has as silly a plot as most musicals but the individual performers do so well that the film provides some sock numbers. (Dir: Andrew L. Stone, 77 mins.)

Story of a Three Day Pass, The (France, 1968)***½ Harry Baird, Nicole Berger, Pierre Doris. The real star of this flawed but touching, honest and rewarding film is its young and talented black writer-director Melvin Van Peebles. (It is a shocking indictment of the American motion picture industry that until this time not a single American movie produced by a major movie company had been directed by a Negro.) Low-budget, independently made entry concerns a bittersweet ro-

mance of a Negro GI in peacetime Paris and a Parisian girl (Berger). The late Miss Berger, killed shortly after completing this film, is most attractive. (87 mins.)

Story of a Woman (U.S.-Italy, 1969)** Robert Stack, Bibi Andersson, Annie Girardot. An involved romance which should please the ladies. Swedish actress Bibi Andersson fluctuates between her American diplomat husband (Robert Stack) and her former flame (James Farentino) and there are many tears and love scenes before the fadeout. (Dir: Leonardo Bercovici, 101 mins.)

Story of Adele H, The (France, 1975)**** Isabelle Adjani, Bruce Robinson, Sylvia Marriott. Director François Truffaut's study of a woman's obsession with a man who doesn't love her is morbidly funny, assisted considerably by the ability of Adjani to play her dour role on several levels of irony. Truffaut makes it deadly clear that obsession is essentially selfish, a dervish spinning of ego about an immaterial object. (Dir: François Truffaut, 97 mins.)

Story of Alexander Graham Bell, The (1939)***½ Don Ameche, Loretta Young, Henry Fonda. Warm, moving story of the man who gave us the telephone. The ending is a bit ridiculous but most of the film, which traces Bell's early disappointments and failures, is top entertainment. (Dir: Irving Pichel, 97 mins.)

Story of David, A (Great Britain, 1960)**½ Jeff Chandler, Basil Sydney, Barbara Shelley, Donald Pleasence. David is unjustly accused of seeking the throne of Israel. Biblical drama originally produced for TV, filmed in Israel. Better than usual production, but generally undistinguished, slow-moving. (Dir: Bob McNaught, 99 mins.)

Story of Dr. Wassell, The (1944)** Gary Cooper, Laraine Day, Signe Hasso. True story of an old doctor who rescued some men from the Japs in Java has been turned into a pulp fiction tale with few facts and little interest. (Dir: Cecil B. De Mille, 136 mins.)

Story of Esther Costello, The (Great Britain, 1957)** Joan Crawford, Rossano Brazzi, Heather Sears. Silly melodrama about a group of greedy promoters who exploit a mute girl as a front for a swindle. The script is cliched and reverts to outrageous melodramatics. (Dir: David Miller, 103 mins.)

Story of G.I. Joe, The (1945)***½ Burgess Meredith, Robert Mitchum. Incidents in the life of famed war correspondent Ernie Pyle, during the bloody Italian campaign. Fine performance, good drama. (Dir: William Wellman, 109 mins.)

Story of Louis Pasteur, The (1936)**** Paul Muni. Not as great as Muni's "Zola" but still a wonderful biographical tribute to the French scientist. Muni is, as usual, superb in this informative and moving film. (Dir: William Dieterle, 87 mins.)

Story of Mankind, The (1957)*½ Ronald Colman, Hedy Lamarr, Groucho Marx, Virginia Mayo, Peter Lorre, Agnes Moorehead, Vincent Price, Chico and Harpo Marx. (Dir: Irwin Allen, 100 mins.)

Story of Pretty Boy Floyd, The (MTV 1974)*** Martin Sheen, Kim Darby, Michael Parks, Ellen Corby. Fine actor Martin Sheen gets a chance to portray the legendary criminal Pretty Boy Floyd in this low-key tale set in the 20's and early 30's, and it's his performance which makes the feature worthwhile. Credit must also go to writer-director Clyde Ware, whose careful attention to period detail adds greatly to the texture of the film. (Dir: Clyde Ware, 72 mins.)

Story of Ruth, The (1960)**½ Elana Eden, Stuart Whitman, Tom Tryon, Viveca Lindfors. Biblical tale of a girl who renounces the worship of pagan gods when she finds the true religion. Stately, interesting drama, despite some dull stretches. (Dir: Henry Koster, 132 mins.)

Story of Seabiscuit (1949)**½ Lon McCallister, Shirley Temple, Barry Fitzgerald. Biography of famous horse is just an excuse for a run-of-the-mill racing picture. Fitzgerald is good as the trainer and there are a few fine racing scenes. (Dir: David Butler, 93 mins.)

Story of the Last Chrysanthemum, The (Japan, 1939)**** Masterwork by director Kenji Mizoguchi is an epic and moving tapestry of ambition, struggle, and sacrifice. A young man in a clan of Kabuki actors turns rebel and seeks fame on his own, only to meet hardship. He reaches acclaim with the help of his completely self-abnegating mistress, the family maid.

Story of Three Loves, The (1953)*** Ethel Barrymore, James Mason, Pier Angeli, Kirk Douglas, Leslie Caron. Each of the three episodes is the flashback of a passenger on an ocean liner; the most interesting is the final episode with Douglas and Angeli. Worth a look. (Dirs: Vincente Minnelli, Gottfried Reinhardt, 122 mins.)

Story of Vernon and Irene Castle (1939)*** Fred Astaire, Ginger Rogers, Walter Brennan. The life and successes of the famous dance team early in the century. Not up to Astaire-Rogers standard, but still entertaining biographical musical. (Dir: H. C. Potter, 93 mins.)

Story of Will Rogers, The (1952)**½ Will Rogers, Jr., Jane Wyman, Eddie Cantor. Slow moving but well done bio-pic of the great humorist Will Rogers. His son, Will Rogers, Jr., looks a great deal like his father, but he inherited none of his dad's charm, talent or wit. (Dir: Michael Curtiz, 109 mins.)

Story on Page One, The (1959)*** Rita Hayworth, Anthony Franciosa, Gig Young. Lawyer agrees to defend two adulterers accused of murdering the lady's husband. Uneven but frequently gripping courtroom drama written and directed by Clifford Odets. Main performances quite good, the legal crossfires dramatically tense. (123 mins.)

Storyteller, The (MTV 1977)**** Martin Balsam, Patty Duke Astin. Balsam plays a Hollywood writer whose TV movie about an arsonist may have resulted in tragedy. A disturbed 12-year-old boy sets fire to his school and dies in the blaze. The question is: Who is to blame? Balsam, given a stimulating script, is splendid as the agonized writer. (Dir: Bob Markowitz, 104 mins.)

Stowaway (1936)*** Shirley Temple, Alice Faye, Robert Young. One of Shirley's best is this tale of a slain Chinese missionary's daughter who stows away on a playboy's yacht and succeeds in solving all problems. (Dir: William A. Seiter, 86 mins.)

Straight on Till Morning (Great Britain, 1972)** Rita Tushingham, Shane Briant, Tom Bell. More style than substance, and few thrills. Young Liverpool lass Tushingham comes to London looking for someone to father a child for her, and meets psycho slayer Briant. Nicely performed, effectively photographed and edited, but that's it. (Dir: Peter Collinson, 96 mins.)

Straight Time (1978)*** Dustin Hoffman, Theresa Russell, Harry Dean Stanton. Interesting but garbled attempt to elucidate the mentality of a hardcore criminal. Hoffman's Max Dembo is a loser who rationalizes his psychotic behavior by a jerk's code of honor. Hoffman makes courageous choices in the role, eschewing charm, but while the performance is true, it never convinces. Excellent supporting cast. (Dir: Ulu Grosbard, 114 mins.)

Strait-Jacket (1964)**½ Joan Crawford, Diane Baker, George Kennedy. Released from a mental hospital years after having committed axe murders, a woman goes to live with her daughter and brother—then axe murders begin again. Unadorned shocker attempts the more flamboyant kind of thrills; mystery fans will see through it, after experiencing a few heart-jumps along the way. (Dir: William Castle, 89 mins.)

Strange Affair, The (Great Britain, 1968)* Michael York, Susan George, Jeremy Kemp. (Dir: David Greene, 106 mins.)

Strange Affection (Great Britain, 1957)**½ Richard Attenborough, Colin Peterson. Boy is accused of murdering his father. Fairly good drama, nice performance by Peterson. (Dir: Wolf Rilla, 84 mins.)

Strange and Deadly Occurrence, The (MTV 1974)** Robert Stack, Vera Miles, L. Q. Jones, Herb Edelman. Homeowners, who think they have headaches, will shudder at the events which throw Robert Stack, Vera Miles and their family into a tailspin when they move into their new home. Fairly clever use of gimmicked suspense ploys. (Dir: John L. Moxey, 72 mins.)

Strange Awakening (Great Britain, 1958)* Lex Barker, Carole Mathews. (Dir: Montgomery Tully, 75 mins.)

Strange Bedfellows (1964)**½ Rock Hudson, Gina Lollobrigida, Gig Young, Terry-Thomas. Wandering business executive tries to reconcile his wife to improve his corporate image. Fairly entertaining comedy based on the unlikely assumption that anyone would desert lovely Lollobrigida for any length of time. Some cute scenes. (Dir: Melvin Frank, 98 mins.)

Strange Cargo (1940)***½ Clark Gable, Joan Crawford, Peter Lorre, Ian Hunter, Albert Dekker, Paul Lukas, Eduardo Ciannelli. Strong, stylized allegory of escapees from Devil's Island. One is remarkably, even mysteriously good (Hunter), one is wholly evil (Lukas). The other characters find themselves having to choose between them. Director Frank Borzage was able to find a style that could accommodate the story's blend of gritty, sweaty realism and semi-fantasy. Film also boasts a fine supporting cast and excellent, committed performances by the leads. (105 mins.)

Strange Case of Dr. Manning (Great Britain, 1958)*½ Ron Randell, Greta Gynt. (Dir: Arthur Crabtree, 75 mins.)

Strange Confession—See: Impostor, The

Strange Countess, The (West Germany, 1961)*½ Joachim Fuchsberger, Marianne Hoppe, Lil Dagover. (Dir: Josef Von Baky, 96 mins.)

Strange Death of Adolf Hitler (1943)** Ludwig Donath, George Dolenz, Gale Sondergaard. Facial double for Hitler is forced by the Gestapo to pose as Der Fuhrer. Doesn't mean much now, but still an intriguing idea. (Dir: James Hogan, 72 mins.)

Strange Door, The (1951)*½ Charles Laughton, Boris Karloff, Sally Forrest. (Dir: Joseph Pevney, 81 mins.)

Strange Homecoming (MTV 1974)** Robert Culp, Barbara Anderson, Glen Campbell. Despite credibility gaps in the story line, star Culp manages to cover up the holes. He plays a murderer who pops up after a long absence and receives a hero's welcome from his sheriff-brother's family. (Dir: Lee H. Katzin, 72 mins.)

Strange Illusion (1945)**½ James Lydon, Warren William, Sally Eilers. An adolescent is suspicious of his widowed mother's boyfriend. This picture has the riveting quality of delirium—framed by dreams, the movie is a nightmare in reel. Director Edgar G. Ulmer's camera tracks and pans through thickets of expressionist shadows, paying only lip service to the action. This is less a movie than a hallucination of a movie—extravagant, and dumbfounding. (80 mins.)

Strange Interlude (1932)*** Norma Shearer, Clark Gable, Robert Young. Interesting screen version of Eugene O'Neill's odd play, in which the characters' thoughts are revealed to the audience through voice-overs. The somber plot concerns a young wife who discovers that insanity runs in her husband's family, and decides to have a child by another man. A bit slow-moving and talky, but the acting is excellent, especially Miss Shearer as the troubled woman. Fine, serious vintage flick. (Dir: Robert Z. Leonard, 110 mins.)

Strange Lady in Town (1955)**½ Greer Garson, Dana Andrews, Cameron Mitchell, Lois Smith. Greer Garson seems out of place in this western. She plays a determined woman whose arrival disturbs Santa Fe's top figures upon her arrival. (Dir: Mervyn LeRoy, 112 mins.)

Strange Love of Martha Ivers, The (1946)*** Barbara Stanwyck, Van Heflin, Kirk Douglas (film debut), Lizabeth Scott, Judith Anderson. In this hard-faced melodrama a woman is haunted by memories of a murder long past. Miss Stanwyck gives a bravura performance as the wealthy neurotic of the title; equally fine is Douglas as her bitter, weak husband. (Dir: Lewis Milestone, 117 mins.)

Strange New World (MTV 1975)*½ John Saxon, Kathleen Miller, Keene Curtis, James Olson. (Dir: Robert Butler, 100 mins.)

Strange One, The (1957)***½ Ben Gazzara, Mark Richman, George Peppard, Pat Hingle, Julie Wilson. Exciting screen version of Calder Willingham's play "End As A Man" about life in a Southern military academy as presided over by a sadistic upper classman. Superb performances by all, with Ben Gazzara a standout in his screen debut. (Dir: Jack Garfein, 97 mins.)

Strange Possession of Mrs. Oliver, The (MTV 1977)**½ Karen Black, George Hamilton. Karen Black is a good actress, and she almost makes this contrived, obvious drama work—but only almost! She plays a housewife who suddenly takes on the personality of a woman who died five years earlier, and it's the split-personality theme which keeps your interest. George Hamilton plays her husband in such a wooden fashion that it makes his wife's search for a new life perfectly understandable. (Dir: Gordon Hessler, 76 mins.)

Strange Shadows in an Empty Room (Italy-Canada, 1977)* Stuart Whitman, Tisa Farrow. (Dir: Martin Herbert, 99 mins.)

Strange World (West Germany-Brazil, 1952)** Angelica Hauff, Alexander Carlos. Man returns to uncharted jungles to search for his father, finds a strange girl living there. Produced by Germans in Brazil, dubbed in English—quite a mixture, but this adventure story turns out fairly well, if a bit on the far-fetched side. Good jungle scenes. (Dir: Franz Eichhorn, 85 mins.)

Stranger, The (1946)***½ Edward G. Robinson, Orson Welles, Loretta Young. A well observed thriller. Robinson stalks a Nazi war criminal to a sleepy college town. His man is director Welles, married to Loretta Young. Welles is especially good at suggesting the menace of connubial domination. (95 mins.)

Stranger, The (Algeria-France-Italy, 1967)

**½ Marcello Mastroianni, Anna Karina, Georges Wilson. Director Luchino Visconti stifles his operatic style to prostrate himself on the altar of literary tribute to Albert Camus. The result is a careful, thematic vulgarization. (104 mins.)

Stranger, The (MTV 1973)**½ Glenn Corbett, Lew Ayres, Cameron Mitchell. Old fugitive plot neatly wrapped up in semi-science-fiction trimmings. Astronaut Corbett crashes on an Earthlike planet known as Terra, and must keep on the run, since his ideas of freedom conflict with the autocratic society called the Perfect Order. (Dir: Lee H. Katzin, 98 mins.)

Stranger and the Gunfighter, The (Italy, 1976)** Lee Van Cleef, Lo Lieh, George Rigaud. Van Cleef brings his monumental ugliness to a spaghetti western with a twist, namely Lieh as a roving kung-fu artist. Some fun but not much. (Dir: Anthony Dawson, 107 mins.)

Stranger at Jefferson High, The (MTV 1981)**½ Stewart Petersen, Dana Kimmell, Philip Brown. Anyone who has moved to a new school and suffered the pains of rejection from established cliques will find this film of special interest. Stewart Petersen plays the new kid at Jefferson High who holds down a job to help his poor widowed mother with the expenses and has to prove himself to the bullies at Jefferson. Familiar but earnest. (Dir: Lyman Dayton, 104 mins.)

Stranger at My Door (1956)*** Macdonald Carey, Patricia Medina, Skip Homeier. Notorious outlaw takes refuge at the home of a preacher, who tries to reform him. Offbeat western is well done. (Dir: William Witney, 85 mins.)

Stranger from Hong Kong (France, 1964)* Dalila, Chin Sing Long. (Dir: Jacques Poitrenaud, 85 mins.)

Stranger from Venus (Great Britain, 1954)**½ Helmut Dantine, Patricia Neal. Remake of "The Day the Earth Stood Still." Dantine replaces Michael Rennie as the alien from another world who brings a message to mankind of peace and brotherhood—or else. Neal repeats her role from the '51 film. (Dir: Burt Balaban, 76 mins.)

Stranger in Between, The (Great Britain, 1952)*** Dirk Bogarde, Jon Whiteley, Elizabeth Sellars. Runaway finds a body and is taken captive by the murderer. Suspenseful, well acted melodrama. (Dir: Charles Crichton, 84 mins.)

Stranger in My Arms, A (1959)** June Allyson, Jeff Chandler, Sandra Dee, Mary Astor. Widow defies her mother-in-law when she meets a man she wants to marry. Good production values, otherwise reminiscent of daytime serials. For the soap fans. (Dir: Helmut Kautner, 88 mins.)

Stranger in Our House (MTV 1978)* Linda Blair, Lee Purcell. (Dir: Wes Craven, 104 mins.)

Stranger in the House—See: **Black Christmas**

Stranger in Town, A (Italy, 1966)*½ Tony Anthony, Frank Wolff. (Dir: Vance Lewis, 86 mins.)

Stranger Knocks, A (Denmark, 1965)***½ Brigitte Federspiel, Preben Rye. A simple, honest, and ultimately extremely moving Danish film that was the subject of a Supreme Court decision in the U.S. The identity of a passing stranger is revealed to a young war widow in a final love scene that is both appropriate and explicit. Without this sequence, this straightforward Danish film is mutilated unfairly and the film is pointless. If your local TV station has the sense to show this film in an evening time slot without cutting it at all, this character study is well worth seeing. (Dir: Johan Jacobsen, 81 mins.)

Stranger on Horseback (1955)*** Joel McCrea, Miroslava, Kevin McCarthy. Fightin' judge cleans up a territory run by one man. Colorful, speedy western, well done. (Dir: Jacques Tourneur, 66 mins.)

Stranger on the Prowl (Italy, 1953)**½ Paul Muni, Joan Lorring. Fugitive from murder is joined by a small boy in his flight from the police. Grim drama, occasionally interesting. (Dir: Joseph Losey, 82 mins.)

Stranger on the Run (MTV 1968)**½ Henry Fonda, Anne Baxter, Michael Parks, Dan Duryea, Sal Mineo. This film is fortunate in having an expert cast to make the characters interesting even when the western drama is pushing to last out the two hours. Henry Fonda is being chased by a band of renegades who've been given badges by a railroad and a free hand to keep things going smoothly in the railroad's town. A first-rate contribution by Michael Parks as the head lawman. (Dir: Don Siegel, 97 mins.)

Stranger on the Third Floor (1940)*** Peter Lorre, John McGuire, Margaret Tallichet, Elisha Cook, Jr. B film done up in High Hollywood Expressionism. It's absurdly overwrought but interesting for it. The director, Boris Ingster, is better with shadows than actors; there's a dream sequence that has to be seen to be disbelieved. A reporter is haunted by the thought that he may have headed an innocent man toward the electric chair, while Lorre creeps around as the embodiment of absolute evil. An effectively creepy, curdled vision (though the ending is a letdown). (Dir: Boris Ingster, 64 mins.)

Stranger Returns, The (Italy-West Germany, 1967)*½ Tony Anthony, Dan Vadis, Jill Banner. (Dir: Vance Lewis, 90 mins.)

Stranger Within, The (MTV 1974)**½ Barbara Eden, George Grizzard. A bizarre tale in the tradition of "Rosemary's Baby." Barbara Eden is quite effective as a normal-appearing woman who finds herself pregnant, though husband George Grizzard has been certified impotent. Thus begins the nightmarish story leading to a suspenseful climax. (Dir: Lee Philips, 72 mins.)

Stranger Who Looks Like Me, The (MTV 1974)**½ Meredith Baxter, Beau Bridges, Whitney Blake. Thoughtful drama about a pair of young people who set out to find their real parents, knowing they are adopted. Whitney Blake who is Miss Baxter's real-life mother, plays the girl's mother in this piece and their confrontation scene is well handled. (Dir: Larry Peerce, 74 mins.)

Strangers—See: **Voyage to Italy**

Strangers, The (Italy, 1954)**½ Ingrid Bergman, George Sanders. An English couple in Italy, rapidly approaching the point of divorce through incompatibility, experiences a miracle that brings them closer together. Despite the presence of the two stars and Roberto Rossellini's direction, this drama remains vague, rather cold. (97 mins.)

Stranger's Hand (Italy-Great Britain, 1954)***½ Trevor Howard, Richard Basehart, Alida Valli. An exciting and tense adventure drama of intrigue acted by an excellent cast. Trevor Howard stands out. (Dir: Mario Soldati, 86 mins.)

Strangers in 7A, The (MTV 1972)** Andy Griffith, Ida Lupino. One of those bank-robbery tales in which the young hoods show their muscle by slapping bystanders around. Griffith and Miss Lupino play the victims, an apartment-house super and his wife, who resist the robbers. Michael Brandon displays some flash as the chief villain, and Susanne Hildur uses her physical charms on the building's super. (Dir: Paul Wendkos, 73 mins.)

Strangers in the City (1962)**½ Robert Gentile, Rosita De Triana, Kenny Delmar. Drama of a Puerto Rican family trying to adjust itself to the pattern of New York life, the resulting tragedy. Has an occasional ragged realism, but is often amateurish, uncertain. (Dir: Rick Carrier, 83 mins.)

Strangers in the Night (1944)**½ William Terry, Virginia Grey, Edith Barrett. A grade B melodrama about pen-pal lovers. (Dir: Anthony Mann, 56 mins.)

Strangers on a Train (1951)***½ Robert Walker, Ruth Roman, Farley Granger. Taut and suspenseful psychological drama directed by the master of suspense Alfred Hitchcock. Walker and Granger meet on a train and form an unholy pact involving murder. Effective performance by the late Robert Walker. Remade as "Once You Kiss a Stranger." (101 mins.)

Strangers: The Story of a Mother and Daughter (MTV 1979)**½ Bette Davis, Gena Rowlands. Deliberately paced study of the strained relationship between a rigid mother and the daughter who left home 21 years ago to seek her independence. The daughter returns to her widowed mother's home hoping to bridge the chasm in their lives. Stalwart performances by Rowlands and Davis. (Dir: Milton Katselas, 104 mins)

Strangers When We Meet (1960)**½ Kirk Douglas, Kim Novak, Ernie Kovacs, Barbara Rush, Walter Matthau, Kent Smith. Glossy, rather humorless version of Evan Hunter's novel exploring love and adultery in an expensive suburb. The stars are attractive (*too* attractive—who lives next door to Kim Novak?) and perform with concentration, but it all seems rather a lot of fuss about nothing. The most interesting character is played by Ernie Kovacs, giving it his inimitable oomph as a successful but unhappy novelist. You might find it involving, at that. (Dir: Richard Quine, 117 mins.)

Stranglehold (Great Britain, 1962)**½ Macdonald Carey, Barbara Shelley, Philip Friend. Temperamental movie actor nears the edge of madness when his gangster roles threaten to invade his private life. Well-acted suspense drama, especially by Carey. (Dir: Lawrence Huntington, 82 mins.)

Strangler, The (1964)**½ Victor Buono, David McLean, Diane Sayer, Ellen Corby. City is in terror and police work frantically to nab a psychotic strangler of women. Grim drama lent some distinction by Buono's fine performance, some good direction. Not for children. (Dir: Burt Topper, 89 mins.)

Strangler of Blackmoor Castle (West Germany, 1963)*½ Karin Dor, Ingmar Zeisberg. (Dir: Harald Reinl, 90 mins.)

Stranglers of Bombay, The (Great Britain, 1960)*** Guy Rolfe, Allan Cuthbertson. Fascinating drama about a cult of evil worshippers in India during the 1800's and their effect on the British trading situation. The scenes of the cultist rites are not for the squeamish. (Dir: Terence Fisher, 81 mins.)

Strangler's Web (Great Britain, 1966)** Griffith Jones, John Stratton. Actor finds himself involved when a woman is found strangled. Routine mystery at least moves quickly. (Dir: John Moxey, 55 mins.)

Strategic Air Command (1955)**½ James Stewart, June Allyson, Frank Lovejoy, Barry Sullivan. Somewhat interesting drama about the workings of the Strategic Air Command: the atom-carrying planes that help to maintain the peace, and the men who are involved. There's a romantic subplot which gives June Allyson a chance to shed a few tears but the highlights of the film are the aerial shots. (Dir: Anthony Mann, 114 mins.)

Strategy of Terror (MTV 1969)* Hugh O'Brian, Barbara Rush. (Dir: Jack Smight, 90 mins.)

Stratton Story, The (1949)*** James Stewart, June Allyson, Frank Morgan, Bill Williams. This is the highly successful film biography based on the true story of baseball pitcher Monty Stratton who lost his leg in a hunting accident. The combination of Allyson and Stewart is used to good advantage in this sentimental comedy drama. Oscar: Douglas Morrow, Best Original Story. (Dir: Sam Wood, 106 mins.)

634

Straw Dogs (Great Britain, 1972)*** Dustin Hoffman, Susan George, David Warner. Controversial film because of a half-hour finale of unrivaled gruesome violence. Hoffman plays a young mathematician who has bought a house on the coast of England in the town where his wife grew up. His taunting and teasing wife (Miss George) is a sexual come-on to the men of the town, and after she has been raped, Hoffman is forced to act. Much of this premise is unbelievable, but the most interesting and effective sequence remains the charged ending where Hoffman gradually begins to enjoy the violence. (Dir: Sam Peckinpah, 113 mins.)

Strawberry Blonde, The (1941)**** James Cagney, Olivia de Havilland, Rita Hayworth, Jack Carson. Cagney is marvelous as a decent young dentist who becomes infatuated with gold digger Hayworth but marries steady, likable de Havilland only to become involved with shady operator Carson and end up a sadder, wiser ex-convict. Director Raoul Walsh achieves a good balance of comedy, nostalgia, and muscular good spirits. (97 mins.)

Strawberry Statement, The (1970)** Kim Darby, Bruce Davison. This tense drama about the college upheavals of the '60s doesn't pack a punch. Darby pushes too hard as the strong-willed girl who turns Davison from a mildly concerned college boy into a radical of sorts. (Dir: Stuart Hagmann, 103 mins.)

Street Is My Beat, The (1966)* Shary Marshall, Todd Lasswell. (Dir: Irvin Berwick, 93 mins.)

Street Killing (MTV 1976)* Andy Griffith, Bradford Dillman, Harry Guardino. (Dir: Harvey Hart, 78 mins.)

Street of Chance (1930)**½ William Powell, Kay Francis, Regis Toomey, Jean Arthur. Powell plays a de-ethnicized character based on Arnold Rothstein, a gambler about town who falls afoul of the boys when he takes his kid brother to the gaming tables to teach him a lesson. Sonny cleans out the pros and the fat is in the fire. (Dir: John Cromwell, 77 mins.)

Street of Chance (1942)*** Burgess Meredith, Claire Trevor. Amnesia victim regains his memory to find he is wanted for murder. Compact mystery melodrama boasts an excellent cast, good script. (Dir: Jack Hively, 74 mins.)

Street of Shame (Japan, 1956)***½ Machiko Kyo, Michiyo Kogure, Ayako Wakao. Director Kenji Mizoguchi's last work was influential in bringing about the outlawing of prostitution in Japan. Kogure is the standout among the actresses playing prostitutes, whose stories are told; Wakao, generally regarded then as a mere sexpot, brings an insouciant recklessness to her role that marks her as a top actress. (96 mins.)

Street Scene (1931)***½ Sylvia Sidney, William Collier, Jr., Beulah Bondi. A stunning film of New York tenement life, adapted from Elmer Rice's play. A young man struggles to escape the constricting values and pressures of slum life. Worth more than one viewing. (Dir: King Vidor, 80 mins.)

Street with No Name, The (1948)***½ Mark Stevens, Richard Widmark, Lloyd Nolan. Another of those exciting semi-documentary films dealing with the FBI. Nothing unusual about the plot of an agent infiltrating the gang but beautifully done. (Dir: William Keighley, 91 mins.)

Streetcar Named Desire, A (1951)**** Vivien Leigh, Marlon Brando, Kim Hunter, Karl Malden. Superb adult drama. Well directed by Elia Kazan. The Tennessee Williams play about a neurotic woman who stays with her sister and her brute of a husband, the resulting tragedy. Explosively potent scenes, powerfully acted. Brando here sets a pattern for a host of poor actors without his prodigious talent. Oscars: Leigh, Best Actress; Malden, Best Supporting Actor; Hunter, Best Supporting Actress; Best Art Direction. (122 mins.)

Streets of L.A., The (MTV 1979)*** Joanne Woodward, Fernando Allende. Woodward shines as a harried Los Angeles realtor, a plucky middle-aged divorcee worn down by life's slaps in the face. When her tires are slashed by Chicanos, she invades the Barrio to demand repayment. Good tale of an encounter between cultures resists the temptation to take sides. (Dir: Jerrold Freedman, 102 mins.)

Streets of Laredo (1949)*** William Holden, Macdonald Carey, William Bendix, Mona Freeman. Two outlaws who have gone straight meet up with their former partner after many years, who is still on the wrong side of the law. Good western with more plot than usual. Remake of "The Texas Rangers." (Dir: Leslie Fenton, 92 mins.)

Streets of San Francisco, The (MTV 1972)**½ Karl Malden, Robert Wagner, Michael Douglas, Kim Darby, Lawrence Dobkin. Good murder mystery, well produced. Pilot film for the police series. Through flashbacks we learn all about a dead girl named Holly, (Darby), and mull over the clues along with Malden and Douglas as they work at solving her murder. (Dir: Walter Grauman, 104 mins.)

Strictly Dishonorable (1951)** Ezio Pinza, Janet Leigh. Noted opera singer takes steps to combat a newspaper's ire, finds himself in a compromising situation. An attempt to draw upon Pinza's "South Pacific" fame, but the comedy lacks punch. (Dir: Melvin Frank, Norman Panama, 94 mins.)

Strike (U.S.S.R., 1924)**** I. Kluvkin, Alexander Antonov, Grigori Alexandrov. One of the great achievements of the Russian directorial genius Sergei M. Eisenstein during the silent-film era. Story concerns a strike in tsarist Russia, spurred by the suicide of one of the workers after he is fired. When peaceful efforts to settle the strike fail, the state sends in cavalrymen who slaughter the strikers and their families. In this new recently released version an obtrusive soundtrack has been added. (82 mins.)

Strike Force (MTV 1975)* Cliff Gorman, Donald Blakely, Richard Gere. (Dir: Barry Shear, 72 mins.)

Strike Me Deadly (1963)*½ Gary Clarke, Jeannine Riley. (81 mins.)

Strike Me Pink (1936)** Eddie Cantor, Ethel Merman, Sally Eilers. Cantor and Merman pair up for a Sam Goldwyn musical, costarring Eilers as a token representative of the human race. Harmless enough. (Dir: Norman Taurog, 100 mins.)

Strike Up the Band (1940)**½ Mickey Rooney, Judy Garland, June Preisser, William Tracy, Paul Whiteman and his orchestra. Big-budget MGM musical is full of energy, but never takes off beyond the level of self-conscious trouping. (Dir: Busby Berkeley, 120 mins.)

Strip, The (1951)**½ Mickey Rooney, Sally Forrest, Vic Damone. Occasionally absorbing drama about an ex-soldier who tries to resume his career as a drummer after he gets out of the service but is sidetracked by a group of racketeers. Good musical numbers by many guest artists, including Vic Damone, Kay Brown, Louis Armstrong, Jack Teagarden, and Monica Lewis. (Dir: Leslie Kardos, 85 mins.)

Stripper, The (1963)**½ Joanne Woodward, Richard Beymer, Claire Trevor, Carol Lynley, Gypsy Rose Lee. Apart from a valiant try by Joanne Woodward in a role that required a Marilyn Monroe-type to carry it off successfully, this film is pure soap opera. Miss Woodward plays a girl working in a run-down road show, who decides to try for a new life and ends up falling for a young lad. Based on William Inge's play "A Loss of Roses," which was a quick, deserved flop on Broadway. (Dir: Franklin Schaffner; 95 mins.)

Stromboli (Italy, 1949)***½ Ingrid Bergman, Mario Vitale, Renzo Cesana. Bergman plays a young woman, displaced by the war, who marries a young fisherman in order to get out of an internment camp. But she doesn't fit into his island society, and the more she tries to escape, the more spiritually isolated she feels. Director Roberto Rossellini's technique is so modern that the film could have been made last week by Jean-Luc Godard. (107 mins.)

Strongest Man in the World, The (1975)** Kurt Russell, Eve Arden, Phil Silvers, Joe Flynn, Cesar Romero. Disney family fare. Simple-minded plot. Russell engagingly plays a college student who comes up with a vitamin formula that gives him superhuman strength. The villains of this piece are execs from a cereal company who try to get the secret formula. (Dir: Vincent McEveety, 92 mins.)

Struggle Continues, The (1971)*** History of the fight of the Mozambique Liberation Front (FRELIMO) against Portuguese colonialism is a concise study of guerrilla warfare. Interesting on-location sequences. In English. (Dir: Robert Van Lieropl.)

Stud, The (Great Britain, 1978)** Joan Collins, Oliver Tobias, Sue Lloyd. Sex, gambling, and swinging London. Adapted from a novel by Joan's sister Jackie, this was a big hit in Britain. The stud is the virile manager of a London nitery whose obligations include service in the club and in the boudoir. High-budget, semisoft-core porno. (Dir: Quentin Masters, 90 mins.)

Student Prince, The (1954)** Ann Blyth, Edmund Purdom. Stuffy prince is sent to Heidelberg U. to learn how to unwind, and he does, falling for a winsome waitress. Corny operetta, with the voice of Mario Lanza on the soundtrack. The famous score by Sigmund Romberg. (Dir: Richard Thorpe, 107 mins.)

Studs Lonigan (1960)** Christopher Knight, Frank Gorshin, Venetia Stevenson, Jack Nicholson. Rambling tale about the life and loves of a young drifter on Chicago's South Side in the '20s, suffers from Knight's stiff acting in the lead role and a trite ending. Visually excellent, captures atmosphere of era. Nicholson has improved a lot! (Dir: Irving Lerner, 103 mins.)

Study in Terror, A (Great Britain-West Germany, 1965)*** John Neville, Donald Houston, Anthony Quayle. Great detective Sherlock Holmes faces the villainous "Jack the Ripper" in this entertaining suspense tale buoyed by a flawless British cast. Action-packed, sly, and full of gore as a counterpoint to Holmes' staid sleuthing. (Dir: James Hill, 94 mins.)

Stump Run (1960)* Edgar Buchanan, Slim Pickens. (Dir: Edward Dew, 78 mins.)

Stunt Man (1980)***½ Peter O'Toole, Steve Railsback, Barbara Hershey. Ambitious, demanding, and remarkably rewarding drama about a fugitive who stumbles into a movie production, is drafted as a stunt man, and begins to lose his grip on reality. O'Toole as an obsessed, dictatorial director gives one of the bravura performances of the decade, and there's good support all along the line. Director-producer Richard Rush worked on the project for nine years and had to wait years after the film was completed to get it released. (129 mins.)

Stunt Seven (MTV 1979)** Christopher Connelly, Christopher Lloyd, Bob Seagren. Action adventure. Seven Hollywood stunt men form a vigilante group to rescue a glamorous movie star who has been snatched for a ransom of $10 million. Comic-book heroics all the way. (Dir: John Peyser, 104 mins.)

Stuntman (Italy, 1968)** Gina Lollobrigida, Robert Viharo, Marisa Mell. Movie stunt man enticed to rob Indian statue by a pair of lovelies. If Miss Lollobrigida entices you, then steal a peek at this one. (Dir: Marcello Baldi, 95 mins.)

Stunts (1977)*** Robert Forster, Fiona Lewis, Joanna Cassidy. Excellent low-budget whodunit about a maniac who systematically kills off stunt persons while a spectacular action film is being shot near San Luis Obispo. Director Mark L. Lester, despite a somewhat indifferent cast, elicits genuine suspense, affectionate humor, inside looks at stunt mechanics, and visual coherence. (89 mins.)

Subject Was Roses, The (1968)***½ Patricia Neal, Jack Albertson, Martin Sheen. Though Frank D. Gilroy's Pulitzer Prize-winning, intensely interesting three-character play is necessarily expanded in its transformation to the screen, it remains an appealing and provocative drama. It is the story of a young man who returns home from his Army duty after WW II, only to find his quarreling parents still engaged in battle. Sheen as the young man and Albertson as the father recreate their Broadway roles successfully. As for Miss Neal, this performance marked her return to acting after her near-fatal illness, playing the difficult role of the mother. (Dir: Ulu Grosbard, 107 mins.)

Submarine Command (1951)**½ William Holden, Nancy Olson, William Bendix. Moderately entertaining war drama (Korean) with good performances by the principals. Holden plays a sub commander who is plagued with self-doubt about his part in a past incident which cost some men their lives. The drama unfolds rather slowly but it should keep your interest. (Dir: John Farrow, 87 mins.)

Submarine Patrol (1938)***½ Richard Greene, Nancy Kelly, Preston Foster. Exciting tale of a World War I tub of a sub-chaser is good fare thanks to John Ford's direction. Nancy Kelly's screen debut, and she makes the most of her role. (Dir: John Ford, 95 mins.)

Submarine Raider (1942)**½ John Howard, Marguerite Chapman, Larry Parks. Exciting, above average "B," supposedly dramatizing some of the events that took place in the Pacific December 6-7, 1941. (Dir: Lew Landers, 64 mins.)

Submarine X-1 (Great Britain, 1968)** James Caan, Rupert Davies. Scenic shenanigans as naval commander Caan trains three crews to man midget submarines and go against a huge German destroyer during WW II. Caan's acting is stoic, and the movie really becomes submerged by the scenes shot on sound stages. (Dir: William Graham, 89 mins.)

Subterfuge (U.S.-Great Britain, 1968)** Gene Barry, Joan Collins, Richard Todd, Suzanna Leigh, Michael Rennie. Barry plays an American agent forced to assist British intelligence in a manhunt for a defector. Slight suspense, OK acting. (Dir: Peter Graham Scott, 92 mins.)

Subterraneans, The (1960)* Leslie Caron,

George Peppard, Janice Rule, Nanette Fabray. (Dir: Ranald MacDougall, 89 mins.)

Subway in the Sky (Great Britain, 1959)** Van Johnson, Hildegarde Neff. Van Johnson stars in this somewhat muddled adventure about an American doctor in post-war Berlin who gets involved with murder, the black market and a glamorous nightclub entertainer. (Dir: Muriel Box, 85 mins.)

Success, The (Italy-France, 1963)***½ Vittorio Gassman, Anouk Aimée, Jean-Louis Trintignant. Real-estate man consumed with the desire for success despite the ordinary comforts sacrifices his happiness in his quest. Well-acted drama tells its story with the moral sharply outlined. Gassman is excellent and again shows that he's an actor with a truly staggering range. (Dir: Dino Risi, 103 mins.)

Such a Gorgeous Kid Like Me (France, 1972)**½ Bernadette Lafont, Charles Denner, Philippe Leotard, André Dussollier. A blanket of clever homages smothers director François Truffaut's film in cinematic cuteness. Dussollier, a boyish wimp of a sociologist, succumbs to the lithe if lumpen charms of an irresponsibly selfish Lafont. And Denner contributes his usual piquant bit as an exterminator who falls (literally) head over heels over the callous Ms. Lafont. (100 mins.)

Such Good Friends (1971)*** Dyan Cannon, James Coco, Jennifer O'Neill, Ken Howard. A sexually frustrated wife (Cannon) discovers that her ailing husband has been philandering with most of their female friends, and sets out to make up for lost time by popping into bed with any willing male. Some scenes and dialogue are sardonic and funny, some witless and vulgar. Director Otto Preminger's penchant for vulgarity is evident throughout. Based on Lois Gould's titillating novel. (101 mins.)

Sudden Danger (1955)*** Bill Elliott, Tom Drake, Beverly Garland. Detective helps a blind man, whose sight is restored after an operation, to track down his mother's murderer. Rates well above the usual grade B run—exceptionally good direction, logical script, good performances. (Dir: Hubert Cornfield, 85 mins.)

Sudden Fear (1952)*** Joan Crawford, Jack Palance, Gloria Grahame, Michael Connors. Wealthy lady playwright marries a worthless actor who plans to murder her. Well acted, smoothly produced suspense thriller. (Dir: David Miller, 110 mins.)

Sudden Terror (Great Britain, 1971)**½ Lionel Jeffries, Susan George, Mark Lester. A fairly well done suspense thriller in the accepted vein. Mark Lester, an adorable child actor from "Oliver," is prone to telling tall tales. So you can't really blame his sister and grandfather when they reject his story about witnessing the assassination of a visiting African president on the island of Malta. It's not boring. (Dir: John Hough, 95 mins.)

Suddenly (1954)***½ Frank Sinatra, Sterling Hayden. A hired killer hits a small town bent on assassination. Sinatra's bravado performance as the cold-blooded thug, plus crisp direction, make this thriller above average. (Dir: Lewis Allen, 77 mins.)

Suddenly It's Spring (1947)*½ Fred MacMurray, Paulette Goddard. (Dir: Mitchell Leisen, 87 mins.)

Suddenly, Last Summer (1959)*** Elizabeth Taylor, Katharine Hepburn, Montgomery Clift. Director Joseph L. Mankiewicz flirts with camp in his adaptation of Tennessee Williams's sweaty gothic study, with Hepburn as a production tool southern dowager brooding over the blossoming relationship between her brain-damaged daughter (Taylor) and Liz's doctor (Clift). Screenplay by Gore Vidal. The cast packs enough sexual ambiguity to satisfy the most rabid Williams fan. (114 mins.)

Suddenly, Love (MTV 1978)**½ Cindy Williams, Paul Shenar, Joan Bennett. Williams proves she can handle drama in Ross Hunter's glossy, sudsy love story. She plays a Brooklyn girl, influenced by John F. Kennedy, who's determined to rise out of the gutter to become an architect. (Dir: Stuart Margolin, 104 mins.)

Suddenly Single (MTV 1971)**½ Hal Holbrook, Barbara Rush, Margot Kidder, Michael Constantine, Cloris Leachman. Holbrook's abundant charm and talent are put to good use in this modern story about an over-35 druggist who finds himself on his own after ten years of marriage. His adjustment to bachelorhood in L.A. is presented within a comedy framework, but he never reduces his character to a stereotype. He gets good support from Rush (who's seldom been better) as a likely candidate for wife number two; Leachman as his ex-wife; and especially Kidder as a complex, emancipated girl of today. (Dir: Jud Taylor, 78 mins.)

Suez (1938)*** Tyrone Power, Loretta Young, Annabella. Well photographed and lavish film which is supposed to tell the true story of how the Suez Canal was built. If it had done that, it might have been a great film instead of another contrived epic. (Dir: Allan Dwan, 104 mins.)

Sugarland Express, The (1974)***½ Goldie Hawn, William Atherton, Michael Sacks, Ben Johnson. Rewarding comedy-drama. Based on a real-life story of a young Texas couple (Hawn and Atherton) running from the law, trying to regain custody of their baby, who has been farmed out to a foster family while they were in prison for some petty thefts. Fine screenplay by Hal Barwood, Mathew Robbins. (Dir: Steven Spielberg, 108 mins.)

Suicide Run (1970)**½ Michael Caine, Cliff Robertson, Henry Fonda, Ian Bannen, Harry Andrews. Theatrically released as "Too Late the Hero," this war drama sports a thoroughly professional cast. The an-

tique plot has British troops led by American Robertson on a suicide mission behind Japanese lines during WW II. Most of the movie concerns the troops escaping after the mission while being pursued by a Japanese officer who doesn't allow the men a moment's rest. Location filming in the Philippines. (Dir: Robert Aldrich, 133 mins.)

Suleiman the Conqueror (Italy, 1961)*½ Edmund Purdom, Giorgia Moll. (Dir: Vatroslav Mimica, 99 mins.)

Sullivans, The (1944)**** Anne Baxter, Thomas Mitchell. The story of the five heroic brothers who died gallantly in Naval service during WW II. Well-made drama pulls the heartstrings in professional fashion. (Dir: Lloyd Bacon, 111 mins.)

Sullivan's Empire (1967)* Martin Milner, Clu Gulager. (Dirs: Harvey Hart and Thomas Carr, 85 mins.)

Sullivan's Travels (1941)**** Joel McCrea, Veronica Lake, William Demarest. Director Preston Sturges's remarkable autobiographical fantasy about a famous comedy director (McCrea) who, after years of turning out things like "Ants in Your Pants of 1940," yearns to create a great social statement, "Brother, Where Art Thou?" The lesson he learns—from a research trip through America's seamy underside—is that the downtrodden masses need Mickey Mouse more than Marx. A dubious proposition, but in Sturges's hands, a charming one, filled out by his unparalleled sense of character. (91 mins.)

Summer and Smoke (1961)***½ Laurence Harvey, Geraldine Page, Rita Moreno. Plain, repressed girl secretly loves a dashing young medical student, but he prefers the wilder life, until it's too late. Somber, powerful Tennessee Williams drama receives superb performances, especially from Page who gives a haunting flawless portrayal, repeating her stage triumph. (Dir: Peter Glenville, 118 mins.)

Summer Holiday (1948)**½ Mickey Rooney, Gloria De Haven, Walter Huston, Frank Morgan, Marilyn Maxwell. Musical version of O'Neill's "Ah, Wilderness!" loses much of the original's quality and receives no aid from a commonplace score. (Dir: Rouben Mamoulian, 92 mins.)

Summer Holiday (Great Britain, 1963)*** Cliff Richards, Lauri Peters, Ron Moody. A pleasant old-fashioned-plot musical. A group of young men travel across Europe in a double decker bus, and before too long they meet pretty young girls who join them. It's an innocent musical spree from then on, and fun for viewers. (Dir: Peter Yates, 107 mins.)

Summer Love (1958)** John Saxon, Molly Bee, Judi Meredith, Jill St. John, Rod McKuen. Teenage romance and complications when a musical combo lands a job at a co-ed summer camp. Okay for the younger set. (Dir: Charles Haas, 85 mins.)

Summer of '42 (1971)**** Jennifer O'Neill, Gary Grimes. A lovely nostalgic evocative film about a 15-year-old boy's coming of sexual age during the summer of '42 in an island vacation community off New England. (Filmed in northern California.) Some could label this simple tale about Grimes's adolescent crush on the beautiful 22-year-old war bride (O'Neill) sentimental . . . but it works beautifully. Screenplay by Herman Raucher is admittedly autobiographical. (Dir: Robert Mulligan, 102 mins.)

Summer of My German Soldier, The (MTV 1978)***½ Kristy McNichol, Bruce Davison, Esther Rolle. There's a sweetness and a sensitivity about this story of the relationship between a Jewish teenager, luminously played by NcNichol, and an escaping anti-Nazi German POW, acted with tender restraint by Davison. Set in a small town in the deep South during WW II, the well-written screenplay deals with the hatred of the townsfolk for the German POWs interned in their midst, and the bonds of friendship that develop between the girl, bewilderingly rejected by her father, and the young man. (Dir: Michael Tuchner, 104 mins.)

Summer Place, A (1959)*½ Richard Egan, Dorothy McGuire, Sandra Dee, Troy Donahue, Arthur Kennedy. (Dir: Delmer Daves, 130 mins.)

Summer Soldiers (Japan, 1971)*** Keith Sykes, Lee Reisen, Kazuo Kitamura. Interesting if partly unrealized story about an American GI stationed in Japan who deserts rather than go to Vietnam. Film is hampered by the unconvincing acting of the deserter (Sykes). Whatever its shortcomings, this Japanese film asks more questions about the American presence in Vietnam than virtually any American feature film of the time. (Dir: Hiroshi Teshigahara, 103 mins.)

Summer Stock (1950)** Judy Garland, Gene Kelly, Gloria De Haven, Eddie Bracken, Phil Silvers. Tuneful musical tailored to the talents of the stars. A farm is invaded by a group of show people who want to turn the barn into a summer theater. Many songs and dances follow, including Judy's big number, "Get Happy." Director Charles Walters' modest but real virtues have been generally overlooked. His clean, straightforward style has its apotheosis in Garland's "Get Happy" finale. (100 mins.)

Summer Storm (1944)***½ George Sanders, Linda Darnell, Anna Lee, Edward Everett Horton. This adaptation of Anton Chekhov's "The Shooting Party" stars Sanders as a dissipating aristocrat undone by his infatuation for a memorably perverse Darnell. (Dir: Douglas Sirk, 106 mins.)

Summer Wishes, Winter Dreams (1973) ***½ Joanne Woodward, Martin Balsam, Sylvia Sidney. Poignant, often perceptive story written by Stewart Stern, about a middle-aged New York couple (Woodward and Balsam) who take a trip to rekindle their flagging marriage, going to Bastogne and other sites of his WW II duty. There is one inexpressibly moving scene where he describes to her his feelings during combat. (Dir: Gilbert Cates, 87 mins.)

Summer Without Boys, A (MTV 1973)*** Barbara Bain, Kay Lenz, Michael Moriarty. Nostalgia runs high in this tale set on the home front during WW II. Drama about an attractive woman and her teen-aged daughter and the romantic confrontations they face during a summer stay at a resort. Both the dialogue and the physical production carefully evoke the tension and loneliness that pervaded the wartime atmosphere. (Dir: Jeannot Szware, 73 mins.)

Summertime (1955)***½ Katharine Hepburn, Rossano Brazzi, Isa Miranda. Hepburn, touching as a lonely spinster on a European vacation, is seduced by the charms of Venice in a melodrama expertly directed by David Lean. The film shifts to mechanical manipulation, though, shortly after Brazzi makes his appearance as Hepburn's swain. Based on Arthur Laurent's play "The Time of the Cuckoo," and filmed in Venice in beautiful color. (99 mins.)

Summertime Killer, The (France-Italy, 1972)** Karl Malden, Christopher Mitchum, Raf Vallone. Confusing revenge tale. Young man plans to punish the men who executed his father several years before. New York ex-cop (Malden) goes after him, providing several good chases, the picture's main asset. (Dir: Antonio Isasi, 109 mins.)

Summertree (1971)** Michael Douglas, Barbara Bel Geddes, Jack Warden, Brenda Vaccaro. A sensitive play mangled in its transfer to film. Douglas plays the young man torn by his parents' beliefs and his own convictions about the Vietnam War and his life in general. Based on the hit off-Broadway play by Ron Cowen, but poorly adapted. Anthony Newley's direction doesn't help either. (88 mins.)

Sun Also Rises, The (1957)**½ Errol Flynn, Ava Gardner, Tyrone Power. Hemingway's sprawling novel about the drifters and dreamers known as the lost generation during the twenties is uneven in its transference to the screen, but contains some good on-location photgraphy and a colorful performance by Flynn as a drunken bon vivant. (Dir: Henry King, 129 mins.)

Sun Comes Up, The (1949)** Jeanette MacDonald, Lassie, Lloyd Nolan, Claude Jarman, Jr. MacDonald's last film was an entry in the Lassie series; she plays a bitter widow warmed by the love of Jarman for his collie. (Dir: Richard Thorpe, 93 mins.)

Sun Shines Bright, The (1953)***½ Charles Winninger, Arleen Whelan, John Russell. Small town judge has a hard time running for re-election. Superb piece of Americana directed by John Ford—one of his best films. (92 mins.)

Sun Valley Serenade (1941)**½ Sonja Henie, John Payne, the Glenn Miller orchestra, Milton Berle, the Nicholas Brothers, Dorothy Dandridge, Joan Davis, Lynn Bari. With a cast like this, who needs a plot? For that matter, who needs Henie as a war refugee or Payne standing in as Glenn's lead trumpet? H. Bruce Humberstone directed this flimsy movie with lots of music and a fair share of laughs. (86 mins.)

Sunburn (Great Britain-U.S., 1979)* Charles Grodin, Farrah Fawcett, Art Carney. (Dir: Richard C. Serafian, 98 mins.)

Sunday Bloody Sunday (Great Britain, 1971)**** Glenda Jackson, Peter Finch, Peggy Ashcroft, Murray Head. A remarkably moving, graceful film about the absence of love, involving a bisexual triangle of Head-Jackson and Head-Finch. Head plays a young sculptor, Bob Elkin. Intelligent screenplay by Penelope Gilliatt; brilliantly directed by John Schlesinger. (110 mins.)

Sunday Encounter (France, 1959)** Bouvril, Danielle Darrieux, Arletty, Jean-Paul Belmondo. An estranged couple find out that true love cannot be denied but not until they bore the audience with endless conversation. (Dir: Marc Allegret, 90 mins.)

Sunday in New York (1964)*** Jane Fonda, Rod Taylor, Cliff Robertson, Robert Culp. A girl still pure meets a dashing young man and quite innocently has her brother thinking the wrong things. Comedy that can be called "cute," but pleasantly so—performances are refreshing, pace is smooth. (Dir: Peter Tewksbury, 105 mins.)

Sundays and Cybele (France, 1962)**** Hardy Kruger, Patricia Gozzi, Nicole Courcel. Touching, beautifully realized story about a troubled young man, an amnesiac who befriends an orphan girl, pretending to be her father and taking her on Sunday excursions in the park. Their relationship builds slowly. The man's psychotic tendencies are revealed as the story builds to a terrifying climax. The undertone of sexual attraction by both parties adds to the tension, and the actors are superb throughout. Oscar: Best Foreign film. (Dir: Serge Bourguignon, 110 mins.)

Sundown (1941)**½ Gene Tierney, Bruce Cabot, George Sanders. The British in Africa receive the aid of a jungle girl in defeating the attempts of the Nazis to take over. Well-produced but second-rate melodrama. (Dir: Henry Hathaway, 91 mins.)

Sundowners, The (1950)***½ Robert Preston, John Barrymore, Jr., Robert Sterling. A renegade gunman rides in to cause trouble for a boy and his father. Topnotch western, well written, acted. (Dir: George Templeton, 83 mins.)

Sundowners, The (1960)**½ Robert Mitchum, Deborah Kerr, Peter Ustinov, Glynis Johns. A long, leisurely, muffled movie, with director Fred Zinnemann lavishing intensive care on character at the expense of even a dollop of dramatic excitement. Mitchum and Kerr are sheepherders in Australia in the '20s, Johns and Ustinov provide some sauce to liven up the show, but it's basically a well-meaning bore. Lovely on-location photography. (113 mins.)

Sunny Side Up (1929)** Janet Gaynor, Charles Farrell, El Brendel. Pleasant antique musical. The DeSylva, Brown, and Henderson score includes such goodies as "If I Had a Talking Picture of You" and "I'm a Dreamer." Jackie Cooper, then seven, in a bit. (Dir: David Butler, 115 mins.)

Sunnyside (1979)* Joey Travolta, Andrew Rubin, John Lansing. (Dir: Timothy Galfas, 100 mins.)

Sunrise at Campobello (1960)**** Ralph Bellamy, Greer Garson. Inspiring story of young FDR, his conquering of the crippling disease of polio enabling him to walk to the rostrum to nominate Al Smith at the Democratic Convention. Based on the stage play, with Bellamy repeating his fine performance as Roosevelt. Greer Garson is surprisingly effective as his wife. Heartwarming drama. Written by Dore Schary. (Dir: Vincent J. Donehue, 143 mins.)

Sunscorched (Spain-Germany, 1965)*½ Mark Stevens, Mario Adorf, Marianne Koch. (Dirs: Mark Stevens, Jesus Jaime Balcazar, 77 mins.)

Sunset Boulevard (1950)**** Gloria Swanson, William Holden, Erich von Stroheim, Jack Webb, Nancy Olson. Director Billy Wilder's searing, funny, morbid look at the "real tinsel beneath the phony tinsel." Aging silent-movie vamp Swanson takes up with a two-bit screenwriter on the make (Holden) and holds him virtual captive in her Hollywood gothic mansion. Von Stroheim, once her director and husband, now her butler, is the only other member of this ménage-à-weird, now that her pet chimp has died. A tour de force by Swanson. (110 mins.)

Sunshine (MTV 1973)*** Cristina Raines, Cliff De Young. An extraordinary tale about a free-spirited young woman, frenetically tied to life, destined to die of bone cancer at the age of 20. No overtones of the accommodating sweetness and resignation as in "Love Story." What is present is an adamant will to live and make every moment count. Based on the true-life diary of a young woman, recorded on tape, it can't help but make you grit your teeth in sympathy. (Dir: Joseph Sargent, 121 mins.)

Sunshine Boys, The (1975)***½ George Burns, Walter Matthau, Richard Benjamin. Neil Simon's funny, touching play about two veteran vaudevillians who have shared a hate-love relationship for decades, works even better on the screen, thanks to Walter Matthau and George Burns' superb timing as the pair of disgruntled show-business codgers. Richard Benjamin also scores as Matthau's nephew who works valiantly to get the pair together for a TV reunion. The dialogue is delicious, and the stars know how to deliver it. George Burns won an Academy Award for this effort and he's wonderful. (Dir: Herbert Ross, 111 mins.)

Sunshine Christmas (MTV 1977)**½ Cliff DeYoung, Pat Hingle, Eileen Heckart. DeYoung plays a footloose musician, Sam Hayden, bringing daughter Jill back to his folks in Texas. Sam's homecoming is full of surprises. (Dir: Glenn Jordan, 104 mins.)

Sunshine Patriot, The (MTV 1968)***½ Cliff Robertson, Dina Merrill, Luther Adler. Good spy story. The familiar plot has an experienced spy, trapped behind the iron curtain, cleverly framing an American businessman and switching identities with him. The excellent cast is headed by Robertson in the dual role of spy and businessman. Merrill as the latter's mistress, and Adler, quite fascinating as the Communist security chief. (Dir: Joseph Sargent, 98 mins.)

Super Cops (1974)**½ Ron Leibman, David Selby. Leibman and Selby are much better than their material in this saga of two real-life New York cops (Greenberg and Hantz) who earned the nicknames of Batman and Robin because of their unorthodox methods in dealing with criminals. The twist here is that the two rookie cops actually work in the traffic division, but they wage their war on drug traffic during their own off-duty hours. Dedicated they certainly are, but the film makes them seem more comic-book heroic than documentary real-life cops. A poor man's version of "Serpico." (Dir: Gordon Parks, Jr., 93 mins.)

Super Fight, The (1969)** Rocky Marciano, Muhammad Ali. Good idea that doesn't come off on screen. All-time heavyweight boxing greats Marciano and Ali, champions from two eras, meet in this computerized "dream fight," supposedly to determine who was the best of all time. (Dir: Murry Voroner, 70 mins.)

Super Fly (1972)** Ron O'Neal, Carl Lee, Sheila Frazier. O'Neal street-hustles heroin, and he's looking to make that one big score. Thoroughly disreputable exploitation piece with some good bits of acting and direction. Curtis Mayfield does the music. (Dir: Gordon Parks, Jr., 97 mins.)

Super Fly T.N.T. (1973)** Ron O'Neal, Roscoe Lee Brown, Jacques Sernas, Sheila Frazier. In this sequel America's favorite coke dealer peddles weapons (in a good cause, of course). Strictly amateur. For connoisseurs of street argot, "T.N.T." is an acronym for "'tain't nothin' to 't." Screenplay by Alex Haley. (Dir: Ron O'Neal, 87 mins.)

Super Vixens (1975)** Shari Eubank, Charles Napier, Vschi Digard, Henry Rowland, Sharon Kelly. Garish, vulgar, grotesque, frenetic, and—for its first two-thirds—fairly entertaining, in director Russ Meyer's wanton style. But the disappearance of the soft-core market has deprived Meyer of his natural audience, forcing him to peddle a parody version of himself, as monstrous women roam through a desert, brutalizing hapless males. (105 mins.)

Superdad (1974)* Bob Crane, Barbara Rush, Kathleen Cody, Kurt Russell, Joe Flynn. (Dir: Vincent McEveety, 95 mins.)

Superdome (MTV 1978)** David Janssen, Donna Mills, Edie Adams. The excitement surrounding a fictional Super Bowl game in New Orleans, particularly the heavy betting, leads to multiple murders in this padded mystery story. Interesting characters, but the suspense dwindles after we learn the identity of the killer. (Dir: Jerry Jameson, 104 mins.)

Superman (1978)***½ Christopher Reeve, Marlon Brando, Valerie Perrine, Glenn Ford, Gene Hackman, Margot Kidder. The elaborate special effects are disappointingly unbeguiling, and Lex Luthor becomes little more than a guest-star nemesis a la TV "Batman," yet the film works as delicious entertainment, largely on the strength of Reeve's Clark Kent and the sophisticated urbanity of the screenplay. With Kidder as the Lois Lane I've always envisioned. (Dir: Richard Donner, 142 mins.)

Superman II (1981)**** Christopher Reeve, Gene Hackman, Margot Kidder, Jackie Cooper, Valerie Perrine, Susannah York. One of the very few movie sequels that is better than the original—terrific fun for the most part, thanks to the superb special effects, and the occasionally droll touches supplied by director Richard Lester. (Some snippets were shot by Richard Donner who directed the first entry.) The screenplay is also more stylish and imaginative than usual thanks to the illustrious trio of Mario Puzo, David Newman and Leslie Newman who based this derring-do tale on an original story by Puzo. The big difference this time around is that the bad guys are meanies from outer space armed with Kryptonite. The unnerving moral to Superman II is that one rhapsodic night of love with Lois Lane can rob even Clark Kent of his special supernatural powers! (Dir: Richard Lester, 127 mins.)

Support Your Local Gunfighter (1971)**½ James Garner, Suzanne Pleshette, Jack Elam, Joan Blondell, Harry Morgan. If you enjoyed James Garner's breezy performance in the previous western spoof, "Support Your Local Sheriff," you'll buy his equally casual playing in this broad tale of a gambler who runs away from a madam with marriage on her mind, and is mistaken for a gunfighter in the troubled town of Purgatory. The supporting cast, which aids and abets his antics, is uniformly hilarious. Garner is a charming farceur by now. (Dir: Burt Kennedy, 92 mins.)

Support Your Local Sheriff (1969)***½ James Garner, Joan Hackett, Walter Brennan, Harry Morgan, Jack Elam, Bruce Dern. Droll western spoof with a funny turn by Garner as an adventurer who stumbles into a town which is feeling the bonanza of a gold rush and becomes its serious sheriff. The rowdy folks in town resent Garner's intrusion and their bouts with him supply many laughs. Miss Hackett impresses as a young miss who wants to be Garner's true love, and Brennan is wonderful as the head of the town's evil clan. If you liked "Cat Ballou" you'll enjoy "Sheriff." (Dir: Burt Kennedy, 93 mins.)

Suppose They Gave a War and Nobody Came (1970)** Brian Keith, Tony Curtis, Ernest Borgnine, Ivan Dixon, Suzanne Pleshette, Tom Ewell. Deceptive title covers a mediocre service comedy about three oldtime Army tankmen who have been stationed in a noncombatant base, and their war with the southern town in which it is located. The screenplay wavers from comedy to drama to satire, never maintaining a clear purpose. A recognizable supporting cast adds vitality. (Dir: Hy Averback, 113 mins.)

Surf Party (1964)* Bobby Vinton, Patricia Morrow. (Dir: Maury Dexter, 68 mins.)

Surgeon's Knife (British, 1957)** Donald Houston, Adrienne Corri. Confusing melodrama about a doctor who believes he has killed a patient through negligence and is being blackmailed for this act. Well acted but talky. (Dir: Gordon Parry, 75 mins.)

Surprise Package (Great Britain, 1960)**½ Yul Brynner, Mitzi Gaynor, Noël Coward. Funny idea on paper, perhaps, but it doesn't smoothly transfer to the screen. Brynner plays a big-time gambler who is deported to his native Greece where he becomes involved with a phony King and some hot jewel dealings. Miss Gaynor hits the right note as a chorine who keeps Brynner company. (Dir: Stanley Donen, 100 mins.)

Surrender—Hell! (1959)*½ Keith Andes, Susan Cabot. (Dir: John Barnwell, 85 mins.)

Survival of Dana, The (MTV 1979)**½ Melissa Sue Anderson, Robert Carradine, Talia Balsam. A drama attempting to explain why kids from affluent families turn to mindless destruction. Anderson plays the new girl in school who runs with the wrong crowd. Parents who drink, divorce, beat each other up, and generally don't care about their offspring get the blame. The kids achieve a realistic flavor unusual in made-for-TV films. (Dir: Jack Starrett, 104 mins.)

Survival Run (1979)** Peter Graves, Ray Milland, Vince Van Patten, Pedro Armendariz, Jr. What some kids won't do, these will. California teenagers are in a

van in Mexico. The van breaks down, bad guys step out from behind the cactus.... (Dir: Larry Spiegel, 90 mins.)

Susan and God (1940)*** Fredric March, Joan Crawford, Ruth Hussey, John Carroll, Rita Hayworth, Nigel Bruce, Gloria DeHaven. From Rachel Crothers' stage hit. Crawford gives one of her best performances as a vapid, selfish socialite when she takes up trendy religious revivalism. (Not as dated as one might once have thought, obviously.) March is splendid as usual as her guilty, alcoholic husband, as is Gloria DeHaven as their suddenly blossoming daughter. Unusual, very well performed and strongly directed by George Cukor. (115 mins.)

Susan Lennox: Her Fall and Rise (1931)**½ Greta Garbo, Clark Gable, Jean Hersholt. There are only two reasons to see the picture: Garbo and Gable. Gable brings out the sex in Garbo as no other leading man did. (Dir: Robert Z. Leonard, 76 mins.)

Susan Slade (1961)** Troy Donahue, Connie Stevens, Dorothy McGuire, Lloyd Nolan, Brian Aherne. Inexperienced girl is seduced, the guy gets himself killed, she finds she's pregnant, pop has a heart attack, the baby has an accident, but all's well as long as faithful stableboy Troy is around. For feminine masochists to take seriously, for others to have a good time keeping ahead of the plot. (Dir: Delmer Daves, 116 mins.)

Susan Slept Here (1954)*** Debbie Reynolds, Dick Powell, Anne Francis. Amusing comedy with Dick Powell, as a Hollywood writer, given custody of "Debbie" for a holiday period. Powell is good in a comedy performance and Debbie sparkles as usual. (Dir: Frank Tashlin, 98 mins.)

Suspect, The (1944)***½ Charles Laughton, Ella Raines, Henry Daniell. Excellent, velvety thriller directed by Robert Siodmak. Laughton gives a consummate performance as a man who falls in love with an ingenue wife (Raines) and murders his shrewish wife, making a sympathetic figure out of a weak man who finds the strength to seek romance at any cost. Daniell is fine as an insidious blackmailer. Good dollops of tension and well-defined atmosphere. Based on the famous Dr. Crippen murder. (85 mins.)

Suspended Alibi (Great Britain, 1957)* Patrick Holt, Honor Blackman. (Dir: Alfred Shaughnessy, 64 mins.)

Suspense (1946)*** Belita, Barry Sullivan, Albert Dekker, Bonita Granville. Small-time sharpie is hired by an ice palace, gets big ideas and plans to kill the owner to get his dough and his wife. Strong melodrama, a good job in all departments. (Dir: Frank Tuttle, 101 mins.)

Suspicion (1941)***½ Cary Grant, Joan Fontaine, Cedric Hardwicke, Nigel Bruce, Heather Angel. The studio imposed the ending that exonerates Grant from being a wifekiller for moral reasons—yet it may be the right choice artistically. Fontaine (Academy Award) is excellent as the wife who thinks her husband is out to murder her. In a sense, the first foray by director Alfred Hitchcock into the arena of the mature and complex artist. (99 mins.)

Suspiria (Italy, 1977)** Jessica Harper, Alida Valli, Joan Bennett. Dario Argento's grossly overstated mise-en-scène adds some perverse interest to a routine (if unusually gory) horror film, with Joan Bennett (cruelly lured out of a serene retirement), in shrieking stereo. (97 mins.)

Suzy (1936)** Jean Harlow, Cary Grant, Franchot Tone. There are hugely satisfying bits in this ill-structured mélange of comedy, romance, action, and sheer star power. Harlow and Grant pair well, and the screenplay (by Dorothy Parker and hubby Alan Campbell among others) provides some bright repartee. George Fitzmaurice directed, with visual flair but not much organization. (99 mins.)

Svengali (1931)***½ John Barrymore, Marian Marsh. A classic version of George Du Maurier's "Trilby," thanks to Barrymore in the title role. The story is far from gripping, but Barrymore's Svengali is like nothing you've ever seen. (Dir: Archie Mayo, 81 mins.)

Svengali (Great Britain, 1955)** Hildegarde Neff, Donald Wolfit. The romantic and compelling drama of Trilby and Svengali is once more on the screen, this time not so successfully due to uneven performances and a mediocre script. (Dir: Noel Langley, 82 mins.)

Swamp of the Lost Monsters, The (Mexico, 1965)* Gaston Santos, Manola Savedra. (Dir: Raphael Baledon, 80 mins.)

Swamp Water (1941)***½ Walter Huston, Dana Andrews, Walter Brennan, Anne Baxter. Director Jean Renoir's first American film (made during his WW II exile from France) was shot on location in Georgia, breaking a then sacred Hollywood rule. A fugitive hides out in the Okefenokee Swamp. Remade as "Lure of the Wilderness." (90 mins.)

Swan, The (1956)**½ Grace Kelly, Alec Guinness, Louis Jourdan. A trio of attractive stars help to make this mild costume romance, based on Ference Molnar's play, entertaining. The plot revolves around Hungary's Crown Prince Albert's required selection of a wife and the intrigues surrounding his reluctant search. This was Princess Grace's last film before she retired from the screen and the U.S. (Dir: Charles Vidor, 112 mins.)

Swan Song (MTV 1980)**½ David Soul, Slim Pickens, Murray Hamilton, Jill Eikenberry. Intense study of a first-rank skier who disqualified himself at the Olympics three years earlier and is back for one last grab at the brass ring. Soul has a handle on the role as country boy Jesse Swan, still struggling with the desire for fame and wealth. Vivid ski-racing

sequences add excitement to this otherwise laid-back drama. (Dir: Jerry London, 104 mins.)

Swanee River (1939)**½ Don Ameche, Al Jolson, Andrea Leeds. Ameche as Stephen Foster in a silly musical biopic enlivened by Jolson's savvy showmanship as E. P. Christy (of the Christy Minstrels). Philip Dunne had a hand in the screenplay. (Dir: Sidney Lanfield, 84 mins.)

Swap, The—See: **Sam's Song**

Swarm, The (1978)** Michael Caine, Katharine Ross, Richard Widmark, Richard Chamberlain. Absurd disaster film sets up the premise that the army and leading scientists can't prevent a takeover by a swarm of killer bees trekking up from South America. Well-known character actors take a back seat to the marauding insects. (Dir: Irwin Allen, 111 mins.)

Sweeney Todd—the Demon Barber of Fleet Street (Great Britain, 1936)** Tod Slaughter, Eve Lister. Slaughter was a hammy melodramatic actor of the old school who made outrageous vanity vehicles. His acting as the demented Sweeney Todd is intense—that is to say, intensely awful. (Dir: George King, 63 mins.)

Sweet and Low Down (1944)*½ Benny Goodman, Lynn Bari, Jack Oakie, Linda Darnell. (Dir: Archie Mayo, 75 mins.)

Sweet Bird of Youth (1962)***½ Paul Newman, Geraldine Page, Ed Begley, Shirley Knight. A no-goodnik causes trouble when he returns to his hometown accompanied by a neurotic, suicidal actress who is wasted in mind and body. It's Tennessee Williams's absorbing play. Page is fabulous in a truly virtuoso turn. Other fine performances, including an Oscar-winning one by Begley, keep things interesting. Williams's harsh ending was altered by MGM in order to unite the lovers. (Dir: Richard Brooks, 120 mins.)

Sweet Charity (1969)*** Shirley MacLaine, John McMartin, Sammy Davis, Jr., Ricardo Montalban, Chita Rivera. MacLaine stars as a prostitute with a heart of mush; McMartin, an estimable actor, makes a hole in the screen. Bob Fosse directed and choreographed, making up for the script and acting. (157 mins.)

Sweet Hostage (MTV 1975)**½ Martin Sheen, Linda Blair. A fine, colorful performance by Sheen as an escaped mental patient lifts this familiar kidnap yarn above the ordinary. He's an eccentric lunatic who spouts poetry, thinks fast on his feet and corrects the poor grammar of his uneducated teenage hostage, well played by Blair. Their scenes together in a remote mountain cabin hideout have an appealing simplicity which grows on you, until the inevitable tragic climax. One for the romanticists. (Dir: Lee Philips, 72 mins.)

Sweet Love, Bitter (1967)** Dick Gregory, Don Murray, Diane Varsi. Interracial friendships are unconvincingly explored in this tale about the downfall of a black jazz musician, partly based on the life of Charlie "Bird" Parker. Movie lacks depth, plausibility; actors flounder in their roles. Gregory, in his first film appearance, does as well as is possible. He's defiant, witty and self-assured in his role as the saxophonist. Based on the novel by John Alfred Williams, "Night Song." Danska co-authored the screenplay with Lewis Jacobs. (Dir: Herbert Danska, 92 mins.)

Sweet November (1968)*** Sandy Dennis, Anthony Newley, Theodore Bikel, Sandy Baron. A frequently touching, but maddening bittersweet comedy with a twist—this time she (Sandy Dennis) just wants to pop into bed with her various boyfriends without regret or apology, but he—or at least **one** of the he's—wants to get married. The reason for her hot pants in cool November is—well, Sandy is worth watching and finding out. Literate screenplay by Herman Raucher. (Dir: Robert Ellis Miller, 114 mins.)

Sweet Revenge (1977)* Stockard Channing, Sam Waterston, Franklyn Ajaye. (Dir: Jerry Schatzberg, 90 mins.)

Sweet Ride, The (1968)** Jacqueline Bisset, Tony Franciosa. The loves of a mod girl who hangs around with too many surfers and tennis bums for her own good. Sleazy tale made worth watching by the beauteous Jacqueline Bisset. With Michael Sarrazin, Bob Denver, Michael Wilding. (Dir: Harvey Hart, 110 mins.)

Sweet Rosie O'Grady (1943)*** Betty Grable, Robert Young, Adolphe Menjou. One of our WW II pin-up queens proves why in this foolish 1890s musical designed to show Betty's legs—which it does. (Dir: Irving Cummings, 74 mins.)

Sweet Saviour (1971)** Troy Donahue, Renay Granville. Distasteful exploitation of the Charles Manson killings. Donahue plays the leader of a "family" that takes over an orgy given by a pregnant actress in suburban New York. In the end, Donahue borrows a few forks and knives from the roast turkey and does in everyone. Makes you wish for Troy's "Hawaiian Eye" days. (Dir: Bob Roberts, 90 mins.)

Sweet Smell of Success (1957)**** Burt Lancaster, Tony Curtis. Biting, no-holds-barred look at the ruthless world of a powerful and evil New York columnist. Lancaster is miscast as the columnist. This is the film in which Tony Curtis emerged as a first rate actor and stopped being considered just another handsome Hollywood face. His slick, opportunistic press agent characterization is the backbone of this powerful drama. A much underrated film at the time of its initial release. (Dir: Alexander Mackendrick, 96 mins.)

Sweet Sweetback's Baadasssss Song (1971)*** Melvin Van Peebles, Simon Chuckster, Hubert Scales. A bitter black fairy tale, where all the blacks are potent studs and fine folks, and the whites are as evil as they are ignorant. Van Peebles plays a black, sexually inexhaustible lady-killer on the lam from the police. Written, directed, and musical score by Van Peebles. (97 mins.)

Sweetheart of the Gods (West Germany, 1960)**½ Peter Van Eyck, Ruth Leuwerik. Tragic drama of an actress who rises to fame during Hitler's time, finds the regime intolerable. Based on fact, this story moves slowly but has a good performance by Miss Leuwerik, realistic picture of the times. Dubbed in English. (Dir: Gottfried Reinhardt, 107 mins.)

Sweethearts (1938)** Nelson Eddy, Jeanette MacDonald, Frank Morgan, Ray Bolger. Eddy-MacDonald musical is for fans only. They play a married couple appearing in a Victor Herbert operetta who are manipulated into a spat by their publicity-hungry producer (Morgan). (Dir: W. S. Van Dyke II, 120 mins.)

Sweethearts on Parade (1953)** Ray Middleton, Lucille Norman. Proprietress of a music school sees her exhusband return to town heading a carnival show. Leisurely turn of the century musical, might please the oldsters. (Dir: Allan Dwan, 90 mins.)

Swept Away by an Unusual Destiny in the Blue Sea of August (Italy, 1975)*** Giancarlo Giannini, Mariangela Melato. A boisterous movie about the comeuppance a hoity-toity bitch receives from a beleaguered working-class hero. It's sexually offensive and hyped up with goggling close-ups and overly stylized long shots. But director Lina Wertmuller thinks movies better than she thinks, and the posturing eventually implies some tender sentiments. (116 mins.)

Swimmer, The (1968)***½ Burt Lancaster, Janice Rule, Janet Landgard, Diana Muldaur, Kim Hunter. Absorbing story about a loser (wonderfully played by Lancaster) gradually flipping out of WASP society because he loathes the life style and mores of affluent executives. He swims his way down various pools in Westport, Conn., and viewers who want something different will follow stroke by stroke. Screenwriter Eleanor Perry had an unusual film problem—expanding a John Cheever short story into a full-length feature. She handled the task with taste and skill. (Dirs: Frank Perry, Sydney Pollack, 94 mins.)

Swindle, The (Italy, 1955)**½ Broderick Crawford, Richard Basehart, Giulietta Masina. English-dubbed drama of three swindlers who con the poor people of Rome out of their money. Directed by Federico Fellini, one of his less successful efforts. Some good moments, mostly confused, wandering drama. (84 mins.)

Swing Time (1936)**** Fred Astaire, Ginger Rogers, Victor Moore, Betty Furness. One of the best of the Astaire-Rogers musicals. Astaire is a depression dandy hopping a freight train and Rogers gets sung

644

to with soapsuds in her hair. Songs by Jerome Kern and Dorothy Fields, including the Oscar winner "The Way You Look Tonight." (Dir: George Stevens, 105 mins.)

Swinger, The (1966)* Ann-Margret, Tony Franciosa, Robert Coote. (Dir: George Sidney, 81 mins.)

Swinger's Paradise (Great Britain, 1964)* Cliff Richards, Walter Slezak, Susan Hampshire. (Dir: Sidney J. Furie, 85 mins.)

Swingin' Along (1962)*½ Tommy Noonan, Peter L. Marshall, Barbara Eden, Ted Knight, Ray Charles. (Dir: Charles Barton, 74 mins.)

Swingin' Summer, A (1965)*½ Raquel Welch, the Righteous Brothers, James Stacy. (Dir: Robert Sparr, 82 mins.)

Swinging Teacher (1974)*½ Lynn Baker, Nancy Nelson, Charlie McCarthy, Michael Montgomery. (Dir: Michael Montgomery.)

Swingtime Johnny (1943)**½ Andrews Sisters, Harriet Hilliard, Peter Cookson. Sister act quit show biz and go to work in a defense plant during WW II. Sprightly little musical, better than the usual run of its kind. Some amusing sequences. (Dir: Edward F. Cline, 61 mins.)

Swiss Family Robinson (1940)*** Thomas Mitchell, Freddie Bartholomew, Tim Holt. The classic of a family marooned on an uninhabited island who find a peaceful existence away from the troubles of the civilized world. Tastefully produced, well acted. (Dir: Edward Ludwig, 93 mins.)

Swiss Family Robinson (1960)*** John Mills, Dorothy McGuire, James MacArthur, Sessue Hayakawa. Living in a tree house with all the conveniences of home, riding ostriches, and playing with elephants on a flowered and fruited island—that's the Robinson family after having left their Swiss home for New Guinea, and being shipwrecked along the way. In this Disney version of the Johann Wyss novel, everything is pleasing, and the rout of the invading pirates is cheered on by all. Fun for families and dreamers alike. (Dir: Ken Annakin, 126 mins.)

Swiss Family Robinson, The (MTV 1975)**½ Martin Milner, Pat Delany, Eric Olson, Michael-James Wixted, Cameron Mitchell. The family-fare adventure-epic which never looks tired, even though it has been done many times before. Irwin Allen (the disaster-film emperor) turned out this handsomely mounted version. Story of the shipwrecked Robinsons and their few friends, circa 19th century. Milner, Delany and youngsters Olson and Wixted go at it with energy. Special effects enhance the production. (Dir: Harry Harris, 74 mins.)

Swiss Miss (1938)** Stan Laurel, Oliver Hardy, Della Lind. The boys are mousetrap salesmen in the Alps. They become foils for an actress who tries to make her composer husband jealous. Too much plot, but the comics manage to get a few laughs. (Dir: John G. Blystone, 73 mins.)

Switch (MTV 1975)** Robert Wagner, Eddie Albert, Charles Durning. Wagner and Albert team up as private eyes in this pilot, playing the old con game to catch their mark, and they aren't hard to take as the smooth operator and the by-the-book ex-cop. With Durning as the chief law officer, the actors are superior to the material. (Dir: Robert Day, 72 mins.)

Sword and the Dragon, The (U.S.S.R., 1958)**½ Boris Andreyev. Legendary hero Ilya Mourometz, armed with a magic sword, goes forth to fight the Mongol hordes. Generally entertaining English-dubbed fantasy, despite some naive scenes, hammy heroics. Lavish production, some good trick camerawork. (Dir: Alexander Ptushko, 84 mins.)

Sword in the Desert (1949)**½ Dana Andrews, Marta Toren, Stephen McNally, Jeff Chandler. Moderately effective drama about the underground movement that smuggled refugees out of Europe to the Palestine coast. The actors play it straight and there's enough suspense to sustain action fans. (Dir: George Sherman, 100 mins.)

Sword of Ali Baba, The (1965)*½ Peter Mann, Jocelyn Lane. (Dir: Virgil Vogel, 81 mins.)

Sword of Damascus (Italy, 1962)* Tony Russel, Gianni Solaro (Dir: Mario Amendola, 93 mins.)

Sword of El Cid, The (Italy, 1962)* Roland Carey, Sandro Moretti. (Dir: Miguel Iglesias, 89 mins.)

Sword of Granada (Mexico, 1953)*½ Cesar Romero, Katy Jurado. (Dirs: Edward Dein, Carlos Vejar, 80 mins.)

Sword of Islam, The (Italy, 1962)* Silvana Pampanini, Abed Elaziz. (Dir: Andrew Marton 90 mins.)

Sword of Justice, Part II (Japan, 1975)** Shintaro Katsu. Top director Yasuzo Masumura made this entry in the popular, brutal series of police dramas starring Katsu as Hanzo "Razor" Itami. Here Razor cleans up an illegal abortion ring with a combination of swordplay and other means of persuasion. The prolific Masumura makes three commercial junk properties for every personal project.

Sword of Lancelot (Great Britain, 1963)*** Cornel Wilde, Jean Wallace, Brian Aherne. The love story of Lancelot, Guinevere, and King Arthur, without the "Camelot" music but with an abundance of action, scope, and fidelity to the old English legend. Better than usual swashbuckling melodramatics, a credit to Wilde as both star and director. (Dir: Cornel Wilde, 116 mins.)

Sword of Sherwood Forest (Great Britain, 1961)**½ Richard Greene, Peter Cushing. Once again brave Robin Hood outwits the evil sheriff of Nottingham. Lively swashbuckler, not a compilation of the TV series but a completely original story. Fun for the kiddies. (Dir: Terence Fisher, 80 mins.)

Sword of the Conqueror (Italy, 1962)*½ Jack Palance, Eleonora Rossi-Drago, Guy Madison. (Dir: Carlo Campogalliani, 85 mins.)

Sword of the Empire (Italy, 1963)* Lang Jeffries, Enzo Tarasci. (Dir: Sergio Grieco, 80 mins.)

Sword Without a Country (Italy, 1961)*½ Jose Jaspe, Leonora Ruffo, Folco Lulli. (Dir: Carlo Veo, 95 mins.)

Swordsman of Siena (France-Italy, 1962)*½ Stewart Granger, Sylva Koscina, Christine Kaufmann. (Dirs: Étienne Perier, Baccio Bandini, 97 mins.)

Sybil (MTV 1976)***½ Joanne Woodward, Sally Field, Brad Davis, Martine Bartlett. Devastating drama about an artistic, troubled young woman who is unable to handle fears originating from a cruel, mentally ill mother. Field is Sybil, a youngster who develops split personalities to cope with the world, finally undergoing treatment from psychiatrist Woodward. Sally changes roles on the screen in the blink of an eye, and never seems to make a false or unbelievable move. An amazing performance which won an Emmy. The material, the cast, and the production are all first-rate. (Dir: Daniel Petrie, 208 mins.)

Sylvia (1965)**½ Carroll Baker, George Maharis, Peter Lawford, Edmond O'Brien, Joanne Dru. An old-fashioned melodrama about a young lady who tries to better her poor lot but takes all the wrong steps. Good performances by the supporting cast, particularly Ann Sothern as a wisecracking ticket taker in a midway amusement gallery, spark this otherwise all too familiar story. (Dir: Gordon Douglas, 115 mins.)

Sylvia Scarlett (1935)*** Katharine Hepburn, Cary Grant, Brian Aherne, Edmund Gwenn. A gently weird pastoral comedy in which Hepburn plays most of the picture in drag and Grant comes into his own as an actor. When the characters get tired of their lives as thieves, they decide to become strolling players— it's that kind of film. A failure in its day, it plays like an estimable failure today, rich with marginal creativity. (Dir: George Cukor, 97 mins.)

Symphony for a Massacre (France-Italy, 1963)**½ Claude Dauphin, Michel Auclair, Jean Rochefort. Excellent acting adds lustre to an interesting crime tale, as a member of a gang decides to go independent with his friends' money. Lack of pat moral ending, and an impassive emotionalism make this an offbeat entry. (Dir: Jacques Deray, 109 mins.)

Sympathy for the Devil (Great Britain, 1969)*** Mick Jagger and the Rolling Stones. The Stones can't get it going at a recording session, and director Jean-Luc Godard intercuts these scenes of frustrated creation in a hostile environment with long sequences of revolutionary rhetoric. Maddening for Stones enthusiasts, and pretty rough going for lovers of Godard's earlier humanistic work, but a most interesting oddity nonetheless. (99 mins.)

Symphony of Six Million (1932)*** Irene Dunne, Ricardo Cortez, Gregory Ratoff. Director Gregory LaCava's masterful melodrama is probably the best of the immigrant success sagas. Cortez is the slum boy who becomes a Park Avenue physician, only to be plagued by social conscience. Superb performance of Ratoff as the hero's father, a multilayered portrayal by an actor who generally did only caricature. Based on Fannie Hurst's novel. (94 mins.)

Symphony of the Don Bas—See: Enthusiasm

Synanon (1965)**½ Chuck Connors, Alex Cord, Stella Stevens, Eartha Kitt, Richard Conte. A bit of truth about drug addicts combined with Hollywood melodrama. This multiplotted story is set in Synanon, a rehabilitation community for drug addicts in California. Some very downbeat characters and situations are depicted, but the film ends on a hopeful note. Alex Cord registers in an overwritten role. (Dir: Richard Quine, 107 mins.)

Syncopation (1942)** Adolphe Menjou, Bonita Granville, Jackie Cooper, Benny Goodman, Harry James. Story of the beginnings of jazz, and of a young trumpeter who wanted to make good. Good jazz music partially makes up for unsure story. (Dir: William Dieterle, 88 mins.)

System, The (1953)** Frank Lovejoy, Joan Weldon, Bob Arthur. A young man discovers that his father is behind a big city's gambling combine. Overacted and clumsily written. (Dir: Lewis Seiler, 90 mins.)

T-Men (1947)***½ Dennis O'Keefe, Alfred Ryder, June Lockhart. Documentary-type story of how Treasury agents broke up a gang of counterfeiters. Excellent; one of the best of its kind, with special mention for a tight script, Anthony Mann's lucid direction, John Alton's superb photography. (96 mins.)

Tabarin (France, 1957)** Sylvia Lopez, Michel Piccoli, Mischa Aner. The saga of a nightclub in Paris, its owners, stars, and patrons. Some music to brighten an otherwise dull film. (Dir: Richard Pottier, 110 mins.)

Tadelloeser and Wolff: Right or Wrong, My Country (West Germany, 1974)*** A portrait of middle-class social conditions under the Third Reich, this sprawling chronicle is based on the biography of Walter Kempowski. (Dir: Eberhard Fechner.)

Taffy and the Jungle Hunter (1965)*½ Jacques Bergerac, Shary Marshall, Manuel Padilla. (Dir: Terry O. Morse, 87 mins.)

Tail Gunner Joe (MTV 1977)**½ Peter Boyle, John Forsythe, Heather Menzies,

Burgess Meredith, Patricia Neal, Jean Stapleton, Tim O'Connor, Ned Beatty, John Carradine. Devastating examination of the rise and fall of Sen. Joseph McCarthy, the demagogue who climbed the road to power in the early '50's with the cry of Communist infiltration. His lack of honesty and talent for smearing opponents built to the point where a president stood aside and the media did nothing. Boyle becomes the Irish, hard-drinking Joe right down to the turn of the head and the rasping voice. Meredith, who won an Emmy for his performance, is a delight playing lawyer Joseph Welch, that fabulous deflater at the televised Senate hearings. (Dir: Jud Taylor, 144 mins.)

Take, The (1974)*½ Eddie Albert, Billy Dee Williams, Vic Morrow. (Dir: Robert Hartford-Davis, 93 mins.)

Take a Giant Step (1959)**** Estelle Hemsley, Ruby Dee, Frederick O'Neal, Ellen Holly, Johnny Nash. Poignant drama and an important one, because "Giant Step," at the time of its release, was the most forthright statement yet made by a major Hollywood film of what it felt like to be a Negro in a white-dominated Northern town. A negro youth (Nash) enters adolescence, and discovers race prejudice. A box-office failure in the theaters at the time, but this beautifully acted drama is a winner on the home screen. Particularly moving scene between Beah Richards and her son (Nash). (Dir: Philip Leacock, 100 mins.)

Take a Hard Ride (1975)** Jim Brown, Lee Van Cleef, Fred Williamson. Routine spaghetti western has interesting Mutt and Jeff routines by Brown and Williamson. Shot in the Canary Islands, the film is offbeat but undistinguished. Van Cleef is the nemesis. (Dir: Anthony Dawson, 103 mins.)

Take a Letter, Darling (1942)**½ Rosalind Russell, Fred MacMurray, Constance Moore, Macdonald Carey, Robert Benchley. Russell is an advertising executive who hires a male secretary (MacMurray) and—it being '42—chucks her career to marry him. Feel free to hiss, but it's still a fairly engaging romantic comedy. Mitchell Leisen directs with his usual polish. (93 mins.)

Take Down (1979)**½ Edward Herrmann, Kathleen Lloyd, Lorenzo Lamas. Comedy-drama of high-school wrestling is worth a look, mainly to see Herrmann's charm as a high-school English teacher unwittingly cast as a coach, and muscular Lamas as the team's real star. The first PG-rated feature from the Disney organization, which had specialized in sexless, violence-free G ratings. But for one or two minor situations, it's really a G movie. (Dir: Kieth Merrill, 107 mins.)

Take Her, She's Mine (1962)** James Stewart, Sandra Dee, Audrey Meadows, Robert Morley, Bob Denver. Once more Stewart appears in one of those father-is-an-idiot domestic comedies beneath his talents. This time concerns his efforts to prevent his daughter from leading a beatnik life, winding up in the soup himself. Some rare funny spots, the rest depressingly trite. (Dir: Henry Koster, 98 mins.)

Take It or Leave It (1944)*½ Phil Baker (Dir: Benjamin Stoloff, 71 mins.)

Take Me Out to the Ball Game (1949)*** Gene Kelly, Frank Sinatra, Esther Williams. Period MGM musical, directed by Busby Berkeley, choreographed by Kelly and Stanley Donen, and scored by Betty Comden and Adolph Green. The plot is typical fluff, with Sinatra and Kelly joining up with Williams's baseball team at the turn of the century, but the production values are excellent.(93 mins.)

Take Me to Town (1953)*** Ann Sheridan, Sterling Hayden. Good fun with Ann Sheridan at the peak of her comedy finesse as a dance hall girl by the name of Vermillion O'Toole (shades of Scarlett O'Hara). Sterling Hayden is equally effective as a preacher whom doubles as a lumberjack. (Dir: Douglas Sirk, 81 mins.)

Take My Life (Great Britain, 1947)*** Hugh Williams, Greta Gynt. Opera star's husband is arrested for the murder of a former sweetheart; she sets out to prove his innocence. Well-made murder mystery is about average for this sort of thing. (Dir: David Lean. 79 mins.)

Take One False Step (1949)**½ William Powell, Shelley Winters. Moderately absorbing drama about a college professor who innocently becomes entangled with the police after a blonde from his past runs into him on a business trip. (Dir: Chester Erskine, 94 mins.)

Take the High Ground (1953)*** Richard Widmark, Karl Malden, Elaine Stewart. Colorful and believable story about the tough sergeants who train raw recruits for the U.S. infantry. Widmark and Malden are good foils for one another and their playing rings true. Elaine Stewart is called upon to look beautiful which she does beautifully. (Dir: Richard Brooks, 101 mins.)

Take the Money and Run (1969)**** Woody Allen, Janet Margolin, Lonny Chapman, Mark Gordon. Woody directed, starred in, and co-authored this lunatic, gloriously funny farce—where he plays a timid fumbling gangster who acquires more jail time than jewels. The plot doesn't matter—what does matter is that this is a fast-paced pot-pourri of frequently inspired sight gags and one-liners. (85 mins.)

Taking of Pelham One Two Three, The (1974)*** Walter Matthau, Robert Shaw, Martin Balsam, Hector Elizondo. A good, solid suspense yarn. Four men get on a New York subway, pull guns, and hold a car full of passengers as hostages, demanding a million-dollar ransom from the mayor's office. The cast is excellent, including Matthau as a transit detective and Shaw as the cold-blooded leader of

647

the heist. Screenplay by Peter Stone based on the novel by John Godey. (Dir: Joseph Sargent, 102 mins.)

Taking Off (1971)**** Lynn Carlin, Buck Henry, Linnea Heacock. Director Milos Forman's first comedy-in-exile about runaway children and their parents is a shrewd adaption of Czech methods to an American subject. A virtuoso serious comedy. (93 mins.)

Tale of Five Women (Great Britain, 1951)*** Bonar Colleano, Gina Lollobrigida, Eva Bartok. Magazine writer helps a man who has lost his memory regain his past by taking him to Europe. Interesting melodrama, well acted. (Dirs: Montgomery Tully, R. Marcellini, M. Stuadte, Emil E. Reinert, Gvon Cziffra, 86 mins.)

Tale of Two Cities, A (1935)*** Ronald Colman, Elizabeth Allan, Basil Rathbone, Edna May Oliver. Rousing MGM version of the Dickens novel, redeemed by brilliant casting. The film's most memorable sequence is the storming of the Bastille. Colman is the dissipated lawyer Sydney Carton (and wisely does not play his double); Blanche Yurka as Madame Defarge, knitting at the guillotine, the rest of the cast is a sturdily etched gallery of types. Jack Conway's direction is strictly of the "Classics Illustrated" school. (128 mins.)

Tale of Two Cities (Great Britain, 1958)**½ Dirk Bogarde, Cecil Parker. Remake is good, but a step down from the '35 version. (Dir: Ralph Thomas, 117 mins.)

Talent for Loving, A (1969)**½ Richard Widmark, Genevieve Page, Topol, Cesar Romero. A lightweight comedy about the Old West which boasts star names in the leading roles and little else. Widmark is the man who comes to Mexico to claim his land and finds that Don Jose (Romero) has a claim on the same land. Disputes, arrangements, and slapstick comedy antics take over from there. There are some good scenes involving an ancient Aztec curse which dooms the Vicuna family regarding their arduous love-making. Didn't get much of a release in this country. From the novel by Richard Condon. (Dir: Richard Quine, 101 mins.)

Tales (1970)**½ Occasionally interesting but overlong low-budget independent film dealing with the sex fantasies of a group of New Yorkers who sit around a living room and discuss them with considerable frankness. (Dir: Cassandra Gerstein, 70 mins.)

Tales from the Crypt (Great Britain, 1972)*** Ralph Richardson, Joan Collins, Richard Greene. Five tales in a horror anthology, attractively mounted and effectively executed. The peg is that five people lost in catacombs encounter an evil monk who shows them their future. Producer Milton Subotsky wrote the script from the comic strips by William Gaines. (Dir: Freddie Francis, 92 mins.)

Tales of Hoffman (Great Britain, 1951)**½ Robert Rounseville, Robert Helpmann,

Pamela Brown, Moira Shearer, Frederick Ashton. Adaptation of Offenbach's opera is hard to take, despite the enormous amount of talent on display in photography, set design, and choreography. Without the dramatic grounding of "The Red Shoes," the voluptuous visuals seem empty. Choreography by Frederick Ashton. (Dirs: Michael Powell, Emeric Pressburger, 118 mins.)

Tales of Manhattan (1942)*** Charles Boyer, Ginger Rogers, Rita Hayworth, Henry Fonda, Cesar Romero, Charles Laughton, Paul Robeson, Edward G. Robinson. Omnibus episode film has an awful pun in its premise—we follow a suit of formal evening clothes from owner to owner. Some of the anecdotes are quite good, notably Robinson's. (Dir: Julien Duvivier, 118 mins.)

Tales of Terror (1962)*** Vincent Price, Basil Rathbone, Peter Lorre, Debra Paget. Good, stylish horror: three tales by Edgar Allan Poe retold by director Roger Corman in his inimitable way. Our favorite is "The Case of M. Valdemar," where Rathbone conducts a horrible experiment in mesmerism. (90 mins.)

Talk of the Town (1942)**½ Cary Grant, Ronald Colman, Jean Arthur. Director George Stevens has taken some serious material for a light comedy, leavened it, and stretched it out to the point of ponderous pointlessness. Anarchist Leopold Dilg (Grant) is on the lam and hiding out in the home of a U.S. Supreme Court nominee (Colman). Arthur, she of the toothy charm and incessant whines, is the landlady. Grievously overblown, with a social worker type of condescension that sinks its high-minded purposes. (118 mins.)

Tall, Dark and Handsome (1941)***½ Cesar Romero, Virginia Gilmore, Milton Berle. Highly amusing comedy about a softhearted gangster, the orphaned son of a deceased mobster and an assortment of crazy characters. Good fun. Remade as "Love That Brute." (Dir: H. Bruce Humberstone, 78 mins.)

Tall in the Saddle (1944)*** John Wayne, Ella Raines, George "Gabby" Hayes, Ward Bond. Woman-hating cowboy takes over as ranch foreman only to find the new owners are a spinster and her young niece. Entertaining, fast paced western. (Dir: Edwin L. Marin, 87 mins.)

Tall Lie, The (1952)*** Paul Henreid, Kathleen Hughes, Margaret Field. College professor exposes brutal hazing incidents in a fraternity. (Dir: Paul Henreid, 93 mins.)

Tall Man Riding (1955)** Randolph Scott, Dorothy Malone, Peggie Castle. All the ingredients for a predictable western—a crooked gambler, a pretty girl, two or three hired guns, another pretty girl and Randolph Scott. (Dir: Lesley Selander, 83 mins.)

Tall Men, The (1955)** Jane Russell, Clark

Gable, Robert Ryan. Routine western fare with big production values and big names to bolster its appeal. Gable plays the granite-fisted cattle driver and Miss Russell decorates the wagon train. Action fans will enjoy the many hazards befalling the cattle drive. (Dir: Raoul Walsh, 122 mins.)

Tall Story (1960)*** Anthony Perkins, Jane Fonda (film debut), Tom Laughlin. This tale of campus athletics and romance is enhanced greatly by the personal charm of the two stars. The plot concerns Tony as a basketball star and Jane's determination to win a degree and a husband. The fine supporting cast includes Ray Walston, Marc Connelly and Anne Jackson. (Dir: Joshua Logan, 91 mins.)

Tall Stranger (1957)*** Joel McCrea, Virginia Mayo. Good western, well-made. Joel joins a wagon train of settlers, helps them fight the bad guys. (Dir: Thomas Carr, 81 mins.)

Tall T, The (1957)**½ Randolph Scott, Richard Boone, Maureen O'Sullivan. Better than average Randolph Scott western tale. A good supporting cast keeps the action believable, as Randy battles Boone and his band of killers. (Dir: Budd Boetticher, 78 mins.)

Tall Target, The (1951)*** Dick Powell, Paula Raymond, Adolphe Menjou. Director Anthony Mann generates suspense from the story of a New York cop who is trying to foil an assassination plot against president-elect Lincoln. Mann understands that mood is more important than plausibility in a thriller, and you can cut the mood here with a knife. (78 mins.)

Tall Texan, The (1953)*** Lloyd Bridges, Marie Windsor, Lee J. Cobb, Luther Adler. A group of assorted people band together on the desert to seek hidden gold which is cached in an Indian burial ground. Suspenseful western, off the beaten track. (Dir: Elmo Williams, 81 mins.)

Tam Lin (Great Britain, 1971)* Ava Gardner, Ian McShane, Cyril Cusack, Stephanie Beacham. (Dir: Roddy McDowall, 104 mins.)

Tamahine (Great Britain, 1963)** Nancy Kwan, John Fraser, Dennis Price, James Fox. Rather foolish, fast-paced froth about lovely Polynesian girl who disrupts routine of a British boys' school. Naive, painless. Written by Denis Cannan, from the book by Thelma Nicklaus. (Dir: Philip Leacock, 85 mins.)

Tamango (France, 1958)** Curt Jurgens, Dorothy Dandridge. Slaves revolt on a ship commanded by a brutal captain. Confused, unpleasant drama, not helped by dubbing of minor roles into English. (Dir: John Berry, 98 mins.)

Tamarind Seed, The (Great Britain, 1974)** Julie Andrews, Omar Sharif, Anthony Quayle. A lush bore. Confused, outdated story of a Cold War Romeo and Juliet. Andrews and Sharif are unconvincing as star-crossed lovers kept apart by international intrigue. (Dir: Blake Edwards, 123 mins.)

Taming of the Shrew, The (U.S.-Italy, 1967)**** Elizabeth Taylor, Richard Burton, Cyril Cusack, Victor Spinetti, Michael York. One of the rare occasions when Shakespeare really works on the screen. Credit director Franco Zeffirelli's exquisite mounting, and the spirited, thoughtful playing by stars Taylor and Burton. Burton seems to have been born to play the wily opportunist Petruchio who comes to Padua to woo and wed the man-hating Kate. Taylor is a rare combination of beauty, fire and luminous femininity as Kate. (126 mins.)

Taming of the Shrew, The (Great Britain, MTV 1980)***½ John Cleese, Sarah Badel, Simon Chandler, Beautifully acted Shakespeare. Jonathan Miller directs with a sure hand; note his offbeat but inspired casting of Monty Python's John Cleese as Petruchio. The subplot involving all those mistaken identities is made clearer than is usual. Badel lacks fire as Katherina, but rises to the occasion in the climactic scenes. (150 mins.)

Tammy and the Bachelor (1957)**½ Debbie Reynolds, Walter Brennan, Leslie Nielsen, Fay Wray. Debbie Reynolds' energetic performance as a backwoods teenager who seems to have a knack for setting things straight is the bright spot of the film. More sophisticated tastes had better not bother but if you like your film comedy laced with corn and hokum, Miss Reynolds and company will oblige. (Dir: Joseph Pevney, 89 mins.)

Tammy and the Doctor (1963)** Sandra Dee, Peter Fonda (film debut), Macdonald Carey. Backwoods girl becomes a nurse's aide, finds romance with a young doctor. Sticky-sweet stuff for the femme-teen set. (Dir: Harry Keller, 88 mins.)

Tammy and the Millionaire (MTV 1967)* Debbie Watson, Frank McGrath, Denver Pyle. (Dirs: Sidney Miller, Ezra Stone and Leslie Goodwins, 87 mins.)

Tammy Tell Me True (1961)**½ Sandra Dee, John Gavin, Beulah Bondi. The country girl decides it's time she got an education and packs off to college. Naive little romantic comedy isn't really as bad as it could have been. Girl teen-agers should take to it, while the rest should find it pleasant if unexceptional. (Dir: Harry Keller, 97 mins.)

Tampico (1944)** Edward G. Robinson, Victor McLaglen, Lynn Bari. Routine war drama about espionage in the merchant marine. Not too much but almost passable, thanks to Robinson. (Dir: Lothar Mendes, 75 mins.)

Tanganyika (1954)** Van Heflin, Ruth Roman, Howard Duff. This jungle drama set in the early 1900's has all the plot ingredients usually found in similar adventure tales —natives, madmen, love, pestilence and massacre. Strictly for adventure fans. (Dir: Andre de Toth, 81 mins.)

Tank Force (Great Britain, 1958)** Victor Mature, Luciana Paluzzi, Leo Genn, Anthony Newley. Average war tale with Victor Mature playing a troubled American soldier who serves with the British in the African campaign. The usual battle scenes with time out for some romantic interludes. (Dir: Terence Young, 81 mins.)

Tap Roots (1948)**½ Susan Hayward, Van Heflin, Boris Karloff, Ward Bond, Julie London. The advent of the Civil War destroys plans for two people to marry, and enables the girl to find her true love. Lavish historical drama has some good moments, but generally the plot never seems to resolve itself; nor is the acting anything to rave about. (Dir: George Marshall, 109 mins.)

Tarantula (1955)**½ John Agar, Mara Corday, Leo G. Carroll. Giant spider escapes from the lab and begins terrorizing the territory. Well-done technically, this horror thriller carries its share of tense situations. Better than usual. (Dir: Jack Arnold, 80 mins.)

Tarantulas: The Deadly Cargo (MTV 1977)** Claude Akins, Pat Hingle. Also features 300 tarantulas. After a plane crashes in the Southwest, the cargo of hairy spiders are free to feed on the local orange crop and the inhabitants. Foolish stuff. (Dir: Stuart Hagmann, 104 mins.)

Taras Bulba (1962)**½ Yul Brynner, Tony Curtis, Christine Kaufmann. Strictly for the undiscriminating action fan. The plot is about the 16th Century Polish revolution which is on a comic book level but the production is lavish and eye-filling. Brynner has the title role of the famed Cossack and Curtis plays one of his sons, bent on revenge against the Poles. (Dir: J. Lee Thompson, 122 mins.)

Target Earth (1954)*½ Richard Denning, Virginia Grey, Kathleen Crowley. Humans are trapped in a deserted city by alien robots. Utterly predictable. With Grey as the archetypal B actress. (Dir: Sherman Rose, 75 mins.)

Target for Killing, A (West Germany, 1966) ** Stewart Granger, Curt Jurgens, Molly Peters. A Lebanese crime syndicate is out to kill a young heiress and an intrepid secret agent is out to stop them. At least the setting has changed. (Dir: Manfred Kohler, 93 mins.)

Target Risk (MTV 1975)** Bo Svenson, Robert Coote, Meredith Baxter. Action piece on the problems of a bonded courier matching wits with jewel thieves who call the early shots. Routine. (Dir: Robert Scheerer, 72 mins.)

Target, Sea of China (1954-66)* Harry Lauter, Lyle Talbot, Aline Towne. (Dir: Franklin Adreon, 100 mins.)

Target Zero (1955)*½ Richard Conte, Peggie Castle, Charles Bronson, Chuck Connors. (Dir: Harmon Jones, 92 mins.)

Targets (1968)***½ Tim O'Kelly, Boris Karloff. Offbeat, occasionally terrifying tale of a psychotic sniper (O'Kelly) and an aging horror-movie star (Karloff) whose paths cross during the most deadly play of all. Low-budget direction by Peter Bogdanovich shows an apt command of the film medium. (92 mins.)

Tarnished Angels, The (1958)***½ Rock Hudson, Dorothy Malone, Robert Stack, Jack Carson. The best film ever made from a William Faulkner novel ("Pylon"). Tawdry tale of stunt fliers during the depression, and of the southern reporter who is fascinated by them. Malone gives the performance of her career. B&W. (Dir: Douglas Sirk, 91 mins.)

Tarnished Heroes (Great Britain, 1961)** Dermot Walsh, Patrick McAlinney. Soldiers with questionable past records are sent on a dangerous mission. Average, familiar war story. (Dir: Ernest Morris, 75 mins.)

Tars and Spars (1946)**½ Sid Caesar, Alfred Drake, Janet Blair. In spite of Caesar and Drake, this is a bore. However, you will see one of Sid's funniest routines, and it almost makes the film worth sitting through. (Dir: Alfred E. Green, 88 mins.)

Tartar Invasion (Italy, 1962)** Akim Tamiroff, Yoko Tani, Joe Robinson. Another Italian-made, English-dubbed, epic for action fans who don't care about accuracy or historical facts. (Dir: Remigio Del Grosso, 85 mins.)

Tartars, The (Italy-Yugoslavia, 1961)* Victor Mature, Orson Welles. (Dirs: Richard Thorpe, Ferdinando Baldi, 83 mins.)

Tarzan and His Mate (1934)*** Johnny Weissmuller, Maureen O'Sullivan. Second Tarzan film with Weissmuller has a decent production and some adult situations. Jane is attempting to make a new home for the couple in the jungle. (Dirs: Cedric Gibbons, Jack Conway, 105 mins.)

Tarzan and the Great River (1967)* Mike Henry, Rafer Johnson, Jan Murray. (Dir: Robert Day, 99 mins.)

Tarzan and the Jungle Boy (U.S.-Switzerland, 1968)* Mike Henry, Rafer Johnson, Alizia Gur. (Dir Robert Gordon, 90 mins.)

Tarzan and the Lost Safari (Great Britain, 1957)** Gordon Scott, Betta St. John, Yolande Donlan. The jungle man has his work cut out for him when he tries to lead the party of a playboy crashed in the jungle to safety. Barely passable Tarzan thriller doesn't have the customary excitement. (Dir: H. Bruce Humberstone, 84 mins.)

Tarzan and the Trappers (1958)*½ Gordon Scott, Eve Brent, Ricky Sorensen. (Dir: H. Bruce Humberstone, 74 mins.)

Tarzan and the Valley of Gold (U.S.-Switzerland, 1966)½ Mike Henry, Nancy Kovack. (Dir: Robert Day, 100 mins.)

Tarzan Goes to India (U.S.-Great Britain-Switzerland, 1962)**½ Jock Mahoney, Mark Dana, Jai. As these jungle epics starring Edgar Rice Burroughs' durable hero go, here's a pretty good one. The locale is shifted from Africa to India. Tarzan does his best to create a sanctuary for elephants and other wild animals, whose existence is threatened by the construction of a dam. Mahoney is a convincing super Ape Man, and the actual Indian locations are impressively mounted. (Dir: John Guillermin, 88 mins.)

Tarzan the Ape Man (1932)**½ Johnny Weissmuller, Maureen O'Sullivan, Neil Hamilton, C. Aubrey Smith. First of one of MGM's most popular series of the '30s. Weissmuller acts Tarzan like the ex-Olympic swimmer he is. (Dir: W. S. Van Dyke, 99 mins.)

Tarzan, the Ape Man (1959)*½ Denny Miller, Joanna Barnes. (Dir: Joseph M. Newman, 82 mins.)

Tarzan the Magnificent (Great Britain, 1960)*** Gordon Scott, Betta St. John, Jock Mahoney, John Carradine. Tarzan captures the murderer of a policeman, but the criminal's family sets out to free him. Good entry in the Tarzan series doesn't let up the fast pace for a moment. Well-made and exciting. Filmed in Africa, which helps make it all believable. (Dir: Robert Day, 88 mins.)

Tarzana (1979)*** Michael C. Gwynne. Elaborate parody of film noir hasn't much of its own to say. An enjoyable curiosity. (Dir: Steve de Jarnatt.)

Tarzan's Fight for Life (1958)** Gordon Scott, Eve Brent. The jungle man incurs the wrath of a tribal witch doctor when he becomes friendly with a doctor running a hospital in the jungle. Just fair Tarzan film, lacks the action and production of some of the better ones. (Dir: H. Bruce Humberstone, 86 mins.)

Tarzan's Greatest Adventure (Great Britain, 1959)*** Gordon Scott, Anthony Quayle, Sean Connery, Sara Shane. Tarzan on the trail of four men, including an old enemy, who don't stop at murder in seeking a diamond mine. One of the better jungle adventures—Tarzan speaks whole sentences, the African locations are beautiful, and the story's loaded with action, some of the more spectacular variety. Good fun. (Dir: John Guillermin, 88 mins.)

Tarzan's New York Adventure (1942)*** Johnny Weissmuller, Maureen O'Sullivan, Charles Bickford. Circus men kidnap Tarzan's boy, and the jungle man follows them to the big city. Lively entrant in the series, with the change of locale amusing, exciting. (Dir: Richard Thorpe, 71 mins.)

Tarzan's Three Challenges (1963)*½ Jock Mahoney, Woody Strode. (Dir: Robert Day, 92 mins.)

Task Force (1949)*** Gary Cooper, Walter Brennan, Jane Wyatt. Story of development of naval aviation and aircraft carriers is too long but contains some interesting scenes and good acting. (Dir: Delmer Daves, 116 mins.)

Taste of Evil, A (MTV 1971)** Barbara Stanwyck, Barbara Parkins, Roddy McDowall. Old-fashioned melodrama set in a big, rambling mansion. Lovely Parkins returns home, cured after years in a sanitarium following a childhood incident which left her catatonic, only to find herself being terrorized. Stanwyck, looking every inch the regal matriarch, gets a chance to rant and rave in the supercharged finale. (Dir: John Llewellyn Moxey, 78 mins.)

Taste of Fear—See: **Scream of Fear**

Taste of Honey, A (Great Britain, 1962)**** Rita Tushingham, Murray Melvin, Dora Bryan, Robert Stephens. Warmly human, drama of an unlovely girl, her sudden entrance into womanhood. It's tops in acting, direction. Miss Tushingham's performance in this, her first film effort, is quite remarkable and deeply moving. Based on the fine British play which also was a hit on Broadway. Beautifully directed by Tony Richardson, this is a lovely, often tender, heartbreaking film. (Dir: Tony Richardson, 100 mins.)

Tattered Dress, The (1957)**½ Jeff Chandler, Jeanne Crain, Jack Carson, Gail Russell. Somewhat muddled but moderately interesting murder drama with a large cast of stars who appear in brief roles. The production is slick and the courtroom scenes add a spark to the proceedings. (Dir: Jack Arnold, 93 mins.)

Tattered Web, A (MTV 1971)**½ Lloyd Bridges, Frank Converse, Sallie Shockley, Broderick Crawford. A detective finds his son-in-law is cheating on his daughter, confronts the other woman and accidentally kills her. Guess who is assigned to the case? The more the detective tries to cover up the clues, the more the finger of suspicion points to his son-in-law. Bridges's performance is not strong enough. (Dir: Paul Wendkos, 78 mins.)

Taur the Mighty (Italy, 1963)* Joe Robinson, Bella Cortez. (Dir: Antonio Leonviola, 89 mins.)

Taxi (1953)** Dan Dailey, Constance Smith, Geraldine Page (film debut). Cab driver helps an Irish immigrant girl with a baby to find her husband. Modest little comedy-drama manages to be quite entertaining; good performances by the leads, New York atmosphere. (Dir: Gregory Ratoff, 77 mins.)

Taxi Driver, The (Greece, 1958)* Mimis Fotopoulos. (Dir: George Tzavellas, 90 mins.)

Taxi Driver (1976)**** Robert De Niro, Cybill Shepherd, Jodie Foster, Peter Boyle, Leonard Harris. A profoundly disturbing story about urban alienation and, finally, madness. Robert De Niro's embittered, lonely Vietnam marine veteran who drives a taxi at night while turning into an urban guerrilla is one of the most chilling, repellent characters in modern films. There are other splendid performances, including Foster playing Iris, a 12-year-old prostitute, who works for a pimp slain by De Niro in his frenzied rage. Scorsese establishes himself as one of the most gifted directors of his generation. Superlative musical score—his last—by Bernard Herrmann. (Dir: Martin Scorsese, 112 mins.)

Taxi for Tobruk (France-Spain-Germany, 1961)**½ Lino Ventura, Hardy Kruger, Charles Aznavour. Group of French soldiers stranded in the North African desert capture a German captain and some supplies, make their way toward safety. World War II drama with an ironic twist at the end; leisurely, but some good performances. Dubbed in English. (Dir: Denys De La Patelliere, 93 mins.)

Tara, Son of Cochise (1954)** Rock Hudson, Barbara Rush. One of the many Western adventure films in which Rock Hudson served his apprenticeship under the Universal banner. The plot concerns the Indian's battle against the invading white man. Production is of high quality, but you've seen it all before. (Dir: Douglas Sirk, 79 mins.)

Tea and Sympathy (1956)***½ Deborah Kerr, John Kerr, Leif Erickson. The successful Broadway play by Robert Anderson is expanded and toned down somewhat in this film version and thereby loses some of its bite. Miss and Mr. Kerr (no relation) repeat their Broadway roles and manage to evoke the sympathy implied in the title. (Dir: Vincente Minnelli, 122 mins.)

Tea for Two (1950)**½ Doris Day, Gordon MacRae, Eve Arden. Mildly diverting musical comedy made long before Doris went dramatic. Based on the 20's play "No, No, Nanette." (Dir: David Bulter, 98 mins.)

Teacher and the Miracle, The (Italy-Spain, 1957)**½ Aldo Fabrizi, Edoardo Nevola. Teacher who has established an art school is crushed by the death of his son, but a miracle encourages him to carry on. Sensitive drama dubbed in English should please viewers who delight in a good cry. (Dir: Aldo Fabrizi, 88 mins.)

Teacher's Pet (1958)***½ Clark Gable, Doris Day, Mamie Van Doren, Gig Young. Rollicking comedy with Gable and Day at their respective best. He plays a hard-boiled city editor who becomes her star pupil in a journalism class. The laughs come often and the supporting cast is fine, especially Gig Young as a tipsy playboy (Dir: George Stevens, 120 mins.)

Teahouse of the August Moon (1956)***½ Marlon Brando, Glenn Ford, Machiko Kyo, Eddie Albert. John Patrick's successful Broadway comedy about the rehabilitation of an Okinawan village by the U.S.Army is brought to the screen with most of the fun intact. Glenn Ford does fairly well as Capt. Fisby, the officer in charge of the military program, but Marlon Brando is miscast in the role of his unpredictable interpreter. (Dir: Daniel Mann, 123 mins.)

Team-Mates (1978)*½ Karen Corrado, Max Goff, Michael Goldfinger. (Dir: Steven Jacobson, 84 mins.)

Teckman Mystery, The (Great Britain, 1954)*** Margaret Leighton, John Justin. Author writing a biography of an airman who crashed is convinced there is something mysterious about the death. Good mystery holds the attention. (Dir: Wendy Toye, 89 mins.)

Teenage Bad Girl (Great Britain, 1956)*** Anna Neagle, Sylvia Syms, Kenneth Haigh, Wilfrid Hyde White. Despite its bad title, this British movie about youth and their wild times is well acted and rewarding. (Dir: Herbert Wilcox, 100 mins.)

Teenage Caveman (1958)** Robert Vaughn, Leslie Bradley, Darrah Marshall. Outrageous quickie shot in someone's backyard with a few plaster boulders added for atmosphere. Vaughn is an antediluvian adolescent who (accompanied by heavy audience identification) defies his parents by journeying to the Land Beyond the River. (Dir: Roger Corman, 65 mins.)

Teenage Crime Wave (1955)*½ Tommy Cook, Mollie McCart. (Dir: Fred F. Sears, 77 mins.)

Teenage Doll (1957)*** June Kenney, Fay Spain, John Brinkley. Magnificent teen film produced and directed by Roger Corman when he did these things best; mood and pace are excellent. The "Variety" review said: "This low-budgeter is ostensibly directed toward the fight against juvenile delinquency. However, the characters talk a stylized jargon and engage in continual brutality and violence, their motivations, delinquent or otherwise, bearing only the slightest resemblance to those of human beings." (68 mins.)

Teenage Millionaire (1961)*½ Jimmy Clanton, Rocky Graziano, Zasu Pitts. (Dir: Lawrence Doheny, 84 mins.)

Teenage Monster—See: Meteor Monster

Teenage Rebel (1956)*½ Ginger Rogers, Michael Rennie, Betty Lou Keim. (Dir: Edmund Goulding, 94 mins.)

Teenage Wolf Pack (Great Britain, 1956)**½ Horst Buchholz, Karin Ball. Strong film about young kids seeking kicks. Acting better than the rest of the production. (Dir: Georg Tressler, 89 mins.)

Teenage Zombies (1960)* Don Sullivan, Katherine Victor, Steve Conte. Thriller; poor. (Dir: Jerry Warren, 73 mins.)

Teenagers from Outer Space (1959)* David Love, Dawn Anderson. (Dir: Tom Graeff, 86 mins.)

Telefon (1977)*** Charles Bronson, Lee Remick, Tyne Daly. Fairly arresting spy story about a Russian KGB agent (Bronson) on assignment in America teamed with a double agent (Remick). Mission: Prevent a psychotic Stalinist from completing a truly deadly series of phone calls aimed at sabotaging U.S. installations all over the land. Daly is effective in a brief role as a CIA agent trying to cope. (Dir: Don Siegel, 100 mins.)

Tell It to the Judge (1949)**½ Rosalind

Russell, Robert Cummings, Gig Young. The stars save this one from total disaster. Corny plot has Roz as a lady lawyer running away from her blonde-chasing husband for most of the film. (Dir: Norman Foster, 87 mins.)

Tell Me Lies (Great Britain, 1968)***½ Glenda Jackson, Peggy Ashcroft, Mark Jones, Robert Lloyd. Produced, directed and conceived by Peter Brook. A mocking, and frequently lacerating attack on the U.S. war policy in Indochina. Original footage, utilizing members of the Royal Shakespeare Company, is mixed with documentary footage of war violence and destruction in Vietnam. It's too bad the film isn't better on a technical level. Your response to this angry, political essay will depend to a large degree on your attitude toward the Vietnam War. (118 mins.)

Tell Me My Name (MTV 1977)*** Arthur Hill, Barbara Barrie, Bernard Hughes. Flawed but sensitive drama. Barrie gives a wonderful performance as a woman who, when she was 18, gave up an illegitimate daughter for adoption. Now, 19 years later, the young lady arrives to see who her real mother is. In the meantime Barrie has married Professor Hill and had two children. Some of the solutions are too pat. (Dir: Delbert Mann, 104 mins.)

Tell Me That You Love Me, Junie Moon (1970)** Liza Minnelli, Ken Howard, Robert Moore. Director Otto Preminger has cheapened Marjorie Kellogg's sensitive novel about three misfits (a physically scarred young girl, an epileptic, and a paraplegic homosexual) who meet in a hospital and decide to live together, commune-style. Ms. Kellogg wrote the rambling screenplay which deals mostly with the trio's sexual hang-ups. Minnelli, miscast, gives a shrill performance; Moore overplays shamelessly as the para-homo; but Howard is touching as the young epileptic. (113 mins.)

Tell-Tale Heart, The (Great Britain, 1960)**½ Laurence Payne, Adrienne Corri, Dermot Walsh. Fair version of Poe's classic tale of horror, about a murderer who is haunted by the sound of his victim's beating heart. Some creepy sequences. (Dir: Ernest Morris, 81 mins.)

Tell Them Willie Boy Is Here (1969)***½ Robert Redford, Robert Blake, Katharine Ross, Susan Clark, Barry Sullivan. Thanks to the thoughtful screenplay and excellent direction by Abraham Polonsky, "Willie Boy" is an exciting western chase story. One of the few major Hollywood films that has dealt sensitively with the question of the American white man's treatment of the Indian. Story, set in '09 during the presidency of Taft, finds sheriff Redford hunting down a young Paiute Indian (well played by Blake). (96 mins.)

Tempest (Italy-Yugoslavia-France, 1958) *** Van Heflin, Silvana Mangano, Viveca Lindfors, Geoffrey Horne. Impressively produced drama of old Russia, as a rebel leader sacrifices his life to protect a soldier who had once saved his own. Mammoth scenes of scope, excellent international cast. English dialogue. (Dir: Alberto Lattuada, 125 mins.)

Tempest, The (Great Britain, MTV 1979)**½ Michael Hordern, Pippa Guard, David Dixon, Warren Clarke, Christopher Guard. The only reason to watch this version of the Shakespeare fantasy is Hordern's perfect portrayal of Prospero, the magician-narrator of the piece. Most of the others overact and posture, making the already complicated plot almost too difficult to follow. Dixon's Ariel is fatally misconceived; and frankly, the inhabitants of the enchanted isle look like the wrong kind of fairies to us. (Dir: John Gorrie, 130 mins.)

Tempestuous Love (West Germany, 1957)** Lilli Palmer, Ivan Desny. Overdone soap opera, with Miss Palmer as the mistress of one of her husband's pupils. Waste of a talented actress. (Dir: Falk Harnack, 89 mins.)

Temple of the White Elephants (Italy, 1963)* Sean Flynn, Marie Versini. (Dir: Umberto Lenzi, 100 mins.)

Temptress, The (1926)*** Greta Garbo, Antonio Moreno. Silent melodrama with Greta playing, of course, the femme fatale, the action zipping back and forth between Europe and South America before Greta's fortune turns sour—she winds up as an impoverished Parisian prostitute. (Dirs: Mauritz Stiller, Fred Niblo, 117 mins.)

"10" (1979)**** Julie Andrews, Bo Derek, Dudley Moore. Hilarious and scintillating, rich, complex, and moving. Moore is a middle-aged songwriter who mourns his own lost sense of possibility, and the film takes him through a diabolically contrived series of misadventures with the object lesson being that possibilities are never lost, only the sense of them. He rates women on a scale from 0 to 10, and Derek, his only 10, is one of the most ravishingly beautiful women who ever stepped in front of a movie camera. (Dir: Blake Edwards, 122 mins.)

Ten Cents a Dance (1931)*** Barbara Stanwyck, Ricardo Cortez, Sally Blane. A tough, sexy early Stanwyck vehicle, directed by the usually stodgy Lionel Barrymore. Uneven, but often remarkable. (80 mins.)

Ten Commandments, The (1956)*** Charlton Heston, Yul Brynner, Edward G. Robinson, Anne Baxter, Yvonne DeCarlo, Vincent Price, John Derek. The last film Cecil B. deMille directed was a remake of his '23 hit, and it was his biggest moneymaker. A model of narrative construction, it is still one of his weaker works, slightly stiff and much too long. The cast enjoy themselves immensely. (220 mins.)

Ten Days' Wonder (France, 1972)* Orson Welles, Anthony Perkins, Michel Piccoli,

653

Marlene Jobert. (Dir: Claude Chabrol, 105 mins.)

Ten from "Your Show of Shows" (1973) ***½ Sid Caesar, Imogene Coca, Carl Reiner. Sketches from the famed TV comedy series of the early '50s. The stars are marvelous in some of their best-remembered routines—including hilarious takeoffs on "From Here to Eternity" and "This Is Your Life." Welcome reminder of Caesar's early, dazzling brilliance. B&W. (Dir: Max Liebman, 92 mins.)

Ten Gentlemen from West Point (1942)*** Laird Cregar, George Montgomery, Maureen O'Hara. Good juvenile drama of the beginning of the U.S.M.A. at West Point. Not true but an exciting adventure story in spite of itself. (Dir: Henry Hathaway, 102 mins.)

Ten Gladiators, The (Italy, 1964)* Roger Browne, Dan Vadis. (Dir: Gianfranco Parolini, 104 mins.)

Ten Little Indians (Great Britain, 1966)**½ Hugh O'Brian, Shirley Eaton, Stanley Holloway, Dennis Price, Daliah Lavi, Fabian, Wilfrid Hyde White. A new version of the marvelous 1945 film "And Then There Were None," but this second mounting of Agatha Christie's famed thriller is not as suspenseful. (And the director of this one, George Pollock, is not as talented as Rene Clair who helmed the first try.) A group is brought to an isolated spot and eliminated one by one. (Dir: George Pollock, 92 mins.)

Ten Little Indians (Italy-France-Spain-West Germany, 1975)**½ Oliver Reed, Elke Sommer, Richard Attenborough, Gert Frobe, Herbert Lom, Stephane Audran, Charles Aznavour. Tediously acted, poorly directed disaster. Third version of Agatha Christie's suspense classic features a bizarre change of location and a hodge-podge of international stars. Ten people are stranded in a hotel in the Iranian desert, while one is slowly doing away with his fellows. See the original "And Then There Were None," directed by Rene Clair, with Walter Huston and Barry Fitzgerald. Another awful film produced by Harry Alan Towers. (Dir: Peter Collinson, 98 mins.)

Ten North Frederick (1958)*** Gary Cooper, Diane Varsi, Suzy Parker, Geraldine Fitzgerald, Stuart Whitman. A good cast overcomes many of the soap-opera tendencies of this script based on John O'Hara's novel about the politics, infidelity, and the ever present struggle between the weak and the strong. Cooper and Suzy Parker are believable in a May-December romantic subplot. (Dir: Philip Dunne, 102 mins.)

10 Rillington Place (Great Britain, 1971)*** Richard Attenborough, Judy Geeson. Absorbing crime film brought to the screen with infinite care for detail and an absence of sensationalism, despite the macabre facts of the real-life multiple murder case on which it is based. Atten-

borough is superb as the mild-mannered man who is in reality a demented murderer of women and children, and the production is first-rate on all counts. (Dir: Richard Fleischer, 102 mins.)

Ten Seconds to Hell (1959)** Jack Palance, Jeff Chandler, Martine Carol. Slow moving adventure yarn about a couple of he-men who pit their strength at work in Europe. Palance and Chandler are victims of a weak script and appear more wooden than ever. (Dir: Robert Aldrich, 93 mins.)

Ten Tall Men (1951)***½ Burt Lancaster, Jody Lawrance, Gilbert Roland. A merry spoof on the Foreign ·Legionnaires and their escapades with harem girls, etc. Lots of fun—played in great tongue-in-cheek style. (Dir: Willis Goldbeck, 97 mins.)

Ten Thousand Bedrooms (1957)**½ Dean Martin, Anna Maria Alberghetti, Walter Slezak. One of those amiably empty musical confections Dino used to be caught in before producers discovered he could act. He's a hotel tycoon, Anna Maria's a stenographer, and after two hours of songs, comedy, and four writers trying to make a script out of nothing, all the right people get together. Harmless fun. (Dir: Richard Thorpe, 114 mins.)

Ten Wanted Men (1955)**½ Randolph Scott, Richard Boone, Jocelyn Brando. Randolph Scott is a cattle baron in Arizona who wants only peace but the desperadoes see it another way. (Dir: H. Bruce Humberstone, 80 mins.)

Ten Who Dared (1960)*½ Brian Keith, John Beal. (Dir: William Beaudine, 92 mins.)

Tenant, The (France U.S., 1976)*** Roman Polanski, Isabelle Adjani, Melvyn Douglas. Through its first half, Director Polanski's most intensely personal work is a cruel and painfully funny black comedy where he plays a timorous Polish expatriate trying to negotiate his way through the intricacies of social intercourse in his adopted Paris. Toward the end it tapers off into an overwrought psychological chiller with disproportionate shock effects, ending up somewhere between Franz Kafka and William Castle. (125 mins.)

Tender Comrade (1943)**½ Ginger Rogers, Robert Ryan. Young wife carries on bravely while her husband goes off to war. Drama pushed the sticky sentiment too much. (Dir: Edward Dmytryk, 102 mins.)

Tender Flesh—See: **Welcome to Arrow Beach**

Tender Is the Night (1962)**½ Jennifer Jones, Jason Robards Jr., Joan Fontaine, Tom Ewell. A lot of care has been lavished on this adaptation of F. Scott Fitzgerald's novel about a psychiatrist who marries one of his patients and enters into the mad whirl of the '20s, eventually finding the marriage will destroy them both. Robards is excellent, Miss Jones less so; and despite the meticulous production, the drama is overlong, superficial all too often. (Dir: Henry King, 146 mins.)

Tender Scoundrel (France-Italy, 1966)** Jean-Paul Belmondo, Nadja Tiller, Robert Morley, Stefania Sandrelli. Frenchman subsists on his attractiveness to women, is worn out by the "demands" of his vocation. Film wears out, too, despite the Belmondo charms. Location scenes in Tahiti. (Dir: Jean Becker, 94 mins.)

Tender Trap, The (1955)*** Frank Sinatra, Debbie Reynolds, David Wayne, Celeste Holm. The successful Broadway comedy is brought to the screen with a great deal of savoir-faire. Sinatra is perfect as the foot loose bachelor who avoids cute Debbie's inviting "trap" of marriage for most of the film's running time. David Wayne and Celeste Holm have some good, funny lines and they deliver them like the pros they are. (Dir: Charles Walters, 111 mins.)

Tennessee Champ (1954)**½ Shelley Winters, Dewey Martin, Keenan Wynn, Earl Holliman. Entertaining tale about the fight game and the various people associated with it. Some nice touches, capable performances. (Dir: Fred M. Wilcox, 73 mins.)

Tennessee Johnson (1942)***½ Van Heflin, Lionel Barrymore, Ruth Hussey. Interesting biography of the man who became President when Lincoln was shot and missed being impeached by one vote. Van Heflin is superb in the title role. (Dir: William Dieterle, 102 mins.)

Tennessee's Partner (1955)*** John Payne, Ronald Reagan, Rhonda Fleming. Stranger steps into the middle of an argument and becomes the friend of a gambler. Entertaining action drama with a good cast. (Dir: Allan Dwan, 87 mins.)

Tension (1949)**½ Richard Basehart, Audrey Totter, Cyd Charisse, Barry Sullivan. Well acted murder mystery thriller. Basehart plays the hen-pecked husband whose wife leaves him for another man. He quietly plans to get even with her but his scheme backfires. (Dir: John Berry, 91 mins.)

Tension at Table Rock (1956)**½ Richard Egan, Dorothy Malone, Cameron Mitchell. Another western dealing with personal problems rather than cattle stampedes. This time a man must prove he has been unjustly labeled a coward. Good performances. (Dir: Charles Marquis Warren, 93 mins.)

Tenspeed and Brown Shoe (MTV 1980)**½ Ben Vereen, Jeff Goldblum, Robert Webber, Jayne Meadows. Pilot film for a TV adventure-caper series. Tenspeed (Vereen) is all quick moves and slick talk as a slippery dude who maneuvers a superheist of a million dollars, and pulls out all the stops to stay one step ahead of the Mafia and the law. He eventually teams up with a young stockbroker, Brown Shoe (Goldblum), who's an innocent bystander at first, (Dir: E. W. Swackhamer, 104 mins.)

Tent of Miracles, The (Brazil, 1978)***½ Director Nelson Pereira dos Santos, a former lawyer and journalist, brings a cosmopolitan sophistication to national subjects. This film, based on a novel by Jorge Amado, is an intricate chronicle of a professor's struggle at the turn of the century to recover and record the culture of Brazil's original black settlers.

Tentacles (1977)* John Huston, Shelley Winters, Bo Hopkins. (Dir: Oliver Hellman, 102 mins.)

Tenth Avenue Angel (1948)* Margaret O'Brien, Angela Lansbury, George Murphy. (Dir: Roy Rowland, 74 mins.)

Tenth Month, The (MTV 1979)*½ Carol Burnett, Keith Michell. (Dir: Joan Tewkesbury, 124 mins.)

Tenth Victim, The (Italy, 1965)***½ Marcello Mastroianni, Ursula Andress. Nightmarish tale of the next century, wherein trained men and women have a license to kill each other for sport. Fantasy is a mixture of suspense thriller and satire, frequently effective because of the unusual sets, photography. Macabre, disturbing, compelling film. Dubbed in English. (Dir: Elio Petri, 92 mins.)

Teresa (1951)***½ Pier Angeli, Ralph Meeker, John Ericson. An exceptionally good film about a mixed-up lad (Ericson) who marries an Italian girl, Pier Angeli, during WW II and brings her home to New York City. The cast is fine, notably Patricia Collinge as the boy's jealous mother and Rod Steiger (film debut) as a psychiatrist. Well written screenplay by Stewart Stern. (Dir: Fred Zinnemann, 102 mins.)

Teresa the Thief (Italy, 1978)*** Monica Vitti, Isa Danieli, Stefano Satta Flores. Waif Vitti survives in Il Duce's Italy. She's well worth watching. Basically the true story of Teresa Numa, who assisted on the production, it's based on the bestseller "Memoirs of a Thief" by Dacia Maraini. (Dir: Carlo Di Palma, 111 mins.)

Term of Trial (Great Britain, 1962)***½ Laurence Olivier, Simone Signoret. Just for Laurence Olivier's remarkable ability to submerge himself into a character, even so seedy a one as the school-teacher he plays here, this film is worth your while. The cast of this downbeat tale about a British teacher in a slum school, victimized by a student (a 16-year-old girl), are all excellent. Simone Signoret plays his slovenly wife; a very young Sarah Miles plays the troublesome girl; and a youthful Terence Stamp plays another brash student. Written and directed by Peter Glenville. Olivier is the greatest actor of his time; he's worth 113 minutes of your time. (113 mins.)

Terminal Man, The (1974)*½ George Segal, Jill Clayburgh, Joan Hackett. Directed by Mike Hodges. (104 mins.)

Terraces (MTV 1977)** Lloyd Bochner, Julie Newmar. It was inevitable that someone would come up with a pilot for a series about tenants in a high-rise apartment building whose only connection is their "terraces" which touch. Vignettes about an ex-Vegas showgirl, a lawyer, a doctor and a bright-eyed newcomer to the building are familiar and hackneyed. Julie Newmar, who is always nice to look at, does what she can as the former chorine. (Dir: Lila Garrett, 72 mins.)

Terrible People, The (West Germany, 1960)** Joachim Fuchsberger, Karin Dor, Fritz Rasp. A condemned criminal promises to return from the grave, and the bloody aftermath makes it appear he has made good his threat. Well produced but involved, unsophisticated Edgar Wallace mystery. Dubbed in English. (Dir: Harald Reinl, 95 mins.)

Terrified (1963)* Rod Lauren, Steve Drexel, Denver Pyle. (Dir: Lew Landers, 81 mins.)

Terror, The (1963)** Boris Karloff, Sandra Khight, Jack Nicholson. Young officer traces a lovely but mysterious girl to a castle inhabited by a madman. Standard horror thriller made quickly and cheaply, gives Boris another chance to say "Boo!" (Dir: Roger Corman, 81 mins.)

Terror After Midnight (West Germany, 1962)** Christine Kaufmann, Martin Held. Teenage girl is kidnaped by a man seeking revenge on her family. Fairly suspenseful melodrama dubbed in English. (Dir: Jurgen Goslar, 76 mins.)

Terror Among Us (MTV 1981)**½ Don Meredith, Sarah Purcell, Jennifer Salt, Ted Shackelford. Routine, occasionally suspenseful drama about a rapist and the judicial system that keeps him out on the streets. Don Meredith is surprisingly good as the police sergeant who tries to get convicted rapist Ted Shackelford back in jail. Jennifer Salt plays the serious-minded but misguided parole officer who believes in the rapist's rehabilitation. (Dir: Paul Krasny, 104 mins.)

Terror at Black Falls (1962)* House Peters Jr., Sandra Knight, Peter Mamakos. (Dir: Richard C. Sarafian, 76 mins.)

Terror by Night (1946)**½ Basil Rathbone, Nigel Bruce, Renee Godfrey. Sherlock Holmes movie made after the series had fallen to B-movie status. Holmes finds himself tied to the back of a shooting gallery cardboard man, with his heart in the center of the bull's-eye. (Dir: Roy William Neill, 60 mins.)

Terror from Year 5,000 (1958)** Ward Costello, Joyce Holden, Salome Jens. Female monster comes from the past to kill. Farfetched horror tale has some scary scenes. (Dir: Robert J. Gurney Jr., 68 mins.)

Terror in the City (1966)*½ Lee Grant, Richard Bray, Sylvia Miles. (Dir: Allen Baron, 86 mins.)

Terror in the Crypt (Spain-Italy, 1963)**½ Christopher Lee. Italian-made horror film that builds slowly and manages some suspense. A strange nobleman, fearing for his daughter's life according to an ancient legend, has a group of scientists come to his home to see what they can do to help. (Dir: Camillo Mastrocinque, 84 mins.)

Terror in the Haunted House (1958)** Gerald Mohr, Cathy O'Donnell. A house on a hill, a newlywed couple spending the night and lightning all over the place. That's the setting and you can take it from there. (Dir: Harold Daniels, 80 mins.)

Terror in the Sky (MTV 1971)** Leif Erickson, Doug McClure, Roddy McDowall, Lois Nettleton. When food poisoning strikes the pilot and passengers on a charter flight, a Vietnam chopper pilot is the only passenger with any experience who can take over the controls. The major scares come during his practice scenes while he follows instructions relayed from a pro on the ground. Plane lurchings are handled realistically indeed. (Dir: Bernard Kowalski, 78 mins.)

Terror in the Wax Museum (1973)** Maurice Evans, John Carradine, Ray Milland, Elsa Lanchester, Louis Hayward. Amiable but silly mystery thriller with a top cast. The museum is filled with wax figures of infamous murderers who have a strange way of coming to life. (Dir: Georg Fenady, 93 mins.)

Terror Is a Man (1959)**½ Francis Lederer, Greta Thyssen, Richard Derr. Above average horror film, mad doctor experiments on turning panthers into humans, is thwarted by a survivor of a shipwreck. Filmed in the Philippines. Good directorial touches, plenty of suspense. (Dir: Gerry DeLeon, 89 mins.)

Terror of Rome Against the Son of Hercules (Italy-France, 1964)* Mark Forest, Marilu Tolo. (Dir: Mario Caiano, 100 mins.)

Terror of the Black Mask (France-Italy, 1960)*½ Pierre Brice, Helene Chanel. (Dir: Umberto Lenzi, 97 mins.)

Terror of the Bloodhunters (1962)* Robert Clarke, Steve Conte. (Dir: Jerry Warren, 72 mins.)

Terror of the Red Mask (Italy, 0000)*½ Lex Barker, Chelo Alonso. (Dir: Piero Pierotti, 92 mins.)

Terror of the Steppe (Italy, 1964)* Kirk Morris, Moira Orfei. (Dir: Amerigo Anton, 97 mins.)

Terror of the Tongs, The (Great Britain, 1961)** Christopher Lee, Yvonne Monlaur, Geoffrey Toone. Sea captain sets out to smash a terrorist Tong society when his daughter is killed. Average melodrama. (Dir: Anthony Bushell, 80 mins.)

Terror of Tiny Town, The (1938)** Billy Curtis, Little Billy, Yvonne Moray, John Bambury. A very ordinary western is enacted by an all-midget cast who ride around on ponies with songs too. It's pleasant enough and should entertain the kids. One of 18—count 'em, 18—films directed in one year by Sam Newfield. (63 mins.)

Terror on a Train (1953)**½ Glenn Ford, Anne Vernon. The best feature of this film is that it is fast paced and wastes no time on incidental plot. Ford plays an armament expert who is called upon to disarm a hidden bomb on a train carrying explosives. (Dir: Ted Tetzlaff, 72 mins.)

Terror on the Beach (MTV 1973)**½ Dennis Weaver, Estelle Parsons, Susan Dey. Hoodlums aboard dune buggies and an old fire truck terrorize a vacationing family camping on an isolated beach. The slow buildup of pranks produces the desired suspense, and the family differences contain the ring of honesty. Although the final plot twists stretch credibility, the cast keep things going smoothly. (Dir: Paul Wendkos, 73 mins.)

Terror on the 40th Floor (MTV 1974)*½ John Forsythe, Anjanette Comer, Joseph Campanella. (Dir: Jerry Jameson, 72 mins.)

Terror out of the Sky (MTV 1978)** Efrem Zimbalist, Jr., Tovah Feldshuh, Dan Haggerty. Another yarn about killer bees on the loose. This one is inept because it takes itself so seriously. Zimbalist is the head of the National Bee Center and it appears that some killer queen bees have infiltrated a hive and the bees have been shipped to beekeepers. It's all plodding, predictable, and juvenile. (Dir: Lee H. Katzin, 104 mins.)

Terror Train (1980)* Ben Johnson, Jamie Lee Curtis, Hart Bochner. (Dir: Roger Spottiswoode,)

Terrornauts, The (Great Britain, 1967)*½ Simon Oates, Zena Marshall, Max Adrian. (Dir: Montgomery Tully, 72 mins.)

Tess (Great Britain, 1980)**** Nastassia Kinski, Peter Firth, Leigh Lawson, John Collin. Director Roman Polanski's faithful rendition of Thomas Hardy's novel exhibits lapidary craft. Kinski reacts with eloquence and stubbornness as the hapless Tess, wedded truly only to her own sense of doom as she is seduced by one man and treated unfairly by another. The ironies, romanticism, and social determinism are dramatized with precision and effectiveness. (170 mins.)

Tess of the Storm Country (1960)** Diane Baker, Lee Philips, Jack Ging. Young girl arrived from Scotland finds herself involved in a feud between the townspeople and a Mennonite family. Leisurely, pleasing costume drama on the old-fashioned side. From the novel by Grace White. (Dir: Paul Guilfoyle, 84 mins.)

Test Pilot (1938)*** Clark Gable, Myrna Loy, Spencer Tracy, Lionel Barrymore. Story of men who risk their lives testing aircraft should be remade today with jets. You'll find the planes funny but good acting makes this a pretty rousing drama. (Dir: Victor Fleming, 120 mins.)

Testament of Dr. Mabuse, The (West Germany, 1960)** Gert Frobe, Alan Dijon. Notorious mad doctor-criminal hypnotizes the head of a sanitarium into carrying out his plans for crime. Remake of the famous old Fritz Lang thriller doesn't compare with the original, but manages to whip up

some weird sequences. Dubbed in English. (Dir: Werner Klinger, 87 mins.)

Texans, The (1938)** Joan Bennett, Randolph Scott, May Robson, Walter Brennan, Robert Cummings. Pretentious class "A" western has little more to offer than a low budget quickie except for a name cast. Story of Texas after the Civil War hasn't got too much action or entertainment value. (Dir: James Hogan, 93 mins.)

Texas (1941)***½ William Holden, Glenn Ford, Claire Trevor, Edgar Buchanan. Two wandering cowpokes take different trails; one with a pretty ranch girl, the other with an outlaw band. Fine lusty western, with some hilarious comedy sequences, good actors. (Dir: George Marshall, 93 mins.)

Texas Across the River (1966)** Dean Martin, Alain Delon, Rosemary Forsyth. This western is geared for belly laughs, but only achieves grins and an occasional titter. Martin is a gun runner who befriends Delon, playing a Spanish nobleman who's having romantic problems. Just to make sure you know what you're to expect from this film, Joey Bishop plays Martin's wise-cracking Indian buddy. (Dir: Michael Gordon, 101 mins.)

Texas Carnival (1951)*** Red Skelton, Esther Williams, Howard Keel, Ann Miller. Carnival barker and a chorus girl become involved in mixups at a swank desert resort. Fast moving musical comedy has the usual funny Skelton clowning and a general air of merriment. (Dir: Charles Walters, 77 mins.)

Texas Detour (1978)* Patrick Wayne, Cameron Mitchell, Priscilla Barnes. (Dir: Hikmet Avedis, 92 mins.)

Texas Lady (1955)** Claudette Colbert, Barry Sullivan. Claudette Colbert, always a lady to her fingertips on the screen, finds herself miscast as a crusading newspaper lady of the old west. (Dir: Tim Whelan, 86 mins.)

Texas Rangers, The (1951)**½ George Montgomery, Gale Storm, Jerome Courtland, Noah Berry, Jr. A band of notorious outlaws get together to fight the Texas Rangers. Enough gunplay for a dozen westerns. (Dir: Phil Karlson, 68 mins.)

Texican, The (U.S.-Spain, 1966)*½ Audie Murphy, Broderick Crawford. (Dir: Lesley Selander, 86 mins.)

Thaddeus Rose and Eddie (MTV 1978)**½ Johnny Cash, Bo Hopkins. Cash works without his guitar in Texas writer William D. Wittliff's story of a pair of country boys who don't want to grow up. Ole Johnny and his sidekick Hopkins clearly love their roles. Cash surprises with his warmth and ease, but the film peters out. (Dir: Jack Starrett, 104 mins.)

Thank God It's Friday (1978)** Jeff Goldblum, Valerie Landsburg, Terri Nunn. A very noisy night in a disco, with only Donna Summer rising above the racket to make a vaguely pleasant impression.

Robert Klane directs abrasively. (100 mins.)

Thank You All Very Much (Great Britain, 1969)*** Sandy Dennis, Eleanor Bron, Ian McKellen. Rosamund (Sandy Dennis), a Ph.D. candidate, finds herself pregnant after her first affair, and decides to have and keep her baby. Touching, unsentimental presentation of a "controversial" subject; the film does not moralize or patronize. It portrays Rosamund as vulnerable, while also capable of taking care of herself and succeeding as an independent person. Refreshing film, with moving performance from Miss Dennis. (Dir: Waris Hussein, 107 mins.)

Thank You, Jeeves (1936)**½ Arthur Treacher, David Niven. You'll love Mr. Treacher as P. G. Wodehouse's butler and David Niven as his tolerant employer. Plot of the film is horribly routine. (Dir: Arthur Greville Collins, 68 mins.)

Thank Your Lucky Stars (1943)*** Eddie Cantor, Dinah Shore, Bette Davis, Ann Sheridan, Humphrey Bogart, Errol Flynn, Olivia de Havilland, John Garfield. Warner Bros.' contribution to the WW II all-star benefit extravaganza. Davis sings "They're Either Too Young or Too Old." (Dir: David Butler, 127 min.)

Thanks a Million (1935)*** Fred Allen, Dick Powell, Ann Dvorak, Patsy Kelly, Paul Whiteman and orchestra. Dated but often amusing musical about a crooner who runs for governor. Fred Allen steals the picture as the campaign manager. (Dir: Roy Del Ruth, 87 mins.)

Thanks for Everything (1938)*** Jack Haley, Jack Oakie, Adolphe Menjou, Tony Martin, Arleen Whelan. Very cute comedy about an advertising agency that discovers the perfect average American. Haley is perfect in the role. (Dir: William A. Seiter, 72 mins.)

That Certain Feeling (1956)***½ Bob Hope, Eva Marie Saint, George Sanders, Pearl Bailey. Artist is hired by a famous syndicated cartoonist to "ghost" a famous comic strip, falls for a secretary. In the better class of Hope comedies with bright lines, witty situations, delightful performances. (Dir: Norman Panama, 103 mins.)

That Certain Summer (MTV 1972)**** Hal Holbrook, Hope Lange, Scott Jacoby, Martin Sheen. Holbrook gives a touching performance as a homosexual who is confronted with the torment of discovering that his 14-year-old son has found out about him. Jacoby, a talented young actor, brings a naturalness to the difficult role of Holbrook's son. Miss Lange as Holbrook's ex-wife, and Sheen as the man he lives with, offer excellent support. Script is tasteful and honest. (Dir: Lamont Johnson, 73 mins.)

That Certain Woman (1937)** Bette Davis, Henry Fonda. Maudlin, sentimental drama of a woman trying desperately to live down her past. Too heavy for modern taste.

Remake of "The Trespasser." (Dir: Edmund Goulding, 93 mins.)

That Cold Day in the Park (Canada, 1969)**½ Sandy Dennis, Michael Burns, Susanne Benton. The first of director Robert Altman's films to bear his unmistakable personal stamp, this is a strange study in sexual gamesmanship pitting spinster Dennis against a seedy hippie (Burns) she picks up in the park. Filmed in Vancouver. From the novel by Richard Miles. (110 mins.)

That Darn Cat! (1965)**½ Dean Jones, Hayley Mills, Dorothy Provine. Jones, Mills and an independent Siamese cat romp through this amusing Disney opus. The plot is thin and convoluted—the cat stumbles on some bad guys—but fast-paced enough to keep the kids involved. The supporting cast includes Elsa Lanchester, Roddy McDowall, William Demarest, Neville Brand, and Frank Gorshin. (Dir: Robert Stevenson, 116 mins.)

That Forsyte Woman (1949)**½ Greer Garson, Errol Flynn, Janet Leigh, Robert Young, Walter Pidgeon. Rather long and on the dull side. Greer Garson falls in love with the man who is engaged to her niece. Acting is good. Based on Galsworthy's "A Man of Property." (Dir: Compton Bennett, 114 mins.)

That Funny Feeling (1965)**½ Sandra Dee, Bobby Darin, Donald O'Connor. Girl who has been working as a maid meets a young executive, gives him her working address as a cover-up, and it's his apartment. Amusing comedy has occasional bright dialogue, pleasant performers. (Dir: Richard Thorpe, 93 mins.)

That Hagan Girl (1947)* Ronald Reagan, Shirley Temple. (Dir: Peter Godfrey, 83 mins.)

That Hamilton Woman (1941)*** Vivien Leigh, Laurence Olivier. The romantic story of the love of Lord Nelson, British naval hero, for the beautiful Lady Hamilton, with its tragic outcome. Two fine stars in a long, but interesting costume drama. (Dir: Alexander Korda, 128 mins.)

That Kind of Woman (1959)** Sophia Loren, Tab Hunter, George Sanders. Fans of Sophia Loren will particularly appreciate this romantic yarn, which was among the first films made in this country by the glamorous Italian star. Despite some excellent New York location shots and the directorial talents of Sidney Lumet, the tale about a beautiful woman who makes an attempt to find true love with a young soldier (Tab Hunter) adds up to glossy soap opera for the ladies. (92 mins.)

That Lady (Great Britain, 1955)** Olivia de Havilland, Gilbert Roland, Paul Scofield. Love of a princess for a commoner is thwarted by the king's love for her and court intrigue. Stodgy costume drama moves slowly. Notable only for a small role well played by the brilliant Scofield. (Dir: Terence Young, 100 mins.)

That Lady In Ermine (1948)*** Betty Grable, Cesar Romero, Douglas Fairbanks, Jr. A mish-mash of dreams and ancestors stepping out of their portraits makes for an entertaining little sophisticated musical comedy. (Dirs: Otto Preminger, Ernst Lubitsch, 89 mins.)

That Man from Rio (France-Italy, 1964)*** Jean-Paul Belmondo, Françoise Dorleac, Jean Servais. Pleasant enough spy spoof, aided by the engaging anarchic presence of Belmondo, hampered by the strenuousness of Philippe de Broca's direction. Filmed in Rio, Paris, Brasilia. (114 mins.)

That Man George (France-Spain-Italy, 1966)*½ George Hamilton, Claudine Auger, Daniel Ivernel. (Dir: Jacques Deray, 90 mins.)

That Man In Istanbul (France-Spain-Italy, 1965)*½ Horst Buchholz, Sylvia Koscina, Klaus Kinski. (Dir: Anthony [Antonio Isasi Isamendi], 117 mins.)

That Midnight Kiss (1949)**½ Kathryn Grayson, Mario Lanza, Ethel Barrymore. Mario Lanza's debut film. Light and romantic story about a patroness of the arts (Ethel Barrymore) and her singing discoveries. Many songs by Lanza and Grayson. (Dir: Norman Taurog, 96 mins.)

That Night (1957)*** John Beal, Augusta Dabney. Dramatic tale of a man suffering a heart attack, the consequences of its aftermath. Well done artistically and technically. (Dir: John Newland, 88 mins.)

That Night In Rio (1941)**½ Alice Faye, Don Ameche, Carman Miranda. Lavish but routine screen musical employing the old mistaken identity plot to no advantage. Carmen is great in her numbers but the film isn't much. (Dir: Irving Cummings, 94 mins.)

That Obscure Object of Desire (France, 1977)**** Fernando Rey, Carole Bouquet, Angela Molina, Julien Bertheau. An aging aristocrat (Rey) yearns after an unattainable young woman, Conchita—who, since she is played by two actresses, is more and less than a standard movie character. Constantly changing, she is unknowable, complicated, perverse, but also an eternal erotic principle. Director Luis Buñuel draws his paradoxes in a perfectly clear style. Based loosely on Pierre Louÿs's 19th-century novel "The Woman and the Puppet." (100 mins.)

That Touch of Mink (1962)***½ Cary Grant, Doris Day, Gig Young. All about how a business tycoon makes a play for an unemployed damsel, and vice versa, until the inevitable climax. Enjoyable comedy, lightly spicy, with some beautiful people romping in beautiful settings; just the thing for audience relaxation. (Dir: Delbert Mann, 99 mins.)

That Uncertain Feeling (1941)*** Merle Oberon, Melvyn Douglas, Burgess Meredith, Eve Arden. A minor but effective late Ernst Lubitsch-directed comedy with Oberon and Douglas a couple whose perfect marriage is disrupted by a deranged concert pianist, played full-tilt by Meredith. (84 mins.)

That Way With Women (1947)** Dane Clark, Martha Vickers, Sydney Greenstreet. Remake of Arliss' "The Millionaire" which has also been released for TV contains none of the flavor or charm of the original. (Dir: Frederick de Cordova, 84 mins.)

That Woman Opposite (Great Britain, 1957)** Phyllis Kirk, Dan O'Herlihy. Insurance investigator solves murder at a French resort. Slow mystery relies upon dialogue at the sacrifice of action. (Dir: Compton Bennett, 84 mins.)

That Wonderful Urge (1948)**½ Tyrone Power, Gene Tierney. Glamour girl has her revenge upon a reporter who's been writing nasty articles about her. Mildly pleasant romantic comedy. Remake of Powers's "Love Is News." (Dir: Robert B. Sinclair, 82 mins.)

That'll Be the Day (Great Britain, 1973)*** David Essex, Ringo Starr, Rosemary Leach. Essex leaves home, learns the ropes, and dead-end-jobs it until he can spring for his first guitar. Finely observed example of kitchen sink realism. Starr gives a well-attuned performance. (Dir: Claude Whatham, 90 mins.)

That's Entertainment (1974)**** Judy Garland, Fred Astaire, Frank Sinatra, Gene Kelly, Esther Williams. The title is right. It is marvelous entertainment: scenes from some of the great MGM musicals released from '29 to '58. They won't be shooting those lavish Esther Williams swimming scenes again, so tune in if you're nostalgic or in search of wonderful entertainers just struttin' their stuff. Written and directed by Jack Haley, Jr. (135 mins.)

That's Entertainment, Part 2 (1976)**** Fred Astaire, Gene Kelly, Judy Garland, Katharine Hepburn, Frank Sinatra, Spencer Tracy. The MGM studio's archives have delivered a spectacular sequel. The 75 films culled are interwoven with new footage of Astaire and Kelly dancing together for the first time in 30 years. Some of the fabulous goodies include the Judy Garland-Gene Kelly number "Be a Clown" from "The Pirate," ravishing Lena Horne singing "The Lady Is a Tramp," and Astaire and Cyd Charisse strutting through "All of You" from Cole Porter's "Silk Stockings." Gene Kelly directed the new sequences. (133 mins.)

That's My Boy (1951)** Dean Martin, Jerry Lewis, Eddie Mayehoff, Polly Bergen. Blustering former athletic hero wants his anemic son to follow in his footsteps. Early Martin & Lewis comedy suffers from hammering repetition of gags. Primarily for their fans. (Dir: Hal Walker, 98 mins.)

That's My Man (1947)**½ Don Ameche, Catherine McLeod, Roscoe Karns. Sloppy script about a compulsive gambler (Ameche) torn between his family and his love for racing. A few scenes—particularly the lovers' first tryst in a hotel room

659

overlooking an amusement park—are nicely realized. (Dir: Frank Borzage, 104 mins.)

That's Right—You're Wrong (1939)**½ Kay Kyser, Lucille Ball, Dennis O'Keefe, Adolphe Menjou. Kyser's orchestra goes to Hollywood to make a picture, where the moguls try to change him. Amusing musical. (Dir: David Butler, 88 mins.)

Theater of Blood (Great Britain, 1973)**** Vincent Price, Diana Rigg. Remarkable British black comedy/horror film about a demented Shakespearean actor (Price) having his macabre revenge on eight critics, including Robert Morley and Jack Hawkins. Gory, imaginative, wildly melodramatic—good fun. Rigg plays Price's helpful daughter. (Dir: Douglas Hickox, 104 mins.)

Theatre of Death (Great Britain, 1966)*** Christopher Lee, Lelia Goldoni, Julian Glover, Jenny Hill, Evelyn Laye. Not a horror flic, but a neat, complex whodunit set in the Grand Guignol theatre in Paris. A perverse director has a strange hold on two girls—when he is murdered (however much he deserved it) the police must decide who did, in fact, do it. Keep watching—you'll never guess. (Dir: Samuel Gallu, 90 mins.)

Their Last Night (France, 1953)** Jean Gabin, Madeleine Robinson. Librarian who is really a notorious gang leader seeks the aid of a girl when the police begin to close in. Flat crime drama dubbed in English is reminiscent of prewar Gabin films, only not as good. (Dir: George Lacombe, 97 mins.)

Them (1954)**½ James Whitmore, Edmund Gwenn, James Arness, Fess Parker, Joan Weldon. Entertaining science fiction thriller about strange creatures who appear suddenly near the Mojave Desert. Treated like a murder mystery rather than the shock approach usually employed in such SF films. (Dir: Gordon Douglas, 94 mins.)

Then Came Bronson (1969)** Michael Parks, Bonnie Bedelia, Akim Tamiroff. Pilot for a TV series. Michael Parks stars as Bronson, a young reporter who chucks it all when his friend commits suicide, leaving him his motorcycle. The film is slow moving and the dialogue, stilted. Parks, an exponent of the slouch and mumble school of acting, is well cast as the rebel searching for (as he puts it) "his piece of the world." Bonnie Bedelia is appealing as a runaway bride who latches on to Bronson and falls in love. (Dir: William Graham, 100 mins.)

Then There Were Three (1962)**½ Frank Latimore, Alex Nicol. German officer infiltrates the American lines to kill an Italian partisan. Neat little combination of WW II and mystery yarn, filmed in Italy. No epic, but well done. (Dir: Alex Nicol, 82 mins.)

Theodora Goes Wild (1936)*** Irene Dunne, Melvyn Douglas, Thomas Mitchell.

Dunne's big breakthrough as a comic actress. Previously a weepie star par excellence, Dunne throws away her dignity and gets laughs as a modest small-town librarian who writes a steamy best-seller about the secret life of small towns. Screwball comedy isn't screwy enough. Screenplay by Sidney Buchman, adapted from a story by Mary McCarthy (that's right). (Dir: Richard Boleslawski, 94 mins.)

Theodora, Slave Empress (Italy, 1954)** Irene Papas, Georges Marchal, Gianna Maria Canale. Lavish but dull epic film about the days of the Roman Empire. Acting is in exaggerated style of Grand Opera. (Dir: Riccardo Freda, 88 mins.)

There Goes Barder (France, 1955)*½ Eddie Constantine, May Britt. (Dir: John Berry, 90 mins.)

There Goes My Girl (1937)*** Gene Raymond, Ann Sothern. Boy and girl reporters love each other, but are bitter rivals when a murder story breaks. Well done comedy, light and amusing. (Dir: Ben Holmes, 74 mins.)

There Goes My Heart (1938)**½ Fredric March, Virginia Bruce. Spoiled heiress skips home and becomes a salesgirl, where a reporter discovers her secret. Pleasant, amusing comedy. (Dir: Norman Z. McLeod, 82 mins.)

There Goes the Groom (1937)**½ Burgess Meredith, Ann Sothern. Man blessed with sudden riches marries, and has in-law trouble. Diverting comedy. (Dir: Joseph Santley, 70 mins.)

There Was a Crooked Man (1970)*** Kirk Douglas, Henry Fonda, Hume Cronyn, Lee Grant, Burgess Meredith. Douglas, as a robber serving time in prison (circa 1880's), and Fonda, as a reform-oriented warden, spark this western tale. Although the script may get too talky at times, director Joseph L. Mankiewicz directs the action with a knowing hand, leading to the film's final confrontation between the two flinty leads. (118 mins.)

There Was an Old Couple (U.S.S.R., 1965)**** Ivan Marin, Vera Kuznetsova, Lyudmila Madsakova. A gentle, touching and moving film about an aged Russian farm couple who go to live with one of their children after their home is destroyed. Sensitively directed by Grigory Choukhrai, who also directed the beautiful "Ballad of a Soldier." Uniformly well acted. English subtitles. (103 mins.)

There's a Girl in My Soup (Great Britain, 1970)*** Peter Sellers, Goldie Hawn, Tony Britton. The delightful combination of confident Sellers as a TV gourmet and scatterbrained Hawn as a girl who disrupts his free-wheeling life-style adds up to fun. Based on the London and Broadway stage comedy, the screen version is better. It ambles along quite nicely, and some of the lines are very funny. (Dir: Roy Boulting, 96 mins.)

There's Always a Price Tag (France, 1957)** Michele Morgan, Daniel Gelin.

Wicked wife draws her lover into a plot to get rid of her husband. Crime drama is bogged down in a welter of conversation. (Dir: Denys De La Patelliere, 102 mins.)

There's Always a Thursday (Great Britain, 1957)** Charles Victor, Frances Day, Jill Ireland. In this lightweight British comedy, a henpecked spouse blossoms into a full fledged louse. Some good acting. (Dir: Charles Saunders, 62 mins.)

There's Always a Woman (1938)*** Joan Blondell, Melvyn Douglas, Mary Astor. Private eye returns to the D.A.'s office and gives his agency to his wife; then they find themselves working on the same murder case. Entertaining comedy-mystery. (Dir: Alexander Hall, 81 mins.)

There's Always Tomorrow (1956)**** Barbara Stanwyck, Fred MacMurray, Joan Bennett. MacMurray is a disaffected toy manufacturer afflicted with a self-absorbed wife (Bennett) and ratty kids. Then old flame Stanwyck reenters his life. Mordant, intelligent soaper. (Dir: Douglas Sirk, 84 mins.)

There's No Business Like Show Business (1954)** Ethel Merman, Dan Dailey, Marilyn Monroe, Donald O'Connor, Johnny Ray, Mitzi Gaynor. A low point in the history of the Hollywood musical. Merman and the talented Dailey are two vaudevillians who spawn a family of showbiz types (O'Connor, Ray, Gaynor) who aren't very entertaining. The film boasts some good Irving Berlin tunes, but the high point is Marilyn Monroe's rendition of "Heat Wave." Lamar Trotti's story was Oscar-nominated, but they hadda be kidding. (Dir: Walter Lang, 117 mins.)

Therese Etienne (France, 1953)** Francoise Arnoul, James Robertson-Justice, Pierre Vaneck. Old plot about the elderly farmer marrying the young servant girl, who is loved by the returning son. Dubbed in English. (Dir: Marcel Carne, 95 mins.)

These Are the Damned (Great Britain, 1963)*** Macdonald Carey, Oliver Reed, Shirley Anne Field, Viveca Lindfors, Alexander Knox, James Villiers. Dark, steely cross between a youth-gang picture and science-fiction. Carey, Reed, and Field are involved in a rather conventional juvenile delinquent wrangle when they come upon a cave inhabited by strangely cold children, loosing a hideous doom. Film was drastically re-cut by the studio, but it's still an unusual, compelling, (if basically over-emotional) vision. (Dir: Joseph Losey, 77 mins.)

These Glamour Girls (1939)*** Lana Turner, Lew Ayres, Anita Louise, Richard Carlson. Good satirical comedy about college life although the film's social implications have lost their bite. You'll still enjoy seeing a sexy Lana make fools out of a pack of debutantes. (Dir: S. Sylvan Simon, 80 mins.)

These Thousand Hills (1959)**½ Don Murray, Richard Egan, Lee Remick, Patricia Owens, Stuart Whitman. Occasionally interesting, frequently meandering western about a young cowpoke who becomes prosperous in the Old West, and the troubles that beset him. Would have been better with more directness, less introspection. (Dir: Richard Fleischer, 96 mins.)

These Three (1936)***½ Merle Oberon, Miriam Hopkins, Joel McCrea. Lillian Hellman's Broadway play "The Children's Hour" caused a scandal with its open treatment of lesbianism, but the censors demanded heterosexuality—and got it in the beefy person of McCrea—for this film version. Director William Wyler handles Hellman's preachy dialogue with some dignity. Remade as "The Children's Hour." (90 mins.)

These Wilder Years (1956)**½ James Cagney, Barbara Stanwyck, Walter Pidgeon. Steel magnate searches for his illegitimate son of 20, runs into unexpected opposition. Trouping by veterans saves this soap opera from becoming too much. (Dir: Roy Rowland, 91 mins.)

They All Kissed the Bride (1942)**½ Joan Crawford, Melvyn Douglas. Career girl learns the importance of love in this familiar, but mildly amusing film. (Dir: Alexander Hall, 87 mins.)

They Call It Murder (MTV 1971)** Jim Hutton, Lloyd Bochner, Jessica Walter. Average murder mystery, as the D.A. finds a corpse in a swimming pool and tries to link the victim to an insurance claim and a car crash. Based on an Erle Stanley Gardner novel. (Dir: Walter Grauman, 97 mins.)

They Call Me Mr. Tibbs (1970)** Sidney Poitier, Martin Landau, Barbara McNair, Juano Hernandez, Norma Crane. Inferior sequel to the first-rate "In the Heat of the Night." Sidney's Virgil Tibbs again, but this time the locale moves from the deep South, and a lot's been lost in the trek to San Francisco. Routine homicide drama, with Poitier looking and acting, quite understandably, very bored. (Dir: Gordon Douglas, 108 mins.)

They Call Me Trinity (Italy, 1972)** Terence Hill, Bud Spencer, Farley Granger. Uneven spaghetti western with tongue-in-cheek comedy. Plot concerns an involved scheme to rustle cattle, dreamed up by bogus sheriff Bambino and freewheeling Trinity. Hill as Trinity and Spencer as his brother Bambino manage to keep the show moving along. (Dir: E. B. Clucher, 110 mins.)

They Came to Cordura (1959)** Gary Cooper, Rita Hayworth, Van Heflin, Tab Hunter. Slow moving tale about six soldiers (circa 1916) and one woman who make an arduous trek across impossible terrain to reach Cordura, a military outpost. The personal feelings of the seven are bared during the interminable journey. Many big stars are wasted in this dry pic. (Dir: Robert Rossen, 123 mins.)

They Came to Rob Las Vegas (Spain-

France-West Germany-Italy, 1968)* Gary Lockwood, Elke Sommer, Lee J. Cobb, Jack Palance. (Dir: Antonio Isasi, 126 mins.)

They Can't Hang Me (Great Britain, 1955)**½ Terence Morgan, Yolande Donlan. Condemned murderer bargains his freedom for information about a vital security leak. Unimportant but fast-moving mystery. (Dir: Val Guest, 75 mins.)

They Died with Their Boots On (1941)***½ Errol Flynn, Olivia de Havilland, Arthur Kennedy, Anthony Quinn, Sydney Greenstreet. Flynn makes a dashing Gen. Custer, maturing from the light romantic comedian of his cadet days to the tragically betrayed figure of Little Big Horn. It's historical nonsense, but the visual style of director Raoul Walsh triumphs over every improbability in this long, expert epic that never drags despite its length. (138 mins.)

They Drive by Night (1940)*** Ida Lupino, George Raft, Humphrey Bogart, Ann Sheridan. For its first half this is a growly social drama about the trucking trade—fast, hard, bitter, brilliantly realized. Then the creaky murder-and-adultery plot gets under way and the rest is tiresome Lupino overacting. Half a masterpiece is better than none. Partial remake of "Bordertown." (Dir: Raoul Walsh, 93 mins.)

They Gave Him a Gun (1937)*½ Spencer Tracy, Gladys George, Franchot Tone. (Dir: W. S. Van Dyke, 94 mins.)

They Got Me Covered (1943)**½ Bob Hope, Dorothy Lamour, Otto Preminger. A typical Hope vs. the German enemy agents chase film, which means it's fun all the way. Hope's favorite brunette, Lamour, is around for the antics and Preminger is cast as a sinister enemy agent, a part he has played many times. (Dir: David Butler, 95 mins.)

They Knew What They Wanted (1940)***½ Charles Laughton, Carole Lombard, William Gargan, Karl Malden. Italian grape-grower takes a lonely waitress as a bride, with tragedy following. Powerful, finely acted drama. Basis for the musical "The Most Happy Fella." (Dir: Garson Kanin, 96 mins.)

They Live by Night (1948)**** Farley Granger, Cathy O'Donnell, Howard da Silva. Perhaps the best debut film of an American director, and I'm not unmindful of "Citizen Kane." Tense, touching story of a doomed fugitive couple (based on Edward Anderson's "Thieves Like Us," later remade by Robert Altman). (Dir: Nicholas Ray, 95 mins.)

They Made Me a Criminal (1939)*** John Garfield, Ann Sheridan, Dead End Kids, Claude Rains. Mr. Garfield's dynamic, yet sensitive, portrayal of a fugitive boxer who thinks he has murdered a man is so stirring that it lifts this commonplace story to the level of entertainment. Remake of "The Life of Jimmy Dolan." (Dir: Busby Berkeley, 92 mins.)

They Made Me a Killer (1946)**½ Robert Lowery, Barbara Britton. Young man is forced to join some bank robbers, but finally outwits them. Fast-moving melodrama with plenty of action. (Dir: William C. Thomas, 64 mins.)

They Met in Bombay (1941)**½ Clark Gable, Rosalind Russell, Peter Lorre. Routine adventure story about a couple of jewel thieves who fall in love and in order to clear his name before the fadeout he joins forces with the English in a battle against the Japs. Confusing? Just another film. (Dir: Clarence Brown, 86 mins.)

They Might Be Giants (1971)*** George C. Scott, Joanne Woodward, Jack Gilford. Bizarre, sentimental fable displaying Scott as Justin Playfair, a retired judge who believes himself to be Sherlock Holmes. The judge's brother calls on a female Dr. Watson (Miss Woodward) to have Scott committed so he can inherit the family fortune. But Scott embraces a world too absurd to be touched by this ploy. Sometimes muddled, often appealing, and Scott and Woodward are splendid. Screenplay by James Goldman. (Dir: Anthony Harvey, 88 mins.)

They Only Come Out at Night (MTV 1975)*½ Jack Warden, Tim O'Connor, Madeline Sherwood, Joe Mantell. (Dir: Daryl Duke, 72 mins.)

They Only Kill Their Masters (1972)**½ James Garner, June Allyson, Peter Lawford, Hal Holbrook, Katharine Ross. James Garner's casual approach to his role as a California town police chief is a diverting note in this offbeat murder mystery. A swinger is found dead on the beach. Prime suspects include June Allyson, as an aging woman with a key to the whole thing; Peter Lawford, as the victim's husband; and Hal Holbrook, as a veterinarian. Some nice moments in original screenplay by Lane Slate. (Dir: James Goldstone, 97 mins.)

They Ran for Their Lives (1968)* John Payne, John Carradine, Jim Davis. (Dir: John Payne, 92 mins.)

They Rode West (1954)*** Robert Francis, Donna Reed, May Wynn, Phil Carey. Better than average western drama dealing with the efforts of a courageous young doctor to maintain peace with the Kiowa Indians. (Dir: Phil Karlson, 84 mins.)

They Shall Have Music (1939)**½ Joel McCrea, Walter Brennan, Marjorie Main, Andrea Leeds. A moderately successful drama about an east side settlement house for young musicians. The highlight of the film is the violin artistry of Jascha Heifetz. (Dir: Archie Mayo, 100 mins.)

They Shall Not Die—See: **Serengeti**

They Shoot Horses, Don't They? (1969) **** Jane Fonda, Michael Sarrazin, Gig Young. Excellent film depicting the madness and desperation of the depression era's marathon dance contests. Based on the '35 novel by Horace McCoy. The cast is perfect., the dance sessions, especially the "sprints," are magnificently staged by director Sydney Pollack. (121 mins.)

They Went That-a-Way and That-a-Way (1978)** Tim Conway, Chuck McCann, Reni Santoni. Dopey comedy about cops and escaped convicts, written by Conway. (Dirs: Edward Montagne, Stuart E. McGowan, 106 mins.)

They Were Expendable (1945)***½ John Wayne, Robert Montgomery, Donna Reed. Director John Ford poured his accumulated emotions about WW II, a combination of personal bitterness and benign acceptance of duty, into this moving account of the fortunes of a PT-boat squadron as its ranks are thinned out during the loss of the Philippines. (135 min.)

They Were Sisters (Great Britain, 1945)*** James Mason, Phyllis Calvert. The love affairs and marital mishaps of three devoted sisters are related. Well acted drama. (Dir: Arthur Crabtree, 108 mins.)

They Were So Young (1955)*** Scott Brady, Johanna Matz, Raymond Burr. Innocent girls are sent to South America as entertainers and killed if they resist. Rather lurid but well-made melodrama with a good cast. Produced in Germany. (Dir: Kurt Neumann, 80 mins.)

They Who Dare (Great Britain, 1954)*** Dirk Bogarde, Akim Tamiroff. Six Englishmen and four Greek soldiers are assigned to blow up air fields in Rhodes when Allied communication lines are being hampered. Well-made, frequently exciting drama of WW II. (Dir: Lewis Milestone, 101 mins.)

They Won't Believe Me (1947)***½ Robert Young, Susan Hayward, Jane Greer. Man intending to kill his wife doesn't succeed, but through a quirk of fate goes on trial anyway. Absorbing ironic melodrama. (Dir: Irving Pichel, 95 mins.)

They Won't Forget (1937)**** Claude Rains, Allyn Joslyn, Lana Turner, Edward Norris. An exceptional drama about a prosecutor in a southern town who turns a murder case into a political stepping stone. Good writing, superb acting, and Mervyn LeRoy's expert direction make this a compelling film. (94 mins.)

Thief, The (1952)*** Ray Milland, Rita Gam, Martin Gabel. Story of how a Communist spy is forced to kill an FBI agent, and how his conscience causes him to give himself up. Unusual in that there is no dialogue; the only sounds are the musical score, and background noises. As such, a novelty; otherwise, the effect is forced, the melodrama routine. (Dir: Russell Rouse, 85 mins.)

Thief (MTV 1971)**½ Richard Crenna, Angie Dickinson, Cameron Mitchell, Hurd Hatfield. Writer John D. F. Black combines suspense with interesting character development as half-hero, half-heel Crenna is in a solid bind when he must rob to pay a gambling debt. Good support from Dickinson as a puzzled lady who wants to know her man better; Mitchell

as a lawyer and Hatfield as a fence for jewelry. (Dir: William Graham, 72 mins.)

Thief of Bagdad, The (Great Britain, 1940)***½ Sabu, John Justin, Rex Ingram, June Duprez, Conrad Veidt. One of the most popular screen fantasies, and deservedly so, this work reflects most of all the flamboyant personality of its producer, Alexander Korda. Enchanting, with superb early Technicolor. Won four Oscars. (Dirs: Michael Powell, Tim Whelan, Ludwig Berger, 106 mins.)

Thief of Bagdad (France-Italy, 1961)** Muscle man Steve Reeves in the Arabian Nights adventure epic—colorful, but on a juvenile level. (Dir: Arthur Lubin, 89 mins.)

Thief of Baghdad, The (MTV 1978)**½ Peter Ustinov, Roddy McDowall, Kabir Bedi. Easy-to-take European-produced version of the Arabian Nights tale. Ustinov helps make things move along as the wily caliph of Baghdad, trying to marry off his daughter, Princess Yasmine, played by Ustinov's real-life daughter Pavla Ustinov. Indian heartthrob Bedi more than fills the bill as the dashing Prince Taj, and McDowall is well cast as the thief of Baghdad who gets about on a flying carpet when the traffic is heavy. (Dir: Clive Donner, 104 mins.)

Thief Who Came to Dinner, The (1973)**½ Ryan O'Neal, Jacqueline Bisset, Warren Oates, Jill Clayburgh. If you are a Ryan O'Neal fan, you'll enjoy this ambling comedy crime film which casts the actor as a computer programmer who happens to be a cat burglar on the side. Some of the plot gets too involved, but you'll enjoy the characters, including beautiful Jacqueline Bisset and especially Jill Clayburgh, in the small role of Ryan's actress ex-wife who decides to look up her former husband again while passing through town with a touring company. (Dir: Bud Yorkin, 103 mins.)

Thieves' Highway (1949)*** Richard Conte, Valentina Cortesa, Lee J. Cobb, Jack Oakie. Action-melodrama concerning truckers, trollops and thugs, on the long haul delivering fresh vegetables to market. Italian actress Valentina Cortesa makes a fine American debut. (Dir: Jules Dassin, 94 mins.)

Thieves' Holiday—See: **Scandal in Paris, A**

Thieves Like Us (1974)**** Keith Carradine, Shelley Duvall, John Schuck, Louise Fletcher, Joan Tewkesbury. A marvelous version, directed beautifully by Robert Altman, of the '37 novel by Edward Anderson, first filmed as "They Live by Night." Story of a pair of doomed lovers during the depression is skillfully adapted by Calder Willingham, Joan Tewkesbury, and Altman. The performances are excellent, especially Carradine and Duvall, who give sensitive, touching performances as the doomed young lovers. (123 mins.)

Thin Air (U.S.-Great Britain, 1969)* George Sanders, Maurice Evans, Robert Flemyng. (Dir: Gerry Levy, 91 mins.)

Thin Ice (1937)*** Sonja Hennie, Tyrone Power. Fast moving, entertaining musical fantasy about the romance of a skating instructor and a prince. Plenty of Sonja's skating and generally a good film. (Dir: Sidney Lanfield, 78 mins.)

Thin Ice (MTV 1981)** Kate Jackson, Gerald Pendergast, Lillian Gish. A blond boy falls for his pretty teacher against a background of high-school classrooms and afternoon sails, in a warm, earnest yarn about young love and small-town priggery. Jackson is the teacher, and Pendergast, though he looks a bit old for the teenage lover, makes it work because of his wholesomeness. Gish, out of Hollywood pioneer days, pleases as a stalwart grandmother. (104 mins.)

Thin Man, The (1934)***½ William Powell, Myrna Loy, Maureen O'Sullivan, Cesar Romero, Edward Ellis (title role). This version of Dashiell Hammett's novel took 16 days to film and is one of the most popular comedies ever made. As Nick and Nora Charles, Powell and Loy are the most sophisticated, insolent, and *healthy* married couple onscreen. (Dir: W.S. Van Dyke II, 93 mins.)

Thin Man Goes Home, The (1944)**½ William Powell, Myrna Loy. Series returns after a three-year hiatus and is way off standard. There's a murder, some good dialogue but it's sadly lacking in the usual fast paced witticisms. (Dir: Richard Thorpe, 101 mins.)

Thin Red Line, The (1964)**½ Keir Dullea, Jack Warden. James Jones' fine novel of the men who fought and died at Guadalcanal made into an uneven film with some fine rugged battle scenes, but a story treatment that never quite jells. (Dir: Andrew Marton, 99 mins.)

Thing, The (1951)*** Kenneth Tobey, Margaret Sheridan, James Arness. Scientific research station in the Arctic comes across a monster from another world. Sufficiently thrilling fantastic melodrama. (Dir: Christian Nyby, 87 mins.)

Thing with Two Heads, The (1972)½ Ray Milland, Rosey Grier. (Dir: Lee Frost, 90 mins.)

Things to Come (Great Britain, 1936)**½ Raymond Massey, Ralph Richardson, Ann Todd, Cedric Hardwicke. A preview of the future by H. G. Wells who, although wildly wrong, had at least the courage to look foolish. Director William Cameron Menzies's camera work is less successful than his intriguingly designed sets. Interesting film shows what the '30s thought about architecture. (100 mins.)

Third Alibi, The (Great Britain, 1961)** Laurence Payne, Patricia Dainton, Jane Griffiths. Husband desiring to rid himself of his wife so he can marry her sister devises an elaborate murder plan. Aver-

age Grade B melodrama. (Dir: Montgomery Tully, 70 mins.)

Third Day, The (1965)**½ George Peppard, Elizabeth Ashley, Roddy McDowall. Fairly engrossing tale about an amnesiac (George Peppard) who has to piece together many events in his past after an auto crash and a possible murder. Peppard looks bewildered enough to carry off his role but it's Roddy McDowall's performance as an oily relative ready to do him in at every turn which is the standout. The competent supporting cast includes Herbert Marshall, Arthur O'Connell and Arte Johnson in a serious role. (Dir: Jack Smight, 119 mins.)

Third Finger, Left Hand (1940)** Melvyn Douglas, Myrna Loy. Not funny in spite of good acting is this sophisticated comedy about a cold cookie who falls for a guy but plays hard to get. (Dir: Robert Z. Leonard, 96 mins.)

Third Girl from the Left, The (MTV 1973)**½ Kim Novak, Tony Curtis, Michael Brandon. Familiar story about an over-the-hill New York chorine who's reached the crossroads in her life—she loses her front-row spot in the chorus; terminates her 13-year engagement to her nightclub singer-comic boyfriend; and finds herself attracted to a very attentive and winning younger man. Dory Previn's script has flashes of truth and insight going for Miss Novak's character, but the men in her life fall into the cliche mold. (Dir: Peter Medak, 74 mins.)

Third Key, The (Great Britain, 1956)***½ Jack Hawkins, Dorothy Alison. Police search for a safecracker, and the chase leads them to murder. Exciting crime drama. (Dir: Charles Frend, 96 mins.)

Third Man, The (Great Britain, 1949)**** Joseph Cotten, Orson Welles, Alida Valli, Trevor Howard, Bernard Lee. Director Carol Reed's thriller is overelaborated visually, in what passed for complexity among critics then. U.S. pulp novelist Cotten foolishly seeks to meet the cynical Old World on his own quixotic terms. Welles steals the show in his brief appearances as the black-market crook thought to be dead, and Howard and Valli are excellent and restrained in support. Photography by Robert Krasker, screenplay by Graham Greene, and that zither music by Anton Karas. (104 mins.)

Third Secret, The (Great Britain, 1964)*** Stephen Boyd, Pamela Franklin, Diane Cilento, Richard Attenborough. Uneven but often interesting psychological drama. When a leading British psychiatrist dies and the coroner's verdict is suicide, his teen-age daughter convinces a TV commentator to investigate further. The film has a surprise ending. (Dir: Charles Crichton, 103 mins.)

Third Voice, The (1960)**** Edmond O'Brien, Laraine Day, Julie London. Fine suspense thriller made economically but excellently about an impostor hired to

664

pose as a murdered financier by his private secretary. Particularly adept direction and script, with top performances make this one a surprise hit. (Dir: Hubert Cornfield, 79 mins.)

Third Walker, The (Canada, 1979)*** Colleen Dewhurst, William Shatner, Frank Moore, David and Tony Meyer. Lensed on picturesque Cape Breton Island and the feature debut of director Teri McLuhan, daughter of the communications expert. The main theme is twins who are mixed up at birth and raised by different mothers. Interesting offbeat entry. (83 mins.)

13 Frightened Girls (1963)½ Kathy Dunn, Murray Hamilton. (Dir: William Castle, 89 mins.)

Thirteen Ghosts (1960)** Charles Herbert, Jo Morrow. A thoroughly gimmicked horror film. Mild entertainment, as a professor and family move into a haunted house. (Dir: William Castle, 88 mins.)

13 Great Disasters That Shook the World, The (1979)** Footage of famous disasters including the crash of the "Hindenburg," the '64 Alaskan earthquake, and the '71 eruption of Sicily's Mt. Etna is fascinating but there is too much filler shot merely to put the film into the "movie" classification. (101 mins.)

13 Rue Madeleine (1946)**½ James Cagney, Annabella, Richard Conte, Karl Malden. Semidocumentary espionage thriller stars Cagney as the leader of a group of secret agents; he goes to France to complete a mission when one of his men is killed by the Nazis. One of a series of "March of Time"-inspired films produced by Louis de Rochemont. (Dir: Henry Hathaway, 95 mins.)

13 West Street (1962)**½ Alan Ladd, Rod Steiger, Michael Callan, Dolores Dorn. Man beaten by a gang of teenagers refuses to cooperate with the police, seeks his own revenge. Tough little crime drama will generally have the viewer on its side; effective use of the it-could-happen-to-you idea. (Dir: Philip Leacock, 80 mins.)

13th Letter, The (1951)*** Charles Boyer, Linda Darnell, Constance Smith, Michael Rennie. Small town in Canada is in turmoil when a series of incriminating letters appear. Suspense, fine performances and direction (by Otto Preminger). (85 mins.)

Thirty-Day Princess (1934)*** Sylvia Sidney, Cary Grant, Edward Arnold. A young actress is hired to take the place of a princess who has come down with mumps on a tour of New York City. Naturally, the ordinary girl falls in love with someone who thinks she is a princess. Sidney convincingly portrays the real and the false princess, and the other performances have great charm. Fine light entertainment. Good script by Preston Sturges. (Dir: Marion Gering, 73 mins.)

30 Foot Bride of Candy Rock, The (1959)* Lou Costello, Dorothy Provine. (Dir: Sidney Miller, 73 mins.)

Thirty Is a Dangerous Age, Cynthia (Great Britain, 1968)***½ Dudley Moore, Suzy Kendall, Eddie Foy, Jr. Moore attempts to attain success and marriage by age 30 (he's got six weeks to go) in this bewitching and eccentric release. Director Joseph McGrath has a flair for portraying the absurd side of sex and marriage. (85 mins.)

39 Steps, The (Great Britain, 1935)**** Robert Donat, Madeleine Carroll. Adaptation of the John Buchan spy thriller, with delightful work by Donat and Carroll, who spend much of the film handcuffed together, with the police and the real spies after them. The suspense is terrific, though the plot resolution is bald contrivance. The fundamental theme of director Alfred Hitchcock—an innocent man plunged into a world of deception, doubt, and chaos—is festooned with more action, humor, suspense, and visual artistry than anyone would have a right to expect. (89 mins.)

39 Steps, The (Great Britain, 1959)**½ Kenneth More, Taina Elg. This remake doesn't measure up to Hitchcock, but suspense fans unfamiliar with the original will find enough here to sustain their interest. Mr. More and Miss Elg play a pair of innocent bystanders who become enmeshed in a tangle of murder and espionage. (Dir: Ralph Thomas, 93 mins.)

Thirty-Nine Steps, The (Great Britain, 1978)*** Robert Powell, John Mills, Karen Dotrice. Third version of the John Buchan novel proves you can't top Alfred Hitchcock's classic, although you can still get some mileage out of the plot. This version is set, like the novel, in London, on the eve of WW I. Powell makes an energetic hero, and Dotrice is lovely and talented. Thrills and laughs in good measure. (Dir: Don Sharp, 102 mins.)

Thirty Seconds Over Tokyo (1944)*** Van Johnson, Spencer Tracy, Robert Walker, Robert Mitchum Phyllis Thaxter. An excellent war film which chronicles the story of our first raid on Japan. Slightly dated but still good entertainment. (Dir: Mervyn LeRoy, 138 mins.)

36 Hours (1964)*** James Garner, Rod Taylor, Eva Marie Saint. Army officer is abducted by the Nazis and made to believe the war has ended, so they can pry secrets from him. First half is excellent; as soon as the plot becomes clear, it gradually deteriorates into a routine WW II spy thriller. Performances quite good. (Dir: George Seaton, 115 mins.)

This Above All (1942)*** Tyrone Power, Joan Fontaine. Eric Knight's novel of the romance between a disillusioned British soldier and a patriotic girl is a powerful love story minus many of the book's values. Superbly directed, it is a bit too slow moving to hold sustained interest. Dated because of subject matter. (Dir: Anatole Litvak, 110 mins.)

This Angry Age (Italy-U.S., 1958)*½ Anthony Perkins, Silvana Mangano, Jo

Van Fleet, Richard Conte, Alida Valli. (Dir: René Clement, 111 mins.)

This Could Be the Night (1957)*** Jean Simmons, Anthony Franciosa, Paul Douglas, Joan Blondell, Julie Wilson. Entertaining comedy about a school teacher charmingly played by Jean Simmons, who takes a part-time job as a secretary to a night club owner, and ends up changing lives left and right. Franciosa comes on strong as the wolf who's tamed by Miss Simmons. (Dir: Robert Wise, 103 mins.)

This Earth Is Mine (1959)**½ Rock Hudson, Jean Simmons, Claude Rains, Dorothy McGuire, Anna Lee. Sprawling family dynasty film set in the Napa Valley wine country. (Dir: Henry King, 125 mins.)

This Gun for Hire (1942)***½ Alan Ladd, Veronica Lake. Exciting, tense tale of a hired killer who is double-crossed and seeks revenge. Ladd's portrayal of the killer made him a star. Based on the Graham Greene novel. (Dir: Frank Tuttle, 80 mins.)

This Happy Breed (Great Britain, 1944) **** Robert Newton, Celia Johnson, John Mills, Stanley Holloway. Noël Coward's panoramic story of a family and of the house in which they live through two wars. Fine drama captures the spirit of England itself; exemplary in all departments. (Dir: David Lean, 114 mins.)

This Happy Feeling (1958)*** Debbie Reynolds, Curt Jurgens, John Saxon, Mary Astor, Alexis Smith. Charming comedy about a young girl who fancies herself in love with a dashing older man. The complications are predictable but the cast plays it in the spirit in which it's intended. (Dir: Blake Edwards, 92 mins.)

This Is My Affair (1937)**½ Robert Taylor, Barbara Stanwyck, Victor McLaglen. Solid studio product, directed by reliable hack William A. Seiter. Taylor is a secret agent assigned by President McKinley to investigate a band of train robbers. He infiltrates the band, gets himself arrested, but then, of course, McKinley is assassinated. (99 mins.)

This Is Not a Test (1962)**½ Mary Morias, Seamon Glass. Tough state trooper takes charge when word comes of an impending nuclear attack, joins a group held up by a roadblock. Grim little drama has the expected rough edges but occasionally whips up some powerful scenes. (Dir: Frederic Gadette, 72 mins.)

This Is the Army (1943)*** George Murphy, Ronald Reagan, Joan Leslie, Kate Smith, Joe Louis. Pleasant Irving Berlin extravaganza is '40's artifact. The Broadway show was entirely cast with men in uniform; some of them appear in the film. Berlin appears at the piano to play his "Oh How I Hate to Get Up in the Morning"; you can tell he's dubbed, since the only key he could play in was F-sharp major, and he's not hitting the black keys. Color. (Dir: Michael Curtiz, 121 mins.)

This Is the West That Was (MTV 1974)*½ Ben Murphy, Kim Darby, Jane Alexander,

Tony Franciosa, Matt Clark. (Dir: Fielder Cook, 74 mins.)

This Island Earth (1955)**½ Jeff Morrow, Faith Domergue, Rex Reason. Science fiction story with nicer plot and special effects than usual. Ends on a planet under heavy attack by meteors being directed at it by an enemy planet. (Dir: Joseph M. Newman, 87 mins.)

This Land Is Mine (1943)***½ Charles Laughton, Maureen O'Hara, George Sanders. A timid schoolteacher becomes a hero when his country is overrun by Nazis. Fine performance by Laughton in this compelling drama. (Dir: Jean Renoir, 103 mins.)

This Love of Ours (1945)**½ Merle Oberon, Claude Rains, Charles Korvin. Maudlin soap opera about an unfaithful wife and mother who returns to her husband's home after 12 years to find resentment and finally love. Good performances by the cast. Remade as "Never Say Goodbye." (Dir: William Dieterle, 90 mins.)

This Man Must Die (France-Italy, 1969) ***½ Michel Duchaussoy, Jean Yanne. Director Claude Chabrol has fashioned another fine crime tale. This time his main character is a man who vows to take revenge on the hit-and-run driver who killed his son. Duchaussoy plays the father, and Yanne plays the insidious and much-hated killer. The inevitability of their mutual destruction is beautifully played against the stunning backgrounds of France. (115 mins.)

This Man Stands Alone (MTV 1979)** Louis Gossett, Jr., Clu Gulager, Lonny Chapman. Gossett is the only reason to watch this pilot film about a minister who becomes the sheriff of a small Alabama town. You've seen the racial strife yarn before. (Dir: Jerrold Freedman, 104 mins.)

This Man's Navy (1945)*** Wallace Beery, Tom Drake, Jan Clayton. Veteran officer in the balloon service "adopts" a lad and urges him to make good in the navy. Familiar but well done melodrama. Good direction, performances. (Dir: William Wellman, 100 mins.)

This Property Is Condemned (1966)**½ Natalie Wood, Robert Redford, Charles Bronson. The allure of stars Redford and Wood, plus the characters created by Tennessee Williams in a one-act play, are the chief inducements in this deep South soap opera about a free spirit of a girl longing for adventure and true love. The film begins interestingly enough, but it soon becomes as uneven as Wood's southern accent. (Dir: Sydney Pollack, 110 mins.)

This Rebel Age—See: **Beat Generation, The**
This Rebel Breed (1960)** Rita Moreno, Mark Damon, Gerald Mohr, Diane (later Dyan) Cannon. Undercover cops deal with narcotics and racial tensions in high school. We've seen it before, since and better! (Dir: Richard L. Bare, 90 mins.)

This Savage Land (MTV 1968)** Barry Sullivan, Glenn Corbett, Kathryn Hays, George C. Scott. Sullivan as an Ohio widower heading out West with his family to start again in the 19th century. Scott guest-starred in these two better-than-average episodes, as the Sullivan clan arrives in a town victimized by a group of vigilantes. (Dir: Vincent McEveety, 97 mins.)

This Side of the Law (1950)** Viveca Lindfors, Kent Smith, Janis Paige. Contrived plot has Kent Smith hired by a shady lawyer to impersonate a missing wealthy man. The complications are as obvious as the outcome. (Dir: Richard L. Bare, 74 mins.)

This Special Friendship (France, 1964)**½ Francis Lacombrade, Didier Haudepin, Lucien Nat. Gallic insights into the delicacy of youthful homoerotic bonds, set of course in a Catholic boarding school and smothering with the requisite sensitivity. Based on Roger Peyrefitte's novel, the m was directed by hack sentimentalist Jean Delannoy. (99 mins.)

This Sporting Life (Great Britain, 1963)***½ Richard Harris, Rachel Roberts, Alan Badel. Strong drama about a bastard of a rugby player, played by Harris, the most mannered of his generation of working-class heroes, as well as the most histrionic—it's still his best performance. The same goes for Roberts as his abused lover. Kitchen sink realism featuring brutal sexuality. From the novel by David Storey. (Dir: Lindsay Anderson, 134 mins.)

This Strange Passion (Mexico, 1952)**** Arturo de Cordova. A study of obsessive, lustful jealousy, this Luis Buñuel-directed film contains some of his most brilliantly conceived moments of black humor. Made cheaply, it towers over more elaborately mounted art with its fiendish, angry wit. (100 mins.)

This Thing Called Love (1941)*** Rosalind Russell, Melvyn Douglas, Lee J. Cobb. Newlyweds agree to a three-month platonic arrangement to test their marriage. Nicely played, amusing, adult comedy. (Dir: Alexander Hall, 98 mins.)

This Time for Keeps (1947)** Esther Williams, Johnnie Johnston, Lauritz Melchior, Jimmy Durante, Xavier Cugat and his orchestra. Lamentable Williams musical. Technicolor work by Karl Freund is insufficient compensation for total lack of artistry. (Dir: Richard Thorpe, 105 mins.)

This Woman Is Dangerous (1952)**½ Joan Crawford, Dennis Morgan, David Brian. A must for Miss Crawford's legion of fans. She plays a typical Crawford role, that of a woman who finds love after she's been through the mill. Brian is quite good as a bigtime mobster who can't let Joan go. (Dir: Felix E. Feist, 97 mins.)

Thomas Crown Affair, The (1968)***½ Steve McQueen, Faye Dunaway. Ingenious caper film with Steve McQueen as the cool operator who masterminds a bank heist which is fascinating to follow. Miss Dunaway, gorgeously costumed, plays an efficient insurance company investigator who falls prey to McQueen's undeniable charm. Fun all the way, aided by sprightly directing of Norman Jewison. (102 mins.)

Thomasine and Bushrod (1974)*½ Max Julien, Vonetta McGee, Juanita Moore, Glynn Turman. (Dir: Gordon Parks, Jr., 95 mins.)

Thor and the Amazon Woman (Italy, 1963)* Joe Robinson, Susy Andersen. (Dir: Antonio Leoviola, 95 mins.)

Thoroughbreds Don't Cry (1937)**½ Mickey Rooney, Judy Garland, Sophie Tucker. Fairly good race track drama thanks to Rooney's expert playing of a jockey. Take a peek if you'd like to see some real early Judy Garland. Good for the kids. (Dir: Alfred E. Green, 80 mins.)

Thoroughly Modern Millie (1967)***½ Julie Andrews, James Fox, Mary Tyler Moore, Carol Channing. Entertaining musical extravaganza with songs, dances, and marvelous comedy sequences, with a '20s setting. Julie Andrews, in the title role, is a delight as the heroine who finds true love in the person of James Fox, but not until she dances and warbles her way through many imaginative production numbers. Carol Channing and Beatrice Lillie are wonderful in the film's chief supporting roles. Oscar: Best Scoring. (Dir: George Roy Hill, 138 mins.)

Those Daring Young Men in Their Jaunty Jalopies (Italy-France-Great Britain, 1969)** Tony Curtis, Susan Hampshire, Peter Cook, Terry-Thomas. A lumbering, disappointing effort by director Ken Annakin to duplicate his triumphant "Those Magnificent Men in Their Flying Machines." About a 1500-mile endurance race in the '20s, all heading for Monte Carlo but starting at five different locales. The big budget, lavish production doesn't turn up much besides a few pretty cars, familiar sight gags and auto crackups. (Dir: Ken Annakin, 93 mins.)

Those Lips, Those Eyes (1980)*** Frank Langella, Glynnis O'Connor, Thomas Hulce. All the clichés about coming of age and about the life of the theater are on blithe display in this sappily sensitive saga of a college junior's summer love affair with a stock operetta company. Langella is the fading matinee lead waiting for the big break that will never come, Hulce captures the callowness of the incredibly innocent young man flunking anatomy while he works as a prop boy, and O'Connor slides into a full adult role with her knowing sensuality in strong bloom. Michael Pressman's direction is reasonably efficient hackwork. (107 mins.)

Those Magnificent Men in Their Flying Machines (Great Britain, 1965)**** Stuart Whitman, Sarah Miles, Terry-Thomas, James Fox, Robert Morley. Just about as perfect as this kind of big-screen family entertainment picture can be. A lavish, wonderfully photographed comedy-adventure about an air race from London to Paris during the early days of aviation. International cast finds Whitman as an American cowboy swapping his horse for an airplane, and Terry-Thomas is one of the most lovable villains movies have ever served up. There's tension concerning the race and some truly inventive hijinks in between. (Dir: Ken Annakin, 133 mins.)

Those Redheads from Seattle (1953)** Rhonda Fleming, Gene Barry, Teresa Brewer, Guy Mitchell. Music and murder try but don't mix in this tale about the Gold Rush in Alaska. Teresa Brewer and Guy Mitchell sing pleasantly. (Dir: Lewis R. Foster, 90 mins.)

Those Were the Days (1940)**½ Bill Holden, Bonita Granville, Ezra Stone. Silly, but often amusing comedy about college back in the horse and buggy days. (Dir: Jay Reed, 76 mins.)

Thou Shalt Not Commit Adultery (MTV 1978)** Louise Fletcher, Robert Reed, Wayne Rogers. Miss Fletcher's character is encouraged by her husband (Reed), after he is incapacitated in an automobile accident, to seek a sexual outlet elsewhere, and the lady picks a golf pro (Rogers). Pure soap opera. (Dir: Delbert Mann, 104 mins.)

Thousand Clowns, A (1965)**** Jason Robards, Jr., Barbara Harris, Martin Balsam, Barry Gordon, Gene Saks. A touching, wacky comedy based on the hit Broadway play by Herb Gardner. Robards winningly re-creates his role of the nonconformist writer, determined to make his teenage nephew (Gordon) charge wise before his time. The supporting characters are beautifully played by Harris as a social worker, Balsam as the hero's successful businessman-brother, and Saks as a TV children's show host whose Chuckles the Chipmunk must be seen to be believed. (Dir: Fred Coe, 118 mins.)

Thousand Eyes of Dr. Mabuse, The (France-Italy-West Germany, 1960)***½ Peter Van Eyck, Gert Frobe, Dawn Addams. The final part of director Fritz Lang's trilogy about Dr. Mabuse. In the comic-book story, the criminal genius has come to life again and detective Frobe is after him. (103 mins.)

Thousand Plane Raid, The (1969)* Christopher George, Laraine Stephens, J. D. Cannon, Garry Marshall, Gavin McLeod. (Dir: Boris Sagal, 94 mins.)

Thousands Cheer (1943)*** Gene Kelly, Kathryn Grayson, Mary Astor, José Iturbi (gak), Kay Kyser and his orchestra (double gak), Lionel Barrymore (triple gak), Margaret O'Brien, Judy Garland, Mickey Rooney, June Allyson, Red Skelton, Lena Horne. Another all-star WW II musical, glossy and patriotic, but full of sappy numbers. (Dir: George Sidney, 126 mins.)

Threat, The (1949)*** Charles McGraw,

Michael O'Shea, Virginia Grey. An escaped killer plans to avenge himself on those who sent him up. Fast, violent melodrama. (Dir: Charles R. Rondeau, 66 mins.)

Three and a Half Musketeers (Mexico, 1957)** Tin Tan, Rosita Arenas. D'Artagnan strives to win full recognition as a King's Musketeer by protecting his Queen from scandal and saving the monarchy. Gagged up version of "The Three Musketeers." (Dir: Gilberto Martinez Solares, 85 mins.)

Three Avengers, The (Italy, 1964)* Alan Steel, Rosalba Neri. (Dir: Gianfranco Parolini, 97 mins.)

Three Bad Sisters (1956)** Maria English, Kathleen Hughes, Sara Shane. Muddled story of three wealthy sisters and their attempts to get what they want. Suicides, accidents, and other mishaps abound in this weak melodrama. (Dir: Gilbert L. Kay, 76 mins.)

Three Bites of the Apple (1967)** David McCallum, Tammy Grimes, Sylva Koscina, Harvey Korman. Tammy Grimes looks tempting enough to peel and bite gently, but the rest of this "Apple" is mostly pits. Glorious location sequences photographed in Switzerland and Italy wasted on hokey story about tour guide (McCallum) winning a fortune at the gambling casino and becoming prey for an adventuress (Koscina). (Dir: Alvin Ganzer, 105 mins.)

Three Blind Mice (1938)**½ Loretta Young, Joel McCrea, David Niven. Pretty good comedy with the all too familiar plot about three girls who try to marry millionaires. (Dir: William A. Seiter, 76 mins.)

Three Blondes in His Life (1960)* Jock Mahoney, Greta Thyssen. (Dir: Leon Chooluck, 81 mins.)

Three Brave Men (1957)**½ Ray Milland, Ernest Borgnine, Frank Lovejoy, Nina Foch. A good story that could have been better presented on the screen. Borgnine portrays a government employee who is asked to resign after years of loyal service because he has been labeled a "security risk." How this affects his life and family and the fight he puts up for reinstatement constitutes the bulk of the plot. (Dir: Philip Dunne, 88 mins.)

Three Came Home (1950)*** Claudette Colbert, Patric Knowles, Sessue Hayakawa. Good drama concerns the tortures undergone by captive women in a Japanese internment camp. Performances effective, particularly Hayakawa as the enemy commandant. (Dir: Jean Negulesco, 106 mins.)

Three Cases of Murder (Great Britain, 1955)***½ Orson Welles, Alan Badel, Elizabeth Sellars. A trio of separate tales: (1) Ghostly doings in an art gallery. (2) Two suspects when a girl is murdered. (3) A powerful lord is plagued by the memory of a House member he has publicly humiliated. The first and third are excellently done. The second, just an average murder mystery. All in all, above average. (Dirs: George More O'Ferrall, David Eady, Wendy Toye, 99 mins.)

Three Cheers for the Irish (1940)**½ Thomas Mitchell, Dennis Morgan, Priscilla Lane, Irene Hervey. Entertaining little film about an Irish cop who is honored after his retirement from the force by being elected alderman. Hold on to your hats—Dennis Morgan plays a Scotsman. (Dir: Lloyd Bacon, 100 mins.)

Three Coins in the Fountain (1954)**½ Clifton Webb, Louis Jourdan, Dorothy McGuire, Jean Peters, Maggie McNamara. Romance is the keynote in this pleasant comedy drama about three American secretaries in the Eternal City, Rome. The gay action unfolds against the beautiful on-location splendor of Rome. (Dir: Jean Negulesco, 102 mins.)

Three Comrades (1938)***½ Robert Taylor, Robert Young, Margaret Sullavan, Franchot Tone. Erich Remarque's novel about postwar (I) Germany is turned into a sensitive film. Not much on plot but deep in mood and character study. Margaret Sullavan is superb as a girl in love with an unsettled, sick veteran of the losing side. (Dir: Frank Borzage, 98 mins.)

Three Daring Daughters (1948)**½ Jeanette MacDonald, Jane Powell, Jose Iturbi, Edward Arnold. Daughters of a lady magazine editor have trouble adjusting themselves to her new husband. Long, mildly amusing musical. (Dir: Fred M. Wilcox, 115 mins.)

Three Days of the Condor (1975)***½ Robert Redford, Faye Dunaway, Cliff Robertson, Max von Sydow, John Houseman. An intriguing, suspenseful spy story involving double agents, all of them, supposedly, working for the CIA. Redford plays a CIA agent paid to read books while working for a cover operation in New York. All Redford's colleagues are murdered one afternoon by von Sydow. Surprising plot twists along the way before "Condor" finds out who was trying to kill him and why. Based on the novel "Six Days of the Condor" by James Grady. Taut screenplay by Lorenzo Semple, Jr., and David Rayfiel. (Dir: Sidney Pollack, 118 mins.)

Three Desperate Men (1951)**½ Preston Foster, Jim Davis, Virginia Grey. Two deputies ride to save their brother from unjust punishment, but circumstances force all three men outside the law. Above average western drama with good characterizations. (Dir: Sam Newfield, 71 mins.)

Three Etc's and the Colonel (France-Italy, 1960)*½ Anita Ekberg, Vittorio De Sica. (Dir: Claude Boissol, 99 mins.)

Three Faces of Eve, The (1957)*** Joanne Woodward, Vince Edwards, David Wayne, Lee J. Cobb. Woodward's Oscar-winning performance as a woman with three separate personalities is so facile that it will remind you of the porridge of Goldilocks's

three bears (this one was too hot, this one was too cold, this one was just right). With narration by Alistair Cooke, a sure signal that the jig is up. (Writer-Dir: Nunnally Johnson, 91 mins.)

Three for Bedroom C (1952)** Gloria Swanson, James Warren, Fred Clark. A glamorous screen star romances a scientist aboard a transcontinental train. Labored comedy never is as funny as it should be. (Dir: Milton Bren, 74 mins.)

Three for the Road (MTV 1975)** Alex Rocco, Julie Sommars, Vincent Van Patten, Lief Garrett. Well-intentioned show, a bit sentimental. The rugged Rocco scores as the photographer-father of two sons who take to the road after the death of Rocco's wife. There is a romance between Rocco and Sommars, who is doomed. (Dir: Boris Sagal, 78 mins.)

Three for the Show (1955)** Betty Grable, Jack Lemmon, Marge and Gower Champion. Downright foolish musical comedy about a Broadway star who believes her first husband dead in the war and marries his best friend. Hubby No. 1 shows up intact and the mad whirl begins. Remake of "Too Many Husbands" with Jean Arthur. Betty sings Gershwin's "I've Got a Crush On You." (Dir: H. C. Potter, 93 mins.)

Three Girls About Town (1941)**½ Joan Blondell, Binnie Barnes, Janet Blair. Three wise girls try to hide a body found in a hotel, to save the hotel's reputation. Senseless but amusing farce. (Dir: Leigh Jason, 73 mins.)

Three Godfathers (1948)**** John Wayne, Pedro Armendariz, Harry Carey, Jr., Ward Bond, Jane Darwell, Mildred Natwick. Ford cuts past the postcard plot to integrate his notions of how society functions and evolves with his view of religion in that scheme of things. The Christmas charm is never cloying, the sense of mortality always palpable, and the film is a masterpiece. Three bad (wise) men, the apostles of civilization, and Mildred Natwick in an impressive turn as the not-so-virgin Mary consigned to a dusty fate, are all delicately, movingly acted. (Dir: John Ford, 105 mins.)

Three Guns for Texas½ Neville Brand, Peter Brown, Bill Smith, Martin Milner. Three episodes of the TV series "Laredo" have been strung together and the result is a fairly amusing western-comedy. Shelley Morrison is very good as a homely Indian maiden who falls madly in love with Texas Ranger Bill Smith, and her devoted pursuit supplies laughs. (Dir: David Lowell Rich, 99 mins.)

Three Guys Named Mike (1951)**½ Jane Wyman, Van Johnson, Howard Keel, Barry Sullivan. Small town girl finds herself the object of assorted Romeos when she becomes an airline stewardess. Pleasing comedy keeps the chuckles coming fairly steadily. (Dir: Charles Walters, 90 mins.)

Three Hearts for Julia (1942)** Ann

Sothern, Melvyn Douglas. Well played, nonsensical farce about a man courting his wife while they're getting a divorce. Not too funny although the performers try hard. (Dir: Richard Thorpe, 89 mins.)

Three Hours to Kill (1954)*** Dana Andrews, Donna Reed, Diane Foster, Carolyn Jones. Dana Andrews rides into town to find the man who killed his former sweetheart's brother. He has three hours to do so. Tight and tense western with good performances. (Dir: Alfred L. Werker, 77 mins.)

300 Spartans, The (1962)**½ Richard Egan, Diane Baker, Ralph Richardson. Relatively small band of soldiers stand against a mighty army of Persia in a fight for free Greece. Slightly better-than-usual production for a costume spectacle, but still stiff and stilted. Filmed in Greece. (Dir: Rudolph Maté, 114 mins.)

Three Husbands (1950)*** Emlyn Williams, Eve Arden, Vanessa Brown. A recently deceased playboy leaves a note saying he was intimate with one of three wives, and their husbands intend to find out which one. Bright, well acted sophisticated comedy. (Dir: Irving Reis, 78 mins.)

Three in the Attic (1969)* Christopher Jones, Yvette Mimieux, Nan Martin. (Dir: Richard Wilson, 92 mins.)

Three Into Two Won't Go (Great Britain, 1969)*** Rod Steiger, Claire Bloom, Judy Geeson, Peggy Ashcroft. Familiar tale of the man approaching 40 who finds his marriage difficult and seeks ego fulfillment with a cooperative young lady. Steiger and Bloom (they were Mr. & Mrs. at the time) play the couple well, and adorable Geeson is the object of Rod's affections. Directed by stage luminary Peter Hall. (93 mins.)

Three Is a Family (1944)*** Everything happens in the household of Fay Bainter and Charlie Ruggles, the home being a melange of married couples, babies, daughter Marjorie Reynolds, many laughs. (Dir: Edward Ludwig, 81 mins.)

Three Little Girls in Blue (1946)**½ June Haver, Vivian Blaine, Vera-Ellen, George Montgomery. A tuneful score, attractive cast and a good production make up for the flimsy tale of the girls in search of millionaires. Celeste Holm makes her screen debut and walks off with the acting honors. (Dir: H. Bruce Humberstone, 90 mins.)

Three Little Words (1950)**½ Fred Astaire, Red Skelton, Vera-Ellen, Arlene Dahl, Debbie Reynolds. MGM got a lot of mileage out of songwriters' biographies. In this late and lesser effort, Burt Kalmar and Harry Ruby are played by Astaire and Skelton. A whole catalog of Tin Pan Alley songs accompanies a sketchy, half-hearted plot line. (Dir: Richard Thorpe, 102 mins.)

Three Lives of Thomasina, The (U.S.-Great Britain, 1963)**½ Patrick McGoohan, Susan Hampshire, Karen Dotrice. Disney story of a veterinarian's daughter who loses her will to live after her cat has been put to sleep, has a nice fairy-tale quality. Trying to bring the cat, Thomasina, back to life, the girl seeks out a mysterious healer living in the woods. The movie's first half has some bite; the ending is too saccharine. For the kiddies. Based on Paul Gallico's "Thomasina, The Cat Who Thought She Was God." (Dir: Don Chaffey, 97 mins.)

Three Loves Has Nancy (1938)**½ Janet Gaynor, Robert Montgomery, Franchot Tone. Two bachelor friends and a girl between them is the focal of this pleasant, well written and played little comedy. (Dir: Richard Thorpe, 70 mins.)

Three Men in a Boat (Great Britain, 1956)*** Laurence Harvey, Martita Hunt, Shirley Eaton, Jill Ireland. Bright British comedy about three young men who have a field day on a gay excursion up the Thames. Martita Hunt is delicious and even Laurence Harvey isn't bad. From the book by Jerome K. Jerome. (Dir: Ken Annakin, 84 mins.)

Three Men in White (1944)** Lionel Barrymore, Van Johnson, Ava Gardner. Routine Dr. Gillespie film with the old boy looking for an assistant and trying to decide between Keye Luke and Van. (Dir: Willis Goldbeck, 85 mins.)

Three Men on a Horse (1936)***½ Sam Levene, Joan Blondell, Frank McHugh. One of our comedy classics. Story of the mild-mannered chap who can pick winners and the characters who try and use him is always good for laughs. Played to the hilt by an expert cast. Holds up very well. (Dir: Mervyn LeRoy, 85 mins.)

Three Murderesses (France, 1959)**½ Alain Delon, Mylene Demongeot, Pascale Petit. Playboy spreads his affections among three beauties, they seek to get even with him. Lightweight amusing English-dubbed comedy with a misleading title. (Dir: Michel Boisrond, 96 mins.)

Three Musketeers (1935)*** Walter Abel, Paul Lukas. Dumas' classic of the dashing D'Artagnan who joins the King's Musketeers. Acceptable version of famous adventure tale. (Dir: Rowland V. Lee, 96 mins.)

Three Musketeers, The (1939)*** Don Ameche, the Ritz Brothers, Lionel Atwill, Binnie Barnes. Yet another go at the Dumas classic, this one strictly for laughs (which develop, even with the wearisome presence of the Ritz Brothers as unsuspecting Musketeers and Ameche as a singing D'Artagnan). Allan Dwan is probably the only director who could bring it off with this much style. (73 mins.)

Three Musketeers, The (1948)*** Lana Turner, Gene Kelly, June Allyson, Van Heflin, Angela Lansbury. A rollicking, if overstuffed MGM rendition of the Dumas classic. Has the courage of its uninhibited vulgarity. (Dir: George Sidney, 125 mins.)

Three Musketeers, The (1973)**** Oliver

Reed, Michael York, Raquel Welch, Richard Chamberlain, Faye Dunaway, Charlton Heston. A joyous whirlwind-paced remake (there may be as many as ten earlier versions of the Dumas classic). In between there are a slew of fabulous sight gags from inventive director Richard Lester and his international cast, with big-name stars playing bit parts. Heston is Cardinal Richelieu and York is D'Artagnan, who understandably wants to seduce the married neighborhood seamstress (Welch). Gorgeous period costumes. (105 mins.)

3 on a Couch (1966)* Jerry Lewis, Janet Leigh, Mary Ann Mobley. (Dir: Jerry Lewis, 109 mins.)

Three on a Date (MTV 1978)** June Allyson, Ray Bolger, Rick Nelson, Forbesy Russell. Adaptation of a book by Stephanie Buffington (played by Russell), a real-life chaperone to winning couples on TV's "The Dating Game," spruced up with guest stars and silly subplots. (Dir: Bill Bixby, 104 mins.)

Three on a Match (1932)*** Joan Blondell, Bette Davis, Ann Dvorak, Edward Arnold, Humphrey Bogart. Three schoolmates take different paths—one a chorine, one a stenographer, the third a millionaire's wife. Interesting melodrama. (Dir: Mervyn LeRoy, 64 mins.)

Three on a Spree (Great Britain, 1961)*½ Jack Watling, Carole Lesley. (Dir: Sidney J. Furie, 83 mins.)

Three Ring Circus (1954)** Dean Martin, Jerry Lewis, Zsa Zsa Gabor. Dean and Jerry join the circus for a mild amount of fun. Not their best, nor their worst. (Dir: Joseph Pevney, 103 mins.)

Three Sailors and a Girl (1953)** Jane Powell, Gordon MacRae, Gene Nelson, Jack E. Leonard. Not to be confused with "Two Girls and a Sailor," "Three Gobs and a Gal," or "Two Sailors and Two Girls," but if you do, it won't matter. It's all the same, anyway. (Dir: Roy Del Ruth, 95 mins.)

Three Secrets (1950)*** Eleanor Parker, Ruth Roman, Patricia Neal. Good drama for the gals. Through flashbacks it tells the story of the three women as they wait word of their loved ones involved in a fatal air crash on a mountain. (Dir: Robert Wise, 99 mins.)

Three Sisters, The (U.S.S.R., 1964)**½ Lyubov Sokolova, Margarita Volodina. Disappointing Russian version of the great Chekhov play about the lives of the daughters of a late Russian officer living in rural Russia early in this century. Filmed in black and white with a couple of good performances. Adapted and directed by Samson Samsonov. Subtitles. (112 mins.)

Three Sisters, The (1965)***½ Kim Stanley, Geraldine Page, Sandy Dennis, Shelley Winters. A movie only by virtue of its being included in a film package, this is a taped version of Anton Chekhov's play as performed in cooperation with the Actors Studio. The drama of loneliness and frustration receives uneven treatment, with some brilliantly acted bits. Worth seeing. (Dir: Lee Strasberg, 168 mins.)

Three Sisters, The (Great Britain, 1970)***½ Laurence Olivier, Joan Plowright, Alan Bates, Jeanne Watts, Louise Purnell. Probably Olivier's best job of direction (with John Sichel). The performances, while shy of the lusty, are impeccable, superbly modulated, and very moving. Joan Plowright is a definitive Masha. Olivier himself plays Dr. Chebutikin. (165 mins.)

Three Smart Girls (1936)***½ Deanna Durbin, Ray Milland. Delightful comedy about three sisters trying to keep their father away from a scheming woman. Miss Durbin's voice is another asset. (Dir: Henry Koster, 90 mins.)

Three Smart Girls Grow Up (1939)*** Deanna Durbin, Robert Cummings, Charles Winninger. Light Deanna Durbin comedy about family involvements, notably the gay romances of three sisters. Charming Deanna is a delight. (Dir: Henry Koster, 73 mins.)

Three Steps North (Italy, 1951)*** Lloyd Bridges, Lea Padovani. Ex-GI returns to Italy to claim hidden loot. Well acted, interesting melodrama. English dialogue. (Dir: W. Lee Wilder, 82 mins.)

Three Stooges Go Around the World in a Daze, The (1963)* The Three Stooges, Jay Sheffield, Jean Freeman. (Dir: Norman Maurer, 94 mins.)

Three Stooges in Orbit, The (1962)** The Three Stooges, Carol Christensen. The boys run across a Martian agent after a professor's new invention. Wild slapstick for the kiddies. (Dir: Edward Bernds, 87 mins.)

Three Stooges Meet Hercules, The (1962)** The Three Stooges, Vicki Trickett. The boys land in a time machine which takes them back to the days of kings and slaves. Amusing burlesque laced with slapstick. (Dir: Edward Bernds, 89 mins.)

Three Strangers (1946)*** Sydney Greenstreet, Geraldine Fitzgerald, Peter Lorre. Warner Bros. melodrama has visual fluency and comic flair from director Jean Negulesco, but is afflicted with one of John Huston's most cynical and misanthropist scripts. The strangers of the title share a winning lottery ticket but eventually come to grief out of greed and bad luck. (92 mins.)

Three Stripes in the Sun (1955)**½ Aldo Ray, Dick York, Phil Carey, Chuck Connors. Formerly prejudiced against the Japanese, a G.I. Sgt. falls in love with a Japanese translator and is torn by his old beliefs. Reasonably interesting. (Dir: Richard Murphy, 93 mins.)

Three Swords of Zorro (Spain-Italy, 1963)*½ Guy Stockwell, Gloria Milland. (Dir: Ricardo Blasco, 88 mins.)

3:10 to Yuma (1957)***½ Glenn Ford, Van Heflin, Felicia Farr. One of the best western dramas, almost in the league of "Shane" and "High Noon." A farmer takes the job of bringing a notorious killer into Yuma because he needs the money. They have to wait together in a hotel room until the train for Yuma arrives. Ford, in the role of the killer, is great as is Heflin as the farmer. (Dir: Delmer Daves, 92 mins.)

Three the Hard Way (1974)**½ Jim Brown, Fred Williamson, Jim Kelly, Shelia Frazier, Jay Robinson. A surprisingly unviolent thriller, highly implausible and stylistically rickety, but well constructed at a pulsating pace. Robinson plays a white supremacist out to exterminate blacks by putting a serum in the water supply; Brown, Williamson, and Kelly are the dudes out to stop him. (Dir: Gordon Parks, Jr., 93 mins.)

3,000 Mile Chase, The (MTV 1977)*½ Cliff DeYoung, Glenn Ford, Blair Brown, David Spielberg. (Dir: Russ Mayberry, 104 mins.)

300 Miles for Stephanie (MTV 1981)**½ Tony Orlando, Edward James Olmos, Pepe Serna. Singer Tony Orlando runs his heart out in this true story about a San Antonio cop. Tony's cop promises God that he will run 300 miles if his ailing daughter is alive for her fifth birthday. Tony is all emotion playing a cop, while the semi-hokey "heart-warming" story benefits from the San Antonio locale. (Dir: Clyde Ware, 104 mins.)

Three Violent People (1956)**½ Charlton Heston, Anne Baxter, Gilbert Roland, Tom Tryon. An action-filled western yarn for horse opera fans. Heston is appropriately cast in the role of a rancher who puts up a valiant fight against the illegal land grabbers. Miss Baxter supplies the love interest. (Dir: Rudolph Mate, 100 mins.)

Three Women (1977)**** Shelley Duvall, Sissy Spacek, Janice Rule, John Cromwell, Robert Fortier. A fascinating, daring film written, produced and directed by Robert Altman. An audacious attempt to create a rich, textured film about two vapid leading characters is rewarded by extraordinarily varied and subtle performances by Duvall and Spacek, playing short roommates in a Palm Springs, Calif., motel. Duvall is a self-assured physical therapist modeling her life on the inspirations she finds in "Good Housekeeping"; Rule has virtually no speeches as spaced-out painter. A remarkable work of art. (125 mins.)

Three Worlds of Gulliver, The (Great Britain, 1960)*** Kerwin Mathews, Jo Morrow. Fast paced adventure fantasy aimed for the juvenile trade. Plenty of visual gimmicks. (Dir: Jack Sher, 100 mins.)

Three Young Texans (1954)** Mitzi Gaynor, Jeffrey Hunter, Keefe Brasselle. Cowboy tries to save his father, in the clutches of crooks, from robbing a train by doing it himself. Cast names can't help this from being anything but an ordinary western. (Dir: Henry Levin, 78 mins.)

ThreePenny Opera (West Germany, 1964)** Curt Jurgens, Hildegarde Neff, Gert Frobe. Draggy, uninspired version of the Kurt Weill-Bertolt Brecht satire about criminal Mack the Knife, who marries the daughter of the King of the Beggars, is trapped by the law, but escapes. Bumpy continuity, below-par performances; Sammy Davis Jr. occasionally appears as a sort of chorus, adding little. Dubbed in English. Too bad. (Dir: Wolfgang Staudte, 83 mins.)

Threepenny Opera, The (Germany, 1931) *** Rudolf Forster, Vladimir Sokoloff, Lotte Lenya, Valeska Gert, Reinhold Schunzel. Film of Bertolt Brecht's musical play, which was inspired by John Gay's "The Beggar's Opera." Brecht strongly disapproved of this version directed by G. W. Pabst, and it's easy to see why: it isn't very pointed, and the mounting is undynamic. Still, the cast is good and the design rich in atmospheric detail. (111 mins.)

Three's a Crowd (1969)**½ Larry Hagman, Jessica Walter, E. J. Peaker. An old bigamy plot, popular in the comedy films of the thirties and forties, is given an uninhibited modern touch in this made-for-TV movie. You'll probably stay with it to see whether husband Larry Hagman chooses wife 1 (E. J. Peaker) or wife 2 (Jessica Walter). The story is obvious, but the last few scenes played in a hotel during Hagman's two separate birthday celebrations provide some laughs. (Dir: Harry Falk, 75 mins.)

Thrill of a Romance (1945)** Van Johnson, Esther Williams, Lauritz Melchior, Tommy Dorsey and orchestra. Air Corps hero romances a pretty swimming instructress at a mountain resort. Cloying, top-heavy musical comedy. (Dir: Richard Thorpe, 104 mins.)

Thrill of It All, The (1963)*** Doris Day, James Garner, Arlene Francis. Some bright moments in this amusing comedy about an obstetrician's wife who becomes a star of television commercials. Carl Reiner's script pokes fun at the TV huckstering business, while Day and Garner are capable funsters themselves. Nice entertainment. (Dir: Norman Jewison, 108 mins.)

Throne of Blood (Japan, 1957)**½ Toshiro Mifune, Isuzu Yamada. Director Akira Kurosawa's interesting version of "Macbeth," flavored with cultural dislocation. Mifune's warlord seems a little opaque to this western mind; Yamada, the first lady of the Japanese screen, is even more incomprehensible and very moving nonetheless. Most of the images tend to slow down the tragic momentum, but the moving woods of Dunsinane are something to remember. (109 mins.)

Through a Glass Darkly (Sweden, 1961) ***½ Harriet Andersson, Gunnar Bjornstrand, Max von Sydow, Lars Possgard. First part of a trilogy (with "Winter Light" and "The Silence") is about a woman (Andersson) who was recently in a sanitarium and who, still mentally disturbed, is on an island with two relatives and her husband. Elaborately rhetorical at the end, the film nevertheless develops its theme lucidly and contains some of writer-director Ingmar Bergman's most unforgettable sequences, like the slow descent of a helicopter as Harriet Andersson screams, "God is a spider!" Academy Award for Best Foreign Film. (91 mins.)

Thunder Afloat (1939)**½ Wallace Beery, Chester Morris. Good comedy-drama about WW I campaign against subs by Naval Reserve. Basic plot is old-hat but Beery is fun to watch. (Dir: George B. Seitz, 100 mins.)

Thunder Alley (1967)* Annette Funicello, Fabian, Jan Murray. (Dir: Richard Rush, 90 mins.)

Thunder and Lightning (1977)** David Carradine, Kate Jackson, Roger C. Carmel. Carrdaine's first line in the film, "Holy shit," is the best writing in this waterlogged rubbish about moonshiners a-cussin' 'n' a-fightin' in the Everglades. (Dir: Corey Allen, 95 mins.)

Thunder Bay (1953)**½ James Stewart, Joanne Dru, Dan Duryea, Gilbert Roland. High spirited adventure yarn about oil prospectors and their run in with shrimp fishermen in Louisiana when an off-shore drilling operation interferes with the routine of a small fishing community. The cast is first rate. (Dir: Anthony Mann, 102 mins.)

Thunder in the East (1953)**½ Deborah Kerr, Alan Ladd, Charles Boyer, Corinne Calvet. Contrived but moderately entertaining film about a group of displaced persons and an American adventurer caught up in the new found independence fever in India. The heroics are heavy handed and Miss Kerr's love story with Alan Ladd may be hard to take. (Dir: Charles Vidor, 98 mins.)

Thunder in the Sun (1959)** Susan Hayward, Jeff Chandler. Wagon train of Basque settlers going to California to cultivate vineyards passes through hostile Indian territory. Triteness of the plot is saved at the last moment by a rousingly staged battle scene, giving this historical action drama the "fair" mark. (Dir: Russell Rouse, 81 mins.)

Thunder in the Valley (1947)**½ Lon McCallister, Edmund Gwenn, Peggy Ann Garner. Good juvenile drama about a boy's love for his dog. (Dir: Louis King, 103 mins.)

Thunder Island (1963)** Gene Nelson, Fay Spain, Brian Kelly. Low-budget suspense tale of assassination plot against an out-of-power South American dictator is told with gusto. Story and screenplay by Jack Nicholson and Don Devlin. (Dir: Jack Leewood, 65 mins.)

Thunder of Drums, A (1961)**½ Richard Boone, George Hamilton, Luana Patten,

Richard Chamberlain. Newly commissioned lieutenant, son of a former general, is treated rough by the captain of a western fort until he can prove he's a soldier. Familiar Cavalry-vs.-Indians actioner benefits from good performances. (Dir: Joseph M. Newman, 97 mins.)

Thunder on the Hill (1951)*** Ann Blyth, Claudette Colbert, Robert Douglas. Mystery yarn set in a British convent during a rainstorm makes absorbing drama when handled as well as it is here. Miss Blyth plays a condemned murderess who is detained at the convent due to the storm and Miss Colbert plays a nun who sets out to prove Miss Blyth's innocence. (Dir: Douglas Sirk, 84 mins.)

Thunder Pass (1954)**½ Dane Clark, Dorothy Patrick, Andy Devine, Raymond Burr. Cavalry captain attempts to lead settlers to safety before the Indians go on the warpath. Generally okay outdoor action melodrama keeps moving at a good rate. (Dir: Frank McDonald, 76 mins.)

Thunder Road (1958)** Robert Mitchum, Keely Smith, Gene Barry. Uneven drama about a group of people in the Kentucky hills who make moonshine whiskey and sell it. Odd little drama with good moments, some weak ones. (Dir: Arthur Ripley, 92 mins.)

Thunder Rock (Great Britain, 1942)**** Michael Redgrave, Lilli Palmer, James Mason. The keeper of an isolated lighthouse hates his fellow man, but is persuaded to return to society by spirits from the past. Thoughtful, excellently acted drama. (Dirs: John and Roy Boulting, 95 mins.)

Thunderball (Great Britain, 1965)***½ Sean Connery, Claudine Auger, Adolfo Celi, Bernard Lee, Luciana Paluzzi. An exciting James Bond adventure in which the villains are delightfully sinister and calculating and Sean Connery is at the top of his form as Agent 007. This time out, the ominous enemy organization, SPECTRE, is out to destroy the city of Miami if SPECTRE is not paid a ransom of 100 million pounds sterling—and super-hero Bond is not about to let all those tourists down. Adolfo Celi strikes the right pose as the arch-villain, and there are enough gorgeous ladies around to make Bond's task worthwhile. (Dir: Terence Young, 132 mins.)

Thunderbolt and Lightfoot (1974)*** Clint Eastwood, Jeff Bridges, George Kennedy. Caper yarn set in the hill country of Montana. Clint, a Vietnam vet with a hankering to pull a big armory robbery and retire forever, teams up with young drifter Bridges. Promising directorial debut for Michael Cimino who also wrote the spirited screenplay. (115 mins.)

Thundercloud (1950)**½ Randolph Scott, Ruth Roman, Zachary Scott. Fast paced western drama with the stress on action. Scott is a gun salesman whose merchandise (Colt .45's) is stolen and used to arm a band of outlaws. (Dir: Edwin L. Marin, 74 mins.)

Thunderhead—Son of Flicka (1945)**½ Roddy McDowall, Preston Foster. Good juvenile film about a boy and a horse. A fair outdoor adventure with little of the fine qualities of "My Friend Flicka." (Dir: Louis King, 78 mins.)

Thursday's Game (MTV 1974)*** Gene Wilder, Bob Newhart, Ellen Burstyn, Cloris Leachman, Valerie Harper, Nancy Walker, Rob Reiner. A cast of top comedy actors adds spark to this tale about two friends (Wilder and Newhart) who decide to lie and continue their weekly night out after their poker game is disbanded. It's a satirical look at marriage and male friendships. Wilder is wonderful as a put-upon guy whose world is suddenly falling apart and Newhart underplays in his pleasing fashion as a successful businessman looking for an out from his marriage and finally finding one. (Dir: Robert Moore, 74 mins.)

THX 1138 (1971)**½ Robert Duvall, Donald Pleasence, Maggie McOmie, Don Pedro Colley, Ian Wolfe. In director George Lucas's feature length expansion of his USC student short, Duvall is a reluctant zombie trying to escape a repressive society of the future, resourcefully evoked through location shooting in underground garages and San Francisco's subway system. Muddled and hopelessly artsy. (88 mins.)

Tiara Tahiti (Great Britain, 1962)**½ James Mason, John Mills, Claude Dauphin. Pompous former officer lands in Tahiti to build a modern hotel, but finds unexpected opposition in the form of an old army enemy, living a life of ease on the isle. Leisurely in pace as befits the climate, this tropical comedy gets its chief lift from the able performances of the leading players. (Dir: William [Ted] Kotcheff, 100 mins.)

...tick...tick...tick (1970)**½ Jim Brown, Fredric March, George Kennedy. Fairly interesting drama about a southern town's sudden shift from a peaceful community to a veritable powder keg. The incident which sets off the situation is the election of the town's first black sheriff, played by Jim Brown. Fine supporting cast. (Dir: Ralph Nelson, 100 mins.)

Ticket to Tomahawk, A (1950)**½ Dan Dailey, Anne Baxter, Rory Calhoun, Walter Brennan. Small-time theatrical group invades the West. Marilyn Monroe has a bit role in this fairly amusing western spoof. (Dir: Richard Sale, 90 mins.)

Tickle Me (1965)** Elvis Presley, Jocelyn Lane, Julie Adams. Elvis as a rodeo star who winds up at a girls' health resort and helps uncover a hidden treasure. His fans won't mind, but he deserves better than this skimpy little nothing. (Dir: Norman Taurog, 90 mins.)

Ticklish Affair, A (1963)** Gig Young, Shirley Jones, Red Buttons, Carolyn Jones.

Naval officer investigating an SOS encounters a widow and her children, and romance blossoms. Watery little comedy doesn't do right by the cast; weak script. (Dir: George Sidney, 89 mins.)

Tidal Wave (Japan, 1975)* Lorne Greene, Keiju Kobayashi, Rhonda Leigh Hopkins. (Dir: Andrew Meyer, 90 mins.)

Tiger and the Pussycat, The (U.S.-Italy, 1967)** Ann-Margret, Vittorio Gassman, Eleanor Parker. This sex drama with comedy thrown in, also throws out the chance to make good use of Gassman's dazzling talent. Gassman is approaching middle age, and he is taken over the coals by Ann-Margret, who laughs at him behind his back. Eleanor Parker suffers quietly as Gassman's wife, and you'll suffer a little too as this soap opera plot offers few surprises. Filmed in Italy. (Dir: Dino Risi, 105 mins.)

Tiger Bay (Great Britain, 1959)**** Horst Buchholz, Hayley Mills, John Mills. Superb suspense yarn with a great plot twist. Hayley Mills is perfect in the role of a little girl who witnesses a murder and ends up protecting the young killer (effectively portrayed by Buchholz) from the authorities. This is the film which launched Miss Mills on her movie career. (Dir: J. Lee Thompson, 105 mins.)

Tiger by the Tail (Great Britain, 1955)** Larry Parks, Constance Smith. An American newspaperman goes to London on an assignment and gets involved with a gang of international thieves. Trite film, poorly acted, except by Parks. (Dir: John Gilling, 83 mins.)

Tiger Makes Out, The (1967)***½ Eli Wallach, Anne Jackson, Charles Nelson Reilly, Elizabeth Wilson. If you pay attention you'll catch Dustin Hoffman in a tiny part. There are other good reasons to watch this wacky tale of a Greenwich Village bachelor who can't cope with the world and turns to kidnapping, the major one being the delicious performances of husband-and-wife team Wallach and Jackson. (Dir: Arthur Hiller, 94 mins.)

Tiger of the Sea (Japan, 1964)* Joe Shishido, Hideaki Nitani. (Dir: Tan Ida, 91 mins.)

Tiger Shark (1932)***½ Edward G. Robinson, J. Carrol Naish, Zita Johann, Richard Arlen. A brutal, stoical film with Robinson as a lively old Portuguese tuna fisherman who marries a younger woman (Johann); Arlen, his best friend, alienates the girl's affections. (Dir: Howard Hawks, 80 mins.)

Tight Little Island (Great Britain, 1949)**** Basil Radford, Joan Greenwood. Scottish islanders low on the spirits take drastic steps when a cargo of whisky is marooned off their shore. This British joy is one of the drollest, most consistently amusing films you can hope to see. A perennial delight, perfectly acted. Alternate title: **Whisky Galore.** (Dir: Alexander Mackendrick, 81 mins.)

Tight Shoes (1941)***½ Broderick Crawford, John Howard, Binnie Barnes. A gangster gets a shoe clerk started on his way in a political career. Surprisingly funny Damon Runyon comedy has a fast pace, good situations. (Dir: Albert S. Rogell, 68 mins.)

Tight Spot (1955)***½ Ginger Rogers, Edward G. Robinson, Brian Keith, Lorne Greene, Kathryn Grant. Well acted crime drama about a girl set up by the police as a trap for a big time gang leader. Witty dialogue. (Dir: Phil Karlson, 97 mins.)

Tijuana Story, The (1957)** James Darren, Joy Stoner. A predictable drama about a youth's involvement with the "drug traffic" in the open city of Tijuana. Some action scenes break up the boredom. (Dir: Leslie Kardos, 72 mins.)

Tiko and the Shark (U.S.-France-Italy, 1962)** Al Kauwe, Marlene Among. Young Polynesian boy raises baby shark; friendship persists into adulthood despite threats from local fishing business. Sometimes trite plea for primitive ways, man and nature, over more "civilized," mechanized modes of life, but generally understated; a well-photographed, pleasant movie—antidote to irrational terror of the "killer" shark. (Dir: Folco Quilici, 88 mins.)

Till Death (1978)** Keith Atkinson, Belinda Balaski. Basically a two-character, one-set film: Atkinson, distraught over the death of wife Balaski on their wedding night, resurrects her from a crypt. A nothing ending, and the fact that most of it takes place in the dark mars the film. Still an OK horror pic. (Dir: Walter Stocker, 89 mins.)

Till Marriage Do Us Part (Italy, 1976)*** Laura Antonelli, Jean Rochefort, Michele Placido. Somewhat dog-eared comedy brought into belated American release to capitalize on the appeal of its star, Antonelli. In early 20th-century Italy, she discovers on her wedding night that she has unknowingly married her illegitimate brother, and she seeks her release and fulfillment as she can. Uneven but frequently funny and poignant. (Dir: Luigi Comencini.)

Till the Clouds Roll By (Great Britain, 1946)** Robert Walker, Judy Garland, Dinah Shore, Van Johnson, Lena Horne, Frank Sinatra. Such a lousy musical biography of Jerome Kern that even his captivating melodies sound short of charm. Stars abound. (Dir: Richard Whorf, 137 mins.)

Till the End of Time (1946)***½ Dorothy McGuire, Guy Madison, Robert Mitchum, Bill Williams. Returned GI tries to readjust himself to civilian life, finds he has changed, falls for a flyer's widow. Potent, excellently produced drama. (Dir: Edward Dmytryk, 105 mins.)

Till We Meet Again (1949)*** Merle Oberon, George Brent, Pat O'Brien, Geraldine Fitzgerald. Remake of "One Way Passage." Story of the criminal and the dying girl is still passable if you like to cry. (Dir: Edmund Goulding, 99 mins.)

Tillie and Gus (1933)*** W.C. Fields, Alison Skipworth, Jacqueline Wells (Julie Bishop), Baby Le Roy. A great team, perfectly cast as crooked gamblers, in a generally routine film. Shows how Fields was one of America's greatest comedy artists. (Dir: Francis Martin, 61 mins.)

Time After Time (1979)**½ Malcolm McDowell, David Warner, Mary Steenburgen, Charles Cioffi. The notion of H. G. Wells pursuing Jack the Ripper to modern-day San Francisco via time machine strikes me as calculatingly commercial, and the film never takes on life of its own except for the tenderness between McDowell (a charming Wells) and Steenburgen. From Karl Alexander's book. (Dir: Nicholas Meyer, 112 mins.)

Time Bomb (France-Italy, 1959)**½ Curt Jurgens, Mylene Demongeot. A French film with some suspense and good production values to recommend it. Curt Jurgens is the captain of a vessel which becomes an important part of a plot of intrigue. (Dir: Yves Clampi, 92 mins.)

Time for Burning, A (1966)**** Rev. William Youngdahl, Ernie Chambers. An honest, extremely moving hour-long documentary about race relations in Omaha, Nebraska, conceived and directed by gifted filmmaker William Jersey, and first seen on the public television network. Nonprofessional actors in their real-life situation, as Jersey's camera crew records what happens when a white minister tries to integrate his lily-white congregation with a nearby Negro Lutheran church. One of the most thoughtful statements about deep-seated American racial prejudice ever captured on film. (Dirs: William C. Jersey, Barbara Connell, 58 mins.)

Time for Killing, A—See: **Long Ride Home, The**

Time for Love, A (MTV 1973)**½ John Davidson, Chris Mitchum, Jack Cassidy. Two introspective, visually handsome love stories for the young by the prolific writer Stirling Silliphant. Davidson's straight-arrow junior exec learns to trust his instincts and buck the patterned corporate-life groove from a questioning beauty (Lauren Hutton) in "No Promises, No Pledges," filmed on location at the Arizona Biltmore. In "Go Sing the Songs, Mark," a sad-faced rock singer loves a teacher of deaf children, but won't relinquish his frenzied life-style. Robert Mitchum's son Christopher and comely Bonnie Bedelia search for answers against California coastline backgrounds. (Dirs: George Schaefer, Joseph Sargent, 99 mins.)

Time, Gentlemen, Please (Great Britain, 1952)**½ Eddie Byrne, Hermione Baddeley, Dora Bryan. The town loafer combats stuffy regulations in his own way, and winds up in clover. Pleasant comedy. (Dir: Lewis Gilbert, 83 mins.)

Time Is My Enemy (Great Britain, 1954)**½ Dennis Price, Renée Asherson. Criminal tries to blackmail his former wife, with murder the result. Interesting melodrama. (Dir: Don Chaffey, 64 mins.)

Time Limit (1957)***½ Richard Widmark, Richard Basehart, June Lockhart, Martin Balsam. The provocative war drama presented on B'way has been brought to the screen with taste and skill. Story concerns the issue of collaboration with enemy during the Korean campaign. Strong drama with excellent performances, notably by Basehart and Widmark. (Dir: Karl Malden, 96 mins.)

Time Lost and Time Remembered (Great Britain, 1966)**½ Sarah Miles, Cyril Cusack. If the screenplay of this tale about a young girl's awakening to life and love matched its sensitive photography and splendid acting by Sarah Miles in the leading role, this would be a winner. But it turns out to be just an average tale, beautifully acted and photographed. (Dir: Desmond Davis, 91 mins.)

Time Machine, The (1960)***½ Rod Taylor, Yvette Mimieux, Alan Young, Sebastian Cabot. Imaginative tale based on the H. G. Wells story of a young inventor who constructs a machine enabling him to travel to the future, and the strange adventures he meets in doing so. Trick work is excellent, the story continually interesting and well acted. Superior fantasy fare. Oscar, Best Special Effects. (Dir: George Pal, 103 mins.)

Time Machine, The (MTV 1978)*½ John Beck, Priscilla Barnes, Andrew Duggan, Rosemary DeCamp. From the story by H. G. Wells. (Dir: Henning Schellerup, 104 mins.)

Time of Indifference (France-Italy, 1964)** Shelley Winters, Rod Steiger, Paulette Goddard, Claudia Cardinale. Grim, unpleasantly executed and played drama about the disintegration of a family in the late '20s. Air of unrelieved gloom with few compensating factors. (Dir: Francisco Maselli, 84 mins.)

Time of Their Lives, The (1946)*** Bud Abbott, Lou Costello, Marjorie Reynolds, Binnie Barnes. A better than average A & C comedy with less stress on slapstick and more on story. Good supporting performances. (Dir: Charles Barton, 82 mins.)

Time of Your Life, The (1948)**** James Cagney, Wayne Morris, Broderick Crawford, Jeanne Cagney, James Barton. A little New York saloon, and the characters who frequent it. From William Saroyan's prize-winning play. Expertly handled. (Dir: H. C. Potter, 109 mins.)

Time Out for Love (France-Italy, 1961)*½ Jean Seberg, Maurice Ronet, Micheline Presle. (Dir: Jean Valere, 91 mins.)

Time Running Out (France-U.S., 1950)** Dane Clark, Simone Signoret. Run of the mill cops and robbers yarn set in France and starring American actor Dane Clark. Simone Signoret, as one of Clark's past mistresses, is totally wasted in a thankless role. (Dirs: Frank Tuttle, Boris Lewin, 90 mins.)

Time to Die, A—See: **Amélie**

Time to Kill (1942)** Lloyd Nolan, Heather Angel. Detective Michael Shayne on the trail of rare coin counterfeiters. Routine film is supported by Nolan's characterization. (Dir: Herbert I. Leeds, 61 mins.)

Time to Love and a Time to Die, A (1958)*** John Gavin, Lilo Pulver, Jock Mahoney, Keenan Wynn. Erich Maria Remarque's novel about young romance during WW II in Nazi Germany comes off well in this screen adaptation. Although the film eventually becomes soap opera, it has some good moments in the earlier scenes. Gavin and Lilo Pulver do nicely in their starring assignments. (Dir: Douglas Sirk, 133 mins.)

Time to Remember (Great Britain, 1962)** Yvonne Monlaur, Harry H. Corbett. Real-estate agent searches for property which holds the key to treasure. Fair mystery based on an Edgar Wallace story. (Dir: Charles Jarrett, 58 mins.)

Time Travelers, The (1964)**½ Preston Foster, Philip Carey, Merry Anders, Joan Woodbury. Scientific team experimenting with time is projected into the future, don't exactly like what they find there. Intriguing scientific idea, handled with a fair amount of skill; some good special effects, capable cast. (Dir: Ib Melchior, 82 mins.)

Time Travelers (MTV 1976)** Sam Groom, Tom Hallick, Richard Basehart. Disaster man Irwin Allen produced this tepid pilot film for another series about scientists who travel through time. It's kid stuff basically as two stalwart men (Groom, Hallick) go back to Chicago on the eve of the famous fire to obtain a cure for "Wood's fever." The action sequences are fairly well done. (Dir: Alex Singer, 74 mins.)

Time Within Memory (Japan, 1973)*** Takahiro Tamura, Atsuko Kaku. Visually stunning, told mostly in flashbacks. After a 30-year absence a man returns to a small island, the scene of his childhood. Directed and photographed by cinematographer Toichiro Narushima. (118 mins.)

Time Without Pity (Great Britain, 1957)** Michael Redgrave, Ann Todd, Joan Plowright, Peter Cushing, Lois Maxwell. A father has 24 hours to save his son from the death sentence. Despite the fine cast, this suspense drama never quite clarifies itself. Some good moments, mostly drab boredom. (Dir: Joseph Losey, 88 mins.)

Timelock (Great Britain, 1957)**½ Robert Beatty, Betty McDowall. Tight British drama about a bank official who accidentally locks his son in the vault, which is set to open sixty-three hours later. The inevitable gimmick about the race against time is used to the breaking point. (Dir: Gerald Thomas, 73 mins.)

Times Square (1980)** Tim Curry, Trini Alvarado, Robin Johnson. Alvarado and Johnson play two teenage girls who run away from a psychiatric hospital in Robert Stigwood's attempt to capitalize on the New Wave market. With Curry as a disk jockey who makes the girls celebrities; screenplay by Jacob Brackman. Dull kind of rock soap opera. (Dir: Alan Moyle, 111 mins.)

Timetable (1956)*** Mark Stevens, Felicia Farr. A streamline train is robbed in a daringly intricate holdup. Neat crime melodrama has many twists. (Dir: Mark Stevens, 79 mins.)

Tin Drum, The (West Germany-France, 1979)**** Angela Winkler, Mario Adorf, Daniel Olbrychski, David Bennent. Director Volker Schlondorff's faithful adaptation of the Günter Grass masterpiece is assisted by the casting coup of young Bennent as the dwarf Oskar, who—from the age of three—refuses to grow. A substantial, entertaining, extraordinary film. Oscar for Best Foreign Language Film. (142 mins.)

Tin Pan Alley (1940)** Alice Faye, Betty Grable, Jack Oakie, John Payne. Undistinguished, pastiche Fox musical does, however, have a winning performance by Oakie, a memorable production number of "The Sheik of Araby" with Billy Gilbert as the sheik, and the amazing Nicholas Brothers. (Dir: Walter Lang, 94 mins.)

Tin Star, The (1957)***½ Henry Fonda, Anthony Perkins, Betsy Palmer. Expertly made western mixes humor with suspense, and a standout performance by Fonda as a wily bounty hunter who helps a young sheriff clean up a town. Superior of its type. (Dir: Anthony Mann, 93 mins.)

Tingler, The (1959)*** Vincent Price, Judith Evelyn. A gimmicked horror film that works. Vincent Price menaces everyone in sight and he's just the one who can do it effectively. Judith Evelyn is very fine as a frightened bystander. (Dir: William Castle, 80 mins.)

Tintorera (Mexico, 1978)½ Susan George, Fiona Lewis, Hugo Stiglitz. (Dir: Rene Cardona, Jr., 91 mins.)

Tip on a Dead Jockey (1957)*** Robert Taylor, Dorothy Malone, Jack Lord, Martin Gabel, Gia Scala. Irwin Shaw's crime story makes a good film with Taylor giving one of his better screen portrayals as a pilot involved with smugglers. The action is fast and believable and the film seldom bogs down despite its length. (Dir: Richard Thorpe, 99 mins.)

Titanic (1953)*** Clifton Webb, Barbara Stanwyck, Robert Wagner, Thelma Ritter, Brian Aherne. Hollywood's version of the famous tragic event, the sinking of the sink-proof Titanic. Personal dramas are unfolded before the climax arrives when the ship hits the inevitable iceberg. Good

performances keep the situation from becoming too maudlin. Oscar: Best Story and Screenplay. (Dir: Jean Negulesco, 98 mins.)

Titfield Thunderbolt, The (Great Britain, 1953)**** Stanley Holloway, George Relph, Hugh Griffith. Villagers resent the closing of their railway line by the government, take over the train themselves. Rollicking, completely delightful comedy, great fun. (Dir: Charles Crichton, 84 mins.)

Titicut Follies (1967)**** This shattering film about a state mental hospital in Massachusetts was brilliantly produced, directed, and edited by Frederick Wiseman, who may be the most gifted documentary filmmaker recording the American scene. There is no commentary in this real-life chamber of horrors and none is needed. The film still cannot be shown in Massachusetts. (87 mins.)

To All My Friends on Shore (MTV 1972)*** Bill Cosby, Gloria Foster. Strong performances and a believable script make this film about a hard-working black man, his sacrificing wife, and their doomed son worthwhile. Cosby completely immerses himself in the difficult role of a determined man with a dream...to get his family out of the small Connecticut ghetto and buy a modest home of their own. His good performance is matched by Miss Foster's commanding portrayal of his loyal, loving, but weary wife. Their plight is compounded by the nature of their son's illness, sickle-cell anemia. Strong drama. (Dir: Gilbert Cates, 74 mins.)

To Be or Not to Be (1942)**** Jack Benny, Carole Lombard, Robert Stack, Stanley Ridges, Lionel Atwill. This story of a Shakespearean troupe in Poland fleeing from the Nazis is one of the greatest film comedies. Benny leads the troupe, and he is as funny impersonating Hamlet as impersonating Hitler. Lombard, who died shortly after the completion of the film, has one of her richest roles as his wife. (Dir: Ernst Lubitsch, 99 mins.)

To Catch a Spy (France, 1957)** Henri Vidal, Barbara Laage, Nicole Maurey. Secret-service man goes after stolen rocket plans. Routine espionage thriller with lots of action, girls, clichés. Dubbed in English (Dir: Irene Chanas, 85 mins.)

To Catch a Thief (1955)***½ Grace Kelly, Cary Grant, Jessie Royce Landis, John Williams. Grant is a retired cat burglar on the Riviera, and Kelly is the spoiled American rich girl who seems to have the perpetual hots for him in this fluffy exercise by director Alfred Hitchcock in light comedy, minimal mystery, and good-natured eroticism (the fireworks scene is a classic). Landis is delightful as Kelly's clearheaded mother; Williams gives expert support as usual. (97 mins.)

To Commit a Murder (France-Italy-West Germany, 1967)*½ Louis Jourdan,

Edmond O'Brien, Senta Berger. (Dir: Edouard Molinaro, 91 mins.)

To Die in Madrid (France, 1963)**** A superb documentary of the Spanish Civil War using newsreel footage from the archives of six different countries. Documents the beginning of the struggle in 1931 to Franco's assumption of complete power in 1939. Scenes of modern Spain skillfully juxtaposed and splendidly edited by Suzanne Baron. One of the best documentaries of its kind ever made. Narrated by John Gielgud, Irene Worth and others. (Dir: Frederic Roussif, 85 mins.)

To Die in Paris (MTV 1968)**½ Louis Jourdan, Kurt Krueger, Philippe Forquet, Robert Ellenstein. Fair suspense tale of French WW II Underground, casts Jourdan as Underground leader jailed by the Nazis, who faces two enemies after his escape: Nazi agents and the Underground itself. He's fearful he will be forced to disclose damning information once his identity is known by the Germans. (Dirs: Charles Dubin, Allen Reisner, 100 mins.)

To Each His Own (1946)*** Olivia de Havilland, John Lund, Roland Culver. Sticky melodrama about a mother of an illegitimate son who meets him during WW II when he is a soldier (and his father's spitting image). Skillfully crafted in high style by director Mitchell Leisen. (100 mins.)

To Find a Man (1972)*** Pamela Martin, Lloyd Bridges, Phyllis Newman, Darren O'Conner. Interesting and occasionally perceptive tale of a young girl in quest of an abortion and the young boy who matures by helping her. Newcomers Martin and O'Conner are excellent as the young couple, and help to overcome the sometimes thin premise. Screenplay by Arnold Schulman (who was the original director), based on the novel by S. J. Wilson. (Dir: Buzz Kulik, 94 mins.)

To Find My Son (MTV 1980)**½ Richard Thomas, Justin Dana, Alyn Ann McLerie, Steve Kanaly, Julie Cobb. Well-meaning drama written by Sandor Stern. Thomas is a young, single man of 23 who becomes attached to an orphan boy with a speech defect and decides to adopt him. Bureaucracy rears its meddling head and he faces prejudices and obstacles in his efforts to give the boy a new life. (Dir: Delbert Mann, 104 mins.)

To Go and Come (Italy, MTV 1972)**½ Laura Betti, Lucia Poll. Occasionally interesting short feature written and directed by Giuseppe Bertolucci. About a young couple who spend the night in a railway station and the fantasies that occur to the young man.

To Have and Have Not (1944)***½ Humphrey Bogart, Lauren Bacall (film debut), Walter Brennan, Hoagy Carmichael. This is when the two lovebirds met and the picture has a good romance and plenty of intrigue to boot. Bogey is a fisherman in this one and between fishing for Nazis he manages to hook Lauren. Supposedly from a Hemingway story but not too accurately. (Dir: Howard Hawks, 100 mins.)

To Hell and Back (1955)*** Audie Murphy, Susan Kohner, Charles Drake, David Janssen, Jack Kelly. Good screen adaptation of Audie Murphy's true heroic war adventures, which earned him the title of the most decorated soldier of WW II. The battle sequences are superior to the personal drama injected throughout the film, and Murphy plays himself with honesty and a surprising absence of arrogance. (Dir: Jesse Hibbs, 106 mins.)

To Kill a Cop (MTV 1978)**½ Joe Don Baker, Lou Gossett, Jr., Desi Arnaz, Jr., Christine Belford. Fine blend of New York street action mixed with backstage political maneuvering in the police department. Pudgy, pig-eyed Baker is thoroughly convincing as a harried chief of detectives, and Gossett is properly menacing as a black intellectual revolutionary. Arnaz and Belford can't shake their Hollywood image as the love interest, but that can be overlooked when writer Ernest Tidyman stages another of his harrowing auto chases up Manhattan's Third Avenue. (Dir: Gary Nelson, 208 mins.)

To Kill a Mockingbird (1962)**** Gregory Peck, Mary Badham, Philip Alford, Brock Peters. Excellent production of Harper Lee's sensitive book about an Alabama lawyer bringing up his two motherless children. Peck (who won an Oscar) was never better, and the two children are most affecting. Superb script (Horton Foote) and direction (Robert Mulligan), together with fine performances. Topnotch. In its own quiet way this is one of the best movies dealing with race relations that the American film industry has ever made. (Dir: Robert Mulligan, 129 mins.)

To Paris with Love (Great Britain, 1955)**½ Alec Guinness. Sometimes witty comedy about a father's lessons in love to his son. Alec Guinness scores again as the fun-loving father. The scenes shot in Paris itself are appealing. One of Guinness's minor films. (Dir: Robert Hamer, 78 mins.)

To Please a Lady (1950)**½ Clark Gable, Barbara Stanwyck. A romantic comedy-drama about a racing car enthusiast and his lady love, who objects to his risking his neck. Adolphe Menjou comes off better than the two stars. (Dir: Clarence Brown, 91 mins.)

To Race the Wind (MTV 1980)*** Steve Guttenberg, Randy Quaid, Mark Taylor. Blind Harold Krents went to Harvard and became a top-drawer law student; his story became the hit play and movie "Butterflies Are Free." This good-humored film adapted from Krents's autobiography retains the same light touch as grinning long-jawed Guttenberg never stops trying to be normal, managing to win girls and sing amusing café songs about his affliction. (Dir: Walter Grauman, 104 mins.)

To Sir, with Love (Great Britain, 1967)**** Sidney Poitier, Judy Geeson, Suzy Kendall. A good humored, touching story of an idealistic ex-engineer (Poitier, of course) and his experiences in teaching a group of rambunctious white high school students from the slums of London's East End. Poitier is particularly appealing in this film based on the novel of E. R. Braithwaite and skillfully produced, adapted and directed by James Clavell. Judy Geeson is particularly affecting as a blonde toughie who comes to have a crush on her teacher. The almost-love scene between them is nicely handled. Lulu had a hit record with the title song. (105 mins.)

To the Devil...a Daughter (Great Britain, 1976)**½ Richard Widmark, Christopher Lee, Nastassa Kinski, Honor Blackman, Denholm Elliott. Defrocked priest Lee, founder of the satanic Children of the Lord cult in Germany, earmarks Kinski for selection as the devil's daughter on her 18th birthday. Her distraught father, Elliott, enlists the aid of occult expert Widmark and the horror begins. Based on the Dennis Wheatley novel. (Dir: Peter Sykes, 93 mins.)

To the Ends of the Earth (1948)**** Dick Powell, Signe Hasso. Government agent chases a narcotic ring around the world. Intricate plotting keeps interest on high in this thrilling melodrama. Excellent. (Dir: Robert Stevenson, 109 mins.)

To the Shores of Hell (1966)* Marshall Thompson, Kiva Lawrence, Richard Arlen. (Dir: Will Zens, 81 mins.)

To the Victor (1948)**½ Dennis Morgan, Viveca Lindfors, Dorothy Malone, Denise Darcel. This film tries to say something but the message gets stuck in its throat. This romance of a black marketeer and a French girl collaborator in post-war Paris never gets off the ground. (Dir: Delmer Daves, 99 mins.)

To Trap a Spy (1966)* Robert Vaughn, Patricia Crowley, David McCallum. (Dir: Don Medford, 92 mins.)

Toast of New Orleans, The (1950)**½ Mario Lanza, Kathryn Grayson, David Niven. This was Mario Lanza's second film and the one in which he sang the popular "Be My Love." He plays a New Orleans fisherman who is converted into an opera star. The buxom Miss Grayson is vocally up to par and looks very attractive. Niven is wasted as a patron of the Arts who adores Miss Grayson. (Dir: Norman Taurog, 97 mins.)

Toast of New York (1937)*** Edward Arnold, Cary Grant, Frances Farmer, Jack Oakie. Story of Jim Fisk, who rose from peddler to a Wall Street tycoon. Interesting biographical drama, well made. (Dir: Rowland V. Lee, 109 mins.)

Tobacco Road (1941)**½ Charlie Grapewin, Marjorie Rambeau, Gene Tierney, Dana Andrews, Ward Bond. Long-run Broadway play has been cleaned up for the screen and emerges as a fair tragicomedy of moral depravity in the impoverished Georgia farmland. (Dir: John Ford, 84 mins.)

Tobruk (1967)** Rock Hudson, George Peppard. Routine WW II adventure with Hudson and Peppard cast as the ready heroes assigned to destroy Rommel's fuel supply at Tobruk. The production is well mounted but you've seen it dozens of times before. (Dir: Arthur Hiller, 110 mins.)

Toby Tyler (1960)*** Kevin Corcoran, Henry Calvin, Bob Sweeney, Mr. Stubbs (the monkey). Popular kids' tale about a boy who runs away to join the circus and finds good pals—animal and people—and success there, is tailor-made for the Disney Studios. They've produced a touching, pleasant film, and young 'uns will adore it. (Dir: Charles Barton, 96 mins.)

Today We Live (1933)** Joan Crawford, Gary Cooper, Franchot Tone, Robert Young. This adaptation of a William Faulkner war story is so loaded with individual heroism and sacrifice that it will strike modern audiences as stupid. (Dir: Howard Hawks, 110 mins.)

Together Again (1944)*** Charles Boyer, Irene Dunne. Straitlaced lady mayor of a small Vermont town falls for a dashing New York sculptor. Amusing, well-acted romantic comedy. (Dir: Charles Vidor, 94 mins.)

Together Brothers (1974)*** Anthony Wilson, Glynn Turman, Richard Yniguez. Acceptable action film about five black youths who stalk the ghetto to revenge the killer of their policeman friend. Commercial considerations are well balanced with character sensitivity. (Dir: William A. Graham, 94 mins.)

Togetherness (1970)** George Hamilton, Peter Lawford, Olinka Berova. Romantic comedy with a contrived plot. Hamilton stars as an American playboy in Greece masquerading as a Mexican journalist so he can trap the woman he loves. Familiar fare. (Dir: Arthur Marks, 98 mins.)

Tokkan (Japan, 1978)**½ Toshitaka Ito, Yusuke Okada. Set during the 19th-century turmoil between the Tokugawa shogunate and the partisans of the Meiji restoration, the film abounds in battle skirmishes, futility, and rampant social chaos. The protagonists are two country boys out for lots of sex and loot, finding all that and plenty else. (Dir: Kihachi Okamoto, 90 mins.)

Tokyo After Dark (1959)** Richard Long, Michi Kobi. Military policeman accidentally kills a Tokyo teenager, breaks jail when he learns he's to be tried in a Japanese court. Fair drama of postwar Japan. (Dir: Norman Herman, 80 mins.)

Tokyo File 212 (1951)*** Robert Peyton, Florence Marly. Army Intelligence officer mops up Communist sabotage in post-war Japan. Fast-moving melodrama aided by on-the-spot backgrounds. (Dirs: Dorrell and Stuart McGowan, 84 mins.)

Tokyo Joe (1949)** Humphrey Bogart, Florence Marly, Sessue Hayakawa. Not one of Bogart's better films. Slow moving story of adventure and intrigue in Japan. (Dir: Stuart Heisler, 88 mins.)

Tokyo Olympiad (Japan, 1965)*** The 1964 Olympics—beautifully, ambitiously recorded in one of the finest photographic monuments to athletics ever made. Though film was originally more comprehensive, a wide-ranging view of athletic endeavor and personal triumphs, picture has been edited by its American distributors to focus on events of interest in this country, making movie appear to be more newsreel reportage than a documentary overview. It is still a magnificent job, worthwhile, stirring. Included is the extraordinary women's volleyball final between Japan and the USSR. (Dir: Kon Ichikawa, 93 mins.)

Tol'able David (1930)** Richard Cromwell, Noah Beery, Joan Peers. A remake of the '21 classic about a gentle mountain boy's fight against his family's oppressors. It's still tol'able! (Dir: John G. Blystone, 82 mins.)

Tom Brown's School Days (Great Britain, 1951)***½ Robert Newton, Diana Wynyard. The adventures of a lad at an exclusive boys' school. Well-done version of classic story. (Dir: Gordon Parry, 93 mins.)

Tom, Dick and Harry (1941)**** Ginger Rogers, George Murphy, Burgess Meredith, Alan Marshal. Telephone operator dreams what life would be like with three eligible suitors. Completely charming, novel comedy, excellent. Remade as "The Girl Most Likely." (Dir: Garson Kanin, 86 mins.)

Tom Horn (1980)**½ Steve McQueen, Richard Farnsworth, Linda Evans. McQueen plays a former Indian fighter drifting through a settled West who falls into a job collaring rustlers for a combine of ranchers. Director William Wiard's lumbering visual plan is as passive as McQueen's acting. (98 mins.)

Tom Jones (Great Britain, 1963)**** Albert Finney, Susannah York, Diane Cilento, Hugh Griffith, Edith Evans. A fantastic, marvelous, hilarious film—one of the films it is hard to overpraise. The remarkable screenplay by John Osborne, based on Henry Fielding's classic novel of life in England, catches the infectious spirit of the novel. Rollicking, bawdy, beautiful England of two centuries ago is brilliantly captured by director Tony Richardson. Finney, clearly a great actor, portrays the rambunctious country boy wenching and winning his way through life. The famous eating scene with the edible Joyce Redman is one of the most riotous and sexy scenes ever filmed. (Won four Oscars.) (131 mins.)

Tom Sawyer (1973)** Johnny Whitaker, Celeste Holm, Warren Oates, Jeff East,

Jodie Foster. Strictly for the kids; the adults will be annoyed by this scrubbed-clean musical version of the Mark Twain classic. Shot entirely on location in Missouri (a plus), the film contains most of the familiar incidents, from the fence whitewashing to the scary chase through the caves. Whitaker and East are too wholesome as Tom and Huck Finn, but Jodie Foster just about steals the movie as the perfect Becky Thatcher. Celeste Holm, as Aunt Polly, and Warren Oates, as Muff Potter, are the adults on hand. (Dir: Don Taylor, 104 mins.)

tom thumb (Great Britain, 1958)*** Russ Tamblyn, Terry-Thomas, Peter Sellers, Alan Young. Grimm's fairy tale brought to life using real actors, puppets, and animation, all cleverly arranged together. Concerns tiny five-inch tom who is forced to help robbers, and then later to capture them. Exemplary family fare. Oscar: Best Special Effects. (Dir: George Pal, 98 mins.)

Toma (1973)**½ Tony Musante, Susan Strasberg. Good police story and pilot for the TV series. Musante is fine as Dave Toma, real-life Newark, N.J., police detective, whose unique approach to his work helped him to crack, almost single-handedly, a big numbers operation connected to the syndicate. The detailed detective work, piling clue upon clue, is interesting to follow and the action is kept at a believable, exciting level, thanks to director Richard T. Heffron. (73 mins.)

Tomahawk (1951)** Van Heflin, Yvonne DeCarlo, Jack Oakie, Rock Hudson. Just another Indian and cowboy film. This time the plot is involved with Indian Affairs treaties and those who fight to protect the enforcement of said treaties. Some action during the proceedings. (Dir: George Sherman, 82 mins.)

Tombstone, the Town Too Tough to Die (1942)*** Richard Dix, Frances Gifford. Routine western rises way above the average thanks to slick production. Story of Wyatt Earp (again), and the infamous duel with the outlaws at Tombstone, Arizona. (Dir: William McGann, 80 mins.)

Tommy (Great Britain, 1975)*** Ann-Margret, Oliver Reed, Jack Nicholson, Roger Daltrey, Elton John, Eric Clapton. A wildly uneven, often visually stunning musical of the Who's rock opera written by composer-guitarist Pete Townshend. Director Ken Russell wrote the screenplay, but the sung dialogue takes a back seat to the music and some crazed, hallucinatory images including an erupting TV set that you won't soon forget. Director Russell's flamboyant style is well-suited to this garish material, and there's a surprisingly good performance by Ann-Margret. (Dir: Ken Russell, 110 mins.)

Tomorrow (1972)***½ Robert Duvall, Olga Bellin, Peter Masterson, Sudie Bond. Respectful, literate, literal transcription of an obscure William Faulkner tale about a handyman who cares for and eventually falls in love with a young pregnant girl. (Dir: Joseph Anthony, 102 mins.)

Tomorrow at 10 (Great Britain, 1962)**½ John Gregson, Robert Shaw, Helen Cherry. Kidnapper leaves his victim in a room with a time bomb, asks for ransom as the police race against time to nab him. Competent crime melodrama has quite a bit of suspense. (Dir: Lance Comfort, 80 mins.)

Tomorrow Is Another Day (1951)*** Ruth Roman, Steve Cochran. Fast paced action drama about hoodlums and their women. Ruth Roman tries to start a new life but her past proves too strong an obstacle. Good performances. (Dir: Felix E. Feist, 90 mins.)

Tomorrow Is Forever (1946)**½ Claudette Colbert, Orson Welles, George Brent, Natalie Wood. Twenty years after he supposedly was killed, a disfigured and crippled chemist comes back to his wife, who remarried. Well-produced but slow drama with an Enoch Arden theme. (Dir: Irving Pichel, 105 mins.)

Tomorrow Is My Turn (France-Italy-Germany, 1960)**½ Charles Aznavour, Georges Rivière. Long, grim saga of two French prisoners of war, their experiences on a farm in Germany. Superior direction, performances—and a wordy script, dubbed in English. (Dir: André Cayatte, 117 mins.)

Tomorrow the World (1944)**** Fredric March, Betty Field, Skip Homeier. An American family adopts a German boy, discovers the Nazi influence has warped the child's mind. Excellent drama, thoughtful, gripping. (Dir: Leslie Fenton, 86 mins.)

Tonight and Every Night (1945)**½ Rita Hayworth, Lee Bowman, Janet Blair, Leslie Brooks. The show must go on despite the London blitz, in this light musical about a gang of troupers who never miss a performance, going down into the underground if they have to. Not very authentic, and the show isn't much, but it passes pleasantly, with a dash of flaming wartime sentiment. Color. (Dir: Victor Saville, 92 mins.)

Tonight at 8:30 (Great Britain, 1952)**** Valerie Hobson, Nigel Patrick, Stanley Holloway. Three of Noël Coward's short plays, all comic gems, sophisticated, worthwhile, stylishly performed for civilized viewers. (Dir: Anthony Pelissier, 81 mins.)

Tonight We Raid Calais (1943)**½ Annabella, John Sutton, Lee J. Cobb. Another of those wartime espionage films. This one is the well-acted, improbable tale of a British agent in France to find a factory the RAF wants to bomb. (Dir: John Brahm, 70 mins.)

Tonight We Sing (1953)** David Wayne, Ezio Pinza, Anne Bancroft, Roberta Peters. The life of Sol Hurok provides the pretext for a hodgepodge of artsy production numbers. Ezio Pinza sports a hilarious accent as the Russian basso Feodor Chaliapin. (Dir: Mitchell Leisen, 109 mins.)

Tonight's the Night (Great Britain, 1954)** David Niven, Yvonne DeCarlo, Barry Fitzgerald. A whimsical comedy filmed in Ireland with authentic settings bolstering the film's appeal. David Niven is funny in his inimitable gentlemanly fashion. (Dir: Mario Zampi, 88 mins.)

Tonio Kroger (West Germany-France, 1964)**½ Jean-Claude Brialy, Nadja Tiller, Gert Frobe. An academic, fairly literal version of Thomas Mann's autobiographical novella about growing up in Germany in the late 19th century. If you haven't got the book handy, this might be a reasonable introduction to the story line, and provide a stimulus to reading the fine Mann work. As a film experience, it's stodgy, picturesque, with some lovely narration directly from the original. English subtitles. (Dir: Rolf Thiele, 90 mins.)

Tonka—See: **Horse Named Comanche, A**

Tony Draws a Horse (Great Britain, 1950)**½ Anne Crawford, Cecil Parker. A psychiatrist and his wife disagree over the treatment of their son, and as a result a happy marriage is nearly terminated. Mildly amusing comedy has some good moments. (Dir: John Paddy Carstairs, 90 mins.)

Tony Rome (1967)** Frank Sinatra, Jill St. John, Richard Conte, Gena Rowlands. Slick production values, tough dialogue, a parade of feminine pulchritrude plus Sinatra as a private eye add up to not a hell of a lot, but with Miami Beach backgrounds, and the familiar plot Rome (Sinatra) is involved in a series of he-man confrontations with an assortment of sordid characters, as he tries to solve a jewel theft and murder. Frankie ain't Bogie! (Dir: Gordon Douglas, 110 mins.)

Too Bad She's Bad (Italy, 1955)**½ Sophia Loren, Vittorio De Sica, Marcello Mastroianni. Taxi driver gets involved with a band of crooks, but falls for one of the pretty ones. Mildly amusing English-dubbed comedy. (Dir: Alessandro Blasetti, 95 mins.)

Too Far to Go (MTV 1979)**** Blythe Danner, Michael Moriarty, Kathryn Walker. One of the standout TV films of the decade. Skillful adaptation by William Hanley of 17 short stories by John Updike, some originally published in the "New Yorker," about the dissolution of a 20-year marriage. Danner is poignant and vulnerable as she both receives and hurls soft-spoken but nonetheless taunting, hurtful barbs at her embattled mate. Music by Elizabeth Swados and perceptive direction by Fielder Cook. (98 mins.)

Too Hot to Handle (1938)***½ Clark Gable, Myrna Loy, Walter Pidgeon. Rival newsreel companies vie with each other for hot news. Big, exciting action melodrama, a most enjoyable show. (Dir: Jack Conway, 107 mins.)

Too Hot to Handle (Great Britain, 1960)*½

Jayne Mansfield, Leo Genn. (Dir: Terence Young, 101 mins.)

Too Late Blues (1961)** Bobby Darin, Stella Stevens. Glum, unpleasant story of a jazz musician who steals the affections of a blonde from his friend. Jazz atmosphere pervades, but it's pretty synthetic. However, Darin gives a good performance. (Dir: John Cassavetes, 100 mins.)

Too Late the Hero (1970)***½ Cliff Robertson, Michael Caine, Henry Fonda, Denholm Elliott. Rugged, complex war story. Caine and Robertson are reluctant men on a tough mission to a south Pacific island occupied by the Japanese in WW II. Elliott gives the performance of his career as the deluded mission leader. Filmed in the Philippines. (Dir: Robert Aldrich, 133 mins.)

Too Late to Love (France, 1958)**½ Michele Morgan, Henri Vidal. Well acted, poorly written drama about the alliance of a news photographer and a lady lawyer, for the purpose of proving a man's innocence. (Dir: Henri Decoin, 90 mins.)

Too Many Crooks (Great Britain, 1959)*** Terry-Thomas, George Cole. Thick-headed gang of crooks try to extort from a businessman. Amusingly daffy comedy. (Dir: Mario Zampi, 85 mins.)

Too Many Girls (1940)*** Lucille Ball, Richard Carlson, Ann Miller, Desi Arnaz (film debut), Eddie Bracken. Small college with ten co-eds to every boy wants badly to win a football game. Entertaining musical comedy. (Dir: George Abbott, 85 mins.)

Too Many Husbands (1940)*** Jean Arthur, Fred MacMurray, Melvyn Douglas. About to marry again, a woman finds her first husband, believed dead, has returned. Pleasing sophisticated comedy. Remade as "Three For The Show." (Dir: Wesley Ruggles, 84 mins.)

Too Many Lovers (France, 1957)** Jeanmaire, Daniel Gelin, Henri Vidal. Lightweight French comedy dealing with a nightclub singer-dancer. The proceedings are enhanced by the dancing of Jeanmaire. Music is by Michel Legrand. (Dir: Henri Decoin, 105 mins.)

Too Many Thieves (1966)** Peter Falk, Britt Ekland, David Carradine. Moderately entertaining caper film with Falk playing an American lawyer who is hired by thieves who stole an art treasure from a Macedonian shrine. The character Falk plays is the same one he played in the short-lived TV series "The Trials of O'Brien." (Dir: Bob Hayes, 95 mins.)

Too Much, Too Soon (1958)**½ Dorothy Malone, Errol Flynn, Martin Milner. Poor Flynn had finally exhausted his tolerance for booze, sex, and drugs by this time, and was reduced to concentrating his erratic attention on acting. Here, he is nothing short of brilliant playing his own late, beloved crony, John Barrymore. His performance alone is worth seeing in this film, and his scenes are unfortunately few

and short. Otherwise, this is a cheap, mawdlin adaptation of the cheap, mawdlin book about John's daughter Diana Barrymore, whose life was apparently one long drunken embarrassment. She seems to blame it all on daddy (which might well be true, though mummy was no prize either). Miss Malone gives it a good try, but it's not worth it. (Dir: Art Napoleon, 121 mins.)

Too Young to Kiss (1951)*** Van Johnson, June Allyson, Gig Young. Young pianist can't get in to see a concert manager, so she poses as a 13-year-old. Bright comedy with plenty of laughs along the way. (Dir: Robert Z. Leonard, 91 mins.)

Too Young to Love (Great Britain, 1960)*½ Thomas Mitchell, Pauline Hahn, Bessie Love. (Dir: Muriel Box, 89 mins.)

Top Banana (1954)***½ Phil Silvers, Rose Marie. A loud burlesque comic becomes a TV star and aids a young romance. From the Broadway stage hit, filmed as it was presented, this has nothing productionwise, but Silvers' yeoman service turns it into a funny show and you will see a couple of those wild sketches that made burlesque such a good training ground years ago for comedians. (Dir: Alfred E. Green, 100 mins.)

Top Floor Girl (Great Britain, 1959)** Kay Callard, Neil Hallett. Ruthless woman stops at nothing to get to the top of the business world. Mildly entertaining "female jungle" type of drama. (Dir: Max Varnel, 71 mins.)

Top Hat (1935)**** Fred Astaire, Ginger Rogers. The best of the Astaire-Rogers films, and that's saying plenty. Fred plays a dancer who pursues the girl of his dreams from London to the Riviera. Irving Berlin tunes: "Cheek to Cheek," "Isn't This A Lovely Day." Isn't this a lovely show? It sure is! (Dir: Mark Sandrich, 100 mins.)

Top Man (1943)**½ Donald O'Connor, Richard Dix, Susanna Foster, Lillian Gish, Noah Beery, Jr. Corny dated comedy about a young man's taking over as head of the family while his father goes to War (WW II). O'Connor is one of our favorites but he can't carry this one. (Dir: Charles Lamont, 74 mins.)

Top o' the Morning (1949)**½ Bing Crosby, Barry Fitzgerald, Ann Blyth. Bing on the Emerald Isle, as he plays an insurance agent out to find who stole the Blarney Stone. Lazily amusing comedy with Bing crooning the songs. (Dir: David Miller, 100 mins.)

Top of the Form (Great Britain, 1953)**½ Ronald Shiner, Jacqueline Pierreux, Anthony Newley. A race track tipster becomes the head of a boys' school by accident. Mildly amusing comedy. (Dir: John Paddy Carstairs, 75 mins.)

Top of the World (1955)**½ Dale Robertson, Evelyn Keyes, Frank Lovejoy. Jet pilot is assigned to an Alaskan observation unit. Typical service melodrama, enlivened by some good scenes in the frozen North. (Dir: Lewis R. Foster, 90 mins.)

Top Secret (Great Britain, 1952)*** George Cole, Oscar Homolka. Sanitary engineer accidentally walks off with atomic secrets, is branded a traitor. Highly amusing topical comedy, good fun. (Dir: Mario Zampi, 94 mins.)

Top Secret (MTV 1978)** Bill Cosby, Tracy Reed, Sheldon Leonard, Gloria Foster. "I Spy" Cosby takes it up again, running through the ruins of southern Italy as a special agent for the U.S. government. Cos is as smooth as ever, the Italian scenery is fetching, but the plot lacks excitement and Bill's female sidekick lacks zip. (Dir: Paul Leaf, 104 mins.)

Top Secret Affair (1957)** Kirk Douglas, Susan Hayward. A tough Major General and a crusading lady publisher slug it out in a slight comedy about Washington politics and the diplomatic service. This could have been a funnier film but it never gets off the ground. From John P. Marquand's Melville Goodwin, Esq. (Dir: H. C. Potter, 90 mins.)

Topaz (1969)**½ John Forsythe, Frederick Stafford. An espionage tale which has agents and double agents jumping around the globe when it is discovered that the Russians have infiltrated into high French government positions. Although Alfred Hitchcock directed this tale, it doesn't have his usual stamp of excitement, but the narrative itself should keep spy fans intrigued. The cast has no real star names in the leads but John Vernon scores as a Castro-type revolutionary and Karin Dor is beautiful and seductive as an undercover agent. (126 mins.)

Topaze (1933)***½ John Barrymore, Myrna Loy, Luis Alberni. Marcel Pagnol's stage play about a shy professor who turns the tables on sharks of industry seeking to exploit his ideas gives Barrymore an opportunity to turn in an actorish performance. He takes such evident relish in the part that his charm is irresistible. (Dir: Harry d'Arrast, 78 mins.)

Topeka (1953)**½ Bill Elliott, Phyllis Coates. Outlaw is offered the job of sheriff, calls in his former gang members to help him clean up the territory. Lively western has plenty of action. (Dir: Thomas Carr, 69 mins.)

Topkapi (1964)**** Melina Mercouri, Maximillian Schell, Peter Ustinov. An exciting jewel of a film about an ingenious theft of a valuable jewel-encrusted dagger from the Topkapi Museum in Istanbul. The color photography is dazzling, whether showing the glories of Istanbul or the treasures of the museum. The big heist scene may strike you as a more elaborate re-shooting of the classic scene in "Rififi," and you'll be right, because they're both the work of ace director Jules Dassin. He has a flawless cast of charming rogues and charlatans assembled, and the film keeps bustling along at a seesaw pace. A delightful, droll adventure film. Oscar: Ustinov, Best Supporting Actor. (119 mins.)

Topper (1937)***½ Cary Grant, Roland Young, Constance Bennett. Of how George and Marian Kirby became involved in their ghostly escapades. Grand fantastic comedy, the original in the "Topper" series. From the novel by Thorne Smith. (Dir: Norman Z. McLeod, 96 mins.)

Topper (MTV 1979)** Kate Jackson, Andrew Stevens, Jack Warden. Jackson and Stevens play those mischievous ghosts who make Cosmo Topper's life a comic shambles. The results are catastrophic since the pair have no flair. Warden also misses the boat as Topper. (Dir: Charles Dubin, 104 mins.)

Topper Returns (1941)**** Roland Young, Joan Blondell, "Rochester" Eddie Anderson, Dennis O'Keefe, Carole Landis. Mr. Cosmo Topper and his ghostly friends are involved in a spooky murder mystery. The best of the Toppers. Hilarious, loaded with laughs, thrills, tip-top performers! (Dir: Roy Del Ruth, 87 mins.)

Topper Takes a Trip (1938)***½ Roland Young, Constance Bennett. Mr. Topper goes to the Riviera for a holiday, only to find the spirit of Marian Kirby in hot pursuit. Amusing comedy. (Dir: Norman Z. McLeod, 80 mins.)

Tops Is the Limit—See: **Anything Goes** (1936)

Tora-San the Matchmaker (Japan, 0000)**½ Kiyoshi Atsumi, Kaori Momoi, Chieko Baisho, Michiyo Kogure. Part of the ever popular series about a lovable tramp, played by Atsumi under the indefatigable direction of Joji Yamada. Tora rescues a wealthy, sheltered young woman (Momoi) from rape, finding that she has fled in fear from an impending marriage. He persuades her to return, only to have her skip out in the middle of the ceremony and seek refuge at the confectionery shop of Tora's aunt and uncle. Tora, the romantic, falls in love with her while she regards him as little more than a friend, and eventually class affinities win out over affairs of the heart.

Tora! Tora! Tora! (1970)*** Jason Robards, Martin Balsam, Joseph Cotten. You'll seldom see a more detailed or expensively mounted battle sequence than the bombing of Pearl Harbor which takes up a good part of the last half of the WW II film. This re-creation of the events leading up to and just after that "day of infamy" has a cast of familiar faces, as well as many Japanese actors. However, they play second fiddle to the Oscar-winning special-effects men who staged the massive Pearl Harbor attack. (Dirs: Richard Fleischer, Toshio Masuda, and Kinji Fukasaku, 142 mins.)

Torch Song (1953)**½ Joan Crawford, Michael Wilding, Gig Young. This film marked Miss Crawford's return to a musical role after years of heavy-weight dramas. She wears tights, dances and sings (dubbed by India Adams) and, of course, cries once or twice, in the role of a Broadway musical comedy star whose personal life leaves much to be desired. Michael Wilding plays a blind pianist who is secretly in love with Miss Crawford. (Dir: Charles Walters, 90 mins.)

Tormented (1960)*½ Richard Carlson, Susan Gordon. (Dir: Bert I. Gordon, 75 mins.)

Torn Between Two Lovers (MTV 1979)**½ Lee Remick, George Peppard, Joseph Bologna. A happily but unexcitingly married woman is accidentally thrown into the company of a divorced, handsome, sophisticated architect who falls in love with her. Contrived story, but her need to be frank with her husband about her affections leads to the most emotionally honest scenes in the drama. (Dir: Delbert Mann, 104 mins.)

Torn Curtain (1966)** Paul Newman, Julie Andrews, Lila Kedrova. The only noteworthy thing about this chiller is that it's the 50th film directed by Alfred Hitchcock, the undisputed master of spy-chase films. But this film is subpar for the master. Newman plays a science professor who gets involved in a fantastic espionage mission while attending a convention in Denmark. Andrews, in a sexy role for a change, is Newman's secretary-lover and she follows him to East Berlin. (119 mins.)

Torpedo Bay (France-Italy, 1963)**½ James Mason, Lilli Palmer, Gabriele Ferzetti. When an Italian sub surfaces in neutral waters, the crew of an antisub craft meets the crew in Tangiers, learn to like each other despite the enmity. Different sort of war drama, with English dialogue, moves leisurely but holds interest for the most part. (Dirs: Bruno Vailati, Charles Frend, 91 mins.)

Torpedo of Doom, The (1938-66)*** Lee Powell, Herman Brix, Bruce Bennett, Eleanor Stewart. Feature version of serial "The Fighting Devil Dogs." Two Marines combat a mysterious hooded figure who wants to rule the world. As a serial, this rated with the best; excellently made for its type. Dated now but should still provide enough thrills for the kids, nostalgia for the elders. (Dirs: William Witney, John English, 100 mins.)

Torpedo Run (1958)**½ Glenn Ford, Ernest Borgnine, Dean Jones. Moderately interesting but slow moving submarine drama with some suspense. Glenn Ford plays the commander of the sub, whose mission is to sink a transport on which his family are passengers. (Dir: Joseph Pevney, 98 mins.)

Torrid Zone (1950)*** Pat O'Brien, Ann Sheridan, James Cagney. Good racy dialogue and the acting of the principals combine to make this a torrid picture. Jim is a no-good, Pat is his foreman and Ann gives out with plenty of oomph as a

night club girl. (Dir: William Keighley, 88 mins.)

Tortilla Flat (1942)** Spencer Tracy, John Garfield, Hedy Lamarr, Frank Morgan. Stale adaptation from the John Steinbeck novel about tramps on the California coast, with some unfortunate set design. Tracy does a good job, but is hopelessly miscast. Garfield and Lamarr look right, but their parts are incompletely written. Only Morgan, as the man with the dogs, comes across. (Dir: Victor Fleming, 104 mins.)

Torture Chamber of Dr. Sadism (West Germany, 1967)** Christopher Lee, Lex Barker, Karin Dor. In Blood Castle an evil count holds a baroness at bay in an effort to gain immortality, or is that immorality? For Lee enthusiasts only. (Dir: Harald Reinl, 85 mins.)

Torture Garden (Great Britain, 1967)**½ Some eerie tales are spun by a sinister doctor (Burgess Meredith) at a sideshow. Best: the first one, about a cat's evil presence. Worst: the last, with a hammy Jack Palance performance. With Peter Cushing, Beverly Adams. (Dir: Freddie Francis, 93 mins.)

Touch, The (Sweden-U.S., 1971)**** Elliott Gould, Bibi Andersson, Max von Sydow. A magnificent, deeply moving melodrama directed in English, by Ingmar Bergman. The film is quiet and subtle, with a visual expressiveness unusual for the dour Swede. Andersson gives one of the most full-bodied emotional performances ever seen onscreen, as the woman who leaves von Sydow for Gould. (113 mins.)

Touch and Go (Great Britain, 1955)*** Jack Hawkins, Margaret Johnston. Funny, sometimes hilarious comedy of a family's decision to pull up stakes and move to Australia. Jack Hawkins shines in the lead role. (Dir: Michael Truman, 84 mins.)

Touch of Class, A (Great Britain, 1972)**** Glenda Jackson, George Segal. A delightful romantic comedy about a pair of clandestine lovers in a London-Spain tryst. Their quarrelsome "brief encounter" in sunny Spain is deft, and Jackson and Segal are enormously charming together. The screenplay by Melvin Frank and Jack Rose is not invariably sophisticated, and overlook the dopey song at the end. Jackson won an Academy Award for her enchanting performance. (Dir: Melvin Frank, 106 mins.)

Touch of Evil (1958)**** Orson Welles, Charlton Heston, Janet Leigh, Joseph Calleia, Marlene Dietrich, Zsa Zsa Gabor, Joseph Cotten. The greatest masterpiece of all sleaze movies, director Orson Welles's baroque thriller was his last Hollywood film. Welles stars as a corrupt sheriff in a seedy border town who matches wits with a Mexican narcotics cop (Heston, on honeymoon with Leigh). Acting honors to Calleia's loyal lieutenant, whose moral quandaries give the drama heart. (108 mins.)

Touch of Larceny, A (Great Britain,

1959)*** James Mason, Vera Miles, George Sanders. Lothariolike military man dreams up a scheme to make it appear that he has defected to the Russians with secrets—so he can sell his memoirs and obtain money to marry. Mason is charming in this clever little comedy with a good portion of sly humor. (Dir: Guy Hamilton, 94 mins.)

Touch of the Sun, A (Great Britain, 1956)*½ Frankie Howerd, Dennis Price. (Dir: Gordon Parry, 80 mins.)

Touch of Treason, A (France, 1961)*½ Roger Hanin, Dany Carrel, Claude Brasseur. (Dir: Edouard Molinaro, 88 mins.)

Touchables, The (Great Britain, 1968)* Judy Huxtable, Esther Anderson, Marilyn Rickard, Kathy Simmonds, David Anthony. (Dir: Robert Freeman, 88 mins.)

Toughest Gun in Tombstone (1958)** George Montgomery, Beverly Tyler, Jim Davis as Ringo. Dull sagebrush saga of a cowboy out to avenge the murder of his wife and bring to justice the villainous outlaw, Johnny Ringo. (Dir: Earl Bellamy, 72 mins.)

Toughest Man Alive (1955)**½ Dane Clark, Lita Milan. Government agent poses as a gun runner to break up a smuggling ring. Fast-moving melodrama. (Dir: Sidney Salkow, 72 mins.)

Tout Va Bien (France, 1972)*** Yves Montand, Jane Fonda, Vittorio Caprioli. Montand as an ex-New Wave filmmaker and Fonda as his wife get involved in a factory takeover in this self-styled "commercial" film, which is only a slight step back from codirector Jean-Luc Godard's previous hard-core political tracts, but the few concessions made—characters and a story, of sorts—make the rhetoric more accessible. (Jean-Pierre Gorin is the other director.) (95 mins.)

Tovarich (1937)***½ Claudette Colbert, Charles Boyer, Basil Rathbone. Top drawer comedy about two royal paupers who are carrying 40 billion francs for the czar but would rather starve than spend it. Translated from Jacques Deval's play by Robert E. Sherwood. (Dir: Anatole Litvak, 98 mins.)

Toward the Unknown (1956)**½ William Holden, Lloyd Nolan, Virginia Leith, James Garner. Fairly interesting drama about the test jet-pilots and their personal involvements. Holden plays a nervous major whose past record makes him overzealous in the performance of his duty. (Dir: Mervyn LeRoy, 115 mins.)

Tower of London (1939)*** Basil Rathbone, Boris Karloff, Vincent Price, Nan Grey, Barbara O'Neill, Ian Hunter, Leo G. Carroll. Atmospheric, witty drama about the rise of the (supposedly) wicked King Richard III, and the various and imaginative murders he committed to gain the British throne. Most of the above stars are among his victims (Price's death is particularly piquant); Karloff is the fiendish assistant. (Dir: Rowland V. Lee, 92 mins.)

Tower of London (1962)** Vincent Price, Michael Pate, Joan Freeman. Melodramatic, lurid retelling of the story of King Richard III. Not as good as the '39 film of the same name. Vince really hams it up. (Dir: Roger Corman, 73 mins.)

Tower of Terror (Great Britain, 1941)** Michael Rennie, Movita, Wilfrid Lawson. OK WW II tale about a lighthouse off the German coast. Its half-mad keeper, Lawson, plays unwitting host to French concentration camp escapee Movita and British spy Rennie, who naturally fall in love. Much of the film takes place in the dark. (Dir: Lawrence Huntington, 80 mins.; cut version, 62 mins.)

Towering Inferno, The (1974)*** Paul Newman, Steve McQueen, Faye Dunaway, Fred Astaire, Jennifer Jones, Richard Chamberlain, Robert Vaughn, William Holden. A multimillion-dollar disaster epic that delivers the goods. Newman is the architect of one of the tallest buildings in the world, erected in San Francisco, and it's grand opening time. But Holden's greedy, selfish son-in-law (Chamberlain) has cut some corners, resulting in unsafe wiring and a big fire which endangers the lives of the guests at the swank opening. Less effective on TV, of course. (Dir: Irwin Allen, 165 mins.)

Town Like Alice, A (Great Britain, 1956)***½ Virginia McKenna, Peter Finch. Powerful film about the tragedy of a group of women who miss being evacuated from Malaya at the outbreak of WW II and suffer many indignities in the hands of the conquering Japanese army. The acting is first rate. (Dir: Jack Lee, 107 mins.)

Town on Trial (Great Britain, 1957)*** John Mills, Charles Coburn. Well done tale of a murder investigation which leads a Scotland Yard man into a town loaded with secrets. The characters are well written and acted thus raising this above the commonplace. (Dir: John Guillermin, 94 mins.)

Town Tamer (1965)* Dana Andrews, Terry Moore, Pat O'Brien, Lon Chaney, Bruce Cabot, Jean Cagney, Barton MacLane, Sonny Tufts. (Dir: Lesley Selander, 89 mins.)

Town Without Pity (U.S.-Switzerland-West Germany, 1961)** Kirk Douglas, E. G. Marshall, Christine Kaufmann, Robert Blake, Richard Jaeckel. Army major in Germany is assigned to defend a quartet of GIs accused of attacking a young girl. Downbeat, grim drama moves stodgily, is obvious in its presentation. Filmed in Germany. (Dir: Gottfried Reinhardt, 105 mins.)

Toy, The (France, 1976)*** Pierre Richard, Michel Bouquet, Fabrice Greco. Engaging, heartwarming comedy about a schnook (Richard) who is hired to be a living "toy" of the spoiled son (Greco) of a wealthy businessman (Bouquet). Richard combines pathos and slapstick to good effect. (Dir: Francis Veber, 90 mins.)

Toy Tiger (1956)**½ Jeff Chandler, Laraine Day, Tim Hovey, David Janssen. Pleasant comedy about a neglected child who plays cupid for his career Mom and selects her new husband, one of her staff commercial artists. The cast is attractive and the pace keeps things hopping. (Dir: Jerry Hopper, 88 mins.)

Toys in the Attic (1963)**½ Dean Martin, Geraldine Page, Wendy Hiller, Yvette Mimieux, Gene Tierney. A no-good rover returns to his New Orleans home with his childlike bride, brings trouble for his spinster sisters. Lillian Hellman's drama becomes commonplace when it should be provoking. Some capable performers, but the general result is disappointing. (Dir: George Roy Hill, 90 mins.)

T. R. Baskin (1971)**½ Candice Bergen, James Caan, Peter Boyle. A romantic, "realistic" view of a working girl's life and loves. Bergen gives a subdued, thoroughly appealing performance as a young woman searching for answers in her formless life. Caan also scores a bull's-eye as a divorced man whose relationships generally add up to a series of one-night stands. (Dir: Herbert Ross, 104 mins.)

Track of the Cat (1954)** Robert Mitchum, Teresa Wright, Diana Lynn, Tab Hunter. A cougar hunt amid family squabbles makes up the action of this otherwise slow-paced movie. Best feature is the fine photography. (Dir: William Wellman, 102 mins.)

Track of the Vampire (1966)*½ William Campbell, Sandra Knight. (Dirs: Jack Hill, Stephanie Rothman, 80 mins.)

Track of Thunder (1967)* Tom Kirk, Ray Stricklyn, H. M. Wynant, Brenda Benet, Faith Domergue. (Dir: Joseph Kane, 83 mins.)

Trackers, The (MTV 1971)*½ Sammy Davis, Jr., Ernest Borgnine, Julie Adams, Jim Davis. (Dir: Earl Bellamy, 72 mins.)

Tracks (1976)*** Dennis Hopper, Dean Stockwell, Taryn Power. Stream-of-consciousness tale about a Vietnam vet (Hopper) who is accompanying his dead buddy's body on a train. Hopper hallucinates about his fellow passengers, who may not be what they seem. (Writer-Dir: Henry Jaglom, 90 mins.)

Trade Winds (1938)***½ Fredric March, Joan Bennett, Ann Sothern, Ralph Bellamy, Thomas Mitchell. Director Tay Garnett had made a trip around the world, and came home with some dynamite travel footage he just *had* to use somehow. So he and co-writer Frank R. Adams concocted this wild, delightful chase around the globe, as wise-cracking detective with a heart-of-gold March trails murder-suspect Bennett. Naturally this becomes a love story (or two), by turning hilarious, suspenseful, and delicately affecting. March is in superb control, Bennett gorgeous (this is the one where she turns from ethereal blonde to exotic brunette on-camera); a sub-romance between Bellamy and Sothern is a scream. Wonderful entertainment. (95 mins.)

Trader Horn (1931)**½ Harry Carey, Edwina Booth, Duncan Renaldo. This exciting jungle thriller scared the daylights out of 1931 audiences. You may find it funny but it was a step forward in realistic movie making. (Dir: W. S. Van Dyke, 120 mins.)

Traffic (France-Italy, 1971)*** Jacques Tati, Maria Kimberly. Not as inspired a bit of tomfoolery as "Mr. Hulot's Holiday," but there are some inventive scenes in this virtually plotless free-form series of running gags about Paris, its traffic and automobile drivers. Tati directed and wrote this slight satire about transporting a model camping car to an automobile show in Holland. (89 mins.)

Trail of Blood (Japan, 1972)**½ Yoshio Harada. The second in a popular series of samurai films. In Japanese films, as in violence films all over the world, bloodshed increased in the '70s, but instead of becoming cynical and ironic as in the spaghetti western, Japanese sentimentality reasserted itself. Harada plays the carefree, roughhouse Jokichi, who tries to reform and become a family man but is forced back into swordplay when gang bosses threaten his woman. The fencing is excellent.

Trail of the Lonesome Pine, The (1936)* Fred MacMurray, Henry Fonda, Sylvia Sidney. Now dated outdoor adventure about feuding and fighting in the backwoods when the railroad first came through. (Dir: Henry Hathaway, 102 mins.)

Trail of the Vigilantes (1940)**** Franchot Tone, Broderick Crawford, Peggy Moran, Warren William. Easterner is sent west to break up an outlaw gang. Excellent western, with emphasis on some hilarious comedy. (Dir: Allan Dwan, 78 mins.)

Train, The (U.S.-France-Italy, 1964)***½ Burt Lancaster, Paul Scofield, Jeanne Moreau. An exciting WW II drama set in Paris during the German occupation which builds scene by scene to a magnificently staged climax in a railroad yard. Lancaster stars as a railroad boss who seeks the aid of the powerful French Resistance fighters when it becomes known that France's valuable art treasures are going to be transported by train to Germany. The cast is first-rate, particularly Scofield as a German officer and marvelous French character actor Michel Simon as a bullheaded train engineer. (Dirs: Arthur Penn, John Frankenheimer, 133 mins.)

Train of Events (Great Britain, 1949)**½ Valerie Hobson, John Clements, Joan Dowling. Various groups of persons aboard a train have their problems, which are resolved in one way or another when the train is involved in an accident. Episodic film manages to hold the attention, with one story line being extremely humorous, another intensely dramatic. (Dirs: Sidney Cole, Charles Crichton, Basil Dearden, 89 mins.)

Train Ride to Hollywood (1975)*½ Guy Marks, Michael Payne. (Dir: Charles Rondeau, 85 mins.)

Train Robbers, The (1973)*½ John Wayne, Ann-Margret, Rod Taylor, Ben Johnson. (Dir: Burt Kennedy, 92 mins.)

Train Robbery Confidential (Brazil, 1962)** Eliezer Gomes, Grande Otelo. A novelty—the true story of six men who perpetrated a payroll robbery on a Brazilian railroad. Technically below par, but the locale, treatment are interesting. Dubbed in English. (Dir: Roberto Farias, 102 mins.)

Tramp Tramp Tramp (1926)*** Harry Langdon, Joan Crawford. An ex-vaudeville comedian, discovered and equipped with a new screen personality by Frank Capra, Langdon rocketed to popularity with a series of shorts made for Mack Sennett. With Capra, Langdon made this first feature, about a cross-country walking race, and followed its success with two more films before canning Capra and striking out on his own. Failure was swift and irreversible, but the Langdon-Capra films still have the mark of a genuine, if rarefied talent. (Dir: Harry Edwards, 65 mins.)

Tramp, Tramp, Tramp (1942)*½ Jackie Gleason, Florence Rice. (Dir: Charles Barton, 70 mins.)

Tramplers, The (Italy, 1966)** Gordon Scott, Joseph Cotton, Jim Mitchum. Confederate soldier returns home to encounter trouble from his father and the problems left by war's aftermath. A Civil War western. Some good moments, some erratic ones. (Dirs: Anthony Wileys [Mario Sequi], Albert Rand, 105 mins.)

Transatlantic (1931)**½ Edmund Lowe, Lois Moran, Myrna Loy. Atmospheric shipboard intrigue. Lowe is top-billed and suave, but the real stars are designer Gordon Wiles and cameraman James Wong Howe, who created a fabric of grids and lights that set standards for much Hollywood style to come. (Dir: William K. Howard, 78 mins.)

Transatlantic Tunnel (Great Britain, 1935)** Richard Dix, Madge Evans, Walter Huston, Leslie Banks, George Arliss. Only the sets retain some interest in this saga. (Dir: Maurice Elvey, 94 mins.)

Transplant (MTV 1979)**½ Kevin Dobson, Granville Van Dusen, Ronny Cox, Melinda Dillon. Story of a heart attack victim—a highly charged man of 35 who smokes like a chimney, drinks like a fish, and loves his family hysterically—and his wife, a vigorous young woman, earthy, strong, loving, enormously appealing and supportive no matter how desperate the situation. Both roles are well played by Dobson and Dillon, who carry the drama through its tensions, despairs, and hopes. (Dir: William A. Graham, 104 mins.)

Trap, The (1959)**½ Richard Widmark, Tina Louise, Lee J. Cobb, Earl Holliman. Head of a crime syndicate trying to flee the country isolates a small desert town. Fairly suspenseful crime melodrama. (Dir: Norman Panama, 84 mins.)

Trap, The (Great Britain-Canada, 1966)*** Rita Tushingham, Oliver Reed. A raw, tough, unusual movie; a fur trapper and the mute girl he has bartered for as wife struggle in the northern wilderness of 19th-century Canada. Authentic, exciting adventure tale, spiced by low-key humor and an off-beat romance. The performances are top-notch. Filmed on location in British Columbia. (Dir: Sidney Hayers, 106 mins.)

Trapeze (1956)**½ Burt Lancaster, Tony Curtis, Gina Lollobrigida. Corny but colorful drama played against a circus background. Lancaster plays a former aerialist who helps a young acrobat achieve fame under the big top. Good European locations, some exciting camera work and Lollobrigida are added assets. (Dir: Carol Reed, 105 mins.)

Trapped (1949)***½ Barbara Payton, Lloyd Bridges, John Hoyt. T-men release a counterfeiter from jail, hoping he will lead them to a big money ring. Excellent documentary-type crime melodrama rates with the best of them. (Dir: Richard Fleischer, 78 mins.)

Trapped (MTV 1973)*½ James Brolin, Susan Clark, Earl Holliman, Robert Hooks. (Dir: Frank De Felitta, 72 mins.)

Trapped Beneath the Sea (1974)**½ Lee J. Cobb, Martin Balsam. Well-made drama about the rescue of an experimental submarine. Good performances and realistic underwater sequences lift this disaster film above the average. Most of the action is told in flashbacks during a Navy inquiry into the incident. The film mirrors a similar real-life story of four men who were trapped in a mini-sub. Made-for-TV. (Dir: William Graham, 72 mins.)

Trapped by Fear (France-Italy, 1969)** Jean-Paul Belmondo, Alexandra Stewart, Sylva Koscina. Ex-soldier becomes a hunted man when he kills a policeman despite efforts of his friend to help. Occasionally interesting, often routine "new-wavish" melodrama dubbed in English. (Dir: Jacques Dupont, 85 mins.)

Trash (1970)**½ Joe Dallesandro, Holly Woodlawn, Geri Miller. You may be able to see this via TV cassettes or on late night cable. A sleazy story, with some improvised dialogue, about various repellent, vapid-minded, foul-mouthed drug addicts. It will have a bizarre fascination for some of you, and there are critics who take this film quite seriously. (Dir: Paul Morrissey, 103 mins.)

Trauma (1962)* John Conte, Lynn Bari, Lorrie Richards. (Dir: Robert Malcolm Young 92 mins.)

Traveling Executioner, The (1970)** Stacy Keach, Marianna Hill, Bud Cort. Keach's performance in the title role (with a portable electric chair, circa 1918) is better than this cheap, contrived movie deserves. Filmed in Alabama. (Dir: Jack Smight, 95 mins.)

Traveling Saleswoman, The (1950)** Joan Davis, Andy Devine. Strictly for slapstick and mugging fans. Joan Davis & Andy Devine vie for laughs in this cornball Western about a soap saleswoman and her rotund fiance. (Dir:Charles F. Reisner, 75 mins.)

Travels with My Aunt (1972)***½ Alec McCowen, Lou Gossett, Robert Stephens, Cindy Williams. Most of the time this is delightful, sophisticated fare, immeasurably aided by Maggie Smith's glowing, winning performance as Aunt Augusta out to ransom her old lover and, in the process, liberate her nephew Henry (McCowen). Screenwriters Jay Presson Allen and Hugh Wheeler scaled down Graham Greene's best-selling novel and added a few not very felicitious plot twists. But the stylish Miss Smith and lively direction from veteran George Cukor keep things moving along briskly and divertingly. (109 mins.)

Travis Logan, D.A. (1971)**½ Vic Morrow, Hal Holbrook, Brenda Vaccaro. Here's another law series TV pilot. Morrow plays a low-keyed small-town district attorney who puzzles over an open killing by a stationer after finding his wife in his best friend's arms. Though a psychiatrist labels the man insane, D.A. Logan believes it is premeditated murder and he faces an uphill battle to prove it. Holbrook plays the stationer, a man who must be clever enough to fool a psychiatrist, and his performance keys the ingenious story by Andy Lewis. (Dir: Paul Wendkos, 100 mins.)

Treasure Island (1934)**½ Wallace Beery, Jackie Cooper, Lionel Barrymore, Lewis Stone, Nigel Bruce. Beery chews the scenery as Long John Silver in this generally enjoyable, visually stodgy MGM-version of Robert Louis Stevenson's adventure story. Cooper is Jim Hawkins and Barrymore has a memorable bit as the black-spotted Billy Bones. (Dir: Victor Fleming, 105 mins.)

Treasure Island (Great Britain, 1972)*** Orson Welles, Kim Burfield, Walter Slezak, Lionel Stander. Welles as Long John Silver eschews the emphasis on roguish charm which Robert Newton and Wallace Beery brought to the role, instead conveying the dangerous, ominous side of the pirate—more what Stevenson intended and dramatically more impressive. The rest of the cast, overshadowed by Welles, are generally fine; the scenery, settings, and costumes are colorful and atmospheric. An entertaining version of the absorbing tale. (Dir: John Hough, 94 mins.)

Treasure of Lost Canyon (1952)*½ William Powell, Julie Adams. A Robert Louis Stevenson story. (Dir: Ted Tetzlaff, 82 mins.)

Treasure of Makuba, The (U.S.-Spain, 1966)½ Cameron Mitchell, Mara Cruz, Todd Martin. Nice backgrounds, but this Spanish-made adventure-drama set in the Polynesian Islands is trash. (Dir: Joe Lacy, 79 mins.)

Treasure of Pancho Villa, The (1955)** Rory Calhoun, Shelley Winters, Gilbert Roland. American adventurer plots a train robbery with the intention of delivering the gold to Villa's forces. Picturesque Mexican backgrounds support a routine plot; standard outdoor drama. (Dir: George Sherman, 96 mins.)

Treasure of Ruby Hills (1955)** Zachary Scott, Carole Mathews. Rancher steps in the middle of a fight to control range land. Undistinguished western. (Dir: Frank McDonald, 71 mins.)

Treasure of San Teresa (Great Britain-West Germany, 1957)** Dawn Addams, Eddie Constantine, Christopher Lee. A predictable espionage yarn with more narrow escapes than you can keep straight. This plot-boiler has all the clichés neatly intact, and the international cast breezes through the proceedings with professional ease. (Dir: Alvin Rakoff, 81 mins.)

Treasure of Sierra Madre, The (1948)**** Humphrey Bogart, Walter Huston, Tim Holt. A group of down-and-outs search the hills for gold only to be undone by their failings. The grizzled prospector of Walter Huston is the capstone of his great and varied career. Bogart brings a conviction to his pathological role that few other actors could supply. Marred only by a god-awful Max Steiner score. Oscars to John Huston, Best Director and Best Original Screenplay; Walter Huston, Best Supporting Actor. (124 mins.)

Treasure of the Golden Condor (1953)** Cornel Wilde, Constance Smith, Anne Bancroft, Fay Wray. Predictable costume adventure film which traps its stars in an 18th century melodrama. Wilde plays the rightful heir to a noble fortune who is cheated and forced to live as a fugitive. Treasure hunting in Central America fills the better half of the movie. Remake of "Son of Fury." (Dir: Delmer Daves, 93 mins.)

Tree Grows in Brooklyn, A (1945)**** Dorothy McGuire, James Dunn, Joan Blondell, Lloyd Nolan, Peggy Ann Garner. Magnificent rendition of Betty Smith's novel, moving and dramatically authentic, though it never leaves the studio sets. McGuire is brilliant as the mother, as are Blondell, Dunn as the alcoholic father (Oscar-winner), and the rest of the cast. (Dir: Elia Kazan, 128 mins.)

Tree Grows in Brooklyn, A (MTV 1974)** Cliff Robertson, Diane Baker, Nancy Malone. Labored remake. Robertson, as the hard-drinking singing waiter and occasional breadwinner of the Nolan family, somehow slips into caricature rather than characterization. Miss Baker is more successful as the brave but stern Katie Nolan, but it's Pamela Ferdin, as the teenage Francine, who delivers the film's best performance. (Dir: Joel Hardy, 74 mins.)

Tree of Wooden Clogs, The (Italy, 1978) **** Luigi Ornaghi, Francesca Moriggi, Omar Brignoli. A turn-of-the-century peasant epic told through the eyes of a young boy in Bergamo. Director Ermanno Olmi is so close to his subject that he is incapable of sentimentality and untruth in art and observation. The pace is measured. (186 mins.)

Trent's Last Case (Great Britain, 1952)*** Margaret Lockwood, Michael Wilding, Hugh McDermott, Miles Malleson, Orson Welles. Film version of the classic that Agatha Christie called "one of the three best detective stories ever written," by E.C. Bentley. A sleuth is called to investigate the mysterious death of a tycoon (played exotically in flashback by Welles, with a nice fake nose). Was it murder, or suicide? And what did the beautiful widow have to do with it? The intricate plot is all talk, but for traditional mystery fans it is most absorbing. (Dir: Herbert Wilcox. 90 mins.)

Trial (1955)***½ Glenn Ford, Dorothy McGuire, Arthur Kennedy, John Hodiak, Katy Jurado. Absorbing drama about the murder trial of a Mexican boy which is fantastically exploited by a Communist-backed organization for their own underhanded purposes. The cast is top notch with Arthur Kennedy the standout as a two-faced legal mind working for the organization. (Dir: Mark Robson, 109 mins.)

Trial, The (France-Italy-West Germany, 1962)***½ Anthony Perkins, Orson Welles, Jeanne Moreau, Romy Schneider. Director Orson Welles's nightmarish version of the Franz Kafka novel was shot mainly in the disused Gare d'Orsay in Paris—a dark, baroque, echoing world of corridors, crannies, and more than a few nooks from which pop startling Wellesian surprises. A magnificently atmospheric film, with the less-than-perfect casting of Perkins as K., and the always welcome presences of Moreau, and Orson himself as Hastler. (120 mins.)

Trial and Error (Great Britain, 1962)**½ Peter Sellers, Beryl Reid, Richard Attenborough, David Lodge. A study in character acting from Peter Sellers and Attenborough, as a bungling barrister and an accused murderer. They're fine, but the film becomes a thespic exhibition at the expense of the narrative, which is thin indeed. (Dir: James Hill, 88 mins.)

Trial at Kampili (Japan, 1963)** Minoru Ohki, Elice Richter. Japanese officer on trial before the War Crimes Commission, but his former prisoners come to his defense. Fairly interesting English-dubbed war drama. (91 mins.)

Trial for Rape (Italy, 1979)*** Extraordinary videotape record of an actual trial in Rome, where several young men are accused of raping a young woman in her early 20s after luring her to a suburban home under the pretext of giving her a job. The male defense counsel for the defendants articulate some astonishing arguments justifying the rape. The production quality is poor and grainy. B&W. (70 mins.)

Trial of Billy Jack, The (1974)½ Tom Laughlin, Delores Taylor, William Wellman, Jr., Sacheen Littlefeather. (170 mins.)

Trial of Chaplain Jensen, The (MTV 1975)**½ James Franciscus, Charles Durning, Joanna Miles, Lynda Day George, Harris Yulin. Offbeat theme, based on a real life incident, given a good mounting here. Franciscus is well cast as the handsome, devout Navy chaplain who is court-martialed when two Navy wives accuse him of adultery. Dialogue is fairly explicit, the story will hold you. (Dir: Robert Day, 72 mins.)

Trial of Lee Harvey Oswald, The (MTV 1977)**½ Ben Gazzara, Lorne Greene, Frances Lee McCain, John Pleshette, Lawrence Pressman. What if Lee Harvey Oswald, President Kennedy's accused assassin, hadn't been shot by Jack Ruby and actually stood trial? Ambitious TV drama painstakingly re-creates the fatal day in Dallas and assumes the fictional events which might have followed. All the facts about the assassination are brought up in the dramatization, such as the possibility of a conspiracy, Oswald's link to Russia, his possible connection with the FBI, the mysterious deaths of various witnesses via suicide and accidents, and the uncovering of a possible Mafia-CIA alliance. (Dir: David Greene, 208 mins.)

Trial of Mary Dugan, The (1929)*½ Norma Shearer, Lewis Stone. (Dir: Bayard Veiller, 000 mins.)

Trial of the Catonsville Nine, The (1972)***½ Ed Flanders, Richard Jordan, Peter Strauss, Douglas Watson, Nancy Malone. Flawed but often moving filmed record of a play by Daniel Berrigan about the trial of a group of anti-Vietnam War protesters, who raided the offices of the draft board in Catonsville, Md., and burned some of the files in May '68. There are many deeply moving statements in this static yet powerful drama. (Dir: Gordon Davidson, 85 mins.)

Trial Run (MTV 1968)**½ Leslie Nielsen, James Franciscus, Janice Rule, Diane Baker. Another slick feature film with the climaxes conveniently constructed to fit the commercial breaks. Nielsen's expert performance as a self-made successful attorney with a troubled personal life makes this one better than most. Familiar fare about the machinations of a young, eager, and somewhat ruthless lawyer (Franciscus) who gets his big chance to shine when he's assigned by his boss (Nielsen) to defend a man who murdered his unfaithful wife. (Dir: William Graham, 98 mins.)

Trials of Alger Hiss, The (1980)***½ Alger Hiss, Richard M. Nixon, Whittaker Chambers. Illuminating, chilling documentary about blacklisting and McCarthyism in America in the '50s. Director John Lowenthal (a law professor) uses some remarkable filmed records of the period, coupled with interviews of principals and observers who are still alive, including of course Hiss himself. A good example of investigative reporting and how filmmakers can contribute to our understanding of history. (166 mins.)

Trials of Oscar Wilde, The (Great Britain, 1960)**** Peter Finch, James Mason, Nigel Patrick, Lionel Jeffries, Yvonne Mitchell. This account of Oscar Wilde's ill-fated libel suit against the Marquis of Queensbury and subsequent trial for sodomy has a handsomer look than most British films of its period. Finch's portrait of the playwright/celebrity is multileveled, capturing the vanity and pomposity along with his sublime incomprehension of how fatally he is going to do himself in. (Writer-Dir: Ken Hughes, 123 mins.)

Trials of Private Schweik (West Germany, 1964)*½ Peter Alexander, Rudolf Prack. (83 mins.)

Triangle Factory Fire Scandal, The (MTV 1979)** Tom Bosley, Tovah Feldshuh, Stephanie Zimbalist. Based on the real-life sweatshop fire in New York which killed 145 garment workers, this drama stars Bosley, who plays a harsh, driving foreman, cracking the whip on immigrant employees, working them mercilessly in crowded, unsafe conditions. Some good scenes. (Dir: Mel Stuart, 104 mins.)

Tribe, The (MTV 1974)* Victor French, Henry Wilcoxon. (Dir: Richard Colla, 72 mins.)

Tribe That Hides from Man, The (Great Britain, 1970)**** Extraordinary feature-length documentary on the efforts of a dedicated anthropologist, Claudio Villas Boas, to establish contact with and help "save" a small band of tribal Indians, the Kreen-Akrore, in the jungles of northern Brazil. Color photography is extraordinary, penetrating areas never before seen by white men, to say nothing of cameramen. (Dir: Adrian Cowell, 43 mins.)

Tribes (MTV 1970)*** Jan-Michael Vincent, Darren McGavin, Earl Holliman. Absorbing, well made film about a drafted hippie in marine boot camp. Marine stories invariably pit a top drill sergeant against a recruit with marine philosophy winning in the end, but not so here. The hippie (Vincent) can't be broken, and his survival methods are adopted by his barracks mates to the consternation of the drill instructor (McGavin). (Dir: Joseph Sargent, 74 mins.)

Tribute (1980)** Jack Lemmon, Lee Remick, Robby Benson. Bernard Slade's emotionally fraudulent play about a show-biz father and his son makes a phonier movie, since Lemmon's skillful hamming hasn't been toned down for the big screen and Benson is out of his depth as the son. Father-son is treated as banally as possible. (Dir: Bob Clark, 125 mins.)

Tribute to a Bad Man (1956)*** James Cagney, Irene Papas, Don Dubbins. A powerful performance by James Cagney as a big horse breeder whose ruthless tactics alienate those closest to him as the bulwark of this under-rated western drama. Greek actress Irene Papas is impressive as the woman who loves him despite his obvious failings. (Dir: Robert Wise, 95 mins.)

Trick Baby—See: **Double Con, The Trilogy** (1969)***½ Maureen Stapleton, Martin Balsam, Geraldine Page, Mildred Natwick. Three short stories by Truman Capote, originally produced for TV, are combined in this rewarding, magnificently acted collection. All three stories were adapted by Capote and writer Eleanor Perry, and directed by Frank Perry. "Among the Paths to Eden" is set in a cemetery and features two lovely performances by Balsam and Stapleton, who hauntingly plays a middle-aged spinster looking for a husband. The last story, "A Christmas Memory," is narrated by Capote and features a lovely performance by Page preparing for the Christmas season. (110 mins.)

Trilogy of Terror (MTV 1975)**½ Karen Black, Robert Burton, John Karlin, George Gaynes. Karen Black, always an interesting actress, has a field day playing four tormented women in three bizarre, off-beat short stories by Richard Matheson. Miss Black's batting average here isn't bad—she's almost scary as the amoral bitch ready to murder her sister in the opener; then becomes more restrained, in a calculating way, as a teacher being blackmailed by a student in the second; and finally lets writer Matheson dominate in the weird finale about a fetish doll coming to life...the best of the trio. (Dir: Dan Curtis, 72 mins.)

Trio (Great Britain, 1950)*** Michael Rennie, Jean Simmons, Wilfrid Hyde White. Second anthology of Somerset Maugham short stories is undistinguished filmmaking. Of the three basically solid yarns, the last, perhaps the most clichéd yet the most affecting, stars Rennie and Simmons as two sanitarium patients. (Dirs: Ken Annakin, Harold French, 91 mins.)

Triple Cross (France-Great Britain, 1966)**½ Christopher Plummer, Romy Schneider, Trevor Howard, Yul Brynner. A no-holds-barred WW II espionage yarn for those who like their escapes narrow, their double agents invincible, and their action pulsating. Plummer plays a double agent who pulls out all stops in his missions crossing from Germany to England with care and know-how, and meeting his attractive cast of co-stars playing various spy types. Based on the real WW II exploits of famed British double-spy Eddie Chapman. (Dir: Terence Young, 126 mins.)

Triple Deception (Great Britain, 1956)***½ Michael Craig, Brenda de Banzie. Sailor poses as a member of a gold smuggling gang to get the goods on them. Rattling good melodrama, heavy on suspense. (Dir: Guy Green, 86 mins.)

Triple Echo (Great Britain, 1972)**½ Glenda Jackson, Brian Deacon, Oliver Reed. British shocker that should have been more atmospheric and tense than it is. Jackson turns in a mild performance as a country war widow who dresses up her young AWOL lover (Deacon) as her sister to keep him around the farm; and Reed is nicely brutish and foul as the sergeant who takes a fancy to the "sister." (Dir: Michael Apted, 90 mins.)

Triple Play (MTV 1971)** William Windom, Rosemary Forsyth, Larry Hagman. With hosting stints performed by Dan Rowan and Dick Martin, three situation comedy pilots comprise this triplet. The best of the three is the third, "Doctor in the House," starring William Windom playing a small-town New England doctor fencing with his new assistant, a big beautiful lady physician (Rosemary Forsyth). Patients are of secondary interest to the budding romance between the M.D.'s in this ingratiating pilot. The second, titled "The Good Life," stars Larry Hagman and Jane Miller. The opener is a slapstick "Mission: Impossible" spoof. (100 mins.)

Tripoli (1950)** Maureen O'Hara, John Payne, Howard da Silva. The year is 1805 and the Marine Forces headed by John Payne defeat the Tripoli pirates but not until Countess Maureen O'Hara gets her man. Howard da Silva gives a very good performance as a Greek captain. (Dir: Will Price, 95 mins.)

Tristana (France-Italy-Spain, 1970)**** Catherine Deneuve, Fernando Rey, Franco Nero. Perhaps the greatest film directed by Luis Buñuel. Adaptation of the novel by Benito Pérez Galdós about a young woman who seeks what little independence is available to a young unmarried woman in turn-of-the-century Spain. The director's touch can be seen when the aging roué of an uncle (Rey) attempts to console the girl after her leg has been amputated by saying she shouldn't despair, some men will find her even more attractive now. (105 mins.)

Triumph of Hercules, The (Italy, 1964)* Dan Vadis, Pierre Cressoy. (Dir: Alberto DeMartino, 90 mins.)

Triumph of Michael Strogoff (France, 1964)*½ Curt Jurgens, Capucine. (Dir: Victor Tourjansky, 118 mins.)

Triumph of Robin Hood (Italy, 1962)*½ Don Burnett, Gia Scala. (Dir: Giancarlo Romiteli, 92 mins.)

Triumph of Sherlock Holmes, The (Great Britain, 1935)*** Arthur Wontner, Ian Fleming, Lyn Harding. Low-budget film stars Wontner as Holmes and Fleming (the Australian-born character actor, not the creator of James Bond) as Dr. Watson in an adaptation of "The Valley of Fear," a neglected novel in the Arthur Conan Doyle canon. Wotner was perhaps more like Doyle's character—not to mention Sidney Paget's original drawings—than any other actor. (Dir: Leslie Hiscott, 84 mins.)

Triumph of the Son of Hercules (Italy, 1963)* Kirk Morris, Cathia Caro. (Dir: Amerigo Anton, 87 mins.)

Triumph of the Ten Gladiators (Italy-Spain, 1964)* Dan Vadis. (Dir: Nick Nostro, 94 mins.)

Triumph of the Will (Germany, 1936)*½ (120 mins.)

Trog (Great Britain, 1970)** Joan Crawford. The superstars of the '30's and '40's all seem to get around to making one of these sci-fi monster epics. In this outing, Joan Crawford gets her turn. She's an anthropologist who has come across what she believes to be the missing link. The only thing missing here is credibility. Crawford's last film. (Dir: Freddie Francis, 91 mins.)

Trojan Women, The (1971)*** Katharine Hepburn, Vanessa Redgrave, Genevieve Bujold, Irene Papas. Director Michael Cacoyannis's stage production of Euripides' play at New York's Circle in the Square in the early '60s was justly famous, but he has no flair for cinema. Here the poetry, aided greatly by splendid performances by Hepburn as ravaged queen mother Hecuba, and Redgrave as Andromache, is sunk by hyperactive cutting. Filmed in Spain. (102 mins.)

Trollenberg Terror, The—See: **The Crawling Eye**

Trooper Hook (1957)**½ Joel McCrea, Barbara Stanwyck, John Kohner, John Dehner, Earl Holliman. Good western drama bolstered by the stars. There are Indian raids and plenty of action sequences for adventure-seeking fans. (Dir: Charles Marquis Warren, 81 mins.)

Tropic Holiday (1938)** Dorothy Lamour, Ray Milland, Martha Raye. Romantic comedy set in Mexico is weak entertainment. Martha's fans may enjoy her bull fighting scenes. (Dir: Theodore Reed, 80 mins.)

Tropic of Cancer (1970)** Rip Torn, Ellen Burstyn, Phil Brown. Director Joseph Strick botches yet another major literary work. Updating Henry Miller's '34 classic of sexual ecstasy, love of art, and prewar Parisian high jinks, and casting the fine but inappropriate Torn as a smirking, not visibly talented Miller, Strick manages to make Miller's life seem actually boring. Originally rated X. (87 mins.)

Tropic Zone (1953)** Ronald Reagan, Rhonda Fleming. The independent banana plantation owners are plagued by a villainous shipping magnate who wants control of the whole works. Ronald Reagan changes horses in mid-stream to join Rhonda Fleming who looks worried but beautiful. You may not care much one way or the other. (Dir: Lewis R. Foster, 94 mins.)

Trouble Along the Way (1953)*½ John Wayne, Donna Reed. (Dir: Michael Curtiz, 110 mins.)

Trouble at 16—See: **Platinum High School**

Trouble Comes to Town (MTV 1974)**½ Lloyd Bridges, Thomas Evans, Pat Hingle. The film tells the story of a black Chicago youngster who goes South to live with a white sheriff, and it's surprisingly effective at times. The three leads give the script a nice realistic touch by not pushing too hard. Young Evans as the gangly kid who enters the small town with a chip on his shoulder proves to be an interesting actor. (Dir: Daniel Petrie, 73 mins.)

Trouble for Father (Greece, 1958)* Basil Logothetidis. (Dir: A. Sakelarios, 100 mins.)

Trouble for Two (1936)*** Robert Montgomery, Rosalind Russell, Frank Morgan, Louis Hayward. Good exciting adventure tale loosely based on Robert Louis Stevenson's "Suicide Club." Scene about the club is as chilling a bit of business as you'll ever see and is not suggested for the youngsters. (Dir: J. Walter Ruben, 75 mins.)

Trouble in Paradise (1932)**** Miriam Hopkins, Herbert Marshall, Kay Francis. Rapid deft, and most elegant comedy about jewel thieves as proficient at lifting hearts as purses. Hilarious from the opening sight gag of a crooning gondolier tenor on a garbage scow. (The voice is that of the legendary Enrico Caruso.) (Dir: Ernst Lubitsch, 83 mins.)

Trouble in the Glen (Great Britain, 1954)** Orson Welles, Margaret Lockwood, Forrest Tucker, Victor McLaglen. Scottish laird returns from South America to land in the middle of a feud over a closed road. Some good players here, but a draggy pace and a script that misfires undermines what was a promising comedy idea. From the novel by Maurice Walsh. (Dir: Herbert Wilcox, 91 mins.)

Trouble in the Sky (Great Britain, 1960)**½ Michael Craig, Bernard Lee, Peter Cushing, George Sanders, Elizabeth Seal. Efforts made to clear a pilot of negligence when his jet crashes. OK English chins-up-pluck. (Dir: Charles Frend, 76 mins.)

Trouble Man (1972)** Robert Hooks, Paul Winfield, Ralph Waite. Hooks turns in a strong if sometimes wooden performance as Mr. T. The male chauvinism of the formula black action film is at its most virulent, and once again the camera lovingly caresses the hero's closetful of $300 suits. During the inevitable shootout, Hooks surveys the "Better Homes and Gardens" chic of a white gangster's penthouse and delivers perhaps the most revealing line in the film: "That honky sonuvabitch sure knows how to live!" Music by Marvin Gaye. (Dir: Ivan Dixon, 99 mins.)

Trouble With Angels, The (1966)** Rosalind Russell, Hayley Mills, June Harding, Gypsy Rose Lee. Unsophisticated comedy geared for family viewing. Two high-spirited young students at St. Francis Academy, played with superabundant energy by Mills and Harding, keep things hopping for the understanding Mother Superior (Russell) and her staff of bewildered Sisters. Episodic, and some of the intended comedy is strained, but the two teenage girls and their pranks have a modest, mindless appeal. (Dir: Ida Lupino, 112 mins.)

Trouble with Girls, The (1969)***½ Elvis Presley, Vincent Price, Marlyn Mason, Joyce Van Patten. Surprisingly sensitive comedy about the effect a traveling Chautauqua show has on the residents of a small midwestern town. Fine performances from Mason and Van Patten, and Presley stays largely in the background. (Dir: Peter Tewksbury, 104 mins.)

Trouble with Harry, The (1955)*** John Forsythe, Shirley MacLaine (film debut), Edmund Gwenn. When a body is discovered in the Vermont woods, various people have a hard time disposing of it. Director Alfred Hitchcock's macabre comic touch deftly makes this kooky little comedy worthwhile. (99 mins.)

Trouble with Women, The (1947)** Ray Milland, Teresa Wright, Brian Donlevy. Psychology professor has his theories on women tested by an enterprising female reporter in this mild comedy. (Dir: Sidney Lanfield, 80 mins.)

Truck Turner (1974)**½ Isaac Hayes, Scatman Crothers, Yaphet Kotto, Annazette Chase. Blaxploitation film features Hayes as a skip tracer, and it has wit, speed, and sharply handled violence. Hayes is a likable personality with a strong screen presence. (Dir: Johnathan Kaplan, 91 mins.)

True Confession (1937)***½ Carole Lombard, Fred MacMurray, John Barrymore. Fast moving, superbly played farce about a girl on trial for murder. Some of it may strike you as dated, but the method has been borrowed for many of our modern film comedies. Remade as "Cross My Heart." (Dir: Wesley Ruggles, 85 mins.)

True Grit (1969)**** John Wayne, Glen Campbell, Kim Darby, Robert Duvall, Dennis Hopper. John Wayne's Academy Award-winning role as Rooster Cogburn, a one-eyed crotchety U.S. marshal who can still shoot straight. Old Duke's never been better. A delightful western chasedown of the bad guys features an appealing performance from Darby as a 14-year-old tomboy out to avenge her murdered father. Campbell is dreary. (Dir: Henry Hathaway, 128 mins.)

True Grit (MTV 1978)**½ Warren Oates, Lisa Pelikan, Lee Meriwether. Not a remake, but a sequel to the '69 "True Grit." Oates is pretty good in the impossible job of filling John Wayne's shoes as Rooster Cogburn, and Pelikan, a talented and charming redhead, plays the Kim Darby role of determined but chattering 16-year-old Hattie. (Dir: Richard T. Heffron, 104 mins.)

True Story of Jesse James, The (1957)**½ Robert Wagner, Jeffrey Hunter, Hope Lange, Agnes Moorehead. Director Nicholas Ray injects the vitality that is evident throughout this umpteenth rehashing of the legend of the James brothers. Bob Wagner as Jesse and Jeff Hunter as Frank offer good performances, and are ably assisted by Miss Moorehead as their mother and Hope Lange as Jesse's wife. (92 mins.)

True Story of Lynn Stuart, The (1958)*½ Betsy Palmer, Jack Lord. (Dir: Lewis Seiler, 78 mins.)

True to Life (1943)**½ Mary Martin, Dick Powell, Victor Moore, Franchot Tone. Cute little comedy about a soap opera writer who goes to live with a nice family and uses their conversations and actions in his scripts. (Dir: George Marshall, 94 mins.)

Trunk to Cairo (Israel-West Germany, 1966)* Audie Murphy, George Sanders, Marianne Koch. (Dir: Menahem Golan, 80 mins.)

Truth, The (France-Italy, 1960)**½ Brigitte Bardot, Charles Vanel, Paul Meurisse. An interesting film; an exploration of justice under France's outdated Napoleonic Code, using as vehicle and foil the uncontrollable sexuality of Miss Bardot, chronicling her trial for a murder which her defense claims was one of passion. Her performance has an unexpected range. The film features the Vanel-Meurisse combination, superb and fiercely combative as the opposing lawyers. (Dir: Henri-Georges Clouzot, 127 mins.)

Truth About Spring, The (1965)**½ Hayley Mills, John Mills, James MacArthur. Daughter of a rascally seaman experiences her first pangs of love when she meets a wealthy young man. Leisurely but entertaining romantic tale, aided by pretty tropic scenery, nice players. Harmless fun. (Dir: Richard Thorpe, 102 mins.)

Truth About Women, The (Great Britain, 1958)**½ Laurence Harvey, Julie Harris, Diane Cilento, Eva Gabor, Mai Zetterling. A fine cast does what it can to make this somewhat contrived comedy romance workable. There are many voluptuous females in the cast and Laurence Harvey plays the roue with a flair. (Dir: Muriel Box, 98 mins.)

Try and Get Me (1950)***½ Frank Lovejoy, Lloyd Bridges, Richard Carlson. Two kidnappers murder their victim, and are themselves victimized by mob violence upon their capture. Dramatic thunderbolt pulls no punches, is morbidly gripping stuff. (Dir: Cyril Endfield, 85 mins.)

Trygon Factor, The (Great Britain, 1967)** Stewart Granger, Susan Hampshire, Robert Morley. If you don't look for logic in this Scotland Yard mystery film, you may enjoy it. Granger is all British cool as the superintendent in charge of a murder investigation. (Dir: Cyril Frankel, 87 mins.)

Tugboat Annie (1933)*** Marie Dressler, Wallace Beery, Robert Young, Maureen O'Sullivan. Norman Reilly Raine's stories of two old sots on the waterfront were a perfect vehicle to reteam Dressler and Beery after their successful "Min and Bill." The film is dated but lively, with Mervyn LeRoy's direction limber and sure. Young and O'Sullivan are the young lovers. (87 mins.)

Tulsa (1949)*** Susan Hayward, Robert Preston. A fiery redhead battles for an oil empire in the early thirties, only to lose it all and become poorer but wiser. Good melodrama of the oil fields, with plenty of action. (Dir: Stuart Heisler, 90 mins.)

Tunes of Glory (Great Britain, 1960)**** John Mills, Alec Guinness. A beautiful film, recommended for the magnificent and memorable performances of its two stars. Story about the bitter struggle between a vicious, careless, goldbricking colonel (Guinness) and the intelligent, disciplined, civilized young officer (Mills) who supersedes him in command. Screenplay by James Kennaway, based on his novel. (Dir: Ronald Neame, 106 mins.)

Tunnel of Love, The (1958)*** Richard Widmark, Doris Day, Gig Young, Gia Scala. Pleasantly performed comedy about a suburban couple who go through all sorts of red tape to adopt a child. Some bright lines of dialogue, fairly steady pace. (Dir: Gene Kelly, 98 mins.)

Tunnelvision (1976)**½ Chevy Chase, Laraine Newman, Phil Proctor, Howard Hesseman, William Schallert. A not-so-funny follow-up to "The Groove Tube," composed of short sketches parodying TV in '85. You saw better, more sardonic material on TV's original "Saturday Night Live." (Dirs: Brad Swirnoff, Neil Israel, 75 mins.)

Turn the Key Softly (Great Britain, 1953)*** Yvonne Mitchell, Joan Collins, Terence Morgan. Concerning the adventure of three women recently released from prison, their attempts to adjust themselves to society. Excellent performances give this drama a lift. (Dir: Jack Lee, 81 mins.)

Turnabout (1940)**½ Adolphe Menjou, John Hubbard, Carole Landis, Mary Astor, William Gargan. Through a mysterious power, husband and wife have a chance to change sexes, with the natural confusion resulting. Risqué comedy has a fair share of laughs. (Dir: Hal Roach, 83 mins.)

Turning Point, The (1952)**½ William

Holden, Alexis Smith, Edmond O'Brien. Reporter learns that the father of the chairman of a crime investigating committee is mixed up with the crooks himself. Familiar crime melodrama competently done. (Dir: William Dieterle, 85 mins.)

Turning Point, The (1977)**** Anne Bancroft, Shirley MacLaine, Mikhail Baryshnikov, Leslie Browne, Tom Skerritt. The venerable tradition of combining ballet with melodrama continues in a story of two old rivals squabbling over the artistic soul of a young danseuse. The musical question, as always, is whether to dance or to love. MacLaine is particularly impressive, and Bancroft's style is for once admirably suited to her role. Eleven Oscar nominations. (Dir: Herbert Ross, 119 mins.)

Turning Point of Jim Mailoy, The (1975)** John Savage, Gig Young, Biff McGuire, Janis Paige, Kathleen Quinlan. John O'Hara's "Gibbsville" stories are the basis for this adaptation by Frank D. Gilroy, who also directed. The result is an ambling, "Peyton Place"-type of soap opera, with some serious overtones. A young man (unevenly played by John Savage) returns to his hometown in Pennsylvania after being expelled from Yale and gets a job on the local newspaper. (Dir: Frank D. Gilroy, 72 mins.)

Turnover Smith (MTV 1980)** William Conrad, Belinda Montgomery, Hilly Hicks. Predictable pilot film starring Conrad as a criminologist, based in San Francisco, who makes the breakthrough in a baffling series of murders of young women. (Dir: Bernard L. Kowalski, 78 mins.)

Tuttles of Tahiti, The (1942)*** Charles Laughton, Jon Hall, Peggy Drake. The easygoing head of a large tropic family takes life as it comes, as long as it doesn't involve work. Pleasing story of the South Seas, pleasant entertainment. (Dir: Charles Vidor, 91 mins.)

Twelfth Night (Great Britain, MTV 1979)***½ Felicity Kendal, Sinead Cusack, Alec McCowan, Robert Hardy, Ronnie Stevens. Shakespeare's deft comedy is given a lively, robust, and thoroughly satisfying production. The play, which deals with Shakespeare's favorite ploys of mistaken identity and unrequited love, has been cast impeccably, with McCowan's foolish, touching Malvolio, Kendal's appealing Viola, Hardy's bawdy Sir Toby Belch, and Stevens's foppish Sir Andrew Aguecheek the standouts. (Dir: John Gorrie, 120 mins.)

Twelve Angry Men (1957)***½ Henry Fonda, Lee J. Cobb, Martin Balsam, Ed Begley, E. G. Marshall. As a period piece of liberal melodrama, this is rousing good fun. Fonda plays the sole holdout on a hanging jury who by dint of sweet reason and native guile turns the case around for the defendant, with a boy accused of killing his father. With a cast of hams, all in top form. (Dir: Sidney Lumet, 95 mins.)

Twelve Chairs, The (1970)*** Mel Brooks, Dom DeLuise, Frank Langella, Ron Moody. Remember the Fred Allen starrer "It's in the Bag"? Well, this romp, filmed in Yugoslavia, written and directed by Mel Brooks, is based on the same Russian comedy-fable, and some of it is quite funny. A few good laughs strewn along the way as an impoverished nobleman (Moody) tries to track down some precious jewel-filled chairs. (94 mins.)

Twelve Hours to Kill (1969)*½ Nico Minardos, Barbara Eden. (Dir: Edward L. Cahn, 83 mins.)

Twelve o'Clock High (1949)*** Gregory Peck, Gary Merrill, Dean Jagger. Peck is a WW II flight commander cracking up under the strain of mission after mission. The film is intelligent and well produced, but the drama is somewhat stillborn. Henry King's direction is precise, direct, and too impersonal. Superb work by cameraman Leon Shamroy. (132 mins.)

Twelve to the Moon (1960)*½ Ken Clark, Michi Kobi. (Dir: David Bradley, 74 mins.)

Twentieth Century (1934)***½ John Barrymore, Carole Lombard, Walter Connolly. Barrymore's Oscar Jaffe is a superb comic incarnation of a demented producer-director, and Lombard emerges as the wackiest comedienne as well as the most beautiful. Set aboard the famous New York-Chicago express train. Best scene: real camels from the Holy Land. (Dir: Howard Hawks, 91 mins.)

25th Hour, The (France-Italy-Yugoslavia, 1967)*** Anthony Quinn, Virna Lisi, Michael Redgrave, Alexander Knox. Sometimes implausible but often affecting drama about Rumanian participation in WW II, and shortly thereafter. Tries to deal with the holocaust of the war in personal, human terms. (Dir: Henri Verneuil, 119 mins.)

24 Eyes (Japan, 1954)**½ Hideko Takamine. Heartwarming story about a young schoolteacher who sees her beloved pupils grow up and go off to war. It is 1928 as the film begins, and young Miss Hisako arrives in the Shodo Island's grammar school. Anti-war messages trotted out in the latter part of the film tend to bog it down a bit, but it's still worthwhile. (Dir: Keisuke Kinoshita, 110 mins.)

24 Hours to Kill (Great Britain, 1965)* Mickey Rooney, Lex Barker, Walter Slezak. (Dir: Peter Bezencenet, 92 mins.)

Twenty Million Miles to Earth (1957)*½ William Hopper, Joan Taylor. (Dir: Nathan Juran, 82 mins.)

21 Days (Great Britain, 1938)**½ Laurence Olivier, Vivien Leigh, Leslie Banks, Robert Newton. Young lawyer has committed murder, finds he has three weeks with his love before justice intervenes. Lot of talent stuck in a drama that doesn't come off; moderate, at best. Film historians will value seeing one of Olivier's early films. (Dir: Basil Dean, 72 mins.)

Twenty-one Hours at Munich (MTV

1976)*** William Holden, Shirley Knight, Franco Nero. A fine re-creation of the dramatic, unforgettable, and terrifying slaughter of the Israeli athletes by Arab terrorists during the 1972 Olympics. The film has been impeccably produced using the actual Munich locations and the cast is very good, especially Nero as the Arab guerrilla leader, Knight as the German member of the Olympic security police who served as an intermediary between the guerrillas and the Munich police, and Holden as the Munich police chief. (Dir: William A. Graham, 105 mins.)

Twenty Plus Two (1961)*½ David Janssen, Jeanne Crain, Dina Merrill, Agnes Moorehead. (Dir: Joseph M. Newman, 102 mins.)

27th Day, The (1957)**½ Gene Barry, Valerie French. A science fiction tale with a few novel twists—at least there are no oversized prehistoric monsters in this one. A selected group of earth people are given capsules which can destroy mankind and our hero has to track them down. (Dir: William Asher, 75 mins.)

20,000 Eyes (1961)** Gene Nelson, Merry Anders. Investment counselor needing ready cash pilots a perfect crime. Passable crime melodrama. (Dir: Jack Leewood, 60 mins.)

20,000 Leagues Across the Land (France-U.S.S.R., 1960)**½ Jean Gaven, Tatiana Samilova. Three Frenchmen seek an old war buddy in Russia. Interesting Franco-Soviet coproduction, dubbed in English; plot is a bit ragged but the novelty makes it an unusual offering. (Dir: Marcello Pagliero, 90 mins.)

20,000 Leagues Under the Sea (1916)*** Allan Holubar, Jane Gail, Matt Moore. Silent with remarkable special effects by J. Earnest Williamson. (Dir: Stuart Paton, 89 mins.)

20,000 Leagues Under the Sea (1954)*** Kirk Douglas, Paul Lukas, James Mason, Peter Lorre. Walt Disney's epic version of Jules Verne's nautical tale. Douglas is the robust harpooner who, along with shipmates Lukas and Lorre, is plunged into a series of exciting events aboard Captain Nemo's (Mason's) cosmic-powered submarine, circa 1860s. It's well produced and entertaining from start to finish. Oscars: Best Special Effects; Best Art Direction. (Dir: Richard Fleischer, 127 mins.)

20,000 Pound Kiss, The (Great Britain, 1963)** Dawn Addams, Michael Goodliffe. Extortion ring tries to blackmail a member of Parliament, which leads to murder. Fair Edgar Wallace mystery. (Dir: John Moxey, 57 mins.)

23 Paces to Baker Street (Great Britain, 1956)*** Van Johnson, Vera Miles. Neat mystery keeps the attention, as a blind man attempts to solve a murder. (Dir: Henry Hathaway, 103 mins.)

Twilight for the Gods (1958)** Rock Hudson, Cyd Charisse, Arthur Kennedy. Ernest Gann's novel is brought to the screen with a strange mixture of miscasting and overdrawn characterizations. The setting is a tramp steamer and the drama unfolds as the passengers begin to distrust each other's reasons for the voyage. (Dir: Joseph Pevney, 120 mins.)

Twilight of Honor (1963)** Richard Chamberlain, Claude Rains, Joey Heatherton, Nick Adams. This film was designed to capitalize on TV's Dr. Kildare fame, but MGM didn't want to demand too much of Chamberlain in his starring debut role on the screen, so they changed him from a sincere young doctor to a sincere young lawyer, defending a murder suspect. Should have been more tightly knit, but isn't, except for Joey Heatherton's gowns. (Dir: Boris Sagal, 115 mins.)

Twilight's Last Gleaming (1977)**½ Burt Lancaster, Richard Widmark, Charles Durning, Melvyn Douglas. Director Robert Aldrich was trying to make a statement condemning the Vietnam War, but he got it mixed up with another theme about a former army general and three other inmates of death row who escape from prison, take over a SAC missile silo, and threaten to launch bombs on Russia and start WW III if their political grievances are not settled. The two stories fundamentally conflict in this flawed, offbeat political thriller based on the novel "Viper Three" by Walter Wager. (144 mins.)

Twin Detectives (MTV 1976)* Jim Hager, Jon Hager, Lillian Gish, Patrick O'Neal, David White. (Dir: Robert Day, 72 mins.)

Twinkle in God's Eye (1955)** Mickey Rooney, Coleen Gray, Hugh O'Brian. Parson arrives in a lawless frontier town to build a church. Offbeat role for Rooney, but still a maudlin drama. (Dir: George Blair, 73 mins.)

Twinkle, Twinkle, Killer Kane (1980)*** Stacy Keach, Scott Wilson, Jason Miller. Thriller, shot in Hungary, about a new "doctor" in an institution for disturbed military men. (Writer-Dir: William Peter Blatty, 105 mins.)

Twist All Night (1961)*½ Louis Prima, June Wilkinson, Gertrude Michael. (Dir: William J. Hole, Jr., 76 mins.)

Twist Around the Clock (1962)**½ Chubby Checker, Dion, Clay Cole. Average musical about the origins of the revolutionary dance and chock-full of early rock standards like "The Wanderer" and "Runaround Sue." Chubby Checker and Dion appear as themselves, and there's a fairly credible story line holding the whole show together. (Dir: Oscar Rudolph, 86 mins.)

Twist of Fate (Great Britain, 1954)** Ginger Rogers, Herbert Lom, Stanley Baker, Jacques Bergerac. Ex-actress on the Riviera learns her husband-to-be is a dangerous criminal. Overdone melodrama has Lom's good performance, little else of distinction. (Dir: David Miller, 89 mins.)

Two and Two Make Six (Great Britain, 1962)** George Chakiris, Janette Scott. American airman, a girl, and a motorbike encounter a similar trio and swap partners. Mild romantic comedy never really gets into gear. (Dir: Freddie Francis, 89 mins.)

Two Colonels, The (Italy, 1962)** Walter Pidgeon, Toto. Captured British officer strikes up a friendship with his enemy opposite member. Mild wartime comedy dubbed in English has good players but doesn't do right by them. (Dir: Steno, 90 mins.)

Two Daughters (India, 1962)***½ Anil Chatterjee, Satyajit Ray, created two gems, each a story about love as experienced by a young woman. The first, "The Postmaster," is a quiet but penetrating story about a young servant girl's devotion to her postmaster employer; the other, "The Conclusion," is a charming tale about a young bride who runs away from her forced marriage to a nice man, only to return to find love. (114 mins.)

Two English Girls (France, 1971)***½ Jean-Pierre Leaud, Kika Markham, Stacey Tendeter. Director François Truffaut said he tried to make a physical film about love. He did that and much more in this graceful, tender tale. Two English sisters are in love with a young Frenchman (Leaud). Based on a novel by Henri-Pierre Roche, who also wrote "Jules and Jim." The setting is Paris before WW I, delicately captured by cinematographer Nestor Almendros. Elegant, tactful, sometimes witty, always involving. (108 mins.)

Two-Faced Woman (1941)*** Greta Garbo, Melvyn Douglas, Constance Bennett, Roland Young, Ruth Gordon. Garbo poses as her own twin sister to test husband Douglas's love. Not a bad comedy, and Garbo does a hell of a rumba. (Dir: George Cukor, 94 mins.)

Two Faces of Dr. Jekyll, The (Great Britain, 1960)** Paul Massie, Christopher Lee. Still another version of the Robert Louis Stevenson story about the tormented Dr. Jekyll whose split personality makes him lead a double life. Massie is the troubled scientist whose life is far from sunny even with Dawn Addams. (Dir: Terence Fisher, 89 mins.)

Two Flags West (1950)** Joseph Cotten, Linda Darnell, Jeff Chandler, Cornel Wilde, Dale Robertson. Spectacular battle scenes make up most of the excitement in this Civil War Western. Inept performances slow down the action. (Dir: Robert Wise, 92 mins.)

Two for the Money (MTV 1972)**½ Robert Hooks, Stephen Brooks, Walter Brennan, Mercedes McCambridge. About ex-cops, one black (Hooks) and one white (Brooks), who open a private detective office. Case involves the search for a mass murderer, at large for over a decade. Good characterizations by competent pros Brennan, McCambridge, and Neville Brand supply substance for an offbeat tale. (Dir: Bernard L. Kowalski, 73 mins.)

Two for the Road (U.S.-Great Britain, 1967)**** Audrey Hepburn, Albert Finney. Refreshing, sophisticated comedydrama about a marriage which isn't working out after a number of years. Audrey Hepburn is not merely a fashion plate in this outing—she gives a convincing portrayal of a woman who loves the man she married and hates what he has become. Albert Finney is great as the husband who has a roving eye but still wants his wife. The flashback technique is used effectively throughout. Directed with great flair by Stanley Donen, and the sprightly screenplay was authored by Frederic Raphael. (112 mins.)

Two for the Seesaw (1962)*** Shirley MacLaine, Robert Mitchum. Essentially a two-character comedy-drama about a disillusioned lawyer from Omaha who meets and loves a tough-tender New York girl. The superb intimacy of the Broadway stage production is negated somewhat by adding characters to the screen version, and rather questionable casting of the leading roles. Mitchum does quite well, Miss MacLaine somewhat less so; but it has its moments, both humorous and poignant. (Dir: Robert Wise, 120 mins.)

Two Girls and a Sailor (1944)***½ Van Johnson, June Allyson, Jimmy Durante, Gloria De Haven. One of those entertaining, first-rate musicals that MGM became famous for. June and Gloria both love Van and Jimmy is around for plenty of laughs. The music is good too and there's plenty of guest stars. (Dir: Richard Thorpe, 124 mins.)

Two Gladiators (Italy, 1964)*½ Richard Harrison. (Dir: Mario Caiano, 97 mins.)

Two Guys from Texas (1948)**½ Jack Carson, Dennis Morgan, Dorothy Malone. Stranded vaudeville team outwits city thugs down in Texas. Mildly amusing musical comedy. Remake of "Cowboy from Brooklyn." Color. (Dir: David Butler, 86 mins.)

Two Headed Spy, The (Great Britain, 1959)*** Jack Hawkins, Gia Scala. Highly suspenseful spy yarn with good performances by Hawkins and Gia Scala as a couple of British agents working inside the German lines. Good climax with an exciting chase sequence. (Dir: André de Toth, 93 mins.)

200 Motels (Great Britain, 1971)*** Ringo Starr, Frank Zappa, Theodore Bikel. Mind trip for those who don't mind plotless films and especially for fans of dynamic rock star Zappa. Supposedly follows the exploits of Zappa's group, the Mothers of Invention, who are stranded in groupie-laden Centerville. When the Mothers play they resort to melting fingers and dissolving faces. Many interesting visual techniques and montages. (Dirs: Frank Zappa and Tony Palmer, 98 mins.)

Two-Lane Blacktop (1971)***½ Warren Oates, James Taylor, Dennis Wilson, Laurie Bird. Although it deals with car freaks, this lean drama is anything but souped-up. Monte Hellman's low-key, rigorously restrained direction is unsentimental about his heroes, who travel a lot but go nowhere. Along the way, they pick up a girl who gradually replaces the cars as the stakes in a race with a GTO (driven by that fine actor, Oates). The point, of course, is that there isn't much point, but the film makes it in an intriguing, intelligent, though somewhat uninvolving way. (101 mins.)

Two Little Bears, The (1961)** Eddie Albert, Brenda Lee, Jane Wyatt, Soupy Sales. Grammar-school principal finds his children can turn themselves into bears. Mild fantasy should be enjoyed best by the younger set. (Dir: Randall Hood, 81 mins.)

Two Lost Worlds (1950)** Laura Elliot, Jim Arness. A colony from Australia lands on a mysterious isle where prehistoric monsters roam. Low grade thriller; if you're a TV movie fan, you'll spot stock footage from "Captain Fury," "One Million B.C." and "Captain Caution" used to stretch the budget. (Dir: Norman Dawn, 61 mins.)

Two Loves (1961)** Shirley MacLaine, Laurence Harvey, Jack Hawkins. Miscasting and mis-scripting combine to throw this drama for a loss. About a teacher in New Zealand and her problems with a mixed up young fatalist who nevertheless brings love to her spinsterish life. Pretty drab going. (Dir: Charles Walters, 99 mins.)

Two Men of Karamoja (1974)**** Iain Ross, Paul Ssalii. Superb color documentary filmed on location in Kidepo Valley National Park in Uganda. White game-park warden trains his black native assistant to take over the park—including protecting the animals from poachers. Director-producer Eugene S. Jones has captured some remarkable animal scenes, including a sequence showing the white warden trapped in a small jeep while besieged by an enraged elephant. Jones honestly records the tensions and friendship as the black man prepares to take over full responsibility for the land's animals and people entrusted to his care. (102 mins.)

Two Minute Warning (1976)* Charlton Heston, John Cassavetes, Martin Balsam, Gena Rowlands, David Janssen. New subplot added for TV version (full length stretched to 156 mins). Gene Palmer directed new footage. (112 mins.)

Two Mrs. Carrolls (1947)** Humphrey Bogart, Barbara Stanwyck, Alexis Smith. Story of a nut who likes to bump off his wives after he paints their portraits is so melodramatic it may make you laugh. (Dir: Peter Godfrey, 99 mins.)

Two Mules for Sister Sara (1970)***½ Clint Eastwood, Shirley MacLaine, Alberto Morin. Good action tale smashingly directed by Don Siegel, with visual verve and a command of storytelling. Eastwood

is the drifter who picks up nun MacLaine in the desert and finds himself drawn into a local war of liberation in Mexico. The final shot, with its pun drawn from the title, is only one of many memorable ones. Filmed in Mexico. (104 mins.)

Two Nights with Cleopatra (Italy, 1954)*½ Sophia Loren, Ettore Manni, Alberto Sordi. (Dir: Mario Mattoli, 80 mins.)

Two of Us, The (France, 1967)**** Michel Simon, Alain Cohen, Luce Fabiole. A beautiful, touching, moving film about racial prejudice and anti-semitism, featuring two near perfect performances from a crusty old bigot (Michel Simon) and the young Jewish boy (Cohen) who comes to board in rural France during the Nazi occupation of Paris during WW II. Wonderfully written and directed by Claude Berri. (Dir: Claude Berri, 86 mins.)

Two on a Bench (MTV 1971)** Patty Duke (Astin), Ted Bessell, John Astin. Gifted Patty turns to light comedy as she and Bessell play two young people who are under suspicion of trafficking with spies, and they're incarcerated for 24 hours while officials look into their backgrounds. Patty's hippie character tries to soften up stuffy bachelor Bessell, and her mobile face makes this contrived comedy look a little better. (Dir: Jerry Paris, 78 mins.)

Two on a Guillotine (1965)* Connie Stevens, Dean Jones, Cesar Romero, (Dir: William Conrad, 107 mins.)

Two Orphans, The (France-Italy, 1965)*½ Mike Marshall, Valeria Ciangottine. (Dir: Riccardo Freda, 97 mins.)

Two People (1973)*½ Peter Fonda, Lindsay Wagner, Estelle Parsons. (110 mins.)

Two Rode Together (1961)**½ James Stewart, Richard Widmark, Shirley Jones. A Texas marshal and a cavalry lieutenant lead a wagon train into Comanche territory to rescue captives of the Indians. A John Ford western—not his best. (Dir: John Ford, 109 mins.)

Two Sisters from Boston (1946)*** Kathryn Grayson, June Allyson, Peter Lawford. A lot to like in this cute musical set at the turn of the century about two well-bred Boston girls who go to work in a joint on New York's Bowery. Jimmy Durante steals the show as owner of the tavern. (Dir: Henry Koster, 112 mins.)

Two Smart People (1946)*½ Lucille Ball, John Hodiak, Lloyd Nolan, Hugo Haas. (Dir: Jules Dassin, 93 mins.)

2001: A Space Odyssey (U.S.-Great Britain, 1968)**** Keir Dullea, Gary Lockwood. Brilliant film; the plot and explanation exist on an almost subliminal level in this tracing of man's history and his contact with new life. In the beginning, the earth heated; the earth cooled; apes moved to man; man to superman and beyond; a space voyage to Jupiter manned by astronauts Bowman (Dullea) and Poole (Lockwood) and computer HAL. The intensity of the landing sequence is blindingly absorbing. This masterpiece by

697

director and co-writer Stanley Kubrick defines film in terms of abstract communication. (138 mins.)

Two Thousand Women (Great Britain, 1944)***½ Phyllis Calvert, Flora Robson, Patricia Roc. Nazis interne British women, but they turn the tables and secretly help downed RAF fliers to escape occupied territory. Suspenseful melodrama, mixing humor and thrills in a skillful blend. (Dir: Frank Launder, 97 mins.)

Two Tickets to Broadway (1951)**½ Janet Leigh, Tony Martin, Ann Miller, Eddie Bracken, Smith and Dale. Small-town girl and a singer arrange a hoax to get them on a TV show. Fairly pleasing musical comedy. (Dir: James V. Kern, 106 mins.)

Two Tickets to London (1943)** Michele Morgan, Alan Curtis, Barry Fitzgerald. Espionage and love don't mix as the hero finds out in this WW II tale of German U-boats and Admiralty dragnets. But Morgan and Fitzgerald are customarily professional. (Dir: Edwin L. Martin, 79 mins.)

Two-Way Stretch (Great Britain, 1960)***½ Peter Sellers, Lionel Jeffries, Wilfrid Hyde White, Bernard Cribbins, Beryl Reid. The pun of the title describes an old movie situation (cons breaking in and out of prison) that goes back to "Up the River." A good cast of British comics keeps the familiar antics amusing, especially Jeffries in one of his funniest roles. (Dir: Robert Day, 87 mins.)

Two Weeks in Another Town (1962)**½ Kirk Douglas, Edward G. Robinson, Cyd Charisse, Claire Trevor, George Hamilton. The sensational best seller about American film makers loving and working in Rome makes a flashy but empty film. Kirk Douglas does what he can in the complex role of a has-been actor who attempts a comeback in the Roman film capital. (Dir: Vincente Minnelli, 107 mins.)

Two Weeks in September (France-Great Britain, 1967)* Brigitte Bardot, Laurent Terzieff, Michael Sarne. (Dir: Serge Bourguignon, 96 mins.)

Two Weeks with Love (1950)**½ Jane Powell, Ricardo Montalban, Debbie Reynolds. Daughter's growing up, parents refuse to realize it. She makes them see the light while on a Catskill vacation. Mildly amusing comedy of the early 1900s. Some enjoyable ricky-tick oldtime turns, cute performance by young Debbie Reynolds. (Dir: Roy Rowland, 92 mins.)

Two Wives at One Wedding (Great Britain, 1961)*½ Gordon Jackson, Christina Gregg, Lisa Daniely. (Dir: Montgomery Tully, 66 mins.)

Two Women (France-Italy, 1960)**** Sophia Loren, Raf Vallone, Jean-Paul Belmondo. Miss Loren won an Oscar for Best Actress for her performance as an Italian mother who faces tragedy with her daughter during WW II. You can see she deserved the accolades. Deeply moving, realistic, well directed. (Dir: Vittorio De Sica, 99 mins.)

Two Worlds of Jennie Logan, The (MTV 1979)**½ Lindsay Wagner, Alan Feinstein, Marc Singer, Linda Gray. Entertaining, offbeat supernatural yarn. Wagner discovers a 19th-century dress in the attic of the old house she and her husband have bought; whenever she puts it on it transports her back in time. After some time travel, she falls in love with a man from the past who she knows is doomed to die in a duel. If you don't pay too much attention to the details of the plot, you'll enjoy the romantic fantasy. (Dir: Frank de Felitta, 104 mins.)

Two Yanks in Trinidad (1942)*** Pat O'Brien, Brian Donlevy, Janet Blair. Two racketeers enlist in the Army, get patriotism when Pearl Harbor happens. Breezy comedy-drama has some bright dialogue, amusing situations. (Dir: Gregory Ratoff, 88 mins.)

Two Years Before the Mast (1946)**½ Alan Ladd, William Bendix, Brian Donlevy, Barry Fitzgerald. A shanghaied crew on a trip around the Horn in the 1800's is the salty background for this famous tale of the sea. Although it has some fine scenes, it never comes close to joining the list of film classics set on the sea. (Dir: John Farrow, 98 mins.)

Twonky, The (1953)** Hans Conried, Gloria Blondell, Trilby Conried. Hans Conried's TV set becomes possessed by a spirit from the future in this lackluster sci-fi satire. (Writer-Dir: Arch Oboler, 72 mins.)

Tycoon (1947)*** John Wayne, Laraine Day, Anthony Quinn, Cedric Hardwicke. Young railroad builder meets with many obstructions before he achieves his goal. Way too long, otherwise nicely made, well acted melodrama. (Dir: Richard Wallace, 128 mins.)

Typhoon over Nagasaki (France, 1957)** Danielle Darrieux, Jean Marais. Engineer in Japan falls for a local girl, then his sweetheart arrives from France. Watery romance not helped by English dubbing; some nice Japanese location scenes, not too much else. (Dir: Yves Ciampi, 90 mins.)

Tyrant of Castile, The (Spain-Italy, 1964)* Mark Damon, Rada Rassimov. (Dir: Ferdinando Baldi, 104 mins.)

Tyrant of Lydia Against the Son of Hercules (Italy, 1963)* Gordon Scott, Massimo Serato. (Dir: Mario Caiavio, 107 mins.)

U-238 and the Witch Doctor (1953-66)* Clay Moore, Phyllis Coates. (Dir: Fred C. Brannon, 100 mins.)

UFO Target Earth (1974)* Nick Plakias, Cynthia Cline. (Dir: Michael A. deGaetano, 90 mins.)

Ugetsu (Japan, 1953)**** Kinuyo Tanaka, Machiko Kyo, Masayuki Mori, Sakae Ozawa. The title can be translated as "Tales of the Pale and Silvery Moon After the Rain." Based on a pair of 16th-century ghost stories, the film is less a study of the supernatural than an embodiment of director Kenji Mizoguchi's perennial theme: the generosity of women and the selfishness of men. Its emotions are delicate and its passions bold, the plot dense and the effect one of enveloping warmth and regret. A formidable work. (96 mins.)

Ugly American, The (1963)*** Marlon Brando, Eiji Okada, Arthur Hill, Jocelyn Brando. The many-faceted Mr. Brando tries the role of a distinguished American Ambassador to an Asian country whose failure to understand differences in policy brings personal and political disaster. He does well in the part, and while the script and direction override some salient story points, the result is a film drama endeavoring to make a serious comment about topical situations. (Dir: George H. Englund, 120 mins.)

Ultimate Chase, The (1974)**½ Barry Brown, Britt Ekland, Eric Braeden. Two lengthy ski chases lift this thriller above the ordinary, as ruthless Braeden pursues wife Britt's lovers to the death. Excellent photography in the ski area of Vail, Colorado, and a nicely underplayed performance by Brown. The musical score is overinsistent. (Dir: Robert Butler, 80 mins.)

Ultimate Impostor, The (MTV 1979)** Joseph Hacker, Keith Andes. Opens with a neat gimmick—a secret agent is chemically brainwashed by the Communists and submits to a unique experiment which feeds him data through a computer which he can only retain for an allotted time. He can scuba dive, race cars, learn Mandarin Chinese. Soon loses suspense. (Dir: Paul Stanley, 104 mins.)

Ulysses (Italy, 1955)*** Kirk Douglas, Silvana Mangano, Anthony Quinn, Rossana Podesta. Lavishly produced version of *some* of the adventures of Homer's King of Ithaca. Douglas is an excellent choice for the title character, who is both vain and glorious; some of the elaborate saga's scenes are particularly well done, especially the den of the Cyclops and the visit to the Underworld. Generally most accurate and entertaining. Though the dialogue is in English, some of the actors' voices are from the Italian "world's worst dubbing" studios, and this does detract somewhat. (Dir: Mario Camerini, 104 mins.)

Ulysses (United States-Great Britain, 1967)*½ Milo O'Shea, Barbara Jefford, Fionnuala Flanagan. (Dir: Joseph Strick, 140 mins.)

Ulysses Against the Son of Hercules— See: **Hercules vs. Ulysses**

Ulzana's Raid (1972)*** Burt Lancaster, Bruce Davison. Deceptively ordinary Indian vs. cavalry yarn turns into a tense, well-acted, and ultimately absorbing film. Lancaster is cast as an Indian scout who assists an inexperienced cavalry officer (Davison) in trying to roust renegade Apache Ulzana and his band out on a rampage of murder, rape, and revenge against the white man. Taut western . . . and one that makes you think. (Dir: Robert Aldrich, 93 mins.)

Umberto D (Italy, 1955)**** Carlo Battisti, Maria Pia Casilio. Italian director De Sica's masterpiece; shattering study of a lonely old man, succumbing to the ravages of age. Packs an uncompromising wallop. One of the remarkable European films of the decade. See it. (Dir: Vittorio De Sica, 89 mins.)

Umbrellas of Cherbourg, The (France-West Germany, 1964)***½ Catherine Deneuve, Nino Castelnuovo, Anne Vernon. A film opera. Director Jacques Demy wrote the lyrics, Michel Legrand the music. The story of simple love thwarted is not as saccharine as contemporary reviews claimed. Deneuve is charming among a fairly pedestrian cast. Filmed in Cherbourg. (95 mins.)

UMC (MTV 1969)** James Daly, Richard Bradford, Maurice Evans. Good acting highlights this routine drama, which served as the pilot film for the TV series "Medical Center." Subplots include malpractice suits; supporting cast boasts Edward G. Robinson and Kim Stanley. (Dir: Boris Sagal, 100 mins.)

Uncanny, The (Great Britain-Canada, 1977)** Peter Cushing, Ray Milland, Donald Pleasence. Horror anthology has Cushing documents a feline conspiracy to dominate the human race. He describes three cat takeovers of the past (shown in flashbacks) to convince a publisher (Milland) to print his material. Low-budget special effects of cat attacks are boring. (Dir: Denis Heroux, 85 mins.)

Uncertain Glory (1944)** Errol Flynn, Paul Lukas, Faye Emerson, Jean Sullivan. Errol is a French crook but he's willing to pretend to be a saboteur and die if it will help France. If that doesn't sound convincing it's because the picture is trite and hackneyed. Paul Lukas is superb as a detective. (Dir: Raoul Walsh, 102 mins.)

Unchained (1955)**** Elroy Hirsch, Chester Morris, Barbara Hale. Warden of an honor prison tames unruly convicts. Based on fact, this is one of the best prison films. Excellently made. Well acted. (Dir: Hall Bartlett, 75 mins.)

Uncle Harry (1945)*** George Sanders, Ella Raines, Geraldine Fitzgerald. Henpecked by his two sisters, a man takes drastic steps when they begin to interfere with his romance. Excellent performances and a suspenseful atmosphere atone for the poor conclusion to this drama. (Dir: Robert Siodmak, 80 mins.)

Uncle Silas—See: **Inheritance, The**

Uncle Vanya (1958)*** Franchot Tone, Dolores Dorn-Heft, George Voskovec, Peggy McCay. Chekhov's atmospheric play about an aging professor and his beautiful wife who visit their country estate is brought to film almost intact from its 1956 Broadway production. Acting is generally excellent, but it is never opened up to utilize the film medium. But Chekhov is a great writer. Adaptation by Stark Young. (Dirs: John Goetz, Franchot Tone, 98 mins.)

Uncle Was a Vampire (Italy, 1961)**½ Renato Rascel, Christopher Lee, Sylva Koscina. Former baron now working as a hotel porter has trouble on his hands when his uncle turns up in vampire form. Amusing spoof of horror films, dubbed in English. Rascel is a likable buffoon. (Dir: Steno, 95 mins.)

Unconquered (1947)***½ Gary Cooper, Paulette Goddard, Boris Karloff. Cooper and Goddard battle Indians in pre-Revolutionary times. Epic directed with brilliant showmanship by Cecil B. deMille Color. (146 mins.)

Undefeated, The (1969)**½ John Wayne, Rock Hudson, Lee Meriwether, Bruce Cabot. Routine western, bolstered somewhat by the presence of Wayne and Hudson. Wayne as an ex-Union officer who is on his way to sell horses to Mexico's emperor and meets up with his former enemy, Confederate officer Hudson. The climax involves their joining forces against Juarez and his bandits. Football fans, note that handsome quarterback Roman Gabriel plays a supporting role in the flick. (Dir: Andrew V. McLaglen, 118 mins.)

Under Capricorn (Great Britain, 1949)**** Ingrid Bergman, Joseph Cotten, Michael Wilding. Senselessly neglected for years because it was directed by Alfred Hitchcock but isn't a thriller. Irish noblewoman (Bergman) and her lower-class husband (Cotten) are in colonial Australia, at a time when many citizens were convicts working off their sentences. Color. (117 mins.)

Under Milk Wood (Great Britain, 1971)***½ Richard Burton, Elizabeth Taylor, Peter O'Toole, Glynis Johns, Sian Phillips, Vivien Merchant, Victor Spinetti, Angharad Rees. The pictures make the great, glorious language of the classic Dylan Thomas radio play seem peripheral, where it should be central. The readings, nonetheless, are first-rate. (Dir: Andrew Sinclair, 90 mins.)

Under My Skin (1950)** John Garfield, Micheline Presle, Luther Adler. An Ernest Hemingway yarn about the racing game and a one-time crooked jockey's efforts to go straight. Involved drama, spotilly acted. Remade as "My Old Man." (Dir: George Blair, 86 mins.)

Under Ten Flags (U.S.-Great Britain-Italy, 1960)** Van Heflin, Charles Laughton, Mylene Demongeot, John Ericson. German raider commanded by a humane captain cleverly thwarts British efforts to capture her. Italian-British coproduction makes

one wonder who really should have won the war—all the sympathy is on the German side. Aside from this, it's well made. (Dir: Duilio Coletti, 92 mins.)

Under the Yum Yum Tree (1963)**½ Jack Lemmon, Carol Lynley, Dean Jones, Edie Adams, Imogene Coca. Good fun, Broadway comedy transfers to the screen with ease, thanks to Jack Lemmon's energetic performance as an amorous landlord. Carol Lynley is cute as one of Lemmon's tenants who is trying to keep her boyfriend at bay. (Dir: David Swift, 110 mins.)

Under Two Flags (1936)**½ Ronald Colman, Claudette Colbert, Rosalind Russell, Victor McLaglen. Creaky, perennial story of love and adventure in the Foreign Legion gets new life in this film but still falls short of top notch entertainment. (Dir: Frank Lloyd, 105 mins.)

Undercover Maisie (1947)** Ann Sothern, Barry Nelson. Blonde chorus girl becomes an undercover investigator for the police. Average comedy in the series. (Dir: Harry Beaumont, 90 mins.)

Undercover Man, The (1949)*** Glenn Ford, Nina Foch, James Whitmore. Tax experts try to pin the goods on a notorious gangster by legal means. Different sort of G-man melodrama with a nice style, some suspenseful moments. (Dir: Joseph H. Lewis, 89 mins.)

Undercover with the KKK (MTV 1979)**½ Don Meredith, James Wainwright. Real-life story of an Alabama redneck (Meredith) who infiltrates the Ku Klux Klan for the FBI. He loses his wife and family, his best friend is murdered, and he must endure three court trials before assuming a new life. Rowe (the real undercover man) was indicted for murder three months after the film was made. (Dir: Barry Shear, 104 mins.)

Undercovers Hero (Great Britain, 1974)** Peter Sellers, Lila Kedrova, Beatrice Romand. (Dir: Roy Boulting, 107 mins.)

Undercurrent (1946)**½ Katharine Hepburn, Robert Taylor, Robert Mitchum. The acting is good but the story of a girl who slowly discovers she has married a villain is not new and, in this case, not too well told. (Dir: Vincente Minnelli, 116 mins.)

Underground (1941)*** Jeffrey Lynn, Phillip Dorn. Exciting melodrama about the underground in Nazi Germany. Not a Grade A film but all involved turn in "A" work in this story of people risking their lives to create secret broadcasts under the Germans' noses. (Dir: Vincent Sherman, 95 mins.)

Underground Commando (1966)* Jose Vergara, Henry Duval. (90 mins.)

Underground Man, The (MTV 1974)**½ Peter Graves, Jack Klugman, Sharon Farrell, Vera Miles, Jim Hutton. Ross Macdonald's best seller is adapted with care and attention by producer Howard Koch. Graves makes a fairly convincing Lew Archer—Macdonald's laconic, compassionate sleuth—and there's a first-class supporting cast including Dame Judith Anderson, Jo Ann Pflug, and Celeste Holm. Archer's task is delving into the murder of a man investigating his father's disappearance. (Dir: Paul Wendkos, 100 mins.)

Undertow (1950)**½ Scott Brady, Peggy Dow, John Russell. Fast-moving, routine chase melodrama about a man who is wrongly accused of murder and has to prove his innocence. Brady makes an effective temporary fugitive and Peggy Dow is lovely as a schoolmarm who aids him. (Dir: William Castle, 71 mins.)

Underwater (1955)**½ Jane Russell, Gilbert Roland, Richard Egan. Two skin-divers brave the perils of the deep to locate sunken treasure. Passable melodrama has good underwater photography. (Dir: John Sturges, 99 mins.)

Underwater City, The (1962)* William Lundigan, Julie Adams. (Dir: Frank McDonald, 78 mins.)

Underwater Warrior (1958)** Dan Dailey, James Gregory, Claire Kelly. Song-and-dance man Dailey has a different role as he dons an underwater diving outfit to play a naval commander in the Korean War. He's left floundering in a dumb script full of heroic deeds and no characterizations. Produced expertly by Ivan Tors. B&W. (Dir: Andrew Marton, 90 mins.)

Underworld Story, The (1950)*** Dan Duryea, Gale Storm, Herbert Marshall. Reporter buys an interest in a small-town newspaper and starts things humming by exposing corruption in back of a murder case. Tightly knit drama with a hard-hitting script, capable performances by a good cast. (Dir: Cy Endfield, 90 mins.)

Underworld, USA (1961)*** Cliff Robertson, Dolores Dorn, Beatrice Kay. Kid who has had a hard road in life grows up determined to get the men who murdered his father in a gang slaying. Crime drama covers familiar ground, but does so expertly. Better than average for its type, good fare for action fans. (Dir: Samuel Fuller, 98 mins.)

Une Femme Douce (France, 1969)*** Dominique Sanda, Guy Frangin. Based on Dostoevski's novella "A Gentle Creature" the film begins with a young wife's suicide and ends with the lid of her coffin being screwed into place. In between is a sharply diffident exposition by the husband of what led up to the suicide. The film is moving in the way that stubborn calm can be in the face of desperation. With Dominique Sanda in her debut. (Dir: Robert Bresson, 87 mins.)

Unearthly Stranger (Great Britain, 1963)**½ John Neville, Gabriella Licudi. Scientist working on a secret project learns other scientists have been killed, then suspects his wife of being not of this earth. Creepy sci-fi thriller handled with finesse. Good for the fans. (Dir: John Krish, 78 mins.)

Unexpected Uncle (1941)**½ Charles Coburn, Anne Shirley, James Craig. Old reprobate aids a shopgirl in her romance with a rich man. Mildly amusing comedy. (Dir: Peter Godfrey, 67 mins.)

Unfaithfully Yours (1948)***½ Rex Harrison, Linda Darnell, Rudy Vallee. Director Preston Sturges's devilish conceit in which an egotistical symphony conductor (limned by Harrison in a parody of Thomas Beecham) imagines the jealous murder of his wife (Darnell) to the strains of the three classical works that are on his program of the evening. (105 mins.)

Unfaithfuls, The (Italy, 1952)*½ May Britt, Gina Lollobrigida, Marina Vlady. (Dir: Stefano Steno, 83 mins.)

Unfinished Business (1941)** Irene Dunne, Robert Montgomery. Irene Dunne, a small town girl, goes to the big city to find adventure and love in this silly comedy romance. (Dir: Gregory LaCava, 96 mins.)

Unfinished Dance, The (1947)**½ Margaret O'Brien, Cyd Charisse, Karin Booth. Remake of the French "La Mort du Cygne" with O'Brien as the talented newcomer to a ballet school and Charisse as the jealous star who causes an accident that injures O'Brien. A few rewarding moments. (Dir: Henry Koster, 101 mins.)

Unforgiven, The (1960)*** Audrey Hepburn, Burt Lancaster, Audie Murphy, Lillian Gish, Charles Bickford. Joseph Wiseman, Albert Salmi, John Saxon, Doug McClure. John Huston's career probably hit its critical nadir with this hysterical western with racial overtones (Audrey Hepburn is suspected of being a half-breed), but if it's viewed in the context of this subgenre of the forties, the film becomes a satisfying and stimulating work. Photographed in a scintillating style by Franz Planer. (Dir: John Huston, 125 mins.)

Unguarded Moment (1956)** Esther Williams, John Saxon, George Nader. Esther Williams doesn't swim in this one—she plays a school teacher who's attacked by one of her pupils (high school boy) and thereby hangs the psychological yarn. Flimsy story (scripted by Rosalind Russell) and unconvincing performances. (Dir: Harry Keller, 95 mins.)

Unholy Garden, The (1931)*** Ronald Colman, Fay Wray, Estelle Taylor, Tully Marshall. Script by Ben Hecht and Charles MacArthur. Colman is incredibly sexy, wistful, and charming in this entertaining if slight melodrama about a gentleman (what else) thief, living in exile in the mysterious desert. Enter the beautiful, innocent Miss Wray. Can he go straight? No surprises, but a lot of engaging romance. (Dir: George Fitzmaurice, 74 mins.)

Unholy Intruders, The (West Germany, 1952)*½ Philip Dorn, Olga Tache (Tschechowa). (Dir: Harald Reinl, 80 mins.)

Unholy Partners (1941)**½ Edward G. Robinson, Edward Arnold, Laraine Day, Marsha Hunt. Well-acted, contrived drama of an editor who is in partnership with a racketeer and decides to expose him in their own paper. (Dir: Mervyn Le Roy, 94 mins.)

Unholy Three, The (1930)***½ Lon Chaney, Sr., Harry Earles, Lila Lee, Ivan Linow. Chaney's only talkie. This quintessentially silent performer shows he could act with his voice too (he died in '30). He plays a ventriloquist who spends much of the movie in drag. (Dir: Jack Conway, 68 mins.)

Unholy Wife (1957)** Diana Dors, Rod Steiger, Tom Tryon, Marie Windsor. Dors is buxom and Steiger chews up the scenery in this muddled story of a wealthy wife's infidelity and plans for murder. (Dir: John Farrow, 94 mins.)

Unidentified Flying Oddball (Great Britain, 1979)**½ Dennis Dugan, Jim Dale, Ron Moody. This Disney feature is a space-age version of Twain's "A Connecticut Yankee in King Arthur's Court." Dale plays a villain, for once, as Modred, while Moody Faginizes Merlin. (Dir: Russ Mayberry, 93 mins.)

Uninhibited, The (Spain-France-Italy, 1965)** Melina Mercouri, James Mason, Hardy Kruger. Incoherent melodrama about a worldly-wise woman, a besotted novelist, and a searching youth in a small Spanish fishing village. Fine seaside atmosphere, but dramatic impact peters out early. (Dir: Juan Antonio Bardem, 104 mins.)

Uninvited, The (1944)*** Ray Milland, Ruth Hussey, Gail Russell. Ghost fans will love this well told chiller about a young couple (brother and sister) who buy a house in England that is haunted. (Dir: Lewis Allen, 98 mins.)

Union Pacific (1939)*** Joel McCrea, Barbara Stanwyck, Akim Tamiroff, Robert Preston, Brian Donlevy. Grandiose western directed by deMille won't be as stupendous on a TV screen, but it's still good entertainment. Saga of linking the east and west by rails has no message, but is well-acted and loaded with action. (Dir: Cecil B. deMille, 135 mins.)

Union Station (1950)*** William Holden, Barry Fitzgerald, Nancy Olson, Jan Sterling. Police join in a manhunt for the kidnaper of a blind girl. Suspenseful crime drama holds the interest. (Dir: Rudolph Mate, 80 mins.)

Unknown Guest, The (1943)***½ Victor Jory, Pamela Blake. A stranger stops in a small village, and is suspected to be an escaped criminal. Tense, exciting melodrama, well acted, far above average. (Dir: Kurt Neumann, 64 mins.)

Unknown Man, The (1951)**½ Walter Pidgeon, Ann Harding, Keefe Brasselle, Barry Sullivan. Honest lawyer defends a murder suspect, finds afterwards his client really was guilty, and finally accomplishes his strange revenge. Involved crime melodrama, with the twists and turns of the plot sustaining interest most of the way. (Dir: Richard Thorpe, 86 mins.)

Unman, Wittering, and Zigo (Great Britain, 1971)**½ David Hemmings, Carolyn Seymour. Hemmings as a schoolteacher at a boys' school who takes over at midterm after his predecessor has taken a suspicious tumble on the stairs. Did the kids have anything to do with the nasty fall? This appears to be the answer. Handsomely mounted, but not terribly interesting. It very much resembles the better-made "Child's Play." (Dir: John MacKenzie, 100 mins.)

Unmarried Woman, An (1978)**** Jill Clayburgh, Alan Bates, Michael Murphy. Poignant, observant, and funny, with a knockout performance by Clayburgh as a woman who seems to be doing all the right things until the day her husband (Murphy) announces he's leaving for another woman. Ms. Clayburgh's realignment of her priorities is fascinating and the film doesn't take preachy stands or offfer pat solutions. Paul Mazursky wrote the intelligent script and directed with careful attention to character details. (124 mins.)

Unseen, The (1945)***½ Joel McCrea, Gail Russell, Herbert Marshall. Exciting chiller-diller about a young girl who comes to a mysterious home to replace a governess who was murdered. Top drawer for fans of this type of fiction. (Dir: Lewis Allen, 81 mins.)

Unsinkable Molly Brown, The (1964)*** Debbie Reynolds, Harve Presnell, Ed Begley, Hermione Baddeley. Rowdy, raucous Meredith Willson musical entertainment for the whole family. Reynolds is all hustle and bustle as Molly, the tough backwoods girl who goes after money, social position, and love with nonstop energy, and she's seldom been better. The musical numbers are deftly staged by Peter Gennaro, and Presnell as Molly's gold-prospecting husband has a good strong voice, and cuts a romantic figure. (Dir: Charles Walters, 128 mins.)

Unstoppable Man, The (Great Britain, 1960)* Cameron Mitchell, Marius Goring, Lois Maxwell. (Dir: Terry Bishop, 68 mins.)

Untamed (1955)** Tyrone Power, Susan Hayward, Richard Egan, Rita Moreno, Agnes Moorehead. Overly romantic adventure yarn about the he-men who pioneered the Zulu territory of Africa. Plenty of action interspersed with a silly quadrangular love interest. The stars go through the paces in a satisfactory professional manner. (Dir: Henry King, 111 mins.)

Untamed Frontier (1952)**½ Joseph Cotton, Shelley Winters, Scott Brady. Sprawling western with a good cast to give the film some added appeal. Story concerns the Texas frontier when cattle barons ran things and range wars were commonplace. (Dir: Hugo Fregonese, 75 mins.)

Untamed Youth (1957)*½ Mamie Van

Doren, Lori Nelson, John Russell. (Dir: Howard W. Koch, 80 mins.)

Until They Sail (1957)*** Paul Newman, Jean Simmons, Joan Fontaine, Piper Laurie, Sandra Dee (film debut). Soap opera made palatable by a good all star cast. Plot revolves around the events in the lives of four sisters living in New Zealand during WW II. Newman and Miss Simmons make an attractive pair of lovers and Miss Laurie handles the heavy dramatics of the story in a most competent fashion. (Dir: Robert Wise, 95 mins.)

Untouched (Mexican, 1956)**½ Ricardo Montalban, Ariadne Welter. Man encounters a recluse in the jungle, falls in love with his beautiful daughter, but has to return to his wife. Inferior English dubbing detracts from a colorful, interesting drama posing the problem of so-called civilized life vs. withdrawal from mankind. Off the beaten path, well directed. (85 mins.)

Unvanquished, The—See: **Aparajito**

Unwed Father (MTV 1974)**½ Joseph Bottoms, Kay Lenz, Beverly Garland, Kim Hunter, Joseph Campanella. Despite the silly title, this has some credible and interesting moments. It tells the story of a principled young man who fights for the custody of his illegitimate child, going against the wishes of his girl friend who wants to put the baby up for adoption. A good cast and an intelligent script. (Dir: Jeremy Kagan, 74 mins.)

Unwed Mother (1958)** Norma Moore, Robert Vaughn, Diana Darrin. Attractive girl gets involved with a lady killer, finds herself pregnant, refuses to give her baby up for adoption. "True confessions" type drama on the sordid side; well acted. (Dir: Walter Doniger, 74 mins.)

Up from the Beach (1965)*** Cliff Robertson, Irina Demick, Broderick Crawford, Red Buttons. Intersting WW II story about a group of American soldiers who liberate a small French village on the day after D-Day. The group, headed by Cliff Robertson, take over a farmhouse where three German SS soldiers are holding hostages. The suspense builds satisfactorily. (Dir: Robert Parrish, 98 mins.)

Up Front (1951)*** David Wayne, Tom Ewell. Bill Mauldin's zany cartoon characters, Willie and Joe, are excellently brought to life by Wayne and Ewell in this amusing film about G.I.'s fighting in Italy during WW II. (Dir: Alexander Knox, 92 mins.)

Up in Arms (1944)*** Danny Kaye, Dinah Shore, Dana Andrews. Kaye made his feature film debut, as a hypochondriac who gets drafted, in this splashy Goldwyn color musical designed to showcase his talents. Kaye's brand of clowning and sentiment doesn't work well in close-up. (Dir: Elliott Nugent, 106 mins.)

Up in Central Park (1948)** Deanna Durbin, Dick Haymes, Vincent Price. Film version of stage musical with Deanna Durbin playing a young Irish colleen during the turn of the century. Strictly for undiscriminating musical fans. (Dir: William A. Seiter, 88 mins.)

Up in Mabel's Room (1944)**½ Dennis O'Keefe, Marjorie Reynolds, Mischa Auer, Charlotte Greenwood, Gail Patrick. A flustered husband tries to retrieve a memento given innocently to his old flame. Farce gets pretty funny at times. (Dir: Allan Dwan, 76 mins.)

Up in Smoke (1978)*** Cheech and Chong, Tom Skeritt, Stacy Keach. A doper movie with a hidden moral, no less. Generally hilarious, well-balanced and rollicking. Two free-spirited bums decide to join forces in their endless search for substances to snort, smoke or drop. They travel in Cheech's ridiculously souped-up car—a good joke in itself—meet lots of weird characters, and eventually invent Punk Rock (Cheech wears a pink tutu). If you're at all tolerant, see it. (Dir: Lou Adler, 85 mins.)

Up Periscope (1959)**½ James Garner, Edmond O'Brien. Routine submarine drama made by Warner Bros. Garner deserved better material as his later career proved. For action fans. (Dir: Gordon Douglas, 111 mins.)

Up the Academy (1980)** Rob Liebman, Wendell Brown, Tom Citera. The first "Mad" magazine movie, set in a boys' military school, is uneven, occasionally inventive. The times may have finally caught up with director Robert Downey's wild brand of humor. (96 mins.)

Up the Creek (Great Britain, 1958)**½ Wilfrid Hyde-White, Peter Sellers, David Tomlinson. Not as funny as some other British naval comedies but many lively moments do come about due to the antics of David Tomlinson as an ingenious Lieutenant. (Dir: Val Guest, 83 mins.)

Up the Down Staircase (1967)**** Sandy Dennis, Patrick Bedford, Elleen Heckart, Jean Stapleton. Bel Kaufman's perceptive best-selling novel about the experiences of a young teacher in a New York high school is transferred to the screen with taste and skill by director Robert Mulligan and screenwriter Tad Mosel. Dennis has never been better and she's very moving, indeed. She's the dedicated teacher who overcomes the bureaucracy of high-school administrators and a series of problems with her students. (124 mins.)

Up the Sandbox (1972)***½ Barbra Streisand, David Selby, Ariane Heller. A funny, wry, and often genuinely touching story about a young New York housewife living on Riverside Drive. One of the first American films to deal with the women's-rights movement. One of Streisand's most observant, restrained performances—she sings nary a note and is delicious delivering various comic monologues or relating to her neighbors. Extremely well adapted by playwright Paul Zindel from the novel by Anne Richardson Roiphe. Nicely handled, except for a clumsy ending, by veteran director Irvin Kershner. (97 mins.)

Up to His Neck (Great Britain, 1954)** Ronald Shiner, Laya Radi, Anthony Newley, Bryan Forbes. Wacky, mixed-up farce with only a few funny moments. (Dir: John Paddy Carstairs, 89 mins.)

Upstairs and Downstairs (Great Britain, 1959)*** Michael Craig, Anne Heywood, Mylene Demongeot, Claudia Cardinale. Charming domestic comedy about a young married couple and their problems in obtaining the right servant girl. Nice chuckling narrative, delightful performance by Demongeot as a Swedish beauty. Good fun. (Dir: Ralph Thomas, 100 mins.)

Uptown Saturday Night (1974)*** Sidney Poitier, Bill Cosby, Harry Belafonte, Flip Wilson, Calvin Lockhart, Richard Pryor, Roscoe Lee Browne. High-spirited fun as Cosby and Poitier play a pair of innocents whose night on the town is interrupted when they're held up at an illegal after-hours nightclub. The duo run into zany characters including Belafonte as a black godfather (made up in a perfect parody of Brando), Pryor as a frenetic private eye, Wilson as the reverend whose sermon on loose lips sinking ships and marriages is a comic tour-de-force and Browne as a phony black-is-beautiful congressman. (Dir: Sidney Poitier, 104 mins.)

Urban Cowboy (1980)***½ John Travolta, Debra Winger, Scott Glenn, Bonnie Raitt, Charlie Daniels Band. Travolta and Winger play two bickering innocents who fall into and out of marriage. Director James Bridges brings off most of the scenes with his visual panache and sensitivity to the expressiveness of his players. (135 mins.)

Urge to Kill (Great Britain, 1960)** Patrick Barr, Ruth Dunning. Police seem to be stymied when a series of girl killings occur. Fair Edgar Wallace mystery. (Dir: Vernon Sewell, 58 mins.)

Us Against the World (MTV 1975)**½ Meredith Baxter Birney, Linda Purl. Interesting but uneven drama about the difficulties young women interns face in the rigorous medical world. A few good scenes of doctor-patient relationships. (Dir: William Asher, 122 mins.)

Used Cars (1980)**½ Kurt Russell, Jack Warden, Gerrit Graham. This nasty, curdled, vicious comedy veers into the grotesque too often to be genuinely funny. About a young go-getter trying to make it to the top any way he can. (Dir: Robert Zemeckis, 113 mins.)

Users, The (MTV 1978)** Jaclyn Smith, Tony Curtis. Hollywood gossip columnist Joyce Haber's sex-ridden book about sinful tinsel town becomes an overproduced, underdressed film. You'll meet the agents, the actors, the writers, the studio heads, the masseurs, and the women who use the bedroom as their boardroom. Smith, decked out in more costume changes than Liberace in his Las Vegas act, does what

she can, which isn't much, as an ex-prostitute who climbs the social ladder until she marries a multimillionaire. (Dir: Joseph E. Hardy, 104 mins.)

Utopia (France-Italy, 1951)*½ Stan Laurel, Oliver Hardy, Suzy Delair. (Dirs: John Berry, Leo Joannon, 86 mins.)

Vacation from Marriage (Great Britain, 1945)*** Robert Donat, Deborah Kerr, Ann Todd, Glynis Johns. Cute little "sleeper" about a mild little English couple who go into service during the war and have their personalities overhauled. Donat and Kerr are a great help as the couple. (Dir: Alexander Korda, 92 mins.)

Vacation in Hell (MTV 1979)** Michael Brandon, Priscilla Barnes, Barbara Feldon. Four vacationing women and the obligatory male flee for their lives in a dense jungle on the outskirts of a posh tropical resort. Peppered liberally with women's lib talk; you've seen it all before. (Dir: David Greene, 104 mins.)

Vagabond King, The (1956)** Kathryn Grayson, Oreste, Rita Moreno. Operetta about Francois Villon, poet and vagabond, and the revolt in Paris. Pretty starchy; the tunes are still pleasant, but the treatment is strictly small-time. (Dir: Michael Curtiz, 86 mins.)

Valachi Papers (France-Italy, 1972)** Charles Bronson, Lino Ventura, Joseph Wiseman. Violent saga of the Cosa Nostra based on Peter Maas's bestseller. Bronson plays the dim-witted Joe Valachi, a Mafia soldier who turned informer. The performances are exaggerated, except for Ventura as Vito Genovese. Wiseman gives the worst performance of his career as a poetry-spouting Mafia leader. (Dir: Terence Young, 125 mins.)

Valdez Is Coming (1971)**½ Burt Lancaster, Susan Clark, Jon Cypher. A lot of Lancaster to watch here, and that's the nimblest aspect of this western-type tale of a Mexican lawman who, after being forced to kill a suspect, tries to provide for his pregnant widow. Clark is more than decoration as land baron Cypher's mistress, whom Lancaster kidnaps. Filmed in Spain. (Dir: Edwin Sherin, 90 mins.)

Valentine (MTV 1979)*** Jack Albertson, Mary Martin, Loretta Swit. Albertson and Martin are lovely as a pair of senior citizens who find romance at an offbeat old-folks' home in Venice, Calif. He's the bragging old codger who keeps everyone at the home on his toes, and she's a widow who finds his blarney appealing. They embark on a rather far-fetched odyssey , and their charm and talent keep this sentimental yarn afloat. (Dir: Lee Philips, 104 mins.)

Valentino (1951)** Anthony Dexter, Eleanor Parker, Richard Carlson. A romanticized version of the Valentino legend; produced in elaborate style. Against a background of gaudy splendor of the early Hollywood days, the phenomenal career of Rudolph Valentino unfolds. Anthony Dexter bears a striking physical resemblance to the original "Sheik of the Silver Screen," but that's where the resemblance ends. (Dir: Lewis Allen, 102 mins.)

Valentino (Great Britain, 1977)**½ Rudolf Nureyev, Leslie Caron, Michelle Phillips, Carol Kane, Huntz Hall. Our own Rudy Nureyev depicts the silent-screen star as a man of dignity and charm if not a whole lot of smarts, beset by baroque horrors that could only arise in a Ken Russell-directed vision of Hollywood. This handsome film is all dressed up with no place to go. (127 mins.)

Valley (Obscured by Clouds), The (France, 1972)*** Bulle Ogier, Jean-Pierre Kalfon, the Mapuga Tribe. Director Barbet Schroeder achieves some bizarre effects in this tale of sophisticated Europeans seeking paradise in the uncharted interiors of Papua New Guinea. Trenchant criticism of how bourgeois the cult of primitivism is. An intelligent film with incidental sensual pleasures. Cinematographer Nestor Almendros's images rival some of Robert Flaherty's. (114 mins.)

Valley of Decision, The (1945)*** Greer Garson, Gregory Peck, Lionel Barrymore. Story of a girl who became a servant in a Pittsburgh industrialist's home and spent the rest of her life there—as a maid and then married to the son. Not a great film but, thanks to cast and production, top screen entertainment. (Dir: Tay Garnett, 111 mins.)

Valley of Gwangi (1969)*½ James Franciscus, Gila Golan, Richard Carlson. (Dir: James O'Connolly, 95 mins.)

Valley of Mystery (1967)* Richard Egan, Peter Graves, Fernando Lamas, Lois Nettleton. (Dir: Joseph Leytes, 94 mins.)

Valley of the Dolls (1967)* Patty Duke, Barbara Parkins, Sharon Tate, Susan Hayward, Lee Grant, Martin Milner. (Dir: Mark Robson, 123 mins.)

Valley of the Doomed (West Germany-Italy, 1962)*½ Don Megowan, Hildegarde Neff. (Dir: Enzo Serafin, 83 mins.)

Valley of the Eagles (Great Britain, 1951)**½ Jack Warner, John McCallum, Nadia Gray. Young scientist has his invention stolen, follows the culprits together with a police inspector to the wastes of Lapland. Up-to-par melodrama with some unusual Northern scenes. (Dir: Terence Young, 83 mins.)

Valley of the Kings (1954)**½ Robert Taylor, Eleanor Parker, Carlos Thompson. Passable adventure set in Egypt. Taylor plays an archeologist who accompanies Eleanor Parker and her villainous husband on an expedition to the tombs of Pharaoh Rahotep. Miss Parker's reasons for the trek are purely for the sake of historical fact while her husband has other ideas. (Dir: Robert Pirosh, 86 mins.)

Valley of the Lions (Italy, 1962)*½ Ed Fury. (Dir: Carlo Ludovico Bragaglia, 94 mins.)

Valley of the Sun (1942)*** Lucille Ball, James Craig, Dean Jagger. Frontiersman finally exposes a crooked Indian agent. Exciting, fast-moving western with a good cast. (Dir: George Marshall, 79 mins.)

Vampire (Great Britain, 1952)*½ Bela Lugosi, Dora Bryan, Richard Wattis. (Writer-Dir: John Gilling.)

Vampire, The—See: **Mark of the Vampire** (1957)

Vampire (MTV 1979)**½ Richard Lynch, Jason Miller, E. G. Marshall. A vampire has been buried lo these many years, when construction begins on the site where his mansion once stood, the earth stirs and he emerges. Lynch has weird, offbeat blond good looks and makes a convincing Prince of Darkness running around the dimly lit streets of San Francisco. A little slow-moving, but fairly well done. (Dir: E. W. Swackhamer, 104 mins.)

Vampire Bat, The (1933)** Melvyn Douglas, Fay Wray, Lionel Atwill. Mad doctor terrorizes a small village with a series of wanton murders. Dated horror thriller. (Dir: Frank Strayer, 71 mins.)

Vampires (Italy, 1965)* Gordon Scott, Gianna Maria, Canale. (Dirs: Giacomo Gentilomo, Sergio Corbucci, 91 mins.)

Vampire's Coffin, The (Mexico, 1959)* Abel Salazar, Ariadne Welter, Jermon Robles. (Dirs: Fernando Mendez, Paul Nagle, 81 mins.)

Vanina Vanini (Italy, 1962)***½ Laurent Terzieff, Sandra Milo, Paolo Stoppa, Martine Carol. Based on a story by Stendhal, the film interpolates his essays and journalism on Italy in the early 19th century, when the Freemasons were in revolt against the Church-dominated order. The political discourse mainly takes the form of bedroom conversations between a firebrand student (Terzieff) and the eponymous princess (Milo), who have become lovers. (Dir: Roberto Rossellini.)

Vanished (MTV 1971)*** Richard Widmark, James Farentino, Robert Young, Eleanor Parker. From the best-selling novel by Fletcher Knebel. Widmark is effective as the president of the United States who faces a major crisis when one of his top advisers is allegedly kidnapped by what appears to be a foreign power. The situation has built-in suspense, and fine production heightens it at every turn. The supporting cast are uniformly good, particularly Farentino as an efficient and likable press secretary; E. G. Marshall as an overly fastidious and dedicated CIA director; and Young as a colorful and shady old senator. (Dir: Buzz Kulik, 196 mins.)

Vanishing Point (1971)** Barry Newman, Dean Jagger, Cleavon Little. The car chases, 80% of this film, are capably handled by director Richard Sarafian. Charlotte Rampling is in the complete 107-minute version of Newman's drive from Colorado to California. (Dir: Richard C. Sarafian, 99 mins.)

Vanishing Virginian, The (1941)** Frank Morgan, Kathryn Grayson. Sentimental, sugary little story which is set back at the beginning of the fight for women's suffrage. (Dir: Frank Borzage, 97 mins.)

Vanishing Wilderness (1973)*** Excellent documentary footage makes this family entertainment appealing. The cameras travel across North America, focusing on wildlife, from the polar bears of the Artic to pelicans, alligators, buffaloes, and whooping cranes. (Dirs: Arthur Dubs, Heinz Seilmann, 93 mins.)

Varan, the Unbelievable (U.S.-Japan, 1962)* Myron Healey, Tsuruko Kobayashi. (Dirs: Jerry A. Baerwitz, Inoshiro Honda, 70 mins.)

Variety Girl (1947)**½ All-star cast. Big mass of stars show their mugs and make this thing passable. Crosby and Hope have the best lines. (Dir: George Marshall, 93 mins.)

Vatican Affair, The (Italy, 1970)*½ Walter Pidgeon, Ira Furstenberg. (Dir: Emilio Miraglia, 94 mins.)

Vegas (MTV 1978)**½ Robert Urich, June Allyson, Tony Curtis, Red Buttons. Las Vegas is again a backdrop for a tale of mystery and murder. In this pilot film Urich is the attractive ex-cop hired to find a runaway teenage girl involved with the underbelly of corruption in the glittering city. (Dir: Richard Lang, 104 mins.)

Veils of Bagdad (1953)** Victor Mature, Mari Blanchard, Virginia Field, James Arness. Mature seems very much at home in his 16th-century costumes of a palace guard in Bagdad. Action fans will get more than their share in this typical Arabian Nights adventure. (Dir: George Sherman, 82 mins.)

Velvet Touch, The (1948)**½ Rosalind Russell, Leo Genn, Claire Trevor, Sydney Greenstreet. Famous stage actress is involved in a murder case. Slick but conventional mystery drama gives Miss Russell a chance to emote in several big scenes. (Dir: John Gage, 98 mins.)

Vendetta (Yugoslavia, 1962)* Alexander Gavrick, Helen Jovan. (Dir: Zivorad Mitrovic, 80 mins.)

Vendetta for the Saint (Great Britain, 1968)** Roger Moore, Ian Hendry, Rosemary Dixter. Remember Roger Moore's Simon Templar, alias the Saint, before he became agent 007 in those James Bond films? Well, here's an episode with added footage from the original series, with dashing Moore playing it cool under pressures coming from his "vendetta" against the syndicate bosses. Naturally, there are plenty of beauteous distractions for Simon along the way. (Dir: James O'Connolly, 98 mins.)

Venetian Affair, The (1967)*½ Robert Vaughn, Boris Karloff, Elke Sommer, Felicia Farr. (Dir: Jerry Thorpe, 92 mins.)

Vengeance of Fu Manchu, The (Great Britain, 1967)* Christopher Lee, Douglas Wilmer, Tony Ferrer, Tsai Chin. (Dir: Jeremy Summers, 91 mins.)

Vengeance of She, The (Great Britain, 1968)*½ Olinka Berova, John Richardson, Edward Judd, Colin Blakely. (Dir: Cliff Owen, 101 mins.)

Vengeance of the Three Musketeers (France, 1963)*½ Gerald Barray, Mylene Demongeot. (Dir: Bernard Borderie, 92 mins.)

Vengeance of Ursus—See: **Revenge of Ursus**

Vengeance Valley (1951)*** Burt Lancaster, Robert Walker, Joanne Dru. Two-fisted western adventure with Burt Lancaster the tall man in the saddle. Robert Walker plays Burt's young brother with an eye for the ladies and a penchant for trouble. Good action, ruggedly presented. (Dir: Richard Thorpe, 83 mins.)

Venice, the Moon and You (Italy, 1959)*½ Alberto Sordi, Marisa Alasio. (Dir: Dino Risi, 106 mins.)

Venus in Furs (Great Britain-Italy-West Germany, 1970)*½ James Darren, Barbara McNair, Maria Rohm, Dennis Price. (Dir: Jess Franco, 86 mins.)

Venusian, The—See: **Stranger from Venus**

Vera Cruz (1954)**½ Gary Cooper, Burt Lancaster, Cesar Romero, Ernest Borgnine, Charles Bronson. The often used western plot of two opportunistic adventurers is on hand once again. This time it's Mexico during the Revolution of 1866. Cooper and Lancaster play the gunmen who inevitably come to grips. Denise Darcel and Sarita Montiel are merely decorative in their brief roles. (Dir: Robert Aldrich, 94 mins.)

Verboten! (1959)*** James Best, Susan Cummings, Tom Pittman. "Their love was VERBOTEN!" screamed the ads, and this sleazy film is no less shrill, beginning with a sniper being tracked down to the motif from Beethoven's Fifth and continuing with the romance of an American soldier and an off-limits fraulein in occupied Germany. Sweaty, claustrophobic, occasionally frenzied, and often brilliant. (Dir: Sam Fuller, 94 mins.)

Verdict, The (1946)***½ Sydney Greenstreet, Peter Lorre, Rosalind Ivan, Joan Lorring, George Coulouris. Donald Siegel directs probably the most enjoyable of the Greenstreet-Lorre vehicles, an amiable Victorian murder mystery where, for once, Greenstreet is on the side of the law, transformed by the daring, ornate camera movements of the young Siegel. Impressive moviemaking by any standard and strong certification of the talent that would not decisively assert itself again until 1954 (with *Riot in Cell Block 11* and *Private Hell 36*). Ernest Haller's camera work is exemplary. (86 mins.)

Verdict, The (Great Britain, 1964)** Cec Linder, Nigel Davenport. International criminal fixes the jury of his murder trial.

Fair crime melodrama. Edgar Wallace story. (Dir: David Eady, 55 mins.)

Vertigo (1958)**** James Stewart, Kim Novak, Barbara Bel Geddes. An Alfred Hitchcock-directed thriller that makes no sense whatsoever but is a dazzling display of directorial finesse, weird situations. A retired San Francisco detective is hired to shadow an old friend's wife, finds himself falling for her—then tragedy occurs. Believable or not, it's excellently done. (120 mins.)

Very Missing Person, A (MTV 1972)** Eve Arden. It's good to have Miss Arden back. Eve plays Hildegarde Withers, spinster sleuth, a character Edna May Oliver played back in a few 1930's movies. Curious Hildegarde, wearing atrocious hats, picks locks with a hatpin and wards off assailants by swinging her handbag, while tracing a wealthy youngster. The story and supporting cast aren't up to the star's level. (Dir: Russell Mayberry, 73 mins.)

Very Private Arrair, A (France-Italy, 1962)*½ Brigitte Bardot, Marcello Mastroianni, Louis Malle. (Dir: Louis Malle, 95 mins.)

Very Special Favor, A (1965)**½ Rock Hudson, Leslie Caron, Charles Boyer. French lawyer persuades Rock, as a favor, to romance his daughter to help her find herself as a woman. Glossy comedy with a pretty production and familiar players; sometimes the intent is funnier than the execution, but the laughs come with fair frequency. (Dir: Michael Gordon, 104 mins.)

Vice and Virtue (Italy-France, 1963)** Annie Girardot, Robert Hossein, Catherine Deneuve. Misguided attempt to update two novels by de Sade ("Juliette," "Justine") and make a relevant comment about contemporary society. Two sisters, one virtuous, one decadent, cope with the Nazi occupation of France. Direction compromised by naive plotting, excessive symbolism. (Dir: Roger Vadim, 108 mins.)

Vice Raid (1959)* Mamie Van Doren, Richard Coogan, Brad Dexter. (Dir: Edward L. Cahn, 71 mins.)

Vice Squad (1953)**½ Edward G. Robinson, Paulette Goddard. A day in the life of a cop, with more plot than you can count on your fingers and toes. Robinson is tough, Goddard is pseudo-sultry, and the result is haphazard. Strictly for the cops-and-robbers crowd. (Dir: Arnold Laven, 87 mins.)

Vicious Circle, The (Great Britain, 1957)*** Johns Mills, Noelle Middleton. Surgeon is suspected of murder when a film star is found dead in his flat. Suspenseful, compact mystery with good performances. (Dir: Gerald Thomas, 84 mins.)

Vicki (1953)** Jeanne Crain, Richard Boone, Jean Peters. Dogged detective tries to pin murder of a local glamour girl on her suitor. This was better as "I Wake Up Screaming" with Grable and Mature.(Dir: Harry Horner, 85 mins.)

Victim (Great Britain, 1961)***½ Dirk Bogarde, Sylvia Syms, Dennis Price. Made by the same talented team of filmmakers responsible for the splendid entry "Saphire." When a lawyer (Bogarde) becomes involved in a case with homosexual implications, his own past jeopardizes his career. Generally thoughtful effort, and one of the earliest movies, to deal with the heretofore forbidden screen subject of homosexuality. Makes an earnest plea for changing the antiquated law making homosexuality a crime. Bogarde is particularly effective. (Dir: Basil Dearden, 100 mins.)

Victim, The (MTV 1972)* Elizabeth Montgomery, George Maharis, Eileen Heckart. (Dir: Herschel Daugherty, 73 mins.)

Victors, The (1963)***½ George Peppard, George Hamilton, Eli Wallach, Jeanne Moreau, Melina Mercouri. Curious, sprawling saga of a squad of American soldiers, following them through Europe during WW II. Uneven results, but done on a broad canvas, commendable in intent. Some splendid sequences, always well acted by a large cast. (Dir: Carl Foreman, 175 mins.)

Victory (1940)**½ Fredric March, Betty Field, Cedric Hardwicke. A fatally bowdlerized adaptation of the Joseph Conrad novel, though many points of interest linger. The lazy performance of Cedric Hardwicke is most damaging. (Dir: John Cromwell, 78 mins.)

Vietnam: An American Journey (1978)***½ For seven weeks director Robert Richter and his crew traveled through Vietnam to record the changes in that country since the end of the war. Richter's eye is one to satisfy our curiosity about what the revolution has wrought other than blatant subcontinental imperialism. An invaluable document.

View from Pompey's Head, The (1955)**½ Richard Egan, Dana Wynter, Cameron Mitchell. Full blown soap opera played in the attractive trappings of the southern social set. Egan plays an executive of a publishing house who goes back home to investigate a claim of money due by an aging author who lives in an air of mystery. A bit slow moving and predictable. Based on Hamilton Basso's best seller. (Dir: Philip Dunne, 97 mins.)

View from the Bridge, A (France-Italy-U.S., 1962)**** Raf Vallone, Maureen Stapleton, Carol Lawrence, Jean Sorel, Raymond Pellegrin. Excellent screen version of Arthur Miller's play about an Italian longshoreman and his eruptive relationships with his wife and niece. The performances are individually exciting and perfectly blended for full dramatic effect. The climactic scene, played in a wee Brooklyn street, is one of the most shattering few minutes ever put on film. Another fine directing job from Sidney Lumet. (114 mins.)

Vigil in the Night (1940)***½ Carole Lombard, Brian Aherne, Anne Shirley. A young nurse in an English hospital makes a fatal mistake, for which her sister takes the blame. Grim but excellently done drama. (Dir: George Stevens, 96 mins.)

Victory at Entebbe (MTV 1976)**½ Elizabeth Taylor, Kirk Douglas, Linda Blair, Burt Lancaster, Helen Hayes. This re-creation of the dramatic Israeli rescue of the 103 hostages at Uganda's Entebbe Airport was hastily put together, and it shows! Taylor and Blair, playing mother and daughter, are laughable, but the rescue itself is a fabulous payoff. (Dir: Marvin Chomsky, 156 mins.)

Victory at Sea (1954)**** Splendid documentary of the course of WW II at sea, adapted from the multi-award winning TV series. One of the best of its kind. Alexander Scourby, narrator. Produced by Henry Salomon. (108 mins.)

Vigilante Force (1976)**½ Jan-Michael Vincent, Kris Kristofferson, Bernadette Peters. The citizens of a small southern California town are under siege from the team of Vietnam veterans they hired for protection. Fast-paced and feverishly funny. (Dir: George Armitage, 89 mins.)

Viking Queen, The (Great Britain, 1967)** Don Murray, Carita. Although made in England, this film very neatly fits the Hollywood adventure category. It is a costumed period piece about the Roman occupation of Britain, and the love that was not meant to be between the Roman military governor and the queen of the local tribe. (Dir: Don Chaffey, 91 mins.)

Vikings, The (1958)**½ Kirk Douglas, Janet Leigh, Tony Curtis, Ernest Borgnine. An all star cast enhances this elaborately mounted adventure epic which places the stress on action. The battle sequences are the highlights of the film which tells the story of the Vikings' invasion of England. On location photography in Norway is another plus factor. (Dir: Richard Fleischer, 114 mins.)

Villa Rides (1968)**½ Yul Brynner, Robert Mitchum, Charles Bronson, Herbert Lom. Action-packed adventure stars Brynner as the famed rebel leader Pancho Villa, and Mitchum as a gun-running aviator who joins forces with Villa to further the revolution in Mexico. (Dir: Buzz Kulik, 122 mins.)

Village, The (Switzerland, 1954)*** John Justin, Eva Dahlbeck. Two teachers at the Pestalozzi school for children of postwar displaced persons fall in love, but she is from behind the Iron Curtain. Frequently touching drama, multi-lingual, with some fine performances from the children. (Dir: Leopold Lindtberg, 98 mins.)

Village of Daughters (Great Britain, 1962)** Eric Sykes, Scilla Gabel. A strained but somewhat funny comedy about a British traveling salesman who encounters hot-blooded Italians in their full passion while stranded in a small town. (Dir: George Pollock, 86 mins.)

Village of the Damned (Great Britain, 1960)**** George Sanders, Barbara Shelley, Martin Stephens. Outstanding low-budget, high-shudder shocker, based on the novel "Cuckoos," by John Wyndham. Fine direction from Wolf Rilla in this chiller about strange kids trying to conquer a village. Reminds us that sometimes the eeriest thrills and chills are the quiet ones. (Dir: Wolf Rilla, 78 mins.)

Village of the Giants (1965)* Tommy Kirk, Johnny Crawford, Beau Bridges, Ron Howard. (Dir: Bert L. Gordon, 82 mins.)

Villain (Great Britain, 1971)**½ Richard Burton, Ian McShane. Uneven crime melodrama with a heavy accent on violence. Burton gives a good account of himself in the offbeat role of a sadistic thief who stops at nothing to get his job done. Burton's character is also a jealous homosexual, which adds some bite to the already heavily plotted film. Lots of blood and gore, some of which will be edited for TV. (Dir: Michael Tuchner, 97 mins.)

Villain, The (1979)** Kirk Douglas, Ann-Margret, Arnold Schwarzenegger. A boo and a hiss to this clumsy western farce which finds cowpoke Douglas caught between the overwhelming chests of Schwarzenegger and Ann-Margret. The film does contain some fancy stunts, courtesy of director Hal Needham, but the characters are slim and the humor is sophomoric. (93 mins.)

Villain Still Pursued Her, The (1940)**½ Buster Keaton, Alan Mowbray, Hugh Herbert, Margaret Hamilton, Billy Gilbert. The able cast burlesque Victorian melodrama in a spoof which, unlike the modern spoofs, is more affectionate than derisive. Only intermittently funny, but worth seeing for the late Keaton performance. (Dir: Edward F. Cline, 66 mins.)

Violent Men, The (1955)**½ Glenn Ford, Barbara Stanwyck, Edward G. Robinson, Brian Keith. A large sprawling Western drama about a ruthless land baron who loses his grip on things due to violent forces opposing him. Good performances by all. (Dir: Rudolph Maté, 96 mins.)

Violent Moment (Great Britain, 1959)** Lyndon Brook, Jane Hylton. Army deserter lives with a woman and her son, commits murder when she intends to place the boy up for adoption. Fairly interesting drama based on a story by Edgar Wallace. (Dir: Sidney Hayers, 61 mins.)

Violent Ones, The (France, 1957)*** Paul Meurisse, Francoise Fabian. Suspenseful drama of a series of murders that sends a whole town into terror. Good acting and fine script. (Dir: Henri Calef, 100 mins.)

Violent Ones, The (1967)* Fernando Lamas, Aldo Ray, David Carradine, Lisa Gaye, Tommy Sands.(84 mins.)

Violent Patriot (Italy, 1957)*½ Vittorio Gassman, Anna Maria Ferrero. (Dir: Sergio Grieco, 90 mins.)

Violent Playground (Great Britain, 1958)*** Stanley Baker, Peter Cushing, David McCallum, Anne Heywood. Policeman tries to prevent crime in a tenement area of Liverpool. Gripping, well-acted drama of juvenile delinquents. (Dir: Basil Dearden, 106 mins.)

Violent Road (1958)** Brian Keith, Efrem Zimbalist, Jr. Average drama about the truck drivers who transport high explosive rocket fuel to a newly built missile base and the dangers they encounter. You can see this sort of thing done better on TV. (Dir: Howard W. Koch, 86 mins.)

Violent Saturday (1955)*** Victor Mature, Richard Egan, Sylvia Sidney, Ernest Borgnine, Stephen McNally, Lee Marvin. A good cast bolsters this episodic yarn about a planned bank robbery in a small town by a trio of hoods. Many of the townspeople's stories come into focus as the bank robbers stake out the town before the heist. (Dir: Richard Fleischer, 91 mins.)

Violent Summer (France-Italy, 1959)**** Eleonora Rossi-Drago, Jean-Louis Trintignant, Jacqueline Sassard. Quiet, perceptive film despite that title. About a frivolous romance solidifying into a passionate, mature affair, set against the upheaval of Mussolini's rotting fascist regime. Trintignant appears to advantage in this early film, his first non-Bardot vehicle, and his performance is complimented by Miss Rossi-Drago's compelling portrait of the older woman drawn to him. Film has delicacy, is well photographed. (Dir: Vallerio Zurlini, 95 mins.)

Violette (France-Canada, 1978)*** Isabelle Huppert, Stephane Audran, Jean Carmet, Bernadette Lafont. The real-life story of a self-centered teenager who poisoned her parents in '33. Huppert plays Violette Noziere, who served time for her father's killing (her mother recovered). Well done, but too long. (Dir: Claude Chabrol, 123 mins.)

V.I.P.'s, The (Great Britain, 1963)*** Elizabeth Taylor, Richard Burton, Louis Jourdan, Margaret Rutherford, Orson Welles. A sort of "Grand Hotel" located at a London airport, as passengers waiting for a delayed flight intercross each other's lives. Practically an all-star cast lends credence to the multi-plots, with an Oscar-winning performance by Rutherford and equally good ones by Rod Taylor and Maggie Smith. (Dir: Anthony Asquith, 119 mins.)

Virgin and the Gypsy, The (Great Britain, 1970)***½ Franco Nero, Joanna Shimkus, Honor Blackman. Shimkus swelters under the Victorian burden of her clerical dad, while the libidinous gypsy clues her in. Lots of rural color, with lust and language in equal measure. Well handled by director Christopher Miles. From the D. H. Lawrence novella. (92 mins.)

Virgin Island (Great Britain, 1958)** John Cassavetes, Virginia Maskell, Sidney Poitier, Ruby Dee. Young writer and his bride buy an island in the Caribbean, live there with the help of a local fisherman. Romantic comedy is pleasant but moves leisurely, uneventfully. (Dir: Pat Jackson, 94 mins.)

Virgin Queen, The (1955)*** Bette Davis, Richard Todd, Joan Collins, Herbert Marshall, Dan O'Herlihy. Davis fans will not want to miss their favorite in the flashy role of the aging Queen Elizabeth and her relationship with Sir Walter Raleigh, gallantly played by Richard Todd. Miss Davis gives a flamboyant performance as the British Queen and the supporting cast is more than competent. TV movie fans might find it interesting to compare this film with the 1939 "Private Lives of Elizabeth & Essex" in which Miss Davis played the same role opposite Errol Flynn. (Dir: Henry Koster, 92 mins.)

Virgin Spring, The (Sweden, 1960)**** Max von Sydow, Brigitta Valberg, Gunnel Lindblom, Brigitta Pettersson. Bergman's quietly chilling morality play, set in the Swedish countryside of the 14th century, about pagan lusts, Christian renewal. Based on a Swedish ballad and legend, a young virgin girl is brutally despoiled and murdered after her sister invokes a pagan curse. Bergman has captured the quality of ancient legends: their primitive passions; human sorrows; abrupt beauty, for one of his most powerful films. Oscar: Best Foreign Film. (Dir: Ingmar Bergman, 88 mins.)

Virginia City (1940)*½ Errol Flynn, Miriam Hopkins, Randolph Scott, Humphrey Bogart. (Dir: Michael Curtiz, 121 mins.)

Virginia Hill Story, The (MTV 1974)** Dyan Cannon, Harvey Keitel, Allen Garfield, Robby Benson. Dyan Cannon stars in this tale about a poor Southern girl who hits the big time as a gangster's moll, and she gives her all to the character of Virginia Hill, the girlfriend of Bugsy Siegel, who was murdered in Beverly Hills back in 1947. Version, based on a true story, is a pale copy of the real thing. (Dir: Joel Schumacher, 72 mins.)

Virginian, The (1929)**** Gary Cooper, Walter Huston, Richard Arlen, Mary Brian. You may find this a bit leaden, but stick around for the ending. With Cooper: "When you call me that...smile." Based on Owen Wister's novel and play. (Dir: Victor Fleming, 90 mins.)

Virginian, The (1946)*** Joel McCrea, Brian Donlevy, Sonny Tufts, Barbara Britton, Fay Bainter. Not exactly powerful, but fairly interesting western about the age old "horse opera" struggle between ranchers and rustlers. (Dir: Stuart Gilmore, 87 mins.)

Viridiana (Mexico-Spain, 1962)**** Silvia Pinal, Francisco Rabal, Fernando Rey. A chaste, charitable girl, Viridiana (Pinal) is about to become a nun. She visits her lovable uncle, who dresses her up in his dead wife's wedding gown, drugs her, and failing to rape her, hangs himself with a child's jump rope. And that's just the first reel of this masterful work directed by Luis Bunuel. (90 mins.)

Virtuous Bigamist, The (France-Italy, 1957)**½ Fernandel, Guilia Rubini, Alberto Sordi. Fernandel helps a mademoiselle in distress—she needs a husband because she is about to become a mother. Both funny and touching. (Dir: Mario Soldati, 90 mins.)

Viscount, The (France-Italy-Spain, 1967)½ Kerwin Mathews, Edmond O'Brien, Jane Fleming. (Dir: Maurice Cloche, 98 mins.)

Visions (MTV 1972)** Monte Markham, Telly Savalas, Barbara Anderson. A good cast and Denver locations add substance to this action film. Clairvoyant professor warns police about impending bombing in Denver. When a building is dynamited, police first suspect the professor. (Dir: Lee Katzin, 73 mins.)

Visions of Eight (1973)***½ A documentary about the 1972 Olympics in Munich lets each of eight of the best directors in the world to film his or her vision of one event. Schlesinger's segment deals with the horrendous massacre of the Israeli athletes. (Dirs: Arthur Penn, Kon Ichikawa, Claude Lelouch, John Schlesinger, Milos Forman, Judi Ozerov, Michael Pfleghar, Mai Zetterling, 110 mins.)

Visit, The (U.S.-West Germany-France-Italy, 1964)** Anthony Quinn, Ingrid Bergman. It took the efforts of four countries to dilute the fascinating play by Swiss playwright Friedrich Durrenmatt. The story line remains intact, but the cynical, brittle cutting edge of the original has been lost in the trip over the Alps. Ingrid is a strong-willed woman who goes to great lengths to wreak vengeance on her former lover. (Dir: Bernhard Wicki, 100 mins.)

Visit to a Small Planet (1960)** Jerry Lewis, Joan Blackman, Earl Holliman. Impish creature from outer space lands on earth to study the ways of us earthlings. Jerry as a spaceman might bring some laughs, but the satiric point of the original Broadway play by Gore Vidal is blunted with slapstick. (Dir: Norman Taurog, 85 mins.)

Visitors, The (1972)***½ Patrick McVey, James Woods, Patricia Joyce. Low-budget (less than $200,000) psychological thriller, often quite moving. Two ex-cons "visit" the home of a prosecution witness who helped send them up. Director Elia Kazan, as always, has a remarkable flair for dealing with actors. (88 mins.)

Vitelloni, I (Italy, 1953)**** Franco Interlenghi, Franco Fabrizi. Young Lothario won't settle down, even after marriage. Penetrating portrait of youth in a small town in Italy. Well worth seeing. (Dir: Federico Fellini, 103 mins.)

Viva Italia!(Italy, 1979)*** Vittorio Gassman, Ugo Tonnazzi, Alberto Sordi, Ornella Muti. Sketch film, necessarily uneven, directed in corporate-collective style

by Ettore Scola, Mario Monicelli, and Dino Risi. The ironies sit as heavily as too many gnocchi, but a delirious food fight between Gassman and Tonnazzi is delightful slapstick, and much messier than anything in "Animal House." A devastating, almost wordless bit by Muti.

Viva Knievel! (1977)** Evel Knievel, Gene Kelly, Marjoe Gortner, Lauren Hutton, Red Buttons. The irrepressible Knievel battles drug smugglers and syndicate hit men while trying to sober up his mechanic (Kelly). Hutton adds sex appeal, under the direction of venerable hack Gordon Douglas. This nonsense wastes a sensitive performance by Kelly. (104 mins.)

Viva Las Vegas (1964)*** Elvis Presley, Ann-Margret, William Demarest. Best of the vulgar Presley musicals. Ann-Margret and director George Sidney enliven the proceedings enormously. Some real visual and behavioral flair and some good dancing. (Dir: George Sidney, 86 mins.)

Viva l'Italia—See: **Garibaldi**

Viva Maria! (France-Italy, 1965)**½ Jeanne Moreau, Brigitte Bardot, George Hamilton. A good try at a turn-of-the-century revolution yarn. The place is Central America and the two gals, both named Maria, are dancers who become involved with the cause of the local revolutionaries when they fall for the charms of the leading revolutionary (Hamilton). Most of the comedy is tongue-in-cheek, and some of it works. (Dir: Louis Malle, 119 mins.)

Viva Max!(1969)**½ Peter Ustinov, Jonathan Winters, Pamela Tiffin, Keenan Wynn. A funny premise never quite takes hold in what promises to be a hilarious romp. In any case, there are plenty of laughs as Ustinov, playing a modern-day Mexican general with a thick accent, leads a scraggly group of men over the border and into the Alamo, reclaiming the tourist attraction for his homeland. The fine supporting cast is led by Winters as a National Guard officer, one of his brilliant bumbler characterizations. (Dir: Jerry Paris, 92 mins.)

Viva Portugal (West Germany-France, 1975)*** A technically crude but generally interesting documentary record of the first year of Portugal's shaky new democracy, which ended in 1974 Europe's longest-lived 20th-century dictatorship. Scenes in Lisbon and of factory workers and farmers who have just taken over land formerly ruled by absentee landlords. Also one remarkable scene about part of the brief fighting filmed by Portuguese TV. Filmed "collectively." (Dirs: Christiane Gerhards, Peer Oliphant, Samuel Schirmbeck, Malte Rauch, Serge July, 99 mins.)

Viva Revolution (Mexico, 1956)***½ Pedro Armendariz, Maria Felix. Well made film about the Mexican Revolution. Armendariz is superb in the leading role. (Dir: Roberto Gavaldon, 106 mins.)

Viva Villa (1934)***½ Wallace Beery, Stuart Erwin, Fay Wray, Leo Carillo, Joseph

Schildkraut, Katherine De Mille. Excellent historical drama of the Mexican bandit-revolutionary. Fast moving screenplay with colorful dialogue, lots of action, and a point; it tries to understand something of the process of revolution, which degenerates so easily into mere power politics. Beery gives one of his best performances as the endearing, ruthless, violent, and ultimately uncomprehending Villa. (Dirs: Jack Conway, Howard Hawks, 115 mins.)

Viva Zapata! (1952)**** Marlon Brando, Jean Peters, Anthony Quinn. Follows the rise of Mexican revolutionary Emiliano Zapata from peon to the presidency. Brando is magnificent as Zapata, and Quinn won a Best Supporting Actor Oscar for a superb depiction of Zapata's brother. John Steinbeck wrote the screenplay, square in the Noble Peasant tradition. (Dir: Elia Kazan, 113 mins.)

Vivacious Lady (1938)***½ Ginger Rogers, James Stewart, James Ellison, Beulah Bondi, Charles Coburn. Delectable comedy directed by George Stevens in a deliberate, measured style that elicits much charm and a bit too much mileage. Professor Stewart goes to Manhattan to rescue his prodigal brother from a chorine. Of course, he stays out all night and marries the selfsame chorine the next morning. Rogers is surprisingly understanding when he takes her home to mother and his tyrannical father, university president Coburn. (90 mins.)

Vivre Sa Vie—See: **My Life to Live**

Vixen (1968)** Erica Gavin, Harrison Page, Jon Evans. Probably the most artistically viable softcore skinflick ever made. (It probably wouldn't even get an R rating today.) Vixen is big, busty, an abrasive fantasy figure who is less the whore with the heart of gold than the bitch with the golden equipment. Director Russ Meyer's color photography is peerless. (71 mins.)

Voice in the Mirror (1958)*** Richard Egan, Julie London, Arthur O'Connell, Walter Matthau, Troy Donahue. With a little more work on the script, this drama about alcoholism and the long road back could have been a very good film. As it is, it's worth your attention. Egan has never been better and Julie London matches his restrained performance, with character actor Arthur O'Connell a standout. (Dir: Harry Keller, 102 mins.)

Voice in the Wind (1943)*** Francis Lederer, Sigrid Gurie. Tragic drama of a mentally-shattered refugee pianist who finds his lost love on a tropical isle. Strange, moody, well acted. Excellent piano interludes. (Dir: Arthur Ripley, 85 mins.)

Voice of Silence, The (Italy, 1952)** Aldo Fabrizi, Jean Marais, Daniel Gelin, Rossana Podesta. Five men go into a religious retreat and try to face their personal problems. Grim, uneven drama, dubbed in English. Some OK performances, but

the story drags. (Dir: G. W. Pabst, 85 mins.)

Voice of the Turtle (1947)***½ Ronald Reagan, Eleanor Parker, Wayne Morris. Broadway play about a week-end romance in a New York apartment between a budding actress and a soldier on leave is throughout amusing. You'll like Eve Arden in a supporting role. (Dir: Irving Rapper, 103 mins.)

Voices (1979)*** Michael Ontkean, Amy Irving, Alex Rocco, Viveca Lindfors. Ontkean plays an aspiring musician who falls in love with Irving, a deaf teacher who wants to be a dancer. Before the characters descend to terminal mutual supportiveness, director Robert Markowitz's feature debut has a pleasant snap to its situations and consistently interesting acting. (107 mins.)

Von Richthofen and Brown (1971)***½ John Phillip Law, Don Stroud, Hurd Hatfield, Corin Redgrave. The aerial dogfights of WW I (shot in the air, not with studio backdrops) are poignantly counterpointed with some good dialogue about the changing nature of war. The aristocrat von Richthofen (Law) is contrasted with the modern man, the reluctant Brown (well played by Stroud), who shot the Red Baron out of the skies forever. (Dir: Roger Corman, 96 mins.)

Von Ryan's Express (1965)*** Frank Sinatra, Trevor Howard. Exciting WW II adventure yarn with Frank Sinatra giving a fine performance as an American Army colonel who goes from heel to hero. Trevor Howard is also excellent as the British officer who is the prisoners' unofficial leader until Ryan takes over. The last quarter of the film follows the escaping prisoners as they commandeer a German train, and you can't ask for a more exciting sequence. (Dir: Mark Robson, 117 mins.)

Voodoo Island (1957)** Boris Karloff, Beverly Tyler, Murvyn Vye. Horror fans will be a bit disappointed by this slow moving tale of witchcraft and monsters. Even Karloff can't make it chilling. (Dir: Reginald Le Borg, 76 mins.)

Voyage of the Damned (Great Britain-Spain, 1976)**½ Faye Dunaway, Oskar Werner, Orson Welles, James Mason, Max von Sydow. About a shipload of Jewish refugees being shuttled back and forth across the Atlantic for Nazi propaganda purposes. An unappealing mix of low melodrama and strained seriousness. Dunaway and Werner head the passenger list, von Sydow sternly captains the ship, and Welles provides the exuberant overacting that always makes him a welcome relief in pictures like this. (Dir: Stuart Rosenberg, 134 mins.)

Voyage of the Yes, The (MTV 1972)** Desi Arnaz, Jr., Mike Evans, Beverly Garland, Skip Homeier, Della Reese. Another opus about whites learning to live with blacks. It's a pedestrian drama about a rich California youngster who sails off to Hawaii with an inexperienced Chicago black on the lam. Storms, sharks, and the black youngster's inability as a seaman keep the action going as the kids work out their prejudices. (Dir: Lee Katzin, 73 mins.)

Voyage to Danger (West Germany, 1962)*½ John Hansen, Karin Baal. (Dir: Wolfgang Schleif, 81 mins.)

Voyage to Italy (Italy, 1954)**** Ingrid Bergman, George Sanders. Director Roberto Rossellini's finest fiction film. Bergman and Sanders play a long married British couple, grown restless and incommunicative. On a trip to Italy to dispose of a piece of property, they find their boredom thrown into relief by the Mediterranean landscape—its vitality (Naples) and its desolation (Pompeii). Suddenly something lights inside them, and their love is renewed as a bond of the spirit. Never shown in America in its original 105-minute version. (75 mins.)

Voyage to the Bottom of the Sea (1961)**½ Walter Pidgeon, Joan Fontaine, Barbara Eden, Frankie Avalon, Peter Lorre. Submarine speeds to explode a radiation belt threatening earth, is hampered by dirty work aboard. Sci-fi melodrama on the juvenile side, enhanced by superb trick photography and special effects. (Dir: Irwin Allen, 105 mins.)

Voyage to the End of the Universe (Czechoslovakia, 1963)*½ Dennis Stephans, Francis Smolen. (Dir: Jack Pollack, 79 mins.)

Vulture, The (U.S.-Great Britain-Canada, 1967)**½ Robert Hutton, Akim Tamiroff, Broderick Crawford. Effective spinetingler. Atomic scientist uses nuclear energy to reincarnate rampaging composite of a sea captain and gigantic, vulturous bird, both buried alive a century earlier. Location scenes filmed in Cornwall, England. (Dir: Lawrence Huntington, 91 mins.)

W—See: I Want Her Dead

Wabash Avenue (1950)*** Betty Grable, Victor Mature, Phil Harris. Typical Betty Grable musical set at the turn of the century. She sings, dances, throws wases at Victor Mature, sings some more, dances some more and ends up in Victor Mature's arms. The musical numbers are fun and Miss Grable, in her prime here, is an able performer. Remake of Grable's "Coney Island." (Dir: Henry Koster, 92 mins.)

Wackiest Ship in the Army, The (1960)*** Jack Lemmon, Ricky Nelson, Chips Rafferty, John Lund. Slightly different mixture of war heroics and comedy blended into an entertaining film, about a sailing expert who's tricked into commanding an aged hulk disguised as a sailing vessel which will secretly land a scout in enemy territory. Some good suspense, effective

lighter moments. (Dir: Richard Murphy, 99 mins.)

Waco (1966)* Howard Keel, Jane Russell, Brian Donlevy, Terry Moore, Wendell Corey. (Dir: R. G. Springsteen, 85 mins.)

Wages of Fear, The (France, 1955)**** Yves Montand, Peter Van Eyck, Vera Clouzot. This existentialist melodrama about four men trucking nitro across the Andes is compelling, exciting, and rather hokey in a '50s French way. (Dir: Henri-Georges Clouzot, 105 mins.)

Wagonmaster (1950)**** Ben Johnson, Harry Carey, Jr., Joanne Dru, Ward Bond. Eloquent masterpiece, directed by John Ford, that eschews pomposity, self-consciousness, and even movie stars. Two drifters (Johnson and Carey), sign on to guide a Mormon wagon train (led by Bond) to the Utah frontier. (86 mins.)

Wagons Roll at Night, The (1941)**½ Eddie Albert, Joan Leslie, Anthony Quinn, Humphrey Bogart, Sylvia Sidney. Carnival comedy gets a big assist from Albert as a fledgling lion tamer but help from other sources, mainly script, never arrives. (Dir: Ray Enright, 84 mins.)

Waikiki (MTV 1980)** Dack Rambo, Steve Marachuck, Donna Mills, Darren McGavin. Pilot of another private-eye show set in the tropical paradise of Oahu. Two young detectives take on a complicated case, the "cane-field murders." The action is swift and predictable, and the psycho is ultimately apprehended. (Dir: Ron Satloff, 104 mins.)

Waikiki Wedding (1937)*** Bing Crosby, Shirley Ross, Martha Raye. Pleasant musical about a pineapple queen's experiences in Hawaii. As Bing is the press agent for the pineapples, we get a nice mixture of romance and comedy. (Dir: Frank Tuttle, 88 mins.)

Wait for the Dawn (1960)**½ Leo Genn. One of director Roberto Rosellini's lesser efforts but worth watching. Genn plays an Englishman who keeps one step ahead of the Nazis in war-torn Italy. His escapes and encounters with a series of helpful strangers form the basis of this adventure drama. (82 mins.)

Wait 'Til the Sun Shines, Nellie (1952)**** David Wayne, Jean Peters. Fine piece of Americana! Tender story of a small town barber, his hopes and disappointments through the early part of the 20th century. Wayne is superb, as is the rest of the cast. Catch this much underrated film. (Dir: Henry King, 108 mins.)

Wait Until Dark (1967)***½ Audrey Hepburn, Alan Arkin, Efrem Zimbalist, Jr. Tense suspense involving a blind woman (Hepburn) who has inadvertently obtained an antique doll full of heroin which Arkin must retrieve. The film is based on Frederick Knott's stage play, and one hardly notices that the action rarely moves from the interior of the house—especially when the lights go out and the pursuer becomes the blind. Arkin is genuinely devilish in his evilness and charm. Sit forward and get some scares. (Dir: Terence Young, 108 mins.)

Wake Island (1942)*** Brian Donlevy, William Bendix, Robert Preston, Macdonald Carey. Dramatic saga of the glorious but bitter defeat suffered by the Marines of Wake Island early in the war. (Dir: John Farrow, 78 mins.)

Wake Me When It's Over (1960)** Dick Shawn, Ernie Kovacs, John Warden, Don Knotts. Mildly amusing service comedy with Dick Shawn working very hard as a WW II vet who gets drafted all over again due to an error. This premise should give you an idea of what to expect. Shawn and his blundering and thundering commanding officer, overplayed by Ernie Kovacs, set up a luxury spa in the middle of the Pacific island and the contrived complications mount up. (Dir: Mervyn LeRoy, 126 mins.)

Wake Me When the War Is Over (MTV 1969)*½ Ken Berry, Eva Gabor, Werner Klemperer. (Dir: Gene Nelson, 73 mins.)

Wake of the Red Witch (1948)**½ John Wayne, Gail Russell, Luther Adler, Gig Young, Adele Mara. A few good action scenes in this confused sea story about a rivalry between a ship's owner and its captain over pearls and a gal. (Dir: Edward Ludwig, 106 mins.)

Wake Up and Dream (1946)** John Payne, June Haver, Charlotte Greenwood. Story of a strange voyage in search of a missing sailor fails long before the fade-out. Confusing adaptation of a Robert Nathan novel. Color. (Dir: Lloyd Bacon, 92 mins.)

Wake Up and Live (1937)**½ Walter Winchell, Ben Bernie, Alice Faye. The mock feud of Winchell and Bernie died some years ago with the untimely death of the "old maestro." This film was made to exploit the feud but even now it's an OK musical film, with Jack Haley stealing the show as a crooner with mike fright. (Dir: Sidney Lanfield, 100 mins.)

Walk a Crooked Mile (1948)**½ Louis Hayward, Dennis O'Keefe, Louise Allbritton. Fine, 100 percent pure American in stealing atomic secrets for the Russians. Routine FBI drama. (Dir: Gordon Douglas, 91 mins.)

Walk, Don't Run (1966)**½ Cary Grant, Samantha Eggar, Jim Hutton. Pedestrian remake of "The More the Merrier." The housing situation is crowded during the 1964 Tokyo Olympics, and Grant plays the kindly older man who gets the youngsters (Hutton and Eggar) together. This role was enough to persuade Grant to retire, alas. (Dir: Charles Walters, 114 mins.)

Walk East on Beacon (1952)*** George Murphy, Virginia Gilmore. FBI cracks a Red spy ring. Documentary-style; earnest, but rather commonplace. (Dir: Alfred L. Werker, 98 mins.)

Walk in the Shadow (Great Britain, 1962)**½ Michael Craig, Patrick McGoohan, Janet Munro. Incisive, refined soap opera; a man who allows his daughter to die because of his inflexible religious beliefs begins to loosen up as grief and realities take hold. Understated, intelligent, well-acted; effectively shot in a bleak coastal setting in northern England. (Dir: Basil Dearden, 93 mins.)

Walk in the Sun, A (1945)***½ Dana Andrews, Richard Conte, John Ireland. War story of a platoon of Texas Division infantrymen in Italy, whose task it is to clear a farmhouse of Germans entrenched there. One of the best WW II dramas. Realistic, well acted. (Dir: Lewis Milestone, 117 mins.)

Walk Into Hell (Australia, 1956)*** Chips Rafferty, Françoise Christophe. New Guinea official and party, investigating oil deposits in the jungle, are captured by savages. Continually interesting, frequently exciting jungle drama. Fine location scenery. (Dir: Lee Robinson, 93 mins.)

Walk Like a Dragon (1960)**½ James Shigeta, Nobu McCarthy, Jack Lord, Mel Torme. Saving a Chinese girl from the San Francisco slave market, a man brings her to his home town, along with a young Chinese immigrant. There's soon plenty of trouble. Drama of racial problems in the early west has the advantage of a different sort of plot and sincere performances, helping it through some of the shaky sections. (Dir: James Clavell, 95 mins.)

Walk on the Wild Side (1962)**½ Laurence Harvey, Jane Fonda, Barbara Stanwyck. A young man finds his childhood love working in a New Orleans brothel during the depression. Nelson Algren's trashy novel at least contained some serious writing, but director Edward Dmytryk is strictly a hack. (114 mins.)

Walk Proud (1979)** Robby Benson, Sarah Holcomb, Henry Darrow. Can you believe boyish Benson as a Chicano who falls in love with well-off WASP Holcomb? Contrived story of a gang member and his conflicts in the Los Angeles barrio, written by Evan Hunter. (Dir: Robert Collins, 102 mins.)

Walk Softly, Stranger (1950)*** Joseph Cotten, Valli. A small-time crook is reformed by the love of a crippled girl. Well written, deftly acted melodrama. (Dir: Robert Stevenson, 81 mins.)

Walk Tall (1960)*½ Willard Parker, Joyce Meadows, Kent Taylor. (Dir: Maury Dexter, 60 mins.)

Walk the Proud Land (1956)*** Audie Murphy, Anne Bancroft, Pat Crowley. Better than average Audie Murphy western. He plays an Indian agent who wins the Apache's friendship and loses the white man's trust in the process. Anne Bancroft is wasted in the role of an Indian maiden. (Dir: Jesse Hibbs, 88 mins.)

Walk with Love and Death, A (1969)**½ Angelica Huston, Assaf Dayan. Set in 14th-century France, about a pair of young

713

lovers caught in the turmoil of war. There is no place to run away, but the lovers find rapture amid the stunning scenery just the same. Director John Huston is not adept enough with character to pull off such a project. With Huston's daughter and Moshe Dayan's son and the director in a small role. Filmed in Austria. Based on a Hans Koningsberger novel. (90 mins.)

Walkabout (1971)***½ Jenny Agutter, Lucien John, David Gumpilil. Stimulating adventure story with disturbing social overtones. Two white Australian children are stranded in the Outback, and must negotiatte their way across the desert. They adapt to the harsh conditions with the help of an aborigine familiar with the terrain. Based on the novel by James Vance Marshall. Directed and photographed on location in Australia by Nicolas Roeg. (95 mins.)

Walking Dead, The (1936)** Boris Karloff, Ricardo Cortez, Warren Hull, Barton MacLane, Edmund Gwenn. This was the height of the Karloff-horror era and in this one they resurrect the excellent actor from the dead. We know today that he outlived those roles. (Dir: Michael Curtiz, 66 mins.)

Walking Hills, The (1949)*** Randolph Scott, Ella Raines, John Ireland, Arthur Kennedy. Ill-assorted group of adventurers seek a lost gold mine. Better than average western with a good script. (Dir: John Sturges, 78 mins.)

Walking My Baby Back Home (1953)**½ Donald O'Connor, Janet Leigh, Buddy Hackett. If you forget the plot in this muddled musical comedy, you'll enjoy the musical numbers and Buddy Hackett's comedy routines. O'Connor and Leigh make an attractive pair and their dancing is easy to take. (Dir: Lloyd Bacon, 95 mins.)

Walking Stick, The (Great Britain, 1970)**½ Samantha Eggar, David Hemmings, Emlyn Williams, Phyllis Calvert. An outstanding, finely etched performance by Samantha Eggar makes this otherwise predictable drama worthwhile. Eggar is a cripple, stricken by polio in childhood, who is befriended by artist-thief David Hemmings. Their developing relationship is sensitively handled. (Dir: Eric Till, 101 mins.)

Walking Tall (1973)**½ Joe Don Baker, Elizabeth Hartman. A real Tennessee sheriff, Buford Pusser, did take a stand against his hometown syndicate-owned gambling operations, and one brutal beating from the mobsters almost cost him his life. But director Phil Karlson, who said he wanted to make a picture in which people will learn respect for a decent lawman, has made a film which glorifies brutal conduct on the part of lawman Pusser. Hartman plays Pusser's wife who gets killed by the local mobsters. (126 mins.)

Walking Tall, Part II (1975)** Bo Svenson,

Luke Askew, Noah Beery. Takes over precisely where Part I left off, not quite as violently. Lawman-extraordinaire Pusser, now played by Svenson, attempts to track down the man who killed his wife in an ambush which left him severely wounded. (Dir: Earl Bellamy, 109 mins.)

Walking Through the Fire (MTV 1979)*** Bess Armstrong, Tom Mason, Richard Masur. An uplifting, engrossing testament to a courageous woman's spirit. Armstrong gives a sensitive performance as Laurel Lee, who discovers she has Hodgkins's disease while carrying her third child, and risks her life to have her baby. The script doesn't flinch from dealing with the disintegration of her marriage during her long, harrowing therapy. (Dir: Robert Day, 104 mins.)

Wall of Death (Great Britain, 1951)** Laurence Harvey, Maxwell Reed, Susan Shaw. A motorcycle rider and a boxer are both in love with the same girl. Thin plot, some suspenseful motorcycle sequences. (Dir: Lewis Gilbert, 85 mins.)

Wall of Fury (West Germany, 1962)*½ Tony Sailer, Richard Goodman. (Dir: Luis Trenker, 97 mins.)

Wall of Noise (1963)**½ Suzanne Pleshette, Ty Hardin, Dorothy Provine, Ralph Meeker. A tough look at horse racing and the people who are closely involved in that world. The story starts off promisingly, but unfortunately, it soon reverts to romantic soap opera with the two female leads vying for Hardin's masculine charms. (Dir: Richard Wilson, 112 mins.)

Wallflower (1948)*** Robert Hutton, Joyce Reynolds, Janis Paige. Pleasant little comedy about a "wallflower" who blossoms out very neatly and gets involved in a scandal. Edward Arnold is particularly good in this one. (Dir: Frederick de Cordova, 77 mins.)

Walls Came Tumbling Down, The (1946)*** Lee Bowman, Marguerite Chapman. Columnist investigates the death of a priest, becomes involved in murder and stolen paintings. Well written, entertaining mystery. (Dir: Lothar Mendes, 82 mins.)

Walls of Fear (France, 1962)** Mouloudji, Louise Carletti, Francis Blanche. Partisan hiding from the Gestapo in an asylum has trouble proving he's not insane. Good idea for a suspense thriller dissipated in routine treatment; rates fair. Dubbed in English. (Dir: Raoul Andre, 81 mins.)

Waltz of the Toreadors (Great Britain, 1962)*** Peter Sellers, Margaret Leighton, Dany Robin. Sellers is oddly cast as the lascivious colonel in the Jean Anouilh play, but is credible, as is everything else in this determinedly adequate film adaptation. Leighton excels as the wronged wife. John Guillermin directed, not badly. (105 mins.)

Wanda (1971)**** Barbara Loden, Michael Higgins. Perceptive, poignant story written and directed by Barbara Loden about a hapless, ill-educated young woman from coal-mining country who goes through a series of brutalizing relationships with itinerant men. Made on a minuscule budget which makes this independent entry even more remarkable. (101 mins.)

Wanda Nevada (1979)** Brooke Shields, Peter Fonda, Fiona Lewis. Director Peter Fonda's blend of moppet comedy and Indian myth doesn't jell, in spite of his visual eloquence. About a drifting cowboy forced to care for a young girl. Among the odd characters encountered along the trail is an unrecognizable Henry Fonda as a bearded old prospector. (105 mins.)

Wanderers, The (1974)** Ken Wahl, Karen Allen, Linda Manz, Nancy Allen. (Dir: Philip Kaufman 113 mins.)

Wanted for Murder (Great Britain, 1946)**½ Eric Portman, Roland Culver, Dulcie Gray, Kieron Moore, Stanley Holloway. While Scotland Yard searches for a demented strangler, a girl falls for him. Competent thriller with the music, Portman's acting being noteworthy. (Dir: Lawrence Huntington, 95 mins.)

Wanted: The Sundance Woman (MTV 1976)**½ Katharine Ross, Stella Stevens. Ross repeats her "Butch Cassidy and the Sundance Kid" role of Etta Place. Ms. Ross is quite good as Sundance's woman, who has to revert to the life of a fugitive every time a Pinkerton detective gets wind of her trail. The film is bolstered by good location photography and a colorful supporting performance by Hector Elizondo as the charismatic Pancho Villa. (Dir: Lee Philips, 105 mins.)

Wanton Contessa, The (Italy, 1954)***½ Alida Valli, Farley Granger, Massimo Girotti. This lush portrait of seduction and betrayal, decadence and deceit in the midst of Italy's resistance to Austrian occupation in the mid-19th century, reveals director Luchino Visconti at his most baroque and the Italian cinema at its most spectacular. Fine performances by Valli and Granger. Color. (125 mins.)

War and Peace (1956)***½ Audrey Hepburn, Henry Fonda, Mel Ferrer, Vittorio Gassman, Oscar Homolka, Herbert Lom (as Napoleon). King Vidor's mounting of the Tolstoy novel (with Mario Soldati) has some spectacularly effective sequences, notably on the battlefield and whenever Hepburn is incandescently onscreen. Filmed in Italy. (208 mins.)

War and Peace (U.S.S.R., 1967)***½ Lyudmila Savelyeva, Sergei Bondarchuk. Here's the epic, multimillion-dollar Russian film adaptation of the great Tolstoy novel. It offers some of the grandest spectacle ever to be put on the screen. Russia's most popular director, Bondarchuk, also plays one of the leading roles, that of Pierre, and Natasha Rostov is played by Savelyeva. As an epic, few films can even touch it. Oscar: Best Foreign Film. (373 mins.)

War Arrow (1953)** Maureen O'Hara, Jeff Chandler. An action-filled western with a predictable plot. Chandler arrives at a Texas cavalry garrison to train Seminole Indians for the purpose of quieting a Kiowa uprising. In between drilling the Redskins, he falls for redheaded Miss O'Hara. (Dir: George Sherman, 78 mins.)

War Between Men and Women, The (1972)**½ Jack Lemmon, Barbara Harris, Jason Robards. Named after a cartoon sequence by humorist James Thurber, this overly sentimental comedy-drama suggested by his life relies on heavy-handed vignettes rather than the excellence of its cast. Lemmon is better than his material playing the Thurber role, as a sardonic but sensitive man who is losing his eyesight. He meets, courts, and marries the wonderful Harris, inheriting her three kids, dog, and ex-husband. (Dir: Melville Shavelson, 104 mins.)

War Between the Tates, The (MTV 1977)**½ Elizabeth Ashley, Richard Crenna, Annette O'Toole. Elizabeth Ashley is unquestionably the star of this film adaptation of Alison Lurie's novel about Mrs. Tate and her war with Mr. Tate over his ridiculous affair with Wendy, a cloying flower child of the '60s. Wendy is luminously played by Annette O'Toole. Uneven and tiresome as this film is, Elizabeth Ashley's Mrs. Tate is wonderfully appealing. (Dir: Lee Philips, 104 mins.)

War Drums (1957)** Lex Barker, Joan Taylor, Ben Johnson. Apache chief takes a Mexican girl for his wife, hopes against hope for peace among his brave brothers and the white man. Meandering western drama has a plot too big for the low budget. (Dir: Reginald Le Borg, 75 mins.)

War Game, The (Great Britain, 1966)**** Enormously powerful "staged" documentary about the horrors of nuclear war after a missile attack. Cleverly, perhaps manipulatively, combines simulated newsreels and various street interviews with a bland narrative. This disturbing, searing short film was made for BBC-TV but not shown by them. A powerful antiwar statement. Written and directed by Peter Watkins. (50 mins.)

War Games—See: **Suppose They Gave a War and Nobody Came**

War Gods of Babylon (Italy, 1962)*½ Howard Duff, Jackie Lane. (Dir: Silvio Amadio, 88 mins.)

War Hunt (1962)***½ John Saxon, Robert Redford (film debut). An offbeat war film with good acting to recommend it. John Saxon does very well as a young soldier in the Korean war who loses his perspective and begins to enjoy killing. Robert Redford is also effective as a young private who sees through Saxon's heroics. (Dir: Denis Sanders, 81 mins.)

War Is Hell (1964)**½ Tony Russel, Baynes Barron. Soldier on Korea patrol stops at nothing, including murder, to grab his share of glory. Grim and violent war drama packs a punch in its own small way. (Dir: Burt Topper, 81 mins.)

War Italian Style (Italy, 1965)*½ Buster Keaton, Martha Hyer. (Dir: Luigi Scattini, 74 mins.)

War Lord, The (1965)*** Charlton Heston, Richard Boone, Rosemary Forsyth, Maurice Evans. Governor of a coastal village in 11th-century England falls in love with a local girl, which starts many conflicts, leading to tragedy. Costume spectacle with some intelligence in production, direction, and script—for a change. Well done, with excellent performances. (Dir: Franklin Schaffner, 123 mins.)

War Lover, The (Great Britain, 1962)**½ Steve McQueen, Robert Wagner, Shirley Ann Field. While it stays in the air, this story of a reckless and unlikable hotshot pilot is graphically absorbing. On the ground, the trite love story involving pilot, copilot, and an English girl is for the birds. Good performances by McQueen and Wagner. (Dir: Philip Leacock, 105 mins.)

War of Children, A (MTV 1972)*** Vivien Merchant, Jenny Agutter. Often poignant drama on the agonizing war between Catholics and Protestants in northern Ireland. James Costigan writes about the emergence of blind hate and the departure of all reason from a sweet Catholic Belfast housewife, after her husband is carted off to prison for a small act of friendship. Even the woman's pigeon-flying little son becomes infected by the ubiquitous hate, for author Costigan's plotting of a tricky situation spares no one. Made in Ireland. (Dir: George Schaefer, 73 mins.)

War of the Monsters (Japan, 1966)* Konjiro Hongo, Kyoko Enami. (Dir: Shigeo Tanaka, 88 mins.)

War of the Wildcats (1943)*** John Wayne, Martha Scott. Ex-cowpuncher fights an oil tycoon for the rights to Indian oil lands. Good melodrama of the oil boom days; plenty of action. (Dir: Albert S. Rogell, 102 mins.)

War of the Worlds, The (1953)*** Gene Barry, Ann Robinson, Les Tremayne. Workmanlike, entertaining sci-fi thriller that highlights the wasting of L.A. by Martians. Good show. Oscar winner, Best Special Effects. Produced by George Pal. Based on an H. G. Wells story. Color. (Dir: Byron Haskin, 85 mins.)

War Paint (1953)*** Robert Stack, Joan Taylor, Peter Graves. Cavalry detachment experiences treachery and danger when they try to deliver a peace treaty to an Indian chief. Exciting outdoor drama has plenty of action, a good story. (Dir: Lesley Selander, 89 mins.)

War Wagon, The (1967)*** John Wayne, Kirk Douglas, Howard Keel. Good, action-filled western with John Wayne playing an ex-con who is bent on revenge for being framed and robbed of his gold-yielding land. The ingredients are familiar for western fans and they won't be disappointed when Wayne teams up with two-fisted Kirk Douglas to steal the gold shipment being transported in a specially armored stage known as the War Wagon. (Dir: Burt Kennedy, 101 mins.)

Warlock (1959)*** Richard Widmark, Henry Fonda, Anthony Quinn, Dorothy Malone. Gunfighter is hired by a town to wipe out outlaws; afterward his own rule is challenged by a cowboy who helped him clean up. Sprawling western has too many plot threads going at the same time, but good performances make it all interesting. (Dir: Edward Dmytryk, 123 mins.)

Warlords of Atlantis (Great Britain, 1978)** Doug McClure, Cyd Charisse, Daniel Massey. Stupid adventure has a diving bell falling to the ocean floor, its researcher passengers discovering the lost Atlantis. The undersea kingdom is a totalitarian state—allied with the red planet Mars—and plans world domination through a master race. (Dir: Keven Connor, 96 mins.)

Warm December, A (Great Britain-U.S., 1972)*½ Sidney Poitier, Esther Anderson, Yvette Curtis. (Dir: Sidney Poitier, 103 mins.)

Warning from Space (Japan, 1956)*½ Keizo Kawa-Saki, Toyomi Karita. (Dir: Koji Shima, 87 mins.)

Warning Shot (1967)**½ Tough, slick, hard-hitting detective yarn with a series of fine performances by a cast of pros—Lillian Gish, Eleanor Parker, Joan Collins, Walter Pidgeon, George Sanders, Stefanie Powers, Steve Allen, Carroll O'Connor, George Grizzard—plus the able playing of star David Janssen. Janssen's a police detective who shoots a seemingly respectable doctor in the line of duty and finds himself in hot water up to his badge. (Dir: Buzz Kulik, 100 mins.)

Warpath (1951)** Edmond O'Brien, Polly Bergen, Dean Jagger. A routine western yarn with enough action to satisfy "cowboys and Indians" fans. The plot has Edmond O'Brien riding a trail of revenge for the murder of his fiancee. The big scene comes at the finale when the Sioux attack the fort. (Dir: Byron Haskin, 95 mins.)

Warrendale (Canada, MTV 1967)**** Powerful documentary about the unique treatment offered to emotionally disturbed teenagers at an innovative treatment center in Warrendale, Ont. Produced and directed by Allan King. Remarkable early cinema verité entry. B&W. (100 mins.)

Warrior Empress, The (France-Italy, 1960)*½ Kerwin Mathews, Tina Louise. (Dir: Pietro Francisci, 87 mins.)

Warriors, The (Great Britain, 1955)**½ Errol Flynn, Joanne Dru, Peter Finch. Flynn swashbuckles his way to lovely Joanne Dru's boudoir and kills many tyrants on the way. Lavish sets and costumes make things easier to watch. (Dir: Henry Levin, 85 mins.)

Warriors, The (1979)***½ Michael Beck,

Thomas Waites, Deborah Van Valkenburgh, James Remar. A disturbing, reckless, but powerful drama which ends up glorifying youth gangs and the cult of mindless violence. A Coney Island gang is trying to return home safely while being besieged by heavily armed rival gangs out to avenge an assassination. Much of the film is so artfully posed and choreographed that it looks more like a ballet than like street warfare. When the film opened, riots broke out in theaters. Loosely based on the 1965 novel by Sol Yurick, who disclaimed any responsibility for the movie. (Dir: Walter Hill, 94 mins.)

Warriors Five (France-Italy, 1962)**½ Jack Palance, Giovanna Ralli, Serge Reggiani. Four Italian liberated prisoners aid an American paratrooper in carrying out sabotage during WW II. Made in Italy and dubbed in English, this war story has several good suspenseful scenes, is well cast, has an ample share of action. (Dir: Leopoldo Savona, 85 mins.)

Washington Story (1952)** Van Johnson, Patricia Neal, Louis Calhern. Writer is assigned to do a hatchet-job on the capital and selects a sincere young Congressman as her target. Well-meant but mild, rather dry drama. (Dir: Robert Pirosh, 81 mins.)

Wasp Woman, The (1959)* Susan Cabot, Anthony Eisley. (Dir: Roger Corman, 73 mins.)

Wastrel, The (Italy, 1961)*½ Van Heflin, Ellie Lambetti. (Dir: Michael Cacoyannis, 84 mins.)

Watch on the Rhine (1943)*** Paul Lukas, Bette Davis, George Coulouris, Lucile Watson. Lillian Hellman's agitprop play is a relic of its time. Lukas, who won as Oscar, is outstanding as an underground patriot, with Coulouris and Watson in effective support as the slimy amoralist and the complacent bystander. (Dir: Herman Shumlin, 114 mins.)

Watch the Birdie (1950)**½ Red Skelton, Arlene Dahl, Ann Miller. Typical Red Skelton comedy. Red's fans will enjoy his crazy antics as a photographer who focuses on trouble. There's a wild chase sequence at the end that makes up for any shortcoming the film might have. Remake of Keaton's "The Cameraman." (Dir: Jack Donohue, 71 mins.)

Watch Your Stern (Great Britain, 1960)*½ Kenneth Connor, Eric Barker. (Dir: Gerald Thomas, 88 mins.)

Watcher in the Woods, The (Great Britain, 1980)**½ Bette Davis, Carroll Baker, Lynn-Holly Johnson, Kyle Richards, David McCallum. Another Walt Disney studio effort to break away from the G-rated kiddie image. Young children may have trouble sleeping after seeing this spooky movie about a young girl's ghost returning to an English manor house after disappearing during a lightning storm 30 years earlier. Beautiful scenery of the English countryside. For adults who like ghost stories. (Dir: John Hough, 108 mins.)

Waterhole No. 3 (1967)*** James Coburn, Carroll O'Connor, Joan Blondell, James Whitmore, Bruce Dern. An attempt to make a zany western that succeeds more than half the time. Coburn is a roguish adventurer who is after a hidden cache of gold. He isn't the only one, as it turns out. Carroll O'Connor's performance is a help too, as is Joan Blondell's, playing the proprietress of a busy bordello. (Dir: William Graham, 95 mins.)

Waterloo (Italy-U.S.S.R., 1970)*½ Rod Steiger, Christopher Plummer, Jack Hawkins, Orson Welles, Virginia McKenna. (123 mins.)

Waterloo Bridge (1931)**½ Mae Clarke, Douglass Montgomery, Bette Davis. Version of the Robert Sherwood play. Sherwood's dramatic situations have aged badly, and director James Whale's command of the medium was shaky. Love story about a prostitute and a naive soldier of genteel background. The acting is uneven. (81 mins.)

Waterloo Bridge (1940)*** Vivien Leigh, Robert Taylor, Lucile Watson, Virginia Field. Tearjerker about a back-row ballerina who has an affair with an upperclass young officer works well. Leigh sinks into prostitution with heart-wrenching trembles of the head and a gallant jaw. Remade as "Gaby." (Dir: Mervyn Le Roy, 103 mins.)

Waterloo Road (Great Britain, 1945)*** John Mills, Stewart Granger, Alastair Sim. An Army private leads everyone a merry chase when he goes AWOL after learning his wife has been seeing an oily rogue. Fast, suspenseful comedy-drama, good fun. (Dir: Sidney Gilliat, 77 mins.)

Watermelon Man (1970)**½ Godfrey Cambridge, Estelle Parsons, Howard Caine. When insurance salesman Jeff Gerber wakes up in his suburban home, he's startled to find he's turned black overnight. That's the intriguing premise of this uneven comedy which features Cambridge as the average racist who must endure the indignities of being a black American. The laughs are broad, but the energies of Melvin Van Peebles, who directed, scored the music, and produced, shine through. (97 mins.)

Watership Down (Great Britain, 1978)*** Voices of John Hurt, Harry Andrews, Ralph Richardson, Michael Hordern, Denholm Elliot, Zero Mostel. Darwinian animated tale, from the Richard Adams novel. The problem of reconciling animation, dramatic forms, and realistic drawing of rabbit protagonists is not really solved. Mostel gives an inspired vocal impression of a Swedish sea gull with Akim Tamiroff inflections. (Dir: Martin Rosen, 97 mins.)

Watts Monster, The (1976)*½ Bernie Casey, Rosalind Cash, Marie O'Henry. (Dir: William Crain, 87 mins.)

Watusi (1959)** George Montgomery, Taina Elg, David Farrar. Slightly altered remake of the highly successful African adventure "King Solomon's Mines." This attempt fails in comparison and offers no surprises in the routine trek through the jungle in search of cached treasure. (Dir: Kurt Neumann, 85 mins.)

Way Ahead, The (Great Britain, 1944)***½ David Niven, Stanley Holloway. A group of civilians are drafted into the infantry during WW II, serve bravely in North Africa. Excellently acted, authentic war drama. (Dir: Carol Reed, 91 mins.)

Way Down East (1920)**** Lillian Gish, Richard Barthelmess, Lowell Sherman. A masterpiece; an outrageously hoary old melodrama. Gish is seduced by a rake (Sherman) by a pretended marriage. When her baby is discovered, she is sent into the frozen wastes by her New England community. (Dir: D. W. Griffith, 119 mins.)

Way Down East (1935)** Henry Fonda, Rochelle Hudson. The D. W. Griffith silent film was far, far better. (Dir: Henry King, 80 mins.)

Way of a Gaucho (1952)** Rory Calhoun, Gene Tierney, Richard Boone, Hugh Marlowe. A slow-moving tale of the people who live in the untamed Argentine territory during the end of the 19th century. There's love, jealousy and murder thrown into this melodrama. (Dir: Jacques Tourneur, 91 mins.)

Way of Youth, The (France, 1960)**½ Francoise Arnoul, Bourvil, Alain Delon. During the Occupation, a father finds his son has been having an affair with a woman whose husband is a prisoner of war. Slow, fairly interesting drama of wartime moral problems. Good performance by Bourvil as the father. Dubbed in English. (Dir: Michel Boisrond, 81 mins.)

Way Out West (1936)**** Stan Laurel, Oliver Hardy. This is the great slapstick pair's version of a western, as Stan and Ollie help a young girl who is being cheated out of her inheritance. Lots of funny gags, better direction than usual—all in all, perhaps their best film; and a must for Laurel and Hardy fans. (Dir: James W. Horne, 65 mins.)

Way to the Gold, The (1957)** Barry Sullivan, Sheree North, Jeffrey Hunter. Moderately suspenseful chase drama concerning a young convict who is the only one who knows where a fortune in stolen gold is hidden. The supporting cast includes veteran Walter Brennan and he's better than the stars. (Dir: Robert D. Webb, 94 mins.)

Way to the Stars, The—See: **Johnny in the Clouds**

Way We Were, The (1973)**** Barbra Streisand, Robert Redford, Bradford Dillman, Lois Chiles. The charismatic appeal of the two stars makes this film an appealing and occasionally touching love story, despite a lot of flaws in the script. Forget the over-simplified political content

as Streisand chases, catches and loses her "gorgeous goyishe guy." Barbra's a college leftist in the late thirties and . . . never mind just sit back and enjoy the two of them together, drunk or sober in and out of bed. (Dir: Sydney Pollack, 118 mins.)

Way West, The (1967)** Kirk Douglas, Robert Mitchum, Richard Widmark, Lola Albright, Sally Field, William Lundigan. The fine novel by A. B. Guthrie, Jr., has been turned into a hackneyed, disappointing saga of a wagon train on the great trek to Oregon in the 1840's. Good cast helps a little but not enough. (Dir: Andrew V. McLaglen, 122 mins.)

Wayward Bus, The (1957)**½ Joan Collins, Jayne Mansfield, Dan Dailey, Rick Jason. John Steinbeck's novel about a group of people who take a short bus ride in California makes an occasionally interesting film. Miss Mansfield plays it straight for a change as a former bubble dancer who wants to go legit and she's not bad. Dan Dailey is ideally cast as the heavy-drinking travelling salesman with a gift of gab. Joan Collins and Rick Jason have some torrid love scenes. (Dir: Victor Vicas, 89 mins.)

Wayward Wife (Italy, 1952)*½ Gina Lollobrigida, Gabriele Ferzetti. (Dir: Mario Soldati, 91 mins.)

W. C. Fields and Me (1976)*** Rod Steiger, Valerie Perrine, John Marley. The "Me" in the title is Fields's mistress for the last 14 years of his life, played by Perrine, and based upon a book by Carlotta Monti who did indeed live with the legendary comic for many years. Rod Steiger is, for him, remarkably restrained, giving an interpretation of Fields rather than trying to imitate or mimic him. Better this flawed tale of the surly genius than none at all. (Dir: Arthur Hiller, 110 mins.)

We All Loved Each Other So Much (Italy, 1977)**** Vittorio Gassman, Nino Manfredi, Stefania Sandrelli, Giovanna Ralli. Moving story of three friends who spend the years mostly apart, meeting occasionally, paralleled by the history of Italian cinema during those years. Gassman's role as a sellout success is a masterful study in slow-budding regret. (Dir: Ettore Scola.)

We Are All Murderers (France, 1957)**** Raymond Pellegrin, Mouloudji. Youth with three strikes against him is tried and convicted for murder. Moving plea against capital punishment, extremely well directed. A disturbing and rewarding film. (Dir: André Cayatte, 113 mins.)

We Are Arab Jews in Israel (France, 1979)***½ Sensitive, moving documentary essay by a Moroccan Jew on the need for a greater understanding between Arabs and Jews in the Middle East. Director Igaal Niddam suggests that the Arab Jews residing in Israel can be "a natural bridge" in bringing together the divergent elements. (120 mins.)

We Are in the Navy Now (Great Britain, 1962)*** Kenneth More, Lloyd Nolan,

Joan O'Brien. Wacky comedy about a naval officer who continually gets himself into hot water, is bounced from post to post, finally winds up hero of a revolution. Nicely played, some funny moments. (Dir: Wendy Toye, 102 mins.)

We Are Not Alone (1939)***½ Paul Muni, Jane Bryan. Beautiful, sensitive adaptation of the James Hilton novel superbly played by Paul Muni, Jane Bryan and Flora Robson. This story, because its prime interest is characters and their motivations, plays more like a fine teleplay than a movie. (Dir: Edmund Goulding, 112 mins.)

We Live Again (1934)*** Fredric March, Anna Sten, Sam Jaffe, Jane Baxter, C. Aubrey Smith. From Tolstoy's novel "Resurrection." March is extraordinary in this weighty nineteenth–century drama. He plays a Russian aristocrat who comes to realize that his life is empty, and that he truly loves a good peasant girl. Though the plot exposition is rather clunky, the hero's gradual discoveries that his family and friends are self-serving hypocrites are extremely well played; there are actual spots of Tolstoy showing through, no mean feat in a Hollywood film. Sten, now almost forgotten, is beautiful and sensitive as the equally troubled girl. Recommended serious viewing. (Dir: Rouben Mamoulian, 82 mins.)

We Shall Return (1963)* Cesar Romero, Linda Libera. (Dir: Philip S. Goodman, 92 mins.)

We Were Dancing (1941)** Norma Shearer, Melvyn Douglas. Contrived rehash of some Noel Coward one-act plays has flashes of wit, is well played but not entertaining. Shearer's last film. (Dir: Robert Z. Leonard, 94 mins.)

We Were Strangers (1949)** John Garfield, Jennifer Jones, Pedro Armendariz. One of director John Huston's most absurd and unsatisfying adventures, about a group of Cuban revolutionaries who build a tunnel through a cemetery as part of a plan to execute a dictator. (106 mins.)

Weapon, The (Great Britain, 1956)**½ Steve Cochran, Lizabeth Scott, Herbert Marshall, Jon Whiteley. Boy flees after accidentally shooting a playmate. Fairly suspenseful melodrama. (Dir: Hal E. Chester, 80 mins.)

Web, The (1947)*** Edmond O'Brien, Ella Raines, William Bendix, Vincent Price. Tight and exciting melodrama about a bodyguard who kills his boss's arch enemy only to find himself involved in a double-cross. Good script and fine performances. (Dir: Michael Gordon, 87 mins.)

Web of Evidence (Great Britain, 1959)**½ Van Johnson, Vera Miles, Emlyn Williams, Bernard Lee. A man's search to find out about his father. Good performances by the American stars and a competent supporting cast add to the film's interest. (Dir: Jack Cardiff, 88 mins.)

Web of Fear (France-Spain, 1964)** Michele Morgan, Claude Rich, Dany Saval. Woman hides a murderer in her apartment, becomes a blackmail victim. Ordinary melodrama with a predictable plot. Dubbed in English. (Dir: François Villiers, 92 mins.)

Web of Passion (France-Italy, 1959)** Madeleine Robinson, Jean-Paul Belmondo, Antonella Lualdi. Mysterious girl next door threatens to disrupt an unhappy family until she's suddenly murdered. Intricate whodunit is visually dazzling, obscure in plot development, unsympathetic in characterization. Dubbed in English. (Dir: Claude Chabrol, 101 mins.)

Web of Suspicion (Great Britain, 1959)** Susan Beaumont, Philip Friend. Man has to prove his innocence when all the evidence points to his guilt. Ordinary suspense drama. (Dir: Max Varnel, 70 mins.)

Wedding, A (1978)***½ Carol Burnett, Lillian Gish, Mia Farrow, Desi Arnaz, Jr. Director Robert Altman's kaleidoscopic view of many characters at a wedding held in a mansion is more clearly expressive work than "Nashville." (125 mins.)

Wedding Night, The (1935)***½ Gary Cooper, Anna Sten, Ralph Bellamy. New York novelist Gary Cooper flees to the Connecticut heartland to finish a book, and falls in love with the daughter of an immigrant Polish farmer. (Dir: King Vidor, 84 mins.)

Wedding of Lilli Marlene, The (Great Britain, 1953)* Lisa Daniely, Hugh McDermott. (Dir: Arthur Crabtree, 87 mins.)

Weddings and Babies (1958)***½ Viveca Lindfors, John Myhers. Momentary, moody affair involving a photographer and a model, both past the age of tender young love. Filmed amid spontaneous New York City activity, this critically acclaimed but neglected feature is worth seeing. (Dir: Morris Engel, 81 mins.)

Wednesday's Child (Great Britain, 1971)***½ Sandy Ratcliff, Bill Dean, Grace Cave, Malcolm Tierney. A harrowing, deeply moving film that is directed like a documentary about a mentally disturbed young woman and her family, but is fictional. Remarkable performances from a nonprofessional cast. Superbly directed by Ken Loach. (108 mins.)

Wee Geordie (Great Britain, 1955)***½ Bill Travers. Charming comedy about a skinny Scottish boy who grows up into a big, brawny man after sending for a "British Charles Atlas" body building correspondence. Travers is perfect, and gets good support from a marvelous cast which includes Alastair Sim. (Dir: Frank Launder, 93 mins.)

Wee Willie Winkie (1937)*** Shirley Temple, Victor McLaglen, June Lang, Cesar Romero. Shirley practically stops a war in India's Khyber Pass as part of the plot in this overly sentimental tale of garrison life in India. Shirley's fans will love it—others beware. (Dir: John Ford, 75 mins.)

Weed of Crime, The (Japan, 1963)** Makoto Sato. Narcotics inspector goes after a dope syndicate. Routine crime drama, with its locale the main attraction. Dubbed in English. (Dir: Jun Fukuda, 90 mins.)

Weekend (France-Italy, 1967)***½ Mireille Darc, Jean-Pierre Kalfon, Jean-Pierre Leaud, Jean Yanne. One of writer-director Jean-Luc Godard's most daring and disturbing diatribes against the capitalist societies of the West. Focuses on a car ride of a couple heading for the countryside and the apathy, anger, and violence they see along the way. They eventually become political guerrillas. (103 mins.)

Weekend at the Waldorf (1945)*** Ginger Rogers, Lana Turner, Walter Pidgeon, Van Johnson, Robert Benchley, Keenan Wynn, Phyllis Thaxter, Edward Arnold. A fun reworking of Vicki Baum's "Grand Hotel," set, obviously, at the Waldorf Hotel in New York City. The various characters are quite cleverly updated—the ballerina is a movie star, the Baron a trench-coated war correspondent; the previous film is slyly mentioned. In fact, some of the subordinate players are better than in the original, less irritatingly Hollywood-European. And Ginger wears a dress with golden ropes hanging on it that is a must-see. (Dir: Robert Z. Leonard, 130 mins.)

Weekend for Three (1941)*** Dennis O'Keefe, Jane Wyatt, Philip Reed. Newlyweds are troubled by a weekend guest who is attracted to the wife. Amusing comedy has good dialogue, pleasant players. (Dir: Irving Reis, 66 mins.)

Weekend in Havana (1941)** Alice Faye, John Payne, Cesar Romero, Carmen Miranda. A romantic triangle, with Faye as the hypotenuse and Miranda as the main source of laughs. Color. (Dir: Walter Lang, 80 mins.)

Weekend, Italian Style (Italy-France-Spain, 1966)** Sandra Milo, Enrico Maria Saterno, Jean Sorel. Fair Italian feature about a marriage that has to test its durability in order to survive. Bored housewife is off to an Adriatic resort for fun in the sun and her businessman husband shows up soon after, bringing along his jealousy. (Dir: Dino Risi, 90 mins.)

Weekend Nun, The (MTV 1972)**½ Joanna Pettet, Vic Morrow, Ann Sothern, Beverly Garland. Based on a true story about Joyce Duco, a former nun who served in an experimental program in which she donned civilian clothes and functioned as a juvenile probation officer by day, returning to the convent each night. Miss Pettet, in the difficult title role, manages to project a combination of naivete and a straightforward sense of duty to her new tasks. (Dir: Jeannot Szwarc, 78 mins.)

Weekend of Terror (MTV 1970)** Lee Majors, Robert Conrad, Lois Nettleton, Carol Lynley, Jane Wyatt. A kidnap yarn with gimmicks to sustain interest. Conrad and Majors play a couple of desperate criminals whose kidnap victim accidentally dies, forcing them to snatch a substitute in order to collect the ransom. As it turns out, along come three nuns with auto trouble and the plot thickens. It's all a fairly predictable yarn but the cast is OK, particularly Nettleton. (Dir: Jud Taylor, 73 mins.)

Weekend with Father (1951)***½ Van Heflin, Patricia Neal, Virginia Field. A widower and widow combine families, get situation comedy responses from the two sets of offspring. (Dir: Douglas Sirk, 83 mins.)

Weird Woman (1944)**½ Lon Chaney, Evelyn Ankers. Chaney comes home with a tropic bride, raised in the South Seas, and finds himself in trouble with an old girl friend. OK melodrama, helped by good production. One of several versions of John Wyndham's "Burn, Witch, Burn." (Dir: Reginald Le Borg, 64 mins.)

Welcome Home, Johnny Bristol (MTV 1972)**½ Martin Landau, Jane Alexander, Pat O'Brien, Martin Sheen, Brock Peters. Perplexing drama that should pique your curiosity. Landau is very good as Johnny Bristol, an army captain who returns to the U.S. after having been a prisoner in Vietnam for two years and discovers there's no trace of the town in Vermont where he grew up. Miss Alexander has the thankless role of the nurse who falls for Johnny; and Forrest Tucker, in a well-written supporting role, is effective. (Dir: George McCowen, 99 mins.)

Welcome Stranger (1947)***½ Bing Crosby, Barry Fitzgerald, Joan Caulfield, Wanda Hendrix. Young carefree doctor arrives to take over practice of conservative country doctor, and thereby hangs this flimsy story. Performances, however, make it a delightful entertainment. (Dir: Elliott Nugent, 107 mins.)

Welcome to Arrow Beach (1973)* Laurence Harvey, Joanna Pettet, Stuart Whitman. (Dir: Laurence Harvey, 108 mins.)

Welcome to Hard Times (1967)**½ Henry Fonda, Janice Rule, Aldo Ray, Janis Paige, Lon Chaney, Jr. With a little more care and a better script this interesting western drama could have been a class film. However it gets bogged down in its effort to mix psychology and basic cowboy film ingredients. Henry Fonda plays a leading citizen of Hard Times who doesn't stand up to a crazed gunman, played with dripping evil by Aldo Ray. A better than average supporting cast helps things along. (Dir: Burt Kennedy, 104 mins.)

Welcome to L.A. (1976)*** Keith Carradine, Sally Kellerman, Geraldine Chaplin, Lauren Hutton, Sissy Spacek. A very promising debut from young (32) writer-director Alan Rudolph about "The City of One-Night Stands," which is the subtitle for the movie. Fragmented and flawed, but one of the most illuminating films ever made about Hollywood and the mystique of movie-Lotus land. An innovative, ambitious film. Many of Producer Robert Altman's movie stock company are in "Welcome." (106 mins.)

Well, The (1951)**** Richard Rober, Barry Kelley, Harry Morgan. Mob violence flares when a child disappears; however, the town bands together when she is discovered trapped in a well. Breathless, gripping drama, excellent in all departments. (Dirs: Leo Popkin, Russell Rouse, 85 mins.)

We'll Bury You (1961)**½ OK documentary tells of the rise of Communism. Contains little unfamiliar material. Should have been much better in all particulars. (Producers: Jack Leewood and Jack Thomas. 72 mins.)

Well Groomed Bride, The (1946)** Olivia de Havilland, Ray Milland, Sonny Tufts. Silly postwar comedy about a bride who wants champagne for her wedding and a naval officer who needs it to launch a ship. (Dir: Sidney Lanfield, 75 mins.)

Wells Fargo (1937)*** Joel McCrea, Bob Burns, Frances Dee, Lloyd Nolan, Robert Cummings. This is a "super" western about the beginnings of the famous company that transports money. Some good adventure but it's heavy with romance and plot. (Dir: Frank Lloyd, 116 mins.)

We're No Angels (1955)**½ Humphrey Bogart, Aldo Ray, Peter Ustinov, Joan Bennett, Basil Rathbone. Three escaped convicts from Devil's Island take over the store of a French shopkeeper, right some wrongs. Comedy has its amusing scenes, but the stage origin is too evident in its talkiness, lack of movement. (Dir: Michael Curtiz, 106 mins.)

We're Not Married (1952)***½ Ginger Rogers, Fred Allen, Marilyn Monroe, Mitzi Gaynor, David Wayne. Five couples are informed that their marriages are not legal. Episodic comedy with some sequences better than others—but the Fred Allen-Ginger Rogers section is a comedy gem. All in all, superior fun. (Dir: Edmund Goulding, 85 mins.)

Werewolf in a Girls' Dormitory (Italy, 1962)* Barbara Lass, Carl Schell. (Dir: Richard Benson, 84 mins.)

Werewolf of London (1935)**½ Henry Hull, Warner Oland, Valerie Hobson, Spring Byington. Leisurely but interesting chiller. A doctor, bitten by a werewolf, turns into a fiend. Good performances by Hull and Oland make this yarn worth staying with, despite the slow spots. (Dir: Stuart Walker, 75 mins.)

West of the Pecos (1945)**½ Robert Mitchum, Barbara Hale, Bill Williams. Zane Grey story of a cowboy who saves a meat packer's daughter, disguised as a boy, from bandits. Pleasing, well-made western. (Dir: Edward Killy, 68 mins.)

West Point Story, The (1950)** James Cagney, Doris Day, Gordon MacRae, Virginia Mayo. Corny musical comedy about a Broadway director who stages a big revue at West Point. It's a delight though to see James Cagney hoofing again. (Dir: Roy Del Ruth, 107 mins.)

West Point Widow (1941)**½ Anne Shirley, Richard Carlson. Nurse marries an Army football star, but the secret union is in jeopardy when she is about to become a mother. Slight romantic tale receives occasional witty dialogue, pleasing performers. (Dir: Robert Siodmak, 64 mins.)

West Side Story (1961)**** Natalie Wood, Rita Moreno, Richard Beymer, George Chakiris, Russ Tamblyn. The celebrated Broadway musical masterpiece about rival white and Puerto Rican gangs in a New York ghetto becomes a spectacular movie musical. Jerome Robbins's brilliant choreography in this modern Romeo and Juliet story is enhanced greatly by the magnificent New York City location photography and the cast is very good. The familiar score by Leonard Bernstein and Stephen Sondheim hasn't diminished in quality or effectiveness. (Dir: Robert Wise, Jerome Robbins, 155 mins.)

Westbound (1959)** Randolph Scott, Virginia Mayo. For Randolph Scott fans only. The leather faced cowboy gives another tight lipped performance in this predictable western. Virginia Mayo is a notch above the usual Scott leading lady. (Dir: Budd Boetticher, 72 mins.)

Western Union (1941)*** Randolph Scott, Robert Young, Dean Jagger. Scott and Young lay the first coast-to-coast telegraph wire. Westerns don't really suit director Fritz Lang; still, he gives the film his best. Color. (94 mins.)

Westerner, The (1940)*** Gary Cooper, Walter Brennan, Doris Davenport, Forrest Tucker (film debut), Dana Andrews (film debut). Brennan's ornery, many-layered performance as Judge Roy Bean dominates the picture, although Cooper is the nominal star. William Wyler's direction is too meticulous, and his comedy relief doesn't play well. (100 mins.)

Westward the Women (1951)**½ Robert Taylor, Denise Darcel, John McIntire. All the elements seem in place in this long, handsome western about 150 Chicago women being led to California in the 1850s to find husbands, but the level of inspiration remains low. (Dir: William A. Wellman, 118 mins.)

Westworld (1973)** Yul Brynner, Richard Benjamin, James Brolin. Two tourists (Benjamin and Brolin) visit Westworld, a fantasyland where robots in human form allow visitors to act out their fantasies. Yul Brynner co-stars as a robot programmed to play the villain in western-style shootouts; as usual in Crichton's tales of the almost possible, science goes haywire. Uneven, disappointing future-schlock! (Dir: Michael Crichton, 88 mins.)

Wet Asphalt (West Germany, 1958)**½ Horst Buchholz, Martin Held, Maria Perschy, Gert Frobe. Young idealist has his illusions shattered when the journalist he idolizes engages in distorting the truth. Wet asphalt becomes soggy drama. (Dir: Frank Wisbar, 90 mins.)

Wet Parade, The (1932)** Myrna Loy, Jimmy Durante, Walter Huston, Robert Young. Prohibition comedy-drama based on Upton Sinclair material, powerhouse cast, and a dog from the word go. Point of view is that while drinking is evil, it's dumb to prohibit it. (Dir: Victor Fleming, 120 mins.)

What! (Italy-France-Great Britain, 1963)** Daliah Lavi, Christopher Lee, Tony Kendall. Grisly murders commence when a dastardly brother returns to his castle after a long absence. Gothic horror thriller dubbed in English is overdone but should satisfy the fans. Some chilling moments. (Dir: John M. Old aka Mario Bava, 92 mins.)

What a Life (1939)*** Jackie Cooper, Betty Field (film debut), Hedda Hopper. The original Henry Aldrich story about the high-school boy who can't stay out of trouble. A chance for all of us to go back nostalgically to our high-school days. Good fun. (Dir: Theodore Reed, 79 mins.)

What a Way to Go (1964)** Shirley MacLaine, Paul Newman, Dick Van Dyke, Robert Mitchum, Gene Kelly, Dean Martin, Bob Cummings. Fair comedy with MacLaine that adds up to very little. Shirley's a simple country girl who marries a succession of wealthy men. (Dir: J. Lee Thompson, 111 mins.)

What Are Best Friends For? (MTV 1973)** Lee Grant, Larry Hagman, Ted Bessell, Barbara Feldon. Wacky, implausible comedy about an immature cuckold (Bessell) who finds a sanctuary with his best friends during his period of adjustment. Enter a liberated divorcee who talks as if she was weaned on TV situation comedies, and love finds a way. Thankless roles for the quartet of actors. (Dir: Jay Sandrich, 74 mins.)

What Did You Do in the War, Daddy? (1966)* James Coburn, Dick Shawn, Harry Morgan, Aldo Ray, Carroll O'Connor. (Dir: Blake Edwards, 116 mins.)

What Do You Say to a Naked Lady? (1970)** Allen Funt. Director Allen ("Candid Camera") Funt's idea of a joke: the title adequately summarizes the premise of this feature-length stunt. Some funny vignettes. (92 mins.)

What Next, Corporal Hargrove? (1945)**½ Robert Walker, Keenan Wynn. Weak follow-up to the original. This is pure slapstick with Hargrove over in France romancing some French cuties. (Dir: Richard Thorpe, 95 mins.)

What Price Glory? (1926)**** Victor McLaglen, Edmund Lowe, Dolores Del Rio. Classic silent film based on the play by Laurence Stallings and Maxwell Anderson. Eloquent antiwar drama with outstanding performances by McLaglen and Lowe as two tough but human marines fighting in the trenches of WW I, and Del Rio as the French country girl who sparks

their intense rivalry. The battle scenes are surreal, stark, and used sparingly. Ironically, the War Department applauded the film, claiming it was responsible for an increase in Marine Corps enlistments. (Dir: Raoul Walsh, 120 mins.)

What Price Glory (1952)**½ James Cagney, Dan Dailey, Corinne Calvet, Robert Wagner. Although not as successful as the original film classic of the same title, this remake is greatly aided by the robust performances of Cagney and Dailey as hard drinking, two-fisted soldiers stationed in France during WW I. (Dir: John Ford, 111 mins.)

What Price Hollywood? (1932)*** Constance Bennett, Lowell Sherman, Neil Hamilton, Gregory Ratoff. Have you heard about the director (Sherman, also a director) who sinks into alcoholism while his discovery (Bennett) rises to stardom? Sherman modeled his performance on in-law John Barrymore. The Hollywood detail is especially piquant, with Ratoff doing an immigrant dealmaker shtick. (Dir: George Cukor, 88 mins.)

What Price Murder (France, 1957)*** Henri Vidal, Mylene Demongeot, Isa Miranda. A French drama of suspense that leads to an exciting climax. Added attraction is provocative Mylene Demongeot. (Dir: Henri Verneuil, 105 mins.)

Whatever Happened to Aunt Alice? (1969)**½ Geraldine Page, Ruth Gordon, Mildred Dunnock. Another in the line of Grand Guignol mellers starring veteran actresses who can chew up the scenery and what little there is of the script as well. Gordon, as dotty as ever, is the prime victim of crazy Page. It's all about housekeepers who keep disappearing after they are hired by Miss Page... (Dir: Lee H. Katzin, 101 mins.)

Whatever Happened to Baby Jane? (1962)*** Bette Davis, Joan Crawford. Grand Guignol in the grand manner, with a chilling performance by Davis as a faded former child movie star who lives in seclusion and gets kicks by mentally torturing her crippled sister. Virtuoso direction by Robert Aldrich, good performances by the stars, and an admirably nasty acting job in a supporting role by Victor Buono. (132 mins.)

What's a Nice Girl Like You...? (MTV 1971)** Brenda Vaccaro, Jack Warden, Vincent Price, Roddy McDowall, Edmond O'Brien. Passable comedy about a Bronx girl who poses as a socialite in an elaborate extortion plot. (Dir: Jerry Paris, 72 mins.)

What's New, Pussycat? (1965)***½ Peter Sellers, Peter O'Toole, Romy Schneider, Woody Allen, Capucine, Paula Prentiss, Ursula Andress. Clive Donner's stylish direction (with Richard Talmadge, here) virtually defined British mod comedy of the '60s with its nervy blend of the elegant and the crass. Woody Allen wrote the screenplay. O'Toole is startlingly effective in his first movie comedy role, as a tireless ladies' man. Standout work by Prentiss. Filmed in Paris. (108 mins.)

What's So Bad About Feeling Good? (1968)** George Peppard, Mary Tyler Moore, Dom DeLuise, Susan Saint James. Silly, harmless little comedy about a bird which spreads a strange virus resulting in "instant happiness." The possibilities are fairly obvious and the film touches on most of them. The attractive stars, Peppard and Mary Tyler Moore and the able supporting cast, are merely stooges for their infectious feathered friends. (Dir: George Seaton, 94 mins.)

What's the Matter with Helen? (1971)**½ Debbie Reynolds, Shelley Winters, Dennis Weaver, Agnes Moorehead. Another Grand Guignol drama. Winters is Helen, and she's a super-loony who, along with Reynolds, moves to Hollywood when their sons become involved in a Leopold-Loeb type of murder. It gets pretty hairy, and sometimes scary. (Dir: Curtis Harrington, 101 mins.)

What's Up Doc? (1972)***½ Barbra Streisand, Ryan O'Neal, Madeline Kahn. Director Peter Bogdanovich resurrects the screwball comedy and invests it with new meanings for our time. O'Neal is an absentminded professor who has many a misadventure with Streisand, ending in an outlandish car chase. (90 mins.)

What's Up Front—See: Fourth for Marriage, A

What's Up, Tiger Lily? (U.S.-Japan, 1966)*** Woody Allen, Lovin' Spoonful. The background of this frequently funny and always wacky film is every bit as crazy as the film itself. The zany Mr. Allen wrote some incongruous English dialogue to accompany a magnificently photographed Japanese ('64) spy story which just happened to be a terrible film without any prospect of a profitable release in the U.S. This juxtaposition of original footage with a new soundtrack has been done before, but a lot of this is quite wild, if you're in the mood for this kind of a romp. (Dirs: Woody Allen, Senkichi Taniguchi, 80 mins.)

Wheeler and Murdock (MTV 1972)*½ Jack Warden, Christopher Stone, Van Johnson, Diane Baker, Jane Powell. (Dir: Joseph Sargent, 53 mins.)

Wheeler Dealers, The (1963)*** James Garner, Lee Remick, Chill Wills, Shelley Berman. Zany comedy about an oil tycoon who comes to New York to raise money for some drilling, runs across a pretty stock analyst. Witty dialogue, performances by a cast filled with funsters like Jim Backus, Phil Harris, John Astin, Louis Nye. (Dir: Arthur Hiller, 106 mins.)

When a Stranger Calls (1979)**½ Carol Kane, Rachel Roberts, Tony Beckley, Colleen Dewhurst, Charles Durning. Three only moderately related episodes. Dewhurst steals the show as the fallen woman trailed by psychopath Beckley through the sleazy streets of downtown L.A. Durning is the detective, and Kane is the terrified baby-sitter who grows into motherhood. Cowriters Steve Feke and (director) Fred Walton expanded their 20-minute short, "The Sitter," into this feature, and the padding shows. (97 mins.)

When a Woman Ascends the Stairs (Japan, 1960)*** Hideko Takamine. A contemporary story, circa 1960, about a Japanese bar girl of the Ginza district in Tokyo. There are subtle touches in the performance of Hideko Takamine as Keiko, a woman who has managed to earn a living as a bar hostess for many years without having to sleep with the customers . . . until she succumbs to one, and then another and another. The scenes in the bar are contrasted nicely with vignettes involving Keiko's friends. (Dir: Mikio Naruse, 111 mins.)

When Comedy Was King (1960)***½ Compilation of scenes from various comedy films featuring the great talents of Charlie Chaplin, Harry Langdon, Fatty Arbuckle, Gloria Swanson, etc. For the nostalgic and those who never have been exposed to the giant comedy stars of yesterday. Quite entertaining. Produced by Robert Youngson. (84 mins.)

When Eight Bells Toll (Great Britain, 1971)** Anthony Hopkins, Robert Morley, Jack Hawkins. Failed attempt to fashion a stylish action picture features a plodding script by Alistair MacLean, and the waste of a superb British cast. Clichés center on Hopkins' underwater search for stolen bullion. (Dir: Étienne Perier, 94 mins.)

When Every Day Was the Fourth of July (MTV 1978)**½ Dean Jones, Louise Sorel. Based on recollections of producer-director Dan Curtis's childhood, this murder mystery offers a solid yarn, with good characters and a suspenseful plot. In '37 in Bridgeport, Conn., a candy store owner is murdered. Though the crime is pinned on a slightly retarded, mute handyman, the efforts of a young girl, her brother, and his friends result in justice. (104 mins.)

When Hell Broke Loose (1958)** Charles Bronson, Violet Rensing. Racketeer in the army has a rough time until the love of a German girl reforms him. Good performance by Bronson in an ordinary war drama. (Dir: Kenneth Crane, 78 mins.)

When Hell Was in Session (MTV 1979)***½ Hal Holbrook, Eva Marie Saint, Mako, Ronny Cox. A moving study of one man's courage and stubbornness, based on the experiences of a navy commander who spent 7½ years as a tortured POW in Vietnam. Taking pounds off to look believable, Holbrook is effective as the haggard Jeremiah Denton, Jr., enduring torture and communicating with other POWs by Morse code. Relief comes in scenes at home with Jane Denton (Saint), family, and POW wives. (In '80 Republican Denton was elected U.S. Senator from Alabama, and his campaign was based on his war hero image.) (Dir: Paul Krasny, 100 mins.)

When I Grow Up (1951)***½ Robert Preston, Martha Scott, Bobby Driscoll, Charley Grapewin. His parents fail to understand a mischievous youngster, until the grandfather takes a hand and straightens things out. Very good drama of a boy's problems, handled with insight and care. (Dir: Michael Kanin, 80 mins.)

When in Rome (1952)**½ Van Johnson, Paul Douglas. During the Holy Year 1950, a con man swipes a priest's clothes, finds the outfit beginning to get him. Dated but fairly amusing comedy-drama, aided by good performances. (Dir: Clarence Brown, 78 mins.)

When Ladies Meet (1941)**½ Joan Crawford, Robert Taylor, Greer Garson, Herbert Marshall, Spring Byington. From the play by Rachel Crothers. A love quadrangle, played by super-professionals. Some once-serious discussion of "Women's Rights" that has dated badly, but on the whole it's an oddly attractive picture. (Dir: Robert Z. Leonard, 108 mins.)

When Michael Calls (MTV 1971)*½ Elizabeth Ashley, Ben Gazzara, Michael Douglas. (Dir: Philip Leacock, 73 mins.)

When My Baby Smiles at Me (1948)**½ Betty Grable, Dan Dailey, Jack Oakie, June Havoc. "Burlesque," the play about a comic and his wife, has been set to music for this routine film. Really not too bad, but so routine. (Dir: Walter Lang, 98 mins.)

When She Was Bad (MTV 1979)**½ Robert Urich, Cheryl Ladd. Ladd plays a troubled wife and mother who lashes out at her young daughter whenever she feels the pressures building. Urich also registers as the upwardly mobile insurance man who doesn't see the cracks in his marriage until it's almost too late. (Dir: Peter Hunt, 104 mins.)

When Strangers Marry—See: **Betrayed**

When the Boys Meet the Girls (1965)** Connie Francis, Harve Presnell, Herman's Hermits. The best thing about this remake of the Judy Garland-Mickey Rooney musical "Girl Crazy" is the songs, such as "I Got Rhythm," "Bidin' My Time," and "Embracable You." The thin plot about a ranch on the verge of bankruptcy which is turned into a dude ranch, serves as a stage wait between musical numbers. The stars are best when vocalizing, and there's a large group of guest stars including Liberace, Louis Armstrong, Sam the Sham and The Pharaohs. (Dir: Alvin Ganzer, 110 mins.)

When the Circus Came to Town (MTV 1981)*** Elizabeth Montgomery, Christopher Plummer, Eileen Brennan. Elizabeth Montgomery and Christopher Plummer are perfectly suited in this romantic yarn about a woman who gives into a life-long ambition to run away and join the circus. Of course, it's not the circus of her childhood dreams, it's a

third-rate, one-ring traveling show with frayed costumes and torn tents but the magic is still there. A nice character study of a woman who almost missed having a fling at life. (Dir: Boris Sagal, 104 mins.)

When the Daltons Rode (1940)*** Randolph Scott, Kay Francis, Brian Donlevy, Broderick Crawford, George Bancroft. Good old-fashioned Western with plenty of action. Supporting players make it better than average. (Dir: George Marshall, 80 mins.)

When the Girls Take Over (1962)* Jackie Coogan, Robert Lowery, James Ellison. (Dir: Russell Hayden, 80 mins.)

When the Legends Die (1972)**** Richard Widmark, Frederic Forrest, Luana Anders. Lovely, understated, perceptive story about a young Indian boy who leaves his reservation to try his luck on the rodeo circuit under the aegis of his hard-drinking guardian (Widmark). Old pro Widmark has never been better. His charge, Tom Black Bull, is played well, if impassively, by newcomer Forrest. Special tribute must be paid to the tact and restraint of director Stuart Miller, who makes an impressive debut. From the lovely opening scenes of mountainous Colorado, there's hardly a false note in this poignant story. (105 mins.)

When the North Wind Blows (1974)** Dan Haggerty, Henry Brandon. In this nature drama an old trapper who hides in the wilderness and befriends wild animals, after accidentally wounding a young boy. Haggerty plays a villager who tries to convince him to come back. (Dir: Stewart Raffill, 108 mins.)

When Time Ran Out (1980)** Paul Newman, Jacqueline Bisset, William Holden, Red Buttons, Ernest Borgnine, James Franciscus. Irwin Allen has churned out another disaster epic filled with high-priced stars. Just plug in a tropical island, a tidal wave, a volcano, and the rest is easy. There are good guys and bad guys. Some of them live, some of them die. (Dir: James Goldstone, 118 mins.)

When Tomorrow Comes (1939)**½ Irene Dunne, Charles Boyer, Barbara O'Neill. A tear jerker for the women; Charles Boyer falls in love with Irene Dunne and understandably asks her to go to Paris with him despite the fact that he is already married. (Dir: John M. Stahl, 82 mins.)

When Willie Comes Marching Home (1950)*** Dan Dailey, Corinne Calvet. Delightful and somewhat touching film about a West Virginian lad who goes into the Army (WW II) and has a series of adventures including an interlude with a beautiful French underground leader. (Dir: John Ford, 81 mins.)

When Worlds Collide (1951)*** Richard Derr, Barbara Rush, Peter Hansson. Good effects and premise sustain this sci-fi piece about choosing the survivors of an impending collision with a planetoid. Oscar to Gordon Jennings for Best Special Effects. (Dir: Rudolph Maté, 81 mins.)

When You Comin' Back, Red Ryder (1979)½ Marjoe Gortner, Peter Firth, Hal Linden, Lee Grant, Pat Hingle. (116 mins.)

When You're Smiling (1950)**½ Frankie Laine, Jerome Courtland, Lola Albright, Bob Crosby, Billy Daniels, Mills Brothers, Kay Starr. Fairly amusing musical comedy about the ups and downs of the record business. Frankie Laine gets a chance to sing several songs. (Dir: Joseph Santley, 75 mins.)

Where Angels Go—Trouble Follows! (1968)** Rosalind Russell, Stella Stevens, Robert Taylor, Van Johnson, Arthur Godfrey. A sequel to Roz Russell's earlier tedious film "The Trouble With Angels," in which she played Mother Superior of St. Francis Academy for Girls. This second outing has Roz, representing the old line religious leadership, opposing new ideas in the person of young nun, Sister George (Stella Stevens). It's contrived and overly cute, but if this is what you're in the mood for, by all means tune in. (Dir: James Neilson, 95 mins.)

Where Do We Go from Here (1945)*** Fred MacMurray, June Haver, Joan Leslie. This fantasy deserves an A for effort but a B for performance. Fred takes us through a cavalcade of American history as a genie grants his request to be in the Army but puts him in the wrong one. Score by Kurt Weill and Ira Gershwin helps. (Dir: Gregory Ratoff, 77 mins.)

Where Does It Hurt? (1972)** Peter Sellers, Jo Ann Pflug, Rick Lenz. Even Sellers, as the corrupt head of a hospital staffed by incompetents, can't save this stumbling slapstick. Based on the book "The Operator" by director Rod Amateau and Budd Robinson. (95 mins.)

Where Eagles Dare (Great Britain, 1968)**½ Richard Burton, Clint Eastwood, Mary Ure. Supercharged superheroics are served up in this adventure yarn about a dangerous mission during WW II. Agents Burton and Eastwood are pawns in the tale; they take turns performing incredible feats against impossible odds, attempting to free an important American officer being held prisoner in one of those supposedly escape-proof prisons. A good round of cliff-hanging exploits. (Dir: Brian G. Hutton, 158 mins.)

Where Have All the People Gone? (MTV 1974)** Peter Graves, Verna Bloom, Michael-James Wixted, Kathleen Quinlan. Another disaster movie, fairly well handled. Concerns a radioactive explosion and the virus it causes, decimating the population and leaving only a few survivors. Among the living are archeologist Steven Anders (Graves) and his children, who come down from the mountain and meet a disturbed woman (Bloom). (Dir: John L. Moxey, 72 mins.)

Where It's At (1969)**½ David Janssen, Robert Drivas, Rosemary Forsyth, Don Rickles. Fairly entertaining comedy examining a father-son relationship. Dad is Janssen, who runs a Las Vegas casino-hotel, and his son (Drivas) is a college student with a different set of moral and ethical standards. When they meet in Vegas, director Garson Kanin's script has them clashing in their efforts to understand one another. A parade of Las Vegas types dot the scene, but Brenda Vaccaro's slightly dumb secretary is tops. (97 mins.)

Where Love Has Gone (1964)*½ Susan Hayward, Bette Davis, Mike Connors, Joey Heatherton, Jane Green. (Dir: Edward Dmytryk, 114 mins.)

Where the Boys Are (1960)**½ Dolores Hart, George Hamilton, Yvette Mimieux, Connie Francis, Paula Prentiss. Or, what college boys and girls do in Fort Lauderdale while on vacation. Combination of songs, comedy, and drama will be best appreciated by the teenage set. (Dir: Henry Levin, 99 mins.)

Where the Bullets Fly (Great Britain, 1966)*½ Tom Adams, Dawn Addams. (Dir: John Gilling, 88 mins.)

Where the Hot Wind Blows (France-Italy, 1960)** Melina Mercouri, Gina Lollobrigida, Marcello Mastroianni, Yves Montand. Gifted director Jules Dassin bombed with this one. A melodrama about the decadence of a small town from the peasants to the aristocracy. Good cast wasted in banal theatrics. English dubbed. (126 mins.)

Where the Ladies Go (MTV 1980)**½ Earl Holliman, Karen Black, Candy Clark, Lisa Hartman. Clever little yarn about housewives and an assorted collection of men who go to a bar which opens at 9 a.m. and closes at 3 p.m. During that time Buck (Holliman), the owner, is host to a group of ladies and gentlemen who turn day into night, complete with music, drinking, and dancing. (Dir: Theodore Flicker, 104 mins.)

Where the Lilies Bloom (1974)**** Julie Gholson, Jan Smithers, Harry Dean Stanton. A lovely, gentle, and altogether superior film for children and adults alike. Filmed on location in rural North Carolina, the touching story is about four children orphaned when their father dies. The plucky 14-year-old daughter (Gholson) assumes command of the household and conspires to keep the news of her father's passing from her neighbors for months. (Dir: William A. Graham, 97 mins.)

Where the Red Fern Grows (1974)**½ James Whitmore, Beverly Garland, Jack Ging, Stewart Petersen. Family fare that borrows liberally from Disney. Stewart Petersen is a young lad who wants nothing more than to own and train redbone hounds to be the best coon hunters in the county. He almost gets his wish. James Whitmore is quite good as the boy's philosophizing grandpa. (Dir: Norman Tokar, 108 mins.)

Where the Sidewalk Ends (1950)***½ Dana

Andrews, Gene Tierney, Gary Merrill. Director Otto Preminger reunited his leads from "Laura"—Andrews and Tierney—in a sizzling, brutal melodrama. Andrews is a hotheaded cop whose temper gets him into trouble when he kills a suspect; he then tries to frame a gangland figure for the crime. (95 mins.)

Where the Spies Are (Great Britain, 1965)*** David Niven, Françoise Dorleac. Diverting and frequently clever spy tale with a rather good performance by Niven as a doctor recruited for espionage service. Although this is hardly a James Bond adventure, Niven manages to acquit himself admirably against all the contrived obstacles the writers have placed in his way. One obstacle, Dorleac, is as appealing as any of the advertised scenery. (Dir: Val Guest, 110 mins.)

Where There's Life (1947)*** Bob Hope, Signe Hasso, William Bendix. Disc jockey becomes ruler of foreign kingdom in this zany Hope film that will appeal mainly to Bob's most ardent fans, and the youngsters. (Dir: Sidney Lanfield, 75 mins.)

Where Were You When the Lights Went Out? (1968)* Doris Day, Robert Morse, Terry-Thomas, Steve Allen, Patrick O'Neal. (Dir: Hy Averback, 95 mins.)

Where's Charley? (Great Britain, 1952)**** Ray Bolger, Allyn McLerie, Robert Shackleton. The musical version of the classic British farce "Charley's Aunt." Broadway hit boasts music and lyrics by Frank Loesser, and old and young alike will enjoy catching Ray Bolger in his show-stopper "Once in Love with Amy." (Dir: David Butler, 97 mins.)

Where's Poppa? (1970)***½ George Segal, Ruth Gordon, Trish Van Devere. Wild, imaginative black comedy about a bachelor (Segal) who schemes to eliminate his aging mother. Director Carl Reiner is a deft hand with sight gags, and septuagenarian scene stealer Gordon is a joy. (84 mins.)

Wherever She Goes (Australia, 1951)**½ Muriel Steinbeck, Suzanne Parrett. The true story of famed pianist Eileen Joyce, who rose to recognition from a childhood filled with hardship. Parrett plays Joyce. Production shortcomings, a sincere film with fine musical interludes played by Miss Joyce. (Dir: Michael S. Gordon, 82 mins.)

Which Way Is Up (1977)** Richard Pryor, Lonette McKee, Margaret Avery, Dewayne Jessie. Director Michael Schultz lacks narrative focus—the story makes no sense whatever. Pryor is a horny farm worker picking oranges in southern California. (84 mins.)

Which Way to the Front? (1970)** Director Jerry Lewis grinds these slapstick efforts out like hamburger. The comedy was left in the trenches. (84 mins.)

While the City Sleeps (1956)***½ Dana Andrews, Ida Lupino, Rhonda Fleming,

George Sanders, Vincent Price. A contest is announced at a New York newspaper: the reporter who catches the notorious Lipstick Killer will become the new editor. The sex killer becomes a sympathetic character, as director Fritz Lang reserves his venom for the desperately competitive reporters. (100 mins.)

Whirlpool (1949)*** Gene Tierney, Richard Conte, José Ferrer, Charles Bickford. An oddball thriller with Tierney as a kleptomaniac who falls under the spell of a mad hypnotist (Ferrer). Director Otto Preminger acquits himself well despite the general aura of absurdity. (97 mins.)

Whirlpool (Great Britain, 1959)*½ Juliette Greco, O. W. Fischer. (Dir: Lewis Allen, 95 mins.)

Whiskey and Sofa (West Germany, 1963)** Maria Schell, Karl Michael. Pretty architect enters a competition, plans to beat out her rival, who is a notorious wolf. Thin romantic comedy, nothing unusual. Dubbed in English. (Dir: Gunter Grawert, 87 mins.)

Whisky Galore—See: **Tight Little Island**

Whispering Footsteps (1943)***½ John Hubbard, Rita Quigley. A bank clerk fits the description of a mad killer, and his friends turn against him in fear and distrust. Excellent suspense melodrama deserves credit for such a neat job done on a small budget. (Dir: Howard Bretherton, 54 mins.)

Whispering Ghosts (1942)** Milton Berle, Brenda Joyce, John Carradine. Milton gets a few laughs out of this film but not enough for success. He's out to solve a sea captain's murder and recover some buried treasure. (Dir: Alfred L. Werker, 75 mins.)

Whispering Smith (1948)*** Alan Ladd, Robert Preston, Brenda Marshall. Railroad detective finds his best friend is in with bandits. Good western is nicely made, actionful. (Dir: Leslie Fenton, 88 mins.)

Whistle at Eaton Falls (1951)**½ Lloyd Bridges, Dorothy Gish, Ernest Borgnine. Union leader suddenly finds himself as manager of a plant, with the necessity of laying off men. Sincere but talky, rather slow drama. (Dir: Robert Slodmak, 96 mins.)

Whistle Down the Wind (Great Britain, 1962)**** Hayley Mills, Alan Bates. An almost perfect film about a trio of children who find an escaped criminal in their barn and mistake him to be Christ. Miss Mills and Alan Bates, as the convict, give excellent performances. Touching, honest, wonderfully directed and altogether recommended. (Dir: Bryan Forbes, 98 mins.)

Whistle Stop (1946)** George Raft, Ava Gardner, Victor McLaglen. Rather glum melodrama with Ava trying to help ne'er-do-well Raft while fighting off villainous nightclub owner McLaglen. (Dir: Leonide Moguy, 84 mins.)

Whistling in Brooklyn (1943)**½ Red Skelton, Ann Rutherford. Another in the fairly amusing comic detective series with Red again playing "The Fox." There's a lot of laughs in the scene where Red pitches against the Dodgers. (Dir: S. Sylvan Simon, 87 mins.)

Whistling in Dixie (1942)**½ Red Skelton, Ann Rutherford. Red's fans and the kids will like this mystery-comedy set in some old southern mansions and abandoned forts. (Dir: S. Sylvan Simon, 74 mins.)

Whistling in the Dark (1941)*** Red Skelton, Ann Rutherford. Red's first starring film and his fans will have a lot of fun with it. He's in the hands of killers and imprisoned in one of those Hollywood houses complete with sliding doors and hidden passageways. (Dir: S. Sylvan Simon, 77 mins.)

White Banners (1938)*** Claude Rains, Fay Bainter, Jackie Cooper, Bonita Granville. Miss Bainter's magnificent acting makes something out of this Lloyd C. Douglas morality fable. Very talky. (Dir: Edmund Goulding, 96 mins.)

White Buffalo, The (1977)*** Charles Bronson, Kim Novak, Clint Walker. Bronson is Wild Bill Hickok, officially retired but plagued by nightmares in which he's charged by a giant white buffalo. Bronson searches out the dream landscape to face what he calls, unflinchingly, his "armageddon." Will Sampson co-stars as an Indian Queequeg. (Dir: J. Lee Thompson, 97 mins.)

White Cargo (1942)** Hedy Lamarr, Walter Pidgeon, Frank Morgan. Boring tale of an Englishman who succumbs to a lovely native girl. Hedy is Tondelayo and she is gorgeous. (Dir: Richard Thorpe, 88 mins.)

White Christmas (1954)*** Bing Crosby, Danny Kaye, Rosemary Clooney, Vera-Ellen. Colorful package of holiday entertainment for the whole family—songs, dances, clowning, plus Irving Berlin's title tune. The cast fits perfectly into the lightweight story which merely serves as a framework for the 15 musical numbers. Remake of Bing's "Holiday Inn." (Dir: Michael Curtiz, 120 mins.)

White Cliffs of Dover, The (1944)*** Irene Dunne, Van Johnson. Well acted, occasionally slow but moving story of en America girl who marries an English lord in 1914. He dies in 1918 and the story, based on Alice Duer Miller's poem "The White Cliffs," follows her life in England. (Dir: Clarence Brown, 126 mins.)

White Corridors (Great Britain, 1951)*** Googie Withers, James Donald, Barry Jones, Petula Clark. Researcher is accidentally infected with disease germs, asks a lady doctor to try a new test on him. Behind-the-scenes medical drama showing routine in a hospital is well done; good performances, subplots tied together nicely. (Dir: Pat Jackson, 82 mins.)

White Dawn, The (1974)***½ Warren Oates, Timothy Bottoms, Lou Gossett. In re-creating the real-life story of a trio of whalers rescued after their boat is swamped, and cared for by a band of Baffin Island Eskimos in 1896, director Philip Kaufman has accomplished a logistical and dramatic miracle, eliciting superb performances from nonprofessional Eskimo hunters, their wives and children, and filming on location with no noticeable compromises. The story is a bit thin, despite its factual basis. (109 mins.)

White Feather (1955)** Robert Wagner, Debra Paget, Jeffrey Hunter, John Lund, Hugh O'Brian. Routine western with some action scenes for cowboys-and-Indian fans. Wagner plays a government man who tries to get a tribe of Cheyenne to move to a reservation. Debra Paget and blue-eyed Jeff Hunter play Indians. (Dir: Robert D. Webb, 102 mins.)

White Heat (1949)**** James Cagney, Virginia Mayo, Edmond O'Brien, Margaret Wycherly. Brutal, brilliant gangster saga with Cagney in his most flamboyant role, as mother-loving Cody Jarrett, the man with the cinema's strongest Oedipus complex. Mayo is the moll, O'Brien the T-man Judas, and Wycherly is mom. (Dir: Raoul Walsh, 114 mins.)

White Huntress (Great Britain, 1954)** Susan Stephen, Robert Urquhart. Good on-location photography in Kenya helps bolster this routine adventure about ivory hunters and their plans to cheat the natives. (Dir: George Breakston, 81 mins.)

White Laager, The (1978)*** White Africaners speak for themselves about their commitment to maintain apartheid, as director Peter Davis tells the history of white settlement from 1652 to the present. A UN-sponsored film.

White Lightning (1973)**½ Burt Reynolds, Jennifer Billingsley, Ned Beatty, Louise Latham, Bo Hopkins. The whole is less than the sum of its parts, which offer some sparkling moments in this fast-paced melodrama about murder, revenge and moonshine in the new South. Reynolds is a convict who's released in order to help the Feds nail sadistic-sheriff Beatty. (Dir: Joseph Sargent, 101 mins.)

White Line Fever (1975)**½ Jan-Michael Vincent, Kay Lenz, Slim Pickens, L. Q. Jones. Blue-collar revenge tragedy sends a young independent trucker (Vincent, stronger than usual) up against the entrenched graft and hoodlumism of the industry. Director Johnathan Kaplan is clearly in control of his pacing and editing. (89 mins.)

White Mama (MTV 1980)**½ Bette Davis, Ernest Harden, Jr., Eileen Heckart. The indomitable Davis as a poor widow forced to take in a young black street thief to make ends meet. Bette's "White Mama" barks out orders, only to make an about-face and to take orders when the going gets tough. Happy ending. (Dir: Jackie Cooper, 104 mins.)

White Nights (Italy, 1959)** Maria Schell, Marcello Mastroianni, Jean Marals. Despite this stellar line-up, this turgid m dodrama fails to generate any excitement. Miss Schell is cast as a very mixed-up creature who has two men's love. The photography strains for artistic effects and only adds to the confusion. (Dir: Luchino Visconti, 94 mins.)

White Slave Ship (France-Italy, 1962)** Pier Angeli, Edmund Purdom. Mutiny on a prison ship carrying girls from London jails en route to the colonies. A young doctor, also a prisoner, aids the captain in quelling it. Passable costume adventure dubbed in English. (Dir: Silvio Amadio, 92 mins.)

White Spider, The (West Germany, 1963)*½ Joachim Fuchsberger, Karin Dor, Horst Frank. (Dir: Harald Reinl, 105 mins.)

White Sun of the Desert, The (U.S.S.R., 1972)* (Dir: V. Motyl.)

White Tie and Tails (1946)**½ Dan Duryea, Ella Raines, William Bendix. A screwy comedy about a butler who takes charge of his employer's mansion when his employer goes on vacation. Deft performances. (Dir: Charles Barton, 81 mins.)

White Tower, The (1950)*** Glenn Ford, Valli, Claude Rains, Lloyd Bridges. Six people risk their lives to scale the Swiss Alps. Thrilling mountain-climbing melodrama. (Dir: Ted Tetzlaff, 98 mins.)

White Wall, The (Sweden, 1975)**** Harriet Andersson, Lena Nyman, Tomas Ponten. Insightful study of the female psyche, directed, written, and coedited by Stig Bjorkman. A 35-year-old divorced housewife anxiously searches for a job and male companionship and affection. Andersson, a familiar presence in Ingmar Bergman films, is profoundly touching. Memorable vignettes include a sensual encounter at a pinball machine and some amused chatter in the ladies' room at a singles dance club. (80 mins.)

White Warrior, The (Italy, Yugoslavia, 1959)*½ Steve Reeves, Giorgia Moll. (Dir: Riccardo Freda, 86 mins.)

White Witch Doctor (1953)**½ Robert Mitchum, Susan Hayward, Walter Slezak. Top Bwana (Mitchum) and his not so trusty second (Slezak) set out with titian-haired nurse (Hayward) into the darkest regions of Bakuba territory. Sweet Susan wants to bring the magic of modern medicine to the hostile savages, but Bad Bob and Wicked Walter are more interested in finding a hidden treasure of gold. The locale and action help some. (Dir: Henry Hathaway, 96 mins.)

White Zombie (1932)*** Bela Lugosi, Madge Bellamy. Sinister Lugosi wants beautiful Bellamy for himself, so they can rule the zombie jungle empire together. Extremely atmospheric, although laughable at times, this archetypical horror thriller still holds some interest. (Dir: Victor Halperin, 73 mins.)

Who Are You, Mr. Sorge? (France, 1960)***½ Jacques Berthier, Thomas Holtzman. Lengthy but frequently fascinating account of the master spy who played both ends against the middle in working for the Russians and the Germans and was involved in obtaining the secret of Japan's attack on Pearl Harbor. Real-life story is superior to most fictional ones. Dubbed in English. (Dir: Yves Ciampi, 135 mins.)

Who Does She Think She Is? (1974)**½ "She" is novelist-painter Rosalyn Drexler, seen improvising scenes for a low-budget movie, at home with her family, and singing at a small New York City nightclub. Through the chaos, glimpses of wit and intelligence are seen. (Dirs: Patricia Lewis Jaffe, Gaby Rodgers, 60 mins.)

Who Done It? (1942)*½ Bud Abbott, Lou Costello, Don Porter, William Gargan. (Dir: Erle C. Kenton, 77 mins.)

Who Is Harry Kellerman and Why Is He Saying Those Terrible Things About Me? (1971)*** Dustin Hoffman, Barbara Harris, Jack Warden. Hoffman is wonderful as a pop composer who is bedeviled by an unknown man who is out to ruin his reputation—or is he? Uneven but often acerbic and funny. (Dir: Ulu Grosbard, 108 mins.)

Who Is Killing the Great Chefs of Europe? (Great Britain, 1978)*** George Segal, Jacqueline Bisset, Robert Morley. Segal is a fast-food businessman in constant pursuit of his lovely master dessert chef ex-wife, while murders on the international cuisine set multiply. As a mystery it's so-so, but as a romantic escapade it's quite digestible. Morley as a gourmet magazine publisher who seems to interrupt every romantic moment shared by the film's leads. Witty screenplay by Peter Stone. (Dir: Ted Kotcheff, 115 mins.)

Who Is Killing the Stuntmen?—See: **Stunts**

Who Is the Black Dahlia? (MTV 1975)**½ Lucie Arnaz, Efrem Zimbalist, Jr., Macdonald Carey, Donna Mills. Sensational 1947 Los Angeles murder is exhumed and receives fairly interesting treatment. Lucie Arnaz stars as the mixed-up, movie-struck girl who ends up a corpse in a vacant lot. Efrem Zimbalist, Jr. portrays detective Harry Hansen, a patient man who must check out every nut in Los Angeles, the many would-be confessors to the lurid crime. (Dir: Joseph Pevney, 96 mins.)

Who Killed Mary Whats'ername? (1971)** Red Buttons, Sylvia Miles, Alice Playten. The murder of a Greenwich Village prostitute leads former lightweight champion, now diabetic Red Buttons, out of the boredom of retirement to play amateur sleuth. Good cast is wasted on a screenplay whose main ingredient is plot loopholes. (Dir: Ernie Pintoff, 90 mins.)

Who Killed Teddy Bear? (1965)** Sal Mineo, Juliet Prowse, Jan Murray, Elaine Stritch. Sexually psychotic busboy preys on disco dancer, as cop trails. Low-key direction creates a portrait of obsession, with some suspense. (Dir: Joseph Cates, 91 mins.)

Who Slew Auntie Roo? (U.S.-Great Britain, 1971)**½ Shelley Winters, Mark Lester, Ralph Richardson, Hugh Griffith, Lionel Jeffries. Another in the line of "who" films casting flamboyant actresses as macabre, slightly mad ladies in gothic tales. Winters as an American widow living in a large house in England, takes her cue from the wicked witch in "Hansel and Gretel" and tries to lure young children into her lair. It gets pretty silly at times, but Miss Winters rolls her eyes and shrieks with the best of them. (Dir: Curtis Harrington, 91 mins.)

Who Stole the Body?—See: Body Is Missing, The

Who Was Maddox? (Great Britain, 1964)** Bernard Lee, Jack Watling, Suzanne Lloyd. Executive rivalry at a publishing house leads to blackmail, murder, and robbery. Ordinary Edgar Wallace mystery. (Dir: Geoffrey Nethercott, 62 mins.)

Who Was That Lady? (1960)**½ Tony Curtis, Dean Martin, Janet Leigh, James Whitmore, Barbara Nichols. Fast-paced comedy romp that fizzles out before the finale. Tony Curtis and Dean Martin play men-about-town, one married and one not, and their adventures lead to complications found only in French farces—especially those based on bad Broadway musicals. (Dir: George Sidney, 115 mins.)

Whole Town's Talking, The (1935)*** Edward G. Robinson, Jean Arthur, Wallace Ford, Donald Meek. Robinson, as a mousy clerk, discovers that he's the look-alike of a notorious gangster. John Ford's direction of comedy has wit and easy grace. (90 mins.)

Whole Truth, The (Great Britain, 1958)** Stewart Granger, Donna Reed, George Sanders. A who-dun-it with very little suspense. Plot concerns an actress' murder which is pinned on an American producer whose wife refuses to believe he did it. (Dir: John Guillermin, 84 mins.)

Whole Truth, The—See: Blind Justice

Whole World Is Watching, The (1969)** Burl Ives, Joseph Campanella, James Farentino, Hal Holbrook. Still another plot film for a TV series. Ives, Campanella, and Farentino play a trio of lawyers, each with a different temperament and style. They take on the defense of a leader of a college student uprising arrested for the murder of a campus policeman. There are numerous scenes in which the students and the faculty get to air their views, but no sensible conclusions emerge. (Dir: Richard Colla, 97 mins.)

Who'll Save Our Children? (MTV 1978)*** Shirley Jones, Len Cariou. A childless couple raise two deserted youngsters in this tale of adjustment. After they fall in love with the kids, they must face the trauma of losing them. Their emotion is believable. (Dir: George Schaefer, 104 mins.)

Who'll Stop the Rain? (1978)*** Nick Nolte, Michael Moriarty, Tuesday Weld. Director Karel Reisz turns from introspective psychodrama to action with fists and machine guns, in a story about two amateur heroin smugglers (Nolte and Moriarty). Reisz's elliptical way with a plot line is more pretentious than helpful. (126 mins.)

Wholly Moses (1980)** Dudley Moore, Richard Pryor, John Houseman, Dom DeLuise, Madeline Kahn. Director Gary Weis's biblical parody is dim and derivative, shot in a bland close-up style that neutralizes Moore's brilliance as a physical performer. Better left in the bulrushes. (104 mins.)

Whoopee (1930)*** Eddie Cantor, Eleanor Hunt. Potent combination of Samuel Goldwyn and Florenz Ziegfeld (producers), Busby Berkely (dance director), and Cantor (in his original Broadway role) will seem awful to some, a lot of fun to others. Worth seeing for the score, including "Making Whoopee," and Cantor himself. Look for Betty Grable and Virginia Bruce among the Goldwyn Girls. Remade as "Up in Arms." (Dir: Thornton Freeland, 92 mins.)

Who's Afraid of Virginia Woolf (1966)**** Elizabeth Taylor, Richard Burton, Sandy Dennis, George Segal. Edward Albee's brilliant, biting play about the love-hate relationship between a middle-aged, resigned college professor and his vitriolic, denigrating, yet seductive wife is turned into a movie experience to be cherished. It's a cinematic feast thanks to Mike Nichols' astute debut as director; Taylor's towering portrayal as the foul-mouthed Martha (Academy Award); Burton's magnificent portrait of the tortured professor; Dennis's Oscar-winning performance as the nervous young bride (129 mins.)

Who's Been Sleeping in My Bed? (1963) **½ Dean Martin, Elizabeth Montgomery, Carol Burnett, Martin Balsam, Jill St. John. The kind of movie that often looks better on TV than it did originally in theaters. It's about a TV idol whose fiancée wants to get him hitched before his affinity for the girls becomes too strong. Carol Burnett in her first movie role has an hilarious scene near the end. The dialogue and situations are frequently amusing, and the supporting cast includes some fine performers. (Dir: Daniel Mann, 103 mins.)

Who's Got the Action? (1962)**½ Dean Martin, Lana Turner, Walter Matthau, Eddie Albert. All the familiar jokes and characters involved in the world of a compulsive horseplayer are trotted out in this occasionally diverting comedy. Lana Turner and Dean Martin are around as attractive window dressing, but Walter Matthau steals the movie with his broad interpretation of an underworld biggie. The plot has Lana trying to curtail hubby Dean's out-of-hand betting habits by secretly joining forces with a bookie. (Dir: Daniel Mann, 93 mins.)

Who's Minding the Mint? (1967)*** Milton Berle, Joey Bishop, Jack Gilford, Walter Brennan, Dorothy Provine, Jim Hutton. Working comic Howard Morris has directed a zany, spirited romp that capitalizes on the performing talents of a large bunch of his second-banana pals. Hutton plays a charming young man who works in the U.S. Mint. When he accidentally burns a large batch of new bills, he sets up an operation to replace them. (97 mins.)

Who's Minding the Store? (1963)*½ Jerry Lewis, Jill St. John, John McGiver, Agnes Moorehead. (Dir: Frank Tashlin, 90 mins.)

Why Bother to Knock? (Great Britain, 1961)** Elke Sommer, Richard Todd, Judith Anderson. Young man on the make indiscrimately gives out keys to his apartment, but all the girls show up at the same time. Lumbering comedy wastes the talents of a fine cast. Some amusing moments, but not enough. (Dir: Cyril Frankel, 88 mins.)

Why Must I Die? (1960)*½ Terry Moore, Debra Paget. (Dir: Roy Del Ruth, 86 mins.)

Why Shoot the Teacher (Canada, 1976)*** Bud Cort, Samantha Eggar, Kenneth Griffith. This drama, set in Saskatchewan, was successful commercially in Canada. It is about a teacher who arrives in a tiny, freezing town and meets with an equally chilly reception. Some tension and romance develop. Cort as the comic-romantic teacher is paired with Eggar. (Dir: Silvio Narizzano, 99 mins.)

Why Would I Lie? (1980)** Treat Williams, Lisa Eichhorn, Jocelyn Brando, Gabriel Swann. Williams plays a free spirit who preaches the joys of therapeutic fabrication; he becomes a social worker, acquires a six-year-old dependent (Swann), and pursues a cranky feminist (Eichhorn) who has a deep, dark secret. Larry Peerce directs, badly. (105 mins.)

Wichita (1955)**½ Joel McCrea, Vera Miles, Lloyd Bridges. Wyatt Earp is once again the lawman who brings law and order to a small western town which is overrun with outlaws. The cast is good and action fans will not feel cheated. (Dir: Jacques Tourneur, 81 mins.)

Wicked Dreams of Paula Schultz, The (1968)* Elke Sommer, Bob Crane, Werner Klemperer. (Dir: George Marshall, 113 mins.)

Wicked Go to Hell, The (France, 1956)* Marina Vlady, Henri Vidal, Serge Reggiani. (Dir: Robert Hossein, 74 mins.)

Wicked Lady, The (Great Britain, 1945)**½ Margaret Lockwood, James Mason, Michael Rennie, Patricia Roc. Scheming woman takes over all the men who cross her path, eventually joins a highwayman as his aide. Theatrical costume drama is lifted a bit by Mason's tongue-in-cheek portrayal of a bandit. (Dir: Leslie Arliss, 98 mins.)

Wicked Ones, The—See: **Teenage Wolf Pack**

Wide Blue Road, The (Italy, 1957)*½ Yves Montand, Alida Valli. (Dir: Gillo Pontecorvo, 90 mins.)

Widow (MTV 1976)**½ Michael Learned, Bradford Dillman, Farley Granger, Robert Lansing. Moderately absorbing drama based on Lynn Caine's autobiographical best-seller. Michael Learned plays the withdrawn widow attempting to cope with two young children, a lack of money, and a new suitor. (Dir: J. Lee Thompson, 98 mins.)

Wife Versus Secretary (1936)** Clark Gable, Jean Harlow, Myrna Loy, James Stewart. Title tells the whole story and, if it wasn't for its big name stars, this would have been an ordinary second feature. (Dir: Clarence Brown, 89 mins.)

Wifemistress (Italy, 1977)*** Laura Antonelli, Marcello Mastroianni, Leonard Mann. A woman confines herself to bed with psychosomatic paralysis while her enlightened husband finances radical causes and writes suffragist pamphlets. She comes into her own after he goes underground after a political murder. In this feminist parable the men are assumed to be responsible for every result. Director Marco Vicario tells his tale well, and the stars are charming in their Latin stubbornness. (106 mins.)

Wilby Conspiracy, The (1975)**½ Michael Caine, Sidney Poitier, Nicol Williamson, Persis Khambatta. Much of this adventure drama set in Africa is predictable, but Caine's glib engineer and his relationship with Poitier's black revolutionary make up for the script's inadequacies. Williamson shines as a racist policeman who sanctions apartheid. (Dir: Ralph Nelson, 104 mins.)

Wild Affair, The (Great Britain, 1965)* Nancy Kwan, Terry-Thomas, Victor Spinetti, Bud Flanagan. (Dir: John Krish, 88 mins.)

Wild and the Free, The (MTV 1980)** Granville Van Dusen, Linda Gray. Light entertainment in which wild chimpanzees steal the show from the humans. Good-looking scientists Van Dusen and Gray (wooden as a butcher's block) save research chimps from radiation experiments by returning them to Africa. (Dir: James Hill, 104 mins.)

Wild and the Innocent, The (1959)**½ Audie Murphy, Sandra Dee, Gilbert Roland, Joanne Dru. Slightly offbeat story of a fur trader, a wild mountain waif and their misadventures in town during a Fourth of July celebration. Never quite makes the top grade but rates credit for a good try. (Dir: Jack Sher, 84 mins.)

Wild and the Willing, The (Great Britain, 1962)*½ Virginia Maskell, Paul Rogers, Ian McShane, Samantha Eggar. (Dir: Ralph Thomas, 113 mins.)

Wild and Wonderful (1964)** Tony Curtis, Christine Kaufmann, Larry Storch, Marty Ingels. When a French poodle with a thirst for liquor is found by an American in Europe, and the owner's pretty daughter goes looking for the pooch—you have a typically uninspired light comedy. The poodle is cute. (Dir: Michael Anderson, 88 mins.)

Wild and Woolly (MTV 1979)** Chris DeLisle, Susan Begelow, Elyssa Davalos. A failed pilot film which hoped to cash in on the success of "Charlie's Angels," series. Set in old frontier days, three lovelies parlay their talents to stem the tide of villainy. (Dir: George Swinson, 104 mins.)

Wild Angels, The (1966)* Peter Fonda, Nancy Sinatra, Bruce Dern, Gayle Hunnicutt, Diane Ladd. (93 mins.)

Wild Bunch, The (1969)***½ William Holden, Ernest Borgnine, Robert Ryan. Holden incarnates weary, honorable cutthroatery, while Ryan plays the consummate man-who-watches. Director Sam Peckinpah delivers violence on the Texas-Mexican border in '13 with cynical band of outlaws joining a rebel Mexican general against law, order, and the Mexican army. (135 mins.)

Wild Child, The (France, 1970)**** Jean-Pierre Cargol, Jean Daste, François Truffaut. A beautiful essay on teaching, and the giving, and eventually receiving, of love. "The Wild Child" is quite literally that—a baby abandoned in the woods of France and discovered years later, around 1797, by a local farmer. Director Truffaut himself portrays, and very gracefully too, the dedicated Dr. Jean Itard, a Frenchman who undertook the formidable task of training the brutish child. (90 mins.)

Wild for Kicks—See: **Beat Girl**

Wild Geese, The (Great Britain, 1978)** Richard Burton, Richard Harris, Roger Moore, Hardy Kruger. Based on a true-story novel, the film is shallow, romanticized, and oversensationalized. The leads are four officers hired by a British banker (Stewart Granger) to command a mercenary force attempting to rescue the president of an emerging African nation. (Dir: Andrew V. McLaglen, 135 mins.)

Wild Geese Calling (1941)** Henry Fonda, Joan Bennett, Warren William. Set in 1890, this story of a man with the wanderlust is sensitively told but is a dull film. Sleep may call before the geese. (Dir: John Brahm, 77 mins.)

Wild Guitar (1962)* Arch Hall, Jr., Cash Flagg, William Watters. (Dir: Ray Dennis Steckler, 87 mins.)

Wild Heart, The—See: **Gone to Earth**

Wild Heritage (1958)**½ Will Rogers, Jr., Maureen O'Sullivan, Troy Donahue, Rod McKuen. Two pioneer families trek west to make their home in a new land, meet with many adventures along the way. Refreshing change from ordinary western fare moves leisurely but pleasantly. (Dir: Charles Haas, 78 mins.)

Wild in the Country (1961)** Elvis Presley, Hope Lange, Tuesday Weld, Millie Perkins, John Ireland. Rural boy is saved from delinquency by a female social worker, who encourages him in his writing talent. Wild in the country is boring at home. (Dir: Philip Dunne, 114 mins.)

Wild in the Sky—See: **Black Jack**

Wild in the Streets (1968)** Christopher Jones, Shelley Winters, Diane Varsi. Inept satire about a rock star (Jones) elected president after the voting age is lowered to 14. Predictable ironies follow—those over 30 are banished to concentration camps and fed LSD, etc. Winters, as Jones's mother, gives the most tasteless performance of her career, while Barry Shear directs as if he'd seen "Dr. Strangelove" too many times. (97 mins.)

Wild Is the Wind (1957)*** Anna Magnani, Anthony Quinn, Anthony Franciosa. Familiar triangle (Magnani is to marry Quinn, but she and his ward, Franciosa, are attracted) is deftly handled by director George Cukor. Locale: a contemporary Nevada sheep ranch. (114 mins.)

Wild 90 (1968)*½ Norman Mailer, Buzz Farber, Mickey Knox. (90 mins.)

Wild North, The (1952)** Stewart Granger, Cyd Charisse, Wendell Corey. He-man adventure drama about fur trappers and their many fights with nature. Cyd Charisse is wasted as the love interest in a very small role. (Dir: Andrew Marton, 97 mins.)

Wild One, The (1954)***½ Marlon Brando, Mary Murphy, Lee Marvin. Good, sleazy movie. Brando and his motorcycle gang invade a small town. Laslo Benedek directed almost as inarticulately as Brando speaks—but lacking the latter's sense of style. (79 mins.)

Wild Party, The (1929)*** Clara Bow, Fredric March, Jack Oakie. Bow is a headstrong college girl out to snag a professor (March), with or without marriage. Film holds the interest and is in the main well directed, considering the newness of the microphone. (Dir: Dorothy Arzner, 78 mins.)

Wild Party, The (1956)** Anthony Quinn, Carol Ohmart, Kathryn Grant. Former football hero on the skids joins a group of beatniks and holds a couple captive. Way-out drama features some hipster dialogue that's practically unintelligible but has some suspense. (Dir: Harry Horner, 81 mins.)

Wild Party, The (1974)**½ James Coco, Raquel Welch, Perry King. A good try that just didn't work. Coco stars as a silent-movie comedy star down on his luck, trying for a comeback by giving a big party at which he plans to show his latest movie. The party turns into a wild, sexual free-for-all, and Coco ends up killing his mistress, played by Welch, and her latest male companion (King). Loosely based on the real-life Fatty Arbuckle scandal. There's good acting here, especially by

Coco and Welch. (Dir: James Ivory, 100 mins.)

Wild Ride, The (1960)* Jack Nicholson, Georgianna Carter. (Dir: Harvey Berman, 63 mins.)

Wild River (1960)**** Montgomery Clift, Lee Remick, Jo Van Fleet, Bruce Dern (debut). TVA agent Clift must evict a matriarch (Van Fleet) from her family island on the Tennessee branch of the Mississippi in order to complete a dam project. Probably director Elia Kazan's finest and deepest film. Remick as Van Fleet's widowed daughter gives an affecting performance. (110 mins.)

Wild Rovers (1971)*** William Holden, Ryan O'Neal, Karl Malden, Joe Don Baker, Rachel Roberts. Holden's crisp, strong performance as a cowboy on the shady side of 50 makes this unusual western drama interesting. He and O'Neal make an unlikely pair as they team up for a bank robbery and the inevitable getaway trek to Mexico. There's a smattering of the expected western ingredients throughout but it's basically a character study of the old and young cowboy, united in their plight. (Dir: Blake Edwards, 109 mins.)

Wild Seed, The (1965)** Michael Parks, Celia Kaye. Young drifter befriends a teen-age girl running away from her foster parents; together they seek happiness. Slow-moving drama uses younger players to advantage, but the story's no help. (Dir: Brian Hutton, 99 mins.)

Wild Stallion (1952)**½ Ben Johnson, Edgar Buchanan, Martha Hyer. Orphan grows up obsessed with the idea of recapturing a wild stallion he lost as a boy. Pleasant outdoor drama, a welcome relief from the usual run western. (Dir: Lewis D. Collins, 72 mins.)

Wild Stampede (Mexico, 1959)** Luis Aguilar, Christiane Martel. Outlaws and revolutionaries fight for a valuable herd of wild horses. Passable outdoor action drama helped by picturesque photography. Dubbed in English. (Dir: Raul de Anda, 77 mins.)

Wild Strawberries (Sweden, 1967)***½ Victor Sjostrom, Ingrid Thulin, Bibi Andersson. Director Ingmar Bergman's landmark film. Valedictory performance of Sweden's first great director and star (Sjostrom) as an old professor taking stock of his life as he rides in a car to get an honorary degree. (A bickering couple in the car presage Edward Albee.) (90 mins.)

Wild, Wild Planet (Italy, 1966)**½ Tony Russel, Lisa Gastoni, Franco Nero. Complicated science fiction about a mad scientist. The deranged man likes to spend his time kidnapping specimens from Earth and grafting and transplanting.... English dubbing better than usual. (Dir: Anthony Dawson [Antonio Margheriti], 93 mins.)

Wild Wild West Revisited, The (MTV 1979)**½ Robert Conrad, Ross Martin, Harry Morgan, René Auberjonois. Return to the old TV series starring Conrad and

Martin as a wily, unorthodox pair of 19th-century government secret agents. Cloning is the subject of this wild and woolly case. (Dir: Burt Kennedy, 104 mins.)

Wild Women (MTV 1970)*½ Hugh O'Brian, Anne Francis, Marilyn Maxwell. (Dir: Don Taylor, 73 mins.)

Wild Youth (1961)*½ Robert Hutton, Steve Rowland, Carol Ohmart. (Dir: John Schreyer, 73 mins.)

Wildcats on the Beach (Italy, 1962)** Alberto Sordi, Rita Gam, Elsa Martinelli, Georges Marchal. Four separate stories taking place on the Côte d'Azur, European playground. Some amusing moments thanks to Sordi, but the plots are insignificant, the pace slow. Dubbed in English. (Dir: Vittorio Sala, 85 mins.)

Wilderness Family, Part 2, The (1978)*** Robert Logan, Susan Damante Shaw, Heather Rattray. Pleasant, harmless outing for the young ones. Sequel to "Adventures of a Wilderness Family," one of the more successful independent features of the '70s. Filmed in Crested Butte, Colo. In part 2 the family, all sunshine and wholesomeness, survive a bitter winter. (Dir: Frank Zuniga, 104 mins.)

Will Penny (1968)***½ Charlton Heston, Joan Hackett, Donald Pleasence, Lee Majors, Bruce Dern. Memorable, a quiet Western with action, not for action's sake, but growing out of the character development.... Saga of a saddle-worn cowboy (Heston) who tries to stay uninvolved and peaceful despite interfering circumstances. Joan Hackett registers strongly as a young frontier woman who wants to build a new life for her son and herself. There's also excellent photographs throughout. Underrated film which never got the attention it deserved, written and directed by Tom Gries. (109 mins.)

Will Success Spoil Rock Hunter? (1957) **** Tony Randall, Jayne Mansfield, Joan Blondell, Groucho Marx. Director Frank Tashlin's brilliant satire of Eisenhower age. Rockwell Hunter (Randall) becomes the hottest ad executive in town by signing up a bosomy movie star (Mansfield) to promote Stay-Put lipstick ("for those oh-so-kissable lips!"). Hilarious from the first frame. (94 mins.)

Willa (MTV 1979)*** Deborah Raffin, Clu Gulager, Diane Ladd, Nancy Marchand. Willa (Raffin), a waitress at a hash joint, mother of two young children and a third on the way, whose husband has left her and whose mother is an alcoholic, is going to be a trucker come hell or high water. It's a little hard to be sympathetic with her dream, since it means leaving her children with her drunken mother and taking her newborn baby along with her on trucking jobs. (Dirs: Joan Darling, Claudio Guzman, 104 mins.)

Willard (1971)** Bruce Davidson, Ernest Borgnine, Sondra Locke. The hit movie about a young man who trains rats to revenge him on those he hates. For hardcore rat fans only. Based on Stephen Gilbert's novel "Ratman's Notebooks." (Dir: Daniel Mann, 95 mins.)

Willy Wonka & The Chocolate Factory (1971)** Gene Wilder, Jack Albertson. One of those boring musicals that kids are taken to by their parents. Based on Roald Dahl's children's book "Charlie and the Chocolate Factory." (Dir: Mel Stuart, 94 mins.)

Wilma (MTV 1977)*** Cicely Tyson, Shirley Jo Finney. When Wilma Rudolph (Finney), triple Olympic gold medal winner in '60, was a little girl, one leg was crippled by pneumonia and scarlet fever. Quietly paced scenes where she is lovingly massaged by her adoring mother (Tyson). The warmth and support Wilma receives from her family give her the necessary drive to exercise her leg until it is not only normally active, but remarkably strong. Some of the later scenes about her marred personal life are sentimental. (Dir: Bud Greenspan, 104 mins.)

Wilmar 8 (1980)***½ Documentary about eight brave women who staged and lost the first bank strike in Minnesota history when they were told they would never earn as much as their male counterparts "because they were women." We see them walking the picket line in −55° weather, getting no support from the townspeople of tiny Wilmar (although the bank closed after two years of picketing), and getting only lukewarm support from the international unions, which staged support demonstrations and gave a little money but refused to sign them up.

Wilson (1944)**** Alexander Knox, Geraldine Fitzgerald, Charles Coburn, Vincent Price. Biography of our WW I president is a powerful story, superbly performed and graphically proving his great philosophy and foresight. Film begins with Wilson at Princeton and follows him all the way to his futile attempts to make us part of the League of Nations. (Dir: Henry King, 154 mins.)

Winchester 73 (1950)***½ James Stewart, Stephen McNally, Shelley Winters, Dan Duryea. Stewart wins one of the legendary rifles in a marksmanship contest, then uses it to track down the man who killed his father (his brother!—McNally). Director Anthony Mann pursues the revenge theme with Elizabethan fury. (92 mins.)

Winchester 73 (MTV 1967)** Tom Tryon, John Saxon, Joan Blondell. Remade, revised version of the exciting Jimmy Stewart western lacks the tautness of the original. Story of a renegade after a valuable rifle moves sluggishly, is just another routine western. (Dir: Herschel Daugherty, 97 mins.)

Wind Across the Everglades (1958)***½ Burl Ives, Christopher Plummer, Gypsy Rose Lee, George Voskovec, Emmett Kelly. Plummer is a Wildlife Service investigator and Ives is the enigmatic king of the swamps in director Nicholas Ray's strange film about Plummer's attempts to save the natural beauty of the Florida wilds in the early part of the century. Screenplay by Budd Schulberg. Color. (93 mins.)

Wind and the Lion, The (1975)*** Sean Connery, Candice Bergen, Brian Keith, John Huston. Excursion into America's protoimperialist era ('04). Bergen is an American lady abducted by Berber bandit, autodidact, and self-proclaimed deity Connery, while Teddy Roosevelt (Keith) dispatches the marines to get her back. Music by Jerry Goldsmith. (Dir: John Milius, 119 mins.)

Wind Cannot Read, The (Great Britain, 1958)**½ Dirk Bogarde, Yoko Tani, Ronald Lewis. Far Eastern color highlights uneven tale of British pilot in WW II and his romance with a Japanese woman training him for language duty. Bogarde and Tani are charming as the lovers. Together with the sensitive direction, they avoid many sentimental pitfalls in the trite plot. (Dir: Ralph Thomas, 115 mins.)

Windjammer (1958)** Capt. Yngvar Kjelstrup and the crew of the S.S. "Christian Radich," Arthur Fiedler and the Boston Pops Orchestra, Pablo Casals, Wilbur de Paris's New Orleans jazz band. The old Cinemiracle adventure tale cut down. Story about sailors on a full-masted training ship at work and at play around the world. (Dirs: Louis de Rochemont III, Bill Colleran, 127 mins.)

Windom's Way (Great Britain, 1957)*** Peter Finch, Mary Ure. Doctor in a remote Malay village tries to prevent the oppressed natives from going Communist. Absorbing drama with some food for thought. (Dir: Ronald Neame, 108 mins.)

Window, The (1949)***½ Bobby Driscoll, Arthur Kennedy, Ruth Roman, Barbara Hale. Child witnesses a murder, but no one will believe him. Terrifically tense, suspenseful melodrama. Special Oscar, Driscoll. (Dir: Ted Tetzlaff, 73 mins.)

Window to the Sky, A—See: **Other Side of the Mountain, The**

Windows (1980)** Talia Shire, Elizabeth Ashley, Joseph Cortese. Cinematographer Gordon Willis ("The Godfather") debuts as a director with a thriller as dim as his patented underlit photography. The lurid plot (with Ashley as a lesbian preying on Shire) plays out with tired predictability. So vague are the characters that Willis's atmosphere shots take precedence over the action—the picture turns into a documentary about the Brooklyn Bridge. (96 mins.)

Winds of Change (Japan, 1978)*** A Japanese animated feature based on themes from Ovid's "Metamorphoses," edited to accommodate American youth audiences. (Dir: Takashi, 86 mins.)

Winds of Kitty Hawk, The (MTV 1978)***½ Michael Moriarty, David Huffman. A loving tribute to the Wright Brothers' first flight. The talented Moriarty holds your attention as dogged dreamer Wilbur, but the real stars are the fragile gliders and facsimiles of the first motor-powered planes. The drama succeeds in re-creating the wonder of the Wrights flying like birds in their flimsy craft. (Dir: E.W. Swackhamer, 104 mins.)

Windwalker (1980)***½ Trevor Howard, Nick Ramus, James Remar. About the rivalry between the Cheyenne and Crow nations. An authentic drama of American Indians before the whites came. Set in the late 18th century with only Indian characters (and actors, except Howard in the title role) and dialogue in Crow and Cheyenne (with English subtitles and narration). Director Kieth Merrill has made an attractive, intelligent low-budget independent film. (108 mins.)

Wing and a Prayer (1944)*** Don Ameche, Dana Andrews. Story of Navy pilots aboard a carrier and their wartime heroism is a good action drama, well acted and directed. (Dir: Henry Hathaway, 97 mins.)

Winged Victory (1944)***½ Lon McCallister, Jeanne Crain, Edmond O'Brien, Judy Holliday. Moss Hart's stirring tribute to the air corps is a well done and entertaining film. You'll get a kick out of watching the all-airmen cast (except for the girls) in action. Watch for Peter Lind Hayes, Red Buttons, Gary Merrill, Barry Nelson and Lee J. Cobb. (Dir: George Cukor, 130 mins.)

Wings (1927)**** Clara Bow, Charles Rogers, Richard Arlen, Gary Cooper, Hedda Hopper. One of the most exciting silent dramas, featuring some of the best aerial photography and dogfighting to be seen. About American pilots in WW I. Cooper is seen briefly but to good advantage, and Bow gets to Europe as a driver to be near her boyfriend. Both director William A. Wellman and screenwriter John Monk Saunders were veterans of the Lafayette Escadrille unit which fought in Europe. Winner of the first Oscar as Best Picture. (130 mins.)

Wings and the Woman (Great Britain, 1942)*** Anna Neagle, Robert Newton. Story of Jim and Amy Mollison, renowned airplane pilots. Good biographical drama. (Dir: Herbert Wilcox, 94 mins.)

Wings in the Dark (1935)**½ Cary Grant, Myrna Loy, Roscoe Karns. Corny but well-acted melodrama about a test pilot who is accidentally blinded. He makes a life for himself and his girl (a lady pilot—what else?), with lots of aerial photography and thrills on the way. (Dir: James Flood, 75 mins.)

Wings of Eagles, The (1957)**½ John Wayne, Dan Dailey, Maureen O'Hara, Ward Bond, Edmund Lowe. He-man Wayne brawls and grins his way through this robust comedy-drama about Commander "Spig" Wead, who started as a barnstormer and ended up a war hero. The first half of the film contains most of the comedy and is by far the best part. Dan Dailey and Wayne's favorite female co-star, Maureen O'Hara, are adequate in support. (Dir: John Ford, 110 mins.)

Wings of Fire (1967)*½ Suzanne Pleshette, James Farentino, Ralph Bellamy, Lloyd Nolan, Juliet Mills. (Dir: David Lowell Rich, 99 mins.)

Wings of the Hawk (1953)** Van Heflin, Julia Adams, Abbe Lane. Predictable adventure set in Mexico involving renegades and their efforts to take over the government. Van Heflin is hardly the dashing hero type and seems rather uncomfortable in that pose. (Dir: Budd Boetticher, 81 mins.)

Wings of the Morning (Great Britain, 1937)**½ Henry Fonda, Annabella. Gypsies, romance and horsemanship in modern Ireland. Studied, often captivating romantic drama. Songs by the great tenor John McCormack. First British film in Technicolor. (Dir: Harold D. Schuster, 89 mins.)

Wings over the World (1978)*** Paul McCartney, Linda McCartney. Former Beatle Paul McCartney and his wife Linda tour with the Wings in '76. Concerts in Australia, the U.K., and the U.S., featuring some of the group's most popular songs, such as "Silly Love Songs" and "Live and Let Die." (78 mins.)

Winner Take All (MTV 1975)**½ Shirley Jones, Laurence Luckinbill, Joan Blondell, Sylvia Sidney. Director Paul Bogart deserves credit for his handling of this story about a compulsive gambler—a housewife this time. Jones plays the addict, frantically attempting to raise the money she has gambled away out of her husband's savings. (100 mins.)

Winning (1969)*** Paul Newman, Joanne Woodward, Robert Wagner, Richard Thomas. A credible drama of professional car racing. Newman, a winner on the track, is less heroic in his personal life after he meets and weds divorcee Woodward. Wagner is the rival driver who servies for Miss Woodward's affection. The racing sequences leading to the Indianapolis 500 are superbly staged, and the cast are first-rate. The massive car crash is the real McCoy from the '68 smashup during the Indianapolis 500. (Dir: James Goldstone, 123 mins.)

Winning Team, The (1952)**½ Doris Day, Ronald Reagan, Frank Lovejoy. Baseball pitcher Grover Cleveland Alexander's biography. Both Doris Day and Ronald Reagan have trouble in this not too convincing film. (Dir: Lewis Seiler, 98 mins.)

Winslow Boy, The (Great Britain, 1948) **** Robert Donat, Margaret Leighton, Cedric Hardwicke. A noted lawyer is engaged to defend a boy accused of stealing at school. Literate, wonderfully well acted drama, excellent. Donat is superb. (Dir: Anthony Asquith, 97 mins.)

Winter Carnival (1939)**½ Ann Sheridan, Richard Carlson. An on-again-off-again romance between a professor and a glamor girl is played against the background of the famous winter carnival at Dartmouth University. Good skiing scenes, not much on story. (Dir: Charles F. Reisner, 100 mins.)

Winter Kills (1979)** Anthony Perkins, Richard Boone, Jeff Bridges, John Huston. Another unenjoyable assassination exploitation thriller. Only the innumerable cameo appearances provide any structure. (Writer-Dir: William Richert, 97 mins.)

Winter Light (Sweden, 1963)***½ Ingrid Thulin, Gunnar Bjornstrand, Max von Sydow. Disillusioned pastor watches his congregation crumble along with his faith. Director Bergman's chilling exploration of man's spiritual debasement, the poverty of human, Christian interdependence, and the relation of love to God. A lean, powerful film. Second in the trilogy of which "Through a Glass Darkly" was first and "The Silence" the third. (Dir: Ingmar Bergman, 80 mins.)

Winter Meeting (1948)**½ Bette Davis, Jim Davis, Janis Paige. Bette is in love with a man who wants to be a priest but a terribly talky script bogs down a potentially dramatic situation. (Dir: Bretaigne Windust, 104 mins.)

Winter Soldier (1972)**** In 1971, in Detroit, the Vietnam Veterans Against the War started several days of hearings. This lacerating reminder of the agonies of the Vietnam War is largely a filmed record of the statements of 28 veterans between ages 20 and 27 who describe the unspeakable horrors they have seen and, in some cases, committed. These veterans all received honorable discharges and many were given medals for their heroism in combat. Made by the Winterfilm Collective. (99 mins.)

Winterkill (MTV 1974)**½ Andy Griffith, Sheree North, Joyce Van Patten. Andy Griffith as a chief of police in a mountain resort area. It's a pretty sound murder yarn with a killer on the loose and a guest star lineup of victims and suspects. Griffith is well cast as the friendly lawman who wants to crack the multiple murder case before big-time outside help is brought in. (Dir: Jud Taylor, 100 mins.)

Winterset (1936)**** Burgess Meredith (film debut), Margo, Eduardo Ciannelli, John Carradine. Twenty years after his father was executed for a crime he didn't commit, his son searches for the real criminal. Fine version of Maxwell Anderson's play; poetic, dramatic, powerful. (Dir: Alfred Santell, 80 mins.)

Wintertime (1943)**½ Sonja Henie, Jack Oakie, Cornel Wilde, Cesar Romero. Sonja's fans may enjoy this musical about a skating star who saves a broken down hotel from bankruptcy. Not much here but Sonja's skating. (Dir: John Brahm, 82 mins.)

Wise Blood (1979)***½ Brad Dourif, Amy Wright, Harry Dean Stanton. Sagacious version of Flannery O'Connor's novella. Dourif is a searingly intense bedeviled psychotic who preaches a gospel of the Church of Jesus Christ Without Christ. Only John Huston could direct a film so simultaneously hilarious and depressing. (108 mins.)

Wishing Well (Great Britain, 1954)**½ Brenda De Banzie, Donald Houston, Petula Clark. Three women use a wishing well to make their dreams come true. Leisurely little comedy-drama, but well acted. (Dir: Maurice Elvey, 78 mins.)

Wistful Widow of Wagon Gap, The (1947)** Bud Abbott, Lou Costello, Marjorie Main. A & C on the range this time with Marjorie Main as the "wishful and willing widow." Not one of the comedy team's best. (Dir: Charles Barton, 78 mins.)

Witch Doctor—See: **Men of Two Worlds**

Witches of Salem—See: **Crucible, The**

Witchfinder General—See: **Conquerer Worm, The**

Witches Curse, The (Italy, 1962)*½ Kirk Morris. (Dir: Riccardo Freda, 78 mins.)

Witch's Mirror, The (Mexico, 1960)* Armando Calvo, Rosita Arenas. (Dir: Chano Urueta, 75 mins.)

With a Song in My Heart (1952)***½ Susan Hayward, David Wayne, Rory Calhoun, Thelma Ritter, Robert Wagner. A very entertaining film despite a bad script. The film biopic of singer Jane Froman and her comeback after a near fatal air crash which left her almost completely crippled. Miss Hayward gives a strong performance with a stress on the dramatics. Many songs are sung by Miss Froman with Susan doing an admirable miming job. Oscar: Alfred Newman, Best Scoring. (Dir: Walter Lang, 117 mins.)

With Fire and Sword (Italy, 1961)** Jeanne Crain, John Drew Barrymore. Lavish but stale English-dubbed epic telling of the Cossacks' revolt against the Poles. Miss Crain looks lovely and is required to do no more than that. (Dir: Fernando Cerchio, 96 mins.)

With Six You Get Eggroll (1968)** Doris Day, Brian Keith, Barbara Hershey. If you weren't positive this was a feature film, you'd swear you tuned in any of a dozen familiar TV situation comedy series. It's one of those bumbling affairs which casts Doris Day as a widow with three kids who teams up with widower Brian Keith who has only one daughter. Howard Morris has coaxed from Doris one of her better, less unctuous performances. (Dir: Howard Morris, 99 mins.)

With This Ring (MTV 1978)**½ Dick Van Patten, Betty White, John Forsythe. Comical if predictable vignettes about weddings. Van Patten is well cast as a harried father of the bride worrying how he's going to pay for the nuptials. White also scores as a social-climbing mother who goes all out for her daughter's wedding and is reunited with her estranged husband (Forsythe). (Dir: James Sheldon, 104 mins.)

Without Love (1945)*** Spencer Tracy, Katharine Hepburn, Lucille Ball, Gloria Grahame, Keenan Wynn. Talky, often amusing comedy about a scientist and a widow who get married just for convenience. You know what happens in the end but the Tracy-Hepburn antics should make the wait pleasant. (Dir: Harold S. Bucquet, 111 mins.)

Without Reservations (1946)**½ Claudette Colbert, John Wayne, Don DeFore. Couple of Marines out for fun and romance encounter a lady novelist on a Hollywood-bound train. Amusing romantic comedy has a couple of cute moments, some funny "guest" appearances. (Dir: Mervyn Le Roy, 107 mins.)

Without Warning (1952)***½ Adam Williams, Meg Randall. Police search for a mad killer who strangles blondes without reason. Sordid tale is surmounted by fine direction of Arnold Laven, giving this documentary-type melodrama a big lift. (75 mins.)

Witness for the Prosecution (1957)**** Tyrone Power, Charles Laughton, Marlene Dietrich, Elsa Lanchester. Agatha Christie's clever and suspenseful play about a sensational London murder trial is excellently recreated on the screen. The cast is uniformly brilliant. Laughton, as an aging barrister, is a standout; Power gives one of his best performances. Even the usually decorative Miss Dietrich gets a chance to emote and is very effective. (Dir: Billy Wilder, 116 mins.)

Witness in the City (France-Italy, 1959)**½ Lino Ventura, Sandra Milo. When a cab driver is murdered, his buddies band together to trap the killer. Pretty fair mystery melodrama keeps a good pace, is well acted. Dubbed in English. (Dir: Edouard Molinaro, 90 mins.)

Witness to Murder (1954)*** Barbara Stanwyck, Gary Merrill, George Sanders. Well-acted, minor little suspense tale. Barbara sees the murder. George commits it and Gary is the cop. (Dir: Roy Rowland, 83 mins.)

Wives (Norway, 1975)***½ Anne Marie Ottersen, Froydis Armand. A perceptive, frequently droll, off-beat look at the by now familiar theme of the awakening woman and her flight from failing marriage. This low-budget, genial story is about three women who meet for the first time since high school and decide to leave their husbands briefly and go on a spree together. There are some lovely scenes as writer-director Breien reverses the usual sex roles. The trio ogles and then tries to pick up men on a busy Oslo street corner. (Dir: Anja Breien, 84 mins.)

Wives and Lovers (1963)*** Van Johnson, Janet Leigh, Shelley Winters, Martha Hyer. A sparkling sophisticated comedy with brittle dialogue and stylish performances. It's all about a "nice-guy" writer whose sudden success changes him into a silly strutting egomaniac, and almost destroys his happy marriage. Credit director John Rich with fashioning a bright comedy about Hollywood and Broadway types. (103 mins.)

Wiz, The (1978)**½ Diana Ross, Nipsey Russell, Ted Ross, Mabel King, Michael Jackson, Richard Pryor, Lena Horne. Hyperexpensive musical derivative of "The Wizard of Oz." With the usual dark disco lighting and romanticizing of urban rubble, it's chipper yet depressing. Ross is indefatigable as Dorothy. (Dir: Sidney Lumet, 133 mins.)

Wizard of Baghdad, The (1960)*½ Dick Shawn, Diane Baker. (Dir: George Sherman, 92 mins.)

Wizard of Oz, The (1939)**** Judy Garland, Frank Morgan, Ray Bolger, Bert Lahr, Jack Haley. This musical fantasy about the farm girl whisked to the incredible land of Oz and her adventures with the scarecrow, the tin woodman, and the cowardly lion has become a TV classic over the years. Just to hear "Over the Rainbow" once again is worth tuning in for. Oscars: Special Award to Judy; Best Original Score (Herbert Stothart); Best Song, "Over the Rainbow," by E. Y. Harburg, Harold Arlen. of course, it's from the book by L. Frank Baum. (Dir: Victor Fleming, 102 mins.)

Wizards (1977)** Director Ralph Bakshi's futuristic fantasy is marred by cut-rate animation techniques and a sloppy screenplay that is offensively and self-righteously pompous. (81 mins.)

Wolf Larsen (1958)** Barry Sullivan, Peter Graves. Brutal sea captain meets his match. If this looks like "The Sea Wolf" it's a remake—in other words, warmed over. (Dir: Harmon Jones, 83 mins.)

Wolf Man, The (1941)*** Lon Chaney, Jr., Claude Rains, Evelyn Ankers, Maria Ouspenskaya, Ralph Bellamy, Bela Lugosi. "Even a man who is pure in heart/And says his prayers by night/Can become a wolf when the wolfbane blooms/And the moon is shining bright" —poor guy. This is one of the second-string classics. Lon is bitten by a werewolf, which gives him paws. Suddenly he starts to feel all funny in the moonlight, and for some reason his father thinks he's crazy. There's also a pretty snappy love story with Ankers, queen of the screamers, good effects, and mist-laden scenery full of those Universal Studios trees that grow straight into the ground—or floor—without any roots. Consistently enjoyable. (Dir: George Waggner, 71 mins.)

Wolves of the Deep (Italy, 1959)**½ Massimo Girotti, Jean-Marc Bory, Horst Frank. Sub crew is trapped on the bottom, with the escape hatch damaged and only one man able to get free. Interesting, frequently suspenseful drama of WW II; good performances. Dubbed in English. (Dir: Silvio Amadio, 85 mins.)

Woman Bait—See: **Inspector Maigret**

Woman Called Moses, A (MTV 1978)***½ Cicely Tyson, Dick Anthony Williams, John Getz. Tyson gives a sparkling, luminous performance as Harriet Ross Tubman, one of the most famous black women in history. Beginning deals with Harriet's early life and her relentless drive to work hard and long in order to save up enough money to buy her freedom. Williams is very effective as John Tubman, the irresponsible free black man Harriet marries. The supporting cast is excellent, and the development of Harriet's character as a slave under duress is wonderfully realized. You won't forget one scene, where her employer, played brilliantly by Getz, forces her to wear a mule harness and pull a wagon to amuse his guests. (Dir: Paul Wendkos, 208 mins.)

Woman Chases Man (1937)*** Joel McCrea, Miriam Hopkins, Broderick Crawford. Vastly entertaining screwball comedy about love among the rich. Played in grand comedy style. (Dir: John G. Blystone, 71 mins.)

Woman for Charley, A—See: **Cockeyed Cowboys of Calico County, The**

Woman in a Dressing Gown (Great Britain, 1957)***½ Yvonne Mitchell, Sylvia Syms, Anthony Quayle. Touching adult story about a married couple who get too used to one another and decide on a divorce. Quayle is wonderful as a man who looks for his lost youth by dating a young, beautiful woman. Extremely well directed by J. Lee Thompson. (93 mins.)

Woman in Hiding (1949)** Ida Lupino, Howard Duff, Peggy Dow. Contrived drama about a ruthless man who stops at nothing, from marriage to murder, to get control of a prosperous mill. Miss Lupino spends most of her time looking terrified and running and the rest of the cast gets caught up in the melodramatics of the piece. (Dir: Michael Gordon, 92 mins.)

Woman in Question, The (Great Britain, 1950)*** Jean Kent, Dirk Bogarde. A questionable fortune teller is found murdered, a police investigation reveals many sides of her character. Neat mystery, more of a character study than a whodunit, with a well-shaded performance by Miss Kent. (Dir: Anthony Asquith, 88 mins.)

Woman in the Dunes (Japan, 1964)**** Eiji Okada, Kyoko Kishida. A haunting, engrossing allegory about a man and a woman trapped in a shack at the bottom of a desolate sand pit amidst isolated dunes. Based on the critically acclaimed Japanese novel by Kobo Abe, who adapted it for the screen. But the impact of the film is due principally to the camerawork of Hiroshi Segawa, and to the extraordinary direction of Hiroshi Teshigahara. The love-making sequences are erotic, involving and deeply moving. (123 mins.)

Woman in the Window, The (1944)***½ Edward G. Robinson, Joan Bennett, Raymond Massey, Dan Duryea. His family on holiday, a professor makes a chance acquaintance with a beautiful woman, becomes involved in murder. Despite a weak, silly ending, this remains a superbly thrilling, tense melodrama. Fine Fritz Lang direction, good performances. (99 mins.)

Woman in White (1948)** Eleanor Parker, Alexis Smith, Sydney Greenstreet, Gig Young, Agnes Moorehead. From the gothic novel by Wilkie Collins. Stormy melodrama about an eccentric household, an emotionally tormented heiress, and the young man who arrives to try to untangle her problems. Good script, nice heavy atmosphere, strong performances, especially by Parker, who was a good actress despite being so beautiful. (Dir: Peter Godfrey, 109 mins.)

Woman Obsessed (1959)** Susan Hayward, Stephen Boyd. Woman finds love again after her husband is accidentally killed. Soapy drama. (Dir: Henry Hathaway, 102 mins.)

Woman of Distinction, A (1950)**½ Ray Milland, Rosalind Russell. A woman Dean of a college finds that she must choose between her career and love. Old stuff nicely played. (Dir: Edward Buzzell, 85 mins.)

Woman of Dolwyn, The (Great Britain, 1949)***½ Huge Griffith, Anthony James. The story of the last days of a Welsh village, which is wiped away by flood at the conclusion. Fine cast includes Emlyn Williams (who also wrote and directed), Dame Edith Evans, Richard Burton (film debut). (95 mins.)

Woman of Paris (1923)**** Edna Purviance, Adolphe Menjou, Carl Miller, Charles Chaplin (cameo as a railway porter). Chaplin wrote and directed this sophisticated comedy-drama for his longtime leading lady, Purviance. The themes are emotional failure and moral blindness, effectively worked out through a tightly structured story of a girl who leaves her provincial hometown to become the mistress of a Parisian millionaire (Menjou). (85 mins.)

Woman of Rome (Italy, 1955)** Gina Lollobrigida, Daniel Gelin. Gina plays a down-trodden girl of easy virtue as she has many times before. Nothing new, plot-wise, but Gina is pleasant to watch. (Dir: Luigi Zampa, 93 mins.)

Woman of Straw (Great Britain, 1964)**½ Gina Lollobrigida, Sean Connery, Ralph Richardson. If you don't examine the plot too closely, you may enjoy this well-dressed murder mystery starring sex symbols Lollobrigida and Connery. However, the two smoldering stars are completely upstaged by veteran pro Richardson, who plays the stuffings out of a wheelchair-bound millionaire with some eccentric views on life. (Dir: Basil Dearden, 117 mins.)

Woman of the Town, The (1943)***½ Claire Trevor, Albert Dekker, Barry Sullivan. The saga of Bat Masterson, frontier marshal whose love for dance hall girl Dora Hand ended tragically when he cleaned up the town. Good western drama with an adult story; well acted. (Dir: George Archainbaud, 89 mins.)

Woman of the Year (1942)*** Spencer Tracy, Katharine Hepburn, Fay Bainter, William Bendix (debut). George Stevens's plodding direction takes much of the edge off the first Hepburn-Tracy vehicle. Tracy is a rumpled sportswriter, Hepburn is a world-famous political columnist, and the opposites duly attract. But the film ends with an embarrassing sequence in which Hepburn is tamed and installed in the kitchen. (112 mins.)

Woman on Pier 13, The (1949)** Laraine Day, Robert Ryan, John Agar, Janis Carter. Simpleminded junk about an American Communist who tries to mend his ways. (Dir: Robert Stevenson, 73 mins.)

Woman on the Beach (1947)***½ Joan Bennett, Robert Ryan, Charles Bickford. Nightmarish, elusive tale of a coast guard officer (Ryan) and his near-tragic dalliance with the fetching wife of a painter (Bennett). (Dir: Jean Renoir, 71 mins.)

Woman on the Run (1950)*** Ann Sheridan, Dennis O'Keefe. When her husband witnesses a murder and flees, his wife and the police try to catch up with him before the real killer does. Compact melodrama, suspenseful. (Dir: Norman Foster, 77 mins.)

Woman Rebels, A (1936)*** Katharine Hepburn, Herbert Marshall, Elizabeth Allan, Van Heflin (film debut). A feminist story given a less than compelling treatment. Hepburn is a rebellious Victorian girl who flaunts convention and becomes a pamphleteer for women's rights. It's all quite crinoline, and though the issues are real and clearly drawn, the treatment lacks insight and passion. (Dir: Mark Sandrich, 88 mins.)

Woman Times Seven (U.S.-France-Italy, 1967)**½ Shirley MacLaine, Michael Caine, Peter Sellers, Alan Arkin, Rossano Brazzi. Shirley MacLaine has an actress' dream in this uneven film—she plays seven different roles with seven different leading men in as many episodes. Miss MacLaine is at her best in the episode which has her playing an ordinary wife who reverts to hysteria in order to capture her novelist-husband's attention. (Dir: Vittorio De Sica, 99 mins.)

Woman Under the Influence, A (1974)**** Gena Rowlands, Peter Falk, Matthew Cassel. An ambitious, harrowing drama focusing on a mad lower-middle-class housewife (quite devastatingly acted by Rowlands) who is searching for her identity. Writer-director John Cassavetes

achieves a remarkable sense of improvisation with his acting troupe. (155 mins.)

Woman Who Wouldn't Die, The (U.S.-Great Britain, 1965)* Gary Merrill, Georgina Cookson. (Dir: Gordon Hessler, 84 mins.)

Woman's Devotion, A (1956)** Ralph Meeker, Janice Rule, Paul Henreid. Artist and his wife in Mexico are implicated in murder. Uneven, confused mystery melodrama. (Dir: Paul Henreid, 88 mins.)

Woman's Face, A (1941)***½ Joan Crawford, Melvyn Douglas, Conrad Veidt. Crawford is an evil woman with a facial scar, and Veidt is her epicene manipulator. When plastic surgery restores her face, her personality improves. (Dir: George Cukor, 105 mins.)

Woman's Secret, A (1949)*** Maureen O'Hara, Melvyn Douglas, Gloria Grahame. Police investigate why a singer should be shot by the woman who made her a success. Interesting melodrama. (Dir: Nicholas Ray, 85 mins.)

Woman's Vengeance, A (1947)***½ Charles Boyer, Ann Blyth, Jessica Tandy. Married man having an affair with a younger woman is placed on trial when his wife is found to have been poisoned. Great performances in this absorbing drama written by Aldous Huxley. (Dir: Zoltan Korda, 96 mins.)

Woman's World, A (1954)**½ June Allyson, Lauren Bacall, Arlene Dahl. As the title suggests, this is strictly a woman's picture. This glossy and ultrasophisticated glimpse into the leatherlined world of big business may not be an accurate one, but it provides the background for some chic fashions worn by the trio of female stars, and some slick dialogue by the male contingent, Van Heflin, Fred MacMurray, Cornel Wilde, and Clifton Webb. (Dir: Jean Negulesco, 94 mins.)

Women, The (1939)***½ Norma Shearer, Joan Crawford, Joan Fontaine, Rosalind Russell, Paulette Goddard. From the delightfully bitchy, marvelously complicated Clare Boothe Luce play. Fearsomely contrived, this MGM paste diamond struts its brittle cattiness with wrenching flair. B&W, with a color fashion show. Remade as "The Opposite Sex." (Dir: George Cukor, 132 mins.)

Women and War (France, 1961)** Bernard Blier, Lucille Saint-Simon. Experiences of a small French town under the yoke of the Germans during WW II, its eventual liberation. War drama tries for deep characterization, doesn't make it—some fair sequences. Dubbed in English. (Dir: Georges Lautner, 100 mins.)

Women Are Like That (France, 1960)*½ Eddie Constantine, Françoise Brion. (Dir: Bernard Borderie.)

Women Are Weak—See: **Three Murderesses**

Women at West Point (MTV 1979)*** Linda Purl, Andrew Stevens, Jameson

Parker. The first women were admitted to West Point in '76 after 174 years of all-male enrollment. Purl, as the young, feisty, determined plebe who is the focus of the movie, gives a thoroughly believable performance, and even looks right in the severe uniforms of the Point. Stevens is also good as an upperclassman who bends the nonfraternization rule and falls in love with Purl. Parker almost steals the film as Palfrey, the by-the-book squad leader who makes all the women plebes' lives tough during the first year. (Dir: Vincent Sherman, 104 mins.)

Women in Chains (MTV 1971)*½ Ida Lupino, Jessica Walter. (Dir: Bernard Kowalski, 73 mins.)

Women in Limbo—See: **Limbo**

Women in Love (Great Britain, 1970)***½ Alan Bates, Glenda Jackson, Oliver Reed, Jennie Linden. Jackson won an Oscar for her multiedged portrayal in this film version of the D. H. Lawrence novel. A bit obscure and hard to follow, the film is sensuously shot and dramatized more for mood and effect than plot and action. Rather like Lawrence, only without the ideas. Bates and Reed co-star and they read the tricky dialogue with spectacular skill. (Dir: Ken Russell, 129 mins.)

Women in Revolt (1972)** Candy Darling, Holly Woodlawn, Jackie Curtis. Three transvestites play females of questionable mettle who become attracted to the rhetoric of the women's movement, go through some astounding moral calisthenics as they go about "organizing," incoherently backslide, fall apart as a group, and end up diversely in certain well-known attitudes taken by the fallen Eve of the legendary Garden. Screamingly funny deadpan farce. (Dir: Andy Warhol, 97 mins.)

Women of Devil's Island (Italy, 1962)* Guy Madison, Michele Morcier. (Dir: Domenico Paolella, 86 mins.)

Women of Pitcairn Island (1957)*½ James Craig, Lynn Bari. (Dir: Jean Yarbrough, 72 mins.)

Women of the Prehistoric Planet (1966)** Wendell Corey, Keith Larsen, John Agar. Studio-bound science fictioner about a spaceship being overpowered by hostages from another planet and crash-landing on an unknown world. Has almost nothing to recommend it. (Dir: Arthur C. Pierce, 87 mins.)

Women's Prison (1955)** Ida Lupino, Jan Sterling, Phyllis Thaxter, Howard Duff, Cleo Moore. Unbelievable account of conditions in a women's prison presided over by a ruthless superintendent. Reminiscent of far superior film on same subject, "Caged." (Dir: Lewis Seiler, 80 mins.)

Women's Room, The (MTV 1980)** Lee Remick, Colleen Dewhurst, Patty Duke Astin, Gregory Harrison, Tyne Daly. Dramatization of Marilyn French's provocative best-seller, with Remick going through the familiar cycle of '50s college girl, blushing bride, harried mother, and divorcee. Then she goes back to college and finds a whole new awareness has sprung up since her campus days. Melodrama gets in the way, as does an unbelievable romance with a younger man, played by Harrison as if he were asleep. Astin as a housewife who can't cope, and Daly as a mother of six who has turned to the bottle for solace give the drama a boost, but their scenes are brief. (Dir: Glenn Jordan, 132 mins.)

Won Ton Ton, The Dog Who Saved Hollywood (1976)* Madeline Kahn, Bruce Dern, Art Carney, Richard Arlen, Billy Barty, Jackie Coogan, Janet Blair, Edgar Bergen, Dennis Day, Andy Devine, Gloria DeHaven, William Demarest, Huntz Hall, Dick Haymes, Keye Luke, Victor Mature, Carmel Myers, Rudy Vallee, and Doodles Weaver. (Dir: Michael Winner, 92 mins.)

Wonder Bar (1934)** Al Jolson, Dick Powell, Kay Francis, Dolores Del Rio. Bizarre Jolson musical mixes murder with a nightclub milieu. At least some of the tasteless facism is cut out on TV. (Dir: Lloyd Bacon, 84 mins.)

Wonder Man (1945)***½ Danny Kaye, Virginia Mayo, Vera-Ellen, Steve Cochran. One of Kaye's best performances—he plays a dual role as twins, one twin is the bookish type while the other is a fast-talking nightclub entertainer. When the gangsters bump off the wrong twin, the bookish Kaye steps into his brother's shoes and the fun begins. (Dir: H. Bruce Humberstone, 99 mins.)

Wonder Women (MTV 1974)** Cathy Lee Crosby, Ricardo Montalban. For devotees of the comic-book adventures of Wonder Woman, here's a film with newcomer Crosby in the title role. Diana Prince, Wonder Woman's other name, leaves her island habitat to take a job as secretary to the Chief of Operations of an intelligence agency. Enter villains and Wonder Woman steps into action. (Dir: Vincent McEveety, 75 mins.)

Wonderful Country, The (1959)**½ Robert Mitchum, Julie London, Jack Oakie, Gary Merrill. Fast action western tale with Mitchum cast as a Texan who has a strange allegiance to the Mexicans and consents to buy arms to be used in the Revolution. Julie London supplies the love interest and Pedro Armendariz fares best in a large supporting cast. (Dir: Robert Parrish, 96 mins.)

Wonderful World of the Brothers Grimm, The (1962)**½ Laurence Harvey, Claire Bloom, Barbara Eden. Children's picture with some biography of Jacob and Wilhelm and some versions of their fairy tales. (Dirs: Henry Levin, George Pal, 129 mins.)

Wonders of Aladdin (France-Italy, 1961)** Donald O'Connor, Noelle Adam, Vittorio De Sica. Strictly for the youngsters—a comedy version of Arabian Nights' adventure complete with magic lamps, genies, and flying carpets. (Dir: Henry Levin, 93 mins.)

Woodstock (1970)**** Jimi Hendrix, Joan Baez, Joe Cocker, Arlo Guthrie, Richie Havens, The Who. An incredible array of rock stars are filmed live at the historic four-day celebration. Shows lots of faces from the crowd. Jimi Hendrix's closing rendition of "The Star-Spangled Banner" is an awesome redefinition of American ideals through the spirituality of music. (Dir: Michael Wadleigh, 184 mins.)

Word of Honor (MTV 1981)*** Karl Malden, Rue McClanahan, Ron Silver. A small town newspaper reporter's world changes when he refuses to name a source in the trial of a leading citizen accused of murder. Karl Malden carries this "man of principle" drama, putting his family through the wringer because he won't go back on his word. The reporter's decent middle class family is emphasized to make the hero's dilemma more poignant; but some of it gets a bit overdone, as does the pat ending. Still, it's an upbeat "American dream" movie in the old-fashioned tradition, a rarity these days. (Dir: Mel Damski, 104 mins.)

Words and Music (1948)*** Mickey Rooney, Tom Drake, Gene Kelly, Vera-Ellen, Mel Tormé, June Allyson, Ann Southern, Betty Garrett, Lena Horne, Perry Como, Allyn Ann McLerie, Cyd Charisse, Janet Leigh. Drake as Richard Rodgers and Rooney as Lorenz Hart in a not-too-accurate biographical pic which is mostly an excuse for musical numbers which range from good to mediocre. Kelly's "Slaughter on Tenth Avenue" ballet with Vera-Ellen is worth the rest of the show. (Dir: Norman Taurog, 119 mins.)

Work is a Four-Letter Word (Great Britain, 1968)**½ David Warner, Cilia Black, Zia Mohyeddin. Even in a future world of utter automation, there is a place for artificial "high." Giant mushrooms make the characters euphoric in this film, based on Henry Livingston's play, "Eh?"—you will be less so. Mildly antic fun. Directed by the illustrious theater director Peter Hall, his first film effort. (87 mins.)

World for Ransom, The (1954)**½ Dan Duryea, Gene Lockhart. Adventurer matches wits with a gang of criminals. A few twists help this one. (Dir: Robert Aldrich, 82 mins.)

World in His Arms, The (1952)*** Gregory Peck, Ann Blyth, Anthony Quinn. Rugged romantic adventure with old fashioned escapes, rescues, brawls and love scenes set amid the raucous, lawless period when fur traders brought cargoes to San Francisco. Peck makes a dashing hero and Ann Blyth is more animated than usual as a Russian countess. (Dir: Raoul Walsh, 104 mins.)

World in My Corner (1956)**½ Audie Murphy, Barbara Rush. Familiar boxing story about the kid from the slums who tastes luxury by fighting in the ring and becomes addicted until it almost ruins his life. Audie Murphy, in a change-of-pace

role from his usual western films, does fairly well as the boxer and a good supporting cast helps. (Dir: Jesse Hibbs, 82 mins.)

World in My Pocket (France-Italy-West Germany, 1961)** Rod Steiger, Nadia Tiller, Ian Bannen, Jean Servais. Another payroll robbery, masterminded by a dame (Tiller). Some suspense. Filmed in Europe. (Dir: Alvin Rakoff, 93 mins.)

World of Abbott and Costello, The (1965)**½ Bud Abbott, Lou Costello. A difficult film to rate, if not describe, because your enjoyment of this film will depend on how you already feel about Bud and Lou. Consists of a mélange of their highlights from many films, and includes their daffy goodie, "Who's On First?" Narration by comic Jack E. Leonard, and clips from A & C flicks. (Dir: Sidney Meyers, 75 mins.)

World of Apu, The (India, 1959)**** Soumitra Chatterjee, Sharmila Tagore. The last part of director Satyajit Ray's great trilogy, certainly the masterpiece of the series. Apu (Chatterjee) marries a young girl (Tagore) through a fluke and grows to love her; when she dies, he undergoes a period of despair and gradual spiritual regeneration. The pace is harsher, faster, but the values that have been percolating throughout the trilogy burgeon into one of the richest, most invaluable humanistic statements in film. (117 mins.)

World of Henry Orient, The (1964)**** Peter Sellers, Tippy Walker, Merrie Spaeth, Angela Lansbury, Paula Prentiss. A rare combination of humor and sensitivity makes this comedy special. It tells a wacky story about a madly egocentric and overly amorous concert pianist (Sellers), who is hilariously pursued around New York City by two teenage fans, brilliantly and naturally portrayed by Walker and Spaeth. New York is photographed to good advantage, in this touching and gay charade. Nice directorial touches by George Roy Hill. (106 mins.)

World of Suzie Wong, The (Great Britain, 1960)** William Holden, Nancy Kwan. Unpleasant and tasteless drama of an American artist and his love for a girl of the streets in Hong Kong. Tries to be daring, succeeds in merely being soap opera. (Dir: Richard Quine, 129 mins.)

World of the Vampires, The (Mexico, 1961)* Mauricio Garces, Silvia Fournier. (Dir: Alfonso Corona Blake, 83 mins.)

World Premiere (1941)*** John Barrymore, Frances Farmer, Daffy satire on Hollywood openings involves some Nazis assigned to see that producer Barrymore's film never opens. Silly, somewhat dated but fun. (Dir: Ted Tetzlaff, 70 mins.)

World, the Flesh and the Devil, The (1959)*** Harry Belafonte, Inger Stevens, Mel Ferrer. Belafonte spends the first part of the film alone on screen, supposedly the last survivor on earth after poisonous gasses have destroyed humanity. The early scenes are skillfully handled by writer-director Ranald MacDougall and should grip your attention. Enter Stevens and Ferrer and conflicts begin, most of which are obvious and pat. (95 mins.)

World Without End (1956)** Hugh Marlowe, Nancy Gates, Rod Taylor. An interesting premise makes this sci-fi tale a bit more absorbing than some comparable films. A space flight intended for Mars goes through the time barrier and ends up on Earth during the 26th century. (Dir: Edward Bernds, 80 mins.)

World Without Sun (France-Italy, 1964)**** Excellent French documentary, showing the experiments of Jacques Ives Cousteau and his men under the Red Sea. Eerily fascinating scenes of underwater life, both human and aquatic, should absorb all viewers. Oscar: Best Documentary. (Dir: Jacques-Yves Cousteau, 93 mins.)

World's Greatest Athlete, The (1973)* Jan-Michael Vincent, Tim Conway, John Amos, Howard Cosell. (Dir: Robert Scheerer, 92 mins.)

World's Greatest Lover, The (1977)***½ Gene Wilder, Carol Kane, Dom DeLuise. Not all the sight gags work, but a great many of them are funny in this maniacal romp which not only stars Wilder but is written, produced, and directed by him. Wilder plays Rudi Valentine—a baker from Milwaukee in the mid-'20s who sets out to achieve recognition as the WGL. (89 mins.)

Worm's Eye View (Great Britain, 1951)**½ Ronald Shiner, Diana Dors. Comic complications when five RAF men are billeted in a suburban villa during WW II. Helter-skelter, rather likeable comedy. (Dir: Jack Raymond, 77 mins.)

Woyzeck (West Germany, 1979)**½ Klaus Kinski, Eva Mattes, Wolfgang Reichmann. Georg Büchner's fragmented masterwork of a play is given a disconcertingly literal treatment by director Werner Herzog, whose visionary style is becoming a matter of holding banal shots too long. Kinski's conceptualization of the simpleminded soldier driven to murder has awesome technical skill, but there is no tragedy or pathos in his performance. Mattes, however, is strikingly authentic. (81 mins.)

WR: Mysteries of the Organism (Yugoslavia-West Germany, 1971)*** Milena Dravic, Jagoda Kaloper, Zoran Radmilovic, Tuli Kupferberg, Jackie Curtis. A cockeyed collage mixes interviews with disciples of Wilhelm Reich with a zany story of a sexually liberated Yugoslav Communist party member who preaches political freedom through sexual energy. While she talks, her roommate does. (Dir: Dusan Makavejev, 86 mins.)

Wrath of God, The (1972)*½ Robert Mitchum, Frank Langella, Rita Hayworth. (Dir: Ralph Nelson, 111 mins.)

Wreck of the Mary Deare, The (U.S.-Great Britain, 1959)**½ Charlton Heston, Gary Cooper, Richard Harris. Rather slow-moving mystery-adventure yarn with good performances by the two stars and an excellent British supporting cast including Emlyn Williams, Michael Redgrave and Virginia McKenna. The plot concerns the strange circumstances surrounding the wreck of the freighter called the Mary Deare. (Dir: Michael Anderson, 105 mins.)

Wrecking Crew, The (1960)** Dean Martin, Elke Sommer, Nancy Kwan, Sharon Tate. Dean plays swinging sleuth Matt Helm again, and it's a tedious carbon copy of his other espionage yarns. This time, Matt has to almost single-handedly save the American and British economies by making certain a gold shipment, en route to London via Denmark, arrives safely. (Dir: Phil Karlson, 104 mins.)

Wrestling Women vs. the Aztec Mummy (Mexico, 1965)* Lorena Velazquez, Armando Sylvestre. (Dir: Rene Cardona, 88 mins.)

Written on the Wind (1956)*** Rock Hudson, Lauren Bacall, Robert Stack, Dorothy Malone. Malone (in the performance of her career) won an Oscar for Best Supporting Actress; she plays a spoiled rich girl who almost destroys her brother (Stack) and the man she covets (Hudson). Director Douglas Sirk's highly imaginative use of color is years ahead of contemporary technique. (99 mins.)

Wrong Arm of the Law, The (Great Britain, 1961)***½ Peter Sellers, Bernard Cribbins, Lionel Jeffries, Nanette Newman. Another British spoof of crime films, with Sellers the Brain planning a very elaborate robbery. It's very funny. (Dir: Cliff Owen, 91 mins.)

Wrong Box, The (Great Britain, 1966)**** John Mills, Ralph Richardson, Michael Caine, Peter Cook, Dudley Moore. Merry, nimble farce, based on a tale co-authored by Robert Louis Stevenson, about Victorian inheritance intrigues and a migratory body, which tumbles between slapstick, black humor and beguiling absurdity, and is played with vigor by an incomparable cast. Utter nonsense, done superbly. Screenplay by Larry Gelbart and Burt Shevelove. (Dir: Bryan Forbes, 98 mins.)

Wrong Kind of Girl, The (1956)*** Marilyn Monroe, Don Murray, Arthur O'Connell, Hope Lange, Betty Field. Naive cowhand meets a sexy entertainer at a bus stop, falls hard for her despite warnings from his pal. Good drama based on the Broadway stage success by William Inge presents Monroe in a good role. Some tender dramatic moments, some funny ones. Good entertainment. Alternate title: "Bus Stop." (Dir: Joshua Logan, 96 mins.)

Wrong Man, The (1957)***½ Henry Fonda, Vera Miles, Anthony Quayle. Frightening account of what happens to a man and his wife when he is wrongly accused of being the man who has performed a series of hold-ups. This story is based on fact. Directed with his customary skill by Alfred Hitchcock. (105 mins.)

Wrong Move, The (West Germany, 1975) ***½ Rudiger Vogler, Hanna Schygulla, Hans Christian Blech, Nastassia Kinski. Director Wim Wenders's free adaptation of Goethe's "Wilhelm Meister" is a dispassionate study of an aspiring writer's pilgrimage through modern Germany in search of truth. Along the way he meets an actress, a poet, an ex-Nazi, and a suicidal industrialist, angst-ridden souls all. This may be Wenders's most dour film, but it has wit, humor, and vision.

Wrong Number (Great Britain, 1959)** Lisa Gastoni, Peter Elliot, Peter Reynolds. Crooks plan a big mail truck robbery, supposedly a "perfect" crime. That it doesn't come off is no news to crime melodrama devotees. (Dir: Vernon Sewell, 67 mins.)

WUSA (1970)* Paul Newman, Joanne Woodward, Laurence Harvey, Anthony Perkins, Cloris Leachman, Wayne Rogers. (Dir: Stuart Rosenberg, 115 mins.)

Wuthering Heights (1939)***½ Laurence Olivier, Merle Oberon, David Niven, Geraldine Fitzgerald (film debut), Flora Robson. Epic piece of romantic tomfoolery about the doomed love affair of a gypsy foundling (Olivier) and the spoiled daughter of the house (Oberon). Director William Wyler strives for a brooding intensity but fails to ignite the material. Olivier begins to show some of the stuff that wowed audiences in his stage career. Rather superb support. Based on the Emily Brontë novel. (103 mins.)

Wuthering Heights (Great Britain, 1970) **½ This remake of the Bronte classic about the epic romance between the wild, dashing, uncontrolled spirit named Heathcliff and his lovely ladylove Catherine falls short of its brilliant predecessor. However, Timothy Dalton as Heathcliff manages better than his lackluster costar Anna Calder-Marshall. Also the physical production is handsome, and the tale remains interesting. (Dir: Robert Fuest, 105 mins.)

W.W. and the Dixie Dancekings (1975)*** Burt Reynolds, Art Carney, Ned Beatty. Reynold's performance as a good ole boy conning his way through the South with a fair-to-middling band (circa '57) is a delight. He gets fine support from country singers Jerry Reed and Conny Van Dyke, and Carney's brief moments as a sheriff-turned-evangelist are inspired. (Dir: John G. Avildsen, 91 mins.)

Wyoming (1940)** Wallace Beery, Ann Rutherford. Typical Beery western which will appeal to his legions of fans. They'll particularly like his "Aw, shucks" romance with Marjorie Main. (Dir: Richard Thorpe, 89 mins.)

Wyoming Kid (1947)** Dennis Morgan, Jane Wyman, Janis Paige, Arthur Kennedy. Gambler is hired to capture a notorious stagecoach robber, falls for the outlaw's wife. Bigger cast than usual in this routine western; few of them look at home in the wide-open spaces. (Dir: Raoul Walsh, 100 mins.)

X-15 (1961)** Charles Bronson, Kenneth Tobey, Mary Tyler Moore. Stilted semi-documentary about test pilots on the X-15 missile project. This one is grade B movie fare with all the clichés, including the patient wives who wait for their husbands while they serve science. Narrated by James Stewart. (Dir: Richard Donner, 105 mins.)

X from Outer Space, The (Japan, 1966)* Eiji Okada, Toshiya Wazaki. (Dir: Kazui Nihonmatsu, 85 mins.)

X-Ray of a Killer (France, 1963)** Jean Servais, Dany Robin, Maurice Teynac. Police inspector suspects a famous surgeon of being a notorious spy, sets a trap for him. Standard espionage melodrama dubbed in English. (Dir: Jean Maley, 79 mins.)

"X": The Man with the X-Ray Eyes (1963)*** Ray Milland, Diana Van Der Vlis. Science fiction horror film about a scientist who is cursed with the ability to see through things. Director Roger Corman demonstrates his special ability to extract maximum mileage from low-cost visuals. (80 mins.)

X—The Unknown (Great Britain, 1956)*½ Dean Jagger, Edward Chapman, Anthony Newley. (Dir: Leslie Norman, 81 mins.)

X, Y and ZEE (Great Britain, 1972)**½ Elizabeth Taylor, Michael Caine, Susannah York. Three troupers put soap opera through the wringer with intelligent dialogue by novelist Edna O'Brien. Taylor and Caine are married; York interferes. Brian G. Hutton, known for mindless action and such, directed this change of pace. (110 mins.)

Yakuza, The (1975)**½ Robert Mitchum, Brian Keith, Keiko Kishi, Takakura Ken. Writer Paul Schrader has cribbed a popular Japanese formula that mixes gangsters and oriental codes of honor. Though Mitchum is in good weary form as an aging American tough guy up against the Japanese underworld, the film is unsettling, intriguing, but ultimately unsatisfying. (Dir: Sydney Pollack, 112 mins.)

Yank at Eton, A (1942)** Mickey Rooney, Peter Lawford. Brash Mickey goes to school in England and the result is forced, not too funny, comedy. (Dir: Norman Taurog, 88 mins.)

Yank at Oxford, A (U.S.-Great Britain, 1938)** Robert Taylor, Vivien Leigh, Maureen O'Sullivan, Lionel Barrymore. The mutual-chauvinistic attitudes of the film have become shopworn. Taylor is the brash youth who encounters an alien culture at the British university. (Dir: Jack Conway, 100 mins.)

Yank in the R.A.F., A (1941)*** Tyrone Power, Betty Grable. Dated but still exciting story of a Yank who joins the R.A.F. just to be near an old girl friend and has some of the cockiness knocked out of him by the R.A.F. spirit. (Dir: Henry King, 97 mins.)

Yank in Viet-Nam, A (1964)** Marshall Thompson, Enrique Magalona. Marine officer is freed from the Communist forces and joins with a soldier to free a kidnapped doctor. Standard war story has the advantage of Viet-Nam locations, adding to the believability. (Dir: Marshall Thompson, 80 mins.)

Yankee Buccaneer (1952)** Jeff Chandler, Scott Brady, Suzan Ball, David Janssen. Strictly for action fans who like swashbuckling yarns. Chandler climbs the mast and commands a decoy U.S. naval ship which is rigged as a private vessel in order to dupe the thieves of the high seas. (Dir: Frederick de Cordova, 86 mins.)

Yankee Doodle Dandy (1942)***½ James Cagney, Walter Huston, Joan Leslie, Jeanne Cagney, Rosemary DeCamp, S. Z. Sakall, Frances Langford. Cagney won an Oscar playing Broadway playwright George M. Cohan in a whopping musical. Much mindless jingoism, but mostly a nice wartime blend of flag waving, family melodrama, and musical numbers (impressively danced by Cagney). (Dir: Michael Curtiz, 126 mins.)

Yankee Pasha (1954)**½ Jeff Chandler, Rhonda Fleming, Lee J. Cobb, Mamie Van Doren, Hal March. Edison Marshall's best selling novel about a man who fights pirates, sultans, harem girls and other obstacles in order to win his lady fair, is elaborately brought to the screen. Action is plentiful and Miss Fleming is lovely to look at. (Dir: Joseph Pevney, 84 mins.)

Yanks (U.S.-Great Britain, 1979)*** Richard Gere, Vanessa Redgrave, William Devane, Lisa Eichborn. Boy meets girl in this story of American GIs in WW II Britain. Director John Schlesinger's meticulous mise-en-scène plays like a well-written textbook. Eichborn is radiant as a middle-class ingenue. (140 mins.)

Yearling, The (1946)**** Gregory Peck, Jane Wyman, Claude Jarman, Jr. For presenting a simple story of a boy's love for a pet fawn which his father must destroy this is one of the finest films of all time. The emotions involved are complex and real, yet this picture has captured all the feelings and depth of the best selling novel without even employing Hollywood tricks. A "must" for the whole family. (Dir: Clarence Brown, 128 mins.)

Years Between, The (Great Britain, 1946)**½ Michael Redgrave, Valerie Hobson. Believed dead, a prisoner of war returns to find his wife remarried. Occasionally interesting drama, despite some

lags. (Dir: Compton Bennett, 98 mins.)

Yellow Balloon (Great Britain, 1952)*** Andrew Ray, Kenneth More, William Sylvester. Small boy is shocked by the accidental death of a playmate, is used for evil purposes by a petty crook. Gripping suspense melodrama, well done. (Dir: J. Lee Thompson, 80 mins.)

Yellow Cab Man, The (1950)**½ Red Skelton, Gloria De Haven, Walter Slezak. Fast and funny frolic for Red Skelton fans. Red's a cab driver who goes out of his way to pick up pretty girls and trouble. Hilarious, slapstick chase is the climax. (Dir: Jack Donohue, 85 mins.)

Yellow Canary (Great Britain, 1943)**½ Anna Neagle, Richard Greene, Margaret Rutherford. English girl poses as a Nazi sympathizer to track down spies. Fairly good espionage melodrama. (Dir: Herbert Wilcox, 84 mins.)

Yellow Canary, The (1963)**½ Pat Boone, Barbara Eden, Steve Forrest, Jack Klugman. Dramatically tight mystery-suspense tale, scripted by Rod Serling, about a singer whose infant son is kidnapped, falls short on characterization. Jack Klugman stands out in supporting role as the frustrated cop. Based on the novel *Evil Come, Evil Go*, by Whit Masterson. (Dir: Buzz Kulik, 93 mins.)

Yellow Fin (1951)*** Wayne Morris, Adrian Booth. Young owner of tuna fishing boat is beset by troubles in the form of a rascally rival and a grasping dame. Good action melodrama. (Dir: Frank McDonald, 74 mins.)

Yellow Jack (1938)***½ Robert Montgomery, Virginia Bruce, Lewis Stone, Buddy Ebsen. Sidney Howard's award winning play is converted into a compelling film. Story of the men who risked their lives to determine the cause of yellow fever is a monument to courage minus the usual phony Hollywood heroics. (Dir: George B. Seitz, 80 mins.)

Yellow Mountain, The (1954)*½ Lex Barker, Mala Powers, Howard Duff. (Dir: Jesse Hibbs, 78 mins.)

Yellow Rolls Royce, The (Great Britain, 1964)**** Rex Harrison, Ingrid Bergman, Shirley MacLaine, Omar Sharif, George C. Scott. Most audiences will enjoy the star-studded cast in this film about the adventures of a fancy Rolls-Royce and the various people who own it. With so much talent before and behind the cameras, it should have been far better than it is. (Dir: Anthony Asquith, 122 mins.)

Yellow Sky (1948)*** Gregory Peck, Richard Widmark, Anne Baxter, James Barton, Harry Morgan. Offbeat, arty western, loosely based on Shakespeare's "The Tempest." Not successful as art. (Dir: William A. Wellman, 98 mins.)

Yellow Submarine (Great Britain, 1968) **** A film treat which shouldn't be missed. It's the delightful, engaging animated fantasy in which the Beatles fight off the Blue Meanies, who have the auacity to disrupt the tranquil amiability of the mythical kingdom of Pepperland of Sgt. Pepper's Lonely Hearts Club Band fame. There are many songs in the film (written and performed by the Beatles), including "All You Need Is Love," "Eleanor Rigby," "Lucy in the Sky with Diamonds," and the title tune, of course. (Dir: George Dunning, 85 mins.)

Yellowneck (1955)*** Lin McCarthy, Stephen Courtleigh. Civil War deserters try to make their way through the Florida Everglades to freedom. Strong drama made in Florida, heavy on the violence, deserves credit as an attempt to be different. (Dir: R. John Hugh, 83 mins.)

Yellowstone Kelly (1959)**½ Clint Walker, John Russell, Edd Byrnes, Ray Danton. Routine western, with most of the Warner Bros. stable of TV western stars. The plot offers nothing new and the cast is very much at home in the saddle and on the trail. (Dir: Gordon Douglas, 91 mins.)

Yes Sir, That's My Baby (1949)**½ Donald O'Connor, Gloria De Haven, Charles Coburn, Jim Davis. Silly but entertaining comedy-musical about the campus life of ex-G.I.'s going to college on the G.I. Bill of Rights. A mixture of football, baby feedings, marital misunderstandings, and nick-of-time victories. (Dir: George Sherman, 82 mins.)

Yesterday, Today and Tomorrow (Italy-France, 1963)***½ Sophia Loren, Marcello Mastroianni. Three spicy stories tailored for the talents of the two stars, especially Loren; in one, she's a black marketeer who takes an unusual method of avoiding the law; in another, she's the flirtatious wife of an industrialist; in the last, she's a call girl whom a seminary student tries to reform. Funny adult fare. Dubbed in English. (Dir: Vittorio De Sica, 119 mins.)

Yesterday's Child (MTV 1977)**½ Shirley Jones, Geraldine Fitzgerald. Shirley Jones and Geraldine Fitzgerald, two good actresses, give this drama its validity. A 17-year-old girl is brought to her wealthy mother and grandmother's house claiming to be the little girl who was kidnapped and believed killed many years before. The device may be slightly old-hat, but the cast, particularly the ladies, keep it from going overboard. Stephanie Zimbalist, Efrem's daughter, plays the young girl who returns from the past. (Dir: Jerry Thorpe, 106 mins.)

Yesterday's Enemy (Great Britain, 1959)**½ Stanley Baker, Guy Rolfe, Bryan Forbes, Philip Ahn. Moderately interesting British war film about a small group of soldiers who take over a Burmese jungle village. The action is believable and the performances are average. (Dir: Val Guest, 95 mins.)

Yojimbo (Japan, 1961)**** Toshiro Mifune, Eijiro Tono, Seizaburo Kawazu, Isuzu Yamada. Director Akira Kurosawa's rendition of Dashiell Hammett's "Red Harvest" in the samurai-movie tradition.

Mifune is incomparable as a masterless samurai who wanders into a war between two gangs in a small town and sets things right by further stirring things up. (110 mins.)

Yokel Boy (1942)*** Albert Dekker, Joan Davis, Eddie Foy Jr. A hick idea man for a Hollywood studio suggests the life of a notorious gangster—with the gangster himself in the lead. Highly amusing comedy. (Dir: Joseph Santley, 69 mins.)

Yolanda and the Thief (1945)***½ Fred Astaire, Lucille Bremer, Frank Morgan. Astaire as a con man and Bremer as an innocent girl. As a musical, it isn't much: the book is trivial and the songs are few and forgettable. But virtuoso director Vincente Minnelli, a superb pictorialist as well as a great director, lets his imagination run wild, and the result is a captivating, dreamlike film full of startling, outrageous, and sometimes sublime images. It has nothing to do with good taste—and that may be the secret of its peculiar appeal. It's kitsch liberated, personalized, and intensified. Photographed in soft Technicolor by the brilliant Charles Rosher. (108 mins.)

You Are Not Alone (Denmark, 1978)**½ Anders Agenso, Peter Bjerg. At an all-male supplementary school, misunderstandings between the headmaster and the students result in an expulsion, a strike, and a brotherhood among the boys. The film finds homosexual phases in young boys' development to be normal. Sensitively handled. (Dirs: Lasse Nielsen, Ernst Johansen, 92 mins.)

You Are What You Eat (1969)** Tiny Tim, Peter Yarrow. An ancestor of the rock concert film, this sleazy-type job gets a number of big names together to do their thing in a rather unimaginative way. The film is interesting for one number only—"The Greta Garbo Home for Wayward Boys and Girls"—it's a knockout! (Dir: Barry Feinstein, 75 mins.)

You Can't Cheat an Honest Man (1939)*** W. C. Fields, Edgar Bergen. Fields runs a traveling show, can't make a buck or stay ahead of the sheriff. Deft performances make this nonsense entertaining. (Dir: George Marshall, 79 mins.)

You Can't Get Away with Murder (1939)*** Humphrey Bogart, Gale Page, Billy Halop. This was made while Bogey was playing crooks and his performance as a killer is so good that it's no wonder he was typed. It's a familiar death-house drama but engrossing and well acted. (Dir: Lewis Seiler, 78 mins.)

You Can't Go Home Again (MTV 1979)*** Lee Grant, Chris Sarandon, Hurd Hatfield. Thomas Wolfe's last long, thinly disguised autobiographical novel is carefully brought to the screen. Sarandon's sharply defined portrait of the writer-hero makes it worthwhile. Wolfe's novel suffers from being trimmed to fit a TV time slot. (Dir: Ralph Nelson, 104 mins.)

You Can't Have Everything (1937)*** Alice Faye, Don Ameche, Ritz Brothers, Tony Martin. The Ritz Brothers supply the comedy and almost succeed in supporting the frail backstage plot. Alice sings well and it's fairly good screen entertainment—if you like the Ritz Brothers. (Dir: Norman Taurog, 99 mins.)

You Can't Run Away from It (1956)** June Allyson, Jack Lemmon. Bad remake of Clark Gable—Claudette Colbert classic "It Happened One Night" with music, no less. Dick Powell produced and directed this so-called comedy about a runaway heiress and a newspaper man. (96 mins.)

You Can't Steal Love—See: Murph the Surf

You Can't Take It with You (1938)***½ James Stewart, Jean Arthur, Lionel Barrymore, Spring Byington, Edward Arnold. Rousing Frank Capra direction of the Kaufman and Hart play about an eccentric family at odds with a stuffy rich one. But Capra overloads this slight farce with intimations of important statements. Using a harmonica-playing motif as a symbol for all that's good and decent about simple people is just too simple by half. (127 mins.)

You Can't Win 'Em All (Great Britain, 1970)*½ Tony Curtis, Charles Bronson, Michele Mercier. (Dir: Peter Collinson, 97 mins.)

You for Me (1952)**½ Peter Lawford, Jane Greer, Gig Young. Two of Hollywood's most suave leading men, Lawford & Young, save this otherwise lightweight romantic comedy from total boredom. The object of their affection is pretty nurse Jane Greer. (Dir: Don Weis, 71 mins.)

You Gotta Stay Happy (1948)**½ James Stewart, Joan Fontaine, Eddie Albert. This could easily be called "The Flyer Takes A Lady"; Joan Fontaine and the flyer, none other than James Stewart. Fast but disappointing comedy. (Dir: H. C. Potter, 99 mins.)

You Lie So Deep, My Love (MTV 1975)* Don Galloway, Barbara Anderson, Angel Tompkins, Walter Pidgeon. (Dir: David Lowell Rich, 72 mins.)

You Light Up My Life (1977)**½ Didi Conn, Joe Silver, Michael Zaslow. Joseph Brooks wrote, scored, produced, and directed this mercifully short study of a singer-songwriter who discovers, after losing two suitors, How to Be Her Own Best Friend and, as she puts it, "Do Her Own Thing." This could be the first EST melodrama, a tearjerker for '70s solipsists. Conn is quite beguiling. The title song won an Oscar. (90 mins.)

You Must Be Joking! (Great Britain, 1965)**½ Michael Callan, Lionel Jeffries, Terry-Thomas, Denholm Elliott. Script has problems, but there's Terry-Thomas as a wacky Army psychiatrist who drafts five equally zany officers to perform a 48-hour "initiative test." Some chuckles. (Dir: Michael Winner, 100 mins.)

You Never Can Tell (1951)*** Dick Powell, Peggy Dow, Joyce Holden. Delightfully wacky film about the reincarnation of a dog and a horse into a private detective (Dick Powell) and a blonde secretary (Joyce Holden) respectively who come to earth to settle an old score concerning murder. Very amusing idea carried off with style. (Dir: Lou Breslow, 78 mins.)

You Only Live Once (1937)***½ Henry Fonda, Sylvia Sidney, William Gargan. In director Fritz Lang's film about an outlaw couple (Fonda and Sidney) on the run, it's always night, usually raining, and the camera hovers over the characters like the heavy hand of fate. (86 mins.)

You Only Live Twice (Great Britain, 1967)**½ Sean Connery, Donald Pleasence, Tetsuro Tampa, Karin Dor. This is tiresome James Bond, set in Japan, with Connery playing the role one last, reluctant time. The evil SPECTRE organization is out to start a war. (Dir: Lewis Gilbert, 116 mins.)

You Were Meant for Me (1948)*** Jeanne Crain, Dan Dailey. A nice score of popular standards, pleasing performances and a routine story of a girl who marries a bandleader she has known one day and then must learn to travel with him and love him. (Dir: Lloyd Bacon, 92 mins.)

You Were Never Lovelier (1942)*** Fred Astaire, Rita Hayworth, Adolphe Menjou. Amiable chica-boom-boom musical with Astaire stranded in Rio, where he walks into a plot that Hayworth's father, Menjou, is hatching to cure her frigidity by fixing her up with an imaginary "unknown admirer." As for dancing, Rita packs a shimmy that would knock Ginger Rogers back to the flatlands. (Dir: William A. Seiter, 97 mins.)

You'll Like My Mother (1972)**½ Patty Duke, Richard Thomas, Rosemary Murphy, Sian Barbara Allen. Satisfying Grand Guignol starring Duke as a harassed pregnant girl menaced by the strange goings-on at a weird house. Filmed in Minnesota. (Dir: Lamont Johnson, 93 mins.)

You'll Never Get Rich (1941)*** Fred Astaire, Rita Hayworth, Robert Benchley. Enjoyable musical features Astaire as a hoofer who knows the show must go on even if he's drafted. The primary source of delight (besides the Cole Porter songs, including "So Near and Then Again So Far") is the young Hayworth, holding her own with Fred and radiating sex appeal. The story bogs down in the second half but the numbers are solid throughout. (Dir: Sidney Lanfield, 88 mins.)

You'll Never See Me Again (MTV 1973)** David Hartman, Jane Wyatt, Ralph Meeker. Suspense thriller. When a couple of newlyweds quarrel, the bride bounces out of the house to visit her mom. Bridegroom Hartman conducts a panicky search, only to wind up as the prime murder suspect. (Dir: Jeannot Szwarc, 73 mins.)

Young and Evil—See: **Cry of the Be-twitched**

Young and Innocent (Great Britain, 1937)**** Derrick de Marney, Nova Pilbeam, Percy Marmont. A young man (de Marney), falsely accused of murder, escapes from the police and sets out after the killer. The very appealing Pilbeam becomes convinced of de Marney's innocence and joins in the search with more fervor than de Marney himself. Much of the film's pleasure lies in the adolescent romance; the suspense of the chase is paralleled with the couple's anxiety about their developing relationship. The film's high point is a tracking shot which begins over a crowded ballroom and ends on an extreme close-up of the twitching eyes of the killer. (Dir: Alfred Hitchcock, 80 mins.)

Young and the Damned, The (Los Olvidados) (Mexico, 1950)**** Estela Inda, Alfonso Mejia. Gripping drama by Spain's great writer-director Luis Buñuel, penetrating portrait of the slum life of Mexico City, with emphasis on the children and how poverty affects them. (88 mins.)

Young and Willing (1942)** William Holden, Eddie Bracken, Susan Hayward, Robert Benchley, Barbara Britton. Some struggling young actors try to interest a big theatrical producer. Mildly amusing madcap comedy. (Dir: Edward Griffith, 82 mins.)

Young and Willing (1962)—See: **Wild and the Willing, The**

Young at Heart (1954)*** Frank Sinatra, Doris Day, Gig Young, Ethel Barrymore, Dorothy Malone. This musical re-make of Fannie Hurst's "Four Daughters" hasn't the classy patina of the '38 original, but has charm and professionalism. Sinatra and Day play the parts originally limned by John Garfield and Priscilla Lane. Gordon Douglas directs capably. (117 mins.)

Young Bess (1953)***½ Jean Simmons, Charles Laughton, Deborah Kerr, Stewart Granger. Handsomely mounted historical drama with two excellent performances by Jean Simmons as the high spirited Bess, and Charles Laughton as her father, Henry VIII. History students may find objections to various aspects of the film but it's entertaining and absorbing. (Dir: George Sidney, 112 mins.)

Young Billy Young (1969)* Robert Mitchum, Angie Dickinson, Robert Walker, David Carradine, Jack Kelly. (Dir: Burt Kennedy, 89 mins.)

Young Captives, The (1959)**½ Steven Marlo, Luana Patten, Ed Nelson. Teenage couple eloping to Mexico run afoul of a crazed killer who holds them captive. Tight little suspense drama made on a small budget, makes its point quickly and excitingly. (Dir: Irvin Kershner, 61 mins.)

Young Cassidy (U.S.-Great Britain, 1965)***½ Rod Taylor, Maggie Smith, Julie Christie. Interesting, if uneven, biographical drama about the early life of playwright Sean O'Casey, depicting his rise from the Dublin slums to the celebrated openings of his early plays. Rod Taylor does well in the central role, and the good cast includes: Flora Robson, Maggie Smith, Michael Redgrave, Edith Evans, and a brief but telling part by Julie Christie. (Dirs: John Ford, Jack Cardiff, 110 mins.)

Young Country, The (MTV 1970)**½ Roger Davis, Joan Hackett, Wally Cox. If you like your western tales with a broad serving of comedy, this feature about a bumbler of a gambler and his adventures in the West will give you a few laughs. Roger Davis is a bewildered hero who gets into trouble trying to earn his keep playing cards. The supporting cast is very good, especially Walter Brennan as a veteran sheriff, and Joan Hackett and Peter Duel as a pair of shady characters. (Dir: Roy Huggins, 73 mins.)

Young Dillinger (1965)*½ Nick Adams, Robert Conrad, Mary Ann Mobley, Victor Buono, Ted Knight. (Dir: Terry D. Morse, 102 mins.)

Young Dr. Kildare (1938)*** Lew Ayres, Lionel Barrymore. Good, sensitive story of a young interne's problems in a big city hospital. First of the MGM series and well played by Ayres and Barrymore. (Dir: Harold S. Bucquet, 82 mins.)

Young Doctors, The (1961)*** Fredric March, Ben Gazzara, Eddie Albert, George Segal (debut), Dick Clark. Routine hospital soap opera elevated to good drama by the earnest playing of a fine cast. March is particularly good as a pathologist of the old school who clashes with the modern approach represented by Gazzara. Many subplots are well integrated into the drama. (Dir: Phil Karlson, 102 mins.)

Young Don't Cry, The (1957)** Sal Mineo, James Whitmore. Confused melodrama about a badly run Georgia orphanage and one teenager in particular who gets involved with an escaped convict. Over-acted. (Dir: Alfred L. Werker, 89 mins.)

Young Frankenstein (1974)**** Gene Wilder, Peter Boyle, Marty Feldman, Madeline Kahn, Gene Hackman. Inspired lunacy written by guffaw wizards Mel Brooks (also directed) and Gene Wilder. Wilder is the grandson of the nefarious Baron Frankenstein; he visits the old family homestead in Transylvania and decides to make a living creature himself. Feldman is hilarious playing a hunchbacked assistant, and Kahn is absolutely delicious having a roll in a hay wagon with the lucky grandson. Some incredibly funny sight gags strewn along the way by maniacal madcap Mel. (98 mins.)

Young Fury (1965)*½ Rory Calhoun, Virginia Mayo, Lon Chaney, Richard Arlen, John Agar, Jody McCrea, William Bendix. Bendix's last film. (Dir: Christian Nyby, 80 mins.)

Young Girls of Good Families (France,

1963)*½ Marie-France Pisier, Ziva Rodann. (Dir: Pierre Montazel, 90 mins.)

Young Girls of Rochefort, The (France, 1967)** Catherine Deneuve, Gene Kelly, Danielle Darrieux. A charming score by Michel Legrand and the lovely Miss Deneuve and her sister, Françoise Dorleac, are the best things about this overly sweet musical. It's a tale about a fair in the quaint French village of Rochefort-sur-Mer where the girls, Gene Kelly, George Chakiris, and a large cast fall in and out of love at the drop of a song cue. (Dir: Jacques Demy, 126 mins.)

Young Guns, The (1956)**½ Russ Tamblyn, Gloria Talbott, Scott Marlowe. A cast of exciting young acting talents make this western yarn seem better than it is. The plot is the familiar one about the boy who has to make a choice between becoming a gunslinger or a law abiding citizen. (Dir: Albert Band, 84 mins.)

Young Guns of Texas (1962)** James Mitchum, Alana Ladd, Jody McCrea, Chill Wills. The chase is on after a group of Confederates as the Civil War ends, with Apaches on the warpath complicating matters. So-so western whose only novelty is the offspring of famous actors in leading roles. (Dir: Maury Dexter, 78 mins.)

Young Hellions—See: **High School Confidential**

Young in Heart, The (1938)***½ A dizzy family of cardsharps and fortune hunters is reformed by the kindness of a sweet old lady, whom they vow to help by leading better lives. Douglas Fairbanks, Jr., Janet Gaynor, Paulette Goddard, and a fine supporting cast—Billie Burke, Roland Young, Richard Carlson. Delightful comedy. (Dir: Richard Wallace, 91 mins.)

Young Jesse James (1960)** Ray Stricklyn, Robert Dix, Willard Parker. Still another version of how Jesse went bad—this time he joined Quantrill's raiders because Union soldiers killed his father. All adds up to just another western. (Dir: William Claxton, 73 mins.)

Young Joe, the Forgotten Kennedy (MTV 1977)**½ Peter Strauss, Barbara Parkins, Simon Oakland. Peter Strauss stars as Joseph Kennedy, Jr., the handsome eldest son of the Kennedy clan, groomed from childhood to be the heir of the family's political dynasty. The young man died during a perilous volunteer mission in WW II. (Dir: Richard T. Heffron, 104 mins.)

Young Land, The (1959)** Pat Wayne, Yvonne Craig, Dan O'Herlihy, Dennis Hopper. In early California, an American is placed on trial for killing a Mexican. Racial problems in the old West—film tries a plea for tolerance but becomes a western minus much action. (Dir: Ted Tetzlaff, 89 mins.)

Young Lawyers, The (1969)*** Jason Evers, Keenan Wynn, Michael Parks. Pilot for a projected TV series. Well produced, well acted, and interesting. A new organization, the Boston Neighborhood Law Office gives student lawyers the opportunity to try cases in court. Three bright young actors, Zalman King, Judy Pace, and Tom Fielding, play the fledgling advocates, and Evers is their director. The focus is on a case which pits cabdriver Wynn against two black musicians accused of assault and theft. (Dir: Harvey Hart, 74 mins.)

Young Lions, The (1958)**½ Marlon Brando, Montgomery Clift, Dean Martin, Maximilian Schell, Hope Lange, Mai Britt. Irwin Shaw's big novel of WW II sprawls across the screen. Director Edward Dmytryk fails to command the material. What merit the film has is in Joe Macdonald's cinematography and the performances, especially by Brando as a poster Aryan, and Clift, whose facial immobility after an auto accident is made use of as a sensitive, stoic mask. (167 mins.)

Young Lovers, The (1949)***½ Sally Forrest, Keefe Brasselle, Hugh O'Brian. The ravages of polio cause a young dancer to readjust herself both physically and mentally. Gripping drama, sensitively directed by Ida Lupino, well acted. (85 mins.)

Young Lovers, The—See: **Chance Meeting (1954)**

Young Lovers, The (1964)* Peter Fonda, Sharon Hugueny, Nick Adams, Deborah Walley. (Dir: Samuel Goldwyn, Jr., 105 mins.)

Young Man with a Horn (1950)***½ Kirk Douglas, Lauren Bacall, Doris Day, Hoagy Carmichael. Kirk Douglas gives an excellent performance in this yarn about a dedicated trumpet player who lived exclusively for his music until it was almost too late. Bacall plays a well-written character who helps Douglas destroy himself in a hurry. Doris Day acts (not too well) and sings (very well). (Dir: Michael Curtiz, 112 mins.)

Young Man with Ideas (1952)**½ Glenn Ford, Ruth Roman, Denise Darcel, Nina Foch. Lawyer moves his family to California and gets a job as a bill collector, which leads to complications. Story never hits any great heights, but the players are pleasant. (Dir: Mitchell Leisen, 84 mins.)

Young Mr. Lincoln (1939)*** Henry Fonda, Alice Brady, Marjorie Weaver. Story of young Abe as a lawyer is not the greatest of Lincoln stories but John Ford's direction and fine acting by Fonda and Alice Brady make it good entertainment. (100 mins.)

Young One, The (Mexico, 1960)** Zachary Scott, Bernie Hamilton, Key Meersman. Negro musician fleeing the law is drawn into a web of danger when he lands on an island inhabited by a young girl and a lecherous older man. Unpleasant mixture of racial theme, "Lolita," and assorted violence. Well acted. Mexican-made. English dialogue. (Dir: Luis Buñuel, 96 mins.)

Young People (1940)** Shirley Temple, Jack Oakie, Charlotte Greenwood. Temple vehicle directed by veteran Allan Dwan, who makes it at least a persuasive sow's ear. Oakie and Greenwood are the show-biz couple who raise orphan Shirley. (78 mins.)

Young Philadelphians, The (1959)*** Paul Newman, Barbara Rush, Alexis Smith, Brian Keith, Billie Burke. Rather long film based on the best seller about people from different levels of Philadelphia society. The performances are better than the screen play, with Robert Vaughn delivering the best one as a rich young man who is framed on a murder charge. (Dir: Vincent Sherman, 136 mins.)

Young Pioneers, The (1976)**½ Linda Purl, Roger Kern. Quality on-location production and two appealing young stars bolster this tale about two young newlyweds who trek to the wilds of Dakota to homestead land given to settlers in the 1870s. The hardships they endure are almost insurmountable. Talented and attractive leads are fresh and believable. Made-for-TV. (Dir: Michael O'Herlihy, 98 mins.)

Young Pioneers' Christmas (MTV 1976)**½ Linda Purl, Roger Kern, Robert Hays. Holiday film about rugged pioneer days in the wilds of Dakota in the 1870s. Sentiment runs high but never becomes sticky, thanks to the appealing young stars. (Dir: Michael O'Herlihy, 104 mins.)

Young Racers, The (1963)** Mark Damon, William Campbell, Luana Anders, Patrick Magee. Former racer turned writer intends to expose a reckless road ace in a book but grows to like him. Plenty of careening autos for the sports fans, all looking pretty much alike; story is slight but holds the interest. Fair result. (Dir: Roger Corman, 87 mins.)

Young Runaways, The (1968)** Brooke Bundy, Kevin Coughlin, Lloyd Bochner, Patty McCormack, Lynn Bari. Predictable, if earnest, attempt to focus on the kids who run away to Chicago's hippie section, in order to find themselves, circa 1968. Best performance is by lovely Bundy, and keen film fans will recognize Richard Dreyfuss in a small role. (Dir: Arthur Dreifuss, 91 mins.)

Young Savages, The (1961)*** Burt Lancaster, Dina Merrill, Shelley Winters, Telly Savalas. Evan Hunter's novel "A Matter of Conviction" makes for a hard-hitting crime drama with Burt Lancaster playing a determined assistant D.A. engaged in the battle against juvenile delinquency. There are many tough and brutally realistic scenes. (Dir: John Frankenheimer, 103 mins.)

Young Scarface (Great Britain, 1947)**½ Richard Attenborough, Hermione Baddeley, William Hartnell. A brave girl whose reporter fiancé has been killed investigates organized gang violence. A shocker in its day. Script by Graham Greene, who adapted it from his novel "Brighton Rock." (Dir: John Boulting, 91 mins.)

Young Sinner, The (1965)*½ Tom Laughlin, Stefanie Powers. (Dir: Tom Laughlin, 82 mins.)

Young Stranger (1957)*** James MacArthur, James Daly, Kim Hunter. A moving story of a boy and his relationship with his father, who doesn't take time from his busy schedule to try and understand his son. Based on a TV play and debut film direction by John Frankenheimer. (84 mins.)

Young, the Evil and the Savage, The (Italy, 1968)** Michael Rennie, Mark Damon, Eleanora Brown. English girls' school provides setting for an unoriginal but painless murder mystery. Fair suspense! (Dir: Antonio Margheriti, 82 mins.)

Young Toerless (France-West Germany, 1966)***½ Matthieu Carriere, Barbara Steele. A very good film, based on the novel by Robert Musil. Beautifully photographed and lovingly written and acted, it is worth seeing for its poetry and dedication. (Dir: Volker Schlondorff, 90 mins.)

Young Tom Edison (1940)*** Mickey Rooney, Fay Bainter. Good biography of the youth of the great inventive genius. Mickey is in rare form and the whole family will enjoy this. (Dir: Norman Taurog, 86 mins.)

Young Warriors, The (1967)** James Drury, Steve Carlson, Norman Fell. An average WW II tale which tries to analyze the effect killing has on a professional soldier and a young newcomer. It begins with some promise but the clichés soon take over. Drury handles the role of the tough sergeant with authority. (Dir: John Peyser, 93 mins.)

Young Winston (Great Britain, 1972)*** Simon Ward, Anne Bancroft, Robert Shaw, John Mills, Jack Hawkins. Interesting, highly enjoyable biography of Winston Churchill as a young man. His lonely childhood, school days, fights in India, and exploits in the Boer War are all rousingly recalled. Battle sequences are particularly stunning. Ward plays Churchill with power, and Bancroft and Shaw are moving as Churchill's inattentive parents. (Dir: Richard Attenborough, 157 mins.)

Youngblood (1978)** Lawrence-Hilton Jacobs, Bryan O'Dell, Ren Woods. Black exploitationer about a ghetto youth gang, the Kingsmen, who war on a local drug ring. Rather well done of its type with a good cast and authentic L.A. ghetto locales. (Dir: Noel Nosseck, 90 mins.)

Youngblood Hawke (1964)*½ James Franciscus, Suzanne Pleshette, Genevieve Page, Mary Astor, Eva Gabor. (Dir: Delmer Daves, 137 mins.)

Youngest Spy, The (U.S.S.R., 1962)*** Kolya Burlyayev. Story of a Russian lad whose parents were killed by the Nazis and became a spy behind the enemy lines. Good observation of child's thoughts, some poetic sequences. English dubbed. (Dir: Andrei Tarkovsky, 94 mins.)

Your Cheatin' Heart (1964)*** George Hamilton, Susan Oliver, Red Buttons, Arthur O'Connell. Hamilton manages to overcome his handsome playboy image to create a solid characterization of the ill-fated country-western singer Hank Williams. Does a straightforward job of telling the public and private story of the country boy who rose to stardom, suffered career setbacks, and died before he was 30. Tunes associated with the singer are mouthed by Hamilton in excellent fashion, and recorded for the soundtrack by Hank Williams, Jr. (Dir: Gene Nelson, 199 mins.)

Your Money or Your Wife (MTV 1972)*½ Ted Bessell, Elizabeth Ashley, Jack Cassidy. (Dir: Allen Reisner, 73 mins.)

Your Past Is Showing (Great Britain, 1957)***½ Peter Sellers, Terry-Thomas, Dennis Price, Shirley Eaton. Price is a blackmailing publisher of a tawdry exposé magazine; Sellers, a nasty TV personality; Terry-Thomas, a racketeering peer; Eaton, a model. The bits are pungently etched and the comedy is pleasantly oddball. (Dir: Mario Zampi, 92 mins.)

'Your Shadow Is Mine (France-Italy, 1962)*½ Jill Haworth, Michel Ruhl. (Dir: André Michel, 91 mins.)

Your Turn, Darling (France, 1963)*½ Eddie Constantine, Elga Andersen, Henri Cogan. (Dir: Bernard Borderie, 93 mins.)

Your Turn, My Turn (France, 1978)*** Marlene Jobert, Philippe Léotard, Micheline Presle. Bright comedy about a neglected wife and a divorced building contractor who literally meet by accident (in a minor traffic collision) and carry on an affair while somehow seeing to their respective children's needs. Stars are pleasant and the eternally beautiful Presle is fine in support as an interior decorator and Jobert's part-time boss, who commits suicide after her young daughter's drug overdose death. The moral seems to be: Live for yourself, not your children. (Dir: François Leterrier, 95 mins.)

You're a Big Boy Now (1967)*** Peter Kastner, Elizabeth Hartman, Geraldine Page, Julie Harris, Karen Black. A fast-paced, often inventive comedy about a contemporary youth (Kastner) who is on the brink of becoming an adult. His escapade with a man-hating go-go dancer, well played by Hartman, leads to some wildly funny scenes. Impressive major directorial debut for young (27) Francis Ford Coppola, who also wrote this screenplay. (96 mins.)

You're in the Army Now (1941)**½ Jimmy Durante, Phil Silvers, Jane Wyman. You'll watch it anyway just to see Phil and Jimmy but don't expect miracles from this frail comedy about two vacuum cleaner salesmen who get into the Army by mistake. (Dir: Lewis Seiler, 79 mins.)

You're in the Navy Now (1951)** Gary Cooper, Jane Greer, Eddie Albert, Jack Webb. Another awkward attempt at trying to make the war funny. A group of misfits led by Cooper (a green officer) are chosen to experiment with a craft outfitted with a steam turbine instead of the conventional diesel engine. The results are supposed to be uproariously funny. (Dir: Henry Hathaway, 93 mins.)

You're My Everything (1949)*** Dan Dailey, Anne Baxter, Shari Robinson, Buster Keaton. When this film is poking fun at the Hollywood heyday of the '20s and '30s, it borders on being great, but when it reverts to the cornball sentiment of the tragic backstage life of the stars, it is only average entertainment. Plenty of songs and dances by Dailey and a Shirley Temple-type moppet, Shari Robinson. (Dir: Walter Lang, 94 mins.)

You're Never Too Young (1955)** Dean Martin, Jerry Lewis, Diana Lynn, Raymond Burr. Jerry as a wacky barber who is forced to pose as a child, with a thief and murderer on his trail. Reworking of "The Major and the Minor" to suit the talents of Martin & Lewis furnishes some laughs but is stretched out; not one of the team's better comedies. (Dir: Norman Taurog, 102 mins.)

You're Only Young Once (1937)**½ Lewis Stone, Mickey Rooney. First in the Stone-Rooney group and a good example of wholesome family comedy which made the Hardy series so popular. (Dir: George B. Seitz, 77 mins.)

You're Telling Me (1934)**** W. C. Fields, Buster Crabbe, Joan Marsh. The "master" appears in almost every hilarious scene of this film and he, and you, have a field day. He's an inventor and you'll hurt your sides laughing at the inventions. Remake of "So's Your Old Man." (Dir: Erle C. Kenton, 70 mins.)

Yours, Mine and Ours (1968)** Henry Fonda, Lucille Ball, Van Johnson, Tom Bosley. You have to love Lucille Ball and Henry Fonda in order to tolerate this farce which has Lucy playing a widow with 8 kids who marries widower Fonda, who has 10 offspring. The result—bedlam, TV-series-style. If your kids aren't very sophisticated they may enjoy this sugar-coated candy. (Dir: Melville Shavelson, 111 mins.)

Yuma (MTV 1970)*½ Clint Walker, Barry Sullivan. (Dir: Ted Post, 73 mins.)

Z (France-Algeria, 1969)**** Yves Montand, Irene Papas, Jean-Louis Trintignant. Marvelous political film. Based on the killing of a peace movement leader in Greece in 1963, the subsequent investigation which uncovered a right-wing terrorist organization with government connections, and the military coup which destroyed democracy. Put in the frame of a thriller; that followed not only fine social protest, but exciting moviemaking. Acting is fine, especially the subdued performance of Trintignant as the government investigator. Oscar: Best Foreign Film. (Dir: Constantin Costa-Gavras, 127 mins.)

Zabriskie Point (1970)* Mark Frechette, Daria Halprin, Rod Taylor, Kathleen Cleaver. (Dir: Michelangelo Antonioni, 112 mins.)

Zandy's Bride—See: **For Better, for Worse**

Zarak (Great Britain, 1957)** Victor Mature, Michael Wilding, Anita Ekberg. Vic becomes an outlaw leader when he's driven from his village, with the British on his trail. Standard adventure opus, with Ekberg looking dazzling but adding little to the plot. (Dir: Terence Young, 99 mins.)

Zardoz (Great Britain, 1974)** Sean Connery, Charlotte Rampling, Sara Kestelman. Science fiction head trip set in 2293. Immortality has led to over-rationalization and boredom. Correction is needed from Connery, who plays a savage. The film examines ideas as if they were to be looked at but not touched. (Dir: John Boorman, 105 mins.)

Zatoichi Enters Again (Japan, 1963)** Shintaro Katsu. Legendary masseur and blind swordsman searches for a kidnapped youth and finds romance with his fencing instructor's daughter in this early entry of a popular series. Katsu is as earthy as ever. (Dir: Tokuzo Tanaka.)

Zebra in the Kitchen (1965)**½ Jay North, Marshall Thompson, Martin Milner, Jim Davis, Andy Devine. If this title intrigues you, you'll find out how it was derived in the final half of this Ivan Tors family movie about an animal-loving lad and his adventures. Jay North stars as the boy who causes an uproar when he frees all the animals from a zoo, including his recently captured pet mountain lion. The animals are the scene stealers here and the kids will enjoy their antics. (Dir: Ivan Tors, 93 mins.)

Zemlya—See: **Earth**

Zeppelin (Great Britain, 1971)** Michael York, Elke Sommer. A rather ridiculous World War I adventure-spy epic which relies on super heroics and a big dirigible which is used in a mission to obtain valuable English documents and thereby destroy British morale. Michael York is surprisingly stiff and Elke Sommer is merely decorative. Good aerial sequences. Okay for kids. (Dir: Etienne Perier, 101 mins.)

Zéro de Conduite (France, 1933)**** Henri Storck. Charts the rebellion of three young boys in a provincial boarding school. On graduation day the boys dump garbage on the assembled dignitaries (some of whom are cardboard cutouts). Director Jean Vigo's grasp of the relationship be-

tween the real and the farcical makes this memorable.(47 mins.)

Zero Hour (1957)** Dana Andrews, Linda Darnell, Sterling Hayden. Predictable tale about a man who was a fighter pilot (WW II). Dana Andrews strikes the right note as the troubled ex-pilot. (Dir: Hall Bartlett, 81 mins.)

Ziegfeld Follies (1946)*** William Powell, Fred Astaire, Gene Kelly, Lucille Bremer. Vincente Minnelli, couldn't have asked for a better vehicle than this unplotted MGM revue featuring every star on the lot with a claim to musical ability, and a few without. The comedy sketches are atrocious, but Minnelli shines in the lavish musical numbers, which include Astaire's only appearance with Kelly (a comic duet). Lucille Ball tames a troupe of tiger girls. Red Skelton, Fanny Brice, Esther Williams, Kathryn Grayson, and Mrs. Minnelli, Judy Garland, also appear. (110 mins.)

Ziegfeld Girl (1941)*** James Stewart, Judy Garland, Hedy Lamarr, Lana Turner. Lavish musical about the girls who were glorified by Ziegfeld is generally routine musical entertainment boasting a lot of attractive stars. (Dir: Robert Z. Leonard, 131 mins.)

Ziegfeld: The Man and His Women (MTV 1978)**½ Paul Shenar, Valerie Perrine, Samantha Eggar, Barbara Parkins, Pamela Peadon. A valentine to those Hollywood movie musical biographies of the '30s and '40s, but the lace on the satin heart is a bit tattered. Story of Florenz Ziegfeld, perhaps the most publicized Broadway entrepreneur of all time, is told through the eyes of the women in his life. (Dir: Buzz Kulik, 156 mins.)

Zigzag (1970)**½ George Kennedy, Anne Jackson, Eli Wallach. Another variation on a murder-for-insurance theme has Kennedy as a terminally ill man who frames himself for a murder to get insurance for his wife. Performances are fine, and especially good is Wallach playing Kennedy's Italian defense lawyer who knows it's a frame, but can't figure out who's doing it and why. (Dir: Richard A. Colla, 104 mins.)

Zita (France, 1968)*** Joanna Shimkus, Katina Paxinou, Jose Maria Flotats. Unusual, appealing film, about a young girl maturing after the double experiences of a loved aunt's death and her own first tastes of love and different sorts of living. Masterfully photographed, with some intriguing scenes of Paris after dark. Well acted, though the pace slackens at times. (Dir: Robert Enrico, 92 mins.)

Zombies of Mora Tau (1957)*½ Gregg Palmer, Allison Hayes. (Dir: Edward L. Cahn, 70 mins.)

Zorba the Greek (U.S.-Greece, 1964)**** Anthony Quinn, Irene Papas, Alan Bates. A marvelous rousing drama set in Crete about a lusty individualist determined to live his own life, free of any restrictions imposed upon him by an unyielding and unchanging Greek society. Noteworthy performance from Quinn, whose magnetism and vitality are perfectly suited to the part. Miss Papas is memorable playing a young widow in a tiny Greek village, and director Michael Cacoyannis captures the mood and brooding spirit of the peasants. Lila Kedrova won an Oscar for her supporting performance as a pitiful, aging courtesan who dwells in the past. (142 mins.)

Zorikan the Barbarian (Italy, 1964)* Dan Vadis, Walter Brandi. (Dir: Roberto Mauri, 92 mins.)

Zorro (France-Italy, 1975)** Alain Delon, Stanley Baker. European version of the popular story of the masked Mexican crusader (Delon) vs. the corrupt aristocracy, presided over by Colonel Huerta (well played by Baker). Lots of action but not very exciting. (Dir: Duccio Tessari, 120 mins.)

Zorro, the Avenger (Spain, 1962)*½ Frank Latimore, Maria Luz Galicia. (Dir: Joaquin Romero Marchent, 90 mins.)

Zotz! (1962)** Tom Poston, Julia Meade, Jim Backus, Fred Clark. Professor finds an old coin with the magical power to make people move in slow motion, becomes a target for spies after the coin. Moderate comedy doesn't have the sparkle necessary to bring it off. (Dir: William Castle, 87 mins.)

Zulu (Great Britain, 1964)*** Stanley Baker, Jack Hawkins, James Booth, Michael Caine. An exciting adventure based on a real-life incident in African history, the massacre in 1879 of a British mission by Zulu warriors. The events leading to the epic battle are depicted in personal terms involving a missionary, his daughter, the mission's commander and his men. The cast is excellent, but the battle sequence is the real star of the film. (Dir.-coauthor: Cy Endfield, 138 mins.)

Zuma Beach (MTV 1978)*½ Suzanne Somers, P. J. Soles, Steven Keats. Routine comedy-drama, used to showcase TV star Somers, relies too heavily on her modest charms. She plays a singer whose career is on the rocks, and who finds a new direction when she becomes friendly with a group of teenage boys. (Dir: Lee H. Katzin, 104 mins.),

ABOUT THE AUTHOR

Steven H. Scheuer is the editor and publisher of TV KEY, the most widely syndicated TV newspaper column in America, appearing daily in over 200 papers, and a new column covering cable television called CABLE KEY. He conceived the idea of previewing television shows, and is the author of numerous critically acclaimed books including *Movies on TV, The Movie Book*, a pictorial history of world cinema and *The Television Annual*, a yearly reference work reporting on both programming and public policy issues. Mr. Scheuer is considered to be one of the most knowledgeable TV critics in the country. *Time* magazine called him "the most influential TV critic." *Access* magazine, published by the National Citizens Committee for Broadcasting, called Mr. Scheuer the best TV critic in the country reporting on questions of television and the public interest.

He is the executive producer of the award-winning weekly series seen on public and cable stations called *All About TV*, the only TV program dealing candidly with TV itself. Mr. Scheuer is the television critic of the CBS Radio Network where he previews programming and comments on public policy issues. Scheuer is currently the president of The Telefilm Databank, a corporation developing a worldwide computer data base of information about motion pictures and television. He is the editor of a forthcoming series of books which will be the first comprehensive *Buyers Guides* about movies and other kinds of programming available on video cassettes and video discs.

Mr. Scheuer is a native New Yorker and a graduate of Yale University. He has done graduate work at the London School of Economics and Political Science, at Columbia University and at New York University. He has served on the faculty of the New School for Social Research where he taught courses in the history of American television. He is a founding member of the Communications Media Committee of the American Civil Liberties Union, and lectures regularly on television and film for colleges and lecture clubs throughout the nation and abroad. He is a trustee of the International Film Seminars.

Mr. Scheuer participates in many sports, and is a nationally ranked squash tennis player.

We Deliver!

And So Do These Bestsellers.

☐	13826	**THE RIGHT STUFF** by Tom Wolfe	$3.50
☐	20229	**LINDA GOODMAN'S SUN SIGNS**	$3.95
☐	14431	**THE THIRD WAVE** by Alvin Toffler	$3.95
☐	14130	**GARY COOPER, AN INTIMATE BIOGRAPHY** by Hector Arce	$2.75
☐	01350	**SOME MEN ARE MORE PERFECT THAN OTHERS** by Merle Shain	$4.95
☐	20506	**WHEN LOVERS ARE FRIENDS** by Merle Shain	$2.50
☐	14965	**I'M DANCING AS FAST AS I CAN** by Barbara Gordon	$2.95
☐	14675	**THE BOOK OF LISTS** by D. Wallechinsky, I. & A. Wallace	$3.50
☐	13101	**THE BOOK OF LISTS #2** by I. Wallace, D. Wallechinsky, A. & S. Wallace	$3.50
☐	20228	**THE COMPLETE SCARSDALE MEDICAL DIET** by Herman Tarnover & S. Baker	$3.25
☐	14481	**THE ONLY INVESTMENT GUIDE YOU'LL EVER NEED** by Andrew Tobias	$2.75
☐	20138	**PASSAGES** by Gail Sheehy	$3.95
☐	14379	**THE GREATEST MIRACLE IN THE WORLD** by Og Mandino	$2.25
☐	20434	**ALL CREATURES GREAT AND SMALL** by James Herriot	$3.95
☐	13406	**THE MEDUSA AND THE SNAIL** Lewis Thomas	$2.95
☐	12942	**JOAN CRAWFORD: A BIOGRAPHY** by Bob Thomas	$2.75
☐	14422	**THE PILL BOOK** by Dr. Gilbert Simon & Dr. Harold Silverman	$2.50
☐	01137	**THE PEOPLE'S ALMANAC #2** by D. Wallechinsky & I. Wallace	$9.95
☐	14500	**GUINNESS BOOK OF WORLD RECORDS— 19th Ed.** by McWhirter	$3.50

Buy them at your local bookstore or use this handy coupon for ordering:

Bantam Books, Inc., Dept. NFB, 414 East Golf Road, Des Plaines, Ill. 60016

Please send me the books I have checked above. I am enclosing $_____
(please add $1.00 to cover postage and handling). Send check or money order
—no cash or C.O.D.'s please.

Mr/Mrs/Miss_____

Address_____

City_____State/Zip_____

NFB—10/81

Please allow four to six weeks for delivery. This offer expires 3/82.